THE ORIENTAL INSTITUTE OF THE UNIVERSITY OF CHICAGO
ASSYRIOLOGICAL STUDIES • NO. 21

ASSYRIOLOGICAL STUDIES • NO. 21

COMPUTER-AIDED ANALYSIS OF AMORITE

IGNACE J. GELB

with the assistance of

JOYCE BARTELS STUART-MORGAN VANCE
ROBERT M. WHITING

THE ORIENTAL INSTITUTE OF THE UNIVERSITY OF CHICAGO
CHICAGO • ILLINOIS

Library of Congress Catalog Card Number: 79-84839
ISBN: 0-918986-21-4
ISSN: 0066-9903

The Oriental Institute, Chicago

TABLE OF CONTENTS

PREFACE

About twenty years have passed since the Amorite computer project was begun. This long period of gestation reflects in some measure the many problems we have faced in all stages of our work: continuous correction of punch cards prepared by inexperienced keypunchers; changes in the analysis of individual names, which had to be entered on white cards, pink cards, punch cards, and in material being prepared for the forthcoming grammar (see below); changes in the new and improved computer programs, which required innumerable test runs; and, finally, the addition over the years of new material, some of which simply complemented the old material, while some forced important changes in the analysis of the data.

My original plan was to publish two volumes on Amorite, one containing the computer-aided analysis of the language and the other the grammar, glossary, and general discussion. I have decided to publish the computer-aided analysis immediately, in case another avalanche of new material should appear while the second volume is being prepared for publication, forcing another long delay in the project.

When completed, the second, much smaller volume will contain a grammar (hereinafter referred to as *Grammar*) in which the data culled from the computer analysis will be reinterpreted and put in the traditional order, in more or less the same form as in my article "Lingua" (see "Abbreviations of Sources"). Unlike the computer analysis, in which all of the data are presented, both the firmly established and the questionable, *Grammar* will deal mainly with ascertainable data. The glossary will consist of a list of free morphemes that occur in Amorite names and will provide translations and annotations whenever possible or necessary. This glossary will also include all the glosses known from the Old Babylonian Mari texts and from other sources. Inasmuch as the present volume may be difficult to use without some immediate help in matters of semantics and morphology, a small preliminary glossary is provided below (under 0.7) to serve as a guide to the computer analysis. This glossary, with its limited critical apparatus, is not intended to stand in place of the full glossary, which will be published in *Grammar*.

The second volume will also contain a brief history of the Amorites, an evaluation of the comparative aspects of the Amorite language, and other general discussion. Since much of the second volume has already been written, there is hope that the entire project may soon be brought to a successful completion.

The title of the present book, *Computer-aided Analysis of Amorite*, does not fully reflect the vast amount of personal, manual work that had to be done at all stages preparatory to the use of the computer. All of the analysis, of course, was done not by the machine but by human effort, and all the good and bad features are ultimately attributable to man. The computer makes no mistakes of its own accord—it merely follows the instructions given by the person in charge. It does, however, add something that no one person could accomplish in a whole lifetime, and that is the vast volume of quantitative documentation.

It must be stressed here, as will be done repeatedly later, that *Computer-aided Analysis of Amorite* is not and cannot be considered to be a grammar of the Amorite language. Rather, it presents a large body of source material, ordered in categories that can be utilized in the study of the non-Akkadian language that we conventionally call Amorite.

The reason why this study cannot be considered a grammar of the Amorite language is obvious. The computer analysis contains a disparate body of material, bringing together not only interpretations which are safe but also others which, owing to the character of the cuneiform writing and human fallibility, must be considered provisional. For example, it places under one heading a meaningful category such as the bound morpheme AH, which stands for the feminine noun. On the other hand, under the bound morpheme A it records a variety of categories which can stand for any morpheme ending in *-a*, be it masculine noun, stative, verb, pronoun, or whatever. Moreover, the computer analysis orders the categories in alphabetical sequence by form (or by rank and form in the case of prefixes and suffixes), rather than by the categories customary in a traditional grammatical analysis. Even the word "Amorite" in the title of this book may be open to question, as the data include not only names identified as Amorite by an ethnic designation or by their context, but also all clearly Semitic but non-Akkadian names of the Old Babylonian period. This problem is discussed further in section 0.1, "Amorite Names."

Despite its weaknesses, the computer analysis makes both a quantitative and a qualitative contribution which in some respects can be considered unique in the field of Semitic linguistics.

Chapter 6, "Index of Names," contains 6,662 entries, including variant forms. As it would have been unduly time-consuming to go through the whole list to ascertain the number of distinct Amorite names, eliminating all variants, I have estimated the number of different names on the basis of a random count of thirty pages. The total obtained by this method was 5,922 different names, a number substantially larger than that found in any of the six published lists of Mesopotamian names.[1] Of the two

1. Knut L. Tallqvist, *Assyrian Personal Names*, Acta Societatis Scientiarum Fennicae, vol. 43, no. 1 (Helsinki, 1914), with about 5,400 entries, comes closest.

large collections of Amorite names published in the past, that by Theo Bauer lists 958 names altogether, including variants, or 786 names excluding variants,[2] while that by H. B. Huffmon lists 1,157 Mari names altogether, including variants, or 879 names excluding variants.[3]

From the quantitative point of view the lists of bound morphemes presented in chapter 3, "Prefixes and Suffixes," outnumber any found in the grammars of Semitic languages. To cite just one example, the computer analysis lists hundreds of examples of the three allomorphs of the feminine singular noun (-AT-, -T-, and -AH), while the most complete Semitic grammars have a few dozen at the most. The complete listing of all the stems (or formations) and the statistical data of the stem and consonant frequencies given in chapter 4, "Stem Count," and in chapter 5, "Phoneme Count," have no parallels in the Semitic field. These two chapters were produced with very little human effort, once the program had been prepared. All the work was done expeditiously by the computer.

From the qualitative point of view it is possible that the grammar of Amorite, reconstructed almost entirely from names, may become better known than that of several Semitic languages attested in thousands of inscriptions, for example, Nabatean, Palmyrenian, or South Arabic. The reason may be not so much the amount of documentation as the structural richness of Amorite names (as opposed to the linguisitic poverty of the preserved inscriptions of some Semitic languages). As an example we may cite the personal pronoun and the verb, attested in the first, second, and third persons singular in Amorite, but only in the third person in the other three languages (the only exception known to me being KTBT for the first person in Palmyrenian).

Included in this volume are names from all Amorite sources available to me up to June 1976.

I wish to express here my heartfelt gratitude to the many persons and institutions who have helped in the course of about twenty years to bring the Amorite project to fruition. The specific contributions of most of them are described in section 0.2, "History of the Computer Project," and section 0.6, "Computer Report."

Professor Stanislav Segert of Prague, now at the University of California in Los Angeles, was constructively involved in the original planning of the Amorite project. Professor Burkhart Kienast of Freiburg, Germany, generously allowed me to use the manuscript of the index of names to his Kisurra publication, which was published recently.[4] Professor David I. Owen of Cornell University provided me with Ur III texts, and Père Marcel Sigrist of the Ecole Biblique Française in Jerusalem with Old Babylonian texts, from which a few scattered references were excerpted.

Financial assistance for the project was provided by the Division of Humanities at the University of Chicago through the kind offices of Professor Robert E. Streeter and Professor Karl J. Weintraub; by the Department of Linguistics with the help of Professor George V. Bobrinskoy and Professor Eric P. Hamp; and by the Oriental Institute with the help of Professor John A. Brinkman, its director. The receipt of a substantial sum of money in 1969-70 from the American Council of Learned Societies is also gratefully acknowledged.

Help with computer programing was given by Professor Victor Yngve and by Messrs. Stephen P. Soulé and Clive A. Church, all of the University of Chicago. Messrs. Allan B. Addleman and Fred H. Harris of the University's Computation Center assisted substantially in technical matters.

The overall contributions of Miss Joyce Bartels and Messrs. Stuart-Morgan Vance and Robert M. Whiting are described in section 0.2, "History of the Computer Project." In acknowledgment of their important contributions their names are listed on the title page.

Statistical evaluations of lists of Semitic names are given in Ignace J. Gelb, Pierre M. Purves, and Allan A. MacRae, *Nuzi Personal Names*, OIP 57 (Chicago, 1943), p. 5 and in Martin Noth, *Die israelitischen Personennamen im Rahmen der gemeinsemitischen Namengebung* (Stuttgart, 1928), p. 87.

2. *Die Ostkanaanäer: Eine philologisch-historische Untersuchung über die Wanderschicht der sogenannten "Amoriter" in Babylonien* (Leipzig, 1926), pp. 9-49 and 92-93.

3. *Amorite Personal Names in the Mari Texts: A Structural and Lexical Study* (Baltimore, 1965), pp. 19-60.

4. *Die altbabylonischen Briefe und Urkunden aus Kisurra*, Freiburger altorientalische Studien, vol. 2 (Wiesbaden, 1978).

POSTSCRIPT OF DECEMBER 1979

As noted above, June 1976 marked the last date at which material from recently published sources could be included in this volume. Since that date, however, a number of publications have appeared, some of which contain important additions to the corpus. The following list contains a few new entries excerpted from scattered publications and also some corrections of the transliteration and analysis offered in this volume. The entries below are numbered in accordance with the corresponding entries in chapter 6, "Index of Names."

Add 66a ʾAB-I+DAŠUR A-BI-DA-ŠU-UR MESOPOTAMIA X-XI P. 27:19

Add 295a ʾAJA+ʿAMM-U-HU [A]-IA-ḪA-AM-MU-U$_2$ TIM II 96:3

Add 476a ḤANAN-UM+ʾIL A-NA-NU-UM-DINGIR FLP 1761, UR III

Add another reference to 426: UET IX 128:1, 6, UR III

Probably correct 693 JA-ʿḎAR+ʿIL AḪ-ZA-AR-I$_3$-DINGIR to JA-ʿḎAR+ʾIL A-AḪ-ZA-AR-I$_3$-DINGIR (Robert M. Whiting)

Correct 1520 ʾIL-I+ʾA-PTAN to ʾIL-A+ʾA-PTAN

Correct 1525 ʾIL-I+DAʿ-AT to ʾIL-A+DAʿ-AT

Correct 1549 ʾIL-I+MAʾD-I+ʾAḪ to ʾIL-A+MAʾD-I+ʾAḪ

Add 1751a QARAʾ+ʾIL GA-RA-DINGIR UET IX 128, UR III

Add 2106a ḪAʾL-U+ŠAMUʿ ḪA-LU-SA-MU-UḪ SYRIA L 279:12

Correct 2237 ḪAN-NA-D-EN-ZU to ḪA-AN-NA-D-EN-ZU

Add 2506a JI-KWUN+ʾEL I-KU-EL TA 1931, 141

Change the present analysis of BAʾB in 2733 ʾIL-I-Š+BAʾB-A to ʾIL-I-Š-BAWB-A

Add 2752a ʾIL-I+ME+JATAR I$_3$-LI$_2$-ME-A-TAR MESOPOTAMIA X-XI P. 10:5

Add 4728a LA+KIWN+PU-HU LA-KI-IN-PU-U$_2$ YOS XIII 459:8

Add 4373a LI+JI-TWUR+ʾAŠD-UM LI-TU-UR-AŠ-DU-UM JCS XXIX P. 147:14 AND SEAL

Add 4650a ME-KWIN-UM ME-KIN$_2$-NU-UM TIM V 23:2,9, AND SEAL

Add 4699a MILK-UM MI-IL-KU-UM TA 1931, 141

Add another reference to 4846: SYRIA L 279:3

Add 5077a NUN-U+RIMŠ-I D-NU-NU-RI-IM-SI? FEM SYRIA LII PL. IV

Delete 5585, since this entry is identical with 5680 (Robert M. Whiting)

Change the present analysis of BAʾB in 5908 ŠU+BAʾB-A to ŠU+BAWB-A

Correct 6639 ZUḪL-AN-UM ZU-UḪ$_3$-LA-NU-U[M] to .... U$_3$-ZU-UḪ$_3$-LA-NU-UM in accordance with a new join (Robert M. Whiting)

This list contains no citations from any of the larger publications listed below—specifically, those under Rouault, Limet, and Dalley et al.—or, of course, from any of the Ibla sources.

Dossin, Georges. *Correspondance féminine.* ARM 10. Paris, 1978. All sources excerpted from ARMT 10 (= TCL 31).

Birot, Maurice; Kupper, Jean-Robert; and Rouault, Olivier. *Répertoire analytique* (2ᵉ volume). *Tomes I-XIV, XVIII et textes divers hors-collection.* Première partie: *Noms propres.* ARM 16/1. Paris, 1979.

Heintz, Jean-Georges. *Index documentaire des textes de Mari*, fasc. 1: *Liste/Codage des textes; Index des ouvrages de référence.* ARM 17. Paris, 1975.

Birot, Maurice. *Lettres de Yaqqim-Addu gouverneur de Sagarâtum.* TCM 1. Paris, 1976. All sources excerpted from ARM 14.

Rouault, Olivier. *Mukannišum: Lettres et documents administratifs.* TCM 2. Paris, 1976 = Idem. *Mukannišum: L'Administration et l'économie palatiales à Mari.* ARM 18. Paris, 1977.

Limet, Henri. *Textes administratifs de l'époque des Šakkanakku.* TCM 3. Paris, 1976 = Idem. *Textes administratifs de l'époque des Šakkanakku.* ARM 19. Paris, 1976.

Dalley, Stephanie; Walker, C. B. F.; and Hawkins, J. D. *The Old Babylonian Tablets from Tell al Rimah.* London, 1976. Some sources were excerpted from earlier scattered publications.

Simmons, Stephen D. *Early Old Babylonian Documents.* YOS 14. New Haven and London, 1978. Harmal names were excerpted from the transliterations published by Simmons in *JCS* 13-15.

SYMBOLS

-	in the standard Assyriological transliterations, to separate graphemes (logographic and syllabic signs), as in *Sa-am-su-i-lu-na* or *Su-mu*-DINGIR
-	in the analysis section, to separate bound morphemes, as in /*Śamś-u+ʾil-u-na*/
-	in discussions only, to separate two or more elements in a name but without indicating the bound morphemes, as in /*Śamśu-ʾiluna*/
+	in the analysis section, to separate two or more elements, as in /*Śamś-u+ʾil-u-na*/
+	in references, to indicate the existence of other occurrences collected but not listed, as in "UCP X p. 56+"
/ /	to indicate a linguistic rather than a graphemic feature, as in /*Śamś-u+ʾil-u-na*/ (in the analysis section) or /*Śamśu-ʾiluna*/ (in discussions); see above
[ ]	in transliterations, to indicate destroyed portions of a name, as in *A-me-ir*-[....]
⸢ ⸣	in transliterations, to indicate partially destroyed portions of a name, as in *A-me-ir*-⸢....⸣
....	in the analysis section, to stand in place of destroyed portions of a name, as in /*ʾAmir*+..../, transliterated as *A-me-ir*-[....]
....	to stand in place of non-Amorite portions of a name, as in /*Śum-u+ʾIl*+..../, transliterated as *Su-mu*-DINGIR-*li-bur-ra-am* (Akkadian); or /*Mut*+..../, transliterated as *Mu-ut*-D-IGI-KUR (*Mu-ut*-^{d}IGI.KUR) (Sumerian)
....	to stand in place of unanalyzable portions of a name, as in /*Ji-jṣiʾ*+..../ (really /*Jīṣiʾ*+..../ or /*Jiṣiʾ*+..../), transliterated as *I-zi-iš-ma-aḫ*

ABBREVIATIONS OF SOURCES

I - XV	Georges Dossin et al. Archives royales de Mari (TCL, vols. 22-31). Paris, 1946-67. Texts in cuneiform.
A	Unpublished tablets in the Oriental Institute, University of Chicago.
A.	D. J. Wiseman. *The Alalakh Tablets*. London, 1953. Some texts published in *JCS* 8 and 13.
ABB	Altbabylonische Briefe in Umschrift und Übersetzung. Leiden, 1964-.
ABL	Robert Francis Harper. *Assyrian and Babylonian Letters Belonging to the Kouyunjik Collections of the British Museum*. Chicago, 1892-1914.
AJSL	*American Journal of Semitic Languages and Literatures*. Chicago, 1884-1941.
Ann. arch. syr.	*Annales archéologiques arabes syriennes* (1951-65 called *Annales archéologiques de Syrie*). Damascus, 1951-.
AOAT	Alter Orient und Altes Testament. Neukirchen-Vluyn and Kevelaer, 1968-.
APN	See Tallqvist, *APN*.
ARMT	Georges Dossin et al. Archives royales de Mari. Paris, 1950-. Texts in transliteration.
B	Theo Bauer. *Die Ostkanaanäer: Eine philologisch-historische Untersuchung über die Wanderschicht der sogenannten "Amoriter" in Babylonien*. Leipzig, 1926.
Bab.	*Babyloniaca*. Paris, 1907-37.
Baghd. Mitt.	*Baghdader Mitteilungen*. Berlin, 1964-.
Bahrein unp.	An unpublished text from Bahrein, discussed in section 0.1.
Balkan, *Letter*	Kemal Balkan. *Letter of King Anum-Hirbi of Mama to King Warshama of Kanish*. Türk Tarih Kurumu, Yayınlarından, ser. 7, vol. 31a. Ankara, 1957.
BASOR	*Bulletin of the American Schools of Oriental Research*. South Hadley, Mass. et al., 1919-.
Bauer	See *B*.
BE	Babylonian Expedition of the University of Pennsylvania. Series A: Cuneiform Texts. Philadelphia, 1893-1914.
BER	Babylonian Expedition of the University of Pennsylvania. Series D: Researches and Treatises. Philadelphia, 1904-10.
BIN	Babylonian Inscriptions in the Collection of James B. Nies. New Haven, Conn., 1917-.
Birot, *TEA*	Maurice Birot. *Tablettes économiques et administratives d'époque babylonienne ancienne*. Paris, 1969.
BM	Unpublished tablets in the collections of the British Museum.
Bottéro	See M.
Buccellati	Giorgio Buccellati. *The Amorites of the Ur III Period*. Pubblicazioni del Seminario di Semitistica. Ricerche, vol. 1. Naples, 1966. See I and U.
Bull. Acad. Belg.	*Bulletin de la classe des lettres ... de l'Académie Royale de Belgique*. Brussels, 1899-.
C	C. J. Gadd. "Tablets from Chagar Bazar and Tall Brak, 1937-38." *Iraq* 7 (1940), pp. 22-66.
C II	Oswald Loretz. "Texte aus Chagar Bazar." In *Lišān mitḫurti: Festschrift Wolfram Freiherr von Soden*, edited by W. Röllig and M. Dietrich, pp. 199-260. AOAT 1. Kevelaer and Neukirchen-Vluyn, 1969. Republished as *Texte aus Chagar Bazar und Tell Brak*. Pt. 1. AOAT 3/1. Kevelaer and Neukirchen-Vluyn, 1969.
Carnegie, *Cat.*	Helen Carnegie. *Catalogue of the Collection of Antique Gems Formed by James, Ninth Earl of Southesk, K.T.* London, 1908.
CCT	Cuneiform Texts from Cappadocian Tablets in the British Museum. London, 1921-.
Chantre	Ernest Chantre. *Recherches archéologiques dans l'Asie Occidentale. Mission en Cappadoce 1893-1894*. Paris, 1898.
Çığ	M. Çığ, H. Kızılyay, and F. R. Kraus. *Eski Babil zamanına ait Nippur hukukî vesikaları. Altbabylonische Rechtsurkunden aus Nippur*. EEMY 3/4. Istanbul, 1952.
Clay, *PNCP*	Albert T. Clay. *Personal Names from Cuneiform Inscriptions of the Cassite Period*. YOSR 1. New Haven, Conn., 1912.
Collon, *Ala. Seals*	Dominique Collon. *The Seal Impressions from Tell Atchana/Alalakh*. AOAT 27. Kevelaer, 1975.
CT	Cuneiform Texts from Babylonian Tablets, &c. in the British Museum. London, 1896-.
De Clercq	Louis de Clercq and A. de Ridder. *Collection de Clercq. Catalogue*. Paris, 1888-1912.
De Gen., *Kich*	Henri de Genouillac. *Fouilles françaises d'el-ᵓAkhymer. Premières recherches archéologiques à Kich, mission d'Henri de Genouillac, 1911-1912*. Paris, 1924-25. Also *Kich*.
Delaporte, *Cat.*	Louis Delaporte. *Catalogue des cylindres orientaux et des cachets assyro-babyloniens, perses et syro-cappadociens de la Bibliothèque Nationale*. Paris, 1910.
Delaporte, *CCL*	Louis Delaporte. *Musée du Louvre. Catalogue des cylindres, cachets et pierres gravées de style oriental*. Paris, 1920-23.
Dossin	See I - XV and ARMT.
Ebeling	See *KAJ*.
EBPN	Hermann Ranke. *Early Babylonian Personal*

	Names from the Published Tablets of the So-Called Hammurabi Dynasty. BER 3. Philadelphia, 1905.
Edzard, *Der*	Dietz Otto Edzard. *Altbabylonische Rechts- und Wirtschaftsurkunden aus Tell ed-Dēr im Iraq Museum, Baghdad*. Bayerische Akademie der Wissenschaften. Philosophisch-historische Klasse. Abhandlungen, n. s. 72. Munich, 1970.
EEMY	Eski Eserler ve Müzeler Genel Müdürlüğü Yayınlarından, ser. 3. Istanbul, 1947-.
Eisser	See *EL*.
EK	S. Langdon and L. Ch. Watelin. *Excavations at Kish*. Vols. 1, 3, 4. Paris, 1924-34.
EL	Georg Eisser and Julius Lewy. *Die altassyrischen Rechtsurkunden vom Kültepe*. MVAG, vol. 33. Leipzig, 1930. MVAG, vol. 35/3. Leipzig, 1935.
Figulla, *Cat.*	H. H. Figulla. *Catalogue of the Babylonian Tablets in the British Museum*. Vol. 1. London, 1961.
Finet	See M.
FLP	Unpublished tablets in the Free Library of Philadelphia.
FM	Ignace J. Gelb. *Old Akkadian Inscriptions in Chicago Natural History Museum: Texts of Legal and Business Interest*. Fieldiana: Anthropology, vol. 44, no. 2. Chicago, 1955.
Frank	See Frank, *SKT*.
Frank, *SKT*	Carl Frank, ed. *Strassburger Keilschrifttexte in sumerischer und babylonischer Sprache*. Berlin and Leipzig, 1928. Also Frank.
Gadd	See *C*.
Gautier	J. E. Gautier. *Archives d'une famille de Dilbat au temps de la première dynastie de Babylone*. Mémoires publiés par les membres de l'Institut Français d'Archéologie Orientale du Caire, vol. 26. Cairo, 1908.
Gelb	See *FM*, *Grammar*, "Lingua," and MAD.
Goetze, *Kizz.*	Albrecht Goetze. *Kizzuwatna and the Problem of Hittite Geography*. YOSR 22. New Haven, Conn., 1940.
Gordon, *SCT*	Cyrus H. Gordon. *Smith College Tablets: 110 Cuneiform Texts Selected from the College Collection*. Smith College Studies in History, vol. 38. Northhampton, Mass., 1952.
Grammar	Ignace J. Gelb. *Grammar of Amorite*. Forthcoming.
Grant, *Hav.*	Elihu Grant. *The Haverford Symposium on Archaeology and the Bible*. New Haven, Conn., 1938. Also *Hav. Symp.*
Hager, *Diss.*	Joseph Hager. *A Dissertation on the Newly Discovered Babylonian Inscriptions*. London, 1801.
Harper	See *ABL*.
Harris	Rivkah Harris. "The Archive of the Sin Temple in Khafajah (Tutub)." *JCS* 9 (1955), pp. 31-58, 59-88, and 91-120.
Hav. Symp.	See Grant, *Hav.*
Hilprecht AV	*Hilprecht Anniversary Volume. Studies in Assyriology and Archaeology Dedicated to Hermann V. Hilprecht* ... Leipzig et al., 1909.
Holma	Harri Holma. *Zehn altbabylonische Tontafeln in Helsingfors*. Acta Societatis Scientiarum Fennicae, vol. 45, no. 3. Helsinki, 1914.
Hrozný	See *ICK*.
HSM	Unpublished tablets in the Harvard Semitic Museum.
Huffmon, *APNMT*	Herbert Bardwell Huffmon. *Amorite Personal Names in the Mari Texts: A Structural and Lexical Study*. Baltimore, 1965.
I	Isin names in Giorgio Buccellati. *The Amorites of the Ur III Period*. Pubblicazioni del Seminario di Semitistica. Ricerche, vol. 1. Naples, 1966. Pp. 125-85. See Buccellati and U.
ICK	Bedřich Hrozný. *Inscriptions cunéiformes du Kultépé*. Vol. 1. Monografie archivu orientálního, vol. 14. Prague, 1952. L. Matouš. *Inscriptions cunéiformes du Kultépé*. Vol. 2. Prague, 1962.
IM	Unpublished tablets in the collections of the Iraq Museum, Baghdad. Also Iraq Museum.
Iraq	*Iraq*. London, 1934-.
Iraq Museum	Unpublished tablets in the collections of the Iraq Museum, Baghdad. Also IM.
ITT	F. Thureau-Dangin, Henri de Genouillac, and L. Delaporte. *Inventaire des tablettes de Tello conservées au Musée Impérial Ottoman*. 5 vols. Paris, 1910-21.
Jacobsen, *CTC*	Thorkild Jacobsen. *Cuneiform Texts in the National Museum, Copenhagen, Chiefly of Economical Contents*. Leiden, 1939.
JAOS	*Journal of the American Oriental Society*. Boston et al., 1843-.
JCS	*Journal of Cuneiform Studies*. New Haven, Conn. et al., 1947-.
JEA	*Journal of Egyptian Archaeology*. London, 1914-.
Jean, *ŠA*	Charles-F. Jean. *Šumer et Akkad*. Paris, 1923.
Jean, *T. Sifr*	Charles-F. Jean. *Tell Sifr: Textes cunéiformes conservés au British Museum*. Paris, 1931.
JNES	*Journal of Near Eastern Studies*. Chicago, 1942-.
KAJ	Erich Ebeling. *Keilschrifttexte aus Assur juristischen Inhalts*. WVDOG 50. Leipzig, 1927.
Kich	See De Gen., *Kich*.
Kienast	See *Kisurra*.
King, *LIH*	L. W. King. *The Letters and Inscriptions of Ḫammurabi, King of Babylon, about B.C. 2200*. London, 1898-1900. Also *LIH*.
Kisurra	Names excerpted from a manuscript that was published as Burkhart Kienast, *Die altbabylonischen Briefe und Urkunden aus Kisurra*, Freiburger Altorientalische Studien, vol. 2 (Wiesbaden, 1978).
Kızılyay	See *Çığ*.
Kraus	See ABB and *Çığ*.

KTS	Julius Lewy. *Die altassyrischen Texte vom Kültepe bei Kaisarīje.* Constantinople, 1926.
Kupper, *L'icon.*	Jean-Robert Kupper. *L'iconographie du dieu Amurru dans la glyptique de la Ire dynastie babylonienne.* Académie Royale de Belgique. Classe des lettres ... Mémoires. Collection in-8°, ser. 2, vol. 55, fasc. 1. Brussels, 1961.
Kupper, *Nom.*	Jean-Robert Kupper. *Les nomades en Mésopotamie au temps des rois de Mari.* Bibliothèque de la Faculté de Philosophie et Lettres de l'Université de Liège. Fasc. 142. Paris, 1957.
Laessøe, *Shemshāra*	Jørgen Laessøe. *The Shemshāra Tablets.* Arkaeologisk-kunsthistoriske Meddelelser, vol. 4, no. 3. Copenhagen, 1959. Also *Shemshāra.*
Langdon	S. Langdon. "Tablets from Kiš." *PSBA* 33 (1911), pp. 185-96 and 232-42.
Legrain, *TRU*	L. Legrain. *Le temps des rois d'Ur.* Paris, 1912.
Lewy	See *EL* and *KTS.*
LIH	See King, *LIH.*
Limet, *Sceaux cass.*	Henri Limet. *Les légendes des sceaux cassites.* Académie Royale de Belgique. Classe des lettres ... Mémoires. Collection in-8°, ser. 2, vol. 60, fasc. 2. Brussels, 1971.
"Lingua"	Ignace J. Gelb. "La lingua degli Amoriti." *Rendiconti della Classe di Scienze morali, storiche e filologiche della Accademia Nazionale dei Lincei,* ser. 8, vol. 13, fasc. 3-4 (1958), pp. 143-64.
Loretz	See *C II.*
M	Mari names excerpted from ARM(T) 1-5 in Jean Bottéro and André Finet. *Répertoire analytique des tomes I à V.* ARMT 15. Paris, 1954. Pp. 120-63.
MAD	I. J. Gelb. Materials for the Assyrian Dictionary. Chicago, 1952-.
MAH	Unpublished tablets in the collection of the Musée d'Art et d'Histoire, Geneva.
MAM	André Parrot. Mission archéologique de Mari. Institut Français d'Archéologie de Beyrouth. Bibliothèque archéologique et historique, vols. 65, 68, 69, 70, 86, 87. Paris, 1956-.
MAOG	Mitteilungen der Altorientalischen Gesellschaft. Leipzig, 1925-43.
Matouš	See *ICK.*
MDP	Délégation en Perse. Mémoires. Paris, 1900-.
Meissner	Bruno Meissner. *Beiträge zum altbabylonischen Privatrecht.* Leipzig, 1893.
Mél. Syr.	*Mélanges syriens offerts à Monsieur René Dussaud.* Haut-Commissariat de la République Française en Syrie et au Liban. Service des Antiquités. Bibliothèque archéologique et historique, vol. 30. Paris, 1939.
Moortgat	Anton Moortgat. *Vorderasiatische Rollsiegel. Ein Beitrag zur Geschichte der Steinschneidekunst.* Berlin, 1940.
MRS	Mission de Ras-Shamra. Paris, 1936-.
MVAG	Mitteilungen der Vorderasiatisch-Aegyptischen Gesellschaft. Berlin and Leipzig, 1896-1944.
MVN	Materiali per il Vocabolario Neosumerico. Rome, 1974-.
NT	Unpublished tablets excavated at Nippur by the Oriental Institute of the University of Chicago and allied institutions.
OIP	Oriental Institute Publications. Chicago, 1924-.
OLZ	*Orientalistische Literaturzeitung.* Berlin, 1898-.
Or. n. s.	*Orientalia,* new series. Rome, 1932-.
Owen	See Totten.
Parrot	See MAM and *SM.*
PBS	University of Pennsylvania. The University Museum. Publications of the Babylonian Section. Philadelphia, 1911-.
Pinches, *Berens*	Theophilus G. Pinches. *The Babylonian Tablets of the Berens Collection.* London, 1915.
Pinches, *Peek*	Theophilus G. Pinches. *Inscribed Babylonian Tablets in the Possession of Sir Henry Peek, Bart.* London, 1888.
PSBA	*Proceedings of the Society of Biblical Archaeology.* London, 1879-1918.
RA	*Revue d'assyriologie et d'archéologie orientale.* Paris, 1884-.
Ranke	See *EBPN.*
Renc. Ass.	Rencontre assyriologique internationale. Leiden et al., 1950-.
RES	*Revue des études sémitiques et Babyloniaca.* Paris, 1934-45.
Riftin	Aleksandr Pavlovich Riftin. *Staro-vavilonskie yuridicheskie i administrativnye dokumenty v sobraniyakh SSSR.* Moscow and Leningrad, 1937.
RLA	*Reallexikon der Assyriologie.* Berlin and Leipzig, 1928-.
RS	*Revue sémitique d'épigraphie et d'histoire anciennes.* Paris, 1893-1914.
Rutten	M. Rutten. "Un lot de tablettes de Mananâ." *RA* 52 (1958), pp. 208-25; 53 (1959), pp. 77-96; 54 (1960), pp. 19-40 and 147-52.
SAKI	F. Thureau-Dangin. *Die sumerischen und akkadischen Königsinschriften.* Vorderasiatische Bibliothek, vol. 1/1. Leipzig, 1907.
Sauren, *WUG*	Herbert Sauren. *Wirtschaftsurkunden aus der Zeit der III. Dynastie von Ur im Besitz des Musée d'Art et d'Histoire in Genf.* Pubblicazioni del Seminario di Semitistica. Ricerche, vol. 6. Naples, 1969.
Scheil	Vincent Scheil. *Une saison de fouilles à Sippar.* Mémoires publiés par les membres de l'Institut Français d'Archéologie Orientale du Caire, vol. 1. Cairo, 1902.
Shemshāra	See Laessøe, *Shemshāra.*
Sigrist unpubl.	Unpublished Old Babylonian texts.
Simmons	Stephen D. Simmons. "Early Old Babylonian Tablets from Ḫarmal and Elsewhere." *JCS* 13 (1959), pp. 71-93, 105-19; 14 (1960), pp. 23-32, 49-55, 75-87, 117-25;

	and 15 (1961), pp. 49-83. Now published as YOS 14.
SM	André Parrot, ed. *Studia Mariana* ... Documenta et monumenta orientis antiqui, vol. 4. Leiden, 1950.
Speleers	Louis Speleers. *Recueil des inscriptions de l'Asie Antérieure des Musées Royaux du Cinquantenaire à Bruxelles*. Brussels, 1925.
Strassm.	J. N. Strassmaier. *Texte altbabylonischer Verträge aus Warka*. Abhandlungen des Fünften Internationalen Orientalisten-Congresses gehalten zu Berlin im September 1881. Beilage. Berlin, 1882.
Sumer	*Sumer*. Baghdad, 1945-.
Symb. Böhl	M. A. Beek et al., eds. *Symbolae biblicae et mesopotamicae Francisco Mario Theodoro de Liagre Böhl dedicatae*. Leiden, 1973.
Syria	*Syria*. Paris, 1920-.
Szlechter, *TJ*	Emile Szlechter. *Tablettes juridiques et administratives de la IIIe Dynastie d'Ur et de la Ire Dynastie de Babylone*. Publications de l'Institut de Droit Romain de l'Université de Paris, vol. 21. Paris, 1963.
TA	Unpublished tablets from Tell Asmar in the Oriental Institute, University of Chicago.
Tallqvist, *APN*	Knut L. Tallqvist. *Assyrian Personal Names*. Acta Societatis Scientiarum Fennicae, vol. 43, no. 1. Helsinki, 1914. Also *APN*.
TCL	Musée du Louvre. Textes cunéiformes. Paris, 1910-.
TCM	Textes cunéiformes de Mari. Paris, 1976-.
Thureau-Dangin	See *ITT* and *SAKI*.
TIM	Texts in the Iraq Museum. Baghdad et al., 1964-.
TLB	Nederlandsch Archeologisch-Philologisch Instituut voor het Nabije Oosten, Leyden. *Tabulae Cuneiformes à F. M. Th. de Liagre Böhl collectae*. Leiden, 1954-.
Totten	Now published by David I. Owen. "Cuneiform Texts in the Collection of Professor Norman Totten." *Mesopotamia* 8-9 (1973-74), pp. 145-66.
TTKB	*Türk Tarih Kurumu. Belleten*. Ankara, 1937-.
U	Ur III names in Giorgio Buccellati. *The Amorites of the Ur III Period*. Pubblicazioni del Seminario di Semitistica. Ricerche, vol. 1. Naples, 1966. Pp. 125-85. See Buccellati and I.
UCP	University of California Publications in Semitic Philology, vols. 9-10. Berkeley, Cal., 1927-40.
UET	Publications of the Joint Expedition of the British Museum and of the Museum of the University of Pennsylvania to Mesopotamia. Ur Excavations. Texts. London, 1928-.
VAS	Vorderasiatische Schriftdenkmäler der Königlichen Museen zu Berlin. Leipzig, 1907-.
Voix	Institut des Hautes Etudes de Belgique. *La voix de l'opposition en Mesopotamie. Colloque organisé par l'Institut des Hautes Etudes de Belgique 19 et 20 mars 1973*. Brussels, n.d.
Walters	Stanley D. Walters. *Water for Larsa: An Old Babylonian Archive Dealing with Irrigation*. Yale Near Eastern Researches, vol. 4. New Haven, Conn. and London, 1970.
Waterman	Leroy Waterman. *Business Documents of the Hammurapi Period from the British Museum*. London, 1916. Also published in *AJSL* 29 and 30.
Wiseman	See *A*.
WVDOG	Wissenschaftliche Veröffentlichung der Deutschen Orient-Gesellschaft. Leipzig and Berlin, 1900-.
YBC	Unpublished tablets in the Babylonian Collection, Yale University Library.
Yondorf	Unpublished tablets belonging to the late Milton Yondorf of Chicago.
YOS	Yale Oriental Series. New Haven, Conn., 1915-.
YOSR	Yale Oriental Series, Researches. New Haven, Conn., 1912-.
ZA	*Zeitschrift für Assyriologie und vorderasiatische Archäologie*. Leipzig et al., 1886-.
ZDPV	*Zeitschrift des Deutschen Palästina-Vereins*. Stuttgart et al., 1878-.

OTHER ABBREVIATIONS AND TERMS

ACC	accusative
ADJ	adjective
ADV	adverb
B	basic stem, Qal
BH	BH stem
BN	BN stem
BŠT	BŠT stem
BT	BT stem
CAPP	Cappadocian
CASE	case tablet
D	double stem, Piel
DATE	year date
DET	determinative (pronoun)
DN	name of a divinity
DŠT	DŠT stem
DT	DT stem
DU	dual
EARLY OB	early Old Babylonian Tell Asmar texts
EDGE	edge of a tablet
FEM	feminine
FIELD	name of a field
FN	feminine name
GEN	genitive
GN	geographical name
IMPV	imperative
INDEF	indefinite (pronoun)
INTERR	interrogative (pronoun)
KING	name of a king
LATE	post-Old Babylonian occurrences from Alalakh IV, Ugarit, Late Assyrian, etc.
L.E.	left edge
LO.E.	lower edge
MASC	masculine
MN	masculine name
MOUNT	name of a mountain
NOM	nominative
OA	Old Assyrian
OB	Old Babylonian
OBV	obverse
OLDER OB	early Old Babylonian Tell Asmar texts
P	page
PART	participle
PASS	passive
PERS	personal (pronoun)
PL	plural
POSS	possessive (pronoun)
POST-U	post-Ur III
PREP	preposition
PRON	pronoun
PSARG	pre-Sargonic
R.E.	right edge
REL	relative (pronoun)
REV	reverse
RIVER	name of a river
Š	Š stem
SARG	Sargonic
SEAL	seal inscription
ŠT	ŠT stem
SUBST	substantive
TRIBE	name of a tribe
U.E.	upper edge
UNPUBL	unpublished

0. INTRODUCTION

0.1. Amorite Names

Our knowledge of Amorite is based almost exclusively on the analysis of proper names. The majority are personal names, but there is also a scattering of geographical names and of names of divinities.

The names are found in cuneiform texts written in the Akkadian (Assyro-Babylonian) language. In content, the texts are mainly letters or administrative and legal documents. The texts may refer to individuals by name or may list them in groups ranging from only a few persons to several hundred. The longest such list, which names 833 individuals, is a Mari administrative text published by G. Dossin[1] and indexed by J.-M. Aynard.[2]

Since 1926, when Bauer's first extended treatment of the Amorite language appeared,[3] the available sources have increased enormously. More important, most of the new sources have come not from Babylonia, the area on which Bauer's study was based, but from sites in the areas where the Amorites lived, such as Mari, Chagar Bazar, and Alalakh (level IX). As expected, these new sources cite Amorite names in a form closer to the original and represent them more consistently than do the Babylonian sources, in which the names are often garbled due to ignorance of the Amorite language on the part of the scribes living in a non-Amorite milieu. Thus the non-Babylonian materials offer a new and more reliable basis for a thorough phonological and morphological analysis.

My interest in Amorite is an outgrowth of the Seminar in Proto-West Semitic, which I held in the spring of 1956 at the University of Chicago. In 1957-58 I prepared a large work on the grammar and lexicon of the Amorite language, a brief digest of which was published as "La lingua degli Amoriti."[4]

In order to achieve a more or less synchronic reconstruction of the language, my work from the beginning was centered on the Old Babylonian period, for which by far the largest number of Amorite names is documented. Names from the few earlier sources, mainly Sumerian administrative texts of the Ur III period, were collected to demonstrate the linguistic unity of the Ur III and Old Babylonian names. Some occurrences from post-Old Babylonian sources, such as Alalakh IV, Ugarit, and Qatna, were adduced, but only in cases where a point weakly documented in the Old Babylonian period needed bolstering from additional evidence.

Before the terms "East Canaanite" or "Canaanite" entered the field with the publication of Bauer's *Ostkanaanäer*, Assyriologists generally applied the term "Amorite" to these Old Babylonian names. Recent studies on this subject employ only the term Amorite.[5]

The Old Babylonian names that we call Amorite generally appear in the Akkadian texts without any ethnolinguistic designation to link them with either the country Amurru or with the Amorite people or language. In the past it was assumed that these names should be called Amorite mainly because they began to appear in mass in Babylonia after, and in consequence of, the Amorite invasions and conquests that took place at the end of the Ur III dynasty and the beginning of the Old Babylonian period.

In contrast to the names of the Old Babylonian period, the Ur III names regularly bear the designation MAR.TU "Amorite." The Old Babylonian names that bear no ethnolinguistic designation are practically identical with the Ur III names. This, as I had noted in 1961,[6] has been demonstrated convincingly by Buccellati.[7]

In addition to the Ur III sources, texts of the early Old Babylonian (Isin-Larsa) period also regularly list names with the MAR.TU "Amorite" designation. These are the several dozen names from Isin, published mainly in BIN IX and collected and analyzed by Buccellati,[8] and many more found in unpublished texts from Tell Asmar (ancient Eshnunna), which Robert Whiting has been studying for the past few years. Perhaps the most important of the latter is the text TA 1930, 615.[9]

Authors of recent studies on the Amorites have stressed the fact that the major Amorite areas lay west of Babylonia, namely, in Upper Mesopotamia (Mari and Chagar Bazar) and Syria (Alalakh).[10] The evidence connecting the Amorites with the areas east and south of Babylonia is discussed by Buccellati.[11] While he called such evidence "quite elusive," he did point out the connection between Dilmun (modern Bahrein) and the Amorites (*Dilmun*^{KI} *ù*

1. Georges Dossin, "Deux listes nominatives du règne de Sûmu-Iamam," *RA* 65 (1971), pp. 40-66.

2. J.-M. Aynard, "Index des noms de personnes de G. Dossin, *RA* 65, 40-66," ibid., pp. 184-90.

3. Theo Bauer, *Die Ostkanaanäer: Eine philologisch-historische Untersuchung über die Wanderschicht der sogenannten "Amoriter" in Babylonien* (Leipzig, 1926).

4. Ignace J. Gelb, "La lingua degli Amoriti," *Rendiconti della Classe di Scienze morali, storiche e filologiche della Accademia Nazionale dei Lincei*, ser. 8, vol. 13, fasc. 3-4 (1958), pp. 143-64.

5. Cf., e.g., I. J. Gelb, "The Early History of the West Semitic Peoples," *JCS* 15 (1961), pp. 27-47, especially pp. 30 ff.; Herbert Bardwell Huffmon, *Amorite Personal Names in the Mari Texts: A Structural and Lexical Study* (Baltimore, 1965); and Giorgio Buccellati, *The Amorites of the Ur III Period*, Pubblicazioni del Seminario di Semitistica, Ricerche, vol. 1 (Naples, 1966).

6. Gelb, *JCS* 15 (1961), pp. 33-34.

7. Buccellati, *Amorites*.

8. Ibid., pp. 23-34.

9. Published in I. J. Gelb, "An Old Babylonian List of Amorites," *JAOS* 88 (1968), pp. 39-46.

10. See, e.g., Buccellati, *Amorites*, pp. 235-47 and 250-52.

11. Ibid., pp. 247-52.

MAR.TU-*ne* in BIN IX 405), a connection which now appears to receive support from a text recently excavated by a Danish expedition at the site of Qalᶜat in Bahrein. The tablet became known to me from a rough copy brought from Denmark by Juris Zarins, a former student of mine. The text, which I would like to date to the post-Ur III or the Isin-Larsa period, is a simple list of three persons, the third being the son of the first. It reads:

1) 1 *Ia-a-bi-na-im* /*Janbiᵓ-naᶜim*/
2) 1 DINGIR-*mi-il-kum* /*ᵓIla-milkum*/
Rev. 3) 1 *I-zi-ta-am-bu* /*Jīṣiᵓ-tambu*/
4) DUMU *I-a-bi-na-im* /*Janbiᵓ-naᶜim*/

All we can say for certain about these three Bahrein names is that they are all clearly Amorite in the sense that we understand and use the term, thus confirming the connection between Dilmun and Amorites deduced from BIN IX 405, cited above. The extension of the Amorites eastward toward the Persian Gulf is also suggested by a passage in the text TA 1930, 615,[12] which notes the derivation of one or more Amorites *a-ab-ba-ta*, "from the Sea," that is, from the Sea-Land or from the land across the Sea, which can be only the Persian Gulf.

To summarize briefly, we find that the geographical distribution of names that are here called Amorite extends from Upper Mesopotamia and Syria in the west, through Babylonia (including the Diyala District) in the center, to areas east of Babylonia as far as Bahrein.

The materials collected from these areas in this volume include all clearly Semitic but non-Akkadian names. Such names may bear an ethnic designation; much more frequently they do not. When they do bear such a designation, it may be Amorite or it may be that of the Ḫanians, Sutians, or some other people, whose relation to the Amorites is as yet unclear. The names listed here may include some which could possibly be Akkadian but which may be justifiably treated as Amorite because they happen to occur in a list of other good West Semitic names, or by virtue of stated family relationships. In doubtful cases, the tendency was to include rather than to disregard.

Considering the very wide area (extending from Syria to Bahrein) from which names have been collected, it is quite possible, nay probable, that the names encompassed in this volume represent more than the one ethnolinguistic unit, the Amorites. On that score, the warning of von Soden against the notion of a monolithic Amorite appears fully justified.[13] In fact, the recent discovery of the Ibla texts in Syria leads one to pause for thought, as it furnishes evidence that the area included a greater linguistic variety than had hitherto been supposed. I hope to discuss these linguistic and dialectal problems in a future article.

12. Gelb, *JAOS* 88 (1968), p. 43.

13. Wolfram von Soden, "Zur Einteilung der semitischen Sprachen," *Wiener Zeitschrift für die Kunde des Morgenlandes* 56 (1960), pp. 177-91, especially pp. 185 ff.

0.2. History of the Computer Project

The early summer of 1976 marked the end of several stages in the history of the Amorite Computer Project, which began to germinate in 1960 and 1963 when I had the occasion, during visits to Prague, to discuss my plans for preparing the Amorite work for publication with Stanislav Segert, then a research fellow in Semitic philology at the Oriental Institute of the Czechoslovak Academy. Because of his own involvement in the preparation of a comparative dictionary of the West Semitic languages, Segert, from the start, showed great interest in my lexical work on Amorite as a part of his overall project. Since the work on his comparative dictionary was based on the use of a computer, he persuaded me to use a computer in the Amorite project. As a result, we began to take steps to enable Segert to come to Chicago for a prolonged stay so that he and I could coordinate our planning. Segert came to Chicago in December 1965 and stayed for about six months. We divided our work in accordance with our interests. I concentrated on the Amorite language, while Segert worked on materials from the South Arabic area. Using the same IBM 7090 computer and a similar program, Segert accepted my code for the Semitic phonemes, with some small changes.

After Segert's return to Prague, I continued my work until early 1967. Professor Victor Yngve and his student Stephen P. Soulé were in charge of the computer programing, and Miss Joyce Bartels supervised the execution of the project.

The procedure followed in collecting and integrating the Amorite materials consisted of three steps. First, all names were transliterated on 3- by 5-inch white cards. Next, the names were copied on pink cards and the analysis was added. And, finally, punch cards were prepared from the pink cards. I will outline briefly the way each of these steps was carried out and will give the reasons for some of the decisions made along the way. A detailed description of the computer processing, written by Vance and Whiting, appears in section 0.6, "Computer Report."

All the names that I considered to be either unquestionably or possibly Amorite were collected in standard Assyriological transliteration on white cards in the following form:

Áš-du-um-la-a-bu-um *Sumer* V 142

Each card contained a single source reference. In addition, many cards contained notes about place of origin, date of source, and family relations of the person bearing the name, as well as discussion of tentative interpretation(s), questionable points of transliteration, and the like. These cards were filed under the first element of the name (in the above case *ᵓaśdum*), with cross references to other elements (in the above case *la* and *ᵓabum*). The entries were filed in the roman order as applied to the Semitic root consonants.

The next step was to rewrite the white cards on pink cards, combining all occurrences of the same name on one pink card and adding the analysis in the following form:

Áš-du-um-la-a-bu-um *ᵓAśd-um+la+ᵓab-um* *Sumer* V 142+

As will be explained in detail in section 0.3, the dash was used to separate graphemic elements in the transliteration, and of bound morphemes in the analysis section; the plus mark was used to separate the different elements of a name in the analysis section and to indicate the existence of additional occurrences in the references section. For some names a helpful abbreviation, symbol, or other information was added to the analysis and reference, such as "FN" for feminine name, "QATNA" for the geographical origin. The pink cards were alphabetized in the same order as the white cards. All the work on the white and pink cards was done by myself exclusively.

The information from the pink cards was next transferred by keypunchers to standard-size computer punch cards, with the order reversed from transliteration-analysis to analysis-transliteration. The 80 spaces available on the punch card were divided in the following way: spaces 1-24 were reserved for the analysis, spaces 25-54 for an asterisk followed by the transliteration, and spaces 55-80 for a period followed by the reference(s). Occasionally, when the transliteration extended beyond the space allotted to it, the part containing the reference(s) was moved to the right by a corresponding number of spaces.

The result of the 1966-67 work was a computer list of about 4,000 names, given in more or less the same form, although not in the same order, as in chapter 6, "Index of Names."

After a brief interval, my work on the Amorite project was resumed in March 1969 and continued throughout 1970. Stuart-Morgan Vance, at that time a student in linguistics, replaced Soulé as the programer, and Robert Whiting, then a student in Assyriology, replaced Miss Bartels as the supervisor of the project. During this stage the list of names was increased to almost 5,000 and the chapters pertaining to stems, roots, prefixes and suffixes, and what was then called "root vocalism" were completed.

Quantitatively, the output may have looked impressive, but it had two shortcomings. First, the list was printed with diacritics placed beside the letters rather than below them, which made it difficult for users unaccustomed to this notation to read it. Second, there were a number of bugs that made extensive corrections necessary. Only a person working with computers is aware of the incredible amount of time that some very simple corrections require. In this study, for instance, a misplaced dot may play havoc with the ordering of entries in at least four to as many as twelve different places, depending on the number of bound and free morphemes in a name. Making the corrections required by such a misplacement of a dot involved not only changing diacritics but also cutting out whole lines and transferring them to the right places.

As it turned out, the correction of these undesirable features in the 1970 material had to be delayed from month to month because of other commitments, and the longer the delay, the more new material accumulated that had to be added. The final setback was when the University of Chicago decided in 1972 to replace the old IBM 7090 with a new, greatly improved IBM 360/65. As a result, our programs, written in Comit II for the earlier computer, had to be adapted to the new computer, a procedure that involved much effort and experimentation. The four-year delay came to an end in October 1974 with the decision to revise and complete the work. The changeover to the new computer was successfully achieved with the help of Professor Yngve, the author of Comit II, and of Miss Eleanor Lewis. Vance and Whiting, both by then Ph.D.'s, continued to carry out their earlier responsibilities.

The work, completed in January of 1975, contained about 6,500 names and approximated in size and content the edition of 1970. Only the chapter that contained the list of names, produced according to the earlier computer program, was left in the old typography. All other chapters have been adapted to the new typography with the help of Mr. Clive Church of the Computation Center. Alas, having eliminated the old bugs, a number of quite disturbing new ones had crept into the program. Among them, one alone —the accidental omission of the suffix NI in the typography program—necessitated some 100 corrections.

The present volume is the result of work done in May-June of 1976, in which Vance and Whiting supervised their respective spheres of competence. In the meantime, Whiting had acquired enough expertise in computer matters to enable him to contribute substantially to the programing of certain sections.

The form and content of the final work underwent a number of important changes. Only the first three chapters —on stems, roots, and prefixes and suffixes—retained their earlier form. The old chapter on root vocalism, equal in form and size to each of the chapters on stems and roots, was completely revised to conform with the new chapter on phoneme count, and was renamed "Stem Count." Whiting and Vance expanded the new chapter on phoneme count, started as an exercise by Peter T. Daniels in my seminar in winter 1975, and made it compatible with the overall presentation.

The old list of names was increased to 6,662 entries by the addition of over 100 names punched with the help of Mr. Peter Steinkeller. More important, the list was accommodated to the new typography program and reordered by Whiting in the strict alphabetical sequence of the transliterations. The bugs of the earlier version were eliminated completely by the new program, and the very few bugs that had crept into the present version have been corrected manually.

0.3. Structure of the Volume

The first six chapters in the volume can be treated in three parts:

Part 1, containing the first three chapters, "Stems," "Roots," and "Prefixes and Suffixes," lists all the names in the same form, but groups them under different topical headings, here called "lemmata." Chapter 1, "Stems," is basic. Chapter 2, "Roots," is derived from chapter 1 by the elimination of stem vowels. Chapter 3, "Prefixes and Suffixes," lists all the bound morphemes shown in the analysis column of chapters 1 and 2.

Part 2, containing chapters 4 and 5, "Stem Count," and "Phoneme Count," synthesizes the results extrapolated from the lemmata of chapters 1 and 2.

Part 3, containing chapter 6, "Index of Names," gives a complete list of the transliterated names in the order of the roman alphabet. Attached to it is a small chapter 7, "Unanalyzed Names," excerpted from the previous chapter.

Before proceeding with the discussion of the structure of the first three chapters, we must explain certain formal differences between the computer output as it appears in chapters 1-7 and the general discussions in the introductory parts of this volume.

As noted below, computer limitations and certain unilateral decisions made by the author to facilitate the use of the materials in a future study forced a certain artificial format in the computer output. In my discussions this format has been changed to conform with the reality and with standard Assyriological or Semitic usage. The forms cited in the discussions in this volume are the same as those in section 0.7, "Glossary," and as they will appear in the *Grammar*.

The most important of these formal changes affects the use of capital letters and of the symbols - and +, as in the following example, in which the first line gives the form as it appears in the computer output, the second as it appears in discussions:

ŚMAᶜ 1 JA ŚMAᶜ HADD U   IA-AŠ$_2$-MA-AḪ-D-IM   M+, C+
*śma*ᵓ 1 *Ja-śma*ᶜ*+Hadd-u*   *Ja-áš-ma-aḫ-*^{d}IM   M+, C+

The computer output gives the form in capital letters exclusively, while the discussions give it in capitals and lowercase letters. In the initial stages of the project, the exclusive use of capitals was governed by the ease in computer programing. Subsequently, the capitals were retained for reasons of legibility, when we discovered, after some experimentation, that capital letters with attached diacritics are easier to read than small letters with attached diacritics. This is especially true in the present volume, with its printout pages greatly reduced in the printing.

The omission of the symbols - and + in the analysis column of the computer output was necessitated by the computer programing.

In the discussions, capital and lowercase letters are differentiated throughout, and the symbols - and + are restored.

Several other differences between the form in the computer output and that in the discussions, which will be treated more fully on the following pages, are the following:

1) in analysis (see pp. 4, 6, below), the fourth element of a name has been restored
2) in analysis (p. 6), the question mark (?) and full brackets ([ ]) have been restored, as also the half brackets (⸢ ⸣) in transliteration (p. 8)
3) in analysis (p. 6), morpheme doubling, as expressed by double consonants (consonantal quantity) and long vowels (vocalic quantity), has been restored
4) in analysis (p. 6), certain prefixes and suffixes, which were run together in the computer output because of space limitations, have been correctly separated by a hyphen
5) in analysis (p. 6), certain types of stems have been reinterpreted
6) in transliteration (pp. 7-8), the form of the determinatives or semantic indicators and of the numbers and diacritics attached to the signs has been changed to conform to standard notation

The first three chapters (chapter 1, "Stems," chapter 2, "Roots," and chapter 3, "Prefixes and Suffixes") constitute the most important and the largest part of the volume. These three chapters can and will be treated here together.

In these three chapters each entry is given in four columns, symbolized here as lemma, analysis, transliteration, and references. Each of the four columns occupies a set number of the 132 spaces that are available on the computer printer (enlarged from the 80 spaces of the punch card). The spaces were allotted in the following way: 11 spaces to the lemma, including the number to indicate whether the lemma is located in the first, second, or third element of the name; 56 spaces to the analysis, with several suballotments; 30 spaces to the transliteration, including some descriptive indications; and 35 spaces to the references, including some descriptive indications.

The use of these space allotments and suballotments is illustrated below by five examples in table 1.

In the computer output, all of the above examples are given in capital letters alone. In the discussion that follows, the examples are given in capitals and lowercase letters, according to standard Assyriological practice. Also incorporated are the other formal changes discussed briefly above, which will be taken up in detail below.

A name may be composed of one, two, three, or as many as four elements.

1. *Lemma.* The first column is occupied by a lemma plus a number. The lemma gives a stem or prefix/suffix in exactly the form that is shown in the second, analysis column. The root is derived from the stem by the omission of all vowels. The number that follows the lemma shows whether the lemma occurs in the first, second, or third element of the name. (Number 4 does not occur after the lemma because the fourth element in the few names that have four elements was not analyzed in the analysis column. See below.) A particular number refers not only to the line in which it occurs but also to all successive lines that contain the same lemma in the same position.

2. *Analysis.* The second column is occupied by the analysis of the name, given in one to three parts: a one-element name appears in the first part of the analysis space; the two elements of a two-element name appear side by side in the first and second parts of the analysis space; in the case of a three-element name, the first two elements appear side by side in the first and second parts of the space, and the third element appears just below the second. The fourth

Table 1. Illustration of Allotment and Suballotment of Spaces

```
         1         2         3         4         5         6         7         8         9         1         1         1         1
                                                                                                   0         1         2         3
12345678901234567890123456789012345678901234567890123456789012345678901234567890123456789012345678901234567890123456789012345678901234567890
```

LEMMA *11 spaces*		ANALYSIS *56 spaces*												TRANSLITERATION *30 spaces*		REFERENCES *35 spaces*
		Element 1 *28 spaces*						Element 2 Element 3 *28 spaces*								
		Pref. *8*		Stem *8*	Suffixes *12*			Pref. *8*		Stem *8*	Suffixes *12*					
		1st	2d		1st	2d	3d	1st	2d		1st	2d	3d			
MLIK	1	JA		MLIK						HADD		U		IA-AM-LIK-D-IM		RA LXV 40 I 31
MULUK	1			ᵓIL		UM				MULUK	AJ	I		DINGIR-MU-LU-KA-JI-KI	GN	XV 127
HU	2			MALIK						ŚUM		U	HU	MA-LIK-SU-MU-U_2		M
MILK	3			LA						ᵓIL		A				
										MILK		I		LA-I-LA-MI-IL-KI		TA 30, 75 2
MALIK	1			MALIK	AT	UM								MA-LI-KA-TUM	FN	EDZARD, DER 91:3

```
         1         2         3         4         5         6         7         8         9         1         1         1         1
                                                                                                   0         1         2         3
12345678901234567890123456789012345678901234567890123456789012345678901234567890123456789012345678901234567890123456789012345678901234567890
```

element in the four-element names has not been analyzed due to limitations connected with computer programing.

The number of names with four elements (all transliterated in full in the transliteration column) is very small —only four in all:

/ᵓAb-ī+mi+ki(+ᵓIl)/
A-bi-mi-ki-DINGIR
/Lāšū+ᵓEl+ka(+ᵓab-im)/
La-ši-El-ka-a-bi-im
/Śamś-u+ᵓil-u-na+kima(+ᵓIl)/
Sa-am-su-i-lu-na-ki-ma-DINGIR
/Śum-u+li+ᵓEl(+dūr-ī)/
Su-mu-li-El-du-ri

Only the first two names are actually composed of four clearly Amorite elements: /ᵓAbī-mi-ki-ᵓIl/ "My-father-is-truly-like-ᵓIl" and /Lāšū-ᵓEl-ka-ᵓabim/ "There-is-no-ᵓEl-like-father." The third and fourth names are composed of the Amorite royal names /Śamśu-ᵓiluna/ and /Śumu-li-ᵓEl/ to which are added the elements *kima*, *ᵓIl* (or *ᵓilim*), and *dūrī*, which may be either Amorite or Akkadian.

Each element of a name consists of a stem, with or without prefixes or suffixes. In the present analysis there are two ranks of prefixes and three ranks of suffixes.

The analysis is the most important and at the same time the most controversial part of this volume. It is the most important because it yields the computer analysis of morphemes on which the whole volume is based. It is also the most controversial due to computer-program limitations and to unilateral decisions made by the author to facilitate the collection of material under some meaningful or workable headings.

No question marks for doubtful readings or interpretations and no brackets for destroyed portions of names are given in the analysis column, although both are shown in the transliteration column that follows.

Nor is the morpheme doubling, as expressed by double consonants (consonantal quantity) or long vowels (vocalic quantity), shown in the analysis column. In contrast, root double consonants are always indicated. Thus the analysis column gives only NATIN, which may stand for *natin*, *nattin*, *nātin*, or *natīn*, but it also gives HADD, which correctly represents the three root consonants H, D, and D.

The decision to omit question marks, brackets, and morphemic doubling in analysis was made only after long experimentation. We decided to omit question marks because we could find no way to distinguish between questionable readings and questionable interpretations. At the same time, we decided not to indicate morpheme doubling in order to avoid the many doubtful interpretations that might have arisen as a result of the imperfect state of our knowledge of Amorite grammar and the vagaries of the Old Babylonian writing, which frequently leaves double consonants and long vowels unexpressed. Moreover, the indication of the morpheme doubling would have played havoc with the root and stem analysis, while the use of symbols for the question mark and brackets would have interfered with the computer analysis, which is based solely on consonants and vowels.

Because of space limitations, certain prefixes and suffixes had to be run together. Thus ATANUM really stands for ATAN UM and ANIJI for ANIJ I. One can deduce the correct segmentation from the columns. For the same reason, the rare single-rank prefix ŠT was introduced, in place of what should properly have been two separate prefixes, Š and T.

It has proved impossible to mark in any way two or more variant forms of the same name, especially in cases which, on the surface, might be perceived as unrelated. Thus the name spelled *Da*-WI-*da-nim*, which theoretically could be read as *Da-wi-da-nim*, was read as *Da-aw-da-nim* because of the variant form *Da-am-da?-nim* for the name of the same person (in all cases, the father of /Etel-pī-Sin/. The variant forms *La-ú-um* and *Li-ú-um*, *Ia-di-a-bu-um* and *Ia-du-a-bu-um*, and *Ma-ah-nu*-KA and *Ma-ah-nu-up-ì-lí* were treated in a similar fashion. All such cases will be fully annotated in *Grammar*.

In order to facilitate the computer analysis, certain radical decisions have been made in the analysis of free and bound morphemes. Often the new analysis has no reality in the grammar of the Semitic languages. This is especially true of the analysis of stems and roots with the so-called weak consonants, as well as of some prefixes and suffixes. Thus the analysis here followed has the verbal stems *nwuḫ* in /Ja-nwuḫ-/ for /Janūḫ-/ or *nwiḫ* in /Ja-nwiḫ-/ for /Janīḫ-/, and the nominal stems *nawḫ*- in /Nawḫ-ān-um/ for /Nāḫānum/, *niwḫ*- in /Niwḫ-at-um/ for /Nīḫatum/, and *nuwḫ*- in /Nuwḫ-um/ for /Nūḫum/, bringing all of them together under the artificial consonantal root NWḪ for *nāḫ*, *nīḫ*, and *nūḫ*. The same kind of analysis resulted in *ḫnun* in /Ja-ḫnun-/ (to bring it into accordance with the standard *qtul* stem), in place of *ḫun* (or *ḫunn*), which occurs in the name spelled *Ia-ḫu-un*-DINGIR /Jaḫun-ᵓIl/.

Similar analysis has been applied to a number of prefixes and suffixes. Thus we have used the prefix N for the N-stem, even though it is realized as NA, NI, NU, or N. The prefix T, used for the T-stem, is always ranked before the stem, as in /Ja-t-baḫar-na/ and /T-baḫr-um/, even though it appears regularly after the first radical consonant in /Jabtaḫarna/ and /Bataḫrum/. The suffix AH is used for the feminine noun, with an artificial H introduced to differentiate this suffix from that of other bound morphemes ending in *-a* and symbolized here as A; the two symbolizations, AH and A, represent two types of commitment: a full commitment under AH, which always stands for the feminine noun, and a zero commitment under A, which can stand for any morpheme ending in *-a*, as in the nouns /Maśīḫa/ "Anointed," /Jadīda/ "Beloved" (masc.) besides /Jadīdah/ (fem.) or /Jadīdatum/ (fem.), and /ᵓAdattah/ "Lady"; the names of the divinities /Hadda/ and /ᵓIrra/; the stative *ṭāba* in /ᵓAbī-ṭāba/ "My-father-is-good";

the verb *mataʿa* in /*Mataʿa-ki-ʾEl*/ "He-has-protected-like-ʾEl"; the pronoun *manna* in /*Manna-baltī-ʾEl*/ "Who-is-without-ʾEl?"; and so forth.

In a superficial analysis of such spellings as *I-la-kab-ka-bu-ú* or *Áš-du-um-la-a-bu-um* one may reach the conclusion that these names are composed of two elements, namely, *ʾIla* plus *kabkabû* and *ʾAšdum* plus *lābum*, and in fact the plene spellings in these and hundreds of parallel examples have regularly been taken to denote vocalic length. However, an analysis of the system of writing Amorite names, based on a complete list of all the plene occurrences, yields different results. The consistency of usage, with but very few exceptions, leads to the important conclusion that the plene spellings indicate not a long vowel but an independent syllable. Thus in the examples cited above, the correct analysis of the system of writing yields /*ʾIla-kabkabuhu*/, in which *-hu* is a bound morpheme with the meaning "his," and /*ʾAšdum-la-ʾabum*/, in which *la* is a free morpheme with asseverative force.[14]

Consonantal clusters are expressed by means of two different signs, the first of which contains the correct vowel plus consonant, the second the correct consonant plus any vowel, which becomes silent, as in /*ʿAbd-ʾEl*/ or /*ʿAbd-ʾIl*/ "Slave-of-ʾEl" written *Ab-da-El*, *Ḫa-ab-di-El*, or *Ab-te-Il*, /*ʿAbd-Ḥamī*/ "Slave-of-Ḥamī" written *Ḫa-ab-du-*^{d}*A-mi*; and /*Kibr-ʾAbba*/ written *Ki-ib-ra-Ab-ba*; or by two different signs containing consonant plus vowel and vowel plus consonant, with both vowels silent, as in *Ki-bi-ir-*^{d}*Ab-ba* /*Kibr-ʾAbba*/ = *Ki-ib-ra-Ab-ba* /*Kibr-ʾAbba*/.

In my analysis of the roots and stems, I tended to place under one root or stem not only the occurrences that belonged there properly but also those with some doubtful or unknown interpretation. This was done in order to facilitate the study of doubtful occurrences by comparing them with those that have an established interpretation. The degree of certainty in these cases will be clarified in *Grammar*, where doubtful interpretations will be either altogether separated from firmly established ones or will be marked by an appropriate question mark, with an annotation.

Dialectal variants have normally been treated separately. Thus the English verb "to give" is listed under both NTN and NDN, and the name of the storm god is given under *Had(d)u*, *Had(d)a*, *Hed(d)a*, *Handu*, and *Handa*, that of the chief god of the Amorites under *ʾEl* and *ʾIl*.

The treatment of allomorphs is not, and it could hardly be, consistent. The English conjunctions "like," "as" are expressed by either *ka* or (rarely) *ki*, depending, I assume, on dialectal distribution, as in /*ʾAḫu-ka-ʾabī*/ "Brother-is-like-my-father" or /*ʾAḫī-ki-Līm*/ "My brother-is-like-(god)-Līm." The name /*Bunu-ki-ʾIl*/ is listed under *ki* without prejudice as to whether *ki* is original in this name, as in /*ʾAḫī-ki-Līm*/ just above, or whether it is derived from *ka* where *a* followed by ʾ with a front vowel would become *i* through morphophonemic change. Similarly, some of the writings of the storm god Hed(d)a cited above may be examples not only of a dialectal distribution but of morphophonemic change as well.

The way in which certain roots have been assigned, baffling on the surface, can be justified by differences in the writing systems. Thus the Ur III name *Ia-gu-na-an* was analyzed as /*Ja-kwun-ān*/ and placed under the root KWN (*kūn*) because the sign GU can be read as *ku* in the Ur III period and it is more plausible to assign the verb to the common root KWN (*kūn*) than to the rare root ʾGN (meaning unknown) of the examples that follow. On the other hand, the Old Babylonian name *Ia-gu-ni-im* was analyzed as /*Ja-ʾgun-im*/ and placed under the root ʾGN because the sign GU does not have the value *ku* in classical Old Babylonian and assigning it to ʾGN can be justified by several spellings *Ia-aḫ-gu-un*. In the root ʾGN, ʾ can be interpreted as ʾ, H, Ḥ, and ʿ, and G as G or Q. (See section 0.4.)

Many elements that appear non-Amorite are included in chapters 1 and 2, "Stems" and "Roots," if they form part of clearly Amorite names. Among them are appellative nouns, such as *ʾandull* in /*ʿAmmī-ʾandullī*/ "My-(paternal) uncle (here deified)-is-my-protection" or *kisibirr* in /*Kisibir-ratum*/ (feminine name) "Coriander"; and names of divinities, deified geographical names, and the like, such as *ʾIšḫara* in /*ʾIšḫara-napšī*/ "Išḫara-is-my-life" or *ʾArrapḫ* in /*Mutu-ʾArrapḫim*/ "Man-of-Arrapḫum (here deified)." In these examples, *ʾandullum* and *kisibirrum* may be foreign words or loanwords in Amorite; *ʾIšḫara* and *ʾArrapḫum* may or may not have been integrated into the Amorite pantheon.

Several practical reasons led to a morphemic analysis that appears to be at variance with the one proposed in my *Sequential Reconstruction of Proto-Akkadian*.[15] In my judgment, both analyses are valid. The analysis proposed here is practical and is close to one that may be offered in a standard grammar. The analysis offered in *Sequential Reconstruction* is theoretical and (as the title indicates) is based on reconstruction.

3. *Transliteration*. The third column is occupied by the transliteration of the name, plus some additional indications. The transliteration here followed is the one generally used in Assyriology, with the following exceptions.

Semantic indicators (determinatives) are placed on the line and joined by a dash, as in D-IM-BA-AḪ-LI for ^{d}IM-*ba-aḫ-li* /*Haddu-baʿlī*/. The determinatives are:

BAD$_2$	fortress
D (for DINGIR)	deity
ḪUR.SAG	mountain
KI	place name
KUR	land
LÚ	person
URU	town

Sumerian elements are joined by a dash rather than by a dot, as in MU-UT-D-IGI-KUR for *Mu-ut-*^{d}IGI.KUR.

14. Cf. Gelb, "Lingua," pp. 143-44.

15. Assyriological Studies, no. 18 (Chicago, 1969).

Index numbers rather than accents are used to differentiate homophones. Thus U_2 is used in place of Ú.

No half-brackets (⌜ ⌝) are used in the transliteration column. In place of half-brackets, transliterations such as [L]A and L[A] are used to serve the purpose, albeit inconsistently.

In the discussions, all of these unconventional features, imposed by computer limitations, have been adapted to conform to the standard Assyriological practice. (See p. 4.)

In many cases a word or an abbreviation is added after the transliteration to help identify a particular type or form of the name. When there is no such special indication, it should be understood that the name is either masculine nominative or that nothing is known about it to define it in any other way. Occasionally a masculine name is designated MN or MN? to point out that despite its unusual form the name nevertheless is or may be masculine.

The following words or abbreviations may appear following a transliteration:

ACC	accusative
DN	name of a divinity
FIELD	name of a field
FN	feminine name
GEN	genitive
GN	geographical name
KING	name of a king
MN	masculine name
MOUNT	name of a mountain
NOM	nominative
PL	plural
RIVER	name of a river
TRIBE	name of a tribe

4. *References.* The fourth column is occupied by references, plus some additional indications. Abbreviations that appear under references are given in the "Abbreviations of Sources." Since the entries have been collected and the cards have been punched over a period of about twenty years by a number of different persons, some careful, some not, there are great variations and discrepancies in the form of the references. Moreover, the limitations in the space allotted to references in the computer program have resulted in some inconsistency in citing abbreviations and accompanying information.

Additional information that supplements the references may indicate the date, place, or kind of occurrence:

Date:	PSARG (pre-Sargonic)
	SARG (Sargonic)
	UR III
	POST-U (post-Ur III)
	CAPP (Cappadocian)
	EARLY OB (early Old Babylonian
	OLDER OB Tell Asmar texts)
	LATE (post-Old Babylonian occurrences from Alalakh IV, Ugarit, Late Assyrian, etc.)
Place:	HANA
	HARMAL
	ISHCHALI
	MARI
	QATNA
	RIMAH
	UGARIT
Kind of occurrence:	DATE (year date)
	SEAL (seal inscription)

The "UR III" indication appears with references that became known after Buccellati's publication.[16] "HARMAL," "ISHCHALI," "MARI," and "UGARIT" appear with references to publications other than the main works, such as ARMT, MRS, and the like. A reference with no supplementary indication is Old Babylonian in date and Babylonian in place. The symbol + at the end of a reference means that there are more occurrences of the name that were collected but not listed.

This ends the discussion of the structure of the first three chapters. For the discussion of chapters 4-7 see the introductory remarks to each of these chapters.

0.4. Consonantal Phonemes

The consonantal phonemes of the Amorite language are: ʾ, ʿ, *b*, *d*, *ḏ*, *g*, *h*, *ḥ*, *ḫ*, *j*, *k*, *l*, *m*, *n*, *p*, *q*, *r*, *s*, *ś*, *š*, *ṣ*, *t*, *ṭ*, *w*, and *z*. These will be fully discussed in *Grammar*. Here we will give only a few facts of relevance to the users of this volume.

The inventory of consonants includes *ḏ*, but does not include *ḍ*, *ġ*, or *ż*.

The consonant ʾ stands not only for the glottal stop (ʾ), but also, more frequently, for ʾ*x*, that is, an uncertain laryngeal or pharyngeal consonant, which could be *h*, *ḥ*, or ʿ.

The consonant Ḫ stands for *ḫ*, but may also include some occurrences of *ḥ* and ʿ.

The consonant Z stands for *z*, but may also include some occurrences of *s*, *ṣ*, and *ḏ*.

Without anticipating the full discussion that is to appear in the forthcoming *Grammar*, I should like to make one brief comment concerning the phoneme here symbolized as Ḏ. This phoneme represents the voiced counterpart of the voiceless interdental spirant here symbolized as Š. A consistent symbolization of this pair should therefore have been either Ṯ and Ḏ or Š and Ž. As will be evident from the material collected in *Grammar*, the support in favor of the latter pair is to be found in the phonemic analysis of Old Akkadian (see provisionally MAD 2^2, pp. 35 and 37-40), Amorite, and Ugaritic.

0.5. Alphabetic Sequence

The alphabetic sequence of the entries in the three columns varies from chapter to chapter, and also within

16. Buccellati, *Amorites*.

each chapter, especially between the first or lemma column and the second or analysis column:

Alphabetic sequence

Chapter	*Lemma column*	*Other columns*
1. Stems	new order	work order
2. Roots	new order	work order
3. Prefixes and Suffixes	roman order	work order
4. Stem Count	roman order	new order
5. Phoneme Count	new order	new order
6. Index of Names	....	roman order (in col. 3)
7. Unanalyzed Names	....	work order

These discrepancies in alphabetic sequence appear more complicated than they are. Actually, since chapters 3 through 7 were derived from chapters 1 and 2, and since using the roman order was the most natural way to present the data in some of the derived chapters, the discrepancies boil down to the difference between the work order and the new order in the first two chapters.

The alphabetic order here called "work order" is the one that was followed on the pink cards and also on the punch cards (see pp. 2-3). I call it "work order" because all of my work on the analysis, certainly in the initial stages, was done on the basis of the pink cards, although in later stages, after the first sets of computer test runs began to appear, I worked from the punch cards as well.

The work order is that of MAD 3. In this order, all names are entered under the consonantal root, disregarding vowels. The stems, which consist of consonants and vowels, are listed under each root in a set order. Nouns are given in the sequence masculine and then feminine, and, under each of these, in the sequence nominative, genitive, accusative. Verbs list the finite forms (such as JAQTUL) first, followed by the verbal nouns in the order QATAL, QATIL, QATUL, QATL; QITAL, QITIL, QITUL, QITL; QUTAL, QUTIL, QUTUL, QUTL; MAQTAL; and so forth.

The alphabetic sequence that I have called "new order" is the one mainly followed in lemmata:

Roots (consonants only) *Stems* (consonants and vowels)

ʾ	H	Ḥ	Ḫ	ʿ	W	J		ʾ	H	Ḥ	Ḫ	ʿ	W	J	
B	D	Ḏ	G					A	B	D	Ḏ	E	G	I	
K	L	M	N	P	Q	R		K	L	M	N	P	Q	R	
S	Ś	Š	Ṣ	T	Ṭ	Z		S	Ś	Š	Ṣ	T	Ṭ	U	Z

In both orders the alphabetization of root consonants begins with the consonants which in Akkadian are called "weak," plus Ḫ, and continues with other consonants in their order in the roman alphabet, with the Semitic consonantal phonemes added. The alphabetization of the stems is the same, except that vowels are included.

N.B.: The characterization of the first seven consonants as "weak" is inappropriate for the Amorite language, as will be shown in *Grammar*.

Essentially the new order is the same as the work order except for the following deviations:

In the work order of the roots, the weak consonants appear all together (as in MAD 3), following one another, and are not separated as in the new order, where roots and stems beginning with ʾ are placed together, followed by roots and stems beginning with H, and so forth. Thus the sequence of the work order is BWʾ, BʾD, BʿD, BʾR, BʿR, while that of the new order is BʾD, BʾR, BʿD, BʿR, BWʾ.

Keeping the weak consonants together, as in the work order, is useful in the interpretation of a little-known language. This can be illustrated by one example among many. If the names transliterated as A-ZI-RUM and ḪA-ZI-RUM are placed in close proximity under the roots ʾZR and ḪZR, one can see at once that they may be related and that Ḫ of ḪA may stand for a phoneme that can be expressed also by A. This leads to the plausible interpretation of the two names as *ʿAzirum* (actually /*ʿAḏirum*/, judging from other evidence).

Another difference in the alphabetization of the roots affects the two-consonantal and three-consonantal (and four-consonantal) roots. In the work order, the two-consonantal roots are grouped together and are separated from the three-consonantal roots. In the new order, the sequence of the roots is not affected by whether they occur in a two-consonantal or a three-consonantal root.

Thus the differences in the sequence of two-consonantal and three-consonantal roots can be illustrated by the following example: ʾḪ ʾJ ʾWJ ʾḪḎ ʾWŠ ʾB ʾBQ in the work order, and ʾḪ ʾḪḎ ʾWJ ʾWŠ ʾJ ʾB ʾBQ in the new order.

The main difference in the alphabetization of the stems is as follows: In the work order, the stems are listed under each root in the morphemic order described above. In the new order, the stems are alphabetized in the same order as the roots, except that the vowels are added.

As can be seen, the differences between the work order and the new order are not serious. Each order has certain advantages. The work order has the advantage of being conducive to new and improved interpretations. The new order has the advantage of being much easier to handle in the computer program.

The justification for using the roman (plus Akkadian) order of letters in the transliteration of cuneiform signs in chapter 6, "Index of Names," is self-evident. I can foresee no objection to the use of the roman order in listing the prefixes and suffixes in chapter 3, "Prefixes and Suffixes," and the patterns or formations in chapter 4, "Stem Count."

0.6. Computer Report, by Stuart-Morgan Vance and Robert M. Whiting

Introduction. As noted above, the project on which this volume is based is a computer-assisted morphological analysis of Amorite names. The ultimate source of the data is cuneiform documents in the Akkadian language. The first step in the project was therefore the recording of these names by now-forgotten scribes several millennia ago. Some of these our earliest colleagues in this endeavor showed a good comprehension of the structure of the names, others were less perspicacious. Of course they were merely writing the names of people involved in commercial or political transactions, not trying to do a scientific analysis.

The first modern step in the project was to transcribe the cuneiform spelling of the names into morphemes of the Amorite language. This was done by I. J. Gelb. Such a task, requiring a thorough knowledge of the ancient Semitic languages and of the cuneiform writing system, cannot be mechanized at the present state of the art.

The next step was to put the transcribed names onto punch cards for input to the computer. Then a computer program was written to perform the required analysis of the morphology of the names. This program is described below.

We wish to express our appreciation to the following people who contributed to this project: First, to those ancient scribes who, by recording the names in the first place, made this project possible at all. Next, to the modern scholars, particularly I. J. Gelb, through whose patient work this mass of data was recovered. We are indebted to V. H. Yngve for instruction in the art of programing computers for nonnumerical applications. We received valuable hints and suggestions from Stephen P. Soulé and Eleanor Lewis. We are also grateful to Clive A. Church for writing the printing program; to Randall Lee, Charles Payne, and Tom Morgan for permission to use the American Library Association print train; and to Ron Skirmont for providing the carbon ribbon and bond paper for the printed output.

Structure of the Names. As noted in section 0.3, each name may consist of one, two, or three roots, each with its associated prefixes and suffixes. The term "root" applies strictly to the consonantal root. The root together with its vocalism is called a "stem."

A stem with its associated prefixes and suffixes is called an "element." Thus a name may have one of the following three structures:

element
element + element
element + element + element

Within each element there may be 0, 1, or 2 prefixes and 0, 1, 2, or 3 suffixes. The possible prefixes and suffixes are divided into mutually exclusive classes: two classes of prefixes and three of suffixes. The structure of an element is therefore the following (the parts that may or may not be present are given in parentheses):

(class 1 prefix) - (class 2 prefix) - stem - (class 1 suffix) - (class 2 suffix) - (class 3 suffix)

Punch-Card Representation of the Names for Input to the Computer Program. The names are punched one to a card. The transcription of the name begins in column 1. The transliteration of the cuneiform begins with an asterisk in column 25. References begin with a period in column 55.

The transcription is punched in the following format: the elements are separated by + signs; within each element the morphemes (prefixes, stems, suffixes) are separated by - signs.

Inasmuch as the keypunch character set does not contain all the characters normally used in transliteration and transcription of cuneiform, certain characters had to be represented by digraphs or "nearest equivalents."

The Output. Each full-name listing appears in the output as many times as there are morphemes in it: once for each stem (consonants and vowels), once for each root (consonants only), and once for each prefix and suffix. All occurrences of the same morpheme are displayed together.

A punch card is 80 characters long. The computer is capable of printing a line 132 characters long. The first item on each line (allotted 11 spaces) is the morpheme being collected, followed by a number that indicates the element in which it occurs. (Such an identifier is not repeated but applies to each successive line until a new identifier appears.) The second item on each line is the transcription in an expanded format: each element is accorded 28 spaces—class 1 prefix in the first 4 spaces of a set, class 2 prefix in the second 4, stem in the next 8, class 1 suffix in the fifth 4 spaces, class 2 suffix in the sixth 4, and class 3 suffix in the seventh 4; the transliteration and reference (65 spaces) complete the line. For one-element names the second 28-space set is left blank; for two-element names both sets are used. Three-element names are too long to fit in one line, so they occupy two: the first two elements appear side by side, as in a two-element name, and the remainder of that first line is left blank; on the next line the third element is aligned directly below the second, and the transliteration and reference(s) follow. (If there be 4 elements, the fourth is not processed. There are only four such names in the entire corpus, and it was not considered worthwhile to provide an additional routine for these *hapax phainomena*.)

In addition to these full-name listings, each consonantal root is also displayed as a function of each consonant in the root, regardless of the position of the root in the name. This information, where X is any given consonant, is given under the heading "Phoneme Count" and is displayed in the following format:

Roots containing X
  First Consonant X
  Second Consonant X
  Third Consonant X
  Fourth Consonant X
  Total Roots Containing X

Under each subheading is printed a list of the roots that contain a given consonant in the designated position. After each root the count of tokens of that root is printed. At the end of each subsection for a particular consonant in a given position is printed the count of the root types, and at the end of the section is printed the total count of these root types for that consonant in all its positions.

Stem vocalization patterns are displayed in a similar format under the heading "Stem Count," but in this case the identifier is a vocalization pattern and the data show a token count of each stem with which the given pattern occurs and a type count of that pattern.

Finally, an index of names is provided which presents the names ordered alphabetically by transliteration, together with the corresponding transcription and reference(s) for each name.

The Programs. The computer program that produced these results consists of six parts: 1) analysis, 2) sorting, 3) stem and phoneme count, 4) index, 5) typography conversion, and 6) printing.

1) *The Analysis Program.* The analysis program takes the data cards as input and produces intermediate files that become the input to the sorting programs. It expands the format of the transcription to that used in the output and makes as many copies of the line as there are morphemes in the name. Each such line is tagged with a code number corresponding to one of the morphemes. These numbers are used by the sorting program to sort the lines into the desired order for output. At the same time the analysis program produces a second file for the stem- and phoneme-count program. Each entry in this file consists of the consonantal-root code number and the vowel-pattern code number, to which latter is appended the full-stem code number. This file is sorted into alphabetical order by another sorting operation.

The principle of operation is as follows. One card is read at a time. Columns 25-80, the transliteration and reference(s), are placed in temporary storage, as they are not involved in the analysis. If columns 1-24 are blank, the name is recognized as unanalyzed and a sort code is assigned to it which causes the name to go to the end of the output in sorting. The name is written into the intermediate file and the next card is read. The first 24 columns (the transcription) are split apart at the + signs, and each resulting element is examined in turn. First it is checked for the presence of - signs. If there be none, then the entire element is a stem and the affix routines may be skipped. Otherwise the examination begins at the left, taking in turn each unit delimited by a - sign. Each such unit (morpheme) is checked against a list of prefixes to explore three possibilities:

1) that it is a class 1 prefix
2) that it is a class 2 prefix
3) that it is not a prefix but a stem

If 1), the morpheme that follows is also checked against the prefix list to see whether it is a class 2 prefix. If 2), the morpheme that follows is taken to be the stem. If 3), the morpheme itself is taken to be the stem. Morphemes that follow the stem are checked against a suffix list in analogous fashion.

For each morpheme (stem, root, prefix, or suffix) a code number is produced and stored, which is later used to prepare a 12-digit sort code. The code number for the stem is produced by converting each letter or digraph of the stem into a 2-digit number from 01 to 29. There are 29 letters in the alphabet used—25 consonants and 4 vowels. This code number is placed in temporary storage. For the root, the code number is produced in the same manner but the vowels are ignored. This code number is also stored but at the same time is used to prepare a 20-digit sort code which is written out into an intermediate file for use in the phoneme- and stem-count program. For the vowel pattern of the stem, the code number is generated by converting each vowel into a single-digit number from 1 to 4 and each consonant into the digit 9. To this code number a copy of the stem code is added and the resulting 20-digit sort code is written into the intermediate file for use in the phoneme- and stem-count program.

Each affix is converted into a predetermined 3-digit code number and placed in temporary storage.

After each morpheme of each element of the name has been converted to a code number, the storage shelves are checked and each code number is used to produce a 12-digit sort code which indicates the class of morpheme, how it is to be alphabetized, and the element of the name in which it occurs.

The transcription is then reassembled in the expanded format described above, and the transliteration and reference(s) are appended. A copy of this line is attached to each sort code and written into an intermediate file. Thus each morpheme in the name is identified by a sort code, with the full name and the reference(s) attached to it. This done, the next card is read and the process repeated.

2) *The Sorting Program.* The intermediate files produced by the analysis program are the input to the sorting program. This is the standard sorting program provided by IBM, which sorts the material in those files in the numerical order of the code numbers produced by the analysis program. The code numbers have been designed to produce the desired alphabetization of the morphemes and their grouping into classes. The sorted outputs appear as further intermediate files on a tape.

3) *The Stem- and Phoneme-Count Program.* The phoneme-count program was adapted from one devised by Peter T. Daniels. The analysis program produces a file of the code numbers for consonantal roots and of root vocalism codes without the appended print line.

Upon sorting, the two classes of code numbers are separated, and each appears in alphabetical order. This sorted file is used as input to the counting program. Depending on whether the first digit be a 1 or a 2, the code number is recognized as a consonantal root or as a vowel pattern. This first digit is then deleted and the remainder is processed according to the class to which it belongs.

In the case of a consonantal root, the consonants are indicated by 2-digit numbers from 01 to 29. Pairs of digits are checked by a list rule and given appropriate subscripts (101 to 125—the four vowels have been deleted). These subscripts are then used to file copies of the root so that they are arranged on shelves 1 through 100 according to the following pattern: 76 through 100 have roots arranged in order by the first consonant ᵓ through Z; 51-75 are arranged in similar order by the second consonant; 26-50 in similar order by the third; and 1-25 in similar order by the fourth. (There are no roots with five or more consonants.)

The subsequent part of the phoneme-count processing counts the number of roots that contain each consonant in each possible position (first through fourth).

After the consonantal phoneme count is completed, the vowel patterns are counted in an analogous manner. The code number in this case has the full stem code appended so that the stems can be printed out. The printed format is similar to that used for the consonantal phonemes.

These count programs supply a file for input to the printing program.

4) *The Index Program*. The index program is a simple three-part program which prepares the transliteration section of each punch card (cols. 25-54) for alphabetization by deleting all determinatives (semantic indicators) and other phonetically nonsignificant characters such as brackets, question marks, and ellipses; sorts the transliterations into the desired order; and converts the original punch-card characters for input to the printing program while adding a line number for each entry.

5) *The Typography-Conversion* and 6) *Printing Programs*. Although these are separate steps, they may be more readily understood if considered together. The printing program is a routine to drive the American Library Association train from the ordinary character set available on the key punch. The print train designed by the ALA contains all the characters needed for the conventional transliteration and transcription of cuneiform. This allows the printing of the output in orthography familiar to Orientalists. Each ALA-train character for output is represented by a digraph on the input. The typography-conversion program makes the appropriate input string for the printing program. Using the sorted morpheme file from the analysis program as input, the typography-conversion program produces the output lines in digraph representation. The code number at the beginning of each line is reconverted to the morpheme it represents by the inverse of the process used by the analysis program to produce the code number. The regenerated morpheme is then printed as an identifier at the beginning of the line.

The output of the typography-conversion program is written on tape. This tape then serves as input to the printing program which produces the printed output. The output of the phoneme- and stem-count and index programs is also used for input to the printing program.

0.7. Glossary

This glossary is presented here as a guide to the morphology and semantics of the computer analysis. The choice of entries is eclectic, and therefore this glossary should not be considered a replacement for the glossary with a full critical apparatus which is to be published later (see p. vii).

From the standpoint of methodology, the decipherment of the Amorite language can be classed as the recovery of an unknown language, on a par with the decipherment of Etruscan, for example. Since in both these cases the writing is known, being cuneiform in the case of Amorite and close to Latin in the case of Etruscan, we are dealing not with a true decipherment, but rather with a linguistic analysis. Luckily, unlike Etruscan, the Amorite language does not stand in complete isolation, as it is closely related to other Semitic languages. Since there are no Amorite texts and no bilinguals, we must rely entirely in our analysis of Amorite on two external processes, comparison with the grammar of other Semitic languages and comparison with the structure of Semitic personal names in general. These processes are much more reliable for the recovery of morphology than semantics. As a result, while the morphology of Amorite is rather well established, the semantics is not, and will remain uncertain until the discovery of extensive lexical or bilingual texts. The following examples will illustrate the problem. Do the verb and the verbal nouns listed under the root ʾMR mean "to see," as in Akkadian, "to say," as in Hebrew, or "to command," as in Arabic? Is the name written *In-bu-um* to be interpreted as *ʾinbum* "fruit" or *ʿinbum* "vine"?

In selecting certain forms and meanings, I was generally guided more by the likelihood of their occurring in personal names than by their overall occurrence in different Semitic languages, be it West or East Semitic. Thus the name /*Manna-baltī-ʾEl*/ is interpreted here as "Who-is-without-ʾEl?" on the basis of such parallels as /*Man-balūm-Dagan*/ "Who-is-without-Dagan?" in Akkadian or /*Mī-kā-ʾEl*/ "Who-is-like-ʾEl?" in Hebrew, and not as "What-is-without-ʾEl?," as proposed by some scholars on the basis of the occurrence of the pronoun *mā* "what?" in Hebrew. An acquaintance with the structure and semantics of Semitic names is a condition *sine qua non* for the correct analysis of the Amorite names.

Entries are organized in two ways, under consonantal roots and under stems consisting of consonants plus vowels. Under roots are found verbs and verbal nouns. Occasionally, related nouns not necessarily of verbal origin are grouped together under a single root for convenience in citation. Under stems all the verbal nouns are listed again, and also primary nouns, primary adjectives, pronouns, and geographical and royal names and names of divinities.

Verbs are organized by stems in the following order: B (basic, Qal), BT, BH, BN, D (double, Piel), DT, Š, ŠT (BŠT), and DŠT.

Because of the uncertainties of cuneiform writing, verbal nouns are often cited with no indication of length and consequently no translation. Thus a form listed as *qatilum* may stand for *qatilum*, *qātilum*, *qatīlum*, and even *qattilum*. (See also p. 6.)

Verbal nouns with the extended stems *-ān*, *-ānum*, *-atān*, *-atānum*, *-atum* (in masculine names), and *-ja* are generally not cited as separate entries because of uncertainties as to whether these bound morphemes belong to the morphology of names or of the language. Exceptionally, some names with an extended stem are included, such as /*Qaqqadān*/ "man with a large head," from *qaqqadum* "head."

Names of the *jaqtulum* formation are generally taken to be hypocoristica of fuller *jaqtul-* names, but they may also represent a deverbal formation in geographical names of tribal origin, as in /*Japṭurum*/ or /*Jaʾrurum*/. Names marked as feminine may either represent nouns occurring in the feminine gender or they may form part of the morphology of feminine names, as in the feminine names /*Kabkaba*/ "Star" or /*Kisibir*(*r*)*atum*/ "Coriander."

Two or more translations of an entry are separated by commas when the meanings are similar (e.g., *bāšum* "shame," "ashamed"), by semicolons when the meanings are unrelated (e.g., *bābum* "gate"; "baby").

I can only repeat here the warnings given above concerning the uncertainties of the phonemic reconstruction (see p. 8) and of the definition of the term "Amorite" (see pp. 1-2).

All entries are listed in the order of the roman alphabet, with certain Semitic phonemes added:

ʾ ʿ A B D Ḏ E G H Ḥ Ḫ I J K
L M N P Q R S Ś Š Ṣ T̄ Ṭ U W Z

ʾ

ʾaʾtamrum, fem. *ʾaʾtamratum*, *ʾaʾtamra*, see ʾMR
ʾababa, see *ʾababum*
ʾabab(*ān*)*um*, fem. *ʾababa*, noun
ʾabaqum, see ʾ?B?Q?
ʾAbba, DN
ʾAbiḫ, GN
ʾAbī-jēšuʿ, an OB king
ʾabnum "stone"
ʾabum "father"
ʾadamum "red," see ʾDM
ʾadanum "lord," "master," fem. *ʾadantum*, *ʾadattum* "lady"
ʾAdmu, DN, see ʾDM
ʾadmum, see ʾDM
ʾadunum, fem. *ʾaduna*, noun
ʾahlum "tent," "house" (deified); cf. also *ʾal*, etc.
ʾAḥlamu, a tribe, see ḤLM
ʾaḫatum, see *ʾaḫum*
ʾāḫizum, see ʾḪD
ʾaḫum "brother," fem. *ʾaḫatum* "sister"
ʾAja, written *ᵈA-a*, fem. DN
ʾajja, *ʾajjan*, *ʾajji*, *ʾijja*, adv., "where?"
ʾajjalum, fem. *ʾajjalatum*, *ʾajjala* "deer"
ʾajjan, see *ʾajja*
ʾajji, see *ʾajja*
ʾakum, noun
ʾal, *ʾali*, *ʾališ*, adv., "where?"; cf. also *ʾahlum*
ʾalaśum, see ʾ?LŚ
ʾ?*alimum*, fem. ʾ?*alima*, noun; root ʾLM or ʿLM
ʾālipum, fem. *ʾālipa*, see ʾ?LP
ʾAlla, DN
ʾalmānum, see ʾ?*almum*
ʾ?*almum*, ʾ?*almānum*, noun; root ʾLM or ʿLM
ʾalpum "bull"
ʾ?*alumum*, noun
ʾalūpum, fem. *ʾalūpatum*, see ʾ?LP
ʾamanum, see ʾMN
ʾaminum, fem. *ʾaminatum*, *ʾamina* "true," see ʾMN
ʾāmirum, fem. *ʾāmiratum*, see ʾMR
ʾAmnān, *ʾAmnānum*, see *ʾAwnān*
ʾamrum, see ʾMR
ʾamtum "slave girl"
ʾAmurrum, a tribe
ʾanā, *ʾanāku*, pers. pron., "I"
ʾanāku, see *ʾanā*
ʾAnnu, DN, mostly in FN's of Mari
ʾaqdamum, see QDM
ʾaraśum, see ʾ?RŚ
ʾarḫum "cow"
ʾariśum, see ʾ?RŚ
ʾarnabum, fem. *ʾarnabatum* "hare"
ʾArrapḫum, GN
ʾarśum, see ʾ?RŚ
ʾarūśum, see ʾ?RŚ
ʾarwijum, fem. *ʾarwītum* "gazelle"
ʾ?*asinum*, noun
ʾaśdum "lion"
ʾaśijum, fem. *ʾaśija* "physician"
ʾ?*aśinum*, noun
ʾaśirum, noun
ʾAśkur, DN, see ŚKR
ʾaśmum, noun
ʾaśqudum "hamster"
ʾaśudum, see ʾ?ŚD
ʾAšar, DN, see ʾŠR
ʾAširatum, *ʾAšira*, *ʾAšratum*, fem. DN, see ʾŠR
ʾašrum, see ʾŠR
ʾAšura, masc. DN, see ʾŠR
ʾ?*atalum*, noun
ʾatta, pers. pron., "thou"
ʾ?*attum*, noun
ʾAwnān, *ʾAwnānum*, *ʾAmnān*, *ʾAmnānum*, GN, a tribe
ʾ?B?Q?, verb
  B *jaʾbuq*
    ʾabaqum
ʾDM "to be red"
  B *jaʾdum*; *ʾadam*
    ʾadamum "red"

ʾadmum
ʾAdmu, GN
ʾEl, see *ʾIl*
ʾ?ellum "pure"
ʾ?ellurum, *ʾ?illurum*, fem. *ʾ?elluratum*, *ʾ?illuratum*, noun
ʾelum "god," see *ʾilum*
ʾEnlil, DN
ʾ?ešb?um, noun
ʾ?GN, verb
B *jaʾgun*
ʾḪḎ "to seize"
B *jaʾḫuḏ*
ʾaḫiḏ(ān)um
BT *taʾḫaḏum* "battle"
BH *jāʾḫiḏ*
mēʾḫiḏum
ʾIblānum "man of ʾIbla"
ʾijja, see *ʾajja*
ʾIl, *ʾIla*, *ʾIlla*, *ʾEl*, DN, see *ʾilum*
ʾillurum, fem. *ʾilluratum*, see *ʾ?ellurum*
ʾiltum "goddess," see *ʾilum*
ʾilum, *ʾillum*, *ʾelum* "god," fem. *ʾiltum*, *ʾillatum* "goddess"; DINGIR regularly rendered as *ʾilī* in the first element, and *ʾIl* (not *ʾEl*) in the second; confusion possible; see also *ʾIl*, DN
ʾIlum-Malik, see *ʾIlum-Muluk*
ʾIlum-Muluk, *ʾIlum-Malik*, GN, see MLK; cf. also *Muluk* DN, and *Malik*, DN
ʾIlum-tuśuʿu, DN
ʾImmer, DN
ʾimmirum, *ʾimmerum* "sheep"
ʾimmum "mother," see *ʾummum*
ʾinbum, see *ʿinbum*
ʾ?ipqum "grace"
ʾ?Irra, DN; cf. also *Jirra*
ʾirśum, see ʾ?RŚ
ʾIršappa, DN
ʾIšḫara, fem. DN
ʾ?ittum, noun
ʾ?K?R, verb
B *jaʾkur*
ʾ?LP, verb
B *jiʾlap*
ʾālipum, fem. *ʾālipa*
ʾalūpum, fem. *ʾalūpatum*
BH *jīʾlip*
ʾ?LŚ, verb
B *jaʾlaś*
ʾalaśum
ʾ?Mʾ?, verb
BH *jāʾmiʾ*
mēʾmiʾum
ʾMN "to be true"
B *ʾamanum*
ʾaminum, fem. *ʾaminatum*, *ʾamina* "true"
BH *māʾminum*
ʾMR "to see," "to command," "to speak"
B *jaʾmur*; *ʾamar*, *ʾamara*
ʾāmirum, fem. *ʾāmiratum*
ʾamrum
BT *jaʾtamar*
ʾaʾtamrum, fem. *ʾaʾtamratum*, *ʾaʾtamra*
ʾ?MR, verb
B *jaʾmar*
ʾ?MW, verb
B *jaʾmū*
ʾ?NP, verb
B *maʾnūpum*
BH *māʾnipum*
ʾ?Q?D, verb
B *jaʾqud*
ʾ?RR, verb
B *Jaʾrurum*, *Jaʾurrum*, a tribe
ʾ?RŚ, verb
B *jaʾruś*
ʾaraśum
ʾariś(ān)
ʾarūśum
ʾarśum
ʾirśum
ʾurāśum
ʾ?ŚD, verb
B *jaʾśud*
ʾaśudum
ʾŠR "to provide (food?)"
B *jaʾšur*
ʾašarum
ʾAšar, DN
ʾaširum
ʾAširatum, *ʾAšira*, *ʾAšratum*, fem. DN
ʾAšura, DN
ʾašrum
ʾTJ? "to come"
B *ʾatā*
ʾuḏḏunān "man with big ears"
ʾummum, *ʾimmum* (very rare) "mother"
ʾ?unāb?um, fem. *ʾ?unāb?atum*, noun
ʾ?unnub?um, fem. *ʾ?unnub?atum*, *ʾ?unnub?tum*, noun; perhaps Akkadian
ʾUpi, *ʾUpum*, Babylonian GN
ʾ?uranum, fem. *ʾ?uranatum*, noun
ʾurāśum, see ʾ?RŚ
ʾūrum "light," see ʾWR
ʾWR "to shine"
ʾūrum "light"
BH *jāʾwir*
mēʾirum, *mīʾirum*

ᵓ?WŠ?, probably ᶜWŠ "to help"
B *jaᵓūš*
BH *jāᵓīš*
mēᵓīšum

ᵓ?Z?W, verb
B *jaᵓzū*
BH *jāᵓzī*

ᶜ

ᶜ*abdum* "slave"

ᶜ*adatum*, see ᶜ*adum*

ᶜ?*adijum*, noun

ᶜ*adnum* "pleasure?," see ᶜDN

ᶜ*adum*, fem. ᶜ*adatum*, noun

ᶜ*aḏarum*, see ᶜḎR

ᶜ*āḏirum*, fem. ᶜ*āḏiratum* "helper," see ᶜḎR

ᶜ*Aḏra*, DN, see ᶜḎR

ᶜ*aḏrum* "help," see ᶜḎR

ᶜ*alijum*, fem. ᶜ*alijatum*, ᶜ*alītum*, ᶜ*alija* "high"

ᶜ*alītum*, see ᶜ*alijum*

ᶜ*Ammī-ditana*, an OB king

ᶜ*Ammī-ṣaduqa*, an OB king

ᶜ*ammum* "paternal uncle," also deified; written regularly *Am-mi/mu-*, *Ḫa-am-mi/mu-*, also *Ḫa-mi/mu-*, but names so written may occasionally have been confused with spellings of *ḫamum*, q.v.

ᶜ*Ammu-rāpi*ᵓ, an OB king

ᶜ*Anat*, DN

ᶜ*Anat*(*a*), see ᶜ*Anum*

ᶜ*anatum*, noun?

ᶜ*Anum*, fem. ᶜ*Anat*(*a*), DN

ᶜ*aqbum*, see ᶜQB

ᶜ*aradum*, ᶜ*ardum*, fem. ᶜ*ardatum* "wild ass"

ᶜ?*arulum*, noun

ᶜ*Aštar*, DN

ᶜ*Aštara*, fem. DN, very rare

ᶜ*a*(*w*)*iqum*, fem. ᶜ*a*(*w*)*iqatum*, see ᶜWQ

ᶜ*azabum*, see ᶜZB

ᶜ*azalum*, fem. ᶜ*azalatum* "gazelle"; cf. also ᶜ*uzālum*

ᶜ*azazum* "strong," see ᶜZZ

ᶜ*azbum*, see ᶜZB

ᶜ*azibum*, fem. ᶜ*aziba*, see ᶜZB

ᶜ*azzum*, fem. ᶜ*azzatum* "strong," see ᶜZZ

ᶜBB "to be pure"
ᶜ*ebbum*, fem. ᶜ*ebbatum* "pure"
ᶜ*ebibum*

ᶜDN "to be pleasant?"
B *jaᶜdun*
ᶜ*adnum* "pleasure?"

ᶜḎR "to help"; cf. also Ḫ?Z?R
B *jaᶜḏar*; ᶜ*aḏar*
ᶜ*aḏarum*
ᶜ*āḏirum*, fem. ᶜ*āḏiratum* "helper"
ᶜ*aḏrum* "help"
ᶜ*Aḏra*, DN
BH *jāᶜḏir*
mēᶜḏirum

ᶜ*ebbum*, fem. ᶜ*ebbatum* "pure," see ᶜBB

ᶜ*ebibum*, see ᶜBB

ᶜ*ināb*(*ān*)*um*; cf. also ᶜ*inbum*

ᶜ*inbum* or ᵓ*inbum*, fem. ᶜ*inbatum* "fruit" or "vine"; cf. also ᶜ*ināb*(*ān*)*um*

ᶜ*iqbum* "protection," see ᶜQB

ᶜ*izbum*, see ᶜZB

ᶜ*izzum* "strength," see ᶜZZ

ᶜLM, see ᵓLM

ᶜMS "to carry"
B *jaᶜmus*
BH *jāᶜmis*

ᶜNW "to be submissive"; "to answer"
B *jaᶜnū*; ᶜ*anā*?
BH *jāᶜnī*
mēᶜnijum

ᶜQB "to protect"
B *jaᶜqub*
ᶜ*aqbum*
ᶜ*iqbum* "protection"
BH *jāᶜqib*
mēᶜqibum

ᶜTQ "to move," "to pass"
BH *jāᶜtiq*

ᶜ*uzābum*, see ᶜZB

ᶜ*uzālum*, fem. ᶜ*uzālatum* "small gazelle"; cf. also ᶜ*azalum*

ᶜ*uz*(*z*)*ubum*, see ᶜZB

ᶜ*uzzum* "strength," see ᶜZZ

ᶜWQ "to hinder"
B *jaᶜūq*
ᶜ*a*(*w*)*iqum*, fem. ᶜ*a*(*w*)*iqatum*

ᶜWŠ, see ᵓ?WŠ?

ᶜZB "to leave," "to abandon"
B *jaᶜzub*
ᶜ*azabum*
ᶜ*azibum*, fem. ᶜ*aziba*
ᶜ*azbum*
ᶜ*izbum*
BH *jāᶜzib*
D ᶜ*uz*(*z*)*ubum*

ᶜZZ "to be strong"
ᶜ*azzum*, fem. ᶜ*azzatum* "strong"
ᶜ*azazum* "strong"
ᶜ*izzum* "strength"
ᶜ*uzzum* "strength"

B

B$^{\supset}$?L, verb
B *jib$^{\supset}$ul*
i-ba-el
ba$^{\supset}$ilum
bu$^{\supset}$lum
D *bu$^{\supset\supset}$ulum*, fem. *bu$^{\supset\supset}$ultum*
B^{c}L, see ŠB^{c}L
ba$^{\supset}$ilum, see B$^{\supset}$?L
bā$^{\supset}$um, see BW$^{\supset}$
ba^{c}dum, *be^{c}dum*, *bi^{c}dum*, noun, "behind"; also prep., "behind"
ba^{c}lum, *be^{c}lum* "lord," fem. *ba^{c}latum*, *ba^{c}la*, *be^{c}latum*, *be^{c}ltum*, *be^{c}la* "lady," also deified
bābum, fem. *bābatum* "gate"; "baby"
baḫīrum "chosen," see BḪR
baḫūrum "chosen"; "young man," see BḪR
bajjānum, see BJN
bakirum, see BKR
bakśatum, fem., see BK?Ś
bakūrum, fem. *bakūratum* "first born," see BKR
bakūśum, see BK?Ś
balāṭum, see BLṬ
baliṭum?, see BLṬ
baltē, *baltī*, prep., "without"
balṭum, see BLṬ
balūṣum, see PLS
banḫatum, see B?NḪ?
baniḫum, see B?NḪ?
bānijum, see BNJ
bānum, see BJN
banūqum, see B?NQ?
baqqum "fly," see BQQ
bārum, fem. *bāratum*, see BJR
Baśar, *Biśir*, name of a mountain, deified
bāšum, fem. *bāštum* "ashamed," "shame," see BWŠ
bataḫrum, fem. *bataḫra*, see BḪR
batanḫum, see B?NḪ?
batūlum "bachelor," fem. *batūlatum* "spinster"
bāzum, noun
be^{c}dum, see *ba^{c}dum*
be^{c}lum, fem. *be^{c}latum*, *be^{c}la*, *be^{c}ltum*, see *ba^{c}lum*
BḪR "to choose"
B *jabḫar*
baḫīrum "chosen"
baḫūrum "chosen"; "young man"
biḫīrum, fem. *biḫīra* "chosen"
biḫrum "choice"
BT *jabtaḫar*
bataḫrum, fem. *bataḫra*

bi^{c}dum, see *ba^{c}dum*
biḫīrum, fem. *biḫīra* "chosen," see BḪR
biḫrum "choice," see BḪR
bikurtum, see BKR
bina, see *binum*
binaḫum, see B?NḪ?
binqum, see B?NQ?
bintum, see *binum*
binum, *bunum* "son," fem. *bintum*, *bittum*, *bina* "daughter"
biqaqum, see BQQ
Biśir, see *Baśar*
bittum, see *binum*
bītum "house"
BJN "to consider"
B *bānum*, fem. *bānatum*
bajjānum
B or BH *jabīn*
BJR, verb
B *bārum*, fem. *bāratum*
B or BH *jabīr*
BKR
bakirum
bakūrum, fem. *bakūratum* "first-born"
bikurtum, masc. name
BK?Ś
bakśatum, fem.
bakūśum
bukś(ān)um
B?LM, verb
B impv. *bulm*
BH *jāblim*
BLṬ "to live"
B *jabluṭ*
baliṭum?
balāṭum
balṭ(ān)
bulāṭum
BLW, verb
B *jablū*
BH *jāblī*
B?NḪ?, verb
B *jabnaḫ*
banḫatum, fem.
baniḫ(ān)
binaḫ(ān)
BT *batanḫum*
BNJ "to build," "to create"
B *jabnī*; *jabannī*
bānijum
B?NQ?, verb
B *banūqum*
binqum
bunāqum
B or BH *jabniq*

BQQ
baqqum "fly"
biqaqum
buqāqum "small fly"
buqqum
BRQ "to shine," "to lighten"
B *jabruq*
burq(ān)um, fem. *burqatum*
BŚJ "to be," "to exist"
B *jabaśśī*
BŚR "to announce"
D *jibaśśir*
buʾʾulum, fem. *buʾʾultum*, see Bʾ?L
Bugaš, DN
bukśum, see BK?Ś
bulāṭum, see BLṬ
bunāqum, see B?NQ?
bunum "son," see *binum*
buqāqum "small fly," see BQQ
buqqum, see BQQ
burqum, fem. *burqatum*, see BRQ
būzum = *būṣum* "hyena?"
BWʾ "to come"
B *jabāʾ*, *jibāʾ*
bāʾum
BH pass. *ʾubāʾ* or *jubāʾ*
BWŠ "to be ashamed"
B *bāš(ān)um*, fem. *bāštum* "shame," "ashamed"
B?Z?W?, verb
B *jabzū*

D

da^{c}um, *di^{c}(atān)um*, fem. *da^{c}atum*, *di^{c}atum* "knowledge," see JD^{c}
dabiʾum "bear"
dādatum, see *dādum*
dadmītum, fem. noun
dadmum, noun
dādum, *dawd(ān)um*, *damdum*, fem. *dādatum* "beloved"; cf. also *dīdum* and *dūdum*
Dagān, DN
dakśatum, fem. noun; cf. also *daśiktum*
dalaqum, see DLQ
dalqum, see DLQ
damdum, see *dādum*
damqum, fem. *damqatum*, *damiqtum* (Akkadian?), *damqa* "good," see DMQ
dannum, fem. *dannatum* "strong," see DNN
Dannum, DN, see DNN
Dāra, DN, see DWR
darikum, see DRK?
darkum, fem. *darkatum*, see DRK?
dārum "eternity," "eternal," see DWR
daśiktum, fem. noun; cf. also *dakśatum*
dašurum, *dušurum*, fem. *dašuratum*, *dašura* "old"
dawdum, see *dādum*
dāwira, see DWR
DBB, see D̲BB
DBR, verb
B *jadbar*
BH *mēdbirum*
di^{c}um, fem. *di^{c}atum*, see *da^{c}um*
Dibir, see *Diwir*
dīdum, noun; cf. also *dādum* and *dūdum*
dīnum "judgment," see DJN
Dīr, *Dīrum*, GN, see DWR
Dīrītum, fem. DN, see DWR
dīrum, noun, see DWR
Dīrum, see *Dīr*
Ditan, DN
ditanum "bison"
Ditanum, *Ditnum*, GN
Diwir, *Dibir*, DN, see DWR
DJN "to judge"
B *jadīn*
dīnum "judgment"
DKR, see D̲KR
DLQ "to burn"
B *jadluq*
dalaqum
dalqum
dulāqum
dulq(ān)um
D *dulluqum*, fem. *dul(l)uqatum*, *dul(l)uqtum*
DLW "to draw water"
B *jadlū*
DMQ "to be good"
damqum, fem. *damqatum*, *damiqtum* (Akkadian?), *damqa* "good"
dumqum "goodness"
DMR, see D̲MR
DNK?, verb
B *jidnik*
DNN "to be strong"
dannum, fem. *dannatum* "strong"
Dannum, DN
dunnum "strength"
DQN, see D̲QN
DRK?, verb
B *jadrak*, *jadruk*
darikum
darkum, fem. *darkatum*
dūdum, noun; cf. also *dādum* and *dīdum*
dulāqum, see DLQ
dulluqum, fem. *dul(l)uqatum*, *dul(l)uqtum*, see DLQ

dulqum, see DLQ
dumqum "goodness," see DMQ
dunnum "strength," see DNN
dūrum "eternity," see DWR
duš(š)ubtum, fem., "sweet"
dušurum, see *dašurum*
DWR "to turn around," "to dwell"
B *jadūr*; impv. *dūr*
dāwira, fem.
dārum "eternity," "eternal"
Dāra, DN
dīrum, noun
Dīr, *Dīrum*, GN
Dīrītum, DN
Diwir, *Dibir*, GN
dūrum "eternity"
BH *jādīr*

Ḏ

(really Ž, see section 0.4)

ḏababum, see ḎBB
ḏabbum, see ḎBB
ḏābibum, see ḎBB
ḏākirum, fem. *ḏākiratum*, see ḎKR
ḏakūrum, fem. *ḏakūra*, see ḎKR
ḏamarum, see ḎMR
ḏāmirum, see ḎMR
ḏamratum, fem., see ḎMR
ḏamūrum, see ḎMR
ḏanabum, see ḎNB
ḏanibum, see ḎNB
ḏanbum, see ḎNB
ḏaqanum, *ḏaqnum* "old," see ḎQN
ḏaqnītum, fem., see ḎQN
ḏar^{c}um, see ḎR^{c}?
ḏara^{c}um, see ḎR^{c}?
ḏari^{c}um, see ḎR^{c}?
ḎBB; written with Z, S, and D signs
ḏababum
ḏābibum
ḏabbum
ḏibibum,
ḏubābum, fem. *ḏubābatum* "little fly"
ḏibbatum "tail," see ḎNB
ḏibibum, see ḎBB
ḏikrum, fem. *ḏikratum* "memory," see ḎKR
ḏimrum "protection," see ḎMR
ḏinubum, see ḎNB
ḏiqnum "old age," see ḎQN
ḏiqunum, see ḎQN
ḎKR "to remember," "to name"; written with Z and D signs; see also ŚKR
B *jaḏkur*
ḏākirum, fem. *ḏākiratum*
ḏakūrum, fem. *ḏakūra*
ḏikrum, fem. *ḏikratum* "memory"
ḏukrum
ḎMR "to guard," "to protect"; written with Z and D signs; see also ŚMR
ḏamarum
ḏāmirum
ḏamratum, fem.
ḏamūr(ān)
ḏimrum "protection"
ḎNB; written with Z and S signs
ḏanab(ān)
ḏanibum
ḏinubum
ḏibbatum, fem., "tail"
ḏunābum "little tail"
ḏun(n)ubum "long-tailed"
ḎQN "to be old"; written with Z and D signs
B *ḏakanum*, *ḏaqnum* "old"
ḏaqnītum, fem.
ḏiqunum
ḏiqnum "old age"
ḎR^{c}? "to sow?," "to seed?"; written with Z signs
B *jaḏra^{c}*, *jiḏru^{c}*; *ḏara^{c}*
ḏari^{c}um; cf. also *śarijum*
ḏar^{c}um
BH *jāḏri^{c}*
mēḏri^{c}um
ḏu (written *zu*), fem. *šāt* (written *ša-at*), det.-rel. pron., "he/she of ...."
ḏubābum, fem. *ḏubābatum* "little fly," see ḎBB
ḏuhhubum "golden"
ḏukrum, see ḎKR
ḏunābum "little tail," see ḎNB
ḏun(n)ubum "long-tailed," see ḎNB

G

G$^{\supset}$L "to redeem"
B *gā$^{\supset}$ilum*, fem. *gā$^{\supset}$ilatum*
ga$^{\supset}$lum
ga$^{\supset}$ūlum
gā$^{\supset}$ilum, fem. *gā$^{\supset}$ilatum*, see G$^{\supset}$L
ga$^{\supset}$jum "people," "clan"
ga$^{\supset}$lum, see G$^{\supset}$L
ga$^{\supset}$ūlum, see G$^{\supset}$L
gaba$^{\supset}$um, see GB$^{\supset}$?
gabbuḫum "bald," see GB$^{\supset}$?
gabi$^{\supset}$um, fem. *gabi$^{\supset}$atum*, see GB$^{\supset}$?
gabu$^{\supset}$um, see GB$^{\supset}$?
gabuhum "high," see GB$^{\supset}$?
gādum, see GJD
gajida, fem., see GJD

gamilum, see GML
gamirum, see GMR
gamlum, see GML
garanum, see GRN
gariśum, noun
gazizum, see GZZ?
GBʾ?
    gabaʾum
    gabiʾum, fem. *gabiʾatum*
    gabuʾum = *gabuhum* "high" or *gabbuḥum* "bald"
    gubʾ(ān)um
gīdum, see GJD
gizzum, see GZZ?
GJD "to be good?"
  B *gād(ān)um*
    gajida, fem.
    gīd(ān)um
  B or BH *jagīd*
GJḤ "to burst forth"
  B or BH *jagīḥ*
GML "to please," "to spare"
  B *gamil*?, impv. *guml*
    gamilum
    gamlum
GMR "to complete," "to finish"
  B *jagmur*
    gamir(ān)um
  BH *jīgmir*
GRN, verb
  B *garanum*
  BH *māgrin*
gubʾum, see GBʾ?
Gubla, GN
GZZ? "to shear"
    gaziz(ān)um
    gizzum

H

Haddu, *Hadu*, *Hadda*, *Hada*, *Hedda*, *Handa*, *Handu*, DN
hālilum, see HLL
Handa, see *Haddu*
Hedda, see *Haddu*
HLL "to shout," "to praise"
  B *ʾahlul*?; *halal*?
    hālilum
  BT impv. *hitlal*
  BH *māhlilum*
HWJ "to be," "to become"; "to desire"
  B or BH *jahwī*

Ḥ

ḥabibum "beloved," see ḤBB
ḥabisum, see Ḥ?BS
ḥabsum, see Ḥ?BS
ḥadūrum "enclosure"
Ḫajja, written *É-a*, DN; this may be the same DN as *Ḫajja* in *Ḫa-ja-il* (*Syria* XVIII 247:32) and ARÁD-*Ḫa-ja* (*Syria* XXVIII 174:26), both Ugaritic
ḥajjum, fem. *ḥajjatum*, *ḥajja* "live," "living," see ḤJJ
ḥakamum, fem. *ḥakamatum* "wise," see ḤKM
Ḥalab, GN, Aleppo
ḥamadum, see ḤMD
ḥamidum, fem. *ḥamida*, see ḤMD
ḥamum "father-in-law," also deified; written regularly ^{d}*A-mi/mu-*, *A-mi/mu-*, but names so written may occasionally have been confused with spellings of *ʿammum*, q.v.
ḥananum, fem. *ḥananatum*, *ḥanana* "gracious," see ḤNN
ḥanḥanum "gracious," see ḤNN
ḥaninum, see ḤNN
ḥannum, see ḤNN
ḥanunum, see ḤNN
ḥaraba, fem., see Ḥ?RB
ḥarbum, fem. *ḥarba*?, see Ḥ?RB
ḥaribum, see Ḥ?RB
ḥarūba, fem., see Ḥ?RB
ḥasīdum "pious"
ḥaṣanum, *ḥaṣnum*, fem. *ḥaṣanatum*, *ḥaṣnatum*, see ḤṢN
Ḥatki, DN
ḥatkum "father?"
ḥazaqum "strong," see ḤZQ
ḥaziqum, see ḤZQ
ḥazūqum, see ḤZQ
ḤBB "to love"
  B *ʾaḥbab*
    ḥabībum "beloved"
Ḥ?BS, verb
  B *jaḥbas*
    ḥabisum
    ḥabs(at)um, masc.
    ḥubāsum
  BH *jāḥbis*
Ḥimārān, GN
ḥimārum "donkey"
ḥimdum "desire," see ḤMD
ḥinanum, see ḤNN
ḥininum, see ḤNN
ḥinnum, fem. *ḥinnatum* "grace," see ḤNN
ḥinunum, see ḤNN
ḥirabum, see Ḥ?RB
ḥirbum, see Ḥ?RB
ḥiṣnum, see ḤṢN
ḤJJ "to live"
  B *jaḥī*
    ḥajjum, fem. *ḥajjatum*, *ḥajja* "living"

ḤKM "to be wise"
B *jaḥkum*
ḥakamum, fem. *ḥakamatum* "wise"
Ḥ?LJ "to be sick?"
B *jiḥlā?*
BH *jāḥlī*, *jīḥlī*
ḤLM
ʾAḥlamu, a tribe
ḤMD "to desire"
B *jaḥmad*
ḥamadum
ḥamidum, fem. *ḥamida*
ḥimdum "desire"
ḥumādum
D *ḥum(m)udum*
ḤNN "to be gracious," "to be merciful"
B *jaḥun*, *jaḥnun*
ḥananum, fem. *ḥananatum*, *ḥanana* "gracious"
ḥaninum
ḥanunum
ḥannum
ḥinanum
ḥininum
ḥinunum
ḥinnum, fem. *ḥinnatum* "grace"
ḥunanum
ḥuninum, fem. *ḥunina*
ḥunnum
ḥanḥanum "gracious"
D *ḥunnunum*
Ḥ?RB, verb
B *ḥaraba*, fem.
ḥarib(ān)um
ḥarūba, fem.
ḥarb(atān)um, fem. *ḥarba?*
ḥirābān
ḥirbum
ḥurbum
ḤRM "to be taboo"
B *ḥaram?*
BH *mēḥrimum*
ḤṢN "to embrace?"
B *jaḥṣun*
ḥaṣanum, fem. *ḥaṣanatum*, *ḥaṣnatum*
ḥiṣnum
ḥuṣānum
BH *jāḥṣin*
ḥubasum, see Ḥ?BS
ḥumādum, see ḤMD
ḥum(m)udum, see ḤMD
ḥunnum, see ḤNN
ḥunnunum, see ḤNN
ḥurbum, see Ḥ?RB
ḥuṣānum, see ḤṢN
ḤZQ "to be strong"
B *jaḥzuq*
ḥazaqum "strong"
ḥaziqum
ḥazuqa(ān)
BH *māḥziqum*, *mēḥziqum*

Ḫ

ḫabadum, see Ḫ?BD
ḫabiʾum, see Ḫ?B?ʾ?
ḫ?ab?irum, noun
Ḫabur, *Ḫubur*, name of a river, deified
ḫālum "maternal uncle," also deified
Ḫ?āna, *Ḫ?iʾ?ana*, GN, a tribe, deified
ḫamaśum, see Ḫ?MŚ
ḫamrum, see Ḫ?MR
ḫamśatum, fem., see Ḫ?MŚ
ḫanpatum, fem. "impious"
ḫarrirum, see Ḫ?RR
ḫ?ašturum, noun
ḫatanum "son-in-law," see ḪTN
Ḫawrān, GN, deified
ḫazimum, see Ḫ?Z?M
Ḫ?B?ʾ?, verb; cf. also Ḫ?P?ʾ?
B *jaḫbaʾ*, *jaḫbuʾ*
ḫabiʾum
BH? *jāḫbiʾ*
Ḫ?BD, verb
B *jaḫbud*
ḫabadum
ḫubādum
ḫubdatum, fem.
Ḫiʾana, see *Ḫ?āna*
ḫ?īlum, fem. *ḫ?īlatum*, noun
ḫimrum, see Ḫ?MR
ḫizrum, see Ḫ?Z?R
Ḫ?MM, verb
B *Jaḫmumum*, GN
Ḫ?MR
ḫamrum, noun
ḫimrum
ḫumrum
Ḫ?MŚ
B *ḫamaś(at)um*, fem. *ḫamśatum*
D *ḫum(m)uś(at)um*, masc.
ḪMṬ, verb
B *jaḫmuṭ*
Jaḫmuṭum, GN
Ḫ?P?ʾ?, verb; cf. also Ḫ?B?ʾ?
B *jaḫappiʾ*
Ḫ?RR, verb
B *ḫarrirum*
D *muḫarrirum*

Ḫ?SJ?, verb
  B or BH *jaḫsī*

Ḫ?ŚM, verb
  BH *māḫśim(ān)um*

Ḫ?T?ʾ?, verb; cf. also ḪṬʾ
  B *jaḫattiʾ*; *ḫataʾ*

ḪTN "to protect?"
  B *jaḫtan*
  ḫatanum "son-in-law"
  ŠT *šataḫtin*

ḪṬʾ "to sin"; cf. also Ḫ?T?ʾ?
  B *jiḫṭaʾ*

ḫubadum, see Ḫ?BD

ḫubdatum, fem., see Ḫ?BD

Ḫubur, see *Ḫabur*

ḫum(m)uśum, see Ḫ?MŚ

ḫumrum, see ḪMR

ḫupšum "freedman"

ḫurśānum "mountain"

ḫuzāmun, see Ḫ?Z?M

ḫuzir(ān)um "pig"

ḫuzmum, see Ḫ?Z?M

Ḫ?Z?M, verb
  B *jaḫzum*
  ḫazimum
  ḫuzāmum
  ḫuzm(ān)um
  BH *jāḫzim*

Ḫ?Z?R, verb; cf. also ᶜḎR
  B *jaḫzur*
  ḫizrum

J

JᶜL "to profit"
  B *jāᶜul*; *jaᶜal*
  BH *jāᶜil*, *jīᶜil*; cf. also *Jaᶜil*

Jaʾrurum, *Jaʾurrum*, a tribe, see ʾ?RR

jaʾum, poss. adj., "my"

Jaʾurrum, see *Jaʾrurum*

Jaᶜil, *Jaᶜilānum*, GN, a tribe

jaᶜilum, fem. *jaᶜilatum*, *jaᶜila* "mountain goat"; cf. also JᶜL

Jabaśiji, a tribe, see JBŚ

jabiśum "dry," see JBŚ

jādiᶜum, fem. *jādiᶜatum*, *jādiᶜa* "knowing," see JDᶜ

jadīdum, fem. *jadīda* "dear," see JDD

jadum, *jidum* "hand"

Jaḥad, DN, see JḤD

jaḥadum "one," "alone," see JḤD

Jaḫmumum, GN, see Ḫ?MM

Jaḫmuṭum, GN, see ḪMṬ

Jakrub-ʾIl, DN, see KRB

Jamʾad, *Jamʾadum*, GN, see Mʾ?D

Jamam, DN

jamamum, fem. *jamama*

Jamin, *Jamina*, *Jaminum*, a tribe

jaminum "right"

jammum "sea"

jamnum, noun

Jamūt-baᶜl, *Jamūt-baᶜlum*, GN, see MWT

Japṭurum, GN, see PṬR

Jāpuᶜ, *Jēpuᶜ*, *Jāpaᶜ*, *Jēpaᶜ*, DN, see JPᶜ

jaqarum, *jaqrum*, fem. *jaqartum*, *jaqra*, *jiqra* "dear," see JQR

Jaraḫ, *Jeraḫ* (or *Jarḫ*, *Jerḫ*), DN

Jaśar, *Jiśar*, DN, see JŚR

jaśarum, *jiśarum*, fem. *jaśara* "straight," see JŚR

Jāšuᶜ, *Jēšuᶜ*, DN, see JŠᶜ

jašunum "old"

jatamum, *jatmum* "orphan"; see also *jatumum*

jatarum, *jatrum*, fem. *jataratum*, *jatara*, *jatratum*, *jatra* "abundant," see JTR

jatašᶜa, fem., see JŠᶜ

jatmum, see *jatamum*

jatrum, fem. *jatratum*, *jatra*, see *jatarum*

jattum, noun

jatum, noun

jatumum, *jitumum* "orphan"; see also *jatamum*

Jatūr-Mēr, see *Jitūr-Mēr*

Jawmaʾ-ᶜammum, GN, see WMʾ

JBL "to carry," "to bring"
  B *jībal*; *jabal*
  BH *jābil*

JBŚ "to be dry"
  B *jībiś*
  jabiśum? "dry"
  Jabaśiji, a tribe
  BH *jābiś*
  mēbiśum
  BN *jinībiś*?

JDᶜ "to know"
  B *jīdaᶜ*; *jadaᶜ*; cf. also *jaṭaᶜ*
  Jīdaᶜ-Maraṣ, GN
  jādiᶜum, fem. *jādiᶜatum*, *jādiᶜa* "knowing"
  daᶜum, *diᶜ(atān)um*, fem. *daᶜatum*, *diᶜatum* "knowledge"
  BH *jādiᶜ*
  mēdiᶜum

JDD "to love"
  B *jadīdum*, fem. *jadīda* "dear"
  BH pass. *mūdadum* "beloved"

Jēpaᶜ, *Jēpuᶜ*, see *Jāpuᶜ*

Jeraḫ, see *Jaraḫ*

Jēšuᶜ, see *Jāšuᶜ*

JḤD "to be one"
  B *jaḥad*

jaḥadum "alone"
Jaḥad, DN
Jida^{c}*-Maraṣ*, GN, see JD^{c}
jidum, see *jadum*
jiqra, fem., see *jaqarum*
Jirra, DN; written WI-*ir-ra*; cf. also $^{\supset}$?*Irra*
Jiśar, see *Jaśar*
jiśarum, see *jaśarum*
jiš^{c}*um*, fem. *jiš*^{c}*atum*, *jiš*^{c}*a* "help," see JŠ^{c}
jitumum, see *jatumum*
Jitūr-Mēr, *Jatūr-Mēr*, DN, see TWR
JP^{c} "to shine"
B *ja(j)pa*^{c}, *jāpa*^{c} or *japa*^{c}
Jāpu^{c}, *Jēpu*^{c}, *Jāpa*^{c}, *Jēpa*^{c}, DN
BH *jāpi*^{c}
mēpi^{c}*um*, *mūpi*^{c}*um*
JQH, WQH "to be obedient?"
B *jīqah*, *jāqah*
BH pass.? $^{\supset}$*ūqah*, *hūqah*, or *jūqah*; also $^{\supset}$*ūqih*? or *jūqih*?
JQR "to be dear"
jaqarum, *jaqrum*, fem. *jaqartum*, *jaqra*, *jiqra* "dear"
BH *jāqir*
mūqir(ān)um
JRD "to descend," "to go down"
B *jīrid*
BH *jārid*
mārid(ān)um
JŚR "to be straight"
B *jīśar*; *jaśar*
jaśarum, *jiśarum*, fem. *jaśara* "straight"
Jaśar, *Jiśar*, DN
BH *jāśir*
BH pass. *mēśarum*
JŠ^{c} "to help," "to save"
B *jāšu*^{c}, *jēšu*^{c}
Jāšu^{c}, *Jēšu*^{c}, DN
jiš^{c}*um*, fem. *jiš*^{c}*atum*, *jiš*^{c}*a* "help"
BT *jataš*^{c}*a*, fem.
BH $^{\supset}$*ūši*^{c} or *jūši*^{c}
mēši^{c}*um*
JŠB "to sit"
B *jašab*
BH *jāwšib*
JṢ$^{\supset}$, WṢ$^{\supset}$ "to go out"
B *jīṣi*$^{\supset}$; impv. *ṣi*$^{\supset}$?
BH *jāwṣi*$^{\supset}$, *jāṣi*$^{\supset}$, $^{\supset}$*ūṣi*$^{\supset}$ or *jūṣi*$^{\supset}$
mūṣi$^{\supset}$*um*
JTR, WTR "to be more," "to be excellent"
B *jītar*
jatarum, *jatrum*, fem. *jataratum*, *jatratum*, *jatara*, *jatra* "abundant"
BH *jātir*
mētirum
BH pass. *jūtar*
mūtar(um)
JṬ^{c}, verb
B *jaṭa*^{c}; cf. also *jada*^{c}

K

ka, *kama*, *ki*, prep., "like," "as"; *kima* is probably Akkadian
kabarum "great," see KBR
kabasum, see KBS
kabdum "heavy," see KBD
Kabid, DN, see KBD
kabidum, fem. *kabida* "heavy," see KBD
kabisum, fem. *kabisatum*, see KBS
kabkabum, fem. *kabkaba* "star"
Kakkabān, GN
kabś(ān)um, fem. *kabśatum*, *kibśatum* "lamb"; cf. also note to *kaśp(ān)um*
kābum, possibly *kāpum* "rock"
kadrum, see *katrum*
kahalum "might?," see KHL
kakka, see *kakkum*
Kakka, DN; cf. also *kakkum*
Kakkabān, GN, see *kabkabum*
kakkum, fem. *kakka* "weapon"; cf. also *Kakka*, DN
kala "all"
kalalum, see KLL
kalbum "dog," fem. *kalbatum*, *kalba*? "bitch"
kama "like," see *ka*
kamanum, see KMN
kaminum, see KMN
kamisum, see KMS
kamnum, see KMN
kanakum, see KNK
kanaśum, see KNŚ
kanikum, see KNK
kaniśum, fem. *kaniśa*, see KNŚ
kānum, see KWN
kāpum, see *kābum*
kasijum?, see K?S?W
kaśp(ān)um; written with BA (not PA), ergo read *kaśb(ān)um* which originated by metathesis from *kabś(ān)um* "lamb"
kašarum, see KŠR
kašerum, fem. *kašera* "proper," see KŠR
katrum or *kadrum*, noun
kazibum, see KZB
KBD "to be heavy," "to be honorable"
kabidum, fem. *kabida* "heavy"
kabdum "heavy"
Kabid, DN
KBR "to be great"

B *jakbur*
kabarum "great," "thick"
kibrum
kubārum
D *kubburum*

KBS "to tread upon"
kabasum
kabisum, fem. *kabisatum*
kabis(ān)
kibsum, fem. *kibsatum* "step"
kubāsum, fem. *kubāsatum*
kubsatum, fem.

KḎB, see KZB

KHL
kahalum "might"
kihilum, fem. *kihila* "mighty?"

ki "like," see *ka*

kibisum, see KBS

kibrum, see KBR

kibsum, fem. *kibsatum* "step," see KBS

kibśatum, see *kabśum*

kihilum, fem. *kihila* "mighty?," see KHL

kima, see *ka*

kīnum "firm," see KWN

kirbum, see KRB

Kiriš, *Kirišu*, DN

kisibir(r)atum, fem., "coriander"

KLL "to comprise"
B *kalalum*
B or BH *jaklil*

KMN, verb
B *kamanum*
kaminum
kamnum
kumānum
B or BH *jakmin*

KMS "to hide"
B *kamisum*
kumis(ān)
kumsum
B or BH *jakmis*

K?NW, verb
B *jaknū*

KNK "to seal"
kanakum
kanikum

KNŚ "to bow down"
kanaśum
kaniśum, fem. *kaniśa*

KRB "to bless," "to pray"
B *jakrub*
Jakrub-ʾIl, DN
kirb(ān)um

K?S?W "to cover?"
B *jiksū*
kasijum?
BH *jāksī*

K?ŚJ, verb
B or BH *jakśī*
D pass. *mukaśśajum*

KŠR "to be proper"
kašarum
kašerum, fem. *kašera* "proper," "kosher"
kušr(ān)um

kubārum, see KBR

kubāsum, fem. *kubāsatum*, see KBS

kubburum, see KBR

kubsatum, see KBS

kūbum, noun

kumānum, see KMN

kumisum, see KMS

kumrum "priest"

kumsum, see KMS

kundulatum, *kundula*, fem., noun

Kupapa, fem. DN

kuśāpum, noun

kušrum, see KŠR

kuwwunum, see KWN

kuzābum, fem. *kuzābatum*, see KZB

KWN "to be firm"
B *jakūn*; impv. *kūn*
kānum
kīnum "firm"
BH *jākīn*; impv. *kīn*?
mēkīnum
D *kuwwunum*

KZB "to be luxuriant"
kazibum
kuzābum, fem. *kuzābatum*

L

Lʾ?ʾ?, verb
B *jilʾaʾ*

LʾJ "to prevail"
B *jalʾē*; *jaleʾʾē*
laʾijum, fem. *laʾītum*; cf. also LWJ

Lʾ?M, verb
B *jalʾum*

Lʾ?P, verb
B *laʾip(ān)*, fem. *laʾipa*
luʾpum
D *luʾʾupum*

Lʾ?Ś, verb
laʾiśum
laʾūśum

la, *li*, *lu*, prep., "to," "for," as in *la-ka* "to you," *lija* "to me," *luhu* "to him" (with exceptions)

la-, *li-*, *lu-*, precative, optative enclitic, "verily," "may ...."
(*lā*, adv., "not"; no clear examples found)
laʾijum, fem. *laʾītum*, see Lʾ J
laʾipum, fem. *laʾipa*, see Lʾ?P
laʾiśum, see Lʾ?Ś
laʾītum, see *laʾijum*
laʾūśum, see Lʾ?Ś
Labā, see *Labwa*
Labana, DN, see LBN
labanum, *labnum* "white," see LBN
labbinum, see LBN
labnum, see *labanum*
labūm, see *labwum*
Labwa, *Labā*, DN
labwum, *labūm* "lion"
laḫm(atān)um, noun
lājum, *lījum*, see LWJ
lalaʾ?um, fem. *lalaʾ?atum* "fullness," "desire"
lālum, noun
lama, adv., "why?" (or *Lama*, DN)
lamassum, fem. *lamassatum*, *lamassa* "(protective) demon"
lāsimum "runner"
lāšū, *lāšī* "there is not"
laṭūpum, noun
LBN "to be white"
  labanum, *labnum* "white"
  Labana, DN
  labbinum
li, *li-*, see *la* and *la-*
libbum "heart"
lījum, see *lājum*
līlum, noun
Līm, DN
līmum "turn"
lu, *lu-*, see *la* and *la-*
luʾʾupum, see Lʾ?P
luʾpum, see Lʾ?P
lūlum, noun
lummum, noun
LWJ "to surround," "to accompany"
  lājum, *lījum*; cf. also Lʾ J

M

Mʾ D "to be plentiful" or Mʿ D "to promise"
 B *Jamʾad*, *Jamʾadum*, GN
  maʾdum
  miʾd(ān)um
 BH *jāmʾid*
Mʿ D, see Mʾ D
mā, see *manna*
-ma, *-mi*, asseverative enclitic, "truly," "verily"
maʾdum, see Mʾ D
māʾnipum, see ʾ?NP
maʾnūpum, see ʾ?NP
maḏmarum, fem. *maḏmaratum*, *maḏmara* "bastard," see ḎMR
maganum, see MGN
māgrin, see GRN
magūnum, fem. *magūnatum*, see MGN
maharum, see MH?R
mahirum, fem. *mahira*, see MH?R
māhlilum, see HLL
mahrum, see MH?R
māḥziqum, *mēḥziqum*, see ḤZQ
māḫśimum, see Ḫ?ŚM
malakum, see MLK
Malik, DN, see MLK; cf. also *ʾIlum-Malik*, GN
malikum "king," fem. *malikatum*, *malika* "queen," see MLK
malkum "king," see MLK
Mama, fem. DN
mammanum, see *manmanum*
manawum, fem. *manawa*, see MNW
manijum, see MNW
manmanum, *mammanum*, indef. pron., "whoever"
manna, *mā*, interr. pron., "who?," "what?"
māntinum, see NTN
manuwum, fem. *manuwatum*, *manūtum*, see MNW
manzalum, see NZL
Maraṣ, DN, see MRṢ
maraṣum, *maruṣum*, fem. *marṣatum*, *marṣa* "sick," see MRṢ
mardapum, see RD?P?
Marduk, DN (Akkadian)
mariʾum, see MRʾ?
māridum, see JRD
marṣatum, *marṣa*, fem., "sick," see *maraṣum*
maruʾum, see MRʾ?
maruṣum, see *maraṣum*
maśalum, noun
maśḥum, fem. *maśḥatum* "anointed," see MŚḤ
maśīḥum, fem. *maśīḥa* "anointed," see MŚḤ
maśiktum, see *maśkum*
māśītum, see ŚJT
maśkarum, see ŚKR
maśkum, fem. *maśiktum*, noun
maśmarum, see ŚMR
maśmiʿum, see ŚMʿ
maśparum, *maśpirum* "envoy," see ŚPR
maṣiʾum, fem. *maṣiʾatum*, see MṢʾ
mataqum, *matiqum*, *matqum* "sweet"

matiᶜum, see MTᶜ
matiqum, see *mataqum*
matqum, see *mataqum*
mātum "land"
Maṭar, DN, see MṬR
maṭarum, see MṬR
mazraqatum, see ZRQ
mēʾḫiḏum, see ʾḪḎ
mēʾirum, *mīʾirum*, see ʾWR
mēʾīšum, see ʾ?WŠ?
mēʾmiʾum, see ʾ?Mʾ?
mēᶜḏirum, see ᶜḎR
mēᶜnijum, see ᶜNW
mēᶜqibum, see ᶜQB
mēbiśum, see JBŚ
mēdbirum, see DBR
mēdiᶜum, see JDᶜ
mēḏriᶜum, see ḎRᶜ?
mēḥrimum, see ḤRM
mēḥziqum, see *māḥziqum*
mēkīnum, see KWN
mēnᶜimum, see NᶜM
mēndibum, see NDB
mēnḥiba, fem., see NḤB
mēnḫijum, see NḪ?J?
mēnḫimum, see *mēnᶜimum*
mēnīḫum, see NWḪ
mēpiᶜum, see JPᶜ
meptūḥum, see PTḤ
mēqīmum, see QWM
Mēr, *Mīrum*, DN
merḫum "governor"
merrum, noun
mēśarum, see JŚR
mēśkinum, see ŚKN
mēśkirum, see ŚKR
mēślibatum, fem., see ŚLB
mēślimum, see ŚLM
mēšiᶜum, see JŠᶜ
meškīnum "serf," "poor," see ŚKN
mēṣīdum, see ṢJD
mētirum, see JTR
mētmihum, see TMH?
MGN "to present," "to donate"
    maganum "shield?"
    magūnum, fem. *magūnatum*
    mignum
MH?R, verb
  B *maharum*
    mahir(ān)um, fem. *mahira*
    mahr(ān)um
    mihrum
    muhrum
-mi, see *-ma*
miʾdum, see MʾD
mīʾirum, see *mēʾirum*
mignum, see MGN
mihrum, see MH?R
milkum "rule," "counsel," see MLK
Miqiṭ, DN (Akkadian), see MQṬ
Mīrum, see *Mēr*
mīśqiḫum, see Ś?QḪ?
mitiᶜum, see MTᶜ
MLʾ "to be full"
  BH *jāmliʾ*
MLK "to rule," "to counsel"
  B *malakum*
    malikum "king," fem. *malikatum*, *malika* "queen"
    Malik, DN
    malkum "king"
    milkum "rule," "counsel"
    mulukum
    Muluk, DN
  B or BH *jamlik*
MNW "to count," "to love"
  B *manawum*, fem. *manawa*
    manijum
    manuwum, fem. *manuwatum*, *manūtum*
MQṬ "to fall"
  B *jamquṭ*
    Miqiṭ, DN
  BT *jamtaqaṭ*
MRʾ?, verb
    mariʾum
    maruʾum
MRṢ "to be sick," "to be angry"
  B *jamraṣ*, *jamruṣ*, *jumraṣ*
    maraṣum, *maruṣum*, fem. *marṣatum*, *marṣa* "sick"
    Maraṣ, DN
MS?R, verb
  B or BH *jamsir*
MŚḤ "to anoint"
  B *maśīḥum*, fem. *maśīḥa* "anointed"
    maśḥum, fem. *maśḥatum* "anointed"
    muśāḥum
  BN? *namśiḥum?*
MŚJ?, verb
  B *jamśī*
MṢʾ "to reach," "to find"
  B *maṣiʾum*, fem. *maṣiʾatum*
  B or BH *jamṣiʾ*
MTᶜ "to protect"
  B *jamattiᶜ*; *mataᶜa*
    matiᶜum
    mitiᶜum?

MṬR "to rain"
B *jamṭar*
maṭarum "rain"
Maṭar, DN
mūbitum, see WB?T?
mūdadum "beloved," see JDD
muhrum, see MH?R
muḫarrirum, see Ḫ?RR
mūḫinum, see WḪ?N
mukaśśajum, see K?ŚJ
Muluk, DN, see MLK; cf. also *ʾIlum-Muluk*, GN
mulukum, see MLK
Mumu, DN
mupaḫḫira, fem., see PḪR
mupattiḥtum, *mupattiḥa*, fem., see PTḤ
mūpiʿum, see JPʿ
muqaddimum, see QDM
muqannitum, see QNT?
mūqirum, see JQR
mūsilatum, fem., see WSL
muśāḥum, see MŚḤ
muśallimum, fem. *muśallimatum*, see ŚLM
muśarrika, fem., see ŚRK
mūṣiʾum, see JṢʾ
mūtarum, see JTR
Muti-jabal, GN
mutum "mate," "man"
MWʾ "to be willing"
B *jamuwwaʾ*
MWŠ? "to depart"
B *jamūš*
MWT "to die"
B *jamūt*
Jamūt-baʿl, *Jamūt-baʿlum*, GN
MZʾ?, see MZW?
MZW?, more probable than MZʾ?, verb
B *jamzū*; *mazā*

N

Nʾ?R, see ŠNʾ?R
Nʿ M "to be pleasant"; some entries may have to be interpreted as NḤM
naʿimum "pleasant"
naʿmum "pleasure"
niʿimatum, *niʿima*, fem., "pleasant"
niʿmum, fem. *niʿmatum* "pleasant"
nuʿāma, fem.
nuʿmum "pleasure"
BH *mēnʿimum*, more plausible than *mēnḥimum*
naʿimum "pleasant," see NʿM
naʿmum "pleasure," see NʿM
nabaʾum, see NBʾ
nabīʾum "prophet," see NBʾ
nabiṭum, see NBṬ
nablum, see NBL
nabuṭum, see NBṬ
nādinum, see NDN
nadūbum, fem. *nadūba*, see NDB
nagihum, fem. *nagiha*, see NGH
nagiś(ān)um, noun
Nahr or *Nahar*, DN
nahrum "river"
naḥalum, *naḥlum* "stream"; "inheritance"
naḫara, fem., see NḪ?R
naḫnum, see NḪ?N
nāḫum, see NWḪ
nakamtum, fem., noun
nakarum, *nakrum*, fem. *nakaratum*, *nakartum*, *nakara*, see NKR
naklum, fem. *naklatum*, noun
nakrum, see *nakarum*
namalum "ant"
namašum, *namišum* "ichneumon?"
namḫ?um, noun
namišum, see *namašum*
namratum, fem., for *nawratum* "shining"?, see NWR
namśiḥum?, see MŚḤ
nanatum, see *nanum*
Nani, *Nanni*, DN
nanum, fem. *nanatum*, noun
Nanum, DN
napśum "breath," "life"
nāp?um, see NWP
nāqimum, see NQM
narbatum, see *narbum*
narbum, see *narbatum*, noun
nasqatum, fem., noun
Naśiʾ, DN, see NŚʾ
naśūʾum, see NŚʾ
našpatum, fem., see NŠP
naṣabum, see NṢB
naṣbum, see NṢB
nāṣirum, see NṢR
natūnum, see NTN
Nawar, GN, see NWR
nawarum, see NWR
nawijum, "nomadic encampment," "oasis"
nērum, see *nīrum*
NBʾ "to call," "to name"
B *janbiʾ*, *jabbiʾ*; *janabbiʾ*
nabaʾ?um
nabīʾum "prophet"
nabūʾum

NBL "to wither"
B *janbul*
nabl(ān)um
NBṬ "to shine," "to appear," "to look"
B *jinbiṭ*, *jibbiṭ*?
nabiṭum
nabuṭum
nubaṭa, fem.
D *nub(b)uṭa*, fem.
NDB "to give generously"; cf. also NṬP
B *nadūbum*, fem. *nadūba*
BH *mēndibum*
NDN "to give"; also NTN
B *jiddin* (never *jaddin*)
nādinum
NDR "to vow"
B *jandur*?
NGH "to shine" or NQJ "to be clear"
B *nagihum*, fem. *nagiha*
nighatum, fem.
B or BH *jangih*
NḤB, verb
B *jaḥḥab*
BH *jāḥḥib*
mēnḥiba, fem.
NḤM, see NʿM
NḪ?J?, verb
BH *mēnḫijum*
NḪ?N, verb
B *janḫan*
naḫnum
BH *jēnḫin*
NḪ?R, verb
B *janḫur*
naḫara, fem.
BH *jānḫir*
niʿimatum, *niʿima*, fem., "pleasant," see NʿM
niʿmum, fem. *niʿmatum* "pleasant," see NʿM
nighatum, fem., see NGH
nīḫum, fem. *nīḫatum*, see NWḪ
nikrum, see NKR
Ningal, DN (Sumerian)
niqmum "vengeance," see NQM
nīrum, *nērum*, *niwrum*, fem. *nīra* "light," see NWR
nišū "people"; written with ŠU sign
niṣbum, see NṢB
niṣrum, see NṢR
niwrum, see *nīrum*
NKR "to be alien, different"
nakarum, *nakrum*, fem. *nakaratum*, *nakartum*, *nakara*
nukr(ān)um
NPḪ "to blow"
B or BH *jippiḫ*

NQJ, see NGH
NQM "to avenge"
B *nāqimum*
niqmum "vengeance"
B or BH *janqim*, *jaqqim*
BT *jantaqim*
NŚʾ "to carry," "to raise"
B *jaśśiʾ*
Naśiʾ, DN
naśūʾum
NŠP, verb
B *našpatum*, fem.
D *nuš(š)upum*
NṢB "to erect," "to set up"
B *naṣab(ān)um*
naṣbum
niṣbum
BH *jānṣib*
NṢR "to guard"
B *jaṣṣur*
nāṣirum
niṣrum
nuṣrum
NTN "to give"; also NDN
B *jantin*
natūnum
BH *māntinum*
NṬʿ "to plant"
BH? *jānṭiʿ*
NṬP "to drip"; cf. also NDB
nuṭupum, fem. *nutupaṭum*, *nutupṭum*
nuʿama, fem., see NʿM
nuʿmum "pleasure," see NʿM
nubaṭa, fem., see NBṬ
nub(b)uṭa, fem., see NBṬ
nūdum, see NWD
nūḫum "rest," see NWḪ
nukrum, see NKR
Numaḫ?a, *Numḫ?a*, GN
numḫ?um, noun
numrum, for *nuwrum*, *nūrum* "light"?, see NWR
Nunu, DN
nūpum, fem. *nūpatum*, see NWP?
nūrum, fem. *nūrtum*, *nūra* "light," see NWR
nuš(š)upum, see NŠP
nuṣābum, see NṢB
nuṣrum, see NṢR
nuṭupum, fem. *nuṭupatum*, *nuṭuptum*, see NṬP
nuwāp?um, see NWP?
NW?B, verb
BN *jinnāb*, *jinnīb*
NWD "to move around"
B *janūd*
nūd(at)um

NWḪ "to rest"
B *janūḫ*
nāḫum
nīḫum, fem. *nīḫatum*
nūḫum "rest"
BH *jānīḫ*
mēnīḫum
BN *jinnāḫ*
NWPʔ "to be exalted"
B *janūpʔ*
nāpʔum
nūpum, fem. *nūpatum*
nuwāpʔum
NWR "to shine"; cf. also *namratum* and *numrum*
B *janūr*
nawarum
Nawar, GN
nīrum, *nērum*, *niwrum*, fem. *nīra* "light"
nūrum, fem. *nūrtum*, *nūra* "light"
NWZʔ, verb
B *janūz*
NZL, verb
ʾanzal
manzal(ān)um

P

pa-, see *pum*
pagirum, noun
paknum "shorn"
palsum, see PLS
palūsum, see PLS
panijum, see PNJ
paqaḥum, see PQḤ
pāqidum, see PQD
paśīqum "cleaved"
pateḥum, fem. *patiḥa*, see PTḤ
paṭarum, see PṬR
paṭirum, see PṬR
paṭrum, see PṬR
pazrum, see PZR
PDJ "to redeem"
B or BH *japdī*
PGʿ, see PQḤ
PḪR "to gather"
B *japḫur*; impv. *puḫ(u)r* (or *puḫrum*, see below)
puḫrum (see above), fem. *puḫurtum*
D *mupaḫḫira*, fem.
pi-, see *pum*
pilaḫum, see PLḪ
pilḫum, see PLḪ
pilsum, see PLS
piqdatum, see PQD
PLḪ "to fear"
B *japlaḫ*
pilaḫum
pilḫum
pulāḫ(ān)
BH *jāpliḫ*?
PLS "to look," "to view"
B *japlus*
palūsum or *balūṣum*
palsum
pilsum
pulsum
BN *jippalis*
PNJ "to turn to," "to face"
B *jipannī*
panijum
PQD "to order"
B *japqid*
pāqidum
piqdatum, fem.
PQḤ "to open" or PGʿ "to fall upon"
B *paqaḥa*
paqaḥ(at)um
PʔRDʔ, verb
B *jiprud*
PRS "to divide," "to break off"
B *japrus*
D *purus(s)atum*, fem.
PTḤ "to open"
B *japtaḥ*; *pataḥa*
pateḥum, fem. *patiḥa*
B pass. *meptūḥum*
BH *jīptiḥ*
D *japattiḥ*?
mupattiḥtum, *mupattiḥa*, fem.
PTN, verb
B *japtun*, *japtan*
PṬR "to solve," "to redeem"
B impv. *puṭr*
Japṭurum, GN
paṭarum
paṭirum
paṭrum
BH *jāpṭir*
pu-, see *pum*
puḫrum, fem. *puḫurtum*, see PḪR
pulāḫum, see PLḪ
pulsum, see PLS
pum (*pu-*, *pi-*, *pa-*) "mouth," "word"
purʿušum "flea" in *purʿušānu* "full of fleas"
purus(s)atum, see PRS
puzārum, see PZR
puz(z)urum, see PZR
PZR "to hide?"
B *pazrum*
puzārum
D? *puz(z)urum*

Q

qabalatum, see QBL

qabilum, see QBL

qadiśum "sacred," see QDŚ

qadmānum "eastern," see QDM

qahilatum, fem., "assembler," "convener"

qālum, see QWL

qāmum, see QWM

qanatum, see QNT?

qanijum, fem. *qanijatum*, see QNJ

qaqqadum "head" in *qaqqadān* "man with a large head"

qariᵓum, see QRᵓ

qariḥum, see QRᵓ

qarnum "horn"

qarradum "hero"

qaṣirum, see QṢR

Qaṭana, *Qaṭanum*, GN

Qaṭar, DN, see QṬR

Qaṭara, GN, see QṬR

qaṭarum, *qaṭrum*, noun, see QṬR

QBJ? "to speak"
  B   *jaqbī*

QBL, verb
      qabalatum, fem.
      qabilum

QDM "to be in front"
  B   *qadimatum*, fem.
      qadm(ān)um "eastern"
      qidm(ān)um "eastern"
      qudmum
      ᵓaqdamum
  D   *muqaddimum*

QDŚ "to be sacred"
  B   *qadiśum* "sacred"
      qudāśum

qidmānum "eastern," see QDM

qīśum, fem. *qīśtum* "given," "gift," see QJŚ

QJŚ "to donate," "to present"
  B   *jaqīś*
      qīśum, fem. *qīśtum* "given," "gift"

QNJ "to create," "to acquire"
  B   *jaqnī*
      qanij(ān)um, fem. *qanijatum*

QNT?, verb
  B   *qanat(ān)um*
  D   *muqannitum*

QRᵓ "to call"
  B   *qaraᵓ*
      qariᵓum or *qariḥum* "bald"
  BH *jāqriᵓ*

QRB "to be near"
  B   *jiqrib*

QṢR "to bind"

B   *jaqṣur*
    qaṣirum

QṬR
      qaṭarum "smoke," "incense"
      Qaṭar, DN
      Qaṭara, GN
      qaṭr(ān)um, noun

qudāśum, see QDŚ

qudmum, see QDM

QWL "to speak"
  B   *qāla*
      qālum

QWM "to stand"
  B   *jaqūm*; *qāma*
      qāmum
  BH *jāqīm*
      mēqīmum

R

RᶜJ "to pasture," "to graze"
  B   *jarᶜī*

RᶜŠ? "to rejoice"
  B   *riᶜštum* "rejoiced over," "joy"
  B or BH *jarᶜiš*

raᵓśum? "head"

rabab(ān)um, noun

rābatum, see *rābum*

rabbum "numerous"

rābum, fem. *rābatum*, see RJB

raḥabum "wide," see RḤB

rāḥatum, see *rāḥum*

raḥibum, see RḤB

raḥimum, fem. *raḥima* "merciful," see RḤM

raḥmum, see RḤM

rāḥum, fem. *rāḥatum*, see RW?Ḥ?

raḥaṣum, see RḤṢ

Rām, *Rāma*, DN, see RWM

ramam(ān)um, noun

ramašum, see RMŠ

rāmatum, see *rāmum*

ramikum, see RMK

ramišum, see RMŠ

rāmum, fem. *rāmatum* "high," see RWM

rapaᵓum, see RPᵓ

Rāpiᵓ, DN, see RPᵓ

rāpiᵓum, fem. *rāpiᵓatum*, *rāpiᵓtum*, *rāpiᵓa* "healer," see RPᵓ

rapš?um "wide"

rapūᵓum "healed," see RPᵓ

Raśap, DN, see RŚP

rašijum, see RŠJ

Raṣijum, GN, see RṢJ

raz?inum, noun

RB?ᶜ?, verb
  B *jarbuᶜ*; *rabaᶜ*?

RBJ "to be large," "to be plentiful"
  BH? *jārbī*

RD?P?, verb
    mardap(ān)um

RGM "to roar," "to speak"
  B *ᵓargam*
    rigm(ān)um "yell," "roar"

RḤB "to be wide," "to be broad"
  B *jarḥab*
    raḥabum "wide"
    raḥibum
    ruḥbatum, fem.
  BH *jārḥib*

RḤM "to have mercy," "to be merciful"
  B *jirḥam, jarḥam*
    raḥimum, fem. *raḥima* "merciful"
    raḥmum

RḤQ "to be far"
  B *jirḥaq*
  BH *jārḥiq*

RḤṢ "to wash," "to inundate"
  B *raḥaṣum*
    riḥṣum "inundation"

riᶜštum "rejoiced over," "joy," see RᶜŠ?

riᶜum "friend"

rībum, fem. *rībatum*, see RJB

rigmum "yell," see RGM

rīḥatum, see *rīḥum*

rīḥum, fem. *rīḥatum*, see RW?Ḥ?

riḥṣum "inundation," see RḤṢ

Rīm, DN, see RWM

rīmatum, see *rīmum*

rimšum, see RMŠ

rīmum, fem. *rīmatum*, see RWM

ripᵓum "healing," see RPᵓ

RJB "to contest"; "to compensate"; cf. also RWB
  B *rābum*, fem. *rābatum*
    rībum, fem. *rībatum*
  B or BH *jarīb*

RKB "to ride upon"
  B *jirkab, jarkab*
    rukābatum, fem.
  BH *jārkib*

RMK, verb
  B *ramik(ān)um*
  BN? *jinirmuk*

RMŠ
    ramašum
    ramišum
    rimšum

RPᵓ "to heal"
  B *jirpaᵓ, jarpaᵓ*; *rapaᵓ*

rapaᵓ(ān)um
rāpiᵓum, fem. *rāpiᵓatum*, *rāpiᵓtum*, *rāpiᵓa* "healer"
Rāpiᵓ, DN
rapūᵓum "healed"
ripᵓum "healing"

RŚP "to flame"
  B *jarśap*
    Raśap, DN
    Ruśpān, DN

RŠJ "to possess," "to acquire"
  B *jaršī*
    rašijum

RṢJ "to be willing"
  B *raṣā*
    Raṣijum, GN

rūbum, fem. *rūbatum*, *rūba*, see RWB

ruḥbatum, fem., see RḤB

rūḥum "wind," see RW?Ḥ?

rukābatum, fem., see RKB

rūmatum, fem., see RWM

Ruśpān, DN, see RŚP

RWB, verb; cf. also RJB
  B *jarūb*
    rūbum, fem. *rūbatum*, *rūba*

RW?Ḥ?, verb
  B *rāḥum*, fem. *rāḥatum*
    rīḥ(ān), fem. *rīḥatum*
    rūḥum "wind"
  BH *jārīḥ*

RWJ "to drink one's fill"
  BH? *jārwī*

RWM "to be high above," "to be lofty"
  B *rāmum*, fem. *rāmatum* "high"
    Rām, Rāma, DN
    rīmum, fem. *rīmatum*
    Rīm, DN
    rūmatum, fem.
  BH *jārīm*

S

saniqum, see SNQ

satūrum, noun

saṭijatum, fem., see S?Ṭ?J?

sikilum, siklum, sikiltum, masc., see SKL

sinaqum, see SNQ

sinuqum, see SNQ

sitrum "cover?," "protection?"; written regularly with ZI, once with SI

SKL
    sikilum, siklum, sikiltum, masc.
    sukilum

SMK, see ŚMK

SNQ, verb
  B *jasniq*

saniqum
sinaqum
sinuqum

S?Ṭ?J?, verb; written three times with ZA, twice with SA, and three times with DI, twice with TI; cf. also Ś?Ṭ?Ḥ?
B *jasaṭṭiʾ*
saṭijatum, fem.

sukilum, see SKL

Sumukan, DN

Ś

Śʾ L "to ask"
B *śaʾalum*
śaʾīlatum, *śaʾīltum*, fem.
śaʾlum, fem. *śaʾlatum*
D *śuʾʾulum*

śaʾalum, see Śʾ L

śaʾīlatum, *śaʾīltum*, fem., see Śʾ L

śaʾlum, fem. *śaʾlatum*, see Śʾ L

śabimum, fem. *śabimatum*, see ŚBM

Śaggaratum, *Śangaratum*, GN

śaggarum, *śangarum*, fem. *śanagratum*, noun

śaḫirum, *śaḫrum*, see Ś?Ḫ?R

śakanum, see ŚKN

śakarum, see ŚKR

śakbum, see ŚKB

śākirum, fem. *śākira*, see ŚKR

śaknum, fem. *śaknatum*, see ŚKN

śakūrum, see ŚKR

śalalum, see ŚLL

śalamum, fem.? *śalamatum*, see ŚLM

śaliḥum, fem. *śaliḥa*, see ŚLḤ

śalilum, see ŚLL

Śalim, DN, see ŚLM

śalimum, fem. *śalimatum*, *śalima* "well," see ŚLM

śalluḥum, see ŚLḤ

śalmum "well," see ŚLM

Śamʾāl, *Śamʾīl*, *Śimʾāl*, deified GN, meaning "left," "north"

śamʿum, see ŚMʿ

śamakum, see ŚMK

śamamum, see ŚMM

Śamar, DN?, see ŚMR

śamarum, see ŚMR

Śam(a)ś, DN, see *śamśum*

śāmiʿum, fem. *śāmiʿa*, see ŚMʿ

śamimum, see ŚMM

śāmirum, see ŚMR

śamkum, see ŚMK

śammum, see ŚMM

Śamśī-Haddu, an OA king

Śamśu-ʾiluna, an OB king

Śamśu-ditana, an OB king

śamśum, *śapśum* "sun"
Śam(a)ś, DN

śamūʿum, see ŚMʿ

śamūkum, see ŚMK

śamulatum, fem., noun

śāmum, fem. *śāmtum*, see ŚJM

śamumum, see ŚMM

śanagratum, fem., see *śaggarum*

Śangaratum, GN, see *Śaggaratum*

śangarum, see *śaggarum*

śapaqum, see ŚPQ

śaparum, see ŚPR

śapiqum, see ŚPQ

śapīrum, fem *śapīratum* "beautiful," see ŚPR

śaprum, see ŚPR

śapśum, see *śamśum*

śapurum, see ŚPR

śaqṭum, see ŚQṬ

śarijum, see ŚRJ?

śarikum, see ŚRK

śarrum "king," fem. *śarratum*, *śarra* "queen"

śāṭiḥum, see Ś?Ṭ?Ḥ?

śaṭūḥum, see Ś?Ṭ?Ḥ?

ŚBB, see ḎBB

ŚBJ "to take captive"
B or BH *jaśbī*

ŚBL, verb; cf. also ZBL
B *śibilum*
D *śub(b)ulum*

ŚB?M, verb
B *jiśbim*
śabimum, fem. *śabimaṭum*

Ś?Ḫ?R, verb
B *jaśḫir*
śaḫirum
śaḫrum
śuḫārum, fem. *śuḫārtum*; written with signs SU and ŠU, not ZU(ṢU)
śuḫrum
BT *śi?taḫra*, fem.

śībatum, see *śībum*

śibilum, see ŚBL

śībum, fem. *śībatum*, *śībtum* "old (person)"

śikirum, see ŚKR

śikrum "memory," see ŚKR

śilibum, see Ś?LB

Śimʾāl, see *Śamʾāl*

śīmatum, see *śīmum*

śimḫum "joy," see ŚMḪ

śimmum, see ŚMM

śimrum "protection," see ŚMR

śīmum, fem. *śīmatum*, *śīmtum*, see ŚJM
śipqum, see ŚPQ
śiprum, see ŚPR
śitaḫra, fem., see Ś?Ḫ?R
śītatum, fem., see ŚJT
ŚJM "to place"
B *jaśīm*; *śāma*
śāmum, fem. *śāmtum*, now under *śamum*
śīmum, fem. *śīmatum*, *śīmtum*
ŚJT "to put," "to place"
B *śītatum*, fem.
BH *jāśīt*
māśītum
ŚKB, verb
B *jaśkub*
śakbum
ŚKḤ, see Ś?Q?Ḫ?
ŚKN "to dwell," "to place"
śakanum
śaknum, fem. *śaknatum*
BH *jāśkin*
mēśkinum or *meśkīnum* "serf," "poor"
ŚKR "to remember"; "to name"; cf. also ḎKR
B *jaśkur*
ᵓAśkur, DN
śakarum
śākirum, fem. *śākira*
śakūr(ān)um
śikrum "memory"
śikirum
maśkarum
BH *mēśkirum*
D *śuk(k)uratum*, fem.
Ś?LB, verb
B *śilibum*
BH *mēślibatum*, fem.
ŚLḤ "to send"
B *jaślaḥ*
śaliḥum, fem. *śaliḥa*
śulāḥ(ān)um, fem. *śulāḥatum*
D *śalluḥum*
śul(l)uḥum
ŚLL "to take booty?"
B *jaślal*
śalalum
śalilum
D *śullalum*
śullulum
DT *juśtallil*
ŚLM "to be well," "to be peaceful"
B *jiślam*
śalamum, fem.? *śalamatum*
śalimum, fem. *śalimatum*, *śalima* "whole," "well"
Śalim, DN
śalmum "well," "whole"
śulāmum
śulmum "peace"
BH *jāślim*
mēślimum
D *muśallimum*, fem. *muśallimatum*
ŚM^{c} "to hear," "to listen to"; some entries may belong to ŚMḪ
B *jiśma^{c}*, *jaśma^{c}*; impv. *śima^{c}*; *śama^{c}*, *śama^{c}*a
śāmi^{c}um, fem. *śāmi^{c}a*
śamū^{c}um
śam^{c}(atān)um
BT *jiśtama^{c}*?
BH *māśmi^{c}(ān)um*
ŚMḪ "to rejoice"; some entries may belong to ŚM^{c}
B *śimḫum* "joy," written mainly with the ŠI sign, not SI as expected
śumḫum "joy"
D *śum(m)uḫum*, fem. *śum(m)uḫatum*, *śum(m)uḫtum* "very joyful"
ŚMK "to support"; not SMK because all entries are written with SA, SU signs, not ZA, ZI signs
B impv. *śum(u)k*
śamakum
śamukum
śamkum
śumk(ān)um
D *śum(m)ukum*
ŚMM, verb
B *śamamum*
śamimum
śamūmum
śammum
śimmum
D *śummumum*
ŚMR "to guard," "to protect"; cf. also ḎMR
B *śamarum*
Śamar, DN?
śāmirum
śimrum "protection"
maśmarum
BT *jiśtamar*
ŚNB, see ḎNB
ŚPQ "to be plentiful"
B *jaśpuq*
śapaqum
śapiqum
śipqum
ŚPR "to be beautiful"; "to send"
B *śaparum*
śapīrum, fem. *śapīratum* "beautiful"
śaprum
śapurum
śiprum
maśparum, *maśpirum* "envoy"
D *śup(p)ur(t)um*
Ś?Q?Ḫ? or ŚKḤ "to forget?"
D *śaqaḫ*
BH *mēśqiḫum*

ŚQṬ "to be undisturbed," "to be quiet"
B *śaqṭum*
BH *jāśqiṭ*
ŚRJ "to contend with"
B *śaraj*
śarijum; cf. also *ḏariʿum*
ŚRK "to give ex-voto"
B *jaśruk*
śarikum
D *muśarrika*, fem.
Ś?Ṭ?Ḥ? "to spread"; cf. also S?Ṭ?J?
B *jaśṭiḥ*
śāṭiḥum
śaṭūḥum
śuʾʾulum, see ŚʾL
śub(b)ulum, see ŚBL
śugāgum "village chief," "sheikh"
śuḫārum, fem. *śuḫārtum*, see Ś?Ḫ?R
śuḫrum, see Ś?Ḫ?R
śuk(k)uratum, see ŚKR
śulāḥum, fem. *śulāḥatum*, see ŚLḤ
śulāmum, see ŚLM
śullalum, see ŚLL
śul(l)uḥum, see ŚLḤ
śul(l)ulum, see ŚLL
śulmum "peace," see ŚLM
śumḫum "joy," see ŚMḪ
śumkum, see ŚMK
śum(m)uḫum, fem. *śum(m)uḫatum*, *śummuḫtum* "very joyful," see ŚMḪ
śum(m)ukum, see ŚMK
śum(m)umum, see ŚMM
Śumu-ʾabum, an OB king
Śumu-ʾEl, an OB king
Śumu-la-ʾIl, an OB king
śumum "name," "(male) progeny"
Śumu-ṣidqum, name of a king?
śup(p)ur(t)um, see ŚPR
śurārum, noun

Š

šābum, see ŠWB
Šadā or *Šadaj*, DN, see *šadūm*
šadūm "mountain," also deified; generally written with ŠA, not SA; cf. also *Šadā* or *Šadaj*, DN
šagišum, see ŠGŠ
Šākim, DN, see ŠKM
šākimum, see ŠKM
šakūmum, see ŠKM
Šala, *Šalaš*, DN
šalgum "snow"
šanijum, see ŠNJ
šaššar(ān)um "chain"
šāt, see *ḏū*
šataqlum, see ŠQL
šatašnijum, see ŠNJ
šaṭpum, see ŠṬP
šaṭūpum, see ŠṬP
šawilum, fem. *šawilatum*, noun
ŠBʿL, quadriconsonantal verb
impv. and/or part. *šuba/iʿl*; collected under BʿL; cf. also ŠNʾ?R
ŠGŠ "to kill"
B *šagišum*
šī, see *šū*
šina, see *šū*
šini, see *šū*
šipṭum "judgment," see ŠPṬ
šiqlum, see ŠQL
ŠKM, verb
B *šākimum*
Šākim, DN
šakūmum
ŠNʾ?R, quadriconsonantal verb
impv. and/or part. *šunuʾr*; collected under Nʾ?R; cf. also ŠBʿL
ŠNJ "to repeat"
B *jišnī*
šanijum
BŠT *jištašnī*
šatašnijum
DT *juštannī*
DŠT *juštašnī*
ŠPṬ "to judge," "to rule"
šipṭum "judgment"
ŠQL "to weigh"
B *šiqlum*
šuqultum, fem.
BT *šataqlum*
ŠṬP, verb
šaṭpum
šaṭūpum
šū, fem. *šī*, pers.-dem. pron. "he," "she"; fem. pl. *šina*, *šini*
šuʿāl(ān)um "fox"
Šulgi, an Ur III king
šuqultum, fem., see ŠQL
šūrum "bull"
ŠWB "to return"
B *jašūb*; impv. *šūb*
šābum
BT *jištāb*?
BH *jāšīb*

Ṣ

ṣabʾum, see ṢBʾ
ṣabaʾum, see ṢBʾ
ṣabiʾum, see ṢBʾ
ṣabrum, see ṢBR
ṣabṭum, see ṢBṬ
ṣabuʾum, see ṢBʾ
ṣadaqa, fem., see ṢDQ
Ṣaduq, *Ṣaduqa*, DN, see ṢDQ
ṣaduqum "just," see ṢDQ
ṣājidum, fem. *ṣājidatum*, see ṢJD
ṣajjādum "hunter," see ṢJD
ṣalilum, see ṢLL
ṣamidum, see ṢMD
ṣarirum, see ṢRR
ṣarrum, see ṢRR
ṢBʾ "to desire"
ṣabaʾum
ṣabiʾum
ṣabuʾum
ṣabʾum
ṣibʾum, fem. *ṣibʾatum* "desire"
ṣubʾum
ṢBR
ṣabrum
ṣibarum
ṢBṬ "to seize"
ṣabṭum
ṣibiṭṭa, fem.
ṢDQ "to be just"
B *jaśduq* (from *jaṣduq*)
ṣadaqa, fem.
ṣaduqum "just"
Ṣaduq, *Ṣaduqa*, DN
ṣidqum "justice"
ṢḤQ "to laugh"
B *jaṣḥaq*
ṣiḥaqum
ṣibʾum, fem. *ṣibʾatum* "desire," see ṢBʾ
ṣibarum, see ṢBR
ṣibiṭṭa, fem., see ṢBṬ
ṣidqum "justice," see ṢDQ
ṣiḥaqum, see ṢḤQ
ṣīḫum, fem. *ṣīḫatum* "rejoiced over," see ṢJḪ
ṣillum "shade," see ṢLL
ṣimidatum?, fem., see ṢMD
ṣirrum, see ṢRR
ṢJD "to nourish"; "to hunt"
B *ṣājidum*, fem. *ṣājidatum*
ṣajjādum "hunter"
BH *jāṣīd*
mēṣīdum
ṢJḪ "to rejoice"
ṣīḫum, fem. *ṣīḫatum* "rejoiced over," "joy"
ṢLL "to shade"
ṣalilum
ṣillum "shade," "protection"
ṢMD "to bind," "to harness"
ṣamidum
ṣimidatum?, fem.
ṢRR
ṣarirum
ṣarrum
ṣirrum
ṣurārum
ṣurrum
ṣubʾum, see ṢBʾ
ṣup?rum "(human) nail"
ṣurārum, see ṢRR
ṣurrum, see ṢRR
ṣūrum "rock"

T

taʾḫadum "battle," see ʾḪḎ
tāʾirum, see TWR
taʾ?um, noun
tabbum, noun
Tabub(*u*), fem. DN
taḥtu, *taḥtun*, prep., "below," "under"
tārum, see TWR
T?Ḫ?J?, verb
B? or BH? *jatḫī*
tinʾ?um, fem. *tinʾ?atum*, noun
tīrum, fem. *tīratum*, see TWR
tispum, fem. *tispatum*, noun
tišanatum, fem., noun
Tišpak, DN
TMH? "to be astounded?"
BH *mētmihum*
T?RM, verb
B impv. *turm*
turmatum, fem.
tuʾ?um, noun
turāḫum "mountain goat"
turmatum, fem., see T?RM
tuśuʿum "ennead," see *ʾIlum-tuśuʿu*, DN
Tutu, DN
TWR "to return"
B *jitūr*; impv. *tūr*
Jitūr-Mēr, *Jatūr-Mēr*, DN
tāʾirum
tārum
tīrum, fem. *tīratum*

Ṭ

ṭābatum, *ṭābtum*, *ṭāba*, fem., "good," see *ṭābum*
ṭābiḫ(at)um, masc.?, "butcher"
ṭābum, fem. *ṭābatum*, *ṭābtum*, *ṭāba* "good"
ṭaḫdum, noun
ṭallum, *ṭillum* "dew," "(light) rain"
ṭaridum, see ṬRD
ṭarudum, see ṬRD
ṬBQ
ṭubqum
ṭubuqa, fem.
ṭillum, see *ṭallum*
ṬRD "to send"
ṭaridum
ṭarudum
ṭubqum, see ṬBQ
ṭubuqa, fem., see ṬBQ
ṭuḫšatum, fem., noun

W

WB?T?, verb
BH *mūbitum*
WDD, see JDD
WDJ "to thank?"
BH pass.? *ᵓawdā* or *hawdā*, *ᵓūdā*, *hūdā*, or *jūdā*
WḤJ "to inspire?"
BH *jāwḥī*
WḪ?N, verb
BH *mūḫinum*
WMᵓ "to swear"
B *jawmaᵓ*, *jūmaᵓ*
Jawmaᵓ-ᶜammum, GN
WPᶜ, see JPᶜ
WQH, see JQH
WQR, see JQR
WSL, verb
BH *mūsilatum*, fem.
WŠB, see JŠB
WṢᵓ, see JṢᵓ
WTᵓ "to search," "to find"
B *ᵓūtaᵓ* or *jūtaᵓ*
WTR, see JTR

Z

zābilum, fem. *zābilatum*, see ZBL
zabūlum, see ZBL
zakkum, noun
zalijum, see ZLJ
zanijatum, see ZNJ
zarqum, see ZRQ
ZBB, see ḎBB
ZBL "to carry"; "to rule"; cf. also ŚBL
zābilum, fem. *zābilatum*
zabūlum
ziblum
zubal(ān), fem. *zubalatum*?
ZHB, see ḎHB
ziblum, see ZBL
z?idarum, noun
zirqum, see ZRQ
ZKR, see ḎKR
Z?LJ?, verb
B *jazlī*
zalijum
ZMR, see ḎMR
ZNB, see ḎNB
ZNJ "to fornicate"
B *zanijatum*, fem.?
BH *māznijatum*, fem.
Z?NR, verb
B *jiznur*
ZQN, see ḎQN
ZRᶜ, see ḎRᶜ?
ZRQ, verb
zarq(atān)um
zirq(ān)um
mazraqatum, fem.
zubālum, fem. *zubālatum*, see ZBL

1. STEMS

The stem, composed of consonants and vowels, is the basic free morpheme of a word without its bound morphemes. It occurs in primary nouns, as in *kalb* of /*Kalb-um*/ "dog"; in several classes of primary conjunctions, prepositions, etc., as in *ka* "like," "as," or *la* of /*La-na-*/ "to us"; and also in the verb and verbal noun *rpaʾ* or *rāpiʾ* of /*Ja-rpaʾ+*/ or /*Rāpiʾ-um*/ from the consonantal root RPʾ "to heal."[1]

For a general discussion of the structure of this chapter and also for a discussion of points of questionable stem analysis see section 0.3.

Consonantal phonemes are discussed briefly in section 0.4.

1. See Ignace J. Gelb, *Sequential Reconstruction of Proto-Akkadian*, Assyriological Studies, no. 18 (Chicago, 1969) and I. M. Diakonoff, "Problems of Root Structure in Proto-Semitic," *Archiv Orientální* 38 (1970), pp. 453 ff.

As will be seen in the introductory remarks to chapter 4, "Stem Count," there are 1,996 consonant-plus-vowel stems.

The alphabetic order of lemmata is the new order of stems:

ʾ	H	Ḥ	Ḫ	ʿ	W	J	
A	B	D	Ḏ	E	G	I	
K	L	M	N	P	Q	R	
S	Ś	Š	Ṣ	T	Ṭ	U	Z

The alphabetic order of parts outside of the lemma is that of my earlier, so-called work order, which is not much different from the new order given above.

For the discussion of the alphabetic sequences see section 0.5.

ʾḪAḎ	2		DANN		UM	TA	ʾḪAḎ			DA-NU-UM-TA-ḪA-AZ		A 7634, M
			DANN		UM	TA	ʾḪAḎ			D-DA-NU-UM-TA-ḪA-[AZ]		TIM V 19 14
ʾḪIḎ	1	JA	ʾḪIḎ		A					IA-E-DA		YOS XIII 343:4
		JA	ʾḪIḎ				ʾUMM	I		IA-ḪI-DU-UM-ME	FN	RA LXV 65 VII 34
		ME	ʾḪIḎ		UM					ME-ḪI-DU-UM		RA LXV 54 XII 64
ʾḪUḎ	1	JA	ʾḪUḎ	AN						IA-ḪU-ZA-AN		RA LXV 43 IV 21
		TA	ʾḪUḎ	AN						TA-ḪU-ZA-AN		RA LXV 52 X 33
ʾWIʾ	2		LA			ʾA	ʾWIʾ					
							ʾIL			LA-WI-IḪ?-DINGIR		TIM IV 33,34,SEALS
ʾWIR	1	JA	ʾWIR		UM					IA-WI-RU-UM		B 31
		MI	ʾWIR		UM					MI-I-RUM		RA LXV 46 V 83
		ME	ʾWIR		I					ME-ḪI-RI		C
		ME	ʾWIR		I		ʾEL			ME-ḪI-RI-E-EL		JCS IV 109 4311 7
	2		LA			ʾA	ʾWIR	UM		LA-WI-RUM		RA XXIV 58 9 4
ʾWIŠ	1	JA	ʾWIŠ				....			IA-ḪI-IŠ-[....]		TIM IV 33 SEAL, 34 SEAL
		ME	ʾWIŠ		UM					ME-I-SU-UM		CT VI 7 21+
ʾWUŠ	1	JA	ʾWUŠ		U					IA-U$_2$-ŠU		B 31
		JA	ʾWUŠ	AN						IA-U$_2$-SA-AN		RA LXV 43 IV 15
		JA	ʾWUŠ				HADD	U		IA-UŠ-D-IM		M+
		JA	ʾWUŠ				HADD	U		IA-U$_2$-UŠ-D-IM		M+
		JA	ʾWUŠ				HADD	U		IA-UŠ$_2$-D-IM		M
		JA	ʾWUŠ				ʾIL			IA-UŠ-DINGIR		M+
		JA	ʾWUŠ				ʾIL			IA-U$_2$-UŠ$_2$-DINGIR		C II 35 28
		JA	ʾWUŠ				ʾIL			IA-U$_2$-UŠ-DINGIR		RA LXV 42 III 10+
		JE	ʾWUŠ				ʾIL			E-WU-ŠI-DINGIR		BIROT, TEA 48:20
		JA	ʾWUŠ				ḪAM	U		IA-U$_2$-UŠ-D-A-MU		M
		JI	ʾWUŠ				ŠALIM			I-UŠ?-SA-LIM		RUTTEN 1 3
ʾAHL	1		ʾAHL		UM		MAʾT	U		[A-LU]-UM-MA-[TU]	FN	M
			ʾAHL		UM		MAʾT	UM		[A-LU-UM]-MA-TUM	FN	M
			ʾAHL		UM		PU		HU	A-LUM-BI-U$_2$		SIMMONS 129 13
			ʾAHL		UM		PU		HU	ḪA-LAM-BU-U$_2$		RLA II 165 17
			ʾAHL		UM		PU		HU	[A]-LI-IN-BU-MU		OLZ 1958 547 N.1
			ʾAHL		UM		PU		HU	A-LUM-BU-MU		OLZ 1958 547 N.1
	2		JAʾ		U		ʾAHL	I		IA-U$_2$-A-LI$_2$		KISURRA 85 19
			JAʾN		A		ʾAHL	UM		JA-NA-A-LUM	GN	MRS VI P.125 61
			BEʿL		I		ʾAHL	I		BE-LI-IA-LI$_2$		KISURRA 112 14
			KAʾB		I		ʾAHL	UM		KA-PI-IA-LUM		UET V 626 11, 702 REV. 5
		JA	KWUN				ʾAHL	I		IA-KU-UN-A-LI		B 92
			MATIʿ				ʾAHL	I		MA-TI-IA-LI		UCP X/1 1 16
		JI	TWUR				ʾAHL	I		I-DUR-A-LI		JCS XXIV 46 NOS. 5, 6
	3		LI			JI	TWUR					
							ʾAHL	I		LI-TU-UR-A-LI		JCS XXIV 62 NO.55+
ʾAḪ	1		ʾAḪ		UM					A-ḪU-UM		M+
			ʾAḪ		IM					A-ḪI-IM	GEN	M
			ʾAḪ		IJA					A-ḪI-IA		M+
			ʾAḪ		AM	ʾA	RŠIJ			A-ḪA-AM-AR-ŠI		I+
			ʾAḪ		I		ḪIʾL			A-ḪI-ḪI-EL		XIII 1 X 17
			ʾAḪ		I		JABAL			A-ḪI-E-BA-AL		M
			ʾAḪ		I		HADD	A		A-ḪI-A-DA		B 12
			ʾAḪ		I		ʾIL			A-ḪI-[I]L		HARRIS 45 11
			ʾAḪ		I		ʾIL	I		A-ḪI-I$_3$-LI$_2$	FN	XIII 1 VIII 20
			ʾAḪ		I		ʾAŠD			A-ḪI-SA-AD		B 12+
			ʾAḪ		I		ʾAŠD			A-ḪI-A-SA-AD		B 12
			ʾAḪ		I		ʾAŠD			A-ḪA-SA-AD		UET V 539 II 19
			ʾAḪ		I		JATAR			A-Ḫ[I]-E?-TAR		RA LXV 46 V 86
			ʾAḪ		I	JI	ʿQUB	A		A-ḪI-I-KU-BA		KISURRA 7A 9
			ʾAḪ		I	JA	JŠUʿ			A-ḪI-IA-ŠU-UḪ		SIMMONS 58 16
			ʾAḪ		I	JA	JŠUʿ			A-ḪI-IA-ŠU		BIROT, TEA 28:17+
			ʾAḪ		I	JE	QWIM			A-ḪI-E-KI-IM		M
			ʾAḪ		I	JA	ŠJIT			A-ḪI-SI-IT		TA 1931, 636
			ʾAḪ		I		DANN	UM		A-ḪI-DA-NU-UM		I
			ʾAḪ		I		DAŠUR			A-ḪI-DA-ŠU-UR$_2$		PBS XI/2 P. 140 NO. 1128
			ʾAḪ		I		KI					
							LIʾM			A-ḪI-KI-LI-IM		JEAN T.SIFR 72 5, 6, 13+
			ʾAḪ		I		KAʾB	I		A-ḪI-KA-PI		YOS VIII 64 18
			ʾAḪ		I		LIʾM			A-ḪI-LI-IM		B 12, M

STEMS													
ʾAḪ	1	ʾAḪ		I			LABAN				A-ḪI-LA-BA-AN		RA LXV 43 IV 5+
		ʾAḪ		I			MAʾJ		UM		A-ḪI-MA-IU-UM		MAM III P. 274
		ʾAḪ		I	JE		MALIK				A-ḪI-E-MA-LIK		M
		ʾAḪ		I			MARAṢ				A-ḪI-MA-RA-AṢ		B 12+, M+
		ʾAḪ		I			MARAṢ				A-ḪI-MA-RA-UṢ		RUTTEN 1 22
		ʾAḪ		I			MARAṢ				A-ḪI-MA-RA-AṢ	FN	XIII 1 IX 24
		ʾAḪ		I			ŠALAŠ				A-ḪI-ŠA-LA-AŠ		EDZARD, DER 104:2
		ʾAḪ		I			ŠUM		U	NA	A-ḪI-SU-MU-NA		SIMMONS 83 5
		ʾAḪ		I		JI	ŠMAʿ			NI	A-ḪI-IŠ-MA-NI		VAS VIII 14:41+
		ʾAḪ		I	Š		TUʾ			JA	A-ḪI-IŠ-TU-IA		A. 86 9
		ʾAḪ		I	Š		TUʾ			KA	A-ḪI-IŠ-DU-KA		A. 98C 1, 6
		ʾAḪ		I		TA	NWUḪ		A		A-ḪI-TA-NU-A		M
		ʾAḪ		I			ṢADUQ				A-ḪI-ZA-DU-UQ		B 12
		ʾAḪ		U			JAḪAD				A-ḪU-IA-ḪA-AD		M+
		ʾAḪ		U			JAT		UM		A-ḪU-IA-TUM	MN	BIN II 98 4
		ʾAḪ		U			JAT		UM		A-ḪU-JA-TUM	MN	M
		ʾAḪ		U			KA						
							ʾAB		I		A-ḪU-KA-A-BI	FN	XIII 1 VIII 60, C+
		ʾAḪ		U			ʾEL				A-ḪU-EL		RA LXV 50 IX 1
		ʾAḪ		UM			LI			JA	A-ḪU-UM-LI-A		M
		ʾAḪ		UM			LA						
							ʾAB		I		A-ḪU-UM-LA-A-BI		YOS XIII 245:17, SEAL
		ʾAḪ		UM			LUʾM		U		A-ḪU-UM-LU-MU		X 166 4+
		ʾAḪ		U			LUʾM		U		A-ḪU-LU-MU		M
		ʾAḪ		UM			MA						
							ʾIL				A-ḪU-UM-MA-DINGIR		M+
		ʾAḪ		UM			MAṬAR		I		A-ḪU-UM-MA-DA-RI		M
		ʾAḪ	AT	UM							A-ḪA-TUM	FN	M+
		ʾAḪ	AT	I							A-ḪA-TI	FN	XIII 1 VIII 6
		ʾAḪ	AT	I			MA				A-ḪA-TI-MA	FN	JCS XXVII 135:1
		ʾAḪ	AT	A	HA						A-ḪA-TA-A	FN	RA LXV 62 V 52
		ʾAḪ	AT	UJA							A-ḪA-TU-IA	FN	SIMMONS 66 4+
		ʾAḪ	AT				JIQR	AH			A-ḪA-AT-IQ-RA	FN	M
		ʾAḪ	AT	A			ʾAB		I		A-ḪA-TA-A-BI	FN	M+
		ʾAḪ	AT	A			NAʿM		I		A-ḪA-TA-NA-AḪ-MI	FN	XIII 1 XI 3
		ʾAḪ	AT	I			JIQR	AT			A-ḪA-TI-IQ-RA-AT	FN	XIII 1 V 5
		ʾAḪ	AT	I			JIQR	AH			A-ḪA-TI-IQ-RA	FN	XIII 1 II 72+
	2	ʾAJA					ʾAḪ		UM		A-IA-A-ḪU-UM		RA LXV 41 II 24
		ʾAJA					ʾAḪ		U		A-IA-A-ḪU		XIII 1 III 52
		ʾAJA					ʾAḪ		U		A-IA-ḪU		A. LATE+
		ʾAJA					ʾAḪ		I		A-IA-A-ḪI		X 166 8'+
		ʾAJA					ʾAḪ		IM		A-IA-A-ḪI-IM		X 166 4
		ʾAJA					ʾAḪ	AT	I		A-IA-A-ḪA-TI	FN	A.
		ʿAḎAR					ʾAḪ				A-ZA-RA-AḪ		JNES XIII 210+ LATE
		ʿAḎR					ʾAḪ		I		ḪA-AZ-RA-ḪI?		CT XLV 54 9
		ʾAL					ʾAḪ	AT	I		AL-A-ḪA-TI	FN	A.
		ʾALI					ʾAḪ		I		A-LI-A-ḪI	FN	M+
		ʾALI					ʾAḪ		I		A-LI_2-A-ḪI	FN	RA LXV 59 II 41
		ʾALI					ʾAḪ	AT	I		A-LI-A-ḪA-TI	FN	XIII 1 IV 71+
		ʾALI					ʾAḪ	AT	I		A-LI-A-ḪA?-TA-TI	FN	M
		ʾALI					ʾAḪ	AT	I		A-LI_2-A-ḪA-TI	FN	RA LXV 59 II 65+
	JA	WMAʾ					ʾAḪ		UM		JA-MA-A-ḪU-UM		RA LXV 52 X 49
		ʿAN		UM			ʾAḪ		I		A-NU-UM-A-ḪI		RA LXV 53 XI 43
		ḪANN		A			ʾAḪ		UM		AN-NA-A-ḪU-UM		RA LXV 52 XI 1
		ḪANN		A			ʾAḪ		IM		AN-NA-A-ḪI-IM	GEN	M
		ḪANN		A			ʾAḪ		I		AN-NA-A-ḪI	GEN	M
		ʿAQB		A			ʾAḪ		UM		AQ-BA-A-ḪU-UM		M+
		ʿAQB		A			ʾAḪ		UM		AQ-BA-ḪU-UM		B 11+
		ʿAQB		A			ʾAḪ		UM		ḪA-AQ-BA-A-ḪU-UM		RA LXV 43 III 57+
		ʿAQB		A			ʾAḪ		U		AQ-BA-A-ḪU		M+, C+
		ʿAQB		A			ʾAḪ		U		AQ-BA-ḪU		BASOR 95 19+
		ʿAQB		A			ʾAḪ		AM		AQ-BA-A-ḪA-AM	ACC	M
		ʿAQB		A			ʾAḪ		IM		AQ-BA-A-ḪI-IM	GEN	M+
		ʿAQB		A			ʾAḪ		IM		ḪA-AQ-BA-A-ḪI-IM	GEN	M+
		ʿAQB		A			ʾAḪ		I		AQ-BA-A-ḪI	GEN	XII 448 5+
		ʿAQB		I			ʾAḪ		U		AQ-BI-A-ḪU		B 11
		ʿIQB		A			ʾAḪ		UM		IQ-BA-A-ḪU-UM		KISURRA 4A 11, M

STEMS

ʾAḪ	2		ʿIQB		A		ʾAḪ	UM		IQ-BA-ḪU-UM		KISURRA 121 6	
			ʾAŠD		A		ʾAḪ	I		AŠ-DA-A-ḪI		VAS XVI 44 3	
		ʾU	WTAʾ				ʾAḪ	I		U_2-TA-A-ḪI		M	
			JATAR				ʾAḪ	UM		JA-TA-AR-ḪU-UM		I	
		JI	JṢIʾ				ʾAḪ	UM		I-ZI-A-ḪU-UM		M+	
		JI	JṢIʾ				ʾAḪ	U		I-ZI-A-ḪU?		X 53:6	
			BIN		A		ʾAḪ	UM		BI-NA-A-ḪU-UM		M+	
			DIWIR				ʾAḪ	I		DI-WI-IR-A-ḪI		PBS XI/1 P. 55+	
			DIWIR				ʾAḪ	I		DI-BI-IR-A-ḪI		PBS XI/1 P. 55+	
			ḎAKUR		A		ʾAḪ	UM		ZA-KU-RA-A-ḪU-UM		M+	
			MUT		I		ʾAḪ	I		MU-TI-A-ḪI	GEN	B 35	
			NAKR				ʾAḪ	UM		NA-AK-RA-ḪU-UM		RUTTEN 2 19+	
		ʾA	RŠIJ				ʾAḪ	UM		AR-ŠI-A-ḪU-UM		M+	
			ŠUM		U		ʾAḪ	I	JA	[SU]-MU-A-ḪI-IA		PBS XI/2 1 I 27	
			ŠAMŠ		I		ʾAḪ	I		SA-AM-SI-A-ḪI		RA LXV 54 XII 26	
			ŠIPṬ		A		ʾAḪ	UM		ŠI-IP-TA-A-ḪU-UM		RA LXV 46 VI 27	
			ṢAMID				ʾAḪ	I		ZA-MI-ID-A-ḪI		CT IV 8B 17	
	3		ʾIL		I		MAʾD	I					
							ʾAḪ			I_3-LI_2-MA-DI-A-AḪ		RUTTEN 1 8	
			ʾIL		I		MAʾD	I					
							ʾAḪ			DINGIR?-MA-DA-AḪ		RA LXV 42 III 21	
			ʾIL		I		MAʾD	I					
							ʾAḪ			I_3-LI_2-MI-DI-AḪ		EDZARD, DER 146:14	
			ʾIL		I		MAʾD	I					
							ʾAḪ	I		I_3-LI_2-MA-DA-ḪI		RUTTEN 14 7	
			ʾIL		I		MAʾD	I					
							ʾAḪ	A		I_3-LI_2-MA-DA-ḪA		VAS VIII 14 4	
			BIN				MA						
							ʾAḪ	IM		BI-IN-MA-A-ḪI-IM		M	
			BIN		I		MA						
							ʾAḪ	UM		BI-IN-NI-MA-ḪU-UM		TLB I 3 28	
			BIN		I		MA						
							ʾAḪ	UM		BI-NI-MA-ḪU-UM		CCT IV 13A 6+	CAPP.
			BUN		I		MA						
							ʾAḪ	UM		BU-NI-MA-ḪU-UM		TCL XX 96 8	
			BUN		U		MA						
							ʾAḪ	UM		BU-NU-MA-A-ḪU-UM		B 16	
			LA			ʾA	HWIJ						
							ʾAḪ	I		LA-AḪ-WI-A-ḪI	FN	XIII 1 VII 3	
			QAWM		U		MA						
							ʾAḪ	UM		QA-MU-MA-A-ḪU-UM		M	
			QAWM		U		MA						
							ʾAḪ	I		QA-MU-MA-A-ḪI		RA LXV 41 II 22	
ʾAḪW	2		ʾAJA				ʾAḪW	I		A-IA-A-ḪU-I		JCS V 133	
ʾAḪAL	1		ʾAḪAL		UM					A-ḪA-LUM		BIROT, TEA 45:12	
ʾAḪIḎ	1		ʾAḪIḎ	AN						A-ḪI-ZA-AN		M	
ʾAḪIL	1		ʾAḪIL	AT	UM					A-ḪI-LA-TUM	FN	XIII 1 I 67	
ʾAḪN	1		ʾAḪN	AN	UM					AḪ-NA-NU-UM		KISURRA 14 4+	
ʾAḪR	1		ʾAḪR		AM					AḪ-RA-AM	ACC	II 43 13	
ʾAWAʾ	1		ʾAWAʾ	AT	UM					A-WA-TUM	FN	M	
			ʾAWAʾ	ATAN						A-WA-TA-AN		RA LXV 47 VII 31+	
			ʾAWAʾ	AT	I		ʾEL			A-WA-TI-EL		RA LXV 41 II 37+	
			ʾAWAʾ	AT	I		ʾIL			A-WA-TI-DINGIR	MN	XIII 1 XI 39	
ʾAWIJ	1		ʾAWIJ		UM					A-WI-U_2-UM		GORDON 38 21+	
			ʾAWIJ	AT	UM					ḪA-WI-IA-TUM		BIROT TEA 39:4	
			ʾAWIJ	AT	UM					A-WI-IA-TUM	MN?	TIM I 11 10+	
			ʾAWIJ	T	UM					ḪA-WI-TUM		BIROT TEA 72 I 28+	
			ʾAWIJ			JA	JṢIʾ			A-WI-IA-ZI		RA LXV 53 XI 49	
			ʾAWIJ				KIRIŠ	U		A-WI-KI-RI-IŠ		XIV 106:18	
ʾAWIN	1		ʾAWIN							A-WI-IN		M+	
			ʾAWIN		UM					A-WI-NU-UM		FLP 516, UR III	
ʾAWN	1		ʾAWN	AN	UM					AM-NA-NU-UM	GN	SAKI P. 222+	
			ʾAWN	AN	UM					AM-NA-NU-UM	PN	SUMER XIV 49	
			ʾAWN	AN	UM					AW-NA-NU-[UM]	TRIBE	M	
			ʾAWN	AN	U					AM-NA-NU		BM 80328 9	
			ʾAWN	AN	IM					AW-NA-NI-[IM]	GEN	MAM III 320, PSARG MARI	

STEMS

ʾAWN	1	ʾAWN	ANIJI							AM-NA-NI-I	TRIBE	M
		ʾAWN	AN		JA	ʾRUR				AM-NA-AN-IA-AḪ-RU-UR	TRIBE	BAGHD. MITT. II 56 I 12+
	2	MUT				ʾAWN	AN			MU-UT-AW-NA-AN		B 35 HANA
		MUT		U		ʾAWN	AN	UM		MU-TU-AM-NA-NU-UM		BM 81641 3, 8
		ŠUM		U		ʾAWN	AN	UM		SU-MU-AM-NA-NU-UM		B 38+
		ŠUM		U		ʾAWN	AN	IM		SU-MU-AW-NA-NIM		SUMER XXIII ARABIC 178
ʾAJ	1	ʾAJ		A		ʿALIJ	AT			D-A-A-ḪA-LI-IA-AT	MN?	CT XLV 92 R. 12
		ʾAJ		A		ʾARR		I		D-A-A-AR-RI	FN	M
ʾAJA	1	ʾAJA				ʾAḪ		UM		A-IA-A-ḪU-UM		RA LXV 41 II 24
		ʾAJA				ʾAḪ		U		A-IA-A-ḪU		XIII 1 III 52
		ʾAJA				ʾAḪ		U		A-IA-ḪU		A. LATE+
		ʾAJA				ʾAḪ		I		A-IA-A-ḪI		X 166 8'+
		ʾAJA				ʾAḪ		IM		A-IA-A-ḪI-IM		X 166 4
		ʾAJA				ʾAḪW		I		A-IA-A-ḪU-I		JCS V 133
		ʾAJA				ʾAḪ	AT	I		A-IA-A-ḪA-TI	FN	A.
		ʾAJA				ḪAʾL		U		A-IA-ḪA-LU		M
		ʾAJA				ʾAB						
						ʾIL				ḪA-IA-AB-DINGIR		B 18
		ʾAJA				ʾAB		I		A-IA-A-BI		A.
		ʾAJA				ʾAB		I		A-IA-BI		A.+
		ʾAJA				ʾAB		I				
						ŠARR		I		A-IA-BI-ŠAR-RI		A.
		ʾAJA				ʾAB		I				
						TALM		A		A-IA-BI-TA-AL-MA		A. 239 15
		ʾAJA				ʾAB		U		A-IA-A?-BU?	FN	C+
		ʾAJA				ʾAB		U		A-IA-BU		A. LATE +
		ʾAJA				ʾAB		U	HU	A-A-A-BU-U_2	FN	DE CLERCQ II 253B
		ʾAJA				ʾAB		UM		ḪA-A-IA-A-BU-UM		M
		ʾAJA				ʾAB		UM		ḪA-IA-BU-UM		B 18+
		ʾAJA				ʾAB		AM		ḪA-A-IA-A-BA-AM	ACC	M+
		ʾAJA				ʾABN		I				
						ʾIL				ḪA-IA-AB-NI-DINGIR		B 18+
		ʾAJA				ʾIL				A-IA-DINGIR		A.+
		ʾAJA				ʾUMM		I		A-IA-UM-MI	FN	RA LXV 59 II 27
		ʾAJA				ʿAMM		U		A-IA-AM-MU		MAOG IV 2 10, 11, A 7740+
		ʾAJA				ʿAMM		U	HU	A-A-ḪA-AM-MU-U_2		BASOR 95 23
		ʾAJA				ʿAMM		U	HU	A-IA-ḪA-MU-U_2		A 7648, M
		ʾAJA				ʿAMM		U	HU	A-IA-AM-MU-U_2		VAS XIII 34:3
		ʾAJA				ʿAMM		U	HU	A-IA-AM-MU-KU		CT XLV 6 33
		ʾAJA				ʿAMM		U	HU	IA-ḪA-AM-MU-U_2		VAS XVIII 100:19
		ʾAJA				ʾAZJ		I		A-IA-ZI		M
		ʾAJA			JE	JŠUʿ				A-A-E-ŠU-UḪ?		TCL X 9 3
		ʾAJA				BAʿL		A	JA	A-A-BA-LA-IA		SIMMONS 63 9
		ʾAJA				DAWD		U		A-IA-DA-DU		M
		ʾAJA				DAWD		U	HU	A-A-DA-DU-U_2		HARRIS 79 5
		ʾAJA				DAWD		U	HU	A-IA-DA-DU-U_2		TIM IV 39 15
		ʾAJA				KALB	AH			A-IA-KA-AL-BA?	FN	C
		ʾAJA				LA						
						ŠUM		U	HU	A-IA-LA-SU-MU-U_2		M, C
		ʾAJA				MA						
						ʾIL				A-IA-MA-DINGIR		M
		ʾAJA				MA						
						ʾIL				ḪA-IA_3-MA-DINGIR		XIV 93:8+
		ʾAJA				MA						
						ʾEL				A-IA-MA-EL		RA LXV 42 III 14
		ʾAJA				MUT		I		ḪA-IA-MU-TI		BAGHD. MITT. II 7 2, 4, 8
		ʾAJA				MAṬAR				ḪA-IA-MA-DAR		YOS XII 360 17
		ʾAJA				MAṬAR				A-IA-MA-[DAR]		YOS XII 360 SEAL
		ʾAJA				NIWR		I		[A]-IA-NI-RI		RA LXV 59 II 36
		ʾAJA				ŠUM				ḪA-IA_3-SU?-UM		M
		ʾAJA				ŠUM		U		ḪA-IA_3-SU-MU		DELAPORTE CCL II A 337+
		ʾAJA				ŠUM		U	HU	ḪA-IA-SU-MU-U_2		XI P.83 N.1+
		ʾAJA				ŠUM		U	HU	ḪA-IA_3-SU-MU-U_2		M+
		ʾAJA				ŠUM		U	HU	ḪA-IA_3-SU-U_2-MU		M+
		ʾAJA				ŠUM		U	HU	ḪA-IA_3-SU-U_2-MU-U_2		X 113 4, 11, 14
		ʾAJA				ŠUM		U				
						ʾAB		IM		ḪA-IA-SU-MU-A-BI-IM		M

STEMS

ʾAJA	1	ʾAJA				ŠARR		UM		ḪA-IA-ŠA-KUM		UCP X P. 56+
ʾAJAK	1	ʾAJAK		UM						A-IA-KU-UM		RA LXV 52 X 51
		ʾAJAK		U						A-JA-KU		RA LXV 52 X 44
ʾAJAL	1	ʾAJAL		UM						A-IA-LU-UM		CT XLV 5 9
		ʾAJAL		UM						A-IA-LUM		M
		ʾAJAL		UM						A-A-LUM		KISURRA 116
		ʾAJAL		IM						A-IA-LIM	GEN	M
		ʾAJAL	AT	UM						A-IA-LA-TUM	FN	VAS VII 3 25
		ʾAJAL	AT	UM						D-A-A-LA-TUM	FN	CT VIII 29C 22+
		ʾAJAL	AH							A-IA-LA	FN	M+
		ʾAJAL	AH							A-JA-LA	FN	XIII 1 IV 37
		ʾAJAL	AN							A-JA-LA-AN		RA LXV 52 X 81
		ʾAJAL		A	HA					A?-IA-LA-A	FN?	M
ʾAJAM	1	ʾAJAM				ʾIL	T	I		A-IA-AM-IL-TI	FN	XIII 1 X 8
		ʾAJAM				DIWD		UM		ḪA-IA-AM-DI-DU-UM		B 18+
		ʾAJAM				DIWD		U		ḪA-IA-AM-DI-DU		B 18
		ʾAJAM			TI	ʾIL				ḪA-IA-AM-TI-DINGIR		BIROT, TEA 72 III 5
	2	ʾANN		U		ʾAJAM				AN-NU-[Ḫ]A-A-AM	FN	XIII 1 II 62
ʾAJAN	1	ʾAJAN				ʾAB		I		A-IA-NA-BI	FN	A.
		ʾAJAN				ʾAB		I				
						ʾILL		A		A-IA-NA-BI-IL-LA		A.
		ʾAJAN				ʾABAL				A-AN-A-BA-AL	FN	XIII 1 IX 38
		ʾAJAN				KURUB				A-AN-KU-RU-UB	FN	RA LXV 51 X 15
		ʾAJAN				LIʾM				A-AN-LI-IM		M+
		ʾAJAN				ŠARR		I		A-IA-AŠ-LUGAL		A. 18 4
		ʾAJAN				ŠARR		I		A-IA-LUGAL-RI		A. 243 22
		ʾAJAN				ŠARR		I		A-IA-LUGAL		A. 274 4
ʾAJI	1	ʾAJI				DAWD		I		A-I-DA-TE	FN	A.
ʾAJIŠ	1	ʾAJIŠ		UM						ḪA-II-ŠUM		KISURRA 101 6+
		ʾAJIŠ				PI			HU	ḪA-II-IŠ-PI$_2$-U$_2$		KISURRA 22+
		ʾAJIŠ				PI			HU	ḪA-A-IŠ-PI$_2$-U$_2$		KISURRA 5+
		ʾAJIŠ				TULL		A		A-JI-IŠ-TU-UL-LA		M
ʾAB	1	ʾAB	AN	UM						A-BA-NU-UM		U+, SIMMONS 51 18
		ʾAB		A		ʾEL				A-BA-EL		TA 31, 221
		ʾAB		A		ʾIL				A-BA-DINGIR	FN	A. 59 5
		ʾAB		A		ʾANN		U		A-BA-AN-NU		M
		ʾAB		A		JARAḪ				A-BA-A-RA-AḪ		KICH II D 8 3
		ʾAB		A		DAWD		UM		A-BA-DA-DUM		HARRIS 95 9
		ʾAB		I		JAʾ		A		A-BI-IA-A		KISURRA 102 7+
		ʾAB		I		JAʾ		UM		A-BI-IA-U$_2$-UM		YOS VIII 10 9
		ʾAB		I		ḪIʾL				A-BI-ḪI-EL		B 10, M
		ʾAB		I		ḪIʾL				A-BI-ḪI-IL		M
		ʾAB		I		ḪIʾL		U		A-BI-ḪE$_2$-LU		MRS VI P. 240 LATE
		ʾAB		I		JAʾAR				A-BI-IA-ḪA-AR		B 10+
		ʾAB		I		JAʾAR				A-BI-A-ḪA-AR		CT XLIII 125 1+
		ʾAB		I		JAʾAR				A-BI-ḪA-AR		B 10+
		ʾAB		I		JABAL				A-BI-A-BA-AL		FIGULLA CAT. I 14206
		ʾAB		I		HADD		U		A-BI-D-IM		B 9, M+
		ʾAB		I		HADD		U		A-BI-A-DU		A.+
		ʾAB		I		HADD		U		A-BI-IA-DU		M+
		ʾAB		I		ʿAḎAR				A-BI-DAR		SIMMONS 58 12
		ʾAB		I		ʿAḎR		I		A-BI-AD-RI		A. LATE
		ʾAB		I		ʾAK		I		A-BI-IA-KI		TCL I 109 3
		ʾAB		I		ʾIL		A		A-BI-LA		CHANTRE 4 13
		ʾAB		I		ʾIL		I		A-BI-I$_3$-LI$_2$	FN	RA LXV 59 II 38+
		ʾAB		I		ʿALAṢ		I		AD-ḪA-LA-ZI	FN	C
		ʾAB		I		ʿALAṢ		I		A-BI-ḪA-LA-ZI	FN	M, C II 49 6
		ʾAB		I		ḪAM		A		A-BI-A-MA		SIMMONS 50 22+
		ʾAB		I		ḪAM		A		A-BI-IA-MA		SIMMONS 54 19+
		ʾAB		I		ʾAMAL				A-BI-A-MA-AL		KISURRA 153 34
		ʾAB		I		ʾANN		IM		A-BI-AN-NIM	GEN	M
		ʾAB		I		ḪUNN		I		A-BI-ḪU-UN?-NI		B 10
		ʾAB		I		JAQAR				A-BI-E-ÇAR		M+
		ʾAB		I		ʾIR		A		AD-I-RA	FN	A.
		ʾAB		I		JARAḪ				A-BI-A-RA-AḪ		B 9+
		ʾAB		I		JARAḪ				A-BI-E-RA-AḪ		B+, M+

ʾAB	1	ʾAB	I				JARAḪ		A-BI-RA-AḪ		B 9+, A. 38 18
		ʾAB	I				JARAḪ		A-BE-RA-AḪ		B 9
		ʾAB	I				ʾAŠD		A-BI-A-SA-AD		B 10+
		ʾAB	I				ʾAŠD		A-BI-SA-AD		B 10+
		ʾAB	I				JAT	UM	A-BI-IA-TUM	FN	WATERMAN 40 R. 5+
		ʾAB	I				ḪATAN		A-BI-ḪA-TA-AN		B 10
		ʾAB	I				JATAR		A-BI$_2$-WA-DAR		U
		ʾAB	I				JATAR		A-BI-IA-TA-AR		B 10+
		ʾAB	I				JATAR		A-BI-E-TAR		BASOR 95 22
		ʾAB	I				ʾAZJ	I	A-BI-A-ZI		A.
		ʾAB	I		ʾA	T	ŠAMAR		A-BI-AŠ-TA-MA-AR		YOS XIII 489:4
		ʾAB	I		JA		MWUT	A	A-BI-IA-MU-TA		BM 80328 15
		ʾAB	I		JA		MWUT	I	A-BI$_2$-A-MU-TI		U
		ʾAB	I		JA		JPAʿ		A-BI-IA-PA-AḪ	FN	XIII 1 II 57
		ʾAB	I		JE		JPUʿ		A-BI-E-PU-UḪ		B 10, M+
		ʾAB	I		JA		JPUʿ		A-BI-IA-PU-UḪ		B 10
		ʾAB	I		JE		JŠUʿ		A-BI-E-ŠU-UḪ		B 10+, XIII 1 III 44
		ʾAB	I		JA		JŠUʿ		A-BI-ŠU-UḪ		B 10
		ʾAB	I		JA		JŠUʿ	A	A-BI-IA-ŠU-ḪA		B 10
		ʾAB	I		JE		JŠUʿ				
							....		A-BI-E-ŠU-UḪ-LI-DI-IŠ		CT XLV 55 11
		ʾAB	I		JE		JŠUʿ				
							....		A-BI-E-ŠU-UḪ-LU-DA-RI		B 10
		ʾAB	I		JA		JŠUʿ				
							....		A-BI-ŠU-UT-LI		B 11
		ʾAB	I				DAGAN		A-BI-D-DA-GAN		M+
		ʾAB	I				DIRAḪ		A-BI?-DI-RA-AḪ		TCL X 41 A/B 4+
		ʾAB	I				DARAB		[A]?-BI-DA-RA-AB		RA LXV 43 III 67
		ʾAB	I				DITAN		A-BI-DI-TA-AN		BM 80328 16
		ʾAB	I				DITAN	UM	A-BI-TI-DA-NU-UM		TA 1931, 538 III,IV
		ʾAB	I				GAʾJ	A	A-BI-GA-A	GN?	A 21919+
		ʾAB	I				KAʾB	I	A-BI-KA-BI		M
		ʾAB	I				KAʾB	I	A-BI-KA-BI	FN	RA LXV 65 VII 42
		ʾAB	I				LUʾL	A	A-BI-LU-LA		SIMMONS 107 13
		ʾAB	I				LIʾM		A-BI-LI-IM		RA LXV 44 IV 60+
		ʾAB	I				LAMA		A-BI-LA-MA		B 10
		ʾAB	I				MA				
							ʾIL	I	A-BI-MA-I$_3$-LI$_2$	FN	RA LXV 64 VI 32
		ʾAB	I		ME		QWIM		A-BI-ME-KI-IM		XIII 34 5+
		ʾAB	I				MI				
							KI		A-BI-MI-KI-DINGIR		M
		ʾAB	I				MULUK	I	A-BI-MU-LU-KI	FN	RA LXV 59 II 26
		ʾAB	I				MARAṢ		A-BI-MA-RA-AṢ		B 10+
		ʾAB	I				MAṬAR		A-BI-MA-DAR		B 10+
		ʾAB	I				MAṬAR		A-BI-MA-DA-AR		TIM II 113 3
		ʾAB	I				NAʿM	I	A-BI-NA-AḪ-MI	FN	XIII 1 VII 43, A.+
		ʾAB	I				NAʿM	I	A-BI-NA-AḪ-ME	FN	RA LXV 59 II 20
		ʾAB	I				NIʿM		A-BI-NI-ḪI-IM		RA LXV 44 IV 31
		ʾAB	I				NIWR	I	A-BI-NI-RI	FN	XIII 1 IX 58+
		ʾAB	I				NAPŠ	I	A-BI-NA-AP-S[I]		XIV 77:7
		ʾAB	I				QAʾD		A-BI-QA-AD		B 11
		ʾAB	I				QAʾD		A-BI-GA-AD		TA 30 237
		ʾAB	I				RAWM		A-BI-RA-AM		RA LXV 43 IV 12
		ʾAB	I				RAPIʾ		A-BI-RA-BI		M
		ʾAB	I				RAPIʾ		A-BI-RA-PI		SYRIA XXXVII 206 6, 7
		ʾAB	I				RAŠAP		A-BI-RA-SA-AP		M
		ʾAB	I	Š			KIWN		A-BI$_2$-IŠ-KI-IN		U
		ʾAB	I	Š			MUM	U	A-BI-IŠ-MU-MU		HARRIS 98 2
		ʾAB	I	Š			TUʾ		A-BI-IŠ-DU		A. LATE
		ʾAB	I		JI	T	ŠAMAR		A-BI-IŠ-TA-MAR		TCL I 226 4, 10+
		ʾAB	I				ŠADW	A	A-BI-SA-DA-A		JCS IV 110 2040
		ʾAB	I				ŠAMAK	U	A-BI-SA-MA-KU		SIMMONS 41 15
		ʾAB	I				ŠAMAR		A-BI-SA-MAR		M+
		ʾAB	I				ŠAMŠ		A-BI-SA-MA-AŠ		M+
		ʾAB	I				ŠAMŠ		A-BI-D-UTU	FN	XIII 24 IV 40
		ʾAB	I				ŠAMŠ	I	A-BI-D-UTU-ŠI	FN	XIII 1 IX 40+

STEMS

ʾAB	1	ʾAB		I		ŠAMAT	A		A-BI-SA-MA-TA		EDZARD, DER 120:4
		ʾAB		I		ŠAPAR			A-BI-SA-PA-AR	FN	C
		ʾAB		I		ŠAPAR			A-BI-SA-PAR_2		CT XLV 82 7+, XIII 1 II 15
		ʾAB		I		ŠARIJ			A-BI-SA-RI		LIMET, SCEAUX CASS. P 114
		ʾAB		I		ŠARIJ		JE	A-BI-SA-RI-E		B 11+; M+
		ʾAB		I		ŠARIJ		JE	A-BI_2-SA-RI-E		BIN VII 93 DATE
		ʾAB		I		ṢUWR	A		A-BE-ZU-RA		TCL IV 87 10 CAPP.
		ʾAB		I		ṢUWR	A		A-BI-ṢU-RA		TIM IV 34 27
		ʾAB		I		ṢUWR	I		A-BI-ZU-RI		M
		ʾAB		I		ṬAJB	A		A-BI-ṬA-BA		A.+
		ʾAB		U		ḪAʾL	UM		A-BU-ḪA-LUM		UCP X P. 53, M
		ʾAB		UM		ḪAʾL	UM		A-BU-UM-ḪA-LUM		B 11+
		ʾAB		UM		ḪAʾL	UM		A-BU-UM-ḪA-LU-UM		B 11+
		ʾAB		U		ḪAʾL	IM		A-BU-ḪA-LIM	GEN	M+
		ʾAB		UM		ḪIʾL	UM		A-BU-UM-ḪI-LUM		B 11
		ʾAB		UM		ʾIL			A-BU-UM-DINGIR		U, M+
		ʾAB		U		JAQAR			A-BU-WA-QAR		M
		ʾAB		U		JAQAR			A-BU-QAR		M
		ʾAB		UM		JAQAR			A-BU-UM-WA-QAR		M
		ʾAB		U		JAT	I	JA	A-BU-IA-TI-IA		TCL I 85 10
		ʾAB		UM	JE	KWIN			A-BU-UM-E-KI-IN		M
		ʾAB		U		KA					
						ʾIL			A-BU-KA-DINGIR		M+
		ʾAB		U		LA		JA	A-BU-LA-IA		XIII 101 6
		ʾAB		U	ME	KWIN			A-BU-ME-KI-IN		X 154 2+
		ʾAB		U	ME	QWIM			A-BU-ME-KI-IM		M+
		ʾAB		U		NIWR	A		A-BU-NI-RA		TIM VI 34, U
		ʾAB		U		NAN	UM		A-BU-NA-NU-UM		B 42+
		ʾAB		U		ŠALIM			A-BU-SA-[LIM]		M
	2	ʾAḪ	AT	A		ʾAB	I		A-ḪA-TA-A-BI	FN	M+
		ʾAJA				ʾAB					
						ʾIL			ḪA-IA-AB-DINGIR		B 18
		ʾAJA				ʾAB	I		A-IA-A-BI		A.
		ʾAJA				ʾAB	I		A-IA-BI		A.+
		ʾAJA				ʾAB	I				
						ŠARR	I		A-IA-BI-ŠAR-RI		A.
		ʾAJA				ʾAB	I				
						TALM	A		A-IA-BI-TA-AL-MA		A. 239 15
		ʾAJA				ʾAB	U		A-IA-A?-BU?	FN	C+
		ʾAJA				ʾAB	U		A-IA-BU		A. LATE +
		ʾAJA				ʾAB	U	HU	A-A-A-BU-U_2	FN	DE CLERCQ II 253B
		ʾAJA				ʾAB	UM		ḪA-A-IA-A-BU-UM		M
		ʾAJA				ʾAB	UM		ḪA-IA-BU-UM		B 18+
		ʾAJA				ʾAB	AM		ḪA-A-IA-A-BA-AM	ACC	M+
		ʾAJAN				ʾAB	I		A-IA-NA-BI	FN	A.
		ʾAJAN				ʾAB	I				
						ʾILL	A		A-IA-NA-BI-IL-LA		A.
		ʾIJA				ʾAB					
						ʾIL			I-A-AB-DINGIR		OIP XXII 262
		ḪAʾN		A		ʾAB	I		ḪA-NA-A-BI		TIM II 113 2, 8
		ḪAWR				ʾAB	I		ḪA-AW-RA-BI		TIM IV 33 21, 34 14
		ḪAWR	AN			ʾAB	I		ḪA-AW-RA-AN-A-BI		M
		ḪAWR	AN			ʾAB	I		ḪA-AW-RA-NA-A-BI		M+
		ʿAD		U	NI	ʾAB	I	JA	A-DU-NI-A-BI-IA		RA XXVII 87 LATE
	JA	JDIʿ				ʾAB	UM		IA-DI-ḪA-BU-UM		B 25+
	JA	JDIʿ				ʾAB	UM		IA-DI-A-BU-UM		M, YOS XII+
	JA	JDIʿ				ʾAB	UM		IA-DU-A-BU-UM		YOS XII+
	JA	JDIʿ				ʾAB	U		IA-DI-ḪA-BU		PBS XIV 1084
	JA	JDIʿ				ʾAB	U		IA-DI-A-BU		YOS XII+
	JA	JDIʿ				ʾAB	UM		IA-DI-ḪA-A-BU-U[M]		RA LXV 45 V 9
	JA	JDIʿ				ʾAB	IM		IA-DI-ḪA-A-BI-IM	GEN	M+
		ʿADN		A		ʾAB	I		ḪA?-AD-NA-A-BI		TTKB XIX 304
		ʾIL		A		ʾAB	I		I-LA-A-BI		C
		ʾIL		UM		ʾAB	I		I-LUM-A-BI		A.
		ʾIL		UM		ʾAB	UM		I-LUM-A-BU-UM		U
		ʾALI				ʾAB	I		A-LI-A-BI	FN	M+

STEMS

ʾAB	2		ʾAMIR	A			ʾAB	UM		A-MI-RA-A-BU-UM		RA LXV 55 XIII 5
		ʾA	JPAʿ				ʾAB	I		A-PA-AḪ-A-BI		YOS VIII 29 13
		JA	JQIR	A			ʾAB	UM		IA-KI-RA-A-BU-UM		RA LXV 47 VII 30
			ʾIRR	A			ʾAB	I		IR$_3$-RA-A-BI		M
			ʾAŚD	UM			ʾAB	I		AŠ$_2$-DU-UM-A-BI		BE VI/1 1 7+
			ʾAŚD	UM			ʾAB	I		D-AŠ-DU-UM-A-BI		UET V 483 4
			ʿAŠTAR				ʾAB	I		AŠ-TAR-A-BI		MRS VI P. 242
			ʿIZZ				ʾAB	I		IZ-ZA-BI		C+
			BILL				ʾAB	I		BI-IL-LA-BI	FN	XIII 1 X 41
		JA	BRUQ				ʾAB	UM		A-AB-RU-UK-A-BU-UM		JCS XXVI 151:13, HARMAL
			DIWIR				ʾAB	I		DI-WI-IR-A-BI		PBS XI/1 P. 55+
			DIWIR				ʾAB	I		DI-BI-IR-A-BI		PBS XI/1 P. 55+
			ḎAKUR				ʾAB	I		ZA-KU-UR-A-BI	GEN	B 41
			ḎAKUR	A			ʾAB	I		ZA-KU-RA-A-BI	GEN	B 41
			ḎAKUR	A			ʾAB	U		ZA-KU-RA-A-BU		M
			ḎAKUR	A			ʾAB	UM		ZA-KU-RA-A-BU-UM		X 79 5
			ḎIMR	I			ʾAB	UM		ZI-IM-RI-A-BU-UM		B 42
			LA				ʾAB	A		LA-A-BA		U
			NUʿM	I			ʾAB	I		NU-UḪ-MI-A-BI		XIII 1 I 38
			NIQM				ʾAB	I		NI-IQ-MA-A-BI		A. 86 7+
		JA	PRUS				ʾAB	I		IA-AP-RU-US-A-BI		BAGHD. MITT. II 23
			QAṬAR				ʾAB	I		GA-TAR-A-BI		BASOR 95 22
		JA	RWIḪ	A			ʾAB	UM		IA-RI-ḪA-A-BU-UM		VII P. 234 N. 4
		JA	RWIḪ	A			ʾAB	AM		IA-RI-ḪA-A-BA-AM	ACC	XIV 101:8
		JA	RWIḪ	A			ʾAB	AM		IA-RI-ḪA-A-BA-AN	ACC	VII P. 234 N. 4
		JA	RWIḪ	A			ʾAB	IM		IA-RI-ḪA-A-BI-IM	GEN	M+
		JI	RPAʾ				ʾAB	I		IR-PA-A-BI		A.+
		JA	ŚJIM				ʾAB	IM		IA-SI-IM-A-BI-IM	GEN	M
		JA	ŚJIT				ʾAB	I		IA-SI-IT-A-BI		M
		JA	ŚJIT				ʾAB	U		IA-SI-IT-A-BU		M+
		JA	ŚJIT		NA		ʾAB	U		IA-SI-IT-NA-A-BU		XIII 1 XII 15
			ŠUBUL				ʾAB	I		ŠU-BU-UL-A-BI		M
			ŚAM	U			ʾAB	IM		SA-MU-A-BI-IM	NOM	RA VIII 71
			ŚAM	U			ʾAB	IM		SA-MU-A-BI-IM	GEN	SUMER XXIII 153+
			ŚUM	I			ʾAB	UM		SU-ME-A-BU-UM		A. 12 4
			ŚUM	U			ʾAB	UM		SU-MU-A-BU-UM		B 38+
			ŚUM	U			ʾAB	UM		D-SU-MU-A-BU-UM		KISURRA 93 22
			ŚUM	U			ʾAB	IM		[S]U-MU-A-BI-IM	NOM	EDZARD, DER 111:5
			ŚUM	U			ʾAB	IM		SU-MU-A-BI-IM	GEN	SUMER XXIII PL. 12 19
			ŚUM	U			ʾAB	I		SU-MA-A-BI		A.
			ŚUM	U			ʾAB	I	JA	[SU]-MU-A-BI-IA		B 38
			ŚUM	U			ʾAB	I				
						JA	RWIM			SU-MU-A-BI-A-RI-IM		TA 30 9, 14, 15+
			ŚUM	UM			ʾAB	I				
						JA	RWIM			SU-MU-UN-A-BI-IA-RI-IM		SUMER XXIII 153:9
			ŚUM	U	NA		ʾAB	I		SU-MU-UN-NA-A-BI	FN	A. 64 7
			ŚUM	U	NA		ʾAB	I		SU-MU-UN-NA-BI	FN	A. 33 3, 34 2+
			ŚUM	U	NA		ʾAB	I		SU-MU-NA-BI	FN	A. 59 8
			ŚUM	U	NA		ʾAB	I		SU-MU-NA-A-BI	FN	A. 244 5, M
			ŚUM	U	NA		ʾAB	I				
						JA	RWIM			SU-MU-NA-BI-IA-RI-IM		SUMER XXIII PL. 7 17+
			ŚUM	U	NA		ʾAB	I				
						JA	RWIM			SU-MU-UN?-A-BI-JA-RI-IM		SUMER XXIII P. 153 9
			ŚAMŚ	I			ʾAB	I		D-UTU-A-BI		M+
			ŚAPŚ	I			ʾAB	I		ŠA-AP-ŠI-A-BI	FN	A.
			ZUMM				ʾAB	U		ZU-UM-MA-BU		BM 80328 7
	3		ʾAḪ	U			KA					
							ʾAB	I		A-ḪU-KA-A-BI	FN	XIII 1 VIII 60, C+
			ʾAḪ	UM			LA					
							ʾAB	I		A-ḪU-UM-LA-A-BI		YOS XIII 245:17, SEAL
			ʾAJA				ŚUM	U				
							ʾAB	IM		ḪA-IA-SU-MU-A-BI-IM		M
			ʾIL	A			KA					
							ʾAB	UM		DINGIR-KA-A-BU-UM		CT XLV 100 17
			ʾIL	A			MA					
							ʾAB	I		DINGIR-MA-A-BI		M

STEMS

ʾAB	3	ʾIL		I		MA				
						ʾAB	I	I_3-LI-MA-A-BI		M+
		ʾUMM		UM		KA				
						ʾAB	IM	UM-MU-UM-KA-A-BI-IM	FN	M
		ʾUMM		UM		KA				
						ʾAB	I	UM-MU-UM-KA-A-BI	FN	XIII 1 VII 56
		ʾUMM		U		KA				
						ʾAB	I	UM-MU-KA-A-BI	FN	RA LXV 62 V 16
		ʾANN		U		KAMA				
						ʾAB	I	AN-NU-KA-MA-BI		CT XLV 116 36
	JA	JPAʿ				ŠUM	U			
						ʾAB	I	IA-PA-AḪ-SU-MU-A-BI		A. 56 47
		ʾIRŠ				MA				
						ʾAB	I	I-RI-IŠ-MA-A-BI		A.
		ʾIRŠ				MA				
						ʾAB	I	I-RI-IŠ-MA-BI		A.
		ʾIRŠ		U		MA				
						ʾAB	I	IR-ŠU-MA-BI		A.
		ʾAŠD		UM		LA				
						ʾAB	UM	AŠ-DU-UM-LA-A-BU-UM		SUMER V 142
		ʾAŠD		UM		LA				
						ʾAB	UM	$AŠ_2$-DU-UM-LA-A-BU-UM		SUMER V 142+
	JI	JṢIʾ				ŠAM	U			
						ʾAB	UM	I-ZI-SA-MU-A-BU-UM		B 23
	JI	JṢIʾ				ŠUM	U			
						ʾAB	UM	I-ZI-SU-MU-A-BU-UM		B 23+
	JI	JṢIʾ				ŠUM	U			
						ʾAB	IM	I-ZI-SU-MU-A-BI-IM	GEN	B 23
	JA	WṢIʾ				ŠUM	U			
						ʾAB	UM	U_2-ṢI-SU-MU-A-BU-UM		AJSL XXVIII 244 19
		ḎU				MA				
						ʾAB	I	ZU-U_2-MA-A-BI		XIV 77:17
		ḎU				MA				
						ʾAB	I	ZU-U_2-MA?-A-BI		M
		ḎIMR		U		LA				
						ʾAB	I	ZI-IM-RU-LA-A-BI		RA LXV 42 III 7
	JA	KWUN				ŠUM	U			
						ʾAB	IM	IA-KU-UN-SU-MU-A-BI-IM		M
		KABD		U		KA				
						ʾAB	I	KA-AB-TU-KA-A-BI		UET V 688:8,12
		LA			ʾA	HWIJ				
						ʾAB	I	LA-AḪ-WI-A-BI	FN	XIII 1 XIII 6
	JA	RWIM				ŠUM	U			
						ʾAB	I	IA-RI-IM-SU-MU-A-BI		RA LXV 42 III 8
		ŠUM		UM		LA				
						ʾAB	I	SU-MU-UM-LA-A-BI	FN	RA LXV 65 VII 24
ʾABAB	1	ʾABAB	AH					A-BA-BA	FN	C+
		ʾABAB		AJA				A-BA-BA-A-IA	FN	M
		ʾABAB	AN	UM				A-BA-BA-NU-UM		B 71+
		ʾABAB	AN	IM				A-BA-BA-NI-IM	GEN	B 42
ʾABAL	2	ʾAJAN				ʾABAL		A-AN-A-BA-AL	FN	XIII 1 IX 38
ʾABAN	1	ʾABAN		UM				ḪA-BA-NU-UM		TA 30, 191+
		ʾABAN		AJA				A-BA-NA-A		BM 81660 2
		ʾABAN	AN					AB-BA-NA?-AN		M
ʾABAQ	1	ʾABAQ		UM				A-BA-GU-UM		KISURRA 82 9
ʾABAŠ	1	ʾABAŠ	IN	UM				A-BA-ŠE-NU-UM		M
ʾABB	1	ʾABB		A				AB-BA		RA LXV 55 XIII 12
		ʾABB		A		ʾIL		D-AB-BA-DINGIR	FN	M
		ʾABB		A		ʾIL		AB-BA-DINGIR		A.+
		ʾABB		A		ʾIL	I	AB-BA-I_3-LI_2	FN	XIII 1 XI 14
		ʾABB		A		ʾIL	I	D-AB-BA-I_3-LI_2	FN	SIMMONS 112:17
		ʾABB		A		ŠARR		AB-BA-LUGAL		A. 86 2
		ʾABB		I		LIʾM				
						MA		AB-BI-LIM-MA		A.+
	2	ʾITT		A		ʾABB	A	ḪI-IT-TA-D-AB-BA		M
		KIBR				ʾABB	A	KI-BI-IR-D-AB-BA		M+

STEMS

ʾABB	2		KIBR				ʾABB		A		KI-IB-RA-AB-BA		CT XXIX 14 16
			KIBR				ʾABB		A		KI-IB-RA-BA		CT XXIX 14 29
		JI	NDIN				ʾABB		A		I-DIN-AB-BA		XIII 1 VIII 46
		JI	NDIN				ʾABB		A		ID-DI-NA-AB-BA		A.
		JI	NDIN				ʾABB		A		ID-DI-NA-BA		A. LATE
		JA	RḤIB				ʾABB		A		IA-AR-IB-D-AB-BA		M
ʾABIḪ	1		ʾABIḪ								A-BI-IḪ-[....]		XIII 79 5
	2		MUT		U		ʾABIḪ				MU-TU-A-BI-I[Ḫ]		M
			MUT		U		ʾABIḪ		IM		MU-TU-A-BI-ḪI-IM		C
			MUT		UM		ʾABIḪ				MU-TUM-A-BI-IḪ		TA 1930, 695
			ŚUM		U		ʾABIḪ				SU-MU-A-BI-IḪ		TIM V 1 16
ʾABIL	1		ʾABIL				TAʾK		U	HU	A-BI-IL-TA-KU-U_2		WALTERS, WL 97:4;105:3+
ʾABIŚ	1		ʾABIŚ	AN	UM						A-BI-SA-NU-UM		CT XLVIII 29 REV.
ʾABN	1		ʾABN		UM						ḪA-AB-NU-UM		GAUTIER 10 R. 10+
			ʾABN		A		JARAḪ				ḪA?-AB-NA-A-RA-AḪ		UET V 476 SEAL 6
			ʾABN		I		ʾIL				ḪA-AB-NI-DINGIR		M
			ʾABN		U		RAPIʾ				AB-NU-RA-BI		C, C II P. 244+
	2		ʾAJA				ʾABN		I				
							ʾIL				ḪA-IA-AB-NI-DINGIR		B 18+
			ʿABD				ʾABN		IM		$ARAD_2$-AB-NIM		BAGHD. MITT. II 72
			ḤANN		A		ʾABN		UM		AN-NA-AB-NU-UM		KISURRA 8A 14
			ḤANN		A		ʾABN		UM		A-NA-AB-NU-UM		HARRIS 57 18
			ḤANN		A		ʾABN	AT			ḪA-AN-NA-AB-NA-AT		A 7763, ISHCHALI
		TA	ʿTIQ				ʾABN		U		TA-TI-QA-AB-NU		RES 1938 128
		TU	WTAR				ʾABN		U		TU-TAR-AB-NU		M
		JI	BAʾEL				ʾABN		U		I-BA-EL-A-AB-NU		III 46 13
ʾADAʾ	2		LAMA				ʾADAʾ		E		LA-MA-A-DA-E	FN	A.
			LAMA				ʾADAʾ		E		LA-MA-TA-E	FN	A.+
ʾADAD	1		ʾADAD		I						A-DA-DI	FN	XIII 1 X 30
ʾADAL	2		KIWN		UM		ʾADAL				KI-NU-UM-A-DA-AL		RA LXV 48 VII 60
ʾADAM	1		ʾADAM		U						ḪA-DA-MU	MN	RUTTEN 19 19+
			ʾADAM		U						A-DA-MU	MN	JNES XIII 210+ LATE
			ʾADAM		U						A-DA-MU	FN	C+
			ʾADAM	AN	U						AD-DA-MA-NU		RUTTEN 28 12
			ʾADAM			TA	ʾAR		U		ḪA-DAM-TA-A-RU		WATERMAN 45 EDGE
			ʾADAM			TI	ʾEL				ḪA-DAM-TI-EL		HARRIS 61 2
			ʾADAM			TI	ʾEL		UM		A-DAM-TE-LUM		GAUTIER 31 6
ʾADAN	1		ʾADAN	AT	UM						ḪA-DA-AN-N[A]?-TUM?	FN	RA LXV 62 V 7
			ʾADAN	T	A						A-DA-AT-TA	FN	C+
			ʾADAN		I	Š	....				ḪA-DA-NI-IŠ-MU-[....]		SIGRIST UNPUBL.
			ʾADAN				ʾIL				ḪA-DA-AN-DINGIR		B 18
			ʾADAN				NUWḪ		UM		ḪA-DA-NU-U_2-UM		M
	2		ʾEŠB		I		ʾADAN	T	A		EŠ-BI-A-DA-AT-TA		A. 455 31, 55
ʾADD	1		ʾADD		I		ŚAMŚ				AD-DI-D-UTU?		RA LXIV 99:23
			ʾADD		I	JA	ʾEL				AD-DI-JA-EL		BAB. III 267 HANA
			ʾADD		I	JA	ʾEL				AD-DI-IA-DINGIR		MAOG IV 2 12 HANA
ʾADID	1		ʾADID		UM						A-DI-DU-UM		B 11+
			ʾADID		UM						A-DI-DUM		SIMMONS 69A 5
			ʾADID		U						A-DI-DU		B 11
ʾADM	1		ʾADM	AN	UM						AD-MA-NU-UM		JCS XXIV 69 NO.3
			ʾADM	AN	UM						ḪA-AD-MA?-NU-UM		VIII 85:29
			ʾADM	AN	IM						ḪA-AD-MA?-NIM	GEN	B 44
			ʾADM		U	HA					AD-MU-A	FN	U
			ʾADM		U		ʿALIJ	AH			D-AD-MU-ḪA-LI-IA	FN	XIII 1 V 55
			ʾADM		U		JIŠʿ	AH			D-AD-MU-IŠ-ḪA	FN	XIII 1 IX 18
			ʾADM		U		JIŠʿ	AH			AD-MU-IŠ-ḪA	FN	XIII 1 IX 57
			ʾADM		U		ḤAṢN		I		D-AD-MU-ḪA-AZ-NI	FN	RA LXV 61 IV 21
			ʾADM		U		BALAṬ		I		D-AD-MU-BA-LA-TI?	FN	M
			ʾADM		U		NIWR		I		AD-MU-NE-RI	FN	XIII 1 VIII 13
			ʾADM		U		NIWR		I		D-AD-MU-NI-RI	FN?	M
			ʾADM		U		QUDM		I		AD-MU-KU-UD-MI	FN	XIII 1 IX 55
			ʾADM		U		RUWB	AH			D-AD-MU-RU-BA	FN	XIII 1 VII 59
			ʾADM		U		ŚIMḪ		I		AD-MU-ŠI-IM-ḪI	FN	XIII 1 IV 6
			ʾADM		U		ŚIMḪ		I		D-AD-MU-ŠI-IM-ḪI	FN	RA LXV 62 V 28
			ʾADM		U	TA	ḤNUN	AN			D-AD-MU-TA-ḪU-NA-AN	FN	RA LXV 61 IV 38
	2	TA	ʾZIJ				ʾADM		U		TA-AḪ-ZI-D-AD-MU	FN	M

STEMS

ʾADM	2	TA	ḪṢIN				ʾADM		U	TA-AḪ-ZI-IN-AD-MU	FN	M
		JA	MʾID				ʾADM		I	IA-AM-I-ID-D-AD-MI		A. 60 4
		JI	NDIN				ʾADM		U	I-DIN-D-AD-MU		M+
			QIJŠ	T	I		ʾADM		U	KI-IŠ-TI-AD-MU		M+
			ṬARID		A		ʾADM		U	TA-RI-DA-AD-MU		XIII 1 16
ʾADUD	1		ʾADUD		U					A-DU-DU	FN	XIII 1 X 7+
ʾADUN	1		ʾADUN							A-DU-UN		A. 237 5+
			ʾADUN		UM					A-DU-NU-UM	FIELD	CT II 23 2
			ʾADUN	AT	UM					A-DU-NA-TUM	MN	TA 30 275
			ʾADUN	AH						ḪA-DU-NA	FN	XIII 1 III 65
			ʾADUN				LUʾM		U	ḪA-DU-UN-LU-MU		M
			ʾADUN				LUʾM		U	ḪA-DU-LU-MU		M
	2		LA				ʾADUN		IM	LA-DU-NIM	GEN	M
ʾAG	2		ʾEN		I	Š	ʾAG		UM	E-NI-IŠ-A-GU-UM		M+
			BAʿL		I	Š	ʾAG		UM	BA-LI-IŠ-A-GU-UM		RA LXV 45 V 36
			QIJŠ				ʾAG		U	KI-IŠ-A-GU	FN	XIII 1 I 70
ʾAGIG	1		ʾAGIG		UM					A-GI-GU-UM		B 12+
			ʾAGIG		U					A-GI-GU		B 12
ʾAK	1		ʾAK		UM					A-KU-UM		U
			ʾAK		I		....			A-KI-[....]	FN	IX 291 13
			ʾAK		IJA					A-KI-IA		M+
			ʾAK		IJAN					A-KI-IA-AN		M, A. LATE+
			ʾAK		I		ʾIL			A-KI-DINGIR		M
			ʾAK		I		ʾEL			A-KI-EL		RA LXV 46 VI 49
			ʾAK		I		JARAḪ			A-KI-E-RA-AḪ		M
			ʾAK		I		LAMA			A-KI-LA-MA		B 12
			ʾAK		UM		LA					
							ʾIL		A	A-KUM-LA-I-LA		RA LXV 55 XIII 1
	2		ʾAB		I		ʾAK		I	A-BI-IA-KI		TCL I 109 3
			ʿAMM		I		ʾAK		I	AM-MI-E-KI		A.
ʾAKAN	1		ʾAKAN	AT	UM					A-KA-NA-TUM		JCS XXIV 62 NO.55+
ʾAKIN	1		ʾAKIN		UM					A-KI-NU-UM		TA 1931, 538 I
ʾAKIR	1		ʾAKIR		UM					A-KI-RU-UM		KISURRA 8 7+
			ʾAKIR		I					A-KI-RI	GEN	VAS VIII 14 37
			ʾAKIR	AH						A-KI-RA	FN	M
ʾAKK	1		ʾAKK		A					AK-KA		XIII 1 IV 27+
			ʾAKK		A		BANIJ			AK-KA-BA-NI		M
			ʾAKK	AT	UM					A-KA-TUM		KISURRA 104 36
			ʾAKK	AT	IJA					A-KA-TI-IA-A		KISURRA 178 1
			ʾAKK	AT	IJA					A-KA-TI-IA	FN	KISURRA 171 1; M+
			ʾAKK	ATANUM						AG-GA-TA-NU-UM		SIMMONS 96 6
			ʾAKK	ATANUM						AG-GA-TA-A-NU-UM		SIMMONS 103 6
			ʾAKK	ATANUM						A-KA-TA-A-NU-UM		SIMMONS 105 7, SEAL
			ʾAKK	ATANUM						AK-KA-TA-A-NU-UM		SIMMONS 106 6, 10 SEAL
			ʾAKK	ATANUM						AK-KA-TA-NU-UM		SIMMONS 112 6, SEAL
			ʾAKK	ATANI						A-GA-DA-NI		TA 1931, 489
			ʾAKK	ATANI						A-GA-TA-NI		TA 1931, 530 I, III
			ʾAKK	ATANIM						AK-KA-TA-NI-IM	GEN	A 32133:6
			ʾAKK	AT			ʾEL			A-GA?-AD-E-EL		I
			ʾAKK	AT			MAʾT		I	AK-KA-AD-MA-TI	FN	A. 409 22
	2	T	HILAL				ʾAKK		A	ḪI-IT-LA-AL-AK-KA		RA LXV 54 XII 36,71
			JATAR				ʾAKK		A	IA-TAR-AK-KA		M
		JI	NDIN				ʾAKK		A	I-DIN-AK-KA		XIII 1 I 54+
			ṢILL				ʾAKK		A	MI-NI-AK-KA		M
ʾAKN	1		ʾAKN	AN	U					AK-NA-NU		B 42
ʾAKUN	1		ʾAKUN		UM					A-KU-NU-UM		KISURRA 58 8
			ʾAKUN		UM					A-KU-NUM$_2$		KISURRA 48 4
			ʾAKUN	AN	IM					A-KU-NA-NIM	GEN	B 92
			ʾAKUN	AT	UM					A-KU-NA-TUM	MN?	M+
			ʾAKUN		IJA					A-KU-NI-IA		CT XLV 5 R. 3
			ʾAKUN		U		QAṬAR			A-KU-NU-GA-DAR		BIN VII 30 5
ʾAL	1		ʾAL				ʾAḪ	AT	I	AL-A-ḪA-TI	FN	A.
			ʾAL		I	Š	TUT		U	A-LI-IŠ-TU-TU		VAS XVI 23 13
ʾALAK	1		ʾALAK		UM					ḪA-LA-KUM		CT XLV 2 22+
ʾALAM	2		MUT				ʾALAM		I	MU-UT-ḪA-LA-MI		C+
ʾALAŠ	1		ʾALAŠ		I		ʾEL			A-LA-SI-E-EL		UCP X/3 3 17

STEMS

ʾALAŠ	2 JA	WṢIʾ				ʾALAŠ		UM		U$_2$-ZI-A-LA-ŠUM		M
ʾALI	1	ʾALI				ʾAḪ		I		A-LI-A-ḪI	FN	M+
		ʾALI				ʾAḪ		I		A-LI$_2$-A-ḪI	FN	RA LXV 59 II 41
		ʾALI				ʾAḪ	AT	I		A-LI-A-ḪA-TI	FN	XIII 1 IV 71+
		ʾALI				ʾAḪ	AT	I		A-LI-A-ḪA?-TA-TI	FN	M
		ʾALI				ʾAḪ	AT	I		A-LI$_2$-A-ḪA-TI	FN	RA LXV 59 II 65+
		ʾALI				ʾAB		I		A-LI-A-BI	FN	M+
		ʾALI				ʾIL				A-LI$_2$-IL		HARRIS 65 16
		ʾALI				ʾUMM		I		A-LI-UM-MI	FN	M
		ʾALI				ʿAMM		U		A-LI$_2$-AM-MU		UCP X/1 52 22
		ʾALI				ʿAMM		U	HU	A-LI$_2$-AM-MU-U$_2$		UCP X/2 58 16
		ʾALI				ʾUP		UM		A-LI$_2$-U$_2$-PU-UM		KISURRA 117 5
		ʾALI				LAMA				A-LI$_2$-LA-MA		SIMMONS 118 17+
		ʾALI				PA						
						ʾIL				A-LI$_2$-PA-DINGIR		RUTTEN 6 21+
		ʾALI				PA						
						ʾIL				A-LI-PA-DINGIR		TIM III 5 18+
		ʾALI				PA						
						ʾIL				ḪA-A-LI-PA-DINGIR		EDZARD,DER 152 REV.16
		ʾALI				PA						
						ʾIL		UM		A-LI$_2$-KA-LUM		RUTTEN 37 19
		ʾALI				PA						
						ŠAMŠ				A-LI$_2$-PA-D-UTU		BE VI/1 15:25
		ʾALI				ŠARAM			NI	A-LI-ŠA-RA-AM-NI	FN	RA LXV 58 I 54
ʾALIK	1	ʾALIK		UM						A-LI-KUM		B+
		ʾALIK		UM						ḪA-LI-KU-UM		B 12+
		ʾALIK		UM						ḪA-LI-KUM		B 12+
ʾALIM	1	ʾALIM								A-LI-IM	NOM	M, TIM III 43 5
		ʾALIM	AH							ḪA-LI-MA	FN	M+
ʾALIP	1	ʾALIP	AH							ḪA-LI-BA	FN	XIII 1 VIII 37
		ʾALIP				ŠAMŠ				A-LI-IB-D-UTU		CT VIII 35B 24+
ʾALL	1	ʾALL	AH							AL-LA	FN	RA LXV 59 II 42
		ʾALL		I		KUPAPA				AL-LI-KU-PA-PA	FN	A.
		ʾALL		I		NIWR		I		AL-LI-NI-RI	FN	A.
		ʾALL		I		TALM		A		AL-LI-TA-AL-MA	FN	A.
		ʾALL		I		TURAḪ				AL-LI-TU-RA-AḪ?	FN	XIII 1 I 10+
		ʾALL		I		TURAḪ		I		AL-LI-TU-RA-ḪI	FN	A.
ʾALLA	1	ʾALLA				MUT	IJ	I		AL-LA-MU-TI-I	TRIBE	4E RENC. ASS. P. 178 9
		ʾALLA				MUT	IJ	I		A-AL-MU-TI-I	TRIBE	M
		ʾALLA				RAPIʾ				AL-LA-RA-PI		TCL XVIII 95 12, 15
		ʾALLA				ŠUʾḪ		U		AL-LA-ŠU-ḪU		U
		ʾALLAI				ḪAṢN		U		AL-LA-I-AṢ-NU	FN	M
ʾALLAI	2	KIʾL		UM		ʾALLAI				KI-LUM-AL-LA-I	FN	XIII 1 XI 49
		ŠIMR				ʾALLA				ŠI-IM-RA-AL-LA		A.
ʾALM	1	ʾALM		U	HU					ḪA-AL-MU-U$_2$		SYRIA XXXVII 206 9 HANA
		ʾALM	AN	UM						AL-MA-NU-UM		TA 1931,148
		ʾALM	AN	UM						ḪA-AL-MA-NU-UM		HARRIS 62 14+
		ʾALM	AT	UM						ḪA-AL-MA-TUM	MN?	HARRIS 66 13
		ʾALM		U	NI					AL-MU-NI		RA LXV 48 VIII 7
ʾALP	1	ʾALP	AN							AL-PA-AN		M+
ʾALUʾ	1	ʾALUʾ		UM						A-LU-U$_2$-UM		VAS XVI 131:1
		ʾALUʾ		U						A-LU?-U$_2$	FN	M
ʾALUN	1	ʾALUN		IJA						A-LU-NI-IA	FN	EDZARD,DER 91:13
		ʾALUN				HADD		U		ḪA-LU-UN-D-IM		M; JCS XIV 203
		ʾALUN				PI						
						JAM		U		ḪA-LU-UN-BI-JA-MU		M
		ʾALUN				PI						
						JAM		U		ḪA-LU-UM-BI-JA-MU		RA LXV 43 III 78
		ʾALUN				PI						
						JAM		U		ḪA-LU-BI-JA-MU		M
		ʾALUN		A		HADD		U		ḪA-LU-NA-D-IM		M
ʾALUP	1	ʾALUP		UM						A-LU-PU-UM		B+
		ʾALUP		I						A-LU-BI	GEN?	CT XLV 92 R. I 14
		ʾALUP	AT	UM						A-LU-PA-TUM	FN	CT XLVII 7 35, 7A 16'
ʾAM	1	ʾAM	T	UM						AM-TUM	FN	XIII 1 II 48
		ʾAM	T			ʾEL				GEME$_2$-E-IL		RIFTIN 44 10

STEMS

ʾAM	1		ʾAM	T			ʿAŠTAR	AH		AM-TI-AŠ-TA-RA	FN?	A. LATE
			ʾAM	T			BAʿL	AH		A-MA-AT-D-BA-A-LA	FN	BAGHD. MITT. II 72 5, 9+
			ʾAM	T			LABW	A		AM-TI-LA-BA	MN	TIM III 7 5
ʾAMAL	2		ʾAB		I		ʾAMAL			A-BI-A-MA-AL		KISURRA 153 34
ʾAMAN	1		ʾAMAN		UM					A-MA-NU-UM		CT XLV 2 24, SEAL
			ʾAMAN		U					ḪA-MA-NU		X 151 4+, KISURRA 21 9
			ʾAMAN		U					ḪA-MA-NU	FN	RA LXV 66 VIII 6
			ʾAMAN	AN	UM					A-MA-NA-NU-UM		B 42+
			ʾAMAN	AN	IM					A-MA-NA-NIM	GEN	B 43
			ʾAMAN				TAʾ	I		AM-MA-AN-TA-ḪI		M
	2		JAT		I		ʾAMAN			IA-TI-ḪA-MA-AN	FN	RA LXV 42 II 55
ʾAMAR	1		ʾAMAR		U					AM-MA-RU		M
			ʾAMAR				HADD	U		AM-MA-RA-DU		A.+
			ʾAMAR		A		HADD	U		AM-MA-RA-A-DU		A.
			ʾAMAR				ʾIL	I		A-MAR-I$_3$-LI$_2$		MAOG IV 2 3 HANA
	TA	T	ʾAMAR							TA-AḪ-TA-MAR		M
	2		NUWR		U		ʾAMAR			NU-RU-A-MA-AR		HARRIS 68 19
ʾAMAT	1		ʾAMAT	AN						A-MA-TA-AN		M+
			ʾAMAT	AN						ḪA-MA-TA-AN		RA LXV 43 III 43
ʾAMIN	1		ʾAMIN		UM					A-MI-NU-UM		B 12+
			ʾAMIN		UM					A-MI-NUM		M
			ʾAMIN		U					A-MI-NU		JNES XIII 210+ LATE
			ʾAMIN	AH						A-MI-NA	FN	RA LXV 64 V 76
			ʾAMIN	AH						AM-MI-IN-NA	FN	RA LXV 64 V 64
			ʾAMIN	AT	UM					A-MI-NA-TUM		B 12
			ʾAMIN	AN	UM					A-MI-NA-NU-UM		B 43
			ʾAMIN		I		ʾANN	U		A-MI-NI-AN-NU		M
ʾAMIR	1		ʾAMIR		UM					A-MI-RU-UM		B 13
			ʾAMIR		UM					A-MI-RUM		M
			ʾAMIR	AT	UM					A-MI-RA-TUM	FN	M
			ʾAMIR		AJA					A-MI-RA-IA	FN	C
			ʾAMIR				....			A-ME-IR-[....]		M
			ʾAMIR		A		ʾAB	UM		A-MI-RA-A-BU-UM		RA LXV 55 XIII 5
			ʾAMIR				KAKK	A		A-ME-IR-KA-AK-KA		XIII 1 V 20
ʾAMR	1	T	ʾAMR		UM					A-TAM-RUM		M+
		T	ʾAMR		UM					A-TA-AM-RU-UM		M+
		T	ʾAMR		IM					A-TAM-RI-IM	GEN	M+
		T	ʾAMR		IM					A-TA-AM-RI-IM	GEN	M+
		T	ʾAMR		AM					A-TAM-RA-AM	ACC	M+
		T	ʾAMR	AT	UM					A-TAM-RA-TUM	FN	M
		T	ʾAMR	AH						A-TAM-RA	FN	M+
		T	ʾAMR		I		ʾIL			A-TAM-RI-DINGIR		M+
			ʾAMR	AT	UM					AM-RA-TUM		YOS XIII 513:4
			ʾAMR				ʿAD	UM		AM-RA-DU-UM		M
	2		ʾANN		U		ʾAMR	I	JA	AN-NU-AM-RI-IA	FN	RA LXV 61 IV 47
ʾAMUM	2 JI		ŠMAʿ				ʾAMUM	I		IŠ-ME-A-MU-MI	FN	M
ʾAMUR	1		ʾAMUR				ŠA					
							DAGAN			A-MUR-ŠA-D-DA-GAN		TCL I 237 31 HANA
			ʾAMUR				ŠA					
							ŠAMŠ			A-MUR-ŠA-D-UTU		A.
ʾAN	1		ʾAN		I	Š	ḪURB	I		A-NI-IŠ-ḪU-UR-BI		M+
			ʾAN		I	Š	KIBAL			A-NI-IŠ-KI-BA-AL		RA LXV 53 XI 37+
			ʾAN		I	Š	KIBEL			A-NI-IŠ-KI-BE-EL		TCL XX 191 33 CAPP.
			ʾAN		A	Š	KIBAL			[A]?-NA-AŠ-KI-BA-AL		VIII 86 23
ʾANA	1		ʾANA		I	Š				A-NA-IŠ		RA LXV 52 X 79
			ʾANA				ḪIJJ	A		A-NA-ḪI?-A?		RUTTEN 20:16
			ʾANA				HADD	U		A-NA-D-IM		MRS XII NO. 24, 6, UGARIT
			ʾANA				ʾIL	I				
							MA			A-NA-I-LIM-MA		A.
			ʾANA				ʿAN	A		A-NA-A-NA		A. 36:11
			ʾANA				ḪANN	I		A-NA-AḪ-ḪA-AN-NI	FN	XIII 1 V 29
			ʾANA				BAʿL	U		A-NA-BA-LU	MN?	CT XLVIII 86 REV
			ʾANA				BAʿL	U		A-NA-BA-LU	FN	M
			ʾANA				DAGAN			A-NA-D-DA-GAN		M
			ʾANA				KIBAL	I		A-NA?-KI-BA-[L]I	FN	M
			ʾANA				MA					
							ʾIL			A-NA-MA-DINGIR		A 29366:9

STEMS

ʾANA	1		ʾANA				RAḪAB		U		A-NA-RA-A-BU		M+
ʾANAKU	1		ʾANAKU				ʾIL		AM				
							MA				A-NA-KU-DINGIR-LAM-MA		XIII 1 II 29
			ʾANAKU				ʾIL		A				
							MA				A-NA-KU-I-LA-MA		SIMMONS 46 7+
ʾANAZ	1		ʾANAZ		UM						AN-NA-ZUM		B 13+
ʾANDUL	2		ʿAMM		I		ʾANDUL		I		ḪA-AM-MI-AN-DUL$_3$-LI$_2$		M+
			ʿAŠTAR		I		ʾANDUL		I		EŠ$_4$-DAR-AN-DUL$_3$-LI$_2$	FN	M
ʾANN	1		ʾANN		U		ʾAJAM				AN-NU-[Ḫ]A-A-AM	FN	XIII 1 II 62
			ʾANN		U		ʾUMM		I		AN-NU-UM-MI	FN	XIII 1 IV 48+
			ʾANN		U		ʾUMM		I		AN-NU-UN-UM-MI		M
			ʾANN		U		ʾAMR		I	JA	AN-NU-AM-RI-IA	FN	RA LXV 61 IV 47
			ʾANN		U		ḪANN		I		AN-NU-ḪA-AN-NI	FN	M+
			ʾANN		U		JAPʿ	AH			AN-NU-IA-AP-ḪA	FN	XIII 1 IV 3+
			ʾANN		U		JIPʿ	AH			AN-NU-IP-ḪA	FN	XIII 1 VIII 29
			ʾANN		U		ʾAŚJ	AH			AN-NU-A-SI-IA	FN	XIII 1 IV 41+
			ʾANN		U		JIŠʿ	AH			AN-NU-IŠ-ḪA	FN	XIII 1 V 46+
			ʾANN		U		ʾAŠR		I		AN-NU-AŠ-RI	FN	M+
			ʾANN		U	T	ḪILAL				AN-NU-ḪI-IT-LA-AL	FN	RA LXV 60 III 18
			ʾANN		U		JATR	AH			AN-NU-IA-AT-RA	FN	XIII 1 VI 53+
			ʾANN		U		ḪAṢN		I		AN-NU-ḪA-AṢ-NI	FN	M+
			ʾANN		U		BAWŠ	T	I		AN-NU-BA-AŠ-TI	FN	RA LXV 65 VII 27
			ʾANN		U		DAMQ	AH			AN-NU-DAM-QA	FN	XIII 1 X 51
			ʾANN		U		DUNN		I		AN-NU-DU-UN-NI	FN	XIII 1 III 37
			ʾANN		U		DUNN		I		AN-NU-DU-NI	FN	RA LXV 65 VII 15
			ʾANN		U		GAMIL	T	I		AN-NU-GA-ME-IL-TI	FN	RA LXV 66 VII 66
			ʾANN		U		KUʾM				AN-NU-KUM	FN	XIII 1 VI 8
			ʾANN		U		KAMA						
							ʾAB		I		AN-NU-KA-MA-BI		CT XLV 116 36
			ʾANN		U		LAMAS		I		AN-NU-LA-MA-ZI	FN	M+
			ʾANN		U		LAMAS		I		AN-NU-D-LAMA	FN	XIII 1 VII 8+
			ʾANN		U		LAMAS	IT	UM		AN-NU-LA-MA-ZI-TUM	FN	RA LXV 59 II 13
			ʾANN		U		MAʾN		A		AN?-NU-MA-NA	FN	M
			ʾANN		U		NIWR		I		AN-NU-NI-RI	FN	M
			ʾANN		U		NABIʾ				AN-NU-NA-BI-IḪ	FN	RA LXV 62 V 24
			ʾANN		U		NABIT		I		AN-NU-NA-BI-TI		XIII 1 VI 61
			ʾANN		U		PUṬR		I		AN-NU-PU-UṬ-RI	FN	RA LXV 58 I 19+
			ʾANN		U		QUDM		I		AN-NU-KU-UD-MI	FN	XIII 1 VIII 77
			ʾANN		U		RAḪM		I		AN-NU-RA-AḪ-MI	FN	XIII 1 V 11+
			ʾANN		U		RIMŠ		I		AN-NU-RI-IM-ŠI	FN	M+
			ʾANN		U		ŠIMḪ		I		[A]N-NU-ŠI-IM-ḪI		XIII 1 XIV 24
			ʾANN		U		ŠATAM				AN?-NU?-ŠA-TAM	FN	XIII 1 IV 46
			ʾANN		U	TA	ḪNUN				AN-NU-TA-AḪ-NU-UN	FN	RA LXV 61 IV 15+
			ʾANN		U	TA	LʾIJ				AN-NU-TA-AL-E	FN	M+
			ʾANN		U	TA	RḪAM				AN-NU-TA-AR-AM	FN	M+
			ʾANN		U	TA	RBIJ				AN-NU-TAR-BI	FN	XIII 1 XI 47
			ʾANN		U	TA	ŠMAʿ				AN-NU-TA-AŠ$_2$-MA-AḪ	FN	M
			ʾANN		U		TIWR		I		AN-NU-TI-RI	FN	M+
			ʾANN		U		TABB		I		AN-NU-TAB-BI	FN	XIII 1 III 36+
			ʾANN		U		TUKUL	T	I		AN-NU-TU-KU-UL-[TI]	FN	M+
			ʾANN		U		TUKUL	T	I		AN-NU-TU-GUL-TI	FN	XIII 1 X 3
			ʾANN		U		TILL	AT	I		AN-NU-TIL-LA-TI	FN	XIII 1 X 2
			ʾANN		U		ṬAJB				AN-NU-DUG$_3$		M+
	2		ʾAB		A		ʾANN		U		A-BA-AN-NU		M
			ʾAB		I		ʾANN		IM		A-BI-AN-NIM	GEN	M
			ʾAMIN		I		ʾANN		U		A-MI-NI-AN-NU		M
			NABIʾ				ʾANN		U		NA-BI-AN-NU		M
		JA	NTIN				ʾANN		I	Š	[IA-AN]-TI-IN-A-NI-IŠ		VII 180 8'
		JI	NDIN				ʾANN		U		I-DIN-AN-NU		M+
		JI	NDIN				ʾANN		UM		I-DIN-AN-NU-UM		M+
		JI	NDIN				ʾANN		U		I-DI-AN-NU		RA LXV 51 IX 31
			RAWḪ		A		ʾANN		UM		RA-ḪA-AN-NU-UM		M
			ṢILL				ʾANN		U		MI-NI-AN-NU		M
			ZAʾZ		I		ʾANN		U		ZA-ZI-AN-NU		B 41+
ʾANT	1		ʾANT	AN	UM						AN-TA-NU-UM		TA 1930, 698
ʾANTAR	1		ʾANTAR		UM						AN-TA-RU-UM		CT VIII 47 B 21

STEMS

ʾANTEL	2	BIN		A		ʾANTEL			BI-NA-AN-TE-EL		TLB I 220 26, M+
ʾANZ	1	ʾANZ	AN	UM					AN-ZA-NU-UM		B 43
ʾAP	1	ʾAP	AN	UM					A-PA-NU-UM		B 43+
		ʾAP		I		ʾAŚAL			A-PI-A-ŠAL		JNES XIII 212F.+ LATE
	2	ʾIL		I		ʾAP	I	JA	I$_3$-LI$_2$-A-PI?-A		TIM III 4 14
ʾAPK	1	ʾAPK	AT	UM					AP-KA-TUM	MN	UCP X/1 4 5
		ʾAPK	AN	UM					AP-KA-NU-UM		SIMMONS 66 28
		ʾAPK	ATAN						AP-KA-TA-AN		M+
ʾAPP	1	ʾAPP	AT	UM					AP-PA-TUM	FN	A.+
		ʾAPP	ATAN						AP-PA-TA-AN		RA LXV 43 IV 18
ʾAPR	1	ʾAPR	AN						AP-RA-AN		A. LATE
		ʾAPR		IJA					AP-RI-A		A.
ʾAR	2	ʾADAM			TA	ʾAR	U		ḪA-DAM-TA-A-RU		WATERMAN 45 EDGE
		ḪATAʾ		A		ʾAR	UM		ḪA-TA-A-A-RUM?		CT XXIX 8A 1
ʾARḪ	1	ʾARḪ		UM					AR-ḪU-UM	FN	XIII 1 VIII 23
		ʾARḪ	AN	UM					AR-ḪA-NU-UM		BM 92657+
		ʾARḪ		I		ŚAMŚ	I		AR-ḪI-D-UTU-ŠI	FN	XIII 1 XIII 2
	2	MUT				ʾARḪ	U		MU-UT-AR-ḪU		M
ʾARWIJ	1	ʾARWIJ		UM					AR-WI-UM		B 13+, M+
		ʾARWIJ		UM					AR-WI-U$_2$-UM		B 13+, M
		ʾARWIJ		U					AR-WI-U$_2$		B 13
		ʾARWIJ		UM					AR-BI$_2$-UM		ITT II/1 P 48, 933, U
		ʾARWIJ		IM					AR-WI-IM	GEN	TIM V 14 23, M
		ʾARWIJ		EM					AR-WI-E-[EM]	GEN	I 30 10
		ʾARWIJ	T	UM					AR-WI-TUM	FN	KISURRA 134 3, M+
		ʾARWIJ	T	UM					AR-BI-TUM		LEGRAIN, TRU 41+, U
		ʾARWIJ	T	UM					AR-BI$_2$-TUM		TCL V 6039 REV 17, U
		ʾARWIJ	ATANUM						AR-WI-TA-NU-UM		B 43
ʾARAḪ	2	ḎIMR		U		ʾARAḪ			ZI-IM-RU-A-RA-AḪ		BM 17045A 13
		ḎIMR		U		ʾARAḪ			ZI-IM-RU-ḪA-RA-AḪ		BM 17045 13
ʾARAM	1	ʾARAM		U					A-RA-MU		M
		ʾARAM		A					A-RA-MA		A.+
		ʾARAM		U					A-RA-AM-MU		A.+
		ʾARAM				MAṬAR	A		A-RA-AM-MA-DA-RA		BM 80328 1
ʾARAPḪ	2	MUT		U		ʾARAPḪ	IM		MU-TU-AR-RA-AP-ḪI-IM		C+
ʾARAŚ	1	ʾARAŚ		UM					ḪA-RA-ŠUM		M
ʾARIŚ	1	ʾARIŚ	AN						ḪA-RI-ŠA-AN		M
ʾARK	1	ʾARK	ATANUM						AR-GA-TA-NU-UM		KISURRA 141 9
		ʾARK	ATANUM						AR-GA-DA-NU-UM		KISURRA 1A 15+
ʾARNAB	1	ʾARNAB		UM					AR-NA-BU-UM	FN	M+
		ʾARNAB	AT	UM					AR-NA-BA-TUM	FN	CT VIII 43C 22+, XIII 1 X 39
		ʾARNAB	AT	IM					AR-NA-BA-TIM	FN? GEN	MEISSNER 18 3
ʾARR	2	ʾAJ		A		ʾARR	I		D-A-A-AR-RI	FN	M
ʾARŚ	1	ʾARŚ		UM		MALIK			ḪA-AR?-ŠUM?-MA-LIK		M
ʾARUḪ	1	ʾARUḪ		UM					A-RU-ḪU-UM		B 13
ʾARUM	1	ʾARUM		A					A-RU-MA	GEN	RA VIII 74 16
ʾARUŚ	1	ʾARUŚ		UM					A-RU-SU-UM		M, JEAN TELL SIFR 72A 3+
		ʾARUŚ		U					A-RU-SU		JEAN TELL SIFR 72 5+
		ʾARUŚ				ʾEL	UM		A-RU-UŠ-E-LUM		UCP X/3 2 25
		ʾARUŚ		I		ʾIL			A-RU-SI-DINGIR		A 7459, M
		ʾARUŚ				PI					
						ʾIL			A-RU-UŠ-BI-DINGIR		M, RA XLI 45 4' HANA
ʾASIN	1	ʾASIN		IM					A-ZI-NIM	GEN	XIII 13 13+
		ʾASIN		I					A-SI-NI		APN P. 31 LATE
		ʾASIN		AM					A-ZI-NA-A[M]	ACC	XIV 33:7
		ʾASIN		U	HU				A-ZI-NU-U$_2$		M
		ʾASIN		U	HU				A-SI-NU-U		APN P. 31 LATE
ʾASUN	1	ʾASUN	AN						A-ZU-NA-AN		RA LXV 48 VIII 29
ʾAŚJ	1	ʾAŚJ		UM					A-SU-UM		M
		ʾAŚJ		IM					A-SI-IM	GEN	C
	2	ʾANN		U		ʾAŚJ	AH		AN-NU-A-SI-IA	FN	XIII 1 IV 41+
		ʾIŚḪAR	AH			ʾAŚJ	AH		D-IŠ-ḪA-RA-A-SI-IA	FN	XIII 1 XI 43
		ʿAŠTAR				ʾAŚJ	AH		EŠ$_4$-DAR-A-SI-IA	FN	XIII 1 IX 3+
		ʿAŠTAR				ʾAŚJ	AH		EŠ$_4$-DAR-A-ZU-IA	FN	M
		KAKK		A		ʾAŚJ	AH		KA-AK-KA-A-SI-IA	FN	XIII 1 VI 11
ʾAŚAL	2	ʾAP		I		ʾAŚAL			A-PI-A-ŠAL		JNES XIII 212F.+ LATE

STEMS

ʾAŠAŠ	1		ʾAŠAŠ		UM						A-SA-ŠUM		BIROT, TEA 72 IV 17
ʾAŠD	1		ʾAŠD		U						D-AŠ-DU		RT XIX 48 SEAL
			ʾAŠD		UM						AŠ-DU-UM		VAS VIII 60 26
			ʾAŠD	AH							ḪA-AŠ-DA	FN	RA LXV 58 I 62
			ʾAŠD		IJA						AŠ-DI-IA		BIN VII 32 4
			ʾAŠD		A			ʾAḪ	I		AŠ-DA-A-ḪI		VAS XVI 44 3
			ʾAŠD		I			JAŠAR			AŠ$_{2}$-DI-E-SA-AR		XIII 1 XI 35
			ʾAŠD		I			JATAR			AŠ-DI-E-TAR		M
			ʾAŠD		I			DAWD	UM		AŠ$_{2}$-DI?-DA-DU-UM		EDZARD, DER 60:11
			ʾAŠD		I		JE	JŠUʿ			AŠ$_{2}$-DI-E-ŠU-UḪ		M
			ʾAŠD		I			KIʾR	U		AŠ-DI-KI-E-RU		BM 92654 A
			ʾAŠD		I			KIʾR	U		AŠ-DI-KI-RU		BM 92654
			ʾAŠD		I			LUMM	A		AŠ-DI-LU-MA		UCP X/3 2 31
			ʾAŠD		I			MAʾK	U	HU	AŠ$_{2}$-DI-MA-KU-U$_{2}$		VAS IX 172 30
			ʾAŠD		I			NIʿM			AŠ$_{2}$-DI-NI-ḪI-IM		M+
			ʾAŠD		I			RAWM			AŠ-DI-RA-AM		RA LXV 55 XIII 42
			ʾAŠD		I		TA	QWIM			AŠ$_{2}$-DI-TA-KI-IM		M+
			ʾAŠD		UM			ʾAB	I		AŠ$_{2}$-DU-UM-A-BI		BE VI/1 1 7+
			ʾAŠD		UM			ʾAB	I		D-AŠ-DU-UM-A-BI		UET V 483 4
			ʾAŠD		UM			LA					
								ʾAB	UM		AŠ-DU-UM-LA-A-BU-UM		SUMER V 142
			ʾAŠD		UM			LA					
								ʾAB	UM		AŠ$_{2}$-DU-UM-LA-A-BU-UM		SUMER V 142+
			ʾAŠD		UM			PI					
								JAD	IM		AŠ-DU-UM-BI-IA-DI-IM		RA LXV 55 XIII 44
			ʾAŠD		U			QAWM	U		AŠ-DU-GA-MU		CT XLV 77 R. 10, 14+
			ʾAŠD		U			QAWM	UM		AŠ$_{2}$-DU-GA-MU-UM		TCL I 130 8+
			ʾAŠD		U			RAPIʾ			AŠ$_{2}$-DU-RA-BI		C+
			ʾAŠD		U	NA	JA	RWIM			[AŠ$_{2}$-D]U-NI-A-RI-IM		CT XXXVI 4 1
			ʾAŠD		U	NA	JE	RWIM			AŠ$_{2}$-DU-NI-E-RI-IM		RA VIII 65 1
	2		ʾAḪ		I			ʾAŠD			A-ḪI-SA-AD		B 12+
			ʾAḪ		I			ʾAŠD			A-ḪI-A-SA-AD		B 12
			ʾAḪ		I			ʾAŠD			A-ḪA-SA-AD		UET V 539 II 19
			ʾAB		I			ʾAŠD			A-BI-A-SA-AD		B 10+
			ʾAB		I			ʾAŠD			A-BI-SA-AD		B 10+
			JARAḪ					ʾAŠD	UM		D-EN-ZU-AŠ-DU-UM		WALTERS, WL 114:2
			JATAR					ʾAŠD	I		IA-TAR-AŠ-DI		M
		JA	KWUN					ʾAŠD	UM		IA-KU-UN-AŠ-DU-UM		B 27
			MUT					ʾAŠD	IM		MU-UT-AŠ-DI-IM		M
			MUT		U			ʾAŠD	I		[MU]-TU-AŠ-DI		VIII 17 13'
			NAʿM		I			ʾAŠD	U		NA-AḪ-ME-AS-DU	FN	RA LXV 60 III 2
		JI	NṢUR					ʾAŠD	UM		I-ZUR-AŠ-DU-UM		A 7685 5
		JI	NṢUR					ʾAŠD	UM		I-ZUR-A-AŠ-DU-UM		CT II 42 25
		JI	TWUR					ʾAŠD	UM		I-DUR-A-AŠ-DU-UM		B 23
		JI	TWUR					ʾAŠD	UM		I-DUR-AŠ-DUM		B 23
		JI	TWUR					ʾAŠD	UM		I-DUR-AŠ-DU-UM		B 23+
		JI	TWUR					ʾAŠD	UM		I-DUR-AŠ$_{2}$-DU-UM		M+
		JI	TWUR					ʾAŠD	U		I-DUR-AŠ-DU		B 23+
		JI	TWUR					ʾAŠD	U		I-DUR-AŠ$_{2}$-DU		VAS IX 172 5, M+
		JI	TWUR					ʾAŠD	U	HU	I-DUR-AŠ-DU-U$_{2}$		SIMMONS 90 4
		JI	TWUR					ʾAŠD	U	HU	I-DUR-AŠ$_{2}$-DU-U$_{2}$		M
	3		LI				JI	JṢIʾ					
								ʾAŠD	UM		LI-ZI-AŠ-DU-UM		VAS XIII 104 R. II 24
ʾAŠIJ	2		ʾIL		I			ʾAŠIJ	AH		I$_{3}$-LI$_{2}$-A-SI-IA	FN	XIII 1 VII 55
ʾAŠIN	1		ʾAŠIN		UM						A-SI-NU-UM		B 14+
			ʾAŠIN		U						A-SI-NU		B 14
ʾAŠIR	1		ʾAŠIR		UM						A-SI-RUM		B 14+, M+
			ʾAŠIR		UM						A-SI-RU-UM		B 14+
			ʾAŠIR	AT	UM						A-SI-RA-TUM		B 14
ʾAŠM	1		ʾAŠM	AN							AŠ-MA-AN		BM 81174 11
			ʾAŠM	AN	UM						ḪA-AŠ-MA-NU-UM		U
			ʾAŠM	AN	I						ḪA-AŠ-MA-NI	GEN	B 44
			ʾAŠM	AT							AŠ-MA-AT	MN	M+
			ʾAŠM	ATEN							AŠ$_{2}$-MA-TI-EN		M
			ʾAŠM		A			HADD	U		AŠ-MA-DU		BM 80328 14
			ʾAŠM		A			HADD	U		AŠ-MA-A-DU		A.+

STEMS

ʾAŠQUD	1		ʾAŠQUD		UM					AŠ-KU-DU-UM		KISURRA 205 7, M+
			ʾAŠQUD		UM					AŠ$_2$-KU-DU-UM		X 59 8
			ʾAŠQUD		UM					AŠ-KU-TU-UM		KISURRA 88 1, 8+
			ʾAŠQUD		U					AŠ-KU-DU		M
			ʾAŠQUD		IM					AŠ-KU-DI-IM	GEN	M+
			ʾAŠQUD		I					AŠ-KU-DI	GEN	M+
			ʾAŠQUD	AN						AŠ-KU-DA-AN		M
			ʾAŠQUD	AN						Ḫ̮A-AŠ-KU-DA-AN		M
			ʾAŠQUD	AN	UM					AŠ-KU-DA-NU-UM		CT XLVIII 86 REV 10+
			ʾAŠQUD	AN	AM					AŠ-KU-DA-NA-AM	ACC	B 43
ʾAŠUD	1		ʾAŠUD		UM					Ḫ̮A-SU-DU-UM		A 7660 2
ʾAŠUL	1		ʾAŠUL		U					A-SU-LU		TA 30 36 3
ʾAŠAR	1		ʾAŠAR		UM					A-ŠA-RU-UM		EDZARD, DER 68 IV 3
			ʾAŠAR			NAṢIR				D-A-ŠAR-NA-ṢIR		M
	2	JA	JṢIʾ			ʾAŠAR				IA-ZI-A-ŠAR		SZLECHTER TJ P. 186
		JI	JṢIʾ			ʾAŠAR				I-ZI-A-ŠAR		B 22+
		JI	JṢIʾ			ʾAŠAR				I-ṢI-A-ŠAR		YOS VIII 108 SEAL
		JA	KWUN			ʾAŠAR				IA-KU-UN-A-ŠAR		B 92+, M+
		JI	KWUN			ʾAŠAR				I-KU-UN-A-ŠAR		GORDON 38 6
		JA	KWUN			ʾAŠAR		I		IA-KU-UN-A-ŠA-RI	NOM	CT XLVIII 10 6
		JA	KWUN			ʾAŠAR		UM		IA-KU-UN-A-ŠA-RU-UM		B 27
		JA	RŠIJ			ʾAŠAR		I		IA-AR-ŠI-A-ŠA-RI		M
		JA	ŠWUB			ʾAŠAR				IA-ŠU-UB-A-ŠAR		M+
			ŠALIM			ʾAŠAR				ŠA-LIM-D-A-ŠAR		M
	3		BUN		U	MA						
						ʾAŠAR				BU-NU-MA-A-ŠA-AR		KISURRA 93 4
			BUN		U	MA						
						ʾAŠAR				BU-NU-MA-ŠAR		B 16+
ʾAŠIḪ̮	1		ʾAŠIḪ̮		UM					A-ŠI-Ḫ̮U-UM	FN	RA LXV 62 V 33
	2		TALM		U	ʾAŠIḪ̮		I		TA-AL-MU-A-ŠI-Ḫ̮I	FN	XIII 1 III 63
ʾAŠIR	1		ʾAŠIR							Ḫ̮A-ŠI-IR?		HARRIS 38 5
			ʾAŠIR	AT	UM					D-A-ŠI-RA-TUM	DN FN	RIFTIN 60 SEAL
			ʾAŠIR			ŠI			JA			
						....				A-ŠE-ER-ŠI-IA-[X]	FN	XIII 1 VIII 2
	2		ʾUMM		I	ʾAŠIR	AH			UM-MI-A-ŠI-RA	FN	VAS XIII 73 6,13
ʾAŠR	1		ʾAŠR		I					Ḫ̮A-AŠ$_2$-RI		CT XLV 92 R. 9
			ʾAŠR		I	JATAR				AŠ-RI-E-TAR		RA XLIX 24 N. 9
			ʾAŠR	AT	UM	ʾUMM		I		D-AŠ-RA-TUM-UM-MI	FN	TCL I P. 16+
	2		Ḫ̮AJJ		A	ʾAŠR		A	JA	E$_2$-A-AŠ-RA-IA		M+
			ʾIL		I	ʾAŠR		A	JA	I$_3$-LI$_2$-AŠ-RA-IA		M+
			ʾANN		U	ʾAŠR		I		AN-NU-AŠ-RI	FN	M+
			DAGAN			ʾAŠR		A	JA	D-DA-GAN-AŠ-RA-IA		M+
			KAKK		A	ʾAŠR		I		KA-AK-KA-AŠ-RI	FN	XIII 1 V 1
ʾAŠUR	2		ʿABD			ʾAŠUR		A		Ḫ̮A-AB-DU-A-ŠU-RA		M
			ṬAJB		A	ʾAŠUR		A		TA-PA-AŠ-ŠU-RA		A.
ʾAŠUZ	1		ʾAŠUZ		I					A-ŠU-ZI		M
ʾATAJ	2		ʾIL		I	ʾATAJ		A	JA	I$_3$-LI$_2$-A-TA-A-IA		RA VIII 69 26
ʾATAL	1		ʾATAL		UM					Ḫ̮A-TA-LU-UM		CT XXXIII 42 23+
			ʾATAL		UM					Ḫ̮A-AT-TA-LUM		CT XXXIII 43A 6
			ʾATAL	AN	UM					A-TA-LA-NU-UM		EDZARD, DER 100:3
			ʾATAL		I	ʾEL				Ḫ̮A-TA-LI-EL		M
ʾATAM	1		ʾATAM		UM					Ḫ̮A-TA-MU-UM		B 20
			ʾATAM	AN	UM					A-TA-MA-NU-UM		UCP X/3 3 22+
			ʾATAM	AN	UM					AT-TA-MA-NU-UM		SIMMONS 122 16
ʾATAR	1		ʾATAR	AN	I					A-TA-RA-NI	GEN	HARRIS 71 12
			ʾATAR		I	ṢADUQ				[A]T-TA-RI-ZA-DU-UQ		I 103 17
ʾATAZ	1		ʾATAZ	AH						AT-TA-ZA	FN	M
			ʾATAZ	AH						AT-TA-AZ-ZA	FN	XIII 1 III 9+
ʾATIM	1		ʾATIM		UM					A-TI-MU-UM		TA 30 7 8, M
			ʾATIM		U					A-TI-MU		M
			ʾATIM		AM					A-TI-M[A-AM]	ACC	M
ʾATT	1		ʾATT		UM					Ḫ̮A-AT-TU-UM		M
			ʾATT		U					Ḫ̮A-AT-TU		C+
			ʾATT		IM					Ḫ̮A-AT-TI-IM	GEN	M+
			ʾATT		A					D-Ḫ̮A-AT-TA	DN	M+
			ʾATT		I					AT-TI	FN	RA LXV 65 VII 6

STEMS

ʾATT	1		ʾATT		I						ḪA-AT-TI		RA LXV 40 I 32
			ʾATT		IJAN						AT-TI-IA-AN		A. 261 14
			ʾATT		I			HADD	U		AT-TI-D-IM		M+
			ʾATT		I			ʿAMM	A		AT-TI-AM-MA		A. LATE
			ʾATT		I			LIʾM	A		AT-TI-LI-MA		A. LATE
			ʾATT		I			MEʾR			AT?-TI-ME-IR?		IX 234 10
	2		ḪAʾR		I			ʾATT	A		ḪA-RI-A-TA		C II 5 7
			BIN	T	A			ʾATT	I		BI-IT-TA-AT-TI	FN	A.+
			KAʾB		I			ʾATT	A		KA-BI-A-TA		M
ʾATTA	1		ʾATTA					BAʿL	I		AT-TA-BA-AḪ-LI		JCS XIII 51 293:8,A. LATE
			ʾATTA					BAʿL	I	JE	AT-TA-BA-AḪ-LI-E		JCS XIII 51 293:15,A.LATE
			ʾATTA					NABIT	I		A-TA-NA-BE-TI		JCS XIII 57 306:5+,A LATE
ʾATUL	1		ʾATUL	AH							ḪA-TU-LA	FN	RA LXV 65 VII 4
ʾAZJ	2		ʾAJA					ʾAZJ	I		A-IA-ZI		M
			ʾAB		I			ʾAZJ	I		A-BI-A-ZI		A.
ʾBUQ	1	JA	ʾBUQ		UM						IA-BU-KUM		KISURRA 83 14
ʾDUM	2		LA				ʾA	ʾDUM	U		LA-AḪ-DU-MU		4E RENC. ASS. P. 178 4
ʾEWIN	1		ʾEWIN		I						E-[W]I-NI		RA LXV 47 VII 22
ʾEB	1		ʾEB	ATAN							E-BA-TA-AN		M+
			ʾEB		I			ʾIL			E-BI-IL		M
			ʾEB		I			DANN	UM		E-BI-DA-NU-UM		U
ʾEDAK	1		ʾEDAK		UM						E-DA-KUM		CT VIII 4A 4
	2	ʾA	RŠIJ					ʾEDAK	U		AR-ŠI-E-DA-KU	FN	M
ʾEDID	1		ʾEDID		UM						E-DI-DU-UM		SIMMONS 138 7
ʾEK	1		ʾEK		I			LA					
							ʾA	HWIJ			E-KI-LA-AḪ-WI		M
ʾEKAL	2		MUT					ʾEKAL	IM		MU-UT-E$_2$-GAL-LIM		M
ʾEL	1		ʾEL	AN	UM						E-LA-NU-UM		U
			ʾEL	AN	I						E-LA-NI		M
			ʾEL					KAWN	UM		EL-GA-NU-UM		TA 1931 238
	2		ʾAḪ		U			ʾEL			A-ḪU-EL		RA LXV 50 IX 1
			ʾAWAʾ	AT	I			ʾEL			A-WA-TI-EL		RA LXV 41 II 37+
			JAḪAD					ʾEL	UM		IA-ḪA-AD-E-LUM		RIFTIN 136 26
			JAḪAD					ʾEL	UM		IA-ḪA-TE-LUM?		UET V 605 13
			ḪAʾL		I			ʾEL			ḪA-LI$_2$-EL		RA LXV 42 III 18+
			ḪAʾL		I			ʾEL			ḪA-A-LI$_2$-EL		RA LXV 42 III 20
		ME	ʾWIR		I			ʾEL			ME-ḪI-RI-E-EL		JCS IV 109 4311 7
			ʾAB		A			ʾEL			A-BA-EL		TA 31, 221
			ʿABD					ʾEL			AB-DA-EL		TA 30, 615 9, 41
			ʿABD					ʾEL			ḪA-AB-DI-EL		KISURRA 74 17
		JI	JBIŠ					ʾEL			I-BI-IŠ-I$_3$-EL		SIMMONS 70 12
			ʿADIJ					ʾEL			ḪA-DI-EL		KISURRA 113 12+
			JADAʿ			TI		ʾEL			IA-DA-AḪ-TE-DINGIR		UNPUBL.
		JA	JDIʿ					ʾEL	UM		IA-DI-ḪI-E-LUM		UNPUBL.
		JA	JDIʿ		A			ʾEL			IA-DI-ḪA-EL		KISURRA 10A 4
			ʾADD		I	JA		ʾEL			AD-DI-JA-EL		BAB. III 267 HANA
			ʾADD		I	JA		ʾEL			AD-DI-IA-DINGIR		MAOG IV 2 12 HANA
			ʾADAM			TI		ʾEL			ḪA-DAM-TI-EL		HARRIS 61 2
			ʾADAM			TI		ʾEL	UM		A-DAM-TE-LUM		GAUTIER 31 6
			ʾAK		I			ʾEL			A-KI-EL		RA LXV 46 VI 49
			ʾAKK	AT				ʾEL			A-GA?-AD-E-EL		I
			ʾIL		A			ʾEL			I-LA-EL		RA LXV 43 IV 3
			ʾALAŠ		I			ʾEL			A-LA-SI-E-EL		UCP X/3 3 17
			ʾAM	T				ʾEL			GEME$_2$-E-IL		RIFTIN 44 10
			ʿAMM		U			ʾEL			AM-MU-E-EL		BM 16931 2
			ʿEMUQ		I			ʾEL			E-[M]U-QI$_2$-EL		RA LXV 40 I 3
			ʿANAJ			TI		ʾEL			A-NI-TE-EL		MOORTGAT 309
			ḪINUN					ʾEL			I-NU-UN-E-EL		UET V 569 2
			ḪUNUN		I			ʾEL			U$_2$-NU-NI-EL		B 40
			ḪUNN		U			ʾEL			U$_3$-NU-EL		TA 31 223
		ʾU	WQIH					ʾEL			U$_2$-QI$_2$-E[L]		RA LXV 41 II 44
			ʿAQAB					ʾEL			A-QA-BE-EL		UET V 839 23
			ʿAQUB		I			ʾEL			A-KU-PI-EL		GORDON 38 16
			ʾARUŠ					ʾEL	UM		A-RU-UŠ-E-LUM		UCP X/3 2 25
			ḪAŠAK			NI		ʾEL			A-SA-AK-NI-EL		RA LXV 52 XI 6
			ʾUŠŠ	AT	I			ʾEL			UŠ-SA-TE-EL		TIM III 43 6

STEMS

ʾEL	2 JA		ḪATIʾ			ʾEL		IA-ḪA-TI-EL		RA LXV 44 IV 46
			ʾATAL	I		ʾEL		ḪA-TA-LI-EL		M
	JA		WṢIʾ			ʾEL		IA-A[W-Z]I-EL?		VIII 87 8'
	JA		ʿZIB	A		ʾEL		IA-AḪ-ZI-BA-EL?		RA LXV 50 VIII 77
			BAʿD	I		ʾEL		[BA]-AḪ-DI-EL		KISURRA 51 10
			BALAṬ	I		ʾEL		BA-LA-TI-EL		RUTTEN 5 21
			BUN	I		ʾEL	UM	BU-UN?-NE-E-LUM		TCL I 220 42
			BUN	UM		ʾEL	UM	BU-NU-UM-E-LU-UM		B 16
			ḎAKUR	I		ʾEL		ZA-KU-RI-E-EL		UCP X/1 86 15
			ḎAKUR	I		ʾEL	UM	ZA-KU-RI-E-LUM		UNPUBL.
			ḎAMAR	I		ʾEL	UM	ZA-MA-RI-E-LUM		B. 92+
			KUʾB	A		ʾEL		KU-BA-EL		X 91 4'
			KUʾB	A		ʾEL		KU-BA-DINGIR		M
			KIʾM	I		ʾEL		KI-MI-EL		UCP X/3 2 2
	JA		KRUB			ʾEL		D-IA-AK-RU-UB-EL	DN	M+
	JI		KRUB			ʾEL		D-IK-RU-UB-EL	DN	M+
			KUŠM	I		ʾEL		KU-UŠ$_2$-MI-EL		RA LXV 48 VII 74
	JI		KSUW			ʾEL		IK-ZU-EL		TA 30 615 10, 20+
			LI		JA	ʾEL		LI-IA-EL		RA LXV 41 II 23
			LAʾL	I		ʾEL		LA-LI-E-EL		SIMMONS 70 15
			LUʾP	U		ʾEL		LU-BU-E-EL		I
			LAŠU			ʾEL KA		LA-ŠI-EL-KA-A-BI-IM		B 33
			MEʾN	I		ʾEL		ME-NI-EL		RA LXV 52 X 18
			MAʾR	A		ʾEL		MA-RA-EL		TA 1931, 298
			MAʾR	A		ʾEL		URU-MA-RA-EL	GN	MRS VI 11830:10
			MAʾR	A		ʾEL		URU-MA-RA-DINGIR	GN	MRS IX 17340:7
			MANIJ			ʾEL		MA-NI-EL		RA VIII 72 7
			MUT	UM		ʾEL		MU-TUM-E-EL		YOS VIII P. 16+
			MUT	UM		ʾEL		MU-TUM-EL		YOS VIII P. 16+
			NAʿM	A		ʾEL		NA-MA-EL		TA 30 615:11+
	JA		NABIʾ			ʾEL		IA-NA-BI-EL		M+
			NADUB			ʾEL	I	NA-DU-BE-LI$_2$		U
			NIṢB	I		ʾEL		NE-IZ-BI-EL		TA 1930, 747 +
			PU	UM		ʾEL		PU-UM-E-EL		BAGH.MITT. IV 291,SEAL
	JI		PANIJ			ʾEL	UM	I-PA-AN-NI-E-LUM		UNPUBL.
			QARIʾ			ʾEL		QA-R[I]-E[L]		M
			RAWM	E		ʾEL		R[A]-ME-EL		RA LXV 42 II 56
	JE		RBUʾ		HU	ʾEL		E-[IR]-BU-U$_2$-[E]L		KISURRA 152 9
	JA		RBIJ			ʾEL		IA-AR-BI-EL		CT XLV 12 23
			SITR	I		ʾEL	UM	ZI-IT-RI-E-LUM		B 42
	JA		SAṬIʾ			ʾEL		[I]A-ZA-AD-DI-EL		M
			ŠU			ʾEL	UM	ŠU-E-LUM		B 40
	JI		ŚKUR			ʾEL	I	IŠ-KUR-E-LI	FN	XIII 1 VII 41
			ŚUM	U		ʾEL		SU-MU-EI		TA 30, 34 6
	JA		ŚMAʿ			ʾEL		IA-AŠ$_2$-MA-AḪ-I$_3$-EL		B 30
			ŚAMUʿ	I		ʾEL		SA-MU-ḪI-EL		M
			ŚAMUK	I		ʾEL		SA-MU-KI-EL		B 38+
	JI	ŠT	ŠNIJ			ʾEL		IŠ-TA-AŠ-NI-EL		SIMMONS 46 30
			ŚARAJ		TI	ʾEL		ŠA-RA-TI-EL		TIM III 59 6
			ŚARAJ		TI	ʾEL		ŠA-RA-TE-EL		TIM III 44 18+
			ŠAṬUP	I		ʾEL		ŠA-TU-BI-EL		RA LXV 44 IV 74
			ṢABAʾ		TI	ʾEL		ZA-BA-TE-EL		UNPUBL.
			ZIZN	I		ʾEL		ZI-IZ-NI-EL		RA LXV 55 XIII 11
	3		ʾAJA			MA ʾEL		A-IA-MA-EL		RA LXV 42 III 14
	JI		JBAL			PI ʾEL		I-BA-AL-BI-EL		M+
	JI		JBAL			PI ʾEL		I-BA-AL-PI-EL		UCP X P. 56+
	ʾA		JDAʿ			PI ʾEL		A-DA-AḪ-[BI]?-EL		SIMMONS 51 21
	JA		ḪNUN			PI ʾEL		IA-ḪU-UN-PI-EL		SIMMONS 54 18
			ḪUNN			PI ʾEL		ḪU-UN-BI-EL		SIMMONS 82 7

STEMS

ʾEL	3 ʾU	WQAH			KI			
					ʾEL		U$_2$-QA-KI-EL	RA LXV 51 IX 69
		JIŠʿ	I		LI			
					ʾEL		IŠ-ḪI-LI-EL	JCS XXIV 69 NO. 3 SEAL
	JA	ʾŚUD			PI			
					ʾEL		IA-SU-UD-PI-EL	SIMMONS 46 31
		BIʿD	I		KI			
					ʾEL		BI-DI-KI-EL	RA LXV 53 XI 54
		BANIJ			ME			
					ʾEL		BA-NI-ME-EL	HARRIS 12 15
		DAWD	I	Š	ME			
					ʾEL		DA-DI-EŠ$_3$-ME-EL	UCP X/3 P. 198+
		DUWD	U	Š	ME			
					ʾEL		DU-DU-UŠ-ME-EL	UCP X/3 P. 198+
		KI			MILK	I		
					ʾEL		KI-MI-II-KI-EL	KISURRA 112:8
	ʾA	KWUN			PI			
					ʾEL		A-KU-PI-EL	GORDON, SCT 38 16
		MILK	I		LA			
					ʾEL		MI-IL-KI-LA-EL	TA 30 615 21
		MILK	I		LI			
					ʾEL		MI-IL-KI-LI-EL	B 34, M+
		MILK	I		LI			
					ʾEL		MIL-KI-LI-EL	VAS VIII 128 16+
		MILK	I		LI			
					ʾEL	UM	MI-IL-KI-LI-E-LUM	A 32065:3
		MANN	A		BALTI			
					ʾEL		MA-NA-BA-AL-TE-EL	B 28+
		MANN	A		BALTI			
					ʾEL		MA-NA-BA-AŠ-TE-EL	M+
		MANN	A		BALTI			
					ʾEL		MA-NA-BA-AL-TI-EL	KISURRA 70A 14+
		MARUʾ			LI			
					ʾEL		MA-RU-LI-EL	SIMMONS 47 18, 49 22
		MUT	I		ME			
					ʾEL		MU-TI-ME-EL	TA 30, 615:4+
		MUT	U		ME			
					ʾEL		MU-TU-ME-EL	CT VIII 31A 25+
		MUT	UM		MA			
					ʾEL		MU-TUM-MA-EL	TA 1931, 456
		MUT	UM		ME			
					ʾEL		MU-TUM-ME-EL	RUTTEN 32 8+
		MATAʿ	A		KI			
					ʾEL		MA-TA-A-KI-EL	RA LXV 50 IX 20;HARRIS 19:5,SEAL+
		PI			KAMA			
					ʾEL		BI-KA-MA-EL	M+
		PI			NAʿM			
					ʾEL		BI-NA-AḪ-ME-EL	B 15
		PU			MA			
					ʾEL		PU-MA-[E]L	TA 1931,538 I
		SITR	I		KI			
					ʾEL		ZI-IT-RI?-KI-EL?	B 42
	ʾA	ŠWUB			LA			
					ʾEL		A-ŠU-UB-LA-EL	TA 1931,765
	ʾA	ŠWUB			LI			
					ʾEL		A-ŠU-UB-LI-EL	OIP XLIII 154 NO. 48+
		ŚAM	A		ME			
					ʾEL		SA-MA-ME-EL	M
		ŚAM	A		ME			
					ʾEL		ŠA-MA-ME-EL	TA 1931, 421
		ŚAM	I		ME			
					ʾEL		SA-MI-ME-EL	CT XLV 117 33
		ŚUM	U		LI			
					ʾEL		SU-MU-LI-EL	B 39+
		ŚUM	U		LA			
					ʾEL		SU-MU-LA-EL	SUMER XXIII 160 5

STEMS

ʾEL	3		ŠUM		U		LI						
							ʾEL				SU-MU-LI-EL-DU-RI		A 7630 3
			ŠUM		U		ME						
							ʾEL				SU-MU-ME-EL		JCS IV 107, YBC 4968
		JI	TWUR				ŠUM		U				
							ʾEL				I-DUR-SU-ME-EL		KISURRA 43 5+
			TIBIʾ		A	Š	ME						
							ʾEL				TI-BI$_2$-AŠ$_2$-ME-EL		CT XXXIII 48A 4
			ZAKK				PI						
							ʾEL				ZA-AK-PI-EL		TA 1931,198 EARLY OB
ʾELAP	1		ʾELAP		I						E-LA-BI	FN	RA LXV 65 VI 62
ʾELIL	1		ʾELIL		I	Š					E-LI-LI-IŠ		M+
			ʾELIL		I	Š					E-LI-LI-ŠA		M
ʾELL	1		ʾELL		UM						E-IL-LUM		RA LXV 50 VIII 70
			ʾELL		I						E-EL-LI		A. 377 8
			ʾELL	AN							EL-LA-AN		M
			ʾELL	AN							E-LA-AN		MAD V, SARG.
			ʾELL	AN	UM						E-EL-LA-NUM		C
			ʾELL	AN	UM						E-LA-NUM		C
			ʾELL	AN	U						E-EL-LA-NU		C
			ʾELL	AT			....				EL-LA-AT-[....]		M
			ʾELL	ATAN							EL-LA-TA-AN		C II 39:8
ʾELM	1		ʾELM	AN	UM						EL-MA?-NU-UM		TA 1931, 538 I
			ʾELM	ATAN							EL-MA-TA-AN		M
ʾELUR	1		ʾELUR		UM						EL-LU-RUM		CT VIII 43B21
			ʾELUR	AT	UM						EL-LU-RA-TUM	MN?	WATERMAN 38 9
ʾEN	1		ʾEN		IJA						E-NI-IA		M+
			ʾEN		I	Š	ʾAG		UM		E-NI-IŠ-A-GU-UM		M+
ʾENLIL	2		ŠUM		I		ʾENLIL				SU-ME-D-EN-LIL$_2$		KISURRA 197A 12
ʾENTIL	2		ŠUM		I		ʾENTIL				SU-ME-EN-TI-[IL]?		B 38
			ŠUM		U		ʾENTIL				SU-MU-EN-TE-IL		B 39
			ŠUM		U		ʾENTIL				SU-MU-EN-TI-[IL]?		KISURRA 95 15
ʾEŠB	1		ʾEŠB		I		HADD		U		EŠ-BI-D-IM		A.+
			ʾEŠB		I		ʾADAN	T	A		EŠ-BI-A-DA-AT-TA		A. 455 31, 55
ʾGUN	1	JA	ʾGUN								IA-AḪ-GU-UN		TCL XVII 25 1
		JA	ʾGUN		UM						IA-AḪ-GU-UN-NU-UM		TCL XVII 24 1
		JA	ʾGUN		UM						IA-AḪ-GU-NU-UM		TLB IV 82:1
		JA	ʾGUN		UM						IA-GU-NU-UM		YOS XII
		JA	ʾGUN		UM						I-IA-GU-NU-UM		YOS XII
		JA	ʾGUN		IM						IA-GU-NI-IM	GEN	BM 16485
		JA	ʾGUN		I						IA-AḪ-GU-UN-NI	GEN	TCL XVII 26 1
ʾIJA	1		ʾIJA				ʾAB						
							ʾIL				I-A-AB-DINGIR		OIP XXII 262
			ʾIJA				ʾUMM		U		I-IA-AMA		MRS VI P. 328+
ʾIB	1		ʾIB		I		JAT		UM		I-BI-IA-TUM		TIM II 27 4
			ʾIB		I		LA						
							ʾIL		UM		I-BI-LA-I$_3$-LUM		U
ʾIBIR	1		ʾIBIR	AN							I-BI-RA-AN		RA LXV XIII 34
ʾIBL	1		ʾIBL	AN	UM						IB-LA-A-NU-UM		HAV. SYMP. 237 13
			ʾIBL	AN	UM						IB-LA-NU-UM		I
ʾIBN	1		ʾIBN	AT	UM						IB-NA-TUM	MN	BM 16939 27+
ʾIDAD	1		ʾIDAD		UM						I-DA-DU-UM		WATERMAN 34 R. 13+
ʾIDAR	1		ʾIDAR	AN							I-DA-RA-AN		M
ʾIDD	1		ʾIDD	AT	UM						ID-DA-TUM	MN	B 21, M
			ʾIDD		I						ID-DI		XIII 1 IX 69+
			ʾIDD		IM						ḪI-ID-DI-IM		XIV 56:28
ʾIDID	1		ʾIDID		UM						I-DI-DUM		XIII 1 I 22
			ʾIDID		A						I-DI-DA	MN	BE VI/1 14 30
ʾIGAR	1		ʾIGAR	AN							I-GA-RA-AN		RA LXV 42 III 15
ʾIL	1		ʾIL	AN	UM						I-LA-NU-UM		I+, B 45+
			ʾIL	AN	UM						I-LA-A-NU-UM		B 93
			ʾIL		A	NI					I-LA-A-NI		A. 279 2
			ʾIL	AT	I						I-LA-TI	MN	M
			ʾIL	ATAN							I-LA-TA-AN		M
			ʾIL		IJA						I$_3$-LI$_2$-IA		M+
			ʾIL		A		ḪAʾL		UM		DINGIR-ḪA-LUM		B 21
			ʾIL		A		ḪAʾL		U	HU	DINGIR-ḪA-LU-U$_2$		XIII 1 IV 18

STEMS

ʾIL	1	ʾIL	A		ʾUWR	I		DINGIR-U$_2$-RI		RA LXVIII 28:13 MARI
		ʾIL	A		ʾAB	I		I-LA-A-BI		C
		ʾIL	A		ḪABAD			DINGIR-ḪA-BA-AD		M+
		ʾIL	A		ʿADN	U	HU	I-LA-ḪA-AD-NU-U$_2$		M
		ʾIL	A		ʿADN	U	HU	I-LA-ḪA-AD-NU-U$_2$	FN	C+
		ʾIL	A		ʿADN	U	HU	DINGIR-ḪA-AD-NU-U$_2$	FN	C+
		ʾIL	A		ʾIL			I-LA-DINGIR		B 21
		ʾIL	A		ʾEL			I-LA-EL		RA LXV 43 IV 3
		ʾIL	A		ʿAMM	U		I-LA-ḪA-MU		RA LXV 42 II 77+
		ʾIL	A		ʾUMM	A		DINGIR-UM-MA		RA LXV 45 V 31
		ʾIL	A		ʾIRR	A		[I-L]A?-IR$_3$-RA		RA LXV 47 VII 18
		ʾIL	A		ʿAŠTAR			I-LA-EŠ$_4$-DAR		RA LXV 42 III 16+
		ʾIL	A	JI	JBAL			DINGIR?-I-BA-AL		M
		ʾIL	A		BAWB	I	JA	DINGIR-BA-BI-A		UET V 263 17
		ʾIL	A		BAʿL	U	HU	I-LA-BA-LU-U$_2$		M
		ʾIL	A		BIN	I		DINGIR-BI-NI		UCP X/3 1 7
		ʾIL	A		BIN	I		I-LA-BI$_2$-NI		I
		ʾIL	A		DAʿ	AT		I-LA-DA-ḪA-AT		SUMER V 141,3+
		ʾIL	A		DAʿ	AT		BAD$_3$-DINGIR-DA-ḪA-AT	GN	A 7650
		ʾIL	A		DAKUL			DINGIR-DA-AK-KU-UL		UET V P. 43
		ʾIL	A		DAKUL			DINGIR-DA-KU-UL		UET V P. 43
		ʾIL	A		DAKUL	UM		DINGIR-DA-AK-KU-UL-LUM		UET V P. 43
		ʾIL	A		DAKUL	UM		DINGIR-DA-KU-UL-LUM		UET V P. 43+
		ʾIL	A		DARAN			DINGIR-DA-RA-AN		M+
		ʾIL	A		GULL	A		DINGIR-GU-UL-LA	FN	C+
		ʾIL	A		GULL	A				
					ʿAḎIR	AT		DINGIR-GUL-LA$_2$-ḪA-ZI-RA-AT	FN	M+
		ʾIL	A		KA					
					ʾAB	UM		DINGIR-KA-A-BU-UM		CT XLV 100 17
		ʾIL	A		KAʾAM			DINGIR-KA-A-AM		TIM III 101 7
		ʾIL	A		KAWN			DINGIR-KA-AN	MN	M+
		ʾIL	A		KAWN			DINGIR-KA-AN	FN	M
		ʾIL	A		KAWN	UM		DINGIR-KA-NU-UM		MAH II/3 P. 188F
		ʾIL	A		KAWN	IM		DINGIR-KA-NIM	GEN	M+
		ʾIL	A		KAWN	IM		DINGIR-KA-NI-IM	GEN	M
		ʾIL	A		KABKAB	I		DINGIR-KAB-KA-BI		JNES XIII 210+ LATE
		ʾIL	A		KABKAB	U	HU	I-LA-KAB-KA-BU-U$_2$		M+
		ʾIL	A		LA					
					ʾIL			DINGIR-LA-IL		U
		ʾIL	A		LA		KA	I-LA-LA-KA		B 21+
		ʾIL	A		LAʾIJ			I-LA-LA-I		TA 1931,395,UR III
		ʾIL	A		LAʾIJ			I-LA-LA-E		TA 1931,609,UR III
		ʾIL	A		LAʾIJ			I-LA-LA-E-KI	GN	LAESSOE,SHEMSHARA P.77
		ʾIL	A		LAʾIJ			I-LA-LA-AḪ		RA LXV IX 38,X 10
		ʾIL	A		MA					
					ʾAB	I		DINGIR-MA-A-BI		M
		ʾIL	A		MA					
					ʾIL	A		DINGIR-MA-I$_3$-LA		B 21+
		ʾIL	A		MA					
					ʾIL	A		DINGIR-MA-D-I-LA		B 21
		ʾIL	A		MAʾD	I		DINGIR-MA-DI		M
		ʾIL	A		MEʾR			DINGIR-ME-IR		JNES XIII 210+ LATE
		ʾIL	A		MALK	I		DINGIR-MA-AL-KI		A. LATE
		ʾIL	A		MILK	UM		DINGIR-MI-IL-KUM		BAHREIN UNP.,POST-UR III
		ʾIL	A		MAṬAR			DINGIR-MA-DA-AR		OR. N.S. XXVI 28 N.4 CAPP
		ʾIL	A		MAṬAR			DINGIR-MA-TAR		M+
		ʾIL	A		NAʿM	A		DINGIR-NA-MA-....		VAS VIII 14 44
		ʾIL	A		NABUṬ			DINGIR-NA-BU-UṬ		VAS VIII 14 31
		ʾIL	A		NUN	U		I-LA-NU-NU		FIGULLA CAT. I 14029
		ʾIL	A		PA	I		I-LA-BA-I		TA 1931, 499
		ʾIL	A		PAʾŠ	I	JA	DINGIR-PA-ŠI-IA		TCL XVIII 106 9
		ʾIL	A		QAʾB			DINGIR-QA-AB		TIM III 130 12, SEAL
		ʾIL	A		RAWḪ	I	JA	DINGIR-RA[Ḫ]I-A		HARRIS 76 21
		ʾIL	A		RAWḪ	I	JA	I-LA-RA-ḪI-IA		M
		ʾIL	A		RAWḪ	I	JE	I-LA-RA-ḪI-E		M
		ʾIL	A		RAWḪ	I	JE	DINGIR-RA-ḪI-E		HARRIS 85 14

ʾIL	1	ʾIL	A			ŠALIM				I-LA-SA-LIM		M, C
		ʾIL	A			ŠAMAR				I-LA-ŠA-MA-AR		U
		ʾIL	A		Š	BAʿL		UM		DINGIR-ŠU-BA-A-LUM		CT II 15 9
		ʾIL	A	TA		RʿIŠ				I-LA-TA-RI-IŠ		B 21
		ʾIL	AM			DIʿ		I		DINGIR-IAM-DI-I		SIMMONS 24 10+
		ʾIL	I			JAʾ		UM		I$_3$-LI$_2$-IA-UM		KISURRA 71A 5+
		ʾIL	I			JAʾ		UM		I$_3$-LI$_2$-I-UM		KISURRA 4A 12+
		ʾIL	I			JAʾ		UM		I$_3$-LI$_2$-I-U$_2$-UM		KISURRA 56 3+
		ʾIL	I			JAʾ		UM		I$_3$-LI$_2$-U$_2$-A-UM		KISURRA 186 5
		ʾIL	I			JAʾ		UM		I$_3$-LI$_2$-A-UM		B 21
		ʾIL	I			ḪAʾL		UM		I$_3$-LI$_2$-ḪA-LU-UM		CT XLV 3 10
		ʾIL	I			ʿIJN		A	JA	I$_3$-LI$_2$-I-NA-A-A		GAUTIER 40 7
		ʾIL	I			JAʾN		UM		I$_3$-LI$_2$-IA-NU-UM		TIM I 29 3
		ʾIL	I			ʾUWR		I		I-LI-U$_2$-RI	FN	A.
		ʾIL	I			HADD		U		I$_3$-LI$_2$-D-IM		M+
		ʾIL	I			HADD		U		I$_3$-LI$_2$-A-DU		A. 57 47
		ʾIL	I			HEDD		A		I$_3$-LI-E-DA		A.
		ʾIL	I			ʿADN		I		I$_3$-LI$_2$-ḪA-AD-NI	FN	M
		ʾIL	I			ʾIL		A		I$_3$-LI$_2$-I-LA		A. LATE
		ʾIL	I			ʾILL		A		I-LI-IL-LA		A. LATE
		ʾIL	I			ʾIMM	AH			I-LI$_2$-IM-MA	FN	C II 41 56, 44 57
		ʾIL	I			ʿAMM		U		I$_3$-LI$_2$-ḪA-MU		RA LVII 178
		ʾIL	I			ḤUMUD		I		I$_3$-LI$_2$-ḪU-MU-DI		M
		ʾIL	I			ḤUNIN		I		I$_3$-LI$_2$-U$_2$-NE-NI		RUTTEN 6 20
		ʾIL	I			ʾAP		I	JA	I$_3$-LI$_2$-A-PI?-A		TIM III 4 14
		ʾIL	I			JAQR		A		I$_3$-LI$_2$-AQ-RA		IRAQ XXX 90, RIMAH
		ʾIL	I			JARAḪ				I$_3$-LI$_2$-IA-RA-AḪ		SIMMONS 131 20
		ʾIL	I			JARAḪ				I$_3$-LI$_2$-E-RA-AḪ		M+, TIM III 133 4, SEAL
		ʾIL	I			ʾAŠIJ	AH			I$_3$-LI$_2$-A-SI-IA	FN	XIII 1 VII 55
		ʾIL	I			ʾAŠR		A	JA	I$_3$-LI$_2$-AŠ-RA-IA		M+
		ʾIL	I			ʿAŠTAR				I$_3$-LI$_2$-EŠ$_4$-DAR		M+
		ʾIL	I			JAT				I$_3$-LI$_2$-A-AT?		TA 1931, 261
		ʾIL	I			JAT		UM		I$_3$-LI$_2$-I-IA-TUM		VAS XVIII 83:15
		ʾIL	I			JAT			KA	I$_3$-LI$_2$-A-AT-KA		TIM III 10 14+
		ʾIL	I			ʾATAJ		A	JA	I$_3$-LI$_2$-A-TA-A-IA		RA VIII 69 26
		ʾIL	I			ʾITEJ			JE	I$_3$-LI$_2$-I-TE-E		MEISSNER 110 20, 23+, M
		ʾIL	I			JATAR				I$_3$-LI$_2$-A-TAR		B 21+
		ʾIL	I			JATAR				I$_3$-LI$_2$-E-TAR		M+
		ʾIL	I			ḪAṢN		A	JA	I$_3$-LI$_2$-ḪA-AṢ-NA-A-IA		M+
		ʾIL	I			ḪAṢN		I	JA	I$_3$-LI$_2$-ḪA-AṢ-NI-IA		XIII 1 IX 8
		ʾIL	I	ʾA		ḪTAN				I$_3$-LI$_2$-AḪ-TA-AN		RUTTEN 6 16+
		ʾIL	I	ʾA		PTAN				I$_3$-LI$_2$-AP-TA-AN		B 21
		ʾIL	I	ʾA		PTAN				DINGIR-AP-TAN		TIM III 150 12
		ʾIL	I	JI		ḪNUW			HU	I$_3$-LI$_2$-IḪ-NU-U$_2$		UCP X/1 19:4+
		ʾIL	I	JE		JPAʿ				I$_3$-LI$_2$-E-PA		A.+
		ʾIL	I	JE		JPUʿ				I$_3$-LI$_2$-E-PU-UḪ		M+
		ʾIL	I	JE		JŠUʿ				I$_3$-LI$_2$-E-ŠU-UḪ		B 21 M
		ʾIL	I	JI		ḪṮAʾ						
						LI			JA	I$_3$-LI$_2$-IḪ-TA-LI-A		BIROT,TEA 69 I 14
		ʾIL	I	JA		MWUT				I$_3$-LI$_2$-IA-MU-[UT]		RA LXV 40 I 29
		ʾIL	I	JA		MLIK				I$_3$-LI$_2$-A-AM-LIK		HARRIS 49 12
		ʾIL	I	JI		ŠMAʿ			NIA	I$_3$-LI$_2$-IŠ-MA-NI-A		TA 1930,399
		ʾIL	I	JI		ŠPIQ				I$_3$-LI$_2$-IŠ-BI-IK		TA 1931, 71
		ʾIL	I	JI	T	ŠAMAR				I$_3$-LI$_2$-IŠ-TA-MAR		EDZARD,DER 67:11
		ʾIL	I			BAWB		UM		I$_3$-LI$_2$-BA-BU-UM		U UNPUBL.
		ʾIL	I			BAWŠ	T	I		I$_3$-LI$_2$-BA-AŠ$_2$-TI	FN	M+
		ʾIL	I			BIN		A	JA	I$_3$-LI$_2$-BI-NA-A-IA		M+
		ʾIL	I			DAʿ	AT			DINGIR-DA-ḪA-AT		A 7650:2
		ʾIL	I			DIʿ	AT			I$_3$-LI$_2$-DI-ḪA-[AT]		HARRIS 39 19
		ʾIL	I			DAGAN				I$_3$-LI$_2$-D-DA-GAN		M+
		ʾIL	I			DITAN				I$_3$-LI$_2$-DI-TA-AN		BM 82424 R. 18
		ʾIL	I			GUML		I	JA	I$_3$-LI$_2$-GU-UM-LI-IA		XIII 1 VIII 45
		ʾIL	I			KAʾB		I		I$_3$-LI$_2$-KA-PI		BIROT, TEA 69:28
		ʾIL	I			KUWN				I$_3$-LI$_2$-KU-UN		RA LXV 55 XIII 32
		ʾIL	I			KABKAB		U		I$_3$-LI$_2$-KA-AB-KA-BU		A 21914 3
		ʾIL	I			KAŠAR				I$_3$-LI$_2$-KA-ŠA-AR		M

STEMS												
ʾIL	1	ʾIL	I			LIʾM				I$_3$-LI$_2$-LI-IM		M+, C
		ʾIL	I			MA						
						ʾAB		I		I$_3$-LI-MA-A-BI		M+
		ʾIL	I			MAʾD		A		I$_3$-LI$_2$-MA-DA		TA 30 615 6
		ʾIL	I			MAʾD		I		I$_3$-LI$_2$-MA-DI		SIMMONS 33 19
		ʾIL	I			MAʾD		I				
						ʾAḪ				I$_3$-LI$_2$-MA-DI-A-AḪ		RUTTEN 1 8
		ʾIL	I			MAʾD		I				
						ʾAḪ				DINGIR?-MA-DA-AḪ		RA LXV 42 III 21
		ʾIL	I			MAʾD		I				
						ʾAḪ				I$_3$-LI$_2$-MI-DI-AḪ		EDZARD, DER 146:14
		ʾIL	I			MAʾD		I				
						ʾAḪ		I		I$_3$-LI$_2$-MA-DA-ḪI		RUTTEN 14 7
		ʾIL	I			MAʾD		I				
						ʾAḪ		A		I$_3$-LI$_2$-MA-DA-ḪA		VAS VIII 14 4
		ʾIL	I			MIWT		I		I$_3$-LI$_2$-MI-TI		I
		ʾIL	I			MALIK				I$_3$-LI$_2$-MA-LIK		M
		ʾIL	I			MILK		U		I$_3$-LI$_2$-MIL-KU	FN	RA LXV 58 I 31
		ʾIL	I			MAṬAR				I$_3$-LI$_2$-MA-DA-AR		M
		ʾIL	I			MAṬAR				I$_3$-LI$_2$-MA-TAR		M
		ʾIL	I			MAṬAR				I$_3$-LI$_2$-MA-TA-AR		B 21
		ʾIL	I			NIʿM				I$_3$-LI$_2$-NE-ḪI-IM		M
		ʾIL	I			NIWR		I		I$_3$-LI$_2$-NE-RI	FN	XIII 1 II 6+
		ʾIL	I			NATUN				I$_3$-LI$_2$-NA-TU-UN		M
		ʾIL	I			PAʾAL		UM		I$_3$-LI$_2$-PA-A-LU-UM		TIM III 44 16+
		ʾIL	I			PAʾAL		UM		I$_3$-LI$_2$-PA-ḪA-LUM		M
		ʾIL	I			QAʾN				I-LI-QA-AN		A. LATE
		ʾIL	I			RAWḪ		I	JE	I$_3$-LI$_2$-RA-AḪ-E		VAS XVI 168 9, FRANK 13 9
		ʾIL	I			RAWM				I$_3$-LI$_2$-RA-AM		M
		ʾIL	I			RIḪṢ		I		I$_3$-LI$_2$-RI-IḪ-ZI	FN	XIII 1 IX 39
		ʾIL	I			RAPIʾ				I$_3$-LI$_2$-RA-BI		M+
		ʾIL	I			RAŠAP				I$_3$-LI$_2$-D-RA-SA-[AP]		XIII 66 5
		ʾIL	I	Š		BAʾB		A		I$_3$-LI$_2$-IŠ-BA-BA		HSM 7934, UR III
		ʾIL	I	Š		GAʾUL		U		I$_3$-LI$_2$-IŠ-GA-U$_2$-LU		KISURRA 70A 17+
		ʾIL	I	Š		KUTUL				I$_3$-LI$_2$-IŠ-KU-TU-UL		KISURRA 75A 18+
		ʾIL	I			ŠAKIM				I$_3$-LI$_2$-ŠA-KI-IM		RA LXV 40 I 44+
		ʾIL	I			ŠUM		U		I$_3$-LI$_2$-SU-U$_2$-MU		M
		ʾIL	I			ŠAMUʿ				I$_3$-LI$_2$-SA-MU-UḪ		XIII 21 11'
		ʾIL	I			ŠIMḪ		I		I$_3$-LI$_2$-ŠI-IM-ḪI		M+
		ʾIL	I			ŠIMḪ		A	JA	I$_3$-LI$_2$-ŠI-IM-ḪA-IA		VIII 57 BIS 16
		ʾIL	I			ŠIMḪ		A	JA	I$_3$-LI$_2$-ŠE-IM-ḪA-IA		VIII 57 14
		ʾIL	I			ŠAMŠ				I$_3$-LI$_2$-SA-MA-AŠ$_2$		M
		ʾIL	I		TA	NWUḪ				I$_3$-LI$_2$-TA-NU-UḪ		XIII 1 IV 19
		ʾIL	I		TA	NWUḪ				I$_3$-LI$_2$-TA-NU		RA LXV 45 V 52
		ʾIL	I			TUWR		A		I$_3$-LI$_2$-TU-RA		M+
		ʾIL	I			TUWR		A	JA	I$_3$-LI$_2$-TU-RA-[I]A		RA LXV 40 I 45
		ʾIL	I			TUWR		I	JA	I$_3$-LI$_2$-TU-RI-IA		XII 115 5+
		ʾIL	I			ṬAJB		A		I$_3$-LI$_2$-DA-[B]A		A. 96 R. 10
		ʾIL	I			ṢADUQ				I$_3$-LI$_2$-ZA-DU-UQ		M+
		ʾIL	I			ṢIDQ		I		I$_3$-LI$_2$-ZI-ID-KI		DELAPORTE CCL II A 337
		ʾIL	I			ṢIDQ		UM		I$_3$-LI$_2$-ZI-ID-KUM		UCP X/1 100 7
		ʾIL	I			ZANN		I		I$_3$-LI$_2$-ZA-AN-NI	FN	M+
		ʾIL	UM			ʾAB		I		I-LUM-A-BI		A.
		ʾIL	UM			ʾAB		UM		I-LUM-A-BU-UM		U
		ʾIL	UM			KATAZ		I		I-LU-UM-KA-TA-ZI		RUTTEN 40 1
		ʾIL	UM			MULUK				DINGIR-MU-LU-UK-KI	GN	XV 127
		ʾIL	UM			MULUK				I-LU-UM-MU-LU-UK-KI	GN	XV 127
		ʾIL	UM			MULUK	AJ	I		DINGIR-MU-LU-KA-JI-KI	GN	XV 127
		ʾIL	U			MALIK	AJ	I		I-LU-MA-LI-KA-JI-KI	GN	XV 127
		ʾIL	UM			ŠALM		A		I-LU-UM-ŠA-AL-MA		RA LXV 45 V 51
		ʾIL	UM			TUŠUʿ		U		D-I-LU-UN-TU-SU-U$_2$	DN	KISURRA
		ʾIL	U	NA						I-LU-NA		RA LXV 43 III 80
		ʾIL	U	NI						I-LU-NI		M+
		ʾIL	U	NA		KIRIŠ		U		I-LU-NA-KI-RI-ŠU		XIII 8 19+
	2	ʾAḪ	I			ʾIL				A-ḪI-[I]L		HARRIS 45 11
		ʾAḪ	I			ʾIL		I		A-ḪI-I$_3$-LI$_2$	FN	XIII 1 VIII 20

STEMS

ʾIL	2		ʾAJA				ʾIL				A-IA-DINGIR		A.+
			JAʾ		U		ʾIL		I		IA-U-I-LI$_2$		SUMER V 143 NO. 2
			JAʾ		UM		ʾIL				IA-U$_2$-UM-DINGIR		B 31
			JAʾ		UM		ʾIL				IA-A-UM-[DINGIR]		B 31
			JAʾ		UM		ʾIL				IA-WU-UM-DINGIR		B 31
			ʾAWAʾ	AT	I		ʾIL				A-WA-TI-DINGIR	MN	XIII 1 XI 39
		JA	HWIJ				ʾIL				IA-WI-DINGIR		B 31+, M+
		JA	HWIJ				ʾIL				JA-AḪ-WI-DINGIR		M
		JA	HWIJ				ʾIL				IA-AḪ-WI-DINGIR		B 27+
		JA	HWIJ				ʾIL		I		IA-AḪ-WI-DINGIR-LI$_2$		KISURRA 6+
		JA	HWIJ				ʾIL		I		IA-WI-LI		A 7695 10
		JA	ḪJIJ				ʾIL				IA-ḪI-DINGIR		B 26+
		JA	ḪJIJ				ʾIL				IA-A-ḪI-DINGIR		XIII 65 5
			ḪAJJ		U		ʾIL				A$_2$-U$_2$-DINGIR		U
		JA	WḪIJ				ʾIL				IA-U$_2$-ḪI-DINGIR		B 31
			JAḪAD				ʾIL				IA-ḪA-AD-DINGIR		M
			ḪAʾL		I		ʾIL				ḪA-LI$_2$-DINGIR		B 18
			ḪAʾL		I		ʾIL		U	HU	ḪA-A-LI$_2$-I-LU-U$_2$		X 146 5
			ḪAʾL		U		ʾIL				ḪA-LU-DINGIR		M
			ʾAJAM				ʾIL	T	I		A-IA-AM-IL-TI	FN	XIII 1 X 8
			ʾAJAM			TI	ʾIL				ḪA-IA-AM-TI-DINGIR		BIROT, TEA 72 III 5
			JAʾAN				ʾIL				IA-AN-DINGIR		M
			ḪAʾR		I		ʾIL				ḪA-RI-DINGIR		BM 82372 27
			JAʾAR				ʾIL				IA-AR-I-I[L-....]		XIII 69 5
		JA	ʾWUŠ				ʾIL				IA-UŠ-DINGIR		M+
		JA	ʾWUŠ				ʾIL				IA-U$_2$-UŠ$_2$-DINGIR		C II 35 28
		JA	ʾWUŠ				ʾIL				IA-U$_2$-UŠ-DINGIR		RA LXV 42 III 10+
		JE	ʾWUŠ				ʾIL				E-WU-ŠI-DINGIR		BIROT, TEA 48:20
			ḪAʾAZ		U		ʾIL				ḪA?-A-ZU-DINGIR		M
			ʾAB		A		ʾIL				A-BA-DINGIR	FN	A. 59 5
			ʾAB		I		ʾIL		A		A-BI-LA		CHANTRE 4 13
			ʾAB		I		ʾIL		I		A-BI-I$_3$-LI$_2$	FN	RA LXV 59 II 38+
			ʾAB		UM		ʾIL				A-BU-UM-DINGIR		U, M+
			ʾEB		I		ʾIL				E-BI-IL		M
		JA	ḪBIʾ				ʾIL		A		IA-AḪ-BI-LA-KI	GN	M+
		JA	ḪAPIʾ				ʾIL				IA-ḪA-AF-PI-I-IL5	GN	JCS XVIII 59 12+
			ʾABB		A		ʾIL				D-AB-BA-DINGIR	FN	M
			ʾABB		A		ʾIL				AB-BA-DINGIR		A.+
			ʾABB		A		ʾIL		I		AB-BA-I$_3$-LI$_2$	FN	XIII 1 XI 14
			ʾABB		A		ʾIL		I		D-AB-BA-I$_3$-LI$_2$	FN	SIMMONS 112:17
			ḪABAD		U		ʾIL				ḪA-BA-DU-DINGIR		M
			ʿABD				ʾIL				AB-TE-IL		I
			ʿABD				ʾIL				ḪA-AB-DI-DINGIR		B 9
			ʿABD				ʾIL				AB-DI-DINGIR		B 9+
			ʿABD				ʾIL		I		AB-DI-LI		A.+
		JI	JBAL				ʾIL				I-BA-AL-DINGIR		EEMY III/4 P. 130, M+
			ʾABN		I		ʾIL				ḪA-AB-NI-DINGIR		M
		JI	JBIŠ				ʾIL				I-BI-IŠ-DINGIR		TA 1930, 261
		JI	JBIŠ				ʾIL				[I-B]I$_2$-IŠ-I$_3$-IL		I
		JA	ḪBAS				ʾIL				IA-AḪ-BA-AZ-DINGIR		CT II 39 18+
			JID		I		ʾIL				I-DI-DINGIR		M
			ʿAD		U	NI	ʾIL		A		A-DU-NI-LA		U
			ʿADIJ				ʾIL				A-DI-DINGIR		M
			ʿADIJ			NA	ʾIL				A-DI-E-NA-DINGIR		M
		ʾA	WDAJ				ʾIL				A-U$_3$-DA-IL		U
		ʾA	WDAJ				ʾIL				A-AW-TE-IL		U
			JADAʿ				ʾIL				IA-DAḪ-DINGIR		B 25+
			JADAʿ				ʾIL				IA-DA-AḪ-DINGIR		CT XLVIII 21 SEAL
			JADAʿ				ʾIL				IA-DA-DINGIR		M
		JA	JDIʿ				ʾIL				IA-DI-IḪ-DINGIR		B 25+
		JA	JDIʿ				ʾIL				IA-DI-DINGIR		M
			ʾADAN				ʾIL				ḪA-DA-AN-DINGIR		B 18
			ʿADN		I		ʾIL				ḪA-AD-NI-DINGIR		M+
			ʿADN		I		ʾIL		U				
							MA				ḪA-AD-NI-DINGIR-MA		M
		JA	ʿḎAR				ʾIL				IA-DAR-DINGIR		RUTTEN 5 9+

STEMS

ʾIL	2 JA	ʿḎAR			ʾIL		IA-AḪ-ZA-AR-DINGIR		B 26
	JA	ʿḎAR			ʾIL		IA-AḪ-ZA-AR-I$_3$-IL		B 26
	JA	ʿḎAR			ʾIL		IA-ZA-AR-DINGIR?		IX 291 II 21,30
	JA	ʿḎAR			ʾIL		AḪ-ZA-AR-I$_3$-DINGIR		VAS XVIII 20:20
	JA	ʿḎIR			ʾIL		IA-AḪ-ZI-IR-DINGIR		B 26+
	JA	ʿḎIR			ʾIL		IA-AḪ-ZI-IR-I$_3$-IL		SUMER V 137
	JA	ʿḎIR			ʾIL		IA-AḪ-ZI-IR-I$_3$-DINGIR		CT XLV 8 6
		ʾAK	I		ʾIL		A-KI-DINGIR		M
		ʾIL	A		ʾIL		I-LA-DINGIR		B 21
		ʾIL	I		ʾIL	A	I$_3$-LI$_2$-I-LA		A. LATE
		ʾALI			ʾIL		A-LI$_2$-IL		HARRIS 65 16
	JA	ḪLIJ			ʾIL		IA-AḪ-LI-DINGIR		B 26
		ʿAMM	I		ʾIL	I	ḪA-MI-I$_3$-LI$_2$		MDP XXIII 307 16
		ʿAMM	U		ʾIL		ḪA-MU-DINGIR		M
		ʿAMM	U		ʾIL		AM-MU-DINGIR		UCP X/1 18 24
	JA	ʾMIʾ			ʾIL		IA-AḪ-MI-DINGIR		PBS XI/2 P. 120 NO. 92
	JA	ʾMIʾ			ʾIL	A	IA-MI-I-LA		M
	JA	ʾMIʾ			ʾIL	A	JA-MI-I-LA		M
	ʾU	WMAʾ			ʾIL		U$_3$-MA-IL		U
	ʾU	WMAʾ			ʾIL	A	U$_2$-MA-D-DINGIR		B 40
		ʾUMM	I		ʾIL	I	UM-MI-I$_3$-LI$_2$	FN	XIII 1 VIII 64
		ʾAMAR			ʾIL	I	A-MAR-I$_3$-LI$_2$		MAOG IV 2 3 HANA
	T	ʾAMR	I		ʾIL		A-TAM-RI-DINGIR		M+
		ʾIMIR			ʾIL	I	IM-ME-IR-I$_3$-LI$_2$		UNPUBL.
	JA	ʿMUS			ʾIL		IA-AḪ-MU-US-DINGIR		M
	JA	ʿMIS			ʾIL		IA-AḪ-MI-IS-DINGIR		RUTTEN 2 23+
	JA	ʿMIS			ʾIL	UM	IA-AḪ-MI-ZI-LUM		RUTTEN 16 17
		ḪAMAṬ	I		ʾIL		ḪA-MA-TI-IL		FIGULLA, CAT. I 14135
		ʾANA			ʾIL	I			
					MA		A-NA-I-LIM-MA		A.
		ʿANAJ		TI	ʾIL		A-NI-TI-DINGIR		M
	JA	ʿNIJ			ʾIL		IA-AḪ-NI-DINGIR		A 7630 6
		ʿINB	I		ʾIL		IN-BI$_2$-IL		U UNPUBL.
	MA	ʾNUP			ʾIL		MA-AḪ-NU-UP-DINGIR		B 33+, M+
	MA	ʾNUP			ʾIL		MA-AḪ-NU-BI-DINGIR		B 33+, M+
	MA	ʾNUP			ʾIL	I	MA-AḪ-NU-UP-I$_3$-LI$_2$		B 33+
		ʾANAKU			ʾIL	AM			
					MA		A-NA-KU-DINGIR-LAM-MA		XIII 1 II 29
		ʾANAKU			ʾIL	A			
					MA		A-NA-KU-I-LA-MA		SIMMONS 46 7+
	JA	ḪNUN			ʾIL		IA-ḪU-UN-DINGIR		M+
	JA	ḪNUN			ʾIL		IA-NU-UN-DINGIR		RA LXV 51 IX 65
		ḪUNUN	I		ʾIL		U$_2$-NU-NI-DINGIR		PBS XI/2 P. 125 NO. 347
		ḪANN	A		ʾIL		AN-NA-DINGIR		B 13+, C+
		ḪANN	I		ʾIL		AN-NI-DINGIR		B 13+, M
		ḪANN	I		ʾIL		ḪA-AN-NI-DINGIR	FN	XIII 1 II 7
		ḪANN	I		ʾIL	A	ḪA-AN-NI-I-LA		A. LATE
		ḪINN	I		ʾIL		ḪI-IN-NE-DINGIR		XIII 1 I 53
		ʾUP			ʾIL	A	UP-I-LA		BULL. ACAD. BELG. 1974 227
	JA	JPAʿ			ʾIL		IA-PA-AḪ-DINGIR		RA LXV 51 IX 74
	JA	JPAʿ			ʾIL		IA-PA-DINGIR		B 29
	JI	JQAH			ʾIL		I-KA-AḪ-DINGIR		B 21
	ʾU	WQAH			ʾIL		U$_2$-QA-DINGIR		M+
	ʾU	WQAH			ʾIL		U$_2$-GA-DINGIR		GAUTIER 41 5
	ʾU	WQAH			ʾIL		U$_3$-QA-DINGIR		SIMMONS 1 3+
	ʾU	WQAH			ʾIL		U$_2$-QA-IL		SYRIA V 274 HANA
	ʾU	WQAH			ʾIL	A	U$_2$-Q[A]-I-LA		A 7699:14, ISHCHALI
	ʾU	WQAH			ʾIL	UM	U$_2$-GA-DINGIR-LUM		FRANK 29 9
	JA	ʿQUB			ʾIL		A-AḪ-KU-UB-DINGIR		HARRIS 12 3+
	JA	ʿQUB			ʾIL		IA-KU-UB-DINGIR		B 27+
	JA	ʿQUB			ʾIL		IA-AḪ-KU-UB-DINGIR		XIII 1 VII 17, C+
	JA	ʿQUB	I		ʾIL		IA-AḪ-KU-BI-DINGIR		CT II 39 18
	JA	ʿQUB	I		ʾIL		IA-KU-BI-DINGIR		KISURRA 41 10
	JA	ʿQIB			ʾIL		IA-KI-IB-DINGIR		TIM V 33 23
		ʿAQUB			ʾIL		A-KU-UB-DINGIR		HARRIS 84 13
		ʿAQB	I		ʾIL		AQ-BI-IL		B 11

ʾIL	2			ʿAQB	I		ʾIL			AQ-BI-DINGIR		BIN VII 156 10+
		JA		ʾKUR			ʾIL			IA-AḪ-KU-UR-DINGIR		CT XLV 6 24
		JA		ʾKUR			ʾIL			A-AḪ-KU-UR$_2$-[DINGIR]?		HARRIS 79 22
				JAQAR			ʾIL			IA-QAR-DINGIR		CT VI 49 A 23
				JAQR	UM		ʾIL			IA-AQ-RUM-DINGIR		A 22010
				WARḪ			ʾIL	A		WA-AR-ḪI-LA$_2$		CCT I 38C 2 CAPP.
				ʾARUŠ	I		ʾIL			A-RU-SI-DINGIR		A 7459, M
		JA		ḪŠIJ			ʾIL			IA-AḪ-SI-DINGIR		OLZ VIII 350 2
		JA		ḪŠIJ			ʾIL			JA-AḪ-SI-DINGIR		M
		JA		JŠUʿ			ʾIL			IA-ŠU-DINGIR		RA LXIV 36 NO. 31
				JIŠʿ	I		ʾIL			IŠ-ḪI-DINGIR		WALTERS, WL 109:5+
				JIŠʿ	I		ʾIL	A				
							MA			IŠ-ḪI-DINGIR-MA		M
				JIŠʿ	I		ʾIL	A				
							MA			IŠ-ḪI-DINGIR-LA-MA		M
				JIŠʿ	I		ʾIL	U				
							MA			IŠ-ḪI-LU-MA		YOS VIII 176 20
				JIŠʿ	I		ʾIL	U	NA	IŠ-ḪI-LU-NA		VII 215 33
				JAŠAR		TI	ʾIL			IA-SA-AR-TI-DINGIR		M
				ʿAŠTAR			ʾIL	I		EŠ$_4$-DAR-I$_3$-LI$_2$	FN	RA LXV 56 I 3
				JAT	I		ʾIL			IA-TI-DINGIR		B 31
		JA		ḪATIʾ			ʾIL			IA-ḪA-AT-TI-DINGIR		M+, C
		JA		ḪATIʾ			ʾIL			IA-ḪA-TI-DINGIR		RUTTEN 15:2+; M
		JA		ḪATIʾ			ʾIL	UM		IA-ḪA-TI-LUM		YOS XII
			ŠT	ḪTIN			ʾIL			(E$_2$-)ŠA-TA-AḪ-TI-IN-DINGIR	GN	KISURRA
				JATAR			ʾIL			IA-TA-AR-DINGIR		B 31+ +
				JATAR			ʾIL			IA-TAR-DINGIR		M
				JATR	A		ʾIL			JA-AT-RA-IL		I
		JI		JTAR			ʾIL	I		I-TAR-I-LI		B 23
				ʾITT	A		ʾIL	I		IT-TA-I$_3$-LI$_2$		M
		JA		JṢIʾ			ʾIL			IA-ZI-DINGIR		M+
		JA		JṢIʾ			ʾIL			IA-ṢI-DINGIR		JCS IV 109 4311 21
		JA		JṢIʾ			ʾIL	UM		IA-ZI-LUM-KI	GN	B 32
		JA		WṢIʾ			ʾIL			IA-AW-ZI-DINGIR		M+
		JA		WṢIʾ			ʾIL			IA-U$_2$-ZI-DINGIR		B 31
		JA		WṢIʾ			ʾIL			IA-U$_2$-ṢI-DINGIR		BAGHD. MITT. II 23
		JA		WṢIʾ			ʾIL	UM		IA-U$_2$-ZI-LUM		B 31
		JI		JṢIʾ			ʾIL	U				
							MA			I-ZI-I-LU-MA		B 23+
		JA		ʾZIJ			ʾIL			IA-AḪ-ZI-DINGIR		M
		JA		ʾZIJ			ʾIL	I		IA-AḪ-ZI-I$_3$-LI$_2$		TCL X 21 13
		JE		ʾZIJ			ʾIL	UM		E-EḪ-ZI-LUM		VIII 3 25
		JA		ʿZUB			ʾIL			IA-AḪ-ZU-UB-DINGIR		B 26+
		JA		ʿZIB			ʾIL			IA-AH-ZI-IB-DINGIR		RUTTEN 21 7+, M
		JA		ʿZIB			ʾIL			A-AḪ-ZI-IB-DINGIR		HARRIS 57 2
		JA		ʿZIB	I		ʾIL			IA-AḪ-ZI-BI-DINGIR		KISURRA 86A 11
		JA		ʿZIB	I		ʾIL			A-AḪ-ZI-BI-DINGIR		SIMMONS 70 5
		JA		ʿZIB	I		ʾIL			IA-A-ZI-BI-DINGIR		KAJ 34 18, 25 LATE
		JA		ḪṢUN			ʾIL			IA-AḪ-ZU-UN-DINGIR		BE VI/1 7 18
				ḪAṢAN			ʾIL	UM		ḪA-ZA-AN-I-LU-UM		M+
		JA		ḪZUQ			ʾIL			IA-AḪ-ZU?-UQ-DINGIR		CT XLVIII 10 3
		JA		ḪZUR			ʾIL			IA-AḪ-ZU-UR-IL		TIM III 34 15A
		JA		ḪZUR			ʾIL			IA-AḪ-ZU-UR-DINGIR		JCS XXIV 57 NO 39 AND 51
				ʿAZZ	I		ʾIL			A-ZI-DINGIR		HARRIS 39 11
		JA		BWAʾ			ʾIL			IA-BA-DINGIR?		MEISSNER 36 25
		JA		BWAʾ			ʾIL			IA-BA-A?-DINGIR		M
		JI		BWAʾ			ʾIL			I-BA-AḪ-DINGIR		KISURRA 6 15
				BAWʾ	U		ʾIL	A		BA-U$_2$-I-LA		MEISSNER 43 45
		ʾU		BWAʾ			ʾIL			U$_2$-BA-DINGIR		M
		ʾU		BWAʾ			ʾIL	A		U$_2$-BA-D-DINGIR		VAS VIII 14:22
				BEʿD	I		ʾIL	UM		BE-DI-LU-UM		TIM III 62 6+
				BEʿD	I		ʾIL	UM		BE-DI-LUM		TIM III 61 15
				BEʿD	I		ʾIL			BE-DI-DINGIR		TIM III 130 11+
				BAʿL	I		ʾIL			BA-AḪ-LI-DINGIR		B 15
				BAʿL	I		ʾIL			BA-LI-DINGIR		EDZARD, DER 68 IV 7
				BAʿL	I		ʾIL	I		BA-AḪ-LI-I$_3$-LI$_2$	FN	M

STEMS

ʾIL	2		BAʿL	UM		ʾIL			BA-AH̲-LU-UM-DINGIR		B 15+
			BEʿL	I		ʾIL	I		BE-LI$_2$-I$_3$-LI$_2$	FN	RA LXV 64 VI 50
			BIJT			ʾIL			D-E$_2$-IL		U
			BIN			ʾIL	A		BI-IN-I-LA		A. LATE
			BIN			ʾIL	I	JA	BI-IN-I-LI$_2$-IA		RA LXIV 24 NO.8
			BUN			ʾIL	UM		BU-NI-LUM		TIM III 33 15+
			BUN	I		ʾIL			BU-NI-DINGIR		B 16
			BUN	I		ʾIL	A		BU-NI-I-LA		B 16+
			BUN	U		ʾIL	A		BU-NU-I-LA		CT XLV 115 24
		JA	BANIJ			ʾIL			IA-BA-AN-NI-DINGIR		M+
		JA	BANIJ			ʾIL			IA-AB-BA-AN-NI-DINGIR		M
		JA	BNIQ			ʾIL			IA-AB-NI-IQ-DINGIR		B 25
		JA	BRUQ			ʾIL			IA-AB-RU-UQ-DINGIR		BASOR 95, 19
		JA	DWUR			ʾIL			IA-DU-UR-DINGIR		M
			DUWR		NI	ʾIL			DU-UR-NI-DINGIR		M+
			DAGAN			ʾIL	I		D-DA-GAN-I$_3$-LI$_2$	FN	RA LXV 62 V 51
			DANN			ʾIL			DAN-DINGIR		U
			DANN	I		ʾIL			DA?-NI-DINGIR		M
			ḎU			ʾIL	A		ZU-I-LA		B 42+
			ḎU			ʾIL	A		ZU-U$_2$-I-LA		B 42
			ḎABIB	I		ʾIL			SA-BI-BI-DINGIR		M
		JA	ḎKUR			ʾIL			A-AD-KU-UR-DINGIR		HARRIS 10 18
		JA	ḎKUR			ʾIL			IA-AD-GUR-DINGIR		SUMER V 142 8+
		JA	ḎKUR			ʾIL			IA-AD-KUR-DINGIR		SUMER V 141
		JA	ḎKUR			ʾIL			A-AD-KUR-DINGIR		SIMMONS 80 13
		JA	ḎKUR			ʾIL			IA-AD-KU?-UR?-DINGIR		VAS IX 58 15
		JI	ḎKUR			ʾIL			II-IZ-KUR-DINGIR		SIMMONS 67 18
			ḎAKUR	A		ʾIL			ZA-KU-RA-DINGIR		M+
			ḎIMR	I		ʾIL			ZI-IM-RI-DINGIR		B 42+
			ḎIMR	I		ʾIL	U				
						MA			ZI-IM-RI-DINGIR-MA		M
			ḎIMR	I		ʾIL	U				
						MA			ZI-IM-RI-I-LU-MA		M
			ḎIMR	I		ʾIL	U				
						MA			ZI-IM-RI-LU-MA		SIMMONS 67 12
			ḎIMR	U		ʾIL	A		ZI-IM-RU-I-L[A]?		II 5 7
			ḎINUB	I		ʾIL			ZI-NU-BI-DINGIR		RA LXV 48 VIII 12
			ḎUNUB	I		ʾIL			ZU-NU-BI-DINGIR		RA LXV 51 X 14
		JI	ḎRUʿ			ʾIL			II-IZ?-RU-UH̲-DINGIR		TCL XI 156 17
		JA	ḎRAʿ			ʾIL			IA-AZ-RA-AH̲-DINGIR		VIII 100 15+
			GABIʾ			ʾIL			GA-BI-DINGIR		C 39+
			GABIʾ			ʾIL			GA-BI-IL		TIM III 12 16A
		JA	GMUR			ʾIL			IA-AG-MU-UR-DINGIR		M
			KIʾL	I		ʾIL			KI-LI-DINGIR		CT IV 33B 19
			KIʾL	I		ʾIL	UM		KI-LI-DINGIR-LUM		XIII 106 14
			KAHAL	I		ʾIL	U				
						MA			KA-A-LI-I-LU-MA		XIV 62:4+
			KAHAL	I		ʾIL	U				
						MA			KA-A-LI-DINGIR-MA		M+
		JA	KWUN			ʾIL			IA-KU-UN-DINGIR		M
		JA	KWIN			ʾIL			JA-KI-IN-DINGIR		JEA VII 196
			KIWN	A		ʾIL	I		KI-NA-I$_3$-LI$_2$		M
			KUWN			ʾIL	A		KU-UN-I-LA		RA LXV 53 XI 31
			KALB			ʾIL			GA-AL-BA-IL		I
			KALB			ʾIL			KA-AL-BA-DINGIR		M
		JA	KRUB			ʾIL			D-IA-AK-RU-UB-DINGIR	DN	M+
		JA	KRUB			ʾIL			D-IA-AK-RU-UB-IL	DN	M+
		JI	KRUB			ʾIL			D-IK-RU-UB-DINGIR	DN	M+
		JI	KRUB			ʾIL			D-IK-RU-UB-IL	DN	M
		JI	KRUB			ʾIL			D-IK-RU-BI-DINGIR	DN	M
		JA	KRUB			ʾIL					
						TILL	AT I		D-IA-AK-RU-UB-DINGIR-TIL-LA-TI		M
		JI	KSUW			ʾIL			IK-ZU-IL		TA 1931 ,435 REV.2
		JA	KSIJ			ʾIL			IA-AK-ZI-DINGIR		SIMMONS 92 16
		JA	KSIJ			ʾIL			A-AK-ZI-DINGIR		FIGULLA CAT I 14029
			LA		KA	ʾIL			LA-KA-DINGIR		KISURRA 111 5

STEMS

ʾIL	2		LA		NA	ʾIL		LA-NA-DINGIR		RUTTEN 27 15+
			LA		NI	ʾIL		LA$_2$-NI-DINGIR		U
			LA			ʾIL	A	[L]A?-I-LA		RA LXV 44 IV 36
			LA			ʾIL	A			
						MILK	I	LA-I-LA-MI-IL-KI		TA 30, 75 2
			LAWUJ			ʾIL		LA-WU-DINGIR		M
			LABAN	A		ʾIL	A	LA-PA-NA-I-LA		ZA XXXVIII 267
			LAMA			ʾIL		LA-MA-DINGIR		B 33+, M+
			LAMA			ʾIL	A	LA-MA-I-LA		YOS XIII 244:2+
			LUMM	A		ʾIL		LUM-MA-IL		M+
			LUMM	A		ʾIL		LUM-MA-DINGIR		KISURRA 100 7+
			LUMM	A		ʾIL		LU-MA-DINGIR		KISURRA 104 29+
			LAŠU			ʾIL		LA-ŠU-IL		U
		JA	MWUŠ	I		ʾIL		IA-MU-ŠI-DINGIR		B 28
		JA	MWUŠ	I		ʾIL		IA-A-MU-ŠI-DINGIR		VAS VII 166 4 LATE
		JA	MLIʾ			ʾIL		A-AM-LI-DINGIR		YOS XIII 63:3, 6
		JA	MLIK			ʾIL		IA-AM-LI-IK-DINGIR		B 28+
		JA	MLIK			ʾIL		IA-AM-LIK-DINGIR		B 28+, M
		JA	MLIK			ʾIL		A-AM-LIK-DINGIR		HARRIS 76 22
		JI	MLIK			ʾIL		II-IM-LIK-DINGIR		B 28+
			MALAK			ʾIL	I	MA-LA-AK-I$_3$-LI$_2$		M
			MALAK	U		ʾIL		MA-LA-KU-IL		M
			MILK	I		ʾIL		MI-IL-KI-DINGIR		B 34
			MILK	I		ʾIL	A	MI-EL-KI-I-[LA]		UCP X/3 1 29
			MILK	I		ʾIL	U	MIL-KI-LU		B 34+
			MILK	I		ʾIL	U	MI-IL-KI-LU		B 34
			MILK	I		ʾIL	UM	MI-IL-KI-LUM		B 34
			MANIJ			ʾIL		MA-NI-IL		U
		JA	MRAṢ			ʾIL		IA-AM-RA-AṢ-DINGIR		M+
		JA	MRAṢ	I		ʾIL		IA-AM-RA-ZI-DINGIR		M
		JA	MRUṢ			ʾIL		IA-AM-RU-UṢ-DINGIR		B 28
		JA	MRUṢ			ʾIL		IA-AM-RU-IṢ-DINGIR		M
		JA	MRUṢ	I		ʾIL	UM	I-IA-AM-RU-UṢ-ZI-I-LU-UM		B 21
		JU	MRAṢ			ʾIL		JU-UM-RA-AṢ-DINGIR		M+
		JA	MŚIJ			ʾIL		IA-AM-SI-DINGIR		B 28+
		JI	MŚIJ			ʾIL		JI-IM-SI-DINGIR		M
			MUT			ʾIL		MU-UT-DINGIR		MAOG IV 2 4 HANA
			MUT	I		ʾIL	UM	MU-TI-LUM		YOS XIII 151:4+
			MUT	U		ʾIL	A	MU-TU-I-LA		RA LXV 43 III 68
			MUT	UM		ʾIL		MU-TUM-DINGIR		FRANK 29 4, 10+ M+
		JA	MATIʿ			ʾIL		IA-MA-AT-TI-DINGIR		M+
		JA	MATIʿ			ʾIL		IA-MA-TI-DINGIR		XII 5 3
			MATIʿ			ʾIL		MA-TI-DINGIR		M
		JA	MṢIʾ			ʾIL		IA-AM-ZI-DINGIR		B 28, M
		JA	MṢIʾ			ʾIL		IA-AM-ṢI-DINGIR		B 28+
		JE	MṢIʾ			ʾIL		IE-E-EM-ZI-DINGIR		B 25
			NAWḪ	I		ʾIL		NA-ḪI-DINGIR		B 35+
			NAWḪ			ʾIL	I	NA-ḪI-LI		B 35
			NAWḪ			ʾIL	UM	NA-ḪI-LUM		B 35+
			NAWḪ			ʾIL	UM	NA-ḪI-LU-UM		B 35
			NAWḪ			ʾIL	IM	NA-ḪI-LI-IM	GEN	B 35
			NUWḪ	I		ʾIL		NU-ḪI-DINGIR		I
		JA	NḪAB			ʾIL		IA-AḪ-ḪA-AB-DINGIR		C+
			NAḤL	I		ʾIL	UM	NA-AḪ-LI-LUM		B 36+
			NUʿM	I		ʾIL		NU-UḪ-MI-DINGIR		M+
			NUʿM	I		ʾIL	I	NU-UḪ-MI-I$_3$-LI$_2$		XIII 1 XIII 26
			NAḪN	I		ʾIL		NA-AḪ-NI-DINGIR		TIM III 86:5
			NUWP	I		ʾIL		NU-BI-DINGIR		C+
		JA	NABIʾ			ʾIL		IA-NA-AB-BI-DINGIR		M+
		JA	NABIʾ			ʾIL		IA-NA-BI-DINGIR		M
		JA	NBIʾ			ʾIL	UM	IA'$_2$-AN-BI$_2$-I$_3$-LUM		U
			NABIʾ			ʾIL	I	NA-BI-I$_3$-LI$_2$		XIII 1 III 61
		JA	NQIM			ʾIL		IA-AN?-KI-IM-DINGIR		RA VIII 69 22
		JA	NQIM			ʾIL		A-AN-KI-IM-DINGIR		HARRIS 9 14+
		JE	NQIM			ʾIL		E-EN-KI-IM-DINGIR		CT VI 49B 4
		JA	NŚIʾ			ʾIL		IA-SI-DINGIR		B 29+

STEMS

ʾIL	2 JA	NŠIʾ			ʾIL	I	IA-SI-LI	B 29+	
	JA	NŠIʾ			ʾIL	I	IA-SI-I-LI$_2$	TCL X 5 3	
	JA	NŠIʾ			ʾIL	UM	IA-SI-LUM	RA IX 22 2+	
	JA	NTIN			ʾIL		IA-AN-TI-IN-DINGIR	B 29+, M+	
	JA	NTIN			ʾIL		IA-AT-TI-IN-DINGIR	M	
	JA	NTIN			ʾIL		[A-A]N-TI-IN-DINGIR	HARRIS 56 15	
	JA	NTIN	I		ʾIL		IA-AN-TI-NI-DINGIR	BM 17084	
	JA	NṢIB			ʾIL		IA-AN-Z[I-I]B-DINGIR	XII 683 4	
		NIṢB	I		ʾIL		NE-IZ-BI-IL	TA 1931, 172	
		PA			ʾIL	A	PA-I-LA	XIII 1 VII 16	
		PA		KA	ʾIL	A	PA-KA-I-LA	B 37+	
		PA		KA	ʾIL	A	PA-KA-DINGIR	B 37	
		PA		KA	ʾIL	A	PA-A-KA-I-LA	B 37	
		PI			ʾIL	A	PI-I-LA	A. LATE	
	JA	PLAḪ			ʾIL		IA-AP-LA-AḪ-DINGIR	M, TIM III 56 5+	
	JA	PLAḪ			ʾIL	IM	IA-AP-LA-AḪ-I-LI-IM GEN	RA LXIV 43	
	JA	PLIḪ			ʾIL		[I]A-AP-LI?-I[Ḫ?-DINGIR]	VII 215 32	
		PANIJ			ʾIL	A	PA-NI-LA	IX 252 17, A.	LATE
		QAWM	I		ʾIL		GA-MI-DINGIR	TIM III 12 16+	
	JA	QNIJ			ʾIL		IA-AQ-NI-DINGIR	CT XLV 92 I 10+	
	JA	QRIʾ			ʾIL		IA-AQ-RI-DINGIR	B 27	
		QAṬAR			ʾIL		GA-TA-AR-DINGIR	B 17	
	JA	QṢUR			ʾIL		IA-AQ-ZU-UR-DINGIR	B 29+	
	JA	RʿIJ			ʾIL		IA-AR-ḪI-DINGIR	CT XLVIII 27	
	JE	RWIḪ	I		ʾIL		E-RI-ḪI-DINGIR	U	
	JA	RWIJ			ʾIL		A-AR-WI-DINGIR	HARRIS 98 R. 7	
	JA	RḪIB			ʾIL		IA-AR-I-IB-DINGIR	M+	
	JA	RḪIB			ʾIL		IA-AR-IB-DINGIR	M+	
	JA	RḪAM	I		ʾIL		IA-AR-ḪA-MI-DINGIR	KISURRA 5A 15+	
	JA	RḪAM			ʾIL		IA-AR-ḪA-AM-DINGIR	B 29	
	JI	RḪAM	I		ʾIL		IR-ḪA-MI-DINGIR	A.	
	JI	RḪAM			ʾIL	A	IR-ḪA-MI-LA	A.+	
		RAḪM	I		ʾIL	I	RA-AḪ-MI-I$_3$-LI$_2$	XIII 1 VIII 79+	
		RIWM			ʾIL	A	RI-IM-I-LA	TCL XIV 54 17	CAPP.
	JA	RBUʾ			ʾIL		IA-AR-BU-DINGIR	KISURRA 9A 9+	
	JA	RBIJ			ʾIL		IA-AR-BI-DINGIR	B 29+	
	JA	RBIJ			ʾIL		I-AR-BI-DINGIR	KISURRA 5A 8+	
	JE	RBIJ			ʾIL		E-IR-BI-DINGIR	KISURRA 22A 15	
		RIMŠ	I		ʾIL		RI-IM-ŠI-DINGIR	M+	
		RIMŠ	I		ʾIL	I	RI-IM-ŠI-I$_3$-LI$_2$	M	
		RIPʾ	A		ʾIL	A	RI-IP-A-DINGIR	M+	
	JA	RŠIJ			ʾIL		IA-AR-ŠI-DINGIR	B 29+, M	
	JA	RŠIJ			ʾIL	I	A-AR-ŠI-DINGIR	TA 1930,7:6	
	JA	RŠIJ			ʾIL	UM	IA-AR-ŠI-DINGIR-UM	UCP X/1 P. 58+	
	JA	SNIQ			ʾIL		IA-AS-NI-IQ-DINGIR	RA LXV 48 VII 66	
	JA	SNIQ			ʾIL		IA-AŠ$_2$-NI-IQ-DINGIR	SIMMONS 55 14	
		SITR	I		ʾIL		ZI-IT-RI-DINGIR	B 42	
	JA	SAṬIʾ			ʾIL		IA-ZA-AD-DI-DINGIR	M+	
	JA	SAṬIʾ			ʾIL		IA-ZA-AT-TI-DINGIR	M	
	JA	SAṬIʾ			ʾIL		IA-SA-AD-DI-DINGIR	M	
	JA	SAṬIʾ			ʾIL		IA-S[A]-TI-DINGIR	M	
	ʾA	ŠWUB			ʾIL	A	A-ŠU-UB-I-LA	A. LATE	
	JA	ŠWUB			ʾIL		IA-ŠU-UB-DINGIR	CT II 23 15+, M+	
	JE	ŠWUB			ʾIL		E-ŠU-UB-DINGIR	BIN VII P. 12+	
	JE	ŠWUB	I		ʾIL		IE-E-ŠU-BI-DINGIR	B 26	
		ŠUWB			ʾIL	A	ŠU-UB-D-I-LA	RA LXV 52 X 66	
		ŠUWB	A		ʾIL	A	ŠU-BA-D-DINGIR	B 23+	
		ŠUWB	A	NI	ʾIL		ŠU-BA-NI-DINGIR	RUTTEN 41 3, 13	
		ŠUWB		NA	ʾIL		ŠU-UB-NA-DINGIR	B 40+, M+	
		ŠUWB		NA	ʾIL		ŠU-UB-NA-IL	B 40	
		ŠUWB		NA	ʾIL	U	ŠU-UB-NA-ḪI-LU	B 40	
	JA	ŠWIB			ʾIL		IA-ŠI-IB-DINGIR	A.	
		ŠAWB	I		ʾIL		ŠA-BI-DINGIR	M, C+	
		ŚAʾL	I		ʾIL		SA-LI-DINGIR	B 37+	
	JA	ŚJIM			ʾIL		IA-SI-IM-DINGIR	M+	
	JA	ŚBIJ			ʾIL		IA-AŠ-BI-DINGIR	B 32	

STEMS

ʾIL	2	JA		ŠBIJ			ʾIL	A		IA-AŠ-BI-I-LA	B 30
				ŠADW	I		ʾIL			SA-DI-DINGIR	JCS IV 110, 2040 16
				ŠADW	U		ʾIL	A		ŠA-DU-[I]-LA	RA LXV 45 V 50
				ŠAKUM	I		ʾIL			SA-KU-MI-DINGIR	M+
		JA		ŠKIN			ʾIL			IA-AŠ$_2$-KI-IN-DINGIR-[....]?	M
		JA		ŠKUR			ʾIL			IA-AŠ$_2$-KU-UR$_2$-DINGIR	B 81
		JA		ŠKUR			ʾIL			IA-AŠ$_2$-KU-UR-DINGIR	B 30+
		JA		ŠKUR			ʾIL			IA-AŠ$_2$-KUR-DINGIR	JNES XIII 210+ LATE
		JA		ŠKUR			ʾIL			[IA]-AŠ-KU-UR-DINGIR	VIII 38 7'
		JA		ŠLAM			ʾIL			IA-AŠ$_2$-LAM-DINGIR	XIV 47:11
				ŠAM	U		ʾIL	A		SA-MU-I-LA	M
				ŠAM	U	HU	ʾIL	A		SA-MU-U$_2$-I-LA	M
				ŠUM	A		ʾIL	A		SU-MA-I-LA	YOS XIII 244:15+
				ŠUM	I		ʾIL	UM		SU-MI-LU-UM	WALTERS, WL 114:13
				ŠUM	U		ʾIL			SU-MU-DINGIR	B 39+
				ŠUM	U		ʾIL			D-SU-MU-DINGIR	KISURRA 85 15, 22+
				ŠUM	U		ʾIL	A		SU-MU-I-LA	B 39; M+
				ŠUM	U		ʾIL				
							BAWB	I	JA	[SU-MU-I]L-BA-BI-IA	PBS XI/2 1 I 11
				ŠUM	U		ʾIL				
							....			SU-MU-DINGIR-LI-BUR-RA-AM	FRANK 27 4
				ŠUM	U		ʾIL				
							ŠARR			SU-MU-[DINGIR]-LUGAL	UCP X/1 17 15
		JA		ŠMAʿ			ʾIL			IA-AŠ$_2$-MA-AḪ-DINGIR	SIMMONS 55 11, M
		JI		ŠMAʿ			ʾIL			IS-MA-AḪ-DINGIR	CT XLV 3 7
		JI		ŠMAʿ			ʾIL			IŠ-ME-EḪ-DINGIR	KISURRA 40 9
				ŠIMAʿ			ʾIL	A		SI-MA-I-LA	X 5 4, 5
				ŠIMAʿ		NI	ʾIL			ŠI-MA-AḪ-NI-DINGIR	VIII 49 BIS 5'
				ŠAMUʿ	I		ʾIL			SA-MU-ḪI-IL	XIV 76:19
				ŠIMḪ	U		ʾIL	UM		ŠI-IM-ḪU-LUM?	A. 265 8
				ŠAMʾAL	A		ʾIL			SA-AM-A-LA-DINGIR	M+
				ŠAMʾIL	I		ʾIL			SA-AM-ḪI-LI-DINGIR	M
				ŠAMAR	I		ʾIL			SA-MA-RI-DINGIR	A. 455 46
				ŠAMŠ	U		ʾIL	U	NA	SA-AM-SU-I-LU-NA	B 38+
				ŠAMŠ	U		ʾIL	U	NA		
							KIMA			SA-AM-SU-I-LU-NA-KI-MA-DINGIR	BM 81047:6
				ŠAMŠ	U		ʾIL	U	NA		
							....			SA-AM-SU-I-LU-NA-QAR-RA-AD	CT XLV 48 5
				ŠUMAT			ʾIL	I		SU-MA-AT-I$_3$-LI$_2$	XIII 1 II 85
				ŠUMUT			ʾIL			SU-MU-UT-DINGIR	VAS VII 148 5+
		JU	T	ŠANIJ			ʾIL	A		UŠ-TA-NI-I-LA	A. 33 22
		JI	ŠT	ŠNIJ			ʾIL			IŠ-TA-AŠ-NI-IL	SYRIA V 274 HANA
		JI	ŠT	ŠNIJ			ʾIL			IŠ-TA-AŠ-NI-DINGIR	VAS IX 156 11+
		JU	ŠT	ŠNIJ			ʾIL			UŠ-TAŠ-NI-DINGIR	VAS IX 130 21+
		JU	ŠT	ŠNIJ			ʾIL			UŠ-TA-AŠ-NI-DINGIR	VAS IX 131 21+
			ŠT	ŠNIJ			ʾIL			ŠA-TA-AŠ-NI-IL	SUMER V 139 NO. 4
		JA		ŠPUQ			ʾIL			IA-AŠ$_2$-PU-UK-DINGIR	M
		JA		ŠQIṬ			ʾIL			IA-AŠ-KI-IṬ-DINGIR	B 30, M+
				ŠARR	A		ʾIL			ŠAR-RA-DINGIR	A. LATE+
				ŠIRṬ	I		ʾIL	I		ŠI-IR-TE-I$_3$-LI$_2$	A. LATE
				ŠITAŠ			ʾIL	I		ŠI-IT-TA-AŠ-I$_3$-LI$_2$	MEL. SYR. 994
		JA		ŠṬIḪ			ʾIL			IA-AŠ-TI-DINGIR	XIII 1 IX 7
				ŠAṬUP	I		ʾIL			ŠA-TU-BI-DINGIR	M+
				ṢUWR	A		ʾIL			ZU-RA-DINGIR	M+
				ṢUWR	I		ʾIL			ZU-RI-DINGIR	M
		JA		ṢDUQ			ʾIL			IA-AŠ-DU-UQ-DINGIR	JEAN 164 R. 4+
		JA		ṢDUQ			ʾIL			[IA]-AŠ$_2$-DU-UQ-DINGIR	BASOR 95, 19
				TAʾK	U		ʾIL			TA-KU-DINGIR	VAS VIII 14 27
				TUWR	A		ʾIL	I		TU-RA-I$_3$-LI$_2$	SAUREN, WUG 285 V, U.
				ṬAJB	A		ʾIL			ṬA-BA-DINGIR	A. 60 11
				ZAKK			ʾIL	I		ZA-AK-I$_3$-LI$_2$	TA 1931,389 UR III
		JA		ZLIJ			ʾIL			IA-AZ-LI-DINGIR	M
				ZALIJ			ʾIL			ZA-LI-DINGIR	B 41
		JI		ZMEʾ			ʾIL			IZ-ME-DINGIR	VAS IX 141 2
	3			ʾAḪ	UM		MA				
							ʾIL			A-ḪU-UM-MA-DINGIR	M+

STEMS

ʾIL	3	ʾAJA			ʾAB					
					ʾIL			ḪA-IA-AB-DINGIR		B 18
		ʾAJA			ʾABN	I				
					ʾIL			ḪA-IA-AB-NI-DINGIR		B 18+
		ʾAJA			MA					
					ʾIL			A-IA-MA-DINGIR		M
		ʾAJA			MA					
					ʾIL			ḪA-IA$_3$-MA-DINGIR		XIV 93:8+
		ʾIJA			ʾAB					
					ʾIL			I-A-AB-DINGIR		OIP XXII 262
		ḪIʾD			LA		KA			
					ʾIL	I		ḪI-ID-LA-KA-I$_3$-LI$_2$		M
		ḪAʾL	I		MA					
					ʾIL			ḪA-LI$_2$-MA-DINGIR		M
		ḪAʾL	U	Š	MI					
					ʾIL			ḪA-LU-UŠ-MI-DINGIR		M
		JAʿAL			PI					
					ʾIL	UM		IA-ḪA-AL-PI-LUM		3NT867:5, 12, 21
	JI	JʿIL			PI					
					ʾIL			I-ḪI-IL-BI-DINGIR		M
		ʾAB	I		MA					
					ʾIL	I		A-BI-MA-I$_3$-LI$_2$	FN	RA LXV 64 VI 32
		ʾAB	U		KA					
					ʾIL			A-BU-KA-DINGIR		M+
		ʾIB	I		LA					
					ʾIL	UM		I-BI-LA-I$_3$-LUM		U
	JI	JBAL			LA					
					ʾIL			I-BA-AL-LA-DINGIR		RA LXV 47 VII 26
	JI	JBAL			PI					
					ʾIL			I-BA-AL-BI-DINGIR		M+
	JI	JDAʿ			PI					
					ʾIL			I-DA-BI$_2$-DINGIR		I
		JADAʿ			PI					
					ʾIL			IA-DA-BI-DINGIR		AJSL XXXIII 224 3
		ʾAK	UM		LA					
					ʾIL	A		A-KUM-LA-I-LA		RA LXV 55 XIII 1
		ʾIL	A		LA					
					ʾIL			DINGIR-LA-IL		U
		ʾIL	A		MA					
					ʾIL	A		DINGIR-MA-I$_3$-LA		B 21+
		ʾIL	A		MA					
					ʾIL	A		DINGIR-MA-D-I-LA		B 21
		ʾALI			PA					
					ʾIL			A-LI$_2$-PA-DINGIR		RUTTEN 6 21+
		ʾALI			PA					
					ʾIL			A-LI-PA-DINGIR		TIM III 5 18+
		ʾALI			PA					
					ʾIL			ḪA-A-LI-PA-DINGIR		EDZARD,DER 152 REV.16
		ʾALI			PA					
					ʾIL	UM		A-LI$_2$-KA-LUM		RUTTEN 37 19
		ʿAMM	U		RAPIʾ					
					ʾIL			ḪA-AM-MU-RA-BI-DINGIR		B 19
		ʿAMM	U	Š	KI					
					ʾIL			AM-MU-US-KI-DINGIR		A.
		ʿAMM	U	Š	KI					
					ʾIL			AM-MU-UŠ-KI-DINGIR		A.+
		ʾANA			MA					
					ʾIL			A-NA-MA-DINGIR		A 29366:9
		ʾARUŠ			PI					
					ʾIL			A-RU-UŠ-BI-DINGIR		M, RA XLI 45 4' HANA
		JATAM			MA					
					ʾIL			IA-TAM-MA-DINGIR		UET V 172 5'
		ḪATAN			PI					
					ʾIL			ḪA-TA-AN-BI-DINGIR		M
		BIN			MA					
					ʾIL			BI-MA-DINGIR		C+

STEMS

ʾIL	3		BIN	I				MA			
								ʾIL		BI-NI-MA-DINGIR	A. LATE
			BUN					TAḪTUN			
								ʾIL	A	BU-UN-TAḪ-UN-I-LA	B 16
			BUN	A				MA			
								ʾIL		BU-NA-MA-DINGIR	XII 1 X 36
			BUN	U				KI			
								ʾIL		BU-NU-KI-DINGIR	M
			BUN	U				KALA			
								ʾIL	I	BU-NU-KA-LA-I-LI	B 16
			BUN	U				KAMA			
								ʾIL	A	BU-NU-KA-MA-I-LA	B 16
			BUN	U				MA			
								ʾIL		BU-NU-MA-DINGIR	M
			BUN	U				TAḪTUN			
								ʾIL	A	BU-NU-TAḪ-TU-UN-I-LA	B 16+
			BUN	U	HU			PI			
								ʾIL	UM	BU-NU-U_2?-BI-I-LUM	UET V 548 2
			DAWD	UM				PI			
								ʾIL		DA-DUM-BI_2-DINGIR	I
			DANN	I	Š			ME			
								ʾIL		DA-NI-IŠ-ME-DINGIR?	I
			ḎARAʿ					LI			
								ʾIL		ZA-RA-AḪ?-LI-DINGIR	M
			KA					ṢUWR	A		
								ʾIL		KA-ZU-RA-DINGIR	M
			KANN	A				MA			
								ʾIL		KA-AN-NA-MA-DINGIR	M
			LA		K			MA			
								ʾIL		LA-AK-MA-AN	B 33
			LA			ʾA		HWIJ			
								ʾIL		LA-WI-DINGIR	XIV 109:7
			LA			ʾA		HWIJ			
								ʾIL		LA-[AḪ]?-WI-DINGIR	M
			LA			ʾA		ʾWIʾ			
								ʾIL		LA-WI-IḪ?-DINGIR	TIM IV 33,34,SEALS
			LA			ʾA		ʾŠUD	I		
								ʾIL		LA-AḪ-SU-DI-DINGIR	XIII 4 14
			LA			ʾA		MLIK			
								ʾIL		LA-AM-LI-IK-DINGIR	RUTTEN 5 22
			LA			ʾA		ŠNIJ			
								ʾIL		LA-AŠ-NI-DINGIR	M
			LI			JI	T	ŠAMAʿ			
								ʾIL		LI?-IŠ?-TA-MI-DINGIR	IX 291 I 18
			LAWUJ					LA			
								ʾIL		LA-WU-LA-DINGIR	M+
			LAMA					LA			
								ʾIL		LA-MA-LA-DINGIR	KAJ 72 18, LATE
		ʾA	MWUT					PA			
								ʾIL		A-MU-UT-PA-DINGIR	SYRIA L 7
		ʾA	MWUT					PA			
								ʾIL		AM-MU-UT-PA-DINGIR	RA XLIII 212 39 QATNA
		ʾA	MWUT					PI			
								ʾIL		A-MU-UT-BI-DINGIR	M+
		ʾA	MWUT					PI			
								ʾIL	A	A-MU-UT-BI-I-LA	M
			MILK	I				LI			
								ʾIL		MI-IL-KI-LI_2-IL	I
			MILK	I				LI			
								ʾIL		[MI]-EL-KI-LI-IL	I
			MILK	I				LU			
								ʾIL	A	MI-IL-KI-LU-I-LA	VAS XVI 10 5, 9
			MILK	U				MA			
								ʾIL		MI-IL-KU-MA-IL	B 35+
			MILK	U				MA			
								ʾIL		MI-IL-KU-MA-DINGIR	C+

STEMS

ʾIL	3		MILK		UM		MA				
							ʾIL		MIL-KUM-MA-DINGIR		A. LATE
			MANN				BALTI				
							ʾIL		MA-AN-BA-AL-TI-DINGIR		RA LXIV 34 NO. 24
			MANN		A		BALTI				
							ʾIL		MA-AN-NA-BA-AL-TI-DINGIR		M
			NIMḪ		AM		PI				
							ʾIL		NI-IM?-ḪA-AM-BI-DINGIR		A. 95 17 (=JCS VIII 8)
			NAPŚ		I		PI				
							ʾIL		NA-AP-SI-BI-DINGIR		SYRIA XLVIII 9:22
			PI				KAMA				
							ʾIL		BI-KA-MA-DINGIR		XIV 111:10+
			PU				ME				
							ʾIL		PU-ME-IL		I
			QAWM		U		MA				
							ʾIL		QA-MU-MA-DINGIR		M
			RAPIʾ				MI				
							ʾIL		RA-BI-MI-IL		BIROT,TEA 72 VI 19
			RAPIʾ				MI				
							ʾIL	UM	RA-BI-MI-LUM		BIROT,TEA 72 IX 29
		JA	RŚAP				LA				
							ʾIL		IA-AR-SA-AP-LA-DINGIR		M+
		JA	RŚAP				LA				
							ʾIL	A	IA-AR-SA-AP-LA-I-[LA]?		M
		ʾA	ŠWUB				LA				
							ʾIL		A-ŠU-UB-LA-DINGIR		C+
		JA	ŚJIM				KI				
							ʾIL		IA-SI-IM-KI-DINGIR		M
			ŠADW		I		MA				
							ʾIL		ŠA-DI-MA-DINGIR		RA LXV 48 VIII 20
			ŚAM		U		LA				
							ʾIL		SA-MU-LA-DINGIR		B 39+
			ŚUM		U		LA				
							ʾIL		SU-MU-LA-DINGIR		B 39+
			ŚUM		U		LA				
							ʾIL	I	SU-MU-LA-I_3-LI_2		UCP X/1 34 2
			ŚAMŚ		I		HADD	U			
							ʾIL	I	SA-AM-SI-D-IM-I_3-LI_2		C+
		JI	TWUR				PI				
							ʾIL		I-DUR-[BI]?-DINGIR		I
			TAḪT		U		PI				
							ʾIL		TA-AḪ-TU-BI-DINGIR		M+
ʾILAP	1		ʾILAP		UM				IL-LA-PU-UM		RA LXV 46 VI 1,10
			ʾILAP	AN					IL-LA-BA-AN		RA LXV 51 X 9
ʾILAR	1		ʾILAR				TAʾ	A	I-LA-AR-TA-A		M
			ʾILAR				TAʾ	A	I-LA-AR-TA-ḪA		M
			ʾILAR				ŠUM		I-LA-AR-ŠUM		I
ʾILL	1		ʾILL		U	NA			IL-LU-NA	FN	A.
			ʾILL	AT	UM				IL-LA-TUM	FN	XIII 1 X 46
			ʾILL		A		JAT	I	IL-LA-I-IA-TI	FN NOM	XIII 1 IX 51
			ʾILL		A		JAT	IM	IL-LA-I-IA-TIM	FN NOM	XIII 1 IV 75
	2		ʾIL		I		ʾILL	A	I-LI-IL-LA		A. LATE
			NABIʾ				ʾILL	I	NA-BI-IL-LI		SYRIA V 274 HANA
		JI	RḪAM				ʾILL	A	IR-ḪA-MI-IL-LA		A. 274 26
		JI	RWIM				ʾILL	A	I-RI-MII-LA		A. 87 30 LATE
		JI	RWIM				ʾILL	A	I-RI-IM-IL-LA		A. LATE
		JI	RWIM				ʾILL	A	I-RI-MI-IL-LA		A. LATE
		JA	ŠWIB		I		ʾILL	A	IA-ŠI-BI-IL-LA		A.
		JI	ŚMAʿ				ʾILL	A	IŠ-MI-IL-LA		A.
	3		ʾAJAN				ʾAB	I			
							ʾILL	A	A-IA-NA-BI-IL-LA		A.
ʾILUL	1		ʾILUL		A				I-LU-UL-LA		M
			ʾILUL		I				I-LU-UL-LI		M
ʾILUR	1		ʾILUR		U				I-LU-RU		B 22
			ʾILUR		IM				I-LU-RI-IM	GEN	B 22
			ʾILUR		A				I-LU-RA	GEN	A.

STEMS

ʾILUR	1		ʾILUR	AT							IL-LU-RA-AT	FN	JACOBSEN CTC P. 48+
			ʾILUR	AT	UM						IL-LU-RA-TUM	FN	CT IV 26A 3+
			ʾILUR	AN							I-LU-RA-AN		A. 378 10
ʾIMAG	1		ʾIMAG		U						I-MA-GU	FN	M
ʾIMIR	1		ʾIMIR		I						IM-ME-RI		A.+
			ʾIMIR		UM						I-MI-RU-UM		UCP X/3 2 21
			ʾIMIR	IN	UM						I-ME-RI-NU-UM		TA 30 615 12
			ʾIMIR				ʾIL		I		IM-ME-IR-I$_3$-LI$_2$		UNPUBL.
			ʾIMIR				ḤUNN		A		IM-ME-IR?-ḪU-UN-NA		A. 43 9
ʾIMM	1		ʾIMM	AH							ḪI-IM-MA	FN	XIII 1 VI 75
			ʾIMM	AN							IM-MA-AN		M
	2		ʾIL		I		ʾIMM	AH			I-LI$_2$-IM-MA	FN	C II 41 56, 44 57
			NAWḪ		I		ʾIMM		I		D-NA-ḪI-IM-MI		YOS II 112 11
ʾINZ	1		ʾINZ	AH							IN-ZA	FN	XIII 1 XII 7
ʾIPQ	1		ʾIPQ	AT	UM						IP-GA-TUM	MN	CT XLV 23 R. 13
			ʾIPQ	AT	UM						IP-QA-TUM	MN	M+
			ʾIPQ	AT	IM						IP-QA-TIM	MN GEN	M+
			ʾIPQ	AT	IM						IP-QA-TI-IM	MN? GEN	M
			ʾIPQ				JARAḪ				I-BI-IQ-D-[EN]-ZU		M
			ʾIPQ				RIʿAJ			HU	I-BI-IQ-RI-E-U$_2$		U
			ʾIPQ		U	JI	TWUR						
							MEʾR				IP-KU-D-I-DUR-ME-ER		M
			ʾIPQ		U		NAZI				IP-KU-D-NA-AZ-ZI		M
			ʾIPQ		U		ŠAL		A		IP-KU-D-ŠA-LA		M
	2		JAʾAR				ʾIPQ				IA-AR-I-BI-IQ		M
ʾIR	2		ʾAB		I		ʾIR		A		AD-I-RA	FN	A.
ʾIRAḪ	1		ʾIRAḪ		I						I-RA-ḪI		RA LXV 47 VII 49+
ʾIRR	1		ʾIRR		A		ʾAB		I		IR$_3$-RA-A-BI		M
			ʾIRR		I		HADD		U		I-RI-A-DU		A.+
			ʾIRR		I		HADD		U		IR-RI-A-DU		A.
			ʾIRR		I		MAʾT		U		I-RI-MA-TU		A.
	2		ʾIL		A		ʾIRR		A		[I-L]A?-IR$_3$-RA		RA LXV 47 VII 18
			ḤIMD				ʾIRR		A		ḪI-ME-ID-IR$_3$-RA		M+
			ḤIMD				ʾIRR		A		ḪI-MI-ID-D-IR$_3$-RA		M+
		JA	ḤṢIN				ʾIRR		A		IA-AḪ-ZI-IN-IR$_3$-RA		M
		JA	RḤIB				ʾIRR		A		IA-AR-IB-D-IR$_3$-RA		M
		JA	RḤIB				ʾIRR		A		IA-AR-I-[IB]-IR$_3$-RA		M
		JA	ŚJIM				ʾIRR		A		IA-ŠI-IM-IR$_3$-RA		M
		JI	ŚBIJ				ʾIRR		A		IŠ-BI-D-IR$_3$-RA		M+
		JI	ŚBIJ				ʾIRR		A		IŠ-BI-IR$_3$-RA		M+
ʾIRŚ	1		ʾIRŚ				MA						
							ʾAB		I		I-RI-IŠ-MA-A-BI		A.
			ʾIRŚ				MA						
							ʾAB		I		I-RI-IŠ-MA-BI		A.
			ʾIRŚ		U		MA						
							ʾAB		I		IR-ŠU-MA-BI		A.
ʾIRŠAP	2		ʿABD				ʾIRŠAP		A		ḪA-AB-DU-IR?-ŠA-PA?		M
ʾIŚAL	1		ʾIŚAL		I						I-SA-LI	GEN	CT VIII 44A+
ʾIŚIM	1		ʾIŚIM	AN	AJA						I-SI-MA-NA-A		B 22
ʾIŚN	1		ʾIŚN	AN	U						IŠ-NA-NU		B 45+
ʾIŚUL	1		ʾIŚUL		UM						ḪI-SU-LUM		SIMMONS 79 4'
ʾIŠḪAR	1		ʾIŠḪAR	AH			ʾUMM		I		D-IŠ-ḪA-RA-UM-MI	FN	XIII 1 II 47+
			ʾIŠḪAR	AH			ʾAŚJ	AH			D-IŠ-ḪA-RA-A-SI-IA	FN	XIII 1 XI 43
			ʾIŠḪAR	AH			DAMQ	AH			D-IŠ-ḪA-RA-DAM-QA	FN	RA LXV 58 I 18
			ʾIŠḪAR	AH			DUMQ		I		D-IŠ-ḪA-RA-DU-UM-KI	FN	XII 265 3
			ʾIŠḪAR	AH			DANN	AT			IŠ-ḪA-RA-DAN-NA-AT	FN	M
			ʾIŠḪAR	AH			ḎAMR	AT	I		D-IŠ-ḪA-RA-ZA-AM-RA-TI	FN	M
			ʾIŠḪAR	AH			GUML		I		D-IŠ-ḪA-RA-GU-UM-LI	FN	XIII 1 IV 39
			ʾIŠḪAR	AH			LAMAS		I		D-IŠ-ḪA-RA-D-LAMA	FN	XIII 1 IX 23
			ʾIŠḪAR	AH			MALAK		I		D-IŠ-ḪA-RA-M[A-L]A-KI	FN	RA LXV 61 IV 61
			ʾIŠḪAR	AH			NAʿM		I		D-IŠ-ḪA-RA-NA-AḪ-ME	FN	RA LXV 64 VI 37
			ʾIŠḪAR	AH			NIWR		I		D-IŠ-ḪA-RA-NI-RI	FN	RA LXV 59 II 22
			ʾIŠḪAR	AH			NAPŚ		I		D-IŠ-ḪA-RA-NA-AP-SI	FN	XIII 1 VII 13
			ʾIŠḪAR	AH			ŚAMŚ		I		D-IŠ-ḪA-RA-D-UTU-ŠI	FN	XII 265 6
			ʾIŠḪAR	AH			ŚARR	AT			D-IŠ-ḪA-RA-ŠAR-RA-AT	FN	M
			ʾIŠḪAR	AH		TA	ŚKUB				D-IŠ-ḪA-RA-TA-AŠ-KU-UB	FN	RA LXV 56 V 21+

STEMS

ʾIŠḪAR	2		ʿABD					ʾIŠḪAR	AH			AB-DI-D-IŠ-ḪA-RA		A.+
			ʿABD					ʾIŠḪAR	AH			ḪA-AB-DU-D-IŠ-ḪA-RA		XIII 1 II 79+
			ʾUMM		I			ʾIŠḪAR	AH			UM-MI-IŠ-ḪA-RA	FN	XIII 1 V 74, A.+
			ḎU					ʾIŠḪAR	AH			ZU-D-IŠ-ḪA-RA		XIII 64 5
			TAʾK		I			ʾIŠḪAR	AH			TA-KI-D-IŠ-ḪA-RA		JCS XIII 52 293 LE,A.LATE
			TAʾK		U			ʾIŠḪAR	AH			TA-KU-D-IŠ-ḪA-R[A]		JCS XIII 52 293 R, A.LATE
ʾIŠAW	1		ʾIŠAW		UM							I-ŠA-WU-UM		M
ʾITEJ	2		ʾIL		I			ʾITEJ			JE	I$_3$-LI$_2$-I-TE-E		MEISSNER 110 20, 23+, M
			ŠAMŠ		I			ʾITEJ			JE	D-UTU-I-TE-E		CT IV 44 B 3, 4
ʾITT	1		ʾITT		A			ʾABB		A		ḪI-IT-TA-D-AB-BA		M
			ʾITT		A			ʾIL		I		IT-TA-I$_3$-LI$_2$		M
ʾIZAM	1		ʾIZAM		U							I-ZA?-MU	FN	M
			ʾIZAM	AN	UM							I-ZA-MA-NU-UM		B 45
ʾKUR	1	JA	ʾKUR		IM							IA-KU-RI?-IM?	GEN	VIII 2 23
		JA	ʾKUR	AN								IA-KU-RA-AN		M
		JA	ʾKUR					ʾIL				IA-AḪ-KU-UR-DINGIR		CT XLV 6 24
		JA	ʾKUR					ʾIL				A-AḪ-KU-UR$_2$-[DINGIR]?		HARRIS 79 22
		JI	ʾKUR					BAʿL		I		I-KU-UR-BA-LI		EDZARD, DER 102:9
		JA	ʾKUR					DAGAN				IA-KU-UR-D-DA-GAN		M+
ʾLAP	1	JI	ʾLAP					HADD		U		IḪ-LA-AP-A-DU		A.
		JI	ʾLAP					ṬALL				I-LA-AP-TI-IL		U
		JI	ʾLAP					ṬALL		U	HU	I-LA-AP-TA-LU-U$_2$		M
ʾLAŠ	2		RAPIʾ				TA	ʾLAŠ				RA-BI-TA-AḪ-LA-AŠ		BASOR 95 22
ʾLIP	1	JI	ʾLIP					HADD		A		IḪ-LI-BA-DA		TCL I 222 13
ʾMAR	1	JA	ʾMAR	AH								IA-MA-RA	FN	XIII 1 XIV 26
	2		LA				ʾA	ʾMAR		UM		LA-MA-RUM		BM 80644
ʾMIʾ	1	JA	ʾMIʾ					ʾIL				IA-AḪ-MI-DINGIR		PBS XI/2 P. 120 NO. 92
		JA	ʾMIʾ					ʾIL		A		IA-MI-I-LA		M
		JA	ʾMIʾ					ʾIL		A		JA-MI-I-LA		M
		ME	ʾMIʾ		IM							ME-MI-ḪI-IM	GEN	C
	2		MUT		I		JE	ʾMIʾ				MU-TI-E-MI-IḪ		M
ʾMIN	1	MA	ʾMIN		UM							MA-AḪ-MI-NU-UM		CT XLVIII 89 REV.
ʾMUW	1	JA	ʾMUW			HU						IA-AḪ-MU-U$_2$		B 26
		JA	ʾMUW					DAGAN				IA-AḪ-MU-D-DA-GAN	GN	B 26
ʾMUR	1	ʾA	ʾMUR		U	HU						A-MU-RU-U$_2$		PBS VIII/1 98 9
		JA	ʾMUR		IM							IA-MU-RI-IM	GEN	B 28+
		JA	ʾMUR					HADD		U		IA-MU-UR-AD-DU		M
		JA	ʾMUR					JARAḪ				IA-MUR-D-EN-ZU		UET V 583 19
		TA	ʾMUR									TA-MU-UR	FN	M
	2		ʿADN		A		ʾA	ʾMUR				ḪA-AD-NA-AM?-MU-UR		X 75 18
			LA				ʾA	ʾMUR		IM		LA-A-MU-RI-IM	GEN	M
			LA				ʾA	ʾMUR		A		LA-MU-RA		B 33+
ʾNIP	1	MA	ʾNIP		UM							MA-NI-PU-UM		SIMMONS 119 10 S
ʾNUP	1	MA	ʾNUP		UM							[MA]-AḪ-NU-KA-UM		VAS IX 192 18
		MA	ʾNUP		U							MA-AḪ-NU-KA		VAS IX 193 18
		MA	ʾNUP		U							MA-AḪ-NU-PU		M
		MA	ʾNUP					ʾIL				MA-AḪ-NU-UP-DINGIR		B 33+, M+
		MA	ʾNUP					ʾIL				MA-AḪ-NU-BI-DINGIR		B 33+, M+
		MA	ʾNUP					ʾIL		I		MA-AḪ-NU-UP-I$_3$-LI$_2$		B 33+
ʾQUD	1	JA	ʾQUD		UM							IA-KU-DU-UM		CT VIII 44A 28, UET V 523
		JA	ʾQUD		UM							IA-AḪ-KU-DU-UM		CT XXXIII 29 14
		JA	ʾQUD		UM							IA-KU-DU-UM-KI	GN	BRM IV 53 III 47+
		JA	ʾQUD		U							IA-KU-DU-KI	GN	UCP IX/4 5 1
		JA	ʾQUD	AN	IM							IA-GU-DA-NIM	GEN	BM 16823A 1
ʾRUR	1	JA	ʾRUR									IA-AḪ-RU-UR-KI	GN	M
		JA	ʾRUR		UM							IA-RU-RUM-KI	GN	YOS XII
		JA	ʾRUR		UM							IA-ḪU-UR-RU-UM-KI	GN	M
		JA	ʾRUR		UM							IA-AḪ-RU-RU-UM	GN	B 26+
		JA	ʾRUR		UM							IA-AḪ-RU-RUM	GN	B 26+
		JA	ʾRUR		UM							IA-AḪ-RU-RUM		BM 80328 10
		JA	ʾRUR		A							IA-AḪ-RU-RA-KI	GN	B 26, M
		JA	ʾRUR		A							IA-ḪU-UR-RA-KI	GN	M+
		JA	ʾRUR	IJ	I							IA-AḪ-RU-RI-I-KI	GN	M
	2		ʾAWN	AN			JA	ʾRUR				AM-NA-AN-IA-AḪ-RU-UR	TRIBE	BAGHD. MITT. II 56 I 12+
			ŠUM		U		JA	ʾRUR		A		[SU-MU-I]A-AḪ-RU-RA		B 39
ʾRUŠ	1	JA	ʾRUŠ									IA-AḪ-RU-UŠ		RA LXV 55 XIII 52

STEMS

ʾŠUʾ	1 JA	ʾŠUʾ				HADD		U		IA-SU-D-IM		TCL I 238 4 HANA+
ʾŠUD	1 JA	ʾŠUD		UM						IA-SU?-DU-UM		CT II 28 19
	JA	ʾŠUD				PI						
						ʾEL				IA-SU-UD-PI-EL		SIMMONS 46 31
	2	LA			ʾA	ʾŠUD		I				
						ʾIL				LA-AḪ-SU-DI-DINGIR		XIII 4 14
ʾŠUR	1 JA	ʾŠUR		UM						IA-ŠU-RU-UM		RA LXV 54 XII 38
ʾUWR	1	ʾUWR		A		HADD		U		U$_2$-RA-A-DU		A.
		ʾUWR		I		HADD		U		U$_2$-RI-A-DU		A.
		ʾUWR		I		HADD		U		WU-RI-A-DU		A.
		ʾUWR		I		JARAḪ				U$_2$-RI-E-RA-AḪ		M
	2	ʾIL		A		ʾUWR		I		DINGIR-U$_2$-RI		RA LXVIII 28:13 MARI
		ʾIL		I		ʾUWR		I		I-LI-U$_2$-RI	FN	A.
ʾUWŠ	1	ʾUWŠ	AN							U$_2$-ŠA-AN		M+
		ʾUWŠ	AN	UM						ḪU-ŠA-NU-UM		B 45+
		ʾUWŠ	AN	UM						ḪU-ŠA-A-NU-UM		KISURRA 48 8
		ʾUWŠ	AN	U						ḪU-SA-NU		4E RENC. ASS. P. 178 4
ʾUBIR	1	ʾUBIR		A						U$_2$-BI-RA		M
ʾUBUŠ	1	ʾUBUŠ		UM						ḪU-BU-ŠUM		UCP X/1 34 13
		ʾUBUŠ		I						U$_2$-BU-SI		M
		ʾUBUŠ				ʿAŠTAR				U$_2$-BU-UŠ$_3$-EŠ$_4$-DAR		RES 1938 P. 129
		ʾUBUŠ				TUʾ			KA	ḪU-BU-UŠ-TU-KA		A. 268 17
ʾUDIN	1	ʾUDIN	AH							U$_2$-DI-NA	FN	XIII 1 IV 67
ʾUDM	1	ʾUDM	AN	UM						ḪU-UD-MA?-NU		XII 712 R 9
ʾUDUD	1	ʾUDUD		UM						ḪU-DU-DU-UM		TLB I/2, 15 18+
ʾUD̲UN	1	ʾUD̲UN	AN							U$_2$-ZU-NA-AN		M+
ʾUGAZ	1	ʾUGAZ		UM						U$_2$-GA-ZUM		TA 30 615 22
ʾUKUL	1	ʾUKUL	IN	UM						U$_2$-KU-LI-NU-UM		RA LXV 43 III 54
ʾULP	1	ʾULP	AH							ḪU-UL-PA	FN	C
ʾUM	1	ʾUM		U		ŠAKIM				U$_2$-MU-ŠA-KI-IM		M+
ʾUMAN	2	ḪATAʾ				ʾUMAN		UM		ḪA-TA-UM-MA-NU-UM		RA VIII 74 19
ʾUMM	1	ʾUMM		IJA						UM?-MI-IA	FN	XIII 1 XIV 18
		ʾUMM		I		ḪAʾT		UM		UM-MI-ḪA-TUM	FN	M+
		ʾUMM		I		ʾIL		I		UM-MI-I$_3$-LI$_2$	FN	XIII 1 VIII 64
		ʾUMM		I		JIQR	AH			UM-MI-IQ-RA	FN	M+
		ʾUMM		I		ʾIŠḪAR	AH			UM-MI-IŠ-ḪA-RA	FN	XIII 1 V 74, A.+
		ʾUMM		I		ʾAŠIR	AH			UM-MI-A-ŠI-RA	FN	VAS XIII 73 6,13
		ʾUMM		I		JAT		UM		UM-MI-IA-TUM		UCP X/1 89 24
		ʾUMM		I		BAʿL	AH			UM-MI-BA-A-LA	FN	A. LATE
		ʾUMM		I		MARṢ	AT			UM-MI-MAR-ṢA-AT	FN	XIII 1 III 5
		ʾUMM		I		NAʿM		I		UM-MI-NA-MI	FN	A.
		ʾUMM		I		NAʿM		I		UM-MI-NA-AḪ-ME	FN	RA LXV 59 II 17
		ʾUMM		I		NAHR		U		UM-MI-NA-RU	FN	M
		ʾUMM		I		NAWAR				UM-MI-NA-WA-AR	FN	XIII 1 IV 73
		ʾUMM		I		ŠAMŠ		I		UM-MI-D-UTU-ŠI	FN	RA LXV 65 VII 38
		ʾUMM		I		ṬAJB	AH			UM-MI-ṬA$_3$-BA	FN	M+
		ʾUMM		I		ṬAJB	AH			UM-MI-ṬA$_3$-BA-NU	FN	RA LXV 64 VI 34
		ʾUMM		U		JARAḪ				U$_2$?-UM-MU-E-RA-AḪ		B 40+
		ʾUMM		UM		KA						
						ʾAB		IM		UM-MU-UM-KA-A-BI-IM	FN	M
		ʾUMM		UM		KA						
						ʾAB		I		UM-MU-UM-KA-A-BI	FN	XIII 1 VII 56
		ʾUMM		U		KA						
						ʾAB		I		UM-MU-KA-A-BI	FN	RA LXV 62 V 16
		ʾUMM		U		ŠARR	AH			UM-MU-ŠAR-RA	FN	IX 291 33
	2	ʾAJA				ʾUMM		I		A-IA-UM-MI	FN	RA LXV 59 II 27
		ʾIJA				ʾUMM		U		I-IA-AMA		MRS VI P. 328+
	JA	ʾḪID̲				ʾUMM		I		IA-ḪI-DU-UM-ME	FN	RA LXV 65 VII 34
		ʾIL		A		ʾUMM		A		DINGIR-UM-MA		RA LXV 45 V 31
		ʾALI				ʾUMM		I		A-LI-UM-MI	FN	M
		ʾANN		U		ʾUMM		I		AN-NU-UM-MI	FN	XIII 1 IV 48+
		ʾANN		U		ʾUMM		I		AN-NU-UN-UM-MI		M
		ʾIŠḪAR	AH			ʾUMM		I		D-IŠ-ḪA-RA-UM-MI	FN	XIII 1 II 47+
		ʾAŠR	AT	UM		ʾUMM		I		D-AŠ-RA-TUM-UM-MI	FN	TCL I P. 16+
		ʿAŠTAR				ʾUMM		I		EŠ$_4$-DAR-UM-MI	FN	XIII 1 II 38 +
		TABUB		U		ʾUMM		I		TA-BU-BU-UM-MI	FN	XIII 1 VI 57

Stem	No.	Pref.	Root	Pattern	Ending	Ext.	Element 2	Ending 2	Spelling	Gram.	Reference
ʾUNAB	1		ʾUNAB		UM				ḪU-NA-BU-UM		KISURRA 17 5
			ʾUNAB		UM				U_2-NA-BU-UM		TIM III 42 13
			ʾUNAB		I				ḪU-NA-BI	NOM	GAUTIER 11 8, R. 2
			ʾUNAB	AH					ḪU-NA-BA	FN	XIII 1 VI 50
			ʾUNAB	AT	UM				U_2-NA-BA-TUM	FN	TIM III 26 7
			ʾUNAB	AT	UM				ḪU-NA-BA-TUM	FN	WATERMAN 54 2, 3+
ʾUNUB	1		ʾUNUB		UM				ḪU-NU-BU-UM		GORDON 39 5, 10
			ʾUNUB		UM				U_2-NU-BU-UM		EDZARD, DER 74:11+
			ʾUNUB		UM				UN-NU-BU-UM		EDZARD, DER 68 III 10
			ʾUNUB		IM				ḪU-NU-BI-I[M]	GEN	M
			ʾUNUB	AT	UM				ḪU-NU-PA-TUM	FN?	BM 17060 35
			ʾUNUB	AT	UM				UN-NU-BA-TUM	FN	WATERMAN 24 R. 24
			ʾUNUB	AT	UM				ḪU-NU-BA-TUM	FN	EDZARD, DER 134:4
			ʾUNUB	T	UM				UN-NU-UB-TUM	FN	EDZARD, DER 33:11+
			ʾUNUB	T	UM				ḪU-NU-UB-TUM	FN	EDZARD, DER 99:8
ʾUP	1		ʾUP				ʾIL	A	UP-I-LA		BULL. ACAD. BELG. 1974 227
	2		ʾALI				ʾUP	UM	A-LI$_2$-U_2-PU-UM		KISURRA 117 5
			ḎIMR		U		ʾUP	I	ZI-IM-RU-UḪ$_2$-KI		TCL VII 23 14 21+
			ŠUM		U		ʾUP	I	SU-MU-UḪ$_2$-KI		JCS XI 23 NO. 10 14+
		JA	ŠMAʿ				ʾUP	I	IA-AŠ$_2$-MA-ḪU-PI		BULL. ACAD. BELG. 1974 228
ʾURAN	1		ʾURAN		UM				U_2-RA-NU-UM		M+
			ʾURAN		UM				U_3-RA-NU-UM		TA 1931, 538 IV
			ʾURAN	AT	UM				U_2-RA-NA-TUM	FN	HARRIS 83 1
ʾURAŠ	1		ʾURAŠ		IJA				U_2-RA-SI-IA		M
ʾURK	1		ʾURK	UTANIM					UR-KU-TA-NIM	GEN	CT VIII 20B 10
ʾURL	1		ʾURL	IJ	UM				UR-LI-U_2-UM		M
ʾURR	1		ʾURR	AN					UR-RA-AN		RA LXV 53 XI 15
ʾURŠAM	1		ʾURŠAM	AN	AM				UR-SA-MA-NAM	ACC	M+
ʾUŠAL	1		ʾUŠAL		UM				U_2-SA?-LUM		WATERMAN 21 R. 10
			ʾUŠAL		UM				ḪU-ŠA-LUM		HARRIS 105 5
ʾUŠAT	1		ʾUŠAT	AN					U_2-SA-TA-AN		M+
ʾUŠIL	2		BEʿL		I		ʾUŠIL	I	BE-LI$_2$-U_2-SI-LI	FN	RA LXV 56 I 10
ʾUŠK	1		ʾUŠK	ATANUM					UŠ-KA-TA-NU-UM		XIII 92 11
			ʾUŠK	ATANIM					UŠ-KA-TA-NIM	MN GEN	XIII 61 5+
ʾUŠM	1		ʾUŠM		A		ʿAMM	I	UŠ-MA-AM-MI		CT XXXIII 46A 4
ʾUŠŠ	1		ʾUŠŠ	AT	I		ʾEL		UŠ-SA-TE-EL		TIM III 43 6
ʾUŠT	1		ʾUŠT		AJA				UŠ-TA-IA		RA LXV 55 XIII 14
ʾUŠAŠ	1		ʾUŠAŠ		UM				U_2-ŠA-ŠUM		I
ʾUTL	2		ʿABD				ʾUTL	I	AB-DU-UT-LI	FN	A. LATE
ʾUZUL	1		ʾUZUL		I				U_2-ZU-UL-LI	FN	XIII 1 III 66
			ʾUZUL		IM				ḪU-UZ-ZU-LIM	GEN	GORDON 38 21+
ʾZIJ	1	JA	ʾZIJ				ʾIL		IA-AḪ-ZI-DINGIR		M
		JA	ʾZIJ				ʾIL	I	IA-AḪ-ZI-I$_3$-LI$_2$		TCL X 21 13
		JE	ʾZIJ				ʾIL	UM	E-EḪ-ZI-LUM		VIII 3 25
		JA	ʾZIJ				DAGAN		IA-AḪ-ZI-D-DA-GAN		RA LXV 54 XII 52
		TA	ʾZIJ				ʾADM	U	TA-AḪ-ZI-D-AD-MU	FN	M
ʾZUW	1	JA	ʾZUW		UM				IA-ZU-UM		UET V 714 +
		JA	ʾZUW				HADD	U	IA-ZU-D-IM		M
		JA	ʾZUW				JARAḪ		IA-ZU-RA-AḪ		M+
		JA	ʾZUW				DAGAN		IA-ZU-D-DA-GAN		M+, SYRIA V 273, HANA
		JA	ʾZUW				RAŠAP		IA-AḪ-ZU-D-RA-SA-AP		M
HWIJ	1	JA	HWIJ		UM				IA?-WI-U_2-UM		M
		JA	HWIJ		UM				IA-AḪ?-WI?-UM?		B 32
		JA	HWIJ			JA			IA-WI-IA		M
		JA	HWIJ				HADD	U	IA-WI-D-IM		M+
		JA	HWIJ				ʾIL		IA-WI-DINGIR		B 31+, M+
		JA	HWIJ				ʾIL		JA-AḪ-WI-DINGIR		M
		JA	HWIJ				ʾIL		IA-AḪ-WI-DINGIR		B 27+
		JA	HWIJ				ʾIL	I	IA-AḪ-WI-DINGIR-LI$_2$		KISURRA 6+
		JA	HWIJ				ʾIL	I	IA-WI-LI		A 7695 10
		JA	HWIJ				DAGAN		IA-WI-D-DA-GAN		B 31
		JA	HWIJ				KI				
							HADD	U	[IA-A]Ḫ-WI-KI-D-IM		M
		JE	HWIJ				MALIK		E-WI-MA-LIK		A.
		JI	HWIJ				MUT	I	I-WI-MU-TI		U
		JA	HWIJ				NAŠIʾ		IA-AḪ-WI-NA-SI		M+

STEMS

HWIJ	1	JA	HWIJ			TA	NWUḪ			IA-WI?-TA-NU		RA LXV 43 III 64
		TA	HWIJ				JARAḪ			TA-AḪ-WI?-D-EN-ZU		RA LXIV 28 NO. 16
		TA	HWIJ				NAPŠ	U		TA-AḪ-WI-NA-AP-SU		RA LXIV 28 NO. 14
	2		ʿAŠTAR			JA	HWIJ			EŠ$_4$-DAR-IA-WI		VAS VII 157 7
			LA			ʾA	HWIJ		JA	LA-WI-IA	FN	RA LXV 60 III 37
			LA			ʾA	HWIJ					
							ʾAḪ	I		LA-AḪ-WI-A-ḪI	FN	XIII 1 VII 3
			LA			ʾA	HWIJ					
							ʾAB	I		LA-AḪ-WI-A-BI	FN	XIII 1 XIII 6
			LA			ʾA	HWIJ					
							HADD	U		LA-AḪ-WI-A-DU		A. 95 36
			LA			ʾA	HWIJ					
							ʾIL			LA-WI-DINGIR		XIV 109:7
			LA			ʾA	HWIJ					
							ʾIL			LA-[AḪ]?-WI-DINGIR		M
			LA			ʾA	HWIJ					
							JAŠAR			LA-AḪ-WI-E-SA-AR		RA LXV 40 I 21
			LA			ʾA	HWIJ					
							BAʿL	U		LA-AḪ-WI-BA-LU		C
			LA			ʾA	HWIJ					
							BAʿL	U		LA-AḪ-WI-BA-AḪ-LU		XIV 29:28
			LA			ʾA	HWIJ					
							BEʿL	I		LA-AḪ-WI-BE-LI$_2$	FN	RA LXV 59 II 73
			LA			ʾA	HWIJ					
							LA		NA	LA-AḪ-WI-LA-NA		RA LXV 65 VII 19
			LA			ʾA	HWIJ					
							MALIK			LA-AḪ-WI-MA-LIK		X 141 2
			LA			ʾA	HWIJ					
							MALIK	U		LA-AḪ-WI-MA-LI-KU		M
			LA			ʾA	HWIJ					
							NIWR	I		LA-AḪ-WI-NE-RI	FN	XIII 1 II 11
	3		ʾEK	I			LA					
						ʾA	HWIJ			E-KI-LA-AḪ-WI		M
HADD	1		HADD	A						AD-DA		M+
			HADD	AJA						A-AD-DA-A		M+
			HADD	AJA						A-DA-A		M
			HADD	U			BAʿL	I		D-IM-BA-AḪ-LI		M+
			HADD	U			BANIJ			D-IM-BA-NI		M+
			HADD	U			DUWR	I		D-IM-DU-RI		M+
			HADD	U			MALIK			AD-DU-MA-LIK		A. 268 4
			HADD	U			MALIK			D-IM-MA-LIK		M+
			HADD	U			NIWR	I		D-IM-NI-RI	FN	RA LXV 61 IV 17
			HADD	U			ŠADW	A		D-IM-ŠA-DA		PSBA XXIX 273 NO. 9 R. 10
	2		ʾAḪ	I			HADD	A		A-ḪI-A-DA		B 12
		JA	HWIJ				HADD	U		IA-WI-D-IM		M+
			ḪAʾL	I			HADD	U		ḪA-LI$_2$-D-IM		M+
			ḪAʾL	I			HADD	U		ḪA-LI-A-DU		A.+
			ḪAʾL	I			HADD	U		ḪA-LI-IA-[D]U		M
			ʾUWR	A			HADD	U		U$_2$-RA-A-DU		A.
			ʾUWR	I			HADD	U		U$_2$-RI-A-DU		A.
			ʾUWR	I			HADD	U		WU-RI-A-DU		A.
			JAʾAR				HADD	U		IA-ḪA-AR-D-IM		M
		JA	ʾWUŠ				HADD	U		IA-UŠ-D-IM		M+
		JA	ʾWUŠ				HADD	U		IA-U$_2$-UŠ-D-IM		M+
		JA	ʾWUŠ				HADD	U		IA-UŠ$_2$-D-IM		M
			ʾAB	I			HADD	U		A-BI-D-IM		B 9, M+
			ʾAB	I			HADD	U		A-BI-A-DU		A.+
			ʾAB	I			HADD	U		A-BI-IA-DU		M+
			ḪABIʾ				HADD	U		ḪA-BI-D-IM		M
			ʿABD				HADD	U		AB-DI-AD-DU		BAGHD. MITT. II 57 28
			ʿABD				HADD	U		ḪA-AB-DU-D-IM		RA LXV 48 VIII 34
		JI	JBAL				HADD	U		I-BA-AL-D-IM		M+, C+
			JABAL				HADD	U		IA-BA-AL-D-IM		M
			ʿAD	U	NA		HADD	U		A-DU-NA-D-IM		SYRIA XIX 109
			ʿAD	U	NI		HADD	U		A-DU-NI-D-U		MRS VI 15, 42 II 20 UGARIT
			JADAʿ				HADD	U		[IA]-ṬA$_3$-AḪ-D-IM		VI 76 10

STEMS

HADD	2		ʿADN	I		HADD	U	ḪA-AD-NI-D-IM	M, C+
			ʿADN	I		HADD	U	ḪA-AD-NI-A-D[U]	DELAPORTE CCL II A 914
			ʿAḎR	I		HADD	U	AD-RI-A-DU	A.+
			ʿAḎR	I		HADD	U	AD-RI-IA-DU	KUPPER, NOM. 231
			ʾIL	I		HADD	U	I$_3$-LI$_2$-D-IM	M+
			ʾIL	I		HADD	U	I$_3$-LI$_2$-A-DU	A. 57 47
		JI	ḪLAJ			HADD	U	IḪ-LA-D-IM	XIII 1 II 76
		JI	ḪLIJ			HADD	U	IḪ-LI-A-DU	A. P. 133+
		JI	ḪLIJ			HADD	U	IḪ-LI$_3$-A-DU	A. P. 133
			ʾALUN			HADD	U	ḪA-LU-UN-D-IM	M; JCS XIV 203
			ʾALUN	A		HADD	U	ḪA-LU-NA-D-IM	M
		JI	ʾLAP			HADD	U	IḪ-LA-AP-A-DU	A.
		JI	ʾLIP			HADD	A	IḪ-LI-BA-DA	TCL I 222 13
			ʿAMM	I		HADD	U	AM-MI-A-DU	A. 60 14
			ʿAMM	I		HADD	U	AM-MI-IA-A-DU	A.
			ʿAMM	I		HADD	U	AM-MI-AD-DU	A. 267 17
			ʿAMM	U		HADD	A	AM-MU-A-DA	A.+
			ʿAMM	U		HADD	A	AM-MU-WA-DA	A.
			ʾAMAR			HADD	U	AM-MA-RA-DU	A.+
			ʾAMAR	A		HADD	U	AM-MA-RA-A-DU	A.
		JA	ʾMUR			HADD	U	IA-MU-UR-AD-DU	M
			ʾANA			HADD	U	A-NA-D-IM	MRS XII NO. 24, 6, UGARIT
			ḪANN	A		HADD	U	AN-NA-D-IM	M+
			ḪANN	A		HADD	U	ḪA-AN-NA-D-IM	M
			ḪINN	I		HADD	U	IN-NI-D-IM	A.
			ḪANZ	A		HADD	U	ḪA-AN-ZA-D-IM	M
		JA	JPAʿ			HADD	U	IA-A-PA-AḪ-D-IM	M+
		JA	JPAʿ			HADD	U	IA-PA-ḪA-D-IM	M
		JA	JPAʿ			HADD	U	IA-PA-AḪ-D-IM	M+
		JA	JPIʿ			HADD	U	IA-BI-IḪ-D-IM	M
		ʾU	WQAH			HADD	U	U$_2$-QA-D-IM	RA LXV 44 IV 51
		ʾU	WQAH			HADD	U	U$_2$-GA-D-IM	BIROT, TEA 24:6
			ʿIQB	I		HADD	U	IQ-BI-D-IM	KISURRA 114 7
			ʾIRR	I		HADD	U	I-RI-A-DU	A.+
			ʾIRR	I		HADD	U	IR-RI-A-DU	A.
		JA	ʾŠUʾ			HADD	U	IA-SU-D-IM	TCL I 238 4 HANA+
			JIŠʿ	I		HADD	U	IŠ-ḪI-D-IM	M+, C+
			ʾEŠB	I		HADD	U	EŠ-BI-D-IM	A.+
			ʾAŠM	A		HADD	U	AŠ-MA-DU	BM 80328 14
			ʾAŠM	A		HADD	U	AŠ-MA-A-DU	A.+
			JATAR			HADD	U	IA-TAR-D-IM	M+
			ʾATT	I		HADD	U	AT-TI-D-IM	M+
			JATT	I		HADD	U	IA-AT-TI-D-IM	M
		JA	JṢIʾ			HADD	U	IA-ZI-D-IM	M
		JA	ʾZUW			HADD	U	IA-ZU-D-IM	M
		JA	ʿZIB			HADD	U	IA-AḪ-ZI-IB-D-IM	M+
		JA	ʿZIB			HADD	U	IA-ZI-IB-D?-IM?	M
		JA	ḪZUR			HADD	U	IA-AḪ-ZU-UR-D-IM	M
			ʿUZZ			HADD	U	U$_2$-ZA-DU	U
			BAʿD	I		HADD	U	BA-AḪ-DI-D-IM	M+
			BUʾL	I		HADD	U	BU-LI-A-DU	A. 60 12
			BAʿL	I		HADD	U	BA-AḪ-LI-D-IM	M+
			BAʿL	I		HADD	U	BA-LI-D-IM	M
			BEʿL	I		HADD	U	BE-LI$_2$-D-IM	RA LXV 52 X 39
		JA	BḪAR			HADD	U	IA-AB-ḪA-AR-D-IM	M
			BULM	A	NA	HADD	U	BU-UL-MA-NA-D-IM	M+
			BIN			HADD	U	DUMU-D-IM	M+
			BIN	A		HADD	U	[B]I-NA-D-IM	M
		JA	BNIJ			HADD	U	IA-AB-NI-D-IM	M
		JI	BNIJ			HADD	U	IB-NI-D-IM	M+
		JA	DJIN			HADD	U	IA-DI-IN-D-IM	RA LXV 44 IV 51+
			DIJN	I		HADD	U	TI-NI-A-DU	A. 59 2
			DIJN	I		HADD	U	DI-NI-A-DU	A.+
			DIJN	I		HADD	U	DI-NA-A-DU	A. LATE
			DUNN	I		HADD	U	DU-NI-A-DU	A. LATE
			ḎIKR	I		HADD	U	ZI-IK-RI-D-IM	M+

STEMS

HADD	2		D̲IMR	I		HADD	U	ZI-IM-RI-D-IM		M+
			D̲IMR	I	JE	HADD	U	ZI-IM-RI-E-D-IM		M
			D̲IMR	U		HADD	U	ZI-IM-RU-D-IM		CT XLVIII 22 REV
		JA	D̲RAʿ			HADD	U	IA-AZ-RA-AḪ-D-IM		M+
		JA	GJIḪ			HADD	U	IA-GI-IḪ-D-IM		M+
		JA	GJIḪ			HADD	U	IA-GI-ḪA-D-IM		M
			GUʾR	U		HADD	U	GU-RU-D-IM		M+
		JI	GMIR			HADD	U	IG-MI-RA-A-DU		A.+
			KAʾB	I		HADD	U	KA-BI-D-IM		B 32, M+, C
			KAHAL	I		HADD	U	KA-A-LI-D-IM		M+
		JA	KWUN			HADD	U	IA-KU-UN-D-IM		B 27, M+
		JA	KWIN			HADD	U	IA-KI-IN-D-IM		M
			KUʾR	U		HADD	U	KU-RU-D-IM		M
			KIBS			HADD	U	KI-IB-ZA-DU	FN	A.
			KIBS	I		HADD	U	KI-IB-ZI-D-IM		M+
			LA		NA	HADD	U	LA-NA-D-IM		XIII 109 15, 16
		JI	LʾAʾ			HADD	U	IL-A-D-IM		X 83 4, 7'
		JI	LʾAʾ			HADD	U	IL-A-DU		A. 78 20
		JI	LEʾEJ			HADD	U	I-LE-E-D-IM		XIII 93 5
			LAWUJ			HADD	U	LA-WU-D-IM		M+
			LAWUJ			HADD	U	LA-U_2-D-IM		A.
			LIʾM	A		HADD	U	LI-MA-A-DU		A.
			LIʾM	I		HADD	U	LI-MI-D-IM		M+
			LIʾM	I		HADD	U	LI-ME-D-IM		M+
			MIHR	I		HADD	U	ME-EḪ-RI-D-IM		C+
		JA	MLIK			HADD	U	IA-AM-LIK-D-IM		RA LXV 40 I 31
			MILK	A		HADD	U	MI-IL-KA-D-IM		SYRIA XXXVII 206 27 HANA
			MILK	I		HADD	U	MIL-KI-D-IM		M
			MILK	I		HADD	U	MI-IL-KI-D-IM		M
			MUŠN	A		HADD	U	MU-UŠ-NA-A-DU		A.+
			MUT			HADD	U	MU-UT-[D]?-IM		RA LXV 41 II 17
			MUT			HADD	I	MU-TA-AD-DI		VAS XVI 165:4
			MUT	I		HADD	U	MU-TI-D-IM		M
			MUT	U		HADD	U	MU-TU-D-IM		M
			NIʿM	A		HADD	U	NI-MA-A-DU		A.
			NAWAR			HADD	U	NA-WA-AR-D-IM		RA LXV 50 VIII 55+
			NIWR	I		HADD	U	NI-IW-RI-A-DU		A.+
		JA	NBIʾ			HADD	U	IA-AB-BI-D-IM		M
			NIMIN	A		HADD	U	NI-MI-NA-A-DU		A.+
			NAPŠ	I		HADD	U	NA-AP-SI-D-IM		M+
			NAPŠ	I		HADD	U	NA-AP-ŠI-A-DU		A.+
			NAPŠ	U		HADD	U	NA-AP-SU-D-IM		M
			NAPŠ	U	NA	HADD	U	NA-AP-SU-NA-D-IM		M+
		JA	NQIM			HADD	U	IA-AK-KI-IM-D-IM		M+
		JA	NQIM			HADD	U	IA-KI-IM-D-IM		M+
			NIQM			HADD	U	NI-IQ-MA-A-DU		A.+
			NIQM			HADD	U	NI-IQ-MA-DU		A.
			NIQM			HADD	U	NI-IQ-MA_2-A-DU		B 36
			NIQM	I		HADD	U	NI-IQ-MI-A-DU		A.+
			NIQM	I		HADD	U	NI-IQ-MI-IA-AD-DU		M
		JA	NŠIʾ			HADD	U	IA-$AŠ_2$-ŠI-D-IM		RA LXV 42 III 13
		JA	NŠIʾ			HADD	U	IA-SI-D-IM		B 29
		JA	NTIN			HADD	U	IA-AN-TI-IN-D-IM		M+
		JA	NTIN			HADD	U	IA-AN-TI-NA-DU		ZDPV XLIX PL. 45 LATE
		JI	NTIN			HADD	U	I-TI-IN-D-IM		M
		JA	NṢIB			HADD	U	IA-AN-ZI-IB-D-IM		M+
		JA	NṢUR			HADD	U	IA-AṢ-ṢU-UR-D-IM		X 12 6, 21+
		JA	PḪUR			HADD	U	IA-AP-Ḫ[U-UR]-A-DU		M
			PILḪ	U		HADD	U	BI-EL-ḪU-D-IM		RA LXV 55 XIII 4
			PILS	I		HADD	U	BI-IL-ZI-D-IM		XIV 41:14
			PULS	I		HADD	U	PU-UL-ZI-D-IM		M+
			PULS	U	NA	HADD	U	PU-UL-ZU-NA-D-IM		UNPUBL.
		TA	PTUN			HADD	A	TAP-TU-NA-A-DA		A. 33 26
		TA	PTAN			HADD	A	TAP-TA-NA-A-DA		A. 206 5
		TA	PTAN			HADD	A	TAP-DA-NA-TA		A. LATE
			QUWJ	U		HADD	U	KU-U_2-D-IM		M

STEMS

HADD	2			QUWJ	UM		HADD	U	KU-UM-D-U	MRS XVI 9:7
		JA		QWIM			HADD	U	IA-KI-IM-D-IM	M+
		JA		QWIM			HADD	U	IA-GI-I[M]?-D-IM	IX 291 III 29'
				QAWM	U		HADD	U	GA-MU-D-IM	M
				QAʾN			HADD	U	QA-AN-A-DU	A.
		JA		QBIJ			HADD	U	IA-AQ-BI-D-IM	RA LXV 43 III 38
		JA		RʿIJ			HADD	U	JA-RI-A-DU	RA LXV 50 VIII 64
		JA		RḤIB			HADD	U	IA-AR-IB-D-IM	M+
		JA		RJIB			HADD	U	IA-RI-IB-D-IM	B 29+
		JA		RWIM			HADD	U	IA-RI-IM-D-IM	M+
				RIWM			HADD	U	RI-IM-D-IM	M+, A. 57 46
				RIWM	U		HADD	U	RI-MU-D-IM	M
		JA		RKAB			HADD	U	IA-AR-KA-AB-D-IM	4E RENCONTRE 23
		JA		RKIB	A		HADD	U	IA-AR-KI-BA-D-IM	XIII 145 6
		JA		RPAʾ			HADD	U	IA-AR-PA-D-IM	M+
		JI		RPAʾ			HADD	A	IR-PA-A-DA	A. 76 8+
		JI		RPAʾ			HADD	A	IR-PA-DA	A. 41 14
		JI		RPAʾ			HADD	U	IR-PA-D-IM	A.+
				RIPʾ	I		HADD	U	RI-IP-I-D-IM	M+
		ʾA		RŠIJ			HADD	A	AR-ŠI-A-DA	M
				SITR	A		HADD	U	ZI-IT-RA-A-DU	A. 456 19
				SITR	I		HADD	U	ZI-IT-RI-D-IM	M
				SITR	I		HADD	U	SI-IT-RI-D-IM	JCS XXIV 60 NO.51 REV.
				SITR	I	JE	HADD	U	ZI-IT-RI-E-D-IM	JCS XXIV 63 NO.56 REV.
				ŠINI			HADD	U	ŠI-NI-D-U	MRS XVI 44:3
		JA		ŠWUB			HADD	U	IA-ŠU-UB-D-IM	LAESSOE P. 90+, C+
				ŠUWB	I		HADD	U	ŠU-BI-D-IM	M
		JA		ŚJIM			HADD	U	IA-SI-IM-D-IM	M
				ŠADW	I		HADD	U	ŠA-DI-D-IM	M
				ŚAKB	I		HADD	U	SA-AK-BI-D-IM	ARMT V P. 123
		ʾA		ŚKUR			HADD	U	AŠ$_2$-KU-UR-D-IM	TCL 1 146 4
		ʾA		ŚKUR			HADD	U	AŠ-KUR-D-IM	M+
				ŚIKR	I		HADD	A	SI-IK-RI-ḪA-DA	BE VI/1 6 19
				ŚAM	U		HADD	U	SA-MU-D-IM	M+
				ŚUM	A		HADD	U	ŠU-MA-A-DU	A.
				ŚUM	I		HADD	U	SU-MI-A-DU	A.+
		JA		ŚMAʿ			HADD	U	IA-AŠ$_2$-MA-AḪ-D-IM	M+, C+
		JA		ŚMAʿ			HADD	U	IA-AŠ$_2$-MI-IḪ-D-IM	M
		JI		ŚMAʿ			HADD	U	IŠ-MA-D-IM	M
		JI		ŚMAʿ			HADD	U	IŠ-ME-D-IM	M+
		JI		ŚMAʿ			HADD	A	IŠ-MA-A-DA	A.+
		ʾA	T	ŚAMAR			HADD	U	AŠ-TA-MAR-D-IM	M+
				ŚAMAR			HADD	U	ŠA-AM-MA-RA-DU	A.
				ŚAMAR	I		HADD	U	SA-MA-RI-A-DU	A. 57 45
				ŚIMAR			HADD	U	ŠI-IM-MA-RA-DU?	A.
				ŚAMŠ	I		HADD	U	SA-AM-SI-D-IM	M+, A.+
				ŚAMŠ	I		HADD	U	SA-AM-SI-A-DU	M+
				ŚAMŠ	I		HADD	U	ŠA-AM-SI-D-IM	M+
				ŚAMŠ	I		HADD	U	D-UTU-ŠI-D-IM	M+, C+
				ŚAMŠ	I		HADD	U	SA-AM-ŠI-D-IM	C
				ŚAMŠ	I		HADD	U	SA-AM-SI-IA-AD-DU	M
				ŚAMŠ	I		HADD	U	D-UTU-ŠI-A-DU	A.
				ŚAPŠ	I		HADD	U	SA-AP-SI-A-DU	A.+
				ŚAMŠ	I		HADD	U		
							ʾIL	I	SA-AM-SI-D-IM-I$_3$-LI$_2$	C+
				ŚAMŠ	I		HADD	U		
							....		SA-AM-SI-D-IM-TU-GUL-TI	M
				ŚAMŠ	U		HADD	U	SA-AM-ŠU-D-IM	COLLON, SEALS NO. 141
		JI		ŠNIJ			HADD	U	IŠ-NI-D-IM	A.
		JU	T	ŠANIJ			HADD	U	UŠ-TI-NI-D-IM?	A. 36 9+
				ŚIPQ	U	NA	HADD	A	SI-IP-KU-NA-D-IM	M
				ŚIPQ	U	NA	HADD	A	SI-IP-KU-NA-DA	M
				ŚAPR	A		HADD	U	SA-AP-RA-A-DU	A. 96 R. 12
				ŠIPṬ	I		HADD	U	ŠI-IP-TI-D-IM	A. LATE
				ṢIJḪ			HADD	A	ZI-ḪA-DA	TA 1933,7 EARLY OB
				ṢUWR	I		HADD	U	ZU-RI-D-IM	M+

STEMS

HADD	2		ṢABAʾ				HADD	U	ZA-BA-AD-DU		M
			ṢIDQ		A		HADD	U	ZI-ID-QA-D-IM		M
			ṢILL				HADD	U	ZI-IL-LA-AD-DU		A. 81
	3	JA	HWIJ				KI				
							HADD	U	[IA-A]Ḫ-WI-KI-D-IM		M
			BIN		U		MA				
							HADD	U	BI-NU-MA-D-IM		4E RENCONTRE 21 NO. 25
			BUN		U		MA				
							HADD	U	BU-NU-MA-D-IM		M+
			LA			ʾA	HWIJ				
							HADD	U	LA-AḪ-WI-A-DU		A. 95 36
			LA			ʾA	ḪJIJ				
							HADD	U	LA-ḪI-A-DU		A. 57 11, 13
			LA				KIWN				
							HADD	U	LA-KI-IN-A-DU		A.
			LAWUJ				LA				
							HADD	A	LA-U_2-LA-A-DA		A.
			LAWUJ				LA				
							HADD	U	LA-WU-LA-D-IM		M+, C
HALAL	2		ŠUM		U	NA	HALAL		SU-MU-NA-ḪA-LA?-AL		UET V 245 11
HALIL	1		HALIL		UM				A-LI-LU-UM		B 18
			HALIL		UM				ḪA-LI-LUM		B 18+, M
			HALIL		UM				ḪA-LI-LU-UM		B 18+
			HALIL		IM				ḪA-LI-LI-IM	GEN	B 18
			HALIL		IM				ḪA-LI-LIM	GEN	SIMMONS 57 14
			HALIL	AT	UM				ḪA-LI-LA-TUM		KISURRA 211 4
			HALIL		IJA				ḪA-LI-LI-IA		B 18+
			HALIL		A		ʿAD	UM	A-LI-LA-ḪA-DU-UM		KISURRA 18 12
HAND	1		HAND		U		MALIK		AN-DU-MA-LIK		A. 252 10
	2		ʿABD				HAND	U	ḪA-AB-DI-IA-AN-DU		KUPPER NOM. P. 231
			ʿABD				HAND	U	AB-DI-IA-DU		KUPPER NOM. P. 231
			ʿABD				HAND	U	AB-DU-IA-AN-DU		KUPPER NOM. P. 231
			ʿAḎR		I		HAND	U	AD-RI-IA-AN-DU		KUPPER, NOM. 231
			ʿAḎR		I		HAND	U	ḪA-AD-RI-IA-AN-DU		KUPPER, NOM. 231
			BAʿL		A		HAND	U	BA-LA-ḪA-AN-DU		VOIX 187:13 MARI
			NAPŠ		I		HAND	U	NA-AP-SI-IA-AN-DU		M
		ʾA	PLAḪ				HAND	A	AP-LA-ḪA-AN-DA		M+
		ʾA	PLAḪ				HAND	A	AP-LI-ḪA-AN-DA		M
		ʾA	PLAḪ				HAND	A	AP-LA-ḪA-DA		M
		ʾA	PLAḪ				HAND	A	AP-LA-AḪ-[AN]-DA		M
		ʾA	PLAḪ				HAND	U	AP-LA-ḪA-AN-DU		RA LXV 42 II 65
		ʾA	RDAK				HAND	A	AR-DA-KA-AN-DA		M
		JA	ŠLIM				HAND	U	IA-AŠ$_2$-LI-IM-IA-[AN-D]U		M
			ŠIPR		I		HAND	A	ŠI-IP-RI-AN-TA		A. LATE
			ŠIPṬ		I		HAND	A	ŠI-IP-TI-AN-TA		A. LATE
			ŠIPṬ		I		HAND	A	ŠI-IP-TI-IA-AN-TA		A. LATE
HEDD	2		ʿABD				HEDD	A	ḪA-AB-DI-E-D-IM		RS XIX 338F.
			ʾIL		I		HEDD	A	I$_3$-LI-E-DA		A.
			ʿAMM		I		HEDD	A	AM-MI-E-DA		A.
		JA	ʿQUB				HEDD	A	IA-AK-KU-UB-E-DA		JEA VIII 207F.
			JIŠʿ		I		HEDD	A	IŠ-ḪI-E-D-IM		TIM IV 33 SEAL, 34 SEAL
		JA	JŠIR				HEDD	A	IA-ŠE-RE-DA		A. 367 5
		JA	JŠIR				HEDD	A	IA-AŠ-RI-E-DA		A.+
		JA	JTIR				HEDD	A	IA-TE-IR-E-DA		A.+
		JA	JTIR				HEDD	A	IA-TE-RI-DA		A.+
			ḎIMR		I		HEDD	A	ZI-IM-RI-E-ID-DA		B 42
			KAʾB		I		HEDD	A	KA-BI-E-D-IM		M+
			KIBS		I		HEDD	A	KI-IB-ZI-E-D-IM		M
		N	MŠIḪ				HEDD	A	NA-AM-SI-E-D-IM		A 7646 6
			RIPʾ		I		HEDD	A	RI-IP-E-D-IM		M
		ʾA	ŠKUR				HEDD	A	AŠ-KUR-E-DA		A. 54 25
			ŠUM		I		HEDD	A	SU-MI-E-DA		YOS XIII 486:1
			ŠAMŠ		I		HEDD	A	SA-AM-SI-E-D-IM		SIMMONS 4 20
			ŠAMŠ		I		HEDD	A	SA-AM-SI-E-DA		A. 455 36
			ŠAPŠ		I		HEDD	A	SA-AP-SI-E-DA		A.+
HELAL	1		HELAL		I				E-LA-LI		RA LXV 50 IX 25

STEMS

HILAL	1	T	HILAL						ʾAKK	A		ḪI-IT-LA-AL-AK-KA		RA LXV 54 XII 36,71
			HILAL		UM							ḪI-IL-LA-LUM		M+
			HILAL		IM							ḪI-LA-LI-IM	GEN	HARRIS 71 10
			HILAL		IM							ḪI-IL-LA-LIM	GEN	M+
	2		ʾANN		U			T	HILAL			AN-NU-ḪI-IT-LA-AL	FN	RA LXV 60 III 18
HILL	1		HILL		U							ḪI-EL-LU		M
HLIL	1	MA	HLIL		UM							MA-AḪ-LI-LUM		SIMMONS 46 34 124 16+
HLUL	1	ʾA	HLUL	AJ	UM							AḪ-LU-LA-UM		CT VIII 38 B 4
HULAL	1		HULAL		UM							ḪU-LA-LUM		M
ḤJIJ	1	JA	ḤJIJ			JA						IA-ḪI-IA		XIV 61:6
		JA	ḤJIJ	AN								[I]A?-Ḫ[I]?-IA-AN		RA LXV 41 II 54
		JA	ḤJIJ						ʾIL			IA-ḪI-DINGIR		B 26+
		JA	ḤJIJ						ʾIL			IA-A-ḪI-DINGIR		XIII 65 5
	2		LA				ʾA		ḤJIJ					
									HADD	U		LA-ḪI-A-DU		A. 57 11, 13
			LA				ʾA		ḤJIJ					
									ʿAN	UM		LA-ḪI-A-NU-UM		U
			LA				ʾA		ḤJIJ					
									BIḪR	U		LA-ḪI-BI-RU		WATERMAN 25 R. 5
			LA				ʾA		ḤJIJ					
									ṢADUQ			LA-ḪI-ZA-DU-UQ		A.+
ḤAJJ	1		ḤAJJ		A				ʾAŠR	A	JA	E$_2$-A-AŠ-RA-IA		M+
			ḤAJJ		A				NIWR	I		E$_2$-A-NI-RI	FN	RA LXV 58 II 2
			ḤAJJ		A				NIWR	I		E$_2$-A-NE-RI	FN	XIII 1 VII 26
			ḤAJJ		A				ŚIMḪ	I		E$_2$-A-ŠI-IM-ḪI	FN	XIII 1 II 44
			ḤAJJ		UM							ḪA-IU-UM		B 18+
			ḤAJJ		UM							ḪA-U$_2$-UM		CT VI 46 5
			ḤAJJ	AT	UM							ḪA-IA-TUM	MN	B 18+
			ḤAJJ	AT	UM							[Ḫ]A-A-A-IA-TUM	FN	XIII 1 XIV 13
			ḤAJJ	AH								A-IA	FN	XIII 1 X 47
			ḤAJJ	AH								A-I-IA	FN	A. LATE+
			ḤAJJ	AT	IJA							A-A-TI-IA		BM 92654 5
			ḤAJJ	AT	IJA							A-IA-TI-IA		BM 82440
			ḤAJJ	ATAN								ḪA-IA-TA-AN		M+
			ḤAJJ	AN	UM							ḪA-IA-NU-UM		VAS XVI 62 12
			ḤAJJ	AN	UM							A-A-NU-UM		M
			ḤAJJ	AN	I							ḪA-IA-A-NI		JNES XIII 210FF.+ LATE
			ḤAJJ		U				ʾIL			A$_2$-U$_2$-DINGIR		U
			ḤAJJ		UM				RAPIʾ			ḪA-JU-UM-RA-BI		M
	2	JI	JṢIʾ						ḤAJJ	UM		I-ZI-A-UM		MOORTGAT 488
		JA	ḤṢIN						ḤAJJ	A		IA-AḪ-ZI-IN-E$_2$-A		XIII 1 VII 23
			BAWB		I				ḤAJJ	A		D-BA-BI-E$_2$-A?		VIII 31 7
			KIBR						ḤAJJ	A		KI-BI-IR-E$_2$-A		XIV 62:23
			LU						ḤAJJ	A				
									ŚAMIʿ	UM		LU-ḪA-A-A-SA-MU-UM		UET V 569 8
			LU						ḤAJJ	A				
									ŚAMIʿ	UM		LU-ḪA-A-A-SA-MI-UM		UET V 569 17
			MILK		I				ḤAJJ	A		MIL-KI-ḪA-A-IA	FN	IRAQ XVI 40 NA
		JA	RḤIB						ḤAJJ	A		IA-AR-IB-D-E$_2$-A		M+
			ŠAWB		A				ḤAJJ	UM		SA-BA-A-U$_2$-UM		OIP XLVII 66
		JA	ŚJIM						ḤAJJ	A		[I]A-ŠI-IM-E$_2$-A		M
		JI	ŚJIM						ḤAJJ	A		I-ŠI-IM-E$_2$-A		M
		JI	TWUR						ḤAJJ	A		I-DUR-E$_2$-A		M
			TIWR						ḤAJJ	A		TI-IR-E$_2$-A		M+
ḤABAS	1		ḤABAS		U							ḪA-BA?-ZU	FN	XIII 1 I 1
ḤABIB	1		ḤABIB		UM							ḪA-BI-BU-UM		RUTTEN 27 14+
			ḤABIB		IM							A-BI-BI-IM	GEN	KISURRA 62
ḤABIS	1		ḤABIS		UM							A-BI-ZUM		TIM II 122 3+
			ḤABIS		UM							A-BI-ZU-UM		TIM III 4 3+
			ḤABIS	AN	I							ḪA-BI-ZA-NI	GEN	CT VIII 42 B 17
ḤABS	1		ḤABS	AT	UM							ḪA-AB-ZA-TUM		BM 17049+
ḪADUR	1		ḪADUR						BAʿL	A		A-DU-UR-BA-LA-IA	GN	SUMER XIV 26
			ḪADUR						BAʿL	A		D-ZA-GAR$_3$-BA-LA-IA	GN	SUMER XIV 26
			ḪADUR						BAʿL	U		A-DU-UR-BA-LU	GN	SUMER XIV 26
			ḪADUR						BEʿL	UM		A-DU-UR-BE-LUM	GN	SIMMONS 138:10
ḤAKAM	1		ḤAKAM	AT	UM							ḪA-KA-MA-TUM	FN	C+

STEMS

ḪAKAM	1		ḪAKAM		AJA					ḪA-KA-MA-A-IA	FN	XIII 1 V 44
ḪALAJ	1		ḪALAJ		A		KUʾM	U		ḪA-LA-A-KU-MU		XIV 79:5+
ḪALAB	2		MUT				ḪALAB			MU-UT-ḪA-LA-AB		A. 271 3
			ŠUM		U		ḪALAB			SU-MU-A-LA-AB		A.
ḪALAṢ	1		ḪALAṢ		UM					A-LA-ZUM		UET V 796 11+
			ḪALAṢ		UM					A-LA-ZU-UM		UET V 397 14
			ḪALAṢ		I					A-LA-ṢI		4E RENC. ASS. P. 178 2
ḪALIṢ	1		ḪALIṢ		UM					A-LI-ZUM		HARRIS 98 R. 5
			ḪALIṢ		UM					ḪA-LI-ZUM		SUMER V 141 3
			ḪALIṢ	IT	UM					A-LI-ZI-TUM?		UET V 534 R. 9
ḪAM	1		ḪAM		I		....			D-A-MI-[....]		M
			ḪAM		I		JATAR			D-A-MI-T[AR]?		M
			ḪAM		I	JI	JBAL			D-A-MI-I-BA-AL		M+
			ḪAM		I	JE	JŠUʿ			D-A-MI-E-ŠU-UḪ		M+
			ḪAM		I	JE	JŠUʿ			A-MI-E-ŠU-UḪ		M+
			ḪAM		I		MALIK			A-MI-MA-LIK		C
			ḪAM		I		ŠAMUʿ			D-A-MI-SA-MU-UḪ		M+
			ḪAM		I	TA	NWUḪ			D-A-MI-TA-NU-UḪ		M+
			ḪAM		I	TA	NWUḪ			D-A-MI-TA-NU		M
			ḪAM		I	TA	NWUḪ	A		D-A-MI-TA-NU-A		M
			ḪAM		I		ṬAJB	I		A-MI-ṬA-BI		RA LXV 45 V 81
			ḪAM		I		ṢABṬ	I		A-MI-ZA-AB-TI	MN	B 13
			ḪAM		I		ṢABṬ	I		A-MI-ZA-AB-TI	FN	CT VIII 35 B 1
			ḪAM		UM	JE	JŠUʿ			D-A-MU-UM-E-ŠU-UḪ		B 13 HANA
			ḪAM		U		DAWD	I		D?-[A?-M]U?-DA-DI		IX 291 16
			ḪAM		U		DAWD	U		D-A-MU-DA-DU		M
			ḪAM		UM		LU		HU	D-A-MU-UM-LU-U$_2$		M
			ḪAM		UM		MALIK			D-A-MU-UM-MA-LIK		M
			ḪAM		U		MALIK			D-A-MU-MA-LIK		M
			ḪAM		U	TA	NWUḪ			D-A-MU-TA-NU		M
			ḪAM		UM	TA	NWUḪ		HU	A-MU-UM-TA-NU-U$_2$		M
	2	JA	ʾWUŠ				ḪAM	U		IA-U$_2$-UŠ-D-A-MU		M
			ʾAB		I		ḪAM	A		A-BI-A-MA		SIMMONS 50 22+
			ʾAB		I		ḪAM	A		A-BI-IA-MA		SIMMONS 54 19+
			ʿABD				ḪAM	I		AB-DI-A-MI		BAGHD. MITT. II 58 III 21
			ʿABD				ḪAM	I		ḪA-AB-DU-D-A-MI		M+
			ʿABD				ḪAM	I		ḪA-AB-DU-A-MI		M
		JI	JBAL				ḪAM	UM		I-BA-AL-D-A-MU-UM		RA LXV 52 X 43
			JATAR				ḪAM	I		IA-TAR-D-A-MI		M+
		JA	JTIR				ḪAM	U		IA-TI-RA-MU		A. 235 4 LATE
			BUN		U		ḪAM	I		BU-NU-D-A-MI		M+
			BUN		U		ḪAM	IM		BU-NU-D-A-MI-IM		RA LXV 41 II 27+
			KALB				ḪAM	I		K[A]-AL-BU-D-A-MI		XIII 1 X 20
			MUT		U		ḪAM	I		MU-TU-D-A-MI		RA LXV 51 IX 49
			QAWL		A		ḪAM	I		QA-LA-D-A-M[I]		M
			QAWL		U		ḪAM	I		QA-L[U]-D-A-MI		M
		JA	RWIḪ		A		ḪAM	U		IA-RI-ḪA-A-MU		M+
			ŠUM		U		ḪAM	I		SU-MU-A-MI		M
			ŠUM		U		ḪAM	IM		SU-MU-D-A-MI-IM		RA LXV 40 I 25+
	3		LA				RIWM					
							ḪAM	I		LA-RI-IM-D-A-MI		M
ḪAMAD	1		ḪAMAD		UM					ḪA-MA-DU-UM	FN	M+
			ḪAMAD		U					ḪA-MA-DU	FN	XIII 1 XIII 20
	2	JA	MWUT				ḪAMAD			IA-MU-UT-ḪA-MA-AD		X 174 18
		JA	MWUT				ḪAMAD	I		IA-MU-UT-ḪA-MA-DI	FN	XIII 1 VI 51
ḪAMID	1		ḪAMID		UM					ḪA-MI-DU-UM		M
			ḪAMID	AH						ḪA-MI-DA	FN	RA LXV 58 I 20
ḪANḪAN	1		ḪANḪAN		UM					ḪA-AN-ḪA-NU-UM		B 48+
			ḪANḪAN		UM					ḪA-ḪA-NU-UM		SPELEERS 224 10
			ḪANḪAN		U					ḪA-AN-ḪA-NU		CT XLV 11 42
ḪANAN	1		ḪANAN		IM					A-NA-NI-IM	GEN	B 43
			ḪANAN		IM					ḪA-NA-NI-IM	GEN	B 44
			ḪANAN		A					A-NA-NA		U
			ḪANAN	AH						ḪA-NA-AN-NA	FN	C
			ḪANAN	AT	UM					A-NA-NA-TUM	FN	EDZARD, DER 97:14
			ḪANAN		A		GAʾJ	A		A-NA-NA-GA-A		RA XLIV 112 5 QATNA

STEMS

ḪANIN	1	ḪANIN		UM						ḪA-NI-NU-UM		B 19+
		ḪANIN		UM						A-NI-NU-UM		EDZARD, DER 73:19
ḪANN	1	ḪANN		AJA						AN-NA-IA	FN	RA LXV 62 V 13
		ḪANN		A		ʾAḪ		UM		AN-NA-A-ḪU-UM		RA LXV 52 XI 1
		ḪANN		A		ʾAḪ		IM		AN-NA-A-ḪI-IM	GEN	M
		ḪANN		A		ʾAḪ		I		AN-NA-A-ḪI	GEN	M
		ḪANN		A		ʾABN		UM		AN-NA-AB-NU-UM		KISURRA 8A 14
		ḪANN		A		ʾABN		UM		A-NA-AB-NU-UM		HARRIS 57 18
		ḪANN		A		ʾABN	AT			ḪA-AN-NA-AB-NA-AT		A 7763, ISHCHALI
		ḪANN		A		HADD		U		AN-NA-D-IM		M+
		ḪANN		A		HADD		U		ḪA-AN-NA-D-IM		M
		ḪANN		A		ʾIL				AN-NA-DINGIR		B 13+, C+
		ḪANN		A		JARAḪ				ḪA-AN-NA-D-EN-ZU		M
		ḪANN		A		JARAḪ				ḪAN-NA-D-EN-ZU		XIII 1 V 27
		ḪANN		A	JI	TWUR						
						MEʾR				ḪA-AN-NA-D-I-DUR-ME-ER		M
		ḪANN		A		KUʾN		I		AN-NA-KU-NI		VAS VIII 14 44
		ḪANN		A		KAʾT		UM		AN-NA-KA-TUM		YOS XIII 509:2
		ḪANN		A		MAʾJ		A		AN-NA-MA-A-A		RUTTEN 14 15
		ḪANN		IJA						ḪA-AN-NI-A	FN	RA LXV 60 III 48
		ḪANN		I		ʾIL				AN-NI-DINGIR		B 13+, M
		ḪANN		I		ʾIL				ḪA-AN-NI-DINGIR	FN	XIII 1 II 7
		ḪANN		I		ʾIL		A		ḪA-AN-NI-I-LA		A. LATE
		ḪANN		I	JI	JŠAR				AN-NI-I-ŠAR?		M
		ḪANN		I		KAʾB		I		A[N-N]I-KA-BI	FN	RA LXV 62 V 17
		ḪANN		I		....				ḪA-AN-NI-D-NIN-ŠE-X-RA?	FN	RA LXV 61 IV 63
	2	ʾANA				ḪANN		I		A-NA-AḪ-ḪA-AN-NI	FN	XIII 1 V 29
		ʾANN		U		ḪANN		I		AN-NU-ḪA-AN-NI	FN	M+
ḪANUN	1	ḪANUN		UM						A-NU-NU-UM		HARRIS 79 16
ḪARAB	1	ḪARAB	AH							ḪA-RA-BA	FN	M
		ḪARAB	AT	UM						A-RA-BA-TUM		YOS XIII 389:4+
	2	MAʾL		I		ḪARAB		A		MA-LI-A-RA-BA?		CT II 30 29
ḪARAM	2	ŠIJB		U	NA	ḪARAM				ŠI-BU-NA-A-RA-AM		M
ḪARB	1	ḪARB	AH							ḪA-AR-B[A]?	FN	RA LXV 62 V 41
		ḪARB	ATANUM							AR-BA-TA-NU-UM		B 43
		ḪARB	ATANU							AR-BA-TA-NU		CT IV 22A 19
		ḪARB		I		TUWR		AM		AR-BI-TU-RA-AM		BIROT, TEA 65:35
ḪARIB	1	ḪARIB	AN							ḪA-RI-BA-AN		M+
		ḪARIB	AN	UM						A-RI-BA-A-NU-UM		SIMMONS 103 13+
		ḪARIB	AN	UM						A-RI-BA-NU-UM		SIMMONS 96 12+
ḪARUB	1	ḪARUB	AH							A-RU-B[A]	FN	XIII 1 III 64+
ḪASAD	1	ḪASAD		UM						A-ZA-DU-UM		CT XLV 77 27
		ḪASAD		UM						ḪA-ZA-DU-U[M]?		M
ḪASID	1	ḪASID		U						ḪA-ZI-DU	FN	XIII 1 VII 42
		ḪASID	AN	U						ḪA-ZI-DA-NU		M+
		ḪASID	AN	IM						ḪA-ZI-DA-NIM	GEN	M+
ḪAŠAK	1	ḪAŠAK			NI	ʾEL				A-SA-AK-NI-EL		RA LXV 52 XI 6
ḪAŠIK	1	ḪAŠIK		UM						ḪA-SI-KUM		B 20+
ḪAṢAN	1	ḪAṢAN		UM						A-ZA-NU-UM		B 43+
		ḪAṢAN	AT	UM						ḪA-[Z]A-NA-TUM	FN	M
		ḪAṢAN		IJA						A-ZA-NI-IA		BM 80363 17
		ḪAṢAN				ʾIL		UM		ḪA-ZA-AN-I-LU-UM		M+
ḪAṢN	1	ḪAṢN	AT	UM						ḪA-AZ-NA-TU[M]	FN	M
		ḪAṢN		U		TABB		I		AZ?-NU-TAB-BI	FN	M
	2	ʾADM		U		ḪAṢN		I		D-AD-MU-ḪA-AZ-NI	FN	RA LXV 61 IV 21
		ʾIL		I		ḪAṢN		A	JA	I$_3$-LI$_2$-ḪA-AṢ-NA-A-IA		M+
		ʾIL		I		ḪAṢN		I	JA	I$_3$-LI$_2$-ḪA-AṢ-NI-IA		XIII 1 IX 8
		ʾALLAI				ḪAṢN		U		AL-LA-I-AṢ-NU	FN	M
		ʾANN		U		ḪAṢN		I		AN-NU-ḪA-AṢ-NI	FN	M+
		ʿAŠTAR				ḪAṢN		I		EŠ$_4$-DAR-ḪA-AZ-NI	FN	XIII 1 II 41
		MAM		A		ḪAṢN		I		D-MA-MA-ḪA-AZ-NI	FN	RA LXV 56 I 7
		TABUB		U		ḪAṢN		I		TA-BU-BU-ḪA-AṢ-NI	FN	RA LXV 60 III 19
ḪATIK	1	ḪATIK		U						ḪA-TI-KU		M
ḪATK	1	ḪATK		UM						ḪA-AT-KU-UM		M
		ḪATK	AN	UM						AT-GA-NU-UM		U
	2	MUT				ḪATK		IM		MU-UT-ḪA-AT-KI-IM		RA LXV 44 IV 57

ḪATK	2		MUT		I		ḪATK		IM	MU-TI-ḪA-AD-KI-IM	NOM	IRAQ XXX 92+ RIMAH
			MUT		U		ḪATK		IM	MU-TU-ḪA-AD-KI-IM		M+
			MUT		U		ḪATK		IM	MU-TU-AD-KI-IM		M
			MUT		U		ḪATK		I	MU-TU-ḪA-AD-KI		M
			TURUM			NA	ḪATK		I	TU-RUM-NA-AT-KI		M+
ḪAZAQ	1		ḪAZAQ	AN						ḪA-ZA-KA-AN-KI	GN	M
			ḪAZAQ	AN	IM					ḪA-ZA-KA-AN-NIM-KI	GN GEN	C
			ḪAZAQ	AN	IM					ḪA-ZA-KA-NIM-KI	GN GEN	C II 39 13
			ḪAZAQ				NAN		UM	A-ZA-AQ-NA-NU-UM		CT IV 50A 21
ḪAZIQ	1		ḪAZIQ		AJA					ḪA-ZI-QA-IA		UCP X/1 87 12
ḪAZUQ	1		ḪAZUQ	AN						ḪA-ZU-GA-AN		RA LXV 54 XII 22
ḪBAB	1	ʾA	ḪBAB		U					AḪ-BA-BU		U
ḪBAS	1	JA	ḪBAS				ʾIL			IA-AḪ-BA-AZ-DINGIR		CT II 39 18+
		TA	ḪBAS		I					TA-AḪ-PA-ZI		A. 28 4, 17
ḪBIS	1	JA	ḪBIS		UM					IA-AḪ-BI-ZUM		GORDON 38 3
ḪIJJ	2		ʾANA				ḪIJJ		A	A-NA-ḪI?-A?		RUTTEN 20:16
			BIN	T	I		ḪIJJ		A	BI-TI-ḪI?-A	FN	HARRIS 85 3
			KUKIM				ḪIJJ		A	KU-UK-KI-IM?-ḪI-IA	FN	X 100 5
ḪILUṢ	1		ḪILUṢ	AT	UM					I-LU-ZA-TUM	FN	CT II 30 29
ḪIMAR	1		ḪIMAR		UM					ḪI-MA-RUM		RA LXV 45 V 56
			ḪIMAR	AN						ḪI-MA-RA-AN-KI	GN	M+
ḪIMD	1		ḪIMD		IJA					ḪI-IM-DI-IA		M+
			ḪIMD				ʾIRR		A	ḪI-ME-ID-IR$_3$-RA		M+
			ḪIMD				ʾIRR		A	ḪI-MI-ID-D-IR$_3$-RA		M+
			ḪIMD				KAKK		A	ḪI-MI-ID-KA-AK-KA		M
			ḪIMD		I		MALIK			ḪI-IM-DI-MA-LIK		M
ḪINAN	1		ḪINAN		UM					I-NA-NU-UM		I
ḪININ	1		ḪININ		UM					EN-NE-NU-UM		B 44+
			ḪININ		UM					EN-NI-NU-UM		SIMMONS 48 5+
ḪINN	1		ḪINN		IJA					ḪI-NI-IA	FN	X 116 3
			ḪINN	AN	U					ḪI-NA-NU		KISURRA 62 SEAL
			ḪINN	AT	UM					ḪI-NA-TUM	FN	RA LXV 59 II 66
			ḪINN	ATAN	UM					IN-NA-TA-NU-UM		TA 1931, 294
			ḪINN		A		BAWŠ	AT		E-NA-BA-ŠA-AT		ICK 63 2+ CAPP.
			ḪINN		A		BAWŠ	AT	A	E-NA-BA-ŠA-TA		EL II P. 171 N. CAPP.
			ḪINN		I		BAWŠ	AT		E-NI-BA-ŠA-AT		ICK 113 10 CAPP.
			ḪINN		I		BAWŠ	AT	A	E-NI-BA-ŠA-TA		KTS 47C 1 CAPP.
			ḪINN		I		HADD		U	IN-NI-D-IM		A.
			ḪINN		I		ʾIL			ḪI-IN-NE-DINGIR		XIII 1 I 53
			ḪINN		I		ʿAŠTAR			EN-NI-D-EŠ$_4$-DAR		A. 247 23
			ḪINN		I		BAJN	AH		IN-NI-BA-NA	FN NOM	X 81 4
	2		NAPŠ		I		ḪINN		I	NA-AP-SI-IN-NI	FN	XIII 1 IV 72
			ŠUM		I		ḪINN		I	ŠU-MI-IN-NI		U
ḪINUN	1		ḪINUN		UM					E-NU-NU-UM		SIMMONS 112 20
			ḪINUN		AM					I-NU-NAM	NOM	SIMMONS 51 3+
			ḪINUN				ʾEL			I-NU-UN-E-EL		UET V 569 2
ḪIRAB	1		ḪIRAB	AN						ḪI-RA-BA-AN		RA LXV 42 II 57
ḪIRB	2		ʿAN		UM		ḪIRB		I	A-NU-UM-ḪI-IR-BI		BALKAN, LETTER P. 6
			MUT				ḪIRB	AN		MU-UT-ḪI-IR-BA?-AN		VIII 11 4
ḪIṢN	1		ḪIṢN		I					ḪI-IZ-NI		B 20 HANA
			ḪIṢN	AN	UM					ḪI-IZ-NA-NU-UM		WALTERS, WL 93:2, 14
			ḪIṢN		I		DAGAN			ḪI-IZ-NI-D-DA-GAN		B 20+ HANA
ḪKUM	1	JA	ḪKUM		UM					IA-AḪ-KU-MU-UM		B 26
ḪLAJ	1	JI	ḪLAJ				HADD		U	IḪ-LA-D-IM		XIII 1 II 76
ḪLAM	1	ʾA	ḪLAM		U					AḪ-LA-MU		M+
		ʾA	ḪLAM		U					AḪ-LA-AM-MU		XII 508 2
		ʾA	ḪLAM		U					AḪ-LA-A-MU		XI 208 2
ḪLIJ	1	JI	ḪLIJ			JA				IḪ-LI-IA		XIII 139 18
		JI	ḪLIJ	AN						IḪ-LI-IA-AN		RA LXV 42 II 73+
		JI	ḪLIJ				HADD		U	IḪ-LI-A-DU		A. P. 133+
		JI	ḪLIJ				HADD		U	IḪ-LI$_3$-A-DU		A. P. 133
		JI	ḪLIJ				ʿAŠTAR			IḪ-LI-AŠ-TAR		A. 55 35
		JI	ḪLIJ				ʿAŠTAR			IḪ-LI-EŠ$_4$-DAR		A. P. 133+
		JA	ḪLIJ				ʾIL			IA-AḪ-LI-DINGIR		B 26
ḪMAD	1	JA	ḪMAD		UM					IA-AḪ-MA-DU-UM		CT XLV 5 7
ḪNUN	1	JA	ḪNUN				ʾIL			IA-ḪU-UN-DINGIR		M+

STEMS

ḪNUN	1	JA	ḪNUN					ʾIL				IA-NU-UN-DINGIR		RA LXV 51 IX 65
		JA	ḪNUN					MAʾT		UM		IA-UN-MA-TUM	FN	RA L 63
		JA	ḪNUN					PI						
								ʾEL				IA-ḪU-UN-PI-EL		SIMMONS 54 18
	2		ʾADM		U		TA	ḪNUN	AN			D-AD-MU-TA-ḪU-NA-AN	FN	RA LXV 61 IV 38
			ʾANN		U		TA	ḪNUN				AN-NU-TA-AḪ-NU-UN	FN	RA LXV 61 IV 15+
ḪRIM	1	ME	ḪRIM		IM							ME-EḪ-RI-MI-IM	GEN	M+
ḪṢIN	1	JA	ḪṢIN					ḪAJJ		A		IA-AḪ-ZI-IN-E_2-A		XIII 1 VII 23
		JA	ḪṢIN					ʾIRR		A		IA-AḪ-ZI-IN-IR_3-RA		M
		JA	ḪṢIN					DAGAN				IA-AḪ-ZI-IN-D-DA-GAN		M
		TA	ḪṢIN					ʾADM		U		TA-AḪ-ZI-IN-AD-MU	FN	M
ḪṢUN	1	JA	ḪṢUN		UM							IA-ZU-NU-UM		SIMMONS 125 13+
		JA	ḪṢUN					ʾIL				IA-AḪ-ZU-UN-DINGIR		BE VI/1 7 18
ḪUBAS	1		ḪUBAS		UM							ḪU-BA-ZU-UM		TA 1931, 218
			ḪUBAS		UM							ḪU-BA-ZUM		VAS VIII 14 33
			ḪUBAS		UM							U_2-BA-ZU-UM		SIMMONS 118 17+
			ḪUBAS		IM							U_2-BA-ZI-IM	GEN	SIMMONS 118 2
			ḪUBAS	AN								ḪU-BA-ZA-AN		M
			ḪUBAS		A							ḪU-BA-AZ-ZA		M+
ḪUBUS	1		ḪUBUS									ḪU-BU-UZ		M
ḪUMAD	1		ḪUMAD		I							ḪU-MA-DI		PINCHES, PEEK 1 4
ḪUMUD	2		ʾIL		I			ḪUMUD		I		I_3-LI_2-ḪU-MU-DI		M
ḪUNIN	1		ḪUNIN	AH								U_2-NI-NA	FN	M+
			ḪUNIN	AN	UM							ḪU-NI-NA-NU-UM		I
	2		ʾIL		I			ḪUNIN		I		I_3-LI_2-U_2-NE-NI		RUTTEN 6 20
ḪUNN	1		ḪUNN	AT	UM							ḪU-UN-NA-TUM	MN	CT XLV 49 8+
			ḪUNN	AN	UM							ḪU-NA-NU-UM		TA 30 615 18+
			ḪUNN	AN	IM							ḪU-NA-NIM	GEN	B 93
			ḪUNN		IJA							ḪU-NI-IA		UCP X/3 2:22; M
			ḪUNN					ḪUPŠ		I		ḪU-UN-ḪU-UP-ŠE		U
			ḪUNN					PI						
								ʾEL				ḪU-UN-BI-EL		SIMMONS 82 7
			ḪUNN					ŠULGI				ḪU-UN-D-ŠUL-GI		U
			ḪUNN					ZANZI				ḪU-UN-ZA-AN-ZI	FN	XIII 1 IX 42
			ḪUNN					ZANZI				ḪU-UN-ZA-ZI	FN	XIII 1 IX 34, C
			ḪUNN		U			ʾEL				U_3-NU-EL		TA 31 223
	2		ʾAB		I			ḪUNN		I		A-BI-ḪU-UN?-NI		B 10
			ʾIMIR					ḪUNN		A		IM-ME-IR?-ḪU-UN-NA		A. 43 9
			ʿAQB		A			ḪUNN		UM		AQ-BA-ḪU-NI-UM		B 11
			LA					ḪUNN		IM		LA-ḪU-NI-IM	GEN	M
ḪUNUN	1		ḪUNUN		U							UN-NU-NU		YOS XIII 139:9+
			ḪUNUN		I			ʾEL				U_2-NU-NI-EL		B 40
			ḪUNUN		I			ʾIL				U_2-NU-NI-DINGIR		PBS XI/2 P. 125 NO. 347
ḪURB	1		ḪURB	ATANU								UR-BA-TA-NU		KISURRA 24 6
	2		ʿAMM		U			ḪURB		I		AM-MU-UR-BI		A.
			ʾAN		I	Š		ḪURB		I		A-NI-IŠ-ḪU-UR-BI		M+
ḪUSUD	1		ḪUSUD		UM							ḪU-ZU-DU-UM	FN	RA LXV 60 III 41
ḪUṢAN	1		ḪUṢAN		U							ḪU-ZA-NU		M
			ḪUṢAN		UM							ḪU-ZA-A-NU-UM		BIN VII 101:3
			ḪUṢAN		I							ḪU-ZA-NI	NOM	B 45
			ḪUṢAN	AH								U_2-ZA-NA	FN	XIII 1 II 68
ḪZIQ	1	MA	ḪZIQ		UM							MA-ZI-GU-UM		CT XLVIII 27 CASE
		ME	ḪZIQ		A							ME-ZI-QA		M
		ME	ḪZIQ	AN								ME-ZI-QA-AN		RA LXV 44 IV 30
ḪZUQ	1	JA	ḪZUQ					ʾIL				IA-AḪ-ZU?-UQ-DINGIR		CT XLVIII 10 3
ḪAʾAN	1		ḪAʾAN	AN								ḪA-A-NA-AN		C+
			ḪAʾAN		A			LA			HA	ḪA-A-NA-LA-A	FN	XIII 1 II 53+
ḪAʾAZ	1		ḪAʾAZ		U			ʾIL				ḪA?-A-ZU-DINGIR		M
ḪAʾD	1		ḪAʾD	ATAN								ḪA-DA-TA-AN		M+
ḪAʾL	1		ḪAʾL		UM							ḪA-LU-UM		B 19
			ḪAʾL		UM							ḪA-A-LUM		UCP X/1 34 12
			ḪAʾL		U							ḪA-A-LU		A
			ḪAʾL		AJA							ḪA-LA-A-A		B 18
			ḪAʾL	AN	UM							ḪA-LA-NU-UM		KISURRA 57 4, SEAL
			ḪAʾL	AN	UM							ḪA-LA-NUM_2		KISURRA 24 2
			ḪAʾL		A	NA						ḪA-LA?-NA	FN	RA LXV 59 II 74

STEMS

ḪAʾL	1		ḪAʾL		IJA						ḪA-LI-IA		C, A. LATE
			ḪAʾL		IJA						ḪA-LI$_2$-IA		C+
			ḪAʾL		IJA						ḪA-LI$_2$-IA		RA LXV 47 VI 64; C+
			ḪAʾL		IJAN						ḪA-LI-IA-AN		A. LATE
			ḪAʾL	ATAN							ḪA-LA-TA-AN		M+
			ḪAʾL	AT	UM						ḪA-LA-TUM		KISURRA 104 8
			ḪAʾL		I			HADD	U		ḪA-LI$_2$-D-IM		M+
			ḪAʾL		I			HADD	U		ḪA-LI-A-DU		A.+
			ḪAʾL		I			HADD	U		ḪA-LI-IA-[D]U		M
			ḪAʾL		I			ʿADN			ḪA-LI-ḪA-DU-UN		M+
			ḪAʾL		I			ʿADN			ḪA-LI$_2$-ḪA-DU-UN		M+
			ḪAʾL		I			ʿADN			ḪA-LI-ḪA-DU-UM?		M
			ḪAʾL		I			ʿADN	U	HU	ḪA-LI-ḪA-AD-NU-U$_2$		M
			ḪAʾL		I			ʿAḎIR	UM		ḪA-LI-A-ṢI-RUM		UNPUBL.
			ḪAʾL		I			ʾIL			ḪA-LI$_2$-DINGIR		B 18
			ḪAʾL		I			ʾEL			ḪA-LI$_2$-EL		RA LXV 42 III 18+
			ḪAʾL		I			ʾEL			ḪA-A-LI$_2$-EL		RA LXV 42 III 20
			ḪAʾL		I			ʾIL	U	HU	ḪA-A-LI$_2$-I-LU-U$_2$		X 146 5
			ḪAʾL		I			ʿAŠTAR			ḪA-LI$_2$-EŠ$_4$-DAR		RA LXV 53 XII 1
			ḪAʾL		I			KUPAPA			ḪA-LI$_2$-KU-BA-BA	FN	RA LXV 58 I 14
			ḪAʾL		I			MA			ḪA-LI-MA	FN	RA LXV 59 II 43
			ḪAʾL		I			MA					
								ʾIL			ḪA-LI$_2$-MA-DINGIR		M
			ḪAʾL		I			MALIK			ḪA-LI$_2$-MA-LIK		M+
			ḪAʾL		I			MAMM	A		ḪA-LI$_2$-D-M[A-A]M-M[A]		M
			ḪAʾL		I			MARAṢ			ḪA-LI-MA-RA-AṢ		GEN, KICH I P. 59 NO. 219
			ḪAʾL		I			MARAṢ			ḪA-LI-MA-RA-AṢ		UET V 521 1
			ḪAʾL		I		MU	WTAR			ḪA-LI$_2$-MU-TAR		M
			ḪAʾL		I			ŠADW	A		ḪA-LI-SA-DA		B 19
			ḪAʾL		I		TA	NWUḪ	A		ḪA-LI-TA-NU-A		A.+
			ḪAʾL		UJAN						ḪA-LU-JA-AN		RA LXV 41 II 33+
			ḪAʾL		U			ʿADN	U		ḪA-LU-ḪA-AD-NU		M+
			ḪAʾL		U			ʾIL			ḪA-LU-DINGIR		M
			ḪAʾL		U			MAṬAR			ḪA-LU-MA-DA-AR		M+
			ḪAʾL		U			NIʿM			ḪA-LU-NI-ḪI-IM		RA LXV 52 X 74
			ḪAʾL		U			RAPIʾ			ḪA-LU-RA-PI		M+
			ḪAʾL		UM			MAṬAR			ḪA-LUM-MA-DAR		C, SIMMONS 67 SEAL
			ḪAʾL		UM			MAṬAR	I		ḪA-LUM-MA-DA-RI		SIMMONS 67 B 11
			ḪAʾL		UM			MAṬAR	I		ḪA-LUM-MA-DAR-RI		SIMMONS 67 11
			ḪAʾL		U	Š		MI					
								ʾIL			ḪA-LU-UŠ-MI-DINGIR		M
	2		ʾAJA					ḪAʾL	U		A-IA-ḪA-LU		M
			ʾAB		U			ḪAʾL	UM		A-BU-ḪA-LUM		UCP X P. 53, M
			ʾAB		UM			ḪAʾL	UM		A-BU-UM-ḪA-LUM		B 11+
			ʾAB		UM			ḪAʾL	UM		A-BU-UM-ḪA-LU-UM		B 11+
			ʾAB		U			ḪAʾL	IM		A-BU-ḪA-LIM	GEN	M+
			JADAʿ					ḪAʾL	UM		IA-DA-AḪ-ḪA-LUM		B 25
			ʾIL		A			ḪAʾL	UM		DINGIR-ḪA-LUM		B 21
			ʾIL		A			ḪAʾL	U	HU	DINGIR-ḪA-LU-U$_2$		XIII 1 IV 18
			ʾIL		I			ḪAʾL	UM		I$_3$-LI$_2$-ḪA-LU-UM		CT XLV 3 10
			ʿAMM		U			ḪAʾL	UM		ḪA-AM-MU-ḪA-LUM		M+
		JI	JṢIʾ					ḪAʾL	U		I-ZI-ḪA-LU		XIV 96:9+
			ʿAZZ		U			ḪAʾL	IM		A-ZU-ḪA-LIM	NOM	M
			ḎIMR		U			ḪAʾL	A		ZI-IM-RU-ḪA-LA		BM 17045
		JA	GJIḪ					ḪAʾL	UM		IA-GI?-ḪA-LUM		RUTTEN 16 18
			MUT					ḪAʾL	I		MU-UT-ḪA-LI		B 35 HANA
			MUT					ḪAʾL	I				
								MA			MU-UT-ḪA-LI-MA		M
		Š	NUʾR					ḪAʾL	I		ŠU-NU-UR-ḪA-LI		KING LIH I 22 4, R. 2
		Š	NUʾR		A			ḪAʾL	U		ŠU-NU-UḪ-RA-ḪA-LU		M+
		Š	NUʾR		A			ḪAʾL	U	HU	ŠU-NU-UḪ-RA-ḪA-LU-U$_2$		M+
		Š	NUʾR		A			ḪAʾL	U	HU	ŠU-NU-ḪU-RA-ḪA-LU-U$_2$		XIV 11:1
		Š	NUʾR		A			ḪAʾL	U	HU	ŠU-NU-UḪ-ḪU-RA-ḪA-LU-U$_2$		XIV 36:1+
		Š	NUʾR		U			ḪAʾL	U		ŠU-NU-UḪ-RU-ḪA-LU		M+
		JA	RWIM					ḪAʾL			IA-RI-IM-ḪA-AL		M+
		JA	ŠWUB					ḪAʾL			IA-ŠU-UB-ḪA-AL		RA LXV 44 IV 28

STEMS

ḪAʾL	2		ŠUWB					ḪAʾL	I	SU-UB-ḪA-LI		A. 268 5
			ŠUWB		A			ḪAʾL	I	ŠU-BA-ḪA-LI		A. 97 16, 18+
			ŠUWB		A			ḪAʾL	I	SU-BA-ḪA-LI		A. 6 29
			ŠUWB		A			ḪAʾL	I	SU-PA-ḪA-LI		A. 252 12+
		JA	ŚLIJ					ḪAʾL		IA-AŠ?-LI?-ḪA-AL		M
			ŚUM		U			ḪAʾL	A	SU-MU-ḪA-LA		B 39
	3		KA					ṢUWR	I			
								ḪAʾL	A	KA-ZU-RI-ḪA-LA		M
ḪAʾN	1		ḪAʾN		A					ḪA-NA-KI	GN	M+
			ḪAʾN	IJ	U					ḪA-NU-U$_2$		JNES XIII 210+ LATE
			ḪAʾN		A			ʾAB	I	ḪA-NA-A-BI		TIM II 113 2, 8
	2		MUT					ḪAʾN	A	MU-UT-ḪA-NA		XIV 47:31
ḪAʾR	1		ḪAʾR		IJA					ḪA-RI-IA		M+
			ḪAʾR		I			ʾIL		ḪA-RI-DINGIR		BM 82372 27
			ḪAʾR		I			ʾATT	A	ḪA-RI-A-TA		C II 5 7
			ḪAʾR		I			MALIK		ḪA-RI-MA-LIK		BE VI/1 46 5
			ḪAʾR		I			MALIK	I	ḪA-RI-MA-LI-KI	GEN	B 20
	2	JI	JṢIʾ					ḪAʾR	U	I-ZI-ḪA-RU		XIV 52:5, 16+
ḪAʾŠ	1		ḪAʾŠ	AT	UM					ḪA-SA-TUM	MN	RUTTEN 15 6 SEAL
			ḪAʾŠ	AN	U					ḪA-SA-NU		M
	2		MUT					ḪAʾŠ	UM	MU-UT-ḪA-SU-UM		A.
ḪAʾT	2		ʿAḎR		I			ḪAʾT	UM	AD-RI-ḪA-TUM		SIMMONS 88 16+
			ʾUMM		I			ḪAʾT	UM	UM-MI-ḪA-TUM	FN	M+
		TA	KWUN					ḪAʾT	UM	TA-KU-UN-ḪA-TUM	FN	M+
		TA	RʿIŠ					ḪAʾT	U	TA-RI-IŠ-ḪA-AT-TU	FN	M+
			ŚAMAʿ					ḪAʾT	IM	ŠA-MA-ḪA-TIM	GEN	XIII 1 VIII 44
		TA	TWUR					ḪAʾT	UM	TA-DUR-ḪA-TUM		TA 1931, 489
ḪAʾZ	1		ḪAʾZ	UT	UM					ḪA-ZU-TUM	FN	RA LXV 58 II 1
ḪAḪUN	1		ḪAḪUN		A					ḪA-ḪU-NA		CT II 23 33
ḪAWIR	1		ḪAWIR			NI				ḪA-WI-IR-NI		RA LXV 45 V 12
ḪAWR	1		ḪAWR					ʾAB	I	ḪA-AW-RA-BI		TIM IV 33 21, 34 14
			ḪAWR	AN	IM					ḪA-AW-RA-NIM	GEN	B 44
			ḪAWR	AN				ʾAB	I	ḪA-AW-RA-AN-A-BI		M
			ḪAWR	AN				ʾAB	I	ḪA-AW-RA-NA-A-BI		M+
ḪABAD	1		ḪABAD		UM					ḪA-BA-TUM	FN	RA LXV 59 II 76
			ḪABAD		U			ʾIL		ḪA-BA-DU-DINGIR		M
	2		ʾIL		A			ḪABAD		DINGIR-ḪA-BA-AD		M+
ḪABIʾ	1		ḪABIʾ			JA				ḪA-BI-IA		RA LXV 52 X 71
			ḪABIʾ	AN	U					ḪA-BI-A-NU		YOS XIII 175:12
			ḪABIʾ					HADD	U	ḪA-BI-D-IM		M
ḪABIR	1		ḪABIR		IM					ḪA-BI-RI-IM	GEN	M
			ḪABIR	AN						ḪA-BI-RA-AN		RA LXV 54 XII 21
ḪABUR	1		ḪABUR		I					ḪA-BU-UR-RI	FN	RA LXV 63 III 1
			ḪABUR				JI	JBAL				
								BUGAŠ		ID$_2$-ḪA-BUR-I-BA-AL-BU-GA-AŠ$_2$		BRM IV 52 HANA
ḪABZUR	1		ḪABZUR	AN						ḪA-AB-ZU-RA-AN		RA LXV 48 VIII 21+
ḪAGIR	1		ḪAGIR		UM					ḪA-GI-RUM		M
ḪAGUR	1		ḪAGUR	AH						ḪA-GU-RA	FN	RA LXV 64 V 63
ḪALAN	1		ḪALAN		I			JATAR		ḪA-LA-NI-E-TAR		M
ḪALD	1		ḪALD		A			MULUK		ḪA?-AL-DA-MU-LU-UK		BASOR 95 21
ḪAMAŚ	1		ḪAMAŚ	AT	UM					ḪA-MA-SA-TUM	MN	CT XLV 91 20
ḪAMAṬ	1		ḪAMAṬ		I			ʾIL		ḪA-MA-TI-IL		FIGULLA, CAT. I 14135
ḪAMBUZ	1		ḪAMBUZ		U	HU				ḪA-AM-BU-ZU-U$_2$		B 19
ḪAMR	1		ḪAMR		U					ḪA-AM-RU		C
			ḪAMR		U			RAPIʾ		ḪA-AM-RU-RA-BI		M
ḪAMŚ	1		ḪAMŚ	AT	UM					ḪA-AM-SA-TUM	FN	BM 16844+
ḪAMUJ	2		LA					ḪAMUJ	IM	LA-ḪA-MU-JI-IM	GEN	M
ḪANAŠ	1		ḪANAŠ		I					ḪA-NA-ŠI	GEN	HARRIS 3916
ḪANB	1		ḪANB	AT	UM					ḪA-AN-BA-TUM	FN	CT XLV 91 18+
ḪAND	1		ḪAND		IJA					ḪA-AN-DI-IA		BIN VII 63 28
ḪANDEN	2		BIN		A			ḪANDEN		BI-NA-ḪA-AN-DI-EN		M
ḪANP	1		ḪANP	AT	UM					ḪA-AN-PA-TUM	FN	A 3521 29
			ḪANP	AT	IM					ḪA-AN-PA-TIM	FN GEN	A 3521 31
ḪANZ	1		ḪANZ		I					ḪA-AN-ZI		TA 1931, 434
			ḪANZ		A			HADD	U	ḪA-AN-ZA-D-IM		M
ḪANZUR	1		ḪANZUR		A					ḪA-AN-ZU-RA		VAS IX 172 39+

STEMS

ḪAPIʾ	1	JA	ḪAPIʾ				ʾIL			IA-ḪA-AP-PI-I-IL5	GN	JCS XVIII 59 12+
ḪAQAT	1		ḪAQAT		A					ḪA-QA-TA		DELAPORTE CCL II A 914
ḪARḪAR	1		ḪARḪAR		U					ḪAR-ḪA-RU		JNES XIII 210+ LATE
ḪARAR	2	JA	KWUN				ḪARAR			IA-KU-UN-ḪA-RA-AR		VAS IX 172 4+
		JA	KWUN				ḪARAR	I		IA-KU-[UN-ḪA]-RA-RI	GEN	BM 81641 6
		JA	KWUN				ḪARAR	I		IA-KUN$_3$-ḪA-RA-RI		CT XLVIII 3:3
		JI	KWUN				ḪARAR	I		I-KU-UN-ḪA-RA-RI?	GEN	TCL I 151 4
ḪARGAL	1		ḪARGAL							ḪA-AR-GA-AL		M
			ḪARGAL		UM					ḪA-AR-GA-LUM		VAS VIII 14 26
ḪARIJ	2		ʿAMM		I	Š	ḪARIJ		JE	AM-MI-IS-ḪA-RI?-E?		JEAN, S'A CLXXXVIII R. 3
ḪARIR	1		ḪARIR		UM					ḪA-RI-RUM		B 20
			ḪARIR		UM					ḪA-AR-RI-RUM		B 20
		MU	ḪARIR		IM					MU-ḪA-RI-RI-IM	GEN	M
ḪAŠAM	2		ḎIMR		I		ḪAŠAM			ZI-IM-RI-ḪA-SA-AM	NOM	C+
ḪAŠIJ	1		ḪAŠIJ	AN	UM					ḪA-ŠI-A-NU-UM		TA 1931, 538 III
ḪAŠT	1		ḪAŠT	AT	UM					ḪA-AŠ-TA-TUM	FN	XIII 1 III 62
ḪAŠḪAŠ	1		ḪAŠḪAŠ		UM					ḪA-AŠ-ḪA-ŠUM		KISURRA 62 3
ḪAŠIŠ	1		ḪAŠIŠ		UM					ḪA-ŠI-ŠUM		B 20+
ḪAŠŠ	1		ḪAŠŠ		UM					ḪA-AŠ-ŠUM		RA LXV 47 VII 27
ḪAŠTUR	1		ḪAŠTUR		UM					ḪA-AŠ-TU-RU-UM		YOS VIII 139 15 CASE 13
ḪATAʾ	1		ḪATAʾ		A		ʾAR	UM		ḪA-TA-A-A-RUM?		CT XXIX 8A 1
			ḪATAʾ				ʾUMAN	UM		ḪA-TA-UM-MA-NU-UM		RA VIII 74 19
ḪATAN	1		ḪATAN				PI					
							ʾIL			ḪA-TA-AN-BI-DINGIR		M
	2		ʾAB		I		ḪATAN			A-BI-ḪA-TA-AN		B 10
ḪATIʾ	1	JA	ḪATIʾ				ʾIL			IA-ḪA-AT-TI-DINGIR		M+, C
		JA	ḪATIʾ				ʾEL			IA-ḪA-TI-EL		RA LXV 44 IV 46
		JA	ḪATIʾ				ʾIL			IA-ḪA-TI-DINGIR		RUTTEN 15:2+; M
		JA	ḪATIʾ				ʾIL	UM		IA-ḪA-TI-LUM		YOS XII
		JA	ḪATIʾ				ŠAMŠ			IA-ḪA-AT-TI-D-UTU		UCP X/1 89 15
ḪAZIM	1		ḪAZIM		UM					ḪA-ZI-MU-UM		HARRIS 63 16
ḪBAʾ	1	JA	ḪBAʾ				RAŠAP			IA-AḪ-BA-D-RA-SA-AP		XIII 94 5
ḪBIʾ	1	JA	ḪBIʾ				ʾIL	A		IA-AḪ-BI-LA-KI	GN	M+
ḪBUʾ	1	JA	ḪBUʾ		UM					IA-AḪ-BU-U$_2$-UM		M
ḪBUD	1	ʾA	ḪBUD	IJ	UM					AḪ-BU-TE-UM		U
ḪIʾAN	1		ḪIʾAN		A					ḪI-A-NA		BM 80328 4
ḪIʾD	1		ḪIʾD	AT	UM					ḪI-DA-TUM	FN	XIII 1 V 54
			ḪIʾD				LA		KA	ḪI-I[D]-LA-A?-KA		XII 141 8
			ḪIʾD				LA		KA			
							ʾIL	I		ḪI-ID-LA-KA-I$_3$-LI$_2$		M
			ḪIʾD				LA			ḪI-ID-L[A]-NAM		XIII 38 27
ḪIʾL	1		ḪIʾL	AT	UM					ḪI-LA-TUM	FN	XIII 1 II 71
	2		ʾAḪ		I		ḪIʾL			A-ḪI-ḪI-EL		XIII 1 X 17
			ʾAB		I		ḪIʾL			A-BI-ḪI-EL		B 10, M
			ʾAB		I		ḪIʾL			A-BI-ḪI-IL		M
			ʾAB		I		ḪIʾL	U		A-BI-ḪE$_2$-LU		MRS VI P. 240 LATE
			ʾAB		UM		ḪIʾL	UM		A-BU-UM-ḪI-LUM		B 11
ḪIBAR	1		ḪIBAR	AT	I					ḪI-BA-RA-TI	MN NOM	VIII 6 31
ḪIBR	1		ḪIBR	AN						Ḫ[I-I]B-RA-AN		RA LXV P. 42 III 6
ḪIGUL	1		ḪIGUL	AH						ḪI-GU-LA	FN	M+
ḪILḪIL	1		ḪILḪIL		UM					ḪI-EL-ḪI-LUM		SIMMONS 111 3
			ḪILḪIL		UM					ḪI-IL-ḪI-LUM		B 48+
ḪILUK	1		ḪILUK	AH						ḪI-LU?-KA	FN	XIII 1 V 81
ḪIMʾ	1		ḪIMʾ	AT	UM					ḪI-IM-A-TUM	FN	XIII 1 X 40
ḪIML	1		ḪIML		UM		....			Ḫ[I-I]M-LU-UM-[....]	FN	M
ḪIMR	2		KUʾŠ		I		ḪIMR	I		KU-ŠI-ḪI-IM-RI		SIMMONS 87 19
ḪINIʾ	1		ḪINIʾ		I					ḪI-NI-I		XII 1 VIII 51
ḪIRD	1		ḪIRD		IJA					ḪI-IR-DI-IA		RA LXV 53 XI 50
ḪIRṢ	1		ḪIRṢ		UM					ḪI-IR-ZU-UM		RA LXV 48 VIII 6
			ḪIRṢ		U	K				ḪI-IR-ZU-UK		RA LXV 51 IX 44
ḪIŠŠ	1		ḪIŠŠ	AT	UM					ḪI-IŠ-ŠA-TUM	FN	WATERMAN
ḪIZR	1		ḪIZR		IJAN					ḪI-IZ-RI-IA-AN		M
ḪMUM	1	JA	ḪMUM		IM					IA-AḪ-MU-MI-IM	GN GEN	M
		JA	ḪMUM		AM					IA-AḪ-MU-MA-AM-KI	GN ACC	M
ḪMUṬ	1	JA	ḪMUṬ		UM					IA-AḪ-MU-TU-UM-KI	GN	UET V 9721
		JA	ḪMUṬ		U					IA-AḪ-MU-TU		JEAN,TELL SIFR 13 15

ḪMUṬ	1	JA	ḪMUṬ	AN						IA-AḪ-MU-DA-AN		M
ḪNUW	2		ʾIL		I	JI	ḪNUW		HU	I_3-LI_2-IḪ-NU-U_2		UCP X/1 19:4+
ḪŠIJ	1	JA	ḪŠIJ				ʾIL			IA-AḪ-SI-DINGIR		OLZ VIII 350 2
		JA	ḪŠIJ				ʾIL			JA-AḪ-SI-DINGIR		M
ḪŠIM	1	MA	ḪŠIM	AN	UM					MA-AḪ-ŠI-MA-NU-UM		B 46+
ḪŠIR	2		LA			ʾA	ḪŠIR	UM		LA-AḪ-SI-RU-UM		BM 80368 2
ḪTAN	2		ʾIL		I	ʾA	ḪTAN			I_3-LI_2-AḪ-TA-AN		RUTTEN 6 16+
ḪTIN	1	ŠT	ḪTIN				ʾIL			(E_2-)ŠA-TA-AḪ-TI-IN-DINGIR	GN	KISURRA
ḪTAʾ	2		ʾIL		I	JI	ḪTAʾ					
							LI		JA	I_3-LI_2-IḪ-TA-LI-A		BIROT,TEA 69 I 14
ḪUʾD	1		ḪUʾD	AN	UM					ḪU-DA-A-NU-UM		SIMMONS 83 8
ḪUʾT	1		ḪUʾT	AN	UM					ḪU-TA-NU-UM		B 45
ḪUʾZ	1		ḪUʾZ	AN	UM					ḪU-ZA-NU-UM		RA LXV 55 XIII 13+
ḪUWAL	1		ḪUWAL		UM					ḪU-WA-LUM		B 20
			ḪUWAL		IM					ḪU-WA-LI-IM	GEN	B 20
ḪUBAD	1		ḪUBAD		UM					ḪU-PA-DU-UM		WATERMAN 14 R. 14
			ḪUBAD		I					ḪU-PA-DI		EDZARD, DER 101:12
ḪUBD	1		ḪUBD	AT	UM					ḪU-UP-DA-T[UM]	FN	XIII 1 VII 65
ḪUBR	1		ḪUBR	AT	UM					ḪU-UB-RA-TUM	FN	XIII 1 IX 31
ḪUBUR	2		MUT				ḪUBUR			MU-UT-ḪU-BUR		SYRIA V 271, 275
ḪUGUL	1		ḪUGUL		UM					ḪU-GU-LU[M]		HARRIS 79 4
ḪULAŠ	1		ḪULAŠ		AJA					ḪU-LA-ŠA-A		HARRIS 75 22
ḪULM	1		ḪULM		EJA					ḪU-UL-ME-I[A]		RA LXV 41 II 46
ḪUMR	1		ḪUMR	AN	UM					ḪU-UM-RA-NU-UM		U
ḪUMUŠ	1		ḪUMUŠ	AT	UM					ḪU-MU-SA-TUM	MN	TCL I 62 3
ḪUNAŠ	1		ḪUNAŠ		UM					ḪU-NA-ŠUM		BM 82432
ḪUPŠ	1		ḪUPŠ		UM					ḪU-UP-ŠUM		CT XLVIII 91 REV.
	2		ḪUNN				ḪUPŠ	I		ḪU-UN-ḪU-UP-ŠE		U
ḪURAṢ	1		ḪURAṢ	AT	UM					ḪU-RA-ZA-TUM	FN	XIII 1 I 73+
			ḪURAṢ		AJA					ḪU-RA-ZA-A-IA	FN	XIII 1 VIII 84
ḪURR	1		ḪURR	AN	UM					ḪU-UR-RA-NU-UM		CT IV 25C 15
ḪURŠAN	2		MUT		I		ḪURŠAN			MU-TI-ḪUR-SAG		YOS XII+
			MUT		I		ḪURŠAN	A		MU-TI-ḪU-UR-ŠA-NA		B 35+
			MUT		I		ḪURŠAN	I		MU-TI-ḪU-UR-ŠA-NI		YOS XII
ḪURṢ	1		ḪURṢ	AN	UM					ḪU-UR-ZA-NU-UM		B 44
			ḪURṢ	AN	U					ḪU-UR-ZA-NU-KI	GN	A.
			ḪURṢ	AN	IM					ḪUR-ZA-NIM	GEN	B 44
			ḪURṢ	AN	IM					ḪUR-ZA-A-NIM	GEN	B 44
			ḪURṢ	AN	IM					ḪU-UR-ZA-NIM	GEN	B 44
ḪURUṢ	1		ḪURUṢ		UM					ḪU-RU-ZUM		RA LXV 53 XI 16
			ḪURUṢ	AN						ḪU-RU-ZA-AN		RA LXV 44 IV 53+
			ḪURUṢ	AN	UM					ḪU-RU-ZA-NU-UM		B 44
ḪUŠŠ	1		ḪUŠŠ	UT	UM					ḪU-ŠU-TUM	FN	CT VI 43 6, 34
			ḪUŠŠ	UT	UM					ḪU-$UŠ_2$-ŠU-TUM	FN	X 96 3
			ḪUŠŠ	UT	IM					ḪU-ŠU-TIM	FN GEN	X 27 8
ḪUZAM	1		ḪUZAM		I					ḪU-ZA-MI		BE VI/2 138 18
ḪUZIR	1		ḪUZIR	AN						ḪU-ZI-RA-AN		RA LXV 50 VIII 67+
			ḪUZIR	AN	UM					ḪU-ZI-RA-NU-UM		B 45
			ḪUZIR	AT	UM					ḪU-ZI-RA-TUM		EDZARD, DER 99 REV 8
ḪUZM	1		ḪUZM	AN	UM					ḪU-UZ-MA-N[U-UM]		TA 1931, 265
			ḪUZM	ATAN						ḪU-IZ-MA-TA-AN		M
ḪZIM	1	JA	ḪZIM				....			IA-AḪ-ZI-IM-[....]		M
ḪZUM	1	JA	ḪZUM		U					IA-AḪ-ZU?-MU		BM 78799 12
ḪZUR	1	JA	ḪZUR				HADD	U		IA-AḪ-ZU-UR-D-IM		M
		JA	ḪZUR				ʾIL			IA-AḪ-ZU-UR-IL		TIM III 34 15A
		JA	ḪZUR				ʾIL			IA-AḪ-ZU-UR-DINGIR		JCS XXIV 57 NO 39 AND 51
ʿWUQ	1	JA	ʿWUQ		UM					IA-U_2-KU-UM		B 31+
ʿAWIQ	1		ʿAWIQ	AN						A-I-GA-AN		RA LXV 52 X 58
			ʿAWIQ	AT	UM					ḪA-I-KA-TUM	FN	SIMMONS 112:17
ʿABD	1		ʿABD		UM					ḪA-AB-DU-UM		B 9+, M+
			ʿABD		IM					AB-DI-IM	GEN	B 9, M
			ʿABD	AN						ḪA-AB-DA-AN		M, C+
			ʿABD	AN						AB-DA-AN		M
			ʿABD	AN	U					AB-DA-NU		CT XLV 59 6
			ʿABD	AN	U					AB-TA-NU		A. LATE
			ʿABD	AN	UM					ḪA-AB-DA-[NUM]?		PBS VIII/2 260 4

STEMS

ʿABD	1	ʿABD	AN	A				AB-TA-NA	NOM	A. LATE
		ʿABD	AT	UM				ḪA-AB-DA-TUM	FN	XIII 1 XIV 39
		ʿABD	ATAN					ḪA-AB-DA-TA-AN		M+
		ʿABD	ATAN					AB-[DA?-T]A-AN		RA LXV 44 IV 62
		ʿABD		AJA				AB-DA-A		GORDON 38 15+
		ʿABD		IJA				ḪA-AB-DI-IA		B 9+, M, C+
		ʿABD		IJA				AB-DI-IA		A.+
		ʿABD			ʾABN		IM	ARAD$_2$-AB-NIM		BAGHD. MITT. II 72
		ʿABD			HAND		U	ḪA-AB-DI-IA-AN-DU		KUPPER NOM. P. 231
		ʿABD			HAND		U	AB-DI-IA-DU		KUPPER NOM. P. 231
		ʿABD			HAND		U	AB-DU-IA-AN-DU		KUPPER NOM. P. 231
		ʿABD			HEDD		A	ḪA-AB-DI-E-D-IM		RS XIX 338F.
		ʿABD			HADD		U	AB-DI-AD-DU		BAGHD. MITT. II 57 28
		ʿABD			HADD		U	ḪA-AB-DU-D-IM		RA LXV 48 VIII 34
		ʿABD			ʿAḎR		A	ḪA-AB-DU-ḪA-AD-RA		M
		ʿABD			ʾEL			AB-DA-EL		TA 30, 615 9, 41
		ʿABD			ʾEL			ḪA-AB-DI-EL		KISURRA 74 17
		ʿABD			ʾIL			AB-TE-IL		I
		ʿABD			ʾIL			ḪA-AB-DI-DINGIR		B 9
		ʿABD			ʾIL			AB-DI-DINGIR		B 9+
		ʿABD			ʾIL		I	AB-DI-LI		A.+
		ʿABD			ḪAM		I	AB-DI-A-MI		BAGHD. MITT. II 58 III 21
		ʿABD			ḪAM		I	ḪA-AB-DU-D-A-MI		M+
		ʿABD			ḪAM		I	ḪA-AB-DU-A-MI		M
		ʿABD			ʿAMM		UM	ḪA-AB-DU-A-MU-UM		M
		ʿABD			ʿAMM		IM	AB-DU-A-MI-IM	NOM	M+
		ʿABD			ʿAMM		IM	AB-DU-A-MI-IM	GEN	M+
		ʿABD			ʿAMM		IM	ḪA-AB-DU-A-MI-IM		M
		ʿABD			ʿAN	AT		ḪA-AB-DU-D-ḪA-NA-AT		M+
		ʿABD			ʿAN	AT	I	AB-TA-NA-TI		A. P. 128A LATE +
		ʿABD			ʿAN	AT	I	AB-DI-A-NA-TI		A. P. 128B LATE +
		ʿABD			ʿAN	AT	I	AB-TI-A-NA-TI		JCS XIII 54 300, A. LATE
		ʿABD			JARAḪ			AB-DI-A-RA-AḪ		B 9+
		ʿABD			JARAḪ			ḪA-AB-DI-A-RA-AḪ		B 9
		ʿABD			JARAḪ			AB-DI-RA-AḪ		B 9+
		ʿABD			JARAḪ			ḪA-AB-DI-E-RA-AḪ		M+, C+
		ʿABD			JARAḪ			AB-DI-E-RA-AḪ		M+, UCP X P. 198+
		ʿABD			JARAḪ			ḪA-AB-DI-RA-AḪ		SUMER XXIII 162 46
		ʿABD			JARAḪ			AB-DI-D-EN-ZU		PBS VII/1 94 III 28
		ʿABD			JARAḪ			AB-DI-D-E-RA-AḪ		YOS XIII 199:22+
		ʿABD			JARAḪ			AB-DU-D-E-RA-AḪ		YOS XIII 218:13+
		ʿABD			JARAḪ			ḪA-AB-DU-E-RA-AḪ		DELAPORTE CCL II A 418 M
		ʿABD			JARAḪ			AB-DU-E-RA-AḪ		M+
		ʿABD			ʾIRŠAP		A	ḪA-AB-DU-IR?-ŠA-PA?		M
		ʿABD			ʾIŠḪAR	AH		AB-DI-D-IŠ-ḪA-RA		A.+
		ʿABD			ʾIŠḪAR	AH		ḪA-AB-DU-D-IŠ-ḪA-RA		XIII 1 II 79+
		ʿABD			ʾAŠUR		A	ḪA-AB-DU-A-ŠU-RA		M
		ʿABD			ʿAŠTAR			AB-DI-D-EŠ$_4$-DAR		A. 19 4, 7
		ʿABD			ʿAŠTAR			AB-DU-EŠ$_4$-DAR		M+
		ʿABD			ʿAŠTAR			ḪA-AB-DU-EŠ$_4$-DAR		M+, C+
		ʿABD			ʿIŠTAR	AH		AB-DU-IŠ-TA-RA?		B 9
		ʿABD			ʾUTL		I	AB-DU-UT-LI	FN	A. LATE
		ʿABD			BAʿL	AH		ḪA-AB-DU-BA-AḪ-LA		M
		ʿABD			BAʿL	AT	I	ḪA-AB-DU-BA-AḪ-LA-TI		M+
		ʿABD			DAGAN			ḪA-AB-DU-D-DA-GAN		M
		ʿABD			DAGAN			AB-DU-D-DA-GAN		M
		ʿABD			KUʾB		I	ḪA-AB-DU-KU-BI		M+
		ʿABD			MA					
					DAGAN			AB-DU-MA-D-DA-GAN		M+
		ʿABD			MA					
					DAGAN			ḪA-AB-DU-MA-D-DA-GAN		M+
		ʿABD			MALIK			ḪA-AB-DU-MA-LIK		M+
		ʿABD			MALIK			AB-DU-MA-LIK		XIII 37 16
		ʿABD			MALIK		I	AB-DU-MA-LI-KI		YOS XIII 54:5
		ʿABD			NAHR			AB-DI-D-ID$_2$		SCHEIL 10 15, 16
		ʿABD			NAWAR			ḪA-AB-DU-NA-WA-AR		M

STEMS

ʿABD	1		ʿABD					NAWAR			AB-DU-NA-W[A-AR]		M
			ʿABD					ŠUWR	I		AB-DU-ŠU-RI		IRAQ XXX 94, RIMAH
			ʿABD		U		TA	RWIM			[ḪA-A]B-DU-TA-RI-IM		M
	2		ŠU					ʿABD	I		ŠU-ḪA-AB-DI		CT XLVIII 43:15,19
ʿAD	1		ʿAD		U						A-DU		A. 269 67, 73+
			ʿAD	AT	UM						A-DA-TUM	MN	I, MEISSNER 51 3
			ʿAD	AT	UM						A-DA-TUM	FN	M+
			ʿAD	AT	IM						A-DA-TIM	MN GEN	XIII 87 5
			ʿAD	AT	IJA						A-DA-TI-A	FN	MRS IX P. 243 UGARIT
			ʿAD	AT	A	HA					A-DA-TA-A	FN	APN P. 12 LATE
			ʿAD		U			RAWM	U		A-DU-RA-MU	FN	U
			ʿAD		U	NA		HADD	U		A-DU-NA-D-IM		SYRIA XIX 109
			ʿAD		U	NI		ʾAB	I	JA	A-DU-NI-A-BI-IA		RA XXVII 87 LATE
			ʿAD		U	NI		HADD	U		A-DU-NI-D-U		MRS VI 15, 42 II 20 UGARIT
			ʿAD		U	NI		ʾIL	A		A-DU-NI-LA		U
	2		HALIL		A			ʿAD	UM		A-LI-LA-ḪA-DU-UM		KISURRA 18 12
			ʾAMR					ʿAD	UM		AM-RA-DU-UM		M
			JARAḪ					ʿAD	U		SIN-A-DU		RA XLIII 8 QATNA
		JI	JṢIʾ					ʿAD	UM		I-ZI-A-DU-UM		M
			ḎU					ʿAD	IM		ZU-ḪA-DI-IM	GEN	M
			LU					ʿAD	UM		LU-ḪA-DU-UM		YOS XIII 497:2
			RABB		U			ʿAD	UM		RU-BU-ḪA-DU-UM		BM 17055 26
			RABB		U			ʿAD	U	HU	RA-AB-BU-ḪA-DU-U$_2$		B 17+
			RABB		U			ʿAD	U	HU	RA-AB-BU-U$_2$-ḪA-DU-U$_2$		BM 17051A 30
		ʾA	RŠIJ					ʿAD	A	HA	AR-ŠI-A-DA?-A	FN	C
			ŠUM		UM			ʿAD	U		SU-MU-UM?-ḪA-DU-KI	GN	YOS II 117:17+
			ŠUM		U			ʿAD	I		SU-MU-ḪA-DI-I	GEN	XIII 13:8
			ŠUM		U			ʿAD	IM		SU-MU-ḪA-DI-IM		X 57 8
			ŠUM		U			ʿAD	U	HU	SU-MU-ḪA-DU-U$_2$		M+
ʿADIJ	1		ʿADIJ		UM						A-DI-UM		M
			ʿADIJ					ʾIL			A-DI-DINGIR		M
			ʿADIJ					ʾEL			ḪA-DI-EL		KISURRA 113 12+
			ʿADIJ			NA		ʾIL			A-DI-E-NA-DINGIR		M
ʿADN	1		ʿADN		U						ḪA-AD-NU		KISURRA 81A 20
			ʿADN	AN							ḪA-AD-NA-AN		M, C
			ʿADN	AN	UM						AD-NA-NU-UM		TIM III 44 19+
			ʿADN		A		ʾA	ʾMUR			ḪA-AD-NA-AM?-MU-UR		X 75 18
			ʿADN		A			ʾAB	I		ḪA?-AD-NA-A-BI		TTKB XIX 304
			ʿADN		I			HADD	U		ḪA-AD-NI-D-IM		M, C+
			ʿADN		I			HADD	U		ḪA-AD-NI-A-D[U]		DELAPORTE CCL II A 914
			ʿADN		I			ʾIL			ḪA-AD-NI-DINGIR		M+
			ʿADN		I			ʾIL	U				
								MA			ḪA-AD-NI-DINGIR-MA		M
			ʿADN		I			ʿAMM	U		ḪA-AD-NI-ḪA-MU		RA LXV 50 VIII 49
			ʿADN		I			JARAḪ			ḪA-AD-NI-E-RA-AḪ		M
			ʿADN		I			DAGAN			ḪA-AD-NI-D-DA-GAN		M
			ʿADN		I			ŠAMŠ			ḪA-AD-NI-SA-MA-AŠ$_2$		M
			ʿADN		U			MA					
								JATAR			ḪA-AD-NU-ME-TAR		M+
			ʿADN		UM			MAZAʾ	A		ḪA-[A]D?-NU-UM-MA-ZA-A		RA LXV 41 II 52
			ʿADN		U			RAPIʾ			ḪA-AD-NU-RA-BI		XIV 109:18+
	2		ḪAʾL		I			ʿADN			ḪA-LI-ḪA-DU-UN		M+
			ḪAʾL		I			ʿADN			ḪA-LI$_2$-ḪA-DU-UN		M+
			ḪAʾL		I			ʿADN			ḪA-LI-ḪA-DU-UM?		M
			ḪAʾL		I			ʿADN	U	HU	ḪA-LI-ḪA-AD-NU-U$_2$		M
			ḪAʾL		U			ʿADN	U		ḪA-LU-ḪA-AD-NU		M+
			ʾIL		A			ʿADN	U	HU	I-LA-ḪA-AD-NU-U$_2$		M
			ʾIL		A			ʿADN	U	HU	I-LA-ḪA-AD-NU-U$_2$	FN	C+
			ʾIL		A			ʿADN	U	HU	DINGIR-ḪA-AD-NU-U$_2$	FN	C+
			ʾIL		I			ʿADN	I		I$_3$-LI$_2$-ḪA-AD-NI	FN	M
			ʿAMM		I			ʿADN	A		AM-MI-ḪA-AD-NA		GOETZE, KIZZ. P. 8, LATE
			JATAR					ʿADN	U		IA-TAR-ḪA-AD-NU		M+
			JATAR					ʿADN	U	HU	IA-TAR-ḪA-AD-NU-U$_2$		RA LXV 54 XII 56
		JI	JTAR					ʿADN	I		I-TAR-AD-AN		WATERMAN 41 R. 10
			DAWD		I			ʿADN			DA-DI-ḪA-DU-UN		M+
			DAWD		I			ʿADN	U	HU	DA-DI-ḪA-AD-NU-U$_2$		18 R.A. P.61 A 3821+

ʿADN	2		ḎU				ʿADN		U		ZU-ḪA-AD-NU		M+
			ḎU				ʿADN		I		ZU-ḪA-AD-NI	NOM	M+
			ḎU				ʿADN		I		ZU-ḪA-AD-NI	GEN	M+
			ḎU				ʿADN		IM		ZU-ḪA-AD-NIM	GEN	M+
			ḎU				ʿADN		IM		ZU-U$_2$-ḪA-AD-NIM		VOIX 187:18 MARI
			LA				ʿADN		I	JA	LA-AD-NI-IA		M
			LA				ʿADN		A				
						ʾA	MWUT				LA-ḪA-AD-NA-A-MU-UT		M
		JA	MṢIʾ				ʿADN		U		IA-AM-ZI-AD-[NU]		CT VI 33A 33
		JA	MṢIʾ				ʿADN		U		IA-AM-ṢI-AD-NU		BM 16914 31
		JA	MṢIʾ				ʿADN		U		IA-AM-ZI-ḪA-AD-NU		M+
		JA	MṢIʾ				ʿADN		U	HU	IA-AM-ZI-AD-NU-U$_2$		BM 81302 4
		JA	MṢIʾ				ʿADN		U	HU	IA-AM-ZI-ḪA-AD-NU-U$_2$		DELAPORTE CCL II A 385, M+
		JA	MZUʾ				ʿADN		IM		[IA?-AM?-Z]U?-ḪA-AD-NIM	GEN	XIII 129 5
		JA	MZUʾ				ʿADN		U	HU	IA-AM-ZU-AD-NU-U$_2$		B 28+
			ŠUM		U		ʿADN		U		SU-MU-ḪA-AD-NU		B 39
			ŠUM		U		ʿADN		U		SU-MU-ḪI-AD-NU		KISURRA 29 12
			ŠARR		UM		ʿADN		U	HU	LUGAL-AI-NU-U$_2$		SIGRIST UNPUBL.
		JI	TWUR				ʿADN		U		I-DUR-ḪA-AD-[NU]		B 24
		JI	TWUR				ʿADN		U	HU	I-DUR-ḪA-AD-NU-U$_2$		TCL XVIII 83 6
ʿAḎAR	1		ʿAḎAR		UM						A-ZA-RU-UM		B 14
			ʿAḎAR		UM						A-DA-RU-UM	FN	RA LXV 60 III 25
			ʿAḎAR		IM						A-ZA-RI-IM	GEN	B 14
			ʿAḎAR	AN	IM						ḪA-ZA-RA-NIM	GEN	B 44
			ʿAḎAR				ʾAḪ				A-ZA-RA-AḪ		JNES XIII 210+ LATE
	2		ʾAB		I		ʿAḎAR				A-BI-DAR		SIMMONS 58 12
			ʿAMM		U		ʿAḎAR				AM-MU-A-DAR		TA 30 59
			ŠUM		U		ʿAḎAR				SU-MU-A-DAR		GORDON 38 DATE+
			ŠUM		U		ʿAḎAR				SU-MU-A-TAR		GORDON 38 DATE+
			ŠUM		U		ʿAḎAR				SU-MA-DAR		SIMMONS 50 26 DATE+
ʿAḎIR	1		ʿAḎIR		UM						ḪA-ZI-RUM	MN	B 20+, M+
			ʿAḎIR		UM						ḪA-ZI-RU-UM		B 20, M
			ʿAḎIR		UM						ḪA-ZI-RUM	FN	M+
			ʿAḎIR		UM						A-ZI-RUM		B 14, M+, C+
			ʿAḎIR		IM						ḪA-ZI-RI-IM	GEN	B 20+
			ʿAḎIR		A						A-ZI-RA	NOM	A. LATE+
			ʿAḎIR	AN							A-ZI-RA-AN		A. P. 131 LATE+
			ʿAḎIR	AH							ḪA-ZI-RA	FN	RA LXV 62 V 26
			ʿAḎIR				ŠAMŠ				ḪA-ZI-IR-D-UTU		M
	2		ḪAʾL		I		ʿAḎIR		UM		ḪA-LI-A-ṢI-RUM		UNPUBL.
	3		ʾIL		A		GULL		A				
							ʿAḎIR	AT			DINGIR-GUL-LA$_2$-ḪA-ZI-RA-AT	FN	M+
			LA				RIWM						
							ʿAḎIR				LA-RI-IM-ḪA-ZI-IR		DELAPORTE, CAT. BN 207
ʿAḎR	1		ʿAḎR	AN							ḪA-AZ-RA-AN		M
			ʿAḎR	AN	UM						AD-RA-NU-UM		I., CT XLVIII 88 REV.
			ʿAḎR		IJA						ḪA-AZ-RI-IA		RA LXV 41 II 21+
			ʿAḎR				ʾAḪ		I		ḪA-AZ-RA-ḪI?		CT XLV 54 9
			ʿAḎR		I		JAḪAD				AD-RI-E-ḪA-AD		M+
			ʿAḎR		I		ḪAʾT		UM		AD-RI-ḪA-TUM		SIMMONS 88 16+
			ʿAḎR		I		HADD		U		AD-RI-A-DU		A.+
			ʿAḎR		I		HADD		U		AD-RI-IA-DU		KUPPER, NOM. 231
			ʿAḎR		I		HAND		U		AD-RI-IA-AN-DU		KUPPER, NOM. 231
			ʿAḎR		I		HAND		U		ḪA-AD-RI-IA-AN-DU		KUPPER, NOM. 231
			ʿAḎR		I		ʿAMM		IM		ḪA-AZ-RI-A-MI-IM	GEN	M
	2		ʾAB		I		ʿAḎR		I		A-BI-AD-RI		A. LATE
			ʿABD				ʿAḎR		A		ḪA-AB-DU-ḪA-AD-RA		M
			ŠINI				ʿAḎR		I		ŠI-NI-AD-RI		M
ʿAGAL	1		ʿAGAL		IM						A-GA-LIM	GEN	YOS XIII 426:9
			ʿAGAL		IM						ḪA-GA-LIM	GEN	M
			ʿAGAL		IJA						ḪA-GA-LI-IA		HARRIS 88:3
ʿAGL	1		ʿAGL	AT	UM						AG-LA-TUM	FN	ABB IV 98:2
ʿALAṢ	2		ʾAB		I		ʿALAṢ		I		AD-ḪA-LA-ZI	FN	C
			ʾAB		I		ʿALAṢ		I		A-BI-ḪA-LA-ZI	FN	M, C II 49 6
		JA	KWUN				ʿALAṢ		I		IA-KU-UN-ḪA-LA-ZI		RA LXV 44 IV 41;43
ʿALIJ	1		ʿALIJ		UM						A-LI-U$_2$-UM		GAUTIER 33 R. 6

STEMS

ʿALIJ	1	ʿALIJ		UM					A-LI-JU-UM		M
		ʿALIJ		UM					A-LI-I-U$_2$-UM		RUTTEN 7 20+
		ʿALIJ		UM					A-LI$_2$-JU-UM		JCS XXIV 52 NO.27+
		ʿALIJ		U					A-LI$_2$-JU-U$_2$		RUTTEN 16 14
		ʿALIJ		UM					ḪA-LI-IU-UM		B 19+
		ʿALIJ		UM					ḪA-LI-U$_2$-UM		B 19+, M
		ʿALIJ		UM					ḪA-LI-JU-UM		B 19+
		ʿALIJ		UM					ḪA-LI-I-JU-UM		CT XLVIII 31 7, 10
		ʿALIJ	AT	UM					ḪA-LI-IA-TUM	FN	B 18+, XIII 1 VII 1
		ʿALIJ	T	UM					A-LI-TUM	FN	M+
		ʿALIJ	T	IM					A-LI-TIM	FN GEN	M
	2	ʾAJ		A		ʿALIJ	AT		D-A-A-ḪA-LI-IA-AT	MN?	CT XLV 92 R. 12
		ʾADM		U		ʿALIJ	AH		D-AD-MU-ḪA-LI-IA	FN	XIII 1 V 55
		TABUB		U		ʿALIJ	AH		D-TA-BU-BU-ḪA-LI-IA	FN	XIII 1 VI 13
ʿAMAS	1	ʿAMAS		UM					A-MA-ZU-UM		KISURRA 98 8
		ʿAMAS		IM					A-MA-ZI-IM	GEN	KISURRA 166 4+
ʿAMIQ	1	ʿAMIQ	AT	IM					ḪA-MI-QA-TIM-KI	GN GEN	M+
ʿAMIS	1	ʿAMIS	AH						ḪA-ME-ZA	FN	RA LXV 58 I 24
		ʿAMIS	AN	U					ḪA-MI-ZA-NU		M
ʿAMM	1	ʿAMM		IJA					AM-MI-IA		B 13+
		ʿAMM		IJA					ḪA-MI-IA		C+
		ʿAMM		IJA					ḪA-AM-MI-IA		M
		ʿAMM		IJAN					AM-MI-IA-AN		A.+
		ʿAMM	AN						ḪA-AM-MA-AN		M+
		ʿAMM	AN	UM					ḪA-AM-MA-NU-UM		M
		ʿAMM	AN	U					ḪA-AM-MA-NU		M
		ʿAMM	AN	IM					ḪA-MA-NIM	GEN	M
		ʿAMM	AN	IM					ḪA-AM-MA-NIM	GEN	M
		ʿAMM	ATAN						ḪA-AM-MA-TA-AN		M+
		ʿAMM		A	JI	ḎRUʿ			ḪA-MA-IZ-RU		RUTTEN 28 5+
		ʿAMM		I		....			AM-MI-....-LU-UB		A. 95 85
		ʿAMM		I		HADD	U		AM-MI-A-DU		A. 60 14
		ʿAMM		I		HADD	U		AM-MI-IA-A-DU		A.
		ʿAMM		I		HADD	U		AM-MI-AD-DU		A. 267 17
		ʿAMM		I		HEDD	A		AM-MI-E-DA		A.
		ʿAMM		I		ʿADN	A		AM-MI-ḪA-AD-NA		GOETZE, KIZZ. P. 8, LATE
		ʿAMM		I		ʾAK	I		AM-MI-E-KI		A.
		ʿAMM		I		ʾIL	I		ḪA-MI-I$_3$-LI$_2$		MDP XXIII 307 16
		ʿAMM		I		ʿAN	AT		ḪA-MI-D-ḪA-NA-AT		M
		ʿAMM		I		ʾANDUL	I		ḪA-AM-MI-AN-DUL$_3$-LI$_2$		M+
		ʿAMM		I		JAŠAR			ḪA-AM-MI-E-SA-AR?		M
		ʿAMM		I		JAT	UM		AM-MI-IA-TUM		A. 273 14
		ʿAMM		I		JATAR			ḪA-AM-MI-A-TAR		B 19+
		ʿAMM		I		JATAR			ḪA-AM-MA-TA-AR		B 19
		ʿAMM		I		JATAR			A-MA-TA-AR		WALTERS, WL 109:9
		ʿAMM		I	JI	JBAL			ḪA-MI-I-BA-AL		M
		ʿAMM		I	JE	JPUʿ			ḪA-MI-E-PU-UḪ		M+
		ʿAMM		I	JE	JPUʿ			ḪA-AM-MI-E-PU-UḪ		M+
		ʿAMM		I	JE	JŠUʿ			ḪA-MI-E-ŠU-UḪ		M
		ʿAMM		I		DAGAN			ḪA-MI-D-DA-GAN		RA LXV 53 XI 33
		ʿAMM		I		DANN	U		AM-MI-DA-NU		YOS XII
		ʿAMM		I		DAŠUR			AM-MI-DA-ŠUR?		A 7894
		ʿAMM		I		DUŠUR			ḪA-MI-DU-ŠU-UR		SIMMONS 46 18+
		ʿAMM		I		DUŠUR			ḪA-MI-DU-ŠU-UR$_2$		SIMMONS 50 14
		ʿAMM		I		DUŠUR			ḪA-AM-MI-DU-ŠU-UR		HARRIS 18 15+
		ʿAMM		I		DUŠUR			ḪA-AM-MI-DU-ŠU-UR$_2$		HARRIS 27 17+
		ʿAMM		I		DUŠUR			AM-MI-DU-ŠU-UR		A7894+
		ʿAMM		I		DITAN	A		AM-MI-DI-TA-NA		B13+
		ʿAMM		I		DITAN	A		AM-MI-TE-TA-NA		CT XLV 44 24
		ʿAMM		I		KUWN			ḪA-MI-KU-UN		RA LXV 54 XII 15
		ʿAMM		I		MAṬAR			AM-MI-MA-DAR		B 13 HANA
		ʿAMM		I		MAṬAR			ḪA-MI-MA-DAR	FN	C
		ʿAMM		I		RAPIʾ			AM-MI-RA-PI		SYRIA XXXVII 206 END HANA
		ʿAMM		I		RAPIʾ			AM-MI-RA-BI-IḪ		RA XXXIV 186 HANA
		ʿAMM		I		RAPIʾ			ḪA-AM-MI-RA-BI		B 19
		ʿAMM		I	Š	ḪARIJ		JE	AM-MI-IS-ḪA-RI?-E?		JEAN, S'A CLXXXVIII R. 3

STEMS

ʿAMM	1	ʿAMM	I		JI	T	ŠAMAR			ḪA-AM-MI-IŠ-TA-MAR		M+
		ʿAMM	I		JI	T	ŠAMAR			AM-MI-IŠ-TA-MAR		M
		ʿAMM	I		JI	T	ŠAMAR	U		AM-MI-IŠ-TAM-RU		MRS VI P. 329 UGARIT+
		ʿAMM	I		JI	T	ŠAMAR	U		AM-MI-IS-TAM-RU		MRS VI P. 239 UGARIT+
		ʿAMM	I				ŠAGIŠ			ḪA-AM-MI-ŠA-GI-IŠ		M+
		ʿAMM	I				ŠAGIŠ			AM-MI-ŠA-GI-IŠ		M
		ʿAMM	I				ŚUM	U		AM-MI-SU-MU		CT XLVIII 61 4,5
		ʿAMM	I				ŚUM	U	HU	ḪA-AM-MI-SU-MU-U_2		CT XLVII 30 44
		ʿAMM	I		TA		QWIM			ḪA-AM-MI-TA-KI-IM	NOM	M
		ʿAMM	I		TA		QWUM			AM-MI-TA-KU-UM		A.+
		ʿAMM	I		TA		QWUM					
							MA			AM-MI-TA-KU-UM-MA		A. +
		ʿAMM	I				ṬAJB	A		AM-MI-ṬA-BA		A.+
		ʿAMM	I				ṬALL	U	HU	ḪA-MI-TI-LU-U_2		M
		ʿAMM	I				ṬALL	U	HU	ḪA-AM-MI-TA-LU-U_2		M+
		ʿAMM	I				ṬALL	U	HU	ḪA-AM-MI-TI-LU-U_2		M+
		ʿAMM	I				ṬILL	U	HU	ḪA-AM-MI-TE-LU-U_2		RA LXVI 118:15
		ʿAMM	I				ZUʾG	U	HU	ḪA-AM-MI-ZU-GU-U_2		BM 17045+
		ʿAMM	I				ṢUWR	A		AM-MI-ZU-RA		CT XLVIII 90 REV.
		ʿAMM	I				ZAʾT	I		ḪA-MI-ZA-TI		HARRIS 103 1
		ʿAMM	I				ṢADUQ			ḪA-MI-ZA-DU-[UQ]		M
		ʿAMM	I				ṢADUQ			ḪA-AM-MI-ZA-DU-UQ		M
		ʿAMM	I				ṢADUQ	A		AM-MI-ZA-DU-GA		B 13+
		ʿAMM	I				ṢADUQ	A				
							....			AM-MI-ZA-DU-GA-I-LU-NI		B 13+
		ʿAMM	I				ZAKK	UM		AM-MI-ZA-KU-UM		IRAQ IV 185, A 385
		ʿAMM	I				ZAKK	U	HU	ḪA-AM-MI-ZA-KU-U_2		M
		ʿAMM	U	HU						A-MU-U_2		EDZARD, DER 90:10+
		ʿAMM	U	HU						ḪA-AM-MU-U_2		EDZARD, DER 68 III 6
		ʿAMM	UJAN							AM-MU-JA-AN		A.+
		ʿAMM	U				ḪAʾL	UM		ḪA-AM-MU-ḪA-LUM		M+
		ʿAMM	U				HADD	A		AM-MU-A-DA		A.+
		ʿAMM	U				HADD	A		AM-MU-WA-DA		A.
		ʿAMM	U				ʿAḎAR			AM-MU-A-DAR		TA 30 59
		ʿAMM	U				ʾEL			AM-MU-E-EL		BM 16931 2
		ʿAMM	U				ʾIL			ḪA-MU-DINGIR		M
		ʿAMM	U				ʾIL			AM-MU-DINGIR		UCP X/1 18 24
		ʿAMM	U				JAQAR			ḪA-MU-IA-QAR		RA LXV 52 X 62
		ʿAMM	U				ḤURB	I		AM-MU-UR-BI		A.
		ʿAMM	U				JAŚAR			ḪA-MU-JA-ŠAR		M
		ʿAMM	U				JATAR			ḪA-MU-TAR		M
		ʿAMM	U				JATAR			[Ḫ]A-AM-MU-TA-[A]R		M
		ʿAMM	U		JE		JPUʿ			ḪA-MU-E-PU-UḪ	FN	C+
		ʿAMM	U				DAGAN			ḪA-AM-MU-D-DA-GAN		M
		ʿAMM	U				DUMAR			ḪA-MU-DU-MAR		RA LXV 51 IX 66
		ʿAMM	U				KUMAR	A		AM-MU-KU-MAR-RA		A.
		ʿAMM	U				LA					
							RIWM			ḪA-MU-L[A]-RI-IM		RA LXV 46 VI 40
		ʿAMM	U				LIʾM			ḪA-MU-LI-IM		RA LXV 52 X 22
		ʿAMM	U				LABW	A		ḪA-AM-MU-LA-BA-A		XIV 114:6
		ʿAMM	U				MAṬAR			ḪA-MU-MA-DAR	FN	C
		ʿAMM	U				NIʿM			ḪA-AM-MU-NI-ḪI-IM	NOM	M
		ʿAMM	U				NIQM	A		AM-MU-NI-IQ-MA		A.+
		ʿAMM	U				PATAḤ	A		ḪA-AM-MU-PA-TA-A		M
		ʿAMM	U				RAWM	A		ḪA-MU-RA-MA		M
		ʿAMM	U				RAPIʾ			ḪA-AM-MU-RA-BI		B 19+, M+, A.+
		ʿAMM	UM				RAPIʾ			ḪA-AM-MU-UM-RA-BI		B 19+
		ʿAMM	U				RAPIʾ			AM-MU-RA-BI		B 19+
		ʿAMM	U				RAPIʾ			D-ḪA-AM-MU-RA-BI		B 19+
		ʿAMM	U				RAPIʾ			ḪA-MU-RA-BI		B 19+, M+
		ʿAMM	U				RAPIʾ			ḪA-AM-MU-RA-BI-IḪ		B 19 HANA
		ʿAMM	U				RAPIʾ			AM-MU-RA-PI		ABL 255 LATE
		ʿAMM	U				RAPIʾ			D-AM-MU-RA-PI		YBC 4362
		ʿAMM	UM				RAPIʾ			ḪA-AM-MU-UM-RA-PI		YBC 6496, 6508
		ʿAMM	UM				RAPIʾ			ḪA-MU-UM-RA-BI		BM 17046+
		ʿAMM	U				RAPIʾ			ḪA-MU-U_2-RA-BI		FIGULLA, CAT. 14138

STEMS										
ʿAMM	1	ʿAMM	U		RAPIʾ	I		AM-MU-RA-BI-I		A+
		ʿAMM	U		RAPIʾ			ḪA-MU-UR$_2$-RA-BI		CT XLVII 31 32+
		ʿAMM	U		RAPIʾ					
					ʾIL			ḪA-AM-MU-RA-BI-DINGIR		B 19
		ʿAMM	U		RAPIʾ					
					BANIJ			ḪA-AM-MU-RA-BI-BA-NI		B 19
		ʿAMM	UM		RAPIʾ					
					....			[ḪA-AM]-MU-UM-RA-PI-LI-WI-IR		UNPUBL.
		ʿAMM	U		RAPIʾ					
					....			ḪA-AM-MU-RA-BI-LU-DA-RI		B 19
		ʿAMM	U		ŠAGIŠ			ḪA-MU-ŠA-KI-IŠ		X 174 13
		ʿAMM	U		ŠALIM			ḪA-MU-SA-L[IM]?		M
		ʿAMM	U		ŠAM	A		AM-MU-SA-MA		A.+
		ʿAMM	U		ŠAMAR			ḪA-MU-SA-MAR		RA LXIV 36 NO. 31
		ʿAMM	U		ŠAMAR			ḪA-MU-SA-MAR	FN	C+
		ʿAMM	U		ŠARR			ḪA-MU-SA-AR		RA LXV 40 I 42
		ʿAMM	U		ŠARR			ḪA-MU-SA-AR	FN	C+
		ʿAMM	U		ŠARR			ḪA-AM-MU-SA-AR		XIV 108:6
		ʿAMM	U		ḎAKAJ	A		Ḫ[A]-MU-ZA-KA-A		RA LXV 43 III 75
		ʿAMM	U	HU	JATAR			ḪA-AM-MU-U$_2$-TAR		M
		ʿAMM	U	HU	RAPIʾ			ḪA-AM-MU-U$_2$-RA-BI		M
		ʿAMM	U	Š	KI					
					ʾIL			AM-MU-US-KI-DINGIR		A.
		ʿAMM	U	Š	KI					
					ʾIL			AM-MU-UŠ-KI-DINGIR		A.+
	2	ʾAJA			ʿAMM	U		A-IA-AM-MU		MAOG IV 2 10, 11, A 7740+
		ʾAJA			ʿAMM	U	HU	A-A-ḪA-AM-MU-U$_2$		BASOR 95 23
		ʾAJA			ʿAMM	U	HU	A-IA-ḪA-MU-U$_2$		A 7648, M
		ʾAJA			ʿAMM	U	HU	A-IA-AM-MU-U$_2$		VAS XIII 34:3
		ʾAJA			ʿAMM	U	HU	A-IA-AM-MU-KU		CT XLV 6 33
		ʾAJA			ʿAMM	U	HU	IA-ḪA-AM-MU-U$_2$		VAS XVIII 100:19
		JAḪAD			ʿAMM	U		IA-ḪA-AD-ḪA-AM-MU		M
		JAḪAD			ʿAMM	U		IA-ḪA-AD-ḪA-MU		M+
		JAḪAD			ʿAMM	U	HU	IA-ḪA-AD-ḪA-MU-U$_2$		M
		ʿABD			ʿAMM	UM		ḪA-AB-DU-A-MU-UM		M
		ʿABD			ʿAMM	IM		AB-DU-A-MI-IM	NOM	M+
		ʿABD			ʿAMM	IM		AB-DU-A-MI-IM	GEN	M+
		ʿABD			ʿAMM	IM		ḪA-AB-DU-A-MI-IM		M
		JADAʿ			ʿAMM	U		IA-DA-AM-MU		C II 5 4
		ʿADN	I		ʿAMM	U		ḪA-AD-NI-ḪA-MU		RA LXV 50 VIII 49
		ʿAḎR	I		ʿAMM	IM		ḪA-AZ-RI-A-MI-IM	GEN	M
		ʾIL	A		ʿAMM	U		I-LA-ḪA-MU		RA LXV 42 II 77+
		ʾIL	I		ʿAMM	U		I$_3$-LI$_2$-ḪA-MU		RA LVII 178
		ʾALI			ʿAMM	U		A-LI$_2$-AM-MU		UCP X/1 52 22
		ʾALI			ʿAMM	U	HU	A-LI$_2$-AM-MU-U$_2$		UCP X/2 58 16
	JA	WMAʾ			ʿAMM	AJ	I	IA-AW-MA-ḪA-MA-JI-KI	GN	M
	JA	WMAʾ			ʿAMM	I		JA-MA-ḪA-MI-KI	GN	M
	JA	WMAʾ			ʿAMM	UM		JA-MA-ḪA-MU-UM		M
	JA	WMAʾ			ʿAMM	UM		IA-MA-ḪA-MU-UM		M
	JA	JQAH			ʿAMM	U		IA-QA-AM-MU		A.+
		ʿAQB	A		ʿAMM	U		AQ-BA-ḪA-MU		M
		ʿAQB	A		ʿAMM	U		AQ-BA-ḪA-AM-MU		IRAQ XXX 91, RIMAH
		ʿAQB	A		ʿAMM	U		ḪA-AQ-BA-ḪA-AM-MU		II 39 19, 58, 80
		ʿAQB	A		ʿAMM	U	HU	ḪA-AQ-BA-ḪA-AM-MU-U$_2$		II 39 14, 16, 24
		ʿAQB	U		ʿAMM	U	HU	AQ-BU-AM-MU-U$_2$		X 174 3
		ʿIQB	A		ʿAMM	U		IQ-BA?-AM-MU		A. 8 35
		ʾUŠM	A		ʿAMM	I		UŠ-MA-AM-MI		CT XXXIII 46A 4
		JATAR			ʿAMM	U		IA-TAR-ḪA-MU		M
		JATAR			ʿAMM	U		IA-TAR-ḪA-MU	FN	C II P. 247+
		ʾATT	I		ʿAMM	A		AT-TI-AM-MA		A. LATE
		ʿAZZ			ʿAMM	I		AZ-ZA-AM-MI		A. 265 19
		BIN	A		ʿAMM	I		BI-NA-AM-MI		B 15
		BUN	U		ʿAMM	I		BU-NU-ḪA-AM-MI	FN	M+
		BUN	U		ʿAMM	U		BU-NU-AM-MU		B 16+
		ḎAKIR	A		ʿAMM	I		ZA-KI-RA-ḪA-MI		M
		ḎAKIR	A		ʿAMM	U		ZA-KI-RA-ḪA-AM-MU		M+

ʿAMM	2			ḎAKIR		A		ʿAMM		U		ZA-KI-RA-ḪA-MU		M
				ḎAKIR		A		ʿAMM		U	HU	ZA-KI-RA-ḪA-AM-MU-U$_2$		M+
				ḎIMR		A		ʿAMM		U		ZI-IM-RA-ḪA-MU		CT XLIV 54 20, C
				ḎIMR		A		ʿAMM		U		ZI-IM-RA-ḪA-AM-MU		M
				ḎIMR		A		ʿAMM		U		ZI-IM-RA-AM-MU		TIM IV 33 20, 34 13
				ḎIMR		A		ʿAMM		U	HU	ZI-IM-RA-ḪA-MU-U$_2$		TIM IV 33 SEAL, 34 SEAL
				ḎIMR		I		ʿAMM		U		ZI-IM-RI-AM-MU		TIM III 94 4
				ḎIMR		I		ʿAMM		U		ZI-IM-RI-ḪA-MU		C
				ḎIMR		I		ʿAMM		U		ZI-IM-RI-ḪA-AM-MU		B 42+, X 35 12
				ḎIMR		U		ʿAMM		I		ZI-IM-RU-ḪA-AM-MI		B 42
				ḎIMR		U		ʿAMM		U		ZI-IM-RU-ḪA-AM-MU		JCS XI 23 10 13
				KIʾL		I		ʿAMM		I		KI-LI-AM-MI	GEN	MRS XVI 12:2
		JA		KWUN				ʿAMM		U		IA-KU-UN-AM-MU		B 27
				KUWN				ʿAMM		U		KU-UN-AM-MU		MRS VI P. 249
				LA				ʿAMM		U		LA-ḪA-AM-MU		HARRIS 18 14
		JA		NḪAB				ʿAMM		U		IA-ḪA-AB-ḪA-MU		M
			Š	NUʾR		A		ʿAMM		U		ŠU-NU-UḪ-RA-AM-MU		B 40 HANA+
		JA		NŠIʾ				ʿAMM		U		IA-SI-ḪA-MU		M
		JA		NTIN				ʿAMM		U		IA-AN-TI-IN-ḪA-MU		M
				RIJB		A		ʿAMM		U		RI-BA-AM-MU		A. 97 4+
		JA		RWIM				ʿAMM		U		IA-RI-IM-ḪA-MU		M
		JA		RWIM				ʿAMM		U		IA-RI-IM-ḪA-AM-MU		M
		JA		RŠIJ				ʿAMM		U		IA-AR-ŠI-ḪA-MU		M, C+
				ŠU				ʿAMM		U		ŠU-ḪA-AM-MU		M+
				ŠUWB				ʿAMM		U		ŠU-UB-AM-MU		MRS VI P. 257+
				ŠUWB		A		ʿAMM		I		ŠU-BA-AM-MI		A. 270 22
		JA		ŚJIM				ʿAMM		U		IA-SI-IM-ḪA-AM-MU		M
		JA		ŚJIM				ʿAMM		U		IA-SI-IM-ḪA-MU		M
				ŚUM		U		ʿAMM		U		SU-MU-ḪA-AM-MU		B 39+
				ŚUM		U		ʿAMM		U		SU-MU-ḪA-MU		M
				ŚUM		U		ʿAMM		U		SU-MU-ḪA-MU	FN	C+
		JA		ŚṬIḪ				ʿAMM		U		IA-AŠ-DI-ḪA-AM-MU		B 30
				ṢUWR		A		ʿAMM		U		ZU-RA-ḪA-AM-MU		M+
				ṢUWR		A		ʿAMM		U		Z[U]-RA-ḪA-M[U]		XIII 132 7
				ṢUWR		A		ʿAMM		U	HU	ZU-RA-ḪA-AM-MU-U$_2$		M
				ṢUWR		I		ʿAMM		U		ZU-RI-ḪA-AM-MU		M
				ṢUWR		I		ʿAMM		U	HU	ZU-RI-ḪA-AM-MU-U$_2$		M+
		JI		TWUR				ʿAMM		U	HU	I-DUR-ḪA-MU-U$_2$		UNPUBL.
				TUWR		U		ʿAMM		I		DUR-RU-AM-MI		MAOG IV 2 6 HANA
				TALM		A		ʿAMM		U		TA-AL-MA-AM-MU		A.+
				ZAʾT				ʿAMM		U		ZA-AT-AM-MU	MN	A. 279 2 3
ʿAN	1			ʿAN		AJA						A-NA-IA		RA LXV 46 VI 17
				ʿAN		AJA						ḪA-NA-IA		RA LXV 50 IX 19
				ʿAN		IJA						A-NI-IA		RUTTEN 31 5+
				ʿAN		UM		ʾAḪ		I		A-NU-UM-A-ḪI		RA LXV 53 XI 43
				ʿAN		UM		ḤIRB		I		A-NU-UM-ḪI-IR-BI		BALKAN, LETTER P. 6
				ʿAN	AT							D-ḪA-NA-AT	DN FN	M+
				ʿAN	AT							ḪA-NA-AT-KI	GN FN	M+
				ʿAN	AT	UM						A-NA-TUM		BIROT, TEA 72 III 58+
				ʿAN	AT	UM						ḪA-NA-TUM	FN	XIII 1:34+
				ʿAN	ATAN							A-NA-TA-AN		RA LXV 53 XI 13
				ʿAN	ATAN							ḪA-NA-TA-AN		M+
				ʿAN	AT	I	JI	JBAL				ḪA-NA-TI-I-BA-AL		RA LXV 40 I 12
				ʿAN	AT			KUʾB		U		A-NA-AT-KU-BU		TCL I 204:11
	2			JAʾ		A		ʿAN		UM		IA-A-A-NU-UM		YOS V 134 16
				ʿABD				ʿAN	AT			ḪA-AB-DU-D-ḪA-NA-AT		M+
				ʿABD				ʿAN	AT	I		AB-TA-NA-TI		A. P. 128A LATE +
				ʿABD				ʿAN	AT	I		AB-DI-A-NA-TI		A. P. 128B LATE +
				ʿABD				ʿAN	AT	I		AB-TI-A-NA-TI		JCS XIII 54 300, A. LATE
				ʿAMM		I		ʿAN	AT			ḪA-MI-D-ḪA-NA-AT		M
				ʾANA				ʿAN		A		A-NA-A-NA		A. 36:11
				JIŠʿ		I		ʿAN		UM		IŠ-ḪI-A-NU-UM		B 45
		JA		BWAʾ				ʿAN		UM		IA-BA-A-NU-UM		B 45
				PALṬ		A		ʿAN		UM		PA-AL?-TA-A-NU-UM		LANGDON IV 15
				BUN		A		ʿAN		UM		BU-NA-A-NU-UM		U
				BUN		U		ʿAN	AT	I		BU-NU-A-NA-TI		B 16

STEMS

ʿAN	2		ḎIKR		I			ʿAN	AT			ZI-IK-RI-ḪA-NA-AT		M
			ḎIKR		I			ʿAN	AT			ZI-IK-RI-D-ḪA-N[A-AT]		M
			ḎIMR		I			ʿAN	AT	A		ZI-IM-RI-ḪA-NA-TA		B 42
			LA					ʿAN		UM		LA-A-NU-UM		U
			LU					ʿAN		UM		LU$_{2}$-A-NU-UM		U
			LASIM					ʿAN		UM		LA-ZE$_{2}$-IM-A-NU-UM		FLP 590:6, U
			LASIM					ʿAN		UM		LA-ZI-MA-NU-UM		MVN III 338:17, U
			MUT					ʿAN	AT			MU-UT-D-ḪA-NA-AT		RA LXV 52 X 65
			MUT		I			ʿAN	AT	A		MU-TI-A-N[A-T]A		B 35
			NAʿM		I			ʿAN		IM		NA-MI-A-NIM		A. 142
			PI					ʿAN		UM		PI-A-NUM$_{2}$		I
			PI					ʿAN		UM		BI$_{2}$-A-NU-UM		I
			PUZUR					ʿAN		A		PUZUR-A-NA		BIN IV 61 29+ CAPP.
		ʾA	RŠIJ					ʿAN		UM		AR-SI?-A-NUM$_{2}$		U
			ŠAT					ʿAN		A		ŠA-AT-A-NA		TCL XXI 220A 4+ CAPP.
			ŠAʾQ		A			ʿAN		UM		SA-GA-A-NU-UM		B 47
		MA	ŠJIT					ʿAN		UM		MA-SI-IT-A-NU-UM		I
			ŠALIM					ʿAN		UM		ŠA-LIM-A-NU-UM		M
			ṢILL					ʿAN	AT			MI-NI-D-ḪA-NA-AT		XIII 83 8
	3		LA				ʾA	ḪJIJ						
								ʿAN		UM		LA-ḪI-A-NU-UM		U
ʿANAJ	1		ʿANAJ			TI		ʾEL				A-NI-TE-EL		MOORTGAT 309
			ʿANAJ			TI		ʾIL				A-NI-TI-DINGIR		M
ʿANAQ	1		ʿANAQ		UM							A-NA-GU-UM		KISURRA 71A 15+
			ʿANAQ		UM							A-NA-KUM		KISURRA 29 8+
ʿANIJ	1	ME	ʿANIJ		U							ME-ḪA-A-NU		KISURRA 81A
		ME	ʿANIJ		IM							ME-ḪA-NI-IM	GEN	KISURRA 80B
		ME	ʿANIJ		I							ME-ḪA-A-NI?	GEN	VAS VIII 14 43
		ME	ʿANIJ			JA						ME-ḪA-NI-IA	FN	RA LXV 58 I 43+
ʿAQAB	1		ʿAQAB					ʾEL				A-QA-BE-EL		UET V 839 23
ʿAQB	1		ʿAQB		UM							AQ-BU-UM		TIM III 82 6
			ʿAQB	AN								ḪA-AQ-BA-AN		M+
			ʿAQB	AN								AQ-BA-AN		M
			ʿAQB	AN	UM							AQ-BA-NU-UM		RUTTEN 40 2+
			ʿAQB		A			ʾAḪ		UM		AQ-BA-A-ḪU-UM		M+
			ʿAQB		A			ʾAḪ		UM		AQ-BA-ḪU-UM		B 11+
			ʿAQB		A			ʾAḪ		UM		ḪA-AQ-BA-A-ḪU-UM		RA LXV 43 III 57+
			ʿAQB		A			ʾAḪ		U		AQ-BA-A-ḪU		M+, C+
			ʿAQB		A			ʾAḪ		U		AQ-BA-ḪU		BASOR 95 19+
			ʿAQB		A			ʾAḪ		AM		AQ-BA-A-ḪA-AM	ACC	M
			ʿAQB		A			ʾAḪ		IM		AQ-BA-A-ḪI-IM	GEN	M+
			ʿAQB		A			ʾAḪ		IM		ḪA-AQ-BA-A-ḪI-IM	GEN	M+
			ʿAQB		A			ʾAḪ		I		AQ-BA-A-ḪI	GEN	XII 448 5+
			ʿAQB		A			ʿAMM		U		AQ-BA-ḪA-MU		M
			ʿAQB		A			ʿAMM		U		AQ-BA-ḪA-AM-MU		IRAQ XXX 91, RIMAH
			ʿAQB		A			ʿAMM		U		ḪA-AQ-BA-ḪA-AM-MU		II 39 19, 58, 80
			ʿAQB		A			ʿAMM		U	HU	ḪA-AQ-BA-ḪA-AM-MU-U$_{2}$		II 39 14, 16, 24
			ʿAQB		A			ḪUNN		UM		AQ-BA-ḪU-NI-UM		B 11
			ʿAQB		I			ʾAḪ		U		AQ-BI-A-ḪU		B 11
			ʿAQB		I			ʾIL				AQ-BI-IL		B 11
			ʿAQB		I			ʾIL				AQ-BI-DINGIR		BIN VII 156 10+
			ʿAQB		I			NAN		UM		AQ-BI-NA-NU-UM		B 42+
			ʿAQB		U	HU						AQ-BU-U$_{2}$		CT IV 50B 24+
			ʿAQB		U			ʿAMM		U	HU	AQ-BU-AM-MU-U$_{2}$		X 174 3
			ʿAQB		U			DAWD		UM		AQ-BU-DA-DU-UM		PBS VIII/2 253 7
			ʿAQB		U			DAWD		A		AQ-BU-DA-DA		B 12
			ʿAQB		U			DAWD		I		ḪA-AQ-BU-DA-DI		M+
			ʿAQB		U			DAWD		I		AQ-BU-DA-DI		M
ʿAQUB	1		ʿAQUB		U							A-KU-BU		VAS VIII 14 14
			ʿAQUB					ʾIL				A-KU-UB-DINGIR		HARRIS 84 13
			ʿAQUB		I			ʾEL				A-KU-PI-EL		GORDON 38 16
ʿARAD	1		ʿARAD	AN								ḪA-RA-DA-AN		M
ʿARD	1		ʿARD		UM							ḪA-AR-DU-UM		M+
			ʿARD		UM							AR-DU-UM		TCL I 168 4+
			ʿARD		U							AR-DU		TCL I 166 2
			ʿARD		IM							ḪA-AR-DI-IM	GEN	M

STEMS

ʿARD	1		ʿARD	AT	UM						ḪA-AR-DA-TUM	FN	M+
			ʿARD		AJA						ḪA-AR-DA-IA	FN	XIII 1 IV 70
			ʿARD	AN	UM						ḪA-AR-DA-NU-UM		M+
ʿARIṢ	1		ʿARIṢ	AN	UM						A-RI-ZA-NU-UM		U
			ʿARIṢ	AN	U						ḪA-RI-ZA-NU		PBS II/1 P. 23+ LATE
ʿARṢ	1		ʿARṢ		U						ḪAR-ṢU		JNES XIII 210+ LATE
			ʿARṢ	AN	UM						AR-ZA-NU-UM		B 43+
			ʿARṢ	AT	UM						AR-ZA-TUM	FN	C
ʿARUL	1		ʿARUL		UM						A-RU-LU-UM		B 13+
			ʿARUL		U						A-RU-LU		STRASSM. 56 29+
ʿAŠTAR	1		ʿAŠTAR				ʾAB		I		AŠ-TAR-A-BI		MRS VI P. 242
			ʿAŠTAR				ʾIL		I		EŠ$_4$-DAR-I$_3$-LI$_2$	FN	RA LXV 56 I 3
			ʿAŠTAR				ʾUMM		I		EŠ$_4$-DAR-UM-MI	FN	XIII 1 II 38 +
			ʿAŠTAR				ʾANDUL		I		EŠ$_4$-DAR-AN-DUL$_3$-LI$_2$	FN	M
			ʿAŠTAR				JIPʿ	AH			EŠ$_4$-DAR-IP-ḪA	FN	XIII 1 VI 19+
			ʿAŠTAR				ʾAŠJ	AH			EŠ$_4$-DAR-A-SI-IA	FN	XIII 1 IX 3+
			ʿAŠTAR				ʾAŠJ	AH			EŠ$_4$-DAR-A-ZU-IA	FN	M
			ʿAŠTAR				JAŠʿ	AH			EŠ$_4$-DAR-IA-AŠ-ḪA	FN	M
			ʿAŠTAR				ḪAṢN		I		EŠ$_4$-DAR-ḪA-AZ-NI	FN	XIII 1 II 41
			ʿAŠTAR			JA	HWIJ				EŠ$_4$-DAR-IA-WI		VAS VII 157 7
			ʿAŠTAR				BAʿL	AH			EŠ$_4$-DAR-BA-AḪ?-LA	FN	M
			ʿAŠTAR				DAMQ	AH			EŠ$_4$-DAR-DAM-QA	FN	XIII 1 V 50+
			ʿAŠTAR				KAWN				EŠ$_4$-DAR-KA-AN		IX 237 II 4+
			ʿAŠTAR				KABAR				EŠ$_4$-DAR-KA-BAR		RA LXV 41 II 39
			ʿAŠTAR				LI			JA	EŠ$_4$-DAR-LI?-IA		YOS XIII 12 REV 14
			ʿAŠTAR				LAMAS		I		EŠ$_4$-DAR-LA-MA-ZI	FN	M
			ʿAŠTAR				LAMAS		I		EŠ$_4$-DAR-D-LAMA	FN	XIII 1 I 69+
			ʿAŠTAR				MILK		I		EŠ$_4$-DAR-ME-IL-KI	FN	RA LXV 62 V 10
			ʿAŠTAR				NIWR		I		EŠ$_4$-DAR-NE-RI	FN	XIII 1 IX 48
			ʿAŠTAR				PUṮR		I		EŠ$_4$-DAR-PU-UṮ-RI	FN	M+
			ʿAŠTAR				RAḪM		I		EŠ$_4$-DAR-RA-AḪ-MI	FN	XIII 1 VIII 83
			ʿAŠTAR				ŠIMḪ		I		EŠ$_4$-DAR-ŠI-IM-ḪI	FN	XIII 1 XII 2
			ʿAŠTAR				ŠAMŠ		I		EŠ$_4$-DAR-D-UTU-ŠI	FN	M
			ʿAŠTAR				ŠARR	AH			EŠ$_4$-DAR-ŠAR-RA	FN	XIII 1 II 67
			ʿAŠTAR			TA	JṢIʾ				EŠ$_4$-DAR-TA-ZI	FN	XIII 1 IV 79
			ʿAŠTAR			TA	LʾIJ				EŠ$_4$-DAR-TA-AL-E	FN	XIII 1 V 41+
			ʿAŠTAR				TIWR	AH			D-EŠ$_4$-DAR-TE-IR-RA		A.
			ʿAŠTAR				TUWR		I	JA	EŠ$_4$-DAR-TU-RI-IA	FN	XIII 1 XIII 33
			ʿAŠTAR				TABB		I		EŠ$_4$-DAR-TAB-BI	FN	M+, C
	2		ḪAʾL		I		ʿAŠTAR				ḪA-LI$_2$-EŠ$_4$-DAR		RA LXV 53 XII 1
			ʿABD				ʿAŠTAR				AB-DI-D-EŠ$_4$-DAR		A. 19 4, 7
			ʿABD				ʿAŠTAR				AB-DU-EŠ$_4$-DAR		M+
			ʿABD				ʿAŠTAR				ḪA-AB-DU-EŠ$_4$-DAR		M+, C+
		JI	JBAL				ʿAŠTAR				I-BA-AL-EŠ$_4$-DAR		M
			ʾUBUŠ				ʿAŠTAR				U$_2$-BU-UŠ$_3$-EŠ$_4$-DAR		RES 1938 P. 129
			ʾIL		A		ʿAŠTAR				I-LA-EŠ$_4$-DAR		RA LXV 42 III 16+
			ʾIL		I		ʿAŠTAR				I$_3$-LI$_2$-EŠ$_4$-DAR		M+
		JI	ḪLIJ				ʿAŠTAR				IḪ-LI-AŠ-TAR		A. 55 35
		JI	ḪLIJ				ʿAŠTAR				IḪ-LI-EŠ$_4$-DAR		A. P. 133+
			ʾAM	T			ʿAŠTAR	AH			AM-TI-AŠ-TA-RA	FN?	A. LATE
			ḪINN		I		ʿAŠTAR				EN-NI-D-EŠ$_4$-DAR		A. 247 23
			BAʿL		A		ʿAŠTAR				BA-LA-EŠ$_4$-DAR		M
			BAʿL		U		ʿAŠTAR				BA-LU-EŠ$_4$-DAR		M+
			BAWZ		I		ʿAŠTAR				BA-ZI-EŠ$_4$-DAR		M
			BIN		A		ʿAŠTAR				BI-NA-EŠ$_4$-DAR		M+
			BUN		A		ʿAŠTAR				BU-NA-D-INNIN		BASOR 95, 19
			BUN		U		ʿAŠTAR				BU-NU-EŠ$_4$-DAR		M+, C+
		TA	BNIJ				ʿAŠTAR				TAB-NI-EŠ$_4$-DAR	FN	XIII 1 XIII 15+
		TA	BRUW				ʿAŠTAR				TAB-RU?-EŠ$_4$-DAR	FN	XIII 1 V 43
			DAŠUR	AH			ʿAŠTAR				DA-ŠU-RA-EŠ$_4$-DAR	FN	YOS VIII 51 5
			ḎIKR		A		ʿAŠTAR				ZI-IK-RA-EŠ$_4$-DAR		M+
			ḎIKR		I		ʿAŠTAR				ZI-IK-RI-EŠ$_4$-DAR		M+
			ḎIKR				ʿAŠTAR				ZI-KI-IR-EŠ$_4$-[DAR]		M
			ḎUKR		A		ʿAŠTAR				[Z]U-UK-RA-EŠ$_4$-DAR		RA LXV 46 VI 21
			ḎIMR		A		ʿAŠTAR				ZI-IM-RA-EŠ$_4$-DAR		M+
			ḎIMR		I		ʿAŠTAR				ZI-IM-RI-D-EŠ$_4$-DAR		M, A.+

STEMS

ʿAŠTAR	2		ḎIMR		U		ʿAŠTAR		ZI-IM-RU-EŠ$_4$-DAR		IRAQ IV 185 A. 385
			KIBR		I		ʿAŠTAR		KI-IB-RI-EŠ$_4$-DAR		M+
		TA	RWIM				ʿAŠTAR		TA-RI-IM-EŠ$_4$-DAR	FN	XIII 1 II 13
		TA	RʿIŠ				ʿAŠTAR		T[A-R]I-IŠ-EŠ$_4$-DAR	FN	RA LXV 65 VII 36
		TA	ŠJIM				ʿAŠTAR		TA-ŠI-IM-EŠ$_4$-DAR	FN	XIII 1 IV 28
			ŠIJM	AT			ʿAŠTAR		ŠI-MA-AT-EŠ$_4$-DAR	FN	XIII 1 V 75+
			ŠUM		U		ʿAŠTAR		SU-MU-EŠ$_4$-DAR		PBS VIII/2 207 5, M
		TA	TWUR				ʿAŠTAR		TA-TU-UR-EŠ$_4$-DAR	FN	M
			TIWR				ʿAŠTAR		TI-IR-EŠ$_4$-DAR		M+
			TUDAR		I		ʿAŠTAR		TU-DA-RI-EŠ$_4$-DAR	FN	EDZARD, DER 58:7
			TUDAR		UM		ʿAŠTAR		TU-DA-RUM-EŠ$_4$-DAR	FN	EDZARD, DER 61:16
			TUPT		U		ʿAŠTAR		TUP-TU-EŠ$_4$-DAR		M
ʿAZAB	1		ʿAZAB		UM				A-ZA-BU-UM		GAUTIER 23 5+
			ʿAZAB	AN	I				A-ZA-BA-NI		TA 1931, 216
ʿAZAL	1		ʿAZAL		UM				A-ZA-LU-UM		B 14
			ʿAZAL		UM				A-ZA-LUM		EDZARD, DER 60:8
			ʿAZAL		UM				AZ-ZA-LUM		GAUTIER 1 R. 9
			ʿAZAL		UM				A-ZA-AL-LUM		KISURRA 26 6
			ʿAZAL		IM				A-ZA-LIM	GEN	VAS VIII 14 23
			ʿAZAL	AH					ḪA-ZA-LA	FN	M+
			ʿAZAL		AJA				A-ZA-LA-IA		B 14
			ʿAZAL		IJA				A-ZA-LI-IA		B 14+
			ʿAZAL		IJA				A-SA-LI-JA		B 14+
ʿAZAZ	1		ʿAZAZ		UM				A-ZA-ZUM		I
			ʿAZAZ	AN	UM				A-ZA-ZA-NU-UM		B 92
ʿAZB	1		ʿAZB		UM				ḪA-AZ-BU-UM		RA LXV 53 XI 20
ʿAZIB	1		ʿAZIB	AH					ḪA-ZI-BA	FN	XIII 1 IV 35
			ʿAZIB	AN					ḪA-ZI-PA-AN		RA LXV 44 IV 25
			ʿAZIB	AT	UM				ḪA-ZI-BA-TUM	MN	GAUTIER 65 5
ʿAZIZ	1		ʿAZIZ	AN					A-ZI-ZA-AN		RA LXV 44 IV 45
ʿAZZ	1		ʿAZZ		U				AZ-ZU	FN	M+, C+
			ʿAZZ		U				ḪA-AZ-ZU		C+
			ʿAZZ	AT	UM				A-ZA-TUM	FN	CT VIII 37D 7, M
			ʿAZZ	AT	AM				A-ZA-TAM	FN ACC	CT VIII 37D 3
			ʿAZZ	ATANIM					ḪA-ZA-TA-NIM	MN GEN	C II 6
			ʿAZZ				ʿAMM	I	AZ-ZA-AM-MI		A. 265 19
			ʿAZZ		I		ʾIL		A-ZI-DINGIR		HARRIS 39 11
			ʿAZZ		I		DAGAN		A-ZI-D-DA-GAN		A. LATE
			ʿAZZ		U		ḪAʾL	IM	A-ZU-ḪA-LIM	NOM	M
			ʿAZZ		U	KA			AZ-ZU-KA	FN	M+, C
			ʿAZZ		U	KI			AZ-ZU-UK-KI	FN	XIII 1 VIII 66
			ʿAZZ		U	NI			AZ-ZU-UN-NI	FN	M
ʿDIJ	1	JA	ʿDIJ				....		JA-AḪ-DI-[....]		M
ʿDUN	1	JA	ʿDUN		UM				IA-AḪ-DU-NU-UM		B 26
		JA	ʿDUN	AN	UM				IA-AḪ-DU-NA-NU-UM		JCS XXIV 60 NO.51 REV.
		JA	ʿDUN				LIʾM		IA-AḪ-DU-UN-LI-IM		M+
		JA	ʿDUN				LIʾM		IA-AḪ-DU-LI-IM		M+
		JA	ʿDUN				LIʾM		IA-AḪ-DU-UL-LI-IM		M
ʿḎAR	1	JA	ʿḎAR				ʾIL		IA-DAR-DINGIR		RUTTEN 5 9+
		JA	ʿḎAR				ʾIL		IA-AḪ-ZA-AR-DINGIR		B 26
		JA	ʿḎAR				ʾIL		IA-AḪ-ZA-AR-I$_3$-IL		B 26
		JA	ʿḎAR				ʾIL		IA-ZA-AR-DINGIR?		IX 291 II 21,30
		JA	ʿḎAR				ʾIL		AḪ-ZA-AR-I$_3$-DINGIR		VAS XVIII 20:20
		TA	ʿḎAR	AH					TA-DA-RA	FN	M
ʿḎIR	1	JA	ʿḎIR						IA-AḪ-ZI-IR		YOS VIII 76 26
		JA	ʿḎIR		UM				IA-AḪ-ZI-RUM		B 26+
		JA	ʿḎIR		U				IA-AḪ-ZI-RU		CT XLV 63 34
		JA	ʿḎIR		I				IA-AḪ-ZI-RI	GEN	BM 16943 34
		JA	ʿḎIR				ʾIL		IA-AḪ-ZI-IR-DINGIR		B 26+
		JA	ʿḎIR				ʾIL		IA-AḪ-ZI-IR-I$_3$-IL		SUMER V 137
		JA	ʿḎIR				ʾIL		IA-AḪ-ZI-IR-I$_3$-DINGIR		CT XLV 8 6
		ME	ʿḎIR		I				ME-ZI-RI		M
ʿEBB	1		ʿEBB		IM				IB-BI-IM	GEN	M+
			ʿEBB	AT	UM				IB-BA-TUM	FN	M+
			ʿEBB	AT	IM				IB-BA-TIM	FN GEN	M
			ʿEBB	ATANUM					IB-BA-TA-NU-UM		BE VI/2 26 III 1

STEMS

ʿEBIB	1		ʿEBIB		UM					E-BI-BU-UM		SIMMONS 76 6
ʿEMES	1		ʿEMES		UM					E-ME-ZUM		I+
ʿEMUQ	1		ʿEMUQ		I		ʾEL			E-[M]U-QI$_2$-EL		RA LXV 40 I 3
ʿIJN	1		ʿIJN				BAʿL	I		IN-BA-AḪ-LI	FN	A.
	2		ʾIL		I		ʿIJN	A	JA	I$_3$-LI$_2$-I-NA-A-A		GAUTIER 40 7
ʿIMD	2		TABUB				ʿIMD	I		TA-BU-UB-IM-[DI]?	FN	VIII 33 7
			TABUB		I		ʿIMD	I		TA-BU-TI?-IM-DI	FN	VIII 31 10 15
ʿIMS	1		ʿIMS		U					IM-ṢU		JNES XIII 210+ LATE
ʿINAB	1		ʿINAB	AN	UM					I-NA-BA-NU-UM		U
ʿINB	1		ʿINB		UM					IN-BU-UM		M
			ʿINB		U					IN-BU	FN	C+
			ʿINB	AT	UM					IN-BA-TUM	FN	BM 78768 3', X 84 3+
			ʿINB		I		ʾIL			IN-BI$_2$-IL		U UNPUBL.
			ʿINB		I		JARAḪ			IN-BI-RA-AḪ		KISURRA 6 15
ʿIQB	1		ʿIQB	AN						ḪI-IQ-BA-AN		M+
			ʿIQB	AN	UM					IQ-BA-NU-UM		I+
			ʿIQB		A		ʾAḪ	UM		IQ-BA-A-ḪU-UM		KISURRA 4A 11, M
			ʿIQB		A		ʾAḪ	UM		IQ-BA-ḪU-UM		KISURRA 121 6
			ʿIQB		A		ʿAMM	U		IQ-BA?-AM-MU		A. 8 35
			ʿIQB		I		HADD	U		IQ-BI-D-IM		KISURRA 114 7
ʿIŠTAR	2		ʿABD				ʿIŠTAR AH			AB-DU-IŠ-TA-RA?		B 9
ʿIZB	1		ʿIZB		A		....			ḪI-IZ-BA-.[....]		VAS XIII 62 R. 1
ʿIZIL	1		ʿIZIL		I					ḪI-ZI-LI		C II 45 II 35
ʿIZIZ	1		ʿIZIZ	AH						I-ZI-ZA	FN	RA LXV 58 I 28
ʿIZL	1		ʿIZL	AH						ḪI-IZ-LA	FN	C+
ʿIZZ	1		ʿIZZ	AN						IZ-ZA-AN		M
			ʿIZZ	AN						I-ZA-AN		RA LXV 44 IV 35
			ʿIZZ	AN	UM					I-ZA-NUM$_2$		U
			ʿIZZ	AN	UM					I-ZA-NU-UM		U
			ʿIZZ	AN	I					IZ-ZA-NI		M
			ʿIZZ		AJA					IZ-ZA-A-IA	FN	XIII 1 III 68
			ʿIZZ		IJA					I-ZI-IA		RA LXV 51 IX 41
			ʿIZZ	AK	UM					I-ZA-KUM		B 24
			ʿIZZ		I					ḪU-IZ-ZI	FN	M
			ʿIZZ				ʾAB	I		IZ-ZA-BI		C+
			ʿIZZ		U	KA				I-ZU-KA		XIII 1 III 50
			ʿIZZ		U		ŠAPAR			I-ZU-SA-PAR$_2$		U+
			ʿIZZ		U		ŠAPAR			IZ?-ZU?-ŠA-PA-AR		BIN II 98 5
			ʿIZZ		U	NI				IZ-ZU-UN-NI		M
ʿMIS	1	JA	ʿMIS				ʾIL			IA-AḪ-MI-IS-DINGIR		RUTTEN 2 23+
		JA	ʿMIS				ʾIL	UM		IA-AḪ-MI-ZI-LUM		RUTTEN 16 17
		JA	ʿMIS				JARAḪ			IA-AḪ-MI-IS-D-SIN		M
ʿMUS	1	JE	ʿMUS		UM					E-MU-ZUM		I UNPUBL.
		JA	ʿMUS				....			IA-AḪ-MU-IS-[....]		XIV 129:5
		JA	ʿMUS				ʾIL			IA-AḪ-MU-US-DINGIR		M
ʿNIJ	1	JA	ʿNIJ				ʾIL			IA-AḪ-NI-DINGIR		A 7630 6
		ME	ʿNIJ		UM					ME-EḪ-NI-JU-UM		M
		ME	ʿNIJ		UM					ME-EḪ-NU-UM		KISURRA 36 4
		ME	ʿNIJ		IM					ME-EḪ-NI-IM	GEN	KISURRA 80A
ʿNUW	1	JA	ʿNUW			HU				IA-AḪ-NU-U$_2$		OIP XLVII 66
ʿQIB	1	JI	ʿQIB		UM					I-KI-BU-UM		CT VIII 19 19+
		JA	ʿQIB				ʾIL			IA-KI-IB-DINGIR		TIM V 33 23
		ME	ʿQIB		UM					ME-KI-BU-UM		U, M+
		ME	ʿQIB		IM					ME-KI-BI-IM	GEN	M+
ʿQUB	1	JA	ʿQUB		U					IA-KU-BU		CT II 9 26
		JI	ʿQUB		UM					I-KU-BU-UM		KISURRA 117 7, 9+
		JA	ʿQUB		AM					IA-KU-BA-[A]M?	NOM	RA LXV 46 V 84
		JA	ʿQUB	AN						IA-KU-B[A]-AN		RA LXV 45 V 57
		JA	ʿQUB				HEDD	A		IA-AK-KU-UB-E-DA		JEA VIII 207F.
		JA	ʿQUB				ʾIL			A-AḪ-KU-UB-DINGIR		HARRIS 12 3+
		JA	ʿQUB				ʾIL			IA-KU-UB-DINGIR		B 27+
		JA	ʿQUB				ʾIL			IA-AḪ-KU-UB-DINGIR		XIII 1 VII 17, C+
		JA	ʿQUB		I		ʾIL			IA-AḪ-KU-BI-DINGIR		CT II 39 18
		JA	ʿQUB		I		ʾIL			IA-KU-BI-DINGIR		KISURRA 41 10
	2		ʾAḪ		I	JI	ʿQUB	A		A-ḪI-I-KU-BA		KISURRA 7A 9
			ŠIMAʿ			TA	ʿQUB			ŠI-ME-TA-GU-UB		M+

STEMS

ʿTIQ	1	TA	ʿTIQ				ʾABN		U	TA-TI-QA-AB-NU		RES 1938 128
ʿUWQ	1		ʿUWQ		UM					ḪU-KU-UM	FN	RA LXV 58 I 51
ʿUMAS	1		ʿUMAS		UM					ḪU-MA-ZUM		VAS VIII 14 33
ʿUMUS	2		MUT				ʿUMUS		IM	MU-UT-ḪU-MU-ZI-IM		XIV 122:6+
ʿUZAB	1		ʿUZAB		UM					U$_2$-ZA-BU-UM		SIMMONS 46 32
			ʿUZAB		UM					U$_2$-SA-BU-UM		SIMMONS 52 16
			ʿUZAB		IM					U$_2$-ZA-BI-IM	GEN	SIMMONS 70 16
			ʿUZAB		U					[ḪU]-ZA-BU	FN	XIII 1 XIV 14
ʿUZAL	1		ʿUZAL		UM					U$_2$-ZA-LUM		CT XXXIII 46A 3+
			ʿUZAL		UM					ḪU-ZA-LUM		UCP X/1 17 14+
			ʿUZAL	AT	UM					ḪU-ZA-LA-TUM	FN	WATERMAN 12 R. 7+
			ʿUZAL	AT	UM					ḪU-ZA-LA-TUM	MN	UCP X/1 86 4+
			ʿUZAL		IJA					ḪU-ZA-LI-IA		BIROT, TEA 70BIS:36'
ʿUZIL	1		ʿUZIL		A					U$_2$-ZI-LA		RA LXV 50 IX 6
ʿUZUB	1		ʿUZUB		UM					ḪU-ZU-BU-UM		RA VIII 75
ʿUZUL	1		ʿUZUL		I					U$_2$-ZU-LI		RA LXV 51 X 6
ʿUZZ	1		ʿUZZ		U					UZ-ZU	FN	XIII 1 XIV 31
			ʿUZZ		AM					ḪU-UZ-ZA-AM	ACC	XIII 100 9
			ʿUZZ				HADD		U	U$_2$-ZA-DU		U
ʿZIB	1	JA	ʿZIB		UM					IA-ZI-BU-UM		M+
		JI	ʿZIB		UM					I-ZI-BU-UM		KISURRA 10A 5+
		JA	ʿZIB		IM					IA-ZI-BI-IM	GEN	XIV 92:26+
		JA	ʿZIB				....			IA-AḪ-ZI-IB-[....]		M
		JA	ʿZIB				HADD		U	IA-AḪ-ZI-IB-D-IM		M+
		JA	ʿZIB				HADD		U	IA-ZI-IB-D?-IM?		M
		JA	ʿZIB				ʾIL			IA-AH-ZI-IB-DINGIR		RUTTEN 21 7+, M
		JA	ʿZIB				ʾIL			A-AḪ-ZI-IB-DINGIR		HARRIS 57 2
		JA	ʿZIB				DAGAN			IA-ZI-IB-D-DA-GAN		M+
		JA	ʿZIB		I		ʾIL			IA-AḪ-ZI-BI-DINGIR		KISURRA 86A 11
		JA	ʿZIB		I		ʾIL			A-AḪ-ZI-BI-DINGIR		SIMMONS 70 5
		JA	ʿZIB		I		ʾIL			IA-A-ZI-BI-DINGIR		KAJ 34 18, 25 LATE
		JA	ʿZIB		A		ʾEL			IA-AḪ-ZI-BA-EL?		RA LXV 50 VIII 77
		JA	ʿZIB		U	HU				IA-AḪ-ZI-BU-U$_2$		M+
		JI	ʿZIB			NA				I-ZI-IB-NA		CT XLV 118 24
ʿZUB	1	JA	ʿZUB				ʾIL			IA-AḪ-ZU-UB-DINGIR		B 26+
WḪIJ	1	JA	WḪIJ				ʾIL			IA-U$_2$-ḪI-DINGIR		B 31
WḪIN	1	MU	WḪIN		UM					MU-ḪI-NU-UM		HAGER DISSERT. PL II/3
WARḪ	1		WARḪ				ʾIL		A	WA-AR-ḪI-LA$_2$		CCT I 38C 2 CAPP.
WBIT	1	MU	WBIT		UM					MU-BI-TU-UM		LANGDON XXVII 4
WDAJ	1	ʾA	WDAJ				ʾIL			A-U$_3$-DA-IL		U
		ʾA	WDAJ				ʾIL			A-AW-TE-IL		U
		ʾU	WDAJ				....			U$_2$-DA-[....]		TA 30, 615 29
		ʾU	WDAJ				MA			U$_2$-DA-MA		I
WDAD	1	MU	WDAD		UM					MU-DA-DU-UM		I, VAS VIII 60 5, 18+
		MU	WDAD		U					MU-DA-DU		YOS XIII 513:9
WMAʾ	1	JA	WMAʾ				ʾAḪ		UM	JA-MA-A-ḪU-UM		RA LXV 52 X 49
		JA	WMAʾ				ʿAMM	AJ	I	IA-AW-MA-ḪA-MA-JI-KI	GN	M
		JA	WMAʾ				ʿAMM		I	JA-MA-ḪA-MI-KI	GN	M
		JA	WMAʾ				ʿAMM		UM	JA-MA-ḪA-MU-UM		M
		JA	WMAʾ				ʿAMM		UM	IA-MA-ḪA-MU-UM		M
		ʾU	WMAʾ				ʾIL			U$_3$-MA-IL		U
		ʾU	WMAʾ				ʾIL		A	U$_2$-MA-D-DINGIR		B 40
WPIʿ	1	MU	WPIʿ		I					MU-BI-ḪI		TA 30, 7 10
WQAH	1	ʾU	WQAH							U$_3$-GA		U
		ʾU	WQAH							U$_3$-GA-A		SAUREN, WUG 114 REV, U
		ʾU	WQAH				HADD		U	U$_2$-QA-D-IM		RA LXV 44 IV 51
		ʾU	WQAH				HADD		U	U$_2$-GA-D-IM		BIROT, TEA 24:6
		ʾU	WQAH				ʾIL			U$_2$-QA-DINGIR		M+
		ʾU	WQAH				ʾIL			U$_2$-GA-DINGIR		GAUTIER 41 5
		ʾU	WQAH				ʾIL			U$_3$-QA-DINGIR		SIMMONS 1 3+
		ʾU	WQAH				ʾIL			U$_2$-QA-IL		SYRIA V 274 HANA
		ʾU	WQAH				ʾIL		A	U$_2$-Q[A]-I-LA		A 7699:14, ISCHCHALI
		ʾU	WQAH				ʾIL		UM	U$_2$-GA-DINGIR-LUM		FRANK 29 9
		ʾU	WQAH				KI					
							ʾEL			U$_2$-QA-KI-EL		RA LXV 51 IX 69
		ʾU	WQAH				ŠAMŠ			U$_2$-GA-A-D-UTU		SZLECHTER TJ 15944 SEAL

STEMS

WQAH	1	ʾU	WQAH				ŠAMŠ			U$_2$-GA-D-UTU		BIROT, TEA 72 V 16'
WQIH	1	ʾU	WQIH				ʾEL			U$_2$-QI$_2$-E[L]		RA LXV 41 II 44
WQIR	1	MU	WQIR	AN	UM					MU-GI-RA-NU-UM		U
WSIL	1	MU	WSIL	AT	UM					MU-ZI-LA-TUM	FN	B 35
WŠIʿ	1	ʾU	WŠIʿ		UM					U$_2$-SI-UM		I
		ʾU	WŠIʿ		I					U$_2$-SI-I		I+
WŠIB	1	JA	WŠIB		U					IA-AW-ŠI-BU		M
WṢIʾ	1	JA	WṢIʾ							I-IA-U$_2$-ZI	FN	XIII 1 X 29
		JA	WṢIʾ							U$_2$-ZI		M
		JA	WṢIʾ				ʾEL			IA-A[W-Z]I-EL?		VIII 87 8'
		JA	WṢIʾ				ʾIL			IA-AW-ZI-DINGIR		M+
		JA	WṢIʾ				ʾIL			IA-U$_2$-ZI-DINGIR		B 31
		JA	WṢIʾ				ʾIL			IA-U$_2$-ṢI-DINGIR		BAGHD. MITT. II 23
		JA	WṢIʾ				ʾIL	UM		IA-U$_2$-ZI-LUM		B 31
		JA	WṢIʾ				ʾALAŠ	UM		U$_2$-ZI-A-LA-ŠUM		M
		MU	WṢIʾ			JA				MU-ZI-IA		M+
		JA	WṢIʾ				ŠUM	U				
							ʾAB	UM		U$_2$-ṢI-SU-MU-A-BU-UM		AJSL XXVIII 244 19
WTAʾ	1	ʾU	WTAʾ	T	UM					U$_2$-TA-TUM	FN	C
		ʾU	WTAʾ				ʾAḪ	I		U$_2$-TA-A-ḪI		M
WTAR	1	TU	WTAR				ʾABN	U		TU-TAR-AB-NU		M
		MU	WTAR							MU?-TA-AR		IX 290 1
	2		ḪAʾL		I	MU	WTAR			ḪA-LI$_2$-MU-TAR		M
JʿIL	1	JA	JʿIL				LIʾM			IA-ḪI-IL-LI-IM		M
		JI	JʿIL				DIJN	I		I-ḪI-IL-DI-NI-X?		RA LXV 48 VIII 1
		JI	JʿIL				PI					
							ʾIL			I-ḪI-IL-BI-DINGIR		M
JʿUL	1	JA	JʿUL				DAGAN			IA-ḪU-UL-D-DA-GAN		RA LXV 48 VII 75
JAʾ	1		JAʾ	AT	UM					IA-A-A-TUM	MN	A 29366:3
			JAʾ		A		ʿAN	UM		IA-A-A-NU-UM		YOS V 134 16
			JAʾ		U		ʾAHL	I		IA-U$_2$-A-LI$_2$		KISURRA 85 19
			JAʾ		U		ʾIL	I		IA-U-I-LI$_2$		SUMER V 143 NO. 2
			JAʾ		U		ŠUM	UM		IA?-U$_2$-SU?-MU-UM?		XIII 146 13
			JAʾ		UM					IA$_3$-A-UM		U
			JAʾ		UM					I-A-UM		U
			JAʾ		UM					IA-A-UM		BIN VII 67 27
			JAʾ		UM		ʾIL			IA-U$_2$-UM-DINGIR		B 31
			JAʾ		UM		ʾIL			IA-A-UM-[DINGIR]		B 31
			JAʾ		UM		ʾIL			IA-WU-UM-DINGIR		B 31
			JAʾ		UM		LU		HU	IA-UM-LU-ḪU		UET V 496:10
	2		ʾAB		I		JAʾ	A		A-BI-IA-A		KISURRA 102 7+
			ʾAB		I		JAʾ	UM		A-BI-IA-U$_2$-UM		YOS VIII 10 9
			ʾIL		I		JAʾ	UM		I$_3$-LI$_2$-IA-UM		KISURRA 71A 5+
			ʾIL		I		JAʾ	UM		I$_3$-LI$_2$-I-UM		KISURRA 4A 12+
			ʾIL		I		JAʾ	UM		I$_3$-LI$_2$-I-U$_2$-UM		KISURRA 56 3+
			ʾIL		I		JAʾ	UM		I$_3$-LI$_2$-U$_2$-A-UM		KISURRA 186 5
			ʾIL		I		JAʾ	UM		I$_3$-LI$_2$-A-UM		B 21
JAʾAN	1		JAʾAN							IA-AN-[....]		IX 257 2
			JAʾAN		UM					IA-A-NU-UM		BIN VII 67 9
			JAʾAN		AM					IA-A-NA-AM		M
			JAʾAN				ʾIL			IA-AN-DINGIR		M
			JAʾAN				ŠARR	I		IA-AN-ŠAR-RI		M XIII 1 X 16
JAʾAR	1		JAʾAR							IA-A-AR		M
			JAʾAR		UM					IA-A-RUM		VAS VII 183 I 7, II 12+
			JAʾAR				HADD	U		IA-ḪA-AR-D-IM		M
			JAʾAR				ʾIL			IA-AR-I-I[I-....]		XIII 69 5
			JAʾAR				ʾIPQ			IA-AR-I-BI-IQ		M
	2		ʾAB		I		JAʾAR			A-BI-IA-ḪA-AR		B 10+
			ʾAB		I		JAʾAR			A-BI-A-ḪA-AR		CT XLIII 125 1+
			ʾAB		I		JAʾAR			A-BI-ḪA-AR		B 10+
			KAʾM		I		JAʾAR	UM		KA-MI-IA-A-RUM		VAS VII 128 46
			ŠIPṬ		I		JAʾAR			ŠI-IP-TI-A-ḪA-AR	FN	C
JAʾIT	1		JAʾIT		I	JI	JBAL			IA-I-TI-I-BA-AL		M
JAʾN	1		JAʾN		UM					IA-NU-UM		B 29
			JAʾN		UM		PI			JA-NU-UM-BI-KI	GN	M
			JAʾN	AN						JA-NA-AN-KI	GN	M+

STEMS

JAʾN	1	JAʾN		A	ʾAHL	UM		JA-NA-A-LUM	GN	MRS VI P.125 61
	2	ʾIL		I	JAʾN	UM		I_3-LI_2-IA-NU-UM		TIM I 29 3
		MUT		I	JAʾN	A		MU-TI-I-IA-NA		B 35
JAḪAD	1	JAḪAD		UM				IA-ḪA-DUM		BIN VII 155 1
		JAḪAD		UM				IA-ḪA?-DU-UM		VII 199 8
		JAḪAD		U				IA-ḪA-TU		B 26
		JAḪAD		U				IA-ḪA-DU		M
		JAḪAD		IM				IA-ḪA-DI-IM	GEN	XIII 1 IX 30
		JAḪAD		A	....			IA-ḪA-DA-[....]		RA LXV 45 V 74
		JAḪAD			ʾEL	UM		IA-ḪA-AD-E-LUM		RIFTIN 136 26
		JAḪAD			ʾEL	UM		IA-ḪA-TE-LUM?		UET V 605 13
		JAḪAD			ʾIL			IA-ḪA-AD-DINGIR		M
		JAḪAD			ʿAMM	U		IA-ḪA-AD-ḪA-AM-MU		M
		JAḪAD			ʿAMM	U		IA-ḪA-AD-ḪA-MU		M+
		JAḪAD			ʿAMM	U	HU	IA-ḪA-AD-ḪA-MU-U_2		M
		JAḪAD			JARAḪ			IA-ḪA-AD-E-RA-AḪ		M
	2	ʾAḪ		U	JAḪAD			A-ḪU-IA-ḪA-AD		M+
		ʿAḎR		I	JAḪAD			AD-RI-E-ḪA-AD		M+
	JA	ŠWUB			JAḪAD			IA-ŠU-UB-IA-ḪA-AD		M
JAʿAL	1	JAʿAL		A				IA-ḪA-LA		YOS XIII 513:9
		JAʿAL			PI					
					ʾIL	UM		IA-ḪA-AL-PI-LUM		3NT867:5, 12, 21
JAʿIL	1	JAʿIL	AT	UM				IA-ḪI-LA-TUM	FN	B 26
		JAʿIL	AT	UM				IA-I-LA?-TUM	FN	B 26
		JAʿIL	AT	IM				IA-ḪI-LA-TIM	GEN	CT XLVIII 27 CASE
		JAʿIL	AH					IA-ḪI-LA	FN	M
		JAʿIL		A				IA-I-LA	MN	RA LXV 40 I 27
		JAʿIL						JA-A-IL-KI	GN	M+
		JAʿIL						JA-I-IL-KI	GN	M+
		JAʿIL	AJ	I				JA-I-LA-JI-KI	GN	M
		JAʿIL	AN					JA-I-LA-AN		M
		JAʿIL	AN	U				JA-I-LA-NU	TRIBE	C
		JAʿIL	AN	IM				JA-I-LA-NIM	TRIBE GEN	M+, SHEMSHARA P. 100+
		JAʿIL	AN	I				JA-I-LA-NI	TRIBE	SHEMSHARA P.100
JAJA	1	JAJA		UM				IA-IA-UM		B 27+
		JAJA	AT	UM				IA-IA-TUM		B 26
JAJAM	1	JAJAM		U				IA-IA-MU		B 26
JABAL	1	JABAL			HADD	U		IA-BA-AL-D-IM		M
	2	ʾAḪ		I	JABAL			A-ḪI-E-BA-AL		M
		ʾAB		I	JABAL			A-BI-A-BA-AL		FIGULLA CAT. I 14206
		JIŠʿ		I	JABAL			IŠ-ḪI-E-BA-AL		M
		DAWD		I	JABAL			DA-DI-E-BA-AL		UNPUBL.
		MUT		I	JABAL			MU-TI-A-BA-AL-KI	GN	B 35+
		MUT		I	JABAL			MU-TI-BA-AL-KI	GN	B 35+
		MUT		I	JABAL			MU-TA-BA-AL-KI	GN	OIP XI 216 IV 3
		MUT		I	JABAL	A		MU-TI-A-BA-LA-KI	GN	B 35
		NUʿM		I	JABAL			NU-UḪ-ME-E-BA-AL	FN	RA LXV 62 V 19
		SITR		I	JABAL			ZI-IT-RI-E-BA-AL		M+
		ŠUMUT		I	JABAL	A		SU-MU-TI-A-BA-LA?		PBS XI/2 1 I 35
	3	ŠUM		U	MUT	I				
					JABAL	A		SU-MU-MU-TI-A-BA-LA		B 39
JABAŠ	1	JABAŠ	IJ	I				JA-BA-SI-JI	TRIBE	M
		JABAŠ	IJ	I				JA-BA-SI-I	TRIBE	M
		JABAŠ	IJ	IM				JA-BA-SI-IM	TRIBE	M
JABS	1	JABS	AT	UM				IA-AB-ZA?-TUM	MN?	VAS VIII 121 5
JABUB	1	JABUB		U				IA-BU-BU		CT XLIII 29 1
JABUS	1	JABUS	AT	UM				IA-BU-ZA-TUM	FN	CT XLVIII 31 5, 9
		JABUS	AT	IM				IA-BU-ZA-TIM	FN GEN	B 25+
JABUŠ	1	JABUŠ						IA-BU-UŠ		CT VIII 29A 28
		JABUŠ		UM				IA-BU-ŠUM	GN	KING LIH II NO. 97 III 1
		JABUŠ		UM				[I]A-BU-SU-UM		VIII 85 41, 44
JAD	1	JAD		IM				IA-DI-IM	GEN	TIM V 35 6
		JAD	AN	UM				IA-DA-NU-UM		SIMMONS 131 17
		JAD		I	NAṢIR			IA-DI-NA-ṢIR		BM 17051, 17052
	3	ʾAŠD		UM	PI					
					JAD	IM		AŠ-DU-UM-BI-IA-DI-IM		RA LXV 55 XIII 44

STEMS

JADAʿ	1	JADAʿ		UM				IA-DA-ḪU-UM		YOS XII
		JADAʿ		UM				IA-ṬA$_3$-ḪU-UM		YOS XII
		JADAʿ				ḪAʾL	UM	IA-DA-AḪ-ḪA-LUM		B 25
		JADAʿ				HADD	U	[IA]-ṬA$_3$-AḪ-D-IM		VI 76 10
		JADAʿ				ʾIL		IA-DAḪ-DINGIR		B 25+
		JADAʿ				ʾIL		IA-DA-AḪ-DINGIR		CT XLVIII 21 SEAL
		JADAʿ				ʾIL		IA-DA-DINGIR		M
		JADAʿ				ʿAMM	U	IA-DA-AM-MU		C II 5 4
		JADAʿ				JAT	UM	IA-DA-A-A-TUM		B 25
		JADAʿ				LIʾM		IA-DAḪ-LI-IM		YOS XII
		JADAʿ				LIʾM		IA-ṬA$_3$-AḪ-LI-IM		YOS XII
		JADAʿ				PI				
						ʾIL		IA-DA-BI-DINGIR		AJSL XXXIII 224 3
		JADAʿ			TI	ʾEL		IA-DA-AḪ-TE-DINGIR		UNPUBL.
	2	KAʾB		I		JADAʿ		KA-BI-E-DA-AḪ		XIII 1 XI 54
		ŠAM		A		JADAʿ	UM	SA-MA-A-DA-ḪU-UM		M+
		ŠAM		A		JADAʿ	U	SA-MA-A-DA-ḪU		M
		ŠAM		A		JADAʿ	IM	SA-MA-A-DA-Ḫ[I-I]M	GEN	M
		ŠUM		U		JADAʿ	UM	SU-MU-A-DA-ḪU-UM		KISURRA 78A 15
JADID	1	JADID		UM				IA-DI-DU-UM		B 25+, M+
		JADID		UM				IA-DI-DUM		CT XLI A 10+
		JADID		U				IA-DI-DU		FIGULLA CAT. I 13371 M
		JADID		IM				IA-DI-DIM	GEN	JCS IV 95 1612 13
		JADID		IM				IA-DI-D[I-IM]	GEN	M
		JADID	AT	UM				IA-DI-DA-TUM	MN	B 25+
		JADID	AT	IM				IA-DI-DA-TIM	MN GEN	B 25+
		JADID		A				IA-DI-DA	MN GEN	VII 206 2, 13
		JADID	AH					IA-DI-DA	FN	M+
JADN	1	JADN		U				IA-AD-NU		M
JAKAL	1	JAKAL	ITIJIM					JA-KA-LI-TE-IM	TRIBE GEN	M
		JAKAL	ITIJI					[JA]-KA-LI-TI-I	TRIBE GEN	M
JAKUK	1	JAKUK		UM				IA-KU?-KU-UM		B 27
JALQUṬ	1	JALQUṬ		UM				IA-AL-GU-TUM		BIN II 68 18
JAM	2	MAʾD		I		JAM	A	MA-DI-IA-MA		UCP X/1 33 10
		MUT		U		JAM	A	MU-TU-IA-MA		M
	3	ʾALUN				PI				
						JAM	U	ḪA-LU-UN-BI-JA-MU		M
		ʾALUN				PI				
						JAM	U	ḪA-LU-UM-BI-JA-MU		RA LXV 43 III 78
		ʾALUN				PI				
						JAM	U	ḪA-LU-BI-JA-MU		M
JAMAM	1	JAMAM	AH					IA-MA-MA?	FN	M
		JAMAM			HU			IA$_3$-MA-AM-U$_2$		U
	2	ŠUM		I		JAMAM		SU-MI-IA-MA-AM		XII 61 5
		ŠUM		U		JAMAM		SU-MU-IA-MA-AM		M+
JAMAN	1	JAMAN						IA?-MA-AN		XII 5 6
JAMIN	1	JAMIN						IA-MI-IN	TRIBE	M
		JAMIN		I				IA-MI-NI	TRIBE	M
		JAMIN		A				IA-MI-NA-A	TRIBE	M
		JAMIN		A				IA-MI-NA	TRIBE	M+
		JAMIN		A				IA-MI-NA	PN	RA LXV 45 V 21
		JAMIN		A				I-IA-MI-NA	TRIBE	M
		JAMIN		A				IA-ME-NA	TRIBE	M
		JAMIN		UM				JA-ME-NU-UM		TA 1931, 538 IV 1, 13
		JAMIN		IM				IA-MI-NIM	TRIBE	M
JAMM	1	JAMM		AJA				IA-AM-MA-A		B 28+
		JAMM		AJA				IA-AM-MA-A-IA	FN	C+
		JAMM	AN					IA-AM-MA-AN		YOS XIII 514:6
		JAMM		U	HU			IA-AM-MU-U$_2$		VAS XVIII 19 R. 6
		JAMM		U		QAʾD	UM	IA-AM-MU?-QA-DU-UM		III 56 7
JAMN	1	JAMN		UM				IA-AM-NU-UM		B 28+
		JAMN		IJA				IA-AM-NI-IA		RA LXV 54 XII 63
		JAMN	ATAN					IA-AM-NA-TA-AN		RA LXV 52 X 48
		JAMN	UN	UM				IA-AM-NU-NU-UM		TIM III 26 13, 39 16
JANIN	1	JANIN		UM				IA-NI-NU-UM		TIM V 18 22
JANT	1	JANT		IJA				IA-AN-TI-IA		M+

STEMS

JAPʿ	1	JAPʿ		UM			IA-AP-ḪU-UM		M+
		JAPʿ	AT	UM			IA-AP-ḪA-TUM	MN	B 24+
		JAPʿ	AT	UM			IA-AP-ḪA-TUM	FN	YOS VIII 12 2+
	2	ʾANN		U	JAPʿ	AH	AN-NU-IA-AP-ḪA	FN	XIII 1 IV 3+
JAPAR	1	JAPAR		IM			IA-PA-RI-IM	GEN	M
	2 JI	JṢIʾ			JAPAR		I-ZI-A-PA-AR		B 22
		ŠUM		U	JAPAR		[SU-MU]-A-PA-AR		B 38
JAQAR	1	JAQAR					IA-QAR		WATERMAN 72 4
		JAQAR		UM			IA-QA-RUM		M+
		JAQAR		UM			IA-GA-RU-UM		KISURRA 59A 24
		JAQAR	T	UM			IA-QAR-TUM	FN	M
		JAQAR			ʾIL		IA-QAR-DINGIR		CT VI 49 A 23
	2	ʾAB		I	JAQAR		A-BI-E-QAR		M+
		ʾAB		U	JAQAR		A-BU-WA-QAR		M
		ʾAB		U	JAQAR		A-BU-QAR		M
		ʾAB		UM	JAQAR		A-BU-UM-WA-QAR		M
		ʿAMM		U	JAQAR		ḪA-MU-IA-QAR		RA LXV 52 X 62
JAQR	1	JAQR		UM	ʾIL		IA-AQ-RUM-DINGIR		A 22010
		JAQR	AN				[I]A-AQ-RA-AN		RA LXV 44 IV 37
		JAQR	IT	UM			IA-AQ-RI-TUM		EDZARD, DER 155 REV 15
	2	ʾIL		I	JAQR	A	I_3-LI_2-AQ-RA		IRAQ XXX 90, RIMAH
		ŠARR		UM	JAQR	AH	LUGAL-JA-AQ-RA	FN	XIII 1 X 45
JARAḪ	1	JARAḪ			ʿAD	U	SIN-A-DU		RA XLIII 8 QATNA
		JARAḪ			ʾAŠD	UM	D-EN-ZU-AŠ-DU-UM		WALTERS, WL 114:2
		JARAḪ			DAŠUR		SIN-DA-ŠUR		VAS IX 185 12+
		JARAḪ			KIWN	A	SIN-KI-NA		TCL I 237 31
		JARAḪ			TIWR	I	D-EN-ZU-TI-RI		M+
		JARAḪ			TIWR	IM	D-EN-ZU-TI-RI-IM	GEN	M
		JARAḪ	T	UM			IA-RA-AḪ-TUM	MN	B 29+
		JARAḪ	T	IM			IA-RA-AḪ-TIM	MN GEN	YOS XII
	2 TA	HWIJ			JARAḪ		TA-AḪ-WI?-D-EN-ZU		RA LXIV 28 NO. 16
		JAḪAD			JARAḪ		IA-ḪA-AD-E-RA-AḪ		M
		ʾUWR		I	JARAḪ		U_2-RI-E-RA-AḪ		M
		ʾAB		A	JARAḪ		A-BA-A-RA-AḪ		KICH II D 8 3
		ʾAB		I	JARAḪ		A-BI-A-RA-AḪ		B 9+
		ʾAB		I	JARAḪ		A-BI-E-RA-AḪ		B+, M+
		ʾAB		I	JARAḪ		A-BI-RA-AḪ		B 9+, A. 38 18
		ʾAB		I	JARAḪ		A-BE-RA-AḪ		B 9
		ʿABD			JARAḪ		AB-DI-A-RA-AḪ		B 9+
		ʿABD			JARAḪ		ḪA-AB-DI-A-RA-AḪ		B 9
		ʿABD			JARAḪ		AB-DI-RA-AḪ		B 9+
		ʿABD			JARAḪ		ḪA-AB-DI-E-RA-AḪ		M+, C+
		ʿABD			JARAḪ		AB-DI-E-RA-AḪ		M+, UCP X P. 198+
		ʿABD			JARAḪ		ḪA-AB-DI-RA-AḪ		SUMER XXIII 162 46
		ʿABD			JARAḪ		AB-DI-D-EN-ZU		PBS VII/1 94 III 28
		ʿABD			JARAḪ		AB-DI-D-E-RA-AḪ		YOS XIII 199:22+
		ʿABD			JARAḪ		AB-DU-D-E-RA-AḪ		YOS XIII 218:13+
		ʿABD			JARAḪ		ḪA-AB-DU-E-RA-AḪ		DELAPORTE CCL II A 418 M
		ʿABD			JARAḪ		AB-DU-E-RA-AḪ		M+
	JI	JBAL			JARAḪ		I-BA-AL-E-RA-AḪ		B 20; RA LXV 52 X 27
		ʾABN		A	JARAḪ		ḪA?-AB-NA-A-RA-AḪ		UET V 476 SEAL 6
	JI	JBIŠ			JARAḪ		I-BI-IŠ-A-RA-AḪ		DELAPORTE CCL I A 446
		ʿADN		I	JARAḪ		ḪA-AD-NI-E-RA-AḪ		M
		ʾAK		I	JARAḪ		A-KI-E-RA-AḪ		M
		ʾIL		I	JARAḪ		I_3-LI_2-IA-RA-AḪ		SIMMONS 131 20
		ʾIL		I	JARAḪ		I_3-LI_2-E-RA-AḪ		M+, TIM III 133 4, SEAL
		ʾUMM		U	JARAḪ		U_2?-UM-MU-E-RA-AḪ		B 40+
	JA	ʾMUR			JARAḪ		IA-MUR-D-EN-ZU		UET V 583 19
	JA	ʿMIS			JARAḪ		IA-AḪ-MI-IS-D-SIN		M
		ʿINB		I	JARAḪ		IN-BI-RA-AḪ		KISURRA 6 15
		ḪANN		A	JARAḪ		ḪA-AN-NA-D-EN-ZU		M
		ḪANN		A	JARAḪ		ḪAN-NA-D-EN-ZU		XIII 1 V 27
		ʾIPQ			JARAḪ		I-BI-IQ-D-[EN]-ZU		M
		JIŠʿ		I	JARAḪ		IŠ-ḪI-E-RA-AḪ		RA LXV 41 II 25
		JIŠʿ		I	JARAḪ		IŠ-I-RA-AḪ		TIM III 28 12
	JA	JṢIʾ			JARAḪ		IA-ZI-E-RA-AḪ		B 32, C

STEMS

JARAḪ	2	JA	ʾZUW			JARAḪ	IA-ZU-RA-AḪ		M+
			BAWʾ			JARAḪ	BA-IA-RA-AḪ		RUTTEN 7 3
			BAWʾ			JARAḪ	BA-A-RA-AḪ		RUTTEN 39 18
			BAWʾ			JARAḪ	PA-IA-RA-AḪ		RUTTEN 7 7
			BAʿL		I	JARAḪ	BA-LI-A-RA-AḪ		SIMMONS 58 11
			BAʿL		I	JARAḪ	BA-LI-E-RA-AḪ		M+, TCL XVIII 92 1+
			BAʿL		I	JARAḪ	BA-LI-RA-AḪ		TCL XVIII 94 1 14+
			BEʿL	T	I	JARAḪ	NIN?-TI-E-RA-AḪ		RA LXV 52 X 54
			BUN		U	JARAḪ	BU-NU-E-RA-AḪ		M
		JI	BNIJ			JARAḪ	IB-NI-E-RA-AḪ		SIMMONS 62 14'+
			BIZZ		I	JARAḪ	BI-IṢ-ṢI-E-RA-AḪ		YOS XIII 245:16
			ḎIKR		I	JARAḪ	ZI-IK-RI-E-RA-AḪ		TIM V 69 7, 17+
			ḎIMR		I	JARAḪ	ZI-IM-RI-E-RA-AḪ		B 42+, C+, M+
			GAʾJ		I	JARAḪ	GA-JI-RA-A[Ḫ]		HARRIS 39 15
			GUMUL			JARAḪ	GU-MU-UL-D-EN-ZU		M+
			KAʾB		I	JARAḪ	KA-BI-E-RA-AḪ		RA LXV 41 II 29+;B 32+
			KIBR			JARAḪ	KI-BI-IR-D-EN-ZU		RUTTEN 11 25
			KIBS		I	JARAḪ	KI-IB-ZI-E-RA-AḪ		RA LXV 43 III 44+
			LAʾR		A	JARAḪ	LA-RA-D-SIN		KAJ 167 23+, LATE
			MILK		I	JARAḪ	MIL-KI-E-RA-AḪ		AJSL XLIV 243 NO. 33
			MUT		I	JARAḪ	MU-TI-A-RA-AḪ		B 35
			MUT		I	JARAḪ	MU-TI-E-RA-AḪ		M; TCL XI 224:69+
			MUT		I	JARAḪ	MU-TE-E-RA-AḪ		A 7804 13
			MUT		U	JARAḪ	MU-TU-E-RA-AḪ		JCS XXIV 60 NO. 51 REV
			NAʿM		I	JARAḪ	NA-AḪ-MI-E-RA-AḪ		JCS XI 29 NO.17 5
			NAPŠ		I	JARAḪ	NA-AP-SI-E-RA-AḪ		M+
		JA	NŠIʾ			JARAḪ	IA-SI-E-RA-AḪ		B 28
		JA	NŠIʾ			JARAḪ	IA-SI-RA-AḪ		B 30
		JA	NŠIʾ			JARAḪ	IA-SI-A-RA-AḪ		GRANT, HAV. 242:2+
		JA	NTIN			JARAḪ	IA-AN-TI-IN-A-RA-AḪ		RA LXV 62 V 34
		JA	NTIN			JARAḪ	IA-AN-TI-NA-RA-AḪ		RUTTEN 11 20+
		JA	NTIN			JARAḪ	IA-AN-TI-LA-RA-AḪ		VAS XVI 91 3
		JA	NTIN			JARAḪ	IA-AN-TI-IN-E-RA-AḪ		M+
		JA	NTIN			JARAḪ	IA-AT-TI-IN-E-RA-AḪ		M+
		JA	NTIN			JARAḪ	IA-T[I-I]N-E-RA-AḪ		M
		JA	PḪUR			JARAḪ	IA-AP-ḪU-UR-SIN		M
			PULS		I	JARAḪ	PU-UL-ZI-RA-AḪ		HARRIS 18 14
			PULS		I	JARAḪ	PU-UL-SI-E-RA-AḪ		TIM V 69 16+
			QUWJ			JARAḪ	KU-WE-RA-AḪ		A 32133 REV.4
			QIMṢ		I	JARAḪ	KI?-IM-ZE_2-RA-AḪ		EDZARD,DER 231:2
		JA	RWIM			JARAḪ	IA-RI-IM-IA-RA-AḪ		RA LXV 41 II 28
		JA	RWIM			JARAḪ	IA-RI-IM-E-RA-AḪ		M
			RABB		I	JARAḪ	RA-AB-BI-E-RA-AḪ		B 37+
			SIMT		I	JARAḪ	ZI-IM-TI-E-RA-AḪ		M+
			ŠAM		I	JARAḪ	SA-ME-E-RA-AḪ		M
			ŠAM		I	JARAḪ	SA-ME-RA-AḪ		YOS VIII 64 19+
			ŠAM		U	JARAḪ	SA-MU-A-RA-AḪ		SIMMONS 98 3
			ŠAM		U	JARAḪ	SA-[M]U-E?-RA-A[Ḫ]?		RA LXV 47 VII 13
			ŠUM		U	JARAḪ	SU-MU-A-RA-AḪ		B 38+
			ŠUM		U	JARAḪ	SU-MU-E-RA-AḪ		M+
			ŠAMŠ		I	JARAḪ	SA-AM-SI-E-RA-AḪ		BASOR 95, 19+, M+
			ŠAMŠ		U	JARAḪ	SA-AM-SU-E-RA-AḪ		B 38
			ŠUMAT			JARAḪ	SU-MA-AT-E-RA-AḪ		M+
			ṢUWR		I	JARAḪ	ZU-RI-E-RA-AḪ		M
			ṢUPR		I	JARAḪ	ZU-UP-RI-E-RA-AḪ		M+
			TINʾ		I	JARAḪ	TI-IN-E-RA-AḪ		C
			TINʾ		I	JARAḪ	TI-IN-I-E-RA-AḪ		C
	3		LA			DJIN			
						JARAḪ	IA-DI-IN-E-RA-AḪ		RA LXV 46 VI 26+
JARAN	1		JARAN		I		JA-RA-A-NI	FN	A. 21 9
JARIN	1		JARIN		IM		JA-RI-NI-IM	GEN	CT XLV 89 III 9
			JARIN				IA-RI-EN		TA 1931, 241
JARIQ	2		MUT		UM	JARIQ	MU-TUM-JA-RI-IQ		TA 1931, 104, 538
JARN	1		JARN		UM		JA-AR-NU-UM		RUTTEN 22 17
JARQ	1		JARQ	AN			IA-AR-QA-A[N]		M
JAŠAR	1		JAŠAR		UM		IA-ŠA-RU-UM		B 30

STEMS

JAŠAR	1		JAŠAR	UM						IA-SA-RU-UM		PINCHES BERENS 101 10, M+
			JAŠAR	AM						IA-SA-RA-AM	ACC	M
			JAŠAR	AH						IA-SA-RA	FN	XIII 1 II 64+
			JAŠAR		TI		)IL			IA-SA-AR-TI-DINGIR		M
	2		(AMM	I			JAŠAR			ḪA-AM-MI-E-SA-AR?		M
			(AMM	U			JAŠAR			ḪA-MU-JA-ŠAR		M
			)AŠD	I			JAŠAR			AŠ$_2$-DI-E-SA-AR		XIII 1 XI 35
			DAWD	I			JAŠAR			DA-DI-E-SA-AR		RA LXV 50 VIII 48+
	3		LA			)A	HWIJ					
							JAŠAR			LA-AḪ-WI-E-SA-AR		RA LXV 40 I 21
JAŠ(	1	T	JAŠ(	AH						IA?-TA-AŠ-ḪA?	FN	M
	2		(AŠTAR				JAŠ(	AH		EŠ$_4$-DAR-IA-AŠ-ḪA	FN	M
			BUN	U			JAŠ(	AH		BU?-NU-IA-AŠ-[ḪA]	FN	XII 1 VII 67
			ŠAMŠ	I			JAŠ(	AH		D-[UT]U-IA-AŠ-ḪA	FN	XIII 1 IV 43
JAŠAB	1		JAŠAB	AN						IA-ŠA-BA-AN		RA LXV 45 V 35
JAŠI(	2		ḎU				JAŠI(	A		ZU-IA-ŠE-IA		A. 64 9
JAŠUN	1		JAŠUN	UM						E-ŠU-NU-UM		U
			JAŠUN	A						IA-ŠU-NA		A.
JAT	1		JAT	UM						I-IA-TUM	FN	RA LXV 64 VI 31
			JAT	IJA						IA-TI-IA		M+
			JAT				KALA			I-IA-AT-KA-LA		VAS XVI 165 5
			JAT	A			DAWD	UM		IA-TA-DA-DUM		B 31
			JAT	I			)IL			IA-TI-DINGIR		B 31
			JAT	I			)AMAN			IA-TI-ḪA-MA-AN	FN	RA LXV 42 II 55
			JAT	U	HU					IA-TU-U$_2$		YOS XIII 426:14
			JAT	UM			MARṢ	AT		I-IA-TUM-MA-AR-ZA-AT	FN	RA LXV 62 V 15
			JAT	UM			MARṢ	AH		IA-TUM-MAR-ZA		A 21899+
			JAT	UM			ṢI)	A		IA-TUM-ZI-A		CT XLV 97 5
	2		)AḪ	U			JAT	UM		A-ḪU-IA-TUM	MN	BIN II 98 4
			)AḪ	U			JAT	UM		A-ḪU-JA-TUM	MN	M
			)AB	I			JAT	UM		A-BI-IA-TUM	FN	WATERMAN 40 R. 5+
			)AB	U			JAT	I	JA	A-BU-IA-TI-IA		TCL I 85 10
			)IB	I			JAT	UM		I-BI-IA-TUM		TIM II 27 4
			JID	I			JAT	UM		I-DI-IA-TUM		M
			JADA(				JAT	UM		IA-DA-A-A-TUM		B 25
			)IL	I			JAT			I$_3$-LI$_2$-A-AT?		TA 1931, 261
			)IL	I			JAT	UM		I$_3$-LI$_2$-I-IA-TUM		VAS XVIII 83:15
			)IL	I			JAT		KA	I$_3$-LI$_2$-A-AT-KA		TIM III 10 14+
			)ILL	A			JAT	I		IL-LA-I-IA-TI	FN NOM	XIII 1 IX 51
			)ILL	A			JAT	IM		IL-LA-I-IA-TIM	FN NOM	XIII 1 IV 75
			(AMM	I			JAT	UM		AM-MI-IA-TUM		A. 273 14
			)UMM	I			JAT	UM		UM-MI-IA-TUM		UCP X/1 89 24
		JI	JṢI)				JAT	UM		I-ZI-IA-TUM		B 23+
			MA)D	I			JAT	UM		MA-DI-IA-TUM		UCP X/1 P. 59+
			MARU)				JAT	UM		MA-RU-IA-TUM		DE GEN., RICH II D 43 R. 2, 4
			MATI(				JAT	U	HU	MA-TI-IA-TU-U$_2$		UCP X/3 107 18
			NA(M	I			JAT	UM		NA-MI-IA-TUM	MN	MEISSNER 100 2
		JI	NDIN				JAT	UM		I-DIN-IA-TUM		M+
		JI	NDIN				JAT	IM		I-DIN-IA-TIM	GEN	M+
		JI	NDIN				JAT	IM		ID-DI-IA-TIM	GEN	M
		JI	NDIN				JAT	AM		I-DIN-IA-TAM	ACC	XIV 64:7
			RAWM	A			JAT	UM		RA-MA-IA-TUM		B 22+
			ŠU)G	U			JAT	UM		ŠU-GU-IA-TUM		B 40
			ŠUM	U			JAT	UM		SU-MU-IA-TUM		TLB IV 40 9, 12, 14
			ŠAMA(				JAT	UM		ŠA-MA-IA-TUM	MN	CT IV 43B 6+
			ŠAMA(	A			JAT	UM		ŠA-MA-A-IA-TUM	MN	WATERMAN 21 R. 6
			ṢABA)				JAT	UM		ZA-BA-IA-TUM	MN	BM 16835 19+
			ZAMA)				JAT	UM		ZA-MA-A-A-TUM	MN?	TCL X 38 1
JATAM	1		JATAM	UM						IA-TA-MU-UM		YOS VIII 153 5
			JATAM	U						IA-TA-MU		JCS XIII 51 292, A. LATE
			JATAM				MA					
							)IL			IA-TAM-MA-DINGIR		UET V 172 5'
JATAR	1		JATAR	UM						IA-TA-RU-UM		B 31
			JATAR	UM						IA-TA-RUM		B 31, M+
			JATAR	U						IA-TA-RU		KISURRA 106 16
			JATAR	UM						IA-TAR-RUM		B 31

STEMS

JATAR	1		JATAR		IM						IA-TA-RI-IM	GEN	B 31, M+
			JATAR		I						IA-TA-RI	GEN	M
			JATAR	AT	UM						IA-TA-RA-TUM	MN	B 31
			JATAR	AT	UM						IA-TA-RA-TUM	FN	B 31
			JATAR	AT	IM						IA-TA-RA-TIM	MN GEN	B 31+
			JATAR	AH							IA-TA-RA	FN	M+
			JATAR		AJA						IA-TA-RA-IA	FN	M
			JATAR		AJA						IA-TA-RA-A-IA	FN	XIII 1 X 54
			JATAR				ʾAḪ		UM		JA-TA-AR-ḪU-UM		I
			JATAR				HADD		U		IA-TAR-D-IM		M+
			JATAR				ʿADN		U		IA-TAR-ḪA-AD-NU		M+
			JATAR				ʿADN		U	HU	IA-TAR-ḪA-AD-NU-U$_2$		RA LXV 54 XII 56
			JATAR				ʾAKK		A		IA-TAR-AK-KA		M
			JATAR				ʾIL				IA-TA-AR-DINGIR		B 31+ +
			JATAR				ʾIL				IA-TAR-DINGIR		M
			JATAR				ḤAM		I		IA-TAR-D-A-MI		M+
			JATAR				ʿAMM		U		IA-TAR-ḪA-MU		M
			JATAR				ʿAMM		U		IA-TAR-ḪA-MU	FN	C II P. 247+
			JATAR				ʾAŠD		I		IA-TAR-AŠ-DI		M
			JATAR				LIʾM				IA-TAR-LI-IM		M+
			JATAR				MALIK				IA-TAR-MA-LIK		A.+
			JATAR				ŠALIM				IA-TAR-SA-LIM		M+
			JATAR				ŠUM		U		IA-TAR-SU-MU		XII 456 10
			JATAR				ŠUM		U	HU	IA-TAR-SU-MU-U$_2$		M+
	2		ʾAḪ		I		JATAR				A-Ḫ[I]-E?-TAR		RA LXV 46 V 86
			ʾAB		I		JATAR				A-BI$_2$-WA-DAR		U
			ʾAB		I		JATAR				A-BI-IA-TA-AR		B 10+
			ʾAB		I		JATAR				A-BI-E-TAR		BASOR 95 22
			ʾIL		I		JATAR				I$_3$-LI$_2$-A-TAR		B 21+
			ʾIL		I		JATAR				I$_3$-LI$_2$-E-TAR		M+
			ḪALAN		I		JATAR				ḪA-LA-NI-E-TAR		M
			ḪAM		I		JATAR				D-A-MI-T[AR]?		M
			ʿAMM		I		JATAR				ḪA-AM-MI-A-TAR		B 19+
			ʿAMM		I		JATAR				ḪA-AM-MA-TA-AR		B 19
			ʿAMM		I		JATAR				A-MA-TA-AR		WALTERS, WL 109:9
			ʿAMM		U		JATAR				ḪA-MU-TAR		M
			ʿAMM		U		JATAR				[Ḫ]A-AM-MU-TA-[A]R		M
			ʿAMM		U	HU	JATAR				ḪA-AM-MU-U$_2$-TAR		M
			ʾAŠD		I		JATAR				AŠ-DI-E-TAR		M
			ʾAŠR		I		JATAR				AŠ-RI-E-TAR		RA XLIX 24 N. 9
			NIQM		I		JATAR				NI-IQ-MI-E-TAR		C II 39 3
			ŠAM		I		JATAR				SA-MI-E-TAR		XII 601 6
			ŠUM			NA	JATAR				SU-UM-NA-IA-TAR		RA LXV 52 X 56
			ŠAMM		I		JATAR				SA-AM-MI-A-TA-AR		TIM I 28 34, 38, 49
			ŠAMM		I		JATAR				SA-AM-ME-TAR		M+
			ŠAMM		I		JATAR				SA-AM-ME-E-TAR		M+
			ŠAMM		I		JATAR				SA-MI-E-TA-AR		M+
			ŠAMM		I		JATAR				SA-AM-MI-E-TAR		M+
			ŠAMM		I		JATAR				SA-AM-MI-TAR		M+
			ŠIMM		I		JATAR				SI-IM-ME-A-TAR		A 7537 16, 21+
			ṢIDQ		I		JATAR				ZI-ID-KI-E-TAR		M+
	3		ʿADN		U		MA						
							JATAR				ḪA-AD-NU-ME-TAR		M+
JATM	1		JATM		UM						WA-AT-MU-UM?		CT XLV 5 R. 4
JATR	1		JATR		IM						IA-AT-RI-IM	GEN	CT XLVIII 29 REV.
			JATR	AT	UM						IA-AT-RA-TUM	MN	VAS VIII 105 4, 7, 12+
			JATR		A		ʾIL				JA-AT-RA-IL		I
	2		ʾANN		U		JATR	AH			AN-NU-IA-AT-RA	FN	XIII 1 VI 53+
JATT	1		JATT		IJA						IA-AT-TI-IA		M
			JATT		A		LIʾM				IA-AT-TA-LI-IM		ZA XXXVI 95, BJ 88 12
			JATT		I		HADD		U		IA-AT-TI-D-IM		M
JATUM	1		JATUM		UM						IA-TU-MU-UM		B 31
			JATUM		U						IA-TU-MU		HARRIS 104 5
JBAL	1	JI	JBAL		UM						I-BA-LUM		B 21, M
		JI	JBAL		U						I-BA-LU		CT VIII 17C 11
		JI	JBAL	AT	UM						JI-BA-LA-TUM	FN	U

STEMS

JBAL	1	JI	JBAL					....			I-BA-AL-[....]	FN	M
		JI	JBAL					....			I-BA-AL-D-[....]		M
		JI	JBAL					....			I-BA-AL-AN-ḪAR		XIII 1 X 43
		JI	JBAL					HADD	U		I-BA-AL-D-IM		M+, C+
		JI	JBAL					ʾIL			I-BA-AL-DINGIR		EEMY III/4 P. 130, M+
		JI	JBAL					ḪAM	UM		I-BA-AL-D-A-MU-UM		RA LXV 52 X 43
		JI	JBAL					JARAḪ			I-BA-AL-E-RA-AḪ		B 20; RA LXV 52 X 27
		JI	JBAL					ʿAŠTAR			I-BA-AL-EŠ$_4$-DAR		M
		JI	JBAL					DAGAN			I-BAL-D-DA-GAN		B 20
		JI	JBAL					DAGAN			I-BA-AL-D-DA-GAN		M
		JI	JBAL					LA					
								ʾIL			I-BA-AL-LA-DINGIR		RA LXV 47 VII 26
		JI	JBAL					PI					
								ʾEL			I-BA-AL-BI-EL		M+
		JI	JBAL					PI					
								ʾEL			I-BA-AL-PI-EL		UCP X P. 56+
		JI	JBAL					PI					
								ʾIL			I-BA-AL-BI-DINGIR		M+
	2		JAʾIT		I	JI		JBAL			IA-I-TI-I-BA-AL		M
			ḪABUR			JI		JBAL					
								BUGAŠ			ID$_2$-ḪA-BUR-I-BA-AL-BU-GA-AŠ$_2$		BRM IV 52 HANA
			ʾIL		A	JI		JBAL			DINGIR?-I-BA-AL		M
			ḪAM		I	JI		JBAL			D-A-MI-I-BA-AL		M+
			ʿAMM		I	JI		JBAL			ḪA-MI-I-BA-AL		M
			ʿAN	AT	I	JI		JBAL			ḪA-NA-TI-I-BA-AL		RA LXV 40 I 12
			SUMUKAN			JI		JBAL			D-GIR$_3$-I-BA-AL		C
	3		LA					RIWM					
						JI		JBAL	U	HU	[L]A?-RI-IM-I-BA-LU-U$_2$		M
JBIL	1	JA	JBIL					JIRR	A		IA-BI-IL-WI-IR-RA		B 24
		JA	JBIL		I			....			IA-BI-LI-[....]		FM 3998 SEAL
JBIŠ	1	JA	JBIŠ		UM						IA-BI-ŠUM		B 24+
		JA	JBIŠ		U						IA-BI-ŠU		A 29366:10
		JI	JBIŠ		U						I-BI-ŠU	FN	BM 82359
		JI	JBIŠ					ʾIL			I-BI-IŠ-DINGIR		TA 1930, 261
		JI	JBIŠ					ʾEL			I-BI-IŠ-I$_3$-EL		SIMMONS 70 12
		JI	JBIŠ					ʾIL			[I-B]I$_2$-IŠ-I$_3$-IL		I
		JI	JBIŠ					JARAḪ			I-BI-IŠ-A-RA-AḪ		DELAPORTE CCL I A 446
		JI	JBIŠ					KABID			I-BI-IŠ-GA-BI-ID		KISURRA 63A
		ME	JBIŠ		UM						ME-BI-ŠUM		M+
		ME	JBIŠ		A						ME-BI-SA	MN	M
	2		LA			JE	N	JBIŠ	U		LA-E-NI-BI-ŠU		YOS XII
JDAʿ	1	JI	JDAʿ					LIʾM					
								MA			I-DA-LIM-MA		B 21
		JI	JDAʿ					MARAṢ			I-DA-MA-RA-AṢ	GN	B 21+, M
		JI	JDAʿ					MARAṢ			A-DA-MA-RA-AṢ	GN	B 11
		JI	JDAʿ					MARAṢ			A-TA-MA-RA-AṢ	PN	CT II 26 3
		JI	JDAʿ					PI					
								ʾIL			I-DA-BI$_2$-DINGIR		I
		JI	JDAʿ					ŠUM			I-DA-SU-UM		M
		ʾA	JDAʿ					PI					
								ʾEL			A-DA-AḪ-[BI]?-EL		SIMMONS 51 21
		JI	JDAʿ					RAWM			I-DAḪ-RA-AM		MEISSNER 91 17
JDIʿ	1	JA	JDIʿ		UM						IA-DI-ḪU-UM		B 25+
		JA	JDIʿ		U						IA-DI-U$_2$		CT VIII 10 B 7+
		JE	JDIʿ		UM						E-TI-UM		I
		JA	JDIʿ		IM						IA-DI-ḪI-IM	GEN	M+
		JA	JDIʿ					....			IA-DI-[....]	FN	M
		JA	JDIʿ	AT	UM						IA-DI-ḪA-TUM	FN	B 25+
		JA	JDIʿ	AH							IA-DI-ḪA	FN	M+
		JA	JDIʿ					ʾAB	UM		IA-DI-ḪA-BU-UM		B 25+
		JA	JDIʿ					ʾAB	UM		IA-DI-A-BU-UM		M, YOS XII+
		JA	JDIʿ					ʾAB	UM		IA-DU-A-BU-UM		YOS XII+
		JA	JDIʿ					ʾAB	U		IA-DI-ḪA-BU		PBS XIV 1084
		JA	JDIʿ					ʾAB	U		IA-DI-A-BU		YOS XII+
		JA	JDIʿ					ʾAB	UM		IA-DI-ḪA-A-BU-U[M]		RA LXV 45 V 9
		JA	JDIʿ					ʾAB	IM		IA-DI-ḪA-A-BI-IM	GEN	M+

STEMS

JDIʿ	1	JA	JDIʿ				ʾEL		UM		IA-DI-ḪI-E-LUM		UNPUBL.
		JA	JDIʿ				ʾIL				IA-DI-IḪ-DINGIR		B 25+
		JA	JDIʿ				ʾIL				IA-DI-DINGIR		M
		JA	JDIʿ				DAGAN				I[A]-DI-D-DA-GAN		B 25
		JA	JDIʿ		A		ʾEL				IA-DI-ḪA-EL		KISURRA 10A 4
		ME	JDIʿ		UM						ME-TE-UM		I
JIBUS	1		JIBUS	AT	UM						I-BU-ZA-TUM		EDZARD,DER 87:11
JID	1		JID	AN	UM						I-DA-NU-UM		I+
			JID		I						I-DI		RA LXV 40 I 22
			JID		IJA						I-DI-IA		M
			JID		IJAN						I-DI-JA-AN		RA LXV 47 VII 54
			JID		U	HU					I-DU-U_2		RA LXV 65 VI 59
			JID		I		ʾIL				I-DI-DINGIR		M
			JID		I		JAT		UM		I-DI-IA-TUM		M
JIPʿ	2		ʾANN		U		JIPʿ	AH			AN-NU-IP-ḪA	FN	XIII 1 VIII 29
			ʿAŠTAR				JIPʿ	AH			$EŠ_4$-DAR-IP-ḪA	FN	XIII 1 VI 19+
JIQR	2		ʾAḪ	AT			JIQR	AH			A-ḪA-AT-IQ-RA	FN	M
			ʾAḪ	AT	I		JIQR	AT			A-ḪA-TI-IQ-RA-AT	FN	XIII 1 V 5
			ʾAḪ	AT	I		JIQR	AH			A-ḪA-TI-IQ-RA	FN	XIII 1 II 72+
			ʾUMM		I		JIQR	AH			UM-MI-IQ-RA	FN	M+
JIRʾ	1		JIRʾ		I						JI-IR-I	TRIBE	IX 248 15'
JIRR	2	JA	JBIL				JIRR		A		IA-BI-IL-WI-IR-RA		B 24
JIŠʿ	1		JIŠʿ	AT	UM						IŠ-ḪA-TUM	FN	RA LXV 60 III 57
			JIŠʿ	AT	I						IŠ-A-TI	MN? GEN	PBS VIII/2 238 5, 8
			JIŠʿ	AT	IJA						IŠ-ḪA-TI-IA	MN?	B 24+
			JIŠʿ	IT	IJA						IŠ-ḪI-TI-IA	MN?	CT XLVIII 91 REV.+
			JIŠʿ	AH							IŠ-ḪA	FN	XIII 1 VIII 25+
			JIŠʿ		IJA						IŠ-HI-IA		M, C
			JIŠʿ				BAʿL		A		E-ŠE-EḪ-BA-LA?		VAS VII 160 7
			JIŠʿ				DAGAN				I-SI-IḪ-D-DA-GAN		RA XLI 43 HANA
			JIŠʿ		A		BAʿL				IŠ-ḪA-B[A-A]L		HARRIS 39 14
			JIŠʿ		A		GAʾL				IŠ-ḪA-GA-AL		A 7459 10
			JIŠʿ		I		JABAL				IŠ-ḪI-E-BA-AL		M
			JIŠʿ		I		HADD		U		IŠ-ḪI-D-IM		M+, C+
			JIŠʿ		I		HEDD		A		IŠ-ḪI-E-D-IM		TIM IV 33 SEAL, 34 SEAL
			JIŠʿ		I		ʾIL				IŠ-ḪI-DINGIR		WALTERS, WL 109:5+
			JIŠʿ		I		ʾIL		A				
							MA				IŠ-ḪI-DINGIR-MA		M
			JIŠʿ		I		ʾIL		A				
							MA				IŠ-ḪI-DINGIR-LA-MA		M
			JIŠʿ		I		ʾIL		U				
							MA				IŠ-ḪI-LU-MA		YOS VIII 176 20
			JIŠʿ		I		ʾIL		U	NA	IŠ-ḪI-LU-NA		VII 215 33
			JIŠʿ		I		ʿAN		UM		IŠ-ḪI-A-NU-UM		B 45
			JIŠʿ		I		JARAḪ				IŠ-ḪI-E-RA-AḪ		RA LXV 41 II 25
			JIŠʿ		I		JARAḪ				IŠ-I-RA-AḪ		TIM III 28 12
			JIŠʿ		I		DAGAN				IŠ-ḪI-D-DA-GAN		M+
			JIŠʿ		I		LI						
							ʾEL				IŠ-ḪI-LI-EL		JCS XXIV 69 NO. 3 SEAL
			JIŠʿ		I		LIʾM				IŠ-ḪI-LI-IM		M
			JIŠʿ		I		MAṬAR				IŠ-ḪI-MA-DAR		V 40 5, 16
			JIŠʿ		I		NABUʾ		UM		IŠ-ḪI-NA-BU-U[M]		EDZARD, DER 68 III 6
	2		ʾADM		U		JIŠʿ	AH			D-AD-MU-IŠ-ḪA	FN	XIII 1 IX 18
			ʾADM		U		JIŠʿ	AH			AD-MU-IŠ-ḪA	FN	XIII 1 IX 57
			ʾANN		U		JIŠʿ	AH			AN-NU-IŠ-ḪA	FN	XIII 1 V 46+
			KAKK		A		JIŠʿ	AH			KA-KA-IŠ-ḪA	FN	M+
JITUM	1		JITUM	AN	IM						I-TU-MA-NIM	GEN	B 45
JPAʿ	1	ʾA	JPAʿ				ʾAB		I		A-PA-AḪ-A-BI		YOS VIII 29 13
		ʾA	JPAʿ				NAN		UM		A-BA-AḪ-NA-NU-UM		TA 1931, 374, EARLY OB
		ʾA	JPAʿ				RAPIʾ				A-PA-AḪ-RA-BI		SUMER XIV 5, IM 52272
		JA	JPAʿ								IA-A-PA-AḪ		M+
		JA	JPAʿ								IA-PA		A.
		JA	JPAʿ		UM						IA-PA-ḪU-UM		RA LXVI 118:16
		JA	JPAʿ		UM						[I]A-PA-ḪU-UM	FN	RA LXV 64 VI 8
		JA	JPAʿ	AT	UM						IA-PA-ḪA-TUM	FN	M+
		JA	JPAʿ	AH							IA-PA-ḪA	FN	M+

STEMS

JPAʿ	1	JA	JPAʿ					HADD		U	IA-A-PA-AḪ-D-IM		M+
		JA	JPAʿ					HADD		U	IA-PA-ḪA-D-IM		M
		JA	JPAʿ					HADD		U	IA-PA-AḪ-D-IM		M+
		JA	JPAʿ					ʾIL			IA-PA-AḪ-DINGIR		RA LXV 51 IX 74
		JA	JPAʿ					ʾIL			IA-PA-DINGIR		B 29
		JA	JPAʿ					DAGAN			IA-PA-AḪ-D-DA-GAN		XIII 58 5+
		JA	JPAʿ					LIʾM			IA-A-PA-AḪ-LI-IM		M+
		JA	JPAʿ					LIʾM			IA-PA-AḪ-LI-IM		M+
		JA	JPAʿ					ŚUM		U			
								ʾAB		I	IA-PA-AḪ-SU-MU-A-BI		A. 56 47
	2		ʾAB		I		JA	JPAʿ			A-BI-IA-PA-AḪ	FN	XIII 1 II 57
			ʾIL		I		JE	JPAʿ			I$_3$-LI$_2$-E-PA		A.+
		JI	JṢIʾ				JA	JPAʿ			I-ZI-A-PA-AḪ		B 22
			BAʿL		I		JE	JPAʿ			BA-LI-E-PA		A.
		JA	LʾIJ				JA	JPAʿ			IA-AL-E-PA-AḪ		M
			NIQM		I		JA	JPAʿ			NI-IQ-MI-PA		A. 27 12
			NIQM		I		JA	JPAʿ			NI-IQ-ME-PA		A.+
			ŚUM		U		JA	JPAʿ			[SU-MU]-A-PA-AḪ		B 38
			ṢIDQ		I		JE	JPAʿ			ZI-ID-KI-E-PA		RA XLIII 37 QATNA
JPIʿ	1	JA	JPIʿ					HADD		U	IA-BI-IḪ-D-IM		M
		ME	JPIʿ		UM						ME-BI-ḪU-UM		M
		ME	JPIʿ		UM						ME-PI-UM		I
JPUʿ	1	JA	JPUʿ		UM						IA-PU-ḪU-UM		B 25+
		JA	JPUʿ		U						IA-PU-ḪU		B 25
		JA	JPUʿ	AT	UM						IA-PU-ḪA-TUM	FN	C+
		JA	JPUʿ		AJA						IA-PU-ḪA-IA	FN	C+
	2		ʾAB		I		JE	JPUʿ			A-BI-E-PU-UḪ		B 10, M+
			ʾAB		I		JA	JPUʿ			A-BI-IA-PU-UḪ		B 10
			ʾIL		I		JE	JPUʿ			I$_3$-LI$_2$-E-PU-UḪ		M+
			ʿAMM		I		JE	JPUʿ			ḪA-MI-E-PU-UḪ		M+
			ʿAMM		I		JE	JPUʿ			ḪA-AM-MI-E-PU-UḪ		M+
			ʿAMM		U		JE	JPUʿ			ḪA-MU-E-PU-UḪ	FN	C+
			BAʿL		I		JA	JPUʿ			BA-LI-A-PU-UḪ		HARRIS 96 6+
			BAʿL		I		JA	JPUʿ			BA-LI-PU-UḪ$_2$		EDZARD, DER 117:38 DATE
			DAGAN				ʾA	JPUʿ			D-DA-GAN-A-PU-UḪ		M
			KAʾB		I		JE	JPUʿ			KA-BI-E-PU-UḪ		M
			NIQM		I		JE	JPUʿ			NI-IQ-MI-E-PU-UḪ		M+, A.+
		JA	ŠWUB				JI	JPUʿ			IA-ŠU-UB-D-I-PU-UḪ		M
			ŚUM		U		JE	JPUʿ			SU-MU-E-PU-UḪ		M+
			ŚUM		U	NA	JA	JPUʿ		A	SU-MU-NA-IA-PU-ḪA-[....]		M
			ŚAMŚ		I		JA	JPUʿ	AT		D-UTU-IA-PU-ḪA-AT	FN?	BM 17075
			ṢIDQ		I		JE	JPUʿ			ZI-ID-KI-E-PU-UḪ		M+, C+
JQAH	1	JI	JQAH					ʾIL			I-KA-AḪ-DINGIR		B 21
		JA	JQAH					ʿAMM		U	IA-QA-AM-MU		A.+
JQIR	1	JA	JQIR	AN	U						IA-KI-RA-NU		M
		JA	JQIR		A			ʾAB		UM	IA-KI-RA-A-BU-UM		RA LXV 47 VII 30
JRID	1	JA	JRID		UM						IA-RI-DU-UM		UCP X/1 109 3
		JI	JRID	AN	UM						I-RI-DA-NU-UM		M
		MA	JRID	UN	UM						MA-RI-DU-NU-UM		SIMMONS 124 17
JŚAR	1	JI	JŚAR		UM						I-ŠA-RUM		C
		JI	JŚAR		I						I-ŠA-RI	FN	A.
		JI	JŚAR					LIʾM			I-ŠAR-LI-IM		M+, C+, CT VI 47B 17
		ME	JŚAR		UM						ME-ŠA-RUM		A.
	2		ḤANN		I		JI	JŚAR			AN-NI-I-ŠAR?		M
			NAWAR				JE	JŚAR			NA-WA-AR-E-ŠAR	FN	XIII 1 VI 40
			ŚAMŚ		U		JI	JŚAR			SA-AM-SU-D-I-[Š]AR		M
			TADAB				JE	JŚAR			TA-DA-AB-E-ŠAR	FN	XIII 1 VI 42
JŚIR	1	JA	JŚIR		UM						IA-SI-RUM		B 30+
		JA	JŚIR		UM						IA-ŠI-RU-[UM]		A 22002
		JA	JŚIR	T	IM						IA-ŠIR-TI-IM	MN GEN	WATERMAN 45 R. 10
		JA	JŚIR					HEDD		A	IA-ŠE-RE-DA		A. 367 5
		JA	JŚIR					HEDD		A	IA-AŠ-RI-E-DA		A.+
JŠIʿ	1	ME	JŠIʿ		UM						ME-SI-UM		SIGRIST UNPUBL.
JŠUʿ	1	JA	JŠUʿ		UM						IA-ŠU-ḪU-UM		B 30+
		JA	JŠUʿ	AT	UM						IA-ŠU-ḪA-TUM	FN	RA LXV 58 I 17; B 30+
		JA	JŠUʿ	AH							IA-ŠU-ḪA	FN	M+

JŠUʿ	1 JA	JŠUʿ			ʾIL			IA-ŠU-DINGIR		RA LXIV 36 NO. 31
	2	ʾAḪ	I	JA	JŠUʿ			A-ḪI-IA-ŠU-UḪ		SIMMONS 58 16
		ʾAḪ	I	JA	JŠUʿ			A-ḪI-IA-ŠU		BIROT, TEA 28:17+
		ʾAJA		JE	JŠUʿ			A-A-E-ŠU-UḪ?		TCL X 9 3
		ʾAB	I	JE	JŠUʿ			A-BI-E-ŠU-UḪ		B 10+, XIII 1 III 44
		ʾAB	I	JA	JŠUʿ			A-BI-ŠU-UḪ		B 10
		ʾAB	I	JA	JŠUʿ	A		A-BI-IA-ŠU-ḪA		B 10
		ʾAB	I	JE	JŠUʿ					
					....			A-BI-E-ŠU-UḪ-LI-DI-IŠ		CT XLV 55 11
		ʾAB	I	JE	JŠUʿ					
					....			A-BI-E-ŠU-UḪ-LU-DA-RI		B 10
		ʾAB	I	JA	JŠUʿ					
					....			A-BI-ŠU-UT-LI		B 11
		ʾIL	I	JE	JŠUʿ			I_3-LI_2-E-ŠU-UḪ		B 21 M
		ḪAM	I	JE	JŠUʿ			D-A-MI-E-ŠU-UḪ		M+
		ḪAM	I	JE	JŠUʿ			A-MI-E-ŠU-UḪ		M+
		ḪAM	UM	JE	JŠUʿ			D-A-MU-UM-E-ŠU-UḪ		B 13 HANA
		ʿAMM	I	JE	JŠUʿ			ḪA-MI-E-ŠU-UḪ		M
		ʾAŠD	I	JE	JŠUʿ			$AŠ_2$-DI-E-ŠU-UḪ		M
		DAWD	I	JE	JŠUʿ			DA-DI-E-ŠU-UḪ		M+
		MUT	A		JŠUʿ			MU-TA-ŠU-UḪ		M+
		MUT	U	JE	JŠUʿ			M[U-T]U-E-ŠU-UḪ		RA LXV 47 VII 21
	JA	NŠIʾ		JA	JŠUʿ			IA-SI-SU-UḪ		BIN II 104 15
JṢIʾ	1 JA	JṢIʾ			HADD	U		IA-ZI-D-IM		M
	JA	JṢIʾ			ʾIL			IA-ZI-DINGIR		M+
	JA	JṢIʾ			ʾIL			IA-ṢI-DINGIR		JCS IV 109 4311 21
	JA	JṢIʾ			ʾIL	UM		IA-ZI-LUM-KI	GN	B 32
	JA	JṢIʾ			JARAḪ			IA-ZI-E-RA-AḪ		B 32, C
	JA	JṢIʾ			ʾAŠAR			IA-ZI-A-ŠAR		SZLECHTER TJ P. 186
	JA	JṢIʾ			DAGAN			IA-ZI-D-DA-GAN		B 31 HANA, M
	JA	JṢIʾ			QAṬAR			IA-ṢI-QA-TAR		B 30
	JI	JṢIʾ			ʾAḪ	UM		I-ZI-A-ḪU-UM		M+
	JI	JṢIʾ			ʾAḪ	U		I-ZI-A-ḪU?		X 53:6
	JI	JṢIʾ			ḪAJJ	UM		I-ZI-A-UM		MOORTGAT 488
	JI	JṢIʾ			ḪAʾL	U		I-ZI-ḪA-LU		XIV 96:9+
	JI	JṢIʾ			ḪAʾR	U		I-ZI-ḪA-RU		XIV 52:5, 16+
	JI	JṢIʾ			ʿAD	UM		I-ZI-A-DU-UM		M
	JI	JṢIʾ			ʾIL	U				
					MA			I-ZI-I-LU-MA		B 23+
	JI	JṢIʾ			ʾAŠAR			I-ZI-A-ŠAR		B 22+
	JI	JṢIʾ			ʾAŠAR			I-ṢI-A-ŠAR		YOS VIII 108 SEAL
	JI	JṢIʾ			JAPAR			I-ZI-A-PA-AR		B 22
	JI	JṢIʾ			JAT	UM		I-ZI-IA-TUM		B 23+
	JI	JṢIʾ		JA	JPAʿ			I-ZI-A-PA-AḪ		B 22
	JI	JṢIʾ			....			I-ZI-ḪI-X		B 23
	JI	JṢIʾ			....			I-ZI-IA-AN?		PBS XI/2 1 IX 16
	JI	JṢIʾ			....			I-ZI-IA-[....]		PBS XI/2 1 IX 15
	JI	JṢIʾ			....			I-ZI-IA-ZI-[....]		B 23
	JI	JṢIʾ			....			I-ZI-IŠ-MA-AḪ		HARRIS 7 11
	JI	JṢIʾ			....			I-ZI-TA?-KAM		B 23
	JI	JṢIʾ			BANIJ	IM		I-ZI-BA-NI-IM	GEN	B 45
	JI	JṢIʾ			DAGAN			I-ZI-D-DA-GAN		B 22 HANA
	JI	JṢIʾ			DAGAN			IS-SI-D-DA-GAN		CT IV 1 14
	JI	JṢIʾ			ḎARIʾ		JE	I-ZI-DA-RI-E		B 22+
	JI	JṢIʾ			ḎARIʾ		JE	I-ṢI-DA-RI-E		B 22+
	JI	JṢIʾ			ḎARIʾ		JE	I-ṢI-DA-RI-E-KI	GN	B 22
	JI	JṢIʾ			ḎARIʾ		JE	I-ṢI-DA-RI-I-KI	GN	B 22
	JI	JṢIʾ			ḎARIʾ		JE	I-ZI-DA-RI		TCL XI 218 9
	JI	JṢIʾ			ḎARIʾ		JE	I-ZI-ZA-RI-E		B 23+, M
	JI	JṢIʾ			ḎARIʾ		JE	I-ZI-IZ-ZA-RI-E		B 23
	JI	JṢIʾ			ḎARIʾ		JE	I-ZA-AR-RI-E		UET V 202 15
	JI	JṢIʾ			KURUB			I-ZI-KU-RU-UB		RA LXV 53 XI 11
	JI	JṢIʾ			MARIʾ		JE	I-ṢI-MA-RI-E		B 22
	JI	JṢIʾ			NABUʾ	UM		I-ZI-NA-B[U-U]M?		VAS IX 79 5
	JI	JṢIʾ			NABUʾ		HU	I-ZI-NA-BU-U_2		B 23+, M+
	JI	JṢIʾ			PU		K	I-ZI-PU-UK	FN?	M+

STEMS

JṢI⁾	1	JI	JṢI⁾				QAṬAR			I-ZI-GA-TA-AR		B 22+
		JI	JṢI⁾				QAṬAR			I-ZI-GA-TAR		B 22+
		JI	JṢI⁾				QAṬAR			I-ṢI-GA-TAR		B 22+
		JI	JṢI⁾				QAṬAR			I-ṢI-GA-TA-AR		B 22+
		JI	JṢI⁾				QAṬAR			I-ZI-GA-DAR		B 22
		JI	JṢI⁾				QAṬAR			I-ZI-QA-TAR		XIII 1 IV 59
		JI	JṢI⁾				QAṬAR	I		I-ZI-GA-DAR-I		B 22
		JI	JṢI⁾				ŠALIM			I-ṢI-SA-LIM		RUTTEN 4 19+
		JI	JṢI⁾				ŠARIJ		JE	I-ZI-SA-RI-E		BIN VII 105 12
		JI	JṢI⁾				ŠUM	UM		I-ZI-SU-MU-UM		B 23, M+
		JI	JṢI⁾				ŠUM	U	JA	I-ZI-SU-MU-A		KISURRA 112 7
		JI	JṢI⁾				ŠUM	U	HU	$I-ZI-SU-MU-U_2$		A 7646 3+
		JI	JṢI⁾				ŠAM	U				
							⁾AB	UM		I-ZI-SA-MU-A-BU-UM		B 23
		JI	JṢI⁾				ŠUM	U				
							⁾AB	UM		I-ZI-SU-MU-A-BU-UM		B 23+
		JI	JṢI⁾				ŠUM	U				
							⁾AB	IM		I-ZI-SU-MU-A-BI-IM	GEN	B 23
		JI	JṢI⁾				ŠARR			I-ZI-ŠAR		B 22
		JI	JṢI⁾				ŠARR			I-ṢI-LUGAL-KI	GN	TIM III 75:3
		JI	JṢI⁾				ŠARR	UM		I-ZI-ŠAR-RUM-KI	GN	SUMER III 79 VI 197+
		JI	JṢI⁾				TAMB	U		I-ZI-TA-AM-BU		BAHREIN UNPUB, POST-U.
		JI	JṢI⁾				ṢARIR	UM		I-ZI-ZA-RI-RUM		CT XLV 115 18
	2		⁾AWIJ			JA	JṢI⁾			A-WI-IA-ZI		RA LXV 53 XI 49
			ʿAŠTAR			TA	JṢI⁾			$EŠ_4$-DAR-TA-ZI	FN	XIII 1 IV 79
			LI			JI	JṢI⁾					
							⁾AŠD	UM		LI-ZI-AŠ-DU-UM		VAS XIII 104 R. II 24
	3		ŠUM				LI					
						JI	JṢI⁾	IM		SU-UM-LI-ZI-IM	GEN	WATERMAN 25 R 9
			ŠUM		U		LI					
						JI	JṢI⁾			SU-MU-LI-ZI		MEISSNER 37 15+
JTAR	1	JI	JTAR		UM					I-TA-RU-UM		B 23+
		JI	JTAR				ʿADN	I		I-TAR-AD-AN		WATERMAN 41 R. 10
		JI	JTAR				⁾IL	I		I-TAR-I-LI		B 23
		JI	JTAR				BEʿL	I		$I-TAR-BE-LI_2$		RA LXV 47 VII 39
		JI	JTAR				....			I-TAR-MA-[....]		AJSL XXXIII 229 SEAL+
		JI	JTAR				MULUK			I-TAR-MU-LU-UK		B 23
JTIR	1	JA	JTIR		A					IA-TE-RA	GEN	A.
		JA	JTIR				HEDD	A		IA-TE-IR-E-DA		A.+
		JA	JTIR				HEDD	A		IA-TE-RI-DA		A.+
		JA	JTIR				ḪAM	U		IA-TI-RA-MU		A. 235 4 LATE
		JA	JTIR				NAN	UM		JA-TI-IR-NA-NU-UM		M+
		JA	JTIR				NAN	AM		JA-TI-IR-NA-NAM	ACC	M
		JA	JTIR				NAN	AM		JA-TE-IR-NA-NAM	ACC	M
		JA	JTIR				NAN	IM		JA-TI-IR-NA-NIM	GEN	M+
		JA	JTIR				NAN	IM		JA-TE-IR-NA-NIM	GEN	M
		JA	JTIR				NAZI			JA-TE-IR-NA-ZI		SYRIA XX 174 MARI
		ME	JTIR	AN	UM					ME-TE-RA-NU-UM		TA 1930, 489
B⁾UL	1	JI	B⁾UL		UM					$IB-U_2-LUM$		I
BḪAR	1	JA	BḪAR		UM					IA-AB-ḪA-RU-UM		B 24
		JA	BḪAR				....			IA-AB-ḪA-AR-[....]		M
		JA	BḪAR				HADD	U		IA-AB-ḪA-AR-D-IM		M
BWA⁾	1	JA	BWA⁾							IA-BA-A		WATERMAN 36 R. 14
		JI	BWA⁾		UM					I-BA-UM		TA 30 615
		JA	BWA⁾	AT	UM					IA-BA-TUM		AJSL XXXIII 237 16
		JI	BWA⁾			JA				I-BA-A-IA		C+
		JI	BWA⁾			JA				I-BA-IA		C II 7 II 3
		JA	BWA⁾				⁾IL			IA-BA-DINGIR?		MEISSNER 36 25
		JA	BWA⁾				⁾IL			IA-BA-A?-DINGIR		M
		JI	BWA⁾				⁾IL			I-BA-AḪ-DINGIR		KISURRA 6 15
		JA	BWA⁾				ʿAN	UM		IA-BA-A-NU-UM		B 45
		⁾U	BWA⁾				⁾IL			U_2-BA-DINGIR		M
		⁾U	BWA⁾				⁾IL	A		U_2-BA-D-DINGIR		VAS VIII 14:22
BJIN	1	JA	BJIN		UM					IA-BI-NU-UM		XIII 38 13
		JA	BJIN		IM					IA-BI-NI-IM	GEN	M+

STEMS

BJIR	1	JA		BJIR		UM						IA-BI-RUM		M
		JI		BJIR		UM						I-BI-RUM		M
BAʾAN	1			BAʾAN		UM						BA-A-NU-UM		TA 1931, 434+
				BAʾAN		IM						BA-ḪA-NIM	GEN	EDZARD, DER 71 IV 3
				BAʾAN	AN	UM						BA-A-NA-NU-UM		B 43
BAʾAT	2			NUʿM		U		BAʾAT		IM		NU-UḪ-MU-BA-A-TIM	FN	C+
BAʾB	2			ʾIL		I	Š	BAʾB		A		I$_3$-LI$_2$-IŠ-BA-BA		HSM 7934, UR III
				ŠU				BAʾB		A		ŠU-BA-BA		U
BAʾEL	1	JI		BAʾEL				ʾABN		U		I-BA-EL-A-AB-NU		III 46 13
BAʾIL	1			BAʾIL		UM						BA-ḪI-LUM		M+
				BAʾIL		IM						BA-ḪI-LIM	NOM	ABB V 157:9'
	2			ŠUʾM		A		BAʾIL				ŠU-UḪ-MA-BA-IL		RA LXV 51 IX 60
BAʾT	2			TATT		I		BAʾT		UM		TA-AT-TI-BA-TUM		TCL I 204:10
BAḤAR	1	JA	T	BAḤAR			NA					IA-AB-TA-ḪA-AR-NA	GN	M+
BAḤIR	1			BAḤIR		UM						BA-I-RUM		M
BAḤR	1		T	BAḤR		UM						BA-TA-AḪ-RUM		M+
			T	BAḤR		IM						BA-TA-AḪ-RI-IM	GEN	M
			T	BAḤR		I						BA-TA-AḪ-RI	GEN	M+
			T	BAḤR	AH							BA-TA-AḪ-RA	FN	RA LXV 59 II 40
BAḤUR	1			BAḤUR		A						BA-ḪU-RA		A. LATE
BAḪŠ	1			BAḪŠ		UM						BA-AḪ-ŠUM		RA LXV 43 III 71
BAʿD	1			BAʿD		IM						BA-AḪ-DI-IM	GEN	RES 1939 69
				BAʿD	AN							BA-AḪ-DA-AN		RUTTEN 7 18+
				BAʿD	AN	UM						BA-AḪ-DA-NUM		HARRIS 106 5
				BAʿD	AN	UM						BA-DA-NU-UM		U
				BAʿD	AN	UM						BA-TA-NUM$_2$		U
				BAʿD	AN	U						BA-AḪ-TA-NU		BM 17060 10
				BAʿD	AN	U	HU					BA-AḪ-TA-NU-U$_2$		BM 17060 2
				BAʿD		IJA						BA-AḪ-DI-IA		RUTTEN 12A 23+
				BAʿD		I		HADD		U		BA-AḪ-DI-D-IM		M+
				BAʿD		I		ʾEL				[BA]-AḪ-DI-EL		KISURRA 51 10
				BAʿD		I		LIʾM				BA-AḪ-DI-LI-IM		M+
	2			BAʿL		U		BAʿD		I		BA-AḪ-LU-BA-DI		EA
BAʿL	1		Š	BAʿL	AN	UM						ŠU-BI-LA-NU-UM		B 47
				BAʿL		UM						BA-LUM		CT II 35 29
				BAʿL	AN							BA-LA-AN		M+
				BAʿL	AN							BA-A-LA-AN		RA LXV 46 VI 48
				BAʿL	AN							BA-AḪ-LA-AN		M
				BAʿL	AN	UM						BA-LA-NU-UM		B 43+
				BAʿL		IJA						BA-AḪ-LI-IA		KISURRA 24 5, 7
				BAʿL		IJA						BA-LI-IA		A.; M
				BAʿL		EJA						BA-LI-E-IA		A.
				BAʿL				TUʾ			KA	BA-AL-DU-UḪ-KA		A.
				BAʿL		A		HAND		U		BA-LA-ḪA-AN-DU		VOIX 187:13 MARI
				BAʿL		A		ʿAŠTAR				BA-LA-EŠ$_4$-DAR		M
				BAʿL		A		MI						
								NAMḪ		U		BA-LA-MI-NA-AM-ḪU		SYRIA XLIV 201 N.1 MARI
				BAʿL		I						BA-AḪ-LI		M
				BAʿL		I		....				BA-AḪ-LI-RA-[....]	FN	M
				BAʿL		I		HADD		U		BA-AḪ-LI-D-IM		M+
				BAʿL		I		HADD		U		BA-LI-D-IM		M
				BAʿL		I		ʾIL				BA-AḪ-LI-DINGIR		B 15
				BAʿL		I		ʾIL				BA-LI-DINGIR		EDZARD, DER 68 IV 7
				BAʿL		I		ʾIL		I		BA-AḪ-LI-I$_3$-LI$_2$	FN	M
				BAʿL		I		JARAḪ				BA-LI-A-RA-AḪ		SIMMONS 58 11
				BAʿL		I		JARAḪ				BA-LI-E-RA-AḪ		M+, TCL XVIII 92 1+
				BAʿL		I		JARAḪ				BA-LI-RA-AḪ		TCL XVIII 94 1 14+
				BAʿL		I	JA	JPUʿ				BA-LI-A-PU-UḪ		HARRIS 96 6+
				BAʿL		I	JA	JPUʿ				BA-LI-PU-UḪ$_2$		EDZARD, DER 117:38 DATE
				BAʿL		I	JE	JPAʿ				BA-LI-E-PA		A.
				BAʿL		I		BAWŠ	T	I		BA-AḪ-LI-BA-AŠ-TI	FN	M+
				BAʿL		I		DIWR		I		BA-AḪ-LI-DI-RI	FN	C+
				BAʿL		I		NIWR		I		BA-AḪ-LI-NI-RI	FN	M+
				BAʿL		I	Š	ʾAG		UM		BA-LI-IŠ-A-GU-UM		RA LXV 45 V 36
				BAʿL		I		ŠAMŠ		I		BA-AḪ-LI-D-UTU-ŠI	FN	M
				BAʿL		I		ŠAPAR				BA-AḪ-LI-SA-PA-AR	FN	M+

STEMS

BAʿL	1	BAʿL		I		ŠAPAR				BA-AḪ-LI-SA-PAR$_2$	FN		M, C+
		BAʿL		I		ṬAJB				BA-LI-SIG5?	FN		XIII 1 VIII 36
		BAʿL		U		ʿAŠTAR				BA-LU-EŠ$_4$-DAR			M+
		BAʿL		U		BAʿD		I		BA-AḪ-LU-BA-DI			EA
		BAʿL		U		GAʾJ		A		BA-AḪ-LU-GA-A	GEN		HOLMA 6 5
		BAʿL		U		GAʾJ		IM		BA-AḪ-LU-GA-JI-IM	GEN		M+
		BAʿL		U		GAʾJ		IM		BA-AḪ-LU-GA-I-IM	GEN		M+
		BAʿL		U		GAʾJ		I		BA-AḪ-LU-GA-I	NOM		M+
		BAʿL		U		GAʾJ		I		BA-AḪ-LU-GA-A-JI	NOM		M
		BAʿL		U		KULIM				BA-AḪ-LU-KU-LI-IM			SYRIA XXXII 7 III 6
		BAʿL		U		LUʾL		I		BA-AḪ-LU-LU-L[I]?			HARRIS 71 14
		BAʿL		U		ME							
						NUMḪ		I		BA-LU-ME-NU-ḪI			M+
		BAʿL		U		ME							
						NUMḪ		I		BA-LU-ME-NU-UM-ḪI			IX 41 2
		BAʿL		U		ŠAMŠ				BA-LU-D-UTU			M
		BAʿL		UM		ʾIL				BA-AḪ-LU-UM-DINGIR			B 15+
		BAʿL		UM		QAWM		UM		BA-LUM-QA-MU-UM			RA LXV 40 I 11
		BAʿL	AT	UM						BA-AḪ-LA-TUM	FN		M+
		BAʿL	AT	UM						BA-LA-TUM	FN		BM 16944 5
		BAʿL	AT	IM						BA-AḪ-LA-TIM	FN	GEN	XIII 1 XIV 37
	2	ʾAJA				BAʿL		A	JA	A-A-BA-LA-IA			SIMMONS 63 9
		ʿIJN				BAʿL		I		IN-BA-AḪ-LI	FN		A.
		ʿABD				BAʿL	AH			ḪA-AB-DU-BA-AḪ-LA			M
		ʿABD				BAʿL	AT	I		ḪA-AB-DU-BA-AḪ-LA-TI			M+
		HADD		U		BAʿL		I		D-IM-BA-AḪ-LI			M+
		ḪADUR				BAʿL		A		A-DU-UR-BA-LA-IA	GN		SUMER XIV 26
		ḪADUR				BAʿL		A		D-ZA-GAR$_3$-BA-LA-IA	GN		SUMER XIV 26
		ḪADUR				BAʿL		U		A-DU-UR-BA-LU	GN		SUMER XIV 26
		ʾIL		A		BAʿL		U	HU	I-LA-BA-LU-U$_2$			M
		ʾIL		A	Š	BAʿL		UM		DINGIR-ŠU-BA-A-LUM			CT II 15 9
		ʾAM	T			BAʿL	AH			A-MA-AT-D-BA-A-LA	FN		BAGHD. MITT. II 72 5, 9+
		ʾUMM		I		BAʿL	AH			UM-MI-BA-A-LA	FN		A. LATE
		ʾANA				BAʿL		U		A-NA-BA-LU	MN?		CT XLVIII 86 REV
		ʾANA				BAʿL		U		A-NA-BA-LU	FN		M
	JI	ʾKUR				BAʿL		I		I-KU-UR-BA-LI			EDZARD, DER 102:9
		JIŠʿ				BAʿL		A		E-ŠE-EḪ-BA-LA?			VAS VII 160 7
		JIŠʿ		A		BAʿL				IŠ-ḪA-B[A-A]L			HARRIS 39 14
		ʿAŠTAR				BAʿL	AH			EŠ$_4$-DAR-BA-AḪ?-LA	FN		M
		ʾATTA				BAʿL		I		AT-TA-BA-AḪ-LI			JCS XIII 51 293:8,A. LATE
		ʾATTA				BAʿL		I	JE	AT-TA-BA-AḪ-LI-E			JCS XIII 51 293:15,A.LATE
		BUN		U		BAʿL		UM		BU-NU-BA-LUM			B 16+
		BUN		U		BAʿL	AN	U		BU-NU-BA-AḪ-LA-NU			M
	JI	KWUN				BAʿL		I		I-KU-UN-BA-LI			A.
	JI	KWUN				BAʿL		I		I-KU-UN-BA-AḪ-LI			A. 246 33
	JA	KWUN				BAʿL				IA-KU-BA-AL			RA LXV 44 V 7
	JA	MWUT				BAʿL				IA-MU-UT-BA-AL	GN		M+
	JA	MWUT				BAʿL		UM		IA-MU-UT-BA-LUM-KI	GN		B 28+
	JA	MWUT				BAʿL		UM		IA-MU-UT-BA-A-LUM-KI	GN		RLA II 194
	JA	MWUT				BAʿL		IM		IA-MU-UT-BA-LI-IM	GN	GEN	YOS II 49 12+
	JA	MWUT				BAʿL		IM		IA-MU-UT-BA-LIM	GN	GEN	BAGHD. MITT. II 56+
	JA	MWUT				BAʿL	AJ	I		IA-MU-UT-BA-LA-I	GN	NOM	M
	JA	MWUT				BAʿL	AJ	I		IA-MU-UT-BA-LA-JI	GN	NOM	M
	JA	MWUT				BAʿL	IJ	I		IA-MU-UT-BA-LI-I	GN	ACC	M
	JE	MWUT				BAʿL		A		E-MU-UT-BA-LA	GN	GEN	SAKI P. 212+
	JE	MWUT				BAʿL		UM		E-MU-UT-BA-LUM-KI	GN		B 28+
	JE	MWUT				BAʿL		UM		E-MU-UT-BA-A-LUM-KI	GN		RLA II 180
	JE	MWUT				BAʿL		UM		IE-E-MU-UT-BA-LUM-KI	GN		SZLECHTER TJ 16 165
	JE	MWUT				BAʿL		IM		E-MU-UT-BA-LI-IM	GN	GEN	KING 34 6+
		MANN		A		BAʿL		A		MA-NA-BA-LA			M
		MUT		U		BAʿL		U	HU	MU-TU-BA-LU-U$_2$			RA LXV 44 IV 26
		ŠUM		U		BAʿL		A		SU-MU-BA-LA			UNPUBL.
	JA	ŠMAʿ				BAʿL				[IA-A]Š$_2$-MA-AḪ-BA-AL			VIII 101 L.E.
	JI	ŠMAʿ				BAʿL				IŠ-ME-EḪ-BA-AL			M
	JI	ŠMAʿ				BAʿL		A		IŠ-ME-BA-LA			TA 30, 122 2
	JI	ŠMAʿ				BAʿL		A		IŠ-ME-EḪ-BA-LA			TA 30, 71

STEMS

BAʿL	2 JI	ŠMAʿ					BAʿL		I		IŠ-ME-BA-LI		HARRIS 71 6+
		ŠUMḪ		U			BAʿL				SU-UM-ḪU-BA-AL		YOS XII 390 2,9
		ŠUMUḪ					BAʿL		A		SU-MU-UḪ-BA-LA		PBS XI/2 1 I 18
		ŠAMIR				Š	BAʿL				ŠA-MI-IR-ŠU-BI-EL		TCL XVIII 125 30
		ŠAMŠ		U			BAʿL		A		SA-AM-SU-BA-LA		SIMMONS 35 14+
		ŠAMŠ		U			BAʿL		I		SA-AM-SU-BA-AḪ-LI		ABB I 59 8
		ŠAMŠ		U	NA		BAʿL		A		SA-AM-SU-NA-BA-LA		A. 77+
		ŠUMUT		I			BAʿL				SU-MU-TI-BA-AL		M
		ṢILL					BAʿL		I		MI-NI-BA-AḪ-LI		M+
	3	LA			ʾA		HWIJ						
							BAʿL		U		LA-AḪ-WI-BA-LU		C
		LA			ʾA		HWIJ						
							BAʿL		U		LA-AḪ-WI-BA-AḪ-LU		XIV 29:28
		LA					RIWM						
							BAʿL		I		LA-RI-IM-BA-AḪ-LI		M+
		ŠUM		U	JA		MWUT						
							BAʿL		A		SU-MU-IA-MU-UT-BA-[LA]		RUTTEN 3 21
		ŠUM		U	JE		MWUT						
							BAʿL		A		SU-MU-E-MU-UT-BA-LA	NOM	JCS IV 66 22
		ŠUM		U	JE		MWUT						
							BAʿL		A		SU-MU-E-MU-UT-BA-LA	GEN	JCS IV 69 17
		ŠUM		U	JE		MWUT						
							BAʿL		IM		SU-MU-E-MU-UT-BA-LIM?	GEN	JCS IV 71 9
		ŠUM		U	JA		MWUT						
							BAʿL		IM		SU-MU-IA-MU-UT-BA-LIM	GEN	CT XLIII 86 1
		ŠUM		U	JA		MWUT		U				
							BAʿL		A		[SU]-MU-IA-MU-TU-BA-LA		PBS XI/2 1 I 19
BAWʾ	1	BAWʾ		UM							BA-A-U_2-UM		KISURRA 94 14
		BAWʾ		UM							BA-IA-UM		CT VI 15 III 19
		BAWʾ					JARAḪ				BA-IA-RA-AḪ		RUTTEN 7 3
		BAWʾ					JARAḪ				BA-A-RA-AḪ		RUTTEN 39 18
		BAWʾ					JARAḪ				BA-IA-RA-AḪ		RUTTEN 7 7
		BAWʾ		U			ʾIL		A		BA-U_2-I-LA		MEISSNER 43 45
	2	LA					BAWʾ		U		LA-BA-U_2		JCS XIII 51 292:5' A.LATE
		LA					BAWʾ		U		LA-BA-ʾU-U		TALLQUIST,APN P.120 LATE
BAWB	1	BAWB	AT	UM							BA-BA-TUM	FN	RA LXV 58 I 59
		BAWB		I			ḪAJJ		A		D-BA-BI-E_2-A?		VIII 31 7
		BAWB		U			QAʾN				BA-BU-QA-AN		M
	2	ʾIL		A			BAWB		I	JA	DINGIR-BA-BI-A		UET V 263 17
		ʾIL		I			BAWB		UM		I_3-LI_2-BA-BU-UM		U UNPUBL.
	3	ŠUM		U			ʾIL						
							BAWB		I	JA	[SU-MU-I]L-BA-BI-IA		PBS XI/2 1 I 11
BAWŠ	1	BAWŠ	AN	UM							BA-ŠA-NU-UM		TA 30 615
		BAWŠ	AN	U							BA-SA-NU		MAOG 4 440 HANA
		BAWŠ	T	UM							BA-AŠ-TUM	FN	M+
		BAWŠ	T	I			NUṢR		I		BA-AŠ-TI-NU-IZ-RI	FN	RA LXV 58 I 45
		BAWŠ	T	I			NUṢR		I		BA-AŠ-TI-UZ-RI		RA LXIV 28 NO. 15
		BAWŠ	T	I			NUṢR		I		BA-$AŠ_2$-TI-NU-UZ-RI	FN	XIII 1 VII 24
	2	ʾIL		I			BAWŠ	T	I		I_3-LI_2-BA-$AŠ_2$-TI	FN	M+
		ʾANN		U			BAWŠ	T	I		AN-NU-BA-AŠ-TI	FN	RA LXV 65 VII 27
		ḤINN		A			BAWŠ	AT			E-NA-BA-ŠA-AT		ICK 63 2+ CAPP.
		ḤINN		A			BAWŠ	AT	A		E-NA-BA-ŠA-TA		EL II P. 171 N. CAPP.
		ḤINN		I			BAWŠ	AT			E-NI-BA-ŠA-AT		ICK 113 10 CAPP.
		ḤINN		I			BAWŠ	AT	A		E-NI-BA-ŠA-TA		KTS 47C 1 CAPP.
		BAʿL		I			BAWŠ	T	I		BA-AḪ-LI-BA-AŠ-TI	FN	M+
		BEʿL		I			BAWŠ	T	I		BE-LI_2-[B]A-AŠ-TI	FN	RA LXV 60 III 42
		DAGAN					BAWŠ	T	I		D-DA-GAN-BA-AŠ-TI	FN	M+
		KIWN		I			BAWŠ		I		KI-NI-BA-ŠI	FN	HARRIS 45 8
		KIWN		U			BAWŠ		I		KI-NU-BA-ŠI		LANGDON XXVIII 12
		MUT		U			BAWŠ		A		MU-TU-BA-SA		B 35+
		ŠARR		UM			BAWŠ	T	I		LUGAL-BA-AŠ-TI	FN	M
		ŠARR		UM			BAWŠ	T	I		LUGAL-BA-$AŠ_2$-TI	FN	M+
BAWZ	1	BAWZ		A							BA-ZA	MN	B 15
		BAWZ	AT	UM							BA-ZA-TUM	FN	B 15+, M+
		BAWZ	AT	IM							BA-ZA-TI[M]	GEN	M+
		BAWZ	AN	UM							BA-ZA-NU-UM		B 43+

STEMS

BAWZ	1		BAWZ		I		ʿAŠTAR		BA-ZI-EŠ$_4$-DAR		M
BAJAN	2		NAHR				BAJAN		D-ID$_2$-BA-IA-AN		A 21929 5,12
BAJN	1		BAJN		UM				BA-NU-UM		M
			BAJN	AN	UM				BA-NA-NU-UM		B 43+
			BAJN	AN	UM				BA-A-NA-NU-UM		B 43
			BAJN	AN	IM				BA-NA-NIM	GEN	B 43
			BAJN	AT	UM				BA-NA-TUM	FN	C; EDZARD 58:3
			BAJN	AT	UM				BA-NA-A-TUM	FN	HARRIS 86 1
			BAJN		U		DAGAN		BA-NU-D-DA-GAN		M+
	2		ḪINN		I		BAJN	AH	IN-NI-BA-NA	FN NOM	X 81 4
BAJR	1		BAJR		UM				BA-RU-UM		HARRIS 89 2
			BAJR	AT	UM				BA-RA-TUM	FN	CT VIII 6A 3+
			BAJR	ATAN					BA-RA-TA-AN	MN	M
BABUL	1		BABUL		UM				BA-BU-LU-[UM]	FN	RA LXV 62 V 8
BADID	1		BADID		UM				BA-DI-DU-UM		B 15+
BAGIN	1		BAGIN		UM				BA-GI-NU-UM		B 15
			BAGIN		U				BA-GI-NU		B 15+
BAKAL	1		BAKAL		UM				BA-KA-LUM		RUTTEN 38 18+
			BAKAL		A				BA-GA-LA		A. LATE
BAKIL	1		BAKIL		UM				BA-KI-LUM		B 15+
			BAKIL		A				BA-KI-LA$_2$		TCL XIX 74:18
			BAKIL	AH					BA-KI-LA	FN	RA LXV 60 III 68
BAKIR	1		BAKIR		UM				BA-KI-RUM		M
BAKS	1		BAKS		I				BA-AK-ZI	NOM	BASOR 95 P.23
BAKŠ	1		BAKŠ	AT	UM				BA-AK-SA-TUM	FN	M
BAKŠIŠ	1		BAKŠIŠ		UM				BA-AK-ŠI-ŠUM		HARRIS 5 3+
BAKUR	1		BAKUR	AT	UM				BA-KU-RA-TUM	FN	B
			BAKUR		AJA				BA-KU?-RA-IA		C
BAKUS	1		BAKUS		I				BA-KU-ZI		RA LXV 55 XIII 43
BAKUŠ	1		BAKUŠ		AJA				BA-KU-SA-A-IA	FN	XIII 1 II 63
BALAL	1		BALAL	AT	I				BA-LA-LA-TI		TA 1930, 399+
BALAṮ	1		BALAṮ		I		ʾEL		BA-LA-TI-EL		RUTTEN 5 21
	2		ʾADM		U		BALAṮ	I	D-AD-MU-BA-LA-TI?	FN	M
			ZAKK		A		BALAṮ		ZA-AK-KA-BA-LA-AṮ?		M+
BALBAL	1		BALBAL		UM				BA-AL-BA-LUM		RUTTEN 37 4 8
BALIK	1		BALIK		I				BA-LI-KI	GEN	A.
			BALIK	AH					BA-LI-KA	FN	A.
BALIL	1		BALIL		UM				BA-LI-LUM		B 15+
			BALIL	AT	UM				BA-LI-LA?-TUM	MN?	VIII 3 5
			BALIL	AH					BA-LI-LA	FN	XIII 1 VIII 72
BALIṮ	2		ŠUM		U		BALIṮ		SU-MU-BA-LI$_2$-IṮ?		RUTTEN 26 12+
			ŠAM		U		BALIṮ		SA-MU-BA-LI$_2$-IṮ?		RUTTEN 34 11
BALK	1		BALK		UM				BA-AL-KUM		TIM V 1 23
			BALK		U	Š	RAḪAB		BA-AL-KU-UŠ$_2$-RA-ḪA-AB	FN	XIII 1 VIII 61
BALTI	2		MANN				BALTI				
							ʾIL		MA-AN-BA-AL-TI-DINGIR		RA LXIV 34 NO. 24
			MANN		A		BALTI				
							ʾEL		MA-NA-BA-AL-TE-EL		B 28+
			MANN		A		BALTI				
							ʾEL		MA-NA-BA-AŠ-TE-EL		M+
			MANN		A		BALTI				
							ʾIL		MA-AN-NA-BA-AL-TI-DINGIR		M
			MANN		A		BALTI				
							ʾEL		MA-NA-BA-AL-TI-EL		KISURRA 70A 14+
BALṮ	1		BALṮ	AN					BA-AL-TA-AN		M
			BALṮ		A	HA			BA-AL-TA-A	FN	XIII 1 IX 32
BALUL	1		BALUL		A				BA-LUL-LA	MN	AJSL XXXIII 224 3, 6
BANḪ	1	T	BANḪ		IM				BA-TA-AN-ḪI-IM	GEN	M
			BANḪ	AT	UM				BA-AN-ḪA-TUM	FN	IX 291 II 19
BANIḪ	1		BANIḪ	AN					BA-NI-ḪA-AN		M
BANIJ	1	JA	BANIJ				ʾIL		IA-BA-AN-NI-DINGIR		M+
		JA	BANIJ				ʾIL		IA-AB-BA-AN-NI-DINGIR		M
			BANIJ		IM				BA-NI-I-IM	GEN	M
			BANIJ				ME				
							ʾEL		BA-NI-ME-EL		HARRIS 12 15
	2		HADD		U		BANIJ		D-IM-BA-NI		M+

STEMS

BANIJ	2		ʾAKK		A		BANIJ			AK-KA-BA-NI		M
		JI	JṢIʾ				BANIJ		IM	I-ZI-BA-NI-IM	GEN	B 45
			MAʾT		U		BANIJ			MA-TU-BA-NI		KISURRA 112 6
	3		ʿAMM		U		RAPIʾ					
							BANIJ			ḪA-AM-MU-RA-BI-BA-NI		B 19
BANN	1		BANN		UM					BA-AN-NU-UM		M+
BANUQ	1		BANUQ		UM					BA-NU-KU-UM		CT XXXIII 48A 3
			BANUQ	AN						BA-NU-KA-AN		RA LXV 55 XIII 46
BAQAQ	1		BAQAQ		UM					BA-GA-KUM		KISURRA 75A 21+
BAQQ	1		BAQQ		UM					BA-AK-KUM		M
			BAQQ		UM					BA-KU-UM		M
			BAQQ		UM					BA-KU-UM	FN	RA LXV 62 V 12
			BAQQ	AN	UM					BA-AQ-QA-NU-UM		M
			BAQQ	AN	IM					BA-AQ-QA-NIM	GEN	M
BARIL	1		BARIL	AT	UM					BA-RI-LA-TUM	FN	CT VI 35A 15
BAŠAJ	1		BAŠAJ	AT	UM					BA-ŠA-A-IA-[TUM]?	FN	M
BAŠAR	1		BAŠAR							HUR-SAG BA-ŠA-AR	MOUNT	RA IX 57,UR III
			BAŠAR							BA-SA-AR KUR	MOUNT	RTC 124,SARGONIC
			BAŠAR	AN						BA-SA-RA-AN		RA LXV 50 VIII 41
	2		BUN				BAŠAR			BU-UN-BA-SAR		EDZARD,DER 68 IV 7
			LA				BAŠAR			LA-BA-ŠA-AR		RA LXV 42 II 58
BAŠIJ	1	JA	BAŠIJ				DAGAN			IA-BA-SI-D-DA-GAN		M
BAŠIR	1	JI	BAŠIR							I-BA-AS$_2$-SI-IR		M
BAŠUM	1		BAŠUM		UM					BA-SU-MU-UM		SIMMONS 46 27+
BATQ	1		BATQ	AN	UM					BA-AT-GA-NU-UM		ZA XLII 41
BATUL	1		BATUL		UM					BA-TU-LUM		HARRIS 15 4+
			BATUL	AT	UM					BA-TU-LA-TUM	FN	XIII 1 II 59
BAZAZ	1		BAZAZ		UM					BA-ZA-ZUM		BM 17072+
BAZBAZ	1		BAZBAZ		UM					BA-AZ-BA-ZUM		B 48
BAZIḪ	1		BAZIḪ	AN	UM					BA-ZI-ḪA-NU-UM		TA 1931, 230 U
BAZIN	1		BAZIN		UM					BA-ZI-NU-UM		B 15+
			BAZIN		U					BA-ZI-NU		B 15
			BAZIN		IM					BA-ZI-NIM	GEN	B 15
BAZUR	1		BAZUR	AT	UM					BA-ZU-RA-TUM	FN	CT XLV 25 11, 20
			BAZUR	AT	IM					BA-ZU-RA-TIM	FN GEN	CT XLV 25 17
			BAZUR	AH						BA-ZU-R[A]	FN	XIII 1 VII 2
BEʿD	1		BEʿD	IT	UM					BE-DI-TUM	MN	EDZARD, DER 145:10
			BEʿD		I		ʾIL		UM	BE-DI-LU-UM		TIM III 62 6+
			BEʿD		I		ʾIL		UM	BE-DI-LUM		TIM III 61 15
			BEʿD		I		ʾIL			BE-DI-DINGIR		TIM III 130 11+
BEʿL	1		BEʿL		UM					BE-E-LUM		KISURRA 36 4
			BEʿL	AN	UM					BE-LA-NU-UM		M+
			BEʿL	AN	IM					BE-LA-NIM	GEN	M+
			BEʿL	AK	UM					BE-LA-KUM		CT VIII 31A 21+
			BEʿL	AK	I					BE-LA-KI	GEN	CT VIII 31B 23+
			BEʿL		I		ʾAHL		I	BE-LI-IA-LI$_2$		KISURRA 112 14
			BEʿL		I		HADD		U	BE-LI$_2$-D-IM		RA LXV 52 X 39
			BEʿL		I		ʾIL		I	BE-LI$_2$-I$_3$-LI$_2$	FN	RA LXV 64 VI 50
			BEʿL		I		ʾUŠIL		I	BE-LI$_2$-U$_2$-SI-LI	FN	RA LXV 56 I 10
			BEʿL		I		BAWŠ	T	I	BE-LI$_2$-[B]A-AŠ-TI	FN	RA LXV 60 III 42
			BEʿL		I		KAʾB		I	BE-LI$_2$-KA-BI	FN	XIII 1 V 28+
			BEʿL		I		KIʾR		I	BE-LI$_2$-KI-RI	FN	RA LXV 58 I 15
			BEʿL		I		NIWR		I	BE-LI$_2$-NI-RI	FN	M+
			BEʿL		I		NIWR		I	BE-LI$_2$-NE-RI	FN	XIII 1 II 55+
			BEʿL		I		NUṢR		I	BE-LI$_2$-NU-IZ-RI	FN	RA LXV 64 V 60
			BEʿL		I		RAWM			BE-LI$_2$-RA-AM		RA LXV 54 XII 60
			BEʿL		I		ŠAPAR			BE-LI$_2$-SA-PAR$_2$	FN	M
			BEʿL		I	TA	LEʾEJ			BE-LI$_2$-TA-LI-IḪ		RA LXV 50 VIII 44
			BEʿL	AT	UM					BE-LA-TUM	FN	M+
			BEʿL	AT	UM					BE-LA-A-TUM	FN	RA LXV 60 III 26
			BEʿL	AT	I					BE-LA-TI	FN? GEN	VIII 63:11
			BEʿL	AT	IM					BE-LA-TI-IM	FN? GEN	VIII 63:2
			BEʿL	AH						BE-LA	FN	IX 291 3 9'
			BEʿL	T	I		JARAḪ			NIN?-TI-E-RA-AḪ		RA LXV 52 X 54
			BEʿL	T	I		MAʾT		I	BE-EL-TI-MA-TI	FN	A. 253 6
	2		ḤADUR				BEʿL		UM	A-DU-UR-BE-LUM	GN	SIMMONS 138:10

STEMS

BEʿL	2 JI	JTAR					BEʿL	I		I-TAR-BE-LI$_2$		RA LXV 47 VII 39
		KAʾB		I			BEʿL			KA-BI-BE-EL		YOS XIII 432:12
	3	LA				ʾA	HWIJ					
							BEʿL	I		LA-AḪ-WI-BE-LI$_2$	FN	RA LXV 59 II 73
		LA					RIWM					
							BEʿL	I		LA-RI-IN-BE-LI$_2$		X 69 5
BELAʾ	2	KIʾL		I			BELAʾ	I		KI-LI-BE-LA-I		M
BELBAN	1	BELBAN		UM						BE-EL-BA-NU-UM		BM 81108 2
BELBIN	1	BELBIN								BE?-EL-BI-IN		HARRIS 108 4
	2	ŠUM		U			BELBIN			SU-MU-BE-EL-BI-IN		JCS IV 108, YBC 5198
BIḪIR	1	BIḪIR		UM						BI-ḪI-RUM		M+
		BIḪIR	AH							BI-ḪI-RA	FN	M
BIḪR	2	LABW		A			BIḪR	I	Š	LA-BA-BI$_2$-RI-IŠ		HSM 7936, UR III
	3	LA				ʾA	ḪJIJ					
							BIḪR	U		LA-ḪI-BI-RU		WATERMAN 25 R. 5
BIʿD	1	BIʿD	AN	UM						BI-DA-NU-UM		SIMMONS 98 9+
		BIʿD		I			KI					
							ʾEL			BI-DI-KI-EL		RA LXV 53 XI 54
	2	MANN		A			BIʿD	IM		MA-NA-BI-IḪ-DI-IM	GEN	HARRIS 3 18
	3	BIN		I			MA					
							BIʿD	I	JE	BI-NI-MA-BI-DI-E		EK I 40
BIJT	1	BIJT	AT	UM						BI-TA-TUM	MN	B 16+
		BIJT					ʾIL			D-E$_2$-IL		U
	2	PALṬ		A			BIJT	U		PA-AL-DA-BI-TU		A. LATE
		DAʾK		A			BIJT	I		DA?-KA-BI-TI		A.
		DANN		A			BIJT			DA-NA-BI$_2$-IT		U
		MILʾ		A			BIJT	I		MI-IL-A-BI-TI		A. 60 2
		ŠAWB		I			BIJT	UM		ŠA-A-BI-E$_2$		SUMER V 142 NO. 6
BIBIJ	1	BIBIJ	AT	UM						BI-BI-IA-TUM	FN	RA LXV 62 V 25
BIDUM	1	BIDUM		U						BI-DU-MU		M
BIKAN	1	BIKAN								BI-GA-AN		YOS XIII 271:6,7+
		BIKAN		UM						BI-KA-NU-UM		KISURRA 47A 10+
		BIKAN		I						BI-KA-NI		KISURRA 30 8
BIKIN	1	BIKIN		UM						BI-KI-IN-NU-UM		VAS VIII 15 16
		BIKIN		UM						BI-IK-KI-NU-UM		YOS XIII 306:4
		BIKIN	AH							BI-KI-IN-NA	FN	XIII 1 VIII 27
		BIKIN		IJA						BI-KI-NI-IA		VAS XIII 20A R. 19
		BIKIN	T	I						BI-IK-KI-IT-TI	MN GEN	A.
BIKN	1	BIKN	AN	UM						BI-IK-NA-NU-UM		VAS VIII 1 21+
BIKUR	1	BIKUR	T	UM						BI-KU-UR-TUM	MN	BASOR 95 P. 24
BILAL	1	BILAL		A			MA			BI-LA-LA-MA		OIP XLIII 135+
BILK	1	BILK	UT	UM						BI-IL-KU-TUM	FN	XIII 1 XIII 17
BILL	1	BILL		UM						BE-EL-LUM		B 15 HANA
		BILL		UM						BIL-LUM		B 15
		BILL	ATAN	UM						BI-LA-TA-NU-UM		HARRIS 49 14
		BILL					ʾAB	I		BI-IL-LA-BI	FN	XIII 1 X 41
		BILL					MAŠIK	A		BI-EL-MA-SI-KA?		M
BILM	1	BILM		U	Š					BI-IL-MU-UŠ$_2$		RA LXV 45 V 80
BILUL	1	BILUL		UM						BI-LU-LU-UM		HARRIS 7 8+
BIN	1	BIN		UM						BI-NU-UM		BM 82360 M+
		BIN		IM						BI-NI-IM	GEN	M
		BIN	AN							BI-NA-AN		RA LXV 43 IV 14
		BIN		IJA						BI-NI-IA		M
		BIN		IJA						BI-IN-NI-IA		CT IV 10 39+
		BIN					HADD	U		DUMU-D-IM		M+
		BIN					ʾIL	A		BI-IN-I-LA		A. LATE
		BIN					ʾIL	I	JA	BI-IN-I-LI$_2$-IA		RA LXIV 24 NO.8
		BIN					DAM	U		BI-IN-DA-MU		RA LXV 42 II 61
		BIN					MA					
							ʾAḪ	IM		BI-IN-MA-A-ḪI-IM		M
		BIN					MA					
							ʾIL			BI-MA-DINGIR		C+
		BIN					NAHR	UM		BI-IN-NA-RUM		CT VI 23 5+
		BIN					NAHR	UM		BI-NA-RU-UM		BIN VII 67 27+
		BIN					NAHR	I		BI-IN-NA-A-R[I]?		M
		BIN					ŠAMŠ			BI-IN-D-UTU		M

STEMS

BIN	1		BIN		A			ʾAḪ		UM		BI-NA-A-ḪU-UM		M+	
			BIN		A			HADD		U		[B]I-NA-D-IM		M	
			BIN		A			ʿAMM		I		BI-NA-AM-MI		B 15	
			BIN		A			ʾANTEL				BI-NA-AN-TE-EL		TLB I 220 26, M+	
			BIN		A			ḪANDEN				BI-NA-ḪA-AN-DI-EN		M	
			BIN		A			ʿAŠTAR				BI-NA-EŠ$_4$-DAR		M+	
			BIN		A			LIʾM				BI-NA-LI-IM		RA LXV 45 V 54	
			BIN		I			MA				BI-NI-MA		A. LATE	
			BIN		I			MA							
								....				BI-NI-MA-D-....		UET V 713 7	
			BIN		I			MA							
								ʾAḪ		UM		BI-IN-NI-MA-ḪU-UM		TLB I 3 28	
			BIN		I			MA							
								ʾAḪ		UM		BI-NI-MA-ḪU-UM		CCT IV 13A 6+	CAPP.
			BIN		I			MA							
								ʾIL				BI-NI-MA-DINGIR		A. LATE	
			BIN		I			MA							
								BIʿD		I	JE	BI-NI-MA-BI-DI-E		EK I 40	
			BIN		I			MARAṢ				BI-NI-MA-RA-AṢ		M	
			BIN		I			MARAṢ		I		BI-NI-MA-RA-ZI	FN	XII 265 2	
			BIN		U			MA							
								HADD		U		BI-NU-MA-D-IM		4E RENCONTRE 21	NO. 25
			BIN	AT	UM							BI-NA-TUM	MN	BM 16820+	
			BIN	AH								BI-[N]A	FN	RA LXV 60 III 62	
			BIN	T	A			ʾATT		I		BI-IT-TA-AT-TI	FN	A.+	
			BIN	T	A			MALK		I		BI-IT-TA-MA-AL-KI	FN	A. LATE	
			BIN	T	E	JE						BI-IT-TE-E	FN	TCL I 52 11	
			BIN	T	I			ḪIJJ		A		BI-TI-ḪI?-A	FN	HARRIS 85 3	
			BIN	T	I			DAGAN				BI-IT-TI-D-DA-GAN	FN	B 16+	
			BIN	T	I			KIʾD		I	JA	BI-IN-TI-KI-DI-IA	FN	A.+	
			BIN	T	U			ṬAJB	AH			BI-IN-DU-ṬA$_3$-BA	FN	RA LXV 65 VII 10	
	2		ʾIL		A			BIN		I		DINGIR-BI-NI		UCP X/3 1 7	
			ʾIL		A			BIN		I		I-LA-BI$_2$-NI		I	
			ʾIL		I			BIN		A	JA	I$_3$-LI$_2$-BI-NA-A-IA		M+	
		JI	NDIN					BIN		UM		I-DIN-BI-NU-UM		UCP X/1 64 2	
			TABʾ		I			BIN		UM		TA-AB-I-BI-NU-UM		BM 82437 4 9	
BINAḪ	1		BINAḪ	AN								BI-NA-ḪA-AN		M	
BINAŠ	2		ŠUM		U			BINAŠ		U		SU-MU-BI-NA-ŠU		A 7630 2	
BINQ	1		BINQ	ATANUM								BI$_2$-GA-TA-NU-UM	MN	TIM III 7:12;39:13	
			BINQ	ATANUM								BI$_2$-IN-GA-TA-NU-UM	MN	TIM III 45:11	
BINZ	1		BINZ		IJA							B[I]-IN-ZI-IA		M	
BIQAQ	1		BIQAQ		UM							BI-GA-GU-UM		YOS VIII 64 19	
			BIQAQ		IM							BI-KA-KI-IM	GEN	CT XLV 79 7	
BIRḪUN	1		BIRḪUN	AH								BI-IR-ḪU-UN-NA	FN	XIII 1 XII 3+	
BIRB	1		BIRB		AJA							BI-IR-BA-IA		RA LXV 52 X 82	
BIRBIR	1		BIRBIR		UM							BI-IR-BI-RU-UM		RUTTEN 7 15+	
			BIRBIR		UM							BIR$_4$-BI$_2$-RU-UM		I	
BIRKIN	1		BIRKIN		UM							BI-IR-KI-NU-UM		TIM V 2 24	
			BIRKIN		U							BI-IR-KI-IN-NU	MN	XIII 1 VI 26	
			BIRKIN	AH								BI-IR-KI-NA	FN	M	
BIRUR	1		BIRUR	UT	UM							BI-RU-RU-TUM	MN	B 15+	
BIŠIR	2		MUT					BIŠIR				MU-UT-BI-SI-IR		M+	
			MUT		U			BIŠIR				MU-TU-BI-SI-IR		M+	
BIZAZ	1		BIZAZ		UM							BI-ZA-ZUM		TA 1931, 327	
BIZKIN	1		BIZKIN	AH								BI-IZ-KI-NA	FN	RA LXV 62 V 22	
BIZZ	1		BIZZ		I			JARAḪ				BI-IṢ-ṢI-E-RA-AḪ		YOS XIII 245:16	
	2		KUʾD		U			BIZZ		U		ḲU-DU-BI-IZ-ZU		A.	
BLIJ	1	JA	BLIJ			JA						IA-AB-LI-IA-KI	GN	M+	
		JA	BLIJ	AT	UM							IA-AB-LI-IA-TUM	FN	B 25+	
BLIM	1	JA	BLIM		UM							JA-AB-LI-MU-UM		RUTTEN 2 17+	
		JI	BLIM		UM							IB-LI-NU-UM		TA 1930, 615:25 +	
BLUW	1	JA	BLUW					DAGAN				IA-AB-LU-D-DA-GAN		M	
BLUṬ	1	JA	BLUṬ	AN	U							IA-AB-LU-TA-NU		MRS VI P. 261+	
	2		BUN		U		ʾA	BLUṬ				BU-NU-AB-LU-UṬ		BIROT,TEA 64:4	
BNAḪ	1	JA	BNAḪ									JA-AB-NA-AḪ		M	
BNIJ	1	JA	BNIJ					HADD		U		IA-AB-NI-D-IM		M	

STEMS

BNIJ	1	JI	BNIJ					HADD		U		IB-NI-D-IM		M+
		JI	BNIJ					JARAḪ				IB-NI-E-RA-AḪ		SIMMONS 62 14'+
		JA	BNIJ					DAGAN				IA-AB-NI-D-DA-GAN		M+
		JI	BNIJ					DAGAN				[I]B?-NI-D-DA-GAN		A. 6 34
		TA	BNIJ	T	UM							TAB-NI-TUM	FN	XIII 1 VI 5+
		TA	BNIJ					ʿAŠTAR				TAB-NI-EŠ$_4$-DAR	FN	XIII 1 XIII 15+
	2		NUN		U		TA	BNIJ				D-NU-NU-TA-AB-NI	FN	XII 265 1
			ŠU				JI	BNIJ			HU	ŠU-U$_2$-IB-NI-U$_2$		TA 1931, 636 REV +
			ŠI				TA	BNIJ				ŠI-TAB-NI	FN	RA LXV 64 VI 18
			ŠI				TA	BNIJ				ŠI-TAB-NI-A-JA	FN	RA LXV 66 VII 57
			ṬALL		I		JI	BNIJ				TA-LI-IB-NI	FN	CT II 5 3 9
BNIQ	1	JA	BNIQ					ʾIL				IA-AB-NI-IQ-DINGIR		B 25
BRUW	1	TA	BRUW					ʿAŠTAR				TAB-RU?-EŠ$_4$-DAR	FN	XIII 1 V 43
BRUQ	1	JA	BRUQ					ʾIL				IA-AB-RU-UQ-DINGIR		BASOR 95, 19
		JA	BRUQ					ʾAB		UM		A-AB-RU-UK-A-BU-UM		JCS XXVI 151:13, HARMAL
		JA	BRUQ					LIʾM				IA-AB-RU-UQ-LI-IM		TCL XI 156 12
BUʾL	1		BUʾL		I			HADD		U		BU-LI-A-DU		A. 60 12
			BUʾL		U	HU						BU-LU-U$_2$		CT XLV 92 II 13
BUʾUL	1		BUʾUL		UM							[B]U-U$_2$-LU-UM		I
			BUʾUL		UM							BU-U$_2$-LUM		TCL I 75 5
			BUʾUL	T	UM							BU-ḪU-UL-TUM	FN	RA LXV 58 I 56
BUḪAZ	1		BUḪAZ		UM							BU-ḪA-ZU-UM		BM 80328 12
BUʿD	1		BUʿD		UM							BU-DU-UM		M
			BUʿD	AN								BU-DA-AN		M
			BUʿD	AT	IM							BU-DA-TIM	GEN	EDZARD, DER 152 REV 6
BUWZ	1		BUWZ		UM							BU-ZU[M]-UM	MN	UCP X/3 2 23
			BUWZ		UM							BU-ZU-UM	FN	C+
			BUWZ		U							BU-ZU		RA LXV 50 VIII 75
			BUWZ		I							BU-ZI	FN	M+, C+
			BUWZ		IJA							BU-ZI-IA		M+
			BUWZ		UJA							BU-ZU-A-IA	FN	RA LXV 62 V 27
			BUWZ		U	HU						BU-ZU-U$_2$		TCL I 59 16+
			BUWZ		U	NA						BU-ZU-NA	FN	RA LXV 58 I 50
	2		KUʾB		A			BUWZ		I		KU-BA-BU-ZI	FN	M
			KIWN					BUWZ	AN	UM		KI-IN-BU-ZA-NU-UM		HARRIS 68 14
BUDAM	1		BUDAM	AN								BU-DA-MA-AN		RA LXV 51 X 4
BUDBUD	1		BUDBUD		UM							BU-UD-BU-DU-UM		BM 16551
BUGAŠ	3		ḪABUR				JI	JBAL						
								BUGAŠ				ID$_2$-ḪA-BUR-I-BA-AL-BU-GA-AŠ$_2$		BRM IV 52 HANA
BUKŠ	1		BUKŠ	AN	UM							BU-UK-SA-NU-UM		PBS XIV 495
BULAṬ	1		BULAṬ		UM							BU-LA-TUM		CT XLV 12 25
			BULAṬ	AT	UM							BU-LA-DA-TUM	MN	BRM III 19E, 22G+
BULM	1		BULM		A	NA		HADD		U		BU-UL-MA-NA-D-IM		M+
BULUK	1		BULUK	AN								B[U]-LU-GA-AN		RA LXV 46 VI 22
BUN	1		BUN	AN	UM							BU-NA-NU-UM		B 44
			BUN	AT	UM							BU-NA-TUM	MN	A 7699 23+
			BUN		IJA							BU-NI-IA		RA LXV 54 XII 31
			BUN					ʾIL		UM		BU-NI-LUM		TIM III 33 15+
			BUN					BAŠAR				BU-UN-BA-SAR		EDZARD,DER 68 IV 7
			BUN					TAḪTUN						
								ʾIL		A		BU-UN-TAḪ-UN-I-LA		B 16
			BUN					TENUT		A		BU-UN-TE-NU?-TA?		MEISSNER 68 13
			BUN		A			ʿAN		UM		BU-NA-A-NU-UM		U
			BUN		A			ʿAŠTAR				BU-NA-D-INNIN		BASOR 95, 19
			BUN		A			MA						
								ʾIL				BU-NA-MA-DINGIR		XII 1 X 36
			BUN		I			ʾIL				BU-NI-DINGIR		B 16
			BUN		I			ʾEL		UM		BU-UN?-NE-E-LUM		TCL I 220 42
			BUN		I			ʾIL		A		BU-NI-I-LA		B 16+
			BUN		I			MA						
								ʾAḪ		UM		BU-NI-MA-ḪU-UM		TCL XX 96 8
			BUN		I			MARAṢ				BU-NI-MA-RA-AṢ		C+
			BUN		U		ʾA	BLUṬ				BU-NU-AB-LU-UṬ		BIROT,TEA 64:4
			BUN		U		ʾA	ŚKUR				BU-NU-AŠ$_2$-KU-UR		SYRIA XXXVII 206 29 HANA
			BUN		U			ʾIL		A		BU-NU-I-LA		CT XLV 115 24
			BUN		U			ḪAM		I		BU-NU-D-A-MI		M+

STEMS

BUN	1		BUN		U		ḪAM		IM	BU-NU-D-A-MI-IM		RA LXV 41 II 27+
			BUN		U		ʿAMM		I	BU-NU-ḪA-AM-MI	FN	M+
			BUN		U		ʿAMM		U	BU-NU-AM-MU		B 16+
			BUN		U		ʿAN	AT	I	BU-NU-A-NA-TI		B 16
			BUN		U		JARAḪ			BU-NU-E-RA-AḪ		M
			BUN		U		JAŠʿ	AH		BU?-NU-IA-AŠ-[ḪA]	FN	XII 1 VII 67
			BUN		U		ʿAŠTAR			BU-NU-EŠ$_4$-DAR		M+, C+
			BUN		U		BAʿL		UM	BU-NU-BA-LUM		B 16+
			BUN		U		BAʿL	AN	U	BU-NU-BA-AḪ-LA-NU		M
			BUN		U		KI					
							ʾIL			BU-NU-KI-DINGIR		M
			BUN		U		KALA					
							ʾIL		I	BU-NU-KA-LA-I-LI		B 16
			BUN		U		KAMA					
							ʾIL		A	BU-NU-KA-MA-I-LA		B 16
			BUN		U		LAʾR		A	BU-NU-LA-RA		B 16
			BUN		U		MA					
							ʾAḪ		UM	BU-NU-MA-A-ḪU-UM		B 16
			BUN		U		MA					
							HADD		U	BU-NU-MA-D-IM		M+
			BUN		U		MA					
							ʾIL			BU-NU-MA-DINGIR		M
			BUN		U		MA					
							ʾAŠAR			BU-NU-MA-A-ŠA-AR		KISURRA 93 4
			BUN		U		MA					
							ʾAŠAR			BU-NU-MA-ŠAR		B 16+
			BUN		U		NAWIJ		E	BU-NU-NA-WI-E		CT XLVIII 56 REV.11
			BUN		UM		ŠAGIŠ			BU-NU-UM-ŠA-GI-IŠ		EDZARD,DER 73:15
			BUN		U		ŠALG		I	BU-NU-ŠA?-AL?-GI		B 16
			BUN		U		TAḪTUN					
							ʾIL		A	BU-NU-TAḪ-TU-UN-I-LA		B 16+
			BUN		UM		ʾEL		UM	BU-NU-UM-E-LU-UM		B 16
			BUN		UM		MA					
							ŠARR			BU-NU-UM-MA-ŠAR		B 16
			BUN		U	HU	PI					
							ʾIL		UM	BU-NU-U$_2$?-BI-I-LUM		UET V 548 2
BUNAQ	1		BUNAQ		UM					BU-NA-GU-UM		TIM III 98 8+
			BUNAQ		UM					BU-NA-KUM		CT XLVIII 87 REV.
BUNZ	1		BUNZ		I					BU-UN-ZI	FN	XIII 1 X 25
BUNZUR	1		BUNZUR		I					BU-UN-ZU-RI	FN	XIII 1 III 13
BUQAQ	1		BUQAQ		UM					BU-QA-KUM		M+
			BUQAQ		UM					BU-QA-KU-UM		M
			BUQAQ		AM					BU-QA-QA-AM	ACC	M
			BUQAQ		IM					BU-QA-KI-IM	GEN	M+
BUQQ	1		BUQQ	AN						BU-QA-AN		C+
			BUQQ	AN						BU-UK-KA-AN		M
			BUQQ	AN	UM					BU-GA-NU-UM		I+
BURAN	1		BURAN	AT	UM					BU-RA-NA-TUM	FN	RA LXV 59 II 70
			BURAN	AH						BU-RA-NA	FN	XIII 1 VI 58
BURBIN	1		BURBIN		UM					BU-UR$_2$-BI-NU-UM		B 16
BURBUR	1		BURBUR		UM					BU-UR$_2$-BU-RU-UM		BIN VII 155 6
			BURBUR		UM					BUR-BUR-RU?-UM		SCHEIL 10 17
			BURBUR	AN						BU-UR-BU-RA-AN		RA LXV 50 VIII 69
BURQ	1		BURQ	AN						BU-UR-QA-AN		M+
			BURQ	AN	U					BU-UR$_2$-GA-NU		BM 17028 5
			BURQ	AN	UM					BU-UR-GA-NU-UM		UET V 482 5
			BURQ	AT	UM					BU-UR-QA-TUM	FN	XIII 1 VII 52+
			BURQ	ATANUM						BU-UR$_2$-GA-TA-NU-UM	MN	SIMMONS 78 11
BURR	1		BURR	AN						BU-UR-RA-AN		RA LXV 47 VII 43
BURŠ	2		KAʾB		I		BURŠ		A	KA-BI-BU-UR-ŠA	FN	XIII 1 XIV 53
BUŠAN	1		BUŠAN	UT	UM					BU?-SA?-NU-TUM	MN?	VIII 13 10'
BUṬUḪ	1		BUṬUḪ		IM					BU-DU-ḪI-IM	GEN	M
BUṬUM	1		BUṬUM	T	UM					BU-TU-UM-TUM	FN	RA LXV 59 II 39
BUZBUZ	1		BUZBUZ		UM					BU-UZ-BU-ZU-UM		B 48+
BUZZ	1		BUZZ	AN	UM					BU-UZ-ZA-NU-UM		M
BZUW	1	JA	BZUW			HU				IA-AB-ZU-U$_2$		CT IV 30D 10+

STEMS

DWIR	1	JA	DWIR		UM						[IA-DI]-RU-U[M]		B 25
		JA	DWIR	AT	UM						[IA-DI]-RA-TUM		B 25
		JA	DWIR		I						IA-DI-RI	NOM	B 25 HANA
DWUR	1	JA	DWUR		IM						IA-DU-RI-IM	GEN	M
		JA	DWUR	AN							IA-DU-RA-AN		M
		JA	DWUR				ʾIL				IA-DU-UR-DINGIR		M
		JA	DWUR				LIʾM				IA-DU-UR-LI-I[M]		RA LXV 45 V 82
		JA	DWUR				NAŠIʾ				IA-DU-UR-NA-SI		M+
DJIN	1	JA	DJIN		IM						IA-DI-NIM	GEN	M+
		JI	DJIN		IM						I-DI-NIM	GEN	M
		JA	DJIN				HADD		U		IA-DI-IN-D-IM		RA LXV 44 IV 51+
	2		LA				DJIN						
							JARAḪ				LA-DI-IN-E-RA-AḪ		RA LXV 46 VI 26+
DAʾK	1		DAʾK		A		BIJT		I		DA?-KA-BI-TI		A.
	2		KUWN		I		DAʾK		A		KU-NI-DA-KA		A. 367 11
			NAʿM		I		DAʾK		A		NA-MI-DA-KA		A. 242 7
DAʾŠ	1		DAʾŠ		U						DA-ŠU		U
DAʿ	1		DAʿ		UM						DA-UM		B 17
	2		ʾIL		A		DAʿ	AT			I-LA-DA-ḪA-AT		SUMER V 141,3+
			ʾIL		A		DAʿ	AT			BAD$_3$-DINGIR-DA-ḪA-AT	GN	A 7650
			ʾIL		I		DAʿ	AT			DINGIR-DA-ḪA-AT		A 7650:2
			ŠAM		I		DAʿ		UM		SA-MI-DA-ḪU-UM		M+
			ŠAM		I		DAʿ		IM		SA-MI-DA-ḪI-IM	GEN	M+
			ŠAM		I		DAʿ	AT	UM		SA-MI-DA-ḪA-TUM	FN	M
			ŠAM		I		DAʿ	AT	IM		SA-MI-DA-ḪA-TIM	FN? GEN	XII 741 6
			ŠAMŠ		I		DAʿ		I		D-UTU-DA-ḪI-I		LANGDON XV 2
DAWD	1		DAWD		UM						DA-DUM		RA LXV 52 XI 3
			DAWD		IM						DA-DI-IM	GEN	M
			DAWD		A						DA-DA	MN	M+, A.
			DAWD		A						DA-A-DA	MN	A.
			DAWD		AJA						DA-DA-A	FN	RA LXV 61 IV 2
			DAWD	AT	UM						DA-DA-TUM	MN	TCL I 109 16+
			DAWD	AT	UM						[D]A-DA-TUM	FN	M
			DAWD	AN	UM						DA-AW-DA-NU-UM		HARRIS 19A 6+
			DAWD	AN	UM						DA-DA-NU-UM		SIMMONS 92 14 M+
			DAWD	AN	U						DA-DA-NU		M
			DAWD	AN	IM						DA-AW-DA-NIM	GEN	B 17+
			DAWD	AN	IM						DA-AM-DA?-NIM	GEN	CT XLVII 78:37
			DAWD	AN	IM						DA-DA-NI-IM	GEN	HARRIS 60:6
			DAWD	AN	I						DA?-DA-NI	FN NOM	M
			DAWD	AK	UM						DA-DA-KUM		KISURRA 39A 4+
			DAWD		IJA						DA-DI-IA		B 16+, M+
			DAWD		IJAN						DA-DI-IA-AN		RA LXV 44 IV 75
			DAWD		I		JABAL				DA-DI-E-BA-AL		UNPUBL.
			DAWD		I		ʿADN				DA-DI-ḪA-DU-UN		M+
			DAWD		I		ʿADN		U	HU	DA-DI-ḪA-AD-NU-U$_2$		18 R.A. P.61 A 3821+
			DAWD		I	Š	ME						
							ʾEL				DA-DI-EŠ$_3$-ME-EL		UCP X/3 P. 198+
			DAWD		I		JAŠAR				DA-DI-E-SA-AR		RA LXV 50 VIII 48+
			DAWD		I	JE	JŠUʿ				DA-DI-E-ŠU-UḪ		M+
			DAWD		I		ŠAMUʿ				DA-DI-SA-MU-UḪ		RA LXV 47 VII 44
			DAWD		UJAN						DA-DU-JA-AN		RA LXV 51 IX 75
			DAWD		U		DANN		UM		DA-AM-DU-DA-NU-UM		HARRIS 92:14+
			DAWD		UM		LU			HU	DA-DU-UM-LU-U$_2$		M
			DAWD		U		MA				DA-DU-MA		HARRIS 49 5
			DAWD		U		MALIK				DA-DU-MA-LIK		XIII 1 VI 27
			DAWD		U		RAPIʾ				DA-DU-RA-BI		B 16+
			DAWD		UM		PI						
							ʾIL				DA-DUM-BI$_2$-DINGIR		I
	2		ʾAJA				DAWD		U		A-IA-DA-DU		M
			ʾAJA				DAWD		U	HU	A-A-DA-DU-U$_2$		HARRIS 79 5
			ʾAJA				DAWD		U	HU	A-IA-DA-DU-U$_2$		TIM IV 39 15
			ʾAJI				DAWD		I		A-I-DA-TE	FN	A.
			ʾAB		A		DAWD		UM		A-BA-DA-DUM		HARRIS 95 9
			ḤAM		U		DAWD		I		D?-[A?-M]U?-DA-DI		IX 291 16
			ḪAM		U		DAWD		U		D-A-MU-DA-DU		M

STEMS

DAWD	2		ʿAQB		U			DAWD		UM		AQ-BU-DA-DU-UM		PBS VIII/2 253 7
			ʿAQB		U			DAWD		A		AQ-BU-DA-DA		B 12
			ʿAQB		U			DAWD		I		ḪA-AQ-BU-DA-DI		M+
			ʿAQB		U			DAWD		I		AQ-BU-DA-DI		M
			ʾAŠD		I			DAWD		UM		AŠ$_2$-DI?-DA-DU-UM		EDZARD, DER 60:11
			JAT		A			DAWD		UM		IA-TA-DA-DUM		B 31
			ḎU					DAWD		A		ZU-E-TA-TA		BIN IV 100 1 CAPP
			ḎU					DAWD		UM		ZU-DA-TUM		I
			ḎU					DAWD		I		ZU-DA-DI		XIV 91:5, 13
		JA	MWUT					DAWD		U		IA-MU-UT-DA-DU		RA LXV 51 X 11
		JA	RWIM					DAWD		U		IA-RI-IM-DA-DU		RA LXV 40 I 38+
			ŠAWB		I			DAWD		I		[Š]A?-BI-DA-DI		RA LXV 43 I 13
			ZAKK					DAWD		I		ZA-AK-DA-TI		TA 1931,377+ EARLY OB
			ZIMM		I			DAWD		I		ZI-IM-MI-DA-DI	FN	C II 44 33+
DAWIR	1		DAWIR	AH								DA-I-RA	FN	M
DAWR	1		DAWR		IJA							DA-RI-IA		M+
	2		NAPŠ		U	NA		DAWR		A		NA-AP-SU-NA-D-DA-RA		CT IV 1 8
			ŠIJM		U			DAWR		A		SI-MU-DA-RA		TA 30, 186+
			ŠUM		I			DAWR		U		SU?-MI-DA-AR-RU		A. 322 9
			ŠUM		I			DAWR		U		ŠU-MI-TA-RU		A. LATE
			ZIʾM		U			DAWR		A		ZI-MU-DA-RA		RA VIII 75 R. 2
DABIʾ	1		DABIʾ		UM							DA-BI-UM		M
DABIN	1		DABIN		UM							DA-BI-NU-UM		TIM III 18 8+
DADM	1		DADM		IM							DA-AD-MI-IM	GEN	M
			DADM	IT	UM							DA-AD-MI-TUM	FN	M
DAGAN	1		DAGAN					ʾIL		I		D-DA-GAN-I$_3$-LI$_2$	FN	RA LXV 62 V 51
			DAGAN					ʾAŠR		A	JA	D-DA-GAN-AŠ-RA-IA		M+
			DAGAN				ʾA	JPUʿ				D-DA-GAN-A-PU-UḪ		M
			DAGAN					BAWŠ	T	I		D-DA-GAN-BA-AŠ-TI	FN	M+
			DAGAN					GAML		I		D-DA-GAN-GA-AM-LI		M
			DAGAN					KIBR		I		D-DA-GAN-KI-IB-RI	FN	M+
			DAGAN					MALAK		U		D-DA-GAN-MA-LA-KU	FN	RA LXV 60 III 3
			DAGAN					MALIK				D-DA-GAN-MA-LIK		M+
			DAGAN					NAʾD		I		D-DA-GAN-NA-DI	FN	XIII 1 III 17+
			DAGAN					NAʿM		I		D-DA-GAN-NA-AḪ-MI	FN	X 116 1, 22
			DAGAN					NIWR		I		D-DA-GAN-NI-RI	MN	RA LXV 47 VII 38
			DAGAN					NIWR		I		D-DA-GAN-NI-RI	FN	M+
			DAGAN					NIWR		I		D-DA-GAN-NE-RI	FN	M+
			DAGAN					NUPAR		A	JA	D-DA-GAN-NU?-PA?-RA-IA		M
			DAGAN					NAṢIR				D-DA-GAN-NA-ṢIR		RA LXV 52 X 76
			DAGAN					ŠAMŠ		I		D-DA-GAN-D-UTU-ŠI	FN	RA LXV 58 I 23+
			DAGAN					TIWR		I		D-DA-GAN-TI-RI	FN	RA LXV 61 IV 51
	2	JA	HWIJ					DAGAN				IA-WI-D-DA-GAN		B 31
		JA	JʿUL					DAGAN				IA-ḪU-UL-D-DA-GAN		RA LXV 48 VII 75
			ʾAB		I			DAGAN				A-BI-D-DA-GAN		M+
			ʿABD					DAGAN				ḪA-AB-DU-D-DA-GAN		M
			ʿABD					DAGAN				AB-DU-D-DA-GAN		M
		JI	JBAL					DAGAN				I-BAL-D-DA-GAN		B 20
		JI	JBAL					DAGAN				I-BA-AL-D-DA-GAN		M
		JA	JDIʿ					DAGAN				I[A]-DI-D-DA-GAN		B 25
			ʿADN		I			DAGAN				ḪA-AD-NI-D-DA-GAN		M
			ʾIL		I			DAGAN				I$_3$-LI$_2$-D-DA-GAN		M+
			ʿAMM		I			DAGAN				ḪA-MI-D-DA-GAN		RA LXV 53 XI 33
			ʿAMM		U			DAGAN				ḪA-AM-MU-D-DA-GAN		M
		JA	ʾMUW					DAGAN				IA-AḪ-MU-D-DA-GAN	GN	B 26
			ʾANA					DAGAN				A-NA-D-DA-GAN		M
		JA	JPAʿ					DAGAN				IA-PA-AḪ-D-DA-GAN		XIII 58 5+
		JA	ʾKUR					DAGAN				IA-KU-UR-D-DA-GAN		M+
			JIŠʿ					DAGAN				I-SI-IḪ-D-DA-GAN		RA XLI 43 HANA
			JIŠʿ		I			DAGAN				IŠ-ḪI-D-DA-GAN		M+
		JA	JṢIʾ					DAGAN				IA-ZI-D-DA-GAN		B 31 HANA, M
		JI	JṢIʾ					DAGAN				I-ZI-D-DA-GAN		B 22 HANA
		JI	JṢIʾ					DAGAN				IS-SI-D-DA-GAN		CT IV 1 14
		JA	ʾZUW					DAGAN				IA-ZU-D-DA-GAN		M+, SYRIA V 273, HANA
		JA	ʾZIJ					DAGAN				IA-AḪ-ZI-D-DA-GAN		RA LXV 54 XII 52
		JA	ʿZIB					DAGAN				IA-ZI-IB-D-DA-GAN		M+

STEMS

DAGAN	2 JA	ḪṢIN				DAGAN	IA-AḪ-ZI-IN-D-DA-GAN		M
		ḪIṢN		I		DAGAN	ḪI-IZ-NI-D-DA-GAN		B 20+ HANA
		ʿAZZ		I		DAGAN	A-ZI-D-DA-GAN		A. LATE
		BAJN		U		DAGAN	BA-NU-D-DA-GAN		M+
	JA	BLUW				DAGAN	IA-AB-LU-D-DA-GAN		M
		BIN	T	I		DAGAN	BI-IT-TI-D-DA-GAN	FN	B 16+
	JA	BNIJ				DAGAN	IA-AB-NI-D-DA-GAN		M+
	JI	BNIJ				DAGAN	[I]B?-NI-D-DA-GAN		A. 6 34
	JA	BAŚIJ				DAGAN	IA-BA-SI-D-DA-GAN		M
		ḎIMR		I		DAGAN	ZI-IM-RI-D-DA-GAN		M+
	JA	ḎRAʿ				DAGAN	IA-AZ-RA-AḪ-D-DA-GAN		XIII 123 26
	JI	ḎRAʿ				DAGAN	IZ-RA-AḪ-D-DA-GAN		B 24 HANA+
		KAʾB		I		DAGAN	KA-BI-D-DA-GAN		M+
	JA	KWUN				DAGAN	IA-KU-UN-D-DA-GAN		X 171 3
		KIʾR		I		DAGAN	KI-RI-D-DA-GAN		RA LXV 52 X 21
		KIBR		I		DAGAN	KI-IB-RI-D-DA-GAN		M+
		LA			NA	DAGAN	LA-NA-D-DA-GAN		M+
	JA	LʾIJ				DAGAN	IA-AL-E-D-DA-GAN		M+
	JA	LʾIJ				DAGAN	IA-[AL]?-I-D-DA-GAN		RA LXV 47 VII 23
	JI	LʾIJ				DAGAN	I-IL-ḪI-D-DA-G[AN]		M
	JE	LʾIJ				DAGAN	EL-I-D-DA-GAN		M
		LIWJ		I		DAGAN	LI-I-D-DA-GAN		M
		MUHR		U		DAGAN	MU-RU-D-DA-GAN		RA LXV 53 XI 53
		MALIK				DAGAN	MA-LI-IK-D-DA-GAN		M
		MILK		I		DAGAN	MIL-KI-D-DA-GAN		TCL I 237 12 HANA
		MANIJ				DAGAN	MA?-NI-D-DA-GAN		A. 6 34
		MUT				DAGAN	MU-UT-D-DA-GAN		M+
		MUT		U		DAGAN	MU-TU-D-DA-GAN		CT XLIII 29 1 M+
		NAWḪ		UM		DAGAN	NA-ḪU-UM-D-DA-GAN		B 36+
		NAʿM		I		DAGAN	NA-AḪ-MI-D-DA-GAN		A.+
		NAʿM		I		DAGAN	NA-MI-D-DA-GAN		A.+
		NAʿM		I		DAGAN	NA-AḪ-ME-D-DA-GAN		RA LXV 48 VIII 33
		NAʿM		UM		DAGAN	NA-AḪ-MU-UM-D-DA-GAN		BM 16824 28+
		NUʿM		I		DAGAN	NU-UḪ-MI-D-DA-GAN		M
	JA	NBIʾ				DAGAN	IA-AB-BI-D-DA-GAN		M+
	JA	NBIʾ				DAGAN	IA-BI-D-DA-GAN		M
	JI	NBIʾ				DAGAN	I-BI-D-DA-GAN		M
		NAPŚ		I		DAGAN	NA-AP-SI-D-DA-GAN		M+
	JA	NŚIʾ				DAGAN	IA-AŠ$_2$-SI-D-DA-GAN		M+
	JA	NŚIʾ				DAGAN	IA-SI-D-DA-GAN		M+
	JI	NŚIʾ				DAGAN	I-SI-IḪ-D-DA-GAN		RA XLI 44 R. 6 HANA
	JI	NŚIʾ				DAGAN	IS-SI-D-DA-GAN		B 22 HANA
	JA	NTIN				DAGAN	IA-AN-TI-IN-D-DA-GAN		M+
	JA	NTIN				DAGAN	IA-TI-IN-D-DA-GAN		M
	JI	NDIN				DAGAN	I-DIN-D-DA-GAN		M+
	JA	NṢIB				DAGAN	IA-AN-ZI-IB-D-DA-GAN		M+
	JA	NṢIB				DAGAN	IA-AZ-ZI-IB-D-DA-GAN		B 29
		PU			KA	DAGAN	PU-KA-D-DA-GAN		M
		PU			HU	DAGAN	PU-U$_2$-D-DA-GAN		M
		QUWJ		U		DAGAN	KU-U$_2$-D-DA-GAN		RA LXV 41 II 43+
	JA	RḪIB				DAGAN	IA-AR-IE-D-DA-GAN		M+
	JA	RJIB				DAGAN	IA-RI-IB-D-D[A-GAN]?		M
		RIJB		U		DAGAN	RI-BU-D-DA-GAN		RA LXV 47 VII 52
	JA	RWIM				DAGAN	IA-RI-IM-D-DA-GAN		M+
	JI	RWIM				DAGAN	I-RI-IM-D-DA-GAN		SYRIA XXXVII 206 2 HANA
		RIWM				DAGAN	RI-IM-D-DA-GAN		M
		RIPʾ		I		DAGAN	RI-IP-I-D-DA-GAN		M+
		RIPʾ		I		DAGAN	RI-BI-D-DA-GAN		M
		RAṢAJ				DAGAN	RA-ZA-D-DA-GAN		M
	JA	ŠWUB				DAGAN	IA-ŠU-UB-D-DA-GAN		B 30 HANA+, M+
	JA	ŚJIM				DAGAN	IA-SI-IM-D-DA-GAN		M+
	JA	ŚJIM				DAGAN	IA-ŠI-IM-D-DA-GAN		VIII 11 33
		ŚIJM	AT			DAGAN	ŠI-MA-AT-D-DA-GAN	FN	XIII 1 VIII 33+
		ŚAM		U		DAGAN	SA-MU-D-DA-GAN		M
		ŚUM		U		DAGAN	SU-MU-D-DA-GAN		B 39+
	JA	ŚMAʿ				DAGAN	IA-AŠ$_2$-MA-AḪ-D-DA-GAN		B 30 HANA+, M+

STEMS

DAGAN	2 JI	ŠMAʿ					DAGAN			IŠ-MA-AḪ-D-DA-GAN		RA XXXIV 186	R. 2 HANA+
	JI	ŠMAʿ					DAGAN			IŠ-ME-D-DA-GAN		M+	
		ŠIMḪ		I			DAGAN			SI-IM-ḪI-D-DA-GAN		M	
		ŠAMŠ		I			DAGAN			SA-AM-SI-D-DA-GAN		M+	
		ṢUWR		I			DAGAN			ZU-RI-D-DA-GAN		M	
	JA	TḪIJ					DAGAN			IA-AT-ḪI-D-DA-GAN		M	
		TUWR		A			DAGAN			TU-RA-D-DA-GAN		M+	
		TUWR		I			DAGAN			TU-RI-D-DA-GAN		B 40+ HANA	
	3	ʿABD					MA						
							DAGAN			AB-DU-MA-D-DA-GAN		M+	
		ʿABD					MA						
							DAGAN			ḪA-AB-DU-MA-D-DA-GAN		M+	
		ʾAMUR					ŠA						
							DAGAN			A-MUR-ŠA-D-DA-GAN		TCL I 237 31 HANA	
DAGAZ	1	DAGAZ		I						DA-GA-ZI	FN	RA LXV 56 I 6	
DAKŠ	1	DAKŠ	AT	UM						DA-AK-SA-TUM	FN	CT IV 45B 6	
DAKUL	1	DAKUL		UM						DA-KUL-LUM		UET V P. 35+	
	2	ʾIL		A			DAKUL			DINGIR-DA-AK-KU-UL		UET V P. 43	
		ʾIL		A			DAKUL			DINGIR-DA-KU-UL		UET V P. 43	
		ʾIL		A			DAKUL		UM	DINGIR-DA-AK-KU-UL-LUM		UET V P. 43	
		ʾIL		A			DAKUL		UM	DINGIR-DA-KU-UL-LUM		UET V P. 43+	
DALAQ	1	DALAQ		UM						DA-LA-KUM		VAS IX 120 13	
DALQ	1	DALQ		UM						DA-AL-KUM		CT VI 28A 24	
DALUM	1	DALUM		UM						DA-LU-MU-UM		MEISSNER 24 15	
DAM	1	DAM	AN	UM						DA-MA-NU-UM		B 44	
		DAM	AT	UM						DA-MA-TUM	FN	XIII 1 V 30	
	2	BIN					DAM		U	BI-IN-DA-MU		RA LXV 42 II 61	
DAMIQ	1	DAMIQ	T	UM						DA-ME-IQ-TUM	FN	RA LXV 59 II 60	
	2	ŠU					DAMIQ			ŠU-DA-ME-IQ		RA LXV 41 II 16	
DAMQ	1	DAMQ	AT	UM						DAM-QA-TUM	FN	CT XLV 2 22+	
		DAMQ	AN	UM						DA-AM-QA-NU-UM		SIMMONS 67 7	
		DAMQ	AN	UM						DAM-QA-NU-UM		SIMMONS PASSIM	
		DAMQ	AN	U						DAM-QA-NU		XIII 1 II 1	
	2	ʾANN		U			DAMQ	AH		AN-NU-DAM-QA	FN	XIII 1 X 51	
		ʾIŠḪAR	AH				DAMQ	AH		D-IŠ-ḪA-RA-DAM-QA	FN	RA LXV 58 I 18	
		ʿAŠTAR					DAMQ	AH		EŠ$_4$-DAR-DAM-QA	FN	XIII 1 V 50+	
		ŠINA					DAMQ		A	ŠI-NA-DAM-QA	FN	XIII 1 IV 29+	
		ŠINI					DAMQ		A	ŠI-NI-DAM-QA	FN	RA LXV 61 IV 48	
DANN	1	DANN					ʾIL			DAN-DINGIR		U	
		DANN		A			BIJT			DA-NA-BI$_2$-IT		U	
		DANN		I			ʾIL			DA?-NI-DINGIR		M	
		DANN		I	Š		ME						
							ʾIL			DA-NI-IŠ-ME-DINGIR?		I	
		DANN		U			MAʾT		UM	DA-NU-MA-TUM		CT XLV 12:24	
		DANN		U		TA	ʾḪAḎ			DAN-NU-TA-ḪA-AZ		M+	
		DANN		U		TA	ʾḪAḎ			DA-NU-TA-ḪA-AZ		SIMMONS 36 23	
		DANN		U		TA	ʾḪAḎ			D-DA-NU-TA-ḪA-AZ		SIMMONS 84 15	
		DANN		UM		TA	ʾḪAḎ			D-DA-AN-NU-UM-TA-ḪA-AZ		SIMMONS 36 A 22	
		DANN		UM		TA	ʾḪAḎ			DA-AN-NU-UM-TA-ḪA-AZ		SIMMONS 36	CASE 22
		DANN		UM		TA	ʾḪAḎ			DA-NU-UM-TA-ḪA-AZ		A 7634, M	
		DANN		UM		TA	ʾḪAḎ			D-DA-NU-UM-TA-ḪA-[AZ]		TIM V 19 14	
	2	ʾAḪ		I			DANN		UM	A-ḪI-DA-NU-UM		I	
		ʾEB		I			DANN		UM	E-BI-DA-NU-UM		U	
		ʿAMM		I			DANN		U	AM-MI-DA-NU		YOS XII	
		ʾIŠḪAR	AH				DANN	AT		IŠ-ḪA-RA-DAN-NA-AT	FN	M	
		DAWD		U			DANN		UM	DA-AM-DU-DA-NU-UM		HARRIS 92:14+	
		KUʾM					DANN		UM	KU-UM-DA-NU-UM		U	
		MILK		U			DANN		UM	MI-IL-KU-DA-NU-UM		UET V 549:8	
		QAWM		A			DANN		UM	QA-MA-[D]A-NUM		M	
		SIKIL					DANN		UM	ZI-GI-IL-DA-NU-UM		M+	
DARAB	2	ʾAB		I			DARAB			[A]?-BI-DA-RA-AB		RA LXV 43 III 67	
DARAN	2	ʾIL		A			DARAN			DINGIR-DA-RA-AN		M+	
DARIK	1	DARIK		UM						DA-RI-KUM		B 17+	
		DARIK		UM						DA-RI-KU-UM		CT XLV 117 27	
		DARIK		UM						DA-AR-RI-KU-[UM]		B 17	
DARK	1	DARK		U						DAR-KU		C	

DARK	1		DARK	AT	UM				DA-AR-KA-TUM	FN	C
			DARK		I	MA			DAR-KI-MA	FN	RA LXV 61 IV 14
DAŠIK	1		DAŠIK	T	UM				DA-SI-IK-TUM	MN	MEISSNER 90 27
DAŠIL	1		DAŠIL		AJA				DA-SI-LA-A-A		HARRIS 79 24
DAŠUR	1		DAŠUR		UM				DA-ŠU-RU-UM		B 17+
			DAŠUR	AT	UM				DA-ŠU-RA-TUM	FN	YOS VIII 51 2,14
			DAŠUR	AH		ʿAŠTAR			DA-ŠU-RA-EŠ$_4$-DAR	FN	YOS VIII 51 5
	2		ʾAḪ		I	DAŠUR			A-ḪI-DA-ŠU-UR$_2$		PBS XI/2 P. 140 NO. 1128
			ʿAMM		I	DAŠUR			AM-MI-DA-ŠUR?		A 7894
			JARAḪ			DAŠUR			SIN-DA-ŠUR		VAS IX 185 12+
DBAR	1	ʾA	DBAR	AT	UM				AD-BA-RA-TUM	MN	A 21946
DBIR	1	ME	DBIR						ME-ED-BI-IR		BASOR 95, 24
DIʾL	1		DIʾL	AN	UM				DI-LA-NU-UM		B 44
DIʿ	1		DIʿ	ATANUM					DI-ḪA-TA-NU-U[M]		CT XLVII 4 3
	2		ʾIL		AM	DIʿ		I	DINGIR-LAM-DI-I		SIMMONS 24 10+
			ʾIL		I	DIʿ	AT		I$_3$-LI$_2$-DI-ḪA-[AT]		HARRIS 39 19
			ŠAMŠ		I	DIʿ	AT		SA-AM-SI-DI-ḪA-AT?		TIM II 49 5
DIWD	1		DIWD		UM				DI-DU-UM		BIN VII 63 24
	2		ʾAJAM			DIWD		UM	ḪA-IA-AM-DI-DU-UM		B 18+
			ʾAJAM			DIWD		U	ḪA-IA-AM-DI-DU		B 18
DIWIR	1		DIWIR			ʾAḪ		I	DI-WI-IR-A-ḪI		PBS XI/1 P. 55+
			DIWIR			ʾAḪ		I	DI-BI-IR-A-ḪI		PBS XI/1 P. 55+
			DIWIR			ʾAB		I	DI-WI-IR-A-BI		PBS XI/1 P. 55+
			DIWIR			ʾAB		I	DI-BI-IR-A-BI		PBS XI/1 P. 55+
			DIWIR			MUT		I	DI-WI-IR-MU-TI		PBS XI/1 P. 55+
			DIWIR			MUT		I	DI-BI-IR-A-MU-TI		PBS XI/1 P. 55+
DIWR	1		DIWR	IT	UM	KAʾB		I	D-DI-RI-IUM-KA-BI		XIII 1 VI 45
	2		BAʿL		I	DIWR		I	BA-AḪ-LI-DI-RI	FN	C+
		JA	KWUN			DIWR		UM	IA-KU-UN-DI-RUM		CT XLVIII 115
		JA	KWUN			DIWR		IM	IA-KU-UN-DI-[R]I-IM	GEN	M
		JA	KWUN			DIWR		I	IA-KU-UN-DI-RI	GEN	CT XLVIII 115 CASE
		JA	KWUN			DIWR			IA-KU-UN-DI-IR		M+
		JA	KWUN			DIWR			IA-KU-DI-IR		RA LXV 45 V 14
		JA	MWUT			DIWR		UM	IA-MU-UT-DI-RUM		WATERMAN 14 9
		JI	NDIN			DIWR	IT	IM	I-DIN-D-DI-RI-TIM	GEN	M
	3		LA			RIWM					
						DIWR			LA-RI-IM-DI-IR		RA LXV 50 IX 22
DIJN	1		DIJN		I	HADD		U	TI-NI-A-DU		A. 59 2
			DIJN		I	HADD		U	DI-NI-A-DU		A.+
			DIJN		I	HADD		U	DI-NA-A-DU		A. LATE
	2	JI	JʿIL			DIJN		I	I-ḪI-IL-DI-NI-X?		RA LXV 48 VIII 1
			LA			DIJN		AM	LA-DI-NAM	ACC	M
			ŠUM		U	DIJN		I	[SU-M]U-DI-NI		PBS XI/2 P. 119
	3	JI	NPIḪ			LI					
						DIJN		I	IB-BI-IḪ-LI-DI-NI	FN	C
DIBDIB	1		DIBDIB		UM				DI-IB-DI-BU-UM		SIMMONS 13 10
DIDAM	1		DIDAM	AN	UM				DI-DA-MA-NU-UM		B 44
DIGAN	1		DIGAN		UM				DI-GA-NU-UM		RUTTEN 11 2
DIGDIG	1		DIGDIG		UM				DI-IG-DI-GU-UM		B 48+
			DIGDIG		UM				DI-DI-GU-UM		UET V 702 R 13
DIMAḪ	1		DIMAḪ		UM				DI-MA-ḪU-UM		B 17
DINIK	1		DINIK			MUʾ		UM	DI-NI-IK-MU-UM		SIMMONS 39 3+
DIRAḪ	2		ʾAB		I	DIRAḪ			A-BI?-DI-RA-AḪ		TCL X 41 A/B 4+
DITAN	1		DITAN		UM				TI-DA-NUM$_2$	GN	GUDEA
			DITAN		U				DI-TA-NU		BM 80328 6
			DITAN		U				DI-DA-A-NU		JNES XIII 210+ LATE
	2		ʾAB		I	DITAN			A-BI-DI-TA-AN		BM 80328 16
			ʾAB		I	DITAN		UM	A-BI-TI-DA-NU-UM		TA 1931, 538 III,IV
			ʾIL		I	DITAN			I$_3$-LI$_2$-DI-TA-AN		BM 82424 R. 18
			ʿAMM		I	DITAN		A	AM-MI-DI-TA-NA		B13+
			ʿAMM		I	DITAN		A	AM-MI-TE-TA-NA		CT XLV 44 24
			....			DITAN			ME-D-DI-TA-AN		UET V 497 11, 581 11
		JI	NWUḪ			DITAN			I-NU-UḪ-DI-TA-AN		GORDON 38 20+
			ŠUM		U	DITAN		A	SU-MU-DI-TA-NA		B 39+, M
			ŠUM		U	DITAN			SU-MU-DI-TA-AN		SIMMONS 126 17+
			ŠUM		U	DITAN			[SU]?-MU?-DI?-TA-A-AN		VAS XVI 24 3

STEMS

DITAN	2	ŠAMŠ		I			DITAN	A		SA-AM-SI-DI-TA-NA		B 38
		ŠAMŠ		U			DITAN	A		SA-AM-SU-DI-TA-NA		B 38+
	3	MA					LA		NA			
							DITAN	A		MA-A-LA-NA-DI-TA-NA		B 34
		ŠUM		U			ṢIDQ	UM				
							DITAN	A		[SU]-MU-ZI-ID-KUM-DI-TA-NA		B 40
DITN	2	....					DITN	IM		MU-RI-IQ-TI-IT-NI-IM	GN GEN	U
		ŠUM		U			DITN	UM		SU-MU-DI-IT-NU-UM		B 39
DLUW	1 JA	DLUW			HU					A-AD-LU-U$_2$		HARRIS 70 15+
DLUQ	1 ʾA	DLUQ		IJA						AD-LU-KI-IA		RES 1939, 69
DNIK	1 JI	DNIK				ʾA	MURR	UM		D-ID-NI-IK-MAR-TU	DN	U
DRAK	1 ʾA	DRAK	AT	UM						AD-RA-KA-TUM	FN	M+
	ʾA	DRAK	AT	IM						AD-RA-KA-TIM	FN GEN	M+
DRUK	1 JA	DRUK		A						IA-AD-RU-QA		A. LATE
DUWD	1	DUWD	AN	UM						DU-DA-NU-UM		CT XLVIII 87
		DUWD	AN	IM						DU-DA-NIM		M
		DUWD		U	HU					DU-DU-U$_2$		M, TCL X 112 8, 22+
		DUWD		U	Š		ME					
							ʾEL			DU-DU-UŠ-ME-EL		UCP X/3 P. 198+
		DUWD	UT	UM						DU-DU-TUM	FN	M
	2	LAMA					DUWD	U		LA-MA-DU-DU		M
DUWR	1	DUWR			NI		ʾIL			DU-UR-NI-DINGIR		M+
	2	HADD		U			DUWR	I		D-IM-DU-RI		M+
		ŠI					DUWR	I		ŠI-DU-RI	FN	RA LXV 58 I 68+
DUDM	2	RABAʿ					DUDM	U		RA-BA?-AḪ-DU-UD-MU		M
DUKUB	1	DUKUB		UM						DU-KU-BU-UM		SUMER XIV 54 28 6
DULAQ	1	DULAQ		UM						DU-LA-KUM		TCL I 56 22+
DULDUL	1	DULDUL		UM						DU-UL-DU-LUM		B 48
DULQ	1	DULQ	AN	UM						TU-UL-GA-NUM$_2$		U
DULUQ	1	DULUQ		UM						DU-LU-KUM		RUTTEN 3 16+
		DULUQ		UM						DU-UL-LU-KUM		RUTTEN 29 5
		DULUQ	AT	UM						DU-LU-GA-TUM	FN	VAS IX 178 2
		DULUQ	T	UM						DU-LU-UQ-TUM	FN	MEISSNER 7 26
DUMAR	2	ʿAMM		U			DUMAR			ḪA-MU-DU-MAR		RA LXV 51 IX 66
DUMAT	1	DUMAT	AN							DU-MA-TA-AN		XIV 47:19
DUMQ	2	ʾIŠḪAR	AH				DUMQ	I		D-IŠ-ḪA-RA-DU-UM-KI	FN	XII 265 3
DUNN	1	DUNN		I			HADD	U		DU-NI-A-DU		A. LATE
		DUNN		I			....			DU-NI-PA-DU		A.
	2	ʾANN		U			DUNN	I		AN-NU-DU-UN-NI	FN	XIII 1 III 37
		ʾANN		U			DUNN	I		AN-NU-DU-NI	FN	RA LXV 65 VII 15
		MAM		A			DUNN	I		D-MA-MA-DU-UN-NI	FN	M
DUŠUB	1	DUŠUB	T	UM						DU-ŠU-UB-TUM	FN	TCL XI 244 11, M
DUŠUR	2	ʿAMM		I			DUŠUR			ḪA-MI-DU-ŠU-UR		SIMMONS 46 18+
		ʿAMM		I			DUŠUR			ḪA-MI-DU-ŠU-UR$_2$		SIMMONS 50 14
		ʿAMM		I			DUŠUR			ḪA-AM-MI-DU-ŠU-UR		HARRIS 18 15+
		ʿAMM		I			DUŠUR			ḪA-AM-MI-DU-ŠU-UR$_2$		HARRIS 27 17+
		ʿAMM		I			DUŠUR			AM-MI-DU-ŠU-UR		A7894+
ḎABAB	1	ḎABAB		UM						ZA-BA-BU-UM		HARRIS 98 R. 5
ḎABB	1	ḎABB		UM						ZA-AB-BU-UM		BM 17051 7
ḎABIB	1	ḎABIB		UM						SA-BI-BU-UM		WATERMAN 24 R. 4+
		ḎABIB		UM						ZA-BI-BU-UM		B 40+
		ḎABIB	IT	UM						SA-BI-BI-TUM	FN?	HARRIS 100 6
		ḎABIB		I			ʾIL			SA-BI-BI-DINGIR		M
ḎABIL	1	ḎABIL		UM						DA-BI-LU-UM		RA LXV 54 XII 20
ḎAKAJ	2	ʿAMM		U			ḎAKAJ	A		Ḫ[A]-MU-ZA-KA-A		RA LXV 43 III 75
ḎAKIR	1	ḎAKIR		UM						DA-KI-RU-UM		B 16
		ḎAKIR		UM						DA-KI-RUM		B 16+
		ḎAKIR		UM						ZA-KI-RUM		RA LXV 53 XI 22; B 41
		ḎAKIR		UM						ZA-KI-RU-UM		M
		ḎAKIR		IM						ZA-KI-RI-IM	GEN	BM 17069 8+, M
		ḎAKIR	AT	UM						ZA-KI-RA-TUM?	FN	C
		ḎAKIR		A			ʿAMM	I		ZA-KI-RA-ḪA-MI		M
		ḎAKIR		A			ʿAMM	U		ZA-KI-RA-ḪA-AM-MU		M+
		ḎAKIR		A			ʿAMM	U		ZA-KI-RA-ḪA-MU		M
		ḎAKIR		A			ʿAMM	U	HU	ZA-KI-RA-ḪA-AM-MU-U$_2$		M+
ḎAKUR	1	ḎAKUR		UM						ZA-KU-RU-UM		B 41+

STEMS

ḎAKUR	1		ḎAKUR		UM					ZA-KU-RUM		B 41+
			ḎAKUR	AH						ZA-KU-RA	FN	XIII 1 II 40
			ḎAKUR		A		ʾAḪ		UM	ZA-KU-RA-A-ḪU-UM		M+
			ḎAKUR				ʾAB		I	ZA-KU-UR-A-BI	GEN	B 41
			ḎAKUR		A		ʾAB		I	ZA-KU-RA-A-BI	GEN	B 41
			ḎAKUR		A		ʾAB		U	ZA-KU-RA-A-BU		M
			ḎAKUR		A		ʾAB		UM	ZA-KU-RA-A-BU-UM		X 79 5
			ḎAKUR		A		ʾIL			ZA-KU-RA-DINGIR		M+
			ḎAKUR		A		KUWN		U	ZA-KU-RA-KU-NU		VII 85 12
			ḎAKUR		I		ʾEL			ZA-KU-RI-E-EL		UCP X/1 86 15
			ḎAKUR		I		ʾEL		UM	ZA-KU-RI-E-LUM		UNPUBL.
ḎAMAR	1		ḎAMAR	AN	UM					ZA-MA-[RA]?-NU-[UM]		TA 1930, 615 28
			ḎAMAR	AN	IM					ZA-AM-MA-RA-NIM-KI	GN GEN	C II 39 8
			ḎAMAR		I		ʾEL		UM	ZA-MA-RI-E-LUM		B. 92+
ḎAMIR	1		ḎAMIR		UM					DA-ME-RU-UM		B 17+
			ḎAMIR		UM					DA-MI-RU-UM		I
			ḎAMIR		IM					DA-ME-RI-IM	GEN	HARRIS 77 13
ḎAMR	2		ʾIŠḪAR	AH			ḎAMR	AT	I	D-IŠ-ḪA-RA-ZA-AM-RA-TI	FN	M
ḎAMUR	1		ḎAMUR	AN						ZA-MU-RA-AN		M
ḎANAB	1		ḎANAB	AN						ZA-NA-BA-AN		RA LXV 41 II 51+
ḎANB	1		ḎANB		UM					ZA-AN-BU-UM		TIM V 33 23
ḎANIB	1		ḎANIB		UM					ZA-NI-BU-UM		BA V 486 NO. 2 5
			ḎANIB		UM					SA-NI-BU-UM		BA V 517 NO. 57 3, 6+
ḎAQAN	1		ḎAQAN		UM					ZA-KA-NU-UM		WALTERS,WL 85:4
ḎAQN	1		ḎAQN		IJA					ZA-AQ-NI-IA		WALTERS,WL 100:4+
			ḎAQN	IT	UM					DA-AQ-NI-TUM	FN	XIII 1 XIII 22
ḎARʿ	1		ḎARʿ		IM					ZA-AR-IM	GEN	M
			ḎARʿ	AN						(E$_2$)-ZA-AR-ḪA-AN-KI	GN	M+
			ḎARʿ	AN	UM					ZA-AR-ḪA-NU-UM	GN	B 48
ḎARAʿ	1		ḎARAʿ		UM					DA-RA-UM		U
			ḎARAʿ				LI					
							ʾIL			ZA-RA-AḪ?-LI-DINGIR		M
ḎARIʾ	2	JI	JṢIʾ				ḎARIʾ		JE	I-ZI-DA-RI-E		B 22+
		JI	JṢIʾ				ḎARIʾ		JE	I-ṢI-DA-RI-E		B 22+
		JI	JṢIʾ				ḎARIʾ		JE	I-ṢI-DA-RI-E-KI	GN	B 22
		JI	JṢIʾ				ḎARIʾ		JE	I-ṢI-DA-RI-I-KI	GN	B 22
		JI	JṢIʾ				ḎARIʾ		JE	I-ZI-DA-RI		TCL XI 218 9
		JI	JṢIʾ				ḎARIʾ		JE	I-ZI-ZA-RI-E		B 23+, M
		JI	JṢIʾ				ḎARIʾ		JE	I-ZI-IZ-ZA-RI-E		B 23
		JI	JṢIʾ				ḎARIʾ		JE	I-ZA-AR-RI-E		UET V 202 15
ḎARIʿ	1		ḎARIʿ		UM					ZA-RI-ḪU-UM		HARRIS 34 12+
			ḎARIʿ		IM					ZA-RI-ḪI-IM	GEN	HARRIS 3 17
ḎIBIB	1		ḎIBIB		UM					SI-BI-BU-UM		PBS VIII/2 228 A4
			ḎIBIB		U					SI-BI-BI-BU		PBS VIII/2 228 4
ḎIKR	1		ḎIKR		IM					ZI-IK-RI-IM	GEN	M
			ḎIKR	AT	UM					ZI-IK-RA-TUM	FN	XIII 1 II 50
			ḎIKR	AT	IM					ZI-IK-RA-TIM	MN? GEN	XII 263 10
			ḎIKR	ATAN						ZI-IK-RA-TA-AN		M+
			ḎIKR	ITANU						ZI-IK-RI-TA-NU		M
			ḎIKR		IJA					ZI-IK-RI-IA		RA LXV 43 IV 20
			ḎIKR	AN						ZI-IK-RA-AN		RA LXV 51 IX 34
			ḎIKR		A		ʿAŠTAR			ZI-IK-RA-EŠ$_4$-DAR		M+
			ḎIKR		I		HADD		U	ZI-IK-RI-D-IM		M+
			ḎIKR		I		ʿAN	AT		ZI-IK-RI-ḪA-NA-AT		M
			ḎIKR		I		ʿAN	AT		ZI-IK-RI-D-ḪA-N[A-AT]		M
			ḎIKR		I		JARAḪ			ZI-IK-RI-E-RA-AḪ		TIM V 69 7, 17+
			ḎIKR		I		ʿAŠTAR			ZI-IK-RI-EŠ$_4$-DAR		M+
			ḎIKR		I		LIʾM			ZI-IK-RI-LI-IM		M+
			ḎIKR		U	HU				ZI-IK-RU-U$_2$		VAS IX 185 12+
			ḎIKR				MARDUK			[Z]I?-IK-RU-D-AMAR-UD		KUPPER, L'ICON PL II NO 8
			ḎIKR				MARAṢ			ZI-IK-RU-MA-RA-AZ	FN	RA LXV 55 XIII 33
			ḎIKR				ʿAŠTAR			ZI-KI-IR-EŠ$_4$-[DAR]		M
ḎIMR	1		ḎIMR	AT	UM					ZI-IM-RA-TUM	MN	B 42+, M
			ḎIMR	AT	IM					ZI-IM-RA-TIM	MN? GEN	M
			ḎIMR	AN						ZI-IM-RA-AN		M+
			ḎIMR	AN	AM					ZI-IM-RA-NAM	ACC	M+

STEMS

ḎIMR	1		ḎIMR	ATAN							ZI-IM-RA-TA-AN		M
			ḎIMR		IJA						ZI-IM-RI-IA		M+, C+
			ḎIMR		IJAN						ZI-IM-RI-IA-AN		RA LXV 44 IV 76
			ḎIMR				RAPIʾ		I		ZI-ME-IR-RA-BI-I		TA 30 34
			ḎIMR				ŠAMŠ				ZI-IM-RU-D-UTU		BIN VII 190 18
			ḎIMR				ŠAMŠ				ZI-IM-RI-D-UTU		BIN VII 206 23+
			ḎIMR				ŠAMŠ				ZI-ME-IR-D-UTU		B 42+
			ḎIMR				ZABABA				ZI-ME-IR-D-ZA-BA$_4$-BA$_4$		CIG P. 155
			ḎIMR		A		ʿAMM		U		ZI-IM-RA-ḪA-MU		CT XLIV 54 20, C
			ḎIMR		A		ʿAMM		U		ZI-IM-RA-ḪA-AM-MU		M
			ḎIMR		A		ʿAMM		U		ZI-IM-RA-AM-MU		TIM IV 33 20, 34 13
			ḎIMR		A		ʿAMM		U	HU	ZI-IM-RA-ḪA-MU-U$_2$		TIM IV 33 SEAL, 34 SEAL
			ḎIMR		A		ʿAŠTAR				ZI-IM-RA-EŠ$_4$-DAR		M+
			ḎIMR		I		....				ZI-IM-RI-D-[....]		M
			ḎIMR		I		ʾAB		UM		ZI-IM-RI-A-BU-UM		B 42
			ḎIMR		I		HADD		U		ZI-IM-RI-D-IM		M+
			ḎIMR		I		HEDD		A		ZI-IM-RI-E-ID-DA		B 42
			ḎIMR		I	JE	HADD		U		ZI-IM-RI-E-D-IM		M
			ḎIMR		I		ʾIL				ZI-IM-RI-DINGIR		B 42+
			ḎIMR		I		ʾIL		U				
							MA				ZI-IM-RI-DINGIR-MA		M
			ḎIMR		I		ʾIL		U				
							MA				ZI-IM-RI-I-LU-MA		M
			ḎIMR		I		ʾIL		U				
							MA				ZI-IM-RI-LU-MA		SIMMONS 67 12
			ḎIMR		I		ʿAMM		U		ZI-IM-RI-AM-MU		TIM III 94 4
			ḎIMR		I		ʿAMM		U		ZI-IM-RI-ḪA-MU		C
			ḎIMR		I		ʿAMM		U		ZI-IM-RI-ḪA-AM-MU		B 42+, X 35 12
			ḎIMR		I		ʿAN	AT	A		ZI-IM-RI-ḪA-NA-TA		B 42
			ḎIMR		I		JARAḪ				ZI-IM-RI-E-RA-AḪ		B 42+, C+, M+
			ḎIMR		I		ḪAŠAM				ZI-IM-RI-ḪA-SA-AM	NOM	C+
			ḎIMR		I		ʿAŠTAR				ZI-IM-RI-D-EŠ$_4$-DAR		M, A.+
			ḎIMR		I		DAGAN				ZI-IM-RI-D-DA-GAN		M+
			ḎIMR		I		LU			HU	ZI-IM-RI-LU-U$_2$	FN	RA LXV 55 XIII 39
			ḎIMR		I		LIʾM				ZI-IM-RI-LI-IM		M+
			ḎIMR		I		RAPUʾ				ZI-IM-RI-RA-BU		M
			ḎIMR		I		ŠAMŠ				ZI-IM-RI-SA-MAŠ		A.
			ḎIMR		I		ŠAMŠ				ZI-IM-RI-SA-MA-AŠ$_2$		M+
			ḎIMR		U		ḪAʾL		A		ZI-IM-RU-ḪA-LA		BM 17045
			ḎIMR		U		HADD		U		ZI-IM-RU-D-IM		CT XLVIII 22 REV
			ḎIMR		U		ʾIL		A		ZI-IM-RU-I-L[A]?		II 5 7
			ḎIMR		U		ʿAMM		I		ZI-IM-RU-ḪA-AM-MI		B 42
			ḎIMR		U		ʿAMM		U		ZI-IM-RU-ḪA-AM-MU		JCS XI 23 10 13
			ḎIMR		U		ʾUP		I		ZI-IM-RU-UḪ$_2$-KI		TCL VII 23 14 21+
			ḎIMR		U		ʾARAḪ				ZI-IM-RU-A-RA-AḪ		BM 17045A 13
			ḎIMR		U		ʾARAḪ				ZI-IM-RU-ḪA-RA-AḪ		BM 17045 13
			ḎIMR		U		ʿAŠTAR				ZI-IM-RU-EŠ$_4$-DAR		IRAQ IV 185 A. 385
			ḎIMR		U		LA						
							ʾAB		I		ZI-IM-RU-LA-A-BI		RA LXV 42 III 7
			ḎIMR		U		RAPIʾ				ZI-IM-RU-RA-BI		TA 30 82
			ḎIMR		U		ŠAMŠ				ZI-IM-RU-D-UTU		BIROT,TEA 70 B I 9
ḎINB	1		ḎINB	AT	UM						ZI-IB-BA-TUM	FN	M+, C P. 38+
ḎINUB	1		ḎINUB		I		ʾIL				ZI-NU-BI-DINGIR		RA LXV 48 VIII 12
ḎIQN	1		ḎIQN		UM						ZI-IQ-NU-UM	FN	RA LXV 61 IV 43
			ḎIQN		U						ZI-IQ-NU	FN	XIII 1 V 36
ḎIQUN	1		ḎIQUN		A		ṬAJB				ZI-KU-NA-ṬA$_3$-AB	FN	RA LXV 59 II 77
ḎKUR	1	JI	ḎKUR		UM						IZ-KUR-RUM		LANGDON XXIX 24
		JA	ḎKUR				ʾIL				A-AD-KU-UR-DINGIR		HARRIS 10 18
		JA	ḎKUR				ʾIL				IA-AD-GUR-DINGIR		SUMER V 142 8+
		JA	ḎKUR				ʾIL				IA-AD-KUR-DINGIR		SUMER V 141
		JA	ḎKUR				ʾIL				A-AD-KUR-DINGIR		SIMMONS 80 13
		JA	ḎKUR				ʾIL				IA-AD-KU?-UR?-DINGIR		VAS IX 58 15
		JI	ḎKUR				ʾIL				II-IZ-KUR-DINGIR		SIMMONS 67 18
		JI	ḎKUR				RAPIʾ				IZ-KUR-RA-BI		BM 81591 7
ḎMAR	1	MA	ḎMAR		UM						MA-AZ-MA-RU-UM		SIMMONS 52 17+, M
		MA	ḎMAR	AT	UM						MA-AZ-MA-RA-TUM	FN	CT VIII 41A 3 4+

STEMS

ḎMAR	1	MA	ḎMAR	AT	UM				MA-IZ-MA-RA-TUM	FN	CT II 30 35	
		MA	ḎMAR	AH					MA-AZ-MA-RA	FN	M+	
ḎRAʿ	1	JA	ḎRAʿ		UM				IA-AZ-RA-ḪU-UM		XIV 77:8	
		JA	ḎRAʿ				HADD	U	IA-AZ-RA-AḪ-D-IM		M+	
		JA	ḎRAʿ				ʾIL		IA-AZ-RA-AḪ-DINGIR		VIII 100 15+	
		JA	ḎRAʿ				DAGAN		IA-AZ-RA-AḪ-D-DA-GAN		XIII 123 26	
		JI	ḎRAʿ				DAGAN		IZ-RA-AḪ-D-DA-GAN		B 24 HANA+	
ḎRIʿ	1	JA	ḎRIʿ		UM				IA-AZ?-RI-ḪU-[UM]		PBS XIII 56:4	
		ME	ḎRIʿ		UM				ME-IZ-RI-JU-UM		M	
ḎRUʿ	1	JI	ḎRUʿ				ʾIL		II-IZ?-RU-UḪ-DINGIR		TCL XI 156 17	
	2		ʿAMM		A	JI	ḎRUʿ		ḪA-MA-IZ-RU		RUTTEN 28 5+	
ḎU	1		ḎU				ʿAD	IM	ZU-ḪA-DI-IM	GEN	M	
			ḎU				ʿADN	U	ZU-ḪA-AD-NU		M+	
			ḎU				ʿADN	I	ZU-ḪA-AD-NI	NOM	M+	
			ḎU				ʿADN	I	ZU-ḪA-AD-NI	GEN	M+	
			ḎU				ʿADN	IM	ZU-ḪA-AD-NIM	GEN	M+	
			ḎU				ʿADN	IM	ZU-U_2-ḪA-AD-NIM		VOIX 187:18 MARI	
			ḎU				ʾIL	A	ZU-I-LA		B 42+	
			ḎU				ʾIL	A	ZU-U_2-I-LA		B 42	
			ḎU				JAŠIʿ	A	ZU-IA-ŠE-IA		A. 64 9	
			ḎU				ʾIŠḪAR	AH	ZU-D-IŠ-ḪA-RA		XIII 64 5	
			ḎU				DAWD	A	ZU-E-TA-TA		BIN IV 100 1 CAPP	
			ḎU				DAWD	UM	ZU-DA-TUM		I	
			ḎU				DAWD	I	ZU-DA-DI		XIV 91:5, 13	
			ḎU				MA					
							ʾAB	I	ZU-U_2-MA-A-BI		XIV 77:17	
			ḎU				MA					
							ʾAB	I	ZU-U_2-MA?-A-BI		M	
			ḎU				ŠUM	IM	ZU-U_2-ŠU?-MI-IM		M	
			ḎU				ŠAT	I	ZU-ŠA-TI		HARRIS 56 12	
ḎUHUB	1		ḎUHUB		UM				ZU-U_2-BU-UM		VII 194 5'	
ḎUBAB	1		ḎUBAB		UM				DU-BA-BU-UM		UET V 208 2+	
			ḎUBAB		U				DU-BA-BU		YOS XII	
			ḎUBAB		UM				SU-BA-BU-UM		TA 30, 30 32+	
			ḎUBAB		UM				SU-PA-BU-UM		RIFTIN 29 23+	
			ḎUBAB		UM				ZU-BA-BU-UM		UET V P. 66+	
			ḎUBAB	AT	UM				DU-BA-BA-TUM	FN	UCP X/1 87 3+	
			ḎUBAB		IJA				SU-BA-BI-IA		SIMMONS P. 71	N. 5 3
			ḎUBAB		IJA				SU-PA-BI-IA		UCP X/1 108 1	
ḎUKR	1		ḎUKR		A		ʿAŠTAR		[Z]U-UK-RA-$EŠ_4$-DAR		RA LXV 46 VI 21	
ḎUMUR	1		ḎUMUR	ATANU					ZU-MUR?-TA-NU		ZA XLII 41	
ḎUNAB	1		ḎUNAB		UM				SU-NA-BU-UM		CT IV 44B 5+	
			ḎUNAB		UM				ZU-NA-BU-UM		BIN VII 150 9	
			ḎUNAB		IM				SU-NA-BI-IM	GEN	SUMER XIV 51 NO. 26 23	
ḎUNUB	1		ḎUNUB		I		ʾIL		ZU-NU-BI-DINGIR		RA LXV 51 X 14	
GJIḪ	1	JA	GJIḪ	AN					IA-G[I]-ḪA-A[N]		M	
		JA	GJIḪ				ḪAʾL	UM	IA-GI?-ḪA-LUM		RUTTEN 16 18	
		JA	GJIḪ				HADD	U	IA-GI-IḪ-D-IM		M+	
		JA	GJIḪ				HADD	U	IA-GI-ḪA-D-IM		M	
		JI	GJIḪ				LUʾ					
							MA		I-GI-IḪ-LU-MA		SIMMONS 60 8, 14+	
		JE	GJIḪ				LUʾ					
							MA		E-GI-IḪ-LU-MA		SUMER XXIII 192	
		JI	GJIḪ				LUʾ					
							MA		I-GI-E-EḪ-LU-MA		JCS XXVI 143:21 HARMAL	
GJID	1	JA	GJID				LIʾM		IA-GI-ID-LI-IM		M+	
		JI	GJID				LIʾM		I-GI-ID-LI-IM		B 21 HANA	
GAʾJ	1		GAʾJ		I		JARAḪ		GA-JI-RA-A[Ḫ]		HARRIS 39 15	
			GAʾJ		I		LAʾL	UM	GA-I-LA-LUM		M	
	2		ʾAB		I		GAʾJ	A	A-BI-GA-A	GN?	A 21919+	
			ḪANAN		A		GAʾJ	A	A-NA-NA-GA-A		RA XLIV 112 5 QATNA	
			BAʿL		U		GAʾJ	A	BA-AḪ-LU-GA-A	GEN	HOLMA 6 5	
			BAʿL		U		GAʾJ	IM	BA-AḪ-LU-GA-JI-IM	GEN	M+	
			BAʿL		U		GAʾJ	IM	BA-AḪ-LU-GA-I-IM	GEN	M+	
			BAʿL		U		GAʾJ	I	BA-AḪ-LU-GA-I	NOM	M+	
			BAʿL		U		GAʾJ	I	BA-AḪ-LU-GA-A-JI	NOM	M	

STEMS												
GAʾAŠ	1		GAʾAŠ		UM					GA-ḪA-ŠUM		XIV 62:25
GAʾG	1		GAʾG		UM					GA-GU-UM		HARRIS 5 18+
			GAʾG	AT	UM					GA-GA-TUM	MN?	HARRIS 13 13+
			GAʾG	AN	UM					GA-GA-NU-UM		B 44+
			GAʾG		IJA					GA-GI-IA		HARRIS 13 12
GAʾIL	1		GAʾIL		UM					GA-JI-LUM		RA LXV 51 IX 54
			GAʾIL	AT	UM					GA-I-LA-TUM	MN?	B 17+
			GAʾIL	AT	UM					GA-I-LA-TUM	FN	EDZARD, DER 224:35
GAʾL	2		JIŠʿ		A		GAʾL			IŠ-ḪA-GA-AL		A 7459 10
GAʾN	1		GAʾN	AN						GA-NA-AN		RA LXV 54 XII 5
GAʾR	1		GAʾR		IJA					GA-RI-IA		RA LXV 44 IV 58
GAʾŠ	1		GAʾŠ		U					GA-AḪ-ŠU		M
GAʾUL	1		GAʾUL		A					GA-U$_2$-LA		JCS XIII 56, ALA. LATE
	2		ʾIL		I	Š	GAʾUL		U	I$_3$-LI$_2$-IŠ-GA-U$_2$-LU		KISURRA 70A 17+
GAʾUŠ	1		GAʾUŠ		UM					GA-U$_2$-ŠUM		I+
GAJD	1		GAJD	AN	IM					GA-DA-NIM	GEN	B 44
GAJID	1		GAJID	AH						GA-I-DA	FN	C; RA LXV 65
			GAJID		E					GA-I-TE		A.
GABAʾ	1		GABAʾ		UM					GA-BA-UM		LANGDON XXX 18
GABIʾ	1		GABIʾ		UM					GA-BI-U[M]		M
			GABIʾ	AT	UM					GA-BI-A-TUM	FN	X 1 3
			GABIʾ	T	UM					GA-BI-TUM		RA LXIV 36 NO. 32
			GABIʾ				ʾIL			GA-BI-DINGIR		C 39+
			GABIʾ				ʾIL			GA-BI-IL		TIM III 12 16A
GABN	1		GABN	AN	UM					GA-AB-NA-NU-UM		SIMMONS 107 14
GABUʾ	1		GABUʾ		UM					GA-BU-UM		B 17
			GABUʾ		UM					GA-BU-U$_2$-UM		M
			GABUʾ		IM					GA-BI-IM	GEN	B 17
			GABUʾ		IM					GA-BI-I-IM	GEN	M+
GALAZ	1		GALAZ		IM					GA-LA-ZI-IM	GEN	HARRIS 83 2
GALD	1		GALD	AN	U					GA-AL-DA-NU		B 44+
GALZ	1		GALZ							GA-AL-ZI-....		M
GAMIL	2		ʾANN		U		GAMIL	T	I	AN-NU-GA-ME-IL-TI	FN	RA LXV 66 VII 66
			ŠIRUN		UM		GAMIL			SI?-RU-NU-UM-GA-MIL?		VII 139 7
			TILIʾ		A	Š	GAMIL			TI-LI-AŠ-GA-MIL		UNPUBL.
			TURUN		U	HU	GAMIL			D-TU-UR-RU-NU-U$_2$-GA-MIL	FN?	XIII 118 14
GAMIR	1		GAMIR	AN	UM					GA-MI-RA-NU-UM		TA 1931, 538 I, V?
GAML	2		DAGAN				GAML		I	D-DA-GAN-GA-AM-LI		M
GANAM	1		GANAM	AN	UM					GA-NA-MA-NU-UM		TA 1931, 438
GANIB	1		GANIB	AN						GA-NI-BA-AN		RA LXV 42 II 80+
GANIN	1		GANIN	AN	UM					GA-NI-NA-NU-UM		BIN VII P. 12+
GANN	1		GANN		I					GA-AN-NI		M
GARAN	1		GARAN		UM					GA-RA-NU-UM		B 44+
GARIŠ	1		GARIŠ		UM					GA-RI-SU-UM		B 17
			GARIŠ		U					GA-RI-SU		B 17
GARUB	1		GARUB		UM					GA-RU-BU-UM		B 17+
GAZIZ	1		GAZIZ	AN	UM					GA-ZI-ZA-NU-[UM]		M
GIJD	1		GIJD	AN	UM					GI-DA-NUM$_2$		BIROT, TEA 70 C REV. I 7
			GIJD	AN	UM					GI-DA-NU-UM		SIMMONS 11 1+
			GIJD	AN	IM					GI-DA-NI-IM	GEN	SIMMONS 12 6
			GIJD	AN	IM					GI-DA-NIM	GEN	M, SIMMONS 16 4
GIZZ	1		GIZZ		I					GI-IZ-ZI		A. 32 3
			GIZZ		I					KI-IZ-ZI		A.+
			GIZZ	IT	IM					GI-ZI-TIM	FN GEN	M
			GIZZ	AN	UM					GI-ZA-NU-UM		B 93
			GIZZ	AN	U					GI-ZA-NU		B 93
			GIZZ	AN	IM					GI-ZA-NI-IM	GEN	B 44
GMIR	1	JI	GMIR				HADD		U	IG-MI-RA-A-DU		A.+
GMUR	1	JA	GMUR				....			IA-AG-MU-UR-[....]		M
		JA	GMUR				ʾIL			IA-AG-MU-UR-DINGIR		M
GRIN	1	MA	GRIN							MA-AG-RI-IN		HARRIS 76 15
GUʾAD	1		GUʾAD		UM					GU-ḪA-DU-UM		JCS XXVI 137:24+ HARMAL
GUʾG	1		GUʾG	AN	UM					GU$_2$-GA-NU-UM		TA 30, 111 6
GUʾR	1		GUʾR		UM					GUR-RU-UM MAR-TU		IRAQ MUS. 43488
			GUʾR		UM					GU-RU-UM		UCP X/3 6A 18+
			GUʾR		I					GU-RI	GEN	B 17

STEMS

GUʾR	1		GUʾR	AT	UM					GU-RA-TUM	FN	C
			GUʾR	AT	IM					GU-RA-TIM	FN GEN	B 17
			GUʾR		IJA					GU-RI-IA		HARRIS 8 5+
			GUʾR		U		HADD	U		GU-RU-D-IM		M+
GUʾUD	1		GUʾUD		A					GU-U$_2$-DA		U
GUʾZ	1		GUʾZ		I					GU-ZI	FN	RA LXV 55 XIII 8
			GUʾZ	AN						GU-ZA-AN		RA LXV 53 XI 57;64
GUBʾ	1		GUBʾ	AN	UM					GU-UB-ḪA-NU-UM		M
GUBL	1		GUBL	AJ	I					GU-UB-LA-A-JI	GN PL NOM	SYRIA XX 111
			GUBL	AJ	I					GU-UB-LA-JI	GN NOM	SYRIA XX 111
			GUBL	AJITUM						GU-UB-LA-JI-TUM	GN FN	SYRIA XX 111
GULAL	1		GULAL	AN						GU-LA-LA-AN		RA LXV 47 VII 55
GULL	1		GULL	AT	UM					GUL-LA-TUM	FN	M+
	2		ʾIL		A		GULL	A		DINGIR-GU-UL-LA	FN	C+
			ʾIL		A		GULL	A				
							ʿAḎIR	AT		DINGIR-GUL-LA$_2$-ḪA-ZI-RA-AT	FN	M+
GULZ	1		GULZ		UM					GUL-ZUM		TA 1931, 538 VI
			GULZ	AT	UM					GU-UL-ZA-TUM		LANGDON XXIX 22
GUML	2		ʾIL		I		GUML	I	JA	I$_3$-LI$_2$-GU-UM-LI-IA		XIII 1 VIII 45
			ʾIŠḪAR	AH			GUML	I		D-IŠ-ḪA-RA-GU-UM-LI	FN	XIII 1 IV 39
GUMUL	1		GUMUL				JARAḪ			GU-MU-UL-D-EN-ZU		M+
GUNGUN	1		GUNGUN		UM					GU-UN-GU-NU-UM		B 48+
GURD	1		GURD	AN						GU-UR-DA-AN		M
GURGUR	1		GURGUR		UM					GU-UR$_2$-GU-RU-UM		KISURRA 202 5
GURUD	1		GURUD		U					GU-RU-DU		XIII 1 III 41
			GURUD		IM					GU-RU-DI-IM	GEN	M
GURUR	1		GURUR		U					GU-UR-RU-RU		M
KWIN	1	JA	KWIN				HADD	U		IA-KI-IN-D-IM		M
		JA	KWIN				ʾIL			JA-KI-IN-DINGIR		JEA VII 196
		JA	KWIN				LU		HU	IA-KI-IN-LU-U$_2$		TALLQUIST APN 95 LATE
		MA	KWIN							MA?-KI-EN		C
		ME	KWIN							ME-KI-IN	FN	A.
		ME	KWIN		UM					ME-KI-NU-UM		M+
	2		ʾAB		UM	JE	KWIN			A-BU-UM-E-KI-IN		M
			ʾAB		U	ME	KWIN			A-BU-ME-KI-IN		X 154 2+
			MUT		A	TA	KWIN			MU-TA-TA-KI-IN		RA LXV 51 IX 78
KWUN	1	ʾA	KWUN				PI					
							ʾEL			A-KU-PI-EL		GORDON, SCT 38 16
		JA	KWUN		UM					IA-KU-NU-UM		B 27+
		JA	KWUN		UM					IA-A-KU-NU-UM		B 27
		JA	KWUN		U					IA-KU-NU		B 27+
		JA	KWUN		AM					IA-KU-NA-AM	ACC	CT VIII 36D 7
		JA	KWUN		IM					IA-KU-NIM	GEN	B 28, M+
		JA	KWUN		I					IA-KU-NI	GEN	TIM III 58 16+
		JA	KWUN	AN						JA-GU-NA-AN		U
		JA	KWUN	AN						IA-KU-NA-AN		M+
		JA	KWUN				ʾAHL	I		IA-KU-UN-A-LI		B 92
		JA	KWUN				HADD	U		IA-KU-UN-D-IM		B 27, M+
		JA	KWUN				ʾIL			IA-KU-UN-DINGIR		M
		JA	KWUN				ʿALAṢ	I		IA-KU-UN-ḪA-LA-ZI		RA LXV 44 IV 41;43
		JA	KWUN				ʿAMM	U		IA-KU-UN-AM-MU		B 27
		JA	KWUN				ḪARAR			IA-KU-UN-ḪA-RA-AR		VAS IX 172 4+
		JA	KWUN				ḪARAR	I		IA-KU-[UN-ḪA]-RA-RI	GEN	BM 81641 6
		JA	KWUN				ḪARAR	I		IA-KUN$_3$-ḪA-RA-RI		CT XLVIII 3:3
		JI	KWUN				ḪARAR	I		I-KU-UN-ḪA-RA-RI?	GEN	TCL I 151 4
		JA	KWUN				ʾAŠD	UM		IA-KU-UN-AŠ-DU-UM		B 27
		JA	KWUN				ʾAŠAR			IA-KU-UN-A-ŠAR		B 92+, M+
		JI	KWUN				ʾAŠAR			I-KU-UN-A-ŠAR		GORDON 38 6
		JA	KWUN				ʾAŠAR	I		IA-KU-UN-A-ŠA-RI	NOM	CT XLVIII 10 6
		JA	KWUN				ʾAŠAR	UM		IA-KU-UN-A-ŠA-RU-UM		B 27
		JI	KWUN				BAʿL	I		I-KU-UN-BA-LI		A.
		JI	KWUN				BAʿL	I		I-KU-UN-BA-AḪ-LI		A. 246 33
		JA	KWUN				BAʿL			IA-KU-BA-AL		RA LXV 44 V 7
		JA	KWUN				DIWR	UM		IA-KU-UN-DI-RUM		CT XLVIII 115
		JA	KWUN				DIWR	IM		IA-KU-UN-DI-[R]I-IM	GEN	M

KWUN	1	JA	KWUN			DIWR	I		IA-KU-UN-DI-RI	GEN	CT XLVIII 115 CASE
		JA	KWUN			DIWR			IA-KU-UN-DI-IR		M+
		JA	KWUN			DIWR			IA-KU-DI-IR		RA LXV 45 V 14
		JA	KWUN			DAGAN			IA-KU-UN-D-DA-GAN		X 171 3
		JA	KWUN			LIʾM			IA-KU-UN-LI-IM		M+
		JA	KWUN			LIʾM			IA-KU-LI-IM		M+
		JA	KWUN			MEʾR			IA-KU-UN-ME-IR		M+
		JA	KWUN			MAṬAR			IA-KU-MA-DAR		SYMB.BCHL P.36?:6
		JA	KWUN			PI			IA-KU-UN-PI		CT VIII 43C 8
		JA	KWUN			PI			IA-KU-BI		B 27
		JA	KWUN			PI			IA-KU-PI		B 27
		JE	KWUN			PI			E-KU-PI		B 17
		JA	KWUN			PI	I	JA	IA-KU-UN-BI-IA		XII 14
		JI	KWUN			PI	I	JA	I-KU-BI-IA		SM P. 54
		JI	KWUN			PI	I		I-KU-UN-BI-I		C II 2 11
		JA	KWUN			PI					
						MAM	A		IA-KU-UN-BI-D-MA-MA	FN	RA LXV 66 VII 61
		JA	KWUN			RAPIʾ			IA-KU-UN-KA-BI		M
		JA	KWUN			ŠUM	U				
						ʾAB	IM		IA-KU-UN-SU-MU-A-BI-IM		M
		JA	KWUN			ŠARR	UM		IA-KU-UN-ŠAR-RU-UM		B 28
		TA	KWUN	AH					TA-KU-NA	FN	XIII 1 VIII 18+
		TA	KWUN	AJA					TA-KU-NA-IA	FN	C
		TA	KWUN			ḪAʾT	UM		TA-KU-UN-ḪA-TUM	FN	M+
		TA	KWUN			MAʾT	UM		TA-KU-UN-MA-TUM	FN	M, C+
		TA	KWUN			MAʾT	I		TA-KUM-MA-TI	FN	A.+
		TA	KWUN			MITEʿ		JE	TA-KU-UN-MI-TE-E		M
		TA	KWUN			ZULAT	UM		TA-KU-UN-ZU?-LA-TUM	FN	RA LXV 62 V 30
KA	1		KA			ṢUWR	A				
						ʾIL			KA-ZU-RA-DINGIR		M
			KA			ṢUWR	I				
						ḪAʾL	A		KA-ZU-RI-ḪA-LA		M
	2		ʾAḪ	U		KA					
						ʾAB	I		A-ḪU-KA-A-BI	FN	XIII 1 VIII 60, C+
			ʾAB	U		KA					
						ʾIL			A-BU-KA-DINGIR		M+
			ʾIL	A		KA					
						ʾAB	UM		DINGIR-KA-A-BU-UM		CT XLV 100 17
			ʾUMM	UM		KA					
						ʾAB	IM		UM-MU-UM-KA-A-BI-IM	FN	M
			ʾUMM	UM		KA					
						ʾAB	I		UM-MU-UM-KA-A-BI	FN	XIII 1 VII 56
			ʾUMM	U		KA					
						ʾAB	I		UM-MU-KA-A-BI	FN	RA LXV 62 V 16
			KABD	U		KA					
						ʾAB	I		KA-AB-TU-KA-A-BI		UET V 688:8,12
	3		LAŠU			ʾEL					
						KA			LA-ŠI-EL-KA-A-BI-IM		B 33
KAʾAM	1		KAʾAM	I					KA-A-MI		A.
	2		ʾIL	A		KAʾAM			DINGIR-KA-A-AM		TIM III 101 7
KAʾB	1		KAʾB	IJA					KA-BI-IA		M+
			KAʾB	I		ʾAHL	UM		KA-PI-IA-LUM		UET V 626 11, 702 REV. 5
			KAʾB	I		JADAʿ			KA-BI-E-DA-AḪ		XIII 1 XI 54
			KAʾB	I		HADD	U		KA-BI-D-IM		B 32, M+, C
			KAʾB	I		HEDD	A		KA-BI-E-D-IM		M+
			KAʾB	I		JARAḪ			KA-BI-E-RA-AḪ		RA LXV 41 II 29+;B 32+
			KAʾB	I		ʾATT	A		KA-BI-A-TA		M
			KAʾB	I	JE	JPUʿ			KA-BI-E-PU-UḪ		M
			KAʾB	I		BEʿL			KA-BI-BE-EL		YOS XIII 432:12
			KAʾB	I		BURŠ	A		KA-BI-BU-UR-ŠA	FN	XIII 1 XIV 53
			KAʾB	I		DAGAN			KA-BI-D-DA-GAN		M+
			KAʾB	I		LA					
						RIWM			KA-BI-LA-RI-IM		RA LXV 47 VI 65+; C+
	2		ʾAḪ	I		KAʾB	I		A-ḪI-KA-PI		YOS VIII 64 18
			ʾAB	I		KAʾB	I		A-BI-KA-BI		M
			ʾAB	I		KAʾB	I		A-BI-KA-BI	FN	RA LXV 65 VII 42

STEMS

KAʾB	2	ʾIL		I		KAʾB	I		I$_3$-LI$_2$-KA-PI		BIROT, TEA 69:28
		ḪANN		I		KAʾB	I		A[N-N]I-KA-BI	FN	RA LXV 62 V 17
		BEʿL		I		KAʾB	I		BE-LI$_2$-KA-BI	FN	XIII 1 V 28+
		DIWR	IT	UM		KAʾB	I		D-DI-RI-TUM-KA-BI		XIII 1 VI 45
KAʾK	1	KAʾK		A					KA-KA		A.
		KAʾK		A					KA-A-KA		A.
KAʾL	1	KAʾL		IJA					KA-LI-IA		RA LXV 53 XI 48
		KAʾL		IJA					KA-LI-IA	FN	C
KAʾM	1	KAʾM	AT	UM					KA-MA-TUM	FN	C
		KAʾM		I		JAʾAR	UM		KA-MI-IA-A-RUM		VAS VII 128 46
		KAʾM		A		ṢILL	UM		KA-MA-ZI-LUM	FN	B 33+
		KAʾM		A		ṢILL	U		KA-MA-ZI-LU?	FN	VAS XIII 9 R. 2
	2 MU	ŠṬUḪ				KAʾM	I		MU-UŠ-TU-KA-M[I]		M+
KAʾR	1	KAʾR		IJA					KA-RI-IA		RA LXV 52 X 25
KAʾŠ	1	KAʾŠ	AN	UM					KA-SA-NU-UM		SIMMONS 128:5
KAʾT	2	ḪANN		A		KAʾT	UM		AN-NA-KA-TUM		YOS XIII 509:2
KAHAL	1	KAHAL	AN						KA-A-LA-AN		M+
		KAHAL		IJA					KA-A-LI-IA		M
		KAHAL		I		HADD	U		KA-A-LI-D-IM		M+
		KAHAL		I		ʾIL	U				
						MA			KA-A-LI-I-LU-MA		XIV 62:4+
		KAHAL		I		ʾIL	U				
						MA			KA-A-LI-DINGIR-MA		M+
KAWJ	1	KAWJ	AN						KA-A-IA-AN		RA LXV 51 IX 58
		KAWJ	AN						KA-A-IA-AN	FN	C
		KAWJ		AJA					KA-A-IA-A-IA		M+
		KAWJ		A		LAʾL	UM		KA-A-LA-LUM		M
KAWN	2	ʾEL				KAWN	UM		EL-GA-NU-UM		TA 1931 238
		ʾIL		A		KAWN			DINGIR-KA-AN	MN	M+
		ʾIL		A		KAWN			DINGIR-KA-AN	FN	M
		ʾIL		A		KAWN	UM		DINGIR-KA-NU-UM		MAH II/3 P. 188F
		ʾIL		A		KAWN	IM		DINGIR-KA-NIM	GEN	M+
		ʾIL		A		KAWN	IM		DINGIR-KA-NI-IM	GEN	M
		ʿAŠTAR				KAWN			EŠ$_4$-DAR-KA-AN		IX 237 II 4+
KABAR	2	ʿAŠTAR				KABAR			EŠ$_4$-DAR-KA-BAR		RA LXV 41 II 39
KABAS	1	KABAS		UM					GA-BA-ZU-UM		HSM 7900, UR III
		KABAS		I	JE				KA-BA-AZ-ZI-E		A.
		KABAS	AN	UM					GA-BA-ZA-NU-UM		TA 1931,262
KABD	1	KABD		U		KA					
						ʾAB	I		KA-AB-TU-KA-A-BI		UET V 688:8,12
KABID	1	KABID	AH						KA-BI-DA	FN	M+
		KABID		AJA					KA-BI-DA-IA	FN	M
		KABID	T	A					KA-BI-IT-TA	MN	C II 6
		KABID	AN	UM					GA-BI-DA-NU-UM		TA 1930,486 OLDER OB
	2 JI	JBIŠ				KABID			I-BI-IŠ-GA-BI-ID		KISURRA 63A
		MUT				KABID			MU-UT-GA-BI-ID		TA 30, 615 24
KABIS	1	KABIS		UM					KA-BI-ZUM		B 32
		KABIS	AT	UM					KA-BI-ZA-TUM	FN	C
KABKAB	1	KABKAB		UM					KA[B-K]A-BU-UM		RA LXV 52 X 77
		KABKAB		IM					KAB-KA-BI-IM	GEN	C
		KABKAB	AH						KA-AB-KA-BA	FN	M+
		KABKAB	AN						GA-GA-BA-AN-KI	GN	IRAQ VII 66 SARGONIC
	2	ʾIL		A		KABKAB	I		DINGIR-KAB-KA-BI		JNES XIII 210+ LATE
		ʾIL		A		KABKAB	U	HU	I-LA-KAB-KA-BU-U$_2$		M+
		ʾIL		I		KABKAB	U		I$_3$-LI$_2$-KA-AB-KA-BU		A 21914 3
KABL	1	KABL	AK	UM					KA-AB-LA-KU-UM		B 32
KABŠ	1	KABŠ	AT	UM					KAB-SA-TUM	FN	M+
		KABŠ	AN	UM					KA-AB-SA-NU-UM		YOS V 18 17
KADAD	1	KADAD		UM					KA-DA-DU-UM	FN	BM 17063A 34
		KADAD		A					KA-DA-DA	GEN	BM 17060 30+
KADUL	1	KADUL		I					KA-DU-LI	FN	M
KAKK	1	KAKK		U					KA-AK-KU	FN	C+
		KAKK	AH						KA-AK-KA	FN	M
		KAKK	ATANUM						KA-KA-TA-NU-UM		SIMMONS 104 6
		KAKK		A		ʾAŠJ	AH		KA-AK-KA-A-SI-IA	FN	XIII 1 VI 11
		KAKK		A		JIŠʿ	AH		KA-KA-IŠ-ḪA	FN	M+

KAKK	1		KAKK		A	ʾAŠR		I		KA-AK-KA-AŠ-RI	FN	XIII 1 V 1
			KAKK		A	LIʾD		I		KA-AK-KA-LI-DI	FN	X 10 5
			KAKK		A	MANN		U		KA-AK-KA-MA-AN-NU		M
			KAKK		A	NAʿM		I		KA-AK-KA-NA-AḪ-MI	FN	XIII 1 VII 30
			KAKK		A	NILŠ		I		KA-A[K]-KA-NI-EL?-ŠI?	FN	XIII 1 VIII 41
			KAKK		A	NIʾŠ		U	JA	KA-AK-KA-NI-ŠU-IA		RA LXV 64 VI 35
			KAKK		A	NIʾŠ		U	JA	KA-KA-NI-ŠU-IA	FN	RA LXV 65 VII 44
			KAKK		A	RIMŠ		I		KA-AK-KA-RI-IM-ŠI	FN	RA LXV 60 III 5
			KAKK		A	TUWR		I	JA	KA-KA-TU-RI-IA	FN	M
	2		ḪIMD			KAKK		A		ḪI-MI-ID-KA-AK-KA		M
			ʾAMIR			KAKK		A		A-ME-IR-KA-AK-KA		XIII 1 V 20
			NABIʾ			KAKK		A		NA-BI-KA-KA		M+
		JI	NDIN			KAKK		A		I-DIN-KA-AK-KA		M+
		JI	NDIN			KAKK		A		I-DIN-D-KA-KA		M+
KAKKAR	1		KAKKAR		I					KA-KA-RI		RA LXV 50 IX 7
KALA	2		JAT			KALA				I-IA-AT-KA-LA		VAS XVI 165 5
			BUN		U	KALA						
						ʾIL		I		BU-NU-KA-LA-I-LI		B 16
KALAL	1		KALAL		UM					KA-LA-LUM		M
			KALAL			TULAʿ			HA	KA-LA-AL-TU-LA-A	FN	M, C
KALB	1		KALB		UM					GA?-[AL]?-BU-UM		BIN IX 410 3
			KALB	AT	UM					KA-AL-BA-TUM	FN	RA LXV 61 IV 46
			KALB			....				GAL-BA-....		MCS V 120
			KALB			ʾIL				GA-AL-BA-IL		I
			KALB			ʾIL				KA-AL-BA-DINGIR		M
			KALB			ḪAM		I		K[A]-AL-BU-D-A-MI		XIII 1 X 20
	2		ʾAJA			KALB	AH			A-IA-KA-AL-BA?	FN	C
KALK	1		KALK	AT	UM					KA-AL-KA-TUM	MN	CT VIII 12C 1 6 9+
			KALK		AJA					KA-AL-KA-IA		CT XLVIII 89 REV.
KAMA	2		ʾANN		U	KAMA						
						ʾAB		I		AN-NU-KA-MA-BI		CT XLV 116 36
			BUN		U	KAMA						
						ʾIL		A		BU-NU-KA-MA-I-LA		B 16
			PI			KAMA						
						ʾIL				BI-KA-MA-DINGIR		XIV 111:10+
			PI			KAMA						
						ʾEL				BI-KA-MA-EL		M+
KAMAN	1		KAMAN		UM					KA-MA-NU-UM		B 45+
			KAMAN	IN	UM					KA-MA-NI-NU-UM		EDZARD,DER 68 IV 11
KAMB	2		KURD		A	KAMB		I		KUR-DA-KA-AM-BI	FN	XIII 1 III 25
KAMIN	1		KAMIN		UM					KA-MI-NU-UM		PBS VIII/1 32 II 6
KAMIS	1		KAMIS		UM					GA-MI-ZUM		I
			KAMIS		UM					KA-MI-ZUM		CT VIII 49A 7
			KAMIS		UM					KA-MI-ZU-UM		AJSL XLIV 243 NO. 32
KAMM	1		KAMM	AT	UM					KAM-MA-TUM	FN	M+
KAMN	1		KAMN		IJA					KA-AM-NI-IA		VAS XVI 78:0
KAMT	1		KAMT	AN						KA-AM-TA-AN		M
KANAK	1		KANAK			RAWḪ		UM		KA-NA-AK-RA-ḪU-UM		VAS XIII 66A R. 5+
			KANAK			RAWḪ		U		KA-NA-AK-RA-ḪU		VAS XIII 66 R. 6
			KANAK			RAWḪ		I		KA-NA-AK-RA-ḪI		VAS XIII 79 R. 7
KANAN	1		KANAN		UM					KA-NA-NU-UM		B 45+
KANAP	1		KANAP	AN						KA-NA-PA-AN		M+
KANAŠ	1		KANAŠ		UM					KA-NA-ŠUM		TIM III 126 15
	2		ŠUM		U	KANAŠ		A		SU-MU-GA-NA-SA		KISURRA 19 9
KANAT	1		KANAT		I					KA-NA-TI		LIMET,SCEAUX CASS. P. 114
	2		MUT		U	KANAT		A		MU-TU-KA-NA-TA		M
KANIK	1		KANIK	AN						KA-NI-KA-AN		M
			KANIK			RUWḪ		UM		KA-NI-IK-RU-UM		B 33+
			KANIK			RUWḪ		UM		KA-NI-IK-RUM		B 33
			KANIK			RUWḪ		IM		KA-NI-IK-RI-IM	GEN	B 33
KANIŠ	1		KANIŠ		UM					KA-NI-ŠUM		RUTTEN 14 23
			KANIŠ	AN						KA-NI-SA-AN		M+
			KANIŠ	AH						KA-NI-SA		RA LXV 60 III 12+
			KANIŠ	IT	UM					KA-NI-SI-T[UM]	FN	M
			KANIŠ	IT	UM					KA-NI-ŠI-TUM	FN	M+
KANN	1		KANN		A	MA						
						ʾIL				KA-AN-NA-MA-DINGIR		M

STEMS

KANN	1		KANN		I					KA-AN-NI		XIII 1 IX 62
KANUK	1		KANUK		A					KA-AN-NU-UK-KA		M
KANUT	1		KANUT		UM					KA-NU-TUM		RA LXIV 43
KANZ	1		KANZ		U					KA-AN-ZU	FN	M+; C II 45 II 40
			KANZ	AN						KA-AN-ZA-AN	FN	C+
			KANZ							KA-AN-ZU-UN-[....]	FN	M
KAPAŠ	1		KAPAŠ		UM					KA?-PA-SU-UM		KISURRA 58 10
KARAN	1		KARAN	AT	UM					KA-RA-NA-TUM	FN	CT II 40B 1, M
			KARAN	AT	IM					KA-RA-NA-[T]IM	FN	M
KARIT	1		KARIT	AN						KA-RI-TA-AN		RA LXV 41 II 36
KARŠ	1		KARŠ	AN						KA-AR-ŠA-AN		RA LXV 54 XII 23
KASIJ	2		MUT				KASIJ			MU-UT-KA-ZI-....		VIII 6 35'
KAŠAJ	1	MU	KAŠAJ		EM					MU-KA-SA-A-JE-EM	ACC	M
KAŠP	1		KAŠP	AN	U					KA-AŠ$_2$-BA-NU		M
KAŠAR	2		ʾIL		I		KAŠAR			I$_3$-LI$_2$-KA-ŠA-AR		M
KAŠER	1		KAŠER		UM					KA-ŠE-RUM		X 30 3
			KAŠER	AH						GA-ŠE-RA	FN	M
KAŠIL	1		KAŠIL		UM					KA-ŠI-LUM		HARRIS 69 9
KATAZ	2		ʾIL		UM		KATAZ	I		I-LU-UM-KA-TA-ZI		RUTTEN 40 1
KATIR	1		KATIR		I					KA-TI-RI	GEN	UET V 88 2,SEAL, A. 37 12
KATR	1		KATR		UM					KA-AT-RU-UM		WATERMAN 14 L.E.+
			KATR		U					KA-AT-RU		B 33+
			KATR		IM					KA-AT-R[I-I]M	GEN	HARRIS 75 17
			KATR		AJA					KA-AT-RA-IA	FN	XIII 1 III 8
KAZIB	1		KAZIB		U					KA-ZI-BU		M
			KAZIB		IM					KA-ZI-BI-IM	GEN	M+
KAZIR	1		KAZIR		AM					KA-ZI-RA-AM	NOM	RA LXV 52 X 24
KBUR	1	JA	KBUR		IM					IA-AK-BU-RI-IM	GEN	B 27
KI	1		KI				MILK	I				
							ʾEL			KI-MI-IL-KI-EL		KISURRA 112:8
			KI				MARUṢ			KI-MA-RU-UṢ		A 3549+
	2		ʾAḪ		I		KI					
							LIʾM			A-ḪI-KI-LI-IM		JEAN T.SIFR 72 5, 6, 13+
		JA	HWIJ				KI					
							HADD	U		[IA-A]Ḫ-WI-KI-D-IM		M
			ʿAMM		U	Š	KI					
							ʾIL			AM-MU-US-KI-DINGIR		A.
			ʿAMM		U	Š	KI					
							ʾIL			AM-MU-UŠ-KI-DINGIR		A.+
		ʾU	WQAH				KI					
							ʾEL			U$_2$-QA-KI-EL		RA LXV 51 IX 69
			BIʿD		I		KI					
							ʾEL			BI-DI-KI-EL		RA LXV 53 XI 54
			BUN		U		KI					
							ʾIL			BU-NU-KI-DINGIR		M
			MATAʿ		A		KI					
							ʾEL			MA-TA-A-KI-EL		RA LXV 50 IX 20;HARRIS 19:5,SEAL+
			SITR		I		KI					
							ʾEL			ZI-IT-RI?-KI-EL?		B 42
		JA	ŠJIM				KI					
							ʾIL			IA-SI-IM-KI-DINGIR		M
	3		ʾAB		I		MI					
							KI			A-BI-MI-KI-DINGIR		M
KIʾD	2		BIN	T	I		KIʾD	I	JA	BI-IN-TI-KI-DI-IA	FN	A.+
KIʾL	1		KIʾL	AN						KI-LA-AN		M
			KIʾL		IJA					KI-LI-IA		RA LXV 45 V 55
			KIʾL		I		ʾIL			KI-LI-DINGIR		CT IV 33B 19
			KIʾL		I		ʾIL	UM		KI-LI-DINGIR-LUM		XIII 106 14
			KIʾL		I		ʿAMM	I		KI-LI-AM-MI	GEN	MRS XVI 12:2
			KIʾL		I		BELAʾ	I		KI-LI-BE-LA-I		M
			KIʾL		UM		ʾALLAI			KI-LUM-AL-LA-I	FN	XIII 1 XI 49
			KIʾL		U		MAʾN	A		KI-LU-MA-NA	FN	RA LXV 56 I 9
	2		LU				KIʾL	A		LU$_2$-KI-LA		BASOR 95, 19
KIʾM	1		KIʾM	AT	IM					KI-MA-TIM	FN GEN	M
			KIʾM		I		ʾEL			KI-MI-EL		UCP X/3 2 2
KIʾR	1		KIʾR		I		DAGAN			KI-RI-D-DA-GAN		RA LXV 52 X 21

KIʾR	2	ʾAŠD		I		KIʾR		U		AŠ-DI-KI-E-RU		BM 92654 A
		ʾAŠD		I		KIʾR		U		AŠ-DI-KI-RU		BM 92654
		BEʿL		I		KIʾR		I		BE-LI$_2$-KI-RI	FN	RA LXV 58 I 15
KIʾZ	1	KIʾZ		UM						KI-ZU-UM		RA LXV 43 IV 16
KIHIL	1	KIHIL		UM						KI-ḪI-LUM		M+
		KIHIL		IM						KI-ḪI-LIM	GEN	M
		KIHIL	AH							KI-ḪI-LA	FN	M+
		KIHIL		A	HA					KI-ḪI-LA-A	FN	M
KIWN	1	KIWN				BUWZ	AN	UM		KI-IN-BU-ZA-NU-UM		HARRIS 68 14
		KIWN				NAHR		IM		KI-IN-NA-RI-IM	GEN	M+
		KIWN		A		ʾIL		I		KI-NA-I$_3$-LI$_2$		M
		KIWN		I		BAWŠ		I		KI-NI-BA-ŠI	FN	HARRIS 45 8
		KIWN		U		BAWŠ		I		KI-NU-BA-ŠI		LANGDON XXVIII 12
		KIWN		UM		ʾADAL				KI-NU-UM-A-DA-AL		RA LXV 48 VII 60
		KIWN		I	Š	LUʾP		A		KI-NI-IŠ-LU-BA		EDZARD,DER 94:17;95:6
		KIWN		I	Š	MAʾT		UM		KI-NI-IŠ-MA-TUM	FN	M+;C
	2	ʾAB		I	Š	KIWN				A-BI$_2$-IŠ-KI-IN		U
		JARAḪ				KIWN		A		SIN-KI-NA		TCL I 237 31
		LA				KIWN		U		LA-K[I]-NU		M
		LA				KIWN						
						HADD		U		LA-KI-IN-A-DU		A.
		LAḪAN		I		KIWN		IM		LA-ḪA-NI-KI-IN-IM	GEN	UCP X/3 2 5
KIBAL	2	ʾAN		I	Š	KIBAL				A-NI-IŠ-KI-BA-AL		RA LXV 53 XI 37+
		ʾAN		A	Š	KIBAL				[A]?-NA-AŠ-KI-BA-AL		VIII 86 23
		ʾANA				KIBAL		I		A-NA?-KI-BA-[L]I	FN	M
KIBAR	1	KIBAR								KI-BA-AR		RA LXV 47 VII 19
KIBEL	2	ʾAN		I	Š	KIBEL				A-NI-IŠ-KI-BE-EL		TCL XX 191 33 CAPF.
KIBIR	1	KIBIR		I						[K]I-BI-RI		RA LXV 43 III 77
KIBIS	1	KIBIS	AN							KI-BI-ZA-AN		M
KIBR	1	KIBR				ḪAJJ		A		KI-BI-IR-E$_2$-A		XIV 62:23
		KIBR				ʾABB		A		KI-BI-IR-D-AB-BA		M+
		KIBR				ʾABB		A		KI-IB-RA-AB-BA		CT XXIX 14 16
		KIBR				ʾABB		A		KI-IB-RA-BA		CT XXIX 14 29
		KIBR				JARAḪ				KI-BI-IR-D-EN-ZU		RUTTEN 11 25
		KIBR		I		ʿAŠTAR				KI-IB-RI-EŠ$_4$-DAR		M+
		KIBR		I		DAGAN				KI-IB-RI-D-DA-GAN		M+
	2	DAGAN				KIBR		I		D-DA-GAN-KI-IB-RI	FN	M+
KIBS	1	KIBS	AT	UM						KI-IB-ZA-TUM	FN	M+
		KIBS				HADD		U		KI-IB-ZA-DU	FN	A.
		KIBS		I		HADD		U		KI-IB-ZI-D-IM		M+
		KIBS		I		HEDD		A		KI-IB-ZI-E-D-IM		M
		KIBS		I		JARAḪ				KI-IB-ZI-E-RA-AḪ		RA LXV 43 III 44+
		KIBS		U	NA					KI-IB-ZU-UN-NA	FN	M+
KIBŠ	1	KIBŠ	AT	UM						KI-IB-SA-TUM	FN	RA LXV 56 I 11
KIBUN	1	KIBUN		UM						KI-BU-NU-UM		TIM III 33 5+
KIKKIN	1	KIKKIN		UM						KI-KI-NU-UM		BM 82437 2 6
		KIKKIN		UM						KI-IK-KI-NUM		B 49
		KIKKIN		U						KI-IK-KI-NU		B 49+
		KIKKIN		IM						KI-KI-NI-IM	GEN	B 49
		KIKKIN		IM						KI-KI-NIM	GEN	B 49+
		KIKKIN		I						KI-IK-KI-NI	GEN	B 49+
		KIKKIR		IM						KI-IK-KI-RI-IM	GEN	M
KIMA	3	ŠAMŠ		U		ʾIL		U	NA			
						KIMA				SA-AM-SU-I-LU-NA-KI-MA-DINGIR		BM 81047:6
KIMM	1	KIMM	AH							KI-IM-MA	FN	M
		KIMM	AN							KI-IM-MA-AN	FN	C
KIMR	1	KIMR	AN	U						KI-IM-RA-NU		M
KINAN	1	KINAN		UM						KI-NA-NU-UM		UCP X/1 P. 58+
		KINAN		U						KI-NA-NU		B 45+
		KINAN	AT	UM						KI-NA-NA-TUM		UCP X/1 27 7+
KINZ	1	KINZ		IJA						KI-IN-ZI-IA		M
KIPT	1	KIPT		UM						KI-IP-TU-UM		M
KIRB	1	KIRB	AN							KI-IR-BA-AN		RA LXV 51 IX 36
		KIRB	AN	UM						GIR$_3$-BA-NUM$_2$		U
KIRIŠ	2	ʾAWIJ				KIRIŠ		U		A-WI-KI-RI-IŠ		XIV 106:18
		ʾIL		U	NA	KIRIŠ		U		I-LU-NA-KI-RI-ŠU		XIII 8 19+

STEMS

KIRUʾ	1		KIRUʾ		UM					KI-RU-UM	FN	M+
			KIRUʾ		U					KI-RU-U$_2$	FN NOM	X 32 3+
			KIRUʾ		IM					KI-RI-E-IM	FN GEN	X 135 3
KIRZ	1		KIRZ		UM					KI-IR-ZU-UM	FN	RA LXV 64 VI 26
KISIBIR	1		KISIBIR	AT	UM					KI-ZI-BI-RA-TUM	FN	RA LXV 61 IV 50
KIŠAM	1		KIŠAM	AN	U					KI-ŠA?-MA-NU		XIII 1 V 60
KITT	1		KITT	AN	IM					KI-IT-TA-NI-IM	GEN	SIMMONS 63 2
KIZUR	1		KIZUR		I					KI-ZU-RI		RA LXV 43 III 41,42
KLIL	1	JA	KLIL		UM					A-AK-LI-LUM		HARRIS 28 11
KMIN	1	JA	KMIN		I					IA-AK-ME-NI		JNES XIII 210+ LATE
KMIS	1	JA	KMIS		I					IA-AK-ME-SI		JCS XIII 210+ LATE
KNUW	1	JA	KNUW			ŠARR		UM		IA-AK-NU-ŠA-RU-UM		KISURRA 47A 4+
		JA	KNUW			ŠARR		U		IA-AK-NU-ŠA-RU		TIM III 133 9
KRUB	1	JA	KRUB			ʾIL				D-IA-AK-RU-UB-DINGIR	DN	M+
		JA	KRUB			ʾEL				D-IA-AK-RU-UB-EL	DN	M+
		JA	KRUB			ʾIL				D-IA-AK-RU-UB-IL	DN	M+
		JI	KRUB			ʾEL				D-IK-RU-UB-EL	DN	M+
		JI	KRUB			ʾIL				D-IK-RU-UB-DINGIR	DN	M+
		JI	KRUB			ʾIL				D-IK-RU-UB-IL	DN	M
		JI	KRUB			ʾIL				D-IK-RU-BI-DINGIR	DN	M
		JA	KRUB			ʾIL						
						TILL	AT	I		D-IA-AK-RU-UB-DINGIR-TIL-LA-TI		M
KSIJ	1	JA	KSIJ			ʾIL				IA-AK-ZI-DINGIR		SIMMONS 92 16
		JA	KSIJ			ʾIL				A-AK-ZI-DINGIR		FIGULLA CAT I 14029
KSUW	1	JI	KSUW			ʾEL				IK-ZU-EL		TA 30 615 10, 20+
		JI	KSUW			ʾIL				IK-ZU-IL		TA 1931 ,435 REV.2
KŠIJ	1	JA	KŠIJ			....				IA-AK-SI-DINGIR-....		DE GEN. KICH II D47+
KUʾB	1		KUʾB		A	ʾEL				KU-BA-EL		X 91 4'
			KUʾB		A	ʾEL				KU-BA-DINGIR		M
			KUʾB		A	BUWZ		I		KU-BA-BU-ZI	FN	M
	2		ʿABD			KUʾB		I		ḪA-AB-DU-KU-BI		M+
			ʿAN	AT		KUʾB		U		A-NA-AT-KU-BU		TCL I 204:11
			MUT		U	KUʾB		I		MU-TU-KU-BI		RA LXV 42 II 66
KUʾD	1		KUʾD		IJA					KU-DI-IA	FN	XIII 1 III 35
			KUʾD		U	BIZZ		U		KU-DU-BI-IZ-ZU		A.
KUʾM	1		KUʾM			DANN		UM		KU-UM-DA-NU-UM		U
			KUʾM			NUWP		I		KU-UM-NU-BI		M
			KUʾM		U	LIʾL		U		KU-MU-LI-LU		CT IV 22A 14
			KUʾM		U	ṢILL		I		KU-MU-ZI-LI	FN	B 33+
	2		ḪALAJ		A	KUʾM		U		ḪA-LA-A-KU-MU		XIV 79:5+
			ʾANN		U	KUʾM				AN-NU-KUM	FN	XIII 1 VI 8
KUʾN	2		ḪANN		A	KUʾN		I		AN-NA-KU-NI		VAS VIII 14 44
		JI	TWUR			KUʾN		U	HU	I-DUR-KU?-NU-U$_2$		VAS XIII 14 R. 10
KUʾR	1		KUʾR		UM					KU-RU-UM		M+
			KUʾR	AN	UM					KU-RA-NU-UM		B 45
			KUʾR	AN	U					KU-RA-NU		B 45, M, C+
			KUʾR		U	HADD		U		KU-RU-D-IM		M
KUʾŠ	1		KUʾŠ	AN						KU-SA-AN		M+
			KUʾŠ		I	ḪIMR		I		KU-ŠI-ḪI-IM-RI		SIMMONS 87 19
KUʾT	1		KUʾT	AN						KU-TA-AN		M
			KUʾT	AN	UM					KU-TA-NU-UM		RUTTEN 38 20+
			KUʾT	AN	UM					KU-TA-A-NU-UM		SIMMONS 98 14
			KUʾT	AT	U					KU-TA-TU	MN	B 33
KUʾUT	1		KUʾUT		UM					KU-ḪU-TUM		UCP X/1 38 9
KUʾZ	1		KUʾZ		UM					KU-ZUM		TA 1931, 327
			KUʾZ	AN						KU-ZA-AN		XIV 86:5+
			KUʾZ	AN	UM					KU-ZA-NU-UM		B 46
			KUʾZ	AN	U					KU-ZA-NU		B 46
KUWN	1		KUWN		UM					KU-NU-UM		RUTTEN 33 6 SEAL+;M
			KUWN	AT	UM					KU-NA-TUM	FN	C
			KUWN	AN	UM					KU-NA-NU-UM		RUTTEN 1 19+
			KUWN	AN	IM					KU-NA-NI-IM	GEN	M
			KUWN		AM					KU-NA-AM	MN NOM	TIM III 17 7, M+
			KUWN			ʾIL		A		KU-UN-I-LA		RA LXV 53 XI 31
			KUWN			ʿAMM		U		KU-UN-AM-MU		MRS VI P. 249
			KUWN		A	MAʾT		UM		KU-NA-MA-TUM		U

STEMS

KUWN	1		KUWN		I	DAʾK	A		KU-NI-DA-KA		A. 367 11
	2		ʾIL		I	KUWN			I$_3$-LI$_2$-KU-UN		RA LXV 55 XIII 32
			ʿAMM		I	KUWN			ḪA-MI-KU-UN		RA LXV 54 XII 15
			ḎAKUR		A	KUWN	U		ZA-KU-RA-KU-NU		VII 85 12
KUWUN	1		KUWUN		UM				KU-U$_2$-NU-UM		UCP X/3 1 35
KUBAR	1		KUBAR		UM				GU-BA-RU-UM		U
KUBAS	1		KUBAS	AT	UM				KU-BA-ZA-TUM	FN	RA LXV 58 I 32
			KUBAS		U	....			KU-BA-ZU-[....]		RA LXV 50 VIII 83
KUBB	1		KUBB		IJA				KU-UB-BI-IA		M
			KUBB	AN	UM				KU-UB-BA-NU-UM		B 45
KUBS	1		KUBS	AT	UM				KU-UB-ZA-TUM		SZLECHTER TJ P. 186
KUBUR	1		KUBUR		UM				KU-UB-BU-RUM		A.
KUDAD	1		KUDAD	AN	UM				KU-DA-DA-NU-UM		U
			KUDAD		I				KU-DA-DI	FN	RA LXV 61 IV 5
KUDD	1		KUDD		I				[K]U-UD-DI		RA LXV 40 I 18
KUKIM	1		KUKIM			ḤIJJ	A		KU-UK-KI-IM?-ḪI-IA	FN	X 100 5
KUKKUB	1		KUKKUB	AT	UM				KU-KU-BA-TUM		VAS IX 175:11
			KUKKUB	AT	UM				KU-KU-BA-TUM	FN	XIII 1 VII 44
			KUKKUN		UM				KU-KU-NU-UM		SIMMONS 111 6 15+
			KUKKUŠ	AN					KU-KU-SA-AN		RA LXV 46 VI 3
			KUKKUŠ	AN	UM				KU-UK-KU-ZA-NU-UM		M
			KUKKUŠ	AN	IM				KU-UK-KU-ZA-NIM	GEN	M
KULIM	2		BAʿL		U	KULIM			BA-AḪ-LU-KU-LI-IM		SYRIA XXXII 7 III 6
		JA	LʾAʾ			KULIM			IA-AL-A-KU-LIM		RA LXV 55 XIII 18
KULP	1		KULP	AN	UM				KU-UL-BA-NU-UM		TA 1931,148
			KULP	AN	UM				GUL-BA-NU-UM		U
			KULP		A	RAWḪ	I	JE	KU-UL-PA-RA-ḪI-E		TCL I 14 1, YOS VIII 141 34
KULUP	2	JA	MWUT			KULUP			IA-MU-UT-KU-LU-UP		DELAPORTE, CCL II A 418
KUMAN	1		KUMAN		UM				KU-MA-NU-UM		B 45
KUMAR	2		ʿAMM		U	KUMAR	A		AM-MU-KU-MAR-RA		A.
KUMIS	1		KUMIS	AN					KU-ME-ZA-AN		RA LXV 50 VIII 53
KUMM	1		KUMM		I	NAʾD	A		KU-UM-MI-NA-DA		JCS IV 113
KUMR	1		KUMR		I				KU-UM-RI		RA LXV 42 II 59
	2		MUT		U	KUMR	I		MU-TU-KU-UM-PI		X 166 10', 13'
KUMS	1		KUMS		AJA				KU-UM-ZA-A-A		HARRIS 66 16
KUMT	1		KUMT	AN	UM				GU-UM-DA-NU-UM		HSM 7936, UR III
KUNAB	1		KUNAB		UM				KU-NA-PU-UM		EDZARD,DER 59:25+
KUNAN	1		KUNAN		UM				KU-NA-A-NU-UM		B 45+
			KUNAN		UM				KU-NA-NU-UM		B 93
			KUNAN	AT	UM				KU-NA-NA-TUM	FN	M
KUND	1		KUND		I				KU-UN-DI	FN	XIII 1 IV 76, C
KUNDUL	1		KUNDUL	AT	UM				KU-UN-DU-LA-TUM	FN	M+
			KUNDUL	AH					KU-UN-DU-LA	FN	XIII 1 III 21, CT XLIV 54 29
KUNN	1		KUNN		I				KU-UN-NI		RA LXV 52 XI 4
			KUNN		A				KU-UN-NA		WO V 59+ ALA. LATE
			KUNN		AM				KU-UN-NAM	NOM	XIV 102:8, 15, 24
			KUNN		A	MA			[K]U-UN-NA-MA		XIV 101:8
KUNZ	1		KUNZ		I				KU-UN-ZI	FN	XIII 1 V 39; C
			KUNZ	AN	UM				KU-UN-ZA-NU-UM		BIROT,TEA 65:17
			KUNZ	AN	UM				KU-UN-ZA-NUM$_2$		TA 1930,181+
			KUNZ	AN	AM				KU-UN-ZA-NAM	ACC	TA 1930,181
KUPAD	1		KUPAD		IM				KU-PA-DI-IM	GEN	M
KUPAPA	2		ḪAʾL		I	KUPAPA			ḪA-LI$_2$-KU-BA-BA	FN	RA LXV 58 I 14
			ʾALL		I	KUPAPA			AL-LI-KU-PA-PA	FN	A.
KURAŠ	1		KURAŠ	AN	UM				KU-RA-ŠA-NU-UM		LAESSOE P. 53+
KURD	1		KURD	AN	UM				KUR-DA-A-NU-UM		RUTTEN 11 26
			KURD		A	KAMB	I		KUR-DA-KA-AM-BI	FN	XIII 1 III 25
KURKUR	1		KURKUR		UM				KU-UR$_2$-KU-RU-UM		B 49+
			KURKUR		IM				KU-UR-KU-RI-IM	GEN	M
			KURKUR	T	UM				KUK$_2$-KUR$_2$-TUM	MN?	PBS VIII/2 178 36
KURŠ	1		KURŠ	AN	UM				KU-UR$_2$-ŠA-NU-UM		B 45
			KURŠ	AN	U				KU-UR-[S]A-NU		M
			KURŠ	AN	I				KU-UR$_2$-SA-NI	NOM	M
KURUB	2		ʾAJAN			KURUB			A-AN-KU-RU-UB	FN	RA LXV 51 X 15
		JI	JṢIʾ			KURUB			I-ZI-KU-RU-UB		RA LXV 53 XI 11
KUŠAP	1		KUŠAP	AN	UM				KU-SA-PA-NU-UM		TIM III 57 6 66 6

STEMS													
KUŠAP	1		KUŠAP		IJA						KU-SA-BI-IA		M
KUŠM	1		KUŠM		I			ʾEL			KU-UŠ$_2$-MI-EL		RA LXV 48 VII 74
KUŠR	1		KUŠR	AN	UM						KU-UŠ-RA-NU-UM		SIMMONS 51 17
KUTKUT	1		KUTKUT		UM						KU-UT-KU-TUM		M, KISURRA 37 8+
KUTUL	1		KUTUL		U	HU					KU-TU-LU-U$_2$		RA LXV 43 III 76
	2		ʾIL		I	Š		KUTUL			I$_3$-LI$_2$-IŠ-KU-TU-UL		KISURRA 75A 18+
KUZAB	1		KUZAB		U						KU-ZA-BU	FN	VAS VII 166 11
			KUZAB	AT	UM						KU-ZA-BA-TUM	MN	CT VI 30B 23+
			KUZAB	AT	UM						KU-ZA-BA-TUM	FN	CT VIII 43A 4, 10+
KUZAR	1		KUZAR		I						KU-ZA-RI		RA LXV 45 V 15+
			KUZAR		I						KU-UZ-ZA-RI		IX 259:5
			KUZAR		I						KU-UZ$_2$-ZA-RI		XIII 90:5
			KUZAR		I	NA					KU-ZA-RI-NA		RA LXV 45 V 22
KUZAZ	1		KUZAZ		I						KU-ZA-AZ-ZI	FN	RA LXV 60 III 52
LʾAʾ	1	JI	LʾAʾ					HADD	U		IL-A-D-IM		X 83 4, 7'
		JI	LʾAʾ					HADD	U		IL-A-DU		A. 78 20
		JA	LʾAʾ					KULIM			IA-AL-A-KU-LIM		RA LXV 55 XIII 18
		JI	LʾAʾ					....			IL-A-KUL$_2$-LAM?		VII 140:10
LʾIJ	1	JA	LʾIJ								IA-AL-E		RA LXV 46 VI 50
		JA	LʾIJ				JA	JPAʿ			IA-AL-E-PA-AḪ		M
		JA	LʾIJ					DAGAN			IA-AL-E-D-DA-GAN		M+
		JA	LʾIJ					DAGAN			IA-[AL]?-I-D-DA-GAN		RA LXV 47 VII 23
		JI	LʾIJ					DAGAN			I-IL-ḪI-D-DA-G[AN]		M
		JE	LʾIJ					DAGAN			EL-I-D-DA-GAN		M
	2		ʾANN		U		TA	LʾIJ			AN-NU-TA-AL-E	FN	M+
			ʿAŠTAR				TA	LʾIJ			EŠ$_4$-DAR-TA-AL-E	FN	XIII 1 V 41+
			MAM		A		TA	LʾIJ			D-MA-MA-TA-AL-E	FN	M
LʾUM	1	JA	LʾUM		U						IA-AL-U$_2$-MU		XIII 36 20
LA	1		LA			KA		ʾIL			LA-KA-DINGIR		KISURRA 111 5
			LA			KA		ṢUBʾ	UM		LA-KA-ZU-BU-UM		M
			LA			K		MA					
								ʾIL			LA-AK-MA-AN		B 33
			LA			NA		HADD	U		LA-NA-D-IM		XIII 109 15, 16
			LA			NA		ʾIL			LA-NA-DINGIR		RUTTEN 27 15+
			LA			NA		DAGAN			LA-NA-D-DA-GAN		M+
			LA			NA		ŠUM	UM		LA-NA-SU-MU-[UM]		CT VIII 26B 22
			LA			NI		ʾIL			LA$_2$-NI-DINGIR		U
			LA				ʾA	HWIJ		JA	LA-WI-IA	FN	RA LXV 60 III 37
			LA				ʾA	HWIJ					
								ʾAḪ	I		LA-AḪ-WI-A-ḪI	FN	XIII 1 VII 3
			LA				ʾA	HWIJ					
								ʾAB	I		LA-AḪ-WI-A-BI	FN	XIII 1 XIII 6
			LA				ʾA	HWIJ					
								HADD	U		LA-AḪ-WI-A-DU		A. 95 36
			LA				ʾA	HWIJ					
								ʾIL			LA-WI-DINGIR		XIV 109:7
			LA				ʾA	HWIJ					
								ʾIL			LA-[AḪ]?-WI-DINGIR		M
			LA				ʾA	HWIJ					
								JAŠAR			LA-AḪ-WI-E-SA-AR		RA LXV 40 I 21
			LA				ʾA	HWIJ					
								BAʿL	U		LA-AḪ-WI-BA-LU		C
			LA				ʾA	HWIJ					
								BAʿL	U		LA-AḪ-WI-BA-AḪ-LU		XIV 29:28
			LA				ʾA	HWIJ					
								BEʿL	I		LA-AḪ-WI-BE-LI$_2$	FN	RA LXV 59 II 73
			LA				ʾA	HWIJ					
								LA		NA	LA-AḪ-WI-LA-NA		RA LXV 65 VII 19
			LA				ʾA	HWIJ					
								MALIK			LA-AḪ-WI-MA-LIK		X 141 2
			LA				ʾA	HWIJ					
								MALIK	U		LA-AḪ-WI-MA-LI-KU		M
			LA				ʾA	HWIJ					
								NIWR	I		LA-AḪ-WI-NE-RI	FN	XIII 1 II 11
			LA				ʾA	ḪJIJ					
								HADD	U		LA-ḪI-A-DU		A. 57 11, 13

STEMS

LA	1	LA	ʾA	ḪJIJ					
				ʿAN	UM		LA-ḪI-A-NU-UM		U
		LA	ʾA	ḪJIJ					
				BIḪR	U		LA-ḪI-BI-RU		WATERMAN 25 R. 5
		LA	ʾA	ḪJIJ					
				ṢADUQ			LA-ḪI-ZA-DU-UQ		A.+
		LA	ʾA	ʾWIʾ					
				ʾIL			LA-WI-IḪ?-DINGIR		TIM IV 33,34,SEALS
		LA	ʾA	ʾWIR	UM		LA-WI-RUM		RA XXIV 58 9 4
		LA	ʾA	ʾDUM	U		LA-AḪ-DU-MU		4E RENC. ASS. P. 178 4
		LA	ʾA	ʾMAR	UM		LA-MA-RUM		BM 80644
		LA	ʾA	ʾMUR	IM		LA-A-MU-RI-IM	GEN	M
		LA	ʾA	ʾMUR	A		LA-MU-RA		B 33+
		LA	ʾA	ʾŠUD	I				
				ʾIL			LA-AḪ-SU-DI-DINGIR		XIII 4 14
		LA	ʾA	ḪŠIR	UM		LA-AḪ-SI-RU-UM		BM 80368 2
		LA	ʾA	MLIK					
				ʾIL			LA-AM-LI-IK-DINGIR		RUTTEN 5 22
		LA	ʾA	RŠIJ	UM		LA-AR-ŠI-U_2-U[M]		TA 1931, 538 IV
		LA	ʾA	ŠNIJ					
				ʾIL			LA-AŠ-NI-DINGIR		M
		LA		ʾAB	A		LA-A-BA		U
		LA		ʿADN	I	JA	LA-AD-NI-IA		M
		LA		ʿADN	A				
			ʾA	MWUT			LA-ḪA-AD-NA-A-MU-UT		M
		LA		ʾADUN	IM		LA-DU-NIM	GEN	M
		LA		ʾIL	A		[L]A?-I-LA		RA LXV 44 IV 36
		LA		ʾIL	A				
				MILK	I		LA-I-LA-MI-IL-KI		TA 30, 75 2
		LA		ʿAMM	U		LA-ḪA-AM-MU		HARRIS 18 14
		LA		ḪAMUJ	IM		LA-ḪA-MU-JI-IM	GEN	M
		LA		ʿAN	UM		LA-A-NU-UM		U
		LA		ḪUNN	IM		LA-ḪU-NI-IM	GEN	M
		LA	JE N	JBIŠ	U		LA-E-NI-BI-ŠU		YOS XII
		LA	JE	RWIḪ	UM		LA-E-RI-ḪU-UM		U
		LA		BAWʾ	U		LA-BA-U_2		JCS XIII 51 292:5' A.LATE
		LA		BAWʾ	U		LA-BA-ʾU-U		TALLQUIST,APN P.120 LATE
		LA		BAŠAR			LA-BA-ŠA-AR		RA LXV 42 II 58
		LA		DIJN	AM		LA-DI-NAM	ACC	M
		LA		DJIN					
				JARAḪ			LA-DI-IN-E-RA-AḪ		RA LXV 46 VI 26+
		LA		KIWN	U		LA-K[I]-NU		M
		LA		KIWN					
				HADD	U		LA-KI-IN-A-DU		A.
		LA		LABW	UM		LA-LA-BU-[UM]?		M
		LA		MANUW	UM		LA-MA-NU-UM		I, TIM III 136 4
		LA		MANUW	IM		LA-MA-NI-IM	GEN	B 46
		LA		NAŠUʾ	UM		LA-NA-SU-U_2-UM		M
		LA		NAŠUʾ	UM		LA-NA-SU-WU-UM		XIV 53:20+
		LA		NAŠUʾ	U		LA-NA-SU-U_2		B 33, 4E RENC. ASS. P. 178 8
		LA		NAŠUʾ	IM		LA-NA-SU-I-IM	GEN	M
		LA		NAŠUʾ	IM		LA-A-NA-SU-I-IM	GEN	M
		LA		NAŠUʾ	I		LA-NA-SU-JI	GEN	M
		LA		NAŠUʾ	I		LA-NI-SU-JI	FN NOM	M
		LA		PAŠIQ	UM		LA-PA-SI-KU-UM		M
		LA		RIWM					
				ḪAM	I		LA-RI-IM-D-A-MI		M
		LA		RIWM					
				ʿAḎIR			LA-RI-IM-ḪA-ZI-IR		DELAPORTE, CAT. BN 207
		LA		RIWM					
			JI	JBAL	U	HU	[L]A?-RI-IM-I-BA-LU-U_2		M
		LA		RIWM					
				BAʿL	I		LA-RI-IM-BA-AḪ-LI		M+
		LA		RIWM					
				BEʿL	I		LA-RI-IM-BE-LI_2		X 69 5
		LA		RIWM					
				DIWR			LA-RI-IM-DI-IR		RA LXV 50 IX 22

LA	1	LA			RIWM						
					LU			HU	LA-RI-IM-LU-U$_2$		M
		LA			RIWM						
					NUMAḪ		A		LA-RI-IM-NU-MA-ḪA-A		M+
		LA			RIWM						
					NUMAḪ		A		LA-RI-IM-NU-MA-A		M
		LA			ŠIJM		A		LA-SI-MA		M
		LA			TEʾḪ		U		LA-TE-ḪU		MRS VI P. 196 22,LATE
		LA			TEBUʾ		U		LA-TE-BU-U$_2$		B 33
		LA			ṬAJB		UM		LA-DA-BU-UM		U
		LA			ṬAJB	T	UM		LA-ṬA$_3$-AB-TUM	FN	XIII 1 VI 44+
		LA			ṢABIʾ		IM		LA-ZA-BI-IM	GEN	M+
		LA			ṢARR		UM		LA-ZA-RU-UM?		B 33
		LA			ṢARR		AJA		LA-ZA-RA-A		YOS XIII 244:14
	2	ʾAḪ	UM		LA						
					ʾAB		I		A-ḪU-UM-LA-A-BI		YOS XIII 245:17, SEAL
		ʾAJA			LA						
					ŠUM		U	HU	A-IA-LA-SU-MU-U$_2$		M, C
		ḪIʾD			LA			KA	ḪI-I[D]-LA-A?-KA		XII 141 8
		ḪIʾD			LA			KA			
					ʾIL		I		ḪI-ID-LA-KA-I$_3$-LI$_2$		M
		ḪIʾD			LA				ḪI-ID-L[A]-NAM		XIII 38 27
		ḪAʾAN	A		LA			HA	ḪA-A-NA-LA-A	FN	XIII 1 II 53+
		ʾAB	U		LA			JA	A-BU-LA-IA		XIII 101 6
		ʾIB	I		LA						
					ʾIL		UM		I-BI-LA-I$_3$-LUM		U
	JI	JBAL			LA						
					ʾIL				I-BA-AL-LA-DINGIR		RA LXV 47 VII 26
		ʾAK	UM		LA						
					ʾIL		A		A-KUM-LA-I-LA		RA LXV 55 XIII 1
		ʾEK	I		LA						
				ʾA	HWIJ				E-KI-LA-AḪ-WI		M
		ʾIL	A		LA						
					ʾIL				DINGIR-LA-IL		U
		ʾIL	A		LA			KA	I-LA-LA-KA		B 21+
		ʿAMM	U		LA						
					RIWM				ḪA-MU-L[A]-RI-IM		RA LXV 46 VI 40
		ʾAŠD	UM		LA						
					ʾAB		UM		AŠ-DU-UM-LA-A-BU-UM		SUMER V 142
		ʾAŠD	UM		LA						
					ʾAB		UM		AŠ$_2$-DU-UM-LA-A-BU-UM		SUMER V 142+
		ḎIMR	U		LA						
					ʾAB		I		ZI-IM-RU-LA-A-BI		RA LXV 42 III 7
		KAʾB	I		LA						
					RIWM				KA-BI-LA-RI-IM		RA LXV 47 VI 65+; C+
		LAWUJ			LA						
					HADD		A		LA-U$_2$-LA-A-DA		A.
		LAWUJ			LA						
					HADD		U		LA-WU-LA-D-IM		M+, C
		LAWUJ			LA						
					ʾIL				LA-WU-LA-DINGIR		M+
		LAMA			LA						
					ʾIL				LA-MA-LA-DINGIR		KAJ 72 18, LATE
		MA			LA			NA			
					DITAN		A		MA-A-LA-NA-DI-TA-NA		B 34
		MILK	I		LA						
					ʾEL				MI-IL-KI-LA-EL		TA 30 615 21
		NIQM	I		LA						
					NAŠIʾ				NI-IQ-MI-LA-NA-SI		M
	JA	RŠAP			LA						
					ʾIL				IA-AR-SA-AP-LA-DINGIR		M+
	JA	RŠAP			LA						
					ʾIL		A		IA-AR-SA-AP-LA-I-[LA]?		M
	ʾA	ŠWUB			LA						
					ʾEL				A-ŠU-UB-LA-EL		TA 1931,765
	ʾA	ŠWUB			LA						
					ʾIL				A-ŠU-UB-LA-DINGIR		C+

STEMS

LA	2	ŠAM		U		LA					
						ʾIL			SA-MU-LA-DINGIR		B 39+
		ŠUM		A		LA					
						LI		JA	SU-MA-LA-LI-A		BM 80363 1
		ŠUM		U		LA		NI	SU-MU-LA-NI		HARRIS 39 11
		ŠUM		U		LA		NIA	SU-MU-LA-NI-A		CT XLVIII 10 1
		ŠUM		UM		LA					
						ʾAB	I		SU-MU-UM-LA-A-BI	FN	RA LXV 65 VII 24
		ŠUM		U		LA					
						ʾIL			SU-MU-LA-DINGIR		B 39+
		ŠUM		U		LA					
						ʾIL	I		SU-MU-LA-I_3-LI_2		UCP X/1 34 2
		ŠUM		U		LA					
						ʾEL			SU-MU-LA-EL		SUMER XXIII 160 5
		ŠIMAʿ				LA		NI	SI-MA-AḪ-LA-NI		SYRIA XLI 54 N. 1
		ŠIMAʿ				LA		NI	SI-MA-AḪ-LA-A-NI		SYRIA XLI 54 N. 1
		ŠIMAʿ				LA		NI	SI-MA-AḪ-I-LA-A-NI		RA LXVI 112 MARI
		ŠIMAʿ				LA		NIE	SI-MA-AḪ-LA-NI-E		SYRIA XLI 54 N. 1+
		ŠIMAʿ				LA		NIE	SI-MA-AḪ-I-LA-A-NI-E		SYRIA XLI 54 N. 1
		ŠIMAʿ				LA		NIE	SU-MU-ḪA-LA-NI-E		SYRIA XLI 54 N. 1
		ŠIMAʿ				LA		NIE	SU-MU?-ḪI-LA-NI-E		SYRIA XLI 54 N. 1
		ŠIMAʿ				LA		NIE	SI-MA-AḪ-LA-A-NI-E		RA LXVI 115:21;117:11 MARI
		ŠIMAʿ				LA		NIE	SI-MA-AḪ-I-LA-NI-E		RA LXVI 112 MARI
		ŠIMAʿ				LA		NIE	SU-MA-AḪ-I-LA-A-NI-E		RA LXVI 120:7 MARI
		ṢIDQ		U		LA					
						NAŠIʾ			ZI-ID-KU-LA-NA-SI		M+
	3	LA			ʾA	HWIJ					
						LA		NA	LA-AḪ-WI-LA-NA		RA LXV 65 VII 19
LAʾJ	1	LAʾJ			JA				LA-A-A		U+
LAʾAT	1	LAʾAT	AN						LA-ḪA-TA-AN		RA LXV 51 IX 68
LAʾIJ	1	LAʾIJ		UM					LA-I-JU-UM		M+
		LAʾIJ	T	UM					LA-I-TUM	FN	RA LXV 58 II 3
		LAʾIJ			JA				LA-I-IA		XIII 1 VII 70+
	2	ʾIL		A		LAʾIJ			I-LA-LA-I		TA 1931,395,UR III
		ʾIL		A		LAʾIJ			I-LA-LA-E		TA 1931,609,UR III
		ʾIL		A		LAʾIJ			I-LA-LA-E-KI	GN	LAESSOE,SHEMSHARA P.77
		ʾIL		A		LAʾIJ			I-LA-LA-AḪ		RA LXV IX 38,X 10
LAʾIP	1	LAʾIP	AH						LA-ḪI-PA	FN	XIII 1 II 65+
		LAʾIP	AN						LA-ḪI-PA-AN		M+
LAʾIŠ	1	LAʾIŠ	T	UM					LA-ḪI-EŠ$_3$-TUM	FN	C
LAʾL	1	LAʾL		UM					LA-LU-UM		HARRIS 76 22
		LAʾL		UM					LA-LUM		HARRIS 76 2
		LAʾL		I		ʾEL			LA-LI-E-EL		SIMMONS 70 15
	2	GAʾJ		I		LAʾL	UM		GA-I-LA-LUM		M
		KAWJ		A		LAʾL	UM		KA-A-LA-LUM		M
		PAQAḪ		A		LAʾL	UM		BA-GA-A-LA-LUM		HARRIS 69 2+
		ŠUM		U		LAʾL	UM		SU-MU-LA-LUM		PBS XI/2 1 I 16
LAʾR	1	LAʾR				MULUK			LA-AR-MU-LU-UK	FN	XIII 1 IX 33
		LAʾR				NAPŠ	U		LA-AR-NA-AP-SU	FN	XIII 1 I 71
		LAʾR		A		JARAḪ			LA-RA-D-SIN		KAJ 167 23+, LATE
	2	BUN		U		LAʾR	A		BU-NU-LA-RA		B 16
LAʾT	1	LAʾT		I		RAWM	E	JE	LA-TI-RA-ME-E		M
LAʾUŠ	1	LAʾUŠ		UM					LA-U_2-ŠUM		I
LAḪM	1	LAḪM	ATANUM						LA-AḪ-MA-TA-NU-UM		SIMMONS 89 10
LAḪAN	1	LAḪAN		UM					LA-ḪA-NU-UM		M+
		LAḪAN		I		KIWN	IM		LA-ḪA-NI-KI-IN-IM	GEN	UCP X/3 2 5
LAḪN	1	LAḪN		UM					LA-AḪ?-NU-UM		M
LAWUJ	1	LAWUJ		UM					LA-U_2-UM		M+
		LAWUJ		IM					LA-I-IM	GEN	M+
		LAWUJ		EM					LA-E-EM	ACC	M+
		LAWUJ				HADD	U		LA-WU-D-IM		M+
		LAWUJ				HADD	U		LA-U_2-D-IM		A.
		LAWUJ				ʾIL			LA-WU-DINGIR		M
		LAWUJ				LA					
						HADD	A		LA-U_2-LA-A-DA		A.
		LAWUJ				LA					
						HADD	U		LA-WU-LA-D-IM		M+, C

STEMS

LAWUJ	1		LAWUJ					LA						
								ʾIL				LA-WU-LA-DINGIR		M+
LABW	1		LABW		A			BIḪR		I	Š	LA-BA-BI$_2$-RI-IŠ		HSM 7936, UR III
			LABW		I			ŠAM		A		LA-BI-SA-MA		UCP X/3 P. 199+
	2		ʾAM	T				LABW		A		AM-TI-LA-BA	MN	TIM III 7 5
			ʿAMM		U			LABW		A		ḪA-AM-MU-LA-BA-A		XIV 114:6
			LA					LABW		UM		LA-LA-BU-[UM]?		M
		JI	NDIN					LABW		A		I-DIN-D-LA-BA		M
			ŠADW		U			LABW		A		ŠA-DU-LA-BA		M
			ŠADW		UM			LABW		A		ŠA-DU-UN-LA-BA		M+
			ŠADW		UM			LABW		A		ŠA-DU-UM-LA-BA		M
			ŠADW		UM			LABW		A		ŠA-DU-UM-LA-BU-A		M
			ŠADW		UM			LABW		I		ŠA-DU-UM-LA-BI		M
			ŠUM		U			LABW		A		SU-MU-LA-BA		M
LABAN	1		LABAN									LA-BA-AN		RA LXV 41 II 32
			LABAN		A			ʾIL		A		LA-PA-NA-I-LA		ZA XXXVIII 267
	2		ʾAḪ		I			LABAN				A-ḪI-LA-BA-AN		RA LXV 43 IV 5+
LABIN	1		LABIN		A							LA-AB-BI-NA		A.+
LABN	1		LABN		UM							LA-AB-NU-UM		TA 1930, 221
LAGIG	1		LAGIG		UM							LA-GI-GU-UM		UET V 719 2
LAKIŠ	1		LAKIŠ		UM							LA-KI-SU-[U]M		UET V 685 28
LALAʾ	1		LALAʾ		IM							LA-LA-I-IM	GEN	XIII 85 5
			LALAʾ	AN	UM							LA-LA-A-NU-UM		UCP X/3 2 27
			LALAʾ	AT	UM							LA-LA-A-TUM	FN	M
			LALAʾ	AT	UM							LA-LA-ḪA-TUM	FN	TCL XVIII 121 9
LAMA	1		LAMA					ʾADAʾ		E		LA-MA-A-DA-E	FN	A.
			LAMA					ʾADAʾ		E		LA-MA-TA-E	FN	A.+
			LAMA					ʾIL				LA-MA-DINGIR		B 33+, M+
			LAMA					ʾIL		A		LA-MA-I-LA		YOS XIII 244:2+
			LAMA					DUWD		U		LA-MA-DU-DU		M
			LAMA					LA						
								ʾIL				LA-MA-LA-DINGIR		KAJ 72 18, LATE
	2		ʾAB		I			LAMA				A-BI-LA-MA		B 10
			ʾAK		I			LAMA				A-KI-LA-MA		B 12
			ʾALI					LAMA				A-LI$_2$-LA-MA		SIMMONS 118 17+
LAMAS	1		LAMAS		I							LA-MA-ZI	GEN	IV 68 18, 20, 21
			LAMAS	AT	UM							[LA]-MA-ZA-TUM	FN	XIII 1 XIV 6
			LAMAS	AH								LA-MA-ZA	FN	M
	2		ʾANN		U			LAMAS		I		AN-NU-LA-MA-ZI	FN	M+
			ʾANN		U			LAMAS		I		AN-NU-D-LAMA	FN	XIII 1 VII 8+
			ʾANN		U			LAMAS	IT	UM		AN-NU-LA-MA-ZI-TUM	FN	RA LXV 59 II 13
			ʾIŠḪAR	AH				LAMAS		I		D-IŠ-ḪA-RA-D-LAMA	FN	XIII 1 IX 23
			ʿAŠTAR					LAMAS		I		EŠ$_4$-DAR-LA-MA-ZI	FN	M
			ʿAŠTAR					LAMAS		I		EŠ$_4$-DAR-D-LAMA	FN	XIII 1 I 69+
LAMM	2		ŠUM		I			LAMM		U		SU-MI-LAM-MU		VAS XVI 24 4, A.+
LAMR	1		LAMR	AT	UM							LA-AM-RA-TUM	FN	YOS XIII 294:18
LAMUM	1		LAMUM	AN	UM							LA-MU-MA-NU-UM		I; TA 1931,148
LAND	1		LAND		U							LA-AN-TU		TA 1931, 148
			LAND	AN								LA-AN-DA-AN		C
LASIM	1		LASIM		A							LA-ZI-MA	NOM	BIN VII 31 6
			LASIM					ʿAN		UM		LA-ZE$_2$-IM-A-NU-UM		FLP 590:6, U
			LASIM					ʿAN		UM		LA-ZI-MA-NU-UM		MVN III 338:17, U
LAŠG	1		LAŠG	AN								LA$_2$-AŠ$_2$-GA-AN		RA XXXIV 176
LAŠIK	1		LAŠIK		U							LA-ŠI-KU	FN	EDZARD,DER 91:17
LAŠU	1		LAŠU					ʾEL						
								KA				LA-ŠI-EL-KA-A-BI-IM		B 33
			LAŠU					ʾIL				LA-ŠU-IL		U
			LAŠU					MIQIṬ				LA-ŠU-MI-GI-IT		B 33
			LAŠU					MIQIṬ				LA-ŠU-MI-KI-IT		B 33
LAṬUP	1		LAṬUP		UM							LA-TU-BU-UM		TA 1931,327
			LAṬUP		UM							LA-DU-BU-UM		TA 31, 297
LEʾEJ	1	JA	LEʾEJ									IA$_3$-LE-E		U
		JI	LEʾEJ					HADD		U		I-LE-E-D-IM		XIII 93 5
	2		BEʿL		I		TA	LEʾEJ				BE-LI$_2$-TA-LI-IḪ		RA LXV 50 VIII 44
LI	1		LI			JA		ʾEL				LI-IA-EL		RA LXV 41 II 23
			LI			JA		SITR		U	HU	LI-IA-ZI-IT-RU-U$_2$		M+
			LI				JI	JṢIʾ						
								ʾAŠD		UM		LI-ZI-AŠ-DU-UM		VAS XIII 104 R. II 24

STEMS

LI	1		LI		JI		MLIK					
							....			LI-IM-LI$_2$-LI-IK-ḪI-LI-GAL$_2$		HSM 7934, UR III
			LI		JI		TWUR					
							ʾAHL	I		LI-TU-UR-A-LI		JCS XXIV 62 NO.55+
			LI		JI	T	ŠAMAʿ					
							ʾIL			LI?-IŠ?-TA-MI-DINGIR		IX 291 I 18
	2		ʾAḪ	UM			LI		JA	A-ḪU-UM-LI-A		M
			JIŠʿ	I			LI					
							ʾEL			IŠ-ḪI-LI-EL		JCS XXIV 69 NO. 3 SEAL
			ʿAŠTAR				LI		JA	EŠ$_4$-DAR-LI?-IA		YOS XIII 12 REV 14
			ḎARAʿ				LI					
							ʾIL			ZA-RA-AḪ?-LI-DINGIR		M
			MILK	I			LI					
							ʾEL			MI-IL-KI-LI-EL		B 34, M+
			MILK	I			LI					
							ʾEL			MIL-KI-LI-EL		VAS VIII 128 16+
			MILK	I			LI					
							ʾIL			MI-IL-KI-LI$_2$-IL		I
			MILK	I			LI					
							ʾIL			[MI]-EL-KI-LI-IL		I
			MILK	I			LI					
							ʾEL	UM		MI-IL-KI-LI-E-LUM		A 32065:3
			MARUʾ				LI					
							ʾEL			MA-RU-LI-EL		SIMMONS 47 18, 49 22
		JI	NPIḪ				LI					
							DIJN	I		IB-BI-IḪ-LI-DI-NI	FN	C
		ʾA	ŠWUB				LI					
							ʾEL			A-ŠU-UB-LI-EL		OIP XLIII 154 NO. 48+
			ŠUM				LI					
					JI		JṢIʾ	IM		SU-UM-LI-ZI-IM	GEN	WATERMAN 25 R 9
			ŠUM	A			LI		KA	SU-MA-LI-KA		BM 80328 13
			ŠUM	U			LI					
							ʾEL			SU-MU-LI-EL		B 39+
			ŠUM	U			LI					
							ʾEL			SU-MU-LI-EL-DU-RI		A 7630 3
			ŠUM	U			LI					
					JI		JṢIʾ			SU-MU-LI-ZI		MEISSNER 37 15+
	3		ʾIL	I	JI		ḪTAʾ					
							LI		JA	I$_3$-LI$_2$-IḪ-TA-LI-A		BIROT,TEA 69 I 14
			ŠUM	A			LA					
							LI		JA	SU-MA-LA-LI-A		BM 80363 1
LIʾD	1		LIʾD	AJA						LI-DA-A-IA		M+
	2		KAKK	A			LIʾD	I		KA-AK-KA-LI-DI	FN	X 10 5
LIʾL	1		LIʾL	IM						LI-LI-IM	GEN	XIII 73 5
	2		KUʾM	U			LIʾL	U		KU-MU-LI-LU		CT IV 22A 14
			QIJŠ T	I			LIʾL	IM		KI-IŠ-TI-LI-LIM	GEN	RA LXIV 34 NO.26
			ŠUM	U			LIʾL	U		SU-MU-LI-LU		B 39
			ṢIBʾ	I			LIʾL	UM		ZE$_2$-BI-LI-LUM		HSM 7900, UR III
LIʾM	1		LIʾM	A			HADD	U		LI-MA-A-DU		A.
			LIʾM	I			HADD	U		LI-MI-D-IM		M+
			LIʾM	I			HADD	U		LI-ME-D-IM		M+
	2		ʾAḪ	I			LIʾM			A-ḪI-LI-IM		B 12, M
			ʾAJAN				LIʾM			A-AN-LI-IM		M+
		JA	JʿIL				LIʾM			IA-ḪI-IL-LI-IM		M
			ʾAB	I			LIʾM			A-BI-LI-IM		RA LXV 44 IV 60+
			ʾABB	I			LIʾM					
							MA			AB-BI-LIM-MA		A.+
		JI	JDAʿ				LIʾM					
							MA			I-DA-LIM-MA		B 21
			JADAʿ				LIʾM			IA-DAḪ-LI-IM		YOS XII
			JADAʿ				LIʾM			IA-ṮA$_3$-AḪ-LI-IM		YOS XII
		JA	ʿDUN				LIʾM			IA-AḪ-DU-UN-LI-IM		M+
		JA	ʿDUN				LIʾM			IA-AḪ-DU-LI-IM		M+
		JA	ʿDUN				LIʾM			IA-AḪ-DU-UL-LI-IM		M
			ʾIL	I			LIʾM			I$_3$-LI$_2$-LI-IM		M+, C
			ʿAMM	U			LIʾM			ḪA-MU-LI-IM		RA LXV 52 X 22

STEMS

LIʾM	2	JA	JPAʿ				LIʾM			IA-A-PA-AḪ-LI-IM		M+
		JA	JPAʿ				LIʾM			IA-PA-AḪ-LI-IM		M+
			JIŠʿ		I		LIʾM			IŠ-ḪI-LI-IM		M
		JI	JŠAR				LIʾM			I-ŠAR-LI-IM		M+, C+, CT VI 47B 17
			JATAR				LIʾM			IA-TAR-LI-IM		M+
			ʾATT		I		LIʾM	A		AT-TI-LI-MA		A. LATE
			JATT		A		LIʾM			IA-AT-TA-LI-IM		ZA XXXVI 95, BJ 88 12
			BAʿD		I		LIʾM			BA-AḪ-DI-LI-IM		M+
			BIN		A		LIʾM			BI-NA-LI-IM		RA LXV 45 V 54
		JA	BRUQ				LIʾM			IA-AB-RU-UQ-LI-IM		TCL XI 156 12
		JA	DWUR				LIʾM			IA-DU-UR-LI-I[M]		RA LXV 45 V 82
			ḎIKR		I		LIʾM			ZI-IK-RI-LI-IM		M+
			ḎIMR		I		LIʾM			ZI-IM-RI-LI-IM		M+
		JA	GJID				LIʾM			IA-GI-ID-LI-IM		M+
		JI	GJID				LIʾM			I-GI-ID-LI-IM		B 21 HANA
		JA	KWUN				LIʾM			IA-KU-UN-LI-IM		M+
		JA	KWUN				LIʾM			IA-KU-LI-IM		M+
		JA	MWUT				LIʾM			IA-MU-UT-LI-IM		B 28+
		JA	MWUT				LIʾM	U		IA-MU-UT-LI-MU		TCL XI 182 10
		JA	NWUḪ				LIʾM			IA-NU-UḪ-LI-IM		RA LXV 44 V 8
		JA	NWUD				LIʾM			IA-NU-UD-LI-IM		M
			NUʿM		I		LIʾM			NU-UḪ-MI-LI-IM		M+
			NAWP				LIʾM					
							MA			NA-AP-LIM-MA		RA XLIV 122+ QATNA
		JI	NBIṮ				LIʾM			I-BI-IṮ-LI-IM		ANN. ARCH. SYR. XX 74:2
		JA	NQIM				LIʾM			IA-AK-KI-IM-LI-IM		M
		JA	NQIM				LIʾM			IA-KI-IM-LI-IM		M
		JA	NŠIʾ				LIʾM			IA$_2$-ŠI-LI-IM		U+
		JA	PḪUR				LIʾM			IA-AP-ḪU-UR-LI-IM		M+, A 7630
		JA	QWIM				LIʾM			IA-KI-IM-LI-IM		M+
			QARN		I		LIʾM			QAR-NI-LI-IM		M+
		JA	RWIM				LIʾM			IA-RI-IM-LI-IM		SIMMONS 66 77, M+, C+, A.+
			RIPʾ		I		LIʾM			RI-IP-I-LI-IM		M
		JA	ŠWUB				LIʾM			IA-ŠU-UB-LI-IM		M+
			ŚUMUK				LIʾM			SU-MU-UK-LI-IM		C P. 42+
			ŚAMŚ		I		LIʾM			SA-AM-SI-LI-IM		M
			ṢIBʾ		I		LIʾM			ZI-BI-LI-IM		M
			ṮAḪD		I		LIʾM			TA-AḪ-DI-LI-IM		M
	3		ʾAḪ		I		KI					
							LIʾM			A-ḪI-KI-LI-IM		JEAN T.SIFR 72 5, 6, 13+
LIʾR	1		LIʾR	AT	UM					LI-RA-TUM	FN	A.
LIʾŠ	1		LIʾŠ	AT	UM					LI-SA-TUM	MN?	TCL X 38 6
LIWJ	1		LIWJ		UM					LI-I-UM		TA 1931, 538
			LIWJ		UM					LI-U$_2$-UM		M
			LIWJ		I		DAGAN			LI-I-D-DA-GAN		M
LIBB	2	JI	NWUḪ				LIBB	I		I-NU-UḪ-LI-BI		M
LILAR	1		LILAR		U					LI-LA-RU		SIMMONS 30 10
LILUR	1		LILUR		I					LI-LU-RI	FN	RA LXV 62 IV 66
LU	1		LU				ḪAJJ	A				
							ŠAMIʿ	UM		LU-ḪA-A-A-SA-MU-UM		UET V 569 8
			LU				ḪAJJ	A				
							ŚAMIʿ	UM		LU-ḪA-A-A-SA-MI-UM		UET V 569 17
			LU				ʿAD	UM		LU-ḪA-DU-UM		YOS XIII 497:2
			LU				ʿAN	UM		LU$_2$-A-NU-UM		U
			LU				KIʾL	A		LU$_2$-KI-LA		BASOR 95, 19
			LU				RAPIʾ			LU$_2$-RA-BI$_2$		I
			LU				RIʿAJ		HU	LU$_2$-RI-E$_2$-U$_2$		U
			LU				RIʿAJ		HU	LU$_2$-RI-ḪU		U
	2		JAʾ		UM		LU		HU	IA-UM-LU-ḪU		UET V 496:10
			ḤAM		UM		LU		HU	D-A-MU-UM-LU-U$_2$		M
			DAWD		UM		LU		HU	DA-DU-UM-LU-U$_2$		M
			ḎIMR		I		LU		HU	ZI-IM-RI-LU-U$_2$	FN	RA LXV 55 XIII 39
		JA	KWIN				LU		HU	IA-KI-IN-LU-U$_2$		TALLQUIST APN 95 LATE
			MILK		I		LU					
							ʾIL	A		MI-IL-KI-LU-I-LA		VAS XVI 10 5, 9
			ŠUWB			NA	LU		HU	ŠU-UB-NA-LU-U$_2$		M+

STEMS

LU	2		TIʾM				LU		HU	TI-IM-LU-U_2	FN	XIII 1 VIII 73+
	3		LA				RIWM					
							LU		HU	LA-RI-IM-LU-U_2		M
LUʾ	2	JI	GJIḤ				LUʾ					
							MA			I-GI-IḪ-LU-MA		SIMMONS 60 8, 14+
		JE	GJIḤ				LUʾ					
							MA			E-GI-IḪ-LU-MA		SUMER XXIII 192
		JI	GJIḤ				LUʾ					
							MA			I-GI-E-EḪ-LU-MA		JCS XXVI 143:21 HARMAL
LUʾL	1		LUʾL	AT	UM					LU-LA-TUM	MN	BM 16820 2, 11
	2		ʾAB		I		LUʾL		A	A-BI-LU-LA		SIMMONS 107 13
			BAʿL		U		LUʾL		I	BA-AḪ-LU-LU-L[I]?		HARRIS 71 14
LUʾM	2		ʾAḪ		UM		LUʾM		U	A-ḪU-UN-LU-MU		X 166 4+
			ʾAḪ		U		LUʾM		U	A-ḪU-LU-MU		M
			ʾADUN				LUʾM		U	ḪA-DU-UN-LU-MU		M
			ʾADUN				LUʾM		U	ḪA-DU-LU-MU		M
			TIʾŠ				LUʾM		U	TI-IŠ-LU-MU		M
LUʾP	1		LUʾP		U		ʾEL			LU-BU-E-EL		I
	2		KIWN		I	Š	LUʾP		A	KI-NI-IŠ-LU-BA		EDZARD, DER 94:17;95:6
LUʾUN	1		LUʾUN		UM					LU-U_2-NU-UM		TOTTEN 26 UNPUBL.
LUʾUP	1		LUʾUP		U					LU-U_2-PU		A.
LUMM	1		LUMM	AN	UM					LU-MA-NU-UM		SIMMONS 94 12+
			LUMM	AN	UM					LU-MA-A-NU-UM		SIMMONS 103 5
			LUMM	AN	UM					LUM-MA-NU-UM		SIMMONS 96 11+
			LUMM	AN	UM					LUM-MA-A-NU-UM		SIMMONS 105 16+
			LUMM		A		ʾIL			LUM-MA-IL		M+
			LUMM		A		ʾIL			LUM-MA-DINGIR		KISURRA 100 7+
			LUMM		A		ʾIL			LU-MA-DINGIR		KISURRA 104 29+
	2		ʾAŠD		I		LUMM		A	AŠ-DI-LU-MA		UCP X/3 2 31
Mʾ AD	1	JA	MʾAD							IA-AM-ḪA-AD-KI	GN	M+
		JA	MʾAD							IA-AM-A-AD	GN	A. 377 8
		JA	MʾAD		U					IA-AM-ḪA-DU	GN	XII 747 4
		JA	MʾAD		U					IA_3-A-MA-TU		U
		JA	MʾAD		UM					IA-AM-ḪA-DU-UM-KI	GN	M+
		JA	MʾAD		I					IA_3-A-MA-TI		U
		JA	MʾAD		IM					IA-AM-ḪA-DI-IM-KI	GN GEN	M+
		JA	MʾAD	AJ	I					IA-AM-ḪA-DA-I-KI	GN GEN	M
		JA	MʾAD	IJ	I					IA-AM-ḪA-DI-I-KI	GN NOM	M
		JA	MʾAD	IJ	I					IA-AM-ḪA-DI-JI	GN NOM	M
		JA	MʾAD	IJ	UM					IA_3-A-MA-TI-UM		U
MʾID	1	JA	MʾID				ʾADM		I	IA-AM-I-ID-D-AD-MI		A. 60 4
MWUʾ	1	JA	MWUʾ		A					IA-MU-U_2-A		KISURRA 33 3
MWUŠ	1	JA	MWUŠ		I		ʾIL			IA-MU-ŠI-DINGIR		B 28
		JA	MWUŠ		I		ʾIL			IA-A-MU-ŠI-DINGIR		VAS VII 166 4 LATE
MWUT	1	ʾA	MWUT				PA					
							ʾIL			A-MU-UT-PA-DINGIR		SYRIA L 7
		ʾA	MWUT				PA					
							ʾIL			AM-MU-UT-PA-DINGIR		RA XLIII 212 39 QATNA
		ʾA	MWUT				PI					
							ʾIL			A-MU-UT-BI-DINGIR		M+
		ʾA	MWUT				PI					
							ʾIL		A	A-MU-UT-BI-I-LA		M
		JA	MWUT		UM					IA_3-A-MU-TUM		U
		JA	MWUT				ḤAMAD			IA-MU-UT-ḪA-MA-AD		X 174 18
		JA	MWUT				ḤAMAD		I	IA-MU-UT-ḪA-MA-DI	FN	XIII 1 VI 51
		JA	MWUT				BAʿL			IA-MU-UT-BA-AL	GN	M+
		JA	MWUT				BAʿL		UM	IA-MU-UT-BA-LUM-KI	GN	B 28+
		JA	MWUT				BAʿL		UM	IA-MU-UT-BA-A-LUM-KI	GN	RLA II 194
		JA	MWUT				BAʿL		IM	IA-MU-UT-BA-LI-IM	GN GEN	YOS II 49 12+
		JA	MWUT				BAʿL		IM	IA-MU-UT-BA-LIM	GN GEN	BAGHD. MITT. II 56+
		JA	MWUT				BAʿL	AJ	I	IA-MU-UT-BA-LA-I	GN NOM	M
		JA	MWUT				BAʿL	AJ	I	IA-MU-UT-BA-LA-JI	GN NOM	M
		JA	MWUT				BAʿL	IJ	I	IA-MU-UT-BA-LI-I	GN ACC	M
		JE	MWUT				BAʿL		A	E-MU-UT-BA-LA	GN GEN	SAKI P. 212+
		JE	MWUT				BAʿL		UM	E-MU-UT-BA-LUM-KI	GN	B 28+
		JE	MWUT				BAʿL		UM	E-MU-UT-BA-A-LUM-KI	GN	RLA II 180

STEMS

MWUT	1	JE	MWUT				BAʿL	UM		IE-E-MU-UT-BA-LUM-KI	GN	SZLECHTER TJ 16 165
		JE	MWUT				BAʿL	IM		E-MU-UT-BA-LI-IM	GN GEN	KING 34 6+
		JA	MWUT				DAWD	U		IA-MU-UT-DA-DU		RA LXV 51 X 11
		JA	MWUT				DIWR	UM		IA-MU-UT-DI-RUM		WATERMAN 14 9
		JA	MWUT				KULUP			IA-MU-UT-KU-LU-UP		DELAPORTE, CCL II A 418
		JA	MWUT				LIʾM			IA-MU-UT-LI-IM		B 28+
		JA	MWUT				LIʾM	U		IA-MU-UT-LI-MU		TCL XI 182 10
		JA	MWUT				MIʾR	UM		IA-MU-UT-MI-RUM		RA LXV 52 X 41
		JA	MWUT				NIWR	I		IA-MU-UT-NI-RI	FN	A.
	2		ʾAB		I	JA	MWUT	A		A-BI-IA-MU-TA		BM 80328 15
			ʾAB		I	JA	MWUT	I		A-BI$_2$-A-MU-TI		U
			ʾIL		I	JA	MWUT			I$_3$-LI$_2$-IA-MU-[UT]		RA LXV 40 I 29
		JI	PTIḪ			JA	MWUT	A		IP-TI-IA-MU-TA		BM 80328 11
			ŠUM		U	JA	MWUT					
							BAʿL	A		SU-MU-IA-MU-UT-BA-[LA]		RUTTEN 3 21
			ŠUM		U	JE	MWUT					
							BAʿL	A		SU-MU-E-MU-UT-BA-LA	NOM	JCS IV 66 22
			ŠUM		U	JE	MWUT					
							BAʿL	A		SU-MU-E-MU-UT-BA-LA	GEN	JCS IV 69 17
			ŠUM		U	JE	MWUT					
							BAʿL	IM		SU-MU-E-MU-UT-BA-LIM?	GEN	JCS IV 71 9
			ŠUM		U	JA	MWUT					
							BAʿL	IM		SU-MU-IA-MU-UT-BA-LIM	GEN	CT XLIII 86 1
			ŠUM		U	JA	MWUT	U				
							BAʿL	A		[SU]-MU-IA-MU-TU-BA-LA		PBS XI/2 1 I 19
			TUPT		I	JA	MWUT	A		TU-UP-TI-IA-MU-TA		BM 80328 2
	3		LA				ʿADN	A				
						ʾA	MWUT			IA-ḪA-AD-NA-A-MU-UT		M
MA	1		MA				LA		NA			
							DITAN	A		MA-A-LA-NA-DI-TA-NA		B 34
			MA				RAʾŠ	UM		MA-A-RA-SU-UM		M
	2		ʾAḪ		UM		MA					
							ʾIL			A-ḪU-UM-MA-DINGIR		M+
			ʾAḪ	AT	I		MA			A-ḪA-TI-MA	FN	JCS XXVII 135:1
			ʾAJA				MA					
							ʾIL			A-IA-MA-DINGIR		M
			ʾAJA				MA					
							ʾIL			ḪA-IA$_3$-MA-DINGIR		XIV 93:8+
			ʾAJA				MA					
							ʾEL			A-IA-MA-EL		RA LXV 42 III 14
			ḪAʾL		I		MA			ḪA-LI-MA	FN	RA LXV 59 II 43
			ḪAʾL		I		MA					
							ʾIL			ḪA-LI$_2$-MA-DINGIR		M
			ʾAB		I		MA					
							ʾIL	I		A-BI-MA-I$_3$-LI$_2$	FN	RA LXV 64 VI 32
			ʿABD				MA					
							DAGAN			AB-DU-MA-D-DA-GAN		M+
			ʿABD				MA					
							DAGAN			ḪA-AB-DU-MA-D-DA-GAN		M+
		ʾU	WDAJ				MA			U$_2$-DA-MA		I
			ʿADN		U		MA					
							JATAR			ḪA-AD-NU-ME-TAR		M+
			ʾIL		A		MA					
							ʾAB	I		DINGIR-MA-A-BI		M
			ʾIL		A		MA					
							ʾIL	A		DINGIR-MA-I$_3$-LA		B 21+
			ʾIL		A		MA					
							ʾIL	A		DINGIR-MA-D-I-LA		B 21
			ʾIL		I		MA					
							ʾAB	I		I$_3$-LI-MA-A-BI		M+
			ʾANA				MA					
							ʾIL			A-NA-MA-DINGIR		A 29366:9
			ʾIRŠ				MA					
							ʾAB	I		I-RI-IŠ-MA-A-BI		A.
			ʾIRŠ				MA					
							ʾAB	I		I-RI-IŠ-MA-BI		A.

STEMS											
MA	2	ʾIRŠ	U		MA						
					ʾAB	I		IR-ŠU-MA-BI		A.	
		JATAM			MA						
					ʾIL			IA-TAM-MA-DINGIR		UET V 172 5'	
		BILAL	A		MA			BI-LA-LA-MA		OIP XLIII 135+	
		BIN			MA						
					ʾAḪ	IM		BI-IN-MA-A-ḪI-IM		M	
		BIN			MA						
					ʾIL			BI-MA-DINGIR		C+	
		BIN	I		MA			BI-NI-MA		A. LATE	
		BIN	I		MA						
					....			BI-NI-MA-D-....		UET V 713 7	
		BIN	I		MA						
					ʾAḪ	UM		BI-IN-NI-MA-ḪU-UM		TLB I 3 28	
		BIN	I		MA						
					ʾAḪ	UM		BI-NI-MA-ḪU-UM		CCT IV 13A 6+	CAPP.
		BIN	I		MA						
					ʾIL			BI-NI-MA-DINGIR		A. LATE	
		BIN	I		MA						
					BIʿD	I	JE	BI-NI-MA-BI-DI-E		EK I 40	
		BIN	U		MA						
					HADD	U		BI-NU-MA-D-IM		4E RENCONTRE 21	NO. 25
		BUN	A		MA						
					ʾIL			BU-NA-MA-DINGIR		XII 1 X 36	
		BUN	I		MA						
					ʾAḪ	UM		BU-NI-MA-ḪU-UM		TCL XX 96 8	
		BUN	U		MA						
					ʾAḪ	UM		BU-NU-MA-A-ḪU-UM		B 16	
		BUN	U		MA						
					HADD	U		BU-NU-MA-D-IM		M+	
		BUN	U		MA						
					ʾIL			BU-NU-MA-DINGIR		M	
		BUN	U		MA						
					ʾAŠAR			BU-NU-MA-A-ŠA-AR		KISURRA 93 4	
		BUN	U		MA						
					ʾAŠAR			BU-NU-MA-ŠAR		B 16+	
		BUN	UM		MA						
					ŠARR			BU-NU-UM-MA-ŠAR		B 16	
		DAWD	U		MA			DA-DU-MA		HARRIS 49 5	
		DARK	I		MA			DAR-KI-MA	FN	RA LXV 61 IV 14	
		ḎU			MA						
					ʾAB	I		ZU-U_2-MA-A-BI		XIV 77:17	
		ḎU			MA						
					ʾAB	I		ZU-U_2-MA?-A-BI		M	
		KANN	A		MA						
					ʾIL			KA-AN-NA-MA-DINGIR		M	
		KUNN	A		MA			[K]U-UN-NA-MA		XIV 101:8	
		LA		K	MA						
					ʾIL			LA-AK-MA-AN		B 33	
		MILK	U		MA			MI-IL-KU-MA		JCS XIII 51 292 R 10,A.LATE	
		MILK	U		MA						
					ʾIL			MI-IL-KU-MA-IL		B 35+	
		MILK	U		MA						
					ʾIL			MI-IL-KU-MA-DINGIR		C+	
		MILK	UM		MA						
					ʾIL			MIL-KUM-MA-DINGIR		A. LATE	
		MUT	UM		MA						
					ʾEL			MU-TUM-MA-EL		TA 1931, 456	
		NANIB	U		MA			NA-NI-BU-MA		SIMMONS 138 4+	
		PU			MA						
					ʾEL			PU-MA-[E]L		TA 1931,538 I	
		QAWM	U		MA						
					ʾAḪ	UM		QA-MU-MA-A-ḪU-UM		M	
		QAWM	U		MA						
					ʾAḪ	I		QA-MU-MA-A-ḪI		RA LXV 41 II 22	
		QAWM	U		MA						
					ʾIL			QA-MU-MA-DINGIR		M	

STEMS

MA	2	ŠADW		I		MA				
						ʾIL		ŠA-DI-MA-DINGIR		RA LXV 48 VIII 20
		ŠADL		U		MA		SA-AD-LU-MA		UCP X/1 P. 61+
		ŠAM		I		MA				
					JA	ŠJIM		SA-MI-MA-IA-SI-IM	FN	C+
		ZUQAT		UM		MA		ZU-KA-TUM-MA		EDZARD,DER 152 REV. 11
	3	ʾABB		I		LIʾM				
						MA		AB-BI-LIM-MA		A.+
	JI	JDAʿ				LIʾM				
						MA		I-DA-LIM-MA		B 21
		ʿADN		I		ʾIL	U			
						MA		ḪA-AD-NI-DINGIR-MA		M
		ʿAMM		I	TA	QWUM				
						MA		AM-MI-TA-KU-UM-MA		A. +
		ʾANA				ʾIL	I			
						MA		A-NA-I-LIM-MA		A.
		ʾANAKU				ʾIL	AM			
						MA		A-NA-KU-DINGIR-LAM-MA		XIII 1 II 29
		ʾANAKU				ʾIL	A			
						MA		A-NA-KU-I-LA-MA		SIMMONS 46 7+
		JIŠʿ		I		ʾIL	A			
						MA		IŠ-ḪI-DINGIR-MA		M
		JIŠʿ		I		ʾIL	A			
						MA		IŠ-ḪI-DINGIR-LA-MA		M
		JIŠʿ		I		ʾIL	U			
						MA		IŠ-ḪI-LU-MA		YOS VIII 176 20
	JI	JṢIʾ				ʾIL	U			
						MA		I-ZI-I-LU-MA		B 23+
		ḎIMR		I		ʾIL	U			
						MA		ZI-IM-RI-DINGIR-MA		M
		ḎIMR		I		ʾIL	U			
						MA		ZI-IM-RI-I-LU-MA		M
		ḎIMR		I		ʾIL	U			
						MA		ZI-IM-RI-LU-MA		SIMMONS 67 12
	JI	GJIḪ				LUʾ				
						MA		I-GI-IḪ-LU-MA		SIMMONS 60 8, 14+
	JE	GJIḪ				LUʾ				
						MA		E-GI-IḪ-LU-MA		SUMER XXIII 192
	JI	GJIḪ				LUʾ				
						MA		I-GI-E-EḪ-LU-MA		JCS XXVI 143:21 HARMAL
		KAHAL		I		ʾIL	U			
						MA		KA-A-LI-I-LU-MA		XIV 62:4+
		KAHAL		I		ʾIL	U			
						MA		KA-A-LI-DINGIR-MA		M+
		MUT				ḪAʾL	I			
						MA		MU-UT-ḪA-LI-MA		M
		NAWP				LIʾM				
						MA		NA-AP-LIM-MA		RA XLIV 122+ QATNA
MAʾJ	1	MAʾJ	AT	UM				MA-IA-TUM	FN	B 34+
	2	ʾAḪ		I		MAʾJ	UM	A-ḪI-MA-IU-UM		MAM III P. 274
		ḪANN		A		MAʾJ	A	AN-NA-MA-A-A		RUTTEN 14 15
MAʾAN	1	MAʾAN		UM				MA-A-NU-UM		KISURRA 22A 17+
		MAʾAN		UM				MA-ḪA-NU-UM		SIMMONS 96 15; M
		MAʾAN		IM				MA-ḪA-NIM	GEN	BM 72766
		MAʾAN		IJA				MA-ḪA-NI-IA	FN	M+
MAʾD	1	MAʾD	AN	UM				MA-AḪ-DA-NU-UM		I
		MAʾD		IJA				MA-DI-IA		RA LXV 55 XIII 49
		MAʾD		I		JAM	A	MA-DI-IA-MA		UCP X/1 33 10
		MAʾD		I		JAT	UM	MA-DI-IA-TUM		UCP X/1 P. 59+
	2	ʾIL		A		MAʾD	I	DINGIR-MA-DI		M
		ʾIL		I		MAʾD	A	I$_3$-LI$_2$-MA-DA		TA 30 615 6
		ʾIL		I		MAʾD	I	I$_3$-LI$_2$-MA-DI		SIMMONS 33 19
		ʾIL		I		MAʾD	I			
						ʾAḪ		I$_3$-LI$_2$-MA-DI-A-AḪ		RUTTEN 1 8
		ʾIL		I		MAʾD	I			
						ʾAḪ		DINGIR?-MA-DA-AḪ		RA LXV 42 III 21

STEMS

MAʾD	2		ʾIL		I		MAʾD	I				
							ʾAḪ			I$_3$-LI$_2$-MI-DI-AḪ		EDZARD, DER 146:14
			ʾIL		I		MAʾD	I				
							ʾAḪ	I		I$_3$-LI$_2$-MA-DA-ḪI		RUTTEN 14 7
			ʾIL		I		MAʾD	I				
							ʾAḪ	A		I$_3$-LI$_2$-MA-DA-ḪA		VAS VIII 14 4
MAʾK	2		ʾAŠD		I		MAʾK	U	HU	AŠ$_2$-DI-MA-KU-U$_2$		VAS IX 172 30
			MUT		I		MAʾK	U	HU	MU-TI-MA-KU-U$_2$		M+
MAʾL	1		MAʾL		IJA					MA-LI-IA		M
			MAʾL		I		ḪARAB	A		MA-LI-A-RA-BA?		CT II 30 29
			MAʾL		I		ŠUM	U	HU	MA-LI-SU-MU-U$_2$		TIM I 29 10
MAʾM	1		MAʾM	AT	UM					MA-MA-TUM		CT XLV 96 18
			MAʾM		IJA					MA-MI-IA		M
MAʾN	1		MAʾN	AN	UM					MA-AḪ-NA-NU-UM		HILPRECHT AV P. 91
	2		ʾANN		U		MAʾN	A		AN?-NU-MA-NA	FN	M
			KIʾL		U		MAʾN	A		KI-LU-MA-NA	FN	RA LXV 56 I 9
MAʾR	1		MAʾR	AT	UM					MA-RA-TUM	MN?	TIM I 14 3
			MAʾR	AT	IJA					MA-RA-TI-IA		HARRIS 99 13
			MAʾR	IT	UM					MA-RI-TUM	FN	XIII 1 XIII 14
			MAʾR		IJAN					MA-RI-IA-AN		RA LXV 43 III 81
			MAʾR		A		ʾEL			MA-RA-EL		TA 1931, 298
			MAʾR		A		ʾEL			URU-MA-RA-EL	GN	MRS VI 11830:10
			MAʾR		A		ʾEL			URU-MA-RA-DINGIR	GN	MRS IX 17340:7
			MAʾR		U		ZAʾT	U	HU	MA-RU-ZA-TU-U$_2$		CT XLVIII 27
MAʾŠ	1		MAʾŠ		UM					MA-ŠUM		M+
			MAʾŠ		IM					MA-ŠI-IM	GEN	M+
			MAʾŠ		AM					MA-ŠA-AM	ACC	M+
			MAʾŠ		IJA					MA-ŠI-IA		M+
			MAʾŠ	AN	IM					MA-SA-NIM	GEN	CT XLV 93 6
MAʾT	1		MAʾT	AT	UM					MA-TA-TUM	FN	CT II 50 6, 18
			MAʾT	AT	UM					MA-TA-TUM	MN?	LIH 29 9
			MAʾT	AT	IM					MA-TA-TIM	MN? GEN	VAS XVI 118 2
			MAʾT		U		BANIJ			MA-TU-BA-NI		KISURRA 112 6
	2		ʾAHL		UM		MAʾT	U		[A-LU]-UM-MA-[TU]	FN	M
			ʾAHL		UM		MAʾT	UM		[A-LU-UM]-MA-TUM	FN	M
			ʾAKK	AT			MAʾT	I		AK-KA-AD-MA-TI	FN	A. 409 22
		JA	ḪNUN				MAʾT	UM		IA-UN-MA-TUM	FN	RA L 63
			ʾIRR		I		MAʾT	U		I-RI-MA-TU		A.
			BEʿL	T	I		MAʾT	I		BE-EL-TI-MA-TI	FN	A. 253 6
			DANN		U		MAʾT	UM		DA-NU-MA-TUM		CT XLV 12:24
		TA	KWUN				MAʾT	UM		TA-KU-UN-MA-TUM	FN	M, C+
		TA	KWUN				MAʾT	I		TA-KUM-MA-TI	FN	A.+
			KIWN		I	Š	MAʾT	UM		KI-NI-IŠ-MA-TUM	FN	M+;C
			KUWN		A		MAʾT	UM		KU-NA-MA-TUM		U
		TA	RʿIŠ				MAʾT	UM		TA-RI-IŠ-MA-TUM	FN	M+, C
			ŠI				MAʾT	UM		ŠI-I-MA-TUM	FN	C+
		TA	TWUR				MAʾT	UM		TA-TU-UR-MA-TUM	FN	M+; C+
		TA	TWUR				MAʾT	UM		TA-DUR-MA-TUM	FN	XIII 1 XIV 34+
MAʾZ	1		MAʾZ	AT	UM					MA-ZA-TUM	FN	KISURRA 21 3, M
			MAʾZ	AN	UM					MA-ZA-NU-UM		UET V 625 9
			MAʾZ	AN	I					MA-ZA-NI		KISURRA 68A 10+
MAHAR	2	JA	ŠJIM				MAHAR			IA-SI-IM-MA-ḪA-AR		M
MAHIR	1		MAHIR	AH						MA-ḪI-RA	FN	XIII 1 VII 34
			MAHIR	AN	IM					MA-ḪI-RA-NIM	GEN	C II 2 8
MAHR	1		MAHR	AN	UM					[M]A-AḪ-RA-NU-UM		U
MADAG	1		MADAG	AT	UM					MA-DA?-GA-TUM	FN	IX 24 III 22
MAGAN	1		MAGAN		UM					MA-GA-NU-UM		U
			MAGAN		I					MA-GA-NI	GEN	MRS XVI P. 329 UGARIT
MAGUN	1		MAGUN	AT	UM					MA-KU-NA-TUM	FN	C+
	2		ŠEʾR		UM		MAGUN	U		ŠE-EḪ-RUM-MA-GU-NU	FN	C
MAKAJ	1		MAKAJ			JA				MA-KA-A		M+
			MAKAJ	AN						MA-KA-A-AN		RA LXV 43 IV 2+
MAKAL	1		MAKAL		UM					MA-KA-LUM		BIROT, TEA 72 V 6+
			MAKAL	AN	U					MA-KA-LA-NU		VAS IX 34 6
MAKIJ	1		MAKIJ	AT	UM					MA-KI-IA-TUM		A 7724 2
			MAKIJ	AH						MA-KI-IA	FN	M

STEMS

MAKIJ	1		MAKIJ	AN	UM							MA-KI-A-NU-UM		TA 31, 223
MALAK	1		MALAK					ʾIL		I		MA-LA-AK-I$_3$-LI$_2$		M
			MALAK		U			ʾIL				MA-LA-KU-IL		M
	2		ʾIŠḪAR	AH				MALAK		I		D-IŠ-ḪA-RA-M[A-L]A-KI	FN	RA LXV 61 IV 61
			DAGAN					MALAK		U		D-DA-GAN-MA-LA-KU	FN	RA LXV 60 III 3
			MUT		U			MALAK		A		MU-TU-MA-LA-KA		M
MALIK	1		MALIK		UM							MA-LI-KUM		U, B 34+
			MALIK		UM							MA-A-LI-KUM		KISURRA 81A 14
			MALIK		I							MA-LI-KI	GEN	B 34, A. 77 6
			MALIK	AT	UM							MA-LI-KA-TUM		BM 17060 35+
			MALIK	AT	UM							MA-LI-KA-TUM	FN	EDZARD, DER 91:3
			MALIK	AH								MA-LI-KA	FN	M
			MALIK					DAGAN				MA-LI-IK-D-DA-GAN		M
			MALIK					ŠUM		U	HU	MA-LIK-SU-MU-U$_2$		M
			MALIK					ZAʾT		UM		MA-LIK-ZA-DU-UM		B 34
	2		ʾAḪ		I	JE		MALIK				A-ḪI-E-MA-LIK		M
		JE	HWIJ					MALIK				E-WI-MA-LIK		A.
			ḪAʾL		I			MALIK				ḪA-LI$_2$-MA-LIK		M+
			ḪAʾR		I			MALIK				ḪA-RI-MA-LIK		BE VI/1 46 5
			ḪAʾR		I			MALIK		I		ḪA-RI-MA-LI-KI	GEN	B 20
			ʿABD					MALIK				ḪA-AB-DU-MA-LIK		M+
			ʿABD					MALIK				AB-DU-MA-LIK		XIII 37 16
			ʿABD					MALIK		I		AB-DU-MA-LI-KI		YOS XIII 54:5
			HADD		U			MALIK				AD-DU-MA-LIK		A. 268 4
			HADD		U			MALIK				D-IM-MA-LIK		M+
			HAND		U			MALIK				AN-DU-MA-LIK		A. 252 10
			ʾIL		I			MALIK				I$_3$-LI$_2$-MA-LIK		M
			ʾIL		U			MALIK	AJ	I		I-LU-MA-LI-KA-JI-KI	GN	XV 127
			ḤAM		I			MALIK				A-MI-MA-LIK		C
			ḤAM		UM			MALIK				D-A-MU-UM-MA-LIK		M
			ḤAM		U			MALIK				D-A-MU-MA-LIK		M
			ḤIMD		I			MALIK				ḪI-IM-DI-MA-LIK		M
			ʾARŠ		UM			MALIK				ḪA-AR?-ŠUM?-MA-LIK		M
			JATAR					MALIK				IA-TAR-MA-LIK		A.+
			DAWD		U			MALIK				DA-DU-MA-LIK		XIII 1 VI 27
			DAGAN					MALIK				D-DA-GAN-MA-LIK		M+
		JA	MZUʾ					MALIK				IA-AM-ZU-MA-LIK		B 28
			NABUʾ			HU		MALIK				D-NA-BU-U$_2$-MA-LIK		M
		JA	RWIM					MALIK				IA-RI-IM-MA-LIK		A 3580:2+
			RIPʾ		A			MALIK				RI-IP-A-MA-LIK		M
			ŠI					MALIK	T	I		ŠI-MA-LI-IK-TI		IX 294:7'
		JA	ŠWUB					MALIK				IA-ŠU-UB-D-MA-[LIK]		M
	3		LA				ʾA	HWIJ						
								MALIK				IA-AḪ-WI-MA-LIK		X 141 2
			LA				ʾA	HWIJ						
								MALIK		U		IA-AḪ-WI-MA-LI-KU		M
MALIL	1		MALIL		UM							MA-LI-LUM		B 34+
MALK	2		ʾIL		A			MALK		I		DINGIR-MA-AL-KI		A. LATE
			BIN	T	A			MALK		I		BI-IT-TA-MA-AL-KI	FN	A. LATE
MAM	1		MAM		A			ḤAṢN		I		D-MA-MA-ḪA-AZ-NI	FN	RA LXV 56 I 7
			MAM		A			DUNN		I		D-MA-MA-DU-UN-NI	FN	M
			MAM		A			NUMR		I		D-MA-MA-NU-UM-RI	FN	RA LXV 65 VII 30
			MAM		A			QUDM		I		D-MA-MA-KU-UD-ME	FN	RA LXV 59 II 18
			MAM		A			ŠARR	AH			D-MA-MA-ŠAR-RA	FN	M
			MAM		A		TA	LʾIJ				D-MA-MA-TA-AL-E	FN	M
			MAM		A			TUʾAL		I		D-MA-MA-TU-ḪA-LI	FN	M
			MAM		A			ṢIJḪ	AT	UM		MA-MA-ZI-A-TUM	FN	RA LXV 61 IV 37
	2	JI	NDIN					MAM		A		I-DIN-D-MA-MA		M+
			QIJŠ	T	I			MAM		A		KI-IŠ-TI-D-MA-MA		M+
			QIJŠ	T	I			MAM		A		KI-IŠ-TI-D-MA-AM-MA		XIV 61:5
			ŠEʾR	AH				MAM		A		ŠE-RA-D-MA-MA	FN	X 110 3
			TIWR					MAM		A		TI-IR-MA-MA		M+
			TABB		I			MAM		A		TA-BI-D-MA-MA	FN	M
	3	JA	KWUN					PI						
								MAM		A		IA-KU-UN-BI-D-MA-MA	FN	RA LXV 66 VII 61
MAMM	1		MAMM	AT	UM							[M]A-A[M]-MA-TUM	FN	RA LXV 64 VI 9

STEMS

MAMM	2			ḪAʾL		I	MAMM	A	ḪA-LI_2-D-M[A-A]M-M[A]		M
MAMN	1			MAMN		UM			MA-AM-NU-UM		I
MANAW	1			MANAW		UM			MA-NA-UM		I
				MANAW	AH				MA-NA-WA	FN	XIII 1 VII 45
MANAN	1			MANAN		UM			MA-NA-NU-UM		I
				MANAN		IM			MA-NA-NI-IM	GEN	B 46+
				MANAN		IM			MA-NA-NIM	GEN	B 46
				MANAN		IM			MA-AN-NA-NIM	GEN	B 46
				MANAN		A			MA-NA-AN-NA		M+
				MANAN	AT	UM			MA-NA-NA-TUM	FN	B 93+
				MANAN		AJA			MA-NA-NA-A		B 34+
MANIJ	1			MANIJ		UM			MA-NI-UM		U; TA 30, 615:40+
				MANIJ	AN	UM			MA?-NI-A-NU-UM		TA 1931, 538 II
				MANIJ			ʾEL		MA-NI-EL		RA VIII 72 7
				MANIJ			ʾIL		MA-NI-IL		U
				MANIJ			DAGAN		MA?-NI-D-DA-GAN		A. 6 34
MANIN	1			MANIN		UM			MA-NI-NU-UM		B 34+
				MANIN		I			MA-NI-NI	GEN	B 34+
MANMAN	1			MANMAN		UM			MA-AN-MA-NU-UM		UCP X/3 P. 199+
				MANMAN		UM			MA-MA-NU-UM		B 46+
MANN	1			MANN		AJA			MA-AN-NA-IA	FN	RA LXV 62 V 49
				MANN		IJA			MA-AN-NI-IA		M+
				MANN	AT	UM			MA-AN-NA-TUM	FN	WATERMAN 52 2+, X 2 6
				MANN	AT	UM			MA-NA-TUM	FN	BM 81479 4
				MANN	ATAN				MA-NA-TA-AN		M+
				MANN	ATANU				MA-NA-TA-NU		M
				MANN		A	....		MA-AN-N[A-....]		M
				MANN		A	BAʿL	A	MA-NA-BA-LA		M
				MANN		A	BIʿD	IM	MA-NA-BI-IḪ-DI-IM	GEN	HARRIS 3 18
				MANN			BALTI				
							ʾIL		MA-AN-BA-AL-TI-DINGIR		RA LXIV 34 NO. 24
				MANN		A	BALTI				
							ʾEL		MA-NA-BA-AL-TE-EL		B 28+
				MANN		A	BALTI				
							ʾEL		MA-NA-BA-AŠ-TE-EL		M+
				MANN		A	BALTI				
							ʾIL		MA-AN-NA-BA-AL-TI-DINGIR		M
				MANN		A	BALTI				
							ʾEL		MA-NA-BA-AL-TI-EL		KISURRA 70A 14+
				MANN		A	TAWR	I	MA-NA-TA-RI		B 34
				MANN		U	ŠAM	A	MA-NU-SA-MA		B 34
	2			KAKK		A	MANN	U	KA-AK-KA-MA-AN-NU		M
MANUW	1			MANUW		UM			MA-NU-UM		M+
				MANUW	T	UM			MA-NU-TUM	FN	CT VIII 28A 2, 4+
				MANUW	AT	UM			MA-NU-A-TUM	FN	I (UNPUBL.)
	2			LA			MANUW	UM	LA-MA-NU-UM		I, TIM III 136 4
				LA			MANUW	IM	LA-MA-NI-IM	GEN	B 46
MAQAṬ	1	JA	T	MAQAṬ					IA-AM-DA-GA-AD		B 28
MAQṬ	1	JA	T	MAQṬ		AM			IA-AM-TA-AQ-TA-AM	ACC	ABB V 39 REV 8'
MARAQ	1			MARAQ		A			MA-RA-QA	GEN	B 34
MARAR	1			MARAR		UM			MA-RA-RU-UM		WATERMAN 45 R. 12
MARAṢ	1			MARAṢ		UM			MA-RA-ZUM		I+, UET V 527 2
	2			ʾAḪ		I	MARAṢ		A-ḪI-MA-RA-AṢ		B 12+, M+
				ʾAḪ		I	MARAṢ		A-ḪI-MA-RA-UṢ		RUTTEN 1 22
				ʾAḪ		I	MARAṢ		A-ḪI-MA-RA-AṢ	FN	XIII 1 IX 24
				ḪAʾL		I	MARAṢ		ḪA-LI-MA-RA-AṢ		GEN, KICH I P. 59 NO. 219
				ḪAʾL		I	MARAṢ		ḪA-LI-MA-RA-AṢ		UET V 521 1
				ʾAB		I	MARAṢ		A-BI-MA-RA-AṢ		B 10+
		JI		JDAʿ			MARAṢ		I-DA-MA-RA-AṢ	GN	B 21+, M
		JI		JDAʿ			MARAṢ		A-DA-MA-RA-AṢ	GN	B 11
		JI		JDAʿ			MARAṢ		A-TA-MA-RA-AṢ	PN	CT II 26 3
				BIN		I	MARAṢ		BI-NI-MA-RA-AṢ		M
				BIN		I	MARAṢ	I	BI-NI-MA-RA-ZI	FN	XII 265 2
				BUN		I	MARAṢ		BU-NI-MA-RA-AṢ		C+
				ḎIKR			MARAṢ		ZI-IK-RU-MA-RA-AZ	FN	RA LXV 55 XIII 33
MARDUK	2			ḎIKR			MARDUK		[Z]I?-IK-RU-D-AMAR-UD		KUPPER, L'ICON PL II NO 8

STEMS

MARIʾ	1		MARIʾ	AN	UM					MA-RI-A-NU-UM		B 46
	2	JI	JṢIʾ			MARIʾ			JE	I-ṢI-MA-RI-E		B 22
MARMAR	1		MARMAR	AN	IM					MA-AR-MA-RA-NIM	GEN	B 93
MARṢ	1		MARṢ	AT	UM					MAR-ZA-TUM	FN	M+
			MARṢ		AJA					MA-AR-ZA-IA	FN	M
	2		ʾUMM		I	MARṢ	AT			UM-MI-MAR-ṢA-AT	FN	XIII 1 III 5
			JAT		UM	MARṢ	AT			I-IA-TUM-MA-AR-ZA-AT	FN	RA LXV 62 V 15
			JAT		UM	MARṢ	AH			IA-TUM-MAR-ZA		A 21899+
MARUʾ	1		MARUʾ			JAT		UM		MA-RU-IA-TUM		DE GEN., KICH II D 43 R. 2, 4
			MARUʾ			LI						
						ʾEL				MA-RU-LI-EL		SIMMONS 47 18, 49 22
MARUṢ	1		MARUṢ		AJA					MA-RU-ZA-IA	FN	RA LXV 61 IV 64
	2		KI			MARUṢ				KI-MA-RU-UṢ		A 3549+
MAŠḪ	1		MAŠḪ		UM					MA-AŠ-ḪU-UM		M+
			MAŠḪ		IM					MA-AŠ-ḪI-IM	GEN	M+
			MAŠḪ	AT	UM					MA-AŠ-ḪA-TUM	FN	M
MAŠAL	1		MAŠAL		UM					MA-SA-LUM		EK I P. 40
			MAŠAL		UM					MA-SA-LU-U[M]		HARRIS 95 10
MAŠD	1		MAŠD	AK	UM					MA-AŠ-DA-KUM		TA 30, 615 6
MAŠIḪ	1		MAŠIḪ		UM					MA-SI-ḪU-UM		M+
			MAŠIḪ		IM					MA-SI-ḪI-IM	GEN	M
			MAŠIḪ		A					MA-SI-ḪA	MN NOM	M
			MAŠIḪ	AN						MA-SI-ḪA-AN		XIII 1 XI 58+
MAŠIK	1		MAŠIK	T	UM					MA-SI-IK-TUM		BM 17063 26+
			MAŠIK	T	UM					MA-SI-IK-TUM	FN	XIII 1 V 73; YOS XIII 453
	2		BILL			MAŠIK		A		BI-EL-MA-SI-KA?		M
MAŠK	1		MAŠK		UM					MA-AŠ$_2$-KUM		BM 16821 8+
			MAŠK		UM					MAŠ-KUM		EBPN 123+
			MAŠK		UM					MA-AŠ$_2$-KU-UM		M
			MAŠK		U					[M]A-AŠ$_2$-KU		M
MAŠUB	1		MAŠUB	AH						MA?-SU-BA?	FN	XIII 1 III 24
MAṢIʾ	1		MAṢIʾ	AT	UM					MA-ZI-A-TUM	FN	WATERMAN 56 R. 8
	2		ṢIDQ		UM	MAṢIʾ				ZI-ID-KUM-MA-ZI		X 131 5+
MATAʿ	1		MATAʿ		A	KI						
						ʾEL				MA-TA-A-KI-EL		RA LXV 50 IX 20;HARRIS 19:5,SEAL+
MATAN	1		MATAN		I					MA-TA-NI	FN	EDZARD, DER 33:3
			MATAN		I					MA-AT-TA-NI		TIM II 99:3
MATAQ	1		MATAQ		I					MA-TA-KI	FN	CT IV 26A 1
MATIʿ	1	JA	MATIʿ			ʾIL				IA-MA-AT-TI-DINGIR		M+
		JA	MATIʿ			ʾIL				IA-MA-TI-DINGIR		XII 5 3
			MATIʿ			ʾAHL		I		MA-TI-IA-LI		UCP X/1 1 16
			MATIʿ			ʾIL				MA-TI-DINGIR		M
			MATIʿ			JAT		U	HU	MA-TI-IA-TU-U$_2$		UCP X/3 107 18
			MATIʿ			....				MA-TI-UT-TA-A-LI		SIMMONS 61 11
			MATIʿ			TIWR		UM		MA-TI-TI-RUM		BM 67281
MATIN	1		MATIN	AT						MA-TI-NA-AT		U
MATIQ	1		MATIQ		I					MA-TI-GI	FN	M+
MATQ	1		MATQ		U	NAN		A		MA-AT-KU-NA-NA	FN	RA LXV 60 III 33
MAṬAR	1		MAṬAR		UM					MA-TA-RUM		M
	2		ʾAḪ		UM	MAṬAR		I		A-ḪU-UM-MA-DA-RI		M
			ʾAJA			MAṬAR				ḪA-IA-MA-DAR		YOS XII 360 17
			ʾAJA			MAṬAR				A-IA-MA-[DAR]		YOS XII 360 SEAL
			ḪAʾL		U	MAṬAR				ḪA-LU-MA-DA-AR		M+
			ḪAʾL		UM	MAṬAR				ḪA-LUM-MA-DAR		C, SIMMONS 67 SEAL
			ḪAʾL		UM	MAṬAR		I		ḪA-LUM-MA-DA-RI		SIMMONS 67 B 11
			ḪAʾL		UM	MAṬAR		I		ḪA-LUM-MA-DAR-RI		SIMMONS 67 11
			ʾAB		I	MAṬAR				A-BI-MA-DAR		B 10+
			ʾAB		I	MAṬAR				A-BI-MA-DA-AR		TIM II 113 3
			ʾIL		A	MAṬAR				DINGIR-MA-DA-AR		OR. N.S. XXVI 28 N.4 CAPP
			ʾIL		A	MAṬAR				DINGIR-MA-TAR		M+
			ʾIL		I	MAṬAR				I$_3$-LI$_2$-MA-DA-AR		M
			ʾIL		I	MAṬAR				I$_3$-LI$_2$-MA-TAR		M
			ʾIL		I	MAṬAR				I$_3$-LI$_2$-MA-TA-AR		B 21
			ʿAMM		I	MAṬAR				AM-MI-MA-DAR		B 13 HANA
			ʿAMM		I	MAṬAR				ḪA-MI-MA-DAR	FN	C
			ʿAMM		U	MAṬAR				ḪA-MU-MA-DAR	FN	C

STEMS

MAṬAR	2		ʾARAM					MAṬAR	A	A-RA-AM-MA-DA-RA		BM 80328 1
			JIŠʿ		I			MAṬAR		IŠ-ḪI-MA-DAR		V 40 5, 16
		JA	KWUN					MAṬAR		IA-KU-MA-DAR		SYMB.BOHL P.36?:6
			ŠAʾL		U			MAṬAR		SA-LU-MA-DAR		RA LXV 52 X 68+
MAZAʾ	2		ʿADN		UM			MAZAʾ	A	ḪA-[A]D?-NU-UM-MA-ZA-A		RA LXV 41 II 52
MAZAL	1		MAZAL	AH						MA-ZA-AL-LA	FN	XIII 1 IV 40+
MAZAZ	2		ŠUM		UM			MAZAZ		ŠU-MU-UM-MA-ZA-AZ		TA 1931, 538 I, IV
MAZN	1		MAZN		UM					MA-AZ-NU-UM		MOORTGAT 345
MAZUM	1		MAZUM	AH						MA-ZU-MA	FN	XIII 1 III 22
ME	2		BAʿL		U			ME				
								NUMḪ	I	BA-LU-ME-NU-ḪI		M+
			BAʿL		U			ME				
								NUMḪ	I	BA-LU-ME-NU-UM-ḪI		IX 41 2
			BANIJ					ME				
								ʾEL		BA-NI-ME-EL		HARRIS 12 15
			DAWD		I	Š		ME				
								ʾEL		DA-DI-EŠ$_3$-ME-EL		UCP X/3 P. 198+
			DUWD		U	Š		ME				
								ʾEL		DU-DU-UŠ-ME-EL		UCP X/3 P. 198+
			DANN		I	Š		ME				
								ʾIL		DA-NI-IŠ-ME-DINGIR?		I
			MUT		I			ME				
								ʾEL		MU-TI-ME-EL		TA 30, 615:4+
			MUT		U			ME				
								ʾEL		MU-TU-ME-EL		CT VIII 31A 25+
			MUT		UM			ME				
								ʾEL		MU-TUM-ME-EL		RUTTEN 32 8+
			PU					ME				
								ʾIL		PU-ME-IL		I
			ŠAM		A			ME				
								ʾEL		SA-MA-ME-EL		M
			ŠAM		A			ME				
								ʾEL		ŠA-MA-ME-EL		TA 1931, 421
			ŠAM		I			ME				
								ʾEL		SA-MI-ME-EL		CT XLV 117 33
			ŠUM		U			ME				
								ʾEL		SU-MU-ME-EL		JCS IV 107, YBC 4968
			TIBIʾ		A	Š		ME				
								ʾEL		TI-BI$_2$-AŠ$_2$-ME-EL		CT XXXIII 48A 4
MEʾM	1		MEʾM	AT	UM					ME-MA-TUM	FN	BASOR 95, 21 I 21
MEʾN	1		MEʾN		I			ʾEL		ME-NI-EL		RA LXV 52 X 18
MEʾR	2		ʾIL		A			MEʾR		DINGIR-ME-IR		JNES XIII 210+ LATE
			ʾATT		I			MEʾR		AT?-TI-ME-IR?		IX 234 10
		JA	KWUN					MEʾR		IA-KU-UN-ME-IR		M+
			MUT		U			MEʾR		MU-TU-ME-ER		M
			NIWR					MEʾR		NI-WA-AR-ME-ER		M
			NUWR					MEʾR		NU-UR-ME-ER		M
		JI	NDIN					MEʾR		I-DIN-D-ME-ER		MAOG IV 2 2 HANA
		JA	TWUR					MEʾR		D-IA-TU-[U]R-ME-I[R]	DN	M
		JI	TWUR					MEʾR		D-I-DUR-ME-IR	DN	M+
	3		ḪANN		A		JI	TWUR				
								MEʾR		ḪA-AN-NA-D-I-DUR-ME-ER		M
			ʾIPQ		U		JI	TWUR				
								MEʾR		IP-KU-D-I-DUR-ME-ER		M
		JI	NDIN				JI	TWUR				
								MEʾR		I-DIN-D-I-DUR-ME-ER		XIII 1 III 49+
MENG	1		MENG		UM					ME-EN-GU-UM		CT XLVIII 86 REV.+
MENIJ	1		MENIJ	T	UM					ME-NI-TUM	FN	M
MENN	1		MENN	AT	UM					ME-EN-NA-TUM	FN	XIII 1 V 32
			MENN	AH						ME-EN-NA	FN	XIII 1 I 68+
			MENN		A	HA				ME-IN-NA-A	FN	X 176:8, 15
MERḪ	1		MERḪ		UM					ME-ER-ḪU-UM		M+; YOS XIII 321+
			MERḪ		IM					ME-ER-ḪI-IM	GEN	M+
MERR	1		MERR		UM					ME-ER-RUM		M+
			MERR		IM					ME-ER-RI-IM	GEN	M+
			MERR		AM					ME-ER-RA-AM	ACC	M

STEMS

MEŠIL	2	MUT			MEŠIL	I	MU-UT-ME-SI-LI		RIFTIN 45 14
MI	2	ḪAʾL		U Š	MI				
					ʾIL		ḪA-LU-UŠ-MI-DINGIR		M
		ʾAB		I	MI				
					KI		A-BI-MI-KI-DINGIR		M
		BAʿL		A	MI				
					NAMḪ	U	BA-LA-MI-NA-AM-ḪU		SYRIA XLIV 201 N.1 MARI
		PAʾAR			MI		PA-ḪA-AR-MI	FN	RA LXV 59 II 23
		RAPIʾ			MI				
					ʾIL		RA-BI-MI-IL		BIROT,TEA 72 VI 19
		RAPIʾ			MI				
					ʾIL	UM	RA-BI-MI-LUM		BIROT,TEA 72 IX 29
MIʾD	1	MIʾD	AN	UM			MI-DA-NU-UM		U+
MIʾR	2 JA	MWUT			MIʾR	UM	IA-MU-UT-MI-RUM		RA LXV 52 X 41
		MUT			MIʾR	UM	MU-UT-MI-RUM?		EDZARD, DER 89:4
MIʾŠ	1	MIʾŠ		AJA			MI-ŠA-IA		M+
MIHR	1	MIHR		I	....		ME-EḪ-RI-[....]		M
		MIHR		I	HADD	U	ME-EḪ-RI-D-IM		C+
MIWT	2	ʾIL		I	MIWT	I	I$_3$-LI$_2$-MI-TI		I
MIJA	1	MIJA			MUT	A	ME-IA-MU-TA		B 34
		MIJA			MUT	U	MI-IA-MU-DU		KISURRA 25 11
		MIJA			NAŠUʾ		MI-IA-NA-SU		XIII 1 I 18
MIGIJ	1	MIGIJ		UM			MI-GI-JU-UM		RA LXV 40 I 9
MIGN	2	ŠI			MIGN	I	ŠI-ME-IG-NI	FN	RA LXV 60 III 24
MILʾ	1	MILʾ		A	BIJT	I	MI-IL-A-BI-TI		A. 60 2
MILAL	1	MILAL		UM			MI-LA-LUM		BM 16943 36
MILK	1	MILK		U			ME-IL-KU	FN	RA LXV 61 IV 3+
		MILK		IM			MI-IL-KI-IM	GEN	B 35
		MILK	AT	UM			MI-IL-KA-TUM		TCL XI 220 11
		MILK	AT	UM			MIL-KA-TUM		YOS XIII 112:16
		MILK	AN	UM			MI-IL-GA-NU-UM		U; TA 31, 148
		MILK	AN	UM			MI-EL-GA-NU-UM		TA 1931, 538 I
		MILK	UN	IM			MI-IL-KU-NI-IM	GEN	SIMMONS 46 33
		MILK	UN	IM			MI-IL-KU-NIM	GEN	SIMMONS 70 17
		MILK		A	HADD	U	MI-IL-KA-D-IM		SYRIA XXXVII 206 27 HANA
		MILK		I	ḪAJJ	A	MIL-KI-ḪA-A-IA	FN	IRAQ XVI 40 NA
		MILK		I	HADD	U	MIL-KI-D-IM		M
		MILK		I	HADD	U	MI-IL-KI-D-IM		M
		MILK		I	ʾIL		MI-IL-KI-DINGIR		B 34
		MILK		I	ʾIL	A	MI-EL-KI-I-[LA]		UCP X/3 1 29
		MILK		I	ʾIL	U	MIL-KI-LU		B 34+
		MILK		I	ʾIL	U	MI-IL-KI-LU		B 34
		MILK		I	ʾIL	UM	MI-IL-KI-LUM		B 34
		MILK		I	JARAḪ		MIL-KI-E-RA-AḪ		AJSL XLIV 243 NO. 33
		MILK		I	DAGAN		MIL-KI-D-DA-GAN		TCL I 237 12 HANA
		MILK		I	LA				
					ʾEL		MI-IL-KI-LA-EL		TA 30 615 21
		MILK		I	LI				
					ʾEL		MI-IL-KI-LI-EL		B 34, M+
		MILK		I	LI				
					ʾEL		MIL-KI-LI-EL		VAS VIII 128 16+
		MILK		I	LI				
					ʾIL		MI-IL-KI-LI$_2$-IL		I
		MILK		I	LI				
					ʾIL		[MI]-EL-KI-LI-IL		I
		MILK		I	LI				
					ʾEL	UM	MI-IL-KI-LI-E-LUM		A 32065:3
		MILK		I	LU				
					ʾIL	A	MI-IL-KI-LU-I-LA		VAS XVI 10 5, 9
		MILK		I	TAʾG	A	MI-IL-KI-TA-GA		A. LATE
		MILK		U	DANN	UM	MI-IL-KU-DA-NU-UM		UET V 549:8
		MILK		U	MA		MI-IL-KU-MA		JCS XIII 51 292 R 10,A.LATE
		MILK		U	MA				
					ʾIL		MI-IL-KU-MA-IL		B 35+
		MILK		U	MA				
					ʾIL		MI-IL-KU-MA-DINGIR		C+

STEMS

MILK	1		MILK	UM		MA					
						ʾIL			MIL-KUM-MA-DINGIR		A. LATE
	2		ʾIL	A		MILK	UM		DINGIR-MI-IL-KUM		BAHREIN UNP.,POST-UR III
			ʾIL	I		MILK	U		I$_3$-LI$_2$-MIL-KU	FN	RA LXV 58 I 31
			ʿAŠTAR			MILK	I		EŠ$_4$-DAR-ME-IL-KI	FN	RA LXV 62 V 10
			KI			MILK	I				
						ʾEL			KI-MI-IL-KI-EL		KISURRA 112:8
			QUWJ			MILK	U		QU-U$_2$-LUGAL		MRS XII 31:24
	3		LA			ʾIL	A				
						MILK	I		LA-I-LA-MI-IL-KI		TA 30, 75 2
MIMEʾ	1		MIMEʾ	UM					MI-ME-U$_2$-UM		M
			MIMEʾ	UM					MI-IM-[ME-U$_2$-UM]		M
MINAN	1		MINAN	UM					MI-NA-NU-UM		B 46+
			MINAN	UM					MI-IN-NA-NU-UM		SIMMONS 18 1, 8
			MINAN	UM					MF-NA-NUM		KISURRA 175A 19
			MINAN	I					MI-NA-NI	GEN	B 46+
			MINAN	AH					ME-NA-AN-NA	FN	RA LXV 60 III 11
MINN	1		MINN	ATANUM					MI-NA-TA-NU-UM		HARRIS 76 11
			MINN	AH		MINN	AH		MI-IN-NA-MI-IN-NA	FN	XIII 1 XII 1
	2		MINN	AH		MINN	AH		MI-IN-NA-MI-IN-NA	FN	XIII 1 XII 1
MIQIṬ	2		LAŠU			MIQIṬ			LA-ŠU-MI-GI-IT		B 33
			LAŠU			MIQIṬ			LA-ŠU-MI-KI-IT		B 33
MISAR	1		MISAR	I					MI?-ZA-RI	FN	RA LXV 65 VI 71
MIŠR	1		MIŠR	IJA					ME-IŠ?-RI-IA	FN	RA LXV 60 III 35
MITEʿ	2	TA	KWUN			MITEʿ		JE	TA-KU-UN-MI-TE-E		M
MKUS	1	JA	MKUS	U		....			IA-AM-KU-UZ-ZU-....		BM 80328 3
MLIʾ	1	JA	MLIʾ			ʾIL			A-AM-LI-DINGIR		YOS XIII 63:3, 6
MLIK	1	JA	MLIK	AN					IA-AM-LI-KA-AN		M
		JA	MLIK			HADD	U		IA-AM-LIK-D-IM		RA LXV 40 I 31
		JA	MLIK			ʾIL			IA-AM-LI-IK-DINGIR		B 28+
		JA	MLIK			ʾIL			IA-AM-LIK-DINGIR		B 28+, M
		JA	MLIK			ʾIL			A-AM-LIK-DINGIR		HARRIS 76 22
		JI	MLIK			ʾIL			II-IM-LIK-DINGIR		B 28+
	2		ʾIL	I	JA	MLIK			I$_3$-LI$_2$-A-AM-LIK		HARRIS 49 12
			LA		ʾA	MLIK					
						ʾIL			LA-AM-LI-IK-DINGIR		RUTTEN 5 22
			LI		JI	MLIK					
						....			LI-IM-LI$_2$-LI-IK-ḪI-LI-GAL$_2$		HSM 7934, UR III
MNID	2		ŠUM	U	ʾA	MNID	IM		[SU-M]U-AM-NI-DI-IM		B 38
MQUṬ	1	JA	MQUṬ	U					IA-AM-KU-DU		M
		JA	MQUṬ	U					I-AM-KU-DU		M
MRAṢ	1	JA	MRAṢ						IA-AM-RA-AṢ		BM 81591 6
		JA	MRAṢ	UM					A-AM-RA-ZUM		HARRIS 45 10
		JA	MRAṢ			ʾIL			IA-AM-RA-AṢ-DINGIR		M+
		JA	MRAṢ	I		ʾIL			IA-AM-RA-ZI-DINGIR		M
		JU	MRAṢ			ʾIL			JU-UM-RA-AṢ-DINGIR		M+
MRUṢ	1	JA	MRUṢ			ʾIL			IA-AM-RU-UṢ-DINGIR		B 28
		JA	MRUṢ			ʾIL			IA-AM-RU-IṢ-DINGIR		M
		JA	MRUṢ	I		ʾIL	UM		I-IA-AM-RU-UṢ-ZI-I-LU-UM		B 21
MSIR	1	JA	MSIR	U					IA-AM-ZI-RU		UCP X/1 50 9
MŠIḪ	1	N	MŠIḪ			HEDD	A		NA-AM-SI-E-D-IM		A 7646 6
MŠIJ	1	JA	MŠIJ			ʾIL			IA-AM-SI-DINGIR		B 28+
		JI	MŠIJ			ʾIL			JI-IM-SI-DINGIR		M
MṢIʾ	1	JA	MṢIʾ	UM					IA-AM-ZI-JU-UM?		M
		JE	MṢIʾ	UM					IE-E-IM-ZU-UM		BIN VII 35:6
		JE	MṢIʾ	UM					E-IM-ṢI-UM		BIN VII P. 11+
		JA	MṢIʾ			ʿADN	U		IA-AM-ZI-AD-[NU]		CT VI 33A 33
		JA	MṢIʾ			ʿADN	U		IA-AM-ṢI-AD-NU		BM 16914 31
		JA	MṢIʾ			ʿADN	U		IA-AM-ZI-ḪA-AD-NU		M+
		JA	MṢIʾ			ʿADN	U	HU	IA-AM-ZI-AD-NU-U$_2$		BM 81302 4
		JA	MṢIʾ			ʿADN	U	HU	IA-AM-ZI-ḪA-AD-NU-U$_2$		DELAPORTE CCL II A 385, M+
		JA	MṢIʾ			ʾIL			IA-AM-ZI-DINGIR		B 28, M
		JA	MṢIʾ			ʾIL			IA-AM-ṢI-DINGIR		B 28+
		JE	MṢIʾ			ʾIL			IE-E-EM-ZI-DINGIR		B 25
MṬAR	1	JA	MṬAR	UM					IA-AM-TA-RU-[UM]		TIM V 63:12
MUʾ	2		DINIK			MUʾ	UM		DI-NI-IK-MU-UM		SIMMONS 39 3+

STEMS													
MUʾ	2		NANN		A			MUʾ		UM	NA-AN-NA-MU-UM		M
MUʾUT	1		MUʾUT		IJA						MU-U$_2$-TI-IA	FN	XIII 1 VII 48
MUʾZ	1		MUʾZ		UM						MU-ZU-[U]M		RA LXV 51 IX 40
			MUʾZ	AN	I						MU-ZA-NI		KISURRA 1A 3+; M
MUHR	1		MUHR	AN	UM						MU-RA-NU-UM		U
			MUHR	AT	UM						MU-UḪ-RA-TUM		BIROT, TEA 72 I 49'+
			MUHR		U			DAGAN			MU-RU-D-DA-GAN		RA LXV 53 XI 53
MUWIʾ	1		MUWIʾ		UM						MU-E-UM		U (MLC 80)
MULUK	1		MULUK	AN							MU-LU-GA-AN		RA LXV 41 II 35
	2		ʾAB		I			MULUK		I	A-BI-MU-LU-KI	FN	RA LXV 59 II 26
			ʾIL		UM			MULUK			DINGIR-MU-LU-UK-KI	GN	XV 127
			ʾIL		UM			MULUK			I-LU-UM-MU-LU-UK-KI	GN	XV 127
			ʾIL		UM			MULUK	AJ	I	DINGIR-MU-LU-KA-JI-KI	GN	XV 127
			ḪALD		A			MULUK			ḪA?-AL-DA-MU-LU-UK		BASOR 95 21
		JI	JTAR					MULUK			I-TAR-MU-LU-UK		B 23
			LAʾR					MULUK			LA-AR-MU-LU-UK	FN	XIII 1 IX 33
MUM	2		ʾAB		I	Š		MUM		U	A-BI-IŠ-MU-MU		HARRIS 98 2
MUNAN	1		MUNAN		UM						MU-NA-NU-UM		I, B 46+
			MUNAN		IM						MU-NA-NIM	GEN	B 46
			MUNAN		IM						MU-NA-NI-IM	GEN	B 46
			MUNAN	AN	UM						MU-NA-NA-NU-UM		B 46
MUNUZ	1		MUNUZ		I						MU-NU-ZI	FN	RA LXV 64 V 59
MURMUR	1		MURMUR	T	IM						MU-UR-MU-UR-TIM	FN GEN	B 49
MURR	1	ʾA	MURR		UM						A-MU-RU-UM		U
		ʾA	MURR		UM						A-MUR-RU-UM		CT II 50 21+
		ʾA	MURR		U						A-MU-UR-RU		M+
		ʾA	MURR								A-MU-RU-UḪ-ḪI		A.
	2	JI	DNIK				ʾA	MURR		UM	D-ID-NI-IK-MAR-TU	DN	U
MUŠAḪ	1		MUŠAḪ		UM						MU-SA-ḪU-UM		UET V P. 50+
			MUŠAḪ		UM						MU-SA-AḪ-ḪU-UM		UET V 722 11
MUŠAR	1		MUŠAR	AN							MU-ŠA-RA-AN		RA LXV 50 VIII 65
MUŠN	1		MUŠN		A			HADD		U	MU-UŠ-NA-A-DU		A.+
MUT	1		MUT	AN	UM						MU-DA-NU-UM		U+
			MUT	AN	UM						MU-TA-NU-UM		B 46
			MUT	AN	I						MU-TA-NI		A. 52 28
			MUT		IJA						MU-TI-IA		B 35, A.+
			MUT		UJAN						MU-TU-JA-AN		C+
			MUT					ḪAʾL		I	MU-UT-ḪA-LI		B 35 HANA
			MUT					ḪAʾL		I			
								MA			MU-UT-ḪA-LI-MA		M
			MUT					ḪAʾN		A	MU-UT-ḪA-NA		XIV 47:31
			MUT					ʾAWN	AN		MU-UT-AW-NA-AN		B 35 HANA
			MUT					ḪAʾŠ		UM	MU-UT-ḪA-SU-UM		A.
			MUT					ḪUBUR			MU-UT-ḪU-BUR		SYRIA V 271, 275
			MUT					HADD		U	MU-UT-[D]?-IM		RA LXV 41 II 17
			MUT					HADD		I	MU-TA-AD-DI		VAS XVI 165:4
			MUT					....			MU-UT-D-IGI-KUR		M
			MUT					ʾEKAL		IM	MU-UT-E$_2$-GAL-LIM		M
			MUT					ʾIL			MU-UT-DINGIR		MAOG IV 2 4 HANA
			MUT					ḪALAB			MU-UT-ḪA-LA-AB		A. 271 3
			MUT					ʾALAM		I	MU-UT-ḪA-LA-MI		C+
			MUT					ʿUMUS		IM	MU-UT-ḪU-MU-ZI-IM		XIV 122:6+
			MUT					ʿAN	AT		MU-UT-D-ḪA-NA-AT		RA LXV 52 X 65
			MUT					ʾARḪ		U	MU-UT-AR-ḪU		M
			MUT					ḪIRB	AN		MU-UT-ḪI-IR-BA?-AN		VIII 11 4
			MUT					ʾAŠD		IM	MU-UT-AŠ-DI-IM		M
			MUT				ʾA	ŠKUR			MU-UT-AŠ-KUR		M+
			MUT					ḪATK		IM	MU-UT-ḪA-AT-KI-IM		RA LXV 44 IV 57
			MUT					BIŠIR			MU-UT-BI-SI-IR		M+
			MUT					DAGAN			MU-UT-D-DA-GAN		M+
			MUT					KABID			MU-UT-GA-BI-ID		TA 30, 615 24
			MUT					KASIJ			MU-UT-KA-ZI-....		VIII 6 35'
			MUT					MIʾR		UM	MU-UT-MI-RUM?		EDZARD, DER 89:4
			MUT					MEŠIL		I	MU-UT-ME-SI-LI		RIFTIN 45 14
			MUT					NAWḪ		A	MU-UT-NA-ḪA		B 35 HANA
			MUT					NAHR		IM	MU-UT-NA-RI-IM		RA LXV 51 IX 59

STEMS

MUT	1	MUT			NAN	UM		MU-UT-NA-NU-UM		TA 30, 615:39+
		MUT			PA					
					NAZI			MU-UT-PA-A-NA-ZI		RA LXV 40 I 10
		MUT			RAWḤ			MU-UT-RA-AḪ		M
		MUT			RAWM	A		MU-UT-RA-MA		CT II 23 13
		MUT			RAWM	E	JE	MU-UT-RA-ME-E		BM 81584 3, M+
		MUT			RAWM	EM		MU-UT-RA-ME-IM		M
		MUT			RAPIʾ			MU-UT-[R]A-BI		M
		MUT			RAPŠ	IM		MU-UT-RA-AP-ŠI-IM		RA LXV 53 XI 7
		MUT			ŠAKIM			MU-UT-ŠA-KI-IM		RA LXV 55 XIII 35
		MUT			ŚALIM			MU-UT-SA-LIM		M
		MUT	A		JŠUʿ			MU-TA-ŠU-UḪ		M+
		MUT	A		NIʿM			MU-TA-NI-ḪI-IM		RA LXV 43 III 51
		MUT	A	TA	KWIN			MU-TA-TA-KI-IN		RA LXV 51 IX 78
		MUT	I		ʾAḪ	I		MU-TI-A-ḪI	GEN	B 35
		MUT	I		JAʾN	A		MU-TI-I-IA-NA		B 35
		MUT	I		JABAL			MU-TI-A-BA-AL-KI	GN	B 35+
		MUT	I		JABAL			MU-TI-BA-AL-KI	GN	B 35+
		MUT	I		JABAL			MU-TA-BA-AL-KI	GN	OIP XI 216 IV 3
		MUT	I		JABAL	A		MU-TI-A-BA-LA-KI	GN	B 35
		MUT	I		HADD	U		MU-TI-D-IM		M
		MUT	I		ʾIL	UM		MU-TI-LUM		YOS XIII 151:4+
		MUT	I		ʿAN	AT	A	MU-TI-A-N[A-T]A		B 35
		MUT	I		JARAḪ			MU-TI-A-RA-AḪ		B 35
		MUT	I		JARAḪ			MU-TI-E-RA-AḪ		M; TCL XI 224:69+
		MUT	I		JARAḪ			MU-TE-E-RA-AḪ		A 7804 13
		MUT	I		ḪURŚAN			MU-TI-ḪUR-SAG		YOS XII+
		MUT	I		ḪURŚAN	A		MU-TI-ḪU-UR-ŠA-NA		B 35+
		MUT	I		ḪURŚAN	I		MU-TI-ḪU-UR-ŠA-NI		YOS XII
		MUT	I		ḤATK	IM		MU-TI-ḪA-AD-KI-IM	NOM	IRAQ XXX 92+ RIMAH
		MUT	I	JE	ʾMIʾ			MU-TI-E-MI-IḪ		M
		MUT	I		....			[M]U?-TI-KA-ṢI-E		PBS XIII 56:8
		MUT	I		....			MU-TI-DA-ZI-U$_2$		TA 1930, 489 I
		MUT	I		ME					
					ʾEL			MU-TI-ME-EL		TA 30, 615:4+
		MUT	I		MAʾK	U	HU	MU-TI-MA-KU-U$_2$		M+
		MUT	I		ŚAMŚ			MU-TI-D-UTU		A.
		MUT	U		ʾAWN	AN	UM	MU-TU-AM-NA-NU-UM		BM 81641 3, 8
		MUT	U		ʾABIḪ			MU-TU-A-BI-I[Ḫ]		M
		MUT	U		ʾABIḪ	IM		MU-TU-A-BI-ḪI-IM		C
		MUT	U		HADD	U		MU-TU-D-IM		M
		MUT	U		ʾIL	A		MU-TU-I-LA		RA LXV 43 III 68
		MUT	U		ḤAM	I		MU-TU-D-A-MI		RA LXV 51 IX 49
		MUT	U		JAM	A		MU-TU-IA-MA		M
		MUT	U		JARAḪ			MU-TU-E-RA-AḪ		JCS XXIV 60 NO. 51 REV
		MUT	U		ʾARAPḪ	IM		MU-TU-AR-RA-AP-ḪI-IM		C+
		MUT	U		ʾAŚD	I		[MU]-TU-AŠ-DI		VIII 17 13'
		MUT	U		ḤATK	IM		MU-TU-ḪA-AD-KI-IM		M+
		MUT	U		ḤATK	IM		MU-TU-AD-KI-IM		M
		MUT	U		ḤATK	I		MU-TU-ḪA-AD-KI		M
		MUT	U	JE	JŠUʿ			M[U-T]U-E-ŠU-UḪ		RA LXV 47 VII 21
		MUT	U	JA	NŠUʾ		HU	MU-TU-A-AN-ŠU-U$_2$		KISURRA 91 24
		MUT	U		BAʿL	U	HU	MU-TU-BA-LU-U$_2$		RA LXV 44 IV 26
		MUT	U		BAWŠ	A		MU-TU-BA-SA		B 35+
		MUT	U		BIŠIR			MU-TU-BI-SI-IR		M+
		MUT	U		DAGAN			MU-TU-D-DA-GAN		CT XLIII 29 1 M+
		MUT	U		KUʾB	I		MU-TU-KU-BI		RA LXV 42 II 66
		MUT	U		KANAT	A		MU-TU-KA-NA-TA		M
		MUT	U		KUMR	I		MU-TU-KU-UM-RI		X 166 10', 13'
		MUT	U		ME					
					ʾEL			MU-TU-ME-EL		CT VIII 31A 25+
		MUT	U		MEʾR			MU-TU-ME-ER		M
		MUT	U		MALAK	A		MU-TU-MA-LA-KA		M
		MUT	U		RAWM	I	JE	MU-TU-RA-MI-E		CT XLV 63 15
		MUT	UM		ʾABIḪ			MU-TUM-A-BI-IḪ		TA 1930, 695
		MUT	UM		ʾEL			MU-TUM-E-EL		YOS VIII P. 16+

STEMS

MUT	1			MUT		UM		ʾEL				MU-TUM-EL		YOS VIII P. 16+
				MUT		UM		ʾIL				MU-TUM-DINGIR		FRANK 29 4, 10+ M+
				MUT		UM		JARIQ				MU-TUM-JA-RI-IQ		TA 1931, 104, 538
				MUT		UM		MA						
								ʾEL				MU-TUM-MA-EL		TA 1931, 456
				MUT		UM		ME						
								ʾEL				MU-TUM-ME-EL		RUTTEN 32 8+
				MUT		UM		NIʾŠ		A		MU-TUM-NI-ŠA		TA 1931, 538 III
	2			ʾAJA				MUT		I		ḪA-IA-MU-TI		BAGHD. MITT. II 7 2, 4, 8
		JI		HWIJ				MUT		I		I-WI-MU-TI		U
				ʾALLA				MUT	IJ	I		AL-LA-MU-TI-I	TRIBE	4E RENC. ASS. P. 178 9
				ʾALLA				MUT	IJ	I		A-AL-MU-TI-I	TRIBE	M
				DIWIR				MUT		I		DI-WI-IR-MU-TI		PBS XI/1 P. 55+
				DIWIR				MUT		I		DI-BI-IR-A-MU-TI		PBS XI/1 P. 55+
				MIJA				MUT		A		ME-IA-MU-TA		B 34
				MIJA				MUT		U		MI-IA-MU-DU		KISURRA 25 11
				ŠUM		U		MUT		I				
								JABAL		A		SU-MU-MU-TI-A-BA-LA		B 39
MUTT	1			MUTT	IJ	UM						MU-UT-TI-JU-UM		M
				MUTT		UJAN						MU-UT-TU-IA-AN		RA LXV 50 IX 18
MZUʾ	1	JE		MZUʾ		UM						E-IM-ZU-UM		BIN VII P. 11+
		JE		MZUʾ		UM						IE-E-EM-ZU-UM		B 25+
		JA		MZUʾ				ʿADN		IM		[IA?-AM?-Z]U?-ḪA-AD-NIM	GEN	XIII 129 5
		JA		MZUʾ				ʿADN		U	HU	IA-AM-ZU-AD-NU-U_2		B 28+
		JA		MZUʾ				MALIK				IA-AM-ZU-MA-LIK		B 28
NḪIM	1	ME		NḪIM		UM						ME-EN-ḪI-MU-UM		HARRIS 57 17
NḪAB	1	JA		NḪAB		UM						IA-ḪA-BU-UM		YOS XII
		JA		NḪAB				ʾIL				IA-AḪ-ḪA-AB-DINGIR		C+
		JA		NḪAB				ʿAMM		U		IA-ḪA-AB-ḪA-MU		M
		TA		NḪAB	AT	UM						TA-ḪA-BA-TUM	FN	VAS VIII 127 2, 29
		TA		NḪAB	AT	I						TA-ḪA-BA-TI	FN GEN	VAS VIII 127 2
NḪAN	1	JA		NḪAN		A						IA-AN-ḪA-NA	GEN	MRS VI P. 334
NḪIJ	1	ME		NḪIJ		UM						ME-EN-ḪI-I-UM		XIII 105 8
NḪIB	1	JA		NḪIB		UM						IA-ḪI-BU-UM		SIMMONS 46 3
		ME		NḪIB	AH							ME-EN-ḪI-BA	FN	XIII 1 I 24
NḪIN	1	JE		NḪIN		UM						IE-EN-ḪI-NU-UM		B 25
NḪIR	1	JA		NḪIR		AJA						A-AN?-ḪI?-RA-A		HARRIS 85 16
NḪUR	1	JA		NḪUR		UM						IA-AN-ḪU-RU-UM		SIMMONS 103 2
NWAḪ	1	JI	N	NWAḪ	AN							IN-NA-ḪA-AN		M+
NWAB	1	JI	N	NWAB	AT	UM						IN-NA-BA-TUM	FN	CT VI 17 13+
		JI	N	NWAB	AT	UM						IN-NA-BA-A-TUM	FN	CT VI 1A 3
		JI	N	NWAB	AT	IM						IN-NA-BA-TIM	FN GEN	CT VI 17 2
NWIḪ	1	JE		NWIḪ		UM						E-NI-ḪU-UM		CT VIII 28C 4
		JA		NWIḪ	AH							IA-NI-ḪA	FN	RA LXV 58 I 55
		ME		NWIḪ		UM						ME-NI-ḪU-UM		BIN II 94 4+
		MI		NWIḪ		UM						MI-NI-ḪU-UM		YOS XII
		MI		NWIḪ		U						MI-NI-ḪU		TIM V 62 13
		MA		NWIḪ	AH							MA-NI-ḪA	FN	RA LXV 58 I 36+
NWIB	1	JI	N	NWIB		UM						IN-NI-BU-UM		M
		JI	N	NWIB		U						IN-NI-BU		YOS XIII 191:2+
		JI	N	NWIB		U						IN-NE-BU		M
		JI	N	NWIB		I						IN-NI-BI		CLAY PNCP 90+
NWUḪ	1	JA		NWUḪ	AN							IA-NU-ḪA-AN		RA LXV 40 I 43
		JI		NWUḪ				DITAN				I-NU-UḪ-DI-TA-AN		GORDON 38 20+
		JA		NWUḪ				LIʾM				IA-NU-UḪ-LI-IM		RA LXV 44 V 8
		JI		NWUḪ				LIBB		I		I-NU-UḪ-LI-BI		M
		JA		NWUḪ				ŠAMAR				IA-NU-UḪ-SA-MAR		CT XLIII 58 3, M
		JI		NWUḪ				ŠAMAR				I-NU-$UḪ_3$-SA-MAR		BIN VII 7 4,9+
		JI		NWUḪ				ŠAMAR				I-NU-UḪ-SA-MAR		TCL I 74 5,18
		TA		NWUḪ	AH							TA-NU-ḪA	FN	M
		TA		NWUḪ				NAWIJ		UM		TA-NU-UḪ-NA-WI-UM	FN	M
	2			ʾAḪ		I	TA	NWUḪ		A		A-ḪI-TA-NU-A		M
		JA		HWIJ			TA	NWUḪ				IA-WI?-TA-NU		RA LXV 43 III 64
				ḪAʾL		I	TA	NWUḪ		A		ḪA-LI-TA-NU-A		A.+
				ʾIL		I	TA	NWUḪ				I_3-LI_2-TA-NU-UḪ		XIII 1 IV 19
				ʾIL		I	TA	NWUḪ				I_3-LI_2-TA-NU		RA LXV 45 V 52

STEMS

NWUḪ	2		ḪAM		I	TA	NWUḪ			D-A-MI-TA-NU-UḪ		M+
			ḪAM		I	TA	NWUḪ			D-A-MI-TA-NU		M
			ḪAM		I	TA	NWUḪ	A		D-A-MI-TA-NU-A		M
			ḪAM		U	TA	NWUḪ			D-A-MU-TA-NU		M
			ḪAM		UM	TA	NWUḪ		HU	A-MU-UM-TA-NU-U_2		M
			ŠAQAḪ			TA	NWUḪ		HU	SA-QA-AḪ-TA-NU-U_2		CT VI 46 2
NWUD	1	JA	NWUD				....			IA-NU-UD-[....]		M
		JA	NWUD				LIʾM			IA-NU-UD-LI-IM		M
		TA	NWUD	AH						TA-NU-DA	FN	RA LXV 61 IV 45
NWUP	1	JA	NWUP		UM					IA-NU-BU-UM		B 29+
NWUR	1	JA	NWUR		UM					IA-NU-RU-UM		RUTTEN 11 10+
NWUZ	1	JA	NWUZ		UM					IA_2-A-NU-ZU-UM		U
		JE	NWUZ		UM					E-NU-ZU-UM		I
NAʾJ	1		NAʾJ	AT	UM					NA-JA-TUM	FN	KISURRA 59A:4
NAʾAŠ	1		NAʾAŠ		UM					NA-A-ŠU-UM	FN	RA LXV 58 I 57
NAʾD	2		DAGAN				NAʾD	I		D-DA-GAN-NA-DI	FN	XIII 1 III 17+
			KUMM		I		NAʾD	A		KU-UM-MI-NA-DA		JCS IV 113
NAʾUL	1		NAʾUL		UM					NA-U_2-LU-UM		TA 1931, 297, 538
NAHR	1		NAHR		IM					NA-RI-IM	GEN	A.
			NAHR	AN	UM					NA-RA-NU-UM		B 47
			NAHR				BAJAN			D-ID_2-BA-IA-AN		A 21929 5,12
			NAHR				ṢUWR	I		D-ID_2-ZU-RI		M
	2		ʿABD				NAHR			AB-DI-D-ID_2		SCHEIL 10 15, 16
			ʾUMM		I		NAHR	U		UM-MI-NA-RU	FN	M
			BIN				NAHR	UM		BI-IN-NA-RUM		CT VI 23 5+
			BIN				NAHR	UM		BI-NA-RU-UM		BIN VII 67 27+
			BIN				NAHR	I		BI-IN-NA-A-R[I]?		M
			KIWN				NAHR	IM		KI-IN-NA-RI-IM	GEN	M+
			MUT				NAHR	IM		MU-UT-NA-RI-IM		RA LXV 51 IX 59
		JA	ŠWUB				NAHR			IA-ŠU-UB-NA-AR		M+
		JA	TWUR				NAHR	UM		IA-DUR-NA-RUM?		RA LXV 48 VII 72
NAḪAL	1		NAḪAL		I					NA-ḪA-LI	FN	IX 291 30
NAḪL	1		NAḪL		I		ʾIL	UM		NA-AḪ-LI-LUM		B 36+
NAḪAR	1		NAḪAR	AH						NA-ḪA-RA	FN	RA LXV 60 III 36
NAḪN	1		NAḪN		I		ʾIL			NA-AḪ-NI-DINGIR		TIM III 86:5
NAʿIM	1		NAʿIM		UM					NA-ḪI-MU-UM		B 36+
			NAʿIM		U					NA-I-MU		B 36+
			NAʿIM		IM					NA-ḪI-MI-IM	GEN	B 36
			NAʿIM		I					NA-ḪI-MI	GEN	B 36
	2	JA	NBIʾ				NAʿIM			I-A-BI-NA-IM	NOM, GEN	BAHREIN UNPUB, POST U.
NAʿM	1		NAʿM		IM					NA-AḪ-MI-IM	GEN	M
			NAʿM		I					NA-AḪ-MI	GEN	M
			NAʿM	AN	U					NA-AḪ-MA-NU		M+
			NAʿM	AN	IM					NA-MA-NI-IM	GEN	TIM III 46 15
			NAʿM		IJA					NA-MI-IA	FN	CT XLV 3 8,15,23
			NAʿM		IJA					NA-AḪ-MI-IA		JCS XXVI 142:8 HARMAL
			NAʿM		A		ʾEL			NA-MA-EL		TA 30 615:11+
			NAʿM		I		ʿAN	IM		NA-MI-A-NIM		A. 142
			NAʿM		I		JARAḪ			NA-AḪ-MI-E-RA-AḪ		JCS XI 29 NO.17 5
			NAʿM		I		ʾAŠD	U		NA-AḪ-ME-AS-DU	FN	RA LXV 60 III 2
			NAʿM		I		JAT	UM		NA-MI-IA-TUM	MN	MEISSNER 100 2
			NAʿM		I		DAʾK	A		NA-MI-DA-KA		A. 242 7
			NAʿM		I		DAGAN			NA-AḪ-MI-D-DA-GAN		A.+
			NAʿM		I		DAGAN			NA-MI-D-DA-GAN		A.+
			NAʿM		I		DAGAN			NA-AḪ-ME-D-DA-GAN		RA LXV 48 VIII 33
			NAʿM		UM		DAGAN			NA-AḪ-MU-UM-D-DA-GAN		BM 16824 28+
	2		ʾAḪ	AT	A		NAʿM	I		A-ḪA-TA-NA-AḪ-MI	FN	XIII 1 XI 3
			ʾAB		I		NAʿM	I		A-BI-NA-AḪ-MI	FN	XIII 1 VII 43, A.+
			ʾAB		I		NAʿM	I		A-BI-NA-AḪ-ME	FN	RA LXV 59 II 20
			ʾIL		A		NAʿM	A		DINGIR-NA-MA-....		VAS VIII 14 44
			ʾUMM		I		NAʿM	I		UM-MI-NA-MI	FN	A.
			ʾUMM		I		NAʿM	I		UM-MI-NA-AḪ-ME	FN	RA LXV 59 II 17
			ʾIŠḪAR	AH			NAʿM	I		D-IŠ-ḪA-RA-NA-AḪ-ME	FN	RA LXV 64 VI 37
			DAGAN				NAʿM	I		D-DA-GAN-NA-AḪ-MI	FN	X 116 1, 22
			KAKK		A		NAʿM	I		KA-AK-KA-NA-AḪ-MI	FN	XIII 1 VII 30
			PI				NAʿM					
							ʾEL			BI-NA-AḪ-ME-EL		B 15

STEMS												
NAWḪ	1		NAWḪ	AN						NA-ḪA-AN	TRIBE	M
			NAWḪ	AN	UM					NA-ḪA-NU-UM		U
			NAWḪ		AJA					NA-ḪA-IA		B 35
			NAWḪ		I		ʾIL			NA-ḪI-DINGIR		B 35+
			NAWḪ				ʾIL	I		NA-ḪI-LI		B 35
			NAWḪ				ʾIL	UM		NA-ḪI-LUM		B 35+
			NAWḪ				ʾIL	UM		NA-ḪI-LU-UM		B 35
			NAWḪ				ʾIL	IM		NA-ḪI-LI-IM	GEN	B 35
			NAWḪ		I		ʾIMM	I		D-NA-ḪI-IM-MI		YOS II 112 11
			NAWḪ		UM		DAGAN			NA-ḪU-UM-D-DA-GAN		B 36+
	2		MUT				NAWḪ	A		MU-UT-NA-ḪA		B 35 HANA
NAWAR	1		NAWAR		I					NA-WA-RI?		RA LXV 53 XI 55
			NAWAR				HADD	U		NA-WA-AR-D-IM		RA LXV 50 VIII 55+
			NAWAR			JE	JŠAR			NA-WA-AR-E-ŠAR	FN	XIII 1 VI 40
	2		ʿABD				NAWAR			ḪA-AB-DU-NA-WA-AR		M
			ʿABD				NAWAR			AB-DU-NA-W[A-AR]		M
			ʾUMM		I		NAWAR			UM-MI-NA-WA-AR	FN	XIII 1 IV 73
NAWIJ	2		BUN		U		NAWIJ	E		BU-NU-NA-WI-E		CT XLVIII 56 REV.11
		TA	NWUḪ				NAWIJ	UM		TA-NU-UḪ-NA-WI-UM	FN	M
NAWP	1		NAWP				LIʾM					
							MA			NA-AP-LIM-MA		RA XLIV 122+ ÇATNA
			NAWP				ŠAMŠ			NA-AP-D-UTU		M
NAJAL	1		NAJAL		AM					NA-JA-LAM		RA LXV 40 I 33
NABAʾ	1		NABAʾ		IM					NA-BA-I-IM	GEN	M+
			NABAʾ		IM					NA-BA-JI-IM	GEN	VIII 39 4
NABAŚ	1		NABAŚ	AN	UM					NA-BA-SA-NUM		BM 17072 9,12+
NABIʾ	1	JA	NABIʾ		IM					IA-NA-BI-IM	GEN	M
		JA	NABIʾ				ʾEL			IA-NA-BI-EL		M+
		JA	NABIʾ				ʾIL			IA-NA-AB-BI-DINGIR		M+
		JA	NABIʾ				ʾIL			IA-NA-BI-DINGIR		M
			NABIʾ		UM					NA-BI-UM		TA 1931, 538 V
			NABIʾ				ʾIL	I		NA-BI-I_3-LI_2		XIII 1 III 61
			NABIʾ				ʾILL	I		NA-BI-IL-LI		SYRIA V 274 HANA
			NABIʾ				ʾANN	U		NA-BI-AN-NU		M
			NABIʾ				KAKK	A		NA-BI-KA-KA		M+
			NABIʾ				ŠAMŠ			NA-BI-D-UTU		M+
	2		ʾANN		U		NABIʾ			AN-NU-NA-BI-IḪ	FN	RA LXV 62 V 24
NABIB	1		NABIB		I					NA-BI-BI		M
NABIT	2		ʾANN		U		NABIT	I		AN-NU-NA-BI-TI		XIII 1 VI 61
			ʾATTA				NABIT	I		A-TA-NA-BE-TI		JCS XIII 57 306:5+,A LATE
NABL	1		NABL	AN	UM					NA-AB-LA-NU-UM		U+, B 46+
			NABL	AN	UM					NA-AB-LA-NUM_2		U+
NABUʾ	1		NABUʾ			HU	MALIK			D-NA-BU-U_2-MA-LIK		M
	2		JIŠʿ		I		NABUʾ	UM		IŠ-ḪI-NA-BU-U[M]		EDZARD, DER 68 III 6
		JI	JṢIʾ				NABUʾ	UM		I-ZI-NA-B[U-U]M?		VAS IX 79 5
		JI	JṢIʾ				NABUʾ		HU	I-ZI-NA-BU-U_2		B 23+, M+
		JI	NBIʾ				NABUʾ		HU	I-BI-NA-BU-U_2		A 7685 13
NABUṬ	1		NABUṬ		UM					NA-BU-TUM		UET V P. 50+
			NABUṬ		IJA					NA-BU-DI-IA		TCL XVIII 125 3
	2		ʾIL		A		NABUṬ			DINGIR-NA-BU-UD		VAS VIII 14 31
NADIN	1		NADIN		A					NA-DI-NA	GEN	A.+
NADUB	1		NADUB		UM					NA-DU-BU-UM		B 35
			NADUB	AH						NA-DU-BA?	FN	XIII 1 VIII 32+
			NADUB				ʾEL	I		NA-DU-BE-LI_2		U
NAGIH	1		NAGIH		UM					NA-KI-ḪU-UM		TIM III 31 17+
			NAGIH		IM					NA-KI-ḪI-IM	GEN	TIM III 77 5A
			NAGIH	AH						NA-GI-IA	FN	XIII 1 V 82
			NAGIH	AN	UM					NA-GI_4-A-NU-UM		TA 30 615 13
NAGIŚ	1		NAGIŚ	AN	UM					NA-GI_4-SA-NU-UM		RUTTEN 2 8+
			NAGIŚ	AN	UM					NA-GI-SA-NU-UM		RUTTEN 5 8
NAKAM	1		NAKAM	T	UM					NA-KA-AM-TUM	FN	M
NAKAR	1		NAKAR		UM					NA-KA-RU-UM		BIROT, TEA 70A II 14+
			NAKAR		UM					NA-KA-RUM		BM 16914 3,11+
			NAKAR	AH						NA-KA-RA	FN	XIII 1 VIII 19
			NAKAR	AT	UM					NA-KA-RA-TUM	FN	RA LXV 59 II 71
			NAKAR	T	UM					NA-KA-AR-TUM	FN	M

STEMS

NAKL	1		NAKL		UM				NA-AK-LUM		BIROT, TEA 69 III 2
			NAKL	AT	UM				NA-AK-LA-TUM	FN	YOS XIII 90 REV 22
NAKR	1		NAKR				ˀAḪ	UM	NA-AK-RA-ḪU-UM		RUTTEN 2 19+
NAMḪ	1		NAMḪ		U	HU			NAM-ḪU-U$_2$		BM 80328 8
	3		BAˁL		A		MI				
							NAMḪ	U	BA-LA-MI-NA-AM-ḪU		SYRIA XLIV 201 N.1 MARI
NAMAL	1		NAMAL		UM				NA-MA-LUM		HARRIS 7 12
			NAMAL	AT	UM				NA-MA-LA-TUM	MN	B 36+
NAMAŠ	1		NAMAŠ		U				NA-MA-ŠU		B 36 HANA
			NAMAŠ		I				NA-MA-ŠI		MAOG IV 3 30 HANA
NAMIŠ	1		NAMIŠ		UM				NA?-MI-ŠUM		XIII 1 VIII 47
			NAMIŠ		U				NA-MI-ŠU		B 36 HANA
			NAMIŠ		A				NA-MI-ŠA	GEN	MAOG IV 3 34 HANA
NAMR	1		NAMR	AT	UM				NA-AM-RA-TUM	FN	YOS XIII 163:7
NAMZ	1		NAMZ		U	HU			NAM-ZU-U$_2$		BM 80328 5
NAN	1		NAN		I				D-NA-NI	DN	M
			NAN	AT	UM				NA-NA-TUM	FN	RA LXV 65 VI 57
			NAN		IJA				NA-NI-IA	FN	RA LXV 60 III 66
	2		ˀAB		U		NAN	UM	A-BU-NA-NU-UM		B 42+
		ˀA	JPAˁ				NAN	UM	A-BA-AḪ-NA-NU-UM		TA 1931, 374, EARLY OB
			ˁAQB		I		NAN	UM	AQ-BI-NA-NU-UM		B 42+
		JA	JTIR				NAN	UM	JA-TI-IR-NA-NU-UM		M+
		JA	JTIR				NAN	AM	JA-TI-IR-NA-NAM	ACC	M
		JA	JTIR				NAN	AM	JA-TE-IR-NA-NAM	ACC	M
		JA	JTIR				NAN	IM	JA-TI-IR-NA-NIM	GEN	M+
		JA	JTIR				NAN	IM	JA-TE-IR-NA-NIM	GEN	M
			ḪAZAQ				NAN	UM	A-ZA-AQ-NA-NU-UM		CT IV 50A 21
			MUT				NAN	UM	MU-UT-NA-NU-UM		TA 30, 615:38+
			MATQ		U		NAN	A	MA-AT-KU-NA-NA	FN	RA LXV 60 III 33
		TA	QJIŠ				NAN	I	TA-KI-IŠ-NA-NI	FN?	TIM III 41 6
NANIB	1		NANIB		UM				NA-NI-BU-UM		SIMMONS 138 29
			NANIB		U		MA		NA-NI-BU-MA		SIMMONS 138 4+
NANN	1		NANN	AH					NA-AN-NA	FN	M+
			NANN	ATAN					NA-NA-TA-AN		M
			NANN		A		MUˀ	UM	NA-AN-NA-MU-UM		M
			NANN		IJA				NA-AN-NI-IA	FN	XIII 1 I 66
			NANN		I		ŠARR	AH	D-NA-AN-NI-ŠAR-RA	FN	XIII 1 V 31
NAPŠ	1		NAPŠ		UM				NA-AP-SU-UM		SIMMONS 36B 6+, M
			NAPŠ		UM				NA-AP-ZUM		SIMMONS 36 7
			NAPŠ		UM				NA-AP-SU-UM	FN	RA LXV 59 II 47
			NAPŠ	AN	UM				NA-AP-SA-NU-UM		U, B 46+
			NAPŠ	AN	UM				NA-AP-ŠA-NU-UM		U+, I+
			NAPŠ	AN	U				NA-AP-SA-NU-KI	GN	B 46
			NAPŠ	AN	UM				NA-AP-ZA-NU-UM		CT XLV 115 14
			NAPŠ		IJA				NA-AP-SI-IA		M
			NAPŠ		I		HADD	U	NA-AP-SI-D-IM		M+
			NAPŠ		I		HADD	U	NA-AP-ŠI-A-DU		A.+
			NAPŠ		I		HAND	U	NA-AP-SI-IA-AN-DU		M
			NAPŠ		I		ḪINN	I	NA-AP-SI-IN-NI	FN	XIII 1 IV 72
			NAPŠ		I		JARAḪ		NA-AP-SI-E-RA-AḪ		M+
			NAPŠ		I		DAGAN		NA-AP-SI-D-DA-GAN		M+
			NAPŠ		I		FI				
							ˀIL		NA-AP-SI-BI-DINGIR		SYRIA XLVIII 9:22
			NAPŠ		I		ŠEˀR	UM	NA-AP-SI-ŠE?-RUM?		M
			NAPŠ		U		HADD	U	NA-AP-SU-D-IM		M
			NAPŠ		U	NA	HADD	U	NA-AP-SU-NA-D-IM		M+
			NAPŠ		U	NA	DAWR	A	NA-AP-SU-NA-D-DA-RA		CT IV 1 8
	2	TA	HWIJ				NAPŠ	U	TA-AḪ-WI-NA-AP-SU		RA LXIV 28 NO. 14
			ˀAB		I		NAPŠ	I	A-BI-NA-AP-S[I]		XIV 77:7
			ˀIŠḪAR	AH			NAPŠ	I	D-IŠ-ḪA-RA-NA-AP-SI	FN	XIII 1 VII 13
			LAˀR				NAPŠ	U	LA-AR-NA-AP-SU	FN	XIII 1 I 71
NAQIM	1	JA T	NAQIM						IA-AN-TA-KI-IM		M+
			NAQIM		UM				NA-KI-MU-UM		B 36+
			NAQIM		U				NA-KI-MU		B 36+
			NAQIM		IM				NA-KI-MI-IM	GEN	B 36+
NARB	1		NARB		U				NA-AR-BU		XIII 1 II 32

STEMS

NARB	1		NARB	AT	UM							NA-AR-BA-TUM	FN	M+
			NARB	AN	IM							NA-AR-BA-NIM	GEN	A 21950
NASQ	1		NASQ	AT	UM							NA-AS-QA-TUM	FN	RA LXV 58 I 38
NAŠʾ	1		NAŠʾ	AT	UM							NA-AŠ-ḪA-TUM	FN	RA LXV 61 IV 33
NAŠIʾ	2	JA	HWIJ					NAŠIʾ				IA-AḪ-WI-NA-SI		M+
		JA	DWUR					NAŠIʾ				IA-DU-UR-NA-SI		M+
	3		NIQM		I			LA						
								NAŠIʾ				NI-IQ-MI-LA-NA-SI		M
			ṢIDQ		U			LA						
								NAŠIʾ				ZI-ID-KU-LA-NA-SI		M+
NAŠUʾ	2		LA					NAŠUʾ		UM		LA-NA-SU-U$_2$-UM		M
			LA					NAŠUʾ		UM		LA-NA-SU-WU-UM		XIV 53:20+
			LA					NAŠUʾ		U		LA-NA-SU-U$_2$		B 33, 4E RENC. ASS. P. 178 8
			LA					NAŠUʾ		IM		LA-NA-SU-I-IM	GEN	M
			LA					NAŠUʾ		IM		LA-A-NA-SU-I-IM	GEN	M
			LA					NAŠUʾ		I		LA-NA-SU-JI	GEN	M
			LA					NAŠUʾ		I		LA-NI-SU-JI	FN NOM	M
			MIJA					NAŠUʾ				MI-IA-NA-SU		XIII 1 I 18
NAŠP	1		NAŠP	AT	UM							NA-AŠ-PA-TUM	FN	CT II 35 28+
NAṢAB	1		NAṢAB	AN	UM							NA-ZA-BA-NU-UM		TCL I 111 3
NAṢB	1		NAṢB		UM							NA-AZ-BU-UM	FN	RA LXV 64 VI 25
NAṢIR	2		JAD		I			NAṢIR				IA-DI-NA-ṢIR		BM 17051, 17052
			ʾAŠAR					NAṢIR				D-A-ŠAR-NA-ṢIR		M
			DAGAN					NAṢIR				D-DA-GAN-NA-ṢIR		RA LXV 52 X 76
NAṢR	1		NAṢR		IJA							NA-AṢ-RI-IA		RA LXV 44 IV 47+
NATT	1		NATT		A							NA-AT-TA		M
NATUN	1		NATUN		UM							NA-TU-NU-UM		B 36
NATUN	2		ʾIL		I			NATUN				I$_3$-LI$_2$-NA-TU-UN		M
NAZI	2		ʾIPQ		U			NAZI				IP-KU-D-NA-AZ-ZI		M
		JA	JTIR					NAZI				JA-TE-IR-NA-ZI		SYRIA XX 174 MARI
	3		MUT					PA						
								NAZI				MU-UT-PA-A-NA-ZI		RA LXV 40 I 10
NBIʾ	1	JA	NBIʾ					HADD		U		IA-AB-BI-D-IM		M
		JA	NBIʾ					ʾIL		UM		IA'$_2$-AN-BI$_2$-I$_3$-LUM		U
		JA	NBIʾ					DAGAN				IA-AB-BI-D-DA-GAN		M+
		JA	NBIʾ					DAGAN				IA-BI-D-DA-GAN		M
		JI	NBIʾ					DAGAN				I-BI-D-DA-GAN		M
		JA	NBIʾ					NAʿIM				I-A-BI-NA-IM	NOM, GEN	BAHREIN UNPUB, POST U.
		JI	NBIʾ					NABUʾ			HU	I-BI-NA-BU-U$_2$		A 7685 13
NBIṬ	1	JI	NBIṬ					LIʾM				I-BI-IṬ-LI-IM		ANN. ARCH. SYR. XX 74:2
		JE	NBIṬ					TIŠPAK				I-EN-BI-IṬ-D-TIŠPAK		JCS XXIV 49 NO. 15:3
NBUL	1	JA	NBUL		I							IA$_2$-AN-BU-LI		U
NDIB	1	ME	NDIB		UM							ME-EN-DI-BU-UM		KING LIH I 25 4
NDIN	1	JI	NDIN		UM							IN-DIN-NU-UM		I
		JI	NDIN		U							ID-DI-NU		XIII 1 I 47
		JI	NDIN		A							ID-DI-NA		A.
		JI	NDIN			JA						I-DIN-IA		M
		JI	NDIN					ʾABB		A		I-DIN-AB-BA		XIII 1 VIII 46
		JI	NDIN					ʾABB		A		ID-DI-NA-AB-BA		A.
		JI	NDIN					ʾABB		A		ID-DI-NA-BA		A. LATE
		JI	NDIN					ʾADM		U		I-DIN-D-AD-MU		M+
		JI	NDIN					....				I-DIN-D-IGI-KUR		M+
		JI	NDIN					ʾAKK		A		I-DIN-AK-KA		XIII 1 I 54+
		JI	NDIN					ʾANN		U		I-DIN-AN-NU		M+
		JI	NDIN					ʾANN		UM		I-DIN-AN-NU-UM		M+
		JI	NDIN					ʾANN		U		I-DI-AN-NU		RA LXV 51 IX 31
		JI	NDIN					JAT		UM		I-DIN-IA-TUM		M+
		JI	NDIN					JAT		IM		I-DIN-IA-TIM	GEN	M+
		JI	NDIN					JAT		IM		ID-DI-IA-TIM	GEN	M
		JI	NDIN					JAT		AM		I-DIN-IA-TAM	ACC	XIV 64:7
		JI	NDIN				ʾA	ŠKUR				I-DIN-D-AŠ$_2$-KU-UR		SYRIA XXXVII 206 8 HANA
		JI	NDIN				JI	TWUR						
								MEʾR				I-DIN-D-I-DUR-ME-ER		XIII 1 III 49+
		JI	NDIN					BIN		UM		I-DIN-BI-NU-UM		UCP X/1 64 2
		JI	NDIN					DIWR	IT	IM		I-DIN-D-DI-RI-TIM	GEN	M
		JI	NDIN					DAGAN				I-DIN-D-DA-GAN		M+

STEMS

NDIN	1	JI	NDIN				KAKK	A		I-DIN-KA-AK-KA		M+
		JI	NDIN				KAKK	A		I-DIN-D-KA-KA		M+
		JI	NDIN				LABW	A		I-DIN-D-LA-BA		M
		JI	NDIN				MEʾR			I-DIN-D-ME-ER		MAOG IV 2 2 HANA
		JI	NDIN				MAM	A		I-DIN-D-MA-MA		M+
		JI	NDIN				RIWM			I-DIN-D-RI-IM		TCL I 238 16 HANA
		JI	NDIN				RUŠP	AN		I-DIN-D-RU-UŠ-PA-AN		MAOG IV 2 5 HANA+
		JI	NDIN				RUŠP	AN		I-DIN-D-RU-UŠ$_2$-PA-AN		MEL. SYR. I 275
		JI	NDIN				TABUB	U		I-DIN-TA-BU-BU		M
NDUB	1	JI	NDUB				ŠALIM			IN-DU-UB-ŠA-LIM		TA 1931, 265:10
NDUR	1	JA	NDUR		UM					IA-AN-DU-RUM?		TIM II 37 1
NEJAL	1		NEJAL	AH						NE-IA-LA	FN	XIII 1 VII 51
NGIH	1	JA	NGIH							IA-AN-GI		JNES XIII 210+ LATE
NIʾG	2		ŠALAŠ				NIʾG	I		ŠA-LA-AŠ-NI-GI	FN	C+
NIʾŠ	1		NIʾŠ		UM					NI-ŠUM		M+
	2		KAKK		A		NIʾŠ	U	JA	KA-AK-KA-NI-ŠU-IA		RA LXV 64 VI 35
			KAKK		A		NIʾŠ	U	JA	KA-KA-NI-ŠU-IA	FN	RA LXV 65 VII 44
			MUT		UM		NIʾŠ	A		MU-TUM-NI-ŠA		TA 1931, 538 III
			ŠUM		U		NIʾŠ	U	JA	SU-MU-NI-ŠU-A		CT VIII 38D:14
NIʿIM	1		NIʿIM	AH						NI-Ḫ͟I-MA	FN	M
			NIʿIM	AT	UM					NI-ḪI-MA-T[UM]	FN?	C II 42 III 31
NIʿM	1		NIʿM		UM					NI-IḪ-MU-UM		M+
			NIʿM	AT	UM					NI-IḪ-MA-TUM	FN	M+
			NIʿM		A		HADD	U		NI-MA-A-DU		A.
	2		ḪAʾL		U		NIʿM			ḪA-LU-NI-ḪI-IM		RA LXV 52 X 74
			ʾAB		I		NIʿM			A-BI-NI-ḪI-IM		RA LXV 44 IV 31
			ʾIL		I		NIʿM			I$_3$-LI$_2$-NE-ḪI-IM		M
			ʿAMM		U		NIʿM			ḪA-AM-MU-NI-ḪI-IM	NOM	M
			ʾAŠD		I		NIʿM			AŠ$_2$-DI-NI-ḪI-IM		M+
			MUT		A		NIʿM			MU-TA-NI-ḪI-IM		RA LXV 43 III 51
			ṢIBʾ		I		NIʿM			ZI-BI-NI-ḪI-I[M]		M
NIWḪ	1		NIWḪ	AT	UM					NI-ḪA-TUM	FN	M+
	2		ŠUM		U		NIWḪ	A		SU-MU-NI-A		GORDON 39 9, 13
			ŠUM		U		NIWḪ	UM		SU-MU-NI-ḪU-UM		B 39
			ŠUM		U		NIWḪ	IM		SU-MU-NI-ḪI-IM	GEN	SIMMONS 121 18, M+
NIWR	1		NIWR		U					NI-E-RU		A.
			NIWR	AH						NI-E-RA	FN	A.
			NIWR				MEʾR			NI-WA-AR-ME-ER		M
			NIWR		I		HADD	U		NI-IW-RI-A-DU		A.+
	2		ʾAJA				NIWR	I		[A]-IA-NI-RI		RA LXV 59 II 36
			ḤAJJ		A		NIWR	I		E$_2$-A-NI-RI	FN	RA LXV 58 II 2
			ḤAJJ		A		NIWR	I		E$_2$-A-NE-RI	FN	XIII 1 VII 26
			ʾAB		I		NIWR	I		A-BI-NI-RI	FN	XIII 1 IX 58+
			ʾAB		U		NIWR	A		A-BU-NI-RA		TIM VI 34, U
			HADD		U		NIWR	I		D-IM-NI-RI	FN	RA LXV 61 IV 17
			ʾADM		U		NIWR	I		AD-MU-NE-RI	FN	XIII 1 VIII 13
			ʾADM		U		NIWR	I		D-AD-MU-NI-RI	FN?	M
			ʾIL		I		NIWR	I		I$_3$-LI$_2$-NE-RI	FN	XIII 1 II 6+
			ʾALL		I		NIWR	I		AL-LI-NI-RI	FN	A.
			ʾANN		U		NIWR	I		AN-NU-NI-RI	FN	M
			ʾIŠḪAR	AH			NIWR	I		D-IŠ-ḪA-RA-NI-RI	FN	RA LXV 59 II 22
			ʿAŠTAR				NIWR	I		EŠ$_4$-DAR-NE-RI	FN	XIII 1 IX 48
			BAʿL		I		NIWR	I		EA-AḪ-LI-NI-RI	FN	M+
			BEʿL		I		NIWR	I		BE-LI$_2$-NI-RI	FN	M+
			BEʿL		I		NIWR	I		BE-LI$_2$-NE-RI	FN	XIII 1 II 55+
			DAGAN				NIWR	I		D-DA-GAN-NI-RI	MN	RA LXV 47 VII 38
			DAGAN				NIWR	I		D-DA-GAN-NI-RI	FN	M+
			DAGAN				NIWR	I		D-DA-GAN-NE-RI	FN	M+
		JA	MWUT				NIWR	I		IA-MU-UT-NI-RI	FN	A.
			NUN		U		NIWR	I		D-NU-NU-NE?-RI	FN	RA LXV 66 VII 56
			ŠUM		U		NIWR	I		SU-MU-NI-RI	FN	XIII 1 XI 46
			ŠARR		UM		NIWR	I		LUGAL-NI-RI	FN	XIII 1 XIII 3+
	3		LA			ʾA	HWIJ					
							NIWR	I		LA-AḪ-WI-NE-RI	FN	XIII 1 II 11
NIGH	1		NIGH	AT	UM					NI-IG-ḪA-TUM	FN	M
NIKID	1		NIKID	AT	UM					NI-KI-DA-TUM		VAS XIII 65 2,3+

STEMS

NIKR	1	NIKR		UM					NI-IK-RU-UM		RA LXV 45 V 40
NILŠ	2	KAKK		A		NILŠ	I		KA-A[K]-KA-NI-EL?-ŠI?FN		XIII 1 VIII 41
NIMḪ	1	NIMḪ		AM		PI					
						ʾIL			NI-IM?-ḪA-AM-BI-DINGIR		A. 95 17 (=JCS VIII 8)
NIMIN	1	NIMIN		A		HADD	U		NI-MI-NA-A-DU		A.+
NINGAL	2 JI	TWUR				NINGAL			I-DUR-D-NIN-GAL		M
NINN	1	NINN		U					NI-IN-NU		M
NIPR	1	NIPR		AM					NI-IP-RA-AM		RA LXV 50IX 26
NIQM	1	NIQM	AN						NI-IQ-MA-AN		M
		NIQM	AN	UM					NI-IQ-MA-NU-UM		B 47+
		NIQM	AN	UM					NI-IQ-MA-A-NU-UM		B 47+
		NIQM		EJA					NI-IQ-ME-IA		M+
		NIQM				ʾAB	I		NI-IQ-MA-A-BI		A. 86 7+
		NIQM				HADD	U		NI-IQ-MA-A-DU		A.+
		NIQM				HADD	U		NI-IQ-MA-DU		A.
		NIQM				HADD	U		NI-IQ-MA$_2$-A-DU		B 36
		NIQM		I		HADD	U		NI-IQ-MI-A-DU		A.+
		NIQM		I		HADD	U		NI-IQ-MI-IA-AD-DU		M
		NIQM		I	JA	JPAʿ			NI-IQ-MI-PA		A. 27 12
		NIQM		I	JA	JPAʿ			NI-IQ-ME-PA		A.+
		NIQM		I	JE	JPUʿ			NI-IQ-MI-E-PU-UḪ		M+, A.+
		NIQM		I		JATAR			NI-IQ-MI-E-TAR		C II 39 3
		NIQM		I		LA					
						NAŜIʾ			NI-IQ-MI-LA-NA-SI		M
		NIQM		U K					NI-IQ-MU-UK	FN	M
	2	ʿAMM		U		NIQM	A		AM-MU-NI-IQ-MA		A.+
NIṢAB	1	NIṢAB	AH						NI-ZA-BA?	FN	RA LXV 68 V 9A
NIṢB	1	NIṢB		I		ʾIL			NE-IZ-BI-IL		TA 1931, 172
		NIṢB		I		ʾEL			NE-IZ-BI-EL		TA 1930, 747 +
NPIḪ	1 JI	NPIḪ		UM					IB-BI$_2$-ḪU-UM?		VIII 3 19
	JI	NPIḪ		U					I-BI-ḪU	FN	C
	JI	NPIḪ				LI					
						DIJN	I		IB-BI-IḪ-LI-DI-NI	FN	C
NQIM	1 JE	NQIM		UM					EN-GI-MU-UM		U+
	JA	NQIM				HADD	U		IA-AK-KI-IM-D-IM		M+
	JA	NQIM				HADD	U		IA-KI-IM-D-IM		M+
	JA	NQIM				ʾIL			IA-AN?-KI-IM-DINGIR		RA VIII 69 22
	JA	NQIM				ʾIL			A-AN-KI-IM-DINGIR		HARRIS 9 14+
	JE	NQIM				ʾIL			E-EN-KI-IM-DINGIR		CT VI 49B 4
	JA	NQIM				LIʾM			IA-AK-KI-IM-LI-IM		M
	JA	NQIM				LIʾM			IA-KI-IM-LI-IM		M
NŜIʾ	1 JA	NŜIʾ	AN						IA-AŠ$_2$-SI-IA-AN		M
	JA	NŜIʾ				HADD	U		IA-AŠ$_2$-ŜI-D-IM		RA LXV 42 III 13
	JA	NŜIʾ				HADD	U		IA-SI-D-IM		B 29
	JA	NŜIʾ				ʾIL			IA-SI-DINGIR		B 29+
	JA	NŜIʾ				ʾIL	I		IA-SI-LI		B 29+
	JA	NŜIʾ				ʾIL	I		IA-SI-I-LI$_2$		TCL X 5 3
	JA	NŜIʾ				ʾIL	UM		IA-SI-LUM		RA IX 22 2+
	JA	NŜIʾ				ʿAMM	U		IA-SI-ḪA-MU		M
	JA	NŜIʾ				JARAḪ			IA-SI-E-RA-AḪ		B 28
	JA	NŜIʾ				JARAḪ			IA-SI-RA-AḪ		B 30
	JA	NŜIʾ				JARAḪ			IA-SI-A-RA-AḪ		GRANT, HAV. 242:2+
	JA	NŜIʾ			JA	JŠUʿ			IA-SI-SU-UḪ		BIN II 104 15
	JA	NŜIʾ				DAGAN			IA-AŠ$_2$-SI-D-DA-GAN		M+
	JA	NŜIʾ				DAGAN			IA-SI-D-DA-GAN		M+
	JI	NŜIʾ				DAGAN			I-SI-IḪ-D-DA-GAN		RA XLI 44 R. 6 HANA
	JI	NŜIʾ				DAGAN			IS-SI-D-DA-GAN		B 22 HANA
	JA	NŜIʾ				LIʾM			IA$_2$-ŠI-LI-IM		U+
NŠUʾ	2	MUT		U	JA	NŠUʾ		HU	MU-TU-A-AN-ŠU-U$_2$		KISURRA 91 24
NṢIB	1 JA	NṢIB		UM					IA-AN-ZI-BU-UM		M+
	JA	NṢIB		IM					IA-AN-ZI-BI-IM	GEN	M+
	JA	NṢIB	AN						IA-AN-ZI-BA-AN		M
	JA	NṢIB	AN						IA-AN-ZI-PA-AN		M
	JA	NṢIB				....			IA-AN-ZI-IB-[....]		M+
	JA	NṢIB				....			IA-AN-ZI-IB-D-[....]		M
	JA	NṢIB				HADD	U		IA-AN-ZI-IB-D-IM		M+

NṢIB	1	JA		NṢIB			ʾIL			IA-AN-Z[I-I]B-DINGIR		XII 683 4
		JA		NṢIB			DAGAN			IA-AN-ZI-IB-D-DA-GAN		M+
		JA		NṢIB			DAGAN			IA-AZ-ZI-IB-D-DA-GAN		B 29
NṢUR	1	JA		NṢUR			HADD	U		IA-AṢ-ṢU-UR-D-IM		X 12 6, 21+
		JI		NṢUR			ʾAŠD	UM		I-ZUR-AŠ-DU-UM		A 7685 5
		JI		NṢUR			ʾAŠD	UM		I-ZUR-A-AŠ-DU-UM		CT II 42 25
NTIN	1	JA		NTIN		UM				IA-AN-TI-NU-UM		B 29+
		JA		NTIN		UM				A-AN-TI-NU-UM		SIMMONS 79 6'
		JA		NTIN		UM				IA-AN-TE-NU-UM		SIMMONS 104 13
		JI		NTIN		UM				IN-TI-NU-UM		I
		JE		NTIN		UM				E-EN-TI-NU-UM		WALTERS,WL 112:25
		JA		NTIN		U				IA-AN-TI-NU		M
		JA		NTIN		U				IA-TI-NU		B 31
		JA		NTIN		U				IA-AT-TI-NU		YOS XIII 280:13
		JA		NTIN		IM				IA-AN-TI-NIM	GEN	M
		JA		NTIN		IM				IA-AT-TI-NIM	GEN	M+
		JI		NTIN						IT-TI-IN		M
		JA		NTIN			....			IA-AN-TI-IN-D-[....]		M
		JA		NTIN			HADD	U		IA-AN-TI-IN-D-IM		M+
		JA		NTIN			HADD	U		IA-AN-TI-NA-DU		ZDPV XLIX PL. 45 LATE
		JI		NTIN			HADD	U		I-TI-IN-D-IM		M
		JA		NTIN			ʾIL			IA-AN-TI-IN-DINGIR		B 29+, M+
		JA		NTIN			ʾIL			IA-AT-TI-IN-DINGIR		M
		JA		NTIN			ʾIL			[A-A]N-TI-IN-DINGIR		HARRIS 56 15
		JA		NTIN		I	ʾIL			IA-AN-TI-NI-DINGIR		BM 17084
		JA		NTIN			ʿAMM	U		IA-AN-TI-IN-ḪA-MU		M
		JA		NTIN			ʾANN	I	Š	[IA-AN]-TI-IN-A-NI-IŠ		VII 180 8'
		JA		NTIN			JARAḪ			IA-AN-TI-IN-A-RA-AḪ		RA LXV 62 V 34
		JA		NTIN			JARAḪ			IA-AN-TI-NA-RA-AḪ		RUTTEN 11 20+
		JA		NTIN			JARAḪ			IA-AN-TI-LA-RA-AḪ		VAS XVI 91 3
		JA		NTIN			JARAḪ			IA-AN-TI-IN-E-RA-AḪ		M+
		JA		NTIN			JARAḪ			IA-AT-TI-IN-E-RA-AḪ		M+
		JA		NTIN			JARAḪ			IA-T[I-I]N-E-RA-AḪ		M
		JA		NTIN			DAGAN			IA-AN-TI-IN-D-DA-GAN		M+
		JA		NTIN			DAGAN			IA-TI-IN-D-DA-GAN		M
		MA		NTIN		UM				MA-AN-TI-NU-UM		HARRIS 31 13+
		MA		NTIN		U				URU MA-AN-TI-NU	GN	BM 16387
NṮIʿ	1	JA		NṮIʿ		A				IA-AN-DI-ḪA-KI	GN	M
NUʾR	1		Š	NUʾR			ḪAʾL	I		ŠU-NU-UR-ḪA-LI		KING LIH I 22 4, R. 2
			Š	NUʾR		A	ḪAʾL	U		ŠU-NU-UḪ-RA-ḪA-LU		M+
			Š	NUʾR		A	ḪAʾL	U	HU	ŠU-NU-UḪ-RA-ḪA-LU-U_2		M+
			Š	NUʾR		A	ḪAʾL	U	HU	ŠU-NU-ḪU-RA-ḪA-LU-U_2		XIV 11:1
			Š	NUʾR		A	ḪAʾL	U	HU	ŠU-NU-UḪ-ḪU-RA-ḪA-LU-U_2		XIV 36:1+
			Š	NUʾR		U	ḪAʾL	U		ŠU-NU-UḪ-RU-ḪA-LU		M+
			Š	NUʾR		A	ʿAMM	U		ŠU-NU-UḪ-RA-AM-MU		B 40 HANA+
NUʿAM	1			NUʿAM	AH					NU-ḪA-MA	FN	M
NUʿM	1			NUʿM		I	ʾAB	I		NU-UḪ-MI-A-BI		XIII 1 I 38
				NUʿM		I	ʾIL			NU-UḪ-MI-DINGIR		M+
				NUʿM		I	ʾIL	I		NU-UḪ-MI-I_3-LI_2		XIII 1 XIII 26
				NUʿM		I	JABAL			NU-UḪ-ME-E-BA-AL	FN	RA LXV 62 V 19
				NUʿM		I	DAGAN			NU-UḪ-MI-D-DA-GAN		M
				NUʿM		I	LIʾM			NU-UḪ-MI-LI-IM		M+
				NUʿM		U	BAʾAT	IM		NU-UḪ-MU-BA-A-TIM	FN	C+
NUWḪ	1			NUWḪ		I	ʾIL			NU-ḪI-DINGIR		I
	2			ʾADAN			NUWḪ	UM		ḪA-DA-NU-U_2-UM		M
NUWAP	1			NUWAP		U				NU-A-BU		JNES XIII 210+ LATE
NUWD	1			NUWD	AT	UM				NU-DA-TUM	MN	U
NUWP	1			NUWP	AN	UM				NU-PA-NU-UM		SIMMONS 95 10+
				NUWP	AN	UM				NU-PA-A-NU-UM		SIMMONS 103 7+
				NUWP	AT	UM				NU-BA-TUM		YOS XIII 191:8
				NUWP	AT	UM				NU-PA-TUM	FN	BIROT, TEA 70C R II 18
				NUWP	AT	IJA				NU-PA-TI-IA	FN	M
				NUWP		AJA				NU-BA-IA		RA LXV 48 VIII 28
				NUWP		I	ʾIL			NU-BI-DINGIR		C+
	2			KUʾM			NUWP	I		KU-UM-NU-BI		M
NUWR	1			NUWR	AH					NU-RA	FN	M

STEMS												
NUWR	1	NUWR	T	UM						NU-UR$_2$-TUM	FN	RA LXV 65 VII 21
		NUWR					MEʾR			NU-UR-ME-ER		M
		NUWR		U			ʾAMAR			NU-RU-A-MA-AR		HARRIS 68 19
	2	ŠI					NUWR	I		ŠI-NU-RI	FN	A. LATE
NUBAṬ	1	NUBAṬ	AH							NU-BA-TA	FN	M
NUBUṬ	1	NUBUṬ	AH							NU-BU-TA	FN	XIII 1 XIV 9
NUKR	1	NUKR	AN	UM						NU-UK-RA-NU-UM		U+
NUMḪ	1	NUMḪ		A						NU-UM-ḪA-A(-KI)	GN	M+
		NUMḪ	AJ	I						NU-UM-ḪA-I	GN	IX 48 3+
		NUMḪ	AJ	I						NU-UM-ḪA-A-JI	GN	X 5 4
	2	ŠUM		U			NUMḪ	A		SU-M[U-N]U-UM-ḪA		RA LXIV 43
		ŠUM		U			NUMḪ	IM		SU-MU-NU-UM-ḪI-IM		RIFTIN 44 12,16+
	3	BAʿL		U			ME					
							NUMḪ	I		BA-LU-ME-NU-ḪI		M+
		BAʿL		U			ME					
							NUMḪ	I		BA-LU-ME-NU-UM-ḪI		IX 41 2
NUMAḪ	1	NUMAḪ		A						NU-MA-ḪA-A	GN	M
	2	ŠUM		U			NUMAḪ	A		SU-MU-NU-MA-ḪA		M
	3	LA					RIWM					
							NUMAḪ	A		LA-RI-IM-NU-MA-ḪA-A		M+
		LA					RIWM					
							NUMAḪ	A		LA-RI-IM-NU-MA-A		M
NUMEN	1	NUMEN	AH							NU-ME-EN-NA	FN	XIII 1 IV 32
NUMN	1	NUMN		UM						NU-UM-NU-UM		BIROT, TEA 65:8
		NUMN		U	HU					NU-UM-NU-U$_2$		M
NUMR	2	MAM		A			NUMR	I		D-MA-MA-NU-UM-RI	FN	RA LXV 65 VII 30
NUN	1	NUN		U			NIWR	I		D-NU-NU-NE?-RI	FN	RA LXV 66 VII 56
		NUN		U		TA	BNIJ			D-NU-NU-TA-AB-NI	FN	XII 265 1
	2	ʾIL		A			NUN	U		I-LA-NU-NU		FIGULLA CAT. I 14029
		PUḪUR					NUN	U		PU-ḪU-UR-D-NU-NU		M
		QIJŠ	T	I			NUN	U		KI-IŠ-TI-D-NU-NU		M+
NUNM	1	NUNM	AN							NU-UN-MA-AN		RUTTEN 26 9
NUPAR	1	NUPAR					ŠARR	IM		NU-BAR-LUGAL		A.
	2	DAGAN					NUPAR	A	JA	D-DA-GAN-NU?-PA?-RA-IA		M
NUPUR	1	NUPUR		I						NU-PU-RI		XIII 1 IV 12
NURNUR	1	NURNUR	AT	UM						NU-UR$_2$-NU-RA-TUM	MN?	BIN VII 157 7
NUŠUP	1	NUŠUP		UM						NU-ŠU-BU-UM		HARRIS 4 9+
NUṢAB	1	NUṢAB		UM						NU-ZA-BU-UM		M
		NUṢAB		U						NU-ZA-BU		XIV 61:7
NUṢR	2	BEʿL		I			NUṢR	I		BE-LI$_2$-NU-IZ-RI	FN	RA LXV 64 V 60
		BAWŠ	T	I			NUṢR	I		BA-AŠ-TI-NU-IZ-RI	FN	RA LXV 58 I 45
		BAWŠ	T	I			NUṢR	I		BA-AŠ-TI-UZ-RI		RA LXIV 28 NO. 15
		BAWŠ	T	I			NUṢR	I		BA-AŠ$_2$-TI-NU-UZ-RI	FN	XIII 1 VII 24
NUṬUP	1	NUṬUP	AT	UM						NU-DU-PA-TUM	FN	FRANK SKT P. 31+
		NUṬUP	T	UM						NU-DU-UB-TUM	FN	UET V P. 53+
		NUṬUP	T	UM						NU-TU-UP-TUM	FN	UET V P. 53+
		NUṬUP		AJA						NU-TU-PA-A-A		UET V 480 3
NUZAM	1	NUZAM	AN							NU-ZA-MA-AN		XIII 1 V 22
NZAL	1 ʾA	NZAL	AT	UM						AN-ZA-LA-TUM	FN?	XIII 1 I 14
	MA	NZAL	AN	UM						MA-AN-ZA-LA-NU-UM		UET V 465 17
PḪUR	1 JA	PḪUR		UM						IA-AP-ḪU-RU-UM		B 24
	JA	PḪUR		UM						IA-AP-ḪU-RUM		TIM IV 33 19, SEAL +
	JA	PḪUR	AN	U						IA-AP-ḪU-RA-NU		M
	JA	PḪUR					HADD	U		IA-AP-Ḫ[U-UR]-A-DU		M
	JA	PḪUR					JARAḪ			IA-AP-ḪU-UR-SIN		M
	JA	PḪUR					LIʾM			IA-AP-ḪU-UR-LI-IM		M+, A 7630
PA	1	PA					ʾIL	A		PA-I-LA		XIII 1 VII 16
		PA			KA		ʾIL	A		PA-KA-I-LA		B 37+
		PA			KA		ʾIL	A		PA-KA-DINGIR		B 37
		PA			KA		ʾIL	A		PA-A-KA-I-LA		B 37
	2	ʾIL		A			PA	I		I-LA-BA-I		TA 1931, 499
		ʾALI					PA					
							ʾIL			A-LI$_2$-PA-DINGIR		RUTTEN 6 21+
		ʾALI					PA					
							ʾIL			A-LI-PA-DINGIR		TIM III 5 18+
		ʾALI					PA					
							ʾIL			ḪA-A-LI-PA-DINGIR		EDZARD, DER 152 REV.16

STEMS

PA	2		ʾALI				PA					
							ʾIL	UM		A-LI$_2$-KA-LUM		RUTTEN 37 19
			ʾALI				PA					
							ŠAMŠ			A-LI$_2$-PA-D-UTU		BE VI/1 15:25
		ʾA	MWUT				PA					
							ʾIL			A-MU-UT-PA-DINGIR		SYRIA L 7
		ʾA	MWUT				PA					
							ʾIL			AM-MU-UT-PA-DINGIR		RA XLIII 212 39 QATNA
			MUT				PA					
							NAZI			MU-UT-PA-A-NA-ZI		RA LXV 40 I 10
PAʾAL	2		ʾIL		I		PAʾAL	UM		I$_3$-LI$_2$-PA-A-LU-UM		TIM III 44 16+
			ʾIL		I		PAʾAL	UM		I$_3$-LI$_2$-PA-ḪA-LUM		M
PAʾAR	1		PAʾAR				MI			PA-ḪA-AR-MI	FN	RA LXV 59 II 23
			PAʾAR	AT	IM					PA-A-RA-TIM	FN GEN	X 170:1
PAʾL	1		PAʾL		A	HA				PA-LA-A	FN	B 37
PAʾP	1		PAʾP	AK	UM					PA-PA-KUM		B 37
PAʾR	1		PAʾR	T	UM					PA-AR-TUM	FN	CT XLV 54 24, M+
			PAʾR	AT	IJA					PA-RA-TI-IA		UCP X/3 3 8
PAʾŠ	2		ʾIL		A		PAʾŠ	I	JA	DINGIR-PA-ŠI-IA		TCL XVIII 106 9
PAʾT	1		PAʾT	AT	UM					PA-TA-TUM	FN	M+
PAḪIR	1	MU	PAḪIR	AH						MU-PA-ḪI-RA	FN	XIII 1 VII 47
PADAL	1		PADAL	AN						PA-DA-LA-AN		RA LXV 51 IX 33
PAGIR	1		PAGIR		UM					PA-GI-RUM		B 36 HANA
			PAGIR		UM					PA-GI-RU-UM		B 36+ HANA
PAKN	1		PAKN		UM					PA-AK-NU-UM		B 37
			PAKN	AN	UM					PA-AK-NA-NU-UM		B 47+
			PAKN	AN	IM					PA-AK-NA-NIM	GEN	B 47
			PAKN	AN	A					PA-AK-NA-NA	GEN	BE VI/2 81 14
PALAṬ	1		PALAṬ		UM					PA-LA-TUM		TIM III 37 14+
PALIS	1	JI N	PALIS		U					IP-PA-LI-ZU?		MAOG IV 2 3 HANA
PALL	1		PALL	AK	UM					PA-AL-LA-KUM		B 37
			PALL	AK	UM					PA-LA-KUM		YOS XIII 164:1
PALS	1		PALS		UM					PA-AL-ZU-UM		HARRIS 65 18
			PALS		IJA					PA-AL-ZI-IA		SIMMONS 44 6+
PALṬ	1		PALṬ		IJA					PA-AL-TI-IA		YONDORF 2
			PALṬ		A		ʿAN	UM		PA-AL?-TA-A-NU-UM		LANGDON IV 15
			PALṬ		A		BIJT	U		PA-AL-DA-BI-TU		A. LATE
PALUS	1		PALUS		UM					BA-LU-ZUM		TA 30 615 26
PANAN	1		PANAN		UM					PA-NA-NU-UM		B 93
			PANAN		UM					PA-NA-NUM		B 47
			PANAN		IM					PA-NA-NIM	GEN	B 47
PANIJ	1	JI	PANIJ				ʾEL	UM		I-PA-AN-NI-E-LUM		UNPUBL.
			PANIJ	AT	UM					PA-NI-IA-TUM	MN?	TIM I 11 11
			PANIJ	AT	UM					PA-AN-NI-IA-TUM	MN	UET V 615 9
			PANIJ				ʾIL	A		PA-NI-LA		IX 252 17, A. LATE
PANN	1		PANN	AT	UM					PA-AN-NA-TUM	MN?	CT XLV 49 11
PAPUZ	1		PAPUZ		I					PA-PU-ZI	FN	XIII 1 III 14
PAQAḪ	1		PAQAḪ	AT	UM					BA-GA-A-TUM	MN	A 29366:17
			PAQAḪ		A		LAʾL	UM		BA-GA-A-LA-LUM		HARRIS 69 2+
PAQID	1		PAQID		UM					PA-GI-DU-UM		CT XLV 89 II 32
PARG	1		PARG	AN	UM					PA-AR-GA-NU-UM		B 47
PARUR	1		PARUR		I					PA-RU-RI		XIII 1 V 64
PASAʿ	1		PASAʿ	T	UM					PA-ZA-AḪ-TUM	FN	XIII 1 VIII 81
			PASAʿ			KA				PA-ZA-AḪ-GA		HARRIS 31 6
PAŠD	1		PAŠD		IJA					PA-AŠ-DI-IA		B 37
PAŠIQ	2		LA				PAŠIQ	UM		LA-PA-SI-KU-UM		M
PATAḪ	2		ʿAMM		U		PATAḪ	A		ḪA-AM-MU-PA-TA-A		M
PATIḪ	1	JA	PATIḪ				....			IA-PA-TE-X		KISURRA 100 8
			PATIḪ		UM					PA-TE-ḪU-UM		HARRIS 53 19+
			PATIḪ		IM					PA-TE-E-IM	GEN	CT IV 21B 6, 22
			PATIḪ	AT	UM					PA-TE-ḪA-TUM	MN?	CARNEGIE CAT. Q B 11
			PATIḪ	AH						PA-TI-ḪA	FN	M+
		MU	PATIḪ	AH						MU-PA-AT-TI-IA	FN	XIII 1 VIII 38+
		MU	PATIḪ	AH						MU-PA-TI-IA	FN	XIII 1 XIII 19+
		MU	PATIḪ	T	UM					MU-PA-AT-TI-TUM	FN	C+
PAṬAR	1		PAṬAR		UM					PA-AT-TA-RUM		B 37

STEMS

PAṮAR	1		PAṮAR	AN	UM					BA-DA-RA-NU-UM		SIMMONS 31 5
PAṮIR	1		PAṮIR		UM					PA-TI-RUM		M
			PAṮIR		UM					BA-DI-RU-UM		HARRIS 26 7
			PAṮIR		UM					BA-TI-RU-UM		TA 1931,377
PAṮR	1		PAṮR		IJA					BA-AṮ-RI-IA		A 21950
PAZR	1		PAZR		I					PA-AZ-RI		M
PDIJ	1	JA	PDIJ		UM					IA-AP?-DI-UM		UNPUBL.
PI	1		PI			HU				BI-U$_3$		U
			PI				ʾIL	A		PI-I-LA		A. LATE
			PI				ʿAN	UM		PI-A-NUM$_2$		I
			PI				ʿAN	UM		BI$_2$-A-NU-UM		I
			PI				KAMA					
							ʾIL			BI-KA-MA-DINGIR		XIV 111:10+
			PI				KAMA					
							ʾEL			BI-KA-MA-EL		M+
			PI				NAʿM					
							ʾEL			BI-NA-AḪ-ME-EL		B 15
	2		JAʿAL				PI					
							ʾIL	UM		IA-ḪA-AL-PI-LUM		3NT867:5, 12, 21
		JI	JʿIL				PI					
							ʾIL			I-ḪI-IL-BI-DINGIR		M
			JAʾN		UM		PI			JA-NU-UM-BI-KI	GN	M
			ʾAJIŠ				PI		HU	ḪA-II-IŠ-PI$_2$-U$_2$		KISURRA 22+
			ʾAJIŠ				PI		HU	ḪA-A-IŠ-PI$_2$-U$_2$		KISURRA 5+
		JI	JBAL				PI					
							ʾEL			I-BA-AL-BI-EL		M+
		JI	JBAL				PI					
							ʾEL			I-BA-AL-PI-EL		UCP X P. 56+
		JI	JBAL				PI					
							ʾIL			I-BA-AL-BI-DINGIR		M+
		JI	JDAʿ				PI					
							ʾIL			I-DA-BI$_2$-DINGIR		I
		ʾA	JDAʿ				PI					
							ʾEL			A-DA-AḪ-[BI]?-EL		SIMMONS 51 21
			JADAʿ				PI					
							ʾIL			IA-DA-BI-DINGIR		AJSL XXXIII 224 3
			ʾALUN				PI					
							JAM	U		ḪA-LU-UN-BI-JA-MU		M
			ʾALUN				PI					
							JAM	U		ḪA-LU-UM-BI-JA-MU		RA LXV 43 III 78
			ʾALUN				PI					
							JAM	U		ḪA-LU-BI-JA-MU		M
		JA	ḪNUN				PI					
							ʾEL			IA-ḪU-UN-PI-EL		SIMMONS 54 18
			ḪUNN				PI					
							ʾEL			ḪU-UN-BI-EL		SIMMONS 82 7
			ʾARUŠ				PI					
							ʾIL			A-RU-UŠ-BI-DINGIR		M, RA XLI 45 4' HANA
			ʾAŠD		UM		PI					
							JAD	IM		AŠ-DU-UM-BI-IA-DI-IM		RA LXV 55 XIII 44
		JA	ʾŠUD				PI					
							ʾEL			IA-SU-UD-PI-EL		SIMMONS 46 31
			ḪATAN				PI					
							ʾIL			ḪA-TA-AN-BI-DINGIR		M
			BUN		U	HU	PI					
							ʾIL	UM		BU-NU-U$_2$?-BI-I-LUM		UET V 548 2
			DAWD		UM		PI					
							ʾIL			DA-DUM-BI$_2$-DINGIR		I
		ʾA	KWUN				PI					
							ʾEL			A-KU-PI-EL		GORDON, SCT 38 16
		JA	KWUN				PI			IA-KU-UN-PI		CT VIII 43C 8
		JA	KWUN				PI			IA-KU-BI		B 27
		JA	KWUN				PI			IA-KU-PI		B 27
		JE	KWUN				PI			E-KU-PI		B 17
		JA	KWUN				PI	I	JA	IA-KU-UN-BI-IA		XII 14
		JI	KWUN				PI	I	JA	I-KU-BI-IA		SM P. 54

STEMS

PI	2	JI	KWUN				PI	I	I-KU-UN-BI-I		C II 2 11
		JA	KWUN				PI				
							MAM	A	IA-KU-UN-BI-D-MA-MA	FN	RA LXV 66 VII 61
		ʾA	MWUT				PI				
							ʾIL		A-MU-UT-BI-DINGIR		M+
		ʾA	MWUT				PI				
							ʾIL	A	A-MU-UT-BI-I-LA		M
			NIMḪ		AM		PI				
							ʾIL		NI-IM?-ḪA-AM-BI-DINGIR		A. 95 17 (=JCS VIII 8)
			NAPŠ		I		PI				
							ʾIL		NA-AP-SI-BI-DINGIR		SYRIA XLVIII 9:22
		JI	TWUR				PI				
							ʾIL		I-DUR-[BI]?-DINGIR		I
			TAḪT		U		PI				
							ʾIL		TA-AḪ-TU-BI-DINGIR		M+
			ZAKK				PI				
							ʾEL		ZA-AK-PI-EL		TA 1931,198 EARLY OB
PILḪ	1		PILḪ		U		HADD	U	BI-EL-ḪU-D-IM		RA LXV 55 XIII 4
PILAḪ	1		PILAḪ		UM				BI-LA-ḪU-[UM]		RA LXV 54 XII 44
PILS	1		PILS	AN	UM				BIL-ZA-NU-UM		BM 80363 8
			PILS		I		HADD	U	BI-IL-ZI-D-IM		XIV 41:14
PIQD	1		PIQD	AT	UM				BI-IQ-DA-TUM	FN	XIII 1 X 27
PLAḪ	1	ʾA	PLAḪ				HAND	A	AP-LA-ḪA-AN-DA		M+
		ʾA	PLAḪ				HAND	A	AP-LI-ḪA-AN-DA		M
		ʾA	PLAḪ				HAND	A	AP-LA-ḪA-DA		M
		ʾA	PLAḪ				HAND	A	AP-LA-AḪ-[AN]-DA		M
		ʾA	PLAḪ				HAND	U	AP-LA-ḪA-AN-DU		RA LXV 42 II 65
		JA	PLAḪ		UM				IA-AP-LA-ḪU-UM		B 24+
		JA	PLAḪ		U				IA-AP-LA-ḪU		B 24+
		JA	PLAḪ				....		IA-AP-LA-[AḪ?-....]		XIII 1 XII 23
		JA	PLAḪ				ʾIL		IA-AP-LA-AḪ-DINGIR		M, TIM III 56 5+
		JA	PLAḪ				ʾIL	IM	IA-AP-LA-AḪ-I-LI-IM	GEN	RA LXIV 43
PLIḪ	1	JA	PLIḪ				ʾIL		[I]A-AP-LI?-I[Ḫ?-DINGIR]		VII 215 32
PLUS	1	JA	PLUS		UM				IA-AP-LU-ZUM		SIMMONS 49 4
		JA	PLUS		I		ŠUM	I	IA-AP-LU-SI-SU-U$_2$-MI		BIROT,TEA 31:6
PQID	1	ʾA	PQID		A				AP-KI-DA		U
		JA	PQID		UM				IA-AP-KI?-DU-UM		CT XLVIII 29:2
		JA	PQID		IM				IA-AP-KI?-DI-IM	GEN	BE VI/1 8 34
PRUD	1	JI	PRUD		U				IP-RU-DU		CT XLV 59 22 SEAL
PRUS	1	JA	PRUS				ʾAB	I	IA-AP-RU-US-A-BI		BAGHD. MITT. II 23
PTAḪ	1	JA	PTAḪ		UM				IA-AP-TA-ḪU-UM		WALTERS,WL 93:1
		JA	PTAḤ		U				IA-AP-TA-ḪU		YOS VIII 156 2, A. LATE
PTAN	1	TA	PTAN				HADD	A	TAP-TA-NA-A-DA		A. 206 5
		TA	PTAN				HADD	A	TAP-DA-NA-TA		A. LATE
		JI	PTAN						IP-TA-AN		C II 39 22; M
	2		ʾIL		I	ʾA	PTAN		I$_3$-LI$_2$-AP-TA-AN		B 21
			ʾIL		I	ʾA	PTAN		DINGIR-AP-TAN		TIM III 150 12
PTIḪ	1	JI	PTIḪ			JA	MWUT	A	IP-TI-IA-MU-TA		BM 80328 11
PTUḤ	1	ME	PTUḤ		UM				ME-EP-TU-U$_2$-UM		M+
		ME	PTUḤ		UM				ME-EP-TU-UM		M+
		ME	PTUḤ		U				ME-EP-TU-U$_2$		M+
		MI	PTUḤ		U				MI-IP-TU-U$_2$		RA LXIV 104:3
		ME	PTUḤ		IM				ME-EP-TI-I-IM	GEN	M+
		ME	PTUḤ		IM				ME-EP-TI-IM	GEN	M+
		ME	PTUḤ		IM				ME-EP-TE-IM	GEN	XIII 43 15
		MI	PTUḤ		IM				MI-IP-TI-IM	GEN	M+
		MI	PTUḤ		I				MI-IP-TI-I	GEN	XII 406 5
PTUN	1	ʾA	PTUN	AN	UM				AP-TU-NA-NU-UM		YOS VIII 176 SEAL
		TA	PTUN				HADD	A	TAP-TU-NA-A-DA		A. 33 26
PṬIR	1	JA	PṬIR		UM				IA-AP-DI-RUM		YOS XII
PṬUR	1	JA	PṬUR		UM				IA-AP-TU-RU-UM	GN	JCS VII 52 II 3
		JA	PṬUR		I				IA-AP-TU-RI	GN GEN	M
		JA	PṬUR	AJ	I				IA-AP-TU-RA-A-JI-KI	GN	M
		JA	PṬUR	AJ	I				IA-AP-TU-RA-JI-KI	GN	M
PU	1		PU			KA	DAGAN		PU-KA-D-DA-GAN		M
			PU			HU	DAGAN		PU-U$_2$-D-DA-GAN		M

STEMS

PU	1		PU				MA				
							ʾEL		PU-MA-[E]L		IA 1931,538 I
			PU				ME				
							ʾIL		PU-ME-IL		I
			PU		UM		ʾEL		PU-UM-E-EL		BAGH.MITT. IV 291,SEAL
	2		ʾAHL		UM		PU	HU	A-LUM-BI-U$_2$		SIMMONS 129 13
			ʾAHL		UM		PU	HU	ḪA-LAM-BU-U$_2$		RLA II 165 17
			ʾAHL		UM		PU	HU	[A]-LI-IM-BU-MU		OLZ 1958 547 N.1
			ʾAHL		UM		PU	HU	A-LUM-BU-MU		OLZ 1958 547 N.1
		JI	JṢIʾ				PU	K	I-ZI-PU-UK	FN?	M+
PUḪR	1		PUḪR		A	NA			PU-UḪ$_3$-RA-NA		YOS VIII 101B 13
PUḪUR	1		PUḪUR	T	UM				PU-ḪU-UR-TUM	FN	M
			PUḪUR				NUN	U	PU-ḪU-UR-D-NU-NU		M
PULAḪ	1		PULAḪ	AN					PU-LA-ḪA-AN		M
PULS	1		PULS	AT	UM				PU-UL-ZA-TUM	MN	TIM III 23 11+
			PULS	AN					PU-UL-ZA-AN		M
			PULS		IJA				PU-UL-ZI-IA		M
			PULS		I		HADD	U	PU-UL-ZI-D-IM		M+
			PULS		I		JARAḪ		PU-UL-ZI-RA-AḪ		HARRIS 18 14
			PULS		I		JARAḪ		PU-UL-SI-E-RA-AḪ		TIM V 69 16+
			PULS		U	NA	HADD	U	PU-UL-ZU-NA-D-IM		UNPUBL.
PURʿUŠ	1		PURʿUŠ	AN	U				PU-UR-ḪU-ŠA-NU		M
PURUS	1		PURUS	AT	UM				PU-RU-ZA-TUM	FN	RA LXV 60 III 60
PUṬR	2		ʾANN		U		PUṬR	I	AN-NU-PU-UṬ-RI	FN	RA LXV 58 I 19+
			ʿAŠTAR				PUṬR	I	EŠ$_4$-DAR-PU-UṬ-RI	FN	M+
PUZAR	1		PUZAR		UM				BU-ZA-RU-UM		TCL I 56 2+
PUZUR	1		PUZUR	AN					BU-ZU-RA-AN		RA LXV 53 XI 10
			PUZUR				ʿAN	A	PUZUR-A-NA		BIN IV 61 29+ CAPP.
QWIM	1	JA	QWIM	AT	UM				IA-KI-MA-TUM	FN	RA LXV 60 III 7
		JA	QWIM	AH					IA-KI-MA	FN	M+
		JA	QWIM				HADD	U	IA-KI-IM-D-IM		M+
		JA	QWIM				HADD	U	IA-GI-I[M]?-D-IM		IX 291 III 29'
		JA	QWIM				LIʾM		IA-KI-IM-LI-IM		M+
		ME	QWIM						ME-KI-IM		RA XXXV 119, MARI
		ME	QWIM						ME-[G]I-IM	GEN	IX 291 III 16'
	2		ʾAḪ		I	JE	QWIM		A-ḪI-E-KI-IM		M
			ʾAB		I	ME	QWIM		A-BI-ME-KI-IM		XIII 34 5+
			ʾAB		U	ME	QWIM		A-BU-ME-KI-IM		M+
			ʿAMM		I	TA	QWIM		ḪA-AM-MI-TA-KI-IM	NOM	M
			ʾAŠD		I	TA	QWIM		AŠ$_2$-DI-TA-KI-IM		M+
			ŠUM		U	TA	QWIM		SU-MU-TA-KI-IM		XIII 131 4'
QWUJ	1	JA	QWUJ		UM				IA-KU-UM		RUTTEN 6:3+; VIII 70:3, 8
		JA	QWUJ		UM				IA-KU-U$_2$-UM		RUTTEN 2:7+
		JA	QWUJ		U				IA-KU-U$_2$		RUTTEN 16:16
		JA	QWUJ			JA			IA-KU-IA		C+
		JA	QWUJ			JA			IA-KU-IA	FN	RA LXV 43 III 49
QWUM	2		ʿAMM		I	TA	QWUM		AM-MI-TA-KU-UM		A.+
			ʿAMM		I	TA	QWUM				
							MA		AM-MI-TA-KU-UM-MA		A. +
QJIŠ	1	TA	QJIŠ				NAN	I	TA-KI-IŠ-NA-NI	FN?	TIM III 41 6
	2		ŠUM		U	TA	QJIŠ		SU-MU-TA-KI-IŠ		M
QAʾB	2		ʾIL		A		QAʾB		DINGIR-QA-AB		TIM III 130 12, SEAL
QAʾD	2		ʾAB		I		QAʾD		A-BI-QA-AD		B 11
			ʾAB		I		QAʾD		A-BI-GA-AD		TA 30 237
			JAMM		U		QAʾD	UM	IA-AM-MU?-QA-DU-UM		III 56 7
QAʾN	1		QAʾN				HADD	U	QA-AN-A-DU		A.
	2		ʾIL		I		QAʾN		I-LI-QA-AN		A. LATE
			BAWB		U		QAʾN		BA-BU-QA-AN		M
QAʾT	1		QAʾT		U	HU			QA-TU-U$_2$	FN	RA LXV 58 I 47
QAHIL	1		QAHIL	AT	UM				QA-ḪI-LA-TUM	FN	C P. 55+
QAWL	1		QAWL		A		ḪAM	I	QA-LA-D-A-M[I]		M
			QAWL		U		ḪAM	I	QA-L[U]-D-A-MI		M
QAWM	1		QAWM		A		DANN	UM	QA-MA-[D]A-NUM		M
			QAWM		I		ʾIL		GA-MI-DINGIR		TIM III 12 16+
			QAWM		U		HADD	U	GA-MU-D-IM		M
			QAWM		U		MA				
							ʾAḪ	UM	QA-MU-MA-A-ḪU-UM		M

QAWM	1		QAWM		U	MA					
						ʾAḪ	I		QA-MU-MA-A-ḪI		RA LXV 41 II 22
			QAWM		U	MA					
						ʾIL			QA-MU-MA-DINGIR		M
	2		ʾAŠD		U	QAWM	U		AŠ-DU-GA-MU		CT XLV 77 R. 10, 14+
			ʾAŠD		U	QAWM	UM		AŠ$_2$-DU-GA-MU-UM		TCL I 130 8+
			BAʿL		UM	QAWM	UM		BA-LUM-QA-MU-UM		RA LXV 40 I 11
QABAL	1		QABAL	AT	UM				GA-BA-LA-TUM	FN	CT XLV 117 36
QABIL	1		QABIL		UM				GA-BI-LUM		KISURRA 106 15
QADIM	1		QADIM	AT	UM				QA-DI-MA-TUM	FN	WATERMAN 39 8+
			QADIM	AT	IM				QA-DI-MA-TIM	FN GEN	WATERMAN 39 11
		MU	QADIM		U				MU-GA-DI-MU		CT XLV 6 33
QADIŠ	1		QADIŠ		UM				KA-DI-ŠUM		RA LXV 52 XI 2
QADM	1		QADM	AN	UM				GA-AD-MA-NU-UM		U
QANAT	1		QANAT	AN	UM				GA-NA-TA-NU-UM		KISURRA 30 7
QANIJ	1		QANIJ	AT	UM				QA-NI-A-TUM	FN	RA LXV 66 VII 52; C+
			QANIJ	AN	U				KA-NI-IA-NU		M
QANIT	1	MU	QANIT		UM				MU-GA-NI-TUM	MN?	TIM III 86 6+
QAQQAD	1		QAQQAD	AN					QA-QA-DA-AN		XIV 47:20
			QAQQAR	AN					QA?-QA-RA?-AN		VII 198:14
QARAʾ	1		QARAʾ			ŠUM	I	JA	QA-RA-SU-MI-IA		CT II 34 5
			QARAʾ			ŠUM	I	JA	GA-RA-SU-MI-IA		CT XLVIII 89 REV.
			QARAʾ			ŠUM	U	JA	QA-RA-SU?-MU-IA		CT VI 43 6
			QARAʾ			ŠUM	U	JA	GA-RA-SU-MU-IA		CT XLV 11 2, 46+
			QARAʾ			ŠUM	U	JA	KA-RA?-SU-MU-IA		CT II 30 3
			QARAʾ			ŠUM	U	JA	KA-RA-SU-LUM		CT II 30 34
QARAD	2		ŠUWB		I	QARAD			ŠU-BI-GA-RA-AD		I
QARIʾ	1		QARIʾ		UM				QA-RI-U$_2$-UM		M+
			QARIʾ			ʾEL			QA-R[I]-E[L]		M
QARN	1		QARN	AN	A				QAR-NA-NA	GEN	SIMMONS 13 5
			QARN	AN	UM				QAR-NA-NU-UM		B 93+
			QARN		I	LIʾM			QAR-NI-LI-IM		M+
QAṢIR	1		QAṢIR		UM				QA-ZI-RUM		RA LXV 53 XI 46
QAṬAN	1		QAṬAN		A				QA-TA-NA-KI	GN	M
			QAṬAN		IM				QA-TA-NIM-KI	GN GEN	M+
			QAṬAN		IM				QA-ṬA$_3$-NIM-KI	GN GEN	M+
			QAṬAN	AJ	I				QA-TA-NA-A-JI-KI	GN	M
			QAṬAN	AJ	I				QA-TA-NA-JI-KI	GN	M+
			QAṬAN	AJ	IM				QA-TA-NA-IM-KI	GN GEN	M
QAṬAR	1		QAṬAR		A				QA-TA-RA-KI	GN	M
			QAṬAR		A				QA-ṬA$_3$-RA-KI	GN	M
			QAṬAR		A				QA-ṬA$_3$-RA-A-KI	GN	M+
			QAṬAR		UM				QA-TA-RU-UM		B 37
			QAṬAR		I				GA?-DA-RI		RA LXV 51 IX 72
			QAṬAR			ʾAB	I		GA-TAR-A-BI		BASOR 95 22
			QAṬAR			ʾIL			GA-TA-AR-DINGIR		B 17
	2		ʾAKUN		U	QAṬAR			A-KU-NU-GA-DAR		BIN VII 30 5
		JA	JṢIʾ			QAṬAR			IA-ṢI-QA-TAR		B 30
		JI	JṢIʾ			QAṬAR			I-ZI-GA-TA-AR		B 22+
		JI	JṢIʾ			QAṬAR			I-ZI-GA-TAR		B 22+
		JI	JṢIʾ			QAṬAR			I-ṢI-GA-TAR		B 22+
		JI	JṢIʾ			QAṬAR			I-ṢI-GA-TA-AR		B 22+
		JI	JṢIʾ			QAṬAR			I-ZI-GA-DAR		B 22
		JI	JṢIʾ			QAṬAR			I-ZI-QA-TAR		XIII 1 IV 59
		JI	JṢIʾ			QAṬAR	I		I-ZI-GA-DAR-I		B 22
QAṬR	1		QAṬR	AN	UM				GA-AT-RA-NU-UM		RUTTEN 14 22
QAZIJ	1		QAZIJ			RAWM	A		QA-ZI-RA-MA		A. LATE
QBIJ	1	JA	QBIJ		UM				IA-AQ-BU?-UM?		CT IV 30D 11
		JA	QBIJ		IM				IA-AQ-BI-IM	GEN	M
		TA	QBIJ		IM				TA-AQ-BI-IM	GEN?	M+
		JA	QBIJ			HADD	U		IA-AQ-BI-D-IM		RA LXV 43 III 38
QDAM	1	ʾA	QDAM		U				AQ-DA-MU		C P. 35+
QIJŠ	1		QIJŠ		IM				KI-ŠI-IM	GEN	M
			QIJŠ	AT	UM				KI-SA-TUM	MN	VAS IX 175 5+, M
			QIJŠ	AT	UM				KI-SA-T[U-U]M	MN	M
			QIJŠ	AT	UM				KI-ŠA-TUM	MN	XIII 1 V 19

STEMS

QIJŠ	1		QIJŠ	AT	IM				KI-ŠA-TIM	MN GEN	M+
			QIJŠ	T	UM				KI-IŠ-TUM	FN	XIII 1 III 16
			QIJŠ				ʾAG	U	KI-IŠ-A-GU	FN	XIII 1 I 70
			QIJŠ	T	I		ʾADM	U	KI-IŠ-TI-AD-MU		M+
			QIJŠ	T	I		LIʾL	IM	KI-IŠ-TI-LI-LIM	GEN	RA LXIV 34 NO.26
			QIJŠ	T	I		MAM	A	KI-IŠ-TI-D-MA-MA		M+
			QIJŠ	T	I		MAM	A	KI-IŠ-TI-D-MA-AM-MA		XIV 61:5
			QIJŠ	T	I		NUN	U	KI-IŠ-TI-D-NU-NU		M+
QIDM	1		QIDM	AN	UM				KI-ID-MA-NU-UM		U
QIMṢ	1		QIMṢ		I		JARAḪ		KI?-IM-ZE$_2$-RA-AḪ		EDZARD,DER 231:2
QNIJ	1	JI	QNIJ		UM				IQ-NI-UM	FN	RA LXV 58 I 34
		JA	QNIJ				ʾIL		IA-AQ-NI-DINGIR		CT XLV 92 I 10+
		TA	QNIJ	T	UM				TA?-AQ-NI-TUM	FN	XIII 1 VIII 74
QRIʾ	1	JA	QRIʾ				ʾIL		IA-AQ-RI-DINGIR		B 27
QRIB	1	JI	QRIB	AN	UM				IQ-RI-BA-NU-UM		I
QṢUR	1	JA	QṢUR		UM				IA-AQ-ZU-RU-UM		BE VI/1 1 22+
		JA	QṢUR				ʾIL		IA-AQ-ZU-UR-DINGIR		B 29+
QUWJ	1		QUWJ		UM				KU-IA-UM		YOS XII +
			QUWJ		UM				KU-WU-UM		EDZARD,DER 94:18
			QUWJ	AT	UM				KU-IA-TUM		CT VIII 29A 29+
			QUWJ				JARAḪ		KU-WE-RA-AḪ		A 32133 REV.4
			QUWJ				MILK	U	QU-U$_2$-LUGAL		MRS XII 31:24
			QUWJ		U		HADD	U	KU-U$_2$-D-IM		M
			QUWJ		UM		HADD	U	KU-UM-D-U		MRS XVI 9:7
			QUWJ		U		DAGAN		KU-U$_2$-D-DA-GAN		RA LXV 41 II 43+
	2		ŠI				QUWJ	I	ŠI-I-KU-WI	FN	A. 8 12, 34
QUDAŠ	1		QUDAŠ		UM				GU-DA-SU-UM		JCS XXIV 60 NO.51+
QUDM	2		ʾADM		U		QUDM	I	AD-MU-KU-UD-MI	FN	XIII 1 IX 55
			ʾANN		U		QUDM	I	AN-NU-KU-UD-MI	FN	XIII 1 VIII 77
			MAM		A		QUDM	I	D-MA-MA-KU-UD-ME	FN	RA LXV 59 II 18
RḪAB	1	JA	RḪAB		UM				IA-AR-ḪA-BU-UM		B 29+
RḪAM	1	JA	RḪAM		UM				IA-AR-A-MU-UM		M+
		JA	RḪAM		U				IA-AR-ḪA-MU		B 29+, M
		JA	RḪAM	AN					IA-AR-ḪA-MA-AN	FN	RA LXV 55 XIII 51
		JA	RḪAM		I		ʾIL		IA-AR-ḪA-MI-DINGIR		KISURRA 5A 15+
		JA	RḪAM				ʾIL		IA-AR-ḪA-AM-DINGIR		B 29
		JI	RḪAM		I		ʾIL		IR-ḪA-MI-DINGIR		A.
		JI	RḪAM				ʾIL	A	IR-ḪA-MI-LA		A.+
		JI	RḪAM				ʾILL	A	IR-ḪA-MI-IL-LA		A. 274 26
	2		ʾANN		U	TA	RḪAM		AN-NU-TA-AR-AM	FN	M+
RḪAQ	1	JI	RḪAQ		UM				IR-ḪA-KUM		B 22
		JI	RḪAQ		UM				II-IR-ḪA-KUM		SIMMONS 86 10+
		JE	RḪAQ		UM				E-ER-ḪA-KUM		SIMMONS 112 7, SEAL
RḪIB	1	JI	RḪIB						IR-IB		U
		JI	RḪIB						I-RI-IB		I
		JA	RḪIB		UM				IA-AR-I-BU-UM		RA LXIV NO.33
		JA	RḪIB		U				IA-AR-I-BU		XIII 1 VI 63
		JA	RḪIB				ḪAJJ	A	IA-AR-IB-D-E$_2$-A		M+
		JA	RḪIB				ʾABB	A	IA-AR-IB-D-AB-BA		M
		JA	RḪIB				HADD	U	IA-AR-IB-D-IM		M+
		JA	RḪIB				ʾIL		IA-AR-I-IB-DINGIR		M+
		JA	RḪIB				ʾIL		IA-AR-IB-DINGIR		M+
		JA	RḪIB				ʾIRR	A	IA-AR-IB-D-IR$_3$-RA		M
		JA	RḪIB				ʾIRR	A	IA-AR-I-[IB]-IR$_3$-RA		M
		JA	RḪIB				DAGAN		IA-AR-IB-D-DA-GAN		M+
RḪIQ	1	JA	RḪIQ		UM				IA-AR-ḪI-KU-UM		A 32133:7
		JI	RḪIQ		A				IR-ḪI-GA		M
RḪAŠ	1	MA	RḪAŠ	AN					MAR-ḪA-ŠA-AN		RA LXV 54 XII 12
RʿIJ	1	JA	RʿIJ				HADD	U	JA-RI-A-DU		RA LXV 50 VIII 64
		JA	RʿIJ				ʾIL		IA-AR-ḪI-DINGIR		CT XLVIII 27
RʿIŠ	1	JA	RʿIŠ		UM				IA-RI-ŠUM		B 29
		TA	RʿIŠ	AH					DA-RI$_2$-ŠA	FN	U
		TA	RʿIŠ				ḪAʾT	U	TA-RI-IŠ-ḪA-AT-TU	FN	M+
		TA	RʿIŠ				ʿAŠTAR		T[A-R]I-IŠ-EŠ$_4$-DAR	FN	RA LXV 65 VII 36
		TA	RʿIŠ				MAʾT	UM	TA-RI-IŠ-MA-TUM	FN	M+, C
	2		ʾIL		A	TA	RʿIŠ		I-IA-TA-RI-IŠ		B 21

STEMS

RWIḪ	1	JA	RWIḪ									IA-RI-IḪ	GN	M
		JA	RWIḪ	AJ	I							IA-RI-ḪA-JI-KI	GN	M
		JA	RWIḪ	IJ	I							IA-RI-ḪI-I-KI	GN	M+
		JA	RWIḪ		A			ʾAB	UM			IA-RI-ḪA-A-BU-UM		VII P. 234 N. 4
		JA	RWIḪ		A			ʾAB	AM			IA-RI-ḪA-A-BA-AM	ACC	XIV 101:8
		JA	RWIḪ		A			ʾAB	AM			IA-RI-ḪA-A-BA-AN	ACC	VII P. 234 N. 4
		JA	RWIḪ		A			ʾAB	IM			IA-RI-ḪA-A-BI-IM	GEN	M+
		JA	RWIḪ		A			ḪAM	U			IA-RI-ḪA-A-MU		M+
		JE	RWIḪ		I			ʾIL				E-RI-ḪI-DINGIR		U
	2		LA				JE	RWIḪ	UM			LA-E-RI-ḪU-UM		U
RWIJ	1	JA	RWIJ		UM							IA-AR-WI-UM	NOM	KUPPER, NOM. P. 199
		JA	RWIJ					ʾIL				A-AR-WI-DINGIR		HARRIS 98 R. 7
RWIM	1	JA	RWIM					ḪAʾL				IA-RI-IM-ḪA-AL		M+
		JA	RWIM					HADD	U			IA-RI-IM-D-IM		M+
		JI	RWIM					ʾILL	A			I-RI-MIL-LA		A. 87 30 LATE
		JI	RWIM					ʾILL	A			I-RI-IM-IL-LA		A. LATE
		JI	RWIM					ʾILL	A			I-RI-MI-IL-LA		A. LATE
		JA	RWIM					ʿAMM	U			IA-RI-IM-ḪA-MU		M
		JA	RWIM					ʿAMM	U			IA-RI-IM-ḪA-AM-MU		M
		JA	RWIM					JARAḪ				IA-RI-IM-IA-RA-AḪ		RA LXV 41 II 28
		JA	RWIM					JARAḪ				IA-RI-IM-E-RA-AḪ		M
		JA	RWIM					DAWD	U			IA-RI-IM-DA-DU		RA LXV 40 I 38+
		JA	RWIM					DAGAN				IA-RI-IM-D-DA-GAN		M+
		JI	RWIM					DAGAN				I-RI-IM-D-DA-GAN		SYRIA XXXVII 206 2 HANA
		JA	RWIM					LIʾM				IA-RI-IM-LI-IM		SIMMONS 66 77, M+, C+, A.+
		JA	RWIM					MALIK				IA-RI-IM-MA-LIK		A 3580:2+
		JA	RWIM					ŠUM	U					
								ʾAB	I			IA-RI-IM-SU-MU-A-BI		RA LXV 42 III 8
		TA	RWIM					ʿAŠTAR				TA-RI-IM-EŠ$_4$-DAR	FN	XIII 1 II 13
		TA	RWIM					ŠAKIM				TA-RI-IM-ŠA-KI-IM		M+
	2		ʿABD		U		TA	RWIM				[ḪA-A]B-DU-TA-RI-IM		M
			ʾAŠD		U	NA	JA	RWIM				[AŠ$_2$-D]U-NI-A-RI-IM		CT XXXVI 4 1
			ʾAŠD		U	NA	JE	RWIM				AŠ$_2$-DU-NI-E-RI-IM		RA VIII 65 1
			ŠUM		U	NA	JA	RWIM				SU-UM-MU-NA-A-RI-IM		HARRIS 57 11
	3		ŠUM		U			ʾAB	I					
							JA	RWIM				SU-MU-A-BI-A-RI-IM		TA 30 9, 14, 15+
			ŠUM		UM			ʾAB	I					
							JA	RWIM				SU-MU-UN-A-BI-IA-RI-IM		SUMER XXIII 153:9
			ŠUM		U	NA		ʾAB	I					
							JA	RWIM				SU-MU-NA-BI-IA-RI-IM		SUMER XXIII PL. 7 17+
			ŠUM		U	NA		ʾAB	I					
							JA	RWIM				SU-MU-UN?-A-BI-JA-RI-IM		SUMER XXIII P. 153 9
RWUB	1	TA	RWUB	AH								TA-RU-BA	FN	M
RJIB	1	JA	RJIB					HADD	U			IA-RI-IB-D-IM		B 29+
		JA	RJIB					DAGAN				IA-RI-IB-D-D[A-GAN]?		M
		TA	RJIB		UM							TA-RI-BU-UM		M
		TA	RJIB		IM							TA-RI-BI-IM	GEN	M
RAʾK	1		RAʾK	AT	UM							RA-KA-TU-UM	FN?	M
RAʾŠ	2		MA					RAʾŠ	UM			MA-A-RA-SU-UM		M
RAʾZ	1		RAʾZ		UM							RA-ZU-UM		TA 1931, 538 IV
RAḪAB	2		ʾANA					RAḪAB	U			A-NA-RA-A-BU		M+
			BALK		U	Š		RAḪAB				BA-AL-KU-UŠ$_2$-RA-ḪA-AB	FN	XIII 1 VIII 61
RAḪIB	1		RAḪIB		UM							RA-I-BU-UM		CT VIII 47A 7
RAḪIM	1		RAḪIM		UM							RA-I-MU-UM		JCS XXVI 151:21 HARMAL
			RAḪIM	AH								RA-ḪI-MA	FN	XIII 1 II 4+
RAḪM	1		RAḪM		AJA							RA-AḪ-MA-IA		M+
			RAḪM		I			....				RA-AḪ-MI-....	FN	M
			RAḪM		I			ʾIL	I			RA-AḪ-MI-I$_3$-LI$_2$		XIII 1 VIII 79+
	2		ʾANN		U			RAḪM	I			AN-NU-RA-AḪ-MI	FN	XIII 1 V 11+
			ʿAŠTAR					RAḪM	I			EŠ$_4$-DAR-RA-AḪ-MI	FN	XIII 1 VIII 83
RAḪAṢ	1		RAḪAṢ		U							RA-ḪA-ZU		WALTERS,WL 114:12
RAWḪ	1		RAWḪ	AT	UM							RA-ḪA-TUM	FN	XIII 1 XII 6
			RAWḪ		A			ʾANN	UM			RA-ḪA-AN-NU-UM		M
	2		ʾIL		A			RAWḪ	I	JA		DINGIR-RA[Ḫ]I-A		HARRIS 76 21
			ʾIL		A			RAWḪ	I	JA		I-LA-RA-ḪI-IA		M
			ʾIL		A			RAWḪ	I	JE		I-LA-RA-ḪI-E		M

STEMS

RAWḤ	2		ʾIL		A	RAWḤ	I	JE	DINGIR-RA-ḪI-E		HARRIS 85 14
			ʾIL		I	RAWḤ	I	JE	I_3-LI_2-RA-AḪ-E		VAS XVI 168 9, FRANK 13 9
			KULP		A	RAWḤ	I	JE	KU-UL-PA-RA-ḪI-E		TCL I 14 1, YOS VIII 141 34
			KANAK			RAWḤ	UM		KA-NA-AK-RA-ḪU-UM		VAS XIII 66A R. 5+
			KANAK			RAWḤ	U		KA-NA-AK-RA-ḪU		VAS XIII 66 R. 6
			KANAK			RAWḤ	I		KA-NA-AK-RA-ḪI		VAS XIII 79 R. 7
			MUT			RAWḤ			MU-UT-RA-AḪ		M
			ŚAM		A	RAWḤ			SA-MA-RA-AḪ		B 38+, XII 385 8
			ŚAM		U	RAWḤ			SA-MU-RA-A-AḪ		SIMMONS 46 28, 47 23
			ŚAM		U	RAWḤ			SA-MU-RA	NOM	CT XLVIII 29 REV.
			ŚUM		U	RAWḤ			SU-MU-RA-A		B 40
			ŚUM		U	RAWḤ			SU-MU-RA-AḪ		B 38+
			ŚUM		U	RAWḤ			SU-MU-RA-A-AḪ		CT II 39 1, 15
			ŚUM		U	RAWḤ	EM		[SU]-MU-RA-ḪI-E-IM		B 40
RAWM	1		RAWM						RA-AM	DN	PBS XIV 360
			RAWM			...			RA-MA-[....]		M
			RAWM	AT	UM				RA-MA-TUM	FN	M, CT VIII 1A 2+
			RAWM	AN	UM				RA-MA-NU-UM		B 47
			RAWM		A	JAT	UM		RA-MA-IA-TUM		B 22+
			RAWM		E	ʾEL			R[A]-ME-EL		RA LXV 42 II 56
	2		ʾAB		I	RAWM			A-BI-RA-AM		RA LXV 43 IV 12
			ʿAD		U	RAWM	U		A-DU-RA-MU	FN	U
		JI	JDAʿ			RAWM			I-DAḪ-RA-AM		MEISSNER 91 17
			ʾIL		I	RAWM			I_3-LI_2-RA-AM		M
			ʿAMM		U	RAWM	A		ḪA-MU-RA-MA		M
			ʾAŚD		I	RAWM			AŠ-DI-RA-AM		RA LXV 55 XIII 42
			BEʿL		I	RAWM			BE-LI_2-RA-AM		RA LXV 54 XII 60
			LAʾT		I	RAWM	E	JE	LA-TI-RA-ME-E		M
			MUT			RAWM	A		MU-UT-RA-MA		CT II 23 13
			MUT			RAWM	E	JE	MU-UT-RA-ME-E		BM 81584 3, M+
			MUT			RAWM	EM		MU-UT-RA-ME-IM		M
			MUT		U	RAWM	I	JE	MU-TU-RA-MI-E		CT XLV 63 15
			QAZIJ			RAWM	A		QA-ZI-RA-MA		A. LATE
			ŠU			RAWM	U		ŠU-RA-MU		A. LATE+
			ŠU			RAWM	A		ŠU-RA-MA		A. LATE+
			ŠI			RAWM	A		SI-I-RA-MA		A. 28 3, 16
			ŚUM		U	RAWM	E	JE	SU-MU-RA-ME-E		B 40+
			ŚUM		U	RAWM	EM		SU-MU-RA-ME-IM		M
RAJB	1		RAJB	AT	UM				RA-BA-TUM	FN	XIII 1 X 59+
			RAJB	AN					RA-[BA]?-AN		RA LXV 47 VI 67
			RAJB	AN	UM				RA-BA-NU-UM		RUTTEN 3 6+
			RAJB	AN	UM				RA-BA-A-NU-UM		RUTTEN 13 3, 8, SEAL+
			RAJB		A	SITR	U	HU	RA-BA-ZI-IT-RU-U_2	FN	M
RABAʿ	1		RABAʿ			DUDM	U		RA-BA?-AḪ-DU-UD-MU		M
RABAB	1		RABAB	AN					RA-BA-BA-AN		M
			RABAB	AN	UM				RA-BA-BA-NU-UM		KISURRA 187 11+
RABB	1		RABB		I	JARAḪ			RA-AB-BI-E-RA-AḪ		B 37+
			RABB		U	ʿAD	UM		RU-BU-ḪA-DU-UM		BM 17055 26
			RABB		U	ʿAD	U	HU	RA-AB-BU-ḪA-DU-U_2		B 17+
			RABB		U	ʿAD	U	HU	RA-AB-BU-U_2-ḪA-DU-U_2		BM 17051A 30
RAMAM	1		RAMAM	AN	UM				RA-MA-MA-NU-UM		B 93
RAMAŠ	1		RAMAŠ		I				RA-MA-ŠI	FN	M
			RAMAŠ		I				RA-MA-A-ŠI	FN	EDZARD,DER 224:42
RAMIK	1		RAMIK	AN	UM				RA-MI-GA-NU-UM		TA 1931, 538 II
RAMIŠ	1		RAMIŠ		UM				RA-MI-ŠUM		TA 1931, 538 III, V
RAPAʾ	1		RAPAʾ	AN	UM				RA-PA-NU-UM		BM 78768
	2		ŚUM		I	RAPAʾ			SU-MI-RA-PA		RA LVI 169, A.+
RAPIʾ	1		RAPIʾ		UM				RA-BI-U_2-UM		M+
			RAPIʾ		UM				RA-BI-JU-[UM]?		M
			RAPIʾ	AT	UM				RA-BI-A-TUM	FN	C+
			RAPIʾ	T	UM				RA-BI-TUM	FN	M
			RAPIʾ	AH					RA-BI-A	FN	XIII 1 VII 32+
			RAPIʾ			MI					
						ʾIL			RA-BI-MI-IL		BIROT,TEA 72 VI 19
			RAPIʾ			MI					
						ʾIL	UM		RA-BI-MI-LUM		BIROT,TEA 72 IX 29

STEMS

RAPIʾ	1		RAPIʾ			TA	ʾLAŠ		RA-BI-TA-AḪ-LA-AŠ		BASOR 95 22
	2		ḪAJJ		UM		RAPIʾ		ḪA-JU-UM-RA-BI		M
			ḪAʾL		U		RAPIʾ		ḪA-LU-RA-PI		M+
			ʾAB		I		RAPIʾ		A-BI-RA-BI		M
			ʾAB		I		RAPIʾ		A-BI-RA-PI		SYRIA XXXVII 206 6, 7
			ʾABN		U		RAPIʾ		AB-NU-RA-BI		C, C II P. 244+
			ʿADN		U		RAPIʾ		ḪA-AD-NU-RA-BI		XIV 109:18+
			ʾIL		I		RAPIʾ		I$_3$-LI$_2$-RA-BI		M+
			ʾALLA				RAPIʾ		AL-LA-RA-PI		TCL XVIII 95 12, 15
			ʿAMM		I		RAPIʾ		AM-MI-RA-PI		SYRIA XXXVII 206 END HANA
			ʿAMM		I		RAPIʾ		AM-MI-RA-BI-IḪ		RA XXXIV 186 HANA
			ʿAMM		I		RAPIʾ		ḪA-AM-MI-RA-BI		B 19
			ʿAMM		U		RAPIʾ		ḪA-AM-MU-RA-BI		B 19+, M+, A.+
			ʿAMM		UM		RAPIʾ		ḪA-AM-MU-UM-RA-BI		B 19+
			ʿAMM		U		RAPIʾ		AM-MU-RA-BI		B 19+
			ʿAMM		U		RAPIʾ		D-ḪA-AM-MU-RA-BI		B 19+
			ʿAMM		U		RAPIʾ		ḪA-MU-RA-BI		B 19+, M+
			ʿAMM		U		RAPIʾ		ḪA-AM-MU-RA-BI-IḪ		B 19 HANA
			ʿAMM		U		RAPIʾ		AM-MU-RA-PI		ABL 255 LATE
			ʿAMM		U		RAPIʾ		D-AM-MU-RA-PI		YBC 4362
			ʿAMM		UM		RAPIʾ		ḪA-AM-MU-UM-RA-PI		YBC 6496, 6508
			ʿAMM		UM		RAPIʾ		ḪA-MU-UM-RA-BI		BM 17046+
			ʿAMM		U		RAPIʾ		ḪA-MU-U$_2$-RA-BI		FIGULLA, CAT. 14138
			ʿAMM		U		RAPIʾ	I	AM-MU-RA-BI-I		A+
			ʿAMM		U		RAPIʾ		ḪA-MU-UR$_2$-RA-BI		CT XLVII 31 32+
			ʿAMM		U		RAPIʾ				
							ʾIL		ḪA-AM-MU-RA-BI-DINGIR		B 19
			ʿAMM		U		RAPIʾ				
							BANIJ		ḪA-AM-MU-RA-BI-BA-NI		B 19
			ʿAMM		UM		RAPIʾ				
							....		[ḪA-AM]-MU-UM-RA-PI-LI-WI-IR		UNPUBL.
			ʿAMM		U		RAPIʾ				
							....		ḪA-AM-MU-RA-BI-LU-DA-RI		B 19
			ʿAMM		U	HU	RAPIʾ		ḪA-AM-MU-U$_2$-RA-BI		M
			ḪAMR		U		RAPIʾ		ḪA-AM-RU-RA-BI		M
		ʾA	JPAʿ				RAPIʾ		A-PA-AḪ-RA-BI		SUMER XIV 5, IM 52272
			ʾAŠD		U		RAPIʾ		AŠ$_2$-DU-RA-BI		C+
			DAWD		U		RAPIʾ		DA-DU-RA-BI		B 16+
		JI	ḎKUR				RAPIʾ		IZ-KUR-RA-BI		BM 81591 7
			ḎIMR				RAPIʾ	I	ZI-ME-IR-RA-BI-I		TA 30 34
			ḎIMR		U		RAPIʾ		ZI-IM-RU-RA-BI		TA 30 82
		JA	KWUN				RAPIʾ		IA-KU-UN-RA-BI		M
			LU				RAPIʾ		LU$_2$-RA-BI$_2$		I
			MUT				RAPIʾ		MU-UT-[R]A-BI		M
		JA	ŠWUB				RAPIʾ		IA-ŠU-UB-RA-BI		A.
			ŠIʾN		U		RAPIʾ		ŠI-NU-RA-BI		A.+
			ŠIʾN		U		RAPIʾ		SI-NU-RA-BI		A.+
			ŚUM		A		RAPIʾ		SU-MA-RA-BI		KAJ 39 17 LATE
			ŚUM		U		RAPIʾ		SU-MU-RA-BI		M
			ŚUMḪ		U		RAPIʾ		SU-UM-ḪU-RA-BI		M+
			ŚAMŠ		I		RAPIʾ		ŠA-AM-[SI]-RA-BI		M
RAPŠ	2		MUT				RAPŠ	IM	MU-UT-RA-AP-ŠI-IM		RA LXV 53 XI 7
RAPUʾ	1		RAPUʾ		UM				RA-PU-U$_2$-UM		RA LXV 41 II 30
			RAPUʾ	AT	UM				RA-PU-A-TUM		A 7660 1
	2		ḎIMR		I		RAPUʾ		ZI-IM-RI-RA-BU		M
			ŠUWB		U		RAPUʾ		ŠU-BU-RA-BU		TCL X 4A 25, B 15
RAŠAP	2		ʾAB		I		RAŠAP		A-BI-RA-SA-AP		M
		JA	ḪBAʾ				RAŠAP		IA-AḪ-BA-D-RA-SA-AP		XIII 94 5
			ʾIL		I		RAŠAP		I$_3$-LI$_2$-D-RA-SA-[AP]		XIII 66 5
		JA	ʾZUW				RAŠAP		IA-AḪ-ZU-D-RA-SA-AP		M
RAŠIJ	1		RAŠIJ			JA			RA-SI-A		TIM III 134 4
RAṢAJ	1		RAṢAJ				DAGAN		RA-ZA-D-DA-GAN		M
RAṢIJ	1		RAṢIJ		IM				RA-ZI-IM-KI	GN	M
			RAṢIJ		EM				RA-ZI-E-IM-KI	GN	M+
	2		ŚUM		U		RAṢIJ	EM	[SU]-MU-RA-ZI-E-IM		B 40
RAZIN	1		RAZIN		IM				RA-ZI-NI-IM	GEN	HARRIS 71 9

STEMS

RBIJ	1	JA	RBIJ				ʾEL			IA-AR-BI-EL		CT XLV 12 23
		JA	RBIJ				ʾIL			IA-AR-BI-DINGIR		B 29+
		JA	RBIJ				ʾIL			I-AR-BI-DINGIR		KISURRA 5A 8+
		JE	RBIJ				ʾIL			E-IR-BI-DINGIR		KISURRA 22A 15
	2		ʾANN		U	TA	RBIJ			AN-NU-TAR-BI	FN	XIII 1 XI 47
RBUʾ	1	JA	RBUʾ				ʾIL			IA-AR-BU-DINGIR		KISURRA 9A 9+
		JE	RBUʾ			HU	ʾEL			E-[IR]-BU-U$_2$-[E]L		KISURRA 152 9
RDAK	1	ʾA	RDAK				HAND	A		AR-DA-KA-AN-DA		M
RDAP	1	MA	RDAP		UM					MAR-DA-BU-UM		BIN III 546; U+
		MA	RDAP	AN						MAR-DA-BA-AN		ITT P.4, 7031 UR III
		MA	RDAP	AN	UM					MAR-DA-BA-NU-UM		U
RGAM	1	ʾA	RGAM	AT	UM					AR-GA-MA-TUM	FN	C
RIḪṢ	2		ʾIL		I		RIḪṢ	I		I$_3$-LI$_2$-RI-IḪ-ZI	FN	XIII 1 IX 39
RIʿAJ	2		ʾIPQ				RIʿAJ		HU	I-BI-IQ-RI-E-U$_2$		U
			LU				RIʿAJ		HU	LU$_2$-RI-E$_2$-U$_2$		U
			LU				RIʿAJ		HU	LU$_2$-RI-ḪU		U
RIʿŠ	1		RIʿŠ	AT			....			RI-ŠA-A[T-....]	FN	I 89 5
RIWḪ	1		RIWḪ	AN						RI-ḪA-AN		C
			RIWḪ	AT	UM					RI-ḪA-DU-UM?		U UNPUBL.
			RIWḪ	AT	UM					RI-ḪA-TUM	FN	XIII 1 I 23+
RIWM	1		RIWM	AT	UM					RI-MA-TUM	FN	M+
			RIWM	AN						[R]I?-MA-AN		RA LXV 41 II 8
			RIWM	AN	UM					RI-MA-NU-UM		U
			RIWM				HADD	U		RI-IM-D-IM		M+, A. 57 46
			RIWM				ʾIL	A		RI-IM-I-LA		TCL XIV 54 17 CAPP.
			RIWM				DAGAN			RI-IM-D-DA-GAN		M
			RIWM		U		HADD	U		RI-MU-D-IM		M
	2		LA				RIWM					
							ḪAM	I		LA-RI-IM-D-A-MI		M
			LA				RIWM					
							ʿAḎIR			LA-RI-IM-ḪA-ZI-IR		DELAPORTE, CAT. BN 207
			LA				RIWM					
						JI	JBAL	U	HU	[L]A?-RI-IM-I-BA-LU-U$_2$		M
			LA				RIWM					
							BAʿL	I		LA-RI-IM-BA-AḪ-LI		M+
			LA				RIWM					
							BEʿL	I		LA-RI-IM-BE-LI$_2$		X 69 5
			LA				RIWM					
							DIWR			LA-RI-IM-DI-IR		RA LXV 50 IX 22
			LA				RIWM					
							LU		HU	LA-RI-IM-LU-U$_2$		M
			LA				RIWM					
							NUMAḪ	A		LA-RI-IM-NU-MA-ḪA-A		M+
			LA				RIWM					
							NUMAḪ	A		LA-RI-IM-NU-MA-A		M
		JI	NDIN				RIWM			I-DIN-D-RI-IM		TCL I 238 16 HANA
	3		ʿAMM		U		LA					
							RIWM			ḪA-MU-L[A]-RI-IM		RA LXV 46 VI 40
			KAʾB		I		LA					
							RIWM			KA-BI-LA-RI-IM		RA LXV 47 VI 65+; C+
RIJB	1		RIJB		UM					RI-I-BU-UM		I
			RIJB	AT	UM					RI-BA-TUM	FN	CT VIII 48B 7+, M+, C+
			RIJB		A		ʿAMM	U		RI-BA-AM-MU		A. 97 4+
			RIJB		U	HU				RI-BU-U$_2$		KISURRA 187 12
			RIJB		U		DAGAN			RI-BU-D-DA-GAN		RA LXV 47 VII 52
	2		ŠUM		I		RIJB	A		SU-MI-RI-BA		A. 98C 10
			ŠUM		I		RIJB	A		ŠU-MI-RI-PA		A. LATE
			ŠUM		I		RIJB	A		ŠU-ME-RI-PA		A. LATE
			TIʾM				RIJB	A		TI-IM-RI-PA		A.
RIBK	1		RIBK		U					RI-IB-KU	FN	XIII 1 IX 56+
RIGM	1		RIGM	AN	U					RI-IG-MA-NU		M
			RIGM	AN	UM					RI-IG-MA-NUM		M
RIMŠ	1		RIMŠ		I		ʾIL			RI-IM-ŠI-DINGIR		M+
			RIMŠ		I		ʾIL	I		RI-IM-ŠI-I$_3$-LI$_2$		M
	2		ʾANN		U		RIMŠ	I		AN-NU-RI-IM-ŠI	FN	M+
			KAKK		A		RIMŠ	I		KA-AK-KA-RI-IM-ŠI	FN	RA LXV 60 III 5

RIPʾ	1			RIPʾ		IM					RI-IP-I-IM	GEN	M+
				RIPʾ		A		ʾIL	A		RI-IP-A-DINGIR		M+
				RIPʾ		A		MALIK			RI-IP-A-MA-LIK		M
				RIPʾ		I		HADD	U		RI-IP-I-D-IM		M+
				RIPʾ		I		HEDD	A		RI-IP-E-D-IM		M
				RIPʾ		I		DAGAN			RI-IP-I-D-DA-GAN		M+
				RIPʾ		I		DAGAN			RI-BI-D-DA-GAN		M
				RIPʾ		I		LIʾM			RI-IP-I-LI-IM		M
RKAB	1	JI		RKAB	T	UM					IR-KAB-TUM	MN	A.+
		JI		RKAB	T	U					IR-KAB-DU	MN	A.+ LATE
		JA		RKAB				HADD	U		IA-AR-KA-AB-D-IM		4E RENCONTRE 23
RKIB	1	JA		RKIB		A		HADD	U		IA-AR-KI-BA-D-IM		XIII 145 6
RMAN	1	ʾA		RMAN	UN	UM					AR-MA-NU-NUM$_2$		TA 1931 , 538 IV
RMUK	1	JI	N	RMUK							I-NI-IR-MU-UK		M+
		JI	N	RMUK							I-NE-IR-MU-UK		M
RPAʾ	1	JA		RPAʾ				HADD	U		IA-AR-PA-D-IM		M+
		JI		RPAʾ				ʾAB	I		IR-PA-A-BI		A.+
		JI		RPAʾ				HADD	A		IR-PA-A-DA		A. 76 8+
		JI		RPAʾ				HADD	A		IR-PA-DA		A. 41 14
		JI		RPAʾ				HADD	U		IR-PA-D-IM		A.+
RŠAP	1	JA		RŠAP				LA					
								ʾIL			IA-AR-SA-AP-LA-DINGIR		M+
		JA		RŠAP				LA					
								ʾIL	A		IA-AR-SA-AP-LA-I-[LA]?		M
		TA		RŠAP	AH						TA-AR-SA-BA	FN	RA LXV 64 VI 28
RŠIJ	1	ʾA		RŠIJ				ʾAḪ	UM		AR-ŠI-A-ḪU-UM		M+
		ʾA		RŠIJ				ʿAD	A	HA	AR-ŠI-A-DA?-A	FN	C
		ʾA		RŠIJ				HADD	A		AR-ŠI-A-DA		M
		ʾA		RŠIJ				ʾEDAK	U		AR-ŠI-E-DA-KU	FN	M
		ʾA		RŠIJ				ʿAN	UM		AR-SI?-A-NUM$_2$		U
		JA		RŠIJ				ʾAŠAR	I		IA-AR-ŠI-A-ŠA-RI		M
		JA		RŠIJ				ʾIL			IA-AR-ŠI-DINGIR		B 29+, M
		JA		RŠIJ				ʾIL	I		A-AR-ŠI-DINGIR		TA 1930,7:6
		JA		RŠIJ				ʾIL	UM		IA-AR-ŠI-DINGIR-UM		UCP X/1 P. 58+
		JA		RŠIJ				ʿAMM	U		IA-AR-ŠI-ḪA-MU		M, C+
	2			ʾAḪ		AM	ʾA	RŠIJ			A-ḪA-AM-AR-ŠI		I+
				LA			ʾA	RŠIJ	UM		LA-AR-ŠI-U$_2$-U[M]		TA 1931, 538 IV
RUḪB	1			RUḪB	AT	UM					RU-UḪ-BA-TUM	FN	XIII 1 IX 46
RUWḪ	2			KANIK				RUWḪ	UM		KA-NI-IK-RU-UM		B 33+
				KANIK				RUWḪ	UM		KA-NI-IK-RUM		B 33
				KANIK				RUWḪ	IM		KA-NI-IK-RI-IM	GEN	B 33
RUWB	1			RUWB	AT	UM					RU-BA-TUM	FN	M+
				RUWB	AT	IM					RU-BA-TIM	FN GEN	M
				RUWB		AJA					RU-BA-IA	FN	XIII 1 II 10+
				RUWB		AJA					RU-BA-A-IA	FN	RA LXIV 43
				RUWB	AN						RU-BA?-AN		RA LXV 45 V 34
	2			ʾADM		U		RUWB	AH		D-AD-MU-RU-BA	FN	XIII 1 VII 59
RUWM	1			RUWM	AT	UM					RU-MA-TUM	FN	XIII 1 VI 10
RUKAB	1			RUKAB	AT	UM					RU-KA-BA-TUM	FN	XIII 1 V 33
RUŠP	2	JI		NDIN				RUŠP	AN		I-DIN-D-RU-UŠ-PA-AN		MAOG IV 2 5 HANA+
		JI		NDIN				RUŠP	AN		I-DIN-D-RU-UŠ$_2$-PA-AN		MEL. SYR. I 275
SANIQ	1			SANIQ		UM					ZA-NI-KUM		M
SATUR	1			SATUR		UM					ZA-TU-RU-UM		RA LXIV 34 NO.24
SAṮIʾ	1	JA		SAṮIʾ				ʾEL			[I]A-ZA-AD-DI-EL		M
		JA		SAṮIʾ				ʾIL			IA-ZA-AD-DI-DINGIR		M+
		JA		SAṮIʾ				ʾIL			IA-ZA-AT-TI-DINGIR		M
		JA		SAṮIʾ				ʾIL			IA-SA-AD-DI-DINGIR		M
		JA		SAṮIʾ				ʾIL			IA-S[A]-TI-DINGIR		M
				SAṮIʾ	AT	UM					ZA-DI-IA-TUM	FN	XIII 1 I 72
SIKIL	1			SIKIL		UM					ṢI-KI-LUM		KISURRA 27 11
				SIKIL		IM					ZI-KI-LI-IM	GEN	TCL I 185 3
				SIKIL		IJA					ZI-KI-LI-IA		CT XLVIII 89
				SIKIL	T	A					ZI-KI-IL-DA	MN	A. 24 3
				SIKIL	T	A					ZI-KI-IL-TA	MN	A. LATE+
				SIKIL	T	A					ZI-KI-EI-TA	MN	A. LATE
				SIKIL	T	E					ZI-GI-II-TE	MN	A.

STEMS													
SIKIL	1		SIKIL					DANN	UM		ZI-GI-IL-DA-NU-UM		M+
SIKL	1		SIKL		UM						ZI-IK-LUM		TIM V 31 19
SIMT	1		SIMT		I			JARAḪ			ZI-IM-TI-E-RA-AḪ		M+
SINAQ	1		SINAQ		I						ZI-NA-GI		M
SINUQ	1		SINUQ		A						SI-NU-GA		BIROT,TEA 16:11
			SINUQ		A						ZI-NU-GA		M+
SITR	1		SITR		IJA						ZI-IT-RI-IA		M+, C+
			SITR		IJA						ZI-IT-RI-JA		M
			SITR		A			HADD	U		ZI-IT-RA-A-DU		A. 456 19
			SITR		I			JABAL			ZI-IT-RI-E-BA-AL		M+
			SITR		I			HADD	U		ZI-IT-RI-D-IM		M
			SITR		I			HADD	U		SI-IT-RI-D-IM		JCS XXIV 60 NO.51 REV.
			SITR		I	JE		HADD	U		ZI-IT-RI-E-D-IM		JCS XXIV 63 NO.56 REV.
			SITR		I			ʾEL	UM		ZI-IT-RI-E-LUM		B 42
			SITR		I			ʾIL			ZI-IT-RI-DINGIR		B 42
			SITR		I			KI					
								ʾEL			ZI-IT-RI?-KI-EL?		B 42
			SITR		U	HU					ZI-IT-RU-U$_2$		DE GEN. KICH II C 82
	2		LI			JA		SITR	U	HU	LI-IA-ZI-IT-RU-U$_2$		M+
			RAJB		A			SITR	U	HU	RA-BA-ZI-IT-RU-U$_2$	FN	M
SNIQ	1	JA	SNIQ	AN							IA-AS-NI-KA-AN		RA LXV 50 VIII 51
		JA	SNIQ					ʾIL			IA-AS-NI-IQ-DINGIR		RA LXV 48 VII 66
		JA	SNIQ					ʾIL			IA-AŠ$_2$-NI-IQ-DINGIR		SIMMONS 55 14
SRID	1	JI	SRID		UM						IZ-RI-TUM		CT XLV 116 16
SUKIL	1		SUKIL		UM						ZU-KI-LUM		KISURRA 38 SEAL
SUMUKAN	1		SUMUKAN				JI	JBAL			D-GIR$_3$-I-BA-AL		C
SUTAR	1		SUTAR	AH							ZU?-TA-RA	FN	RA LXV 61 IV 42
SUṮIʾ	1		SUṮIʾ	AN	UM						ZUM-TI-A-NU-U[M]		TA 1930, 6
ŠḪIR	1	JA	ŠḪIR		UM						IA-AŠ-ḪI-RUM		M
ŠJIM	1	JA	ŠJIM	AT	UM						IA-SI-MA-TUM	FN	RA LXV 60 III 8
		JA	ŠJIM					ḤAJJ	A		[I]A-ŠI-IM-E$_2$-A		M
		JI	ŠJIM					ḤAJJ	A		I-ŠI-IM-E$_2$-A		M
		JA	ŠJIM					ʾAB	IM		IA-SI-IM-A-BI-IM	GEN	M
		JA	ŠJIM					HADD	U		IA-SI-IM-D-IM		M
		JA	ŠJIM					ʾIL			IA-SI-IM-DINGIR		M+
		JA	ŠJIM					ʿAMM	U		IA-SI-IM-ḪA-AM-MU		M
		JA	ŠJIM					ʿAMM	U		IA-SI-IM-ḪA-MU		M
		JA	ŠJIM					ʾIRR	A		IA-ŠI-IM-IR$_3$-RA		M
		JA	ŠJIM					DAGAN			IA-SI-IM-D-DA-GAN		M+
		JA	ŠJIM					DAGAN			IA-ŠI-IM-D-DA-GAN		VIII 11 33
		JA	ŠJIM					KI					
								ʾIL			IA-SI-IM-KI-DINGIR		M
		JA	ŠJIM					MAHAR			IA-SI-IM-MA-ḪA-AR		M
		JA	ŠJIM					ŠUM	U	HU	IA-SI-IM-SU-MU-U$_2$		M+
		TA	ŠJIM					ʿAŠTAR			TA-ŠI-IM-EŠ$_4$-DAR	FN	XIII 1 IV 28
	2		ŠUM		U		JA	ŠJIM			SU-MU-IA-SI-IM		M+
	3		ŠAM		I			MA					
							JA	ŠJIM			SA-MI-MA-IA-SI-IM	FN	C+
ŠJIT	1	JA	ŠJIT		UM						IA-SI-TUM		XIII 98 3+
		JA	ŠJIT	AN							IA-SI-TA-AN		M+
		JA	ŠJIT	AN							IA-SI-IT-TA-AN		M
		JA	ŠJIT					ʾAB	I		IA-SI-IT-A-BI		M
		JA	ŠJIT					ʾAB	U		IA-SI-IT-A-BU		M+
		JA	ŠJIT			NA					IA-SI-IT-NA		TIM IV 20 SEAL, M
		JI	ŠJIT			NA					I-SI-IT-NA		UCP X/1 58 3
		JA	ŠJIT			NA		ʾAB	U		IA-SI-IT-NA-A-BU		XIII 1 XII 15
		MA	ŠJIT					ʿAN	UM		MA-SI-IT-A-NU-UM		I
	2		ʾAḪ		I		JA	ŠJIT			A-ḪI-SI-IT		TA 1931, 636
			ŠUM		U		JA	ŠJIT			SU-MU-IA-SI-IT		B 39
ŠAʾAD	1		ŠAʾAD		IJA						SA-A-DI-IA		C+
ŠAʾAL	1		ŠAʾAL		A						SA-A-LA	NOM	CT II 42 2, 5
ŠAʾB	1		ŠAʾB	AT	UM						SA-BA-TUM		JCS XXIV 57 NO. 42,44
ŠAʾIL	1		ŠAʾIL	AT	UM						SA-I-LA-TUM	FN	B 37, TIM IV 53 7
			ŠAʾIL	T	UM						ŠA-IL-TUM	FN	U+
ŠAʾIQ	1		ŠAʾIQ		UM						ŠA-I-GU-UM		RA LXV 54 XII 27
ŠAʾIR	1		ŠAʾIR	AT	UM						SA-E-RA-TUM	FN	B 37

STEMS

ŚAʾIR	1			ŚAʾIR	AT	IM				SA-E-RA-TIM	FN GEN	B 37+
ŚAʾL	1			ŚAʾL	AT	UM				SA-LA-TUM	FN	CT VIII 20B 9+, M+, C+
				ŚAʾL	AN	UM				ŠA-LA-NU-UM		TA 30, 615 23
				ŚAʾL		IJA				SA-LI-IA		B 37
				ŚAʾL		I		ʾIL		SA-LI-DINGIR		B 37+
				ŚAʾL		U		MAṬAR		SA-LU-MA-DAR		RA LXV 52 X 68+
ŚAʾQ	1			ŚAʾQ		UM				SA-KUM		UCP X/1 P. 61+, M
				ŚAʾQ	AT	UM				SA-QA?-TUM	FN	XIII 1 VI 59
				ŚAʾQ		IJAN				ŠA-GI-IA-AN		RA LXV 54 XII 11+
				ŚAʾQ		U	HU			SA-GU-U_2		SIMMONS 60 31
				ŚAʾQ		A		ʿAN	UM	SA-GA-A-NU-UM		B 47
ŚAʾR	1			ŚAʾR		UM				SA-RU-UM		TIM II 89 2, M
				ŚAʾR		I				SA-RI	GEN	VAS VIII 14 28
				ŚAʾR		IJA				SA-RI-IA		UCP X/1 108 10+
				ŚAʾR	AN	UM				SA-RA-NU-UM		TIM V 19 4
ŚAḪIR	1			ŚAḪIR		A				ŠA-ḪI-RA	NOM	CT VIII 37D 1, 9
				ŚAḪIR		A				ŠA-ḪI-RA	GEN	CT VIII 37D 6, 13
ŚAḪR	1		T	ŚAḪR	AH					SI?-TA-AḪ-RA	FN	IX 291 III 29'
ŚAWIR	1			ŚAWIR	AT	UM				SA-WI-RA-TUM		UET V 378 5
				ŚAWIR	AN	IM				SA-WI-RA-NI-IM	GEN	TA 1930, 558
ŚABAŚ	2			ŚUM		U	JA	ŚABAŚ	UM	SU-MU-IA-SA-BA-SU-UM		PBS XI/2 1 I 34
ŚABIM	1			ŚABIM		UM				SA-BI-MU-UM		M+
				ŚABIM		U				SA-BI-MU		C+
				ŚABIM	AT	IM				SA-BI-MA-TIM	FN NOM	RA LXIV 43
ŚADID	1			ŚADID		UM				SA-DI-DU-UM		HARRIS 76 17
ŚADIR	1			ŚADIR	AT	UM				SA-DI-RA-TUM?	FN	BM 80485 7, 18
ŚADL	1			ŚADL		U		MA		SA-AD-LU-MA		UCP X/1 P. 61+
ŚADR	1			ŚADR		UM				SA-AD-[RU]?-UM		RA LXV 53 XI 34
ŚAGAR	1			ŚAGAR		UM				SA-GA-RU-UM		GAUTIER 4 R. 4+
				ŚAGAR		UM				SAG-GA-RU-UM		UET V 534 R. 6+
				ŚAGAR		UM				SA-AN-GA-RU-UM		BIN VII 45 12
				ŚAGAR	AT	UM				SA-GA-RA-TUM-KI	GN	M+
				ŚAGAR	AT	IM				SA-GA-RA-TIM-KI	GN GEN	M+
				ŚAGAR	AT	IM				SAG-GA-RA-TIM	MN GEN	M
				ŚAGAR	AT	IM				SAG-GA-RA-TIM	GN GEN	M+
				ŚAGAR	AT	IM				SA-AN-GA-RA-TIM-KI	GN GEN	M
ŚAKAN	1			ŚAKAN		UM				SA-KA-NU-UM		B 93
ŚAKAR	1			ŚAKAR		UM				SA-KA-RU-UM		HARRIS 39 13
				ŚAKAR		UM				SA-KA-RUM		BIN VII 90 12+
ŚAKB	1			ŚAKB		IJA				SA-[A]K-BI-IA		RA LXV 44 IV 34
				ŚAKB		I		HADD	U	SA-AK-BI-D-IM		ARMT V P. 123
ŚAKIR	1			ŚAKIR		UM				SA-KI-RUM		M+
				ŚAKIR		UM				SA-KI-RU-UM		RUTTEN 35 6, SEAL+
				ŚAKIR		U				SA-KI-RU		B 37
				ŚAKIR		AM				SA-KI-RA-AM	ACC	M
				ŚAKIR	AH					SA-KI-RA	FN	M
ŚAKN	1			ŚAKN		UM				SA-AK-NU-UM		TA 30, 36 2
				ŚAKN		U				SA-AK-NU	FN	M
				ŚAKN		U				ŠA-AK-NU		M
				ŚAKN	AT	UM				SA-AK-NA-TUM	FN	RA LXV 58 I 27
ŚAKUN	1			ŚAKUN	UN	UM				SA-KU-NU-NU-UM		RUTTEN 26 4
ŚAKUR	1			ŚAKUR	AN					SA-KU-RA-AN		RA LXV 54 XII 24
				ŚAKUR	AN	U				SA-KU-RA-NU		M+
ŚALAL	1			ŚALAL		UM				ŠA-LA-LUM		XIII 1 VII 29
ŚALAM	1			ŚALAM		UM				ŠA-LA-MU-UM		EDZARD, DER 100:16
				ŚALAM	AT	UM				SA-LA-MA-TUM	FN?	M
				ŚALAM	AN					SA-LA-MA-AN		RA LXV 43 III 55
ŚALD	1			ŚALD		IJA				SA-AL-DI-IA		TCL I 80 16
ŚALIḪ	1			ŚALIḪ		UM				SA-LI-ḪU-UM		M
				ŚALIḪ		U				SA-LI-ḪU		M, SYRIA V 274+ HANA
				ŚALIḪ	AH					SA-LI-ḪA	FN	M+
ŚALIL	1	JU	T	ŚALIL		I				UŠ-TA-LI-LI	NOM	M+
				ŚALIL		UM				SA-LI-LUM		TIM III 131 9
ŚALIM	1	MU		ŚALIM		UM				MU-SA-LI-MU-UM		CT XLVIII 57 2, 3
		MU		ŚALIM		U				MU-SA-LI-MU		CT IV 47B 28
		MU		ŚALIM		I				MU-SA-LI-MI	NOM	UCP X/1 87 11

STEMS											
ŠALIM	1	MU	ŠALIM		IM				MU-SA-LI-MI-IM	GEN	CT VIII 47B 28
		MU	ŠALIM	AT	IM				MU-SA-LI-MA-TIM	FN GEN	BE VI/1 8 14
			ŠALIM	AT	UM				SA-LI-MA-TUM	MN?	CT VIII 49A 46+
			ŠALIM	AT	UM				SA-LI-MA-TUM	FN	XIII 1 VI 46
			ŠALIM	AT	IM				SA-LI-MA-TIM	FN GEN	CT VIII 28C 13
			ŠALIM	AH					SA-LI-MA	FN	XIII 1 III 29+
			ŠALIM	AN					SA-LI-MA-AN		M+
			ŠALIM	AN	U				SA-LI-MA-NU		A 7733 4, C+
			ŠALIM	AN	IM				SA-LI-MA-NIM	GEN	M
			ŠALIM				ʿAN	UM	ŠA-LIM-A-NU-UM		M
			ŠALIM				ʾAŠAR		ŠA-LIM-D-A-ŠAR		M
	2	JI	ʾWUŠ				ŠALIM		I-UŠ?-SA-LIM		RUTTEN 1 3
			ʾAB		U		ŠALIM		A-BU-SA-[LIM]		M
			ʾIL		A		ŠALIM		I-LA-SA-LIM		M, C
			ʿAMM		U		ŠALIM		ḪA-MU-SA-L[IM]?		M
			JATAR				ŠALIM		IA-TAR-SA-LIM		M+
		JI	JṢIʾ				ŠALIM		I-ṢI-SA-LIM		RUTTEN 4 19+
			MUT				ŠALIM		MU-UT-SA-LIM		M
		JI	NDUB				ŠALIM		IN-DU-UB-ŠA-LIM		TA 1931, 265:10
		JI	TWUR				ŠALIM		I-DUR-SA-LIM		YOS II 84 21 22
ŠALM	1		ŠALM		U		ṬAJB	A	ŠA-AL-MU-ṬA$_3$-BA	FN	RA LXV 66 VII 64
	2		ʾIL		UM		ŠALM	A	I-LU-UM-ŠA-AL-MA		RA LXV 45 V 51
ŠALUḪ	1		ŠALUḪ		I				SA-AL-LU-ḪI	GEN	BE VI/2 138 2, 5
ŠAM	1		ŠAM		UM				SA-MU-UM		EBPN 141+, M
			ŠAM		IM				SA-MI-IM	GEN	CT XLVIII 91, XIII 142 40+
			ŠAM		AM				SA-MA-AM	ACC	XIII 38 7+
			ŠAM	AN					SA-MA-AN		B 39+, M
			ŠAM	AN	UM				SA-MA-NU-UM		B 47
			ŠAM	AN	UM				ŠA-MA-NUM$_2$		U
			ŠAM	AN	UM				ŠA-MA-NU-UM		I
			ŠAM	AN	U				SA-MA-NU		JNES XIII 212F. LATE
			ŠAM	AN	I				SA-MA-A-NI		JNES XIII 212F.+ LATE
			ŠAM		IJA				SA-MI-IA		EBPN 140+, MAM II/3 PL. XXXIX+
			ŠAM	T	UM				SA-AM-TUM	FN	TCL I 189 17, M+
			ŠAM		A		JADAʿ	UM	SA-MA-A-DA-ḪU-UM		M+
			ŠAM		A		JADAʿ	U	SA-MA-A-DA-ḪU		M
			ŠAM		A		JADAʿ	IM	SA-MA-A-DA-Ḫ[I-I]M	GEN	M
			ŠAM		A		ME				
							ʾEL		SA-MA-ME-EL		M
			ŠAM		A		ME				
							ʾEL		ŠA-MA-ME-EL		TA 1931, 421
			ŠAM		A		RAWḪ		SA-MA-RA-AḪ		B 38+, XII 385 8
			ŠAM		I		JARAḪ		SA-ME-E-RA-AḪ		M
			ŠAM		I		JARAḪ		SA-ME-RA-AḪ		YOS VIII 64 19+
			ŠAM		I		JATAR		SA-MI-E-TAR		XII 601 6
			ŠAM		I		DAʿ	UM	SA-MI-DA-ḪU-UM		M+
			ŠAM		I		DAʿ	IM	SA-MI-DA-ḪI-IM	GEN	M+
			ŠAM		I		DAʿ AT	UM	SA-MI-DA-ḪA-TUM	FN	M
			ŠAM		I		DAʿ AT	IM	SA-MI-DA-ḪA-TIM	FN? GEN	XII 741 6
			ŠAM		I		MA				
						JA	ŠJIM		SA-MI-MA-IA-SI-IM	FN	C+
			ŠAM		I		ME				
							ʾEL		SA-MI-ME-EL		CT XLV 117 33
			ŠAM		U		ʾAB	IM	SA-MU-A-BI-IM	NOM	RA VIII 71
			ŠAM		U		ʾAB	IM	SA-MU-A-BI-IM	GEN	SUMER XXIII 153+
			ŠAM		U		HADD	U	SA-MU-D-IM		M+
			ŠAM		U		ʾIL	A	SA-MU-I-LA		M
			ŠAM		U		JARAḪ		SA-MU-A-RA-AḪ		SIMMONS 98 3
			ŠAM		U		JARAḪ		SA-[M]U-E?-RA-A[Ḫ]?		RA LXV 47 VII 13
			ŠAM		U		DAGAN		SA-MU-D-DA-GAN		M
			ŠAM		U		LA				
							ʾIL		SA-MU-LA-DINGIR		B 39+
			ŠAM		U		RAWḪ		SA-MU-RA-A-AḪ		SIMMONS 46 28, 47 23
			ŠAM		U		RAWḪ		SA-MU-RA	NOM	CT XLVIII 29 REV.
			ŠAM		U	HU			SA-MU-U$_2$		M+
			ŠAM		U	HU	ʾIL	A	SA-MU-U$_2$-I-LA		M

STEMS

ŚAM	1		ŚAM		U			BALIṬ		SA-MU-BA-LI$_2$-IṬ?		RUTTEN 34 11
	2		ʿAMM		U			ŚAM	A	AM-MU-SA-MA		A.+
		JI	JṢIʾ					ŚAM	U			
								ʾAB	UM	I-ZI-SA-MU-A-BU-UM		B 23
			LABW		I			ŚAM	A	LA-BI-SA-MA		UCP X/3 P. 199+
			MANN		U			ŚAM	A	MA-NU-SA-MA		B 34
ŚAMʾAL	1		ŚAMʾAL							SA-AM-A-AL		M
			ŚAMʾAL		A			ʾIL		SA-AM-A-LA-DINGIR		M+
ŚAMʾIL	1		ŚAMʾIL		I			ʾIL		SA-AM-ḪI-LI-DINGIR		M
ŚAMḪ	1		ŚAMḪ	ATANI						SA-AM-ḪA-TA-NI		VAS VIII 14 5
ŚAMʿ	1		ŚAMʿ	AN	UM					SA-AM-ḪA-NU-UM		TCL X 21 21
			ŚAMʿ	AN	UM					ŠA-AM-ḪA-NU-UM		B 93+
ŚAMAʿ	1		ŚAMAʿ					ḪAʾT	IM	ŠA-MA-ḪA-TIM	GEN	XIII 1 VIII 44
			ŚAMAʿ					JAT	UM	ŠA-MA-IA-TUM	MN	CT IV 43B 6+
			ŚAMAʿ		A			JAT	UM	ŠA-MA-A-IA-TUM	MN	WATERMAN 21 R. 6
	2		LI				JI T	ŚAMAʿ				
								ʾIL		LI?-IŠ?-TA-MI-DINGIR		IX 291 I 18
ŚAMAK	1		ŚAMAK		UM					SA-MA-GU-UM		AJSL XLIV 242 NO. 29
			ŚAMAK	T	UM					ŠA-M[A]-AK-T[UM]	MN	TA 1931, 527
	2		ʾAB		I			ŚAMAK	U	A-BI-SA-MA-KU		SIMMONS 41 15
ŚAMAM	1		ŚAMAM		UM					SA-MA-MU-UM		I+, CT VI 44B 12
			ŚAMAM		UM					ŠA-MA-MU-UM		I+
ŚAMAR	1	ʾA T	ŚAMAR					HADD	U	AŠ-TA-MAR-D-IM		M+
			ŚAMAR		A					SA-MA-RA?		HARRIS 35 11
			ŚAMAR	AN	U					SA-MA-RA?-NU		X 20 11
			ŚAMAR					HADD	U	ŠA-AM-MA-RA-DU		A.
			ŚAMAR		I			HADD	U	SA-MA-RI-A-DU		A. 57 45
			ŚAMAR		I			ʾIL		SA-MA-RI-DINGIR		A. 455 46
	2		ʾAB		I		ʾA T	ŚAMAR		A-BI-AŠ-TA-MA-AR		YOS XIII 489:4
			ʾAB		I		JI T	ŚAMAR		A-BI-IŠ-TA-MAR		TCL I 226 4, 10+
			ʾAB		I			ŚAMAR		A-BI-SA-MAR		M+
			ʾIL		A			ŚAMAR		I-LA-ŠA-MA-AR		U
			ʾIL		I		JI T	ŚAMAR		I$_3$-LI$_2$-IŠ-TA-MAR		EDZARD,DER 67:11
			ʿAMM		U			ŚAMAR		ḪA-MU-SA-MAR		RA LXIV 36 NO. 31
			ʿAMM		U			ŚAMAR		ḪA-MU-SA-MAR	FN	C+
		JA	NWUḪ					ŚAMAR		IA-NU-UḪ-SA-MAR		CT XLIII 58 3, M
		JI	NWUḪ					ŚAMAR		I-NU-UḪ$_3$-SA-MAR		BIN VII 7 4,9+
		JI	NWUḪ					ŚAMAR		I-NU-UḪ-SA-MAR		TCL I 74 5,18
			ŚUM		U		JI T	ŚAMAR		SU-MU-UŠ-TA-MAR		TIM II 14 21
ŚAMAŚ	1		ŚAMAŚ		I					ŠA-MA-ŠI		CT IV 43B 7
ŚAMAT	2		ʾAB		I			ŚAMAT	A	A-BI-SA-MA-TA		EDZARD, DER 120:4
ŚAMIʿ	1		ŚAMIʿ		UM					SA-ME-ḪU-UM		B 38
			ŚAMIʿ		UM					SA-MI-UM		LARSA, KING
			ŚAMIʿ		UM					SA-MU-UM		LARSA, KING
			ŚAMIʿ		UM					SA-MU-U$_2$-UM		RA LII 235, KING
			ŚAMIʿ	AH						SA-ME-ḪA	FN	RA LXV 60 III 54
	3		LU					ḪAJJ	A			
								ŚAMIʿ	UM	LU-ḪA-A-A-SA-MU-UM		UET V 569 8
			LU					ḪAJJ	A			
								ŚAMIʿ	UM	LU-ḪA-A-A-SA-MI-UM		UET V 569 17
ŚAMIB	1		ŚAMIB	AT	UM					SA-MI-BA-TUM	FN	M
ŚAMID	1		ŚAMID		UM					SA-MI-TUM		U
			ŚAMID		U					SA-MI-DU		CT VIII 9A 1
ŚAMIM	1		ŚAMIM		UM					SA-MI-MU-UM		BIN VII 154:4+
			ŚAMIM		U					SA-MI-MU		WALTERS, WL 109:10
ŚAMIN	1		ŚAMIN		U	HU				SA-MI-NU-U$_2$	FN	CT II 46 4
ŚAMIR	1		ŚAMIR				Š	BAʿL		ŠA-MI-IR-ŠU-BI-EL		TCL XVIII 125 30
ŚAMK	1		ŚAMK	AN	IM					ŠA-AM-KA-NIM	GEN	LIH 81 7,17, 23
			ŚAMK		AJA					SA-AM-KA-IA		RA LXV 53 XII 4
			ŚAMK	AN	UM					ZA-AM?-GA-NU-UM		TA 1931, 538 V
ŚAMM	1		ŚAMM		I			JATAR		SA-AM-MI-A-TA-AR		TIM I 28 34, 38, 49
			ŚAMM		I			JATAR		SA-AM-ME-TAR		M+
			ŚAMM		I			JATAR		SA-AM-ME-E-TAR		M+
			ŚAMM		I			JATAR		SA-MI-E-TA-AR		M+
			ŚAMM		I			JATAR		SA-AM-MI-E-TAR		M+
			ŚAMM		I			JATAR		SA-AM-MI-TAR		M+

STEMS

ŠAMŠ	1	ŠAMŠ		UM						ZA-AM-ZUM		CT IV 47B 20
		ŠAMŠ		U						SA-AM-SU		YOS XII
		ŠAMŠ	AN	UM						SA-AM-SA-NU-UM		SIMMONS 119 23+
		ŠAMŠ	AN	U						ZA-AM-ZA-NU		M
		ŠAMŠ		IJA						SA-AM-SI-IA		X 166 9, 13
		ŠAMŠ		I		ʾAḪ		I		SA-AM-SI-A-ḪI		RA LXV 54 XII 26
		ŠAMŠ		I		ʾAB		I		D-UTU-A-BI		M+
		ŠAMŠ		I		HADD		U		SA-AM-SI-D-IM		M+, A.+
		ŠAMŠ		I		HADD		U		SA-AM-SI-A-DU		M+
		ŠAMŠ		I		HADD		U		ŠA-AM-SI-D-IM		M+
		ŠAMŠ		I		HADD		U		D-UTU-ŠI-D-IM		M+, C+
		ŠAMŠ		I		HADD		U		SA-AM-ŠI-D-IM		C
		ŠAMŠ		I		HADD		U		SA-AM-SI-IA-AD-DU		M
		ŠAMŠ		I		HADD		U		D-UTU-ŠI-A-DU		A.
		ŠAMŠ		I		HADD		U				
						ʾIL		I		SA-AM-SI-D-IM-I$_3$-LI$_2$		C+
		ŠAMŠ		I		HADD		U				
						....				SA-AM-SI-D-IM-TU-GUL-TI		M
		ŠAMŠ		I		HEDD		A		SA-AM-SI-E-D-IM		SIMMONS 4 20
		ŠAMŠ		I		HEDD		A		SA-AM-SI-E-DA		A. 455 36
		ŠAMŠ		I		JARAḪ				SA-AM-SI-E-RA-AḪ		BASOR 95, 19+, M+
		ŠAMŠ		I		JAŠʿ	AH			D-[UT]U-IA-AŠ-ḪA	FN	XIII 1 IV 43
		ŠAMŠ		I		ʾITEJ			JE	D-UTU-I-TE-E		CT IV 44 B 3, 4
		ŠAMŠ		I	JA	JPUʿ	AT			D-UTU-IA-PU-ḪA-AT	FN?	BM 17075
		ŠAMŠ		I		DAʿ		I		D-UTU-DA-ḪI-I		LANGDON XV 2
		ŠAMŠ		I		DIʿ	AT			SA-AM-SI-DI-ḪA-AT?		TIM II 49 5
		ŠAMŠ		I		DAGAN				SA-AM-SI-D-DA-GAN		M+
		ŠAMŠ		I		DITAN		A		SA-AM-SI-DI-TA-NA		B 38
		ŠAMŠ		I		LIʾM				SA-AM-SI-LI-IM		M
		ŠAMŠ		I		RAPIʾ				ŠA-AM-[SI]-RA-PI		M
		ŠAMŠ		I		ŠAMŠ				ZA-AM-SI-D-UTU		YOS XII 39 END
		ŠAMŠ		U		HADD		U		SA-AM-ŠU-D-IM		COLLON, SEALS NO. 141
		ŠAMŠ		U		ʾIL		U	NA	SA-AM-SU-I-LU-NA		B 38+
		ŠAMŠ		U		ʾIL		U	NA			
						KIMA				SA-AM-SU-I-LU-NA-KI-MA-DINGIR		BM 81047:6
		ŠAMŠ		U		ʾIL		U	NA			
						....				SA-AM-SU-I-LU-NA-QAR-RA-AD		CT XLV 48 5
		ŠAMŠ		U		JARAḪ				SA-AM-SU-E-RA-AḪ		B 38
		ŠAMŠ		U	JI	JŚAR				SA-AM-SU-D-I-[Š]AR		M
		ŠAMŠ		U		BAʿL		A		SA-AM-SU-BA-LA		SIMMONS 35 14+
		ŠAMŠ		U		BAʿL		I		SA-AM-SU-BA-AḪ-LI		ABB I 59 8
		ŠAMŠ		U		DITAN		A		SA-AM-SU-DI-TA-NA		B 38+
		ŠAMŠ		U		....				SA-AM-SU-MA-[....]		YOS XIII 446:3
		ŠAMŠ		U	NA					SA-AM-SU-NA		HARRIS 58 14+
		ŠAMŠ		U	NA	BAʿL		A		SA-AM-SU-NA-BA-LA		A. 77+
	2	ʾAB		I		ŠAMŠ				A-BI-SA-MA-AŠ		M+
		ʾAB		I		ŠAMŠ				A-BI-D-UTU	FN	XIII 24 IV 40
		ʾAB		I		ŠAMŠ		I		A-BI-D-UTU-ŠI	FN	XIII 1 IX 40+
		ʾADD		I		ŠAMŠ				AD-DI-D-UTU?		RA LXIV 99:23
		ʿADN		I		ŠAMŠ				ḪA-AD-NI-SA-MA-AŠ$_2$		M
		ʿAḎIR				ŠAMŠ				ḪA-ZI-IR-D-UTU		M
		ʾIL		I		ŠAMŠ				I$_3$-LI$_2$-SA-MA-AŠ$_2$		M
		ʾALIP				ŠAMŠ				A-LI-IB-D-UTU		CT VIII 35B 24+
		ʾUMM		I		ŠAMŠ		I		UM-MI-D-UTU-ŠI	FN	RA LXV 65 VII 38
	ʾU	WQAH				ŠAMŠ				U$_2$-GA-A-D-UTU		SZLECHTER TJ 15944 SEAL
	ʾU	WQAH				ŠAMŠ				U$_2$-GA-D-UTU		BIROT, TEA 72 V 16'
		ʾARḪ		I		ŠAMŠ		I		AR-ḪI-D-UTU-ŠI	FN	XIII 1 XIII 2
		ʾIŠḪAR	AH			ŠAMŠ		I		D-IŠ-ḪA-RA-D-UTU-ŠI	FN	XII 265 6
		ʿAŠTAR				ŠAMŠ		I		EŠ$_4$-DAR-D-UTU-ŠI	FN	M
	JA	ḪATIʾ				ŠAMŠ				IA-ḪA-AT-TI-D-UTU		UCP X/1 89 15
		BAʿL		I		ŠAMŠ		I		BA-AḪ-LI-D-UTU-ŠI	FN	M
		BAʿL		U		ŠAMŠ				BA-LU-D-UTU		M
		BIN				ŠAMŠ				BI-IN-D-UTU		M
		DAGAN				ŠAMŠ		I		D-DA-GAN-D-UTU-ŠI	FN	RA LXV 58 I 23+
		ḎIMR				ŠAMŠ				ZI-IM-RU-D-UTU		BIN VII 190 18
		ḎIMR				ŠAMŠ				ZI-IM-RI-D-UTU		BIN VII 206 23+

ŠAMŠ	2	ḎIMR				ŠAMŠ			ZI-ME-IR-D-UTU		B 42+
		ḎIMR		I		ŠAMŠ			ZI-IM-RI-SA-MAŠ		A.
		ḎIMR		I		ŠAMŠ			ZI-IM-RI-SA-MA-AŠ$_2$		M+
		ḎIMR		U		ŠAMŠ			ZI-IM-RU-D-UTU		BIROT, TEA 70 B I 9
		MUT		I		ŠAMŠ			MU-TI-D-UTU		A.
		NAWP				ŠAMŠ			NA-AP-D-UTU		M
		NABIʾ				ŠAMŠ			NA-BI-D-UTU		M+
		ŠUM		U		ŠAMŠ			SU-MU-D-UTU		CT XLVIII 83 SEAL
		ŠAMŠ		I		ŠAMŠ			ZA-AM-SI-D-UTU		YOS XII 39 END
	3	ʾALI				PA					
						ŠAMŠ			A-LI$_2$-PA-D-UTU		BE VI/1 15:25
		ʾAMUR				ŠA					
						ŠAMŠ			A-MUR-ŠA-D-UTU		A.
ŠAMUʿ	1	ŠAMUʿ		I		ʾIL			SA-MU-ḪI-IL		XIV 76:19
		ŠAMUʿ		I		ʾEL			SA-MU-ḪI-EL		M
	2	ʾIL		I		ŠAMUʿ			I$_3$-LI$_2$-SA-MU-UḪ		XIII 21 11'
		ḪAM		I		ŠAMUʿ			E-A-MI-SA-MU-UḪ		M+
		DAWD		I		ŠAMUʿ			DA-DI-SA-MU-UḪ		RA LXV 47 VII 44
ŠAMUK	1	ŠAMUK		UM					SA-MU-KUM		CT XLVIII 90 REV.
		ŠAMUK							SA-MU-UK		HARRIS 41 12
		ŠAMUK		IM					SA-MU-KI-IM	GEN	CT VIII 47B 22
		ŠAMUK	AN	UM					SA-MU-KA-NU-[UM]		HARRIS 68 21
		ŠAMUK		I		ʾEL			SA-MU-KI-EL		B 38+
ŠAMUL	1	ŠAMUL	AT	UM					SA-MU-LA-TUM	FN	M
ŠAMUM	1	ŠAMUM		U	HU				SA-MU-MU-U$_2$		M
		ŠAMUM	AN	IM					SA-MU-MA-NIM	GEN	PBS XIV 357
ŠAMUŠ	1	ŠAMUŠ		IM					SA-MU-SI-IM	GEN	BM 78366 3
		ŠAMUŠ		A					SA-MU-ŠA	NOM	M+
ŠANAG	1	ŠANAG		UM					SA-NA-GU-UM		JCS IV 109, 3328 2+
		ŠANAGR	AT	UM					SA-NA-AG-RA-TUM	FN	CT IV 47B 27+, M+
ŠANIN	1	ŠANIN		UM					ŠA-NI-NU-UM		SIMMONS 55 13
ŠANQAM	1	ŠANQAM		UM					SA-AN-QA-MU-UM		JCS V 89, MAH 15882
ŠAPAQ	1	ŠAPAQ		UM					SA-BA-KUM		TA 30 28
ŠAPAR	1	ŠAPAR	AN						[S]A-PA-RA-AN		RA LXV 40 I 7
		ŠAPAR	AK	UM					ŠA-BA-AR-KUM		U
	2	ʾAB		I		ŠAPAR			A-BI-SA-PA-AR	FN	C
		ʾAB		I		ŠAPAR			A-BI-SA-PAR$_2$		CT XLV 82 7+, XIII 1 II 15
		ʿIZZ		U		ŠAPAR			I-ZU-SA-PAR$_2$		U+
		ʿIZZ		U		ŠAPAR			IZ?-ZU?-ŠA-PA-AR		BIN II 98 5
		BAʿL		I		ŠAPAR			BA-AḪ-LI-SA-PA-AR	FN	M+
		BAʿL		I		ŠAPAR			BA-AḪ-LI-SA-PAR$_2$	FN	M, C+
		BEʿL		I		ŠAPAR			BE-LI$_2$-SA-PAR$_2$	FN	M
ŠAPIQ	1	ŠAPIQ		UM					SA-BI-KUM		TCL I 190 4, 5
ŠAPIR	1	ŠAPIR		UM					ŠA-BI-RU-UM		I+
		ŠAPIR		UM					SA-BI-RU-UM		B 37+
		ŠAPIR		U					SA-BI-RU		YOS XIII 166:14
		ŠAPIR	AT	UM					SA-BI-RA-TUM	FN	B 37+
		ŠAPIR	AT	UM					SA-PI-RA-TUM		B 37
		ŠAPIR		AJA					SA-BI-RA-A-IA	FN	X 166 11, 12+
ŠAPR	1	ŠAPR		AJA					SA-AP-RA-IA		A.
		ŠAPR	AK	UM					ŠA-AP-RA-KUM		M
		ŠAPR		A		HADD	U		SA-AP-RA-A-DU		A. 96 R. 12
ŠAPŠ	1	ŠAPŠ		I					ŠA-AP-ŠI		A.
		ŠAPŠ		IJA					SA-AP-SI-IA		A. 53 R. 9
		ŠAPŠ		I		ʾAB	I		ŠA-AP-ŠI-A-BI	FN	A.
		ŠAPŠ		I		HADD	U		SA-AP-SI-A-DU		A.+
		ŠAPŠ		I		HEDD	A		SA-AP-SI-E-DA		A.+
ŠAPUR	1	ŠAPUR		UM					SA-PU-RU-UM		TIM V 19 5
ŠAQAḪ	1	ŠAQAḪ			TA	NWUḪ		HU	SA-QA-AḪ-TA-NU-U$_2$		CT VI 46 2
ŠAQṬ	1	ŠAQṬ		I					ŠA-AQ-TI	GEN	CT VIII 10B 7+
ŠARAJ	1	ŠARAJ				ṢIDQ	UM		ŠA-RA-ZI-ID-K[UM]		MEISSNER 36 22
		ŠARAJ				ṢUWR	UM		ŠA-RA-ṢUR-RU-UM		KISURRA 111 6
		ŠARAJ			TI	ʾEL			ŠA-RA-TI-EL		TIM III 59 6
		ŠARAJ			TI	ʾEL			ŠA-RA-TE-EL		TIM III 44 18+
ŠARAM	1	ŠARAM		UM					SA-RA-MU-UM		YOS XII
		ŠARAM	AN	U					SA-RA-MA-NU		SZLECHTER TJ P. 25

STEMS

ŠARAM	1		ŠARAM		AJA					ŠA-RA-MA-A		M
	2		ʾALI			ŠARAM			NI	A-LI-ŠA-RA-AM-NI	FN	RA LXV 58 I 54
ŠARB	1		ŠARB	AN						SA-AR-BA-AN		M
ŠARIḪ	1		ŠARIḪ	AH						SA-RI-ḪA	FN	RA LXV 60 III 39
ŠARIJ	2		ʾAB		I	ŠARIJ				A-BI-SA-RI		LIMET, SCEAUX CASS. P 114
			ʾAB		I	ŠARIJ			JE	A-BI-SA-RI-E		B 11+; M+
			ʾAB		I	ŠARIJ			JE	A-BI_2-SA-RI-E		BIN VII 93 DATE
		JI	JṢIʾ			ŠARIJ			JE	I-ZI-SA-RI-E		BIN VII 105 12
ŠARIK	1		ŠARIK		UM					SA-RI-KUM		B 38+
		MU	ŠARIK	AH						MU-SA-AR-RI-KA	FN	XIII 1 VIII 75
ŠARR	1		ŠARR		AJA					ŠAR-RA-A-IA		M
			ŠARR		AJA					ŠAR-RA-IA		M+
			ŠARR		IJA					ŠAR-RI-IA		M+
			ŠARR		A	ʾIL				ŠAR-RA-DINGIR		A. LATE+
			ŠARR		UM	ʿADN		U	HU	LUGAL-AD-NU-U_2		SIGRIST UNPUBL.
			ŠARR		UM	JAQR	AH			LUGAL-JA-AQ-RA	FN	XIII 1 X 45
			ŠARR		UM	BAWŠ	T	I		LUGAL-BA-AŠ-TI	FN	M
			ŠARR		UM	BAWŠ	T	I		LUGAL-BA-$AŠ_2$-TI	FN	M+
			ŠARR		UM	NIWR		I		LUGAL-NI-RI	FN	XIII 1 XIII 3+
	2		ʾAJA			ŠARR		UM		ḪA-IA-ŠA-RUM		UCP X P. 56+
			ʾAJAN			ŠARR		I		A-IA-AŠ-LUGAL		A. 18 4
			ʾAJAN			ŠARR		I		A-IA-LUGAL-RI		A. 243 22
			ʾAJAN			ŠARR		I		A-IA-LUGAL		A. 274 4
			JAʾAN			ŠARR		I		IA-AN-ŠAR-RI		M XIII 1 X 16
			ʾABB		A	ŠARR				AB-BA-LUGAL		A. 86 2
			ʿAMM		U	ŠARR				ḪA-MU-SA-AR		RA LXV 40 I 42
			ʿAMM		U	ŠARR				ḪA-MU-SA-AR	FN	C+
			ʿAMM		U	ŠARR				ḪA-AM-MU-SA-AR		XIV 108:6
			ʾUMM		U	ŠARR	AH			UM-MU-ŠAR-RA	FN	IX 291 33
			ʾIŠḪAR	AH		ŠARR	AT			D-IŠ-ḪA-RA-ŠAR-RA-AT	FN	M
			ʿAŠTAR			ŠARR	AH			$EŠ_4$-DAR-ŠAR-RA	FN	XIII 1 II 67
		JI	JṢIʾ			ŠARR				I-ZI-ŠAR		B 22
		JI	JṢIʾ			ŠARR				I-ṢI-LUGAL-KI	GN	TIM III 75:3
		JI	JṢIʾ			ŠARR		UM		I-ZI-ŠAR-RUM-KI	GN	SUMER III 79 VI 197+
		JA	KWUN			ŠARR		UM		IA-KU-UN-ŠAR-RU-UM		B 28
		JA	KNUW			ŠARR		UM		IA-AK-NU-ŠA-RU-UM		KISURRA 47A 4+
		JA	KNUW			ŠARR		U		IA-AK-NU-ŠA-RU		TIM III 133 9
			MAM		A	ŠARR	AH			D-MA-MA-ŠAR-RA	FN	M
			NANN		I	ŠARR	AH			D-NA-AN-NI-ŠAR-RA	FN	XIII 1 V 31
			NUPAR			ŠARR		IM		NU-BAR-LUGAL		A.
			ŠADW		UM	ŠARR		I		[Š]A-DU-UM-ŠAR-RI		XIV 106:10, 17
			ŠADW		U	ŠARR		I		ŠA-DU-ŠAR-RI		XIV 109:6
			ŠADW		U	ŠARR		I		ŠA-DU-ŠA-AR-RI		M
			ŠADW		U	ŠARR		I		ŠA-DU-LUGAL		M
			ŠADW		UM	ŠARR		I		ŠA-DU-UN-ŠAR-RI		M
	3		ʾAJA			ʾAB		I				
						ŠARR		I		A-IA-BI-ŠAR-RI		A.
			BUN		UM	MA						
						ŠARR				BU-NU-UM-MA-ŠAR		B 16
			ŠUM		U	ʾIL						
						ŠARR				SU-MU-[DINGIR]-LUGAL		UCP X/1 17 15
ŠATAM	2		ʾANN		U	ŠATAM				AN?-NU?-ŠA-TAM	FN	XIII 1 IV 46
ŠAṬAR	1		ŠAṬAR	AH						ŠA-$ṬA_3$-AR-RA	FN	M
ŠAṬIḪ	1		ŠAṬIḪ		I					SA-TI-I	GEN	SYRIA XXXVII 206 10 HANA
ŠAṬUḪ	1		ŠAṬUḪ		UM					SA-TU-ḪU-UM		UCP X/1 89 28
ŠBIJ	1	JA	ŠBIJ			ʾIL				IA-AŠ-BI-DINGIR		B 32
		JA	ŠBIJ			ʾIL		A		IA-AŠ-BI-I-LA		B 30
		JI	ŠBIJ			ʾIRR		A		IŠ-BI-D-IR_3-RA		M+
		JI	ŠBIJ			ʾIRR		A		IŠ-BI-IR_3-RA		M+
ŠBIM	1	JI	ŠBIM		U					IŠ-BI-MU		CT IV 30D 10
ŠIJB	1		ŠIJB	AT	UM					ŠI-BA-TUM	FN	M
			ŠIJB	T	UM					ŠI-IB-TU-UM	FN	RA LXV 62 V 50
			ŠIJB	T	UM					ŠI-IB-TUM	FN	M
			ŠIJB	T	U					ŠI-IB-TU	FN	M+
			ŠIJB	AT	IJA					SI-BA-TI-IA	FN?	BM 80363 7
			ŠIJB	ATANU						SI-BA-TA-NU		SIMMONS 88 1

STEMS

ŚIJB	1		ŚIJB		U	NA		ḤARAM				ŠI-BU-NA-A-RA-AM		M
ŚIJM	1		ŚIJM	AT	UM							ŠI-MA-TUM	FN	M+
			ŚIJM	AT	IM							ŠI-MA-TIM	FN GEN	XIII 1 V 15+
			ŚIJM	AT				ʿAŠTAR				ŠI-MA-AT-EŠ$_4$-DAR	FN	XIII 1 V 75+
			ŚIJM	AT				DAGAN				ŠI-MA-AT-D-DA-GAN	FN	XIII 1 VIII 33+
			ŚIJM		U			DAWR		A		SI-MU-DA-RA		TA 30, 186+
	2		LA					ŚIJM		A		LA-SI-MA		M
			ṬAJB					ŚIJM	T	UM		TA-AB-SI-IM-TUM	FN	A. 8 4
ŚIJT	1		ŚIJT	AT	UM							SI-TA-TUM	FN	XIII 1 IV 74+
ŚIBIL	1		ŚIBIL		UM							SI-BI-LU-UM		A 21941
ŚIKIR	1		ŚIKIR		UM							SI-KI-RUM		YOS XIII 294:4+
ŚIKR	1		ŚIKR		I			HADD		A		SI-IK-RI-ḪA-DA		BE VI/1 6 19
ŚILIB	1		ŚILIB		UM							ŠI-LI-BU-UM		HARRIS 36 5
ŚIMʾAL	1		ŚIMʾAL									SI-IM-ḪA-AL	TRIBE	M
			ŚIMʾAL									SI-IM-A-AL	TRIBE	M+
			ŚIMʾAL									SI-MA-AL	TRIBE	M
			ŚIMʾAL		UM							SI-IM-A-LU-UM	TRIBE	M
ŚIMḪ	1		ŚIMḪ		AJA							ŠI-IM-ḪA-A-IA	FN	M
			ŚIMḪ		I			DAGAN				SI-IM-ḪI-D-DA-GAN		M
			ŚIMḪ		U			ʾIL		UM		ŠI-IM-ḪU-LUM?		A. 265 8
	2		ḤAJJ		A			ŚIMḪ		I		E$_2$-A-ŠI-IM-ḪI	FN	XIII 1 II 44
			ʾADM		U			ŚIMḪ		I		AD-MU-ŠI-IM-ḪI	FN	XIII 1 IV 6
			ʾADM		U			ŚIMḪ		I		D-AD-MU-ŠI-IM-ḪI	FN	RA LXV 62 V 28
			ʾIL		I			ŚIMḪ		I		I$_3$-LI$_2$-ŠI-IM-ḪI		M+
			ʾIL		I			ŚIMḪ		A	JA	I$_3$-LI$_2$-ŠI-IM-ḪA-IA		VIII 57 BIS 16
			ʾIL		I			ŚIMḪ		A	JA	I$_3$-LI$_2$-ŠE-IM-ḪA-IA		VIII 57 14
			ʾANN		U			ŚIMḪ		I		[A]N-NU-ŠI-IM-ḪI		XIII 1 XIV 24
			ʿAŠTAR					ŚIMḪ		I		EŠ$_4$-DAR-ŠI-IM-ḪI	FN	XIII 1 XII 2
			TABUB		U			ŚIMḪ		I		TA-BU-BU-ŠI-IM-ḪI	FN	XII 265 4
ŚIMAʿ	1		ŚIMAʿ					ʾIL		A		SI-MA-I-LA		X 5 4, 5
			ŚIMAʿ					LA			NI	SI-MA-AḪ-LA-NI		SYRIA XLI 54 N. 1
			ŚIMAʿ					LA			NI	SI-MA-AḪ-LA-A-NI		SYRIA XLI 54 N. 1
			ŚIMAʿ					LA			NI	SI-MA-AḪ-I-LA-A-NI		RA LXVI 112 MARI
			ŚIMAʿ					LA			NIE	SI-MA-AḪ-LA-NI-E		SYRIA XLI 54 N. 1+
			ŚIMAʿ					LA			NIE	SI-MA-AḪ-I-LA-A-NI-E		SYRIA XLI 54 N. 1
			ŚIMAʿ					LA			NIE	SU-MU-ḪA-LA-NI-E		SYRIA XLI 54 N. 1
			ŚIMAʿ					LA			NIE	SU-MU?-ḪI-LA-NI-E		SYRIA XLI 54 N. 1
			ŚIMAʿ					LA			NIE	SI-MA-AḪ-LA-A-NI-E		RA LXVI 115:21;117:11 MARI
			ŚIMAʿ					LA			NIE	SI-MA-AḪ-I-LA-NI-E		RA LXVI 112 MARI
			ŚIMAʿ					LA			NIE	SU-MA-AḪ-I-LA-A-NI-E		RA LXVI 120:7 MARI
			ŚIMAʿ			NI		ʾIL				ŠI-MA-AḪ-NI-DINGIR		VIII 49 BIS 5'
			ŚIMAʿ				TA	ʿQUB				ŠI-ME-TA-GU-UB		M+
ŚIMAR	1		ŚIMAR					HADD		U		ŠI-IM-MA-RA-DU?		A.
ŚIMM	1		ŚIMM		I			JATAR				SI-IM-ME-A-TAR		A 7537 16, 21+
ŚIMR	1		ŚIMR					ʾALLA				ŠI-IM-RA-AL-LA		A.
ŚINAN	1		ŚINAN		UM							SI-NA-NU-UM		SIMMONS 114 7
			ŚINAN		A							ŠI-NA-AN-NA		XIII 1 I 19
ŚININ	1		ŚININ	AH								SI-NE-NA	FN	XIII 1 V 51+
			ŚININ	AH								SI-NI-NA	FN	M+
			ŚININ		AJA							SI-NI-NA-A-IA	FN	X 166 1+
ŚINN	1		ŚINN	AH								SI-IN-NA	FN	RA LXV 58 I 61
ŚIPQ	1		ŚIPQ		U	NA		HADD		A		SI-IP-KU-NA-D-IM		M
			ŚIPQ		U	NA		HADD		A		SI-IP-KU-NA-DA		M
ŚIPR	1		ŚIPR	AT	U							ŠE-IP-RA-TU	MN	LAESSOE P. 99+
			ŚIPR	AN								ŠI-IP-RA-AN		A. LATE
			ŚIPR	AN	UM							ŠE?-IP?-[RA]?-NU-UM		I
			ŚIPR	AN	UM							ŠI-IP?-RA?-NU-UM		I
			ŚIPR		I			HAND		A		ŠI-IP-RI-AN-TA		A. LATE
ŚIRIB	1		ŚIRIB		I							SI-RI-BI		SYRIA XXXVII 206 29 HANA
ŚIRUN	1		ŚIRUN		UM			GAMIL				SI?-RU-NU-UM-GA-MIL?		VII 139 7
ŚKAR	1	MA	ŚKAR		UM							MAŠ-GA-RU-UM		RUTTEN 33 5, SEAL
ŚKIN	1	ʾA	ŚKIN	AN	UM							AŠ$_2$-KI-NA-NU-UM		TA 30 87+
		JA	ŚKIN					ʾIL				IA-AŠ$_2$-KI-IN-DINGIR-[....]?		M
		ME	ŚKIN		UM							ME-EŠ$_3$-KI-NU-UM		WALTERS, WL 95:2
		ME	ŚKIN		IM							ME-EŠ$_3$-KI-NIM	GEN	M+
ŚKIR	1	ME	ŚKIR		UM							ME-IŠ-KI-RUM		B 34

ŠKIR	1	MI	ŠKIR		UM					MI-IŠ-KI-RUM		VAS IX 172 13
ŠKUB	2		ʾIŠḪAR	AH		TA	ŠKUB			D-IŠ-ḪA-RA-TA-AŠ-KU-UB	FN	RA LXV 56 V 21+
ŠKUR	1	ʾA	ŠKUR	AN						AŠ-KU-RA-AN		RA LXV 50 IX 15
		ʾA	ŠKUR				HADD	U		AŠ$_2$-KU-UR-D-IM		TCL 1 146 4
		ʾA	ŠKUR				HADD	U		AŠ-KUR-D-IM		M+
		ʾA	ŠKUR				HEDD	A		AŠ-KUR-E-DA		A. 54 25
		JA	ŠKUR		UM					IA-AŠ$_2$-KU-RUM		XIII 1 XI 13
		JA	ŠKUR		UM					IA-AŠ-KU-RUM		XIII 1 XI 19
		JA	ŠKUR		UM					IA-UŠ-KU-RU-UM		TIM III 133 11
		JA	ŠKUR		IM					IA-AŠ$_2$-KU-RI-IM	GEN	M+
		JA	ŠKUR				ʾIL			IA-AŠ$_2$-KU-UR$_2$-DINGIR		B 81
		JA	ŠKUR				ʾIL			IA-AŠ$_2$-KU-UR-DINGIR		B 30+
		JA	ŠKUR				ʾIL			IA-AŠ$_2$-KUR-DINGIR		JNES XIII 210+ LATE
		JA	ŠKUR				ʾIL			[IA]-AŠ-KU-UR-DINGIR		VIII 38 7'
		JI	ŠKUR				ʾEL	I		IŠ-KUR-E-LI	FN	XIII 1 VII 41
	2		BUN		U	ʾA	ŠKUR			BU-NU-AŠ$_2$-KU-UR		SYRIA XXXVII 206 29 HANA
			MUT			ʾA	ŠKUR			MU-UT-AŠ-KUR		M+
		JI	NDIN			ʾA	ŠKUR			I-DIN-D-AŠ$_2$-KU-UR		SYRIA XXXVII 206 8 HANA
			ŠUM		U	ʾA	ŠKUR	A		ŠU-MU-AŠ$_2$-KU-RA		TA 30, 299
ŠLAḪ	1	JA	ŠLAḪ				....			IA-AŠ$_2$-LA-A[Ḫ-....]		M
ŠLAL	1	TA	ŠLAL		UM					DA-AŠ-LA-LUM		TA 1931, 538 II
		TA	ŠLAL		UM					DA-AŠ-LA-LU-UM		TA 1931, 435
ŠLAM	1	JI	ŠLAM	AN	A					IŠ-LA-MA-NA	GEN	MRS VI P. 202 UGARIT
		JA	ŠLAM				ʾIL			IA-AŠ$_2$-LAM-DINGIR		XIV 47:11
ŠLIJ	1	JA	ŠLIJ				ḪAʾL			IA-AŠ?-LI?-ḪA-AL		M
ŠLIB	1	ME	ŠLIB	AT	UM					ME-EŠ$_3$-LI-BA-TUM	FN	YOS V 117 1
ŠLIM	1	JA	ŠLIM				HAND	U		IA-AŠ$_2$-LI-IM-IA-[AN-D]U		M
		ME	ŠLIM		UM					ME-IŠ-LI-MU-UM		HARRIS 31 18
ŠMAʿ	1	JA	ŠMAʿ		UM					IA-AŠ$_2$-MA-ḪU-UM		M
		JA	ŠMAʿ		U					IA-AŠ$_2$-MA-ḪU		B 30 HANA
		JA	ŠMAʿ				HADD	U		IA-AŠ$_2$-MA-AḪ-D-IM		M+, C+
		JA	ŠMAʿ				HADD	U		IA-AŠ$_2$-MI-IḪ-D-IM		M
		JI	ŠMAʿ				HADD	U		IŠ-MA-D-IM		M
		JI	ŠMAʿ				HADD	U		IŠ-ME-D-IM		M+
		JI	ŠMAʿ				HADD	A		IŠ-MA-A-DA		A.+
		JA	ŠMAʿ				ʾEL			IA-AŠ$_2$-MA-AḪ-I$_3$-EL		B 30
		JA	ŠMAʿ				ʾIL			IA-AŠ$_2$-MA-AḪ-DINGIR		SIMMONS 55 11, M
		JI	ŠMAʿ				ʾIL			IS-MA-AḪ-DINGIR		CT XLV 3 7
		JI	ŠMAʿ				ʾIL			IŠ-ME-EḪ-DINGIR		KISURRA 40 9
		JI	ŠMAʿ				ʾILL	A		IŠ-MI-IL-LA		A.
		JI	ŠMAʿ				ʾAMUM	I		IŠ-ME-A-MU-MI	FN	M
		JA	ŠMAʿ				ʾUP	I		IA-AŠ$_2$-MA-ḪU-PI		BULL. ACAD. BELG. 1974 228
		JA	ŠMAʿ				BAʿL			[IA-A]Š$_2$-MA-AḪ-BA-AL		VIII 101 L.E.
		JI	ŠMAʿ				BAʿL			IŠ-ME-EḪ-BA-AL		M
		JI	ŠMAʿ				BAʿL	A		IŠ-ME-BA-LA		TA 30, 122 2
		JI	ŠMAʿ				BAʿL	A		IŠ-ME-EḪ-BA-LA		TA 30, 71
		JI	ŠMAʿ				BAʿL	I		IŠ-ME-BA-LI		HARRIS 71 6+
		JA	ŠMAʿ				DAGAN			IA-AŠ$_2$-MA-AḪ-D-DA-GAN		B 30 HANA+, M+
		JI	ŠMAʿ				DAGAN			IŠ-MA-AḪ-D-DA-GAN		RA XXXIV 186 R. 2 HANA+
		JI	ŠMAʿ				DAGAN			IŠ-ME-D-DA-GAN		M+
	2		ʾAḪ		I	JI	ŠMAʿ		NI	A-ḪI-IŠ-MA-NI		VAS VIII 14:41+
			ʾIL		I	JI	ŠMAʿ		NIA	I$_3$-LI$_2$-IŠ-MA-NI-A		TA 1930,399
			ʾANN		U	TA	ŠMAʿ			AN-NU-TA-AŠ$_2$-MA-AḪ	FN	M
ŠMAR	1	MA	ŠMAR		IM					MA-AŠ-MA-RI-IM	GEN	M
ŠMIʿ	1	MA	ŠMIʿ	AN	AM					MA-AŠ-MI-A-NA-AM	ACC	M
ŠNUL	1	JI	ŠNUL		UM					IŠ-NU-LU-UM	TRIBE	M
ŠPAR	1	MA	ŠPAR		UM					MAŠ-PA-RU-UM		B 49+
		MA	ŠPAR		UM					MA-AŠ$_2$-PA-RU-UM		SUMER XXIII 153 8, 17, 23
ŠPIQ	2		ʾIL		I	JI	ŠPIQ			I$_3$-LI$_2$-IŠ-BI-IK		TA 1931, 71
ŠPIR	1	MA	ŠPIR		UM					MAŠ-PI-RU-UM		CT VI 49B 12
ŠPUQ	1	JA	ŠPUQ		UM					IA-AŠ$_2$-PU-KU-UM		B 30+
		JA	ŠPUQ		UM					IA-AŠ-PU-KUM		VAS XIII 3 15+
		JA	ŠPUQ				ʾIL			IA-AŠ$_2$-PU-UK-DINGIR		M
ŠQIḪ	1	MI	ŠQIḪ		I					MI-IS-KI-ḪI	NOM	UET V 605 20
ŠQIṬ	1	JA	ŠQIṬ				ʾIL			IA-AŠ-KI-IṬ-DINGIR		B 30, M+
ŠRUK	1	JA	ŠRUK	AN						IA-AŠ$_2$-RU-KA-AN		RA XLI 45 6' HANA+

STEMS

ŠṬAḪ	1	MU	ŠṬAḪ	AT	UM								MU-UŠ-TA-ḪA-[TUM]?	MN	M
ŠṬIḪ	1	JA	ŠṬIḪ						ʾIL				IA-AŠ-TI-DINGIR		XIII 1 IX 7
		JA	ŠṬIḪ						ʿAMM		U		IA-AŠ-DI-ḪA-AM-MU		B 30
ŠṬUḪ	1	MU	ŠṬUḪ	AT	UM								MU-UŠ-TU-A-TUM	FN	C
		MU	ŠṬUḪ						KAʾM		I		MU-UŠ-TU-KA-M[I]		M+
ŠUʾQ	1		ŠUʾQ	AN	UM								ŠU-GA-NU-UM		EDZARD, DER 90:14
ŠUʾUL	1		ŠUʾUL		UM								SU-U_2-LU-UM		M
ŠUḪ	1		ŠUḪ	IT	UM								SU?-ḪI-TUM	FN	XIII 1 II 52
ŠUḪAR	1		ŠUḪAR		UM								SU-ḪA-RU-UM		TA 30, 249 4
			ŠUḪAR	T	UM								ŠU-ḪA-AR-TUM	FN	M
ŠUḪR	1		ŠUḪR		AJA								ŠU-UḪ-RA-IA	FN	SIMMONS 138 5, 14
ŠUBUL	1		ŠUBUL		UM								SU-BU-LU-UM		AJSL XXXII 227 4
			ŠUBUL		UM								SU-BU-LUM	FN	RA LXV 58 I 65
ŠUGAG	1		ŠUGAG		UM								SU-GA-GU-UM		CT IV 42A 1, 8+
			ŠUGAG		UM								ZU-GA-GU-UM		SIMMONS 72 11+
			ŠUGAG		I								SU-GA-GI	GEN	CT IV 31A 5+
ŠUKUR	1		ŠUKUR	AT	UM								ŠU-KU-[R]A-TUM	FN	XIII 1 V 78
ŠUKUŠ	1		ŠUKUŠ		UM								SU-KU-SU-UM		M
ŠULAḪ	1		ŠULAḪ	AT	UM								SU-LA-A-TUM	FN	RA LXV 66 VII 62
			ŠULAḪ	AN	U								SU-LA-ḪA-NU		A 7702 13
ŠULAL	1		ŠULAL		I								SU-UL-LA-LI	GEN	TCL XVIII 95 1
ŠULAM	1		ŠULAM		UM								SU-LA-MU-UM		UET V 608 3
ŠULAP	1		ŠULAP		UM								SU-LA-PU-UM		PBS XI/2 P. 119
			ŠULAP		I								SU-LA-PI		PBS XI/2 P. 119
ŠULM	1		ŠULM	AN	UM								ŠU-U[L]-MA-NU-U[M]		I
ŠULUḪ	1		ŠULUḪ		UM								SU-LU?-ḪU-UM		UET V 169 18
			ŠULUḪ		U								SU-LU-ḪU		UET V 427 16
ŠULUK	1		ŠULUK		UM								SU-LU-KUM		PBS XI/2 P. 119
ŠULUL	1		ŠULUL		UM								SU-UL-LU-LUM		PBS XI/2 P. 119
ŠUM	1		ŠUM		UM								ŠU-MU-UM		TA 30, 615 5
			ŠUM	AN									SU-MA-AN		B 39
			ŠUM		IJA								SU-MI-IA		M+
			ŠUM		U	JA							SU-MU-IA		B 39+
			ŠUM		U	JA							SU-MU-U_2-A		PBS XI/2 1 32
			ŠUM						LI						
							JI		JSIʾ		IM		SU-UM-LI-ZI-IM	GEN	WATERMAN 25 R 9
			ŠUM		A				HADD		U		ŠU-MA-A-DU		A.
			ŠUM		A				ʾIL		A		SU-MA-I-LA		YOS XIII 244:15+
			ŠUM		A				LA						
									LI			JA	SU-MA-LA-LI-A		BM 80363 1
			ŠUM		A				LI			KA	SU-MA-LI-KA		BM 80328 13
			ŠUM		A				RAPIʾ				SU-MA-RA-BI		KAJ 39 17 LATE
			ŠUM		I				ʾAB		UM		SU-ME-A-BU-UM		A. 12 4
			ŠUM		I				HADD		U		SU-MI-A-DU		A.+
			ŠUM		I				HEDD		A		SU-MI-E-DA		YOS XIII 486:1
			ŠUM		I				ʾIL		UM		SU-MI-LU-UM		WALTERS, WL 114:13
			ŠUM		I				JAMAM				SU-MI-IA-MA-AM		XII 61 5
			ŠUM		I				ʾENLIL				SU-ME-D-EN-LIL_2		KISURRA 197A 12
			ŠUM		I				ḪINN		I		ŠU-MI-IN-NI		U
			ŠUM		I				ʾENTIL				SU-ME-EN-TI-[IL]?		B 38
			ŠUM		I				DAWR		U		SU?-MI-DA-AR-RU		A. 322 9
			ŠUM		I				DAWR		U		ŠU-MI-TA-RU		A. LATE
			ŠUM		I				LAMM		U		SU-MI-LAM-MU		VAS XVI 24 4, A.+
			ŠUM		I				RIJB		A		SU-MI-RI-BA		A. 98C 10
			ŠUM		I				RIJB		A		ŠU-MI-RI-PA		A. LATE
			ŠUM		I				RIJB		A		ŠU-ME-RI-PA		A. LATE
			ŠUM		I				RAPAʾ				SU-MI-RA-PA		RA LVI 169, A.+
			ŠUM		I				ṬAJB		A		SU?-MI-DA-BA		A. 7 44+
			ŠUM			NA			JATAR				SU-UM-NA-IA-TAR		RA LXV 52 X 56
			ŠUM		U				ʾAḪ		I	JA	[SU]-MU-A-ḪI-IA		PBS XI/2 1 I 27
			ŠUM		U		ʾA		MNID		IM		[SU-M]U-AM-NI-DI-IM		B 38
			ŠUM		U		ʾA		ŠKUR		A		ŠU-MU-$AŠ_2$-KU-RA		TA 30, 299
			ŠUM		U		JI	T	ŠAMAR				SU-MU-UŠ-TA-MAR		TIM II 14 21
			ŠUM		U				ḪAʾL		A		SU-MU-ḪA-LA		B 39
			ŠUM		U				ʾAWN	AN	UM		SU-MU-AM-NA-NU-UM		B 38+
			ŠUM		U				ʾAWN	AN	IM		SU-MU-AW-NA-NIM		SUMER XXIII ARABIC 178

STEMS

ŠUM 1

ŠUM	U		ʾAB	UM		SU-MU-A-BU-UM		B 38+
ŠUM	U		ʾAB	UM		D-SU-MU-A-BU-UM		KISURRA 93 22
ŠUM	U		ʾAB	IM		[S]U-MU-A-BI-IM	NOM	EDZARD, DER 111:5
ŠUM	U		ʾAB	IM		SU-MU-A-BI-IM	GEN	SUMER XXIII PL. 12 19
ŠUM	U		ʾAB	I		SU-MA-A-BI		A.
ŠUM	U		ʾAB	I	JA	[SU]-MU-A-BI-IA		B 38
ŠUM	U		ʾAB	I				
		JA	RWIM			SU-MU-A-BI-A-RI-IM		TA 30 9, 14, 15+
ŠUM	UM		ʾAB	I				
		JA	RWIM			SU-MU-UN-A-BI-IA-RI-IM		SUMER XXIII 153:9
ŠUM	U		ʾABIḪ			SU-MU-A-BI-IḪ		TIM V 1 16
ŠUM	UM		ʿAD	U		SU-MU-UM?-ḪA-DU-KI	GN	YOS II 117:17+
ŠUM	U		ʿAD	I		SU-MU-ḪA-DI-I	GEN	XIII 13:8
ŠUM	U		ʿAD	IM		SU-MU-ḪA-DI-IM		X 57 8
ŠUM	U		ʿAD	U	HU	SU-MU-ḪA-DU-U$_2$		M+
ŠUM	U		JADAʿ	UM		SU-MU-A-DA-ḪU-UM		KISURRA 78A 15
ŠUM	U		ʿADN	U		SU-MU-ḪA-AD-NU		B 39
ŠUM	U		ʿADN	U		SU-MU-ḪI-AD-NU		KISURRA 29 12
ŠUM	U		ʿAḎAR			SU-MU-A-DAR		GORDON 38 DATE+
ŠUM	U		ʿAḎAR			SU-MU-A-TAR		GORDON 38 DATE+
ŠUM	U		ʿAḎAR			SU-MA-DAR		SIMMONS 50 26 DATE+
ŠUM	U		ʾEL			SU-MU-EL		TA 30, 34 6
ŠUM	U		ʾIL			SU-MU-DINGIR		B 39+
ŠUM	U		ʾIL			D-SU-MU-DINGIR		KISURRA 85 15, 22+
ŠUM	U		ʾIL	A		SU-MU-I-LA		B 39; M+
ŠUM	U		ʾIL					
			BAWB	I	JA	[SU-MU-I]L-BA-BI-IA		PBS XI/2 1 I 11
ŠUM	U		ʾIL					
			....			SU-MU-DINGIR-LI-BUR-RA-AM		FRANK 27 4
ŠUM	U		ʾIL					
			ŠARR			SU-MU-[DINGIR]-LUGAL		UCP X/1 17 15
ŠUM	U		ḪALAB			SU-MU-A-LA-AB		A.
ŠUM	U		ḪAM	I		SU-MU-A-MI		M
ŠUM	U		ḪAM	IM		SU-MU-D-A-MI-IM		RA LXV 40 I 25+
ŠUM	U		ʿAMM	U		SU-MU-ḪA-AM-MU		B 39+
ŠUM	U		ʿAMM	U		SU-MU-ḪA-MU		M
ŠUM	U		ʿAMM	U		SU-MU-ḪA-MU	FN	C+
ŠUM	U		JAMAM			SU-MU-IA-MA-AM		M+
ŠUM	U		....			[SU-M]U-A-NI-....		PBS XI/2 1 I 12
ŠUM	U		ʾENTIL			SU-MU-EN-TE-IL		B 39
ŠUM	U		ʾENTIL			SU-MU-EN-TI-[IL]?		KISURRA 95 15
ŠUM	U		ʾUP	I		SU-MU-UḪ$_2$-KI		JCS XI 23 NO. 10 14+
ŠUM	U		JAPAR			[SU-MU]-A-PA-AR		B 38
ŠUM	U		JARAḪ			SU-MU-A-RA-AḪ		B 38+
ŠUM	U		JARAḪ			SU-MU-E-RA-AḪ		M+
ŠUM	U		ʿAŠTAR			SU-MU-EŠ$_4$-DAR		PBS VIII/2 207 5, M
ŠUM	U		JAT	UM		SU-MU-IA-TUM		TLB IV 40 9. 12, 14
ŠUM	U	JA	ʾRUR	A		[SU-MU-I]A-AḪ-RU-RA		B 39
ŠUM	U	JA	MWUT					
			BAʿL	A		SU-MU-IA-MU-UT-BA-[LA]		RUTTEN 3 21
ŠUM	U	JE	MWUT					
			BAʿL	A		SU-MU-E-MU-UT-BA-LA	NOM	JCS IV 66 22
ŠUM	U	JE	MWUT					
			BAʿL	A		SU-MU-E-MU-UT-BA-LA	GEN	JCS IV 69 17
ŠUM	U	JE	MWUT					
			BAʿL	IM		SU-MU-E-MU-UT-BA-LIM?	GEN	JCS IV 71 9
ŠUM	U	JA	MWUT					
			BAʿL	IM		SU-MU-IA-MU-UT-BA-LIM	GEN	CT XLIII 86 1
ŠUM	U	JA	MWUT	U				
			BAʿL	A		[SU]-MU-IA-MU-TU-BA-LA		PBS XI/2 1 I 19
ŠUM	U	JA	JPAʿ			[SU-MU]-A-PA-AḪ		B 38
ŠUM	U	JE	JPUʿ			SU-MU-E-PU-UḪ		M+
ŠUM	U	JA	ŠJIM			SU-MU-IA-SI-IM		M+
ŠUM	U	JA	ŠJIT			SU-MU-IA-SI-IT		B 39
ŠUM	U	JA	ŠABAŠ	UM		SU-MU-IA-SA-BA-SU-UM		PBS XI/2 1 I 34
ŠUM	U		BAʿL	A		SU-MU-BA-LA		UNPUBL.

STEMS

ŠUM	1	ŠUM	U			BALIṬ			SU-MU-BA-LI$_2$-IṬ?		RUTTEN 26 12+
		ŠUM	U			BELBIN			SU-MU-BE-EL-BI-IN		JCS IV 108, YBC 5198
		ŠUM	U			BINAŠ	U		SU-MU-BI-NA-ŠU		A 7630 2
		ŠUM	U			DAGAN			SU-MU-D-DA-GAN		B 39+
		ŠUM	U			....			SU-MU-DI-NA-....		B 39
		ŠUM	U			DIJN	I		[SU-M]U-DI-NI		PBS XI/2 P. 119
		ŠUM	U			DITAN	A		SU-MU-DI-TA-NA		B 39+, M-
		ŠUM	U			DITAN			SU-MU-DI-TA-AN		SIMMONS 126 17+
		ŠUM	U			DITAN			[SU]?-MU?-DI?-TA-A-AN		VAS XVI 24 3
		ŠUM	U			DITN	UM		SU-MU-DI-IT-NU-UM		B 39
		ŠUM	U			KANAŠ	A		SU-MU-GA-NA-SA		KISURRA 19 9
		ŠUM	U			LA		NI	SU-MU-LA-NI		HARRIS 39 11
		ŠUM	U			LA		NIA	SU-MU-LA-NI-A		CT XLVIII 10 1
		ŠUM	UM			LA					
						ʾAB	I		SU-MU-UM-LA-A-BI	FN	RA LXV 65 VII 24
		ŠUM	U			LA					
						ʾIL			SU-MU-LA-DINGIR		B 39+
		ŠUM	U			LA					
						ʾIL	I		SU-MU-LA-I$_3$-LI$_2$		UCP X/1 34 2
		ŠUM	U			LI					
						ʾEL			SU-MU-LI-EL		B 39+
		ŠUM	U			LA					
						ʾEL			SU-MU-LA-EL		SUMER XXIII 160 5
		ŠUM	U			LI					
						ʾEL			SU-MU-LI-EL-DU-RI		A 7630 3
		ŠUM	U			LI					
					JI	JṢIʾ			SU-MU-LI-ZI		MEISSNER 37 15+
		ŠUM	U			LAʾL	UM		SU-MU-LA-LUM		PBS XI/2 1 I 16
		ŠUM	U			LIʾL	U		SU-MU-LI-LU		B 39
		ŠUM	U			LABW	A		SU-MU-LA-BA		M
		ŠUM	U			ME					
						ʾEL			SU-MU-ME-EL		JCS IV 107, YBC 4968
		ŠUM	U			MUT	I				
						JABAL	A		SU-MU-MU-TI-A-BA-LA		B 39
		ŠUM	UM			MAZAZ			ŠU-MU-UM-MA-ZA-AZ		TA 1931, 538 I, IV
		ŠUM	U	NA		ʾAB	I		SU-MU-UN-NA-A-BI	FN	A. 64 7
		ŠUM	U	NA		ʾAB	I		SU-MU-UN-NA-BI	FN	A. 33 3, 34 2+
		ŠUM	U	NA		ʾAB	I		SU-MU-NA-BI	FN	A. 59 8
		ŠUM	U	NA		ʾAB	I		SU-MU-NA-A-BI	FN	A. 244 5, M
		ŠUM	U	NA		ʾAB	I				
					JA	RWIM			SU-MU-NA-BI-IA-RI-IM		SUMER XXIII PL. 7 17+
		ŠUM	U	NA		ʾAB	I				
					JA	RWIM			SU-MU-UN?-A-BI-JA-RI-IM		SUMER XXIII P. 153 9
		ŠUM	U	NA		HALAL			SU-MU-NA-ḪA-LA?-AL		UET V 245 11
		ŠUM	U	NA	JA	JPUʿ	A		SU-MU-NA-IA-PU-ḪA-[....]		M
		ŠUM	U	NA	JA	RWIM			SU-UM-MU-NA-A-RI-IM		HARRIS 57 11
		ŠUM	U	NI					SU-MU-NI		B 39
		ŠUM	U			NIWḪ	A		SU-MU-NI-A		GORDON 39 9, 13
		ŠUM	U			NIWḪ	UM		SU-MU-NI-ḪU-UM		B 39
		ŠUM	U			NIWḪ	IM		SU-MU-NI-ḪI-IM	GEN	SIMMONS 121 18, M+
		ŠUM	U			NIWR	I		SU-MU-NI-RI	FN	XIII 1 XI 46
		ŠUM	U			NIʾŠ	U	JA	SU-MU-NI-ŠU-A		CT VIII 38D:14
		ŠUM	U			NUMAḪ	A		SU-MU-NU-MA-ḪA		M
		ŠUM	U			NUMḪ	A		SU-M[U-N]U-UM-ḪA		RA LXIV 43
		ŠUM	U			NUMḪ	IM		SU-MU-NU-UM-ḪI-IM		RIFTIN 44 12,16+
		ŠUM	U			RAWḪ			SU-MU-RA-A		B 40
		ŠUM	U			RAWḪ			SU-MU-RA-AḪ		B 38+
		ŠUM	U			RAWḪ			SU-MU-RA-A-AḪ		CT II 39 1, 15
		ŠUM	U			RAWḪ	EM		[SU]-MU-RA-ḪI-E-IM		B 40
		ŠUM	U			RAWM	E	JE	SU-MU-RA-ME-E		B 40+
		ŠUM	U			RAWM	EM		SU-MU-RA-ME-IM		M
		ŠUM	U			RAPIʾ			SU-MU-RA-BI		M
		ŠUM	U			RAṢIJ	EM		[SU]-MU-RA-ZI-E-IM		B 40
		ŠUM	U			....			SU-MU-SI-MU-....		A 7457 3
		ŠUM	U			ŠAMŠ			SU-MU-D-UTU		CT XLVIII 83 SEAL
		ŠUM	U		TA	QWIM			SU-MU-TA-KI-IM		XIII 131 4'

STEMS												
ŠUM	1		ŠUM		U	TA	QJIŠ			SU-MU-TA-KI-IŠ		M
			ŠUM		U		TAMAR			SU-MU-TA-MAR		B 40+
			ŠUM		U		TAMAR	U		SU-MU-TA-MA-RU		RA LXIV 43
			ŠUM		U		ṬAJB	I		SU-MU-DA-BI		X 90 10+
			ŠUM		U		ṢIDQ	UM		[SU]-MU-ZI-ID-KUM		B 40
			ŠUM		U		ṢIDQ	UM				
							DITAN	A		[SU]-MU-ZI-ID-KUM-DI-TA-NA		B 40
	2		ʾAḪ		I		ŠUM	U	NA	A-ḪI-SU-MU-NA		SIMMONS 83 5
			ʾAJA				ŠUM			ḪA-IA$_3$-SU?-UM		M
			ʾAJA				ŠUM	U		ḪA-IA$_3$-SU-MU		DELAPORTE CCL II A 337+
			ʾAJA				ŠUM	U	HU	ḪA-IA-SU-MU-U$_2$		XI P.83 N.1+
			ʾAJA				ŠUM	U	HU	ḪA-IA$_3$-SU-MU-U$_2$		M+
			ʾAJA				ŠUM	U	HU	ḪA-IA$_3$-SU-U$_2$-MU		M+
			ʾAJA				ŠUM	U	HU	ḪA-IA$_3$-SU-U$_2$-MU-U$_2$		X 113 4, 11, 14
			ʾAJA				ŠUM	U				
							ʾAB	IM		ḪA-IA-SU-MU-A-BI-IM		M
			JAʾ		U		ŠUM	UM		IA?-U$_2$-SU?-MU-UM?		XIII 146 13
		JI	JDAʿ				ŠUM			I-DA-SU-UM		M
			ʾIL		I		ŠUM	U		I$_3$-LI$_2$-SU-U$_2$-MU		M
			ʾILAR				ŠUM			I-LA-AR-ŠUM		I
			ʿAMM		I		ŠUM	U		AM-MI-SU-MU		CT XLVIII 61 4,5
			ʿAMM		I		ŠUM	U	HU	ḪA-AM-MI-SU-MU-U$_2$		CT XLVII 30 44
		JA	JPAʿ				ŠUM	U				
							ʾAB	I		IA-PA-AḪ-SU-MU-A-BI		A. 56 47
			JATAR				ŠUM	U		IA-TAR-SU-MU		XII 456 10
			JATAR				ŠUM	U	HU	IA-TAR-SU-MU-U$_2$		M+
		JI	JṢIʾ				ŠUM	UM		I-ZI-SU-MU-UM		B 23, M+
		JI	JṢIʾ				ŠUM	U	JA	I-ZI-SU-MU-A		KISURRA 112 7
		JI	JṢIʾ				ŠUM	U	HU	I-ZI-SU-MU-U$_2$		A 7646 3+
		JI	JṢIʾ				ŠUM	U				
							ʾAB	UM		I-ZI-SU-MU-A-BU-UM		B 23+
		JI	JṢIʾ				ŠUM	U				
							ʾAB	IM		I-ZI-SU-MU-A-BI-IM	GEN	B 23
		JA	WṢIʾ				ŠUM	U				
							ʾAB	UM		U$_2$-ṢI-SU-MU-A-BU-UM		AJSL XXVIII 244 19
			ḎU				ŠUM	IM		ZU-U$_2$-ŠU?-MI-IM		M
		JA	KWUN				ŠUM	U				
							ʾAB	IM		IA-KU-UN-SU-MU-A-BI-IM		M
			LA			NA	ŠUM	UM		LA-NA-SU-MU-[UM]		CT VIII 26B 22
			MAʾL		I		ŠUM	U	HU	MA-LI-SU-MU-U$_2$		TIM I 29 10
			MALIK				ŠUM	U	HU	MA-LIK-SU-MU-U$_2$		M
		JA	PLUS		I		ŠUM	I		IA-AP-LU-SI-SU-U$_2$-MI		BIROT,TEA 31:6
			QARAʾ				ŠUM	I	JA	QA-RA-SU-MI-IA		CT II 34 5
			QARAʾ				ŠUM	I	JA	GA-RA-SU-MI-IA		CT XLVIII 89 REV.
			QARAʾ				ŠUM	U	JA	QA-RA-SU?-MU-IA		CT VI 43 6
			QARAʾ				ŠUM	U	JA	GA-RA-SU-MU-IA		CT XLV 11 2, 46+
			QARAʾ				ŠUM	U	JA	KA-RA?-SU-MU-IA		CT II 30 3
			QARAʾ				ŠUM	U	JA	KA-RA-SU-LUM		CT II 30 34
		JA	RWIM				ŠUM	U				
							ʾAB	I		IA-RI-IM-SU-MU-A-BI		RA LXV 42 III 8
		JA	ŠJIM				ŠUM	U	HU	IA-SI-IM-SU-MU-U$_2$		M+
		JI	TWUR				ŠUM	U				
							ʾEL			I-DUR-SU-ME-EL		KISURRA 43 5+
			ṬAJB				ŠUM	U	HU	ṬA$_3$-AB-SU-MU-U$_2$		M+
	3		ʾAJA				LA					
							ŠUM	U	HU	A-IA-LA-SU-MU-U$_2$		M, C
ŠUMḪ	1		ŠUMḪ		U		BAʿL			SU-UM-ḪU-BA-AL		YOS XII 390 2,9
			ŠUMḪ		U		RAPIʾ			SU-UM-ḪU-RA-BI		M+
ŠUMAT	1		ŠUMAT	AN						SU-MA-TA-AN		M
			ŠUMAT	AN	UM					SU-MA-TA-A-NU-UM		GORDON 38 2, 5
			ŠUMAT				ʾIL	I		SU-MA-AT-I$_3$-LI$_2$		XIII 1 II 85
			ŠUMAT				JARAḪ			SU-MA-AT-E-RA-AḪ		M+
ŠUMK	1		ŠUMK	AN	UM					ZUM-GA-NU-UM		TA 1931, 538 IV
ŠUMUḪ	1		ŠUMUḪ		UM					SU-MU-ḪU-UM		BM 16852
			ŠUMUḪ		UM					ZU-MU-ḪU-UM		M
			ŠUMUḪ	AT	UM					ŠU-MU-ḪA-TUM	FN	RA LXV 64 V 58

STEMS

ŚUMUḪ	1			ŚUMUḪ	T	UM				ŠU-MU-UḪ-TUM	FN	XIII 1 X 49+
				ŚUMUḪ				BAʿL	A	SU-MU-UḪ-BA-LA		PBS XI/2 1 I 18
ŚUMUK	1			ŚUMUK				LIʾM		SU-MU-UK-LI-IM		C P. 42+
ŚUMUM	1			ŚUMUM		U				SU-MU-MU		RA LXIV 22 NO. 2+
ŚUMUT	1			ŚUMUT		I				SU-MU-TI		B 40
				ŚUMUT	AN					SU-MU-TA-AN		RA LXV 46 VI 4+
				ŚUMUT				ʾIL		SU-MU-UT-DINGIR		VAS VII 148 5+
				ŚUMUT		I		BAʿL		SU-MU-TI-BA-AL		M
				ŚUMUT		I		JABAL	A	SU-MU-TI-A-BA-LA?		PBS XI/2 1 I 35
ŚUNAḪ	1			ŚUNAḪ		UM				SU-NA-ḪU-UM		UET V 572 2
ŚUNAN	1			ŚUNAN		UM				SU-NA-NU-UM		TA 30, 30 29
ŚUPUR	1			ŚUPUR	T	UM				SU-PU-UR-TUM		PBS VIII/1 45 17
ŚURAR	1			ŚURAR		UM				SU-RA-RU-UM		TIM III 133 14
ŠWIB	1	JA		ŠWIB				ʾIL		IA-ŠI-IB-DINGIR		A.
		JA		ŠWIB		I		ʾILL	A	IA-ŠI-BI-IL-LA		A.
ŠWUB	1	ʾA		ŠWUB				ʾIL	A	A-ŠU-UB-I-LA		A. LATE
		ʾA		ŠWUB				LA				
								ʾEL		A-ŠU-UB-LA-EL		TA 1931,765
		ʾA		ŠWUB				LA				
								ʾIL		A-ŠU-UB-LA-DINGIR		C+
		ʾA		ŠWUB				LI				
								ʾEL		A-ŠU-UB-LI-EL		OIP XLIII 154 NO. 48+
		JA		ŠWUB		UM				IA-ŠU-BU-UM		B 30+
		JA		ŠWUB		IM				IA-ŠU-BI-IM	GEN	M+
		JA		ŠWUB	AN					IA-ŠU-BA-AN		M
		JA		ŠWUB				....		IA-ŠU-UB-[....]		A.
		JA		ŠWUB				JAḪAD		IA-ŠU-UB-IA-ḪA-AD		M
		JA		ŠWUB				ḪAʾL		IA-ŠU-UB-ḪA-AL		RA LXV 44 IV 28
		JA		ŠWUB				HADD	U	IA-ŠU-UB-D-IM		LAESSOE P. 90+, C+
		JA		ŠWUB				ʾIL		IA-ŠU-UB-DINGIR		CT II 23 15+, M+
		JE		ŠWUB				ʾIL		E-ŠU-UB-DINGIR		BIN VII P. 12+
		JE		ŠWUB		I		ʾIL		IE-E-ŠU-BI-DINGIR		B 26
		JA		ŠWUB				ʾAŠAR		IA-ŠU-UB-A-ŠAR		M+
		JA		ŠWUB			JI	JPUʿ		IA-ŠU-UB-D-I-PU-UḪ		M
		JA		ŠWUB				DAGAN		IA-ŠU-UB-D-DA-GAN		B 30 HANA+, M+
		JA		ŠWUB				LIʾM		IA-ŠU-UB-LI-IM		M+
		JA		ŠWUB				MALIK		IA-ŠU-UB-D-MA-[LIK]		M
		JA		ŠWUB				NAHR		IA-ŠU-UB-NA-AR		M+
		JA		ŠWUB				RAPIʾ		IA-ŠU-UB-RA-BI		A.
		TA		ŠWUB	AT	UM				TA-ŠU-BA-TUM	FN	M
		TA		ŠWUB	AH					TA-ŠU-BA	FN	M+
ŠA	2			ʾAMUR				ŠA				
								DAGAN		A-MUR-ŠA-D-DA-GAN		TCL I 237 31 HANA
				ʾAMUR				ŠA				
								ŚAMŠ		A-MUR-ŠA-D-UTU		A.
ŠAʾḪ	1			ŠAʾḪ	AT	UM				ŠA-ḪA-TUM	FN	RA LXV 59 II 75
ŠAʾUM	1			ŠAʾUM		I				ŠA-U$_2$-MI		BAB. III 267 HANA
ŠAWAB	1	JI	T	ŠAWAB		U				IŠ-TA-BU		B 24 HANA
		JI	T	ŠAWAB		U				IŠ-TA-A-BU		MAOG IV 3 36 HANA
ŠAWB	1			ŠAWB		A		ḪAJJ	UM	SA-BA-A-U$_2$-UM		OIP XLVII 66
				ŠAWB		I		ʾIL		ŠA-BI-DINGIR		M, C+
				ŠAWB		I		BIJT	UM	ŠA-A-BI-E$_2$		SUMER V 142 NO. 6
				ŠAWB		I		DAWD	I	[Š]A?-BI-DA-DI		RA LXV 43 I 13
ŠAWIL	1			ŠAWIL		UM				ŠA-WI-LUM		M
				ŠAWIL	AT	UM				ŠA-WI-LA-TUM	FN	M
ŠAWUʾ	1			ŠAWUʾ		UM				ŠA-WU-U$_2$-UM		RA LXV 48 VIII 16
ŠADW	1			ŠADW		IJA				ŠA?-DI?-IA		XIII 1 I 3
				ŠADW		I		HADD	U	ŠA-DI-D-IM		M
				ŠADW		I		ʾIL		SA-DI-DINGIR		JCS IV 110, 2040 16
				ŠADW		I		MA				
								ʾIL		ŠA-DI-MA-DINGIR		RA LXV 48 VIII 20
				ŠADW		U		ʾIL	A	ŠA-DU-[I]-LA		RA LXV 45 V 50
				ŠADW		U		LABW	A	ŠA-DU-LA-BA		M
				ŠADW		UM		LABW	A	ŠA-DU-UN-LA-BA		M+
				ŠADW		UM		LABW	A	ŠA-DU-UM-LA-BA		M
				ŠADW		UM		LABW	A	ŠA-DU-UM-LA-BU-A		M

STEMS

ŠADW	1			ŠADW		UM				LABW		I		ŠA-DU-UM-LA-BI		M
				ŠADW		UM				ŚARR		I		[Š]A-DU-UM-ŠAR-RI		XIV 106:10, 17
				ŠADW		U				ŚARR		I		ŠA-DU-ŠAR-RI		XIV 109:6
				ŠADW		U				ŚARR		I		ŠA-DU-ŠA-AR-RI		M
				ŠADW		U				ŚARR		I		ŠA-DU-LUGAL		M
				ŠADW		UM				ŚARR		I		ŠA-DU-UN-ŠAR-RI		M
	2			ḪAʾL		I				ŠADW		A		ḪA-LI-SA-DA		B 19
				ʾAB		I				ŠADW		A		A-BI-SA-DA-A		JCS IV 110 2040
				HADD		U				ŠADW		A		D-IM-ŠA-DA		PSBA XXIX 273 NO. 9 R. 10
ŠAGIŠ	2			ʿAMM		I				ŠAGIŠ				ḪA-AM-MI-ŠA-GI-IŠ		M+
				ʿAMM		I				ŠAGIŠ				AM-MI-ŠA-GI-IŠ		M
				ʿAMM		U				ŠAGIŠ				ḪA-MU-ŠA-KI-IŠ		X 174 13
				BUN		UM				ŠAGIŠ				BU-NU-UM-ŠA-GI-IŠ		EDZARD,DER 73:15
ŠAKIM	1			ŠAKIM		UM								ŠA-KI-MU-UM		HARRIS 91 17+
				ŠAKIM	AN	UM								ŠA-KI-MA-NUM		C
	2			ʾIL		I				ŠAKIM				I_3-LI_2-ŠA-KI-IM		RA LXV 40 I 44+
				ʾUM		U				ŠAKIM				U_2-MU-ŠA-KI-IM		M+
				MUT						ŠAKIM				MU-UT-ŠA-KI-IM		RA LXV 55 XIII 35
		TA		RWIM						ŠAKIM				TA-RI-IM-ŠA-KI-IM		M+
ŠAKK	1			ŠAKK		I								ŠA-AK-KI		RA LXV 45 V 13
ŠAKUM	1			ŠAKUM		UM								SA-KU-MU-UM		B 37+
				ŠAKUM		I				ʾIL				SA-KU-MI-DINGIR		M+
ŠAL	2			ʾIPQ		U				ŠAL		A		IP-KU-D-ŠA-LA		M
ŠALAŠ	1			ŠALAŠ						NIʾG		I		ŠA-LA-AŠ-NI-GI	FN	C+
				ŠALAŠ						TUWR		A	JA	ŠA-LA-AŠ-TU-RA-IA	FN	C
				ŠALAŠ						TABB		I		D-ŠA-LA-AŠ-TAB-BI	FN	XIII 1 III 26
	2			ʾAḪ		I				ŠALAŠ				A-ḪI-ŠA-LA-AŠ		EDZARD, DER 104:2
ŠALG	1			ŠALG	AN									ŠA-AL-GA-AN		RA LXV 40 I 49
	2			BUN		U				ŠALG		I		BU-NU-ŠA?-AL?-GI		B 16
ŠAMAR	2			ʿAMM		I		JI	T	ŠAMAR				ḪA-AM-MI-IŠ-TA-MAR		M+
				ʿAMM		I		JI	T	ŠAMAR				AM-MI-IŠ-TA-MAR		M
				ʿAMM		I		JI	T	ŠAMAR		U		AM-MI-IŠ-TAM-RU		MRS VI P. 329 UGARIT+
				ʿAMM		I		JI	T	ŠAMAR		U		AM-MI-IS-TAM-RU		MRS VI P. 239 UGARIT+
ŠANIJ	1	JU	T	ŠANIJ										UŠ-TA-AN-NI		RA LXV 44 IV 55; A.+
		JU	T	ŠANIJ						HADD		U		UŠ-TI-NI-D-IM?		A. 36 9+
		JU	T	ŠANIJ						ʾIL		A		UŠ-TA-NI-I-LA		A. 33 22
				ŠANIJ		UM								SA-NI-U_2-UM		M
				ŠANIJ		I								SA-NI-I		YOS II 139 3
ŠAPAṮ	1			ŠAPAṮ	AN									ŠA-PA-TA-AN		M
ŠAQL	1		T	ŠAQL		UM								ŠA-TA-AQ-LUM		RA LXV 43 III 50
ŠARŠAR	1			ŠARŠAR	AN	UM								ŠA-ŠA-RA-NU-UM		M
				ŠARŠAR	AN	U								ŠA-ŠA-RA-NU		M
				ŠARŠAR	AN	IM								ŠA-ŠA-RA-NIM	GEN	M+
ŠAT	1			ŠAT						ʿAN		A		ŠA-AT-A-NA		TCL XXI 220A 4+ CAPP.
	2			ḎU						ŠAT		I		ZU-ŠA-TI		HARRIS 56 12
ŠAṮP	1			ŠAṮP	AH									ŠA-AṮ-BA	FN	RA LXV 65 VII 39
ŠAṮUP	1			ŠAṮUP		I				ʾIL				ŠA-TU-BI-DINGIR		M+
				ŠAṮUP		I				ʾEL				ŠA-TU-BI-EL		RA LXV 44 IV 74
ŠEʾR	1			ŠEʾR	AH					MAM		A		ŠE-RA-D-MA-MA	FN	X 110 3
				ŠEʾR		UM				MAGUN		U		ŠE-EḪ-RUM-MA-GU-NU	FN	C
	2			NAPŚ		I				ŠEʾR		UM		NA-AP-SI-ŠE?-RUM?		M
ŠERIR	1			ŠERIR	AN	IM								ŠE-RI-RA-NIM	GEN	M
ŠI	1			ŠI						DUWR		I		ŠI-DU-RI	FN	RA LXV 58 I 68+
				ŠI						QUWJ		I		ŠI-I-KU-WI	FN	A. 8 12, 34
				ŠI						MAʾT		UM		ŠI-I-MA-TUM	FN	C+
				ŠI						MIGN		I		ŠI-ME-IG-NI	FN	RA LXV 60 III 24
				ŠI						MALIK	T	I		ŠI-MA-LI-IK-TI		IX 294:7'
				ŠI						NUWR		I		ŠI-NU-RI	FN	A. LATE
				ŠI						RAWM		A		SI-I-RA-MA		A. 28 3, 16
				ŠI				TA		BNIJ				ŠI-TAB-NI	FN	RA LXV 64 VI 18
				ŠI				TA		BNIJ				ŠI-TAB-NI-A-JA	FN	RA LXV 66 VII 57
				ŠI			JA			....				ŠI-IA-N[A-....]	FN	M
				ŠI			JA			TAKAL				ŠI-IA-TA-KA-AL	MN	IX 291 III 37'
	2			ʾAŠIR						ŠI			JA			
										....				A-ŠE-ER-ŠI-IA-[X]	FN	XIII 1 VIII 2
ŠIʾN	1			ŠIʾN	AT	IM								ŠI-NA-TIM	FN GEN	XIII 1 V 83

STEMS

ŠIʾN	1			ŠIʾN		U			RAPIʾ			ŠI-NU-RA-BI		A.+
				ŠIʾN		U			RAPIʾ			SI-NU-RA-BI		A.+
ŠIMGIN	1			ŠIMGIN	AH							ŠI-IM-GI-IN-NA	FN	M
				ŠIMGIN	AH							ŠI-IM-GI-EN-NA	FN	M
				ŠIMGIN	AH							ŠI-IM-GI-NA	FN	M+, C
ŠINA	1			ŠINA					DAMQ	A		ŠI-NA-DAM-QA	FN	XIII 1 IV 29+
ŠINI	1			ŠINI					HADD	U		ŠI-NI-D-U		MRS XVI 44:3
				ŠINI					ʿAḎR	I		ŠI-NI-AD-RI		M
				ŠINI					DAMQ	A		ŠI-NI-DAM-QA	FN	RA LXV 61 IV 48
ŠIPṬ	1			ŠIPṬ		A			ʾAḪ	UM		ŠI-IP-TA-A-ḪU-UM		RA LXV 46 VI 27
				ŠIPṬ		I			JAʾAR			ŠI-IP-TI-A-ḪA-AR	FN	C
				ŠIPṬ		I			HADD	U		ŠI-IP-TI-D-IM		A. LATE
				ŠIPṬ		I			HAND	A		ŠI-IP-TI-AN-TA		A. LATE
				ŠIPṬ		I			HAND	A		ŠI-IP-TI-IA-AN-TA		A. LATE
ŠIQL	1			ŠIQL		IM						ŠI-IQ-LI-IM	GEN	CT XLVIII 90
				ŠIQL	AN	U						ŠI-IQ-LA-NU		B 47
				ŠIQL	AN	UM						SI-IQ-LA-NU-UM		TA 30, 231+
				ŠIQL	AN	UM						ŠI-IQ-LA-NU-UM		TA 30, 2 4
				ŠIQL	AN	IM						SI-IQ-LA-NIM	GEN	TA 1930, 189
ŠIRṬ	1			ŠIRṬ		IJA						ŠE-ER-DI-IA		A.
				ŠIRṬ		I			ʾIL	I		ŠI-IR-TE-I$_3$-LI$_2$		A. LATE
ŠITAŠ	1			ŠITAŠ					ʾIL	I		ŠI-IT-TA-AŠ-I$_3$-LI$_2$		MEL. SYR. 994
ŠKAK	1	MA		ŠKAK		IM						MA-AŠ-KA-KI-[I]M	GEN	M
ŠNIJ	1	JI		ŠNIJ					HADD	U		IŠ-NI-D-IM		A.
		JI	ŠT	ŠNIJ					ʾEL			IŠ-TA-AŠ-NI-EL		SIMMONS 46 30
		JI	ŠT	ŠNIJ					ʾIL			IŠ-TA-AŠ-NI-IL		SYRIA V 274 HANA
		JI	ŠT	ŠNIJ					ʾIL			IŠ-TA-AŠ-NI-DINGIR		VAS IX 156 11+
		JU	ŠT	ŠNIJ					ʾIL			UŠ-TAŠ-NI-DINGIR		VAS IX 130 21+
		JU	ŠT	ŠNIJ					ʾIL			UŠ-TA-AŠ-NI-DINGIR		VAS IX 131 21+
			ŠT	ŠNIJ					ʾIL			ŠA-TA-AŠ-NI-IL		SUMER V 139 NO. 4
	2			LA				ʾA	ŠNIJ					
									ʾIL			LA-AŠ-NI-DINGIR		M
ŠU	1			ŠU					ʿABD	I		ŠU-ḪA-AB-DI		CT XLVIII 43:15,19
				ŠU					ʾEL	UM		ŠU-E-LUM		B 40
				ŠU					ʿAMM	U		ŠU-ḪA-AN-MU		M+
				ŠU				JI	BNIJ		HU	ŠU-U$_2$-IB-NI-U$_2$		TA 1931, 636 REV +
				ŠU					BAʾB	A		ŠU-BA-BA		U
				ŠU					DAMIQ			ŠU-DA-ME-IQ		RA LXV 41 II 16
				ŠU					RAWM	U		ŠU-RA-MU		A. LATE+
				ŠU					RAWM	A		ŠU-RA-MA		A. LATE+
ŠUʾḪ	1			ŠUʾḪ		UM						ŠU-ḪU-UM		RUTTEN 29 3, 6 SEAL+
				ŠUʾḪ	AT	UM						ŠU-ḪA-TUM		HARRIS 1 3, 6+
	2			ʾALLA					ŠUʾḪ	U		AL-LA-ŠU-ḪU		U
ŠUʾAR	1			ŠUʾAR		I			....			ŠU-A-RI-[....]		M
ŠUʾG	1			ŠUʾG		U			JAT	UM		ŠU-GU-IA-TUM		B 40
ŠUʾM	1			ŠUʾM		A			HAʾIL			ŠU-UḪ-MA-BA-IL		RA LXV 51 IX 60
ŠUʿAL	1			ŠUʿAL	AN							ŠU-ḪA-LA-AN		M
				ŠUʿAL	AN	U						ŠU-ḪA-LA-NU		M
ŠUWB	1			ŠUWB					ḪAʾL	I		SU-UB-ḪA-LI		A. 268 5
				ŠUWB		A			ḪAʾL	I		ŠU-BA-ḪA-LI		A. 97 16, 18+
				ŠUWB		A			ḪAʾL	I		SU-BA-ḪA-LI		A. 6 29
				ŠUWB		A			ḪAʾL	I		SU-PA-ḪA-LI		A. 252 12+
				ŠUWB					ʾIL	A		ŠU-UB-D-I-LA		RA LXV 52 X 66
				ŠUWB					ʿAMM	U		ŠU-UB-AM-MU		MRS VI P. 257+
				ŠUWB		A			ʾIL	A		ŠU-BA-D-DINGIR		B 23+
				ŠUWB		A			ʿAMM	I		ŠU-BA-AM-MI		A. 270 22
				ŠUWB		A	NI		ʾIL			ŠU-BA-NI-DINGIR		RUTTEN 41 3, 13
				ŠUWB		I			HADD	U		ŠU-BI-D-IM		M
				ŠUWB		I			QARAD			ŠU-BI-GA-RA-AD		I
				ŠUWB			NA		ʾIL			ŠU-UB-NA-DINGIR		B 40+, M+
				ŠUWB			NA		ʾIL			ŠU-UB-NA-IL		B 40
				ŠUWB			NA		ʾIL	U		ŠU-UB-NA-ḪI-LU		B 40
				ŠUWB			NA		LU		HU	ŠU-UB-NA-LU-U$_2$		M+
				ŠUWB		U			RAPUʾ			ŠU-BU-RA-BU		TCL X 4A 25, B 15
ŠUWR	2			ʿABD					ŠUWR	I		AB-DU-ŠU-RI		IRAQ XXX 94, RIMAH
ŠUBUL	1			ŠUBUL	T	UM						ŠU-BU-UL-TUM	FN	M, C

STEMS

ŠUBUL	1		ŠUBUL				ʾAB	I		ŠU-BU-UL-A-BI		M
ŠUKUD	1		ŠUKUD		UM					ŠU-KU-DU-UM		M
ŠULGI	2		ḪUNN				ŠULGI			ḪU-UN-D-ŠUL-GI		U
ŠUQUL	1		ŠUQUL	T	UM					ŠU-GUL-TUM	FN	XIII 1 XI 9
ŠURAN	1		ŠURAN	AT	UM					ŠU-RA-NA-TUM	FN	M
ŠUŠAG	1		ŠUŠAG		I					ŠU-ŠA-GI	FN	M
ṢḪAQ	1	JA	ṢḪAQ		IM					IA-AZ-ḪA-KI?-IM	GEN	IX 291 I 38
ṢJID	1	JE	ṢJID	AN	UM					E-ZI-DA-NU-UM		I
		TA	ṢJID		UM					TA-ZI-TUM	FN	M
		ME	ṢJID		UM					ME-ṢI-TUM		B 34
		ME	ṢJID		UM					ME-ZI-TUM		XIII 1 VI 29
		ME	ṢJID		UM					ME-ZI-[T]U-UM		M
ṢAJAD	1		ṢAJAD		UM					ZA-IA-DU-UM		CT XLV 97 16
			ṢAJAD	AN						ZA-A-DA-AN		RA LXV 43 III 45; C+
			ṢAJAD	AN						ZA-JA-DA-AN		M+
ṢAJID	1		ṢAJID		IM					ZA-I-DI-IM	GEN	VAS IX 172 18+
			ṢAJID	AT	UM					ZA-I-DA-TUM	FN	EDZARD, DER 90:2+
ṢABʾ	1		ṢABʾ		I					ZA-BI$_2$	FN	U
			ṢABʾ	AN	UM					ZA-AB-ḪA-NU-UM		CT XLVIII 88 REV.
ṢABAʾ	1		ṢABAʾ				HADD	U		ZA-BA-AD-DU		M
			ṢABAʾ				JAT	UM		ZA-BA-IA-TUM	MN	BM 16835 19+
			ṢABAʾ			TI	ʾEL			ZA-BA-TE-EL		UNPUBL.
ṢABIʾ	1		ṢABIʾ		UM					ZA-BI-UM		OB KING
			ṢABIʾ		UM					ZA-BU-UM		OB KING
			ṢABIʾ		UM					ZA-BI-ḪU-UM		M+
			ṢABIʾ		IM					ZA-BI-ḪI-IM	GEN	M+
			ṢABIʾ		IM					ZA-BI-I-IM	GEN	C P.39 N. 8+
	2		LA				ṢABIʾ	IM		LA-ZA-BI-IM	GEN	M+
ṢABR	1		ṢABR		UM					ZA-AB-RUM		YOS VIII 29 3
			ṢABR		IJA					ZA-AB-RI-IA		YOS VIII 120 22
			ṢABR	AN	UM					ZA-AB-RA-NU-UM		I
ṢABṬ	2		ḪAM		I		ṢABṬ	I		A-MI-ZA-AB-TI	MN	B 13
			ḪAM		I		ṢABṬ	I		A-MI-ZA-AB-TI	FN	CT VIII 35 B 1
ṢABUʾ	1		ṢABUʾ		UM					ZA-BU-UM	FN	M
			ṢABUʾ		UM					ZA-BU-U$_2$-UM	MN	M
ṢADAQ	1		ṢADAQ	AH						ZA-DA-GA	FN	U
ṢADUQ	1		ṢADUQ		UM					ZA-DU-KUM		B 41
	2		ʾAḪ		I		ṢADUQ			A-ḪI-ZA-DU-UQ		B 12
			ʾIL		I		ṢADUQ			I$_3$-LI$_2$-ZA-DU-UQ		M+
			ʿAMM		I		ṢADUQ			ḪA-MI-ZA-DU-[UQ]		M
			ʿAMM		I		ṢADUQ			ḪA-AM-MI-ZA-DU-UQ		M
			ʿAMM		I		ṢADUQ	A		AM-MI-ZA-DU-GA		B 13+
			ʿAMM		I		ṢADUQ	A				
							....			AM-MI-ZA-DU-GA-I-LU-NI		B 13+
			ʾATAR		I		ṢADUQ			[A]T-TA-RI-ZA-DU-UQ		I 103 17
	3		LA			ʾA	ḪJIJ					
							ṢADUQ			LA-ḪI-ZA-DU-UQ		A.+
ṢALIL	1		ṢALIL		UM					ZA-LI-LUM		B 41+
			ṢALIL		I					ZA-LI-LI	GEN	B 41
ṢAMID	1		ṢAMID		UM					ZA-MI-DU-UM	FN	B 41+
			ṢAMID				ʾAḪ	I		ZA-MI-ID-A-ḪI		CT IV 8B 17
ṢARIP	1		ṢARIP	AT	UM					ZA-RI-PA-TUM	FN	RA LXV 60 III 49
ṢARIR	1		ṢARIR		UM					ZA-RI-RU-UM		A 7688
	2	JI	JṢIʾ				ṢARIR	UM		I-ZI-ZA-RI-RUM		CT XLV 115 18
ṢARP	1		ṢARP		I		....			ZA-AR-BI-[....]		M
ṢARR	1		ṢARR		UM					ZA-AR-RUM		XIII 1 I 52
			ṢARR		UM					ZA-AR-RU-[UM]		IX 285 1
	2		LA				ṢARR	UM		LA-ZA-RU-UM?		B 33
			LA				ṢARR	AJA		LA-ZA-RA-A		YOS XIII 244:14
ṢDUQ	1	JA	ṢDUQ		UM					IA-AŠ-DU-KUM		B 30
		JA	ṢDUQ				ʾIL			IA-AŠ-DU-UQ-DINGIR		JEAN 164 R. 4+
		JA	ṢDUQ				ʾIL			[IA]-AŠ$_2$-DU-UQ-DINGIR		BASOR 95, 19
ṢIʾ	2		JAT		UM		ṢIʾ	A		IA-TUM-ZI-A		CT XLV 97 5
ṢIḪAQ	1		ṢIḪAQ		AJA					ZI-ḪA-KA-A-A		KISURRA 82 2
ṢIḪAR	1		ṢIḪAR				ṬALL	U	K	ṢI-ḪAR-TI-LU-UK	FN	PBS VIII/2 252 9, 18
ṢIJḪ	1		ṢIJḪ	AT	UM					ZI-ḪA-TUM	FN	XIII 1 VII 35

STEMS

ṢIJḪ	1	ṢIJḪ				HADD		A		ZI-ḪA-DA		TA 1933,7 EARLY OB
	2	MAM		A		ṢIJḪ	AT	UM		MA-MA-ZI-A-TUM	FN	RA LXV 61 IV 37
ṢIBʾ	1	ṢIBʾ		U						ZI-BU		B 42
		ṢIBʾ	AT	UM						ZI-IB-A-TUM	FN	XIII 1 III 2
		ṢIBʾ		IJA						ZI-BI-IA		XIV 106:6
		ṢIBʾ		IJAN						ZI-BI-IA-AN		RA LXV 42 III 24
		ṢIBʾ	AN							ZI-BA-AN		BM 16836 27; M+
		ṢIBʾ	ATAN							[Z]I-BA-TA-AN		VII 185 10
		ṢIBʾ		I		LIʾL		UM		ZE$_2$-BI-LI-LUM		HSM 7900, UR III
		ṢIBʾ		I		LIʾM				ZI-BI-LI-IM		M
		ṢIBʾ		I		NIʿM				ZI-BI-NI-ḪI-I[M]		M
ṢIBAR	1	ṢIBAR		UM						ZI-BA-RU-UM		RA VIII 69 21+
		ṢIBAR	AT	UM						ṢI-BA-RA-TUM	MN?	OLZ VIII 351 16
ṢIBIṬ	1	ṢIBIṬ	AH							ZI-BI-IT-TA	FN	C P. 41+
ṢIDQ	1	ṢIDQ		UM						ZI-ID-KUM		TCL XI 198 23
		ṢIDQ	AN							ZI-ID-QA-AN		M
		ṢIDQ	AN	UM						ṢI-ID-GA-NU-UM		EDZARD, DER 85:45+
		ṢIDQ		IJA						ZI-ID-KI-IA		RA LXV 55 XIII 9
		ṢIDQ		A		HADD		U		ZI-ID-QA-D-IM		M
		ṢIDQ		I		JATAR				ZI-ID-KI-E-TAR		M+
		ṢIDQ		I	JE	JPAʿ				ZI-ID-KI-E-PA		RA XLIII 37 QATNA
		ṢIDQ		I	JE	JPUʿ				ZI-ID-KI-E-PU-UḪ		M+, C+
		ṢIDQ		U		LA						
						NAŠIʾ				ZI-ID-KU-LA-NA-SI		M+
		ṢIDQ		UM		MAṢIʾ				ZI-ID-KUM-MA-ZI		X 131 5+
	2	ʾIL		I		ṢIDQ		I		I$_3$-LI$_2$-ZI-ID-KI		DELAPORTE CCL II A 337
		ʾIL		I		ṢIDQ		UM		I$_3$-LI$_2$-ZI-ID-KUM		UCP X/1 100 7
		ŠUM		U		ṢIDQ		UM		[SU]-MU-ZI-ID-KUM		B 40
		ŠUM		U		ṢIDQ		UM				
						DITAN		A		[SU]-MU-ZI-ID-KUM-DI-TA-NA		B 40
		ŠARAJ				ṢIDQ		UM		ŠA-RA-ZI-ID-K[UM]		MEISSNER 36 22
ṢILL	1	ṢILL	AN							Z[I]-IL-LA-AN		RA LXV 55 XIII 15
		ṢILL	AN							ZI-LA-AN		RA LXV 55 XIII 47
		ṢILL				HADD		U		ZI-IL-LA-AD-DU		A. 81
		ṢILL				ʾAKK		A		MI-NI-AK-KA		M
		ṢILL				ʿAN	AT			MI-NI-D-ḪA-NA-AT		XIII 83 8
		ṢILL				ʾANN		U		MI-NI-AN-NU		M
		ṢILL				BAʿL		I		MI-NI-BA-AḪ-LI		M+
	2	KAʾM		A		ṢILL		UM		KA-MA-ZI-LUM	FN	B 33+
		KAʾM		A		ṢILL		U		KA-MA-ZI-LU?	FN	VAS XIII 9 R. 2
		KUʾM		U		ṢILL		I		KU-MU-ZI-LI	FN	B 33+
		ṬAJB				ṢILL		U	HU	ṬA$_3$-AB-ṢI-LU-U$_2$		TCL X 38 7
ṢIMID	1	ṢIMID	AT	UM						ZI-MI-DA?-TUM	FN	M
ṢIRR	1	ṢIRR		I						ZI-IR-RI	NOM	M, A.+
ṢUWR	1	ṢUWR		AJA						ZU-RA-A		M
		ṢUWR		IJA						ZU-RI-IA		XIV 98:11
		ṢUWR	AT	IM						ZU?-RA?-TIM	GEN	M
		ṢUWR	ATANU							ZU-RA-TA-NU		M
		ṢUWR		A		ʾIL				ZU-RA-DINGIR		M+
		ṢUWR		A		ʿAMM		U		ZU-RA-ḪA-AM-MU		M+
		ṢUWR		A		ʿAMM		U		Z[U]-RA-ḪA-M[U]		XIII 132 7
		ṢUWR		A		ʿAMM		U	HU	ZU-RA-ḪA-AM-MU-U$_2$		M
		ṢUWR		I		HADD		U		ZU-RI-D-IM		M+
		ṢUWR		I		ʾIL				ZU-RI-DINGIR		M
		ṢUWR		I		ʿAMM		U		ZU-RI-ḪA-AM-MU		M
		ṢUWR		I		ʿAMM		U	HU	ZU-RI-ḪA-AM-MU-U$_2$		M+
		ṢUWR		I		JARAḪ				ZU-RI-E-RA-AḪ		M
		ṢUWR		I		DAGAN				ZU-RI-D-DA-GAN		M
	2	ʾAB		I		ṢUWR		A		A-BE-ZU-RA		TCL IV 87 10 CAPP.
		ʾAB		I		ṢUWR		A		A-BI-ṢU-RA		TIM IV 34 27
		ʾAB		I		ṢUWR		I		A-BI-ZU-RI		M
		ʿAMM		I		ṢUWR		A		AM-MI-ZU-RA		CT XLVIII 90 REV.
		KA				ṢUWR		A				
						ʾIL				KA-ZU-RA-DINGIR		M
		KA				ṢUWR		I				
						ḪAʾL		A		KA-ZU-RI-ḪA-LA		M

STEMS											
ṢUWR	2		NAHR			ṢUWR	I		D-ID$_2$-ZU-RI		M
			ŠARAJ			ṢUWR	UM		ŠA-RA-ṢUR-RU-UM		KISURRA 111 6
ṢUBʾ	2		LA		KA	ṢUBʾ	UM		LA-KA-ZU-BU-UM		M
ṢUBUʾ	1		ṢUBUʾ	UM					ZU-BU-UM		SIMMONS 50 23+
			ṢUBUʾ	UM					ZU-BU-U$_2$-UM		SIMMONS 47 21
ṢUPR	1		ṢUPR	UM					ZU-UP-RUM	FN	RA LXV 62 V 9
			ṢUPR	AM					ZU-UP-RA-AM		RA LXV 51 IX 70
			ṢUPR	I		JARAḪ			ZU-UP-RI-E-RA-AḪ		M+
ṢURAR	1		ṢURAR	UM					ZU-RA-RUM		PBS VIII/2 198 8
			ṢURAR	U					ṢU-RA-RU		KISURRA 104 36
ṢURR	1		ṢURR	I					ZU-UR-RI	NOM	M
			ṢURR	UM					ZU-UR-R[U-UM]?		M
TḪIJ	1	JA	TḪIJ			DAGAN			IA-AT-ḪI-D-DA-GAN		M
TWUR	1	JI	TWUR			ḪAJJ	A		I-DUR-E$_2$-A		M
		JI	TWUR			ʾAHL	I		I-DUR-A-LI		JCS XXIV 46 NOS. 5, 6
		JI	TWUR			ʿADN	U		I-DUR-ḪA-AD-[NU]		B 24
		JI	TWUR			ʿADN	U	HU	I-DUR-ḪA-AD-NU-U$_2$		TCL XVIII 83 6
		JI	TWUR			ʿAMM	U	HU	I-DUR-ḪA-MU-U$_2$		UNPUBL.
		JI	TWUR			ʾAŠD	UM		I-DUR-A-AŠ-DU-UM		B 23
		JI	TWUR			ʾAŠD	UM		I-DUR-AŠ-DUM		B 23
		JI	TWUR			ʾAŠD	UM		I-DUR-AŠ-DU-UM		B 23+
		JI	TWUR			ʾAŠD	UM		I-DUR-AŠ$_2$-DU-UM		M+
		JI	TWUR			ʾAŠD	U		I-DUR-AŠ-DU		B 23+
		JI	TWUR			ʾAŠD	U		I-DUR-AŠ$_2$-DU		VAS IX 172 5, M+
		JI	TWUR			ʾAŠD	U	HU	I-DUR-AŠ-DU-U$_2$		SIMMONS 90 4
		JI	TWUR			ʾAŠD	U	HU	I-DUR-AŠ$_2$-DU-U$_2$		M
		JI	TWUR			KUʾN	U	HU	I-DUR-KU?-NU-U$_2$		VAS XIII 14 R. 10
		JA	TWUR			MEʾR			D-IA-TU-[U]R-ME-I[R]	DN	M
		JI	TWUR			MEʾR			D-I-DUR-ME-IR	DN	M+
		JA	TWUR			NAHR	UM		IA-DUR-NA-RUM?		RA LXV 48 VII 72
		JI	TWUR			NINGAL			I-DUR-D-NIN-GAL		M
		JI	TWUR			PI					
						ʾIL			I-DUR-[BI]?-DINGIR		I
		JI	TWUR			ŠALIM			I-DUR-SA-LIM		YOS II 84 21 22
		JI	TWUR			ŠUM	U				
						ʾEL			I-DUR-SU-ME-EL		KISURRA 43 5+
		TA	TWUR			ʿAŠTAR			TA-TU-UR-EŠ$_4$-DAR	FN	M
		TA	TWUR			ḪAʾT	UM		TA-DUR-ḪA-TUM		TA 1931, 489
		TA	TWUR			MAʾT	UM		TA-TU-UR-MA-TUM	FN	M+; C+
		TA	TWUR			MAʾT	UM		TA-DUR-MA-TUM	FN	XIII 1 XIV 34+
	2		ḪANN	A	JI	TWUR					
						MEʾR			ḪA-AN-NA-D-I-DUR-ME-ER		M
			ʾIPQ	U	JI	TWUR					
						MEʾR			IP-KU-D-I-DUR-ME-ER		M
			LI		JI	TWUR					
						ʾAHL	I		LI-TU-UR-A-LI		JCS XXIV 62 NO.55+
		JI	NDIN		JI	TWUR					
						MEʾR			I-DIN-D-I-DUR-ME-ER		XIII 1 III 49+
TAʾ	1		TAʾ	I					TA-ḪI		M+
	2		ʾILAR			TAʾ	A		I-LA-AR-TA-A		M
			ʾILAR			TAʾ	A		I-LA-AR-TA-ḪA		M
			ʾAMAN			TAʾ	I		AM-MA-AN-TA-ḪI		M
TAʾG	1		TAʾG	I					TA-GI		RA LXV 43 III 40+
			TAʾG	IT UM					TA-GI-TUM	FN	XIII 1 II 45
	2		MILK	I		TAʾG	A		MI-IL-KI-TA-GA		A. LATE
TAʾIL	1		TAʾIL	U					TA-ḪI-LU?	FN	RA LXV 65 VII 33
TAʾK	1		TAʾK	I					TA-KI		RA LXV 55 XIII 19
			TAʾK	U		ʾIL			TA-KU-DINGIR		VAS VIII 14 27
			TAʾK	I		ʾIŠḪAR	AH		TA-KI-D-IŠ-ḪA-RA		JCS XIII 52 293 LE,A.LATE
			TAʾK	U		ʾIŠḪAR	AH		TA-KU-D-IŠ-ḪA-R[A]		JCS XIII 52 293 R, A. LATE
	2		ʾABIL			TAʾK	U	HU	A-BI-IL-TA-KU-U$_2$		WALTERS, WL 97:4;105:3+
TAʾL	1		TAʾL	UM					TA-LU-UM		EDZARD, DER 112:23
TAʾM	1		TAʾM	I					TA-MI		RA LXV 50 IX 13
TAḪT	1		TAḪT	U		PI					
						ʾIL			TA-AḪ-TU-BI-DINGIR		M+
TAḪTUN	2		BUN			TAḪTUN					
						ʾIL	A		BU-UN-TAḪ-UN-I-LA		B 16

STEMS

TAḪTUN	2	BUN		U		TAḪTUN						
						ʾIL		A		BU-NU-TAḪ-TU-UN-I-LA		B 16+
TAḪTAḪ	1	TAḪTAḪ		UM						TA-AḪ-TA-ḪU-UM		BIN VII 116 3
TAWIR	1	TAWIR		UM						TA-E-RUM		KISURRA 73 2+
		TAWIR		U						TA-E-RU		KISURRA 81A 4+
TAWR	2	MANN		A		TAWR		I		MA-NA-TA-RI		B 34
TABʾ	1	TABʾ		I		BIN		UM		TA-AB-I-BI-NU-UM		BM 82437 4 9
TABB	1	TABB		I		MAM		A		TA-BI-D-MA-MA	FN	M
	2	ʾANN		U		TABB		I		AN-NU-TAB-BI	FN	XIII 1 III 36+
		ʿAŠTAR				TABB		I		EŠ$_4$-DAR-TAB-BI	FN	M+, C
		ḪAṢN		U		TABB		I		AZ?-NU-TAB-BI	FN	M
		ŠALAŠ				TABB		I		D-ŠA-LA-AŠ-TAB-BI	FN	XIII 1 III 26
TABIN	1	TABIN		UM						TA-BI-NU-UM		BM 82359
TABUB	1	TABUB		U						TA-BU-BU	FN	XIII 1 VIII 35
		TABUB				ʿIMD		I		TA-BU-UB-IM-[DI]?	FN	VIII 33 7
		TABUB		I		ʿIMD		I		TA-BU-TI?-IM-DI	FN	VIII 31 10 15
		TABUB		U		ʿALIJ	AH			D-TA-BU-BU-ḪA-LI-IA	FN	XIII 1 VI 13
		TABUB		U		ʾUMM		I		TA-BU-BU-UM-MI	FN	XIII 1 VI 57
		TABUB		U		ḪAṢN		I		TA-BU-BU-ḪA-AṢ-NI	FN	RA LXV 60 III 19
		TABUB		U		ŠIMḪ		I		TA-BU-BU-ŠI-IM-ḪI	FN	XII 265 4
	2 JI	NDIN				TABUB		U		I-DIN-TA-BU-BU		M
TABUZ	1	TABUZ		I						TA-BU-ZI		RA LXV 45 V 33
TADAB	1	TADAB			JE	JŠAR				TA-DA-AB-E-ŠAR	FN	XIII 1 VI 42
TAKAL	2	ŠI			JA	TAKAL				ŠI-IA-TA-KA-AL	MN	IX 291 III 37'
TALAʾ	1	TALAʾ		UM						TA-LA-ḪU-UM		BE VI/2 80 29
TALIʾ	1	TALIʾ	AN	UM						TA-LI-A-NU-UM		TA 1931, 538 VI
TALM	1	TALM		A		ʿAMM		U		TA-AL-MA-AM-MU		A.+
		TALM		U		ʾAŠIḪ		I		TA-AL-MU-A-ŠI-ḪI	FN	XIII 1 III 63
	2	ʾALL		I		TALM		A		AL-LI-TA-AL-MA	FN	A.
	3	ʾAJA				ʾAB		I				
						TALM		A		A-IA-BI-TA-AL-MA		A. 239 15
TAMAR	1	TAMAR		U						TA-MA-RU		RA LXV 50 VIII 71
	2	ŠUM		U		TAMAR				SU-MU-TA-MAR		B 40+
		ŠUM		U		TAMAR		U		SU-MU-TA-MA-RU		RA LXIV 43
TAMB	2 JI	JṢIʾ				TAMB		U		I-ZI-TA-AM-BU		BAHREIN UNPUB, POST-U.
TANTAN	1	TANTAN		UM						TA-AN-TA-NU-UM		SUMER V 141
		TANTAN		UM						TA-TA-NU-UM		HARRIS 11 17, 14 14+
TARAJ	1	TARAJ	AT	UM						TA-RA-IA-TUM	FN	VAS XIII 14 5+
TATT	1	TATT	AH							TA-AT-TA	FN	RA LXV 62 V 55
		TATT		A	HA					TA-AT-TA-A	FN	RA LXV 60 III 73
		TATT		I		BAʾT		UM		TA-AT-TI-BA-TUM		TCL I 204:10
TEʾḪ	2	LA				TEʾḪ		U		LA-TE-ḪU		MRS VI P. 196 22,LATE
TEBUʾ	2	LA				TEBUʾ		U		LA-TE-BU-U$_2$		B 33
TENUT	2	BUN				TENUT		A		BU-UN-TE-NU?-TA?		MEISSNER 68 13
TIʾAR	1	TIʾAR		UM						TI-A-RUM		B 40
TIʾL	1	TIʾL	AN	UM						TI-LA-NU-UM		B 47
TIʾM	1	TIʾM				LU			HU	TI-IM-LU-U$_2$	FN	XIII 1 VIII 73+
		TIʾM				RIJB		A		TI-IM-RI-PA		A.
TIʾŠ	1	TIʾŠ	AT	UM						TI-ŠA-TUM	FN	M
		TIʾŠ				LUʾM		U		TI-IŠ-LU-MU		M
TIʾT	1	TIʾT		AJA						TI-TA-A-A		RUTTEN 28 10+
TIWR	1	TIWR	AT	UM						TI-RA-TUM	FN	M
		TIWR				ḪAJJ		A		TI-IR-E$_2$-A		M+
		TIWR				ʿAŠTAR				TI-IR-EŠ$_4$-DAR		M+
		TIWR				MAM		A		TI-IR-MA-MA		M+
		TIWR		I	Š	TUWR				TE-RI-IŠ-TU-UR$_2$		C+
	2	ʾANN		U		TIWR		I		AN-NU-TI-RI	FN	M+
		JARAḪ				TIWR		I		D-EN-ZU-TI-RI		M+
		JARAḪ				TIWR		IM		D-EN-ZU-TI-RI-IM	GEN	M
		ʿAŠTAR				TIWR	AH			D-EŠ$_4$-DAR-TE-IR-RA		A.
		DAGAN				TIWR		I		D-DA-GAN-TI-RI	FN	RA LXV 61 IV 51
		MATIʿ				TIWR		UM		MA-TI-TI-RUM		BM 67281
TIBIʾ	1	TIBIʾ		A	Š	ME						
						ʾEL				TI-BI$_2$-AŠ$_2$-ME-EL		CT XXXIII 48A 4
TIDIQ	1	TIDIQ	AN							TI-DI-QA-AN		RA LXV 48 VIII 18+
TILIʾ	1	TILIʾ		A	Š	GAMIL				TI-LI-AŠ-GA-MIL		UNPUBL.

TILL	2		ʾANN		U		TILL	AT	I		AN-NU-TIL-LA-TI	FN	XIII 1 X 2
	3	JA	KRUB				ʾIL						
							TILL	AT	I		D-IA-AK-RU-UB-DINGIR-TIL-LA-TI		M
TIMAN	1		TIMAN		AJA						TI-MA-NA-A-A		HARRIS 66 14
TINʾ	1		TINʾ	AT	UM						TI-IN-A-TUM	FN	XIII 1 VI 4
			TINʾ		IJAN						TI-IN-I-IA-AN		RA LXV 51 IX 76+
			TINʾ		I		JARAḪ				TI-IN-E-RA-AḪ		C
			TINʾ		I		JARAḪ				TI-IN-I-E-RA-AḪ		C
TIRR	1		TIRR		U						TE-IR-RU		M+
			TIRR		U						TI-IR-RU		M
TISP	1		TISP		UM						[T]I-IS-PU-UM		RA XLI 45 8', HANA
			TISP	AT	UM						TI-IS-PA-TUM	FN	M+, C
			TISP	AT	UM						TI-IS-PA-A-TUM	FN	X 105 3
TIŠAN	1		TIŠAN	AT	UM						TI-ŠA-NA-TUM	MN	VAS VIII 58 34+
			TIŠAN	AT	UM						TI-ŠA-NA-TUM	FN	BM 82372, M
TIŠPAK	2	JE	NBIṬ				TIŠPAK				I-EN-BI-IṬ-D-TIŠPAK		JCS XXIV 49 NO. 15:3
TMIH	1	ME	TMIH		UM						ME-IT-ME-U_2-UM		M
		ME	TMIH		UM						ME-IT-MU-UM		M
		ME	TMIH		U						ME-IT-MI-JU		M+
TUʾ	1		TUʾ		I						TU-I		XIII 60 5
			TUʾ	AN	UM						TU-ḪA-NU-UM		UCP X/3 2 26
			TUʾ	ATAN							TU-ḪA-TA-AN		M
	2		ʾAḪ		I	Š	TUʾ			JA	A-ḪI-IŠ-TU-IA		A. 86 9
			ʾAḪ		I	Š	TUʾ			KA	A-ḪI-IŠ-DU-KA		A. 98C 1, 6
			ʾAB		I	Š	TUʾ				A-BI-IŠ-DU		A. LATE
			ʾUBUŠ				TUʾ			KA	ḪU-BU-UŠ-TU-KA		A. 268 17
			BAʿL				TUʾ			KA	BA-AL-DU-UḪ-KA		A.
TUʾAL	1		TUʾAL		U						TU-A-LU		RA LXV 48 VIII 17
	2		MAM		A		TUʾAL		I		D-MA-MA-TU-ḪA-LI	FN	M
TUʾM	1		TUʾM	AN	UM						TU-MA-NU-UM		B 47
TUʾN	1		TUʾN	AN	UM						TU-NA-NU-UM		TCL XVIII 118 7
			TUʾN	AN	U						TU-NA-NU		BM 81617 5
			TUʾN	AK	UM						TU-NA-KUM		UET V 285 22
TUʾZ	1		TUʾZ		AJA						TU-ZA-A	FN	XIII 1 XIII 29
			TUʾZ		AJA						TU-ZA-[I]A	FN	M
			TUʾZ	ATAN							TU-ZA-TA-AN		M
TUḪT	1		TUḪT		U		....				TU-UḪ-TU-[....]		M
TUWR	1		TUWR		A		ʾIL		I		TU-RA-I_3-LI_2		SAUREN, WUG 285 V, U.
			TUWR		A		DAGAN				TU-RA-D-DA-GAN		M+
			TUWR		I		DAGAN				TU-RI-D-DA-GAN		B 40+ HANA
			TUWR		U		ʿAMM		I		DUR-RU-AM-MI		MAOG IV 2 6 HANA
	2		ʾIL		I		TUWR		A		I_3-LI_2-TU-RA		M+
			ʾIL		I		TUWR		A	JA	I_3-LI_2-TU-RA-[I]A		RA LXV 40 I 45
			ʾIL		I		TUWR		I	JA	I_3-LI_2-TU-RI-IA		XII 115 5+
			ḪARB		I		TUWR		AM		AR-BI-TU-RA-AM		BIROT, TEA 65:35
			ʿAŠTAR				TUWR		I	JA	$EŠ_4$-DAR-TU-RI-IA	FN	XIII 1 XIII 33
			KAKK		A		TUWR		I	JA	KA-KA-TU-RI-IA	FN	M
			ŠALAŠ				TUWR		A	JA	ŠA-LA-AŠ-TU-RA-IA	FN	C
			TIWR		I	Š	TUWR				TE-RI-IŠ-TU-UR_2		C+
TUBAB	1		TUBAB		I						TU-BA-BI		RA LXV 41 II 26
TUBIN	1		TUBIN		UM						TU-BI-NU-UM		TA 30 103
TUDAR	1		TUDAR		I		ʿAŠTAR				TU-DA-RI-$EŠ_4$-DAR	FN	EDZARD, DER 58:7
			TUDAR		UM		ʿAŠTAR				TU-DA-RUM-$EŠ_4$-DAR	FN	EDZARD, DER 61:16
TUKR	1		TUKR	ATIJI							TUK-RA-TI-I	GEN	UCP X/3 2 19
TUKUL	2		ʾANN		U		TUKUL	T	I		AN-NU-TU-KU-UL-[TI]	FN	M+
			ʾANN		U		TUKUL	T	I		AN-NU-TU-GUL-TI	FN	XIII 1 X 3
TULAʿ	2		KALAL				TULAʿ			HA	KA-LA-AL-TU-LA-A	FN	M, C
TULL	2		ʾAJIŠ				TULL		A		A-JI-IŠ-TU-UL-LA		M
TUND	1		TUND		I						TU-UN-DI	FN	M+
TUPT	1		TUPT		I	JA	MWUT		A		TU-UP-TI-IA-MU-TA		BM 80328 2
			TUPT		U		ʿAŠTAR				TUP-TU-$EŠ_4$-DAR		M
TUQAR	1		TUQAR		UM						TU-GA-RU-UM		UET V 625 10+
			TUQAR		UM						TU-QA-RU-UM		CT XXXIII 42 21
			TUQAR		IM						TU-GA-RI-IM	GEN	HARRIS 64 7
TURAḪ	2		ʾALL		I		TURAḪ				AL-LI-TU-RA-AḪ?	FN	XIII 1 I 10+
			ʾALL		I		TURAḪ		I		AL-LI-TU-RA-ḪI	FN	A.

STEMS

TURBIN	1		TURBIN	AH								TU-UR-BI-NA	FN	IX 291 II 17
TURM	1		TURM	AT	UM							TU-UR-MA-TUM	FN	M
TURTUR	1		TURTUR	AH								TU-TU-RA	FN	RA LXV 60 III 67
			TURTUR	AN								TU-UR-TU-RA-AN		RA LXV 42 II 76
TURUM	1		TURUM			NA		ḪATK		I		TU-RUM-NA-AT-KI		M+
TURUN	1		TURUN		U	HU		GAMIL				D-TU-UR-RU-NU-U$_2$-GA-MIL	FN?	XIII 118 14
TUŠUʿ	2		ʾIL		UM			TUŠUʿ		U		D-I-LU-UN-TU-SU-U$_2$	DN	KISURRA
TUŠAR	1		TUŠAR		UM							TU-ŠA-RU-UM	FN	BM 82212 3
TUŠER	1		TUŠER		U							TU-ŠE?-RU?		M
TUŠIM	1		TUŠIM		UM							DU-SI-MU-UM		I
			TUŠIM	AT	UM							TU-ŠI-MA-TUM	FN	RA LXV 61 III 77
TUT	2		ʾAL		I	Š		TUT		U		A-LI-IŠ-TU-TU		VAS XVI 23 13
TUTUG	1		TUTUG		UM							TU-TU-GU-UM		SIMMONS 119 21+
TUZAL	1		TUZAL		UM							TU-ZA-LUM		BM 17049 19+
ṬAḪD	1		ṬAḪD		I			LIʾM				TA-AḪ-DI-LI-IM		M
ṬAJB	1		ṬAJB	AT	UM							DA-BA-TUM	FN	U
			ṬAJB	AT	UM							ṬA$_3$-BA-TUM	FN	M+
			ṬAJB	AH								ṬA$_3$-BA	FN	M+
			ṬAJB	AH								TA-A-BA	FN	M+
			ṬAJB		IJA							ṬA$_3$-BI-A	FN	RA LXV 66 VII 54
			ṬAJB					ŠIJM	T	UM		TA-AB-SI-IM-TUM	FN	A. 8 4
			ṬAJB					ŠUM		U	HU	ṬA$_3$-AB-SU-MU-U$_2$		M+
			ṬAJB					ṢILL		U	HU	ṬA$_3$-AB-ṢI-LU-U$_2$		TCL X 38 7
			ṬAJB		A			ʾIL				ṬA-BA-DINGIR		A. 60 11
			ṬAJB		A			ʾAŠUR		A		TA-PA-AŠ-ŠU-RA		A.
	2		ʾAB		I			ṬAJB		A		A-BI-ṬA-BA		A.+
			ʾIL		I			ṬAJB		A		I$_3$-LI$_2$-DA-[B]A		A. 96 R. 10
			ḪAM		I			ṬAJB		I		A-MI-ṬA-BI		RA LXV 45 V 81
			ʿAMM		I			ṬAJB		A		AM-MI-ṬA-BA		A.+
			ʾUMM		I			ṬAJB	AH			UM-MI-ṬA$_3$-BA	FN	M+
			ʾUMM		I			ṬAJB	AH			UM-MI-ṬA$_3$-BA-NU	FN	RA LXV 64 VI 34
			ʾANN		U			ṬAJB				AN-NU-DUG$_3$		M+
			BAʿL		I			ṬAJB				BA-LI-SIG5?	FN	XIII 1 VIII 36
			BIN	T	U			ṬAJB	AH			BI-IN-DU-ṬA$_3$-BA	FN	RA LXV 65 VII 10
			ḎIQUN		A			ṬAJB				ZI-KU-NA-ṬA$_3$-AB	FN	RA LXV 59 II 77
			LA					ṬAJB		UM		LA-DA-BU-UM		U
			LA					ṬAJB	T	UM		LA-ṬA$_3$-AB-TUM	FN	XIII 1 VI 44+
			ŠALM		U			ṬAJB		A		ŠA-AL-MU-ṬA$_3$-BA	FN	RA LXV 66 VII 64
			ŠUM		I			ṬAJB		A		SU?-MI-DA-BA		A. 7 44+
			ŠUM		U			ṬAJB		I		SU-MU-DA-BI		X 90 10+
ṬABIḪ	1		ṬABIḪ	AT	UM							TA-BI-ḪA-TUM	MN?	BE VI/1 3 3 11
ṬALL	1		ṬALL		I		JI	BNIJ				TA-LI-IB-NI	FN	CT II 5 3 9
	2	JI	ʾLAP					ṬALL				I-LA-AP-TI-IL		U
		JI	ʾLAP					ṬALL		U	HU	I-LA-AP-TA-LU-U$_2$		M
			ʿAMM		I			ṬALL		U	HU	ḪA-MI-TI-LU-U$_2$		M
			ʿAMM		I			ṬALL		U	HU	ḪA-AM-MI-TA-LU-U$_2$		M+
			ʿAMM		I			ṬALL		U	HU	ḪA-AM-MI-TI-LU-U$_2$		M+
			ṢIḪAR					ṬALL		U	K	ṢI-ḪAR-TI-LU-UK	FN	PBS VIII/2 252 9, 18
ṬARID	1		ṬARID		UM							DA-RI-DU-UM		B 17+
			ṬARID		UM							TA-RI-DU-UM		BM 17049 26+
			ṬARID		A			ʾADM		U		TA-RI-DA-AD-MU		XIII 1 16
ṬARUD	1		ṬARUD		UM							DA-RU-DU-UM		TCL X 30 11
ṬILL	2		ʿAMM		I			ṬILL		U	HU	ḪA-AM-MI-TE-LU-U$_2$		RA LXVI 118:15
ṬUḪŠ	1		ṬUḪŠ	AT	UM							DU-UḪ-ŠA-TUM	FN	TCL X 12 12, M
			ṬUḪŠ	AT	UM							TU-UḪ$_3$-ŠA-TUM		UET V 290 2
ṬUBQ	1		ṬUBQ		I							TU-UB-KI		RA LXV 40 I 24
			ṬUBQ	AT	UM							TU-UB-GA-TUM	MN	MEISSNER 11 3
ṬUBUQ	1		ṬUBUQ	AH								TU-BU-QA	FN	M
ṬUQM	1		ṬUQM	AT	UM							TU-UK-MA-TUM	FN	RA LXV 65 VII 25
ZAʾAN	1		ZAʾAN		UM							ZA-A-NU-UM		SIMMONS 98 8 SEAL
			ZAʾAN		UM							ZA-ḪA-NU-UM		M+
			ZAʾAN		IM							ZA-ḪA-NIM	GEN	M
ZAʾAZ	1		ZAʾAZ	AH								ZA-ḪA-AZ-ZA	FN	XIII 1 IX 22
ZAʾN	1		ZAʾN	AN								ZA-AḪ-NA-AN		M
ZAʾR	1		ZAʾR		UM							ZA-RUM		XIII 1 IV 17
			ZAʾR	T	UM							ZA-AR-TUM	FN	M

STEMS

ZA'T	1	ZA'T	AN					ZA-TA-AN		RA LXV 45 V 38
		ZA'T			ʿAMM	U		ZA-AT-AM-MU	MN	A. 279 2 3
	2	ʿAMM		I	ZA'T	I		ḪA-MI-ZA-TI		HARRIS 103 1
		MA'R		U	ZA'T	U	HU	MA-RU-ZA-TU-U$_2$		CT XLVIII 27
		MALIK			ZA'T	UM		MA-LIK-ZA-DU-UM		B 34
ZA'Z	1	ZA'Z	AN	UM				ZA-ZA-NU-UM		RA LXV 47 VII 28; B 48+
		ZA'Z	AN	UM				ZA-ZA-NUM$_2$		KISURRA 2A:7+
		ZA'Z	AN	IM				ZA-ZA-NI-IM	GEN	B 48
		ZA'Z	AN	AJA				ZA-ZA-NA-IA	FN	RA LXV 58 I 52
		ZA'Z	UN	UM				ZA-ZU-NU-UM		M
		ZA'Z		IJA				ZA-ZI-IA		M+
		ZA'Z		I	'ANN	U		ZA-ZI-AN-NU		B 41+
ZAḪIL	1	ZAḪIL		UM				ZA-ḪI-LUM		HARRIS 12 30
ZAḪL	1	ZAḪL	AT	IM				ZA-AḪ-LA-TIM	GEN	CT VIII 31B 25
ZAḪZAḪ	1	ZAḪZAḪ		UM				ZA-AḪ-ZA-ḪU-UM		B 49
ZABABA	2	D̲IMR			ZABABA			ZI-ME-IR-D-ZA-BA$_4$-BA$_4$		CIG P. 155
ZABAN	1	ZABAN		UM				ZA-BA-NU-UM		U UNPUBL., B 47+
ZABIL	1	ZABIL		IM				ZA-BI-LIM	GEN	M+
		ZABIL	AT	UM				ZA-BI-LA-TUM	FN	RA LXV 60 III 50
ZABIN	1	ZABIN		UM				ZA-BI-NU-UM		M
ZABIZ	1	ZABIZ	AT	UM				ZA-BI-ZA-TUM		YOS XIII 175:11
ZABUG	1	ZABUG		A				ZA-BU-GA		JCS XIII 57 NO.305 A.LATE
		ZABUG	AN					ZA-BU-GA-AN		RA LXV 45 V 23,30
ZABUL	1	ZABUL		UM				ZA-BU-LUM		A 21950 4 5
ZABZAB	1	ZABZAB		UM				ZA-AB-ZA-BU-UM		B 49
ZAKK	1	ZAKK		U				ZA-AK-KU		M
		ZAKK		U HU				ZA-AK-KU-U$_2$		M+
		ZAKK		U HU				ZA-KU-U$_2$		M
		ZAKK			'IL	I		ZA-AK-I$_3$-LI$_2$		TA 1931,389 UR III
		ZAKK			DAWD	I		ZA-AK-DA-TI		TA 1931,377+ EARLY OB
		ZAKK			PI					
					'EL			ZA-AK-PI-EL		TA 1931,198 EARLY OB
		ZAKK		A	BALAṬ			ZA-AK-KA-BA-LA-AṬ?		M+
	2	ʿAMM		I	ZAKK	UM		AM-MI-ZA-KU-UM		IRAQ IV 185, A 385
		ʿAMM		I	ZAKK	U	HU	ḪA-AM-MI-ZA-KU-U$_2$		M
ZAKZAK	1	ZAKZAK		UM				ZA-AK-ZA-KU-UM		UNPUBL.
		ZAKZAK		UM				ZA-AK-ZA-KUM		B 49
ZALḪ	1	ZALḪ		UM				ZA-AL-ḪU-UM		RUTTEN 6 23
ZALAT	1	ZALAT	AN					ZA-LA-TA-AN		RA LXV 55 XIII 38
		ZALAT		IJA				ZA-LA-TI-IA		BM 17060 35+
ZALIJ	1	ZALIJ			'IL			ZA-LI-DINGIR		B 41
ZALUḪ	1	ZALUḪ		UM				ZA-LU-ḪU-UM		BIN VII 8 5
ZALZAL	1	ZALZAL		UM				ZA-AL-ZA-LUM		B 49+
		ZALZAL		IM				ZA-AL-ZA-LIM	GEN	M+
ZAMA'	1	ZAMA'			JAT	UM		ZA-MA-A-A-TUM	MN?	TCL X 38 1
ZAMIN	1	ZAMIN		UM				ZA-MI-NU-UM		YOS VIII P. 25+
		ZAMIN		UM				ZA-MI-NUM$_2$		YOS VIII P. 25
ZAMM	1	ZAMM	AN	UM				ZA-AM-MA-A-NU-UM		B 48
		ZAMM	AN	UM				ZA-AM-MA-NU-UM		B 48+
ZANAN	1	ZANAN		I				ZA-NA-NI	GEN	B 48
		ZANAN	AH					ZA-NA-NA	FN	RA LXV 64 V 61
ZANIJ	1	ZANIJ	AT	UM				ZA-NI-IA-TUM		BM 80496 3'
ZANN	1	ZANN		UM				ZA-AN-NU-UM		BIN VII 186 22, M
		ZANN	AT	UM				ZA-AN-NA-TUM	FN	M+
		ZANN		I				ZA-AN-NI		B 41
	2	'IL		I	ZANN	I		I$_3$-LI$_2$-ZA-AN-NI	FN	M+
ZANZI	2	ḪUNN			ZANZI			ḪU-UN-ZA-AN-ZI	FN	XIII 1 IX 42
		ḪUNN			ZANZI			ḪU-UN-ZA-ZI	FN	XIII 1 IX 34, C
ZAQAT	1	ZAQAT		UM				ZA-KA-TUM		B 41
		ZAQAT		UM				ZA-GA-TUM		KISURRA 112 5+
		ZAQAT		UM				ZA-KA-TUM	FN	RA LXV 61 IV 63
		ZAQAT		I				ZA-GA-TI	GEN	B 41
ZARAM	1	ZARAM		UM				ZA-AR-RA-MU-UM		TIM III 131 4
		ZARAM	AN	UM				ZA-RA-MA-NU-UM		TIM III 24 14
		ZARAM	AN	UM				ZA-RA-MA-A-NU-UM		SIMMONS 99 8 SEAL
ZARNAB	1	ZARNAB		UM				ZA-AR-NA-BU-UM		B 41

STEMS

ZARQ	1		ZARQ	ATANUM						ZA-AR-GA-TA-NU-UM		JCS IV 110A 19
ZARZAR	1		ZARZAR		UM					ZA-AR-ZA-RU-UM		BM 16835 26+
ZIʾM	1		ZIʾM		U		DAWR	A		ZI-MU-DA-RA		RA VIII 75 R. 2
ZIʾN	1		ZIʾN	ATANU						ZI-NA-TA-NU		BM 16984 24
ZIʾQ	1		ZIʾQ	AN						ZI-QA-AN		RA LXV 54 XII 14
ZIʾZ	1		ZIʾZ		U					ZI-ZU	FN	RA LXV 65 VII 43
			ZIʾZ	AN	UM					ZI-ZA-NU-UM		B 48+
ZIJAD	1		ZIJAD	AH						ZI?-IA?-DA	FN	XIII 1 XIII 25
ZIJAN	1		ZIJAN		I					ZI-JA-NI	FN	M
			ZIJAN		I					ZI-IA-NI		KISURRA 4A:11+
			ZIJAN		I					D-EN-ZU-I-A-NI		KISURRA 72:6
ZIBIN	1		ZIBIN		I					ZI-BI-NI		B 42
ZIBL	1		ZIBL	AN	UM					ZI-IB-LA-NU--M		BASOR 95 23
ZIDAR	1		ZIDAR		U	HU				ZI-DA-RU-U$_2$		VAS XIII 93A R. 8+
ZIKZIK	1		ZIKZIK		UM					ZI-IK-ZI-KUM		B 49
ZILḪ	1		ZILḪ	AN						ZI-IL-ḪA-AN		M+, C
ZILIB	1		ZILIB		UM					ZI-LI-BU-UM		M
			ZILIB	AN						ZI-LI-BA-AN		I 14 10
			ZILIB		IJA					ZI-LI-BI-IA		RUTTEN 19 21
ZIMM	1		ZIMM		I		DAWD	I		ZI-IM-MI-DA-DI	FN	C II 44 33+
ZINAN	1		ZINAN		UM					ZI-NA-NU-UM		CT XLV 117 32
ZIPP	1		ZIPP	ATANIM						ZI-IP-PA-TA-NIM	GEN	M
ZIRIT	1		ZIRIT	AN						ZI-RI-IT-TA-A[N]		M
ZIRQ	1		ZIRQ	AN	UM					ZE$_2$-IR-GA-NU-UM		TA 1931,438
			ZIRQ	AN	IM					ZI-IR-GA-NIM	GEN	TA 1930,221 EARLY OB
ZIZAB	1		ZIZAB	AN						ZI-ZA-BA-AN		RA LXV 52 X 38
ZIZN	1		ZIZN		I		ʾEL			ZI-IZ-NI-EL		RA LXV 55 XIII 11
ZLIJ	1	JA	ZLIJ				ʾIL			IA-AZ-LI-DINGIR		M
ZMEʾ	1	JI	ZMEʾ				ʾIL			IZ-ME-DINGIR		VAS IX 141 2
ZNIJ	1	MA	ZNIJ	AT	UM					MA-AZ-NI-A-T[UM]	FN	JCS XIX 56
ZNUR	1	JI	ZNUR		UM					IZ-NU-RU-UM		SIMMONS 48 20+
		JI	ZNUR		UM					IZ-NU-RUM		CT XLV 82 7 25
ZRAQ	1	MA	ZRAQ	AT	UM					MA-AZ-RA-QA-TUM	FN	XIII 1 II 37
ZUʾG	2		ʿAMM		I		ZUʾG	U	HU	ḪA-AM-MI-ZU-GU-U$_2$		BM 17045+
ZUʾUM	1		ZUʾUM		IM					ZU-U$_2$-MI-IM	GEN	M
			ZUʾUM		IM					ZU-[U$_2$]?-MI-IM	GEN	M
			ZUʾUM		I					ZU-U$_2$-MI	GEN	PBS VIII/2 236 6
ZUʾUZ	1		ZUʾUZ		U					ZU-U$_2$-ZU		M
ZUʾZ	1		ZUʾZ	AN						ZU-ZA-AN		M+
			ZUʾZ	AN	U					ZU-ZA-NU		B 48
			ZUʾZ	AN	UM					ZU-ZA-NU-UM		B 48
			ZUʾZ	AN	UM					ZU-ZA-NUM$_2$		RUTTEN 9 16
			ZUʾZ	AN	UM					ZU-ZA-A-NUM$_2$		KISURRA 48:12
ZUḪAL	1		ZUḪAL	AN						ZU-ḪA-LA-AN		RA LXV 51 X 2
ZUḪIR	1		ZUḪIR		I					ZU-ḪI-RI		M
ZUḪL	1		ZUḪL	AN	UM					ZU-UḪ$_3$-LA-NU-U[M]		TA 1931, 141
ZUJAN	1		ZUJAN							ZU-I-IA-AN		RA LXV 50 IX 3
			ZUJAN		I					ZU-JA-NI	FN	C
			ZUJAN		E					ZU-JA-NE	FN	XIII 1 VIII 11
ZUBAL	1		ZUBAL		IM					ZU-BA-LI-IM	GEN	EDZARD,DER 152:18
			ZUBAL	AN						ZU-BA-LA-AN		M
			ZUBAL	AT	UM					ZU?-BA-LA-TUM	FN	U
ZULAN	1		ZULAN		UM					ZU-LA-NU-UM		TA 30 35 6
ZULAT	2	TA	KWUN				ZULAT	UM		TA-KU-UN-ZU?-LA-TUM	FN	RA LXV 62 V 30
ZUMM	1		ZUMM	AN						ZU-UM-MA-AN		XIII 95 6
			ZUMM				ʾAB	U		ZU-UM-MA-BU		BM 80328 7
ZUNAN	1		ZUNAN							ZU-NA-AN		M
			ZUNAN		UM					ZU-NA-NU-UM		KISURRA 94 5
			ZUNAN		U					ZU-NA-NU		B 48
ZUNN	1		ZUNN	AH						ZU-UN-NA	FN	XIII 1 IV 51
ZUNZ	1		ZUNZ		UM					ZU-UN-ZU-UM		RA LXV 48 VIII 4
ZUNZUN	1		ZUNZUN		UM					ZU-UN-ZU-NU-UM		RUTTEN 1 9
			ZUNZUN		A					ZU-UN-ZU-NA		B 49
ZUQAT	1		ZUQAT		UM		MA			ZU-KA-TUM-MA		EDZARD,DER 152 REV. 11
ZURZUR	1		ZURZUR		UM					ZU-UR-ZU-RU-UM		CT XLV 5 R. 6
			ZURZUR		UM					ZU-UR$_2$-ZU-RU-UM		KISURRA 20 13+
ZURZUR	1		ZURZUR	T	UM					ZU-UR$_2$-ZU-UR-TUM	FN	KISURRA 187 5
			ZURZUR	T	UM					ZU-UR$_2$-ZU-UR-TUM	FN	KISURRA 187 5

2. ROOTS

The root lemmata are derived from the stems in chapter 1, "Stems," by omitting all vowels.

According to the definition proposed by me[1] and by Diakonoff,[2] the consonantal root appears only in verbs and in nouns derived from verbs (verbal nouns), as in /*Ja-rpa*ʾ+/ and /*Rāpi*ʾ-*um*/ from the consonantal root RPʾ "to heal."

The reduction of stems to roots by computer analysis, however, resulted in the listing of not only verbs and verbal nouns but also of several classes of primary elements with an artificial consonantal root analysis. Among the latter are KLB in /*Kalbum*/ "dog," ʾNK in /*Anāku-ʾila-ma*/ "I-am-truly-god," and foreign names, as in ʾŠḪR for the divinity ʾ*Išḫara* in /ʾ*Išḫara-napšī*/ "ʾIšḫara-is-my-life."

For a general discussion of the structure of this chapter and also for a discussion of points of questionable root analysis see section 0.3.

1. *Sequential Reconstruction of Proto-Akkadian*, Assyriological Studies, no. 18 (Chicago, 1969), p. 164.

2. I. M. Diakonoff, "Problems of Root Structure in Proto-Semitic," *Archiv Orientální* 38 (1970), pp. 453 ff.

Consonantal phonemes are discussed briefly in section 0.4.

We find that there are 1,020 consonantal roots altogether, distributed among 1,996 consonant-plus-vowel stems. See the introductory remarks to chapter 4, "Stem Count."

The alphabetic order of lemmata is the new order of roots:

ʾ	H	Ḥ	Ḫ	ʿ	W	J
B	D	Ḏ	G			
K	L	M	N	P	Q	R
S	Ś	Š	Ṣ	T	Ṭ	Z

The alphabetic order of parts outside of the lemma is that of my work order, which does not differ much from the order given above.

For the discussion of alphabetic sequences see section 0.5.

ROOTS (Consonants only)

ʾHL	1		ʾAHL	UM			MAʾT	U		[A-LU]-UM-MA-[TU]	FN	M
			ʾAHL	UM			MAʾT	UM		[A-LU-UM]-MA-TUM	FN	M
			ʾAHL	UM			PU		HU	A-LUM-BI-U$_2$		SIMMONS 129 13
			ʾAHL	UM			PU		HU	ḪA-LAM-BU-U$_2$		RLA II 165 17
			ʾAHL	UM			PU		HU	[A]-LI-IM-BU-MU		OLZ 1958 547 N.1
			ʾAHL	UM			PU		HU	A-LUM-BU-MU		OLZ 1958 547 N.1
	2		JAʾ	U			ʾAHL	I		IA-U$_2$-A-LI$_2$		KISURRA 85 19
			JAʾN	A			ʾAHL	UM		JA-NA-A-LUM	GN	MRS VI P.125 61
			BEʿL	I			ʾAHL	I		BE-LI-IA-LI$_2$		KISURRA 112 14
			KAʾB	I			ʾAHL	UM		KA-PI-IA-LUM		UET V 626 11, 702 REV. 5
		JA	KWUN				ʾAHL	I		IA-KU-UN-A-LI		B 92
			MATIʿ				ʾAHL	I		MA-TI-IA-LI		UCP X/1 1 16
		JI	TWUR				ʾAHL	I		I-DUR-A-LI		JCS XXIV 46 NOS. 5, 6
	3		LI			JI	TWUR					
							ʾAHL	I		LI-TU-UR-A-LI		JCS XXIV 62 NO.55+
ʾḪ	1		ʾAḪ	UM						A-ḪU-UM		M+
			ʾAḪ	IM						A-ḪI-IM	GEN	M
			ʾAḪ	IJA						A-ḪI-IA		M+
			ʾAḪ	AM		ʾA	RŠIJ			A-ḪA-AM-AR-ŠI		I+
			ʾAḪ	I			ḪIʾL			A-ḪI-ḪI-EL		XIII 1 X 17
			ʾAḪ	I			JABAL			A-ḪI-E-BA-AL		M
			ʾAḪ	I			HADD	A		A-ḪI-A-DA		B 12
			ʾAḪ	I			ʾIL			A-ḪI-[I]L		HARRIS 45 11
			ʾAḪ	I			ʾIL	I		A-ḪI-I$_3$-LI$_2$	FN	XIII 1 VIII 20
			ʾAḪ	I			ʾAŠD			A-ḪI-SA-AD		B 12+
			ʾAḪ	I			ʾAŠD			A-ḪI-A-SA-AD		B 12
			ʾAḪ	I			ʾAŠD			A-ḪA-SA-AD		UET V 539 II 19
			ʾAḪ	I			JATAR			A-Ḫ[I]-E?-TAR		RA LXV 46 V 86
			ʾAḪ	I		JI	ʿQUB	A		A-ḪI-I-KU-BA		KISURRA 7A 9
			ʾAḪ	I		JA	JŠUʿ			A-ḪI-IA-ŠU-UḪ		SIMMONS 58 16
			ʾAḪ	I		JA	JŠUʿ			A-ḪI-IA-ŠU		BIROT, TEA 28:17+
			ʾAḪ	I		JE	QWIM			A-ḪI-E-KI-IM		M
			ʾAḪ	I		JA	ŠJIT			A-ḪI-SI-IT		TA 1931, 636
			ʾAḪ	I			DANN	UM		A-ḪI-DA-NU-UM		I
			ʾAḪ	I			DAŠUR			A-ḪI-DA-ŠU-UR$_2$		PBS XI/2 P. 140 NO. 1128
			ʾAḪ	I			KI					
							LIʾM			A-ḪI-KI-LI-IM		JEAN T.SIFR 72 5, 6, 13+
			ʾAḪ	I			KAʾB	I		A-ḪI-KA-PI		YOS VIII 64 18
			ʾAḪ	I			LIʾM			A-ḪI-LI-IM		B 12, M
			ʾAḪ	I			LABAN			A-ḪI-LA-BA-AN		RA LXV 43 IV 5+
			ʾAḪ	I			MAʾJ	UM		A-ḪI-MA-IU-UM		MAM III P. 274
			ʾAḪ	I	JE		MALIK			A-ḪI-E-MA-LIK		M
			ʾAḪ	I			MARAṢ			A-ḪI-MA-RA-AṢ		B 12+, M+
			ʾAḪ	I			MARAṢ			A-ḪI-MA-RA-UṢ		RUTTEN 1 22
			ʾAḪ	I			MARAṢ			A-ḪI-MA-RA-AṢ	FN	XIII 1 IX 24
			ʾAḪ	I			ŠALAŠ			A-ḪI-ŠA-LA-AŠ		EDZARD, DER 104:2
			ʾAḪ	I			ŠUM	U	NA	A-ḪI-SU-MU-NA		SIMMONS 83 5
			ʾAḪ	I		JI	ŠMAʿ		NI	A-ḪI-IŠ-MA-NI		VAS VIII 14:41+
			ʾAḪ	I	Š		TUʾ		JA	A-ḪI-IŠ-TU-IA		A. 86 9
			ʾAḪ	I	Š		TUʾ		KA	A-ḪI-IŠ-DU-KA		A. 98C 1, 6
			ʾAḪ	I		TA	NWUḪ	A		A-ḪI-TA-NU-A		M
			ʾAḪ	I			ṢADUQ			A-ḪI-ZA-DU-UQ		B 12
			ʾAḪ	U			JAḪAD			A-ḪU-IA-ḪA-AD		M+
			ʾAḪ	U			JAT	UM		A-ḪU-IA-TUM	MN	BIN II 98 4
			ʾAḪ	U			JAT	UM		A-ḪU-JA-TUM	MN	M
			ʾAḪ	U			KA					
							ʾAB	I		A-ḪU-KA-A-BI	FN	XIII 1 VIII 60, C+
			ʾAḪ	U			ʾEL			A-ḪU-EL		RA LXV 50 IX 1
			ʾAḪ	UM			LI		JA	A-ḪU-UM-LI-A		M
			ʾAḪ	UM			LA					
							ʾAB	I		A-ḪU-UM-LA-A-BI		YOS XIII 245:17, SEAL
			ʾAḪ	UM			LUʾM	U		A-ḪU-UM-LU-MU		X 166 4+
			ʾAḪ	U			LUʾM	U		A-ḪU-LU-MU		M
			ʾAḪ	UM			MA					
							ʾIL			A-ḪU-UM-MA-DINGIR		M+
			ʾAḪ	UM			MAṬAR	I		A-ḪU-UM-MA-DA-RI		M

ROOTS (Consonants only)

ʾḪ	1	ʾAḪ	AT	UM						A-ḪA-TUM	FN	M+
		ʾAḪ	AT	I						A-ḪA-TI	FN	XIII 1 VIII 6
		ʾAḪ	AT	I		MA				A-ḪA-TI-MA	FN	JCS XXVII 135:1
		ʾAḪ	AT	A	HA					A-ḪA-TA-A	FN	RA LXV 62 V 52
		ʾAḪ	AT	UJA						A-ḪA-TU-IA	FN	SIMMONS 66 4+
		ʾAḪ	AT			JIQR	AH			A-ḪA-AT-IQ-RA	FN	M
		ʾAḪ	AT	A		ʾAB		I		A-ḪA-TA-A-BI	FN	M+
		ʾAḪ	AT	A		NAʿM		I		A-ḪA-TA-NA-AḪ-MI	FN	XIII 1 XI 3
		ʾAḪ	AT	I		JIQR	AT			A-ḪA-TI-IQ-RA-AT	FN	XIII 1 V 5
		ʾAḪ	AT	I		JIQR	AH			A-ḪA-TI-IQ-RA	FN	XIII 1 II 72+
	2	ʾAJA				ʾAḪ		UM		A-IA-A-ḪU-UM		RA LXV 41 II 24
		ʾAJA				ʾAḪ		U		A-IA-A-ḪU		XIII 1 III 52
		ʾAJA				ʾAḪ		U		A-IA-ḪU		A. LATE+
		ʾAJA				ʾAḪ		I		A-IA-A-ḪI		X 166 8'+
		ʾAJA				ʾAḪ		IM		A-IA-A-ḪI-IM		X 166 4
		ʾAJA				ʾAḪ	AT	I		A-IA-A-ḪA-TI	FN	A.
		ʿAḎAR				ʾAḪ				A-ZA-RA-AḪ		JNES XIII 210+ LATE
		ʿAḎR				ʾAḪ		I		ḪA-AZ-RA-ḪI?		CT XLV 54 9
		ʾAL				ʾAḪ	AT	I		AL-A-ḪA-TI	FN	A.
		ʾALI				ʾAḪ		I		A-LI-A-ḪI	FN	M+
		ʾALI				ʾAḪ		I		A-LI$_2$-A-ḪI	FN	RA LXV 59 II 41
		ʾALI				ʾAḪ	AT	I		A-LI-A-ḪA-TI	FN	XIII 1 IV 71+
		ʾALI				ʾAḪ	AT	I		A-LI-A-ḪA?-TA-TI	FN	M
		ʾALI				ʾAḪ	AT	I		A-LI$_2$-A-ḪA-TI	FN	RA LXV 59 II 65+
	JA	WMAʾ				ʾAḪ		UM		JA-MA-A-ḪU-UM		RA LXV 52 X 49
		ʿAN		UM		ʾAḪ		I		A-NU-UM-A-ḪI		RA LXV 53 XI 43
		ḪANN		A		ʾAḪ		UM		AN-NA-A-ḪU-UM		RA LXV 52 XI 1
		ḪANN		A		ʾAḪ		IM		AN-NA-A-ḪI-IM	GEN	M
		ḪANN		A		ʾAḪ		I		AN-NA-A-ḪI	GEN	M
		ʿAQB		A		ʾAḪ		UM		AQ-BA-A-ḪU-UM		M+
		ʿAQB		A		ʾAḪ		UM		AQ-BA-ḪU-UM		B 11+
		ʿAQB		A		ʾAḪ		UM		ḪA-AQ-BA-A-ḪU-UM		RA LXV 43 III 57+
		ʿAQB		A		ʾAḪ		U		AQ-BA-A-ḪU		M+, C+
		ʿAQB		A		ʾAḪ		U		AQ-BA-ḪU		BASOR 95 19+
		ʿAQB		A		ʾAḪ		AM		AQ-BA-A-ḪA-AM	ACC	M
		ʿAQB		A		ʾAḪ		IM		AQ-BA-A-ḪI-IM	GEN	M+
		ʿAQB		A		ʾAḪ		IM		ḪA-AQ-BA-A-ḪI-IM	GEN	M+
		ʿAQB		A		ʾAḪ		I		AQ-BA-A-ḪI	GEN	XII 448 5+
		ʿAQB		I		ʾAḪ		U		AQ-BI-A-ḪU		B 11
		ʿIQB		A		ʾAḪ		UM		IQ-BA-A-ḪU-UM		KISURRA 4A 11, M
		ʿIQB		A		ʾAḪ		UM		IQ-BA-ḪU-UM		KISURRA 121 6
		ʾAŠD		A		ʾAḪ		I		AŠ-DA-A-ḪI		VAS XVI 44 3
	ʾU	WTAʾ				ʾAḪ		I		U$_2$-TA-A-ḪI		M
		JATAR				ʾAḪ		UM		JA-TA-AR-ḪU-UM		I
	JI	JṢIʾ				ʾAḪ		UM		I-ZI-A-ḪU-UM		M+
	JI	JṢIʾ				ʾAḪ		U		I-ZI-A-ḪU?		X 53:6
		BIN		A		ʾAḪ		UM		BI-NA-A-ḪU-UM		M+
		DIWIR				ʾAḪ		I		DI-WI-IR-A-ḪI		PBS XI/1 P. 55+
		DIWIR				ʾAḪ		I		DI-BI-IR-A-ḪI		PBS XI/1 P. 55+
		ḎAKUR		A		ʾAḪ		UM		ZA-KU-RA-A-ḪU-UM		M+
		MUT		I		ʾAḪ		I		MU-TI-A-ḪI	GEN	B 35
		NAKR				ʾAḪ		UM		NA-AK-RA-ḪU-UM		RUTTEN 2 19+
	ʾA	RŠIJ				ʾAḪ		UM		AR-ŠI-A-ḪU-UM		M+
		ŠUM		U		ʾAḪ		I	JA	[SU]-MU-A-ḪI-IA		PBS XI/2 1 I 27
		ŠAMŠ		I		ʾAḪ		I		SA-AM-SI-A-ḪI		RA LXV 54 XII 26
		ŠIPṬ		A		ʾAḪ		UM		ŠI-IP-TA-A-ḪU-UM		RA LXV 46 VI 27
		ṢAMID				ʾAḪ		I		ZA-MI-ID-A-ḪI		CT IV 8B 17
	3	ʾIL		I		MAʾD		I				
						ʾAḪ				I$_3$-LI$_2$-MA-DI-A-AḪ		RUTTEN 1 8
		ʾIL		I		MAʾD		I				
						ʾAḪ				DINGIR?-MA-DA-AḪ		RA LXV 42 III 21
		ʾIL		I		MAʾD		I				
						ʾAḪ				I$_3$-LI$_2$-MI-DI-AḪ		EDZARD, DER 146:14
		ʾIL		I		MAʾD		I				
						ʾAḪ		I		I$_3$-LI$_2$-MA-DA-ḪI		RUTTEN 14 7
		ʾIL		I		MAʾD		I				
						ʾAḪ		A		I$_3$-LI$_2$-MA-DA-ḪA		VAS VIII 14 4

ROOTS (Consonants only)

ʾḪ	3		BIN				MA					
							ʾAḪ		IM	BI-IN-MA-A-ḪI-IM		M
			BIN		I		MA					
							ʾAḪ		UM	BI-IN-NI-MA-ḪU-UM		TLB I 3 28
			BIN		I		MA					
							ʾAḪ		UM	BI-NI-MA-ḪU-UM		CCT IV 13A 6+ CAPP.
			BUN		I		MA					
							ʾAḪ		UM	BU-NI-MA-ḪU-UM		TCL XX 96 8
			BUN		U		MA					
							ʾAḪ		UM	BU-NU-MA-A-ḪU-UM		B 16
			LA			ʾA	ḪWIJ					
							ʾAḪ		I	IA-AḪ-WI-A-ḪI	FN	XIII 1 VII 3
			QAWM		U		MA					
							ʾAḪ		UM	QA-MU-MA-A-ḪU-UM		M
			QAWM		U		MA					
							ʾAḪ		I	QA-MU-MA-A-ḪI		RA LXV 41 II 22
ʾḪW	2		ʾAJA				ʾAḪW		I	A-IA-A-ḪU-I		JCS V 133
ʾḪḎ	1		ʾAḪIḎ	AN						A-ḪI-ZA-AN		M
		JA	ʾḪUḎ	AN						IA-ḪU-ZA-AN		RA LXV 43 IV 21
		TA	ʾḪUḎ	AN						TA-ḪU-ZA-AN		RA LXV 52 X 33
		JA	ʾḪIḎ		A					IA-E-DA		YOS XIII 343:4
		JA	ʾḪIḎ				ʾUMM		I	IA-ḪI-DU-UM-ME	FN	RA LXV 65 VII 34
		ME	ʾḪIḎ		UM					ME-ḪI-DU-UM		RA LXV 54 XII 64
		ME	ʾḪAḎ		UM					ME-ḪA-DUM		UCP X/3 3:18; YONDORF 4
		MI	ʾḪAḎ		UM					MI-ḪA-[TUM]?	TRIBE	IX 244:5
	2		DANN		U	TA	ʾḪAḎ			DAN-NU-TA-ḪA-AZ		M+
			DANN		U	TA	ʾḪAḎ			DA-NU-TA-ḪA-AZ		SIMMONS 36 23
			DANN		U	TA	ʾḪAḎ			D-DA-NU-TA-ḪA-AZ		SIMMONS 84 15
			DANN		UM	TA	ʾḪAḎ			D-DA-AN-NU-UM-TA-ḪA-AZ		SIMMONS 36 A 22
			DANN		UM	TA	ʾḪAḎ			DA-AN-NU-UM-TA-ḪA-AZ		SIMMONS 36 CASE 22
			DANN		UM	TA	ʾḪAḎ			DA-NU-UM-TA-ḪA-AZ		A 7634, M
			DANN		UM	TA	ʾḪAḎ			D-DA-NU-UM-TA-ḪA-[AZ]		TIM V 19 14
ʾḪL	1		ʾAḪAL		UM					A-ḪA-LUM		BIROT, TEA 45:12
			ʾAḪIL	AT	UM					A-ḪI-LA-TUM	FN	XIII 1 I 67
ʾḪN	1		ʾAḪN	AN	UM					AḪ-NA-NU-UM		KISURRA 14 4+
ʾḪR	1		ʾAḪR		AM					AḪ-RA-AM	ACC	II 43 13
ʾWʾ	1		ʾAWAʾ	AT	UM					A-WA-TUM	FN	M
			ʾAWAʾ	ATAN						A-WA-TA-AN		RA LXV 47 VII 31+
			ʾAWAʾ	AT	I		ʾEL			A-WA-TI-EL		RA LXV 41 II 37+
			ʾAWAʾ	AT	I		ʾIL			A-WA-TI-DINGIR	MN	XIII 1 XI 39
	2		LA			ʾA	ʾWIʾ					
							ʾIL			LA-WI-IḪ?-DINGIR		TIM IV 33,34,SEALS
ʾWJ	1		ʾAWIJ		UM					A-WI-U_2-UM		GORDON 38 21+
			ʾAWIJ	AT	UM					ḪA-WI-IA-TUM		BIROT TEA 39:4
			ʾAWIJ	AT	UM					A-WI-IA-TUM	MN?	TIM I 11 10+
			ʾAWIJ	T	UM					ḪA-WI-TUM		BIROT TEA 72 I 28+
			ʾAWIJ			JA	JṢIʾ			A-WI-IA-ZI		RA LXV 53 XI 49
			ʾAWIJ				KIRIŠ		U	A-WI-KI-RI-IŠ		XIV 106:18
ʾWN	1		ʾAWIN							A-WI-IN		M+
			ʾAWIN		UM					A-WI-NU-UM		FLP 516, UR III
			ʾEWIN		I					E-[W]I-NI		RA LXV 47 VII 22
			ʾAWN	AN	UM					AM-NA-NU-UM	GN	SAKI P. 222+
			ʾAWN	AN	UM					AM-NA-NU-UM	PN	SUMER XIV 49
			ʾAWN	AN	UM					AW-NA-NU-[UM]	TRIBE	M
			ʾAWN	AN	U					AM-NA-NU		BM 80328 9
			ʾAWN	AN	IM					AW-NA-NI-[IM]	GEN	MAM III 320, PSARG MARI
			ʾAWN	ANIJI						AM-NA-NI-I	TRIBE	M
			ʾAWN	AN		JA	ʾRUR			AM-NA-AN-IA-AḪ-RU-UR	TRIBE	BAGHD. MITT. II 56 I 12+
	2		MUT				ʾAWN	AN		MU-UT-AW-NA-AN		B 35 HANA
			MUT		U		ʾAWN	AN	UM	MU-TU-AM-NA-NU-UM		BM 81641 3, 8
			ŠUM		U		ʾAWN	AN	UM	SU-MU-AM-NA-NU-UM		B 38+
			ŠUM		U		ʾAWN	AN	IM	SU-MU-AW-NA-NIM		SUMER XXIII ARABIC 178
ʾWR	1	JA	ʾWIR		UM					IA-WI-RU-UM		B 31
		MI	ʾWIR		UM					MI-I-RUM		RA LXV 46 V 83
		ME	ʾWIR		I					ME-ḪI-RI		C
		ME	ʾWIR		I		ʾEL			ME-ḪI-RI-E-EL		JCS IV 109 4311 7

ROOTS (Consonants only)

ʾWR	1		ʾUWR		A		HADD		U		U_2-RA-A-DU		A.
			ʾUWR		I		HADD		U		U_2-RI-A-DU		A.
			ʾUWR		I		HADD		U		WU-RI-A-DU		A.
			ʾUWR		I		JARAḪ				U_2-RI-E-RA-AḪ		M
	2		ʾIL		A		ʾUWR		I		DINGIR-U_2-RI		RA LXVIII 28:13 MARI
			ʾIL		I		ʾUWR		I		I-LI-U_2-RI	FN	A.
			LA			ʾA	ʾWIR		UM		LA-WI-RUM		RA XXIV 58 9 4
ʾWŠ	1	JA	ʾWUŠ		U						IA-U_2-ŠU		B 31
		JA	ʾWUŠ	AN							IA-U_2-SA-AN		RA LXV 43 IV 15
		JA	ʾWUŠ				HADD		U		IA-UŠ-D-IM		M+
		JA	ʾWUŠ				HADD		U		IA-U_2-UŠ-D-IM		M+
		JA	ʾWUŠ				HADD		U		IA-$UŠ_2$-D-IM		M
		JA	ʾWUŠ				ʾIL				IA-UŠ-DINGIR		M+
		JA	ʾWUŠ				ʾIL				IA-U_2-$UŠ_2$-DINGIR		C II 35 28
		JA	ʾWUŠ				ʾIL				IA-U_2-UŠ-DINGIR		RA LXV 42 III 10+
		JE	ʾWUŠ				ʾIL				E-WU-ŠI-DINGIR		BIROT, TEA 48:20
		JA	ʾWUŠ				ḤAM		U		IA-U_2-UŠ-D-A-MU		M
		JI	ʾWUŠ				ŠALIM				I-UŠ?-SA-LIM		RUTTEN 1 3
		JA	ʾWIŠ				....				IA-ḪI-IŠ-[....]		TIM IV 33 SEAL, 34 SEAL
		ME	ʾWIŠ		UM						ME-I-SU-UM		CT VI 7 21+
			ʾUWŠ	AN							U_2-ŠA-AN		M+
			ʾUWŠ	AN	UM						ḪU-ŠA-NU-UM		B 45+
			ʾUWŠ	AN	UM						ḪU-ŠA-A-NU-UM		KISURRA 48 8
			ʾUWŠ	AN	U						ḪU-SA-NU		4E RENC. ASS. P. 178 4
ʾJ	1		ʾAJ		A		ʿALIJ	AT			D-A-A-ḪA-LI-IA-AT	MN?	CT XLV 92 R. 12
			ʾAJ		A		ʾARR		I		D-A-A-AR-RI	FN	M
			ʾAJA				ʾAḪ		UM		A-IA-A-ḪU-UM		RA LXV 41 II 24
			ʾAJA				ʾAḪ		U		A-IA-A-ḪU		XIII 1 III 52
			ʾAJA				ʾAḪ		U		A-IA-ḪU		A. LATE+
			ʾAJA				ʾAḪ		I		A-IA-A-ḪI		X 166 8'+
			ʾAJA				ʾAḪ		IM		A-IA-A-ḪI-IM		X 166 4
			ʾAJA				ʾAḪW		I		A-IA-A-ḪU-I		JCS V 133
			ʾAJA				ʾAḪ	AT	I		A-IA-A-ḪA-TI	FN	A.
			ʾAJA				ḪAʾL		U		A-IA-ḪA-LU		M
			ʾAJA				ʾAB						
							ʾIL				ḪA-IA-AB-DINGIR		B 18
			ʾAJA				ʾAB		I		A-IA-A-BI		A.
			ʾAJA				ʾAB		I		A-IA-BI		A.+
			ʾAJA				ʾAB		I				
							ŠARR		I		A-IA-BI-ŠAR-RI		A.
			ʾAJA				ʾAB		I				
							TALM		A		A-IA-BI-TA-AL-MA		A. 239 15
			ʾAJA				ʾAB		U		A-IA-A?-BU?	FN	C+
			ʾAJA				ʾAB		U		A-IA-BU		A. LATE +
			ʾAJA				ʾAB		U	HU	A-A-A-BU-U_2	FN	DE CLERCQ II 253B
			ʾAJA				ʾAB		UM		ḪA-A-IA-A-BU-UM		M
			ʾAJA				ʾAB		UM		ḪA-IA-BU-UM		B 18+
			ʾAJA				ʾAB		AM		ḪA-A-IA-A-BA-AM	ACC	M+
			ʾAJA				ʾABN		I				
							ʾIL				ḪA-IA-AB-NI-DINGIR		B 18+
			ʾAJA				ʾIL				A-IA-DINGIR		A.+
			ʾAJA				ʾUMM		I		A-IA-UM-MI	FN	RA LXV 59 II 27
			ʾAJA				ʿAMM		U		A-IA-AM-MU		MAOG IV 2 10, 11, A 7740+
			ʾAJA				ʿAMM		U	HU	A-A-ḪA-AM-MU-U_2		BASOR 95 23
			ʾAJA				ʿAMM		U	HU	A-IA-ḪA-MU-U_2		A 7648, M
			ʾAJA				ʿAMM		U	HU	A-IA-AM-MU-U_2		VAS XIII 34:3
			ʾAJA				ʿAMM		U	HU	A-IA-AM-MU-KU		CT XLV 6 33
			ʾAJA				ʿAMM		U	HU	IA-ḪA-AM-MU-U_2		VAS XVIII 100:19
			ʾAJA				ʾAZJ		I		A-IA-ZI		M
			ʾAJA			JE	JŠUʿ				A-A-E-ŠU-UḪ?		TCL X 9 3
			ʾAJA				BAʿL		A	JA	A-A-BA-IA-IA		SIMMONS 63 9
			ʾAJA				DAWD		U		A-IA-DA-DU		M
			ʾAJA				DAWD		U	HU	A-A-DA-DU-U_2		HARRIS 79 5
			ʾAJA				DAWD		U	HU	A-IA-DA-DU-U_2		TIM IV 39 15
			ʾAJA				KALB	AB			A-IA-KA-AL-BA?	FN	C
			ʾAJA				LA						
							ŠUM		U	HU	A-IA-LA-SU-MU-U_2		M, C

ROOTS (Consonants only)

ʾJ	1	ʾAJA				MA						
						ʾIL				A-IA-MA-DINGIR		M
		ʾAJA				MA						
						ʾIL				ḪA-IA$_3$-MA-DINGIR		XIV 93:8+
		ʾAJA				MA						
						ʾEL				A-IA-MA-EL		RA LXV 42 III 14
		ʾAJA				MUT		I		ḪA-IA-MU-TI		BAGHD. MITT. II 7 2, 4, 8
		ʾAJA				MAṬAR				ḪA-IA-MA-DAR		YOS XII 360 17
		ʾAJA				MAṬAR				A-IA-MA-[DAR]		YOS XII 360 SEAL
		ʾAJA				NIWR		I		[A]-IA-NI-RI		RA LXV 59 II 36
		ʾAJA				ŠUM				ḪA-IA$_3$-SU?-UM		M
		ʾAJA				ŠUM		U		ḪA-IA$_3$-SU-MU		DELAPORTE CCL II A 337+
		ʾAJA				ŠUM		U	HU	ḪA-IA-SU-MU-U$_2$		XI P.83 N.1+
		ʾAJA				ŠUM		U	HU	ḪA-IA$_3$-SU-MU-U$_2$		M+
		ʾAJA				ŠUM		U	HU	ḪA-IA$_3$-SU-U$_2$-MU		M+
		ʾAJA				ŠUM		U	HU	ḪA-IA$_3$-SU-U$_2$-MU-U$_2$		X 113 4, 11, 14
		ʾAJA				ŠUM		U				
						ʾAB		IM		ḪA-IA-SU-MU-A-BI-IM		M
		ʾAJA				ŠARR		UM		ḪA-IA-ŠA-RUM		UCP X P. 56+
		ʾAJI				DAWD		I		A-I-DA-TE	FN	A.
		ʾIJA				ʾAB						
						ʾIL				I-A-AB-DINGIR		OIP XXII 262
		ʾIJA				ʾUMM		U		I-IA-AMA		MRS VI P. 328+
ʾJK	1	ʾAJAK		UM						A-IA-KU-UM		RA LXV 52 X 51
		ʾAJAK		U						A-JA-KU		RA LXV 52 X 44
ʾJL	1	ʾAJAL		UM						A-IA-LU-UM		CT XLV 5 9
		ʾAJAL		UM						A-IA-LUM		M
		ʾAJAL		UM						A-A-LUM		KISURRA 116
		ʾAJAL		IM						A-IA-LIM	GEN	M
		ʾAJAL	AT	UM						A-IA-LA-TUM	FN	VAS VII 3 25
		ʾAJAL	AT	UM						D-A-A-LA-TUM	FN	CT VIII 29C 22+
		ʾAJAL	AH							A-IA-LA	FN	M+
		ʾAJAL	AH							A-JA-LA	FN	XIII 1 IV 37
		ʾAJAL	AN							A-JA-LA-AN		RA LXV 52 X 81
		ʾAJAL		A	HA					A?-IA-LA-A	FN?	M
ʾJM	1	ʾAJAM				ʾIL	T	I		A-IA-AM-IL-TI	FN	XIII 1 X 8
		ʾAJAM				DIWD		UM		ḪA-IA-AM-DI-DU-UM		B 18+
		ʾAJAM				DIWD		U		ḪA-IA-AM-DI-DU		B 18
		ʾAJAM			TI	ʾIL				ḪA-IA-AM-TI-DINGIR		BIROT, TEA 72 III 5
	2	ʾANN		U		ʾAJAM				AN-NU-[Ḫ]A-A-AM	FN	XIII 1 II 62
ʾJN	1	ʾAJAN				ʾAB		I		A-IA-NA-BI	FN	A.
		ʾAJAN				ʾAB		I				
						ʾILL		A		A-IA-NA-BI-IL-LA		A.
		ʾAJAN				ʾABAL				A-AN-A-BA-AL	FN	XIII 1 IX 38
		ʾAJAN				KURUB				A-AN-KU-RU-UB	FN	RA LXV 51 X 15
		ʾAJAN				IIʾM				A-AN-LI-IM		M+
		ʾAJAN				ŠARR		I		A-IA-AŠ-LUGAL		A. 18 4
		ʾAJAN				ŠARR		I		A-IA-LUGAL-RI		A. 243 22
		ʾAJAN				ŠARR		I		A-IA-LUGAL		A. 274 4
ʾJŠ	1	ʾAJIŠ		UM						ḪA-II-ŠUM		KISURRA 101 6+
		ʾAJIŠ				PI			HU	ḪA-II-IŠ-PI$_2$-U$_2$		KISURRA 22+
		ʾAJIŠ				PI			HU	ḪA-A-IŠ-PI$_2$-U$_2$		KISURRA 5+
		ʾAJIŠ				TULL		A		A-JI-IŠ-TU-UL-LA		M
ʾB	1	ʾAB	AN	UM						A-BA-NU-UM		U+, SIMMONS 51 18
		ʾAB		A		ʾEL				A-BA-EL		TA 31, 221
		ʾAB		A		ʾIL				A-BA-DINGIR	FN	A. 59 5
		ʾAB		A		ʾANN		U		A-BA-AN-NU		M
		ʾAB		A		JARAḪ				A-BA-A-RA-AḪ		KICH II D 8 3
		ʾAB		A		DAWD		UM		A-BA-DA-DUM		HARRIS 95 9
		ʾAB		I		JAʾ		A		A-BI-IA-A		KISURRA 102 7+
		ʾAB		I		JAʾ		UM		A-BI-IA-U$_2$-UM		YOS VIII 10 9
		ʾAB		I		ḪIʾL				A-BI-ḪI-EL		B 10, M
		ʾAB		I		ḪIʾL				A-BI-ḪI-IL		M
		ʾAB		I		ḪIʾL		U		A-BI-ḪE$_2$-LU		MRS VI P. 240 LATE
		ʾAB		I		JAʾAR				A-BI-IA-ḪA-AR		B 10+
		ʾAB		I		JAʾAR				A-BI-A-ḪA-AR		CT XLIII 125 1+

ROOTS (Consonants only)

ʾB	1	ʾAB	I		JAʾAR		A-BI-ḪA-AR		B 10+
		ʾAB	I		JABAL		A-BI-A-BA-AL		FIGULLA CAT. I 14206
		ʾAB	I		HADD	U	A-BI-D-IM		B 9, M+
		ʾAB	I		HADD	U	A-BI-A-DU		A.+
		ʾAB	I		HADD	U	A-BI-IA-DU		M+
		ʾAB	I		ʿAḎAR		A-BI-DAR		SIMMONS 58 12
		ʾAB	I		ʿAḎR	I	A-BI-AD-RI		A. LATE
		ʾAB	I		ʾAK	I	A-BI-IA-KI		TCL I 109 3
		ʾAB	I		ʾIL	A	A-BI-LA		CHANTRE 4 13
		ʾAB	I		ʾIL	I	A-BI-I$_3$-LI$_2$	FN	RA LXV 59 II 38+
		ʾAB	I		ʿALAṢ	I	AD-ḪA-LA-ZI	FN	C
		ʾAB	I		ʿALAṢ	I	A-BI-ḪA-LA-ZI	FN	M, C II 49 6
		ʾAB	I		ḤAM	A	A-BI-A-MA		SIMMONS 50 22+
		ʾAB	I		ḤAM	A	A-BI-IA-MA		SIMMONS 54 19+
		ʾAB	I		ʾAMAL		A-BI-A-MA-AL		KISURRA 153 34
		ʾAB	I		ʾANN	IM	A-BI-AN-NIM	GEN	M
		ʾAB	I		ḪUNN	I	A-BI-ḪU-UN?-NI		B 10
		ʾAB	I		JAQAR		A-BI-E-QAR		M+
		ʾAB	I		ʾIR	A	AD-I-RA	FN	A.
		ʾAB	I		JARAḪ		A-BI-A-RA-AḪ		B 9+
		ʾAB	I		JARAḪ		A-BI-E-RA-AḪ		B+, M+
		ʾAB	I		JARAḪ		A-BI-RA-AḪ		B 9+, A. 38 18
		ʾAB	I		JARAḪ		A-BE-RA-AḪ		B 9
		ʾAB	I		ʾAŠD		A-BI-A-SA-AD		B 10+
		ʾAB	I		ʾAŠD		A-BI-SA-AD		B 10+
		ʾAB	I		JAT	UM	A-BI-IA-TUM	FN	WATERMAN 40 R. 5+
		ʾAB	I		ḪATAN		A-BI-ḪA-TA-AN		B 10
		ʾAB	I		JATAR		A-BI$_2$-WA-DAR		U
		ʾAB	I		JATAR		A-BI-IA-TA-AR		B 10+
		ʾAB	I		JATAR		A-BI-E-TAR		BASOR 95 22
		ʾAB	I		ʾAZJ	I	A-BI-A-ZI		A.
		ʾAB	I	ʾA T	ŠAMAR		A-BI-AŠ-TA-MA-AR		YOS XIII 489:4
		ʾAB	I	JA	MWUT	A	A-BI-IA-MU-TA		BM 80328 15
		ʾAB	I	JA	MWUT	I	A-BI$_2$-A-MU-TI		U
		ʾAB	I	JA	JPAʿ		A-BI-IA-PA-AḪ	FN	XIII 1 II 57
		ʾAB	I	JE	JPUʿ		A-BI-E-PU-UḪ		B 10, M+
		ʾAB	I	JA	JPUʿ		A-BI-IA-PU-UḪ		B 10
		ʾAB	I	JE	JŠUʿ		A-BI-E-ŠU-UḪ		B 10+, XIII 1 III 44
		ʾAB	I	JA	JŠUʿ		A-BI-ŠU-UḪ		B 10
		ʾAB	I	JA	JŠUʿ	A	A-BI-IA-ŠU-ḪA		B 10
		ʾAB	I	JE	JŠUʿ				
					....		A-BI-E-ŠU-UḪ-LI-DI-IŠ		CT XLV 55 11
		ʾAB	I	JE	JŠUʿ				
					....		A-BI-E-ŠU-UḪ-LU-DA-RI		B 10
		ʾAB	I	JA	JŠUʿ				
					....		A-BI-ŠU-UT-LI		B 11
		ʾAB	I		DAGAN		A-BI-D-DA-GAN		M+
		ʾAB	I		DIRAḪ		A-BI?-DI-RA-AḪ		TCL X 41 A/B 4+
		ʾAB	I		DARAB		[A]?-BI-DA-RA-AB		RA LXV 43 III 67
		ʾAB	I		DITAN		A-BI-DI-TA-AN		BM 80328 16
		ʾAB	I		DITAN	UM	A-BI-TI-DA-NU-UM		TA 1931, 538 III,IV
		ʾAB	I		GAʾJ	A	A-BI-GA-A	GN?	A 21919+
		ʾAB	I		KAʾB	I	A-BI-KA-BI		M
		ʾAB	I		KAʾB	I	A-BI-KA-BI	FN	RA LXV 65 VII 42
		ʾAB	I		LUʾL	A	A-BI-LU-LA		SIMMONS 107 13
		ʾAB	I		LIʾM		A-BI-LI-IM		RA LXV 44 IV 60+
		ʾAB	I		LAMA		A-BI-LA-MA		B 10
		ʾAB	I		MA				
					ʾIL	I	A-BI-MA-I$_3$-LI$_2$	FN	RA LXV 64 VI 32
		ʾAB	I	ME	QWIM		A-BI-ME-KI-IM		XIII 34 5+
		ʾAB	I		MI				
					KI		A-BI-MI-KI-DINGIR		M
		ʾAB	I		MULUK	I	A-BI-MU-LU-KI	FN	RA LXV 59 II 26
		ʾAB	I		MARAṢ		A-BI-MA-RA-AṢ		B 10+
		ʾAB	I		MAṬAR		A-BI-MA-DAR		B 10+
		ʾAB	I		MAṬAR		A-BI-MA-DA-AR		TIM II 113 3

ROOTS (Consonants only)

ʾB	1	ʾAB	I				NAʿM	I		A-BI-NA-AḪ-MI	FN	XIII 1 VII 43, A.+
		ʾAB	I				NAʿM	I		A-BI-NA-AḪ-ME	FN	RA LXV 59 II 20
		ʾAB	I				NIʿM			A-BI-NI-ḪI-IM		RA LXV 44 IV 31
		ʾAB	I				NIWR	I		A-BI-NI-RI	FN	XIII 1 IX 58+
		ʾAB	I				NAPŠ	I		A-BI-NA-AP-S[I]		XIV 77:7
		ʾAB	I				QAʾD			A-BI-QA-AD		B 11
		ʾAB	I				QAʾD			A-BI-GA-AD		TA 30 237
		ʾAB	I				RAWM			A-BI-RA-AM		RA LXV 43 IV 12
		ʾAB	I				RAPIʾ			A-BI-RA-BI		M
		ʾAB	I				RAPIʾ			A-BI-RA-PI		SYRIA XXXVII 206 6, 7
		ʾAB	I				RAŠAP			A-BI-RA-SA-AP		M
		ʾAB	I	Š			KIWN			$A-BI_2-IŠ-KI-IN$		U
		ʾAB	I	Š			MUM	U		A-BI-IŠ-MU-MU		HARRIS 98 2
		ʾAB	I	Š			TUʾ			A-BI-IŠ-DU		A. LATE
		ʾAB	I		JI	T	ŠAMAR			A-BI-IŠ-TA-MAR		TCL I 226 4, 10+
		ʾAB	I				ŠADW	A		A-BI-SA-DA-A		JCS IV 110 2040
		ʾAB	I				ŠAMAK	U		A-BI-SA-MA-KU		SIMMONS 41 15
		ʾAB	I				ŠAMAR			A-BI-SA-MAR		M+
		ʾAB	I				ŠAMŠ			A-BI-SA-MA-AŠ		M+
		ʾAB	I				ŠAMŠ			A-BI-D-UTU	FN	XIII 24 IV 40
		ʾAB	I				ŠAMŠ	I		A-BI-D-UTU-ŠI	FN	XIII 1 IX 40+
		ʾAB	I				ŠAMAT	A		A-BI-SA-MA-TA		EDZARD, DER 120:4
		ʾAB	I				ŠAPAR			A-BI-SA-PA-AR	FN	C
		ʾAB	I				ŠAPAR			$A-BI-SA-PAR_2$		CT XLV 82 7+, XIII 1 II 15
		ʾAB	I				ŠARIJ			A-BI-SA-RI		LIMET, SCEAUX CASS. P 114
		ʾAB	I				ŠARIJ		JE	A-BI-SA-RI-E		B 11+; M+
		ʾAB	I				ŠARIJ		JE	$A-BI_2-SA-RI-E$		BIN VII 93 DATE
		ʾAB	I				ṢUWR	A		A-BE-ZU-RA		TCL IV 87 10 CAPP.
		ʾAB	I				ṢUWR	A		A-BI-ṢU-RA		TIM IV 34 27
		ʾAB	I				ṢUWR	I		A-BI-ZU-RI		M
		ʾAB	I				ṬAJB	A		A-BI-ṬA-BA		A.+
		ʾAB	U				ḪAʾL	UM		A-BU-ḪA-LUM		UCP X P. 53, M
		ʾAB	UM				ḪAʾL	UM		A-BU-UM-ḪA-LUM		B 11+
		ʾAB	UM				ḪAʾL	UM		A-BU-UM-ḪA-LU-UM		B 11+
		ʾAB	U				ḪAʾL	IM		A-BU-ḪA-LIM	GEN	M+
		ʾAB	UM				ḪIʾL	UM		A-BU-UM-ḪI-LUM		B 11
		ʾAB	UM				ʾIL			A-BU-UM-DINGIR		U, M+
		ʾAB	U				JAQAR			A-BU-WA-QAR		M
		ʾAB	U				JAQAR			A-BU-QAR		M
		ʾAB	UM				JAQAR			A-BU-UM-WA-QAR		M
		ʾAB	U				JAT	I	JA	A-BU-IA-TI-IA		TCL I 85 10
		ʾAB	UM		JE		KWIN			A-BU-UM-E-KI-IN		M
		ʾAB	U				KA					
							ʾIL			A-BU-KA-DINGIR		M+
		ʾAB	U				LA		JA	A-BU-LA-IA		XIII 101 6
		ʾAB	U		ME		KWIN			A-BU-ME-KI-IN		X 154 2+
		ʾAB	U		ME		QWIM			A-BU-ME-KI-IM		M+
		ʾAB	U				NIWR	A		A-BU-NI-RA		TIM VI 34, U
		ʾAB	U				NAN	UM		A-BU-NA-NU-UM		B 42+
		ʾAB	U				ŠALIM			A-BU-SA-[LIM]		M
		ʾEB	ATAN							E-BA-TA-AN		M+
		ʾEB	I				ʾIL			E-BI-IL		M
		ʾEB	I				DANN	UM		E-BI-DA-NU-UM		U
		ʾIB	I				JAT	UM		I-BI-IA-TUM		TIM II 27 4
		ʾIB	I				LA					
							ʾIL	UM		$I-BI-LA-I_3-LUM$		U
	2	ʾAḪ	AT A				ʾAB	I		A-ḪA-TA-A-BI	FN	M+
		ʾAJA					ʾAB					
							ʾIL			ḪA-IA-AB-DINGIR		B 18
		ʾAJA					ʾAB	I		A-IA-A-BI		A.
		ʾAJA					ʾAB	I		A-IA-BI		A.+
		ʾAJA					ʾAB	I				
							ŠARR	I		A-IA-BI-ŠAR-RI		A.
		ʾAJA					ʾAB	I				
							TALM	A		A-IA-BI-TA-AL-MA		A. 239 15
		ʾAJA					ʾAB	U		A-IA-A?-BU?	FN	C+

ROOTS (Consonants only)

ʾB	2		ʾAJA				ʾAB	U		A-IA-BU		A. LATE +
			ʾAJA				ʾAB	U	HU	A-A-A-BU-U$_2$	FN	DE CLERCQ II 253B
			ʾAJA				ʾAB	UM		ḪA-A-IA-A-BU-UM		M
			ʾAJA				ʾAB	UM		ḪA-IA-BU-UM		B 18+
			ʾAJA				ʾAB	AM		ḪA-A-IA-A-BA-AM	ACC	M+
			ʾAJAN				ʾAB	I		A-IA-NA-BI	FN	A.
			ʾAJAN				ʾAB	I				
							ʾILL	A		A-IA-NA-BI-IL-LA		A.
			ʾIJA				ʾAB					
							ʾIL			I-A-AB-DINGIR		OIP XXII 262
			ḪAʾN		A		ʾAB	I		ḪA-NA-A-BI		TIM II 113 2, 8
			ḪAWR				ʾAB	I		ḪA-AW-RA-BI		TIM IV 33 21, 34 14
			ḪAWR	AN			ʾAB	I		ḪA-AW-RA-AN-A-BI		M
			ḪAWR	AN			ʾAB	I		ḪA-AW-RA-NA-A-BI		M+
			ʿAD		U	NI	ʾAB	I	JA	A-DU-NI-A-BI-IA		RA XXVII 87 LATE
		JA	JDIʿ				ʾAB	UM		IA-DI-ḪA-BU-UM		B 25+
		JA	JDIʿ				ʾAB	UM		IA-DI-A-BU-UM		M, YOS XII+
		JA	JDIʿ				ʾAB	UM		IA-DU-A-BU-UM		YOS XII+
		JA	JDIʿ				ʾAB	U		IA-DI-ḪA-BU		PBS XIV 1084
		JA	JDIʿ				ʾAB	U		IA-DI-A-BU		YOS XII+
		JA	JDIʿ				ʾAB	UM		IA-DI-ḪA-A-BU-U[M]		RA LXV 45 V 9
		JA	JDIʿ				ʾAB	IM		IA-DI-ḪA-A-BI-IM	GEN	M+
			ʿADN		A		ʾAB	I		ḪA?-AD-NA-A-BI		TTKB XIX 304
			ʾIL		A		ʾAB	I		I-LA-A-BI		C
			ʾIL		UM		ʾAB	I		I-LUM-A-BI		A.
			ʾIL		UM		ʾAB	UM		I-LUM-A-BU-UM		U
			ʾALI				ʾAB	I		A-LI-A-BI	FN	M+
			ʾAMIR		A		ʾAB	UM		A-MI-RA-A-BU-UM		RA LXV 55 XIII 5
		ʾA	JPAʿ				ʾAB	I		A-PA-AḪ-A-BI		YOS VIII 29 13
		JA	JQIR		A		ʾAB	UM		IA-KI-RA-A-BU-UM		RA LXV 47 VII 30
			ʾIRR		A		ʾAB	I		IR$_3$-RA-A-BI		M
			ʾAŠD		UM		ʾAB	I		AŠ$_2$-DU-UM-A-BI		BE VI/1 1 7+
			ʾAŠD		UM		ʾAB	I		D-AŠ-DU-UM-A-BI		UET V 483 4
			ʿAŠTAR				ʾAB	I		AŠ-TAR-A-BI		MRS VI P. 242
			ʿIZZ				ʾAB	I		IZ-ZA-BI		C+
			BILL				ʾAB	I		BI-IL-LA-BI	FN	XIII 1 X 41
		JA	BRUQ				ʾAB	UM		A-AB-RU-UK-A-BU-UM		JCS XXVI 151:13, HARMAL
			DIWIR				ʾAB	I		DI-WI-IR-A-BI		PBS XI/1 P. 55+
			DIWIR				ʾAB	I		DI-BI-IR-A-BI		PBS XI/1 P. 55+
			ḎAKUR				ʾAB	I		ZA-KU-UR-A-BI	GEN	B 41
			ḎAKUR		A		ʾAB	I		ZA-KU-RA-A-BI	GEN	B 41
			ḎAKUR		A		ʾAB	U		ZA-KU-RA-A-BU		M
			ḎAKUR		A		ʾAB	UM		ZA-KU-RA-A-BU-UM		X 79 5
			ḎIMR		I		ʾAB	UM		ZI-IM-RI-A-BU-UM		B 42
			LA				ʾAB	A		LA-A-BA		U
			NUʿM		I		ʾAB	I		NU-UḪ-MI-A-BI		XIII 1 I 38
			NIQM				ʾAB	I		NI-IQ-MA-A-BI		A. 86 7+
		JA	PRUS				ʾAB	I		IA-AP-RU-US-A-BI		BAGHD. MITT. II 23
			QAṬAR				ʾAB	I		GA-TAR-A-BI		BASOR 95 22
		JA	RWIḪ		A		ʾAB	UM		IA-RI-ḪA-A-BU-UM		VII P. 234 N. 4
		JA	RWIḪ		A		ʾAB	AM		IA-RI-ḪA-A-BA-AM	ACC	XIV 101:8
		JA	RWIḪ		A		ʾAB	AM		IA-RI-ḪA-A-BA-AN	ACC	VII P. 234 N. 4
		JA	RWIḪ		A		ʾAB	IM		IA-RI-ḪA-A-BI-IM	GEN	M+
		JI	RPAʾ				ʾAB	I		IR-PA-A-BI		A.+
		JA	ŚJIM				ʾAB	IM		IA-SI-IM-A-BI-IM	GEN	M
		JA	ŚJIT				ʾAB	I		IA-SI-IT-A-BI		M
		JA	ŚJIT				ʾAB	U		IA-SI-IT-A-BU		M+
		JA	ŚJIT			NA	ʾAB	U		IA-SI-IT-NA-A-BU		XIII 1 XII 15
			ŠUBUL				ʾAB	I		ŠU-BU-UL-A-BI		M
			ŚAM		U		ʾAB	IM		SA-MU-A-BI-IM	NOM	RA VIII 71
			ŚAM		U		ʾAB	IM		SA-MU-A-BI-IM	GEN	SUMER XXIII 153+
			ŚUM		I		ʾAB	UM		SU-ME-A-BU-UM		A. 12 4
			ŚUM		U		ʾAB	UM		SU-MU-A-BU-UM		B 38+
			ŚUM		U		ʾAB	UM		D-SU-MU-A-BU-UM		KISURRA 93 22
			ŚUM		U		ʾAB	IM		[S]U-MU-A-BI-IM	NOM	EDZARD, DER 111:5
			ŚUM		U		ʾAB	IM		SU-MU-A-BI-IM	GEN	SUMER XXIII PL. 12 19

ROOTS (Consonants only)

ʾB	2	ŠUM	U			ʾAB	I		SU-MA-A-BI		A.
		ŠUM	U			ʾAB	I	JA	[SU]-MU-A-BI-IA		B 38
		ŠUM	U			ʾAB	I				
					JA	RWIM			SU-MU-A-BI-A-RI-IM		TA 30 9, 14, 15+
		ŠUM	UM			ʾAB	I				
					JA	RWIM			SU-MU-UN-A-BI-IA-RI-IM		SUMER XXIII 153:9
		ŠUM	U	NA		ʾAB	I		SU-MU-UN-NA-A-BI	FN	A. 64 7
		ŠUM	U	NA		ʾAB	I		SU-MU-UN-NA-BI	FN	A. 33 3, 34 2+
		ŠUM	U	NA		ʾAB	I		SU-MU-NA-BI	FN	A. 59 8
		ŠUM	U	NA		ʾAB	I		SU-MU-NA-A-BI	FN	A. 244 5, M
		ŠUM	U	NA		ʾAB	I				
					JA	RWIM			SU-MU-NA-BI-IA-RI-IM		SUMER XXIII PL. 7 17+
		ŠUM	U	NA		ʾAB	I				
					JA	RWIM			SU-MU-UN?-A-BI-JA-RI-IM		SUMER XXIII P. 153 9
		ŠAMŠ	I			ʾAB	I		D-UTU-A-BI		M+
		ŠAPŠ	I			ʾAB	I		ŠA-AP-ŠI-A-BI	FN	A.
		ZUMM				ʾAB	U		ZU-UM-MA-BU		BM 80328 7
	3	ʾAḪ	U			KA					
						ʾAB	I		A-ḪU-KA-A-BI	FN	XIII 1 VIII 60, C+
		ʾAḪ	UM			LA					
						ʾAB	I		A-ḪU-UM-LA-A-BI		YOS XIII 245:17, SEAL
		ʾAJA				ŠUM	U				
						ʾAB	IM		ḪA-IA-SU-MU-A-BI-IM		M
		ʾIL	A			KA					
						ʾAB	UM		DINGIR-KA-A-BU-UM		CT XLV 100 17
		ʾIL	A			MA					
						ʾAB	I		DINGIR-MA-A-BI		M
		ʾIL	I			MA					
						ʾAB	I		I_3-LI-MA-A-BI		M+
		ʾUMM	UM			KA					
						ʾAB	IM		UM-MU-UM-KA-A-BI-IM	FN	M
		ʾUMM	UM			KA					
						ʾAB	I		UM-MU-UM-KA-A-BI	FN	XIII 1 VII 56
		ʾUMM	U			KA					
						ʾAB	I		UM-MU-KA-A-BI	FN	RA LXV 62 V 16
		ʾANN	U			KAMA					
						ʾAB	I		AN-NU-KA-MA-BI		CT XLV 116 36
	JA	JPAʿ				ŠUM	U				
						ʾAB	I		IA-PA-AḪ-SU-MU-A-BI		A. 56 47
		ʾIRŠ				MA					
						ʾAB	I		I-RI-IŠ-MA-A-BI		A.
		ʾIRŠ				MA					
						ʾAB	I		I-RI-IŠ-MA-BI		A.
		ʾIRŠ	U			MA					
						ʾAB	I		IR-ŠU-MA-BI		A.
		ʾAŠD	UM			LA					
						ʾAB	UM		AŠ-DU-UM-LA-A-BU-UM		SUMER V 142
		ʾAŠD	UM			LA					
						ʾAB	UM		$AŠ_2$-DU-UM-LA-A-BU-UM		SUMER V 142+
	JI	JṢIʾ				ŠAM	U				
						ʾAB	UM		I-ZI-SA-MU-A-BU-UM		B 23
	JI	JṢIʾ				ŠUM	U				
						ʾAB	UM		I-ZI-SU-MU-A-BU-UM		B 23+
	JI	JṢIʾ				ŠUM	U				
						ʾAB	IM		I-ZI-SU-MU-A-BI-IM	GEN	B 23
	JA	WṢIʾ				ŠUM	U				
						ʾAB	UM		U_2-ṢI-SU-MU-A-BU-UM		AJSL XXVIII 244 19
		ḎU				MA					
						ʾAB	I		ZU-U_2-MA-A-BI		XIV 77:17
		ḎU				MA					
						ʾAB	I		ZU-U_2-MA?-A-BI		M
		ḎIMR	U			LA					
						ʾAB	I		ZI-IM-RU-LÀ-A-BI		RA LXV 42 III 7
	JA	KWUN				ŠUM	U				
						ʾAB	IM		IA-KU-UN-SU-MU-A-BI-IM		M
		KABD	U			KA					
						ʾAB	I		KA-AB-TU-KA-A-BI		UET V 688:8,12

ROOTS (Consonants only)

ʾB	3		LA			ʾA	HWIJ						
							ʾAB		I		LA-AḪ-WI-A-BI	FN	XIII 1 XIII 6
		JA	RWIM				ŠUM		U				
							ʾAB		I		IA-RI-IM-SU-MU-A-BI		RA LXV 42 III 8
			ŠUM		UM		LA						
							ʾAB		I		SU-MU-UM-LA-A-BI	FN	RA LXV 65 VII 24
ʾBḪ	1		ʾABIḪ								A-BI-IḪ-[....]		XIII 79 5
	2		MUT		U		ʾABIḪ				MU-TU-A-BI-I[Ḫ]		M
			MUT		U		ʾABIḪ		IM		MU-TU-A-BI-ḪI-IM		C
			MUT		UM		ʾABIḪ				MU-TUM-A-BI-IḪ		TA 1930, 695
			ŠUM		U		ʾABIḪ				SU-MU-A-BI-IḪ		TIM V 1 16
ʾBB	1		ʾABAB	AH							A-BA-BA	FN	C+
			ʾABAB		AJA						A-BA-BA-A-IA	FN	M
			ʾABAB	AN	UM						A-BA-BA-NU-UM		B 71+
			ʾABAB	AN	IM						A-BA-BA-NI-IM	GEN	B 42
			ʾABB		A						AB-BA		RA LXV 55 XIII 12
			ʾABB		A		ʾIL				D-AB-BA-DINGIR	FN	M
			ʾABB		A		ʾIL				AB-BA-DINGIR		A.+
			ʾABB		A		ʾIL		I		AB-BA-I$_3$-LI$_2$	FN	XIII 1 XI 14
			ʾABB		A		ʾIL		I		D-AB-BA-I$_3$-LI$_2$	FN	SIMMONS 112:17
			ʾABB		A		ŠARR				AB-BA-LUGAL		A. 86 2
			ʾABB		I		LIʾM						
							MA				AB-BI-LIM-MA		A.+
	2		ʾITT		A		ʾABB		A		ḪI-IT-TA-D-AB-BA		M
			KIBR				ʾABB		A		KI-BI-IR-D-AB-BA		M+
			KIBR				ʾABB		A		KI-IB-RA-AB-BA		CT XXIX 14 16
			KIBR				ʾABB		A		KI-IB-RA-BA		CT XXIX 14 29
		JI	NDIN				ʾABB		A		I-DIN-AB-BA		XIII 1 VIII 46
		JI	NDIN				ʾABB		A		ID-DI-NA-AB-BA		A.
		JI	NDIN				ʾABB		A		ID-DI-NA-BA		A. LATE
		JA	RḪIB				ʾABB		A		IA-AR-IB-D-AB-BA		M
ʾBL	1		ʾABIL				TAʾK		U	HU	A-BI-IL-TA-KU-U$_2$		WALTERS, WL 97:4;105:3+
			ʾIBL	AN	UM						IB-LA-A-NU-UM		HAV. SYMP. 237 13
			ʾIBL	AN	UM						IB-LA-NU-UM		I
	2		ʾAJAN				ʾABAL				A-AN-A-BA-AL	FN	XIII 1 IX 38
ʾBN	1		ʾABAN		UM						ḪA-BA-NU-UM		TA 30, 191+
			ʾABAN		AJA						A-BA-NA-A		BM 81660 2
			ʾABAN	AN							AB-BA-NA?-AN		M
			ʾABN		UM						ḪA-AB-NU-UM		GAUTIER 10 R. 10+
			ʾABN		A		JARAḪ				ḪA?-AB-NA-A-RA-AḪ		UET V 476 SEAL 6
			ʾABN		I		ʾIL				ḪA-AB-NI-DINGIR		M
			ʾABN		U		RAPIʾ				AB-NU-RA-BI		C, C II P. 244+
			ʾIBN	AT	UM						IB-NA-TUM	MN	BM 16939 27+
	2		ʾAJA				ʾABN		I				
							ʾIL				ḪA-IA-AB-NI-DINGIR		B 18+
			ʿABD				ʾABN		IM		ARAD$_2$-AB-NIM		BAGHD. MITT. II 72
			ḪANN		A		ʾABN		UM		AN-NA-AB-NU-UM		KISURRA 8A 14
			ḪANN		A		ʾABN		UM		A-NA-AB-NU-UM		HARRIS 57 18
			ḪANN		A		ʾABN	AT			ḪA-AN-NA-AB-NA-AT		A 7763, ISHCHALI
		TA	ʿTIQ				ʾABN		U		TA-TI-QA-AB-NU		RES 1938 128
		TU	WTAR				ʾABN		U		TU-TAR-AB-NU		M
		JI	BAʾEL				ʾABN		U		I-BA-EL-A-AB-NU		III 46 13
ʾBQ	1	JA	ʾBUQ		UM						IA-BU-KUM		KISURRA 83 14
			ʾABAQ		UM						A-BA-GU-UM		KISURRA 82 9
ʾBR	1		ʾIBIR	AN							I-BI-RA-AN		RA LXV XIII 34
			ʾUBIR		A						U$_2$-BI-RA		M
ʾBŠ	1		ʾABAŠ	IN	UM						A-BA-ŠE-NU-UM		M
			ʾABIŠ	AN	UM						A-BI-SA-NU-UM		CT XLVIII 29 REV.
			ʾUBUŠ		UM						ḪU-BU-ŠUM		UCP X/1 34 13
			ʾUBUŠ		I						U$_2$-BU-SI		M
			ʾUBUŠ				ʿAŠTAR				U$_2$-BU-UŠ$_3$-EŠ$_4$-DAR		RES 1938 P. 129
			ʾUBUŠ				TUʾ			KA	ḪU-BU-UŠ-TU-KA		A. 268 17
ʾDʾ	2		LAMA				ʾADAʾ		E		LA-MA-A-DA-E	FN	A.
			LAMA				ʾADAʾ		E		LA-MA-TA-E	FN	A.+
ʾDD	1		ʾADAD		I						A-DA-DI	FN	XIII 1 X 30
			ʾADID		UM						A-DI-DU-UM		B 11+

ROOTS (Consonants only)

ʾDD	1		ʾADID		UM						A-DI-DUM		SIMMONS 69A 5
			ʾADID		U						A-DI-DU		B 11
			ʾEDID		UM						E-DI-DU-UM		SIMMONS 138 7
			ʾADUD		U						A-DU-DU	FN	XIII 1 X 7+
			ʾADD		I			ŠAMŠ			AD-DI-D-UTU?		RA LXIV 99:23
			ʾADD		I	JA		ʾEL			AD-DI-JA-EL		BAB. III 267 HANA
			ʾADD		I	JA		ʾEL			AD-DI-IA-DINGIR		MAOG IV 2 12 HANA
			ʾIDAD		UM						I-DA-DU-UM		WATERMAN 34 R. 13+
			ʾIDID		UM						I-DI-DUM		XIII 1 I 22
			ʾIDID		A						I-DI-DA	MN	BE VI/1 14 30
			ʾIDD	AT	UM						ID-DA-TUM	MN	B 21, M
			ʾIDD		I						ID-DI		XIII 1 IX 69+
			ʾIDD		IM						ḪI-ID-DI-IM		XIV 56:28
			ʾUDUD		UM						ḪU-DU-DU-UM		TLB I/2, 15 18+
ʾDK	1		ʾEDAK		UM						E-DA-KUM		CT VIII 4A 4
	2	ʾA	RŠIJ					ʾEDAK		U	AR-ŠI-E-DA-KU	FN	M
ʾDL	2		KIWN		UM			ʾADAL			KI-NU-UM-A-DA-AL		RA LXV 48 VII 60
ʾDM	1		ʾADAM		U						ḪA-DA-MU	MN	RUTTEN 19 19+
			ʾADAM		U						A-DA-MU	MN	JNES XIII 210+ LATE
			ʾADAM		U						A-DA-MU	FN	C+
			ʾADAM	AN	U						AD-DA-MA-NU		RUTTEN 28 12
			ʾADAM			TA		ʾAR		U	ḪA-DAM-TA-A-RU		WATERMAN 45 EDGE
			ʾADAM			TI		ʾEL			ḪA-DAM-TI-EL		HARRIS 61 2
			ʾADAM			TI		ʾEL		UM	A-DAM-TE-LUM		GAUTIER 31 6
			ʾADM	AN	UM						AD-MA-NU-UM		JCS XXIV 69 NO.3
			ʾADM	AN	UM						ḪA-AD-MA?-NU-UM		VIII 85:29
			ʾADM	AN	IM						ḪA-AD-MA?-NIM	GEN	B 44
			ʾADM		U	HA					AD-MU-A	FN	U
			ʾADM		U			ʿALIJ	AH		D-AD-MU-ḪA-LI-IA	FN	XIII 1 V 55
			ʾADM		U			JIŠʿ	AH		D-AD-MU-IŠ-ḪA	FN	XIII 1 IX 18
			ʾADM		U			JIŠʿ	AH		AD-MU-IŠ-ḪA	FN	XIII 1 IX 57
			ʾADM		U			ḪAṢN		I	D-AD-MU-ḪA-AZ-NI	FN	RA LXV 61 IV 21
			ʾADM		U			BALAṬ		I	D-AD-MU-BA-LA-TI?	FN	M
			ʾADM		U			NIWR		I	AD-MU-NE-RI	FN	XIII 1 VIII 13
			ʾADM		U			NIWR		I	D-AD-MU-NI-RI	FN?	M
			ʾADM		U			QUDM		I	AD-MU-KU-UD-MI	FN	XIII 1 IX 55
			ʾADM		U			RUWB	AH		D-AD-MU-RU-BA	FN	XIII 1 VII 59
			ʾADM		U			ŠIMḪ		I	AD-MU-ŠI-IM-ḪI	FN	XIII 1 IV 6
			ʾADM		U			ŠIMḪ		I	D-AD-MU-ŠI-IM-ḪI	FN	RA LXV 62 V 28
			ʾADM		U		TA	ḪNUN	AN		D-AD-MU-TA-ḪU-NA-AN	FN	RA LXV 61 IV 38
			ʾUDM	AN	UM						ḪU-UD-MA?-NU		XII 712 R 9
	2	TA	ʾZIJ					ʾADM		U	TA-AḪ-ZI-D-AD-MU	FN	M
		TA	ḪṢIN					ʾADM		U	TA-AḪ-ZI-IN-AD-MU	FN	M
			LA				ʾA	ʾDUM		U	LA-AḪ-DU-MU		4E RENC. ASS. P. 178 4
		JA	MʾID					ʾADM		I	IA-AM-I-ID-D-AD-MI		A. 60 4
		JI	NDIN					ʾADM		U	I-DIN-D-AD-MU		M+
			QIJŠ	T	I			ʾADM		U	KI-IŠ-TI-AD-MU		M+
			ṮARID		A			ʾADM		U	TA-RI-DA-AD-MU		XIII 1 16
ʾDN	1		ʾADAN	AT	UM						ḪA-DA-AN-N[A]?-TUM?	FN	RA LXV 62 V 7
			ʾADAN	T	A						A-DA-AT-TA	FN	C+
			ʾADAN		I	Š		....			ḪA-DA-NI-IŠ-MU-[....]		SIGRIST UNPUBL.
			ʾADAN					ʾIL			ḪA-DA-AN-DINGIR		B 18
			ʾADAN					NUWḪ		UM	ḪA-DA-NU-U$_2$-UM		M
			ʾADUN								A-DU-UN		A. 237 5+
			ʾADUN		UM						A-DU-NU-UM	FIELD	CT II 23 2
			ʾADUN	AT	UM						A-DU-NA-TUM	MN	TA 30 275
			ʾADUN	AH							ḪA-DU-NA	FN	XIII 1 III 65
			ʾADUN					LUʾM		U	ḪA-DU-UN-LU-MU		M
			ʾADUN					LUʾM		U	ḪA-DU-LU-MU		M
			ʾUDIN	AH							U$_2$-DI-NA	FN	XIII 1 IV 67
	2		ʾEŠB		I			ʾADAN	T	A	EŠ-BI-A-DA-AT-TA		A. 455 31, 55
			LA					ʾADUN		IM	LA-DU-NIM	GEN	M
ʾDR	1		ʾIDAR	AN							I-DA-RA-AN		M
ʾḎN	1		ʾUḎUN	AN							U$_2$-ZU-NA-AN		M+
ʾG	2		ʾEN		I	Š		ʾAG		UM	E-NI-IŠ-A-GU-UM		M+
			BAʿL		I	Š		ʾAG		UM	BA-LI-IŠ-A-GU-UM		RA LXV 45 V 36

ROOTS (Consonants only)

ʾG	2		QIJŠ				ʾAG	U	KI-IŠ-A-GU	FN	XIII 1 I 70
ʾGG	1		ʾAGIG		UM				A-GI-GU-UM		B 12+
			ʾAGIG		U				A-GI-GU		B 12
ʾGN	1	JA	ʾGUN						IA-AḪ-GU-UN		TCL XVII 25 1
		JA	ʾGUN		UM				IA-AḪ-GU-UN-NU-UM		TCL XVII 24 1
		JA	ʾGUN		UM				IA-AḪ-GU-NU-UM		TLB IV 82:1
		JA	ʾGUN		UM				IA-GU-NU-UM		YOS XII
		JA	ʾGUN		UM				I-IA-GU-NU-UM		YOS XII
		JA	ʾGUN		IM				IA-GU-NI-IM	GEN	BM 16485
		JA	ʾGUN		I				IA-AḪ-GU-UN-NI	GEN	TCL XVII 26 1
ʾGR	1		ʾIGAR	AN					I-GA-RA-AN		RA LXV 42 III 15
ʾGZ	1		ʾUGAZ		UM				U_2-GA-ZUM		TA 30 615 22
ʾK	1		ʾAK		UM				A-KU-UM		U
			ʾAK		I		....		A-KI-[....]	FN	IX 291 13
			ʾAK		IJA				A-KI-IA		M+
			ʾAK		IJAN				A-KI-IA-AN		M, A. LATE+
			ʾAK		I		ʾIL		A-KI-DINGIR		M
			ʾAK		I		ʾEL		A-KI-EL		RA LXV 46 VI 49
			ʾAK		I		JARAḪ		A-KI-E-RA-AḪ		M
			ʾAK		I		LAMA		A-KI-LA-MA		B 12
			ʾAK		UM		LA				
							ʾIL	A	A-KUM-LA-I-LA		RA LXV 55 XIII 1
			ʾEK		I		LA				
						ʾA	HWIJ		E-KI-LA-AḪ-WI		M
	2		ʾAB		I		ʾAK	I	A-BI-IA-KI		TCL I 109 3
			ʿAMM		I		ʾAK	I	AM-MI-E-KI		A.
ʾKK	1		ʾAKK		A				AK-KA		XIII 1 IV 27+
			ʾAKK		A		BANIJ		AK-KA-BA-NI		M
			ʾAKK	AT	UM				A-KA-TUM		KISURRA 104 36
			ʾAKK	AT	IJA				A-KA-TI-IA-A		KISURRA 178 1
			ʾAKK	AT	IJA				A-KA-TI-IA	FN	KISURRA 171 1; M+
			ʾAKK	ATANUM					AG-GA-TA-NU-UM		SIMMONS 96 6
			ʾAKK	ATANUM					AG-GA-TA-A-NU-UM		SIMMONS 103 6
			ʾAKK	ATANUM					A-KA-TA-A-NU-UM		SIMMONS 105 7, SEAL
			ʾAKK	ATANUM					AK-KA-TA-A-NU-UM		SIMMONS 106 6, 10 SEAL
			ʾAKK	ATANUM					AK-KA-TA-NU-UM		SIMMONS 112 6, SEAL
			ʾAKK	ATANI					A-GA-DA-NI		TA 1931, 489
			ʾAKK	ATANI					A-GA-TA-NI		TA 1931, 530 I, III
			ʾAKK	ATANIM					AK-KA-TA-NI-IM	GEN	A 32133:6
			ʾAKK	AT			ʾEL		A-GA?-AD-E-EL		I
			ʾAKK	AT			MAʾT	I	AK-KA-AD-MA-TI	FN	A. 409 22
	2	T	HILAL				ʾAKK	A	ḪI-IT-LA-AL-AK-KA		RA LXV 54 XII 36,71
			JATAR				ʾAKK	A	IA-TAR-AK-KA		M
		JI	NDIN				ʾAKK	A	I-DIN-AK-KA		XIII 1 I 54+
			ṢILL				ʾAKK	A	MI-NI-AK-KA		M
ʾKL	1		ʾUKUL	IN	UM				U_2-KU-LI-NU-UM		RA LXV 43 III 54
	2		MUT				ʾEKAL	IM	MU-UT-E_2-GAL-LIM		M
ʾKN	1		ʾAKAN	AT	UM				A-KA-NA-TUM		JCS XXIV 62 NO.55+
			ʾAKIN		UM				A-KI-NU-UM		TA 1931, 538 I
			ʾAKUN		UM				A-KU-NU-UM		KISURRA 58 8
			ʾAKUN		UM				A-KU-NUM_2		KISURRA 48 4
			ʾAKUN	AN	IM				A-KU-NA-NIM	GEN	B 92
			ʾAKUN	AT	UM				A-KU-NA-TUM	MN?	M+
			ʾAKUN		IJA				A-KU-NI-IA		CT XLV 5 R. 3
			ʾAKUN		U		QAṬAR		A-KU-NU-GA-DAR		BIN VII 30 5
			ʾAKN	AN	U				AK-NA-NU		B 42
ʾKR	1		ʾAKIR		UM				A-KI-RU-UM		KISURRA 8 7+
			ʾAKIR		I				A-KI-RI	GEN	VAS VIII 14 37
			ʾAKIR	AH					A-KI-RA	FN	M
		JA	ʾKUR		IM				IA-KU-RI?-IM?	GEN	VIII 2 23
		JA	ʾKUR	AN					IA-KU-RA-AN		M
		JA	ʾKUR				ʾIL		IA-AḪ-KU-ÚR-DINGIR		CT XLV 6 24
		JA	ʾKUR				ʾIL		A-AḪ-KU-UR_2-[DINGIR]?		HARRIS 79 22
		JI	ʾKUR				BAʿL	I	I-KU-UR-BA-LI		EDZARD, DER 102:9
		JA	ʾKUR				DAGAN		IA-KU-UR-D-DA-GAN		M+
ʾL	1		ʾEL	AN	UM				E-LA-NU-UM		U
			ʾIL	AN	UM				I-LA-NU-UM		I+, B 45+

ROOTS (Consonants only)

ʾL	1	ʾIL	AN	UM						I-LA-A-NU-UM		B 93
		ʾEL	AN	I						E-LA-NI		M
		ʾIL		A	NI					I-LA-A-NI		A. 279 2
		ʾIL	AT	I						I-LA-TI	MN	M
		ʾIL	ATAN							I-LA-TA-AN		M
		ʾIL		IJA						I$_3$-LI$_2$-IA		M+
		ʾEL				KAWN		UM		EL-GA-NU-UM		TA 1931 238
		ʾIL		A		ḪAʾL		UM		DINGIR-ḪA-LUM		B 21
		ʾIL		A		ḪAʾL		U	HU	DINGIR-ḪA-LU-U$_2$		XIII 1 IV 18
		ʾIL		A		ʾUWR		I		DINGIR-U$_2$-RI		RA LXVIII 28:13 MARI
		ʾIL		A		ʾAB		I		I-LA-A-BI		C
		ʾIL		A		ḪABAD				DINGIR-ḪA-BA-AD		M+
		ʾIL		A		ʿADN		U	HU	I-LA-ḪA-AD-NU-U$_2$		M
		ʾIL		A		ʿADN		U	HU	I-LA-ḪA-AD-NU-U$_2$	FN	C+
		ʾIL		A		ʿADN		U	HU	DINGIR-ḪA-AD-NU-U$_2$	FN	C+
		ʾIL		A		ʾIL				I-LA-DINGIR		B 21
		ʾIL		A		ʾEL				I-LA-EL		RA LXV 43 IV 3
		ʾIL		A		ʿAMM		U		I-LA-ḪA-MU		RA LXV 42 II 77+
		ʾIL		A		ʾUMM		A		DINGIR-UM-MA		RA LXV 45 V 31
		ʾIL		A		ʾIRR		A		[I-L]A?-IR$_3$-RA		RA LXV 47 VII 18
		ʾIL		A		ʿAŠTAR				I-LA-EŠ$_4$-DAR		RA LXV 42 III 16+
		ʾIL		A	JI	JBAL				DINGIR?-I-BA-AL		M
		ʾIL		A		BAWB		I	JA	DINGIR-BA-BI-A		UET V 263 17
		ʾIL		A		BAʿL		U	HU	I-LA-BA-LU-U$_2$		M
		ʾIL		A		BIN		I		DINGIR-BI-NI		UCP X/3 1 7
		ʾIL		A		BIN		I		I-LA-BI$_2$-NI		I
		ʾIL		A		DAʿ	AT			I-LA-DA-ḪA-AT		SUMER V 141,3+
		ʾIL		A		DAʿ	AT			BAD$_3$-DINGIR-DA-ḪA-AT	GN	A 7650
		ʾIL		A		DAKUL				DINGIR-DA-AK-KU-UL		UET V P. 43
		ʾIL		A		DAKUL				DINGIR-DA-KU-UL		UET V P. 43
		ʾIL		A		DAKUL		UM		DINGIR-DA-AK-KU-UL-LUM		UET V P. 43
		ʾIL		A		DAKUL		UM		DINGIR-DA-KU-UL-LUM		UET V P. 43+
		ʾIL		A		DARAN				DINGIR-DA-RA-AN		M+
		ʾIL		A		GULL		A		DINGIR-GU-UL-LA	FN	C+
		ʾIL		A		GULL		A				
						ʿAḎIR	AT			DINGIR-GUL-LA$_2$-ḪA-ZI-RA-AT	FN	M+
		ʾIL		A		KA						
						ʾAB		UM		DINGIR-KA-A-BU-UM		CT XLV 100 17
		ʾIL		A		KAʾAM				DINGIR-KA-A-AM		TIM III 101 7
		ʾIL		A		KAWN				DINGIR-KA-AN	MN	M+
		ʾIL		A		KAWN				DINGIR-KA-AN	FN	M
		ʾIL		A		KAWN		UM		DINGIR-KA-NU-UM		MAH II/3 P. 188F
		ʾIL		A		KAWN		IM		DINGIR-KA-NIM	GEN	M+
		ʾIL		A		KAWN		IM		DINGIR-KA-NI-IM	GEN	M
		ʾIL		A		KABKAB		I		DINGIR-KAB-KA-BI		JNES XIII 210+ LATE
		ʾIL		A		KABKAB		U	HU	I-LA-KAB-KA-BU-U$_2$		M+
		ʾIL		A		LA						
						ʾIL				DINGIR-LA-IL		U
		ʾIL		A		LA			KA	I-LA-LA-KA		B 21+
		ʾIL		A		LAʾIJ				I-LA-LA-I		TA 1931,395,UR III
		ʾIL		A		LAʾIJ				I-LA-LA-E		TA 1931,609,UR III
		ʾIL		A		LAʾIJ				I-LA-LA-E-KI	GN	LAESSOE,SHEMSHARA P.77
		ʾIL		A		LAʾIJ				I-LA-LA-AḪ		RA LXV IX 38,X 10
		ʾIL		A		MA						
						ʾAB		I		DINGIR-MA-A-BI		M
		ʾIL		A		MA						
						ʾIL		A		DINGIR-MA-I$_3$-LA		B 21+
		ʾIL		A		MA						
						ʾIL		A		DINGIR-MA-D-I-LA		B 21
		ʾIL		A		MAʾD		I		DINGIR-MA-DI		M
		ʾIL		A		MEʾR				DINGIR-ME-IR		JNES XIII 210+ LATE
		ʾIL		A		MALK		I		DINGIR-MA-AL-KI		A. LATE
		ʾIL		A		MILK		UM		DINGIR-MI-IL-KUM		BAHREIN UNP.,POST-UR III
		ʾIL		A		MAṬAR				DINGIR-MA-DA-AR		OR. N.S. XXVI 28 N.4 CAPP
		ʾIL		A		MAṬAR				DINGIR-MA-TAR		M+
		ʾIL		A		NAʿM		A		DINGIR-NA-MA-....		VAS VIII 14 44

ROOTS (Consonants only)

ʾL	1	ʾIL	A			NABUṬ				DINGIR-NA-BU-UṬ		VAS VIII 14 31
		ʾIL	A			NUN		U		I-LA-NU-NU		FIGULLA CAT. I 14029
		ʾIL	A			PA		I		I-LA-BA-I		TA 1931, 499
		ʾIL	A			PAʾŠ		I	JA	DINGIR-PA-ŠI-IA		TCL XVIII 106 9
		ʾIL	A			QAʾB				DINGIR-QA-AB		TIM III 130 12, SEAL
		ʾIL	A			RAWḪ		I	JA	DINGIR-RA[Ḫ]I-A		HARRIS 76 21
		ʾIL	A			RAWḪ		I	JA	I-LA-RA-ḪI-IA		M
		ʾIL	A			RAWḪ		I	JE	I-LA-RA-ḪI-E		M
		ʾIL	A			RAWḪ		I	JE	DINGIR-RA-ḪI-E		HARRIS 85 14
		ʾIL	A			ŠALIM				I-LA-SA-LIM		M, C
		ʾIL	A			ŠAMAR				I-LA-ŠA-MA-AR		U
		ʾIL	A	Š		BAʿL		UM		DINGIR-ŠU-BA-A-LUM		CT II 15 9
		ʾIL	A	TA		RʿIŠ				I-LA-TA-RI-IŠ		B 21
		ʾIL	AM			DIʿ		I		DINGIR-LAM-DI-I		SIMMONS 24 10+
		ʾIL	I			JAʾ		UM		I$_3$-LI$_2$-IA-UM		KISURRA 71A 5+
		ʾIL	I			JAʾ		UM		I$_3$-LI$_2$-I-UM		KISURRA 4A 12+
		ʾIL	I			JAʾ		UM		I$_3$-LI$_2$-I-U$_2$-UM		KISURRA 56 3+
		ʾIL	I			JAʾ		UM		I$_3$-LI$_2$-U$_2$-A-UM		KISURRA 186 5
		ʾIL	I			JAʾ		UM		I$_3$-LI$_2$-A-UM		B 21
		ʾIL	I			ḪAʾL		UM		I$_3$-LI$_2$-ḪA-LU-UM		CT XLV 3 10
		ʾIL	I			ʿIJN		A	JA	I$_3$-LI$_2$-I-NA-A-A		GAUTIER 40 7
		ʾIL	I			JAʾN		UM		I$_3$-LI$_2$-IA-NU-UM		TIM I 29 3
		ʾIL	I			ʾUWR		I		I-LI-U$_2$-RI	FN	A.
		ʾIL	I			HADD		U		I$_3$-LI$_2$-D-IM		M+
		ʾIL	I			HADD		U		I$_3$-LI$_2$-A-DU		A. 57 47
		ʾIL	I			HEDD		A		I$_3$-LI-E-DA		A.
		ʾIL	I			ʿADN		I		I$_3$-LI$_2$-ḪA-AD-NI	FN	M
		ʾIL	I			ʾIL		A		I$_3$-LI$_2$-I-LA		A. LATE
		ʾIL	I			ʾILL		A		I-LI-IL-LA		A. LATE
		ʾIL	I			ʾIMM	AH			I-LI$_2$-IM-MA	FN	C II 41 56, 44 57
		ʾIL	I			ʿAMM		U		I$_3$-LI$_2$-ḪA-MU		RA LVII 178
		ʾIL	I			ḪUMUD		I		I$_3$-LI$_2$-ḪU-MU-DI		M
		ʾIL	I			ḪUNIN		I		I$_3$-LI$_2$-U$_2$-NE-NI		RUTTEN 6 20
		ʾIL	I			ʾAP		I	JA	I$_3$-LI$_2$-A-PI?-A		TIM III 4 14
		ʾIL	I			JAQR		A		I$_3$-LI$_2$-AQ-RA		IRAQ XXX 90, RIMAH
		ʾIL	I			JARAḪ				I$_3$-LI$_2$-IA-RA-AḪ		SIMMONS 131 20
		ʾIL	I			JARAḪ				I$_3$-LI$_2$-E-RA-AḪ		M+, TIM III 133 4, SEAL
		ʾIL	I			ʾAŠIJ	AH			I$_3$-LI$_2$-A-SI-IA	FN	XIII 1 VII 55
		ʾIL	I			ʾAŠR		A	JA	I$_3$-LI$_2$-AŠ-RA-IA		M+
		ʾIL	I			ʿAŠTAR				I$_3$-LI$_2$-EŠ$_4$-DAR		M+
		ʾIL	I			JAT				I$_3$-LI$_2$-A-AT?		TA 1931, 261
		ʾIL	I			JAT		UM		I$_3$-LI$_2$-I-IA-TUM		VAS XVIII 83:15
		ʾIL	I			JAT			KA	I$_3$-LI$_2$-A-AT-KA		TIM III 10 14+
		ʾIL	I			ʾATAJ		A	JA	I$_3$-LI$_2$-A-TA-A-IA		RA VIII 69 26
		ʾIL	I			ʾITEJ			JE	I$_3$-LI$_2$-I-TE-E		MEISSNER 110 20, 23+, M
		ʾIL	I			JATAR				I$_3$-LI$_2$-A-TAR		B 21+
		ʾIL	I			JATAR				I$_3$-LI$_2$-E-TAR		M+
		ʾIL	I			ḪAṢN		A	JA	I$_3$-LI$_2$-ḪA-AṢ-NA-A-IA		M+
		ʾIL	I			ḪAṢN		I	JA	I$_3$-LI$_2$-ḪA-AṢ-NI-IA		XIII 1 IX 8
		ʾIL	I	ʾA		ḪTAN				I$_3$-LI$_2$-AḪ-TA-AN		RUTTEN 6 16+
		ʾIL	I	ʾA		PTAN				I$_3$-LI$_2$-AP-TA-AN		B 21
		ʾIL	I	ʾA		PTAN				DINGIR-AP-TAN		TIM III 150 12
		ʾIL	I	JI		ḪNUW			HU	I$_3$-LI$_2$-IḪ-NU-U$_2$		UCP X/1 19:4+
		ʾIL	I	JE		JPAʿ				I$_3$-LI$_2$-E-PA		A.+
		ʾIL	I	JE		JPUʿ				I$_3$-LI$_2$-E-PU-UḪ		M+
		ʾIL	I	JE		JŠUʿ				I$_3$-LI$_2$-E-ŠU-UḪ		B 21 M
		ʾIL	I	JI		ḪṬAʾ						
						LI			JA	I$_3$-LI$_2$-IḪ-TA-LI-A		BIROT,TEA 69 I 14
		ʾIL	I	JA		MWUT				I$_3$-LI$_2$-IA-MU-[UT]		RA LXV 40 I 29
		ʾIL	I	JA		MLIK				I$_3$-LI$_2$-A-AM-LIK		HARRIS 49 12
		ʾIL	I	JI		ŠMAʿ			NIA	I$_3$-LI$_2$-IŠ-MA-NI-A		TA 1930,399
		ʾIL	I	JI		ŠPIQ				I$_3$-LI$_2$-IŠ-BI-IK		TA 1931, 71
		ʾIL	I	JI	T	ŠAMAR				I$_3$-LI$_2$-IŠ-TA-MAR		EDZARD,DER 67:11
		ʾIL	I			BAWB		UM		I$_3$-LI$_2$-BA-BU-UM		U UNPUBL.
		ʾIL	I			BAWŠ	T	I		I$_3$-LI$_2$-BA-AŠ$_2$-TI	FN	M+
		ʾIL	I			BIN		A	JA	I$_3$-LI$_2$-BI-NA-A-IA		M+

ROOTS (Consonants only)

ʾL	1	ʾIL	I			DAʿ	AT		DINGIR-DA-ḪA-AT		A 7650:2
		ʾIL	I			DIʿ	AT		I$_3$-LI$_2$-DI-ḪA-[AT]		HARRIS 39 19
		ʾIL	I			DAGAN			I$_3$-LI$_2$-D-DA-GAN		M+
		ʾIL	I			DITAN			I$_3$-LI$_2$-DI-TA-AN		BM 82424 R. 18
		ʾIL	I			GUML	I	JA	I$_3$-LI$_2$-GU-UM-LI-IA		XIII 1 VIII 45
		ʾIL	I			KAʾB	I		I$_3$-LI$_2$-KA-PI		BIROT, TEA 69:28
		ʾIL	I			KUWN			I$_3$-LI$_2$-KU-UN		RA LXV 55 XIII 32
		ʾIL	I			KABKAB	U		I$_3$-LI$_2$-KA-AB-KA-BU		A 21914 3
		ʾIL	I			KAŠAR			I$_3$-LI$_2$-KA-ŠA-AR		M
		ʾIL	I			LIʾM			I$_3$-LI$_2$-LI-IM		M+, C
		ʾIL	I			MA					
						ʾAB	I		I$_3$-LI-MA-A-BI		M+
		ʾIL	I			MAʾD	A		I$_3$-LI$_2$-MA-DA		TA 30 615 6
		ʾIL	I			MAʾD	I		I$_3$-LI$_2$-MA-DI		SIMMONS 33 19
		ʾIL	I			MAʾD	I				
						ʾAḪ			I$_3$-LI$_2$-MA-DI-A-AḪ		RUTTEN 1 8
		ʾIL	I			MAʾD	I				
						ʾAḪ			DINGIR?-MA-DA-AḪ		RA LXV 42 III 21
		ʾIL	I			MAʾD	I				
						ʾAḪ			I$_3$-LI$_2$-MI-DI-AḪ		EDZARD,DER 146:14
		ʾIL	I			MAʾD	I				
						ʾAḪ	I		I$_3$-LI$_2$-MA-DA-ḪI		RUTTEN 14 7
		ʾIL	I			MAʾD	I				
						ʾAḪ	A		I$_3$-LI$_2$-MA-DA-ḪA		VAS VIII 14 4
		ʾIL	I			MIWT	I		I$_3$-LI$_2$-MI-TI		I
		ʾIL	I			MALIK			I$_3$-LI$_2$-MA-LIK		M
		ʾIL	I			MILK	U		I$_3$-LI$_2$-MIL-KU	FN	RA LXV 58 I 31
		ʾIL	I			MAṬAR			I$_3$-LI$_2$-MA-DA-AR		M
		ʾIL	I			MAṬAR			I$_3$-LI$_2$-MA-TAR		M
		ʾIL	I			MAṬAR			I$_3$-LI$_2$-MA-TA-AR		B 21
		ʾIL	I			NIʿM			I$_3$-LI$_2$-NE-ḪI-IM		M
		ʾIL	I			NIWR	I		I$_3$-LI$_2$-NE-RI	FN	XIII 1 II 6+
		ʾIL	I			NATUN			I$_3$-LI$_2$-NA-TU-UN		M
		ʾIL	I			PAʾAL	UM		I$_3$-LI$_2$-PA-A-LU-UM		TIM III 44 16+
		ʾIL	I			PAʾAL	UM		I$_3$-LI$_2$-PA-ḪA-LUM		M
		ʾIL	I			QAʾN			I-LI-QA-AN		A. LATE
		ʾIL	I			RAWḪ	I	JE	I$_3$-LI$_2$-RA-AḪ-E		VAS XVI 168 9, FRANK 13 9
		ʾIL	I			RAWM			I$_3$-LI$_2$-RA-AM		M
		ʾIL	I			RIḪṢ	I		I$_3$-LI$_2$-RI-IḪ-ZI	FN	XIII 1 IX 39
		ʾIL	I			RAPIʾ			I$_3$-LI$_2$-RA-BI		M+
		ʾIL	I			RAŠAP			I$_3$-LI$_2$-D-RA-SA-[AP]		XIII 66 5
		ʾIL	I	Š		BAʾB	A		I$_3$-LI$_2$-IŠ-BA-BA		HSM 7934, UR III
		ʾIL	I	Š		GAʾUL	U		I$_3$-LI$_2$-IŠ-GA-U$_2$-LU		KISURRA 70A 17+
		ʾIL	I	Š		KUTUL			I$_3$-LI$_2$-IŠ-KU-TU-UL		KISURRA 75A 18+
		ʾIL	I			ŠAKIM			I$_3$-LI$_2$-ŠA-KI-IM		RA LXV 40 I 44+
		ʾIL	I			ŠUM	U		I$_3$-LI$_2$-SU-U$_2$-MU		M
		ʾIL	I			ŠAMUʿ			I$_3$-LI$_2$-SA-MU-UḪ		XIII 21 11'
		ʾIL	I			ŠIMḪ	I		I$_3$-LI$_2$-ŠI-IM-ḪI		M+
		ʾIL	I			ŠIMḪ	A	JA	I$_3$-LI$_2$-ŠI-IM-ḪA-IA		VIII 57 BIS 16
		ʾIL	I			ŠIMḪ	A	JA	I$_3$-LI$_2$-ŠE-IM-ḪA-IA		VIII 57 14
		ʾIL	I			ŠAMŠ			I$_3$-LI$_2$-SA-MA-AŠ$_2$		M
		ʾIL	I		TA	NWUḪ			I$_3$-LI$_2$-TA-NU-UḪ		XIII 1 IV 19
		ʾIL	I		TA	NWUḪ			I$_3$-LI$_2$-TA-NU		RA LXV 45 V 52
		ʾIL	I			TUWR	A		I$_3$-LI$_2$-TU-RA		M+
		ʾIL	I			TUWR	A	JA	I$_3$-LI$_2$-TU-RA-[I]A		RA LXV 40 I 45
		ʾIL	I			TUWR	I	JA	I$_3$-LI$_2$-TU-RI-IA		XII 115 5+
		ʾIL	I			ṬAJB	A		I$_3$-LI$_2$-DA-[B]A		A. 96 R. 10
		ʾIL	I			ṢADUQ			I$_3$-LI$_2$-ZA-DU-UQ		M+
		ʾIL	I			ṢIDQ	I		I$_3$-LI$_2$-ZI-ID-KI		DELAPORTE CCL II A 337
		ʾIL	I			ṢIDQ	UM		I$_3$-LI$_2$-ZI-ID-KUM		UCP X/1 100 7
		ʾIL	I			ZANN	I		I$_3$-LI$_2$-ZA-AN-NI	FN	M+
		ʾIL	UM			ʾAB	I		I-LUM-A-BI		A.
		ʾIL	UM			ʾAB	UM		I-LUM-A-BU-UM		U
		ʾIL	UM			KATAZ	I		I-LU-UM-KA-TA-ZI		RUTTEN 40 1
		ʾIL	UM			MULUK			DINGIR-MU-LU-UK-KI	GN	XV 127
		ʾIL	UM			MULUK			I-LU-UM-MU-LU-UK-KI	GN	XV 127

ROOTS (Consonants only)

ʾL	1		ʾIL		UM		MULUK	AJ	I		DINGIR-MU-LU-KA-JI-KI	GN	XV 127
			ʾIL		U		MALIK	AJ	I		I-LU-MA-LI-KA-JI-KI	GN	XV 127
			ʾIL		UM		ŠALM		A		I-LU-UM-ŠA-AL-MA		RA LXV 45 V 51
			ʾIL		UM		TUŠUʿ		U		D-I-LU-UN-TU-SU-U$_2$	DN	KISURRA
			ʾIL		U	NA					I-LU-NA		RA LXV 43 III 80
			ʾIL		U	NI					I-LU-NI		M+
			ʾIL		U	NA	KIRIŠ		U		I-LU-NA-KI-RI-ŠU		XIII 8 19+
			ʾAL				ʾAḪ	AT	I		AL-A-ḪA-TI	FN	A.
			ʾALI				ʾAḪ		I		A-LI-A-ḪI	FN	M+
			ʾALI				ʾAḪ		I		A-LI$_2$-A-ḪI	FN	RA LXV 59 II 41
			ʾALI				ʾAḪ	AT	I		A-LI-A-ḪA-TI	FN	XIII 1 IV 71+
			ʾALI				ʾAḪ	AT	I		A-LI-A-ḪA?-TA-TI	FN	M
			ʾALI				ʾAḪ	AT	I		A-LI$_2$-A-ḪA-TI	FN	RA LXV 59 II 65+
			ʾALI				ʾAB		I		A-LI-A-BI	FN	M+
			ʾALI				ʾIL				A-LI$_2$-IL		HARRIS 65 16
			ʾALI				ʾUMM		I		A-LI-UM-MI	FN	M
			ʾALI				ʿAMM		U		A-LI$_2$-AM-MU		UCP X/1 52 22
			ʾALI				ʿAMM		U	HU	A-LI$_2$-AM-MU-U$_2$		UCP X/2 58 16
			ʾALI				ʾUP		UM		A-LI$_2$-U$_2$-PU-UM		KISURRA 117 5
			ʾALI				LAMA				A-LI$_2$-LA-MA		SIMMONS 118 17+
			ʾALI				PA						
							ʾIL				A-LI$_2$-PA-DINGIR		RUTTEN 6 21+
			ʾALI				PA						
							ʾIL				A-LI-PA-DINGIR		TIM III 5 18+
			ʾALI				PA						
							ʾIL				ḪA-A-LI-PA-DINGIR		EDZARD,DER 152 REV.16
			ʾALI				PA						
							ʾIL		UM		A-LI$_2$-KA-LUM		RUTTEN 37 19
			ʾALI				PA						
							ŠAMŠ				A-LI$_2$-PA-D-UTU		BE VI/1 15:25
			ʾALI				ŠARAM			NI	A-LI-ŠA-RA-AM-NI	FN	RA LXV 58 I 54
			ʾAL		I	Š	TUT		U		A-LI-IŠ-TU-TU		VAS XVI 23 13
	2		ʾAḪ		I		ʾIL				A-ḪI-[I]L		HARRIS 45 11
			ʾAḪ		I		ʾIL		I		A-ḪI-I$_3$-LI$_2$	FN	XIII 1 VIII 20
			ʾAḪ		U		ʾEL				A-ḪU-EL		RA LXV 50 IX 1
			ʾAJA				ʾIL				A-IA-DINGIR		A.+
			JAʾ		U		ʾIL		I		IA-U-I-LI$_2$		SUMER V 143 NO. 2
			JAʾ		UM		ʾIL				IA-U$_2$-UM-DINGIR		B 31
			JAʾ		UM		ʾIL				IA-A-UM-[DINGIR]		B 31
			JAʾ		UM		ʾIL				IA-WU-UM-DINGIR		B 31
			ʾAWAʾ	AT	I		ʾEL				A-WA-TI-EL		RA LXV 41 II 37+
			ʾAWAʾ	AT	I		ʾIL				A-WA-TI-DINGIR	MN	XIII 1 XI 39
		JA	HWIJ				ʾIL				IA-WI-DINGIR		B 31+, M+
		JA	HWIJ				ʾIL				JA-AḪ-WI-DINGIR		M
		JA	HWIJ				ʾIL				IA-AḪ-WI-DINGIR		B 27+
		JA	HWIJ				ʾIL		I		IA-AḪ-WI-DINGIR-LI$_2$		KISURRA 6+
		JA	HWIJ				ʾIL		I		IA-WI-LI		A 7695 10
		JA	ḤJIJ				ʾIL				IA-ḪI-DINGIR		B 26+
		JA	ḤJIJ				ʾIL				IA-A-ḪI-DINGIR		XIII 65 5
			ḤAJJ		U		ʾIL				A$_2$-U$_2$-DINGIR		U
		JA	WḤIJ				ʾIL				IA-U$_2$-ḪI-DINGIR		B 31
			JAḤAD				ʾEL		UM		IA-ḪA-AD-E-LUM		RIFTIN 136 26
			JAḤAD				ʾEL		UM		IA-ḪA-TE-LUM?		UET V 605 13
			JAḤAD				ʾIL				IA-ḪA-AD-DINGIR		M
			ḪAʾL		I		ʾIL				ḪA-LI$_2$-DINGIR		B 18
			ḪAʾL		I		ʾEL				ḪA-LI$_2$-EL		RA LXV 42 III 18+
			ḪAʾL		I		ʾEL				ḪA-A-LI$_2$-EL		RA LXV 42 III 20
			ḪAʾL		I		ʾIL		U	HU	ḪA-A-LI$_2$-I-LU-U$_2$		X 146 5
			ḪAʾL		U		ʾIL				ḪA-LU-DINGIR		M
			ʾAJAM				ʾIL	T	I		A-IA-AM-IL-TI	FN	XIII 1 X 8
			ʾAJAM			TI	ʾIL				ḪA-IA-AM-TI-DINGIR		BIROT, TEA 72 III 5
			JAʾAN				ʾIL				IA-AN-DINGIR		M
		ME	ʾWIR		I		ʾEL				ME-ḪI-RI-E-EL		JCS IV 109 4311 7
			ḪAʾR		I		ʾIL				ḪA-RI-DINGIR		BM 82372 27
			JAʾAR				ʾIL				IA-AR-I-I[L-....]		XIII 69 5
		JA	ʾWUŠ				ʾIL				IA-UŠ-DINGIR		M+

ROOTS (Consonants only)

ʾL	2	JA	ʾWUŠ			ʾIL		IA-U$_2$-UŠ$_2$-DINGIR		C II 35 28
		JA	ʾWUŠ			ʾIL		IA-U$_2$-UŠ-DINGIR		RA LXV 42 III 10+
		JE	ʾWUŠ			ʾIL		E-WU-ŠI-DINGIR		BIROT, TEA 48:20
			ḪAʾAZ	U		ʾIL		ḪA?-A-ZU-DINGIR		M
			ʾAB	A		ʾEL		A-BA-EL		TA 31, 221
			ʾAB	A		ʾIL		A-BA-DINGIR	FN	A. 59 5
			ʾAB	I		ʾIL	A	A-BI-LA		CHANTRE 4 13
			ʾAB	I		ʾIL	I	A-BI-I$_3$-LI$_2$	FN	RA LXV 59 II 38+
			ʾAB	UM		ʾIL		A-BU-UM-DINGIR		U, M+
			ʾEB	I		ʾIL		E-BI-IL		M
		JA	ḪBIʾ			ʾIL	A	IA-AḪ-BI-LA-KI	GN	M+
		JA	ḪAPIʾ			ʾIL		IA-ḪA-AP-PI-I-IL$_5$	GN	JCS XVIII 59 12+
			ʾABB	A		ʾIL		D-AB-BA-DINGIR	FN	M
			ʾABB	A		ʾIL		AB-BA-DINGIR		A.+
			ʾABB	A		ʾIL	I	AB-BA-I$_3$-LI$_2$	FN	XIII 1 XI 14
			ʾABB	A		ʾIL	I	D-AB-BA-I$_3$-LI$_2$	FN	SIMMONS 112:17
			ḪABAD	U		ʾIL		ḪA-BA-DU-DINGIR		M
			ʿABD			ʾEL		AB-DA-EL		TA 30, 615 9, 41
			ʿABD			ʾEL		ḪA-AB-DI-EL		KISURRA 74 17
			ʿABD			ʾIL		AB-TE-IL		I
			ʿABD			ʾIL		ḪA-AB-DI-DINGIR		B 9
			ʿABD			ʾIL		AB-DI-DINGIR		B 9+
			ʿABD			ʾIL	I	AB-DI-LI		A.+
		JI	JBAL			ʾIL		I-BA-AL-DINGIR		EEMY III/4 P. 130, M+
			ʾABN	I		ʾIL		ḪA-AB-NI-DINGIR		M
		JI	JBIŠ			ʾIL		I-BI-IŠ-DINGIR		TA 1930, 261
		JI	JBIŠ			ʾEL		I-BI-IŠ-I$_3$-EL		SIMMONS 70 12
		JI	JBIŠ			ʾIL		[I-B]I$_2$-IŠ-I$_3$-IL		I
		JA	ḪBAS			ʾIL		IA-AḪ-BA-AZ-DINGIR		CT II 39 18+
			JID	I		ʾIL		I-DI-DINGIR		M
			ʿAD	U	NI	ʾIL	A	A-DU-NI-LA		U
			ʿADIJ			ʾIL		A-DI-DINGIR		M
			ʿADIJ			ʾEL		ḪA-DI-EL		KISURRA 113 12+
			ʿADIJ		NA	ʾIL		A-DI-E-NA-DINGIR		M
		ʾA	WDAJ			ʾIL		A-U$_3$-DA-IL		U
		ʾA	WDAJ			ʾIL		A-AW-TE-IL		U
			JADAʿ			ʾIL		IA-DAḪ-DINGIR		B 25+
			JADAʿ			ʾIL		IA-DA-AḪ-DINGIR		CT XLVIII 21 SEAL
			JADAʿ			ʾIL		IA-DA-DINGIR		M
			JADAʿ		TI	ʾEL		IA-DA-AḪ-TE-DINGIR		UNPUBL.
		JA	JDIʿ			ʾEL	UM	IA-DI-ḪI-E-LUM		UNPUBL.
		JA	JDIʿ			ʾIL		IA-DI-IḪ-DINGIR		B 25+
		JA	JDIʿ			ʾIL		IA-DI-DINGIR		M
		JA	JDIʿ	A		ʾEL		IA-DI-ḪA-EL		KISURRA 10A 4
			ʾADD	I	JA	ʾEL		AD-DI-JA-EL		BAB. III 267 HANA
			ʾADD	I	JA	ʾEL		AD-DI-IA-DINGIR		MAOG IV 2 12 HANA
			ʾADAM		TI	ʾEL		ḪA-DAM-TI-EL		HARRIS 61 2
			ʾADAM		TI	ʾEL	UM	A-DAM-TE-LUM		GAUTIER 31 6
			ʾADAN			ʾIL		ḪA-DA-AN-DINGIR		B 18
			ʿADN	I		ʾIL		ḪA-AD-NI-DINGIR		M+
			ʿADN	I		ʾIL	U			
						MA		ḪA-AD-NI-DINGIR-MA		M
		JA	ʿḎAR			ʾIL		IA-DAR-DINGIR		RUTTEN 5 9+
		JA	ʿḎAR			ʾIL		IA-AḪ-ZA-AR-DINGIR		B 26
		JA	ʿḎAR			ʾIL		IA-AḪ-ZA-AR-I$_3$-IL		B 26
		JA	ʿḎAR			ʾIL		IA-ZA-AR-DINGIR?		IX 291 II 21,30
		JA	ʿḎAR			ʾIL		AḪ-ZA-AR-I$_3$-DINGIR		VAS XVIII 20:20
		JA	ʿḎIR			ʾIL		IA-AḪ-ZI-IR-DINGIR		B 26+
		JA	ʿḎIR			ʾIL		IA-AḪ-ZI-IR-I$_3$-IL		SUMER V 137
		JA	ʿḎIR			ʾIL		IA-AḪ-ZI-IR-I$_3$-DINGIR		CT XLV 8 6
			ʾAK	I		ʾIL		A-KI-DINGIR		M
			ʾAK	I		ʾEL		A-KI-EL		RA LXV 46 VI 49
			ʾAKK	AT		ʾEL		A-GA?-AD-Ȩ-EL		I
			ʾIL	A		ʾIL		I-LA-DINGIR		B 21
			ʾIL	A		ʾEL		I-LA-EL		RA LXV 43 IV 3
			ʾIL	I		ʾIL	A	I$_3$-LI$_2$-I-LA		A. LATE

ROOTS (Consonants only)

ʾL	2	ʾALI			ʾIL		A-LI$_2$-IL		HARRIS 65 16
JA		ḪLIJ			ʾIL		IA-AḪ-LI-DINGIR		B 26
		ʾALAŠ	I		ʾEL		A-LA-SI-E-EL		UCP X/3 3 17
		ʾAM		T	ʾEL		GEME$_2$-E-IL		RIFTIN 44 10
		ʿAMM	I		ʾIL	I	ḪA-MI-I$_3$-LI$_2$		MDP XXIII 307 16
		ʿAMM	U		ʾEL		AM-MU-E-EL		BM 16931 2
		ʿAMM	U		ʾIL		ḪA-MU-DINGIR		M
		ʿAMM	U		ʾIL		AM-MU-DINGIR		UCP X/1 18 24
JA		ʾMIʾ			ʾIL		IA-AḪ-MI-DINGIR		PBS XI/2 P. 120 NO. 92
JA		ʾMIʾ			ʾIL	A	IA-MI-I-LA		M
JA		ʾMIʾ			ʾIL	A	JA-MI-I-LA		M
ʾU		WMAʾ			ʾIL		U$_3$-MA-IL		U
ʾU		WMAʾ			ʾIL	A	U$_2$-MA-D-DINGIR		B 40
		ʾUMM	I		ʾIL	I	UM-MI-I$_3$-LI$_2$	FN	XIII 1 VIII 64
		ʿEMUQ	I		ʾEL		E-[M]U-QI$_2$-EL		RA LXV 40 I 3
		ʾAMAR			ʾIL	I	A-MAR-I$_3$-LI$_2$		MAOG IV 2 3 HANA
	T	ʾAMR	I		ʾIL		A-TAM-RI-DINGIR		M+
		ʾIMIR			ʾIL	I	IM-ME-IR-I$_3$-LI$_2$		UNPUBL.
JA		ʿMUS			ʾIL		IA-AḪ-MU-US-DINGIR		M
JA		ʿMIS			ʾIL		IA-AḪ-MI-IS-DINGIR		RUTTEN 2 23+
JA		ʿMIS			ʾIL	UM	IA-AḪ-MI-ZI-LUM		RUTTEN 16 17
		ḪAMAṮ	I		ʾIL		ḪA-MA-TI-IL		FIGULLA, CAT. I 14135
		ʾANA			ʾIL	I			
					MA		A-NA-I-LIM-MA		A.
		ʿANAJ		TI	ʾEL		A-NI-TE-EL		MOORTGAT 309
		ʿANAJ		TI	ʾIL		A-NI-TI-DINGIR		M
JA		ʿNIJ			ʾIL		IA-AḪ-NI-DINGIR		A 7630 6
		ʿINB	I		ʾIL		IN-BI$_2$-IL		U UNPUBL.
MA		ʾNUP			ʾIL		MA-AḪ-NU-UP-DINGIR		B 33+, M+
MA		ʾNUP			ʾIL		MA-AḪ-NU-BI-DINGIR		B 33+, M+
MA		ʾNUP			ʾIL	I	MA-AḪ-NU-UP-I$_3$-LI$_2$		B 33+
		ʾANAKU			ʾIL	AM			
					MA		A-NA-KU-DINGIR-LAM-MA		XIII 1 II 29
		ʾANAKU			ʾIL	A			
					MA		A-NA-KU-I-LA-MA		SIMMONS 46 7+
JA		ḪNUN			ʾIL		IA-ḪU-UN-DINGIR		M+
JA		ḪNUN			ʾIL		IA-NU-UN-DINGIR		RA LXV 51 IX 65
		ḪINUN			ʾEL		I-NU-UN-E-EL		UET V 569 2
		ḪUNUN	I		ʾEL		U$_2$-NU-NI-EL		B 40
		ḪUNUN	I		ʾIL		U$_2$-NU-NI-DINGIR		PBS XI/2 P. 125 NO. 347
		ḪANN	A		ʾIL		AN-NA-DINGIR		B 13+, C+
		ḪANN	I		ʾIL		AN-NI-DINGIR		B 13+, M
		ḪANN	I		ʾIL		ḪA-AN-NI-DINGIR	FN	XIII 1 II 7
		ḪANN	I		ʾIL	A	ḪA-AN-NI-I-LA		A. LATE
		ḪINN	I		ʾIL		ḪI-IN-NE-DINGIR		XIII 1 I 53
		ḪUNN	U		ʾEL		U$_3$-NU-EL		TA 31 223
		ʾUP			ʾIL	A	UP-I-LA		BULL. ACAD. BELG. 1974 227
JA		JPAʿ			ʾIL		IA-PA-AḪ-DINGIR		RA LXV 51 IX 74
JA		JPAʿ			ʾIL		IA-PA-DINGIR		B 29
JI		JQAH			ʾIL		I-KA-AḪ-DINGIR		B 21
ʾU		WQAH			ʾIL		U$_2$-QA-DINGIR		M+
ʾU		WQAH			ʾIL		U$_2$-GA-DINGIR		GAUTIER 41 5
ʾU		WQAH			ʾIL		U$_3$-QA-DINGIR		SIMMONS 1 3+
ʾU		WQAH			ʾIL		U$_2$-QA-IL		SYRIA V 274 HANA
ʾU		WQAH			ʾIL	A	U$_2$-Q[A]-I-LA		A 7699:14, ISHCHALI
ʾU		WQAH			ʾIL	UM	U$_2$-GA-DINGIR-LUM		FRANK 29 9
ʾU		WQIH			ʾEL		U$_2$-QI$_2$-E[L]		RA LXV 41 II 44
JA		ʿQUB			ʾIL		A-AḪ-KU-UB-DINGIR		HARRIS 12 3+
JA		ʿQUB			ʾIL		IA-KU-UB-DINGIR		B 27+
JA		ʿQUB			ʾIL		IA-AḪ-KU-UB-DINGIR		XIII 1 VII 17, C+
JA		ʿQUB	I		ʾIL		IA-AḪ-KU-BI-DINGIR		CT II 39 18
JA		ʿQUB	I		ʾIL		IA-KU-BI-DINGIR		KISURRA 41 10
JA		ʿQIB			ʾIL		IA-KI-IB-DINGIR		TIM V 33 23
		ʿAQAB			ʾEL		A-QA-BE-EL		UET V 839 23
		ʿAQUB			ʾIL		A-KU-UB-DINGIR		HARRIS 84 13
		ʿAQUB	I		ʾEL		A-KU-PI-EL		GORDON 38 16

ROOTS (Consonants only)

ʾL	2		ʿAQB		I		ʾIL			AQ-BI-IL		B 11
			ʿAQB		I		ʾIL			AQ-BI-DINGIR		BIN VII 156 10+
	JA		ʾKUR				ʾIL			IA-AḪ-KU-UR-DINGIR		CT XLV 6 24
	JA		ʾKUR				ʾIL			A-AḪ-KU-UR$_2$-[DINGIR]?		HARRIS 79 22
			JAQAR				ʾIL			IA-QAR-DINGIR		CT VI 49 A 23
			JAQR		UM		ʾIL			IA-AQ-RUM-DINGIR		A 22010
			WARḪ				ʾIL	A		WA-AR-ḪI-LA$_2$		CCT I 38C 2 CAPP.
			ʾARUŠ				ʾEL	UM		A-RU-UŠ-E-LUM		UCP X/3 2 25
			ʾARUŠ		I		ʾIL			A-RU-SI-DINGIR		A 7459, M
	JA		ḪŠIJ				ʾIL			IA-AḪ-SI-DINGIR		OLZ VIII 350 2
	JA		ḪŠIJ				ʾIL			JA-AḪ-SI-DINGIR		M
	JA		JŠUʿ				ʾIL			IA-ŠU-DINGIR		RA LXIV 36 NO. 31
			JIŠʿ		I		ʾIL			IŠ-ḪI-DINGIR		WALTERS, WL 109:5+
			JIŠʿ		I		ʾIL	A				
							MA			IŠ-ḪI-DINGIR-MA		M
			JIŠʿ		I		ʾIL	A				
							MA			IŠ-ḪI-DINGIR-LA-MA		M
			JIŠʿ		I		ʾIL	U				
							MA			IŠ-ḪI-LU-MA		YOS VIII 176 20
			JIŠʿ		I		ʾIL	U	NA	IŠ-ḪI-LU-NA		VII 215 33
			ḪAŠAK			NI	ʾEL			A-SA-AK-NI-EL		RA LXV 52 XI 6
			JAŠAR			TI	ʾIL			IA-SA-AR-TI-DINGIR		M
			ʾUŠŠ	AT	I		ʾEL			UŠ-SA-TE-EL		TIM III 43 6
			ʿAŠTAR				ʾIL	I		EŠ$_4$-DAR-I$_3$-LI$_2$	FN	RA LXV 56 I 3
			JAT		I		ʾIL			IA-TI-DINGIR		B 31
	JA		ḪATIʾ				ʾIL			IA-ḪA-AT-TI-DINGIR		M+, C
	JA		ḪATIʾ				ʾEL			IA-ḪA-TI-EL		RA LXV 44 IV 46
	JA		ḪATIʾ				ʾIL			IA-ḪA-TI-DINGIR		RUTTEN 15:2+; M
	JA		ḪATIʾ				ʾIL	UM		IA-ḪA-TI-LUM		YOS XII
			ʾATAL		I		ʾEL			ḪA-TA-LI-EL		M
		ŠT	ḪTIN				ʾIL			(E$_2$-)ŠA-TA-AḪ-TI-IN-DINGIR	GN	KISURRA
			JATAR				ʾIL			IA-TA-AR-DINGIR		B 31+ +
			JATAR				ʾIL			IA-TAR-DINGIR		M
			JATR		A		ʾIL			JA-AT-RA-IL		I
	JI		JTAR				ʾIL	I		I-TAR-I-LI		B 23
			ʾITT		A		ʾIL	I		IT-TA-I$_3$-LI$_2$		M
	JA		JṢIʾ				ʾIL			IA-ZI-DINGIR		M+
	JA		JṢIʾ				ʾIL			IA-ṢI-DINGIR		JCS IV 109 4311 21
	JA		JṢIʾ				ʾIL	UM		IA-ZI-LUM-KI	GN	B 32
	JA		WṢIʾ				ʾEL			IA-A[W-Z]I-EL?		VIII 87 8'
	JA		WṢIʾ				ʾIL			IA-AW-ZI-DINGIR		M+
	JA		WṢIʾ				ʾIL			IA-U$_2$-ZI-DINGIR		B 31
	JA		WṢIʾ				ʾIL			IA-U$_2$-ṢI-DINGIR		BAGHD. MITT. II 23
	JA		WṢIʾ				ʾIL	UM		IA-U$_2$-ZI-LUM		B 31
	JI		JṢIʾ				ʾIL	U				
							MA			I-ZI-I-LU-MA		B 23+
	JA		ʾZIJ				ʾIL			IA-AḪ-ZI-DINGIR		M
	JA		ʾZIJ				ʾIL	I		IA-AḪ-ZI-I$_3$-LI$_2$		TCL X 21 13
	JE		ʾZIJ				ʾIL	UM		E-EḪ-ZI-LUM		VIII 3 25
	JA		ʿZUB				ʾIL			IA-AḪ-ZU-UB-DINGIR		B 26+
	JA		ʿZIB				ʾIL			IA-AH-ZI-IB-DINGIR		RUTTEN 21 7+, M
	JA		ʿZIB				ʾIL			A-AḪ-ZI-IB-DINGIR		HARRIS 57 2
	JA		ʿZIB		I		ʾIL			IA-AḪ-ZI-BI-DINGIR		KISURRA 86A 11
	JA		ʿZIB		I		ʾIL			A-AḪ-ZI-BI-DINGIR		SIMMONS 70 5
	JA		ʿZIB		I		ʾIL			IA-A-ZI-BI-DINGIR		KAJ 34 18, 25 LATE
	JA		ʿZIB		A		ʾEL			IA-AḪ-ZI-BA-EL?		RA LXV 50 VIII 77
	JA		ḪṢUN				ʾIL			IA-AḪ-ZU-UN-DINGIR		BE VI/1 7 18
			ḪAṢAN				ʾIL	UM		ḪA-ZA-AN-I-LU-UM		M+
	JA		ḪZUQ				ʾIL			IA-AḪ-ZU?-UQ-DINGIR		CT XLVIII 10 3
	JA		ḪZUR				ʾIL			IA-AḪ-ZU-UR-IL		TIM III 34 15A
	JA		ḪZUR				ʾIL			IA-AḪ-ZU-UR-DINGIR		JCS XXIV 57 NO 39 AND 51
			ʿAZZ		I		ʾIL			A-ZI-DINGIR		HARRIS 39 11
	JA		BWAʾ				ʾIL			IA-BA-DINGIR?		MEISSNER 36 25
	JA		BWAʾ				ʾIL			IA-BA-A?-DINGIR		M
	JI		BWAʾ				ʾIL			I-BA-AḪ-DINGIR		KISURRA 6 15
			BAWʾ		U		ʾIL	A		BA-U$_2$-I-LA		MEISSNER 43 45

ROOTS (Consonants only)

ʾL	2 ʾU	BWAʾ			ʾIL			U$_2$-BA-DINGIR		M
	ʾU	BWAʾ			ʾIL	A		U$_2$-BA-D-DINGIR		VAS VIII 14:22
		BAʿD	I		ʾEL			[BA]-AḪ-DI-EL		KISURRA 51 10
		BEʿD	I		ʾIL	UM		BE-DI-LU-UM		TIM III 62 6+
		BEʿD	I		ʾIL	UM		BE-DI-LUM		TIM III 61 15
		BEʿD	I		ʾIL			BE-DI-DINGIR		TIM III 130 11+
		BAʿL	I		ʾIL			BA-AḪ-LI-DINGIR		B 15
		BAʿL	I		ʾIL			BA-LI-DINGIR		EDZARD, DER 68 IV 7
		BAʿL	I		ʾIL	I		BA-AḪ-LI-I$_3$-LI$_2$	FN	M
		BAʿL	UM		ʾIL			BA-AḪ-LU-UM-DINGIR		B 15+
		BEʿL	I		ʾIL	I		BE-LI$_2$-I$_3$-LI$_2$	FN	RA LXV 64 VI 50
		BIJT			ʾIL			D-E$_2$-IL		U
		BALAṬ	I		ʾEL			BA-LA-TI-EL		RUTTEN 5 21
		BIN			ʾIL	A		BI-IN-I-LA		A. LATE
		BIN			ʾIL	I	JA	BI-IN-I-LI$_2$-IA		RA LXIV 24 NO.8
		BUN			ʾIL	UM		BU-NI-LUM		TIM III 33 15+
		BUN	I		ʾIL			BU-NI-DINGIR		B 16
		BUN	I		ʾEL	UM		BU-UN?-NE-E-LUM		TCL I 220 42
		BUN	I		ʾIL	A		BU-NI-I-LA		B 16+
		BUN	U		ʾIL	A		BU-NU-I-LA		CT XLV 115 24
		BUN	UM		ʾEL	UM		BU-NU-UM-E-LU-UM		B 16
	JA	BANIJ			ʾIL			IA-BA-AN-NI-DINGIR		M+
	JA	BANIJ			ʾIL			IA-AB-BA-AN-NI-DINGIR		M
	JA	BNIQ			ʾIL			IA-AB-NI-IQ-DINGIR		B 25
	JA	BRUQ			ʾIL			IA-AB-RU-UQ-DINGIR		BASOR 95, 19
	JA	DWUR			ʾIL			IA-DU-UR-DINGIR		M
		DUWR		NI	ʾIL			DU-UR-NI-DINGIR		M+
		DAGAN			ʾIL	I		D-DA-GAN-I$_3$-LI$_2$	FN	RA LXV 62 V 51
		DANN			ʾIL			DAN-DINGIR		U
		DANN	I		ʾIL			DA?-NI-DINGIR		M
		ḎU			ʾIL	A		ZU-I-LA		B 42+
		ḎU			ʾIL	A		ZU-U$_2$-I-LA		B 42
		ḎABIB	I		ʾIL			SA-BI-BI-DINGIR		M
	JA	ḎKUR			ʾIL			A-AD-KU-UR-DINGIR		HARRIS 10 18
	JA	ḎKUR			ʾIL			IA-AD-GUR-DINGIR		SUMER V 142 8+
	JA	ḎKUR			ʾIL			IA-AD-KUR-DINGIR		SUMER V 141
	JA	ḎKUR			ʾIL			A-AD-KUR-DINGIR		SIMMONS 80 13
	JA	ḎKUR			ʾIL			IA-AD-KU?-UR?-DINGIR		VAS IX 58 15
	JI	ḎKUR			ʾIL			II-IZ-KUR-DINGIR		SIMMONS 67 18
		ḎAKUR	A		ʾIL			ZA-KU-RA-DINGIR		M+
		ḎAKUR	I		ʾEL			ZA-KU-RI-E-EL		UCP X/1 86 15
		ḎAKUR	I		ʾEL	UM		ZA-KU-RI-E-LUM		UNPUBL.
		ḎAMAR	I		ʾEL	UM		ZA-MA-RI-E-LUM		B. 92+
		ḎIMR	I		ʾIL			ZI-IM-RI-DINGIR		B 42+
		ḎIMR	I		ʾIL	U				
					MA			ZI-IM-RI-DINGIR-MA		M
		ḎIMR	I		ʾIL	U				
					MA			ZI-IM-RI-I-LU-MA		M
		ḎIMR	I		ʾIL	U				
					MA			ZI-IM-RI-LU-MA		SIMMONS 67 12
		ḎIMR	U		ʾIL	A		ZI-IM-RU-I-L[A]?		II 5 7
		ḎINUB	I		ʾIL			ZI-NU-BI-DINGIR		RA LXV 48 VIII 12
		ḎUNUB	I		ʾIL			ZU-NU-BI-DINGIR		RA LXV 51 X 14
	JI	ḎRUʿ			ʾIL			II-IZ?-RU-UḪ-DINGIR		TCL XI 156 17
	JA	ḎRAʿ			ʾIL			IA-AZ-RA-AḪ-DINGIR		VIII 100 15+
		GABIʾ			ʾIL			GA-BI-DINGIR		C 39+
		GABIʾ			ʾIL			GA-BI-IL		TIM III 12 16A
	JA	GMUR			ʾIL			IA-AG-MU-UR-DINGIR		M
		KUʾB	A		ʾEL			KU-BA-EL		X 91 4'
		KUʾB	A		ʾEL			KU-BA-DINGIR		M
		KIʾL	I		ʾIL			KI-LI-DINGIR		CT IV 33B 19
		KIʾL	I		ʾIL	UM		KI-LI-DINGIR-LUM		XIII 106 14
		KAHAL	I		ʾIL	U				
					MA			KA-A-LI-I-LU-MA		XIV 62:4+
		KAHAL	I		ʾIL	U				
					MA			KA-A-LI-DINGIR-MA		M+

ROOTS (Consonants only)

ʾL	2	KIʾM	I		ʾEL			KI-MI-EL		UCP X/3 2 2
	JA	KWUN			ʾIL			IA-KU-UN-DINGIR		M
	JA	KWIN			ʾIL			JA-KI-IN-DINGIR		JEA VII 196
		KIWN	A		ʾIL		I	KI-NA-I_3-LI_2		M
		KUWN			ʾIL		A	KU-UN-I-LA		RA LXV 53 XI 31
		KALB			ʾIL			GA-AL-BA-IL		I
		KALB			ʾIL			KA-AL-BA-DINGIR		M
	JA	KRUB			ʾIL			D-IA-AK-RU-UB-DINGIR	DN	M+
	JA	KRUB			ʾEL			D-IA-AK-RU-UB-EL	DN	M+
	JA	KRUB			ʾIL			D-IA-AK-RU-UB-IL	DN	M+
	JI	KRUB			ʾEL			D-IK-RU-UB-EL	DN	M+
	JI	KRUB			ʾIL			D-IK-RU-UB-DINGIR	DN	M+
	JI	KRUB			ʾIL			D-IK-RU-UB-IL	DN	M
	JI	KRUB			ʾIL			D-IK-RU-BI-DINGIR	DN	M
	JA	KRUB			ʾIL					
					TILL	AT	I	D-IA-AK-RU-UB-DINGIR-TIL-LA-TI		M
		KUŠM	I		ʾEL			KU-UŠ$_2$-MI-EL		RA LXV 48 VII 74
	JI	KSUW			ʾEL			IK-ZU-EL		TA 30 615 10, 20+
	JI	KSUW			ʾIL			IK-ZU-IL		TA 1931 ,435 REV.2
	JA	KSIJ			ʾIL			IA-AK-ZI-DINGIR		SIMMONS 92 16
	JA	KSIJ			ʾIL			A-AK-ZI-DINGIR		FIGULLA CAT I 14029
		LI		JA	ʾEL			LI-IA-EL		RA LXV 41 II 23
		LA		KA	ʾIL			LA-KA-DINGIR		KISURRA 111 5
		LA		NA	ʾIL			LA-NA-DINGIR		RUTTEN 27 15+
		LA		NI	ʾIL			IA_2-NI-DINGIR		U
		LA			ʾIL		A	[L]A?-I-LA		RA LXV 44 IV 36
		LA			ʾIL		A			
					MILK		I	LA-I-LA-MI-IL-KI		TA 30, 75 2
		LAWUJ			ʾIL			LA-WU-DINGIR		M
		LAʾL	I		ʾEL			LA-LI-E-EL		SIMMONS 70 15
		LUʾP	U		ʾEL			LU-BU-E-EL		I
		LABAN	A		ʾIL		A	LA-PA-NA-I-LA		ZA XXXVIII 267
		LAMA			ʾIL			LA-MA-DINGIR		B 33+, M+
		LAMA			ʾIL		A	LA-MA-I-LA		YOS XIII 244:2+
		LUMM	A		ʾIL			LUM-MA-IL		M+
		LUMM	A		ʾIL			LUM-MA-DINGIR		KISURRA 100 7+
		LUMM	A		ʾIL			LU-MA-DINGIR		KISURRA 104 29+
		LAŠU			ʾEL					
					KA			LA-ŠI-EL-KA-A-BI-IM		B 33
		LAŠU			ʾIL			LA-ŠU-IL		U
		MEʾN	I		ʾEL			ME-NI-EL		RA LXV 52 X 18
		MAʾR	A		ʾEL			MA-RA-EL		TA 1931, 298
		MAʾR	A		ʾEL			URU-MA-RA-EL	GN	MRS VI 11830:10
		MAʾR	A		ʾEL			URU-MA-RA-DINGIR	GN	MRS IX 17340:7
	JA	MWUŠ	I		ʾIL			IA-MU-ŠI-DINGIR		B 28
	JA	MWUŠ	I		ʾIL			IA-A-MU-ŠI-DINGIR		VAS VII 166 4 LATE
	JA	MLIʾ			ʾIL			A-AM-LI-DINGIR		YOS XIII 63:3, 6
	JA	MLIK			ʾIL			IA-AM-LI-IK-DINGIR		B 28+
	JA	MLIK			ʾIL			IA-AM-LIK-DINGIR		B 28+, M
	JA	MLIK			ʾIL			A-AM-LIK-DINGIR		HARRIS 76 22
	JI	MLIK			ʾIL			II-IM-LIK-DINGIR		B 28+
		MALAK			ʾIL		I	MA-LA-AK-I_3-LI_2		M
		MALAK	U		ʾIL			MA-LA-KU-IL		M
		MILK	I		ʾIL			MI-IL-KI-DINGIR		B 34
		MILK	I		ʾIL		A	MI-EL-KI-I-[LA]		UCP X/3 1 29
		MILK	I		ʾIL		U	MIL-KI-LU		B 34+
		MILK	I		ʾIL		U	MI-IL-KI-LU		B 34
		MILK	I		ʾIL		UM	MI-IL-KI-LUM		B 34
		MANIJ			ʾEL			MA-NI-EL		RA VIII 72 7
		MANIJ			ʾIL			MA-NI-IL		U
	JA	MRAṢ			ʾIL			IA-AM-RA-AṢ-DINGIR		M+
	JA	MRAṢ	I		ʾIL			IA-AM-RA-ZI-DINGIR		M
	JA	MRUṢ			ʾIL			IA-AM-RU-UṢ-DINGIR		B 28
	JA	MRUṢ			ʾIL			IA-AM-RU-IṢ-DINGIR		M
	JA	MRUṢ	I		ʾIL		UM	I-IA-AM-RU-UṢ-ZI-I-LU-UM		B 21
	JU	MRAṢ			ʾIL			JU-UM-RA-AṢ-DINGIR		M+

ROOTS (Consonants only)

ʾL	2 JA	MŚIJ			ʾIL		IA-AM-SI-DINGIR		B 28+
	JI	MŚIJ			ʾIL		JI-IM-SI-DINGIR		M
		MUT			ʾIL		MU-UT-DINGIR		MAOG IV 2 4 HANA
		MUT	I		ʾIL	UM	MU-TI-LUM		YOS XIII 151:4+
		MUT	U		ʾIL	A	MU-TU-I-LA		RA LXV 43 III 68
		MUT	UM		ʾEL		MU-TUM-E-EL		YOS VIII P. 16+
		MUT	UM		ʾEL		MU-TUM-EL		YOS VIII P. 16+
		MUT	UM		ʾIL		MU-TUM-DINGIR		FRANK 29 4, 10+ M+
	JA	MATIʿ			ʾIL		IA-MA-AT-TI-DINGIR		M+
	JA	MATIʿ			ʾIL		IA-MA-TI-DINGIR		XII 5 3
		MATIʿ			ʾIL		MA-TI-DINGIR		M
	JA	MṢIʾ			ʾIL		IA-AM-ZI-DINGIR		B 28, M
	JA	MṢIʾ			ʾIL		IA-AM-ṢI-DINGIR		B 28+
	JE	MṢIʾ			ʾIL		IE-E-EM-ZI-DINGIR		B 25
		NAWḪ	I		ʾIL		NA-ḪI-DINGIR		B 35+
		NAWḪ			ʾIL	I	NA-ḪI-LI		B 35
		NAWḪ			ʾIL	UM	NA-ḪI-LUM		B 35+
		NAWḪ			ʾIL	UM	NA-ḪI-LU-UM		B 35
		NAWḪ			ʾIL	IM	NA-ḪI-LI-IM	GEN	B 35
		NUWḪ	I		ʾIL		NU-ḪI-DINGIR		I
	JA	NḪAB			ʾIL		IA-AḪ-ḪA-AB-DINGIR		C+
		NAḤL	I		ʾIL	UM	NA-AḪ-LI-LUM		B 36+
		NAʿM	A		ʾEL		NA-MA-EL		TA 30 615:11+
		NUʿM	I		ʾIL		NU-UḪ-MI-DINGIR		M+
		NUʿM	I		ʾIL	I	NU-UḪ-MI-I_3-LI_2		XIII 1 XIII 26
		NAḪN	I		ʾIL		NA-AḪ-NI-DINGIR		TIM III 86:5
		NUWP	I		ʾIL		NU-BI-DINGIR		C+
	JA	NABIʾ			ʾEL		IA-NA-BI-EL		M+
	JA	NABIʾ			ʾIL		IA-NA-AB-BI-DINGIR		M+
	JA	NABIʾ			ʾIL		IA-NA-BI-DINGIR		M
	JA	NBIʾ			ʾIL	UM	IA$'_2$-AN-BI_2-I_3-LUM		U
		NABIʾ			ʾIL	I	NA-BI-I_3-LI_2		XIII 1 III 61
		NADUB			ʾEL	I	NA-DU-BE-LI_2		U
	JA	NQIM			ʾIL		IA-AN?-KI-IM-DINGIR		RA VIII 69 22
	JA	NQIM			ʾIL		A-AN-KI-IM-DINGIR		HARRIS 9 14+
	JE	NQIM			ʾIL		E-EN-KI-IM-DINGIR		CT VI 49B 4
	JA	NŚIʾ			ʾIL		IA-SI-DINGIR		B 29+
	JA	NŚIʾ			ʾIL	I	IA-SI-LI		B 29+
	JA	NŚIʾ			ʾIL	I	IA-SI-I-LI_2		TCL X 5 3
	JA	NŚIʾ			ʾIL	UM	IA-SI-LUM		RA IX 22 2+
	JA	NTIN			ʾIL		IA-AN-TI-IN-DINGIR		B 29+, M+
	JA	NTIN			ʾIL		IA-AT-TI-IN-DINGIR		M
	JA	NTIN			ʾIL		[A-A]N-TI-IN-DINGIR		HARRIS 56 15
	JA	NTIN	I		ʾIL		IA-AN-TI-NI-DINGIR		BM 17084
	JA	NṢIB			ʾIL		IA-AN-Z[I-I]B-DINGIR		XII 683 4
		NIṢB	I		ʾIL		NE-IZ-BI-IL		TA 1931, 172
		NIṢB	I		ʾEL		NE-IZ-BI-EL		TA 1930, 747 +
		PA			ʾIL	A	PA-I-LA		XIII 1 VII 16
		PA		KA	ʾIL	A	PA-KA-I-LA		B 37+
		PA		KA	ʾIL	A	PA-KA-DINGIR		B 37
		PA		KA	ʾIL	A	PA-A-KA-I-LA		B 37
		PI			ʾIL	A	PI-I-LA		A. LATE
		PU	UM		ʾEL		PU-UM-E-EL		BAGH.MITT. IV 291,SEAL
	JA	PLAḪ			ʾIL		IA-AP-LA-AḪ-DINGIR		M, TIM III 56 5+
	JA	PLAḪ			ʾIL	IM	IA-AP-LA-AḪ-I-LI-IM	GEN	RA LXIV 43
	JA	PLIḪ			ʾIL		[I]A-AP-LI?-I[Ḫ?-DINGIR]		VII 215 32
	JI	PANIJ			ʾEL	UM	I-PA-AN-NI-E-LUM		UNPUBL.
		PANIJ			ʾIL	A	PA-NI-LA		IX 252 17, A. LATE
		QAWM	I		ʾIL		GA-MI-DINGIR		TIM III 12 16+
	JA	QNIJ			ʾIL		IA-AQ-NI-DINGIR		CT XLV 92 I 10+
	JA	QRIʾ			ʾIL		IA-AQ-RI-DINGIR		B 27
		QARIʾ			ʾEL		QA-R[I]-E[L]		M
		QAṬAR			ʾIL		GA-TA-AR-DINGIR		B 17
	JA	QṢUR			ʾIL		IA-AQ-ZU-UR-DINGIR		B 29+
	JA	RʿIJ			ʾIL		IA-AR-ḪI-DINGIR		CT XLVIII 27
	JE	RWIḤ	I		ʾIL		E-RI-ḪI-DINGIR		U

ROOTS (Consonants only)

ʾL	2 JA	RWIJ			ʾIL		A-AR-WI-DINGIR	HARRIS 98 R. 7	
	JA	RḪIB			ʾIL		IA-AR-I-IB-DINGIR	M+	
	JA	RḪIB			ʾIL		IA-AR-IB-DINGIR	M+	
	JA	RḪAM	I		ʾIL		IA-AR-ḪA-MI-DINGIR	KISURRA 5A 15+	
	JA	RḪAM			ʾIL		IA-AR-ḪA-AM-DINGIR	B 29	
	JI	RḪAM	I		ʾIL		IR-ḪA-MI-DINGIR	A.	
	JI	RḪAM			ʾIL	A	IR-ḪA-MI-LA	A.+	
		RAḪM	I		ʾIL	I	RA-AḪ-MI-I$_3$-LI$_2$	XIII 1 VIII 79+	
		RAWM	E		ʾEL		R[A]-ME-EL	RA LXV 42 II 56	
		RIWM			ʾIL	A	RI-IM-I-LA	TCL XIV 54 17	CAPP.
	JA	RBUʾ			ʾIL		IA-AR-BU-DINGIR	KISURRA 9A 9+	
	JE	RBUʾ		HU	ʾEL		E-[IR]-BU-U$_2$-[E]L	KISURRA 152 9	
	JA	RBIJ			ʾEL		IA-AR-BI-EL	CT XLV 12 23	
	JA	RBIJ			ʾIL		IA-AR-BI-DINGIR	B 29+	
	JA	RBIJ			ʾIL		I-AR-BI-DINGIR	KISURRA 5A 8+	
	JE	RBIJ			ʾIL		E-IR-BI-DINGIR	KISURRA 22A 15	
		RIMŠ	I		ʾIL		RI-IM-ŠI-DINGIR	M+	
		RIMŠ	I		ʾIL	I	RI-IM-ŠI-I$_3$-LI$_2$	M	
		RIPʾ	A		ʾIL	A	RI-IP-A-DINGIR	M+	
	JA	RŠIJ			ʾIL		IA-AR-ŠI-DINGIR	B 29+, M	
	JA	RŠIJ			ʾIL	I	A-AR-ŠI-DINGIR	TA 1930,7:6	
	JA	RŠIJ			ʾIL	UM	IA-AR-ŠI-DINGIR-UM	UCP X/1 P. 58+	
	JA	SNIQ			ʾIL		IA-AS-NI-IQ-DINGIR	RA LXV 48 VII 66	
	JA	SNIQ			ʾIL		IA-AŠ$_2$-NI-IQ-DINGIR	SIMMONS 55 14	
		SITR	I		ʾEL	UM	ZI-IT-RI-E-LUM	B 42	
		SITR	I		ʾIL		ZI-IT-RI-DINGIR	B 42	
	JA	SAṬIʾ			ʾEL		[I]A-ZA-AD-DI-EL	M	
	JA	SAṬIʾ			ʾIL		IA-ZA-AD-DI-DINGIR	M+	
	JA	SAṬIʾ			ʾIL		IA-ZA-AT-TI-DINGIR	M	
	JA	SAṬIʾ			ʾIL		IA-SA-AD-DI-DINGIR	M	
	JA	SAṬIʾ			ʾIL		IA-S[A]-TI-DINGIR	M	
		ŠU			ʾEL	UM	ŠU-E-LUM	B 40	
	ʾA	ŠWUB			ʾIL	A	A-ŠU-UB-I-LA	A. LATE	
	JA	ŠWUB			ʾIL		IA-ŠU-UB-DINGIR	CT II 23 15+, M+	
	JE	ŠWUB			ʾIL		E-ŠU-UB-DINGIR	BIN VII P. 12+	
	JE	ŠWUB	I		ʾIL		IE-E-ŠU-BI-DINGIR	B 26	
		ŠUWB			ʾIL	A	ŠU-UB-D-I-LA	RA LXV 52 X 66	
		ŠUWB	A		ʾIL	A	ŠU-BA-D-DINGIR	B 23+	
		ŠUWB	A	NI	ʾIL		ŠU-BA-NI-DINGIR	RUTTEN 41 3, 13	
		ŠUWB		NA	ʾIL		ŠU-UB-NA-DINGIR	B 40+, M+	
		ŠUWB		NA	ʾIL		ŠU-UB-NA-IL	B 40	
		ŠUWB		NA	ʾIL	U	ŠU-UB-NA-ḪI-LU	B 40	
	JA	ŠWIB			ʾIL		IA-ŠI-IB-DINGIR	A.	
		ŠAWB	I		ʾIL		ŠA-BI-DINGIR	M, C+	
		ŚAʾL	I		ʾIL		SA-LI-DINGIR	B 37+	
	JA	ŚJIM			ʾIL		IA-SI-IM-DINGIR	M+	
	JA	ŚBIJ			ʾIL		IA-AŠ-BI-DINGIR	B 32	
	JA	ŚBIJ			ʾIL	A	IA-AŠ-BI-I-LA	B 30	
		ŠADW	I		ʾIL		SA-DI-DINGIR	JCS IV 110, 2040 16	
		ŠADW	U		ʾIL	A	ŠA-DU-[I]-LA	RA LXV 45 V 50	
		ŠAKUM	I		ʾIL		SA-KU-MI-DINGIR	M+	
	JA	ŚKIN			ʾIL		IA-AŠ$_2$-KI-IN-DINGIR-[....]?	M	
	JA	ŚKUR			ʾIL		IA-AŠ$_2$-KU-UR$_2$-DINGIR	B 81	
	JA	ŚKUR			ʾIL		IA-AŠ$_2$-KU-UR-DINGIR	B 30+	
	JA	ŚKUR			ʾIL		IA-AŠ$_2$-KUR-DINGIR	JNES XIII 210+	LATE
	JA	ŚKUR			ʾIL		[IA]-AŠ-KU-UR-DINGIR	VIII 38 7'	
	JI	ŚKUR			ʾEL	I	IŠ-KUR-E-LI FN	XIII 1 VII 41	
	JA	ŚLAM			ʾIL		IA-AŠ$_2$-LAM-DINGIR	XIV 47:11	
		ŚAM	U		ʾIL	A	SA-MU-I-LA	M	
		ŚAM	U	HU	ʾIL	A	SA-MU-U$_2$-I-LA	M	
		ŚUM	A		ʾIL	A	SU-MA-I-LA	YOS XIII 244:15+	
		ŚUM	I		ʾIL	UM	SU-MI-LU-UM	WALTERS, WL 114:13	
		ŚUM	U		ʾEL		SU-MU-EL	TA 30, 34 6	
		ŚUM	U		ʾIL		SU-MU-DINGIR	B 39+	
		ŚUM	U		ʾIL		D-SU-MU-DINGIR	KISURRA 85 15, 22+	
		ŚUM	U		ʾIL	A	SU-MU-I-LA	B 39; M+	

ROOTS (Consonants only)

ʾL	2			ŠUM	U		ʾIL				
							BAWB	I	JA	[SU-MU-I]L-BA-BI-IA	PBS XI/2 1 I 11
				ŠUM	U		ʾIL				
							....			SU-MU-DINGIR-LI-BUR-RA-AM	FRANK 27 4
				ŠUM	U		ʾIL				
							ŠARR			SU-MU-[DINGIR]-LUGAL	UCP X/1 17 15
		JA		ŠMAʿ			ʾEL			IA-AŠ$_2$-MA-AḪ-I$_3$-EL	B 30
		JA		ŠMAʿ			ʾIL			IA-AŠ$_2$-MA-AḪ-DINGIR	SIMMONS 55 11, M
		JI		ŠMAʿ			ʾIL			IS-MA-AḪ-DINGIR	CT XLV 3 7
		JI		ŠMAʿ			ʾIL			IŠ-ME-EḪ-DINGIR	KISURRA 40 9
				ŠIMAʿ			ʾIL	A		SI-MA-I-LA	X 5 4, 5
				ŠIMAʿ		NI	ʾIL			ŠI-MA-AḪ-NI-DINGIR	VIII 49 BIS 5'
				ŠAMUʿ	I		ʾIL			SA-MU-ḪI-IL	XIV 76:19
				ŠAMUʿ	I		ʾEL			SA-MU-ḪI-EL	M
				ŠIMḪ	U		ʾIL	UM		ŠI-IM-ḪU-LUM?	A. 265 8
				ŠAMʾAL	A		ʾIL			SA-AM-A-LA-DINGIR	M+
				ŠAMʾIL	I		ʾIL			SA-AM-ḪI-LI-DINGIR	M
				ŠAMUK	I		ʾEL			SA-MU-KI-EL	B 38+
				ŠAMAR	I		ʾIL			SA-MA-RI-DINGIR	A. 455 46
				ŠAMŠ	U		ʾIL	U	NA	SA-AM-SU-I-LU-NA	B 38+
				ŠAMŠ	U		ʾIL	U	NA		
							KIMA			SA-AM-SU-I-LU-NA-KI-MA-DINGIR	BM 81047:6
				ŠAMŠ	U		ʾIL	U	NA		
							....			SA-AM-SU-I-LU-NA-QAR-RA-AD	CT XLV 48 5
				ŠUMAT			ʾIL	I		SU-MA-AT-I$_3$-LI$_2$	XIII 1 II 85
				ŠUMUT			ʾIL			SU-MU-UT-DINGIR	VAS VII 148 5+
		JU	T	ŠANIJ			ʾIL	A		UŠ-TA-NI-I-LA	A. 33 22
		JI	ŠT	ŠNIJ			ʾEL			IŠ-TA-AŠ-NI-EL	SIMMONS 46 30
		JI	ŠT	ŠNIJ			ʾIL			IŠ-TA-AŠ-NI-IL	SYRIA V 274 HANA
		JI	ŠT	ŠNIJ			ʾIL			IŠ-TA-AŠ-NI-DINGIR	VAS IX 156 11+
		JU	ŠT	ŠNIJ			ʾIL			UŠ-TAŠ-NI-DINGIR	VAS IX 130 21+
		JU	ŠT	ŠNIJ			ʾIL			UŠ-TA-AŠ-NI-DINGIR	VAS IX 131 21+
			ŠT	ŠNIJ			ʾIL			ŠA-TA-AŠ-NI-IL	SUMER V 139 NO. 4
		JA		ŠPUQ			ʾIL			IA-AŠ$_2$-PU-UK-DINGIR	M
		JA		ŠQIṬ			ʾIL			IA-AŠ-KI-IṬ-DINGIR	B 30, M+
				ŠARAJ		TI	ʾEL			ŠA-RA-TI-EL	TIM III 59 6
				ŠARAJ		TI	ʾEL			ŠA-RA-TE-EL	TIM III 44 18+
				ŠARR	A		ʾIL			ŠAR-RA-DINGIR	A. LATE+
				ŠIRṬ	I		ʾIL	I		ŠI-IR-TE-I$_3$-LI$_2$	A. LATE
				ŠITAŠ			ʾIL	I		ŠI-IT-TA-AŠ-I$_3$-LI$_2$	MEL. SYR. 994
		JA		ŠṬIḪ			ʾIL			IA-AŠ-TI-DINGIR	XIII 1 IX 7
				ŠAṬUP	I		ʾIL			ŠA-TU-BI-DINGIR	M+
				ŠAṬUP	I		ʾEL			ŠA-TU-BI-EL	RA LXV 44 IV 74
				ṢUWR	A		ʾIL			ZU-RA-DINGIR	M+
				ṢUWR	I		ʾIL			ZU-RI-DINGIR	M
				ṢABAʾ		TI	ʾEL			ZA-BA-TE-EL	UNPUBL.
		JA		ṢDUQ			ʾIL			IA-AŠ-DU-UQ-DINGIR	JEAN 164 R. 4+
		JA		ṢDUQ			ʾIL			[IA]-AŠ$_2$-DU-UQ-DINGIR	BASOR 95, 19
				TAʾK	U		ʾIL			TA-KU-DINGIR	VAS VIII 14 27
				TUWR	A		ʾIL	I		TU-RA-I$_3$-LI$_2$	SAUREN, WUG 285 V, U.
				ṬAJB	A		ʾIL			ṬA-BA-DINGIR	A. 60 11
				ZAKK			ʾIL	I		ZA-AK-I$_3$-LI$_2$	TA 1931,389 UR III
		JA		ZLIJ			ʾIL			IA-AZ-LI-DINGIR	M
				ZALIJ			ʾIL			ZA-LI-DINGIR	B 41
		JI		ZMEʾ			ʾIL			IZ-ME-DINGIR	VAS IX 141 2
				ZIZN	I		ʾEL			ZI-IZ-NI-EL	RA LXV 55 XIII 11
	3			ʾAḪ	UM		MA				
							ʾIL			A-ḪU-UM-MA-DINGIR	M+
				ʾAJA			ʾAB				
							ʾIL			ḪA-IA-AB-DINGIR	B 18
				ʾAJA			ʾABN	I			
							ʾIL			ḪA-IA-AB-NI-DINGIR	B 18+
				ʾAJA			MA				
							ʾIL			A-IA-MA-DINGIR	M
				ʾAJA			MA				
							ʾIL			ḪA-IA$_3$-MA-DINGIR	XIV 93:8+

ROOTS (Consonants only)

ʾL	3	ʾAJA			MA				
					ʾEL		A-IA-MA-EL		RA LXV 42 III 14
		ʾIJA			ʾAB				
					ʾIL		I-A-AB-DINGIR		OIP XXII 262
		ḪIʾD			LA	KA			
					ʾIL	I	ḪI-ID-LA-KA-I_3-LI_2		M
		ḪAʾL	I		MA				
					ʾIL		ḪA-LI_2-MA-DINGIR		M
		ḪAʾL	U	Š	MI				
					ʾIL		ḪA-LU-UŠ-MI-DINGIR		M
		JAʿAL			PI				
					ʾIL	UM	IA-ḪA-AL-PI-LUM		3NT867:5, 12, 21
	JI	JʿIL			PI				
					ʾIL		I-ḪI-IL-BI-DINGIR		M
		ʾAB	I		MA				
					ʾIL	I	A-BI-MA-I_3-LI_2	FN	RA LXV 64 VI 32
		ʾAB	U		KA				
					ʾIL		A-BU-KA-DINGIR		M+
		ʾIB	I		LA				
					ʾIL	UM	I-BI-LA-I_3-LUM		U
	JI	JBAL			LA				
					ʾIL		I-BA-AL-LA-DINGIR		RA LXV 47 VII 26
	JI	JBAL			PI				
					ʾEL		I-BA-AL-BI-EL		M+
	JI	JBAL			PI				
					ʾEL		I-BA-AL-PI-EL		UCP X P. 56+
	JI	JBAL			PI				
					ʾIL		I-BA-AL-BI-DINGIR		M+
	JI	JDAʿ			PI				
					ʾIL		I-DA-BI_2-DINGIR		I
	ʾA	JDAʿ			PI				
					ʾEL		A-DA-AḪ-[BI]?-EL		SIMMONS 51 21
		JADAʿ			PI				
					ʾIL		IA-DA-BI-DINGIR		AJSL XXXIII 224 3
		ʾAK	UM		LA				
					ʾIL	A	A-KUM-LA-I-LA		RA LXV 55 XIII 1
		ʾIL	A		LA				
					ʾIL		DINGIR-LA-IL		U
		ʾIL	A		MA				
					ʾIL	A	DINGIR-MA-I_3-LA		B 21+
		ʾIL	A		MA				
					ʾIL	A	DINGIR-MA-D-I-LA		B 21
		ʾALI			PA				
					ʾIL		A-LI_2-PA-DINGIR		RUTTEN 6 21+
		ʾALI			PA				
					ʾIL		A-LI-PA-DINGIR		TIM III 5 18+
		ʾALI			PA				
					ʾIL		ḪA-A-LI-PA-DINGIR		EDZARD,DER 152 REV.16
		ʾALI			PA				
					ʾIL	UM	A-LI_2-KA-LUM		RUTTEN 37 19
		ʿAMM	U		RAPIʾ				
					ʾIL		ḪA-AM-MU-RA-BI-DINGIR		B 19
		ʿAMM	U	Š	KI				
					ʾIL		AM-MU-US-KI-DINGIR		A.
		ʿAMM	U	Š	KI				
					ʾIL		AM-MU-UŠ-KI-DINGIR		A.+
		ʾANA			MA				
					ʾIL		A-NA-MA-DINGIR		A 29366:9
	JA	ḪNUN			PI				
					ʾEL		IA-ḪU-UN-PI-EL		SIMMONS 54 18
		ḪUNN			PI				
					ʾEL		ḪU-UN-BI-EL		SIMMONS 82 7
	ʾU	WQAH			KI				
					ʾEL		U_2-QA-KI-EL		RA LXV 51 IX 69
		ʾARUŠ			PI				
					ʾIL		A-RU-UŠ-BI-DINGIR		M, RA XLI 45 4' HANA

ROOTS (Consonants only)

ʾL	3	JIŠʿ	I				LI			
							ʾEL		IŠ-ḪI-LI-EL	JCS XXIV 69 NO. 3 SEAL
	JA	ʾŠUD					PI			
							ʾEL		IA-SU-UD-PI-EL	SIMMONS 46 31
		JATAM					MA			
							ʾIL		IA-TAM-MA-DINGIR	UET V 172 5'
		ḪATAN					PI			
							ʾIL		ḪA-TA-AN-BI-DINGIR	M
		BIʿD	I				KI			
							ʾEL		BI-DI-KI-EL	RA LXV 53 XI 54
		BIN					MA			
							ʾIL		BI-MA-DINGIR	C+
		BIN	I				MA			
							ʾIL		BI-NI-MA-DINGIR	A. LATE
		BUN					TAḪTUN			
							ʾIL	A	BU-UN-TAḪ-UN-I-LA	B 16
		BUN	A				MA			
							ʾIL		BU-NA-MA-DINGIR	XII 1 X 36
		BUN	U				KI			
							ʾIL		BU-NU-KI-DINGIR	M
		BUN	U				KALA			
							ʾIL	I	BU-NU-KA-LA-I-LI	B 16
		BUN	U				KAMA			
							ʾIL	A	BU-NU-KA-MA-I-LA	B 16
		BUN	U				MA			
							ʾIL		BU-NU-MA-DINGIR	M
		BUN	U				TAḪTUN			
							ʾIL	A	BU-NU-TAḪ-TU-UN-I-LA	B 16+
		BUN	U	HU			PI			
							ʾIL	UM	BU-NU-U$_2$?-BI-I-LUM	UET V 548 2
		BANIJ					ME			
							ʾEL		BA-NI-ME-EL	HARRIS 12 15
		DAWD	I	Š			ME			
							ʾEL		DA-DI-EŠ$_3$-ME-EL	UCP X/3 P. 198+
		DAWD	UM				PI			
							ʾIL		DA-DUM-BI$_2$-DINGIR	I
		DUWD	U	Š			ME			
							ʾEL		DU-DU-UŠ-ME-EL	UCP X/3 P. 198+
		DANN	I	Š			ME			
							ʾIL		DA-NI-IŠ-ME-DINGIR?	I
		ḎARAʿ					LI			
							ʾIL		ZA-RA-AḪ?-LI-DINGIR	M
		KA					ṢUWR	A		
							ʾIL		KA-ZU-RA-DINGIR	M
		KI					MILK	I		
							ʾEL		KI-MI-IL-KI-EL	KISURRA 112:8
	ʾA	KWUN					PI			
							ʾEL		A-KU-PI-EL	GORDON, SCT 38 16
		KANN	A				MA			
							ʾIL		KA-AN-NA-MA-DINGIR	M
		LA		K			MA			
							ʾIL		LA-AK-MA-AN	B 33
		LA			ʾA		HWIJ			
							ʾIL		LA-WI-DINGIR	XIV 109:7
		LA			ʾA		HWIJ			
							ʾIL		LA-[AḪ]?-WI-DINGIR	M
		LA			ʾA		ʾWIʾ			
							ʾIL		LA-WI-IḪ?-DINGIR	TIM IV 33,34,SEALS
		LA			ʾA		ʾŠUD	I		
							ʾIL		LA-AḪ-SU-DI-DINGIR	XIII 4 14
		LA			ʾA		MLIK			
							ʾIL		LA-AM-LI-IK-DINGIR	RUTTEN 5 22
		LA			ʾA		ŠNIJ			
							ʾIL		LA-AŠ-NI-DINGIR	M
		LI			JI	T	ŠAMAʿ			
							ʾIL		LI?-IŠ?-TA-MI-DINGIR	IX 291 I 18

ROOTS (Consonants only)

ʾL	3		LAWUJ		LA	ʾIL		LA-WU-LA-DINGIR	M+
			LAMA		LA	ʾIL		LA-MA-LA-DINGIR	KAJ 72 18, LATE
		ʾA	MWUT		PA	ʾIL		A-MU-UT-PA-DINGIR	SYRIA L 7
		ʾA	MWUT		PA	ʾIL		AM-MU-UT-PA-DINGIR	RA XLIII 212 39 QATNA
		ʾA	MWUT		PI	ʾIL		A-MU-UT-BI-DINGIR	M+
		ʾA	MWUT		PI	ʾIL	A	A-MU-UT-BI-I-LA	M
			MILK	I	LA	ʾEL		MI-IL-KI-LA-EL	TA 30 615 21
			MILK	I	LI	ʾEL		MI-IL-KI-LI-EL	B 34, M+
			MILK	I	LI	ʾEL		MIL-KI-LI-EL	VAS VIII 128 16+
			MILK	I	LI	ʾIL		MI-IL-KI-LI_2-IL	I
			MILK	I	LI	ʾIL		[MI]-EL-KI-LI-IL	I
			MILK	I	LI	ʾEL	UM	MI-IL-KI-LI-E-LUM	A 32065:3
			MILK	I	LU	ʾIL	A	MI-IL-KI-LU-I-LA	VAS XVI 10 5, 9
			MILK	U	MA	ʾIL		MI-IL-KU-MA-IL	B 35+
			MILK	U	MA	ʾIL		MI-IL-KU-MA-DINGIR	C+
			MILK	UM	MA	ʾIL		MIL-KUM-MA-DINGIR	A. LATE
			MANN		BALTI	ʾIL		MA-AN-BA-AL-TI-DINGIR	RA LXIV 34 NO. 24
			MANN	A	BALTI	ʾEL		MA-NA-BA-AL-TE-EL	B 28+
			MANN	A	BALTI	ʾEL		MA-NA-BA-AŠ-TE-EL	M+
			MANN	A	BALTI	ʾIL		MA-AN-NA-BA-AL-TI-DINGIR	M
			MANN	A	BALTI	ʾEL		MA-NA-BA-AL-TI-EL	KISURRA 70A 14+
			MARUʾ		LI	ʾEL		MA-RU-LI-EL	SIMMONS 47 18, 49 22
			MUT	I	ME	ʾEL		MU-TI-ME-EL	TA 30, 615:4+
			MUT	U	ME	ʾEL		MU-TU-ME-EL	CT VIII 31A 25+
			MUT	UM	MA	ʾEL		MU-TUM-MA-EL	TA 1931, 456
			MUT	UM	ME	ʾEL		MU-TUM-ME-EL	RUTTEN 32 8+
			MATAʿ	A	KI	ʾEL		MA-TA-A-KI-EL	RA LXV 50 IX 20;HARRIS 19:5,SEAL+
			NIMḪ	AM	PI	ʾIL		NI-IM?-ḪA-AM-BI-DINGIR	A. 95 17 (=JCS VIII 8)
			NAPŠ	I	PI	ʾIL		NA-AP-SI-BI-DINGIR	SYRIA XLVIII 9:22
			PI		KAMA	ʾIL		BI-KA-MA-DINGIR	XIV 111:10+
			PI		KAMA	ʾEL		BI-KA-MA-EL	M+
			PI		NAʿM	ʾEL		BI-NA-AḪ-ME-EL	B 15
			PU		MA	ʾEL		PU-MA-[E]L	TA 1931,538 I

ROOTS (Consonants only)

ʾL	3		PU			ME						
						ʾIL			PU-ME-IL		I	
			QAWM	U		MA						
						ʾIL			QA-MU-MA-DINGIR		M	
			RAPIʾ			MI						
						ʾIL			RA-BI-MI-IL		BIROT,TEA 72 VI 19	
			RAPIʾ			MI						
						ʾIL		UM	RA-BI-MI-LUM		BIROT,TEA 72 IX 29	
		JA	RŠAP			LA						
						ʾIL			IA-AR-SA-AP-LA-DINGIR		M+	
		JA	RŠAP			LA						
						ʾIL		A	IA-AR-SA-AP-LA-I-[LA]?		M	
			SITR	I		KI						
						ʾEL			ZI-IT-RI?-KI-EL?		B 42	
		ʾA	ŠWUB			LA						
						ʾEL			A-ŠU-UB-LA-EL		TA 1931,765	
		ʾA	ŠWUB			LA						
						ʾIL			A-ŠU-UB-LA-DINGIR		C+	
		ʾA	ŠWUB			LI						
						ʾEL			A-ŠU-UB-LI-EL		OIP XLIII 154	NO. 48+
		JA	ŚJIM			KI						
						ʾIL			IA-SI-IM-KI-DINGIR		M	
			ŠADW	I		MA						
						ʾIL			ŠA-DI-MA-DINGIR		RA LXV 48 VIII 20	
			ŚAM	A		ME						
						ʾEL			SA-MA-ME-EL		M	
			ŚAM	A		ME						
						ʾEL			ŠA-MA-ME-EL		TA 1931, 421	
			ŚAM	I		ME						
						ʾEL			SA-MI-ME-EL		CT XLV 117 33	
			ŚAM	U		LA						
						ʾIL			SA-MU-LA-DINGIR		B 39+	
			ŚUM	U		LA						
						ʾIL			SU-MU-LA-DINGIR		B 39+	
			ŚUM	U		LA						
						ʾIL		I	SU-MU-LA-I_3-LI_2		UCP X/1 34 2	
			ŚUM	U		LI						
						ʾEL			SU-MU-LI-EL		B 39+	
			ŚUM	U		LA						
						ʾEL			SU-MU-LA-EL		SUMER XXIII 160 5	
			ŚUM	U		LI						
						ʾEL			SU-MU-LI-EL-DU-RI		A 7630 3	
			ŚUM	U		ME						
						ʾEL			SU-MU-ME-EL		JCS IV 107,	YBC 4968
			ŚAMŚ	I		HADD		U				
						ʾIL		I	SA-AM-SI-D-IM-I_3-LI_2		C+	
		JI	TWUR			PI						
						ʾIL			I-DUR-[BI]?-DINGIR		I	
		JI	TWUR			ŚUM		U				
						ʾEL			I-DUR-SU-ME-EL		KISURRA 43 5+	
			TAḪT	U		PI						
						ʾIL			TA-AḪ-TU-BI-DINGIR		M+	
			TIBIʾ	A	Š	ME						
						ʾEL			TI-BI_2-$AŠ_2$-ME-EL		CT XXXIII 48A 4	
			ZAKK			PI						
						ʾEL			ZA-AK-PI-EL		TA 1931,198 EARLY OB	
ʾLʾ	1		ʾALUʾ	UM					A-LU-U_2-UM		VAS XVI 131:1	
			ʾALUʾ	U					A-LU?-U_2	FN	M	
ʾLK	1		ʾALAK	UM					ḪA-LA-KUM		CT XLV 2 22+	
			ʾALIK	UM					A-LI-KUM		B+	
			ʾALIK	UM					ḪA-LI-KU-UM		B 12+	
			ʾALIK	UM					ḪA-LI-KUM		B 12+	
ʾLL	1		ʾILL	U	NA				IL-LU-NA	FN	A.	
			ʾALL	AH					AL-LA	FN	RA LXV 59 II 42	
			ʾALLA			MUT	IJ	I	AL-LA-MU-TI-I	TRIBE	4E RENC. ASS. P. 178 9	
			ʾALLA			MUT	IJ	I	A-AL-MU-TI-I	TRIBE	M	

ROOTS (Consonants only)

ʾLL	1		ʾALLA				RAPIʾ			AL-LA-RA-PI		TCL XVIII 95 12, 15
			ʾALLA				ŠUʾḪ	U		AL-LA-ŠU-ḪU		U
			ʾALLAI				ḪAṢN	U		AL-LA-I-AṢ-NU	FN	M
			ʾALL		I		KUPAPA			AL-LI-KU-PA-PA	FN	A.
			ʾALL		I		NIWR	I		AL-LI-NI-RI	FN	A.
			ʾALL		I		TALM	A		AL-LI-TA-AL-MA	FN	A.
			ʾALL		I		TURAḪ			AL-LI-TU-RA-AḪ?	FN	XIII 1 I 10+
			ʾALL		I		TURAḪ	I		AL-LI-TU-RA-ḪI	FN	A.
			ʾELL		UM					E-IL-LUM		RA LXV 50 VIII 70
			ʾELL		I					E-EL-LI		A. 377 8
			ʾELL	AN						EL-LA-AN		M
			ʾELL	AN						E-LA-AN		MAD V, SARG.
			ʾELL	AN	UM					E-EL-LA-NUM		C
			ʾELL	AN	UM					E-LA-NUM		C
			ʾELL	AN	U					E-EL-LA-NU		C
			ʾELL	AT			....			EL-LA-AT-[....]		M
			ʾELL	ATAN						EL-LA-TA-AN		C II 39:8
			ʾELIL		I	Š				E-LI-LI-IŠ		M+
			ʾELIL		I	Š				E-LI-LI-ŠA		M
			ʾILL	AT	UM					IL-LA-TUM	FN	XIII 1 X 46
			ʾILL		A		JAT	I		IL-LA-I-IA-TI	FN NOM	XIII 1 IX 51
			ʾILL		A		JAT	IM		IL-LA-I-IA-TIM	FN NOM	XIII 1 IV 75
			ʾILUL		A					I-LU-UL-LA		M
			ʾILUL		I					I-LU-UL-LI		M
	2		ʾIL		I		ʾILL	A		I-LI-IL-LA		A. LATE
			KIʾL		UM		ʾALLAI			KI-LUM-AL-LA-I	FN	XIII 1 XI 49
			NABIʾ				ʾILL	I		NA-BI-IL-LI		SYRIA V 274 HANA
		JI	RḪAM				ʾILL	A		IR-ḪA-MI-IL-LA		A. 274 26
		JI	RWIM				ʾILL	A		I-RI-MI-LA		A. 87 30 LATE
		JI	RWIM				ʾILL	A		I-RI-IM-IL-LA		A. LATE
		JI	RWIM				ʾILL	A		I-RI-MI-IL-LA		A. LATE
		JA	ŠWIB		I		ʾILL	A		IA-ŠI-BI-IL-LA		A.
		JI	ŠMAʿ				ʾILL	A		IŠ-MI-IL-LA		A.
			ŠIMR				ʾALLA			ŠI-IM-RA-AL-LA		A.
	3		ʾAJAN				ʾAB	I				
							ʾILL	A		A-IA-NA-BI-IL-LA		A.
ʾLM	1		ʾALM		U	HU				ḪA-AL-MU-U$_2$		SYRIA XXXVII 206 8 HANA
			ʾALM	AN	UM					AL-MA-NU-UM		TA 1931,148
			ʾALM	AN	UM					ḪA-AL-MA-NU-UM		HARRIS 62 14+
			ʾALM	AT	UM					ḪA-AL-MA-TUM	MN?	HARRIS 66 13
			ʾALIM							A-LI-IM	NOM	M, TIM III 43 5
			ʾALIM	AH						ḪA-LI-MA	FN	M+
			ʾALM		U	NI				AL-MU-NI		RA LXV 48 VIII 7
			ʾELM	AN	UM					EL-MA?-NU-UM		TA 1931, 538 I
			ʾELM	ATAN						EL-MA-TA-AN		M
	2		MUT				ʾALAM	I		MU-UT-ḪA-LA-MI		C+
ʾLN	1		ʾALUN		IJA					A-LU-NI-IA	FN	EDZARD,DER 91:13
			ʾALUN				HADD	U		ḪA-LU-UN-D-IM		M; JCS XIV 203
			ʾALUN				PI					
							JAM	U		ḪA-LU-UN-BI-JA-MU		M
			ʾALUN				PI					
							JAM	U		ḪA-LU-UM-BI-JA-MU		RA LXV 43 III 78
			ʾALUN				PI					
							JAM	U		ḪA-LU-BI-JA-MU		M
			ʾALUN		A		HADD	U		ḪA-LU-NA-D-IM		M
ʾLP	1	JI	ʾLAP				HADD	U		IḪ-LA-AP-A-DU		A.
		JI	ʾLAP				ṬALL			I-LA-AP-TI-IL		U
		JI	ʾLAP				ṬALL	U	HU	I-LA-AP-TA-LU-U$_2$		M
		JI	ʾLIP				HADD	A		IḪ-LI-BA-DA		TCL I 222 13
			ʾALIP	AH						ḪA-LI-BA	FN	XIII 1 VIII 37
			ʾALIP				ŠAMŠ			A-LI-IB-D-UTU		CT VIII 35B 24+
			ʾALUP		UM					A-LU-PU-UM		B+
			ʾALUP		I					A-LU-BI	GEN?	CT XLV 92 R. I 14
			ʾALUP	AT	UM					A-LU-PA-TUM	FN	CT XLVII 7 35, 7A 16'
			ʾALP	AN						AL-PA-AN		M+
			ʾELAP		I					E-LA-BI	FN	RA LXV 65 VI 62

ROOTS (Consonants only)

ʾLP	1		ʾILAP		UM					IL-LA-PU-UM		RA LXV 46 VI 1,10
			ʾILAP	AN						IL-LA-BA-AN		RA LXV 51 X 9
			ʾULP	AH						ḪU-UL-PA	FN	C
ʾLR	1		ʾILAR				TAʾ		A	I-LA-AR-TA-A		M
			ʾILAR				TAʾ		A	I-LA-AR-TA-ḪA		M
			ʾILAR				ŠUM			I-LA-AR-ŠUM		I
			ʾELUR		UM					EL-LU-RUM		CT VIII 43B21
			ʾILUR		U					I-LU-RU		B 22
			ʾILUR		IM					I-LU-RI-IM	GEN	B 22
			ʾILUR		A					I-LU-RA	GEN	A.
			ʾILUR	AT						IL-LU-RA-AT	FN	JACOBSEN CTC P. 49+
			ʾELUR	AT	UM					EL-LU-RA-TUM	MN?	WATERMAN 38 9
			ʾILUR	AT	UM					IL-LU-RA-TUM	FN	CT IV 26A 3+
			ʾILUR	AN						I-LU-RA-AN		A. 378 10
ʾLŠ	1		ʾALAŠ		I		ʾEL			A-LA-SI-E-EL		UCP X/3 3 17
	2	JA	WṢIʾ				ʾALAŠ		UM	U$_2$-ZI-A-LA-ŠUM		M
			RAPIʾ			TA	ʾLAŠ			RA-BI-TA-AḪ-LA-AŠ		BASOR 95 22
ʾM	1		ʾAM	T	UM					AM-TUM	FN	XIII 1 II 48
			ʾAM	T			ʾEL			GEME$_2$-E-IL		RIFTIN 44 10
			ʾAM	T			ʿAŠTAR	AH		AM-TI-AŠ-TA-RA	FN?	A. LATE
			ʾAM	T			BAʿL	AH		A-MA-AT-D-BA-A-LA	FN	BAGHD. MITT. II 72 5, 9+
			ʾAM	T			LABW		A	AM-TI-LA-BA	MN	TIM III 7 5
			ʾUM		U		ŠAKIM			U$_2$-MU-ŠA-KI-IM		M+
ʾMʾ	1	JA	ʾMIʾ				ʾIL			IA-AḪ-MI-DINGIR		PBS XI/2 P. 120 NO. 92
		JA	ʾMIʾ				ʾIL		A	IA-MI-I-LA		M
		JA	ʾMIʾ				ʾIL		A	JA-MI-I-LA		M
		ME	ʾMIʾ		IM					ME-MI-ḪI-IM	GEN	C
	2		MUT		I	JE	ʾMIʾ			MU-TI-E-MI-IḪ		M
ʾMW	1	JA	ʾMUW			HU				IA-AḪ-MU-U$_2$		B 26
		JA	ʾMUW				DAGAN			IA-AḪ-MU-D-DA-GAN	GN	B 26
ʾMG	1		ʾIMAG		U					I-MA-GU	FN	M
ʾML	2		ʾAB		I		ʾAMAL			A-BI-A-MA-AL		KISURRA 153 34
ʾMM	1		ʾIMM	AH						ḪI-IM-MA	FN	XIII 1 VI 75
			ʾIMM	AN						IM-MA-AN		M
			ʾUMM		IJA					UM?-MI-IA	FN	XIII 1 XIV 18
			ʾUMM		I		ḪAʾT		UM	UM-MI-ḪA-TUM	FN	M+
			ʾUMM		I		ʾIL		I	UM-MI-I$_3$-LI$_2$	FN	XIII 1 VIII 64
			ʾUMM		I		JIQR	AH		UM-MI-IQ-RA	FN	M+
			ʾUMM		I		ʾIŠḪAR	AH		UM-MI-IŠ-ḪA-RA	FN	XIII 1 V 74, A.+
			ʾUMM		I		ʾAŠIR	AH		UM-MI-A-ŠI-RA	FN	VAS XIII 73 6,13
			ʾUMM		I		JAT		UM	UM-MI-IA-TUM		UCP X/1 89 24
			ʾUMM		I		BAʿL	AH		UM-MI-BA-A-LA	FN	A. LATE
			ʾUMM		I		MARṢ	AT		UM-MI-MAR-ṢA-AT	FN	XIII 1 III 5
			ʾUMM		I		NAʿM		I	UM-MI-NA-MI	FN	A.
			ʾUMM		I		NAʿM		I	UM-MI-NA-AḪ-ME	FN	RA LXV 59 II 17
			ʾUMM		I		NAHR		U	UM-MI-NA-RU	FN	M
			ʾUMM		I		NAWAR			UM-MI-NA-WA-AR	FN	XIII 1 IV 73
			ʾUMM		I		ŠAMŠ		I	UM-MI-D-UTU-ŠI	FN	RA LXV 65 VII 38
			ʾUMM		I		ṬAJB	AH		UM-MI-ṬA$_3$-BA	FN	M+
			ʾUMM		I		ṬAJB	AH		UM-MI-ṬA$_3$-BA-NU	FN	RA LXV 64 VI 34
			ʾUMM		U		JARAḪ			U$_2$?-UM-MU-E-RA-AḪ		B 40+
			ʾUMM		UM		KA					
							ʾAB		IM	UM-MU-UM-KA-A-BI-IM	FN	M
			ʾUMM		UM		KA					
							ʾAB		I	UM-MU-UM-KA-A-BI	FN	XIII 1 VII 56
			ʾUMM		U		KA					
							ʾAB		I	UM-MU-KA-A-BI	FN	RA LXV 62 V 16
			ʾUMM		U		ŠARR	AH		UM-MU-ŠAR-RA	FN	IX 291 33
	2		ʾAJA				ʾUMM		I	A-IA-UM-MI	FN	RA LXV 59 II 27
			ʾIJA				ʾUMM		U	I-IA-AMA		MRS VI P. 328+
		JA	ʾḪIḎ				ʾUMM		I	IA-ḪI-DU-UM-ME	FN	RA LXV 65 VII 34
			ʾIL		A		ʾUMM		A	DINGIR-UM-MA		RA LXV 45 V 31
			ʾIL		I		ʾIMM	AH		I-LI$_2$-IM-MA	FN	C II 41 56, 44 57
			ʾALI				ʾUMM		I	A-LI-UM-MI	FN	M
			ʾANN		U		ʾUMM		I	AN-NU-UM-MI	FN	XIII 1 IV 48+
			ʾANN		U		ʾUMM		I	AN-NU-UN-UM-MI		M

ROOTS (Consonants only)

ʾMM	2			ʾIŠḪAR	AH				ʾUMM	I		D-IŠ-ḪA-RA-UM-MI	FN	XIII 1 II 47+
				ʾAŠR	AT	UM			ʾUMM	I		D-AŠ-RA-TUM-UM-MI	FN	TCL I P. 16+
				ʿAŠTAR					ʾUMM	I		EŠ$_4$-DAR-UM-MI	FN	XIII 1 II 38 +
				NAWḪ		I			ʾIMM	I		D-NA-ḪI-IM-MI		YOS II 112 11
		JI		ŚMAʿ					ʾAMUM	I		IŠ-ME-A-MU-MI	FN	M
				TABUB		U			ʾUMM	I		TA-BU-BU-UM-MI	FN	XIII 1 VI 57
ʾMN	1	MA		ʾMIN		UM						MA-AḪ-MI-NU-UM		CT XLVIII 89 REV.
				ʾAMAN		UM						A-MA-NU-UM		CT XLV 2 24,SEAL
				ʾAMAN		U						ḪA-MA-NU		X 151 4+, KISURRA 21 9
				ʾAMAN		U						ḪA-MA-NU	FN	RA LXV 66 VIII 6
				ʾAMAN	AN	UM						A-MA-NA-NU-UM		B 42+
				ʾAMAN	AN	IM						A-MA-NA-NIM	GEN	B 43
				ʾAMAN					TAʾ	I		AM-MA-AN-TA-ḪI		M
				ʾAMIN		UM						A-MI-NU-UM		B 12+
				ʾAMIN		UM						A-MI-NUM		M
				ʾAMIN		U						A-MI-NU		JNES XIII 210+ LATE
				ʾAMIN	AH							A-MI-NA	FN	RA LXV 64 V 76
				ʾAMIN	AH							AM-MI-IN-NA	FN	RA LXV 64 V 64
				ʾAMIN	AT	UM						A-MI-NA-TUM		B 12
				ʾAMIN	AN	UM						A-MI-NA-NU-UM		B 43
				ʾAMIN		I			ʾANN	U		A-MI-NI-AN-NU		M
	2			JAT		I			ʾAMAN			IA-TI-ḪA-MA-AN	FN	RA LXV 42 II 55
				ḪATAʾ					ʾUMAN	UM		ḪA-TA-UM-MA-NU-UM		RA VIII 74 19
ʾMR	1	JA		ʾMAR	AH							IA-MA-RA	FN	XIII 1 XIV 26
				ʾAMAR		U						AM-MA-RU		M
				ʾAMAR					HADD	U		AM-MA-RA-DU		A.+
				ʾAMAR		A			HADD	U		AM-MA-RA-A-DU		A.
				ʾAMAR					ʾIL	I		A-MAR-I$_3$-LI$_2$		MAOG IV 2 3 HANA
		ʾA		ʾMUR		U	HU					A-MU-RU-U$_2$		PBS VIII/1 98 9
		JA		ʾMUR		IM						IA-MU-RI-IM	GEN	B 28+
		JA		ʾMUR					HADD	U		IA-MU-UR-AD-DU		M
		JA		ʾMUR					JARAḪ			IA-MUR-D-EN-ZU		UET V 583 19
		TA		ʾMUR								TA-MU-UR	FN	M
				ʾAMUR					ŠA					
									DAGAN			A-MUR-ŠA-D-DA-GAN		TCL I 237 31 HANA
				ʾAMUR					ŠA					
									ŚAMŚ			A-MUR-ŠA-D-UTU		A.
		TA	T	ʾAMAR								TA-AḪ-TA-MAR		M
			T	ʾAMR		UM						A-TAM-RUM		M+
			T	ʾAMR		UM						A-TA-AM-RU-UM		M+
			T	ʾAMR		IM						A-TAM-RI-IM	GEN	M+
			T	ʾAMR		IM						A-TA-AM-RI-IM	GEN	M+
			T	ʾAMR		AM						A-TAM-RA-AM	ACC	M+
			T	ʾAMR	AT	UM						A-TAM-RA-TUM	FN	M
			T	ʾAMR	AH							A-TAM-RA	FN	M+
			T	ʾAMR		I			ʾIL			A-TAM-RI-DINGIR		M+
				ʾAMIR		UM						A-MI-RU-UM		B 13
				ʾAMIR		UM						A-MI-RUM		M
				ʾAMIR	AT	UM						A-MI-RA-TUM	FN	M
				ʾAMIR		AJA						A-MI-RA-IA	FN	C
				ʾAMIR					....			A-ME-IR-[....]		M
				ʾAMIR		A			ʾAB	UM		A-MI-RA-A-BU-UM		RA LXV 55 XIII 5
				ʾAMIR					KAKK	A		A-ME-IR-KA-AK-KA		XIII 1 V 20
				ʾAMR	AT	UM						AM-RA-TUM		YOS XIII 513:4
				ʾAMR					ʿAD	UM		AM-RA-DU-UM		M
				ʾIMIR		I						IM-ME-RI		A.+
				ʾIMIR		UM						I-MI-RU-UM		UCP X/3 2 21
				ʾIMIR	IN	UM						I-ME-RI-NU-UM		TA 30 615 12
				ʾIMIR					ʾIL	I		IM-ME-IR-I$_3$-LI$_2$		UNPUBL.
				ʾIMIR					ḪUNN	A		IM-ME-IR?-ḪU-UN-NA		A. 43 9
	2			ʿADN		A		ʾA	ʾMUR			ḪA-AD-NA-AM?-MU-UR		X 75 18
				ʾANN		U			ʾAMR	I	JA	AN-NU-AM-RI-IA	FN	RA LXV 61 IV 47
				LA				ʾA	ʾMAR	UM		LA-MA-RUM		BM 80644
				LA				ʾA	ʾMUR	IM		LA-A-MU-RI-IM	GEN	M
				LA				ʾA	ʾMUR	A		LA-MU-RA		B 33+
				NUWR		U			ʾAMAR			NU-RU-A-MA-AR		HARRIS 68 19

ROOTS (Consonants only)

ʾMT	1	ʾAMAT	AN								A-MA-TA-AN		M+
		ʾAMAT	AN								ḪA-MA-TA-AN		RA LXV 43 III 43
ʾN	1	ʾAN		I	Š		ḪURB		I		A-NI-IŠ-ḪU-UR-BI		M+
		ʾAN		I	Š		KIBAL				A-NI-IŠ-KI-BA-AL		RA LXV 53 XI 37+
		ʾAN		I	Š		KIBEL				A-NI-IŠ-KI-BE-EL		TCL XX 191 33 CAPP.
		ʾAN		A	Š		KIBAL				[A]?-NA-AŠ-KI-BA-AL		VIII 86 23
		ʾANA		I	Š						A-NA-IŠ		RA LXV 52 X 79
		ʾANA					ḪIJJ		A		A-NA-ḪI?-A?		RUTTEN 20:16
		ʾANA					HADD		U		A-NA-D-IM		MRS XII NO. 24, 6, UGARIT
		ʾANA					ʾIL		I				
							MA				A-NA-I-LIM-MA		A.
		ʾANA					ʿAN		A		A-NA-A-NA		A. 36:11
		ʾANA					ḪANN		I		A-NA-AḪ-ḪA-AN-NI	FN	XIII 1 V 29
		ʾANA					BAʿL		U		A-NA-BA-LU	MN?	CT XLVIII 86 REV
		ʾANA					BAʿL		U		A-NA-BA-LU	FN	M
		ʾANA					DAGAN				A-NA-D-LA-GAN		M
		ʾANA					KIBAL		I		A-NA?-KI-BA-[L]I	FN	M
		ʾANA					MA						
							ʾIL				A-NA-MA-DINGIR		A 29366:9
		ʾANA					RAḪAB		U		A-NA-RA-A-BU		M+
		ʾEN		IJA							E-NI-IA		M+
		ʾEN		I	Š		ʾAG		UM		E-NI-IŠ-A-GU-UM		M+
ʾNB	1	ʾUNAB		UM							ḪU-NA-BU-UM		KISURRA 17 5
		ʾUNAB		UM							U$_2$-NA-BU-UM		TIM III 42 13
		ʾUNAB		I							ḪU-NA-BI	NOM	GAUTIER 11 8, R. 2
		ʾUNAB	AH								ḪU-NA-BA	FN	XIII 1 VI 50
		ʾUNAB	AT	UM							U$_2$-NA-BA-TUM	FN	TIM III 26 7
		ʾUNAB	AT	UM							ḪU-NA-BA-TUM	FN	WATERMAN 54 2, 3+
		ʾUNUB		UM							ḪU-NU-BU-UM		GORDON 39 5, 10
		ʾUNUB		UM							U$_2$-NU-BU-UM		EDZARD, DER 74:11+
		ʾUNUB		UM							UN-NU-BU-UM		EDZARD, DER 68 III 10
		ʾUNUB		IM							ḪU-NU-BI-I[M]	GEN	M
		ʾUNUB	AT	UM							ḪU-NU-PA-TUM	FN?	BM 17060 35
		ʾUNUB	AT	UM							UN-NU-BA-TUM	FN	WATERMAN 24 R. 24
		ʾUNUB	AT	UM							ḪU-NU-BA-TUM	FN	EDZARD, DER 134:4
		ʾUNUB	T	UM							UN-NU-UB-TUM	FN	EDZARD, DER 33:11+
		ʾUNUB	T	UM							ḪU-NU-UP-TUM	FN	EDZARD, DER 99:8
ʾNDL	2	ʿAMM		I			ʾANDUL		I		ḪA-AM-MI-AN-DUL$_3$-LI$_2$		M+
		ʿAŠTAR					ʾANDUL		I		EŠ$_4$-DAR-AN-DUL$_3$-LI$_2$	FN	M
ʾNK	1	ʾANAKU					ʾIL		AM				
							MA				A-NA-KU-DINGIR-LAM-MA		XIII 1 II 29
		ʾANAKU					ʾIL		A				
							MA				A-NA-KU-I-LA-MA		SIMMONS 46 7+
ʾNLL	2	ŠUM		I			ʾENLIL				SU-ME-D-EN-LIL$_2$		KISURRA 197A 12
ʾNN	1	ʾANN		U			ʾAJAM				AN-NU-[Ḫ]A-A-AM	FN	XIII 1 II 62
		ʾANN		U			ʾUMM		I		AN-NU-UM-MI	FN	XIII 1 IV 48+
		ʾANN		U			ʾUMM		I		AN-NU-UN-UM-MI		M
		ʾANN		U			ʾAMR		I	JA	AN-NU-AM-RI-IA	FN	RA LXV 61 IV 47
		ʾANN		U			ḪANN		I		AN-NU-ḪA-AN-NI	FN	M+
		ʾANN		U			JAPʿ	AH			AN-NU-IA-AP-ḪA	FN	XIII 1 IV 3+
		ʾANN		U			JIPʿ	AH			AN-NU-IP-ḪA	FN	XIII 1 VIII 29
		ʾANN		U			ʾAŚJ	AH			AN-NU-A-SI-IA	FN	XIII 1 IV 41+
		ʾANN		U			JIŠʿ	AH			AN-NU-IŠ-ḪA	FN	XIII 1 V 46+
		ʾANN		U			ʾAŠR		I		AN-NU-AŠ-RI	FN	M+
		ʾANN		U		T	HILAL				AN-NU-ḪI-IT-LA-AL	FN	RA LXV 60 III 18
		ʾANN		U			JATR	AH			AN-NU-IA-AT-RA	FN	XIII 1 VI 53+
		ʾANN		U			ḪAṢN		I		AN-NU-ḪA-AṢ-NI	FN	M+
		ʾANN		U			BAWŠ	T	I		AN-NU-BA-AŠ-TI	FN	RA LXV 65 VII 27
		ʾANN		U			DAMQ	AH			AN-NU-DAM-QA	FN	XIII 1 X 51
		ʾANN		U			DUNN		I		AN-NU-DU-UN-NI	FN	XIII 1 III 37
		ʾANN		U			DUNN		I		AN-NU-DU-NI	FN	RA LXV 65 VII 15
		ʾANN		U			GAMIL	T	I		AN-NU-GA-ME-IL-TI	FN	RA LXV 66 VII 66
		ʾANN		U			KUʾM				AN-NU-KUM	FN	XIII 1 VI 8
		ʾANN		U			KAMA						
							ʾAB		I		AN-NU-KA-MA-BI		CT XLV 116 36
		ʾANN		U			LAMAS		I		AN-NU-LA-MA-ZI	FN	M+

ROOTS (Consonants only)

ʾNN	1		ʾANN		U		LAMAS		I		AN-NU-D-LAMA	FN	XIII 1 VII 8+
			ʾANN		U		LAMAS	IT	UM		AN-NU-LA-MA-ZI-TUM	FN	RA LXV 59 II 13
			ʾANN		U		MAʾN		A		AN?-NU-MA-NA	FN	M
			ʾANN		U		NIWR		I		AN-NU-NI-RI	FN	M
			ʾANN		U		NABIʾ				AN-NU-NA-BI-IḪ	FN	RA LXV 62 V 24
			ʾANN		U		NABIT		I		AN-NU-NA-BI-TI		XIII 1 VI 61
			ʾANN		U		PUṬR		I		AN-NU-PU-UṬ-RI	FN	RA LXV 58 I 19+
			ʾANN		U		QUDM		I		AN-NU-KU-UD-MI	FN	XIII 1 VIII 77
			ʾANN		U		RAḪM		I		AN-NU-RA-AḪ-MI	FN	XIII 1 V 11+
			ʾANN		U		RIMŠ		I		AN-NU-RI-IM-ŠI	FN	M+
			ʾANN		U		ŚIMḪ		I		[A]N-NU-ŠI-IM-ḪI		XIII 1 XIV 24
			ʾANN		U		ŚATAM				AN?-NU?-ŠA-TAM	FN	XIII 1 IV 46
			ʾANN		U	TA	ḪNUN				AN-NU-TA-AḪ-NU-UN	FN	RA LXV 61 IV 15+
			ʾANN		U	TA	LʾIJ				AN-NU-TA-AL-E	FN	M+
			ʾANN		U	TA	RḪAM				AN-NU-TA-AR-AM	FN	M+
			ʾANN		U	TA	RBIJ				AN-NU-TAR-BI	FN	XIII 1 XI 47
			ʾANN		U	TA	ŠMAʿ				AN-NU-TA-AŠ$_2$-MA-AḪ	FN	M
			ʾANN		U		TIWR		I		AN-NU-TI-RI	FN	M+
			ʾANN		U		TABB		I		AN-NU-TAB-BI	FN	XIII 1 III 36+
			ʾANN		U		TUKUL	T	I		AN-NU-TU-KU-UL-[TI]	FN	M+
			ʾANN		U		TUKUL	T	I		AN-NU-TU-GUL-TI	FN	XIII 1 X 3
			ʾANN		U		TILL	AT	I		AN-NU-TIL-LA-TI	FN	XIII 1 X 2
			ʾANN		U		ṬAJB				AN-NU-DUG$_3$		M+
	2		ʾAB		A		ʾANN		U		A-BA-AN-NU		M
			ʾAB		I		ʾANN		IM		A-BI-AN-NIM	GEN	M
			ʾAMIN		I		ʾANN		U		A-MI-NI-AN-NU		M
			NABIʾ				ʾANN		U		NA-BI-AN-NU		M
		JA	NTIN				ʾANN		I	Š	[IA-AN]-TI-IN-A-NI-IŠ		VII 180 8'
		JI	NDIN				ʾANN		U		I-DIN-AN-NU		M+
		JI	NDIN				ʾANN		UM		I-DIN-AN-NU-UM		M+
		JI	NDIN				ʾANN		U		I-DI-AN-NU		RA LXV 51 IX 31
			RAWḪ		A		ʾANN		UM		RA-ḪA-AN-NU-UM		M
			ṢILL				ʾANN		U		MI-NI-AN-NU		M
			ZAʾZ		I		ʾANN		U		ZA-ZI-AN-NU		B 41+
ʾNP	1	MA	ʾNIP		UM						MA-NI-PU-UM		SIMMONS 119 10 S
		MA	ʾNUP		UM						[MA]-AḪ-NU-KA-UM		VAS IX 192 18
		MA	ʾNUP		U						MA-AḪ-NU-KA		VAS IX 193 18
		MA	ʾNUP		U						MA-AḪ-NU-PU		M
		MA	ʾNUP				ʾIL				MA-AḪ-NU-UP-DINGIR		B 33+, M+
		MA	ʾNUP				ʾIL				MA-AḪ-NU-BI-DINGIR		B 33+, M+
		MA	ʾNUP				ʾIL		I		MA-AḪ-NU-UP-I$_3$-LI$_2$		B 33+
ʾNT	1		ʾANT	AN	UM						AN-TA-NU-UM		TA 1930, 698
ʾNTL	2		BIN		A		ʾANTEL				BI-NA-AN-TE-EL		TLB I 220 26, M+
			ŚUM		I		ʾENTIL				SU-ME-EN-TI-[IL]?		B 38
			ŚUM		U		ʾENTIL				SU-MU-EN-TE-IL		B 39
			ŚUM		U		ʾENTIL				SU-MU-EN-TI-[IL]?		KISURRA 95 15
ʾNTR	1		ʾANTAR		UM						AN-TA-RU-UM		CT VIII 47 B 21
ʾNZ	1		ʾANAZ		UM						AN-NA-ZUM		B 13+
			ʾINZ	AH							IN-ZA	FN	XIII 1 XII 7
			ʾANZ	AN	UM						AN-ZA-NU-UM		B 43
ʾP	1		ʾAP	AN	UM						A-PA-NU-UM		B 43+
			ʾAP		I		ʾAŠAL				A-PI-A-ŠAL		JNES XIII 212F.+ LATE
			ʾUP				ʾIL		A		UP-I-LA		BULL. ACAD. BELG. 1974 227
	2		ʾIL		I		ʾAP		I	JA	I$_3$-LI$_2$-A-PI?-A		TIM III 4 14
			ʾALI				ʾUP		UM		A-LI$_2$-U$_2$-PU-UM		KISURRA 117 5
			ḎIMR		U		ʾUP		I		ZI-IM-RU-UḪ$_2$-KI		TCL VII 23 14 21+
			ŚUM		U		ʾUP		I		SU-MU-UḪ$_2$-KI		JCS XI 23 NO. 10 14+
		JA	ŚMAʿ				ʾUP		I		IA-AŠ$_2$-MA-ḪU-PI		BULL. ACAD. BELG. 1974 228
ʾPK	1		ʾAPK	AT	UM						AP-KA-TUM	MN	UCP X/1 4 5
			ʾAPK	AN	UM						AP-KA-NU-UM		SIMMONS 66 28
			ʾAPK	ATAN							AP-KA-TA-AN		M+
ʾPP	1		ʾAPP	AT	UM						AP-PA-TUM	FN	A.+
			ʾAPP	ATAN							AP-PA-TA-AN		RA LXV 43 IV 18
ʾPQ	1		ʾIPQ	AT	UM						IP-GA-TUM	MN	CT XLV 23 R. 13
			ʾIPQ	AT	UM						IP-QA-TUM	MN	M+
			ʾIPQ	AT	IM						IP-QA-TIM	MN GEN	M+

ROOTS (Consonants only)

ʾPQ	1		ʾIPQ	AT	IM					IP-QA-TI-IM	MN? GEN	M
			ʾIPQ				JARAḪ			I-BI-IQ-D-[EN]-ZU		M
			ʾIPQ				RIʿAJ		HU	I-BI-IQ-RI-E-U_2		U
			ʾIPQ		U	JI	TWUR					
							MEʾR			IP-KU-D-I-DUR-ME-ER		M
			ʾIPQ		U		NAZI			IP-KU-D-NA-AZ-ZI		M
			ʾIPQ		U		ŠAL	A		IP-KU-D-ŠA-LA		M
	2		JAʾAR				ʾIPQ			IA-AR-I-BI-IQ		M
ʾPR	1		ʾAPR	AN						AP-RA-AN		A. LATE
			ʾAPR		IJA					AP-RI-A		A.
ʾQD	1	JA	ʾQUD		UM					IA-KU-DU-UM		CT VIII 44A 28, UET V 523
		JA	ʾQUD		UM					IA-AḪ-KU-DU-UM		CT XXXIII 29 14
		JA	ʾQUD		UM					IA-KU-DU-UM-KI	GN	BRM IV 53 III 47+
		JA	ʾQUD		U					IA-KU-DU-KI	GN	UCP IX/4 5 1
		JA	ʾQUD	AN	IM					IA-GU-DA-NIM	GEN	BM 16823A 1
ʾR	2		ʾAB		I		ʾIR	A		AD-I-RA	FN	A.
			ʾADAM			TA	ʾAR	U		ḪA-DAM-TA-A-RU		WATERMAN 45 EDGE
			ḪATAʾ		A		ʾAR	UM		ḪA-TA-A-A-RUM?		CT XXIX 8A 1
ʾRḪ	1		ʾARḪ		UM					AR-ḪU-UM	FN	XIII 1 VIII 23
			ʾARḪ	AN	UM					AR-ḪA-NU-UM		BM 92657+
			ʾARḪ		I		ŠAMŠ	I		AR-ḪI-D-UTU-ŠI	FN	XIII 1 XIII 2
			ʾARUḪ		UM					A-RU-ḪU-UM		B 13
			ʾIRAḪ		I					I-RA-ḪI		RA LXV 47 VII 49+
	2		DIMR		U		ʾARAḪ			ZI-IM-RU-A-RA-AḪ		BM 17045A 13
			DIMR		U		ʾARAḪ			ZI-IM-RU-ḪA-RA-AḪ		BM 17045 13
			MUT				ʾARḪ	U		MU-UT-AR-ḪU		M
ʾRWJ	1		ʾARWIJ		UM					AR-WI-UM		B 13+, M+
			ʾARWIJ		UM					AR-WI-U_2-UM		B 13+, M
			ʾARWIJ		U					AR-WI-U_2		B 13
			ʾARWIJ		UM					AR-BI_2-UM		ITT II/1 P 48, 933, U
			ʾARWIJ		IM					AR-WI-IM	GEN	TIM V 14 23, M
			ʾARWIJ		EM					AR-WI-E-[EM]	GEN	I 30 10
			ʾARWIJ	T	UM					AR-WI-TUM	FN	KISURRA 134 3, M+
			ʾARWIJ	T	UM					AR-BI-TUM		LEGRAIN, TRU 41+, U
			ʾARWIJ	T	UM					AR-BI_2-TUM		TCL V 6039 REV 17, U
			ʾARWIJ	ATANUM						AR-WI-TA-NU-UM		B 43
ʾRK	1		ʾARK	ATANUM						AR-GA-TA-NU-UM		KISURRA 141 9
			ʾARK	ATANUM						AR-GA-DA-NU-UM		KISURRA 1A 15+
			ʾURK	UTANIM						UR-KU-TA-NIM	GEN	CT VIII 20B 10
ʾRL	1		ʾURL	IJ	UM					UR-LI-U_2-UM		M
ʾRM	1		ʾARAM		U					A-RA-MU		M
			ʾARAM		A					A-RA-MA		A.+
			ʾARAM		U					A-RA-AM-MU		A.+
			ʾARAM				MAṬAR	A		A-RA-AM-MA-DA-RA		BM 80328 1
			ʾARUM		A					A-RU-MA	GEN	RA VIII 74 16
ʾRN	1		ʾURAN		UM					U_2-RA-NU-UM		M+
			ʾURAN		UM					U_3-RA-NU-UM		TA 1931, 538 IV
			ʾURAN	AT	UM					U_2-RA-NA-TUM	FN	HARRIS 83 1
ʾRNB	1		ʾARNAB		UM					AR-NA-BU-UM	FN	M+
			ʾARNAB	AT	UM					AR-NA-BA-TUM	FN	CT VIII 43C 22+, XIII 1 X 39
			ʾARNAB	AT	IM					AR-NA-BA-TIM	FN? GEN	MEISSNER 18 3
ʾRPḪ	2		MUT		U		ʾARAPḪ	IM		MU-TU-AR-RA-AP-ḪI-IM		C+
ʾRR	1		ʾIRR		A		ʾAB	I		IR_3-RA-A-BI		M
			ʾIRR		I		HADD	U		I-RI-A-DU		A.+
			ʾIRR		I		HADD	U		IR-RI-A-DU		A.
			ʾIRR		I		MAʾT	U		I-RI-MA-TU		A.
		JA	ʾRUR							IA-AḪ-RU-UR-KI	GN	M
		JA	ʾRUR		UM					IA-RU-RUM-KI	GN	YOS XII
		JA	ʾRUR		UM					IA-ḪU-UR-RU-UM-KI	GN	M
		JA	ʾRUR		UM					IA-AḪ-RU-RU-UM	GN	B 26+
		JA	ʾRUR		UM					IA-AḪ-RU-RUM	GN	B 26+
		JA	ʾRUR		UM					IA-AḪ-RU-RUM		BM 80328 10
		JA	ʾRUR		A					IA-AḪ-RU-RA-KI	GN	B 26, M
		JA	ʾRUR		A					IA-ḪU-UR-RA-KI	GN	M+
		JA	ʾRUR	IJ	I					IA-AḪ-RU-RI-I-KI	GN	M
			ʾURR	AN						UR-RA-AN		RA LXV 53 XI 15

ROOTS (Consonants only)

ʾRR	2		ʾAJ		A		ʾARR		I		D-A-A-AR-RI	FN	M
			ʾAWN	AN		JA	ʾRUR				AM-NA-AN-IA-AḪ-RU-UR TRIBE		BAGHD. MITT. II 56 I 12+
			ʾIL		A		ʾIRR		A		[I-L]A?-IR$_3$-RA		RA LXV 47 VII 18
			ḪIMD				ʾIRR		A		ḪI-ME-ID-IR$_3$-RA		M+
			ḪIMD				ʾIRR		A		ḪI-MI-ID-D-IR$_3$-RA		M+
		JA	ḪṢIN				ʾIRR		A		IA-AḪ-ZI-IN-IR$_3$-RA		M
		JA	RḪIB				ʾIRR		A		IA-AR-IB-D-IR$_3$-RA		M
		JA	RḪIB				ʾIRR		A		IA-AR-I-[IB]-IR$_3$-RA		M
		JA	ŠJIM				ʾIRR		A		IA-ŠI-IM-IR$_3$-RA		M
		JI	ŠBIJ				ʾIRR		A		IŠ-BI-D-IR$_3$-RA		M+
		JI	ŠBIJ				ʾIRR		A		IŠ-BI-IR$_3$-RA		M+
			ŠUM		U	JA	ʾRUR		A		[SU-MU-I]A-AḪ-RU-RA		B 39
ʾRŠ	1	JA	ʾRUŠ								IA-AḪ-RU-UŠ		RA LXV 55 XIII 52
			ʾARAŠ		UM						ḪA-RA-ŠUM		M
			ʾARIŠ	AN							ḪA-RI-ŠA-AN		M
			ʾARUŠ		UM						A-RU-SU-UM		M, JEAN TELL SIFR 72A 3+
			ʾARUŠ		U						A-RU-SU		JEAN TELL SIFR 72 5+
			ʾARUŠ				ʾEL		UM		A-RU-UŠ-E-LUM		UCP X/3 2 25
			ʾARUŠ		I		ʾIL				A-RU-SI-DINGIR		A 7459, M
			ʾARUŠ				PI						
							ʾIL				A-RU-UŠ-BI-DINGIR		M, RA XLI 45 4' HANA
			ʾARŠ		UM		MALIK				ḪA-AR?-ŠUM?-MA-LIK		M
			ʾIRŠ				MA						
							ʾAB		I		I-RI-IŠ-MA-A-BI		A.
			ʾIRŠ				MA						
							ʾAB		I		I-RI-IŠ-MA-BI		A.
			ʾIRŠ		U		MA						
							ʾAB		I		IR-ŠU-MA-BI		A.
			ʾURAŠ		IJA						U$_2$-RA-SI-IA		M
ʾRŠM	1		ʾURŠAM	AN	AM						UR-SA-MA-NAM	ACC	M+
ʾRŠP	2		ʿABD				ʾIRŠAP		A		ḪA-AB-DU-IR?-ŠA-PA?		M
ʾSN	1		ʾASIN		IM						A-ZI-NIM	GEN	XIII 13 13+
			ʾASIN		I						A-SI-NI		APN P. 31 LATE
			ʾASIN		AM						A-ZI-NA-A[M]	ACC	XIV 33:7
			ʾASIN		U	HU					A-ZI-NU-U$_2$		M
			ʾASIN		U	HU					A-SI-NU-U		APN P. 31 LATE
			ʾASUN	AN							A-ZU-NA-AN		RA LXV 48 VIII 29
ʾŠʾ	1	JA	ʾŠUʾ				HADD		U		IA-SU-D-IM		TCL I 238 4 HANA+
ʾŠJ	1		ʾAŠJ		UM						A-SU-UM		M
			ʾAŠJ		IM						A-SI-IM	GEN	C
	2		ʾIL		I		ʾAŠIJ	AH			I$_3$-LI$_2$-A-SI-IA	FN	XIII 1 VII 55
			ʾANN		U		ʾAŠJ	AH			AN-NU-A-SI-IA	FN	XIII 1 IV 41+
			ʾIŠḪAR	AH			ʾAŠJ	AH			D-IŠ-ḪA-RA-A-SI-IA	FN	XIII 1 XI 43
			ʿAŠTAR				ʾAŠJ	AH			EŠ$_4$-DAR-A-SI-IA	FN	XIII 1 IX 3+
			ʿAŠTAR				ʾAŠJ	AH			EŠ$_4$-DAR-A-ZU-IA	FN	M
			KAKK		A		ʾAŠJ	AH			KA-AK-KA-A-SI-IA	FN	XIII 1 VI 11
ʾŠD	1		ʾAŠD		U						D-AŠ-DU		RT XIX 48 SEAL
			ʾAŠD		UM						AŠ-DU-UM		VAS VIII 60 26
			ʾAŠD	AH							ḪA-AŠ-DA	FN	RA LXV 58 I 62
			ʾAŠD		IJA						AŠ-DI-IA		BIN VII 32 4
			ʾAŠD		A		ʾAḪ		I		AŠ-DA-A-ḪI		VAS XVI 44 3
			ʾAŠD		I		JAŠAR				AŠ$_2$-DI-E-SA-AR		XIII 1 XI 35
			ʾAŠD		I		JATAR				AŠ-DI-E-TAR		M
			ʾAŠD		I		DAWD		UM		AŠ$_2$-DI?-DA-DU-UM		EDZARD, DER 60:11
			ʾAŠD		I	JE	JŠUʿ				AŠ$_2$-DI-E-ŠU-UḪ		M
			ʾAŠD		I		KIʾR		U		AŠ-DI-KI-E-RU		BM 92654 A
			ʾAŠD		I		KIʾR		U		AŠ-DI-KI-RU		BM 92654
			ʾAŠD		I		LUMM		A		AŠ-DI-LU-MA		UCP X/3 2 31
			ʾAŠD		I		MAʾK		U	HU	AŠ$_2$-DI-MA-KU-U$_2$		VAS IX 172 30
			ʾAŠD		I		NIʿM				AŠ$_2$-DI-NI-ḪI-IM		M+
			ʾAŠD		I		RAWM				AŠ-DI-RA-AM		RA LXV 55 XIII 42
			ʾAŠD		I	TA	QWIM				AŠ$_2$-DI-TA-KI-IM		M+
			ʾAŠD		UM		ʾAB		I		AŠ$_2$-DU-UM-A-BI		BE VI/1 1 7+
			ʾAŠD		UM		ʾAB		I		D-AŠ-DU-UM-A-BI		UET V 483 4
			ʾAŠD		UM		LA						
							ʾAB		UM		AŠ-DU-UM-LA-A-BU-UM		SUMER V 142

ʾŠD	1		ʾAŠD		UM			LA					
								ʾAB	UM		AŠ$_2$-DU-UM-LA-A-BU-UM		SUMER V 142+
			ʾAŠD		UM			PI					
								JAD	IM		AŠ-DU-UM-BI-IA-DI-IM		RA LXV 55 XIII 44
			ʾAŠD		U			QAWM	U		AŠ-DU-GA-MU		CT XLV 77 R. 10, 14+
			ʾAŠD		U			QAWM	UM		AŠ$_2$-DU-GA-MU-UM		TCL I 130 8+
			ʾAŠD		U			RAPIʾ			AŠ$_2$-DU-RA-BI		C+
			ʾAŠD		U	NA	JA	RWIM			[AŠ$_2$-D]U-NI-A-RI-IM		CT XXXVI 4 1
			ʾAŠD		U	NA	JE	RWIM			AŠ$_2$-DU-NI-E-RI-IM		RA VIII 65 1
		JA	ʾŠUD		UM						IA-SU?-DU-UM		CT II 28 19
		JA	ʾŠUD					PI					
								ʾEL			IA-SU-UD-PI-EL		SIMMONS 46 31
			ʾAŠUD		UM						ḪA-SU-DU-UM		A 7660 2
	2		ʾAḪ		I			ʾAŠD			A-ḪI-SA-AD		B 12+
			ʾAḪ		I			ʾAŠD			A-ḪI-A-SA-AD		B 12
			ʾAḪ		I			ʾAŠD			A-ḪA-SA-AD		UET V 539 II 19
			ʾAB		I			ʾAŠD			A-BI-A-SA-AD		B 10+
			ʾAB		I			ʾAŠD			A-BI-SA-AD		B 10+
			JARAḪ					ʾAŠD	UM		D-EN-ZU-AŠ-DU-UM		WALTERS, WL 114:2
			JATAR					ʾAŠD	I		IA-TAR-AŠ-DI		M
		JA	KWUN					ʾAŠD	UM		IA-KU-UN-AŠ-DU-UM		B 27
			LA				ʾA	ʾŠUD	I				
								ʾIL			LA-AḪ-SU-DI-DINGIR		XIII 4 14
			MUT					ʾAŠD	IM		MU-UT-AŠ-DI-IM		M
			MUT		U			ʾAŠD	I		[MU]-TU-AŠ-DI		VIII 17 13'
			NAʿM		I			ʾAŠD	U		NA-AḪ-ME-AS-DU	FN	RA LXV 60 III 2
		JI	NṢUR					ʾAŠD	UM		I-ZUR-AŠ-DU-UM		A 7685 5
		JI	NṢUR					ʾAŠD	UM		I-ZUR-A-AŠ-DU-UM		CT II 42 25
		JI	TWUR					ʾAŠD	UM		I-DUR-A-AŠ-DU-UM		B 23
		JI	TWUR					ʾAŠD	UM		I-DUR-AŠ-DUM		B 23
		JI	TWUR					ʾAŠD	UM		I-DUR-AŠ-DU-UM		B 23+
		JI	TWUR					ʾAŠD	UM		I-DUR-AŠ$_2$-DU-UM		M+
		JI	TWUR					ʾAŠD	U		I-DUR-AŠ-DU		B 23+
		JI	TWUR					ʾAŠD	U		I-DUR-AŠ$_2$-DU		VAS IX 172 5, M+
		JI	TWUR					ʾAŠD	U	HU	I-DUR-AŠ-DU-U$_2$		SIMMONS 90 4
		JI	TWUR					ʾAŠD	U	HU	I-DUR-AŠ$_2$-DU-U$_2$		M
	3		LI				JI	JṢIʾ					
								ʾAŠD	UM		LI-ZI-AŠ-DU-UM		VAS XIII 104 R. II 24
ʾŠK	1		ʾUŠK	ATANUM							UŠ-KA-TA-NU-UM		XIII 92 11
			ʾUŠK	ATANIM							UŠ-KA-TA-NIM	MN GEN	XIII 61 5+
ʾŠL	1		ʾAŠUL		U						A-SU-LU		TA 30 36 3
			ʾIŠAL		I						I-SA-LI	GEN	CT VIII 44A+
			ʾIŠUL		UM						ḪI-SU-LUM		SIMMONS 79 4'
			ʾUŠAL		UM						U$_2$-SA?-LUM		WATERMAN 21 R. 10
			ʾUŠAL		UM						ḪU-ŠA-LUM		HARRIS 105 5
	2		ʾAP		I			ʾAŠAL			A-PI-A-ŠAL		JNES XIII 212F.+ LATE
			BEʿL		I			ʾUŠIL	I		BE-LI$_2$-U$_2$-SI-LI	FN	RA LXV 56 I 10
ʾŠM	1		ʾAŠM	AN							AŠ-MA-AN		BM 81174 11
			ʾAŠM	AN	UM						ḪA-AŠ-MA-NU-UM		U
			ʾAŠM	AN	I						ḪA-AŠ-MA-NI	GEN	B 44
			ʾAŠM	AT							AŠ-MA-AT	MN	M+
			ʾAŠM	ATEN							AŠ$_2$-MA-TI-EN		M
			ʾAŠM		A			HADD	U		AŠ-MA-DU		BM 80328 14
			ʾAŠM		A			HADD	U		AŠ-MA-A-DU		A.+
			ʾIŠIM	AN	AJA						I-SI-MA-NA-A		B 22
			ʾUŠM		A			ʿAMM	I		UŠ-MA-AM-MI		CT XXXIII 46A 4
ʾŠN	1		ʾAŠIN		UM						A-SI-NU-UM		B 14+
			ʾAŠIN		U						A-SI-NU		B 14
			ʾIŠN	AN	U						IŠ-NA-NU		B 45+
ʾŠQD	1		ʾAŠQUD		UM						AŠ-KU-DU-UM		KISURRA 205 7, M+
			ʾAŠQUD		UM						AŠ$_2$-KU-DU-UM		X 59 8
			ʾAŠQUD		UM						AŠ-KU-TU-UM		KISURRA 88 1, 8+
			ʾAŠQUD		U						AŠ-KU-DU		M
			ʾAŠQUD		IM						AŠ-KU-DI-IM	GEN	M+
			ʾAŠQUD		I						AŠ-KU-DI	GEN	M+
			ʾAŠQUD	AN							AŠ-KU-DA-AN		M

ROOTS (Consonants only)

ʾŚQD	1		ʾAŚQUD	AN							ḪA-AŠ-KU-DA-AN		M
			ʾAŚQUD	AN	UM						AŠ-KU-DA-NU-UM		CT XLVIII 86 REV 10+
			ʾAŚQUD	AN	AM						AŠ-KU-DA-NA-AM	ACC	B 43
ʾŚR	1		ʾAŚIR		UM						A-SI-RUM		B 14+, M+
			ʾAŚIR		UM						A-SI-RU-UM		B 14+
			ʾAŚIR	AT	UM						A-SI-RA-TUM		B 14
ʾŚŚ	1		ʾAŚAŚ		UM						A-SA-ŠUM		BIROT, TEA 72 IV 17
			ʾUŚŚ	AT	I		ʾEL				UŠ-SA-TE-EL		TIM III 43 6
ʾŚT	1		ʾUŚAT	AN							U_2-SA-TA-AN		M+
			ʾUŚT		AJA						UŠ-TA-IA		RA LXV 55 XIII 14
ʾŠḪ	1		ʾAŠIḪ		UM						A-ŠI-ḪU-UM	FN	RA LXV 62 V 33
	2		TALM		U		ʾAŠIḪ		I		TA-AL-MU-A-ŠI-ḪI	FN	XIII 1 III 63
ʾŠḪR	1		ʾIŠḪAR	AH			ʾUMM		I		D-IŠ-ḪA-RA-UM-MI	FN	XIII 1 II 47+
			ʾIŠḪAR	AH			ʾAŠJ	AH			D-IŠ-ḪA-RA-A-SI-IA	FN	XIII 1 XI 43
			ʾIŠḪAR	AH			DAMQ	AH			D-IŠ-ḪA-RA-DAM-QA	FN	RA LXV 58 I 18
			ʾIŠḪAR	AH			DUMQ		I		D-IŠ-ḪA-RA-DU-UM-KI	FN	XII 265 3
			ʾIŠḪAR	AH			DANN	AT			IŠ-ḪA-RA-DAN-NA-AT	FN	M
			ʾIŠḪAR	AH			ḎAMR	AT	I		D-IŠ-ḪA-RA-ZA-AM-RA-TI	FN	M
			ʾIŠḪAR	AH			GUML		I		D-IŠ-ḪA-RA-GU-UM-LI	FN	XIII 1 IV 39
			ʾIŠḪAR	AH			LAMAS		I		D-IŠ-ḪA-RA-D-LAMA	FN	XIII 1 IX 23
			ʾIŠḪAR	AH			MALAK		I		D-IŠ-ḪA-RA-M[A-L]A-KI	FN	RA LXV 61 IV 61
			ʾIŠḪAR	AH			NAʿM		I		D-IŠ-ḪA-RA-NA-AḪ-ME	FN	RA LXV 64 VI 37
			ʾIŠḪAR	AH			NIWR		I		D-IŠ-ḪA-RA-NI-RI	FN	RA LXV 59 II 22
			ʾIŠḪAR	AH			NAPŠ		I		D-IŠ-ḪA-RA-NA-AP-SI	FN	XIII 1 VII 13
			ʾIŠḪAR	AH			ŠAMŠ		I		D-IŠ-ḪA-RA-D-UTU-ŠI	FN	XII 265 6
			ʾIŠḪAR	AH			ŠARR	AT			D-IŠ-ḪA-RA-ŠAR-RA-AT	FN	M
			ʾIŠḪAR	AH		TA	ŠKUB				D-IŠ-ḪA-RA-TA-AŠ-KU-UB	FN	RA LXV 56 V 21+
	2		ʿABD				ʾIŠḪAR	AH			AB-DI-D-IŠ-ḪA-RA		A.+
			ʿABD				ʾIŠḪAR	AH			ḪA-AB-DU-D-IŠ-ḪA-RA		XIII 1 II 79+
			ʾUMM		I		ʾIŠḪAR	AH			UM-MI-IŠ-ḪA-RA	FN	XIII 1 V 74, A.+
			ḎU				ʾIŠḪAR	AH			ZU-D-IŠ-ḪA-RA		XIII 64 5
			TAʾK		I		ʾIŠḪAR	AH			TA-KI-D-IŠ-ḪA-RA		JCS XIII 52 293 LE,A.LATE
			TAʾK		U		ʾIŠḪAR	AH			TA-KU-D-IŠ-ḪA-R[A]		JCS XIII 52 293 R, A. LATE
ʾŠW	1		ʾIŠAW		UM						I-ŠA-WU-UM		M
ʾŠB	1		ʾEŠB		I		HADD		U		EŠ-BI-D-IM		A.+
			ʾEŠB		I		ʾADAN	T	A		EŠ-BI-A-DA-AT-TA		A. 455 31, 55
ʾŠR	1	JA	ʾŠUR		UM						IA-ŠU-RU-UM		RA LXV 54 XII 38
			ʾAŠAR		UM						A-ŠA-RU-UM		EDZARD, DER 68 IV 3
			ʾAŠAR				NAṢIR				D-A-ŠAR-NA-ṢIR		M
			ʾAŠIR								ḪA-ŠI-IR?		HARRIS 38 5
			ʾAŠIR	AT	UM						D-A-ŠI-RA-TUM	DN FN	RIFTIN 60 SEAL
			ʾAŠR		I						ḪA-$AŠ_2$-RI		CT XLV 92 R. 9
			ʾAŠR		I		JATAR				AŠ-RI-E-TAR		RA XLIX 24 N. 9
			ʾAŠR	AT	UM		ʾUMM		I		D-AŠ-RA-TUM-UM-MI	FN	TCL I P. 16+
			ʾAŠIR				ŠI			JA			
							....				A-ŠE-ER-ŠI-IA-[X]	FN	XIII 1 VIII 2
	2		ḤAJJ		A		ʾAŠR		A	JA	E_2-A-AŠ-RA-IA		M+
			ʿABD				ʾAŠUR		A		ḪA-AB-DU-A-ŠU-RA		M
			ʾIL		I		ʾAŠR		A	JA	I_3-LI_2-AŠ-RA-IA		M+
			ʾUMM		I		ʾAŠIR	AH			UM-MI-A-ŠI-RA	FN	VAS XIII 73 6,13
			ʾANN		U		ʾAŠR		I		AN-NU-AŠ-RI	FN	M+
		JA	JṢIʾ				ʾAŠAR				IA-ZI-A-ŠAR		SZLECHTER TJ P. 186
		JI	JṢIʾ				ʾAŠAR				I-ZI-A-ŠAR		B 22+
		JI	JṢIʾ				ʾAŠAR				I-ṢI-A-ŠAR		YOS VIII 108 SEAL
			DAGAN				ʾAŠR		A	JA	D-DA-GAN-AŠ-RA-IA		M+
		JA	KWUN				ʾAŠAR				IA-KU-UN-A-ŠAR		B 92+, M+
		JI	KWUN				ʾAŠAR				I-KU-UN-A-ŠAR		GORDON 38 6
		JA	KWUN				ʾAŠAR		I		IA-KU-UN-A-ŠA-RI	NOM	CT XLVIII 10 6
		JA	KWUN				ʾAŠAR		UM		IA-KU-UN-A-ŠA-RU-UM		B 27
			KAKK		A		ʾAŠR		I		KA-AK-KA-AŠ-RI	FN	XIII 1 V 1
		JA	RŠIJ				ʾAŠAR		I		IA-AR-ŠI-A-ŠA-RI		M
		JA	ŠWUB				ʾAŠAR				IA-ŠU-UB-A-ŠAR		M+
			ŠALIM				ʾAŠAR				ŠA-LIM-D-A-ŠAR		M
			ṬAJB		A		ʾAŠUR		A		TA-PA-AŠ-ŠU-RA		A.
	3		BUN		U		MA						
							ʾAŠAR				BU-NU-MA-A-ŠA-AR		KISURRA 93 4

ROOTS (Consonants only)

Root	No.	Prefix	Stem	Affix	Vowel	Suffix	Element 2	Vowel 2	Suffix 2	Spelling	Note	Reference
ʾŠR	3		BUN		U		MA					
							ʾAŠAR			BU-NU-MA-ŠAR		B 16+
ʾŠŠ	1		ʾUŠAŠ		UM					U$_2$-ŠA-ŠUM		I
ʾŠZ	1		ʾAŠUZ		I					A-ŠU-ZI		M
ʾTJ	2		ʾIL		I		ʾATAJ	A	JA	I$_3$-LI$_2$-A-TA-A-IA		RA VIII 69 26
			ʾIL		I		ʾITEJ		JE	I$_3$-LI$_2$-I-TE-E		MEISSNER 110 20, 23+, M
			ŠAMŠ		I		ʾITEJ		JE	D-UTU-I-TE-E		CT IV 44 B 3, 4
ʾTL	1		ʾATAL		UM					ḪA-TA-LU-UM		CT XXXIII 42 23+
			ʾATAL		UM					ḪA-AT-TA-LUM		CT XXXIII 43A 6
			ʾATAL	AN	UM					A-TA-LA-NU-UM		EDZARD, DER 100:3
			ʾATAL		I		ʾEL			ḪA-TA-LI-EL		M
			ʾATUL	AH						ḪA-TU-LA	FN	RA LXV 65 VII 4
	2		ʿABD				ʾUTL	I		AB-DU-UT-LI	FN	A. LATE
ʾTM	1		ʾATAM		UM					ḪA-TA-MU-UM		B 20
			ʾATAM	AN	UM					A-TA-MA-NU-UM		UCP X/3 3 22+
			ʾATAM	AN	UM					AT-TA-MA-NU-UM		SIMMONS 122 16
			ʾATIM		UM					A-TI-MU-UM		TA 30 7 8, M
			ʾATIM		U					A-TI-MU		M
			ʾATIM		AM					A-TI-M[A-AM]	ACC	M
ʾTR	1		ʾATAR	AN	I					A-TA-RA-NI	GEN	HARRIS 71 12
			ʾATAR		I		ṢADUQ			[A]T-TA-RI-ZA-DU-UQ		I 103 17
ʾTT	1		ʾATT		UM					ḪA-AT-TU-UM		M
			ʾATT		U					ḪA-AT-TU		C+
			ʾATT		IM					ḪA-AT-TI-IM	GEN	M+
			ʾATT		A					D-ḪA-AT-TA	DN	M+
			ʾATTA				BAʿL	I		AT-TA-BA-AḪ-LI		JCS XIII 51 293:8,A. LATE
			ʾATTA				BAʿL	I	JE	AT-TA-BA-AḪ-LI-E		JCS XIII 51 293:15,A.LATE
			ʾATTA				NABIT	I		A-TA-NA-BE-TI		JCS XIII 57 306:5+,A LATE
			ʾATT		I					AT-TI	FN	RA LXV 65 VII 6
			ʾATT		I					ḪA-AT-TI		RA LXV 40 I 32
			ʾATT		IJAN					AT-TI-IA-AN		A. 261 14
			ʾATT		I		HADD	U		AT-TI-D-IM		M+
			ʾATT		I		ʿAMM	A		AT-TI-AM-MA		A. LATE
			ʾATT		I		LIʾM	A		AT-TI-LI-MA		A. LATE
			ʾATT		I		MEʾR			AT?-TI-ME-IR?		IX 234 10
			ʾITT		A		ʾABB	A		ḪI-IT-TA-D-AB-BA		M
			ʾITT		A		ʾIL	I		IT-TA-I$_3$-LI$_2$		M
	2		ḪAʾR		I		ʾATT	A		ḪA-RI-A-TA		C II 5 7
			BIN	T	A		ʾATT	I		BI-IT-TA-AT-TI	FN	A.+
			KAʾB		I		ʾATT	A		KA-BI-A-TA		M
ʾTZ	1		ʾATAZ	AH						AT-TA-ZA	FN	M
			ʾATAZ	AH						AT-TA-AZ-ZA	FN	XIII 1 III 9+
ʾZW	1	JA	ʾZUW		UM					IA-ZU-UM		UET V 714 +
		JA	ʾZUW				HADD	U		IA-ZU-D-IM		M
		JA	ʾZUW				JARAḪ			IA-ZU-RA-AḪ		M+
		JA	ʾZUW				DAGAN			IA-ZU-D-DA-GAN		M+, SYRIA V 273, HANA
		JA	ʾZUW				RAŠAP			IA-AḪ-ZU-D-RA-SA-AP		M
ʾZJ	1	JA	ʾZIJ				ʾIL			IA-AḪ-ZI-DINGIR		M
		JA	ʾZIJ				ʾIL	I		IA-AḪ-ZI-I$_3$-LI$_2$		TCL X 21 13
		JE	ʾZIJ				ʾIL	UM		E-EḪ-ZI-LUM		VIII 3 25
		JA	ʾZIJ				DAGAN			IA-AḪ-ZI-D-DA-GAN		RA LXV 54 XII 52
		TA	ʾZIJ				ʾADM	U		TA-AḪ-ZI-D-AD-MU	FN	M
	2		ʾAJA				ʾAZJ	I		A-IA-ZI		M
			ʾAB		I		ʾAZJ	I		A-BI-A-ZI		A.
ʾZL	1		ʾUZUL		I					U$_2$-ZU-UL-LI	FN	XIII 1 III 66
			ʾUZUL		IM					ḪU-UZ-ZU-LIM	GEN	GORDON 38 21+
ʾZM	1		ʾIZAM		U					I-ZA?-MU	FN	M
			ʾIZAM	AN	UM					I-ZA-MA-NU-UM		B 45
HWJ	1	JA	HWIJ		UM					IA?-WI-U$_2$-UM		M
		JA	HWIJ		UM					IA-AḪ?-WI?-UM?		B 32
		JA	HWIJ			JA				IA-WI-IA		M
		JA	HWIJ				HADD	U		IA-WI-D-IM		M+
		JA	HWIJ				ʾIL			IA-WI-DINGIR		B 31+, M+
		JA	HWIJ				ʾIL			JA-AḪ-WI-DINGIR		M
		JA	HWIJ				ʾIL			IA-AḪ-WI-DINGIR		B 27+
		JA	HWIJ				ʾIL	I		IA-AḪ-WI-DINGIR-LI$_2$		KISURRA 6+

HWJ	1	JA	HWIJ			ʾIL	I		IA-WI-LI		A 7695 10
		JA	HWIJ			DAGAN			IA-WI-D-DA-GAN		B 31
		JA	HWIJ			KI					
						HADD	U		[IA-A]Ḫ-WI-KI-D-IM		M
		JE	HWIJ			MALIK			E-WI-MA-LIK		A.
		JI	HWIJ			MUT	I		I-WI-MU-TI		U
		JA	HWIJ			NAŠIʾ			IA-AḪ-WI-NA-SI		M+
		JA	HWIJ		TA	NWUḪ			IA-WI?-TA-NU		RA LXV 43 III 64
		TA	HWIJ			JARAḪ			TA-AḪ-WI?-D-EN-ZU		RA LXIV 28 NO. 16
		TA	HWIJ			NAPŠ	U		TA-AḪ-WI-NA-AP-SU		RA LXIV 28 NO. 14
	2		ʿAŠTAR		JA	HWIJ			EŠ$_4$-DAR-IA-WI		VAS VII 157 7
			LA		ʾA	HWIJ		JA	LA-WI-IA	FN	RA LXV 60 III 37
			LA		ʾA	HWIJ					
						ʾAḪ	I		LA-AḪ-WI-A-ḪI	FN	XIII 1 VII 3
			LA		ʾA	HWIJ					
						ʾAB	I		LA-AḪ-WI-A-BI	FN	XIII 1 XIII 6
			LA		ʾA	HWIJ					
						HADD	U		LA-AḪ-WI-A-DU		A. 95 36
			LA		ʾA	HWIJ					
						ʾIL			LA-WI-DINGIR		XIV 109:7
			LA		ʾA	HWIJ					
						ʾIL			LA-[AḪ]?-WI-DINGIR		M
			LA		ʾA	HWIJ					
						JAŠAR			LA-AḪ-WI-E-SA-AR		RA LXV 40 I 21
			LA		ʾA	HWIJ					
						BAʿL	U		LA-AḪ-WI-BA-LU		C
			LA		ʾA	HWIJ					
						BAʿL	U		LA-AḪ-WI-BA-AḪ-LU		XIV 29:28
			LA		ʾA	HWIJ					
						BEʿL	I		LA-AḪ-WI-BE-LI$_2$	FN	RA LXV 59 II 73
			LA		ʾA	HWIJ					
						LA		NA	LA-AḪ-WI-LA-NA		RA LXV 65 VII 19
			LA		ʾA	HWIJ					
						MALIK			LA-AḪ-WI-MA-LIK		X 141 2
			LA		ʾA	HWIJ					
						MALIK	U		LA-AḪ-WI-MA-LI-KU		M
			LA		ʾA	HWIJ					
						NIWR	I		LA-AḪ-WI-NE-RI	FN	XIII 1 II 11
	3		ʾEK	I		LA					
					ʾA	HWIJ			E-KI-LA-AḪ-WI		M
HDD	1		HADD	A					AD-DA		M+
			HADD	AJA					A-AD-DA-A		M+
			HADD	AJA					A-DA-A		M
			HADD	U		BAʿL	I		D-IM-BA-AḪ-LI		M+
			HADD	U		BANIJ			D-IM-BA-NI		M+
			HADD	U		DUWR	I		D-IM-DU-RI		M+
			HADD	U		MALIK			AD-DU-MA-LIK		A. 268 4
			HADD	U		MALIK			D-IM-MA-LIK		M+
			HADD	U		NIWR	I		D-IM-NI-RI	FN	RA LXV 61 IV 17
			HADD	U		ŠADW	A		D-IM-ŠA-DA		PSBA XXIX 273 NO. 9 R. 10
	2		ʾAḪ	I		HADD	A		A-ḪI-A-DA		B 12
		JA	HWIJ			HADD	U		IA-WI-D-IM		M+
			ḪAʾL	I		HADD	U		ḪA-LI$_2$-D-IM		M+
			ḪAʾL	I		HADD	U		ḪA-LI-A-DU		A.+
			ḪAʾL	I		HADD	U		ḪA-LI-IA-[D]U		M
			ʾUWR	A		HADD	U		U$_2$-RA-A-DU		A.
			ʾUWR	I		HADD	U		U$_2$-RI-A-DU		A.
			ʾUWR	I		HADD	U		WU-RI-A-DU		A.
			JAʾAR			HADD	U		IA-ḪA-AR-D-IM		M
		JA	ʾWUŠ			HADD	U		IA-UŠ-D-IM		M+
		JA	ʾWUŠ			HADD	U		IA-U$_2$-UŠ-D-IM		M+
		JA	ʾWUŠ			HADD	U		IA-UŠ$_2$-D-IM		M
			ʾAB	I		HADD	U		A-BI-D-IM		B 9, M+
			ʾAB	I		HADD	U		A-BI-A-DU		A.+
			ʾAB	I		HADD	U		A-BI-IA-DU		M+
			ḪABIʾ			HADD	U		ḪA-BI-D-IM		M

ROOTS (Consonants only)

HDD	2	ʿABD			HEDD	A	ḪA-AB-DI-E-D-IM	RS XIX 338F.
		ʿABD			HADD	U	AB-DI-AD-DU	BAGHD. MITT. II 57 28
		ʿABD			HADD	U	ḪA-AB-DU-D-IM	RA LXV 48 VIII 34
	JI	JBAL			HADD	U	I-BA-AL-D-IM	M+, C+
		JABAL			HADD	U	IA-BA-AL-D-IM	M
		ʿAD	U	NA	HADD	U	A-DU-NA-D-IM	SYRIA XIX 109
		ʿAD	U	NI	HADD	U	A-DU-NI-D-U	MRS VI 15, 42 II 20 UGARIT
		JADAʿ			HADD	U	[IA]-ṬA$_3$-AḪ-D-IM	VI 76 10
		ʿADN	I		HADD	U	ḪA-AD-NI-D-IM	M, C+
		ʿADN	I		HADD	U	ḪA-AD-NI-A-D[U]	DELAPORTE CCL II A 914
		ʿAḎR	I		HADD	U	AD-RI-A-DU	A.+
		ʿAḎR	I		HADD	U	AD-RI-IA-DU	KUPPER, NOM. 231
		ʾIL	I		HADD	U	I$_3$-LI$_2$-D-IM	M+
		ʾIL	I		HADD	U	I$_3$-LI$_2$-A-DU	A. 57 47
		ʾIL	I		HEDD	A	I$_3$-LI-E-DA	A.
	JI	ḪLAJ			HADD	U	IḪ-LA-D-IM	XIII 1 II 76
	JI	ḪLIJ			HADD	U	IḪ-LI-A-DU	A. P. 133+
	JI	ḪLIJ			HADD	U	IḪ-LI$_3$-A-DU	A. P. 133
		ʾALUN			HADD	U	ḪA-LU-UN-D-IM	M; JCS XIV 203
		ʾALUN	A		HADD	U	ḪA-LU-NA-D-IM	M
	JI	ʾLAP			HADD	U	IḪ-LA-AP-A-DU	A.
	JI	ʾLIP			HADD	A	IḪ-LI-BA-DA	TCL I 222 13
		ʿAMM	I		HADD	U	AM-MI-A-DU	A. 60 14
		ʿAMM	I		HADD	U	AM-MI-IA-A-DU	A.
		ʿAMM	I		HADD	U	AM-MI-AD-DU	A. 267 17
		ʿAMM	I		HEDD	A	AM-MI-E-DA	A.
		ʿAMM	U		HADD	A	AM-MU-A-DA	A.+
		ʿAMM	U		HADD	A	AM-MU-WA-DA	A.
		ʾAMAR			HADD	U	AM-MA-RA-DU	A.+
		ʾAMAR	A		HADD	U	AM-MA-RA-A-DU	A.
	JA	ʾMUR			HADD	U	IA-MU-UR-AD-DU	M
		ʾANA			HADD	U	A-NA-D-IM	MRS XII NO. 24, 6, UGARIT
		ḪANN	A		HADD	U	AN-NA-D-IM	M+
		ḪANN	A		HADD	U	ḪA-AN-NA-D-IM	M
		ḤINN	I		HADD	U	IN-NI-D-IM	A.
		ḪANZ	A		HADD	U	ḪA-AN-ZA-D-IM	M
	JA	JPAʿ			HADD	U	IA-A-PA-AḪ-D-IM	M+
	JA	JPAʿ			HADD	U	IA-PA-ḪA-D-IM	M
	JA	JPAʿ			HADD	U	IA-PA-AḪ-D-IM	M+
	JA	JPIʿ			HADD	U	IA-BI-IḪ-D-IM	M
	ʾU	WQAH			HADD	U	U$_2$-QA-D-IM	RA LXV 44 IV 51
	ʾU	WQAH			HADD	U	U$_2$-GA-D-IM	BIROT, TEA 24:6
	JA	ʿQUB			HEDD	A	IA-AK-KU-UB-E-DA	JEA VIII 207F.
		ʿIQB	I		HADD	U	IQ-BI-D-IM	KISURRA 114 7
		ʾIRR	I		HADD	U	I-RI-A-DU	A.+
		ʾIRR	I		HADD	U	IR-RI-A-DU	A.
	JA	ʾŠUʾ			HADD	U	IA-SU-D-IM	TCL I 238 4 HANA+
		JIŠʿ	I		HADD	U	IŠ-ḪI-D-IM	M+, C+
		JIŠʿ	I		HEDD	A	IŠ-ḪI-E-D-IM	TIM IV 33 SEAL, 34 SEAL
		ʾEŠB	I		HADD	U	EŠ-BI-D-IM	A.+
		ʾAŠM	A		HADD	U	AŠ-MA-DU	BM 80328 14
		ʾAŠM	A		HADD	U	AŠ-MA-A-DU	A.+
	JA	JŠIR			HEDD	A	IA-ŠE-RE-DA	A. 367 5
	JA	JŠIR			HEDD	A	IA-AŠ-RI-E-DA	A.+
		JATAR			HADD	U	IA-TAR-D-IM	M+
	JA	JTIR			HEDD	A	IA-TE-IR-E-DA	A.+
	JA	JTIR			HEDD	A	IA-TE-RI-DA	A.+
		ʾATT	I		HADD	U	AT-TI-D-IM	M+
		JATT	I		HADD	U	IA-AT-TI-D-IM	M
	JA	JṢIʾ			HADD	U	IA-ZI-D-IM	M
	JA	ʾZUW			HADD	U	IA-ZU-D-IM	M
	JA	ʿZIB			HADD	U	IA-AḪ-ZI-IB-D-IM	M+
	JA	ʿZIB			HADD	U	IA-ZI-IB-D?-IM?	M
	JA	ḪZUR			HADD	U	IA-AḪ-ZU-UR-D-IM	M
		ʿUZZ			HADD	U	U$_2$-ZA-DU	U
		BAʿD	I		HADD	U	BA-AḪ-DI-D-IM	M+

ROOTS (Consonants only)

HDD	2		BUʾL	I		HADD	U	BU-LI-A-DU		A. 60 12
			BAʿL	I		HADD	U	BA-AḪ-LI-D-IM		M+
			BAʿL	I		HADD	U	BA-LI-D-IM		M
			BEʿL	I		HADD	U	BE-LI_2-D-IM		RA LXV 52 X 39
		JA	BḪAR			HADD	U	IA-AB-ḪA-AR-D-IM		M
			BULM	A	NA	HADD	U	BU-UL-MA-NA-D-IM		M+
			BIN			HADD	U	DUMU-D-IM		M+
			BIN	A		HADD	U	[B]I-NA-D-IM		M
		JA	BNIJ			HADD	U	IA-AB-NI-D-IM		M
		JI	BNIJ			HADD	U	IB-NI-D-IM		M+
		JA	DJIN			HADD	U	IA-DI-IN-D-IM		RA LXV 44 IV 51+
			DIJN	I		HADD	U	TI-NI-A-DU		A. 59 2
			DIJN	I		HADD	U	DI-NI-A-DU		A.+
			DIJN	I		HADD	U	DI-NA-A-DU		A. LATE
			DUNN	I		HADD	U	DU-NI-A-DU		A. LATE
			ḎIKR	I		HADD	U	ZI-IK-RI-D-IM		M+
			ḎIMR	I		HADD	U	ZI-IM-RI-D-IM		M+
			ḎIMR	I		HEDD	A	ZI-IM-RI-E-ID-DA		B 42
			ḎIMR	I	JE	HADD	U	ZI-IM-RI-E-D-IM		M
			ḎIMR	U		HADD	U	ZI-IM-RU-D-IM		CT XLVIII 22 REV
		JA	ḎRAʿ			HADD	U	IA-AZ-RA-AḪ-D-IM		M+
		JA	GJIḪ			HADD	U	IA-GI-IḪ-D-IM		M+
		JA	GJIḪ			HADD	U	IA-GI-ḪA-D-IM		M
			GUʾR	U		HADD	U	GU-RU-D-IM		M+
		JI	GMIR			HADD	U	IG-MI-RA-A-DU		A.+
			KAʾB	I		HADD	U	KA-BI-D-IM		B 32, M+, C
			KAʾB	I		HEDD	A	KA-BI-E-D-IM		M+
			KAHAL	I		HADD	U	KA-A-LI-D-IM		M+
		JA	KWUN			HADD	U	IA-KU-UN-D-IM		B 27, M+
		JA	KWIN			HADD	U	IA-KI-IN-D-IM		M
			KUʾR	U		HADD	U	KU-RU-D-IM		M
			KIBS			HADD	U	KI-IB-ZA-DU	FN	A.
			KIBS	I		HADD	U	KI-IB-ZI-D-IM		M+
			KIBS	I		HEDD	A	KI-IB-ZI-E-D-IM		M
			LA		NA	HADD	U	LA-NA-D-IM		XIII 109 15, 16
		JI	LʾAʾ			HADD	U	IL-A-D-IM		X 83 4, 7'
		JI	LʾAʾ			HADD	U	IL-A-DU		A. 78 20
		JI	LEʾEJ			HADD	U	I-LE-E-D-IM		XIII 93 5
			LAWUJ			HADD	U	LA-WU-D-IM		M+
			LAWUJ			HADD	U	LA-U_2-D-IM		A.
			LIʾM	A		HADD	U	LI-MA-A-DU		A.
			LIʾM	I		HADD	U	LI-MI-D-IM		M+
			LIʾM	I		HADD	U	LI-ME-D-IM		M+
			MIHR	I		HADD	U	ME-EḪ-RI-D-IM		C+
		JA	MLIK			HADD	U	IA-AM-LIK-D-IM		RA LXV 40 I 31
			MILK	A		HADD	U	MI-IL-KA-D-IM		SYRIA XXXVII 206 27 HANA
			MILK	I		HADD	U	MIL-KI-D-IM		M
			MILK	I		HADD	U	MI-IL-KI-D-IM		M
		N	MŠIḪ			HEDD	A	NA-AM-SI-E-D-IM		A 7646 6
			MUŠN	A		HADD	U	MU-UŠ-NA-A-DU		A.+
			MUT			HADD	U	MU-UT-[D]?-IM		RA LXV 41 II 17
			MUT			HADD	I	MU-TA-AD-DI		VAS XVI 165:4
			MUT	I		HADD	U	MU-TI-D-IM		M
			MUT	U		HADD	U	MU-TU-D-IM		M
			NIʿM	A		HADD	U	NI-MA-A-DU		A.
			NAWAR			HADD	U	NA-WA-AR-D-IM		RA LXV 50 VIII 55+
			NIWR	I		HADD	U	NI-IW-RI-A-DU		A.+
		JA	NBIʾ			HADD	U	IA-AB-BI-D-IM		M
			NIMIN	A		HADD	U	NI-MI-NA-A-DU		A.+
			NAPŠ	I		HADD	U	NA-AP-SI-D-IM		M+
			NAPŠ	I		HADD	U	NA-AP-ŠI-A-DU		A.+
			NAPŠ	U		HADD	U	NA-AP-SU-D-IM		M
			NAPŠ	U	NA	HADD	U	NA-AP-SU-NA-D-IM		M+
		JA	NQIM			HADD	U	IA-AK-KI-IM-D-IM		M+
		JA	NQIM			HADD	U	IA-KI-IM-D-IM		M+
			NIQM			HADD	U	NI-IQ-MA-A-DU		A.+

ROOTS (Consonants only)

HDD	2		NIQM			HADD	U	NI-IQ-MA-DU	A.
			NIQM			HADD	U	NI-IQ-MA$_2$-A-DU	B 36
			NIQM	I		HADD	U	NI-IQ-MI-A-DU	A.+
			NIQM	I		HADD	U	NI-IQ-MI-IA-AD-DU	M
		JA	NŠIʾ			HADD	U	IA-AŠ$_2$-ŠI-D-IM	RA LXV 42 III 13
		JA	NŠIʾ			HADD	U	IA-SI-D-IM	B 29
		JA	NTIN			HADD	U	IA-AN-TI-IN-D-IM	M+
		JA	NTIN			HADD	U	IA-AN-TI-NA-DU	ZDPV XLIX PL. 45 LATE
		JI	NTIN			HADD	U	I-TI-IN-D-IM	M
		JA	NṢIB			HADD	U	IA-AN-ZI-IB-D-IM	M+
		JA	NṢUR			HADD	U	IA-AṢ-ṢU-UR-D-IM	X 12 6, 21+
		JA	PḪUR			HADD	U	IA-AP-Ḫ[U-UR]-A-DU	M
			PILḪ	U		HADD	U	BI-EL-ḪU-D-IM	RA LXV 55 XIII 4
			PILS	I		HADD	U	BI-IL-ZI-D-IM	XIV 41:14
			PULS	I		HADD	U	PU-UL-ZI-D-IM	M+
			PULS	U	NA	HADD	U	PU-UL-ZU-NA-D-IM	UNPUBL.
		TA	PTUN			HADD	A	TAP-TU-NA-A-DA	A. 33 26
		TA	PTAN			HADD	A	TAP-TA-NA-A-DA	A. 206 5
		TA	PTAN			HADD	A	TAP-DA-NA-TA	A. LATE
			QUWJ	U		HADD	U	KU-U$_2$-D-IM	M
			QUWJ	UM		HADD	U	KU-UM-D-U	MRS XVI 9:7
		JA	QWIM			HADD	U	IA-KI-IM-D-IM	M+
		JA	QWIM			HADD	U	IA-GI-I[M]?-D-IM	IX 291 III 29'
			QAWM	U		HADD	U	GA-MU-D-IM	M
			QAʾN			HADD	U	QA-AN-A-DU	A.
		JA	QBIJ			HADD	U	IA-AQ-BI-D-IM	RA LXV 43 III 38
		JA	RʿIJ			HADD	U	JA-RI-A-DU	RA LXV 50 VIII 64
		JA	RḤIB			HADD	U	IA-AR-IB-D-IM	M+
		JA	RJIB			HADD	U	IA-RI-IB-D-IM	B 29+
		JA	RWIM			HADD	U	IA-RI-IM-D-IM	M+
			RIWM			HADD	U	RI-IM-D-IM	M+, A. 57 46
			RIWM	U		HADD	U	RI-MU-D-IM	M
		JA	RKAB			HADD	U	IA-AR-KA-AB-D-IM	4E RENCONTRE 23
		JA	RKIB	A		HADD	U	IA-AR-KI-BA-D-IM	XIII 145 6
		JA	RPAʾ			HADD	U	IA-AR-PA-D-IM	M+
		JI	RPAʾ			HADD	A	IR-PA-A-DA	A. 76 8+
		JI	RPAʾ			HADD	A	IR-PA-DA	A. 41 14
		JI	RPAʾ			HADD	U	IR-PA-D-IM	A.+
			RIPʾ	I		HADD	U	RI-IP-I-D-IM	M+
			RIPʾ	I		HEDD	A	RI-IP-E-D-IM	M
		ʾA	RŠIJ			HADD	A	AR-ŠI-A-DA	M
			SITR	A		HADD	U	ZI-IT-RA-A-DU	A. 456 19
			SITR	I		HADD	U	ZI-IT-RI-D-IM	M
			SITR	I		HADD	U	SI-IT-RI-D-IM	JCS XXIV 60 NO.51 REV.
			SITR	I	JE	HADD	U	ZI-IT-RI-E-D-IM	JCS XXIV 63 NO.56 REV.
			ŠINI			HADD	U	ŠI-NI-D-U	MRS XVI 44:3
		JA	ŠWUB			HADD	U	IA-ŠU-UB-D-IM	LAESSOE P. 90+, C+
			ŠUWB	I		HADD	U	ŠU-BI-D-IM	M
		JA	ŠJIM			HADD	U	IA-SI-IM-D-IM	M
			ŠADW	I		HADD	U	ŠA-DI-D-IM	M
			ŠAKB	I		HADD	U	SA-AK-BI-D-IM	ARMT V P. 123
		ʾA	ŠKUR			HADD	U	AŠ$_2$-KU-UR-D-IM	TCL 1 146 4
		ʾA	ŠKUR			HADD	U	AŠ-KUR-D-IM	M+
		ʾA	ŠKUR			HEDD	A	AŠ-KUR-E-DA	A. 54 25
			ŠIKR	I		HADD	A	SI-IK-RI-ḪA-DA	BE VI/1 6 19
			ŠAM	U		HADD	U	SA-MU-D-IM	M+
			ŠUM	A		HADD	U	ŠU-MA-A-DU	A.
			ŠUM	I		HADD	U	SU-MI-A-DU	A.+
			ŠUM	I		HEDD	A	SU-MI-E-DA	YOS XIII 486:1
		JA	ŠMAʿ			HADD	U	IA-AŠ$_2$-MA-AḪ-D-IM	M+, C+
		JA	ŠMAʿ			HADD	U	IA-AŠ$_2$-MI-IḪ-D-IM	M
		JI	ŠMAʿ			HADD	U	IŠ-MA-D-IM	M
		JI	ŠMAʿ			HADD	U	IŠ-ME-D-IM	M+
		JI	ŠMAʿ			HADD	A	IŠ-MA-A-DA	A.+
		ʾA T	ŠAMAR			HADD	U	AŠ-TA-MAR-D-IM	M+
			ŠAMAR			HADD	U	ŠA-AM-MA-RA-DU	A.

ROOTS (Consonants only)

HDD	2			ŠAMAR		I				HADD	U	SA-MA-RI-A-DU		A. 57 45
				ŠIMAR						HADD	U	ŠI-IM-MA-RA-DU?		A.
				ŠAMŠ		I				HADD	U	SA-AM-SI-D-IM		M+, A.+
				ŠAMŠ		I				HADD	U	SA-AM-SI-A-DU		M+
				ŠAMŠ		I				HADD	U	ŠA-AM-SI-D-IM		M+
				ŠAMŠ		I				HADD	U	D-UTU-ŠI-D-IM		M+, C+
				ŠAMŠ		I				HADD	U	SA-AM-ŠI-D-IM		C
				ŠAMŠ		I				HADD	U	SA-AM-SI-IA-AD-DU		M
				ŠAMŠ		I				HADD	U	D-UTU-ŠI-A-DU		A.
				ŠAPŠ		I				HADD	U	SA-AP-SI-A-DU		A.+
				ŠAMŠ		I				HADD	U			
										ʾIL	I	SA-AM-SI-D-IM-I_3-LI_2		C+
				ŠAMŠ		I				HADD	U			
										....		SA-AM-SI-D-IM-TU-GUL-TI		M
				ŠAMŠ		I				HEDD	A	SA-AM-SI-E-D-IM		SIMMONS 4 20
				ŠAMŠ		I				HEDD	A	SA-AM-SI-E-DA		A. 455 36
				ŠAPŠ		I				HEDD	A	SA-AP-SI-E-DA		A.+
				ŠAMŠ		U				HADD	U	SA-AM-ŠU-D-IM		COLLON, SEALS NO. 141
		JI		ŠNIJ						HADD	U	IŠ-NI-D-IM		A.
		JU	T	ŠANIJ						HADD	U	UŠ-TI-NI-D-IM?		A. 36 9+
				ŠIPQ		U	NA			HADD	A	SI-IP-KU-NA-D-IM		M
				ŠIPQ		U	NA			HADD	A	SI-IP-KU-NA-DA		M
				ŠAPR		A				HADD	U	SA-AP-RA-A-DU		A. 96 R. 12
				ŠIPṬ		I				HADD	U	ŠI-IP-TI-D-IM		A. LATE
				ṢIJḪ						HADD	A	ZI-ḪA-DA		TA 1933,7 EARLY OB
				ṢUWR		I				HADD	U	ZU-RI-D-IM		M+
				ṢABAʾ						HADD	U	ZA-BA-AD-DU		M
				ṢIDQ		A				HADD	U	ZI-ID-QA-D-IM		M
				ṢILL						HADD	U	ZI-IL-LA-AD-DU		A. 81
	3	JA		HWIJ						KI				
										HADD	U	[IA-A]Ḫ-WI-KI-D-IM		M
				BIN		U				MA				
										HADD	U	BI-NU-MA-D-IM		4E RENCONTRE 21 NO. 25
				BUN		U				MA				
										HADD	U	BU-NU-MA-D-IM		M+
				LA				ʾA		HWIJ				
										HADD	U	LA-AḪ-WI-A-DU		A. 95 36
				LA				ʾA		ḪJIJ				
										HADD	U	LA-ḪI-A-DU		A. 57 11, 13
				LA						KIWN				
										HADD	U	LA-KI-IN-A-DU		A.
				LAWUJ						LA				
										HADD	A	LA-U_2-LA-A-DA		A.
				LAWUJ						LA				
										HADD	U	LA-WU-LA-D-IM		M+, C
HLL	1	ʾA		HLUL	AJ	UM						AḪ-LU-LA-UM		CT VIII 38 B 4
			T	HILAL						ʾAKK	A	ḪI-IT-LA-AL-AK-KA		RA LXV 54 XII 36,71
		MA		HLIL		UM						MA-AḪ-LI-LUM		SIMMONS 46 34 124 16+
				HALIL		UM						A-LI-LU-UM		B 18
				HALIL		UM						ḪA-LI-LUM		B 18+, M
				HALIL		UM						ḪA-LI-LU-UM		B 18+
				HALIL		IM						ḪA-LI-LI-IM	GEN	B 18
				HALIL		IM						ḪA-LI-LIM	GEN	SIMMONS 57 14
				HALIL	AT	UM						ḪA-LI-LA-TUM		KISURRA 211 4
				HALIL		IJA						ḪA-LI-LI-IA		B 18+
				HALIL		A				ʿAD	UM	A-LI-LA-ḪA-DU-UM		KISURRA 18 12
				HELAL		I						E-LA-LI		RA LXV 50 IX 25
				HILAL		UM						ḪI-IL-LA-LUM		M+
				HILAL		IM						ḪI-LA-LI-IM	GEN	HARRIS 71 10
				HILAL		IM						ḪI-IL-LA-LIM	GEN	M+
				HILL		U						ḪI-EL-LU		M
				HULAL		UM						ḪU-LA-LUM		M
	2			ʾANN		U			T	HILAL		AN-NU-ḪI-ÌT-LA-AL	FN	RA LXV 60 III 18
				ŠUM		U	NA			HALAL		SU-MU-NA-ḪA-LA?-AL		UET V 245 11
HND	1			HAND		U				MALIK		AN-DU-MA-LIK		A. 252 10
	2			ʿABD						HAND	U	ḪA-AB-DI-IA-AN-DU		KUPPER NOM. P. 231

ROOTS (Consonants only)

HND	2		ʿABD				HAND	U		AB-DI-IA-DU		KUPPER NOM. P. 231
			ʿABD				HAND	U		AB-DU-IA-AN-DU		KUPPER NOM. P. 231
			ʿAḎR		I		HAND	U		AD-RI-IA-AN-DU		KUPPER, NOM. 231
			ʿAḎR		I		HAND	U		ḪA-AD-RI-IA-AN-DU		KUPPER, NOM. 231
			BAʿL		A		HAND	U		BA-LA-ḪA-AN-DU		VOIX 187:13 MARI
			NAPŠ		I		HAND	U		NA-AP-SI-IA-AN-DU		M
		ʾA	PLAḪ				HAND	A		AP-LA-ḪA-AN-DA		M+
		ʾA	PLAḪ				HAND	A		AP-LI-ḪA-AN-DA		M
		ʾA	PLAḪ				HAND	A		AP-LA-ḪA-DA		M
		ʾA	PLAḪ				HAND	A		AP-LA-AḪ-[AN]-DA		M
		ʾA	PLAḪ				HAND	U		AP-LA-ḪA-AN-DU		RA LXV 42 II 65
		ʾA	RDAK				HAND	A		AR-DA-KA-AN-DA		M
		JA	ŠLIM				HAND	U		IA-AŠ$_2$-LI-IM-IA-[AN-D]U		M
			ŠIPR		I		HAND	A		ŠI-IP-RI-AN-TA		A. LATE
			ŠIPṬ		I		HAND	A		ŠI-IP-TI-AN-TA		A. LATE
			ŠIPṬ		I		HAND	A		ŠI-IP-TI-IA-AN-TA		A. LATE
ḪJJ	1	JA	ḪJIJ			JA				IA-ḪI-IA		XIV 61:6
		JA	ḪJIJ	AN						[I]A?-Ḫ[I]?-IA-AN		RA LXV 41 II 54
		JA	ḪJIJ				ʾIL			IA-ḪI-DINGIR		B 26+
		JA	ḪJIJ				ʾIL			IA-A-ḪI-DINGIR		XIII 65 5
			ḪAJJ		A		ʾAŠR	A	JA	E$_2$-A-AŠ-RA-IA		M+
			ḪAJJ		A		NIWR	I		E$_2$-A-NI-RI	FN	RA LXV 58 II 2
			ḪAJJ		A		NIWR	I		E$_2$-A-NE-RI	FN	XIII 1 VII 26
			ḪAJJ		A		ŠIMḪ	I		E$_2$-A-ŠI-IM-ḪI	FN	XIII 1 II 44
			ḪAJJ		UM					ḪA-IU-UM		B 18+
			ḪAJJ		UM					ḪA-U$_2$-UM		CT VI 46 5
			ḪAJJ	AT	UM					ḪA-IA-TUM	MN	B 18+
			ḪAJJ	AT	UM					[Ḫ]A-A-A-IA-TUM	FN	XIII 1 XIV 13
			ḪAJJ	AH						A-IA	FN	XIII 1 X 47
			ḪAJJ	AH						A-I-IA	FN	A. LATE+
			ḪAJJ	AT	IJA					A-A-TI-IA		BM 92654 5
			ḪAJJ	AT	IJA					A-IA-TI-IA		BM 82440
			ḪAJJ	ATAN						ḪA-IA-TA-AN		M+
			ḪAJJ	AN	UM					ḪA-IA-NU-UM		VAS XVI 62 12
			ḪAJJ	AN	UM					A-A-NU-UM		M
			ḪAJJ	AN	I					ḪA-IA-A-NI		JNES XIII 210FF.+ LATE
			ḪAJJ		U		ʾIL			A$_2$-U$_2$-DINGIR		U
			ḪAJJ		UM		RAPIʾ			ḪA-JU-UM-RA-BI		M
	2		ʾANA				ḪIJJ	A		A-NA-ḪI?-A?		RUTTEN 20:16
		JI	JṢIʾ				ḪAJJ	UM		I-ZI-A-UM		MOORTGAT 488
		JA	ḪṢIN				ḪAJJ	A		IA-AḪ-ZI-IN-E$_2$-A		XIII 1 VII 23
			BAWB		I		ḪAJJ	A		D-BA-BI-E$_2$-A?		VIII 31 7
			BIN	T	I		ḪIJJ	A		BI-TI-ḪI?-A	FN	HARRIS 85 3
			KIBR				ḪAJJ	A		KI-BI-IR-E$_2$-A		XIV 62:23
			KUKIM				ḪIJJ	A		KU-UK-KI-IM?-ḪI-IA	FN	X 100 5
			LA			ʾA	ḪJIJ					
							HADD	U		LA-ḪI-A-DU		A. 57 11, 13
			LA			ʾA	ḪJIJ					
							ʿAN	UM		LA-ḪI-A-NU-UM		U
			LA			ʾA	ḪJIJ					
							BIḪR	U		LA-ḪI-BI-RU		WATERMAN 25 R. 5
			LA			ʾA	ḪJIJ					
							ṢADUQ			LA-ḪI-ZA-DU-UQ		A.+
			LU				ḪAJJ	A				
							ŠAMIʿ	UM		LU-ḪA-A-A-SA-MU-UM		UET V 569 8
			LU				ḪAJJ	A				
							ŠAMIʿ	UM		LU-ḪA-A-A-SA-MI-UM		UET V 569 17
			MILK		I		ḪAJJ	A		MIL-KI-ḪA-A-IA	FN	IRAQ XVI 40 NA
		JA	RḪIB				ḪAJJ	A		IA-AR-IB-D-E$_2$-A		M+
			ŠAWB		A		ḪAJJ	UM		SA-BA-A-U$_2$-UM		OIP XLVII 66
		JA	ŠJIM				ḪAJJ	A		[I]A-ŠI-IM-E$_2$-A		M
		JI	ŠJIM				ḪAJJ	A		I-ŠI-IM-E$_2$-A		M
		JI	TWUR				ḪAJJ	A		I-DUR-E$_2$-A		M
			TIWR				ḪAJJ	A		TI-IR-E$_2$-A		M+
ḪBB	1	ʾA	ḪBAB		U					AḪ-BA-BU		U
			ḪABIB		UM					ḪA-BI-BU-UM		RUTTEN 27 14+

ROOTS (Consonants only)

ḤBB	1		ḤABIB		IM					A-BI-BI-IM	GEN	KISURRA 62
ḤBS	1	JA	ḤBAS				ʾIL			IA-AḪ-BA-AZ-DINGIR		CT II 39 18+
		TA	ḤBAS		I					TA-AḪ-PA-ZI		A. 28 4, 17
		JA	ḤBIS		UM					IA-AḪ-BI-ZUM		GORDON 38 3
			ḤABAS		U					ḪA-BA?-ZU	FN	XIII 1 I 1
			ḤABIS		UM					A-BI-ZUM		TIM II 122 3+
			ḤABIS		UM					A-BI-ZU-UM		TIM III 4 3+
			ḤABIS	AN	I					ḪA-BI-ZA-NI	GEN	CT VIII 42 B 17
			ḤABS	AT	UM					ḪA-AB-ZA-TUM		BM 17049+
			ḤUBAS		UM					ḪU-BA-ZU-UM		TA 1931, 218
			ḤUBAS		UM					ḪU-BA-ZUM		VAS VIII 14 33
			ḤUBAS		UM					U_2-BA-ZU-UM		SIMMONS 118 17+
			ḤUBAS		IM					U_2-BA-ZI-IM	GEN	SIMMONS 118 2
			ḤUBAS	AN						ḪU-BA-ZA-AN		M
			ḤUBAS		A					ḪU-BA-AZ-ZA		M+
			ḤUBUS							ḪU-BU-UZ		M
ḤDR	1		ḤADUR				BAʿL	A		A-DU-UR-BA-LA-IA	GN	SUMER XIV 26
			ḤADUR				BAʿL	A		D-ZA-GAR$_3$-BA-LA-IA	GN	SUMER XIV 26
			ḤADUR				BAʿL	U		A-DU-UR-BA-LU	GN	SUMER XIV 26
			ḤADUR				BEʿL	UM		A-DU-UR-BE-LUM	GN	SIMMONS 138:10
ḤKM	1	JA	ḤKUM		UM					IA-AḪ-KU-MU-UM		B 26
			ḤAKAM	AT	UM					ḪA-KA-MA-TUM	FN	C+
			ḤAKAM		AJA					ḪA-KA-MA-A-IA	FN	XIII 1 V 44
ḤLJ	1		ḤALAJ		A		KUʾM	U		ḪA-LA-A-KU-MU		XIV 79:5+
		JI	ḤLAJ				HADD	U		IḪ-LA-D-IM		XIII 1 II 76
		JI	ḤLIJ			JA				IḪ-LI-IA		XIII 139 18
		JI	ḤLIJ	AN						IḪ-LI-IA-AN		RA LXV 42 II 73+
		JI	ḤLIJ				HADD	U		IḪ-LI-A-DU		A. P. 133+
		JI	ḤLIJ				HADD	U		IḪ-LI$_3$-A-DU		A. P. 133
		JI	ḤLIJ				ʿAŠTAR			IḪ-LI-AŠ-TAR		A. 55 35
		JI	ḤLIJ				ʿAŠTAR			IḪ-LI-EŠ$_4$-DAR		A. P. 133+
		JA	ḤLIJ				ʾIL			IA-AḪ-LI-DINGIR		B 26
ḤLB	2		MUT				ḤALAB			MU-UT-ḪA-LA-AB		A. 271 3
			ŠUM		U		ḤALAB			SU-MU-A-LA-AB		A.
ḤLM	1	ʾA	ḤLAM		U					AḪ-LA-MU		M+
		ʾA	ḤLAM		U					AḪ-LA-AM-MU		XII 508 2
		ʾA	ḤLAM		U					AḪ-LA-A-MU		XI 208 2
ḤLṢ	1		ḤALAṢ		UM					A-LA-ZUM		UET V 796 11+
			ḤALAṢ		UM					A-LA-ZU-UM		UET V 397 14
			ḤALAṢ		I					A-LA-ṢI		4E RENC. ASS. P. 178 2
			ḤALIṢ		UM					A-LI-ZUM		HARRIS 98 R. 5
			ḤALIṢ		UM					ḪA-LI-ZUM		SUMER V 141 3
			ḤALIṢ	IT	UM					A-LI-ZI-TUM?		UET V 534 R. 9
			ḤILUṢ	AT	UM					I-LU-ZA-TUM	FN	CT II 30 29
ḤM	1		ḤAM		I		....			D-A-MI-[....]		M
			ḤAM		I		JATAR			D-A-MI-T[AR]?		M
			ḤAM		I	JI	JBAL			D-A-MI-I-BA-AL		M+
			ḤAM		I	JE	JŠUʿ			D-A-MI-E-ŠU-UḪ		M+
			ḤAM		I	JE	JŠUʿ			A-MI-E-ŠU-UḪ		M+
			ḤAM		I		MALIK			A-MI-MA-LIK		C
			ḤAM		I		ŠAMUʿ			D-A-MI-SA-MU-UḪ		M+
			ḤAM		I	TA	NWUḪ			D-A-MI-TA-NU-UḪ		M+
			ḤAM		I	TA	NWUḪ			D-A-MI-TA-NU		M
			ḤAM		I	TA	NWUḪ	A		D-A-MI-TA-NU-A		M
			ḤAM		I		ṬAJB	I		A-MI-ṬA-BI		RA LXV 45 V 81
			ḤAM		I		ṢABṬ	I		A-MI-ZA-AB-TI	MN	B 13
			ḤAM		I		ṢABṬ	I		A-MI-ZA-AB-TI	FN	CT VIII 35 B 1
			ḤAM		UM	JE	JŠUʿ			D-A-MU-UM-E-ŠU-UḪ		B 13 HANA
			ḤAM		U		DAWD	I		D?-[A?-M]U?-DA-DI		IX 291 16
			ḤAM		U		DAWD	U		D-A-MU-DA-DU		M
			ḤAM		UM		LU		HU	D-A-MU-UM-LU-U_2		M
			ḤAM		UM		MALIK			D-A-MU-UM-MA-LIK		M
			ḤAM		U		MALIK			D-A-MU-MA-LIK		M
			ḤAM		U	TA	NWUḪ			D-A-MU-TA-NU		M
			ḤAM		UM	TA	NWUḪ		HU	A-MU-UM-TA-NU-U_2		M
	2	JA	ʾWUŠ				ḤAM	U		IA-U_2-UŠ-D-A-MU		M

ROOTS (Consonants only)

ḪM	2		ʾAB		I	ḪAM	A	A-BI-A-MA		SIMMONS 50 22+
			ʾAB		I	ḪAM	A	A-BI-IA-MA		SIMMONS 54 19+
			ʿABD			ḪAM	I	AB-DI-A-MI		BAGHD. MITT. II 58 III 21
			ʿABD			ḪAM	I	ḪA-AB-DU-D-A-MI		M+
			ʿABD			ḪAM	I	ḪA-AB-DU-A-MI		M
		JI	JBAL			ḪAM	UM	I-BA-AL-D-A-MU-UM		RA LXV 52 X 43
			JATAR			ḪAM	I	IA-TAR-D-A-MI		M+
		JA	JTIR			ḪAM	U	IA-TI-RA-MU		A. 235 4 LATE
			BUN		U	ḪAM	I	BU-NU-D-A-MI		M+
			BUN		U	ḪAM	IM	BU-NU-D-A-MI-IM		RA LXV 41 II 27+
			KALB			ḪAM	I	K[A]-AL-BU-D-A-MI		XIII 1 X 20
			MUT		U	ḪAM	I	MU-TU-D-A-MI		RA LXV 51 IX 49
			QAWL		A	ḪAM	I	QA-LA-D-A-M[I]		M
			QAWL		U	ḪAM	I	QA-L[U]-D-A-MI		M
		JA	RWIḪ		A	ḪAM	U	IA-RI-ḪA-A-MU		M+
			ŚUM		U	ḪAM	I	SU-MU-A-MI		M
			ŚUM		U	ḪAM	IM	SU-MU-D-A-MI-IM		RA LXV 40 I 25+
	3		LA			RIWM				
						ḪAM	I	IA-RI-IM-D-A-MI		M
ḪMD	1	JA	ḪMAD		UM			IA-AḪ-MA-DU-UM		CT XLV 5 7
			ḪAMAD		UM			ḪA-MA-DU-UM	FN	M+
			ḪAMAD		U			ḪA-MA-DU	FN	XIII 1 XIII 20
			ḪAMID		UM			ḪA-MI-DU-UM		M
			ḪAMID	AH				ḪA-MI-DA	FN	RA LXV 58 I 20
			ḪIMD		IJA			ḪI-IM-DI-IA		M+
			ḪIMD			ʾIRR	A	ḪI-ME-ID-IR$_3$-RA		M+
			ḪIMD			ʾIRR	A	ḪI-MI-ID-D-IR$_3$-RA		M+
			ḪIMD			KAKK	A	ḪI-MI-ID-KA-AK-KA		M
			ḪIMD		I	MALIK		ḪI-IM-DI-MA-LIK		M
			ḪUMAD		I			ḪU-MA-DI		PINCHES, PEEK 1 4
	2		ʾIL		I	ḪUMUD	I	I$_3$-LI$_2$-ḪU-MU-DI		M
		JA	MWUT			ḪAMAD		IA-MU-UT-ḪA-MA-AD		X 174 18
		JA	MWUT			ḪAMAD	I	IA-MU-UT-ḪA-MA-DI	FN	XIII 1 VI 51
ḪMR	1		ḪIMAR		UM			ḪI-MA-RUM		RA LXV 45 V 56
			ḪIMAR	AN				ḪI-MA-RA-AN-KI	GN	M+
ḪNḪN	1		ḪANḪAN		UM			ḪA-AN-ḪA-NU-UM		B 48+
			ḪANḪAN		UM			ḪA-ḪA-NU-UM		SPELEERS 224 10
			ḪANḪAN		U			ḪA-AN-ḪA-NU		CT XLV 11 42
ḪNN	1	JA	ḪNUN			ʾIL		IA-ḪU-UN-DINGIR		M+
		JA	ḪNUN			ʾIL		IA-NU-UN-DINGIR		RA LXV 51 IX 65
		JA	ḪNUN			MAʾT	UM	IA-UN-MA-TUM	FN	RA L 63
		JA	ḪNUN			PI				
						ʾEL		IA-ḪU-UN-PI-EL		SIMMONS 54 18
			ḪANAN		IM			A-NA-NI-IM	GEN	B 43
			ḪANAN		IM			ḪA-NA-NI-IM	GEN	B 44
			ḪANAN		A			A-NA-NA		U
			ḪANAN	AH				ḪA-NA-AN-NA	FN	C
			ḪANAN	AT	UM			A-NA-NA-TUM	FN	EDZARD, DER 87:14
			ḪANAN		A	GAʾJ	A	A-NA-NA-GA-A		RA XLIV 112 5 QATNA
			ḪANIN		UM			ḪA-NI-NU-UM		B 19+
			ḪANIN		UM			A-NI-NU-UM		EDZARD, DER 73:19
			ḪANUN		UM			A-NU-NU-UM		HARRIS 79 16
			ḪINAN		UM			I-NA-NU-UM		I
			ḪININ		UM			EN-NE-NU-UM		B 44+
			ḪININ		UM			EN-NI-NU-UM		SIMMONS 48 5+
			ḪINUN		UM			E-NU-NU-UM		SIMMONS 112 20
			ḪINUN		AM			I-NU-NAM	NOM	SIMMONS 51 3+
			ḪINUN			ʾEL		I-NU-UN-E-EL		UET V 569 2
			ḪUNIN	AH				U$_2$-NI-NA	FN	M+
			ḪUNIN	AN	UM			ḪU-NI-NA-NU-UM		I
			ḪUNUN		U			UN-NU-NU		YOS XIII 139:9+
			ḪUNUN		I	ʾEL		U$_2$-NU-NI-EL		B 40
			ḪUNUN		I	ʾIL		U$_2$-NU-NI-DINGIR		PBS XI/2 P. 125 NO. 347
			ḪANN		AJA			AN-NA-IA	FN	RA LXV 62 V 13
			ḪANN		A	ʾAḪ	UM	AN-NA-A-ḪU-UM		RA LXV 52 XI 1
			ḪANN		A	ʾAḪ	IM	AN-NA-A-ḪI-IM	GEN	M

ROOTS (Consonants only)

ḤNN	1	ḤANN		A		ʾAḪ		I	AN-NA-A-ḪI	GEN	M
		ḤANN		A		ʾABN		UM	AN-NA-AB-NU-UM		KISURRA 8A 14
		ḤANN		A		ʾABN		UM	A-NA-AB-NU-UM		HARRIS 57 18
		ḤANN		A		ʾABN	AT		ḪA-AN-NA-AB-NA-AT		A 7763, ISHCHALI
		ḤANN		A		HADD		U	AN-NA-D-IM		M+
		ḤANN		A		HADD		U	ḪA-AN-NA-D-IM		M
		ḤANN		A		ʾIL			AN-NA-DINGIR		B 13+, C+
		ḤANN		A		JARAḪ			ḪA-AN-NA-D-EN-ZU		M
		ḤANN		A		JARAḪ			ḪAN-NA-D-EN-ZU		XIII 1 V 27
		ḤANN		A	JI	TWUR					
						MEʾR			ḪA-AN-NA-D-I-DUR-ME-ER		M
		ḤANN		A		KUʾN		I	AN-NA-KU-NI		VAS VIII 14 44
		ḤANN		A		KAʾT		UM	AN-NA-KA-TUM		YOS XIII 509:2
		ḤANN		A		MAʾJ		A	AN-NA-MA-A-A		RUTTEN 14 15
		ḤANN		IJA					ḪA-AN-NI-A	FN	RA LXV 60 III 48
		ḤANN		I		ʾIL			AN-NI-DINGIR		B 13+, M
		ḤANN		I		ʾIL			ḪA-AN-NI-DINGIR	FN	XIII 1 II 7
		ḤANN		I		ʾIL		A	ḪA-AN-NI-I-LA		A. LATE
		ḤANN		I	JI	JŠAR			AN-NI-I-ŠAR?		M
		ḤANN		I		KAʾB		I	A[N-N]I-KA-BI	FN	RA LXV 62 V 17
		ḤANN		I		....			ḪA-AN-NI-D-NIN-ŠE-X-RA?	FN	RA LXV 61 IV 63
		ḤINN		IJA					ḪI-NI-IA	FN	X 116 3
		ḤINN	AN	U					ḪI-NA-NU		KISURRA 62 SEAL
		ḤINN	AT	UM					ḪI-NA-TUM	FN	RA LXV 59 II 66
		ḤINN	ATANUM						IN-NA-TA-NU-UM		TA 1931, 294
		ḤINN		A		BAWŠ	AT		E-NA-BA-ŠA-AT		ICK 63 2+ CAPP.
		ḤINN		A		BAWŠ	AT	A	E-NA-BA-ŠA-TA		EL II P. 171 N. CAPP.
		ḤINN		I		BAWŠ	AT		E-NI-BA-ŠA-AT		ICK 113 10 CAPP.
		ḤINN		I		BAWŠ	AT	A	E-NI-BA-ŠA-TA		KTS 47C 1 CAPP.
		ḤINN		I		HADD		U	IN-NI-D-IM		A.
		ḤINN		I		ʾIL			ḪI-IN-NE-DINGIR		XIII 1 I 53
		ḤINN		I		ʿAŠTAR			EN-NI-D-EŠ$_4$-DAR		A. 247 23
		ḤINN		I		BAJN	AH		IN-NI-BA-NA	FN NOM	X 81 4
		ḤUNN	AT	UM					ḪU-UN-NA-TUM	MN	CT XLV 49 8+
		ḤUNN	AN	UM					ḪU-NA-NU-UM		TA 30 615 18+
		ḤUNN	AN	IM					ḪU-NA-NIM	GEN	B 93
		ḤUNN		IJA					ḪU-NI-IA		UCP X/3 2:22; M
		ḤUNN				ḪUPŠ		I	ḪU-UN-ḪU-UP-ŠE		U
		ḤUNN				PI					
						ʾEL			ḪU-UN-BI-EL		SIMMONS 82 7
		ḤUNN				ŠULGI			ḪU-UN-D-ŠUL-GI		U
		ḤUNN				ZANZI			ḪU-UN-ZA-AN-ZI	FN	XIII 1 IX 42
		ḤUNN				ZANZI			ḪU-UN-ZA-ZI	FN	XIII 1 IX 34, C
		ḤUNN		U		ʾEL			U$_3$-NU-EL		TA 31 223
	2	ʾAB		I		ḤUNN		I	A-BI-ḪU-UN?-NI		B 10
		ʾADM		U	TA	ḤNUN	AN		D-AD-MU-TA-ḪU-NA-AN	FN	RA LXV 61 IV 38
		ʾIL		I		ḤUNIN		I	I$_3$-LI$_2$-U$_2$-NE-NI		RUTTEN 6 20
		ʾIMIR				ḤUNN		A	IM-ME-IR?-ḪU-UN-NA		A. 43 9
		ʾANA				ḤANN		I	A-NA-AḪ-ḪA-AN-NI	FN	XIII 1 V 29
		ʾANN		U		ḤANN		I	AN-NU-ḪA-AN-NI	FN	M+
		ʾANN		U	TA	ḤNUN			AN-NU-TA-AḪ-NU-UN	FN	RA LXV 61 IV 15+
		ʿAQB		A		ḤUNN		UM	AQ-BA-ḪU-NI-UM		B 11
		LA				ḤUNN		IM	LA-ḪU-NI-IM	GEN	M
		NAPŠ		I		ḤINN		I	NA-AP-SI-IN-NI	FN	XIII 1 IV 72
		ŠUM		I		ḤINN		I	ŠU-MI-IN-NI		U
ḤRB	1	ḤARAB	AH						ḪA-RA-BA	FN	M
		ḤARAB	AT	UM					A-RA-BA-TUM		YOS XIII 389:4+
		ḤARIB	AN						ḪA-RI-BA-AN		M+
		ḤARIB	AN	UM					A-RI-BA-A-NU-UM		SIMMONS 103 13+
		ḤARIB	AN	UM					A-RI-BA-NU-UM		SIMMONS 96 12+
		ḤARUB	AH						A-RU-B[A]	FN	XIII 1 III 64+
		ḤARB	AH						ḪA-AR-B[A]?	FN	RA LXV 62 V 41
		ḤARB	ATANUM						AR-BA-TA-NU-UM		B 43
		ḤARB	ATANU						AR-BA-TA-NU		CT IV 22A 19
		ḤARB		I		TUWR		AM	AR-BI-TU-RA-AM		BIROT, TEA 65:35
		ḤIRAB	AN						ḪI-RA-BA-AN		RA LXV 42 II 57

ROOTS (Consonants only)

ḪRB	1		ḪURB	ATANU						UR-BA-TA-NU		KISURRA 24 6
	2		ʿAMM		U		ḪURB	I		AM-MU-UR-BI		A.
			ʿAN		UM		ḪIRB	I		A-NU-UM-ḪI-IR-BI		BALKAN, LETTER P. 6
			ʾAN		I	Š	ḪURB	I		A-NI-IŠ-ḪU-UR-BI		M+
			MAʾL		I		ḪARAB	A		MA-LI-A-RA-BA?		CT II 30 29
			MUT				ḪIRB	AN		MU-UT-ḪI-IR-BA?-AN		VIII 11 4
ḪRM	1	ME	ḪRIM		IM					ME-EḪ-RI-MI-IM	GEN	M+
	2		ŠIJB		U	NA	ḪARAM			ŠI-BU-NA-A-RA-AM		M
ḪSD	1		ḪASAD		UM					A-ZA-DU-UM		CT XLV 77 27
			ḪASAD		UM					ḪA-ZA-DU-U[M]?		M
			ḪASID		U					ḪA-ZI-DU	FN	XIII 1 VII 42
			ḪASID	AN	U					ḪA-ZI-DA-NU		M+
			ḪASID	AN	IM					ḪA-ZI-DA-NIM	GEN	M+
			ḪUSUD		UM					ḪU-ZU-DU-UM	FN	RA LXV 60 III 41
ḪŠK	1		ḪAŠAK			NI	ʾEL			A-SA-AK-NI-EL		RA LXV 52 XI 6
			ḪAŠIK		UM					ḪA-SI-KUM		B 20+
ḪṢN	1	JA	ḪṢUN		UM					IA-ZU-NU-UM		SIMMONS 125 13+
		JA	ḪṢUN				ʾIL			IA-AḪ-ZU-UN-DINGIR		BE VI/1 7 18
		JA	ḪṢIN				ḪAJJ	A		IA-AḪ-ZI-IN-E$_2$-A		XIII 1 VII 23
		JA	ḪṢIN				ʾIRR	A		IA-AḪ-ZI-IN-IR$_3$-RA		M
		JA	ḪṢIN				DAGAN			IA-AḪ-ZI-IN-D-DA-GAN		M
		TA	ḪṢIN				ʾADM	U		TA-AḪ-ZI-IN-AD-MU	FN	M
			ḪAṢAN		UM					A-ZA-NU-UM		B 43+
			ḪAṢAN	AT	UM					ḪA-[Z]A-NA-TUM	FN	M
			ḪAṢAN		IJA					A-ZA-NI-IA		BM 80363 17
			ḪAṢAN				ʾIL	UM		ḪA-ZA-AN-I-LU-UM		M+
			ḪAṢN	AT	UM					ḪA-AZ-NA-TU[M]	FN	M
			ḪAṢN		U		TABB	I		AZ?-NU-TAB-BI	FN	M
			ḪIṢN		I					ḪI-IZ-NI		B 20 HANA
			ḪIṢN	AN	UM					ḪI-IZ-NA-NU-UM		WALTERS, WL 93:2, 14
			ḪIṢN		I		DAGAN			ḪI-IZ-NI-D-DA-GAN		B 20+ HANA
			ḪUṢAN		U					ḪU-ZA-NU		M
			ḪUṢAN		UM					ḪU-ZA-A-NU-UM		BIN VII 101:3
			ḪUṢAN		I					ḪU-ZA-NI	NOM	B 45
			ḪUṢAN	AH						U$_2$-ZA-NA	FN	XIII 1 II 68
	2		ʾADM		U		ḪAṢN	I		D-AD-MU-ḪA-AZ-NI	FN	RA LXV 61 IV 21
			ʾIL		I		ḪAṢN	A	JA	I$_3$-LI$_2$-ḪA-AṢ-NA-A-IA		M+
			ʾIL		I		ḪAṢN	I	JA	I$_3$-LI$_2$-ḪA-AṢ-NI-IA		XIII 1 IX 8
			ʾALLAI				ḪAṢN	U		AL-LA-I-AṢ-NU	FN	M
			ʾANN		U		ḪAṢN	I		AN-NU-ḪA-AṢ-NI	FN	M+
			ʿAŠTAR				ḪAṢN	I		EŠ$_4$-DAR-ḪA-AZ-NI	FN	XIII 1 II 41
			MAM		A		ḪAṢN	I		D-MA-MA-ḪA-AZ-NI	FN	RA LXV 56 I 7
			TABUB		U		ḪAṢN	I		TA-BU-BU-ḪA-AṢ-NI	FN	RA LXV 60 III 19
ḪTK	1		ḪATIK		U					ḪA-TI-KU		M
			ḪATK		UM					ḪA-AT-KU-UM		M
			ḪATK	AN	UM					AT-GA-NU-UM		U
	2		MUT				ḪATK	IM		MU-UT-ḪA-AT-KI-IM		RA LXV 44 IV 57
			MUT		I		ḪATK	IM		MU-TI-ḪA-AD-KI-IM	NOM	IRAQ XXX 92+ RIMAH
			MUT		U		ḪATK	IM		MU-TU-ḪA-AD-KI-IM		M+
			MUT		U		ḪATK	IM		MU-TU-AD-KI-IM		M
			MUT		U		ḪATK	I		MU-TU-ḪA-AD-KI		M
			TURUM			NA	ḪATK	I		TU-RUM-NA-AT-KI		M+
ḪZQ	1	JA	ḪZUQ				ʾIL			IA-AḪ-ZU?-UQ-DINGIR		CT XLVIII 10 3
			ḪAZAQ	AN						ḪA-ZA-KA-AN-KI	GN	M
			ḪAZAQ	AN	IM					ḪA-ZA-KA-AN-NIM-KI	GN GEN	C
			ḪAZAQ	AN	IM					ḪA-ZA-KA-NIM-KI	GN GEN	C II 39 13
			ḪAZAQ				NAN	UM		A-ZA-AQ-NA-NU-UM		CT IV 50A 21
			ḪAZIQ		AJA					ḪA-ZI-QA-IA		UCP X/1 87 12
			ḪAZUQ	AN						ḪA-ZU-GA-AN		RA LXV 54 XII 22
		MA	ḪZIQ		UM					MA-ZI-GU-UM		CT XLVIII 27 CASE
		ME	ḪZIQ		A					ME-ZI-QA		M
		ME	ḪZIQ	AN						ME-ZI-QA-AN		RA LXV 44 IV 30
Ḫʾ D	1		ḪAʾD	ATAN						ḪA-DA-TA-AN		M+
			ḪIʾD	AT	UM					ḪI-DA-TUM	FN	XIII 1 V 54
			ḪIʾD				LA		KA	ḪI-I[D]-LA-A?-KA		XII 141 8

ROOTS (Consonants only)

Ḫʾ D	1	ḪIʾD				LA		KA			
						ʾIL	I		ḪI-ID-LA-KA-I$_3$-LI$_2$		M
		ḪIʾD				LA			ḪI-ID-L[A]-NAM		XIII 38 27
		ḪUʾD	AN	UM					ḪU-DA-A-NU-UM		SIMMONS 83 8
Ḫʾ L	1	ḪAʾL		UM					ḪA-LU-UM		B 19
		ḪAʾL		UM					ḪA-A-LUM		UCP X/1 34 12
		ḪAʾL		U					ḪA-A-LU		A
		ḪAʾL		AJA					ḪA-LA-A-A		B 18
		ḪAʾL	AN	UM					ḪA-LA-NU-UM		KISURRA 57 4, SEAL
		ḪAʾL	AN	UM					ḪA-LA-NUM$_2$		KISURRA 24 2
		ḪAʾL		A	NA				ḪA-LA?-NA	FN	RA LXV 59 II 74
		ḪAʾL		IJA					ḪA-LI-IA		C, A. LATE
		ḪAʾL		IJA					ḪA-LI$_2$-IA		C+
		ḪAʾL		IJA					ḪA-LI$_2$-IA		RA LXV 47 VI 64; C+
		ḪAʾL		IJAN					ḪA-LI-IA-AN		A. LATE
		ḪAʾL	ATAN						ḪA-LA-TA-AN		M+
		ḪAʾL	AT	UM					ḪA-LA-TUM		KISURRA 104 8
		ḪAʾL		I		HADD	U		ḪA-LI$_2$-D-IM		M+
		ḪAʾL		I		HADD	U		ḪA-LI-A-DU		A.+
		ḪAʾL		I		HADD	U		ḪA-LI-IA-[D]U		M
		ḪAʾL		I		ʿADN			ḪA-LI-ḪA-DU-UN		M+
		ḪAʾL		I		ʿADN			ḪA-LI$_2$-ḪA-DU-UN		M+
		ḪAʾL		I		ʿADN			ḪA-LI-ḪA-DU-UM?		M
		ḪAʾL		I		ʿADN	U	HU	ḪA-LI-ḪA-AD-NU-U$_2$		M
		ḪAʾL		I		ʿAḌIR	UM		ḪA-LI-A-ṢI-RUM		UNPUBL.
		ḪAʾL		I		ʾIL			ḪA-LI$_2$-DINGIR		B 18
		ḪAʾL		I		ʾEL			ḪA-LI$_2$-EL		RA LXV 42 III 18+
		ḪAʾL		I		ʾEL			ḪA-A-LI$_2$-EL		RA LXV 42 III 20
		ḪAʾL		I		ʾIL	U	HU	ḪA-A-LI$_2$-I-LU-U$_2$		X 146 5
		ḪAʾL		I		ʿAŠTAR			ḪA-LI$_2$-EŠ$_4$-DAR		RA LXV 53 XII 1
		ḪAʾL		I		KUPAPA			ḪA-LI$_2$-KU-BA-BA	FN	RA LXV 58 I 14
		ḪAʾL		I		MA			ḪA-LI-MA	FN	RA LXV 59 II 43
		ḪAʾL		I		MA					
						ʾIL			ḪA-LI$_2$-MA-DINGIR		M
		ḪAʾL		I		MALIK			ḪA-LI$_2$-MA-LIK		M+
		ḪAʾL		I		MAMM	A		ḪA-LI$_2$-D-M[A-A]M-M[A]		M
		ḪAʾL		I		MARAṢ			ḪA-LI-MA-RA-AṢ		GEN, KICH I P. 59 NO. 219
		ḪAʾL		I		MARAṢ			ḪA-LI-MA-RA-AṢ		UET V 521 1
		ḪAʾL		I	MU	WTAR			ḪA-LI$_2$-MU-TAR		M
		ḪAʾL		I		ŠADW	A		ḪA-LI-SA-DA		B 19
		ḪAʾL		I	TA	NWUḪ	A		ḪA-LI-TA-NU-A		A.+
		ḪAʾL		UJAN					ḪA-LU-JA-AN		RA LXV 41 II 33+
		ḪAʾL		U		ʿADN	U		ḪA-LU-ḪA-AD-NU		M+
		ḪAʾL		U		ʾIL			ḪA-LU-DINGIR		M
		ḪAʾL		U		MAṬAR			ḪA-LU-MA-DA-AR		M+
		ḪAʾL		U		NIʿM			ḪA-LU-NI-ḪI-IM		RA LXV 52 X 74
		ḪAʾL		U		RAPIʾ			ḪA-LU-RA-PI		M+
		ḪAʾL		UM		MAṬAR			ḪA-LUM-MA-DAR		C, SIMMONS 67 SEAL
		ḪAʾL		UM		MAṬAR	I		ḪA-LUM-MA-DA-RI		SIMMONS 67 B 11
		ḪAʾL		UM		MAṬAR	I		ḪA-LUM-MA-DAR-RI		SIMMONS 67 11
		ḪAʾL		U	Š	MI					
						ʾIL			ḪA-LU-UŠ-MI-DINGIR		M
		ḪIʾL	AT	UM					ḪI-LA-TUM	FN	XIII 1 II 71
	2	ʾAḪ		I		ḪIʾL			A-ḪI-ḪI-EL		XIII 1 X 17
		ʾAJA				ḪAʾL	U		A-IA-ḪA-LU		M
		ʾAB		I		ḪIʾL			A-BI-ḪI-EL		B 10, M
		ʾAB		I		ḪIʾL			A-BI-ḪI-IL		M
		ʾAB		I		ḪIʾL	U		A-BI-ḪE$_2$-LU		MRS VI P. 240 LATE
		ʾAB		U		ḪAʾL	UM		A-BU-ḪA-LUM		UCP X P. 53, M
		ʾAB		UM		ḪAʾL	UM		A-BU-UM-ḪA-LUM		B 11+
		ʾAB		UM		ḪAʾL	UM		A-BU-UM-ḪA-LU-UM		B 11+
		ʾAB		U		ḪAʾL	IM		A-BU-ḪA-LIM	GEN	M+
		ʾAB		UM		ḪIʾL	UM		A-BU-UM-ḪI-LUM		B 11
		JADAʿ				ḪAʾL	UM		IA-DA-AḪ-ḪA-LUM		B 25
		ʾIL		A		ḪAʾL	UM		DINGIR-ḪA-LUM		B 21
		ʾIL		A		ḪAʾL	U	HU	DINGIR-ḪA-LU-U$_2$		XIII 1 IV 18

ROOTS (Consonants only)

ḪʾL	2		ʾIL		I		ḪAʾL	UM		I$_3$-LI$_2$-ḪA-LU-UM		CT XLV 3 10
			ʿAMM		U		ḪAʾL	UM		ḪA-AM-MU-ḪA-LUM		M+
		JI	JṢIʾ				ḪAʾL	U		I-ZI-ḪA-LU		XIV 96:9+
			ʿAZZ		U		ḪAʾL	IM		A-ZU-ḪA-LIM	NOM	M
			ḎIMR		U		ḪAʾL	A		ZI-IM-RU-ḪA-LA		BM 17045
		JA	GJIḤ				ḪAʾL	UM		IA-GI?-ḪA-LUM		RUTTEN 16 18
			MUT				ḪAʾL	I		MU-UT-ḪA-LI		B 35 HANA
			MUT				ḪAʾL	I				
							MA			MU-UT-ḪA-LI-MA		M
		Š	NUʾR				ḪAʾL	I		ŠU-NU-UR-ḪA-LI		KING LIH I 22 4, R. 2
		Š	NUʾR		A		ḪAʾL	U		ŠU-NU-UḪ-RA-ḪA-LU		M+
		Š	NUʾR		A		ḪAʾL	U	HU	ŠU-NU-UḪ-RA-ḪA-LU-U$_2$		M+
		Š	NUʾR		A		ḪAʾL	U	HU	ŠU-NU-ḪU-RA-ḪA-LU-U$_2$		XIV 11:1
		Š	NUʾR		A		ḪAʾL	U	HU	ŠU-NU-UḪ-ḪU-RA-ḪA-LU-U$_2$		XIV 36:1+
		Š	NUʾR		U		ḪAʾL	U		ŠU-NU-UḪ-RU-ḪA-LU		M+
		JA	RWIM				ḪAʾL			IA-RI-IM-ḪA-AL		M+
		JA	ŠWUB				ḪAʾL			IA-ŠU-UB-ḪA-AL		RA LXV 44 IV 28
			ŠUWB				ḪAʾL	I		SU-UB-ḪA-LI		A. 268 5
			ŠUWB		A		ḪAʾL	I		ŠU-BA-ḪA-LI		A. 97 16, 18+
			ŠUWB		A		ḪAʾL	I		SU-BA-ḪA-LI		A. 6 29
			ŠUWB		A		ḪAʾL	I		SU-PA-ḪA-LI		A. 252 12+
		JA	ŠLIJ				ḪAʾL			IA-AŠ?-LI?-ḪA-AL		M
			ŠUM		U		ḪAʾL	A		SU-MU-ḪA-LA		B 39
	3		KA				ṢUWR	I				
							ḪAʾI	A		KA-ZU-RI-ḪA-LA		M
ḪʾN	1		ḪAʾN		A					ḪA-NA-KI	GN	M+
			ḪAʾN	IJ	U					ḪA-NU-U$_2$		JNES XIII 210+ LATE
			ḪAʾAN	AN						ḪA-A-NA-AN		C+
			ḪAʾN		A		ʾAB	I		ḪA-NA-A-BI		TIM II 113 2, 8
			ḪAʾAN		A		LA		HA	ḪA-A-NA-LA-A	FN	XIII 1 II 53+
			ḪIʾAN		A					ḪI-A-NA		BM 80328 4
	2		MUT				ḪAʾN	A		MU-UT-ḪA-NA		XIV 47:31
ḪʾR	1		ḪAʾR		IJA					ḪA-RI-IA		M+
			ḪAʾR		I		ʾIL			ḪA-RI-DINGIR		BM 82372 27
			ḪAʾR		I		ʾATT	A		ḪA-RI-A-TA		C II 5 7
			ḪAʾR		I		MALIK			ḪA-RI-MA-LIK		BE VI/1 46 5
			ḪAʾR		I		MALIK	I		ḪA-RI-MA-LI-KI	GEN	B 20
	2	JI	JṢIʾ				ḪAʾR	U		I-ZI-ḪA-RU		XIV 52:5, 16+
ḪʾŠ	1		ḪAʾŠ	AT	UM					ḪA-SA-TUM	MN	RUTTEN 15 6 SEAL
			ḪAʾŠ	AN	U					ḪA-SA-NU		M
	2		MUT				ḪAʾŠ	UM		MU-UT-ḪA-SU-UM		A.
ḪʾT	1		ḪUʾT	AN	UM					ḪU-TA-NU-UM		B 45
	2		ʿAḎR		I		ḪAʾT	UM		AD-RI-ḪA-TUM		SIMMONS 88 16+
			ʾUMM		I		ḪAʾT	UM		UM-MI-ḪA-TUM	FN	M+
		TA	KWUN				ḪAʾT	UM		TA-KU-UN-ḪA-TUM	FN	M+
		TA	RʿIŠ				ḪAʾT	U		TA-RI-IŠ-ḪA-AT-TU	FN	M+
			ŠAMAʿ				ḪAʾT	IM		ŠA-MA-ḪA-TIM	GEN	XIII 1 VIII 44
		TA	TWUR				ḪAʾT	UM		TA-DUR-ḪA-TUM		TA 1931, 489
ḪʾZ	1		ḪAʾZ	UT	UM					ḪA-ZU-TUM	FN	RA LXV 58 II 1
			ḪAʾAZ		U		ʾIL			ḪA?-A-ZU-DINGIR		M
			ḪUʾZ	AN	UM					ḪU-ZA-NU-UM		RA LXV 55 XIII 13+
ḪḪN	1		ḪAḪUN		A					ḪA-ḪU-NA		CT II 23 33
ḪWL	1		ḪUWAL		UM					ḪU-WA-LUM		B 20
			ḪUWAL		IM					ḪU-WA-LI-IM	GEN	B 20
ḪWR	1		ḪAWR				ʾAB	I		ḪA-AW-RA-BI		TIM IV 33 21, 34 14
			ḪAWR	AN	IM					ḪA-AW-RA-NIM	GEN	B 44
			ḪAWR	AN			ʾAB	I		ḪA-AW-RA-AN-A-BI		M
			ḪAWR	AN			ʾAB	I		ḪA-AW-RA-NA-A-BI		M+
			ḪAWIR			NI				ḪA-WI-IR-NI		RA LXV 45 V 12
ḪBʾ	1	JA	ḪBAʾ				RAŠAP			IA-AḪ-BA-D-RA-SA-AP		XIII 94 5
		JA	ḪBUʾ		UM					IA-AḪ-BU-U$_2$-UM		M
		JA	ḪBIʾ				ʾIL	A		IA-AḪ-BI-LA-KI	GN	M+
			ḪABIʾ			JA				ḪA-BI-IA		RA LXV 52 X 71
			ḪABIʾ	AN	U					ḪA-BI-A-NU		YOS XIII 175:12
			ḪABIʾ				HADD	U		ḪA-BI-D-IM		M
ḪBD	1	ʾA	ḪBUD	IJ	UM					AḪ-BU-TE-UM		U

ROOTS (Consonants only)

ḪBD	1		ḪABAD		UM				ḪA-BA-TUM	FN	RA LXV 59 II 76
			ḪABAD		U		ʾIL		ḪA-BA-DU-DINGIR		M
			ḪUBAD		UM				ḪU-PA-DU-UM		WATERMAN 14 R. 14
			ḪUBAD		I				ḪU-PA-DI		EDZARD, DER 101:12
			ḪUBD	AT	UM				ḪU-UP-DA-T[UM]	FN	XIII 1 VII 65
	2		ʾIL		A		ḪABAD		DINGIR-ḪA-BA-AD		M+
ḪBR	1		ḪABIR		IM				ḪA-BI-RI-IM	GEN	M
			ḪABIR	AN					ḪA-BI-RA-AN		RA LXV 54 XII 21
			ḪABUR		I				ḪA-BU-UR-RI	FN	RA LXV 63 III 1
			ḪABUR			JI	JBAL				
							BUGAŠ		ID$_2$-ḪA-BUR-I-BA-AL-BU-GA-AŠ$_2$		BRM IV 52 HANA
			ḪIBAR	AT	I				ḪI-BA-RA-TI	MN NOM	VIII 6 31
			ḪIBR	AN					Ḫ[I-I]B-RA-AN		RA LXV P. 42 III 6
			ḪUBR	AT	UM				ḪU-UB-RA-TUM	FN	XIII 1 IX 31
	2		MUT				ḪUBUR		MU-UT-ḪU-BUR		SYRIA V 271, 275
ḪBZR	1		ḪABZUR	AN					ḪA-AB-ZU-RA-AN		RA LXV 48 VIII 21+
ḪGL	1		ḪIGUL	AH					ḪI-GU-LA	FN	M+
			ḪUGUL		UM				ḪU-GU-LU[M]		HARRIS 79 4
ḪGR	1		ḪAGIR		UM				ḪA-GI-RUM		M
			ḪAGUR	AH					ḪA-GU-RA	FN	RA LXV 64 V 63
ḪLḪL	1		ḪILḪIL		UM				ḪI-EL-ḪI-LUM		SIMMONS 111 3
			ḪILḪIL		UM				ḪI-IL-ḪI-LUM		B 48+
ḪLD	1		ḪALD		A		MULUK		ḪA?-AL-DA-MU-LU-UK		BASOR 95 21
ḪLK	1		ḪILUK	AH					ḪI-LU?-KA	FN	XIII 1 V 81
ḪLM	1		ḪULM		EJA				ḪU-UL-ME-I[A]		RA LXV 41 II 46
ḪLN	1		ḪALAN		I		JATAR		ḪA-LA-NI-E-TAR		M
ḪLŠ	1		ḪULAŠ		AJA				ḪU-LA-ŠA-A		HARRIS 75 22
ḪMʾ	1		ḪIMʾ	AT	UM				ḪI-IM-A-TUM	FN	XIII 1 X 40
ḪMJ	2		LA				ḪAMUJ	IM	LA-ḪA-MU-JI-IM	GEN	M
ḪMBZ	1		ḪAMBUZ		U	HU			ḪA-AM-BU-ZU-U$_2$		B 19
ḪML	1		ḪIML		UM		....		Ḫ[I-I]M-LU-UM-[....]	FN	M
ḪMM	1	JA	ḪMUM		IM				IA-AḪ-MU-MI-IM	GN GEN	M
		JA	ḪMUM		AM				IA-AḪ-MU-MA-AM-KI	GN ACC	M
ḪMR	1		ḪAMR		U				ḪA-AM-RU		C
			ḪAMR		U		RAPIʾ		ḪA-AM-RU-RA-BI		M
			ḪUMR	AN	UM				ḪU-UM-RA-NU-UM		U
	2		KUʾŠ		I		ḪIMR	I	KU-ŠI-ḪI-IM-RI		SIMMONS 87 19
ḪMŠ	1		ḪAMAŠ	AT	UM				ḪA-MA-SA-TUM	MN	CT XLV 91 20
			ḪAMŠ	AT	UM				ḪA-AM-SA-TUM	FN	BM 16844+
			ḪUMUŠ	AT	UM				ḪU-MU-SA-TUM	MN	TCL I 62 3
ḪMṬ	1		ḪAMAṬ		I		ʾIL		ḪA-MA-TI-IL		FIGULLA, CAT. I 14135
		JA	ḪMUṬ		UM				IA-AḪ-MU-TU-UM-KI	GN	UET V 9721
		JA	ḪMUṬ		U				IA-AḪ-MU-TU		JEAN,TELL SIFR 13 15
		JA	ḪMUṬ	AN					IA-AḪ-MU-DA-AN		M
ḪNʾ	1		ḪINIʾ		I				ḪI-NI-I		XII 1 VIII 51
ḪNW	2		ʾIL		I	JI	ḪNUW	HU	I$_3$-LI$_2$-IḪ-NU-U$_2$		UCP X/1 19:4+
ḪNB	1		ḪANB	AT	UM				ḪA-AN-BA-TUM	FN	CT XLV 91 18+
ḪND	1		ḪAND		IJA				ḪA-AN-DI-IA		BIN VII 63 28
ḪNDN	2		BIN		A		ḪANDEN		BI-NA-ḪA-AN-DI-EN		M
ḪNP	1		ḪANP	AT	UM				ḪA-AN-PA-TUM	FN	A 3521 29
			ḪANP	AT	IM				ḪA-AN-PA-TIM	FN GEN	A 3521 31
ḪNŠ	1		ḪANAŠ		I				ḪA-NA-ŠI	GEN	HARRIS 3916
			ḪUNAŠ		UM				ḪU-NA-ŠUM		BM 82432
ḪNZ	1		ḪANZ		I				ḪA-AN-ZI		TA 1931, 434
			ḪANZ		A		HADD	U	ḪA-AN-ZA-D-IM		M
ḪNZR	1		ḪANZUR		A				ḪA-AN-ZU-RA		VAS IX 172 39+
ḪPʾ	1	JA	ḪAPIʾ				ʾIL		IA-ḪA-AP-PI-I-IL5	GN	JCS XVIII 59 12+
ḪPŠ	1		ḪUPŠ		UM				ḪU-UP-ŠUM		CT XLVIII 81 REV.
	2		ḪUNN				ḪUPŠ	I	ḪU-UN-ḪU-UP-ŠE		U
ḪQT	1		ḪAQAT		A				ḪA-QA-TA		DELAPORTE CCL II A 914
ḪRḪR	1		ḪARḪAR		U				ḪAR-ḪA-RU		JNES XIII 210+ LATE
ḪRJ	2		ʿAMM		I	Š	ḪARIJ	JE	AM-MI-IS-ḪA-RI?-E?		JEAN, S'A CLXXXVIII R. 3
ḪRD	1		ḪIRD		IJA				ḪI-IR-DI-IA		RA LXV 53 XI 50
ḪRGL	1		ḪARGAL						ḪA-AR-GA-AL		M
			ḪARGAL		UM				ḪA-AR-GA-LUM		VAS VIII 14 26
ḪRR	1		ḪARIR		UM				ḪA-RI-RUM		B 20

ḪRR	1		ḪARIR		UM						ḪA-AR-RI-RUM		B 20
			ḪURR	AN	UM						ḪU-UR-RA-NU-UM		CT IV 25C 15
		MU	ḪARIR		IM						MU-ḪA-RI-RI-IM	GEN	M
	2	JA	KWUN					ḪARAR			IA-KU-UN-ḪA-RA-AR		VAS IX 172 4+
		JA	KWUN					ḪARAR	I		IA-KU-[UN-ḪA]-RA-RI	GEN	BM 81641 6
		JA	KWUN					ḪARAR	I		IA-KUN$_3$-ḪA-RA-RI		CT XLVIII 3:3
		JI	KWUN					ḪARAR	I		I-KU-UN-ḪA-RA-RI?	GEN	TCL I 151 4
ḪRŠN	2		MUT		I			ḪURŠAN			MU-TI-ḪUR-SAG		YOS XII+
			MUT		I			ḪURŠAN	A		MU-TI-ḪU-UR-ŠA-NA		B 35+
			MUT		I			ḪURŠAN	I		MU-TI-ḪU-UR-ŠA-NI		YOS XII
ḪRṢ	1		ḪIRṢ		UM						ḪI-IR-ZU-UM		RA LXV 48 VIII 6
			ḪIRṢ		U	K					ḪI-IR-ZU-UK		RA LXV 51 IX 44
			ḪURAṢ	AT	UM						ḪU-RA-ZA-TUM	FN	XIII 1 I 73+
			ḪURAṢ		AJA						ḪU-RA-ZA-A-IA	FN	XIII 1 VIII 84
			ḪURUṢ		UM						ḪU-RU-ZUM		RA LXV 53 XI 16
			ḪURUṢ	AN							ḪU-RU-ZA-AN		RA LXV 44 IV 53+
			ḪURUṢ	AN	UM						ḪU-RU-ZA-NU-UM		B 44
			ḪURṢ	AN	UM						ḪU-UR-ZA-NU-UM		B 44
			ḪURṢ	AN	U						ḪU-UR-ZA-NU-KI	GN	A.
			ḪURṢ	AN	IM						ḪUR-ZA-NIM	GEN	B 44
			ḪURṢ	AN	IM						ḪUR-ZA-A-NIM	GEN	B 44
			ḪURṢ	AN	IM						ḪU-UR-ZA-NIM	GEN	B 44
ḪŠJ	1	JA	ḪŠIJ					ʾIL			IA-AḪ-SI-DINGIR		OLZ VIII 350 2
		JA	ḪŠIJ					ʾIL			JA-AḪ-SI-DINGIR		M
			ḪAŠIJ	AN	UM						ḪA-ŠI-A-NU-UM		TA 1931, 538 III
ḪŠM	1	MA	ḪŠIM	AN	UM						MA-AḪ-ŠI-MA-NU-UM		B 46+
	2		ḎIMR		I			ḪAŠAM			ZI-IM-RI-ḪA-SA-AM	NOM	C+
ḪŠR	2		LA				ʾA	ḪŠIR	UM		LA-AḪ-SI-RU-UM		BM 80368 2
ḪŠT	1		ḪAŠT	AT	UM						ḪA-AŠ-TA-TUM	FN	XIII 1 III 62
ḪŠḪŠ	1		ḪAŠḪAŠ		UM						ḪA-AŠ-ḪA-ŠUM		KISURRA 62 3
ḪŠŠ	1		ḪAŠIŠ		UM						ḪA-ŠI-ŠUM		B 20+
			ḪAŠŠ		UM						ḪA-AŠ-ŠUM		RA LXV 47 VII 27
			ḪIŠŠ	AT	UM						ḪI-IŠ-ŠA-TUM	FN	WATERMAN
			ḪUŠŠ	UT	UM						ḪU-ŠU-TUM	FN	CT VI 43 6, 34
			ḪUŠŠ	UT	UM						ḪU-UŠ$_2$-ŠU-TUM	FN	X 96 3
			ḪUŠŠ	UT	IM						ḪU-ŠU-TIM	FN GEN	X 27 8
ḪŠTR	1		ḪAŠTUR		UM						ḪA-AŠ-TU-RU-UM		YOS VIII 139 15 CASE 13
ḪTʾ	1	JA	ḪATIʾ					ʾIL			IA-ḪA-AT-TI-DINGIR		M+, C
		JA	ḪATIʾ					ʾEL			IA-ḪA-TI-EL		RA LXV 44 IV 46
		JA	ḪATIʾ					ʾIL			IA-ḪA-TI-DINGIR		RUTTEN 15:2+; M
		JA	ḪATIʾ					ʾIL	UM		IA-ḪA-TI-LUM		YOS XII
		JA	ḪATIʾ					ŠAMŠ			IA-ḪA-AT-TI-D-UTU		UCP X/1 89 15
			ḪATAʾ		A			ʾAR	UM		ḪA-TA-A-A-RUM?		CT XXIX 8A 1
			ḪATAʾ					ʾUMAN	UM		ḪA-TA-UM-MA-NU-UM		RA VIII 74 19
ḪTN	1		ḪATAN					PI					
								ʾIL			ḪA-TA-AN-BI-DINGIR		M
		ŠT	ḪTIN					ʾIL			(E$_2$-)ŠA-TA-AḪ-TI-IN-DINGIR	GN	KISURRA
	2		ʾAB		I			ḪATAN			A-BI-ḪA-TA-AN		B 10
			ʾIL		I		ʾA	ḪTAN			I$_3$-LI$_2$-AḪ-TA-AN		RUTTEN 6 16+
ḪṬʾ	2		ʾIL		I		JI	ḪṬAʾ					
								LI		JA	I$_3$-LI$_2$-IḪ-TA-LI-A		BIROT,TEA 69 I 14
ḪZM	1	JA	ḪZUM		U						IA-AḪ-ZU?-MU		BM 78799 12
		JA	ḪZIM					....			IA-AḪ-ZI-IM-[....]		M
			ḪAZIM		UM						ḪA-ZI-MU-UM		HARRIS 63 16
			ḪUZAM		I						ḪU-ZA-MI		BE VI/2 138 18
			ḪUZM	AN	UM						ḪU-UZ-MA-N[U-UM]		TA 1931, 265
			ḪUZM	ATAN							ḪU-IZ-MA-TA-AN		M
ḪZR	1	JA	ḪZUR					HADD	U		IA-AḪ-ZU-UR-D-IM		M
		JA	ḪZUR					ʾIL			IA-AḪ-ZU-UR-IL		TIM III 34 15A
		JA	ḪZUR					ʾIL			IA-AḪ-ZU-UR-DINGIR		JCS XXIV 57 NO 39 AND 51
			ḪIZR		IJAN						ḪI-IZ-RI-IA-AN		M
			ḪUZIR	AN							ḪU-ZI-RA-AN		RA LXV 50 VIII 67+
			ḪUZIR	AN	UM						ḪU-ZI-RA-NU-UM		B 45
			ḪUZIR	AT	UM						ḪU-ZI-RA-TUM		EDZARD, DER 99 REV 8
ʿWQ	1	JA	ʿWUQ		UM						IA-U$_2$-KU-UM		B 31+
			ʿAWIQ	AN							A-I-GA-AN		RA LXV 52 X 58

ROOTS (Consonants only)

ʿWQ	1	ʿAWIQ	AT	UM				ḪA-I-KA-TUM	FN	SIMMONS 112:17
		ʿUWQ		UM				ḪU-KU-UM	FN	RA LXV 58 I 51
ʿJN	1	ʿIJN			BAʿL	I		IN-BA-AḪ-LI	FN	A.
	2	ʾIL		I	ʿIJN	A	JA	I$_3$-LI$_2$-I-NA-A-A		GAUTIER 40 7
ʿBB	1	ʿEBIB		UM				E-BI-BU-UM		SIMMONS 76 6
		ʿEBB		IM				IB-BI-IM	GEN	M+
		ʿEBB	AT	UM				IB-BA-TUM	FN	M+
		ʿEBB	AT	IM				IB-BA-TIM	FN GEN	M
		ʿEBB	ATANUM					IB-BA-TA-NU-UM		BE VI/2 26 III 1
ʿBD	1	ʿABD		UM				ḪA-AB-DU-UM		B 9+, M+
		ʿABD		IM				AB-DI-IM	GEN	B 9, M
		ʿABD	AN					ḪA-AB-DA-AN		M, C+
		ʿABD	AN					AB-DA-AN		M
		ʿABD	AN	U				AB-DA-NU		CT XLV 59 6
		ʿABD	AN	U				AB-TA-NU		A. LATE
		ʿABD	AN	UM				ḪA-AB-DA-[NUM]?		PBS VIII/2 260 4
		ʿABD	AN	A				AB-TA-NA	NOM	A. LATE
		ʿABD	AT	UM				ḪA-AB-DA-TUM	FN	XIII 1 XIV 39
		ʿABD	ATAN					ḪA-AB-DA-TA-AN		M+
		ʿABD	ATAN					AB-[DA?-T]A-AN		RA LXV 44 IV 62
		ʿABD		AJA				AB-DA-A		GORDON 38 15+
		ʿABD		IJA				ḪA-AB-DI-IA		B 9+, M, C+
		ʿABD		IJA				AB-DI-IA		A.+
		ʿABD			ʾABN	IM		ARAD$_2$-AB-NIM		BAGHD. MITT. II 72
		ʿABD			HAND	U		ḪA-AB-DI-IA-AN-DU		KUPPER NOM. P. 231
		ʿABD			HAND	U		AB-DI-IA-DU		KUPPER NOM. P. 231
		ʿABD			HAND	U		AB-DU-IA-AN-DU		KUPPER NOM. P. 231
		ʿABD			HEDD	A		ḪA-AB-DI-E-D-IM		RS XIX 338F.
		ʿABD			HADD	U		AB-DI-AD-DU		BAGHD. MITT. II 57 28
		ʿABD			HADD	U		ḪA-AB-DU-D-IM		RA LXV 48 VIII 34
		ʿABD			ʿAḎR	A		ḪA-AB-DU-ḪA-AD-RA		M
		ʿABD			ʾEL			AB-DA-EL		TA 30, 615 9, 41
		ʿABD			ʾEL			ḪA-AB-DI-EL		KISURRA 74 17
		ʿABD			ʾIL			AB-TE-IL		I
		ʿABD			ʾIL			ḪA-AB-DI-DINGIR		B 9
		ʿABD			ʾIL			AB-DI-DINGIR		B 9+
		ʿABD			ʾIL	I		AB-DI-LI		A.+
		ʿABD			ḪAM	I		AB-DI-A-MI		BAGHD. MITT. II 58 III 21
		ʿABD			ḪAM	I		ḪA-AB-DU-D-A-MI		M+
		ʿABD			ḪAM	I		ḪA-AB-DU-A-MI		M
		ʿABD			ʿAMM	UM		ḪA-AB-DU-A-MU-UM		M
		ʿABD			ʿAMM	IM		AB-DU-A-MI-IM	NOM	M+
		ʿABD			ʿAMM	IM		AB-DU-A-MI-IM	GEN	M+
		ʿABD			ʿAMM	IM		ḪA-AB-DU-A-MI-IM		M
		ʿABD			ʿAN	AT		ḪA-AB-DU-D-ḪA-NA-AT		M+
		ʿABD			ʿAN	AT	I	AB-TA-NA-TI		A. P. 128A LATE +
		ʿABD			ʿAN	AT	I	AB-DI-A-NA-TI		A. P. 128B LATE +
		ʿABD			ʿAN	AT	I	AB-TI-A-NA-TI		JCS XIII 54 300, A. LATE
		ʿABD			JARAḪ			AB-DI-A-RA-AḪ		B 9+
		ʿABD			JARAḪ			ḪA-AB-DI-A-RA-AḪ		B 9
		ʿABD			JARAḪ			AB-DI-RA-AḪ		B 9+
		ʿABD			JARAḪ			ḪA-AB-DI-E-RA-AḪ		M+, C+
		ʿABD			JARAḪ			AB-DI-E-RA-AḪ		M+, UCP X P. 198+
		ʿABD			JARAḪ			ḪA-AB-DI-RA-AḪ		SUMER XXIII 162 46
		ʿABD			JARAḪ			AB-DI-D-EN-ZU		PBS VII/1 94 III 28
		ʿABD			JARAḪ			AB-DI-D-E-RA-AḪ		YOS XIII 199:22+
		ʿABD			JARAḪ			AB-DU-D-E-RA-AḪ		YOS XIII 218:13+
		ʿABD			JARAḪ			ḪA-AB-DU-E-RA-AḪ		DELAPORTE CCL II A 418 M
		ʿABD			JARAḪ			AB-DU-E-RA-AḪ		M+
		ʿABD			ʾIRŠAP	A		ḪA-AB-DU-IR?-ŠA-PA?		M
		ʿABD			ʾIŠḪAR	AH		AB-DI-D-IŠ-ḪA-RA		A.+
		ʿABD			ʾIŠḪAR	AH		ḪA-AB-DU-D-IŠ-ḪA-RA		XIII 1 II 79+
		ʿABD			ʾAŠUR	A		ḪA-AB-DU-A-ŠU-RA		M
		ʿABD			ʿAŠTAR			AB-DI-D-EŠ$_4$-DAR		A. 19 4, 7
		ʿABD			ʿAŠTAR			AB-DU-EŠ$_4$-DAR		M+
		ʿABD			ʿAŠTAR			ḪA-AB-DU-EŠ$_4$-DAR		M+, C+

ROOTS (Consonants only)

ʿBD	1		ʿABD					ʿIŠTAR	AH			AB-DU-IŠ-TA-RA?		B 9
			ʿABD					ʾUTL		I		AB-DU-UT-LI	FN	A. LATE
			ʿABD					BAʿL	AH			ḪA-AB-DU-BA-AḪ-LA		M
			ʿABD					BAʿL	AT	I		ḪA-AB-DU-BA-AḪ-LA-TI		M+
			ʿABD					DAGAN				ḪA-AB-DU-D-DA-GAN		M
			ʿABD					DAGAN				AB-DU-D-DA-GAN		M
			ʿABD					KUʾB		I		ḪA-AB-DU-KU-BI		M+
			ʿABD					MA						
								DAGAN				AB-DU-MA-D-DA-GAN		M+
			ʿABD					MA						
								DAGAN				ḪA-AB-DU-MA-D-DA-GAN		M+
			ʿABD					MALIK				ḪA-AB-DU-MA-LIK		M+
			ʿABD					MALIK				AB-DU-MA-LIK		XIII 37 16
			ʿABD					MALIK		I		AB-DU-MA-LI-KI		YOS XIII 54:5
			ʿABD					NAHR				AB-DI-D-ID$_2$		SCHEIL 10 15, 16
			ʿABD					NAWAR				ḪA-AB-DU-NA-WA-AR		M
			ʿABD					NAWAR				AB-DU-NA-W[A-AR]		M
			ʿABD					ŠUWR		I		AB-DU-ŠU-RI		IRAQ XXX 94, RIMAH
			ʿABD		U		TA	RWIM				[ḪA-A]B-DU-TA-RI-IM		M
	2		ŠU					ʿABD		I		ŠU-ḪA-AB-DI		CT XLVIII 43:15,19
ʿD	1		ʿAD		U							A-DU		A. 269 67, 73+
			ʿAD	AT	UM							A-DA-TUM	MN	I, MEISSNER 51 3
			ʿAD	AT	UM							A-DA-TUM	FN	M+
			ʿAD	AT	IM							A-DA-TIM	MN GEN	XIII 87 5
			ʿAD	AT	IJA							A-DA-TI-A	FN	MRS IX P. 243 UGARIT
			ʿAD	AT	A	HA						A-DA-TA-A	FN	APN P. 12 LATE
			ʿAD		U			RAWM		U		A-DU-RA-MU	FN	U
			ʿAD		U	NA		HADD		U		A-DU-NA-D-IM		SYRIA XIX 109
			ʿAD		U	NI		ʾAB		I	JA	A-DU-NI-A-BI-IA		RA XXVII 87 LATE
			ʿAD		U	NI		HADD		U		A-DU-NI-D-U		MRS VI 15, 42 II 20 UGARIT
			ʿAD		U	NI		ʾIL		A		A-DU-NI-LA		U
	2		HALIL		A			ʿAD		UM		A-LI-LA-ḪA-DU-UM		KISURRA 18 12
			ʾAMR					ʿAD		UM		AM-RA-DU-UM		M
			JARAḪ					ʿAD		U		SIN-A-DU		RA XLIII 8 QATNA
		JI	JṢIʾ					ʿAD		UM		I-ZI-A-DU-UM		M
			ḎU					ʿAD		IM		ZU-ḪA-DI-IM	GEN	M
			LU					ʿAD		UM		LU-ḪA-DU-UM		YOS XIII 497:2
			RABB		U			ʿAD		UM		RU-BU-ḪA-DU-UM		BM 17055 26
			RABB		U			ʿAD		U	HU	RA-AB-BU-ḪA-DU-U$_2$		B 17+
			RABB		U			ʿAD		U	HU	RA-AB-BU-U$_2$-ḪA-DU-U$_2$		BM 17051A 30
		ʾA	RŠIJ					ʿAD		A	HA	AR-ŠI-A-DA?-A	FN	C
			ŠUM		UM			ʿAD		U		SU-MU-UM?-ḪA-DU-KI	GN	YOS II 117:17+
			ŠUM		U			ʿAD		I		SU-MU-ḪA-DI-I	GEN	XIII 13:8
			ŠUM		U			ʿAD		IM		SU-MU-ḪA-DI-IM		X 57 8
			ŠUM		U			ʿAD		U	HU	SU-MU-ḪA-DU-U$_2$		M+
ʿDJ	1	JA	ʿDIJ					....				JA-AḪ-DI-[....]		M
			ʿADIJ		UM							A-DI-UM		M
			ʿADIJ					ʾIL				A-DI-DINGIR		M
			ʿADIJ					ʾEL				ḪA-DI-EL		KISURRA 113 12+
			ʿADIJ			NA		ʾIL				A-DI-E-NA-DINGIR		M
ʿDN	1	JA	ʿDUN		UM							IA-AḪ-DU-NU-UM		B 26
		JA	ʿDUN	AN	UM							IA-AḪ-DU-NA-NU-UM		JCS XXIV 60 NO.51 REV.
		JA	ʿDUN					LIʾM				IA-AḪ-DU-UN-LI-IM		M+
		JA	ʿDUN					LIʾM				IA-AḪ-DU-LI-IM		M+
		JA	ʿDUN					LIʾM				IA-AḪ-DU-UL-LI-IM		M
			ʿADN		U							ḪA-AD-NU		KISURRA 81A 20
			ʿADN	AN								ḪA-AD-NA-AN		M, C
			ʿADN	AN	UM							AD-NA-NU-UM		TIM III 44 19+
			ʿADN		A		ʾA	ʾMUR				ḪA-AD-NA-AM?-MU-UR		X 75 18
			ʿADN		A			ʾAB		I		ḪA?-AD-NA-A-BI		TTKB XIX 304
			ʿADN		I			HADD		U		ḪA-AD-NI-D-IM		M, C+
			ʿADN		I			HADD		U		ḪA-AD-NI-A-D[U]		DELAPORTE CCL II A 914
			ʿADN		I			ʾIL				ḪA-AD-NI-DINGIR		M+
			ʿADN		I			ʾIL		U				
								MA				ḪA-AD-NI-DINGIR-MA		M
			ʿADN		I			ʿAMM		U		ḪA-AD-NI-ḪA-MU		RA LXV 50 VIII 49

ROOTS (Consonants only)

ʿDN	1		ʿADN		I		JARAḪ			ḪA-AD-NI-E-RA-AḪ		M
			ʿADN		I		DAGAN			ḪA-AD-NI-D-DA-GAN		M
			ʿADN		I		ŠAMŠ			ḪA-AD-NI-SA-MA-AŠ$_2$		M
			ʿADN		U		MA					
							JATAR			ḪA-AD-NU-ME-TAR		M+
			ʿADN		UM		MAZAʾ	A		ḪA-[A]D?-NU-UM-MA-ZA-A		RA LXV 41 II 52
			ʿADN		U		RAPIʾ			ḪA-AD-NU-RA-BI		XIV 109:18+
	2		ḪAʾL		I		ʿADN			ḪA-LI-ḪA-DU-UN		M+
			ḪAʾL		I		ʿADN			ḪA-LI$_2$-ḪA-DU-UN		M+
			ḪAʾL		I		ʿADN			ḪA-LI-ḪA-DU-UM?		M
			ḪAʾL		I		ʿADN	U	HU	ḪA-LI-ḪA-AD-NU-U$_2$		M
			ḪAʾL		U		ʿADN	U		ḪA-LU-ḪA-AD-NU		M+
			ʾIL		A		ʿADN	U	HU	I-LA-ḪA-AD-NU-U$_2$		M
			ʾIL		A		ʿADN	U	HU	I-LA-ḪA-AD-NU-U$_2$	FN	C+
			ʾIL		A		ʿADN	U	HU	DINGIR-ḪA-AD-NU-U$_2$	FN	C+
			ʾIL		I		ʿADN	I		I$_3$-LI$_2$-ḪA-AD-NI	FN	M
			ʿAMM		I		ʿADN	A		AM-MI-ḪA-AD-NA		GOETZE, KIZZ. P. 8, LATE
			JATAR				ʿADN	U		IA-TAR-ḪA-AD-NU		M+
			JATAR				ʿADN	U	HU	IA-TAR-ḪA-AD-NU-U$_2$		RA LXV 54 XII 56
		JI	JTAR				ʿADN	I		I-TAR-AD-AN		WATERMAN 41 R. 10
			DAWD		I		ʿADN			DA-DI-ḪA-DU-UN		M+
			DAWD		I		ʿADN	U	HU	DA-DI-ḪA-AD-NU-U$_2$		18 R.A. P.61 A 3821+
			ḎU				ʿADN	U		ZU-ḪA-AD-NU		M+
			ḎU				ʿADN	I		ZU-ḪA-AD-NI	NOM	M+
			ḎU				ʿADN	I		ZU-ḪA-AD-NI	GEN	M+
			ḎU				ʿADN	IM		ZU-ḪA-AD-NIM	GEN	M+
			ḎU				ʿADN	IM		ZU-U$_2$-ḪA-AD-NIM		VOIX 187:18 MARI
			LA				ʿADN	I	JA	LA-AD-NI-IA		M
			LA				ʿADN	A				
						ʾA	MWUT			LA-ḪA-AD-NA-A-MU-UT		M
		JA	MṢIʾ				ʿADN	U		IA-AM-ZI-AD-[NU]		CT VI 33A 33
		JA	MṢIʾ				ʿADN	U		IA-AM-ṢI-AD-NU		BM 16914 31
		JA	MṢIʾ				ʿADN	U		IA-AM-ZI-ḪA-AD-NU		M+
		JA	MṢIʾ				ʿADN	U	HU	IA-AM-ZI-AD-NU-U$_2$		BM 81302 4
		JA	MṢIʾ				ʿADN	U	HU	IA-AM-ZI-ḪA-AD-NU-U$_2$		DELAPORTE CCL II A 385, M+
		JA	MZUʾ				ʿADN	IM		[IA?-AM?-Z]U?-ḪA-AD-NIM	GEN	XIII 129 5
		JA	MZUʾ				ʿADN	U	HU	IA-AM-ZU-AD-NU-U$_2$		B 28+
			ŠUM		U		ʿADN	U		SU-MU-ḪA-AD-NU		B 39
			ŠUM		U		ʿADN	U		SU-MU-ḪI-AD-NU		KISURRA 29 12
			ŠARR		UM		ʿADN	U	HU	LUGAL-AD-NU-U$_2$		SIGRIST UNPUBL.
		JI	TWUR				ʿADN	U		I-DUR-ḪA-AD-[NU]		B 24
		JI	TWUR				ʿADN	U	HU	I-DUR-ḪA-AD-NU-U$_2$		TCL XVIII 83 6
ʿḎR	1	JA	ʿḎAR				ʾIL			IA-DAR-DINGIR		RUTTEN 5 9+
		JA	ʿḎAR				ʾIL			IA-AḪ-ZA-AR-DINGIR		B 26
		JA	ʿḎAR				ʾIL			IA-AḪ-ZA-AR-I$_3$-IL		B 26
		JA	ʿḎAR				ʾIL			IA-ZA-AR-DINGIR?		IX 291 II 21,30
		JA	ʿḎAR				ʾIL			AḪ-ZA-AR-I$_3$-DINGIR		VAS XVIII 20:20
		TA	ʿḎAR	AH						TA-DA-RA	FN	M
		JA	ʿḎIR							IA-AḪ-ZI-IR		YOS VIII 76 26
		JA	ʿḎIR		UM					IA-AḪ-ZI-RUM		B 26+
		JA	ʿḎIR		U					IA-AḪ-ZI-RU		CT XLV 63 34
		JA	ʿḎIR		I					IA-AḪ-ZI-RI	GEN	BM 16943 34
		JA	ʿḎIR				ʾIL			IA-AḪ-ZI-IR-DINGIR		B 26+
		JA	ʿḎIR				ʾIL			IA-AḪ-ZI-IR-I$_3$-IL		SUMER V 137
		JA	ʿḎIR				ʾIL			IA-AḪ-ZI-IR-I$_3$-DINGIR		CT XLV 8 6
		ME	ʿḎIR		I					ME-ZI-RI		M
			ʿAḎAR		UM					A-ZA-RU-UM		B 14
			ʿAḎAR		UM					A-DA-RU-UM	FN	RA LXV 60 III 25
			ʿAḎAR		IM					A-ZA-RI-IM	GEN	B 14
			ʿAḎAR	AN	IM					ḪA-ZA-RA-NIM	GEN	B 44
			ʿAḎAR				ʾAḪ			A-ZA-RA-AḪ		JNES XIII 210+ LATE
			ʿAḎIR		UM					ḪA-ZI-RUM	MN	B 20+, M+
			ʿAḎIR		UM					ḪA-ZI-RU-UM		B 20, M
			ʿAḎIR		UM					ḪA-ZI-RUM	FN	M+
			ʿAḎIR		UM					A-ZI-RUM		B 14, M+, C+
			ʿAḎIR		IM					ḪA-ZI-RI-IM	GEN	B 20+

ROOTS (Consonants only)

ʿḎR	1	ʿAḎIR		A					A-ZI-RA	NOM	A. LATE+
		ʿAḎIR	AN						A-ZI-RA-AN		A. P. 131 LATE+
		ʿAḎIR	AH						ḪA-ZI-RA	FN	RA LXV 62 V 26
		ʿAḎIR				ŠAMŠ			ḪA-ZI-IR-D-UTU		M
		ʿAḎR	AN						ḪA-AZ-RA-AN		M
		ʿAḎR	AN	UM					AD-RA-NU-UM		I., CT XLVIII 88 REV.
		ʿAḎR		IJA					ḪA-AZ-RI-IA		RA LXV 41 II 21+
		ʿAḎR				ʾAḪ		I	ḪA-AZ-RA-ḪI?		CT XLV 54 9
		ʿAḎR		I		JAḪAD			AD-RI-E-ḪA-AD		M+
		ʿAḎR		I		ḪAʾT		UM	AD-RI-ḪA-TUM		SIMMONS 88 16+
		ʿAḎR		I		HADD		U	AD-RI-A-DU		A.+
		ʿAḎR		I		HADD		U	AD-RI-IA-DU		KUPPER, NOM. 231
		ʿAḎR		I		HAND		U	AD-RI-IA-AN-DU		KUPPER, NOM. 231
		ʿAḎR		I		HAND		U	ḪA-AD-RI-IA-AN-DU		KUPPER, NOM. 231
		ʿAḎR		I		ʿAMM		IM	ḪA-AZ-RI-A-MI-IM	GEN	M
	2	ḪAʾL		I		ʿAḎIR		UM	ḪA-LI-A-ṢI-RUM		UNPUBL.
		ʾAB		I		ʿAḎAR			A-BI-DAR		SIMMONS 58 12
		ʾAB		I		ʿAḎR		I	A-BI-AD-RI		A. LATE
		ʿABD				ʿAḎR		A	ḪA-AB-DU-ḪA-AD-RA		M
		ʿAMM		U		ʿAḎAR			AM-MU-A-DAR		TA 30 59
		ŠINI				ʿAḎR		I	ŠI-NI-AD-RI		M
		ŠUM		U		ʿAḎAR			SU-MU-A-DAR		GORDON 38 DATE+
		ŠUM		U		ʿAḎAR			SU-MU-A-TAR		GORDON 38 DATE+
		ŠUM		U		ʿAḎAR			SU-MA-DAR		SIMMONS 50 26 DATE+
	3	ʾIL		A		GULL		A			
						ʿAḎIR	AT		DINGIR-GUL-LA$_2$-ḪA-ZI-RA-AT	FN	M+
		LA				RIWM					
						ʿAḎIR			LA-RI-IM-ḪA-ZI-IR		DELAPORTE, CAT. BN 207
ʿGL	1	ʿAGAL		IM					A-GA-LIM	GEN	YOS XIII 426:9
		ʿAGAL		IM					ḪA-GA-LIM	GEN	M
		ʿAGAL		IJA					ḪA-GA-LI-IA		HARRIS 88:3
		ʿAGL	AT	UM					AG-LA-TUM	FN	ABB IV 98:2
ʿLJ	1	ʿALIJ		UM					A-LI-U$_2$-UM		GAUTIER 33 R. 6
		ʿALIJ		UM					A-LI-JU-UM		M
		ʿALIJ		UM					A-LI-I-U$_2$-UM		RUTTEN 7 20+
		ʿALIJ		UM					A-LI$_2$-JU-UM		JCS XXIV 52 NO.27+
		ʿALIJ		U					A-LI$_2$-JU-U$_2$		RUTTEN 16 14
		ʿALIJ		UM					ḪA-LI-IU-UM		B 19+
		ʿALIJ		UM					ḪA-LI-U$_2$-UM		B 19+, M
		ʿALIJ		UM					ḪA-LI-JU-UM		B 19+
		ʿALIJ		UM					ḪA-LI-I-JU-UM		CT XLVIII 31 7, 10
		ʿALIJ	AT	UM					ḪA-LI-IA-TUM	FN	B 18+, XIII 1 VII 1
		ʿALIJ	T	UM					A-LI-TUM	FN	M+
		ʿALIJ	T	IM					A-LI-TIM	FN GEN	M
	2	ʾAJ		A		ʿALIJ	AT		D-A-A-ḪA-LI-IA-AT	MN?	CT XLV 92 R. 12
		ʾADM		U		ʿALIJ	AH		D-AD-MU-ḪA-LI-IA	FN	XIII 1 V 55
		TABUB		U		ʿALIJ	AH		D-TA-BU-BU-ḪA-LI-IA	FN	XIII 1 VI 13
ʿLṢ	2	ʾAB		I		ʿALAṢ		I	AD-ḪA-LA-ZI	FN	C
		ʾAB		I		ʿALAṢ		I	A-BI-ḪA-LA-ZI	FN	M, C II 49 6
	JA	KWUN				ʿALAṢ		I	IA-KU-UN-ḪA-LA-ZI		RA LXV 44 IV 41;43
ʿMD	2	TABUB				ʿIMD		I	TA-BU-UB-IM-[DI]?	FN	VIII 33 7
		TABUB		I		ʿIMD		I	TA-BU-TI?-IM-DI	FN	VIII 31 10 15
ʿMM	1	ʿAMM		IJA					AM-MI-IA		B 13+
		ʿAMM		IJA					ḪA-MI-IA		C+
		ʿAMM		IJA					ḪA-AM-MI-IA		M
		ʿAMM		IJAN					AM-MI-IA-AN		A.+
		ʿAMM	AN						ḪA-AM-MA-AN		M+
		ʿAMM	AN	UM					ḪA-AM-MA-NU-UM		M
		ʿAMM	AN	U					ḪA-AM-MA-NU		M
		ʿAMM	AN	IM					ḪA-MA-NIM	GEN	M
		ʿAMM	AN	IM					ḪA-AM-MA-NIM	GEN	M
		ʿAMM	ATAN						ḪA-AM-MA-TA-AN		M+
		ʿAMM		A	JI	ḎRUʿ			ḪA-MA-IZ-RU		RUTTEN 28 5+
		ʿAMM		I		....			AM-MI-....-LU-UB		A. 95 85
		ʿAMM		I		HADD		U	AM-MI-A-DU		A. 60 14
		ʿAMM		I		HADD		U	AM-MI-IA-A-DU		A.

ROOTS (Consonants only)

ᶜMM	1	ᶜAMM	I				HADD		U		AM-MI-AD-DU		A. 267 17
		ᶜAMM	I				HEDD		A		AM-MI-E-DA		A.
		ᶜAMM	I				ᶜADN		A		AM-MI-ḪA-AD-NA		GOETZE, KIZZ. P. 8, LATE
		ᶜAMM	I				ʾAK		I		AM-MI-E-KI		A.
		ᶜAMM	I				ʾIL		I		ḪA-MI-I$_3$-LI$_2$		MDP XXIII 307 16
		ᶜAMM	I				ᶜAN	AT			ḪA-MI-D-ḪA-NA-AT		M
		ᶜAMM	I				ʾANDUL		I		ḪA-AM-MI-AN-DUL$_3$-LI$_2$		M+
		ᶜAMM	I				JAŚAR				ḪA-AM-MI-E-SA-AR?		M
		ᶜAMM	I				JAT		UM		AM-MI-IA-TUM		A. 273 14
		ᶜAMM	I				JATAR				ḪA-AM-MI-A-TAR		B 19+
		ᶜAMM	I				JATAR				ḪA-AM-MA-TA-AR		B 19
		ᶜAMM	I				JATAR				A-MA-TA-AR		WALTERS, WL 109:9
		ᶜAMM	I		JI		JBAL				ḪA-MI-I-BA-AL		M
		ᶜAMM	I		JE		JPUᶜ				ḪA-MI-E-PU-UḪ		M+
		ᶜAMM	I		JE		JPUᶜ				ḪA-AM-MI-E-PU-UḪ		M+
		ᶜAMM	I		JE		JŠUᶜ				ḪA-MI-E-ŠU-UḪ		M
		ᶜAMM	I				DAGAN				ḪA-MI-D-DA-GAN		RA LXV 53 XI 33
		ᶜAMM	I				DANN		U		AM-MI-DA-NU		YOS XII
		ᶜAMM	I				DAŠUR				AM-MI-DA-ŠUR?		A 7894
		ᶜAMM	I				DUŠUR				ḪA-MI-DU-ŠU-UR		SIMMONS 46 18+
		ᶜAMM	I				DUŠUR				ḪA-MI-DU-ŠU-UR$_2$		SIMMONS 50 14
		ᶜAMM	I				DUŠUR				ḪA-AM-MI-DU-ŠU-UR		HARRIS 18 15+
		ᶜAMM	I				DUŠUR				ḪA-AM-MI-DU-ŠU-UR$_2$		HARRIS 27 17+
		ᶜAMM	I				DUŠUR				AM-MI-DU-ŠU-UR		A7894+
		ᶜAMM	I				DITAN		A		AM-MI-DI-TA-NA		B13+
		ᶜAMM	I				DITAN		A		AM-MI-TE-TA-NA		CT XLV 44 24
		ᶜAMM	I				KUWN				ḪA-MI-KU-UN		RA LXV 54 XII 15
		ᶜAMM	I				MAṬAR				AM-MI-MA-DAR		B 13 HANA
		ᶜAMM	I				MAṬAR				ḪA-MI-MA-DAR	FN	C
		ᶜAMM	I				RAPIʾ				AM-MI-RA-PI		SYRIA XXXVII 206 END HANA
		ᶜAMM	I				RAPIʾ				AM-MI-RA-BI-IḪ		RA XXXIV 186 HANA
		ᶜAMM	I				RAPIʾ				ḪA-AM-MI-RA-BI		B 19
		ᶜAMM	I	Š			ḪARIJ			JE	AM-MI-IS-ḪA-RI?-E?		JEAN, S'A CLXXXVIII R. 3
		ᶜAMM	I		JI	T	ŠAMAR				ḪA-AM-MI-IŠ-TA-MAR		M+
		ᶜAMM	I		JI	T	ŠAMAR				AM-MI-IŠ-TA-MAR		M
		ᶜAMM	I		JI	T	ŠAMAR		U		AM-MI-IŠ-TAM-RU		MRS VI P. 329 UGARIT+
		ᶜAMM	I		JI	T	ŠAMAR		U		AM-MI-IS-TAM-RU		MRS VI P. 239 UGARIT+
		ᶜAMM	I				ŠAGIŠ				ḪA-AM-MI-ŠA-GI-IŠ		M+
		ᶜAMM	I				ŠAGIŠ				AM-MI-ŠA-GI-IŠ		M
		ᶜAMM	I				ŠUM		U		AM-MI-SU-MU		CT XLVIII 61 4,5
		ᶜAMM	I				ŠUM		U	HU	ḪA-AM-MI-SU-MU-U$_2$		CT XLVII 30 44
		ᶜAMM	I		TA		QWIM				ḪA-AM-MI-TA-KI-IM	NOM	M
		ᶜAMM	I		TA		QWUM				AM-MI-TA-KU-UM		A.+
		ᶜAMM	I		TA		QWUM						
							MA				AM-MI-TA-KU-UM-MA		A. +
		ᶜAMM	I				ṬAJB		A		AM-MI-ṬA-BA		A.+
		ᶜAMM	I				ṬALL		U	HU	ḪA-MI-TI-LU-U$_2$		M
		ᶜAMM	I				ṬALL		U	HU	ḪA-AM-MI-TA-LU-U$_2$		M+
		ᶜAMM	I				ṬALL		U	HU	ḪA-AM-MI-TI-LU-U$_2$		M+
		ᶜAMM	I				ṬILL		U	HU	ḪA-AM-MI-TE-LU-U$_2$		RA LXVI 118:15
		ᶜAMM	I				ZUʾG		U	HU	ḪA-AM-MI-ZU-GU-U$_2$		BM 17045+
		ᶜAMM	I				ṢUWR		A		AM-MI-ZU-RA		CT XLVIII 90 REV.
		ᶜAMM	I				ZAʾT		I		ḪA-MI-ZA-TI		HARRIS 103 1
		ᶜAMM	I				ṢADUQ				ḪA-MI-ZA-DU-[UQ]		M
		ᶜAMM	I				ṢADUQ				ḪA-AM-MI-ZA-DU-UQ		M
		ᶜAMM	I				ṢADUQ		A		AM-MI-ZA-DU-GA		B 13+
		ᶜAMM	I				ṢADUQ		A				
							....				AM-MI-ZA-DU-GA-I-LU-NI		B 13+
		ᶜAMM	I				ZAKK		UM		AM-MI-ZA-KU-UM		IRAQ IV 185, A 385
		ᶜAMM	I				ZAKK		U	HU	ḪA-AM-MI-ZA-KU-U$_2$		M
		ᶜAMM	U	HU							A-MU-U$_2$		EDZARD, DER 90:10+
		ᶜAMM	U	HU							ḪA-AM-MU-U$_2$		EDZARD, DER 68 III 6
		ᶜAMM	UJAN								AM-MU-JA-AN		A.+
		ᶜAMM	U				ḪAʾL		UM		ḪA-AM-MU-ḪA-LUM		M+
		ᶜAMM	U				HADD		A		AM-MU-A-DA		A.+
		ᶜAMM	U				HADD		A		AM-MU-WA-DA		A.

ROOTS (Consonants only)

ʿMM	1	ʿAMM	U		ʿAḎAR			AM-MU-A-DAR		TA 30 59
		ʿAMM	U		ʾEL			AM-MU-E-EL		BM 16931 2
		ʿAMM	U		ʾIL			ḪA-MU-DINGIR		M
		ʿAMM	U		ʾIL			AM-MU-DINGIR		UCP X/1 18 24
		ʿAMM	U		JAQAR			ḪA-MU-IA-QAR		RA LXV 52 X 62
		ʿAMM	U		ḪURB	I		AM-MU-UR-BI		A.
		ʿAMM	U		JAŠAR			ḪA-MU-JA-ŠAR		M
		ʿAMM	U		JATAR			ḪA-MU-TAR		M
		ʿAMM	U		JATAR			[Ḫ]A-AM-MU-TA-[A]R		M
		ʿAMM	U	JE	JPUʿ			ḪA-MU-E-PU-UḪ	FN	C+
		ʿAMM	U		DAGAN			ḪA-AM-MU-D-DA-GAN		M
		ʿAMM	U		DUMAR			ḪA-MU-DU-MAR		RA LXV 51 IX 66
		ʿAMM	U		KUMAR	A		AM-MU-KU-MAR-RA		A.
		ʿAMM	U		LA					
					RIWM			ḪA-MU-L[A]-RI-IM		RA LXV 46 VI 40
		ʿAMM	U		LIʾM			ḪA-MU-LI-IM		RA LXV 52 X 22
		ʿAMM	U		LABW	A		ḪA-AM-MU-LA-BA-A		XIV 114:6
		ʿAMM	U		MAṮAR			ḪA-MU-MA-DAR	FN	C
		ʿAMM	U		NIʿM			ḪA-AM-MU-NI-ḪI-IM	NOM	M
		ʿAMM	U		NIQM	A		AM-MU-NI-IQ-MA		A.+
		ʿAMM	U		PATAḪ	A		ḪA-AM-MU-PA-TA-A		M
		ʿAMM	U		RAWM	A		ḪA-MU-RA-MA		M
		ʿAMM	U		RAPIʾ			ḪA-AM-MU-RA-BI		B 19+, M+, A.+
		ʿAMM	UM		RAPIʾ			ḪA-AM-MU-UM-RA-BI		B 19+
		ʿAMM	U		RAPIʾ			AM-MU-RA-BI		B 19+
		ʿAMM	U		RAPIʾ			D-ḪA-AM-MU-RA-BI		B 19+
		ʿAMM	U		RAPIʾ			ḪA-MU-RA-BI		B 19+, M+
		ʿAMM	U		RAPIʾ			ḪA-AM-MU-RA-BI-IḪ		B 19 HANA
		ʿAMM	U		RAPIʾ			AM-MU-RA-PI		ABL 255 LATE
		ʿAMM	U		RAPIʾ			D-AM-MU-RA-PI		YBC 4362
		ʿAMM	UM		RAPIʾ			ḪA-AM-MU-UM-RA-PI		YBC 6496, 6508
		ʿAMM	UM		RAPIʾ			ḪA-MU-UM-RA-BI		BM 17046+
		ʿAMM	U		RAPIʾ			ḪA-MU-U_2-RA-BI		FIGULLA, CAT. 14138
		ʿAMM	U		RAPIʾ	I		AM-MU-RA-BI-I		A+
		ʿAMM	U		RAPIʾ			ḪA-MU-UR_2-RA-BI		CT XLVII 31 32+
		ʿAMM	U		RAPIʾ					
					ʾIL			ḪA-AM-MU-RA-BI-DINGIR		B 19
		ʿAMM	U		RAPIʾ					
					BANIJ			ḪA-AM-MU-RA-BI-BA-NI		B 19
		ʿAMM	UM		RAPIʾ					
					....			[ḪA-AM]-MU-UM-RA-PI-LI-WI-IR		UNPUBL.
		ʿAMM	U		RAPIʾ					
					....			ḪA-AM-MU-RA-BI-LU-DA-RI		B 19
		ʿAMM	U		ŠAGIŠ			ḪA-MU-ŠA-KI-IŠ		X 174 13
		ʿAMM	U		ŠALIM			ḪA-MU-SA-L[IM]?		M
		ʿAMM	U		ŠAM	A		AM-MU-SA-MA		A.+
		ʿAMM	U		ŠAMAR			ḪA-MU-SA-MAR		RA LXIV 36 NO. 31
		ʿAMM	U		ŠAMAR			ḪA-MU-SA-MAR	FN	C+
		ʿAMM	U		ŠARR			ḪA-MU-SA-AR		RA LXV 40 I 42
		ʿAMM	U		ŠARR			ḪA-MU-SA-AR	FN	C+
		ʿAMM	U		ŠARR			ḪA-AM-MU-SA-AR		XIV 108:6
		ʿAMM	U		ḎAKAJ	A		Ḫ[A]-MU-ZA-KA-A		RA LXV 43 III 75
		ʿAMM	U	HU	JATAR			ḪA-AM-MU-U_2-TAR		M
		ʿAMM	U	HU	RAPIʾ			ḪA-AM-MU-U_2-RA-BI		M
		ʿAMM	U	Š	KI					
					ʾIL			AM-MU-US-KI-DINGIR		A.
		ʿAMM	U	Š	KI					
					ʾIL			AM-MU-UŠ-KI-DINGIR		A.+
	2	ʾAJA			ʿAMM	U		A-IA-AM-MU		MAOG IV 2 10, 11, A 7740+
		ʾAJA			ʿAMM	U	HU	A-A-ḪA-AM-MU-U_2		BASOR 95 23
		ʾAJA			ʿAMM	U	HU	A-IA-ḪA-MU-U_2		A 7648, M
		ʾAJA			ʿAMM	U	HU	A-IA-AM-MU-U_2		VAS XIII 34:3
		ʾAJA			ʿAMM	U	HU	A-IA-AM-MU-KU		CT XLV 6 33
		ʾAJA			ʿAMM	U	HU	IA-ḪA-AM-MU-U_2		VAS XVIII 100:19
		JAḪAD			ʿAMM	U		IA-ḪA-AD-ḪA-AM-MU		M
		JAḪAD			ʿAMM	U		IA-ḪA-AD-ḪA-MU		M+

ROOTS (Consonants only)

ᶜMM	2		JAḪAD		ᶜAMM		U	HU	IA-ḪA-AD-ḪA-MU-U$_2$		M
			ᶜABD		ᶜAMM		UM		ḪA-AB-DU-A-MU-UM		M
			ᶜABD		ᶜAMM		IM		AB-DU-A-MI-IM	NOM	M+
			ᶜABD		ᶜAMM		IM		AB-DU-A-MI-IM	GEN	M+
			ᶜABD		ᶜAMM		IM		ḪA-AB-DU-A-MI-IM		M
			JADAᶜ		ᶜAMM		U		IA-DA-AM-MU		C II 5 4
			ᶜADN	I	ᶜAMM		U		ḪA-AD-NI-ḪA-MU		RA LXV 50 VIII 49
			ᶜAḎR	I	ᶜAMM		IM		ḪA-AZ-RI-A-MI-IM	GEN	M
			ʾIL	A	ᶜAMM		U		I-LA-ḪA-MU		RA LXV 42 II 77+
			ʾIL	I	ᶜAMM		U		I$_3$-LI$_2$-ḪA-MU		RA LVII 178
			ʾALI		ᶜAMM		U		A-LI$_2$-AM-MU		UCP X/1 52 22
			ʾALI		ᶜAMM		U	HU	A-LI$_2$-AM-MU-U$_2$		UCP X/2 58 16
	JA		WMAʾ		ᶜAMM	AJ	I		IA-AW-MA-ḪA-MA-JI-KI	GN	M
	JA		WMAʾ		ᶜAMM		I		JA-MA-ḪA-MI-KI	GN	M
	JA		WMAʾ		ᶜAMM		UM		JA-MA-ḪA-MU-UM		M
	JA		WMAʾ		ᶜAMM		UM		IA-MA-ḪA-MU-UM		M
	JA		JQAH		ᶜAMM		U		IA-QA-AM-MU		A.+
			ᶜAQB	A	ᶜAMM		U		AQ-BA-ḪA-MU		M
			ᶜAQB	A	ᶜAMM		U		AQ-BA-ḪA-AM-MU		IRAQ XXX 91, RIMAH
			ᶜAQB	A	ᶜAMM		U		ḪA-AQ-BA-ḪA-AM-MU		II 39 19, 58, 80
			ᶜAQB	A	ᶜAMM		U	HU	ḪA-AQ-BA-ḪA-AM-MU-U$_2$		II 39 14, 16, 24
			ᶜAQB	U	ᶜAMM		U	HU	AQ-BU-AM-MU-U$_2$		X 174 3
			ᶜIQB	A	ᶜAMM		U		IQ-BA?-AM-MU		A. 8 35
			ʾUŠM	A	ᶜAMM		I		UŠ-MA-AM-MI		CT XXXIII 46A 4
			JATAR		ᶜAMM		U		IA-TAR-ḪA-MU		M
			JATAR		ᶜAMM		U		IA-TAR-ḪA-MU	FN	C II P. 247+
			ʾATT	I	ᶜAMM		A		AT-TI-AM-MA		A. LATE
			ᶜAZZ		ᶜAMM		I		AZ-ZA-AM-MI		A. 265 19
			BIN	A	ᶜAMM		I		BI-NA-AM-MI		B 15
			BUN	U	ᶜAMM		I		BU-NU-ḪA-AM-MI	FN	M+
			BUN	U	ᶜAMM		U		BU-NU-AM-MU		B 16+
			ḎAKIR	A	ᶜAMM		I		ZA-KI-RA-ḪA-MI		M
			ḎAKIR	A	ᶜAMM		U		ZA-KI-RA-ḪA-AM-MU		M+
			ḎAKIR	A	ᶜAMM		U		ZA-KI-RA-ḪA-MU		M
			ḎAKIR	A	ᶜAMM		U	HU	ZA-KI-RA-ḪA-AM-MU-U$_2$		M+
			ḎIMR	A	ᶜAMM		U		ZI-IM-RA-ḪA-MU		CT XLIV 54 20, C
			ḎIMR	A	ᶜAMM		U		ZI-IM-RA-ḪA-AM-MU		M
			ḎIMR	A	ᶜAMM		U		ZI-IM-RA-AM-MU		TIM IV 33 20, 34 13
			ḎIMR	A	ᶜAMM		U	HU	ZI-IM-RA-ḪA-MU-U$_2$		TIM IV 33 SEAL, 34 SEAL
			ḎIMR	I	ᶜAMM		U		ZI-IM-RI-AM-MU		TIM III 94 4
			ḎIMR	I	ᶜAMM		U		ZI-IM-RI-ḪA-MU		C
			ḎIMR	I	ᶜAMM		U		ZI-IM-RI-ḪA-AM-MU		B 42+, X 35 12
			ḎIMR	U	ᶜAMM		I		ZI-IM-RU-ḪA-AM-MI		B 42
			ḎIMR	U	ᶜAMM		U		ZI-IM-RU-ḪA-AM-MU		JCS XI 23 10 13
			KIʾL	I	ᶜAMM		I		KI-LI-AM-MI	GEN	MRS XVI 12:2
	JA		KWUN		ᶜAMM		U		IA-KU-UN-AM-MU		B 27
			KUWN		ᶜAMM		U		KU-UN-AM-MU		MRS VI P. 249
			LA		ᶜAMM		U		LA-ḪA-AM-MU		HARRIS 18 14
	JA		NḪAB		ᶜAMM		U		IA-ḪA-AB-ḪA-MU		M
		Š	NUʾR	A	ᶜAMM		U		ŠU-NU-UḪ-RA-AM-MU		B 40 HANA+
	JA		NŠIʾ		ᶜAMM		U		IA-SI-ḪA-MU		M
	JA		NTIN		ᶜAMM		U		IA-AN-TI-IN-ḪA-MU		M
			RIJB	A	ᶜAMM		U		RI-BA-AM-MU		A. 97 4+
	JA		RWIM		ᶜAMM		U		IA-RI-IM-ḪA-MU		M
	JA		RWIM		ᶜAMM		U		IA-RI-IM-ḪA-AM-MU		M
	JA		RŠIJ		ᶜAMM		U		IA-AR-ŠI-ḪA-MU		M, C+
			ŠU		ᶜAMM		U		ŠU-ḪA-AM-MU		M+
			ŠUWB		ᶜAMM		U		ŠU-UB-AM-MU		MRS VI P. 257+
			ŠUWB	A	ᶜAMM		I		ŠU-BA-AM-MI		A. 270 22
	JA		ŚJIM		ᶜAMM		U		IA-SI-IM-ḪA-AM-MU		M
	JA		ŚJIM		ᶜAMM		U		IA-SI-IM-ḪA-MU		M
			ŚUM	U	ᶜAMM		U		SU-MU-ḪA-AM-MU		B 39+
			ŚUM	U	ᶜAMM		U		SU-MU-ḪA-MU		M
			ŚUM	U	ᶜAMM		U		SU-MU-ḪA-MU	FN	C+
	JA		ŠṬIḪ		ᶜAMM		U		IA-AŠ-DI-ḪA-AM-MU		B 30
			ṢUWR	A	ᶜAMM		U		ZU-RA-ḪA-AM-MU		M+

ROOTS (Consonants only)

ʿMM	2		ṢUWR		A		ʿAMM		U		Z[U]-RA-ḪA-M[U]		XIII 132 7
			ṢUWR		A		ʿAMM		U	HU	ZU-RA-ḪA-AM-MU-U$_2$		M
			ṢUWR		I		ʿAMM		U		ZU-RI-ḪA-AM-MU		M
			ṢUWR		I		ʿAMM		U	HU	ZU-RI-ḪA-AM-MU-U$_2$		M+
		JI	TWUR				ʿAMM		U	HU	I-DUR-ḪA-MU-U$_2$		UNPUBL.
			TUWR		U		ʿAMM		I		DUR-RU-AM-MI		MAOG IV 2 6 HANA
			TALM		A		ʿAMM		U		TA-AL-MA-AM-MU		A.+
			ZAʾT				ʿAMM		U		ZA-AT-AM-MU	MN	A. 279 2 3
ʿMQ	1		ʿAMIQ	AT	IM						ḪA-MI-QA-TIM-KI	GN GEN	M+
			ʿEMUQ		I		ʾEL				E-[M]U-QI$_2$-EL		RA LXV 40 I 3
ʿMS	1	JE	ʿMUS		UM						E-MU-ZUM		I UNPUBL.
		JA	ʿMUS				....				IA-AḪ-MU-IS-[....]		XIV 129:5
		JA	ʿMUS				ʾIL				IA-AḪ-MU-US-DINGIR		M
		JA	ʿMIS				ʾIL				IA-AḪ-MI-IS-DINGIR		RUTTEN 2 23+
		JA	ʿMIS				ʾIL		UM		IA-AḪ-MI-ZI-LUM		RUTTEN 16 17
		JA	ʿMIS				JARAḪ				IA-AḪ-MI-IS-D-SIN		M
			ʿAMAS		UM						A-MA-ZU-UM		KISURRA 98 8
			ʿAMAS		IM						A-MA-ZI-IM	GEN	KISURRA 166 4+
			ʿAMIS	AH							ḪA-ME-ZA	FN	RA LXV 58 I 24
			ʿAMIS	AN	U						ḪA-MI-ZA-NU		M
			ʿEMES		UM						E-ME-ZUM		I+
			ʿIMS		U						IM-ṢU		JNES XIII 210+ LATE
			ʿUMAS		UM						ḪU-MA-ZUM		VAS VIII 14 33
	2		MUT				ʿUMUS		IM		MU-UT-ḪU-MU-ZI-IM		XIV 122:6+
ʿN	1		ʿAN		AJA						A-NA-IA		RA LXV 46 VI 17
			ʿAN		AJA						ḪA-NA-IA		RA LXV 50 IX 19
			ʿAN		IJA						A-NI-IA		RUTTEN 31 5+
			ʿAN		UM		ʾAḪ		I		A-NU-UM-A-ḪI		RA LXV 53 XI 43
			ʿAN		UM		ḪIRB		I		A-NU-UM-ḪI-IR-BI		BALKAN, LETTER P. 6
			ʿAN	AT							D-ḪA-NA-AT	DN FN	M+
			ʿAN	AT							ḪA-NA-AT-KI	GN FN	M+
			ʿAN	AT	UM						A-NA-TUM		BIROT, TEA 72 III 58+
			ʿAN	AT	UM						ḪA-NA-TUM	FN	XIII 1:34+
			ʿAN	ATAN							A-NA-TA-AN		RA LXV 53 XI 13
			ʿAN	ATAN							ḪA-NA-TA-AN		M+
			ʿAN	AT	I	JI	JBAL				ḪA-NA-TI-I-BA-AL		RA LXV 40 I 12
			ʿAN	AT			KUʾB		U		A-NA-AT-KU-BU		TCL I 204:11
	2		JAʾ		A		ʿAN		UM		IA-A-A-NU-UM		YOS V 134 16
			ʿABD				ʿAN	AT			ḪA-AB-DU-D-ḪA-NA-AT		M+
			ʿABD				ʿAN	AT	I		AB-TA-NA-TI		A. P. 128A LATE +
			ʿABD				ʿAN	AT	I		AB-DI-A-NA-TI		A. P. 128B LATE +
			ʿABD				ʿAN	AT	I		AB-TI-A-NA-TI		JCS XIII 54 300, A. LATE
			ʿAMM		I		ʿAN	AT			ḪA-MI-D-ḪA-NA-AT		M
			ʾANA				ʿAN		A		A-NA-A-NA		A. 36:11
			JIŠʿ		I		ʿAN		UM		IŠ-ḪI-A-NU-UM		B 45
		JA	BWAʾ				ʿAN		UM		IA-BA-A-NU-UM		B 45
			PALṬ		A		ʿAN		UM		PA-AL?-TA-A-NU-UM		LANGDON IV 15
			BUN		A		ʿAN		UM		BU-NA-A-NU-UM		U
			BUN		U		ʿAN	AT	I		BU-NU-A-NA-TI		B 16
			ḎIKR		I		ʿAN	AT			ZI-IK-RI-ḪA-NA-AT		M
			ḎIKR		I		ʿAN	AT			ZI-IK-RI-D-ḪA-N[A-AT]		M
			ḎIMR		I		ʿAN	AT	A		ZI-IM-RI-ḪA-NA-TA		B 42
			LA				ʿAN		UM		LA-A-NU-UM		U
			LU				ʿAN		UM		LU$_2$-A-NU-UM		U
			LASIM				ʿAN		UM		LA-ZE$_2$-IM-A-NU-UM		FLP 590:6, U
			LASIM				ʿAN		UM		LA-ZI-MA-NU-UM		MVN III 338:17, U
			MUT				ʿAN	AT			MU-UT-D-ḪA-NA-AT		RA LXV 52 X 65
			MUT		I		ʿAN	AT	A		MU-TI-A-N[A-T]A		B 35
			NAʿM		I		ʿAN		IM		NA-MI-A-NIM		A. 142
			PI				ʿAN		UM		PI-A-NUM$_2$		I
			PI				ʿAN		UM		BI$_2$-A-NU-UM		I
			PUZUR				ʿAN		A		PUZUR-A-NA		BIN IV 61 29+ CAPP.
		ʾA	RŠIJ				ʿAN		UM		AR-SI?-A-NUM$_2$		U
			ŠAT				ʿAN		A		ŠA-AT-A-NA		TCL XXI 220A 4+ CAPP.
			ŠAʾQ		A		ʿAN		UM		SA-GA-A-NU-UM		B 47
		MA	ŠJIT				ʿAN		UM		MA-SI-IT-A-NU-UM		I

ROOTS (Consonants only)

ʿN	2		ŠALIM					ʿAN		UM		ŠA-LIM-A-NU-UM		M
			ṢILL					ʿAN	AT			MI-NI-D-ḪA-NA-AT		XIII 83 8
	3		LA				ʾA	ḪJIJ						
								ʿAN		UM		LA-ḪI-A-NU-UM		U
ʿNW	1	JA	ʿNUW			HU						IA-AḪ-NU-U$_2$		OIP XLVII 66
ʿNJ	1		ʿANAJ			TI		ʾEL				A-NI-TE-EL		MOORTGAT 309
			ʿANAJ			TI		ʾIL				A-NI-TI-DINGIR		M
		JA	ʿNIJ					ʾIL				IA-AḪ-NI-DINGIR		A 7630 6
		ME	ʿNIJ		UM							ME-EḪ-NI-JU-UM		M
		ME	ʿNIJ		UM							ME-EḪ-NU-UM		KISURRA 36 4
		ME	ʿNIJ		IM							ME-EḪ-NI-IM	GEN	KISURRA 80A
		ME	ʿANIJ		U							ME-ḪA-A-NU		KISURRA 81A
		ME	ʿANIJ		IM							ME-ḪA-NI-IM	GEN	KISURRA 80B
		ME	ʿANIJ		I							ME-ḪA-A-NI?	GEN	VAS VIII 14 43
		ME	ʿANIJ			JA						ME-ḪA-NI-IA	FN	RA LXV 58 I 43+
ʿNB	1		ʿINAB	AN	UM							I-NA-BA-NU-UM		U
			ʿINB		UM							IN-BU-UM		M
			ʿINB		U							IN-BU	FN	C+
			ʿINB	AT	UM							IN-BA-TUM	FN	BM 78768 3', X 84 3+
			ʿINB		I			ʾIL				IN-BI$_2$-IL		U UNPUBL.
			ʿINB		I			JARAḪ				IN-BI-RA-AḪ		KISURRA 6 15
ʿNQ	1		ʿANAQ		UM							A-NA-GU-UM		KISURRA 71A 15+
			ʿANAQ		UM							A-NA-KUM		KISURRA 29 8+
ʿQB	1	JA	ʿQUB		U							IA-KU-BU		CT II 9 26
		JI	ʿQUB		UM							I-KU-BU-UM		KISURRA 117 7, 9+
		JA	ʿQUB		AM							IA-KU-BA-[A]M?	NOM	RA LXV 46 V 84
		JA	ʿQUB	AN								IA-KU-B[A]-AN		RA LXV 45 V 57
		JA	ʿQUB					HEDD		A		IA-AK-KU-UB-E-DA		JEA VIII 207F.
		JA	ʿQUB					ʾIL				A-AḪ-KU-UB-DINGIR		HARRIS 12 3+
		JA	ʿQUB					ʾIL				IA-KU-UB-DINGIR		B 27+
		JA	ʿQUB					ʾIL				IA-AḪ-KU-UB-DINGIR		XIII 1 VII 17, C+
		JA	ʿQUB		I			ʾIL				IA-AḪ-KU-BI-DINGIR		CT II 39 18
		JA	ʿQUB		I			ʾIL				IA-KU-BI-DINGIR		KISURRA 41 10
		JI	ʿQIB		UM							I-KI-BU-UM		CT VIII 19 19+
		JA	ʿQIB					ʾIL				IA-KI-IB-DINGIR		TIM V 33 23
		ME	ʿQIB		UM							ME-KI-BU-UM		U, M+
		ME	ʿQIB		IM							ME-KI-BI-IM	GEN	M+
			ʿAQAB					ʾEL				A-QA-BE-EL		UET V 839 23
			ʿAQUB		U							A-KU-BU		VAS VIII 14 14
			ʿAQUB					ʾIL				A-KU-UB-DINGIR		HARRIS 84 13
			ʿAQUB		I			ʾEL				A-KU-PI-EL		GORDON 38 16
			ʿAQB		UM							AQ-BU-UM		TIM III 82 6
			ʿAQB	AN								ḪA-AQ-BA-AN		M+
			ʿAQB	AN								AQ-BA-AN		M
			ʿAQB	AN	UM							AQ-BA-NU-UM		RUTTEN 40 2+
			ʿAQB		A			ʾAḪ		UM		AQ-BA-A-ḪU-UM		M+
			ʿAQB		A			ʾAḪ		UM		AQ-BA-ḪU-UM		B 11+
			ʿAQB		A			ʾAḪ		UM		ḪA-AQ-BA-A-ḪU-UM		RA LXV 43 III 57+
			ʿAQB		A			ʾAḪ		U		AQ-BA-A-ḪU		M+, C+
			ʿAQB		A			ʾAḪ		U		AQ-BA-ḪU		BASOR 95 19+
			ʿAQB		A			ʾAḪ		AM		AQ-BA-A-ḪA-AM	ACC	M
			ʿAQB		A			ʾAḪ		IM		AQ-BA-A-ḪI-IM	GEN	M+
			ʿAQB		A			ʾAḪ		IM		ḪA-AQ-BA-A-ḪI-IM	GEN	M+
			ʿAQB		A			ʾAḪ		I		AQ-BA-A-ḪI	GEN	XII 448 5+
			ʿAQB		A			ʿAMM		U		AQ-BA-ḪA-MU		M
			ʿAQB		A			ʿAMM		U		AQ-BA-ḪA-AM-MU		IRAQ XXX 91, RIMAH
			ʿAQB		A			ʿAMM		U		ḪA-AQ-BA-ḪA-AM-MU		II 39 19, 58, 80
			ʿAQB		A			ʿAMM		U	HU	ḪA-AQ-BA-ḪA-AM-MU-U$_2$		II 39 14, 16, 24
			ʿAQB		A			ḪUNN		UM		AQ-BA-ḪU-NI-UM		B 11
			ʿAQB		I			ʾAḪ		U		AQ-BI-A-ḪU		B 11
			ʿAQB		I			ʾIL				AQ-BI-IL		B 11
			ʿAQB		I			ʾIL				AQ-BI-DINGIR		BIN VII 156 10+
			ʿAQB		I			NAN		UM		AQ-BI-NA-NU-UM		B 42+
			ʿAQB		U	HU						AQ-BU-U$_2$		CT IV 50B 24+
			ʿAQB		U			ʿAMM		U	HU	AQ-BU-AM-MU-U$_2$		X 174 3
			ʿAQB		U			DAWD		UM		AQ-BU-DA-DU-UM		PBS VIII/2 253 7

ROOTS (Consonants only)

ʿQB	1		ʿAQB		U		DAWD		A		AQ-BU-DA-DA		B 12
			ʿAQB		U		DAWD		I		ḪA-AQ-BU-DA-DI		M+
			ʿAQB		U		DAWD		I		AQ-BU-DA-DI		M
			ʿIQB	AN							ḪI-IQ-BA-AN		M+
			ʿIQB	AN	UM						IQ-BA-NU-UM		I+
			ʿIQB		A		ʾAḪ		UM		IQ-BA-A-ḪU-UM		KISURRA 4A 11, M
			ʿIQB		A		ʾAḪ		UM		IQ-BA-ḪU-UM		KISURRA 121 6
			ʿIQB		A		ʿAMM		U		IQ-BA?-AM-MU		A. 8 35
			ʿIQB		I		HADD		U		IQ-BI-D-IM		KISURRA 114 7
	2		ʾAḪ		I	JI	ʿQUB		A		A-ḪI-I-KU-BA		KISURRA 7A 9
			ŠIMAʿ			TA	ʿQUB				ŠI-ME-TA-GU-UB		M+
ʿRD	1		ʿARAD	AN							ḪA-RA-DA-AN		M
			ʿARD		UM						ḪA-AR-DU-UM		M+
			ʿARD		UM						AR-DU-UM		TCL I 168 4+
			ʿARD		U						AR-DU		TCL I 166 2
			ʿARD		IM						ḪA-AR-DI-IM	GEN	M
			ʿARD	AT	UM						ḪA-AR-DA-TUM	FN	M+
			ʿARD		AJA						ḪA-AR-DA-IA	FN	XIII 1 IV 70
			ʿARD	AN	UM						ḪA-AR-DA-NU-UM		M+
ʿRL	1		ʿARUL		UM						A-RU-LU-UM		B 13+
			ʿARUL		U						A-RU-LU		STRASSM. 56 29+
ʿRṢ	1		ʿARIṢ	AN	UM						A-RI-ZA-NU-UM		U
			ʿARIṢ	AN	U						ḪA-RI-ZA-NU		PBS II/1 P. 23+ LATE
			ʿARṢ		U						ḪAR-ṢU		JNES XIII 210+ LATE
			ʿARṢ	AN	UM						AR-ZA-NU-UM		B 43+
			ʿARṢ	AT	UM						AR-ZA-TUM	FN	C
ʿŠTR	1		ʿAŠTAR				ʾAB		I		AŠ-TAR-A-BI		MRS VI P. 242
			ʿAŠTAR				ʾIL		I		EŠ$_4$-DAR-I$_3$-LI$_2$	FN	RA LXV 56 I 3
			ʿAŠTAR				ʾUMM		I		EŠ$_4$-DAR-UM-MI	FN	XIII 1 II 38 +
			ʿAŠTAR				ʾANDUL		I		EŠ$_4$-DAR-AN-DUL$_3$-LI$_2$	FN	M
			ʿAŠTAR				JIPʿ	AH			EŠ$_4$-DAR-IP-ḪA	FN	XIII 1 VI 19+
			ʿAŠTAR				ʾAŠJ	AH			EŠ$_4$-DAR-A-SI-IA	FN	XIII 1 IX 3+
			ʿAŠTAR				ʾAŠJ	AH			EŠ$_4$-DAR-A-ZU-IA	FN	M
			ʿAŠTAR				JAŠʿ	AH			EŠ$_4$-DAR-IA-AŠ-ḪA	FN	M
			ʿAŠTAR				ḪAṢN		I		EŠ$_4$-DAR-ḪA-AZ-NI	FN	XIII 1 II 41
			ʿAŠTAR			JA	HWIJ				EŠ$_4$-DAR-IA-WI		VAS VII 157 7
			ʿAŠTAR				BAʿL	AH			EŠ$_4$-DAR-BA-AḪ?-LA	FN	M
			ʿAŠTAR				DAMQ	AH			EŠ$_4$-DAR-DAM-QA	FN	XIII 1 V 50+
			ʿAŠTAR				KAWN				EŠ$_4$-DAR-KA-AN		IX 237 II 4+
			ʿAŠTAR				KABAR				EŠ$_4$-DAR-KA-BAR		RA LXV 41 II 39
			ʿAŠTAR				LI			JA	EŠ$_4$-DAR-LI?-IA		YOS XIII 12 REV 14
			ʿAŠTAR				LAMAS		I		EŠ$_4$-DAR-LA-MA-ZI	FN	M
			ʿAŠTAR				LAMAS		I		EŠ$_4$-DAR-D-LAMA	FN	XIII 1 I 69+
			ʿAŠTAR				MILK		I		EŠ$_4$-DAR-ME-IL-KI	FN	RA LXV 62 V 10
			ʿAŠTAR				NIWR		I		EŠ$_4$-DAR-NE-RI	FN	XIII 1 IX 48
			ʿAŠTAR				PUṬR		I		EŠ$_4$-DAR-PU-UṬ-RI	FN	M+
			ʿAŠTAR				RAḪM		I		EŠ$_4$-DAR-RA-AḪ-MI	FN	XIII 1 VIII 83
			ʿAŠTAR				ŠIMḪ		I		EŠ$_4$-DAR-ŠI-IM-ḪI	FN	XIII 1 XII 2
			ʿAŠTAR				ŠAMŠ		I		EŠ$_4$-DAR-D-UTU-ŠI	FN	M
			ʿAŠTAR				ŠARR	AH			EŠ$_4$-DAR-ŠAR-RA	FN	XIII 1 II 67
			ʿAŠTAR			TA	JṢIʾ				EŠ$_4$-DAR-TA-ZI	FN	XIII 1 IV 79
			ʿAŠTAR			TA	LʾIJ				EŠ$_4$-DAR-TA-AL-E	FN	XIII 1 V 41+
			ʿAŠTAR				TIWR	AH			D-EŠ$_4$-DAR-TE-IR-RA		A.
			ʿAŠTAR				TUWR		I	JA	EŠ$_4$-DAR-TU-RI-IA	FN	XIII 1 XIII 33
			ʿAŠTAR				TABB		I		EŠ$_4$-DAR-TAB-BI	FN	M+, C
	2		ḪAʾL		I		ʿAŠTAR				ḪA-LI$_2$-EŠ$_4$-DAR		RA LXV 53 XII 1
			ʿABD				ʿAŠTAR				AB-DI-D-EŠ$_4$-DAR		A. 19 4, 7
			ʿABD				ʿAŠTAR				AB-DU-EŠ$_4$-DAR		M+
			ʿABD				ʿAŠTAR				ḪA-AB-DU-EŠ$_4$-DAR		M+, C+
			ʿABD				ʿIŠTAR	AH			AB-DU-IŠ-TA-RA?		B 9
		JI	JBAL				ʿAŠTAR				I-BA-AL-EŠ$_4$-DAR		M
			ʾUBUŠ				ʿAŠTAR				U$_2$-BU-UŠ$_3$-EŠ$_4$-DAR		RES 1938 P. 129
			ʾIL		A		ʿAŠTAR				I-LA-EŠ$_4$-DAR		RA LXV 42 III 16+
			ʾIL		I		ʿAŠTAR				I$_3$-LI$_2$-EŠ$_4$-DAR		M+
		JI	ḪLIJ				ʿAŠTAR				IḪ-LI-AŠ-TAR		A. 55 35
		JI	ḪLIJ				ʿAŠTAR				IḪ-LI-EŠ$_4$-DAR		A. P. 133+

ROOTS (Consonants only)

ʿŠTR	2		ʾAM	T			ʿAŠTAR	AH	AM-TI-AŠ-TA-RA	FN?	A. LATE	
			ḪINN		I		ʿAŠTAR		EN-NI-D-EŠ$_4$-DAR		A. 247 23	
			BAʿL		A		ʿAŠTAR		BA-LA-EŠ$_4$-DAR		M	
			BAʿL		U		ʿAŠTAR		BA-LU-EŠ$_4$-DAR		M+	
			BAWZ		I		ʿAŠTAR		BA-ZI-EŠ$_4$-DAR		M	
			BIN		A		ʿAŠTAR		BI-NA-EŠ$_4$-DAR		M+	
			BUN		A		ʿAŠTAR		BU-NA-D-INNIN		BASOR 95, 19	
			BUN		U		ʿAŠTAR		BU-NU-EŠ$_4$-DAR		M+, C+	
		TA	BNIJ				ʿAŠTAR		TAB-NI-EŠ$_4$-DAR	FN	XIII 1 XIII 15+	
		TA	BRUW				ʿAŠTAR		TAB-RU?-EŠ$_4$-DAR	FN	XIII 1 V 43	
			DAŠUR	AH			ʿAŠTAR		DA-ŠU-RA-EŠ$_4$-DAR	FN	YOS VIII 51 5	
			ḎIKR		A		ʿAŠTAR		ZI-IK-RA-EŠ$_4$-DAR		M+	
			ḎIKR		I		ʿAŠTAR		ZI-IK-RI-EŠ$_4$-DAR		M+	
			ḎIKR				ʿAŠTAR		ZI-KI-IR-EŠ$_4$-[DAR]		M	
			ḎUKR		A		ʿAŠTAR		[Z]U-UK-RA-EŠ$_4$-DAR		RA LXV 46 VI 21	
			ḎIMR		A		ʿAŠTAR		ZI-IM-RA-EŠ$_4$-DAR		M+	
			ḎIMR		I		ʿAŠTAR		ZI-IM-RI-D-EŠ$_4$-DAR		M, A.+	
			ḎIMR		U		ʿAŠTAR		ZI-IM-RU-EŠ$_4$-DAR		IRAQ IV 185	A. 385
			KIBR		I		ʿAŠTAR		KI-IB-RI-EŠ$_4$-DAR		M+	
		TA	RWIM				ʿAŠTAR		TA-RI-IM-EŠ$_4$-DAR	FN	XIII 1 II 13	
		TA	RʿIŠ				ʿAŠTAR		T[A-R]I-IŠ-EŠ$_4$-DAR	FN	RA LXV 65 VII 36	
		TA	ŠJIM				ʿAŠTAR		TA-ŠI-IM-EŠ$_4$-DAR	FN	XIII 1 IV 28	
			ŠIJM	AT			ʿAŠTAR		ŠI-MA-AT-EŠ$_4$-DAR	FN	XIII 1 V 75+	
			ŠUM		U		ʿAŠTAR		SU-MU-EŠ$_4$-DAR		PBS VIII/2 207 5, M	
		TA	TWUR				ʿAŠTAR		TA-TU-UR-EŠ$_4$-DAR	FN	M	
			TIWR				ʿAŠTAR		TI-IR-EŠ$_4$-DAR		M+	
			TUDAR		I		ʿAŠTAR		TU-DA-RI-EŠ$_4$-DAR	FN	EDZARD, DER 58:7	
			TUDAR		UM		ʿAŠTAR		TU-DA-RUM-EŠ$_4$-DAR	FN	EDZARD, DER 61:16	
			TUPT		U		ʿAŠTAR		TUP-TU-EŠ$_4$-DAR		M	
ʿTQ	1	TA	ʿTIQ				ʾABN	U	TA-TI-QA-AB-NU		RES 1938 128	
ʿZB	1	JA	ʿZUB				ʾIL		IA-AḪ-ZU-UB-DINGIR		B 26+	
		JA	ʿZIB		UM				IA-ZI-BU-UM		M+	
		JI	ʿZIB		UM				I-ZI-BU-UM		KISURRA 10A 5+	
		JA	ʿZIB		IM				IA-ZI-BI-IM	GEN	XIV 92:26+	
		JA	ʿZIB				....		IA-AḪ-ZI-IB-[....]		M	
		JA	ʿZIB				HADD	U	IA-AḪ-ZI-IB-D-IM		M+	
		JA	ʿZIB				HADD	U	IA-ZI-IB-D?-IM?		M	
		JA	ʿZIB				ʾIL		IA-AH-ZI-IB-DINGIR		RUTTEN 21 7+, M	
		JA	ʿZIB				ʾIL		A-AḪ-ZI-IB-DINGIR		HARRIS 57 2	
		JA	ʿZIB				DAGAN		IA-ZI-IB-D-DA-GAN		M+	
		JA	ʿZIB		I		ʾIL		IA-AḪ-ZI-BI-DINGIR		KISURRA 86A 11	
		JA	ʿZIB		I		ʾIL		A-AḪ-ZI-BI-DINGIR		SIMMONS 70 5	
		JA	ʿZIB		I		ʾIL		IA-A-ZI-BI-DINGIR		KAJ 34 18, 25 LATE	
		JA	ʿZIB		A		ʾEL		IA-AḪ-ZI-BA-EL?		RA LXV 50 VIII 77	
		JA	ʿZIB		U	HU			IA-AḪ-ZI-BU-U$_2$		M+	
		JI	ʿZIB			NA			I-ZI-IB-NA		CT XLV 118 24	
			ʿAZAB		UM				A-ZA-BU-UM		GAUTIER 23 5+	
			ʿAZAB	AN	I				A-ZA-BA-NI		TA 1931, 216	
			ʿAZIB	AH					ḪA-ZI-BA	FN	XIII 1 IV 35	
			ʿAZIB	AN					ḪA-ZI-PA-AN		RA LXV 44 IV 25	
			ʿAZIB	AT	UM				ḪA-ZI-BA-TUM	MN	GAUTIER 65 5	
			ʿAZB		UM				ḪA-AZ-BU-UM		RA LXV 53 XI 20	
			ʿIZB		A		....		ḪI-IZ-BA-.[....]		VAS XIII 62 R. 1	
			ʿUZAB		UM				U$_2$-ZA-BU-UM		SIMMONS 46 32	
			ʿUZAB		UM				U$_2$-SA-BU-UM		SIMMONS 52 16	
			ʿUZAB		IM				U$_2$-ZA-BI-IM	GEN	SIMMONS 70 16	
			ʿUZAB		U				[ḪU]-ZA-BU	FN	XIII 1 XIV 14	
			ʿUZUB		UM				ḪU-ZU-BU-UM		RA VIII 75	
ʿZL	1		ʿAZAL		UM				A-ZA-LU-UM		B 14	
			ʿAZAL		UM				A-ZA-LUM		EDZARD, DER 60:8	
			ʿAZAL		UM				AZ-ZA-LUM		GAUTIER 1 R. 9	
			ʿAZAL		UM				A-ZA-AL-LUM		KISURRA 26 6	
			ʿAZAL		IM				A-ZA-LIM'	GEN	VAS VIII 14 23	
			ʿAZAL	AH					ḪA-ZA-LA	FN	M+	
			ʿAZAL		AJA				A-ZA-LA-IA		B 14	
			ʿAZAL		IJA				A-ZA-LI-IA		B 14+	

ROOTS (Consonants only)

ʿZL	1		ʿAZAL		IJA					A-SA-LI-JA		B 14+
			ʿIZIL		I					ḪI-ZI-LI		C II 45 II 35
			ʿIZL	AH						ḪI-IZ-LA	FN	C+
			ʿUZAL		UM					U$_2$-ZA-LUM		CT XXXIII 46A 3+
			ʿUZAL		UM					ḪU-ZA-LUM		UCP X/1 17 14+
			ʿUZAL	AT	UM					ḪU-ZA-LA-TUM	FN	WATERMAN 12 R. 7+
			ʿUZAL	AT	UM					ḪU-ZA-LA-TUM	MN	UCP X/1 86 4+
			ʿUZAL		IJA					ḪU-ZA-LI-IA		BIROT, TEA 70BIS:36'
			ʿUZIL		A					U$_2$-ZI-LA		RA LXV 50 IX 6
			ʿUZUL		I					U$_2$-ZU-LI		RA LXV 51 X 6
ʿZZ	1		ʿAZAZ		UM					A-ZA-ZUM		I
			ʿAZAZ	AN	UM					A-ZA-ZA-NU-UM		B 92
			ʿAZIZ	AN						A-ZI-ZA-AN		RA LXV 44 IV 45
			ʿIZIZ	AH						I-ZI-ZA	FN	RA LXV 58 I 28
			ʿAZZ		U					AZ-ZU	FN	M+, C+
			ʿAZZ		U					ḪA-AZ-ZU		C+
			ʿAZZ	AT	UM					A-ZA-TUM	FN	CT VIII 37D 7, M
			ʿAZZ	AT	AM					A-ZA-TAM	FN ACC	CT VIII 37D 3
			ʿAZZ	ATANIM						ḪA-ZA-TA-NIM	MN GEN	C II 6
			ʿAZZ				ʿAMM		I	AZ-ZA-AM-MI		A. 265 19
			ʿAZZ		I		ʾIL			A-ZI-DINGIR		HARRIS 39 11
			ʿAZZ		I		DAGAN			A-ZI-D-DA-GAN		A. LATE
			ʿAZZ		U		ḪAʾL		IM	A-ZU-ḪA-LIM	NOM	M
			ʿAZZ		U	KA				AZ-ZU-KA	FN	M+, C
			ʿAZZ		U	KI				AZ-ZU-UK-KI	FN	XIII 1 VIII 66
			ʿAZZ		U	NI				AZ-ZU-UN-NI	FN	M
			ʿIZZ	AN						IZ-ZA-AN		M
			ʿIZZ	AN						I-ZA-AN		RA LXV 44 IV 35
			ʿIZZ	AN	UM					I-ZA-NUM$_2$		U
			ʿIZZ	AN	UM					I-ZA-NU-UM		U
			ʿIZZ	AN	I					IZ-ZA-NI		M
			ʿIZZ		AJA					IZ-ZA-A-IA	FN	XIII 1 III 68
			ʿIZZ		IJA					I-ZI-IA		RA LXV 51 IX 41
			ʿIZZ	AK	UM					I-ZA-KUM		B 24
			ʿIZZ		I					ḪU-IZ-ZI	FN	M
			ʿIZZ				ʾAB		I	IZ-ZA-BI		C+
			ʿIZZ		U	KA				I-ZU-KA		XIII 1 III 50
			ʿIZZ		U		ŠAPAR			I-ZU-SA-PAR$_2$		U+
			ʿIZZ		U		ŠAPAR			IZ?-ZU?-ŠA-PA-AR		BIN II 98 5
			ʿIZZ		U	NI				IZ-ZU-UN-NI		M
			ʿUZZ		U					UZ-ZU	FN	XIII 1 XIV 31
			ʿUZZ		AM					ḪU-UZ-ZA-AM	ACC	XIII 100 9
			ʿUZZ				HADD		U	U$_2$-ZA-DU		U
WḪJ	1	JA	WḪIJ				ʾIL			IA-U$_2$-ḪI-DINGIR		B 31
WḪN	1	MU	WḪIN		UM					MU-ḪI-NU-UM		HAGER DISSERT. PL II/3
WBT	1	MU	WBIT		UM					MU-BI-TU-UM		LANGDON XXVII 4
WDJ	1	ʾA	WDAJ				ʾIL			A-U$_3$-DA-IL		U
		ʾA	WDAJ				ʾIL			A-AW-TE-IL		U
		ʾU	WDAJ				....			U$_2$-DA-[....]		TA 30, 615 29
		ʾU	WDAJ				MA			U$_2$-DA-MA		I
WDD	1	MU	WDAD		UM					MU-DA-DU-UM		I, VAS VIII 60 5, 18+
		MU	WDAD		U					MU-DA-DU		YOS XIII 513:9
WMʾ	1	JA	WMAʾ				ʾAḪ		UM	JA-MA-A-ḪU-UM		RA LXV 52 X 49
		JA	WMAʾ				ʿAMM	AJ	I	IA-AW-MA-ḪA-MA-JI-KI	GN	M
		JA	WMAʾ				ʿAMM		I	JA-MA-ḪA-MI-KI	GN	M
		JA	WMAʾ				ʿAMM		UM	JA-MA-ḪA-MU-UM		M
		JA	WMAʾ				ʿAMM		UM	IA-MA-ḪA-MU-UM		M
		ʾU	WMAʾ				ʾIL			U$_3$-MA-IL		U
		ʾU	WMAʾ				ʾIL		A	U$_2$-MA-D-DINGIR		B 40
WPʿ	1	MU	WPIʿ		I					MU-BI-ḪI		TA 30, 7 10
WQH	1	ʾU	WQAH							U$_3$-GA		U
		ʾU	WQAH							U$_3$-GA-A		SAUREN, WUG 114 REV, U
		ʾU	WQAH				HADD		U	U$_2$-QA-D-IM		RA LXV 44 IV 51
		ʾU	WQAH				HADD		U	U$_2$-GA-D-IM		BIROT, TEA 24:6
		ʾU	WQAH				ʾIL			U$_2$-QA-DINGIR		M+
		ʾU	WQAH				ʾIL			U$_2$-GA-DINGIR		GAUTIER 41 5

ROOTS (Consonants only)

WQH	1	ʾU	WQAH				ʾIL			U_3-QA-DINGIR		SIMMONS 1 3+
		ʾU	WQAH				ʾIL			U_2-QA-IL		SYRIA V 274 HANA
		ʾU	WQAH				ʾIL	A		U_2-Q[A]-I-LA		A 7699:14, ISHCHALI
		ʾU	WQAH				ʾIL	UM		U_2-GA-DINGIR-LUM		FRANK 29 9
		ʾU	WQAH				KI					
							ʾEL			U_2-QA-KI-EL		RA LXV 51 IX 69
		ʾU	WQAH				ŠAMŠ			U_2-GA-A-D-UTU		SZLECHTER TJ 15944 SEAL
		ʾU	WQAH				ŠAMŠ			U_2-GA-D-UTU		BIROT, TEA 72 V 16'
		ʾU	WQIH				ʾEL			U_2-QI_2-E[L]		RA LXV 41 II 44
WQR	1	MU	WQIR	AN	UM					MU-GI-RA-NU-UM		U
WRḪ	1		WARḪ				ʾIL	A		WA-AR-ḪI-LA_2		CCT I 38C 2 CAPP.
WSL	1	MU	WSIL	AT	UM					MU-ZI-LA-TUM	FN	B 35
WŠʿ	1	ʾU	WŠIʿ		UM					U_2-SI-UM		I
		ʾU	WŠIʿ		I					U_2-SI-I		I+
WŠB	1	JA	WŠIB		U					IA-AW-ŠI-BU		M
WṢʾ	1	JA	WṢIʾ							I-IA-U_2-ZI	FN	XIII 1 X 29
		JA	WṢIʾ							U_2-ZI		M
		JA	WṢIʾ				ʾEL			IA-A[W-Z]I-EL?		VIII 87 8'
		JA	WṢIʾ				ʾIL			IA-AW-ZI-DINGIR		M+
		JA	WṢIʾ				ʾIL			IA-U_2-ZI-DINGIR		B 31
		JA	WṢIʾ				ʾIL			IA-U_2-ṢI-DINGIR		BAGHD. MITT. II 23
		JA	WṢIʾ				ʾIL	UM		IA-U_2-ZI-LUM		B 31
		JA	WṢIʾ				ʾALAŠ	UM		U_2-ZI-A-LA-ŠUM		M
		MU	WṢIʾ			JA				MU-ZI-IA		M+
		JA	WṢIʾ				ŠUM	U				
							ʾAB	UM		U_2-ṢI-SU-MU-A-BU-UM		AJSL XXVIII 244 19
WTʾ	1	ʾU	WTAʾ	T	UM					U_2-TA-TUM	FN	C
		ʾU	WTAʾ				ʾAḪ	I		U_2-TA-A-ḪI		M
WTR	1	TU	WTAR				ʾABN	U		TU-TAR-AB-NU		M
		MU	WTAR							MU?-TA-AR		IX 290 1
	2		ḪAʾL		I	MU	WTAR			ḪA-LI_2-MU-TAR		M
Jʾ	1		JAʾ	AT	UM					IA-A-A-TUM	MN	A 29366:3
			JAʾ		A		ʿAN	UM		IA-A-A-NU-UM		YOS V 134 16
			JAʾ		U		ʾAHL	I		IA-U_2-A-LI_2		KISURRA 85 19
			JAʾ		U		ʾIL	I		IA-U-I-LI_2		SUMER V 143 NO. 2
			JAʾ		U		ŠUM	UM		IA?-U_2-SU?-MU-UM?		XIII 146 13
			JAʾ		UM					IA_3-A-UM		U
			JAʾ		UM					I-A-UM		U
			JAʾ		UM					IA-A-UM		BIN VII 67 27
			JAʾ		UM		ʾIL			IA-U_2-UM-DINGIR		B 31
			JAʾ		UM		ʾIL			IA-A-UM-[DINGIR]		B 31
			JAʾ		UM		ʾIL			IA-WU-UM-DINGIR		B 31
			JAʾ		UM		LU		HU	IA-UM-LU-ḪU		UET V 496:10
	2		ʾAB		I		JAʾ	A		A-BI-IA-A		KISURRA 102 7+
			ʾAB		I		JAʾ	UM		A-BI-IA-U_2-UM		YOS VIII 10 9
			ʾIL		I		JAʾ	UM		I_3-LI_2-IA-UM		KISURRA 71A 5+
			ʾIL		I		JAʾ	UM		I_3-LI_2-I-UM		KISURRA 4A 12+
			ʾIL		I		JAʾ	UM		I_3-LI_2-I-U_2-UM		KISURRA 56 3+
			ʾIL		I		JAʾ	UM		I_3-LI_2-U_2-A-UM		KISURRA 186 5
			ʾIL		I		JAʾ	UM		I_3-LI_2-A-UM		B 21
JʾN	1		JAʾN		UM					IA-NU-UM		B 29
			JAʾN		UM		PI			JA-NU-UM-BI-KI	GN	M
			JAʾN	AN						JA-NA-AN-KI	GN	M+
			JAʾN		A		ʾAHL	UM		JA-NA-A-LUM	GN	MRS VI P.125 61
			JAʾAN							IA-AN-[....]		IX 257 2
			JAʾAN		UM					IA-A-NU-UM		BIN VII 67 9
			JAʾAN		AM					IA-A-NA-AM		M
			JAʾAN				ʾIL			IA-AN-DINGIR		M
			JAʾAN				ŠARR	I		IA-AN-ŠAR-RI		M XIII 1 X 16
JʾN	2		ʾIL		I		JAʾN	UM		I_3-LI_2-IA-NU-UM		TIM I 29 3
			MUT		I		JAʾN	A		MU-TI-I-IA-NA		B 35
JʾR	1		JAʾAR							IA-A-AR		M
			JAʾAR		UM					IA-A-RUM		VAS VII 183 I 7, II 12+
			JAʾAR				HADD	U		IA-ḪA-AR-D-IM		M
			JAʾAR				ʾIL			IA-AR-I-I[L-....]		XIII 69 5
			JAʾAR				ʾIPQ			IA-AR-I-BI-IQ		M

ROOTS (Consonants only)

JʾR	2		ʾAB		I		JAʾAR			A-BI-IA-ḪA-AR		B 10+
			ʾAB		I		JAʾAR			A-BI-A-ḪA-AR		CT XLIII 125 1+
			ʾAB		I		JAʾAR			A-BI-ḪA-AR		B 10+
			KAʾM		I		JAʾAR	UM		KA-MI-IA-A-RUM		VAS VII 128 46
			ŠIPṬ		I		JAʾAR			ŠI-IP-TI-A-ḪA-AR	FN	C
JʾT	1		JAʾIT		I	JI	JBAL			IA-I-TI-I-BA-AL		M
JḪD	1		JAḪAD		UM					IA-ḪA-DUM		BIN VII 155 1
			JAḪAD		UM					IA-ḪA?-DU-UM		VII 199 8
			JAḪAD		U					IA-ḪA-TU		B 26
			JAḪAD		U					IA-ḪA-DU		M
			JAḪAD		IM					IA-ḪA-DI-IM	GEN	XIII 1 IX 30
			JAḪAD		A		....			IA-ḪA-DA-[....]		RA LXV 45 V 74
			JAḪAD				ʾEL	UM		IA-ḪA-AD-E-LUM		RIFTIN 136 26
			JAḪAD				ʾEL	UM		IA-ḪA-TE-LUM?		UET V 605 13
			JAḪAD				ʾIL			IA-ḪA-AD-DINGIR		M
			JAḪAD				ʿAMM	U		IA-ḪA-AD-ḪA-AM-MU		M
			JAḪAD				ʿAMM	U		IA-ḪA-AD-ḪA-MU		M+
			JAḪAD				ʿAMM	U	HU	IA-ḪA-AD-ḪA-MU-U$_2$		M
			JAḪAD				JARAḪ			IA-ḪA-AD-E-RA-AḪ		M
	2		ʾAḪ		U		JAḪAD			A-ḪU-IA-ḪA-AD		M+
			ʿAḎR		I		JAḪAD			AD-RI-E-ḪA-AD		M+
		JA	ŠWUB				JAḪAD			IA-ŠU-UB-IA-ḪA-AD		M
JʿL	1		JAʿAL		A					IA-ḪA-LA		YOS XIII 513:9
			JAʿAL				PI					
							ʾIL	UM		IA-ḪA-AL-PI-LUM		3NT867:5, 12, 21
		JA	JʿIL				LIʾM			IA-ḪI-IL-LI-IM		M
		JI	JʿIL				DIJN	I		I-ḪI-IL-DI-NI-X?		RA LXV 48 VIII 1
		JI	JʿIL				PI					
							ʾIL			I-ḪI-IL-BI-DINGIR		M
			JAʿIL	AT	UM					IA-ḪI-LA-TUM	FN	B 26
			JAʿIL	AT	UM					IA-I-LA?-TUM	FN	B 26
			JAʿIL	AT	IM					IA-ḪI-LA-TIM	GEN	CT XLVIII 27 CASE
			JAʿIL	AH						IA-ḪI-LA	FN	M
			JAʿIL		A					IA-I-LA	MN	RA LXV 40 I 27
			JAʿIL							JA-A-IL-KI	GN	M+
			JAʿIL							JA-I-IL-KI	GN	M+
			JAʿIL	AJ	I					JA-I-LA-JI-KI	GN	M
			JAʿIL	AN						JA-I-LA-AN		M
			JAʿIL	AN	U					JA-I-LA-NU	TRIBE	C
			JAʿIL	AN	IM					JA-I-LA-NIM	TRIBE GEN	M+, SHEMSHARA P. 100+
			JAʿIL	AN	I					JA-I-LA-NI	TRIBE	SHEMSHARA P.100
		JA	JʿUL				DAGAN			IA-ḪU-UL-D-DA-GAN		RA LXV 48 VII 75
JJ	1		JAJA		UM					IA-IA-UM		B 27+
			JAJA	AT	UM					IA-IA-TUM		B 26
JJM	1		JAJAM		U					IA-IA-MU		B 26
JBB	1		JABUB		U					IA-BU-BU		CT XLIII 29 1
JBL	1	JI	JBAL		UM					I-BA-LUM		B 21, M
		JI	JBAL		U					I-BA-LU		CT VIII 17C 11
		JI	JBAL	AT	UM					JI-BA-LA-TUM	FN	U
		JI	JBAL				....			I-BA-AL-[....]	FN	M
		JI	JBAL				....			I-BA-AL-D-[....]		M
		JI	JBAL				....			I-BA-AL-AN-ḪAR		XIII 1 X 43
		JI	JBAL				HADD	U		I-BA-AL-D-IM		M+, C+
		JI	JBAL				ʾIL			I-BA-AL-DINGIR		EEMY III/4 P. 130, M+
		JI	JBAL				ḪAM	UM		I-BA-AL-D-A-MU-UM		RA LXV 52 X 43
		JI	JBAL				JARAḪ			I-BA-AL-E-RA-AḪ		B 20; RA LXV 52 X 27
		JI	JBAL				ʿAŠTAR			I-BA-AL-EŠ$_4$-DAR		M
		JI	JBAL				DAGAN			I-BAL-D-DA-GAN		B 20
		JI	JBAL				DAGAN			I-BA-AL-D-DA-GAN		M
		JI	JBAL				LA					
							ʾIL			I-BA-AL-LA-DINGIR		RA LXV 47 VII 26
		JI	JBAL				PI					
							ʾEL			I-BA-AL-BI-EL		M+
		JI	JBAL				PI					
							ʾEL			I-BA-AL-PI-EL		UCP X P. 56+
		JI	JBAL				PI					
							ʾIL			I-BA-AL-BI-DINGIR		M+

ROOTS (Consonants only)

JBL	1	JA	JBIL						JIRR	A		IA-BI-IL-WI-IR-RA		B 24
		JA	JBIL		I				....			IA-BI-LI-[....]		FM 3998 SEAL
			JABAL						HADD	U		IA-BA-AL-D-IM		M
	2		ʾAḪ		I				JABAL			A-ḪI-E-BA-AL		M
			JAʾIT		I		JI		JBAL			IA-I-TI-I-BA-AL		M
			ʾAB		I				JABAL			A-BI-A-BA-AL		FIGULLA CAT. I 14206
			ḪABUR				JI		JBAL					
									BUGAŠ			ID$_2$-ḪA-BUR-I-BA-AL-BU-GA-AŠ$_2$		BRM IV 52 HANA
			ʾIL		A		JI		JBAL			DINGIR?-I-BA-AL		M
			ḪAM		I		JI		JBAL			D-A-MI-I-BA-AL		M+
			ʿAMM		I		JI		JBAL			ḪA-MI-I-BA-AL		M
			ʿAN	AT	I		JI		JBAL			ḪA-NA-TI-I-BA-AL		RA LXV 40 I 12
			JIŠʿ		I				JABAL			IŠ-ḪI-E-BA-AL		M
			DAWD		I				JABAL			DA-DI-E-BA-AL		UNPUBL.
			MUT		I				JABAL			MU-TI-A-BA-AI-KI	GN	B 35+
			MUT		I				JABAL			MU-TI-BA-AL-KI	GN	B 35+
			MUT		I				JABAL			MU-TA-BA-AI-KI	GN	OIP XI 216 IV 3
			MUT		I				JABAL	A		MU-TI-A-BA-LA-KI	GN	B 35
			NUʿM		I				JABAL			NU-UḪ-ME-E-BA-AL	FN	RA LXV 62 V 19
			SUMUKAN				JI		JBAL			D-GIR$_3$-I-BA-AL		C
			SITR		I				JABAL			ZI-IT-RI-E-BA-AL		M+
			ŠUMUT		I				JABAL	A		SU-MU-TI-A-BA-LA?		PBS XI/2 1 I 35
	3		LA						RIWM					
							JI		JBAL	U	HU	[L]A?-RI-IM-I-BA-LU-U$_2$		M
			ŠUM		U				MUT	I				
									JABAL	A		SU-MU-MU-TI-A-BA-LA		B 39
JBS	1		JABUS	AT	UM							IA-BU-ZA-TUM	FN	CT XLVIII 31 5, 9
			JABUS	AT	IM							IA-BU-ZA-TIM	FN GEN	B 25+
			JIBUS	AT	UM							I-BU-ZA-TUM		EDZARD, DER 87:11
			JABS	AT	UM							IA-AB-ZA?-TUM	MN?	VAS VIII 121 5
JBŚ	1	JA	JBIŚ		UM							IA-BI-ŠUM		B 24+
		JA	JBIŚ		U							IA-BI-ŠU		A 29366:10
		JI	JBIŚ		U							I-BI-ŠU	FN	BM 82359
		JI	JBIŚ						ʾIL			I-BI-IŠ-DINGIR		TA 1930, 261
		JI	JBIŚ						ʾEL			I-BI-IŠ-I$_3$-EL		SIMMONS 70 12
		JI	JBIŚ						ʾIL			[I-B]I$_2$-IŠ-I$_3$-IL		I
		JI	JBIŚ						JARAḪ			I-BI-IŠ-A-RA-AḪ		DELAPORTE CCL I A 446
		JI	JBIŚ						KABID			I-BI-IŠ-GA-BI-ID		KISURRA 63A
		ME	JBIŚ		UM							ME-BI-ŠUM		M+
		ME	JBIŚ		A							ME-BI-SA	MN	M
			JABAŚ	IJ	I							JA-BA-SI-JI	TRIBE	M
			JABAŚ	IJ	I							JA-BA-SI-I	TRIBE	M
			JABAŚ	IJ	IM							JA-BA-SI-IM	TRIBE	M
			JABUŚ									IA-BU-UŠ		CT VIII 29A 28
			JABUŚ		UM							IA-BU-ŠUM	GN	KING LIH II NO. 97 III 1
			JABUŚ		UM							[I]A-BU-SU-UM		VIII 85 41, 44
	2		LA				JE	N	JBIŚ	U		LA-E-NI-BI-ŠU		YOS XII
JD	1		JAD		IM							IA-DI-IM	GEN	TIM V 35 6
			JAD	AN	UM							IA-DA-NU-UM		SIMMONS 131 17
			JAD		I				NAṢIR			IA-DI-NA-ṢIR		BM 17051, 17052
			JID	AN	UM							I-DA-NU-UM		I+
			JID		I							I-DI		RA LXV 40 I 22
			JID		IJA							I-DI-IA		M
			JID		IJAN							I-DI-JA-AN		RA LXV 47 VII 54
			JID		U	HU						I-DU-U$_2$		RA LXV 65 VI 59
			JID		I				ʾIL			I-DI-DINGIR		M
			JID		I				JAT	UM		I-DI-IA-TUM		M
	3		ʾAŠD		UM				PI					
									JAD	IM		AŠ-DU-UM-BI-IA-DI-IM		RA LXV 55 XIII 44
JDʿ	1	JI	JDAʿ						LIʾM					
									MA			I-DA-LIM-MA		B 21
		JI	JDAʿ						MARAṢ			I-DA-MA-RA-AṢ	GN	B 21+, M
		JI	JDAʿ						MARAṢ			A-DA-MA-RA-AṢ	GN	B 11
		JI	JDAʿ						MARAṢ			A-TA-MA-RA-AṢ	PN	CT II 26 3
		JI	JDAʿ						PI					
									ʾIL			I-DA-BI$_2$-DINGIR		I

ROOTS (Consonants only)

JDʿ	1	JI	JDAʿ				ŠUM		I-DA-SU-UM		M
		ʾA	JDAʿ				PI				
							ʾEL		A-DA-AḪ-[BI]?-EL		SIMMONS 51 21
			JADAʿ		UM				IA-DA-ḪU-UM		YOS XII
			JADAʿ		UM				IA-ṬA₃-ḪU-UM		YOS XII
			JADAʿ				ḪAʾL	UM	IA-DA-AḪ-ḪA-LUM		B 25
			JADAʿ				HADD	U	[IA]-ṬA₃-AḪ-D-IM		VI 76 10
			JADAʿ				ʾIL		IA-DAḪ-DINGIR		B 25+
			JADAʿ				ʾIL		IA-DA-AḪ-DINGIR		CT XLVIII 21 SEAL
			JADAʿ				ʾIL		IA-DA-DINGIR		M
			JADAʿ				ʿAMM	U	IA-DA-AM-MU		C II 5 4
			JADAʿ				JAT	UM	IA-DA-A-A-TUM		B 25
			JADAʿ				LIʾM		IA-DAḪ-LI-IM		YOS XII
			JADAʿ				LIʾM		IA-ṬA₃-AḪ-LI-IM		YOS XII
			JADAʿ				PI				
							ʾIL		IA-DA-BI-DINGIR		AJSL XXXIII 224 3
			JADAʿ			TI	ʾEL		IA-DA-AḪ-TE-DINGIR		UNPUBL.
		JI	JDAʿ				RAWM		I-DAḪ-RA-AM		MEISSNER 91 17
		JA	JDIʿ		UM				IA-DI-ḪU-UM		B 25+
		JA	JDIʿ		U				IA-DI-U₂		CT VIII 10 B 7+
		JE	JDIʿ		UM				E-TI-UM		I
		JA	JDIʿ		IM				IA-DI-ḪI-IM	GEN	M+
		JA	JDIʿ				....		IA-DI-[....]	FN	M
		JA	JDIʿ	AT	UM				IA-DI-ḪA-TUM	FN	B 25+
		JA	JDIʿ	AH					IA-DI-ḪA	FN	M+
		JA	JDIʿ				ʾAB	UM	IA-DI-ḪA-BU-UM		B 25+
		JA	JDIʿ				ʾAB	UM	IA-DI-A-BU-UM		M, YOS XII+
		JA	JDIʿ				ʾAB	UM	IA-DU-A-BU-UM		YOS XII+
		JA	JDIʿ				ʾAB	U	IA-DI-ḪA-BU		PBS XIV 1084
		JA	JDIʿ				ʾAB	U	IA-DI-A-BU		YOS XII+
		JA	JDIʿ				ʾAB	UM	IA-DI-ḪA-A-BU-U[M]		RA LXV 45 V 9
		JA	JDIʿ				ʾAB	IM	IA-DI-ḪA-A-BI-IM	GEN	M+
		JA	JDIʿ				ʾEL	UM	IA-DI-ḪI-E-LUM		UNPUBL.
		JA	JDIʿ				ʾIL		IA-DI-IḪ-DINGIR		B 25+
		JA	JDIʿ				ʾIL		IA-DI-DINGIR		M
		JA	JDIʿ				DAGAN		I[A]-DI-D-DA-GAN		B 25
		JA	JDIʿ		A		ʾEL		IA-DI-ḪA-EL		KISURRA 10A 4
		ME	JDIʿ		UM				ME-TE-UM		I
	2		KAʾB		I		JADAʿ		KA-BI-E-DA-AḪ		XIII 1 XI 54
			ŠAM		A		JADAʿ	UM	SA-MA-A-DA-ḪU-UM		M+
			ŠAM		A		JADAʿ	U	SA-MA-A-DA-ḪU		M
			ŠAM		A		JADAʿ	IM	SA-MA-A-DA-Ḫ[I-I]M	GEN	M
			ŠUM		U		JADAʿ	UM	SU-MU-A-DA-ḪU-UM		KISURRA 78A 15
JDD	1		JADID		UM				IA-DI-DU-UM		B 25+, M+
			JADID		UM				IA-DI-DUM		CT XLI A 10+
			JADID		U				IA-DI-DU		FIGULLA CAT. I 13371 M
			JADID		IM				IA-DI-DIM	GEN	JCS IV 95 1612 13
			JADID		IM				IA-DI-D[I-IM]	GEN	M
			JADID	AT	UM				IA-DI-DA-TUM	MN	B 25+
			JADID	AT	IM				IA-DI-DA-TIM	MN GEN	B 25+
			JADID		A				IA-DI-DA	MN GEN	VII 206 2, 13
			JADID	AH					IA-DI-DA	FN	M+
JDN	1		JADN		U				IA-AD-NU		M
JKK	1		JAKUK		UM				IA-KU?-KU-UM		B 27
JKL	1		JAKAL	ITIJIM					JA-KA-LI-TE-IM	TRIBE GEN	M
			JAKAL	ITIJI					[JA]-KA-LI-TI-I	TRIBE GEN	M
JLQṬ	1		JALQUṬ		UM				IA-AL-GU-TUM		BIN II 68 18
JM	2		MAʾD		I		JAM	A	MA-DI-IA-MA		UCP X/1 33 10
			MUT		U		JAM	A	MU-TU-IA-MA		M
	3		ʾALUN				PI				
							JAM	U	ḪA-LU-UN-BI-JA-MU		M
			ʾALUN				PI				
							JAM	U	ḪA-LU-UM-BI-JA-MU		RA LXV 43 III 78
			ʾALUN				PI				
							JAM	U	ḪA-LU-BI-JA-MU		M
JMM	1		JAMAM	AH					IA-MA-MA?	FN	M

ROOTS (Consonants only)

JMM	1		JAMAM			HU			IA$_3$-MA-AM-U$_2$		U
			JAMM		AJA				IA-AM-MA-A		B 28+
			JAMM		AJA				IA-AM-MA-A-IA	FN	C+
			JAMM	AN					IA-AM-MA-AN		YOS XIII 514:6
			JAMM		U	HU			IA-AM-MU-U$_2$		VAS XVIII 19 R. 6
			JAMM		U		QAʾD	UM	IA-AM-MU?-QA-DU-UM		III 56 7
	2		ŠUM		I		JAMAM		SU-MI-IA-MA-AM		XII 61 5
			ŠUM		U		JAMAM		SU-MU-IA-MA-AM		M+
JMN	1		JAMAN						IA?-MA-AN		XII 5 6
			JAMIN						IA-MI-IN	TRIBE	M
			JAMIN		I				IA-MI-NI	TRIBE	M
			JAMIN		A				IA-MI-NA-A	TRIBE	M
			JAMIN		A				IA-MI-NA	TRIBE	M+
			JAMIN		A				IA-MI-NA	PN	RA LXV 45 V 21
			JAMIN		A				I-IA-MI-NA	TRIBE	M
			JAMIN		A				IA-ME-NA	TRIBE	M
			JAMIN		UM				JA-ME-NU-UM		TA 1931, 538 IV 1, 13
			JAMIN		IM				IA-MI-NIM	TRIBE	M
			JAMN		UM				IA-AM-NU-UM		B 28+
			JAMN		IJA				IA-AM-NI-IA		RA LXV 54 XII 63
			JAMN	ATAN					IA-AM-NA-TA-AN		RA LXV 52 X 48
			JAMN	UN	UM				IA-AM-NU-NU-UM		TIM III 26 13, 39 16
JNN	1		JANIN		UM				IA-NI-NU-UM		TIM V 18 22
JNT	1		JANT		IJA				IA-AN-TI-IA		M+
JPʿ	1	ʾA	JPAʿ				ʾAB	I	A-PA-AḪ-A-BI		YOS VIII 29 13
		ʾA	JPAʿ				NAN	UM	A-BA-AḪ-NA-NU-UM		TA 1931, 374, EARLY OB
		ʾA	JPAʿ				RAPIʾ		A-PA-AḪ-RA-BI		SUMER XIV 5, IM 52272
		JA	JPAʿ						IA-A-PA-AḪ		M+
		JA	JPAʿ						IA-PA		A.
		JA	JPAʿ		UM				IA-PA-ḪU-UM		RA LXVI 118:16
		JA	JPAʿ		UM				[I]A-PA-ḪU-UM	FN	RA LXV 64 VI 8
		JA	JPAʿ	AT	UM				IA-PA-ḪA-TUM	FN	M+
		JA	JPAʿ	AH					IA-PA-ḪA	FN	M+
		JA	JPAʿ				HADD	U	IA-A-PA-AḪ-D-IM		M+
		JA	JPAʿ				HADD	U	IA-PA-ḪA-D-IM		M
		JA	JPAʿ				HADD	U	IA-PA-AḪ-D-IM		M+
		JA	JPAʿ				ʾIL		IA-PA-AḪ-DINGIR		RA LXV 51 IX 74
		JA	JPAʿ				ʾIL		IA-PA-DINGIR		B 29
		JA	JPAʿ				DAGAN		IA-PA-AḪ-D-DA-GAN		XIII 58 5+
		JA	JPAʿ				LIʾM		IA-A-PA-AḪ-LI-IM		M+
		JA	JPAʿ				LIʾM		IA-PA-AḪ-LI-IM		M+
		JA	JPAʿ				ŠUM	U			
							ʾAB	I	IA-PA-AḪ-SU-MU-A-BI		A. 56 47
		JA	JPUʿ		UM				IA-PU-ḪU-UM		B 25+
		JA	JPUʿ		U				IA-PU-ḪU		B 25
		JA	JPUʿ	AT	UM				IA-PU-ḪA-TUM	FN	C+
		JA	JPUʿ		AJA				IA-PU-ḪA-IA	FN	C+
			JAPʿ		UM				IA-AP-ḪU-UM		M+
			JAPʿ	AT	UM				IA-AP-ḪA-TUM	MN	B 24+
			JAPʿ	AT	UM				IA-AP-ḪA-TUM	FN	YOS VIII 12 2+
		JA	JPIʿ				HADD	U	IA-BI-IḪ-D-IM		M
		ME	JPIʿ		UM				ME-BI-ḪU-UM		M
		ME	JPIʿ		UM				ME-PI-UM		I
	2		ʾAB		I	JA	JPAʿ		A-BI-IA-PA-AḪ	FN	XIII 1 II 57
			ʾAB		I	JE	JPUʿ		A-BI-E-PU-UḪ		B 10, M+
			ʾAB		I	JA	JPUʿ		A-BI-IA-PU-UḪ		B 10
			ʾIL		I	JE	JPAʿ		I$_3$-LI$_2$-E-PA		A.+
			ʾIL		I	JE	JPUʿ		I$_3$-LI$_2$-E-PU-UḪ		M+
			ʿAMM		I	JE	JPUʿ		ḪA-MI-E-PU-UḪ		M+
			ʿAMM		I	JE	JPUʿ		ḪA-AM-MI-E-PU-UḪ		M+
			ʿAMM		U	JE	JPUʿ		ḪA-MU-E-PU-UḪ	FN	C+
			ʾANN		U		JAPʿ	AH	AN-NU-IA-AP-ḪA	FN	XIII 1 IV 3+
			ʾANN		U		JIPʿ	AH	AN-NU-IP-ḪA	FN	XIII 1 VIII 29
			ʿAŠTAR				JIPʿ	AH	EŠ$_4$-DAR-IP-ḪA	FN	XIII 1 VI 19+
		JI	JṢIʾ			JA	JPAʿ		I-ZI-A-PA-AḪ		B 22
			BAʿL		I	JA	JPUʿ		BA-LI-A-PU-UḪ		HARRIS 96 6+

JPʿ	2	BAʿL		I		JA	JPUʿ			BA-LI-PU-UḪ$_2$		EDZARD, DER 117:38 DATE
		BAʿL		I		JE	JPAʿ			BA-LI-E-PA		A.
		DAGAN				ʾA	JPUʿ			D-DA-GAN-A-PU-UḪ		M
		KAʾB		I		JE	JPUʿ			KA-BI-E-PU-UḪ		M
	JA	LʾIJ				JA	JPAʿ			IA-AL-E-PA-AḪ		M
		NIQM		I		JA	JPAʿ			NI-IQ-MI-PA		A. 27 12
		NIQM		I		JA	JPAʿ			NI-IQ-ME-PA		A.+
		NIQM		I		JE	JPUʿ			NI-IQ-MI-E-PU-UḪ		M+, A.+
	JA	ŠWUB				JI	JPUʿ			IA-ŠU-UB-D-I-PU-UḪ		M
		ŠUM		U		JA	JPAʿ			[SU-MU]-A-PA-AḪ		B 38
		ŠUM		U		JE	JPUʿ			SU-MU-E-PU-UḪ		M+
		ŠUM		U	NA	JA	JPUʿ		A	SU-MU-NA-IA-PU-ḪA-[....]		M
		ŠAMŠ		I		JA	JPUʿ	AT		D-UTU-IA-PU-ḪA-AT	FN?	BM 17075
		ṢIDQ		I		JE	JPAʿ			ZI-ID-KI-E-PA		RA XLIII 37 QATNA
		ṢIDQ		I		JE	JPUʿ			ZI-ID-KI-E-PU-UḪ		M+, C+
JPR	1	JAPAR		IM						IA-PA-RI-IM	GEN	M
	2 JI	JṢIʾ					JAPAR			I-ZI-A-PA-AR		B 22
		ŠUM		U			JAPAR			[SU-MU]-A-PA-AR		B 38
JQH	1 JI	JQAH					ʾIL			I-KA-AḪ-DINGIR		B 21
	JA	JQAH					ʿAMM		U	IA-QA-AM-MU		A.+
JQR	1	JAQAR								IA-QAR		WATERMAN 72 4
		JAQAR		UM						IA-QA-RUM		M+
		JAQAR		UM						IA-GA-RU-UM		KISURRA 59A 24
		JAQAR	T	UM						IA-QAR-TUM	FN	M
		JAQAR					ʾIL			IA-QAR-DINGIR		CT VI 49 A 23
	JA	JQIR	AN	U						IA-KI-RA-NU		M
	JA	JQIR		A			ʾAB		UM	IA-KI-RA-A-BU-UM		RA LXV 47 VII 30
		JAQR		UM			ʾIL			IA-AQ-RUM-DINGIR		A 22010
		JAQR	AN							[I]A-AQ-RA-AN		RA LXV 44 IV 37
		JAQR	IT	UM						IA-AQ-RI-TUM		EDZARD, DER 155 REV 15
	2	ʾAḪ	AT				JIQR	AH		A-ḪA-AT-IQ-RA	FN	M
		ʾAḪ	AT	I			JIQR	AT		A-ḪA-TI-IQ-RA-AT	FN	XIII 1 V 5
		ʾAḪ	AT	I			JIQR	AH		A-ḪA-TI-IQ-RA	FN	XIII 1 II 72+
		ʾAB		I			JAQAR			A-BI-E-QAR		M+
		ʾAB		U			JAQAR			A-BU-WA-QAR		M
		ʾAB		U			JAQAR			A-BU-QAR		M
		ʾAB		UM			JAQAR			A-BU-UM-WA-QAR		M
		ʾIL		I			JAQR		A	I$_3$-LI$_2$-AQ-RA		IRAQ XXX 90, RIMAH
		ʿAMM		U			JAQAR			ḪA-MU-IA-QAR		RA LXV 52 X 62
		ʾUMM		I			JIQR	AH		UM-MI-IQ-RA	FN	M+
		ŠARR		UM			JAQR	AH		LUGAL-JA-AQ-RA	FN	XIII 1 X 45
JRʾ	1	JIRʾ		I						JI-IR-I	TRIBE	IX 248 15'
JRḪ	1	JARAḪ					ʿAD		U	SIN-A-DU		RA XLIII 8 QATNA
		JARAḪ					ʾAŠD		UM	D-EN-ZU-AŠ-DU-UM		WALTERS, WL 114:2
		JARAḪ					DAŠUR			SIN-DA-ŠUR		VAS IX 185 12+
		JARAḪ					KIWN		A	SIN-KI-NA		TCL I 237 31
		JARAḪ					TIWR		I	D-EN-ZU-TI-RI		M+
		JARAḪ					TIWR		IM	D-EN-ZU-TI-RI-IM	GEN	M
		JARAḪ	T	UM						IA-RA-AḪ-TUM	MN	B 29+
		JARAḪ	T	IM						IA-RA-AḪ-TIM	MN GEN	YOS XII
	2 TA	HWIJ					JARAḪ			TA-AḪ-WI?-D-EN-ZU		RA LXIV 28 NO. 16
		JAḪAD					JARAḪ			IA-ḪA-AD-E-RA-AḪ		M
		ʾUWR		I			JARAḪ			U$_2$-RI-E-RA-AḪ		M
		ʾAB		A			JARAḪ			A-BA-A-RA-AḪ		KICH II D 8 3
		ʾAB		I			JARAḪ			A-BI-A-RA-AḪ		B 9+
		ʾAB		I			JARAḪ			A-BI-E-RA-AḪ		B+, M+
		ʾAB		I			JARAḪ			A-BI-RA-AḪ		B 9+, A. 38 18
		ʾAB		I			JARAḪ			A-BE-RA-AḪ		B 9
		ʿABD					JARAḪ			AB-DI-A-RA-AḪ		B 9+
		ʿABD					JARAḪ			ḪA-AB-DI-A-RA-AḪ		B 9
		ʿABD					JARAḪ			AB-DI-RA-AḪ		B 9+
		ʿABD					JARAḪ			ḪA-AB-DI-E-RA-AḪ		M+, C+
		ʿABD					JARAḪ			AB-DI-E-RA-AḪ		M+, UCP X P. 198+
		ʿABD					JARAḪ			ḪA-AB-DI-RA-AḪ		SUMER XXIII 162 46
		ʿABD					JARAḪ			AB-DI-D-EN-ZU		PBS VII/1 94 III 28
		ʿABD					JARAḪ			AB-DI-D-E-RA-AḪ		YOS XIII 199:22+

ROOTS (Consonants only)

JRḪ	2		ʿABD			JARAḪ	AB-DU-D-E-RA-AḪ	YOS XIII 218:13+
			ʿABD			JARAḪ	ḪA-AB-DU-E-RA-AḪ	DELAPORTE CCL II A 418 M
			ʿABD			JARAḪ	AB-DU-E-RA-AḪ	M+
		JI	JBAL			JARAḪ	I-BA-AL-E-RA-AḪ	B 20; RA LXV 52 X 27
			ʾABN		A	JARAḪ	ḪA?-AB-NA-A-RA-AḪ	UET V 476 SEAL 6
		JI	JBIŠ			JARAḪ	I-BI-IŠ-A-RA-AḪ	DELAPORTE CCL I A 446
			ʿADN		I	JARAḪ	ḪA-AD-NI-E-RA-AḪ	M
			ʾAK		I	JARAḪ	A-KI-E-RA-AḪ	M
			ʾIL		I	JARAḪ	I$_3$-LI$_2$-IA-RA-AḪ	SIMMONS 131 20
			ʾIL		I	JARAḪ	I$_3$-LI$_2$-E-RA-AḪ	M+, TIM III 133 4, SEAL
			ʾUMM		U	JARAḪ	U$_2$?-UM-MU-E-RA-AḪ	B 40+
		JA	ʾMUR			JARAḪ	IA-MUR-D-EN-ZU	UET V 583 19
		JA	ʿMIS			JARAḪ	IA-AḪ-MI-IS-D-SIN	M
			ʿINB		I	JARAḪ	IN-BI-RA-AḪ	KISURRA 6 15
			ḪANN		A	JARAḪ	ḪA-AN-NA-D-EN-ZU	M
			ḪANN		A	JARAḪ	ḪAN-NA-D-EN-ZU	XIII 1 V 27
			ʾIPQ			JARAḪ	I-BI-IQ-D-[EN]-ZU	M
			JIŠʿ		I	JARAḪ	IŠ-ḪI-E-RA-AḪ	RA LXV 41 II 25
			JIŠʿ		I	JARAḪ	IŠ-I-RA-AḪ	TIM III 28 12
		JA	JṢIʾ			JARAḪ	IA-ZI-E-RA-AḪ	B 32, C
		JA	ʾZUW			JARAḪ	IA-ZU-RA-AḪ	M+
			BAWʾ			JARAḪ	BA-IA-RA-AḪ	RUTTEN 7 3
			BAWʾ			JARAḪ	BA-A-RA-AḪ	RUTTEN 39 18
			BAWʾ			JARAḪ	PA-IA-RA-AḪ	RUTTEN 7 7
			BAʿL		I	JARAḪ	BA-LI-A-RA-AḪ	SIMMONS 58 11
			BAʿL		I	JARAḪ	BA-LI-E-RA-AḪ	M+, TCL XVIII 92 1+
			BAʿL		I	JARAḪ	BA-LI-RA-AḪ	TCL XVIII 94 1 14+
			BEʿL	T	I	JARAḪ	NIN?-TI-E-RA-AḪ	RA LXV 52 X 54
			BUN		U	JARAḪ	BU-NU-E-RA-AḪ	M
		JI	BNIJ			JARAḪ	IB-NI-E-RA-AḪ	SIMMONS 62 14'+
			BIZZ		I	JARAḪ	BI-IṢ-ṢI-E-RA-AḪ	YOS XIII 245:16
			ḎIKR		I	JARAḪ	ZI-IK-RI-E-RA-AḪ	TIM V 69 7, 17+
			ḎIMR		I	JARAḪ	ZI-IM-RI-E-RA-AḪ	B 42+, C+, M+
			GAʾJ		I	JARAḪ	GA-JI-RA-A[Ḫ]	HARRIS 39 15
			GUMUL			JARAḪ	GU-MU-UL-D-EN-ZU	M+
			KAʾB		I	JARAḪ	KA-BI-E-RA-AḪ	RA LXV 41 II 29+;B 32+
			KIBR			JARAḪ	KI-BI-IR-D-EN-ZU	RUTTEN 11 25
			KIBS		I	JARAḪ	KI-IB-ZI-E-RA-AḪ	RA LXV 43 III 44+
			LAʾR		A	JARAḪ	LA-RA-D-SIN	KAJ 167 23+, LATE
			MILK		I	JARAḪ	MIL-KI-E-RA-AḪ	AJSL XLIV 243 NO. 33
			MUT		I	JARAḪ	MU-TI-A-RA-AḪ	B 35
			MUT		I	JARAḪ	MU-TI-E-RA-AḪ	M; TCL XI 224:69+
			MUT		I	JARAḪ	MU-TE-E-RA-AḪ	A 7804 13
			MUT		U	JARAḪ	MU-TU-E-RA-AḪ	JCS XXIV 60 NO. 51 REV
			NAʿM		I	JARAḪ	NA-AḪ-MI-E-RA-AḪ	JCS XI 29 NO.17 5
			NAPŠ		I	JARAḪ	NA-AP-SI-E-RA-AḪ	M+
		JA	NŠIʾ			JARAḪ	IA-SI-E-RA-AḪ	B 28
		JA	NŠIʾ			JARAḪ	IA-SI-RA-AḪ	B 30
		JA	NŠIʾ			JARAḪ	IA-SI-A-RA-AḪ	GRANT, HAV. 242:2+
		JA	NTIN			JARAḪ	IA-AN-TI-IN-A-RA-AḪ	RA LXV 62 V 34
		JA	NTIN			JARAḪ	IA-AN-TI-NA-RA-AḪ	RUTTEN 11 20+
		JA	NTIN			JARAḪ	IA-AN-TI-LA-RA-AḪ	VAS XVI 91 3
		JA	NTIN			JARAḪ	IA-AN-TI-IN-E-RA-AḪ	M+
		JA	NTIN			JARAḪ	IA-AT-TI-IN-E-RA-AḪ	M+
		JA	NTIN			JARAḪ	IA-T[I-I]N-E-RA-AḪ	M
		JA	PḪUR			JARAḪ	IA-AP-ḪU-UR-SIN	M
			PULS		I	JARAḪ	PU-UL-ZI-RA-AḪ	HARRIS 18 14
			PULS		I	JARAḪ	PU-UL-SI-E-RA-AḪ	TIM V 69 16+
			QUWJ			JARAḪ	KU-WE-RA-AḪ	A 32133 REV.4
			QIMṢ		I	JARAḪ	KI?-IM-ZE$_2$-RA-AḪ	EDZARD,DER 231:2
		JA	RWIM			JARAḪ	IA-RI-IM-IA-RA-AḪ	RA LXV 41 II 28
		JA	RWIM			JARAḪ	IA-RI-IM-E-RA-AḪ	M
			RABB		I	JARAḪ	RA-AB-BI-E-RA-AḪ	B 37+
			SIMT		I	JARAḪ	ZI-IM-TI-E-RA-AḪ	M+
			ŠAM		I	JARAḪ	SA-ME-E-RA-AḪ	M
			ŠAM		I	JARAḪ	SA-ME-RA-AḪ	YOS VIII 64 19+

ROOTS (Consonants only)

JRḪ	2		ŠAM		U		JARAḪ		SA-MU-A-RA-AḪ		SIMMONS 98 3
			ŠAM		U		JARAḪ		SA-[M]U-E?-RA-A[Ḫ]?		RA LXV 47 VII 13
			ŠUM		U		JARAḪ		SU-MU-A-RA-AḪ		B 38+
			ŠUM		U		JARAḪ		SU-MU-E-RA-AḪ		M+
			ŠAMŠ		I		JARAḪ		SA-AM-SI-E-RA-AḪ		BASOR 95, 19+, M+
			ŠAMŠ		U		JARAḪ		SA-AM-SU-E-RA-AḪ		B 38
			ŠUMAT				JARAḪ		SU-MA-AT-E-RA-AḪ		M+
			ṢUWR		I		JARAḪ		ZU-RI-E-RA-AḪ		M
			ṢUPR		I		JARAḪ		ZU-UP-RI-E-RA-AḪ		M+
			TINʾ		I		JARAḪ		TI-IN-E-RA-AḪ		C
			TINʾ		I		JARAḪ		TI-IN-I-E-RA-AḪ		C
	3		LA				DJIN				
							JARAḪ		LA-DI-IN-E-RA-AḪ		RA LXV 46 VI 26+
JRD	1	JA	JRID		UM				IA-RI-DU-UM		UCP X/1 109 3
		JI	JRID	AN	UM				I-RI-DA-NU-UM		M
		MA	JRID	UN	UM				MA-RI-DU-NU-UM		SIMMONS 124 17
JRN	1		JARAN		I				JA-RA-A-NI	FN	A. 21 9
			JARIN		IM				JA-RI-NI-IM	GEN	CT XLV 89 III 9
			JARIN						IA-RI-EN		TA 1931, 241
			JARN		UM				JA-AR-NU-UM		RUTTEN 22 17
JRQ	1		JARQ	AN					IA-AR-QA-A[N]		M
	2		MUT		UM		JARIQ		MU-TUM-JA-RI-IQ		TA 1931, 104, 538
JRR	2	JA	JBIL				JIRR	A	IA-BI-IL-WI-IR-RA		B 24
JŠR	1		JAŠAR		UM				IA-ŠA-RU-UM		B 30
			JAŠAR		UM				IA-SA-RU-UM		PINCHES BERENS 101 10, M+
			JAŠAR		AM				IA-SA-RA-AM	ACC	M
			JAŠAR	AH					IA-SA-RA	FN	XIII 1 II 64+
			JAŠAR			TI	ʾIL		IA-SA-AR-TI-DINGIR		M
		JA	JŠIR		UM				IA-SI-RUM		B 30+
		JA	JŠIR		UM				IA-ŠI-RU-[UM]		A 22002
		JA	JŠIR	T	IM				IA-ŠIR-TI-IM	MN GEN	WATERMAN 45 R. 10
		JA	JŠIR				HEDD	A	IA-ŠE-RE-DA		A. 367 5
		JA	JŠIR				HEDD	A	IA-AŠ-RI-E-DA		A.+
		JI	JŠAR		UM				I-ŠA-RUM		C
		JI	JŠAR		I				I-ŠA-RI	FN	A.
		JI	JŠAR				LIʾM		I-ŠAR-LI-IM		M+, C+, CT VI 47B 17
		ME	JŠAR		UM				ME-ŠA-RUM		A.
	2		ʿAMM		I		JAŠAR		ḪA-AM-MI-E-SA-AR?		M
			ʿAMM		U		JAŠAR		ḪA-MU-JA-ŠAR		M
			ḪANN		I	JI	JŠAR		AN-NI-I-ŠAR?		M
			ʾAŠD		I		JAŠAR		AŠ$_2$-DI-E-SA-AR		XIII 1 XI 35
			DAWD		I		JAŠAR		DA-DI-E-SA-AR		RA LXV 50 VIII 48+
			NAWAR			JE	JŠAR		NA-WA-AR-E-ŠAR	FN	XIII 1 VI 40
			ŠAMŠ		U	JI	JŠAR		SA-AM-SU-D-I-[Š]AR		M
			TADAB			JE	JŠAR		TA-DA-AB-E-ŠAR	FN	XIII 1 VI 42
	3		LA			ʾA	HWIJ				
							JAŠAR		LA-AḪ-WI-E-SA-AR		RA LXV 40 I 21
JŠʿ	1	JA	JŠUʿ		UM				IA-ŠU-ḪU-UM		B 30+
		JA	JŠUʿ	AT	UM				IA-ŠU-ḪA-TUM	FN	RA LXV 58 I 17; B 30+
		JA	JŠUʿ	AH					IA-ŠU-ḪA	FN	M+
		JA	JŠUʿ				ʾIL		IA-ŠU-DINGIR		RA LXIV 36 NO. 31
		T	JAŠʿ	AH					IA?-TA-AŠ-ḪA?	FN	M
		ME	JŠIʿ		UM				ME-SI-UM		SIGRIST UNPUBL.
			JIŠʿ	AT	UM				IŠ-ḪA-TUM	FN	RA LXV 60 III 57
			JIŠʿ	AT	I				IŠ-A-TI	MN? GEN	PBS VIII/2 238 5, 8
			JIŠʿ	AT	IJA				IŠ-ḪA-TI-IA	MN?	B 24+
			JIŠʿ	IT	IJA				IŠ-ḪI-TI-IA	MN?	CT XLVIII 91 REV.+
			JIŠʿ	AH					IŠ-ḪA	FN	XIII 1 VIII 25+
			JIŠʿ		IJA				IŠ-HI-IA		M, C
			JIŠʿ				BAʿL	A	E-ŠE-EḪ-BA-LA?		VAS VII 160 7
			JIŠʿ				DAGAN		I-SI-IḪ-D-DA-GAN		RA XLI 43 HANA
			JIŠʿ		A		BAʿL		IŠ-ḪA-B[A-A]L		HARRIS 39 14
			JIŠʿ		A		GAʾL		IŠ-ḪA-GA-AL		A 7459 10
			JIŠʿ		I		JABAL		IŠ-ḪI-E-BA-AL		M
			JIŠʿ		I		HADD	U	IŠ-ḪI-D-IM		M+, C+
			JIŠʿ		I		HEDD	A	IŠ-ḪI-E-D-IM		TIM IV 33 SEAL, 34 SEAL

ROOTS (Consonants only)

JŠʿ	1		JIŠʿ	I		ʾIL			IŠ-ḪI-DINGIR		WALTERS, WL 109:5+
			JIŠʿ	I		ʾIL	A				
						MA			IŠ-ḪI-DINGIR-MA		M
			JIŠʿ	I		ʾIL	A				
						MA			IŠ-ḪI-DINGIR-LA-MA		M
			JIŠʿ	I		ʾIL	U				
						MA			IŠ-ḪI-LU-MA		YOS VIII 176 20
			JIŠʿ	I		ʾIL	U	NA	IŠ-ḪI-LU-NA		VII 215 33
			JIŠʿ	I		ʿAN	UM		IŠ-ḪI-A-NU-UM		B 45
			JIŠʿ	I		JARAḪ			IŠ-ḪI-E-RA-AḪ		RA LXV 41 II 25
			JIŠʿ	I		JARAḪ			IŠ-I-RA-AḪ		TIM III 28 12
			JIŠʿ	I		DAGAN			IŠ-ḪI-D-DA-GAN		M+
			JIŠʿ	I		LI					
						ʾEL			IŠ-ḪI-LI-EL		JCS XXIV 69 NO. 3 SEAL
			JIŠʿ	I		LIʾM			IŠ-ḪI-LI-IM		M
			JIŠʿ	I		MAṬAR			IŠ-ḪI-MA-DAR		V 40 5, 16
			JIŠʿ	I		NABUʾ	UM		IŠ-ḪI-NA-BU-U[M]		EDZARD, DER 68 III 6
	2		ʾAḪ	I	JA	JŠUʿ			A-ḪI-IA-ŠU-UḪ		SIMMONS 58 16
			ʾAḪ	I	JA	JŠUʿ			A-ḪI-IA-ŠU		BIROT, TEA 28:17+
			ʾAJA		JE	JŠUʿ			A-A-E-ŠU-UḪ?		TCL X 9 3
			ʾAB	I	JE	JŠUʿ			A-BI-E-ŠU-UḪ		B 10+, XIII 1 III 44
			ʾAB	I	JA	JŠUʿ			A-BI-ŠU-UḪ		B 10
			ʾAB	I	JA	JŠUʿ	A		A-BI-IA-ŠU-ḪA		B 10
			ʾAB	I	JE	JŠUʿ					
						....			A-BI-E-ŠU-UḪ-LI-DI-IŠ		CT XLV 55 11
			ʾAB	I	JE	JŠUʿ					
						....			A-BI-E-ŠU-UḪ-LU-DA-RI		B 10
			ʾAB	I	JA	JŠUʿ					
						....			A-BI-ŠU-UT-LI		B 11
			ʾADM	U		JIŠʿ	AH		D-AD-MU-IŠ-ḪA	FN	XIII 1 IX 18
			ʾADM	U		JIŠʿ	AH		AD-MU-IŠ-ḪA	FN	XIII 1 IX 57
			ʾIL	I	JE	JŠUʿ			I_{3}-LI_{2}-E-ŠU-UḪ		B 21 M
			ḪAM	I	JE	JŠUʿ			D-A-MI-E-ŠU-UḪ		M+
			ḪAM	I	JE	JŠUʿ			A-MI-E-ŠU-UḪ		M+
			ḪAM	UM	JE	JŠUʿ			D-A-MU-UM-E-ŠU-UḪ		B 13 HANA
			ʿAMM	I	JE	JŠUʿ			ḪA-MI-E-ŠU-UḪ		M
			ʾANN	U		JIŠʿ	AH		AN-NU-IŠ-ḪA	FN	XIII 1 V 46+
			ʾAŠD	I	JE	JŠUʿ			$AŠ_{2}$-DI-E-ŠU-UḪ		M
			ʿAŠTAR			JAŠʿ	AH		$EŠ_{4}$-DAR-IA-AŠ-ḪA	FN	M
			BUN	U		JAŠʿ	AH		BU?-NU-IA-AŠ-[ḪA]	FN	XII 1 VII 67
			DAWD	I	JE	JŠUʿ			DA-DI-E-ŠU-UḪ		M+
			ḎU			JAŠIʿ	A		ZU-IA-ŠE-IA		A. 64 9
			KAKK	A		JIŠʿ	AH		KA-KA-IŠ-ḪA	FN	M+
			MUT	A		JŠUʿ			MU-TA-ŠU-UḪ		M+
			MUT	U	JE	JŠUʿ			M[U-T]U-E-ŠU-UḪ		RA LXV 47 VII 21
		JA	NŠIʾ		JA	JŠUʿ			IA-SI-SU-UḪ		BIN II 104 15
			ŠAMŠ	I		JAŠʿ	AH		D-[UT]U-IA-AŠ-ḪA	FN	XIII 1 IV 43
JŠB	1		JAŠAB	AN					IA-ŠA-BA-AN		RA LXV 45 V 35
JŠN	1		JAŠUN	UM					E-ŠU-NU-UM		U
			JAŠUN	A					IA-ŠU-NA		A.
JṢʾ	1	JA	JṢIʾ			HADD	U		IA-ZI-D-IM		M
		JA	JṢIʾ			ʾIL			IA-ZI-DINGIR		M+
		JA	JṢIʾ			ʾIL			IA-ṢI-DINGIR		JCS IV 109 4311 21
		JA	JṢIʾ			ʾIL	UM		IA-ZI-LUM-KI	GN	B 32
		JA	JṢIʾ			JARAḪ			IA-ZI-E-RA-AḪ		B 32, C
		JA	JṢIʾ			ʾAŠAR			IA-ZI-A-ŠAR		SZLECHTER TJ P. 186
		JA	JṢIʾ			DAGAN			IA-ZI-D-DA-GAN		B 31 HANA, M
		JA	JṢIʾ			QAṬAR			IA-ṢI-QA-TAR		B 30
		JI	JṢIʾ			ʾAḪ	UM		I-ZI-A-ḪU-UM		M+
		JI	JṢIʾ			ʾAḪ	U		I-ZI-A-ḪU?		X 53:6
		JI	JṢIʾ			ḪAJJ	UM		I-ZI-A-UM		MOORTGAT 488
		JI	JṢIʾ			ḪAʾL	U		I-ZI-ḪA-LU		XIV 96:9+
		JI	JṢIʾ			ḪAʾR	U		I-ZI-ḪA-RU		XIV 52:5, 16+
		JI	JṢIʾ			ʿAD	UM		I-ZI-A-DU-UM		M
		JI	JṢIʾ			ʾIL	U				
						MA			I-ZI-I-LU-MA		B 23+

ROOTS (Consonants only)

JṢʾ	1	JI	JṢIʾ				ʾAŠAR				I-ZI-A-ŠAR		B 22+
		JI	JṢIʾ				ʾAŠAR				I-ṢI-A-ŠAR		YOS VIII 108 SEAL
		JI	JṢIʾ				JAPAR				I-ZI-A-PA-AR		B 22
		JI	JṢIʾ				JAT		UM		I-ZI-IA-TUM		B 23+
		JI	JṢIʾ			JA	JPAʿ				I-ZI-A-PA-AḪ		B 22
		JI	JṢIʾ				....				I-ZI-ḪI-X		B 23
		JI	JṢIʾ				....				I-ZI-IA-AN?		PBS XI/2 1 IX 16
		JI	JṢIʾ				....				I-ZI-IA-[....]		PBS XI/2 1 IX 15
		JI	JṢIʾ				....				I-ZI-IA-ZI-[....]		B 23
		JI	JṢIʾ				....				I-ZI-IŠ-MA-AḪ		HARRIS 7 11
		JI	JṢIʾ				....				I-ZI-TA?-KAM		B 23
		JI	JṢIʾ				BANIJ		IM		I-ZI-BA-NI-IM	GEN	B 45
		JI	JṢIʾ				DAGAN				I-ZI-D-DA-GAN		B 22 HANA
		JI	JṢIʾ				DAGAN				IS-SI-D-DA-GAN		CT IV 1 14
		JI	JṢIʾ				ḎARIʾ			JE	I-ZI-DA-RI-E		B 22+
		JI	JṢIʾ				ḎARIʾ			JE	I-ṢI-DA-RI-E		B 22+
		JI	JṢIʾ				ḎARIʾ			JE	I-ṢI-DA-RI-E-KI	GN	B 22
		JI	JṢIʾ				ḎARIʾ			JE	I-ṢI-DA-RI-I-KI	GN	B 22
		JI	JṢIʾ				ḎARIʾ			JE	I-ZI-DA-RI		TCL XI 218 9
		JI	JṢIʾ				ḎARIʾ			JE	I-ZI-ZA-RI-E		B 23+, M
		JI	JṢIʾ				ḎARIʾ			JE	I-ZI-IZ-ZA-RI-E		B 23
		JI	JṢIʾ				ḎARIʾ			JE	I-ZA-AR-RI-E		UET V 202 15
		JI	JṢIʾ				KURUB				I-ZI-KU-RU-UB		RA LXV 53 XI 11
		JI	JṢIʾ				MARIʾ			JE	I-ṢI-MA-RI-E		B 22
		JI	JṢIʾ				NABUʾ		UM		I-ZI-NA-B[U-U]M?		VAS IX 79 5
		JI	JṢIʾ				NABUʾ			HU	I-ZI-NA-BU-U$_2$		B 23+, M+
		JI	JṢIʾ				PU			K	I-ZI-PU-UK	FN?	M+
		JI	JṢIʾ				QAṮAR				I-ZI-GA-TA-AR		B 22+
		JI	JṢIʾ				QAṮAR				I-ZI-GA-TAR		B 22+
		JI	JṢIʾ				QAṮAR				I-ṢI-GA-TAR		B 22+
		JI	JṢIʾ				QAṮAR				I-ṢI-GA-TA-AR		B 22+
		JI	JṢIʾ				QAṮAR				I-ZI-GA-DAR		B 22
		JI	JṢIʾ				QAṮAR				I-ZI-QA-TAR		XIII 1 IV 59
		JI	JṢIʾ				QAṮAR		I		I-ZI-GA-DAR-I		B 22
		JI	JṢIʾ				ŠALIM				I-ṢI-SA-LIM		RUTTEN 4 19+
		JI	JṢIʾ				ŠARIJ			JE	I-ZI-SA-RI-E		BIN VII 105 12
		JI	JṢIʾ				ŠUM		UM		I-ZI-SU-MU-UM		B 23, M+
		JI	JṢIʾ				ŠUM		U	JA	I-ZI-SU-MU-A		KISURRA 112 7
		JI	JṢIʾ				ŠUM		U	HU	I-ZI-SU-MU-U$_2$		A 7646 3+
		JI	JṢIʾ				ŠAM		U				
							ʾAB		UM		I-ZI-SA-MU-A-BU-UM		B 23
		JI	JṢIʾ				ŠUM		U				
							ʾAB		UM		I-ZI-SU-MU-A-BU-UM		B 23+
		JI	JṢIʾ				ŠUM		U				
							ʾAB		IM		I-ZI-SU-MU-A-BI-IM	GEN	B 23
		JI	JṢIʾ				ŠARR				I-ZI-ŠAR		B 22
		JI	JṢIʾ				ŠARR				I-ṢI-LUGAL-KI	GN	TIM III 75:3
		JI	JṢIʾ				ŠARR		UM		I-ZI-ŠAR-RUM-KI	GN	SUMER III 79 VI 197+
		JI	JṢIʾ				TAMB		U		I-ZI-TA-AM-BU		BAHREIN UNPUB, POST-U.
		JI	JṢIʾ				ṢARIR		UM		I-ZI-ZA-RI-RUM		CT XLV 115 18
	2		ʾAWIJ			JA	JṢIʾ				A-WI-IA-ZI		RA LXV 53 XI 49
			ʿAŠTAR			TA	JṢIʾ				EŠ$_4$-DAR-TA-ZI	FN	XIII 1 IV 79
			LI			JI	JṢIʾ						
							ʾAŠD		UM		LI-ZI-AŠ-DU-UM		VAS XIII 104 R. II 24
	3		ŠUM				LI						
						JI	JṢIʾ		IM		SU-UM-LI-ZI-IM	GEN	WATERMAN 25 R 9
			ŠUM	U			LI						
						JI	JṢIʾ				SU-MU-LI-ZI		MEISSNER 37 15+
JT	1		JAT	UM							I-IA-TUM	FN	RA LXV 64 VI 31
			JAT	IJA							IA-TI-IA		M+
			JAT				KALA				I-IA-AT-KA-LA		VAS XVI 165 5
			JAT	A			DAWD		UM		IA-TA-DA-DUM		B 31
			JAT	I			ʾIL				IA-TI-DINGIR		B 31
			JAT	I			ʾAMAN				IA-TI-ḪA-MA-AN	FN	RA LXV 42 II 55
			JAT	U	HU						IA-TU-U$_2$		YOS XIII 426:14
			JAT	UM			MARṢ	AT			I-IA-TUM-MA-AR-ZA-AT	FN	RA LXV 62 V 15

ROOTS (Consonants only)

JT	1		JAT		UM	MARṢ	AH			IA-TUM-MAR-ZA			A 21899+
			JAT		UM	ṢIʾ		A		IA-TUM-ZI-A			CT XLV 97 5
	2		ʾAḪ		U	JAT		UM		A-ḪU-IA-TUM	MN		BIN II 98 4
			ʾAḪ		U	JAT		UM		A-ḪU-JA-TUM	MN		M
			ʾAB		I	JAT		UM		A-BI-IA-TUM	FN		WATERMAN 40 R. 5+
			ʾAB		U	JAT		I	JA	A-BU-IA-TI-IA			TCL I 85 10
			ʾIB		I	JAT		UM		I-BI-IA-TUM			TIM II 27 4
			JID		I	JAT		UM		I-DI-IA-TUM			M
			JADAʿ			JAT		UM		IA-DA-A-A-TUM			B 25
			ʾIL		I	JAT				I$_3$-LI$_2$-A-AT?			TA 1931, 261
			ʾIL		I	JAT		UM		I$_3$-LI$_2$-I-IA-TUM			VAS XVIII 83:15
			ʾIL		I	JAT			KA	I$_3$-LI$_2$-A-AT-KA			TIM III 10 14+
			ʾILL		A	JAT		I		IL-LA-I-IA-TI	FN	NOM	XIII 1 IX 51
			ʾILL		A	JAT		IM		IL-LA-I-IA-TIM	FN	NOM	XIII 1 IV 75
			ʿAMM		I	JAT		UM		AM-MI-IA-TUM			A. 273 14
			ʾUMM		I	JAT		UM		UM-MI-IA-TUM			UCP X/1 89 24
		JI	JṢIʾ			JAT		UM		I-ZI-IA-TUM			B 23+
			MAʾD		I	JAT		UM		MA-DI-IA-TUM			UCP X/1 P. 59+
			MARUʾ			JAT		UM		MA-RU-IA-TUM			DE GEN., KICH II D 43 R. 2, 4
			MATIʿ			JAT		U	HU	MA-TI-IA-TU-U$_2$			UCP X/3 107 18
			NAʿM		I	JAT		UM		NA-MI-IA-TUM	MN		MEISSNER 100 2
		JI	NDIN			JAT		UM		I-DIN-IA-TUM			M+
		JI	NDIN			JAT		IM		I-DIN-IA-TIM	GEN		M+
		JI	NDIN			JAT		IM		ID-DI-IA-TIM	GEN		M
		JI	NDIN			JAT		AM		I-DIN-IA-TAM	ACC		XIV 64:7
			RAWM		A	JAT		UM		RA-MA-IA-TUM			B 22+
			ŠUʾG		U	JAT		UM		ŠU-GU-IA-TUM			B 40
			ŠUM		U	JAT		UM		SU-MU-IA-TUM			TLB IV 40 9, 12, 14
			ŠAMAʿ			JAT		UM		ŠA-MA-IA-TUM	MN		CT IV 43B 6+
			ŠAMAʿ		A	JAT		UM		ŠA-MA-A-IA-TUM	MN		WATERMAN 21 R. 6
			ṢABAʾ			JAT		UM		ZA-BA-IA-TUM	MN		BM 16835 19+
			ZAMAʾ			JAT		UM		ZA-MA-A-A-TUM	MN?		TCL X 38 1
JTM	1		JATAM		UM					IA-TA-MU-UM			YOS VIII 153 5
			JATAM		U					IA-TA-MU			JCS XIII 51 292, A. LATE
			JATUM		UM					IA-TU-MU-UM			B 31
			JATUM		U					IA-TU-MU			HARRIS 104 5
			JITUM	AN	IM					I-TU-MA-NIM	GEN		B 45
			JATAM			MA							
						ʾIL				IA-TAM-MA-DINGIR			UET V 172 5'
			JATM		UM					WA-AT-MU-UM?			CT XLV 5 R. 4
JTR	1		JATAR		UM					IA-TA-RU-UM			B 31
			JATAR		UM					IA-TA-RUM			B 31, M+
			JATAR		U					IA-TA-RU			KISURRA 106 16
			JATAR		UM					IA-TAR-RUM			B 31
			JATAR		IM					IA-TA-RI-IM	GEN		B 31, M+
			JATAR		I					IA-TA-RI	GEN		M
			JATAR	AT	UM					IA-TA-RA-TUM	MN		B 31
			JATAR	AT	UM					IA-TA-RA-TUM	FN		B 31
			JATAR	AT	IM					IA-TA-RA-TIM	MN	GEN	B 31+
			JATAR	AH						IA-TA-RA	FN		M+
			JATAR		AJA					IA-TA-RA-IA	FN		M
			JATAR		AJA					IA-TA-RA-A-IA	FN		XIII 1 X 54
			JATAR			ʾAḪ		UM		JA-TA-AR-ḪU-UM			I
			JATAR			HADD		U		IA-TAR-D-IM			M+
			JATAR			ʿADN		U		IA-TAR-ḪA-AD-NU			M+
			JATAR			ʿADN		U	HU	IA-TAR-ḪA-AD-NU-U$_2$			RA LXV 54 XII 56
			JATAR			ʾAKK		A		IA-TAR-AK-KA			M
			JATAR			ʾIL				IA-TA-AR-DINGIR			B 31+ +
			JATAR			ʾIL				IA-TAR-DINGIR			M
			JATAR			ḪAM		I		IA-TAR-D-A-MI			M+
			JATAR			ʿAMM		U		IA-TAR-ḪA-MU			M
			JATAR			ʿAMM		U		IA-TAR-ḪA-MU	FN		C II P. 247+
			JATAR			ʾAŠD		I		IA-TAR-AŠ-DI			M
			JATAR			LIʾM				IA-TAR-LI-IM			M+
			JATAR			MALIK				IA-TAR-MA-LIK			A.+
			JATAR			ŠALIM				IA-TAR-SA-LIM			M+

ROOTS (Consonants only)

JTR	1		JATAR				ŠUM		U		IA-TAR-SU-MU		XII 456 10
			JATAR				ŠUM		U	HU	IA-TAR-SU-MU-U$_2$		M+
			JATR		IM						IA-AT-RI-IM	GEN	CT XLVIII 29 REV.
			JATR	AT	UM						IA-AT-RA-TUM	MN	VAS VIII 105 4, 7, 12+
			JATR		A		ʾIL				JA-AT-RA-IL		I
		JI	JTAR		UM						I-TA-RU-UM		B 23+
		JI	JTAR				ʿADN		I		I-TAR-AD-AN		WATERMAN 41 R. 10
		JI	JTAR				ʾIL		I		I-TAR-I-LI		B 23
		JI	JTAR				BEʿL		I		I-TAR-BE-LI$_2$		RA LXV 47 VII 39
		JI	JTAR				....				I-TAR-MA-[....]		AJSL XXXIII 229 SEAL+
		JI	JTAR				MULUK				I-TAR-MU-LU-UK		B 23
		JA	JTIR		A						IA-TE-RA	GEN	A.
		JA	JTIR				HEDD		A		IA-TE-IR-E-DA		A.+
		JA	JTIR				HEDD		A		IA-TE-RI-DA		A.+
		JA	JTIR				ḤAM		U		IA-TI-RA-MU		A. 235 4 LATE
		JA	JTIR				NAN		UM		JA-TI-IR-NA-NU-UM		M+
		JA	JTIR				NAN		AM		JA-TI-IR-NA-NAM	ACC	M
		JA	JTIR				NAN		AM		JA-TE-IR-NA-NAM	ACC	M
		JA	JTIR				NAN		IM		JA-TI-IR-NA-NIM	GEN	M+
		JA	JTIR				NAN		IM		JA-TE-IR-NA-NIM	GEN	M
		JA	JTIR				NAZI				JA-TE-IR-NA-ZI		SYRIA XX 174 MARI
		ME	JTIR	AN	UM						ME-TE-RA-NU-UM		TA 1930, 489
	2		ʾAḪ		I		JATAR				A-Ḫ[I]-E?-TAR		RA LXV 46 V 86
			ʾAB		I		JATAR				A-BI$_2$-WA-DAR		U
			ʾAB		I		JATAR				A-BI-IA-TA-AR		B 10+
			ʾAB		I		JATAR				A-BI-E-TAR		BASOR 95 22
			ʾIL		I		JATAR				I$_3$-LI$_2$-A-TAR		B 21+
			ʾIL		I		JATAR				I$_3$-LI$_2$-E-TAR		M+
			ḪALAN		I		JATAR				ḪA-LA-NI-E-TAR		M
			ḤAM		I		JATAR				E-A-MI-T[AR]?		M
			ʿAMM		I		JATAR				ḪA-AM-MI-A-TAR		B 19+
			ʿAMM		I		JATAR				ḪA-AM-MA-TA-AR		B 19
			ʿAMM		I		JATAR				A-MA-TA-AR		WALTERS, WL 109:9
			ʿAMM		U		JATAR				ḪA-MU-TAR		M
			ʿAMM		U		JATAR				[Ḫ]A-AM-MU-TA-[A]R		M
			ʿAMM		U	HU	JATAR				ḪA-AM-MU-U$_2$-TAR		M
			ʾANN		U		JATR	AH			AN-NU-IA-AT-RA	FN	XIII 1 VI 53+
			ʾAŠD		I		JATAR				AŠ-DI-E-TAR		M
			ʾAŠR		I		JATAR				AŠ-RI-E-TAR		RA XLIX 24 N. 9
			NIQM		I		JATAR				NI-IQ-MI-E-TAR		C II 39 3
			ŠAM		I		JATAR				SA-MI-E-TAR		XII 601 6
			ŠUM			NA	JATAR				SU-UM-NA-IA-TAR		RA LXV 52 X 56
			ŠAMM		I		JATAR				SA-AM-MI-A-TA-AR		TIM I 28 34, 38, 49
			ŠAMM		I		JATAR				SA-AM-ME-TAR		M+
			ŠAMM		I		JATAR				SA-AM-ME-E-TAR		M+
			ŠAMM		I		JATAR				SA-MI-E-TA-AR		M+
			ŠAMM		I		JATAR				SA-AM-MI-E-TAR		M+
			ŠAMM		I		JATAR				SA-AM-MI-TAR		M+
			ŠIMM		I		JATAR				SI-IM-ME-A-TAR		A 7537 16, 21+
			ṢIDQ		I		JATAR				ZI-ID-KI-E-TAR		M+
	3		ʿADN		U		MA						
							JATAR				ḪA-AD-NU-ME-TAR		M+
JTT	1		JATT		IJA						IA-AT-TI-IA		M
			JATT		A		LIʾM				IA-AT-TA-LI-IM		ZA XXXVI 95, BJ 88 12
			JATT		I		HADD		U		IA-AT-TI-D-IM		M
BʾB	2		ʾIL		I	Š	BAʾB		A		I$_3$-LI$_2$-IŠ-BA-BA		HSM 7934, UR III
			ŠU				BAʾB		A		ŠU-BA-BA		U
BʾL	1	JI	BʾUL		UM						IB-U$_2$-LUM		I
		JI	BAʾEL				ʾABN		U		I-BA-EL-A-AB-NU		III 46 13
			BAʾIL		UM						BA-ḪI-LUM		M+
			BAʾIL		IM						BA-ḪI-LIM	NOM	ABB V 157:9'
			BUʾUL		UM						[B]U-U$_2$-LU-UM		I
			BUʾUL		UM						BU-U$_2$-LUM		TCL I 75 5
			BUʾUL	T	UM						BU-ḪU-UL-TUM	FN	RA LXV 58 I 56
			BUʾL		I		HADD		U		BU-LI-A-DU		A. 60 12
			BUʾL		U	HU					BU-LU-U$_2$		CT XLV 92 II 13

ROOTS (Consonants only)

BʾL	2			ŠUʾM		A			BAʾIL			ŠU-UḪ-MA-BA-IL		RA LXV 51 IX 60
BʾN	1			BAʾAN		UM						BA-A-NU-UM		TA 1931, 434+
				BAʾAN		IM						BA-ḪA-NIM	GEN	EDZARD,DER 71 IV 3
				BAʾAN	AN	UM						BA-A-NA-NU-UM		B 43
BʾT	2			NUʿM		U			BAʾAT	IM		NU-UḪ-MU-BA-A-TIM	FN	C+
				TATT		I			BAʾT	UM		TA-AT-TI-BA-TUM		TCL I 204:10
BḪR	1	JA		BḪAR		UM						IA-AB-ḪA-RU-UM		B 24
		JA		BḪAR					....			IA-AB-ḪA-AR-[....]		M
		JA		BḪAR					HADD	U		IA-AB-ḪA-AR-D-IM		M
		JA	T	BAḪAR			NA					IA-AB-TA-ḪA-AR-NA	GN	M+
			T	BAḪR		UM						BA-TA-AḪ-RUM		M+
			T	BAḪR		IM						BA-TA-AḪ-RI-IM	GEN	M
			T	BAḪR		I						BA-TA-AḪ-RI	GEN	M+
			T	BAḪR	AH							BA-TA-AḪ-RA	FN	RA LXV 59 II 40
				BAḪIR		UM						BA-I-RUM		M
				BAḪUR		A						BA-ḪU-RA		A. LATE
				BIḪIR		UM						BI-ḪI-RUM		M+
				BIḪIR	AH							BI-ḪI-RA	FN	M
	2			LABW		A			BIḪR	I	Š	LA-BA-BI$_2$-RI-IŠ		HSM 7936, UR III
	3			LA				ʾA	ḪJIJ					
									BIḪR	U		LA-ḪI-BI-RU		WATERMAN 25 R. 5
BḪŠ	1			BAḪŠ		UM						BA-AḪ-ŠUM		RA LXV 43 III 71
BḪZ	1			BUḪAZ		UM						BU-ḪA-ZU-UM		BM 80328 12
BʿD	1			BAʿD		IM						BA-AḪ-DI-IM	GEN	RES 1939 69
				BAʿD	AN							BA-AḪ-DA-AN		RUTTEN 7 18+
				BAʿD	AN	UM						BA-AḪ-DA-NUM		HARRIS 106 5
				BAʿD	AN	UM						BA-DA-NU-UM		U
				BAʿD	AN	UM						BA-TA-NUM$_2$		U
				BAʿD	AN	U						BA-AḪ-TA-NU		BM 17060 10
				BAʿD	AN	U	HU					BA-AḪ-TA-NU-U$_2$		BM 17060 2
				BAʿD		IJA						BA-AḪ-DI-IA		RUTTEN 12A 23+
				BAʿD		I			HADD	U		BA-AḪ-DI-D-IM		M+
				BAʿD		I			ʾEL			[BA]-AḪ-DI-EL		KISURRA 51 10
				BAʿD		I			LIʾM			BA-AḪ-DI-LI-IM		M+
				BEʿD	IT	UM						BE-DI-TUM	MN	EDZARD, DER 145:10
				BEʿD		I			ʾIL	UM		BE-DI-LU-UM		TIM III 62 6+
				BEʿD		I			ʾIL	UM		BE-DI-LUM		TIM III 61 15
				BEʿD		I			ʾIL			BE-DI-DINGIR		TIM III 130 11+
				BIʿD	AN	UM						BI-DA-NU-UM		SIMMONS 98 9+
				BIʿD		I			KI					
									ʾEL			BI-DI-KI-EL		RA LXV 53 XI 54
				BUʿD		UM						BU-DU-UM		M
				BUʿD	AN							BU-DA-AN		M
				BUʿD	AT	IM						BU-DA-TIM	GEN	EDZARD, DER 152 REV 6
	2			BAʿL		U			BAʿD	I		BA-AḪ-LU-BA-DI		EA
				MANN		A			BIʿD	IM		MA-NA-BI-IḪ-DI-IM	GEN	HARRIS 3 18
	3			BIN		I			MA					
									BIʿD	I	JE	BI-NI-MA-BI-DI-E		EK I 40
BʿL	1		Š	BAʿL	AN	UM						ŠU-BI-LA-NU-UM		B 47
				BAʿL		UM						BA-LUM		CT II 35 29
				BAʿL	AN							BA-LA-AN		M+
				BAʿL	AN							BA-A-LA-AN		RA LXV 46 VI 48
				BAʿL	AN							BA-AḪ-LA-AN		M
				BAʿL	AN	UM						BA-LA-NU-UM		B 43+
				BAʿL		IJA						BA-AḪ-LI-IA		KISURRA 24 5, 7
				BAʿL		IJA						BA-LI-IA		A.; M
				BAʿL		EJA						BA-LI-E-IA		A.
				BAʿL					TUʾ		KA	BA-AL-DU-UḪ-KA		A.
				BAʿL		A			HAND	U		BA-LA-ḪA-AN-DU		VOIX 187:13 MARI
				BAʿL		A			ʿAŠTAR			BA-LA-EŠ$_4$-DAR		M
				BAʿL		A			MI					
									NAMḪ	U		BA-LA-MI-NA-AM-ḪU		SYRIA XLIV 201 N.1 MARI
				BAʿL		I						BA-AḪ-LI		M
				BAʿL		I			....			BA-AḪ-LI-RA-[....]	FN	M
				BAʿL		I			HADD	U		BA-AḪ-LI-D-IM		M+
				BAʿL		I			HADD	U		BA-LI-D-IM		M

ROOTS (Consonants only)

BʿL	1	BAʿL		I			ʾIL				BA-AḪ-LI-DINGIR		B 15
		BAʿL		I			ʾIL				BA-LI-DINGIR		EDZARD, DER 68 IV 7
		BAʿL		I			ʾIL		I		BA-AḪ-LI-I$_3$-LI$_2$	FN	M
		BAʿL		I			JARAḪ				BA-LI-A-RA-AḪ		SIMMONS 58 11
		BAʿL		I			JARAḪ				BA-LI-E-RA-AḪ		M+, TCL XVIII 92 1+
		BAʿL		I			JARAḪ				BA-LI-RA-AḪ		TCL XVIII 94 1 14+
		BAʿL		I		JA	JPUʿ				BA-LI-A-PU-UḪ		HARRIS 96 6+
		BAʿL		I		JA	JPUʿ				BA-LI-PU-UḪ$_2$		EDZARD, DER 117:38 DATE
		BAʿL		I		JE	JPAʿ				BA-LI-E-PA		A.
		BAʿL		I			BAWŠ	T	I		BA-AḪ-LI-BA-AŠ-TI	FN	M+
		BAʿL		I			DIWR		I		BA-AḪ-LI-DI-RI	FN	C+
		BAʿL		I			NIWR		I		BA-AḪ-LI-NI-RI	FN	M+
		BAʿL		I	Š		ʾAG		UM		BA-LI-IŠ-A-GU-UM		RA LXV 45 V 36
		BAʿL		I			ŚAMŚ		I		BA-AḪ-LI-D-UTU-ŠI	FN	M
		BAʿL		I			ŚAPAR				BA-AḪ-LI-SA-PA-AR	FN	M+
		BAʿL		I			ŚAPAR				BA-AḪ-LI-SA-PAR$_2$	FN	M, C+
		BAʿL		I			ṬAJB				BA-LI-SIG5?	FN	XIII 1 VIII 36
		BAʿL		U			ʿAŠTAR				BA-LU-EŠ$_4$-DAR		M+
		BAʿL		U			BAʿD		I		BA-AḪ-LU-BA-DI		EA
		BAʿL		U			GAʾJ		A		BA-AḪ-LU-GA-A	GEN	HOLMA 6 5
		BAʿL		U			GAʾJ		IM		BA-AḪ-LU-GA-JI-IM	GEN	M+
		BAʿL		U			GAʾJ		IM		BA-AḪ-LU-GA-I-IM	GEN	M+
		BAʿL		U			GAʾJ		I		BA-AḪ-LU-GA-I	NOM	M+
		BAʿL		U			GAʾJ		I		BA-AḪ-LU-GA-A-JI	NOM	M
		BAʿL		U			KULIM				BA-AḪ-LU-KU-LI-IM		SYRIA XXXII 7 III 6
		BAʿL		U			LUʾL		I		BA-AḪ-LU-LU-L[I]?		HARRIS 71 14
		BAʿL		U			ME						
							NUMḪ		I		BA-LU-ME-NU-ḪI		M+
		BAʿL		U			ME						
							NUMḪ		I		BA-LU-ME-NU-UM-ḪI		IX 41 2
		BAʿL		U			ŚAMŚ				BA-LU-D-UTU		M
		BAʿL		UM			ʾIL				BA-AḪ-LU-UM-DINGIR		B 15+
		BAʿL		UM			QAWM		UM		BA-LUM-QA-NU-UM		RA LXV 40 I 11
		BAʿL	AT	UM							BA-AḪ-LA-TUM	FN	M+
		BAʿL	AT	UM							BA-LA-TUM	FN	BM 16944 5
		BAʿL	AT	IM							BA-AḪ-LA-TIM	FN GEN	XIII 1 XIV 37
		BEʿL		UM							BE-E-LUM		KISURRA 36 4
		BEʿL	AN	UM							BE-LA-NU-UM		M+
		BEʿL	AN	IM							BE-LA-NIM	GEN	M+
		BEʿL	AK	UM							BE-LA-KUM		CT VIII 31A 21+
		BEʿL	AK	I							BE-LA-KI	GEN	CT VIII 31B 23+
		BEʿL		I			ʾAHL		I		BE-LI-IA-LI$_2$		KISURRA 112 14
		BEʿL		I			HADD		U		BE-LI$_2$-D-IM		RA LXV 52 X 39
		BEʿL		I			ʾIL		I		BE-LI$_2$-I$_3$-LI$_2$	FN	RA LXV 64 VI 50
		BEʿL		I			ʾUŠIL		I		BE-LI$_2$-U$_2$-SI-LI	FN	RA LXV 56 I 10
		BEʿL		I			BAWŠ	T	I		BE-LI$_2$-[B]A-AŠ-TI	FN	RA LXV 60 III 42
		BEʿL		I			KAʾB		I		BE-LI$_2$-KA-BI	FN	XIII 1 V 28+
		BEʿL		I			KIʾR		I		BE-LI$_2$-KI-RI	FN	RA LXV 58 I 15
		BEʿL		I			NIWR		I		BE-LI$_2$-NI-RI	FN	M+
		BEʿL		I			NIWR		I		BE-LI$_2$-NE-RI	FN	XIII 1 II 55+
		BEʿL		I			NUṢR		I		BE-LI$_2$-NU-IZ-RI	FN	RA LXV 64 V 60
		BEʿL		I			RAWM				BE-LI$_2$-RA-AM		RA LXV 54 XII 60
		BEʿL		I			ŚAPAR				BE-LI$_2$-SA-PAR$_2$	FN	M
		BEʿL		I		TA	LEʾEJ				BE-LI$_2$-TA-LI-IḪ		RA LXV 50 VIII 44
		BEʿL	AT	UM							BE-LA-TUM	FN	M+
		BEʿL	AT	UM							BE-LA-A-TUM	FN	RA LXV 60 III 26
		BEʿL	AT	I							BE-LA-TI	FN? GEN	VIII 63:11
		BEʿL	AT	IM							BE-LA-TI-IM	FN? GEN	VIII 63:2
		BEʿL	AH								BE-LA	FN	IX 291 3 9'
		BEʿL	T	I			JARAḪ				NIN?-TI-E-RA-AḪ		RA LXV 52 X 54
		BEʿL	T	I			MAʾT		I		BE-EL-TI-MA-TI	FN	A. 253 6
	2	ʾAJA					BAʿL		A	JA	A-A-BA-LA-IA		SIMMONS 63 9
		ʿIJN					BAʿL		I		IN-BA-AḪ-LI	FN	A.
		ʿABD					BAʿL	AH			ḪA-AB-DU-BA-AḪ-LA		M
		ʿABD					BAʿL	AT	I		ḪA-AB-DU-BA-AḪ-LA-TI		M+
		HADD		U			BAʿL		I		D-IM-BA-AḪ-LI		M+

ROOTS (Consonants only)

BʿL	2		ḪADUR					BAʿL		A		A-DU-UR-BA-LA-IA	GN	SUMER XIV 26
			ḪADUR					BAʿL		A		D-ZA-GAR$_3$-BA-LA-IA	GN	SUMER XIV 26
			ḪADUR					BAʿL		U		A-DU-UR-BA-LU	GN	SUMER XIV 26
			ḪADUR					BEʿL		UM		A-DU-UR-BE-LUM	GN	SIMMONS 138:10
			ʾIL		A			BAʿL		U	HU	I-LA-BA-LU-U$_2$		M
			ʾIL		A		Š	BAʿL		UM		DINGIR-ŠU-BA-A-LUM		CT II 15 9
			ʾAM	T				BAʿL	AH			A-MA-AT-D-BA-A-LA	FN	BAGHD. MITT. II 72 5, 9+
			ʾUMM		I			BAʿL	AH			UM-MI-BA-A-LA	FN	A. LATE
			ʾANA					BAʿL		U		A-NA-BA-LU	MN?	CT XLVIII 86 REV
			ʾANA					BAʿL		U		A-NA-BA-LU	FN	M
		JI	ʾKUR					BAʿL		I		I-KU-UR-BA-LI		EDZARD, DER 102:9
			JIŠʿ					BAʿL		A		E-ŠE-EḪ-BA-LA?		VAS VII 160 7
			JIŠʿ		A			BAʿL				IŠ-ḪA-B[A-A]L		HARRIS 39 14
			ʿAŠTAR					BAʿL	AH			EŠ$_4$-DAR-BA-AḪ?-LA	FN	M
		JI	JTAR					BEʿL		I		I-TAR-BE-LI$_2$		RA LXV 47 VII 39
			ʾATTA					BAʿL		I		AT-TA-BA-AḪ-LI		JCS XIII 51 293:8,A. LATE
			ʾATTA					BAʿL		I	JE	AT-TA-BA-AḪ-LI-E		JCS XIII 51 293:15,A.LATE
			BUN		U			BAʿL		UM		BU-NU-BA-LUM		B 16+
			BUN		U			BAʿL	AN	U		BU-NU-BA-AḪ-LA-NU		M
			KAʾB		I			BEʿL				KA-BI-BE-EL		YOS XIII 432:12
		JI	KWUN					BAʿL		I		I-KU-UN-BA-LI		A.
		JI	KWUN					BAʿL		I		I-KU-UN-BA-AḪ-LI		A. 246 33
		JA	KWUN					BAʿL				IA-KU-BA-AL		RA LXV 44 V 7
		JA	MWUT					BAʿL				IA-MU-UT-BA-AL	GN	M+
		JA	MWUT					BAʿL		UM		IA-MU-UT-BA-LUM-KI	GN	B 28+
		JA	MWUT					BAʿL		UM		IA-MU-UT-BA-A-LUM-KI	GN	RLA II 194
		JA	MWUT					BAʿL		IM		IA-MU-UT-BA-LI-IM	GN GEN	YOS II 49 12+
		JA	MWUT					BAʿL		IM		IA-MU-UT-BA-LIM	GN GEN	BAGHD. MITT. II 56+
		JA	MWUT					BAʿL	AJ	I		IA-MU-UT-BA-LA-I	GN NOM	M
		JA	MWUT					BAʿL	AJ	I		IA-MU-UT-BA-LA-JI	GN NOM	M
		JA	MWUT					BAʿL	IJ	I		IA-MU-UT-BA-LI-I	GN ACC	M
		JE	MWUT					BAʿL		A		E-MU-UT-BA-LA	GN GEN	SAKI P. 212+
		JE	MWUT					BAʿL		UM		E-MU-UT-BA-LUM-KI	GN	B 28+
		JE	MWUT					BAʿL		UM		E-MU-UT-BA-A-LUM-KI	GN	RLA II 180
		JE	MWUT					BAʿL		UM		IE-E-MU-UT-BA-LUM-KI	GN	SZLECHTER TJ 16 165
		JE	MWUT					BAʿL		IM		E-MU-UT-BA-LI-IM	GN GEN	KING 34 6+
			MANN		A			BAʿL		A		MA-NA-BA-LA		M
			MUT		U			BAʿL		U	HU	MU-TU-BA-LU-U$_2$		RA LXV 44 IV 26
			ŚUM		U			BAʿL		A		SU-MU-BA-LA		UNPUBL.
		JA	ŚMAʿ					BAʿL				[IA-A]S$_2$-MA-AḪ-BA-AL		VIII 101 L.E.
		JI	ŚMAʿ					BAʿL				IŠ-ME-EḪ-BA-AL		M
		JI	ŚMAʿ					BAʿL		A		IŠ-ME-BA-LA		TA 30, 122 2
		JI	ŚMAʿ					BAʿL		A		IŠ-ME-EḪ-BA-LA		TA 30, 71
		JI	ŚMAʿ					BAʿL		I		IŠ-ME-BA-LI		HARRIS 71 6+
			ŚUMḪ		U			BAʿL				SU-UM-ḪU-BA-AL		YOS XII 390 2,9
			ŚUMUḪ					BAʿL		A		SU-MU-UḪ-BA-LA		PBS XI/2 1 I 18
			ŚAMIR				Š	BAʿL				ŠA-MI-IR-ŠU-BI-EL		TCL XVIII 125 30
			ŚAMŚ		U			BAʿL		A		SA-AM-SU-BA-LA		SIMMONS 35 14+
			ŚAMŚ		U			BAʿL		I		SA-AM-SU-BA-AḪ-LI		ABB I 59 8
			ŚAMŚ		U	NA		BAʿL		A		SA-AM-SU-NA-BA-LA		A. 77+
			ŚUMUT		I			BAʿL				SU-MU-TI-BA-AL		M
			ṢILL					BAʿL		I		MI-NI-BA-AḪ-LI		M+
	3		LA				ʾA	HWIJ						
								BAʿL		U		LA-AḪ-WI-BA-LU		C
			LA				ʾA	HWIJ						
								BAʿL		U		LA-AḪ-WI-BA-AḪ-LU		XIV 29:28
			LA				ʾA	HWIJ						
								BEʿL		I		LA-AḪ-WI-BE-LI$_2$	FN	RA LXV 59 II 73
			LA					RIWM						
								BAʿL		I		LA-RI-IM-BA-AḪ-LI		M+
			LA					RIWM						
								BEʿL		I		LA-RI-IM-BE-LI$_2$		X 69 5
			ŚUM		U		JA	MWUT						
								BAʿL		A		SU-MU-IA-MU-UT-BA-[LA]		RUTTEN 3 21
			ŚUM		U		JE	MWUT						
								BAʿL		A		SU-MU-E-MU-UT-BA-LA	NOM	JCS IV 66 22

ROOTS (Consonants only)

BʿL	3		ŠUM		U	JE	MWUT						
							BAʿL		A		SU-MU-E-MU-UT-BA-LA	GEN	JCS IV 69 17
			ŠUM		U	JE	MWUT						
							BAʿL		IM		SU-MU-E-MU-UT-BA-LIM?	GEN	JCS IV 71 9
			ŠUM		U	JA	MWUT						
							BAʿL		IM		SU-MU-IA-MU-UT-BA-LIM	GEN	CT XLIII 86 1
			ŠUM		U	JA	MWUT		U				
							BAʿL		A		[SU]-MU-IA-MU-TU-BA-LA		PBS XI/2 1 I 19
BWʾ	1	JA	BWAʾ								IA-BA-A		WATERMAN 36 R. 14
		JI	BWAʾ		UM						I-BA-UM		TA 30 615
		JA	BWAʾ	AT	UM						IA-BA-TUM		AJSL XXXIII 237 16
		JI	BWAʾ			JA					I-BA-A-IA		C+
		JI	BWAʾ			JA					I-BA-IA		C II 7 II 3
		JA	BWAʾ				ʾIL				IA-BA-DINGIR?		MEISSNER 36 25
		JA	BWAʾ				ʾIL				IA-BA-A?-DINGIR		M
		JI	BWAʾ				ʾIL				I-BA-AḪ-DINGIR		KISURRA 6 15
		JA	BWAʾ				ʿAN		UM		IA-BA-A-NU-UM		B 45
			BAWʾ		UM						BA-A-U_2-UM		KISURRA 94 14
			BAWʾ		UM						BA-IA-UM		CT VI 15 III 19
			BAWʾ				JARAḪ				BA-IA-RA-AḪ		RUTTEN 7 3
			BAWʾ				JARAḪ				BA-A-RA-AḪ		RUTTEN 39 18
			BAWʾ				JARAḪ				PA-IA-RA-AḪ		RUTTEN 7 7
			BAWʾ		U		ʾIL		A		BA-U_2-I-LA		MEISSNER 43 45
		ʾU	BWAʾ				ʾIL				U_2-BA-DINGIR		M
		ʾU	BWAʾ				ʾIL		A		U_2-BA-D-DINGIR		VAS VIII 14:22
	2		LA				BAWʾ		U		LA-BA-U_2		JCS XIII 51 292:5' A.LATE
			LA				BAWʾ		U		LA-BA-ʾU-U		TALLQUIST,APN P.120 LATE
BWB	1		BAWB	AT	UM						BA-BA-TUM	FN	RA LXV 58 I 59
			BAWB		I		ḪAJJ		A		D-BA-BI-E_2-A?		VIII 31 7
			BAWB		U		QAʾN				BA-BU-QA-AN		M
	2		ʾIL		A		BAWB		I	JA	DINGIR-BA-BI-A		UET V 263 17
			ʾIL		I		BAWB		UM		I_3-LI_2-BA-BU-UM		U UNPUBL.
	3		ŠUM		U		ʾIL						
							BAWB		I	JA	[SU-MU-I]L-BA-BI-IA		PBS XI/2 1 I 11
BWŠ	1		BAWŠ	AN	UM						BA-ŠA-NU-UM		TA 30 615
			BAWŠ	AN	U						BA-SA-NU		MAOG 4 440 HANA
			BAWŠ	T	UM						BA-AŠ-TUM	FN	M+
			BAWŠ	T	I		NUṢR		I		BA-AŠ-TI-NU-IZ-RI	FN	RA LXV 58 I 45
			BAWŠ	T	I		NUṢR		I		BA-AŠ-TI-UZ-RI		RA LXIV 28 NO. 15
			BAWŠ	T	I		NUṢR		I		BA-$AŠ_2$-TI-NU-UZ-RI	FN	XIII 1 VII 24
	2		ʾIL		I		BAWŠ	T	I		I_3-LI_2-BA-$AŠ_2$-TI	FN	M+
			ʾANN		U		BAWŠ	T	I		AN-NU-BA-AŠ-TI	FN	RA LXV 65 VII 27
			ḪINN		A		BAWŠ	AT			E-NA-BA-ŠA-AT		ICK 63 2+ CAPP.
			ḪINN		A		BAWŠ	AT	A		E-NA-BA-ŠA-TA		EL II P. 171 N. CAPP.
			ḪINN		I		BAWŠ	AT			E-NI-BA-ŠA-AT		ICK 113 10 CAPP.
			ḪINN		I		BAWŠ	AT	A		E-NI-BA-ŠA-TA		KTS 47C 1 CAPP.
			BAʿL		I		BAWŠ	T	I		BA-AḪ-LI-BA-AŠ-TI	FN	M+
			BEʿL		I		BAWŠ	T	I		BE-LI_2-[B]A-AŠ-TI	FN	RA LXV 60 III 42
			DAGAN				BAWŠ	T	I		D-DA-GAN-BA-AŠ-TI	FN	M+
			KIWN		I		BAWŠ		I		KI-NI-BA-ŠI	FN	HARRIS 45 8
			KIWN		U		BAWŠ		I		KI-NU-BA-ŠI		LANGDON XXVIII 12
			MUT		U		BAWŠ		A		MU-TU-BA-SA		B 35+
			ŠARR		UM		BAWŠ	T	I		LUGAL-BA-AŠ-TI	FN	M
			ŠARR		UM		BAWŠ	T	I		LUGAL-BA-$AŠ_2$-TI	FN	M+
BWZ	1		BAWZ		A						BA-ZA	MN	B 15
			BAWZ	AT	UM						BA-ZA-TUM	FN	B 15+, M+
			BAWZ	AT	IM						BA-ZA-TI[M]	GEN	M+
			BAWZ	AN	UM						BA-ZA-NU-UM		B 43+
			BAWZ		I		ʿAŠTAR				BA-ZI-$EŠ_4$-DAR		M
			BUWZ		UM						BU-ZU[M]-UM	MN	UCP X/3 2 23
			BUWZ		UM						BU-ZU-UM	FN	C+
			BUWZ		U						BU-ZU		RA LXV 50 VIII 75
			BUWZ		I						BU-ZI	FN	M+, C+
			BUWZ		IJA						BU-ZI-IA		M+
			BUWZ		UJA						BU-ZU-A-IA	FN	RA LXV 62 V 27
			BUWZ		U	HU					BU-ZU-U_2		TCL I 59 16+

ROOTS (Consonants only)

BWZ	1	BUWZ		U	NA				BU-ZU-NA	FN	RA LXV 58 I 50
	2	KUʾB		A		BUWZ		I	KU-BA-BU-ZI	FN	M
		KIWN				BUWZ	AN	UM	KI-IN-BU-ZA-NU-UM		HARRIS 68 14
BJN	1 JA	BJIN		UM					IA-BI-NU-UM		XIII 38 13
	JA	BJIN		IM					IA-BI-NI-IM	GEN	M+
		BAJN		UM					BA-NU-UM		M
		BAJN	AN	UM					BA-NA-NU-UM		B 43+
		BAJN	AN	UM					BA-A-NA-NU-UM		B 43
		BAJN	AN	IM					BA-NA-NIM	GEN	B 43
		BAJN	AT	UM					BA-NA-TUM	FN	C; EDZARD 58:3
		BAJN	AT	UM					BA-NA-A-TUM	FN	HARRIS 86 1
		BAJN		U		DAGAN			BA-NU-D-DA-GAN		M+
	2	ḪINN		I		BAJN	AH		IN-NI-BA-NA	FN NOM	X 81 4
		NAHR				BAJAN			D-ID$_2$-BA-IA-AN		A 21929 5,12
BJR	1 JA	BJIR		UM					IA-BI-RUM		M
	JI	BJIR		UM					I-BI-RUM		M
		BAJR		UM					BA-RU-UM		HARRIS 89 2
		BAJR	AT	UM					BA-RA-TUM	FN	CT VIII 6A 3+
		BAJR	ATAN						BA-RA-TA-AN	MN	M
BJT	1	BIJT	AT	UM					BI-TA-TUM	MN	B 16+
		BIJT				ʾIL			D-E$_2$-IL		U
	2	PALṬ		A		BIJT		U	PA-AL-DA-BI-TU		A. LATE
		DAʾK		A		BIJT		I	DA?-KA-BI-TI		A.
		DANN		A		BIJT			DA-NA-BI$_2$-IT		U
		MILʾ		A		BIJT		I	MI-IL-A-BI-TI		A. 60 2
		ŠAWB		I		BIJT		UM	ŠA-A-BI-E$_2$		SUMER V 142 NO. 6
BBJ	1	BIBIJ	AT	UM					BI-BI-IA-TUM	FN	RA LXV 62 V 25
BBL	1	BABUL		UM					BA-BU-LU-[UM]	FN	RA LXV 62 V 8
BDBD	1	BUDBUD		UM					BU-UD-BU-DU-UM		BM 16551
BDD	1	BADID		UM					BA-DI-DU-UM		B 15+
BDM	1	BIDUM		U					BI-DU-MU		M
		BUDAM	AN						BU-DA-MA-AN		RA LXV 51 X 4
BGN	1	BAGIN		UM					BA-GI-NU-UM		B 15
		BAGIN		U					BA-GI-NU		B 15+
BGŠ	3	ḪABUR			JI	JBAL					
						BUGAŠ			ID$_2$-ḪA-BUR-I-BA-AL-BU-GA-AŠ$_2$		BRM IV 52 HANA
BKL	1	BAKAL		UM					BA-KA-LUM		RUTTEN 38 18+
		BAKAL		A					BA-GA-LA		A. LATE
		BAKIL		UM					BA-KI-LUM		B 15+
		BAKIL		A					BA-KI-LA$_2$		TCL XIX 74:18
		BAKIL	AH						BA-KI-LA	FN	RA LXV 60 III 68
BKN	1	BIKAN							BI-GA-AN		YOS XIII 271:6,7+
		BIKAN		UM					BI-KA-NU-UM		KISURRA 47A 10+
		BIKAN		I					BI-KA-NI		KISURRA 30 8
		BIKIN		UM					BI-KI-IN-NU-UM		VAS VIII 15 16
		BIKIN		UM					BI-IK-KI-NU-UM		YOS XIII 306:4
		BIKIN	AH						BI-KI-IN-NA	FN	XIII 1 VIII 27
		BIKIN		IJA					BI-KI-NI-IA		VAS XIII 20A R. 19
		BIKIN	T	I					BI-IK-KI-IT-TI	MN GEN	A.
		BIKN	AN	UM					BI-IK-NA-NU-UM		VAS VIII 1 21+
BKR	1	BAKIR		UM					BA-KI-RUM		M
		BAKUR	AT	UM					BA-KU-RA-TUM	FN	B
		BAKUR		AJA					BA-KU?-RA-IA		C
		BIKUR	T	UM					BI-KU-UR-TUM	MN	BASOR 95 P. 24
BKS	1	BAKUS		I					BA-KU-ZI		RA LXV 55 XIII 43
		BAKS		I					BA-AK-ZI	NOM	BASOR 95 P.23
BKŠ	1	BAKUŠ		AJA					BA-KU-SA-A-IA	FN	XIII 1 II 63
		BAKŠ	AT	UM					BA-AK-SA-TUM	FN	M
		BUKŠ	AN	UM					BU-UK-SA-NU-UM		PBS XIV 495
BKŠŠ	1	BAKŠIŠ		UM					BA-AK-ŠI-ŠUM		HARRIS 5 3+
BLʾ	2	KIʾL		I		BELAʾ		I	KI-LI-BE-LA-I		M
BLW	1 JA	BLUW				DAGAN			IA-AB-LU-D-DA-GAN		M
BLJ	1 JA	BLIJ			JA				IA-AB-LI-IA-KI	GN	M+
	JA	BLIJ	AT	UM					IA-AB-LI-IA-TUM	FN	B 25+
BLBL	1	BALBAL		UM					BA-AL-BA-LUM		RUTTEN 37 4 8
BLBN	1	BELBAN		UM					BE-EL-BA-NU-UM		BM 81108 2

ROOTS (Consonants only)

BLBN	1	BELBIN							BE?-EL-BI-IN		HARRIS 108 4	
	2	ŠUM		U		BELBIN			SU-MU-BE-EL-BI-IN		JCS IV 108,	YBC 5198
BLK	1	BALIK		I					BA-LI-KI	GEN	A.	
		BALIK	AH						BA-LI-KA	FN	A.	
		BALK		UM					BA-AL-KUM		TIM V 1 23	
		BALK		U	Š	RAḪAB			BA-AL-KU-UŠ$_2$-RA-ḪA-AB	FN	XIII 1 VIII 61	
		BILK	UT	UM					BI-IL-KU-TUM	FN	XIII 1 XIII 17	
		BULUK	AN						B[U]-LU-GA-AN		RA LXV 46 VI 22	
BLL	1	BALAL	AT	I					BA-LA-LA-TI		TA 1930, 399+	
		BALIL		UM					BA-LI-LUM		B 15+	
		BALIL	AT	UM					BA-LI-LA?-TUM	MN?	VIII 3 5	
		BALIL	AH						BA-LI-LA	FN	XIII 1 VIII 72	
		BALUL		A					BA-LUL-LA	MN	AJSL XXXIII	224 3, 6
		BILAL		A		MA			BI-LA-LA-MA		OIP XLIII 135+	
		BILUL		UM					BI-LU-LU-UM		HARRIS 7 8+	
		BILL		UM					BE-EL-LUM		B 15 HANA	
		BILL		UM					BIL-LUM		B 15	
		BILL	ATANUM						BI-LA-TA-NU-UM		HARRIS 49 14	
		BILL				ʾAB	I		BI-IL-LA-BI	FN	XIII 1 X 41	
		BILL				MAŠIK	A		BI-EL-MA-SI-KA?		M	
BLM	1 JA	BLIM		UM					JA-AB-LI-MU-UM		RUTTEN 2 17+	
	JI	BLIM		UM					IB-LI-NU-UM		TA 1930, 615:25 +	
		BILM		U	Š				BI-IL-MU-UŠ$_2$		RA LXV 45 V 80	
		BULM		A	NA	HADD	U		BU-UL-MA-NA-D-IM		M+	
BLT	2	MANN				BALTI						
						ʾIL			MA-AN-BA-AL-TI-DINGIR		RA LXIV 34 NO. 24	
		MANN		A		BALTI						
						ʾEL			MA-NA-BA-AL-TE-EL		B 28+	
		MANN		A		BALTI						
						ʾEL			MA-NA-BA-AŠ-TE-EL		M+	
		MANN		A		BALTI						
						ʾIL			MA-AN-NA-BA-AL-TI-DINGIR		M	
		MANN		A		BALTI						
						ʾEL			MA-NA-BA-AL-TI-EL		KISURRA 70A 14+	
BLṮ	1 JA	BLUṮ	AN	U					IA-AB-LU-TA-NU		MRS VI P. 261+	
		BALAṮ		I		ʾEL			BA-LA-TI-EL		RUTTEN 5 21	
		BALṮ	AN						BA-AL-TA-AN		M	
		BALṮ		A	HA				BA-AL-TA-A	FN	XIII 1 IX 32	
		BULAṮ		UM					BU-LA-TUM		CT XLV 12 25	
		BULAṮ	AT	UM					BU-LA-DA-TUM	MN	BRM III 19E, 22G+	
	2	ʾADM		U		BALAṮ	I		D-AD-MU-BA-LA-TI?	FN	M	
		BUN		U	ʾA	BLUṮ			BU-NU-AB-LU-UṮ		BIROT,TEA 64:4	
		ŠUM		U		BALIṮ			SU-MU-BA-LI$_2$-IṮ?		RUTTEN 26 12+	
		ŠAM		U		BALIṮ			SA-MU-BA-LI$_2$-IṮ?		RUTTEN 34 11	
		ZAKK		A		BALAṮ			ZA-AK-KA-BA-LA-AṮ?		M+	
BN	1	BIN		UM					BI-NU-UM		BM 82360 M+	
		BIN		IM					BI-NI-IM	GEN	M	
		BIN	AN						BI-NA-AN		RA LXV 43 IV 14	
		BIN		IJA					BI-NI-IA		M	
		BIN		IJA					BI-IN-NI-IA		CT IV 10 39+	
		BIN				HADD	U		DUMU-D-IM		M+	
		BIN				ʾIL	A		BI-IN-I-LA		A. LATE	
		BIN				ʾIL	I	JA	BI-IN-I-LI$_2$-IA		RA LXIV 24 NO.8	
		BIN				DAM	U		BI-IN-DA-MU		RA LXV 42 II 61	
		BIN				MA						
						ʾAḪ	IM		BI-IN-MA-A-ḪI-IM		M	
		BIN				MA						
						ʾIL			BI-MA-DINGIR		C+	
		BIN				NAHR	UM		BI-IN-NA-RUM		CT VI 23 5+	
		BIN				NAHR	UM		BI-NA-RU-UM		BIN VII 67 27+	
		BIN				NAHR	I		BI-IN-NA-A-R[I]?		M	
		BIN				ŠAMŠ			BI-IN-D-UTU		M	
		BIN		A		ʾAḪ	UM		BI-NA-A-ḪU-UM		M+	
		BIN		A		HADD	U		[B]I-NA-D-IM		M	
		BIN		A		ʿAMM	I		BI-NA-AM-MI		B 15	
		BIN		A		ʾANTEL			BI-NA-AN-TE-EL		TLB I 220 26, M+	

ROOTS (Consonants only)

BN	1	BIN		A		ḪANDEN				BI-NA-ḪA-AN-DI-EN		M	
		BIN		A		ʿAŠTAR				BI-NA-EŠ$_4$-DAR		M+	
		BIN		A		LIʾM				BI-NA-LI-IM		RA LXV 45 V 54	
		BIN		I		MA				BI-NI-MA		A. LATE	
		BIN		I		MA							
						....				BI-NI-MA-D-....		UET V 713 7	
		BIN		I		MA							
						ʾAḪ		UM		BI-IN-NI-MA-ḪU-UM		TLB I 3 28	
		BIN		I		MA							
						ʾAḪ		UM		BI-NI-MA-ḪU-UM		CCT IV 13A 6+	CAPP.
		BIN		I		MA							
						ʾIL				BI-NI-MA-DINGIR		A. LATE	
		BIN		I		MA							
						BIʿD		I	JE	BI-NI-MA-BI-DI-E		EK I 40	
		BIN		I		MARAṢ				BI-NI-MA-RA-AṢ		M	
		BIN		I		MARAṢ		I		BI-NI-MA-RA-ZI	FN	XII 265 2	
		BIN		U		MA							
						HADD		U		BI-NU-MA-D-IM		4E RENCONTRE 21 NO. 25	
		BUN	AN	UM						BU-NA-NU-UM		B 44	
		BUN	AT	UM						BU-NA-TUM	MN	A 7699 23+	
		BUN		IJA						BU-NI-IA		RA LXV 54 XII 31	
		BUN				ʾIL		UM		BU-NI-LUM		TIM III 33 15+	
		BUN				BAŠAR				BU-UN-BA-SAR		EDZARD,DER 68 IV 7	
		BUN				TAḪTUN							
						ʾIL		A		BU-UN-TAḪ-UN-I-LA		B 16	
		BUN				TENUT		A		BU-UN-TE-NU?-TA?		MEISSNER 68 13	
		BUN		A		ʿAN		UM		BU-NA-A-NU-UM		U	
		BUN		A		ʿAŠTAR				BU-NA-D-INNIN		BASOR 95, 19	
		BUN		A		MA							
						ʾIL				BU-NA-MA-DINGIR		XII 1 X 36	
		BUN		I		ʾIL				BU-NI-DINGIR		B 16	
		BUN		I		ʾEL		UM		BU-UN?-NE-E-LUM		TCL I 220 42	
		BUN		I		ʾIL		A		BU-NI-I-LA		B 16+	
		BUN		I		MA							
						ʾAḪ		UM		BU-NI-MA-ḪU-UM		TCL XX 96 8	
		BUN		I		MARAṢ				BU-NI-MA-RA-AṢ		C+	
		BUN		U	ʾA	BLUṬ				BU-NU-AB-LU-UṬ		BIROT,TEA 64:4	
		BUN		U	ʾA	ŚKUR				BU-NU-AŠ$_2$-KU-UR		SYRIA XXXVII 206 29 HANA	
		BUN		U		ʾIL		A		BU-NU-I-LA		CT XLV 115 24	
		BUN		U		ḪAM		I		BU-NU-D-A-MI		M+	
		BUN		U		ḪAM		IM		BU-NU-D-A-MI-IM		RA LXV 41 II 27+	
		BUN		U		ʿAMM		I		BU-NU-ḪA-AM-MI	FN	M+	
		BUN		U		ʿAMM		U		BU-NU-AM-MU		B 16+	
		BUN		U		ʿAN	AT	I		BU-NU-A-NA-TI		B 16	
		BUN		U		JARAḪ				BU-NU-E-RA-AḪ		M	
		BUN		U		JAŠʿ	AB			BU?-NU-IA-AŠ-[ḪA]	FN	XII 1 VII 67	
		BUN		U		ʿAŠTAR				BU-NU-EŠ$_4$-DAR		M+, C+	
		BUN		U		BAʿL		UM		BU-NU-BA-LUM		B 16+	
		BUN		U		BAʿL	AN	U		BU-NU-BA-AḪ-LA-NU		M	
		BUN		U		KI							
						ʾIL				BU-NU-KI-DINGIR		M	
		BUN		U		KALA							
						ʾIL		I		BU-NU-KA-LA-I-LI		B 16	
		BUN		U		KAMA							
						ʾIL		A		BU-NU-KA-MA-I-LA		B 16	
		BUN		U		LAʾR		A		BU-NU-LA-RA		B 16	
		BUN		U		MA							
						ʾAḪ		UM		BU-NU-MA-A-ḪU-UM		B 16	
		BUN		U		MA							
						HADD		U		BU-NU-MA-D-IM		M+	
		BUN		U		MA							
						ʾIL				BU-NU-MA-DINGIR		M	
		BUN		U		MA							
						ʾAŠAR				BU-NU-MA-A-ŠA-AR		KISURRA 93 4	
		BUN		U		MA							
						ʾAŠAR				BU-NU-MA-ŠAR		B 16+	

ROOTS (Consonants only)

BN	1			BUN		U		NAWIJ		E		BU-NU-NA-WI-E		CT XLVIII 56 REV.11
				BUN		UM		ŠAGIŠ				BU-NU-UM-ŠA-GI-IŠ		EDZARD,DER 73:15
				BUN		U		ŠALG		I		BU-NU-ŠA?-AL?-GI		B 16
				BUN		U		TAḤTUN						
								ʾIL		A		BU-NU-TAḪ-TU-UN-I-LA		B 16+
				BUN		UM		ʾEL		UM		BU-NU-UM-E-LU-UM		B 16
				BUN		UM		MA						
								ŠARR				BU-NU-UM-MA-ŠAR		B 16
				BUN		U	HU	PI						
								ʾIL		UM		BU-NU-U$_2$?-BI-I-LUM		UET V 548 2
				BIN	AT	UM						BI-NA-TUM	MN	BM 16820+
				BIN	AH							BI-[N]A	FN	RA LXV 60 III 62
				BIN	T	A		ʾATT		I		BI-IT-TA-AT-TI	FN	A.+
				BIN	T	A		MALK		I		BI-IT-TA-MA-AL-KI	FN	A. LATE
				BIN	T	E	JE					BI-IT-TE-E	FN	TCL I 52 11
				BIN	T	I		ḪIJJ		A		BI-TI-ḪI?-A	FN	HARRIS 85 3
				BIN	T	I		DAGAN				BI-IT-TI-D-DA-GAN	FN	B 16+
				BIN	T	I		KIʾD		I	JA	BI-IN-TI-KI-DI-IA	FN	A.+
				BIN	T	U		ṬAJB	AH			BI-IN-DU-ṬA$_3$-BA	FN	RA LXV 65 VII 10
	2			ʾIL		A		BIN		I		DINGIR-BI-NI		UCP X/3 1 7
				ʾIL		A		BIN		I		I-LA-BI$_2$-NI		I
				ʾIL		I		BIN		A	JA	I$_3$-LI$_2$-BI-NA-A-IA		M+
		JI		NDIN				BIN		UM		I-DIN-BI-NU-UM		UCP X/1 64 2
				TABʾ		I		BIN		UM		TA-AB-I-BI-NU-UM		BM 82437 4 9
BNḪ	1	JA		BNAḪ								JA-AB-NA-AḪ		M
			T	BANḪ		IM						BA-TA-AN-ḪI-IM	GEN	M
				BANḪ	AT	UM						BA-AN-ḪA-TUM	FN	IX 291 II 19
				BANIḪ	AN							BA-NI-ḪA-AN		M
				BINAḪ	AN							BI-NA-ḪA-AN		M
BNJ	1	JA		BANIJ				ʾIL				IA-BA-AN-NI-DINGIR		M+
		JA		BANIJ				ʾIL				IA-AB-BA-AN-NI-DINGIR		M
		JA		BNIJ				HADD		U		IA-AB-NI-D-IM		M
		JI		BNIJ				HADD		U		IB-NI-D-IM		M+
		JI		BNIJ				JARAḪ				IB-NI-E-RA-AḪ		SIMMONS 62 14'+
		JA		BNIJ				DAGAN				IA-AB-NI-D-DA-GAN		M+
		JI		BNIJ				DAGAN				[I]B?-NI-D-DA-GAN		A. 6 34
		TA		BNIJ	T	UM						TAB-NI-TUM	FN	XIII 1 VI 5+
		TA		BNIJ				ʿAŠTAR				TAB-NI-EŠ$_4$-DAR	FN	XIII 1 XIII 15+
				BANIJ		IM						BA-NI-I-IM	GEN	M
				BANIJ				ME						
								ʾEL				BA-NI-ME-EL		HARRIS 12 15
	2			HADD		U		BANIJ				D-IM-BA-NI		M+
				ʾAKK		A		BANIJ				AK-KA-BA-NI		M
		JI		JṢIʾ				BANIJ		IM		I-ZI-BA-NI-IM	GEN	B 45
				MAʾT		U		BANIJ				MA-TU-BA-NI		KISURRA 112 6
				NUN		U	TA	BNIJ				D-NU-NU-TA-AB-NI	FN	XII 265 1
				ŠU			JI	BNIJ			HU	ŠU-U$_2$-IB-NI-U$_2$		TA 1931, 636 REV +
				ŠI			TA	BNIJ				ŠI-TAB-NI	FN	RA LXV 64 VI 18
				ŠI			TA	BNIJ				ŠI-TAB-NI-A-JA	FN	RA LXV 66 VII 57
				ṬALL		I	JI	BNIJ				TA-LI-IB-NI	FN	CT II 5 3 9
	3			ʿAMM		U		RAPIʾ						
								BANIJ				ḪA-AM-MU-RA-BI-BA-NI		B 19
BNN	1			BANN		UM						BA-AN-NU-UM		M+
BNQ	1	JA		BNIQ				ʾIL				IA-AB-NI-IQ-DINGIR		B 25
				BANUQ		UM						BA-NU-KU-UM		CT XXXIII 48A 3
				BANUQ	AN							BA-NU-KA-AN		RA LXV 55 XIII 46
				BINQ	ATANUM							BI$_2$-GA-TA-NU-UM	MN	TIM III 7:12;39:13
				BINQ	ATANUM							BI$_2$-IN-GA-TA-NU-UM	MN	TIM III 45:11
				BUNAQ		UM						BU-NA-GU-UM		TIM III 98 8+
				BUNAQ		UM						BU-NA-KUM		CT XLVIII 87 REV.
BNŠ	2			ŠUM		U		BINAŠ		U		SU-MU-BI-NA-ŠU		A 7630 2
BNZ	1			BINZ		IJA						B[I]-IN-ZI-IA		M
				BUNZ		I						BU-UN-ZI	FN	XIII 1 X 25
BNZR	1			BUNZUR		I						BU-UN-ZU-RI	FN	XIII 1 III 13
BQQ	1			BAQQ		UM						BA-AK-KUM		M
				BAQQ		UM						BA-KU-UM		M

ROOTS (Consonants only)

BQQ	1		BAQQ		UM				BA-KU-UM	FN	RA LXV 62 V 12
			BAQAQ		UM				BA-GA-KUM		KISURRA 75A 21+
			BAQQ	AN	UM				BA-AQ-QA-NU-UM		M
			BAQQ	AN	IM				BA-AQ-QA-NIM	GEN	M
			BIQAQ		UM				BI-GA-GU-UM		YOS VIII 64 19
			BIQAQ		IM				BI-KA-KI-IM	GEN	CT XLV 79 7
			BUQAQ		UM				BU-QA-KUM		M+
			BUQAQ		UM				BU-QA-KU-UM		M
			BUQAQ		AM				BU-QA-QA-AM	ACC	M
			BUQAQ		IM				BU-QA-KI-IM	GEN	M+
			BUQQ	AN					BU-QA-AN		C+
			BUQQ	AN					BU-UK-KA-AN		M
			BUQQ	AN	UM				BU-GA-NU-UM		I+
BRḪN	1		BIRḪUN	AH					BI-IR-ḪU-UN-NA	FN	XIII 1 XII 3+
BRW	1	TA	BRUW				ʿAŠTAR		TAB-RU?-EŠ$_4$-DAR	FN	XIII 1 V 43
BRB	1		BIRB		AJA				BI-IR-BA-IA		RA LXV 52 X 82
BRBN	1		BURBIN		UM				BU-UR$_2$-BI-NU-UM		B 16
BRBR	1		BIRBIR		UM				BI-IR-BI-RU-UM		RUTTEN 7 15+
			BIRBIR		UM				BIR$_4$-BI$_2$-RU-UM		I
			BURBUR		UM				BU-UR$_2$-BU-RU-UM		BIN VII 155 6
			BURBUR		UM				BUR-BUR-RU?-UM		SCHEIL 10 17
			BURBUR	AN					BU-UR-BU-RA-AN		RA LXV 50 VIII 69
BRKN	1		BIRKIN		UM				BI-IR-KI-NU-UM		TIM V 2 24
			BIRKIN		U				BI-IR-KI-IN-NU	MN	XIII 1 VI 26
			BIRKIN	AH					BI-IR-KI-NA	FN	M
BRL	1		BARIL	AT	UM				BA-RI-LA-TUM	FN	CT VI 35A 15
BRN	1		BURAN	AT	UM				BU-RA-NA-TUM	FN	RA LXV 59 II 70
			BURAN	AH					BU-RA-NA	FN	XIII 1 VI 58
BRQ	1	JA	BRUQ				ʾIL		IA-AB-RU-UQ-DINGIR		BASOR 95, 19
		JA	BRUQ				ʾAB	UM	A-AB-RU-UK-A-BU-UM		JCS XXVI 151:13, HARMAL
		JA	BRUQ				LIʾM		IA-AB-RU-UQ-LI-IM		TCL XI 156 12
			BURQ	AN					BU-UR-QA-AN		M+
			BURQ	AN	U				BU-UR$_2$-GA-NU		BM 17028 5
			BURQ	AN	UM				BU-UR-GA-NU-UM		UET V 482 5
			BURQ	AT	UM				BU-UR-QA-TUM	FN	XIII 1 VII 52+
			BURQ	ATANUM					BU-UR$_2$-GA-TA-NU-UM	MN	SIMMONS 78 11
BRR	1		BIRUR	UT	UM				BI-RU-RU-TUM	MN	B 15+
			BURR	AN					BU-UR-RA-AN		RA LXV 47 VII 43
BRŠ	2		KAʾB		I		BURŠ	A	KA-BI-BU-UR-ŠA	FN	XIII 1 XIV 53
BŠJ	1	JA	BAŠIJ				DAGAN		IA-BA-SI-D-DA-GAN		M
			BAŠAJ	AT	UM				BA-ŠA-A-IA-[TUM]?	FN	M
BŠM	1		BAŠUM		UM				BA-SU-MU-UM		SIMMONS 46 27+
BŠN	1		BUŠAN	UT	UM				BU?-SA?-NU-TUM	MN?	VIII 13 10'
BŠR	1	JI	BAŠIR						I-BA-AS$_2$-SI-IR		M
			BAŠAR						HUR-SAG BA-ŠA-AR	MOUNT	RA IX 57, UR III
			BAŠAR						BA-SA-AR KUR	MOUNT	RTC 124, SARGONIC
			BAŠAR	AN					BA-SA-RA-AN		RA LXV 50 VIII 41
	2		BUN				BAŠAR		BU-UN-BA-SAR		EDZARD, DER 68 IV 7
			LA				BAŠAR		LA-BA-ŠA-AR		RA LXV 42 II 58
			MUT				BIŠIR		MU-UT-BI-SI-IR		M+
			MUT		U		BIŠIR		MU-TU-BI-SI-IR		M+
BTL	1		BATUL		UM				BA-TU-LUM		HARRIS 15 4+
			BATUL	AT	UM				BA-TU-LA-TUM	FN	XIII 1 II 59
BTQ	1		BATQ	AN	UM				BA-AT-GA-NU-UM		ZA XLII 41
BṬḪ	1		BUṬUḪ		IM				BU-DU-ḪI-IM	GEN	M
BṬM	1		BUṬUM	T	UM				BU-TU-UM-TUM	FN	RA LXV 59 II 39
BZḪ	1		BAZIḪ	AN	UM				BA-ZI-ḪA-NU-UM		TA 1931, 230 U
BZW	1	JA	BZUW			HU			IA-AB-ZU-U$_2$		CT IV 30D 10+
BZBZ	1		BAZBAZ		UM				BA-AZ-BA-ZUM		B 48
			BUZBUZ		UM				BU-UZ-BU-ZU-UM		B 48+
BZKN	1		BIZKIN	AH					BI-IZ-KI-NA	FN	RA LXV 62 V 22
BZN	1		BAZIN		UM				BA-ZI-NU-UM		B 15+
			BAZIN		U				BA-ZI-NU		B 15
			BAZIN		IM				BA-ZI-NIM	GEN	B 15
BZR	1		BAZUR	AT	UM				BA-ZU-RA-TUM	FN	CT XLV 25 11, 20
			BAZUR	AT	IM				BA-ZU-RA-TIM	FN GEN	CT XLV 25 17

ROOTS (Consonants only)

BZR	1	BAZUR	AH							BA-ZU-R[A]	FN	XIII 1 VII 2
BZZ	1	BAZAZ		UM						BA-ZA-ZUM		BM 17072+
		BIZAZ		UM						BI-ZA-ZUM		TA 1931, 327
		BIZZ		I		JARAḪ				BI-IṢ-ṢI-E-RA-AḪ		YOS XIII 245:16
		BUZZ	AN	UM						BU-UZ-ZA-NU-UM		M
	2	KUʾD		U		BIZZ		U		KU-DU-BI-IZ-ZU		A.
Dʾk	1	DAʾK		A		BIJT		I		DA?-KA-BI-TI		A.
	2	KUWN		I		DAʾK		A		KU-NI-DA-KA		A. 367 11
		NAʿM		I		DAʾK		A		NA-MI-DA-KA		A. 242 7
Dʾl	1	DIʾL	AN	UM						DI-LA-NU-UM		B 44
DʾŠ	1	DAʾŠ		U						DA-ŠU		U
Dʿ	1	DAʿ		UM						DA-UM		B 17
		DIʿ	ATANUM							DI-ḪA-TA-NU-U[M]		CT XLVII 4 3
	2	ʾIL		A		DAʿ	AT			I-LA-DA-ḪA-AT		SUMER V 141,3+
		ʾIL		A		DAʿ	AT			BAD$_3$-DINGIR-DA-ḪA-AT	GN	A 7650
		ʾIL		AM		DIʿ		I		DINGIR-LAM-DI-I		SIMMONS 24 10+
		ʾIL		I		DAʿ	AT			DINGIR-DA-ḪA-AT		A 7650:2
		ʾIL		I		DIʿ	AT			I$_3$-LI$_2$-DI-ḪA-[AT]		HARRIS 39 19
		ŠAM		I		DAʿ		UM		SA-MI-DA-ḪU-UM		M+
		ŠAM		I		DAʿ		IM		SA-MI-DA-ḪI-IM	GEN	M+
		ŠAM		I		DAʿ	AT	UM		SA-MI-DA-ḪA-TUM	FN	M
		ŠAM		I		DAʿ	AT	IM		SA-MI-DA-ḪA-TIM	FN? GEN	XII 741 6
		ŠAMŠ		I		DAʿ		I		D-UTU-DA-ḪI-I		LANGDON XV 2
		ŠAMŠ		I		DIʿ	AT			SA-AM-SI-DI-ḪA-AT?		TIM II 49 5
DWD	1	DAWD		UM						DA-DUM		RA LXV 52 XI 3
		DAWD		IM						DA-DI-IM	GEN	M
		DAWD		A						DA-DA	MN	M+, A.
		DAWD		A						DA-A-DA	MN	A.
		DAWD		AJA						DA-DA-A	FN	RA LXV 61 IV 2
		DAWD	AT	UM						DA-DA-TUM	MN	TCL I 109 16+
		DAWD	AT	UM						[D]A-DA-TUM	FN	M
		DAWD	AN	UM						DA-AW-DA-NU-UM		HARRIS 19A 6+
		DAWD	AN	UM						DA-DA-NU-UM		SIMMONS 92 14 M+
		DAWD	AN	U						DA-DA-NU		M
		DAWD	AN	IM						DA-AW-DA-NIM	GEN	B 17+
		DAWD	AN	IM						DA-AM-DA?-NIM	GEN	CT XLVII 78:37
		DAWD	AN	IM						DA-DA-NI-IM	GEN	HARRIS 60:6
		DAWD	AN	I						DA?-DA-NI	FN NOM	M
		DAWD	AK	UM						DA-DA-KUM		KISURRA 39A 4+
		DAWD		IJA						DA-DI-IA		B 16+, M+
		DAWD		IJAN						DA-DI-IA-AN		RA LXV 44 IV 75
		DAWD		I		JABAL				DA-DI-E-BA-AL		UNPUBL.
		DAWD		I		ʿADN				DA-DI-ḪA-DU-UN		M+
		DAWD		I		ʿADN		U	HU	DA-DI-ḪA-AD-NU-U$_2$		18 R.A. P.61 A 3821+
		DAWD		I	Š	ME						
						ʾEL				DA-DI-EŠ$_3$-ME-EL		UCP X/3 P. 198+
		DAWD		I		JAŠAR				DA-DI-E-SA-AR		RA LXV 50 VIII 48+
		DAWD		I	JE	JŠUʿ				DA-DI-E-ŠU-UḪ		M+
		DAWD		I		ŠAMUʿ				DA-DI-SA-MU-UḪ		RA LXV 47 VII 44
		DAWD		UJAN						DA-DU-JA-AN		RA LXV 51 IX 75
		DAWD		U		DANN		UM		DA-AM-DU-DA-NU-UM		HARRIS 92:14+
		DAWD		UM		LU			HU	DA-DU-UM-LU-U$_2$		M
		DAWD		U		MA				DA-DU-MA		HARRIS 49 5
		DAWD		U		MALIK				DA-DU-MA-LIK		XIII 1 VI 27
		DAWD		U		RAPIʾ				DA-DU-RA-BI		B 16+
		DAWD		UM		PI						
						ʾIL				DA-DUM-BI$_2$-DINGIR		I
		DIWD		UM						DI-DU-UM		BIN VII 63 24
		DUWD	AN	UM						DU-DA-NU-UM		CT XLVIII 87
		DUWD	AN	IM						DU-DA-NIM		M
		DUWD		U	HU					DU-DU-U$_2$		M, TCL X 112 8, 22+
		DUWD		U	Š	ME						
						ʾEL				DU-DU-UŠ-ME-EL		UCP X/3 P. 198+
		DUWD	UT	UM						DU-DU-TUM	FN	M
	2	ʾAJA				DAWD		U		A-IA-DA-DU		M
		ʾAJA				DAWD		U	HU	A-A-DA-DU-U$_2$		HARRIS 79 5

DWD	2		ʾAJA				DAWD		U	HU	A-IA-DA-DU-U_2		TIM IV 39 15
			ʾAJI				DAWD		I		A-I-DA-TE	FN	A.
			ʾAJAM				DIWD		UM		ḪA-IA-AM-DI-DU-UM		B 18+
			ʾAJAM				DIWD		U		ḪA-IA-AM-DI-DU		B 18
			ʾAB		A		DAWD		UM		A-BA-DA-DUM		HARRIS 95 9
			ḪAM		U		DAWD		I		D?-[A?-M]U?-DA-DI		IX 291 16
			ḪAM		U		DAWD		U		D-A-MU-DA-DU		M
			ʿAQB		U		DAWD		UM		AQ-BU-DA-DU-UM		PBS VIII/2 253 7
			ʿAQB		U		DAWD		A		AQ-BU-DA-DA		B 12
			ʿAQB		U		DAWD		I		ḪA-AQ-BU-DA-DI		M+
			ʿAQB		U		DAWD		I		AQ-BU-DA-DI		M
			ʾAŠD		I		DAWD		UM		A$Š_2$-DI?-DA-DU-UM		EDZARD, DER 60:11
			JAT		A		DAWD		UM		IA-TA-DA-DUM		B 31
			ḎU				DAWD		A		ZU-E-TA-TA		BIN IV 100 1 CAPP
			ḎU				DAWD		UM		ZU-DA-TUM		I
			ḎU				DAWD		I		ZU-DA-DI		XIV 91:5, 13
			LAMA				DUWD		U		LA-MA-DU-DU		M
		JA	MWUT				DAWD		U		IA-MU-UT-DA-DU		RA LXV 51 X 11
		JA	RWIM				DAWD		U		IA-RI-IM-DA-DU		RA LXV 40 I 38+
			ŠAWB		I		DAWD		I		[Š]A?-BI-DA-DI		RA LXV 43 I 13
			ZAKK				DAWD		I		ZA-AK-DA-TI		TA 1931,377+ EARLY OB
			ZIMM		I		DAWD		I		ZI-IM-MI-DA-DI	FN	C II 44 33+
DWR	1	JA	DWUR		IM						IA-DU-RI-IM	GEN	M
		JA	DWUR	AN							IA-DU-RA-AN		M
		JA	DWUR				ʾIL				IA-DU-UR-DINGIR		M
		JA	DWUR				LIʾM				IA-DU-UR-LI-I[M]		RA LXV 45 V 82
		JA	DWUR				NAŠIʾ				IA-DU-UR-NA-SI		M+
			DUWR			NI	ʾIL				DU-UR-NI-DINGIR		M+
		JA	DWIR		UM						[IA-DI]-RU-U[M]		B 25
		JA	DWIR	AT	UM						[IA-DI]-RA-TUM		B 25
		JA	DWIR		I						IA-DI-RI	NOM	B 25 HANA
			DAWIR	AH							DA-I-RA	FN	M
			DAWR		IJA						DA-RI-IA		M+
			DIWR	IT	UM		KAʾB		I		D-DI-RI-TUM-KA-BI		XIII 1 VI 45
			DIWIR				ʾAḪ		I		DI-WI-IR-A-ḪI		PBS XI/1 P. 55+
			DIWIR				ʾAḪ		I		DI-BI-IR-A-ḪI		PBS XI/1 P. 55+
			DIWIR				ʾAB		I		DI-WI-IR-A-BI		PBS XI/1 P. 55+
			DIWIR				ʾAB		I		DI-BI-IR-A-BI		PBS XI/1 P. 55+
			DIWIR				MUT		I		DI-WI-IR-MU-TI		PBS XI/1 P. 55+
			DIWIR				MUT		I		DI-BI-IR-A-MU-TI		PBS XI/1 P. 55+
	2		HADD		U		DUWR		I		D-IM-DU-RI		M+
			BAʿL		I		DIWR		I		BA-AḪ-LI-DI-RI	FN	C+
		JA	KWUN				DIWR		UM		IA-KU-UN-DI-RUM		CT XLVIII 115
		JA	KWUN				DIWR		IM		IA-KU-UN-DI-[R]I-IM	GEN	M
		JA	KWUN				DIWR		I		IA-KU-UN-DI-RI	GEN	CT XLVIII 115 CASE
		JA	KWUN				DIWR				IA-KU-UN-DI-IR		M+
		JA	KWUN				DIWR				IA-KU-DI-IR		RA LXV 45 V 14
		JA	MWUT				DIWR		UM		IA-MU-UT-DI-RUM		WATERMAN 14 9
			NAPŠ		U	NA	DAWR		A		NA-AP-SU-NA-D-DA-RA		CT IV 1 8
		JI	NDIN				DIWR	IT	IM		I-DIN-D-DI-RI-TIM	GEN	M
			ŠI				DUWR		I		ŠI-DU-RI	FN	RA LXV 58 I 68+
			ŠIJM		U		DAWR		A		SI-MU-DA-RA		TA 30, 186+
			ŠUM		I		DAWR		U		SU?-MI-DA-AR-RU		A. 322 9
			ŠUM		I		DAWR		U		ŠU-MI-TA-RU		A. LATE
			ZIʾM		U		DAWR		A		ZI-MU-DA-RA		RA VIII 75 R. 2
	3		LA				RIWM						
							DIWR				LA-RI-IM-DI-IR		RA LXV 50 IX 22
DJN	1	JA	DJIN		IM						IA-DI-NIM	GEN	M+
		JI	DJIN		IM						I-DI-NIM	GEN	M
		JA	DJIN				HADD		U		IA-DI-IN-D-IM		RA LXV 44 IV 51+
			DIJN		I		HADD		U		TI-NI-A-DU		A. 59 2
			DIJN		I		HADD		U		DI-NI-A-DU		A.+
			DIJN		I		HADD		U		DI-NA-A-DU		A. LATE
	2	JI	JʿIL				DIJN		I		I-ḪI-IL-DI-NI-X?		RA LXV 48 VIII 1
			LA				DIJN		AM		LA-DI-NAM	ACC	M
			LA				DJIN						
							JARAḪ				LA-DI-IN-E-RA-AḪ		RA LXV 46 VI 26+

ROOTS (Consonants only)

DJN	2		ŚUM		U		DIJN		I		[SU-M]U-DI-NI		PBS XI/2 P. 119
	3	JI	NPIḪ				LI						
							DIJN		I		IB-BI-IḪ-LI-DI-NI	FN	C
DBʾ	1		DABIʾ		UM						DA-BI-UM		M
DBDB	1		DIBDIB		UM						DI-IB-DI-BU-UM		SIMMONS 13 10
DBN	1		DABIN		UM						DA-BI-NU-UM		TIM III 18 8+
DBR	1	ʾA	DBAR	AT	UM						AD-BA-RA-TUM	MN	A 21946
		ME	DBIR								ME-ED-BI-IR		BASOR 95, 24
DDM	1		DADM		IM						DA-AD-MI-IM	GEN	M
			DADM	IT	UM						DA-AD-MI-TUM	FN	M
			DIDAM	AN	UM						DI-DA-MA-NU-UM		B 44
	2		RABAʿ				DUDM		U		RA-BA?-AḪ-DU-UD-MU		M
DGDG	1		DIGDIG		UM						DI-IG-DI-GU-UM		B 48+
			DIGDIG		UM						DI-DI-GU-UM		UET V 702 R 13
DGN	1		DAGAN				ʾIL		I		D-DA-GAN-I_3-LI_2	FN	RA LXV 62 V 51
			DAGAN				ʾAŠR		A	JA	D-DA-GAN-AŠ-RA-IA		M+
			DAGAN			ʾA	JPUʿ				D-DA-GAN-A-PU-UḪ		M
			DAGAN				BAWŠ	T	I		D-DA-GAN-BA-AŠ-TI	FN	M+
			DAGAN				GAML		I		D-DA-GAN-GA-AM-LI		M
			DAGAN				KIBR		I		D-DA-GAN-KI-IB-RI	FN	M+
			DAGAN				MALAK		U		D-DA-GAN-MA-LA-KU	FN	RA LXV 60 III 3
			DAGAN				MALIK				D-DA-GAN-MA-LIK		M+
			DAGAN				NAʾD		I		D-DA-GAN-NA-DI	FN	XIII 1 III 17+
			DAGAN				NAʿM		I		D-DA-GAN-NA-AḪ-MI	FN	X 116 1, 22
			DAGAN				NIWR		I		D-DA-GAN-NI-RI	MN	RA LXV 47 VII 38
			DAGAN				NIWR		I		D-DA-GAN-NI-RI	FN	M+
			DAGAN				NIWR		I		D-DA-GAN-NE-RI	FN	M+
			DAGAN				NUPAR		A	JA	D-DA-GAN-NU?-PA?-RA-IA		M
			DAGAN				NAṢIR				D-DA-GAN-NA-ṢIR		RA LXV 52 X 76
			DAGAN				ŚAMŠ		I		D-DA-GAN-D-UTU-ŠI	FN	RA LXV 58 I 23+
			DAGAN				TIWR		I		D-DA-GAN-TI-RI	FN	RA LXV 61 IV 51
			DIGAN		UM						DI-GA-NU-UM		RUTTEN 11 2
	2	JA	HWIJ				DAGAN				IA-WI-D-DA-GAN		B 31
		JA	JʿUL				DAGAN				IA-ḪU-UL-D-DA-GAN		RA LXV 48 VII 75
			ʾAB		I		DAGAN				A-BI-D-DA-GAN		M+
			ʿABD				DAGAN				ḪA-AB-DU-D-DA-GAN		M
			ʿABD				DAGAN				AB-DU-D-DA-GAN		M
		JI	JBAL				DAGAN				I-BAL-D-DA-GAN		B 20
		JI	JBAL				DAGAN				I-BA-AL-D-DA-GAN		M
		JA	JDIʿ				DAGAN				I[A]-DI-D-DA-GAN		B 25
			ʿADN		I		DAGAN				ḪA-AD-NI-D-DA-GAN		M
			ʾIL		I		DAGAN				I_3-LI_2-D-DA-GAN		M+
			ʿAMM		I		DAGAN				ḪA-MI-D-DA-GAN		RA LXV 53 XI 33
			ʿAMM		U		DAGAN				ḪA-AM-MU-D-DA-GAN		M
		JA	ʾMUW				DAGAN				IA-AḪ-MU-D-DA-GAN	GN	B 26
			ʾANA				DAGAN				A-NA-D-DA-GAN		M
		JA	JPAʿ				DAGAN				IA-PA-AḪ-D-DA-GAN		XIII 58 5+
		JA	ʾKUR				DAGAN				IA-KU-UR-D-DA-GAN		M+
			JIŠʿ				DAGAN				I-SI-IḪ-D-DA-GAN		RA XLI 43 HANA
			JIŠʿ		I		DAGAN				IŠ-ḪI-D-DA-GAN		M+
		JA	JṢIʾ				DAGAN				IA-ZI-D-DA-GAN		B 31 HANA, M
		JI	JṢIʾ				DAGAN				I-ZI-D-DA-GAN		B 22 HANA
		JI	JṢIʾ				DAGAN				IS-SI-D-DA-GAN		CT IV 1 14
		JA	ʾZUW				DAGAN				IA-ZU-D-DA-GAN		M+, SYRIA V 273, HANA
		JA	ʾZIJ				DAGAN				IA-AḪ-ZI-D-DA-GAN		RA LXV 54 XII 52
		JA	ʿZIB				DAGAN				IA-ZI-IB-D-DA-GAN		M+
		JA	ḤṢIN				DAGAN				IA-AḪ-ZI-IN-D-DA-GAN		M
			ḤIṢN		I		DAGAN				ḪI-IZ-NI-D-DA-GAN		B 20+ HANA
			ʿAZZ		I		DAGAN				A-ZI-D-DA-GAN		A. LATE
			BAJN		U		DAGAN				BA-NU-D-DA-GAN		M+
		JA	BLUW				DAGAN				IA-AB-LU-D-DA-GAN		M
			BIN	T	I		DAGAN				BI-IT-TI-D-DA-GAN	FN	B 16+
		JA	BNIJ				DAGAN				IA-AB-NI-D-DA-GAN		M+
		JI	BNIJ				DAGAN				[I]B?-NI-D-DA-GAN		A. 6 34
		JA	BAŚIJ				DAGAN				IA-BA-SI-D-DA-GAN		M
			ḎIMR		I		DAGAN				ZI-IM-RI-D-DA-GAN		M+

ROOTS (Consonants only)

DGN	2	JA	ḎRAʿ			DAGAN	IA-AZ-RA-AḪ-D-DA-GAN		XIII 123 26
		JI	ḎRAʿ			DAGAN	IZ-RA-AḪ-D-DA-GAN		B 24 HANA+
			KAʾB	I		DAGAN	KA-BI-D-DA-GAN		M+
		JA	KWUN			DAGAN	IA-KU-UN-D-DA-GAN		X 171 3
			KIʾR	I		DAGAN	KI-RI-D-DA-GAN		RA LXV 52 X 21
			KIBR	I		DAGAN	KI-IB-RI-D-DA-GAN		M+
			LA		NA	DAGAN	LA-NA-D-DA-GAN		M+
		JA	LʾIJ			DAGAN	IA-AL-E-D-DA-GAN		M+
		JA	LʾIJ			DAGAN	IA-[AL]?-I-D-DA-GAN		RA LXV 47 VII 23
		JI	LʾIJ			DAGAN	I-IL-ḪI-D-DA-G[AN]		M
		JE	LʾIJ			DAGAN	EL-I-D-DA-GAN		M
			LIWJ	I		DAGAN	LI-I-D-DA-GAN		M
			MUHR	U		DAGAN	MU-RU-D-DA-GAN		RA LXV 53 XI 53
			MALIK			DAGAN	MA-LI-IK-D-DA-GAN		M
			MILK	I		DAGAN	MIL-KI-D-DA-GAN		TCL I 237 12 HANA
			MANIJ			DAGAN	MA?-NI-D-DA-GAN		A. 6 34
			MUT			DAGAN	MU-UT-D-DA-GAN		M+
			MUT	U		DAGAN	MU-TU-D-DA-GAN		CT XLIII 29 1 M+
			NAWḪ	UM		DAGAN	NA-ḪU-UM-D-DA-GAN		B 36+
			NAʿM	I		DAGAN	NA-AḪ-MI-D-DA-GAN		A.+
			NAʿM	I		DAGAN	NA-MI-D-DA-GAN		A.+
			NAʿM	I		DAGAN	NA-AḪ-ME-D-DA-GAN		RA LXV 48 VIII 33
			NAʿM	UM		DAGAN	NA-AḪ-MU-UM-D-DA-GAN		BM 16824 28+
			NUʿM	I		DAGAN	NU-UḪ-MI-D-DA-GAN		M
		JA	NBIʾ			DAGAN	IA-AB-BI-D-DA-GAN		M+
		JA	NBIʾ			DAGAN	IA-BI-D-DA-GAN		M
		JI	NBIʾ			DAGAN	I-BI-D-DA-GAN		M
			NAPŠ	I		DAGAN	NA-AP-SI-D-DA-GAN		M+
		JA	NŠIʾ			DAGAN	IA-AŠ$_2$-SI-D-DA-GAN		M+
		JA	NŠIʾ			DAGAN	IA-SI-D-DA-GAN		M+
		JI	NŠIʾ			DAGAN	I-SI-IḪ-D-DA-GAN		RA XLI 44 R. 6 HANA
		JI	NŠIʾ			DAGAN	IS-SI-D-DA-GAN		B 22 HANA
		JA	NTIN			DAGAN	IA-AN-TI-IN-D-DA-GAN		M+
		JA	NTIN			DAGAN	IA-TI-IN-D-DA-GAN		M
		JI	NDIN			DAGAN	I-DIN-D-DA-GAN		M+
		JA	NṢIB			DAGAN	IA-AN-ZI-IB-D-DA-GAN		M+
		JA	NṢIB			DAGAN	IA-AZ-ZI-IB-D-DA-GAN		B 29
			PU		KA	DAGAN	PU-KA-D-DA-GAN		M
			PU		HU	DAGAN	PU-U$_2$-D-DA-GAN		M
			QUWJ	U		DAGAN	KU-U$_2$-D-DA-GAN		RA LXV 41 II 43+
		JA	RḤIB			DAGAN	IA-AR-IB-D-DA-GAN		M+
		JA	RJIB			DAGAN	IA-RI-IB-D-D[A-GAN]?		M
			RIJB	U		DAGAN	RI-BU-D-DA-GAN		RA LXV 47 VII 52
		JA	RWIM			DAGAN	IA-RI-IM-D-DA-GAN		M+
		JI	RWIM			DAGAN	I-RI-IM-D-DA-GAN		SYRIA XXXVII 206 2 HANA
			RIWM			DAGAN	RI-IM-D-DA-GAN		M
			RIPʾ	I		DAGAN	RI-IP-I-D-DA-GAN		M+
			RIPʾ	I		DAGAN	RI-BI-D-DA-GAN		M
			RAṢAJ			DAGAN	RA-ZA-D-DA-GAN		M
		JA	ŠWUB			DAGAN	IA-ŠU-UB-D-DA-GAN		B 30 HANA+, M+
		JA	ŚJIM			DAGAN	IA-SI-IM-D-DA-GAN		M+
		JA	ŚJIM			DAGAN	IA-ŠI-IM-D-DA-GAN		VIII 11 33
			ŚIJM	AT		DAGAN	ŠI-MA-AT-D-DA-GAN	FN	XIII 1 VIII 33+
			ŚAM	U		DAGAN	SA-MU-D-DA-GAN		M
			ŚUM	U		DAGAN	SU-MU-D-DA-GAN		B 39+
		JA	ŚMAʿ			DAGAN	IA-AŠ$_2$-MA-AḪ-D-DA-GAN		B 30 HANA+, M+
		JI	ŚMAʿ			DAGAN	IŠ-MA-AḪ-D-DA-GAN		RA XXXIV 186 R. 2 HANA+
		JI	ŚMAʿ			DAGAN	IŠ-ME-D-DA-GAN		M+
			ŚIMḪ	I		DAGAN	SI-IM-ḪI-D-DA-GAN		M
			ŚAMŠ	I		DAGAN	SA-AM-SI-D-DA-GAN		M+
			ṢUWR	I		DAGAN	ZU-RI-D-DA-GAN		M
		JA	TḪIJ			DAGAN	IA-AT-ḪI-D-DA-GAN		M
			TUWR	A		DAGAN	TU-RA-D-DA-GAN		M+
			TUWR	I		DAGAN	TU-RI-D-DA-GAN		B 40+ HANA
	3		ʿABD			MA			
						DAGAN	AB-DU-MA-D-DA-GAN		M+

ROOTS (Consonants only)

DGN	3	ʿABD				MA DAGAN			ḪA-AB-DU-MA-D-DA-GAN		M+	
		ʾAMUR				ŠA DAGAN			A-MUR-ŠA-D-DA-GAN		TCL I 237 31 HANA	
DGZ	1	DAGAZ		I					DA-GA-ZI	FN	RA LXV 56 I 6	
DKB	1	DUKUB		UM					DU-KU-BU-UM		SUMER XIV 54 28 6	
DKL	1	DAKUL		UM					DA-KUL-LUM		UET V P. 35+	
	2	ʾIL		A		DAKUL			DINGIR-DA-AK-KU-UL		UET V P. 43	
		ʾIL		A		DAKUL			DINGIR-DA-KU-UL		UET V P. 43	
		ʾIL		A		DAKUL		UM	DINGIR-DA-AK-KU-UL-LUM		UET V P. 43	
		ʾIL		A		DAKUL		UM	DINGIR-DA-KU-UL-LUM		UET V P. 43+	
DKŠ	1	DAKŠ	AT	UM					DA-AK-SA-TUM	FN	CT IV 45B 6	
DLW	1 JA	DLUW			HU				A-AD-LU-U$_2$		HARRIS 70 15+	
DLDL	1	DULDUL		UM					DU-UL-DU-LUM		B 48	
DLM	1	DALUM		UM					DA-LU-MU-UM		MEISSNER 24 15	
DLQ	1 ʾA	DLUQ		IJA					AD-LU-KI-IA		RES 1939, 69	
		DALAQ		UM					DA-LA-KUM		VAS IX 120 13	
		DALQ		UM					DA-AL-KUM		CT VI 28A 24	
		DULAQ		UM					DU-LA-KUM		TCL I 56 22+	
		DULUQ		UM					DU-LU-KUM		RUTTEN 3 16+	
		DULUQ		UM					DU-UL-LU-KUM		RUTTEN 29 5	
		DULUQ	AT	UM					DU-LU-GA-TUM	FN	VAS IX 178 2	
		DULUQ	T	UM					DU-LU-UQ-TUM	FN	MEISSNER 7 26	
		DULQ	AN	UM					TU-UL-GA-NUM$_2$		U	
DM	1	DAM	AN	UM					DA-MA-NU-UM		B 44	
		DAM	AT	UM					DA-MA-TUM	FN	XIII 1 V 30	
	2	BIN				DAM		U	BI-IN-DA-MU		RA LXV 42 II 61	
DMḪ	1	DIMAḪ		UM					DI-MA-ḪU-UM		B 17	
DMQ	1	DAMIQ	T	UM					DA-ME-IQ-TUM	FN	RA LXV 59 II 60	
		DAMQ	AT	UM					DAM-QA-TUM	FN	CT XLV 2 22+	
		DAMQ	AN	UM					DA-AM-QA-NU-UM		SIMMONS 67 7	
		DAMQ	AN	UM					DAM-QA-NU-UM		SIMMONS PASSIM	
		DAMQ	AN	U					DAM-QA-NU		XIII 1 II 1	
	2	ʾANN		U		DAMQ	AH		AN-NU-DAM-QA	FN	XIII 1 X 51	
		ʾIŠḪAR	AH			DAMQ	AH		D-IŠ-ḪA-RA-DAM-QA	FN	RA LXV 58 I 18	
		ʾIŠḪAR	AH			DUMQ		I	D-IŠ-ḪA-RA-DU-UM-KI	FN	XII 265 3	
		ʿAŠTAR				DAMQ	AH		EŠ$_4$-DAR-DAM-QA	FN	XIII 1 V 50+	
		ŠU				DAMIQ			ŠU-DA-ME-IQ		RA LXV 41 II 16	
		ŠINA				DAMQ		A	ŠI-NA-DAM-QA	FN	XIII 1 IV 29+	
		ŠINI				DAMQ		A	ŠI-NI-DAM-QA	FN	RA LXV 61 IV 48	
DMR	2	ʿAMM		U		DUMAR			ḪA-MU-DU-MAR		RA LXV 51 IX 66	
DMT	1	DUMAT	AN						DU-MA-TA-AN		XIV 47:19	
DNK	1 JI	DNIK			ʾA	MURR		UM	D-ID-NI-IK-MAR-TU	DN	U	
		DINIK				MUʾ		UM	DI-NI-IK-MU-UM		SIMMONS 39 3+	
DNN	1	DANN				ʾIL			DAN-DINGIR		U	
		DANN		A		BIJT			DA-NA-BI$_2$-IT		U	
		DANN		I		ʾIL			DA?-NI-DINGIR		M	
		DANN		I	Š	ME ʾIL			DA-NI-IŠ-ME-DINGIR?		I	
		DANN		U		MAʾT		UM	DA-NU-MA-TUM		CT XLV 12:24	
		DANN		U	TA	ʾḪAḎ			DAN-NU-TA-ḪA-AZ		M+	
		DANN		U	TA	ʾḪAḎ			DA-NU-TA-ḪA-AZ		SIMMONS 36 23	
		DANN		U	TA	ʾḪAḎ			D-DA-NU-TA-ḪA-AZ		SIMMONS 84 15	
		DANN		UM	TA	ʾḪAḎ			D-DA-AN-NU-UM-TA-ḪA-AZ		SIMMONS 36 A 22	
		DANN		UM	TA	ʾḪAḎ			DA-AN-NU-UM-TA-ḪA-AZ		SIMMONS 36	CASE 22
		DANN		UM	TA	ʾḪAḎ			DA-NU-UM-TA-ḪA-AZ		A 7634, M	
		DANN		UM	TA	ʾḪAḎ			D-DA-NU-UM-TA-ḪA-[AZ]		TIM V 19 14	
		DUNN		I		HADD		U	DU-NI-A-DU		A. LATE	
		DUNN		I		....			DU-NI-PA-DU		A.	
	2	ʾAḪ		I		DANN		UM	A-ḪI-DA-NU-UM		I	
		ʾEB		I		DANN		UM	E-BI-DA-NU-UM		U	
		ʿAMM		I		DANN		U	AM-MI-DA-NU		YOS XII	
		ʾANN		U		DUNN		I	AN-NU-DU-UN-NI	FN	XIII 1 III 37	
		ʾANN		U		DUNN		I	AN-NU-DU-NI	FN	RA LXV 65 VII 15	
		ʾIŠḪAR	AH			DANN	AT		IŠ-ḪA-RA-DAN-NA-AT	FN	M	
		DAWD		U		DANN		UM	DA-AM-DU-DA-NU-UM		HARRIS 92:14+	

ROOTS (Consonants only)

DNN	2		KUʾM			DANN	UM		KU-UM-DA-NU-UM		U
			MILK		U	DANN	UM		MI-IL-KU-DA-NU-UM		UET V 549:8
			MAM		A	DUNN	I		D-MA-MA-DU-UN-NI	FN	M
			QAWM		A	DANN	UM		QA-MA-[D]A-NUM		M
			SIKIL			DANN	UM		ZI-GI-IL-DA-NU-UM		M+
DRḪ	2		ʾAB		I	DIRAḪ			A-BI?-DI-RA-AḪ		TCL X 41 A/B 4+
DRB	2		ʾAB		I	DARAB			[A]?-BI-DA-RA-AB		RA LXV 43 III 67
DRK	1	ʾA	DRAK	AT	UM				AD-RA-KA-TUM	FN	M+
		ʾA	DRAK	AT	IM				AD-RA-KA-TIM	FN GEN	M+
		JA	DRUK		A				IA-AD-RU-QA		A. LATE
			DARIK		UM				DA-RI-KUM		B 17+
			DARIK		UM				DA-RI-KU-UM		CT XLV 117 27
			DARIK		UM				DA-AR-RI-KU-[UM]		B 17
			DARK		U				DAR-KU		C
			DARK	AT	UM				DA-AR-KA-TUM	FN	C
			DARK		I	MA			DAR-KI-MA	FN	RA LXV 61 IV 14
DRN	2		ʾIL		A	DARAN			DINGIR-DA-RA-AN		M+
DŠB	1		DUŠUB	T	UM				DU-ŠU-UB-TUM	FN	TCL XI 244 11, M
DŠK	1		DAŠIK	T	UM				DA-SI-IK-TUM	MN	MEISSNER 90 27
DŠL	1		DAŠIL		AJA				DA-SI-LA-A-A		HARRIS 79 24
DŠR	1		DAŠUR		UM				DA-ŠU-RU-UM		B 17+
			DAŠUR	AT	UM				DA-ŠU-RA-TUM	FN	YOS VIII 51 2,14
			DAŠUR	AH		ʿAŠTAR			DA-ŠU-RA-EŠ$_4$-DAR	FN	YOS VIII 51 5
	2		ʾAḪ		I	DAŠUR			A-ḪI-DA-ŠU-UR$_2$		PBS XI/2 P. 140 NO. 1128
			ʿAMM		I	DAŠUR			AM-MI-DA-ŠUR?		A 7894
			ʿAMM		I	DUŠUR			ḪA-MI-DU-ŠU-UR		SIMMONS 46 18+
			ʿAMM		I	DUŠUR			ḪA-MI-DU-ŠU-UR$_2$		SIMMONS 50 14
			ʿAMM		I	DUŠUR			ḪA-AM-MI-DU-ŠU-UR		HARRIS 18 15+
			ʿAMM		I	DUŠUR			ḪA-AM-MI-DU-ŠU-UR$_2$		HARRIS 27 17+
			ʿAMM		I	DUŠUR			AM-MI-DU-ŠU-UR		A7894+
			JARAḪ			DAŠUR			SIN-DA-ŠUR		VAS IX 185 12+
DTN	1		DITAN		UM				TI-DA-NUM$_2$	GN	GUDEA
			DITAN		U				DI-TA-NU		BM 80328 6
			DITAN		U				DI-DA-A-NU		JNES XIII 210+ LATE
	2		ʾAB		I	DITAN			A-BI-DI-TA-AN		BM 80328 16
			ʾAB		I	DITAN	UM		A-BI-TI-DA-NU-UM		TA 1931, 538 III,IV
			ʾIL		I	DITAN			I$_3$-LI$_2$-DI-TA-AN		BM 82424 R. 18
			ʿAMM		I	DITAN	A		AM-MI-DI-TA-NA		B13+
			ʿAMM		I	DITAN	A		AM-MI-TE-TA-NA		CT XLV 44 24
			....			DITN	IM		MU-RI-IQ-TI-IT-NI-IM	GN GEN	U
			....			DITAN			ME-D-DI-TA-AN		UET V 497 11, 581 11
		JI	NWUḪ			DITAN			I-NU-UḪ-DI-TA-AN		GORDON 38 20+
			ŠUM		U	DITAN	A		SU-MU-DI-TA-NA		B 39+, M
			ŠUM		U	DITAN			SU-MU-DI-TA-AN		SIMMONS 126 17+
			ŠUM		U	DITAN			[SU]?-MU?-DI?-TA-A-AN		VAS XVI 24 3
			ŠUM		U	DITN	UM		SU-MU-DI-IT-NU-UM		B 39
			ŠAMŠ		I	DITAN	A		SA-AM-SI-DI-TA-NA		B 38
			ŠAMŠ		U	DITAN	A		SA-AM-SU-DI-TA-NA		B 38+
	3		MA			LA		NA			
						DITAN	A		MA-A-LA-NA-DI-TA-NA		B 34
			ŠUM		U	ṢIDQ	UM				
						DITAN	A		[SU]-MU-ZI-ID-KUM-DI-TA-NA		B 40
Ḏ	1		ḎU			ʿAD	IM		ZU-ḪA-DI-IM	GEN	M
			ḎU			ʿADN	U		ZU-ḪA-AD-NU		M+
			ḎU			ʿADN	I		ZU-ḪA-AD-NI	NOM	M+
			ḎU			ʿADN	I		ZU-ḪA-AD-NI	GEN	M+
			ḎU			ʿADN	IM		ZU-ḪA-AD-NIM	GEN	M+
			ḎU			ʿADN	IM		ZU-U$_2$-ḪA-AD-NIM		VOIX 187:18 MARI
			ḎU			ʾIL	A		ZU-I-LA		B 42+
			ḎU			ʾIL	A		ZU-U$_2$-I-LA		B 42
			ḎU			JAŠIʿ	A		ZU-IA-ŠE-IA		A. 64 9
			ḎU			ʾIŠḪAR AH			ZU-D-IŠ-ḪA-RA		XIII 64 5
			ḎU			DAWD	A		ZU-E-TA-TA		BIN IV 100 1 CAPP
			ḎU			DAWD	UM		ZU-DA-TUM		I
			ḎU			DAWD	I		ZU-DA-DI		XIV 91:5, 13
			ḎU			MA					
						ʾAB	I		ZU-U$_2$-MA-A-BI		XIV 77:17

ROOTS (Consonants only)

Ḏ	1		ḎU			MA						
						ʾAB	I		ZU-U_2-MA?-A-BI		M	
			ḎU			ŠUM	IM		ZU-U_2-ŠU?-MI-IM		M	
			ḎU			ŠAT	I		ZU-ŠA-TI		HARRIS 56 12	
ḎHB	1		ḎUHUB		UM				ZU-U_2-BU-UM		VII 194 5'	
ḎBB	1		ḎABAB		UM				ZA-BA-BU-UM		HARRIS 98 R. 5	
			ḎABIB		UM				SA-BI-BU-UM		WATERMAN 24 R. 4+	
			ḎABIB		UM				ZA-BI-BU-UM		B 40+	
			ḎABIB	IT	UM				SA-BI-BI-TUM	FN?	HARRIS 100 6	
			ḎABIB		I	ʾIL			SA-BI-BI-DINGIR		M	
			ḎABB		UM				ZA-AB-BU-UM		BM 17051 7	
			ḎIBIB		UM				SI-BI-BU-UM		PBS VIII/2 228 A4	
			ḎIBIB		U				SI-BI-BI-BU		PBS VIII/2 228 4	
			ḎUBAB		UM				DU-BA-BU-UM		UET V 208 2+	
			ḎUBAB		U				DU-BA-BU		YOS XII	
			ḎUBAB		UM				SU-BA-BU-UM		TA 30, 30 32+	
			ḎUBAB		UM				SU-PA-BU-UM		RIFTIN 29 23+	
			ḎUBAB		UM				ZU-BA-BU-UM		UET V P. 66+	
			ḎUBAB	AT	UM				DU-BA-BA-TUM	FN	UCP X/1 87 3+	
			ḎUBAB		IJA				SU-BA-BI-IA		SIMMONS P. 71	N. 5 3
			ḎUBAB		IJA				SU-PA-BI-IA		UCP X/1 108 1	
ḎBL	1		ḎABIL		UM				DA-BI-LU-UM		RA LXV 54 XII 20	
ḎKJ	2		ʿAMM		U	ḎAKAJ	A		Ḫ[A]-MU-ZA-KA-A		RA LXV 43 III 75	
ḎKR	1	JI	ḎKUR		UM				IZ-KUR-RUM		LANGDON XXIX 24	
		JA	ḎKUR			ʾIL			A-AD-KU-UR-DINGIR		HARRIS 10 18	
		JA	ḎKUR			ʾIL			IA-AD-GUR-DINGIR		SUMER V 142 8+	
		JA	ḎKUR			ʾIL			IA-AD-KUR-DINGIR		SUMER V 141	
		JA	ḎKUR			ʾIL			A-AD-KUR-DINGIR		SIMMONS 80 13	
		JA	ḎKUR			ʾIL			IA-AD-KU?-UR?-DINGIR		VAS IX 58 15	
		JI	ḎKUR			ʾIL			II-IZ-KUR-DINGIR		SIMMONS 67 18	
		JI	ḎKUR			RAPIʾ			IZ-KUR-RA-BI		BM 81591 7	
			ḎAKIR		UM				DA-KI-RU-UM		B 16	
			ḎAKIR		UM				DA-KI-RUM		B 16+	
			ḎAKIR		UM				ZA-KI-RUM		RA LXV 53 XI 22; B 41	
			ḎAKIR		UM				ZA-KI-RU-UM		M	
			ḎAKIR		IM				ZA-KI-RI-IM	GEN	BM 17069 8+, M	
			ḎAKIR	AT	UM				ZA-KI-RA-TUM?	FN	C	
			ḎAKIR		A	ʿAMM	I		ZA-KI-RA-ḪA-MI		M	
			ḎAKIR		A	ʿAMM	U		ZA-KI-RA-ḪA-AM-MU		M+	
			ḎAKIR		A	ʿAMM	U		ZA-KI-RA-ḪA-MU		M	
			ḎAKIR		A	ʿAMM	U	HU	ZA-KI-RA-ḪA-AM-MU-U_2		M+	
			ḎAKUR		UM				ZA-KU-RU-UM		B 41+	
			ḎAKUR		UM				ZA-KU-RUM		B 41+	
			ḎAKUR	AH					ZA-KU-RA	FN	XIII 1 II 40	
			ḎAKUR		A	ʾAḪ	UM		ZA-KU-RA-A-ḪU-UM		M+	
			ḎAKUR			ʾAB	I		ZA-KU-UR-A-BI	GEN	B 41	
			ḎAKUR		A	ʾAB	I		ZA-KU-RA-A-BI	GEN	B 41	
			ḎAKUR		A	ʾAB	U		ZA-KU-RA-A-BU		M	
			ḎAKUR		A	ʾAB	UM		ZA-KU-RA-A-BU-UM		X 79 5	
			ḎAKUR		A	ʾIL			ZA-KU-RA-DINGIR		M+	
			ḎAKUR		A	KUWN	U		ZA-KU-RA-KU-NU		VII 85 12	
			ḎAKUR		I	ʾEL			ZA-KU-RI-E-EL		UCP X/1 86 15	
			ḎAKUR		I	ʾEL	UM		ZA-KU-RI-E-LUM		UNPUBL.	
			ḎIKR		IM				ZI-IK-RI-IM	GEN	M	
			ḎIKR	AT	UM				ZI-IK-RA-TUM	FN	XIII 1 II 50	
			ḎIKR	AT	IM				ZI-IK-RA-TIM	MN? GEN	XII 263 10	
			ḎIKR	ATAN					ZI-IK-RA-TA-AN		M+	
			ḎIKR	ITANU					ZI-IK-RI-TA-NU		M	
			ḎIKR		IJA				ZI-IK-RI-IA		RA LXV 43 IV 20	
			ḎIKR	AN					ZI-IK-RA-AN		RA LXV 51 IX 34	
			ḎIKR		A	ʿAŠTAR			ZI-IK-RA-EŠ$_4$-DAR		M+	
			ḎIKR		I	HADD	U		ZI-IK-RI-D-IM		M+	
			ḎIKR		I	ʿAN	AT		ZI-IK-RI-ḪA-NA-AT		M	
			ḎIKR		I	ʿAN	AT		ZI-IK-RI-D-ḪA-N[A-AT]		M	
			ḎIKR		I	JARAḪ			ZI-IK-RI-E-RA-AḪ		TIM V 69 7, 17+	
			ḎIKR		I	ʿAŠTAR			ZI-IK-RI-EŠ$_4$-DAR		M+	

ROOTS (Consonants only)

ḎKR	1	ḎIKR		I		LIʾM				ZI-IK-RI-LI-IM		M+	
		ḎIKR		U	HU					ZI-IK-RU-U$_2$		VAS IX 185 12+	
		ḎIKR				MARDUK				[Z]I?-IK-RU-D-AMAR-UD		KUPPER, L'ICON PL II NO 8	
		ḎIKR				MARAṢ				ZI-IK-RU-MA-RA-AZ	FN	RA LXV 55 XIII 33	
		ḎIKR				ʿAŠTAR				ZI-KI-IR-EŠ$_4$-[DAR]		M	
		ḎUKR		A		ʿAŠTAR				[Z]U-UK-RA-EŠ$_4$-DAR		RA LXV 46 VI 21	
ḎMR	1	ḎAMAR	AN	UM						ZA-MA-[RA]?-NU-[UM]		TA 1930, 615 28	
		ḎAMAR	AN	IM						ZA-AM-MA-RA-NIM-KI	GN GEN	C II 39 8	
		ḎAMAR		I		ʾEL		UM		ZA-MA-RI-E-LUM		B. 92+	
		ḎAMIR		UM						DA-ME-RU-UM		B 17+	
		ḎAMIR		UM						DA-MI-RU-UM		I	
		ḎAMIR		IM						DA-ME-RI-IM	GEN	HARRIS 77 13	
		ḎAMUR	AN							ZA-MU-RA-AN		M	
		ḎIMR	AT	UM						ZI-IM-RA-TUM	MN	B 42+, M	
		ḎIMR	AT	IM						ZI-IM-RA-TIM	MN? GEN	M	
		ḎIMR	AN							ZI-IM-RA-AN		M+	
		ḎIMR	AN	AM						ZI-IM-RA-NAM	ACC	M+	
		ḎIMR	ATAN							ZI-IM-RA-TA-AN		M	
		ḎIMR		IJA						ZI-IM-RI-IA		M+, C+	
		ḎIMR		IJAN						ZI-IM-RI-IA-AN		RA LXV 44 IV 76	
		ḎIMR				RAPIʾ		I		ZI-ME-IR-RA-BI-I		TA 30 34	
		ḎIMR				ŚAMŚ				ZI-IM-RU-D-UTU		BIN VII 190 18	
		ḎIMR				ŚAMŚ				ZI-IM-RI-D-UTU		BIN VII 206 23+	
		ḎIMR				ŚAMŚ				ZI-ME-IR-D-UTU		B 42+	
		ḎIMR				ZABABA				ZI-ME-IR-D-ZA-BA$_4$-BA$_4$		CIG P. 155	
		ḎIMR		A		ʿAMM		U		ZI-IM-RA-ḪA-MU		CT XLIV 54 20, C	
		ḎIMR		A		ʿAMM		U		ZI-IM-RA-ḪA-AM-MU		M	
		ḎIMR		A		ʿAMM		U		ZI-IM-RA-AM-MU		TIM IV 33 20, 34 13	
		ḎIMR		A		ʿAMM		U	HU	ZI-IM-RA-ḪA-MU-U$_2$		TIM IV 33 SEAL, 34 SEAL	
		ḎIMR		A		ʿAŠTAR				ZI-IM-RA-EŠ$_4$-DAR		M+	
		ḎIMR		I		....				ZI-IM-RI-D-[....]		M	
		ḎIMR		I		ʾAB		UM		ZI-IM-RI-A-BU-UM		B 42	
		ḎIMR		I		HADD		U		ZI-IM-RI-D-IM		M+	
		ḎIMR		I		HEDD		A		ZI-IM-RI-E-ID-DA		B 42	
		ḎIMR		I	JE	HADD		U		ZI-IM-RI-E-D-IM		M	
		ḎIMR		I		ʾIL				ZI-IM-RI-DINGIR		B 42+	
		ḎIMR		I		ʾIL		U					
						MA				ZI-IM-RI-DINGIR-MA		M	
		ḎIMR		I		ʾIL		U					
						MA				ZI-IM-RI-I-LU-MA		M	
		ḎIMR		I		ʾIL		U					
						MA				ZI-IM-RI-LU-MA		SIMMONS 67 12	
		ḎIMR		I		ʿAMM		U		ZI-IM-RI-AM-MU		TIM III 94 4	
		ḎIMR		I		ʿAMM		U		ZI-IM-RI-ḪA-MU		C	
		ḎIMR		I		ʿAMM		U		ZI-IM-RI-ḪA-AM-MU		B 42+, X 35 12	
		ḎIMR		I		ʿAN	AT	A		ZI-IM-RI-ḪA-NA-TA		B 42	
		ḎIMR		I		JARAḪ				ZI-IM-RI-E-RA-AḪ		B 42+, C+, M+	
		ḎIMR		I		ḪAŚAM				ZI-IM-RI-ḪA-SA-AM	NOM	C+	
		ḎIMR		I		ʿAŠTAR				ZI-IM-RI-D-EŠ$_4$-DAR		M, A.+	
		ḎIMR		I		DAGAN				ZI-IM-RI-D-DA-GAN		M+	
		ḎIMR		I		LU			HU	ZI-IM-RI-LU-U$_2$	FN	RA LXV 55 XIII 39	
		ḎIMR		I		LIʾM				ZI-IM-RI-LI-IM		M+	
		ḎIMR		I		RAPUʾ				ZI-IM-RI-RA-BU		M	
		ḎIMR		I		ŚAMŚ				ZI-IM-RI-SA-MAŠ		A.	
		ḎIMR		I		ŚAMŚ				ZI-IM-RI-SA-MA-AŠ$_2$		M+	
		ḎIMR		U		ḪAʾL		A		ZI-IM-RU-ḪA-LA		BM 17045	
		ḎIMR		U		HADD		U		ZI-IM-RU-D-IM		CT XLVIII 22 REV	
		ḎIMR		U		ʾIL		A		ZI-IM-RU-I-L[A]?		II 5 7	
		ḎIMR		U		ʿAMM		I		ZI-IM-RU-ḪA-AM-MI		B 42	
		ḎIMR		U		ʿAMM		U		ZI-IM-RU-ḪA-AM-MU		JCS XI 23 10 13	
		ḎIMR		U		ʾUP		I		ZI-IM-RU-UḪ$_2$-KI		TCL VII 23 14 21+	
		ḎIMR		U		ʾARAḪ				ZI-IM-RU-A-RA-AḪ		BM 17045A 13	
		ḎIMR		U		ʾARAḪ				ZI-IM-RU-ḪA-RA-AḪ		BM 17045 13	
		ḎIMR		U		ʿAŠTAR				ZI-IM-RU-EŠ$_4$-DAR		IRAQ IV 185	A. 385
		ḎIMR		U		LA							
						ʾAB		I		ZI-IM-RU-LA-A-BI		RA LXV 42 III 7	

ROOTS (Consonants only)

ḎMR	1		ḎIMR		U		RAPIʾ				ZI-IM-RU-RA-BI		TA 30 82
			ḎIMR		U		ŠAMŠ				ZI-IM-RU-D-UTU		BIROT,TEA 70 B I 9
			ḎUMUR	ATANU							ZU-MUR?-TA-NU		ZA XLII 41
		MA	ḎMAR		UM						MA-AZ-MA-RU-UM		SIMMONS 52 17+, M
		MA	ḎMAR	AT	UM						MA-AZ-MA-RA-TUM	FN	CT VIII 41A 3 4+
		MA	ḎMAR	AT	UM						MA-IZ-MA-RA-TUM	FN	CT II 30 35
		MA	ḎMAR	AH							MA-AZ-MA-RA	FN	M+
	2		ʾIŠḪAR	AH			ḎAMR	AT	I		D-IŠ-ḪA-RA-ZA-AM-RA-TI	FN	M
ḎNB	1		ḎANAB	AN							ZA-NA-BA-AN		RA LXV 41 II 51+
			ḎANIB		UM						ZA-NI-BU-UM		BA V 486 NO. 2 5
			ḎANIB		UM						SA-NI-BU-UM		BA V 517 NO. 57 3, 6+
			ḎANB		UM						ZA-AN-BU-UM		TIM V 33 23
			ḎINUB		I		ʾIL				ZI-NU-BI-DINGIR		RA LXV 48 VIII 12
			ḎINB	AT	UM						ZI-IB-BA-TUM	FN	M+, C P. 38+
			ḎUNAB		UM						SU-NA-BU-UM		CT IV 44B 5+
			ḎUNAB		UM						ZU-NA-BU-UM		BIN VII 150 9
			ḎUNAB		IM						SU-NA-BI-IM	GEN	SUMER XIV 51 NO. 26 23
			ḎUNUB		I		ʾIL				ZU-NU-BI-DINGIR		RA LXV 51 X 14
ḎQN	1		ḎAQAN		UM						ZA-KA-NU-UM		WALTERS,WL 85:4
			ḎAQN		IJA						ZA-AQ-NI-IA		WALTERS,WL 100:4+
			ḎAQN	IT	UM						DA-AQ-NI-TUM	FN	XIII 1 XIII 22
			ḎIQUN		A		ṬAJB				ZI-KU-NA-ṬA$_3$-AB	FN	RA LXV 59 II 77
			ḎIQN		UM						ZI-IQ-NU-UM	FN	RA LXV 61 IV 43
			ḎIQN		U						ZI-IQ-NU	FN	XIII 1 V 36
ḎRʾ	2	JI	JṢIʾ				ḎARIʾ			JE	I-ZI-DA-RI-E		B 22+
		JI	JṢIʾ				ḎARIʾ			JE	I-ṢI-DA-RI-E		B 22+
		JI	JṢIʾ				ḎARIʾ			JE	I-ṢI-DA-RI-E-KI	GN	B 22
		JI	JṢIʾ				ḎARIʾ			JE	I-ṢI-DA-RI-I-KI	GN	B 22
		JI	JṢIʾ				ḎARIʾ			JE	I-ZI-DA-RI		TCL XI 218 9
		JI	JṢIʾ				ḎARIʾ			JE	I-ZI-ZA-RI-E		B 23+, M
		JI	JṢIʾ				ḎARIʾ			JE	I-ZI-IZ-ZA-RI-E		B 23
		JI	JṢIʾ				ḎARIʾ			JE	I-ZA-AR-RI-E		UET V 202 15
ḎRʿ	1	JA	ḎRAʿ		UM						IA-AZ-RA-ḪU-UM		XIV 77:8
		JI	ḎRUʿ				ʾIL				II-IZ?-RU-UḪ-DINGIR		TCL XI 156 17
		JA	ḎRAʿ				HADD		U		IA-AZ-RA-AḪ-D-IM		M+
		JA	ḎRAʿ				ʾIL				IA-AZ-RA-AḪ-DINGIR		VIII 100 15+
		JA	ḎRAʿ				DAGAN				IA-AZ-RA-AḪ-D-DA-GAN		XIII 123 26
		JI	ḎRAʿ				DAGAN				IZ-RA-AḪ-D-DA-GAN		B 24 HANA+
		JA	ḎRIʿ		UM						IA-AZ?-RI-ḪU-[UM]		PBS XIII 56:4
		ME	ḎRIʿ		UM						ME-IZ-RI-JU-UM		M
			ḎARAʿ		UM						DA-RA-UM		U
			ḎARAʿ				LI						
							ʾIL				ZA-RA-AḪ?-LI-DINGIR		M
			ḎARIʿ		UM						ZA-RI-ḪU-UM		HARRIS 34 12+
			ḎARIʿ		IM						ZA-RI-ḪI-IM	GEN	HARRIS 3 17
			ḎARʿ		IM						ZA-AR-IM	GEN	M
			ḎARʿ	AN							(E$_2$)-ZA-AR-ḪA-AN-KI	GN	M+
			ḎARʿ	AN	UM						ZA-AR-ḪA-NU-UM	GN	B 48
	2		ʿAMM		A	JI	ḎRUʿ				ḪA-MA-IZ-RU		RUTTEN 28 5+
GʾJ	1		GAʾJ		I		JARAḪ				GA-JI-RA-A[Ḫ]		HARRIS 39 15
			GAʾJ		I		LAʾL		UM		GA-I-LA-LUM		M
	2		ʾAB		I		GAʾJ		A		A-BI-GA-A	GN?	A 21919+
			ḪANAN		A		GAʾJ		A		A-NA-NA-GA-A		RA XLIV 112 5 QATNA
			BAʿL		U		GAʾJ		A		BA-AḪ-LU-GA-A	GEN	HOLMA 6 5
			BAʿL		U		GAʾJ		IM		BA-AḪ-LU-GA-JI-IM	GEN	M+
			BAʿL		U		GAʾJ		IM		BA-AḪ-LU-GA-I-IM	GEN	M+
			BAʿL		U		GAʾJ		I		BA-AḪ-LU-GA-I	NOM	M+
			BAʿL		U		GAʾJ		I		BA-AḪ-LU-GA-A-JI	NOM	M
GʾD	1		GUʾAD		UM						GU-ḪA-DU-UM		JCS XXVI 137:24+ HARMAL
			GUʾUD		A						GU-U$_2$-DA		U
GʾG	1		GAʾG		UM						GA-GU-UM		HARRIS 5 18+
			GAʾG	AT	UM						GA-GA-TUM	MN?	HARRIS 13 13+
			GAʾG	AN	UM						GA-GA-NU-UM		B 44+
			GAʾG		IJA						GA-GI-IA		HARRIS 13 12
			GUʾG	AN	UM						GU$_2$-GA-NU-UM		TA 30, 111 6
GʾL	1		GAʾIL		UM						GA-JI-LUM		RA LXV 51 IX 54

ROOTS (Consonants only)

GʾL	1		GAʾIL	AT	UM						GA-I-LA-TUM	MN?	B 17+
			GAʾIL	AT	UM						GA-I-LA-TUM	FN	EDZARD,DER 224:35
			GAʾUL		A						GA-U$_2$-LA		JCS XIII 56, ALA. LATE
	2		ʾIL		I	Š	GAʾUL		U		I$_3$-LI$_2$-IŠ-GA-U$_2$-LU		KISURRA 70A 17+
			JIŠʿ		A		GAʾL				IŠ-ḪA-GA-AL		A 7459 10
GʾN	1		GAʾN	AN							GA-NA-AN		RA LXV 54 XII 5
GʾR	1		GAʾR		IJA						GA-RI-IA		RA LXV 44 IV 58
			GUʾR		UM						GUR-RU-UM MAR-TU		IRAQ MUS. 43488
			GUʾR		UM						GU-RU-UM		UCP X/3 6A 18+
			GUʾR		I						GU-RI	GEN	B 17
			GUʾR	AT	UM						GU-RA-TUM	FN	C
			GUʾR	AT	IM						GU-RA-TIM	FN GEN	B 17
			GUʾR		IJA						GU-RI-IA		HARRIS 8 5+
			GUʾR		U		HADD		U		GU-RU-D-IM		M+
GʾŠ	1		GAʾAŠ		UM						GA-ḪA-ŠUM		XIV 62:25
			GAʾUŠ		UM						GA-U$_2$-ŠUM		I+
			GAʾŠ		U						GA-AḪ-ŠU		M
GʾZ	1		GUʾZ		I						GU-ZI	FN	RA LXV 55 XIII 8
			GUʾZ	AN							GU-ZA-AN		RA LXV 53 XI 57;64
GJḪ	1	JA	GJIḪ	AN							IA-G[I]-ḪA-A[N]		M
		JA	GJIḪ				ḪAʾL		UM		IA-GI?-ḪA-LUM		RUTTEN 16 18
		JA	GJIḪ				HADD		U		IA-GI-IḪ-D-IM		M+
		JA	GJIḪ				HADD		U		IA-GI-ḪA-D-IM		M
		JI	GJIḪ				LUʾ						
							MA				I-GI-IḪ-LU-MA		SIMMONS 60 8, 14+
		JE	GJIḪ				LUʾ						
							MA				E-GI-IḪ-LU-MA		SUMER XXIII 192
		JI	GJIḪ				LUʾ						
							MA				I-GI-E-EḪ-LU-MA		JCS XXVI 143:21 HARMAL
GJD	1	JA	GJID				LIʾM				IA-GI-ID-LI-IM		M+
		JI	GJID				LIʾM				I-GI-ID-LI-IM		B 21 HANA
			GAJID	AH							GA-I-DA	FN	C; RA LXV 65
			GAJID		E						GA-I-TE		A.
			GAJD	AN	IM						GA-DA-NIM	GEN	B 44
			GIJD	AN	UM						GI-DA-NUM$_2$		BIROT,TEA 70 C REV. I 7
			GIJD	AN	UM						GI-DA-NU-UM		SIMMONS 11 1+
			GIJD	AN	IM						GI-DA-NI-IM	GEN	SIMMONS 12 6
			GIJD	AN	IM						GI-DA-NIM	GEN	M, SIMMONS 16 4
GBʾ	1		GABAʾ		UM						GA-BA-UM		LANGDON XXX 18
			GABIʾ		UM						GA-BI-U[M]		M
			GABIʾ	AT	UM						GA-BI-A-TUM	FN	X 1 3
			GABIʾ	T	UM						GA-BI-TUM		RA LXIV 36 NO. 32
			GABIʾ				ʾIL				GA-BI-DINGIR		C 39+
			GABIʾ				ʾIL				GA-BI-IL		TIM III 12 16A
			GABUʾ		UM						GA-BU-UM		B 17
			GABUʾ		UM						GA-BU-U$_2$-UM		M
			GABUʾ		IM						GA-BI-IM	GEN	B 17
			GABUʾ		IM						GA-BI-I-IM	GEN	M+
			GUBʾ	AN	UM						GU-UB-ḪA-NU-UM		M
GBL	1		GUBL	AJ	I						GU-UB-LA-A-JI	GN PL NOM	SYRIA XX 111
			GUBL	AJ	I						GU-UB-LA-JI	GN NOM	SYRIA XX 111
			GUBL	AJITUM							GU-UB-LA-JI-TUM	GN FN	SYRIA XX 111
GBN	1		GABN	AN	UM						GA-AB-NA-NU-UM		SIMMONS 107 14
GLD	1		GALD	AN	U						GA-AL-DA-NU		B 44+
GLL	1		GULAL	AN							GU-LA-LA-AN		RA LXV 47 VII 55
			GULL	AT	UM						GUL-LA-TUM	FN	M+
	2		ʾIL		A		GULL		A		DINGIR-GU-UL-LA	FN	C+
			ʾIL		A		GULL		A				
							ʿAḎIR	AT			DINGIR-GUL-LA$_2$-ḪA-ZI-RA-AT	FN	M+
GLZ	1		GALAZ		IM						GA-LA-ZI-IM	GEN	HARRIS 83 2
			GALZ								GA-AL-ZI-....		M
			GULZ		UM						GUL-ZUM		TA 1931, 538 VI
			GULZ	AT	UM						GU-UL-ZA-TUM		LANGDON XXIX 22
GML	1		GUMUL				JARAḪ				GU-MU-UL-D-EN-ZU		M+
	2		ʾIL		I		GUML		I	JA	I$_3$-LI$_2$-GU-UM-LI-IA		XIII 1 VIII 45
			ʾANN		U		GAMIL	T	I		AN-NU-GA-ME-IL-TI	FN	RA LXV 66 VII 66

ROOTS (Consonants only)

GML	2		ʾIŠḪAR	AH			GUML	I	D-IŠ-ḪA-RA-GU-UM-LI	FN	XIII 1 IV 39
			DAGAN				GAML	I	D-DA-GAN-GA-AM-LI		M
			ŠIRUN		UM		GAMIL		SI?-RU-NU-UM-GA-MIL?		VII 139 7
			TILIʾ		A	Š	GAMIL		TI-LI-AŠ-GA-MIL		UNPUBL.
			TURUN		U	HU	GAMIL		D-TU-UR-RU-NU-U_2-GA-MIL	FN?	XIII 118 14
GMR	1	JA	GMUR				....		IA-AG-MU-UR-[....]		M
		JA	GMUR				ʾIL		IA-AG-MU-UR-DINGIR		M
		JI	GMIR				HADD	U	IG-MI-RA-A-DU		A.+
			GAMIR	AN	UM				GA-MI-RA-NU-UM		TA 1931, 538 I, V?
GNB	1		GANIB	AN					GA-NI-BA-AN		RA LXV 42 II 80+
GNGN	1		GUNGUN		UM				GU-UN-GU-NU-UM		B 48+
GNM	1		GANAM	AN	UM				GA-NA-MA-NU-UM		TA 1931, 438
GNN	1		GANIN	AN	UM				GA-NI-NA-NU-UM		BIN VII P. 12+
			GANN		I				GA-AN-NI		M
GRB	1		GARUB		UM				GA-RU-BU-UM		B 17+
GRD	1		GURUD		U				GU-RU-DU		XIII 1 III 41
			GURUD		IM				GU-RU-DI-IM	GEN	M
			GURD	AN					GU-UR-DA-AN		M
GRGR	1		GURGUR		UM				GU-UR_2-GU-RU-UM		KISURRA 202 5
GRN	1		GARAN		UM				GA-RA-NU-UM		B 44+
		MA	GRIN						MA-AG-RI-IN		HARRIS 76 15
GRR	1		GURUR		U				GU-UR-RU-RU		M
GRŠ	1		GARIŠ		UM				GA-RI-SU-UM		B 17
			GARIŠ		U				GA-RI-SU		B 17
GZZ	1		GAZIZ	AN	UM				GA-ZI-ZA-NU-[UM]		M
			GIZZ		I				GI-IZ-ZI		A. 32 3
			GIZZ		I				KI-IZ-ZI		A.+
			GIZZ	IT	IM				GI-ZI-TIM	FN GEN	M
			GIZZ	AN	UM				GI-ZA-NU-UM		B 93
			GIZZ	AN	U				GI-ZA-NU		B 93
			GIZZ	AN	IM				GI-ZA-NI-IM	GEN	B 44
K	1		KA				ṢUWR	A			
							ʾIL		KA-ZU-RA-DINGIR		M
			KA				ṢUWR	I			
							ḪAʾL	A	KA-ZU-RI-ḪA-LA		M
			KI				MILK	I			
							ʾEL		KI-MI-IL-KI-EL		KISURRA 112:8
			KI				MARUṢ		KI-MA-RU-UṢ		A 3549+
	2		ʾAḪ		I		KI				
							LIʾM		A-ḪI-KI-LI-IM		JEAN T.SIFR 72 5, 6, 13+
			ʾAḪ		U		KA				
							ʾAB	I	A-ḪU-KA-A-BI	FN	XIII 1 VIII 60, C+
		JA	HWIJ				KI				
							HADD	U	[IA-A]Ḫ-WI-KI-D-IM		M
			ʾAB		U		KA				
							ʾIL		A-BU-KA-DINGIR		M+
			ʾIL		A		KA				
							ʾAB	UM	DINGIR-KA-A-BU-UM		CT XLV 100 17
			ʿAMM		U	Š	KI				
							ʾIL		AM-MU-US-KI-DINGIR		A.
			ʿAMM		U	Š	KI				
							ʾIL		AM-MU-UŠ-KI-DINGIR		A.+
			ʾUMM		UM		KA				
							ʾAB	IM	UM-MU-UM-KA-A-BI-IM	FN	M
			ʾUMM		UM		KA				
							ʾAB	I	UM-MU-UM-KA-A-BI	FN	XIII 1 VII 56
			ʾUMM		U		KA				
							ʾAB	I	UM-MU-KA-A-BI	FN	RA LXV 62 V 16
		ʾU	WQAH				KI				
							ʾEL		U_2-QA-KI-EL		RA LXV 51 IX 69
			BIʿD		I		KI				
							ʾEL		BI-DI-KI-EL		RA LXV 53 XI 54
			BUN		U		KI				
							ʾIL		BU-NU-KI-DINGIR		M
			KABD		U		KA				
							ʾAB	I	KA-AB-TU-KA-A-BI		UET V 688:8,12

ROOTS (Consonants only)

K	2		MATAʿ		A		KI					
							ʾEL			MA-TA-A-KI-EL		RA LXV 50 IX 20;HARRIS 19:5,SEAL+
			SITR		I		KI					
							ʾEL			ZI-IT-RI?-KI-EL?		B 42
		JA	ŠJIM				KI					
							ʾIL			IA-SI-IN-KI-DINGIR		M
	3		ʾAB		I		MI					
							KI			A-BI-MI-KI-DINGIR		M
			LAŠU				ʾEL					
							KA			LA-ŠI-EL-KA-A-BI-IM		B 33
Kʾ B	1		KAʾB		IJA					KA-BI-IA		M+
			KAʾB		I		ʾAHL	UM		KA-PI-IA-LUM		UET V 626 11, 702 REV. 5
			KAʾB		I		JADAʿ			KA-BI-E-DA-AḪ		XIII 1 XI 54
			KAʾB		I		HADD	U		KA-BI-D-IM		B 32, M+, C
			KAʾB		I		HEDD	A		KA-BI-E-D-IM		M+
			KAʾB		I		JARAḪ			KA-BI-E-RA-AḪ		RA LXV 41 II 29+;B 32+
			KAʾB		I		ʾATT	A		KA-BI-A-TA		M
			KAʾB		I	JE	JPUʿ			KA-BI-E-PU-UḪ		M
			KAʾB		I		BEʿL			KA-BI-BE-EL		YOS XIII 432:12
			KAʾB		I		BURŠ	A		KA-BI-BU-UR-ŠA	FN	XIII 1 XIV 53
			KAʾB		I		DAGAN			KA-BI-D-DA-GAN		M+
			KAʾB		I		LA					
							RIWM			KA-BI-LA-RI-IM		RA LXV 47 VI 65+; C+
			KUʾB		A		ʾEL			KU-BA-EL		X 91 4'
			KUʾB		A		ʾEL			KU-BA-DINGIR		M
			KUʾB		A		BUWZ	I		KU-BA-BU-ZI	FN	M
	2		ʾAḪ		I		KAʾB	I		A-ḪI-KA-PI		YOS VIII 64 18
			ʾAB		I		KAʾB	I		A-BI-KA-BI		M
			ʾAB		I		KAʾB	I		A-BI-KA-BI	FN	RA LXV 65 VII 42
			ʿABD				KUʾB	I		ḪA-AB-DU-KU-BI		M+
			ʾIL		I		KAʾB	I		I_3-LI_2-KA-PI		BIROT, TEA 69:28
			ʿAN	AT			KUʾB	U		A-NA-AT-KU-BU		TCL I 204:11
			ḪANN		I		KAʾB	I		A[N-N]I-KA-BI	FN	RA LXV 62 V 17
			BEʿL		I		KAʾB	I		BE-LI_2-KA-BI	FN	XIII 1 V 28+
			DIWR	IT	UM		KAʾB	I		D-DI-RI-TUM-KA-BI		XIII 1 VI 45
			MUT		U		KUʾB	I		MU-TU-KU-BI		RA LXV 42 II 66
KʾD	1		KUʾD		IJA					KU-DI-IA	FN	XIII 1 III 35
			KUʾD		U		BIZZ	U		KU-DU-BI-IZ-ZU		A.
	2		BIN	T	I		KIʾD	I	JA	BI-IN-TI-KI-DI-IA	FN	A.+
KʾK	1		KAʾK		A					KA-KA		A.
			KAʾK		A					KA-A-KA		A.
KʾL	1		KAʾL		IJA					KA-LI-IA		RA LXV 53 XI 48
			KAʾL		IJA					KA-LI-IA	FN	C
			KIʾL	AN						KI-LA-AN		M
			KIʾL		IJA					KI-LI-IA		RA LXV 45 V 55
			KIʾL		I		ʾIL			KI-LI-DINGIR		CT IV 33B 19
			KIʾL		I		ʾIL	UM		KI-LI-DINGIR-LUM		XIII 106 14
			KIʾL		I		ʿAMM	I		KI-LI-AM-MI	GEN	MRS XVI 12:2
			KIʾL		I		BELAʾ	I		KI-LI-BE-LA-I		M
			KIʾL		UM		ʾALLAI			KI-LUM-AL-LA-I	FN	XIII 1 XI 49
			KIʾL		U		MAʾN	A		KI-LU-MA-NA	FN	RA LXV 56 I 9
	2		LU				KIʾL	A		LU_2-KI-LA		BASOR 95, 19
KʾM	1		KAʾAM		I					KA-A-MI		A.
			KAʾM	AT	UM					KA-MA-TUM	FN	C
			KAʾM		I		JAʾAR	UM		KA-MI-IA-A-RUM		VAS VII 128 46
			KAʾM		A		ṢILL	UM		KA-MA-ZI-LUM	FN	B 33+
			KAʾM		A		ṢILL	U		KA-MA-ZI-LU?	FN	VAS XIII 9 R. 2
			KIʾM	AT	IM					KI-MA-TIM	FN GEN	M
			KIʾM		I		ʾEL			KI-MI-EL		UCP X/3 2 2
			KUʾM				DANN	UM		KU-UM-DA-NU-UM		U
			KUʾM				NUWP	I		KU-UM-NU-BI		M
			KUʾM		U		LIʾL	U		KU-MU-LI-LU		CT IV 22A 14
			KUʾM		U		ṢILL	I		KU-MU-ZI-LI	FN	B 33+
	2		ʾIL		A		KAʾAM			DINGIR-KA-A-AM		TIM III 101 7
			ḪALAJ		A		KUʾM	U		ḪA-LA-A-KU-MU		XIV 79:5+
			ʾANN		U		KUʾM			AN-NU-KUM	FN	XIII 1 VI 8

ROOTS (Consonants only)

KʾM	2	MU	ŠTUḪ				KAʾM	I		MU-UŠ-TU-KA-M[I]		M+
KʾN	2		ḪANN		A		KUʾN	I		AN-NA-KU-NI		VAS VIII 14 44
		JI	TWUR				KUʾN	U	HU	I-DUR-KU?-NU-U_2		VAS XIII 14 R. 10
KʾR	1		KAʾR		IJA					KA-RI-IA		RA LXV 52 X 25
			KIʾR		I		DAGAN			KI-RI-D-DA-GAN		RA LXV 52 X 21
			KUʾR		UM					KU-RU-UM		M+
			KUʾR	AN	UM					KU-RA-NU-UM		B 45
			KUʾR	AN	U					KU-RA-NU		B 45, M, C+
			KUʾR		U		HADD	U		KU-RU-D-IM		M
	2		ʾAŠD		I		KIʾR	U		AŠ-DI-KI-E-RU		BM 92654 A
			ʾAŠD		I		KIʾR	U		AŠ-DI-KI-RU		BM 92654
			BEʿL		I		KIʾR	I		BE-LI_2-KI-RI	FN	RA LXV 58 I 15
KʾŠ	1		KAʾŠ	AN	UM					KA-SA-NU-UM		SIMMONS 128:5
			KUʾŠ	AN						KU-SA-AN		M+
			KUʾŠ		I		ḪIMR	I		KU-ŠI-ḪI-IM-RI		SIMMONS 87 19
KʾT	1		KUʾUT		UM					KU-ḪU-TUM		UCP X/1 38 9
			KUʾT	AN						KU-TA-AN		M
			KUʾT	AN	UM					KU-TA-NU-UM		RUTTEN 38 20+
			KUʾT	AN	UM					KU-TA-A-NU-UM		SIMMONS 98 14
			KUʾT	AT	U					KU-TA-TU	MN	B 33
	2		ḪANN		A		KAʾT	UM		AN-NA-KA-TUM		YOS XIII 509:2
KʾZ	1		KIʾZ		UM					KI-ZU-UM		RA LXV 43 IV 16
			KUʾZ		UM					KU-ZUM		TA 1931, 327
			KUʾZ	AN						KU-ZA-AN		XIV 86:5+
			KUʾZ	AN	UM					KU-ZA-NU-UM		B 46
			KUʾZ	AN	U					KU-ZA-NU		B 46
KHL	1		KAHAL	AN						KA-A-LA-AN		M+
			KAHAL		IJA					KA-A-LI-IA		M
			KAHAL		I		HADD	U		KA-A-LI-D-IM		M+
			KAHAL		I		ʾIL	U				
							MA			KA-A-LI-I-LU-MA		XIV 62:4+
			KAHAL		I		ʾIL	U				
							MA			KA-A-LI-DINGIR-MA		M+
			KIHIL		UM					KI-ḪI-LUM		M+
			KIHIL		IM					KI-ḪI-LIM	GEN	M
			KIHIL	AH						KI-ḪI-LA	FN	M+
			KIHIL		A	HA				KI-ḪI-LA-A	FN	M
KWJ	1		KAWJ	AN						KA-A-IA-AN		RA LXV 51 IX 58
			KAWJ	AN						KA-A-IA-AN	FN	C
			KAWJ		AJA					KA-A-IA-A-IA		M+
			KAWJ		A		LAʾL	UM		KA-A-LA-LUM		M
KWN	1	ʾA	KWUN				PI					
							ʾEL			A-KU-PI-EL		GORDON, SCT 38 16
		JA	KWUN		UM					IA-KU-NU-UM		B 27+
		JA	KWUN		UM					IA-A-KU-NU-UM		B 27
		JA	KWUN		U					IA-KU-NU		B 27+
		JA	KWUN		AM					IA-KU-NA-AM	ACC	CT VIII 36D 7
		JA	KWUN		IM					IA-KU-NIM	GEN	B 28, M+
		JA	KWUN		I					IA-KU-NI	GEN	TIM III 58 16+
		JA	KWUN	AN						JA-GU-NA-AN		U
		JA	KWUN	AN						IA-KU-NA-AN		M+
		JA	KWUN				ʾAHL	I		IA-KU-UN-A-LI		B 92
		JA	KWUN				HADD	U		IA-KU-UN-D-IM		B 27, M+
		JA	KWUN				ʾIL			IA-KU-UN-DINGIR		M
		JA	KWUN				ʿALAṢ	I		IA-KU-UN-ḪA-LA-ZI		RA LXV 44 IV 41;43
		JA	KWUN				ʿAMM	U		IA-KU-UN-AM-MU		B 27
		JA	KWUN				ḪARAR			IA-KU-UN-ḪA-RA-AR		VAS IX 172 4+
		JA	KWUN				ḪARAR	I		IA-KU-[UN-ḪA]-RA-RI	GEN	BM 81641 6
		JA	KWUN				ḪARAR	I		IA-KUN_3-ḪA-RA-RI		CT XLVIII 3:3
		JI	KWUN				ḪARAR	I		I-KU-UN-ḪA-RA-RI?	GEN	TCL I 151 4
		JA	KWUN				ʾAŠD	UM		IA-KU-UN-AŠ-DU-UM		B 27
		JA	KWUN				ʾAŠAR			IA-KU-UN-A-ŠAR		B 92+, M+
		JI	KWUN				ʾAŠAR			I-KU-UN-A-ŠAR		GORDON 38 6
		JA	KWUN				ʾAŠAR	I		IA-KU-UN-A-ŠA-RI	NOM	CT XLVIII 10 6
		JA	KWUN				ʾAŠAR	UM		IA-KU-UN-A-ŠA-RU-UM		B 27

ROOTS (Consonants only)

KWN	1	JI	KWUN					BAʿL		I		I-KU-UN-BA-LI		A.
		JI	KWUN					BAʿL		I		I-KU-UN-BA-AḪ-LI		A. 246 33
		JA	KWUN					BAʿL				IA-KU-BA-AL		RA LXV 44 V 7
		JA	KWUN					DIWR		UM		IA-KU-UN-DI-RUM		CT XLVIII 115
		JA	KWUN					DIWR		IM		IA-KU-UN-DI-[R]I-IM	GEN	M
		JA	KWUN					DIWR		I		IA-KU-UN-DI-RI	GEN	CT XLVIII 115 CASE
		JA	KWUN					DIWR				IA-KU-UN-DI-IR		M+
		JA	KWUN					DIWR				IA-KU-DI-IR		RA LXV 45 V 14
		JA	KWUN					DAGAN				IA-KU-UN-D-DA-GAN		X 171 3
		JA	KWUN					LIʾM				IA-KU-UN-LI-IM		M+
		JA	KWUN					LIʾM				IA-KU-LI-IM		M+
		JA	KWUN					MEʾR				IA-KU-UN-ME-IR		M+
		JA	KWUN					MAṬAR				IA-KU-MA-DAR		SYMB.BCHL P.36?:6
		JA	KWUN					PI				IA-KU-UN-PI		CT VIII 43C 8
		JA	KWUN					PI				IA-KU-BI		B 27
		JA	KWUN					PI				IA-KU-PI		B 27
		JE	KWUN					PI				E-KU-PI		B 17
		JA	KWUN					PI		I	JA	IA-KU-UN-BI-IA		XII 14
		JI	KWUN					PI		I	JA	I-KU-BI-IA		SM P. 54
		JI	KWUN					PI		I		I-KU-UN-BI-I		C II 2 11
		JA	KWUN					PI						
								MAM		A		IA-KU-UN-BI-D-MA-MA	FN	RA LXV 66 VII 61
		JA	KWUN					RAPIʾ				IA-KU-UN-RA-BI		M
		JA	KWUN					ŠUM		U				
								ʾAB		IM		IA-KU-UN-SU-MU-A-BI-IM		M
		JA	KWUN					ŠARR		UM		IA-KU-UN-ŠAR-RU-UM		B 28
		TA	KWUN	AH								TA-KU-NA	FN	XIII 1 VIII 18+
		TA	KWUN		AJA							TA-KU-NA-IA	FN	C
		TA	KWUN					ḪAʾT		UM		TA-KU-UN-ḪA-TUM	FN	M+
		TA	KWUN					MAʾT		UM		TA-KU-UN-MA-TUM	FN	M, C+
		TA	KWUN					MAʾT		I		TA-KUM-MA-TI	FN	A.+
		TA	KWUN					MITEʿ			JE	TA-KU-UN-MI-TE-E		M
		TA	KWUN					ZULAT		UM		TA-KU-UN-ZU?-LA-TUM	FN	RA LXV 62 V 30
		JA	KWIN					HADD		U		IA-KI-IN-D-IM		M
		JA	KWIN					ʾIL				JA-KI-IN-DINGIR		JEA VII 196
		JA	KWIN					LU			HU	IA-KI-IN-LU-U$_2$		TALLQUIST APN 95 LATE
		MA	KWIN									MA?-KI-EN		C
		ME	KWIN									ME-KI-IN	FN	A.
		ME	KWIN		UM							ME-KI-NU-UM		M+
			KIWN					BUWZ	AN	UM		KI-IN-BU-ZA-NU-UM		HARRIS 68 14
			KIWN					NAHR		IM		KI-IN-NA-RI-IM	GEN	M+
			KIWN		A			ʾIL		I		KI-NA-I$_3$-LI$_2$		M
			KIWN		I			BAWŠ		I		KI-NI-BA-ŠI	FN	HARRIS 45 8
			KIWN		U			BAWŠ		I		KI-NU-BA-ŠI		LANGDON XXVIII 12
			KIWN		UM			ʾADAL				KI-NU-UM-A-DA-AL		RA LXV 48 VII 60
			KIWN		I	Š		LUʾP		A		KI-NI-IŠ-LU-BA		EDZARD,DER 94:17;95:6
			KIWN		I	Š		MAʾT		UM		KI-NI-IŠ-MA-TUM	FN	M+;C
			KUWUN		UM							KU-U$_2$-NU-UM		UCP X/3 1 35
			KUWN		UM							KU-NU-UM		RUTTEN 33 6 SEAL+;M
			KUWN	AT	UM							KU-NA-TUM	FN	C
			KUWN	AN	UM							KU-NA-NU-UM		RUTTEN 1 19+
			KUWN	AN	IM							KU-NA-NI-IM	GEN	M
			KUWN		AM							KU-NA-AM	MN NOM	TIM III 17 7, M+
			KUWN					ʾIL		A		KU-UN-I-LA		RA LXV 53 XI 31
			KUWN					ʿAMM		U		KU-UN-AM-MU		MRS VI P. 249
			KUWN		A			MAʾT		UM		KU-NA-MA-TUM		U
			KUWN		I			DAʾK		A		KU-NI-DA-KA		A. 367 11
	2		ʾAB		I	Š		KIWN				A-BI$_2$-IŠ-KI-IN		U
			ʾAB		UM		JE	KWIN				A-BU-UM-E-KI-IN		M
			ʾAB		U		ME	KWIN				A-BU-ME-KI-IN		X 154 2+
			ʾEL					KAWN		UM		EL-GA-NU-UM		TA 1931 238
			ʾIL		A			KAWN				DINGIR-KA-AN	MN	M+
			ʾIL		A			KAWN				DINGIR-KA-AN	FN	M
			ʾIL		A			KAWN		UM		DINGIR-KA-NU-UM		MAH II/3 P. 188F
			ʾIL		A			KAWN		IM		DINGIR-KA-NIM	GEN	M+
			ʾIL		A			KAWN		IM		DINGIR-KA-NI-IM	GEN	M

KWN	2	ʾIL		I		KUWN			I$_3$-LI$_2$-KU-UN		RA LXV 55 XIII 32
		ʿAMM		I		KUWN			ḪA-MI-KU-UN		RA LXV 54 XII 15
		JARAḪ				KIWN	A		SIN-KI-NA		TCL I 237 31
		ʿAŠTAR				KAWN			EŠ$_4$-DAR-KA-AN		IX 237 II 4+
		ḎAKUR		A		KUWN	U		ZA-KU-RA-KU-NU		VII 85 12
		LA				KIWN	U		LA-K[I]-NU		M
		LA				KIWN					
						HADD	U		LA-KI-IN-A-DU		A.
		LAḪAN		I		KIWN	IM		LA-ḪA-NI-KI-IN-IM	GEN	UCP X/3 2 5
		MUT		A	TA	KWIN			MU-TA-TA-KI-IN		RA LXV 51 IX 78
KBB	1	KUBB		IJA					KU-UB-BI-IA		M
		KUBB	AN	UM					KU-UB-BA-NU-UM		B 45
KBD	1	KABID	AH						KA-BI-DA	FN	M+
		KABID		AJA					KA-BI-DA-IA	FN	M
		KABID	T	A					KA-BI-IT-TA	MN	C II 6
		KABID	AN	UM					GA-BI-DA-NU-UM		TA 1930,486 OLDER OB
		KABD		U		KA					
						ʾAB	I		KA-AB-TU-KA-A-BI		UET V 688:8,12
	2 JI	JBIŠ				KABID			I-BI-IŠ-GA-BI-ID		KISURRA 63A
		MUT				KABID			MU-UT-GA-BI-ID		TA 30, 615 24
KBKB	1	KABKAB		UM					KA[B-K]A-BU-UM		RA LXV 52 X 77
		KABKAB		IM					KAB-KA-BI-IM	GEN	C
		KABKAB	AH						KA-AB-KA-BA	FN	M+
		KABKAB	AN						GA-GA-BA-AN-KI	GN	IRAQ VII 66 SARGONIC
	2	ʾIL		A		KABKAB	I		DINGIR-KAB-KA-BI		JNES XIII 210+ LATE
		ʾIL		A		KABKAB	U	HU	I-LA-KAB-KA-BU-U$_2$		M+
		ʾIL		I		KABKAB	U		I$_3$-LI$_2$-KA-AB-KA-BU		A 21914 3
KBL	1	KABL	AK	UM					KA-AB-LA-KU-UM		B 32
	2	ʾAN		I	Š	KIBAL			A-NI-IŠ-KI-BA-AL		RA LXV 53 XI 37+
		ʾAN		I	Š	KIBEL			A-NI-IŠ-KI-BE-EL		TCL XX 191 33 CAPP.
		ʾAN		A	Š	KIBAL			[A]?-NA-AŠ-KI-BA-AL		VIII 86 23
		ʾANA				KIBAL	I		A-NA?-KI-BA-[L]I	FN	M
KBN	1	KIBUN		UM					KI-BU-NU-UM		TIM III 33 5+
KBR	1 JA	KBUR		IM					IA-AK-BU-RI-IM	GEN	B 27
		KIBR				ḪAJJ	A		KI-BI-IR-E$_2$-A		XIV 62:23
		KIBR				ʾABB	A		KI-BI-IR-D-AB-BA		M+
		KIBR				ʾABB	A		KI-IB-RA-AB-BA		CT XXIX 14 16
		KIBR				ʾABB	A		KI-IB-RA-BA		CT XXIX 14 29
		KIBR				JARAḪ			KI-BI-IR-D-EN-ZU		RUTTEN 11 25
		KIBR		I		ʿAŠTAR			KI-IB-RI-EŠ$_4$-DAR		M+
		KIBR		I		DAGAN			KI-IB-RI-D-DA-GAN		M+
		KIBAR							KI-BA-AR		RA LXV 47 VII 19
		KIBIR		I					[K]I-BI-RI		RA LXV 43 III 77
		KUBAR		UM					GU-BA-RU-UM		U
		KUBUR		UM					KU-UB-BU-RUM		A.
	2	ʿAŠTAR				KABAR			EŠ$_4$-DAR-KA-BAR		RA LXV 41 II 39
		DAGAN				KIBR	I		D-DA-GAN-KI-IB-RI	FN	M+
KBS	1	KABAS		UM					GA-BA-ZU-UM		HSM 7900, UR III
		KABAS		I	JE				KA-BA-AZ-ZI-E		A.
		KABAS	AN	UM					GA-BA-ZA-NU-UM		TA 1931,262
		KABIS		UM					KA-BI-ZUM		B 32
		KABIS	AT	UM					KA-BI-ZA-TUM	FN	C
		KIBIS	AN						KI-BI-ZA-AN		M
		KIBS	AT	UM					KI-IB-ZA-TUM	FN	M+
		KIBS				HADD	U		KI-IB-ZA-DU	FN	A.
		KIBS		I		HADD	U		KI-IB-ZI-D-IM		M+
		KIBS		I		HEDD	A		KI-IB-ZI-E-D-IM		M
		KIBS		I		JARAḪ			KI-IB-ZI-E-RA-AḪ		RA LXV 43 III 44+
		KIBS		U	NA				KI-IB-ZU-UN-NA	FN	M+
		KUBAS	AT	UM					KU-BA-ZA-TUM	FN	RA LXV 58 I 32
		KUBAS		U		....			KU-BA-ZU-[....]		RA LXV 50 VIII 83
		KUBS	AT	UM					KU-UB-ZA-TUM		SZLECHTER TJ P. 186
KBŠ	1	KABŠ	AT	UM					KAB-SA-TUM	FN	M+
		KABŠ	AN	UM					KA-AB-SA-NU-UM		YOS V 18 17
		KIBŠ	AT	UM					KI-IB-SA-TUM	FN	RA LXV 56 I 11
KDD	1	KADAD		UM					KA-DA-DU-UM	FN	BM 17063A 34

KDD	1		KADAD		A					KA-DA-DA	GEN	BM 17060 30+
			KUDAD	AN	UM					KU-DA-DA-NU-UM		U
			KUDAD		I					KU-DA-DI	FN	RA LXV 61 IV 5
			KUDD		I					[K]U-UD-DI		RA LXV 40 I 18
KDL	1		KADUL		I					KA-DU-LI	FN	M
KKK	1		KAKK		U					KA-AK-KU	FN	C+
			KAKK	AH						KA-AK-KA	FN	M
			KAKK	ATANUM						KA-KA-TA-NU-UM		SIMMONS 104 6
			KAKK		A	ʾAŠJ	AH			KA-AK-KA-A-SI-IA	FN	XIII 1 VI 11
			KAKK		A	JIŠʿ	AH			KA-KA-IŠ-ḪA	FN	M+
			KAKK		A	ʾAŠR		I		KA-AK-KA-AŠ-RI	FN	XIII 1 V 1
			KAKK		A	LIʾD		I		KA-AK-KA-LI-DI	FN	X 10 5
			KAKK		A	MANN		U		KA-AK-KA-MA-AN-NU		M
			KAKK		A	NAʿM		I		KA-AK-KA-NA-AḪ-MI	FN	XIII 1 VII 30
			KAKK		A	NILŠ		I		KA-A[K]-KA-NI-EL?-ŠI?	FN	XIII 1 VIII 41
			KAKK		A	NIʾŠ		U	JA	KA-AK-KA-NI-ŠU-IA		RA LXV 64 VI 35
			KAKK		A	NIʾŠ		U	JA	KA-KA-NI-ŠU-IA	FN	RA LXV 65 VII 44
			KAKK		A	RIMŠ		I		KA-AK-KA-RI-IM-ŠI	FN	RA LXV 60 III 5
			KAKK		A	TUWR		I	JA	KA-KA-TU-RI-IA	FN	M
	2		ḪIMD			KAKK		A		ḪI-MI-ID-KA-AK-KA		M
			ʾAMIR			KAKK		A		A-ME-IR-KA-AK-KA		XIII 1 V 20
			NABIʾ			KAKK		A		NA-BI-KA-KA		M+
		JI	NDIN			KAKK		A		I-DIN-KA-AK-KA		M+
		JI	NDIN			KAKK		A		I-DIN-D-KA-KA		M+
KKKB	1		KUKKUB	AT	UM					KU-KU-BA-TUM		VAS IX 175:11
			KUKKUB	AT	UM					KU-KU-BA-TUM	FN	XIII 1 VII 44
KKKN	1		KIKKIN		UM					KI-KI-NU-UM		BM 82437 2 6
			KIKKIN		UM					KI-IK-KI-NUM		B 49
			KIKKIN		U					KI-IK-KI-NU		B 49+
			KIKKIN		IM					KI-KI-NI-IM	GEN	B 49
			KIKKIN		IM					KI-KI-NIM	GEN	B 49+
			KIKKIN		I					KI-IK-KI-NI	GEN	B 49+
			KUKKUN		UM					KU-KU-NU-UM		SIMMONS 111 6 15+
KKKR	1		KAKKAR		I					KA-KA-RI		RA LXV 50 IX 7
			KIKKIR		IM					KI-IK-KI-RI-IM	GEN	M
KKKŠ	1		KUKKUŠ	AN						KU-KU-SA-AN		RA LXV 46 VI 3
			KUKKUŠ	AN	UM					KU-UK-KU-ZA-NU-UM		M
			KUKKUŠ	AN	IM					KU-UK-KU-ZA-NIM	GEN	M
KKM	1		KUKIM			ḪIJJ		A		KU-UK-KI-IM?-ḪI-IA	FN	X 100 5
KL	2		JAT			KALA				I-IA-AT-KA-LA		VAS XVI 165 5
			BUN		U	KALA						
						ʾIL		I		BU-NU-KA-LA-I-LI		B 16
KLB	1		KALB		UM					GA?-[AL]?-BU-UM		BIN IX 410 3
			KALB	AT	UM					KA-AL-BA-TUM	FN	RA LXV 61 IV 46
			KALB			....				GAL-BA-....		MCS V 120
			KALB			ʾIL				GA-AL-BA-IL		I
			KALB			ʾIL				KA-AL-BA-DINGIR		M
			KALB			ḪAM		I		K[A]-AL-BU-D-A-MI		XIII 1 X 20
	2		ʾAJA			KALB	AH			A-IA-KA-AL-BA?	FN	C
KLK	1		KALK	AT	UM					KA-AL-KA-TUM	MN	CT VIII 12C 1 6 9+
			KALK		AJA					KA-AL-KA-IA		CT XLVIII 89 REV.
KLL	1	JA	KLIL		UM					A-AK-LI-LUM		HARRIS 28 11
			KALAL		UM					KA-LA-LUM		M
			KALAL			TULAʿ			HA	KA-LA-AL-TU-LA-A	FN	M, C
KLM	2		BAʿL		U	KULIM				BA-AḪ-LU-KU-LI-IM		SYRIA XXXII 7 III 6
		JA	LʾAʾ			KULIM				IA-AL-A-KU-LIM		RA LXV 55 XIII 18
KLP	1		KULP	AN	UM					KU-UL-BA-NU-UM		TA 1931,148
			KULP	AN	UM					GUL-BA-NU-UM		U
			KULP		A	RAWḪ		I	JE	KU-UL-PA-RA-ḪI-E		TCL I 14 1, YOS VIII 141 34
	2	JA	MWUT			KULUP				IA-MU-UT-KU-LU-UP		DELAPORTE, CCL II A 418
KM	2		ʾANN		U	KAMA						
						ʾAB		I		AN-NU-KA-MA-BI		CT XLV 116 36
			BUN		U	KAMA						
						ʾIL		A		BU-NU-KA-MA-I-LA		B 16
			PI			KAMA						
						ʾIL				BI-KA-MA-DINGIR		XIV 111:10+

KM	2	PI			KAMA				
					ʾEL		BI-KA-MA-EL		M+
	3	ŠAMŠ		U	ʾIL	U NA			
					KIMA		SA-AM-SU-I-LU-NA-KI-MA-DINGIR		BM 81047:6
KMB	2	KURD		A	KAMB	I	KUR-DA-KA-AM-BI	FN	XIII 1 III 25
KMM	1	KAMM	AT	UM			KAM-MA-TUM	FN	M+
		KIMM	AH				KI-IM-MA	FN	M
		KIMM	AN				KI-IM-MA-AN	FN	C
		KUMM		I	NAʾD	A	KU-UM-MI-NA-DA		JCS IV 113
KMN	1 JA	KMIN		I			IA-AK-ME-NI		JNES XIII 210+ LATE
		KAMAN		UM			KA-MA-NU-UM		B 45+
		KAMAN	IN	UM			KA-MA-NI-NU-UM		EDZARD,DER 68 IV 11
		KAMIN		UM			KA-MI-NU-UM		PBS VIII/1 32 II 6
		KAMN		IJA			KA-AM-NI-IA		VAS XVI 78:0
		KUMAN		UM			KU-MA-NU-UM		B 45
KMR	1	KIMR	AN	U			KI-IM-RA-NU		M
		KUMR		I			KU-UM-RI		RA LXV 42 II 59
	2	ʿAMM		U	KUMAR	A	AM-MU-KU-MAR-RA		A.
		MUT		U	KUMR	I	MU-TU-KU-UM-RI		X 166 10', 13'
KMS	1 JA	KMIS		I			IA-AK-ME-SI		JCS XIII 210+ LATE
		KAMIS		UM			GA-MI-ZUM		I
		KAMIS		UM			KA-MI-ZUM		CT VIII 49A 7
		KAMIS		UM			KA-MI-ZU-UM		AJSL XLIV 243 NO. 32
		KUMIS	AN				KU-ME-ZA-AN		RA LXV 50 VIII 53
		KUMS		AJA			KU-UM-ZA-A-A		HARRIS 66 16
KMT	1	KAMT	AN				KA-AM-TA-AN		M
		KUMT	AN	UM			GU-UM-DA-NU-UM		HSM 7936, UR III
KNW	1 JA	KNUW			ŠARR	UM	IA-AK-NU-ŠA-RU-UM		KISURRA 47A 4+
	JA	KNUW			ŠARR	U	IA-AK-NU-ŠA-RU		TIM III 133 9
KNB	1	KUNAB		UM			KU-NA-PU-UM		EDZARD,DER 59:25+
KND	1	KUND		I			KU-UN-DI	FN	XIII 1 IV 76, C
KNDL	1	KUNDUL	AT	UM			KU-UN-DU-LA-TUM	FN	M+
		KUNDUL	AH				KU-UN-DU-LA	FN	XIII 1 III 21, CT XLIV 54 29
KNK	1	KANAK			RAWḪ	UM	KA-NA-AK-RA-ḪU-UM		VAS XIII 66A R. 5+
		KANAK			RAWḪ	U	KA-NA-AK-RA-ḪU		VAS XIII 66 R. 6
		KANAK			RAWḪ	I	KA-NA-AK-RA-ḪI		VAS XIII 79 R. 7
		KANIK	AN				KA-NI-KA-AN		M
		KANIK			RUWḪ	UM	KA-NI-IK-RU-UM		B 33+
		KANIK			RUWḪ	UM	KA-NI-IK-RUM		B 33
		KANIK			RUWḪ	IM	KA-NI-IK-RI-IM	GEN	B 33
		KANUK		A			KA-AN-NU-UK-KA		M
KNN	1	KANAN		UM			KA-NA-NU-UM		B 45+
		KANN		A	MA				
					ʾIL		KA-AN-NA-MA-DINGIR		M
		KANN		I			KA-AN-NI		XIII 1 IX 62
		KINAN		UM			KI-NA-NU-UM		UCP X/1 P. 58+
		KINAN		U			KI-NA-NU		B 45+
		KINAN	AT	UM			KI-NA-NA-TUM		UCP X/1 27 7+
		KUNAN		UM			KU-NA-A-NU-UM		B 45+
		KUNAN		UM			KU-NA-NU-UM		B 93
		KUNAN	AT	UM			KU-NA-NA-TUM	FN	M
		KUNN		I			KU-UN-NI		RA LXV 52 XI 4
		KUNN		A			KU-UN-NA		WO V 59+ ALA. LATE
		KUNN		AM			KU-UN-NAM	NOM	XIV 102:8, 15, 24
		KUNN		A	MA		[K]U-UN-NA-MA		XIV 101:8
KNP	1	KANAP	AN				KA-NA-PA-AN		M+
KNŠ	1	KANAŠ		UM			KA-NA-ŠUM		TIM III 126 15
		KANIŠ		UM			KA-NI-ŠUM		RUTTEN 14 23
		KANIŠ	AN				KA-NI-SA-AN		M+
		KANIŠ	AH				KA-NI-SA		RA LXV 60 III 12+
		KANIŠ	IT	UM			KA-NI-SI-T[UM]	FN	M
		KANIŠ	IT	UM			KA-NI-ŠI-TUM	FN	M+
	2	ŠUM		U	KANAŠ	A	SU-MU-GA-NA-SA		KISURRA 19 9
KNT	1	KANAT		I			KA-NA-TI		LIMET,SCEAUX CASS. P. 114
		KANUT		UM			KA-NU-TUM		RA LXIV 43
	2	MUT		U	KANAT	A	MU-TU-KA-NA-TA		M

ROOTS (Consonants only)

KNZ	1		KANZ		U					KA-AN-ZU	FN		M+; C II 45 II 40
			KANZ	AN						KA-AN-ZA-AN	FN		C+
			KANZ							KA-AN-ZU-UN-[....]	FN		M
			KINZ		IJA					KI-IN-ZI-IA			M
			KUNZ		I					KU-UN-ZI	FN		XIII 1 V 39; C
			KUNZ	AN	UM					KU-UN-ZA-NU-UM			BIROT,TEA 65:17
			KUNZ	AN	UM					KU-UN-ZA-NUM$_2$			TA 1930,181+
			KUNZ	AN	AM					KU-UN-ZA-NAM	ACC		TA 1930,181
KPD	1		KUPAD		IM					KU-PA-DI-IM	GEN		M
KPP	2		ḪAʾL		I		KUPAPA			ḪA-LI$_2$-KU-BA-BA	FN		RA LXV 58 I 14
			ʾALL		I		KUPAPA			AL-LI-KU-PA-PA	FN		A.
KPŚ	1		KAPAŚ		UM					KA?-PA-SU-UM			KISURRA 58 10
KPT	1		KIPT		UM					KI-IP-TU-UM			M
KRʾ	1		KIRUʾ		UM					KI-RU-UM	FN		M+
			KIRUʾ		U					KI-RU-U$_2$	FN	NOM	X 32 3+
			KIRUʾ		IM					KI-RI-E-IM	FN	GEN	X 135 3
KRB	1	JA	KRUB				ʾIL			D-IA-AK-RU-UB-DINGIR	DN		M+
		JA	KRUB				ʾEL			D-IA-AK-RU-UB-EL	DN		M+
		JA	KRUB				ʾIL			D-IA-AK-RU-UB-IL	DN		M+
		JI	KRUB				ʾEL			D-IK-RU-UE-EL	DN		M+
		JI	KRUB				ʾIL			D-IK-RU-UB-DINGIR	DN		M+
		JI	KRUB				ʾIL			D-IK-RU-UB-IL	DN		M
		JI	KRUB				ʾIL			D-IK-RU-BI-DINGIR	DN		M
		JA	KRUB				ʾIL						
							TILL	AT	I	D-IA-AK-RU-UB-DINGIR-TIL-LA-TI			M
			KIRB	AN						KI-IR-BA-AN			RA LXV 51 IX 36
			KIRB	AN	UM					GIR$_3$-BA-NUM$_2$			U
	2		ʾAJAN				KURUB			A-AN-KU-RU-UB	FN		RA LXV 51 X 15
		JI	JṢIʾ				KURUB			I-ZI-KU-RU-UB			RA LXV 53 XI 11
KRD	1		KURD	AN	UM					KUR-DA-A-NU-UM			RUTTEN 11 26
			KURD		A		KAMB		I	KUR-DA-KA-AM-BI	FN		XIII 1 III 25
KRKR	1		KURKUR		UM					KU-UR$_2$-KU-RU-UM			B 49+
			KURKUR		IM					KU-UR-KU-RI-IM	GEN		M
			KURKUR	T	UM					KUR$_2$-KUR$_2$-TUM	MN?		PBS VIII/2 178 36
KRN	1		KARAN	AT	UM					KA-RA-NA-TUM	FN		CT II 40B 1, M
			KARAN	AT	IM					KA-RA-NA-[T]IM	FN		M
KRŚ	1		KARŚ	AN						KA-AR-ŠA-AN			RA LXV 54 XII 23
			KURAŚ	AN	UM					KU-RA-ŠA-NU-UM			LAESSOE P. 53+
			KURŚ	AN	UM					KU-UR$_2$-ŠA-NU-UM			B 45
			KURŚ	AN	U					KU-UR-[S]A-NU			M
			KURŚ	AN	I					KU-UR$_2$-SA-NI	NOM		M
KRŠ	2		ʾAWIJ				KIRIŠ		U	A-WI-KI-RI-IŠ			XIV 106:18
			ʾIL		U	NA	KIRIŠ		U	I-LU-NA-KI-RI-ŠU			XIII 8 19+
KRT	1		KARIT	AN						KA-RI-TA-AN			RA LXV 41 II 36
KRZ	1		KIRZ		UM					KI-IR-ZU-UM	FN		RA LXV 64 VI 26
KSW	1	JI	KSUW				ʾEL			IK-ZU-EL			TA 30 615 10, 20+
		JI	KSUW				ʾIL			IK-ZU-IL			TA 1931 ,435 REV.2
KSJ	1	JA	KSIJ				ʾIL			IA-AK-ZI-DINGIR			SIMMONS 92 16
		JA	KSIJ				ʾIL			A-AK-ZI-DINGIR			FIGULLA CAT I 14029
	2		MUT				KASIJ			MU-UT-KA-ZI-....			VIII 6 35'
KSBR	1		KISIBIR	AT	UM					KI-ZI-BI-RA-TUM	FN		RA LXV 61 IV 50
KŚJ	1	JA	KŚIJ				....			IA-AK-SI-DINGIR-....			DE GEN. KICH II D47+
		MU	KAŚAJ		EM					MU-KA-SA-A-JE-EM	ACC		M
KŚP	1		KAŚP	AN	U					KA-AŠ$_2$-BA-NU			M
			KUŚAP	AN	UM					KU-SA-PA-NU-UM			TIM III 57 6 66 6
			KUŚAP		IJA					KU-SA-BI-IA			M
KŠL	1		KAŠIL		UM					KA-ŠI-LUM			HARRIS 69 9
KŠM	1		KIŠAM	AN	U					KI-ŠA?-MA-NU			XIII 1 V 60
			KUŠM		I		ʾEL			KU-UŠ$_2$-MI-EL			RA LXV 48 VII 74
KŠR	1		KAŠER		UM					KA-ŠE-RUM			X 30 3
			KAŠER	AH						GA-ŠE-RA	FN		M
			KUŠR	AN	UM					KU-UŠ-RA-NU-UM			SIMMONS 51 17
	2		ʾIL		I		KAŠAR			I$_3$-LI$_2$-KA-ŠA-AR			M
KTKT	1		KUTKUT		UM					KU-UT-KU-TUM			M, KISURRA 37 8+
KTL	1		KUTUL		U	HU				KU-TU-LU-U$_2$			RA LXV 43 III 76
	2		ʾIL		I	Š	KUTUL			I$_3$-LI$_2$-IŠ-KU-TU-UL			KISURRA 75A 18+

ROOTS (Consonants only)

KTR	1	KATIR		I						KA-TI-RI	GEN	UET V 88 2,SEAL, A. 37 12
		KATR		UM						KA-AT-RU-UM		WATERMAN 14 L.E.+
		KATR		U						KA-AT-RU		B 33+
		KATR		IM						KA-AT-R[I-I]M	GEN	HARRIS 75 17
		KATR		AJA						KA-AT-RA-IA	FN	XIII 1 III 8
KTT	1	KITT	AN	IM						KI-IT-TA-NI-IM	GEN	SIMMONS 63 2
KTZ	2	ʾIL		UM			KATAZ	I		I-LU-UM-KA-TA-ZI		RUTTEN 40 1
KZB	1	KAZIB		U						KA-ZI-BU		M
		KAZIB		IM						KA-ZI-BI-IM	GEN	M+
		KUZAB		U						KU-ZA-BU	FN	VAS VII 166 11
		KUZAB	AT	UM						KU-ZA-BA-TUM	MN	CT VI 30B 23+
		KUZAB	AT	UM						KU-ZA-BA-TUM	FN	CT VIII 43A 4, 10+
KZR	1	KAZIR		AM						KA-ZI-RA-AM	NOM	RA LXV 52 X 24
		KIZUR		I						KI-ZU-RI		RA LXV 43 III 41,42
		KUZAR		I						KU-ZA-RI		RA LXV 45 V 15+
		KUZAR		I						KU-UZ-ZA-RI		IX 259:5
		KUZAR		I						KU-UZ$_2$-ZA-RI		XIII 90:5
		KUZAR		I	NA					KU-ZA-RI-NA		RA LXV 45 V 22
KZZ	1	KUZAZ		I						KU-ZA-AZ-ZI	FN	RA LXV 60 III 52
L	1	LI			JA		ʾEL			LI-IA-EL		RA LXV 41 II 23
		LI			JA		SITR	U	HU	LI-IA-ZI-IT-RU-U$_2$		M+
		LA			KA		ʾIL			LA-KA-DINGIR		KISURRA 111 5
		LA			KA		ṢUBʾ	UM		LA-KA-ZU-BU-UM		M
		LA			K		MA					
							ʾIL			LA-AK-MA-AN		B 33
		LA			NA		HADD	U		LA-NA-D-IM		XIII 109 15, 16
		LA			NA		ʾIL			LA-NA-DINGIR		RUTTEN 27 15+
		LA			NA		DAGAN			LA-NA-D-DA-GAN		M+
		LA			NA		ŠUM	UM		LA-NA-SU-MU-[UM]		CT VIII 26B 22
		LA			NI		ʾIL			LA$_2$-NI-DINGIR		U
		LA				ʾA	HWIJ		JA	LA-WI-IA	FN	RA LXV 60 III 37
		LA				ʾA	HWIJ					
							ʾAḪ	I		LA-AḪ-WI-A-ḪI	FN	XIII 1 VII 3
		LA				ʾA	HWIJ					
							ʾAB	I		LA-AḪ-WI-A-BI	FN	XIII 1 XIII 6
		LA				ʾA	HWIJ					
							HADD	U		LA-AḪ-WI-A-DU		A. 95 36
		LA				ʾA	HWIJ					
							ʾIL			IA-WI-DINGIR		XIV 109:7
		LA				ʾA	HWIJ					
							ʾIL			IA-[AḪ]?-WI-DINGIR		M
		LA				ʾA	HWIJ					
							JAŠAR			LA-AḪ-WI-E-SA-AR		RA LXV 40 I 21
		LA				ʾA	HWIJ					
							BAʿL	U		LA-AḪ-WI-BA-LU		C
		LA				ʾA	HWIJ					
							BAʿL	U		LA-AḪ-WI-BA-AḪ-LU		XIV 29:28
		LA				ʾA	HWIJ					
							BEʿL	I		LA-AḪ-WI-BE-LI$_2$	FN	RA LXV 59 II 73
		LA				ʾA	HWIJ					
							LA		NA	LA-AḪ-WI-LA-NA		RA LXV 65 VII 19
		LA				ʾA	HWIJ					
							MALIK			LA-AḪ-WI-MA-LIK		X 141 2
		LA				ʾA	HWIJ					
							MALIK	U		LA-AḪ-WI-MA-LI-KU		M
		LA				ʾA	HWIJ					
							NIWR	I		LA-AḪ-WI-NE-RI	FN	XIII 1 II 11
		LA				ʾA	ḪJIJ					
							HADD	U		LA-ḪI-A-DU		A. 57 11, 13
		LA				ʾA	ḪJIJ					
							ʿAN	UM		LA-ḪI-A-NU-UM		U
		LA				ʾA	ḪJIJ					
							BIḪR	U		LA-ḪI-BI-RU		WATERMAN 25 R. 5
		LA				ʾA	ḪJIJ					
							ṢADUQ			LA-ḪI-ZA-DU-UQ		A.+
		LA				ʾA	ʾWIʾ					
							ʾIL			LA-WI-IḪ?-DINGIR		TIM IV 33,34,SEALS

ROOTS (Consonants only)

L	1	LA	ʾA		ʾWIR	UM		LA-WI-RUM		RA XXIV 58 9 4
		LA	ʾA		ʾDUM	U		LA-AḪ-DU-MU		4E RENC. ASS. P. 178 4
		LA	ʾA		ʾMAR	UM		LA-MA-RUM		BM 80644
		LA	ʾA		ʾMUR	IM		LA-A-MU-RI-IM	GEN	M
		LA	ʾA		ʾMUR	A		LA-MU-RA		B 33+
		LA	ʾA		ʾŠUD	I				
					ʾIL			LA-AḪ-SU-DI-DINGIR		XIII 4 14
		LA	ʾA		ḪŠIR	UM		LA-AḪ-SI-RU-UM		BM 80368 2
		LA	ʾA		MLIK					
					ʾIL			LA-AM-LI-IK-DINGIR		RUTTEN 5 22
		LA	ʾA		RŠIJ	UM		LA-AR-ŠI-U_2-U[M]		TA 1931, 538 IV
		LA	ʾA		ŠNIJ					
					ʾIL			LA-AŠ-NI-DINGIR		M
		LA			ʾAB	A		LA-A-BA		U
		LA			ʿADN	I	JA	LA-AD-NI-IA		M
		LA			ʿADN	A				
			ʾA		MWUT			LA-ḪA-AD-NA-A-MU-UT		M
		LA			ʾADUN	IM		LA-DU-NIM	GEN	M
		LA			ʾIL	A		[L]A?-I-LA		RA LXV 44 IV 36
		LA			ʾIL	A				
					MILK	I		LA-I-LA-MI-IL-KI		TA 30, 75 2
		LA			ʿAMM	U		LA-ḪA-AM-MU		HARRIS 18 14
		LA			ḪAMUJ	IM		LA-ḪA-MU-JI-IM	GEN	M
		LA			ʿAN	UM		LA-A-NU-UM		U
		LA			ḪUNN	IM		LA-ḪU-NI-IM	GEN	M
		LA	JE	N	JBIŠ	U		LA-E-NI-BI-ŠU		YOS XII
		LA	JE		RWIḪ	UM		LA-E-RI-ḪU-UM		U
		LA			BAWʾ	U		LA-BA-U_2		JCS XIII 51 292:5' A.LATE
		LA			BAWʾ	U		LA-BA-ʾU-U		TALLQUIST,APN P.120 LATE
		LA			BAŠAR			LA-BA-ŠA-AR		RA LXV 42 II 58
		LA			DIJN	AM		LA-DI-NAM	ACC	M
		LA			DJIN					
					JARAḪ			LA-DI-IN-E-RA-AḪ		RA LXV 46 VI 26+
		LA			KIWN	U		LA-K[I]-NU		M
		LA			KIWN					
					HADD	U		LA-KI-IN-A-DU		A.
		LA			LABW	UM		LA-LA-BU-[UM]?		M
		LA			MANUW	UM		LA-MA-NU-UM		I, TIM III 136 4
		LA			MANUW	IM		LA-MA-NI-IM	GEN	B 46
		LA			NAŠUʾ	UM		LA-NA-SU-U_2-UM		M
		LA			NAŠUʾ	UM		LA-NA-SU-WU-UM		XIV 53:20+
		LA			NAŠUʾ	U		LA-NA-SU-U_2		B 33, 4E RENC. ASS. P. 178
		LA			NAŠUʾ	IM		LA-NA-SU-I-IM	GEN	M
		LA			NAŠUʾ	IM		LA-A-NA-SU-I-IM	GEN	M
		LA			NAŠUʾ	I		LA-NA-SU-JI	GEN	M
		LA			NAŠUʾ	I		LA-NI-SU-JI	FN NOM	M
		LA			PAŠIQ	UM		LA-PA-SI-KU-UM		M
		LA			RIWM					
					ḪAM	I		LA-RI-IM-D-A-MI		M
		LA			RIWM					
					ʿAḎIR			LA-RI-IM-ḪA-ZI-IR		DELAPORTE, CAT. BN 207
		LA			RIWM					
			JI		JBAL	U	HU	[L]A?-RI-IM-I-BA-LU-U_2		M
		LA			RIWM					
					BAʿL	I		LA-RI-IM-BA-AḪ-LI		M+
		LA			RIWM					
					BEʿL	I		LA-RI-IM-BE-LI_2		X 69 5
		LA			RIWM					
					DIWR			LA-RI-IM-DI-IR		RA LXV 50 IX 22
		LA			RIWM					
					LU		HU	LA-RI-IM-LU-U_2		M
		LA			RIWM					
					NUMAḪ	A		LA-RI-IM-NU-MA-ḪA-A		M+
		LA			RIWM					
					NUMAḪ	A		LA-RI-IM-NU-MA-A		M
		LA			ŠIJM	A		LA-SI-MA		M

ROOTS (Consonants only)

L	1	LA				TEʾḪ		U		LA-TE-ḪU		MRS VI P. 196 22,LATE
		LA				TEBUʾ		U		LA-TE-BU-U$_2$		B 33
		LA				ṬAJB		UM		LA-DA-BU-UM		U
		LA				ṬAJB	T	UM		LA-ṬA$_3$-AB-TUM	FN	XIII 1 VI 44+
		LA				ṢABIʾ		IM		LA-ZA-BI-IM	GEN	M+
		LA				ṢARR		UM		LA-ZA-RU-UM?		B 33
		LA				ṢARR		AJA		LA-ZA-RA-A		YOS XIII 244:14
		LI		JI		JṢIʾ						
						ʾAŠD		UM		LI-ZI-AŠ-DU-UM		VAS XIII 104 R. II 24
		LI		JI		MLIK						
						....				LI-IM-LI$_2$-LI-IK-ḪI-LI-GAL$_2$		HSM 7934, UR III
		LI		JI		TWUR						
						ʾAHL		I		LI-TU-UR-A-LI		JCS XXIV 62 NO.55+
		LI		JI	T	ŠAMAʿ						
						ʾIL				LI?-IŠ?-TA-MI-DINGIR		IX 291 I 18
		LU				ḤAJJ		A				
						ŠAMIʿ		UM		LU-ḪA-A-A-SA-MU-UM		UET V 569 8
		LU				ḤAJJ		A				
						ŠAMIʿ		UM		LU-ḪA-A-A-SA-MI-UM		UET V 569 17
		LU				ʿAD		UM		LU-ḪA-DU-UM		YOS XIII 497:2
		LU				ʿAN		UM		LU$_2$-A-NU-UM		U
		LU				KIʾL		A		LU$_2$-KI-LA		BASOR 95, 19
		LU				RAPIʾ				LU$_2$-RA-BI$_2$		I
		LU				RIʿAJ			HU	LU$_2$-RI-E$_2$-U$_2$		U
		LU				RIʿAJ			HU	LU$_2$-RI-ḪU		U
	2	ʾAḪ	UM			LI			JA	A-ḪU-UM-LI-A		M
		ʾAḪ	UM			LA						
						ʾAB		I		A-ḪU-UM-LA-A-BI		YOS XIII 245:17, SEAL
		ʾAJA				LA						
						ŠUM		U	HU	A-IA-LA-SU-MU-U$_2$		M, C
		JAʾ	UM			LU			HU	IA-UM-LU-ḪU		UET V 496:10
		ḪIʾD				LA			KA	ḪI-I[D]-LA-A?-KA		XII 141 8
		ḪIʾD				LA			KA			
						ʾIL		I		ḪI-ID-LA-KA-I$_3$-LI$_2$		M
		ḪIʾD				LA				ḪI-ID-L[A]-NAM		XIII 38 27
		ḪAʾAN	A			LA			HA	ḪA-A-NA-LA-A	FN	XIII 1 II 53+
		ʾAB	U			LA			JA	A-BU-LA-IA		XIII 101 6
		ʾIB	I			LA						
						ʾIL		UM		I-BI-LA-I$_3$-LUM		U
	JI	JBAL				LA						
						ʾIL				I-BA-AL-LA-DINGIR		RA LXV 47 VII 26
		ʾAK	UM			LA						
						ʾIL		A		A-KUM-LA-I-LA		RA LXV 55 XIII 1
		ʾEK	I			LA						
				ʾA		HWIJ				E-KI-LA-AḪ-WI		M
		ʾIL	A			LA						
						ʾIL				DINGIR-LA-IL		U
		ʾIL	A			LA			KA	I-LA-LA-KA		B 21+
		ḪAM	UM			LU			HU	D-A-MU-UM-LU-U$_2$		M
		ʿAMM	U			LA						
						RIWM				ḪA-MU-L[A]-RI-IM		RA LXV 46 VI 40
		JIŠʿ	I			LI						
						ʾEL				IŠ-ḪI-LI-EL		JCS XXIV 69 NO. 3 SEAL
		ʾAŠD	UM			LA						
						ʾAB		UM		AŠ-DU-UM-LA-A-BU-UM		SUMER V 142
		ʾAŠD	UM			LA						
						ʾAB		UM		AŠ$_2$-DU-UM-LA-A-BU-UM		SUMER V 142+
		ʿAŠTAR				LI			JA	EŠ$_4$-DAR-LI?-IA		YOS XIII 12 REV 14
		DAWD	UM			LU			HU	DA-DU-UM-LU-U$_2$		M
		ḎIMR	I			LU			HU	ZI-IM-RI-LU-U$_2$	FN	RA LXV 55 XIII 39
		ḎIMR	U			LA						
						ʾAB		I		ZI-IM-RU-LA-A-BI		RA LXV 42 III 7
		ḎARAʿ				LI						
						ʾIL				ZA-RA-AḪ?-LI-DINGIR		M
		KAʾB	I			LA						
						RIWM				KA-BI-LA-RI-IM		RA LXV 47 VI 65+; C+

ROOTS (Consonants only)

L	2 JA	KWIN			LU		HU	IA-KI-IN-LU-U_2		TALLQUIST APN 95 LATE
		LAWUJ			LA					
					HADD	A		LA-U_2-LA-A-DA		A.
		LAWUJ			LA					
					HADD	U		LA-WU-LA-D-IM		M+, C
		LAWUJ			LA					
					ʾIL			LA-WU-LA-DINGIR		M+
		LAMA			LA					
					ʾIL			LA-MA-LA-DINGIR		KAJ 72 18, LATE
		MA			LA		NA			
					DITAN	A		MA-A-LA-NA-DI-TA-NA		B 34
		MILK	I		LA					
					ʾEL			MI-IL-KI-LA-EL		TA 30 615 21
		MILK	I		LI					
					ʾEL			MI-IL-KI-LI-EL		B 34, M+
		MILK	I		LI					
					ʾEL			MIL-KI-LI-EL		VAS VIII 128 16+
		MILK	I		LI					
					ʾIL			MI-IL-KI-LI_2-IL		I
		MILK	I		LI					
					ʾIL			[MI]-EL-KI-LI-IL		I
		MILK	I		LI					
					ʾEL	UM		MI-IL-KI-LI-E-LUM		A 32065:3
		MILK	I		LU					
					ʾIL	A		MI-IL-KI-LU-I-LA		VAS XVI 10 5, 9
		MARUʾ			LI					
					ʾEL			MA-RU-LI-EL		SIMMONS 47 18, 49 22
	JI	NPIḪ			LI					
					DIJN	I		IB-BI-IḪ-LI-DI-NI	FN	C
		NIQM	I		LA					
					NAŠIʾ			NI-IQ-MI-LA-NA-SI		M
	JA	RŠAP			LA					
					ʾIL			IA-AR-SA-AP-LA-DINGIR		M+
	JA	RŠAP			LA					
					ʾIL	A		IA-AR-SA-AP-LA-I-[LA]?		M
	ʾA	ŠWUB			LA					
					ʾEL			A-ŠU-UB-LA-EL		TA 1931,765
	ʾA	ŠWUB			LA					
					ʾIL			A-ŠU-UB-LA-DINGIR		C+
	ʾA	ŠWUB			LI					
					ʾEL			A-ŠU-UB-LI-EL		OIP XLIII 154 NO. 48+
		ŠUWB		NA	LU		HU	ŠU-UB-NA-LU-U_2		M+
		ŚAM	U		LA					
					ʾIL			SA-MU-LA-DINGIR		B 39+
		ŚUM			LI					
				JI	JṢIʾ	IM		SU-UM-LI-ZI-IM	GEN	WATERMAN 25 R 9
		ŚUM	A		LA					
					LI		JA	SU-MA-LA-LI-A		BM 80363 1
		ŚUM	A		LI		KA	SU-MA-LI-KA		BM 80328 13
		ŚUM	U		LA		NI	SU-MU-LA-NI		HARRIS 39 11
		ŚUM	U		LA		NIA	SU-MU-LA-NI-A		CT XLVIII 10 1
		ŚUM	UM		LA					
					ʾAB	I		SU-MU-UM-LA-A-BI	FN	RA LXV 65 VII 24
		ŚUM	U		LA					
					ʾIL			SU-MU-LA-DINGIR		B 39+
		ŚUM	U		LA					
					ʾIL	I		SU-MU-LA-I_3-LI_2		UCP X/1 34 2
		ŚUM	U		LI					
					ʾEL			SU-MU-LI-EL		B 39+
		ŚUM	U		LA					
					ʾEL			SU-MU-LA-EL		SUMER XXIII 160 5
		ŚUM	U		LI					
					ʾEL			SU-MU-LI-EĹ-DU-RI		A 7630 3
		ŚUM	U		LI					
				JI	JṢIʾ			SU-MU-LI-ZI		MEISSNER 37 15+
		ŚIMAʿ			LA		NI	SI-MA-AḪ-LA-NI		SYRIA XLI 54 N. 1

L	2		ŠIMAʿ				LA	NI	SI-MA-AḪ-LA-A-NI		SYRIA XLI 54 N. 1
			ŠIMAʿ				LA	NI	SI-MA-AḪ-I-LA-A-NI		RA LXVI 112 MARI
			ŠIMAʿ				LA	NIE	SI-MA-AḪ-LA-NI-E		SYRIA XLI 54 N. 1+
			ŠIMAʿ				LA	NIE	SI-MA-AḪ-I-LA-A-NI-E		SYRIA XLI 54 N. 1
			ŠIMAʿ				LA	NIE	SU-MU-ḪA-LA-NI-E		SYRIA XLI 54 N. 1
			ŠIMAʿ				LA	NIE	SU-MU?-ḪI-LA-NI-E		SYRIA XLI 54 N. 1
			ŠIMAʿ				LA	NIE	SI-MA-AḪ-LA-A-NI-E		RA LXVI 115:21;117:11 MARI
			ŠIMAʿ				LA	NIE	SI-MA-AḪ-I-LA-NI-E		RA LXVI 112 MARI
			ŠIMAʿ				LA	NIE	SU-MA-AḪ-I-LA-A-NI-E		RA LXVI 120:7 MARI
			ṢIDQ		U		LA				
							NAŠIʾ		ZI-ID-KU-LA-NA-SI		M+
			TIʾM				LU	HU	TI-IM-LU-U_2	FN	XIII 1 VIII 73+
	3		ʾIL		I	JI	ḪTAʾ				
							LI	JA	I_3-LI_2-IḪ-TA-LI-A		BIROT,TEA 69 I 14
			LA			ʾA	HWIJ				
							LA	NA	LA-AḪ-WI-LA-NA		RA LXV 65 VII 19
			LA				RIWM				
							LU	HU	LA-RI-IM-LU-U_2		M
			ŠUM		A		LA				
							LI	JA	SU-MA-LA-LI-A		BM 80363 1
Lʾ	2	JI	GJIḪ				LUʾ				
							MA		I-GI-IḪ-LU-MA		SIMMONS 60 8, 14+
		JE	GJIḪ				LUʾ				
							MA		E-GI-IḪ-LU-MA		SUMER XXIII 192
		JI	GJIḪ				LUʾ				
							MA		I-GI-E-EḪ-LU-MA		JCS XXVI 143:21 HARMAL
Lʾʾ	1	JI	LʾAʾ				HADD	U	IL-A-D-IM		X 83 4, 7'
		JI	LʾAʾ				HADD	U	IL-A-DU		A. 78 20
		JA	LʾAʾ				KULIM		IA-AL-A-KU-LIM		RA LXV 55 XIII 18
		JI	LʾAʾ				....		IL-A-KUL_2-LAM?		VII 140:10
LʾJ	1	JA	LʾIJ						IA-AL-E		RA LXV 46 VI 50
		JA	LʾIJ			JA	JPAʿ		IA-AL-E-PA-AḪ		M
		JA	LʾIJ				DAGAN		IA-AL-E-D-DA-GAN		M+
		JA	LʾIJ				DAGAN		IA-[AL]?-I-D-DA-GAN		RA LXV 47 VII 23
		JI	LʾIJ				DAGAN		I-IL-ḪI-D-DA-G[AN]		M
		JE	LʾIJ				DAGAN		EL-I-D-DA-GAN		M
		JA	LEʾEJ						IA_3-LE-E		U
		JI	LEʾEJ				HADD	U	I-LE-E-D-IM		XIII 93 5
			LAʾIJ		UM				LA-I-JU-UM		M+
			LAʾIJ	T	UM				LA-I-TUM	FN	RA LXV 58 II 3
			LAʾIJ			JA			LA-I-IA		XIII 1 VII 70+
			LAʾJ			JA			LA-A-A		U+
	2		ʾIL		A		LAʾIJ		I-LA-LA-I		TA 1931,395,UR III
			ʾIL		A		LAʾIJ		I-LA-LA-E		TA 1931,609,UR III
			ʾIL		A		LAʾIJ		I-LA-LA-E-KI	GN	LAESSOE,SHEMSHARA P.77
			ʾIL		A		LAʾIJ		I-LA-LA-AḪ		RA LXV IX 38,X 10
			ʾANN		U	TA	LʾIJ		AN-NU-TA-AL-E	FN	M+
			ʿAŠTAR			TA	LʾIJ		$EŠ_4$-DAR-TA-AL-E	FN	XIII 1 V 41+
			MAM		A	TA	LʾIJ		D-MA-MA-TA-AL-E	FN	M
			BEʿL		I	TA	LEʾEJ		BE-LI_2-TA-LI-IḪ		RA LXV 50 VIII 44
LʾD	1		LIʾD		AJA				LI-DA-A-IA		M+
	2		KAKK		A		LIʾD	I	KA-AK-KA-LI-DI	FN	X 10 5
LʾL	1		LAʾL		UM				LA-LU-UM		HARRIS 76 22
			LAʾL		UM				LA-LUM		HARRIS 76 2
			LAʾL		I		ʾEL		LA-LI-E-EL		SIMMONS 70 15
			LIʾL		IM				LI-LI-IM	GEN	XIII 73 5
			LUʾL	AT	UM				LU-LA-TUM	MN	BM 16820 2, 11
	2		ʾAB		I		LUʾL	A	A-BI-LU-LA		SIMMONS 107 13
			BAʿL		U		LUʾL	I	BA-AḪ-LU-LU-L[I]?		HARRIS 71 14
			GAʾJ		I		LAʾL	UM	GA-I-LA-LUM		M
			KAWJ		A		LAʾL	UM	KA-A-LA-LUM		M
			KUʾM		U		LIʾL	U	KU-MU-LI-LU		CT IV 22A 14
			PAQAḪ		A		LAʾL	UM	BA-GA-A-LA-LUM		HARRIS 69 2+
			QIJŠ	T	I		LIʾL	IM	KI-IŠ-TI-LI-LIM	GEN	RA LXIV 34 NO.26
			ŠUM		U		LAʾL	UM	SU-MU-LA-LUM		PBS XI/2 1 I 16
			ŠUM		U		LIʾL	U	SU-MU-LI-LU		B 39

ROOTS (Consonants only)

LʾL	2		ṢIBʾ	I	LIʾL	UM	ZE$_2$-BI-LI-LUM	HSM 7900, UR III
LʾM	1	JA	LʾUM	U			IA-AL-U$_2$-MU	XIII 36 20
			LIʾM	A	HADD	U	LI-MA-A-DU	A.
			LIʾM	I	HADD	U	LI-MI-D-IM	M+
			LIʾM	I	HADD	U	LI-ME-D-IM	M+
	2		ʾAḪ	I	LIʾM		A-ḪI-LI-IM	B 12, M
			ʾAḪ	UM	LUʾM	U	A-ḪU-UM-LU-MU	X 166 4+
			ʾAḪ	U	LUʾM	U	A-ḪU-LU-MU	M
			ʾAJAN		LIʾM		A-AN-LI-IM	M+
		JA	JʿIL		LIʾM		IA-ḪI-IL-LI-IM	M
			ʾAB	I	LIʾM		A-BI-LI-IM	RA LXV 44 IV 60+
			ʾABB	I	LIʾM			
					MA		AB-BI-LIM-MA	A.+
		JI	JDAʿ		LIʾM			
					MA		I-DA-LIM-MA	B 21
			JADAʿ		LIʾM		IA-DAḪ-LI-IM	YOS XII
			JADAʿ		LIʾM		IA-ṬA$_3$-AḪ-LI-IM	YOS XII
			ʾADUN		LUʾM	U	ḪA-DU-UN-LU-MU	M
			ʾADUN		LUʾM	U	ḪA-DU-LU-MU	M
		JA	ʿDUN		LIʾM		IA-AḪ-DU-UN-LI-IM	M+
		JA	ʿDUN		LIʾM		IA-AḪ-DU-LI-IM	M+
		JA	ʿDUN		LIʾM		IA-AḪ-DU-UL-LI-IM	M
			ʾIL	I	LIʾM		I$_3$-LI$_2$-LI-IM	M+, C
			ʿAMM	U	LIʾM		ḪA-MU-LI-IM	RA LXV 52 X 22
		JA	JPAʿ		LIʾM		IA-A-PA-AḪ-LI-IM	M+
		JA	JPAʿ		LIʾM		IA-PA-AḪ-LI-IM	M+
			JIŠʿ	I	LIʾM		IŠ-ḪI-LI-IM	M
		JI	JŚAR		LIʾM		I-ŠAR-LI-IM	M+, C+, CT VI 47B 17
			JATAR		LIʾM		IA-TAR-LI-IM	M+
			ʾATT	I	LIʾM	A	AT-TI-LI-MA	A. LATE
			JATT	A	LIʾM		IA-AT-TA-LI-IM	ZA XXXVI 95, BJ 88 12
			BAʿD	I	LIʾM		BA-AḪ-DI-LI-IM	M+
			BIN	A	LIʾM		BI-NA-LI-IM	RA LXV 45 V 54
		JA	BRUQ		LIʾM		IA-AB-RU-UQ-LI-IM	TCL XI 156 12
		JA	DWUR		LIʾM		IA-DU-UR-LI-I[M]	RA LXV 45 V 82
			ḎIKR	I	LIʾM		ZI-IK-RI-LI-IM	M+
			ḎIMR	I	LIʾM		ZI-IM-RI-LI-IM	M+
		JA	GJID		LIʾM		IA-GI-ID-LI-IM	M+
		JI	GJID		LIʾM		I-GI-ID-LI-IM	B 21 HANA
		JA	KWUN		LIʾM		IA-KU-UN-LI-IM	M+
		JA	KWUN		LIʾM		IA-KU-LI-IM	M+
		JA	MWUT		LIʾM		IA-MU-UT-LI-IM	B 28+
		JA	MWUT		LIʾM	U	IA-MU-UT-LI-MU	TCL XI 182 10
		JA	NWUḪ		LIʾM		IA-NU-UḪ-LI-IM	RA LXV 44 V 8
		JA	NWUD		LIʾM		IA-NU-UD-LI-IM	M
			NUʿM	I	LIʾM		NU-UḪ-MI-LI-IM	M+
			NAWP		LIʾM			
					MA		NA-AP-LIM-MA	RA XLIV 122+ QATNA
		JI	NBIṬ		LIʾM		I-BI-IṬ-LI-IM	ANN. ARCH. SYR. XX 74:2
		JA	NQIM		LIʾM		IA-AK-KI-IM-LI-IM	M
		JA	NQIM		LIʾM		IA-KI-IM-LI-IM	M
		JA	NŚIʾ		LIʾM		IA$_2$-ŠI-LI-IM	U+
		JA	PḪUR		LIʾM		IA-AP-ḪU-UR-LI-IM	M+, A 7630
		JA	QWIM		LIʾM		IA-KI-IM-LI-IM	M+
			QARN	I	LIʾM		QAR-NI-LI-IM	M+
		JA	RWIM		LIʾM		IA-RI-IM-LI-IM	SIMMONS 66 77, M+, C+, A.+
			RIPʾ	I	LIʾM		RI-IP-I-LI-IM	M
		JA	ŠWUB		LIʾM		IA-ŠU-UB-LI-IM	M+
			ŚUMUK		LIʾM		SU-MU-UK-LI-IM	C P. 42+
			ŚAMŚ	I	LIʾM		SA-AM-SI-LI-IM	M
			ṢIBʾ	I	LIʾM		ZI-BI-LI-IM	M
			TIʾŠ		LUʾM	U	TI-IŠ-LU-MU	M
			ṬAḪD	I	LIʾM		TA-AḪ-DI-LI-IM	M
	3		ʾAḪ	I	KI			
					LIʾM		A-ḪI-KI-LI-IM	JEAN T.SIFR 72 5, 6, 13+
LʾN	1		LUʾUN	UM			LU-U$_2$-NU-UM	TOTTEN 26 UNPUBL.

ROOTS (Consonants only)

Lʾ P	1		LAʾIP	AH						LA-ḪI-PA	FN	XIII 1 II 65+
			LAʾIP	AN						LA-ḪI-PA-AN		M+
			LUʾUP		U					LU-U$_2$-PU		A.
			LUʾP		U		ʾEL			LU-BU-E-EL		I
	2		KIWN		I	Š	LUʾP	A		KI-NI-IŠ-LU-BA		EDZARD,DER 94:17;95:6
LʾR	1		LAʾR				MULUK			LA-AR-MU-LU-UK	FN	XIII 1 IX 33
			LAʾR				NAPŠ	U		LA-AR-NA-AP-SU	FN	XIII 1 I 71
			LAʾR		A		JARAḪ			LA-RA-D-SIN		KAJ 167 23+, LATE
			LIʾR	AT	UM					LI-RA-TUM	FN	A.
	2		BUN		U		LAʾR	A		BU-NU-LA-RA		B 16
LʾŠ	1		LAʾIŠ	T	UM					LA-ḪI-EŠ$_3$-TUM	FN	C
			LAʾUŠ		UM					LA-U$_2$-ŠUM		I
			LIʾŠ	AT	UM					LI-SA-TUM	MN?	TCL X 38 6
LʾT	1		LAʾAT	AN						LA-ḪA-TA-AN		RA LXV 51 IX 68
			LAʾT		I		RAWM	E	JE	LA-TI-RA-ME-E		M
LḪM	1		LAḪM	ATANUM						LA-AḪ-MA-TA-NU-UM		SIMMONS 89 10
LḪN	1		LAḪAN		UM					LA-ḪA-NU-UM		M+
			LAḪAN		I		KIWN	IM		LA-ḪA-NI-KI-IN-IM	GEN	UCP X/3 2 5
			LAḪN		UM					LA-AḪ?-NU-UM		M
LWJ	1		LAWUJ		UM					LA-U$_2$-UM		M+
			LAWUJ		IM					LA-I-IM	GEN	M+
			LAWUJ		EM					LA-E-EM	ACC	M+
			LAWUJ				HADD	U		LA-WU-D-IM		M+
			LAWUJ				HADD	U		LA-U$_2$-D-IM		A.
			LAWUJ				ʾIL			LA-WU-DINGIR		M
			LAWUJ				LA					
							HADD	A		LA-U$_2$-LA-A-DA		A.
			LAWUJ				LA					
							HADD	U		LA-WU-LA-D-IM		M+, C
			LAWUJ				LA					
							ʾIL			LA-WU-LA-DINGIR		M+
			LIWJ		UM					LI-I-UM		TA 1931, 538
			LIWJ		UM					LI-U$_2$-UM		M
			LIWJ		I		DAGAN			LI-I-D-DA-GAN		M
LBW	1		LABW		A		BIḪR	I	Š	LA-BA-BI$_2$-RI-IŠ		HSM 7936, UR III
			LABW		I		ŠAM	A		LA-BI-SA-MA		UCP X/3 P. 199+
	2		ʾAM	T			LABW	A		AM-TI-LA-BA	MN	TIM III 7 5
			ʿAMM		U		LABW	A		ḪA-AM-MU-LA-BA-A		XIV 114:6
			LA				LABW	UM		LA-LA-BU-[UM]?		M
		JI	NDIN				LABW	A		I-DIN-D-LA-BA		M
			ŠADW		U		LABW	A		ŠA-DU-LA-BA		M
			ŠADW		UM		LABW	A		ŠA-DU-UN-LA-BA		M+
			ŠADW		UM		LABW	A		ŠA-DU-UM-LA-BA		M
			ŠADW		UM		LABW	A		ŠA-DU-UM-LA-BU-A		M
			ŠADW		UM		LABW	I		ŠA-DU-UM-LA-BI		M
			ŠUM		U		LABW	A		SU-MU-LA-BA		M
LBB	2	JI	NWUḪ				LIBB	I		I-NU-UḪ-LI-BI		M
LBN	1		LABAN							LA-BA-AN		RA LXV 41 II 32
			LABAN		A		ʾIL	A		LA-PA-NA-I-LA		ZA XXXVIII 267
			LABIN		A					LA-AB-BI-NA		A.+
			LABN		UM					LA-AB-NU-UM		TA 1930, 221
	2		ʾAḪ		I		LABAN			A-ḪI-LA-BA-AN		RA LXV 43 IV 5+
LGG	1		LAGIG		UM					LA-GI-GU-UM		UET V 719 2
LKŠ	1		LAKIŠ		UM					LA-KI-SU-[U]M		UET V 685 28
LLʾ	1		LALAʾ		IM					LA-LA-I-IM	GEN	XIII 85 5
			LALAʾ	AN	UM					LA-LA-A-NU-UM		UCP X/3 2 27
			LALAʾ	AT	UM					LA-LA-A-TUM	FN	M
			LALAʾ	AT	UM					LA-LA-ḪA-TUM	FN	TCL XVIII 121 9
LLR	1		LILAR		U					LI-LA-RU		SIMMONS 30 10
			LILUR		I					LI-LU-RI	FN	RA LXV 62 IV 66
LM	1		LAMA				ʾADAʾ	E		LA-MA-A-DA-E	FN	A.
			LAMA				ʾADAʾ	E		LA-MA-TA-E	FN	A.+
			LAMA				ʾIL			LA-MA-DINGIR		B 33+, M+
			LAMA				ʾIL	A		LA-MA-I-LA		YOS XIII 244:2+
			LAMA				DUWD	U		LA-MA-DU-DU		M
			LAMA				LA					
							ʾIL			LA-MA-LA-DINGIR		KAJ 72 18, LATE

ROOTS (Consonants only)

LM	2	ʾAB		I		LAMA				A-BI-LA-MA		B 10
		ʾAK		I		LAMA				A-KI-LA-MA		B 12
		ʾALI				LAMA				A-LI$_2$-LA-MA		SIMMONS 118 17+
LMM	1	LAMUM	AN	UM						LA-MU-MA-NU-UM		I; TA 1931,148
		LUMM	AN	UM						LU-MA-NU-UM		SIMMONS 94 12+
		LUMM	AN	UM						LU-MA-A-NU-UM		SIMMONS 103 5
		LUMM	AN	UM						LUM-MA-NU-UM		SIMMONS 96 11+
		LUMM	AN	UM						LUM-MA-A-NU-UM		SIMMONS 105 16+
		LUMM		A		ʾIL				LUM-MA-IL		M+
		LUMM		A		ʾIL				LUM-MA-DINGIR		KISURRA 100 7+
		LUMM		A		ʾIL				LU-MA-DINGIR		KISURRA 104 29+
	2	ʾAŠD		I		LUMM		A		AŠ-DI-LU-MA		UCP X/3 2 31
		ŠUM		I		LAMM		U		SU-MI-LAM-MU		VAS XVI 24 4, A.+
LMR	1	LAMR	AT	UM						LA-AM-RA-TUM	FN	YOS XIII 294:18
LMS	1	LAMAS		I						LA-MA-ZI	GEN	IV 68 18, 20, 21
		LAMAS	AT	UM						[LA]-MA-ZA-TUM	FN	XIII 1 XIV 6
		LAMAS	AH							LA-MA-ZA	FN	M
	2	ʾANN		U		LAMAS		I		AN-NU-LA-MA-ZI	FN	M+
		ʾANN		U		LAMAS		I		AN-NU-D-LAMA	FN	XIII 1 VII 8+
		ʾANN		U		LAMAS	IT	UM		AN-NU-LA-MA-ZI-TUM	FN	RA LXV 59 II 13
		ʾIŠḪAR	AH			LAMAS		I		D-IŠ-ḪA-RA-D-LAMA	FN	XIII 1 IX 23
		ʿAŠTAR				LAMAS		I		EŠ$_4$-DAR-LA-MA-ZI	FN	M
		ʿAŠTAR				LAMAS		I		EŠ$_4$-DAR-D-LAMA	FN	XIII 1 I 69+
LND	1	LAND		U						LA-AN-TU		TA 1931, 148
		LAND	AN							LA-AN-DA-AN		C
LSM	1	LASIM		A						LA-ZI-MA	NOM	BIN VII 31 6
		LASIM				ʿAN		UM		LA-ZE$_2$-IM-A-NU-UM		FLP 590:6, U
		LASIM				ʿAN		UM		LA-ZI-MA-NU-UM		MVN III 338:17, U
LŠ	1	LAŠU				ʾEL						
						KA				LA-ŠI-EL-KA-A-BI-IM		B 33
		LAŠU				ʾIL				LA-ŠU-IL		U
		LAŠU				MIQIṬ				LA-ŠU-MI-GI-IT		B 33
		LAŠU				MIQIṬ				LA-ŠU-MI-KI-IT		B 33
LŠG	1	LAŠG	AN							LA$_2$-AŠ$_2$-GA-AN		RA XXXIV 176
LŠK	1	LAŠIK		U						LA-ŠI-KU	FN	EDZARD,DER 91:17
LṬP	1	LAṬUP		UM						LA-TU-BU-UM		TA 1931,327
		LAṬUP		UM						LA-DU-BU-UM		TA 31, 297
M	1	MA				LA			NA			
						DITAN		A		MA-A-LA-NA-DI-TA-NA		B 34
		MA				RAʾŠ		UM		MA-A-RA-SU-UM		M
	2	ʾAḪ		UM		MA						
						ʾIL				A-ḪU-UM-MA-DINGIR		M+
		ʾAḪ	AT	I		MA				A-ḪA-TI-MA	FN	JCS XXVII 135:1
		ʾAJA				MA						
						ʾIL				A-IA-MA-DINGIR		M
		ʾAJA				MA						
						ʾIL				ḪA-IA$_3$-MA-DINGIR		XIV 93:8+
		ʾAJA				MA						
						ʾEL				A-IA-MA-EL		RA LXV 42 III 14
		ḪAʾL		I		MA				ḪA-LI-MA	FN	RA LXV 59 II 43
		ḪAʾL		I		MA						
						ʾIL				ḪA-LI$_2$-MA-DINGIR		M
		ḪAʾL		U	Š	MI						
						ʾIL				ḪA-LU-UŠ-MI-DINGIR		M
		ʾAB		I		MA						
						ʾIL		I		A-BI-MA-I$_3$-LI$_2$	FN	RA LXV 64 VI 32
		ʾAB		I		MI						
						KI				A-BI-MI-KI-DINGIR		M
		ʿABD				MA						
						DAGAN				AB-DU-MA-D-DA-GAN		M+
		ʿABD				MA						
						DAGAN				ḪA-AB-DU-MA-D-DA-GAN		M+
	ʾU	WDAJ				MA				U$_2$-DA-MA		I
		ʿADN		U		MA						
						JATAR				ḪA-AD-NU-ME-TAR		M+
		ʾIL		A		MA						
						ʾAB		I		DINGIR-MA-A-BI		M

ROOTS (Consonants only)

M	2	ʾIL	A		MA					
					ʾIL	A		DINGIR-MA-I$_3$-LA		B 21+
		ʾIL	A		MA					
					ʾIL	A		DINGIR-MA-D-I-LA		B 21
		ʾIL	I		MA					
					ʾAB	I		I$_3$-LI-MA-A-BI		M+
		ʾANA			MA					
					ʾIL			A-NA-MA-DINGIR		A 29366:9
		ʾIRŠ			MA					
					ʾAB	I		I-RI-IŠ-MA-A-BI		A.
		ʾIRŠ			MA					
					ʾAB	I		I-RI-IŠ-MA-BI		A.
		ʾIRŠ	U		MA					
					ʾAB	I		IR-ŠU-MA-BI		A.
		JATAM			MA					
					ʾIL			IA-TAM-MA-DINGIR		UET V 172 5'
		BAʿL	A		MI					
					NAMḪ	U		BA-LA-MI-NA-AM-ḪU		SYRIA XLIV 201 N.1 MARI
		BAʿL	U		ME					
					NUMḪ	I		BA-LU-ME-NU-ḪI		M+
		BAʿL	U		ME					
					NUMḪ	I		BA-LU-ME-NU-UM-ḪI		IX 41 2
		BILAL	A		MA			BI-LA-LA-MA		OIP XLIII 135+
		BIN			MA					
					ʾAḪ	IM		BI-IN-MA-A-ḪI-IM		M
		BIN			MA					
					ʾIL			BI-MA-DINGIR		C+
		BIN	I		MA			BI-NI-MA		A. LATE
		BIN	I		MA					
					....			BI-NI-MA-D-....		UET V 713 7
		BIN	I		MA					
					ʾAḪ	UM		BI-IN-NI-MA-ḪU-UM		TLB I 3 28
		BIN	I		MA					
					ʾAḪ	UM		BI-NI-MA-ḪU-UM		CCT IV 13A 6+ CAPP.
		BIN	I		MA					
					ʾIL			BI-NI-MA-DINGIR		A. LATE
		BIN	I		MA					
					BIʿD	I	JE	BI-NI-MA-BI-DI-E		EK I 40
		BIN	U		MA					
					HADD	U		BI-NU-MA-D-IM		4E RENCONTRE 21 NO. 25
		BUN	A		MA					
					ʾIL			BU-NA-MA-DINGIR		XII 1 X 36
		BUN	I		MA					
					ʾAḪ	UM		BU-NI-MA-ḪU-UM		TCL XX 96 8
		BUN	U		MA					
					ʾAḪ	UM		BU-NU-MA-A-ḪU-UM		B 16
		BUN	U		MA					
					HADD	U		BU-NU-MA-D-IM		M+
		BUN	U		MA					
					ʾIL			BU-NU-MA-DINGIR		M
		BUN	U		MA					
					ʾAŠAR			BU-NU-MA-A-ŠA-AR		KISURRA 93 4
		BUN	U		MA					
					ʾAŠAR			BU-NU-MA-ŠAR		B 16+
		BUN	UM		MA					
					ŠARR			BU-NU-UM-MA-ŠAR		B 16
		BANIJ			ME					
					ʾEL			BA-NI-ME-EL		HARRIS 12 15
		DAWD	I	Š	ME					
					ʾEL			DA-DI-EŠ$_3$-ME-EL		UCP X/3 P. 198+
		DAWD	U		MA			DA-DU-MA		HARRIS 49 5
		DUWD	U	Š	ME					
					ʾEL			DU-DU-UŠ-ME-EL		UCP X/3 P. 198+
		DANN	I	Š	ME					
					ʾIL			DA-NI-IŠ-ME-DINGIR?		I
		DARK	I		MA			DAR-KI-MA	FN	RA LXV 61 IV 14

ROOTS (Consonants only)

M	2	ḎU			MA				
					ʾAB	I	ZU-U$_2$-MA-A-BI		XIV 77:17
		ḎU			MA				
					ʾAB	I	ZU-U$_2$-MA?-A-BI		M
		KANN	A		MA				
					ʾIL		KA-AN-NA-MA-DINGIR		M
		KUNN	A		MA		[K]U-UN-NA-MA		XIV 101:8
		LA		K	MA				
					ʾIL		LA-AK-MA-AN		B 33
		MILK	U		MA		MI-IL-KU-MA		JCS XIII 51 292 R 10,A.LATE
		MILK	U		MA				
					ʾIL		MI-IL-KU-MA-IL		B 35+
		MILK	U		MA				
					ʾIL		MI-IL-KU-MA-DINGIR		C+
		MILK	UM		MA				
					ʾIL		MIL-KUM-MA-DINGIR		A. LATE
		MUT	I		ME				
					ʾEL		MU-TI-ME-EL		TA 30, 615:4+
		MUT	U		ME				
					ʾEL		MU-TU-ME-EL		CT VIII 31A 25+
		MUT	UM		MA				
					ʾEL		MU-TUM-MA-EL		TA 1931, 456
		MUT	UM		ME				
					ʾEL		MU-TUM-ME-EL		RUTTEN 32 8+
		NANIB	U		MA		NA-NI-BU-MA		SIMMONS 138 4+
		PU			MA				
					ʾEL		PU-MA-[E]L		TA 1931,538 I
		PU			ME				
					ʾIL		PU-ME-IL		I
		PAʾAR			MI		PA-ḪA-AR-MI	FN	RA LXV 59 II 23
		QAWM	U		MA				
					ʾAḪ	UM	QA-MU-MA-A-ḪU-UM		M
		QAWM	U		MA				
					ʾAḪ	I	QA-MU-MA-A-ḪI		RA LXV 41 II 22
		QAWM	U		MA				
					ʾIL		QA-MU-MA-DINGIR		M
		RAPIʾ			MI				
					ʾIL		RA-BI-MI-IL		BIROT,TEA 72 VI 19
		RAPIʾ			MI				
					ʾIL	UM	RA-BI-MI-LUM		BIROT,TEA 72 IX 29
		ŠADW	I		MA				
					ʾIL		ŠA-DI-MA-DINGIR		RA LXV 48 VIII 20
		ŚADL	U		MA		SA-AD-LU-MA		UCP X/1 P. 61+
		ŚAM	A		ME				
					ʾEL		SA-MA-ME-EL		M
		ŚAM	A		ME				
					ʾEL		ŠA-MA-ME-EL		TA 1931, 421
		ŚAM	I		MA				
				JA	ŚJIM		SA-MI-MA-IA-SI-IM	FN	C+
		ŚAM	I		ME				
					ʾEL		SA-MI-ME-EL		CT XLV 117 33
		ŚUM	U		ME				
					ʾEL		SU-MU-ME-EL		JCS IV 107, YBC 4968
		TIBIʾ	A	Š	ME				
					ʾEL		TI-BI$_2$-AŠ$_2$-ME-EL		CT XXXIII 48A 4
		ZUQAT	UM		MA		ZU-KA-TUM-MA		EDZARD,DER 152 REV. 11
	3	ʾABB	I		LIʾM				
					MA		AB-BI-LIM-MA		A.+
	JI	JDAʿ			LIʾM				
					MA		I-DA-LIM-MA		B 21
		ʿADN	I		ʾIL	U			
					MA		ḪA-AD-NI-DINGIR-MA		M
		ʿAMM	I	TA	QWUM				
					MA		AM-MI-TA-KU-UM-MA		A. +
		ʾANA			ʾIL	I			
					MA		A-NA-I-LIM-MA		A.

ROOTS (Consonants only)

M	3		ʾANAKU			ʾIL	AM					
						MA		A-NA-KU-DINGIR-LAM-MA			XIII 1 II 29	
			ʾANAKU			ʾIL	A					
						MA		A-NA-KU-I-LA-MA			SIMMONS 46 7+	
			JIŠʿ		I	ʾIL	A					
						MA		IŠ-ḪI-DINGIR-MA			M	
			JIŠʿ		I	ʾIL	A					
						MA		IŠ-ḪI-DINGIR-LA-MA			M	
			JIŠʿ		I	ʾIL	U					
						MA		IŠ-ḪI-LU-MA			YOS VIII 176 20	
		JI	JṢIʾ			ʾIL	U					
						MA		I-ZI-I-LU-MA			B 23+	
			ḎIMR		I	ʾIL	U					
						MA		ZI-IM-RI-DINGIR-MA			M	
			ḎIMR		I	ʾIL	U					
						MA		ZI-IM-RI-I-LU-MA			M	
			ḎIMR		I	ʾIL	U					
						MA		ZI-IM-RI-LU-MA			SIMMONS 67 12	
		JI	GJIḪ			LUʾ						
						MA		I-GI-IḪ-LU-MA			SIMMONS 60 8, 14+	
		JE	GJIḪ			LUʾ						
						MA		E-GI-IḪ-LU-MA			SUMER XXIII 192	
		JI	GJIḪ			LUʾ						
						MA		I-GI-E-EḪ-LU-MA			JCS XXVI 143:21 HARMAL	
			KAHAL		I	ʾIL	U					
						MA		KA-A-LI-I-LU-MA			XIV 62:4+	
			KAHAL		I	ʾIL	U					
						MA		KA-A-LI-DINGIR-MA			M+	
			MUT			ḪAʾL	I					
						MA		MU-UT-ḪA-LI-MA			M	
			NAWP			LIʾM						
						MA		NA-AP-LIM-MA			RA XLIV 122+	QATNA
Mʾ	2		DINIK			MUʾ	UM	DI-NI-IK-MU-UM			SIMMONS 39 3+	
			NANN		A	MUʾ	UM	NA-AN-NA-MU-UM			M	
MʾJ	1		MAʾJ	AT	UM			MA-IA-TUM	FN		B 34+	
	2		ʾAḪ		I	MAʾJ	UM	A-ḪI-MA-IU-UM			MAM III P. 274	
			ḪANN		A	MAʾJ	A	AN-NA-MA-A-A			RUTTEN 14 15	
MʾD	1	JA	MʾID			ʾADM	I	IA-AM-I-ID-D-AD-MI			A. 60 4	
			MAʾD	AN	UM			MA-AḪ-DA-NU-UM			I	
			MAʾD		IJA			MA-DI-IA			RA LXV 55 XIII 49	
			MAʾD		I	JAM	A	MA-DI-IA-MA			UCP X/1 33 10	
			MAʾD		I	JAT	UM	MA-DI-IA-TUM			UCP X/1 P. 59+	
			MIʾD	AN	UM			MI-DA-NU-UM			U+	
		JA	MʾAD					IA-AM-ḪA-AD-KI	GN		M+	
		JA	MʾAD					IA-AM-A-AD	GN		A. 377 8	
		JA	MʾAD		U			IA-AM-ḪA-DU	GN		XII 747 4	
		JA	MʾAD		U			IA$_3$-A-MA-TU			U	
		JA	MʾAD		UM			IA-AM-ḪA-DU-UM-KI	GN		M+	
		JA	MʾAD		I			IA$_3$-A-MA-TI			U	
		JA	MʾAD		IM			IA-AM-ḪA-DI-IM-KI	GN	GEN	M+	
		JA	MʾAD	AJ	I			IA-AM-ḪA-DA-I-KI	GN	GEN	M	
		JA	MʾAD	IJ	I			IA-AM-ḪA-DI-I-KI	GN	NOM	M	
		JA	MʾAD	IJ	I			IA-AM-ḪA-DI-JI	GN	NOM	M	
		JA	MʾAD	IJ	UM			IA$_3$-A-MA-TI-UM			U	
	2		ʾIL		A	MAʾD	I	DINGIR-MA-DI			M	
			ʾIL		I	MAʾD	A	I$_3$-LI$_2$-MA-DA			TA 30 615 6	
			ʾIL		I	MAʾD	I	I$_3$-LI$_2$-MA-DI			SIMMONS 33 19	
			ʾIL		I	MAʾD	I					
						ʾAḪ		I$_3$-LI$_2$-MA-DI-A-AḪ			RUTTEN 1 8	
			ʾIL		I	MAʾD	I					
						ʾAḪ		DINGIR?-MA-DA-AḪ			RA LXV 42 III 21	
			ʾIL		I	MAʾD	I					
						ʾAḪ		I$_3$-LI$_2$-MI-DI-AḪ			EDZARD, DER 146:14	
			ʾIL		I	MAʾD	I					
						ʾAḪ	I	I$_3$-LI$_2$-MA-DA-ḪI			RUTTEN 14 7	
			ʾIL		I	MAʾD	I					
						ʾAḪ	A	I$_3$-LI$_2$-MA-DA-ḪA			VAS VIII 14 4	

Mʾ K	2		ʾAŠD		I		MAʾK	U	HU	AŠ$_2$-DI-MA-KU-U$_2$		VAS IX 172 30
			MUT		I		MAʾK	U	HU	MU-TI-MA-KU-U$_2$		M+
Mʾ L	1		MAʾL		IJA					MA-LI-IA		M
			MAʾL		I		ḪARAB	A		MA-LI-A-RA-BA?		CT II 30 29
			MAʾL		I		ŠUM	U	HU	MA-LI-SU-MU-U$_2$		TIM I 29 10
Mʾ M	1		MAʾM	AT	UM					MA-MA-TUM		CT XLV 96 18
			MAʾM		IJA					MA-MI-IA		M
			MEʾM	AT	UM					ME-MA-TUM	FN	BASOR 95, 21 I 21
Mʾ N	1		MAʾAN		UM					MA-A-NU-UM		KISURRA 22A 17+
			MAʾAN		UM					MA-ḪA-NU-UM		SIMMONS 96 15; M
			MAʾAN		IM					MA-ḪA-NIM	GEN	BM 72766
			MAʾAN		IJA					MA-ḪA-NI-IA	FN	M+
			MAʾN	AN	UM					MA-AḪ-NA-NU-UM		HILPRECHT AV P. 91
			MEʾN		I		ʾEL			ME-NI-EL		RA LXV 52 X 18
	2		ʾANN		U		MAʾN	A		AN?-NU-MA-NA	FN	M
			KIʾL		U		MAʾN	A		KI-LU-MA-NA	FN	RA LXV 56 I 9
Mʾ R	1		MAʾR	AT	UM					MA-RA-TUM	MN?	TIM I 14 3
			MAʾR	AT	IJA					MA-RA-TI-IA		HARRIS 99 13
			MAʾR	IT	UM					MA-RI-TUM	FN	XIII 1 XIII 14
			MAʾR		IJAN					MA-RI-IA-AN		RA LXV 43 III 81
			MAʾR		A		ʾEL			MA-RA-EL		TA 1931, 298
			MAʾR		A		ʾEL			URU-MA-RA-EL	GN	MRS VI 11830:10
			MAʾR		A		ʾEL			URU-MA-RA-DINGIR	GN	MRS IX 17340:7
			MAʾR		U		ZAʾT	U	HU	MA-RU-ZA-TU-U$_2$		CT XLVIII 27
	2		ʾIL		A		MEʾR			DINGIR-ME-IR		JNES XIII 210+ LATE
			ʾATT		I		MEʾR			AT?-TI-ME-IR?		IX 234 10
		JA	KWUN				MEʾR			IA-KU-UN-ME-IR		M+
		JA	MWUT				MIʾR	UM		IA-MU-UT-MI-RUM		RA LXV 52 X 41
			MUT				MIʾR	UM		MU-UT-MI-RUM?		EDZARD, DER 89:4
			MUT		U		MEʾR			MU-TU-ME-ER		M
			NIWR				MEʾR			NI-WA-AR-ME-ER		M
			NUWR				MEʾR			NU-UR-ME-ER		M
		JI	NDIN				MEʾR			I-DIN-D-ME-ER		MAOG IV 2 2 HANA
		JA	TWUR				MEʾR			D-IA-TU-[U]R-ME-I[R]	DN	M
		JI	TWUR				MEʾR			D-I-DUR-ME-IR	DN	M+
	3		ḪANN		A	JI	TWUR					
							MEʾR			ḪA-AN-NA-D-I-DUR-ME-ER		M
			ʾIPQ		U	JI	TWUR					
							MEʾR			IP-KU-D-I-DUR-ME-ER		M
		JI	NDIN			JI	TWUR					
							MEʾR			I-DIN-D-I-DUR-ME-ER		XIII 1 III 49+
Mʾ Š	1		MAʾŠ		UM					MA-ŠUM		M+
			MAʾŠ		IM					MA-ŠI-IM	GEN	M+
			MAʾŠ		AM					MA-ŠA-AM	ACC	M+
			MAʾŠ		IJA					MA-ŠI-IA		M+
			MAʾŠ	AN	IM					MA-SA-NIM	GEN	CT XLV 93 6
			MIʾŠ		AJA					MI-ŠA-IA		M+
Mʾ T	1		MAʾT	AT	UM					MA-TA-TUM	FN	CT II 50 6, 18
			MAʾT	AT	UM					MA-TA-TUM	MN?	LIH 29 9
			MAʾT	AT	IM					MA-TA-TIM	MN? GEN	VAS XVI 118 2
			MAʾT		U		BANIJ			MA-TU-BA-NI		KISURRA 112 6
			MUʾUT		IJA					MU-U$_2$-TI-IA	FN	XIII 1 VII 48
	2		ʾAHL		UM		MAʾT	U		[A-LU]-UM-MA-[TU]	FN	M
			ʾAHL		UM		MAʾT	UM		[A-LU-UM]-MA-TUM	FN	M
			ʾAKK	AT			MAʾT	I		AK-KA-AD-MA-TI	FN	A. 409 22
		JA	ḪNUN				MAʾT	UM		IA-UN-MA-TUM	FN	RA L 63
			ʾIRR		I		MAʾT	U		I-RI-MA-TU		A.
			BEʿL	T	I		MAʾT	I		BE-EL-TI-MA-TI	FN	A. 253 6
			DANN		U		MAʾT	UM		DA-NU-MA-TUM		CT XLV 12:24
		TA	KWUN				MAʾT	UM		TA-KU-UN-MA-TUM	FN	M, C+
		TA	KWUN				MAʾT	I		TA-KUM-MA-TI	FN	A.+
			KIWN		I	Š	MAʾT	UM		KI-NI-IŠ-MA-TUM	FN	M+;C
			KUWN		A		MAʾT	UM		KU-NA-MA-TUM		U
		TA	RʿIŠ				MAʾT	UM		TA-RI-IŠ-MA-TUM	FN	M+, C
			ŠI				MAʾT	UM		ŠI-I-MA-TUM	FN	C+
		TA	TWUR				MAʾT	UM		TA-TU-UR-MA-TUM	FN	M+; C+

ROOTS (Consonants only)

MʾT	2	TA	TWUR				MAʾT		UM	TA-DUR-MA-TUM	FN		XIII 1 XIV 34+
MʾZ	1		MAʾZ	AT	UM					MA-ZA-TUM	FN		KISURRA 21 3, M
			MAʾZ	AN	UM					MA-ZA-NU-UM			UET V 625 9
			MAʾZ	AN	I					MA-ZA-NI			KISURRA 68A 10+
			MUʾZ		UM					MU-ZU-[U]M			RA LXV 51 IX 40
			MUʾZ	AN	I					MU-ZA-NI			KISURRA 1A 3+; M
MHR	1		MAHIR	AH						MA-ḪI-RA	FN		XIII 1 VII 34
			MAHIR	AN	IM					MA-ḪI-RA-NIM	GEN		C II 2 8
			MAHR	AN	UM					[M]A-AḪ-RA-NU-UM			U
			MIHR		I		....			ME-EḪ-RI-[....]			M
			MIHR		I		HADD		U	ME-EḪ-RI-D-IM			C+
			MUHR	AN	UM					MU-RA-NU-UM			U
			MUHR	AT	UM					MU-UḪ-RA-TUM			BIROT, TEA 72 I 49'+
			MUHR		U		DAGAN			MU-RU-D-DA-GAN			RA LXV 53 XI 53
	2	JA	ŠJIM				MAHAR			IA-SI-IM-MA-ḪA-AR			M
MWʾ	1	JA	MWUʾ		A					IA-MU-U$_2$-A			KISURRA 33 3
			MUWIʾ		UM					MU-E-UM			U (MLC 80)
MWŠ	1	JA	MWUŠ		I		ʾIL			IA-MU-ŠI-DINGIR			B 28
		JA	MWUŠ		I		ʾIL			IA-A-MU-ŠI-DINGIR			VAS VII 166 4 LATE
MWT	1	ʾA	MWUT				PA						
							ʾIL			A-MU-UT-PA-DINGIR			SYRIA L 7
		ʾA	MWUT				PA						
							ʾIL			AM-MU-UT-PA-DINGIR			RA XLIII 212 39 QATNA
		ʾA	MWUT				PI						
							ʾIL			A-MU-UT-BI-DINGIR			M+
		ʾA	MWUT				PI						
							ʾIL		A	A-MU-UT-BI-I-LA			M
		JA	MWUT		UM					IA$_3$-A-MU-TUM			U
		JA	MWUT				ḪAMAD			IA-MU-UT-ḪA-MA-AD			X 174 18
		JA	MWUT				ḪAMAD		I	IA-MU-UT-ḪA-MA-DI	FN		XIII 1 VI 51
		JA	MWUT				BAʿL			IA-MU-UT-BA-AL	GN		M+
		JA	MWUT				BAʿL		UM	IA-MU-UT-BA-LUM-KI	GN		B 28+
		JA	MWUT				BAʿL		UM	IA-MU-UT-BA-A-LUM-KI	GN		RLA II 194
		JA	MWUT				BAʿL		IM	IA-MU-UT-BA-LI-IM	GN	GEN	YOS II 49 12+
		JA	MWUT				BAʿL		IM	IA-MU-UT-BA-LIM	GN	GEN	BAGHD. MITT. II 56+
		JA	MWUT				BAʿL	AJ	I	IA-MU-UT-BA-LA-I	GN	NOM	M
		JA	MWUT				BAʿL	AJ	I	IA-MU-UT-BA-LA-JI	GN	NOM	M
		JA	MWUT				BAʿL	IJ	I	IA-MU-UT-BA-LI-I	GN	ACC	M
		JE	MWUT				BAʿL		A	E-MU-UT-BA-LA	GN	GEN	SAKI P. 212+
		JE	MWUT				BAʿL		UM	E-MU-UT-BA-LUM-KI	GN		B 28+
		JE	MWUT				BAʿL		UM	E-MU-UT-BA-A-LUM-KI	GN		RLA II 180
		JE	MWUT				BAʿL		UM	IE-E-MU-UT-BA-LUM-KI	GN		SZLECHTER TJ 16 165
		JE	MWUT				BAʿL		IM	E-MU-UT-BA-LI-IM	GN	GEN	KING 34 6+
		JA	MWUT				DAWD		U	IA-MU-UT-DA-DU			RA LXV 51 X 11
		JA	MWUT				DIWR		UM	IA-MU-UT-DI-RUM			WATERMAN 14 9
		JA	MWUT				KULUP			IA-MU-UT-KU-LU-UP			DELAPORTE, CCL II A 418
		JA	MWUT				LIʾM			IA-MU-UT-LI-IM			B 28+
		JA	MWUT				LIʾM		U	IA-MU-UT-LI-MU			TCL XI 182 10
		JA	MWUT				MIʾR		UM	IA-MU-UT-MI-RUM			RA LXV 52 X 41
		JA	MWUT				NIWR		I	IA-MU-UT-NI-RI	FN		A.
	2		ʾAB		I	JA	MWUT		A	A-BI-IA-MU-TA			BM 80328 15
			ʾAB		I	JA	MWUT		I	A-BI$_2$-A-MU-TI			U
			ʾIL		I	JA	MWUT			I$_3$-LI$_2$-IA-MU-[UT]			RA LXV 40 I 29
			ʾIL		I		MIWT		I	I$_3$-LI$_2$-MI-TI			I
		JI	PTIḪ			JA	MWUT		A	IP-TI-IA-MU-TA			BM 80328 11
			ŠUM		U	JA	MWUT						
							BAʿL		A	SU-MU-IA-MU-UT-BA-[LA]			RUTTEN 3 21
			ŠUM		U	JE	MWUT						
							BAʿL		A	SU-MU-E-MU-UT-BA-LA	NOM		JCS IV 66 22
			ŠUM		U	JE	MWUT						
							BAʿL		A	SU-MU-E-MU-UT-BA-LA	GEN		JCS IV 69 17
			ŠUM		U	JE	MWUT						
							BAʿL		IM	SU-MU-E-MU-UT-BA-LIM?	GEN		JCS IV 71 9
			ŠUM		U	JA	MWUT						
							BAʿL		IM	SU-MU-IA-MU-UT-BA-LIM	GEN		CT XLIII 86 1
			ŠUM		U	JA	MWUT		U				
							BAʿL		A	[SU]-MU-IA-MU-TU-BA-LA			PBS XI/2 1 I 19

ROOTS (Consonants only)

MWT	2	TUPT		I	JA	MWUT	A		TU-UP-TI-IA-MU-TA		BM 80328 2
	3	LA				ʿADN	A				
					ʾA	MWUT			LA-ḪA-AD-NA-A-MU-UT		M
MJ	1	MIJA				MUT	A		ME-IA-MU-TA		B 34
		MIJA				MUT	U		MI-IA-MU-DU		KISURRA 25 11
		MIJA				NAŠUʾ			MI-IA-NA-SU		XIII 1 I 18
MDG	1	MADAG	AT	UM					MA-DA?-GA-TUM	FN	IX 24 III 22
MGJ	1	MIGIJ		UM					MI-GI-JU-UM		RA LXV 40 I 9
MGN	1	MAGAN		UM					MA-GA-NU-UM		U
		MAGAN		I					MA-GA-NI	GEN	MRS XVI P. 329 UGARIT
		MAGUN	AT	UM					MA-KU-NA-TUM	FN	C+
	2	ŠI				MIGN	I		ŠI-ME-IG-NI	FN	RA LXV 60 III 24
		ŠEʾR		UM		MAGUN	U		ŠE-EḪ-RUM-MA-GU-NU	FN	C
MKJ	1	MAKAJ			JA				MA-KA-A		M+
		MAKAJ	AN						MA-KA-A-AN		RA LXV 43 IV 2+
		MAKIJ	AT	UM					MA-KI-IA-TUM		A 7724 2
		MAKIJ	AH						MA-KI-IA	FN	M
		MAKIJ	AN	UM					MA-KI-A-NU-UM		TA 31, 223
MKL	1	MAKAL		UM					MA-KA-LUM		BIROT, TEA 72 V 6+
		MAKAL	AN	U					MA-KA-LA-NU		VAS IX 34 6
MKS	1 JA	MKUS		U		....			IA-AM-KU-UZ-ZU-....		BM 80328 3
MLʾ	1	MILʾ		A		BIJT	I		MI-IL-A-BI-TI		A. 60 2
	JA	MLIʾ				ʾIL			A-AM-LI-DINGIR		YOS XIII 63:3, 6
MLK	1 JA	MLIK	AN						IA-AM-LI-KA-AN		M
	JA	MLIK				HADD	U		IA-AM-LIK-D-IM		RA LXV 40 I 31
	JA	MLIK				ʾIL			IA-AM-LI-IK-DINGIR		B 28+
	JA	MLIK				ʾIL			IA-AM-LIK-DINGIR		B 28+, M
	JA	MLIK				ʾIL			A-AM-LIK-DINGIR		HARRIS 76 22
	JI	MLIK				ʾIL			II-IM-LIK-DINGIR		B 28+
		MALAK				ʾIL	I		MA-LA-AK-I_3-LI_2		M
		MALAK		U		ʾIL			MA-LA-KU-IL		M
		MALIK		UM					MA-LI-KUM		U, B 34+
		MALIK		UM					MA-A-LI-KUM		KISURRA 81A 14
		MALIK		I					MA-LI-KI	GEN	B 34, A. 77 6
		MALIK	AT	UM					MA-LI-KA-TUM		BM 17060 35+
		MALIK	AT	UM					MA-LI-KA-TUM	FN	EDZARD, DER 91:3
		MALIK	AH						MA-LI-KA	FN	M
		MALIK				DAGAN			MA-LI-IK-D-DA-GAN		M
		MALIK				ŠUM	U	HU	MA-LIK-SU-MU-U_2		M
		MALIK				ZAʾT	UM		MA-LIK-ZA-DU-UM		B 34
		MILK		U					ME-IL-KU	FN	RA LXV 61 IV 3+
		MILK		IM					MI-IL-KI-IM	GEN	B 35
		MILK	AT	UM					MI-IL-KA-TUM		TCL XI 220 11
		MILK	AT	UM					MIL-KA-TUM		YOS XIII 112:16
		MILK	AN	UM					MI-IL-GA-NU-UM		U; TA 31, 148
		MILK	AN	UM					MI-EL-GA-NU-UM		TA 1931, 538 I
		MILK	UN	IM					MI-IL-KU-NI-IM	GEN	SIMMONS 46 33
		MILK	UN	IM					MI-IL-KU-NIM	GEN	SIMMONS 70 17
		MILK		A		HADD	U		MI-IL-KA-D-IM		SYRIA XXXVII 206 27 HANA
		MILK		I		ḤAJJ	A		MIL-KI-ḪA-A-IA	FN	IRAQ XVI 40 NA
		MILK		I		HADD	U		MIL-KI-D-IM		M
		MILK		I		HADD	U		MI-IL-KI-D-IM		M
		MILK		I		ʾIL			MI-IL-KI-DINGIR		B 34
		MILK		I		ʾIL	A		MI-EL-KI-I-[LA]		UCP X/3 1 29
		MILK		I		ʾIL	U		MIL-KI-LU		B 34+
		MILK		I		ʾIL	U		MI-IL-KI-LU		B 34
		MILK		I		ʾIL	UM		MI-IL-KI-LUM		B 34
		MILK		I		JARAḪ			MIL-KI-E-RA-AḪ		AJSL XLIV 243 NO. 33
		MILK		I		DAGAN			MIL-KI-D-DA-GAN		TCL I 237 12 HANA
		MILK		I		LA					
						ʾEL			MI-IL-KI-LA-EL		TA 30 615 21
		MILK		I		LI					
						ʾEL			MI-IL-KI-LI-EL		B 34, M+
		MILK		I		LI					
						ʾEL			MIL-KI-II-EL		VAS VIII 128 16+
		MILK		I		LI					
						ʾIL			MI-IL-KI-LI_2-IL		I

ROOTS (Consonants only)

MLK	1	MILK		I		LI					
						ʾIL			[MI]-EL-KI-LI-IL		I
		MILK		I		LI					
						ʾEL		UM	MI-IL-KI-LI-E-LUM		A 32065:3
		MILK		I		LU					
						ʾIL		A	MI-IL-KI-LU-I-LA		VAS XVI 10 5, 9
		MILK		I		TAʾG		A	MI-IL-KI-TA-GA		A. LATE
		MILK		U		DANN		UM	MI-IL-KU-DA-NU-UM		UET V 549:8
		MILK		U		MA			MI-IL-KU-MA		JCS XIII 51 292 R 10,A.LATE
		MILK		U		MA					
						ʾIL			MI-IL-KU-MA-IL		B 35+
		MILK		U		MA					
						ʾIL			MI-IL-KU-MA-DINGIR		C+
		MILK		UM		MA					
						ʾIL			MIL-KUM-MA-DINGIR		A. LATE
		MULUK	AN						MU-LU-GA-AN		RA LXV 41 II 35
	2	ʾAḪ		I	JE	MALIK			A-ḪI-E-MA-LIK		M
	JE	HWIJ				MALIK			E-WI-MA-LIK		A.
		ḪAʾL		I		MALIK			ḪA-LI$_2$-MA-LIK		M+
		ḪAʾR		I		MALIK			ḪA-RI-MA-LIK		BE VI/1 46 5
		ḪAʾR		I		MALIK		I	ḪA-RI-MA-LI-KI	GEN	B 20
		ʾAB		I		MULUK		I	A-BI-MU-LU-KI	FN	RA LXV 59 II 26
		ʿABD				MALIK			ḪA-AB-DU-MA-LIK		M+
		ʿABD				MALIK			AB-DU-MA-LIK		XIII 37 16
		ʿABD				MALIK		I	AB-DU-MA-LI-KI		YOS XIII 54:5
		HADD		U		MALIK			AD-DU-MA-LIK		A. 268 4
		HADD		U		MALIK			D-IM-MA-LIK		M+
		HAND		U		MALIK			AN-DU-MA-LIK		A. 252 10
		ʾIL		A		MALK		I	DINGIR-MA-AL-KI		A. LATE
		ʾIL		A		MILK		UM	DINGIR-MI-IL-KUM		BAHREIN UNP., POST-UR III
		ʾIL		I	JA	MLIK			I$_3$-LI$_2$-A-AM-LIK		HARRIS 49 12
		ʾIL		I		MALIK			I$_3$-LI$_2$-MA-LIK		M
		ʾIL		I		MILK		U	I$_3$-LI$_2$-MIL-KU	FN	RA LXV 58 I 31
		ʾIL		UM		MULUK			DINGIR-MU-LU-UK-KI	GN	XV 127
		ʾIL		UM		MULUK			I-LU-UM-MU-LU-UK-KI	GN	XV 127
		ʾIL		UM		MULUK	AJ	I	DINGIR-MU-LU-KA-JI-KI	GN	XV 127
		ʾIL		U		MALIK	AJ	I	I-LU-MA-LI-KA-JI-KI	GN	XV 127
		ḪALD		A		MULUK			ḪA?-AL-DA-MU-LU-UK		BASOR 95 21
		ḤAM		I		MALIK			A-MI-MA-LIK		C
		ḤAM		UM		MALIK			D-A-MU-UM-MA-LIK		M
		ḤAM		U		MALIK			D-A-MU-MA-LIK		M
		ḤIMD		I		MALIK			ḪI-IM-DI-MA-LIK		M
		ʾARŠ		UM		MALIK			ḪA-AR?-ŠUM?-MA-LIK		M
		ʾIŠḪAR	AH			MALAK		I	D-IŠ-ḪA-RA-M[A-L]A-KI	FN	RA LXV 61 IV 61
		ʿAŠTAR				MILK		I	EŠ$_4$-DAR-ME-IL-KI	FN	RA LXV 62 V 10
		JATAR				MALIK			IA-TAR-MA-LIK		A.+
	JI	JTAR				MULUK			I-TAR-MU-LU-UK		B 23
		BIN	T	A		MALK		I	BI-IT-TA-MA-AL-KI	FN	A. LATE
		DAWD		U		MALIK			DA-DU-MA-LIK		XIII 1 VI 27
		DAGAN				MALAK		U	D-DA-GAN-MA-LA-KU	FN	RA LXV 60 III 3
		DAGAN				MALIK			D-DA-GAN-MA-LIK		M+
		KI				MILK		I			
						ʾEL			KI-MI-IL-KI-EL		KISURRA 112:8
		LA			ʾA	MLIK					
						ʾIL			LA-AM-LI-IK-DINGIR		RUTTEN 5 22
		LI			JI	MLIK					
						....			LI-IM-LI$_2$-LI-IK-ḪI-LI-GAL$_2$		HSM 7934, UR III
		LAʾR				MULUK			LA-AR-MU-LU-UK	FN	XIII 1 IX 33
		MUT		U		MALAK		A	MU-TU-MA-LA-KA		M
	JA	MZUʾ				MALIK			IA-AM-ZU-MA-LIK		B 28
		NABUʾ			HU	MALIK			D-NA-BU-U$_2$-MA-LIK		M
		QUWJ				MILK		U	QU-U$_2$-LUGAL		MRS XII 31:24
	JA	RWIM				MALIK			IA-RI-IM-MA-LIK		A 3580:2+
		RIPʾ		A		MALIK			RI-IP-A-MA-LIK		M
		ŠI				MALIK	T	I	ŠI-MA-LI-IK-TI		IX 294:7'
	JA	ŠWUB				MALIK			IA-ŠU-UB-D-MA-[LIK]		M

MLK	3	LA				ʾA	HWIJ					
							MALIK			LA-AḪ-WI-MA-LIK		X 141 2
		LA				ʾA	HWIJ					
							MALIK		U	LA-AḪ-WI-MA-LI-KU		M
		LA					ʾIL		A			
							MILK		I	LA-I-LA-MI-IL-KI		TA 30, 75 2
MLL	1	MALIL		UM						MA-LI-LUM		B 34+
		MILAL		UM						MI-LA-LUM		BM 16943 36
MM	1	MAM		A			ḪAṢN		I	D-MA-MA-ḪA-AZ-NI	FN	RA LXV 56 I 7
		MAM		A			DUNN		I	D-MA-MA-DU-UN-NI	FN	M
		MAM		A			NUMR		I	D-MA-MA-NU-UM-RI	FN	RA LXV 65 VII 30
		MAM		A			QUDM		I	D-MA-MA-KU-UD-ME	FN	RA LXV 59 II 18
		MAM		A			ŚARR	AH		D-MA-MA-ŠAR-RA	FN	M
		MAM		A		TA	LʾIJ			D-MA-MA-TA-AL-E	FN	M
		MAM		A			TUʾAL		I	D-MA-MA-TU-ḪA-LI	FN	M
		MAM		A			ṢIJḪ	AT	UM	MA-MA-ZI-A-TUM	FN	RA LXV 61 IV 37
	2	ʾAB		I	Š		MUM		U	A-BI-IŠ-MU-MU		HARRIS 98 2
	JI	NDIN					MAM		A	I-DIN-D-MA-MA		M+
		QIJŚ	T	I			MAM		A	KI-IŠ-TI-D-MA-MA		M+
		QIJŚ	T	I			MAM		A	KI-IŠ-TI-D-MA-AM-MA		XIV 61:5
		ŠEʾR	AH				MAM		A	ŠE-RA-D-MA-MA	FN	X 110 3
		TIWR					MAM		A	TI-IR-MA-MA		M+
		TAB3		I			MAM		A	TA-BI-D-MA-MA	FN	M
	3 JA	KWUN					PI					
							MAM		A	IA-KU-UN-BI-D-MA-MA	FN	RA LXV 66 VII 61
MMʾ	1	MIMEʾ		UM						MI-ME-U_2-UM		M
		MIMEʾ		UM						MI-IM-[ME-U_2-UM]		M
MMM	1	MAMM	AT	UM						[M]A-A[M]-MA-TUM	FN	RA LXV 64 VI 9
	2	ḪAʾL		I			MAMM		A	ḪA-LI_2-D-M[A-A]M-M[A]		M
MMN	1	MAMN		UM						MA-AM-NU-UM		I
MNW	1	MANAW		UM						MA-NA-UM		I
		MANAW	AH							MA-NA-WA	FN	XIII 1 VII 45
		MANUW		UM						MA-NU-UM		M+
		MANUW	T	UM						MA-NU-TUM	FN	CT VIII 28A 2, 4+
		MANUW	AT	UM						MA-NU-A-TUM	FN	I (UNPUBL.)
	2	LA					MANUW		UM	LA-MA-NU-UM		I, TIM III 136 4
		LA					MANUW		IM	LA-MA-NI-IM	GEN	B 46
MNJ	1	MANIJ		UM						MA-NI-UM		U; TA 30, 615:40+
		MANIJ	AN	UM						MA?-NI-A-NU-UM		TA 1931, 538 II
		MANIJ					ʾEL			MA-NI-EL		RA VIII 72 7
		MANIJ					ʾIL			MA-NI-IL		U
		MANIJ					DAGAN			MA?-NI-D-DA-GAN		A. 6 34
		MENIJ	T	UM						ME-NI-TUM	FN	M
MND	2	ŠUM		U		ʾA	MNID		IM	[SU-M]U-AM-NI-DI-IM		B 38
MNG	1	MENG		UM						ME-EN-GU-UM		CT XLVIII 86 REV.+
MNMN	1	MANMAN		UM						MA-AN-MA-NU-UM		UCP X/3 P. 199+
		MANMAN		UM						MA-MA-NU-UM		B 46+
MNN	1	MANAN		UM						MA-NA-NU-UM		I
		MANAN		IM						MA-NA-NI-IM	GEN	B 46+
		MANAN		IM						MA-NA-NIM	GEN	B 46
		MANAN		IM						MA-AN-NA-NIM	GEN	B 46
		MANAN		A						MA-NA-AN-NA		M+
		MANAN	AT	UM						MA-NA-NA-TUM	FN	B 93+
		MANAN		AJA						MA-NA-NA-A		B 34+
		MANIN		UM						MA-NI-NU-UM		B 34+
		MANIN		I						MA-NI-NI	GEN	B 34+
		MANN		AJA						MA-AN-NA-IA	FN	RA LXV 62 V 49
		MANN		IJA						MA-AN-NI-IA		M+
		MANN	AT	UM						MA-AN-NA-TUM	FN	WATERMAN 52 2+, X 2 6
		MANN	AT	UM						MA-NA-TUM	FN	BM 81479 4
		MANN	ATAN							MA-NA-TA-AN		M+
		MANN	ATANU							MA-NA-TA-NU		M
		MANN		A			....			MA-AN-N[A-....]		M
		MANN		A			BAʿL		A	MA-NA-BA-LA		M
		MANN		A			BIʿD		IM	MA-NA-BI-IḪ-DI-IM	GEN	HARRIS 3 18
		MANN					BALTI					
							ʾIL			MA-AN-BA-AL-TI-DINGIR		RA LXIV 34 NO. 24

ROOTS (Consonants only)

MNN	1			MANN		A			BALTI						
									ʾEL				MA-NA-BA-AL-TE-EL		B 28+
				MANN		A			BALTI						
									ʾEL				MA-NA-BA-AŠ-TE-EL		M+
				MANN		A			BALTI						
									ʾIL				MA-AN-NA-BA-AL-TI-DINGIR		M
				MANN		A			BALTI						
									ʾEL				MA-NA-BA-AL-TI-EL		KISURRA 70A 14+
				MANN		A			TAWR		I		MA-NA-TA-RI		B 34
				MANN		U			ŠAM		A		MA-NU-SA-MA		B 34
				MINAN		UM							MI-NA-NU-UM		B 46+
				MINAN		UM							MI-IN-NA-NU-UM		SIMMONS 18 1, 8
				MINAN		UM							ME-NA-NUM		KISURRA 175A 19
				MINAN		I							MI-NA-NI	GEN	B 46+
				MINAN	AH								ME-NA-AN-NA	FN	RA LXV 60 III 11
				MENN	AT	UM							ME-EN-NA-TUM	FN	XIII 1 V 32
				MENN	AH								ME-EN-NA	FN	XIII 1 I 68+
				MENN		A	HA						ME-IN-NA-A	FN	X 176:8, 15
				MINN	ATANUM								MI-NA-TA-NU-UM		HARRIS 76 11
				MINN	AH				MINN	AH			MI-IN-NA-MI-IN-NA	FN	XIII 1 XII 1
				MUNAN		UM							MU-NA-NU-UM		I, B 46+
				MUNAN		IM							MU-NA-NIM	GEN	B 46
				MUNAN		IM							MU-NA-NI-IM	GEN	B 46
				MUNAN	AN	UM							MU-NA-NA-NU-UM		B 46
	2			KAKK		A			MANN		U		KA-AK-KA-MA-AN-NU		M
				MINN	AH				MINN	AH			MI-IN-NA-MI-IN-NA	FN	XIII 1 XII 1
MNZ	1			MUNUZ		I							MU-NU-ZI	FN	RA LXV 64 V 59
MQṬ	1	JA		MQUṬ		U							IA-AM-KU-DU		M
		JA		MQUṬ		U							I-AM-KU-DU		M
		JA	T	MAQAṬ									IA-AM-DA-GA-AD		B 28
		JA	T	MAQṬ		AM							IA-AM-TA-AQ-TA-AM	ACC	ABB V 39 REV 8'
	2			LAŠU					MIQIṬ				LA-ŠU-MI-GI-IT		B 33
				LAŠU					MIQIṬ				LA-ŠU-MI-KI-IT		B 33
MRʾ	1			MARIʾ	AN	UM							MA-RI-A-NU-UM		B 46
				MARUʾ					JAT		UM		MA-RU-IA-TUM		DE GEN., KICH II D 43 R. 2, 4
				MARUʾ					LI						
									ʾEL				MA-RU-LI-EL		SIMMONS 47 18, 49 22
	2	JI		JṢIʾ					MARIʾ			JE	I-ṢI-MA-RI-E		B 22
MRḪ	1			MERḪ		UM							ME-ER-ḪU-UM		M+; YOS XIII 321+
				MERḪ		IM							ME-ER-ḪI-IM	GEN	M+
MRDK	2			DIKR					MARDUK				[Z]I?-IK-RU-D-AMAR-UD		KUPPER, L'ICON PL II NO 8
MRMR	1			MARMAR	AN	IM							MA-AR-MA-RA-NIM	GEN	B 93
				MURMUR	T	IM							MU-UR-MU-UR-TIM	FN GEN	B 49
MRQ	1			MARAQ		A							MA-RA-QA	GEN	B 34
MRR	1			MARAR		UM							MA-RA-RU-UM		WATERMAN 45 R. 12
				MERR		UM							ME-ER-RUM		M+
				MERR		IM							ME-ER-RI-IM	GEN	M+
				MERR		AM							ME-ER-RA-AM	ACC	M
		ʾA		MURR		UM							A-MU-RU-UM		U
		ʾA		MURR		UM							A-MUR-RU-UM		CT II 50 21+
		ʾA		MURR		U							A-MU-UR-RU		M+
		ʾA		MURR									A-MU-PU-UḪ-ḪI		A.
	2	JI		DNIK				ʾA	MURR		UM		D-ID-NI-IK-MAR-TU	DN	U
MRṢ	1	JA		MRAṢ									IA-AM-RA-AṢ		BM 81591 6
		JA		MRAṢ		UM							A-AM-RA-ZUM		HARRIS 45 10
		JA		MRAṢ					ʾIL				IA-AM-RA-AṢ-DINGIR		M+
		JA		MRAṢ		I			ʾIL				IA-AM-RA-ZI-DINGIR		M
		JA		MRUṢ					ʾIL				IA-AM-RU-UṢ-DINGIR		B 28
		JA		MRUṢ					ʾIL				IA-AM-RU-IṢ-DINGIR		M
		JA		MRUṢ		I			ʾIL		UM		I-IA-AM-RU-UṢ-ZI-I-LU-UM		B 21
		JU		MRAṢ					ʾIL				JU-UM-RA-AṢ-DINGIR		M+
				MARAṢ		UM							MA-RA-ZUM		I+, UET V 527 2
				MARUṢ		AJA							MA-RU-ZA-IA	FN	RA LXV 61 IV 64
				MARṢ	AT	UM							MAR-ZA-TUM	FN	M+
				MARṢ		AJA							MA-AR-ZA-IA	FN	M
	2			ʾAḪ		I			MARAṢ				A-ḪI-MA-RA-AṢ		B 12+, M+

ROOTS (Consonants only)

MRṢ	2			ʾAḪ		I	MARAṢ				A-ḪI-MA-RA-UṢ		RUTTEN 1 22
				ʾAḪ		I	MARAṢ				A-ḪI-MA-RA-AṢ	FN	XIII 1 IX 24
				ḪAʾL		I	MARAṢ				ḪA-LI-MA-RA-AṢ		GEN, KICH I P. 59 NO. 219
				ḪAʾL		I	MARAṢ				ḪA-LI-MA-RA-AṢ		UET V 521 1
				ʾAB		I	MARAṢ				A-BI-MA-RA-AṢ		B 10+
		JI		JDAʿ			MARAṢ				I-DA-MA-RA-AṢ	GN	B 21+, M
		JI		JDAʿ			MARAṢ				A-DA-MA-RA-AṢ	GN	B 11
		JI		JDAʿ			MARAṢ				A-TA-MA-RA-AṢ	PN	CT II 26 3
				ʾUMM		I	MARṢ	AT			UM-MI-MAR-ṢA-AT	FN	XIII 1 III 5
				JAT		UM	MARṢ	AT			I-IA-TUM-MA-AR-ZA-AT	FN	RA LXV 62 V 15
				JAT		UM	MARṢ	AH			IA-TUM-MAR-ZA		A 21899+
				BIN		I	MARAṢ				BI-NI-MA-RA-AṢ		M
				BIN		I	MARAṢ		I		BI-NI-MA-RA-ZI	FN	XII 265 2
				BUN		I	MARAṢ				BU-NI-MA-RA-AṢ		C+
				D̲IKR			MARAṢ				ZI-IK-RU-MA-RA-AZ	FN	RA LXV 55 XIII 33
				KI			MARUṢ				KI-MA-RU-UṢ		A 3549+
MSR	1	JA		MSIR		U					IA-AN-ZI-RU		UCP X/1 50 9
				MISAR		I					MI?-ZA-RI	FN	RA LXV 65 VI 71
MŠḪ	1			MAŠIḪ		UM					MA-SI-ḪU-UM		M+
				MAŠIḪ		IM					MA-SI-ḪI-IM	GEN	M
				MAŠIḪ		A					MA-SI-ḪA	MN NOM	M
				MAŠIḪ	AN						MA-SI-ḪA-AN		XIII 1 XI 58+
				MAŠḪ		UM					MA-AŠ-ḪU-UM		M+
				MAŠḪ		IM					MA-AŠ-ḪI-IM	GEN	M+
				MAŠḪ	AT	UM					MA-AŠ-ḪA-TUM	FN	M
				MUŠAḪ		UM					MU-SA-ḪU-UM		UET V P. 50+
				MUŠAḪ		UM					MU-SA-AḪ-ḪU-UM		UET V 722 11
			N	MŠIḪ			HEDD		A		NA-AM-SI-E-D-IM		A 7646 6
MŠJ	1	JA		MŠIJ			ʾIL				IA-AM-SI-DINGIR		B 28+
		JI		MŠIJ			ʾIL				JI-IM-SI-DINGIR		M
MŠB	1			MAŠUB	AH						MA?-SU-BA?	FN	XIII 1 III 24
MŠD	1			MAŠD	AK	UM					MA-AŠ-DA-KUM		TA 30, 615 6
MŠK	1			MAŠK		UM					MA-AŠ$_2$-KUM		BM 16821 8+
				MAŠK		UM					MAŠ-KUM		EBPN 123+
				MAŠK		UM					MA-AŠ$_2$-KU-UM		M
				MAŠK		U					[M]A-AŠ$_2$-KU		M
				MAŠIK	T	UM					MA-SI-IK-TUM		BM 17063 26+
				MAŠIK	T	UM					MA-SI-IK-TUM	FN	XIII 1 V 73; YOS XIII 453
	2			BILL			MAŠIK		A		BI-EL-MA-SI-KA?		M
MŠL	1			MAŠAL		UM					MA-SA-LUM		EK I P. 40
				MAŠAL		UM					MA-SA-LU-U[M]		HARRIS 95 10
	2			MUT			MEŠIL		I		MU-UT-ME-SI-LI		RIFTIN 45 14
MŠN	1			MUŠN		A	HADD		U		MU-UŠ-NA-A-DU		A.+
MŠR	1			MIŠR		IJA					ME-IŠ?-RI-IA	FN	RA LXV 60 III 35
				MUŠAR	AN						MU-ŠA-RA-AN		RA LXV 50 VIII 65
MṢʾ	1	JA		MṢIʾ		UM					IA-AM-ZI-JU-UM?		M
		JE		MṢIʾ		UM					IE-E-IM-ZU-UM		BIN VII 35:6
		JE		MṢIʾ		UM					E-IM-ṢI-UM		BIN VII P. 11+
		JA		MṢIʾ			ʿADN		U		IA-AM-ZI-AD-[NU]		CT VI 33A 33
		JA		MṢIʾ			ʿADN		U		IA-AM-ṢI-AD-NU		BM 16914 31
		JA		MṢIʾ			ʿADN		U		IA-AM-ZI-ḪA-AD-NU		M+
		JA		MṢIʾ			ʿADN		U	HU	IA-AM-ZI-AD-NU-U$_2$		BM 81302 4
		JA		MṢIʾ			ʿADN		U	HU	IA-AM-ZI-ḪA-AD-NU-U$_2$		DELAPORTE CCL II A 385, M+
		JA		MṢIʾ			ʾIL				IA-AM-ZI-DINGIR		B 28, M
		JA		MṢIʾ			ʾIL				IA-AM-ṢI-DINGIR		B 28+
		JE		MṢIʾ			ʾIL				IE-E-EM-ZI-DINGIR		B 25
				MAṢIʾ	AT	UM					MA-ZI-A-TUM	FN	WATERMAN 56 R. 8
	2			ṢIDQ		UM	MAṢIʾ				ZI-ID-KUM-MA-ZI		X 131 5+
MT	1			MUT	AN	UM					MU-DA-NU-UM		U+
				MUT	AN	UM					MU-TA-NU-UM		B 46
				MUT	AN	I					MU-TA-NI		A. 52 28
				MUT		IJA					MU-TI-IA		B 35, A.+
				MUT		UJAN					MU-TU-JA-AN		C+
				MUT			ḪAʾL		I		MU-UT-ḪA-LI		B 35 HANA
				MUT			ḪAʾL		I				
							MA				MU-UT-ḪA-LI-MA		M

ROOTS (Consonants only)

MT	1	MUT			ḪAʾN		A		MU-UT-ḪA-NA		XIV 47:31
		MUT			ʾAWN	AN			MU-UT-AW-NA-AN		B 35 HANA
		MUT			ḪAʾŠ		UM		MU-UT-ḪA-SU-UM		A.
		MUT			ḪUBUR				MU-UT-ḪU-BUR		SYRIA V 271, 275
		MUT			HADD		U		MU-UT-[D]?-IM		RA LXV 41 II 17
		MUT			HADD		I		MU-TA-AD-DI		VAS XVI 165:4
		MUT			....				MU-UT-D-IGI-KUR		M
		MUT			ʾEKAL		IM		MU-UT-E$_2$-GAL-LIM		M
		MUT			ʾIL				MU-UT-DINGIR		MAOG IV 2 4 HANA
		MUT			ḪALAB				MU-UT-ḪA-LA-AB		A. 271 3
		MUT			ʾALAM		I		MU-UT-ḪA-LA-MI		C+
		MUT			ʿUMUS		IM		MU-UT-ḪU-MU-ZI-IM		XIV 122:6+
		MUT			ʿAN	AT			MU-UT-D-ḪA-NA-AT		RA LXV 52 X 65
		MUT			ʾARḪ		U		MU-UT-AR-ḪU		M
		MUT			ḪIRB	AN			MU-UT-ḪI-IR-BA?-AN		VIII 11 4
		MUT			ʾAŠD		IM		MU-UT-AŠ-DI-IM		M
		MUT		ʾA	ŠKUR				MU-UT-AŠ-KUR		M+
		MUT			ḪATK		IM		MU-UT-ḪA-AT-KI-IM		RA LXV 44 IV 57
		MUT			BIŠIR				MU-UT-BI-SI-IR		M+
		MUT			DAGAN				MU-UT-D-DA-GAN		M+
		MUT			KABID				MU-UT-GA-BI-ID		TA 30, 615 24
		MUT			KASIJ				MU-UT-KA-ZI-....		VIII 6 35'
		MUT			MIʾR		UM		MU-UT-MI-RUM?		EDZARD, DER 89:4
		MUT			MEŠIL		I		MU-UT-ME-SI-LI		RIFTIN 45 14
		MUT			NAWḪ		A		MU-UT-NA-ḪA		B 35 HANA
		MUT			NAHR		IM		MU-UT-NA-RI-IM		RA LXV 51 IX 59
		MUT			NAN		UM		MU-UT-NA-NU-UM		TA 30, 615:39+
		MUT			PA						
					NAZI				MU-UT-PA-A-NA-ZI		RA LXV 40 I 10
		MUT			RAWḪ				MU-UT-RA-AḪ		M
		MUT			RAWM		A		MU-UT-RA-MA		CT II 23 13
		MUT			RAWM		E	JE	MU-UT-RA-ME-E		BM 81584 3, M+
		MUT			RAWM		EM		MU-UT-RA-ME-IM		M
		MUT			RAPIʾ				MU-UT-[R]A-BI		M
		MUT			RAPŠ		IM		MU-UT-RA-AP-ŠI-IM		RA LXV 53 XI 7
		MUT			ŠAKIM				MU-UT-ŠA-KI-IM		RA LXV 55 XIII 35
		MUT			ŠALIM				MU-UT-SA-LIM		M
		MUT	A		JŠUʿ				MU-TA-ŠU-UḪ		M+
		MUT	A		NIʿM				MU-TA-NI-ḪI-IM		RA LXV 43 III 51
		MUT	A	TA	KWIN				MU-TA-TA-KI-IN		RA LXV 51 IX 78
		MUT	I		ʾAḪ		I		MU-TI-A-ḪI	GEN	B 35
		MUT	I		JAʾN		A		MU-TI-I-IA-NA		B 35
		MUT	I		JABAL				MU-TI-A-BA-AL-KI	GN	B 35+
		MUT	I		JABAL				MU-TI-BA-AL-KI	GN	B 35+
		MUT	I		JABAL				MU-TA-BA-AL-KI	GN	OIP XI 216 IV 3
		MUT	I		JABAL		A		MU-TI-A-BA-LA-KI	GN	B 35
		MUT	I		HADD		U		MU-TI-D-IM		M
		MUT	I		ʾIL		UM		MU-TI-LUM		YOS XIII 151:4+
		MUT	I		ʿAN	AT	A		MU-TI-A-N[A-T]A		B 35
		MUT	I		JARAḪ				MU-TI-A-RA-AḪ		B 35
		MUT	I		JARAḪ				MU-TI-E-RA-AḪ		M; TCL XI 224:69+
		MUT	I		JARAḪ				MU-TE-E-RA-AḪ		A 7804 13
		MUT	I		ḪURŠAN				MU-TI-ḪUR-SAG		YOS XII+
		MUT	I		ḪURŠAN		A		MU-TI-ḪU-UR-ŠA-NA		B 35+
		MUT	I		ḪURŠAN		I		MU-TI-ḪU-UR-ŠA-NI		YOS XII
		MUT	I		ḪATK		IM		MU-TI-ḪA-AD-KI-IM	NOM	IRAQ XXX 92+ RIMAH
		MUT	I	JE	ʾMIʾ				MU-TI-E-MI-IḪ		M
		MUT	I		....				[M]U?-TI-KA-ṢI-E		PBS XIII 56:8
		MUT	I		....				MU-TI-DA-ZI-U$_2$		TA 1930, 489 I
		MUT	I		ME						
					ʾEL				MU-TI-ME-EL		TA 30, 615:4+
		MUT	I		MAʾK		U	HU	MU-TI-MA-KU-U$_2$		M+
		MUT	I		ŠAMŠ				MU-TI-D-UTU		A.
		MUT	U		ʾAWN	AN	UM		MU-TU-AM-NA-NU-UM		BM 81641 3, 8
		MUT	U		ʾABIḪ				MU-TU-A-BI-I[Ḫ]		M
		MUT	U		ʾABIḪ		IM		MU-TU-A-BI-ḪI-IM		C

ROOTS (Consonants only)

MT	1		MUT		U		HADD		U		MU-TU-D-IM		M
			MUT		U		ʾIL		A		MU-TU-I-LA		RA LXV 43 III 68
			MUT		U		ḪAM		I		MU-TU-D-A-MI		RA LXV 51 IX 49
			MUT		U		JAM		A		MU-TU-IA-MA		M
			MUT		U		JARAḪ				MU-TU-E-RA-AḪ		JCS XXIV 60 NO. 51 REV
			MUT		U		ʾARAPḪ		IM		MU-TU-AR-RA-AP-ḪI-IM		C+
			MUT		U		ʾAŠD		I		[MU]-TU-AŠ-DI		VIII 17 13'
			MUT		U		ḪATK		IM		MU-TU-ḪA-AD-KI-IM		M+
			MUT		U		ḪATK		IM		MU-TU-AD-KI-IM		M
			MUT		U		ḪATK		I		MU-TU-ḪA-AD-KI		M
			MUT		U	JE	JŠUʿ				M[U-T]U-E-ŠU-UḪ		RA LXV 47 VII 21
			MUT		U	JA	NŠUʾ			HU	MU-TU-A-AN-ŠU-U_2		KISURRA 91 24
			MUT		U		BAʿL		U	HU	MU-TU-BA-LU-U_2		RA LXV 44 IV 26
			MUT		U		BAWŠ		A		MU-TU-BA-SA		B 35+
			MUT		U		BIŠIR				MU-TU-BI-SI-IR		M+
			MUT		U		DAGAN				MU-TU-D-DA-GAN		CT XLIII 29 1 M+
			MUT		U		KUʾB		I		MU-TU-KU-BI		RA LXV 42 II 66
			MUT		U		KANAT		A		MU-TU-KA-NA-TA		M
			MUT		U		KUMR		I		MU-TU-KU-UM-RI		X 166 10', 13'
			MUT		U		ME						
							ʾEL				MU-TU-ME-EL		CT VIII 31A 25+
			MUT		U		MEʾR				MU-TU-ME-ER		M
			MUT		U		MALAK		A		MU-TU-MA-LA-KA		M
			MUT		U		RAWM		I	JE	MU-TU-RA-MI-E		CT XLV 63 15
			MUT		UM		ʾABIḪ				MU-TUM-A-BI-IḪ		TA 1930, 695
			MUT		UM		ʾEL				MU-TUM-E-EL		YOS VIII P. 16+
			MUT		UM		ʾEL				MU-TUM-EL		YOS VIII P. 16+
			MUT		UM		ʾIL				MU-TUM-DINGIR		FRANK 29 4, 10+ M+
			MUT		UM		JARIQ				MU-TUM-JA-RI-IQ		TA 1931, 104, 538
			MUT		UM		MA						
							ʾEL				MU-TUM-MA-EL		TA 1931, 456
			MUT		UM		ME						
							ʾEL				MU-TUM-ME-EL		RUTTEN 32 8+
			MUT		UM		NIʾŠ		A		MU-TUM-NI-ŠA		TA 1931, 538 III
	2		ʾAJA				MUT		I		ḪA-IA-MU-TI		BAGHD. MITT. II 7 2, 4, 8
		JI	HWIJ				MUT		I		I-WI-MU-TI		U
			ʾALLA				MUT	IJ	I		AL-LA-MU-TI-I	TRIBE	4E RENC. ASS. P. 178 9
			ʾALLA				MUT	IJ	I		A-AL-MU-TI-I	TRIBE	M
			DIWIR				MUT		I		DI-WI-IR-MU-TI		PBS XI/1 P. 55+
			DIWIR				MUT		I		DI-BI-IR-A-MU-TI		PBS XI/1 P. 55+
			MIJA				MUT		A		ME-IA-MU-TA		B 34
			MIJA				MUT		U		MI-IA-MU-DU		KISURRA 25 11
			ŠUM		U		MUT		I				
							JABAL		A		SU-MU-MU-TI-A-BA-LA		B 39
MTʿ	1		MATAʿ		A		KI						
							ʾEL				MA-TA-A-KI-EL		RA LXV 50 IX 20;HARRIS 19:5,SEAL+
		JA	MATIʿ				ʾIL				IA-MA-AT-TI-DINGIR		M+
		JA	MATIʿ				ʾIL				IA-MA-TI-DINGIR		XII 5 3
			MATIʿ				ʾAHL		I		MA-TI-IA-LI		UCP X/1 1 16
			MATIʿ				ʾIL				MA-TI-DINGIR		M
			MATIʿ				JAT		U	HU	MA-TI-IA-TU-U_2		UCP X/3 107 18
			MATIʿ				....				MA-TI-UT-TA-A-LI		SIMMONS 61 11
			MATIʿ				TIWR		UM		MA-TI-TI-RUM		BM 67281
	2	TA	KWUN				MITEʿ			JE	TA-KU-UN-MI-TE-E		M
MTN	1		MATAN		I						MA-TA-NI	FN	EDZARD, DER 33:3
			MATAN		I						MA-AT-TA-NI		TIM II 99:3
			MATIN	AT							MA-TI-NA-AT		U
MTQ	1		MATAQ		I						MA-TA-KI	FN	CT IV 26A 1
			MATIQ		I						MA-TI-GI	FN	M+
			MATQ		U		NAN		A		MA-AT-KU-NA-NA	FN	RA LXV 60 III 33
MTT	1		MUTT	IJ	UM						MU-UT-TI-JU-UM		M
			MUTT		UJAN						MU-UT-TU-IA-AN		RA LXV 50 IX 18
MṬR	1	JA	MṬAR		UM						IA-AM-TA-RU-[UM]		TIM V 63:12
			MAṬAR		UM						MA-TA-RUM		M
	2		ʾAḪ		UM		MAṬAR		I		A-ḪU-UM-MA-DA-RI		M
			ʾAJA				MAṬAR				ḪA-IA-MA-DAR		YOS XII 360 17

MṬR	2			ʾAJA			MAṬAR			A-IA-MA-[DAR]		YOS XII 360 SEAL
				ḪAʾL		U	MAṬAR			ḪA-LU-MA-DA-AR		M+
				ḪAʾL		UM	MAṬAR			ḪA-LUM-MA-DAR		C, SIMMONS 67 SEAL
				ḪAʾL		UM	MAṬAR	I		ḪA-LUM-MA-DA-RI		SIMMONS 67 B 11
				ḪAʾL		UM	MAṬAR	I		ḪA-LUM-MA-DAR-RI		SIMMONS 67 11
				ʾAB		I	MAṬAR			A-BI-MA-DAR		B 10+
				ʾAB		I	MAṬAR			A-BI-MA-DA-AR		TIM II 113 3
				ʾIL		A	MAṬAR			DINGIR-MA-DA-AR		OR. N.S. XXVI 28 N.4 CAPP
				ʾIL		A	MAṬAR			DINGIR-MA-TAR		M+
				ʾIL		I	MAṬAR			I$_3$-LI$_2$-MA-DA-AR		M
				ʾIL		I	MAṬAR			I$_3$-LI$_2$-MA-TAR		M
				ʾIL		I	MAṬAR			I$_3$-LI$_2$-MA-TA-AR		B 21
				ʿAMM		I	MAṬAR			AM-MI-MA-DAR		B 13 HANA
				ʿAMM		I	MAṬAR			ḪA-MI-MA-DAR	FN	C
				ʿAMM		U	MAṬAR			ḪA-MU-MA-DAR	FN	C
				ʾARAM			MAṬAR	A		A-RA-AM-MA-DA-RA		BM 80328 1
				JIŠʿ		I	MAṬAR			IŠ-ḪI-MA-DAR		V 40 5, 16
		JA		KWUN			MAṬAR			IA-KU-MA-DAR		SYMB.BOHL P.36?:6
				ŠAʾL		U	MAṬAR			SA-LU-MA-DAR		RA LXV 52 X 68+
MZʾ	1	JE		MZUʾ		UM				E-IM-ZU-UM		BIN VII P. 11+
		JE		MZUʾ		UM				IE-E-EM-ZU-UM		B 25+
		JA		MZUʾ			ʿADN	IM		[IA?-AM?-Z]U?-ḪA-AD-NIM	GEN	XIII 129 5
		JA		MZUʾ			ʿADN	U	HU	IA-AM-ZU-AD-NU-U$_2$		B 28+
		JA		MZUʾ			MALIK			IA-AM-ZU-MA-LIK		B 28
	2			ʿADN		UM	MAZAʾ	A		ḪA-[A]D?-NU-UM-MA-ZA-A		RA LXV 41 II 52
MZL	1			MAZAL	AH					MA-ZA-AL-LA	FN	XIII 1 IV 40+
MZM	1			MAZUM	AH					MA-ZU-MA	FN	XIII 1 III 22
MZN	1			MAZN		UM				MA-AZ-NU-UM		MOORTGAT 345
MZZ	2			ŠUM		UM	MAZAZ			ŠU-MU-UM-MA-ZA-AZ		TA 1931, 538 I, IV
NʾJ	1			NAʾJ	AT	UM				NA-JA-TUM	FN	KISURRA 59A:4
NʾD	2			DAGAN			NAʾD	I		D-DA-GAN-NA-DI	FN	XIII 1 III 17+
				KUMM		I	NAʾD	A		KU-UM-MI-NA-DA		JCS IV 113
NʾG	2			ŠALAŠ			NIʾG	I		ŠA-LA-AŠ-NI-GI	FN	C+
NʾL	1			NAʾUL		UM				NA-U$_2$-LU-UM		TA 1931, 297, 538
NʾR	1		Š	NUʾR			ḪAʾL	I		ŠU-NU-UR-ḪA-LI		KING LIH I 22 4, R. 2
			Š	NUʾR		A	ḪAʾL	U		ŠU-NU-UḪ-RA-ḪA-LU		M+
			Š	NUʾR		A	ḪAʾL	U	HU	ŠU-NU-UḪ-RA-ḪA-LU-U$_2$		M+
			Š	NUʾR		A	ḪAʾL	U	HU	ŠU-NU-ḪU-RA-ḪA-LU-U$_2$		XIV 11:1
			Š	NUʾR		A	ḪAʾL	U	HU	ŠU-NU-UḪ-ḪU-RA-ḪA-LU-U$_2$		XIV 36:1+
			Š	NUʾR		U	ḪAʾL	U		ŠU-NU-UḪ-RU-ḪA-LU		M+
			Š	NUʾR		A	ʿAMM	U		ŠU-NU-UḪ-RA-AM-MU		B 40 HANA+
NʾŠ	1			NAʾAŠ		UM				NA-A-ŠU-UM	FN	RA LXV 58 I 57
				NIʾŠ		UM				NI-ŠUM		M+
	2			KAKK		A	NIʾŠ	U	JA	KA-AK-KA-NI-ŠU-IA		RA LXV 64 VI 35
				KAKK		A	NIʾŠ	U	JA	KA-KA-NI-ŠU-IA	FN	RA LXV 65 VII 44
				MUT		UM	NIʾŠ	A		MU-TUM-NI-ŠA		TA 1931, 538 III
				ŠUM		U	NIʾŠ	U	JA	SU-MU-NI-ŠU-A		CT VIII 38D:14
NHR	1			NAHR		IM				NA-RI-IM	GEN	A.
				NAHR	AN	UM				NA-RA-NU-UM		B 47
				NAHR			BAJAN			D-ID$_2$-BA-IA-AN		A 21929 5,12
				NAHR			ṢUWR	I		D-ID$_2$-ZU-RI		M
	2			ʿABD			NAHR			AB-DI-D-ID$_2$		SCHEIL 10 15, 16
				ʾUMM		I	NAHR	U		UM-MI-NA-RU	FN	M
				BIN			NAHR	UM		BI-IN-NA-RUM		CT VI 23 5+
				BIN			NAHR	UM		BI-NA-RU-UM		BIN VII 67 27+
				BIN			NAHR	I		BI-IN-NA-A-R[I]?		M
				KIWN			NAHR	IM		KI-IN-NA-RI-IM	GEN	M+
				MUT			NAHR	IM		MU-UT-NA-RI-IM		RA LXV 51 IX 59
		JA		ŠWUB			NAHR			IA-ŠU-UB-NA-AR		M+
		JA		TWUR			NAHR	UM		IA-DUR-NA-RUM?		RA LXV 48 VII 72
NḪL	1			NAḪAL		I				NA-ḪA-LI	FN	IX 291 30
				NAḪL		I	ʾIL	UM		NA-AḪ-LI-LUM		B 36+
NḪM	1	ME		NḪIM		UM				ME-EN-ḪI-MU-UM		HARRIS 57 17
NḪJ	1	ME		NḪIJ		UM				ME-EN-ḪI-I-UM		XIII 105 8
NḪB	1	JA		NḪAB		UM				IA-ḪA-BU-UM		YOS XII
		JA		NḪAB			ʾIL			IA-AḪ-ḪA-AB-DINGIR		C+

ROOTS (Consonants only)

NḪB	1	JA	NḪAB			ʿAMM	U	IA-ḪA-AB-ḪA-MU		M
		TA	NḪAB	AT	UM			TA-ḪA-BA-TUM	FN	VAS VIII 127 2, 29
		TA	NḪAB	AT	I			TA-ḪA-BA-TI	FN GEN	VAS VIII 127 2
		JA	NḪIB		UM			IA-ḪI-BU-UM		SIMMONS 46 3
		ME	NḪIB	AH				ME-EN-ḪI-BA	FN	XIII 1 I 24
NḪN	1	JA	NḪAN		A			IA-AN-ḪA-NA	GEN	MRS VI P. 334
		JE	NḪIN		UM			IE-EN-ḪI-NU-UM		B 25
			NAḪN		I	ʾIL		NA-AḪ-NI-DINGIR		TIM III 86:5
NḪR	1	JA	NḪUR		UM			IA-AN-ḪU-RU-UM		SIMMONS 103 2
		JA	NḪIR		AJA			A-AN?-ḪI?-RA-A		HARRIS 85 16
			NAḪAR	AH				NA-ḪA-RA	FN	RA LXV 60 III 36
Nʿ M	1		NAʿIM		UM			NA-ḪI-MU-UM		B 36+
			NAʿIM		U			NA-I-MU		B 36+
			NAʿIM		IM			NA-ḪI-MI-IM	GEN	B 36
			NAʿIM		I			NA-ḪI-MI	GEN	B 36
			NAʿM		IM			NA-AḪ-MI-IM	GEN	M
			NAʿM		I			NA-AḪ-MI	GEN	M
			NAʿM	AN	U			NA-AḪ-MA-NU		M+
			NAʿM	AN	IM			NA-MA-NI-IM	GEN	TIM III 46 15
			NAʿM		IJA			NA-MI-IA	FN	CT XLV 3 8,15,23
			NAʿM		IJA			NA-AḪ-MI-IA		JCS XXVI 142:8 HARMAL
			NAʿM		A	ʾEL		NA-MA-EL		TA 30 615:11+
			NAʿM		I	ʿAN	IM	NA-MI-A-NIM		A. 142
			NAʿM		I	JARAḪ		NA-AḪ-MI-E-RA-AḪ		JCS XI 29 NO.17 5
			NAʿM		I	ʾAŠD	U	NA-AḪ-ME-AS-DU	FN	RA LXV 60 III 2
			NAʿM		I	JAT	UM	NA-MI-IA-TUM	MN	MEISSNER 100 2
			NAʿM		I	DAʾK	A	NA-MI-DA-KA		A. 242 7
			NAʿM		I	DAGAN		NA-AḪ-MI-D-DA-GAN		A.+
			NAʿM		I	DAGAN		NA-MI-D-DA-GAN		A.+
			NAʿM		I	DAGAN		NA-AḪ-ME-D-DA-GAN		RA LXV 48 VIII 33
			NAʿM		UM	DAGAN		NA-AḪ-MU-UM-D-DA-GAN		BM 16824 28+
			NIʿIM	AH				NI-ḪI-MA	FN	M
			NIʿIM	AT	UM			NI-ḪI-MA-T[UM]	FN?	C II 42 III 31
			NIʿM		UM			NI-IḪ-MU-UM		M+
			NIʿM	AT	UM			NI-IḪ-MA-TUM	FN	M+
			NIʿM		A	HADD	U	NI-MA-A-DU		A.
			NUʿAM	AH				NU-ḪA-MA	FN	M
			NUʿM		I	ʾAB	I	NU-UḪ-MI-A-BI		XIII 1 I 38
			NUʿM		I	ʾIL		NU-UḪ-MI-DINGIR		M+
			NUʿM		I	ʾIL	I	NU-UḪ-MI-I_3-LI_2		XIII 1 XIII 26
			NUʿM		I	JABAL		NU-UḪ-ME-E-BA-AL	FN	RA LXV 62 V 19
			NUʿM		I	DAGAN		NU-UḪ-MI-D-DA-GAN		M
			NUʿM		I	LIʾM		NU-UḪ-MI-LI-IM		M+
			NUʿM		U	BAʾAT	IM	NU-UḪ-MU-BA-A-TIM	FN	C+
	2		ʾAḪ	AT	A	NAʿM	I	A-ḪA-TA-NA-AḪ-MI	FN	XIII 1 XI 3
			ḪAʾL		U	NIʿM		ḪA-LU-NI-ḪI-IM		RA LXV 52 X 74
			ʾAB		I	NAʿM	I	A-BI-NA-AḪ-MI	FN	XIII 1 VII 43, A.+
			ʾAB		I	NAʿM	I	A-BI-NA-AḪ-ME	FN	RA LXV 59 II 20
			ʾAB		I	NIʿM		A-BI-NI-ḪI-IM		RA LXV 44 IV 31
			ʾIL		A	NAʿM	A	DINGIR-NA-MA-....		VAS VIII 14 44
			ʾIL		I	NIʿM		I_3-LI_2-NE-ḪI-IM		M
			ʿAMM		U	NIʿM		ḪA-AM-MU-NI-ḪI-IM	NOM	M
			ʾUMM		I	NAʿM	I	UM-MI-NA-MI	FN	A.
			ʾUMM		I	NAʿM	I	UM-MI-NA-AḪ-ME	FN	RA LXV 59 II 17
			ʾIŠḪAR	AH		NAʿM	I	D-IŠ-ḪA-RA-NA-AḪ-ME	FN	RA LXV 64 VI 37
			ʾAŠD		I	NIʿM		AŠ$_2$-DI-NI-ḪI-IM		M+
			DAGAN			NAʿM	I	D-DA-GAN-NA-AḪ-MI	FN	X 116 1, 22
			KAKK		A	NAʿM	I	KA-AK-KA-NA-AḪ-MI	FN	XIII 1 VII 30
			MUT		A	NIʿM		MU-TA-NI-ḪI-IM		RA LXV 43 III 51
		JA	NBIʾ			NAʿIM		I-A-BI-NA-IM	NOM, GEN	BAHREIN UNPUB, POST U.
			PI			NAʿM				
						ʾEL		BI-NA-AḪ-ME-EL		B 15
			ṢIBʾ		I	NIʿM		ZI-BI-NI-ḪI-I[M]		M
NWḪ	1	JA	NWUḪ	AN				IA-NU-ḪA-AN		RA LXV 40 I 43
		JI	NWUḪ			DITAN		I-NU-UḪ-DI-TA-AN		GORDON 38 20+
		JA	NWUḪ			LIʾM		IA-NU-UḪ-LI-IM		RA LXV 44 V 8

ROOTS (Consonants only)

NWḪ	1	JI		NWUḪ				LIBB	I		I-NU-UḪ-LI-BI		M	
		JA		NWUḪ				ŠAMAR			IA-NU-UḪ-SA-MAR		CT XLIII 58 3, M	
		JI		NWUḪ				ŠAMAR			I-NU-UḪ$_3$-SA-MAR		BIN VII 7 4,9+	
		JI		NWUḪ				ŠAMAR			I-NU-UḪ-SA-MAR		TCL I 74 5,18	
		TA		NWUḪ	AH						TA-NU-ḪA	FN	M	
		TA		NWUḪ				NAWIJ	UM		TA-NU-UḪ-NA-WI-UM	FN	M	
		JE		NWIḪ		UM					E-NI-ḪU-UM		CT VIII 28C 4	
		JA		NWIḪ	AH						IA-NI-ḪA	FN	RA LXV 58 I 55	
		ME		NWIḪ		UM					ME-NI-ḪU-UM		BIN II 94 4+	
		MI		NWIḪ		UM					MI-NI-ḪU-UM		YOS XII	
		MI		NWIḪ		U					MI-NI-ḪU		TIM V 62 13	
		MA		NWIḪ	AH						MA-NI-ḪA	FN	RA LXV 58 I 36+	
				NAWḪ	AN						NA-ḪA-AN	TRIBE	M	
				NAWḪ	AN	UM					NA-ḪA-NU-UM		U	
				NAWḪ		AJA					NA-ḪA-IA		B 35	
				NAWḪ		I		ʾIL			NA-ḪI-DINGIR		B 35+	
				NAWḪ				ʾIL	I		NA-ḪI-LI		B 35	
				NAWḪ				ʾIL	UM		NA-ḪI-LUM		B 35+	
				NAWḪ				ʾIL	UM		NA-ḪI-LU-UM		B 35	
				NAWḪ				ʾIL	IM		NA-ḪI-LI-IM	GEN	B 35	
				NAWḪ		I		ʾIMM	I		D-NA-ḪI-IM-MI		YOS II 112 11	
				NAWḪ		UM		DAGAN			NA-ḪU-UM-D-DA-GAN		B 36+	
				NIWḪ	AT	UM					NI-ḪA-TUM	FN	M+	
				NUWḪ		I		ʾIL			NU-ḪI-DINGIR		I	
		JI	N	NWAḪ	AN						IN-NA-ḪA-AN		M+	
	2			ʾAḪ		I	TA	NWUḪ	A		A-ḪI-TA-NU-A		M	
		JA		HWIJ			TA	NWUḪ			IA-WI?-TA-NU		RA LXV 43 III 64	
				ḪAʾL		I	TA	NWUḪ	A		ḪA-LI-TA-NU-A		A.+	
				ʾADAN				NUWḪ	UM		ḪA-DA-NU-U$_2$-UM		M	
				ʾIL		I	TA	NWUḪ			I$_3$-LI$_2$-TA-NU-UḪ		XIII 1 IV 19	
				ʾIL		I	TA	NWUḪ			I$_3$-LI$_2$-TA-NU		RA LXV 45 V 52	
				ḪAM		I	TA	NWUḪ			D-A-MI-TA-NU-UḪ		M+	
				ḪAM		I	TA	NWUḪ			D-A-MI-TA-NU		M	
				ḪAM		I	TA	NWUḪ	A		D-A-MI-TA-NU-A		M	
				ḪAM		U	TA	NWUḪ			D-A-MU-TA-NU		M	
				ḪAM		UM	TA	NWUḪ		HU	A-MU-UM-TA-NU-U$_2$		M	
				MUT				NAWḪ	A		MU-UT-NA-ḪA		B 35 HANA	
				ŠUM		U		NIWḪ	A		SU-MU-NI-A		GORDON 39 9, 13	
				ŠUM		U		NIWḪ	UM		SU-MU-NI-ḪU-UM		B 39	
				ŠUM		U		NIWḪ	IM		SU-MU-NI-ḪI-IM	GEN	SIMMONS 121 18, M+	
				ŠAQAḪ			TA	NWUḪ		HU	SA-QA-AḪ-TA-NU-U$_2$		CT VI 46 2	
NWJ	2			BUN		U		NAWIJ	E		BU-NU-NA-WI-E		CT XLVIII 56 REV.11	
		TA		NWUḪ				NAWIJ	UM		TA-NU-UḪ-NA-WI-UM	FN	M	
NWB	1	JI	N	NWAB	AT	UM					IN-NA-BA-TUM	FN	CT VI 17 13+	
		JI	N	NWAB	AT	UM					IN-NA-BA-A-TUM	FN	CT VI 1A 3	
		JI	N	NWAB	AT	IM					IN-NA-BA-TIM	FN GEN	CT VI 17 2	
		JI	N	NWIB		UM					IN-NI-BU-UM		M	
		JI	N	NWIB		U					IN-NI-BU		YOS XIII 191:2+	
		JI	N	NWIB		U					IN-NE-BU		M	
		JI	N	NWIB		I					IN-NI-BI		CLAY PNCP 90+	
NWD	1	JA		NWUD				....			IA-NU-UD-[....]		M	
		JA		NWUD				LIʾM			IA-NU-UD-LI-IM		M	
		TA		NWUD	AH						TA-NU-DA	FN	RA LXV 61 IV 45	
				NUWD	AT	UM					NU-DA-TUM	MN	U	
NWP	1	JA		NWUP		UM					IA-NU-BU-UM		B 29+	
				NAWP				LIʾM MA			NA-AP-LIM-MA		RA XLIV 122+	QATNA
				NAWP				ŠAMŠ			NA-AP-D-UTU		M	
				NUWP	AN	UM					NU-PA-NU-UM		SIMMONS 95 10+	
				NUWP	AN	UM					NU-PA-A-NU-UM		SIMMONS 103 7+	
				NUWP	AT	UM					NU-BA-TUM		YOS XIII 191:8	
				NUWP	AT	UM					NU-PA-TUM	FN	BIROT, TEA 70C R II 18	
				NUWP	AT	IJA					NU-PA-TI-IA	FN	M	
				NUWP		AJA					NU-BA-IA		RA LXV 48 VIII 28	
				NUWP		I		ʾIL			NU-BI-DINGIR		C+	
				NUWAP		U					NU-A-BU		JNES XIII 210+	LATE

ROOTS (Consonants only)

NWP	2	KUʾM			NUWP	I	KU-UM-NU-BI		M
NWR	1 JA	NWUR	UM				IA-NU-RU-UM		RUTTEN 11 10+
		NAWAR	I				NA-WA-RI?		RA LXV 53 XI 55
		NAWAR			HADD	U	NA-WA-AR-D-IM		RA LXV 50 VIII 55+
		NAWAR		JE	JŠAR		NA-WA-AR-E-ŠAR	FN	XIII 1 VI 40
		NIWR	U				NI-E-RU		A.
		NIWR	AH				NI-E-RA	FN	A.
		NIWR			MEʾR		NI-WA-AR-ME-ER		M
		NIWR	I		HADD	U	NI-IW-RI-A-DU		A.+
		NUWR	AH				NU-RA	FN	M
		NUWR	T UM				NU-UR$_2$-TUM	FN	RA LXV 65 VII 21
		NUWR			MEʾR		NU-UR-ME-ER		M
		NUWR	U		ʾAMAR		NU-RU-A-MA-AR		HARRIS 68 19
	2	ʾAJA			NIWR	I	[A]-IA-NI-RI		RA LXV 59 II 36
		ḪAJJ	A		NIWR	I	E$_2$-A-NI-RI	FN	RA LXV 58 II 2
		ḪAJJ	A		NIWR	I	E$_2$-A-NE-RI	FN	XIII 1 VII 26
		ʾAB	I		NIWR	I	A-BI-NI-RI	FN	XIII 1 IX 58+
		ʾAB	U		NIWR	A	A-BU-NI-RA		TIM VI 34, U
		ʿABD			NAWAR		ḪA-AB-DU-NA-WA-AR		M
		ʿABD			NAWAR		AB-DU-NA-W[A-AR]		M
		HADD	U		NIWR	I	D-IM-NI-RI	FN	RA LXV 61 IV 17
		ʾADM	U		NIWR	I	AD-MU-NE-RI	FN	XIII 1 VIII 13
		ʾADM	U		NIWR	I	D-AD-MU-NI-RI	FN?	M
		ʾIL	I		NIWR	I	I$_3$-LI$_2$-NE-RI	FN	XIII 1 II 6+
		ʾALL	I		NIWR	I	AL-LI-NI-RI	FN	A.
		ʾUMM	I		NAWAR		UM-MI-NA-WA-AR	FN	XIII 1 IV 73
		ʾANN	U		NIWR	I	AN-NU-NI-RI	FN	M
		ʾIŠḪAR	AH		NIWR	I	D-IŠ-ḪA-RA-NI-RI	FN	RA LXV 59 II 22
		ʿAŠTAR			NIWR	I	EŠ$_4$-DAR-NE-RI	FN	XIII 1 IX 48
		BAʿL	I		NIWR	I	BA-AḪ-LI-NI-RI	FN	M+
		BEʿL	I		NIWR	I	BE-LI$_2$-NI-RI	FN	M+
		BEʿL	I		NIWR	I	BE-LI$_2$-NE-RI	FN	XIII 1 II 55+
		DAGAN			NIWR	I	D-DA-GAN-NI-RI	MN	RA LXV 47 VII 38
		DAGAN			NIWR	I	D-DA-GAN-NI-RI	FN	M+
		DAGAN			NIWR	I	D-DA-GAN-NE-RI	FN	M+
	JA	MWUT			NIWR	I	IA-MU-UT-NI-RI	FN	A.
		NUN	U		NIWR	I	D-NU-NU-NE?-RI	FN	RA LXV 66 VII 56
		ŠI			NUWR	I	ŠI-NU-RI	FN	A. LATE
		ŠUM	U		NIWR	I	SU-MU-NI-RI	FN	XIII 1 XI 46
		ŠARR	UM		NIWR	I	LUGAL-NI-RI	FN	XIII 1 XIII 3+
	3	LA		ʾA	HWIJ				
					NIWR	I	LA-AḪ-WI-NE-RI	FN	XIII 1 II 11
NWZ	1 JA	NWUZ	UM				IA$_2$-A-NU-ZU-UM		U
	JE	NWUZ	UM				E-NU-ZU-UM		I
NJL	1	NAJAL	AM				NA-JA-LAM		RA LXV 40 I 33
		NEJAL	AH				NE-IA-LA	FN	XIII 1 VII 51
NBʾ	1 JA	NABIʾ	IM				IA-NA-BI-IM	GEN	M
	JA	NABIʾ			ʾEL		IA-NA-BI-EL		M+
	JA	NABIʾ			ʾIL		IA-NA-AB-BI-DINGIR		M+
	JA	NABIʾ			ʾIL		IA-NA-BI-DINGIR		M
	JA	NBIʾ			HADD	U	IA-AB-BI-D-IM		M
	JA	NBIʾ			ʾIL	UM	IA$_2$-AN-BI$_2$-I$_3$-LUM		U
	JA	NBIʾ			DAGAN		IA-AB-BI-D-DA-GAN		M+
	JA	NBIʾ			DAGAN		IA-BI-D-DA-GAN		M
	JI	NBIʾ			DAGAN		I-BI-D-DA-GAN		M
	JA	NBIʾ			NAʿIM		I-A-BI-NA-IM	NOM, GEN	BAHREIN UNPUB, POST U.
	JI	NBIʾ			NABUʾ	HU	I-BI-NA-BU-U$_2$		A 7685 13
		NABAʾ	IM				NA-BA-I-IM	GEN	M+
		NABAʾ	IM				NA-BA-JI-IM	GEN	VIII 39 4
		NABIʾ	UM				NA-BI-UM		TA 1931, 538 V
		NABIʾ			ʾIL	I	NA-BI-I$_3$-LI$_2$		XIII 1 III 61
		NABIʾ			ʾILL	I	NA-BI-IL-LI		SYRIA V 274 HANA
		NABIʾ			ʾANN	U	NA-BI-AN-NU		M
		NABIʾ			KAKK	A	NA-BI-KA-KA		M+
		NABIʾ			ŠAMŠ		NA-BI-D-UTU		M+
		NABUʾ	HU		MALIK		D-NA-BU-U$_2$-MA-LIK		M

ROOTS (Consonants only)

NBʾ	2		ʾANN		U			NABIʾ				AN-NU-NA-BI-IḪ	FN	RA LXV 62 V 24
			JIŠʿ		I			NABUʾ		UM		IŠ-ḪI-NA-BU-U[M]		EDZARD, DER 68 III 6
		JI	JṢIʾ					NABUʾ		UM		I-ZI-NA-B[U-U]M?		VAS IX 79 5
		JI	JṢIʾ					NABUʾ			HU	I-ZI-NA-BU-U$_2$		B 23+, M+
		JI	NBIʾ					NABUʾ			HU	I-BI-NA-BU-U$_2$		A 7685 13
NBB	1		NABIB		I							NA-BI-BI		M
NBL	1	JA	NBUL		I							IA$_2$-AN-BU-LI		U
			NABL	AN	UM							NA-AB-LA-NU-UM		U+, B 46+
			NABL	AN	UM							NA-AB-LA-NUM$_2$		U+
NBŠ	1		NABAŠ	AN	UM							NA-BA-SA-NUM		BM 17072 9,12+
NBT	2		ʾANN		U			NABIT		I		AN-NU-NA-BI-TI		XIII 1 VI 61
			ʾATTA					NABIT		I		A-TA-NA-BE-TI		JCS XIII 57 306:5+,A LATE
NBṬ	1	JI	NBIṬ					LIʾM				I-BI-IṬ-LI-IM		ANN. ARCH. SYR. XX 74:2
		JE	NBIṬ					TIŠPAK				I-EN-BI-IṬ-D-TIŠPAK		JCS XXIV 49 NO. 15:3
			NABUṬ		UM							NA-BU-TUM		UET V P. 50+
			NABUṬ		IJA							NA-BU-DI-IA		TCL XVIII 125 3
			NUBAṬ	AH								NU-BA-TA	FN	M
			NUBUṬ	AH								NU-BU-TA	FN	XIII 1 XIV 9
	2		ʾIL		A			NABUṬ				DINGIR-NA-BU-UṬ		VAS VIII 14 31
NDB	1	JI	NDUB					ŠALIM				IN-DU-UB-ŠA-LIM		TA 1931, 265:10
		ME	NDIB		UM							ME-EN-DI-BU-UM		KING LIH I 25 4
			NADUB		UM							NA-DU-BU-UM		B 35
			NADUB	AH								NA-DU-BA?	FN	XIII 1 VIII 32+
			NADUB					ʾEL		I		NA-DU-BE-LI$_2$		U
NDN	1	JI	NDIN		UM							IN-DIN-NU-UM		I
		JI	NDIN		U							ID-DI-NU		XIII 1 I 47
		JI	NDIN		A							ID-DI-NA		A.
		JI	NDIN			JA						I-DIN-IA		M
		JI	NDIN					ʾABB		A		I-DIN-AB-BA		XIII 1 VIII 46
		JI	NDIN					ʾABB		A		ID-DI-NA-AB-BA		A.
		JI	NDIN					ʾABB		A		ID-DI-NA-BA		A. LATE
		JI	NDIN					ʾADM		U		I-DIN-D-AD-MU		M+
		JI	NDIN					....				I-DIN-D-IGI-KUR		M+
		JI	NDIN					ʾAKK		A		I-DIN-AK-KA		XIII 1 I 54+
		JI	NDIN					ʾANN		U		I-DIN-AN-NU		M+
		JI	NDIN					ʾANN		UM		I-DIN-AN-NU-UM		M+
		JI	NDIN					ʾANN		U		I-DI-AN-NU		RA LXV 51 IX 31
		JI	NDIN					JAT		UM		I-DIN-IA-TUM		M+
		JI	NDIN					JAT		IM		I-DIN-IA-TIM	GEN	M+
		JI	NDIN					JAT		IM		ID-DI-IA-TIM	GEN	M
		JI	NDIN					JAT		AM		I-DIN-IA-TAM	ACC	XIV 64:7
		JI	NDIN				ʾA	ŠKUR				I-DIN-D-AŠ$_2$-KU-UR		SYRIA XXXVII 206 8 HANA
		JI	NDIN				JI	TWUR						
								MEʾR				I-DIN-D-I-DUR-ME-ER		XIII 1 III 49+
		JI	NDIN					BIN		UM		I-DIN-BI-NU-UM		UCP X/1 64 2
		JI	NDIN					DIWR	IT	IM		I-DIN-D-DI-RI-TIM	GEN	M
		JI	NDIN					DAGAN				I-DIN-D-DA-GAN		M+
		JI	NDIN					KAKK		A		I-DIN-KA-AK-KA		M+
		JI	NDIN					KAKK		A		I-DIN-D-KA-KA		M+
		JI	NDIN					LABW		A		I-DIN-D-LA-BA		M
		JI	NDIN					MEʾR				I-DIN-D-ME-ER		MAOG IV 2 2 HANA
		JI	NDIN					MAM		A		I-DIN-D-MA-MA		M+
		JI	NDIN					RIWM				I-DIN-D-RI-IM		TCL I 238 16 HANA
		JI	NDIN					RUŠP	AN			I-DIN-D-RU-UŠ-PA-AN		MAOG IV 2 5 HANA+
		JI	NDIN					RUŠP	AN			I-DIN-D-RU-UŠ$_2$-PA-AN		MEL. SYR. I 275
		JI	NDIN					TABUB		U		I-DIN-TA-BU-BU		M
			NADIN		A							NA-DI-NA	GEN	A.+
NDR	1	JA	NDUR		UM							IA-AN-DU-RUM?		TIM II 37 1
NGH	1	JA	NGIH									IA-AN-GI		JNES XIII 210+ LATE
			NAGIH		UM							NA-KI-ḪU-UM		TIM III 31 17+
			NAGIH		IM							NA-KI-ḪI-IM	GEN	TIM III 77 5A
			NAGIH	AH								NA-GI-IA	FN	XIII 1 V 82
			NAGIH	AN	UM							NA-GI$_4$-A-NU-UM		TA 30 615 13
			NIGH	AT	UM							NI-IG-ḪA-TUM	FN	M
NGŠ	1		NAGIŠ	AN	UM							NA-GI$_4$-SA-NU-UM		RUTTEN 2 8+
			NAGIŠ	AN	UM							NA-GI-SA-NU-UM		RUTTEN 5 8

ROOTS (Consonants only)

NKD	1		NIKID	AT	UM					NI-KI-DA-TUM		VAS XIII 65 2,3+
NKL	1		NAKL		UM					NA-AK-LUM		BIROT, TEA 69 III 2
			NAKL	AT	UM					NA-AK-LA-TUM	FN	YOS XIII 90 REV 22
NKM	1		NAKAM	Ī	UM					NA-KA-AM-TUM	FN	M
NKR	1		NAKAR		UM					NA-KA-RU-UM		BIROT, TEA 70A II 14+
			NAKAR		UM					NA-KA-RUM		BM 16914 3,11+
			NAKAR	AH						NA-KA-RA	FN	XIII 1 VIII 19
			NAKAR	AT	UM					NA-KA-RA-TUM	FN	RA LXV 59 II 71
			NAKAR	Ī	UM					NA-KA-AR-TUM	FN	M
			NAKR					ʾAḪ	UM	NA-AK-RA-ḪU-UM		RUTTEN 2 19+
			NIKR		UM					NI-IK-RU-UM		RA LXV 45 V 40
			NUKR	AN	UM					NU-UK-RA-NU-UM		U+
NLŠ	2		KAKK		A			NILŠ	I	KA-A[K]-KA-NI-EL?-ŠI?	FN	XIII 1 VIII 41
NMḪ	1		NAMḪ		U	HU				NAM-ḪU-U$_2$		BM 80328 8
			NIMḪ		AM			PI				
								ʾIL		NI-IM?-ḪA-AM-BI-DINGIR		A. 95 17 (=JCS VIII 8)
			NUMAḪ		A					NU-MA-ḪA-A	GN	M
			NUMḪ		A					NU-UM-ḪA-A(-KI)	GN	M+
			NUMḪ	AJ	I					NU-UM-ḪA-I	GN	IX 48 3+
			NUMḪ	AJ	I					NU-UM-ḪA-A-JI	GN	X 5 4
	2		ŠUM		U			NUMAḪ	A	SU-MU-NU-MA-ḪA		M
			ŠUM		U			NUMḪ	A	SU-M[U-N]U-UM-ḪA		RA LXIV 43
			ŠUM		U			NUMḪ	IM	SU-MU-NU-UM-ḪI-IM		RIFTIN 44 12,16+
	3		BAʿL		A			MI				
								NAMḪ	U	BA-LA-MI-NA-AM-ḪU		SYRIA XLIV 201 N.1 MARI
			BAʿL		U			ME				
								NUMḪ	I	BA-LU-ME-NU-ḪI		M+
			BAʿL		U			ME				
								NUMḪ	I	BA-LU-ME-NU-UM-ḪI		IX 41 2
			LA					RIWM				
								NUMAḪ	A	LA-RI-IM-NU-MA-ḪA-A		M+
			LA					RIWM				
								NUMAḪ	A	LA-RI-IM-NU-MA-A		M
NML	1		NAMAL		UM					NA-MA-LUM		HARRIS 7 12
			NAMAL	AT	UM					NA-MA-LA-TUM	MN	B 36+
NMN	1		NIMIN		A			HADD	U	NI-MI-NA-A-DU		A.+
			NUMEN	AH						NU-ME-EN-NA	FN	XIII 1 IV 32
			NUMN		UM					NU-UM-NU-UM		BIROT, TEA 65:8
			NUMN		U	HU				NU-UM-NU-U$_2$		M
NMR	1		NAMR	AT	UM					NA-AM-RA-TUM	FN	YOS XIII 163:7
	2		MAM		A			NUMR	I	D-MA-MA-NU-UM-RI	FN	RA LXV 65 VII 30
NMŠ	1		NAMAŠ		U					NA-MA-ŠU		B 36 HANA
			NAMAŠ		I					NA-MA-ŠI		MAOG IV 3 30 HANA
			NAMIŠ		UM					NA?-MI-ŠUM		XIII 1 VIII 47
			NAMIŠ		U					NA-MI-ŠU		B 36 HANA
			NAMIŠ		A					NA-MI-ŠA	GEN	MAOG IV 3 34 HANA
NMZ	1		NAMZ		U	HU				NAM-ZU-U$_2$		BM 80328 5
NN	1		NAN		I					D-NA-NI	DN	M
			NAN	AT	UM					NA-NA-TUM	FN	RA LXV 65 VI 57
			NAN		IJA					NA-NI-IA	FN	RA LXV 60 III 66
			NUN		U			NIWR	I	D-NU-NU-NE?-RI	FN	RA LXV 66 VII 56
			NUN		U		TA	BNIJ		D-NU-NU-TA-AB-NI	FN	XII 265 1
	2		ʾAB		U			NAN	UM	A-BU-NA-NU-UM		B 42+
			ʾIL		A			NUN	U	I-LA-NU-NU		FIGULLA CAT. I 14029
		ʾA	JPAʿ					NAN	UM	A-BA-AḪ-NA-NU-UM		TA 1931, 374, EARLY OB
			ʿAQB		I			NAN	UM	AQ-BI-NA-NU-UM		B 42+
		JA	JTIR					NAN	UM	JA-TI-IR-NA-NU-UM		M+
		JA	JTIR					NAN	AM	JA-TI-IR-NA-NAM	ACC	M
		JA	JTIR					NAN	AM	JA-TE-IR-NA-NAM	ACC	M
		JA	JTIR					NAN	IM	JA-TI-IR-NA-NIM	GEN	M+
		JA	JTIR					NAN	IM	JA-TE-IR-NA-NIM	GEN	M
			ḪAZAQ					NAN	UM	A-ZA-AQ-NA-NU-UM		CT IV 50A 21
			MUT					NAN	UM	MU-UT-NA-NU-UM		TA 30, 615:39+
			MATQ		U			NAN	A	MA-AT-KU-NA-NA	FN	RA LXV 60 III 33
			PUḪUR					NUN	U	PU-ḪU-UR-D-NU-NU		M
		TA	QJIŠ					NAN	I	TA-KI-IŠ-NA-NI	FN?	TIM III 41 6

ROOTS (Consonants only)

NN	2		QIJŠ	T	I		NUN		U		KI-IŠ-TI-D-NU-NU		M+
NNB	1		NANIB		UM						NA-NI-BU-UM		SIMMONS 138 29
			NANIB		U		MA				NA-NI-BU-MA		SIMMONS 138 4+
NNGL	2	JI	TWUR				NINGAL				I-DUR-D-NIN-GAL		M
NNM	1		NUNM	AN							NU-UN-MA-AN		RUTTEN 26 9
NNN	1		NANN	AH							NA-AN-NA	FN	M+
			NANN	ATAN							NA-NA-TA-AN		M
			NANN		A		MUʾ		UM		NA-AN-NA-MU-UM		M
			NANN		IJA						NA-AN-NI-IA	FN	XIII 1 I 66
			NANN		I		ŠARR	AH			D-NA-AN-NI-ŠAR-RA	FN	XIII 1 V 31
			NINN		U						NI-IN-NU		M
NPḪ	1	JI	NPIḪ		UM						IB-BI$_2$-ḪU-UM?		VIII 3 19
		JI	NPIḪ		U						I-BI-ḪU	FN	C
		JI	NPIḪ				LI						
							DIJN		I		IB-BI-IḪ-LI-DI-NI	FN	C
NPR	1		NIPR		AM						NI-IP-RA-AM		RA LXV 50IX 26
			NUPAR				ŠARR		IM		NU-BAR-LUGAL		A.
			NUPUR		I						NU-PU-RI		XIII 1 IV 12
	2		DAGAN				NUPAR		A	JA	D-DA-GAN-NU?-PA?-RA-IA		M
NPŠ	1		NAPŠ		UM						NA-AP-SU-UM		SIMMONS 36B 6+, M
			NAPŠ		UM						NA-AP-ZUM		SIMMONS 36 7
			NAPŠ		UM						NA-AP-SU-UM	FN	RA LXV 59 II 47
			NAPŠ	AN	UM						NA-AP-SA-NU-UM		U, B 46+
			NAPŠ	AN	UM						NA-AP-ŠA-NU-UM		U+, I+
			NAPŠ	AN	U						NA-AP-SA-NU-KI	GN	B 46
			NAPŠ	AN	UM						NA-AP-ZA-NU-UM		CT XLV 115 14
			NAPŠ		IJA						NA-AP-SI-IA		M
			NAPŠ		I		HADD		U		NA-AP-SI-D-IM		M+
			NAPŠ		I		HADD		U		NA-AP-ŠI-A-DU		A.+
			NAPŠ		I		HAND		U		NA-AP-SI-IA-AN-DU		M
			NAPŠ		I		ḪINN		I		NA-AP-SI-IN-NI	FN	XIII 1 IV 72
			NAPŠ		I		JARAḪ				NA-AP-SI-E-RA-AḪ		M+
			NAPŠ		I		DAGAN				NA-AP-SI-D-DA-GAN		M+
			NAPŠ		I		PI						
							ʾIL				NA-AP-SI-BI-DINGIR		SYRIA XLVIII 9:22
			NAPŠ		I		ŠEʾR		UM		NA-AP-SI-ŠE?-RUM?		M
			NAPŠ		U		HADD		U		NA-AP-SU-D-IM		M
			NAPŠ		U	NA	HADD		U		NA-AP-SU-NA-D-IM		M+
			NAPŠ		U	NA	DAWR		A		NA-AP-SU-NA-D-DA-RA		CT IV 1 8
	2	TA	HWIJ				NAPŠ		U		TA-AḪ-WI-NA-AP-SU		RA LXIV 28 NO. 14
			ʾAB		I		NAPŠ		I		A-BI-NA-AP-S[I]		XIV 77:7
			ʾIŠḪAR	AH			NAPŠ		I		D-IŠ-ḪA-RA-NA-AP-SI	FN	XIII 1 VII 13
			LAʾR				NAPŠ		U		LA-AR-NA-AP-SU	FN	XIII 1 I 71
NQM	1	JE	NQIM		UM						EN-GI-MU-UM		U+
		JA	NQIM				HADD		U		IA-AK-KI-IM-D-IM		M+
		JA	NQIM				HADD		U		IA-KI-IM-D-IM		M+
		JA	NQIM				ʾIL				IA-AN?-KI-IM-DINGIR		RA VIII 69 22
		JA	NQIM				ʾIL				A-AN-KI-IM-DINGIR		HARRIS 9 14+
		JE	NQIM				ʾIL				E-EN-KI-IM-DINGIR		CT VI 49B 4
		JA	NQIM				LIʾM				IA-AK-KI-IM-LI-IM		M
		JA	NQIM				LIʾM				IA-KI-IM-LI-IM		M
		JA T	NAQIM								IA-AN-TA-KI-IM		M+
			NAQIM		UM						NA-KI-MU-UM		B 36+
			NAQIM		U						NA-KI-MU		B 36+
			NAQIM		IM						NA-KI-MI-IM	GEN	B 36+
			NIQM	AN							NI-IQ-MA-AN		M
			NIQM	AN	UM						NI-IQ-MA-NU-UM		B 47+
			NIQM	AN	UM						NI-IQ-MA-A-NU-UM		B 47+
			NIQM		EJA						NI-IQ-ME-IA		M+
			NIQM				ʾAB		I		NI-IQ-MA-A-BI		A. 86 7+
			NIQM				HADD		U		NI-IQ-MA-A-DU		A.+
			NIQM				HADD		U		NI-IQ-MA-DU		A.
			NIQM				HADD		U		NI-IQ-MA$_2$-A-DU		B 36
			NIQM		I		HADD		U		NI-IQ-MI-A-DU		A.+
			NIQM		I		HADD		U		NI-IQ-MI-IA-AD-DU		M
			NIQM		I	JA	JPAʿ				NI-IQ-MI-PA		A. 27 12

ROOTS (Consonants only)

NQM	1		NIQM		I		JA	JPAʿ			NI-IQ-ME-PA		A.+
			NIQM		I		JE	JPUʿ			NI-IQ-MI-E-PU-UḪ		M+, A.+
			NIQM		I			JATAR			NI-IQ-MI-E-TAR		C II 39 3
			NIQM		I			LA					
								NAŠIʾ			NI-IQ-MI-LA-NA-SI		M
			NIQM		U	K					NI-IQ-MU-UK	FN	M
	2		ʿAMM		U			NIQM	A		AM-MU-NI-IQ-MA		A.+
NRB	1		NARB		U						NA-AR-BU		XIII 1 II 32
			NARB	AT	UM						NA-AR-BA-TUM	FN	M+
			NARB	AN	IM						NA-AR-BA-NIM	GEN	A 21950
NRNR	1		NURNUR	AT	UM						NU-UR$_2$-NU-RA-TUM	MN?	BIN VII 157 7
NSQ	1		NASQ	AT	UM						NA-AS-QA-TUM	FN	RA LXV 58 I 38
NŠʾ	1	JA	NŠIʾ	AN							IA-AŠ$_2$-SI-IA-AN		M
		JA	NŠIʾ					HADD	U		IA-AŠ$_2$-ŠI-D-IM		RA LXV 42 III 13
		JA	NŠIʾ					HADD	U		IA-SI-D-IM		B 29
		JA	NŠIʾ					ʾIL			IA-SI-DINGIR		B 29+
		JA	NŠIʾ					ʾIL	I		IA-SI-LI		B 29+
		JA	NŠIʾ					ʾIL	I		IA-SI-I-LI$_2$		TCL X 5 3
		JA	NŠIʾ					ʾIL	UM		IA-SI-LUM		RA IX 22 2+
		JA	NŠIʾ					ʿAMM	U		IA-SI-ḪA-MU		M
		JA	NŠIʾ					JARAḪ			IA-SI-E-RA-AḪ		B 28
		JA	NŠIʾ					JARAḪ			IA-SI-RA-AḪ		B 30
		JA	NŠIʾ					JARAḪ			IA-SI-A-RA-AḪ		GRANT, HAV. 242:2+
		JA	NŠIʾ				JA	JŠUʿ			IA-SI-SU-UḪ		BIN II 104 15
		JA	NŠIʾ					DAGAN			IA-AŠ$_2$-SI-D-DA-GAN		M+
		JA	NŠIʾ					DAGAN			IA-SI-D-DA-GAN		M+
		JI	NŠIʾ					DAGAN			I-SI-IḪ-D-DA-GAN		RA XLI 44 R. 6 HANA
		JI	NŠIʾ					DAGAN			IS-SI-D-DA-GAN		B 22 HANA
		JA	NŠIʾ					LIʾM			IA$_2$-ŠI-LI-IM		U+
			NAŠʾ	AT	UM						NA-AŠ-ḪA-TUM	FN	RA LXV 61 IV 33
	2	JA	HWIJ					NAŠIʾ			IA-AḪ-WI-NA-SI		M+
		JA	DWUR					NAŠIʾ			IA-DU-UR-NA-SI		M+
			LA					NAŠUʾ	UM		LA-NA-SU-U$_2$-UM		M
			LA					NAŠUʾ	UM		LA-NA-SU-WU-UM		XIV 53:20+
			LA					NAŠUʾ	U		LA-NA-SU-U$_2$		B 33, 4E RENC. ASS. P. 178 8
			LA					NAŠUʾ	IM		LA-NA-SU-I-IM	GEN	M
			LA					NAŠUʾ	IM		LA-A-NA-SU-I-IM	GEN	M
			LA					NAŠUʾ	I		LA-NA-SU-JI	GEN	M
			LA					NAŠUʾ	I		LA-NI-SU-JI	FN NOM	M
			MIJA					NAŠUʾ			MI-IA-NA-SU		XIII 1 I 18
	3		NIQM		I			LA					
								NAŠIʾ			NI-IQ-MI-LA-NA-SI		M
			ṢIDQ		U			LA					
								NAŠIʾ			ZI-ID-KU-LA-NA-SI		M+
NŠʾ	2		MUT		U		JA	NŠUʾ		HU	MU-TU-A-AN-ŠU-U$_2$		KISURRA 91 24
NŠP	1		NAŠP	AT	UM						NA-AŠ-PA-TUM	FN	CT II 35 28+
			NUŠUP		UM						NU-ŠU-BU-UM		HARRIS 4 9+
NṢB	1	JA	NṢIB		UM						IA-AN-ZI-BU-UM		M+
		JA	NṢIB		IM						IA-AN-ZI-BI-IM	GEN	M+
		JA	NṢIB	AN							IA-AN-ZI-BA-AN		M
		JA	NṢIB	AN							IA-AN-ZI-PA-AN		M
		JA	NṢIB					....			IA-AN-ZI-IB-[....]		M+
		JA	NṢIB					....			IA-AN-ZI-IB-D-[....]		M
		JA	NṢIB					HADD	U		IA-AN-ZI-IB-D-IM		M+
		JA	NṢIB					ʾIL			IA-AN-Z[I-I]B-DINGIR		XII 683 4
		JA	NṢIB					DAGAN			IA-AN-ZI-IB-D-DA-GAN		M+
		JA	NṢIB					DAGAN			IA-AZ-ZI-IB-D-DA-GAN		B 29
			NAṢAB	AN	UM						NA-ZA-BA-NU-UM		TCL I 111 3
			NAṢB		UM						NA-AZ-BU-UM	FN	RA LXV 64 VI 25
			NIṢAB	AH							NI-ZA-BA?	FN	RA LXV 68 V 9A
			NIṢB		I			ʾIL			NE-IZ-BI-IL		TA 1931, 172
			NIṢB		I			ʾEL			NE-IZ-BI-EL		TA 1930, 747 +
			NUṢAB		UM						NU-ZA-BU-UM		M
			NUṢAB		U						NU-ZA-BU		XIV 61:7
NṢR	1	JA	NṢUR					HADD	U		IA-AṢ-ṢU-UR-D-IM		X 12 6, 21+
		JI	NṢUR					ʾAŠD	UM		I-ZUR-AŠ-DU-UM		A 7685 5

ROOTS (Consonants only)

NṢR	1	JI	NṢUR				ʾAŚD	UM		I-ZUR-A-AŠ-DU-UM		CT II 42 25
			NAṢR		IJA					NA-AṢ-RI-IA		RA LXV 44 IV 47+
	2		JAD		I		NAṢIR			IA-DI-NA-ṢIR		BM 17051, 17052
			ʾAŠAR				NAṢIR			D-A-ŠAR-NA-ṢIR		M
			BEʿL		I		NUṢR	I		BE-LI$_2$-NU-IZ-RI	FN	RA LXV 64 V 60
			BAWŠ	T	I		NUṢR	I		BA-AŠ-TI-NU-IZ-RI	FN	RA LXV 58 I 45
			BAWŠ	T	I		NUṢR	I		BA-AŠ-TI-UZ-RI		RA LXIV 28 NO. 15
			BAWŠ	T	I		NUṢR	I		BA-AŠ$_2$-TI-NU-UZ-RI	FN	XIII 1 VII 24
			DAGAN				NAṢIR			D-DA-GAN-NA-ṢIR		RA LXV 52 X 76
NTN	1	JA	NTIN		UM					IA-AN-TI-NU-UM		B 29+
		JA	NTIN		UM					A-AN-TI-NU-UM		SIMMONS 79 6'
		JA	NTIN		UM					IA-AN-TE-NU-UM		SIMMONS 104 13
		JI	NTIN		UM					IN-TI-NU-UM		I
		JE	NTIN		UM					E-EN-TI-NU-UM		WALTERS,WL 112:25
		JA	NTIN		U					IA-AN-TI-NU		M
		JA	NTIN		U					IA-TI-NU		B 31
		JA	NTIN		U					IA-AT-TI-NU		YOS XIII 280:13
		JA	NTIN		IM					IA-AN-TI-NIM	GEN	M
		JA	NTIN		IM					IA-AT-TI-NIM	GEN	M+
		JI	NTIN							IT-TI-IN		M
		JA	NTIN				....			IA-AN-TI-IN-D-[....]		M
		JA	NTIN				HADD	U		IA-AN-TI-IN-D-IM		M+
		JA	NTIN				HADD	U		IA-AN-TI-NA-DU		ZDPV XLIX PL. 45 LATE
		JI	NTIN				HADD	U		I-TI-IN-D-IM		M
		JA	NTIN				ʾIL			IA-AN-TI-IN-DINGIR		B 29+, M+
		JA	NTIN				ʾIL			IA-AT-TI-IN-DINGIR		M
		JA	NTIN				ʾIL			[A-A]N-TI-IN-DINGIR		HARRIS 56 15
		JA	NTIN		I		ʾIL			IA-AN-TI-NI-DINGIR		BM 17084
		JA	NTIN				ʿAMM	U		IA-AN-TI-IN-ḪA-MU		M
		JA	NTIN				ʾANN	I	Š	[IA-AN]-TI-IN-A-NI-IŠ		VII 180 8'
		JA	NTIN				JARAḪ			IA-AN-TI-IN-A-RA-AḪ		RA LXV 62 V 34
		JA	NTIN				JARAḪ			IA-AN-TI-NA-RA-AḪ		RUTTEN 11 20+
		JA	NTIN				JARAḪ			IA-AN-TI-LA-RA-AḪ		VAS XVI 91 3
		JA	NTIN				JARAḪ			IA-AN-TI-IN-E-RA-AḪ		M+
		JA	NTIN				JARAḪ			IA-AT-TI-IN-E-RA-AḪ		M+
		JA	NTIN				JARAḪ			IA-T[I-I]N-E-RA-AḪ		M
		JA	NTIN				DAGAN			IA-AN-TI-IN-D-DA-GAN		M+
		JA	NTIN				DAGAN			IA-TI-IN-D-DA-GAN		M
			NATUN		UM					NA-TU-NU-UM		B 36
		MA	NTIN		UM					MA-AN-TI-NU-UM		HARRIS 31 13+
		MA	NTIN		U					URU MA-AN-TI-NU	GN	BM 16387
	2		ʾIL		I		NATUN			I$_3$-LI$_2$-NA-TU-UN		M
NTT	1		NATT		A					NA-AT-TA		M
NTʿ	1	JA	NTIʿ		A					IA-AN-DI-ḪA-KI	GN	M
NṬP	1		NUṬUP	AT	UM					NU-DU-PA-TUM	FN	FRANK SKT P. 31+
			NUṬUP	T	UM					NU-DU-UB-TUM	FN	UET V P. 53+
			NUṬUP	T	UM					NU-TU-UP-TUM	FN	UET V P. 53+
			NUṬUP		AJA					NU-TU-PA-A-A		UET V 480 3
NZ	2		ʾIPQ		U		NAZI			IP-KU-D-NA-AZ-ZI		M
		JA	JTIR				NAZI			JA-TE-IR-NA-ZI		SYRIA XX 174 MARI
	3		MUT				PA					
							NAZI			MU-UT-PA-A-NA-ZI		RA LXV 40 I 10
NZL	1	ʾA	NZAL	AT	UM					AN-ZA-LA-TUM	FN?	XIII 1 I 14
		MA	NZAL	AN	UM					MA-AN-ZA-LA-NU-UM		UET V 465 17
NZM	1		NUZAM	AN						NU-ZA-MA-AN		XIII 1 V 22
P	1		PA				ʾIL	A		PA-I-LA		XIII 1 VII 16
			PA			KA	ʾIL	A		PA-KA-I-LA		B 37+
			PA			KA	ʾIL	A		PA-KA-DINGIR		B 37
			PA			KA	ʾIL	A		PA-A-KA-I-LA		B 37
			PI			HU				BI-U$_3$		U
			PI				ʾIL	A		PI-I-LA		A. LATE
			PI				ʿAN	UM		PI-A-NUM$_2$		I
			PI				ʿAN	UM		BI$_2$-A-NU-UM		I
			PI				KAMA					
							ʾIL			BI-KA-MA-DINGIR		XIV 111:10+
			PI				KAMA					
							ʾEL			BI-KA-MA-EL		M+

ROOTS (Consonants only)

P	1	PI			NAʿM					
					ʾEL			BI-NA-AḪ-ME-EL		B 15
		PU		KA	DAGAN			PU-KA-D-DA-GAN		M
		PU		HU	DAGAN			PU-U$_2$-D-DA-GAN		M
		PU			MA					
					ʾEL			PU-MA-[E]L		TA 1931,538 I
		PU			ME					
					ʾIL			PU-ME-IL		I
		PU	UM		ʾEL			PU-UM-E-EL		BAGH.MITT. IV 291,SEAL
	2	ʾAHL	UM		PU		HU	A-LUM-BI-U$_2$		SIMMONS 129 13
		ʾAHL	UM		PU		HU	ḪA-LAM-BU-U$_2$		RLA II 165 17
		ʾAHL	UM		PU		HU	[A]-LI-IM-BU-MU		OLZ 1958 547 N.1
		ʾAHL	UM		PU		HU	A-LUM-BU-MU		OLZ 1958 547 N.1
		JAʿAL			PI					
					ʾIL	UM		IA-ḪA-AL-PI-LUM		3NT867:5, 12, 21
	JI	JʿIL			PI					
					ʾIL			I-ḪI-IL-BI-DINGIR		M
		JAʾN	UM		PI			JA-NU-UM-BI-KI	GN	M
		ʾAJIŠ			PI		HU	ḪA-II-IŠ-PI$_2$-U$_2$		KISURRA 22+
		ʾAJIŠ			PI		HU	ḪA-A-IŠ-PI$_2$-U$_2$		KISURRA 5+
	JI	JBAL			PI					
					ʾEL			I-BA-AL-BI-EL		M+
	JI	JBAL			PI					
					ʾEL			I-BA-AL-PI-EL		UCP X P. 56+
	JI	JBAL			PI					
					ʾIL			I-BA-AL-BI-DINGIR		M+
	JI	JDAʿ			PI					
					ʾIL			I-DA-BI$_2$-DINGIR		I
	ʾA	JDAʿ			PI					
					ʾEL			A-DA-AḪ-[BI]?-EL		SIMMONS 51 21
		JADAʿ			PI					
					ʾIL			IA-DA-BI-DINGIR		AJSL XXXIII 224 3
		ʾIL	A		PA	I		I-LA-BA-I		TA 1931, 499
		ʾALI			PA					
					ʾIL			A-LI$_2$-PA-DINGIR		RUTTEN 6 21+
		ʾALI			PA					
					ʾIL			A-LI-PA-DINGIR		TIM III 5 18+
		ʾALI			PA					
					ʾIL			ḪA-A-LI-PA-DINGIR		EDZARD,DER 152 REV.16
		ʾALI			PA					
					ʾIL	UM		A-LI$_2$-KA-LUM		RUTTEN 37 19
		ʾALI			PA					
					ŠAMŠ			A-LI$_2$-PA-D-UTU		BE VI/1 15:25
		ʾALUN			PI					
					JAM	U		ḪA-LU-UN-BI-JA-MU		M
		ʾALUN			PI					
					JAM	U		ḪA-LU-UM-BI-JA-MU		RA LXV 43 III 78
		ʾALUN			PI					
					JAM	U		ḪA-LU-BI-JA-MU		M
	JA	ḪNUN			PI					
					ʾEL			IA-ḪU-UN-PI-EL		SIMMONS 54 18
		ḪUNN			PI					
					ʾEL			ḪU-UN-BI-EL		SIMMONS 82 7
		ʾARUŠ			PI					
					ʾIL			A-RU-UŠ-BI-DINGIR		M, RA XLI 45 4' HANA
		ʾAŠD	UM		PI					
					JAD	IM		AŠ-DU-UM-BI-IA-DI-IM		RA LXV 55 XIII 44
	JA	ʾŠUD			PI					
					ʾEL			IA-SU-UD-PI-EL		SIMMONS 46 31
		ḪATAN			PI					
					ʾIL			ḪA-TA-AN-BI-DINGIR		M
	JI	JṢIʾ			PU		K	I-ZI-PU-UK	FN?	M+
		BUN	U	HU	PI					
					ʾIL	UM		BU-NU-U$_2$?-BI-I-LUM		UET V 548 2
		DAWD	UM		PI					
					ʾIL			DA-DUM-BI$_2$-DINGIR		I

ROOTS (Consonants only)

P	2	ʾA	KWUN				PI					
							ʾEL			A-KU-PI-EL		GORDON, SCT 38 16
		JA	KWUN				PI			IA-KU-UN-PI		CT VIII 43C 8
		JA	KWUN				PI			IA-KU-BI		B 27
		JA	KWUN				PI			IA-KU-PI		B 27
		JE	KWUN				PI			E-KU-PI		B 17
		JA	KWUN				PI	I	JA	IA-KU-UN-BI-IA		XII 14
		JI	KWUN				PI	I	JA	I-KU-BI-IA		SM P. 54
		JI	KWUN				PI	I		I-KU-UN-BI-I		C II 2 11
		JA	KWUN				PI					
							MAM	A		IA-KU-UN-BI-D-MA-MA	FN	RA LXV 66 VII 61
		ʾA	MWUT				PA					
							ʾIL			A-MU-UT-PA-DINGIR		SYRIA L 7
		ʾA	MWUT				PA					
							ʾIL			AM-MU-UT-PA-DINGIR		RA XLIII 212 39 QATNA
		ʾA	MWUT				PI					
							ʾIL			A-MU-UT-BI-DINGIR		M+
		ʾA	MWUT				PI					
							ʾIL	A		A-MU-UT-BI-I-LA		M
			MUT				PA					
							NAZI			MU-UT-PA-A-NA-ZI		RA LXV 40 I 10
			NIMḪ		AM		PI					
							ʾIL			NI-IM?-ḪA-AM-BI-DINGIR		A. 95 17 (=JCS VIII 8)
			NAPŠ		I		PI					
							ʾIL			NA-AP-SI-BI-DINGIR		SYRIA XLVIII 9:22
		JI	TWUR				PI					
							ʾIL			I-DUR-[BI]?-DINGIR		I
			TAḪT		U		PI					
							ʾIL			TA-AḪ-TU-BI-DINGIR		M+
			ZAKK				PI					
							ʾEL			ZA-AK-PI-EL		TA 1931,198 EARLY OB
PʾL	1		PAʾL		A	HA				PA-LA-A	FN	B 37
	2		ʾIL		I		PAʾAL	UM		I_3-LI_2-PA-A-LU-UM		TIM III 44 16+
			ʾIL		I		PAʾAL	UM		I_3-LI_2-PA-ḪA-LUM		M
PʾP	1		PAʾP	AK	UM					PA-PA-KUM		B 37
PʾR	1		PAʾAR				MI			PA-ḪA-AR-MI	FN	RA LXV 59 II 23
			PAʾAR	AT	IM					PA-A-RA-TIM	FN GEN	X 170:1
			PAʾR	T	UM					PA-AR-TUM	FN	CT XLV 54 24, M+
			PAʾR	AT	IJA					PA-RA-TI-IA		UCP X/3 3 8
PʾŠ	2		ʾIL		A		PAʾŠ	I	JA	DINGIR-PA-ŠI-IA		TCL XVIII 106 9
PʾT	1		PAʾT	AT	UM					PA-TA-TUM	FN	M+
PḪR	1	JA	PḪUR		UM					IA-AP-ḪU-RU-UM		B 24
		JA	PḪUR		UM					IA-AP-ḪU-RUM		TIM IV 33 19, SEAL +
		JA	PḪUR	AN	U					IA-AP-ḪU-RA-NU		M
		JA	PḪUR				HADD	U		IA-AP-Ḫ[U-UR]-A-DU		M
		JA	PḪUR				JARAḪ			IA-AP-ḪU-UR-SIN		M
		JA	PḪUR				LIʾM			IA-AP-ḪU-UR-LI-IM		M+, A 7630
			PUḪR		A	NA				PU-UḪ$_3$-RA-NA		YOS VIII 101B 13
			PUḪUR	T	UM					PU-ḪU-UR-TUM	FN	M
			PUḪUR				NUN	U		PU-ḪU-UR-D-NU-NU		M
		MU	PAḪIR	AH						MU-PA-ḪI-RA	FN	XIII 1 VII 47
PDJ	1	JA	PDIJ		UM					IA-AP?-DI-UM		UNPUBL.
PDL	1		PADAL	AN						PA-DA-LA-AN		RA LXV 51 IX 33
PGR	1		PAGIR		UM					PA-GI-RUM		B 36 HANA
			PAGIR		UM					PA-GI-RU-UM		B 36+ HANA
PKN	1		PAKN		UM					PA-AK-NU-UM		B 37
			PAKN	AN	UM					PA-AK-NA-NU-UM		B 47+
			PAKN	AN	IM					PA-AK-NA-NIM	GEN	B 47
			PAKN	AN	A					PA-AK-NA-NA	GEN	BE VI/2 81 14
PLḪ	1	ʾA	PLAḪ				HAND	A		AP-LA-ḪA-AN-DA		M+
		ʾA	PLAḪ				HAND	A		AP-LI-ḪA-AN-DA		M
		ʾA	PLAḪ				HAND	A		AP-LA-ḪA-DA		M
		ʾA	PLAḪ				HAND	A		AP-LA-AḪ-[AN]-DA		M
		ʾA	PLAḪ				HAND	U		AP-LA-ḪA-AN-DU		RA LXV 42 II 65
		JA	PLAḪ		UM					IA-AP-LA-ḪU-UM		B 24+
		JA	PLAḪ		U					IA-AP-LA-ḪU		B 24+

PLḪ	1	JA		PLAḪ				....		IA-AP-LA-[AḪ?-....]		XIII 1 XII 23
		JA		PLAḪ				ʾIL		IA-AP-LA-AḪ-DINGIR		M, TIM III 56 5+
		JA		PLAḪ				ʾIL	IM	IA-AP-LA-AḪ-I-LI-IM	GEN	RA LXIV 43
		JA		PLIḪ				ʾIL		[I]A-AP-LI?-I[Ḫ?-DINGIR]		VII 215 32
				PILAḪ		UM				BI-LA-ḪU-[UM]		RA LXV 54 XII 44
				PILḪ		U		HADD	U	BI-EL-ḪU-D-IM		RA LXV 55 XIII 4
				PULAḪ	AN					PU-LA-ḪA-AN		M
PLL	1			PALL	AK	UM				PA-AL-LA-KUM		B 37
				PALL	AK	UM				PA-LA-KUM		YOS XIII 164:1
PLS	1	JA		PLUS		UM				IA-AP-LU-ZUM		SIMMONS 49 4
		JA		PLUS		I		ŠUM	I	IA-AP-LU-SI-SU-U_2-MI		BIROT,TEA 31:6
		JI	N	PALIS		U				IP-PA-LI-ZU?		MAOG IV 2 3 HANA
				PALUS		UM				BA-LU-ZUM		TA 30 615 26
				PALS		UM				PA-AL-ZU-UM		HARRIS 65 18
				PALS		IJA				PA-AL-ZI-IA		SIMMONS 44 6+
				PILS	AN	UM				BIL-ZA-NU-UM		BM 80363 8
				PILS		I		HADD	U	BI-IL-ZI-D-IM		XIV 41:14
				PULS	AT	UM				PU-UL-ZA-TUM	MN	TIM III 23 11+
				PULS	AN					PU-UL-ZA-AN		M
				PULS		IJA				PU-UL-ZI-IA		M
				PULS		I		HADD	U	PU-UL-ZI-D-IM		M+
				PULS		I		JARAḪ		PU-UL-ZI-RA-AḪ		HARRIS 18 14
				PULS		I		JARAḪ		PU-UL-SI-E-RA-AḪ		TIM V 69 16+
				PULS		U	NA	HADD	U	PU-UL-ZU-NA-D-IM		UNPUBL.
PLṬ	1			PALAṬ		UM				PA-LA-TUM		TIM III 37 14+
				PALṬ		IJA				PA-AL-TI-IA		YONDORF 2
				PALṬ		A		ʿAN	UM	PA-AL?-TA-A-NU-UM		LANGDON IV 15
				PALṬ		A		BIJT	U	PA-AL-DA-BI-TU		A. LATE
PNJ	1	JI		PANIJ				ʾEL	UM	I-PA-AN-NI-E-LUM		UNPUBL.
				PANIJ	AT	UM				PA-NI-IA-TUM	MN?	TIM I 11 11
				PANIJ	AT	UM				PA-AN-NI-IA-TUM	MN	UET V 615 9
				PANIJ				ʾIL	A	PA-NI-LA		IX 252 17, A. LATE
PNN	1			PANAN		UM				PA-NA-NU-UM		B 93
				PANAN		UM				PA-NA-NUM		B 47
				PANAN		IM				PA-NA-NIM	GEN	B 47
				PANN	AT	UM				PA-AN-NA-TUM	MN?	CT XLV 49 11
PPZ	1			PAPUZ		I				PA-PU-ZI	FN	XIII 1 III 14
PQḪ	1			PAQAḪ	AT	UM				BA-GA-A-TUM	MN	A 29366:17
				PAQAḪ		A		LAʾL	UM	BA-GA-A-LA-LUM		HARRIS 69 2+
PQD	1	ʾA		PQID		A				AP-KI-DA		U
		JA		PQID		UM				IA-AP-KI?-DU-UM		CT XLVIII 29:2
		JA		PQID		IM				IA-AP-KI?-DI-IM	GEN	BE VI/1 8 34
				PAQID		UM				PA-GI-DU-UM		CT XLV 89 II 32
				PIQD	AT	UM				BI-IQ-DA-TUM	FN	XIII 1 X 27
PRʿŠ	1			PURʿUŠ	AN	U				PU-UR-ḪU-ŠA-NU		M
PRD	1	JI		PRUD		U				IP-RU-DU		CT XLV 59 22 SEAL
PRG	1			PARG	AN	UM				PA-AR-GA-NU-UM		B 47
PRR	1			PARUR		I				PA-RU-RI		XIII 1 V 64
PRS	1	JA		PRUS				ʾAB	I	IA-AP-RU-US-A-BI		BAGHD. MITT. II 23
				PURUS	AT	UM				PU-RU-ZA-TUM	FN	RA LXV 60 III 60
PSʿ	1			PASAʿ	T	UM				PA-ZA-AḪ-TUM	FN	XIII 1 VIII 81
				PASAʿ			KA			PA-ZA-AḪ-GA		HARRIS 31 6
PŠD	1			PAŠD		IJA				PA-AŠ-DI-IA		B 37
PŠQ	2			LA				PAŠIQ	UM	LA-PA-SI-KU-UM		M
PTḪ	1	JA		PTAḪ		UM				IA-AP-TA-ḪU-UM		WALTERS,WL 93:1
		JA		PTAḪ		U				IA-AP-TA-ḪU		YOS VIII 156 2, A. LATE
		JI		PTIḪ			JA	MWUT	A	IP-TI-IA-MU-TA		BM 80328 11
		JA		PATIḪ				....		IA-PA-TE-X		KISURRA 100 8
				PATIḪ		UM				PA-TE-ḪU-UM		HARRIS 53 19+
				PATIḪ		IM				PA-TE-E-IM	GEN	CT IV 21B 6, 22
				PATIḪ	AT	UM				PA-TE-ḪA-TUM	MN?	CARNEGIE CAT. Q B 11
				PATIḪ	AH					PA-TI-ḪA	FN	M+
		ME		PTUḪ		UM				ME-EP-TU-U_2-UM		M+
		ME		PTUḪ		UM				ME-EP-TU-UM		M+
		ME		PTUḪ		U				ME-EP-TU-U_2		M+
		MI		PTUḪ		U				MI-IP-TU-U_2		RA LXIV 104:3

ROOTS (Consonants only)

PTḪ	1	ME	PTUḪ		IM				ME-EP-TI-I-IM	GEN	M+
		ME	PTUḪ		IM				ME-EP-TI-IM	GEN	M+
		ME	PTUḪ		IM				ME-EP-TE-IM	GEN	XIII 43 15
		MI	PTUḪ		IM				MI-IP-TI-IM	GEN	M+
		MI	PTUḪ		I				MI-IP-TI-I	GEN	XII 406 5
		MU	PATIḪ	AH					MU-PA-AT-TI-IA	FN	XIII 1 VIII 38+
		MU	PATIḪ	AH					MU-PA-TI-IA	FN	XIII 1 XIII 19+
		MU	PATIḪ	T	UM				MU-PA-AT-TI-TUM	FN	C+
	2		ʿAMM		U		PATAḪ	A	ḪA-AM-MU-PA-TA-A		M
PTN	1	ʾA	PTUN	AN	UM				AP-TU-NA-NU-UM		YOS VIII 176 SEAL
		TA	PTUN				HADD	A	TAP-TU-NA-A-DA		A. 33 26
		TA	PTAN				HADD	A	TAP-TA-NA-A-DA		A. 206 5
		TA	PTAN				HADD	A	TAP-DA-NA-TA		A. LATE
		JI	PTAN						IP-TA-AN		C II 39 22; M
	2		ʾIL		I	ʾA	PTAN		I$_3$-LI$_2$-AP-TA-AN		B 21
			ʾIL		I	ʾA	PTAN		DINGIR-AP-TAN		TIM III 150 12
PṬR	1	JA	PṬUR		UM				IA-AP-TU-RU-UM	GN	JCS VII 52 II 3
		JA	PṬUR		I				IA-AP-TU-RI	GN GEN	M
		JA	PṬUR	AJ	I				IA-AP-TU-RA-A-JI-KI	GN	M
		JA	PṬUR	AJ	I				IA-AP-TU-RA-JI-KI	GN	M
		JA	PṬIR		UM				IA-AP-DI-RUM		YOS XII
			PAṬAR		UM				PA-AT-TA-RUM		B 37
			PAṬAR	AN	UM				BA-DA-RA-NU-UM		SIMMONS 31 5
			PAṬIR		UM				PA-TI-RUM		M
			PAṬIR		UM				BA-DI-RU-UM		HARRIS 26 7
			PAṬIR		UM				BA-TI-RU-UM		TA 1931,377
			PAṬR		IJA				BA-AṬ-RI-IA		A 21950
	2		ʾANN		U		PUṬR	I	AN-NU-PU-UṬ-RI	FN	RA LXV 58 I 19+
			ʿAŠTAR				PUṬR	I	EŠ$_4$-DAR-PU-UṬ-RI	FN	M+
PZR	1		PAZR		I				PA-AZ-RI		M
			PUZAR		UM				BU-ZA-RU-UM		TCL I 56 2+
			PUZUR	AN					BU-ZU-RA-AN		RA LXV 53 XI 10
			PUZUR				ʿAN	A	PUZUR-A-NA		BIN IV 61 29+ CAPP.
QʾB	2		ʾIL		A		QAʾB		DINGIR-QA-AB		TIM III 130 12, SEAL
QʾD	2		ʾAB		I		QAʾD		A-BI-QA-AD		B 11
			ʾAB		I		QAʾD		A-BI-GA-AD		TA 30 237
			JAMM		U		QAʾD	UM	IA-AM-MU?-QA-DU-UM		III 56 7
QʾN	1		QAʾN				HADD	U	QA-AN-A-DU		A.
	2		ʾIL		I		QAʾN		I-LI-QA-AN		A. LATE
			BAWB		U		QAʾN		BA-BU-QA-AN		M
QʾT	1		QAʾT		U	HU			QA-TU-U$_2$	FN	RA LXV 58 I 47
QHL	1		QAHIL	AT	UM				QA-ḪI-LA-TUM	FN	C P. 55+
QWJ	1	JA	QWUJ		UM				IA-KU-UM		RUTTEN 6:3+; VIII 70:3, 8
		JA	QWUJ		UM				IA-KU-U$_2$-UM		RUTTEN 2:7+
		JA	QWUJ		U				IA-KU-U$_2$		RUTTEN 16:16
		JA	QWUJ			JA			IA-KU-IA		C+
		JA	QWUJ			JA			IA-KU-IA	FN	RA LXV 43 III 49
			QUWJ		UM				KU-IA-UM		YOS XII +
			QUWJ		UM				KU-WU-UM		EDZARD,DER 94:18
			QUWJ	AT	UM				KU-IA-TUM		CT VIII 29A 29+
			QUWJ				JARAḪ		KU-WE-RA-AḪ		A 32133 REV.4
			QUWJ				MILK	U	QU-U$_2$-LUGAL		MRS XII 31:24
			QUWJ		U		HADD	U	KU-U$_2$-D-IM		M
			QUWJ		UM		HADD	U	KU-UM-D-U		MRS XVI 9:7
			QUWJ		U		DAGAN		KU-U$_2$-D-DA-GAN		RA LXV 41 II 43+
	2		ŠI				QUWJ	I	ŠI-I-KU-WI	FN	A. 8 12, 34
QWL	1		QAWL		A		ḪAM	I	QA-LA-D-A-M[I]		M
			QAWL		U		ḪAM	I	QA-L[U]-D-A-MI		M
QWM	1	JA	QWIM	AT	UM				IA-KI-MA-TUM	FN	RA LXV 60 III 7
		JA	QWIM	AH					IA-KI-MA	FN	M+
		JA	QWIM				HADD	U	IA-KI-IM-D-IM		M+
		JA	QWIM				HADD	U	IA-GI-I[M]?-D-IM		IX 291 III 29'
		JA	QWIM				LIʾM		IA-KI-IM-LI-IM		M+
		ME	QWIM						ME-KI-IM		RA XXXV 119, MARI
		ME	QWIM						ME-[G]I-IM	GEN	IX 291 III 16'
			QAWM		A		DANN	UM	QA-MA-[D]A-NUM		M

ROOTS (Consonants only)

QWM	1		QAWM		I		ʾIL			GA-MI-DINGIR		TIM III 12 16+
			QAWM		U		HADD	U		GA-MU-D-IM		M
			QAWM		U		MA					
							ʾAḪ	UM		QA-MU-MA-A-ḪU-UM		M
			QAWM		U		MA					
							ʾAḪ	I		QA-MU-MA-A-ḪI		RA LXV 41 II 22
			QAWM		U		MA					
							ʾIL			QA-MU-MA-DINGIR		M
	2		ʾAḪ		I	JE	QWIM			A-ḪI-E-KI-IM		M
			ʾAB		I	ME	QWIM			A-BI-ME-KI-IM		XIII 34 5+
			ʾAB		U	ME	QWIM			A-BU-ME-KI-IM		M+
			ʿAMM		I	TA	QWIM			ḪA-AM-MI-TA-KI-IM	NOM	M
			ʿAMM		I	TA	QWUM			AM-MI-TA-KU-UM		A.+
			ʿAMM		I	TA	QWUM					
							MA			AM-MI-TA-KU-UM-MA		A. +
			ʾAŠD		I	TA	QWIM			AŠ$_2$-DI-TA-KI-IM		M+
			ʾAŠD		U		QAWM	U		AŠ-DU-GA-MU		CT XLV 77 R. 10, 14+
			ʾAŠD		U		QAWM	UM		AŠ$_2$-DU-GA-MU-UM		TCL I 130 8+
			BAʿL		UM		QAWM	UM		BA-LUM-QA-MU-UM		RA LXV 40 I 11
			ŠUM		U	TA	QWIM			SU-MU-TA-KI-IM		XIII 131 4'
QJŠ	1	TA	QJIŠ				NAN	I		TA-KI-IŠ-NA-NI	FN?	TIM III 41 6
			QIJŠ		IM					KI-ŠI-IM	GEN	M
			QIJŠ	AT	UM					KI-SA-TUM	MN	VAS IX 175 5+, M
			QIJŠ	AT	UM					KI-SA-T[U-U]M	MN	M
			QIJŠ	AT	UM					KI-ŠA-TUM	MN	XIII 1 V 19
			QIJŠ	AT	IM					KI-ŠA-TIM	MN GEN	M+
			QIJŠ	T	UM					KI-IŠ-TUM	FN	XIII 1 III 16
			QIJŠ				ʾAG	U		KI-IŠ-A-GU	FN	XIII 1 I 70
			QIJŠ	T	I		ʾADM	U		KI-IŠ-TI-AD-MU		M+
			QIJŠ	T	I		LIʾL	IM		KI-IŠ-TI-LI-LIM	GEN	RA LXIV 34 NO.26
			QIJŠ	T	I		MAM	A		KI-IŠ-TI-D-MA-MA		M+
			QIJŠ	T	I		MAM	A		KI-IŠ-TI-D-MA-AM-MA		XIV 61:5
			QIJŠ	T	I		NUN	U		KI-IŠ-TI-D-NU-NU		M+
	2		ŠUM		U	TA	QJIŠ			SU-MU-TA-KI-IŠ		M
QBJ	1	JA	QBIJ		UM					IA-AQ-BU?-UM?		CT IV 30D 11
		JA	QBIJ		IM					IA-AQ-BI-IM	GEN	M
		TA	QBIJ		IM					TA-AQ-BI-IM	GEN?	M+
		JA	QBIJ				HADD	U		IA-AQ-BI-D-IM		RA LXV 43 III 38
QBL	1		QABAL	AT	UM					GA-BA-LA-TUM	FN	CT XLV 117 36
			QABIL		UM					GA-BI-LUM		KISURRA 106 15
QDM	1		QADIM	AT	UM					QA-DI-MA-TUM	FN	WATERMAN 39 8+
			QADIM	AT	IM					QA-DI-MA-TIM	FN GEN	WATERMAN 39 11
			QADM	AN	UM					GA-AD-MA-NU-UM		U
			QIDM	AN	UM					KI-ID-MA-NU-UM		U
		ʾA	QDAM		U					AQ-DA-MU		C P. 35+
		MU	QADIM		U					MU-GA-DI-MU		CT XLV 6 33
	2		ʾADM		U		QUDM	I		AD-MU-KU-UD-MI	FN	XIII 1 IX 55
			ʾANN		U		QUDM	I		AN-NU-KU-UD-MI	FN	XIII 1 VIII 77
			MAM		A		QUDM	I		D-MA-MA-KU-UD-ME	FN	RA LXV 59 II 18
QDŠ	1		QADIŠ		UM					KA-DI-ŠUM		RA LXV 52 XI 2
			QUDAŠ		UM					GU-DA-SU-UM		JCS XXIV 60 NO.51+
QMṢ	1		QIMṢ		I		JARAḪ			KI?-IM-ZE$_2$-RA-AḪ		EDZARD,DER 231:2
QNJ	1	JI	QNIJ		UM					IQ-NI-UM	FN	RA LXV 58 I 34
		JA	QNIJ				ʾIL			IA-AQ-NI-DINGIR		CT XLV 92 I 10+
		TA	QNIJ	T	UM					TA?-AQ-NI-TUM	FN	XIII 1 VIII 74
			QANIJ	AT	UM					QA-NI-A-TUM	FN	RA LXV 66 VII 52; C+
			QANIJ	AN	U					KA-NI-IA-NU		M
QNT	1	MU	QANIT		UM					MU-GA-NI-TUM	MN?	TIM III 86 6+
			QANAT	AN	UM					GA-NA-TA-NU-UM		KISURRA 30 7
QQQD	1		QAQQAD	AN						QA-QA-DA-AN		XIV 47:20
QQQR	1		QAQQAR	AN						QA?-QA-RA?-AN		VII 198:14
QRʾ	1	JA	QRIʾ				ʾIL			IA-AQ-RI-DINGIR		B 27
			QARAʾ				ŠUM	I	JA	QA-RA-SU-MI-IA		CT II 34 5
			QARAʾ				ŠUM	I	JA	GA-RA-SU-MI-IA		CT XLVIII 89 REV.
			QARAʾ				ŠUM	U	JA	QA-RA-SU?-MU-IA		CT VI 43 6
			QARAʾ				ŠUM	U	JA	GA-RA-SU-MU-IA		CT XLV 11 2, 46+

ROOTS (Consonants only)

QRʾ	1		QARAʾ				ŠUM	U	JA	KA-RA?-SU-MU-IA		CT II 30 3
			QARAʾ				ŠUM	U	JA	KA-RA-SU-LUM		CT II 30 34
			QARIʾ		UM					QA-RI-U$_2$-UM		M+
			QARIʾ				ʾEL			QA-R[I]-E[L]		M
QRB	1	JI	QRIB	AN	UM					IQ-RI-BA-NU-UM		I
QRD	2		ŠUWB		I		QARAD			ŠU-BI-GA-RA-AD		I
QRN	1		QARN	AN	A					QAR-NA-NA	GEN	SIMMONS 13 5
			QARN	AN	UM					QAR-NA-NU-UM		B 93+
			QARN		I		LIʾM			QAR-NI-LI-IM		M+
QṢR	1	JA	QṢUR		UM					IA-AQ-ZU-RU-UM		BE VI/1 1 22+
		JA	QṢUR				ʾIL			IA-AQ-ZU-UR-DINGIR		B 29+
			QAṢIR		UM					QA-ZI-RUM		RA LXV 53 XI 46
QṬN	1		QAṬAN		A					QA-TA-NA-KI	GN	M
			QAṬAN		IM					QA-TA-NIM-KI	GN GEN	M+
			QAṬAN		IM					QA-ṬA$_3$-NIM-KI	GN GEN	M+
			QAṬAN	AJ	I					QA-TA-NA-A-JI-KI	GN	M
			QAṬAN	AJ	I					QA-TA-NA-JI-KI	GN	M+
			QAṬAN	AJ	IM					QA-TA-NA-IM-KI	GN GEN	M
QṬR	1		QAṬAR		A					QA-TA-RA-KI	GN	M
			QAṬAR		A					QA-ṬA$_3$-RA-KI	GN	M
			QAṬAR		A					QA-ṬA$_3$-RA-A-KI	GN	M+
			QAṬAR		UM					QA-TA-RU-UM		B 37
			QAṬAR		I					GA?-DA-RI		RA LXV 51 IX 72
			QAṬAR				ʾAB	I		GA-TAR-A-BI		BASOR 95 22
			QAṬAR				ʾIL			GA-TA-AR-DINGIR		B 17
			QAṬR	AN	UM					GA-AT-RA-NU-UM		RUTTEN 14 22
	2		ʾAKUN		U		QAṬAR			A-KU-NU-GA-DAR		BIN VII 30 5
		JA	JṢIʾ				QAṬAR			IA-ṢI-QA-TAR		B 30
		JI	JṢIʾ				QAṬAR			I-ZI-GA-TA-AR		B 22+
		JI	JṢIʾ				QAṬAR			I-ZI-GA-TAR		B 22+
		JI	JṢIʾ				QAṬAR			I-ṢI-GA-TAR		B 22+
		JI	JṢIʾ				QAṬAR			I-ṢI-GA-TA-AR		B 22+
		JI	JṢIʾ				QAṬAR			I-ZI-GA-DAR		B 22
		JI	JṢIʾ				QAṬAR			I-ZI-QA-TAR		XIII 1 IV 59
		JI	JṢIʾ				QAṬAR	I		I-ZI-GA-DAR-I		B 22
QZJ	1		QAZIJ				RAWM	A		QA-ZI-RA-MA		A. LATE
Rʾ K	1		RAʾK	AT	UM					RA-KA-TU-UM	FN?	M
RʾŠ	2		MA				RAʾŠ	UM		MA-A-RA-SU-UM		M
RʾZ	1		RAʾZ		UM					RA-ZU-UM		TA 1931, 538 IV
RḪB	1	JA	RḪAB		UM					IA-AR-ḪA-BU-UM		B 29+
		JI	RḪIB							IR-IB		U
		JI	RḪIB							I-RI-IB		I
		JA	RḪIB		UM					IA-AR-I-BU-UM		RA LXIV NO.33
		JA	RḪIB		U					IA-AR-I-BU		XIII 1 VI 63
		JA	RḪIB				ḪAJJ	A		IA-AR-IB-D-E$_2$-A		M+
		JA	RḪIB				ʾABB	A		IA-AR-IB-D-AB-BA		M
		JA	RḪIB				HADD	U		IA-AR-IB-D-IM		M+
		JA	RḪIB				ʾIL			IA-AR-I-IB-DINGIR		M+
		JA	RḪIB				ʾIL			IA-AR-IB-DINGIR		M+
		JA	RḪIB				ʾIRR	A		IA-AR-IB-D-IR$_3$-RA		M
		JA	RḪIB				ʾIRR	A		IA-AR-I-[IB]-IR$_3$-RA		M
		JA	RḪIB				DAGAN			IA-AR-IB-D-DA-GAN		M+
			RAḪIB		UM					RA-I-BU-UM		CT VIII 47A 7
			RUḪB	AT	UM					RU-UḪ-BA-TUM	FN	XIII 1 IX 46
	2		ʾANA				RAḪAB	U		A-NA-RA-A-BU		M+
			BALK		U	Š	RAḪAB			BA-AL-KU-UŠ$_2$-RA-ḪA-AB	FN	XIII 1 VIII 61
RḪM	1	JA	RḪAM		UM					IA-AR-A-MU-UM		M+
		JA	RḪAM		U					IA-AR-ḪA-MU		B 29+, M
		JA	RḪAM	AN						IA-AR-ḪA-MA-AN	FN	RA LXV 55 XIII 51
		JA	RḪAM		I		ʾIL			IA-AR-ḪA-MI-DINGIR		KISURRA 5A 15+
		JA	RḪAM				ʾIL			IA-AR-ḪA-AM-DINGIR		B 29
		JI	RḪAM		I		ʾIL			IR-ḪA-MI-DINGIR		A.
		JI	RḪAM				ʾIL	A		IR-ḪA-MI-LA		A.+
		JI	RḪAM				ʾILL	A		IR-ḪA-MI-IL-LA		A. 274 26
			RAḪIM		UM					RA-I-MU-UM		JCS XXVI 151:21 HARMAL
			RAḪIM	AH						RA-ḪI-MA	FN	XIII 1 II 4+

ROOTS (Consonants only)

RḪM	1		RAḪM		AJA					RA-AḪ-MA-IA		M+
			RAḪM		I		....			RA-AḪ-MI-....	FN	M
			RAḪM		I		ʾIL	I		RA-AḪ-MI-I$_3$-LI$_2$		XIII 1 VIII 79+
	2		ʾANN		U		RAḪM	I		AN-NU-RA-AḪ-MI	FN	XIII 1 V 11+
			ʾANN		U	TA	RḪAM			AN-NU-TA-AR-AM	FN	M+
			ʿAŠTAR				RAḪM	I		EŠ$_4$-DAR-RA-AḪ-MI	FN	XIII 1 VIII 83
RḪQ	1	JI	RḪAQ		UM					IR-ḪA-KUM		B 22
		JI	RḪAQ		UM					II-IR-ḪA-KUM		SIMMONS 86 10+
		JE	RḪAQ		UM					E-ER-ḪA-KUM		SIMMONS 112 7, SEAL
		JA	RḪIQ		UM					IA-AR-ḪI-KU-UM		A 32133:7
		JI	RḪIQ		A					IR-ḪI-GA		M
RḪŠ	1	MA	RḪAŠ	AN						MAR-ḪA-ŠA-AN		RA LXV 54 XII 12
RḪṢ	1		RAḪAṢ		U					RA-ḪA-ZU		WALTERS,WL 114:12
	2		ʾIL		I		RIḪṢ	I		I$_3$-LI$_2$-RI-IḪ-ZI	FN	XIII 1 IX 39
RʿJ	1	JA	RʿIJ				HADD	U		JA-RI-A-DU		RA LXV 50 VIII 64
		JA	RʿIJ				ʾIL			IA-AR-ḪI-DINGIR		CT XLVIII 27
	2		ʾIPQ				RIʿAJ		HU	I-BI-IQ-RI-E-U$_2$		U
			LU				RIʿAJ		HU	LU$_2$-RI-E$_2$-U$_2$		U
			LU				RIʿAJ		HU	LU$_2$-RI-ḪU		U
RʿŠ	1	JA	RʿIŠ		UM					IA-RI-ŠUM		B 29
		TA	RʿIŠ	AH						DA-RI$_2$-ŠA	FN	U
		TA	RʿIŠ				ḪAʾT	U		TA-RI-IŠ-ḪA-AT-TU	FN	M+
		TA	RʿIŠ				ʿAŠTAR			T[A-R]I-IŠ-EŠ$_4$-DAR	FN	RA LXV 65 VII 36
		TA	RʿIŠ				MAʾT	UM		TA-RI-IŠ-MA-TUM	FN	M+, C
			RIʿŠ	AT			....			RI-ŠA-A[T-....]	FN	I 89 5
	2		ʾIL		A	TA	RʿIŠ			I-LA-TA-RI-IŠ		B 21
RWḪ	1	JA	RWIḪ							IA-RI-IḪ	GN	M
		JA	RWIḪ	AJ	I					IA-RI-ḪA-JI-KI	GN	M
		JA	RWIḪ	IJ	I					IA-RI-ḪI-I-KI	GN	M+
		JA	RWIḪ		A		ʾAB	UM		IA-RI-ḪA-A-BU-UM		VII P. 234 N. 4
		JA	RWIḪ		A		ʾAB	AM		IA-RI-ḪA-A-BA-AM	ACC	XIV 101:8
		JA	RWIḪ		A		ʾAB	AM		IA-RI-ḪA-A-BA-AN	ACC	VII P. 234 N. 4
		JA	RWIḪ		A		ʾAB	IM		IA-RI-ḪA-A-BI-IM	GEN	M+
		JA	RWIḪ		A		ḪAM	U		IA-RI-ḪA-A-MU		M+
		JE	RWIḪ		I		ʾIL			E-RI-ḪI-DINGIR		U
			RAWḪ	AT	UM					RA-ḪA-TUM	FN	XIII 1 XII 6
			RAWḪ		A		ʾANN	UM		RA-ḪA-AN-NU-UM		M
			RIWḪ	AN						RI-ḪA-AN		C
			RIWḪ	AT	UM					RI-ḪA-DU-UM?		U UNPUBL.
			RIWḪ	AT	UM					RI-ḪA-TUM	FN	XIII 1 I 23+
	2		ʾIL		A		RAWḪ	I	JA	DINGIR-RA[Ḫ]I-A		HARRIS 76 21
			ʾIL		A		RAWḪ	I	JA	I-LA-RA-ḪI-IA		M
			ʾIL		A		RAWḪ	I	JE	I-LA-RA-ḪI-E		M
			ʾIL		A		RAWḪ	I	JE	DINGIR-RA-ḪI-E		HARRIS 85 14
			ʾIL		I		RAWḪ	I	JE	I$_3$-LI$_2$-RA-AḪ-E		VAS XVI 168 9, FRANK 13 9
			KULP		A		RAWḪ	I	JE	KU-UL-PA-RA-ḪI-E		TCL I 14 1, YOS VIII 141 34
			KANAK				RAWḪ	UM		KA-NA-AK-RA-ḪU-UM		VAS XIII 66A R. 5+
			KANAK				RAWḪ	U		KA-NA-AK-RA-ḪU		VAS XIII 66 R. 6
			KANAK				RAWḪ	I		KA-NA-AK-RA-ḪI		VAS XIII 79 R. 7
			KANIK				RUWḪ	UM		KA-NI-IK-RU-UM		B 33+
			KANIK				RUWḪ	UM		KA-NI-IK-RUM		B 33
			KANIK				RUWḪ	IM		KA-NI-IK-RI-IM	GEN	B 33
			LA			JE	RWIḪ	UM		LA-E-RI-ḪU-UM		U
			MUT				RAWḪ			MU-UT-RA-AḪ		M
			ŠAM		A		RAWḪ			SA-MA-RA-AḪ		B 38+, XII 385 8
			ŠAM		U		RAWḪ			SA-MU-RA-A-AḪ		SIMMONS 46 28, 47 23
			ŠAM		U		RAWḪ			SA-MU-RA	NOM	CT XLVIII 29 REV.
			ŠUM		U		RAWḪ			SU-MU-RA-A		B 40
			ŠUM		U		RAWḪ			SU-MU-RA-AḪ		B 38+
			ŠUM		U		RAWḪ			SU-MU-RA-A-AḪ		CT II 39 1, 15
			ŠUM		U		RAWḪ	EM		[SU]-MU-RA-ḪI-E-IM		B 40
RWJ	1	JA	RWIJ		UM					IA-AR-WI-UM	NOM	KUPPER, NOM. P. 199
		JA	RWIJ				ʾIL			A-AR-WI-DINGIR		HARRIS 98 R. 7
RWB	1	TA	RWUB	AH						TA-RU-BA	FN	M
			RUWB	AT	UM					RU-BA-TUM	FN	M+
			RUWB	AT	IM					RU-BA-TIM	FN GEN	M

ROOTS (Consonants only)

RWB	1		RUWB		AJA						RU-BA-IA	FN	XIII 1 II 10+
			RUWB		AJA						RU-BA-A-IA	FN	RA LXIV 43
			RUWB	AN							RU-BA?-AN		RA LXV 45 V 34
	2		ʾADM		U			RUWB	AH		D-AD-MU-RU-BA	FN	XIII 1 VII 59
RWM	1	JA	RWIM					ḪAʾL			IA-RI-IM-ḪA-AL		M+
		JA	RWIM					HADD	U		IA-RI-IM-D-IM		M+
		JI	RWIM					ʾILL	A		I-RI-MII-LA		A. 87 30 LATE
		JI	RWIM					ʾILL	A		I-RI-IM-IL-LA		A. LATE
		JI	RWIM					ʾILL	A		I-RI-MI-IL-LA		A. LATE
		JA	RWIM					ʿAMM	U		IA-RI-IM-ḪA-MU		M
		JA	RWIM					ʿAMM	U		IA-RI-IM-ḪA-AM-MU		M
		JA	RWIM					JARAḪ			IA-RI-IM-IA-RA-AḪ		RA LXV 41 II 28
		JA	RWIM					JARAḪ			IA-RI-IM-E-RA-AḪ		M
		JA	RWIM					DAWD	U		IA-RI-IM-DA-DU		RA LXV 40 I 38+
		JA	RWIM					DAGAN			IA-RI-IM-D-DA-GAN		M+
		JI	RWIM					DAGAN			I-RI-IM-D-DA-GAN		SYRIA XXXVII 206 2 HANA
		JA	RWIM					LIʾM			IA-RI-IM-LI-IM		SIMMONS 66 77, M+, C+, A.+
		JA	RWIM					MALIK			IA-RI-IM-MA-LIK		A 3580:2+
		JA	RWIM					ŠUM	U				
								ʾAB	I		IA-RI-IM-SU-MU-A-BI		RA LXV 42 III 8
		TA	RWIM					ʿAŠTAR			TA-RI-IM-EŠ$_4$-DAR	FN	XIII 1 II 13
		TA	RWIM					ŠAKIM			TA-RI-IM-ŠA-KI-IM		M+
			RAWM								RA-AM	DN	PBS XIV 360
			RAWM					...			RA-MA-[....]		M
			RAWM	AT	UM						RA-MA-TUM	FN	M, CT VIII 1A 2+
			RAWM	AN	UM						RA-MA-NU-UM		B 47
			RAWM		A			JAT	UM		RA-MA-IA-TUM		B 22+
			RAWM		E			ʾEL			R[A]-ME-EL		RA LXV 42 II 56
			RIWM	AT	UM						RI-MA-TUM	FN	M+
			RIWM	AN							[R]I?-MA-AN		RA LXV 41 II 8
			RIWM	AN	UM						RI-MA-NU-UM		U
			RIWM					HADD	U		RI-IM-D-IM		M+, A. 57 46
			RIWM					ʾIL	A		RI-IM-I-LA		TCL XIV 54 17 CAPP.
			RIWM					DAGAN			RI-IM-D-DA-GAN		M
			RIWM		U			HADD	U		RI-MU-D-IM		M
			RUWM	AT	UM						RU-MA-TUM	FN	XIII 1 VI 10
	2		ʾAB		I			RAWM			A-BI-RA-AM		RA LXV 43 IV 12
			ʿABD		U		TA	RWIM			[ḪA-A]B-DU-TA-RI-IM		M
			ʿAD		U			RAWM	U		A-DU-RA-MU	FN	U
		JI	JDAʿ					RAWM			I-DAḪ-RA-AM		MEISSNER 91 17
			ʾIL		I			RAWM			I$_3$-LI$_2$-RA-AM		M
			ʿAMM		U			RAWM	A		ḪA-MU-RA-MA		M
			ʾAŠD		I			RAWM			AŠ-DI-RA-AM		RA LXV 55 XIII 42
			ʾAŠD		U	NA	JA	RWIM			[AŠ$_2$-D]U-NI-A-RI-IM		CT XXXVI 4 1
			ʾAŠD		U	NA	JE	RWIM			AŠ$_2$-DU-NI-E-RI-IM		RA VIII 65 1
			BEʿL		I			RAWM			BE-LI$_2$-RA-AM		RA LXV 54 XII 60
			LA					RIWM					
								ḪAM	I		LA-RI-IM-D-A-MI		M
			LA					RIWM					
								ʿAḎIR			LA-RI-IM-ḪA-ZI-IR		DELAPORTE, CAT. BN 207
			LA					RIWM					
							JI	JBAL	U	HU	[L]A?-RI-IM-I-BA-LU-U$_2$		M
			LA					RIWM					
								BAʿL	I		LA-RI-IM-BA-AḪ-LI		M+
			LA					RIWM					
								BEʿL	I		LA-RI-IM-BE-LI$_2$		X 69 5
			LA					RIWM					
								DIWR			LA-RI-IM-DI-IR		RA LXV 50 IX 22
			LA					RIWM					
								LU		HU	LA-RI-IM-LU-U$_2$		M
			LA					RIWM					
								NUMAḪ	A		LA-RI-IM-NU-MA-ḪA-A		M+
			LA					RIWM					
								NUMAḪ	A		LA-RI-IM-NU-MA-A		M
			LAʾT		I			RAWM	E	JE	LA-TI-RA-ME-E		M
			MUT					RAWM	A		MU-UT-RA-MA		CT II 23 13

RWM	2		MUT					RAWM	E	JE	MU-UT-RA-ME-E		BM 81584 3, M+
			MUT					RAWM	EM		MU-UT-RA-ME-IM		M
			MUT		U			RAWM	I	JE	MU-TU-RA-MI-E		CT XLV 63 15
		JI	NDIN					RIWM			I-DIN-D-RI-IM		TCL I 238 16 HANA
			QAZIJ					RAWM	A		QA-ZI-RA-MA		A. LATE
			ŠU					RAWM	U		ŠU-RA-MU		A. LATE+
			ŠU					RAWM	A		ŠU-RA-MA		A. LATE+
			ŠI					RAWM	A		SI-I-RA-MA		A. 28 3, 16
			ŚUM		U	NA	JA	RWIM			SU-UM-MU-NA-A-RI-IM		HARRIS 57 11
			ŚUM		U			RAWM	E	JE	SU-MU-RA-ME-E		B 40+
			ŚUM		U			RAWM	EM		SU-MU-RA-ME-IM		M
	3		ʿAMM		U			LA					
								RIWM			ḪA-MU-L[A]-RI-IM		RA LXV 46 VI 40
			KAʾB		I			LA					
								RIWM			KA-BI-LA-RI-IM		RA LXV 47 VI 65+; C+
			ŚUM		U			ʾAB	I				
							JA	RWIM			SU-MU-A-BI-A-RI-IM		TA 30 9, 14, 15+
			ŚUM		UM			ʾAB	I				
							JA	RWIM			SU-MU-UN-A-BI-IA-RI-IM		SUMER XXIII 153:9
			ŚUM		U	NA		ʾAB	I				
							JA	RWIM			SU-MU-NA-BI-IA-RI-IM		SUMER XXIII PL. 7 17+
			ŚUM		U	NA		ʾAB	I				
							JA	RWIM			SU-MU-UN?-A-BI-JA-RI-IM		SUMER XXIII P. 153 9
RJB	1	JA	RJIB					HADD	U		IA-RI-IB-D-IM		B 29+
		JA	RJIB					DAGAN			IA-RI-IB-D-D[A-GAN]?		M
		TA	RJIB		UM						TA-RI-BU-UM		M
		TA	RJIB		IM						TA-RI-BI-IM	GEN	M
			RAJB	AT	UM						RA-BA-TUM	FN	XIII 1 X 59+
			RAJB	AN							RA-[BA]?-AN		RA LXV 47 VI 67
			RAJB	AN	UM						RA-BA-NU-UM		RUTTEN 3 6+
			RAJB	AN	UM						RA-BA-A-NU-UM		RUTTEN 13 3, 8, SEAL+
			RAJB		A			SITR	U	HU	RA-BA-ZI-IT-RU-U$_2$	FN	M
			RIJB		UM						RI-I-BU-UM		I
			RIJB	AT	UM						RI-BA-TUM	FN	CT VIII 48B 7+, M+, C+
			RIJB		A			ʿAMM	U		RI-BA-AM-MU		A. 97 4+
			RIJB		U	HU					RI-BU-U$_2$		KISURRA 187 12
			RIJB		U			DAGAN			RI-BU-D-DA-GAN		RA LXV 47 VII 52
	2		ŚUM		I			RIJB	A		SU-MI-RI-BA		A. 98C 10
			ŚUM		I			RIJB	A		ŠU-MI-RI-PA		A. LATE
			ŚUM		I			RIJB	A		ŠU-ME-RI-PA		A. LATE
			TIʾM					RIJB	A		TI-IM-RI-PA		A.
RBʾ	1	JA	RBUʾ					ʾIL			IA-AR-BU-DINGIR		KISURRA 9A 9+
		JE	RBUʾ			HU		ʾEL			E-[IR]-BU-U$_2$-[E]L		KISURRA 152 9
RBʿ	1		RABAʿ					DUDM	U		RA-BA?-AḪ-DU-UD-MU		M
RBJ	1	JA	RBIJ					ʾEL			IA-AR-BI-EL		CT XLV 12 23
		JA	RBIJ					ʾIL			IA-AR-BI-DINGIR		B 29+
		JA	RBIJ					ʾIL			I-AR-BI-DINGIR		KISURRA 5A 8+
		JE	RBIJ					ʾIL			E-IR-BI-DINGIR		KISURRA 22A 15
	2		ʾANN		U		TA	RBIJ			AN-NU-TAR-BI	FN	XIII 1 XI 47
RBB	1		RABAB	AN							RA-BA-BA-AN		M
			RABAB	AN	UM						RA-BA-BA-NU-UM		KISURRA 187 11+
			RABB		I			JARAḪ			RA-AB-BI-E-RA-AḪ		B 37+
			RABB		U			ʿAD	UM		RU-BU-ḪA-DU-UM		BM 17055 26
			RABB		U			ʿAD	U	HU	RA-AB-BU-ḪA-DU-U$_2$		B 17+
			RABB		U			ʿAD	U	HU	RA-AB-BU-U$_2$-ḪA-DU-U$_2$		BM 17051A 30
RBK	1		RIBK		U						RI-IB-KU	FN	XIII 1 IX 56+
RDK	1	ʾA	RDAK					HAND	A		AR-DA-KA-AN-DA		M
RDP	1	MA	RDAP		UM						MAR-DA-BU-UM		BIN III 546; U+
		MA	RDAP	AN							MAR-DA-BA-AN		ITT P.4, 7031 UR III
		MA	RDAP	AN	UM						MAR-DA-BA-NU-UM		U
RGM	1	ʾA	RGAM	AT	UM						AR-GA-MA-TUM	FN	C
			RIGM	AN	U						RI-IG-MA-NU		M
			RIGM	AN	UM						RI-IG-MA-NUM		M
RKB	1	JI	RKAB	T	UM						IR-KAB-TUM	MN	A.+
		JI	RKAB	T	U						IR-KAB-DU	MN	A.+ LATE
		JA	RKAB					HADD	U		IA-AR-KA-AB-D-IM		4E RENCONTRE 23

ROOTS (Consonants only)

RKB	1	JA		RKIB		A		HADD	U	IA-AR-KI-BA-D-IM		XIII 145 6
				RUKAB	AT	UM				RU-KA-BA-TUM	FN	XIII 1 V 33
RMK	1	JI	N	RMUK						I-NI-IR-MU-UK		M+
		JI	N	RMUK						I-NE-IR-MU-UK		M
				RAMIK	AN	UM				RA-MI-GA-NU-UM		TA 1931, 538 II
RMM	1			RAMAM	AN	UM				RA-MA-MA-NU-UM		B 93
RMN	1	ʾA		RMAN	UN	UM				AR-MA-NU-NUM$_2$		TA 1931 , 538 IV
RMŠ	1			RAMAŠ		I				RA-MA-ŠI	FN	M
				RAMAŠ		I				RA-MA-A-ŠI	FN	EDZARD,DER 224:42
				RAMIŠ		UM				RA-MI-ŠUM		TA 1931, 538 III, V
				RIMŠ		I		ʾIL		RI-IM-ŠI-DINGIR		M+
				RIMŠ		I		ʾIL	I	RI-IM-ŠI-I$_3$-LI$_2$		M
	2			ʾANN		U		RIMŠ	I	AN-NU-RI-IM-ŠI	FN	M+
				KAKK		A		RIMŠ	I	KA-AK-KA-RI-IM-ŠI	FN	RA LXV 60 III 5
RPʾ	1	JA		RPAʾ				HADD	U	IA-AR-PA-D-IM		M+
		JI		RPAʾ				ʾAB	I	IR-PA-A-BI		A.+
		JI		RPAʾ				HADD	A	IR-PA-A-DA		A. 76 8+
		JI		RPAʾ				HADD	A	IR-PA-DA		A. 41 14
		JI		RPAʾ				HADD	U	IR-PA-D-IM		A.+
				RAPAʾ	AN	UM				RA-PA-NU-UM		BM 78768
				RAPIʾ		UM				RA-BI-U$_2$-UM		M+
				RAPIʾ		UM				RA-BI-JU-[UM]?		M
				RAPIʾ	AT	UM				RA-BI-A-TUM	FN	C+
				RAPIʾ	T	UM				RA-BI-TUM	FN	M
				RAPIʾ	AH					RA-BI-A	FN	XIII 1 VII 32+
				RAPIʾ				MI				
								ʾIL		RA-BI-MI-IL		BIROT,TEA 72 VI 19
				RAPIʾ				MI				
								ʾIL	UM	RA-BI-MI-LUM		BIROT,TEA 72 IX 29
				RAPIʾ			TA	ʾLAŠ		RA-BI-TA-AḪ-LA-AŠ		BASOR 95 22
				RAPUʾ		UM				RA-PU-U$_2$-UM		RA LXV 41 II 30
				RAPUʾ	AT	UM				RA-PU-A-TUM		A 7660 1
				RIPʾ		IM				RI-IP-I-IM	GEN	M+
				RIPʾ		A		ʾIL	A	RI-IP-A-DINGIR		M+
				RIPʾ		A		MALIK		RI-IP-A-MA-LIK		M
				RIPʾ		I		HADD	U	RI-IP-I-D-IM		M+
				RIPʾ		I		HEDD	A	RI-IP-E-D-IM		M
				RIPʾ		I		DAGAN		RI-IP-I-D-DA-GAN		M+
				RIPʾ		I		DAGAN		RI-BI-D-DA-GAN		M
				RIPʾ		I		LIʾM		RI-IP-I-LI-IM		M
	2			ḪAJJ		UM		RAPIʾ		ḪA-JU-UM-RA-BI		M
				ḪAʾL		U		RAPIʾ		ḪA-LU-RA-PI		M+
				ʾAB		I		RAPIʾ		A-BI-RA-BI		M
				ʾAB		I		RAPIʾ		A-BI-RA-PI		SYRIA XXXVII 206 6, 7
				ʾABN		U		RAPIʾ		AB-NU-RA-BI		C, C II P. 244+
				ʿADN		U		RAPIʾ		ḪA-AD-NU-RA-BI		XIV 109:18+
				ʾIL		I		RAPIʾ		I$_3$-LI$_2$-RA-BI		M+
				ʾALLA				RAPIʾ		AL-LA-RA-PI		TCL XVIII 95 12, 15
				ʿAMM		I		RAPIʾ		AM-MI-RA-PI		SYRIA XXXVII 206 END HANA
				ʿAMM		I		RAPIʾ		AM-MI-RA-BI-IḪ		RA XXXIV 186 HANA
				ʿAMM		I		RAPIʾ		ḪA-AM-MI-RA-BI		B 19
				ʿAMM		U		RAPIʾ		ḪA-AM-MU-RA-BI		B 19+, M+, A.+
				ʿAMM		UM		RAPIʾ		ḪA-AM-MU-UM-RA-BI		B 19+
				ʿAMM		U		RAPIʾ		AM-MU-RA-BI		B 19+
				ʿAMM		U		RAPIʾ		D-ḪA-AM-MU-RA-BI		B 19+
				ʿAMM		U		RAPIʾ		ḪA-MU-RA-BI		B 19+, M+
				ʿAMM		U		RAPIʾ		ḪA-AM-MU-RA-BI-IḪ		B 19 HANA
				ʿAMM		U		RAPIʾ		AM-MU-RA-PI		ABL 255 LATE
				ʿAMM		U		RAPIʾ		D-AM-MU-RA-PI		YBC 4362
				ʿAMM		UM		RAPIʾ		ḪA-AM-MU-UM-RA-PI		YBC 6496, 6508
				ʿAMM		UM		RAPIʾ		ḪA-MU-UM-RA-BI		BM 17046+
				ʿAMM		U		RAPIʾ		ḪA-MU-U$_2$-RA-BI		FIGULLA, CAT. 14138
				ʿAMM		U		RAPIʾ	I	AM-MU-RA-BI-I		A+
				ʿAMM		U		RAPIʾ		ḪA-MU-UR$_2$-RA-BI		CT XLVII 31 32+
				ʿAMM		U		RAPIʾ				
								ʾIL		ḪA-AM-MU-RA-BI-DINGIR		B 19

ROOTS (Consonants only)

RPʾ	2		ʿAMM		U			RAPIʾ						
								BANIJ				ḪA-AM-MU-RA-BI-BA-NI		B 19
			ʿAMM		UM			RAPIʾ						
								....				[ḪA-AM]-MU-UM-RA-PI-LI-WI-IR		UNPUBL.
			ʿAMM		U			RAPIʾ						
								....				ḪA-AM-MU-RA-BI-LU-DA-RI		B 19
			ʿAMM		U	HU		RAPIʾ				ḪA-AM-MU-U$_2$-RA-BI		M
			ḪAMR		U			RAPIʾ				ḪA-AM-RU-RA-BI		M
		ʾA	JPAʿ					RAPIʾ				A-PA-AḪ-RA-BI		SUMER XIV 5, IM 52272
			ʾAŠD		U			RAPIʾ				AŠ$_2$-DU-RA-BI		C+
			DAWD		U			RAPIʾ				DA-DU-RA-BI		B 16+
		JI	ḎKUR					RAPIʾ				IZ-KUR-RA-BI		BM 81591 7
			ḎIMR					RAPIʾ		I		ZI-ME-IR-RA-BI-I		TA 30 34
			ḎIMR		I			RAPUʾ				ZI-IM-RI-RA-BU		M
			ḎIMR		U			RAPIʾ				ZI-IM-RU-RA-BI		TA 30 82
		JA	KWUN					RAPIʾ				IA-KU-UN-RA-BI		M
			LU					RAPIʾ				LU$_2$-RA-BI$_2$		I
			MUT					RAPIʾ				MU-UT-[R]A-BI		M
		JA	ŠWUB					RAPIʾ				IA-ŠU-UB-RA-BI		A.
			ŠUWB		U			RAPUʾ				ŠU-BU-RA-BU		TCL X 4A 25, B 15
			ŠIʾN		U			RAPIʾ				ŠI-NU-RA-BI		A.+
			ŠIʾN		U			RAPIʾ				SI-NU-RA-BI		A.+
			ŚUM		A			RAPIʾ				SU-MA-RA-BI		KAJ 39 17 LATE
			ŚUM		I			RAPAʾ				SU-MI-RA-PA		RA LVI 169, A.+
			ŚUM		U			RAPIʾ				SU-MU-RA-BI		M
			ŚUMḪ		U			RAPIʾ				SU-UM-ḪU-RA-BI		M+
			ŚAMŚ		I			RAPIʾ				ŠA-AM-[SI]-RA-BI		M
RPŠ	2		MUT					RAPŠ		IM		MU-UT-RA-AP-ŠI-IM		RA LXV 53 XI 7
RŚP	1	JA	RŚAP					LA						
								ʾIL				IA-AR-SA-AP-LA-DINGIR		M+
		JA	RŚAP					LA						
								ʾIL		A		IA-AR-SA-AP-LA-I-[LA]?		M
		TA	RŚAP	AH								TA-AR-SA-BA	FN	RA LXV 64 VI 28
	2		ʾAB		I			RAŚAP				A-BI-RA-SA-AP		M
		JA	ḪBAʾ					RAŚAP				IA-AḪ-BA-D-RA-SA-AP		XIII 94 5
			ʾIL		I			RAŚAP				I$_3$-LI$_2$-D-RA-SA-[AP]		XIII 66 5
		JA	ʾZUW					RAŚAP				IA-AḪ-ZU-D-RA-SA-AP		M
		JI	NDIN					RUŚP	AN			I-DIN-D-RU-UŠ-PA-AN		MAOG IV 2 5 HANA+
		JI	NDIN					RUŚP	AN			I-DIN-D-RU-UŠ$_2$-PA-AN		MEL. SYR. I 275
RŠJ	1	ʾA	RŠIJ					ʾAḪ		UM		AR-ŠI-A-ḪU-UM		M+
		ʾA	RŠIJ					ʿAD		A	HA	AR-ŠI-A-DA?-A	FN	C
		ʾA	RŠIJ					HADD		A		AR-ŠI-A-DA		M
		ʾA	RŠIJ					ʾEDAK		U		AR-ŠI-E-DA-KU	FN	M
		ʾA	RŠIJ					ʿAN		UM		AR-SI?-A-NUM$_2$		U
		JA	RŠIJ					ʾAŠAR		I		IA-AR-ŠI-A-ŠA-RI		M
		JA	RŠIJ					ʾIL				IA-AR-ŠI-DINGIR		B 29+, M
		JA	RŠIJ					ʾIL		I		A-AR-ŠI-DINGIR		TA 1930,7:6
		JA	RŠIJ					ʾIL		UM		IA-AR-ŠI-DINGIR-UM		UCP X/1 P. 58+
		JA	RŠIJ					ʿAMM		U		IA-AR-ŠI-ḪA-MU		M, C+
			RAŠIJ			JA						RA-SI-A		TIM III 134 4
	2		ʾAḪ		AM		ʾA	RŠIJ				A-ḪA-AM-AR-ŠI		I+
			LA				ʾA	RŠIJ		UM		LA-AR-ŠI-U$_2$-U[M]		TA 1931, 538 IV
RṢJ	1		RAṢIJ		IM							RA-ZI-IM-KI	GN	M
			RAṢIJ		EM							RA-ZI-E-IM-KI	GN	M+
			RAṢAJ					DAGAN				RA-ZA-D-DA-GAN		M
	2		ŚUM		U			RAṢIJ		EM		[SU]-MU-RA-ZI-E-IM		B 40
RZN	1		RAZIN		IM							RA-ZI-NI-IM	GEN	HARRIS 71 9
SKL	1		SIKIL		UM							ṢI-KI-LUM		KISURRA 27 11
			SIKIL		IM							ZI-KI-LI-IM	GEN	TCL I 185 3
			SIKIL		IJA							ZI-KI-LI-IA		CT XLVIII 89
			SIKIL	T	A							ZI-KI-IL-DA	MN	A. 24 3
			SIKIL	T	A							ZI-KI-IL-TA	MN	A. LATE+
			SIKIL	T	A							ZI-KI-EL-TA	MN	A. LATE
			SIKIL	T	E							ZI-GI-IL-TE	MN	A.
			SIKIL					DANN		UM		ZI-GI-IL-DA-NU-UM		M+
			SIKL		UM							ZI-IK-LUM		TIM V 31 19

ROOTS (Consonants only)

SKL	1			SUKIL		UM					ZU-KI-LUM		KISURRA 38 SEAL
SMKN	1			SUMUKAN			JI	JBAL			D-GIR$_3$-I-BA-AL		C
SMT	1			SIMT		I		JARAḪ			ZI-IM-TI-E-RA-AḪ		M+
SNQ	1	JA		SNIQ	AN						IA-AS-NI-KA-AN		RA LXV 50 VIII 51
		JA		SNIQ				ʾIL			IA-AS-NI-IQ-DINGIR		RA LXV 48 VII 66
		JA		SNIQ				ʾIL			IA-AŠ$_2$-NI-IQ-DINGIR		SIMMONS 55 14
				SANIQ		UM					ZA-NI-KUM		M
				SINAQ		I					ZI-NA-GI		M
				SINUQ		A					SI-NU-GA		BIROT,TEA 16:11
				SINUQ		A					ZI-NU-GA		M+
SRD	1	JI		SRID		UM					IZ-RI-TUM		CT XLV 116 16
STR	1			SATUR		UM					ZA-TU-RU-UM		RA LXIV 34 NO.24
				SITR		IJA					ZI-IT-RI-IA		M+, C+
				SITR		IJA					ZI-IT-RI-JA		M
				SITR		A		HADD	U		ZI-IT-RA-A-DU		A. 456 19
				SITR		I		JABAL			ZI-IT-RI-E-BA-AL		M+
				SITR		I		HADD	U		ZI-IT-RI-D-IM		M
				SITR		I		HADD	U		SI-IT-RI-D-IM		JCS XXIV 60 NO.51 REV.
				SITR		I	JE	HADD	U		ZI-IT-RI-E-D-IM		JCS XXIV 63 NO.56 REV.
				SITR		I		ʾEL	UM		ZI-IT-RI-E-LUM		B 42
				SITR		I		ʾIL			ZI-IT-RI-DINGIR		B 42
				SITR		I		KI					
								ʾEL			ZI-IT-RI?-KI-EL?		B 42
				SITR		U	HU				ZI-IT-RU-U$_2$		DE GEN. KICH II C 82
				SUTAR	AH						ZU?-TA-RA	FN	RA LXV 61 IV 42
	2			LI			JA	SITR	U	HU	LI-IA-ZI-IT-RU-U$_2$		M+
				RAJB		A		SITR	U	HU	RA-BA-ZI-IT-RU-U$_2$	FN	M
SṬʾ	1	JA		SAṬIʾ				ʾEL			[I]A-ZA-AD-DI-EL		M
		JA		SAṬIʾ				ʾIL			IA-ZA-AD-DI-DINGIR		M+
		JA		SAṬIʾ				ʾIL			IA-ZA-AT-TI-DINGIR		M
		JA		SAṬIʾ				ʾIL			IA-SA-AD-DI-DINGIR		M
		JA		SAṬIʾ				ʾIL			IA-S[A]-TI-DINGIR		M
				SAṬIʾ	AT	UM					ZA-DI-IA-TUM	FN	XIII 1 I 72
				SUṬIʾ	AN	UM					ZUM-TI-A-NU-U[M]		TA 1930, 6
ŠʾB	1			ŠAʾB	AT	UM					SA-BA-TUM		JCS XXIV 57 NO. 42,44
ŠʾD	1			ŠAʾAD		IJA					SA-A-DI-IA		C+
ŠʾL	1			ŠAʾAL		A					SA-A-LA	NOM	CT II 42 2, 5
				ŠAʾIL	AT	UM					SA-I-LA-TUM	FN	B 37, TIM IV 53 7
				ŠAʾIL	T	UM					ŠA-IL-TUM	FN	U+
				ŠAʾL	AT	UM					SA-LA-TUM	FN	CT VIII 20B 9+, M+, C+
				ŠAʾL	AN	UM					ŠA-LA-NU-UM		TA 30, 615 23
				ŠAʾL		IJA					SA-LI-IA		B 37
				ŠAʾL		I		ʾIL			SA-LI-DINGIR		B 37+
				ŠAʾL		U		MAṬAR			SA-LU-MA-DAR		RA LXV 52 X 68+
				ŠUʾUL		UM					SU-U$_2$-LU-UM		M
ŠʾQ	1			ŠAʾIQ		UM					ŠA-I-GU-UM		RA LXV 54 XII 27
				ŠAʾQ		UM					SA-KUM		UCP X/1 P. 61+, M
				ŠAʾQ	AT	UM					SA-QA?-TUM	FN	XIII 1 VI 59
				ŠAʾQ		IJAN					ŠA-GI-IA-AN		RA LXV 54 XII 11+
				ŠAʾQ		U	HU				SA-GU-U$_2$		SIMMONS 60 31
				ŠAʾQ		A		ʿAN	UM		SA-GA-A-NU-UM		B 47
				ŠUʾQ	AN	UM					ŠU-GA-NU-UM		EDZARD, DER 90:14
ŠʾR	1			ŠAʾR		UM					SA-RU-UM		TIM II 89 2, M
				ŠAʾR		I					SA-RI	GEN	VAS VIII 14 28
				ŠAʾR		IJA					SA-RI-IA		UCP X/1 108 10+
				ŠAʾIR	AT	UM					SA-E-RA-TUM	FN	B 37
				ŠAʾIR	AT	IM					SA-E-RA-TIM	FN GEN	B 37+
				ŠAʾR	AN	UM					SA-RA-NU-UM		TIM V 19 4
ŠḪ	1			ŠUḪ	IT	UM					SU?-ḪI-TUM	FN	XIII 1 II 52
ŠḪR	1	JA		ŠḪIR		UM					IA-AŠ-ḪI-RUM		M
			T	ŠAḪR	AH						SI?-TA-AḪ-RA	FN	IX 291 III 29'
				ŠAḪIR		A					ŠA-ḪI-RA	NOM	CT VIII 37D 1, 9
				ŠAḪIR		A					ŠA-ḪI-RA	GEN	CT VIII 37D 6, 13
				ŠUḪAR		UM					SU-ḪA-RU-UM		TA 30, 249 4
				ŠUḪAR	T	UM					ŠU-ḪA-AR-TUM	FN	M
				ŠUḪR		AJA					ŠU-UḪ-RA-IA	FN	SIMMONS 138 5, 14

ROOTS (Consonants only)

ŚWR	1		ŚAWIR	AT	UM							SA-WI-RA-TUM		UET V 378 5
			ŚAWIR	AN	IM							SA-WI-RA-NI-IM	GEN	TA 1930, 558
ŚJB	1		ŚIJB	AT	UM							ŠI-BA-TUM	FN	M
			ŚIJB	T	UM							ŠI-IB-TU-UM	FN	RA LXV 62 V 50
			ŚIJB	T	UM							ŠI-IB-TUM	FN	M
			ŚIJB	T	U							ŠI-IB-TU	FN	M+
			ŚIJB	AT	IJA							SI-BA-TI-IA	FN?	BM 80363 7
			ŚIJB	ATANU								SI-BA-TA-NU		SIMMONS 88 1
			ŚIJB		U	NA		ḪARAM				ŠI-BU-NA-A-RA-AM		M
ŚJM	1	JA	ŚJIM	AT	UM							IA-SI-MA-TUM	FN	RA LXV 60 III 8
		JA	ŚJIM					ḪAJJ		A		[I]A-ŠI-IM-E$_2$-A		M
		JI	ŚJIM					ḪAJJ		A		I-ŠI-IM-E$_2$-A		M
		JA	ŚJIM					ʾAB		IM		IA-SI-IM-A-BI-IM	GEN	M
		JA	ŚJIM					HADD		U		IA-SI-IM-D-IM		M
		JA	ŚJIM					ʾIL				IA-SI-IM-DINGIR		M+
		JA	ŚJIM					ʿAMM		U		IA-SI-IM-ḪA-AM-MU		M
		JA	ŚJIM					ʿAMM		U		IA-SI-IM-ḪA-MU		M
		JA	ŚJIM					ʾIRR		A		IA-ŠI-IM-IR$_3$-RA		M
		JA	ŚJIM					DAGAN				IA-SI-IM-D-DA-GAN		M+
		JA	ŚJIM					DAGAN				IA-ŠI-IM-D-DA-GAN		VIII 11 33
		JA	ŚJIM					KI						
								ʾIL				IA-SI-IM-KI-DINGIR		M
		JA	ŚJIM					MAHAR				IA-SI-IM-MA-ḪA-AR		M
		JA	ŚJIM					ŚUM		U	HU	IA-SI-IM-SU-MU-U$_2$		M+
		TA	ŚJIM					ʿAŠTAR				TA-ŠI-IM-EŠ$_4$-DAR	FN	XIII 1 IV 28
			ŚIJM	AT	UM							ŠI-MA-TUM	FN	M+
			ŚIJM	AT	IM							ŠI-MA-TIM	FN GEN	XIII 1 V 15+
			ŚIJM	AT				ʿAŠTAR				ŠI-MA-AT-EŠ$_4$-DAR	FN	XIII 1 V 75+
			ŚIJM	AT				DAGAN				ŠI-MA-AT-D-DA-GAN	FN	XIII 1 VIII 33+
			ŚIJM		U			DAWR		A		SI-MU-DA-RA		TA 30, 186+
	2		LA					ŚIJM		A		LA-SI-MA		M
			ŚUM		U		JA	ŚJIM				SU-MU-IA-SI-IM		M+
			ṮAJB					ŚIJM	T	UM		TA-AB-SI-IM-TUM	FN	A. 8 4
	3		ŚAM		I			MA						
							JA	ŚJIM				SA-MI-MA-IA-SI-IM	FN	C+
ŚJT	1	JA	ŚJIT		UM							IA-SI-TUM		XIII 98 3+
		JA	ŚJIT	AN								IA-SI-TA-AN		M+
		JA	ŚJIT	AN								IA-SI-IT-TA-AN		M
		JA	ŚJIT					ʾAB		I		IA-SI-IT-A-BI		M
		JA	ŚJIT					ʾAB		U		IA-SI-IT-A-BU		M+
		JA	ŚJIT			NA						IA-SI-IT-NA		TIM IV 20 SEAL, M
		JI	ŚJIT			NA						I-SI-IT-NA		UCP X/1 58 3
		JA	ŚJIT			NA		ʾAB		U		IA-SI-IT-NA-A-BU		XIII 1 XII 15
		MA	ŚJIT					ʿAN		UM		MA-SI-IT-A-NU-UM		I
			ŚIJT	AT	UM							SI-TA-TUM	FN	XIII 1 IV 74+
	2		ʾAḪ		I		JA	ŚJIT				A-ḪI-SI-IT		TA 1931, 636
			ŚUM		U		JA	ŚJIT				SU-MU-IA-SI-IT		B 39
ŚBJ	1	JA	ŚBIJ					ʾIL				IA-AŠ-BI-DINGIR		B 32
		JA	ŚBIJ					ʾIL		A		IA-AŠ-BI-I-LA		B 30
		JI	ŚBIJ					ʾIRR		A		IŠ-BI-D-IR$_3$-RA		M+
		JI	ŚBIJ					ʾIRR		A		IŠ-BI-IR$_3$-RA		M+
ŚBL	1		ŚIBIL		UM							SI-BI-LU-UM		A 21941
			ŚUBUL		UM							SU-BU-LU-UM		AJSL XXXII 227 4
			ŚUBUL		UM							SU-BU-LUM	FN	RA LXV 58 I 65
ŚBM	1	JI	ŚBIM		U							IŠ-BI-MU		CT IV 30D 10
			ŚABIM		UM							SA-BI-MU-UM		M+
			ŚABIM		U							SA-BI-MU		C+
			ŚABIM	AT	IM							SA-BI-MA-TIM	FN NOM	RA LXIV 43
ŚBŠ	2		ŚUM		U		JA	ŚABAŠ		UM		SU-MU-IA-SA-BA-SU-UM		PBS XI/2 1 I 34
ŚDD	1		ŚADID		UM							SA-DI-DU-UM		HARRIS 76 17
ŚDL	1		ŚADL		U			MA				SA-AD-LU-MA		UCP X/1 P. 61+
ŚDR	1		ŚADIR	AT	UM							SA-DI-RA-TUM?	FN	BM 80485 7, 18
			ŚADR		UM							SA-AD-[RU]?-UM		RA LXV 53 XI 34
ŚGG	1		ŚUGAG		UM							SU-GA-GU-UM		CT IV 42A 1, 8+
			ŚUGAG		UM							ZU-GA-GU-UM		SIMMONS 72 11+
			ŚUGAG		I							SU-GA-GI	GEN	CT IV 31A 5+

ROOTS (Consonants only)

ŚGR	1		ŚAGAR		UM				SA-GA-RU-UM		GAUTIER 4 R. 4+
			ŚAGAR		UM				SAG-GA-RU-UM		UET V 534 R. 6+
			ŚAGAR		UM				SA-AN-GA-RU-UM		BIN VII 45 12
			ŚAGAR	AT	UM				SA-GA-RA-TUM-KI	GN	M+
			ŚAGAR	AT	IM				SA-GA-RA-TIM-KI	GN GEN	M+
			ŚAGAR	AT	IM				SAG-GA-RA-TIM	MN GEN	M
			ŚAGAR	AT	IM				SAG-GA-RA-TIM	GN GEN	M+
			ŚAGAR	AT	IM				SA-AN-GA-RA-TIM-KI	GN GEN	M
ŚKB	1		ŚAKB		IJA				SA-[A]K-BI-IA		RA LXV 44 IV 34
			ŚAKB		I		HADD	U	SA-AK-BI-D-IM		ARMT V P. 123
	2		ʾIŠḪAR	AH		TA	ŚKUB		D-IŠ-ḪA-RA-TA-AŠ-KU-UB	FN	RA LXV 56 V 21+
ŚKN	1	ʾA	ŚKIN	AN	UM				AŠ$_2$-KI-NA-NU-UM		TA 30 87+
		JA	ŚKIN				ʾIL		IA-AŠ$_2$-KI-IN-DINGIR-[....]?		M
		ME	ŚKIN		UM				ME-EŠ$_3$-KI-NU-UM		WALTERS, WL 95:2
		ME	ŚKIN		IM				ME-EŠ$_3$-KI-NIM	GEN	M+
			ŚAKAN		UM				SA-KA-NU-UM		B 93
			ŚAKUN	UN	UM				SA-KU-NU-NU-UM		RUTTEN 26 4
			ŚAKN		UM				SA-AK-NU-UM		TA 30, 36 2
			ŚAKN		U				SA-AK-NU	FN	M
			ŚAKN		U				ŠA-AK-NU		M
			ŚAKN	AT	UM				SA-AK-NA-TUM	FN	RA LXV 58 I 27
ŚKR	1	ʾA	ŚKUR	AN					AŠ-KU-RA-AN		RA LXV 50 IX 15
		ʾA	ŚKUR				HADD	U	AŠ$_2$-KU-UR-D-IM		TCL 1 146 4
		ʾA	ŚKUR				HADD	U	AŠ-KUR-D-IM		M+
		ʾA	ŚKUR				HEDD	A	AŠ-KUR-E-DA		A. 54 25
		JA	ŚKUR		UM				IA-AŠ$_2$-KU-RUM		XIII 1 XI 13
		JA	ŚKUR		UM				IA-AŠ-KU-RUM		XIII 1 XI 19
		JA	ŚKUR		UM				IA-UŠ-KU-RU-UM		TIM III 133 11
		JA	ŚKUR		IM				IA-AŠ$_2$-KU-RI-IM	GEN	M+
		JA	ŚKUR				ʾIL		IA-AŠ$_2$-KU-UR$_2$-DINGIR		B 81
		JA	ŚKUR				ʾIL		IA-AŠ$_2$-KU-UR-DINGIR		B 30+
		JA	ŚKUR				ʾIL		IA-AŠ$_2$-KUR-DINGIR		JNES XIII 210+ LATE
		JA	ŚKUR				ʾIL		[IA]-AŠ-KU-UR-DINGIR		VIII 38 7'
		JI	ŚKUR				ʾEL	I	IŠ-KUR-E-LI	FN	XIII 1 VII 41
		ME	ŚKIR		UM				ME-IŠ-KI-RUM		B 34
		MI	ŚKIR		UM				MI-IŠ-KI-RUM		VAS IX 172 13
			ŚAKAR		UM				SA-KA-RU-UM		HARRIS 39 13
			ŚAKAR		UM				SA-KA-RUM		BIN VII 90 12+
			ŚAKIR		UM				SA-KI-RUM		M+
			ŚAKIR		UM				SA-KI-RU-UM		RUTTEN 35 6, SEAL+
			ŚAKIR		U				SA-KI-RU		B 37
			ŚAKIR		AM				SA-KI-RA-AM	ACC	M
			ŚAKIR	AH					SA-KI-RA	FN	M
			ŚAKUR	AN					SA-KU-RA-AN		RA LXV 54 XII 24
			ŚAKUR	AN	U				SA-KU-RA-NU		M+
			ŚIKR		I		HADD	A	SI-IK-RI-ḪA-DA		BE VI/1 6 19
			ŚIKIR		UM				SI-KI-RUM		YOS XIII 294:4+
			ŚUKUR	AT	UM				ŠU-KU-[R]A-TUM	FN	XIII 1 V 78
		MA	ŚKAR		UM				MAŠ-GA-RU-UM		RUTTEN 33 5, SEAL
	2		BUN		U	ʾA	ŚKUR		BU-NU-AŠ$_2$-KU-UR		SYRIA XXXVII 206 29 HANA
			MUT			ʾA	ŚKUR		MU-UT-AŠ-KUR		M+
		JI	NDIN			ʾA	ŚKUR		I-DIN-D-AŠ$_2$-KU-UR		SYRIA XXXVII 206 8 HANA
			ŚUM		U	ʾA	ŚKUR	A	ŠU-MU-AŠ$_2$-KU-RA		TA 30, 299
ŚKŚ	1		ŚUKUŚ		UM				SU-KU-SU-UM		M
ŚLḤ	1	JA	ŚLAḤ				....		IA-AŠ$_2$-LA-A[Ḫ-....]		M
			ŚALIḤ		UM				SA-LI-ḪU-UM		M
			ŚALIḤ		U				SA-LI-ḪU		M, SYRIA V 274+ HANA
			ŚALIḤ	AH					SA-LI-ḪA	FN	M+
			ŚALUḤ		I				SA-AL-LU-ḪI	GEN	BE VI/2 138 2, 5
			ŚULAḤ	AT	UM				SU-LA-A-TUM	FN	RA LXV 66 VII 62
			ŚULAḤ	AN	U				SU-LA-ḪA-NU		A 7702 13
			ŚULUḤ		UM				SU-LU?-ḪU-UM		UET V 169 18
			ŚULUḤ		U				SU-LU-ḪU		UET V 427 16
ŚLJ	1	JA	ŚLIJ				ḪAʾL		IA-AŠ?-LI?-ḪA-AL		M
ŚLB	1	ME	ŚLIB	AT	UM				ME-EŠ$_3$-LI-BA-TUM	FN	YOS V 117 1
			ŚILIB		UM				ŠI-LI-BU-UM		HARRIS 36 5

ROOTS (Consonants only)

ŚLD	1			ŚALD		IJA			SA-AL-DI-IA		TCL I 80 16
ŚLK	1			ŚULUK		UM			SU-LU-KUM		PBS XI/2 P. 119
ŚLL	1	TA		ŚLAL		UM			DA-AŠ-LA-LUM		TA 1931, 538 II
		TA		ŚLAL		UM			DA-AŠ-LA-LU-UM		TA 1931, 435
		JU	T	ŚALIL		I			UŠ-TA-LI-LI	NOM	M+
				ŚALAL		UM			ŠA-LA-LUM		XIII 1 VII 29
				ŚALIL		UM			SA-LI-LUM		TIM III 131 9
				ŚULAL		I			SU-UL-LA-LI	GEN	TCL XVIII 95 1
				ŚULUL		UM			SU-UL-LU-LUM		PBS XI/2 P. 119
ŚLM	1	JI		ŚLAM	AN	A			IŠ-LA-MA-NA	GEN	MRS VI P. 202 UGARIT
		JA		ŚLAM			ʾIL		IA-AŠ$_2$-LAM-DINGIR		XIV 47:11
		JA		ŚLIM			HAND	U	IA-AŠ$_2$-LI-IM-IA-[AN-D]U		M
		ME		ŚLIM		UM			ME-IŠ-LI-MU-UM		HARRIS 31 18
		MU		ŚALIM		UM			MU-SA-LI-MU-UM		CT XLVIII 57 2, 3
		MU		ŚALIM		U			MU-SA-LI-MU		CT IV 47B 28
		MU		ŚALIM		I			MU-SA-LI-MI	NOM	UCP X/1 87 11
		MU		ŚALIM		IM			MU-SA-LI-MI-IM	GEN	CT VIII 47B 28
		MU		ŚALIM	AT	IM			MU-SA-LI-MA-TIM	FN GEN	BE VI/1 8 14
				ŚALAM		UM			ŠA-LA-MU-UM		EDZARD, DER 100:16
				ŚALAM	AT	UM			SA-LA-MA-TUM	FN?	M
				ŚALAM	AN				SA-LA-MA-AN		RA LXV 43 III 55
				ŚALIM	AT	UM			SA-LI-MA-TUM	MN?	CT VIII 49A 46+
				ŚALIM	AT	UM			SA-LI-MA-TUM	FN	XIII 1 VI 46
				ŚALIM	AT	IM			SA-LI-MA-TIM	FN GEN	CT VIII 28C 13
				ŚALIM	AH				SA-LI-MA	FN	XIII 1 III 29+
				ŚALIM	AN				SA-LI-MA-AN		M+
				ŚALIM	AN	U			SA-LI-MA-NU		A 7733 4, C+
				ŚALIM	AN	IM			SA-LI-MA-NIM	GEN	M
				ŚALIM			ʿAN	UM	ŠA-LIM-A-NU-UM		M
				ŚALIM			ʾAŠAR		ŠA-LIM-D-A-ŠAR		M
				ŚALM		U	ṬAJB	A	ŠA-AL-MU-ṬA$_3$-BA	FN	RA LXV 66 VII 64
				ŚULAM		UM			SU-LA-MU-UM		UET V 608 3
				ŚULM	AN	UM			ŠU-U[L]-MA-NU-U[M]		I
	2	JI		ʾWUŠ			ŚALIM		I-UŠ?-SA-LIM		RUTTEN 1 3
				ʾAB		U	ŚALIM		A-BU-SA-[LIM]		M
				ʾIL		A	ŚALIM		I-LA-SA-LIM		M, C
				ʾIL		UM	ŚALM	A	I-LU-UM-ŠA-AL-MA		RA LXV 45 V 51
				ʿAMM		U	ŚALIM		ḪA-MU-SA-L[IM]?		M
				JATAR			ŚALIM		IA-TAR-SA-LIM		M+
		JI		JṢIʾ			ŚALIM		I-ṢI-SA-LIM		RUTTEN 4 19+
				MUT			ŚALIM		MU-UT-SA-LIM		M
		JI		NDUB			ŚALIM		IN-DU-UB-ŠA-LIM		TA 1931, 265:10
		JI		TWUR			ŚALIM		I-DUR-SA-LIM		YOS II 84 21 22
ŚLP	1			ŚULAP		UM			SU-LA-PU-UM		PBS XI/2 P. 119
				ŚULAP		I			SU-LA-PI		PBS XI/2 P. 119
ŚM	1			ŚAM		UM			SA-MU-UM		EBPN 141+, M
				ŚAM		IM			SA-MI-IM	GEN	CT XLVIII 91, XIII 142 40+
				ŚAM		AM			SA-MA-AM	ACC	XIII 38 7+
				ŚAM	AN				SA-MA-AN		B 39+, M
				ŚAM	AN	UM			SA-MA-NU-UM		B 47
				ŚAM	AN	UM			ŠA-MA-NUM$_2$		U
				ŚAM	AN	UM			ŠA-MA-NU-UM		I
				ŚAM	AN	U			SA-MA-NU		JNES XIII 212F. LATE
				ŚAM	AN	I			SA-MA-A-NI		JNES XIII 212F.+ LATE
				ŚAM		IJA			SA-MI-IA		EBPN 140+, MAM II/3 PL. XXXIX+
				ŚAM	T	UM			SA-AM-TUM	FN	TCL I 189 17, M+
				ŚAM		A	JADAʿ	UM	SA-MA-A-DA-ḪU-UM		M+
				ŚAM		A	JADAʿ	U	SA-MA-A-DA-ḪU		M
				ŚAM		A	JADAʿ	IM	SA-MA-A-DA-Ḫ[I-I]M	GEN	M
				ŚAM		A	ME				
							ʾEL		SA-MA-ME-EL		M
				ŚAM		A	ME				
							ʾEL		ŠA-MA-ME-EL		TA 1931, 421
				ŚAM		A	RAWḪ		SA-MA-RA-AḪ		B 38+, XII 385 8
				ŚAM		I	JARAḪ		SA-ME-E-RA-AḪ		M
				ŚAM		I	JARAḪ		SA-ME-RA-AḪ		YOS VIII 64 19+

ROOTS (Consonants only)

ŠM	1	ŠAM		I				JATAR				SA-MI-E-TAR		XII 601 6
		ŠAM		I				DAʿ		UM		SA-MI-DA-ḪU-UM		M+
		ŠAM		I				DAʿ		IM		SA-MI-DA-ḪI-IM	GEN	M+
		ŠAM		I				DAʿ	AT	UM		SA-MI-DA-ḪA-TUM	FN	M
		ŠAM		I				DAʿ	AT	IM		SA-MI-DA-ḪA-TIM	FN? GEN	XII 741 6
		ŠAM		I				MA						
						JA		ŠJIM				SA-MI-MA-IA-SI-IM	FN	C+
		ŠAM		I				ME						
								ʾEL				SA-MI-ME-EL		CT XLV 117 33
		ŠAM		U				ʾAB		IM		SA-MU-A-BI-IM	NOM	RA VIII 71
		ŠAM		U				ʾAB		IM		SA-MU-A-BI-IM	GEN	SUMER XXIII 153+
		ŠAM		U				HADD		U		SA-MU-D-IM		M+
		ŠAM		U				ʾIL		A		SA-MU-I-LA		M
		ŠAM		U				JARAḪ				SA-MU-A-RA-AḪ		SIMMONS 98 3
		ŠAM		U				JARAḪ				SA-[M]U-E?-RA-A[Ḫ]?		RA LXV 47 VII 13
		ŠAM		U				DAGAN				SA-MU-D-DA-GAN		M
		ŠAM		U				LA						
								ʾIL				SA-MU-LA-DINGIR		B 39+
		ŠAM		U				RAWḪ				SA-MU-RA-A-AḪ		SIMMONS 46 28, 47 23
		ŠAM		U				RAWḪ				SA-MU-RA	NOM	CT XLVIII 29 REV.
		ŠAM		U	HU							SA-MU-U$_2$		M+
		ŠAM		U	HU			ʾIL		A		SA-MU-U$_2$-I-LA		M
		ŠUM		UM								ŠU-MU-UM		TA 30, 615 5
		ŠUM	AN									SU-MA-AN		B 39
		ŠUM		IJA								SU-MI-IA		M+
		ŠUM		U	JA							SU-MU-IA		B 39+
		ŠUM		U	JA							SU-MU-U$_2$-A		PBS XI/2 1 32
		ŠUM						LI						
						JI		JṢIʾ		IM		SU-UM-LI-ZI-IM	GEN	WATERMAN 25 R 9
		ŠUM		A				HADD		U		ŠU-MA-A-DU		A.
		ŠUM		A				ʾIL		A		SU-MA-I-LA		YOS XIII 244:15+
		ŠUM		A				LA						
								LI			JA	SU-MA-LA-LI-A		BM 80363 1
		ŠUM		A				LI			KA	SU-MA-LI-KA		BM 80328 13
		ŠUM		A				RAPIʾ				SU-MA-RA-BI		KAJ 39 17 LATE
		ŠUM		I				ʾAB		UM		SU-ME-A-BU-UM		A. 12 4
		ŠUM		I				HADD		U		SU-MI-A-DU		A.+
		ŠUM		I				HEDD		A		SU-MI-E-DA		YOS XIII 486:1
		ŠUM		I				ʾIL		UM		SU-MI-LU-UM		WALTERS, WL 114:13
		ŠUM		I				JAMAM				SU-MI-IA-MA-AM		XII 61 5
		ŠUM		I				ʾENLIL				SU-ME-D-EN-LIL$_2$		KISURRA 197A 12
		ŠUM		I				ḪINN		I		ŠU-MI-IN-NI		U
		ŠUM		I				ʾENTIL				SU-ME-EN-TI-[IL]?		B 38
		ŠUM		I				DAWR		U		SU?-MI-DA-AR-RU		A. 322 9
		ŠUM		I				DAWR		U		ŠU-MI-TA-RU		A. LATE
		ŠUM		I				LAMM		U		SU-MI-LAM-MU		VAS XVI 24 4, A.+
		ŠUM		I				RIJB		A		SU-MI-RI-BA		A. 98C 10
		ŠUM		I				RIJB		A		ŠU-MI-RI-PA		A. LATE
		ŠUM		I				RIJB		A		ŠU-ME-RI-PA		A. LATE
		ŠUM		I				RAPAʾ				SU-MI-RA-PA		RA LVI 169, A.+
		ŠUM		I				ṬAJB		A		SU?-MI-DA-BA		A. 7 44+
		ŠUM			NA			JATAR				SU-UM-NA-IA-TAR		RA LXV 52 X 56
		ŠUM		U				ʾAḪ		I	JA	[SU]-MU-A-ḪI-IA		PBS XI/2 1 I 27
		ŠUM		U		ʾA		MNID		IM		[SU-M]U-AM-NI-DI-IM		B 38
		ŠUM		U		ʾA		ŠKUR		A		ŠU-MU-AŠ$_2$-KU-RA		TA 30, 299
		ŠUM		U		JI	T	ŠAMAR				SU-MU-UŠ-TA-MAR		TIM II 14 21
		ŠUM		U				ḪAʾL		A		SU-MU-ḪA-LA		B 39
		ŠUM		U				ʾAWN	AN	UM		SU-MU-AM-NA-NU-UM		B 38+
		ŠUM		U				ʾAWN	AN	IM		SU-MU-AW-NA-NIM		SUMER XXIII ARABIC 178
		ŠUM		U				ʾAB		UM		SU-MU-A-BU-UM		B 38+
		ŠUM		U				ʾAB		UM		D-SU-MU-A-BU-UM		KISURRA 93 22
		ŠUM		U				ʾAB		IM		[S]U-MU-A-BI-IM	NOM	EDZARD, DER 111:5
		ŠUM		U				ʾAB		IM		SU-MU-A-BI-IM	GEN	SUMER XXIII PL. 12 19
		ŠUM		U				ʾAB		I		SU-MA-A-BI		A.
		ŠUM		U				ʾAB		I	JA	[SU]-MU-A-BI-IA		B 38
		ŠUM		U				ʾAB		I				
						JA		RWIM				SU-MU-A-BI-A-RI-IM		TA 30 9, 14, 15+

ROOTS (Consonants only)

ŠM	1	ŠUM	UM		ʾAB	I				
				JA	RWIM			SU-MU-UN-A-BI-IA-RI-IM		SUMER XXIII 153:9
		ŠUM	U		ʾABIḪ			SU-MU-A-BI-IḪ		TIM V 1 16
		ŠUM	UM		ʿAD	U		SU-MU-UM?-ḪA-DU-KI	GN	YOS II 117:17+
		ŠUM	U		ʿAD	I		SU-MU-ḪA-DI-I	GEN	XIII 13:8
		ŠUM	U		ʿAD	IM		SU-MU-ḪA-DI-IM		X 57 8
		ŠUM	U		ʿAD	U	HU	SU-MU-ḪA-DU-U$_2$		M+
		ŠUM	U		JADAʿ	UM		SU-MU-A-DA-ḪU-UM		KISURRA 78A 15
		ŠUM	U		ʿADN	U		SU-MU-ḪA-AD-NU		B 39
		ŠUM	U		ʿADN	U		SU-MU-ḪI-AD-NU		KISURRA 29 12
		ŠUM	U		ʿAḎAR			SU-MU-A-DAR		GORDON 38 DATE+
		ŠUM	U		ʿAḎAR			SU-MU-A-TAR		GORDON 38 DATE+
		ŠUM	U		ʿAḎAR			SU-MA-DAR		SIMMONS 50 26 DATE+
		ŠUM	U		ʾEL			SU-MU-EL		TA 30, 34 6
		ŠUM	U		ʾIL			SU-MU-DINGIR		B 39+
		ŠUM	U		ʾIL			D-SU-MU-DINGIR		KISURRA 85 15, 22+
		ŠUM	U		ʾIL	A		SU-MU-I-LA		B 39; M+
		ŠUM	U		ʾIL					
					BAWB	I	JA	[SU-MU-I]L-BA-BI-IA		PBS XI/2 1 I 11
		ŠUM	U		ʾIL					
					....			SU-MU-DINGIR-LI-BUR-RA-AM		FRANK 27 4
		ŠUM	U		ʾIL					
					ŠARR			SU-MU-[DINGIR]-LUGAL		UCP X/1 17 15
		ŠUM	U		HALAB			SU-MU-A-LA-AB		A.
		ŠUM	U		ḪAM	I		SU-MU-A-MI		M
		ŠUM	U		ḪAM	IM		SU-MU-D-A-MI-IM		RA LXV 40 I 25+
		ŠUM	U		ʿAMM	U		SU-MU-ḪA-AM-MU		B 39+
		ŠUM	U		ʿAMM	U		SU-MU-ḪA-MU		M
		ŠUM	U		ʿAMM	U		SU-MU-ḪA-MU	FN	C+
		ŠUM	U		JAMAM			SU-MU-IA-MA-AM		M+
		ŠUM	U		....			[SU-M]U-A-NI-....		PBS XI/2 1 I 12
		ŠUM	U		ʾENTIL			SU-MU-EN-TE-IL		B 39
		ŠUM	U		ʾENTIL			SU-MU-EN-TI-[IL]?		KISURRA 95 15
		ŠUM	U		ʾUP	I		SU-MU-UḪ$_2$-KI		JCS XI 23 NO. 10 14+
		ŠUM	U		JAPAR			[SU-MU]-A-PA-AR		B 38
		ŠUM	U		JARAḪ			SU-MU-A-RA-AḪ		B 38+
		ŠUM	U		JARAḪ			SU-MU-E-RA-AḪ		M+
		ŠUM	U		ʿAŠTAR			SU-MU-EŠ$_4$-DAR		PBS VIII/2 207 5, M
		ŠUM	U		JAT	UM		SU-MU-IA-TUM		TLB IV 40 9, 12, 14
		ŠUM	U	JA	ʾRUR	A		[SU-MU-I]A-AḪ-RU-RA		B 39
		ŠUM	U	JA	MWUT					
					BAʿL	A		SU-MU-IA-MU-UT-BA-[LA]		RUTTEN 3 21
		ŠUM	U	JE	MWUT					
					BAʿL	A		SU-MU-E-MU-UT-BA-LA	NOM	JCS IV 66 22
		ŠUM	U	JE	MWUT					
					BAʿL	A		SU-MU-E-MU-UT-BA-LA	GEN	JCS IV 69 17
		ŠUM	U	JE	MWUT					
					BAʿL	IM		SU-MU-E-MU-UT-BA-LIM?	GEN	JCS IV 71 9
		ŠUM	U	JA	MWUT					
					BAʿL	IM		SU-MU-IA-MU-UT-BA-LIM	GEN	CT XLIII 86 1
		ŠUM	U	JA	MWUT	U				
					BAʿL	A		[SU]-MU-IA-MU-TU-BA-LA		PBS XI/2 1 I 19
		ŠUM	U	JA	JPAʿ			[SU-MU]-A-PA-AḪ		B 38
		ŠUM	U	JE	JPUʿ			SU-MU-E-PU-UḪ		M+
		ŠUM	U	JA	ŠJIM			SU-MU-IA-SI-IM		M+
		ŠUM	U	JA	ŠJIT			SU-MU-IA-SI-IT		B 39
		ŠUM	U	JA	ŠABAŠ	UM		SU-MU-IA-SA-BA-SU-UM		PBS XI/2 1 I 34
		ŠUM	U		BAʿL	A		SU-MU-BA-LA		UNPUBL.
		ŠUM	U		BALIṬ			SU-MU-BA-LI$_2$-IṬ?		RUTTEN 26 12+
		ŠAM	U		BALIṬ			SA-MU-BA-LI$_2$-IṬ?		RUTTEN 34 11
		ŠUM	U		BELBIN			SU-MU-BE-EL-BI-IN		JCS IV 108, YBC 5198
		ŠUM	U		BINAŠ	U		SU-MU-BI-NA-ŠU		A 7630 2
		ŠUM	U		DAGAN			SU-MU-D-DA-GAN		B 39+
		ŠUM	U		....			SU-MU-DI-NA-....		B 39
		ŠUM	U		DIJN	I		[SU-M]U-DI-NI		PBS XI/2 P. 119
		ŠUM	U		DITAN	A		SU-MU-DI-TA-NA		B 39+, M

ROOTS (Consonants only)

ŠM	1	ŠUM	U			DITAN			SU-MU-DI-TA-AN		SIMMONS 126 17+	
		ŠUM	U			DITAN			[SU]?-MU?-DI?-TA-A-AN		VAS XVI 24 3	
		ŠUM	U			DITN	UM		SU-MU-DI-IT-NU-UM		B 39	
		ŠUM	U			KANAŠ	A		SU-MU-GA-NA-SA		KISURRA 19 9	
		ŠUM	U			LA		NI	SU-MU-LA-NI		HARRIS 39 11	
		ŠUM	U			LA		NIA	SU-MU-LA-NI-A		CT XLVIII 10 1	
		ŠUM	UM			LA						
						ʾAB	I		SU-MU-UM-LA-A-BI	FN	RA LXV 65 VII 24	
		ŠUM	U			LA						
						ʾIL			SU-MU-LA-DINGIR		B 39+	
		ŠUM	U			LA						
						ʾIL	I		SU-MU-LA-I_3-LI_2		UCP X/1 34 2	
		ŠUM	U			LI						
						ʾEL			SU-MU-LI-EL		B 39+	
		ŠUM	U			LA						
						ʾEL			SU-MU-LA-EL		SUMER XXIII 160 5	
		ŠUM	U			LI						
						ʾEL			SU-MU-LI-EL-DU-RI		A 7630 3	
		ŠUM	U			LI						
					JI	JṢIʾ			SU-MU-LI-ZI		MEISSNER 37 15+	
		ŠUM	U			LAʾL	UM		SU-MU-LA-LUM		PBS XI/2 1 I 16	
		ŠUM	U			LIʾL	U		SU-MU-LI-LU		B 39	
		ŠUM	U			LABW	A		SU-MU-LA-BA		M	
		ŠUM	U			ME						
						ʾEL			SU-MU-ME-EL		JCS IV 107,	YBC 4968
		ŠUM	U			MUT	I					
						JABAL	A		SU-MU-MU-TI-A-BA-LA		B 39	
		ŠUM	UM			MAZAZ			ŠU-MU-UM-MA-ZA-AZ		TA 1931, 538 I, IV	
		ŠUM	U	NA		ʾAB	I		SU-MU-UN-NA-A-BI	FN	A. 64 7	
		ŠUM	U	NA		ʾAB	I		SU-MU-UN-NA-BI	FN	A. 33 3, 34 2+	
		ŠUM	U	NA		ʾAB	I		SU-MU-NA-BI	FN	A. 59 8	
		ŠUM	U	NA		ʾAB	I		SU-MU-NA-A-BI	FN	A. 244 5, M	
		ŠUM	U	NA		ʾAB	I					
					JA	RWIM			SU-MU-NA-BI-IA-RI-IM		SUMER XXIII PL. 7 17+	
		ŠUM	U	NA		ʾAB	I					
					JA	RWIM			SU-MU-UN?-A-BI-JA-RI-IM		SUMER XXIII P. 153 9	
		ŠUM	U	NA		HALAL			SU-MU-NA-ḪA-LA?-AL		UET V 245 11	
		ŠUM	U	NA	JA	JPUʿ	A		SU-MU-NA-IA-PU-ḪA-[....]		M	
		ŠUM	U	NA	JA	RWIM			SU-UM-MU-NA-A-RI-IM		HARRIS 57 11	
		ŠUM	U	NI					SU-MU-NI		B 39	
		ŠUM	U			NIWḪ	A		SU-MU-NI-A		GORDON 39 9, 13	
		ŠUM	U			NIWḪ	UM		SU-MU-NI-ḪU-UM		B 39	
		ŠUM	U			NIWḪ	IM		SU-MU-NI-ḪI-IM	GEN	SIMMONS 121 18,	M+
		ŠUM	U			NIWR	I		SU-MU-NI-RI	FN	XIII 1 XI 46	
		ŠUM	U			NIʾŠ	U	JA	SU-MU-NI-ŠU-A		CT VIII 38D:14	
		ŠUM	U			NUMAḪ	A		SU-MU-NU-MA-ḪA		M	
		ŠUM	U			NUMḪ	A		SU-M[U-N]U-UM-ḪA		RA LXIV 43	
		ŠUM	U			NUMḪ	IM		SU-MU-NU-UM-ḪI-IM		RIFTIN 44 12,16+	
		ŠUM	U			RAWḤ			SU-MU-RA-A		B 40	
		ŠUM	U			RAWḤ			SU-MU-RA-AḪ		B 38+	
		ŠUM	U			RAWḤ			SU-MU-RA-A-AḪ		CT II 39 1, 15	
		ŠUM	U			RAWḤ	EM		[SU]-MU-RA-ḪI-E-IM		B 40	
		ŠUM	U			RAWM	E	JE	SU-MU-RA-ME-E		B 40+	
		ŠUM	U			RAWM	EM		SU-MU-RA-ME-IM		M	
		ŠUM	U			RAPIʾ			SU-MU-RA-BI		M	
		ŠUM	U			RAṢIJ	EM		[SU]-MU-RA-ZI-E-IM		B 40	
		ŠUM	U			....			SU-MU-SI-MU-....		A 7457 3	
		ŠUM	U			ŠAMŠ			SU-MU-D-UTU		CT XLVIII 83 SEAL	
		ŠUM	U		TA	QWIM			SU-MU-TA-KI-IM		XIII 131 4'	
		ŠUM	U		TA	QJIŠ			SU-MU-TA-KI-IŠ		M	
		ŠUM	U			TAMAR			SU-MU-TA-MAR		B 40+	
		ŠUM	U			TAMAR	U		SU-MU-TA-MA-RU		RA LXIV 43	
		ŠUM	U			ṬAJB	I		SU-MU-DA-BI		X 90 10+	
		ŠUM	U			ṢIDQ	UM		[SU]-MU-ZI-ID-KUM		B 40	
		ŠUM	U			ṢIDQ	UM					
						DITAN	A		[SU]-MU-ZI-ID-KUM-DI-TA-NA		B 40	

ROOTS (Consonants only)

ŠM	2	ʾAḪ	I	ŠUM	U	NA	A-ḪI-SU-MU-NA		SIMMONS 83 5
		ʾAJA		ŠUM			ḪA-IA3-SU?-UM		M
		ʾAJA		ŠUM	U		ḪA-IA3-SU-MU		DELAPORTE CCL II A 337+
		ʾAJA		ŠUM	U	HU	ḪA-IA-SU-MU-U2		XI P.83 N.1+
		ʾAJA		ŠUM	U	HU	ḪA-IA3-SU-MU-U2		M+
		ʾAJA		ŠUM	U	HU	ḪA-IA3-SU-U2-MU		M+
		ʾAJA		ŠUM	U	HU	ḪA-IA3-SU-U2-MU-U2		X 113 4, 11, 14
		ʾAJA		ŠUM	U				
				ʾAB	IM		ḪA-IA-SU-MU-A-BI-IM		M
		JAʾ	U	ŠUM	UM		IA?-U2-SU?-MU-UM?		XIII 146 13
	JI	JDAʿ		ŠUM			I-DA-SU-UM		M
		ʾIL	I	ŠUM	U		I3-LI2-SU-U2-MU		M
		ʾILAR		ŠUM			I-LA-AR-ŠUM		I
		ʿAMM	I	ŠUM	U		AM-MI-SU-MU		CT XLVIII 61 4,5
		ʿAMM	I	ŠUM	U	HU	ḪA-AM-MI-SU-MU-U2		CT XLVII 30 44
		ʿAMM	U	ŠAM	A		AM-MU-SA-MA		A.+
	JA	JPAʿ		ŠUM	U				
				ʾAB	I		IA-PA-AḪ-SU-MU-A-BI		A. 56 47
		JATAR		ŠUM	U		IA-TAR-SU-MU		XII 456 10
		JATAR		ŠUM	U	HU	IA-TAR-SU-MU-U2		M+
	JI	JṢIʾ		ŠUM	UM		I-ZI-SU-MU-UM		B 23, M+
	JI	JṢIʾ		ŠUM	U	JA	I-ZI-SU-MU-A		KISURRA 112 7
	JI	JṢIʾ		ŠUM	U	HU	I-ZI-SU-MU-U2		A 7646 3+
	JI	JṢIʾ		ŠAM	U				
				ʾAB	UM		I-ZI-SA-MU-A-BU-UM		B 23
	JI	JṢIʾ		ŠUM	U				
				ʾAB	UM		I-ZI-SU-MU-A-BU-UM		B 23+
	JI	JṢIʾ		ŠUM	U				
				ʾAB	IM		I-ZI-SU-MU-A-BI-IM	GEN	B 23
	JA	WṢIʾ		ŠUM	U				
				ʾAB	UM		U2-ṢI-SU-MU-A-BU-UM		AJSL XXVIII 244 19
		ḌU		ŠUM	IM		ZU-U2-ŠU?-MI-IM		M
	JA	KWUN		ŠUM	U				
				ʾAB	IM		IA-KU-UN-SU-MU-A-BI-IM		M
		LA	NA	ŠUM	UM		LA-NA-SU-MU-[UM]		CT VIII 26B 22
		LABW	I	ŠAM	A		LA-BI-SA-MA		UCP X/3 P. 199+
		MAʾL	I	ŠUM	U	HU	MA-LI-SU-MU-U2		TIM I 29 10
		MALIK		ŠUM	U	HU	MA-LIK-SU-MU-U2		M
		MANN	U	ŠAM	A		MA-NU-SA-MA		B 34
	JA	PLUS	I	ŠUM	I		IA-AP-LU-SI-SU-U2-MI		BIROT,TEA 31:6
		QARAʾ		ŠUM	I	JA	QA-RA-SU-MI-IA		CT II 34 5
		QARAʾ		ŠUM	I	JA	GA-RA-SU-MI-IA		CT XLVIII 89 REV.
		QARAʾ		ŠUM	U	JA	QA-RA-SU?-MU-IA		CT VI 43 6
		QARAʾ		ŠUM	U	JA	GA-RA-SU-MU-IA		CT XLV 11 2, 46+
		QARAʾ		ŠUM	U	JA	KA-RA?-SU-MU-IA		CT II 30 3
		QARAʾ		ŠUM	U	JA	KA-RA-SU-LUM		CT II 30 34
	JA	RWIM		ŠUM	U				
				ʾAB	I		IA-RI-IM-SU-MU-A-BI		RA LXV 42 III 8
	JA	ŠJIM		ŠUM	U	HU	IA-SI-IM-SU-MU-U2		M+
	JI	TWUR		ŠUM	U				
				ʾEL			I-DUR-SU-ME-EL		KISURRA 43 5+
		ṬAJB		ŠUM	U	HU	ṬA3-AB-SU-MU-U2		M+
	3	ʾAJA		LA					
				ŠUM	U	HU	A-IA-LA-SU-MU-U2		M, C
ŠMʾL	1	ŠAMʾAL					SA-AM-A-AL		M
		ŠAMʾAL	A	ʾIL			SA-AM-A-LA-DINGIR		M+
		ŠAMʾIL	I	ʾIL			SA-AM-ḪI-LI-DINGIR		M
		ŠIMʾAL					SI-IM-ḪA-AL	TRIBE	M
		ŠIMʾAL					SI-IM-A-AL	TRIBE	M+
		ŠIMʾAL					SI-MA-AL	TRIBE	M
		ŠIMʾAL	UM				SI-IM-A-LU-UM	TRIBE	M
ŠMḪ	1	ŠAMḪ	ATANI				SA-AM-ḪA-TA-NI		VAS VIII 14 5
		ŠIMḪ	AJA				ŠI-IM-ḪA-A-IA	FN	M
		ŠIMḪ	I	DAGAN			SI-IM-ḪI-D-DA-GAN		M
		ŠIMḪ	U	ʾIL	UM		ŠI-IM-ḪU-LUM?		A. 265 8
		ŠUMḪ	U	BAʿL			SU-UM-ḪU-BA-AL		YOS XII 390 2,9

ROOTS (Consonants only)

ŠMḪ	1		ŠUMḪ		U			RAPIʾ			SU-UM-ḪU-RA-BI		M+
			ŠUMUḪ		UM						SU-MU-ḪU-UM		BM 16852
			ŠUMUḪ		UM						ZU-MU-ḪU-UM		M
			ŠUMUḪ	AT	UM						ŠU-MU-ḪA-TUM	FN	RA LXV 64 V 58
			ŠUMUḪ	T	UM						ŠU-MU-UḪ-TUM	FN	XIII 1 X 49+
			ŠUMUḪ					BAʿL	A		SU-MU-UḪ-EA-LA		PBS XI/2 1 I 18
	2		ḪAJJ		A			ŠIMḪ	I		E$_2$-A-ŠI-IM-ḪI	FN	XIII 1 II 44
			ʾADM		U			ŠIMḪ	I		AD-MU-ŠI-IM-ḪI	FN	XIII 1 IV 6
			ʾADM		U			ŠIMḪ	I		D-AD-MU-ŠI-IM-ḪI	FN	RA LXV 62 V 28
			ʾIL		I			ŠIMḪ	I		I$_3$-LI$_2$-ŠI-IM-ḪI		M+
			ʾIL		I			ŠIMḪ	A	JA	I$_3$-LI$_2$-ŠI-IM-ḪA-IA		VIII 57 BIS 16
			ʾIL		I			ŠIMḪ	A	JA	I$_3$-LI$_2$-ŠE-IM-ḪA-IA		VIII 57 14
			ʾANN		U			ŠIMḪ	I		[A]N-NU-ŠI-IM-ḪI		XIII 1 XIV 24
			ʿAŠTAR					ŠIMḪ	I		EŠ$_4$-DAR-ŠI-IM-ḪI	FN	XIII 1 XII 2
			TABUB		U			ŠIMḪ	I		TA-BU-BU-ŠI-IM-ḪI	FN	XII 265 4
ŠMʿ	1	JA	ŠMAʿ		UM						IA-AŠ$_2$-MA-ḪU-UM		M
		JA	ŠMAʿ		U						IA-AŠ$_2$-MA-ḪU		B 30 HANA
		JA	ŠMAʿ					HADD	U		IA-AŠ$_2$-MA-AḪ-D-IM		M+, C+
		JA	ŠMAʿ					HADD	U		IA-AŠ$_2$-NI-IḪ-D-IM		M
		JI	ŠMAʿ					HADD	U		IŠ-MA-D-IM		M
		JI	ŠMAʿ					HADD	U		IŠ-ME-D-IM		M+
		JI	ŠMAʿ					HADD	A		IŠ-MA-A-DA		A.+
		JA	ŠMAʿ					ʾEL			IA-AŠ$_2$-MA-AḪ-I$_3$-EL		B 30
		JA	ŠMAʿ					ʾIL			IA-AŠ$_2$-MA-AḪ-DINGIR		SIMMONS 55 11, M
		JI	ŠMAʿ					ʾIL			IS-MA-AḪ-DINGIR		CT XLV 3 7
		JI	ŠMAʿ					ʾIL			IŠ-ME-EḪ-DINGIR		KISURRA 40 9
		JI	ŠMAʿ					ʾILL	A		IŠ-MI-IL-LA		A.
		JI	ŠMAʿ					ʾAMUM	I		IŠ-ME-A-MU-MI	FN	M
		JA	ŠMAʿ					ʾUP	I		IA-AŠ$_2$-MA-ḪU-PI		BULL. ACAD. BELG. 1974 228
		JA	ŠMAʿ					BAʿL			[IA-A]Š$_2$-MA-AḪ-BA-AL		VIII 101 L.E.
		JI	ŠMAʿ					BAʿL			IŠ-ME-EḪ-BA-AL		M
		JI	ŠMAʿ					BAʿL	A		IŠ-ME-BA-LA		TA 30, 122 2
		JI	ŠMAʿ					BAʿL	A		IŠ-ME-EḪ-BA-LA		TA 30, 71
		JI	ŠMAʿ					BAʿL	I		IŠ-ME-BA-LI		HARRIS 71 6+
		JA	ŠMAʿ					DAGAN			IA-AŠ$_2$-MA-AḪ-D-DA-GAN		B 30 HANA+, M+
		JI	ŠMAʿ					DAGAN			IŠ-MA-AḪ-D-DA-GAN		RA XXXIV 186 R. 2 HANA+
		JI	ŠMAʿ					DAGAN			IŠ-ME-D-DA-GAN		M+
			ŠIMAʿ					ʾIL	A		SI-MA-I-LA		X 5 4, 5
			ŠIMAʿ					LA		NI	SI-MA-AḪ-LA-NI		SYRIA XLI 54 N. 1
			ŠIMAʿ					LA		NI	SI-MA-AḪ-LA-A-NI		SYRIA XLI 54 N. 1
			ŠIMAʿ					LA		NI	SI-MA-AḪ-I-LA-A-NI		RA LXVI 112 MARI
			ŠIMAʿ					LA		NIE	SI-MA-AḪ-LA-NI-E		SYRIA XLI 54 N. 1+
			ŠIMAʿ					LA		NIE	SI-MA-AḪ-I-LA-A-NI-E		SYRIA XLI 54 N. 1
			ŠIMAʿ					LA		NIE	SU-MU-ḪA-LA-NI-E		SYRIA XLI 54 N. 1
			ŠIMAʿ					LA		NIE	SU-MU?-ḪI-LA-NI-E		SYRIA XLI 54 N. 1
			ŠIMAʿ					LA		NIE	SI-MA-AḪ-LA-A-NI-E		RA LXVI 115:21;117:11 MARI
			ŠIMAʿ					LA		NIE	SI-MA-AḪ-I-LA-NI-E		RA LXVI 112 MARI
			ŠIMAʿ					LA		NIE	SU-MA-AḪ-I-LA-A-NI-E		RA LXVI 120:7 MARI
			ŠIMAʿ			NI		ʾIL			ŠI-MA-AḪ-NI-DINGIR		VIII 49 BIS 5'
			ŠIMAʿ				TA	ʿQUB			ŠI-ME-TA-GU-UB		M+
			ŠAMAʿ					ḪAʾT	IM		ŠA-MA-ḪA-TIM	GEN	XIII 1 VIII 44
			ŠAMAʿ					JAT	UM		ŠA-MA-IA-TUM	MN	CT IV 43B 6+
			ŠAMAʿ		A			JAT	UM		ŠA-MA-A-IA-TUM	MN	WATERMAN 21 R. 6
			ŠAMIʿ		UM						SA-ME-ḪU-UM		B 38
			ŠAMIʿ		UM						SA-MI-UM		LARSA, KING
			ŠAMIʿ		UM						SA-MU-UM		LARSA, KING
			ŠAMIʿ		UM						SA-MU-U$_2$-UM		RA LII 235, KING
			ŠAMIʿ	AB							SA-ME-ḪA	FN	RA LXV 60 III 54
			ŠAMUʿ		I			ʾIL			SA-MU-ḪI-IL		XIV 76:19
			ŠAMUʿ		I			ʾEL			SA-MU-ḪI-EL		M
			ŠAMʿ	AN	UM						SA-AM-ḪA-NU-UM		TCL X 21 21
			ŠAMʿ	AN	UM						ŠA-AM-ḪA-NU-UM		B 93+
		MA	ŠMIʿ	AN	AM						MA-AŠ-MI-A-NA-AM	ACC	M
	2		ʾAḪ		I		JI	ŠMAʿ		NI	A-ḪI-IŠ-MA-NI		VAS VIII 14:41+
			ʾIL		I		JI	ŠMAʿ		NIA	I$_3$-LI$_2$-IŠ-MA-NI-A		TA 1930,399
			ʾIL		I			ŠAMUʿ			I$_3$-LI$_2$-SA-MU-UḪ		XIII 21 11'

ROOTS (Consonants only)

ŚMʿ	2		ḤAM		I				ŚAMUʿ		D-A-MI-SA-MU-UḪ		M+
			ʾANN		U		TA		ŚMAʿ		AN-NU-TA-AŠ$_2$-MA-AḪ	FN	M
			DAWD		I				ŚAMUʿ		DA-DI-SA-MU-UḪ		RA LXV 47 VII 44
			LI				JI	T	ŚAMAʿ				
									ʾIL		LI?-IŠ?-TA-MI-DINGIR		IX 291 I 18
	3		LU						ḤAJJ	A			
									ŚAMIʿ	UM	LU-ḪA-A-A-SA-MU-UM		UET V 569 8
			LU						ḤAJJ	A			
									ŚAMIʿ	UM	LU-ḪA-A-A-SA-MI-UM		UET V 569 17
ŚMB	1		ŚAMIB	AT	UM						SA-MI-BA-TUM	FN	M
ŚMD	1		ŚAMID		UM						SA-MI-TUM		U
			ŚAMID		U						SA-MI-DU		CT VIII 9A 1
ŚMK	1		ŚAMAK		UM						SA-MA-GU-UM		AJSL XLIV 242 NO. 29
			ŚAMAK	T	UM						ŠA-M[A]-AK-T[UM]	MN	TA 1931, 527
			ŚAMUK		UM						SA-MU-KUM		CT XLVIII 90 REV.
			ŚAMUK								SA-MU-UK		HARRIS 41 12
			ŚAMUK		IM						SA-MU-KI-IM	GEN	CT VIII 47B 22
			ŚAMUK	AN	UM						SA-MU-KA-NU-[UM]		HARRIS 68 21
			ŚAMUK		I				ʾEL		SA-MU-KI-EL		B 38+
			ŚAMK	AN	IM						ŠA-AM-KA-NIM	GEN	LIH 81 7,17, 23
			ŚAMK		AJA						SA-AM-KA-IA		RA LXV 53 XII 4
			ŚAMK	AN	UM						ZA-AM?-GA-NU-UM		TA 1931, 538 V
			ŚUMUK						LIʾM		SU-MU-UK-LI-IM		C P. 42+
			ŚUMK	AN	UM						ZUM-GA-NU-UM		TA 1931, 538 IV
	2		ʾAB		I				ŚAMAK	U	A-BI-SA-MA-KU		SIMMONS 41 15
ŚML	1		ŚAMUL	AT	UM						SA-MU-LA-TUM	FN	M
ŚMM	1		ŚAMAM		UM						SA-MA-MU-UM		I+, CT VI 44B 12
			ŚAMAM		UM						ŠA-MA-MU-UM		I+
			ŚAMIM		UM						SA-MI-MU-UM		BIN VII 154:4+
			ŚAMIM		U						SA-MI-MU		WALTERS, WL 109:10
			ŚAMUM		U	HU					SA-MU-MU-U$_2$		M
			ŚAMUM	AN	IM						SA-MU-MA-NIM	GEN	PBS XIV 357
			ŚAMM		I				JATAR		SA-AM-MI-A-TA-AR		TIM I 28 34, 38, 49
			ŚAMM		I				JATAR		SA-AM-ME-TAR		M+
			ŚAMM		I				JATAR		SA-AM-ME-E-TAR		M+
			ŚAMM		I				JATAR		SA-MI-E-TA-AR		M+
			ŚAMM		I				JATAR		SA-AM-MI-E-TAR		M+
			ŚAMM		I				JATAR		SA-AM-MI-TAR		M+
			ŚIMM		I				JATAR		SI-IM-ME-A-TAR		A 7537 16, 21+
			ŚUMUM		U						SU-MU-MU		RA LXIV 22 NO. 2+
ŚMN	1		ŚAMIN		U	HU					SA-MI-NU-U$_2$	FN	CT II 46 4
ŚMR	1	ʾA T	ŚAMAR						HADD	U	AŠ-TA-MAR-D-IM		M+
			ŚAMAR		A						SA-MA-RA?		HARRIS 35 11
			ŚAMAR	AN	U						SA-MA-RA?-NU		X 20 11
			ŚAMAR						HADD	U	ŠA-AM-MA-RA-DU		A.
			ŚAMAR		I				HADD	U	SA-MA-RI-A-DU		A. 57 45
			ŚAMAR		I				ʾIL		SA-MA-RI-DINGIR		A. 455 46
			ŚAMIR					Š	BAʿL		ŠA-MI-IR-ŠU-BI-EL		TCL XVIII 125 30
			ŚIMAR						HADD	U	ŠI-IM-MA-RA-DU?		A.
			ŚIMR						ʾALLA		ŠI-IM-RA-AL-LA		A.
		MA	ŚMAR		IM						MA-AŠ-MA-RI-IM	GEN	M
	2		ʾAB		I		ʾA	T	ŚAMAR		A-BI-AŠ-TA-MA-AR		YOS XIII 489:4
			ʾAB		I		JI	T	ŚAMAR		A-BI-IŠ-TA-MAR		TCL I 226 4, 10+
			ʾAB		I				ŚAMAR		A-BI-SA-MAR		M+
			ʾIL		A				ŚAMAR		I-LA-ŠA-MA-AR		U
			ʾIL		I		JI	T	ŚAMAR		I$_3$-LI$_2$-IŠ-TA-MAR		EDZARD,DER 67:11
			ʿAMM		U				ŚAMAR		ḪA-MU-SA-MAR		RA LXIV 36 NO. 31
			ʿAMM		U				ŚAMAR		ḪA-MU-SA-MAR	FN	C+
		JA	NWUḪ						ŚAMAR		IA-NU-UḪ-SA-MAR		CT XLIII 58 3, M
		JI	NWUḪ						ŚAMAR		I-NU-UḪ$_3$-SA-MAR		BIN VII 7 4,9+
		JI	NWUḪ						ŚAMAR		I-NU-UḪ-SA-MAR		TCL I 74 5,18
			ŚUM		U		JI	T	ŚAMAR		SU-MU-UŠ-TA-MAR		TIM II 14 21
ŚMŚ	1		ŚAMŚ		UM						ZA-AM-ZUM		CT IV 47B 20
			ŚAMŚ		U						SA-AM-SU		YOS XII
			ŚAMŚ	AN	UM						SA-AM-SA-NU-UM		SIMMONS 119 23+
			ŚAMŚ	AN	U						ZA-AM-ZA-NU		M

ROOTS (Consonants only)

ŜMŜ	1	ŜAMŜ	IJA					SA-AM-SI-IA		X 166 9, 13
		ŜAMŜ	I		ʾAḪ	I		SA-AM-SI-A-ḪI		RA LXV 54 XII 26
		ŜAMŜ	I		ʾAB	I		D-UTU-A-BI		M+
		ŜAMŜ	I		HADD	U		SA-AM-SI-D-IM		M+, A.+
		ŜAMŜ	I		HADD	U		SA-AM-SI-A-DU		M+
		ŜAMŜ	I		HADD	U		ŠA-AM-SI-D-IM		M+
		ŜAMŜ	I		HADD	U		D-UTU-ŠI-D-IM		M+, C+
		ŜAMŜ	I		HADD	U		SA-AM-ŠI-D-IM		C
		ŜAMŜ	I		HADD	U		SA-AM-SI-IA-AD-DU		M
		ŜAMŜ	I		HADD	U		D-UTU-ŠI-A-DU		A.
		ŜAMŜ	I		HADD	U				
					ʾIL	I		SA-AM-SI-D-IM-I$_3$-LI$_2$		C+
		ŜAMŜ	I		HADD	U				
					....			SA-AM-SI-D-IM-TU-GUL-TI		M
		ŜAMŜ	I		HEDD	A		SA-AM-SI-E-D-IM		SIMMONS 4 20
		ŜAMŜ	I		HEDD	A		SA-AM-SI-E-DA		A. 455 36
		ŜAMŜ	I		JARAḪ			SA-AM-SI-E-RA-AḪ		BASOR 95, 19+, M+
		ŜAMŜ	I		JAŠʿ	AH		D-[UT]U-IA-AŠ-ḪA	FN	XIII 1 IV 43
		ŜAMŜ	I		ʾITEJ		JE	D-UTU-I-TE-E		CT IV 44 B 3, 4
		ŜAMŜ	I	JA	JPUʿ	AT		D-UTU-IA-PU-ḪA-AT	FN?	BM 17075
		ŜAMŜ	I		DAʿ	I		D-UTU-DA-ḪI-I		LANGDON XV 2
		ŜAMŜ	I		DIʿ	AT		SA-AM-SI-DI-ḪA-AT?		TIM II 49 5
		ŜAMŜ	I		DAGAN			SA-AM-SI-D-DA-GAN		M+
		ŜAMŜ	I		DITAN	A		SA-AM-SI-DI-TA-NA		B 38
		ŜAMŜ	I		LIʾM			SA-AM-SI-LI-IM		M
		ŜAMŜ	I		RAPIʾ			ŠA-AM-[SI]-RA-BI		M
		ŜAMŜ	I		ŜAMŜ			ZA-AM-SI-D-UTU		YOS XII 39 END
		ŜAMŜ	U		HADD	U		SA-AM-ŠU-D-IM		COLLON, SEALS NO. 141
		ŜAMŜ	U		ʾIL	U	NA	SA-AM-SU-I-LU-NA		B 38+
		ŜAMŜ	U		ʾIL	U	NA			
					KIMA			SA-AM-SU-I-LU-NA-KI-MA-DINGIR		BM 81047:6
		ŜAMŜ	U		ʾIL	U	NA			
					....			SA-AM-SU-I-LU-NA-QAR-RA-AD		CT XLV 48 5
		ŜAMŜ	U		JARAḪ			SA-AM-SU-E-RA-AḪ		B 38
		ŜAMŜ	U	JI	JŜAR			SA-AM-SU-D-I-[Š]AR		M
		ŜAMŜ	U		BAʿL	A		SA-AM-SU-BA-LA		SIMMONS 35 14+
		ŜAMŜ	U		BAʿL	I		SA-AM-SU-BA-AḪ-LI		ABB I 59 8
		ŜAMŜ	U		DITAN	A		SA-AM-SU-DI-TA-NA		B 38+
		ŜAMŜ	U		....			SA-AM-SU-MA-[....]		YOS XIII 446:3
		ŜAMŜ	U	NA				SA-AM-SU-NA		HARRIS 58 14+
		ŜAMŜ	U	NA	BAʿL	A		SA-AM-SU-NA-BA-LA		A. 77+
		ŜAMAŜ	I					ŠA-MA-ŠI		CT IV 43B 7
		ŜAMUŜ	IM					SA-MU-SI-IM	GEN	BM 78366 3
		ŜAMUŜ	A					SA-MU-ŠA	NOM	M+
	2	ʾAB	I		ŜAMŜ			A-BI-SA-MA-AŠ		M+
		ʾAB	I		ŜAMŜ			A-BI-D-UTU	FN	XIII 24 IV 40
		ʾAB	I		ŜAMŜ	I		A-BI-D-UTU-ŠI	FN	XIII 1 IX 40+
		ʾADD	I		ŜAMŜ			AD-DI-D-UTU?		RA LXIV 99:23
		ʿADN	I		ŜAMŜ			ḪA-AD-NI-SA-MA-AŠ$_2$		M
		ʿAḎIR			ŜAMŜ			ḪA-ZI-IR-D-UTU		M
		ʾIL	I		ŜAMŜ			I$_3$-LI$_2$-SA-MA-AŠ$_2$		M
		ʾALIP			ŜAMŜ			A-LI-IB-D-UTU		CT VIII 35B 24+
		ʾUMM	I		ŜAMŜ	I		UM-MI-D-UTU-ŠI	FN	RA LXV 65 VII 38
	ʾU	WQAH			ŜAMŜ			U$_2$-GA-A-D-UTU		SZLECHTER TJ 15944 SEAL
	ʾU	WQAH			ŜAMŜ			U$_2$-GA-D-UTU		BIROT, TEA 72 V 16'
		ʾARḪ	I		ŜAMŜ	I		AR-ḪI-D-UTU-ŠI	FN	XIII 1 XIII 2
		ʾIŠḪAR		AH	ŜAMŜ	I		D-IŠ-ḪA-RA-D-UTU-ŠI	FN	XII 265 6
		ʿAŠTAR			ŜAMŜ	I		EŠ$_4$-DAR-D-UTU-ŠI	FN	M
	JA	ḪATIʾ			ŜAMŜ			IA-ḪA-AT-TI-D-UTU		UCP X/1 89 15
		BAʿL	I		ŜAMŜ	I		BA-AḪ-LI-D-UTU-ŠI	FN	M
		BAʿL	U		ŜAMŜ			BA-LU-D-UTU		M
		BIN			ŜAMŜ			BI-IN-D-UTU		M
		DAGAN			ŜAMŜ	I		D-DA-GAN-D-UTU-ŠI	FN	RA LXV 58 I 23+
		ḎIMR			ŜAMŜ			ZI-IM-RU-D-UTU		BIN VII 190 18
		ḎIMR			ŜAMŜ			ZI-IM-RI-D-UTU		BIN VII 206 23+
		ḎIMR			ŜAMŜ			ZI-ME-IR-D-UTU		B 42+

ROOTS (Consonants only)

ŚMŚ	2		ḎIMR		I			ŚAMŚ		ZI-IM-RI-SA-MAŠ		A.
			ḎIMR		I			ŚAMŚ		ZI-IM-RI-SA-MA-AŠ$_2$		M+
			ḎIMR		U			ŚAMŚ		ZI-IM-RU-D-UTU		BIROT,TEA 70 B I 9
			MUT		I			ŚAMŚ		MU-TI-D-UTU		A.
			NAWP					ŚAMŚ		NA-AP-D-UTU		M
			NABIʾ					ŚAMŚ		NA-BI-D-UTU		M+
			ŚUM		U			ŚAMŚ		SU-MU-D-UTU		CT XLVIII 83 SEAL
			ŚAMŚ		I			ŚAMŚ		ZA-AM-SI-D-UTU		YOS XII 39 END
	3		ʾALI					PA				
								ŚAMŚ		A-LI$_2$-PA-D-UTU		BE VI/1 15:25
			ʾAMUR					ŠA				
								ŚAMŚ		A-MUR-ŠA-D-UTU		A.
ŚMT	1		ŚUMAT	AN						SU-MA-TA-AN		M
			ŚUMAT	AN	UM					SU-MA-TA-A-NU-UM		GORDON 38 2, 5
			ŚUMAT					ʾIL	I	SU-MA-AT-I$_3$-LI$_2$		XIII 1 II 85
			ŚUMAT					JARAḪ		SU-MA-AT-E-RA-AḪ		M+
			ŚUMUT		I					SU-MU-TI		B 40
			ŚUMUT	AN						SU-MU-TA-AN		RA LXV 46 VI 4+
			ŚUMUT					ʾIL		SU-MU-UT-DINGIR		VAS VII 148 5+
			ŚUMUT		I			BAʿL		SU-MU-TI-BA-AL		M
			ŚUMUT		I			JABAL	A	SU-MU-TI-A-BA-LA?		PBS XI/2 1 I 35
	2		ʾAB		I			ŚAMAT	A	A-BI-SA-MA-TA		EDZARD, DER 120:4
ŚNḪ	1		ŚUNAḪ		UM					SU-NA-ḪU-UM		UET V 572 2
ŚNG	1		ŚANAG		UM					SA-NA-GU-UM		JCS IV 109, 3328 2+
ŚNGR	1		ŚANAGR	AT	UM					SA-NA-AG-RA-TUM	FN	CT IV 47B 27+, M+
ŚNL	1	JI	ŚNUL		UM					IŠ-NU-LU-UM	TRIBE	M
ŚNN	1		ŚANIN		UM					ŠA-NI-NU-UM		SIMMONS 55 13
			ŚINAN		UM					SI-NA-NU-UM		SIMMONS 114 7
			ŚINAN		A					ŠI-NA-AN-NA		XIII 1 I 19
			ŚININ	AH						SI-NE-NA	FN	XIII 1 V 51+
			ŚININ	AH						SI-NI-NA	FN	M+
			ŚININ		AJA					SI-NI-NA-A-IA	FN	X 166 1+
			ŚINN	AH						SI-IN-NA	FN	RA LXV 58 I 61
			ŚUNAN		UM					SU-NA-NU-UM		TA 30, 30 29
ŚNQM	1		ŚANQAM		UM					SA-AN-QA-MU-UM		JCS V 89, MAH 15882
ŚPQ	1	JA	ŚPUQ		UM					IA-AŠ$_2$-PU-KU-UM		B 30+
		JA	ŚPUQ		UM					IA-AŠ-PU-KUM		VAS XIII 3 15+
		JA	ŚPUQ					ʾIL		IA-AŠ$_2$-PU-UK-DINGIR		M
			ŚAPAQ		UM					SA-BA-KUM		TA 30 28
			ŚAPIQ		UM					SA-BI-KUM		TCL I 190 4, 5
			ŚIPQ		U	NA		HADD	A	SI-IP-KU-NA-D-IM		M
			ŚIPQ		U	NA		HADD	A	SI-IP-KU-NA-DA		M
	2		ʾIL		I		JI	ŚPIQ		I$_3$-LI$_2$-IŠ-BI-IK		TA 1931, 71
ŚPR	1		ŚAPAR	AN						[S]A-PA-RA-AN		RA LXV 40 I 7
			ŚAPIR		UM					ŠA-BI-RU-UM		I+
			ŚAPIR		UM					SA-BI-RU-UM		B 37+
			ŚAPIR		U					SA-BI-RU		YOS XIII 166:14
			ŚAPIR	AT	UM					SA-BI-RA-TUM	FN	B 37+
			ŚAPIR	AT	UM					SA-PI-RA-TUM		B 37
			ŚAPIR		AJA					SA-BI-RA-A-IA	FN	X 166 11, 12+
			ŚAPUR		UM					SA-PU-RU-UM		TIM V 19 5
			ŚAPR		AJA					SA-AP-RA-IA		A.
			ŚAPR	AK	UM					ŠA-AP-RA-KUM		M
			ŚAPAR	AK	UM					ŠA-BA-AR-KUM		U
			ŚAPR		A			HADD	U	SA-AP-RA-A-DU		A. 96 R. 12
			ŚIPR	AT	U					ŠE-IP-RA-TU	MN	LAESSOE P. 99+
			ŚIPR	AN						ŠI-IP-RA-AN		A. LATE
			ŚIPR	AN	UM					ŠE?-IP?-[RA]?-NU-UM		I
			ŚIPR	AN	UM					ŠI-IP?-RA?-NU-UM		I
			ŚIPR		I			HAND	A	ŠI-IP-RI-AN-TA		A. LATE
			ŚUPUR	T	UM					SU-PU-UR-TUM		PBS VIII/1 45 17
		MA	ŚPAR		UM					MAŠ-PA-RU-UM		B 49+
		MA	ŚPAR		UM					MA-AŠ$_2$-PA-RU-UM		SUMER XXIII 153 8, 17, 23
		MA	ŚPIR		UM					MAŠ-PI-RU-UM		CT VI 49B 12
	2		ʾAB		I			ŚAPAR		A-BI-SA-PA-AR	FN	C
			ʾAB		I			ŚAPAR		A-BI-SA-PAR$_2$		CT XLV 82 7+, XIII 1 II 15

ROOTS (Consonants only)

ŠPR	2		ʿIZZ		U		ŠAPAR				I-ZU-SA-PAR$_2$		U+
			ʿIZZ		U		ŠAPAR				IZ?-ZU?-ŠA-PA-AR		BIN II 98 5
			BAʿL		I		ŠAPAR				BA-AḪ-LI-SA-PA-AR	FN	M+
			BAʿL		I		ŠAPAR				BA-AḪ-LI-SA-PAR$_2$	FN	M, C+
			BEʿL		I		ŠAPAR				BE-LI$_2$-SA-PAR$_2$	FN	M
ŠPŠ	1		ŠAPŠ		I						ŠA-AP-ŠI		A.
			ŠAPŠ		IJA						SA-AP-SI-IA		A. 53 R. 9
			ŠAPŠ		I		ʾAB		I		ŠA-AP-ŠI-A-BI	FN	A.
			ŠAPŠ		I		HADD		U		SA-AP-SI-A-DU		A.+
			ŠAPŠ		I		HEDD		A		SA-AP-SI-E-DA		A.+
ŠQḪ	1		ŠAQAḪ			TA	NWUḪ			HU	SA-QA-AḪ-TA-NU-U$_2$		CT VI 46 2
		MI	ŠQIḪ		I						MI-IS-KI-ḪI	NOM	UET V 605 20
ŠQṬ	1	JA	ŠQIṬ				ʾIL				IA-AŠ-KI-IṬ-DINGIR		B 30, M+
			ŠAQṬ		I						ŠA-AQ-TI	GEN	CT VIII 10B 7+
ŠRḪ	1		ŠARIḪ	AH							SA-RI-ḪA	FN	RA LXV 60 III 39
ŠRJ	1		ŠARAJ				ṢIDQ		UM		ŠA-RA-ZI-ID-K[UM]		MEISSNER 36 22
			ŠARAJ				ṢUWR		UM		ŠA-RA-ṢUR-RU-UM		KISURRA 111 6
			ŠARAJ			TI	ʾEL				ŠA-RA-TI-EL		TIM III 59 6
			ŠARAJ			TI	ʾEL				ŠA-RA-TE-EL		TIM III 44 18+
	2		ʾAB		I		ŠARIJ				A-BI-SA-RI		LIMET, SCEAUX CASS. P 114
			ʾAB		I		ŠARIJ			JE	A-BI-SA-RI-E		B 11+; M+
			ʾAB		I		ŠARIJ			JE	A-BI$_2$-SA-RI-E		BIN VII 93 DATE
		JI	JṢIʾ				ŠARIJ			JE	I-ZI-SA-RI-E		BIN VII 105 12
ŠRB	1		ŠARB	AN							SA-AR-BA-AN		M
			ŠIRIB		I						SI-RI-BI		SYRIA XXXVII 206 29 HANA
ŠRK	1	JA	ŠRUK	AN							IA-AŠ$_2$-RU-KA-AN		RA XLI 45 6' HANA+
			ŠARIK		UM						SA-RI-KUM		B 38+
		MU	ŠARIK	AH							MU-SA-AR-RI-KA	FN	XIII 1 VIII 75
ŠRM	1		ŠARAM		UM						SA-RA-MU-UM		YOS XII
			ŠARAM	AN	U						SA-RA-MA-NU		SZLECHTER TJ P. 25
			ŠARAM		AJA						ŠA-RA-MA-A		M
	2		ʾALI				ŠARAM			NI	A-LI-ŠA-RA-AM-NI	FN	RA LXV 58 I 54
ŠRN	1		ŠIRUN		UM		GAMIL				SI?-RU-NU-UM-GA-MIL?		VII 139 7
ŠRR	1		ŠARR		AJA						ŠAR-RA-A-IA		M
			ŠARR		AJA						ŠAR-RA-IA		M+
			ŠARR		IJA						ŠAR-RI-IA		M+
			ŠARR		A		ʾIL				ŠAR-RA-DINGIR		A. LATE+
			ŠARR		UM		ʿADN		U	HU	LUGAL-AD-NU-U$_2$		SIGRIST UNPUBL.
			ŠARR		UM		JAQR	AH			LUGAL-JA-AQ-RA	FN	XIII 1 X 45
			ŠARR		UM		BAWŠ	T	I		LUGAL-BA-AŠ-TI	FN	M
			ŠARR		UM		BAWŠ	T	I		LUGAL-BA-AŠ$_2$-TI	FN	M+
			ŠARR		UM		NIWR		I		LUGAL-NI-RI	FN	XIII 1 XIII 3+
			ŠURAR		UM						SU-RA-RU-UM		TIM III 133 14
	2		ʾAJA				ŠARR		UM		ḪA-IA-ŠA-RUM		UCP X P. 56+
			ʾAJAN				ŠARR		I		A-IA-AŠ-LUGAL		A. 18 4
			ʾAJAN				ŠARR		I		A-IA-LUGAL-RI		A. 243 22
			ʾAJAN				ŠARR		I		A-IA-LUGAL		A. 274 4
			JAʾAN				ŠARR		I		IA-AN-ŠAR-RI		M XIII 1 X 16
			ʾABB		A		ŠARR				AB-BA-LUGAL		A. 86 2
			ʿAMM		U		ŠARR				ḪA-MU-SA-AR		RA LXV 40 I 42
			ʿAMM		U		ŠARR				ḪA-MU-SA-AR	FN	C+
			ʿAMM		U		ŠARR				ḪA-AM-MU-SA-AR		XIV 108:6
			ʾUMM		U		ŠARR	AH			UM-MU-ŠAR-RA	FN	IX 291 33
			ʾIŠḪAR	AH			ŠARR	AT			D-IŠ-ḪA-RA-ŠAR-RA-AT	FN	M
			ʿAŠTAR				ŠARR	AH			EŠ$_4$-DAR-ŠAR-RA	FN	XIII 1 II 67
		JI	JṢIʾ				ŠARR				I-ZI-ŠAR		B 22
		JI	JṢIʾ				ŠARR				I-ṢI-LUGAL-KI	GN	TIM III 75:3
		JI	JṢIʾ				ŠARR		UM		I-ZI-ŠAR-RUM-KI	GN	SUMER III 79 VI 197+
		JA	KWUN				ŠARR		UM		IA-KU-UN-ŠAR-RU-UM		B 28
		JA	KNUW				ŠARR		UM		IA-AK-NU-ŠA-RU-UM		KISURRA 47A 4+
		JA	KNUW				ŠARR		U		IA-AK-NU-ŠA-RU		TIM III 133 9
			MAM		A		ŠARR	AH			D-MA-MA-ŠAR-RA	FN	M
			NANN		I		ŠARR	AH			D-NA-AN-NI-ŠAR-RA	FN	XIII 1 V 31
			NUPAR				ŠARR		IM		NU-BAR-LUGAL		A.
			ŠADW		UM		ŠARR		I		[Š]A-DU-UM-ŠAR-RI		XIV 106:10, 17
			ŠADW		U		ŠARR		I		ŠA-DU-ŠAR-RI		XIV 109:6

ROOTS (Consonants only)

ŠRR	2		ŠADW		U			ŠARR		I		ŠA-DU-ŠA-AR-RI			M
			ŠADW		U			ŠARR		I		ŠA-DU-LUGAL			M
			ŠADW		UM			ŠARR		I		ŠA-DU-UN-ŠAR-RI			M
	3		ʾAJA					ʾAB		I					
								ŠARR		I		A-IA-BI-ŠAR-RI			A.
			BUN		UM			MA							
								ŠARR				BU-NU-UM-MA-ŠAR			B 16
			ŠUM		U			ʾIL							
								ŠARR				SU-MU-[DINGIR]-LUGAL			UCP X/1 17 15
ŠTM	2		ʾANN		U			ŠATAM				AN?-NU?-ŠA-TAM	FN		XIII 1 IV 46
ŠṮḪ	1	JA	ŠṮIḪ					ʾIL				IA-AŠ-TI-DINGIR			XIII 1 IX 7
		JA	ŠṮIḪ					ʿAMM		U		IA-AŠ-DI-ḪA-AM-MU			B 30
			ŠAṮIḪ		I							SA-TI-I	GEN		SYRIA XXXVII 206 10 HANA
			ŠAṮUḪ		UM							SA-TU-ḪU-UM			UCP X/1 89 28
		MU	ŠṮAḪ	AT	UM							MU-UŠ-TA-ḪA-[TUM]?	MN		M
		MU	ŠṮUḪ	AT	UM							MU-UŠ-TU-A-TUM	FN		C
		MU	ŠṮUḪ					KAʾM		I		MU-UŠ-TU-KA-M[I]			M+
ŠṮR	1		ŠAṮAR	AH								ŠA-ṮA$_3$-AR-RA	FN		M
Š	1		ŠU					ʿABD		I		ŠU-ḪA-AB-DI			CT XLVIII 43:15,19
			ŠU					ʾEL		UM		ŠU-E-LUM			B 40
			ŠU					ʿAMM		U		ŠU-ḪA-AM-MU			M+
			ŠU				JI	BNIJ			HU	ŠU-U$_2$-IB-NI-U$_2$			TA 1931, 636 REV +
			ŠU					BAʾB		A		ŠU-BA-BA			U
			ŠU					DAMIQ				ŠU-DA-ME-IQ			RA LXV 41 II 16
			ŠU					RAWM		U		ŠU-RA-MU			A. LATE+
			ŠU					RAWM		A		ŠU-RA-MA			A. LATE+
			ŠI					DUWR		I		ŠI-DU-RI	FN		RA LXV 58 I 68+
			ŠI					QUWJ		I		ŠI-I-KU-WI	FN		A. 8 12, 34
			ŠI					MAʾT		UM		ŠI-I-MA-TUM	FN		C+
			ŠI					MIGN		I		ŠI-ME-IG-NI	FN		RA LXV 60 III 24
			ŠI					MALIK	T	I		ŠI-MA-LI-IK-TI			IX 294:7'
			ŠI					NUWR		I		ŠI-NU-RI	FN		A. LATE
			ŠI					RAWM		A		SI-I-RA-MA			A. 28 3, 16
			ŠI				TA	BNIJ				ŠI-TAB-NI	FN		RA LXV 64 VI 18
			ŠI				TA	BNIJ				ŠI-TAB-NI-A-JA	FN		RA LXV 66 VII 57
			ŠI			JA		....				ŠI-IA-N[A-....]	FN		M
			ŠI			JA		TAKAL				ŠI-IA-TA-KA-AL	MN		IX 291 III 37'
	2		ʾAMUR					ŠA							
								DAGAN				A-MUR-ŠA-D-DA-GAN			TCL I 237 31 HANA
			ʾAMUR					ŠA							
								ŠAMŠ				A-MUR-ŠA-D-UTU			A.
			ʾAŠIR					ŠI			JA				
								....				A-ŠE-ER-ŠI-IA-[X]	FN		XIII 1 VIII 2
ŠʾḪ	1		ŠAʾḪ	AT	UM							ŠA-ḪA-TUM	FN		RA LXV 59 II 75
			ŠUʾḪ		UM							ŠU-ḪU-UM			RUTTEN 29 3, 6 SEAL+
			ŠUʾḪ	AT	UM							ŠU-ḪA-TUM			HARRIS 1 3, 6+
	2		ʾALLA					ŠUʾḪ		U		AL-LA-ŠU-ḪU			U
ŠʾG	1		ŠUʾG		U			JAT		UM		ŠU-GU-IA-TUM			B 40
ŠʾM	1		ŠAʾUM		I							ŠA-U$_2$-MI			BAB. III 267 HANA
			ŠUʾM		A			BAʾIL				ŠU-UḪ-MA-BA-IL			RA LXV 51 IX 60
ŠʾN	1		ŠIʾN	AT	IM							ŠI-NA-TIM	FN	GEN	XIII 1 V 83
			ŠIʾN		U			RAPIʾ				ŠI-NU-RA-BI			A.+
			ŠIʾN		U			RAPIʾ				SI-NU-RA-BI			A.+
ŠʾR	1		ŠEʾR	AH				MAM		A		ŠE-RA-D-MA-MA	FN		X 110 3
			ŠEʾR		UM			MAGUN		U		ŠE-EḪ-RUM-MA-GU-NU	FN		C
			ŠUʾAR		I			....				ŠU-A-RI-[....]			M
	2		NAPŠ		I			ŠEʾR		UM		NA-AP-SI-ŠE?-RUM?			M
ŠʿL	1		ŠUʿAL	AN								ŠU-ḪA-LA-AN			M
			ŠUʿAL	AN	U							ŠU-ḪA-LA-NU			M
ŠWʾ	1		ŠAWUʾ		UM							ŠA-WU-U$_2$-UM			RA LXV 48 VIII 16
ŠWB	1	ʾA	ŠWUB					ʾIL		A		A-ŠU-UB-I-LA			A. LATE
		ʾA	ŠWUB					LA							
								ʾEL				A-ŠU-UB-LA-EL			TA 1931,765
		ʾA	ŠWUB					LA							
								ʾIL				A-ŠU-UB-LA-DINGIR			C+
		ʾA	ŠWUB					LI							
								ʾEL				A-ŠU-UB-LI-EL			OIP XLIII 154 NO. 48+

ROOTS (Consonants only)

ŠWB	1	JA		ŠWUB		UM						IA-ŠU-BU-UM		B 30+	
		JA		ŠWUB		IM						IA-ŠU-BI-IM	GEN	M+	
		JA		ŠWUB	AN							IA-ŠU-BA-AN		M	
		JA		ŠWUB					....			IA-ŠU-UB-[....]		A.	
		JA		ŠWUB					JAḪAD			IA-ŠU-UB-IA-ḪA-AD		M	
		JA		ŠWUB					ḪAʾL			IA-ŠU-UB-ḪA-AL		RA LXV 44 IV 28	
		JA		ŠWUB					HADD	U		IA-ŠU-UB-D-IM		LAESSOE P. 90+, C+	
		JA		ŠWUB					ʾIL			IA-ŠU-UB-DINGIR		CT II 23 15+, M+	
		JE		ŠWUB					ʾIL			E-ŠU-UB-DINGIR		BIN VII P. 12+	
		JE		ŠWUB		I			ʾIL			IE-E-ŠU-BI-DINGIR		B 26	
		JA		ŠWUB					ʾAŠAR			IA-ŠU-UB-A-ŠAR		M+	
		JA		ŠWUB				JI	JPUʿ			IA-ŠU-UB-D-I-PU-UḪ		M	
		JA		ŠWUB					DAGAN			IA-ŠU-UB-D-DA-GAN		B 30 HANA+, M+	
		JA		ŠWUB					LIʾM			IA-ŠU-UB-LI-IM		M+	
		JA		ŠWUB					MALIK			IA-ŠU-UB-D-MA-[LIK]		M	
		JA		ŠWUB					NAHR			IA-ŠU-UB-NA-AR		M+	
		JA		ŠWUB					RAPIʾ			IA-ŠU-UB-RA-BI		A.	
		TA		ŠWUB	AT	UM						TA-ŠU-BA-TUM	FN	M	
		TA		ŠWUB	AH							TA-ŠU-BA	FN	M+	
				ŠUWB					ḪAʾL	I		SU-UB-ḪA-LI		A. 268 5	
				ŠUWB		A			ḪAʾL	I		ŠU-BA-ḪA-LI		A. 97 16, 18+	
				ŠUWB		A			ḪAʾL	I		SU-BA-ḪA-LI		A. 6 29	
				ŠUWB		A			ḪAʾL	I		SU-PA-ḪA-LI		A. 252 12+	
				ŠUWB					ʾIL	A		ŠU-UB-D-I-LA		RA LXV 52 X 66	
				ŠUWB					ʿAMM	U		ŠU-UB-AM-MU		MRS VI P. 257+	
				ŠUWB		A			ʾIL	A		ŠU-BA-D-DINGIR		B 23+	
				ŠUWB		A			ʿAMM	I		ŠU-BA-AM-MI		A. 270 22	
				ŠUWB		A	NI		ʾIL			ŠU-BA-NI-DINGIR		RUTTEN 41 3, 13	
				ŠUWB		I			HADD	U		ŠU-BI-D-IM		M	
				ŠUWB		I			ÇARAD			ŠU-BI-GA-RA-AD		I	
				ŠUWB			NA		ʾIL			ŠU-UB-NA-DINGIR		B 40+, M+	
				ŠUWB			NA		ʾIL			ŠU-UB-NA-IL		B 40	
				ŠUWB			NA		ʾIL	U		ŠU-UB-NA-ḪI-LU		B 40	
				ŠUWB			NA		LU		HU	ŠU-UB-NA-LU-U_2		M+	
				ŠUWB		U			RAPUʾ			ŠU-BU-RA-BU		TCL X 4A 25, B 15	
		JA		ŠWIB					ʾIL			IA-ŠI-IB-DINGIR		A.	
		JA		ŠWIB		I			ʾILL	A		IA-ŠI-BI-IL-LA		A.	
				ŠAWB		A			ḪAJJ	UM		SA-BA-A-U_2-UM		OIP XLVII 66	
				ŠAWB		I			ʾIL			ŠA-BI-DINGIR		M, C+	
				ŠAWB		I			BIJT	UM		ŠA-A-BI-E_2		SUMER V 142 NO. 6	
				ŠAWB		I			DAWD	I		[Š]A?-BI-DA-DI		RA LXV 43 I 13	
		JI	T	ŠAWAB		U						IŠ-TA-BU		B 24 HANA	
		JI	T	ŠAWAB		U						IŠ-TA-A-BU		MAOG IV 3 36	HANA
ŠWL	1			ŠAWIL		UM						ŠA-WI-LUM		M	
				ŠAWIL	AT	UM						ŠA-WI-LA-TUM	FN	M	
ŠWR	2			ʿABD					ŠUWR	I		AB-DU-ŠU-RI		IRAQ XXX 94, RIMAH	
ŠBL	1			ŠUBUL	T	UM						ŠU-BU-UL-TUM	FN	M, C	
				ŠUBUL					ʾAB	I		ŠU-BU-UL-A-BI		M	
ŠDW	1			ŠADW		IJA						ŠA?-DI?-IA		XIII 1 I 3	
				ŠADW		I			HADD	U		ŠA-DI-D-IM		M	
				ŠADW		I			ʾIL			SA-DI-DINGIR		JCS IV 110, 2040 16	
				ŠADW		I			MA						
									ʾIL			ŠA-DI-MA-DINGIR		RA LXV 48 VIII 20	
				ŠADW		U			ʾIL	A		ŠA-DU-[I]-LA		RA LXV 45 V 50	
				ŠADW		U			LABW	A		ŠA-DU-LA-BA		M	
				ŠADW		UM			LABW	A		ŠA-DU-UN-LA-BA		M+	
				ŠADW		UM			LABW	A		ŠA-DU-UM-LA-BA		M	
				ŠADW		UM			LABW	A		ŠA-DU-UM-LA-BU-A		M	
				ŠADW		UM			LABW	I		ŠA-DU-UM-LA-BI		M	
				ŠADW		UM			ŚARR	I		[Š]A-DU-UM-ŠAR-RI		XIV 106:10, 17	
				ŠADW		U			ŚARR	I		ŠA-DU-ŠAR-RI		XIV 109:6	
				ŠADW		U			ŚARR	I		ŠA-DU-ŠA-AR-RI		M	
				ŠADW		U			ŚARR	I		ŠA-DU-LUĢAL		M	
				ŠADW		UM			ŚARR	I		ŠA-DU-UN-ŠAR-RI		M	
	2			ḪAʾL		I			ŠADW	A		ḪA-LI-SA-DA		B 19	
				ʾAB		I			ŠADW	A		A-BI-SA-DA-A		JCS IV 110 2040	

ROOTS (Consonants only)

ŠDW	2			HADD		U			ŠADW	A		D-IM-ŠA-DA		PSBA XXIX 273 NO. 9 R. 10
ŠGŠ	2			ʿAMM		I			ŠAGIŠ			ḪA-AM-MI-ŠA-GI-IŠ		M+
				ʿAMM		I			ŠAGIŠ			AM-MI-ŠA-GI-IŠ		M
				ʿAMM		U			ŠAGIŠ			ḪA-MU-ŠA-KI-IŠ		X 174 13
				BUN		UM			ŠAGIŠ			BU-NU-UM-ŠA-GI-IŠ		EDZARD,DER 73:15
ŠKD	1			ŠUKUD		UM						ŠU-KU-DU-UM		M
ŠKK	1			ŠAKK		I						ŠA-AK-KI		RA LXV 45 V 13
		MA		ŠKAK		IM						MA-AŠ-KA-KI-[I]M	GEN	M
ŠKM	1			ŠAKIM		UM						ŠA-KI-MU-UM		HARRIS 91 17+
				ŠAKIM	AN	UM						ŠA-KI-MA-NUM		C
				ŠAKUM		UM						SA-KU-MU-UM		B 37+
				ŠAKUM		I			ʾIL			SA-KU-MI-DINGIR		M+
	2			ʾIL		I			ŠAKIM			I$_3$-LI$_2$-ŠA-KI-IM		RA LXV 40 I 44+
				ʾUM		U			ŠAKIM			U$_2$-MU-ŠA-KI-IM		M+
				MUT					ŠAKIM			MU-UT-ŠA-KI-IM		RA LXV 55 XIII 35
		TA		RWIM					ŠAKIM			TA-RI-IM-ŠA-KI-IM		M+
ŠL	2			ʾIPQ		U			ŠAL	A		IP-KU-D-ŠA-LA		M
ŠLG	1			ŠALG	AN							ŠA-AL-GA-AN		RA LXV 40 I 49
	2			ḪUNN					ŠULGI			ḪU-UN-D-ŠUL-GI		U
				BUN		U			ŠALG	I		BU-NU-ŠA?-AL?-GI		B 16
ŠLŠ	1			ŠALAŠ					NIʾG	I		ŠA-LA-AŠ-NI-GI	FN	C+
				ŠALAŠ					TUWR	A	JA	ŠA-LA-AŠ-TU-RA-IA	FN	C
				ŠALAŠ					TABB	I		D-ŠA-LA-AŠ-TAB-BI	FN	XIII 1 III 26
	2			ʾAḪ		I			ŠALAŠ			A-ḪI-ŠA-LA-AŠ		EDZARD, DER 104:2
ŠMGN	1			ŠIMGIN	AH							ŠI-IM-GI-IN-NA	FN	M
				ŠIMGIN	AH							ŠI-IM-GI-EN-NA	FN	M
				ŠIMGIN	AH							ŠI-IM-GI-NA	FN	M+, C
ŠMR	2			ʿAMM		I	JI	T	ŠAMAR			ḪA-AM-MI-IŠ-TA-MAR		M+
				ʿAMM		I	JI	T	ŠAMAR			AM-MI-IŠ-TA-MAR		M
				ʿAMM		I	JI	T	ŠAMAR	U		AM-MI-IŠ-TAM-RU		MRS VI P. 329 UGARIT+
				ʿAMM		I	JI	T	ŠAMAR	U		AM-MI-IS-TAM-RU		MRS VI P. 239 UGARIT+
ŠN	1			ŠINA					DAMQ	A		ŠI-NA-DAM-QA	FN	XIII 1 IV 29+
				ŠINI					HADD	U		ŠI-NI-D-U		MRS XVI 44:3
				ŠINI					ʿAḎR	I		ŠI-NI-AD-RI		M
				ŠINI					DAMQ	A		ŠI-NI-DAM-QA	FN	RA LXV 61 IV 48
ŠNJ	1	JI		ŠNIJ					HADD	U		IŠ-NI-D-IM		A.
		JU	T	ŠANIJ								UŠ-TA-AN-NI		RA LXV 44 IV 55; A.+
		JU	T	ŠANIJ					HADD	U		UŠ-TI-NI-D-IM?		A. 36 9+
		JU	T	ŠANIJ					ʾIL	A		UŠ-TA-NI-I-LA		A. 33 22
		JI	ŠT	ŠNIJ					ʾEL			IŠ-TA-AŠ-NI-EL		SIMMONS 46 30
		JI	ŠT	ŠNIJ					ʾIL			IŠ-TA-AŠ-NI-IL		SYRIA V 274 HANA
		JI	ŠT	ŠNIJ					ʾIL			IŠ-TA-AŠ-NI-DINGIR		VAS IX 156 11+
		JU	ŠT	ŠNIJ					ʾIL			UŠ-TAŠ-NI-DINGIR		VAS IX 130 21+
		JU	ŠT	ŠNIJ					ʾIL			UŠ-TA-AŠ-NI-DINGIR		VAS IX 131 21+
			ŠT	ŠNIJ					ʾIL			ŠA-TA-AŠ-NI-IL		SUMER V 139 NO. 4
				ŠANIJ		UM						SA-NI-U$_2$-UM		M
				ŠANIJ		I						SA-NI-I		YOS II 139 3
	2			LA			ʾA		ŠNIJ					
									ʾIL			LA-AŠ-NI-DINGIR		M
ŠPṬ	1			ŠAPAṬ	AN							ŠA-PA-TA-AN		M
				ŠIPṬ		A			ʾAḪ	UM		ŠI-IP-TA-A-ḪU-UM		RA LXV 46 VI 27
				ŠIPṬ		I			JAʾAR			ŠI-IP-TI-A-ḪA-AR	FN	C
				ŠIPṬ		I			HADD	U		ŠI-IP-TI-D-IM		A. LATE
				ŠIPṬ		I			HAND	A		ŠI-IP-TI-AN-TA		A. LATE
				ŠIPṬ		I			HAND	A		ŠI-IP-TI-IA-AN-TA		A. LATE
ŠQL	1		T	ŠAQL		UM						ŠA-TA-AQ-LUM		RA LXV 43 III 50
				ŠIQL		IM						ŠI-IQ-LI-IM	GEN	CT XLVIII 90
				ŠIQL	AN	U						ŠI-IQ-LA-NU		B 47
				ŠIQL	AN	UM						SI-IQ-LA-NU-UM		TA 30, 231+
				ŠIQL	AN	UM						ŠI-IQ-LA-NU-UM		TA 30, 2 4
				ŠIQL	AN	IM						SI-IQ-LA-NIM	GEN	TA 1930, 189
				ŠUQUL	T	UM						ŠU-GUL-TUM	FN	XIII 1 XI 9
ŠRN	1			ŠURAN	AT	UM						ŠU-RA-NA-TUM	FN	M
ŠRR	1			ŠERIR	AN	IM						ŠE-RI-RA-NIM	GEN	M
ŠRŠR	1			ŠARŠAR	AN	UM						ŠA-ŠA-RA-NU-UM		M
				ŠARŠAR	AN	U						ŠA-ŠA-RA-NU		M

ROOTS (Consonants only)

ŠRŠR	1		ŠARŠAR	AN	IM					ŠA-ŠA-RA-NIM	GEN	M+
ŠRṬ	1		ŠIRṬ		IJA					ŠE-ER-DI-IA		A.
			ŠIRṬ		I		ʾIL	I		ŠI-IR-TE-I_3-LI_2		A. LATE
ŠŠG	1		ŠUŠAG		I					ŠU-ŠA-GI	FN	M
ŠT	1		ŠAT				ʿAN	A		ŠA-AT-A-NA		TCL XXI 220A 4+ CAPP.
	2		ḎU				ŠAT	I		ZU-ŠA-TI		HARRIS 56 12
ŠTŠ	1		ŠITAŠ				ʾIL	I		ŠI-IT-TA-AŠ-I_3-LI_2		MEL. SYR. 994
ŠṬP	1		ŠAṬUP		I		ʾIL			ŠA-TU-BI-DINGIR		M+
			ŠAṬUP		I		ʾEL			ŠA-TU-BI-EL		RA LXV 44 IV 74
			ŠAṬP	AH						ŠA-AṬ-BA	FN	RA LXV 65 VII 39
Ṣʾ	2		JAT		UM		ṢIʾ	A		IA-TUM-ZI-A		CT XLV 97 5
ṢḪQ	1	JA	ṢḪAQ		IM					IA-AZ-ḪA-KI?-IM	GEN	IX 291 I 38
			ṢIḪAQ		AJA					ZI-ḪA-KA-A-A		KISURRA 82 2
ṢḪR	1		ṢIḪAR				ṬALL	U	K	ṢI-ḪAR-TI-LU-UK	FN	PBS VIII/2 252 9, 18
ṢWR	1		ṢUWR		AJA					ZU-RA-A		M
			ṢUWR		IJA					ZU-RI-IA		XIV 98:11
			ṢUWR	AT	IM					ZU?-RA?-TIM	GEN	M
			ṢUWR	ATANU						ZU-RA-TA-NU		M
			ṢUWR		A		ʾIL			ZU-RA-DINGIR		M+
			ṢUWR		A		ʿAMM	U		ZU-RA-ḪA-AM-MU		M+
			ṢUWR		A		ʿAMM	U		Z[U]-RA-ḪA-M[U]		XIII 132 7
			ṢUWR		A		ʿAMM	U	HU	ZU-RA-ḪA-AM-MU-U_2		M
			ṢUWR		I		HADD	U		ZU-RI-D-IM		M+
			ṢUWR		I		ʾIL			ZU-RI-DINGIR		M
			ṢUWR		I		ʿAMM	U		ZU-RI-ḪA-AM-MU		M
			ṢUWR		I		ʿAMM	U	HU	ZU-RI-ḪA-AM-MU-U_2		M+
			ṢUWR		I		JARAḪ			ZU-RI-E-RA-AḪ		M
			ṢUWR		I		DAGAN			ZU-RI-D-DA-GAN		M
	2		ʾAB		I		ṢUWR	A		A-BE-ZU-RA		TCL IV 87 10 CAPP.
			ʾAB		I		ṢUWR	A		A-BI-ṢU-RA		TIM IV 34 27
			ʾAB		I		ṢUWR	I		A-BI-ZU-RI		M
			ʿAMM		I		ṢUWR	A		AM-MI-ZU-RA		CT XLVIII 90 REV.
			KA				ṢUWR	A				
							ʾIL			KA-ZU-RA-DINGIR		M
			KA				ṢUWR	I				
							ḪAʾL	A		KA-ZU-RI-ḪA-LA		M
			NAHR				ṢUWR	I		D-ID_2-ZU-RI		M
			ŠARAJ				ṢUWR	UM		ŠA-RA-ṢUR-RU-UM		KISURRA 111 6
ṢJḪ	1		ṢIJḪ	AT	UM					ZI-ḪA-TUM	FN	XIII 1 VII 35
			ṢIJḪ				HADD	A		ZI-ḪA-DA		TA 1933,7 EARLY OB
	2		MAM		A		ṢIJḪ AT	UM		MA-MA-ZI-A-TUM	FN	RA LXV 61 IV 37
ṢJD	1	JE	ṢJID	AN	UM					E-ZI-DA-NU-UM		I
		TA	ṢJID		UM					TA-ZI-TUM	FN	M
		ME	ṢJID		UM					ME-ṢI-TUM		B 34
		ME	ṢJID		UM					ME-ZI-TUM		XIII 1 VI 29
		ME	ṢJID		UM					ME-ZI-[T]U-UM		M
			ṢAJAD		UM					ZA-IA-DU-UM		CT XLV 97 16
			ṢAJAD	AN						ZA-A-DA-AN		RA LXV 43 III 45; C+
			ṢAJAD	AN						ZA-JA-DA-AN		M+
			ṢAJID		IM					ZA-I-DI-IM	GEN	VAS IX 172 18+
			ṢAJID	AT	UM					ZA-I-DA-TUM	FN	EDZARD, DER 90:2+
ṢBʾ	1		ṢABAʾ				HADD	U		ZA-BA-AD-DU		M
			ṢABAʾ				JAT	UM		ZA-BA-IA-TUM	MN	BM 16835 19+
			ṢABAʾ			TI	ʾEL			ZA-BA-TE-EL		UNPUBL.
			ṢABIʾ		UM					ZA-BI-UM		OB KING
			ṢABIʾ		UM					ZA-BU-UM		OB KING
			ṢABIʾ		UM					ZA-BI-ḪU-UM		M+
			ṢABIʾ		IM					ZA-BI-ḪI-IM	GEN	M+
			ṢABIʾ		IM					ZA-BI-I-IM	GEN	C P.39 N. 8+
			ṢABUʾ		UM					ZA-BU-UM	FN	M
			ṢABUʾ		UM					ZA-BU-U_2-UM	MN	M
			ṢABʾ		I					ZA-BI_2	FN	U
			ṢABʾ	AN	UM					ZA-AB-ḪA-NU-UM		CT XLVIII 88 REV.
			ṢIBʾ		U					ZI-BU		B 42
			ṢIBʾ	AT	UM					ZI-IB-A-TUM	FN	XIII 1 III 2
			ṢIBʾ		IJA					ZI-BI-IA		XIV 106:6

ROOTS (Consonants only)

ṢBʾ	1		ṢIBʾ		IJAN						ZI-BI-IA-AN		RA LXV 42 III 24
			ṢIBʾ	AN							ZI-BA-AN		BM 16836 27; M+
			ṢIBʾ	ATAN							[Z]I-BA-TA-AN		VII 185 10
			ṢIBʾ		I		LIʾL		UM		ZE$_2$-BI-LI-LUM		HSM 7900, UR III
			ṢIBʾ		I		LIʾM				ZI-BI-LI-IM		M
			ṢIBʾ		I		NIʿM				ZI-BI-NI-ḪI-I[M]		M
			ṢUBUʾ		UM						ZU-BU-UM		SIMMONS 50 23+
			ṢUBUʾ		UM						ZU-BU-U$_2$-UM		SIMMONS 47 21
	2		LA			KA	ṢUBʾ		UM		LA-KA-ZU-BU-UM		M
			LA				ṢABIʾ		IM		LA-ZA-BI-IM	GEN	M+
ṢBR	1		ṢABR		UM						ZA-AB-RUM		YOS VIII 29 3
			ṢABR		IJA						ZA-AB-RI-IA		YOS VIII 120 22
			ṢABR	AN	UM						ZA-AB-RA-NU-UM		I
			ṢIBAR		UM						ZI-BA-RU-UM		RA VIII 69 21+
			ṢIBAR	AT	UM						ṢI-BA-RA-TUM	MN?	OLZ VIII 351 16
ṢBṬ	1		ṢIBIṬ	AH							ZI-BI-IT-TA	FN	C P. 41+
	2		ḪAM		I		ṢABṬ		I		A-MI-ZA-AB-TI	MN	B 13
			ḪAM		I		ṢABṬ		I		A-MI-ZA-AB-TI	FN	CT VIII 35 B 1
ṢDQ	1	JA	ṢDUQ		UM						IA-AŠ-DU-KUM		B 30
		JA	ṢDUQ				ʾIL				IA-AŠ-DU-UQ-DINGIR		JEAN 164 R. 4+
		JA	ṢDUQ				ʾIL				[IA]-AŠ$_2$-DU-UQ-DINGIR		BASOR 95, 19
			ṢADAQ	AH							ZA-DA-GA	FN	U
			ṢADUQ		UM						ZA-DU-KUM		B 41
			ṢIDQ		UM						ZI-ID-KUM		TCL XI 198 23
			ṢIDQ	AN							ZI-ID-QA-AN		M
			ṢIDQ	AN	UM						ṢI-ID-GA-NU-UM		EDZARD, DER 85:45+
			ṢIDQ		IJA						ZI-ID-KI-IA		RA LXV 55 XIII 9
			ṢIDQ		A		HADD		U		ZI-ID-QA-D-IM		M
			ṢIDQ		I		JATAR				ZI-ID-KI-E-TAR		M+
			ṢIDQ		I	JE	JPAʿ				ZI-ID-KI-E-PA		RA XLIII 37 QATNA
			ṢIDQ		I	JE	JPUʿ				ZI-ID-KI-E-PU-UḪ		M+, C+
			ṢIDQ		U		LA						
							NAŠIʾ				ZI-ID-KU-LA-NA-SI		M+
			ṢIDQ		UM		MAṢIʾ				ZI-ID-KUM-MA-ZI		X 131 5+
	2		ʾAḪ		I		ṢADUQ				A-ḪI-ZA-DU-UQ		B 12
			ʾIL		I		ṢADUQ				I$_3$-LI$_2$-ZA-DU-UQ		M+
			ʾIL		I		ṢIDQ		I		I$_3$-LI$_2$-ZI-ID-KI		DELAPORTE CCL II A 337
			ʾIL		I		ṢIDQ		UM		I$_3$-LI$_2$-ZI-ID-KUM		UCP X/1 100 7
			ʿAMM		I		ṢADUQ				ḪA-MI-ZA-DU-[UQ]		M
			ʿAMM		I		ṢADUQ				ḪA-AM-MI-ZA-DU-UQ		M
			ʿAMM		I		ṢADUQ		A		AM-MI-ZA-DU-GA		B 13+
			ʿAMM		I		ṢADUQ		A				
							....				AM-MI-ZA-DU-GA-I-LU-NI		B 13+
			ʾATAR		I		ṢADUQ				[A]T-TA-RI-ZA-DU-UQ		I 103 17
			ŠUM		U		ṢIDQ		UM		[SU]-MU-ZI-ID-KUM		B 40
			ŠUM		U		ṢIDQ		UM				
							DITAN		A		[SU]-MU-ZI-ID-KUM-DI-TA-NA		B 40
			ŠARAJ				ṢIDQ		UM		ŠA-RA-ZI-ID-K[UM]		MEISSNER 36 22
	3		LA			ʾA	ḪJIJ						
							ṢADUQ				LA-ḪI-ZA-DU-UQ		A.+
ṢLL	1		ṢALIL		UM						ZA-LI-LUM		B 41+
			ṢALIL		I						ZA-LI-LI	GEN	B 41
			ṢILL	AN							Z[I]-IL-LA-AN		RA LXV 55 XIII 15
			ṢILL	AN							ZI-LA-AN		RA LXV 55 XIII 47
			ṢILL				HADD		U		ZI-IL-LA-AD-DU		A. 81
			ṢILL				ʾAKK		A		MI-NI-AK-KA		M
			ṢILL				ʿAN	AT			MI-NI-D-ḪA-NA-AT		XIII 83 8
			ṢILL				ʾANN		U		MI-NI-AN-NU		M
			ṢILL				BAʿL		I		MI-NI-BA-AḪ-LI		M+
	2		KAʾM		A		ṢILL		UM		KA-MA-ZI-LUM	FN	B 33+
			KAʾM		A		ṢILL		U		KA-MA-ZI-LU?	FN	VAS XIII 9 R. 2
			KUʾM		U		ṢILL		I		KU-MU-ZI-LI	FN	B 33+
			ṬAJB				ṢILL		U	HU	ṬA$_3$-AB-ṢI-LU-U$_2$		TCL X 38 7
ṢMD	1		ṢAMID		UM						ZA-MI-DU-UM	FN	B 41+
			ṢAMID				ʾAḪ		I		ZA-MI-ID-A-ḪI		CT IV 8B 17
			ṢIMID	AT	UM						ZI-MI-DA?-TUM	FN	M

ROOTS (Consonants only)

ṢPR	1	ṢUPR		UM					ZU-UP-RUM	FN	RA LXV 62 V 9
		ṢUPR		AM					ZU-UP-RA-AM		RA LXV 51 IX 70
		ṢUPR		I		JARAḪ			ZU-UP-RI-E-RA-AḪ		M+
ṢRP	1	ṢARIP	AT	UM					ZA-RI-PA-TUM	FN	RA LXV 60 III 49
		ṢARP		I		....			ZA-AR-BI-[....]		M
ṢRR	1	ṢARIR		UM					ZA-RI-RU-UM		A 7688
		ṢARR		UM					ZA-AR-RUM		XIII 1 I 52
		ṢARR		UM					ZA-AR-RU-[UM]		IX 285 1
		ṢIRR		I					ZI-IR-RI	NOM	M, A.+
		ṢURAR		UM					ZU-RA-RUM		PBS VIII/2 198 8
		ṢURAR		U					ṢU-RA-RU		KISURRA 104 36
		ṢURR		I					ZU-UR-RI	NOM	M
		ṢURR		UM					ZU-UR-R[U-UM]?		M
	2 JI	JṢIʾ				ṢARIR	UM		I-ZI-ZA-RI-RUM		CT XLV 115 18
		LA				ṢARR	UM		LA-ZA-RU-UM?		B 33
		LA				ṢARR	AJA		LA-ZA-RA-A		YOS XIII 244:14
Tʾ	1	TAʾ		I					TA-ḪI		M+
		TUʾ		I					TU-I		XIII 60 5
		TUʾ	AN	UM					TU-ḪA-NU-UM		UCP X/3 2 26
		TUʾ	ATAN						TU-ḪA-TA-AN		M
	2	ʾAḪ		I	Š	TUʾ		JA	A-ḪI-IŠ-TU-IA		A. 86 9
		ʾAḪ		I	Š	TUʾ		KA	A-ḪI-IŠ-DU-KA		A. 98C 1, 6
		ʾAB		I	Š	TUʾ			A-BI-IŠ-DU		A. LATE
		ʾUBUŠ				TUʾ		KA	ḪU-BU-UŠ-TU-KA		A. 268 17
		ʾILAR				TAʾ	A		I-LA-AR-TA-A		M
		ʾILAR				TAʾ	A		I-LA-AR-TA-ḪA		M
		ʾAMAN				TAʾ	I		AM-MA-AN-TA-ḪI		M
		BAʿL				TUʾ		KA	BA-AL-DU-UḪ-KA		A.
TʾḪ	2	LA				TEʾḪ	U		LA-TE-ḪU		MRS VI P. 196 22,LATE
TʾG	1	TAʾG		I					TA-GI		RA LXV 43 III 40+
		TAʾG	IT	UM					TA-GI-TUM	FN	XIII 1 II 45
	2	MILK		I		TAʾG	A		MI-IL-KI-TA-GA		A. LATE
TʾK	1	TAʾK		I					TA-KI		RA LXV 55 XIII 19
		TAʾK		U		ʾIL			TA-KU-DINGIR		VAS VIII 14 27
		TAʾK		I		ʾIŠḪAR	AH		TA-KI-D-IŠ-ḪA-RA		JCS XIII 52 293 LE,A.LATE
		TAʾK		U		ʾIŠḪAR	AH		TA-KU-D-IŠ-ḪA-R[A]		JCS XIII 52 293 R, A. LATE
	2	ʾABIL				TAʾK	U	HU	A-BI-IL-TA-KU-U_2		WALTERS, WL 97:4;105:3+
TʾL	1	TAʾIL		U					TA-ḪI-LU?	FN	RA LXV 65 VII 33
		TAʾL		UM					TA-LU-UM		EDZARD, DER 112:23
		TIʾL	AN	UM					TI-LA-NU-UM		B 47
		TUʾAL		U					TU-A-LU		RA LXV 48 VIII 17
	2	MAM		A		TUʾAL	I		D-MA-MA-TU-ḪA-LI	FN	M
TʾM	1	TAʾM		I					TA-MI		RA LXV 50 IX 13
		TIʾM				LU		HU	TI-IM-LU-U_2	FN	XIII 1 VIII 73+
		TIʾM				RIJB	A		TI-IM-RI-PA		A.
		TUʾM	AN	UM					TU-MA-NU-UM		B 47
TʾN	1	TUʾN	AN	UM					TU-NA-NU-UM		TCL XVIII 118 7
		TUʾN	AN	U					TU-NA-NU		BM 81617 5
		TUʾN	AK	UM					TU-NA-KUM		UET V 285 22
TʾR	1	TIʾAR		UM					TI-A-RUM		B 40
TʾŠ	1	TIʾŠ	AT	UM					TI-ŠA-TUM	FN	M
		TIʾŠ				LUʾM	U		TI-IŠ-LU-MU		M
TʾT	1	TIʾT		AJA					TI-TA-A-A		RUTTEN 28 10+
TʾZ	1	TUʾZ		AJA					TU-ZA-A	FN	XIII 1 XIII 29
		TUʾZ		AJA					TU-ZA-[I]A	FN	M
		TUʾZ	ATAN						TU-ZA-TA-AN		M
TḪT	1	TAḪT		U		PI					
						ʾIL			TA-AḪ-TU-BI-DINGIR		M+
		TUḪT		U		....			TU-UḪ-TU-[....]		M
TḪTN	2	BUN				TAḪTUN					
						ʾIL	A		BU-UN-TAḪ-UN-I-LA		B 16
		BUN		U		TAḪTUN					
						ʾIL	A		BU-NU-TAḪ-TU-UN-I-LA		B 16+
TḪJ	1 JA	TḪIJ				DAGAN			IA-AT-ḪI-D-DA-GAN		M
TḪTḪ	1	TAḪTAḪ		UM					TA-AḪ-TA-ḪU-UM		BIN VII 116 3
TWR	1 JI	TWUR				ḪAJJ	A		I-DUR-E_2-A		M

ROOTS (Consonants only)

TWR	1	JI-	TWUR					ʾAHL		I		I-DUR-A-LI		JCS XXIV 46 NCS. 5, 6
		JI	TWUR					ʿADN		U		I-DUR-ḪA-AD-[NU]		B 24
		JI	TWUR					ʿADN		U	HU	I-DUR-ḪA-AD-NU-U$_2$		TCL XVIII 83 6
		JI	TWUR					ʿAMM		U	HU	I-DUR-ḪA-MU-U$_2$		UNPUBL.
		JI	TWUR					ʾAŠD		UM		I-DUR-A-AŠ-DU-UM		B 23
		JI	TWUR					ʾAŠD		UM		I-DUR-AŠ-DUM		B 23
		JI	TWUR					ʾAŠD		UM		I-DUR-AŠ-DU-UM		B 23+
		JI	TWUR					ʾAŠD		UM		I-DUR-AŠ$_2$-DU-UM		M+
		JI	TWUR					ʾAŠD		U		I-DUR-AŠ-DU		B 23+
		JI	TWUR					ʾAŠD		U		I-DUR-AŠ$_2$-DU		VAS IX 172 5, M+
		JI	TWUR					ʾAŠD		U	HU	I-DUR-AŠ-DU-U$_2$		SIMMONS 90 4
		JI	TWUR					ʾAŠD		U	HU	I-DUR-AŠ$_2$-DU-U$_2$		M
		JI	TWUR					KUʾN		U	HU	I-DUR-KU?-NU-U$_2$		VAS XIII 14 R. 10
		JA	TWUR					MEʾR				D-IA-TU-[U]R-ME-I[R]	DN	M
		JI	TWUR					MEʾR				D-I-DUR-ME-IR	DN	M+
		JA	TWUR					NAHR		UM		IA-DUR-NA-RUM?		RA LXV 48 VII 72
		JI	TWUR					NINGAL				I-DUR-D-NIN-GAL		M
		JI	TWUR					PI						
								ʾIL				I-DUR-[BI]?-DINGIR		I
		JI	TWUR					ŠALIM				I-DUR-SA-LIM		YOS II 84 21 22
		JI	TWUR					ŠUM		U				
								ʾEL				I-DUR-SU-ME-EL		KISURRA 43 5+
		TA	TWUR					ʿAŠTAR				TA-TU-UR-EŠ$_4$-DAR	FN	M
		TA	TWUR					ḪAʾT		UM		TA-DUR-ḪA-TUM		TA 1931, 489
		TA	TWUR					MAʾT		UM		TA-TU-UR-MA-TUM	FN	M+; C+
		TA	TWUR					MAʾT		UM		TA-DUR-MA-TUM	FN	XIII 1 XIV 34+
			TUWR		A			ʾIL		I		TU-RA-I$_3$-LI$_2$		SAUREN, WUG 285 V, U.
			TUWR		A			DAGAN				TU-RA-D-DA-GAN		M+
			TUWR		I			DAGAN				TU-RI-D-DA-GAN		B 40+ HANA
			TUWR		U			ʿAMM		I		DUR-RU-AM-MI		MAOG IV 2 6 HANA
			TAWIR		UM							TA-E-RUM		KISURRA 73 2+
			TAWIR		U							TA-E-RU		KISURRA 81A 4+
			TIWR	AT	UM							TI-RA-TUM	FN	M
			TIWR					ḪAJJ		A		TI-IR-E$_2$-A		M+
			TIWR					ʿAŠTAR				TI-IR-EŠ$_4$-DAR		M+
			TIWR					MAM		A		TI-IR-MA-MA		M+
			TIWR		I	Š		TUWR				TE-RI-IŠ-TU-UR$_2$		C+
	2		ʾIL		I			TUWR		A		I$_3$-LI$_2$-TU-RA		M+
			ʾIL		I			TUWR		A	JA	I$_3$-LI$_2$-TU-RA-[I]A		RA LXV 40 I 45
			ʾIL		I			TUWR		I	JA	I$_3$-LI$_2$-TU-RI-IA		XII 115 5+
			ʾANN		U			TIWR		I		AN-NU-TI-RI	FN	M+
			ḪANN		A		JI	TWUR						
								MEʾR				ḪA-AN-NA-D-I-DUR-ME-ER		M
			ʾIPQ		U		JI	TWUR						
								MEʾR				IP-KU-D-I-DUR-ME-ER		M
			JARAḪ					TIWR		I		D-EN-ZU-TI-RI		M+
			JARAḪ					TIWR		IM		D-EN-ZU-TI-RI-IM	GEN	M
			ḤARB		I			TUWR		AM		AR-BI-TU-RA-AM		BIROT, TEA 65:35
			ʿAŠTAR					TIWR	AH			D-EŠ$_4$-DAR-TE-IR-RA		A.
			ʿAŠTAR					TUWR		I	JA	EŠ$_4$-DAR-TU-RI-IA	FN	XIII 1 XIII 33
			DAGAN					TIWR		I		D-DA-GAN-TI-RI	FN	RA LXV 61 IV 51
			KAKK		A			TUWR		I	JA	KA-KA-TU-RI-IA	FN	M
			LI				JI	TWUR						
								ʾAHL		I		LI-TU-UR-A-LI		JCS XXIV 62 NO.55+
			MANN		A			TAWR		I		MA-NA-TA-RI		B 34
			MATIʿ					TIWR		UM		MA-TI-TI-RUM		BM 67281
		JI	NDIN				JI	TWUR						
								MEʾR				I-DIN-D-I-DUR-ME-ER		XIII 1 III 48+
			ŠALAŠ					TUWR		A	JA	ŠA-LA-AŠ-TU-RA-IA	FN	C
			TIWR		I	Š		TUWR				TE-RI-IŠ-TU-UR$_2$		C+
TBʾ	1		TABʾ		I			BIN		UM		TA-AB-I-BI-NU-UM		BM 82437 4 9
			TIBIʾ		A	Š		ME						
								ʾEL				TI-BI$_2$-AŠ$_2$-ME-EL		CT XXXIII 48A 4
	2		LA					TEBUʾ		U		LA-TE-BU-U$_2$		B 33
TBB	1		TABUB		U							TA-BU-BU	FN	XIII 1 VIII 35
			TABUB					ʿIMD		I		TA-BU-UB-IM-[DI]?	FN	VIII 33 7

TBB	1	TABUB		I		ʿIMD		I		TA-BU-TI?-IM-DI	FN	VIII 31 10 15
		TABUB		U		ʿALIJ	AH			D-TA-BU-BU-ḪA-LI-IA	FN	XIII 1 VI 13
		TABUB		U		ʾUMM		I		TA-BU-BU-UM-MI	FN	XIII 1 VI 57
		TABUB		U		ḪAṢN		I		TA-BU-BU-ḪA-AṢ-NI	FN	RA LXV 60 III 19
		TABUB		U		ŠIMḪ		I		TA-BU-BU-ŠI-IM-ḪI	FN	XII 265 4
		TABB		I		MAM		A		TA-BI-D-MA-MA	FN	M
		TUBAB		I						TU-BA-BI		RA LXV 41 II 26
	2	ʾANN		U		TABB		I		AN-NU-TAB-BI	FN	XIII 1 III 36+
		ʿAŠTAR				TABB		I		EŠ$_4$-DAR-TAB-BI	FN	M+, C
		ḪAṢN		U		TABB		I		AZ?-NU-TAB-BI	FN	M
	JI	NDIN				TABUB		U		I-DIN-TA-BU-BU		M
		ŠALAŠ				TABB		I		D-ŠA-LA-AŠ-TAB-BI	FN	XIII 1 III 26
TBN	1	TABIN		UM						TA-BI-NU-UM		BM 82359
		TUBIN		UM						TU-BI-NU-UM		TA 30 103
TBZ	1	TABUZ		I						TA-BU-ZI		RA LXV 45 V 33
TDB	1	TADAB			JE	JŠAR				TA-DA-AB-E-ŠAR	FN	XIII 1 VI 42
TDQ	1	TIDIQ	AN							TI-DI-QA-AN		RA LXV 48 VIII 18+
TDR	1	TUDAR		I		ʿAŠTAR				TU-DA-RI-EŠ$_4$-DAR	FN	EDZARD, DER 58:7
		TUDAR		UM		ʿAŠTAR				TU-DA-RUM-EŠ$_4$-DAR	FN	EDZARD, DER 61:16
TKL	2	ʾANN		U		TUKUL	T	I		AN-NU-TU-KU-UL-[TI]	FN	M+
		ʾANN		U		TUKUL	T	I		AN-NU-TU-GUL-TI	FN	XIII 1 X 3
		ŠI			JA	TAKAL				ŠI-IA-TA-KA-AL	MN	IX 291 III 37'
TKR	1	TUKR	ATIJI							TUK-RA-TI-I	GEN	UCP X/3 2 19
TLʾ	1	TALAʾ		UM						TA-LA-ḪU-UM		BE VI/2 80 29
		TALIʾ	AN	UM						TA-LI-A-NU-UM		TA 1931, 538 VI
		TILIʾ		A	Š	GAMIL				TI-LI-AŠ-GA-MIL		UNPUBL.
TLʿ	2	KALAL				TULAʿ			HA	KA-LA-AL-TU-LA-A	FN	M, C
TLL	2	ʾAJIŠ				TULL		A		A-JI-IŠ-TU-UL-LA		M
		ʾANN		U		TILL	AT	I		AN-NU-TIL-LA-TI	FN	XIII 1 X 2
	3 JA	KRUB				ʾIL						
						TILL	AT	I		D-IA-AK-RU-UB-DINGIR-TIL-LA-TI		M
TLM	1	TALM		A		ʿAMM		U		TA-AL-MA-AM-MU		A.+
		TALM		U		ʾAŠIḪ		I		TA-AL-MU-A-ŠI-ḪI	FN	XIII 1 III 63
	2	ʾALL		I		TALM		A		AL-LI-TA-AL-MA	FN	A.
	3	ʾAJA				ʾAB		I				
						TALM		A		A-IA-BI-TA-AL-MA		A. 239 15
TMH	1 ME	TMIH		UM						ME-IT-ME-U$_2$-UM		M
	ME	TMIH		UM						ME-IT-MU-UM		M
	ME	TMIH		U						ME-IT-MI-JU		M+
TMB	2 JI	JṢIʾ				TAMB		U		I-ZI-TA-AM-BU		BAHREIN UNPUB, POST-U.
TMN	1	TIMAN		AJA						TI-MA-NA-A-A		HARRIS 66 14
TMR	1	TAMAR		U						TA-MA-RU		RA LXV 50 VIII 71
	2	ŠUM		U		TAMAR				SU-MU-TA-MAR		B 40+
		ŠUM		U		TAMAR		U		SU-MU-TA-MA-RU		RA LXIV 43
TNʾ	1	TINʾ	AT	UM						TI-IN-A-TUM	FN	XIII 1 VI 4
		TINʾ		IJAN						TI-IN-I-IA-AN		RA LXV 51 IX 76+
		TINʾ		I		JARAḪ				TI-IN-E-RA-AḪ		C
		TINʾ		I		JARAḪ				TI-IN-I-E-RA-AḪ		C
TND	1	TUND		I						TU-UN-DI	FN	M+
TNT	2	BUN				TENUT		A		BU-UN-TE-NU?-TA?		MEISSNER 68 13
TNTN	1	TANTAN		UM						TA-AN-TA-NU-UM		SUMER V 141
		TANTAN		UM						TA-TA-NU-UM		HARRIS 11 17, 14 14+
TPT	1	TUPT		I	JA	MWUT		A		TU-UP-TI-IA-MU-TA		BM 80328 2
		TUPT		U		ʿAŠTAR				TUP-TU-EŠ$_4$-DAR		M
TQR	1	TUQAR		UM						TU-GA-RU-UM		UET V 625 10+
		TUQAR		UM						TU-QA-RU-UM		CT XXXIII 42 21
		TUQAR		IM						TU-GA-RI-IM	GEN	HARRIS 64 7
TRḪ	2	ʾALL		I		TURAḪ				AL-LI-TU-RA-AḪ?	FN	XIII 1 I 10+
		ʾALL		I		TURAḪ		I		AL-LI-TU-RA-ḪI	FN	A.
TRJ	1	TARAJ	AT	UM						TA-RA-IA-TUM	FN	VAS XIII 14 5+
TRBN	1	TURBIN	AH							TU-UR-BI-NA	FN	IX 291 II 17
TRM	1	TURUM			NA	ḪATK		I		TU-RUM-NA-AT-KI		M+
		TURM	AT	UM						TU-UR-MA-⸢TUM	FN	M
TRN	1	TURUN		U	HU	GAMIL				D-TU-UR-RU-NU-U$_2$-GA-MIL	FN?	XIII 118 14
TRR	1	TIRR		U						TE-IR-RU		M+
		TIRR		U						TI-IR-RU		M

ROOTS (Consonants only)

TRTR	1		TURTUR	AH							TU-TU-RA	FN	RA LXV 60 III 67
			TURTUR	AN							TU-UR-TU-RA-AN		RA LXV 42 II 76
TSP	1		TISP		UM						[T]I-IS-PU-UM		RA XLI 45 8', HANA
			TISP	AT	UM						TI-IS-PA-TUM	FN	M+, C
			TISP	AT	UM						TI-IS-PA-A-TUM	FN	X 105 3
TŠʿ	2		ʾIL		UM		TUŠUʿ		U		D-I-LU-UN-TU-SU-U$_2$	DN	KISURRA
TŠM	1		TUŠIM		UM						DU-SI-MU-UM		I
			TUŠIM	AT	UM						TU-ŠI-MA-TUM	FN	RA LXV 61 III 77
TŠN	1		TIŠAN	AT	UM						TI-ŠA-NA-TUM	MN	VAS VIII 58 34+
			TIŠAN	AT	UM						TI-ŠA-NA-TUM	FN	BM 82372, M
TŠPK	2	JE	NBIṬ				TIŠPAK				I-EN-BI-IṬ-D-TIŠPAK		JCS XXIV 49 NO. 15:3
TŠR	1		TUŠAR		UM						TU-ŠA-RU-UM	FN	BM 82212 3
			TUŠER		U						TU-ŠE?-RU?		M
TT	2		ʾAL		I	Š	TUT		U		A-LI-IŠ-TU-TU		VAS XVI 23 13
TTG	1		TUTUG		UM						TU-TU-GU-UM		SIMMONS 119 21+
TTT	1		TATT	AH							TA-AT-TA	FN	RA LXV 62 V 55
			TATT		A	HA					TA-AT-TA-A	FN	RA LXV 60 III 73
			TATT		I		BAʾT		UM		TA-AT-TI-BA-TUM		TCL I 204:10
TZL	1		TUZAL		UM						TU-ZA-LUM		BM 17049 19+
ṬḪD	1		ṬAḪD		I		LIʾM				TA-AḪ-DI-LI-IM		M
ṬḪŠ	1		ṬUḪŠ	AT	UM						DU-UḪ-ŠA-TUM	FN	TCL X 12 12, M
			ṬUḪŠ	AT	UM						TU-UḪ$_3$-ŠA-TUM		UET V 290 2
ṬJB	1		ṬAJB	AT	UM						DA-BA-TUM	FN	U
			ṬAJB	AT	UM						ṬA$_3$-BA-TUM	FN	M+
			ṬAJB	AH							ṬA$_3$-BA	FN	M+
			ṬAJB	AH							TA-A-BA	FN	M+
			ṬAJB		IJA						ṬA$_3$-BI-A	FN	RA LXV 66 VII 54
			ṬAJB				ŠIJM	T	UM		TA-AB-SI-IM-TUM	FN	A. 8 4
			ṬAJB				ŠUM		U	HU	ṬA$_3$-AB-SU-MU-U$_2$		M+
			ṬAJB				ṢILL		U	HU	ṬA$_3$-AB-ṢI-LU-U$_2$		TCL X 38 7
			ṬAJB		A		ʾIL				ṬA-BA-DINGIR		A. 60 11
			ṬAJB		A		ʾAŠUR		A		TA-PA-AŠ-ŠU-RA		A.
	2		ʾAB		I		ṬAJB		A		A-BI-ṬA-BA		A.+
			ʾIL		I		ṬAJB		A		I$_3$-LI$_2$-DA-[B]A		A. 96 R. 10
			ḪAM		I		ṬAJB		I		A-MI-ṬA-BI		RA LXV 45 V 81
			ʿAMM		I		ṬAJB		A		AN-MI-ṬA-BA		A.+
			ʾUMM		I		ṬAJB	AH			UM-MI-ṬA$_3$-BA	FN	M+
			ʾUMM		I		ṬAJB	AH			UM-MI-ṬA$_3$-BA-NU	FN	RA LXV 64 VI 34
			ʾANN		U		ṬAJB				AN-NU-DUG$_3$		M+
			BAʿL		I		ṬAJB				BA-LI-SIG5?	FN	XIII 1 VIII 36
			BIN	T	U		ṬAJB	AH			BI-IN-DU-ṬA$_3$-BA	FN	RA LXV 65 VII 10
			ḎIQUN		A		ṬAJB				ZI-KU-NA-ṬA$_3$-AB	FN	RA LXV 59 II 77
			LA				ṬAJB		UM		LA-DA-BU-UM		U
			LA				ṬAJB	T	UM		LA-ṬA$_3$-AB-TUM	FN	XIII 1 VI 44+
			ŠALM		U		ṬAJB		A		ŠA-AL-MU-ṬA$_3$-BA	FN	RA LXV 66 VII 64
			ŠUM		I		ṬAJB		A		SU?-MI-DA-BA		A. 7 44+
			ŠUM		U		ṬAJB		I		SU-MU-DA-BI		X 90 10+
TBḪ	1		TABIḪ	AT	UM						TA-BI-ḪA-TUM	MN?	BE VI/1 3 3 11
ṬBQ	1		ṬUBUQ	AH							TU-BU-QA	FN	M
			ṬUBQ		I						TU-UB-KI		RA LXV 40 I 24
			ṬUBQ	AT	UM						TU-UB-GA-TUM	MN	MEISSNER 11 3
ṬLL	1		ṬALL		I	JI	BNIJ				TA-LI-IB-NI	FN	CT II 5 3 9
	2	JI	ʾLAP				ṬALL				I-LA-AP-TI-IL		U
		JI	ʾLAP				ṬALL		U	HU	I-LA-AP-TA-LU-U$_2$		M
			ʿAMM		I		ṬALL		U	HU	ḪA-MI-TI-LU-U$_2$		M
			ʿAMM		I		ṬALL		U	HU	ḪA-AM-MI-TA-LU-U$_2$		M+
			ʿAMM		I		ṬALL		U	HU	ḪA-AM-MI-TI-LU-U$_2$		M+
			ʿAMM		I		ṬILL		U	HU	ḪA-AM-MI-TE-LU-U$_2$		RA LXVI 118:15
			ṢIḪAR				ṬALL		U	K	ṢI-ḪAR-TI-LU-UK	FN	PBS VIII/2 252 9, 18
ṬQM	1		ṬUQM	AT	UM						TU-UK-MA-TUM	FN	RA LXV 65 VII 25
ṬRD	1		ṬARID		UM						DA-RI-DU-UM		B 17+
			ṬARID		UM						TA-RI-DU-UM		BM 17049 26+
			ṬARID		A		ʾADM		U		TA-RI-DA-AD-MU		XIII 1 16
			ṬARUD		UM						DA-RU-DU-UM		TCL X 30 11
ZʾG	2		ʿAMM		I		ZUʾG		U	HU	ḪA-AM-MI-ZU-GU-U$_2$		BM 17045+
ZʾM	1		ZIʾM		U		DAWR		A		ZI-MU-DA-RA		RA VIII 75 R. 2

ROOTS (Consonants only)

ZʾM	1	ZUʾUM		IM				ZU-U$_2$-MI-IM	GEN	M
		ZUʾUM		IM				ZU-[U$_2$]?-MI-IM	GEN	M
		ZUʾUM		I				ZU-U$_2$-MI	GEN	PBS VIII/2 236 6
ZʾN	1	ZAʾAN		UM				ZA-A-NU-UM		SIMMONS 98 8 SEAL
		ZAʾAN		UM				ZA-ḪA-NU-UM		M+
		ZAʾAN		IM				ZA-ḪA-NIM	GEN	M
		ZAʾN	AN					ZA-AḪ-NA-AN		M
		ZIʾN	ATANU					ZI-NA-TA-NU		BM 16984 24
ZʾQ	1	ZIʾQ	AN					ZI-QA-AN		RA LXV 54 XII 14
ZʾR	1	ZAʾR		UM				ZA-RUM		XIII 1 IV 17
		ZAʾR	T	UM				ZA-AR-TUM	FN	M
ZʾT	1	ZAʾT	AN					ZA-TA-AN		RA LXV 45 V 38
		ZAʾT			ʿAMM	U		ZA-AT-AM-MU	MN	A. 279 2 3
	2	ʿAMM		I	ZAʾT	I		ḪA-MI-ZA-TI		HARRIS 103 1
		MAʾR		U	ZAʾT	U	HU	MA-RU-ZA-TU-U$_2$		CT XLVIII 27
		MALIK			ZAʾT	UM		MA-LIK-ZA-DU-UM		B 34
ZʾZ	1	ZAʾAZ	AH					ZA-ḪA-AZ-ZA	FN	XIII 1 IX 22
		ZAʾZ	AN	UM				ZA-ZA-NU-UM		RA LXV 47 VII 28; B 48+
		ZAʾZ	AN	UM				ZA-ZA-NUM$_2$		KISURRA 2A:7+
		ZAʾZ	AN	IM				ZA-ZA-NI-IM	GEN	B 48
		ZAʾZ	AN	AJA				ZA-ZA-NA-IA	FN	RA LXV 58 I 52
		ZAʾZ	UN	UM				ZA-ZU-NU-UM		M
		ZAʾZ		IJA				ZA-ZI-IA		M+
		ZAʾZ		I	ʾANN	U		ZA-ZI-AN-NU		B 41+
		ZIʾZ		U				ZI-ZU	FN	RA LXV 65 VII 43
		ZIʾZ	AN	UM				ZI-ZA-NU-UM		B 48+
		ZUʾUZ		U				ZU-U$_2$-ZU		M
		ZUʾZ	AN					ZU-ZA-AN		M+
		ZUʾZ	AN	U				ZU-ZA-NU		B 48
		ZUʾZ	AN	UM				ZU-ZA-NU-UM		B 48
		ZUʾZ	AN	UM				ZU-ZA-NUM$_2$		RUTTEN 9 16
		ZUʾZ	AN	UM				ZU-ZA-A-NUM$_2$		KISURRA 48:12
ZḪL	1	ZAḪIL		UM				ZA-ḪI-LUM		HARRIS 12 30
		ZAḪL	AT	IM				ZA-AḪ-LA-TIM	GEN	CT VIII 31B 25
		ZUḪAL	AN					ZU-ḪA-LA-AN		RA LXV 51 X 2
		ZUḪL	AN	UM				ZU-UḪ$_3$-IA-NU-U[M]		TA 1931, 141
ZḪR	1	ZUḪIR		I				ZU-ḪI-RI		M
ZḪZḪ	1	ZAḪZAḪ		UM				ZA-AḪ-ZA-ḪU-UM		B 49
ZJD	1	ZIJAD	AH					ZI?-IA?-DA	FN	XIII 1 XIII 25
ZJN	1	ZIJAN		I				ZI-JA-NI	FN	M
		ZIJAN		I				ZI-IA-NI		KISURRA 4A:11+
		ZIJAN		I				D-EN-ZU-I-A-NI		KISURRA 72:6
		ZUJAN						ZU-I-IA-AN		RA LXV 50 IX 3
		ZUJAN		I				ZU-JA-NI	FN	C
		ZUJAN		E				ZU-JA-NE	FN	XIII 1 VIII 11
ZBB	2	D̲IMR			ZABABA			ZI-ME-IR-D-ZA-BA$_4$-BA$_4$		CIG P. 155
ZBG	1	ZABUG		A				ZA-BU-GA		JCS XIII 57 NO.305 A.LATE
		ZABUG	AN					ZA-BU-GA-AN		RA LXV 45 V 23,30
ZBL	1	ZABIL		IM				ZA-BI-LIM	GEN	M+
		ZABIL	AT	UM				ZA-BI-LA-TUM	FN	RA LXV 60 III 50
		ZABUL		UM				ZA-BU-LUM		A 21950 4 5
		ZIBL	AN	UM				ZI-IB-LA-NU--M		BASOR 95 23
		ZUBAL		IM				ZU-BA-LI-IM	GEN	EDZARD,DER 152:18
		ZUBAL	AN					ZU-BA-LA-AN		M
		ZUBAL	AT	UM				ZU?-BA-LA-TUM	FN	U
ZBN	1	ZABAN		UM				ZA-BA-NU-UM		U UNPUBL., B 47+
		ZABIN		UM				ZA-BI-NU-UM		M
		ZIBIN		I				ZI-BI-NI		B 42
ZBZ	1	ZABIZ	AT	UM				ZA-BI-ZA-TUM		YOS XIII 175:11
ZBZB	1	ZABZAB		UM				ZA-AB-ZA-BU-UM		B 49
ZDR	1	ZIDAR		U	HU			ZI-DA-RU-U$_2$		VAS XIII 93A R. 8+
ZKK	1	ZAKK		U				ZA-AK-KU		M
		ZAKK		U	HU			ZA-AK-KU-U$_2$		M+
		ZAKK		U	HU			ZA-KU-U$_2$		M
		ZAKK			ʾIL	I		ZA-AK-I$_3$-LI$_2$		TA 1931,389 UR III
		ZAKK			DAWD	I		ZA-AK-DA-TI		TA 1931,377+ EARLY OB

ZKK	1		ZAKK			PI					
						ʾEL			ZA-AK-PI-EL		TA 1931,198 EARLY OB
			ZAKK		A	BALAṬ			ZA-AK-KA-BA-LA-AṬ?		M+
	2		ʿAMM		I	ZAKK	UM		AM-MI-ZA-KU-UM		IRAQ IV 185, A 385
			ʿAMM		I	ZAKK	U	HU	ḪA-AM-MI-ZA-KU-U_2		M
ZKZK	1		ZAKZAK		UM				ZA-AK-ZA-KU-UM		UNPUBL.
			ZAKZAK		UM				ZA-AK-ZA-KUM		B 49
			ZIKZIK		UM				ZI-IK-ZI-KUM		B 49
ZLḪ	1		ZALUḪ		UM				ZA-LU-ḪU-UM		BIN VII 8 5
			ZALḪ		UM				ZA-AL-ḪU-UM		RUTTEN 6 23
			ZILḪ	AN					ZI-IL-ḪA-AN		M+, C
ZLJ	1	JA	ZLIJ			ʾIL			IA-AZ-LI-DINGIR		M
			ZALIJ			ʾIL			ZA-LI-DINGIR		B 41
ZLB	1		ZILIB		UM				ZI-LI-BU-UM		M
			ZILIB	AN					ZI-LI-BA-AN		I 14 10
			ZILIB		IJA				ZI-LI-BI-IA		RUTTEN 19 21
ZLN	1		ZULAN		UM				ZU-LA-NU-UM		TA 30 35 6
ZLT	1		ZALAT	AN					ZA-LA-TA-AN		RA LXV 55 XIII 38
			ZALAT		IJA				ZA-LA-TI-IA		BM 17060 35+
	2	TA	KWUN			ZULAT	UM		TA-KU-UN-ZU?-LA-TUM	FN	RA LXV 62 V 30
ZLZL	1		ZALZAL		UM				ZA-AL-ZA-LUM		B 49+
			ZALZAL		IM				ZA-AL-ZA-LIM	GEN	M+
Zmʾ	1	JI	ZMEʾ			ʾIL			IZ-ME-DINGIR		VAS IX 141 2
			ZAMAʾ			JAT	UM		ZA-MA-A-A-TUM	MN?	TCL X 38 1
ZMM	1		ZAMM	AN	UM				ZA-AM-MA-A-NU-UM		B 48
			ZAMM	AN	UM				ZA-AM-MA-NU-UM		B 48+
			ZIMM		I	DAWD	I		ZI-IM-MI-DA-DI	FN	C II 44 33+
			ZUMM	AN					ZU-UM-MA-AN		XIII 95 6
			ZUMM			ʾAB	U		ZU-UM-MA-BU		BM 80328 7
ZMN	1		ZAMIN		UM				ZA-MI-NU-UM		YOS VIII P. 25+
			ZAMIN		UM				ZA-MI-NUM_2		YOS VIII P. 25
ZNJ	1		ZANIJ	AT	UM				ZA-NI-IA-TUM		BM 80496 3'
		MA	ZNIJ	AT	UM				MA-AZ-NI-A-T[UM]	FN	JCS XIX 56
ZNN	1		ZANAN		I				ZA-NA-NI	GEN	B 48
			ZANAN	AH					ZA-NA-NA	FN	RA LXV 64 V 61
			ZANN		UM				ZA-AN-NU-UM		BIN VII 186 22, M
			ZANN	AT	UM				ZA-AN-NA-TUM	FN	M+
			ZANN		I				ZA-AN-NI		B 41
			ZINAN		UM				ZI-NA-NU-UM		CT XLV 117 32
			ZUNAN						ZU-NA-AN		M
			ZUNAN		UM				ZU-NA-NU-UM		KISURRA 94 5
			ZUNAN		U				ZU-NA-NU		B 48
			ZUNN	AH					ZU-UN-NA	FN	XIII 1 IV 51
	2		ʾIL		I	ZANN	I		I_3-LI_2-ZA-AN-NI	FN	M+
ZNR	1	JI	ZNUR		UM				IZ-NU-RU-UM		SIMMONS 48 20+
		JI	ZNUR		UM				IZ-NU-RUM		CT XLV 82 7 26
ZNZ	1		ZUNZ		UM				ZU-UN-ZU-UM		RA LXV 48 VIII 4
ZNZ	2		ḪUNN			ZANZI			ḪU-UN-ZA-AN-ZI	FN	XIII 1 IX 42
			ḪUNN			ZANZI			ḪU-UN-ZA-ZI	FN	XIII 1 IX 34, C
ZNZN	1		ZUNZUN		UM				ZU-UN-ZU-NU-UM		RUTTEN 1 9
			ZUNZUN		A				ZU-UN-ZU-NA		B 49
ZPP	1		ZIPP	ATANIM					ZI-IP-PA-TA-NIM	GEN	M
ZQT	1		ZAQAT		UM				ZA-KA-TUM		B 41
			ZAQAT		UM				ZA-GA-TUM		KISURRA 112 5+
			ZAQAT		UM				ZA-KA-TUM	FN	RA LXV 61 IV 63
			ZAQAT		I				ZA-GA-TI	GEN	B 41
			ZUQAT		UM	MA			ZU-KA-TUM-MA		EDZARD,DER 152 REV. 11
ZRM	1		ZARAM		UM				ZA-AR-RA-MU-UM		TIM III 131 4
			ZARAM	AN	UM				ZA-RA-MA-NU-UM		TIM III 24 14
			ZARAM	AN	UM				ZA-RA-MA-A-NU-UM		SIMMONS 99 8 SEAL
ZRNB	1		ZARNAB		UM				ZA-AR-NA-BU-UM		B 41
ZRQ	1		ZARQ	ATANUM					ZA-AR-GA-TA-NU-UM		JCS IV 110A 19
			ZIRQ	AN	UM				ZE_2-IR-GA-NU-UM		TA 1931,438
			ZIRQ	AN	IM				ZI-IR-GA-NIM	GEN	TA 1930,221 EARLY OB
		MA	ZRAQ	AT	UM				MA-AZ-RA-QA-TUM	FN	XIII 1 II 37
ZRT	1		ZIRIT	AN					ZI-RI-IT-TA-A[N]		M

ZRZR	1	ZARZAR		UM		ZA-AR-ZA-RU-UM		BM 16835 26+
		ZURZUR		UM		ZU-UR-ZU-RU-UM		CT XLV 5 R. 6
		ZURZUR		UM		ZU-UR$_2$-ZU-RU-UM		KISURRA 20 13+
		ZURZUR	T	UM		ZU-UR$_2$-ZU-UR-TUM	FN	KISURRA 187 5
		ZURZUR		UM		ZU-UR$_2$-ZU-RU-UM		KISURRA 20 13+
ZZB	1	ZIZAB	AN			ZI-ZA-BA-AN		RA LXV 52 X 38
ZZN	1	ZIZN		I	ʾEL	ZI-IZ-NI-EL		RA LXV 55 XIII 11

3. PREFIXES AND SUFFIXES

The lemmata correspond to the prefixes and suffixes of the analysis column given in chapter 1, "Stems."

For a general discussion of the structure of this chapter see section 0.3. Two important points are noted there: that the morphemic analysis of the prefixes and suffixes in the present study does not correspond to the results that can be obtained on the basis of the sequential reconstruction; and that because of space limitations imposed by the computer program, certain morpheme sequences are run together. Thus the two suffixes ATAN UM appear as ATANUM, and ANIJ I as ANIJI. The correct segmentation of the two suffixes can be reconstructed by noting the columns in which they appear.

There are 16 prefixes in ranks 1 and 2, and 47 suffixes in ranks 1, 2, and 3—altogether 63 prefixes and suffixes.

PREFIXES

Rank 1

ᵓA	Conjugational prefix; nominal formative
ᵓU	Conjugational prefix
JA	Conjugational prefix
JE	Conjugational prefix
JI	Conjugational prefix
JU	Conjugational prefix
MA	Participial prefix; nominal formative
ME	Participial prefix; nominal formative
MI	Participial prefix; nominal formative
MU	Participial prefix; nominal formative
TA	Conjugational prefix; nominal formative
TU	Conjugational prefix

Rank 2

N	N-stem (BN)
Š	Š-stem
ŠT	ŠT-stem (BŠT and DŠT)
T	T-stem (BT and DT)

SUFFIXES

Rank 1

AH	Noun/verb, feminine suffix
AJ	Noun, gentilic formative
AJIT	Noun, gentilic formative *-aj-* + feminine gentilic *-īt*
AK	Name formative
AN	Noun/name formative *-ān-*
ANIJ	Noun/name formative *-ān-* + gentilic *-ij*
AT	Noun/verb, feminine suffix; name, masculine formative
ATAN	Noun/name formative *-at-* + noun/name formative *-ān*
ATEN	Noun/name formative *-at-* + noun/name formative *-ēn*; hapax
ATIJ	Noun/name formative *-at-* + gentilic *-ij*; hapax
IJ	Noun, gentilic formative
IN	Noun/name formative
IT	Noun, feminine gentilic *-īt*
ITAN	Unclear; hapax
ITIJ	Unclear; hapax
T	Noun/verb feminine suffix; name, masculine formative
UN	Noun/name formative
UT	Unclear
UTAN	Unclear; hapax

Rank 2

A	Declensional suffix; many other functions
AJA	Name formative
AM	Declensional suffix; other functions
E	Declensional suffix; other functions
EJA	Name formative
EM	Declensional suffix
I	Declensional suffix; pronominal suffix
IJA	Name formative
IJAN	Name formative *-ija-* + name formative *-ān*
IM	Declensional suffix
U	Declensional suffix
UJA	Name formative
UJAN	Name formative *-uja-* + name formative *-ān*
UM	Declensional suffix

Rank 3

HA	Pronominal suffix
HU	Pronominal suffix
JA	Pronominal suffix
JE	Pronominal suffix
K	Pronominal suffix
KA	Pronominal suffix
KI	Pronominal suffix
NA	Pronominal suffix
NI	Pronominal suffix
NIA	Pronominal suffix
NIE	Pronominal suffix
Š	Declensional suffix *-iš*, *-aš*, *-uš*
TA	Conjugational suffix; hapax
TI	Conjugational suffix

The alphabetic order of lemmata is that of the roman alphabet.

The alphabetic order of the parts outside of the lemma is that of my work order, discussed in section 0.5.

ʾA	2		LA				ʾA	ʾWIʾ					
								ʾIL			LA-WI-IḪ?-DINGIR		TIM IV 33,34,SEALS
	2		LA				ʾA	ʾWIR	UM		LA-WI-RUM		RA XXIV 58 9 4
	2		LA				ʾA	ʾDUM	U		LA-AḪ-DU-MU		4E RENC. ASS. P. 178 4
	2		LA				ʾA	ʾMAR	UM		LA-MA-RUM		BM 80644
	1	ʾA	ʾMUR		U	HU					A-MU-RU-U_2		PBS VIII/1 98 9
	2		ʿADN		A		ʾA	ʾMUR			ḪA-AD-NA-AM?-MU-UR		X 75 18
			LA				ʾA	ʾMUR	IM		LA-A-MU-RI-IM	GEN	M
			LA				ʾA	ʾMUR	A		LA-MU-RA		B 33+
	2		LA				ʾA	ʾŠUD	I				
								ʾIL			LA-AḪ-SU-DI-DINGIR		XIII 4 14
	2		LA				ʾA	HWIJ		JA	LA-WI-IA	FN	RA LXV 60 III 37
			LA				ʾA	HWIJ					
								ʾAḪ	I		LA-AḪ-WI-A-ḪI	FN	XIII 1 VII 3
			LA				ʾA	HWIJ					
								ʾAB	I		LA-AḪ-WI-A-BI	FN	XIII 1 XIII 6
			LA				ʾA	HWIJ					
								HADD	U		LA-AḪ-WI-A-DU		A. 95 36
			LA				ʾA	HWIJ					
								ʾIL			LA-WI-DINGIR		XIV 109:7
			LA				ʾA	HWIJ					
								ʾIL			LA-[AḪ]?-WI-DINGIR		M
			LA				ʾA	HWIJ					
								JAŠAR			LA-AḪ-WI-E-SA-AR		RA LXV 40 I 21
			LA				ʾA	HWIJ					
								BAʿL	U		LA-AḪ-WI-BA-LU		C
			LA				ʾA	HWIJ					
								BAʿL	U		LA-AḪ-WI-BA-AḪ-LU		XIV 29:28
			LA				ʾA	HWIJ					
								BEʿL	I		LA-AḪ-WI-BE-LI_2	FN	RA LXV 59 II 73
			LA				ʾA	HWIJ					
								LA		NA	LA-AḪ-WI-LA-NA		RA LXV 65 VII 19
			LA				ʾA	HWIJ					
								MALIK			LA-AḪ-WI-MA-LIK		X 141 2
			LA				ʾA	HWIJ					
								MALIK	U		LA-AḪ-WI-MA-LI-KU		M
			LA				ʾA	HWIJ					
								NIWR	I		LA-AḪ-WI-NE-RI	FN	XIII 1 II 11
	3		ʾEK		I			LA					
							ʾA	HWIJ			E-KI-LA-AḪ-WI		M
	1	ʾA	HLUL	AJ	UM						AḪ-LU-LA-UM		CT VIII 38 B 4
	2		LA				ʾA	ḤJIJ					
								HADD	U		LA-ḪI-A-DU		A. 57 11, 13
			LA				ʾA	ḤJIJ					
								ʿAN	UM		LA-ḪI-A-NU-UM		U
			LA				ʾA	ḤJIJ					
								BIḪR	U		LA-ḪI-BI-RU		WATERMAN 25 R. 5
			LA				ʾA	ḤJIJ					
								ṢADUQ			LA-ḪI-ZA-DU-UQ		A.+
	1	ʾA	ḪBAB		U						AḪ-BA-BU		U
	1	ʾA	ḪLAM		U						AḪ-LA-MU		M+
		ʾA	ḪLAM		U						AḪ-LA-AM-MU		XII 508 2
		ʾA	ḪLAM		U						AḪ-LA-A-MU		XI 208 2
	1	ʾA	ḪBUD	IJ	UM						AḪ-BU-TE-UM		U
	2		LA				ʾA	ḪŠIR	UM		LA-AḪ-SI-RU-UM		BM 80368 2
	2		ʾIL		I		ʾA	ḪTAN			I_3-LI_2-AḪ-TA-AN		RUTTEN 6 16+
	1	ʾA	WDAJ					ʾIL			A-U_3-DA-IL		U
		ʾA	WDAJ					ʾIL			A-AW-TE-IL		U
	1	ʾA	JDAʿ					PI					
								ʾEL			A-DA-AḪ-[BI]?-EL		SIMMONS 51 21
	1	ʾA	JPAʿ					ʾAB	I		A-PA-AḪ-A-BI		YOS VIII 29 13
		ʾA	JPAʿ					NAN	UM		A-BA-AḪ-NA-NU-UM		TA 1931, 374, EARLY OB
		ʾA	JPAʿ					RAPIʾ			A-PA-AḪ-RA-BI		SUMER XIV 5, IM 52272
	2		DAGAN				ʾA	JPUʿ			D-DA-GAN-A-PU-UḪ		M
	2		BUN		U		ʾA	BLUṬ			BU-NU-AB-LU-UṬ		BIROT,TEA 64:4
	1	ʾA	DBAR	AT	UM						AD-BA-RA-TUM	MN	A 21946

PREFIXES, Class 1

ʾA	1 ʾA	DLUQ		IJA					AD-LU-KI-IA		RES 1939, 69
	1 ʾA	DRAK	AT	UM					AD-RA-KA-TUM	FN	M+
	ʾA	DRAK	AT	IM					AD-RA-KA-TIM	FN GEN	M+
	1 ʾA	KWUN				PI					
						ʾEL			A-KU-PI-EL		GORDON, SCT 38 16
	1 ʾA	MWUT				PA					
						ʾIL			A-MU-UT-PA-DINGIR		SYRIA L 7
	ʾA	MWUT				PA					
						ʾIL			AM-MU-UT-PA-DINGIR		RA XLIII 212 39 QATNA
	ʾA	MWUT				PI					
						ʾIL			A-MU-UT-BI-DINGIR		M+
	ʾA	MWUT				PI					
						ʾIL	A		A-MU-UT-BI-I-LA		M
	3	LA				ʿADN	A				
					ʾA	MWUT			LA-ḪA-AD-NA-A-MU-UT		M
	2	LA			ʾA	MLIK					
						ʾIL			LA-AM-LI-IK-DINGIR		RUTTEN 5 22
	2	ŠUM		U	ʾA	MNID	IM		[SU-M]U-AM-NI-DI-IM		B 38
	1 ʾA	MURR		UM					A-MU-RU-UM		U
	ʾA	MURR		UM					A-MUR-RU-UM		CT II 50 21+
	ʾA	MURR		U					A-MU-UR-RU		M+
	ʾA	MURR							A-MU-RU-UḪ-ḪI		A.
	2 JI	DNIK			ʾA	MURR	UM		D-ID-NI-IK-MAR-TU	DN	U
	1 ʾA	NZAL	AT	UM					AN-ZA-LA-TUM	FN?	XIII 1 I 14
	1 ʾA	PLAḪ				HAND	A		AP-LA-ḪA-AN-DA		M+
	ʾA	PLAḪ				HAND	A		AP-LI-ḪA-AN-DA		M
	ʾA	PLAḪ				HAND	A		AP-LA-ḪA-DA		M
	ʾA	PLAḪ				HAND	A		AP-LA-AḪ-[AN]-DA		M
	ʾA	PLAḪ				HAND	U		AP-LA-ḪA-AN-DU		RA LXV 42 II 65
	1 ʾA	PQID		A					AP-KI-DA		U
	2	ʾIL		I	ʾA	PTAN			I$_3$-LI$_2$-AP-TA-AN		B 21
		ʾIL		I	ʾA	PTAN			DINGIR-AP-TAN		TIM III 150 12
	1 ʾA	PTUN	AN	UM					AP-TU-NA-NU-UM		YOS VIII 176 SEAL
	1 ʾA	QDAM		U					AQ-DA-MU		C P. 35+
	1 ʾA	RDAK				HAND	A		AR-DA-KA-AN-DA		M
	1 ʾA	RGAM	AT	UM					AR-GA-MA-TUM	FN	C
	1 ʾA	RMAN	UN	UM					AR-MA-NU-NUM$_2$		TA 1931 , 538 IV
	1 ʾA	RŠIJ				ʾAḪ	UM		AR-ŠI-A-ḪU-UM		M+
	ʾA	RŠIJ				ʿAD	A	HA	AR-ŠI-A-DA?-A	FN	C
	ʾA	RŠIJ				HADD	A		AR-ŠI-A-DA		M
	ʾA	RŠIJ				ʾEDAK	U		AR-ŠI-E-DA-KU	FN	M
	ʾA	FŠIJ				ʿAN	UM		AR-SI?-A-NUM$_2$		U
	2	ʾAḪ		AM	ʾA	RŠIJ			A-ḪA-AM-AR-ŠI		I+
		LA			ʾA	RŠIJ	UM		LA-AR-ŠI-U$_2$-U[M]		TA 1931, 538 IV
	1 ʾA T	ŠAMAR				HADD	U		AŠ-TA-MAR-D-IM		M+
	2	ʾAB		I	ʾA T	ŠAMAR			A-BI-AŠ-TA-MA-AR		YOS XIII 489:4
	1 ʾA	ŠKIN	AN	UM					AŠ$_2$-KI-NA-NU-UM		TA 30 87+
	1 ʾA	ŠKUR	AN						AŠ-KU-RA-AN		RA LXV 50 IX 15
	ʾA	ŠKUR				HADD	U		AŠ$_2$-KU-UR-D-IM		TCL 1 146 4
	ʾA	ŠKUR				HADD	U		AŠ-KUR-D-IM		M+
	ʾA	ŠKUR				HEDD	A		AŠ-KUR-E-DA		A. 54 25
	2	BUN		U	ʾA	ŠKUR			BU-NU-AŠ$_2$-KU-UR		SYRIA XXXVII 206 29 HANA
		MUT			ʾA	ŠKUR			MU-UT-AŠ-KUR		M+
	JI	NDIN			ʾA	ŠKUR			I-DIN-D-AŠ$_2$-KU-UR		SYRIA XXXVII 206 8 HANA
		ŠUM		U	ʾA	ŠKUR	A		ŠU-MU-AŠ$_2$-KU-RA		TA 30, 299
	1 ʾA	ŠWUB				ʾIL	A		A-ŠU-UB-I-LA		A. LATE
	ʾA	ŠWUB				LA					
						ʾEL			A-ŠU-UB-LA-EL		TA 1931,765
	ʾA	ŠWUB				LA					
						ʾIL			A-ŠU-UB-LA-DINGIR		C+
	ʾA	ŠWUB				LI					
						ʾEL			A-ŠU-UB-LI-EL		OIP XLIII 154 NO. 48+
	2	LA			ʾA	ŠNIJ					
						ʾIL			LA-AŠ-NI-DINGIR		M
ʾU	1 ʾU	WDAJ				....			U$_2$-DA-[....]		TA 30, 615 29
	ʾU	WDAJ				MA			U$_2$-DA-MA		I

PREFIXES, Class 1

ʾU	1	ʾU	WMAʾ				ʾIL		U_3-MA-IL		U
		ʾU	WMAʾ				ʾIL	A	U_2-MA-D-DINGIR		B 40
	1	ʾU	WQAH						U_3-GA		U
		ʾU	WQAH						U_3-GA-A		SAUREN, WUG 114 REV, U
		ʾU	WQAH				HADD	U	U_2-QA-D-IM		RA LXV 44 IV 51
		ʾU	WQAH				HADD	U	U_2-GA-D-IM		BIROT, TEA 24:6
		ʾU	WQAH				ʾIL		U_2-QA-DINGIR		M+
		ʾU	WQAH				ʾIL		U_2-GA-DINGIR		GAUTIER 41 5
		ʾU	WQAH				ʾIL		U_3-QA-DINGIR		SIMMONS 1 3+
		ʾU	WQAH				ʾIL		U_2-QA-IL		SYRIA V 274 HANA
		ʾU	WQAH				ʾIL	A	U_2-Q[A]-I-LA		A 7699:14, ISHCHALI
		ʾU	WQAH				ʾIL	UM	U_2-GA-DINGIR-LUM		FRANK 29 9
		ʾU	WQAH				KI				
							ʾEL		U_2-QA-KI-EL		RA LXV 51 IX 69
		ʾU	WQAH				ŠAMŠ		U_2-GA-A-D-UTU		SZLECHTER TJ 15944 SEAL
		ʾU	WQAH				ŠAMŠ		U_2-GA-D-UTU		BIROT, TEA 72 V 16'
	1	ʾU	WQIH				ʾEL		U_2-QI_2-E[L]		RA LXV 41 II 44
	1	ʾU	WŠIʿ		UM				U_2-SI-UM		I
		ʾU	WŠIʿ		I				U_2-SI-I		I+
	1	ʾU	WTAʾ	T	UM				U_2-TA-TUM	FN	C
		ʾU	WTAʾ				ʾAḪ	I	U_2-TA-A-ḪI		M
	1	ʾU	BWAʾ				ʾIL		U_2-BA-DINGIR		M
		ʾU	BWAʾ				ʾIL	A	U_2-BA-D-DINGIR		VAS VIII 14:22
JA	1	JA	ʾḪIḎ		A				IA-E-DA		YOS XIII 343:4
		JA	ʾḪIḎ				ʾUMM	I	IA-ḪI-DU-UM-ME	FN	RA LXV 65 VII 34
	1	JA	ʾḪUḎ	AN					IA-ḪU-ZA-AN		RA LXV 43 IV 21
	1	JA	ʾWIR		UM				IA-WI-RU-UM		B 31
	1	JA	ʾWIŠ				....		IA-ḪI-IŠ-[....]		TIM IV 33 SEAL, 34 SEAL
	1	JA	ʾWUŠ		U				IA-U_2-ŠU		B 31
		JA	ʾWUŠ	AN					IA-U_2-SA-AN		RA LXV 43 IV 15
		JA	ʾWUŠ				HADD	U	IA-UŠ-D-IM		M+
		JA	ʾWUŠ				HADD	U	IA-U_2-UŠ-D-IM		M+
		JA	ʾWUŠ				HADD	U	IA-$UŠ_2$-D-IM		M
		JA	ʾWUŠ				ʾIL		IA-UŠ-DINGIR		M+
		JA	ʾWUŠ				ʾIL		IA-U_2-$UŠ_2$-DINGIR		C II 35 28
		JA	ʾWUŠ				ʾIL		IA-U_2-UŠ-DINGIR		RA LXV 42 III 10+
		JA	ʾWUŠ				ḪAM	U	IA-U_2-UŠ-D-A-MU		M
	1	JA	ʾBUQ		UM				IA-BU-KUM		KISURRA 83 14
	1	JA	ʾGUN						IA-AḪ-GU-UN		TCL XVII 25 1
		JA	ʾGUN		UM				IA-AḪ-GU-UN-NU-UM		TCL XVII 24 1
		JA	ʾGUN		UM				IA-AḪ-GU-NU-UM		TLB IV 82:1
		JA	ʾGUN		UM				IA-GU-NU-UM		YOS XII
		JA	ʾGUN		UM				I-IA-GU-NU-UM		YOS XII
		JA	ʾGUN		IM				IA-GU-NI-IM	GEN	BM 16485
		JA	ʾGUN		I				IA-AḪ-GU-UN-NI	GEN	TCL XVII 26 1
	1	JA	ʾKUR		IM				IA-KU-RI?-IM?	GEN	VIII 2 23
		JA	ʾKUR	AN					IA-KU-RA-AN		M
		JA	ʾKUR				ʾIL		IA-AḪ-KU-UR-DINGIR		CT XLV 6 24
		JA	ʾKUR				ʾIL		A-AḪ-KU-UR_2-[DINGIR]?		HARRIS 79 22
		JA	ʾKUR				DAGAN		IA-KU-UR-D-DA-GAN		M+
	1	JA	ʾMAR	AH					IA-MA-RA	FN	XIII 1 XIV 26
	1	JA	ʾMIʾ				ʾIL		IA-AḪ-MI-DINGIR		PBS XI/2 P. 120 NO. 92
		JA	ʾMIʾ				ʾIL	A	IA-MI-I-LA		M
		JA	ʾMIʾ				ʾIL	A	JA-MI-I-LA		M
	1	JA	ʾMUW			HU			IA-AḪ-MU-U_2		B 26
		JA	ʾMUW				DAGAN		IA-AḪ-MU-D-DA-GAN	GN	B 26
	1	JA	ʾMUR		IM				IA-MU-RI-IM	GEN	B 28+
		JA	ʾMUR				HADD	U	IA-MU-UR-AD-DU		M
		JA	ʾMUR				JARAḪ		IA-MUR-D-EN-ZU		UET V 583 19
	1	JA	ʾQUD		UM				IA-KU-DU-UM		CT VIII 44A 28, UET V 523
		JA	ʾQUD		UM				IA-AḪ-KU-DU-UM		CT XXXIII 29 14
		JA	ʾQUD		UM				IA-KU-DU-UM-KI	GN	BRM IV 53 III 47+
		JA	ʾQUD		U				IA-KU-DU-KI	GN	UCP IX/4 5 1
		JA	ʾQUD	AN	IM				IA-GU-DA-NIM	GEN	BM 16823A 1
	1	JA	ʾRUR						IA-AḪ-RU-UR-KI	GN	M
		JA	ʾRUR		UM				IA-RU-RUM-KI	GN	YOS XII
		JA	ʾRUR		UM				IA-ḪU-UR-RU-UM-KI	GN	M

PREFIXES, Class 1

Prefix	No.	Element	Root				Element 2		Form		Reference
JA	1	JA	ʾRUR		UM				IA-AḪ-RU-RU-UM	GN	B 26+
		JA	ʾRUR		UM				IA-AḪ-RU-RUM	GN	B 26+
		JA	ʾRUR		UM				IA-AḪ-RU-RUM		BM 80328 10
		JA	ʾRUR		A				IA-AḪ-RU-RA-KI	GN	B 26, M
		JA	ʾRUR		A				IA-ḪU-UR-RA-KI	GN	M+
		JA	ʾRUR	IJ	I				IA-AḪ-RU-RI-I-KI	GN	M
	2		ʾAWN	AN		JA	ʾRUR		AN-NA-AN-IA-AḪ-RU-UR	TRIBE	BAGHD. MITT. II 56 I 12+
			ŠUM		U	JA	ʾRUR	A	[SU-MU-I]A-AḪ-RU-RA		B 39
	1	JA	ʾRUŠ						IA-AḪ-RU-UŠ		RA LXV 55 XIII 52
	1	JA	ʾŠUʾ				HADD	U	IA-SU-D-IM		TCL I 238 4 HANA+
	1	JA	ʾŠUD		UM				IA-SU?-DU-UM		CT II 28 19
		JA	ʾŠUD				PI				
							ʾEL		IA-SU-UD-PI-EL		SIMMONS 46 31
	1	JA	ʾŠUR		UM				IA-ŠU-RU-UM		RA LXV 54 XII 38
	1	JA	ʾZIJ				ʾIL		IA-AḪ-ZI-DINGIR		M
		JA	ʾZIJ				ʾIL	I	IA-AḪ-ZI-I$_3$-LI$_2$		TCL X 21 13
		JA	ʾZIJ				DAGAN		IA-AḪ-ZI-D-DA-GAN		RA LXV 54 XII 52
	1	JA	ʾZUW		UM				IA-ZU-UM		UET V 714 +
		JA	ʾZUW				HADD	U	IA-ZU-D-IM		M
		JA	ʾZUW				JARAḪ		IA-ZU-RA-AḪ		M+
		JA	ʾZUW				DAGAN		IA-ZU-D-DA-GAN		M+, SYRIA V 273, HANA
		JA	ʾZUW				RAŠAP		IA-AḪ-ZU-D-RA-SA-AP		M
	1	JA	HWIJ		UM				IA?-WI-U$_2$-UM		M
		JA	HWIJ		UM				IA-AḪ?-WI?-UM?		B 32
		JA	HWIJ			JA			IA-WI-IA		M
		JA	HWIJ				HADD	U	IA-WI-D-IM		M+
		JA	HWIJ				ʾIL		IA-WI-DINGIR		B 31+, M+
		JA	HWIJ				ʾIL		JA-AḪ-WI-DINGIR		M
		JA	HWIJ				ʾIL		IA-AḪ-WI-DINGIR		B 27+
		JA	HWIJ				ʾIL	I	IA-AḪ-WI-DINGIR-LI$_2$		KISURRA 6+
		JA	HWIJ				ʾIL	I	IA-WI-LI		A 7695 10
		JA	HWIJ				DAGAN		IA-WI-D-DA-GAN		B 31
		JA	HWIJ				KI				
							HADD	U	[IA-A]Ḫ-WI-KI-D-IM		M
		JA	HWIJ				NAŠIʾ		IA-AḪ-WI-NA-SI		M+
		JA	HWIJ			TA	NWUḪ		IA-WI?-TA-NU		RA LXV 43 III 64
	2		ʿAŠTAR			JA	HWIJ		EŠ$_4$-DAR-IA-WI		VAS VII 157 7
	1	JA	ḪJIJ			JA			IA-ḪI-IA		XIV 61:6
		JA	ḪJIJ	AN					[I]A?-Ḫ[I]?-IA-AN		RA LXV 41 II 54
		JA	ḪJIJ				ʾIL		IA-ḪI-DINGIR		B 26+
		JA	ḪJIJ				ʾIL		IA-A-ḪI-DINGIR		XIII 65 5
	1	JA	ḪBAS				ʾIL		IA-AḪ-BA-AZ-DINGIR		CT II 39 18+
	1	JA	ḪBIS		UM				IA-AḪ-BI-ZUM		GORDON 38 3
	1	JA	ḪKUM		UM				IA-AḪ-KU-MU-UM		B 26
	1	JA	ḪLIJ				ʾIL		IA-AḪ-LI-DINGIR		B 26
	1	JA	ḪMAD		UM				IA-AḪ-MA-DU-UM		CT XLV 5 7
	1	JA	ḪNUN				ʾIL		IA-ḪU-UN-DINGIR		M+
		JA	ḪNUN				ʾIL		IA-NU-UN-DINGIR		RA LXV 51 IX 65
		JA	ḪNUN				MAʾT	UM	IA-UN-MA-TUM	FN	RA L 63
		JA	ḪNUN				PI				
							ʾEL		IA-ḪU-UN-PI-EL		SIMMONS 54 18
	1	JA	ḪṢIN				ḪAJJ	A	IA-AḪ-ZI-IN-E$_2$-A		XIII 1 VII 23
		JA	ḪṢIN				ʾIRR	A	IA-AḪ-ZI-IN-IR$_3$-RA		M
		JA	ḪṢIN				DAGAN		IA-AḪ-ZI-IN-D-DA-GAN		M
	1	JA	ḪṢUN		UM				IA-ZU-NU-UM		SIMMONS 125 13+
		JA	ḪṢUN				ʾIL		IA-AḪ-ZU-UN-DINGIR		BE VI/1 7 18
	1	JA	ḪZUQ				ʾIL		IA-AḪ-ZU?-UQ-DINGIR		CT XLVIII 10 3
	1	JA	ḪAPIʾ				ʾIL		IA-ḪA-AP-PI-I-IL5	GN	JCS XVIII 59 12+
	1	JA	ḪATIʾ				ʾIL		IA-ḪA-AT-TI-DINGIR		M+, C
		JA	ḪATIʾ				ʾEL		IA-ḪA-TI-EL		RA LXV 44 IV 46
		JA	ḪATIʾ				ʾIL		IA-ḪA-TI-DINGIR		RUTTEN 15:2+; M
		JA	ḪATIʾ				ʾIL	UM	IA-ḪA-TI-LUM		YOS XII
		JA	ḪATIʾ				ŠAMŠ		IA-ḪA-AT-TI-D-UTU		UCP X/1 89 15
	1	JA	ḪBAʾ				RAŠAP		IA-AḪ-BA-D-RA-SA-AP		XIII 94 5
	1	JA	ḪBIʾ				ʾIL	A	IA-AḪ-BI-LA-KI	GN	M+
	1	JA	ḪBUʾ		UM				IA-AḪ-BU-U$_2$-UM		M

PREFIXES, Class 1

JA	1	JA	ḪMUM		IM					IA-AḪ-MU-MI-IM	GN GEN	M
		JA	ḪMUM		AM					IA-AḪ-MU-MA-AM-KI	GN ACC	M
	1	JA	ḪMUṬ		UM					IA-AḪ-MU-TU-UM-KI	GN	UET V 9721
		JA	ḪMUṬ		U					IA-AḪ-MU-TU		JEAN,TELL SIFR 13 15
		JA	ḪMUṬ	AN						IA-AḪ-MU-DA-AN		M
	1	JA	ḪŚIJ				ʾIL			IA-AḪ-SI-DINGIR		OLZ VIII 350 2
		JA	ḪŚIJ				ʾIL			JA-AḪ-SI-DINGIR		M
	1	JA	ḪZIM				....			IA-AḪ-ZI-IM-[....]		M
	1	JA	ḪZUM		U					IA-AḪ-ZU?-MU		BM 78799 12
	1	JA	ḪZUR				HADD		U	IA-AḪ-ZU-UR-D-IM		M
		JA	ḪZUR				ʾIL			IA-AḪ-ZU-UR-IL		TIM III 34 15A
		JA	ḪZUR				ʾIL			IA-AḪ-ZU-UR-DINGIR		JCS XXIV 57 NO 39 AND 51
	1	JA	ʿWUQ		UM					IA-U_2-KU-UM		B 31+
	1	JA	ʿDIJ				....			JA-AḪ-DI-[....]		M
	1	JA	ʿDUN		UM					IA-AḪ-DU-NU-UM		B 26
		JA	ʿDUN	AN	UM					IA-AḪ-DU-NA-NU-UM		JCS XXIV 60 NO.51 REV.
		JA	ʿDUN				LIʾM			IA-AḪ-DU-UN-LI-IM		M+
		JA	ʿDUN				LIʾM			IA-AḪ-DU-LI-IM		M+
		JA	ʿDUN				LIʾM			IA-AḪ-DU-UL-LI-IM		M
	1	JA	ʿḎAR				ʾIL			IA-DAR-DINGIR		RUTTEN 5 9+
		JA	ʿḎAR				ʾIL			IA-AḪ-ZA-AR-DINGIR		B 26
		JA	ʿḎAR				ʾIL			IA-AḪ-ZA-AR-I_3-IL		B 26
		JA	ʿḎAR				ʾIL			IA-ZA-AR-DINGIR?		IX 291 II 21,30
		JA	ʿḎAR				ʾIL			AḪ-ZA-AR-I_3-DINGIR		VAS XVIII 20:20
	1	JA	ʿḎIR							IA-AḪ-ZI-IR		YOS VIII 76 26
		JA	ʿḎIR		UM					IA-AḪ-ZI-RUM		B 26+
		JA	ʿḎIR		U					IA-AḪ-ZI-RU		CT XLV 63 34
		JA	ʿḎIR		I					IA-AḪ-ZI-RI	GEN	BM 16943 34
		JA	ʿḎIR				ʾIL			IA-AḪ-ZI-IR-DINGIR		B 26+
		JA	ʿḎIR				ʾIL			IA-AḪ-ZI-IR-I_3-IL		SUMER V 137
		JA	ʿḎIR				ʾIL			IA-AḪ-ZI-IR-I_3-DINGIR		CT XLV 8 6
	1	JA	ʿMIS				ʾIL			IA-AḪ-MI-IS-DINGIR		RUTTEN 2 23+
		JA	ʿMIS				ʾIL		UM	IA-AḪ-MI-ZI-LUM		RUTTEN 16 17
		JA	ʿMIS				JARAḪ			IA-AḪ-MI-IS-D-SIN		M
	1	JA	ʿMUS				....			IA-AḪ-MU-IS-[....]		XIV 129:5
		JA	ʿMUS				ʾIL			IA-AḪ-MU-US-DINGIR		M
	1	JA	ʿNIJ				ʾIL			IA-AḪ-NI-DINGIR		A 7630 6
	1	JA	ʿNUW			HU				IA-AḪ-NU-U_2		OIP XLVII 66
	1	JA	ʿQIB				ʾIL			IA-KI-IB-DINGIR		TIM V 33 23
	1	JA	ʿQUB		U					IA-KU-BU		CT II 9 26
		JA	ʿQUB		AM					IA-KU-BA-[A]M?	NOM	RA LXV 46 V 84
		JA	ʿQUB	AN						IA-KU-B[A]-AN		RA LXV 45 V 57
		JA	ʿQUB				HEDD		A	IA-AK-KU-UB-E-DA		JEA VIII 207F.
		JA	ʿQUB				ʾIL			A-AḪ-KU-UB-DINGIR		HARRIS 12 3+
		JA	ʿQUB				ʾIL			IA-KU-UB-DINGIR		B 27+
		JA	ʿQUB				ʾIL			IA-AḪ-KU-UB-DINGIR		XIII 1 VII 17, C+
		JA	ʿQUB		I		ʾIL			IA-AḪ-KU-BI-DINGIR		CT II 39 18
		JA	ʿQUB		I		ʾIL			IA-KU-BI-DINGIR		KISURRA 41 10
	1	JA	ʿZIB		UM					IA-ZI-BU-UM		M+
		JA	ʿZIB		IM					IA-ZI-BI-IM	GEN	XIV 92:26+
		JA	ʿZIB				....			IA-AḪ-ZI-IB-[....]		M
		JA	ʿZIB				HADD		U	IA-AḪ-ZI-IB-D-IM		M+
		JA	ʿZIB				HADD		U	IA-ZI-IB-D?-IM?		M
		JA	ʿZIB				ʾIL			IA-AH-ZI-IB-DINGIR		RUTTEN 21 7+, M
		JA	ʿZIB				ʾIL			A-AḪ-ZI-IB-DINGIR		HARRIS 57 2
		JA	ʿZIB				DAGAN			IA-ZI-IB-D-DA-GAN		M+
		JA	ʿZIB		I		ʾIL			IA-AḪ-ZI-BI-DINGIR		KISURRA 86A 11
		JA	ʿZIB		I		ʾIL			A-AḪ-ZI-BI-DINGIR		SIMMONS 70 5
		JA	ʿZIB		I		ʾIL			IA-A-ZI-BI-DINGIR		KAJ 34 18, 25 LATE
		JA	ʿZIB		A		ʾEL			IA-AḪ-ZI-BA-EL?		RA LXV 50 VIII 77
		JA	ʿZIB		U	HU				IA-AḪ-ZI-BU-U_2		M+
	1	JA	ʿZUB				ʾIL			IA-AḪ-ZU-UB-DINGIR		B 26+
	1	JA	WḪIJ				ʾIL			IA-U_2-ḪI-DINGIR		B 31
	1	JA	WMAʾ				ʾAḪ		UM	JA-MA-A-ḪU-UM		RA LXV 52 X 49
		JA	WMAʾ				ʿAMM	AJ	I	IA-AW-MA-ḪA-MA-JI-KI	GN	M
		JA	WMAʾ				ʿAMM		I	JA-MA-ḪA-MI-KI	GN	M

JA	1	JA	WMAʾ				ʿAMM	UM	JA-MA-ḪA-MU-UM		M
		JA	WMAʾ				ʿAMM	UM	IA-MA-ḪA-MU-UM		M
	1	JA	WŠIB		U				IA-AW-ŠI-BU		M
	1	JA	WṢIʾ						I-IA-U$_2$-ZI	FN	XIII 1 X 29
		JA	WṢIʾ						U$_2$-ZI		M
		JA	WṢIʾ				ʾEL		IA-A[W-Z]I-EL?		VIII 87 8'
		JA	WṢIʾ				ʾIL		IA-AW-ZI-DINGIR		M+
		JA	WṢIʾ				ʾIL		IA-U$_2$-ZI-DINGIR		B 31
		JA	WṢIʾ				ʾIL		IA-U$_2$-ṢI-DINGIR		BAGHD. MITT. II 23
		JA	WṢIʾ				ʾIL	UM	IA-U$_2$-ZI-LUM		B 31
		JA	WṢIʾ				ʾALAŠ	UM	U$_2$-ZI-A-LA-ŠUM		M
		JA	WṢIʾ				ŠUM	U			
							ʾAB	UM	U$_2$-ṢI-SU-MU-A-BU-UM		AJSL XXVIII 244 19
	1	JA	JʿIL				LIʾM		IA-ḪI-IL-LI-IM		M
	1	JA	JʿUL				DAGAN		IA-ḪU-UL-D-DA-GAN		RA LXV 48 VII 75
	1	JA	JBIL				JIRR	A	IA-BI-IL-WI-IR-RA		B 24
		JA	JBIL		I		....		IA-BI-LI-[....]		FM 3998 SEAL
	1	JA	JBIŠ		UM				IA-BI-ŠUM		B 24+
		JA	JBIŠ		U				IA-BI-ŠU		A 29366:10
	1	JA	JDIʿ		UM				IA-DI-ḪU-UM		B 25+
		JA	JDIʿ		U				IA-DI-U$_2$		CT VIII 10 B 7+
		JA	JDIʿ		IM				IA-DI-ḪI-IM	GEN	M+
		JA	JDIʿ				....		IA-DI-[....]	FN	M
		JA	JDIʿ	AT	UM				IA-DI-ḪA-TUM	FN	B 25+
		JA	JDIʿ	AH					IA-DI-ḪA	FN	M+
		JA	JDIʿ				ʾAB	UM	IA-DI-ḪA-BU-UM		B 25+
		JA	JDIʿ				ʾAB	UM	IA-DI-A-BU-UM		M, YOS XII+
		JA	JDIʿ				ʾAB	UM	IA-DU-A-BU-UM		YOS XII+
		JA	JDIʿ				ʾAB	U	IA-DI-ḪA-BU		PBS XIV 1084
		JA	JDIʿ				ʾAB	U	IA-DI-A-BU		YOS XII+
		JA	JDIʿ				ʾAB	UM	IA-DI-ḪA-A-BU-U[M]		RA LXV 45 V 9
		JA	JDIʿ				ʾAB	IM	IA-DI-ḪA-A-BI-IM	GEN	M+
		JA	JDIʿ				ʾFL	UM	IA-DI-ḪI-E-LUM		UNPUBL.
		JA	JDIʿ				ʾIL		IA-DI-IḪ-DINGIR		B 25+
		JA	JDIʿ				ʾIL		IA-DI-DINGIR		M
		JA	JDIʿ				DAGAN		I[A]-DI-D-DA-GAN		B 25
		JA	JDIʿ		A		ʾEL		IA-DI-ḪA-EL		KISURRA 10A 4
	1	JA	JPAʿ						IA-A-PA-AḪ		M+
		JA	JPAʿ						IA-PA		A.
		JA	JPAʿ		UM				IA-PA-ḪU-UM		RA LXVI 118:16
		JA	JPAʿ		UM				[I]A-PA-ḪU-UM	FN	RA LXV 64 VI 8
		JA	JPAʿ	AT	UM				IA-PA-ḪA-TUM	FN	M+
		JA	JPAʿ	AH					IA-PA-ḪA	FN	M+
		JA	JPAʿ				HADD	U	IA-A-PA-AḪ-D-IM		M+
		JA	JPAʿ				HADD	U	IA-PA-ḪA-D-IM		M
		JA	JPAʿ				HADD	U	IA-PA-AḪ-D-IM		M+
		JA	JPAʿ				ʾIL		IA-PA-AḪ-DINGIR		RA LXV 51 IX 74
		JA	JPAʿ				ʾIL		IA-PA-DINGIR		B 29
		JA	JPAʿ				DAGAN		IA-PA-AḪ-D-DA-GAN		XIII 58 5+
		JA	JPAʿ				LIʾM		IA-A-PA-AḪ-LI-IM		M+
		JA	JPAʿ				LIʾM		IA-PA-AḪ-LI-IM		M+
		JA	JPAʿ				ŠUM	U			
							ʾAB	I	IA-PA-AḪ-SU-MU-A-BI		A. 56 47
	2		ʾAB		I	JA	JPAʿ		A-BI-IA-PA-AḪ	FN	XIII 1 II 57
		JI	JṢIʾ			JA	JPAʿ		I-ZI-A-PA-AḪ		B 22
		JA	LʾIJ			JA	JPAʿ		IA-AL-E-PA-AḪ		M
			NIQM		I	JA	JPAʿ		NI-IQ-MI-PA		A. 27 12
			NIQM		I	JA	JPAʿ		NI-IQ-ME-PA		A.+
			ŠUM		U	JA	JPAʿ		[SU-MU]-A-PA-AḪ		B 38
	1	JA	JPIʿ				HADD	U	IA-BI-IḪ-D-IM		M
	1	JA	JPUʿ		UM				IA-PU-ḪU-UM		B 25+
		JA	JPUʿ		U				IA-PU-ḪU		B 25
		JA	JPUʿ	AT	UM				IA-PU-ḪA-TUM	FN	C+
		JA	JPUʿ		AJA				IA-PU-ḪA-IA	FN	C+
	2		ʾAB		I	JA	JPUʿ		A-BI-IA-PU-UḪ		B 10
			BAʿL		I	JA	JPUʿ		BA-LI-A-PU-UḪ		HARRIS 96 6+

JA	2			BAʿL		I		JA	JPUʿ			BA-LI-PU-UḪ$_2$		EDZARD, DER 117:38 DATE
				ŠUM		U	NA	JA	JPUʿ		A	SU-MU-NA-IA-PU-ḪA-[....]		M
				ŠAMŠ		I		JA	JPUʿ	AT		D-UTU-IA-PU-ḪA-AT	FN?	BM 17075
	1	JA		JQAH					ʿAMM		U	IA-QA-AM-MU		A.+
	1	JA		JQIR	AN	U						IA-KI-RA-NU		M
		JA		JQIR		A			ʾAB		UM	IA-KI-RA-A-BU-UM		RA LXV 47 VII 30
	1	JA		JRID		UM						IA-RI-DU-UM		UCP X/1 109 3
	1	JA		JŠIR		UM						IA-SI-RUM		B 30+
		JA		JŠIR		UM						IA-ŠI-RU-[UM]		A 22002
		JA		JŠIR	T	IM						IA-ŠIR-TI-IM	MN GEN	WATERMAN 45 R. 10
		JA		JŠIR					HEDD		A	IA-ŠE-RE-DA		A. 367 5
		JA		JŠIR					HEDD		A	IA-AŠ-RI-E-DA		A.+
	1	JA		JŠUʿ		UM						IA-ŠU-ḪU-UM		B 30+
		JA		JŠUʿ	AT	UM						IA-ŠU-ḪA-TUM	FN	RA LXV 58 I 17; B 30+
		JA		JŠUʿ	AH							IA-ŠU-ḪA	FN	M+
		JA		JŠUʿ					ʾIL			IA-ŠU-DINGIR		RA LXIV 36 NO. 31
	2			ʾAḪ		I		JA	JŠUʿ			A-ḪI-IA-ŠU-UḪ		SIMMONS 58 16
				ʾAḪ		I		JA	JŠUʿ			A-ḪI-IA-ŠU		BIROT, TEA 28:17+
				ʾAB		I		JA	JŠUʿ			A-BI-ŠU-UḪ		B 10
				ʾAB		I		JA	JŠUʿ		A	A-BI-IA-ŠU-ḪA		B 10
				ʾAB		I		JA	JŠUʿ					
									....			A-BI-ŠU-UT-LI		B 11
		JA		NŠIʾ				JA	JŠUʿ			IA-SI-SU-UḪ		BIN II 104 15
	1	JA		JṢIʾ					HADD		U	IA-ZI-D-IM		M
		JA		JṢIʾ					ʾIL			IA-ZI-DINGIR		M+
		JA		JṢIʾ					ʾIL			IA-ṢI-DINGIR		JCS IV 109 4311 21
		JA		JṢIʾ					ʾIL		UM	IA-ZI-LUM-KI	GN	B 32
		JA		JṢIʾ					JARAḪ			IA-ZI-E-RA-AḪ		B 32, C
		JA		JṢIʾ					ʾAŠAR			IA-ZI-A-ŠAR		SZLECHTER TJ P. 186
		JA		JṢIʾ					DAGAN			IA-ZI-D-DA-GAN		B 31 HANA, M
		JA		JṢIʾ					QAṬAR			IA-ṢI-QA-TAR		B 30
	2			ʾAWIJ				JA	JṢIʾ			A-WI-IA-ZI		RA LXV 53 XI 49
	1	JA		JTIR		A						IA-TE-RA	GEN	A.
		JA		JTIR					HEDD		A	IA-TE-IR-E-DA		A.+
		JA		JTIR					HEDD		A	IA-TE-RI-DA		A.+
		JA		JTIR					ḤAM		U	IA-TI-RA-MU		A. 235 4 LATE
		JA		JTIR					NAN		UM	JA-TI-IR-NA-NU-UM		M+
		JA		JTIR					NAN		AM	JA-TI-IR-NA-NAM	ACC	M
		JA		JTIR					NAN		AM	JA-TE-IR-NA-NAM	ACC	M
		JA		JTIR					NAN		IM	JA-TI-IR-NA-NIM	GEN	M+
		JA		JTIR					NAN		IM	JA-TE-IR-NA-NIM	GEN	M
		JA		JTIR					NAZI			JA-TE-IR-NA-ZI		SYRIA XX 174 MARI
	1	JA		BḤAR		UM						IA-AB-ḪA-RU-UM		B 24
		JA		BḤAR					....			IA-AB-ḪA-AR-[....]		M
		JA		BḤAR					HADD		U	IA-AB-ḪA-AR-D-IM		M
	1	JA		BWAʾ								IA-BA-A		WATERMAN 36 R. 14
		JA		BWAʾ	AT	UM						IA-BA-TUM		AJSL XXXIII 237 16
		JA		BWAʾ					ʾIL			IA-BA-DINGIR?		MEISSNER 36 25
		JA		BWAʾ					ʾIL			IA-BA-A?-DINGIR		M
		JA		EWAʾ					ʿAN		UM	IA-BA-A-NU-UM		B 45
	1	JA		BJIN		UM						IA-BI-NU-UM		XIII 38 13
		JA		BJIN		IM						IA-BI-NI-IM	GEN	M+
	1	JA		BJIR		UM						IA-BI-RUM		M
	1	JA	T	BAḤAR			NA					IA-AB-TA-ḪA-AR-NA	GN	M+
	1	JA		BANIJ					ʾIL			IA-BA-AN-NI-DINGIR		M+
		JA		BANIJ					ʾIL			IA-AB-BA-AN-NI-DINGIR		M
	1	JA		BAŠIJ					DAGAN			IA-BA-SI-D-DA-GAN		M
	1	JA		BLIJ			JA					IA-AB-LI-IA-KI	GN	M+
		JA		BLIJ	AT	UM						IA-AB-LI-IA-TUM	FN	B 25+
	1	JA		BLIM		UM						JA-AB-LI-MU-UM		RUTTEN 2 17+
	1	JA		BLUW					DAGAN			IA-AB-LU-D-DA-GAN		M
	1	JA		BLUṬ	AN	U						IA-AB-LU-TA-NU		MRS VI P. 261+
	1	JA		BNAḪ								JA-AB-NA-AḪ		M
	1	JA		BNIJ					HADD		U	IA-AB-NI-D-IM		M
		JA		BNIJ					DAGAN			IA-AB-NI-D-DA-GAN		M+
	1	JA		BNIQ					ʾIL			IA-AB-NI-IQ-DINGIR		B 25

JA	1 JA	BRUQ				ʾIL			IA-AB-RU-UQ-DINGIR		BASOR 95, 19
	JA	BRUQ				ʾAB	UM		A-AB-RU-UK-A-BU-UM		JCS XXVI 151:13, HARMAL
	JA	BRUQ				LIʾM			IA-AB-RU-UQ-LI-IM		TCL XI 156 12
	1 JA	BZUW			HU				IA-AB-ZU-U$_2$		CT IV 30D 10+
	1 JA	DWIR		UM					[IA-DI]-RU-U[M]		B 25
	JA	DWIR	AT	UM					[IA-DI]-RA-TUM		B 25
	JA	DWIR		I					IA-DI-RI	NOM	B 25 HANA
	1 JA	DWUR		IM					IA-DU-RI-IM	GEN	M
	JA	DWUR	AN						IA-DU-RA-AN		M
	JA	DWUR				ʾIL			IA-DU-UR-DINGIR		M
	JA	DWUR				LIʾM			IA-DU-UR-LI-I[M]		RA LXV 45 V 82
	JA	DWUR				NAŠIʾ			IA-DU-UR-NA-SI		M+
	1 JA	DJIN		IM					IA-DI-NIM	GEN	M+
	JA	DJIN				HADD	U		IA-DI-IN-D-IM		RA LXV 44 IV 51+
	1 JA	DLUW			HU				A-AD-LU-U$_2$		HARRIS 70 15+
	1 JA	DRUK		A					IA-AD-RU-QA		A. LATE
	1 JA	D̲KUR				ʾIL			A-AD-KU-UR-DINGIR		HARRIS 10 18
	JA	D̲KUR				ʾIL			IA-AD-GUR-DINGIR		SUMER V 142 8+
	JA	D̲KUR				ʾIL			IA-AD-KUR-DINGIR		SUMER V 141
	JA	D̲KUR				ʾIL			A-AD-KUR-DINGIR		SIMMONS 80 13
	JA	D̲KUR				ʾIL			IA-AD-KU?-UR?-DINGIR		VAS IX 58 15
	1 JA	D̲RAʿ		UM					IA-AZ-RA-ḪU-UM		XIV 77:8
	JA	D̲RAʿ				HADD	U		IA-AZ-RA-AḪ-D-IM		M+
	JA	D̲RAʿ				ʾIL			IA-AZ-RA-AḪ-DINGIR		VIII 100 15+
	JA	D̲RAʿ				DAGAN			IA-AZ-RA-AḪ-D-DA-GAN		XIII 123 26
	1 JA	D̲RIʿ		UM					IA-AZ?-RI-ḪU-[UM]		PBS XIII 56:4
	1 JA	GJIḪ	AN						IA-G[I]-ḪA-A[N]		M
	JA	GJIḪ				ḪAʾL	UM		IA-GI?-ḪA-LUM		RUTTEN 16 18
	JA	GJIḪ				HADD	U		IA-GI-IḪ-D-IM		M+
	JA	GJIḪ				HADD	U		IA-GI-ḪA-D-IM		M
	1 JA	GJID				LIʾM			IA-GI-ID-LI-IM		M+
	1 JA	GMUR				....			IA-AG-MU-UR-[....]		M
	JA	GMUR				ʾIL			IA-AG-MU-UR-DINGIR		M
	1 JA	KWIN				HADD	U		IA-KI-IN-D-IM		M
	JA	KWIN				ʾIL			JA-KI-IN-DINGIR		JEA VII 196
	JA	KWIN				LU		HU	IA-KI-IN-LU-U$_2$		TALLQUIST APN 95 LATE
	1 JA	KWUN		UM					IA-KU-NU-UM		B 27+
	JA	KWUN		UM					IA-A-KU-NU-UM		B 27
	JA	KWUN		U					IA-KU-NU		B 27+
	JA	KWUN		AM					IA-KU-NA-AM	ACC	CT VIII 36D 7
	JA	KWUN		IM					IA-KU-NIM	GEN	B 28, M+
	JA	KWUN	AN						JA-GU-NA-AN		U
	JA	KWUN	AN						IA-KU-NA-AN		M+
	JA	KWUN				ʾAHL	I		IA-KU-UN-A-LI		B 92
	JA	KWUN				HADD	U		IA-KU-UN-D-IM		B 27, M+
	JA	KWUN				ʾIL			IA-KU-UN-DINGIR		M
	JA	KWUN				ʿALAṢ	I		IA-KU-UN-ḪA-LA-ZI		RA LXV 44 IV 41;43
	JA	KWUN				ʿAMM	U		IA-KU-UN-AM-MU		B 27
	JA	KWUN				ḪARAR			IA-KU-UN-ḪA-RA-AR		VAS IX 172 4+
	JA	KWUN				ḪARAR	I		IA-KU-[UN-ḪA]-RA-RI	GEN	BM 81641 6
	JA	KWUN				ḪARAR	I		IA-KUN$_3$-ḪA-RA-RI		CT XLVIII 3:3
	JA	KWUN				ʾAŠD	UM		IA-KU-UN-AŠ-DU-UM		B 27
	JA	KWUN				ʾAŠAR			IA-KU-UN-A-ŠAR		B 92+, M+
	JA	KWUN				ʾAŠAR	I		IA-KU-UN-A-ŠA-RI	NOM	CT XLVIII 10 6
	JA	KWUN				ʾAŠAR	UM		IA-KU-UN-A-ŠA-RU-UM		B 27
	JA	KWUN				BAʿL			IA-KU-BA-AL		RA LXV 44 V 7
	JA	KWUN				DIWR	UM		IA-KU-UN-DI-RUM		CT XLVIII 115
	JA	KWUN				DIWR	IM		IA-KU-UN-DI-[R]I-IM	GEN	M
	JA	KWUN				DIWR	I		IA-KU-UN-DI-RI	GEN	CT XLVIII 115 CASE
	JA	KWUN				DIWR			IA-KU-UN-DI-IR		M+
	JA	KWUN				DIWR			IA-KU-DI-IR		RA LXV 45 V 14
	JA	KWUN				DAGAN			IA-KU-UN-D-DA-GAN		X 171 3
	JA	KWUN				LIʾM			IA-KU-UN-LI-IM		M+
	JA	KWUN				LIʾM			IA-KU-LI-IM		M+

PREFIXES, Class 1

JA	1	JA	KWUN				MEʾR				IA-KU-UN-ME-IR			M+	
		JA	KWUN				MAṬAR				IA-KU-MA-DAR			SYMB.BOHL P.36?:6	
		JA	KWUN				PI				IA-KU-UN-PI			CT VIII 43C 8	
		JA	KWUN				PI				IA-KU-BI			B 27	
		JA	KWUN				PI				IA-KU-PI			B 27	
		JA	KWUN				PI		I	JA	IA-KU-UN-BI-IA			XII 14	
		JA	KWUN				PI								
							MAM		A		IA-KU-UN-BI-D-MA-MA	FN		RA LXV 66 VII 61	
		JA	KWUN				RAPIʾ				IA-KU-UN-RA-BI			M	
		JA	KWUN				ŠUM		U						
							ʾAB		IM		IA-KU-UN-SU-MU-A-BI-IM			M	
		JA	KWUN				ŠARR		UM		IA-KU-UN-ŠAR-RU-UM			B 28	
	1	JA	KBUR		IM						IA-AK-BU-RI-IM	GEN		B 27	
	1	JA	KLIL		UM						A-AK-LI-LUM			HARRIS 28 11	
	1	JA	KMIN		I						IA-AK-ME-NI			JNES XIII 210+	LATE
	1	JA	KMIS		I						IA-AK-ME-SI			JCS XIII 210+	LATE
	1	JA	KNUW				ŠARR		UM		IA-AK-NU-ŠA-RU-UM			KISURRA 47A 4+	
		JA	KNUW				ŠARR		U		IA-AK-NU-ŠA-RU			TIM III 133 9	
	1	JA	KRUB				ʾIL				D-IA-AK-RU-UB-DINGIR	DN		M+	
		JA	KRUB				ʾEL				D-IA-AK-RU-UB-EL	DN		M+	
		JA	KRUB				ʾIL				D-IA-AK-RU-UB-IL	DN		M+	
		JA	KRUB				ʾIL								
							TILL	AT	I		D-IA-AK-RU-UB-DINGIR-TIL-LA-TI			M	
	1	JA	KSIJ				ʾIL				IA-AK-ZI-DINGIR			SIMMONS 92 16	
		JA	KSIJ				ʾIL				A-AK-ZI-DINGIR			FIGULLA CAT I 14029	
	1	JA	KŠIJ				....				IA-AK-SI-DINGIR-....			DE GEN. KICH II D47+	
	1	JA	LʾAʾ				KULIM				IA-AL-A-KU-LIM			RA LXV 55 XIII 18	
	1	JA	LʾIJ								IA-AL-E			RA LXV 46 VI 50	
		JA	LʾIJ			JA	JPAʿ				IA-AL-E-PA-AḪ			M	
		JA	LʾIJ				DAGAN				IA-AL-E-D-DA-GAN			M+	
		JA	LʾIJ				DAGAN				IA-[AL]?-I-D-DA-GAN			RA LXV 47 VII 23	
	1	JA	LʾUM		U						IA-AL-U$_2$-MU			XIII 36 20	
	1	JA	LEʾEJ								IA$_3$-LE-E			U	
	1	JA	MʾAD								IA-AM-ḪA-AD-KI	GN		M+	
		JA	MʾAD								IA-AM-A-AD	GN		A. 377 8	
		JA	MʾAD		U						IA-AM-ḪA-DU	GN		XII 747 4	
		JA	MʾAD		U						IA$_3$-A-MA-TU			U	
		JA	MʾAD		UM						IA-AM-ḪA-DU-UM-KI	GN		M+	
		JA	MʾAD		I						IA$_3$-A-MA-TI			U	
		JA	MʾAD		IM						IA-AM-ḪA-DI-IM-KI	GN	GEN	M+	
		JA	MʾAD	AJ	I						IA-AM-ḪA-DA-I-KI	GN	GEN	M	
		JA	MʾAD	IJ	I						IA-AM-ḪA-DI-I-KI	GN	NOM	M	
		JA	MʾAD	IJ	I						IA-AM-ḪA-DI-JI	GN	NOM	M	
		JA	MʾAD	IJ	UM						IA$_3$-A-MA-TI-UM			U	
	1	JA	MʾID				ʾADM		I		IA-AM-I-ID-D-AD-MI			A. 60 4	
	1	JA	MWUʾ		A						IA-MU-U$_2$-A			KISURRA 33 3	
	1	JA	MWUŠ		I		ʾIL				IA-MU-ŠI-DINGIR			B 28	
		JA	MWUŠ		I		ʾIL				IA-A-MU-ŠI-DINGIR			VAS VII 166 4 LATE	
	1	JA	MWUT		UM						IA$_3$-A-MU-TUM			U	
		JA	MWUT				ḤAMAD				IA-MU-UT-ḪA-MA-AD			X 174 18	
		JA	MWUT				ḤAMAD		I		IA-MU-UT-ḪA-MA-DI	FN		XIII 1 VI 51	
		JA	MWUT				BAʿL				IA-MU-UT-BA-AL	GN		M+	
		JA	MWUT				BAʿL		UM		IA-MU-UT-BA-LUM-KI	GN		B 28+	
		JA	MWUT				BAʿL		UM		IA-MU-UT-BA-A-LUM-KI	GN		RLA II 194	
		JA	MWUT				BAʿL		IM		IA-MU-UT-BA-LI-IM	GN	GEN	YOS II 49 12+	
		JA	MWUT				BAʿL		IM		IA-MU-UT-BA-LIM	GN	GEN	BAGHD. MITT. II 56+	
		JA	MWUT				BAʿL	AJ	I		IA-MU-UT-BA-LA-I	GN	NOM	M	
		JA	MWUT				BAʿL	AJ	I		IA-MU-UT-BA-LA-JI	GN	NOM	M	
		JA	MWUT				BAʿL	IJ	I		IA-MU-UT-BA-LI-I	GN	ACC	M	
		JA	MWUT				DAWD		U		IA-MU-UT-DA-DU			RA LXV 51 X 11	
		JA	MWUT				DIWR		UM		IA-MU-UT-DI-RUM			WATERMAN 14 9	
		JA	MWUT				KULUP				IA-MU-UT-KU-LU-UP			DELAPORTE, CCL II A 418	
		JA	MWUT				LIʾM				IA-MU-UT-LI-IM			B 28+	
		JA	MWUT				LIʾM		U		IA-MU-UT-LI-MU			TCL XI 182 10	
		JA	MWUT				MIʾR		UM		IA-MU-UT-MI-RUM			RA LXV 52 X 41	
		JA	MWUT				NIWR		I		IA-MU-UT-NI-RI	FN		A.	

PREFIXES, Class 1

JA	2			ʾAB		I	JA	MWUT	A		A-BI-IA-MU-TA		BM 80328 15
				ʾAB		I	JA	MWUT	I		A-BI$_2$-A-MU-TI		U
				ʾIL		I	JA	MWUT			I$_3$-LI$_2$-IA-MU-[UT]		RA LXV 40 I 29
		JI		PTIḤ			JA	MWUT	A		IP-TI-IA-MU-TA		BM 80328 11
				ŠUM		U	JA	MWUT					
								BAʿL	A		SU-MU-IA-MU-UT-BA-[LA]		RUTTEN 3 21
				ŠUM		U	JA	MWUT					
								BAʿL	IM		SU-MU-IA-MU-UT-BA-LIM	GEN	CT XLIII 86 1
				ŠUM		U	JA	MWUT	U				
								BAʿL	A		[SU]-MU-IA-MU-TU-BA-LA		PBS XI/2 1 I 19
				TUPT		I	JA	MWUT	A		TU-UP-TI-IA-MU-TA		BM 80328 2
	1	JA	T	MAQAṬ							IA-AM-DA-GA-AD		B 28
	1	JA	T	MAQṬ		AM					IA-AM-TA-AQ-TA-AM	ACC	ABB V 39 REV 8'
	1	JA		MATIʿ				ʾIL			IA-MA-AT-TI-DINGIR		M+
		JA		MATIʿ				ʾIL			IA-MA-TI-DINGIR		XII 5 3
	1	JA		MKUS		U		....			IA-AM-KU-UZ-ZU-....		BM 80328 3
	1	JA		MLIʾ				ʾIL			A-AM-LI-DINGIR		YOS XIII 63:3, 6
	1	JA		MLIK	AN						IA-AM-LI-KA-AN		M
		JA		MLIK				HADD	U		IA-AM-LIK-D-IM		RA LXV 40 I 31
		JA		MLIK				ʾIL			IA-AM-LI-IK-DINGIR		B 28+
		JA		MLIK				ʾIL			IA-AM-LIK-DINGIR		B 28+, M
		JA		MLIK				ʾIL			A-AM-LIK-DINGIR		HARRIS 76 22
	2			ʾIL		I	JA	MLIK			I$_3$-LI$_2$-A-AM-LIK		HARRIS 49 12
	1	JA		MQUṬ		U					IA-AM-KU-DU		M
		JA		MQUṬ		U					I-AM-KU-DU		M
	1	JA		MRAṢ							IA-AM-RA-AṢ		BM 81591 6
		JA		MRAṢ		UM					A-AM-RA-ZUM		HARRIS 45 10
		JA		MRAṢ				ʾIL			IA-AM-RA-AṢ-DINGIR		M+
		JA		MRAṢ		I		ʾIL			IA-AM-RA-ZI-DINGIR		M
	1	JA		MRUṢ				ʾIL			IA-AM-RU-UṢ-DINGIR		B 28
		JA		MRUṢ				ʾIL			IA-AM-RU-IṢ-DINGIR		M
		JA		MRUṢ		I		ʾIL	UM		I-IA-AM-RU-UṢ-ZI-I-LU-UM		B 21
	1	JA		MSIR		U					IA-AM-ZI-RU		UCP X/1 50 9
	1	JA		MŠIJ				ʾIL			IA-AM-SI-DINGIR		B 28+
	1	JA		MṢIʾ		UM					IA-AM-ZI-JU-UM?		M
		JA		MṢIʾ				ʿADN	U		IA-AM-ZI-AD-[NU]		CT VI 33A 33
		JA		MṢIʾ				ʿADN	U		IA-AM-ṢI-AD-NU		BM 16914 31
		JA		MṢIʾ				ʿADN	U		IA-AM-ZI-ḪA-AD-NU		M+
		JA		MṢIʾ				ʿADN	U	HU	IA-AM-ZI-AD-NU-U$_2$		BM 81302 4
		JA		MṢIʾ				ʿADN	U	HU	IA-AM-ZI-ḪA-AD-NU-U$_2$		DELAPORTE CCL II A 385, M+
		JA		MṢIʾ				ʾIL			IA-AM-ZI-DINGIR		B 28, M
		JA		MṢIʾ				ʾIL			IA-AM-ṢI-DINGIR		B 28+
	1	JA		MṬAR		UM					IA-AM-TA-RU-[UM]		TIM V 63:12
	1	JA		MZUʾ				ʿADN	IM		[IA?-AM?-Z]U?-ḪA-AD-NIM	GEN	XIII 129 5
		JA		MZUʾ				ʿADN	U	HU	IA-AM-ZU-AD-NU-U$_2$		B 28+
		JA		MZUʾ				MALIK			IA-AM-ZU-MA-LIK		B 28
	1	JA		NḪAB		UM					IA-ḪA-BU-UM		YOS XII
		JA		NḪAB				ʾIL			IA-AḪ-ḪA-AB-DINGIR		C+
		JA		NḪAB				ʿAMM	U		IA-ḪA-AB-ḪA-MU		M
	1	JA		NḪAN		A					IA-AN-ḪA-NA	GEN	MRS VI P. 334
	1	JA		NḪIB		UM					IA-ḪI-BU-UM		SIMMONS 46 3
	1	JA		NḪIR		AJA					A-AN?-ḪI?-RA-A		HARRIS 85 16
	1	JA		NḪUR		UM					IA-AN-ḪU-RU-UM		SIMMONS 103 2
	1	JA		NWIḪ	AH						IA-NI-ḪA	FN	RA LXV 58 I 55
	1	JA		NWUḪ	AN						IA-NU-ḪA-AN		RA LXV 40 I 43
		JA		NWUḪ				LIʾM			IA-NU-UḪ-LI-IM		RA LXV 44 V 8
		JA		NWUḪ				ŠAMAR			IA-NU-UḪ-SA-MAR		CT XLIII 58 3, M
	1	JA		NWUD				....			IA-NU-UD-[....]		M
		JA		NWUD				LIʾM			IA-NU-UD-LI-IM		M
	1	JA		NWUP		UM					IA-NU-BU-UM		B 29+
	1	JA		NWUR		UM					IA-NU-RU-UM		RUTTEN 11 10+
	1	JA		NWUZ		UM					IA$_2$-A-NU-ZU-UM		U
	1	JA		NABIʾ		IM					IA-NA-BI-IM	GEN	M
		JA		NABIʾ				ʾEL			IA-NA-BI-EL		M+
		JA		NABIʾ				ʾIL			IA-NA-AB-BI-DINGIR		M+
		JA		NABIʾ				ʾIL			IA-NA-BI-DINGIR		M

PREFIXES, Class 1

JA	1	JA	T	NAQIM						IA-AN-TA-KI-IM		M+
	1	JA		NBIʾ			HADD	U		IA-AB-BI-D-IM		M
		JA		NBIʾ			ʾIL	UM		IA'$_2$-AN-BI$_2$-I$_3$-LUM		U
		JA		NBIʾ			DAGAN			IA-AB-BI-D-DA-GAN		M+
		JA		NBIʾ			DAGAN			IA-BI-D-DA-GAN		M
		JA		NBIʾ			NAʿIM			I-A-BI-NA-IM	NOM, GEN	BAHREIN UNPUB, POST U.
	1	JA		NBUL	I					IA$_2$-AN-BU-LI		U
	1	JA		NDUR	UM					IA-AN-DU-RUM?		TIM II 37 1
	1	JA		NGIH						IA-AN-GI		JNES XIII 210+ LATE
	1	JA		NQIM			HADD	U		IA-AK-KI-IM-D-IM		M+
		JA		NQIM			HADD	U		IA-KI-IM-D-IM		M+
		JA		NQIM			ʾIL			IA-AN?-KI-IM-DINGIR		RA VIII 69 22
		JA		NQIM			ʾIL			A-AN-KI-IM-DINGIR		HARRIS 9 14+
		JA		NQIM			LIʾM			IA-AK-KI-IM-LI-IM		M
		JA		NQIM			LIʾM			IA-KI-IM-LI-IM		M
	1	JA		NŠIʾ	AN					IA-AŠ$_2$-SI-IA-AN		M
		JA		NŠIʾ			HADD	U		IA-AŠ$_2$-ŠI-D-IM		RA LXV 42 III 13
		JA		NŠIʾ			HADD	U		IA-SI-D-IM		B 29
		JA		NŠIʾ			ʾIL			IA-SI-DINGIR		B 29+
		JA		NŠIʾ			ʾIL	I		IA-SI-LI		B 29+
		JA		NŠIʾ			ʾIL	I		IA-SI-I-LI$_2$		TCL X 5 3
		JA		NŠIʾ			ʾIL	UM		IA-SI-LUM		RA IX 22 2+
		JA		NŠIʾ			ʿAMM	U		IA-SI-ḪA-MU		M
		JA		NŠIʾ			JARAḪ			IA-SI-E-RA-AḪ		B 28
		JA		NŠIʾ			JARAḪ			IA-SI-RA-AḪ		B 30
		JA		NŠIʾ			JARAḪ			IA-SI-A-RA-AḪ		GRANT, HAV. 242:2+
		JA		NŠIʾ		JA	JŠUʿ			IA-SI-SU-UḪ		BIN II 104 15
		JA		NŠIʾ			DAGAN			IA-AŠ$_2$-SI-D-DA-GAN		M+
		JA		NŠIʾ			DAGAN			IA-SI-D-DA-GAN		M+
		JA		NŠIʾ			LIʾM			IA$_2$-ŠI-LI-IM		U+
	2			MUT	U	JA	NŠUʾ		HU	MU-TU-A-AN-ŠU-U$_2$		KISURRA 91 24
	1	JA		NṢIB	UM					IA-AN-ZI-BU-UM		M+
		JA		NṢIB	IM					IA-AN-ZI-BI-IM	GEN	M+
		JA		NṢIB	AN					IA-AN-ZI-BA-AN		M
		JA		NṢIB	AN					IA-AN-ZI-PA-AN		M
		JA		NṢIB			....			IA-AN-ZI-IB-[....]		M+
		JA		NṢIB			....			IA-AN-ZI-IB-D-[....]		M
		JA		NṢIB			HADD	U		IA-AN-ZI-IB-D-IM		M+
		JA		NṢIB			ʾIL			IA-AN-Z[I-I]B-DINGIR		XII 683 4
		JA		NṢIB			DAGAN			IA-AN-ZI-IB-D-DA-GAN		M+
		JA		NṢIB			DAGAN			IA-AZ-ZI-IB-D-DA-GAN		B 29
	1	JA		NṢUR			HADD	U		IA-AṢ-ṢU-UR-D-IM		X 12 6, 21+
	1	JA		NTIN	UM					IA-AN-TI-NU-UM		B 29+
		JA		NTIN	UM					A-AN-TI-NU-UM		SIMMONS 79 6'
		JA		NTIN	UM					IA-AN-TE-NU-UM		SIMMONS 104 13
		JA		NTIN	U					IA-AN-TI-NU		M
		JA		NTIN	U					IA-TI-NU		B 31
		JA		NTIN	U					IA-AT-TI-NU		YOS XIII 280:13
		JA		NTIN	IM					IA-AN-TI-NIM	GEN	M
		JA		NTIN	IM					IA-AT-TI-NIM	GEN	M+
		JA		NTIN			....			IA-AN-TI-IN-D-[....]		M
		JA		NTIN			HADD	U		IA-AN-TI-IN-D-IM		M+
		JA		NTIN			HADD	U		IA-AN-TI-NA-DU		ZDPV XLIX PL. 45 LATE
		JA		NTIN			ʾIL			IA-AN-TI-IN-DINGIR		B 29+, M+
		JA		NTIN			ʾIL			IA-AT-TI-IN-DINGIR		M
		JA		NTIN			ʾIL			[A-A]N-TI-IN-DINGIR		HARRIS 56 15
		JA		NTIN	I		ʾIL			IA-AN-TI-NI-DINGIR		BM 17084
		JA		NTIN			ʿAMM	U		IA-AN-TI-IN-ḪA-MU		M
		JA		NTIN			ʾANN	I	Š	[IA-AN]-TI-IN-A-NI-IŠ		VII 180 8'
		JA		NTIN			JARAḪ			IA-AN-TI-IN-A-RA-AḪ		RA LXV 62 V 34
		JA		NTIN			JARAḪ			IA-AN-TI-NA-RA-AḪ		RUTTEN 11 20+
		JA		NTIN			JARAḪ			IA-AN-TI-LA-RA-AḪ		VAS XVI 91 3
		JA		NTIN			JARAḪ			IA-AN-TI-IN-E-RA-AḪ		M+
		JA		NTIN			JARAḪ			IA-AT-TI-IN-E-RA-AḪ		M+
		JA		NTIN			JARAḪ			IA-T[I-I]N-E-RA-AḪ		M
		JA		NTIN			DAGAN			IA-AN-TI-IN-D-DA-GAN		M+

PREFIXES, Class 1

JA	1 JA	NTIN				DAGAN		IA-TI-IN-D-DA-GAN		M
	1 JA	NṮIᶜ		A				IA-AN-DI-ḪA-KI	GN	M
	1 JA	PḪUR		UM				IA-AP-ḪU-RU-UM		B 24
	JA	PḪUR		UM				IA-AP-ḪU-RUM		TIM IV 33 19, SEAL +
	JA	PḪUR	AN	U				IA-AP-ḪU-RA-NU		M
	JA	PḪUR				HADD	U	IA-AP-Ḫ[U-UR]-A-DU		M
	JA	PḪUR				JARAḪ		IA-AP-ḪU-UR-SIN		M
	JA	PḪUR				LIʾM		IA-AP-ḪU-UR-LI-IM		M+, A 7630
	1 JA	PATIḪ				....		IA-PA-TE-X		KISURRA 100 8
	1 JA	PDIJ		UM				IA-AP?-DI-UM		UNPUBL.
	1 JA	PLAḪ		UM				IA-AP-LA-ḪU-UM		B 24+
	JA	PLAḪ		U				IA-AP-LA-ḪU		B 24+
	JA	PLAḪ				....		IA-AP-LA-[AḪ?-....]		XIII 1 XII 23
	JA	PLAḪ				ʾIL		IA-AP-LA-AḪ-DINGIR		M, TIM III 56 5+
	JA	PLAḪ				ʾIL	IM	IA-AP-LA-AḪ-I-LI-IM	GEN	RA LXIV 43
	1 JA	PLIḪ				ʾIL		[I]A-AP-LI?-I[Ḫ?-DINGIR]		VII 215 32
	1 JA	PLUS		UM				IA-AP-LU-ZUM		SIMMONS 49 4
	JA	PLUS		I		ŠUM	I	IA-AP-LU-SI-SU-U_2-MI		BIROT,TEA 31:6
	1 JA	PQID		UM				IA-AP-KI?-DU-UM		CT XLVIII 29:2
	JA	PQID		IM				IA-AP-KI?-DI-IM	GEN	BE VI/1 8 34
	1 JA	PRUS				ʾAB	I	IA-AP-RU-US-A-BI		BAGHD. MITT. II 23
	1 JA	PTAḤ		UM				IA-AP-TA-ḪU-UM		WALTERS,WL 93:1
	JA	PTAḤ		U				IA-AP-TA-ḪU		YOS VIII 156 2, A. LATE
	1 JA	PṬIR		UM				IA-AP-DI-RUM		YOS XII
	1 JA	PṬUR		UM				IA-AP-TU-RU-UM	GN	JCS VII 52 II 3
	JA	PṬUR		I				IA-AP-TU-RI	GN GEN	M
	JA	PṬUR	AJ	I				IA-AP-TU-RA-A-JI-KI	GN	M
	JA	PṬUR	AJ	I				IA-AP-TU-RA-JI-KI	GN	M
	1 JA	QWIM	AT	UM				IA-KI-MA-TUM	FN	RA LXV 60 III 7
	JA	QWIM	AH					IA-KI-MA	FN	M+
	JA	QWIM				HADD	U	IA-KI-IN-D-IM		M+
	JA	QWIM				HADD	U	IA-GI-I[M]?-D-IM		IX 291 III 29'
	JA	QWIM				LIʾM		IA-KI-IM-LI-IM		M+
	1 JA	QWUJ		UM				IA-KU-UM		RUTTEN 6:3+; VIII 70:3, 8
	JA	QWUJ		UM				IA-KU-U_2-UM		RUTTEN 2:7+
	JA	QWUJ		U				IA-KU-U_2		RUTTEN 16:16
	JA	QWUJ			JA			IA-KU-IA		C+
	JA	QWUJ			JA			IA-KU-IA	FN	RA LXV 43 III 49
	1 JA	QBIJ		UM				IA-AQ-BU?-UM?		CT IV 30D 11
	JA	QBIJ		IM				IA-AQ-BI-IM	GEN	M
	JA	QBIJ				HADD	U	IA-AQ-BI-D-IM		RA LXV 43 III 38
	1 JA	QNIJ				ʾIL		IA-AQ-NI-DINGIR		CT XLV 92 I 10+
	1 JA	QRIʾ				ʾIL		IA-AQ-RI-DINGIR		B 27
	1 JA	QṢUR		UM				IA-AQ-ZU-RU-UM		BE VI/1 1 22+
	JA	QṢUR				ʾIL		IA-AQ-ZU-UR-DINGIR		B 29+
	1 JA	RḤAB		UM				IA-AR-ḪA-BU-UM		B 29+
	1 JA	RḤAM		UM				IA-AR-A-MU-UM		M+
	JA	RḤAM		U				IA-AR-ḪA-MU		B 29+, M
	JA	RḤAM	AN					IA-AR-ḪA-MA-AN	FN	RA LXV 55 XIII 51
	JA	RḤAM		I		ʾIL		IA-AR-ḪA-MI-DINGIR		KISURRA 5A 15+
	JA	RḤAM				ʾIL		IA-AR-ḪA-AN-DINGIR		B 29
	1 JA	RḤIB		UM				IA-AR-I-BU-UM		RA LXIV NO.33
	JA	RḤIB		U				IA-AR-I-BU		XIII 1 VI 63
	JA	RḤIB				ḪAJJ	A	IA-AR-IB-D-E_2-A		M+
	JA	RḤIB				ʾABB	A	IA-AR-IB-D-AB-BA		M
	JA	RḤIB				HADD	U	IA-AR-IB-D-IM		M+
	JA	RḤIB				ʾIL		IA-AR-I-IB-DINGIR		M+
	JA	RḤIB				ʾIL		IA-AR-IB-DINGIR		M+
	JA	RḤIB				ʾIRR	A	IA-AR-IB-D-IR_3-RA		M
	JA	RḤIB				ʾIRR	A	IA-AR-I-[IB]-IR_3-RA		M
	JA	RḤIB				DAGAN		IA-AR-IB-D-DA-GAN		M+
	1 JA	RḤIQ		UM				IA-AR-ḪI-KU-UM		A 32133:7
	1 JA	RᶜIJ				HADD	U	JA-RI-A-DU		RA LXV 50 VIII 64
	JA	RᶜIJ				ʾIL		IA-AR-ḪI-DINGIR		CT XLVIII 27
	1 JA	RᶜIŠ		UM				IA-RI-ŠUM		B 29
	1 JA	RWIḤ						IA-RI-IḪ	GN	M

JA	1 JA	RWIḪ	AJ	I					IA-RI-ḪA-JI-KI	GN	M
	JA	RWIḪ	IJ	I					IA-RI-ḪI-I-KI	GN	M+
	JA	RWIḪ		A			ʾAB	UM	IA-RI-ḪA-A-BU-UM		VII P. 234 N. 4
	JA	RWIḪ		A			ʾAB	AM	IA-RI-ḪA-A-BA-AM	ACC	XIV 101:8
	JA	RWIḪ		A			ʾAB	AM	IA-RI-ḪA-A-BA-AN	ACC	VII P. 234 N. 4
	JA	RWIḪ		A			ʾAB	IM	IA-RI-ḪA-A-BI-IM	GEN	M+
	JA	RWIḪ		A			ḪAM	U	IA-RI-ḪA-A-MU		M+
	1 JA	RWIJ		UM					IA-AR-WI-UM	NOM	KUPPER, NOM. P. 199
	JA	RWIJ					ʾIL		A-AR-WI-DINGIR		HARRIS 98 R. 7
	1 JA	RWIM					ḪAʾL		IA-RI-IM-ḪA-AL		M+
	JA	RWIM					HADD	U	IA-RI-IM-D-IM		M+
	JA	RWIM					ʿAMM	U	IA-RI-IM-ḪA-MU		M
	JA	RWIM					ʿAMM	U	IA-RI-IM-ḪA-AM-MU		M
	JA	RWIM					JARAḪ		IA-RI-IM-IA-RA-AḪ		RA LXV 41 II 28
	JA	RWIM					JARAḪ		IA-RI-IM-E-RA-AḪ		M
	JA	RWIM					DAWD	U	IA-RI-IM-DA-DU		RA LXV 40 I 38+
	JA	RWIM					DAGAN		IA-RI-IM-D-DA-GAN		M+
	JA	RWIM					LIʾM		IA-RI-IM-LI-IM		SIMMONS 66 77, M+, C+, A.+
	JA	RWIM					MALIK		IA-RI-IM-MA-LIK		A 3580:2+
	JA	RWIM					ŠUM	U			
							ʾAB	I	IA-RI-IM-SU-MU-A-BI		RA LXV 42 III 8
	2	ʾAŠD		U	NA	JA	RWIM		[AŠ$_2$-D]U-NI-A-RI-IM		CT XXXVI 4 1
		ŠUM		U	NA	JA	RWIM		SU-UM-MU-NA-A-RI-IM		HARRIS 57 11
	3	ŠUM		U			ʾAB	I			
						JA	RWIM		SU-MU-A-BI-A-RI-IM		TA 30 9, 14, 15+
		ŠUM		UM			ʾAB	I			
						JA	RWIM		SU-MU-UN-A-BI-IA-RI-IM		SUMER XXIII 153:9
		ŠUM		U	NA		ʾAB	I			
						JA	RWIM		SU-MU-NA-BI-IA-RI-IM		SUMER XXIII PL. 7 17+
		ŠUM		U	NA		ʾAB	I			
						JA	RWIM		SU-MU-UN?-A-BI-JA-RI-IM		SUMER XXIII P. 153 9
	1 JA	RJIB					HADD	U	IA-RI-IB-D-IM		B 29+
	JA	RJIB					DAGAN		IA-RI-IB-D-D[A-GAN]?		M
	1 JA	RBIJ					ʾEL		IA-AR-BI-EL		CT XLV 12 23
	JA	RBIJ					ʾIL		IA-AR-BI-DINGIR		B 29+
	JA	RBIJ					ʾIL		I-AR-BI-DINGIR		KISURRA 5A 8+
	1 JA	RBUʾ					ʾIL		IA-AR-BU-DINGIR		KISURRA 9A 9+
	1 JA	RKAB					HADD	U	IA-AR-KA-AB-D-IM		4E RENCONTRE 23
	1 JA	RKIB		A			HADD	U	IA-AR-KI-BA-D-IM		XIII 145 6
	1 JA	RPAʾ					HADD	U	IA-AR-PA-D-IM		M+
	1 JA	RŠAP					LA				
							ʾIL		IA-AR-SA-AP-LA-DINGIR		M+
	JA	RŠAP					LA				
							ʾIL	A	IA-AR-SA-AP-LA-I-[LA]?		M
	1 JA	RŠIJ					ʾAŠAR	I	IA-AR-ŠI-A-ŠA-RI		M
	JA	RŠIJ					ʾIL		IA-AR-ŠI-DINGIR		B 29+, M
	JA	RŠIJ					ʾIL	I	A-AR-ŠI-DINGIR		TA 1930,7:6
	JA	RŠIJ					ʾIL	UM	IA-AR-ŠI-DINGIR-UM		UCP X/1 P. 58+
	JA	RŠIJ					ʿAMM	U	IA-AR-ŠI-ḪA-MU		M, C+
	1 JA	SAṬIʾ					ʾEL		[I]A-ZA-AD-DI-EL		M
	JA	SAṬIʾ					ʾIL		IA-ZA-AD-DI-DINGIR		M+
	JA	SAṬIʾ					ʾIL		IA-ZA-AT-TI-DINGIR		M
	JA	SAṬIʾ					ʾIL		IA-SA-AD-DI-DINGIR		M
	JA	SAṬIʾ					ʾIL		IA-S[A]-TI-DINGIR		M
	1 JA	SNIQ	AN·						IA-AS-NI-KA-AN		RA LXV 50 VIII 51
	JA	SNIQ					ʾIL		IA-AS-NI-IQ-DINGIR		RA LXV 48 VII 66
	JA	SNIQ					ʾIL		IA-AŠ$_2$-NI-IQ-DINGIR		SIMMONS 55 14
	1 JA	ŠḪIR		UM					IA-AŠ-ḪI-RUM		M
	1 JA	ŠJIM	AT	UM					IA-SI-MA-TUM	FN	RA LXV 60 III 8
	JA	ŠJIM					ḪAJJ	A	[I]A-ŠI-IM-E$_2$-A		M
	JA	ŠJIM					ʾAB	IM	IA-SI-IM-A-BI-IM	GEN	M
	JA	ŠJIM					HADD	U	IA-SI-IM-D-IM		M
	JA	ŠJIM					ʾIL		IA-SI-IM-DINGIR		M+
	JA	ŠJIM					ʿAMM	U	IA-SI-IM-ḪA-AM-MU		M
	JA	ŠJIM					ʿAMM	U	IA-SI-IM-ḪA-MU		M
	JA	ŠJIM					ʾIRR	A	IA-ŠI-IM-IR$_3$-RA		M

PREFIXES, Class 1

JA	1 JA	ŚJIM					DAGAN			IA-SI-IM-D-DA-GAN		M+	
	JA	ŚJIM					DAGAN			IA-ŠI-IM-D-DA-GAN		VIII 11 33	
	JA	ŚJIM					KI						
							ʾIL			IA-SI-IM-KI-DINGIR		M	
	JA	ŚJIM					MAHAR			IA-SI-IM-MA-ḪA-AR		M	
	JA	ŚJIM					ŚUM	U	HU	IA-SI-IM-SU-MU-U$_2$		M+	
	2	ŚUM		U		JA	ŚJIM			SU-MU-IA-SI-IM		M+	
	3	ŚAM		I			MA						
						JA	ŚJIM			SA-MI-MA-IA-SI-IM	FN	C+	
	1 JA	ŚJIT		UM						IA-SI-TUM		XIII 98 3+	
	JA	ŚJIT	AN							IA-SI-TA-AN		M+	
	JA	ŚJIT	AN							IA-SI-IT-TA-AN		M	
	JA	ŚJIT					ʾAB	I		IA-SI-IT-A-BI		M	
	JA	ŚJIT					ʾAB	U		IA-SI-IT-A-BU		M+	
	JA	ŚJIT			NA					IA-SI-IT-NA		TIM IV 20 SEAL, M	
	JA	ŚJIT			NA		ʾAB	U		IA-SI-IT-NA-A-BU		XIII 1 XII 15	
	2	ʾAḪ		I		JA	ŚJIT			A-ḪI-SI-IT		TA 1931, 636	
		ŚUM		U		JA	ŚJIT			SU-MU-IA-SI-IT		B 39	
	2	ŚUM		U		JA	ŚABAŚ	UM		SU-MU-IA-SA-BA-SU-UM		PBS XI/2 1 I 34	
	1 JA	ŚBIJ					ʾIL			IA-AŠ-BI-DINGIR		B 32	
	JA	ŚBIJ					ʾIL	A		IA-AŠ-BI-I-LA		B 30	
	1 JA	ŚKIN					ʾIL			IA-AŠ$_2$-KI-IN-DINGIR-[....]?		M	
	1 JA	ŚKUR		UM						IA-AŠ$_2$-KU-RUM		XIII 1 XI 13	
	JA	ŚKUR		UM						IA-AŠ-KU-RUM		XIII 1 XI 19	
	JA	ŚKUR		UM						IA-UŠ-KU-RU-UM		TIM III 133 11	
	JA	ŚKUR		IM						IA-AŠ$_2$-KU-RI-IM	GEN	M+	
	JA	ŚKUR					ʾIL			IA-AŠ$_2$-KU-UR$_2$-DINGIR		B 81	
	JA	ŚKUR					ʾIL			IA-AŠ$_2$-KU-UR-DINGIR		B 30+	
	JA	ŚKUR					ʾIL			IA-AŠ$_2$-KUR-DINGIR		JNES XIII 210+	LATE
	JA	ŚKUR					ʾIL			[IA]-AŠ-KU-UR-DINGIR		VIII 38 7'	
	1 JA	ŚLAḪ					....			IA-AŠ$_2$-LA-A[Ḫ-....]		M	
	1 JA	ŚLAM					ʾIL			IA-AŠ$_2$-LAM-DINGIR		XIV 47:11	
	1 JA	ŚLIJ					ḪAʾL			IA-AŠ?-LI?-ḪA-AL		M	
	1 JA	ŚLIM					HAND	U		IA-AŠ$_2$-LI-IM-IA-[AN-D]U		M	
	1 JA	ŚMAʿ		UM						IA-AŠ$_2$-MA-ḪU-UM		M	
	JA	ŚMAʿ		U						IA-AŠ$_2$-MA-ḪU		B 30 HANA	
	JA	ŚMAʿ					HADD	U		IA-AŠ$_2$-MA-AḪ-D-IM		M+, C+	
	JA	ŚMAʿ					HADD	U		IA-AŠ$_2$-MI-IḪ-D-IM		M	
	JA	ŚMAʿ					ʾEL			IA-AŠ$_2$-MA-AḪ-I$_3$-EL		B 30	
	JA	ŚMAʿ					ʾIL			IA-AŠ$_2$-MA-AḪ-DINGIR		SIMMONS 55 11, M	
	JA	ŚMAʿ					ʾUP	I		IA-AŠ$_2$-MA-ḪU-PI		BULL. ACAD. BELG. 1974 228	
	JA	ŚMAʿ					BAʿL			[IA-A]Š$_2$-MA-AḪ-BA-AL		VIII 101 L.E.	
	JA	ŚMAʿ					DAGAN			IA-AŠ$_2$-MA-AḪ-D-DA-GAN		B 30 HANA+, M+	
	1 JA	ŚPUQ		UM						IA-AŠ$_2$-PU-KU-UM		B 30+	
	JA	ŚPUQ		UM						IA-AŠ-PU-KUM		VAS XIII 3 15+	
	JA	ŚPUQ					ʾIL			IA-AŠ$_2$-PU-UK-DINGIR		M	
	1 JA	ŚQIṬ					ʾIL			IA-AŠ-KI-IṬ-DINGIR		B 30, M+	
	1 JA	ŚRUK	AN							IA-AŠ$_2$-RU-KA-AN		RA XLI 45 6'	HANA+
	1 JA	ŚṬIḪ					ʾIL			IA-AŠ-TI-DINGIR		XIII 1 IX 7	
	JA	ŚṬIḪ					ʿAMM	U		IA-AŠ-DI-ḪA-AM-MU		B 30	
	1 JA	ŠWIB					ʾIL			IA-ŠI-IB-DINGIR		A.	
	JA	ŠWIB		I			ʾILL	A		IA-ŠI-BI-IL-LA		A.	
	1 JA	ŠWUB		UM						IA-ŠU-BU-UM		B 30+	
	JA	ŠWUB		IM						IA-ŠU-BI-IM	GEN	M+	
	JA	ŠWUB	AN							IA-ŠU-BA-AN		M	
	JA	ŠWUB					....			IA-ŠU-UB-[....]		A.	
	JA	ŠWUB					JAḪAD			IA-ŠU-UB-IA-ḪA-AD		M	
	JA	ŠWUB					ḪAʾL			IA-ŠU-UB-ḪA-AL		RA LXV 44 IV 28	
	JA	ŠWUB					HADD	U		IA-ŠU-UB-D-IM		LAESSOE P. 90+, C+	
	JA	ŠWUB					ʾIL			IA-ŠU-UB-DINGIR		CT II 23 15+, M+	
	JA	ŠWUB					ʾAŠAR			IA-ŠU-UB-A-ŠAR		M+	
	JA	ŠWUB				JI	JPUʿ			IA-ŠU-UB-D-I-PU-UḪ		M	
	JA	ŠWUB					DAGAN			IA-ŠU-UB-D-DA-GAN		B 30 HANA+, M+	
	JA	ŠWUB					LIʾM			IA-ŠU-UB-LI-IM		M+	
	JA	ŠWUB					MALIK			IA-ŠU-UB-D-MA-[LIK]		M	
	JA	ŠWUB					NAHR			IA-ŠU-UB-NA-AR		M+	

PREFIXES, Class 1

JA	1 JA	ŠWUB				RAPIʾ		IA-ŠU-UB-RA-BI		A.
	1 JA	ṢḪAQ	IM					IA-AZ-ḪA-KI?-IM	GEN	IX 291 I 38
	1 JA	ṢDUQ	UM					IA-AŠ-DU-KUM		B 30
	JA	ṢDUQ				ʾIL		IA-AŠ-DU-UQ-DINGIR		JEAN 164 R. 4+
	JA	ṢDUQ				ʾIL		[IA]-AŠ$_2$-DU-UQ-DINGIR		BASOR 95, 19
	1 JA	TḪIJ				DAGAN		IA-AT-ḪI-D-DA-GAN		M
	1 JA	TWUR				MEʾR		D-IA-TU-[U]R-ME-I[R]	DN	M
	JA	TWUR				NAHR	UM	IA-DUR-NA-RUM?		RA LXV 48 VII 72
	1 JA	ZLIJ				ʾIL		IA-AZ-LI-DINGIR		M
JE	1 JE	ʾWUŠ				ʾIL		E-WU-ŠI-DINGIR		BIROT, TEA 48:20
	2	MUT	I	JE		ʾMIʾ		MU-TI-E-MI-IḪ		M
	1 JE	ʾZIJ				ʾIL	UM	E-EḪ-ZI-LUM		VIII 3 25
	1 JE	HWIJ				MALIK		E-WI-MA-LIK		A.
	1 JE	ʿMUS	UM					E-MU-ZUM		I UNPUBL.
	2	LA		JE	N	JBIŚ	U	LA-E-NI-BI-ŠU		YOS XII
	1 JE	JDIʿ	UM					E-TI-UM		I
	2	ʾIL	I	JE		JPAʿ		I$_3$-LI$_2$-E-PA		A.+
		BAʿL	I	JE		JPAʿ		BA-LI-E-PA		A.
		ṢIDQ	I	JE		JPAʿ		ZI-ID-KI-E-PA		RA XLIII 37 QATNA
	2	ʾAB	I	JE		JPUʿ		A-BI-E-PU-UḪ		B 10, M+
		ʾIL	I	JE		JPUʿ		I$_3$-LI$_2$-E-PU-UḪ		M+
		ʿAMM	I	JE		JPUʿ		ḪA-MI-E-PU-UḪ		M+
		ʿAMM	I	JE		JPUʿ		ḪA-AM-MI-E-PU-UḪ		M+
		ʿAMM	U	JE		JPUʿ		ḪA-MU-E-PU-UḪ	FN	C+
		KAʾB	I	JE		JPUʿ		KA-BI-E-PU-UḪ		M
		NIQM	I	JE		JPUʿ		NI-IQ-MI-E-PU-UḪ		M+, A.+
		ŚUM	U	JE		JPUʿ		SU-MU-E-PU-UḪ		M+
		ṢIDQ	I	JE		JPUʿ		ZI-ID-KI-E-PU-UḪ		M+, C+
	2	NAWAR		JE		JŚAR		NA-WA-AR-E-ŠAR	FN	XIII 1 VI 40
		TADAB		JE		JŚAR		TA-DA-AB-E-ŠAR	FN	XIII 1 VI 42
	2	ʾAJA		JE		JŠUʿ		A-A-E-ŠU-UḪ?		TCL X 9 3
		ʾAB	I	JE		JŠUʿ		A-BI-E-ŠU-UḪ		B 10+, XIII 1 III 44
		ʾAB	I	JE		JŠUʿ				
						....		A-BI-E-ŠU-UḪ-LI-DI-IŠ		CT XLV 55 11
		ʾAB	I	JE		JŠUʿ				
						....		A-BI-E-ŠU-UḪ-LU-DA-RI		B 10
		ʾIL	I	JE		JŠUʿ		I$_3$-LI$_2$-E-ŠU-UḪ		B 21 M
		ḤAM	I	JE		JŠUʿ		D-A-MI-E-ŠU-UḪ		M+
		ḤAM	I	JE		JŠUʿ		A-MI-E-ŠU-UḪ		M+
		ḤAM	UM	JE		JŠUʿ		D-A-MU-UM-E-ŠU-UḪ		B 13 HANA
		ʿAMM	I	JE		JŠUʿ		ḪA-MI-E-ŠU-UḪ		M
		ʾAŚD	I	JE		JŠUʿ		AŠ$_2$-DI-E-ŠU-UḪ		M
		DAWD	I	JE		JŠUʿ		DA-DI-E-ŠU-UḪ		M+
		MUT	U	JE		JŠUʿ		M[U-T]U-E-ŠU-UḪ		RA LXV 47 VII 21
	1 JE	GJIḤ				LUʾ				
						MA		E-GI-IḪ-LU-MA		SUMER XXIII 192
	2	ʾAB	UM	JE		KWIN		A-BU-UM-E-KI-IN		M
	1 JE	KWUN				PI		E-KU-PI		B 17
	1 JE	LʾIJ				DAGAN		EL-I-D-DA-GAN		M
	1 JE	MWUT				BAʿL	A	E-MU-UT-BA-LA	GN GEN	SAKI P. 212+
	JE	MWUT				BAʿL	UM	E-MU-UT-BA-LUM-KI	GN	B 28+
	JE	MWUT				BAʿL	UM	E-MU-UT-BA-A-LUM-KI	GN	RLA II 180
	JE	MWUT				BAʿL	UM	IE-E-MU-UT-BA-LUM-KI	GN	SZLECHTER TJ 16 165
	JE	MWUT				BAʿL	IM	E-MU-UT-BA-LI-IM	GN GEN	KING 34 6+
	2	ŚUM	U	JE		MWUT				
						BAʿL	A	SU-MU-E-MU-UT-BA-LA	NOM	JCS IV 66 22
		ŚUM	U	JE		MWUT				
						BAʿL	A	SU-MU-E-MU-UT-BA-LA	GEN	JCS IV 69 17
		ŚUM	U	JE		MWUT				
						BAʿL	IM	SU-MU-E-MU-UT-BA-LIM?	GEN	JCS IV 71 9
	1 JE	MṢIʾ	UM					IE-E-IM-ZU-UM		BIN VII 35:6
	JE	MṢIʾ	UM					E-IM-ṢI-UM		BIN VII P. 11+
	JE	MṢIʾ				ʾIL		IE-E-EM-ZÍ-DINGIR		B 25
	1 JE	MZUʾ	UM					E-IM-ZU-UM		BIN VII P. 11+
	JE	MZUʾ	UM					IE-E-EM-ZU-UM		B 25+
	1 JE	NḪIN	UM					IE-EN-ḪI-NU-UM		B 25

PREFIXES, Class 1

JE	1 JE	NWIḪ		UM						E-NI-ḪU-UM		CT VIII 28C 4
	1 JE	NWUZ		UM						E-NU-ZU-UM		I
	1 JE	NBIṬ					TIŠPAK			I-EN-BI-IṬ-D-TIŠPAK		JCS XXIV 49 NO. 15:3
	1 JE	NQIM		UM						EN-GI-MU-UM		U+
	JE	NQIM					ʾIL			E-EN-KI-IM-DINGIR		CT VI 49B 4
	1 JE	NTIN		UM						E-EN-TI-NU-UM		WALTERS,WL 112:25
	2	ʾAḪ		I		JE	QWIM			A-ḪI-E-KI-IM		M
	1 JE	RḪAQ		UM						E-ER-ḪA-KUM		SIMMONS 112 7, SEAL
	1 JE	RWIḪ		I			ʾIL			E-RI-ḪI-DINGIR		U
	2	LA				JE	RWIḪ	UM		LA-E-RI-ḪU-UM		U
	2	ʾAŠD		U	NA	JE	RWIM			AŠ$_2$-DU-NI-E-RI-IM		RA VIII 65 1
	1 JE	RBIJ					ʾIL			E-IR-BI-DINGIR		KISURRA 22A 15
	1 JE	RBUʾ			HU		ʾEL			E-[IR]-BU-U$_2$-[E]L		KISURRA 152 9
	1 JE	ŠWUB					ʾIL			E-ŠU-UB-DINGIR		BIN VII P. 12+
	JE	ŠWUB		I			ʾIL			IE-E-ŠU-BI-DINGIR		B 26
	1 JE	ṢJID	AN	UM						E-ZI-DA-NU-UM		I
JI	1 JI	ʾWUŠ					ŠALIM			I-UŠ?-SA-LIM		RUTTEN 1 3
	1 JI	ʾKUR					BAʿL	I		I-KU-UR-BA-LI		EDZARD, DER 102:9
	1 JI	ʾLAP					HADD	U		IḪ-LA-AP-A-DU		A.
	JI	ʾLAP					ṬALL			I-LA-AP-TI-IL		U
	JI	ʾLAP					ṬALL	U	HU	I-LA-AP-TA-LU-U$_2$		M
	1 JI	ʾLIP					HADD	A		IḪ-LI-BA-DA		TCL I 222 13
	1 JI	HWIJ					MUT	I		I-WI-MU-TI		U
	1 JI	ḪLAJ					HADD	U		IḪ-LA-D-IM		XIII 1 II 76
	1 JI	ḪLIJ			JA					IḪ-LI-IA		XIII 139 18
	JI	ḪLIJ	AN							IḪ-LI-IA-AN		RA LXV 42 II 73+
	JI	ḪLIJ					HADD	U		IḪ-LI-A-DU		A. P. 133+
	JI	ḪLIJ					HADD	U		IḪ-LI$_3$-A-DU		A. P. 133
	JI	ḪLIJ					ʿAŠTAR			IḪ-LI-AŠ-TAR		A. 55 35
	JI	ḪLIJ					ʿAŠTAR			IḪ-LI-EŠ$_4$-DAR		A. P. 133+
	2	ʾIL		I		JI	ḪNUW		HU	I$_3$-LI$_2$-IḪ-NU-U$_2$		UCP X/1 19:4+
	2	ʾIL		I		JI	ḪṬAʾ					
							LI		JA	I$_3$-LI$_2$-IḪ-TA-LI-A		BIROT,TEA 69 I 14
	1 JI	ʿQIB		UM						I-KI-BU-UM		CT VIII 19 19+
	1 JI	ʿQUB		UM						I-KU-BU-UM		KISURRA 117 7, 9+
	2	ʾAḪ		I		JI	ʿQUB	A		A-ḪI-I-KU-BA		KISURRA 7A 9
	1 JI	ʿZIB		UM						I-ZI-BU-UM		KISURRA 10A 5+
	JI	ʿZIB			NA					I-ZI-IB-NA		CT XLV 118 24
	1 JI	JʿIL					DIJN	I		I-ḪI-IL-DI-NI-X?		RA LXV 48 VIII 1
	JI	JʿIL					PI					
							ʾIL			I-ḪI-IL-BI-DINGIR		M
	1 JI	JBAL		UM						I-BA-LUM		B 21, M
	JI	JBAL		U						I-BA-LU		CT VIII 17C 11
	JI	JBAL	AT	UM						JI-BA-LA-TUM	FN	U
	JI	JBAL					....			I-BA-AL-[....]	FN	M
	JI	JBAL					....			I-BA-AL-D-[....]		M
	JI	JBAL					....			I-BA-AL-AN-ḪAR		XIII 1 X 43
	JI	JBAL					HADD	U		I-BA-AL-D-IM		M+, C+
	JI	JBAL					ʾIL			I-BA-AL-DINGIR		EEMY III/4 P. 130, M+
	JI	JBAL					ḪAM	UM		I-BA-AL-D-A-MU-UM		RA LXV 52 X 43
	JI	JBAL					JARAḪ			I-BA-AL-E-RA-AḪ		B 20; RA LXV 52 X 27
	JI	JBAL					ʿAŠTAR			I-BA-AL-EŠ$_4$-DAR		M
	JI	JBAL					DAGAN			I-BAL-D-DA-GAN		B 20
	JI	JBAL					DAGAN			I-BA-AL-D-DA-GAN		M
	JI	JBAL					LA					
							ʾIL			I-BA-AL-LA-DINGIR		RA LXV 47 VII 26
	JI	JBAL					PI					
							ʾEL			I-BA-AL-BI-EL		M+
	JI	JBAL					PI					
							ʾEL			I-BA-AL-PI-EL		UCP X P. 56+
	JI	JBAL					PI					
							ʾIL			I-BA-AL-BI-DINGIR		M+
	2	JAʾIT		I		JI	JBAL			IA-I-TI-I-BA-AL		M
		ḪABUR				JI	JBAL					
							BUGAŠ			ID$_2$-ḪA-BUR-I-BA-AL-BU-GA-AŠ$_2$		BRM IV 52 HANA
		ʾIL		A		JI	JBAL			DINGIR?-I-BA-AL		M

PREFIXES, Class 1

JI	2		ḪAM		I	JI	JBAL			D-A-MI-I-BA-AL		M+
			ʿAMM		I	JI	JBAL			ḪA-MI-I-BA-AL		M
			ʿAN	AT	I	JI	JBAL			ḪA-NA-TI-I-BA-AL		RA LXV 40 I 12
			SUMUKAN			JI	JBAL			D-GIR_3-I-BA-AL		C
	3		LA				RIWM					
						JI	JBAL	U	HU	[L]A?-RI-IM-I-BA-LU-U_2		M
	1	JI	JBIŠ		U					I-BI-ŠU	FN	BM 82359
		JI	JBIŠ				ʾIL			I-BI-IŠ-DINGIR		TA 1930, 261
		JI	JBIŠ				ʾEL			I-BI-IŠ-I_3-EL		SIMMONS 70 12
		JI	JBIŠ				ʾIL			[I-B]I_2-IŠ-I_3-IL		I
		JI	JBIŠ				JARAḪ			I-BI-IŠ-A-RA-AḪ		DELAPORTE CCL I A 446
		JI	JBIŠ				KABID			I-BI-IŠ-GA-BI-ID		KISURRA 63A
	1	JI	JDAʿ				LIʾM					
							MA			I-DA-LIM-MA		B 21
		JI	JDAʿ				MARAṢ			I-DA-MA-RA-AṢ	GN	B 21+, M
		JI	JDAʿ				MARAṢ			A-DA-MA-RA-AṢ	GN	B 11
		JI	JDAʿ				MARAṢ			A-TA-MA-RA-AṢ	PN	CT II 26 3
		JI	JDAʿ				PI					
							ʾIL			I-DA-BI_2-DINGIR		I
		JI	JDAʿ				ŠUM			I-DA-SU-UM		M
		JI	JDAʿ				RAWM			I-DAḪ-RA-AM		MEISSNER 91 17
	2	JA	ŠWUB			JI	JPUʿ			IA-ŠU-UB-D-I-PU-UḪ		M
	1	JI	JQAH				ʾIL			I-KA-AḪ-DINGIR		B 21
	1	JI	JRID	AN	UM					I-RI-DA-NU-UM		M
	1	JI	JŠAR		UM					I-ŠA-RUM		C
		JI	JŠAR		I					I-ŠA-RI	FN	A.
		JI	JŠAR				LIʾM			I-ŠAR-LI-IM		M+, C+, CT VI 47B 17
	2		ḪANN		I	JI	JŠAR			AN-NI-I-ŠAR?		M
			ŠAMŠ		U	JI	JŠAR			SA-AM-SU-D-I-[Š]AR		M
	1	JI	JṢIʾ				ʾAḪ	UM		I-ZI-A-ḪU-UM		M+
		JI	JṢIʾ				ʾAḪ	U		I-ZI-A-ḪU?		X 53:6
		JI	JṢIʾ				ḪAJJ	UM		I-ZI-A-UM		MOORTGAT 488
		JI	JṢIʾ				ḪAʾL	U		I-ZI-ḪA-LU		XIV 96:9+
		JI	JṢIʾ				ḪAʾR	U		I-ZI-ḪA-RU		XIV 52:5, 16+
		JI	JṢIʾ				ʿAD	UM		I-ZI-A-DU-UM		M
		JI	JṢIʾ				ʾIL	U				
							MA			I-ZI-I-LU-MA		B 23+
		JI	JṢIʾ				ʾAŠAR			I-ZI-A-ŠAR		B 22+
		JI	JṢIʾ				ʾAŠAR			I-ṢI-A-ŠAR		YOS VIII 108 SEAL
		JI	JṢIʾ				JAPAR			I-ZI-A-PA-AR		B 22
		JI	JṢIʾ				JAT	UM		I-ZI-IA-TUM		B 23+
		JI	JṢIʾ			JA	JPAʿ			I-ZI-A-PA-AḪ		B 22
		JI	JṢIʾ				....			I-ZI-ḪI-X		B 23
		JI	JṢIʾ				....			I-ZI-IA-AN?		PBS XI/2 1 IX 16
		JI	JṢIʾ				....			I-ZI-IA-[....]		PBS XI/2 1 IX 15
		JI	JṢIʾ				....			I-ZI-IA-ZI-[....]		B 23
		JI	JṢIʾ				....			I-ZI-IŠ-MA-AḪ		HARRIS 7 11
		JI	JṢIʾ				....			I-ZI-TA?-KAM		B 23
		JI	JṢIʾ				BANIJ	IM		I-ZI-BA-NI-IM	GEN	B 45
		JI	JṢIʾ				DAGAN			I-ZI-D-DA-GAN		B 22 HANA
		JI	JṢIʾ				DAGAN			IS-SI-D-DA-GAN		CT IV 1 14
		JI	JṢIʾ				ḎARIʾ		JE	I-ZI-DA-RI-E		B 22+
		JI	JṢIʾ				ḎARIʾ		JE	I-ṢI-DA-RI-E		B 22+
		JI	JṢIʾ				ḎARIʾ		JE	I-ṢI-DA-RI-E-KI	GN	B 22
		JI	JṢIʾ				ḎARIʾ		JE	I-ṢI-DA-RI-I-KI	GN	B 22
		JI	JṢIʾ				ḎARIʾ		JE	I-ZI-DA-RI		TCL XI 218 9
		JI	JṢIʾ				ḎARIʾ		JE	I-ZI-ZA-RI-E		B 23+, M
		JI	JṢIʾ				ḎARIʾ		JE	I-ZI-IZ-ZA-RI-E		B 23
		JI	JṢIʾ				ḎARIʾ		JE	I-ZA-AR-RI-E		UET V 202 15
		JI	JṢIʾ				KURUB			I-ZI-KU-RU-UB		RA LXV 53 XI 11
		JI	JṢIʾ				MARIʾ		JE	I-ṢI-MA-RI-E		B 22
		JI	JṢIʾ				NABUʾ	UM		I-ZI-NA-B[U-U]M?		VAS IX 79 5
		JI	JṢIʾ				NABUʾ		HU	I-ZI-NA-BU-U_2		B 23+, M+
		JI	JṢIʾ				PU		K	I-ZI-PU-UḲ	FN?	M+
		JI	JṢIʾ				QAṬAR			I-ZI-GA-TA-AR		B 22+
		JI	JṢIʾ				QAṬAR			I-ZI-GA-TAR		B 22+

JI	1	JI	JṢIʾ			QAṬAR			I-ṢI-GA-TAR		B 22+
		JI	JṢIʾ			QAṬAR			I-ṢI-GA-TA-AR		B 22+
		JI	JṢIʾ			QAṬAR			I-ZI-GA-DAR		B 22
		JI	JṢIʾ			QAṬAR			I-ZI-QA-TAR		XIII 1 IV 59
		JI	JṢIʾ			QAṬAR	I		I-ZI-GA-DAR-I		B 22
		JI	JṢIʾ			ŠALIM			I-ṢI-SA-LIM		RUTTEN 4 19+
		JI	JṢIʾ			ŠARIJ		JE	I-ZI-SA-RI-E		BIN VII 105 12
		JI	JṢIʾ			ŠUM	UM		I-ZI-SU-MU-UM		B 23, M+
		JI	JṢIʾ			ŠUM	U	JA	I-ZI-SU-MU-A		KISURRA 112 7
		JI	JṢIʾ			ŠUM	U	HU	I-ZI-SU-MU-U$_2$		A 7646 3+
		JI	JṢIʾ			ŠAM	U				
						ʾAB	UM		I-ZI-SA-MU-A-BU-UM		B 23
		JI	JṢIʾ			ŠUM	U				
						ʾAB	UM		I-ZI-SU-MU-A-BU-UM		B 23+
		JI	JṢIʾ			ŠUM	U				
						ʾAB	IM		I-ZI-SU-MU-A-BI-IM	GEN	B 23
		JI	JṢIʾ			ŠARR			I-ZI-ŠAR		B 22
		JI	JṢIʾ			ŠARR			I-ṢI-LUGAL-KI	GN	TIM III 75:3
		JI	JṢIʾ			ŠARR	UM		I-ZI-ŠAR-RUM-KI	GN	SUMER III 79 VI 197+
		JI	JṢIʾ			TAMB	U		I-ZI-TA-AM-BU		BAHREIN UNPUB, POST-U.
		JI	JṢIʾ			ṢARIR	UM		I-ZI-ZA-RI-RUM		CT XLV 115 18
	2		LI		JI	JṢIʾ					
						ʾAŠD	UM		LI-ZI-AŠ-DU-UM		VAS XIII 104 R. II 24
	3		ŠUM			LI					
					JI	JṢIʾ	IM		SU-UM-LI-ZI-IM	GEN	WATERMAN 25 R 9
			ŠUM	U		LI					
					JI	JṢIʾ			SU-MU-LI-ZI		MEISSNER 37 15+
	1	JI	JTAR	UM					I-TA-RU-UM		B 23+
		JI	JTAR			ʿADN	I		I-TAR-AD-AN		WATERMAN 41 R. 10
		JI	JTAR			ʾIL	I		I-TAR-I-LI		B 23
		JI	JTAR			BEʿL	I		I-TAR-BE-LI$_2$		RA LXV 47 VII 39
		JI	JTAR			....			I-TAR-MA-[....]		AJSL XXXIII 229 SEAL+
		JI	JTAR			MULUK			I-TAR-MU-LU-UK		B 23
	1	JI	BʾUL	UM					IB-U$_2$-LUM		I
	1	JI	BWAʾ	UM					I-BA-UM		TA 30 615
		JI	BWAʾ		JA				I-BA-A-IA		C+
		JI	BWAʾ		JA				I-BA-IA		C II 7 II 3
		JI	BWAʾ			ʾIL			I-BA-AḪ-DINGIR		KISURRA 6 15
	1	JI	BJIR	UM					I-BI-RUM		M
	1	JI	BAʾEL			ʾABN	U		I-BA-EL-A-AB-NU		III 46 13
	1	JI	BAŠIR						I-BA-AS$_2$-SI-IR		M
	1	JI	BLIM	UM					IB-LI-NU-UM		TA 1930, 615:25 +
	1	JI	BNIJ			HADD	U		IB-NI-D-IM		M+
		JI	BNIJ			JARAḪ			IB-NI-E-RA-AḪ		SIMMONS 62 14'+
		JI	BNIJ			DAGAN			[I]B?-NI-D-DA-GAN		A. 6 34
	2		ŠU		JI	BNIJ		HU	ŠU-U$_2$-IB-NI-U$_2$		TA 1931, 636 REV +
			ṬALL	I	JI	BNIJ			TA-LI-IB-NI	FN	CT II 5 3 9
	1	JI	DJIN	IM					I-DI-NIM	GEN	M
	1	JI	DNIK		ʾA	MURR	UM		D-ID-NI-IK-MAR-TU	DN	U
	1	JI	ḎKUR	UM					IZ-KUR-RUM		LANGDON XXIX 24
		JI	ḎKUR			ʾIL			II-IZ-KUR-DINGIR		SIMMONS 67 18
		JI	ḎKUR			RAPIʾ			IZ-KUR-RA-BI		BM 81591 7
	1	JI	ḎRAʿ			DAGAN			IZ-RA-AḪ-D-DA-GAN		B 24 HANA+
	1	JI	ḎRUʿ			ʾIL			II-IZ?-RU-UḪ-DINGIR		TCL XI 156 17
	2		ʿAMM	A	JI	ḎRUʿ			ḪA-MA-IZ-RU		RUTTEN 28 5+
	1	JI	GJIḪ			LUʾ					
						MA			I-GI-IḪ-LU-MA		SIMMONS 60 8, 14+
		JI	GJIḪ			LUʾ					
						MA			I-GI-E-EḪ-LU-MA		JCS XXVI 143:21 HARMAL
	1	JI	GJID			LIʾM			I-GI-ID-LI-IM		B 21 HANA
	1	JI	GMIR			HADD	U		IG-MI-RA-A-DU		A.+
	1	JI	KWUN			ḪARAR	I		I-KU-UN-ḪA-RA-RI?	GEN	TCL I 151 4
		JI	KWUN			ʾAŠAR			I-KU-UN-A-ŠAR		GORDON 38 6
		JI	KWUN			BAʿL	I		I-KU-UN-BA-LI		A.
		JI	KWUN			BAʿL	I		I-KU-UN-BA-AḪ-LI		A. 246 33
		JI	KWUN			PI	I	JA	I-KU-BI-IA		SM P. 54

JI	1 JI		KWUN				PI		I		I-KU-UN-BI-I		C II 2 11
	1 JI		KRUB				ʾEL				D-IK-RU-UB-EL	DN	M+
	JI		KRUB				ʾIL				D-IK-RU-UB-DINGIR	DN	M+
	JI		KRUB				ʾIL				D-IK-RU-UB-IL	DN	M
	JI		KRUB				ʾIL				D-IK-RU-BI-DINGIR	DN	M
	1 JI		KSUW				ʾEL				IK-ZU-EL		TA 30 615 10, 20+
	JI		KSUW				ʾIL				IK-ZU-IL		TA 1931 ,435 REV.2
	1 JI		LʾAʾ				HADD		U		IL-A-D-IM		X 83 4, 7'
	JI		LʾAʾ				HADD		U		IL-A-DU		A. 78 20
	JI		LʾAʾ				....				IL-A-KUL$_2$-LAM?		VII 140:10
	1 JI		LʾIJ				DAGAN				I-IL-ḪI-D-DA-G[AN]		M
	1 JI		LEʾEJ				HADD		U		I-LE-E-D-IM		XIII 93 5
	1 JI		MLIK				ʾIL				II-IM-LIK-DINGIR		B 28+
	2		LI			JI	MLIK						
							....				LI-IM-LI$_2$-LI-IK-ḪI-LI-GAL$_2$		HSM 7934, UR III
	1 JI		MŠIJ				ʾIL				JI-IM-SI-DINGIR		M
	1 JI	N	NWAḪ	AN							IN-NA-ḪA-AN		M+
	1 JI	N	NWAB	AT	UM						IN-NA-BA-TUM	FN	CT VI 17 13+
	JI	N	NWAB	AT	UM						IN-NA-BA-A-TUM	FN	CT VI 1A 3
	JI	N	NWAB	AT	IM						IN-NA-BA-TIM	FN GEN	CT VI 17 2
	1 JI	N	NWIB		UM						IN-NI-BU-UM		M
	JI	N	NWIB		U						IN-NI-BU		YOS XIII 191:2+
	JI	N	NWIB		U						IN-NE-BU		M
	JI	N	NWIB		I						IN-NI-BI		CLAY PNCP 90+
	1 JI		NWUḪ				DITAN				I-NU-UḪ-DI-TA-AN		GORDON 38 20+
	JI		NWUḪ				LIBB		I		I-NU-UḪ-LI-BI		M
	JI		NWUḪ				ŠAMAR				I-NU-UḪ$_3$-SA-MAR		BIN VII 7 4,9+
	JI		NWUḪ				ŠAMAR				I-NU-UḪ-SA-MAR		TCL I 74 5,18
	1 JI		NBIʾ				DAGAN				I-BI-D-DA-GAN		M
	JI		NBIʾ				NABUʾ			HU	I-BI-NA-BU-U$_2$		A 7685 13
	1 JI		NBIṮ				LIʾM				I-BI-IṮ-LI-IM		ANN. ARCH. SYR. XX 74:2
	1 JI		NDIN		UM						IN-DIN-NU-UM		I
	JI		NDIN		U						ID-DI-NU		XIII 1 I 47
	JI		NDIN		A						ID-DI-NA		A.
	JI		NDIN			JA					I-DIN-IA		M
	JI		NDIN				ʾABB		A		I-DIN-AB-BA		XIII 1 VIII 46
	JI		NDIN				ʾABB		A		ID-DI-NA-AB-BA		A.
	JI		NDIN				ʾABB		A		ID-DI-NA-BA		A. LATE
	JI		NDIN				ʾADM		U		I-DIN-D-AD-MU		M+
	JI		NDIN				....				I-DIN-D-IGI-KUR		M+
	JI		NDIN				ʾAKK		A		I-DIN-AK-KA		XIII 1 I 54+
	JI		NDIN				ʾANN		U		I-DIN-AN-NU		M+
	JI		NDIN				ʾANN		UM		I-DIN-AN-NU-UM		M+
	JI		NDIN				ʾANN		U		I-DI-AN-NU		RA LXV 51 IX 31
	JI		NDIN				JAT		UM		I-DIN-IA-TUM		M+
	JI		NDIN				JAT		IM		I-DIN-IA-TIM	GEN	M+
	JI		NDIN				JAT		IM		ID-DI-IA-TIM	GEN	M
	JI		NDIN				JAT		AM		I-DIN-IA-TAM	ACC	XIV 64:7
	JI		NDIN			ʾA	ŠKUR				I-DIN-D-AŠ$_2$-KU-UR		SYRIA XXXVII 206 8 HANA
	JI		NDIN			JI	TWUR						
							MEʾR				I-DIN-D-I-DUR-ME-ER		XIII 1 III 49+
	JI		NDIN				BIN		UM		I-DIN-BI-NU-UM		UCP X/1 64 2
	JI		NDIN				DIWR	IT	IM		I-DIN-D-DI-RI-TIM	GEN	M
	JI		NDIN				DAGAN				I-DIN-D-DA-GAN		M+
	JI		NDIN				KAKK		A		I-DIN-KA-AK-KA		M+
	JI		NDIN				KAKK		A		I-DIN-D-KA-KA		M+
	JI		NDIN				LABW		A		I-DIN-D-LA-BA		M
	JI		NDIN				MEʾR				I-DIN-D-ME-ER		MAOG IV 2 2 HANA
	JI		NDIN				MAM		A		I-DIN-D-MA-MA		M+
	JI		NDIN				RIWM				I-DIN-D-RI-IM		TCL I 238 16 HANA
	JI		NDIN				RUŠP	AN			I-DIN-D-RU-UŠ-PA-AN		MAOG IV 2 5 HANA+
	JI		NDIN				RUŠP	AN			I-DIN-D-RU-UŠ$_2$-PA-AN		MEL. SYR. I 275
	JI		NDIN				TABUB		U		I-DIN-TA-BŪ-BU		M
	1 JI		NDUB				ŠALIM				IN-DU-UB-ŠA-LIM		TA 1931, 265:10
	1 JI		NPIḪ		UM						IB-BI$_2$-ḪU-UM?		VIII 3 19
	JI		NPIḪ		U						I-BI-ḪU	FN	C

JI	1 JI		NPIḪ						LI					
									DIJN	I		IB-BI-IḪ-LI-DI-NI	FN	C
	1 JI		NŠIʾ						DAGAN			I-SI-IḪ-D-DA-GAN		RA XLI 44 R. 6 HANA
	JI		NŠIʾ						DAGAN			IS-SI-D-DA-GAN		B 22 HANA
	1 JI		NṢUR						ʾAŠD	UM		I-ZUR-AŠ-DU-UM		A 7685 5
	JI		NṢUR						ʾAŠD	UM		I-ZUR-A-AŠ-DU-UM		CT II 42 25
	1 JI		NTIN		UM							IN-TI-NU-UM		I
	JI		NTIN									IT-TI-IN		M
	JI		NTIN						HADD	U		I-TI-IN-D-IM		M
	1 JI	N	PALIS		U							IP-PA-LI-ZU?		MAOG IV 2 3 HANA
	1 JI		PANIJ						ʾEL	UM		I-PA-AN-NI-E-LUM		UNPUBL.
	1 JI		PRUD		U							IP-RU-DU		CT XLV 59 22 SEAL
	1 JI		PTAN									IP-TA-AN		C II 39 22; M
	1 JI		PTIḤ				JA		MWUT	A		IP-TI-IA-MU-TA		BM 80328 11
	1 JI		QNIJ		UM							IQ-NI-UM	FN	RA LXV 58 I 34
	1 JI		QRIB	AN	UM							IQ-RI-BA-NU-UM		I
	1 JI		RḤAM		I				ʾIL			IR-ḪA-MI-DINGIR		A.
	JI		RḤAM						ʾIL	A		IR-ḪA-MI-LA		A.+
	JI		RḤAM						ʾILL	A		IR-ḪA-MI-IL-LA		A. 274 26
	1 JI		RḤAQ		UM							IR-ḪA-KUM		B 22
	JI		RḤAQ		UM							II-IR-ḪA-KUM		SIMMONS 96 10+
	1 JI		RḤIB									IR-IB		U
	JI		RḤIB									I-RI-IB		I
	1 JI		RḤIQ		A							IR-ḪI-GA		M
	1 JI		RWIM						ʾILL	A		I-RI-MIL-LA		A. 87 30 LATE
	JI		RWIM						ʾILL	A		I-RI-IM-IL-LA		A. LATE
	JI		RWIM						ʾILL	A		I-RI-MI-IL-LA		A. LATE
	JI		RWIM						DAGAN			I-RI-IM-D-DA-GAN		SYRIA XXXVII 206 2 HANA
	1 JI		RKAB	T	UM							IR-KAB-TUM	MN	A.+
	JI		RKAB	T	U							IR-KAB-DU	MN	A.+ LATE
	1 JI	N	RMUK									I-NI-IR-MU-UK		M+
	JI	N	RMUK									I-NE-IR-MU-UK		M
	1 JI		RPAʾ						ʾAB	I		IR-PA-A-BI		A.+
	JI		RPAʾ						HADD	A		IR-PA-A-DA		A. 76 8+
	JI		RPAʾ						HADD	A		IR-PA-DA		A. 41 14
	JI		RPAʾ						HADD	U		IR-PA-D-IM		A.+
	1 JI		SRID		UM							IZ-RI-TUM		CT XLV 116 16
	1 JI		ŠJIM						ḪAJJ	A		I-ŠI-IM-E$_2$-A		M
	1 JI		ŠJIT			NA						I-SI-IT-NA		UCP X/1 58 3
	2		ʾAB		I		JI	T	ŠAMAR			A-BI-IŠ-TA-MAR		TCL I 226 4, 10+
			ʾIL		I		JI	T	ŠAMAR			I$_3$-LI$_2$-IŠ-TA-MAR		EDZARD,DER 67:11
			LI				JI	T	ŠAMAʿ					
									ʾIL			LI?-IŠ?-TA-MI-DINGIR		IX 291 I 18
			ŠUM		U		JI	T	ŠAMAR			SU-MU-UŠ-TA-MAR		TIM II 14 21
	1 JI		ŠBIJ						ʾIRR	A		IŠ-BI-D-IR$_3$-RA		M+
	JI		ŠBIJ						ʾIRR	A		IŠ-BI-IR$_3$-RA		M+
	1 JI		ŠBIM		U							IŠ-BI-MU		CT IV 30D 10
	1 JI		ŠKUR						ʾEL	I		IŠ-KUR-E-LI	FN	XIII 1 VII 41
	1 JI		ŠLAM	AN	A							IŠ-LA-MA-NA	GEN	MRS VI P. 202 UGARIT
	1 JI		ŠMAʿ						HADD	U		IŠ-MA-D-IM		M
	JI		ŠMAʿ						HADD	U		IŠ-ME-D-IM		M+
	JI		ŠMAʿ						HADD	A		IŠ-MA-A-DA		A.+
	JI		ŠMAʿ						ʾIL			IS-MA-AḪ-DINGIR		CT XLV 3 7
	JI		ŠMAʿ						ʾIL			IŠ-ME-EḪ-DINGIR		KISURRA 40 9
	JI		ŠMAʿ						ʾILL	A		IŠ-MI-IL-LA		A.
	JI		ŠMAʿ						ʾAMUM	I		IŠ-ME-A-MU-MI	FN	M
	JI		ŠMAʿ						BAʿL			IŠ-ME-EḪ-BA-AL		M
	JI		ŠMAʿ						BAʿL	A		IŠ-ME-BA-LA		TA 30, 122 2
	JI		ŠMAʿ						BAʿL	A		IŠ-ME-EḪ-BA-LA		TA 30, 71
	JI		ŠMAʿ						BAʿL	I		IŠ-ME-BA-LI		HARRIS 71 6+
	JI		ŠMAʿ						DAGAN			IŠ-MA-AḪ-D-DA-GAN		RA XXXIV 186 R. 2 HANA+
	JI		ŠMAʿ						DAGAN			IŠ-ME-D-DA-GAN		M+
	2		ʾAḪ		I		JI		ŠMAʿ		NI	A-ḪI-IŠ-MA-NI		VAS VIII 14:41+
			ʾIL		I		JI		ŠMAʿ		NIA	I$_3$-LI$_2$-IŠ-MA-NI-A		TA 1930,399
	1 JI		ŠNUL		UM							IŠ-NU-LU-UM	TRIBE	M
	2		ʾIL		I		JI		ŠPIQ			I$_3$-LI$_2$-IŠ-BI-IK		TA 1931, 71

JI	1	JI	T	ŠAWAB		U						IŠ-TA-BU		B 24 HANA
		JI	T	ŠAWAB		U						IŠ-TA-A-BU		MAOG IV 3 36 HANA
	2			ʿAMM		I	JI	T	ŠAMAR			ḪA-AM-MI-IŠ-TA-MAR		M+
				ʿAMM		I	JI	T	ŠAMAR			AM-MI-IŠ-TA-MAR		M
				ʿAMM		I	JI	T	ŠAMAR	U		AM-MI-IŠ-TAM-RU		MRS VI P. 329 UGARIT+
				ʿAMM		I	JI	T	ŠAMAR	U		AM-MI-IS-TAM-RU		MRS VI P. 239 UGARIT+
	1	JI		ŠNIJ					HADD	U		IŠ-NI-D-IM		A.
		JI	ŠT	ŠNIJ					ʾEL			IŠ-TA-AŠ-NI-EL		SIMMONS 46 30
		JI	ŠT	ŠNIJ					ʾIL			IŠ-TA-AŠ-NI-IL		SYRIA V 274 HANA
		JI	ŠT	ŠNIJ					ʾIL			IŠ-TA-AŠ-NI-DINGIR		VAS IX 156 11+
	1	JI		TWUR					ḪAJJ	A		I-DUR-E$_2$-A		M
		JI		TWUR					ʾAHL	I		I-DUR-A-LI		JCS XXIV 46 NOS. 5, 6
		JI		TWUR					ʿADN	U		I-DUR-ḪA-AD-[NU]		B 24
		JI		TWUR					ʿADN	U	HU	I-DUR-ḪA-AD-NU-U$_2$		TCL XVIII 83 6
		JI		TWUR					ʿAMM	U	HU	I-DUR-ḪA-MU-U$_2$		UNPUBL.
		JI		TWUR					ʾAŠD	UM		I-DUR-A-AŠ-DU-UM		B 23
		JI		TWUR					ʾAŠD	UM		I-DUR-AŠ-DUM		B 23
		JI		TWUR					ʾAŠD	UM		I-DUR-AŠ-DU-UM		B 23+
		JI		TWUR					ʾAŠD	UM		I-DUR-AŠ$_2$-DU-UM		M+
		JI		TWUR					ʾAŠD	U		I-DUR-AŠ-DU		B 23+
		JI		TWUR					ʾAŠD	U		I-DUR-AŠ$_2$-DU		VAS IX 172 5, M+
		JI		TWUR					ʾAŠD	U	HU	I-DUR-AŠ-DU-U$_2$		SIMMONS 90 4
		JI		TWUR					ʾAŠD	U	HU	I-DUR-AŠ$_2$-DU-U$_2$		M
		JI		TWUR					KUʾN	U	HU	I-DUR-KU?-NU-U$_2$		VAS XIII 14 R. 10
		JI		TWUR					MEʾR			D-I-DUR-ME-IR	DN	M+
		JI		TWUR					NINGAL			I-DUR-D-NIN-GAL		M
		JI		TWUR					FI					
									ʾIL			I-DUR-[BI]?-DINGIR		I
		JI		TWUR					ŠALIM			I-DUR-SA-LIM		YOS II 84 21 22
		JI		TWUR					ŠUM	U				
									ʾEL			I-DUR-SU-ME-EL		KISURRA 43 5+
	2			ḤANN		A	JI		TWUR					
									MEʾR			ḪA-AN-NA-D-I-DUR-ME-ER		M
				ʾIPQ		U	JI		TWUR					
									MEʾR			IP-KU-D-I-DUR-ME-ER		M
				LI			JI		TWUR					
									ʾAHL	I		LI-TU-UR-A-LI		JCS XXIV 62 NO.55+
		JI		NDIN			JI		TWUR					
									MEʾR			I-DIN-D-I-DUR-ME-ER		XIII 1 III 49+
	1	JI		ZMEʾ					ʾIL			IZ-ME-DINGIR		VAS IX 141 2
	1	JI		ZNUR		UM						IZ-NU-RU-UM		SIMMONS 48 20+
		JI		ZNUR		UM						IZ-NU-RUM		CT XLV 82 7 25
JU	1	JU		MRAṢ					ʾIL			JU-UM-RA-AṢ-DINGIR		M+
	1	JU	T	ŠALIL		I						UŠ-TA-LI-LI	NOM	M+
	1	JU	T	ŠANIJ								UŠ-TA-AN-NI		RA LXV 44 IV 55; A.+
		JU	T	ŠANIJ					HADD	U		UŠ-TI-NI-D-IM?		A. 36 9+
		JU	T	ŠANIJ					ʾIL	A		UŠ-TA-NI-I-LA		A. 33 22
	1	JU	ŠT	ŠNIJ					ʾIL			UŠ-TAŠ-NI-DINGIR		VAS IX 130 21+
		JU	ŠT	ŠNIJ					ʾIL			UŠ-TA-AŠ-NI-DINGIR		VAS IX 131 21+
MA	1	MA		ʾMIN		UM						MA-AḪ-MI-NU-UM		CT XLVIII 89 REV.
	1	MA		ʾNIP		UM						MA-NI-PU-UM		SIMMONS 119 10 S
	1	MA		ʾNUP		UM						[MA]-AḪ-NU-KA-UM		VAS IX 192 18
		MA		ʾNUP		U						MA-AḪ-NU-KA		VAS IX 193 18
		MA		ʾNUP		U						MA-AḪ-NU-PU		M
		MA		ʾNUP					ʾIL			MA-AḪ-NU-UP-DINGIR		B 33+, M+
		MA		ʾNUP					ʾIL			MA-AḪ-NU-BI-DINGIR		B 33+, M+
		MA		ʾNUP					ʾIL	I		MA-AḪ-NU-UP-I$_3$-LI$_2$		B 33+
	1	MA		HLIL		UM						MA-AḪ-LI-LUM		SIMMONS 46 34 124 16+
	1	MA		ḪZIQ		UM						MA-ZI-GU-UM		CT XLVIII 27 CASE
	1	MA		ḪŚIM	AN	UM						MA-AḪ-ŠI-MA-NU-UM		B 46+
	1	MA		JRID	UN	UM						MA-RI-DU-NU-UM		SIMMONS 124 17
	1	MA		ḎMAR		UM						MA-AZ-MA-RU-UM		SIMMONS 52 17+, M
		MA		ḎMAR	AT	UM						MA-AZ-MA-RA-TUM	FN	CT VIII 41A 3 4+
		MA		ḎMAR	AT	UM						MA-IZ-MA-RA-TUM	FN	CT II 30 35
		MA		ḎMAR	AH							MA-AZ-MA-RA	FN	M+
	1	MA		GRIN								MA-AG-RI-IN		HARRIS 76 15

PREFIXES, Class 1

MA	1	MA	KWIN							MA?-KI-EN		C
	1	MA	NWIḪ	AH						MA-NI-ḪA	FN	RA LXV 58 I 36+
	1	MA	NTIN		UM					MA-AN-TI-NU-UM		HARRIS 31 13+
		MA	NTIN		U					URU MA-AN-TI-NU	GN	BM 16387
	1	MA	NZAL	AN	UM					MA-AN-ZA-LA-NU-UM		UET V 465 17
	1	MA	RḪAŠ	AN						MAR-ḪA-ŠA-AN		RA LXV 54 XII 12
	1	MA	RDAP		UM					MAR-DA-BU-UM		BIN III 546; U+
		MA	RDAP	AN						MAR-DA-BA-AN		ITT P.4, 7031 UR III
		MA	RDAP	AN	UM					MAR-DA-BA-NU-UM		U
	1	MA	ŚJIT					ʿAN	UM	MA-SI-IT-A-NU-UM		I
	1	MA	ŚKAR		UM					MAŠ-GA-RU-UM		RUTTEN 33 5, SEAL
	1	MA	ŚMAR		IM					MA-AŠ-MA-RI-IM	GEN	M
	1	MA	ŚMIʿ	AN	AM					MA-AŠ-MI-A-NA-AM	ACC	M
	1	MA	ŚPAR		UM					MAŠ-PA-RU-UM		B 49+
		MA	ŚPAR		UM					MA-AŠ$_2$-PA-RU-UM		SUMER XXIII 153 8, 17, 23
	1	MA	ŚPIR		UM					MAŠ-PI-RU-UM		CT VI 49B 12
	1	MA	ŠKAK		IM					MA-AŠ-KA-KI-[I]M	GEN	M
	1	MA	ZNIJ	AT	UM					MA-AZ-NI-A-T[UM]	FN	JCS XIX 56
	1	MA	ZRAQ	AT	UM					MA-AZ-RA-QA-TUM	FN	XIII 1 II 37
ME	1	ME	ʾḪAḎ		UM					ME-ḪA-DUM		UCP X/3 3:18; YONDORF 4
	1	ME	ʾḪIḎ		UM					ME-ḪI-DU-UM		RA LXV 54 XII 64
	1	ME	ʾWIR		I					ME-ḪI-RI		C
		ME	ʾWIR		I			ʾEL		ME-ḪI-RI-E-EL		JCS IV 109 4311 7
	1	ME	ʾWIŠ		UM					ME-I-SU-UM		CT VI 7 21+
	1	ME	ʾMIʾ		IM					ME-MI-ḪI-IM	GEN	C
	1	ME	ḪRIM		IM					ME-EḪ-RI-MI-IM	GEN	M+
	1	ME	ḪZIQ		A					ME-ZI-QA		M
		ME	ḪZIQ	AN						ME-ZI-QA-AN		RA LXV 44 IV 30
	1	ME	ʿANIJ		U					ME-ḪA-A-NU		KISURRA 81A
		ME	ʿANIJ		IM					ME-ḪA-NI-IM	GEN	KISURRA 80B
		ME	ʿANIJ		I					ME-ḪA-A-NI?	GEN	VAS VIII 14 43
		ME	ʿANIJ			JA				ME-ḪA-NI-IA	FN	RA LXV 58 I 43+
	1	ME	ʿḎIR		I					ME-ZI-RI		M
	1	ME	ʿNIJ		UM					ME-EḪ-NI-JU-UM		M
		ME	ʿNIJ		UM					ME-EḪ-NU-UM		KISURRA 36 4
		ME	ʿNIJ		IM					ME-EḪ-NI-IM	GEN	KISURRA 80A
	1	ME	ʿQIB		UM					ME-KI-BU-UM		U, M+
		ME	ʿQIB		IM					ME-KI-BI-IM	GEN	M+
	1	ME	JBIŚ		UM					ME-BI-ŠUM		M+
		ME	JBIŚ		A					ME-BI-SA	MN	M
	1	ME	JDIʿ		UM					ME-TE-UM		I
	1	ME	JPIʿ		UM					ME-BI-ḪU-UM		M
		ME	JPIʿ		UM					ME-PI-UM		I
	1	ME	JŚAR		UM					ME-ŠA-RUM		A.
	1	ME	JŠIʿ		UM					ME-SI-UM		SIGRIST UNPUBL.
	1	ME	JTIR	AN	UM					ME-TE-RA-NU-UM		TA 1930, 489
	1	ME	DBIR							ME-ED-BI-IR		BASOR 95, 24
	1	ME	ḎRIʿ		UM					ME-IZ-RI-JU-UM		M
	1	ME	KWIN							ME-KI-IN	FN	A.
		ME	KWIN		UM					ME-KI-NU-UM		M+
	2		ʾAB		U		ME	KWIN		A-BU-ME-KI-IN		X 154 2+
	1	ME	NḪIM		UM					ME-EN-ḪI-MU-UM		HARRIS 57 17
	1	ME	NḪIJ		UM					ME-EN-ḪI-I-UM		XIII 105 8
	1	ME	NḪIB	AH						ME-EN-ḪI-BA	FN	XIII 1 I 24
	1	ME	NWIḪ		UM					ME-NI-ḪU-UM		BIN II 94 4+
	1	ME	NDIB		UM					ME-EN-DI-BU-UM		KING LIH I 25 4
	1	ME	PTUḪ		UM					ME-EP-TU-U$_2$-UM		M+
		ME	PTUḪ		UM					ME-EP-TU-UM		M+
		ME	PTUḪ		U					ME-EP-TU-U$_2$		M+
		ME	PTUḪ		IM					ME-EP-TI-I-IM	GEN	M+
		ME	PTUḪ		IM					ME-EP-TI-IM	GEN	M+
		ME	PTUḪ		IM					ME-EP-TE-IM	GEN	XIII 43 15
	1	ME	QWIM							ME-KI-IM		RA XXXV 119, MARI
		ME	QWIM							ME-[G]I-IM	GEN	IX 291 III 16'
	2		ʾAB		I		ME	QWIM		A-BI-ME-KI-IM		XIII 34 5+
			ʾAB		U		ME	QWIM		A-BU-ME-KI-IM		M+

PREFIXES, Class 1

ME	1	ME		ŚKIN		UM						ME-EŠ$_3$-KI-NU-UM		WALTERS, WL 95:2
		ME		ŚKIN		IM						ME-EŠ$_3$-KI-NIM	GEN	M+
	1	ME		ŚKIR		UM						ME-IŠ-KI-RUM		B 34
	1	ME		ŚLIB	AT	UM						ME-EŠ$_3$-LI-BA-TUM	FN	YOS V 117 1
	1	ME		ŚLIM		UM						ME-IŠ-LI-MU-UM		HARRIS 31 18
	1	ME		ṢJID		UM						MF-ṢI-TUM		B 34
		ME		ṢJID		UM						ME-ZI-TUM		XIII 1 VI 29
		ME		ṢJID		UM						ME-ZI-[T]U-UM		M
	1	ME		TMIH		UM						ME-IT-ME-U$_2$-UM		M
		ME		TMIH		UM						ME-IT-MU-UM		M
		ME		TMIH		U						ME-IT-MI-JU		M+
MI	1	MI		ʾḪAḎ		UM						MI-ḪA-[TUM]?	TRIBE	IX 244:5
	1	MI		ʾWIR		UM						MI-I-RUM		RA LXV 46 V 83
	1	MI		NWIḪ		UM						MI-NI-ḪU-UM		YOS XII
		MI		NWIḪ		U						MI-NI-ḪU		TIM V 62 13
	1	MI		PTUḤ		U						MI-IP-TU-U$_2$		RA LXIV 104:3
		MI		PTUḤ		IM						MI-IP-TI-IM	GEN	M+
		MI		PTUḤ		I						MI-IP-TI-I	GEN	XII 406 5
	1	MI		ŚKIR		UM						MI-IŠ-KI-RUM		VAS IX 172 13
	1	MI		ŚQIḪ		I						MI-IS-KI-ḪI	NOM	UET V 605 20
MU	1	MU		ḪARIR		IM						MU-ḪA-RI-RI-IM	GEN	M
	1	MU		WḪIN		UM						MU-ḪI-NU-UM		HAGER DISSERT. PL II/3
	1	MU		WBIT		UM						MU-BI-TU-UM		LANGDON XXVII 4
	1	MU		WDAD		UM						MU-DA-DU-UM		I, VAS VIII 60 5, 18+
		MU		WDAD		U						MU-DA-DU		YOS XIII 513:9
	1	MU		WPIʿ		I						MU-BI-ḪI		TA 30, 7 10
	1	MU		WQIR	AN	UM						MU-GI-RA-NU-UM		U
	1	MU		WSIL	AT	UM						MU-ZI-LA-TUM	FN	B 35
	1	MU		WṢIʾ			JA					MU-ZI-IA		M+
	1	MU		WTAR								MU?-TA-AR		IX 290 1
	2			ḪAʾL		I		MU	WTAR			ḪA-LI$_2$-MU-TAR		M
	1	MU		KAŚAJ		EM						MU-KA-SA-A-JE-EM	ACC	M
	1	MU		PAḪIR	AH							MU-PA-ḪI-RA	FN	XIII 1 VII 47
	1	MU		PATIḤ	AH							MU-PA-AT-TI-IA	FN	XIII 1 VIII 38+
		MU		PATIḤ	AH							MU-PA-TI-IA	FN	XIII 1 XIII 19+
		MU		PATIḤ	T	UM						MU-PA-AT-TI-TUM	FN	C+
	1	MU		QADIM		U						MU-GA-DI-MU		CT XLV 6 33
	1	MU		QANIT		UM						MU-GA-NI-TUM	MN?	TIM III 86 6+
	1	MU		ŚALIM		UM						MU-SA-LI-MU-UM		CT XLVIII 57 2, 3
		MU		ŚALIM		U						MU-SA-LI-MU		CT IV 47B 28
		MU		ŚALIM		I						MU-SA-LI-MI	NOM	UCP X/1 87 11
		MU		ŚALIM		IM						MU-SA-LI-MI-IM	GEN	CT VIII 47B 28
		MU		ŚALIM	AT	IM						MU-SA-LI-MA-TIM	FN GEN	BE VI/1 8 14
	1	MU		ŚARIK	AH							MU-SA-AR-RI-KA	FN	XIII 1 VIII 75
	1	MU		ŚṬAḤ	AT	UM						MU-UŠ-TA-ḪA-[TUM]?	MN	M
	1	MU		ŚṬUḤ	AT	UM						MU-UŠ-TU-A-TUM	FN	C
		MU		ŚṬUḤ					KAʾM		I	MU-UŠ-TU-KA-M[I]		M+
TA	2			DANN		U		TA	ʾḪAḎ			DAN-NU-TA-ḪA-AZ		M+
				DANN		U		TA	ʾḪAḎ			DA-NU-TA-ḪA-AZ		SIMMONS 36 23
				DANN		U		TA	ʾḪAḎ			D-DA-NU-TA-ḪA-AZ		SIMMONS 84 15
				DANN		UM		TA	ʾḪAḎ			D-DA-AN-NU-UM-TA-ḪA-AZ		SIMMONS 36 A 22
				DANN		UM		TA	ʾḪAḎ			DA-AN-NU-UM-TA-ḪA-AZ		SIMMONS 36 CASE 22
				DANN		UM		TA	ʾḪAḎ			DA-NU-UM-TA-ḪA-AZ		A 7634, M
				DANN		UM		TA	ʾḪAḎ			D-DA-NU-UM-TA-ḪA-[AZ]		TIM V 19 14
	1	TA		ʾḪUḎ	AN							TA-ḪU-ZA-AN		RA LXV 52 X 33
	1	TA	T	ʾAMAR								TA-AḪ-TA-MAR		M
	2			RAPIʾ				TA	ʾLAŚ			RA-BI-TA-AḪ-LA-AŠ		BASOR 95 22
	1	TA		ʾMUR								TA-MU-UR	FN	M
	1	TA		ʾZIJ					ʾADM		U	TA-AḪ-ZI-D-AD-MU	FN	M
	1	TA		HWIJ					JARAḪ			TA-AḪ-WI?-D-EN-ZU		RA LXIV 28 NO. 16
		TA		HWIJ					NAPŚ		U	TA-AḪ-WI-NA-AP-SU		RA LXIV 28 NO. 14
	1	TA		ḤBAS		I						TA-AḪ-PA-ZI		A. 28 4, 17
	2			ʾADM		U		TA	ḤNUN	AN		D-AD-MU-TA-ḪU-NA-AN	FN	RA LXV 61 IV 38
				ʾANN		U		TA	ḤNUN			AN-NU-TA-AḪ-NU-UN	FN	RA LXV 61 IV 15+
	1	TA		ḪṢIN					ʾADM		U	TA-AḪ-ZI-IN-AD-MU	FN	M
	1	TA		ʿḎAR	AH							TA-DA-RA	FN	M

PREFIXES, Class 1

TA	2		ŠIMAʿ			TA	ʿQUB			ŠI-ME-TA-GU-UB		M+
	1	TA	ʿTIQ				ʾABN	U		TA-TI-QA-AB-NU		RES 1938 128
	2		ʿAŠTAR			TA	JS̱Iʾ			EŠ$_4$-DAR-TA-ZI	FN	XIII 1 IV 79
	1	TA	BNIJ	T	UM					TAB-NI-TUM	FN	XIII 1 VI 5+
		TA	BNIJ				ʿAŠTAR			TAB-NI-EŠ$_4$-DAR	FN	XIII 1 XIII 15+
	2		NUN		U	TA	BNIJ			D-NU-NU-TA-AB-NI	FN	XII 265 1
			ŠI			TA	BNIJ			ŠI-TAB-NI	FN	RA LXV 64 VI 18
			ŠI			TA	BNIJ			ŠI-TAB-NI-A-JA	FN	RA LXV 66 VII 57
	1	TA	BRUW				ʿAŠTAR			TAB-RU?-EŠ$_4$-DAR	FN	XIII 1 V 43
	2		MUT		A	TA	KWIN			MU-TA-TA-KI-IN		RA LXV 51 IX 78
	1	TA	KWUN	AH						TA-KU-NA	FN	XIII 1 VIII 18+
		TA	KWUN		AJA					TA-KU-NA-IA	FN	C
		TA	KWUN				ḪAʾT	UM		TA-KU-UN-ḪA-TUM	FN	M+
		TA	KWUN				MAʾT	UM		TA-KU-UN-MA-TUM	FN	M, C+
		TA	KWUN				MAʾT	I		TA-KUM-MA-TI	FN	A.+
		TA	KWUN				MITEʿ		JE	TA-KU-UN-MI-TE-E		M
		TA	KWUN				ZULAT	UM		TA-KU-UN-ZU?-LA-TUM	FN	RA LXV 62 V 30
	2		BEʿL		I	TA	LEʾEJ			BE-LI$_2$-TA-LI-IḪ		RA LXV 50 VIII 44
	2		ʾANN		U	TA	LʾIJ			AN-NU-TA-AL-E	FN	M+
			ʿAŠTAR			TA	LʾIJ			EŠ$_4$-DAR-TA-AL-E	FN	XIII 1 V 41+
			MAM		A	TA	LʾIJ			D-MA-MA-TA-AL-E	FN	M
	1	TA	NḪAB	AT	UM					TA-ḪA-BA-TUM	FN	VAS VIII 127 2, 29
		TA	NḪAB	AT	I					TA-ḪA-BA-TI	FN GEN	VAS VIII 127 2
	1	TA	NWUḪ	AH						TA-NU-ḪA	FN	M
		TA	NWUḪ				NAWIJ	UM		TA-NU-UḪ-NA-WI-UM	FN	M
	2		ʾAḪ		I	TA	NWUḪ	A		A-ḪI-TA-NU-A		M
		JA	HWIJ			TA	NWUḪ			IA-WI?-TA-NU		RA LXV 43 III 64
			ḪAʾL		I	TA	NWUḪ	A		ḪA-LI-TA-NU-A		A.+
			ʾIL		I	TA	NWUḪ			I$_3$-LI$_2$-TA-NU-UḪ		XIII 1 IV 19
			ʾIL		I	TA	NWUḪ			I$_3$-LI$_2$-TA-NU		RA LXV 45 V 52
			ḪAM		I	TA	NWUḪ			D-A-MI-TA-NU-UḪ		M+
			ḪAM		I	TA	NWUḪ			D-A-MI-TA-NU		M
			ḪAM		I	TA	NWUḪ	A		D-A-MI-TA-NU-A		M
			ḪAM		U	TA	NWUḪ			D-A-MU-TA-NU		M
			ḪAM		UM	TA	NWUḪ		HU	A-MU-UM-TA-NU-U$_2$		M
			ŠAQAḪ			TA	NWUḪ		HU	SA-QA-AḪ-TA-NU-U$_2$		CT VI 46 2
	1	TA	NWUD	AH						TA-NU-DA	FN	RA LXV 61 IV 45
	1	TA	PTAN				HADD	A		TAP-TA-NA-A-DA		A. 206 5
		TA	PTAN				HADD	A		TAP-DA-NA-TA		A. LATE
	1	TA	PTUN				HADD	A		TAP-TU-NA-A-DA		A. 33 26
	2		ʿAMM		I	TA	QWIM			ḪA-AM-MI-TA-KI-IM	NOM	M
			ʾAŠD		I	TA	QWIM			AŠ$_2$-DI-TA-KI-IM		M+
			ŠUM		U	TA	QWIM			SU-MU-TA-KI-IM		XIII 131 4'
	2		ʿAMM		I	TA	QWUM			AM-MI-TA-KU-UM		A.+
			ʿAMM		I	TA	QWUM					
							MA			AM-MI-TA-KU-UM-MA		A. +
	1	TA	QJIŠ				NAN	I		TA-KI-IŠ-NA-NI	FN?	TIM III 41 6
	2		ŠUM		U	TA	QJIŠ			SU-MU-TA-KI-IŠ		M
	1	TA	QBIJ		IM					TA-AQ-BI-IM	GEN?	M+
	1	TA	QNIJ	T	UM					TA?-AQ-NI-TUM	FN	XIII 1 VIII 74
	2		ʾANN		U	TA	RḪAM			AN-NU-TA-AR-AM	FN	M+
	1	TA	RʿIŠ	AH						DA-RI$_2$-ŠA	FN	U
		TA	RʿIŠ				ḪAʾT	U		TA-RI-IŠ-ḪA-AT-TU	FN	M+
		TA	RʿIŠ				ʿAŠTAR			T[A-R]I-IŠ-EŠ$_4$-DAR	FN	RA LXV 65 VII 36
		TA	RʿIŠ				MAʾT	UM		TA-RI-IŠ-MA-TUM	FN	M+, C
	2		ʾIL		A	TA	RʿIŠ			I-LA-TA-RI-IŠ		B 21
	1	TA	RWIM				ʿAŠTAR			TA-RI-IM-EŠ$_4$-DAR	FN	XIII 1 II 13
		TA	RWIM				ŠAKIM			TA-RI-IM-ŠA-KI-IM		M+
	2		ʿABD		U	TA	RWIM			[ḪA-A]B-DU-TA-RI-IM		M
	1	TA	RWUB	AH						TA-RU-BA	FN	M
	1	TA	RJIB		UM					TA-RI-BU-UM		M
		TA	RJIB		IM					TA-RI-BI-IM	GEN	M
	2		ʾANN		U	TA	RBIJ			AN-NU-TAR-BI	FN	XIII 1 XI 47
	1	TA	RŠAP	AH						TA-AR-SA-BA	FN	RA LXV 64 VI 28
	1	TA	ŠJIM				ʿAŠTAR			TA-ŠI-IM-EŠ$_4$-DAR	FN	XIII 1 IV 28
	2		ʾIŠḪAR	AH		TA	ŠKUB			D-IŠ-ḪA-RA-TA-AŠ-KU-UB	FN	RA LXV 56 V 21+

TA	1	TA	ŚLAL		UM				DA-AŠ-LA-LUM		TA 1931, 538 II
		TA	ŚLAL		UM				DA-AŠ-LA-LU-UM		TA 1931, 435
	2		ʾANN		U	TA	ŚMAʿ		AN-NU-TA-AŠ$_2$-MA-AḪ	FN	M
	1	TA	ŠWUB	AT	UM				TA-ŠU-BA-TUM	FN	M
		TA	ŠWUB	AH					TA-ŠU-BA	FN	M+
	1	TA	ṢJID		UM				TA-ZI-TUM	FN	M
	1	TA	TWUR				ʿAŠTAR		TA-TU-UR-EŠ$_4$-DAR	FN	M
		TA	TWUR				ḪAʾT	UM	TA-DUR-ḪA-TUM		TA 1931, 489
		TA	TWUR				MAʾT	UM	TA-TU-UR-MA-TUM	FN	M+; C+
		TA	TWUR				MAʾT	UM	TA-DUR-MA-TUM	FN	XIII 1 XIV 34+
TU	1	TU	WTAR				ʾABN	U	TU-TAR-AB-NU		M

N	2		LA			JE	N	JBIŠ	U		LA-E-NI-BI-ŠU		YOS XII
	1	N	MŠIḤ					HEDD	A		NA-AM-SI-E-D-IM		A 7646 6
	1 JI	N	NWAḪ	AN							IN-NA-ḪA-AN		M+
	1 JI	N	NWAB	AT	UM						IN-NA-BA-TUM	FN	CT VI 17 13+
	JI	N	NWAB	AT	UM						IN-NA-BA-A-TUM	FN	CT VI 1A 3
	JI	N	NWAB	AT	IM						IN-NA-BA-TIM	FN GEN	CT VI 17 2
	1 JI	N	NWIB		UM						IN-NI-BU-UM		M
	JI	N	NWIB		U						IN-NI-BU		YOS XIII 191:2+
	JI	N	NWIB		U						IN-NE-BU		M
	JI	N	NWIB		I						IN-NI-BI		CLAY PNCP 90+
	1 JI	N	PALIS		U						IP-PA-LI-ZU?		MAOG IV 2 3 HANA
	1 JI	N	RMUK								I-NI-IR-MU-UK		M+
	JI	N	RMUK								I-NE-IR-MU-UK		M
Š	1	Š	BAʿL	AN	UM						ŠU-BI-LA-NU-UM		B 47
	2		ʾIL		A		Š	BAʿL	UM		DINGIR-ŠU-BA-A-LUM		CT II 15 9
			ŠAMIR				Š	BAʿL			ŠA-MI-IR-ŠU-BI-EL		TCL XVIII 125 30
	1	Š	NUʾR					ḪAʾL	I		ŠU-NU-UR-ḪA-LI		KING LIH I 22 4, R. 2
		Š	NUʾR		A			ḪAʾL	U		ŠU-NU-UḪ-RA-ḪA-LU		M+
		Š	NUʾR		A			ḪAʾL	U	HU	ŠU-NU-UḪ-RA-ḪA-LU-U_2		M+
		Š	NUʾR		A			ḪAʾL	U	HU	ŠU-NU-ḪU-RA-ḪA-LU-U_2		XIV 11:1
		Š	NUʾR		A			ḪAʾL	U	HU	ŠU-NU-UḪ-ḪU-RA-ḪA-LU-U_2		XIV 36:1+
		Š	NUʾR		U			ḪAʾL	U		ŠU-NU-UḪ-RU-ḪA-LU		M+
		Š	NUʾR		A			ʿAMM	U		ŠU-NU-UḪ-RA-AM-MU		B 40 HANA+
ŠT	1	ŠT	ḪTIN					ʾIL			(E_2-)ŠA-TA-AḪ-TI-IN-DINGIR	GN	KISURRA
	1 JI	ŠT	ŠNIJ					ʾEL			IŠ-TA-AŠ-NI-EL		SIMMONS 46 30
	JI	ŠT	ŠNIJ					ʾIL			IŠ-TA-AŠ-NI-IL		SYRIA V 274 HANA
	JI	ŠT	ŠNIJ					ʾIL			IŠ-TA-AŠ-NI-DINGIR		VAS IX 156 11+
	JU	ŠT	ŠNIJ					ʾIL			UŠ-TAŠ-NI-DINGIR		VAS IX 130 21+
	JU	ŠT	ŠNIJ					ʾIL			UŠ-TA-AŠ-NI-DINGIR		VAS IX 131 21+
		ŠT	ŠNIJ					ʾIL			ŠA-TA-AŠ-NI-IL		SUMER V 139 NO. 4
T	1 TA	T	ʾAMAR								TA-AḪ-TA-MAR		M
	1	T	ʾAMR		UM						A-TAM-RUM		M+
		T	ʾAMR		UM						A-TA-AM-RU-UM		M+
		T	ʾAMR		IM						A-TAM-RI-IM	GEN	M+
		T	ʾAMR		IM						A-TA-AM-RI-IM	GEN	M+
		T	ʾAMR		AM						A-TAM-RA-AM	ACC	M+
		T	ʾAMR	AT	UM						A-TAM-RA-TUM	FN	M
		T	ʾAMR	AH							A-TAM-RA	FN	M+
		T	ʾAMR		I			ʾIL			A-TAM-RI-DINGIR		M+
	1	T	HILAL					ʾAKK	A		ḪI-IT-LA-AL-AK-KA		RA LXV 54 XII 36,71
	2		ʾANN		U		T	HILAL			AN-NU-ḪI-IT-LA-AL	FN	RA LXV 60 III 18
	1	T	JAŠʿ	AH							IA?-TA-AŠ-ḪA?	FN	M
	1 JA	T	BAḪAR		NA						IA-AB-TA-ḪA-AR-NA	GN	M+
	1	T	BAḪR		UM						BA-TA-AḪ-RUM		M+
		T	BAḪR		IM						BA-TA-AḪ-RI-IM	GEN	M
		T	BAḪR		I						BA-TA-AḪ-RI	GEN	M+
		T	BAḪR	AH							BA-TA-AḪ-RA	FN	RA LXV 59 II 40
	1	T	BANḪ		IM						BA-TA-AN-ḪI-IM	GEN	M
	1 JA	T	MAQAṬ								IA-AM-DA-GA-AD		B 28
	1 JA	T	MAQṬ		AM						IA-AM-TA-AQ-TA-AM	ACC	ABB V 39 REV 8'
	1 JA	T	NAQIM								IA-AN-TA-KI-IM		M+
	1	T	ŠAḪR	AH							SI?-TA-AḪ-RA	FN	IX 291 III 29'
	1 JU	T	ŠALIL		I						UŠ-TA-LI-LI	NOM	M+
	1 ʾA	T	ŠAMAR					HADD	U		AŠ-TA-MAR-D-IM		M+
	2		ʾAB		I	ʾA	T	ŠAMAR			A-BI-AŠ-TA-MA-AR		YOS XIII 489:4
			ʾAB		I	JI	T	ŠAMAR			A-BI-IŠ-TA-MAR		TCL I 226 4, 10+
			ʾIL		I	JI	T	ŠAMAR			I_3-LI_2-IŠ-TA-MAR		EDZARD,DER 67:11
			LI			JI	T	ŠAMAʿ					
								ʾIL			LI?-IŠ?-TA-MI-DINGIR		IX 291 I 18
			ŠUM		U	JI	T	ŠAMAR			SU-MU-UŠ-TA-MAR		TIM II 14 21
	1 JI	T	ŠAWAB		U						IŠ-TA-BU		B 24 HANA
	JI	T	ŠAWAB		U						IŠ-TA-A-BU		MAOG IV 3 36 HANA
	2		ʿAMM		I	JI	T	ŠAMAR			ḪA-AM-MI-IŠ-TA-MAR		M+
			ʿAMM		I	JI	T	ŠAMAR			AM-MI-IŠ-TA-MAR		M
			ʿAMM		I	JI	T	ŠAMAR	U		AM-MI-IŠ-TAM-RU		MRS VI P. 329 UGARIT+
			ʿAMM		I	JI	T	ŠAMAR	U		AM-MI-IS-TAM-RU		MRS VI P. 239 UGARIT+

T	1	JU	T	ŠANIJ				UŠ-TA-AN-NI	RA LXV 44 IV 55; A.+
		JU	T	ŠANIJ		HADD	U	UŠ-TI-NI-D-IM?	A. 36 9+
		JU	T	ŠANIJ		ᵓIL	A	UŠ-TA-NI-I-LA	A. 33 22
	1		T	ŠAQL	UM			ŠA-TA-AQ-LUM	RA LXV 43 III 50

SUFFIXES, Class 1

AH	1		ʾAJAL	AH						A-IA-LA	FN	M+
			ʾAJAL	AH						A-JA-LA	FN	XIII 1 IV 37
	1		ʾABAB	AH						A-BA-BA	FN	C+
	1		ʾADUN	AH						ḪA-DU-NA	FN	XIII 1 III 65
	1		ʾAKIR	AH						A-KI-RA	FN	M
	1		ʾALIM	AH						ḪA-LI-MA	FN	M+
			ʾALIP	AH						ḪA-LI-BA	FN	XIII 1 VIII 37
	1		ʾALL	AH						AL-LA	FN	RA LXV 59 II 42
	1		ʾAMIN	AH						A-MI-NA	FN	RA LXV 64 V 76
			ʾAMIN	AH						AM-MI-IN-NA	FN	RA LXV 64 V 64
	1	T	ʾAMR	AH						A-TAM-RA	FN	M+
	2		ʾANN		U		ʾAŚJ	AH		AN-NU-A-SI-IA	FN	XIII 1 IV 41+
			ʾIŠḪAR	AH			ʾAŚJ	AH		D-IŠ-ḪA-RA-A-SI-IA	FN	XIII 1 XI 43
			ʿAŠTAR				ʾAŚJ	AH		$EŠ_4$-DAR-A-SI-IA	FN	XIII 1 IX 3+
			ʿAŠTAR				ʾAŚJ	AH		$EŠ_4$-DAR-A-ZU-IA	FN	M
			KAKK		A		ʾAŚJ	AH		KA-AK-KA-A-SI-IA	FN	XIII 1 VI 11
	1		ʾAŚD	AH						ḪA-AŠ-DA	FN	RA LXV 58 I 62
	2		ʾIL		I		ʾAŚIJ	AH		I_3-LI_2-A-SI-IA	FN	XIII 1 VII 55
	2		ʾUMM		I		ʾAŠIR	AH		UM-MI-A-ŠI-RA	FN	VAS XIII 73 6,13
	1		ʾATAZ	AH						AT-TA-ZA	FN	M
			ʾATAZ	AH						AT-TA-AZ-ZA	FN	XIII 1 III 9+
	1		ʾATUL	AH						ḪA-TU-LA	FN	RA LXV 65 VII 4
	1		ʾIMM	AH						ḪI-IM-MA	FN	XIII 1 VI 75
	2		ʾIL		I		ʾIMM	AH		I-LI_2-IM-MA	FN	C II 41 56, 44 57
	1		ʾINZ	AH						IN-ZA	FN	XIII 1 XII 7
	1		ʾIŠḪAR	AH			ʾUMM		I	D-IŠ-ḪA-RA-UM-MI	FN	XIII 1 II 47+
			ʾIŠḪAR	AH			ʾAŚJ	AH		D-IŠ-ḪA-RA-A-SI-IA	FN	XIII 1 XI 43
			ʾIŠḪAR	AH			DAMQ	AH		D-IŠ-ḪA-RA-DAM-QA	FN	RA LXV 58 I 18
			ʾIŠḪAR	AH			DUMQ		I	D-IŠ-ḪA-RA-DU-UM-KI	FN	XII 265 3
			ʾIŠḪAR	AH			DANN	AT		IŠ-ḪA-RA-DAN-NA-AT	FN	M
			ʾIŠḪAR	AH			ḎAMR	AT	I	D-IŠ-ḪA-RA-ZA-AM-RA-TI	FN	M
			ʾIŠḪAR	AH			GUML		I	D-IŠ-ḪA-RA-GU-UM-LI	FN	XIII 1 IV 39
			ʾIŠḪAR	AH			LAMAS		I	D-IŠ-ḪA-RA-D-LAMA	FN	XIII 1 IX 23
			ʾIŠḪAR	AH			MALAK		I	D-IŠ-ḪA-RA-M[A-L]A-KI	FN	RA LXV 61 IV 61
			ʾIŠḪAR	AH			NAʿM		I	D-IŠ-ḪA-RA-NA-AḪ-ME	FN	RA LXV 64 VI 37
			ʾIŠḪAR	AH			NIWR		I	D-IŠ-ḪA-RA-NI-RI	FN	RA LXV 59 II 22
			ʾIŠḪAR	AH			NAPŚ		I	D-IŠ-ḪA-RA-NA-AP-SI	FN	XIII 1 VII 13
			ʾIŠḪAR	AH			ŚAMŚ		I	D-IŠ-ḪA-RA-D-UTU-ŠI	FN	XII 265 6
			ʾIŠḪAR	AH			ŚARR	AT		D-IŠ-ḪA-RA-ŠAR-RA-AT	FN	M
			ʾIŠḪAR	AH		TA	ŚKUB			D-IŠ-ḪA-RA-TA-AŠ-KU-UB	FN	RA LXV 56 V 21+
	2		ʿABD				ʾIŠḪAR	AH		AB-DI-D-IŠ-ḪA-RA		A.+
			ʿABD				ʾIŠḪAR	AH		ḪA-AB-DU-D-IŠ-ḪA-RA		XIII 1 II 79+
			ʾUMM		I		ʾIŠḪAR	AH		UM-MI-IŠ-ḪA-RA	FN	XIII 1 V 74, A.+
			ḎU				ʾIŠḪAR	AH		ZU-D-IŠ-ḪA-RA		XIII 64 5
			TAʾK		I		ʾIŠḪAR	AH		TA-KI-D-IŠ-ḪA-RA		JCS XIII 52 293 LE,A.LATE
			TAʾK		U		ʾIŠḪAR	AH		TA-KU-D-IŠ-ḪA-R[A]		JCS XIII 52 293 R, A. LAT
	1	JA	ʾMAR	AH						IA-MA-RA	FN	XIII 1 XIV 26
	1		ʾUDIN	AH						U_2-DI-NA	FN	XIII 1 IV 67
	1		ʾULP	AH						ḪU-UL-PA	FN	C
	1		ʾUNAB	AH						ḪU-NA-BA	FN	XIII 1 VI 50
	1		ḤAJJ	AH						A-IA	FN	XIII 1 X 47
			ḤAJJ	AH						A-I-IA	FN	A. LATE+
	1		ḤAMID	AH						ḪA-MI-DA	FN	RA LXV 58 I 20
	1		ḤANAN	AH						ḪA-NA-AN-NA	FN	C
	1		ḤARAB	AH						ḪA-RA-BA	FN	M
	1		ḤARB	AH						ḪA-AR-B[A]?	FN	RA LXV 62 V 41
	1		ḤARUB	AH						A-RU-B[A]	FN	XIII 1 III 64+
	1		ḤUNIN	AH						U_2-NI-NA	FN	M+
	1		ḤUṢAN	AH						U_2-ZA-NA	FN	XIII 1 II 68
	1		ḪAGUR	AH						ḪA-GU-RA	FN	RA LXV 64 V 63
	1		ḪIGUL	AH						ḪI-GU-LA	FN	M+
	1		ḪILUK	AH						ḪI-LU?-KA	FN	XIII 1 V 81
	1		ʿAḎIR	AH						ḪA-ZI-RA	FN	RA LXV 62 V 26
	2		ʾADM		U		ʿALIJ	AH		D-AD-MU-ḪA-LI-IA	FN	XIII 1 V 55
			TABUB		U		ʿALIJ	AH		D-TA-BU-BU-ḪA-LI-IA	FN	XIII 1 VI 13
	1		ʿAMIS	AH						ḪA-ME-ZA	FN	RA LXV 58 I 24

SUFFIXES, Class 1

AH	2			ʾAM	T		ʿAŠTAR	AH	AM-TI-AŠ-TA-RA	FN?		A. LATE
	1			ʿAZAL	AH				ḪA-ZA-LA	FN		M+
	1			ʿAZIB	AH				ḪA-ZI-BA	FN		XIII 1 IV 35
	1	TA		ʿḎAR	AH				TA-DA-RA	FN		M
	2			ʿABD			ʿIŠTAR	AH	AB-DU-IŠ-TA-RA?			B 9
	1			ʿIZIZ	AH				I-ZI-ZA	FN		RA LXV 58 I 28
	1			ʿIZL	AH				ḪI-IZ-LA	FN		C+
	1			JAʿIL	AH				IA-ḪI-LA	FN		M
	1			JADID	AH				IA-DI-DA	FN		M+
	1			JAMAM	AH				IA-MA-MA?	FN		M
	2			ʾANN		U	JAPʿ	AH	AN-NU-IA-AP-ḪA	FN		XIII 1 IV 3+
	2			ŠARR		UM	JAQR	AH	LUGAL-JA-AQ-RA	FN		XIII 1 X 45
	1			JAŠAR	AH				IA-SA-RA	FN		XIII 1 II 64+
	1		T	JAŠʿ	AH				IA?-TA-AŠ-ḪA?	FN		M
	2			ʿAŠTAR			JAŠʿ	AH	EŠ$_4$-DAR-IA-AŠ-ḪA	FN		M
				BUN		U	JAŠʿ	AH	BU?-NU-IA-AŠ-[ḪA]	FN		XII 1 VII 67
				ŠAMŠ		I	JAŠʿ	AH	D-[UT]U-IA-AŠ-ḪA	FN		XIII 1 IV 43
	1			JATAR	AH				IA-TA-RA	FN		M+
	2			ʾANN		U	JATR	AH	AN-NU-IA-AT-RA	FN		XIII 1 VI 53+
	1	JA		JDIʿ	AH				IA-DI-ḪA	FN		M+
	2			ʾANN		U	JIPʿ	AH	AN-NU-IP-ḪA	FN		XIII 1 VIII 29
				ʿAŠTAR			JIPʿ	AH	EŠ$_4$-DAR-IP-ḪA	FN		XIII 1 VI 19+
	2			ʾAḪ	AT		JIQR	AH	A-ḪA-AT-IQ-RA	FN		M
				ʾAḪ	AT	I	JIQR	AH	A-ḪA-TI-IQ-RA	FN		XIII 1 II 72+
				ʾUMM		I	JIQR	AH	UM-MI-IQ-RA	FN		M+
	1			JIŠʿ	AH				IŠ-ḪA	FN		XIII 1 VIII 25+
	2			ʾADM		U	JIŠʿ	AH	D-AD-MU-IŠ-ḪA	FN		XIII 1 IX 18
				ʾADM		U	JIŠʿ	AH	AD-MU-IŠ-ḪA	FN		XIII 1 IX 57
				ʾANN		U	JIŠʿ	AH	AN-NU-IŠ-ḪA	FN		XIII 1 V 46+
				KAKK		A	JIŠʿ	AH	KA-KA-IŠ-ḪA	FN		M+
	1	JA		JPAʿ	AH				IA-PA-ḪA	FN		M+
	1	JA		JŠUʿ	AH				IA-ŠU-ḪA	FN		M+
	1		T	BAḪR	AH				BA-TA-AḪ-RA	FN		RA LXV 59 II 40
	2			ʿABD			BAʿL	AH	ḪA-AB-DU-BA-AḪ-LA			M
				ʾAM	T		BAʿL	AH	A-MA-AT-D-BA-A-LA	FN		BAGHD. MITT. II 72 5, 9+
				ʾUMM		I	BAʿL	AH	UM-MI-BA-A-LA	FN		A. LATE
				ʿAŠTAR			BAʿL	AH	EŠ$_4$-DAR-BA-AḪ?-LA	FN		M
	2			ḪINN		I	BAJN	AH	IN-NI-BA-NA	FN	NOM	X 81 4
	1			BAKIL	AH				BA-KI-LA	FN		RA LXV 60 III 68
	1			BALIK	AH				BA-LI-KA	FN		A.
				BALIL	AH				BA-LI-LA	FN		XIII 1 VIII 72
	1			BAZUR	AH				BA-ZU-R[A]	FN		XIII 1 VII 2
	1			BEʿL	AH				BE-LA	FN		IX 291 3 9'
	1			BIḪIR	AH				BI-ḪI-RA	FN		M
	1			BIKIN	AH				BI-KI-IN-NA	FN		XIII 1 VIII 27
	1			BIN	AH				BI-[N]A	FN		RA LXV 60 III 62
	1			BIRḪUN	AH				BI-IR-ḪU-UN-NA	FN		XIII 1 XII 3+
	1			BIRKIN	AH				BI-IR-KI-NA	FN		M
	1			BIZKIN	AH				BI-IZ-KI-NA	FN		RA LXV 62 V 22
	1			BURAN	AH				BU-RA-NA	FN		XIII 1 VI 58
	1			DAWIR	AH				DA-I-RA	FN		M
	2			ʾANN		U	DAMQ	AH	AN-NU-DAM-QA	FN		XIII 1 X 51
				ʾIŠḪAR	AH		DAMQ	AH	D-IŠ-ḪA-RA-DAM-QA	FN		RA LXV 58 I 18
				ʿAŠTAR			DAMQ	AH	EŠ$_4$-DAR-DAM-QA	FN		XIII 1 V 50+
	1			DAŠUR	AH		ʿAŠTAR		DA-ŠU-RA-EŠ$_4$-DAR	FN		YOS VIII 51 5
	1			ḎAKUR	AH				ZA-KU-RA	FN		XIII 1 II 40
	1	MA		ḎMAR	AH				MA-AZ-MA-RA	FN		M+
	1			GAJID	AH				GA-I-DA	FN		C; RA LXV 65
	1	TA		KWUN	AH				TA-KU-NA	FN		XIII 1 VIII 18+
	1			KABID	AH				KA-BI-DA	FN		M+
	1			KABKAB	AH				KA-AB-KA-BA	FN		M+
	1			KAKK	AH				KA-AK-KA	FN		M
	2			ʾAJA			KALB	AH	A-IA-KA-AL-BA?	FN		C
	1			KANIŠ	AH				KA-NI-SA			RA LXV 60 III 12+
	1			KAŠER	AH				GA-ŠE-RA	FN		M
	1			KIHIL	AH				KI-ḪI-LA	FN		M+

SUFFIXES, Class 1

AH	1			KIMM	AH					KI-IM-MA	FN	M
	1			KUNDUL	AH					KU-UN-DU-LA	FN	XIII 1 III 21, CT XLIV 54 29
	1			LAʾIP	AH					LA-ḪI-PA	FN	XIII 1 II 65+
	1			LAMAS	AH					LA-MA-ZA	FN	M
	1			MAHIR	AH					MA-ḪI-RA	FN	XIII 1 VII 34
	1			MAKIJ	AH					MA-KI-IA	FN	M
	1			MALIK	AH					MA-LI-KA	FN	M
	1			MANAW	AH					MA-NA-WA	FN	XIII 1 VII 45
	2			JAT		UM	MARṢ	AH		IA-TUM-MAR-ZA		A 21899+
	1			MAŚUB	AH					MA?-SU-BA?	FN	XIII 1 III 24
	1			MAZAL	AH					MA-ZA-AL-LA	FN	XIII 1 IV 40+
	1			MAZUM	AH					MA-ZU-MA	FN	XIII 1 III 22
	1			MENN	AH					ME-EN-NA	FN	XIII 1 I 68+
	1			MINAN	AH					ME-NA-AN-NA	FN	RA LXV 60 III 11
	1			MINN	AH		MINN	AH		MI-IN-NA-MI-IN-NA	FN	XIII 1 XII 1
	2			MINN	AH		MINN	AH		MI-IN-NA-MI-IN-NA	FN	XIII 1 XII 1
	1	ME		NḪIB	AH					ME-EN-ḪI-BA	FN	XIII 1 I 24
	1	JA		NWIḪ	AH					IA-NI-ḪA	FN	RA LXV 58 I 55
		MA		NWIḪ	AH					MA-NI-ḪA	FN	RA LXV 58 I 36+
	1	TA		NWUḪ	AH					TA-NU-ḪA	FN	M
	1	TA		NWUD	AH					TA-NU-DA	FN	RA LXV 61 IV 45
	1			NAḪAR	AH					NA-ḪA-RA	FN	RA LXV 60 III 36
	1			NADUB	AH					NA-DU-BA?	FN	XIII 1 VIII 32+
	1			NAGIH	AH					NA-GI-IA	FN	XIII 1 V 82
	1			NAKAR	AH					NA-KA-RA	FN	XIII 1 VIII 19
	1			NANN	AH					NA-AN-NA	FN	M+
	1			NEJAL	AH					NE-IA-LA	FN	XIII 1 VII 51
	1			NIʿIM	AH					NI-ḪI-MA	FN	M
	1			NIWR	AH					NI-E-RA	FN	A.
	1			NIṢAB	AH					NI-ZA-BA?	FN	RA LXV 68 V 9A
	1			NUʿAM	AH					NU-ḪA-MA	FN	M
	1			NUWR	AH					NU-RA	FN	M
	1			NUBAṬ	AH					NU-BA-TA	FN	M
	1			NUBUṬ	AH					NU-BU-TA	FN	XIII 1 XIV 9
	1			NUMEN	AH					NU-ME-EN-NA	FN	XIII 1 IV 32
	1	MU		PAḪIR	AH					MU-PA-ḪI-RA	FN	XIII 1 VII 47
	1			PATIḤ	AH					PA-TI-ḪA	FN	M+
		MU		PATIḤ	AH					MU-PA-AT-TI-IA	FN	XIII 1 VIII 38+
		MU		PATIḤ	AH					MU-PA-TI-IA	FN	XIII 1 XIII 19+
	1	JA		QWIM	AH					IA-KI-MA	FN	M+
	1	TA		RʿIŠ	AH					DA-RI$_2$-ŠA	FN	U
	1	TA		RWUB	AH					TA-RU-BA	FN	M
	1			RAḤIM	AH					RA-ḪI-MA	FN	XIII 1 II 4+
	1			RAPIʾ	AH					RA-BI-A	FN	XIII 1 VII 32+
	1	TA		RŚAP	AH					TA-AR-SA-BA	FN	RA LXV 64 VI 28
	2			ʾADM		U	RUWB	AH		D-AD-MU-RU-BA	FN	XIII 1 VII 59
	1			SUTAR	AH					ZU?-TA-RA	FN	RA LXV 61 IV 42
	1		T	ŠAḪR	AH					SI?-TA-AḪ-RA	FN	IX 291 III 29'
	1			ŚAKIR	AH					SA-KI-RA	FN	M
	1			ŚALIḤ	AH					SA-LI-ḪA	FN	M+
				ŠALIM	AH					SA-LI-MA	FN	XIII 1 III 29+
	1			ŚAMIʿ	AH					SA-ME-ḪA	FN	RA LXV 60 III 54
	1			ŚARIḤ	AH					SA-RI-ḪA	FN	RA LXV 60 III 39
		MU		ŚARIK	AH					MU-SA-AR-RI-KA	FN	XIII 1 VIII 75
	2			ʾUMM		U	ŚARR	AH		UM-MU-ŠAR-RA	FN	IX 291 33
				ʿAŠTAR			ŚARR	AH		EŠ$_4$-DAR-ŠAR-RA	FN	XIII 1 II 67
				MAM		A	ŚARR	AH		D-MA-MA-ŠAR-RA	FN	M
				NANN		I	ŚARR	AH		D-NA-AN-NI-ŠAR-RA	FN	XIII 1 V 31
	1			ŚAṬAR	AH					ŠA-ṬA$_3$-AR-RA	FN	M
	1			ŚININ	AH					SI-NE-NA	FN	XIII 1 V 51+
				ŚININ	AH					SI-NI-NA	FN	M+
	1			ŚINN	AH					SI-IN-NA	FN	RA LXV 58 I 61
	1	TA		ŠWUB	AH					TA-ŠU-BA	FN	M+
	1			ŠAṬP	AH					ŠA-AṬ-BA	FN	RA LXV 65 VII 39
	1			ŠEʾR	AH		MAM		A	ŠE-RA-D-MA-MA	FN	X 110 3
	1			ŠIMGIN	AH					ŠI-IM-GI-IN-NA	FN	M

SUFFIXES, Class 1

AH	1		ŠIMGIN	AH						ŠI-IM-GI-EN-NA	FN	M
			ŠIMGIN	AH						ŠI-IM-GI-NA	FN	M+, C
	1		ṢADAQ	AH						ZA-DA-GA	FN	U
	1		ṢIBIṬ	AH						ZI-BI-IT-TA	FN	C P. 41+
	1		TATT	AH						TA-AT-TA	FN	RA LXV 62 V 55
	2		ʿAŠTAR				TIWR	AH		D-EŠ$_{4}$-DAR-TE-IR-RA		A.
	1		TURBIN	AH						TU-UR-BI-NA	FN	IX 291 II 17
	1		TURTUR	AH						TU-TU-RA	FN	RA LXV 60 III 67
	1		ṬAJB	AH						ṬA$_{3}$-BA	FN	M+
			ṬAJB	AH						TA-A-BA	FN	M+
	2		ʾUMM		I		ṬAJB	AH		UM-MI-ṬA$_{3}$-BA	FN	M+
			ʾUMM		I		ṬAJB	AH		UM-MI-ṬA$_{3}$-BA-NU	FN	RA LXV 64 VI 34
			BIN	T	U		ṬAJB	AH		BI-IN-DU-ṬA$_{3}$-BA	FN	RA LXV 65 VII 10
	1		ṬUBUQ	AH						TU-BU-QA	FN	M
	1		ZAʾAZ	AH						ZA-ḪA-AZ-ZA	FN	XIII 1 IX 22
	1		ZANAN	AH						ZA-NA-NA	FN	RA LXV 64 V 61
	1		ZIJAD	AH						ZI?-IA?-DA	FN	XIII 1 XIII 25
	1		ZUNN	AH						ZU-UN-NA	FN	XIII 1 IV 51
AJ	1	ʾA	HLUL	AJ	UM					AḪ-LU-LA-UM		CT VIII 38 B 4
	2	JA	WMAʾ				ʿAMM	AJ	I	IA-AW-MA-ḪA-MA-JI-KI	GN	M
	1		JAʿIL	AJ	I					JA-I-LA-JI-KI	GN	M
	2	JA	MWUT				BAʿL	AJ	I	IA-MU-UT-BA-LA-I	GN NOM	M
		JA	MWUT				BAʿL	AJ	I	IA-MU-UT-BA-LA-JI	GN NOM	M
	1		GUBL	AJ	I					GU-UB-LA-A-JI	GN PL NOM	SYRIA XX 111
			GUBL	AJ	I					GU-UB-LA-JI	GN NOM	SYRIA XX 111
	1	JA	MʾAD	AJ	I					IA-AM-ḪA-DA-I-KI	GN GEN	M
	2		ʾIL		U		MALIK	AJ	I	I-LU-MA-LI-KA-JI-KI	GN	XV 127
	2		ʾIL		UM		MULUK	AJ	I	DINGIR-MU-LU-KA-JI-KI	GN	XV 127
	1		NUMḪ	AJ	I					NU-UM-ḪA-I	GN	IX 48 3+
			NUMḪ	AJ	I					NU-UM-ḪA-A-JI	GN	X 5 4
	1	JA	PṬUR	AJ	I					IA-AP-TU-RA-A-JI-KI	GN	M
		JA	PṬUR	AJ	I					IA-AP-TU-RA-JI-KI	GN	M
	1		QAṬAN	AJ	I					QA-TA-NA-A-JI-KI	GN	M
			QAṬAN	AJ	I					QA-TA-NA-JI-KI	GN	M+
			QAṬAN	AJ	IM					QA-TA-NA-IM-KI	GN GEN	M
	1	JA	RWIḤ	AJ	I					IA-RI-ḪA-JI-KI	GN	M
AJIT	1		GUBL	AJITUM						GU-UB-LA-JI-TUM	GN FN	SYRIA XX 111
AK	1		ʿIZZ	AK	UM					I-ZA-KUM		B 24
	1		BEʿL	AK	UM					BE-LA-KUM		CT VIII 31A 21+
			BEʿL	AK	I					BE-LA-KI	GEN	CT VIII 31B 23+
	1		DAWD	AK	UM					DA-DA-KUM		KISURRA 39A 4+
	1		KABL	AK	UM					KA-AB-LA-KU-UM		B 32
	1		MAŚD	AK	UM					MA-AŠ-DA-KUM		TA 30, 615 6
	1		PAʾP	AK	UM					PA-PA-KUM		B 37
	1		PALL	AK	UM					PA-AL-LA-KUM		B 37
			PALL	AK	UM					PA-LA-KUM		YOS XIII 164:1
	1		ŚAPAR	AK	UM					ŠA-BA-AR-KUM		U
	1		ŚAPR	AK	UM					ŠA-AP-RA-KUM		M
	1		TUʾN	AK	UM					TU-NA-KUM		UET V 285 22
AN	1	JA	ʾḪUḎ	AN						IA-ḪU-ZA-AN		RA LXV 43 IV 21
		TA	ʾḪUḎ	AN						TA-ḪU-ZA-AN		RA LXV 52 X 33
	1	JA	ʾWUŠ	AN						IA-U$_{2}$-SA-AN		RA LXV 43 IV 15
	1		ʾAḪIḎ	AN						A-ḪI-ZA-AN		M
	1		ʾAḪN	AN	UM					AḪ-NA-NU-UM		KISURRA 14 4+
	1		ʾAWN	AN	UM					AM-NA-NU-UM	GN	SAKI P. 222+
			ʾAWN	AN	UM					AM-NA-NU-UM	PN	SUMER XIV 49
			ʾAWN	AN	UM					AW-NA-NU-[UM]	TRIBE	M
			ʾAWN	AN	U					AM-NA-NU		BM 80328 9
			ʾAWN	AN	IM					AW-NA-NI-[IM]	GEN	MAM III 320, PSARG MARI
			ʾAWN	AN		JA	ʾRUR			AM-NA-AN-IA-AḪ-RU-UR	TRIBE	BAGHD. MITT. II 56 I 12+
	2		MUT				ʾAWN	AN		MU-UT-AW-NA-AN		B 35 HANA
			MUT		U		ʾAWN	AN	UM	MU-TU-AM-NA-NU-UM		BM 81641 3, 8
			ŚUM		U		ʾAWN	AN	UM	SU-MU-AM-NA-NU-UM		B 38+
			ŚUM		U		ʾAWN	AN	IM	SU-MU-AW-NA-NIM		SUMER XXIII ARABIC 178
	1		ʾAJAL	AN						A-JA-LA-AN		RA LXV 52 X 81
	1		ʾAB	AN	UM					A-BA-NU-UM		U+, SIMMONS 51 18

AN	1	ʾABAB	AN	UM	A-BA-BA-NU-UM		B 71+
		ʾABAB	AN	IM	A-BA-BA-NI-IM	GEN	B 42
		ʾABAN	AN		AB-BA-NA?-AN		M
	1	ʾABIŠ	AN	UM	A-BI-SA-NU-UM		CT XLVIII 29 REV.
	1	ʾADAM	AN	U	AD-DA-MA-NU		RUTTEN 28 12
	1	ʾADM	AN	UM	AD-MA-NU-UM		JCS XXIV 69 NO.3
		ʾADM	AN	UM	ḪA-AD-MA?-NU-UM		VIII 85:29
		ʾADM	AN	IM	ḪA-AD-MA?-NIM	GEN	B 44
	1	ʾAKN	AN	U	AK-NA-NU		B 42
	1	ʾAKUN	AN	IM	A-KU-NA-NIM	GEN	B 92
	1	ʾALM	AN	UM	AL-MA-NU-UM		TA 1931,148
		ʾALM	AN	UM	ḪA-AL-MA-NU-UM		HARRIS 62 14+
	1	ʾALP	AN		AL-PA-AN		M+
	1	ʾAMAN	AN	UM	A-MA-NA-NU-UM		B 42+
		ʾAMAN	AN	IM	A-MA-NA-NIM	GEN	B 43
		ʾAMAT	AN		A-MA-TA-AN		M+
		ʾAMAT	AN		ḪA-MA-TA-AN		RA LXV 43 III 43
	1	ʾAMIN	AN	UM	A-MI-NA-NU-UM		B 43
	1	ʾANT	AN	UM	AN-TA-NU-UM		TA 1930, 698
	1	ʾANZ	AN	UM	AN-ZA-NU-UM		B 43
	1	ʾAP	AN	UM	A-PA-NU-UM		B 43+
	1	ʾAPK	AN	UM	AP-KA-NU-UM		SIMMONS 66 28
	1	ʾAPR	AN		AP-RA-AN		A. LATE
	1	ʾARḪ	AN	UM	AR-ḪA-NU-UM		BM 92657+
	1	ʾARIŠ	AN		ḪA-RI-ŠA-AN		M
	1	ʾASUN	AN		A-ZU-NA-AN		RA LXV 48 VIII 29
	1	ʾAŠM	AN		AŠ-MA-AN		BM 81174 11
		ʾAŠM	AN	UM	ḪA-AŠ-MA-NU-UM		U
		ʾAŠM	AN	I	ḪA-AŠ-MA-NI	GEN	B 44
	1	ʾAŠQUD	AN		AŠ-KU-DA-AN		M
		ʾAŠQUD	AN		ḪA-AŠ-KU-DA-AN		M
		ʾAŠQUD	AN	UM	AŠ-KU-DA-NU-UM		CT XLVIII 86 REV 10+
		ʾAŠQUD	AN	AM	AŠ-KU-DA-NA-AM	ACC	B 43
	1	ʾATAL	AN	UM	A-TA-LA-NU-UM		EDZARD, DER 100:3
		ʾATAM	AN	UM	A-TA-MA-NU-UM		UCP X/3 3 22+
		ʾATAM	AN	UM	AT-TA-MA-NU-UM		SIMMONS 122 16
		ʾATAR	AN	I	A-TA-RA-NI	GEN	HARRIS 71 12
	1	ʾEL	AN	UM	E-LA-NU-UM		U
		ʾEL	AN	I	E-LA-NI		M
	1	ʾELL	AN		EL-LA-AN		M
		ʾELL	AN		E-LA-AN		MAD V, SARG.
		ʾELL	AN	UM	E-EL-LA-NUM		C
		ʾELL	AN	UM	E-LA-NUM		C
		ʾELL	AN	U	E-EL-LA-NU		C
	1	ʾELM	AN	UM	EL-MA?-NU-UM		TA 1931, 538 I
	1	ʾIBIR	AN		I-BI-RA-AN		RA LXV XIII 34
	1	ʾIBL	AN	UM	IB-LA-A-NU-UM		HAV. SYMP. 237 13
		ʾIBL	AN	UM	IB-LA-NU-UM		I
	1	ʾIDAR	AN		I-DA-RA-AN		M
	1	ʾIGAR	AN		I-GA-RA-AN		RA LXV 42 III 15
	1	ʾIL	AN	UM	I-LA-NU-UM		I+, B 45+
		ʾIL	AN	UM	I-LA-A-NU-UM		B 93
	1	ʾILAP	AN		IL-LA-BA-AN		RA LXV 51 X 9
	1	ʾILUR	AN		I-LU-RA-AN		A. 378 10
	1	ʾIMM	AN		IM-MA-AN		M
	1	ʾIŠIM	AN	AJA	I-SI-MA-NA-A		B 22
	1	ʾIŠN	AN	U	IŠ-NA-NU		B 45+
	1	ʾIZAM	AN	UM	I-ZA-MA-NU-UM		B 45
	1 JA	ʾKUR	AN		IA-KU-RA-AN		M
	1 JA	ʾQUD	AN	IM	IA-GU-DA-NIM	GEN	BM 16823A 1
	1	ʾUWŠ	AN		U_2-ŠA-AN		M+
		ʾUWŠ	AN	UM	ḪU-ŠA-NU-UM		B 45+
		ʾUWŠ	AN	UM	ḪU-ŠA-A-NU-UM		KISURRA 48 8
		ʾUWŠ	AN	U	ḪU-SA-NU		4E RENC. ASS. P. 178 4
	1	ʾUDM	AN	UM	ḪU-UD-MA?-NU		XII 712 R 9
	1	ʾUḎUN	AN		U_2-ZU-NA-AN		M+

SUFFIXES, Class 1

AN	1		ʾURR	AN					UR-RA-AN		RA LXV 53 XI 15
	1		ʾURŠAM	AN	AM				UR-SA-MA-NAM	ACC	M+
	1		ʾUŠAT	AN					U_2-SA-TA-AN		M+
	1	JA	ḪJIJ	AN					[I]A?-Ḫ[I]?-IA-AN		RA LXV 41 II 54
	1		ḪAJJ	AN	UM				ḪA-IA-NU-UM		VAS XVI 62 12
			ḪAJJ	AN	UM				A-A-NU-UM		M
			ḪAJJ	AN	I				ḪA-IA-A-NI		JNES XIII 210FF.+ LATE
	1		ḪABIS	AN	I				ḪA-BI-ZA-NI	GEN	CT VIII 42 B 17
	1		ḪARIB	AN					ḪA-RI-BA-AN		M+
			ḪARIB	AN	UM				A-RI-BA-A-NU-UM		SIMMONS 103 13+
			ḪARIB	AN	UM				A-RI-BA-NU-UM		SIMMONS 96 12+
	1		ḪASID	AN	U				ḪA-ZI-DA-NU		M+
			ḪASID	AN	IM				ḪA-ZI-DA-NIM	GEN	M+
	1		ḪATK	AN	UM				AT-GA-NU-UM		U
	1		ḪAZAQ	AN					ḪA-ZA-KA-AN-KI	GN	M
			ḪAZAQ	AN	IM				ḪA-ZA-KA-AN-NIM-KI	GN GEN	C
			ḪAZAQ	AN	IM				ḪA-ZA-KA-NIM-KI	GN GEN	C II 39 13
	1		ḪAZUQ	AN					ḪA-ZU-GA-AN		RA LXV 54 XII 22
	1		ḪIMAR	AN					ḪI-MA-RA-AN-KI	GN	M+
	1		ḪINN	AN	U				ḪI-NA-NU		KISURRA 62 SEAL
	1		ḪIRAB	AN					ḪI-RA-BA-AN		RA LXV 42 II 57
	2		MUT				ḪIRB	AN	MU-UT-ḪI-IR-BA?-AN		VIII 11 4
	1		ḪIṢN	AN	UM				ḪI-IZ-NA-NU-UM		WALTERS, WL 93:2, 14
	1	JI	ḪLIJ	AN					IḪ-LI-IA-AN		RA LXV 42 II 73+
	2		ʾADM		U	TA	ḪNUN	AN	E-AD-MU-TA-ḪU-NA-AN	FN	RA LXV 61 IV 38
	1		ḪUBAS	AN					ḪU-BA-ZA-AN		M
	1		ḪUNIN	AN	UM				ḪU-NI-NA-NU-UM		I
	1		ḪUNN	AN	UM				ḪU-NA-NU-UM		TA 30 615 18+
			ḪUNN	AN	IM				ḪU-NA-NIM	GEN	B 93
	1	ME	ḪZIQ	AN					ME-ZI-QA-AN		RA LXV 44 IV 30
	1		ḪAʾAN	AN					ḪA-A-NA-AN		C+
	1		ḪAʾL	AN	UM				ḪA-LA-NU-UM		KISURRA 57 4, SEAL
			ḪAʾL	AN	UM				ḪA-LA-NUM_2		KISURRA 24 2
	1		ḪAʾŠ	AN	U				ḪA-SA-NU		M
	1		ḪAWR	AN	IM				ḪA-AW-RA-NIM	GEN	B 44
			ḪAWR	AN			ʾAB	I	ḪA-AW-RA-AN-A-BI		M
			ḪAWR	AN			ʾAB	I	ḪA-AW-RA-NA-A-BI		M+
	1		ḪABIʾ	AN	U				ḪA-BI-A-NU		YOS XIII 175:12
			ḪABIR	AN					ḪA-BI-RA-AN		RA LXV 54 XII 21
	1		ḪABZUR	AN					ḪA-AB-ZU-RA-AN		RA LXV 48 VIII 21+
	1		ḪAŠIJ	AN	UM				ḪA-ŠI-A-NU-UM		TA 1931, 538 III
	1		ḪIBR	AN					Ḫ[I-I]B-RA-AN		RA LXV P. 42 III 6
	1	JA	ḪMUṬ	AN					IA-AḪ-MU-DA-AN		M
	1	MA	ḪŠIM	AN	UM				MA-AḪ-ŠI-MA-NU-UM		B 46+
	1		ḪUʾD	AN	UM				ḪU-DA-A-NU-UM		SIMMONS 83 8
	1		ḪUʾT	AN	UM				ḪU-TA-NU-UM		B 45
	1		ḪUʾZ	AN	UM				ḪU-ZA-NU-UM		RA LXV 55 XIII 13+
	1		ḪUMR	AN	UM				ḪU-UM-RA-NU-UM		U
	1		ḪURR	AN	UM				ḪU-UR-RA-NU-UM		CT IV 25C 15
	1		ḪURṢ	AN	UM				ḪU-UR-ZA-NU-UM		B 44
			ḪURṢ	AN	U				ḪU-UR-ZA-NU-KI	GN	A.
			ḪURṢ	AN	IM				ḪUR-ZA-NIM	GEN	B 44
			ḪURṢ	AN	IM				ḪUR-ZA-A-NIM	GEN	B 44
			ḪURṢ	AN	IM				ḪU-UR-ZA-NIM	GEN	B 44
	1		ḪURUṢ	AN					ḪU-RU-ZA-AN		RA LXV 44 IV 53+
			ḪURUṢ	AN	UM				ḪU-RU-ZA-NU-UM		B 44
	1		ḪUZIR	AN					ḪU-ZI-RA-AN		RA LXV 50 VIII 67+
			ḪUZIR	AN	UM				ḪU-ZI-RA-NU-UM		B 45
	1		ḪUZM	AN	UM				ḪU-UZ-MA-N[U-UM]		TA 1931, 265
	1		ʿAWIQ	AN					A-I-GA-AN		RA LXV 52 X 58
	1		ʿABD	AN					ḪA-AB-DA-AN		M, C+
			ʿABD	AN					AB-DA-AN		M
			ʿABD	AN	U				AB-DA-NU		CT XLV 59 6
			ʿABD	AN	U				AB-TA-NU		A. LATE
			ʿABD	AN	UM				ḪA-AB-DA-[NUM]?		PBS VIII/2 260 4
			ʿABD	AN	A				AB-TA-NA	NOM	A. LATE

AN	1		ʿADN	AN						ḪA-AD-NA-AN		M, C
			ʿADN	AN	UM					AD-NA-NU-UM		TIM III 44 19+
	1		ʿAḎAR	AN	IM					ḪA-ZA-RA-NIM	GEN	B 44
	1		ʿAḎIR	AN						A-ZI-RA-AN		A. P. 131 LATE+
	1		ʿAḎR	AN						ḪA-AZ-RA-AN		M
			ʿAḎR	AN	UM					AD-RA-NU-UM		I., CT XLVIII 88 REV.
	1		ʿAMIS	AN	U					ḪA-MI-ZA-NU		M
	1		ʿAMM	AN						ḪA-AM-MA-AN		M+
			ʿAMM	AN	UM					ḪA-AN-MA-NU-UM		M
			ʿAMM	AN	U					ḪA-AM-MA-NU		M
			ʿAMM	AN	IM					ḪA-MA-NIM	GEN	M
			ʿAMM	AN	IM					ḪA-AM-MA-NIM	GEN	M
	1		ʿAQB	AN						ḪA-AQ-BA-AN		M+
			ʿAQB	AN						AQ-BA-AN		M
			ʿAQB	AN	UM					AQ-BA-NU-UM		RUTTEN 40 2+
	1		ʿARAD	AN						ḪA-RA-DA-AN		M
	1		ʿARD	AN	UM					ḪA-AR-DA-NU-UM		M+
	1		ʿARIṢ	AN	UM					A-RI-ZA-NU-UM		U
			ʿARIṢ	AN	U					ḪA-RI-ZA-NU		PBS II/1 P. 23+ LATE
	1		ʿARṢ	AN	UM					AR-ZA-NU-UM		B 43+
	1		ʿAZAB	AN	I					A-ZA-BA-NI		TA 1931, 216
			ʿAZAZ	AN	UM					A-ZA-ZA-NU-UM		B 92
	1		ʿAZIB	AN						ḪA-ZI-PA-AN		RA LXV 44 IV 25
			ʿAZIZ	AN						A-ZI-ZA-AN		RA LXV 44 IV 45
	1 JA		ʿDUN	AN	UM					IA-AḪ-DU-NA-NU-UM		JCS XXIV 60 NO.51 REV.
	1		ʿINAB	AN	UM					I-NA-BA-NU-UM		U
	1		ʿIQB	AN						ḪI-IQ-BA-AN		M+
			ʿIQB	AN	UM					IQ-BA-NU-UM		I+
	1		ʿIZZ	AN						IZ-ZA-AN		M
			ʿIZZ	AN						I-ZA-AN		RA LXV 44 IV 35
			ʿIZZ	AN	UM					I-ZA-NUM_2		U
			ʿIZZ	AN	UM					I-ZA-NU-UM		U
			ʿIZZ	AN	I					IZ-ZA-NI		M
	1 JA		ʿQUB	AN						IA-KU-B[A]-AN		RA LXV 45 V 57
	1 MU		WQIR	AN	UM					MU-GI-RA-NU-UM		U
	1		JAʾN	AN						JA-NA-AN-KI	GN	M+
	1		JAʿIL	AN						JA-I-LA-AN		M
			JAʿIL	AN	U					JA-I-LA-NU	TRIBE	C
			JAʿIL	AN	IM					JA-I-LA-NIM	TRIBE GEN	M+, SHEMSHARA P. 100+
			JAʿIL	AN	I					JA-I-LA-NI	TRIBE	SHEMSHARA P.100
	1		JAD	AN	UM					IA-DA-NU-UM		SIMMONS 131 17
	1		JAMM	AN						IA-AM-MA-AN		YOS XIII 514:6
	1		JAQR	AN						[I]A-AQ-RA-AN		RA LXV 44 IV 37
	1		JARQ	AN						IA-AR-QA-A[N]		M
	1		JAŠAB	AN						IA-ŠA-BA-AN		RA LXV 45 V 35
	1		JID	AN	UM					I-DA-NU-UM		I+
	1		JITUM	AN	IM					I-TU-MA-NIM	GEN	B 45
	1 JA		JQIR	AN	U					IA-KI-RA-NU		M
	1 JI		JRID	AN	UM					I-RI-DA-NU-UM		M
	1 ME		JTIR	AN	UM					ME-TE-RA-NU-UM		TA 1930, 489
	1		BAʾAN	AN	UM					BA-A-NA-NU-UM		B 43
	1		BAʿD	AN						BA-AḪ-DA-AN		RUTTEN 7 18+
			BAʿD	AN	UM					BA-AḪ-DA-NUM		HARRIS 106 5
			BAʿD	AN	UM					BA-DA-NU-UM		U
			BAʿD	AN	UM					BA-TA-NUM_2		U
			BAʿD	AN	U					BA-AḪ-TA-NU		BM 17060 10
			BAʿD	AN	U	HU				BA-AḪ-TA-NU-U_2		BM 17060 2
	1	Š	BAʿL	AN	UM					ŠU-BI-LA-NU-UM		B 47
			BAʿL	AN						BA-LA-AN		M+
			BAʿL	AN						BA-A-LA-AN		RA LXV 46 VI 48
			BAʿL	AN						BA-AḪ-LA-AN		M
			BAʿL	AN	UM					BA-LA-NU-UM		B 43+
	2		BUN		U		BAʿL	AN	U	BU-NU-BA-AḪ-LA-NU		M
	1		BAWŠ	AN	UM					BA-ŠA-NU-UM		TA 30 615
			BAWŠ	AN	U					BA-SA-NU		MAOG 4 440 HANA
	1		BAWZ	AN	UM					BA-ZA-NU-UM		B 43+

AN	1		BAJN	AN	UM				BA-NA-NU-UM		B 43+
			BAJN	AN	UM				BA-A-NA-NU-UM		B 43
			BAJN	AN	IM				BA-NA-NIM	GEN	B 43
	1		BALṬ	AN					BA-AL-TA-AN		M
	1		BANIḪ	AN					BA-NI-ḪA-AN		M
	1		BANUQ	AN					BA-NU-KA-AN		RA LXV 55 XIII 46
	1		BAQQ	AN	UM				BA-AQ-QA-NU-UM		M
			BAQQ	AN	IM				BA-AQ-QA-NIM	GEN	M
	1		BAŠAR	AN					BA-SA-RA-AN		RA LXV 50 VIII 41
	1		BATQ	AN	UM				BA-AT-GA-NU-UM		ZA XLII 41
	1		BAZIḪ	AN	UM				BA-ZI-ḪA-NU-UM		TA 1931, 230 U
	1		BEʿL	AN	UM				BE-LA-NU-UM		M+
			BEʿL	AN	IM				BE-LA-NIM	GEN	M+
	1		BIʿD	AN	UM				BI-DA-NU-UM		SIMMONS 98 9+
	1		BIKN	AN	UM				BI-IK-NA-NU-UM		VAS VIII 1 21+
	1		BIN	AN					BI-NA-AN		RA LXV 43 IV 14
	1		BINAḪ	AN					BI-NA-ḪA-AN		M
	1	JA	BLUṬ	AN	U				IA-AB-LU-TA-NU		MRS VI P. 261+
	1		BUʿD	AN					BU-DA-AN		M
	2		KIWN			BUWZ	AN	UM	KI-IN-BU-ZA-NU-UM		HARRIS 68 14
	1		BUDAM	AN					BU-DA-MA-AN		RA LXV 51 X 4
	1		BUKŠ	AN	UM				BU-UK-SA-NU-UM		PBS XIV 495
	1		BULUK	AN					B[U]-LU-GA-AN		RA LXV 46 VI 22
	1		BUN	AN	UM				BU-NA-NU-UM		B 44
	1		BUQQ	AN					BU-QA-AN		C+
			BUQQ	AN					BU-UK-KA-AN		M
			BUQQ	AN	UM				BU-GA-NU-UM		I+
	1		BURBUR	AN					BU-UR-BU-RA-AN		RA LXV 50 VIII 69
	1		BURQ	AN					BU-UR-QA-AN		M+
			BURQ	AN	U				BU-UR$_2$-GA-NU		BM 17028 5
			BURQ	AN	UM				BU-UR-GA-NU-UM		UET V 482 5
	1		BURR	AN					BU-UR-RA-AN		RA LXV 47 VII 43
	1		BUZZ	AN	UM				BU-UZ-ZA-NU-UM		M
	1	JA	DWUR	AN					IA-DU-RA-AN		M
	1		DAWD	AN	UM				DA-AW-DA-NU-UM		HARRIS 19A 6+
			DAWD	AN	UM				DA-DA-NU-UM		SIMMONS 92 14 M+
			DAWD	AN	U				DA-DA-NU		M
			DAWD	AN	IM				DA-AW-DA-NIM	GEN	B 17+
			DAWD	AN	IM				DA-AM-DA?-NIM	GEN	CT XLVII 78:37
			DAWD	AN	IM				DA-DA-NI-IM	GEN	HARRIS 60:6
			DAWD	AN	I				DA?-DA-NI	FN NOM	M
	1		DAM	AN	UM				DA-MA-NU-UM		B 44
	1		DAMQ	AN	UM				DA-AM-QA-NU-UM		SIMMONS 67 7
			DAMQ	AN	UM				DAM-QA-NU-UM		SIMMONS PASSIM
			DAMQ	AN	U				DAM-QA-NU		XIII 1 II 1
	1		DIʾL	AN	UM				DI-LA-NU-UM		B 44
	1		DIDAM	AN	UM				DI-DA-MA-NU-UM		B 44
	1		DUWD	AN	UM				DU-DA-NU-UM		CT XLVIII 87
			DUWD	AN	IM				DU-DA-NIM		M
	1		DULQ	AN	UM				TU-UL-GA-NUM$_2$		U
	1		DUMAT	AN					DU-MA-TA-AN		XIV 47:19
	1		ḎAMAR	AN	UM				ZA-MA-[RA]?-NU-[UM]		TA 1930, 615 28
			ḎAMAR	AN	IM				ZA-AM-MA-RA-NIM-KI	GN GEN	C II 39 8
	1		ḎAMUR	AN					ZA-MU-RA-AN		M
	1		ḎANAB	AN					ZA-NA-BA-AN		RA LXV 41 II 51+
	1		ḎARʿ	AN					(E$_2$)-ZA-AR-ḪA-AN-KI	GN	M+
			ḎARʿ	AN	UM				ZA-AR-ḪA-NU-UM	GN	B 48
	1		ḎIKR	AN					ZI-IK-RA-AN		RA LXV 51 IX 34
	1		ḎIMR	AN					ZI-IM-RA-AN		M+
			ḎIMR	AN	AM				ZI-IM-RA-NAM	ACC	M+
	1	JA	GJIḪ	AN					IA-G[I]-ḪA-A[N]		M
	1		GAʾG	AN	UM				GA-GA-NU-UM		B 44+
	1		GAʾN	AN					GA-NA-AN		RA LXV 54 XII 5
	1		GAJD	AN	IM				GA-DA-NIM	GEN	B 44
	1		GABN	AN	UM				GA-AB-NA-NU-UM		SIMMONS 107 14
	1		GALD	AN	U				GA-AL-DA-NU		B 44+

AN	1	GAMIR	AN	UM	GA-MI-RA-NU-UM		TA 1931, 538 I, V?
	1	GANAM	AN	UM	GA-NA-MA-NU-UM		TA 1931, 438
	1	GANIB	AN		GA-NI-BA-AN		RA LXV 42 II 80+
		GANIN	AN	UM	GA-NI-NA-NU-UM		BIN VII P. 12+
	1	GAZIZ	AN	UM	GA-ZI-ZA-NU-[UM]		M
	1	GIJD	AN	UM	GI-DA-NUM$_2$		BIROT,TEA 70 C REV. I 7
		GIJD	AN	UM	GI-DA-NU-UM		SIMMONS 11 1+
		GIJD	AN	IM	GI-DA-NI-IM	GEN	SIMMONS 12 6
		GIJD	AN	IM	GI-DA-NIM	GEN	M, SIMMONS 16 4
	1	GIZZ	AN	UM	GI-ZA-NU-UM		B 93
		GIZZ	AN	U	GI-ZA-NU		B 93
		GIZZ	AN	IM	GI-ZA-NI-IM	GEN	B 44
	1	GUʾG	AN	UM	GU$_2$-GA-NU-UM		TA 30, 111 6
	1	GUʾZ	AN		GU-ZA-AN		RA LXV 53 XI 57;64
	1	GUBʾ	AN	UM	GU-UB-ḪA-NU-UM		M
	1	GULAL	AN		GU-LA-LA-AN		RA LXV 47 VII 55
	1	GURD	AN		GU-UR-DA-AN		M
	1 JA	KWUN	AN		JA-GU-NA-AN		U
	JA	KWUN	AN		IA-KU-NA-AN		M+
	1	KAʾŠ	AN	UM	KA-SA-NU-UM		SIMMONS 128:5
	1	KAHAL	AN		KA-A-LA-AN		M+
	1	KAWJ	AN		KA-A-IA-AN		RA LXV 51 IX 58
		KAWJ	AN		KA-A-IA-AN	FN	C
	1	KABAS	AN	UM	GA-BA-ZA-NU-UM		TA 1931,262
	1	KABID	AN	UM	GA-BI-DA-NU-UM		TA 1930,486 OLDER OB
	1	KABKAB	AN		GA-GA-BA-AN-KI	GN	IRAQ VII 66 SARGONIC
	1	KABŠ	AN	UM	KA-AB-SA-NU-UM		YOS V 18 17
	1	KAMT	AN		KA-AM-TA-AN		M
	1	KANAP	AN		KA-NA-PA-AN		M+
	1	KANIK	AN		KA-NI-KA-AN		M
		KANIŠ	AN		KA-NI-SA-AN		M+
	1	KANZ	AN		KA-AN-ZA-AN	FN	C+
	1	KARIT	AN		KA-RI-TA-AN		RA LXV 41 II 36
	1	KARŠ	AN		KA-AR-ŠA-AN		RA LXV 54 XII 23
	1	KAŠP	AN	U	KA-AŠ$_2$-BA-NU		M
	1	KIʾL	AN		KI-LA-AN		M
	1	KIBIS	AN		KI-BI-ZA-AN		M
	1	KIMM	AN		KI-IM-MA-AN	FN	C
	1	KIMR	AN	U	KI-IM-RA-NU		M
	1	KIRB	AN		KI-IR-BA-AN		RA LXV 51 IX 36
		KIRB	AN	UM	GIR$_3$-BA-NUM$_2$		U
	1	KIŠAM	AN	U	KI-ŠA?-MA-NU		XIII 1 V 60
	1	KITT	AN	IM	KI-IT-TA-NI-IM	GEN	SIMMONS 63 2
	1	KUʾR	AN	UM	KU-RA-NU-UM		B 45
		KUʾR	AN	U	KU-RA-NU		B 45, M, C+
	1	KUʾŠ	AN		KU-SA-AN		M+
	1	KUʾT	AN		KU-TA-AN		M
		KUʾT	AN	UM	KU-TA-NU-UM		RUTTEN 38 20+
		KUʾT	AN	UM	KU-TA-A-NU-UM		SIMMONS 98 14
	1	KUʾZ	AN		KU-ZA-AN		XIV 86:5+
		KUʾZ	AN	UM	KU-ZA-NU-UM		B 46
		KUʾZ	AN	U	KU-ZA-NU		B 46
	1	KUWN	AN	UM	KU-NA-NU-UM		RUTTEN 1 19+
		KUWN	AN	IM	KU-NA-NI-IM	GEN	M
	1	KUBB	AN	UM	KU-UB-BA-NU-UM		B 45
	1	KUDAD	AN	UM	KU-DA-DA-NU-UM		U
	1	KUKKUŠ	AN		KU-KU-SA-AN		RA LXV 46 VI 3
		KUKKUŠ	AN	UM	KU-UK-KU-ZA-NU-UM		M
		KUKKUŠ	AN	IM	KU-UK-KU-ZA-NIM	GEN	M
	1	KULP	AN	UM	KU-UL-BA-NU-UM		TA 1931,148
		KULP	AN	UM	GUL-BA-NU-UM		U
	1	KUMIS	AN		KU-ME-ZA-AN		RA LXV 50 VIII 53
	1	KUMT	AN	UM	GU-UM-DA-NU-UM		HSM 7936, UR III
	1	KUNZ	AN	UM	KU-UN-ZA-NU-UM		BIROT,TEA 65:17
		KUNZ	AN	UM	KU-UN-ZA-NUM$_2$		TA 1930,181+
		KUNZ	AN	AM	KU-UN-ZA-NAM	ACC	TA 1930,181

AN	1	KURAŠ	AN	UM	KU-RA-ŠA-NU-UM		LAESSOE P. 53+
	1	KURD	AN	UM	KUR-DA-A-NU-UM		RUTTEN 11 26
	1	KURŠ	AN	UM	KU-UR$_2$-ŠA-NU-UM		B 45
		KURŠ	AN	U	KU-UR-[S]A-NU		M
		KURŠ	AN	I	KU-UR$_2$-SA-NI	NOM	M
	1	KUŠAP	AN	UM	KU-SA-PA-NU-UM		TIM III 57 6 66 6
	1	KUŠR	AN	UM	KU-UŠ-RA-NU-UM		SIMMONS 51 17
	1	LAʾAT	AN		LA-ḪA-TA-AN		RA LXV 51 IX 68
	1	LAʾIP	AN		LA-ḪI-PA-AN		M+
	1	LALAʾ	AN	UM	LA-LA-A-NU-UM		UCP X/3 2 27
	1	LAMUM	AN	UM	LA-MU-MA-NU-UM		I; TA 1931,148
	1	LAND	AN		LA-AN-DA-AN		C
	1	LAŠG	AN		LA$_2$-AŠ$_2$-GA-AN		RA XXXIV 176
	1	LUMM	AN	UM	LU-MA-NU-UM		SIMMONS 94 12+
		LUMM	AN	UM	LU-MA-A-NU-UM		SIMMONS 103 5
		LUMM	AN	UM	LUM-MA-NU-UM		SIMMONS 96 11+
		LUMM	AN	UM	LUM-MA-A-NU-UM		SIMMONS 105 16+
	1	MAʾD	AN	UM	MA-AḪ-DA-NU-UM		I
	1	MAʾN	AN	UM	MA-AḪ-NA-NU-UM		HILPRECHT AV P. 91
	1	MAʾŠ	AN	IM	MA-SA-NIM	GEN	CT XLV 93 6
	1	MAʾZ	AN	UM	MA-ZA-NU-UM		UET V 625 9
		MAʾZ	AN	I	MA-ZA-NI		KISURRA 68A 10+
	1	MAHIR	AN	IM	MA-ḪI-RA-NIM	GEN	C II 2 8
	1	MAHR	AN	UM	[M]A-AḪ-RA-NU-UM		U
	1	MAKAJ	AN		MA-KA-A-AN		RA LXV 43 IV 2+
		MAKAL	AN	U	MA-KA-LA-NU		VAS IX 34 6
	1	MAKIJ	AN	UM	MA-KI-A-NU-UM		TA 31, 223
	1	MANIJ	AN	UM	MA?-NI-A-NU-UM		TA 1931, 538 II
	1	MARIʾ	AN	UM	MA-RI-A-NU-UM		B 46
	1	MARMAR	AN	IM	MA-AR-MA-RA-NIM	GEN	B 93
	1	MAŠIḪ	AN		MA-SI-ḪA-AN		XIII 1 XI 58+
	1	MIʾD	AN	UM	MI-DA-NU-UM		U+
	1	MILK	AN	UM	MI-IL-GA-NU-UM		U; TA 31, 148
		MILK	AN	UM	MI-EL-GA-NU-UM		TA 1931, 538 I
	1 JA	MLIK	AN		IA-AM-LI-KA-AN		M
	1	MUʾZ	AN	I	MU-ZA-NI		KISURRA 1A 3+; M
	1	MUHR	AN	UM	MU-RA-NU-UM		U
	1	MULUK	AN		MU-LU-GA-AN		RA LXV 41 II 35
	1	MUNAN	AN	UM	MU-NA-NA-NU-UM		B 46
	1	MUŠAR	AN		MU-ŠA-RA-AN		RA LXV 50 VIII 65
	1	MUT	AN	UM	MU-DA-NU-UM		U+
		MUT	AN	UM	MU-TA-NU-UM		B 46
		MUT	AN	I	MU-TA-NI		A. 52 28
	1 JI N	NWAḪ	AN		IN-NA-ḪA-AN		M+
	1 JA	NWUḪ	AN		IA-NU-ḪA-AN		RA LXV 40 I 43
	1	NAHR	AN	UM	NA-RA-NU-UM		B 47
	1	NAʿM	AN	U	NA-AḪ-MA-NU		M+
		NAʿM	AN	IM	NA-MA-NI-IM	GEN	TIM III 46 15
	1	NAWḪ	AN		NA-ḪA-AN	TRIBE	M
		NAWḪ	AN	UM	NA-ḪA-NU-UM		U
	1	NABAŠ	AN	UM	NA-BA-SA-NUM		BM 17072 9,12+
	1	NABL	AN	UM	NA-AB-LA-NU-UM		U+, B 46+
		NABL	AN	UM	NA-AB-LA-NUM$_2$		U+
	1	NAGIH	AN	UM	NA-GI$_4$-A-NU-UM		TA 30 615 13
		NAGIŠ	AN	UM	NA-GI$_4$-SA-NU-UM		RUTTEN 2 8+
		NAGIŠ	AN	UM	NA-GI-SA-NU-UM		RUTTEN 5 8
	1	NAPŠ	AN	UM	NA-AP-SA-NU-UM		U, B 46+
		NAPŠ	AN	UM	NA-AP-ŠA-NU-UM		U+, I+
		NAPŠ	AN	U	NA-AP-SA-NU-KI	GN	B 46
		NAPŠ	AN	UM	NA-AP-ZA-NU-UM		CT XLV 115 14
	1	NARB	AN	IM	NA-AR-BA-NIM	GEN	A 21950
	1	NAṢAB	AN	UM	NA-ZA-BA-NU-UM		TCL I 111 3
	1	NIQM	AN		NI-IQ-MA-AN		M
		NIQM	AN	UM	NI-IQ-MA-NU-UM		B 47+
		NIQM	AN	UM	NI-IQ-MA-A-NU-UM		B 47+
	1 JA	NŠIʾ	AN		IA-AŠ$_2$-SI-IA-AN		M

AN	1 JA	NṢIB	AN				IA-AN-ZI-BA-AN		M
	JA	NṢIB	AN				IA-AN-ZI-PA-AN		M
	1	NUWP	AN	UM			NU-PA-NU-UM		SIMMONS 95 10+
		NUWP	AN	UM			NU-PA-A-NU-UM		SIMMONS 103 7+
	1	NUKR	AN	UM			NU-UK-RA-NU-UM		U+
	1	NUNM	AN				NU-UN-MA-AN		RUTTEN 26 9
	1	NUZAM	AN				NU-ZA-MA-AN		XIII 1 V 22
	1 MA	NZAL	AN	UM			MA-AN-ZA-LA-NU-UM		UET V 465 17
	1 JA	PḪUR	AN	U			IA-AP-ḪU-RA-NU		M
	1	PADAL	AN				PA-DA-LA-AN		RA LXV 51 IX 33
	1	PAKN	AN	UM			PA-AK-NA-NU-UM		B 47+
		PAKN	AN	IM			PA-AK-NA-NIM	GEN	B 47
		PAKN	AN	A			PA-AK-NA-NA	GEN	BE VI/2 81 14
	1	PARG	AN	UM			PA-AR-GA-NU-UM		B 47
	1	PAṬAR	AN	UM			BA-DA-RA-NU-UM		SIMMONS 31 5
	1	PILS	AN	UM			BIL-ZA-NU-UM		BM 80363 8
	1 ʾA	PTUN	AN	UM			AP-TU-NA-NU-UM		YOS VIII 176 SEAL
	1	PULAḪ	AN				PU-LA-ḪA-AN		M
	1	PULS	AN				PU-UL-ZA-AN		M
	1	PURʿUŠ	AN	U			PU-UR-ḪU-ŠA-NU		M
	1	PUZUR	AN				BU-ZU-RA-AN		RA LXV 53 XI 10
	1	QADM	AN	UM			GA-AD-MA-NU-UM		U
	1	QANAT	AN	UM			GA-NA-TA-NU-UM		KISURRA 30 7
	1	QANIJ	AN	U			KA-NI-IA-NU		M
	1	QAQQAD	AN				QA-QA-DA-AN		XIV 47:20
		QAQQAR	AN				QA?-QA-RA?-AN		VII 198:14
	1	QARN	AN	A			QAR-NA-NA	GEN	SIMMONS 13 5
		QARN	AN	UM			QAR-NA-NU-UM		B 93+
	1	QAṬR	AN	UM			GA-AT-RA-NU-UM		RUTTEN 14 22
	1	QIDM	AN	UM			KI-ID-MA-NU-UM		U
	1 JI	QRIB	AN	UM			IQ-RI-BA-NU-UM		I
	1 JA	RḪAM	AN				IA-AR-ḪA-MA-AN	FN	RA LXV 55 XIII 51
	1 MA	RḪAŠ	AN				MAR-ḪA-ŠA-AN		RA LXV 54 XII 12
	1	RAWM	AN	UM			RA-MA-NU-UM		B 47
	1	RAJB	AN				RA-[BA]?-AN		RA LXV 47 VI 67
		RAJB	AN	UM			RA-BA-NU-UM		RUTTEN 3 6+
		RAJB	AN	UM			RA-BA-A-NU-UM		RUTTEN 13 3, 8, SEAL+
	1	RABAB	AN				RA-BA-BA-AN		M
		RABAB	AN	UM			RA-BA-BA-NU-UM		KISURRA 187 11+
	1	RAMAM	AN	UM			RA-MA-MA-NU-UM		B 93
	1	RAMIK	AN	UM			RA-MI-GA-NU-UM		TA 1931, 538 II
	1	RAPAʾ	AN	UM			RA-PA-NU-UM		BM 78768
	1 MA	RDAP	AN				MAR-DA-BA-AN		ITT P.4, 7031 UR III
	MA	RDAP	AN	UM			MAR-DA-BA-NU-UM		U
	1	RIWḪ	AN				RI-ḪA-AN		C
	1	RIWM	AN				[R]I?-MA-AN		RA LXV 41 II 8
		RIWM	AN	UM			RI-MA-NU-UM		U
	1	RIGM	AN	U			RI-IG-MA-NU		M
		RIGM	AN	UM			RI-IG-MA-NUM		M
	1	RUWB	AN				RU-BA?-AN		RA LXV 45 V 34
	2 JI	NDIN			RUŠP	AN	I-DIN-D-RU-UŠ-PA-AN		MAOG IV 2 5 HANA+
	JI	NDIN			RUŠP	AN	I-DIN-D-RU-UŠ$_2$-PA-AN		MEL. SYR. I 275
	1 JA	SNIQ	AN				IA-AS-NI-KA-AN		RA LXV 50 VIII 51
	1	SUṬIʾ	AN	UM			ZUM-TI-A-NU-U[M]		TA 1930, 6
	1 JA	ŠJIT	AN				IA-SI-TA-AN		M+
	JA	ŠJIT	AN				IA-SI-IT-TA-AN		M
	1	ŠAʾL	AN	UM			ŠA-LA-NU-UM		TA 30, 615 23
	1	ŠAʾR	AN	UM			SA-RA-NU-UM		TIM V 19 4
	1	ŠAWIR	AN	IM			SA-WI-RA-NI-IM	GEN	TA 1930, 558
	1	ŠAKUR	AN				SA-KU-RA-AN		RA LXV 54 XII 24
		ŠAKUR	AN	U			SA-KU-RA-NU		M+
	1	ŠALAM	AN				SA-LA-MA-AN		RA LXV 43 III 55
	1	ŠALIM	AN				SA-LI-MA-AN		M+
		ŠALIM	AN	U			SA-LI-MA-NU		A 7733 4, C+
		ŠALIM	AN	IM			SA-LI-MA-NIM	GEN	M
	1	ŠAM	AN				SA-MA-AN		B 39+, M

AN	1		ŚAM	AN	UM	SA-MA-NU-UM		B 47
			ŚAM	AN	UM	ŠA-MA-NUM$_2$		U
			ŚAM	AN	UM	ŠA-MA-NU-UM		I
			ŚAM	AN	U	SA-MA-NU		JNES XIII 212F. LATE
			ŚAM	AN	I	SA-MA-A-NI		JNES XIII 212F.+ LATE
	1		ŚAMʿ	AN	UM	SA-AM-Ḫ̮A-NU-UM		TCL X 21 21
			ŚAMʿ	AN	UM	ŠA-AM-Ḫ̮A-NU-UM		B 93+
	1		ŚAMAR	AN	U	SA-MA-RA?-NU		X 20 11
	1		ŚAMK	AN	IM	ŠA-AM-KA-NIM	GEN	LIH 81 7,17, 23
			ŚAMK	AN	UM	ZA-AM?-GA-NU-UM		TA 1931, 538 V
	1		ŚAMŚ	AN	UM	SA-AM-SA-NU-UM		SIMMONS 119 23+
			ŚAMŚ	AN	U	ZA-AM-ZA-NU		M
	1		ŚAMUK	AN	UM	SA-MU-KA-NU-[UM]		HARRIS 68 21
			ŚAMUM	AN	IM	SA-MU-MA-NIM	GEN	PBS XIV 357
	1		ŚAPAR	AN		[S]A-PA-RA-AN		RA LXV 40 I 7
	1		ŚARAM	AN	U	SA-RA-MA-NU		SZLECHTER TJ P. 25
	1		ŚARB	AN		SA-AR-BA-AN		M
	1		ŚIPR	AN		ŠI-IP-RA-AN		A. LATE
			ŚIPR	AN	UM	ŠE?-IP?-[RA]?-NU-UM		I
			ŚIPR	AN	UM	ŠI-IP?-RA?-NU-UM		I
	1	ʾA	ŚKIN	AN	UM	AŠ$_2$-KI-NA-NU-UM		TA 30 87+
	1	ʾA	ŚKUR	AN		AŠ-KU-RA-AN		RA LXV 50 IX 15
	1	JI	ŚLAM	AN	A	IŠ-LA-MA-NA	GEN	MRS VI P. 202 UGARIT
	1	MA	ŚMIʿ	AN	AM	MA-AŠ-MI-A-NA-AM	ACC	M
	1	JA	ŚRUK	AN		IA-AŠ$_2$-RU-KA-AN		RA XLI 45 6' HANA+
	1		ŚUʾQ	AN	UM	ŠU-GA-NU-UM		EDZARD, DER 90:14
	1		ŚULAḪ̮	AN	U	SU-LA-Ḫ̮A-NU		A 7702 13
	1		ŚULM	AN	UM	ŠU-U[L]-MA-NU-U[M]		I
	1		ŚUM	AN		SU-MA-AN		B 39
	1		ŚUMAT	AN		SU-MA-TA-AN		M
			ŚUMAT	AN	UM	SU-MA-TA-A-NU-UM		GORDON 38 2, 5
	1		ŚUMK	AN	UM	ZUM-GA-NU-UM		TA 1931, 538 IV
	1		ŚUMUT	AN		SU-MU-TA-AN		RA LXV 46 VI 4+
	1	JA	ŠWUB	AN		IA-ŠU-BA-AN		M
	1		ŠAKIM	AN	UM	ŠA-KI-MA-NUM		C
	1		ŠALG	AN		ŠA-AL-GA-AN		RA LXV 40 I 49
	1		ŠAPAṮ	AN		ŠA-PA-TA-AN		M
	1		ŠARŠAR	AN	UM	ŠA-ŠA-RA-NU-UM		M
			ŠARŠAR	AN	U	ŠA-ŠA-RA-NU		M
			ŠARŠAR	AN	IM	ŠA-ŠA-RA-NIM	GEN	M+
	1		ŠERIR	AN	IM	ŠE-RI-RA-NIM	GEN	M
	1		ŠIQL	AN	U	ŠI-IQ-LA-NU		B 47
			ŠIQL	AN	UM	SI-IQ-LA-NU-UM		TA 30, 231+
			ŠIQL	AN	UM	ŠI-IQ-LA-NU-UM		TA 30, 2 4
			ŠIQL	AN	IM	SI-IQ-LA-NIM	GEN	TA 1930, 189
	1		ŠUʿAL	AN		ŠU-Ḫ̮A-LA-AN		M
			ŠUʿAL	AN	U	ŠU-Ḫ̮A-LA-NU		M
	1	JE	ṢJID	AN	UM	E-ZI-DA-NU-UM		I
	1		ṢAJAD	AN		ZA-A-DA-AN		RA LXV 43 III 45; C+
			ṢAJAD	AN		ZA-JA-DA-AN		M+
	1		ṢABʾ	AN	UM	ZA-AB-Ḫ̮A-NU-UM		CT XLVIII 88 REV.
	1		ṢABR	AN	UM	ZA-AB-RA-NU-UM		I
	1		ṢIBʾ	AN		ZI-BA-AN		BM 16836 27; M+
	1		ṢIDQ	AN		ZI-ID-QA-AN		M
			ṢIDQ	AN	UM	ṢI-ID-GA-NU-UM		EDZARD, DER 85:45+
	1		ṢILL	AN		Z[I]-IL-LA-AN		RA LXV 55 XIII 15
			ṢILL	AN		ZI-LA-AN		RA LXV 55 XIII 47
	1		TALIʾ	AN	UM	TA-LI-A-NU-UM		TA 1931, 538 VI
	1		TIʾL	AN	UM	TI-LA-NU-UM		B 47
	1		TIDIQ	AN		TI-DI-QA-AN		RA LXV 48 VIII 18+
	1		TUʾ	AN	UM	TU-Ḫ̮A-NU-UM		UCP X/3 2 26
	1		TUʾM	AN	UM	TU-MA-NU-UM		B 47
	1		TUʾN	AN	UM	TU-NA-NU-UM		TCL XVIII 118 7
			TUʾN	AN	U	TU-NA-NU		BM 81617 5
	1		TURTUR	AN		TU-UR-TU-RA-AN		RA LXV 42 II 76
	1		ZAʾN	AN		ZA-AḪ̮-NA-AN		M

AN	1	ZAʾT	AN						ZA-TA-AN		RA LXV 45 V 38
	1	ZAʾZ	AN	UM					ZA-ZA-NU-UM		RA LXV 47 VII 28; B 48+
		ZAʾZ	AN	UM					ZA-ZA-NUM$_2$		KISURRA 2A:7+
		ZAʾZ	AN	IM					ZA-ZA-NI-IM	GEN	B 48
		ZAʾZ	AN	AJA					ZA-ZA-NA-IA	FN	RA LXV 58 I 52
	1	ZABUG	AN						ZA-BU-GA-AN		RA LXV 45 V 23,30
	1	ZALAT	AN						ZA-LA-TA-AN		RA LXV 55 XIII 38
	1	ZAMM	AN	UM					ZA-AM-MA-A-NU-UM		B 48
		ZAMM	AN	UM					ZA-AM-MA-NU-UM		B 48+
	1	ZARAM	AN	UM					ZA-RA-MA-NU-UM		TIM III 24 14
		ZARAM	AN	UM					ZA-RA-MA-A-NU-UM		SIMMONS 99 8 SEAL
	1	ZIʾQ	AN						ZI-QA-AN		RA LXV 54 XII 14
	1	ZIʾZ	AN	UM					ZI-ZA-NU-UM		B 48+
	1	ZIBL	AN	UM					ZI-IB-LA-NU--M		BASOR 95 23
	1	ZILḪ	AN						ZI-IL-ḪA-AN		M+, C
	1	ZILIB	AN						ZI-LI-BA-AN		I 14 10
	1	ZIRIT	AN						ZI-RI-IT-TA-A[N]		M
	1	ZIRQ	AN	UM					ZE$_2$-IR-GA-NU-UM		TA 1931,438
		ZIRQ	AN	IM					ZI-IR-GA-NIM	GEN	TA 1930,221 EARLY OB
	1	ZIZAB	AN						ZI-ZA-BA-AN		RA LXV 52 X 38
	1	ZUʾZ	AN						ZU-ZA-AN		M+
		ZUʾZ	AN	U					ZU-ZA-NU		B 48
		ZUʾZ	AN	UM					ZU-ZA-NU-UM		B 48
		ZUʾZ	AN	UM					ZU-ZA-NUM$_2$		RUTTEN 9 16
		ZUʾZ	AN	UM					ZU-ZA-A-NUM$_2$		KISURRA 48:12
	1	ZUḪAL	AN						ZU-ḪA-LA-AN		RA LXV 51 X 2
	1	ZUḪL	AN	UM					ZU-UḪ$_3$-LA-NU-U[M]		TA 1931, 141
	1	ZUBAL	AN						ZU-BA-LA-AN		M
	1	ZUMM	AN						ZU-UM-MA-AN		XIII 95 6
ANIJ	1	ʾAWN	ANIJI						AM-NA-NI-I	TRIBE	M
AT	1	ʾAḪ	AT	UM					A-ḪA-TUM	FN	M+
		ʾAḪ	AT	I					A-ḪA-TI	FN	XIII 1 VIII 6
		ʾAḪ	AT	I		MA			A-ḪA-TI-MA	FN	JCS XXVII 135:1
		ʾAḪ	AT	A	HA				A-ḪA-TA-A	FN	RA LXV 62 V 52
		ʾAḪ	AT	UJA					A-ḪA-TU-IA	FN	SIMMONS 66 4+
		ʾAḪ	AT			JIQR	AH		A-ḪA-AT-IQ-RA	FN	M
		ʾAḪ	AT	A		ʾAB		I	A-ḪA-TA-A-BI	FN	M+
		ʾAḪ	AT	A		NAʿM		I	A-ḪA-TA-NA-AḪ-MI	FN	XIII 1 XI 3
		ʾAḪ	AT	I		JIQR	AT		A-ḪA-TI-IQ-RA-AT	FN	XIII 1 V 5
		ʾAḪ	AT	I		JIQR	AH		A-ḪA-TI-IQ-RA	FN	XIII 1 II 72+
	2	ʾAJA				ʾAḪ	AT	I	A-IA-A-ḪA-TI	FN	A.
		ʾAL				ʾAḪ	AT	I	AL-A-ḪA-TI	FN	A.
		ʾALI				ʾAḪ	AT	I	A-LI-A-ḪA-TI	FN	XIII 1 IV 71+
		ʾALI				ʾAḪ	AT	I	A-LI-A-ḪA?-TA-TI	FN	M
		ʾALI				ʾAḪ	AT	I	A-LI$_2$-A-ḪA-TI	FN	RA LXV 59 II 65+
	1	ʾAḪIL	AT	UM					A-ḪI-LA-TUM	FN	XIII 1 I 67
	1	ʾAWAʾ	AT	UM					A-WA-TUM	FN	M
		ʾAWAʾ	AT	I		ʾEL			A-WA-TI-EL		RA LXV 41 II 37+
		ʾAWAʾ	AT	I		ʾIL			A-WA-TI-DINGIR	MN	XIII 1 XI 39
	1	ʾAWIJ	AT	UM					ḪA-WI-IA-TUM		BIROT TEA 39:4
		ʾAWIJ	AT	UM					A-WI-IA-TUM	MN?	TIM I 11 10+
	1	ʾAJAL	AT	UM					A-IA-LA-TUM	FN	VAS VII 3 25
		ʾAJAL	AT	UM					D-A-A-LA-TUM	FN	CT VIII 29C 22+
	2	ḪANN		A		ʾABN	AT		ḪA-AN-NA-AB-NA-AT		A 7763, ISHCHALI
	1	ʾADAN	AT	UM					ḪA-DA-AN-N[A]?-TUM?	FN	RA LXV 62 V 7
	1	ʾADUN	AT	UM					A-DU-NA-TUM	MN	TA 30 275
	1	ʾAKAN	AT	UM					A-KA-NA-TUM		JCS XXIV 62 NO.55+
	1	ʾAKK	AT	UM					A-KA-TUM		KISURRA 104 36
		ʾAKK	AT	IJA					A-KA-TI-IA-A		KISURRA 178 1
		ʾAKK	AT	IJA					A-KA-TI-IA	FN	KISURRA 171 1; M+
		ʾAKK	AT			ʾEL			A-GA?-AD-E-EL		I
		ʾAKK	AT			MAʾT		I	AK-KA-AD-MA-TI	FN	A. 409 22
	1	ʾAKUN	AT	UM					A-KU-NA-TUM	MN?	M+
	1	ʾALM	AT	UM					ḪA-AL-MA-TUM	MN?	HARRIS 66 13
	1	ʾALUP	AT	UM					A-LU-PA-TUM	FN	CT XLVII 7 35, 7A 16'
	1	ʾAMIN	AT	UM					A-MI-NA-TUM		B 12

AT	1		ʾAMIR	AT	UM			A-MI-RA-TUM	FN	M
	1	T	ʾAMR	AT	UM			A-TAM-RA-TUM	FN	M
			ʾAMR	AT	UM			AM-RA-TUM		YOS XIII 513:4
	1		ʾAPK	AT	UM			AP-KA-TUM	MN	UCP X/1 4 5
	1		ʾAPP	AT	UM			AP-PA-TUM	FN	A.+
	1		ʾARNAB	AT	UM			AR-NA-BA-TUM	FN	CT VIII 43C 22+, XIII 1 X 39
			ʾARNAB	AT	IM			AR-NA-BA-TIM	FN? GEN	MEISSNER 18 3
	1		ʾAŠIR	AT	UM			A-SI-RA-TUM		B 14
	1		ʾAŠM	AT				AŠ-MA-AT	MN	M+
	1		ʾAŠIR	AT	UM			D-A-ŠI-RA-TUM	DN FN	RIFTIN 60 SEAL
	1		ʾAŠR	AT	UM	ʾUMM	I	D-AŠ-RA-TUM-UM-MI	FN	TCL I P. 16+
	1		ʾELL	AT		....		EL-LA-AT-[....]		M
	1		ʾELUR	AT	UM			EL-LU-RA-TUM	MN?	WATERMAN 38 9
	1		ʾIBN	AT	UM			IB-NA-TUM	MN	BM 16939 27+
	1		ʾIDD	AT	UM			ID-DA-TUM	MN	B 21, M
	1		ʾIL	AT	I			I-LA-TI	MN	M
	1		ʾILL	AT	UM			IL-LA-TUM	FN	XIII 1 X 46
	1		ʾILUR	AT				IL-LU-RA-AT	FN	JACOBSEN CTC P. 49+
			ʾILUR	AT	UM			IL-LU-RA-TUM	FN	CT IV 26A 3+
	1		ʾIPQ	AT	UM			IP-GA-TUM	MN	CT XLV 23 R. 13
			ʾIPQ	AT	UM			IP-QA-TUM	MN	M+
			ʾIPQ	AT	IM			IP-QA-TIM	MN GEN	M+
			ʾIPQ	AT	IM			IP-QA-TI-IM	MN? GEN	M
	1		ʾUNAB	AT	UM			U_2-NA-BA-TUM	FN	TIM III 26 7
			ʾUNAB	AT	UM			ḪU-NA-BA-TUM	FN	WATERMAN 54 2, 3+
	1		ʾUNUB	AT	UM			ḪU-NU-PA-TUM	FN?	BM 17060 35
			ʾUNUB	AT	UM			UN-NU-BA-TUM	FN	WATERMAN 24 R. 24
			ʾUNUB	AT	UM			ḪU-NU-BA-TUM	FN	EDZARD, DER 134:4
	1		ʾURAN	AT	UM			U_2-RA-NA-TUM	FN	HARRIS 83 1
	1		ʾUŠŠ	AT	I	ʾEL		UŠ-SA-TE-EL		TIM III 43 6
	1		HALIL	AT	UM			ḪA-LI-LA-TUM		KISURRA 211 4
	1		ḤAJJ	AT	UM			ḪA-IA-TUM	MN	B 18+
			ḤAJJ	AT	UM			[Ḫ]A-A-A-IA-TUM	FN	XIII 1 XIV 13
			ḤAJJ	AT	IJA			A-A-TI-IA		BM 92654 5
			ḤAJJ	AT	IJA			A-IA-TI-IA		BM 82440
	1		ḤABS	AT	UM			ḪA-AB-ZA-TUM		BM 17049+
	1		ḤAKAM	AT	UM			ḪA-KA-MA-TUM	FN	C+
	1		ḤANAN	AT	UM			A-NA-NA-TUM	FN	EDZARD, DER 97:14
	1		ḤARAB	AT	UM			A-RA-BA-TUM		YOS XIII 389:4+
	1		ḤAṢAN	AT	UM			ḪA-[Z]A-NA-TUM	FN	M
	1		ḤAṢN	AT	UM			ḪA-AZ-NA-TU[M]	FN	M
	1		ḤILUṢ	AT	UM			I-LU-ZA-TUM	FN	CT II 30 29
	1		ḤINN	AT	UM			ḪI-NA-TUM	FN	RA LXV 59 II 66
	1		ḤUNN	AT	UM			ḪU-UN-NA-TUM	MN	CT XLV 49 8+
	1		ḪAʾL	AT	UM			ḪA-LA-TUM		KISURRA 104 8
	1		ḪAʾŠ	AT	UM			ḪA-SA-TUM	MN	RUTTEN 15 6 SEAL
	1		ḪAMAŠ	AT	UM			ḪA-MA-SA-TUM	MN	CT XLV 91 20
	1		ḪAMŠ	AT	UM			ḪA-AM-SA-TUM	FN	BM 16844+
	1		ḪANB	AT	UM			ḪA-AN-BA-TUM	FN	CT XLV 91 18+
	1		ḪANP	AT	UM			ḪA-AN-PA-TUM	FN	A 3521 29
			ḪANP	AT	IM			ḪA-AN-PA-TIM	FN GEN	A 3521 31
	1		ḪAŠT	AT	UM			ḪA-AŠ-TA-TUM	FN	XIII 1 III 62
	1		ḪIʾD	AT	UM			ḪI-DA-TUM	FN	XIII 1 V 54
	1		ḪIʾL	AT	UM			ḪI-LA-TUM	FN	XIII 1 II 71
	1		ḪIBAR	AT	I			ḪI-BA-RA-TI	MN NOM	VIII 6 31
	1		ḪIMʾ	AT	UM			ḪI-IM-A-TUM	FN	XIII 1 X 40
	1		ḪIŠŠ	AT	UM			ḪI-IŠ-ŠA-TUM	FN	WATERMAN
	1		ḪUBD	AT	UM			ḪU-UP-DA-T[UM]	FN	XIII 1 VII 65
	1		ḪUBR	AT	UM			ḪU-UB-RA-TUM	FN	XIII 1 IX 31
	1		ḪUMUŠ	AT	UM			ḪU-MU-SA-TUM	MN	TCL I 62 3
	1		ḪURAṢ	AT	UM			ḪU-RA-ZA-TUM	FN	XIII 1 I 73+
	1		ḪUZIR	AT	UM			ḪU-ZI-RA-TUM		EDZARD, DER 99 REV 8
	1		ʿAWIQ	AT	UM			ḪA-I-KA-TÙM	FN	SIMMONS 112:17
	1		ʿABD	AT	UM			ḪA-AB-DA-TUM	FN	XIII 1 XIV 39
	1		ʿAD	AT	UM			A-DA-TUM	MN	I, MEISSNER 51 3
			ʿAD	AT	UM			A-DA-TUM	FN	M+

AT	1	ʿAD	AT	IM					A-DA-TIM	MN GEN	XIII 87 5
		ʿAD	AT	IJA					A-DA-TI-A	FN	MRS IX P. 243 UGARIT
		ʿAD	AT	A	HA				A-DA-TA-A	FN	APN P. 12 LATE
	3	ʾIL		A		GULL		A			
						ʿAḎIR	AT		DINGIR-GUL-LA_2-ḪA-ZI-RA-AT	FN	M+
	1	ʿAGL	AT	UM					AG-LA-TUM	FN	ABB IV 98:2
	1	ʿALIJ	AT	UM					ḪA-LI-IA-TUM	FN	B 18+, XIII 1 VII 1
	2	ʾAJ		A		ʿALIJ	AT		D-A-A-ḪA-LI-IA-AT	MN?	CT XLV 92 R. 12
	1	ʿAMIQ	AT	IM					ḪA-MI-QA-TIM-KI	GN GEN	M+
	1	ʿAN	AT						D-ḪA-NA-AT	DN FN	M+
		ʿAN	AT						ḪA-NA-AT-KI	GN FN	M+
		ʿAN	AT	UM					A-NA-TUM		BIROT, TEA 72 III 58+
		ʿAN	AT	UM					ḪA-NA-TUM	FN	XIII 1:34+
		ʿAN	AT	I	JI	JBAL			ḪA-NA-TI-I-BA-AL		RA LXV 40 I 12
		ʿAN	AT			KUʾB		U	A-NA-AT-KU-BU		TCL I 204:11
	2	ʿABD				ʿAN	AT		ḪA-AB-DU-D-ḪA-NA-AT		M+
		ʿABD				ʿAN	AT	I	AB-TA-NA-TI		A. P. 128A LATE +
		ʿABD				ʿAN	AT	I	AB-DI-A-NA-TI		A. P. 128B LATE +
		ʿABD				ʿAN	AT	I	AB-TI-A-NA-TI		JCS XIII 54 300, A. LATE
		ʿAMM		I		ʿAN	AT		ḪA-MI-D-ḪA-NA-AT		M
		BUN		U		ʿAN	AT	I	BU-NU-A-NA-TI		B 16
		ḎIKR		I		ʿAN	AT		ZI-IK-RI-ḪA-NA-AT		M
		ḎIKR		I		ʿAN	AT		ZI-IK-RI-D-ḪA-N[A-AT]		M
		ḎIMR		I		ʿAN	AT	A	ZI-IM-RI-ḪA-NA-TA		B 42
		MUT				ʿAN	AT		MU-UT-D-ḪA-NA-AT		RA LXV 52 X 65
		MUT		I		ʿAN	AT	A	MU-TI-A-N[A-T]A		B 35
		ṢILL				ʿAN	AT		MI-NI-D-ḪA-NA-AT		XIII 83 8
	1	ʿARD	AT	UM					ḪA-AR-DA-TUM	FN	M+
	1	ʿARṢ	AT	UM					AR-ZA-TUM	FN	C
	1	ʿAZIB	AT	UM					ḪA-ZI-BA-TUM	MN	GAUTIER 65 5
	1	ʿAZZ	AT	UM					A-ZA-TUM	FN	CT VIII 37D 7, M
		ʿAZZ	AT	AM					A-ZA-TAM	FN ACC	CT VIII 37D 3
	1	ʿEBB	AT	UM					IB-BA-TUM	FN	M+
		ʿEBB	AT	IM					IB-BA-TIM	FN GEN	M
	1	ʿINB	AT	UM					IN-BA-TUM	FN	BM 78768 3', X 84 3+
	1	ʿUZAL	AT	UM					ḪU-ZA-LA-TUM	FN	WATERMAN 12 R. 7+
		ʿUZAL	AT	UM					ḪU-ZA-LA-TUM	MN	UCP X/1 86 4+
	1 MU	WSIL	AT	UM					MU-ZI-LA-TUM	FN	B 35
	1	JAʾ	AT	UM					IA-A-A-TUM	MN	A 29366:3
	1	JAʿIL	AT	UM					IA-ḪI-LA-TUM	FN	B 26
		JAʿIL	AT	UM					IA-I-LA?-TUM	FN	B 26
		JAʿIL	AT	IM					IA-ḪI-LA-TIM	GEN	CT XLVIII 27 CASE
	1	JAJA	AT	UM					IA-IA-TUM		B 26
	1	JABS	AT	UM					IA-AB-ZA?-TUM	MN?	VAS VIII 121 5
	1	JABUS	AT	UM					IA-BU-ZA-TUM	FN	CT XLVIII 31 5, 9
		JABUS	AT	IM					IA-BU-ZA-TIM	FN GEN	B 25+
	1	JADID	AT	UM					IA-DI-DA-TUM	MN	B 25+
		JADID	AT	IM					IA-DI-DA-TIM	MN GEN	B 25+
	1	JAPʿ	AT	UM					IA-AP-ḪA-TUM	MN	B 24+
		JAPʿ	AT	UM					IA-AP-ḪA-TUM	FN	YOS VIII 12 2+
	1	JATAR	AT	UM					IA-TA-RA-TUM	MN	B 31
		JATAR	AT	UM					IA-TA-RA-TUM	FN	B 31
		JATAR	AT	IM					IA-TA-RA-TIM	MN GEN	B 31+
	1	JATR	AT	UM					IA-AT-RA-TUM	MN	VAS VIII 105 4, 7, 12+
	1 JI	JBAL	AT	UM					JI-BA-LA-TUM	FN	U
	1 JA	JDIʿ	AT	UM					IA-DI-ḪA-TUM	FN	B 25+
	1	JIBUS	AT	UM					I-BU-ZA-TUM		EDZARD,DER 87:11
	2	ʾAḪ	AT	I		JIQR	AT		A-ḪA-TI-IQ-RA-AT	FN	XIII 1 V 5
	1	JIŠʿ	AT	UM					IŠ-ḪA-TUM	FN	RA LXV 60 III 57
		JIŠʿ	AT	I					IŠ-A-TI	MN? GEN	PBS VIII/2 238 5, 8
		JIŠʿ	AT	IJA					IŠ-ḪA-TI-IA	MN?	B 24+
	1 JA	JPAʿ	AT	UM					IA-PA-ḪA-TUM	FN	M+
	1 JA	JPUʿ	AT	UM					IA-PU-ḪA-TUM	FN	C+
	2	ŠAMŠ		I	JA	JPUʿ	AT		D-UTU-IA-PU-ḪA-AT	FN?	BM 17075
	1 JA	JŠUʿ	AT	UM					IA-ŠU-ḪA-TUM	FN	RA LXV 58 I 17; B 30+
	1 JA	BWAʾ	AT	UM					IA-BA-TUM		AJSL XXXIII 237 16

AT	1		BAʿL	AT	UM				BA-AḪ-LA-TUM	FN	M+
			BAʿL	AT	UM				BA-LA-TUM	FN	BM 16944 5
			BAʿL	AT	IM				BA-AḪ-LA-TIM	FN GEN	XIII 1 XIV 37
	2		ʿABD			BAʿL	AT	I	ḪA-AB-DU-BA-AḪ-LA-TI		M+
	1		BAWB	AT	UM				BA-BA-TUM	FN	RA LXV 58 I 59
	2		ḤINN		A	BAWŠ	AT		E-NA-BA-ŠA-AT		ICK 63 2+ CAPP.
			ḤINN		A	BAWŠ	AT	A	E-NA-BA-ŠA-TA		EL II P. 171 N. CAPP.
			ḤINN		I	BAWŠ	AT		E-NI-BA-ŠA-AT		ICK 113 10 CAPP.
			ḤINN		I	BAWŠ	AT	A	E-NI-BA-ŠA-TA		KTS 47C 1 CAPP.
	1		BAWZ	AT	UM				BA-ZA-TUM	FN	B 15+, M+
			BAWZ	AT	IM				BA-ZA-TI[M]	GEN	M+
	1		BAJN	AT	UM				BA-NA-TUM	FN	C; EDZARD 58:3
			BAJN	AT	UM				BA-NA-A-TUM	FN	HARRIS 86 1
	1		BAJR	AT	UM				BA-RA-TUM	FN	CT VIII 6A 3+
	1		BAKŠ	AT	UM				BA-AK-SA-TUM	FN	M
	1		BAKUR	AT	UM				BA-KU-RA-TUM	FN	B
	1		BALAL	AT	I				BA-LA-LA-TI		TA 1930, 399+
	1		BALIL	AT	UM				BA-LI-LA?-TUM	MN?	VIII 3 5
	1		BANḪ	AT	UM				BA-AN-ḪA-TUM	FN	IX 291 II 19
	1		BARIL	AT	UM				BA-RI-LA-TUM	FN	CT VI 35A 15
	1		BAŠAJ	AT	UM				BA-ŠA-A-IA-[TUM]?	FN	M
	1		BATUL	AT	UM				BA-TU-LA-TUM	FN	XIII 1 II 59
	1		BAZUR	AT	UM				BA-ZU-RA-TUM	FN	CT XLV 25 11, 20
			BAZUR	AT	IM				BA-ZU-RA-TIM	FN GEN	CT XLV 25 17
	1		BEʿL	AT	UM				BE-LA-TUM	FN	M+
			BEʿL	AT	UM				BE-LA-A-TUM	FN	RA LXV 60 III 26
			BEʿL	AT	I				BE-LA-TI	FN? GEN	VIII 63:11
			BEʿL	AT	IM				BE-LA-TI-IM	FN? GEN	VIII 63:2
	1		BIJT	AT	UM				BI-TA-TUM	MN	B 16+
	1		BIBIJ	AT	UM				BI-BI-IA-TUM	FN	RA LXV 62 V 25
	1		BIN	AT	UM				BI-NA-TUM	MN	BM 16820+
	1	JA	BLIJ	AT	UM				IA-AB-LI-IA-TUM	FN	B 25+
	1		BUʿD	AT	IM				BU-DA-TIM	GEN	EDZARD, DER 152 REV 6
	1		BULAṬ	AT	UM				BU-LA-DA-TUM	MN	BRM III 19B, 22G+
	1		BUN	AT	UM				BU-NA-TUM	MN	A 7699 23+
	1		BURAN	AT	UM				BU-RA-NA-TUM	FN	RA LXV 59 II 70
	1		BURQ	AT	UM				BU-UR-QA-TUM	FN	XIII 1 VII 52+
	1	JA	DWIR	AT	UM				[IA-DI]-RA-TUM		B 25
	2		ʾIL		A	DAʿ	AT		I-LA-DA-ḪA-AT		SUMER V 141,3+
			ʾIL		A	DAʿ	AT		BAD$_3$-DINGIR-DA-ḪA-AT	GN	A 7650
			ʾIL		I	DAʿ	AT		DINGIR-DA-ḪA-AT		A 7650:2
			ŠAM		I	DAʿ	AT	UM	SA-MI-DA-ḪA-TUM	FN	M
			ŠAM		I	DAʿ	AT	IM	SA-MI-DA-ḪA-TIM	FN? GEN	XII 741 6
	1		DAWD	AT	UM				DA-DA-TUM	MN	TCL I 109 16+
			DAWD	AT	UM				[D]A-DA-TUM	FN	M
	1		DAKŠ	AT	UM				DA-AK-SA-TUM	FN	CT IV 45B 6
	1		DAM	AT	UM				DA-MA-TUM	FN	XIII 1 V 30
	1		DAMQ	AT	UM				DAM-QA-TUM	FN	CT XLV 2 22+
	2		ʾIŠḪAR	AH		DANN	AT		IŠ-ḪA-RA-DAN-NA-AT	FN	M
	1		DARK	AT	UM				DA-AR-KA-TUM	FN	C
	1		DAŠUR	AT	UM				DA-ŠU-RA-TUM	FN	YOS VIII 51 2,14
	1	ʾA	DBAR	AT	UM				AD-BA-RA-TUM	MN	A 21946
	2		ʾIL		I	DIʿ	AT		I$_3$-LI$_2$-DI-ḪA-[AT]		HARRIS 39 19
			ŠAMŠ		I	DIʿ	AT		SA-AM-SI-DI-ḪA-AT?		TIM II 49 5
	1	ʾA	DRAK	AT	UM				AD-RA-KA-TUM	FN	M+
		ʾA	DRAK	AT	IM				AD-RA-KA-TIM	FN GEN	M+
	1		DULUQ	AT	UM				DU-LU-GA-TUM	FN	VAS IX 178 2
	1		ḎAKIR	AT	UM				ZA-KI-RA-TUM?	FN	C
	2		ʾIŠḪAR	AH		ḎAMR	AT	I	D-IŠ-ḪA-RA-ZA-AM-RA-TI	FN	M
	1		ḎIKR	AT	UM				ZI-IK-RA-TUM	FN	XIII 1 II 50
			ḎIKR	AT	IM				ZI-IK-RA-TIM	MN? GEN	XII 263 10
	1		ḎIMR	AT	UM				ZI-IM-RA-TUM	MN	B 42+, M
			ḎIMR	AT	IM				ZI-IM-RA-TIM	MN? GEN	M
	1		ḎINB	AT	UM				ZI-IB-BA-TUM	FN	M+, C P. 38+
	1	MA	ḎMAR	AT	UM				MA-AZ-MA-RA-TUM	FN	CT VIII 41A 3 4+
		MA	ḎMAR	AT	UM				MA-IZ-MA-RA-TUM	FN	CT II 30 35

AT	1	ḎUBAB	AT	UM			DU-BA-BA-TUM	FN	UCP X/1 87 3+
	1	GAʾG	AT	UM			GA-GA-TUM	MN?	HARRIS 13 13+
	1	GAʾIL	AT	UM			GA-I-LA-TUM	MN?	B 17+
		GAʾIL	AT	UM			GA-I-LA-TUM	FN	EDZARD, DER 224:35
	1	GABIʾ	AT	UM			GA-BI-A-TUM	FN	X 1 3
	1	GUʾR	AT	UM			GU-RA-TUM	FN	C
		GUʾR	AT	IM			GU-RA-TIM	FN GEN	B 17
	1	GULL	AT	UM			GUL-LA-TUM	FN	M+
	1	GULZ	AT	UM			GU-UL-ZA-TUM		LANGDON XXIX 22
	1	KAʾM	AT	UM			KA-MA-TUM	FN	C
	1	KABIS	AT	UM			KA-BI-ZA-TUM	FN	C
	1	KABŠ	AT	UM			KAB-SA-TUM	FN	M+
	1	KALB	AT	UM			KA-AL-BA-TUM	FN	RA LXV 61 IV 46
	1	KALK	AT	UM			KA-AL-KA-TUM	MN	CT VIII 12C 1 6 9+
	1	KAMM	AT	UM			KAM-MA-TUM	FN	M+
	1	KARAN	AT	UM			KA-RA-NA-TUM	FN	CT II 40B 1, M
		KARAN	AT	IM			KA-RA-NA-[T]IM	FN	M
	1	KIʾM	AT	IM			KI-MA-TIM	FN GEN	M
	1	KIBS	AT	UM			KI-IB-ZA-TUM	FN	M+
	1	KIBŠ	AT	UM			KI-IB-SA-TUM	FN	RA LXV 56 I 11
	1	KINAN	AT	UM			KI-NA-NA-TUM		UCP X/1 27 7+
	1	KISIBIR	AT	UM			KI-ZI-BI-RA-TUM	FN	RA LXV 61 IV 50
	1	KUʾT	AT	U			KU-TA-TU	MN	B 33
	1	KUWN	AT	UM			KU-NA-TUM	FN	C
	1	KUBAS	AT	UM			KU-BA-ZA-TUM	FN	RA LXV 58 I 32
	1	KUBS	AT	UM			KU-UB-ZA-TUM		SZLECHTER TJ P. 186
	1	KUKKUB	AT	UM			KU-KU-BA-TUM		VAS IX 175:11
		KUKKUB	AT	UM			KU-KU-BA-TUM	FN	XIII 1 VII 44
	1	KUNAN	AT	UM			KU-NA-NA-TUM	FN	M
	1	KUNDUL	AT	UM			KU-UN-DU-LA-TUM	FN	M+
	1	KUZAB	AT	UM			KU-ZA-BA-TUM	MN	CT VI 30B 23+
		KUZAB	AT	UM			KU-ZA-BA-TUM	FN	CT VIII 43A 4, 10+
	1	LALAʾ	AT	UM			LA-LA-A-TUM	FN	M
		LALAʾ	AT	UM			LA-LA-ḪA-TUM	FN	TCL XVIII 121 9
	1	LAMAS	AT	UM			[LA]-MA-ZA-TUM	FN	XIII 1 XIV 6
	1	LAMR	AT	UM			LA-AM-RA-TUM	FN	YOS XIII 294:18
	1	LIʾR	AT	UM			LI-RA-TUM	FN	A.
	1	LIʾŠ	AT	UM			LI-SA-TUM	MN?	TCL X 38 6
	1	LUʾL	AT	UM			LU-LA-TUM	MN	BM 16820 2, 11
	1	MAʾJ	AT	UM			MA-IA-TUM	FN	B 34+
	1	MAʾM	AT	UM			MA-MA-TUM		CT XLV 96 18
	1	MAʾR	AT	UM			MA-RA-TUM	MN?	TIM I 14 3
		MAʾR	AT	IJA			MA-RA-TI-IA		HARRIS 99 13
	1	MAʾT	AT	UM			MA-TA-TUM	FN	CT II 50 6, 18
		MAʾT	AT	UM			MA-TA-TUM	MN?	LIH 29 9
		MAʾT	AT	IM			MA-TA-TIM	MN? GEN	VAS XVI 118 2
	1	MAʾZ	AT	UM			MA-ZA-TUM	FN	KISURRA 21 3, M
	1	MADAG	AT	UM			MA-DA?-GA-TUM	FN	IX 24 III 22
	1	MAGUN	AT	UM			MA-KU-NA-TUM	FN	C+
	1	MAKIJ	AT	UM			MA-KI-IA-TUM		A 7724 2
	1	MALIK	AT	UM			MA-LI-KA-TUM		BM 17060 35+
		MALIK	AT	UM			MA-LI-KA-TUM	FN	EDZARD, DER 91:3
	1	MAMM	AT	UM			[M]A-A[M]-MA-TUM	FN	RA LXV 64 VI 9
	1	MANAN	AT	UM			MA-NA-NA-TUM	FN	B 93+
	1	MANN	AT	UM			MA-AN-NA-TUM	FN	WATERMAN 52 2+, X 2 6
		MANN	AT	UM			MA-NA-TUM	FN	BM 81479 4
	1	MANUW	AT	UM			MA-NU-A-TUM	FN	I (UNPUBL.)
	1	MARṢ	AT	UM			MAR-ZA-TUM	FN	M+
	2	ʾUMM		I	MARṢ	AT	UM-MI-MAR-ṢA-AT	FN	XIII 1 III 5
		JAT		UM	MARṢ	AT	I-IA-TUM-MA-AR-ZA-AT	FN	RA LXV 62 V 15
	1	MAŠḪ	AT	UM			MA-AŠ-ḪA-TUM	FN	M
	1	MAṢIʾ	AT	UM			MA-ZI-A-TUM	FN	WATERMAN 56 R. 8
	1	MATIN	AT				MA-TI-NA-AT		U
	1	MEʾM	AT	UM			ME-MA-TUM	FN	BASOR 95, 21 I 21
	1	MENN	AT	UM			ME-EN-NA-TUM	FN	XIII 1 V 32
	1	MILK	AT	UM			MI-IL-KA-TUM		TCL XI 220 11

SUFFIXES, Class 1

AT	1			MILK	AT	UM		MIL-KA-TUM		YOS XIII 112:16
	1			MUHR	AT	UM		MU-UḪ-RA-TUM		BIROT, TEA 72 I 49'+
	1	TA		NḪAB	AT	UM		TA-ḪA-BA-TUM	FN	VAS VIII 127 2, 29
		TA		NḪAB	AT	I		TA-ḪA-BA-TI	FN GEN	VAS VIII 127 2
	1	JI	N	NWAB	AT	UM		IN-NA-BA-TUM	FN	CT VI 17 13+
		JI	N	NWAB	AT	UM		IN-NA-BA-A-TUM	FN	CT VI 1A 3
		JI	N	NWAB	AT	IM		IN-NA-BA-TIM	FN GEN	CT VI 17 2
	1			NAʾJ	AT	UM		NA-JA-TUM	FN	KISURRA 59A:4
	1			NAKAR	AT	UM		NA-KA-RA-TUM	FN	RA LXV 59 II 71
	1			NAKL	AT	UM		NA-AK-LA-TUM	FN	YOS XIII 90 REV 22
	1			NAMAL	AT	UM		NA-MA-LA-TUM	MN	B 36+
	1			NAMR	AT	UM		NA-AM-RA-TUM	FN	YOS XIII 163:7
	1			NAN	AT	UM		NA-NA-TUM	FN	RA LXV 65 VI 57
	1			NARB	AT	UM		NA-AR-BA-TUM	FN	M+
	1			NASQ	AT	UM		NA-AS-QA-TUM	FN	RA LXV 58 I 38
	1			NAŠʾ	AT	UM		NA-AŠ-ḪA-TUM	FN	RA LXV 61 IV 33
	1			NAŠP	AT	UM		NA-AŠ-PA-TUM	FN	CT II 35 28+
	1			NIʿIM	AT	UM		NI-ḪI-MA-T[UM]	FN?	C II 42 III 31
	1			NIʿM	AT	UM		NI-IḪ-MA-TUM	FN	M+
	1			NIWḪ	AT	UM		NI-ḪA-TUM	FN	M+
	1			NIGH	AT	UM		NI-IG-ḪA-TUM	FN	M
	1			NIKID	AT	UM		NI-KI-DA-TUM		VAS XIII 65 2,3+
	1			NUWD	AT	UM		NU-DA-TUM	MN	U
	1			NUWP	AT	UM		NU-BA-TUM		YOS XIII 191:8
				NUWP	AT	UM		NU-PA-TUM	FN	BIROT, TEA 70C R II 18
				NUWP	AT	IJA		NU-PA-TI-IA	FN	M
	1			NURNUR	AT	UM		NU-UR$_2$-NU-RA-TUM	MN?	BIN VII 157 7
	1			NUṬUP	AT	UM		NU-DU-PA-TUM	FN	FRANK SKT P. 31+
	1	ʾA		NZAL	AT	UM		AN-ZA-LA-TUM	FN?	XIII 1 I 14
	1			PAʾAR	AT	IM		PA-A-RA-TIM	FN GEN	X 170:1
	1			PAʾR	AT	IJA		PA-RA-TI-IA		UCP X/3 3 8
	1			PAʾT	AT	UM		PA-TA-TUM	FN	M+
	1			PANIJ	AT	UM		PA-NI-IA-TUM	MN?	TIM I 11 11
				PANIJ	AT	UM		PA-AN-NI-IA-TUM	MN	UET V 615 9
	1			PANN	AT	UM		PA-AN-NA-TUM	MN?	CT XLV 49 11
	1			PAQAḪ	AT	UM		BA-GA-A-TUM	MN	A 29366:17
	1			PATIḪ	AT	UM		PA-TE-ḪA-TUM	MN?	CARNEGIE CAT. Q B 11
	1			PIQD	AT	UM		BI-IQ-DA-TUM	FN	XIII 1 X 27
	1			PULS	AT	UM		PU-UL-ZA-TUM	MN	TIM III 23 11+
	1			PURUS	AT	UM		PU-RU-ZA-TUM	FN	RA LXV 60 III 60
	1	JA		QWIM	AT	UM		IA-KI-MA-TUM	FN	RA LXV 60 III 7
	1			QAHIL	AT	UM		QA-ḪI-LA-TUM	FN	C P. 55+
	1			QABAL	AT	UM		GA-BA-LA-TUM	FN	CT XLV 117 36
	1			QADIM	AT	UM		QA-DI-MA-TUM	FN	WATERMAN 39 8+
				QADIM	AT	IM		QA-DI-MA-TIM	FN GEN	WATERMAN 39 11
	1			QANIJ	AT	UM		QA-NI-A-TUM	FN	RA LXV 66 VII 52; C+
	1			QIJŠ	AT	UM		KI-SA-TUM	MN	VAS IX 175 5+, M
				QIJŠ	AT	UM		KI-SA-T[U-U]M	MN	M
				QIJŠ	AT	UM		KI-ŠA-TUM	MN	XIII 1 V 19
				QIJŠ	AT	IM		KI-ŠA-TIM	MN GEN	M+
	1			QUWJ	AT	UM		KU-IA-TUM		CT VIII 29A 29+
	1			RAʾK	AT	UM		RA-KA-TU-UM	FN?	M
	1			RAWḪ	AT	UM		RA-ḪA-TUM	FN	XIII 1 XII 6
	1			RAWM	AT	UM		RA-MA-TUM	FN	M, CT VIII 1A 2+
	1			RAJB	AT	UM		RA-BA-TUM	FN	XIII 1 X 59+
	1			RAPIʾ	AT	UM		RA-BI-A-TUM	FN	C+
	1			RAPUʾ	AT	UM		RA-PU-A-TUM		A 7660 1
	1	ʾA		RGAM	AT	UM		AR-GA-MA-TUM	FN	C
	1			RIʿŠ	AT		....	RI-ŠA-A[T-....]	FN	I 89 5
	1			RIWḪ	AT	UM		RI-ḪA-DU-UM?		U UNPUBL.
				RIWḪ	AT	UM		RI-ḪA-TUM	FN	XIII 1 I 23+
	1			RIWM	AT	UM		RI-MA-TUM	FN	M+
	1			RIJB	AT	UM		RI-BA-TUM	FN	CT VIII 48B 7+, M+, C+
	1			RUḪB	AT	UM		RU-UḪ-BA-TUM	FN	XIII 1 IX 46
	1			RUWB	AT	UM		RU-BA-TUM	FN	M+
				RUWB	AT	IM		RU-BA-TIM	FN GEN	M

SUFFIXES, Class 1

AT	1		RUWM	AT	UM				RU-MA-TUM	FN	XIII 1 VI 10
	1		RUKAB	AT	UM				RU-KA-BA-TUM	FN	XIII 1 V 33
	1		SAṬIʾ	AT	UM				ZA-DI-IA-TUM	FN	XIII 1 I 72
	1	JA	ŚJIM	AT	UM				IA-SI-MA-TUN	FN	RA LXV 60 III 8
	1		ŚAʾB	AT	UM				SA-BA-TUM		JCS XXIV 57 NO. 42,44
	1		ŚAʾIL	AT	UM				SA-I-LA-TUM	FN	B 37, TIM IV 53 7
			ŚAʾIR	AT	UM				SA-E-RA-TUM	FN	B 37
			ŚAʾIR	AT	IM				SA-E-RA-TIM	FN GEN	B 37+
	1		ŚAʾL	AT	UM				SA-LA-TUM	FN	CT VIII 20B 9+, M+, C+
	1		ŚAʾQ	AT	UM				SA-QA?-TUM	FN	XIII 1 VI 59
	1		ŚAWIR	AT	UM				SA-WI-RA-TUM		UET V 378 5
	1		ŚABIM	AT	IM				SA-BI-MA-TIM	FN NOM	RA LXIV 43
	1		ŚADIR	AT	UM				SA-DI-RA-TUM?	FN	BM 80485 7, 18
	1		ŚAGAR	AT	UM				SA-GA-RA-TUM-KI	GN	M+
			ŚAGAR	AT	IM				SA-GA-RA-TIM-KI	GN GEN	M+
			ŚAGAR	AT	IM				SAG-GA-RA-TIM	MN GEN	M
			ŚAGAR	AT	IM				SAG-GA-RA-TIM	GN GEN	M+
			ŚAGAR	AT	IM				SA-AN-GA-RA-TIM-KI	GN GEN	M
	1		ŚAKN	AT	UM				SA-AK-NA-TUM	FN	RA LXV 58 I 27
	1		ŚALAM	AT	UM				SA-LA-MA-TUM	FN?	M
	1	MU	ŚALIM	AT	IM				MU-SA-LI-MA-TIM	FN GEN	BE VI/1 8 14
			ŚALIM	AT	UM				SA-LI-MA-TUM	MN?	CT VIII 49A 46+
			ŚALIM	AT	UM				SA-LI-MA-TUM	FN	XIII 1 VI 46
			ŚALIM	AT	IM				SA-LI-MA-TIM	FN GEN	CT VIII 28C 13
	1		ŚAMIB	AT	UM				SA-MI-BA-TUM	FN	M
	1		ŚAMUL	AT	UM				SA-MU-LA-TUM	FN	M
	1		ŚANAGR	AT	UM				SA-NA-AG-RA-TUM	FN	CT IV 47B 27+, M+
	1		ŚAPIR	AT	UM				SA-BI-RA-TUM	FN	B 37+
			ŚAPIR	AT	UM				SA-PI-RA-TUM		B 37
	2		ʾIŠḪAR	AH		ŚARR	AT		D-IŠ-ḪA-RA-ŠAR-RA-AT	FN	M
	1		ŚIJB	AT	UM				ŠI-BA-TUM	FN	M
			ŚIJB	AT	IJA				SI-BA-TI-IA	FN?	BM 80363 7
	1		ŚIJM	AT	UM				ŠI-MA-TUM	FN	M+
			ŚIJM	AT	IM				ŠI-MA-TIM	FN GEN	XIII 1 V 15+
			ŚIJM	AT		ʿAŠTAR			ŠI-MA-AT-EŠ$_4$-DAR	FN	XIII 1 V 75+
			ŚIJM	AT		DAGAN			ŠI-MA-AT-D-DA-GAN	FN	XIII 1 VIII 33+
	1		ŚIJT	AT	UM				SI-TA-TUM	FN	XIII 1 IV 74+
	1		ŚIPR	AT	U				ŠE-IP-RA-TU	MN	LAESSOE P. 99+
	1	ME	ŚLIB	AT	UM				ME-EŠ$_3$-LI-BA-TUM	FN	YOS V 117 1
	1	MU	ŚṬAḪ	AT	UM				MU-UŠ-TA-ḪA-[TUM]?	MN	M
	1	MU	ŚṬUḪ	AT	UM				MU-UŠ-TU-A-TUM	FN	C
	1		ŚUKUR	AT	UM				ŠU-KU-[R]A-TUM	FN	XIII 1 V 78
	1		ŚULAḪ	AT	UM				SU-LA-A-TUM	FN	RA LXV 66 VII 62
	1		ŚUMUḪ	AT	UM				ŠU-MU-ḪA-TUM	FN	RA LXV 64 V 58
	1	TA	ŠWUB	AT	UM				TA-ŠU-BA-TUM	FN	M
	1		ŠAʾḪ	AT	UM				ŠA-ḪA-TUM	FN	RA LXV 59 II 75
	1		ŠAWIL	AT	UM				ŠA-WI-LA-TUM	FN	M
	1		ŠIʾN	AT	IM				ŠI-NA-TIM	FN GEN	XIII 1 V 83
	1		ŠUʾḪ	AT	UM				ŠU-ḪA-TUM		HARRIS 1 3, 6+
	1		ŠURAN	AT	UM				ŠU-RA-NA-TUM	FN	M
	1		ṢAJID	AT	UM				ZA-I-DA-TUM	FN	EDZARD, DER 90:2+
	1		ṢARIP	AT	UM				ZA-RI-PA-TUM	FN	RA LXV 60 III 49
	1		ṢIJḪ	AT	UM				ZI-ḪA-TUM	FN	XIII 1 VII 35
	2		MAM		A	ṢIJḪ	AT	UM	MA-MA-ZI-A-TUM	FN	RA LXV 61 IV 37
	1		ṢIBʾ	AT	UM				ZI-IB-A-TUM	FN	XIII 1 III 2
	1		ṢIBAR	AT	UM				ṢI-BA-RA-TUM	MN?	OLZ VIII 351 16
	1		ṢIMID	AT	UM				ZI-MI-DA?-TUM	FN	M
	1		ṢUWR	AT	IM				ZU?-RA?-TIM	GEN	M
	1		TARAJ	AT	UM				TA-RA-IA-TUM	FN	VAS XIII 14 5+
	1		TIʾŠ	AT	UM				TI-ŠA-TUM	FN	M
	1		TIWR	AT	UM				TI-RA-TUM	FN	M
	2		ʾANN		U	TILL	AT	I	AN-NU-TIL-LA-TI	FN	XIII 1 X 2
	3	JA	KRUB			ʾIL					
						TILL	AT	I	D-IA-AK-RU-UB-DINGIR-TIL-LA-TI		M
	1		TINʾ	AT	UM				TI-IN-A-TUM	FN	XIII 1 VI 4
	1		TISP	AT	UM				TI-IS-PA-TUM	FN	M+, C

SUFFIXES, Class 1

AT	1		TISP	AT UM	TI-IS-PA-A-TUM	FN	X 105 3
	1		TIŠAN	AT UM	TI-ŠA-NA-TUM	MN	VAS VIII 58 34+
			TIŠAN	AT UM	TI-ŠA-NA-TUM	FN	BM 82372, M
	1		TURM	AT UM	TU-UR-MA-TUM	FN	M
	1		TUŠIM	AT UM	TU-ŠI-MA-TUM	FN	RA LXV 61 III 77
	1		ṬAJB	AT UM	DA-BA-TUM	FN	U
			ṬAJB	AT UM	ṬA$_3$-BA-TUM	FN	M+
	1		ṬABIḪ	AT UM	TA-BI-ḪA-TUM	MN?	BE VI/1 3 3 11
	1		ṬUḪŠ	AT UM	DU-UḪ-ŠA-TUM	FN	TCL X 12 12, M
			ṬUḪŠ	AT UM	TU-UḪ$_3$-ŠA-TUM		UET V 290 2
	1		ṬUBQ	AT UM	TU-UB-GA-TUM	MN	MEISSNER 11 3
	1		ṬUQM	AT UM	TU-UK-MA-TUM	FN	RA LXV 65 VII 25
	1		ZAḪL	AT IM	ZA-AḪ-LA-TIM	GEN	CT VIII 31B 25
	1		ZABIL	AT UM	ZA-BI-LA-TUM	FN	RA LXV 60 III 50
			ZABIZ	AT UM	ZA-BI-ZA-TUM		YOS XIII 175:11
	1		ZANIJ	AT UM	ZA-NI-IA-TUM		BM 80496 3'
	1		ZANN	AT UM	ZA-AN-NA-TUM	FN	M+
	1	MA	ZNIJ	AT UM	MA-AZ-NI-A-T[UM]	FN	JCS XIX 56
	1	MA	ZRAQ	AT UM	MA-AZ-RA-QA-TUM	FN	XIII 1 II 37
	1		ZUBAL	AT UM	ZU?-BA-LA-TUM	FN	U
ATAN	1		ʾAWAʾ	ATAN	A-WA-TA-AN		RA LXV 47 VII 31+
	1		ʾAKK	ATANUM	AG-GA-TA-NU-UM		SIMMONS 96 6
			ʾAKK	ATANUM	AG-GA-TA-A-NU-UM		SIMMONS 103 6
			ʾAKK	ATANUM	A-KA-TA-A-NU-UM		SIMMONS 105 7, SEAL
			ʾAKK	ATANUM	AK-KA-TA-A-NU-UM		SIMMONS 106 6, 10 SEAL
			ʾAKK	ATANUM	AK-KA-TA-NU-UM		SIMMONS 112 6, SEAL
			ʾAKK	ATANI	A-GA-DA-NI		TA 1931, 489
			ʾAKK	ATANI	A-GA-TA-NI		TA 1931, 530 I, III
			ʾAKK	ATANIM	AK-KA-TA-NI-IM	GEN	A 32133:6
	1		ʾAPK	ATAN	AP-KA-TA-AN		M+
	1		ʾAPP	ATAN	AP-PA-TA-AN		RA LXV 43 IV 18
	1		ʾARWIJ	ATANUM	AR-WI-TA-NU-UM		B 43
	1		ʾARK	ATANUM	AR-GA-TA-NU-UM		KISURRA 141 9
			ʾARK	ATANUM	AR-GA-DA-NU-UM		KISURRA 1A 15+
	1		ʾEB	ATAN	E-BA-TA-AN		M+
	1		ʾELL	ATAN	EL-LA-TA-AN		C II 39:8
	1		ʾELM	ATAN	EL-MA-TA-AN		M
	1		ʾIL	ATAN	I-LA-TA-AN		M
	1		ʾUŠK	ATANUM	UŠ-KA-TA-NU-UM		XIII 92 11
			ʾUŠK	ATANIM	UŠ-KA-TA-NIM	MN GEN	XIII 61 5+
	1		ḪAJJ	ATAN	ḪA-IA-TA-AN		M+
	1		ḪARB	ATANUM	AR-BA-TA-NU-UM		B 43
			ḪARB	ATANU	AR-BA-TA-NU		CT IV 22A 19
	1		ḪINN	ATANUM	IN-NA-TA-NU-UM		TA 1931, 294
	1		ḪURB	ATANU	UR-BA-TA-NU		KISURRA 24 6
	1		ḪAʾD	ATAN	ḪA-DA-TA-AN		M+
	1		ḪAʾL	ATAN	ḪA-LA-TA-AN		M+
	1		ḪUZM	ATAN	ḪU-IZ-MA-TA-AN		M
	1		ʿABD	ATAN	ḪA-AB-DA-TA-AN		M+
			ʿABD	ATAN	AB-[DA?-T]A-AN		RA LXV 44 IV 62
	1		ʿAMM	ATAN	ḪA-AM-MA-TA-AN		M+
	1		ʿAN	ATAN	A-NA-TA-AN		RA LXV 53 XI 13
			ʿAN	ATAN	ḪA-NA-TA-AN		M+
	1		ʿAZZ	ATANIM	ḪA-ZA-TA-NIM	MN GEN	C II 6
	1		ʿEBB	ATANUM	IB-BA-TA-NU-UM		BE VI/2 26 III 1
	1		JAMN	ATAN	IA-AM-NA-TA-AN		RA LXV 52 X 48
	1		BAJR	ATAN	BA-RA-TA-AN	MN	M
	1		BILL	ATANUM	BI-LA-TA-NU-UM		HARRIS 49 14
	1		BINQ	ATANUM	BI$_2$-GA-TA-NU-UM	MN	TIM III 7:12;39:13
			BINQ	ATANUM	BI$_2$-IN-GA-TA-NU-UM	MN	TIM III 45:11
	1		BURQ	ATANUM	BU-UR$_2$-GA-TA-NU-UM	MN	SIMMONS 78 11
	1		DIʿ	ATANUM	DI-ḪA-TA-NU-U[M]		CT XLVII 4 3
	1		ḎIKR	ATAN	ZI-IK-RA-TA-AN		M+
	1		ḎIMR	ATAN	ZI-IM-RA-TA-AN		M
	1		ḎUMUR	ATANU	ZU-MUR?-TA-NU		ZA XLII 41
	1		KAKK	ATANUM	KA-KA-TA-NU-UM		SIMMONS 104 6

SUFFIXES, Class 1

ATAN	1		LAḤM	ATANUM					LA-AḪ-MA-TA-NU-UM		SIMMONS 89 10
	1		MANN	ATAN					MA-NA-TA-AN		M+
			MANN	ATANU					MA-NA-TA-NU		M
	1		MINN	ATANUM					MI-NA-TA-NU-UM		HARRIS 76 11
	1		NANN	ATAN					NA-NA-TA-AN		M
	1		ŚAMḪ	ATANI					SA-AM-ḪA-TA-NI		VAS VIII 14 5
	1		ŚIJB	ATANU					SI-BA-TA-NU		SIMMONS 88 1
	1		ṢIBʾ	ATAN					[Z]I-BA-TA-AN		VII 185 10
	1		ṢUWR	ATANU					ZU-RA-TA-NU		M
	1		TUʾ	ATAN					TU-ḪA-TA-AN		M
	1		TUʾZ	ATAN					TU-ZA-TA-AN		M
	1		ZARQ	ATANUM					ZA-AR-GA-TA-NU-UM		JCS IV 110A 19
	1		ZIʾN	ATANU					ZI-NA-TA-NU		BM 16984 24
	1		ZIPP	ATANIM					ZI-IP-PA-TA-NIM	GEN	M
ATEN	1		ʾAŚM	ATEN					AŠ$_2$-MA-TI-EN		M
ATIJ	1		TUKR	ATIJI					TUK-RA-TI-I	GEN	UCP X/3 2 19
IJ	1	JA	ʾRUR	IJ	I				IA-AḪ-RU-RI-I-KI	GN	M
	1		ʾURL	IJ	UM				UR-LI-U$_2$-UM		M
	1		ḪAʾN	IJ	U				ḪA-NU-U$_2$		JNES XIII 210+ LATE
	1	ʾA	ḪBUD	IJ	UM				AḪ-BU-TE-UM		U
	1		JABAŚ	IJ	I				JA-BA-SI-JI	TRIBE	M
			JABAŚ	IJ	I				JA-BA-SI-I	TRIBE	M
			JABAŚ	IJ	IM				JA-BA-SI-IM	TRIBE	M
	2	JA	MWUT			BAʿL	IJ	I	IA-MU-UT-BA-LI-I	GN ACC	M
	1	JA	MʾAD	IJ	I				IA-AM-ḪA-DI-I-KI	GN NOM	M
		JA	MʾAD	IJ	I				IA-AM-ḪA-DI-JI	GN NOM	M
		JA	MʾAD	IJ	UM				IA$_3$-A-MA-TI-UM		U
	2		ʾALLA			MUT	IJ	I	AL-LA-MU-TI-I	TRIBE	4E RENC. ASS. P. 178 9
			ʾALLA			MUT	IJ	I	A-AL-MU-TI-I	TRIBE	M
	1		MUTT	IJ	UM				MU-UT-TI-JU-UM		M
	1	JA	RWIḤ	IJ	I				IA-RI-ḪI-I-KI	GN	M+
IN	1		ʾABAŚ	IN	UM				A-BA-ŠE-NU-UM		M
	1		ʾIMIR	IN	UM				I-ME-RI-NU-UM		TA 30 615 12
	1		ʾUKUL	IN	UM				U$_2$-KU-LI-NU-UM		RA LXV 43 III 54
	1		KAMAN	IN	UM				KA-MA-NI-NU-UM		EDZARD,DER 68 IV 11
IT	1		ḤALIṢ	IT	UM				A-LI-ZI-TUM?		UET V 534 R. 9
	1		JAQR	IT	UM				IA-AQ-RI-TUM		EDZARD, DER 155 REV 15
	1		JIŠʿ	IT	IJA				IŠ-ḪI-TI-IA	MN?	CT XLVIII 91 REV.+
	1		BEʿD	IT	UM				BE-DI-TUM	MN	EDZARD, DER 145:10
	1		DADM	IT	UM				DA-AD-MI-TUM	FN	M
	1		DIWR	IT	UM	KAʾB		I	D-DI-RI-TUM-KA-BI		XIII 1 VI 45
	2	JI	NDIN			DIWR	IT	IM	I-DIN-D-DI-RI-TIM	GEN	M
	1		ḎABIB	IT	UM				SA-BI-BI-TUM	FN?	HARRIS 100 6
	1		ḎAQN	IT	UM				DA-AQ-NI-TUM	FN	XIII 1 XIII 22
	1		GIZZ	IT	IM				GI-ZI-TIM	FN GEN	M
	1		KANIŚ	IT	UM				KA-NI-SI-T[UM]	FN	M
			KANIŚ	IT	UM				KA-NI-ŠI-TUM	FN	M+
	2		ʾANN		U	LAMAS	IT	UM	AN-NU-LA-MA-ZI-TUM	FN	RA LXV 59 II 13
	1		MAʾR	IT	UM				MA-RI-TUM	FN	XIII 1 XIII 14
	1		ŚUḪ	IT	UM				SU?-ḪI-TUM	FN	XIII 1 II 52
	1		TAʾG	IT	UM				TA-GI-TUM	FN	XIII 1 II 45
ITAN	1		ḎIKR	ITANU					ZI-IK-RI-TA-NU		M
ITIJ	1		JAKAL	ITIJIM					JA-KA-LI-TE-IM	TRIBE GEN	M
			JAKAL	ITIJI					[JA]-KA-LI-TI-I	TRIBE GEN	M
T	1		ʾAWIJ	T	UM				ḪA-WI-TUM		BIROT TEA 72 I 28+
	1		ʾADAN	T	A				A-DA-AT-TA	FN	C+
	2		ʾEŠB		I	ʾADAN	T	A	EŠ-BI-A-DA-AT-TA		A. 455 31, 55
	1		ʾAM	T	UM				AM-TUM	FN	XIII 1 II 48
			ʾAM	T		ʾEL			GEME$_2$-E-IL		RIFTIN 44 10
			ʾAM	T		ʿAŠTAR	AH		AM-TI-AŠ-TA-RA	FN?	A. LATE
			ʾAM	T		BAʿL	AH		A-MA-AT-D-BA-A-IA	FN	BAGHD. MITT. II 72 5, 9+
			ʾAM	T		LABW		A	AM-TI-LA-BA	MN	TIM III 7 5
	1		ʾARWIJ	T	UM				AR-WI-TUM	FN	KISURRA 134 3, M+
			ʾARWIJ	T	UM				AR-BI-TUM		LEGRAIN, TRU 41+, U
			ʾARWIJ	T	UM				AR-BI$_2$-TUM		TCL V 6039 REV 17, U
	2		ʾAJAM			ʾIL	T	I	A-IA-AM-IL-TI	FN	XIII 1 X 8

SUFFIXES, Class 1

T	1		ʾUNUB	T	UM						UN-NU-UB-TUM	FN	EDZARD, DER 33:11+
			ʾUNUB	T	UM						Ḫ̮U-NU-UB-TUM	FN	EDZARD, DER 99:8
	1		ʿALIJ	T	UM						A-LI-TUM	FN	M+
			ʿALIJ	T	IM						A-LI-TIM	FN GEN	M
	1	ʾU	WTAʾ	T	UM						U$_2$-TA-TUM	FN	C
	1		JAQAR	T	UM						IA-QAR-TUM	FN	M
	1		JARAḪ	T	UM						IA-RA-AḪ-TUM	MN	B 29+
			JARAḪ	T	IM						IA-RA-AḪ-TIM	MN GEN	YOS XII
	1	JA	JŠIR	T	IM						IA-ŠIR-TI-IM	MN GEN	WATERMAN 45 R. 10
	1		BAWŠ	T	UM						BA-AŠ-TUM	FN	M+
			BAWŠ	T	I		NUṢR		I		BA-AŠ-TI-NU-IZ-RI	FN	RA LXV 58 I 45
			BAWŠ	T	I		NUṢR		I		BA-AŠ-TI-UZ-RI		RA LXIV 28 NO. 15
			BAWŠ	T	I		NUṢR		I		BA-AŠ$_2$-TI-NU-UZ-RI	FN	XIII 1 VII 24
	2		ʾIL		I		BAWŠ	T	I		I$_3$-LI$_2$-BA-AŠ$_2$-TI	FN	M+
			ʾANN		U		BAWŠ	T	I		AN-NU-BA-AŠ-TI	FN	RA LXV 65 VII 27
			BAʿL		I		BAWŠ	T	I		BA-AḪ-LI-BA-AŠ-TI	FN	M+
			BEʿL		I		BAWŠ	T	I		BE-LI$_2$-[B]A-AŠ-TI	FN	RA LXV 60 III 42
			DAGAN				BAWŠ	T	I		D-DA-GAN-BA-AŠ-TI	FN	M+
			ŠARR		UM		BAWŠ	T	I		LUGAL-BA-AŠ-TI	FN	M
			ŠARR		UM		BAWŠ	T	I		LUGAL-BA-AŠ$_2$-TI	FN	M+
	1		BEʿL	T	I		JARAḪ				NIN?-TI-E-RA-AḪ		RA LXV 52 X 54
			BEʿL	T	I		MAʾT		I		BE-EL-TI-MA-TI	FN	A. 253 6
	1		BIKIN	T	I						BI-IK-KI-IT-TI	MN GEN	A.
	1		BIKUR	T	UM						BI-KU-UR-TUM	MN	BASOR 95 P. 24
	1		BIN	T	A		ʾATT		I		BI-IT-TA-AT-TI	FN	A.+
			BIN	T	A		MALK		I		BI-IT-TA-MA-AL-KI	FN	A. LATE
			BIN	T	E	JE					BI-IT-TE-E	FN	TCL I 52 11
			BIN	T	I		ḪIJJ		A		BI-TI-ḪI?-A	FN	HARRIS 85 3
			BIN	T	I		DAGAN				BI-IT-TI-D-DA-GAN	FN	B 16+
			BIN	T	I		KIʾD		I	JA	BI-IN-TI-KI-DI-IA	FN	A.+
			BIN	T	U		ṬAJB		AH		BI-IN-DU-ṬA$_3$-BA	FN	RA LXV 65 VII 10
	1	TA	BNIJ	T	UM						TAB-NI-TUM	FN	XIII 1 VI 5+
	1		BUʾUL	T	UM						BU-ḪU-UL-TUM	FN	RA LXV 58 I 56
	1		BUṬUM	T	UM						BU-TU-UM-TUM	FN	RA LXV 59 II 39
	1		DAMIQ	T	UM						DA-ME-IQ-TUM	FN	RA LXV 59 II 60
	1		DAŠIK	T	UM						DA-SI-IK-TUM	MN	MEISSNER 90 27
	1		DULUQ	T	UM						DU-LU-UQ-TUM	FN	MEISSNER 7 26
	1		DUŠUB	T	UM						DU-ŠU-UB-TUM	FN	TCL XI 244 11, M
	1		GABIʾ	T	UM						GA-BI-TUM		RA LXIV 36 NO. 32
	2		ʾANN		U		GAMIL	T	I		AN-NU-GA-ME-IL-TI	FN	RA LXV 66 VII 66
	1		KABID	T	A						KA-BI-IT-TA	MN	C II 6
	1		KURKUR	T	UM						KUR$_2$-KUR$_2$-TUM	MN?	PBS VIII/2 178 36
	1		LAʾIJ	T	UM						LA-I-TUM	FN	RA LXV 58 II 3
			LAʾIŠ	T	UM						LA-ḪI-EŠ$_3$-TUM	FN	C
	2		ŠI				MALIK	T	I		ŠI-MA-LI-IK-TI		IX 294:7'
	1		MANUW	T	UM						MA-NU-TUM	FN	CT VIII 28A 2, 4+
	1		MAŠIK	T	UM						MA-SI-IK-TUM		BM 17063 26+
			MAŠIK	T	UM						MA-SI-IK-TUM	FN	XIII 1 V 73; YOS XIII 453
	1		MENIJ	T	UM						ME-NI-TUM	FN	M
	1		MURMUR	T	IM						MU-UR-MU-UR-TIM	FN GEN	B 49
	1		NAKAM	T	UM						NA-KA-AM-TUM	FN	M
			NAKAR	T	UM						NA-KA-AR-TUM	FN	M
	1		NUWR	T	UM						NU-UR$_2$-TUM	FN	RA LXV 65 VII 21
	1		NUṬUP	T	UM						NU-DU-UB-TUM	FN	UET V P. 53+
			NUṬUP	T	UM						NU-TU-UP-TUM	FN	UET V P. 53+
	1		PAʾR	T	UM						PA-AR-TUM	FN	CT XLV 54 24, M+
	1		PASAʿ	T	UM						PA-ZA-AḪ-TUM	FN	XIII 1 VIII 81
	1	MU	PATIḪ	T	UM						MU-PA-AT-TI-TUM	FN	C+
	1		PUḪUR	T	UM						PU-ḪU-UR-TUM	FN	M
	1		QIJŠ	T	UM						KI-IŠ-TUM	FN	XIII 1 III 16
			QIJŠ	T	I		ʾADM		U		KI-IŠ-TI-AD-MU		M+
			QIJŠ	T	I		LIʾL		IM		KI-IŠ-TI-LI-LIM	GEN	RA LXIV 34 NO.26
			QIJŠ	T	I		MAM		A		KI-IŠ-TI-D-MA-MA		M+
			QIJŠ	T	I		MAM		A		KI-IŠ-TI-D-MA-AM-MA		XIV 61:5
			QIJŠ	T	I		NUN		U		KI-IŠ-TI-D-NU-NU		M+
	1	TA	QNIJ	T	UM						TA?-AQ-NI-TUM	FN	XIII 1 VIII 74

T	1	RAPIʾ	T	UM				RA-BI-TUM	FN	M
	1 JI	RKAB	T	UM				IR-KAB-TUM	MN	A.+
	JI	RKAB	T	U				IR-KAB-DU	MN	A.+ LATE
	1	SIKIL	T	A				ZI-KI-IL-DA	MN	A. 24 3
		SIKIL	T	A				ZI-KI-IL-TA	MN	A. LATE+
		SIKIL	T	A				ZI-KI-EL-TA	MN	A. LATE
		SIKIL	T	E				ZI-GI-IL-TE	MN	A.
	1	ŠAʾIL	T	UM				ŠA-IL-TUM	FN	U+
	1	ŠAM	T	UM				SA-AM-TUM	FN	TCL I 189 17, M+
	1	ŠAMAK	T	UM				ŠA-M[A]-AK-T[UM]	MN	TA 1931, 527
	1	ŠIJB	T	UM				ŠI-IB-TU-UM	FN	RA LXV 62 V 50
		ŠIJB	T	UM				ŠI-IB-TUM	FN	M
		ŠIJB	T	U				ŠI-IB-TU	FN	M+
	2	ṬAJB			ŠIJM	T	UM	TA-AB-SI-IM-TUM	FN	A. 8 4
	1	ŠUḪAR	T	UM				ŠU-ḪA-AR-TUM	FN	M
	1	ŠUMUḪ	T	UM				ŠU-MU-UḪ-TUM	FN	XIII 1 X 49+
	1	ŠUPUR	T	UM				SU-PU-UR-TUM		PBS VIII/1 45 17
	1	ŠUBUL	T	UM				ŠU-BU-UL-TUM	FN	M, C
	1	ŠUQUL	T	UM				ŠU-GUL-TUM	FN	XIII 1 XI 9
	2	ʾANN		U	TUKUL	T	I	AN-NU-TU-KU-UL-[TI]	FN	M+
		ʾANN		U	TUKUL	T	I	AN-NU-TU-GUL-TI	FN	XIII 1 X 3
	2	LA			ṬAJB	T	UM	LA-ṬA_3-AB-TUM	FN	XIII 1 VI 44+
	1	ZAʾR	T	UM				ZA-AR-TUM	FN	M
	1	ZURZUR	T	UM				ZU-UR_2-ZU-UR-TUM	FN	KISURRA 187 5
		ZURZUR	T	UM				ZU-UR_2-ZU-UR-TUM	FN	KISURRA 187 5
UN	1	JAMN	UN	UM				IA-AM-NU-NU-UM		TIM III 26 13, 39 16
	1 MA	JRID	UN	UM				MA-RI-DU-NU-UM		SIMMONS 124 17
	1	MILK	UN	IM				MI-IL-KU-NI-IM	GEN	SIMMONS 46 33
		MILK	UN	IM				MI-IL-KU-NIM	GEN	SIMMONS 70 17
	1 ʾA	RMAN	UN	UM				AR-MA-NU-NUM_2		TA 1931 , 538 IV
	1	ŠAKUN	UN	UM				SA-KU-NU-NU-UM		RUTTEN 26 4
	1	ZAʾZ	UN	UM				ZA-ZU-NU-UM		M
UT	1	ḪAʾZ	UT	UM				ḪA-ZU-TUM	FN	RA LXV 58 II 1
	1	ḪUŠŠ	UT	UM				ḪU-ŠU-TUM	FN	CT VI 43 6, 34
		ḪUŠŠ	UT	UM				ḪU-U$Š_2$-ŠU-TUM	FN	X 96 3
		ḪUŠŠ	UT	IM				ḪU-ŠU-TIM	FN GEN	X 27 8
	1	BILK	UT	UM				BI-IL-KU-TUM	FN	XIII 1 XIII 17
	1	BIRUR	UT	UM				BI-RU-RU-TUM	MN	B 15+
	1	BUŠAN	UT	UM				BU?-SA?-NU-TUM	MN?	VIII 13 10'
	1	DUWD	UT	UM				DU-DU-TUM	FN	M
UTAN	1	ʾURK	UTANIM					UR-KU-TA-NIM	GEN	CT VIII 20B 10

A	1	JA		ʾḪIḎ		A						IA-E-DA		YOS XIII 343:4
	1			ʾAḪ	AT	A	HA					A-ḪA-TA-A	FN	RA LXV 62 V 52
				ʾAḪ	AT	A		ʾAB		I		A-ḪA-TA-A-BI	FN	M+
				ʾAḪ	AT	A		NAʿM		I		A-ḪA-TA-NA-AḪ-MI	FN	XIII 1 XI 3
	3			ʾIL		I		MAʾD		I				
								ʾAḪ		A		I$_3$-LI$_2$-MA-DA-ḪA		VAS VIII 14 4
	1			ʾAJ		A		ʿALIJ	AT			D-A-A-ḪA-LI-IA-AT	MN?	CT XLV 92 R. 12
				ʾAJ		A		ʾARR		I		D-A-A-AR-RI	FN	M
	1			ʾAJAL		A	HA					A?-IA-LA-A	FN?	M
	1			ʾAB		A		ʾEL				A-BA-EL		TA 31, 221
				ʾAB		A		ʾIL				A-BA-DINGIR	FN	A. 59 5
				ʾAB		A		ʾANN		U		A-BA-AN-NU		M
				ʾAB		A		JARAḪ				A-BA-A-RA-AḪ		KICH II D 8 3
				ʾAB		A		DAWD		UM		A-BA-DA-DUM		HARRIS 95 9
	2			LA				ʾAB		A		LA-A-BA		U
	1			ʾABB		A						AB-BA		RA LXV 55 XIII 12
				ʾABB		A		ʾIL				D-AB-BA-DINGIR	FN	M
				ʾABB		A		ʾIL				AB-BA-DINGIR		A.+
				ʾABB		A		ʾIL		I		AB-BA-I$_3$-LI$_2$	FN	XIII 1 XI 14
				ʾABB		A		ʾIL		I		D-AB-BA-I$_3$-LI$_2$	FN	SIMMONS 112:17
				ʾABB		A		ŠARR				AB-BA-LUGAL		A. 86 2
	2			ʾITT		A		ʾABB		A		ḪI-IT-TA-D-AB-BA		M
				KIBR				ʾABB		A		KI-BI-IR-D-AB-BA		M+
				KIBR				ʾABB		A		KI-IB-RA-AB-BA		CT XXIX 14 16
				KIBR				ʾABB		A		KI-IB-RA-BA		CT XXIX 14 29
		JI		NDIN				ʾABB		A		I-DIN-AB-BA		XIII 1 VIII 46
		JI		NDIN				ʾABB		A		ID-DI-NA-AB-BA		A.
		JI		NDIN				ʾABB		A		ID-DI-NA-BA		A. LATE
		JA		RḪIB				ʾABB		A		IA-AR-IB-D-AB-BA		M
	1			ʾABN		A		JARAḪ				ḪA?-AB-NA-A-RA-AḪ		UET V 476 SEAL 6
	1			ʾADAN	T	A						A-DA-AT-TA	FN	C+
	2			ʾEŠB		I		ʾADAN	T	A		EŠ-BI-A-DA-AT-TA		A. 455 31, 55
	1			ʾAKK		A						AK-KA		XIII 1 IV 27+
				ʾAKK		A		BANIJ				AK-KA-BA-NI		M
	2		T	HILAL				ʾAKK		A		ḪI-IT-LA-AL-AK-KA		RA LXV 54 XII 36,71
				JATAR				ʾAKK		A		IA-TAR-AK-KA		M
		JI		NDIN				ʾAKK		A		I-DIN-AK-KA		XIII 1 I 54+
				ṢILL				ʾAKK		A		MI-NI-AK-KA		M
	1			ʾALUN		A		HADD		U		ḪA-LU-NA-D-IM		M
	1			ʾAMAR		A		HADD		U		AM-MA-RA-A-DU		A.
	1			ʾAMIR		A		ʾAB		UM		A-MI-RA-A-BU-UM		RA LXV 55 XIII 5
	1			ʾAN		A	Š	KIBAL				[A]?-NA-AŠ-KI-BA-AL		VIII 86 23
	1			ʾARAM		A						A-RA-MA		A.+
	1			ʾARUM		A						A-RU-MA	GEN	RA VIII 74 16
	1			ʾAŠD		A		ʾAḪ		I		AŠ-DA-A-ḪI		VAS XVI 44 3
	1			ʾAŠM		A		HADD		U		AŠ-MA-DU		BM 80328 14
				ʾAŠM		A		HADD		U		AŠ-MA-A-DU		A.+
	2			ḪAJJ		A		ʾAŠR		A	JA	E$_2$-A-AŠ-RA-IA		M+
				ʾIL		I		ʾAŠR		A	JA	I$_3$-LI$_2$-AŠ-RA-IA		M+
				DAGAN				ʾAŠR		A	JA	D-DA-GAN-AŠ-RA-IA		M+
	2			ʿABD				ʾAŠUR		A		ḪA-AB-DU-A-ŠU-RA		M
				ṬAJB		A		ʾAŠUR		A		TA-PA-AŠ-ŠU-RA		A.
	2			ʾIL		I		ʾATAJ		A	JA	I$_3$-LI$_2$-A-TA-A-IA		RA VIII 69 26
	1			ʾATT		A						D-ḪA-AT-TA	DN	M+
	2			ḪAʾR		I		ʾATT		A		ḪA-RI-A-TA		C II 5 7
				KAʾB		I		ʾATT		A		KA-BI-A-TA		M
	1			ʾIDID		A						I-DI-DA	MN	BE VI/1 14 30
	1			ʾIL		A	NI					I-LA-A-NI		A. 279 2
				ʾIL		A		ḪAʾL		UM		DINGIR-ḪA-LUM		B 21
				ʾIL		A		ḪAʾL		U	HU	DINGIR-ḪA-LU-U$_2$		XIII 1 IV 18
				ʾIL		A		ʾUWR		I		DINGIR-U$_2$-RI		RA LXVIII 28:13 MARI
				ʾIL		A		ʾAB		I		I-LA-A-BI		C
				ʾIL		A		ḪABAD				DINGIR-ḪA-BA-AD		M+
				ʾIL		A		ʿADN		U	HU	I-LA-ḪA-AD-NU-U$_2$		M
				ʾIL		A		ʿADN		U	HU	I-LA-ḪA-AD-NU-U$_2$	FN	C+
				ʾIL		A		ʿADN		U	HU	DINGIR-ḪA-AD-NU-U$_2$	FN	C+

SUFFIXES, Class 2

A	1	ʾIL	A		ʾIL			I-LA-DINGIR		B 21
		ʾIL	A		ʾEL			I-LA-EL		RA LXV 43 IV 3
		ʾIL	A		ʿAMM	U		I-LA-ḪA-MU		RA LXV 42 II 77+
		ʾIL	A		ʾUMM	A		DINGIR-UM-MA		RA LXV 45 V 31
		ʾIL	A		ʾIRR	A		[I-L]A?-IR$_3$-RA		RA LXV 47 VII 18
		ʾIL	A		ʿAŠTAR			I-LA-EŠ$_4$-DAR		RA LXV 42 III 16+
		ʾIL	A	JI	JBAL			DINGIR?-I-BA-AL		M
		ʾIL	A		BAWB	I	JA	DINGIR-BA-BI-A		UET V 263 17
		ʾIL	A		BAʿL	U	HU	I-LA-BA-LU-U$_2$		M
		ʾIL	A		BIN	I		DINGIR-BI-NI		UCP X/3 1 7
		ʾIL	A		BIN	I		I-LA-BI$_2$-NI		I
		ʾIL	A		DAʿ	AT		I-LA-DA-ḪA-AT		SUMER V 141,3+
		ʾIL	A		DAʿ	AT		BAD$_3$-DINGIR-DA-ḪA-AT GN		A 7650
		ʾIL	A		DAKUL			DINGIR-DA-AK-KU-UL		UET V P. 43
		ʾIL	A		DAKUL			DINGIR-DA-KU-UL		UET V P. 43
		ʾIL	A		DAKUL	UM		DINGIR-DA-AK-KU-UL-LUM		UET V P. 43
		ʾIL	A		DAKUL	UM		DINGIR-DA-KU-UL-LUM		UET V P. 43+
		ʾIL	A		DARAN			DINGIR-DA-RA-AN		M+
		ʾIL	A		GULL	A		DINGIR-GU-UL-LA	FN	C+
		ʾIL	A		GULL	A				
					ʿAḎIR	AT		DINGIR-GUL-LA$_2$-ḪA-ZI-RA-AT	FN	M+
		ʾIL	A		KA					
					ʾAB	UM		DINGIR-KA-A-BU-UM		CT XLV 100 17
		ʾIL	A		KAʾAM			DINGIR-KA-A-AM		TIM III 101 7
		ʾIL	A		KAWN			DINGIR-KA-AN	MN	M+
		ʾIL	A		KAWN			DINGIR-KA-AN	FN	M
		ʾIL	A		KAWN	UM		DINGIR-KA-NU-UM		MAH II/3 P. 188F
		ʾIL	A		KAWN	IM		DINGIR-KA-NIM	GEN	M+
		ʾIL	A		KAWN	IM		DINGIR-KA-NI-IM	GEN	M
		ʾIL	A		KABKAB	I		DINGIR-KAB-KA-BI		JNES XIII 210+ LATE
		ʾIL	A		KABKAB	U	HU	I-LA-KAB-KA-BU-U$_2$		M+
		ʾIL	A		LA					
					ʾIL			DINGIR-LA-IL		U
		ʾIL	A		LA		KA	I-LA-LA-KA		B 21+
		ʾIL	A		LAʾIJ			I-LA-LA-I		TA 1931,395,UR III
		ʾIL	A		LAʾIJ			I-LA-LA-E		TA 1931,609,UR III
		ʾIL	A		LAʾIJ			I-LA-LA-E-KI	GN	LAESSOE, SHEMSHARA P.77
		ʾIL	A		LAʾIJ			I-LA-LA-AḪ		RA LXV IX 38,X 10
		ʾIL	A		MA					
					ʾAB	I		DINGIR-MA-A-BI		M
		ʾIL	A		MA					
					ʾIL	A		DINGIR-MA-I$_3$-LA		B 21+
		ʾIL	A		MA					
					ʾIL	A		DINGIR-MA-D-I-LA		B 21
		ʾIL	A		MAʾD	I		DINGIR-MA-DI		M
		ʾIL	A		MEʾR			DINGIR-ME-IR		JNES XIII 210+ LATE
		ʾIL	A		MALK	I		DINGIR-MA-AL-KI		A. LATE
		ʾIL	A		MILK	UM		DINGIR-MI-IL-KUM		BAHREIN UNP., POST-UR III
		ʾIL	A		MAṬAR			DINGIR-MA-DA-AR		OR. N.S. XXVI 28 N.4 CAPP
		ʾIL	A		MAṬAR			DINGIR-MA-TAR		M+
		ʾIL	A		NAʿM	A		DINGIR-NA-MA-....		VAS VIII 14 44
		ʾIL	A		NABUṬ			DINGIR-NA-BU-UD		VAS VIII 14 31
		ʾIL	A		NUN	U		I-LA-NU-NU		FIGULLA CAT. I 14029
		ʾIL	A		PA	I		I-LA-BA-I		TA 1931, 499
		ʾIL	A		PAʾŠ	I	JA	DINGIR-PA-ŠI-IA		TCL XVIII 106 9
		ʾIL	A		QAʾB			DINGIR-QA-AB		TIM III 130 12, SEAL
		ʾIL	A		RAWḤ	I	JA	DINGIR-RA[Ḫ]I-A		HARRIS 76 21
		ʾIL	A		RAWḤ	I	JA	I-LA-RA-ḪI-IA		M
		ʾIL	A		RAWḤ	I	JE	I-LA-RA-ḪI-E		M
		ʾIL	A		RAWḤ	I	JE	DINGIR-RA-ḪI-E		HARRIS 85 14
		ʾIL	A		ŚALIM			I-LA-SA-LIM		M, C
		ʾIL	A		ŚAMAR			I-LA-ŠA-MA-AR		U
		ʾIL	A	Š	BAʿL	UM		DINGIR-ŠU-BA-A-LUM		CT II 15 9
		ʾIL	A	TA	RʿIŠ			I-LA-TA-RI-IŠ		B 21
	2	ʾAB	I		ʾIL	A		A-BI-LA		CHANTRE 4 13
JA		ḪBIʾ			ʾIL	A		IA-AḪ-BI-LA-KI	GN	M+

A	2		ʿAD	U	NI	ʾIL	A	A-DU-NI-LA	U
			ʾIL	I		ʾIL	A	I$_3$-LI$_2$-I-LA	A. LATE
		JA	ʾMIʾ			ʾIL	A	IA-MI-I-LA	M
		JA	ʾMIʾ			ʾIL	A	JA-MI-I-LA	M
		ʾU	WMAʾ			ʾIL	A	U$_2$-MA-D-DINGIR	B 40
			ʾANAKU			ʾIL	A		
						MA		A-NA-KU-I-LA-MA	SIMMONS 46 7+
			ḪANN	I		ʾIL	A	ḪA-AN-NI-I-LA	A. LATE
			ʾUP			ʾIL	A	UP-I-LA	BULL. ACAD. BELG. 1974 227
		ʾU	WQAH			ʾIL	A	U$_2$-Q[A]-I-LA	A 7699:14, ISHCHALI
			WARḪ			ʾIL	A	WA-AR-ḪI-LA$_2$	CCT I 38C 2 CAPP.
			JIŠʿ	I		ʾIL	A		
						MA		IŠ-ḪI-DINGIR-MA	M
			JIŠʿ	I		ʾIL	A		
						MA		IŠ-ḪI-DINGIR-LA-MA	M
			BAWʾ	U		ʾIL	A	BA-U$_2$-I-LA	MEISSNER 43 45
		ʾU	BWAʾ			ʾIL	A	U$_2$-BA-D-DINGIR	VAS VIII 14:22
			BIN			ʾIL	A	BI-IN-I-LA	A. LATE
			BUN	I		ʾIL	A	BU-NI-I-LA	B 16+
			BUN	U		ʾIL	A	BU-NU-I-LA	CT XLV 115 24
			ḎU			ʾIL	A	ZU-I-LA	B 42+
			ḎU			ʾIL	A	ZU-U$_2$-I-LA	B 42
			ḎIMR	U		ʾIL	A	ZI-IM-RU-I-L[A]?	II 5 7
			KUWN			ʾIL	A	KU-UN-I-LA	RA LXV 53 XI 31
			LA			ʾIL	A	[L]A?-I-LA	RA LXV 44 IV 36
			LA			ʾIL	A		
						MILK	I	LA-I-LA-MI-IL-KI	TA 30, 75 2
			LABAN	A		ʾIL	A	LA-PA-NA-I-LA	ZA XXXVIII 267
			LAMA			ʾIL	A	LA-MA-I-LA	YOS XIII 244:2+
			MILK	I		ʾIL	A	MI-EL-KI-I-[LA]	UCP X/3 1 29
			MUT	U		ʾIL	A	MU-TU-I-LA	RA LXV 43 III 68
			PA			ʾIL	A	PA-I-LA	XIII 1 VII 16
			PA		KA	ʾIL	A	PA-KA-I-LA	B 37+
			PA		KA	ʾIL	A	PA-KA-DINGIR	B 37
			PA		KA	ʾIL	A	PA-A-KA-I-LA	B 37
			PI			ʾIL	A	PI-I-LA	A. LATE
			PANIJ			ʾIL	A	PA-NI-LA	IX 252 17, A. LATE
		JI	RḪAM			ʾIL	A	IR-ḪA-MI-LA	A.+
			RIWM			ʾIL	A	RI-IM-I-LA	TCL XIV 54 17 CAPP.
			RIPʾ	A		ʾIL	A	RI-IP-A-DINGIR	M+
		ʾA	ŠWUB			ʾIL	A	A-ŠU-UB-I-LA	A. LATE
			ŠUWB			ʾIL	A	ŠU-UB-D-I-LA	RA LXV 52 X 66
			ŠUWB	A		ʾIL	A	ŠU-BA-D-DINGIR	B 23+
		JA	ŠBIJ			ʾIL	A	IA-AŠ-BI-I-LA	B 30
			ŠADW	U		ʾIL	A	ŠA-DU-[I]-LA	RA LXV 45 V 50
			ŚAM	U		ʾIL	A	SA-MU-I-LA	M
			ŚAM	U	HU	ʾIL	A	SA-MU-U$_2$-I-LA	M
			ŚUM	A		ʾIL	A	SU-MA-I-LA	YOS XIII 244:15+
			ŚUM	U		ʾIL	A	SU-MU-I-LA	B 39; M+
			ŚIMAʿ			ʾIL	A	SI-MA-I-LA	X 5 4, 5
		JU T	ŠANIJ			ʾIL	A	UŠ-TA-NI-I-LA	A. 33 22
	3		ʾAK	UM		LA			
						ʾIL	A	A-KUM-LA-I-LA	RA LXV 55 XIII 1
			ʾIL	A		MA			
						ʾIL	A	DINGIR-MA-I$_3$-LA	B 21+
			ʾIL	A		MA			
						ʾIL	A	DINGIR-MA-D-I-LA	B 21
			BUN			TAḪTUN			
						ʾIL	A	BU-UN-TAḪ-UN-I-LA	B 16
			BUN	U		KAMA			
						ʾIL	A	BU-NU-KA-MA-I-LA	B 16
			BUN	U		TAḪTUN			
						ʾIL	A	BU-NU-TAḪ-TU-UN-I-LA	B 16+
		ʾA	MWUT			PI			
						ʾIL	A	A-MU-UT-BI-I-LA	M
			MILK	I		LU			
						ʾIL	A	MI-IL-KI-LU-I-LA	VAS XVI 10 5, 9

A	3	JA	RŠAP				LA				
							ʾIL	A	IA-AR-SA-AP-LA-I-[LA]?		M
	1		ʾILL	A			JAT	I	IL-LA-I-IA-TI	FN NOM	XIII 1 IX 51
			ʾILL	A			JAT	IM	IL-LA-I-IA-TIM	FN NOM	XIII 1 IV 75
	2		ʾIL	I			ʾILL	A	I-LI-IL-LA		A. LATE
		JI	RḤAM				ʾILL	A	IR-ḪA-MI-IL-LA		A. 274 26
		JI	RWIM				ʾILL	A	I-RI-MIL-LA		A. 87 30 LATE
		JI	RWIM				ʾILL	A	I-RI-IM-IL-LA		A. LATE
		JI	RWIM				ʾILL	A	I-RI-MI-IL-LA		A. LATE
		JA	ŠWIB	I			ʾILL	A	IA-ŠI-BI-IL-LA		A.
		JI	ŚMAʿ				ʾILL	A	IŠ-MI-IL-LA		A.
	3		ʾAJAN				ʾAB	I			
							ʾILL	A	A-IA-NA-BI-IL-LA		A.
	1		ʾILUL	A					I-LU-UL-LA		M
			ʾILUR	A					I-LU-RA	GEN	A.
	2		ʾAB	I			ʾIR	A	AD-I-RA	FN	A.
	1		ʾIRR	A			ʾAB	I	IR$_3$-RA-A-BI		M
	2		ʾIL	A			ʾIRR	A	[I-L]A?-IR$_3$-RA		RA LXV 47 VII 18
			ḤIMD				ʾIRR	A	ḪI-ME-ID-IR$_3$-RA		M+
			ḤIMD				ʾIRR	A	ḪI-MI-ID-D-IR$_3$-RA		M+
		JA	ḪṢIN				ʾIRR	A	IA-AḪ-ZI-IN-IR$_3$-RA		M
		JA	RḤIB				ʾIRR	A	IA-AR-IB-D-IR$_3$-RA		M
		JA	RḤIB				ʾIRR	A	IA-AR-I-[IB]-IR$_3$-RA		M
		JA	ŚJIM				ʾIRR	A	IA-ŠI-IM-IR$_3$-RA		M
		JI	ŚBIJ				ʾIRR	A	IŠ-BI-D-IR$_3$-RA		M+
		JI	ŚBIJ				ʾIRR	A	IŠ-BI-IR$_3$-RA		M+
	2		ʿABD				ʾIRŠAP	A	ḪA-AB-DU-IR?-ŠA-PA?		M
	1		ʾITT	A			ʾABB	A	ḪI-IT-TA-D-AB-BA		M
			ʾITT	A			ʾIL	I	IT-TA-I$_3$-LI$_2$		M
	2		LA			ʾA	ʾMUR	A	LA-MU-RA		B 33+
	1	JA	ʾRUR	A					IA-AḪ-RU-RA-KI	GN	B 26, M
		JA	ʾRUR	A					IA-ḪU-UR-RA-KI	GN	M+
	2		ŚUM	U		JA	ʾRUR	A	[SU-MU-I]A-AḪ-RU-RA		B 39
	1		ʾUWR	A			HADD	U	U$_2$-RA-A-DU		A.
	1		ʾUBIR	A					U$_2$-BI-RA		M
	2		ʾIL	A			ʾUMM	A	DINGIR-UM-MA		RA LXV 45 V 31
	1		ʾUŠM	A			ʿAMM	I	UŠ-MA-AM-MI		CT XXXIII 46A 4
	1		HADD	A					AD-DA		M+
	2		ʾAḪ	I			HADD	A	A-ḪI-A-DA		B 12
		JI	ʾLIP				HADD	A	IḪ-LI-BA-DA		TCL I 222 13
			ʿAMM	U			HADD	A	AM-MU-A-DA		A.+
			ʿAMM	U			HADD	A	AM-MU-WA-DA		A.
		TA	PTUN				HADD	A	TAP-TU-NA-A-DA		A. 33 26
		TA	PTAN				HADD	A	TAP-TA-NA-A-DA		A. 206 5
		TA	PTAN				HADD	A	TAP-DA-NA-TA		A. LATE
		JI	RPAʾ				HADD	A	IR-PA-A-DA		A. 76 8+
		JI	RPAʾ				HADD	A	IR-PA-DA		A. 41 14
		ʾA	RŠIJ				HADD	A	AR-ŠI-A-DA		M
			ŚIKR	I			HADD	A	SI-IK-RI-ḪA-DA		BE VI/1 6 19
		JI	ŚMAʿ				HADD	A	IŠ-MA-A-DA		A.+
			ŚIPQ	U	NA		HADD	A	SI-IP-KU-NA-D-IM		M
			ŚIPQ	U	NA		HADD	A	SI-IP-KU-NA-DA		M
			ṢIJḪ				HADD	A	ZI-ḪA-DA		TA 1933,7 EARLY OB
	3		LAWUJ				LA				
							HADD	A	LA-U$_2$-LA-A-DA		A.
	1		HALIL	A			ʿAD	UM	A-LI-LA-ḪA-DU-UM		KISURRA 18 12
	2	ʾA	PLAḪ				HAND	A	AP-LA-ḪA-AN-DA		M+
		ʾA	PLAḪ				HAND	A	AP-LI-ḪA-AN-DA		M
		ʾA	PLAḪ				HAND	A	AP-LA-ḪA-DA		M
		ʾA	PLAḪ				HAND	A	AP-LA-AḪ-[AN]-DA		M
		ʾA	RDAK				HAND	A	AR-DA-KA-AN-DA		M
			ŚIPR	I			HAND	A	ŠI-IP-RI-AN-TA		A. LATE
			ŠIPṬ	I			HAND	A	ŠI-IP-TI-AN-TA		A. LATE
			ŠIPṬ	I			HAND	A	ŠI-IP-TI-IA-AN-TA		A. LATE
	2		ʿABD				HEDD	A	ḪA-AB-DI-E-D-IM		RS XIX 338F.
			ʾIL	I			HEDD	A	I$_3$-LI-E-DA		A.

A	2			ʿAMM		I		HEDD		A		AM-MI-E-DA		A.
		JA		ʿQUB				HEDD		A		IA-AK-KU-UB-E-DA		JEA VIII 207F.
				JIŠʿ		I		HEDD		A		IŠ-ḪI-E-D-IM		TIM IV 33 SEAL, 34 SEAL
		JA		JŠIR				HEDD		A		IA-ŠE-RE-DA		A. 367 5
		JA		JŠIR				HEDD		A		IA-AŠ-RI-E-DA		A.+
		JA		JTIR				HEDD		A		IA-TE-IR-E-DA		A.+
		JA		JTIR				HEDD		A		IA-TE-RI-DA		A.+
				ḎIMR		I		HEDD		A		ZI-IM-RI-E-ID-DA		B 42
				KAʾB		I		HEDD		A		KA-BI-E-D-IM		M+
				KIBS		I		HEDD		A		KI-IB-ZI-E-D-IM		M
			N	MŠIḪ				HEDD		A		NA-AM-SI-E-D-IM		A 7646 6
				RIPʾ		I		HEDD		A		RI-IP-E-D-IM		M
		ʾA		ŠKUR				HEDD		A		AŠ-KUR-E-DA		A. 54 25
				ŠUM		I		HEDD		A		SU-MI-E-DA		YOS XIII 486:1
				ŠAMŠ		I		HEDD		A		SA-AM-SI-E-D-IM		SIMMONS 4 20
				ŠAMŠ		I		HEDD		A		SA-AM-SI-E-DA		A. 455 36
				ŠAPŠ		I		HEDD		A		SA-AP-SI-E-DA		A.+
	1			ḪAJJ		A		ʾAŠR		A	JA	E$_2$-A-AŠ-RA-IA		M+
				ḪAJJ		A		NIWR		I		E$_2$-A-NI-RI	FN	RA LXV 58 II 2
				ḪAJJ		A		NIWR		I		E$_2$-A-NE-RI	FN	XIII 1 VII 26
				ḪAJJ		A		ŠIMḪ		I		E$_2$-A-ŠI-IM-ḪI	FN	XIII 1 II 44
	2	JA		ḪṢIN				ḪAJJ		A		IA-AḪ-ZI-IN-E$_2$-A		XIII 1 VII 23
				BAWB		I		ḪAJJ		A		D-BA-BI-E$_2$-A?		VIII 31 7
				KIBR				ḪAJJ		A		KI-BI-IR-E$_2$-A		XIV 62:23
				LU				ḪAJJ		A				
								ŠAMIʿ		UM		LU-ḪA-A-A-SA-MU-UM		UET V 569 8
				LU				ḪAJJ		A				
								ŠAMIʿ		UM		LU-ḪA-A-A-SA-MI-UM		UET V 569 17
				MILK		I		ḪAJJ		A		MIL-KI-ḪA-A-IA	FN	IRAQ XVI 40 NA
		JA		RḤIB				ḪAJJ		A		IA-AR-IB-D-E$_2$-A		M+
		JA		ŠJIM				ḪAJJ		A		[I]A-ŠI-IM-E$_2$-A		M
		JI		ŠJIM				ḪAJJ		A		I-ŠI-IM-E$_2$-A		M
		JI		TWUR				ḪAJJ		A		I-DUR-E$_2$-A		M
				TIWR				ḪAJJ		A		TI-IR-E$_2$-A		M+
	1			ḪALAJ		A		KUʾM		U		ḪA-LA-A-KU-MU		XIV 79:5+
	2			ʾAB		I		ḪAM		A		A-BI-A-MA		SIMMONS 50 22+
				ʾAB		I		ḪAM		A		A-BI-IA-MA		SIMMONS 54 19+
	1			ḪANAN		A						A-NA-NA		U
				ḪANAN		A		GAʾJ		A		A-NA-NA-GA-A		RA XLIV 112 5 QATNA
	1			ḪANN		A		ʾAḪ		UM		AN-NA-A-ḪU-UM		RA LXV 52 XI 1
				ḪANN		A		ʾAḪ		IM		AN-NA-A-ḪI-IM	GEN	M
				ḪANN		A		ʾAḪ		I		AN-NA-A-ḪI	GEN	M
				ḪANN		A		ʾABN		UM		AN-NA-AB-NU-UM		KISURRA 8A 14
				ḪANN		A		ʾABN		UM		A-NA-AB-NU-UM		HARRIS 57 18
				ḪANN		A		ʾABN	AT			ḪA-AN-NA-AB-NA-AT		A 7763, ISHCHALI
				ḪANN		A		HADD		U		AN-NA-D-IM		M+
				ḪANN		A		HADD		U		ḪA-AN-NA-D-IM		M
				ḪANN		A		ʾIL				AN-NA-DINGIR		B 13+, C+
				ḪANN		A		JARAḪ				ḪA-AN-NA-D-EN-ZU		M
				ḪANN		A		JARAḪ				ḪAN-NA-D-EN-ZU		XIII 1 V 27
				ḪANN		A	JI	TWUR						
								MEʾR				ḪA-AN-NA-D-I-DUR-ME-ER		M
				ḪANN		A		KUʾN		I		AN-NA-KU-NI		VAS VIII 14 44
				ḪANN		A		KAʾT		UM		AN-NA-KA-TUM		YOS XIII 508:2
				ḪANN		A		MAʾJ		A		AN-NA-MA-A-A		RUTTEN 14 15
	2			MAʾL		I		ḪARAB		A		MA-LI-A-RA-BA?		CT II 30 29
	2			ʾIL		I		ḪAṢN		A	JA	I$_3$-LI$_2$-ḪA-AṢ-NA-A-IA		M+
	2			ʾANA				ḪIJJ		A		A-NA-ḪI?-A?		RUTTEN 20:16
				BIN	T	I		ḪIJJ		A		BI-TI-ḪI?-A	FN	HARRIS 85 3
				KUKIM				ḪIJJ		A		KU-UK-KI-IM?-ḪI-IA	FN	X 100 5
	1			ḪINN		A		BAWŠ	AT			E-NA-BA-ŠA-AT		ICK 63 2+ CAPP.
				ḪINN		A		BAWŠ	AT	A		E-NA-BA-ŠA-TA		EL II P. 171 N. CAPP.
	1			ḪUBAS		A						ḪU-BA-AZ-ZA		M+
	2			ʾIMIR				ḪUNN		A		IM-ME-IR?-ḪU-UN-NA		A. 43 9
	1	ME		ḪZIQ		A						ME-ZI-QA		M
	1			ḪAʾAN		A		LA			HA	ḪA-A-NA-LA-A	FN	XIII 1 II 53+

SUFFIXES, Class 2

A	1		ḪAʾL		A	NA					ḪA-LA?-NA	FN	RA LXV 59 II 74
	2		ḎIMR		U		ḪAʾL		A		ZI-IM-RU-ḪA-LA		BM 17045
			ŠUM		U		ḪAʾL		A		SU-MU-ḪA-LA		B 39
	3		KA				ṢUWR		I				
							ḪAʾL		A		KA-ZU-RI-ḪA-LA		M
	1		ḪAʾN		A						ḪA-NA-El	GN	M+
			ḪAʾN		A		ʾAB		I		ḪA-NA-A-BI		TIM II 113 2, 8
	2		MUT				ḪAʾN		A		MU-UT-ḪA-NA		XIV 47:31
	1		ḪAḪUN		A						ḪA-ḪU-NA		CT II 23 33
	1		ḪALD		A		MULUK				ḪA?-AL-DA-MU-LU-UK		BASOR 95 21
	1		ḪANZ		A		HADD		U		ḪA-AN-ZA-D-IM		M
			ḪANZUR		A						ḪA-AN-ZU-RA		VAS IX 172 39+
	1		ḪAQAT		A						ḪA-QA-TA		DELAPORTE CCL II A 914
	1		ḪATAʾ		A		ʾAR		UM		ḪA-TA-A-A-RUM?		CT XXIX 8A '
	1		ḪIʾAN		A						ḪI-A-NA		BM 80328 4
	2		MUT		I		ḪURŠAN		A		MU-TI-ḪU-UR-ŠA-NA		B 35+
	1		ʿABD	AN	A						AB-TA-NA	NOM	A. LATE
	1		ʿAD	AT	A	HA					A-DA-TA-A	FN	APN P. 12 LATE
	2	ʾA	RŠIJ				ʿAD		A	HA	AR-ŠI-A-DA?-A	FN	C
	1		ʿADN		A	ʾA	ʾMUR				ḪA-AD-NA-AM?-MU-UR		X 75 18
			ʿADN		A		ʾAB		I		ḪA?-AD-NA-A-BI		TTKB XIX 304
	2		ʿAMM		I		ʿADN		A		AM-MI-ḪA-AD-NA		GOETZE, KIZZ. P. 8, LATE
			LA				ʿADN		A				
						ʾA	MWUT				IA-ḪA-AD-NA-A-MU-UT		M
	1		ʿAḎIR		A						A-ZI-RA	NOM	A. LATE+
	2		ʿABD				ʿAḎR		A		ḪA-AB-DU-ḪA-AD-RA		M
	1		ʿAMM		A	JI	ḎRUʿ				ḪA-MA-IZ-RU		RUTTEN 28 5+
	2		ʾATT		I		ʿAMM		A		AT-TI-AM-MA		A. LATE
	2		ʾANA				ʿAN		A		A-NA-A-NA		A. 36:11
			ḎIMR		I		ʿAN	AT	A		ZI-IM-RI-ḪA-NA-TA		B 42
			MUT		I		ʿAN	AT	A		MU-TI-A-N[A-T]A		B 35
			PUZUR				ʿAN		A		PUZUR-A-NA		BIN IV 61 29+ CAPP.
			ŠAT				ʿAN		A		ŠA-AT-A-NA		TCL XXI 220A 4+ CAPP.
	1		ʿAQB		A		ʾAḪ		UM		AQ-BA-A-ḪU-UM		M+
			ʿAQB		A		ʾAḪ		UM		AQ-BA-ḪU-UM		B 11+
			ʿAQB		A		ʾAḪ		UM		ḪA-AQ-BA-A-ḪU-UM		RA LXV 43 III 57+
			ʿAQB		A		ʾAḪ		U		AQ-BA-A-ḪU		M+, C+
			ʿAQB		A		ʾAḪ		U		AQ-BA-ḪU		BASOR 95 19+
			ʿAQB		A		ʾAḪ		AM		AQ-BA-A-ḪA-AM	ACC	M
			ʿAQB		A		ʾAḪ		IM		AQ-BA-A-ḪI-IM	GEN	M+
			ʿAQB		A		ʾAḪ		IM		ḪA-AQ-BA-A-ḪI-IM	GEN	M+
			ʿAQB		A		ʾAḪ		I		AQ-BA-A-ḪI	GEN	XII 448 5+
			ʿAQB		A		ʿAMM		U		AQ-BA-ḪA-MU		M
			ʿAQB		A		ʿAMM		U		AQ-BA-ḪA-AM-MU		IRAQ XXX 91, RIMAH
			ʿAQB		A		ʿAMM		U		ḪA-AQ-BA-ḪA-AM-MU		II 39 19, 58, 80
			ʿAQB		A		ʿAMM		U	HU	ḪA-AQ-BA-ḪA-AM-MU-U_2		II 39 14, 16, 24
			ʿAQB		A		ḪUNN		UM		AQ-BA-ḪU-NI-UM		B 11
	2		ʾIL		I		ʿIJN		A	JA	I_3-LI_2-I-NA-A-A		GAUTIER 40 7
	1		ʿIQB		A		ʾAḪ		UM		IQ-BA-A-ḪU-UM		KISURRA 4A 11, M
			ʿIQB		A		ʾAḪ		UM		IQ-BA-ḪU-UM		KISURRA 121 6
			ʿIQB		A		ʿAMM		U		IQ-BA?-AM-MU		A. 8 35
	1		ʿIZB		A		....				ḪI-IZ-BA-.[....]		VAS XIII 62 R. 1
	2		ʾAḪ		I	JI	ʿQUB		A		A-ḪI-I-KU-BA		KISURRA 7A 9
	1		ʿUZIL		A						U_2-ZI-LA		RA LXV 50 IX 6
	1	JA	ʿZIB		A		ʾEL				IA-AḪ-ZI-BA-EL?		RA LXV 50 VIII 77
	1		JAʾ		A		ʿAN		UM		IA-A-A-NU-UM		YOS V 134 16
	2		ʾAB		I		JAʾ		A		A-BI-IA-A		KISURRA 102 7+
	1		JAʾN		A		ʾAHL		UM		JA-NA-A-LUM	GN	MRS VI P.125 61
	2		MUT		I		JAʾN		A		MU-TI-I-IA-NA		B 35
	1		JAḪAD		A		....				IA-ḪA-DA-[....]		RA LXV 45 V 74
	1		JAʿAL		A						IA-ḪA-LA		YOS XIII 513:9
	1		JAʿIL		A						IA-I-LA	MN	RA LXV 40 I 27
	2		MUT		I		JABAL		A		MU-TI-A-BA-LA-KI	GN	B 35
			ŠUMUT		I		JABAL		A		SU-MU-TI-A-BA-LA?		PBS XI/2 1 I 35
	3		ŠUM		U		MUT		I				
							JABAL		A		SU-MU-MU-TI-A-BA-LA		B 39

A	1		JADID	A							IA-DI-DA	MN GEN	VII 206 2, 13
	2		MAʾD	I			JAM		A		MA-DI-IA-MA		UCP X/1 33 10
			MUT	U			JAM		A		MU-TU-IA-MA		M
	1		JAMIN	A							IA-MI-NA-A	TRIBE	M
			JAMIN	A							IA-MI-NA	TRIBE	M+
			JAMIN	A							IA-MI-NA	PN	RA LXV 45 V 21
			JAMIN	A							I-IA-MI-NA	TRIBE	M
			JAMIN	A							IA-ME-NA	TRIBE	M
	2		ʾIL	I			JAQR		A		I$_3$-LI$_2$-AQ-RA		IRAQ XXX 90, RIMAH
	2		ḎU				JAŠIʿ		A		ZU-IA-ŠE-IA		A. 64 9
	1		JAŠUN	A							IA-ŠU-NA		A.
	1		JAT	A			DAWD		UM		IA-TA-DA-DUM		B 31
	1		JATR	A			ʾIL				JA-AT-RA-IL		I
	1		JATT	A			LIʾM				IA-AT-TA-LI-IM		ZA XXXVI 95, BJ 88 12
	1	ME	JBIŠ	A							ME-BI-SA	MN	M
	1	JA	JDIʿ	A			ʾEL				IA-DI-ḪA-EL		KISURRA 10A 4
	2	JA	JBIL				JIRR		A		IA-BI-II-WI-IR-RA		B 24
	1		JIŠʿ	A			BAʿL				IŠ-ḪA-B[A-A]L		HARRIS 39 14
			JIŠʿ	A			GAʾL				IŠ-ḪA-GA-AL		A 7459 10
	2		ŠUM	U	NA	JA	JPUʿ		A		SU-MU-NA-IA-PU-ḪA-[....]		M
	1	JA	JQIR	A			ʾAB		UM		IA-KI-RA-A-BU-UM		RA LXV 47 VII 30
	2		ʾAB	I		JA	JŠUʿ		A		A-BI-IA-ŠU-ḪA		B 10
	1	JA	JTIR	A							IA-TE-RA	GEN	A.
	2		ʾIL	I	Š		BAʾB		A		I$_3$-LI$_2$-IŠ-BA-BA		HSM 7934, UR III
			ŠU				BAʾB		A		ŠU-BA-BA		U
	1		BAḪUR	A							BA-ḪU-RA		A. LATE
	1		BAʿL	A			HAND		U		BA-LA-ḪA-AN-DU		VOIX 187:13 MARI
			BAʿL	A			ʿAŠTAR				BA-LA-EŠ$_4$-DAR		M
			BAʿL	A			MI						
							NAMḪ		U		BA-LA-MI-NA-AM-ḪU		SYRIA XLIV 201 N.1 MARI
	2		ʾAJA				BAʿL		A	JA	A-A-BA-LA-IA		SIMMONS 63 9
			ḪADUR				BAʿL		A		A-DU-UR-BA-LA-IA	GN	SUMER XIV 26
			ḪADUR				BAʿL		A		D-ZA-GAR$_3$-BA-LA-IA	GN	SUMER XIV 26
			JIŠʿ				BAʿL		A		E-ŠE-EḪ-BA-LA?		VAS VII 160 7
		JE	MWUT				BAʿL		A		E-MU-UT-BA-LA	GN GEN	SAKI P. 212+
			MANN	A			BAʿL		A		MA-NA-BA-LA		M
			ŠUM	U			BAʿL		A		SU-MU-BA-LA		UNPUBL.
		JI	ŠMAʿ				BAʿL		A		IŠ-ME-BA-LA		TA 30, 122 2
		JI	ŠMAʿ				BAʿL		A		IŠ-ME-EḪ-BA-LA		TA 30, 71
			ŠUMUḪ				BAʿL		A		SU-MU-UḪ-BA-LA		PBS XI/2 1 I 18
			ŠAMŠ	U			BAʿL		A		SA-AM-SU-BA-LA		SIMMONS 35 14+
			ŠAMŠ	U	NA		BAʿL		A		SA-AM-SU-NA-BA-LA		A. 77+
	3		ŠUM	U		JA	MWUT						
							BAʿL		A		SU-MU-IA-MU-UT-BA-[LA]		RUTTEN 3 21
			ŠUM	U		JE	MWUT						
							BAʿL		A		SU-MU-E-MU-UT-BA-LA	NOM	JCS IV 66 22
			ŠUM	U		JE	MWUT						
							BAʿL		A		SU-MU-E-MU-UT-BA-LA	GEN	JCS IV 69 17
			ŠUM	U		JA	MWUT		U				
							BAʿL		A		[SU]-MU-IA-MU-TU-BA-LA		PBS XI/2 1 I 19
	2		ḪINN	A			BAWŠ	AT	A		E-NA-BA-ŠA-TA		EL II P. 171 N. CAPP.
			ḪINN	I			BAWŠ	AT	A		E-NI-BA-ŠA-TA		KTS 47C 1 CAPP.
			MUT	U			BAWŠ		A		MU-TU-BA-SA		B 35+
	1		BAWZ	A							BA-ZA	MN	B 15
	1		BAKAL	A							BA-GA-LA		A. LATE
	1		BAKIL	A							BA-KI-LA$_2$		TCL XIX 74:18
	1		BALṮ	A	HA						BA-AL-TA-A	FN	XIII 1 IX 32
	1		BALUL	A							BA-LUL-IA	MN	AJSL XXXIII 224 3, 6
	1		BILAL	A			MA				BI-LA-LA-MA		OIP XLIII 135+
	1		BIN	A			ʾAḪ		UM		BI-NA-A-ḪU-UM		M+
			BIN	A			HADD		U		[B]I-NA-D-IM		M
			BIN	A			ʿAMM		I		BI-NA-AM-MI		B 15
			BIN	A			ʾANTEL				BI-NA-AN-TE-EL		TLB I 220 26, M+
			BIN	A			ḪANDEN				BI-NA-ḪA-AN-DI-EN		M
			BIN	A			ʿAŠTAR				BI-NA-EŠ$_4$-DAR		M+
			BIN	A			LIʾM				BI-NA-LI-IM		RA LXV 45 V 54

A	1	BIN	T	A		ʾATT	I		BI-IT-TA-AT-TI	FN	A.+
		BIN	T	A		MALK	I		BI-IT-TA-MA-AL-KI	FN	A. LATE
	2	ʾIL		I		BIN	A	JA	I$_3$-LI$_2$-BI-NA-A-IA		M+
	1	BULM		A	NA	HADD	U		BU-UL-MA-NA-D-IM		M+
	1	BUN		A		ʿAN	UM		BU-NA-A-NU-UM		U
		BUN		A		ʿAŠTAR			BU-NA-D-INNIN		BASOR 95, 19
		BUN		A		MA					
						ʾIL			BU-NA-MA-DINGIR		XII 1 X 36
	2	KAʾB		I		BURŠ	A		KA-BI-BU-UR-ŠA	FN	XIII 1 XIV 53
	1	DAʾK		A		BIJT	I		DA?-KA-BI-TI		A.
	2	KUWN		I		DAʾK	A		KU-NI-DA-KA		A. 367 11
		NAʿM		I		DAʾK	A		NA-MI-DA-KA		A. 242 7
	1	DAWD		A					DA-DA	MN	M+, A.
		DAWD		A					DA-A-DA	MN	A.
	2	ʿAQB		U		DAWD	A		AQ-BU-DA-DA		B 12
		ḎU				DAWD	A		ZU-E-TA-TA		BIN IV 100 1 CAPP
	2	NAPŠ		U	NA	DAWR	A		NA-AP-SU-NA-D-DA-RA		CT IV 1 8
		ŠIJM		U		DAWR	A		SI-MU-DA-RA		TA 30, 186+
		ZIʾM		U		DAWR	A		ZI-MU-DA-RA		RA VIII 75 R. 2
	2	ŠINA				DAMQ	A		ŠI-NA-DAM-QA	FN	XIII 1 IV 29+
		ŠINI				DAMQ	A		ŠI-NI-DAM-QA	FN	RA LXV 61 IV 48
	1	DANN		A		BIJT			DA-NA-BI$_2$-IT		U
	2	ʿAMM		I		DITAN	A		AM-MI-DI-TA-NA		B13+
		ʿAMM		I		DITAN	A		AM-MI-TE-TA-NA		CT XLV 44 24
		ŠUM		U		DITAN	A		SU-MU-DI-TA-NA		B 39+, M
		ŠAMŠ		I		DITAN	A		SA-AM-SI-DI-TA-NA		B 38
		ŠAMŠ		U		DITAN	A		SA-AM-SU-DI-TA-NA		B 38+
	3	MA				LA		NA			
						DITAN	A		MA-A-LA-NA-DI-TA-NA		B 34
		ŠUM		U		ṢIDQ	UM				
						DITAN	A		[SU]-MU-ZI-ID-KUM-DI-TA-NA		B 40
	1 JA	DRUK		A					IA-AD-RU-QA		A. LATE
	2	ʿAMM		U		ḎAKAJ	A		Ḫ[A]-MU-ZA-KA-A		RA LXV 43 III 75
	1	ḎAKIR		A		ʿAMM	I		ZA-KI-RA-ḪA-MI		M
		ḎAKIR		A		ʿAMM	U		ZA-KI-RA-ḪA-AM-MU		M+
		ḎAKIR		A		ʿAMM	U		ZA-KI-RA-ḪA-MU		M
		ḎAKIR		A		ʿAMM	U	HU	ZA-KI-RA-ḪA-AM-MU-U$_2$		M+
	1	ḎAKUR		A		ʾAḪ	UM		ZA-KU-RA-A-ḪU-UM		M+
		ḎAKUR		A		ʾAB	I		ZA-KU-RA-A-BI	GEN	B 41
		ḎAKUR		A		ʾAB	U		ZA-KU-RA-A-BU		M
		ḎAKUR		A		ʾAB	UM		ZA-KU-RA-A-BU-UM		X 79 5
		ḎAKUR		A		ʾIL			ZA-KU-RA-DINGIR		M+
		ḎAKUR		A		KUWN	U		ZA-KU-RA-KU-NU		VII 85 12
	1	ḎIKR		A		ʿAŠTAR			ZI-IK-RA-EŠ$_4$-DAR		M+
	1	ḎIMR		A		ʿAMM	U		ZI-IM-RA-ḪA-MU		CT XLIV 54 20, C
		ḎIMR		A		ʿAMM	U		ZI-IM-RA-ḪA-AM-MU		M
		ḎIMR		A		ʿAMM	U		ZI-IM-RA-AM-MU		TIM IV 33 20, 34 13
		ḎIMR		A		ʿAMM	U	HU	ZI-IM-RA-ḪA-MU-U$_2$		TIM IV 33 SEAL, 34 SEAL
		ḎIMR		A		ʿAŠTAR			ZI-IM-RA-EŠ$_4$-DAR		M+
	1	ḎIQUN		A		ṬAJB			ZI-KU-NA-ṬA$_3$-AB	FN	RA LXV 59 II 77
	1	ḎUKR		A		ʿAŠTAR			[Z]U-UK-RA-EŠ$_4$-DAR		RA LXV 46 VI 21
	2	ʾAB		I		GAʾJ	A		A-BI-GA-A	GN?	A 21919+
		ḪANAN		A		GAʾJ	A		A-NA-NA-GA-A		RA XLIV 112 5 QATNA
		BAʿL		U		GAʾJ	A		BA-AḪ-LU-GA-A	GEN	HOLMA 6 5
	1	GAʾUL		A					GA-U$_2$-LA		JCS XIII 56, ALA. LATE
	1	GUʾUD		A					GU-U$_2$-DA		U
	2	ʾIL		A		GULL	A		DINGIR-GU-UL-LA	FN	C+
		ʾIL		A		GULL	A				
						ʿAḎIR	AT		DINGIR-GUL-LA$_2$-ḪA-ZI-KA-AT	FN	M+
	1	KAʾK		A					KA-KA		A.
		KAʾK		A					KA-A-KA		A.
	1	KAʾM		A		ṢILL	UM		KA-MA-ZI-LUM	FN	B 33+
		KAʾM		A		ṢILL	U		KA-MA-ZI-LU?	FN	VAS XIII 9 R. 2
	1	KAWJ		A		LAʾL	UM		KA-A-LA-LUM		M
	1	KABID	T	A					KA-BI-IT-TA	MN	C II 6
	1	KADAD		A					KA-DA-DA	GEN	BM 17060 30+

A	1	KAKK	A		ʾAŠJ	AH		KA-AK-KA-A-SI-IA	FN	XIII 1 VI 11
		KAKK	A		JIŠʿ	AH		KA-KA-IŠ-ḪA	FN	M+
		KAKK	A		ʾAŠR	I		KA-AK-KA-AŠ-RI	FN	XIII 1 V 1
		KAKK	A		LIʾD	I		KA-AK-KA-LI-DI	FN	X 10 5
		KAKK	A		MANN	U		KA-AK-KA-MA-AN-NU		M
		KAKK	A		NAʿM	I		KA-AK-KA-NA-AḪ-MI	FN	XIII 1 VII 30
		KAKK	A		NILŠ	I		KA-A[K]-KA-NI-EL?-ŠI?	FN	XIII 1 VIII 41
		KAKK	A		NIʾŠ	U	JA	KA-AK-KA-NI-ŠU-IA		RA LXV 64 VI 35
		KAKK	A		NIʾŠ	U	JA	KA-KA-NI-ŠU-IA	FN	RA LXV 65 VII 44
		KAKK	A		RIMŠ	I		KA-AK-KA-RI-IM-ŠI	FN	RA LXV 60 III 5
		KAKK	A		TUWR	I	JA	KA-KA-TU-RI-IA	FN	M
	2	ḪIMD			KAKK	A		ḪI-MI-ID-KA-AK-KA		M
		ʾAMIR			KAKK	A		A-ME-IR-KA-AK-KA		XIII 1 V 20
		NABIʾ			KAKK	A		NA-BI-KA-KA		M+
	JI	NDIN			KAKK	A		I-DIN-KA-AK-KA		M+
	JI	NDIN			KAKK	A		I-DIN-D-KA-KA		M+
	2	MUT	U		KANAT	A		MU-TU-KA-NA-TA		M
		ŠUM	U		KANAŠ	A		SU-MU-GA-NA-SA		KISURRA 19 9
	1	KANN	A		MA					
					ʾIL			KA-AN-NA-MA-DINGIR		M
	1	KANUK	A					KA-AN-NU-UK-KA		M
	2	LU			KIʾL	A		LU$_2$-KI-LA		BASOR 95, 19
	1	KIHIL	A	HA				KI-ḪI-LA-A	FN	M
	1	KIWN	A		ʾIL	I		KI-NA-I$_3$-LI$_2$		M
	2	JARAḪ			KIWN	A		SIN-KI-NA		TCL I 237 31
	1	KUʾB	A		ʾEL			KU-BA-EL		X 91 4'
		KUʾB	A		ʾEL			KU-BA-DINGIR		M
		KUʾB	A		BUWZ	I		KU-BA-BU-ZI	FN	M
	1	KUWN	A		MAʾT	UM		KU-NA-MA-TUM		U
	1	KULP	A		RAWḤ	I	JE	KU-UL-PA-RA-ḪI-E		TCL I 14 1, YCS VIII 141 34
	2	ʿAMM	U		KUMAR	A		AM-MU-KU-MAR-RA		A.
	1	KUNN	A					KU-UN-NA		WO V 59+ ALA. LATE
		KUNN	A		MA			[K]U-UN-NA-MA		XIV 101:8
	1	KURD	A		KAMB	I		KUR-DA-KA-AM-BI	FN	XIII 1 III 25
	1	LAʾR	A		JARAḪ			LA-RA-D-SIN		KAJ 167 23+, LATE
	2	BUN	U		LAʾR	A		BU-NU-LA-RA		B 16
	1	LABW	A		BIḪR	I	Š	LA-BA-BI$_2$-RI-IŠ		HSM 7936, UR III
	2	ʾAM	T		LABW	A		AM-TI-LA-BA	MN	TIM III 7 5
		ʿAMM	U		LABW	A		ḪA-AM-MU-LA-BA-A		XIV 114:6
	JI	NDIN			LABW	A		I-DIN-D-LA-BA		M
		ŠADW	U		LABW	A		ŠA-DU-LA-BA		M
		ŠADW	UM		LABW	A		ŠA-DU-UN-LA-BA		M+
		ŠADW	UM		LABW	A		ŠA-DU-UM-LA-BA		M
		ŠADW	UM		LABW	A		ŠA-DU-UM-LA-BU-A		M
		ŠUM	U		LABW	A		SU-MU-LA-BA		M
	1	LABAN	A		ʾIL	A		LA-PA-NA-I-LA		ZA XXXVIII 267
	1	LABIN	A					LA-AB-BI-NA		A.+
	1	LASIM	A					LA-ZI-MA	NOM	BIN VII 31 6
	1	LIʾM	A		HADD	U		LI-MA-A-DU		A.
	2	ʾATT	I		LIʾM	A		AT-TI-LI-MA		A. LATE
	2	ʾAB	I		LUʾL	A		A-BI-LU-LA		SIMMONS 107 13
	2	KIWN	I	Š	LUʾP	A		KI-NI-IŠ-LU-BA		EDZARD,DER 94:17;95:6
	1	LUMM	A		ʾIL			LUM-MA-IL		M+
		LUMM	A		ʾIL			LUM-MA-DINGIR		KISURRA 100 7+
		LUMM	A		ʾIL			LU-MA-DINGIR		KISURRA 104 29+
	2	ʾAŠD	I		LUMM	A		AŠ-DI-LU-MA		UCP X/3 2 31
	1 JA	MWUʾ	A					IA-MU-U$_2$-A		KISURRA 33 3
	2	ʾAB	I	JA	MWUT	A		A-BI-IA-MU-TA		BM 80328 15
	JI	PTIḤ		JA	MWUT	A		IP-TI-IA-MU-TA		BM 80328 11
		TUPT	I	JA	MWUT	A		TU-UP-TI-IA-MU-TA		BM 80328 2
	2	ḪANN	A		MAʾJ	A		AN-NA-MA-A-A		RUTTEN 14 15
	2	ʾIL	I		MAʾD	A		I$_3$-LI$_2$-MA-DA		TA 30 615 6
	2	ʾANN	U		MAʾN	A		AN?-NU-MA-NA	FN	M
		KIʾL	U		MAʾN	A		KI-LU-MA-NA	FN	RA LXV 56 I 9
	1	MAʾR	A		ʾEL			MA-RA-EL		TA 1931, 298
		MAʾR	A		ʾEL			URU-MA-RA-EL	GN	MRS VI 11830:10

A	1	MAʾR		A		ʾEL			URU-MA-RA-DINGIR	GN	MRS IX 17340:7
	2	MUT		U		MALAK		A	MU-TU-MA-LA-KA		M
	1	MAM		A		ḪAṢN		I	D-MA-MA-ḪA-AZ-NI	FN	RA LXV 56 I 7
		MAM		A		DUNN		I	D-MA-MA-DU-UN-NI	FN	M
		MAM		A		NUMR		I	D-MA-MA-NU-UM-RI	FN	RA LXV 65 VII 30
		MAM		A		QUDM		I	D-MA-MA-KU-UD-ME	FN	RA LXV 59 II 18
		MAM		A		ŠARR	AH		D-MA-MA-ŠAR-RA	FN	M
		MAM		A	TA	LʾIJ			D-MA-MA-TA-AL-E	FN	M
		MAM		A		TUʾAL		I	D-MA-MA-TU-ḪA-LI	FN	M
		MAM		A		ṢIJḪ	AT	UM	MA-MA-ZI-A-TUM	FN	RA LXV 61 IV 37
	2 JI	NDIN				MAM		A	I-DIN-D-MA-MA		M+
		QIJŠ	T	I		MAM		A	KI-IŠ-TI-D-MA-MA		M+
		QIJŠ	T	I		MAM		A	KI-IŠ-TI-D-MA-AM-MA		XIV 61:5
		ŠEʾR	AH			MAM		A	ŠE-RA-D-MA-MA	FN	X 110 3
		TIWR				MAM		A	TI-IR-MA-MA		M+
		TABB		I		MAM		A	TA-BI-D-MA-MA	FN	M
	3 JA	KWUN				PI					
						MAM		A	IA-KU-UN-BI-D-MA-MA	FN	RA LXV 66 VII 61
	2	ḪAʾL		I		MAMM		A	ḪA-LI$_2$-D-M[A-A]M-M[A]		M
	1	MANAN		A					MA-NA-AN-NA		M+
	1	MANN		A		....			MA-AN-N[A-....]		M
		MANN		A		BAʿL		A	MA-NA-BA-LA		M
		MANN		A		BIʿD		IM	MA-NA-BI-IḪ-DI-IM	GEN	HARRIS 3 18
		MANN		A		BALTI					
						ʾEL			MA-NA-BA-AL-TE-EL		B 28+
		MANN		A		BALTI					
						ʾEL			MA-NA-BA-AŠ-TE-EL		M+
		MANN		A		BALTI					
						ʾIL			MA-AN-NA-BA-AL-TI-DINGIR		M
		MANN		A		BALTI					
						ʾEL			MA-NA-BA-AL-TI-EL		KISURRA 70A 14+
		MANN		A		TAWR		I	MA-NA-TA-RI		B 34
	1	MARAQ		A					MA-RA-QA	GEN	B 34
	1	MAŠIḤ		A					MA-SI-ḪA	MN NOM	M
	2	BILL				MAŠIK		A	BI-EL-MA-SI-KA?		M
	1	MATAʿ		A		KI					
						ʾEL			MA-TA-A-KI-EL		RA LXV 50 IX 20;HARRIS 19:5,SEAL+
	2	ʾARAM				MAṬAR		A	A-RA-AM-MA-DA-RA		BM 80328 1
	2	ʿADN		UM		MAZAʾ		A	ḪA-[A]D?-NU-UM-MA-ZA-A		RA LXV 41 II 52
	1	MENN		A	HA				ME-IN-NA-A	FN	X 176:8, 15
	1	MILʾ		A		BIJT		I	MI-IL-A-BI-TI		A. 60 2
	1	MILK		A		HADD		U	MI-IL-KA-D-IM		SYRIA XXXVII 206 27 HANA
	1	MUŠN		A		HADD		U	MU-UŠ-NA-A-DU		A.+
	1	MUT		A		JŠUʿ			MU-TA-ŠU-UḪ		M+
		MUT		A		NIʿM			MU-TA-NI-ḪI-IM		RA LXV 43 III 51
		MUT		A	TA	KWIN			MU-TA-TA-KI-IN		RA LXV 51 IX 78
	2	MIJA				MUT		A	ME-IA-MU-TA		B 34
	1 JA	NḪAN		A					IA-AN-ḪA-NA	GEN	MRS VI P. 334
	2	ʾAḪ		I	TA	NWUḪ		A	A-ḪI-TA-NU-A		M
		ḪAʾL		I	TA	NWUḪ		A	ḪA-LI-TA-NU-A		A.+
		ḤAM		I	TA	NWUḪ		A	D-A-MI-TA-NU-A		M
	2	KUMM		I		NAʾD		A	KU-UM-MI-NA-DA		JCS IV 113
	1	NAʿM		A		ʾEL			NA-MA-EL		TA 30 615:11+
	2	ʾIL		A		NAʿM		A	DINGIR-NA-MA-....		VAS VIII 14 44
	2	MUT				NAWḪ		A	MU-UT-NA-ḪA		B 35 HANA
	1	NADIN		A					NA-DI-NA	GEN	A.+
	1	NAMIŠ		A					NA-MI-ŠA	GEN	MAOG IV 3 34 HANA
	2	MATQ		U		NAN		A	MA-AT-KU-NA-NA	FN	RA LXV 60 III 33
	1	NANN		A		MUʾ		UM	NA-AN-NA-MU-UM		M
	1	NATT		A					NA-AT-TA		M
	1 JI	NDIN		A					ID-DI-NA		A.
	2	MUT		UM		NIʾŠ		A	MU-TUM-NI-ŠA		TA 1931, 538 III
	1	NIʿM		A		HADD		U	NI-MA-A-DU		A.
	2	ŠUM		U		NIWḪ		A	SU-MU-NI-A		GORDON 39 9, 13
	2	ʾAB		U		NIWR		A	A-BU-NI-RA		TIM VI 34, U
	1	NIMIN		A		HADD		U	NI-MI-NA-A-DU		A.+

A	2		ʿAMM		U		NIQM	A		AM-MU-NI-IQ-MA		A.+
	1	JA	NṮIʿ		A					IA-AN-DI-ḪA-KI	GN	M
	1	Š	NUʾR		A		ḪAʾL	U		ŠU-NU-UḪ-RA-ḪA-LU		M+
		Š	NUʾR		A		ḪAʾL	U	HU	ŠU-NU-UḪ-RA-ḪA-LU-U$_2$		M+
		Š	NUʾR		A		ḪAʾL	U	HU	ŠU-NU-ḪU-RA-ḪA-LU-U$_2$		XIV 11:1
		Š	NUʾR		A		ḪAʾL	U	HU	ŠU-NU-UḪ-ḪU-RA-ḪA-LU-U$_2$		XIV 36:1+
		Š	NUʾR		A		ʿAMM	U		ŠU-NU-UḪ-RA-AM-MU		B 40 HANA+
	1		NUMḪ		A					NU-UM-ḪA-A(-KI)	GN	M+
	2		ŠUM		U		NUMḪ	A		SU-M[U-N]U-UM-ḪA		RA LXIV 43
	1		NUMAḪ		A					NU-MA-ḪA-A	GN	M
	2		ŠUM		U		NUMAḪ	A		SU-MU-NU-MA-ḪA		M
	3		LA				RIWM					
							NUMAḪ	A		LA-RI-IM-NU-MA-ḪA-A		M+
			LA				RIWM					
							NUMAḪ	A		LA-RI-IM-NU-MA-A		M
	2		DAGAN				NUPAR	A	JA	D-DA-GAN-NU?-PA?-RA-IA		M
	1		PAʾL		A	HA				PA-LA-A	FN	B 37
	1		PAKN	AN	A					PA-AK-NA-NA	GEN	BE VI/2 81 14
	1		PALṬ		A		ʿAN	UM		PA-AL?-TA-A-NU-UM		LANGDON IV 15
			PALṬ		A		BIJT	U		PA-AL-DA-BI-TU		A. LATE
	1		PAQAḪ		A		LAʾL	UM		BA-GA-A-LA-LUM		HARRIS 69 2+
	2		ʿAMM		U		PATAḪ	A		ḪA-AM-MU-PA-TA-A		M
	1	ʾA	PQID		A					AP-KI-DA		U
	1		PUḪR		A	NA				PU-UḪ$_3$-RA-NA		YOS VIII 101B 13
	1		QAWL		A		ḪAM	I		QA-LA-D-A-M[I]		M
	1		QAWM		A		DANN	UM		QA-MA-[D]A-NUM		M
	1		QARN	AN	A					QAR-NA-NA	GEN	SIMMONS 13 5
	1		QAṬAN		A					QA-TA-NA-KI	GN	M
			QAṬAR		A					QA-TA-RA-KI	GN	M
			QAṬAR		A					QA-ṬA$_3$-RA-KI	GN	M
			QAṬAR		A					QA-ṬA$_3$-RA-A-KI	GN	M+
	1	JI	RḪIQ		A					IR-ḪI-GA		M
	1	JA	RWIḪ		A		ʾAB	UM		IA-RI-ḪA-A-BU-UM		VII P. 234 N. 4
		JA	RWIḪ		A		ʾAB	AM		IA-RI-ḪA-A-BA-AM	ACC	XIV 101:8
		JA	RWIḪ		A		ʾAB	AM		IA-RI-ḪA-A-BA-AN	ACC	VII P. 234 N. 4
		JA	RWIḪ		A		ʾAB	IM		IA-RI-ḪA-A-BI-IM	GEN	M+
		JA	RWIḪ		A		ḪAM	U		IA-RI-ḪA-A-MU		M+
	1		RAWḪ		A		ʾANN	UM		RA-ḪA-AN-NU-UM		M
	1		RAWM		A		JAT	UM		RA-MA-IA-TUM		B 22+
	2		ʿAMM		U		RAWM	A		ḪA-MU-RA-MA		M
			MUT				RAWM	A		MU-UT-RA-MA		CT II 23 13
			QAZIJ				RAWM	A		QA-ZI-RA-MA		A. LATE
			ŠU				RAWM	A		ŠU-RA-MA		A. LATE+
			ŠI				RAWM	A		SI-I-RA-MA		A. 28 3, 16
	1		RAJB		A		SITR	U	HU	RA-BA-ZI-IT-RU-U$_2$	FN	M
	1		RIJB		A		ʿAMM	U		RI-BA-AM-MU		A. 97 4+
	2		ŠUM		I		RIJB	A		SU-MI-RI-BA		A. 98C 10
			ŠUM		I		RIJB	A		ŠU-MI-RI-PA		A. LATE
			ŠUM		I		RIJB	A		ŠU-ME-RI-PA		A. LATE
			TIʾM				RIJB	A		TI-IM-RI-PA		A.
	1		RIPʾ		A		ʾIL	A		RI-IP-A-DINGIR		M+
			RIPʾ		A		MALIK			RI-IP-A-MA-LIK		M
	1	JA	RKIB		A		HADD	U		IA-AR-KI-BA-D-IM		XIII 145 6
	1		SIKIL	T	A					ZI-KI-IL-DA	MN	A. 24 3
			SIKIL	T	A					ZI-KI-IL-TA	MN	A. LATE+
			SIKIL	T	A					ZI-KI-EL-TA	MN	A. LATE
	1		SINUQ		A					SI-NU-GA		BIROT,TEA 16:11
			SINUQ		A					ZI-NU-GA		M+
	1		SITR		A		HADD	U		ZI-IT-RA-A-DU		A. 456 19
	1		ŠAʾAL		A					SA-A-LA	NOM	CT II 42 2, 5
	1		ŠAʾQ		A		ʿAN	UM		SA-GA-A-NU-UM		B 47
	1		ŠAḪIR		A					ŠA-ḪI-RA	NOM	CT VIII 37D 1, 9
			ŠAḪIR		A					ŠA-ḪI-RA	GEN	CT VIII 37D 6, 13
	2		ʾIL		UM		ŠALM	A		I-LU-UM-ŠA-AL-MA		RA LXV 45 V 51
	1		ŠAM		A		JADAʿ	UM		SA-MA-A-DA-ḪU-UM		M+
			ŠAM		A		JADAʿ	U		SA-MA-A-DA-ḪU		M

SUFFIXES, Class 2

A	1	ŚAM		A		JADAʿ	IM		SA-MA-A-DA-Ḫ[I-I]M	GEN	M
		ŚAM		A		ME					
						ʾEL			SA-MA-ME-EL		M
		ŚAM		A		ME					
						ʾEL			ŠA-MA-ME-EL		TA 1931, 421
		ŚAM		A		RAWḤ			SA-MA-RA-AḪ		B 38+, XII 385 8
	2	ʿAMM		U		ŚAM	A		AM-MU-SA-MA		A.+
		LABW		I		ŚAM	A		LA-BI-SA-MA		UCP X/3 P. 199+
		MANN		U		ŚAM	A		MA-NU-SA-MA		B 34
	1	ŚAMʾAL		A		ʾIL			SA-AM-A-LA-DINGIR		M+
	1	ŚAMAʿ		A		JAT	UM		ŠA-MA-A-IA-TUM	MN	WATERMAN 21 R. 6
		ŚAMAR		A					SA-MA-RA?		HARRIS 35 11
	2	ʾAB		I		ŚAMAT	A		A-BI-SA-MA-TA		EDZARD, DER 120:4
	1	ŚAMUŚ		A					SA-MU-ŠA	NOM	M+
	1	ŚAPR		A		HADD	U		SA-AP-RA-A-DU		A. 96 R. 12
	1	ŚARR		A		ʾIL			ŠAR-RA-DINGIR		A. LATE+
	2	LA				ŚIJM	A		LA-SI-MA		M
	2	ʾIL		I		ŚIMḪ	A	JA	I_3-LI_2-ŠI-IM-ḪA-IA		VIII 57 BIS 16
		ʾIL		I		ŚIMḪ	A	JA	I_3-LI_2-ŠE-IM-ḪA-IA		VIII 57 14
	1	ŚINAN		A					ŠI-NA-AN-NA		XIII 1 I 19
	2	ŚUM		U	ʾA	ŚKUR	A		ŠU-MU-$AŠ_2$-KU-RA		TA 30, 299
	1 JI	ŚLAM	AN	A					IŠ-LA-MA-NA	GEN	MRS VI P. 202 UGARIT
	1	ŚUM		A		HADD	U		ŠU-MA-A-DU		A.
		ŚUM		A		ʾIL	A		SU-MA-I-LA		YOS XIII 244:15+
		ŚUM		A		LA					
						LI		JA	SU-MA-LA-LI-A		BM 80363 1
		ŚUM		A		LI		KA	SU-MA-LI-KA		BM 80328 13
		ŚUM		A		RAPIʾ			SU-MA-RA-BI		KAJ 39 17 LATE
	1	ŠAWB		A		ḤAJJ	UM		SA-BA-A-U_2-UM		OIP XLVII 66
	2	ḪAʾL		I		ŠADW	A		ḪA-LI-SA-DA		B 19
		ʾAB		I		ŠADW	A		A-BI-SA-DA-A		JCS IV 110 2040
		HADD		U		ŠADW	A		D-IM-ŠA-DA		PSBA XXIX 273 NO. 9 R. 10
	2	ʾIPQ		U		ŠAL	A		IP-KU-D-ŠA-LA		M
	1	ŠIPṬ		A		ʾAḪ	UM		ŠI-IP-TA-A-ḪU-UM		RA LXV 46 VI 27
	1	ŠUʾM		A		BAʾIL			ŠU-UḪ-MA-BA-IL		RA LXV 51 IX 60
	1	ŠUWB		A		ḪAʾL	I		ŠU-BA-ḪA-LI		A. 97 16, 18+
		ŠUWB		A		ḪAʾL	I		SU-BA-ḪA-LI		A. 6 29
		ŠUWB		A		ḪAʾL	I		SU-PA-ḪA-LI		A. 252 12+
		ŠUWB		A		ʾIL	A		ŠU-BA-D-DINGIR		B 23+
		ŠUWB		A		ʿAMM	I		ŠU-BA-AM-MI		A. 270 22
		ŠUWB		A	NI	ʾIL			ŠU-BA-NI-DINGIR		RUTTEN 41 3, 13
	2	ʿAMM		I		ṢADUQ	A		AM-MI-ZA-DU-GA		B 13+
		ʿAMM		I		ṢADUQ	A				
						....			AM-MI-ZA-DU-GA-I-LU-NI		B 13+
	2	JAT		UM		ṢIʾ	A		IA-TUM-ZI-A		CT XLV 97 5
	1	ṢIDQ		A		HADD	U		ZI-ID-QA-D-IM		M
	1	ṢUWR		A		ʾIL			ZU-RA-DINGIR		M+
		ṢUWR		A		ʿAMM	U		ZU-RA-ḪA-AM-MU		M+
		ṢUWR		A		ʿAMM	U		Z[U]-RA-ḪA-M[U]		XIII 132 7
		ṢUWR		A		ʿAMM	U	HU	ZU-RA-ḪA-AM-MU-U_2		M
	2	ʾAB		I		ṢUWR	A		A-BE-ZU-RA		TCL IV 87 10 CAPP.
		ʾAB		I		ṢUWR	A		A-BI-ṢU-RA		TIM IV 34 27
		ʿAMM		I		ṢUWR	A		AM-MI-ZU-RA		CT XLVIII 90 REV.
		KA				ṢUWR	A				
						ʾIL			KA-ZU-RA-DINGIR		M
	2	ʾILAR				TAʾ	A		I-LA-AR-TA-A		M
		ʾILAR				TAʾ	A		I-LA-AR-TA-ḪA		M
	2	MILK		I		TAʾG	A		MI-IL-KI-TA-GA		A. LATE
	1	TALM		A		ʿAMM	U		TA-AL-MA-AM-MU		A.+
	2	ʾALL		I		TALM	A		AL-LI-TA-AL-MA	FN	A.
	3	ʾAJA				ʾAB	I				
						TALM	A		A-IA-BI-TA-AL-MA		A. 239 15
	1	TATT		A	HA				TA-AT-TA-A	FN	RA LXV 60 III 73
	2	BUN				TENUT	A		BU-UN-TE-NU?-TA?		MEISSNER 68 13
	1	TIBIʾ		A	Š	ME					
						ʾEL			TI-BI_2-$AŠ_2$-ME-EL		CT XXXIII 48A 4

A	1	TILIʾ		A	Š	GAMIL			TI-LI-AŠ-GA-MIL		UNPUBL.
	1	TUWR		A		ʾIL	I		TU-RA-I$_3$-LI$_2$		SAUREN, WUG 285 V, U.
		TUWR		A		DAGAN			TU-RA-D-DA-GAN		M+
	2	ʾIL		I		TUWR	A		I$_3$-LI$_2$-TU-RA		M+
		ʾIL		I		TUWR	A	JA	I$_3$-LI$_2$-TU-RA-[I]A		RA LXV 40 I 45
		ŠALAŠ				TUWR	A	JA	ŠA-LA-AŠ-TU-RA-IA	FN	C
	2	ʾAJIŠ				TULL	A		A-JI-IŠ-TU-UL-LA		M
	1	ṬAJB		A		ʾIL			ṬA-BA-DINGIR		A. 60 11
		ṬAJB		A		ʾAŠUR	A		TA-PA-AŠ-ŠU-RA		A.
	2	ʾAB		I		ṬAJB	A		A-BI-ṬA-BA		A.+
		ʾIL		I		ṬAJB	A		I$_3$-LI$_2$-DA-[B]A		A. 96 R. 10
		ʿAMM		I		ṬAJB	A		AM-MI-ṬA-BA		A.+
		ŠALM		U		ṬAJB	A		ŠA-AL-MU-ṬA$_3$-BA	FN	RA LXV 66 VII 64
		ŠUM		I		ṬAJB	A		SU?-MI-DA-BA		A. 7 44+
	1	ṬARID		A		ʾADM	U		TA-RI-DA-AD-MU		XIII 1 16
	1	ZABUG		A					ZA-BU-GA		JCS XIII 57 NO.305 A.LATE
	1	ZAKK		A		BALAṬ			ZA-AK-KA-BA-LA-AṬ?		M+
	1	ZUNZUN		A					ZU-UN-ZU-NA		B 49
AJA	1	ʾABAB		AJA					A-BA-BA-A-IA	FN	M
		ʾABAN		AJA					A-BA-NA-A		BM 81660 2
	1	ʾAMIR		AJA					A-MI-RA-IA	FN	C
	1	ʾIŠIM	AN	AJA					I-SI-MA-NA-A		B 22
	1	ʾUŠT		AJA					UŠ-TA-IA		RA LXV 55 XIII 14
	1	HADD		AJA					A-AD-DA-A		M+
		HADD		AJA					A-DA-A		M
	1	ḪAKAM		AJA					ḪA-KA-MA-A-IA	FN	XIII 1 V 44
	1	ḪANN		AJA					AN-NA-IA	FN	RA LXV 62 V 13
	1	ḪAZIQ		AJA					ḪA-ZI-QA-IA		UCP X/1 87 12
	1	ḪAʾL		AJA					ḪA-LA-A-A		B 18
	1	ḪULAŠ		AJA					ḪU-LA-ŠA-A		HARRIS 75 22
	1	ḪURAṢ		AJA					ḪU-RA-ZA-A-IA	FN	XIII 1 VIII 84
	1	ʿABD		AJA					AB-DA-A		GORDON 38 15+
	1	ʿAN		AJA					A-NA-IA		RA LXV 46 VI 17
		ʿAN		AJA					ḪA-NA-IA		RA LXV 50 IX 19
	1	ʿARD		AJA					ḪA-AR-DA-IA	FN	XIII 1 IV 70
	1	ʿAZAL		AJA					A-ZA-LA-IA		B 14
	1	ʿIZZ		AJA					IZ-ZA-A-IA	FN	XIII 1 III 68
	1	JAMM		AJA					IA-AM-MA-A		B 28+
		JAMM		AJA					IA-AM-MA-A-IA	FN	C+
	1	JATAR		AJA					IA-TA-RA-IA	FN	M
		JATAR		AJA					IA-TA-RA-A-IA	FN	XIII 1 X 54
	1 JA	JPUʿ		AJA					IA-PU-ḪA-IA	FN	C+
	1	BAKUR		AJA					BA-KU?-RA-IA		C
		BAKUŠ		AJA					BA-KU-SA-A-IA	FN	XIII 1 II 63
	1	BIRB		AJA					BI-IR-BA-IA		RA LXV 52 X 82
	1	DAWD		AJA					DA-DA-A	FN	RA LXV 61 IV 2
	1	DAŠIL		AJA					DA-SI-LA-A-A		HARRIS 79 24
	1 TA	KWUN		AJA					TA-KU-NA-IA	FN	C
	1	KAWJ		AJA					KA-A-IA-A-IA		M+
	1	KABID		AJA					KA-BI-DA-IA	FN	M
	1	KALK		AJA					KA-AL-KA-IA		CT XLVIII 89 REV.
	1	KATR		AJA					KA-AT-RA-IA	FN	XIII 1 III 8
	1	KUMS		AJA					KU-UM-ZA-A-A		HARRIS 66 16
	1	LIʾD		AJA					LI-DA-A-IA		M+
	1	MANAN		AJA					MA-NA-NA-A		B 34+
	1	MANN		AJA					MA-AN-NA-IA	FN	RA LXV 62 V 49
	1	MARṢ		AJA					MA-AR-ZA-IA	FN	M
	1	MARUṢ		AJA					MA-RU-ZA-IA	FN	RA LXV 61 IV 64
	1	MIʾŠ		AJA					MI-ŠA-IA		M+
	1 JA	NḪIR		AJA					A-AN?-ḪI?-RA-A		HARRIS 85 16
	1	NAWḪ		AJA					NA-ḪA-IA		B 35
	1	NUWP		AJA					NU-BA-IA		RA LXV 48 VIII 28
	1	NUṬUP		AJA					NU-TU-PA-A-A		UET V 480 3
	1	RAḪM		AJA					RA-AḪ-MA-IA		M+
	1	RUWB		AJA					RU-BA-IA	FN	XIII 1 II 10+
		RUWB		AJA					RU-BA-A-IA	FN	RA LXIV 43

SUFFIXES, Class 2

AJA	1			ŠAMK		AJA				SA-AM-KA-IA		RA LXV 53 XII 4
	1			ŠAPIR		AJA				SA-BI-RA-A-IA	FN	X 166 11, 12+
	1			ŠAPR		AJA				SA-AP-RA-IA		A.
	1			ŠARAM		AJA				ŠA-RA-MA-A		M
	1			ŠARR		AJA				ŠAR-RA-A-IA		M
				ŠARR		AJA				ŠAR-RA-IA		M+
	1			ŠIMḪ		AJA				ŠI-IM-ḪA-A-IA	FN	M
	1			ŠININ		AJA				SI-NI-NA-A-IA	FN	X 166 1+
	1			ŠUḪR		AJA				ŠU-UḪ-RA-IA	FN	SIMMONS 138 5, 14
	2			LA				ṢARR	AJA	LA-ZA-RA-A		YOS XIII 244:14
	1			ṢIḪAQ		AJA				ZI-ḪA-KA-A-A		KISURRA 82 2
	1			ṢUWR		AJA				ZU-RA-A		M
	1			TIʾT		AJA				TI-TA-A-A		RUTTEN 28 10+
	1			TIMAN		AJA				TI-MA-NA-A-A		HARRIS 66 14
	1			TUʾZ		AJA				TU-ZA-A	FN	XIII 1 XIII 29
				TUʾZ		AJA				TU-ZA-[I]A	FN	M
	1			ZAʾZ	AN	AJA				ZA-ZA-NA-IA	FN	RA LXV 58 I 52
AM	1			ʾAḪ		AM	ʾA	RŠIJ		A-ḪA-AM-AR-ŠI		I+
	2			ʿAQB		A		ʾAḪ	AM	AQ-BA-A-ḪA-AM	ACC	M
	1			ʾAḪR		AM				AḪ-RA-AM	ACC	II 43 13
	2			ʾAJA				ʾAB	AM	ḪA-A-IA-A-BA-AM	ACC	M+
		JA		RWIḪ		A		ʾAB	AM	IA-RI-ḪA-A-BA-AM	ACC	XIV 101:8
		JA		RWIḪ		A		ʾAB	AM	IA-RI-ḪA-A-BA-AN	ACC	VII P. 234 N. 4
	1		T	ʾAMK		AM				A-TAM-RA-AM	ACC	M+
	1			ʾASIN		AM				A-ZI-NA-A[M]	ACC	XIV 33:7
	1			ʾAŠQUD	AN	AM				AŠ-KU-DA-NA-AM	ACC	B 43
	1			ʾATIM		AM				A-TI-M[A-AM]	ACC	M
	1			ʾIL		AM		DIʿ	I	DINGIR-IAM-DI-I		SIMMONS 24 10+
	2			ʾANAKU				ʾIL	AM			
								MA		A-NA-KU-DINGIR-LAM-MA		XIII 1 II 29
	1			ʾURŠAM	AN	AM				UR-SA-MA-NAM	ACC	M+
	1			ḪINUN		AM				I-NU-NAM	NOM	SIMMONS 51 3+
	1	JA		ḪMUM		AM				IA-AḪ-MU-MA-AM-KI	GN ACC	M
	1			ʿAZZ	AT	AM				A-ZA-TAM	FN ACC	CT VIII 37D 3
	1	JA		ʿQUB		AM				IA-KU-BA-[A]M?	NOM	RA LXV 46 V 84
	1			ʿUZZ		AM				ḪU-UZ-ZA-AM	ACC	XIII 100 9
	1			JAʾAN		AM				IA-A-NA-AM		M
	1			JAŠAR		AM				IA-SA-RA-AM	ACC	M
	2	JI		NDIN				JAT	AM	I-DIN-IA-TAM	ACC	XIV 64:7
	1			BUQAQ		AM				BU-QA-OA-AM	ACC	M
	2			LA				DIJN	AM	LA-DI-NAM	ACC	M
	1			ḎIMR	AN	AM				ZI-IM-RA-NAM	ACC	M+
	1	JA		KWUN		AM				IA-KU-NA-AM	ACC	CT VIII 36D 7
	1			KAZIR		AM				KA-ZI-RA-AM	NOM	RA LXV 52 X 24
	1			KUWN		AM				KU-NA-AM	MN NOM	TIM III 17 7, M+
	1			KUNN		AM				KU-UN-NAM	NOM	XIV 102:8, 15, 24
	1			KUNZ	AN	AM				KU-UN-ZA-NAM	ACC	TA 1930,181
	1			MAʾŠ		AM				MA-ŠA-AM	ACC	M+
	1	JA	T	MAQṬ		AM				IA-AM-TA-AQ-TA-AM	ACC	ABB V 39 REV 8'
	1			MERR		AM				ME-ER-RA-AM	ACC	M
	1			NAJAL		AM				NA-JA-LAM		RA LXV 40 I 33
	2	JA		JTIR				NAN	AM	JA-TI-IR-NA-NAM	ACC	M
		JA		JTIR				NAN	AM	JA-TE-IR-NA-NAM	ACC	M
	1			NIMḪ		AM		PI				
								ʾIL		NI-IM?-ḪA-AM-BI-DINGIR		A. 95 17 (=JCS VIII 8)
	1			NIPR		AM				NI-IP-RA-AM		RA LXV 50IX 26
	1			ŠAKIR		AM				SA-KI-RA-AM	ACC	M
	1			ŠAM		AM				SA-MA-AM	ACC	XIII 38 7+
	1	MA		ŠMIʿ	AN	AM				MA-AŠ-MI-A-NA-AM	ACC	M
	1			ṢUPR		AM				ZU-UP-RA-AM		RA LXV 51 IX 70
	2			ḪARB		I		TUWR	AM	AR-BI-TU-RA-AM		BIROT, TEA 65:35
E	2			LAMA				ʾADAʾ	E	LA-MA-A-DA-E	FN	A.
				LAMA				ʾADAʾ	E	LA-MA-TA-E	FN	A.+
	1			BIN	T	E	JE			BI-IT-TE-E	FN	TCL I 52 11
	1			GAJID		E				GA-I-TE		A.
	2			BUN		U		NAWIJ	E	BU-NU-NA-WI-E		CT XLVIII 56 REV.11

SUFFIXES, Class 2

E	1		RAWM		E		ʾEL				R[A]-ME-EL		RA LXV 42 II 56
	2		LAʾT		I		RAWM		E	JE	LA-TI-RA-ME-E		M
			MUT				RAWM		E	JE	MU-UT-RA-ME-E		BM 81584 3, M+
			ŠUM		U		RAWM		E	JE	SU-MU-RA-ME-E		B 40+
	1		SIKIL	T	E						ZI-GI-IL-TE	MN	A.
	1		ZUJAN		E						ZU-JA-NE	FN	XIII 1 VIII 11
EJA	1		ḪULM		EJA						ḪU-UL-ME-I[A]		RA LXV 41 II 46
	1		BAʿL		EJA						BA-LI-E-IA		A.
	1		NIQM		EJA						NI-IQ-ME-IA		M+
EM	1		ʾARWIJ		EM						AR-WI-E-[EM]	GEN	I 30 10
	1	MU	KAŠAJ		EM						MU-KA-SA-A-JE-EM	ACC	M
	1		LAWUJ		EM						LA-E-EM	ACC	M+
	2		ŠUM		U		RAWḪ		EM		[SU]-MU-RA-ḪI-E-IM		B 40
	2		MUT				RAWM		EM		MU-UT-RA-ME-IM		M
			ŠUM		U		RAWM		EM		SU-MU-RA-ME-IM		M
	1		RAṢIJ		EM						RA-ZI-E-IM-KI	GN	M+
	2		ŠUM		U		RAṢIJ		EM		[SU]-MU-RA-ZI-E-IM		B 40
I	1	ME	ʾWIR		I						ME-ḪI-RI		C
		ME	ʾWIR		I		ʾEL				ME-ḪI-RI-E-EL		JCS IV 109 4311 7
	2		JAʾ		U		ʾAHL		I		IA-U$_{2}$-A-LI$_{2}$		KISURRA 85 19
			BEʿL		i		ʾAHL		I		BE-LI-IA-LI$_{2}$		KISURRA 112 14
		JA	KWUN				ʾAHL		I		IA-KU-UN-A-LI		B 92
			MATIʿ				ʾAHL		I		MA-TI-IA-LI		UCP X/1 1 16
		JI	TWUR				ʾAHL		I		I-DUR-A-LI		JCS XXIV 46 NOS. 5, 6
	3		LI			JI	TWUR						
							ʾAHL		I		LI-TU-UR-A-LI		JCS XXIV 62 NO.55+
	1		ʾAḪ		I		ḪIʾL				A-ḪI-ḪI-EL		XIII 1 X 17
			ʾAḪ		I		JABAL				A-ḪI-E-BA-AL		M
			ʾAḪ		I		HADD		A		A-ḪI-A-DA		B 12
			ʾAḪ		I		ʾIL				A-ḪI-[I]L		HARRIS 45 11
			ʾAḪ		I		ʾIL		I		A-ḪI-I$_{3}$-LI$_{2}$	FN	XIII 1 VIII 20
			ʾAḪ		I		ʾAŠD				A-ḪI-SA-AD		B 12+
			ʾAḪ		I		ʾAŠD				A-ḪI-A-SA-AD		B 12
			ʾAḪ		I		ʾAŠD				A-ḪA-SA-AD		UET V 539 II 19
			ʾAḪ		I		JATAR				A-Ḫ[I]-E?-TAR		RA LXV 46 V 86
			ʾAḪ		I	JI	ʿQUB		A		A-ḪI-I-KU-BA		KISURRA 7A 9
			ʾAḪ		I	JA	JŠUʿ				A-ḪI-IA-ŠU-UḪ		SIMMONS 58 16
			ʾAḪ		I	JA	JŠUʿ				A-ḪI-IA-ŠU		BIROT, TEA 28:17+
			ʾAḪ		I	JE	QWIM				A-ḪI-E-KI-IM		M
			ʾAḪ		I	JA	ŠJIT				A-ḪI-SI-IT		TA 1931, 636
			ʾAḪ		I		DANN		UM		A-ḪI-DA-NU-UM		I
			ʾAḪ		I		DAŠUR				A-ḪI-DA-ŠU-UR$_{2}$		PBS XI/2 P. 140 NO. 1128
			ʾAḪ		I		KI						
							LIʾM				A-ḪI-KI-LI-IM		JEAN T.SIFR 72 5, 6, 13+
			ʾAḪ		I		KAʾB		I		A-ḪI-KA-PI		YOS VIII 64 18
			ʾAḪ		I		LIʾM				A-ḪI-LI-IM		B 12, M
			ʾAḪ		I		LABAN				A-ḪI-LA-BA-AN		RA LXV 43 IV 5+
			ʾAḪ		I		MAʾJ		UM		A-ḪI-MA-IU-UM		MAM III P. 274
			ʾAḪ		I	JE	MALIK				A-ḪI-E-MA-LIK		M
			ʾAḪ		I		MARAṢ				A-ḪI-MA-RA-AṢ		B 12+, M+
			ʾAḪ		I		MARAṢ				A-ḪI-MA-RA-UṢ		RUTTEN 1 22
			ʾAḪ		I		MARAṢ				A-ḪI-MA-RA-AṢ	FN	XIII 1 IX 24
			ʾAḪ		I		ŠALAŠ				A-ḪI-ŠA-LA-AŠ		EDZARD, DER 104:2
			ʾAḪ		I		ŠUM		U	NA	A-ḪI-SU-MU-NA		SIMMONS 83 5
			ʾAḪ		I	JI	ŠMAʿ			NI	A-ḪI-IŠ-MA-NI		VAS VIII 14:41+
			ʾAḪ		I	Š	TUʾ			JA	A-ḪI-IŠ-TU-IA		A. 86 9
			ʾAḪ		I	Š	TUʾ			KA	A-ḪI-IŠ-DU-KA		A. 98C 1, 6
			ʾAḪ		I	TA	NWUḪ		A		A-ḪI-TA-NU-A		M
			ʾAḪ		I		ṢADUQ				A-ḪI-ZA-DU-UQ		B 12
			ʾAḪ	AT	I						A-ḪA-TI	FN	XIII 1 VIII 6
			ʾAḪ	AT	I		MA				A-ḪA-TI-MA	FN	JCS XXVII 135:1
			ʾAḪ	AT	I		JIQR	AT			A-ḪA-TI-IQ-RA-AT	FN	XIII 1 V 5
			ʾAḪ	AT	I		JIQR	AB			A-ḪA-TI-IQ-RA	FN	XIII 1 II 72+
	2		ʾAJA				ʾAḪ		I		A-IA-A-ḪI		X 166 8'+
			ʾAJA				ʾAḪ	AT	I		A-IA-A-ḪA-TI	FN	A.
			ʿAḎR				ʾAḪ		I		ḪA-AZ-RA-ḪI?		CT XLV 54 9

I	2		ʾAL					ʾAḪ	AT	I		AL-A-ḪA-TI	FN	A.
			ʾALI					ʾAḪ		I		A-LI-A-ḪI	FN	M+
			ʾALI					ʾAḪ	AT	I		A-LI-A-ḪA-TI	FN	XIII 1 IV 71+
			ʾALI					ʾAḪ	AT	I		A-LI-A-ḪA?-TA-TI	FN	M
			ʾALI					ʾAḪ	AT	I		A-LI_2-A-ḪA-TI	FN	RA LXV 59 II 65+
			ʿAN		UM			ʾAḪ		I		A-NU-UM-A-ḪI		RA LXV 53 XI 43
			ḪANN		A			ʾAḪ		I		AN-NA-A-ḪI	GEN	M
			ʿAQB		A			ʾAḪ		I		AQ-BA-A-ḪI	GEN	XII 448 5+
			ʾAŠD		A			ʾAḪ		I		AŠ-DA-A-ḪI		VAS XVI 44 3
		ʾU	WTAʾ					ʾAḪ		I		U_2-TA-A-ḪI		M
			DIWIR					ʾAḪ		I		DI-WI-IR-A-ḪI		PBS XI/1 P. 55+
			DIWIR					ʾAḪ		I		DI-BI-IR-A-ḪI		PBS XI/1 P. 55+
			MUT		I			ʾAḪ		I		MU-TI-A-ḪI	GEN	B 35
			ŠUM		U			ʾAḪ		I	JA	[SU]-MU-A-ḪI-IA		PBS XI/2 1 I 27
			ŠAMŠ		I			ʾAḪ		I		SA-AM-SI-A-ḪI		RA LXV 54 XII 26
			ṢAMID					ʾAḪ		I		ZA-MI-ID-A-ḪI		CT IV 8B 17
	3		ʾIL		I			MAʾD		I				
								ʾAḪ		I		I_3-LI_2-MA-DA-ḪI		RUTTEN 14 7
			LA			ʾA		HWIJ						
								ʾAḪ		I		LA-AḪ-WI-A-ḪI	FN	XIII 1 VII 3
			QAWM		U			MA						
								ʾAḪ		I		QA-MU-MA-A-ḪI		RA LXV 41 II 22
	2		ʾAJA					ʾAḪW		I		A-IA-A-ḪU-I		JCS V 133
	1		ʾAWAʾ	AT	I			ʾEL				A-WA-TI-EL		RA LXV 41 II 37+
			ʾAWAʾ	AT	I			ʾIL				A-WA-TI-DINGIR	MN	XIII 1 XI 39
	1		ʾAWN	ANIJI								AM-NA-NI-I	TRIBE	M
	1		ʾAB		I			JAʾ		A		A-BI-IA-A		KISURRA 102 7+
			ʾAB		I			JAʾ		UM		A-BI-IA-U_2-UM		YOS VIII 10 9
			ʾAB		I			ḪIʾL				A-BI-ḪI-EL		B 10, M
			ʾAB		I			ḪIʾL				A-BI-ḪI-IL		M
			ʾAB		I			ḪIʾL		U		A-BI-ḪE_2-LU		MRS VI P. 240 LATE
			ʾAB		I			JAʾAR				A-BI-IA-ḪA-AR		B 10+
			ʾAB		I			JAʾAR				A-BI-A-ḪA-AR		CT XLIII 125 1+
			ʾAB		I			JAʾAR				A-BI-ḪA-AR		B 10+
			ʾAB		I			JABAL				A-BI-A-BA-AL		FIGULLA CAT. I 14206
			ʾAB		I			HADD		U		A-BI-D-IM		B 9, M+
			ʾAB		I			HADD		U		A-BI-A-DU		A.+
			ʾAB		I			HADD		U		A-BI-IA-DU		M+
			ʾAB		I			ʿAḎAR				A-BI-DAR		SIMMONS 58 12
			ʾAB		I			ʿAḎR		I		A-BI-AD-RI		A. LATE
			ʾAB		I			ʾAK		I		A-BI-IA-KI		TCL I 109 3
			ʾAB		I			ʾIL		A		A-BI-LA		CHANTRE 4 13
			ʾAB		I			ʾIL		I		A-BI-I_3-LI_2	FN	RA LXV 59 II 38+
			ʾAB		I			ʿALAṢ		I		AD-ḪA-LA-ZI	FN	C
			ʾAB		I			ʿALAṢ		I		A-BI-ḪA-LA-ZI	FN	M, C II 49 6
			ʾAB		I			ḪAM		A		A-BI-A-MA		SIMMONS 50 22+
			ʾAB		I			ḪAM		A		A-BI-IA-MA		SIMMONS 54 19+
			ʾAB		I			ʾAMAL				A-BI-A-MA-AL		KISURRA 153 34
			ʾAB		I			ʾANN		IM		A-BI-AN-NIM	GEN	M
			ʾAB		I			ḪUNN		I		A-BI-ḪU-UN?-NI		B 10
			ʾAB		I			JAQAR				A-BI-E-QAR		M+
			ʾAB		I			ʾIR		A		AD-I-RA	FN	A.
			ʾAB		I			JARAḪ				A-BI-A-RA-AḪ		B 9+
			ʾAB		I			JARAḪ				A-BI-E-RA-AḪ		B+, M+
			ʾAB		I			JARAḪ				A-BI-RA-AḪ		B 9+, A. 38 18
			ʾAB		I			JARAḪ				A-BE-RA-AḪ		B 9
			ʾAB		I			ʾAŠD				A-BI-A-SA-AD		B 10+
			ʾAB		I			ʾAŠD				A-BI-SA-AD		B 10+
			ʾAB		I			JAT		UM		A-BI-IA-TUM	FN	WATERMAN 40 R. 5+
			ʾAB		I			ḪATAN				A-BI-ḪA-TA-AN		B 10
			ʾAB		I			JATAR				A-BI_2-WA-DAR		U
			ʾAB		I			JATAR				A-BI-IA-TA-AR		B 10+
			ʾAB		I			JATAR				A-BI-E-TAR		BASOR 95 22
			ʾAB		I			ʾAZJ		I		A-BI-A-ZI		A.
			ʾAB		I	ʾA	T	ŠAMAR				A-BI-AŠ-TA-MA-AR		YOS XIII 489:4
			ʾAB		I	JA		MWUT		A		A-BI-IA-MU-TA		BM 80328 15

I	1	ʾAB		I		JA		MWUT	I		A-BI$_2$-A-MU-TI		U
		ʾAB		I		JA		JPAʿ			A-BI-IA-PA-AḪ	FN	XIII 1 II 57
		ʾAB		I		JE		JPUʿ			A-BI-E-PU-UḪ		B 10, M+
		ʾAB		I		JA		JPUʿ			A-BI-IA-PU-UḪ		B 10
		ʾAB		I		JE		JŠUʿ			A-BI-E-ŠU-UḪ		B 10+, XIII 1 III 44
		ʾAB		I		JA		JŠUʿ			A-BI-ŠU-UḪ		B 10
		ʾAB		I		JA		JŠUʿ	A		A-BI-IA-ŠU-ḪA		B 10
		ʾAB		I		JE		JŠUʿ					
								....			A-BI-E-ŠU-UḪ-LI-DI-IŠ		CT XLV 55 11
		ʾAB		I		JE		JŠUʿ					
								....			A-BI-E-ŠU-UḪ-LU-DA-RI		B 10
		ʾAB		I		JA		JŠUʿ					
								....			A-BI-ŠU-UT-LI		B 11
		ʾAB		I				DAGAN			A-BI-D-DA-GAN		M+
		ʾAB		I				DIRAḪ			A-BI?-DI-RA-AḪ		TCL X 41 A/B 4+
		ʾAB		I				DARAB			[A]?-BI-DA-RA-AB		RA LXV 43 III 67
		ʾAB		I				DITAN			A-BI-DI-TA-AN		BM 80328 16
		ʾAB		I				DITAN	UM		A-BI-TI-DA-NU-UM		TA 1931, 538 III,IV
		ʾAB		I				GAʾJ	A		A-BI-GA-A	GN?	A 21919+
		ʾAB		I				KAʾB	I		A-BI-KA-BI		M
		ʾAB		I				KAʾB	I		A-BI-KA-BI	FN	RA LXV 65 VII 42
		ʾAB		I				LUʾL	A		A-BI-LU-LA		SIMMONS 107 13
		ʾAB		I				LIʾM			A-BI-LI-IM		RA LXV 44 IV 60+
		ʾAB		I				LAMA			A-BI-LA-MA		B 10
		ʾAB		I				MA					
								ʾIL	I		A-BI-MA-I$_3$-LI$_2$	FN	RA LXV 64 VI 32
		ʾAB		I		ME		QWIM			A-BI-ME-KI-IM		XIII 34 5+
		ʾAB		I				MI					
								KI			A-BI-MI-KI-DINGIR		M
		ʾAB		I				MULUK	I		A-BI-MU-LU-KI	FN	RA LXV 59 II 26
		ʾAB		I				MARAṢ			A-BI-MA-RA-AṢ		B 10+
		ʾAB		I				MAṬAR			A-BI-MA-DAR		B 10+
		ʾAB		I				MAṬAR			A-BI-MA-DA-AR		TIM II 113 3
		ʾAB		I				NAʿM	I		A-BI-NA-AḪ-MI	FN	XIII 1 VII 43, A.+
		ʾAB		I				NAʿM	I		A-BI-NA-AḪ-ME	FN	RA LXV 59 II 20
		ʾAB		I				NIʿM			A-BI-NI-ḪI-IM		RA LXV 44 IV 31
		ʾAB		I				NIWR	I		A-BI-NI-RI	FN	XIII 1 IX 58+
		ʾAB		I				NAPŠ	I		A-BI-NA-AP-S[I]		XIV 77:7
		ʾAB		I				QAʾD			A-BI-QA-AD		B 11
		ʾAB		I				QAʾD			A-BI-GA-AD		TA 30 237
		ʾAB		I				RAWM			A-BI-RA-AM		RA LXV 43 IV 12
		ʾAB		I				RAPIʾ			A-BI-RA-BI		M
		ʾAB		I				RAPIʾ			A-BI-RA-PI		SYRIA XXXVII 206 6, 7
		ʾAB		I				RAŠAP			A-BI-RA-SA-AP		M
		ʾAB		I	Š			KIWN			A-BI$_2$-IŠ-KI-IN		U
		ʾAB		I	Š			MUM	U		A-BI-IŠ-MU-MU		HARRIS 98 2
		ʾAB		I	Š			TUʾ			A-BI-IŠ-DU		A. LATE
		ʾAB		I		JI	T	ŠAMAR			A-BI-IŠ-TA-MAR		TCL I 226 4, 10+
		ʾAB		I				ŠADW	A		A-BI-SA-DA-A		JCS IV 110 2040
		ʾAB		I				ŠAMAK	U		A-BI-SA-MA-KU		SIMMONS 41 15
		ʾAB		I				ŠAMAR			A-BI-SA-MAR		M+
		ʾAB		I				ŠAMŠ			A-BI-SA-MA-AŠ		M+
		ʾAB		I				ŠAMŠ			A-BI-D-UTU	FN	XIII 24 IV 40
		ʾAB		I				ŠAMŠ	I		A-BI-D-UTU-ŠI	FN	XIII 1 IX 40+
		ʾAB		I				ŠAMAT	A		A-BI-SA-MA-TA		EDZARD, DER 120:4
		ʾAB		I				ŠAPAR			A-BI-SA-PA-AR	FN	C
		ʾAB		I				ŠAPAR			A-BI-SA-PAR$_2$		CT XLV 82 7+, XIII 1 II 15
		ʾAB		I				ŠARIJ			A-BI-SA-RI		LIMET, SCEAUX CASS. P 114
		ʾAB		I				ŠARIJ		JE	A-BI-SA-RI-E		B 11+; M+
		ʾAB		I				ŠARIJ		JE	A-BI$_2$-SA-RI-E		BIN VII 93 DATE
		ʾAB		I				ṢUWR	A		A-BE-ZU-RA		TCL IV 87 10 CAPP.
		ʾAB		I				ṢUWR	A		A-BI-ṢU-RA		TIM IV 34 27
		ʾAB		I				ṢUWR	I		A-BI-ZU-RI		M
		ʾAB		I				ṬAJB	A		A-BI-ṬA-BA		A.+
	2	ʾAḪ	AT	A				ʾAB	I		A-ḪA-TA-A-BI	FN	M+
		ʾAJA						ʾAB	I		A-IA-A-BI		A.

I	2		ʾAJA				ʾAB	I		A-IA-BI		A.+
			ʾAJA				ʾAB	I				
							ŠARR	I		A-IA-BI-ŠAR-RI		A.
			ʾAJA				ʾAB	I				
							TALM	A		A-IA-BI-TA-AL-MA		A. 239 15
			ʾAJAN				ʾAB	I		A-IA-NA-BI	FN	A.
			ʾAJAN				ʾAB	I				
							ʾILL	A		A-IA-NA-BI-IL-LA		A.
			ḪAʾN	A			ʾAB	I		ḪA-NA-A-BI		TIM II 113 2, 8
			ḪAWR				ʾAB	I		ḪA-AW-RA-BI		TIM IV 33 21, 34 14
			ḪAWR	AN			ʾAB	I		ḪA-AW-RA-AN-A-BI		M
			ḪAWR	AN			ʾAB	I		ḪA-AW-RA-NA-A-BI		M+
			ʿAD	U	NI		ʾAB	I	JA	A-DU-NI-A-BI-IA		RA XXVII 87 LATE
			ʿADN	A			ʾAB	I		ḪA?-AD-NA-A-BI		TTKB XIX 304
			ʾIL	A			ʾAB	I		I-LA-A-BI		C
			ʾIL	UM			ʾAB	I		I-LUM-A-BI		A.
			ʾALI				ʾAB	I		A-LI-A-BI	FN	M+
		ʾA	JPAʿ				ʾAB	I		A-PA-AḪ-A-BI		YOS VIII 29 13
			ʾIRR	A			ʾAB	I		IR$_{3}$-RA-A-BI		M
			ʾAŚD	UM			ʾAB	I		AŠ$_{2}$-DU-UM-A-BI		BE VI/1 1 7+
			ʾAŚD	UM			ʾAB	I		D-AŠ-DU-UM-A-BI		UET V 483 4
			ʿAŠTAR				ʾAB	I		AŠ-TAR-A-BI		MRS VI P. 242
			ʿIZZ				ʾAB	I		IZ-ZA-BI		C+
			BILL				ʾAB	I		BI-IL-LA-BI	FN	XIII 1 X 41
			DIWIR				ʾAB	I		DI-WI-IR-A-BI		PBS XI/1 P. 55+
			DIWIR				ʾAB	I		DI-BI-IR-A-BI		PBS XI/1 P. 55+
			ḎAKUR				ʾAB	I		ZA-KU-UR-A-BI	GEN	B 41
			ḎAKUR	A			ʾAB	I		ZA-KU-RA-A-BI	GEN	B 41
			NUʿM	I			ʾAB	I		NU-UḪ-MI-A-BI		XIII 1 I 38
			NIQM				ʾAB	I		NI-IQ-MA-A-BI		A. 86 7+
		JA	PRUS				ʾAB	I		IA-AP-RU-US-A-BI		BAGHD. MITT. II 23
			QAṬAR				ʾAB	I		GA-TAR-A-BI		BASOR 95 22
		JI	RPAʾ				ʾAB	I		IR-PA-A-BI		A.+
		JA	ŚJIT				ʾAB	I		IA-SI-IT-A-BI		M
			ŠUBUL				ʾAB	I		ŠU-BU-UL-A-BI		M
			ŚUM	U			ʾAB	I		SU-MA-A-BI		A.
			ŚUM	U			ʾAB	I	JA	[SU]-MU-A-BI-IA		B 38
			ŚUM	U			ʾAB	I				
						JA	RWIM			SU-MU-A-BI-A-RI-IM		TA 30 9, 14, 15+
			ŚUM	UM			ʾAB	I				
						JA	RWIM			SU-MU-UN-A-BI-IA-RI-IM		SUMER XXIII 153:9
			ŚUM	U	NA		ʾAB	I		SU-MU-UN-NA-A-BI	FN	A. 64 7
			ŚUM	U	NA		ʾAB	I		SU-MU-UN-NA-BI	FN	A. 33 3, 34 2+
			ŚUM	U	NA		ʾAB	I		SU-MU-NA-BI	FN	A. 59 8
			ŚUM	U	NA		ʾAB	I		SU-MU-NA-A-BI	FN	A. 244 5, M
			ŚUM	U	NA		ʾAB	I				
						JA	RWIM			SU-MU-NA-BI-IA-RI-IM		SUMER XXIII PL. 7 17+
			ŚUM	U	NA		ʾAB	I				
						JA	RWIM			SU-MU-UN?-A-BI-JA-RI-IM		SUMER XXIII P. 153 9
			ŚAMŚ	I			ʾAB	I		D-UTU-A-BI		M+
			ŚAPŚ	I			ʾAB	I		ŠA-AP-ŠI-A-BI	FN	A.
	3		ʾAḪ	U			KA					
							ʾAB	I		A-ḪU-KA-A-BI	FN	XIII 1 VIII 60, C+
			ʾAḪ	UM			LA					
							ʾAB	I		A-ḪU-UM-LA-A-BI		YOS XIII 245:17, SEAL
			ʾIL	A			MA					
							ʾAB	I		DINGIR-MA-A-BI		M
			ʾIL	I			MA					
							ʾAB	I		I$_{3}$-LI-MA-A-BI		M+
			ʾUMM	UM			KA					
							ʾAB	I		UM-MU-UM-KA-A-BI	FN	XIII 1 VII 56
			ʾUMM	U			KA					
							ʾAB	I		UM-MU-KA-A-BI	FN	RA LXV 62 V 16
			ʾANN	U			KAMA					
							ʾAB	I		AN-NU-KA-MA-BI		CT XLV 116 36
		JA	JPAʿ				ŠUM	U				
							ʾAB	I		IA-PA-AḪ-SU-MU-A-BI		A. 56 47

SUFFIXES, Class 2

I	3		ʾIRŠ				MA					
							ʾAB	I		I-RI-IŠ-MA-A-BI		A.
			ʾIRŠ				MA					
							ʾAB	I		I-RI-IŠ-MA-BI		A.
			ʾIRŠ	U			MA					
							ʾAB	I		IR-ŠU-MA-BI		A.
			ḎU				MA					
							ʾAB	I		ZU-U$_2$-MA-A-BI		XIV 77:17
			ḎU				MA					
							ʾAB	I		ZU-U$_2$-MA?-A-BI		M
			ḎIMR	U			LA					
							ʾAB	I		ZI-IM-RU-LA-A-BI		RA LXV 42 III 7
			KABD	U			KA					
							ʾAB	I		KA-AB-TU-KA-A-BI		UET V 688:8,12
			LA			ʾA	HWIJ					
							ʾAB	I		LA-AḪ-WI-A-BI	FN	XIII 1 XIII 6
		JA	RWIM				ŠUM	U				
							ʾAB	I		IA-RI-IM-SU-MU-A-BI		RA LXV 42 III 8
			ŠUM	UM			LA					
							ʾAB	I		SU-MU-UM-LA-A-BI	FN	RA LXV 65 VII 24
	1		ʾABB	I			LIʾM					
							MA			AB-BI-LIM-MA		A.+
	1		ʾABN	I			ʾIL			ḪA-AB-NI-DINGIR		M
	2		ʾAJA				ʾABN	I				
							ʾIL			ḪA-IA-AB-NI-DINGIR		B 18+
	1		ʾADAD	I						A-DA-DI	FN	XIII 1 X 30
			ʾADAN	I	Š		....			ḪA-DA-NI-IŠ-MU-[....]		SIGRIST UNPUBL.
	1		ʾADD	I			ŠAMŠ			AD-DI-D-UTU?		RA LXIV 99:23
			ʾADD	I	JA		ʾEL			AD-DI-JA-EL		BAB. III 267 HANA
			ʾADD	I	JA		ʾEL			AD-DI-IA-DINGIR		MAOG IV 2 12 HANA
	2	JA	MʾID				ʾADM	I		IA-AM-I-ID-D-AD-MI		A. 60 4
	1		ʾAK	I			....			A-KI-[....]	FN	IX 291 13
			ʾAK	I			ʾIL			A-KI-DINGIR		M
			ʾAK	I			ʾEL			A-KI-EL		RA LXV 46 VI 49
			ʾAK	I			JARAḪ			A-KI-E-RA-AḪ		M
			ʾAK	I			LAMA			A-KI-LA-MA		B 12
	2		ʾAB	I			ʾAK	I		A-BI-IA-KI		TCL I 109 3
			ʿAMM	I			ʾAK	I		AM-MI-E-KI		A.
	1		ʾAKIR	I						A-KI-RI	GEN	VAS VIII 14 37
	1		ʾAKK	ATANI						A-GA-DA-NI		TA 1931, 489
			ʾAKK	ATANI						A-GA-TA-NI		TA 1931, 530 I, III
	1		ʾAL	I	Š		TUT	U		A-LI-IŠ-TU-TU		VAS XVI 23 13
	1		ʾALAŠ	I			ʾEL			A-IA-SI-E-EL		UCP X/3 3 17
	2		MUT				ʾALAM	I		MU-UT-ḪA-LA-MI		C+
	1		ʾALL	I			KUPAPA			AL-LI-KU-PA-PA	FN	A.
			ʾALL	I			NIWR	I		AL-LI-NI-RI	FN	A.
			ʾALL	I			TALM	A		AL-LI-TA-AL-MA	FN	A.
			ʾALL	I			TURAḪ			AL-LI-TU-RA-AḪ?	FN	XIII 1 I 10+
			ʾALL	I			TURAḪ	I		AL-LI-TU-RA-ḪI	FN	A.
	1		ʾALUP	I						A-LU-BI	GEN?	CT XLV 92 R. I 14
	1		ʾAMIN	I			ʾANN	U		A-MI-NI-AN-NU		M
	1	T	ʾAMR	I			ʾIL			A-TAM-RI-DINGIR		M+
	2		ʾANN	U			ʾAMR	I	JA	AN-NU-AM-RI-IA	FN	RA LXV 61 IV 47
	2	JI	ŠMAʿ				ʾAMUM	I		IŠ-ME-A-MU-MI	FN	M
	1		ʾAN	I	Š		ḪURB	I		A-NI-IŠ-ḪU-UR-BI		M+
			ʾAN	I	Š		KIBAL			A-NI-IŠ-KI-BA-AL		RA LXV 53 XI 37+
			ʾAN	I	Š		KIBEL			A-NI-IŠ-KI-BE-EL		TCL XX 191 33 CAPP.
	1		ʾANA	I	Š					A-NA-IŠ		RA LXV 52 X 79
	2		ʿAMM	I			ʾANDUL	I		ḪA-AM-MI-AN-DUL$_3$-LI$_2$		M+
			ʿAŠTAR				ʾANDUL	I		EŠ$_4$-DAR-AN-DUL$_3$-LI$_2$	FN	M
	2	JA	NTIN				ʾANN	I	Š	[IA-AN]-TI-IN-A-NI-IŠ		VII 180 8'
	1		ʾAP	I			ʾAŠAL			A-PI-A-ŠAL		JNES XIII 212F.+ LATE
	2		ʾIL	I			ʾAP	I	JA	I$_3$-LI$_2$-A-PI?-A		TIM III 4 14
	1		ʾARḪ	I			ŠAMŠ	I		AR-ḪI-D-UTU-ŠI	FN	XIII 1 XIII 2
	2		ʾAJ	A			ʾARR	I		D-A-A-AR-RI	FN	M
	1		ʾARUŠ	I			ʾIL			A-RU-SI-DINGIR		A 7459, M

I	1		ʾASIN		I							A-SI-NI		APN P. 31 LATE
	1		ʾAŠD		I			JAŠAR				AŠ$_2$-DI-E-SA-AR		XIII 1 XI 35
			ʾAŠD		I			JATAR				AŠ-DI-E-TAR		M
			ʾAŠD		I			DAWD		UM		AŠ$_2$-DI?-DA-DU-UM		EDZARD, DER 60:11
			ʾAŠD		I		JE	JŠUʿ				AŠ$_2$-DI-E-ŠU-UḪ		M
			ʾAŠD		I			KIʾR		U		AŠ-DI-KI-E-RU		BM 92654 A
			ʾAŠD		I			KIʾR		U		AŠ-DI-KI-RU		BM 92654
			ʾAŠD		I			LUMM		A		AŠ-DI-LU-MA		UCP X/3 2 31
			ʾAŠD		I			MAʾK		U	HU	AŠ$_2$-DI-MA-KU-U$_2$		VAS IX 172 30
			ʾAŠD		I			NIʿM				AŠ$_2$-DI-NI-ḪI-IM		M+
			ʾAŠD		I			RAWM				AŠ-DI-RA-AM		RA LXV 55 XIII 42
			ʾAŠD		I		TA	QWIM				AŠ$_2$-DI-TA-KI-IM		M+
	2		JATAR					ʾAŠD		I		IA-TAR-AŠ-DI		M
			MUT		U			ʾAŠD		I		[MU]-TU-AŠ-DI		VIII 17 13'
	1		ʾAŠM	AN	I							ḪA-AŠ-MA-NI	GEN	B 44
	1		ʾAŠQUD		I							AŠ-KU-DI	GEN	M+
	2	JA	KWUN					ʾAŠAR		I		IA-KU-UN-A-ŠA-RI	NOM	CT XLVIII 10 6
		JA	RŠIJ					ʾAŠAR		I		IA-AR-ŠI-A-ŠA-RI		M
	2		TALM		U			ʾAŠIḪ		I		TA-AL-MU-A-ŠI-ḪI	FN	XIII 1 III 63
	1		ʾAŠR		I							ḪA-AŠ$_2$-RI		CT XLV 92 R. 9
			ʾAŠR		I			JATAR				AŠ-RI-E-TAR		RA XLIX 24 N. 9
	2		ʾANN		U			ʾAŠR		I		AN-NU-AŠ-RI	FN	M+
			KAKK		A			ʾAŠR		I		KA-AK-KA-AŠ-RI	FN	XIII 1 V 1
	1		ʾAŠUZ		I							A-ŠU-ZI		M
	1		ʾATAL		I			ʾEL				ḪA-TA-LI-EL		M
			ʾATAR	AN	I							A-TA-RA-NI	GEN	HARRIS 71 12
			ʾATAR		I			ṢADUQ				[A]T-TA-RI-ZA-DU-UQ		I 103 17
	1		ʾATT		I							AT-TI	FN	RA LXV 65 VII 6
			ʾATT		I							ḪA-AT-TI		RA LXV 40 I 32
			ʾATT		I			HADD		U		AT-TI-D-IM		M+
			ʾATT		I			ʿAMM		A		AT-TI-AM-MA		A. LATE
			ʾATT		I			LIʾM		A		AT-TI-LI-MA		A. LATE
			ʾATT		I			MEʾR				AT?-TI-ME-IR?		IX 234 10
	2		BIN	T	A			ʾATT		I		BI-IT-TA-AT-TI	FN	A.+
	2		ʾAJA					ʾAZJ		I		A-IA-ZI		M
			ʾAB		I			ʾAZJ		I		A-BI-A-ZI		A.
	1		ʾEWIN		I							E-[W]I-NI		RA LXV 47 VII 22
	1		ʾEB		I			ʾIL				E-BI-IL		M
			ʾEB		I			DANN		UM		E-BI-DA-NU-UM		U
	1		ʾEK		I			LA						
							ʾA	HWIJ				E-KI-LA-AḪ-WI		M
	1		ʾEL	AN	I							E-LA-NI		M
	2		NADUB					ʾEL		I		NA-DU-BE-LI$_2$		U
		JI	ŠKUR					ʾEL		I		IŠ-KUR-E-LI	FN	XIII 1 VII 41
	1		ʾELAP		I							E-LA-BI	FN	RA LXV 65 VI 62
	1		ʾELIL		I	Š						E-LI-LI-IŠ		M+
			ʾELIL		I	Š						E-LI-LI-ŠA		M
	1		ʾELL		I							E-EL-LI		A. 377 8
	1		ʾEN		I	Š		ʾAG		UM		E-NI-IŠ-A-GU-UM		M+
	1		ʾEŠB		I			HADD		U		EŠ-BI-D-IM		A.+
			ʾEŠB		I			ʾADAN	T	A		EŠ-BI-A-DA-AT-TA		A. 455 31, 55
	1	JA	ʾGUN		I							IA-AḪ-GU-UN-NI	GEN	TCL XVII 26 1
	1		ʾIB		I			JAT		UM		I-BI-IA-TUM		TIM II 27 4
			ʾIB		I			LA						
								ʾIL		UM		I-BI-LA-I$_3$-LUM		U
	1		ʾIDD		I							ID-DI		XIII 1 IX 69+
	1		ʾIL	AT	I							I-LA-TI	MN	M
			ʾIL		I			JAʾ		UM		I$_3$-LI$_2$-IA-UM		KISURRA 71A 5+
			ʾIL		I			JAʾ		UM		I$_3$-LI$_2$-I-UM		KISURRA 4A 12+
			ʾIL		I			JAʾ		UM		I$_3$-LI$_2$-I-U$_2$-UM		KISURRA 56 3+
			ʾIL		I			JAʾ		UM		I$_3$-LI$_2$-U$_2$-A-UM		KISURRA 186 5
			ʾIL		I			JAʾ		UM		I$_3$-LI$_2$-A-UM		B 21
			ʾIL		I			ḪAʾL		UM		I$_3$-LI$_2$-ḪA-LU-UM		CT XLV 3 10
			ʾIL		I			ʿIJN		A	JA	I$_3$-LI$_2$-I-NA-A-A		GAUTIER 40 7
			ʾIL		I			JAʾN		UM		I$_3$-LI$_2$-IA-NU-UM		TIM I 29 3
			ʾIL		I			ʾUWR		I		I-LI-U$_2$-RI	FN	A.

I	1	ʾIL	I			HADD		U		I$_3$-LI$_2$-D-IM		M+
		ʾIL	I			HADD		U		I$_3$-LI$_2$-A-DU		A. 57 47
		ʾIL	I			HEDD		A		I$_3$-LI-E-DA		A.
		ʾIL	I			ʿADN		I		I$_3$-LI$_2$-ḪA-AD-NI	FN	M
		ʾIL	I			ʾIL		A		I$_3$-LI$_2$-I-LA		A. LATE
		ʾIL	I			ʾILL		A		I-LI-IL-LA		A. LATE
		ʾIL	I			ʾIMM	AH			I-LI$_2$-IM-MA	FN	C II 41 56, 44 57
		ʾIL	I			ʿAMM		U		I$_3$-LI$_2$-ḪA-MU		RA LVII 178
		ʾIL	I			ḪUMUD		I		I$_3$-LI$_2$-ḪU-MU-DI		M
		ʾIL	I			ḪUNIN		I		I$_3$-LI$_2$-U$_2$-NE-NI		RUTTEN 6 20
		ʾIL	I			ʾAP		I	JA	I$_3$-LI$_2$-A-PI?-A		TIM III 4 14
		ʾIL	I			JAQR		A		I$_3$-LI$_2$-AQ-RA		IRAQ XXX 90, RIMAH
		ʾIL	I			JARAḪ				I$_3$-LI$_2$-IA-RA-AḪ		SIMMONS 131 20
		ʾIL	I			JARAḪ				I$_3$-LI$_2$-E-RA-AḪ		M+, TIM III 133 4, SEAL
		ʾIL	I			ʾAŠIJ	AH			I$_3$-LI$_2$-A-SI-IA	FN	XIII 1 VII 55
		ʾIL	I			ʾAŠR		A	JA	I$_3$-LI$_2$-AŠ-RA-IA		M+
		ʾIL	I			ʿAŠTAR				I$_3$-LI$_2$-EŠ$_4$-DAR		M+
		ʾIL	I			JAT				I$_3$-LI$_2$-A-AT?		TA 1931, 261
		ʾIL	I			JAT		UM		I$_3$-LI$_2$-I-IA-TUM		VAS XVIII 83:15
		ʾIL	I			JAT			KA	I$_3$-LI$_2$-A-AT-KA		TIM III 10 14+
		ʾIL	I			ʾATAJ		A	JA	I$_3$-LI$_2$-A-TA-A-IA		RA VIII 69 26
		ʾIL	I			ʾITEJ			JE	I$_3$-LI$_2$-I-TE-E		MEISSNER 110 20, 23+, M
		ʾIL	I			JATAR				I$_3$-LI$_2$-A-TAR		B 21+
		ʾIL	I			JATAR				I$_3$-LI$_2$-E-TAR		M+
		ʾIL	I			ḪAṢN		A	JA	I$_3$-LI$_2$-ḪA-AṢ-NA-A-IA		M+
		ʾIL	I			ḪAṢN		I	JA	I$_3$-LI$_2$-ḪA-AṢ-NI-IA		XIII 1 IX 8
		ʾIL	I	ʾA		ḪTAN				I$_3$-LI$_2$-AḪ-TA-AN		RUTTEN 6 16+
		ʾIL	I	ʾA		PTAN				I$_3$-LI$_2$-AP-TA-AN		B 21
		ʾIL	I	ʾA		PTAN				DINGIR-AP-TAN		TIM III 150 12
		ʾIL	I	JI		ḪNUW			HU	I$_3$-LI$_2$-IḪ-NU-U$_2$		UCP X/1 19:4+
		ʾIL	I	JE		JPAʿ				I$_3$-LI$_2$-E-PA		A.+
		ʾIL	I	JE		JPUʿ				I$_3$-LI$_2$-E-PU-UḪ		M+
		ʾIL	I	JE		JŠUʿ				I$_3$-LI$_2$-E-ŠU-UḪ		B 21 M
		ʾIL	I	JI		ḪTAʾ						
						LI			JA	I$_3$-LI$_2$-IḪ-TA-LI-A		BIROT,TEA 69 I 14
		ʾIL	I	JA		MWUT				I$_3$-LI$_2$-IA-MU-[UT]		RA LXV 40 I 29
		ʾIL	I	JA		MLIK				I$_3$-LI$_2$-A-AM-LIK		HARRIS 49 12
		ʾIL	I	JI		ŠMAʿ			NIA	I$_3$-LI$_2$-IŠ-MA-NI-A		TA 1930,399
		ʾIL	I	JI		ŠPIQ				I$_3$-LI$_2$-IŠ-BI-IK		TA 1931, 71
		ʾIL	I	JI	T	ŠAMAR				I$_3$-LI$_2$-IŠ-TA-MAR		EDZARD,DER 67:11
		ʾIL	I			BAWB		UM		I$_3$-LI$_2$-BA-BU-UM		U UNPUBL.
		ʾIL	I			BAWŠ	T	I		I$_3$-LI$_2$-BA-AŠ$_2$-TI	FN	M+
		ʾIL	I			BIN		A	JA	I$_3$-LI$_2$-BI-NA-A-IA		M+
		ʾIL	I			DAʿ	AT			DINGIR-DA-ḪA-AT		A 7650:2
		ʾIL	I			DIʿ	AT			I$_3$-LI$_2$-DI-ḪA-[AT]		HARRIS 39 19
		ʾIL	I			DAGAN				I$_3$-LI$_2$-D-DA-GAN		M+
		ʾIL	I			DITAN				I$_3$-LI$_2$-DI-TA-AN		BM 82424 R. 18
		ʾIL	I			GUML		I	JA	I$_3$-LI$_2$-GU-UM-LI-IA		XIII 1 VIII 45
		ʾIL	I			KAʾB		I		I$_3$-LI$_2$-KA-PI		BIROT, TEA 69:28
		ʾIL	I			KUWN				I$_3$-LI$_2$-KU-UN		RA LXV 55 XIII 32
		ʾIL	I			KABKAB		U		I$_3$-LI$_2$-KA-AB-KA-BU		A 21914 3
		ʾIL	I			KAŠAR				I$_3$-LI$_2$-KA-ŠA-AR		M
		ʾIL	I			LIʾM				I$_3$-LI$_2$-LI-IM		M+, C
		ʾIL	I			MA						
						ʾAB		I		I$_3$-LI-MA-A-BI		M+
		ʾIL	I			MAʾD		A		I$_3$-LI$_2$-MA-DA		TA 30 615 6
		ʾIL	I			MAʾD		I		I$_3$-LI$_2$-MA-DI		SIMMONS 33 19
		ʾIL	I			MAʾD		I				
						ʾAḪ				I$_3$-LI$_2$-MA-DI-A-AḪ		RUTTEN 1 8
		ʾIL	I			MAʾD		I				
						ʾAḪ				DINGIR?-MA-DA-AḪ		RA LXV 42 III 21
		ʾIL	I			MAʾD		I				
						ʾAḪ				I$_3$-LI$_2$-MI-DI-AḪ		EDZARD,DER 146:14
		ʾIL	I			MAʾD		I				
						ʾAḪ		I		I$_3$-LI$_2$-MA-DA-ḪI		RUTTEN 14 7
		ʾIL	I			MAʾD		I				
						ʾAḪ		A		I$_3$-LI$_2$-MA-DA-ḪA		VAS VIII 14 4

I	1		ʾIL	I			MIWT		I		I$_3$-LI$_2$-MI-TI		I
			ʾIL	I			MALIK				I$_3$-LI$_2$-MA-LIK		M
			ʾIL	I			MILK		U		I$_3$-LI$_2$-MIL-KU	FN	RA LXV 58 I 31
			ʾIL	I			MAṬAR				I$_3$-LI$_2$-MA-DA-AR		M
			ʾIL	I			MAṬAR				I$_3$-LI$_2$-MA-TAR		M
			ʾIL	I			MAṬAR				I$_3$-LI$_2$-MA-TA-AR		B 21
			ʾIL	I			NIʿM				I$_3$-LI$_2$-NE-ḪI-IM		M
			ʾIL	I			NIWR		I		I$_3$-LI$_2$-NE-RI	FN	XIII 1 II 6+
			ʾIL	I			NATUN				I$_3$-LI$_2$-NA-TU-UN		M
			ʾIL	I			PAʾAL		UM		I$_3$-LI$_2$-PA-A-LU-UM		TIM III 44 16+
			ʾIL	I			PAʾAL		UM		I$_3$-LI$_2$-PA-ḪA-LUM		M
			ʾIL	I			QAʾN				I-LI-QA-AN		A. LATE
			ʾIL	I			RAWḪ		I	JE	I$_3$-LI$_2$-RA-AḪ-E		VAS XVI 168 9, FRANK 13 9
			ʾIL	I			RAWM				I$_3$-LI$_2$-RA-AM		M
			ʾIL	I			RIḪṢ		I		I$_3$-LI$_2$-RI-IḪ-ZI	FN	XIII 1 IX 39
			ʾIL	I			RAPIʾ				I$_3$-LI$_2$-RA-BI		M+
			ʾIL	I			RAŠAP				I$_3$-LI$_2$-D-RA-SA-[AP]		XIII 66 5
			ʾIL	I	Š		BAʾB		A		I$_3$-LI$_2$-IŠ-BA-BA		HSM 7934, UR III
			ʾIL	I	Š		GAʾUL		U		I$_3$-LI$_2$-IŠ-GA-U$_2$-LU		KISURRA 70A 17+
			ʾIL	I	Š		KUTUL				I$_3$-LI$_2$-IŠ-KU-TU-UL		KISURRA 75A 18+
			ʾIL	I			ŠAKIM				I$_3$-LI$_2$-ŠA-KI-IM		RA LXV 40 I 44+
			ʾIL	I			ŠUM		U		I$_3$-LI$_2$-SU-U$_2$-MU		M
			ʾIL	I			ŠAMUʿ				I$_3$-LI$_2$-SA-MU-UḪ		XIII 21 11'
			ʾIL	I			ŠIMḪ		I		I$_3$-LI$_2$-ŠI-IM-ḪI		M+
			ʾIL	I			ŠIMḪ		A	JA	I$_3$-LI$_2$-ŠI-IM-ḪA-IA		VIII 57 BIS 16
			ʾIL	I			ŠIMḪ		A	JA	I$_3$-LI$_2$-ŠE-IM-ḪA-IA		VIII 57 14
			ʾIL	I			ŠAMŠ				I$_3$-LI$_2$-SA-MA-AŠ$_2$		M
			ʾIL	I		TA	NWUḪ				I$_3$-LI$_2$-TA-NU-UḪ		XIII 1 IV 19
			ʾIL	I		TA	NWUḪ				I$_3$-LI$_2$-TA-NU		RA LXV 45 V 52
			ʾIL	I			TUWR		A		I$_3$-LI$_2$-TU-RA		M+
			ʾIL	I			TUWR		A	JA	I$_3$-LI$_2$-TU-RA-[I]A		RA LXV 40 I 45
			ʾIL	I			TUWR		I	JA	I$_3$-LI$_2$-TU-RI-IA		XII 115 5+
			ʾIL	I			ṬAJB		A		I$_3$-LI$_2$-DA-[B]A		A. 96 R. 10
			ʾIL	I			ṢADUQ				I$_3$-LI$_2$-ZA-DU-UQ		M+
			ʾIL	I			ṢIDQ		I		I$_3$-LI$_2$-ZI-ID-KI		DELAPORTE CCL II A 337
			ʾIL	I			ṢIDQ		UM		I$_3$-LI$_2$-ZI-ID-KUM		UCP X/1 100 7
			ʾIL	I			ZANN		I		I$_3$-LI$_2$-ZA-AN-NI	FN	M+
	2		ʾAḪ	I			ʾIL		I		A-ḪI-I$_3$-LI$_2$	FN	XIII 1 VIII 20
			JAʾ	U			ʾIL		I		IA-U-I-LI$_2$		SUMER V 143 NO. 2
		JA	HWIJ				ʾIL		I		IA-AḪ-WI-DINGIR-LI$_2$		KISURRA 6+
		JA	HWIJ				ʾIL		I		IA-WI-LI		A 7695 10
			ʾAJAM				ʾIL	T	I		A-IA-AM-IL-TI	FN	XIII 1 X 8
			ʾAB	I			ʾIL		I		A-BI-I$_3$-LI$_2$	FN	RA LXV 59 II 38+
			ʾABB	A			ʾIL		I		AB-BA-I$_3$-LI$_2$	FN	XIII 1 XI 14
			ʾABB	A			ʾIL		I		D-AB-BA-I$_3$-LI$_2$	FN	SIMMONS 112:17
			ʿABD				ʾIL		I		AB-DI-LI		A.+
			ʿAMM	I			ʾIL		I		ḪA-MI-I$_3$-LI$_2$		MDP XXIII 307 16
			ʾUMM	I			ʾIL		I		UM-MI-I$_3$-LI$_2$	FN	XIII 1 VIII 64
			ʾAMAR				ʾIL		I		A-MAR-I$_3$-LI$_2$		MAOG IV 2 3 HANA
			ʾIMIR				ʾIL		I		IM-ME-IR-I$_3$-LI$_2$		UNPUBL.
			ʾANA				ʾIL		I				
							MA				A-NA-I-LIM-MA		A.
		MA	ʾNUP				ʾIL		I		MA-AḪ-NU-UP-I$_3$-LI$_2$		B 33+
			ʿAŠTAR				ʾIL		I		EŠ$_4$-DAR-I$_3$-LI$_2$	FN	RA LXV 56 I 3
		JI	JTAR				ʾIL		I		I-TAR-I-LI		B 23
			ʾITT	A			ʾIL		I		IT-TA-I$_3$-LI$_2$		M
		JA	ʾZIJ				ʾIL		I		IA-AḪ-ZI-I$_3$-LI$_2$		TCL X 21 13
			BAʿL	I			ʾIL		I		BA-AḪ-LI-I$_3$-LI$_2$	FN	M
			BEʿL	I			ʾIL		I		BE-LI$_2$-I$_3$-LI$_2$	FN	RA LXV 64 VI 50
			BIN				ʾIL		I	JA	BI-IN-I-LI$_2$-IA		RA LXIV 24 NO.8
			DAGAN				ʾIL		I		D-DA-GAN-I$_3$-LI$_2$	FN	RA LXV 62 V 51
			KIWN	A			ʾIL		I		KI-NA-I$_3$-LI$_2$		M
			MALAK				ʾIL		I		MA-LA-AK-I$_3$-LI$_2$		M
			NAWḪ				ʾIL		I		NA-ḪI-LI		B 35
			NUʿM	I			ʾIL		I		NU-UḪ-MI-I$_3$-LI$_2$		XIII 1 XIII 26
			NABIʾ				ʾIL		I		NA-BI-I$_3$-LI$_2$		XIII 1 III 61

I	2	JA	NŠIʾ				ʾIL		I		IA-SI-LI		B 29+
		JA	NŠIʾ				ʾIL		I		IA-SI-I-LI$_2$		TCL X 5 3
			RAḤM		I		ʾIL		I		RA-AḪ-MI-I$_3$-LI$_2$		XIII 1 VIII 79+
			RIMŠ		I		ʾIL		I		RI-IM-ŠI-I$_3$-LI$_2$		M
		JA	RŠIJ				ʾIL		I		A-AR-ŠI-DINGIR		TA 1930,7:6
			ŚUMAT				ʾIL		I		SU-MA-AT-I$_3$-LI$_2$		XIII 1 II 85
			ŠIRṬ		I		ʾIL		I		ŠI-IR-TE-I$_3$-LI$_2$		A. LATE
			ŠITAŠ				ʾIL		I		ŠI-IT-TA-AŠ-I$_3$-LI$_2$		MEL. SYR. 994
			TUWR		A		ʾIL		I		TU-RA-I$_3$-LI$_2$		SAUREN, WUG 285 V, U.
			ZAKK				ʾIL		I		ZA-AK-I$_3$-LI$_2$		TA 1931,389 UR III
	3		ḪIʾD				LA			KA			
							ʾIL		I		ḪI-ID-LA-KA-I$_3$-LI$_2$		M
			ʾAB		I		MA						
							ʾIL		I		A-BI-MA-I$_3$-LI$_2$	FN	RA LXV 64 VI 32
			BUN		U		KALA						
							ʾIL		I		BU-NU-KA-LA-I-LI		B 16
			ŚUM		U		LA						
							ʾIL		I		SU-MU-LA-I$_3$-LI$_2$		UCP X/1 34 2
			ŚAMŠ		I		HADD		U				
							ʾIL		I		SA-AM-SI-D-IM-I$_3$-LI$_2$		C+
	2		NABIʾ				ʾILL		I		NA-BI-IL-LI		SYRIA V 274 HANA
	1		ʾILUL		I						I-LU-UL-LI		M
	1		ʾIMIR		I						IM-ME-RI		A.+
	2		NAWḪ		I		ʾIMM		I		D-NA-ḪI-IM-MI		YOS II 112 11
	1		ʾIRAḪ		I						I-RA-ḪI		RA LXV 47 VII 49+
	1		ʾIRR		I		HADD		U		I-RI-A-DU		A.+
			ʾIRR		I		HADD		U		IR-RI-A-DU		A.
			ʾIRR		I		MAʾT		U		I-RI-MA-TU		A.
	1		ʾIŚAL		I						I-SA-LI	GEN	CT VIII 44A+
	1	JA	ʾRUR	IJ	I						IA-AḪ-RU-RI-I-KI	GN	M
	2		LA			ʾA	ʾŚUD		I				
							ʾIL				LA-AḪ-SU-DI-DINGIR		XIII 4 14
	1		ʾUWR		I		HADD		U		U$_2$-RI-A-DU		A.
			ʾUWR		I		HADD		U		WU-RI-A-DU		A.
			ʾUWR		I		JARAḪ				U$_2$-RI-E-RA-AḪ		M
	2		ʾIL		A		ʾUWR		I		DINGIR-U$_2$-RI		RA LXVIII 28:13 MARI
			ʾIL		I		ʾUWR		I		I-LI-U$_2$-RI	FN	A.
	1		ʾUBUŚ		I						U$_2$-BU-SI		M
	1		ʾUMM		I		ḪAʾT		UM		UM-MI-ḪA-TUM	FN	M+
			ʾUMM		I		ʾIL		I		UM-MI-I$_3$-LI$_2$	FN	XIII 1 VIII 64
			ʾUMM		I		JIQR	AH			UM-MI-IQ-RA	FN	M+
			ʾUMM		I		ʾIŠḪAR	AH			UM-MI-IŠ-ḪA-RA	FN	XIII 1 V 74, A.+
			ʾUMM		I		ʾAŠIR	AH			UM-MI-A-ŠI-RA	FN	VAS XIII 73 6,13
			ʾUMM		I		JAT		UM		UM-MI-IA-TUM		UCP X/1 89 24
			ʾUMM		I		BAʿL	AH			UM-MI-BA-A-LA	FN	A. LATE
			ʾUMM		I		MARṢ	AT			UM-MI-MAR-ṢA-AT	FN	XIII 1 III 5
			ʾUMM		I		NAʿM		I		UM-MI-NA-MI	FN	A.
			ʾUMM		I		NAʿM		I		UM-MI-NA-AḪ-ME	FN	RA LXV 59 II 17
			ʾUMM		I		NAHR		U		UM-MI-NA-RU	FN	M
			ʾUMM		I		NAWAR				UM-MI-NA-WA-AR	FN	XIII 1 IV 73
			ʾUMM		I		ŚAMŠ		I		UM-MI-D-UTU-ŠI	FN	RA LXV 65 VII 38
			ʾUMM		I		ṬAJB	AH			UM-MI-ṬA$_3$-BA	FN	M+
			ʾUMM		I		ṬAJB	AH			UM-MI-ṬA$_3$-BA-NU	FN	RA LXV 64 VI 34
	2		ʾAJA				ʾUMM		I		A-IA-UM-MI	FN	RA LXV 59 II 27
		JA	ʾḪIḎ				ʾUMM		I		IA-ḪI-DU-UM-ME	FN	RA LXV 65 VII 34
			ʾALI				ʾUMM		I		A-LI-UM-MI	FN	M
			ʾANN		U		ʾUMM		I		AN-NU-UM-MI	FN	XIII 1 IV 48+
			ʾANN		U		ʾUMM		I		AN-NU-UN-UM-MI		M
			ʾIŠḪAR	AH			ʾUMM		I		D-IŠ-ḪA-RA-UM-MI	FN	XIII 1 II 47+
			ʾAŠR	AT	UM		ʾUMM		I		D-AŠ-RA-TUM-UM-MI	FN	TCL I P. 16+
			ʿAŠTAR				ʾUMM		I		EŠ$_4$-DAR-UM-MI	FN	XIII 1 II 38 +
			TABUB		U		ʾUMM		I		TA-BU-BU-UM-MI	FN	XIII 1 VI 57
	1		ʾUNAB		I						ḪU-NA-BI	NOM	GAUTIER 11 8, R. 2
	2		ḎIMR		U		ʾUP		I		ZI-IM-RU-UḪ$_2$-KI		TCL VII 23 14 21+
			ŚUM		U		ʾUP		I		SU-MU-UḪ$_2$-KI		JCS XI 23 NO. 10 14+
		JA	ŚMAʿ				ʾUP		I		IA-AŠ$_2$-MA-ḪU-PI		BULL. ACAD. BELG. 1974 228

SUFFIXES, Class 2

I	2	BEʿL		I		ʾUŠIL		I		BE-LI$_2$-U$_2$-SI-LI	FN	RA LXV 56 I 10
	1	ʾUŠŠ	AT	I		ʾEL				UŠ-SA-TE-EL		TIM III 43 6
	2	ʿABD				ʾUTL		I		AB-DU-UT-LI	FN	A. LATE
	1	ʾUZUL		I						U$_2$-ZU-UL-LI	FN	XIII 1 III 66
	2	MUT				HADD		I		MU-TA-AD-DI		VAS XVI 165:4
	1	HELAL		I						E-LA-LI		RA LXV 50 IX 25
	1	ḪAJJ	AN	I						ḪA-IA-A-NI		JNES XIII 210FF.+ LATE
	1	ḪABIS	AN	I						ḪA-BI-ZA-NI	GEN	CT VIII 42 B 17
	1	ḪALAṢ		I						A-LA-ṢI		4E RENC. ASS. P. 178 2
	1	ḪAM		I		....				D-A-MI-[....]		M
		ḪAM		I		JATAR				D-A-MI-I[AR]?		M
		ḪAM		I	JI	JBAL				D-A-MI-I-BA-AL		M+
		ḪAM		I	JE	JŠUʿ				D-A-MI-E-ŠU-UḪ		M+
		ḪAM		I	JE	JŠUʿ				A-MI-E-ŠU-UḪ		M+
		ḪAM		I		MALIK				A-MI-MA-LIK		C
		ḪAM		I		ŠAMUʿ				D-A-MI-SA-MU-UḪ		M+
		ḪAM		I	TA	NWUḪ				D-A-MI-TA-NU-UḪ		M+
		ḪAM		I	TA	NWUḪ				D-A-MI-TA-NU		M
		ḪAM		I	TA	NWUḪ		A		D-A-MI-TA-NU-A		M
		ḪAM		I		ṬAJB		I		A-MI-ṬA-BI		RA LXV 45 V 81
		ḪAM		I		ṢABṬ		I		A-MI-ZA-AB-TI	MN	B 13
		ḪAM		I		ṢABṬ		I		A-MI-ZA-AB-TI	FN	CT VIII 35 B 1
	2	ʿABD				ḪAM		I		AB-DI-A-MI		BAGHD. MITT. II 58 III 21
		ʿABD				ḪAM		I		ḪA-AB-DU-D-A-MI		M+
		ʿABD				ḪAM		I		ḪA-AB-DU-A-MI		M
		JATAR				ḪAM		I		IA-TAR-D-A-MI		M+
		BUN		U		ḪAM		I		BU-NU-D-A-MI		M+
		KALB				ḪAM		I		K[A]-AL-BU-D-A-MI		XIII 1 X 20
		MUT		U		ḪAM		I		MU-TU-D-A-MI		RA LXV 51 IX 49
		QAWL		A		ḪAM		I		QA-LA-D-A-M[I]		M
		QAWL		U		ḪAM		I		QA-L[U]-D-A-MI		M
		ŠUM		U		ḪAM		I		SU-MU-A-MI		M
	3	LA				RIWM						
						ḪAM		I		LA-RI-IM-D-A-MI		M
	2 JA	MWUT				ḪAMAD		I		IA-MU-UT-ḪA-MA-DI	FN	XIII 1 VI 51
	1	ḪANN		I		ʾIL				AN-NI-DINGIR		B 13+, M
		ḪANN		I		ʾIL				ḪA-AN-NI-DINGIR	FN	XIII 1 II 7
		ḪANN		I		ʾIL		A		ḪA-AN-NI-I-LA		A. LATE
		ḪANN		I	JI	JŠAR				AN-NI-I-ŠAR?		M
		ḪANN		I		KAʾB		I		A[N-N]I-KA-BI	FN	RA LXV 62 V 17
		ḪANN		I		....				ḪA-AN-NI-D-NIN-ŠE-X-RA?	FN	RA LXV 61 IV 63
	2	ʾANA				ḪANN		I		A-NA-AḪ-ḪA-AN-NI	FN	XIII 1 V 29
		ʾANN		U		ḪANN		I		AN-NU-ḪA-AN-NI	FN	M+
	1	ḪARB		I		TUWR		AM		AR-BI-TU-RA-AM		BIROT, TEA 65:35
	2	ʾADM		U		ḪAṢN		I		D-AD-MU-ḪA-AZ-NI	FN	RA LXV 61 IV 21
		ʾIL		I		ḪAṢN		I	JA	I$_3$-LI$_2$-ḪA-AṢ-NI-IA		XIII 1 IX 8
		ʾANN		U		ḪAṢN		I		AN-NU-ḪA-AṢ-NI	FN	M+
		ʿAŠTAR				ḪAṢN		I		EŠ$_4$-DAR-ḪA-AZ-NI	FN	XIII 1 II 41
		MAM		A		ḪAṢN		I		D-MA-MA-ḪA-AZ-NI	FN	RA LXV 56 I 7
		TABUB		U		ḪAṢN		I		TA-BU-BU-ḪA-AṢ-NI	FN	RA LXV 60 III 19
	2	MUT		U		ḪATK		I		MU-TU-ḪA-AD-KI		M
		TURUM			NA	ḪATK		I		TU-RUM-NA-AT-KI		M+
	1 TA	ḪBAS		I						TA-AḪ-PA-ZI		A. 28 4, 17
	1	ḪIMD		I		MALIK				ḪI-IM-DI-MA-LIK		M
	1	ḪINN		I		BAWŠ	AT			E-NI-BA-ŠA-AT		ICK 113 10 CAPP.
		ḪINN		I		BAWŠ	AT	A		E-NI-BA-ŠA-TA		KTS 47C 1 CAPP.
		ḪINN		I		HADD		U		IN-NI-D-IM		A.
		ḪINN		I		ʾIL				ḪI-IN-NE-DINGIR		XIII 1 I 53
		ḪINN		I		ʿAŠTAR				EN-NI-D-EŠ$_4$-DAR		A. 247 23
		ḪINN		I		BAJN	AH			IN-NI-BA-NA	FN NOM	X 81 4
	2	NAPŠ		I		ḪINN		I		NA-AP-SI-IN-NI	FN	XIII 1 IV 72
		ŠUM		I		ḪINN		I		ŠU-MI-IN-NI		U
	2	ʿAN		UM		ḪIRB		I		A-NU-UM-ḪI-IR-BI		BALKAN, LETTER P. 6
	1	ḪIṢN		I						ḪI-IZ-NI		B 20 HANA
		ḪIṢN		I		DAGAN				ḪI-IZ-NI-D-DA-GAN		B 20+ HANA
	1	ḪUMAD		I						ḪU-MA-DI		PINCHES, PEEK 1 4

I	2		ʾIL		I		ḪUMUD	I		I$_3$-LI$_2$-ḪU-MU-DI		M
	2		ʾIL		I		ḪUNIN	I		I$_3$-LI$_2$-U$_2$-NE-NI		RUTTEN 6 20
	2		ʾAB		I		ḪUNN	I		A-BI-ḪU-UN?-NI		B 10
	1		ḪUNUN		I		ʾEL			U$_2$-NU-NI-EL		B 40
			ḪUNUN		I		ʾIL			U$_2$-NU-NI-DINGIR		PBS XI/2 P. 125 NO. 347
	2		ʿAMM		U		ḪURB	I		AM-MU-UR-BI		A.
			ʾAN		I	Š	ḪURB	I		A-NI-IŠ-ḪU-UR-BI		M+
	1		ḪUṢAN		I					ḪU-ZA-NI	NOM	B 45
	1		ḪAʾL		I		HADD	U		ḪA-LI$_2$-D-IM		M+
			ḪAʾL		I		HADD	U		ḪA-LI-A-DU		A.+
			ḪAʾL		I		HADD	U		ḪA-LI-IA-[D]U		M
			ḪAʾL		I		ʿADN			ḪA-LI-ḪA-DU-UN		M+
			ḪAʾL		I		ʿADN			ḪA-LI$_2$-ḪA-DU-UN		M+
			ḪAʾL		I		ʿADN			ḪA-LI-ḪA-DU-UM?		M
			ḪAʾL		I		ʿADN	U	HU	ḪA-LI-ḪA-AD-NU-U$_2$		M
			ḪAʾL		I		ʿAḎIR	UM		ḪA-LI-A-ṢI-RUM		UNPUBL.
			ḪAʾL		I		ʾIL			ḪA-LI$_2$-DINGIR		B 18
			ḪAʾL		I		ʾEL			ḪA-LI$_2$-EL		RA LXV 42 III 18+
			ḪAʾL		I		ʾEL			ḪA-A-LI$_2$-EL		RA LXV 42 III 20
			ḪAʾL		I		ʾIL	U	HU	ḪA-A-LI$_2$-I-LU-U$_2$		X 146 5
			ḪAʾL		I		ʿAŠTAR			ḪA-LI$_2$-EŠ$_4$-DAR		RA LXV 53 XII 1
			ḪAʾL		I		KUPAPA			ḪA-LI$_2$-KU-BA-BA	FN	RA LXV 58 I 14
			ḪAʾL		I		MA			ḪA-LI-MA	FN	RA LXV 59 II 43
			ḪAʾL		I		MA					
							ʾIL			ḪA-LI$_2$-MA-DINGIR		M
			ḪAʾL		I		MALIK			ḪA-LI$_2$-MA-LIK		M+
			ḪAʾL		I		MAMM	A		ḪA-LI$_2$-D-M[A-A]M-M[A]		M
			ḪAʾL		I		MARAṢ			ḪA-LI-MA-RA-AṢ		GEN, KICH I P. 59 NO. 219
			ḪAʾL		I		MARAṢ			ḪA-LI-MA-RA-AṢ		UET V 521 1
			ḪAʾL		I	MU	WTAR			ḪA-LI$_2$-MU-TAR		M
			ḪAʾL		I		ŠADW	A		ḪA-LI-SA-DA		B 19
			ḪAʾL		I	TA	NWUḪ	A		ḪA-LI-TA-NU-A		A.+
	2		MUT				ḪAʾL	I		MU-UT-ḪA-LI		B 35 HANA
			MUT				ḪAʾL	I				
							MA			MU-UT-ḪA-LI-MA		M
		Š	NUʾR				ḪAʾL	I		ŠU-NU-UR-ḪA-LI		KING LIH I 22 4, R. 2
			ŠUWB				ḪAʾL	I		SU-UB-ḪA-LI		A. 268 5
			ŠUWB		A		ḪAʾL	I		ŠU-BA-ḪA-LI		A. 97 16, 18+
			ŠUWB		A		ḪAʾL	I		SU-BA-ḪA-LI		A. 6 29
			ŠUWB		A		ḪAʾL	I		SU-PA-ḪA-LI		A. 252 12+
	1		ḪAʾR		I		ʾIL			ḪA-RI-DINGIR		BM 82372 27
			ḪAʾR		I		ʾATT	A		ḪA-RI-A-TA		C II 5 7
			ḪAʾR		I		MALIK			ḪA-RI-MA-LIK		BE VI/1 46 5
			ḪAʾR		I		MALIK	I		ḪA-RI-MA-LI-KI	GEN	B 20
	1		ḪABUR		I					ḪA-BU-UR-RI	FN	RA LXV 63 III 1
	1		ḪALAN		I		JATAR			ḪA-LA-NI-E-TAR		M
	1		ḪAMAṮ		I		ʾIL			ḪA-MA-TI-IL		FIGULLA, CAT. I 14135
	1		ḪANAŠ		I					ḪA-NA-ŠI	GEN	HARRIS 3916
	1		ḪANZ		I					ḪA-AN-ZI		TA 1931, 434
	2 JA		KWUN				ḪARAR	I		IA-KU-[UN-ḪA]-RA-RI	GEN	BM 81641 6
	JA		KWUN				ḪARAR	I		IA-KUN$_3$-ḪA-RA-RI		CT XLVIII 3:3
	JI		KWUN				ḪARAR	I		I-KU-UN-ḪA-RA-RI?	GEN	TCL I 151 4
	1		ḪIBAR	AT	I					ḪI-BA-RA-TI	MN NOM	VIII 6 31
	2		KUʾŠ		I		ḪIMR	I		KU-ŠI-ḪI-IM-RI		SIMMONS 87 19
	1		ḪINIʾ		I					ḪI-NI-I		XII 1 VIII 51
	1		ḪUBAD		I					ḪU-PA-DI		EDZARD, DER 101:12
	2		ḪUNN				ḪUPŠ	I		ḪU-UN-ḪU-UP-ŠE		U
	2		MUT		I		ḪURŠAN	I		MU-TI-ḪU-UR-ŠA-NI		YOS XII
	1		ḪUZAM		I					ḪU-ZA-MI		BE VI/2 138 18
	2		ŠU				ʿABD	I		ŠU-ḪA-AB-DI		CT XLVIII 43:15,19
	2		ŠUM		U		ʿAD	I		SU-MU-ḪA-DI-I	GEN	XIII 13:8
	1		ʿADN		I		HADD	U		ḪA-AD-NI-D-IM		M, C+
			ʿADN		I		HADD	U		ḪA-AD-NI-A-D[U]		DELAPORTE CCL II A 914
			ʿADN		I		ʾIL			ḪA-AD-NI-DINGIR		M+
			ʿADN		I		ʾIL	U				
							MA			ḪA-AD-NI-DINGIR-MA		M

I	1	ʿADN	I				ʿAMM		U		ḪA-AD-NI-ḪA-MU		RA LXV 50 VIII 49
		ʿADN	I				JARAḪ				ḪA-AD-NI-E-RA-AḪ		M
		ʿADN	I				DAGAN				ḪA-AD-NI-D-DA-GAN		M
		ʿADN	I				ŠAMŠ				ḪA-AD-NI-SA-MA-AŠ$_2$		M
	2	ʾIL	I				ʿADN		I		I$_3$-LI$_2$-ḪA-AD-NI	FN	M
	JI	JTAR					ʿADN		I		I-TAR-AD-AN		WATERMAN 41 R. 10
		D̲U					ʿADN		I		ZU-ḪA-AD-NI	NOM	M+
		D̲U					ʿADN		I		ZU-ḪA-AD-NI	GEN	M+
		LA					ʿADN		I	JA	LA-AD-NI-IA		M
	1	ʿAD̲R	I				JAḪAD				AD-RI-E-ḪA-AD		M+
		ʿAD̲R	I				ḪAʾT		UM		AD-RI-ḪA-TUM		SIMMONS 88 16+
		ʿAD̲R	I				HADD		U		AD-RI-A-DU		A.+
		ʿAD̲R	I				HADD		U		AD-RI-IA-DU		KUPPER, NOM. 231
		ʿAD̲R	I				HAND		U		AD-RI-IA-AN-DU		KUPPER, NOM. 231
		ʿAD̲R	I				HAND		U		ḪA-AD-RI-IA-AN-DU		KUPPER, NOM. 231
		ʿAD̲R	I				ʿAMM		IM		ḪA-AZ-RI-A-MI-IM	GEN	M
	2	ʾAB	I				ʿAD̲R		I		A-BI-AD-RI		A. LATE
		ŠINI					ʿAD̲R		I		ŠI-NI-AD-RI		M
	2	ʾAB	I				ʿALAṢ		I		AD-ḪA-LA-ZI	FN	C
		ʾAB	I				ʿALAṢ		I		A-BI-ḪA-LA-ZI	FN	M, C II 49 6
	JA	KWUN					ʿALAṢ		I		IA-KU-UN-ḪA-LA-ZI		RA LXV 44 IV 41;43
	1	ʿAMM	I				....				AM-MI-....-LU-UB		A. 95 85
		ʿAMM	I				HADD		U		AM-MI-A-DU		A. 60 14
		ʿAMM	I				HADD		U		AM-MI-IA-A-DU		A.
		ʿAMM	I				HADD		U		AM-MI-AD-DU		A. 267 17
		ʿAMM	I				HEDD		A		AM-MI-E-DA		A.
		ʿAMM	I				ʿADN		A		AM-MI-ḪA-AD-NA		GOETZE, KIZZ. P. 8, LATE
		ʿAMM	I				ʾAK		I		AM-MI-E-KI		A.
		ʿAMM	I				ʾIL		I		ḪA-MI-I$_3$-LI$_2$		MDP XXIII 307 16
		ʿAMM	I				ʿAN	AT			ḪA-MI-D-ḪA-NA-AT		M
		ʿAMM	I				ʾANDUL		I		ḪA-AM-MI-AN-DUL$_3$-LI$_2$		M+
		ʿAMM	I				JAŠAR				ḪA-AM-MI-E-SA-AR?		M
		ʿAMM	I				JAT		UM		AM-MI-IA-TUM		A. 273 14
		ʿAMM	I				JATAR				ḪA-AM-MI-A-TAR		B 19+
		ʿAMM	I				JATAR				ḪA-AM-MA-TA-AR		B 19
		ʿAMM	I				JATAR				A-MA-TA-AR		WALTERS, WL 109:9
		ʿAMM	I		JI		JBAL				ḪA-MI-I-BA-AL		M
		ʿAMM	I		JE		JPUʿ				ḪA-MI-E-PU-UḪ		M+
		ʿAMM	I		JE		JPUʿ				ḪA-AM-MI-E-PU-UḪ		M+
		ʿAMM	I		JE		JŠUʿ				ḪA-MI-E-ŠU-UḪ		M
		ʿAMM	I				DAGAN				ḪA-MI-D-DA-GAN		RA LXV 53 XI 33
		ʿAMM	I				DANN		U		AM-MI-DA-NU		YOS XII
		ʿAMM	I				DAŠUR				AM-MI-DA-ŠUR?		A 7894
		ʿAMM	I				DUŠUR				ḪA-MI-DU-ŠU-UR		SIMMONS 46 18+
		ʿAMM	I				DUŠUR				ḪA-MI-DU-ŠU-UR$_2$		SIMMONS 50 14
		ʿAMM	I				DUŠUR				ḪA-AM-MI-DU-ŠU-UR		HARRIS 18 15+
		ʿAMM	I				DUŠUR				ḪA-AM-MI-DU-ŠU-UR$_2$		HARRIS 27 17+
		ʿAMM	I				DUŠUR				AM-MI-DU-ŠU-UR		A7894+
		ʿAMM	I				DITAN		A		AM-MI-DI-TA-NA		B13+
		ʿAMM	I				DITAN		A		AM-MI-TE-TA-NA		CT XLV 44 24
		ʿAMM	I				KUWN				ḪA-MI-KU-UN		RA LXV 54 XII 15
		ʿAMM	I				MAṬAR				AM-MI-MA-DAR		B 13 HANA
		ʿAMM	I				MAṬAR				ḪA-MI-MA-DAR	FN	C
		ʿAMM	I				RAPIʾ				AM-MI-RA-PI		SYRIA XXXVII 206 END HANA
		ʿAMM	I				RAPIʾ				AM-MI-RA-BI-IḪ		RA XXXIV 186 HANA
		ʿAMM	I				RAPIʾ				ḪA-AM-MI-RA-BI		B 19
		ʿAMM	I	Š			ḪARIJ			JE	AM-MI-IS-ḪA-RI?-E?		JEAN, S'A CLXXXVIII R. 3
		ʿAMM	I		JI	T	ŠAMAR				ḪA-AM-MI-IŠ-TA-MAR		M+
		ʿAMM	I		JI	T	ŠAMAR				AM-MI-IŠ-TA-MAR		M
		ʿAMM	I		JI	T	ŠAMAR		U		AM-MI-IŠ-TAM-RU		MRS VI P. 329 UGARIT+
		ʿAMM	I		JI	T	ŠAMAR		U		AM-MI-IS-TAM-RU		MRS VI P. 239 UGARIT+
		ʿAMM	I				ŠAGIŠ				ḪA-AM-MI-ŠA-GI-IŠ		M+
		ʿAMM	I				ŠAGIŠ				AM-MI-ŠA-GI-IŠ		M
		ʿAMM	I				ŠUM		U		AM-MI-SU-MU		CT XLVIII 61 4,5
		ʿAMM	I				ŠUM		U	HU	ḪA-AM-MI-SU-MU-U$_2$		CT XLVII 30 44
		ʿAMM	I		TA		QWIM				ḪA-AM-MI-TA-KI-IM	NOM	M

SUFFIXES, Class 2

I	1	ʿAMM		I	TA	QWUM				AM-MI-TA-KU-UM		A.+
		ʿAMM		I	TA	QWUM						
						MA				AM-MI-TA-KU-UM-MA		A. +
		ʿAMM		I		ṬAJB		A		AM-MI-ṬA-BA		A.+
		ʿAMM		I		ṬALL		U	HU	ḪA-MI-TI-LU-U_2		M
		ʿAMM		I		ṬALL		U	HU	ḪA-AM-MI-TA-LU-U_2		M+
		ʿAMM		I		ṬALL		U	HU	ḪA-AM-MI-TI-LU-U_2		M+
		ʿAMM		I		ṬILL		U	HU	ḪA-AM-MI-TE-LU-U_2		RA LXVI 118:15
		ʿAMM		I		ZUʾG		U	HU	ḪA-AM-MI-ZU-GU-U_2		BM 17045+
		ʿAMM		I		ṢUWR		A		AM-MI-ZU-RA		CT XLVIII 90 REV.
		ʿAMM		I		ZAʾT		I		ḪA-MI-ZA-TI		HARRIS 103 1
		ʿAMM		I		ṢADUQ				ḪA-MI-ZA-DU-[UQ]		M
		ʿAMM		I		ṢADUQ				ḪA-AM-MI-ZA-DU-UQ		M
		ʿAMM		I		ṢADUQ		A		AM-MI-ZA-DU-GA		B 13+
		ʿAMM		I		ṢADUQ		A				
						....				AM-MI-ZA-DU-GA-I-LU-NI		B 13+
		ʿAMM		I		ZAKK		UM		AM-MI-ZA-KU-UM		IRAQ IV 185, A 385
		ʿAMM		I		ZAKK		U	HU	ḪA-AM-MI-ZA-KU-U_2		M
	2 JA	WMAʾ				ʿAMM	AJ	I		IA-AW-MA-ḪA-MA-JI-KI	GN	M
	JA	WMAʾ				ʿAMM		I		JA-MA-ḪA-MI-KI	GN	M
		ʾUŠM		A		ʿAMM		I		UŠ-MA-AM-MI		CT XXXIII 46A 4
		ʿAZZ				ʿAMM		I		AZ-ZA-AM-MI		A. 265 19
		BIN		A		ʿAMM		I		BI-NA-AM-MI		B 15
		BUN		U		ʿAMM		I		BU-NU-ḪA-AM-MI	FN	M+
		ḎAKIR		A		ʿAMM		I		ZA-KI-RA-ḪA-MI		M
		ḎIMR		U		ʿAMM		I		ZI-IM-RU-ḪA-AM-MI		B 42
		KIʾL		I		ʿAMM		I		KI-LI-AM-MI	GEN	MRS XVI 12:2
		ŠUWB		A		ʿAMM		I		ŠU-BA-AM-MI		A. 270 22
		TUWR		U		ʿAMM		I		DUR-RU-AM-MI		MAOG IV 2 6 HANA
	1	ʿAN	AT	I	JI	JBAL				ḪA-NA-TI-I-BA-AL		RA LXV 40 I 12
	2	ʿABD				ʿAN	AT	I		AB-TA-NA-TI		A. P. 128A LATE +
		ʿABD				ʿAN	AT	I		AB-DI-A-NA-TI		A. P. 128B LATE +
		ʿABD				ʿAN	AT	I		AB-TI-A-NA-TI		JCS XIII 54 300, A. LATE
		BUN		U		ʿAN	AT	I		BU-NU-A-NA-TI		B 16
	1 ME	ʿANIJ		I						ME-ḪA-A-NI?	GEN	VAS VIII 14 43
	1	ʿAQB		I		ʾAḪ		U		AQ-BI-A-ḪU		B 11
		ʿAQB		I		ʾIL				AQ-BI-IL		B 11
		ʿAQB		I		ʾIL				AQ-BI-DINGIR		BIN VII 156 10+
		ʿAQB		I		NAN		UM		AQ-BI-NA-NU-UM		B 42+
	1	ʿAQUB		I		ʾEL				A-KU-PI-EL		GORDON 38 16
	1	ʿAZAB	AN	I						A-ZA-BA-NI		TA 1931, 216
	1	ʿAZZ		I		ʾIL				A-ZI-DINGIR		HARRIS 39 11
		ʿAZZ		I		DAGAN				A-ZI-D-DA-GAN		A. LATE
	1 JA	ʿḎIR		I						IA-AḪ-ZI-RI	GEN	BM 16943 34
	ME	ʿḎIR		I						ME-ZI-RI		M
	1	ʿEMUQ		I		ʾEL				E-[M]U-QI_2-EL		RA LXV 40 I 3
	2	TABUB				ʿIMD		I		TA-BU-UB-IM-[DI]?	FN	VIII 33 7
		TABUB		I		ʿIMD		I		TA-BU-TI?-IM-DI	FN	VIII 31 10 15
	1	ʿINB		I		ʾIL				IN-BI_2-IL		U UNPUBL.
		ʿINB		I		JARAḪ				IN-BI-RA-AḪ		KISURRA 6 15
	1	ʿIQB		I		HADD		U		IQ-BI-D-IM		KISURRA 114 7
	1	ʿIZIL		I						ḪI-ZI-LI		C II 45 II 35
	1	ʿIZZ	AN	I						IZ-ZA-NI		M
		ʿIZZ		I						ḪU-IZ-ZI	FN	M
	1 JA	ʿQUB		I		ʾIL				IA-AḪ-KU-BI-DINGIR		CT II 39 18
	JA	ʿQUB		I		ʾIL				IA-KU-BI-DINGIR		KISURRA 41 10
	1	ʿUZUL		I						U_2-ZU-LI		RA LXV 51 X 6
	1 JA	ʿZIB		I		ʾIL				IA-AḪ-ZI-BI-DINGIR		KISURRA 86A 11
	JA	ʿZIB		I		ʾIL				A-AḪ-ZI-BI-DINGIR		SIMMONS 70 5
	JA	ʿZIB		I		ʾIL				IA-A-ZI-BI-DINGIR		KAJ 34 18, 25 LATE
	1 MU	WPIʿ		I						MU-BI-ḪI		TA 30, 7 10
	1 ʾU	WŠIʿ		I						U_2-SI-I		I+
	1	JAʾIT		I	JI	JBAL				IA-I-TI-I-BA-AL		M
	1	JAʿIL	AJ	I						JA-I-LA-JI-KI	GN	M
		JAʿIL	AN	I						JA-I-LA-NI	TRIBE	SHEMSHARA F.100
	1	JABAŠ	IJ	I						JA-BA-SI-JI	TRIBE	M

I	1		JABAŠ	IJ	I							JA-BA-SI-I	TRIBE	M
	1		JAD		I			NAṢIR				IA-DI-NA-ṢIR		BM 17051, 17052
	1		JAKAL	ITIJI								[JA]-KA-LI-TI-I	TRIBE GEN	M
	1		JAMIN		I							IA-MI-NI	TRIBE	M
	1		JARAN		I							JA-RA-A-NI	FN	A. 21 9
	1		JAT		I			ʾIL				IA-TI-DINGIR		B 31
			JAT		I			ʾAMAN				IA-TI-ḪA-MA-AN	FN	RA LXV 42 II 55
	2		ʾAB		U			JAT		I	JA	A-BU-IA-TI-IA		TCL I 85 10
			ʾILL		A			JAT		I		IL-LA-I-IA-TI	FN NOM	XIII 1 IX 51
	1		JATAR		I							IA-TA-RI	GEN	M
	1		JATT		I			HADD		U		IA-AT-TI-D-IM		M
	1 JA		JBIL		I			....				IA-BI-LI-[....]		FM 3998 SEAL
	1		JID		I							I-DI		RA LXV 40 I 22
			JID		I			ʾIL				I-DI-DINGIR		M
			JID		I			JAT		UM		I-DI-IA-TUM		M
	1		JIRʾ		I							JI-IR-I	TRIBE	IX 248 15'
	1		JIŠʿ	AT	I							IŠ-A-TI	MN? GEN	PBS VIII/2 238 5, 8
			JIŠʿ		I			JABAL				IŠ-ḪI-E-BA-AL		M
			JIŠʿ		I			HADD		U		IŠ-ḪI-D-IM		M+, C+
			JIŠʿ		I			HEDD		A		IŠ-ḪI-E-D-IM		TIM IV 33 SEAL, 34 SEAL
			JIŠʿ		I			ʾIL				IŠ-ḪI-DINGIR		WALTERS, WL 109:5+
			JIŠʿ		I			ʾIL		A				
								MA				IŠ-ḪI-DINGIR-MA		M
			JIŠʿ		I			ʾIL		A				
								MA				IŠ-ḪI-DINGIR-LA-MA		M
			JIŠʿ		I			ʾIL		U				
								MA				IŠ-ḪI-LU-MA		YOS VIII 176 20
			JIŠʿ		I			ʾIL		U	NA	IŠ-ḪI-LU-NA		VII 215 33
			JIŠʿ		I			ʿAN		UM		IŠ-ḪI-A-NU-UM		B 45
			JIŠʿ		I			JARAḪ				IŠ-ḪI-E-RA-AḪ		RA LXV 41 II 25
			JIŠʿ		I			JARAḪ				IŠ-I-RA-AḪ		TIM III 28 12
			JIŠʿ		I			DAGAN				IŠ-ḪI-D-DA-GAN		M+
			JIŠʿ		I			LI						
								ʾEL				IŠ-ḪI-LI-EL		JCS XXIV 69 NO. 3 SEAL
			JIŠʿ		I			LIʾM				IŠ-ḪI-LI-IM		M
			JIŠʿ		I			MAṬAR				IŠ-ḪI-MA-DAR		V 40 5, 16
			JIŠʿ		I			NABUʾ		UM		IŠ-ḪI-NA-BU-U[M]		EDZARD, DER 68 III 6
	1 JI		JŠAR		I							I-ŠA-RI	FN	A.
	2		ʾALI					ʾAḪ		I		A-LI_2-A-ḪI	FN	RA LXV 59 II 41
	1	T	BAḪR		I							BA-TA-AḪ-RI	GEN	M+
	1		BAʿD		I			HADD		U		BA-AḪ-DI-D-IM		M+
			BAʿD		I			ʾEL				[BA]-AḪ-DI-EL		KISURRA 51 10
			BAʿD		I			LIʾM				BA-AḪ-DI-LI-IM		M+
	2		BAʿL		U			BAʿD		I		BA-AḪ-LU-BA-DI		EA
	1		BAʿL		I							BA-AḪ-LI		M
			BAʿL		I			....				BA-AḪ-LI-RA-[....]	FN	M
			BAʿL		I			HADD		U		BA-AḪ-LI-D-IM		M+
			BAʿL		I			HADD		U		BA-LI-D-IM		M
			BAʿL		I			ʾIL				BA-AḪ-LI-DINGIR		B 15
			BAʿL		I			ʾIL				BA-LI-DINGIR		EDZARD, DER 68 IV 7
			BAʿL		I			ʾIL		I		BA-AḪ-LI-I_3-LI_2	FN	M
			BAʿL		I			JARAḪ				BA-LI-A-RA-AḪ		SIMMONS 58 11
			BAʿL		I			JARAḪ				BA-LI-E-RA-AḪ		M+, TCL XVIII 92 1+
			BAʿL		I			JARAḪ				BA-LI-RA-AḪ		TCL XVIII 94 1 14+
			BAʿL		I		JA	JPUʿ				BA-LI-A-PU-UḪ		HARRIS 96 6+
			BAʿL		I		JA	JPUʿ				BA-LI-PU-$UḪ_2$		EDZARD, DER 117:38 DATE
			BAʿL		I		JE	JPAʿ				BA-LI-E-PA		A.
			BAʿL		I			BAWŠ	T	I		BA-AḪ-LI-BA-AŠ-TI	FN	M+
			BAʿL		I			DIWR		I		BA-AḪ-LI-DI-RI	FN	C+
			BAʿL		I			NIWR		I		BA-AḪ-LI-NI-RI	FN	M+
			BAʿL		I	Š		ʾAG		UM		BA-LI-IŠ-A-GU-UM		RA LXV 45 V 36
			BAʿL		I			ŠAMŠ		I		BA-AḪ-LI-D-UTU-ŠI	FN	M
			BAʿL		I			ŠAPAR				BA-AḪ-LI-SA-PA-AR	FN	M+
			BAʿL		I			ŠAPAR				BA-AḪ-LI-SA-PAR_2	FN	M, C+
			BAʿL		I			ṬAJB				BA-LI-SIG5?	FN	XIII 1 VIII 36
	2		ʿIJN					BAʿL		I		IN-BA-AḪ-LI	FN	A.

I	2	ʿABD				BAʿL	AT	I		ḪA-AB-DU-BA-AḪ-LA-TI		M+
		HADD		U		BAʿL		I		D-IM-BA-AḪ-LI		M+
	JI	ʾKUR				BAʿL		I		I-KU-UR-BA-LI		EDZARD, DER 102:9
		ʾATTA				BAʿL		I		AT-TA-BA-AḪ-LI		JCS XIII 51 293:8,A. LATE
		ʾATTA				BAʿL		I	JE	AT-TA-BA-AḪ-LI-E		JCS XIII 51 293:15,A.LATE
	JI	KWUN				BAʿL		I		I-KU-UN-BA-LI		A.
	JI	KWUN				BAʿL		I		I-KU-UN-BA-AḪ-LI		A. 246 33
	JA	MWUT				BAʿL	AJ	I		IA-MU-UT-BA-LA-I	GN NOM	M
	JA	MWUT				BAʿL	AJ	I		IA-MU-UT-BA-LA-JI	GN NOM	M
	JA	MWUT				BAʿL	IJ	I		IA-MU-UT-BA-LI-I	GN ACC	M
	JI	ŠMAʿ				BAʿL		I		IŠ-ME-BA-LI		HARRIS 71 6+
		ŠAMŠ		U		BAʿL		I		SA-AM-SU-BA-AḪ-LI		ABB I 59 8
		ṢILL				BAʿL		I		MI-NI-BA-AḪ-LI		M+
	3	LA				RIWM						
						BAʿL		I		LA-RI-IM-BA-AḪ-LI		M+
	1	BAWB		I		ḪAJJ		A		D-BA-BI-E$_2$-A?		VIII 31 7
	2	ʾIL		A		BAWB		I	JA	DINGIR-BA-BI-A		UET V 263 17
	3	ŠUM		U		ʾIL						
						BAWB		I	JA	[SU-MU-I]L-BA-BI-IA		PBS XI/2 1 I 11
	1	BAWŠ	T	I		NUṢR		I		BA-AŠ-TI-NU-IZ-RI	FN	RA LXV 58 I 45
		BAWŠ	T	I		NUṢR		I		BA-AŠ-TI-UZ-RI		RA LXIV 28 NO. 15
		BAWŠ	T	I		NUṢR		I		BA-AŠ$_2$-TI-NU-UZ-RI	FN	XIII 1 VII 24
	2	ʾIL		I		BAWŠ	T	I		I$_3$-LI$_2$-BA-AŠ$_2$-TI	FN	M+
		ʾANN		U		BAWŠ	T	I		AN-NU-BA-AŠ-TI	FN	RA LXV 65 VII 27
		BAʿL		I		BAWŠ	T	I		BA-AḪ-LI-BA-AŠ-TI	FN	M+
		BEʿL		I		BAWŠ	T	I		BE-LI$_2$-[B]A-AŠ-TI	FN	RA LXV 60 III 42
		DAGAN				BAWŠ	T	I		D-DA-GAN-BA-AŠ-TI	FN	M+
		KIWN		I		BAWŠ		I		KI-NI-BA-ŠI	FN	HARRIS 45 8
		KIWN		U		BAWŠ		I		KI-NU-BA-ŠI		LANGDON XXVIII 12
		ŠARR		UM		BAWŠ	T	I		LUGAL-BA-AŠ-TI	FN	M
		ŠARR		UM		BAWŠ	T	I		LUGAL-BA-AŠ$_2$-TI	FN	M+
	1	BAWZ		I		ʿAŠTAR				BA-ZI-EŠ$_4$-DAR		M
	1	BAKS		I						BA-AK-ZI	NOM	BASOR 95 P.23
	1	BAKUS		I						BA-KU-ZI		RA LXV 55 XIII 43
	1	BALAL	AT	I						BA-LA-LA-TI		TA 1930, 399+
		BALAṮ		I		ʾEL				BA-LA-TI-EL		RUTTEN 5 21
	2	ʾADM		U		BALAṮ		I		D-AD-MU-BA-LA-TI?	FN	M
	1	BALIK		I						BA-LI-KI	GEN	A.
	1	BEʿD		I		ʾIL	UM			BE-DI-LU-UM		TIM III 62 6+
		BEʿD		I		ʾIL	UM			BE-DI-LUM		TIM III 61 15
		BEʿD		I		ʾIL				BE-DI-DINGIR		TIM III 130 11+
	1	BEʿL	AK	I						BE-LA-KI	GEN	CT VIII 31B 23+
		BEʿL		I		ʾAHL		I		BE-LI-IA-LI$_2$		KISURRA 112 14
		BEʿL		I		HADD		U		BE-LI$_2$-D-IM		RA LXV 52 X 39
		BEʿL		I		ʾIL		I		BE-LI$_2$-I$_3$-LI$_2$	FN	RA LXV 64 VI 50
		BEʿL		I		ʾUŠIL		I		BE-LI$_2$-U$_2$-SI-LI	FN	RA LXV 56 I 10
		BEʿL		I		BAWŠ	T	I		BE-LI$_2$-[B]A-AŠ-TI	FN	RA LXV 60 III 42
		BEʿL		I		KAʾB		I		BE-LI$_2$-KA-BI	FN	XIII 1 V 28+
		BEʿL		I		KIʾR		I		BE-LI$_2$-KI-RI	FN	RA LXV 58 I 15
		BEʿL		I		NIWR		I		BE-LI$_2$-NI-RI	FN	M+
		BEʿL		I		NIWR		I		BE-LI$_2$-NE-RI	FN	XIII 1 II 55+
		BEʿL		I		NUṢR		I		BE-LI$_2$-NU-IZ-RI	FN	RA LXV 64 V 60
		BEʿL		I		RAWM				BE-LI$_2$-RA-AM		RA LXV 54 XII 60
		BEʿL		I		ŠAPAR				BE-LI$_2$-SA-PAR$_2$	FN	M
		BEʿL		I	TA	LEʾEJ				BE-LI$_2$-TA-LI-IḪ		RA LXV 50 VIII 44
		BEʿL	AT	I						BE-LA-TI	FN? GEN	VIII 63:11
		BEʿL	T	I		JAKAḪ				NIN?-TI-E-RA-AḪ		RA LXV 52 X 54
		BEʿL	T	I		MAʾT		I		BE-EL-TI-MA-TI	FN	A. 253 6
	2 JI	JTAR				BEʿL		I		I-TAR-BE-LI$_2$		RA LXV 47 VII 39
	3	LA			ʾA	HWIJ						
						BEʿL		I		LA-AḪ-WI-BE-LI$_2$	FN	RA LXV 59 II 73
		LA				RIWM						
						BEʿL		I		LA-RI-IM-BE-LI$_2$		X 69 5
	2	KIʾL		I		BELAʾ		I		KI-LI-BE-LA-I		M
	2	LABW		A		BIḪR		I	Š	LA-BA-BI$_2$-RI-IŠ		HSM 7936, UR III
	1	BIʿD		I		KI						
						ʾEL				BI-DI-KI-EL		RA LXV 53 XI 54

I	3	BIN		I		MA						
						BIʿD	I	JE	BI-NI-MA-BI-DI-E		EK I 40	
	2	DAʾK		A		BIJT	I		DA?-KA-BI-TI		A.	
		MILʾ		A		BIJT	I		MI-IL-A-BI-TI		A. 60 2	
	1	BIKAN		I					BI-KA-NI		KISURRA 30 8	
	1	BIKIN	T	I					BI-IK-KI-IT-TI	MN GEN	A.	
	1	BIN		I		MA			BI-NI-MA		A. LATE	
		BIN		I		MA						
						....			BI-NI-MA-D-....		UET V 713 7	
		BIN		I		MA						
						ʾAḪ	UM		BI-IN-NI-MA-ḪU-UM		TLB I 3 28	
		BIN		I		MA						
						ʾAḪ	UM		BI-NI-MA-ḪU-UM		CCT IV 13A 6+	CAPP.
		BIN		I		MA						
						ʾIL			BI-NI-MA-DINGIR		A. LATE	
		BIN		I		MA						
						BIʿD	I	JE	BI-NI-MA-BI-DI-E		EK I 40	
		BIN		I		MARAṢ			BI-NI-MA-RA-AṢ		M	
		BIN		I		MARAṢ	I		BI-NI-MA-RA-ZI	FN	XII 265 2	
		BIN	T	I		ḪIJJ	A		BI-TI-ḪI?-A	FN	HARRIS 85 3	
		BIN	T	I		DAGAN			BI-IT-TI-D-DA-GAN	FN	B 16+	
		BIN	T	I		KIʾD	I	JA	BI-IN-TI-KI-DI-IA	FN	A.+	
	2	ʾIL		A		BIN	I		DINGIR-BI-NI		UCP X/3 1 7	
		ʾIL		A		BIN	I		I-LA-BI$_2$-NI		I	
	1	BIZZ		I		JARAḪ			BI-IṢ-ṢI-E-RA-AḪ		YOS XIII 245:16	
	1	BUʾL		I		HADD	U		BU-LI-A-DU		A. 60 12	
	1	BUWZ		I					BU-ZI	FN	M+, C+	
	2	KUʾB		A		BUWZ	I		KU-BA-BU-ZI	FN	M	
	1	BUN		I		ʾIL			BU-NI-DINGIR		B 16	
		BUN		I		ʾEL	UM		BU-UN?-NE-E-LUM		TCL I 220 42	
		BUN		I		ʾIL	A		BU-NI-I-LA		B 16+	
		BUN		I		MA						
						ʾAḪ	UM		BU-NI-MA-ḪU-UM		TCL XX 96 8	
		BUN		I		MARAṢ			BU-NI-MA-RA-AṢ		C+	
	1	BUNZ		I					BU-UN-ZI	FN	XIII 1 X 25	
		BUNZUR		I					BU-UN-ZU-RI	FN	XIII 1 III 13	
	1 JA	DWIR		I					IA-DI-RI	NOM	B 25 HANA	
	2	ŚAMŚ		I		DAʿ	I		D-UTU-DA-ḪI-I		LANGDON XV 2	
	1	DAWD	AN	I					DA?-DA-NI	FN NOM	M	
		DAWD		I		JABAL			DA-DI-E-BA-AL		UNPUBL.	
		DAWD		I		ʿADN			DA-DI-ḪA-DU-UN		M+	
		DAWD		I		ʿADN	U	HU	DA-DI-ḪA-AD-NU-U$_2$		18 R.A. P.61 A 3821+	
		DAWD		I	Š	ME						
						ʾEL			DA-DI-EŠ$_3$-ME-EL		UCP X/3 P. 198+	
		DAWD		I		JAŠAR			DA-DI-E-SA-AR		RA LXV 50 VIII 48+	
		DAWD		I	JE	JŠUʿ			DA-DI-E-ŠU-UḪ		M+	
		DAWD		I		ŚAMUʿ			DA-DI-SA-MU-UḪ		RA LXV 47 VII 44	
	2	ʾAJI				DAWD	I		A-I-DA-TE	FN	A.	
		ḪAM		U		DAWD	I		D?-[A?-M]U?-DA-DI		IX 291 16	
		ʿAQB		U		DAWD	I		ḪA-AQ-BU-DA-DI		M+	
		ʿAQB		U		DAWD	I		AQ-BU-DA-DI		M	
		ḎU				DAWD	I		ZU-DA-DI		XIV 91:5, 13	
		ŠAWB		I		DAWD	I		[Š]A?-BI-DA-DI		RA LXV 43 I 13	
		ZAKK				DAWD	I		ZA-AK-DA-TI		TA 1931,377+ EARLY OB	
		ZIMM		I		DAWD	I		ZI-IM-MI-DA-DI	FN	C II 44 33+	
	1	DAGAZ		I					DA-GA-ZI	FN	RA LXV 56 I 6	
	1	DANN		I		ʾIL			DA?-NI-DINGIR		M	
		DANN		I	Š	ME						
						ʾIL			DA-NI-IŠ-ME-DINGIR?		I	
	1	DARK		I		MA			DAR-KI-MA	FN	RA LXV 61 IV 14	
	2	ʾIL		AM		DIʿ	I		DINGIR-LAM-DI-I		SIMMONS 24 10+	
	2	BAʿL		I		DIWR	I		BA-AḪ-LI-DI-RI	FN	C+	
	JA	KWUN				DIWR	I		IA-KU-UN-DI-RI	GEN	CT XLVIII 115 CASE	
	1	DIJN		I		HADD	U		TI-NI-A-DU		A. 59 2	
		DIJN		I		HADD	U		DI-NI-A-DU		A.+	
		DIJN		I		HADD	U		DI-NA-A-DU		A. LATE	

SUFFIXES, Class 2

I	2 JI	JʿIL				DIJN		I		I-ḪI-IL-DI-NI-X?		RA LXV 48 VIII 1
		ŠUM		U		DIJN		I		[SU-M]U-DI-NI		PBS XI/2 P. 119
	3 JI	NPIḪ				LI						
						DIJN		I		IB-BI-IḪ-LI-DI-NI	FN	C
	2	HADD		U		DUWR		I		D-IM-DU-RI		M+
		ŠI				DUWR		I		ŠI-DU-RI	FN	RA LXV 58 I 68+
	2	ʾIŠḪAR	AH			DUMQ		I		D-IŠ-ḪA-RA-DU-UM-KI	FN	XII 265 3
	1	DUNN		I		HADD		U		DU-NI-A-DU		A. LATE
		DUNN		I		....				DU-NI-PA-DU		A.
	2	ʾANN		U		DUNN		I		AN-NU-DU-UN-NI	FN	XIII 1 III 37
		ʾANN		U		DUNN		I		AN-NU-DU-NI	FN	RA LXV 65 VII 15
		MAM		A		DUNN		I		D-MA-MA-DU-UN-NI	FN	M
	1	ḎABIB		I		ʾIL				SA-BI-BI-DINGIR		M
	1	ḎAKUR		I		ʾEL				ZA-KU-RI-E-EL		UCP X/1 86 15
		ḎAKUR		I		ʾEL		UM		ZA-KU-RI-E-LUM		UNPUBL.
	1	ḎAMAR		I		ʾEL		UM		ZA-MA-RI-E-LUM		B. 92+
	2	ʾIŠḪAR	AH			ḎAMR	AT	I		D-IŠ-ḪA-RA-ZA-AM-RA-TI	FN	M
	1	ḎIKR		I		HADD		U		ZI-IK-RI-D-IM		M+
		ḎIKR		I		ʿAN	AT			ZI-IK-RI-ḪA-NA-AT		M
		ḎIKR		I		ʿAN	AT			ZI-IK-RI-D-ḪA-N[A-AT]		M
		ḎIKR		I		JARAḪ				ZI-IK-RI-E-RA-AḪ		TIM V 69 7, 17+
		ḎIKR		I		ʿAŠTAR				ZI-IK-RI-EŠ$_4$-DAR		M+
		ḎIKR		I		LIʾM				ZI-IK-RI-LI-IM		M+
	1	ḎIMR		I		....				ZI-IM-RI-D-[....]		M
		ḎIMR		I		ʾAB		UM		ZI-IM-RI-A-BU-UM		B 42
		ḎIMR		I		HADD		U		ZI-IM-RI-D-IM		M+
		ḎIMR		I		HEDD		A		ZI-IM-RI-E-ID-DA		B 42
		ḎIMR		I	JE	HADD		U		ZI-IM-RI-E-D-IM		M
		ḎIMR		I		ʾIL				ZI-IM-RI-DINGIR		B 42+
		ḎIMR		I		ʾIL		U				
						MA				ZI-IM-RI-DINGIR-MA		M
		ḎIMR		I		ʾIL		U				
						MA				ZI-IM-RI-I-LU-MA		M
		ḎIMR		I		ʾIL		U				
						MA				ZI-IM-RI-LU-MA		SIMMONS 67 12
		ḎIMR		I		ʿAMM		U		ZI-IM-RI-AM-MU		TIM III 94 4
		ḎIMR		I		ʿAMM		U		ZI-IM-RI-ḪA-MU		C
		ḎIMR		I		ʿAMM		U		ZI-IM-RI-ḪA-AM-MU		B 42+, X 35 12
		ḎIMR		I		ʿAN	AT	A		ZI-IM-RI-ḪA-NA-TA		B 42
		ḎIMR		I		JARAḪ				ZI-IM-RI-E-RA-AḪ		B 42+, C+, M+
		ḎIMR		I		ḪAŠAM				ZI-IM-RI-ḪA-SA-AM	NOM	C+
		ḎIMR		I		ʿAŠTAR				ZI-IM-RI-D-EŠ$_4$-DAR		M, A.+
		ḎIMR		I		DAGAN				ZI-IM-RI-D-DA-GAN		M+
		ḎIMR		I		LU			HU	ZI-IM-RI-LU-U$_2$	FN	RA LXV 55 XIII 39
		ḎIMR		I		LIʾM				ZI-IM-RI-LI-IM		M+
		ḎIMR		I		RAPUʾ				ZI-IM-RI-RA-BU		M
		ḎIMR		I		ŠAMŠ				ZI-IM-RI-SA-MAŠ		A.
		ḎIMR		I		ŠAMŠ				ZI-IM-RI-SA-MA-AŠ$_2$		M+
	1	ḎINUB		I		ʾIL				ZI-NU-BI-DINGIR		RA LXV 48 VIII 12
	1	ḎUNUB		I		ʾIL				ZU-NU-BI-DINGIR		RA LXV 51 X 14
	1	GAʾJ		I		JARAḪ				GA-JI-RA-A[Ḫ]		HARRIS 39 15
		GAʾJ		I		LAʾL		UM		GA-I-LA-LUM		M
	2	BAʿL		U		GAʾJ		I		BA-AḪ-LU-GA-I	NOM	M+
		BAʿL		U		GAʾJ		I		BA-AḪ-LU-GA-A-JI	NOM	M
	2	ʾANN		U		GAMIL	T	I		AN-NU-GA-ME-IL-TI	FN	RA LXV 66 VII 66
	2	DAGAN				GAML		I		D-DA-GAN-GA-AM-LI		M
	1	GANN		I						GA-AN-NI		M
	1	GIZZ		I						GI-IZ-ZI		A. 32 3
		GIZZ		I						KI-IZ-ZI		A.+
	1	GUʾR		I						GU-RI	GEN	B 17
	1	GUʾZ		I						GU-ZI	FN	RA LXV 55 XIII 8
	1	GUBL	AJ	I						GU-UB-LA-A-JI	GN PL NOM	SYRIA XX 111
		GUBL	AJ	I						GU-UB-LA-JI	GN NOM	SYRIA XX 111
	2	ʾIL		I		GUML		I	JA	I$_3$-LI$_2$-GU-UM-LI-IA		XIII 1 VIII 45
		ʾIŠḪAR	AH			GUML		I		D-IŠ-ḪA-RA-GU-UM-LI	FN	XIII 1 IV 39
	1 JA	KWUN		I						IA-KU-NI	GEN	TIM III 58 16+

SUFFIXES, Class 2

I	1	KAʾAM		I					KA-A-MI		A.
	1	KAʾB		I		ʾAHL	UM		KA-PI-IA-LUM		UET V 626 11, 702 REV. 5
		KAʾB		I		JADAʿ			KA-BI-E-DA-AḪ		XIII 1 XI 54
		KAʾB		I		HADD	U		KA-BI-D-IM		B 32, M+, C
		KAʾB		I		HEDD	A		KA-BI-E-D-IM		M+
		KAʾB		I		JARAḪ			KA-BI-E-RA-AḪ		RA LXV 41 II 29+;B 32+
		KAʾB		I		ʾATT	A		KA-BI-A-TA		M
		KAʾB		I	JE	JPUʿ			KA-BI-E-PU-UḪ		M
		KAʾB		I		BEʿL			KA-BI-BE-EL		YOS XIII 432:12
		KAʾB		I		BURŠ	A		KA-BI-BU-UR-ŠA	FN	XIII 1 XIV 53
		KAʾB		I		DAGAN			KA-BI-D-DA-GAN		M+
		KAʾB		I		LA					
						RIWM			KA-BI-LA-RI-IM		RA LXV 47 VI 65+; C+
	2	ʾAḪ		I		KAʾB	I		A-ḪI-KA-PI		YOS VIII 64 18
		ʾAB		I		KAʾB	I		A-BI-KA-BI		M
		ʾAB		I		KAʾB	I		A-BI-KA-BI	FN	RA LXV 65 VII 42
		ʾIL		I		KAʾB	I		I$_3$-LI$_2$-KA-PI		BIROT, TEA 69:28
		ḪANN		I		KAʾB	I		A[N-N]I-KA-BI	FN	RA LXV 62 V 17
		BEʿL		I		KAʾB	I		BE-LI$_2$-KA-BI	FN	XIII 1 V 28+
		DIWR	IT	UM		KAʾB	I		D-DI-RI-TUM-KA-BI		XIII 1 VI 45
	1	KAʾM		I		JAʾAR	UM		KA-MI-IA-A-RUM		VAS VII 128 46
	2 MU	ṢTUḪ				KAʾM	I		MU-UŠ-TU-KA-M[I]		M+
	1	KAHAL		I		HADD	U		KA-A-LI-D-IM		M+
		KAHAL		I		ʾIL	U				
						MA			KA-A-LI-I-LU-MA		XIV 62:4+
		KAHAL		I		ʾIL	U				
						MA			KA-A-LI-DINGIR-MA		M+
	1	KABAS		I	JE				KA-BA-AZ-ZI-E		A.
	2	ʾIL		A		KABKAB	I		DINGIR-KAB-KA-BI		JNES XIII 210+ LATE
	1	KADUL		I					KA-DU-LI	FN	M
	1	KAKKAR		I					KA-KA-RI		RA LXV 50 IX 7
	2	KURD		A		KAMB	I		KUR-DA-KA-AM-BI	FN	XIII 1 III 25
	1	KANAT		I					KA-NA-TI		LIMET,SCEAUX CASS. P. 114
	1	KANN		I					KA-AN-NI		XIII 1 IX 62
	2	ʾIL		UM		KATAZ	I		I-LU-UM-KA-TA-ZI		RUTTEN 40 1
	1	KATIR		I					KA-TI-RI	GEN	UET V 88 2,SEAL, A. 37 12
	2	BIN	T	I		KIʾD	I	JA	BI-IN-TI-KI-DI-IA	FN	A.+
	1	KIʾL		I		ʾIL			KI-LI-DINGIR		CT IV 33B 19
		KIʾL		I		ʾIL	UM		KI-LI-DINGIR-LUM		XIII 106 14
		KIʾL		I		ʿAMM	I		KI-LI-AM-MI	GEN	MRS XVI 12:2
		KIʾL		I		BELAʾ	I		KI-LI-BE-LA-I		M
	1	KIʾM		I		ʾEL			KI-MI-EL		UCP X/3 2 2
	1	KIʾR		I		DAGAN			KI-RI-D-DA-GAN		RA LXV 52 X 21
	2	BEʿL		I		KIʾR	I		BE-LI$_2$-KI-RI	FN	RA LXV 58 I 15
	1	KIWN		I		BAWŠ	I		KI-NI-BA-ŠI	FN	HARRIS 45 8
		KIWN		I	Š	LUʾP	A		KI-NI-IŠ-LU-BA		EDZARD,DER 94:17;95:6
		KIWN		I	Š	MAʾT	UM		KI-NI-IŠ-MA-TUM	FN	M+;C
	2	ʾANA				KIBAL	I		A-NA?-KI-BA-[L]I	FN	M
	1	KIBIR		I					[K]I-BI-RI		RA LXV 43 III 77
	1	KIBR		I		ʿAŠTAR			KI-IB-RI-EŠ$_4$-DAR		M+
		KIBR		I		DAGAN			KI-IB-RI-D-DA-GAN		M+
	2	DAGAN				KIBR	I		D-DA-GAN-KI-IB-RI	FN	M+
	1	KIBS		I		HADD	U		KI-IB-ZI-D-IM		M+
		KIBS		I		HEDD	A		KI-IB-ZI-E-D-IM		M
		KIBS		I		JARAḪ			KI-IB-ZI-E-RA-AḪ		RA LXV 43 III 44+
	1	KIKKIN		I					KI-IK-KI-NI	GEN	B 49+
	1	KIZUR		I					KI-ZU-RI		RA LXV 43 III 41,42
	1 JA	KMIN		I					IA-AK-ME-NI		JNES XIII 210+ LATE
	1 JA	KMIS		I					IA-AK-ME-SI		JCS XIII 210+ LATE
	2	ʿABD				KUʾB	I		ḪA-AB-DU-KU-BI		M+
		MUT		U		KUʾB	I		MU-TU-KU-BI		RA LXV 42 II 66
	2	ḪANN		A		KUʾN	I		AN-NA-KU-NI		VAS VIII 14 44
	1	KUʾŠ		I		ḪIMR	I		KU-ŠI-ḪI-IM-RI		SIMMONS 87 19
	1	KUWN		I		DAʾK	A		KU-NI-DA-KA		A. 367 11
	1	KUDAD		I					KU-DA-DI	FN	RA LXV 61 IV 5
	1	KUDD		I					[K]U-UD-DI		RA LXV 40 I 18

SUFFIXES, Class 2

I	1		KUMM		I		NAʾD		A		KU-UM-MI-NA-DA		JCS IV 113
	1		KUMR		I						KU-UM-RI		RA LXV 42 II 59
	2		MUT		U		KUMR		I		MU-TU-KU-UM-RI		X 166 10', 13'
	1		KUND		I						KU-UN-DI	FN	XIII 1 IV 76, C
	1		KUNN		I						KU-UN-NI		RA LXV 52 XI 4
	1		KUNZ		I						KU-UN-ZI	FN	XIII 1 V 39; C
	1		KURŠ	AN	I						KU-UR$_2$-SA-NI	NOM	M
	1		KUŠM		I		ʾEL				KU-UŠ$_2$-MI-EL		RA LXV 48 VII 74
	1		KUZAR		I						KU-ZA-RI		RA LXV 45 V 15+
			KUZAR		I						KU-UZ-ZA-RI		IX 259:5
			KUZAR		I						KU-UZ$_2$-ZA-RI		XIII 90:5
			KUZAR		I	NA					KU-ZA-RI-NA		RA LXV 45 V 22
			KUZAZ		I						KU-ZA-AZ-ZI	FN	RA LXV 60 III 52
	1		LAʾL		I		ʾEL				LA-LI-E-EL		SIMMONS 70 15
	1		LAʾT		I		RAWM		E	JE	LA-TI-RA-ME-E		M
	1		LAḪAN		I		KIWN		IM		LA-ḪA-NI-KI-IN-IM	GEN	UCP X/3 2 5
	1		LABW		I		ŚAM		A		LA-BI-SA-MA		UCP X/3 P. 199+
	2		ŠADW		UM		LABW		I		ŠA-DU-UM-LA-BI		M
	1		LAMAS		I						LA-MA-ZI	GEN	IV 68 18, 20, 21
	2		ʾANN		U		LAMAS		I		AN-NU-LA-MA-ZI	FN	M+
			ʾANN		U		LAMAS		I		AN-NU-D-LAMA	FN	XIII 1 VII 8+
			ʾIŠḪAR	AH			LAMAS		I		D-IŠ-ḪA-RA-D-LAMA	FN	XIII 1 IX 23
			ʿAŠTAR				LAMAS		I		EŠ$_4$-DAR-LA-MA-ZI	FN	M
			ʿAŠTAR				LAMAS		I		EŠ$_4$-DAR-D-LAMA	FN	XIII 1 I 69+
	2		KAKK		A		LIʾD		I		KA-AK-KA-LI-DI	FN	X 10 5
	1		LIʾM		I		HADD		U		LI-MI-D-IM		M+
			LIʾM		I		HADD		U		LI-ME-D-IM		M+
	1		LIWJ		I		DAGAN				LI-I-D-DA-GAN		M
	2	JI	NWUḪ				LIBB		I		I-NU-UḪ-LI-BI		M
	1		LILUR		I						LI-LU-RI	FN	RA LXV 62 IV 66
	2		BAʿL		U		LUʾL		I		BA-AḪ-LU-LU-L[I]?		HARRIS 71 14
	1	JA	MʾAD		I						IA$_3$-A-MA-TI		U
		JA	MʾAD	AJ	I						IA-AM-ḪA-DA-I-KI	GN GEN	M
		JA	MʾAD	IJ	I						IA-AM-ḪA-DI-I-KI	GN NOM	M
		JA	MʾAD	IJ	I						IA-AM-ḪA-DI-JI	GN NOM	M
	1	JA	MWUŠ		I		ʾIL				IA-MU-ŠI-DINGIR		B 28
		JA	MWUŠ		I		ʾIL				IA-A-MU-ŠI-DINGIR		VAS VII 166 4 LATE
	2		ʾAB		I	JA	MWUT		I		A-BI$_2$-A-MU-TI		U
	1		MAʾD		I		JAM		A		MA-DI-IA-MA		UCP X/1 33 10
			MAʾD		I		JAT		UM		MA-DI-IA-TUM		UCP X/1 P. 59+
	2		ʾIL		A		MAʾD		I		DINGIR-MA-DI		M
			ʾIL		I		MAʾD		I		I$_3$-LI$_2$-MA-DI		SIMMONS 33 19
			ʾIL		I		MAʾD		I				
							ʾAḪ				I$_3$-LI$_2$-MA-DI-A-AḪ		RUTTEN 1 8
			ʾIL		I		MAʾD		I				
							ʾAḪ				DINGIR?-MA-DA-AḪ		RA LXV 42 III 21
			ʾIL		I		MAʾD		I				
							ʾAḪ				I$_3$-LI$_2$-MI-DI-AḪ		EDZARD,DER 146:14
			ʾIL		I		MAʾD		I				
							ʾAḪ		I		I$_3$-LI$_2$-MA-DA-ḪI		RUTTEN 14 7
			ʾIL		I		MAʾD		I				
							ʾAḪ		A		I$_3$-LI$_2$-MA-DA-ḪA		VAS VIII 14 4
	1		MAʾL		I		ḤARAB		A		MA-LI-A-RA-BA?		CT II 30 29
			MAʾL		I		ŚUM		U	HU	MA-LI-SU-MU-U$_2$		TIM I 29 10
	2		ʾAKK	AT			MAʾT		I		AK-KA-AD-MA-TI	FN	A. 409 22
			BEʿL	T	I		MAʾT		I		BE-EL-TI-MA-TI	FN	A. 253 6
		TA	KWUN				MAʾT		I		TA-KUM-MA-TI	FN	A.+
	1		MAʾZ	AN	I						MA-ZA-NI		KISURRA 68A 10+
	1		MAGAN		I						MA-GA-NI	GEN	MRS XVI P. 329 UGARIT
	2		ʾIŠḪAR	AH			MALAK		I		D-IŠ-ḪA-RA-M[A-L]A-KI	FN	RA LXV 61 IV 61
	1		MALIK		I						MA-LI-KI	GEN	B 34, A. 77 6
	2		ḪAʾR		I		MALIK		I		ḪA-RI-MA-LI-KI	GEN	B 20
			ʿABD				MALIK		I		AB-DU-MA-LI-KI		YOS XIII 54:5
			ʾIL		U		MALIK	AJ	I		I-LU-MA-LI-KA-JI-KI	GN	XV 127
			ŠI				MALIK	T	I		ŠI-MA-LI-IK-TI		IX 294:7'
	2		ʾIL		A		MALK		I		DINGIR-MA-AL-KI		A. LATE

I	2	BIN	T	A	MALK		I	BI-IT-TA-MA-AL-KI	FN	A. LATE
	1	MANIN		I				MA-NI-NI	GEN	B 34+
	2	BIN		I	MARAṢ		I	BI-NI-MA-RA-ZI	FN	XII 265 2
	1	MATAN		I				MA-TA-NI	FN	EDZARD, DER 33:3
		MATAN		I				MA-AT-TA-NI		TIM II 99:3
		MATAQ		I				MA-TA-KI	FN	CT IV 26A 1
	1	MATIQ		I				MA-TI-GI	FN	M+
	2	ʾAḪ		UM	MAṬAR		I	A-ḪU-UM-MA-DA-RI		M
		ḪAʾL		UM	MAṬAR		I	ḪA-LUM-MA-DA-RI		SIMMONS 67 B 11
		ḪAʾL		UM	MAṬAR		I	ḪA-LUM-MA-DAR-RI		SIMMONS 67 11
	1	MEʾN		I	ʾEL			ME-NI-EL		RA LXV 52 X 18
	2	MUT			MEŠIL		I	MU-UT-ME-SI-LI		RIFTIN 45 14
	1	MIHR		I	....			ME-EḪ-RI-[....]		M
		MIHR		I	HADD		U	ME-EḪ-RI-D-IM		C+
	2	ʾIL		I	MIWT		I	I_3-LI_2-MI-TI		I
	2	ŠI			MIGN		I	ŠI-ME-IG-NI	FN	RA LXV 60 III 24
	1	MILK		I	ḪAJJ		A	MIL-KI-ḪA-A-IA	FN	IRAQ XVI 40 NA
		MILK		I	HADD		U	MIL-KI-D-IM		M
		MILK		I	HADD		U	MI-IL-KI-D-IM		M
		MILK		I	ʾIL			MI-IL-KI-DINGIR		B 34
		MILK		I	ʾIL		A	MI-EL-KI-I-[LA]		UCP X/3 1 29
		MILK		I	ʾIL		U	MIL-KI-LU		B 34+
		MILK		I	ʾIL		U	MI-IL-KI-LU		B 34
		MILK		I	ʾIL		UM	MI-IL-KI-LUM		B 34
		MILK		I	JARAḪ			MIL-KI-E-RA-AḪ		AJSL XLIV 243 NO. 33
		MILK		I	DAGAN			MIL-KI-D-DA-GAN		TCL I 237 12 HANA
		MILK		I	LA					
					ʾEL			MI-IL-KI-LA-EL		TA 30 615 21
		MILK		I	LI					
					ʾEL			MI-IL-KI-LI-EL		B 34, M+
		MILK		I	LI					
					ʾEL			MIL-KI-LI-EL		VAS VIII 128 16+
		MILK		I	LI					
					ʾIL			MI-IL-KI-LI_2-IL		I
		MILK		I	LI					
					ʾIL			[MI]-EL-KI-LI-IL		I
		MILK		I	LI					
					ʾEL		UM	MI-IL-KI-LI-E-LUM		A 32065:3
		MILK		I	LU					
					ʾIL		A	MI-IL-KI-LU-I-LA		VAS XVI 10 5, 9
		MILK		I	TAʾG		A	MI-IL-KI-TA-GA		A. LATE
	2	ʿAŠTAR			MILK		I	$EŠ_4$-DAR-ME-IL-KI	FN	RA LXV 62 V 10
		KI			MILK		I			
					ʾEL			KI-MI-IL-KI-EL		KISURRA 112:8
	3	LA			ʾIL		A			
					MILK		I	LA-I-LA-MI-IL-KI		TA 30, 75 2
	1	MINAN		I				MI-NA-NI	GEN	B 46+
	1	MISAR		I				MI?-ZA-RI	FN	RA LXV 65 VI 71
	1 JA	MRAṢ		I	ʾIL			IA-AM-RA-ZI-DINGIR		M
	1 JA	MRUṢ		I	ʾIL		UM	I-IA-AM-RU-UṢ-ZI-I-LU-UM		B 21
	1	MUʾZ	AN	I				MU-ZA-NI		KISURRA 1A 3+; M
	2	ʾAB		I	MULUK		I	A-BI-MU-LU-KI	FN	RA LXV 59 II 26
		ʾIL		UM	MULUK	AJ	I	DINGIR-MU-LU-KA-JI-KI	GN	XV 127
	1	MUNUZ		I				MU-NU-ZI	FN	RA LXV 64 V 59
	1	MUT	AN	I				MU-TA-NI		A. 52 28
		MUT		I	ʾAḪ		I	MU-TI-A-ḪI	GEN	B 35
		MUT		I	JAʾN		A	MU-TI-I-IA-NA		B 35
		MUT		I	JABAL			MU-TI-A-BA-AL-KI	GN	B 35+
		MUT		I	JABAL			MU-TI-BA-AL-KI	GN	B 35+
		MUT		I	JABAL			MU-TA-BA-AL-KI	GN	OIP XI 216 IV 3
		MUT		I	JABAL		A	MU-TI-A-BA-LA-KI	GN	B 35
		MUT		I	HADD		U	MU-TI-D-IM		M
		MUT		I	ʾIL		UM	MU-TI-LUM		YOS XIII 151:4+
		MUT		I	ʿAN	AT	A	MU-TI-A-N[A-T]A		B 35
		MUT		I	JARAḪ			MU-TI-A-RA-AḪ		B 35
		MUT		I	JARAḪ			MU-TI-E-RA-AḪ		M; TCL XI 224:69+

I	1	MUT	I		JARAḪ			MU-TE-E-RA-AḪ		A 7804 13
		MUT	I		ḪURŠAN			MU-TI-ḪUR-SAG		YOS XII+
		MUT	I		ḪURŠAN	A		MU-TI-ḪU-UR-ŠA-NA		B 35+
		MUT	I		ḪURŠAN	I		MU-TI-ḪU-UR-ŠA-NI		YOS XII
		MUT	I		ḪATK	IM		MU-TI-ḪA-AD-KI-IM	NOM	IRAQ XXX 92+ RIMAH
		MUT	I	JE	ʾMIʾ			MU-TI-E-MI-IḪ		M
		MUT	I		....			[M]U?-TI-KA-ṢI-E		PBS XIII 56:8
		MUT	I		....			MU-TI-DA-ZI-U_2		TA 1930, 489 I
		MUT	I		ME					
					ʾEL			MU-TI-ME-EL		TA 30, 615:4+
		MUT	I		MAʾK	U	HU	MU-TI-MA-KU-U_2		M+
		MUT	I		ŠAMŠ			MU-TI-D-UTU		A.
	2	ʾAJA			MUT	I		ḪA-IA-MU-TI		BAGHD. MITT. II 7 2, 4, 8
	JI	HWIJ			MUT	I		I-WI-MU-TI		U
		ʾALLA			MUT	IJ I		AL-LA-MU-TI-I	TRIBE	4E RENC. ASS. P. 178 9
		ʾALLA			MUT	IJ I		A-AL-MU-TI-I	TRIBE	M
		DIWIR			MUT	I		DI-WI-IR-MU-TI		PBS XI/1 P. 55+
		DIWIR			MUT	I		DI-BI-IR-A-MU-TI		PBS XI/1 P. 55+
		ŠUM	U		MUT	I				
					JABAL	A		SU-MU-MU-TI-A-BA-LA		B 39
	1 TA	NḪAB	AT I					TA-ḪA-BA-TI	FN GEN	VAS VIII 127 2
	1 JI N	NWIB	I					IN-NI-BI		CLAY PNCP 90+
	2	DAGAN			NAʾD	I		D-DA-GAN-NA-DI	FN	XIII 1 III 17+
	2	BIN			NAHR	I		BI-IN-NA-A-R[I]?		M
	1	NAḪAL	I					NA-ḪA-LI	FN	IX 291 30
	1	NAḪL	I		ʾIL	UM		NA-AḪ-LI-LUM		B 36+
	1	NAḪN	I		ʾIL			NA-AḪ-NI-DINGIR		TIM III 86:5
	1	NAʿIM	I					NA-ḪI-MI	GEN	B 36
	1	NAʿM	I					NA-AḪ-MI	GEN	M
		NAʿM	I		ʿAN	IM		NA-MI-A-NIM		A. 142
		NAʿM	I		JARAḪ			NA-AḪ-MI-E-RA-AḪ		JCS XI 29 NO.17 5
		NAʿM	I		ʾAŠD	U		NA-AḪ-ME-AS-DU	FN	RA LXV 60 III 2
		NAʿM	I		JAT	UM		NA-MI-IA-TUM	MN	MEISSNER 100 2
		NAʿM	I		DAʾK	A		NA-MI-DA-KA		A. 242 7
		NAʿM	I		DAGAN			NA-AḪ-MI-D-DA-GAN		A.+
		NAʿM	I		DAGAN			NA-MI-D-DA-GAN		A.+
		NAʿM	I		DAGAN			NA-AḪ-ME-D-DA-GAN		RA LXV 48 VIII 33
	2	ʾAḪ	AT A		NAʿM	I		A-ḪA-TA-NA-AḪ-MI	FN	XIII 1 XI 3
		ʾAB	I		NAʿM	I		A-BI-NA-AḪ-MI	FN	XIII 1 VII 43, A.+
		ʾAB	I		NAʿM	I		A-BI-NA-AḪ-ME	FN	RA LXV 59 II 20
		ʾUMM	I		NAʿM	I		UM-MI-NA-MI	FN	A.
		ʾUMM	I		NAʿM	I		UM-MI-NA-AḪ-ME	FN	RA LXV 59 II 17
		ʾIŠḪAR	AH		NAʿM	I		D-IŠ-ḪA-RA-NA-AḪ-ME	FN	RA LXV 64 VI 37
		DAGAN			NAʿM	I		D-DA-GAN-NA-AḪ-MI	FN	X 116 1, 22
		KAKK	A		NAʿM	I		KA-AK-KA-NA-AḪ-MI	FN	XIII 1 VII 30
	1	NAWḪ	I		ʾIL			NA-ḪI-DINGIR		B 35+
		NAWḪ	I		ʾIMM	I		D-NA-ḪI-IM-MI		YOS II 112 11
	1	NAWAR	I					NA-WA-RI?		RA LXV 53 XI 55
	1	NABIB	I					NA-BI-BI		M
	2	ʾANN	U		NABIT	I		AN-NU-NA-BI-TI		XIII 1 VI 61
		ʾATTA			NABIT	I		A-TA-NA-BE-TI		JCS XIII 57 306:5+,A LATE
	1	NAMAŠ	I					NA-MA-ŠI		MAOG IV 3 30 HANA
	1	NAN	I					D-NA-NI	DN	M
	2 TA	QJIŠ			NAN	I		TA-KI-IŠ-NA-NI	FN?	TIM III 41 6
	1	NANN	I		ŠARR	AH		D-NA-AN-NI-ŠAR-RA	FN	XIII 1 V 31
	1	NAPŠ	I		HADD	U		NA-AP-SI-D-IM		M+
		NAPŠ	I		HADD	U		NA-AP-ŠI-A-DU		A.+
		NAPŠ	I		HAND	U		NA-AP-SI-IA-AN-DU		M
		NAPŠ	I		ḪINN	I		NA-AP-SI-IN-NI	FN	XIII 1 IV 72
		NAPŠ	I		JARAḪ			NA-AP-SI-E-RA-AḪ		M+
		NAPŠ	I		DAGAN			NA-AP-SI-D-DA-GAN		M+
		NAPŠ	I		PI					
					ʾIL			NA-AP-SI-BI-DINGIR		SYRIA XLVIII 9:22
		NAPŠ	I		ŠEʾR	UM		NA-AP-SI-ŠE?-RUM?		M
	2	ʾAB	I		NAPŠ	I		A-BI-NA-AP-S[I]		XIV 77:7
		ʾIŠḪAR	AH		NAPŠ	I		D-IŠ-ḪA-RA-NA-AP-SI	FN	XIII 1 VII 13

I	2	LA				NAŠUʾ	I		LA-NA-SU-JI	GEN	M
		LA				NAŠUʾ	I		LA-NI-SU-JI	FN NOM	M
	1 JA	NBUL		I					IA$_2$-AN-BU-LI		U
	2	ŠALAŠ				NIʾG	I		ŠA-LA-AŠ-NI-GI	FN	C+
	1	NIWR		I		HADD	U		NI-IW-RI-A-DU		A.+
	2	ʾAJA				NIWR	I		[A]-IA-NI-RI		RA LXV 59 II 36
		ḪAJJ		A		NIWR	I		E$_2$-A-NI-RI	FN	RA LXV 58 II 2
		ḪAJJ		A		NIWR	I		E$_2$-A-NE-RI	FN	XIII 1 VII 26
		ʾAB		I		NIWR	I		A-BI-NI-RI	FN	XIII 1 IX 58+
		HADD		U		NIWR	I		D-IM-NI-RI	FN	RA LXV 61 IV 17
		ʾADM		U		NIWR	I		AD-MU-NE-RI	FN	XIII 1 VIII 13
		ʾADM		U		NIWR	I		D-AD-MU-NI-RI	FN?	M
		ʾIL		I		NIWR	I		I$_3$-LI$_2$-NE-RI	FN	XIII 1 II 6+
		ʾALL		I		NIWR	I		AL-LI-NI-RI	FN	A.
		ʾANN		U		NIWR	I		AN-NU-NI-RI	FN	M
		ʾIŠḪAR	AH			NIWR	I		D-IŠ-ḪA-RA-NI-RI	FN	RA LXV 59 II 22
		ʿAŠTAR				NIWR	I		EŠ$_4$-DAR-NE-RI	FN	XIII 1 IX 48
		BAʿL		I		NIWR	I		BA-AḪ-LI-NI-RI	FN	M+
		BEʿL		I		NIWR	I		BE-LI$_2$-NI-RI	FN	M+
		BEʿL		I		NIWR	I		BE-LI$_2$-NE-RI	FN	XIII 1 II 55+
		DAGAN				NIWR	I		D-DA-GAN-NI-RI	MN	RA LXV 47 VII 38
		DAGAN				NIWR	I		D-DA-GAN-NI-RI	FN	M+
		DAGAN				NIWR	I		D-DA-GAN-NE-RI	FN	M+
	JA	MWUT				NIWR	I		IA-MU-UT-NI-RI	FN	A.
		NUN		U		NIWR	I		D-NU-NU-NE?-RI	FN	RA LXV 66 VII 56
		ŠUM		U		NIWR	I		SU-MU-NI-RI	FN	XIII 1 XI 46
		ŠARR		UM		NIWR	I		LUGAL-NI-RI	FN	XIII 1 XIII 3+
	3	LA			ʾA	HWIJ					
						NIWR	I		LA-AḪ-WI-NE-RI	FN	XIII 1 II 11
	2	KAKK		A		NILŠ	I		KA-A[K]-KA-NI-EL?-ŠI?FN		XIII 1 VIII 41
	1	NIQM		I		HADD	U		NI-IQ-MI-A-DU		A.+
		NIQM		I		HADD	U		NI-IQ-MI-IA-AD-DU		M
		NIQM		I	JA	JPAʿ			NI-IQ-MI-PA		A. 27 12
		NIQM		I	JA	JPAʿ			NI-IQ-ME-PA		A.+
		NIQM		I	JE	JPUʿ			NI-IQ-MI-E-PU-UḪ		M+, A.+
		NIQM		I		JATAR			NI-IQ-MI-E-TAR		C II 39 3
		NIQM		I		LA					
						NAŠIʾ			NI-IQ-MI-LA-NA-SI		M
	1	NIṢB		I		ʾIL			NE-IZ-BI-IL		TA 1931, 172
		NIṢB		I		ʾEL			NE-IZ-BI-EL		TA 1930, 747 +
	1 JA	NTIN		I		ʾIL			IA-AN-TI-NI-DINGIR		BM 17084
	1	NUʿM		I		ʾAB	I		NU-UḪ-MI-A-BI		XIII 1 I 38
		NUʿM		I		ʾIL			NU-UḪ-MI-DINGIR		M+
		NUʿM		I		ʾIL	I		NU-UḪ-MI-I$_3$-LI$_2$		XIII 1 XIII 26
		NUʿM		I		JABAL			NU-UḪ-ME-E-BA-AL	FN	RA LXV 62 V 19
		NUʿM		I		DAGAN			NU-UḪ-MI-D-DA-GAN		M
		NUʿM		I		LIʾM			NU-UḪ-MI-LI-IM		M+
	1	NUWḪ		I		ʾIL			NU-ḪI-DINGIR		I
	1	NUWP		I		ʾIL			NU-BI-DINGIR		C+
	2	KUʾM				NUWP	I		KU-UM-NU-BI		M
	2	ŠI				NUWR	I		ŠI-NU-RI	FN	A. LATE
	1	NUMḪ	AJ	I					NU-UM-ḪA-I	GN	IX 48 3+
		NUMḪ	AJ	I					NU-UM-ḪA-A-JI	GN	X 5 4
	3	BAʿL		U		ME					
						NUMḪ	I		BA-LU-ME-NU-ḪI		M+
		BAʿL		U		ME					
						NUMḪ	I		BA-LU-ME-NU-UM-ḪI		IX 41 2
	2	MAM		A		NUMR	I		D-MA-MA-NU-UM-RI	FN	RA LXV 65 VII 30
	1	NUPUR		I					NU-PU-RI		XIII 1 IV 12
	2	BEʿL		I		NUṢR	I		BE-LI$_2$-NU-IZ-RI	FN	RA LXV 64 V 60
		BAWŠ	T	I		NUṢR	I		BA-AŠ-TI-NU-IZ-RI	FN	RA LXV 58 I 45
		BAWŠ	T	I		NUṢR	I		BA-AŠ-TI-UZ-RI		RA LXIV 28 NO. 15
		BAWŠ	T	I		NUṢR	I		BA-AŠ$_2$-TI-NU-UZ-RI	FN	XIII 1 VII 24
	2	ʾIL		A		PA	I		I-LA-BA-I		TA 1931, 499
	2	ʾIL		A		PAʾŠ	I	JA	DINGIR-PA-ŠI-IA		TCL XVIII 106 9
	1	PAPUZ		I					PA-PU-ZI	FN	XIII 1 III 14

I	1	PARUR		I				PA-RU-RI		XIII 1 V 64
	1	PAZR		I				PA-AZ-RI		M
	2 JA	KWUN			PI	I	JA	IA-KU-UN-BI-IA		XII 14
	JI	KWUN			PI	I	JA	I-KU-BI-IA		SM P. 54
	JI	KWUN			PI	I		I-KU-UN-BI-I		C II 2 11
	1	PILS		I	HADD	U		BI-IL-ZI-D-IM		XIV 41:14
	1 JA	PLUS		I	ŠUM	I		IA-AP-LU-SI-SU-U$_2$-MI		BIROT,TEA 31:6
	1 MI	PTUḪ		I				MI-IP-TI-I	GEN	XII 406 5
	1 JA	PṬUR		I				IA-AP-TU-RI	GN GEN	M
	JA	PṬUR	AJ	I				IA-AP-TU-RA-A-JI-KI	GN	M
	JA	PṬUR	AJ	I				IA-AP-TU-RA-JI-KI	GN	M
	1	PULS		I	HADD	U		PU-UL-ZI-D-IM		M+
		PULS		I	JARAḪ			PU-UL-ZI-RA-AḪ		HARRIS 18 14
		PULS		I	JARAḪ			PU-UL-SI-E-RA-AḪ		TIM V 69 16+
	2	ʾANN		U	PUṬR	I		AN-NU-PU-UṬ-RI	FN	RA LXV 58 I 19+
		ʿAŠTAR			PUṬR	I		EŠ$_4$-DAR-PU-UṬ-RI	FN	M+
	1	QAWM		I	ʾIL			GA-MI-DINGIR		TIM III 12 16+
	1	QARN		I	LIʾM			QAR-NI-LI-IM		M+
	1	QAṬAN	AJ	I				QA-TA-NA-A-JI-KI	GN	M
		QAṬAN	AJ	I				QA-TA-NA-JI-KI	GN	M+
		QAṬAR		I				GA?-DA-RI		RA LXV 51 IX 72
	2 JI	JṢIʾ			QAṬAR	I		I-ZI-GA-DAR-I		B 22
	1	QIJŠ	T	I	ʾADM	U		KI-IŠ-TI-AD-MU		M+
		QIJŠ	T	I	LIʾL	IM		KI-IŠ-TI-LI-LIM	GEN	RA LXIV 34 NO.26
		QIJŠ	T	I	MAM	A		KI-IŠ-TI-D-MA-MA		M+
		QIJŠ	T	I	MAM	A		KI-IŠ-TI-D-MA-AM-MA		XIV 61:5
		QIJŠ	T	I	NUN	U		KI-IŠ-TI-D-NU-NU		M+
	1	QIMṢ		I	JARAḪ			KI?-IM-ZE$_2$-RA-AḪ		EDZARD,DER 231:2
	2	ŠI			QUWJ	I		ŠI-I-KU-WI	FN	A. 8 12, 34
	2	ʾADM		U	QUDM	I		AD-MU-KU-UD-MI	FN	XIII 1 IX 55
		ʾANN		U	QUDM	I		AN-NU-KU-UD-MI	FN	XIII 1 VIII 77
		MAM		A	QUDM	I		D-MA-MA-KU-UD-ME	FN	RA LXV 59 II 18
	1 JA	RḤAM		I	ʾIL			IA-AR-ḪA-MI-DINGIR		KISURRA 5A 15+
	JI	RḤAM		I	ʾIL			IR-ḪA-MI-DINGIR		A.
	1 JA	RWIḪ	AJ	I				IA-RI-ḪA-JI-KI	GN	M
	JA	RWIḤ	IJ	I				IA-RI-ḪI-I-KI	GN	M+
	JE	RWIḪ		I	ʾIL			E-RI-ḪI-DINGIR		U
	1	RAḤM		I	....			RA-AḪ-MI-....	FN	M
		RAḤM		I	ʾIL	I		RA-AḪ-MI-I$_3$-LI$_2$		XIII 1 VIII 79+
	2	ʾANN		U	RAḤM	I		AN-NU-RA-AḪ-MI	FN	XIII 1 V 11+
		ʿAŠTAR			RAḤM	I		EŠ$_4$-DAR-RA-AḪ-MI	FN	XIII 1 VIII 83
	2	ʾIL		A	RAWḤ	I	JA	DINGIR-RA[Ḫ]I-A		HARRIS 76 21
		ʾIL		A	RAWḤ	I	JA	I-LA-RA-ḪI-IA		M
		ʾIL		A	RAWḤ	I	JE	I-LA-RA-ḪI-E		M
		ʾIL		A	RAWḤ	I	JE	DINGIR-RA-ḪI-E		HARRIS 85 14
		ʾIL		I	RAWḤ	I	JE	I$_3$-LI$_2$-RA-AḪ-E		VAS XVI 168 9, FRANK 13 9
		KULP		A	RAWḤ	I	JE	KU-UL-PA-RA-ḪI-E		TCL I 14 1, YOS VIII 141 34
		KANAK			RAWḤ	I		KA-NA-AK-RA-ḪI		VAS XIII 79 R. 7
	2	MUT		U	RAWM	I	JE	MU-TU-RA-MI-E		CT XLV 63 15
	1	RABB		I	JARAḪ			RA-AB-BI-E-RA-AḪ		B 37+
	1	RAMAŠ		I				RA-MA-ŠI	FN	M
		RAMAŠ		I				RA-MA-A-ŠI	FN	EDZARD,DER 224:42
	2	ʿAMM		U	RAPIʾ	I		AM-MU-RA-BI-I		A+
		ḎIMR			RAPIʾ	I		ZI-ME-IR-RA-BI-I		TA 30 34
	2	ʾIL		I	RIḪṢ	I		I$_3$-LI$_2$-RI-IḪ-ZI	FN	XIII 1 IX 39
	1	RIMŠ		I	ʾIL			RI-IM-ŠI-DINGIR		M+
		RIMŠ		I	ʾIL	I		RI-IM-ŠI-I$_3$-LI$_2$		M
	2	ʾANN		U	RIMŠ	I		AN-NU-RI-IM-ŠI	FN	M+
		KAKK		A	RIMŠ	I		KA-AK-KA-RI-IM-ŠI	FN	RA LXV 60 III 5
	1	RIPʾ		I	HADD	U		RI-IP-I-D-IM		M+
		RIPʾ		I	HEDD	A		RI-IP-E-D-IM		M
		RIPʾ		I	DAGAN			RI-IP-I-D-DA-GAN		M+
		RIPʾ		I	DAGAN			RI-BI-D-DA-GAN		M
		RIPʾ		I	LIʾM			RI-IP-I-LI-IM		M
	1	SIMT		I	JARAḪ			ZI-IM-TI-E-RA-AḪ		M+
	1	SINAQ		I				ZI-NA-GI		M

SUFFIXES, Class 2

I	1			SITR		I		JABAL				ZI-IT-RI-E-BA-AL		M+
				SITR		I		HADD		U		ZI-IT-RI-D-IM		M
				SITR		I		HADD		U		SI-IT-RI-D-IM		JCS XXIV 60 NO.51 REV.
				SITR		I	JE	HADD		U		ZI-IT-RI-E-D-IM		JCS XXIV 63 NO.56 REV.
				SITR		I		ʾEL		UM		ZI-IT-RI-E-LUM		B 42
				SITR		I		ʾIL				ZI-IT-RI-DINGIR		B 42
				SITR		I		KI						
								ʾEL				ZI-IT-RI?-KI-EL?		B 42
	1			ŠAʾL		I		ʾIL				SA-LI-DINGIR		B 37+
	1			ŠAʾR		I						SA-RI	GEN	VAS VIII 14 28
	1			ŠAKB		I		HADD		U		SA-AK-BI-D-IM		ARMT V P. 123
	1	JU	T	ŠALIL		I						UŠ-TA-LI-LI	NOM	M+
		MU		ŠALIM		I						MU-SA-LI-MI	NOM	UCP X/1 87 11
	1			ŠALUḪ		I						SA-AL-LU-ḪI	GEN	BE VI/2 138 2, 5
	1			ŠAM	AN	I						SA-MA-A-NI		JNES XIII 212F.+ LATE
				ŠAM		I		JARAḪ				SA-ME-E-RA-AḪ		M
				ŠAM		I		JARAḪ				SA-ME-RA-AḪ		YOS VIII 64 19+
				ŠAM		I		JATAR				SA-MI-E-TAR		XII 601 6
				ŠAM		I		DAʿ		UM		SA-MI-DA-ḪU-UM		M+
				ŠAM		I		DAʿ		IM		SA-MI-DA-ḪI-IM	GEN	M+
				ŠAM		I		DAʿ	AT	UM		SA-MI-DA-ḪA-TUM	FN	M
				ŠAM		I		DAʿ	AT	IM		SA-MI-DA-ḪA-TIM	FN? GEN	XII 741 6
				ŠAM		I		MA						
							JA	ŠJIM				SA-MI-MA-IA-SI-IM	FN	C+
				ŠAM		I		ME						
								ʾEL				SA-MI-ME-EL		CT XLV 117 33
	1			ŠAMʾIL		I		ʾIL				SA-AM-ḪI-LI-DINGIR		M
	1			ŠAMḪ	ATANI							SA-AM-ḪA-TA-NI		VAS VIII 14 5
	1			ŠAMAR		I		HADD		U		SA-MA-RI-A-DU		A. 57 45
				ŠAMAR		I		ʾIL				SA-MA-RI-DINGIR		A. 455 46
				ŠAMAŠ		I						ŠA-MA-ŠI		CT IV 43B 7
	1			ŠAMM		I		JATAR				SA-AM-MI-A-TA-AR		TIM I 28 34, 38, 49
				ŠAMM		I		JATAR				SA-AM-ME-TAR		M+
				ŠAMM		I		JATAR				SA-AM-ME-E-TAR		M+
				ŠAMM		I		JATAR				SA-MI-E-TA-AR		M+
				ŠAMM		I		JATAR				SA-AM-MI-E-TAR		M+
				ŠAMM		I		JATAR				SA-AM-MI-TAR		M+
	1			ŠAMŠ		I		ʾAḪ		I		SA-AM-SI-A-ḪI		RA LXV 54 XII 26
				ŠAMŠ		I		ʾAB		I		D-UTU-A-BI		M+
				ŠAMŠ		I		HADD		U		SA-AM-SI-D-IM		M+, A.+
				ŠAMŠ		I		HADD		U		SA-AM-SI-A-DU		M+
				ŠAMŠ		I		HADD		U		ŠA-AM-SI-D-IM		M+
				ŠAMŠ		I		HADD		U		D-UTU-ŠI-D-IM		M+, C+
				ŠAMŠ		I		HADD		U		SA-AM-ŠI-D-IM		C
				ŠAMŠ		I		HADD		U		SA-AM-SI-IA-AD-DU		M
				ŠAMŠ		I		HADD		U		D-UTU-ŠI-A-DU		A.
				ŠAMŠ		I		HADD		U				
								ʾIL		I		SA-AM-SI-D-IM-I_3-LI_2		C+
				ŠAMŠ		I		HADD		U				
								....				SA-AM-SI-D-IM-TU-GUL-TI		M
				ŠAMŠ		I		HEDD		A		SA-AM-SI-E-D-IM		SIMMONS 4 20
				ŠAMŠ		I		HEDD		A		SA-AM-SI-E-DA		A. 455 36
				ŠAMŠ		I		JARAḪ				SA-AM-SI-E-RA-AḪ		BASOR 95, 19+, M+
				ŠAMŠ		I		JAŠʿ	AH			D-[UT]U-IA-AŠ-ḪA	FN	XIII 1 IV 43
				ŠAMŠ		I		ʾITEJ			JE	D-UTU-I-TE-E		CT IV 44 B 3, 4
				ŠAMŠ		I	JA	JPUʿ	AT			D-UTU-IA-PU-ḪA-AT	FN?	BM 17075
				ŠAMŠ		I		DAʿ		I		D-UTU-DA-ḪI-I		LANGDON XV 2
				ŠAMŠ		I		DIʿ	AT			SA-AM-SI-DI-ḪA-AT?		TIM II 49 5
				ŠAMŠ		I		DAGAN				SA-AM-SI-D-DA-GAN		M+
				ŠAMŠ		I		DITAN		A		SA-AM-SI-DI-TA-NA		B 38
				ŠAMŠ		I		LIʾM				SA-AM-SI-LI-IM		M
				ŠAMŠ		I		RAPIʾ				ŠA-AM-[SI]-RA-BI		M
				ŠAMŠ		I		ŠAMŠ				ZA-AM-SI-D-UTU		YOS XII 39 END
	2			ʾAB		I		ŠAMŠ		I		A-BI-D-UTU-ŠI	FN	XIII 1 IX 40+
				ʾUMM		I		ŠAMŠ		I		UM-MI-D-UTU-ŠI	FN	RA LXV 65 VII 38
				ʾARḪ		I		ŠAMŠ		I		AR-ḪI-D-UTU-ŠI	FN	XIII 1 XIII 2

I	2	ʾIŠḪAR	AH	ŠAMŠ	I		D-IŠ-ḪA-RA-D-UTU-ŠI	FN	XII 265 6
		ʿAŠTAR		ŠAMŠ	I		EŠ$_4$-DAR-D-UTU-ŠI	FN	M
		BAʿL	I	ŠAMŠ	I		BA-AḪ-LI-D-UTU-ŠI	FN	M
		DAGAN		ŠAMŠ	I		D-DA-GAN-D-UTU-ŠI	FN	RA LXV 58 I 23+
	1	ŠAMUʿ	I	ʾIL			SA-MU-ḪI-IL		XIV 76:19
		ŠAMUʿ	I	ʾEL			SA-MU-ḪI-EL		M
		ŠAMUK	I	ʾEL			SA-MU-KI-EL		B 38+
	1	ŠAPŠ	I				ŠA-AP-ŠI		A.
		ŠAPŠ	I	ʾAB	I		ŠA-AP-ŠI-A-BI	FN	A.
		ŠAPŠ	I	HADD	U		SA-AP-SI-A-DU		A.+
		ŠAPŠ	I	HEDD	A		SA-AP-SI-E-DA		A.+
	1	ŠAQṮ	I				ŠA-AQ-TI	GEN	CT VIII 10B 7+
	2	ʾAJAN		ŠARR	I		A-IA-AŠ-LUGAL		A. 18 4
		ʾAJAN		ŠARR	I		A-IA-LUGAL-RI		A. 243 22
		ʾAJAN		ŠARR	I		A-IA-LUGAL		A. 274 4
		JAʾAN		ŠARR	I		IA-AN-ŠAR-RI		M XIII 1 X 16
		ŠADW	UM	ŠARR	I		[Š]A-DU-UM-ŠAR-RI		XIV 106:10, 17
		ŠADW	U	ŠARR	I		ŠA-DU-ŠAR-RI		XIV 109:6
		ŠADW	U	ŠARR	I		ŠA-DU-ŠA-AR-RI		M
		ŠADW	U	ŠARR	I		ŠA-DU-LUGAL		M
		ŠADW	UM	ŠARR	I		ŠA-DU-UN-ŠAR-RI		M
	3	ʾAJA		ʾAB	I				
				ŠARR	I		A-IA-BI-ŠAR-RI		A.
	1	ŠAṮIḪ	I				SA-TI-I	GEN	SYRIA XXXVII 206 10 HANA
	1	ŠIKR	I	HADD	A		SI-IK-RI-ḪA-DA		BE VI/1 6 19
	1	ŠIMḪ	I	DAGAN			SI-IM-ḪI-D-DA-GAN		M
	2	ḪAJJ	A	ŠIMḪ	I		E$_2$-A-ŠI-IM-ḪI	FN	XIII 1 II 44
		ʾADM	U	ŠIMḪ	I		AD-MU-ŠI-IM-ḪI	FN	XIII 1 IV 6
		ʾADM	U	ŠIMḪ	I		D-AD-MU-ŠI-IM-ḪI	FN	RA LXV 62 V 28
		ʾIL	I	ŠIMḪ	I		I$_3$-LI$_2$-ŠI-IM-ḪI		M+
		ʾANN	U	ŠIMḪ	I		[A]N-NU-ŠI-IM-ḪI		XIII 1 XIV 24
		ʿAŠTAR		ŠIMḪ	I		EŠ$_4$-DAR-ŠI-IM-ḪI	FN	XIII 1 XII 2
		TABUB	U	ŠIMḪ	I		TA-BU-BU-ŠI-IM-ḪI	FN	XII 265 4
	1	ŠIMM	I	JATAR			SI-IM-ME-A-TAR		A 7537 16, 21+
	1	ŠIPR	I	HAND	A		ŠI-IP-RI-AN-TA		A. LATE
	1	ŠIRIB	I				SI-RI-BI		SYRIA XXXVII 206 29 HANA
	1 MI	ŠQIḪ	I				MI-IS-KI-ḪI	NOM	UET V 605 20
	1	ŠUGAG	I				SU-GA-GI	GEN	CT IV 31A 5+
	1	ŠULAL	I				SU-UL-LA-LI	GEN	TCL XVIII 95 1
		ŠULAP	I				SU-LA-PI		PBS XI/2 P. 119
	1	ŠUM	I	ʾAB	UM		SU-ME-A-BU-UM		A. 12 4
		ŠUM	I	HADD	U		SU-MI-A-DU		A.+
		ŠUM	I	HEDD	A		SU-MI-E-DA		YOS XIII 486:1
		ŠUM	I	ʾIL	UM		SU-MI-LU-UM		WALTERS, WL 114:13
		ŠUM	I	JAMAM			SU-MI-IA-MA-AM		XII 61 5
		ŠUM	I	ʾENLIL			SU-ME-D-EN-LIL$_2$		KISURRA 197A 12
		ŠUM	I	ḪINN	I		ŠU-MI-IN-NI		U
		ŠUM	I	ʾENTIL			SU-ME-EN-TI-[IL]?		B 38
		ŠUM	I	DAWR	U		SU?-MI-DA-AR-RU		A. 322 9
		ŠUM	I	DAWR	U		ŠU-MI-TA-RU		A. LATE
		ŠUM	I	LAMM	U		SU-MI-LAM-MU		VAS XVI 24 4, A.+
		ŠUM	I	RIJB	A		SU-MI-RI-BA		A. 98C 10
		ŠUM	I	RIJB	A		ŠU-MI-RI-PA		A. LATE
		ŠUM	I	RIJB	A		ŠU-ME-RI-PA		A. LATE
		ŠUM	I	RAPAʾ			SU-MI-RA-PA		RA LVI 169, A.+
		ŠUM	I	ṮAJB	A		SU?-MI-DA-BA		A. 7 44+
	2 JA	PLUS	I	ŠUM	I		IA-AP-LU-SI-SU-U$_2$-MI		BIROT,TEA 31:6
		QARAʾ		ŠUM	I	JA	QA-RA-SU-MI-IA		CT II 34 5
		QARAʾ		ŠUM	I	JA	GA-RA-SU-MI-IA		CT XLVIII 89 REV.
	1	ŠUMUT	I				SU-MU-TI		B 40
		ŠUMUT	I	BAʿL			SU-MU-TI-BA-AL		M
		ŠUMUT	I	JABAL	A		SU-MU-TI-A-BA-LA?		PBS XI/2 1 I 35
	1 JA	ŠWIB	I	ʾILL	A		IA-ŠI-BI-IL-LA		A.
	1 JE	ŠWUB	I	ʾIL			IE-E-ŠU-BI-DINGIR		B 26
	1	ŠAʾUM	I				ŠA-U$_2$-MI		BAB. III 267 HANA
	1	ŠAWB	I	ʾIL			ŠA-BI-DINGIR		M, C+

I	1	ŠAWB	I		BIJT	UM		ŠA-A-BI-E$_2$		SUMER V 142 NO. 6
		ŠAWB	I		DAWD	I		[Š]A?-BI-DA-DI		RA LXV 43 I 13
	1	ŠADW	I		HADD	U		ŠA-DI-D-IM		M
		ŠADW	I		ʾIL			SA-DI-DINGIR		JCS IV 110, 2040 16
		ŠADW	I		MA					
					ʾIL			ŠA-DI-MA-DINGIR		RA LXV 48 VIII 20
	1	ŠAKK	I					ŠA-AK-KI		RA LXV 45 V 13
	1	ŠAKUM	I		ʾIL			SA-KU-MI-DINGIR		M+
	2	BUN	U		ŠALG	I		BU-NU-ŠA?-AL?-GI		B 16
	1	ŠANIJ	I					SA-NI-I		YOS II 139 3
	2	ḎU			ŠAT	I		ZU-ŠA-TI		HARRIS 56 12
	1	ŠAṬUP	I		ʾIL			ŠA-TU-BI-DINGIR		M+
		ŠAṬUP	I		ʾEL			ŠA-TU-BI-EL		RA LXV 44 IV 74
	1	ŠIPṬ	I		JAʾAR			ŠI-IP-TI-A-ḪA-AR	FN	C
		ŠIPṬ	I		HADD	U		ŠI-IP-TI-D-IM		A. LATE
		ŠIPṬ	I		HAND	A		ŠI-IP-TI-AN-TA		A. LATE
		ŠIPṬ	I		HAND	A		ŠI-IP-TI-IA-AN-TA		A. LATE
	1	ŠIRṬ	I		ʾIL	I		ŠI-IR-TE-I$_3$-LI$_2$		A. LATE
	1	ŠUʾAR	I		....			ŠU-A-RI-[....]		M
	1	ŠUWB	I		HADD	U		ŠU-BI-D-IM		M
		ŠUWB	I		QARAD			ŠU-BI-GA-RA-AD		I
	2	ʿABD			ŠUWR	I		AB-DU-ŠU-RI		IRAQ XXX 94, RIMAH
	1	ŠUŠAG	I					ŠU-ŠA-GI	FN	M
	1	ṢABʾ	I					ZA-BI$_2$	FN	U
	2	ḤAM	I		ṢABṬ	I		A-MI-ZA-AB-TI	MN	B 13
		ḤAM	I		ṢABṬ	I		A-MI-ZA-AB-TI	FN	CT VIII 35 B 1
	1	ṢALIL	I					ZA-LI-LI	GEN	B 41
	1	ṢARP	I		....			ZA-AR-BI-[....]		M
	1	ṢIBʾ	I		LIʾL	UM		ZE$_2$-BI-LI-LUM		HSM 7900, UR III
		ṢIBʾ	I		LIʾM			ZI-BI-LI-IM		M
		ṢIBʾ	I		NIʿM			ZI-BI-NI-ḪI-I[M]		M
	1	ṢIDQ	I		JATAR			ZI-ID-KI-E-TAR		M+
		ṢIDQ	I	JE	JPAʿ			ZI-ID-KI-E-PA		RA XLIII 37 QATNA
		ṢIDQ	I	JE	JPUʿ			ZI-ID-KI-E-PU-UḪ		M+, C+
	2	ʾIL	I		ṢIDQ	I		I$_3$-LI$_2$-ZI-ID-KI		DELAPORTE CCL II A 337
	2	KUʾM	U		ṢILL	I		KU-MU-ZI-LI	FN	B 33+
	1	ṢIRP	I					ZI-IR-RI	NOM	M, A.+
	1	ṢUWR	I		HADD	U		ZU-RI-D-IM		M+
		ṢUWR	I		ʾIL			ZU-RI-DINGIR		M
		ṢUWR	I		ʿAMM	U		ZU-RI-ḪA-AM-MU		M
		ṢUWR	I		ʿAMM	U	HU	ZU-RI-ḪA-AM-MU-U$_2$		M+
		ṢUWR	I		JARAḪ			ZU-RI-E-RA-AḪ		M
		ṢUWR	I		DAGAN			ZU-RI-D-DA-GAN		M
	2	ʾAB	I		ṢUWR	I		A-BI-ZU-RI		M
		KA			ṢUWR	I				
					ḪAʾL	A		KA-ZU-RI-ḪA-LA		M
		NAHR			ṢUWR	I		D-ID$_2$-ZU-RI		M
	1	ṢUPR	I		JARAḪ			ZU-UP-RI-E-RA-AḪ		M+
	1	ṢURR	I					ZU-UR-RI	NOM	M
	1	TAʾ	I					TA-ḪI		M+
	2	ʾAMAN			TAʾ	I		AM-MA-AN-TA-ḪI		M
	1	TAʾG	I					TA-GI		RA LXV 43 III 40+
	1	TAʾK	I					TA-KI		RA LXV 55 XIII 19
		TAʾK	I		ʾIŠḪAR AH			TA-KI-D-IŠ-ḪA-RA		JCS XIII 52 293 LE,A.LATE
	1	TAʾM	I					TA-MI		RA LXV 50 IX 13
	2	MANN	A		TAWR	I		MA-NA-TA-RI		B 34
	1	TABʾ	I		BIN	UM		TA-AB-I-BI-NU-UM		BM 82437 4 9
	1	TABB	I		MAM	A		TA-BI-D-MA-MA	FN	M
	2	ʾANN	U		TABB	I		AN-NU-TAB-BI	FN	XIII 1 III 36+
		ʿAŠTAR			TABB	I		EŠ$_4$-DAR-TAB-BI	FN	M+, C
		ḤAṢN	U		TABB	I		AZ?-NU-TAB-BI	FN	M
		ŠALAŠ			TABB	I		D-ŠA-LA-AŠ-TAB-BI	FN	XIII 1 III 26
	1	TABUB	I		ʿIMD	I		TA-BU-TI?-IM-DI	FN	VIII 31 10 15
		TABUZ	I					TA-BU-ZI		RA LXV 45 V 33
	1	TATT	I		BAʾT	UM		TA-AT-TI-BA-TUM		TCL I 204:10
	1	TIWR	I	Š	TUWR			TE-RI-IŠ-TU-UR$_2$		C+

I	2	ʾANN	U		TIWR		I		AN-NU-TI-RI	FN	M+
		JARAḪ			TIWR		I		D-EN-ZU-TI-RI		M+
		DAGAN			TIWR		I		D-DA-GAN-TI-RI	FN	RA LXV 61 IV 51
	2	ʾANN	U		TILL	AT	I		AN-NU-TIL-LA-TI	FN	XIII 1 X 2
	3 JA	KRUB			ʾIL						
					TILL	AT	I		D-IA-AK-RU-UB-DINGIR-TIL-LA-TI		M
	1	TINʾ	I		JARAḪ				TI-IN-E-RA-AḪ		C
		TINʾ	I		JARAḪ				TI-IN-I-E-RA-AḪ		C
	1	TUʾ	I						TU-I		XIII 60 5
	2	MAM	A		TUʾAL		I		D-MA-MA-TU-ḪA-LI	FN	M
	1	TUWR	I		DAGAN				TU-RI-D-DA-GAN		B 40+ HANA
	2	ʾIL	I		TUWR		I	JA	I_3-LI_2-TU-RI-IA		XII 115 5+
		ʿAŠTAR			TUWR		I	JA	$EŠ_4$-DAR-TU-RI-IA	FN	XIII 1 XIII 33
		KAKK	A		TUWR		I	JA	KA-KA-TU-RI-IA	FN	M
	1	TUBAB	I						TU-BA-BI		RA LXV 41 II 26
	1	TUDAR	I		ʿAŠTAR				TU-DA-RI-$EŠ_4$-DAR	FN	EDZARD, DER 58:7
	1	TUKR	ATIJI						TUK-RA-TI-I	GEN	UCP X/3 2 19
	2	ʾANN	U		TUKUL	T	I		AN-NU-TU-KU-UL-[TI]	FN	M+
		ʾANN	U		TUKUL	T	I		AN-NU-TU-GUL-TI	FN	XIII 1 X 3
	1	TUND	I						TU-UN-DI	FN	M+
	1	TUPT	I	JA	MWUT		A		TU-UP-TI-IA-MU-TA		BM 80328 2
	2	ʾALL	I		TURAḪ		I		AL-LI-TU-RA-ḪI	FN	A.
	1	ṬAḪD	I		LIʾM				TA-AḪ-DI-LI-IM		M
	2	ḪAM	I		ṬAJB		I		A-MI-ṬA-BI		RA LXV 45 V 81
		ŠUM	U		ṬAJB		I		SU-MU-DA-BI		X 90 10+
	1	ṬALL	I	JI	BNIJ				TA-LI-IB-NI	FN	CT II 5 3 9
	1	ṬUBQ	I						TU-UB-KI		RA LXV 40 I 24
	2	ʿAMM	I		ZAʾT		I		ḪA-MI-ZA-TI		HARRIS 103 1
	1	ZAʾZ	I		ʾANN		U		ZA-ZI-AN-NU		B 41+
	1	ZANAN	I						ZA-NA-NI	GEN	B 48
	1	ZANN	I						ZA-AN-NI		B 41
	2	ʾIL	I		ZANN		I		I_3-LI_2-ZA-AN-NI	FN	M+
	1	ZAQAT	I						ZA-GA-TI	GEN	B 41
	1	ZIJAN	I						ZI-JA-NI	FN	M
		ZIJAN	I						ZI-IA-NI		KISURRA 4A:11+
		ZIJAN	I						D-EN-ZU-I-A-NI		KISURRA 72:6
	1	ZIBIN	I						ZI-BI-NI		B 42
	1	ZIMM	I		DAWD		I		ZI-IM-MI-DA-DI	FN	C II 44 33+
	1	ZIZN	I		ʾEL				ZI-IZ-NI-EL		RA LXV 55 XIII 11
	1	ZUʾUM	I						ZU-U_2-MI	GEN	PBS VIII/2 236 6
	1	ZUḪIR	I						ZU-ḪI-RI		M
	1	ZUJAN	I						ZU-JA-NI	FN	C
IJA	1	ʾAḪ	IJA						A-ḪI-IA		M+
	1	ʾAK	IJA						A-KI-IA		M+
	1	ʾAKK	AT	IJA					A-KA-TI-IA-A		KISURRA 178 1
		ʾAKK	AT	IJA					A-KA-TI-IA	FN	KISURRA 171 1; M+
	1	ʾAKUN	IJA						A-KU-NI-IA		CT XLV 5 R. 3
	1	ʾALUN	IJA						A-LU-NI-IA	FN	EDZARD, DER 91:13
	1	ʾAPR	IJA						AP-RI-A		A.
	1	ʾAŠD	IJA						AŠ-DI-IA		BIN VII 32 4
	1	ʾEN	IJA						E-NI-IA		M+
	1	ʾIL	IJA						I_3-LI_2-IA		M+
	1	ʾUMM	IJA						UM?-MI-IA	FN	XIII 1 XIV 18
	1	ʾURAŠ	IJA						U_2-RA-SI-IA		M
	1	HALIL	IJA						ḪA-LI-LI-IA		B 18+
	1	ḤAJJ	AT	IJA					A-A-TI-IA		BM 92654 5
		ḤAJJ	AT	IJA					A-IA-TI-IA		BM 82440
	1	ḤANN	IJA						ḪA-AN-NI-A	FN	RA LXV 60 III 48
	1	ḤAṢAN	IJA						A-ZA-NI-IA		BM 80363 17
	1	ḤIMD	IJA						ḪI-IM-DI-IA		M+
	1	ḤINN	IJA						ḪI-NI-IA	FN	X 116 3
	1	ḤUNN	IJA						ḪU-NI-IA		UCP X/3 2:22; M
	1	ḪAʾL	IJA						ḪA-LI-IA		C, A. LATE
		ḪAʾL	IJA						ḪA-LI_2-IA		C+
		ḪAʾL	IJA						ḪA-LI_2-IA		RA LXV 47 VI 64; C+
	1	ḪAʾR	IJA						ḪA-RI-IA		M+

IJA	1	ḪAND		IJA	ḪA-AN-DI-IA		BIN VII 63 28
	1	ḪIRD		IJA	ḪI-IR-DI-IA		RA LXV 53 XI 50
	1	ʿABD		IJA	ḪA-AB-DI-IA		B 9+, M, C+
		ʿABD		IJA	AB-DI-IA		A.+
	1	ʿAD	AT	IJA	A-DA-TI-A	FN	MRS IX P. 243 UGARIT
	1	ʿAḎR		IJA	ḪA-AZ-RI-IA		RA LXV 41 II 21+
	1	ʿAGAL		IJA	ḪA-GA-LI-IA		HARRIS 88:3
	1	ʿAMM		IJA	AM-MI-IA		B 13+
		ʿAMM		IJA	ḪA-MI-IA		C+
		ʿAMM		IJA	ḪA-AM-MI-IA		M
	1	ʿAN		IJA	A-NI-IA		RUTTEN 31 5+
	1	ʿAZAL		IJA	A-ZA-LI-IA		B 14+
		ʿAZAL		IJA	A-SA-LI-JA		B 14+
	1	ʿIZZ		IJA	I-ZI-IA		RA LXV 51 IX 41
	1	ʿUZAL		IJA	ḪU-ZA-LI-IA		BIROT, TEA 70BIS:36'
	1	JAMN		IJA	IA-AM-NI-IA		RA LXV 54 XII 63
	1	JANT		IJA	IA-AN-TI-IA		M+
	1	JAT		IJA	IA-TI-IA		M+
	1	JATT		IJA	IA-AT-TI-IA		M
	1	JID		IJA	I-DI-IA		M
	1	JIŠʿ	AT	IJA	IŠ-ḪA-TI-IA	MN?	B 24+
		JIŠʿ	IT	IJA	IŠ-ḪI-TI-IA	MN?	CT XLVIII 91 REV.+
		JIŠʿ		IJA	IŠ-HI-IA		M, C
	1	BAʿD		IJA	BA-AḪ-DI-IA		RUTTEN 12A 23+
	1	BAʿL		IJA	BA-AḪ-LI-IA		KISURRA 24 5, 7
		BAʿL		IJA	BA-LI-IA		A.; M
	1	BIKIN		IJA	BI-KI-NI-IA		VAS XIII 20A R. 19
	1	BIN		IJA	BI-NI-IA		M
		BIN		IJA	BI-IN-NI-IA		CT IV 10 39+
	1	BINZ		IJA	B[I]-IN-ZI-IA		M
	1	BUWZ		IJA	BU-ZI-IA		M+
	1	BUN		IJA	BU-NI-IA		RA LXV 54 XII 31
	1	DAWD		IJA	DA-DI-IA		B 16+, M+
	1	DAWR		IJA	DA-RI-IA		M+
	1 ʾA	DLUQ		IJA	AD-LU-KI-IA		RES 1939, 69
	1	ḎAQN		IJA	ZA-AQ-NI-IA		WALTERS,WL 100:4+
	1	ḎIKR		IJA	ZI-IK-RI-IA		RA LXV 43 IV 20
	1	ḎIMR		IJA	ZI-IM-RI-IA		M+, C+
	1	ḎUBAB		IJA	SU-BA-BI-IA		SIMMONS P. 71 N. 5 3
		ḎUBAB		IJA	SU-PA-BI-IA		UCP X/1 108 1
	1	GAʾG		IJA	GA-GI-IA		HARRIS 13 12
	1	GAʾR		IJA	GA-RI-IA		RA LXV 44 IV 58
	1	GUʾR		IJA	GU-RI-IA		HARRIS 8 5+
	1	KAʾB		IJA	KA-BI-IA		M+
	1	KAʾL		IJA	KA-LI-IA		RA LXV 53 XI 48
		KAʾL		IJA	KA-LI-IA	FN	C
	1	KAʾR		IJA	KA-RI-IA		RA LXV 52 X 25
	1	KAHAL		IJA	KA-A-LI-IA		M
	1	KAMN		IJA	KA-AM-NI-IA		VAS XVI 78:0
	1	KIʾL		IJA	KI-LI-IA		RA LXV 45 V 55
	1	KINZ		IJA	KI-IN-ZI-IA		M
	1	KUʾD		IJA	KU-DI-IA	FN	XIII 1 III 35
	1	KUBB		IJA	KU-UB-BI-IA		M
	1	KUŠAP		IJA	KU-SA-BI-IA		M
	1	MAʾAN		IJA	MA-ḪA-NI-IA	FN	M+
	1	MAʾD		IJA	MA-DI-IA		RA LXV 55 XIII 49
	1	MAʾL		IJA	MA-LI-IA		M
	1	MAʾM		IJA	MA-MI-IA		M
	1	MAʾR	AT	IJA	MA-RA-TI-IA		HARRIS 99 13
	1	MAʾŠ		IJA	MA-ŠI-IA		M+
	1	MANN		IJA	MA-AN-NI-IA		M+
	1	MIŠR		IJA	ME-IŠ?-RI-IA	FN	RA LXV 60 III 35
	1	MUʾUT		IJA	MU-U_2-TI-IA	FN	XIII 1 VII 48
	1	MUT		IJA	MU-TI-IA		B 35, A.+
	1	NAʿM		IJA	NA-MI-IA	FN	CT XLV 3 8,15,23
		NAʿM		IJA	NA-AḪ-MI-IA		JCS XXVI 142:8 HARMAL

IJA	1	NABUṬ		IJA			NA-BU-DI-IA		TCL XVIII 125 3
	1	NAN		IJA			NA-NI-IA	FN	RA LXV 60 III 66
	1	NANN		IJA			NA-AN-NI-IA	FN	XIII 1 I 66
	1	NAPŠ		IJA			NA-AP-SI-IA		M
	1	NAṢR		IJA			NA-AṢ-RI-IA		RA LXV 44 IV 47+
	1	NUWP	AT	IJA			NU-PA-TI-IA	FN	M
	1	PAʾR	AT	IJA			PA-RA-TI-IA		UCP X/3 3 8
	1	PALS		IJA			PA-AL-ZI-IA		SIMMONS 44 6+
	1	PALṬ		IJA			PA-AL-TI-IA		YONDORF 2
	1	PAŠD		IJA			PA-AŠ-DI-IA		B 37
	1	PAṬR		IJA			BA-AṬ-RI-IA		A 21950
	1	PULS		IJA			PU-UL-ZI-IA		M
	1	SIKIL		IJA			ZI-KI-LI-IA		CT XLVIII 89
	1	SITR		IJA			ZI-IT-RI-IA		M+, C+
		SITR		IJA			ZI-IT-RI-JA		M
	1	ŠAʾAD		IJA			SA-A-DI-IA		C+
	1	ŠAʾL		IJA			SA-LI-IA		B 37
	1	ŠAʾR		IJA			SA-RI-IA		UCP X/1 108 10+
	1	ŠAKB		IJA			SA-[A]K-BI-IA		RA LXV 44 IV 34
	1	ŠALD		IJA			SA-AL-DI-IA		TCL I 80 16
	1	ŠAM		IJA			SA-MI-IA		EBPN 140+, MAM II/3 PL. XXXIX+
	1	ŠAMŠ		IJA			SA-AM-SI-IA		X 166 9, 13
	1	ŠAPŠ		IJA			SA-AP-SI-IA		A. 53 R. 9
	1	ŠARR		IJA			ŠAR-RI-IA		M+
	1	ŠIJB	AT	IJA			SI-BA-TI-IA	FN?	BM 80363 7
	1	ŠUM		IJA			SU-MI-IA		M+
	1	ŠADW		IJA			ŠA?-DI?-IA		XIII 1 I 3
	1	ŠIRṬ		IJA			ŠE-ER-DI-IA		A.
	1	ṢABR		IJA			ZA-AB-RI-IA		YOS VIII 120 22
	1	ṢIBʾ		IJA			ZI-BI-IA		XIV 106:6
	1	ṢIDQ		IJA			ZI-ID-KI-IA		RA LXV 55 XIII 9
	1	ṢUWR		IJA			ZU-RI-IA		XIV 98:11
	1	ṬAJB		IJA			ṬA$_3$-BI-A	FN	RA LXV 66 VII 54
	1	ZAʾZ		IJA			ZA-ZI-IA		M+
	1	ZALAT		IJA			ZA-LA-TI-IA		BM 17060 35+
	1	ZILIB		IJA			ZI-LI-BI-IA		RUTTEN 19 21
IJAN	1	ʾAK		IJAN			A-KI-IA-AN		M, A. LATE+
	1	ʾATT		IJAN			AT-TI-IA-AN		A. 261 14
	1	ḪAʾL		IJAN			ḪA-LI-IA-AN		A. LATE
	1	ḪIZR		IJAN			ḪI-IZ-RI-IA-AN		M
	1	ʿAMM		IJAN			AM-MI-IA-AN		A.+
	1	JID		IJAN			I-DI-JA-AN		RA LXV 47 VII 54
	1	DAWD		IJAN			DA-DI-IA-AN		RA LXV 44 IV 75
	1	ḎIMR		IJAN			ZI-IM-RI-IA-AN		RA LXV 44 IV 76
	1	MAʾR		IJAN			MA-RI-IA-AN		RA LXV 43 III 81
	1	ŠAʾQ		IJAN			ŠA-GI-IA-AN		RA LXV 54 XII 11+
	1	ṢIBʾ		IJAN			ZI-BI-IA-AN		RA LXV 42 III 24
	1	TINʾ		IJAN			TI-IN-I-IA-AN		RA LXV 51 IX 76+
IM	1	ʾAḪ		IM			A-ḪI-IM	GEN	M
	2	ʾAJA			ʾAḪ	IM	A-IA-A-ḪI-IM		X 166 4
		ḪANN		A	ʾAḪ	IM	AN-NA-A-ḪI-IM	GEN	M
		ʿAQB		A	ʾAḪ	IM	AQ-BA-A-ḪI-IM	GEN	M+
		ʿAQB		A	ʾAḪ	IM	ḪA-AQ-BA-A-ḪI-IM	GEN	M+
	3	BIN			MA				
					ʾAḪ	IM	BI-IN-MA-A-ḪI-IM		M
	1	ʾAWN	AN	IM			AW-NA-NI-[IM]	GEN	MAM III 320, PSARG MARI
	2	ŠUM		U	ʾAWN AN	IM	SU-MU-AW-NA-NIM		SUMER XXIII ARABIC 178
	1	ʾAJAL		IM			A-IA-LIM	GEN	M
	2 JA	JDIʿ			ʾAB	IM	IA-DI-ḪA-A-BI-IM	GEN	M+
	JA	RWIḪ		A	ʾAB	IM	IA-RI-ḪA-A-BI-IM	GEN	M+
	JA	ŠJIM			ʾAB	IM	IA-SI-IM-A-BI-IM	GEN	M
		ŠAM		U	ʾAB	IM	SA-MU-A-BI-IM	NOM	RA VIII 71
		ŠAM		U	ʾAB	IM	SA-MU-A-BI-IM	GEN	SUMER XXIII 153+
		ŠUM		U	ʾAB	IM	[S]U-MU-A-BI-IM	NOM	EDZARD, DER 111:5
		ŠUM		U	ʾAB	IM	SU-MU-A-BI-IM	GEN	SUMER XXIII PL. 12 19
	3	ʾAJA			ŠUM	U			
					ʾAB	IM	ḪA-IA-SU-MU-A-BI-IM		M

IM	3			ʾUMM		UM		KA				
								ʾAB	IM	UM-MU-UM-KA-A-BI-IM	FN	M
		JI		JṢIʾ				ŠUM	U			
								ʾAB	IM	I-ZI-SU-MU-A-BI-IM	GEN	B 23
		JA		KWUN				ŠUM	U			
								ʾAB	IM	IA-KU-UN-SU-MU-A-BI-IM		M
	1			ʾABAB	AN	IM				A-BA-BA-NI-IM	GEN	B 42
	2			MUT		U		ʾABIḪ	IM	MU-TU-A-BI-ḪI-IM		C
	2			ʿABD				ʾABN	IM	ARAD$_2$-AB-NIM		BAGHD. MITT. II 72
	1			ʾADM	AN	IM				ḪA-AD-MA?-NIM	GEN	B 44
	2			LA				ʾADUN	IM	LA-DU-NIM	GEN	M
		JA		ʾGUN		IM				IA-GU-NI-IM	GEN	BM 16485
	1			ʾAKK	ATANIM					AK-KA-TA-NI-IM	GEN	A 32133:6
	1			ʾAKUN	AN	IM				A-KU-NA-NIM	GEN	B 92
	1			ʾAMAN	AN	IM				A-MA-NA-NIM	GEN	B 43
	1		T	ʾAMR		IM				A-TAM-RI-IM	GEN	M+
			T	ʾAMR		IM				A-TA-AM-RI-IM	GEN	M+
	2			ʾAB		I		ʾANN	IM	A-BI-AN-NIM	GEN	M
	1			ʾARWIJ		IM				AR-WI-IM	GEN	TIM V 14 23, M
	2			MUT		U		ʾARAPḪ	IM	MU-TU-AR-RA-AP-ḪI-IM		C+
	1			ʾARNAB	AT	IM				AR-NA-BA-TIM	FN? GEN	MEISSNER 18 3
	1			ʾASIN		IM				A-ZI-NIM	GEN	XIII 13 13+
	1			ʾAŠJ		IM				A-SI-IM	GEN	C
	2			MUT				ʾAŠD	IM	MU-UT-AŠ-DI-IM		M
	1			ʾAŠQUD		IM				AŠ-KU-DI-IM	GEN	M+
	1			ʾATT		IM				ḪA-AT-TI-IM	GEN	M+
	2			MUT				ʾEKAL	IM	MU-UT-E$_2$-GAL-LIM		M
	1			ʾIDD		IM				ḪI-ID-DI-IM		XIV 56:28
	2			NAWḪ				ʾIL	IM	NA-ḪI-LI-IM	GEN	B 35
		JA		PLAḪ				ʾIL	IM	IA-AP-LA-AḪ-I-LI-IM	GEN	RA LXIV 43
	1			ʾILUR		IM				I-LU-RI-IM	GEN	B 22
	1			ʾIPQ	AT	IM				IP-QA-TIM	MN GEN	M+
				ʾIPQ	AT	IM				IP-QA-TI-IM	MN? GEN	M
	1	JA		ʾKUR		IM				IA-KU-RI?-IM?	GEN	VIII 2 23
	1	ME		ʾMIʾ		IM				ME-MI-ḪI-IM	GEN	C
	1	JA		ʾMUR		IM				IA-MU-RI-IM	GEN	B 28+
	2			LA			ʾA	ʾMUR	IM	LA-A-MU-RI-IM	GEN	M
	1	JA		ʾQUD	AN	IM				IA-GU-DA-NIM	GEN	BM 16823A 1
	1			ʾUNUB		IM				ḪU-NU-BI-I[M]	GEN	M
	1			ʾÚRK	UTANIM					UR-KU-TA-NIM	GEN	CT VIII 20B 10
	1			ʾUŠK	ATANIM					UŠ-KA-TA-NIM	MN GEN	XIII 61 5+
	1			ʾUZUL		IM				ḪU-UZ-ZU-LIM	GEN	GORDON 38 21+
	1			HALIL		IM				ḪA-LI-LI-IM	GEN	B 18
				HALIL		IM				ḪA-LI-LIM	GEN	SIMMONS 57 14
	1			HILAL		IM				ḪI-LA-LI-IM	GEN	HARRIS 71 10
				HILAL		IM				ḪI-IL-LA-LIM	GEN	M+
	1			ḪABIB		IM				A-BI-BI-IM	GEN	KISURRA 62
	2			BUN		U		ḪAM	IM	BU-NU-D-A-MI-IM		RA LXV 41 II 27+
				ŠUM		U		ḪAM	IM	SU-MU-D-A-MI-IM		RA LXV 40 I 25+
	1			ḪANAN		IM				A-NA-NI-IM	GEN	B 43
				ḪANAN		IM				ḪA-NA-NI-IM	GEN	B 44
	1			ḪASID	AN	IM				ḪA-ZI-DA-NIM	GEN	M+
	2			MUT				ḪATK	IM	MU-UT-ḪA-AT-KI-IM		RA LXV 44 IV 57
				MUT		I		ḪATK	IM	MU-TI-ḪA-AD-KI-IM	NOM	IRAQ XXX 92+ RIMAH
				MUT		U		ḪATK	IM	MU-TU-ḪA-AD-KI-IM		M+
				MUT		U		ḪATK	IM	MU-TU-AD-KI-IM		M
	1			ḪAZAQ	AN	IM				ḪA-ZA-KA-AN-NIM-KI	GN GEN	C
				ḪAZAQ	AN	IM				ḪA-ZA-KA-NIM-KI	GN GEN	C II 39 13
	1	ME		ḪRIM		IM				ME-EḪ-RI-MI-IM	GEN	M+
	1			ḪUBAS		IM				U$_2$-BA-ZI-IM	GEN	SIMMONS 118 2
	1			ḪUNN	AN	IM				ḪU-NA-NIM	GEN	B 93
	2			LA				ḪUNN	IM	LA-ḪU-NI-IM	GEN	M
	2			ʾAB		U		ḪAʾL	IM	A-BU-ḪA-LIM	GEN	M+
				ʿAZZ		U		ḪAʾL	IM	A-ZU-ḪA-LIM	NOM	M
	2			ŠAMAʿ				ḪAʾT	IM	ŠA-MA-ḪA-TIM	GEN	XIII 1 VIII 44
	1			ḪAWR	AN	IM				ḪA-AW-RA-NIM	GEN	B 44
	1			ḪABIR		IM				ḪA-BI-RI-IM	GEN	M

IM	2		LA			ḪAMUJ	IM	LA-ḪA-MU-JI-IM	GEN	M
	1		ḪANP	AT	IM			ḪA-AN-PA-TIM	FN GEN	A 3521 31
	1	MU	ḪARIR		IM			MU-ḪA-RI-RI-IM	GEN	M
	1	JA	ḪMUM		IM			IA-AḪ-MU-MI-IM	GN GEN	M
	1		ḪUWAL		IM			ḪU-WA-LI-IM	GEN	B 20
	1		ḪURṢ	AN	IM			ḪUR-ZA-NIM	GEN	B 44
			ḪURṢ	AN	IM			ḪUR-ZA-A-NIM	GEN	B 44
			ḪURṢ	AN	IM			ḪU-UR-ZA-NIM	GEN	B 44
	1		ḪUŠŠ	UT	IM			ḪU-ŠU-TIM	FN GEN	X 27 8
	1		ʿABD		IM			AB-DI-IM	GEN	B 9, M
	1		ʿAD	AT	IM			A-DA-TIM	MN GEN	XIII 87 5
	2		ḎU			ʿAD	IM	ZU-ḪA-DI-IM	GEN	M
			ŠUM		U	ʿAD	IM	SU-MU-ḪA-DI-IM		X 57 8
	2		ḎU			ʿADN	IM	ZU-ḪA-AD-NIM	GEN	M+
			ḎU			ʿADN	IM	ZU-U$_2$-ḪA-AD-NIM		VOIX 187:18 MARI
		JA	MZUʾ			ʿADN	IM	[IA?-AM?-Z]U?-ḪA-AD-NIM	GEN	XIII 129 5
	1		ʿAḎAR		IM			A-ZA-RI-IM	GEN	B 14
			ʿAḎAR	AN	IM			ḪA-ZA-RA-NIM	GEN	B 44
	1		ʿAḎIR		IM			ḪA-ZI-RI-IM	GEN	B 20+
	1		ʿAGAL		IM			A-GA-LIM	GEN	YOS XIII 426:9
			ʿAGAL		IM			ḪA-GA-LIM	GEN	M
	1		ʿALIJ	T	IM			A-LI-TIM	FN GEN	M
	1		ʿAMAS		IM			A-MA-ZI-IM	GEN	KISURRA 166 4+
	1		ʿAMIQ	AT	IM			ḪA-MI-QA-TIM-KI	GN GEN	M+
	1		ʿAMM	AN	IM			ḪA-MA-NIM	GEN	M
			ʿAMM	AN	IM			ḪA-AM-MA-NIM	GEN	M
	2		ʿABD			ʿAMM	IM	AB-DU-A-MI-IM	NOM	M+
			ʿABD			ʿAMM	IM	AB-DU-A-MI-IM	GEN	M+
			ʿABD			ʿAMM	IM	ḪA-AB-DU-A-MI-IM		M
			ʿAḎR		I	ʿAMM	IM	ḪA-AZ-RI-A-MI-IM	GEN	M
	2		NAʿM		I	ʿAN	IM	NA-MI-A-NIM		A. 142
	1	ME	ʿANIJ		IM			ME-ḪA-NI-IM	GEN	KISURRA 80B
	1		ʿARD		IM			ḪA-AR-DI-IM	GEN	M
	1		ʿAZAL		IM			A-ZA-LIM	GEN	VAS VIII 14 23
	1		ʿAZZ	ATANIM				ḪA-ZA-TA-NIM	MN GEN	C II 6
	1		ʿEBB		IM			IB-BI-IM	GEN	M+
			ʿEBB	AT	IM			IB-BA-TIM	FN GEN	M
	1	ME	ʿNIJ		IM			ME-EḪ-NI-IM	GEN	KISURRA 80A
	1	ME	ʿQIB		IM			ME-KI-BI-IM	GEN	M+
	2		MUT			ʿUMUS	IM	MU-UT-ḪU-MU-ZI-IM		XIV 122:6+
	1		ʿUZAB		IM			U$_2$-ZA-BI-IM	GEN	SIMMONS 70 16
	1	JA	ʿZIB		IM			IA-ZI-BI-IM	GEN	XIV 92:26+
	1		JAḪAD		IM			IA-ḪA-DI-IM	GEN	XIII 1 IX 30
	1		JAʿIL	AT	IM			IA-ḪI-LA-TIM	GEN	CT XLVIII 27 CASE
			JAʿIL	AN	IM			JA-I-LA-NIM	TRIBE GEN	M+, SHEMSHARA P. 100+
	1		JABAŠ	IJ	IM			JA-BA-SI-IM	TRIBE	M
	1		JABUS	AT	IM			IA-BU-ZA-TIM	FN GEN	B 25+
	1		JAD		IM			IA-DI-IM	GEN	TIM V 35 6
	3		ʾAŠD		UM	PI				
						JAD	IM	AŠ-DU-UM-BI-IA-DI-IM		RA LXV 55 XIII 44
	2		ŠAM		A	JADAʿ	IM	SA-MA-A-DA-Ḫ[I-I]M	GEN	M
	1		JADID		IM			IA-DI-DIM	GEN	JCS IV 95 1612 13
			JADID		IM			IA-DI-D[I-IM]	GEN	M
			JADID	AT	IM			IA-DI-DA-TIM	MN GEN	B 25+
	1		JAKAL	ITIJIM				JA-KA-LI-TE-IM	TRIBE GEN	M
	1		JAMIN		IM			IA-MI-NIM	TRIBE	M
	1		JAPAR		IM			IA-PA-RI-IM	GEN	M
	1		JARAḪ	T	IM			IA-RA-AḪ-TIM	MN GEN	YOS XII
	1		JARIN		IM			JA-RI-NI-IM	GEN	CT XLV 89 III 9
	2		ʾILL		A	JAT	IM	IL-LA-I-IA-TIM	FN NOM	XIII 1 IV 75
		JI	NDIN			JAT	IM	I-DIN-IA-TIM	GEN	M+
		JI	NDIN			JAT	IM	ID-DI-IA-TIM	GEN	M
	1		JATAR		IM			IA-TA-RI-IM	GEN	B 31, M+
			JATAR	AT	IM			IA-TA-RA-TIM	MN GEN	B 31+
	1		JATR		IM			IA-AT-RI-IM	GEN	CT XLVIII 29 REV.
	1	JA	JDIʿ		IM			IA-DI-ḪI-IM	GEN	M+

IM	1		JITUM	AN	IM					I-TU-MA-NIM	GEN	B 45
	1 JA		JŠIR	T	IM					IA-ŠIR-TI-IM	MN GEN	WATERMAN 45 R. 10
	3		ŠUM				LI					
						JI	JṢIʾ		IM	SU-UM-LI-ZI-IM	GEN	WATERMAN 25 R 9
	1 JA		BJIN		IM					IA-BI-NI-IM	GEN	M+
	1		BAʾAN		IM					BA-ḪA-NIM	GEN	EDZARD,DER 71 IV 3
	2		NUʿM		U		BAʾAT		IM	NU-UḪ-MU-BA-A-TIM	FN	C+
	1		BAʾIL		IM					BA-ḪI-LIM	NOM	ABB V 157:9'
	1	T	BAḪR		IM					BA-TA-AḪ-RI-IM	GEN	M
	1		BAʿD		IM					BA-AḪ-DI-IM	GEN	RES 1939 69
	1		BAʿL	AT	IM					BA-AḪ-LA-TIM	FN GEN	XIII 1 XIV 37
	2 JA		MWUT				BAʿL		IM	IA-MU-UT-BA-LI-IM	GN GEN	YOS II 49 12+
	JA		MWUT				BAʿL		IM	IA-MU-UT-BA-LIM	GN GEN	BAGHD. MITT. II 56+
	JE		MWUT				BAʿL		IM	E-MU-UT-BA-LI-IM	GN GEN	KING 34 6+
	3		ŠUM		U	JE	MWUT					
							BAʿL		IM	SU-MU-E-MU-UT-BA-LIM?	GEN	JCS IV 71 9
			ŠUM		U	JA	MWUT					
							BAʿL		IM	SU-MU-IA-MU-UT-BA-LIM	GEN	CT XLIII 86 1
	1		BAWZ	AT	IM					BA-ZA-TI[M]	GEN	M+
	1		BAJN	AN	IM					BA-NA-NIM	GEN	B 43
	1	T	BANḪ		IM					BA-TA-AN-ḪI-IM	GEN	M
	1		BANIJ		IM					BA-NI-I-IM	GEN	M
	2 JI		JṢIʾ				BANIJ		IM	I-ZI-BA-NI-IM	GEN	B 45
	1		BAQQ	AN	IM					BA-AQ-QA-NIM	GEN	M
	1		BAZIN		IM					BA-ZI-NIM	GEN	B 15
	1		BAZUR	AT	IM					BA-ZU-RA-TIM	FN GEN	CT XLV 25 17
	1		BEʿL	AN	IM					BE-LA-NIM	GEN	M+
			BEʿL	AT	IM					BE-LA-TI-IM	FN? GEN	VIII 63:2
	2		MANN		A		BIʿD		IM	MA-NA-BI-IḪ-DI-IM	GEN	HARRIS 3 18
	1		BIN		IM					BI-NI-IM	GEN	M
	1		BIQAQ		IM					BI-KA-KI-IM	GEN	CT XLV 79 7
	1		BUʿD	AT	IM					BU-DA-TIM	GEN	EDZARD, DER 152 REV 6
	1		BUQAQ		IM					BU-QA-KI-IM	GEN	M+
	1		BUṬUḪ		IM					BU-DU-ḪI-IM	GEN	M
	1 JA		DWUR		IM					IA-DU-RI-IM	GEN	M
	1 JA		DJIN		IM					IA-DI-NIM	GEN	M+
	JI		DJIN		IM					I-DI-NIM	GEN	M
	2		ŠAM		I		DAʿ		IM	SA-MI-DA-ḪI-IM	GEN	M+
			ŠAM		I		DAʿ	AT	IM	SA-MI-DA-ḪA-TIM	FN? GEN	XII 741 6
	1		DAWD		IM					DA-DI-IM	GEN	M
			DAWD	AN	IM					DA-AW-DA-NIM	GEN	B 17+
			DAWD	AN	IM					DA-AM-DA?-NIM	GEN	CT XLVII 78:37
			DAWD	AN	IM					DA-DA-NI-IM	GEN	HARRIS 60:6
	1		DADM		IM					DA-AD-MI-IM	GEN	M
	2 JA		KWUN				DIWR		IM	IA-KU-UN-DI-[R]I-IM	GEN	M
	JI		NDIN				DIWR	IT	IM	I-DIN-D-DI-RI-TIM	GEN	M
	2		....				DITN		IM	MU-RI-IQ-TI-IT-NI-IM	GN GEN	U
	1 ʾA		DRAK	AT	IM					AD-RA-KA-TIM	FN GEN	M+
	1		DUWD	AN	IM					DU-DA-NIM		M
	1		ḎAKIR		IM					ZA-KI-RI-IM	GEN	BM 17069 8+, M
	1		ḎAMAR	AN	IM					ZA-AM-MA-RA-NIM-KI	GN GEN	C II 39 8
	1		ḎAMIR		IM					DA-ME-RI-IM	GEN	HARRIS 77 13
	1		ḎARʿ		IM					ZA-AR-IM	GEN	M
	1		ḎARIʿ		IM					ZA-RI-ḪI-IM	GEN	HARRIS 3 17
	1		ḎIKR		IM					ZI-IK-RI-IM	GEN	M
			ḎIKR	AT	IM					ZI-IK-RA-TIM	MN? GEN	XII 263 10
	1		ḎIMR	AT	IM					ZI-IM-RA-TIM	MN? GEN	M
	1		ḎUNAB		IM					SU-NA-BI-IM	GEN	SUMER XIV 51 NO. 26 23
	2		BAʿL		U		GAʾJ		IM	BA-AḪ-LU-GA-JI-IM	GEN	M+
			BAʿL		U		GAʾJ		IM	BA-AḪ-LU-GA-I-IM	GEN	M+
	1		GAJD	AN	IM					GA-DA-NIM	GEN	B 44
	1		GABUʾ		IM					GA-BI-IM	GEN	B 17
			GABUʾ		IM					GA-BI-I-ÍM	GEN	M+
	1		GALAZ		IM					GA-LA-ZI-IM	GEN	HARRIS 83 2
	1		GIJD	AN	IM					GI-DA-NI-IM	GEN	SIMMONS 12 6
			GIJD	AN	IM					GI-DA-NIM	GEN	M, SIMMONS 16 4

IM	1		GIZZ	IT	IM				GI-ZI-TIM	FN GEN	M
			GIZZ	AN	IM				GI-ZA-NI-IM	GEN	B 44
	1		GUʾR	AT	IM				GU-RA-TIM	FN GEN	B 17
	1		GURUD		IM				GU-RU-DI-IM	GEN	M
	1	JA	KWUN		IM				IA-KU-NIM	GEN	B 28, M+
	2		ʾIL		A		KAWN	IM	DINGIR-KA-NIM	GEN	M+
			ʾIL		A		KAWN	IM	DINGIR-KA-NI-IM	GEN	M
	1		KABKAB		IM				KAB-KA-BI-IM	GEN	C
	1		KARAN	AT	IM				KA-RA-NA-[T]IM	FN	M
	1		KATR		IM				KA-AT-R[I-I]M	GEN	HARRIS 75 17
	1		KAZIB		IM				KA-ZI-BI-IM	GEN	M+
	1	JA	KBUR		IM				IA-AK-BU-RI-IM	GEN	B 27
	1		KIʾM	AT	IM				KI-MA-TIM	FN GEN	M
	1		KIHIL		IM				KI-ḪI-LIM	GEN	M
	2		LAḪAN		I		KIWN	IM	LA-ḪA-NI-KI-IN-IM	GEN	UCP X/3 2 5
	1		KIKKIN		IM				KI-KI-NI-IM	GEN	B 49
			KIKKIN		IM				KI-KI-NIM	GEN	B 49+
			KIKKIR		IM				KI-IK-KI-RI-IM	GEN	M
	1		KIRUʾ		IM				KI-RI-E-IM	FN GEN	X 135 3
	1		KITT	AN	IM				KI-IT-TA-NI-IM	GEN	SIMMONS 63 2
	1		KUWN	AN	IM				KU-NA-NI-IM	GEN	M
	1		KUKKUŠ	AN	IM				KU-UK-KU-ZA-NIM	GEN	M
	1		KUPAD		IM				KU-PA-DI-IM	GEN	M
	1		KURKUR		IM				KU-UR-KU-RI-IM	GEN	M
	1		LAWUJ		IM				LA-I-IM	GEN	M+
	1		LALAʾ		IM				LA-LA-I-IM	GEN	XIII 85 5
	1		LIʾL		IM				LI-LI-IM	GEN	XIII 73 5
	2		QIJŠ	T	I		LIʾL	IM	KI-IŠ-TI-LI-LIM	GEN	RA LXIV 34 NO.26
	1	JA	MʾAD		IM				IA-AM-ḪA-DI-IM-KI	GN GEN	M+
	1		MAʾAN		IM				MA-ḪA-NIM	GEN	BM 72766
	1		MAʾŠ		IM				MA-ŠI-IM	GEN	M+
			MAʾŠ	AN	IM				MA-SA-NIM	GEN	CT XLV 93 6
	1		MAʾT	AT	IM				MA-TA-TIM	MN? GEN	VAS XVI 118 2
	1		MAHIR	AN	IM				MA-ḪI-RA-NIM	GEN	C II 2 8
	1		MANAN		IM				MA-NA-NI-IM	GEN	B 46+
			MANAN		IM				MA-NA-NIM	GEN	B 46
			MANAN		IM				MA-AN-NA-NIM	GEN	B 46
	2		LA				MANUW	IM	LA-MA-NI-IM	GEN	B 46
	1		MARMAR	AN	IM				MA-AR-MA-RA-NIM	GEN	B 93
	1		MAŠḪ		IM				MA-AŠ-ḪI-IM	GEN	M+
	1		MAŠIḪ		IM				MA-SI-ḪI-IM	GEN	M
	1		MERḪ		IM				ME-ER-ḪI-IM	GEN	M+
	1		MERR		IM				ME-ER-RI-IM	GEN	M+
	1		MILK		IM				MI-IL-KI-IM	GEN	B 35
			MILK	UN	IM				MI-IL-KU-NI-IM	GEN	SIMMONS 46 33
			MILK	UN	IM				MI-IL-KU-NIM	GEN	SIMMONS 70 17
	2		ŠUM		U	ʾA	MNID	IM	[SU-M]U-AM-NI-DI-IM		B 38
	1		MUNAN		IM				MU-NA-NIM	GEN	B 46
			MUNAN		IM				MU-NA-NI-IM	GEN	B 46
	1		MURMUR	T	IM				MU-UR-MU-UR-TIM	FN GEN	B 49
	1	JI N	NWAB	AT	IM				IN-NA-BA-TIM	FN GEN	CT VI 17 2
	1		NAHR		IM				NA-RI-IM	GEN	A.
	2		KIWN				NAHR	IM	KI-IN-NA-RI-IM	GEN	M+
			MUT				NAHR	IM	MU-UT-NA-RI-IM		RA LXV 51 IX 59
	1		NAʿIM		IM				NA-ḪI-MI-IM	GEN	B 36
	1		NAʿM		IM				NA-AḪ-MI-IM	GEN	M
			NAʿM	AN	IM				NA-MA-NI-IM	GEN	TIM III 46 15
	1		NABAʾ		IM				NA-BA-I-IM	GEN	M+
			NABAʾ		IM				NA-BA-JI-IM	GEN	VIII 39 4
	1	JA	NABIʾ		IM				IA-NA-BI-IM	GEN	M
	1		NAGIH		IM				NA-KI-ḪI-IM	GEN	TIM III 77 5A
	2	JA	JTIR				NAN	IM	JA-TI-IR-NA-NIM	GEN	M+
		JA	JTIR				NAN	IM	JA-TE-IR-NA-NIM	GEN	M
	1		NAQIM		IM				NA-KI-MI-IM	GEN	B 36+
	1		NARB	AN	IM				NA-AR-BA-NIM	GEN	A 21950

IM	2		LA			NAŠUʾ	IM	LA-NA-SU-I-IM	GEN	M
			LA			NAŠUʾ	IM	LA-A-NA-SU-I-IM	GEN	M
	2		ŚUM		U	NIWḪ	IM	SU-MU-NI-ḪI-IM	GEN	SIMMONS 121 18, M+
	1	JA	NṢIB		IM			IA-AN-ZI-BI-IM	GEN	M+
	1	JA	NTIN		IM			IA-AN-TI-NIM	GEN	M
		JA	NTIN		IM			IA-AT-TI-NIM	GEN	M+
	2		ŚUM		U	NUMḪ	IM	SU-MU-NU-UM-ḪI-IM		RIFTIN 44 12,16+
	1		PAʾAR	AT	IM			PA-A-RA-TIM	FN GEN	X 170:1
	1		PAKN	AN	IM			PA-AK-NA-NIM	GEN	B 47
	1		PANAN		IM			PA-NA-NIM	GEN	B 47
	1		PATIḤ		IM			PA-TE-E-IM	GEN	CT IV 21B 6, 22
	1	JA	PQID		IM			IA-AP-KI?-DI-IM	GEN	BE VI/1 8 34
	1	ME	PTUḤ		IM			ME-EP-TI-I-IM	GEN	M+
		ME	PTUḤ		IM			ME-EP-TI-IM	GEN	M+
		ME	PTUḤ		IM			ME-EP-TE-IM	GEN	XIII 43 15
		MI	PTUḤ		IM			MI-IP-TI-IM	GEN	M+
	1		QADIM	AT	IM			QA-DI-MA-TIM	FN GEN	WATERMAN 39 11
	1		QAṬAN		IM			QA-TA-NIM-KI	GN GEN	M+
			QAṬAN		IM			QA-ṬA$_3$-NIM-KI	GN GEN	M+
			QAṬAN	AJ	IM			QA-TA-NA-IM-KI	GN GEN	M
	1	JA	QBIJ		IM			IA-AQ-BI-IM	GEN	M
		TA	QBIJ		IM			TA-AQ-BI-IM	GEN?	M+
	1		QIJŚ		IM			KI-ŠI-IM	GEN	M
			QIJŚ	AT	IM			KI-ŠA-TIM	MN GEN	M+
	1	TA	RJIB		IM			TA-RI-BI-IM	GEN	M
	2		MUT			RAPŠ	IM	MU-UT-RA-AP-ŠI-IM		RA LXV 53 XI 7
	1		RAṢIJ		IM			RA-ZI-IM-KI	GN	M
	1		RAZIN		IM			RA-ZI-NI-IM	GEN	HARRIS 71 9
	1		RIPʾ		IM			RI-IP-I-IM	GEN	M+
	2		KANIK			RUWḤ	IM	KA-NI-IK-KI-IM	GEN	B 33
	1		RUWB	AT	IM			RU-BA-TIM	FN GEN	M
	1		SIKIL		IM			ZI-KI-LI-IM	GEN	TCL I 185 3
	1		ŚAʾIR	AT	IM			SA-E-RA-TIM	FN GEN	B 37+
	1		ŚAWIR	AN	IM			SA-WI-RA-NI-IM	GEN	TA 1930, 558
	1		ŚABIM	AT	IM			SA-BI-MA-TIM	FN NOM	RA LXIV 43
	1		ŚAGAR	AT	IM			SA-GA-RA-TIM-KI	GN GEN	M+
			ŚAGAR	AT	IM			SAG-GA-RA-TIM	MN GEN	M
			ŚAGAR	AT	IM			SAG-GA-RA-TIM	GN GEN	M+
			ŚAGAR	AT	IM			SA-AN-GA-RA-TIM-KI	GN GEN	M
	1	MU	ŚALIM		IM			MU-SA-LI-MI-IM	GEN	CT VIII 47B 28
		MU	ŚALIM	AT	IM			MU-SA-LI-MA-TIM	FN GEN	BE VI/1 8 14
			ŚALIM	AT	IM			SA-LI-MA-TIM	FN GEN	CT VIII 28C 13
			ŚALIM	AN	IM			SA-LI-MA-NIM	GEN	M
	1		ŚAM		IM			SA-MI-IM	GEN	CT XLVIII 91, XIII 142 40+
	1		ŚAMK	AN	IM			ŠA-AM-KA-NIM	GEN	LIH 81 7,17, 23
	1		ŚAMUK		IM			SA-MU-KI-IM	GEN	CT VIII 47B 22
			ŚAMUM	AN	IM			SA-MU-MA-NIM	GEN	PBS XIV 357
			ŚAMUŚ		IM			SA-MU-SI-IM	GEN	BM 78366 3
	2		NUPAR			ŚARR	IM	NU-BAR-LUGAL		A.
	1		ŚIJM	AT	IM			ŠI-MA-TIM	FN GEN	XIII 1 V 15+
	1	ME	ŚKIN		IM			ME-EŠ$_3$-KI-NIM	GEN	M+
	1	JA	ŚKUR		IM			IA-AŠ$_2$-KU-RI-IM	GEN	M+
	1	MA	ŚMAR		IM			MA-AŠ-MA-RI-IM	GEN	M
	2		D̲U			ŚUM	IM	ZU-U$_2$-ŠU?-MI-IM		M
	1	JA	ŠWUB		IM			IA-ŠU-BI-IM	GEN	M+
	1		ŠARŠAR	AN	IM			ŠA-ŠA-RA-NIM	GEN	M+
	1		ŠERIR	AN	IM			ŠE-RI-RA-NIM	GEN	M
	1		ŠIʾN	AT	IM			ŠI-NA-TIM	FN GEN	XIII 1 V 83
	1		ŠIQL		IM			ŠI-IQ-LI-IM	GEN	CT XLVIII 90
			ŠIQL	AN	IM			SI-IQ-LA-NIM	GEN	TA 1930, 189
	1	MA	ŠKAK		IM			MA-AŠ-KA-KI-[I]M	GEN	M
	1	JA	ṢḪAQ		IM			IA-AZ-ḪA-KI?-IM	GEN	IX 291 I 38
	1		ṢAJID		IM			ZA-I-DI-IM	GEN	VAS IX 172 18+
	1		ṢABIʾ		IM			ZA-BI-ḪI-IM	GEN	M+
			ṢABIʾ		IM			ZA-BI-I-IM	GEN	C P.39 N. 8+
	2		LA			ṢABIʾ	IM	LA-ZA-BI-IM	GEN	M+

IM	1		ṢUWR	AT	IM					ZU?-RA?-TIM	GEN	M
	2		JARAḪ				TIWR	IM		D-EN-ZU-TI-RI-IM	GEN	M
	1		TUQAR		IM					TU-GA-RI-IM	GEN	HARRIS 64 7
	1		ZAʾAN		IM					ZA-ḪA-NIM	GEN	M
	1		ZAʾZ	AN	IM					ZA-ZA-NI-IM	GEN	B 48
	1		ZAḪL	AT	IM					ZA-AḪ-LA-TIM	GEN	CT VIII 31B 25
	1		ZABIL		IM					ZA-BI-LIM	GEN	M+
	1		ZALZAL		IM					ZA-AL-ZA-LIM	GEN	M+
	1		ZIPP	ATAN	IM					ZI-IP-PA-TA-NIM	GEN	M
	1		ZIRQ	AN	IM					ZI-IR-GA-NIM	GEN	TA 1930,221 EARLY OB
	1		ZUʾUM		IM					ZU-U_2-MI-IM	GEN	M
			ZUʾUM		IM					ZU-[U_2]?-MI-IM	GEN	M
	1		ZUBAL		IM					ZU-BA-LI-IM	GEN	EDZARD,DER 152:18
U	1	JA	ʾWUŠ		U					IA-U_2-ŠU		B 31
	1		ʾAḪ		U		JAḤAD			A-ḪU-IA-ḪA-AD		M+
			ʾAḪ		U		JAT	UM		A-ḪU-IA-TUM	MN	BIN II 98 4
			ʾAḪ		U		JAT	UM		A-ḪU-JA-TUM	MN	M
			ʾAḪ		U		KA					
							ʾAB	I		A-ḪU-KA-A-BI	FN	XIII 1 VIII 60, C+
			ʾAḪ		U		ʾEL			A-ḪU-EL		RA LXV 50 IX 1
			ʾAḪ		U		LUʾM	U		A-ḪU-LU-MU		M
	2		ʾAJA				ʾAḪ	U		A-IA-A-ḪU		XIII 1 III 52
			ʾAJA				ʾAḪ	U		A-IA-ḪU		A. LATE+
			ʿAQB		A		ʾAḪ	U		AQ-BA-A-ḪU		M+, C+
			ʿAQB		A		ʾAḪ	U		AQ-BA-ḪU		BASOR 95 19+
			ʿAQB		I		ʾAḪ	U		AQ-BI-A-ḪU		B 11
		JI	JṢIʾ				ʾAḪ	U		I-ZI-A-ḪU?		X 53:6
	1		ʾAWN	AN	U					AM-NA-NU		BM 80328 9
	1		ʾAJAK		U					A-JA-KU		RA LXV 52 X 44
	1		ʾAB		U		ḪAʾL	UM		A-BU-ḪA-LUM		UCP X P. 53, M
			ʾAB		U		ḪAʾL	IM		A-BU-ḪA-LIM	GEN	M+
			ʾAB		U		JAQAR			A-BU-WA-QAR		M
			ʾAB		U		JAQAR			A-BU-QAR		M
			ʾAB		U		JAT	I	JA	A-BU-IA-TI-IA		TCL I 85 10
			ʾAB		U		KA					
							ʾIL			A-BU-KA-DINGIR		M+
			ʾAB		U		LA		JA	A-BU-LA-IA		XIII 101 6
			ʾAB		U	ME	KWIN			A-BU-ME-KI-IN		X 154 2+
			ʾAB		U	ME	QWIM			A-BU-ME-KI-IM		M+
			ʾAB		U		NIWR	A		A-BU-NI-RA		TIM VI 34, U
			ʾAB		U		NAN	UM		A-BU-NA-NU-UM		B 42+
			ʾAB		U		ŚALIM			A-BU-SA-[LIM]		M
	2		ʾAJA				ʾAB	U		A-IA-A?-BU?	FN	C+
			ʾAJA				ʾAB	U		A-IA-BU		A. LATE +
			ʾAJA				ʾAB	U	HU	A-A-A-BU-U_2	FN	DE CLERCQ II 253B
		JA	JDIʿ				ʾAB	U		IA-DI-ḪA-BU		PBS XIV 1084
		JA	JDIʿ				ʾAB	U		IA-DI-A-BU		YOS XII+
			ḎAKUR		A		ʾAB	U		ZA-KU-RA-A-BU		M
		JA	ŚJIT				ʾAB	U		IA-SI-IT-A-BU		M+
		JA	ŚJIT			NA	ʾAB	U		IA-SI-IT-NA-A-BU		XIII 1 XII 15
			ZUMM				ʾAB	U		ZU-UM-MA-BU		BM 80328 7
	1		ʾABN		U		RAPIʾ			AB-NU-RA-BI		C, C II P. 244+
	2	TA	ʿTIQ				ʾABN	U		TA-TI-QA-AB-NU		RES 1938 128
		TU	WTAR				ʾABN	U		TU-TAR-AB-NU		M
		JI	BAʾEL				ʾABN	U		I-BA-EL-A-AB-NU		III 46 13
	1		ʾADAM		U					ḪA-DA-MU	MN	RUTTEN 19 19+
			ʾADAM		U					A-DA-MU	MN	JNES XIII 210+ LATE
			ʾADAM		U					A-DA-MU	FN	C+
			ʾADAM	AN	U					AD-DA-MA-NU		RUTTEN 28 12
	1		ʾADID		U					A-DI-DU		B 11
	1		ʾADM		U	HA				AD-MU-A	FN	U
			ʾADM		U		ʿALIJ	AH		D-AD-MU-ḪA-LI-IA	FN	XIII 1 V 55
			ʾADM		U		JIŠʿ	AH		D-AD-MU-IŠ-ḪA	FN	XIII 1 IX 18
			ʾADM		U		JIŠʿ	AH		AD-MU-IŠ-ḪA	FN	XIII 1 IX 57
			ʾADM		U		ḪAṢN	I		D-AD-MU-ḪA-AZ-NI	FN	RA LXV 61 IV 21
			ʾADM		U		BALAṬ	I		D-AD-MU-BA-LA-TI?	FN	M

U	1		ʾADM		U				NIWR		I		AD-MU-NE-RI	FN	XIII 1 VIII 13
			ʾADM		U				NIWR		I		D-AD-MU-NI-RI	FN?	M
			ʾADM		U				QUDM		I		AD-MU-KU-UD-MI	FN	XIII 1 IX 55
			ʾADM		U				RUWB	AH			D-AD-MU-RU-BA	FN	XIII 1 VII 59
			ʾADM		U				ŠIMḪ		I		AD-MU-ŠI-IM-ḪI	FN	XIII 1 IV 6
			ʾADM		U				ŠIMḪ		I		D-AD-MU-ŠI-IM-ḪI	FN	RA LXV 62 V 28
			ʾADM		U		TA		ḪNUN	AN			D-AD-MU-TA-ḪU-NA-AN	FN	RA LXV 61 IV 38
	2	TA	ʾZIJ						ʾADM		U		TA-AḪ-ZI-D-AD-MU	FN	M
		TA	ḪṢIN						ʾADM		U		TA-AḪ-ZI-IN-AD-MU	FN	M
		JI	NDIN						ʾADM		U		I-DIN-D-AD-MU		M+
			QIJŠ	T	I				ʾADM		U		KI-IŠ-TI-AD-MU		M+
			ṬARID		A				ʾADM		U		TA-RI-DA-AD-MU		XIII 1 16
	1		ʾADUD		U								A-DU-DU	FN	XIII 1 X 7+
	2		QIJŠ						ʾAG		U		KI-IŠ-A-GU	FN	XIII 1 I 70
	1		ʾAGIG		U								A-GI-GU		B 12
	1		ʾAKN	AN	U								AK-NA-NU		B 42
	1		ʾAKUN		U				QAṬAR				A-KU-NU-GA-DAR		BIN VII 30 5
	1		ʾALM		U	HU							ḪA-AL-MU-U$_2$		SYRIA XXXVII 206 9 HANA
			ʾALM		U	NI							AL-MU-NI		RA LXV 48 VIII 7
	1		ʾALUʾ		U								A-LU?-U$_2$	FN	M
	1		ʾAMAN		U								ḪA-MA-NU		X 151 4+, KISURRA 21 9
			ʾAMAN		U								ḪA-MA-NU	FN	RA LXV 66 VIII 6
			ʾAMAR		U								AM-MA-RU		M
	1		ʾAMIN		U								A-MI-NU		JNES XIII 210+ LATE
	1		ʾANN		U				ʾAJAM				AN-NU-[Ḫ]A-A-AM	FN	XIII 1 II 62
			ʾANN		U				ʾUMM		I		AN-NU-UM-MI	FN	XIII 1 IV 48+
			ʾANN		U				ʾUMM		I		AN-NU-UN-UM-MI		M
			ʾANN		U				ʾAMR		I	JA	AN-NU-AM-RI-IA	FN	RA LXV 61 IV 47
			ʾANN		U				ḪANN		I		AN-NU-ḪA-AN-NI	FN	M+
			ʾANN		U				JAPʿ	AH			AN-NU-IA-AP-ḪA	FN	XIII 1 IV 3+
			ʾANN		U				JIPʿ	AH			AN-NU-IP-ḪA	FN	XIII 1 VIII 29
			ʾANN		U				ʾAŠJ	AH			AN-NU-A-SI-IA	FN	XIII 1 IV 41+
			ʾANN		U				JIŠʿ	AH			AN-NU-IŠ-ḪA	FN	XIII 1 V 46+
			ʾANN		U				ʾAŠR		I		AN-NU-AŠ-RI	FN	M+
			ʾANN		U			T	HILAL				AN-NU-ḪI-IT-LA-AL	FN	RA LXV 60 III 18
			ʾANN		U				JATR	AH			AN-NU-IA-AT-RA	FN	XIII 1 VI 53+
			ʾANN		U				ḪAṢN		I		AN-NU-ḪA-AṢ-NI	FN	M+
			ʾANN		U				BAWŠ	T	I		AN-NU-BA-AŠ-TI	FN	RA LXV 65 VII 27
			ʾANN		U				DAMQ	AH			AN-NU-DAM-QA	FN	XIII 1 X 51
			ʾANN		U				DUNN		I		AN-NU-DU-UN-NI	FN	XIII 1 III 37
			ʾANN		U				DUNN		I		AN-NU-DU-NI	FN	RA LXV 65 VII 15
			ʾANN		U				GAMIL	T	I		AN-NU-GA-ME-IL-TI	FN	RA LXV 66 VII 66
			ʾANN		U				KUʾM				AN-NU-KUM	FN	XIII 1 VI 8
			ʾANN		U				KAMA						
									ʾAB		I		AN-NU-KA-MA-BI		CT XLV 116 36
			ʾANN		U				LAMAS		I		AN-NU-LA-MA-ZI	FN	M+
			ʾANN		U				LAMAS		I		AN-NU-D-LAMA	FN	XIII 1 VII 8+
			ʾANN		U				LAMAS	IT	UM		AN-NU-LA-MA-ZI-TUM	FN	RA LXV 59 II 13
			ʾANN		U				MAʾN		A		AN?-NU-MA-NA	FN	M
			ʾANN		U				NIWR		I		AN-NU-NI-RI	FN	M
			ʾANN		U				NABIʾ				AN-NU-NA-BI-IḪ	FN	RA LXV 62 V 24
			ʾANN		U				NABIT		I		AN-NU-NA-BI-TI		XIII 1 VI 61
			ʾANN		U				PUṬR		I		AN-NU-PU-UṬ-RI	FN	RA LXV 58 I 19+
			ʾANN		U				QUDM		I		AN-NU-KU-UD-MI	FN	XIII 1 VIII 77
			ʾANN		U				RAḪM		I		AN-NU-RA-AḪ-MI	FN	XIII 1 V 11+
			ʾANN		U				RIMŠ		I		AN-NU-RI-IM-ŠI	FN	M+
			ʾANN		U				ŠIMḪ		I		[A]N-NU-ŠI-IM-ḪI		XIII 1 XIV 24
			ʾANN		U				ŠATAM				AN?-NU?-ŠA-TAM	FN	XIII 1 IV 46
			ʾANN		U		TA		ḪNUN				AN-NU-TA-AḪ-NU-UN	FN	RA LXV 61 IV 15+
			ʾANN		U		TA		LʾIJ				AN-NU-TA-AL-E	FN	M+
			ʾANN		U		TA		RḪAM				AN-NU-TA-AR-AM	FN	M+
			ʾANN		U		TA		RBIJ				AN-NU-TAR-BI	FN	XIII 1 XI 47
			ʾANN		U		TA		ŠMAʿ				AN-NU-TA-AŠ$_2$-MA-AḪ	FN	M
			ʾANN		U				TIWR		I		AN-NU-TI-RI	FN	M+
			ʾANN		U				TABB		I		AN-NU-TAB-BI	FN	XIII 1 III 36+
			ʾANN		U				TUKUL	T	I		AN-NU-TU-KU-UL-[TI]	FN	M+

U	1		ʾANN	U			TUKUL	T	I		AN-NU-TU-GUL-TI	FN	XIII 1 X 3
			ʾANN	U			TILL	AT	I		AN-NU-TIL-LA-TI	FN	XIII 1 X 2
			ʾANN	U			ṬAJB				AN-NU-DUG$_3$		M+
	2		ʾAB	A			ʾANN		U		A-BA-AN-NU		M
			ʾAMIN	I			ʾANN		U		A-MI-NI-AN-NU		M
			NABIʾ				ʾANN		U		NA-BI-AN-NU		M
		JI	NDIN				ʾANN		U		I-DIN-AN-NU		M+
		JI	NDIN				ʾANN		U		I-DI-AN-NU		RA LXV 51 IX 31
			ṢILL				ʾANN		U		MI-NI-AN-NU		M
			ZAʾZ	I			ʾANN		U		ZA-ZI-AN-NU		B 41+
	2		ʾADAM		TA		ʾAR		U		ḪA-DAM-TA-A-RU		WATERMAN 45 EDGE
	2		MUT				ʾARḪ		U		MU-UT-AR-ḪU		M
	1		ʾARWIJ	U							AR-WI-U$_2$		B 13
	1		ʾARAM	U							A-RA-MU		M
			ʾARAM	U							A-RA-AM-MU		A.+
	1		ʾARUŠ	U							A-RU-SU		JEAN TELL SIFR 72 5+
	1		ʾASIN	U	HU						A-ZI-NU-U$_2$		M
			ʾASIN	U	HU						A-SI-NU-U		APN P. 31 LATE
	1		ʾAŚD	U							D-AŠ-DU		RT XIX 48 SEAL
			ʾAŚD	U			QAWM		U		AŠ-DU-GA-MU		CT XLV 77 R. 10, 14+
			ʾAŚD	U			QAWM		UM		AŠ$_2$-DU-GA-MU-UM		TCL I 130 8+
			ʾAŚD	U			RAPIʾ				AŠ$_2$-DU-RA-BI		C+
			ʾAŚD	U	NA	JA	RWIM				[AŠ$_2$-D]U-NI-A-RI-IM		CT XXXVI 4 1
			ʾAŚD	U	NA	JE	RWIM				AŠ$_2$-DU-NI-E-RI-IM		RA VIII 65 1
	2		NAʿM	I			ʾAŚD		U		NA-AḪ-ME-AS-DU	FN	RA LXV 60 III 2
		JI	TWUR				ʾAŚD		U		I-DUR-AŠ-DU		B 23+
		JI	TWUR				ʾAŚD		U		I-DUR-AŠ$_2$-DU		VAS IX 172 5, M+
		JI	TWUR				ʾAŚD		U	HU	I-DUR-AŠ-DU-U$_2$		SIMMONS 90 4
		JI	TWUR				ʾAŚD		U	HU	I-DUR-AŠ$_2$-DU-U$_2$		M
	1		ʾAŚIN	U							A-SI-NU		B 14
	1		ʾAŚQUD	U							AŠ-KU-DU		M
	1		ʾAŚUL	U							A-SU-LU		TA 30 36 3
	1		ʾATIM	U							A-TI-MU		M
	1		ʾATT	U							ḪA-AT-TU		C+
	2		LA			ʾA	ʾDUM		U		LA-AḪ-DU-MU		4E RENC. ASS. P. 178 4
	2	ʾA	RŠIJ				ʾEDAK		U		AR-ŠI-E-DA-KU	FN	M
	1		ʾELL AN	U							E-EL-LA-NU		C
	1		ʾIL	U			MALIK	AJ	I		I-LU-MA-LI-KA-JI-KI	GN	XV 127
			ʾIL	U	NA						I-LU-NA		RA LXV 43 III 80
			ʾIL	U	NI						I-LU-NI		M+
			ʾIL	U	NA		KIRIŠ		U		I-LU-NA-KI-RI-ŠU		XIII 8 19+
	2		ḪAʾL	I			ʾIL		U	HU	ḪA-A-LI$_2$-I-LU-U$_2$		X 146 5
			ʿADN	I			ʾIL		U				
							MA				ḪA-AD-NI-DINGIR-MA		M
			JIŠʿ	I			ʾIL		U				
							MA				IŠ-ḪI-LU-MA		YOS VIII 176 20
			JIŠʿ	I			ʾIL		U	NA	IŠ-ḪI-LU-NA		VII 215 33
		JI	JṢIʾ				ʾIL		U				
							MA				I-ZI-I-LU-MA		B 23+
			ḎIMR	I			ʾIL		U				
							MA				ZI-IM-RI-DINGIR-MA		M
			ḎIMR	I			ʾIL		U				
							MA				ZI-IM-RI-I-LU-MA		M
			ḎIMR	I			ʾIL		U				
							MA				ZI-IM-RI-LU-MA		SIMMONS 67 12
			KAHAL	I			ʾIL		U				
							MA				KA-A-LI-I-LU-MA		XIV 62:4+
			KAHAL	I			ʾIL		U				
							MA				KA-A-LI-DINGIR-MA		M+
			MILK	I			ʾIL		U		MIL-KI-LU		B 34+
			MILK	I			ʾIL		U		MI-IL-KI-LU		B 34
			ŠUWB		NA		ʾIL		U		ŠU-UB-NA-ḪI-LU		B 40
			ŚAMŠ	U			ʾIL		U	NA	SA-AM-SU-I-LU-NA		B 38+
			ŚAMŠ	U			ʾIL		U	NA			
							KIMA				SA-AM-SU-I-LU-NA-KI-MA-DINGIR		BM 81047:6
			ŚAMŠ	U			ʾIL		U	NA			
							....				SA-AM-SU-I-LU-NA-QAR-RA-AD		CT XLV 48 5

SUFFIXES, Class 2

U	1		ʾILL		U	NA					IL-LU-NA	FN	A.
	1		ʾILUR		U						I-LU-RU		B 22
	1		ʾIMAG		U						I-MA-GU	FN	M
	1		ʾIPQ		U		JI	TWUR					
								MEʾR			IP-KU-D-I-DUR-ME-ER		M
			ʾIPQ		U			NAZI			IP-KU-D-NA-AZ-ZI		M
			ʾIPQ		U			ŠAL		A	IP-KU-D-ŠA-LA		M
	1		ʾIRŠ		U			MA					
								ʾAB		I	IR-ŠU-MA-BI		A.
	1		ʾIŚN	AN	U						IŠ-NA-NU		B 45+
	1		ʾIZAM		U						I-ZA?-MU	FN	M
	1	ʾA	ʾMUR		U	HU					A-MU-RU-U$_2$		PBS VIII/1 98 9
	1	MA	ʾNUP		U						MA-AḪ-NU-KA		VAS IX 193 18
		MA	ʾNUP		U						MA-AḪ-NU-PU		M
	1	JA	ʾQUD		U						IA-KU-DU-KI	GN	UCP IX/4 5 1
	1		ʾUWŠ	AN	U						ḪU-SA-NU		4E RENC. ASS. P. 178 4
	1		ʾUM		U			ŠAKIM			U$_2$-MU-ŠA-KI-IM		M+
	1		ʾUMM		U			JARAḪ			U$_2$?-UM-MU-E-RA-AḪ		B 40+
			ʾUMM		U			KA					
								ʾAB		I	UM-MU-KA-A-BI	FN	RA LXV 62 V 16
			ʾUMM		U			ŠARR	AH		UM-MU-ŠAR-RA	FN	IX 291 33
	2		ʾIJA					ʾUMM		U	I-IA-AMA		MRS VI P. 328+
	1		HADD		U			BAʿL		I	D-IM-BA-AḪ-LI		M+
			HADD		U			BANIJ			D-IM-BA-NI		M+
			HADD		U			DUWR		I	D-IM-DU-RI		M+
			HADD		U			MALIK			AD-DU-MA-LIK		A. 268 4
			HADD		U			MALIK			D-IM-MA-LIK		M+
			HADD		U			NIWR		I	D-IM-NI-RI	FN	RA LXV 61 IV 17
			HADD		U			ŠADW		A	D-IM-ŠA-DA		PSBA XXIX 273 NO. 9 R. 10
	2	JA	HWIJ					HADD		U	IA-WI-D-IM		M+
			ḪAʾL		I			HADD		U	ḪA-LI$_2$-D-IM		M+
			ḪAʾL		I			HADD		U	ḪA-LI-A-DU		A.+
			ḪAʾL		I			HADD		U	ḪA-LI-IA-[D]U		M
			ʾUWR		A			HADD		U	U$_2$-RA-A-DU		A.
			ʾUWR		I			HADD		U	U$_2$-RI-A-DU		A.
			ʾUWR		I			HADD		U	WU-RI-A-DU		A.
			JAʾAR					HADD		U	IA-ḪA-AR-D-IM		M
		JA	ʾWUŠ					HADD		U	IA-UŠ-D-IM		M+
		JA	ʾWUŠ					HADD		U	IA-U$_2$-UŠ-D-IM		M+
		JA	ʾWUŠ					HADD		U	IA-UŠ$_2$-D-IM		M
			ʾAB		I			HADD		U	A-BI-D-IM		B 9, M+
			ʾAB		I			HADD		U	A-BI-A-DU		A.+
			ʾAB		I			HADD		U	A-BI-IA-DU		M+
			ḪABIʾ					HADD		U	ḪA-BI-D-IM		M
			ʿABD					HADD		U	AB-DI-AD-DU		BAGHD. MITT. II 57 28
			ʿABD					HADD		U	ḪA-AB-DU-D-IM		RA LXV 48 VIII 34
		JI	JBAL					HADD		U	I-BA-AL-D-IM		M+, C+
			JABAL					HADD		U	IA-BA-AL-D-IM		M
			ʿAD		U	NA		HADD		U	A-DU-NA-D-IM		SYRIA XIX 109
			ʿAD		U	NI		HADD		U	A-DU-NI-D-U		MRS VI 15, 42 II 20 UGARIT
			JADAʿ					HADD		U	[IA]-ṬA$_3$-AḪ-D-IM		VI 76 10
			ʿADN		I			HADD		U	ḪA-AD-NI-D-IM		M, C+
			ʿADN		I			HADD		U	ḪA-AD-NI-A-D[U]		DELAPORTE CCL II A 914
			ʿAḎR		I			HADD		U	AD-RI-A-DU		A.+
			ʿAḎR		I			HADD		U	AD-RI-IA-DU		KUPPER, NOM. 231
			ʾIL		I			HADD		U	I$_3$-LI$_2$-D-IM		M+
			ʾIL		I			HADD		U	I$_3$-LI$_2$-A-DU		A. 57 47
		JI	ḤLAJ					HADD		U	IḪ-LA-D-IM		XIII 1 II 76
		JI	ḤLIJ					HADD		U	IḪ-LI-A-DU		A. P. 133+
		JI	ḤLIJ					HADD		U	IḪ-LI$_3$-A-DU		A. P. 133
			ʾALUN					HADD		U	ḪA-LU-UN-D-IM		M; JCS XIV 203
			ʾALUN		A			HADD		U	ḪA-LU-NA-D-IM		M
		JI	ʾLAP					HADD		U	IḪ-LA-AP-A-DU		A.
			ʿAMM		I			HADD		U	AM-MI-A-DU		A. 60 14
			ʿAMM		I			HADD		U	AM-MI-IA-A-DU		A.
			ʿAMM		I			HADD		U	AM-MI-AD-DU		A. 267 17

SUFFIXES, Class 2

U	2		ʾAMAR			HADD	U	AM-MA-RA-DU		A.+
			ʾAMAR	A		HADD	U	AM-MA-RA-A-DU		A.
		JA	ʾMUR			HADD	U	IA-MU-UR-AD-DU		M
			ʾANA			HADD	U	A-NA-D-IM		MRS XII NO. 24, 6, UGARIT
			ḤANN	A		HADD	U	AN-NA-D-IM		M+
			ḤANN	A		HADD	U	Ḫ̮A-AN-NA-D-IM		M
			ḤINN	I		HADD	U	IN-NI-D-IM		A.
			Ḫ̮ANZ	A		HADD	U	Ḫ̮A-AN-ZA-D-IM		M
		JA	JPAʿ			HADD	U	IA-A-PA-AḪ̮-D-IM		M+
		JA	JPAʿ			HADD	U	IA-PA-Ḫ̮A-D-IM		M
		JA	JPAʿ			HADD	U	IA-PA-AḪ̮-D-IM		M+
		JA	JPIʿ			HADD	U	IA-BI-IḪ̮-D-IM		M
		ʾU	WQAH			HADD	U	U_2-QA-D-IM		RA LXV 44 IV 51
		ʾU	WQAH			HADD	U	U_2-GA-D-IM		BIROT, TEA 24:6
			ʿIQB	I		HADD	U	IQ-BI-D-IM		KISURRA 114 7
			ʾIRR	I		HADD	U	I-RI-A-DU		A.+
			ʾIRR	I		HADD	U	IR-RI-A-DU		A.
		JA	ʾŚUʾ			HADD	U	IA-SU-D-IM		TCL I 238 4 HANA+
			JIŠʿ	I		HADD	U	IŠ-Ḫ̮I-D-IM		M+, C+
			ʾEŠB	I		HADD	U	EŠ-BI-D-IM		A.+
			ʾAŚM	A		HADD	U	AŠ-MA-DU		BM 80328 14
			ʾAŚM	A		HADD	U	AŠ-MA-A-DU		A.+
			JATAR			HADD	U	IA-TAR-D-IM		M+
			ʾATT	I		HADD	U	AT-TI-D-IM		M+
			JATT	I		HADD	U	IA-AT-TI-D-IM		M
		JA	JṢIʾ			HADD	U	IA-ZI-D-IM		M
		JA	ʾZUW			HADD	U	IA-ZU-D-IM		M
		JA	ʿZIB			HADD	U	IA-AḪ̮-ZI-IB-D-IM		M+
		JA	ʿZIB			HADD	U	IA-ZI-IB-D?-IM?		M
		JA	Ḫ̮ZUR			HADD	U	IA-AḪ̮-ZU-UR-D-IM		M
			ʿUZZ			HADD	U	U_2-ZA-DU		U
			BAʿD	I		HADD	U	BA-AḪ̮-DI-D-IM		M+
			BUʾL	I		HADD	U	BU-LI-A-DU		A. 60 12
			BAʿL	I		HADD	U	BA-AḪ̮-LI-D-IM		M+
			BAʿL	I		HADD	U	BA-LI-D-IM		M
			BEʿL	I		HADD	U	BE-LI_2-D-IM		RA LXV 52 X 39
		JA	BḤAR			HADD	U	IA-AB-Ḫ̮A-AR-D-IM		M
			BULM	A	NA	HADD	U	BU-UL-MA-NA-D-IM		M+
			BIN			HADD	U	DUMU-D-IM		M+
			BIN	A		HADD	U	[B]I-NA-D-IM		M
		JA	BNIJ			HADD	U	IA-AB-NI-D-IM		M
		JI	BNIJ			HADD	U	IB-NI-D-IM		M+
		JA	DJIN			HADD	U	IA-DI-IN-D-IM		RA LXV 44 IV 51+
			DIJN	I		HADD	U	TI-NI-A-DU		A. 59 2
			DIJN	I		HADD	U	DI-NI-A-DU		A.+
			DIJN	I		HADD	U	DI-NA-A-DU		A. LATE
			DUNN	I		HADD	U	DU-NI-A-DU		A. LATE
			ḎIKR	I		HADD	U	ZI-IK-RI-D-IM		M+
			ḎIMR	I		HADD	U	ZI-IM-RI-D-IM		M+
			ḎIMR	I	JE	HADD	U	ZI-IM-RI-E-D-IM		M
			ḎIMR	U		HADD	U	ZI-IM-RU-D-IM		CT XLVIII 22 REV
		JA	ḎRAʿ			HADD	U	IA-AZ-RA-AḪ̮-D-IM		M+
		JA	GJIḤ			HADD	U	IA-GI-IḪ̮-D-IM		M+
		JA	GJIḤ			HADD	U	IA-GI-Ḫ̮A-D-IM		M
			GUʾR	U		HADD	U	GU-RU-D-IM		M+
		JI	GMIR			HADD	U	IG-MI-RA-A-DU		A.+
			KAʾB	I		HADD	U	KA-BI-D-IM		B 32, M+, C
			KAHAL	I		HADD	U	KA-A-LI-D-IM		M+
		JA	KWUN			HADD	U	IA-KU-UN-D-IM		B 27, M+
		JA	KWIN			HADD	U	IA-KI-IN-D-IM		M
			KUʾR	U		HADD	U	KU-RU-D-IM		M
			KIBS			HADD	U	KI-IB-ZA-DU	FN	A.
			KIBS	I		HADD	U	KI-IB-ZI-D-IM		M+
			LA		NA	HADD	U	LA-NA-D-IM		XIII 109 15, 16
		JI	LʾAʾ			HADD	U	IL-A-D-IM		X 83 4, 7'
		JI	LʾAʾ			HADD	U	IL-A-DU		A. 78 20

U	2	JI	LEʾEJ			HADD	U	I-LE-E-D-IM	XIII 93 5
			LAWUJ			HADD	U	LA-WU-D-IM	M+
			LAWUJ			HADD	U	LA-U$_2$-D-IM	A.
			LIʾM	A		HADD	U	LI-MA-A-DU	A.
			LIʾM	I		HADD	U	LI-MI-D-IM	M+
			LIʾM	I		HADD	U	LI-ME-D-IM	M+
			MIHR	I		HADD	U	ME-EḪ-RI-D-IM	C+
		JA	MLIK			HADD	U	IA-AM-LIK-D-IM	RA LXV 40 I 31
			MILK	A		HADD	U	MI-IL-KA-D-IM	SYRIA XXXVII 206 27 HANA
			MILK	I		HADD	U	MIL-KI-D-IM	M
			MILK	I		HADD	U	MI-IL-KI-D-IM	M
			MUŠN	A		HADD	U	MU-UŠ-NA-A-DU	A.+
			MUT			HADD	U	MU-UT-[D]?-IM	RA LXV 41 II 17
			MUT	I		HADD	U	MU-TI-D-IM	M
			MUT	U		HADD	U	MU-TU-D-IM	M
			NIʿM	A		HADD	U	NI-MA-A-DU	A.
			NAWAR			HADD	U	NA-WA-AR-D-IM	RA LXV 50 VIII 55+
			NIWR	I		HADD	U	NI-IW-RI-A-DU	A.+
		JA	NBIʾ			HADD	U	IA-AB-BI-D-IM	M
			NIMIN	A		HADD	U	NI-MI-NA-A-DU	A.+
			NAPŠ	I		HADD	U	NA-AP-SI-D-IM	M+
			NAPŠ	I		HADD	U	NA-AP-ŠI-A-DU	A.+
			NAPŠ	U		HADD	U	NA-AP-SU-D-IM	M
			NAPŠ	U	NA	HADD	U	NA-AP-SU-NA-D-IM	M+
		JA	NQIM			HADD	U	IA-AK-KI-IM-D-IM	M+
		JA	NQIM			HADD	U	IA-KI-IM-D-IM	M+
			NIQM			HADD	U	NI-IQ-MA-A-DU	A.+
			NIQM			HADD	U	NI-IQ-MA-DU	A.
			NIQM			HADD	U	NI-IQ-MA$_2$-A-DU	B 36
			NIQM	I		HADD	U	NI-IQ-MI-A-DU	A.+
			NIQM	I		HADD	U	NI-IQ-MI-IA-AD-DU	M
		JA	NŠIʾ			HADD	U	IA-AŠ$_2$-ŠI-D-IM	RA LXV 42 III 13
		JA	NŠIʾ			HADD	U	IA-SI-D-IM	B 29
		JA	NTIN			HADD	U	IA-AN-TI-IN-D-IM	M+
		JA	NTIN			HADD	U	IA-AN-TI-NA-DU	ZDPV XLIX PL. 45 LATE
		JI	NTIN			HADD	U	I-TI-IN-D-IM	M
		JA	NṢIB			HADD	U	IA-AN-ZI-IB-D-IM	M+
		JA	NṢUR			HADD	U	IA-AṢ-ṢU-UR-D-IM	X 12 6, 21+
		JA	PḪUR			HADD	U	IA-AP-Ḫ[U-UR]-A-DU	M
			PILḪ	U		HADD	U	BI-EL-ḪU-D-IM	RA LXV 55 XIII 4
			PILS	I		HADD	U	BI-IL-ZI-D-IM	XIV 41:14
			PULS	I		HADD	U	PU-UL-ZI-D-IM	M+
			PULS	U	NA	HADD	U	PU-UL-ZU-NA-D-IM	UNPUBL.
			QUWJ	U		HADD	U	KU-U$_2$-D-IM	M
			QUWJ	UM		HADD	U	KU-UM-D-U	MRS XVI 9:7
		JA	QWIM			HADD	U	IA-KI-IM-D-IM	M+
		JA	QWIM			HADD	U	IA-GI-I[M]?-D-IM	IX 291 III 29'
			QAWM	U		HADD	U	GA-MU-D-IM	M
			QAʾN			HADD	U	QA-AN-A-DU	A.
		JA	QBIJ			HADD	U	IA-AQ-BI-D-IM	RA LXV 43 III 38
		JA	RʿIJ			HADD	U	JA-RI-A-DU	RA LXV 50 VIII 64
		JA	RḤIB			HADD	U	IA-AR-IB-D-IM	M+
		JA	RJIB			HADD	U	IA-RI-IB-D-IM	B 29+
		JA	RWIM			HADD	U	IA-RI-IM-D-IM	M+
			RIWM			HADD	U	RI-IM-D-IM	M+, A. 57 46
			RIWM	U		HADD	U	RI-MU-D-IM	M
		JA	RKAB			HADD	U	IA-AR-KA-AB-D-IM	4E RENCONTRE 23
		JA	RKIB	A		HADD	U	IA-AR-KI-BA-D-IM	XIII 145 6
		JA	RPAʾ			HADD	U	IA-AR-PA-D-IM	M+
		JI	RPAʾ			HADD	U	IR-PA-D-IM	A.+
			RIPʾ	I		HADD	U	RI-IP-I-D-IM	M+
			SITR	A		HADD	U	ZI-IT-RA-A-DU	A. 456 19
			SITR	I		HADD	U	ZI-IT-RI-D-IM	M
			SITR	I		HADD	U	SI-IT-RI-D-IM	JCS XXIV 60 NO.51 REV.
			SITR	I	JE	HADD	U	ZI-IT-RI-E-D-IM	JCS XXIV 63 NO.56 REV.
			ŠINI			HADD	U	ŠI-NI-D-U	MRS XVI 44:3

SUFFIXES, Class 2

U	2	JA		ŠWUB			HADD	U	IA-ŠU-UB-D-IM		LAESSOE P. 90+, C+
				ŠUWB	I		HADD	U	ŠU-BI-D-IM		M
		JA		ŚJIM			HADD	U	IA-SI-IM-D-IM		M
				ŠADW	I		HADD	U	ŠA-DI-D-IM		M
				ŚAKB	I		HADD	U	SA-AK-BI-D-IM		ARMT V P. 123
		ʾA		ŚKUR			HADD	U	AŠ$_{2}$-KU-UR-D-IM		TCL 1 146 4
		ʾA		ŚKUR			HADD	U	AŠ-KUR-D-IM		M+
				ŚAM	U		HADD	U	SA-MU-D-IM		M+
				ŚUM	A		HADD	U	ŠU-MA-A-DU		A.
				ŚUM	I		HADD	U	SU-MI-A-DU		A.+
		JA		ŚMAʿ			HADD	U	IA-AŠ$_{2}$-MA-AḪ-D-IM		M+, C+
		JA		ŚMAʿ			HADD	U	IA-AŠ$_{2}$-MI-IḪ-D-IM		M
		JI		ŚMAʿ			HADD	U	IŠ-MA-D-IM		M
		JI		ŚMAʿ			HADD	U	IŠ-ME-D-IM		M+
		ʾA	T	ŚAMAR			HADD	U	AŠ-TA-MAR-D-IM		M+
				ŚAMAR			HADD	U	ŠA-AM-MA-RA-DU		A.
				ŚAMAR	I		HADD	U	SA-MA-RI-A-DU		A. 57 45
				ŚIMAR			HADD	U	ŠI-IM-MA-RA-DU?		A.
				ŚAMŚ	I		HADD	U	SA-AM-SI-D-IM		M+, A.+
				ŚAMŚ	I		HADD	U	SA-AM-SI-A-DU		M+
				ŚAMŚ	I		HADD	U	ŠA-AM-SI-D-IM		M+
				ŚAMŚ	I		HADD	U	D-UTU-ŠI-D-IM		M+, C+
				ŚAMŚ	I		HADD	U	SA-AM-ŠI-D-IM		C
				ŚAMŚ	I		HADD	U	SA-AM-SI-IA-AD-DU		M
				ŚAMŚ	I		HADD	U	D-UTU-ŠI-A-DU		A.
				ŚAPŚ	I		HADD	U	SA-AP-SI-A-DU		A.+
				ŚAMŚ	I		HADD	U			
							ʾIL	I	SA-AM-SI-D-IM-I$_{3}$-LI$_{2}$		C+
				ŚAMŚ	I		HADD	U			
							....		SA-AM-SI-D-IM-TU-GUL-TI		M
				ŚAMŚ	U		HADD	U	SA-AM-ŠU-D-IM		COLLON, SEALS NO. 141
		JI		ŠNIJ			HADD	U	IŠ-NI-D-IM		A.
		JU	T	ŠANIJ			HADD	U	UŠ-TI-NI-D-IM?		A. 36 9+
				ŚAPR	A		HADD	U	SA-AP-RA-A-DU		A. 96 R. 12
				ŠIPṬ	I		HADD	U	ŠI-IP-TI-D-IM		A. LATE
				ṢUWR	I		HADD	U	ZU-RI-D-IM		M+
				ṢABAʾ			HADD	U	ZA-BA-AD-DU		M
				ṢIDQ	A		HADD	U	ZI-ID-QA-D-IM		M
				ṢILL			HADD	U	ZI-IL-LA-AD-DU		A. 81
	3	JA		HWIJ			KI				
							HADD	U	[IA-A]Ḫ-WI-KI-D-IM		M
				BIN	U		MA				
							HADD	U	BI-NU-MA-D-IM		4E RENCONTRE 21 NO. 25
				BUN	U		MA				
							HADD	U	BU-NU-MA-D-IM		M+
				LA		ʾA	HWIJ				
							HADD	U	LA-AḪ-WI-A-DU		A. 95 36
				LA		ʾA	ḪJIJ				
							HADD	U	LA-ḪI-A-DU		A. 57 11, 13
				LA			KIWN				
							HADD	U	LA-KI-IN-A-DU		A.
				LAWUJ			LA				
							HADD	U	LA-WU-LA-D-IM		M+, C
	1			HAND	U		MALIK		AN-DU-MA-LIK		A. 252 10
	2			ʿABD			HAND	U	ḪA-AB-DI-IA-AN-DU		KUPPER NOM. P. 231
				ʿABD			HAND	U	AB-DI-IA-DU		KUPPER NOM. P. 231
				ʿABD			HAND	U	AB-DU-IA-AN-DU		KUPPER NOM. P. 231
				ʿAḎR	I		HAND	U	AD-RI-IA-AN-DU		KUPPER, NOM. 231
				ʿAḎR	I		HAND	U	ḪA-AD-RI-IA-AN-DU		KUPPER, NOM. 231
				BAʿL	A		HAND	U	BA-LA-ḪA-AN-DU		VOIX 187:13 MARI
				NAPŠ	I		HAND	U	NA-AP-SI-IA-AN-DU		M
		ʾA		PLAḪ			HAND	U	AP-LA-ḪA-AN-DU		RA LXV 42 II 65
		JA		ŚLIM			HAND	U	IA-AŠ$_{2}$-LI-IM-IA-[AN-D]U		M
	1			HILL	U				ḪI-EL-LU		M
	1			ḪAJJ	U		ʾIL		A$_{2}$-U$_{2}$-DINGIR		U
	1			ḪABAS	U				ḪA-BA?-ZU	FN	XIII 1 I 1

U	1		ḪAM		U		DAWD	I		D?-[A?-M]U?-DA-DI		IX 291 16
			ḪAM		U		DAWD	U		D-A-MU-DA-DU		M
			ḪAM		U		MALIK			D-A-MU-MA-LIK		M
			ḪAM		U	TA	NWUḪ			D-A-MU-TA-NU		M
	2 JA		ʾWUŠ				ḪAM	U		IA-U$_2$-UŠ-D-A-MU		M
	JA		JTIR				ḪAM	U		IA-TI-RA-MU		A. 235 4 LATE
	JA		RWIḪ		A		ḪAM	U		IA-RI-ḪA-A-MU		M+
	1		ḪAMAD		U					ḪA-MA-DU	FN	XIII 1 XIII 20
	1		ḪANḪAN		U					ḪA-AN-ḪA-NU		CT XLV 11 42
	1		ḪARB	ATANU						AR-BA-TA-NU		CT IV 22A 19
	1		ḪASID		U					ḪA-ZI-DU	FN	XIII 1 VII 42
			ḪASID	AN	U					ḪA-ZI-DA-NU		M+
	1		ḪAṢN		U		TABB	I		AZ?-NU-TAB-BI	FN	M
	2		ʾALLAI				ḪAṢN	U		AL-LA-I-AṢ-NU	FN	M
	1		ḪATIK		U					ḪA-TI-KU		M
	1 ʾA		ḪBAB		U					AḪ-BA-BU		U
	1		ḪINN	AN	U					ḪI-NA-NU		KISURRA 62 SEAL
	1 ʾA		ḪLAM		U					AḪ-LA-MU		M+
	ʾA		ḪLAM		U					AḪ-LA-AM-MU		XII 508 2
	ʾA		ḪLAM		U					AḪ-LA-A-MU		XI 208 2
	1		ḪUNN		U		ʾEL			U$_3$-NU-EL		TA 31 223
	1		ḪUNUN		U					UN-NU-NU		YOS XIII 139:9+
	1		ḪURB	ATANU						UR-BA-TA-NU		KISURRA 24 6
	1		ḪUṢAN		U					ḪU-ZA-NU		M
	1		ḪAʾAZ		U		ʾIL			ḪA?-A-ZU-DINGIR		M
	1		ḪAʾL		U					ḪA-A-LU		A
			ḪAʾL		U		ʿADN	U		ḪA-LU-ḪA-AD-NU		M+
			ḪAʾL		U		ʾIL			ḪA-LU-DINGIR		M
			ḪAʾL		U		MAṬAR			ḪA-LU-MA-DA-AR		M+
			ḪAʾL		U		NIʿM			ḪA-LU-NI-ḪI-IM		RA LXV 52 X 74
			ḪAʾL		U		RAPIʾ			ḪA-LU-RA-PI		M+
			ḪAʾL		U	Š	MI					
							ʾIL			ḪA-LU-UŠ-MI-DINGIR		M
	2		ʾAJA				ḪAʾL	U		A-IA-ḪA-LU		M
			ʾIL		A		ḪAʾL	U	HU	DINGIR-ḪA-LU-U$_2$		XIII 1 IV 18
	JI		JṢIʾ				ḪAʾL	U		I-ZI-ḪA-LU		XIV 96:9+
		Š	NUʾR		A		ḪAʾL	U		ŠU-NU-UḪ-RA-ḪA-LU		M+
		Š	NUʾR		A		ḪAʾL	U	HU	ŠU-NU-UḪ-RA-ḪA-LU-U$_2$		M+
		Š	NUʾR		A		ḪAʾL	U	HU	ŠU-NU-ḪU-RA-ḪA-LU-U$_2$		XIV 11:1
		Š	NUʾR		A		ḪAʾL	U	HU	ŠU-NU-UḪ-ḪU-RA-ḪA-LU-U$_2$		XIV 36:1+
		Š	NUʾR		U		ḪAʾL	U		ŠU-NU-UḪ-RU-ḪA-LU		M+
	1		ḪAʾN	IJ	U					ḪA-NU-U$_2$		JNES XIII 210+ LATE
	2 JI		JṢIʾ				ḪAʾR	U		I-ZI-ḪA-RU		XIV 52:5, 16+
	1		ḪAʾŠ	AN	U					ḪA-SA-NU		M
	2 TA		RʿIŠ				ḪAʾT	U		TA-RI-IŠ-ḪA-AT-TU	FN	M+
	1		ḪABAD		U		ʾIL			ḪA-BA-DU-DINGIR		M
	1		ḪABIʾ	AN	U					ḪA-BI-A-NU		YOS XIII 175:12
	1		ḪAMBUZ		U	HU				ḪA-AM-BU-ZU-U$_2$		B 19
	1		ḪAMR		U					ḪA-AM-RU		C
			ḪAMR		U		RAPIʾ			ḪA-AM-RU-RA-BI		M
	1		ḪARḪAR		U					ḪAR-ḪA-RU		JNES XIII 210+ LATE
	2		ʾAB		I		ḪIʾL	U		A-BI-ḪE$_2$-LU		MRS VI P. 240 LATE
	1		ḪIRṢ		U	K				ḪI-IR-ZU-UK		RA LXV 51 IX 44
	1 JA		ḪMUṬ		U					IA-AḪ-MU-TU		JEAN,TELL SIFR 13 15
	1		ḪURṢ	AN	U					ḪU-UR-ZA-NU-KI	GN	A.
	1 JA		ḪZUM		U					IA-AḪ-ZU?-MU		BM 78799 12
	1		ʿABD	AN	U					AB-DA-NU		CT XLV 59 6
			ʿABD	AN	U					AB-TA-NU		A. LATE
			ʿABD		U	TA	RWIM			[ḪA-A]B-DU-TA-RI-IM		M
	1		ʿAD		U					A-DU		A. 269 67, 73+
			ʿAD		U		RAWM	U		A-DU-RA-MU	FN	U
			ʿAD		U	NA	HADD	U		A-DU-NA-D-IM		SYRIA XIX 109
			ʿAD		U	NI	ʾAB	I	JA	A-DU-NI-A-BI-IA		RA XXVII 87 LATE
			ʿAD		U	NI	HADD	U		A-DU-NI-D-U		MRS VI 15, 42 II 20 UGARIT
			ʿAD		U	NI	ʾIL	A		A-DU-NI-LA		U
	2		JARAḪ				ʿAD	U		SIN-A-DU		RA XLIII 8 QATNA

U	2		RABB		U			ʿAD	U	HU	RA-AB-BU-ḪA-DU-U$_2$		B 17+
			RABB		U			ʿAD	U	HU	RA-AB-BU-U$_2$-ḪA-DU-U$_2$		BM 17051A 30
			ŠUM		UM			ʿAD	U		SU-MU-UM?-ḪA-DU-KI	GN	YOS II 117:17+
			ŠUM		U			ʿAD	U	HU	SU-MU-ḪA-DU-U$_2$		M+
	1		ʿADN		U						ḪA-AD-NU		KISURRA 81A 20
			ʿADN		U			MA					
								JATAR			ḪA-AD-NU-ME-TAR		M+
			ʿADN		U			RAPIʾ			ḪA-AD-NU-RA-BI		XIV 109:18+
	2		ḪAʾL		I			ʿADN	U	HU	ḪA-LI-ḪA-AD-NU-U$_2$		M
			ḪAʾL		U			ʿADN	U		ḪA-LU-ḪA-AD-NU		M+
			ʾIL		A			ʿADN	U	HU	I-LA-ḪA-AD-NU-U$_2$		M
			ʾIL		A			ʿADN	U	HU	I-LA-ḪA-AD-NU-U$_2$	FN	C+
			ʾIL		A			ʿADN	U	HU	DINGIR-ḪA-AD-NU-U$_2$	FN	C+
			JATAR					ʿADN	U		IA-TAR-ḪA-AD-NU		M+
			JATAR					ʿADN	U	HU	IA-TAR-ḪA-AD-NU-U$_2$		RA LXV 54 XII 56
			DAWD		I			ʿADN	U	HU	DA-DI-ḪA-AD-NU-U$_2$		18 R.A. P.61 A 3821+
			ḎU					ʿADN	U		ZU-ḪA-AD-NU		M+
		JA	MṢIʾ					ʿADN	U		IA-AM-ZI-AD-[NU]		CT VI 33A 33
		JA	MṢIʾ					ʿADN	U		IA-AM-ṢI-AD-NU		BM 16914 31
		JA	MṢIʾ					ʿADN	U		IA-AM-ZI-ḪA-AD-NU		M+
		JA	MṢIʾ					ʿADN	U	HU	IA-AM-ZI-AD-NU-U$_2$		BM 81302 4
		JA	MṢIʾ					ʿADN	U	HU	IA-AM-ZI-ḪA-AD-NU-U$_2$		DELAPORTE CCL II A 385, M+
		JA	MZUʾ					ʿADN	U	HU	IA-AM-ZU-AD-NU-U$_2$		B 28+
			ŠUM		U			ʿADN	U		SU-MU-ḪA-AD-NU		B 39
			ŠUM		U			ʿADN	U		SU-MU-ḪI-AD-NU		KISURRA 29 12
			ŠARR		UM			ʿADN	U	HU	LUGAL-AD-NU-U$_2$		SIGRIST UNPUBL.
		JI	TWUR					ʿADN	U		I-DUR-ḪA-AD-[NU]		B 24
		JI	TWUR					ʿADN	U	HU	I-DUR-ḪA-AD-NU-U$_2$		TCL XVIII 83 6
	1		ʿALIJ		U						A-LI$_2$-JU-U$_2$		RUTTEN 16 14
	1		ʿAMIS	AN	U						ḪA-MI-ZA-NU		M
	1		ʿAMM	AN	U						ḪA-AM-MA-NU		M
			ʿAMM		U	HU					A-MU-U$_2$		EDZARD, DER 80:10+
			ʿAMM		U	HU					ḪA-AM-MU-U$_2$		EDZARD, DER 68 III 6
			ʿAMM		U			ḪAʾL	UM		ḪA-AM-MU-ḪA-LUM		M+
			ʿAMM		U			HADD	A		AM-MU-A-DA		A.+
			ʿAMM		U			HADD	A		AM-MU-WA-DA		A.
			ʿAMM		U			ʿAḎAR			AM-MU-A-DAR		TA 30 59
			ʿAMM		U			ʾEL			AM-MU-E-EL		BM 16931 2
			ʿAMM		U			ʾIL			ḪA-MU-DINGIR		M
			ʿAMM		U			ʾIL			AM-MU-DINGIR		UCP X/1 18 24
			ʿAMM		U			JAQAR			ḪA-MU-IA-QAR		RA LXV 52 X 62
			ʿAMM		U			ḪURB	I		AM-MU-UR-BI		A.
			ʿAMM		U			JAŠAR			ḪA-MU-JA-ŠAR		M
			ʿAMM		U			JATAR			ḪA-MU-TAR		M
			ʿAMM		U			JATAR			[Ḫ]A-AM-MU-TA-[A]R		M
			ʿAMM		U		JE	JPUʿ			ḪA-MU-E-PU-UḪ	FN	C+
			ʿAMM		U			DAGAN			ḪA-AM-MU-D-DA-GAN		M
			ʿAMM		U			DUMAR			ḪA-MU-DU-MAR		RA LXV 51 IX 66
			ʿAMM		U			KUMAR	A		AM-MU-KU-MAR-RA		A.
			ʿAMM		U			LA					
								RIWM			ḪA-MU-L[A]-RI-IM		RA LXV 46 VI 40
			ʿAMM		U			LIʾM			ḪA-MU-LI-IM		RA LXV 52 X 22
			ʿAMM		U			LABW	A		ḪA-AM-MU-LA-BA-A		XIV 114:6
			ʿAMM		U			MAṮAR			ḪA-MU-MA-DAR	FN	C
			ʿAMM		U			NIʿM			ḪA-AM-MU-NI-ḪI-IM	NOM	M
			ʿAMM		U			NIQM	A		AM-MU-NI-IQ-MA		A.+
			ʿAMM		U			PATAḪ	A		ḪA-AM-MU-PA-TA-A		M
			ʿAMM		U			RAWM	A		ḪA-MU-RA-MA		M
			ʿAMM		U			RAPIʾ			ḪA-AM-MU-RA-BI		B 19+, M+, A.+
			ʿAMM		U			RAPIʾ			AM-MU-RA-BI		B 19+
			ʿAMM		U			RAPIʾ			D-ḪA-AM-MU-RA-BI		B 19+
			ʿAMM		U			RAPIʾ			ḪA-MU-RA-BI		B 19+, M+
			ʿAMM		U			RAPIʾ			ḪA-AM-MU-RA-BI-IḪ		B 19 HANA
			ʿAMM		U			RAPIʾ			AM-MU-RA-PI		ABL 255 LATE
			ʿAMM		U			RAPIʾ			D-AM-MU-RA-PI		YBC 4362
			ʿAMM		U			RAPIʾ			ḪA-MU-U$_2$-RA-BI		FIGULLA, CAT. 14138

U	1		ʿAMM	U		RAPIʾ	I		AM-MU-RA-BI-I		A+
			ʿAMM	U		RAPIʾ			ḪA-MU-UR$_2$-RA-BI		CT XLVII 31 32+
			ʿAMM	U		RAPIʾ					
						ʾIL			ḪA-AM-MU-RA-BI-DINGIR		B 19
			ʿAMM	U		RAPIʾ					
						BANIJ			ḪA-AM-MU-RA-BI-BA-NI		B 19
			ʿAMM	U		RAPIʾ					
						....			ḪA-AM-MU-RA-BI-LU-DA-RI		B 19
			ʿAMM	U		ŠAGIŠ			ḪA-MU-ŠA-KI-IŠ		X 174 13
			ʿAMM	U		ŠALIM			ḪA-MU-SA-L[IM]?		M
			ʿAMM	U		ŠAM	A		AM-MU-SA-MA		A.+
			ʿAMM	U		ŠAMAR			ḪA-MU-SA-MAR		RA LXIV 36 NO. 31
			ʿAMM	U		ŠAMAR			ḪA-MU-SA-MAR	FN	C+
			ʿAMM	U		ŠARR			ḪA-MU-SA-AR		RA LXV 40 I 42
			ʿAMM	U		ŠARR			ḪA-MU-SA-AR	FN	C+
			ʿAMM	U		ŠARR			ḪA-AM-MU-SA-AR		XIV 108:6
			ʿAMM	U		ḎAKAJ	A		Ḫ[A]-MU-ZA-KA-A		RA LXV 43 III 75
			ʿAMM	U	HU	JATAR			ḪA-AM-MU-U$_2$-TAR		M
			ʿAMM	U	HU	RAPIʾ			ḪA-AM-MU-U$_2$-RA-BI		M
			ʿAMM	U	Š	KI					
						ʾIL			AM-MU-US-KI-DINGIR		A.
			ʿAMM	U	Š	KI					
						ʾIL			AM-MU-UŠ-KI-DINGIR		A.+
	2		ʾAJA			ʿAMM	U		A-IA-AM-MU		MAOG IV 2 10, 11, A 7740+
			ʾAJA			ʿAMM	U	HU	A-A-ḪA-AM-MU-U$_2$		BASOR 95 23
			ʾAJA			ʿAMM	U	HU	A-IA-ḪA-MU-U$_2$		A 7648, M
			ʾAJA			ʿAMM	U	HU	A-IA-AM-MU-U$_2$		VAS XIII 34:3
			ʾAJA			ʿAMM	U	HU	A-IA-AM-MU-KU		CT XLV 6 33
			ʾAJA			ʿAMM	U	HU	IA-ḪA-AM-MU-U$_2$		VAS XVIII 100:19
			JAḤAD			ʿAMM	U		IA-ḪA-AD-ḪA-AM-MU		M
			JAḤAD			ʿAMM	U		IA-ḪA-AD-ḪA-MU		M+
			JAḤAD			ʿAMM	U	HU	IA-ḪA-AD-ḪA-MU-U$_2$		M
			JADAʿ			ʿAMM	U		IA-DA-AM-MU		C II 5 4
			ʿADN	I		ʿAMM	U		ḪA-AD-NI-ḪA-MU		RA LXV 50 VIII 49
			ʾIL	A		ʿAMM	U		I-LA-ḪA-MU		RA LXV 42 II 77+
			ʾIL	I		ʿAMM	U		I$_3$-LI$_2$-ḪA-MU		RA LVII 178
			ʾALI			ʿAMM	U		A-LI$_2$-AM-MU		UCP X/1 52 22
			ʾALI			ʿAMM	U	HU	A-LI$_2$-AM-MU-U$_2$		UCP X/2 58 16
	JA		JQAH			ʿAMM	U		IA-QA-AM-MU		A.+
			ʿAQB	A		ʿAMM	U		AQ-BA-ḪA-MU		M
			ʿAQB	A		ʿAMM	U		AQ-BA-ḪA-AM-MU		IRAQ XXX 91, RIMAH
			ʿAQB	A		ʿAMM	U		ḪA-AQ-BA-ḪA-AM-MU		II 39 19, 58, 80
			ʿAQB	A		ʿAMM	U	HU	ḪA-AQ-BA-ḪA-AM-MU-U$_2$		II 39 14, 16, 24
			ʿAQB	U		ʿAMM	U	HU	AQ-BU-AM-MU-U$_2$		X 174 3
			ʿIQB	A		ʿAMM	U		IQ-BA?-AM-MU		A. 8 35
			JATAR			ʿAMM	U		IA-TAR-ḪA-MU		M
			JATAR			ʿAMM	U		IA-TAR-ḪA-MU	FN	C II P. 247+
			BUN	U		ʿAMM	U		BU-NU-AM-MU		B 16+
			ḎAKIR	A		ʿAMM	U		ZA-KI-RA-ḪA-AM-MU		M+
			ḎAKIR	A		ʿAMM	U		ZA-KI-RA-ḪA-MU		M
			ḎAKIR	A		ʿAMM	U	HU	ZA-KI-RA-ḪA-AM-MU-U$_2$		M+
			ḎIMR	A		ʿAMM	U		ZI-IM-RA-ḪA-MU		CT XLIV 54 20, C
			ḎIMR	A		ʿAMM	U		ZI-IM-RA-ḪA-AM-MU		M
			ḎIMR	A		ʿAMM	U		ZI-IM-RA-AM-MU		TIM IV 33 20, 34 13
			ḎIMR	A		ʿAMM	U	HU	ZI-IM-RA-ḪA-MU-U$_2$		TIM IV 33 SEAL, 34 SEAL
			ḎIMR	I		ʿAMM	U		ZI-IM-RI-AM-MU		TIM III 94 4
			ḎIMR	I		ʿAMM	U		ZI-IM-RI-ḪA-MU		C
			ḎIMR	I		ʿAMM	U		ZI-IM-RI-ḪA-AM-MU		B 42+, X 35 12
			ḎIMR	U		ʿAMM	U		ZI-IM-RU-ḪA-AM-MU		JCS XI 23 10 13
	JA		KWUN			ʿAMM	U		IA-KU-UN-AM-MU		B 27
			KUWN			ʿAMM	U		KU-UN-AM-MU		MRS VI P. 249
			LA			ʿAMM	U		LA-ḪA-AM-MU		HARRIS 18 14
	JA		NḪAB			ʿAMM	U		IA-ḪA-AB-ḪA-MU		M
		Š	NUʾR	A		ʿAMM	U		ŠU-NU-UḪ-RA-AM-MU		B 40 HANA+
	JA		NŠIʾ			ʿAMM	U		IA-SI-ḪA-MU		M
	JA		NTIN			ʿAMM	U		IA-AN-TI-IN-ḪA-MU		M

U	2		RIJB		A		ʿAMM	U		RI-BA-AM-MU		A. 97 4+
		JA	RWIM				ʿAMM	U		IA-RI-IM-ḪA-MU		M
		JA	RWIM				ʿAMM	U		IA-RI-IM-ḪA-AM-MU		M
		JA	RŠIJ				ʿAMM	U		IA-AR-ŠI-ḪA-MU		M, C+
			ŠU				ʿAMM	U		ŠU-ḪA-AM-MU		M+
			ŠUWB				ʿAMM	U		ŠU-UB-AM-MU		MRS VI P. 257+
		JA	ŚJIM				ʿAMM	U		IA-SI-IM-ḪA-AM-MU		M
		JA	ŚJIM				ʿAMM	U		IA-SI-IM-ḪA-MU		M
			ŚUM		U		ʿAMM	U		SU-MU-ḪA-AM-MU		B 39+
			ŚUM		U		ʿAMM	U		SU-MU-ḪA-MU		M
			ŚUM		U		ʿAMM	U		SU-MU-ḪA-MU	FN	C+
		JA	ŠṬIḪ				ʿAMM	U		IA-AŠ-DI-ḪA-AM-MU		B 30
			ṢUWR		A		ʿAMM	U		ZU-RA-ḪA-AM-MU		M+
			ṢUWR		A		ʿAMM	U		Z[U]-RA-ḪA-M[U]		XIII 132 7
			ṢUWR		A		ʿAMM	U	HU	ZU-RA-ḪA-AM-MU-U_2		M
			ṢUWR		I		ʿAMM	U		ZU-RI-ḪA-AM-MU		M
			ṢUWR		I		ʿAMM	U	HU	ZU-RI-ḪA-AM-MU-U_2		M+
		JI	TWUR				ʿAMM	U	HU	I-DUR-ḪA-MU-U_2		UNPUBL.
			TALM		A		ʿAMM	U		TA-AL-MA-AM-MU		A.+
			ZAʾT				ʿAMM	U		ZA-AT-AM-MU	MN	A. 279 2 3
	1	ME	ʿANIJ		U					ME-ḪA-A-NU		KISURRA 81A
	1		ʿAQB		U	HU				AQ-BU-U_2		CT IV 50B 24+
			ʿAQB		U		ʿAMM	U	HU	AQ-BU-AM-MU-U_2		X 174 3
			ʿAQB		U		DAWD	UM		AQ-BU-DA-DU-UM		PBS VIII/2 253 7
			ʿAQB		U		DAWD	A		AQ-BU-DA-DA		B 12
			ʿAQB		U		DAWD	I		ḪA-AQ-BU-DA-DI		M+
			ʿAQB		U		DAWD	I		AQ-BU-DA-DI		M
	1		ʿAQUB		U					A-KU-BU		VAS VIII 14 14
	1		ʿARD		U					AR-DU		TCL I 166 2
	1		ʿARIṢ	AN	U					ḪA-RI-ZA-NU		PBS II/1 P. 23+ LATE
	1		ʿARṢ		U					ḪAR-ṢU		JNES XIII 210+ LATE
	1		ʿARUL		U					A-RU-LU		STRASSM. 56 29+
	1		ʿAZZ		U					AZ-ZU	FN	M+, C+
			ʿAZZ		U					ḪA-AZ-ZU		C+
			ʿAZZ		U		ḪAʾL	IM		A-ZU-ḪA-LIM	NOM	M
			ʿAZZ		U	KA				AZ-ZU-KA	FN	M+, C
			ʿAZZ		U	KI				AZ-ZU-UK-KI	FN	XIII 1 VIII 66
			ʿAZZ		U	NI				AZ-ZU-UN-NI	FN	M
	1	JA	ʿḎIR		U					IA-AḪ-ZI-RU		CT XLV 63 34
	1		ʿIMS		U					IM-ṢU		JNES XIII 210+ LATE
	1		ʿINB		U					IN-BU	FN	C+
	1		ʿIZZ		U	KA				I-ZU-KA		XIII 1 III 50
			ʿIZZ		U		ŠAPAR			I-ZU-SA-PAR_2		U+
			ʿIZZ		U		ŠAPAR			IZ?-ZU?-ŠA-PA-AR		BIN II 98 5
			ʿIZZ		U	NI				IZ-ZU-UN-NI		M
	1	JA	ʿQUB		U					IA-KU-BU		CT II 9 26
	1		ʿUZAB		U					[ḪU]-ZA-BU	FN	XIII 1 XIV 14
	1		ʿUZZ		U					UZ-ZU	FN	XIII 1 XIV 31
	1	JA	ʿZIB		U	HU				IA-AḪ-ZI-BU-U_2		M+
	1	MU	WDAD		U					MU-DA-DU		YOS XIII 513:9
	1	JA	WŠIB		U					IA-AW-ŠI-BU		M
	1		JAʾ		U		ʾAHL	I		IA-U_2-A-LI_2		KISURRA 85 19
			JAʾ		U		ʾIL	I		IA-U-I-LI_2		SUMER V 143 NO. 2
			JAʾ		U		ŚUM	UM		IA?-U_2-SU?-MU-UM?		XIII 146 13
	1		JAḤAD		U					IA-ḪA-TU		B 26
			JAḤAD		U					IA-ḪA-DU		M
	1		JAʿIL	AN	U					JA-I-LA-NU	TRIBE	C
	1		JAJAM		U					IA-IA-MU		B 26
	1		JABUB		U					IA-BU-BU		CT XLIII 29 1
	2		ŚAM		A		JADAʿ	U		SA-MA-A-DA-ḪU		M
	1		JADID		U					IA-DI-DU		FIGULLA CAT. I 13371 M
	1		JADN		U					IA-AD-NU		M
	3		ʾALUN				PI					
							JAM	U		ḪA-LU-UN-BI-JA-MU		M
			ʾALUN				PI					
							JAM	U		ḪA-LU-UM-BI-JA-MU		RA LXV 43 III 78

U	3	ʾALUN						PI						
								JAM		U		ḪA-LU-BI-JA-MU		M
	1	JAMM		U	HU							IA-AM-MU-U$_2$		VAS XVIII 19 R. 6
		JAMM		U				QAʾD		UM		IA-AM-MU?-QA-DU-UM		III 56 7
	1	JAT		U	HU							IA-TU-U$_2$		YOS XIII 426:14
	2	MATIʿ						JAT		U	HU	MA-TI-IA-TU-U$_2$		UCP X/3 107 18
	1	JATAM		U								IA-TA-MU		JCS XIII 51 292, A. LATE
		JATAR		U								IA-TA-RU		KISURRA 106 16
	1	JATUM		U								IA-TU-MU		HARRIS 104 5
	1 JI	JBAL		U								I-BA-LU		CT VIII 17C 11
	3	LA						RIWM						
						JI		JBAL		U	HU	[L]A?-RI-IM-I-BA-LU-U$_2$		M
	1 JA	JBIŠ		U								IA-BI-ŠU		A 29366:10
	JI	JBIŠ		U								I-BI-ŠU	FN	BM 82359
	2	LA				JE	N	JBIŠ		U		LA-E-NI-BI-ŠU		YOS XII
	1 JA	JDIʿ		U								IA-DI-U$_2$		CT VIII 10 B 7+
	1	JID		U	HU							I-DU-U$_2$		RA LXV 65 VI 59
	1 JA	JPUʿ		U								IA-PU-ḪU		B 25
	1 JA	JQIR	AN	U								IA-KI-RA-NU		M
	1	BAʿD	AN	U								BA-AḪ-TA-NU		BM 17060 10
		BAʿD	AN	U	HU							BA-AḪ-TA-NU-U$_2$		BM 17060 2
	1	BAʿL		U				ʿAŠTAR				BA-LU-EŠ$_4$-DAR		M+
		BAʿL		U				BAʿD		I		BA-AḪ-LU-BA-DI		EA
		BAʿL		U				GAʾJ		A		BA-AḪ-LU-GA-A	GEN	HOLMA 6 5
		BAʿL		U				GAʾJ		IM		BA-AḪ-LU-GA-JI-IM	GEN	M+
		BAʿL		U				GAʾJ		IM		BA-AḪ-LU-GA-I-IM	GEN	M+
		BAʿL		U				GAʾJ		I		BA-AḪ-LU-GA-I	NOM	M+
		BAʿL		U				GAʾJ		I		BA-AḪ-LU-GA-A-JI	NOM	M
		BAʿL		U				KULIM				BA-AḪ-LU-KU-LI-IM		SYRIA XXXII 7 III 6
		BAʿL		U				LUʾL		I		BA-AḪ-LU-LU-L[I]?		HARRIS 71 14
		BAʿL		U				ME						
								NUMḪ		I		BA-LU-ME-NU-ḪI		M+
		BAʿL		U				ME						
								NUMḪ		I		BA-LU-ME-NU-UM-ḪI		IX 41 2
		BAʿL		U				ŠAMŠ				BA-LU-D-UTU		M
	2	ḪADUR						BAʿL		U		A-DU-UR-BA-LU	GN	SUMER XIV 26
		ʾIL		A				BAʿL		U	HU	I-IA-BA-LU-U$_2$		M
		ʾANA						BAʿL		U		A-NA-BA-LU	MN?	CT XLVIII 86 REV
		ʾANA						BAʿL		U		A-NA-BA-LU	FN	M
		BUN		U				BAʿL	AN	U		BU-NU-BA-AḪ-LA-NU		M
		MUT		U				BAʿL		U	HU	MU-TU-BA-LU-U$_2$		RA LXV 44 IV 26
	3	LA				ʾA		HWIJ						
								BAʿL		U		LA-AḪ-WI-BA-LU		C
		LA				ʾA		HWIJ						
								BAʿL		U		LA-AḪ-WI-BA-AḪ-LU		XIV 29:28
	1	BAWʾ		U				ʾIL		A		BA-U$_2$-I-LA		MEISSNER 43 45
	2	LA						BAWʾ		U		LA-BA-U$_2$		JCS XIII 51 292:5' A.LATE
		LA						BAWʾ		U		LA-BA-ʾU-U		TALLQUIST,APN P.120 LATE
	1	BAWB		U				QAʾN				BA-BU-QA-AN		M
	1	BAWŠ	AN	U								BA-SA-NU		MAOG 4 440 HANA
	1	BAJN		U				DAGAN				BA-NU-D-DA-GAN		M+
	1	BAGIN		U								BA-GI-NU		B 15+
	1	BALK		U	Š			RAḪAB				BA-AL-KU-UŠ$_2$-RA-ḪA-AB	FN	XIII 1 VIII 61
	1	BAZIN		U								BA-ZI-NU		B 15
	3	LA				ʾA		ḪJIJ						
								BIḪR		U		LA-ḪI-BI-RU		WATERMAN 25 R. 5
	2	PALṬ		A				BIJT		U		PA-AL-DA-BI-TU		A. LATE
	1	BIDUM		U								BI-DU-MU		M
	1	BILM		U	Š							BI-IL-MU-UŠ$_2$		RA LXV 45 V 80
	1	BIN		U				MA						
								HADD		U		BI-NU-MA-D-IM		4E RENCONTRE 21 NO. 25
		BIN	T	U				ṬAJB	AH			BI-IN-DU-ṬA$_3$-BA	FN	RA LXV 65 VII 10
	2	ŠUM		U				BINAŠ		U		SU-MU-BI-NA-ŠU		A 7630 2
	1	BIRKIN		U								BI-IR-KI-IN-NU	MN	XIII 1 VI 26
	2	KUʾD		U				BIZZ		U		KU-DU-BI-IZ-ZU		A.
	1 JA	BLUṬ	AN	U								IA-AB-LU-TA-NU		MRS VI P. 261+

U		1	BUʾL		U	HU						BU-LU-U$_2$		CT XLV 92 II 13
		1	BUWZ		U							BU-ZU		RA LXV 50 VIII 75
			BUWZ		U	HU						BU-ZU-U$_2$		TCL I 59 16+
			BUWZ		U	NA						BU-ZU-NA	FN	RA LXV 58 I 50
		1	BUN		U		ʾA	BLUṮ				BU-NU-AB-LU-UṮ		BIROT,TEA 64:4
			BUN		U		ʾA	ŠKUR				BU-NU-AŠ$_2$-KU-UR		SYRIA XXXVII 206 29 HANA
			BUN		U			ʾIL		A		BU-NU-I-LA		CT XLV 115 24
			BUN		U			ḪAM		I		BU-NU-D-A-MI		M+
			BUN		U			ḪAM		IM		BU-NU-D-A-MI-IM		RA LXV 41 II 27+
			BUN		U			ʿAMM		I		BU-NU-ḪA-AM-MI	FN	M+
			BUN		U			ʿAMM		U		BU-NU-AM-MU		B 16+
			BUN		U			ʿAN	AT	I		BU-NU-A-NA-TI		B 16
			BUN		U			JARAḪ				BU-NU-E-RA-AḪ		M
			BUN		U			JAŠʿ	AH			BU?-NU-IA-AŠ-[ḪA]	FN	XII 1 VII 67
			BUN		U			ʿAŠTAR				BU-NU-EŠ$_4$-DAR		M+, C+
			BUN		U			BAʿL		UM		BU-NU-BA-LUM		B 16+
			BUN		U			BAʿL	AN	U		BU-NU-BA-AḪ-LA-NU		M
			BUN		U			KI						
								ʾIL				BU-NU-KI-DINGIR		M
			BUN		U			KALA						
								ʾIL		I		BU-NU-KA-LA-I-LI		B 16
			BUN		U			KAMA						
								ʾIL		A		BU-NU-KA-MA-I-LA		B 16
			BUN		U			LAʾR		A		BU-NU-LA-RA		B 16
			BUN		U			MA						
								ʾAḪ		UM		BU-NU-MA-A-ḪU-UM		B 16
			BUN		U			MA						
								HADD		U		BU-NU-MA-D-IM		M+
			BUN		U			MA						
								ʾIL				BU-NU-MA-DINGIR		M
			BUN		U			MA						
								ʾAŠAR				BU-NU-MA-A-ŠA-AR		KISURRA 93 4
			BUN		U			MA						
								ʾAŠAR				BU-NU-MA-ŠAR		B 16+
			BUN		U			NAWIJ		E		BU-NU-NA-WI-E		CT XLVIII 56 REV.11
			BUN		U			ŠALG		I		BU-NU-ŠA?-AL?-GI		B 16
			BUN		U			TAḪTUN						
								ʾIL		A		BU-NU-TAḪ-TU-UN-I-LA		B 16+
			BUN		U	HU		PI						
								ʾIL		UM		BU-NU-U$_2$?-BI-I-LUM		UET V 548 2
		1	BURQ	AN	U							BU-UR$_2$-GA-NU		BM 17028 5
		1	DAʾŠ		U							DA-ŠU		U
		1	DAWD	AN	U							DA-DA-NU		M
			DAWD		U			DANN		UM		DA-AM-DU-DA-NU-UM		HARRIS 92:14+
			DAWD		U			MA				DA-DU-MA		HARRIS 49 5
			DAWD		U			MALIK				DA-DU-MA-LIK		XIII 1 VI 27
			DAWD		U			RAPIʾ				DA-DU-RA-BI		B 16+
		2	ʾAJA					DAWD		U		A-IA-DA-DU		M
			ʾAJA					DAWD		U	HU	A-A-DA-DU-U$_2$		HARRIS 79 5
			ʾAJA					DAWD		U	HU	A-IA-DA-DU-U$_2$		TIM IV 39 15
			ḪAM		U			DAWD		U		D-A-MU-DA-DU		M
	JA		MWUT					DAWD		U		IA-MU-UT-DA-DU		RA LXV 51 X 11
	JA		RWIM					DAWD		U		IA-RI-IM-DA-DU		RA LXV 40 I 38+
		2	ŠUM		I			DAWR		U		SU?-MI-DA-AR-RU		A. 322 9
			ŠUM		I			DAWR		U		ŠU-MI-TA-RU		A. LATE
		2	BIN					DAM		U		BI-IN-DA-MU		RA LXV 42 II 61
		1	DAMQ	AN	U							DAM-QA-NU		XIII 1 II 1
		1	DANN		U			MAʾT		UM		DA-NU-MA-TUM		CT XLV 12:24
			DANN		U		TA	ʾḪAḎ				DAN-NU-TA-ḪA-AZ		M+
			DANN		U		TA	ʾḪAḎ				DA-NU-TA-ḪA-AZ		SIMMONS 36 23
			DANN		U		TA	ʾḪAḎ				D-DA-NU-TA-ḪA-AZ		SIMMONS 84 15
		2	ʿAMM		I			DANN		U		AM-MI-DA-NU		YOS XII
		1	DARK		U							DAR-KU		C
		2	ʾAJAM					DIWD		U		ḪA-IA-AM-DI-DU		B 18
		1	DITAN		U							DI-TA-NU		BM 80328 6
			DITAN		U							DI-DA-A-NU		JNES XIII 210+ LATE

U	1	DUWD		U	HU				DU-DU-U$_2$		M, TCL X 112	8, 22+
		DUWD		U	Š	ME						
						ʾEL			DU-DU-UŠ-ME-EL		UCP X/3 P. 198+	
	2	LAMA				DUWD	U		LA-MA-DU-DU		M	
	2	RABAʿ				DUDM	U		RA-BA?-AḪ-DU-UD-MU		M	
	1	ḎIBIB		U					SI-BI-BI-BU		PBS VIII/2 228 4	
	1	ḎIKR	ITANU						ZI-IK-RI-TA-NU		M	
		ḎIKR		U	HU				ZI-IK-RU-U$_2$		VAS IX 185 12+	
	1	ḎIMR		U		ḪAʾL	A		ZI-IM-RU-ḪA-LA		BM 17045	
		ḎIMR		U		HADD	U		ZI-IM-RU-D-IM		CT XLVIII 22 REV	
		ḎIMR		U		ʾIL	A		ZI-IM-RU-I-L[A]?		II 5 7	
		ḎIMR		U		ʿAMM	I		ZI-IM-RU-ḪA-AM-MI		B 42	
		ḎIMR		U		ʿAMM	U		ZI-IM-RU-ḪA-AM-MU		JCS XI 23 10 13	
		ḎIMR		U		ʾUP	I		ZI-IM-RU-UḪ$_2$-KI		TCL VII 23 14 21+	
		ḎIMR		U		ʾARAḪ			ZI-IM-RU-A-RA-AḪ		BM 17045A 13	
		ḎIMR		U		ʾARAḪ			ZI-IM-RU-ḪA-RA-AḪ		BM 17045 13	
		ḎIMR		U		ʿAŠTAR			ZI-IM-RU-EŠ$_4$-DAR		IRAQ IV 185	A. 385
		ḎIMR		U		LA						
						ʾAB	I		ZI-IM-RU-LA-A-BI		RA LXV 42 III 7	
		ḎIMR		U		RAPIʾ			ZI-IM-RU-RA-BI		TA 30 82	
		ḎIMR		U		ŚAMŚ			ZI-IM-RU-D-UTU		BIROT,TEA 70 B I 9	
	1	ḎIQN		U					ZI-IQ-NU	FN	XIII 1 V 36	
	1	ḎUBAB		U					DU-BA-BU		YOS XII	
	1	ḎUMUR	ATANU						ZU-MUR?-TA-NU		ZA XLII 41	
	1	GAʾŠ		U					GA-AḪ-ŠU		M	
	2	ʾIL		I	Š	GAʾUL	U		I$_3$-LI$_2$-IŠ-GA-U$_2$-LU		KISURRA 70A 17+	
	1	GALD	AN	U					GA-AL-DA-NU		B 44+	
	1	GARIŠ		U					GA-RI-SU		B 17	
	1	GIZZ	AN	U					GI-ZA-NU		B 93	
	1	GUʾR		U		HADD	U		GU-RU-D-IM		M+	
	1	GURUD		U					GU-RU-DU		XIII 1 III 41	
		GURUR		U					GU-UR-RU-RU		M	
	1 JA	KWUN		U					IA-KU-NU		B 27+	
	1	KABD		U		KA						
						ʾAB	I		KA-AB-TU-KA-A-BI		UET V 688:8,12	
	2	ʾIL		A		KABKAB	U	HU	I-LA-KAB-KA-BU-U$_2$		M+	
		ʾIL		I		KABKAB	U		I$_3$-LI$_2$-KA-AB-KA-BU		A 21914 3	
	1	KAKK		U					KA-AK-KU	FN	C+	
	1	KANZ		U					KA-AN-ZU	FN	M+; C II 45 II 40	
	1	KAŠP	AN	U					KA-AŠ$_2$-BA-NU		M	
	1	KATR		U					KA-AT-RU		B 33+	
	1	KAZIB		U					KA-ZI-BU		M	
	1	KIʾL		U		MAʾN	A		KI-LU-MA-NA	FN	RA LXV 56 I 9	
	2	ʾAŠD		I		KIʾR	U		AŠ-DI-KI-E-RU		BM 92654 A	
		ʾAŠD		I		KIʾR	U		AŠ-DI-KI-RU		BM 92654	
	1	KIWN		U		BAWŠ	I		KI-NU-BA-ŠI		LANGDON XXVIII 12	
	2	LA				KIWN	U		LA-K[I]-NU		M	
	1	KIBS		U	NA				KI-IB-ZU-UN-NA	FN	M+	
	1	KIKKIN		U					KI-IK-KI-NU		B 49+	
	1	KIMR	AN	U					KI-IM-RA-NU		M	
	1	KINAN		U					KI-NA-NU		B 45+	
	2	ʾAWIJ				KIRIŠ	U		A-WI-KI-RI-IŠ		XIV 106:18	
		ʾIL		U	NA	KIRIŠ	U		I-LU-NA-KI-RI-ŠU		XIII 8 19+	
	1	KIRUʾ		U					KI-RU-U$_2$	FN NOM	X 32 3+	
	1	KIŠAM	AN	U					KI-ŠA?-MA-NU		XIII 1 V 60	
	2	ʿAN	AT			KUʾB	U		A-NA-AT-KU-BU		TCL I 204:11	
	1	KUʾD		U		BIZZ	U		KU-DU-BI-IZ-ZU		A.	
	1	KUʾM		U		LIʾL	U		KU-MU-LI-LU		CT IV 22A 14	
		KUʾM		U		ṢILL	I		KU-MU-ZI-LI	FN	B 33+	
	2	ḪALAJ		A		KUʾM	U		ḪA-LA-A-KU-MU		XIV 79:5+	
	2 JI	TWUR				KUʾN	U	HU	I-DUR-KU?-NU-U$_2$		VAS XIII 14 R. 10	
	1	KUʾR	AN	U					KU-RA-NU		B 45, M, C+	
		KUʾR		U		HADD	U		KU-RU-D-IM		M	
	1	KUʾT	AT	U					KU-TA-TU	MN	B 33	
	1	KUʾZ	AN	U					KU-ZA-NU		B 46	
	2	ḎAKUR		A		KUWN	U		ZA-KU-RA-KU-NU		VII 85 12	

SUFFIXES, Class 2

U	1		KUBAS		U		....				KU-BA-ZU-[....]		RA LXV 50 VIII 83
	1		KURŠ	AN	U						KU-UR-[S]A-NU		M
	1		KUTUL		U	HU					KU-TU-LU-U_2		RA LXV 43 III 76
	1		KUZAB		U						KU-ZA-BU	FN	VAS VII 166 11
	1	JA	LʾUM		U						IA-AL-U_2-MU		XIII 36 20
	2		ŠUM		I		LAMM		U		SU-MI-LAM-MU		VAS XVI 24 4, A.+
	1		LAND		U						LA-AN-TU		TA 1931, 148
	1		LAŠIK		U						LA-ŠI-KU	FN	EDZARD, DER 91:17
	2		KUʾM		U		LIʾL		U		KU-MU-LI-LU		CT IV 22A 14
			ŠUM		U		LIʾL		U		SU-MU-LI-LU		B 39
	2	JA	MWUT				LIʾM		U		IA-MU-UT-LI-MU		TCL XI 182 10
	1		LILAR		U						LI-LA-RU		SIMMONS 30 10
	2		ʾAḪ		UM		LUʾM		U		A-ḪU-UM-LU-MU		X 166 4+
			ʾAḪ		U		LUʾM		U		A-ḪU-LU-MU		M
			ʾADUN				LUʾM		U		ḪA-DU-UN-LU-MU		M
			ʾADUN				LUʾM		U		ḪA-DU-LU-MU		M
			TIʾŠ				LUʾM		U		TI-IŠ-LU-MU		M
	1		LUʾP		U		ʾEL				LU-BU-E-EL		I
	1		LUʾUP		U						LU-U_2-PU		A.
	1	JA	MʾAD		U						IA-AM-ḪA-DU	GN	XII 747 4
		JA	MʾAD		U						IA_3-A-MA-TU		U
	2		ŠUM		U	JA	MWUT		U				
							BAʿL		A		[SU]-MU-IA-MU-TU-BA-LA		PBS XI/2 1 I 19
	2		ʾAŠD		I		MAʾK		U	HU	$AŠ_2$-DI-MA-KU-U_2		VAS IX 172 30
			MUT		I		MAʾK		U	HU	MU-TI-MA-KU-U_2		M+
	1		MAʾR		U		ZAʾT		U	HU	MA-RU-ZA-TU-U_2		CT XLVIII 27
	1		MAʾT		U		BANIJ				MA-TU-BA-NI		KISURRA 112 6
	2		ʾAHL		UM		MAʾT		U		[A-LU]-UM-MA-[TU]	FN	M
			ʾIRR		I		MAʾT		U		I-RI-MA-TU		A.
	2		ŠEʾR		UM		MAGUN		U		ŠE-EḪ-RUM-MA-GU-NU	FN	C
	1		MAKAL	AN	U						MA-KA-LA-NU		VAS IX 34 6
	1		MALAK		U		ʾIL				MA-LA-KU-IL		M
	2		DAGAN				MALAK		U		D-DA-GAN-MA-LA-KU	FN	RA LXV 60 III 3
	3		LA			ʾA	HWIJ						
							MALIK		U		LA-AḪ-WI-MA-LI-KU		M
	1		MANN	ATANU							MA-NA-TA-NU		M
			MANN		U		ŠAM		A		MA-NU-SA-MA		B 34
	2		KAKK		A		MANN		U		KA-AK-KA-MA-AN-NU		M
	1		MAŠK		U						[M]A-$AŠ_2$-KU		M
	1		MATQ		U		NAN		A		MA-AT-KU-NA-NA	FN	RA LXV 60 III 33
	1		MILK		U						MF-IL-KU	FN	RA LXV 61 IV 3+
			MILK		U		DANN		UM		MI-IL-KU-DA-NU-UM		UET V 549:8
			MILK		U		MA				MI-IL-KU-MA		JCS XIII 51 292 R 10,A.LATE
			MILK		U		MA						
							ʾIL				MI-IL-KU-MA-IL		B 35+
			MILK		U		MA						
							ʾIL				MI-IL-KU-MA-DINGIR		C+
	2		ʾIL		I		MILK		U		I_3-LI_2-MIL-KU	FN	RA LXV 58 I 31
			QUWJ				MILK		U		QU-U_2-LUGAL		MRS XII 31:24
	1	JA	MKUS		U		....				IA-AM-KU-UZ-ZU-....		BM 80328 3
	1	JA	MQUṮ		U						IA-AM-KU-DU		M
		JA	MQUṮ		U						I-AM-KU-DU		M
	1	JA	MSIR		U						IA-AM-ZI-RU		UCP X/1 50 9
	1		MUHR		U		DAGAN				MU-RU-D-DA-GAN		RA LXV 53 XI 53
	2		ʾAB		I	Š	MUM		U		A-BI-IŠ-MU-MU		HARRIS 98 2
	1	ʾA	MURR		U						A-MU-UR-RU		M+
	1		MUT		U		ʾAWN	AN	UM		MU-TU-AM-NA-NU-UM		BM 81641 3, 8
			MUT		U		ʾABIḪ				MU-TU-A-BI-I[Ḫ]		M
			MUT		U		ʾABIḪ		IM		MU-TU-A-BI-ḪI-IM		C
			MUT		U		HADD		U		MU-TU-D-IM		M
			MUT		U		ʾIL		A		MU-TU-I-LA		RA LXV 43 III 68
			MUT		U		ḪAM		I		MU-TU-D-A-MI		RA LXV 51 IX 49
			MUT		U		JAM		A		MU-TU-IA-MA		M
			MUT		U		JARAḪ				MU-TU-E-RA-AḪ		JCS XXIV 60 NO. 51 REV
			MUT		U		ʾARAPḪ		IM		MU-TU-AR-RA-AP-ḪI-IM		C+
			MUT		U		ʾAŠD		I		[MU]-TU-AŠ-DI		VIII 17 13'

U	1			MUT		U			ḪATK	IM		MU-TU-ḪA-AD-KI-IM		M+
				MUT		U			ḪATK	IM		MU-TU-AD-KI-IM		M
				MUT		U			ḪATK	I		MU-TU-ḪA-AD-KI		M
				MUT		U		JE	JŠUʿ			M[U-T]U-E-ŠU-UḪ		RA LXV 47 VII 21
				MUT		U		JA	NŠUʾ		HU	MU-TU-A-AN-ŠU-U$_2$		KISURRA 91 24
				MUT		U			BAʿL	U	HU	MU-TU-BA-LU-U$_2$		RA LXV 44 IV 26
				MUT		U			BAWŠ	A		MU-TU-BA-SA		B 35+
				MUT		U			BIŠIR			MU-TU-BI-SI-IR		M+
				MUT		U			DAGAN			MU-TU-D-DA-GAN		CT XLIII 29 1 M+
				MUT		U			KUʾB	I		MU-TU-KU-BI		RA LXV 42 II 66
				MUT		U			KANAT	A		MU-TU-KA-NA-TA		M
				MUT		U			KUMR	I		MU-TU-KU-UM-RI		X 166 10', 13'
				MUT		U			ME					
									ʾEL			MU-TU-ME-EL		CT VIII 31A 25+
				MUT		U			MEʾR			MU-TU-ME-ER		M
				MUT		U			MALAK	A		MU-TU-MA-LA-KA		M
				MUT		U			RAWM	I	JE	MU-TU-RA-MI-E		CT XLV 63 15
	2			MIJA					MUT	U		MI-IA-MU-DU		KISURRA 25 11
	1	MI		NWIḪ		U						MI-NI-ḪU		TIM V 62 13
	1	JI	N	NWIB		U						IN-NI-BU		YOS XIII 191:2+
		JI	N	NWIB		U						IN-NE-BU		M
	2			ʾUMM		I			NAHR	U		UM-MI-NA-RU	FN	M
	1			NAʿIM		U						NA-I-MU		B 36+
	1			NAʿM	AN	U						NA-AḪ-MA-NU		M+
	1			NAMḪ		U	HU					NAM-ḪU-U$_2$		BM 80328 8
	3			BAʿL		A			MI					
									NAMḪ	U		BA-LA-MI-NA-AM-ḪU		SYRIA XLIV 201 N.1 MARI
	1			NAMAŠ		U						NA-MA-ŠU		B 36 HANA
	1			NAMIŠ		U						NA-MI-ŠU		B 36 HANA
	1			NAMZ		U	HU					NAM-ZU-U$_2$		BM 80328 5
	1			NANIB		U			MA			NA-NI-BU-MA		SIMMONS 138 4+
	1			NAPŠ	AN	U						NA-AP-SA-NU-KI	GN	B 46
				NAPŠ		U			HADD	U		NA-AP-SU-D-IM		M
				NAPŠ		U	NA		HADD	U		NA-AP-SU-NA-D-IM		M+
				NAPŠ		U	NA		DAWR	A		NA-AP-SU-NA-D-DA-RA		CT IV 1 8
	2	TA		HWIJ					NAPŠ	U		TA-AḪ-WI-NA-AP-SU		RA LXIV 28 NO. 14
				LAʾR					NAPŠ	U		LA-AR-NA-AP-SU	FN	XIII 1 I 71
	1			NAQIM		U						NA-KI-MU		B 36+
	1			NARB		U						NA-AR-BU		XIII 1 II 32
	2			LA					NAŠUʾ	U		LA-NA-SU-U$_2$		B 33, 4E RENC. ASS. P. 178 8
	1	JI		NDIN		U						ID-DI-NU		XIII 1 I 47
	2			KAKK		A			NIʾŠ	U	JA	KA-AK-KA-NI-ŠU-IA		RA LXV 64 VI 35
				KAKK		A			NIʾŠ	U	JA	KA-KA-NI-ŠU-IA	FN	RA LXV 65 VII 44
				ŠUM		U			NIʾŠ	U	JA	SU-MU-NI-ŠU-A		CT VIII 38D:14
	1			NIWR		U						NI-E-RU		A.
	1			NINN		U						NI-IN-NU		M
	1			NIQM		U	K					NI-IQ-MU-UK	FN	M
	1	JI		NPIḪ		U						I-BI-ḪU	FN	C
	1	JA		NTIN		U						IA-AN-TI-NU		M
		JA		NTIN		U						IA-TI-NU		B 31
		JA		NTIN		U						IA-AT-TI-NU		YOS XIII 280:13
		MA		NTIN		U						URU MA-AN-TI-NU	GN	BM 16387
	1		Š	NUʾR		U			ḪAʾL	U		ŠU-NU-UḪ-RU-ḪA-LU		M+
	1			NUʿM		U			BAʾAT	IM		NU-UḪ-MU-BA-A-TIM	FN	C+
	1			NUWAP		U						NU-A-BU		JNES XIII 210+ LATE
	1			NUWR		U			ʾAMAR			NU-RU-A-MA-AR		HARRIS 68 19
	1			NUMN		U	HU					NU-UM-NU-U$_2$		M
	1			NUN		U			NIWR	I		D-NU-NU-NE?-RI	FN	RA LXV 66 VII 56
				NUN		U		TA	BNIJ			D-NU-NU-TA-AB-NI	FN	XII 265 1
	2			ʾIL		A			NUN	U		I-LA-NU-NU		FIGULLA CAT. I 14029
				PUḪUR					NUN	U		PU-ḪU-UR-D-NU-NU		M
				QIJŠ	T	I			NUN	U		KI-IŠ-TI-D-NU-NU		M+
	1			NUṢAB		U						NU-ZA-BU		XIV 61:7
	1	JA		PḪUR	AN	U						IA-AP-ḪU-RA-NU		M
	1	JI	N	PALIS		U						IP-PA-LI-ZU?		MAOG IV 2 3 HANA
	1			PILḪ		U			HADD	U		BI-EL-ḪU-D-IM		RA LXV 55 XIII 4

U	1 JA	PLAḪ		U					IA-AP-LA-ḪU		B 24+
	1 JI	PRUD		U					IP-RU-DU		CT XLV 59 22 SEAL
	1 JA	PTAḪ		U					IA-AP-TA-ḪU		YOS VIII 156 2, A. LATE
	1 ME	PTUḪ		U					ME-EP-TU-U_2		M+
	MI	PTUḪ		U					MI-IP-TU-U_2		RA LXIV 104:3
	1	PULS		U	NA	HADD	U		PU-UL-ZU-NA-D-IM		UNPUBL.
	1	PURʿUŠ	AN	U					PU-UR-ḪU-ŠA-NU		M
	1 JA	QWUJ		U					IA-KU-U_2		RUTTEN 16:16
	1	QAʾT		U	HU				QA-TU-U_2	FN	RA LXV 58 I 47
	1	QAWL		U		ḪAM	I		QA-L[U]-D-A-MI		M
	1	QAWM		U		HADD	U		GA-MU-D-IM		M
		QAWM		U		MA					
						ʾAḪ	UM		QA-MU-MA-A-ḪU-UM		M
		QAWM		U		MA					
						ʾAḪ	I		QA-MU-MA-A-ḪI		RA LXV 41 II 22
		QAWM		U		MA					
						ʾIL			QA-MU-MA-DINGIR		M
	2	ʾAŚD		U		QAWM	U		AŠ-DU-GA-MU		CT XLV 77 R. 10, 14+
	1 MU	QADIM		U					MU-GA-DI-MU		CT XLV 6 33
	1	QANIJ	AN	U					KA-NI-IA-NU		M
	1 ʾA	QDAM		U					AQ-DA-MU		C P. 35+
	1	QUWJ		U		HADD	U		KU-U_2-D-IM		M
		QUWJ		U		DAGAN			KU-U_2-D-DA-GAN		RA LXV 41 II 43+
	1 JA	RḤAM		U					IA-AR-ḪA-MU		B 29+, M
	1 JA	RḤIB		U					IA-AR-I-BU		XIII 1 VI 63
	2	ʾANA				RAḤAB	U		A-NA-RA-A-BU		M+
	1	RAḪAṢ		U					RA-ḪA-ZU		WALTERS,WL 114:12
	2	KANAK				RAWḤ	U		KA-NA-AK-RA-ḪU		VAS XIII 66 R. 6
	2	ʿAD		U		RAWM	U		A-DU-RA-MU	FN	U
		ŠU				RAWM	U		ŠU-RA-MU		A. LATE+
	1	RABB		U		ʿAD	UM		RU-BU-ḪA-DU-UM		BM 17055 26
		RABB		U		ʿAD	U	HU	RA-AB-BU-ḪA-DU-U_2		B 17+
		RABB		U		ʿAD	U	HU	RA-AB-BU-U_2-ḪA-DU-U_2		BM 17051A 30
	1	RIWM		U		HADD	U		RI-MU-D-IM		M
	1	RIJB		U	HU				RI-BU-U_2		KISURRA 187 12
		RIJB		U		DAGAN			RI-BU-D-DA-GAN		RA LXV 47 VII 52
	1	RIBK		U					RI-IB-KU	FN	XIII 1 IX 56+
	1	RIGM	AN	U					RI-IG-MA-NU		M
	1 JI	RKAB	T	U					IR-KAB-DU	MN	A.+ LATE
	1	SITR		U	HU				ZI-IT-RU-U_2		DE GEN. KICH II C 82
	2	LI			JA	SITR	U	HU	LI-IA-ZI-IT-RU-U_2		M+
		RAJB		A		SITR	U	HU	RA-BA-ZI-IT-RU-U_2	FN	M
	1	ŚAʾL		U		MAṬAR			SA-LU-MA-DAR		RA LXV 52 X 68+
	1	ŚAʾQ		U	HU				SA-GU-U_2		SIMMONS 60 31
	1	ŚABIM		U					SA-BI-MU		C+
	1	ŚADL		U		MA			SA-AD-LU-MA		UCP X/1 P. 61+
	1	ŚAKIR		U					SA-KI-RU		B 37
	1	ŚAKN		U					SA-AK-NU	FN	M
		ŚAKN		U					ŠA-AK-NU		M
	1	ŚAKUR	AN	U					SA-KU-RA-NU		M+
	1	ŚALIḤ		U					SA-LI-ḪU		M, SYRIA V 274+ HANA
	MU	ŚALIM		U					MU-SA-LI-MU		CT IV 47B 28
		ŚALIM	AN	U					SA-LI-MA-NU		A 7733 4, C+
	1	ŚALM		U		ṬAJB	A		ŠA-AL-MU-$ṬA_3$-BA	FN	RA LXV 66 VII 64
	1	ŚAM	AN	U					SA-MA-NU		JNES XIII 212F. LATE
		ŚAM		U		ʾAB	IM		SA-MU-A-BI-IM	NOM	RA VIII 71
		ŚAM		U		ʾAB	IM		SA-MU-A-BI-IM	GEN	SUMER XXIII 153+
		ŚAM		U		HADD	U		SA-MU-D-IM		M+
		ŚAM		U		ʾIL	A		SA-MU-I-LA		M
		ŚAM		U		JARAḪ			SA-MU-A-RA-AḪ		SIMMONS 98 3
		ŚAM		U		JARAḪ			SA-[M]U-E?-RA-A[Ḫ]?		RA LXV 47 VII 13
		ŚAM		U		DAGAN			SA-MU-D-DA-GAN		M
		ŚAM		U		LA					
						ʾIL			SA-MU-LA-DINGIR		B 39+
		ŚAM		U		RAWḤ			SA-MU-RA-A-AḪ		SIMMONS 46 28, 47 23
		ŚAM		U		RAWḤ			SA-MU-RA	NOM	CT XLVIII 29 REV.

U	1	ŠAM		U	HU							SA-MU-U$_2$		M+
		ŠAM		U	HU			ʾIL		A		SA-MU-U$_2$-I-LA		M
		ŠAM		U				BALIṬ				SA-MU-BA-LI$_2$-IṬ?		RUTTEN 34 11
	2 JI	JṢIʾ						ŠAM		U				
								ʾAB		UM		I-ZI-SA-MU-A-BU-UM		B 23
	1	ŠAMAR	AN	U								SA-MA-RA?-NU		X 20 11
	2	ʾAB		I				ŠAMAK		U		A-BI-SA-MA-KU		SIMMONS 41 15
	1	ŠAMID		U								SA-MI-DU		CT VIII 9A 1
		ŠAMIM		U								SA-MI-MU		WALTERS, WL 109:10
		ŠAMIN		U	HU							SA-MI-NU-U$_2$	FN	CT II 46 4
	1	ŠAMŠ		U								SA-AM-SU		YOS XII
		ŠAMŠ	AN	U								ZA-AM-ZA-NU		M
		ŠAMŠ		U				HADD		U		SA-AM-ŠU-D-IM		COLLON, SEALS NO. 141
		ŠAMŠ		U				ʾIL		U	NA	SA-AM-SU-I-LU-NA		B 38+
		ŠAMŠ		U				ʾIL		U	NA			
								KIMA				SA-AM-SU-I-LU-NA-KI-MA-DINGIR		BM 81047:6
		ŠAMŠ		U				ʾIL		U	NA			
								....				SA-AM-SU-I-LU-NA-QAR-RA-AD		CT XLV 48 5
		ŠAMŠ		U				JARAḪ				SA-AM-SU-E-RA-AḪ		B 38
		ŠAMŠ		U		JI		JŠAR				SA-AM-SU-D-I-[Š]AR		M
		ŠAMŠ		U				BAʿL		A		SA-AM-SU-BA-LA		SIMMONS 35 14+
		ŠAMŠ		U				BAʿL		I		SA-AM-SU-BA-AḪ-LI		ABB I 59 8
		ŠAMŠ		U				DITAN		A		SA-AM-SU-DI-TA-NA		B 38+
		ŠAMŠ		U				....				SA-AM-SU-MA-[....]		YOS XIII 446:3
		ŠAMŠ		U	NA							SA-AM-SU-NA		HARRIS 58 14+
		ŠAMŠ		U	NA			BAʿL		A		SA-AM-SU-NA-BA-LA		A. 77+
	1	ŠAMUM		U	HU							SA-MU-MU-U$_2$		M
	1	ŠAPIR		U								SA-BI-RU		YOS XIII 166:14
	1	ŠARAM	AN	U								SA-RA-MA-NU		SZLECHTER TJ P. 25
	2 JA	KNUW						ŠARR		U		IA-AK-NU-ŠA-RU		TIM III 133 9
	1 JI	ŠBIM		U								IŠ-BI-MU		CT IV 30D 10
	1	ŠIJB	T	U								ŠI-IB-TU	FN	M+
		ŠIJB	ATANU									SI-BA-TA-NU		SIMMONS 88 1
		ŠIJB		U	NA			ḪARAM				ŠI-BU-NA-A-RA-AM		M
	1	ŠIJM		U				DAWR		A		SI-MU-DA-RA		TA 30, 186+
	1	ŠIMḪ		U				ʾIL		UM		ŠI-IM-ḪU-LUM?		A. 265 8
	1	ŠIPQ		U	NA			HADD		A		SI-IP-KU-NA-D-IM		M
		ŠIPQ		U	NA			HADD		A		SI-IP-KU-NA-DA		M
	1	ŠIPR	AT	U								ŠE-IP-RA-TU	MN	LAESSOE P. 99+
	1 JA	ŠMAʿ		U								IA-AŠ$_2$-MA-ḪU		B 30 HANA
	1	ŠULAḪ	AN	U								SU-LA-ḪA-NU		A 7702 13
	1	ŠULUḪ		U								SU-LU-ḪU		UET V 427 16
	1	ŠUM		U	JA							SU-MU-IA		B 39+
		ŠUM		U	JA							SU-MU-U$_2$-A		PBS XI/2 1 32
		ŠUM		U				ʾAḪ		I	JA	[SU]-MU-A-ḪI-IA		PBS XI/2 1 I 27
		ŠUM		U		ʾA		MNID		IM		[SU-M]U-AM-NI-DI-IM		B 38
		ŠUM		U		ʾA		ŠKUR		A		ŠU-MU-AŠ$_2$-KU-RA		TA 30, 299
		ŠUM		U		JI	T	ŠAMAR				SU-MU-UŠ-TA-MAR		TIM II 14 21
		ŠUM		U				ḪAʾL		A		SU-MU-ḪA-LA		B 39
		ŠUM		U				ʾAWN	AN	UM		SU-MU-AM-NA-NU-UM		B 38+
		ŠUM		U				ʾAWN	AN	IM		SU-MU-AW-NA-NIM		SUMER XXIII ARABIC 178
		ŠUM		U				ʾAB		UM		SU-MU-A-BU-UM		B 38+
		ŠUM		U				ʾAB		UM		D-SU-MU-A-BU-UM		KISURRA 93 22
		ŠUM		U				ʾAB		IM		[S]U-MU-A-BI-IM	NOM	EDZARD, DER 111:5
		ŠUM		U				ʾAB		IM		SU-MU-A-BI-IM	GEN	SUMER XXIII PL. 12 19
		ŠUM		U				ʾAB		I		SU-MA-A-BI		A.
		ŠUM		U				ʾAB		I	JA	[SU]-MU-A-BI-IA		B 38
		ŠUM		U				ʾAB		I				
						JA		RWIM				SU-MU-A-BI-A-RI-IM		TA 30 9, 14, 15+
		ŠUM		U				ʾABIḪ				SU-MU-A-BI-IḪ		TIM V 1 16
		ŠUM		U				ʿAD		I		SU-MU-ḪA-DI-I	GEN	XIII 13:8
		ŠUM		U				ʿAD		IM		SU-MU-ḪA-DI-IM		X 57 8
		ŠUM		U				ʿAD		U	HU	SU-MU-ḪA-DU-U$_2$		M+
		ŠUM		U				JADAʿ		UM		SU-MU-A-DA-ḪU-UM		KISURRA 78A 15
		ŠUM		U				ʿADN		U		SU-MU-ḪA-AD-NU		B 39
		ŠUM		U				ʿADN		U		SU-MU-ḪI-AD-NU		KISURRA 29 12

U	1	ŠUM	U		ʿAḎAR			SU-MU-A-DAR		GORDON 38 DATE+
		ŠUM	U		ʿAḎAR			SU-MU-A-TAR		GORDON 38 DATE+
		ŠUM	U		ʿAḎAR			SU-MA-DAR		SIMMONS 50 26 DATE+
		ŠUM	U		ʾEL			SU-MU-EL		TA 30, 34 6
		ŠUM	U		ʾIL			SU-MU-DINGIR		B 39+
		ŠUM	U		ʾIL			D-SU-MU-DINGIR		KISURRA 85 15, 22+
		ŠUM	U		ʾIL	A		SU-MU-I-LA		B 39; M+
		ŠUM	U		ʾIL					
					BAWB	I	JA	[SU-MU-I]L-BA-BI-IA		PBS XI/2 1 I 11
		ŠUM	U		ʾIL					
					....			SU-MU-DINGIR-LI-BUR-RA-AM		FRANK 27 4
		ŠUM	U		ʾIL					
					ŠARR			SU-MU-[DINGIR]-LUGAL		UCP X/1 17 15
		ŠUM	U		ḪALAB			SU-MU-A-LA-AB		A.
		ŠUM	U		ḪAM	I		SU-MU-A-MI		M
		ŠUM	U		ḪAM	IM		SU-MU-D-A-MI-IM		RA LXV 40 I 25+
		ŠUM	U		ʿAMM	U		SU-MU-ḪA-AM-MU		B 39+
		ŠUM	U		ʿAMM	U		SU-MU-ḪA-MU		M
		ŠUM	U		ʿAMM	U		SU-MU-ḪA-MU	FN	C+
		ŠUM	U		JAMAM			SU-MU-IA-MA-AM		M+
		ŠUM	U		....			[SU-M]U-A-NI-....		PBS XI/2 1 I 12
		ŠUM	U		ʾENTIL			SU-MU-EN-TE-IL		B 39
		ŠUM	U		ʾENTIL			SU-MU-EN-TI-[IL]?		KISURRA 95 15
		ŠUM	U		ʾUP	I		SU-MU-UḪ$_2$-KI		JCS XI 23 NO. 10 14+
		ŠUM	U		JAPAR			[SU-MU]-A-PA-AR		B 38
		ŠUM	U		JARAḪ			SU-MU-A-RA-AḪ		B 38+
		ŠUM	U		JARAḪ			SU-MU-E-RA-AḪ		M+
		ŠUM	U		ʿAŠTAR			SU-MU-EŠ$_4$-DAR		PBS VIII/2 207 5, M
		ŠUM	U		JAT	UM		SU-MU-IA-TUM		TLB IV 40 9, 12, 14
		ŠUM	U	JA	ʾRUR	A		[SU-MU-I]A-AḪ-RU-RA		B 39
		ŠUM	U	JA	MWUT					
					BAʿL	A		SU-MU-IA-MU-UT-BA-[LA]		RUTTEN 3 21
		ŠUM	U	JE	MWUT					
					BAʿL	A		SU-MU-E-MU-UT-BA-LA	NOM	JCS IV 66 22
		ŠUM	U	JE	MWUT					
					BAʿL	A		SU-MU-E-MU-UT-BA-LA	GEN	JCS IV 69 17
		ŠUM	U	JE	MWUT					
					BAʿL	IM		SU-MU-E-MU-UT-BA-LIM?	GEN	JCS IV 71 9
		ŠUM	U	JA	MWUT					
					BAʿL	IM		SU-MU-IA-MU-UT-BA-LIM	GEN	CT XLIII 86 1
		ŠUM	U	JA	MWUT	U				
					BAʿL	A		[SU]-MU-IA-MU-TU-BA-LA		PBS XI/2 1 I 19
		ŠUM	U	JA	JPAʿ			[SU-MU]-A-PA-AḪ		B 38
		ŠUM	U	JE	JPUʿ			SU-MU-E-PU-UḪ		M+
		ŠUM	U	JA	ŠJIM			SU-MU-IA-SI-IM		M+
		ŠUM	U	JA	ŠJIT			SU-MU-IA-SI-IT		B 39
		ŠUM	U	JA	ŠABAŠ	UM		SU-MU-IA-SA-BA-SU-UM		PBS XI/2 1 I 34
		ŠUM	U		BAʿL	A		SU-MU-BA-LA		UNPUBL.
		ŠUM	U		BALIṬ			SU-MU-BA-LI$_2$-IṬ?		RUTTEN 26 12+
		ŠUM	U		BELBIN			SU-MU-BE-EL-BI-IN		JCS IV 108, YBC 5198
		ŠUM	U		BINAŠ	U		SU-MU-BI-NA-ŠU		A 7630 2
		ŠUM	U		DAGAN			SU-MU-D-DA-GAN		B 39+
		ŠUM	U		....			SU-MU-DI-NA-....		B 39
		ŠUM	U		DIJN	I		[SU-M]U-DI-NI		PBS XI/2 P. 119
		ŠUM	U		DITAN	A		SU-MU-DI-TA-NA		B 39+, M
		ŠUM	U		DITAN			SU-MU-DI-TA-AN		SIMMONS 126 17+
		ŠUM	U		DITAN			[SU]?-MU?-DI?-TA-A-AN		VAS XVI 24 3
		ŠUM	U		DITN	UM		SU-MU-DI-IT-NU-UM		B 39
		ŠUM	U		KANAŠ	A		SU-MU-GA-NA-SA		KISURRA 19 9
		ŠUM	U		LA		NI	SU-MU-LA-NI		HARRIS 39 11
		ŠUM	U		LA		NIA	SU-MU-LA-NI-A		CT XLVIII 10 1
		ŠUM	U		LA					
					ʾIL			SU-MU-LA-DINGIR		B 39+
		ŠUM	U		LA					
					ʾIL	I		SU-MU-LA-I$_3$-LI$_2$		UCP X/1 34 2
		ŠUM	U		LI					
					ʾEL			SU-MU-LI-EL		B 39+

SUFFIXES, Class 2

U	1	ŠUM	U			LA					
						ʾEL			SU-MU-LA-EL		SUMER XXIII 160 5
		ŠUM	U			LI					
						ʾEL			SU-MU-LI-EL-DU-RI		A 7630 3
		ŠUM	U			LI					
					JI	JṢIʾ			SU-MU-LI-ZI		MEISSNER 37 15+
		ŠUM	U			LAʾL	UM		SU-MU-LA-LUM		PBS XI/2 1 I 16
		ŠUM	U			LIʾL	U		SU-MU-LI-LU		B 39
		ŠUM	U			LABW	A		SU-MU-LA-BA		M
		ŠUM	U			ME					
						ʾEL			SU-MU-ME-EL		JCS IV 107, YBC 4968
		ŠUM	U			MUT	I				
						JABAL	A		SU-MU-MU-TI-A-BA-LA		B 39
		ŠUM	U	NA		ʾAB	I		SU-MU-UN-NA-A-BI	FN	A. 64 7
		ŠUM	U	NA		ʾAB	I		SU-MU-UN-NA-BI	FN	A. 33 3, 34 2+
		ŠUM	U	NA		ʾAB	I		SU-MU-NA-BI	FN	A. 59 8
		ŠUM	U	NA		ʾAB	I		SU-MU-NA-A-BI	FN	A. 244 5, M
		ŠUM	U	NA		ʾAB	I				
					JA	RWIM			SU-MU-NA-BI-IA-RI-IM		SUMER XXIII PL. 7 17+
		ŠUM	U	NA		ʾAB	I				
					JA	RWIM			SU-MU-UN?-A-BI-JA-RI-IM		SUMER XXIII P. 153 9
		ŠUM	U	NA		HALAL			SU-MU-NA-ḪA-LA?-AL		UET V 245 11
		ŠUM	U	NA	JA	JPUʿ	A		SU-MU-NA-IA-PU-ḪA-[....]		M
		ŠUM	U	NA	JA	RWIM			SU-UM-MU-NA-A-RI-IM		HARRIS 57 11
		ŠUM	U	NI					SU-MU-NI		B 39
		ŠUM	U			NIWḪ	A		SU-MU-NI-A		GORDON 39 9, 13
		ŠUM	U			NIWḪ	UM		SU-MU-NI-ḪU-UM		B 39
		ŠUM	U			NIWḪ	IM		SU-MU-NI-ḪI-IM	GEN	SIMMONS 121 18, M+
		ŠUM	U			NIWR	I		SU-MU-NI-RI	FN	XIII 1 XI 46
		ŠUM	U			NIʾŠ	U	JA	SU-MU-NI-ŠU-A		CT VIII 38D:14
		ŠUM	U			NUMAḪ	A		SU-MU-NU-MA-ḪA		M
		ŠUM	U			NUMḪ	A		SU-M[U-N]U-UM-ḪA		RA LXIV 43
		ŠUM	U			NUMḪ	IM		SU-MU-NU-UM-ḪI-IM		RIFTIN 44 12,16+
		ŠUM	U			RAWḪ			SU-MU-RA-A		B 40
		ŠUM	U			RAWḪ			SU-MU-RA-AḪ		B 38+
		ŠUM	U			RAWḪ			SU-MU-RA-A-AḪ		CT II 39 1, 15
		ŠUM	U			RAWḪ	EM		[SU]-MU-RA-ḪI-E-IM		B 40
		ŠUM	U			RAWM	E	JE	SU-MU-RA-ME-E		B 40+
		ŠUM	U			RAWM	EM		SU-MU-RA-ME-IM		M
		ŠUM	U			RAPIʾ			SU-MU-RA-BI		M
		ŠUM	U			RAṢIJ	EM		[SU]-MU-RA-ZI-E-IM		B 40
		ŠUM	U			....			SU-MU-SI-MU-....		A 7457 3
		ŠUM	U			ŠAMŠ			SU-MU-D-UTU		CT XLVIII 83 SEAL
		ŠUM	U		TA	QWIM			SU-MU-TA-KI-IM		XIII 131 4'
		ŠUM	U		TA	QJIŠ			SU-MU-TA-KI-IŠ		M
		ŠUM	U			TAMAR			SU-MU-TA-MAR		B 40+
		ŠUM	U			TAMAR	U		SU-MU-TA-MA-RU		RA LXIV 43
		ŠUM	U			ṬAJB	I		SU-MU-DA-BI		X 90 10+
		ŠUM	U			ṢIDQ	UM		[SU]-MU-ZI-ID-KUM		B 40
		ŠUM	U			ṢIDQ	UM				
						DITAN	A		[SU]-MU-ZI-ID-KUM-DI-TA-NA		B 40
	2	ʾAḪ	I			ŠUM	U	NA	A-ḪI-SU-MU-NA		SIMMONS 83 5
		ʾAJA				ŠUM	U		ḪA-IA$_3$-SU-MU		DELAPORTE CCL II A 337+
		ʾAJA				ŠUM	U	HU	ḪA-IA-SU-MU-U$_2$		XI P.83 N.1+
		ʾAJA				ŠUM	U	HU	ḪA-IA$_3$-SU-MU-U$_2$		M+
		ʾAJA				ŠUM	U	HU	ḪA-IA$_3$-SU-U$_2$-MU		M+
		ʾAJA				ŠUM	U	HU	ḪA-IA$_3$-SU-U$_2$-MU-U$_2$		X 113 4, 11, 14
		ʾAJA				ŠUM	U				
						ʾAB	IM		ḪA-IA-SU-MU-A-BI-IM		M
		ʾIL	I			ŠUM	U		I$_3$-LI$_2$-SU-U$_2$-MU		M
		ʿAMM	I			ŠUM	U		AM-MI-SU-MU		CT XLVIII 61 4,5
		ʿAMM	I			ŠUM	U	HU	ḪA-AM-MI-SU-MU-U$_2$		CT XLVII 30 44
	JA	JPAʿ				ŠUM	U				
						ʾAB	I		IA-PA-AḪ-SU-MU-A-BI		A. 56 47
		JATAR				ŠUM	U		IA-TAR-SU-MU		XII 456 10
		JATAR				ŠUM	U	HU	IA-TAR-SU-MU-U$_2$		M+

U	2	JI		JṢIʾ				ŠUM	U	JA	I-ZI-SU-MU-A		KISURRA 112 7
		JI		JṢIʾ				ŠUM	U	HU	I-ZI-SU-MU-U_2		A 7646 3+
		JI		JṢIʾ				ŠUM	U				
								ʾAB	UM		I-ZI-SU-MU-A-BU-UM		B 23+
		JI		JṢIʾ				ŠUM	U				
								ʾAB	IM		I-ZI-SU-MU-A-BI-IM	GEN	B 23
		JA		WṢIʾ				ŠUM	U				
								ʾAB	UM		U_2-ṢI-SU-MU-A-BU-UM		AJSL XXVIII 244 19
		JA		KWUN				ŠUM	U				
								ʾAB	IM		IA-KU-UN-SU-MU-A-BI-IM		M
				MAʾL	I			ŠUM	U	HU	MA-LI-SU-MU-U_2		TIM I 29 10
				MALIK				ŠUM	U	HU	MA-LIK-SU-MU-U_2		M
				QARAʾ				ŠUM	U	JA	QA-RA-SU?-MU-IA		CT VI 43 6
				QARAʾ				ŠUM	U	JA	GA-RA-SU-MU-IA		CT XLV 11 2, 46+
				QARAʾ				ŠUM	U	JA	KA-RA?-SU-MU-IA		CT II 30 3
				QARAʾ				ŠUM	U	JA	KA-RA-SU-LUM		CT II 30 34
		JA		RWIM				ŠUM	U				
								ʾAB	I		IA-RI-IM-SU-MU-A-BI		RA LXV 42 III 8
		JA		ŠJIM				ŠUM	U	HU	IA-SI-IM-SU-MU-U_2		M+
		JI		TWUR				ŠUM	U				
								ʾEL			I-DUR-SU-ME-EL		KISURRA 43 5+
				ṬAJB				ŠUM	U	HU	ṬA_3-AB-SU-MU-U_2		M+
	3			ʾAJA				LA					
								ŠUM	U	HU	A-IA-LA-SU-MU-U_2		M, C
	1			ŠUMḪ	U			BAʿL			SU-UM-ḪU-BA-AL		YOS XII 390 2,9
				ŠUMḪ	U			RAPIʾ			SU-UM-ḪU-RA-BI		M+
	1			ŠUMUM	U						SU-MU-MU		RA LXIV 22 NO. 2+
	1	JI	T	ŠAWAB	U						IŠ-TA-BU		B 24 HANA
		JI	T	ŠAWAB	U						IŠ-TA-A-BU		MAOG IV 3 36 HANA
	1			ŠADW	U			ʾIL	A		ŠA-DU-[I]-LA		RA LXV 45 V 50
				ŠADW	U			LABW	A		ŠA-DU-LA-BA		M
				ŠADW	U			ŠARR	I		ŠA-DU-ŠAR-RI		XIV 109:6
				ŠADW	U			ŠARR	I		ŠA-DU-ŠA-AR-RI		M
				ŠADW	U			ŠARR	I		ŠA-DU-LUGAL		M
	2			ʿAMM	I	JI	T	ŠAMAR	U		AM-MI-IŠ-TAM-RU		MRS VI P. 329 UGARIT+
				ʿAMM	I	JI	T	ŠAMAR	U		AM-MI-IS-TAM-RU		MRS VI P. 239 UGARIT+
	1			ŠARŠAR	AN U						ŠA-ŠA-RA-NU		M
	1			ŠIʾN	U			RAPIʾ			ŠI-NU-RA-BI		A.+
				ŠIʾN	U			RAPIʾ			SI-NU-RA-BI		A.+
	1			ŠIQL	AN U						ŠI-IQ-LA-NU		B 47
	2			ʾALLA				ŠUʾḪ	U		AL-LA-ŠU-ḪU		U
	1			ŠUʾG	U			JAT	UM		ŠU-GU-IA-TUM		B 40
	1			ŠUʿAL	AN U						ŠU-ḪA-LA-NU		M
	1			ŠUWB	U			RAPUʾ			ŠU-BU-RA-BU		TCL X 4A 25, B 15
	1			ṢIBʾ	U						ZI-BU		B 42
	1			ṢIDQ	U			LA					
								NAŠIʾ			ZI-ID-KU-LA-NA-SI		M+
	2			KAʾM	A			ṢILL	U		KA-MA-ZI-LU?	FN	VAS XIII 9 R. 2
				ṬAJB				ṢILL	U	HU	ṬA_3-AB-ṢI-LU-U_2		TCL X 38 7
	1			ṢUWR	ATANU						ZU-RA-TA-NU		M
	1			ṢURAR	U						ṢU-RA-RU		KISURRA 104 36
	1			TAʾIL	U						TA-ḪI-LU?	FN	RA LXV 65 VII 33
	1			TAʾK	U			ʾIL			TA-KU-DINGIR		VAS VIII 14 27
				TAʾK	U			ʾIŠḪAR	AH		TA-KU-D-IŠ-ḪA-R[A]		JCS XIII 52 293 R, A. LATE
	2			ʾABIL				TAʾK	U	HU	A-BI-IL-TA-KU-U_2		WALTERS, WL 97:4;105:3+
	1			TAḪT	U			PI					
								ʾIL			TA-AḪ-TU-BI-DINGIR		M+
	1			TAWIR	U						TA-E-RU		KISURRA 81A 4+
	1			TABUB	U						TA-BU-BU	FN	XIII 1 VIII 35
				TABUB	U			ʿALIJ	AH		D-TA-BU-BU-ḪA-LI-IA	FN	XIII 1 VI 13
				TABUB	U			ʾUMM	I		TA-BU-BU-UM-MI	FN	XIII 1 VI 57
				TABUB	U			ḪAṢN	I		TA-BU-BU-ḪA-AṢ-NI	FN	RA LXV 60 III 19
				TABUB	U			ŠIMḪ	I		TA-BU-BU-ŠI-IM-ḪI	FN	XII 265 4
	2	JI		NDIN				TABUB	U		I-DIN-TA-BU-BU		M
	1			TALM	U			ʾAŠIḪ	I		TA-AL-MU-A-ŠI-ḪI	FN	XIII 1 III 63
	1			TAMAR	U						TA-MA-RU		RA LXV 50 VIII 71

U	2	ŠUM		U			TAMAR	U		SU-MU-TA-MA-RU		RA LXIV 43
	2 JI	JṢIʾ					TAMB	U		I-ZI-TA-AM-BU		BAHREIN UNPUB, POST-U.
	2	LA					TEʾḪ	U		LA-TE-ḪU		MRS VI P. 196 22,LATE
	2	LA					TEBUʾ	U		LA-TE-BU-U$_2$		B 33
	1	TIRR		U						TE-IR-RU		M+
		TIRR		U						TI-IR-RU		M
	1 ME	TMIH		U						ME-IT-MI-JU		M+
	1	TUʾAL		U						TU-A-LU		RA LXV 48 VIII 17
	1	TUʾN	AN	U						TU-NA-NU		BM 81617 5
	1	TUḪT		U			....			TU-UḪ-TU-[....]		M
	1	TUWR		U			ʿAMM	I		DUR-RU-AM-MI		MAOG IV 2 6 HANA
	1	TUPT		U			ʿAŠTAR			TUP-TU-EŠ$_4$-DAR		M
	1	TURUN		U	HU		GAMIL			D-TU-UR-RU-NU-U$_2$-GA-MIL	FN?	XIII 118 14
	2	ʾIL		UM			TUŠUʿ	U		D-I-LU-UN-TU-SU-U$_2$	DN	KISURRA
	1	TUŠER		U						TU-ŠE?-RU?		M
	2	ʾAL		I	Š		TUT	U		A-LI-IŠ-TU-TU		VAS XVI 23 13
	2 JI	ʾLAP					ṬALL	U	HU	I-LA-AP-TA-LU-U$_2$		M
		ʿAMM		I			ṬALL	U	HU	ḪA-MI-TI-LU-U$_2$		M
		ʿAMM		I			ṬALL	U	HU	ḪA-AM-MI-TA-LU-U$_2$		M+
		ʿAMM		I			ṬALL	U	HU	ḪA-AM-MI-TI-LU-U$_2$		M+
		ṢIḪAR					ṬALL	U	K	ṢI-ḪAR-TI-LU-UK	FN	PBS VIII/2 252 9, 18
	2	ʿAMM		I			ṬILL	U	HU	ḪA-AM-MI-TE-LU-U$_2$		RA LXVI 118:15
	2	MAʾR		U			ZAʾT	U	HU	MA-RU-ZA-TU-U$_2$		CT XLVIII 27
	1	ZAKK		U						ZA-AK-KU		M
		ZAKK		U	HU					ZA-AK-KU-U$_2$		M+
		ZAKK		U	HU					ZA-KU-U$_2$		M
	2	ʿAMM		I			ZAKK	U	HU	ḪA-AM-MI-ZA-KU-U$_2$		M
	1	ZIʾM		U			DAWR	A		ZI-MU-DA-RA		RA VIII 75 R. 2
	1	ZIʾN	ATAN	U						ZI-NA-TA-NU		BM 16984 24
	1	ZIʾZ		U						ZI-ZU	FN	RA LXV 65 VII 43
	1	ZIDAR		U	HU					ZI-DA-RU-U$_2$		VAS XIII 93A R. 8+
	2	ʿAMM		I			ZUʾG	U	HU	ḪA-AM-MI-ZU-GU-U$_2$		BM 17045+
	1	ZUʾUZ		U						ZU-U$_2$-ZU		M
	1	ZUʾZ	AN	U						ZU-ZA-NU		B 48
	1	ZUNAN		U						ZU-NA-NU		B 48
UJA	1	ʾAḪ	AT	UJA						A-ḪA-TU-IA	FN	SIMMONS 66 4+
	1	BUWZ		UJA						BU-ZU-A-IA	FN	RA LXV 62 V 27
UJAN	1	ḪAʾL		UJAN						ḪA-LU-JA-AN		RA LXV 41 II 33+
	1	ʿAMM		UJAN						AM-MU-JA-AN		A.+
	1	DAWD		UJAN						DA-DU-JA-AN		RA LXV 51 IX 75
	1	MUT		UJAN						MU-TU-JA-AN		C+
	1	MUTT		UJAN						MU-UT-TU-IA-AN		RA LXV 50 IX 18
UM	1 ME	ʾḪAḎ		UM						ME-ḪA-DUM		UCP X/3 3:18; YONDORF 4
	MI	ʾḪAḎ		UM						MI-ḪA-[TUM]?	TRIBE	IX 244:5
	1 ME	ʾḪIḎ		UM						ME-ḪI-DU-UM		RA LXV 54 XII 64
	1 JA	ʾWIR		UM						IA-WI-RU-UM		B 31
	MI	ʾWIR		UM						MI-I-RUM		RA LXV 46 V 83
	2	LA				ʾA	ʾWIR	UM		LA-WI-RUM		RA XXIV 58 9 4
	1 ME	ʾWIŠ		UM						ME-I-SU-UM		CT VI 7 21+
	1	ʾAHL		UM			MAʾT	U		[A-LU]-UM-MA-[TU]	FN	M
		ʾAHL		UM			MAʾT	UM		[A-LU-UM]-MA-TUM	FN	M
		ʾAHL		UM			PU		HU	A-LUM-BI-U$_2$		SIMMONS 129 13
		ʾAHL		UM			PU		HU	ḪA-LAM-BU-U$_2$		RLA II 165 17
		ʾAHL		UM			PU		HU	[A]-LI-IM-BU-MU		OLZ 1958 547 N.1
		ʾAHL		UM			PU		HU	A-LUM-BU-MU		OLZ 1958 547 N.1
	2	JAʾN		A			ʾAHL	UM		JA-NA-A-LUM	GN	MRS VI P.125 61
		KAʾB		I			ʾAHL	UM		KA-PI-IA-LUM		UET V 626 11, 702 REV. 5
	1	ʾAḪ		UM						A-ḪU-UM		M+
		ʾAḪ		UM			LI		JA	A-ḪU-UM-LI-A		M
		ʾAḪ		UM			LA					
							ʾAB	I		A-ḪU-UM-LA-A-BI		YOS XIII 245:17, SEAL
		ʾAḪ		UM			LUʾM	U		A-ḪU-UM-LU-MU		X 166 4+
		ʾAḪ		UM			MA					
							ʾIL			A-ḪU-UM-MA-DINGIR		M+
		ʾAḪ		UM			MAṬAR	I		A-ḪU-UM-MA-DA-RI		M
		ʾAḪ	AT	UM						A-ḪA-TUM	FN	M+

SUFFIXES, Class 2

UM	2		ʾAJA				ʾAḪ		UM	A-IA-A-ḪU-UM		RA LXV 41 II 24	
		JA	WMAʾ				ʾAḪ		UM	JA-MA-A-ḪU-UM		RA LXV 52 X 49	
			ḪANN		A		ʾAḪ		UM	AN-NA-A-ḪU-UM		RA LXV 52 XI 1	
			ʿAQB		A		ʾAḪ		UM	AQ-BA-A-ḪU-UM		M+	
			ʿAQB		A		ʾAḪ		UM	AQ-BA-ḪU-UM		B 11+	
			ʿAQB		A		ʾAḪ		UM	ḪA-AQ-BA-A-ḪU-UM		RA LXV 43 III 57+	
			ʿIQB		A		ʾAḪ		UM	IQ-BA-A-ḪU-UM		KISURRA 4A 11, M	
			ʿIQB		A		ʾAḪ		UM	IQ-BA-ḪU-UM		KISURRA 121 6	
			JATAR				ʾAḪ		UM	JA-TA-AR-ḪU-UM		I	
		JI	JṢIʾ				ʾAḪ		UM	I-ZI-A-ḪU-UM		M+	
			BIN		A		ʾAḪ		UM	BI-NA-A-ḪU-UM		M+	
			ḎAKUR		A		ʾAḪ		UM	ZA-KU-RA-A-ḪU-UM		M+	
			NAKR				ʾAḪ		UM	NA-AK-RA-ḪU-UM		RUTTEN 2 19+	
		ʾA	RŠIJ				ʾAḪ		UM	AR-ŠI-A-ḪU-UM		M+	
			ŠIPṬ		A		ʾAḪ		UM	ŠI-IP-TA-A-ḪU-UM		RA LXV 46 VI 27	
	3		BIN		I		MA						
							ʾAḪ		UM	BI-IN-NI-MA-ḪU-UM		TLB I 3 28	
			BIN		I		MA						
							ʾAḪ		UM	BI-NI-MA-ḪU-UM		CCT IV 13A 6+	CAPP.
			BUN		I		MA						
							ʾAḪ		UM	BU-NI-MA-ḪU-UM		TCL XX 96 8	
			BUN		U		MA						
							ʾAḪ		UM	BU-NU-MA-A-ḪU-UM		B 16	
			QAWM		U		MA						
							ʾAḪ		UM	QA-MU-MA-A-ḪU-UM		M	
	1		ʾAḪAL		UM					A-ḪA-LUM		BIROT, TEA 45:12	
	1		ʾAḪIL	AT	UM					A-ḪI-LA-TUM	FN	XIII 1 I 67	
	1		ʾAḪN	AN	UM					AḪ-NA-NU-UM		KISURRA 14 4+	
	1		ʾAWAʾ	AT	UM					A-WA-TUM	FN	M	
	1		ʾAWIJ		UM					A-WI-U$_2$-UM		GORDON 38 21+	
			ʾAWIJ	AT	UM					ḪA-WI-IA-TUM		BIROT TEA 39:4	
			ʾAWIJ	AT	UM					A-WI-IA-TUM	MN?	TIM I 11 10+	
			ʾAWIJ	T	UM					ḪA-WI-TUM		BIROT TEA 72 I 28+	
			ʾAWIN		UM					A-WI-NU-UM		FLP 516, UR III	
	1		ʾAWN	AN	UM					AM-NA-NU-UM	GN	SAKI P. 222+	
			ʾAWN	AN	UM					AM-NA-NU-UM	PN	SUMER XIV 49	
			ʾAWN	AN	UM					AW-NA-NU-[UM]	TRIBE	M	
	2		MUT		U		ʾAWN	AN	UM	MU-TU-AM-NA-NU-UM		BM 81641 3, 8	
			ŠUM		U		ʾAWN	AN	UM	SU-MU-AM-NA-NU-UM		B 38+	
	1		ʾAJAK		UM					A-IA-KU-UM		RA LXV 52 X 51	
			ʾAJAL		UM					A-IA-LU-UM		CT XLV 5 9	
			ʾAJAL		UM					A-IA-LUM		M	
			ʾAJAL		UM					A-A-LUM		KISURRA 116	
			ʾAJAL	AT	UM					A-IA-LA-TUM	FN	VAS VII 3 25	
			ʾAJAL	AT	UM					D-A-A-LA-TUM	FN	CT VIII 29C 22+	
	1		ʾAJIŠ		UM					ḪA-II-ŠUM		KISURRA 101 6+	
	1		ʾAB	AN	UM					A-BA-NU-UM		U+, SIMMONS 51 18	
			ʾAB		UM		ḪAʾL		UM	A-BU-UM-ḪA-LUM		B 11+	
			ʾAB		UM		ḪAʾL		UM	A-BU-UM-ḪA-LU-UM		B 11+	
			ʾAB		UM		ḪIʾL		UM	A-BU-UM-ḪI-LUM		B 11	
			ʾAB		UM		ʾIL			A-BU-UM-DINGIR		U, M+	
			ʾAB		UM		JAQAR			A-BU-UM-WA-QAR		M	
			ʾAB		UM	JE	KWIN			A-BU-UM-E-KI-IN		M	
	2		ʾAJA				ʾAB		UM	ḪA-A-IA-A-BU-UM		M	
			ʾAJA				ʾAB		UM	ḪA-IA-BU-UM		B 18+	
		JA	JDIʿ				ʾAB		UM	IA-DI-ḪA-BU-UM		B 25+	
		JA	JDIʿ				ʾAB		UM	IA-DI-A-BU-UM		M, YOS XII+	
		JA	JDIʿ				ʾAB		UM	IA-DU-A-BU-UM		YOS XII+	
		JA	JDIʿ				ʾAB		UM	IA-DI-ḪA-A-BU-U[M]		RA LXV 45 V 9	
			ʾIL		UM		ʾAB		UM	I-LUM-A-BU-UM		U	
			ʾAMIR		A		ʾAB		UM	A-MI-RA-A-BU-UM		RA LXV 55 XIII 5	
		JA	JQIR		A		ʾAB		UM	IA-KI-RA-A-BU-UM		RA LXV 47 VII 30	
		JA	BRUQ				ʾAB		UM	A-AB-RU-UK-A-BU-UM		JCS XXVI 151:13, HARMAL	
			ḎAKUR		A		ʾAB		UM	ZA-KU-RA-A-BU-UM		X 79 5	
			ḎIMR		I		ʾAB		UM	ZI-IM-RI-A-BU-UM		B 42	
		JA	RWIḪ		A		ʾAB		UM	IA-RI-ḪA-A-BU-UM		VII P. 234 N. 4	

UM	2	ŠUM		I		ʾAB	UM	SU-ME-A-BU-UM		A. 12 4
		ŠUM		U		ʾAB	UM	SU-MU-A-BU-UM		B 38+
		ŠUM		U		ʾAB	UM	D-SU-MU-A-BU-UM		KISURRA 93 22
	3	ʾIL		A		KA				
						ʾAB	UM	DINGIR-KA-A-BU-UM		CT XLV 100 17
		ʾAŠD		UM		LA				
						ʾAB	UM	AŠ-DU-UM-LA-A-BU-UM		SUMER V 142
		ʾAŠD		UM		LA				
						ʾAB	UM	$AŠ_2$-DU-UM-LA-A-BU-UM		SUMER V 142+
	JI	JṢIʾ				ŠAM	U			
						ʾAB	UM	I-ZI-SA-MU-A-BU-UM		B 23
	JI	JṢIʾ				ŠUM	U			
						ʾAB	UM	I-ZI-SU-MU-A-BU-UM		B 23+
	JA	WṢIʾ				ŠUM	U			
						ʾAB	UM	U_2-ṢI-SU-MU-A-BU-UM		AJSL XXVIII 244 18
	1	ʾABAB	AN	UM				A-BA-BA-NU-UM		B 71+
		ʾABAN		UM				ḪA-BA-NU-UM		TA 30, 191+
		ʾABAQ		UM				A-BA-GU-UM		KISURRA 82 9
		ʾABAŠ	IN	UM				A-BA-ŠE-NU-UM		M
	1	ʾABIŠ	AN	UM				A-BI-SA-NU-UM		CT XLVIII 29 REV.
	1	ʾABN		UM				ḪA-AB-NU-UM		GAUTIER 10 R. 10+
	2	ḪANN		A		ʾABN	UM	AN-NA-AB-NU-UM		KISURRA 8A 14
		ḪANN		A		ʾABN	UM	A-NA-AB-NU-UM		HARRIS 57 18
	1	ʾADAN	AT	UM				ḪA-DA-AN-N[A]?-TUM?	FN	RA LXV 62 V 7
	1	ʾADID		UM				A-DI-DU-UM		B 11+
		ʾADID		UM				A-DI-DUM		SIMMONS 69A 5
	1	ʾADM	AN	UM				AD-MA-NU-UM		JCS XXIV 69 NO.3
		ʾADM	AN	UM				ḪA-AD-MA?-NU-UM		VIII 85:29
	1	ʾADUN		UM				A-DU-NU-UM	FIELD	CT II 23 2
		ʾADUN	AT	UM				A-DU-NA-TUM	MN	TA 30 275
	2	ʾEN		I	Š	ʾAG	UM	E-NI-IŠ-A-GU-UM		M+
		BAʿL		I	Š	ʾAG	UM	BA-LI-IŠ-A-GU-UM		RA LXV 45 V 36
	1	ʾAGIG		UM				A-GI-GU-UM		B 12+
	1	ʾAK		UM				A-KU-UM		U
		ʾAK		UM		LA				
						ʾIL	A	A-KUM-LA-I-LA		RA LXV 55 XIII 1
	1	ʾAKAN	AT	UM				A-KA-NA-TUM		JCS XXIV 62 NO.55+
	1	ʾAKIN		UM				A-KI-NU-UM		TA 1931, 538 I
		ʾAKIR		UM				A-KI-RU-UM		KISURRA 8 7+
	1	ʾAKK	AT	UM				A-KA-TUM		KISURRA 104 36
		ʾAKK	ATANUM					AG-GA-TA-NU-UM		SIMMONS 96 6
		ʾAKK	ATANUM					AG-GA-TA-A-NU-UM		SIMMONS 103 6
		ʾAKK	ATANUM					A-KA-TA-A-NU-UM		SIMMONS 105 7, SEAL
		ʾAKK	ATANUM					AK-KA-TA-A-NU-UM		SIMMONS 106 6, 10 SEAL
		ʾAKK	ATANUM					AK-KA-TA-NU-UM		SIMMONS 112 6, SEAL
	1	ʾAKUN		UM				A-KU-NU-UM		KISURRA 58 8
		ʾAKUN		UM				A-KU-NUM_2		KISURRA 48 4
		ʾAKUN	AT	UM				A-KU-NA-TUM	MN?	M+
	1	ʾALAK		UM				ḪA-LA-KUM		CT XLV 2 22+
	2 JA	WṢIʾ				ʾALAŠ	UM	U_2-ZI-A-LA-ŠUM		M
	1	ʾALIK		UM				A-LI-KUM		B+
		ʾALIK		UM				ḪA-LI-KU-UM		B 12+
		ʾALIK		UM				ḪA-LI-KUM		B 12+
	1	ʾALM	AN	UM				AL-MA-NU-UM		TA 1931,148
		ʾALM	AN	UM				ḪA-AL-MA-NU-UM		HARRIS 62 14+
		ʾALM	AT	UM				ḪA-AL-MA-TUM	MN?	HARRIS 66 13
	1	ʾALUʾ		UM				A-LU-U_2-UM		VAS XVI 131:1
		ʾALUP		UM				A-LU-PU-UM		B+
		ʾALUP	AT	UM				A-LU-PA-TUM	FN	CT XLVII 7 35, 7A 16'
	1	ʾAM	T	UM				AM-TUM	FN	XIII 1 II 48
	1	ʾAMAN		UM				A-MA-NU-UM		CT XLV 2 24,SEAL
		ʾAMAN	AN	UM				A-MA-NA-NU-UM		B 42+
	1	ʾAMIN		UM				A-MI-NU-UM		B 12+
		ʾAMIN		UM				A-MI-NUM		M
		ʾAMIN	AT	UM				A-MI-NA-TUM		B 12
		ʾAMIN	AN	UM				A-MI-NA-NU-UM		B 43

UM	1		ʾAMIR		UM				A-MI-RU-UM		B 13
			ʾAMIR		UM				A-MI-RUM		M
			ʾAMIR	AT	UM				A-MI-RA-TUM	FN	M
	1	T	ʾAMR		UM				A-TAM-RUM		M+
		T	ʾAMR		UM				A-TA-AM-RU-UM		M+
		T	ʾAMR	AT	UM				A-TAM-RA-TUM	FN	M
			ʾAMR	AT	UM				AM-RA-TUM		YOS XIII 513:4
	1		ʾANAZ		UM				AN-NA-ZUM		B 13+
	2 JI		NDIN				ʾANN	UM	I-DIN-AN-NU-UM		M+
			RAWḪ		A		ʾANN	UM	RA-ḪA-AN-NU-UM		M
	1		ʾANT	AN	UM				AN-TA-NU-UM		TA 1930, 698
			ʾANTAR		UM				AN-TA-RU-UM		CT VIII 47 B 21
	1		ʾANZ	AN	UM				AN-ZA-NU-UM		B 43
	1		ʾAP	AN	UM				A-PA-NU-UM		B 43+
	1		ʾAPK	AT	UM				AP-KA-TUM	MN	UCP X/1 4 5
			ʾAPK	AN	UM				AP-KA-NU-UM		SIMMONS 66 28
	1		ʾAPP	AT	UM				AP-PA-TUM	FN	A.+
	2		ḪATAʾ		A		ʾAR	UM	ḪA-TA-A-A-RUM?		CT XXIX 8A 1
	1		ʾARḪ		UM				AR-ḪU-UM	FN	XIII 1 VIII 23
			ʾARḪ	AN	UM				AR-ḪA-NU-UM		BM 92657+
	1		ʾARWIJ		UM				AR-WI-UM		B 13+, M+
			ʾARWIJ		UM				AR-WI-U$_2$-UM		B 13+, M
			ʾARWIJ		UM				AR-BI$_2$-UM		ITT II/1 P 48, 933, U
			ʾARWIJ	T	UM				AR-WI-TUM	FN	KISURRA 134 3, M+
			ʾARWIJ	T	UM				AR-BI-TUM		LEGRAIN, TRU 41+, U
			ʾARWIJ	T	UM				AR-BI$_2$-TUM		TCL V 6039 REV 17, U
			ʾARWIJ	ATANUM					AR-WI-TA-NU-UM		B 43
	1		ʾARAŠ		UM				ḪA-RA-ŠUM		M
	1		ʾARK	ATANUM					AR-GA-TA-NU-UM		KISURRA 141 9
			ʾARK	ATANUM					AR-GA-DA-NU-UM		KISURRA 1A 15+
	1		ʾARNAB		UM				AR-NA-BU-UM	FN	M+
			ʾARNAB	AT	UM				AR-NA-BA-TUM	FN	CT VIII 43C 22+, XIII 1 X 39
	1		ʾARŠ		UM		MALIK		ḪA-AR?-ŠUM?-MA-LIK		M
	1		ʾARUḪ		UM				A-RU-ḪU-UM		B 13
			ʾARUŠ		UM				A-RU-SU-UM		M, JEAN TELL SIFR 72A 3+
	1		ʾAŠJ		UM				A-SU-UM		M
	1		ʾAŠAŠ		UM				A-SA-ŠUM		BIROT, TEA 72 IV 17
	1		ʾAŠD		UM				AŠ-DU-UM		VAS VIII 60 26
			ʾAŠD		UM		ʾAB	I	AŠ$_2$-DU-UM-A-BI		BE VI/1 1 7+
			ʾAŠD		UM		ʾAB	I	D-AŠ-DU-UM-A-BI		UET V 483 4
			ʾAŠD		UM		LA				
							ʾAB	UM	AŠ-DU-UM-LA-A-BU-UM		SUMER V 142
			ʾAŠD		UM		LA				
							ʾAB	UM	AŠ$_2$-DU-UM-LA-A-BU-UM		SUMER V 142+
			ʾAŠD		UM		PI				
							JAD	IM	AŠ-DU-UM-BI-IA-DI-IM		RA LXV 55 XIII 44
	2		JARAḪ				ʾAŠD	UM	D-EN-ZU-AŠ-DU-UM		WALTERS, WL 114:2
	JA		KWUN				ʾAŠD	UM	IA-KU-UN-AŠ-DU-UM		B 27
	JI		NṢUR				ʾAŠD	UM	I-ZUR-AŠ-DU-UM		A 7685 5
	JI		NṢUR				ʾAŠD	UM	I-ZUR-A-AŠ-DU-UM		CT II 42 25
	JI		TWUR				ʾAŠD	UM	I-DUR-A-AŠ-DU-UM		B 23
	JI		TWUR				ʾAŠD	UM	I-DUR-AŠ-DUM		B 23
	JI		TWUR				ʾAŠD	UM	I-DUR-AŠ-DU-UM		B 23+
	JI		TWUR				ʾAŠD	UM	I-DUR-AŠ$_2$-DU-UM		M+
	3		LI			JI	JṢIʾ				
							ʾAŠD	UM	LI-ZI-AŠ-DU-UM		VAS XIII 104 R. II 24
	1		ʾAŠIN		UM				A-SI-NU-UM		B 14+
			ʾAŠIR		UM				A-SI-RUM		B 14+, M+
			ʾAŠIR		UM				A-SI-RU-UM		B 14+
			ʾAŠIR	AT	UM				A-SI-RA-TUM		B 14
	1		ʾAŠM	AN	UM				ḪA-AŠ-MA-NU-UM		U
	1		ʾAŠQUD		UM				AŠ-KU-DU-UM		KISURRA 205 7, M+
			ʾAŠQUD		UM				AŠ$_2$-KU-DU-UM		X 59 8
			ʾAŠQUD		UM				AŠ-KU-TU-UM		KISURRA 88 1, 8+
			ʾAŠQUD	AN	UM				AŠ-KU-DA-NU-UM		CT XLVIII 86 REV 10+
	1		ʾAŠUD		UM				ḪA-SU-DU-UM		A 7660 2

UM	1	ʾAŠAR		UM				A-ŠA-RU-UM		EDZARD, DER 68 IV 3
	2 JA	KWUN			ʾAŠAR		UM	IA-KU-UN-A-ŠA-RU-UM		B 27
	1	ʾAŠIḪ		UM				A-ŠI-ḪU-UM	FN	RA LXV 62 V 33
		ʾAŠIR	AT	UM				D-A-ŠI-RA-TUM	DN FN	RIFTIN 60 SEAL
	1	ʾAŠR	AT	UM	ʾUMM		I	D-AŠ-RA-TUM-UM-MI	FN	TCL I P. 16+
	1	ʾATAL		UM				ḪA-TA-LU-UM		CT XXXIII 42 23+
		ʾATAL		UM				ḪA-AT-TA-LUM		CT XXXIII 43A 6
		ʾATAL	AN	UM				A-TA-LA-NU-UM		EDZARD, DER 100:3
		ʾATAM		UM				ḪA-TA-MU-UM		B 20
		ʾATAM	AN	UM				A-TA-MA-NU-UM		UCP X/3 3 22+
		ʾATAM	AN	UM				AT-TA-MA-NU-UM		SIMMONS 122 16
	1	ʾATIM		UM				A-TI-MU-UM		TA 30 7 8, M
	1	ʾATT		UM				ḪA-AT-TU-UM		M
	1 JA	ʾBUQ		UM				IA-BU-KUM		KISURRA 83 14
	1	ʾEDAK		UM				E-DA-KUM		CT VIII 4A 4
	1	ʾEDID		UM				E-DI-DU-UM		SIMMONS 138 7
	1	ʾEL	AN	UM				E-LA-NU-UM		U
	2	JAḪAD			ʾEL		UM	IA-ḪA-AD-E-LUM		RIFTIN 136 26
		JAḪAD			ʾEL		UM	IA-ḪA-TE-LUM?		UET V 605 13
	JA	JDIʿ			ʾEL		UM	IA-DI-ḪI-E-LUM		UNPUBL.
		ʾADAM		TI	ʾEL		UM	A-DAM-TE-LUM		GAUTIER 31 6
		ʾARUŠ			ʾEL		UM	A-RU-UŠ-E-LUM		UCP X/3 2 25
		BUN		I	ʾEL		UM	BU-UN?-NE-E-LUM		TCL I 220 42
		BUN		UM	ʾEL		UM	BU-NU-UM-E-LU-UM		B 16
		ḎAKUR		I	ʾEL		UM	ZA-KU-RI-E-LUM		UNPUBL.
		ḎAMAR		I	ʾEL		UM	ZA-MA-RI-E-LUM		B. 92+
	JI	PANIJ			ʾEL		UM	I-PA-AN-NI-E-LUM		UNPUBL.
		SITR		I	ʾEL		UM	ZI-IT-RI-E-LUM		B 42
		ŠU			ʾEL		UM	ŠU-E-LUM		B 40
	3	MILK		I	LI					
					ʾEL		UM	MI-IL-KI-LI-E-LUM		A 32065:3
	1	ʾELL		UM				E-IL-LUM		RA LXV 50 VIII 70
		ʾELL	AN	UM				E-EL-LA-NUM		C
		ʾELL	AN	UM				E-LA-NUM		C
	1	ʾELM	AN	UM				EL-MA?-NU-UM		TA 1931, 538 I
	1	ʾELUR		UM				EL-LU-RUM		CT VIII 43B21
		ʾELUR	AT	UM				EL-LU-RA-TUM	MN?	WATERMAN 38 9
	1 JA	ʾGUN		UM				IA-AḪ-GU-UN-NU-UM		TCL XVII 24 1
	JA	ʾGUN		UM				IA-AḪ-GU-NU-UM		TLB IV 82:1
	JA	ʾGUN		UM				IA-GU-NU-UM		YOS XII
	JA	ʾGUN		UM				I-IA-GU-NU-UM		YOS XII
	1	ʾIBL	AN	UM				IB-LA-A-NU-UM		HAV. SYMP. 237 13
		ʾIBL	AN	UM				IB-LA-NU-UM		I
	1	ʾIBN	AT	UM				IB-NA-TUM	MN	BM 16939 27+
	1	ʾIDAD		UM				I-DA-DU-UM		WATERMAN 34 R. 13+
	1	ʾIDD	AT	UM				ID-DA-TUM	MN	B 21, M
	1	ʾIDID		UM				I-DI-DUM		XIII 1 I 22
	1	ʾIL	AN	UM				I-LA-NU-UM		I+, B 45+
		ʾIL	AN	UM				I-LA-A-NU-UM		B 93
		ʾIL		UM	ʾAB		I	I-LUM-A-BI		A.
		ʾIL		UM	ʾAB		UM	I-LUM-A-BU-UM		U
		ʾIL		UM	KATAZ		I	I-LU-UM-KA-TA-ZI		RUTTEN 40 1
		ʾIL		UM	MULUK			DINGIR-MU-LU-UK-KI	GN	XV 127
		ʾIL		UM	MULUK			I-LU-UM-MU-LU-UK-KI	GN	XV 127
		ʾIL		UM	MULUK	AJ	I	DINGIR-MU-LU-KA-JI-KI	GN	XV 127
		ʾIL		UM	ŠALM		A	I-LU-UM-ŠA-AL-MA		RA LXV 45 V 51
		ʾIL		UM	TUŠUʿ		U	D-I-LU-UN-TU-SU-U_2	DN	KISURRA
	2 JA	ʿMIS			ʾIL		UM	IA-AḪ-MI-ZI-LUM		RUTTEN 16 17
	ʾU	WQAH			ʾIL		UM	U_2-GA-DINGIR-LUM		FRANK 29 9
	JA	ḪATIʾ			ʾIL		UM	IA-ḪA-TI-LUM		YOS XII
	JA	JṢIʾ			ʾIL		UM	IA-ZI-LUM-KI	GN	B 32
	JA	WṢIʾ			ʾIL		UM	IA-U_2-ZI-LUM		B 31
	JE	ʾZIJ			ʾIL		UM	E-EḪ-ZI-LUM		VIII 3 25
		ḪAṢAN			ʾIL		UM	ḪA-ZA-AN-I-LU-UM		M+
		BEʿD		I	ʾIL		UM	BE-DI-LU-UM		TIM III 62 6+
		BEʿD		I	ʾIL		UM	BE-DI-LUM		TIM III 61 15

SUFFIXES, Class 2

UM	2		BUN					ʾIL	UM	BU-NI-LUM		TIM III 33 15+
			KIʾL		I			ʾIL	UM	KI-LI-DINGIR-LUM		XIII 106 14
			MILK		I			ʾIL	UM	MI-IL-KI-LUM		B 34
		JA	MRUṢ		I			ʾIL	UM	I-IA-AM-RU-UṢ-ZI-I-LU-UM		B 21
			MUT		I			ʾIL	UM	MU-TI-LUM		YOS XIII 151:4+
			NAWḪ					ʾIL	UM	NA-ḪI-LUM		B 35+
			NAWḪ					ʾIL	UM	NA-ḪI-LU-UM		B 35
			NAḪL		I			ʾIL	UM	NA-AḪ-LI-LUM		B 36+
		JA	NBIʾ					ʾIL	UM	IA$_2$-AN-BI$_2$-I$_3$-LUM		U
		JA	NŠIʾ					ʾIL	UM	IA-SI-LUM		RA IX 22 2+
		JA	RŠIJ					ʾIL	UM	IA-AR-ŠI-DINGIR-UM		UCP X/1 P. 58+
			ŠUM		I			ʾIL	UM	SU-MI-LU-UM		WALTERS, WL 114:13
			ŠIMḪ		U			ʾIL	UM	ŠI-IM-ḪU-LUM?		A. 265 8
	3		JAʿAL					PI				
								ʾIL	UM	IA-ḪA-AL-PI-LUM		3NT867:5, 12, 21
			ʾIB		I			LA				
								ʾIL	UM	I-BI-LA-I$_3$-LUM		U
			ʾALI					FA				
								ʾIL	UM	A-LI$_2$-KA-LUM		RUTTEN 37 19
			BUN		U	BU		PI				
								ʾIL	UM	BU-NU-U$_2$?-BI-I-LUM		UET V 548 2
			RAPIʾ					MI				
								ʾIL	UM	RA-BI-MI-LUM		BIROT, TEA 72 IX 29
	1		ʾILAP		UM					IL-LA-PU-UM		RA LXV 46 VI 1,10
	1		ʾILL	AT	UM					IL-LA-TUM	FN	XIII 1 X 46
	1		ʾILUR	AT	UM					IL-LU-RA-TUM	FN	CT IV 26A 3+
	1		ʾIMIR		UM					I-MI-RU-UM		UCP X/3 2 21
			ʾIMIR	IN	UM					I-ME-RI-NU-UM		TA 30 615 12
	1		ʾIPQ	AT	UM					IP-GA-TUM	MN	CT XLV 23 R. 13
			ʾIPQ	AT	UM					IP-QA-TUM	MN	M+
	1		ʾIŠUL		UM					ḪI-SU-LUM		SIMMONS 79 4'
	1		ʾIŠAW		UM					I-ŠA-WU-UM		M
	1		ʾIZAM	AN	UM					I-ZA-MA-NU-UM		B 45
	2		LA				ʾA	ʾMAR	UM	LA-MA-RUM		BM 80644
	1	MA	ʾMIN		UM					MA-AḪ-MI-NU-UM		CT XLVIII 89 REV.
	1	MA	ʾNIP		UM					MA-NI-PU-UM		SIMMONS 119 10 S
	1	MA	ʾNUP		UM					[MA]-AḪ-NU-KA-UM		VAS IX 192 18
	1	JA	ʾQUD		UM					IA-KU-DU-UM		CT VIII 44A 28, UET V 523
		JA	ʾQUD		UM					IA-AḪ-KU-DU-UM		CT XXXIII 29 14
		JA	ʾQUD		UM					IA-KU-DU-UM-KI	GN	BRM IV 53 III 47+
	1	JA	ʾRUR		UM					IA-RU-RUM-KI	GN	YOS XII
		JA	ʾRUR		UM					IA-ḪU-UR-RU-UM-KI	GN	M
		JA	ʾRUR		UM					IA-AḪ-RU-RU-UM	GN	B 26+
		JA	ʾRUR		UM					IA-AḪ-RU-RUM	GN	B 26+
		JA	ʾRUR		UM					IA-AḪ-RU-RUM		BM 80328 10
	1	JA	ʾŠUD		UM					IA-SU?-DU-UM		CT II 28 19
	1	JA	ʾŠUR		UM					IA-ŠU-RU-UM		RA LXV 54 XII 38
	1		ʾUWŠ	AN	UM					ḪU-ŠA-NU-UM		B 45+
			ʾUWŠ	AN	UM					ḪU-ŠA-A-NU-UM		KISURRA 48 8
	1		ʾUBUŠ		UM					ḪU-BU-ŠUM		UCP X/1 34 13
	1		ʾUDM	AN	UM					ḪU-UD-MA?-NU		XII 712 R 9
	1		ʾUDUD		UM					ḪU-DU-DU-UM		TLB I/2, 15 18+
	1		ʾUGAZ		UM					U$_2$-GA-ZUM		TA 30 615 22
	1		ʾUKUL	IN	UM					U$_2$-KU-LI-NU-UM		RA LXV 43 III 54
	2		ḪATAʾ					ʾUMAN	UM	ḪA-TA-UM-MA-NU-UM		RA VIII 74 19
	1		ʾUMM		UM			KA				
								ʾAB	IM	UM-MU-UM-KA-A-BI-IM	FN	M
			ʾUMM		UM			KA				
								ʾAB	I	UM-MU-UM-KA-A-BI	FN	XIII 1 VII 56
	1		ʾUNAB		UM					ḪU-NA-BU-UM		KISURRA 17 5
			ʾUNAB		UM					U$_2$-NA-BU-UM		TIM III 42 13
			ʾUNAB	AT	UM					U$_2$-NA-BA-TUM	FN	TIM III 26 7
			ʾUNAB	AT	UM					ḪU-NA-BA-TUM	FN	WATERMAN 54 2, 3+
	1		ʾUNUB		UM					ḪU-NU-BU-UM		GORDON 39 5, 10
			ʾUNUB		UM					U$_2$-NU-BU-UM		EDZARD, DER 74:11+
			ʾUNUB		UM					UN-NU-BU-UM		EDZARD, DER 68 III 10

UM	1	ʾUNUB	AT	UM					ḪU-NU-PA-TUM	FN?	BM 17060 35
		ʾUNUB	AT	UM					UN-NU-BA-TUM	FN	WATERMAN 24 R. 24
		ʾUNUB	AT	UM					ḪU-NU-BA-TUM	FN	EDZARD, DER 134:4
		ʾUNUB	T	UM					UN-NU-UB-TUM	FN	EDZARD, DER 33:11+
		ʾUNUB	T	UM					ḪU-NU-UB-TUM	FN	EDZARD, DER 99:8
	2	ʾALI				ʾUP	UM		A-LI$_2$-U$_2$-PU-UM		KISURRA 117 5
	1	ʾURAN		UM					U$_2$-RA-NU-UM		M+
		ʾURAN		UM					U$_3$-RA-NU-UM		TA 1931, 538 IV
		ʾURAN	AT	UM					U$_2$-RA-NA-TUM	FN	HARRIS 83 1
	1	ʾURL	IJ	UM					UR-LI-U$_2$-UM		M
	1	ʾUŠAL		UM					U$_2$-SA?-LUM		WATERMAN 21 R. 10
		ʾUŠAL		UM					ḪU-ŠA-LUM		HARRIS 105 5
	1	ʾUŠK	ATANUM						UŠ-KA-TA-NU-UM		XIII 92 11
	1	ʾUŠAŠ		UM					U$_2$-ŠA-ŠUM		I
	1 JA	ʾZUW		UM					IA-ZU-UM		UET V 714 +
	1 JA	HWIJ		UM					IA?-WI-U$_2$-UM		M
	JA	HWIJ		UM					IA-AḪ?-WI?-UM?		B 32
	1	HALIL		UM					A-LI-LU-UM		B 18
		HALIL		UM					ḪA-LI-LUM		B 18+, M
		HALIL		UM					ḪA-LI-LU-UM		B 18+
		HALIL	AT	UM					ḪA-LI-LA-TUM		KISURRA 211 4
	1	HILAL		UM					ḪI-IL-LA-LUM		M+
	1 MA	HLIL		UM					MA-AḪ-LI-LUM		SIMMONS 46 34 124 16+
	1 ʾA	HLUL	AJ	UM					AḪ-LU-IA-UM		CT VIII 38 B 4
	1	HULAL		UM					ḪU-LA-LUM		M
	1	ḤAJJ		UM					ḪA-IU-UM		B 18+
		ḤAJJ		UM					ḪA-U$_2$-UM		CT VI 46 5
		ḤAJJ	AT	UM					ḪA-IA-TUM	MN	B 18+
		ḤAJJ	AT	UM					[Ḫ]A-A-A-IA-TUM	FN	XIII 1 XIV 13
		ḤAJJ	AN	UM					ḪA-IA-NU-UM		VAS XVI 62 12
		ḤAJJ	AN	UM					A-A-NU-UM		M
		ḤAJJ		UM		RAPIʾ			ḪA-JU-UM-RA-BI		M
	2 JI	JṢIʾ				ḤAJJ	UM		I-ZI-A-UM		MOORTGAT 488
		ŠAWB		A		ḤAJJ	UM		SA-BA-A-U$_2$-UM		OIP XLVII 66
	1	ḤABIB		UM					ḪA-BI-BU-UM		RUTTEN 27 14+
		ḤABIS		UM					A-BI-ZUM		TIM II 122 3+
		ḤABIS		UM					A-BI-ZU-UM		TIM III 4 3+
	1	ḤABS	AT	UM					ḪA-AB-ZA-TUM		BM 17049+
	1	ḤAKAM	AT	UM					ḪA-KA-MA-TUM	FN	C+
	1	ḤALAṢ		UM					A-LA-ZUM		UET V 796 11+
		ḤALAṢ		UM					A-LA-ZU-UM		UET V 397 14
	1	ḤALIṢ		UM					A-LI-ZUM		HARRIS 98 R. 5
		ḤALIṢ		UM					ḪA-LI-ZUM		SUMER V 141 3
		ḤALIṢ	IT	UM					A-LI-ZI-TUM?		UET V 534 R. 9
	1	ḤAM		UM	JE	JŠUʿ			D-A-MU-UM-E-ŠU-UḪ		B 13 HANA
		ḤAM		UM		LU		HU	D-A-MU-UM-LU-U$_2$		M
		ḤAM		UM		MALIK			D-A-MU-UM-MA-LIK		M
		ḤAM		UM	TA	NWUḪ		HU	A-MU-UM-TA-NU-U$_2$		M
	2 JI	JBAL				ḤAM	UM		I-BA-AL-D-A-MU-UM		RA LXV 52 X 43
	1	ḤAMAD		UM					ḪA-MA-DU-UM	FN	M+
	1	ḤAMID		UM					ḪA-MI-DU-UM		M
	1	ḤANḪAN		UM					ḪA-AN-ḪA-NU-UM		B 48+
		ḤANḪAN		UM					ḪA-ḪA-NU-UM		SPELEERS 224 10
	1	ḤANAN	AT	UM					A-NA-NA-TUM	FN	EDZARD, DER 97:14
	1	ḤANIN		UM					ḪA-NI-NU-UM		B 19+
		ḤANIN		UM					A-NI-NU-UM		EDZARD, DER 73:19
	1	ḤANUN		UM					A-NU-NU-UM		HARRIS 79 16
	1	ḤARAB	AT	UM					A-RA-BA-TUM		YOS XIII 389:4+
	1	ḤARB	ATANUM						AR-BA-TA-NU-UM		B 43
	1	ḤARIB	AN	UM					A-RI-BA-A-NU-UM		SIMMONS 103 13+
		ḤARIB	AN	UM					A-RI-BA-NU-UM		SIMMONS 96 12+
	1	ḤASAD		UM					A-ZA-DU-UM		CT XLV 77 27
		ḤASAD		UM					ḪA-ZA-DU-U[M]?		M
	1	ḤAŠIK		UM					ḪA-SI-KUM		B 20+
	1	ḤAṢAN		UM					A-ZA-NU-UM		B 43+
		ḤAṢAN	AT	UM					ḪA-[Z]A-NA-TUM	FN	M

SUFFIXES, Class 2

UM	1		ḪAṢN	AT	UM			ḪA-AZ-NA-TU[M]	FN	M
	1		ḤATK		UM			ḪA-AT-KU-UM		M
			ḤATK	AN	UM			AT-GA-NU-UM		U
	1	JA	ḪBIS		UM			IA-AḪ-BI-ZUM		GORDON 38 3
	1		ḤILUṢ	AT	UM			I-LU-ZA-TUM	FN	CT II 30 29
	1		ḪIMAR		UM			ḪI-MA-RUM		RA LXV 45 V 56
	1		ḤINAN		UM			I-NA-NU-UM		I
	1		ḤININ		UM			EN-NE-NU-UM		B 44+
			ḤININ		UM			EN-NI-NU-UM		SIMMONS 48 5+
	1		ḪINN	AT	UM			ḪI-NA-TUM	FN	RA LXV 59 II 66
			ḤINN	ATAN	UM			IN-NA-TA-NU-UM		TA 1931, 294
	1		ḤINUN		UM			E-NU-NU-UM		SIMMONS 112 20
	1		ḪIṢN	AN	UM			ḪI-IZ-NA-NU-UM		WALTERS, WL 93:2, 14
	1	JA	ḪKUM		UM			IA-AḪ-KU-MU-UM		B 26
	1	JA	ḤMAD		UM			IA-AḪ-MA-DU-UM		CT XLV 5 7
	1	JA	ḤṢUN		UM			IA-ZU-NU-UM		SIMMONS 125 13+
	1		ḪUBAS		UM			ḪU-BA-ZU-UM		TA 1931, 218
			ḤUBAS		UM			ḪU-BA-ZUM		VAS VIII 14 33
			ḤUBAS		UM			U_2-BA-ZU-UM		SIMMONS 118 17+
	1		ḤUNIN	AN	UM			ḪU-NI-NA-NU-UM		I
	1		ḤUNN	AT	UM			ḪU-UN-NA-TUM	MN	CT XLV 49 8+
			ḤUNN	AN	UM			ḪU-NA-NU-UM		TA 30 615 18+
	2		ʿAQB		A	ḤUNN	UM	AQ-BA-ḪU-NI-UM		B 11
	1		ḤUSUD		UM			ḪU-ZU-DU-UM	FN	RA LXV 60 III 41
	1		ḤUṢAN		UM			ḪU-ZA-A-NU-UM		BIN VII 101:3
	1	MA	ḤZIQ		UM			MA-ZI-GU-UM		CT XLVIII 27 CASE
	1		ḪAʾL		UM			ḪA-LU-UM		B 19
			ḪAʾL		UM			ḪA-A-LUM		UCP X/1 34 12
			ḪAʾL	AN	UM			ḪA-LA-NU-UM		KISURRA 57 4, SEAL
			ḪAʾL	AN	UM			ḪA-LA-NUM_2		KISURRA 24 2
			ḪAʾL	AT	UM			ḪA-LA-TUM		KISURRA 104 8
			ḪAʾL		UM	MAṬAR		ḪA-LUM-MA-DAR		C, SIMMONS 67 SEAL
			ḪAʾL		UM	MAṬAR	I	ḪA-LUM-MA-DA-RI		SIMMONS 67 B 11
			ḪAʾL		UM	MAṬAR	I	ḪA-LUM-MA-DAR-RI		SIMMONS 67 11
	2		ʾAB		U	ḪAʾL	UM	A-BU-ḪA-LUM		UCP X P. 53, M
			ʾAB		UM	ḪAʾL	UM	A-BU-UM-ḪA-LUM		B 11+
			ʾAB		UM	ḪAʾL	UM	A-BU-UM-ḪA-LU-UM		B 11+
			JADAʿ			ḪAʾL	UM	IA-DA-AḪ-ḪA-LUM		B 25
			ʾIL		A	ḪAʾL	UM	DINGIR-ḪA-LUM		B 21
			ʾIL		I	ḪAʾL	UM	I_3-LI_2-ḪA-LU-UM		CT XLV 3 10
			ʿAMM		U	ḪAʾL	UM	ḪA-AM-MU-ḪA-LUM		M+
		JA	GJIḤ			ḪAʾL	UM	IA-GI?-ḪA-LUM		RUTTEN 16 18
	1		ḪAʾŚ	AT	UM			ḪA-SA-TUM	MN	RUTTEN 15 6 SEAL
	2		MUT			ḪAʾŚ	UM	MU-UT-ḪA-SU-UM		A.
	2		ʿAḎR		I	ḪAʾT	UM	AD-RI-ḪA-TUM		SIMMONS 88 16+
			ʾUMM		I	ḪAʾT	UM	UM-MI-ḪA-TUM	FN	M+
		TA	KWUN			ḪAʾT	UM	TA-KU-UN-ḪA-TUM	FN	M+
		TA	TWUR			ḪAʾT	UM	TA-DUR-ḪA-TUM		TA 1931, 489
	1		ḪAʾZ	UT	UM			ḪA-ZU-TUM	FN	RA LXV 58 II 1
	1		ḪABAD		UM			ḪA-BA-TUM	FN	RA LXV 59 II 76
	1		ḪAGIR		UM			ḪA-GI-RUM		M
	1		ḪAMAŚ	AT	UM			ḪA-MA-SA-TUM	MN	CT XLV 91 20
	1		ḪAMŚ	AT	UM			ḪA-AM-SA-TUM	FN	BM 16844+
	1		ḪANB	AT	UM			ḪA-AN-BA-TUM	FN	CT XLV 91 18+
	1		ḪANP	AT	UM			ḪA-AN-PA-TUM	FN	A 3521 29
	1		ḪARGAL		UM			ḪA-AR-GA-LUM		VAS VIII 14 26
	1		ḪARIR		UM			ḪA-RI-RUM		B 20
			ḪARIR		UM			ḪA-AR-RI-RUM		B 20
	1		ḪAŚIJ	AN	UM			ḪA-ŠI-A-NU-UM		TA 1931, 538 III
	1		ḪAŚT	AT	UM			ḪA-AŠ-TA-TUM	FN	XIII 1 III 62
	1		ḪAŠḪAŠ		UM			ḪA-AŠ-ḪA-ŠUM		KISURRA 62 3
	1		ḪAŠIŠ		UM			ḪA-ŠI-ŠUM		B 20+
	1		ḪAŠŠ		UM			ḪA-AŠ-ŠUM		RA LXV 47 VII 27
	1		ḪAŠTUR		UM			ḪA-AŠ-TU-RU-UM		YOS VIII 139 15 CASE 13
	1		ḪAZIM		UM			ḪA-ZI-MU-UM		HARRIS 63 16
	1	JA	ḪBUʾ		UM			IA-AḪ-BU-U_2-UM		M

SUFFIXES, Class 2

UM	1	ʾA	ḪBUD	IJ	UM				AḪ-BU-TE-UM		U
	1		ḪIʾD	AT	UM				ḪI-DA-TUM	FN	XIII 1 V 54
	1		ḪIʾL	AT	UM				ḪI-LA-TUM	FN	XIII 1 II 71
	2		ʾAB		UM		ḪIʾL	UM	A-BU-UM-ḪI-LUM		B 11
	1		ḪILḪIL		UM				ḪI-EL-ḪI-LUM		SIMMONS 111 3
			ḪILḪIL		UM				ḪI-IL-ḪI-LUM		B 48+
	1		ḪIMʾ	AT	UM				ḪI-IM-A-TUM	FN	XIII 1 X 40
	1		ḪIML		UM		....		Ḫ[I-I]M-LU-UM-[....]	FN	M
	1		ḪIRṢ		UM				ḪI-IR-ZU-UM		RA LXV 48 VIII 6
	1		ḪIŠŠ	AT	UM				ḪI-IŠ-ŠA-TUM	FN	WATERMAN
	1	JA	ḪMUṬ		UM				IA-AḪ-MU-TU-UM-KI	GN	UET V 9721
	1	MA	ḪŠIM	AN	UM				MA-AḪ-ŠI-MA-NU-UM		B 46+
	2		LA			ʾA	ḪŠIR	UM	LA-AḪ-SI-RU-UM		BM 80368 2
	1		ḪUʾD	AN	UM				ḪU-DA-A-NU-UM		SIMMONS 83 8
	1		ḪUʾT	AN	UM				ḪU-TA-NU-UM		B 45
	1		ḪUʾZ	AN	UM				ḪU-ZA-NU-UM		RA LXV 55 XIII 13+
	1		ḪUWAL		UM				ḪU-WA-LUM		B 20
	1		ḪUBAD		UM				ḪU-PA-DU-UM		WATERMAN 14 R. 14
	1		ḪUBD	AT	UM				ḪU-UP-DA-T[UM]	FN	XIII 1 VII 65
	1		ḪUBR	AT	UM				ḪU-UB-RA-TUM	FN	XIII 1 IX 31
	1		ḪUGUL		UM				ḪU-GU-LU[M]		HARRIS 79 4
	1		ḪUMR	AN	UM				ḪU-UM-RA-NU-UM		U
	1		ḪUMUŠ	AT	UM				ḪU-MU-SA-TUM	MN	TCL I 62 3
	1		ḪUNAŠ		UM				ḪU-NA-ŠUM		BM 82432
	1		ḪUPŠ		UM				ḪU-UP-ŠUM		CT XLVIII 91 REV.
	1		ḪURAṢ	AT	UM				ḪU-RA-ZA-TUM	FN	XIII 1 I 73+
	1		ḪURR	AN	UM				ḪU-UR-RA-NU-UM		CT IV 25C 15
	1		ḪURṢ	AN	UM				ḪU-UR-ZA-NU-UM		B 44
	1		ḪURUṢ		UM				ḪU-RU-ZUM		RA LXV 53 XI 16
			ḪURUṢ	AN	UM				ḪU-RU-ZA-NU-UM		B 44
	1		ḪUŠŠ	UT	UM				ḪU-ŠU-TUM	FN	CT VI 43 6, 34
			ḪUŠŠ	UT	UM				ḪU-UŠ$_2$-ŠU-TUM	FN	X 96 3
	1		ḪUZIR	AN	UM				ḪU-ZI-RA-NU-UM		B 45
			ḪUZIR	AT	UM				ḪU-ZI-RA-TUM		EDZARD, DER 99 REV 8
	1		ḪUZM	AN	UM				ḪU-UZ-MA-N[U-UM]		TA 1931, 265
	1	JA	ʿWUQ		UM				IA-U$_2$-KU-UM		B 31+
	1		ʿAWIQ	AT	UM				ḪA-I-KA-TUM	FN	SIMMONS 112:17
	1		ʿABD		UM				ḪA-AB-DU-UM		B 9+, M+
			ʿABD	AN	UM				ḪA-AB-DA-[NUM]?		PBS VIII/2 260 4
			ʿABD	AT	UM				ḪA-AB-DA-TUM	FN	XIII 1 XIV 39
	1		ʿAD	AT	UM				A-DA-TUM	MN	I, MEISSNER 51 3
			ʿAD	AT	UM				A-DA-TUM	FN	M+
	2		HALIL		A		ʿAD	UM	A-LI-LA-ḪA-DU-UM		KISURRA 18 12
			ʾAMR				ʿAD	UM	AM-RA-DU-UM		M
		JI	JṢIʾ				ʿAD	UM	I-ZI-A-DU-UM		M
			LU				ʿAD	UM	LU-ḪA-DU-UM		YOS XIII 497:2
			RABB		U		ʿAD	UM	RU-BU-ḪA-DU-UM		BM 17055 26
	1		ʿADIJ		UM				A-DI-UM		M
	1		ʿADN	AN	UM				AD-NA-NU-UM		TIM III 44 19+
			ʿADN		UM		MAZAʾ	A	ḪA-[A]D?-NU-UM-MA-ZA-A		RA LXV 41 II 52
	1		ʿAḎAR		UM				A-ZA-RU-UM		B 14
			ʿAḎAR		UM				A-DA-RU-UM	FN	RA LXV 60 III 25
	1		ʿAḎIR		UM				ḪA-ZI-RUM	MN	B 20+, M+
			ʿAḎIR		UM				ḪA-ZI-RU-UM		B 20, M
			ʿAḎIR		UM				ḪA-ZI-RUM	FN	M+
			ʿAḎIR		UM				A-ZI-RUM		B 14, M+, C+
	2		ḪAʾL		I		ʿAḎIR	UM	ḪA-LI-A-ṢI-RUM		UNPUBL.
	1		ʿAḎR	AN	UM				AD-RA-NU-UM		I., CT XLVIII 88 REV.
	1		ʿAGL	AT	UM				AG-LA-TUM	FN	ABB IV 98:2
	1		ʿALIJ		UM				A-LI-U$_2$-UM		GAUTIER 33 R. 6
			ʿALIJ		UM				A-LI-JU-UM		M
			ʿALIJ		UM				A-LI-I-U$_2$-UM		RUTTEN 7 20+
			ʿALIJ		UM				A-LI$_2$-JU-UM		JCS XXIV 52 NO.27+
			ʿALIJ		UM				ḪA-LI-IU-UM		B 19+
			ʿALIJ		UM				ḪA-LI-U$_2$-UM		B 19+, M
			ʿALIJ		UM				ḪA-LI-JU-UM		B 19+

UM	1		ʿALIJ		UM				ḪA-LI-I-JU-UM		CT XLVIII 31 7, 10
			ʿALIJ	AT	UM				ḪA-LI-IA-TUM	FN	B 18+, XIII 1 VII 1
			ʿALIJ	T	UM				A-LI-TUM	FN	M+
	1		ʿAMAS		UM				A-MA-ZU-UM		KISURRA 98 8
	1		ʿAMM	AN	UM				ḪA-AM-MA-NU-UM		M
			ʿAMM		UM		RAPIʾ		ḪA-AM-MU-UM-RA-BI		B 19+
			ʿAMM		UM		RAPIʾ		ḪA-AM-MU-UM-RA-PI		YBC 6496, 6508
			ʿAMM		UM		RAPIʾ		ḪA-MU-UM-RA-BI		BM 17046+
			ʿAMM		UM		RAPIʾ				
							....		[ḪA-AM]-MU-UM-RA-PI-LI-WI-IR		UNPUBL.
	2		ʿABD				ʿAMM	UM	ḪA-AB-DU-A-MU-UM		M
		JA	WMAʾ				ʿAMM	UM	JA-MA-ḪA-MU-UM		M
		JA	WMAʾ				ʿAMM	UM	IA-MA-ḪA-MU-UM		M
	1		ʿAN		UM		ʾAḪ	I	A-NU-UM-A-ḪI		RA LXV 53 XI 43
			ʿAN		UM		ḤIRB	I	A-NU-UM-ḪI-IR-BI		BALKAN, LETTER P. 6
			ʿAN	AT	UM				A-NA-TUM		BIROT, TEA 72 III 58+
			ʿAN	AT	UM				ḪA-NA-TUM	FN	XIII 1:34+
	2		JAʾ		A		ʿAN	UM	IA-A-A-NU-UM		YOS V 134 16
			JIŠʿ		I		ʿAN	UM	IŠ-ḪI-A-NU-UM		B 45
		JA	BWAʾ				ʿAN	UM	IA-BA-A-NU-UM		B 45
			PALṬ		A		ʿAN	UM	PA-AL?-TA-A-NU-UM		LANGDON IV 15
			BUN		A		ʿAN	UM	BU-NA-A-NU-UM		U
			LA				ʿAN	UM	LA-A-NU-UM		U
			LU				ʿAN	UM	LU$_2$-A-NU-UM		U
			LASIM				ʿAN	UM	LA-ZE$_2$-IM-A-NU-UM		FLP 590:6, U
			LASIM				ʿAN	UM	LA-ZI-MA-NU-UM		MVN III 338:17, U
			PI				ʿAN	UM	PI-A-NUM$_2$		I
			PI				ʿAN	UM	BI$_2$-A-NU-UM		I
		ʾA	RŠIJ				ʿAN	UM	AR-SI?-A-NUM$_2$		U
			ŚAʾQ		A		ʿAN	UM	SA-GA-A-NU-UM		B 47
		MA	ŚJIT				ʿAN	UM	MA-SI-IT-A-NU-UM		I
			ŚALIM				ʿAN	UM	ŠA-LIM-A-NU-UM		M
	3		LA			ʾA	ḤJIJ				
							ʿAN	UM	LA-ḪI-A-NU-UM		U
	1		ʿANAQ		UM				A-NA-GU-UM		KISURRA 71A 15+
			ʿANAQ		UM				A-NA-KUM		KISURRA 29 8+
	1		ʿAQB		UM				AQ-BU-UM		TIM III 82 6
			ʿAQB	AN	UM				AQ-BA-NU-UM		RUTTEN 40 2+
	1		ʿARD		UM				ḪA-AR-DU-UM		M+
			ʿARD		UM				AR-DU-UM		TCL I 168 4+
			ʿARD	AT	UM				ḪA-AR-DA-TUM	FN	M+
			ʿARD	AN	UM				ḪA-AR-DA-NU-UM		M+
	1		ʿARIṢ	AN	UM				A-RI-ZA-NU-UM		U
	1		ʿARṢ	AN	UM				AR-ZA-NU-UM		B 43+
			ʿARṢ	AT	UM				AR-ZA-TUM	FN	C
	1		ʿARUL		UM				A-RU-LU-UM		B 13+
	1		ʿAZAB		UM				A-ZA-BU-UM		GAUTIER 23 5+
			ʿAZAL		UM				A-ZA-LU-UM		B 14
			ʿAZAL		UM				A-ZA-LUM		EDZARD, DER 60:8
			ʿAZAL		UM				AZ-ZA-LUM		GAUTIER 1 R. 9
			ʿAZAL		UM				A-ZA-AL-LUM		KISURRA 26 6
			ʿAZAZ		UM				A-ZA-ZUM		I
			ʿAZAZ	AN	UM				A-ZA-ZA-NU-UM		B 92
	1		ʿAZB		UM				ḪA-AZ-BU-UM		RA LXV 53 XI 20
	1		ʿAZIB	AT	UM				ḪA-ZI-BA-TUM	MN	GAUTIER 65 5
	1		ʿAZZ	AT	UM				A-ZA-TUM	FN	CT VIII 37D 7, M
	1	JA	ʿDUN		UM				IA-AḪ-DU-NU-UM		B 26
		JA	ʿDUN	AN	UM				IA-AḪ-DU-NA-NU-UM		JCS XXIV 60 NO.51 REV.
	1	JA	ʿḎIR		UM				IA-AḪ-ZI-RUM		B 26+
	1		ʿEBB	AT	UM				IB-BA-TUM	FN	M+
			ʿEBB	ATAN	UM				IB-BA-TA-NU-UM		BE VI/2 26 III 1
	1		ʿEBIB		UM				E-BI-BU-UM		SIMMONS 76 6
	1		ʿEMES		UM				E-ME-ZUM		I+
	1		ʿINAB	AN	UM				I-NA-BA-NU-UM		U
	1		ʿINB		UM				IN-BU-UM		M
			ʿINB	AT	UM				IN-BA-TUM	FN	BM 78768 3', X 84 3+

UM	1	ʿIQB	AN	UM				IQ-BA-NU-UM		I+
	1	ʿIZZ	AN	UM				I-ZA-NUM$_2$		U
		ʿIZZ	AN	UM				I-ZA-NU-UM		U
		ʿIZZ	AK	UM				I-ZA-KUM		B 24
	1 JE	ʿMUS		UM				E-MU-ZUM		I UNPUBL.
	1 ME	ʿNIJ		UM				ME-EḪ-NI-JU-UM		M
	ME	ʿNIJ		UM				ME-EḪ-NU-UM		KISURRA 36 4
	1 JI	ʿQIB		UM				I-KI-BU-UM		CT VIII 19 19+
	ME	ʿQIB		UM				ME-KI-BU-UM		U, M+
	1 JI	ʿQUB		UM				I-KU-BU-UM		KISURRA 117 7, 9+
	1	ʿUWQ		UM				ḪU-KU-UM	FN	RA LXV 58 I 51
	1	ʿUMAS		UM				ḪU-MA-ZUM		VAS VIII 14 33
	1	ʿUZAB		UM				U$_2$-ZA-BU-UM		SIMMONS 46 32
		ʿUZAB		UM				U$_2$-SA-BU-UM		SIMMONS 52 16
		ʿUZAL		UM				U$_2$-ZA-LUM		CT XXXIII 46A 3+
		ʿUZAL		UM				ḪU-ZA-LUM		UCP X/1 17 14+
		ʿUZAL	AT	UM				ḪU-ZA-LA-TUM	FN	WATERMAN 12 R. 7+
		ʿUZAL	AT	UM				ḪU-ZA-LA-TUM	MN	UCP X/1 86 4+
	1	ʿUZUB		UM				ḪU-ZU-BU-UM		RA VIII 75
	1 JA	ʿZIB		UM				IA-ZI-BU-UM		M+
	JI	ʿZIB		UM				I-ZI-BU-UM		KISURRA 10A 5+
	1 MU	WḪIN		UM				MU-ḪI-NU-UM		HAGER DISSERT. PL II/3
	1 MU	WBIT		UM				MU-BI-TU-UM		LANGDON XXVII 4
	1 MU	WDAD		UM				MU-DA-DU-UM		I, VAS VIII 60 5, 18+
	1 MU	WQIR	AN	UM				MU-GI-RA-NU-UM		U
	1 MU	WSIL	AT	UM				MU-ZI-LA-TUM	FN	B 35
	1 ʾU	WŠIʿ		UM				U$_2$-SI-UM		I
	1 ʾU	WTAʾ	T	UM				U$_2$-TA-TUM	FN	C
	1	JAʾ	AT	UM				IA-A-A-TUM	MN	A 29366:3
		JAʾ		UM				IA$_3$-A-UM		U
		JAʾ		UM				I-A-UM		U
		JAʾ		UM				IA-A-UM		BIN VII 67 27
		JAʾ		UM	ʾIL			IA-U$_2$-UM-DINGIR		B 31
		JAʾ		UM	ʾIL			IA-A-UM-[DINGIR]		B 31
		JAʾ		UM	ʾIL			IA-WU-UM-DINGIR		B 31
		JAʾ		UM	LU		HU	IA-UM-LU-ḪU		UET V 496:10
	2	ʾAB	I	JAʾ	UM			A-BI-IA-U$_2$-UM		YOS VIII 10 9
		ʾIL	I	JAʾ	UM			I$_3$-LI$_2$-IA-UM		KISURRA 71A 5+
		ʾIL	I	JAʾ	UM			I$_3$-LI$_2$-I-UM		KISURRA 4A 12+
		ʾIL	I	JAʾ	UM			I$_3$-LI$_2$-I-U$_2$-UM		KISURRA 56 3+
		ʾIL	I	JAʾ	UM			I$_3$-LI$_2$-U$_2$-A-UM		KISURRA 186 5
		ʾIL	I	JAʾ	UM			I$_3$-LI$_2$-A-UM		B 21
	1	JAʾAN		UM				IA-A-NU-UM		BIN VII 67 9
		JAʾAR		UM				IA-A-RUM		VAS VII 183 I 7, II 12+
	2	KAʾM	I	JAʾAR	UM			KA-MI-IA-A-RUM		VAS VII 128 46
	1	JAʾN		UM				IA-NU-UM		B 29
		JAʾN		UM	PI			JA-NU-UM-BI-KI	GN	M
	2	ʾIL	I	JAʾN	UM			I$_3$-LI$_2$-IA-NU-UM		TIM I 29 3
	1	JAḪAD		UM				IA-ḪA-DUM		BIN VII 155 1
		JAḪAD		UM				IA-ḪA?-DU-UM		VII 199 8
	1	JAʿIL	AT	UM				IA-ḪI-LA-TUM	FN	B 26
		JAʿIL	AT	UM				IA-I-LA?-TUM	FN	B 26
	1	JAJA		UM				IA-IA-UM		B 27+
		JAJA	AT	UM				IA-IA-TUM		B 26
	1	JABS	AT	UM				IA-AB-ZA?-TUM	MN?	VAS VIII 121 5
	1	JABUŠ		UM				IA-BU-ŠUM	GN	KING LIH II NO. 97 III 1
		JABUŠ		UM				[I]A-BU-SU-UM		VIII 85 41, 44
		JABUS	AT	UM				IA-BU-ZA-TUM	FN	CT XLVIII 31 5, 9
	1	JAD	AN	UM				IA-DA-NU-UM		SIMMONS 131 17
	1	JADAʿ		UM				IA-DA-ḪU-UM		YOS XII
		JADAʿ		UM				IA-ṬA$_3$-ḪU-UM		YOS XII
	2	ŠAM	A	JADAʿ	UM			SA-MA-A-DA-ḪU-UM		M+
		ŠUM	U	JADAʿ	UM			SU-MU-A-ḊA-ḪU-UM		KISURRA 78A 15
	1	JADID		UM				IA-DI-DU-UM		B 25+, M+
		JADID		UM				IA-DI-DUM		CT XLI A 10+
		JADID	AT	UM				IA-DI-DA-TUM	MN	B 25+

UM	1		JAKUK		UM				IA-KU?-KU-UM		B 27
	1		JALQUṬ		UM				IA-AL-GU-TUM		BIN II 68 18
	1		JAMIN		UM				JA-ME-NU-UM		TA 1931, 538 IV 1, 13
	1		JAMN		UM				IA-AM-NU-UM		B 28+
			JAMN	UN	UM				IA-AM-NU-NU-UM		TIM III 26 13, 39 16
	1		JANIN		UM				IA-NI-NU-UM		TIM V 18 22
	1		JAPʿ		UM				IA-AP-ḪU-UM		M+
			JAPʿ	AT	UM				IA-AP-ḪA-TUM	MN	B 24+
			JAPʿ	AT	UM				IA-AP-ḪA-TUM	FN	YOS VIII 12 2+
	1		JAQAR		UM				IA-QA-RUM		M+
			JAQAR		UM				IA-GA-RU-UM		KISURRA 59A 24
			JAQAR	T	UM				IA-QAR-TUM	FN	M
	1		JAQR		UM	ʾIL			IA-AQ-RUM-DINGIR		A 22010
			JAQR	IT	UM				IA-AQ-RI-TUM		EDZARD, DER 155 REV 15
	1		JARAḪ	T	UM				IA-RA-AḪ-TUM	MN	B 29+
	1		JARN		UM				JA-AR-NU-UM		RUTTEN 22 17
	1		JAŚAR		UM				IA-ŠA-RU-UM		B 30
			JAŚAR		UM				IA-SA-RU-UM		PINCHES BERENS 101 10, M+
	1		JAŠUN		UM				E-ŠU-NU-UM		U
	1		JAT		UM				I-IA-TUM	FN	RA LXV 64 VI 31
			JAT		UM	MARṢ	AT		I-IA-TUM-MA-AR-ZA-AT	FN	RA LXV 62 V 15
			JAT		UM	MARṢ	AH		IA-TUM-MAR-ZA		A 21899+
			JAT		UM	ṢIʾ		A	IA-TUM-ZI-A		CT XLV 97 5
	2		ʾAḪ		U	JAT		UM	A-ḪU-IA-TUM	MN	BIN II 98 4
			ʾAḪ		U	JAT		UM	A-ḪU-JA-TUM	MN	M
			ʾAB		I	JAT		UM	A-BI-IA-TUM	FN	WATERMAN 40 R. 5+
			ʾIB		I	JAT		UM	I-BI-IA-TUM		TIM II 27 4
			JID		I	JAT		UM	I-DI-IA-TUM		M
			JADAʿ			JAT		UM	IA-DA-A-A-TUM		B 25
			ʾIL		I	JAT		UM	I_3-LI_2-I-IA-TUM		VAS XVIII 83:15
			ʿAMM		I	JAT		UM	AM-MI-IA-TUM		A. 273 14
			ʾUMM		I	JAT		UM	UM-MI-IA-TUM		UCP X/1 89 24
		JI	JṢIʾ			JAT		UM	I-ZI-IA-TUM		B 23+
			MAʾD		I	JAT		UM	MA-DI-IA-TUM		UCP X/1 P. 59+
			MARUʾ			JAT		UM	MA-RU-IA-TUM		DE GEN., KICH II D 43 R. 2, 4
			NAʿM		I	JAT		UM	NA-MI-IA-TUM	MN	MEISSNER 100 2
		JI	NDIN			JAT		UM	I-DIN-IA-TUM		M+
			RAWM		A	JAT		UM	RA-MA-IA-TUM		B 22+
			ŠUʾG		U	JAT		UM	ŠU-GU-IA-TUM		B 40
			ŚUM		U	JAT		UM	SU-MU-IA-TUM		TLB IV 40 9, 12, 14
			ŚAMAʿ			JAT		UM	ŠA-MA-IA-TUM	MN	CT IV 43B 6+
			ŚAMAʿ		A	JAT		UM	ŠA-MA-A-IA-TUM	MN	WATERMAN 21 R. 6
			ṢABAʾ			JAT		UM	ZA-BA-IA-TUM	MN	BM 16835 19+
			ZAMAʾ			JAT		UM	ZA-MA-A-A-TUM	MN?	TCL X 38 1
	1		JATAM		UM				IA-TA-MU-UM		YOS VIII 153 5
			JATAR		UM				IA-TA-RU-UM		B 31
			JATAR		UM				IA-TA-RUM		B 31, M+
			JATAR		UM				IA-TAR-RUM		B 31
			JATAR	AT	UM				IA-TA-RA-TUM	MN	B 31
			JATAR	AT	UM				IA-TA-RA-TUM	FN	B 31
	1		JATM		UM				WA-AT-MU-UM?		CT XLV 5 R. 4
	1		JATR	AT	UM				IA-AT-RA-TUM	MN	VAS VIII 105 4, 7, 12+
	1		JATUM		UM				IA-TU-MU-UM		B 31
	1	JI	JBAL		UM				I-BA-LUM		B 21, M
		JI	JBAL	AT	UM				JI-BA-LA-TUM	FN	U
	1	JA	JBIŚ		UM				IA-BI-ŠUM		B 24+
		ME	JBIŚ		UM				ME-BI-ŠUM		M+
	1	JA	JDIʿ		UM				IA-DI-ḪU-UM		B 25+
		JE	JDIʿ		UM				E-TI-UM		I
		JA	JDIʿ	AT	UM				IA-DI-ḪA-TUM	FN	B 25+
		ME	JDIʿ		UM				ME-TE-UM		I
	1		JIBUS	AT	UM				I-BU-ZA-TUM		EDZARD, DER 87:11
	1		JID	AN	UM				I-DA-NU-UM		I+
	1		JIŠʿ	AT	UM				IŠ-ḪA-TUM	FN	RA LXV 60 III 57
	1	JA	JPAʿ		UM				IA-PA-ḪU-UM		RA LXVI 118:16
		JA	JPAʿ		UM				[I]A-PA-ḪU-UM	FN	RA LXV 64 VI 8

UM	1	JA		JPAʿ	AT	UM				IA-PA-ḪA-TUM	FN	M+
	1	ME		JPIʿ		UM				ME-BI-ḪU-UM		M
		ME		JPIʿ		UM				ME-PI-UM		I
	1	JA		JPUʿ		UM				IA-PU-ḪU-UM		B 25+
		JA		JPUʿ	AT	UM				IA-PU-ḪA-TUM	FN	C+
	1	JA		JRID		UM				IA-RI-DU-UM		UCP X/1 109 3
		JI		JRID	AN	UM				I-RI-DA-NU-UM		M
		MA		JRID	UN	UM				MA-RI-DU-NU-UM		SIMMONS 124 17
	1	JI		JŠAR		UM				I-ŠA-RUM		C
		ME		JŠAR		UM				ME-ŠA-RUM		A.
	1	JA		JŚIR		UM				IA-SI-RUM		B 30+
		JA		JŚIR		UM				IA-ŠI-RU-[UM]		A 22002
	1	ME		JŠIʿ		UM				ME-SI-UM		SIGRIST UNPUBL.
	1	JA		JŠUʿ		UM				IA-ŠU-ḪU-UM		B 30+
		JA		JŠUʿ	AT	UM				IA-ŠU-ḪA-TUM	FN	RA LXV 58 I 17; B 30+
	1	JI		JTAR		UM				I-TA-RU-UM		B 23+
	1	ME		JTIR	AN	UM				ME-TE-RA-NU-UM		TA 1930, 489
	1	JI		Bʾ UL		UM				IB-U_2-LUM		I
	1	JA		BḪAR		UM				IA-AB-ḪA-RU-UM		B 24
	1	JI		BWAʾ		UM				I-BA-UM		TA 30 615
		JA		BWAʾ	AT	UM				IA-BA-TUM		AJSL XXXIII 237 16
	1	JA		BJIN		UM				IA-BI-NU-UM		XIII 38 13
	1	JA		BJIR		UM				IA-BI-RUM		M
		JI		BJIR		UM				I-BI-RUM		M
	1			BAʾAN		UM				BA-A-NU-UM		TA 1931, 434+
				BAʾAN	AN	UM				BA-A-NA-NU-UM		B 43
	1			BAʾIL		UM				BA-ḪI-LUM		M+
	2			TATT	I			BAʾT	UM	TA-AT-TI-BA-TUM		TCL I 204:10
	1			BAḪIR		UM				BA-I-RUM		M
	1		T	BAḪR		UM				BA-TA-AḪ-RUM		M+
	1			BAḪŠ		UM				BA-AḪ-ŠUM		RA LXV 43 III 71
	1			BAʿD	AN	UM				BA-AḪ-DA-NUM		HARRIS 106 5
				BAʿD	AN	UM				BA-DA-NU-UM		U
				BAʿD	AN	UM				BA-TA-NUM_2		U
	1		Š	BAʿL	AN	UM				ŠU-BI-LA-NU-UM		B 47
				BAʿL		UM				BA-LUM		CT II 35 29
				BAʿL	AN	UM				BA-LA-NU-UM		B 43+
				BAʿL		UM		ʾIL		BA-AḪ-LU-UM-DINGIR		B 15+
				BAʿL		UM		QAWM	UM	BA-LUM-QA-MU-UM		RA LXV 40 I 11
				BAʿL	AT	UM				BA-AḪ-LA-TUM	FN	M+
				BAʿL	AT	UM				BA-LA-TUM	FN	BM 16944 5
	2			ʾIL	A		Š	BAʿL	UM	DINGIR-ŠU-BA-A-LUM		CT II 15 9
				BUN	U			BAʿL	UM	BU-NU-BA-LUM		B 16+
		JA		MWUT				BAʿL	UM	IA-MU-UT-BA-LUM-KI	GN	B 28+
		JA		MWUT				BAʿL	UM	IA-MU-UT-BA-A-LUM-KI	GN	RLA II 194
		JE		MWUT				BAʿL	UM	E-MU-UT-BA-LUM-KI	GN	B 28+
		JE		MWUT				BAʿL	UM	E-MU-UT-BA-A-LUM-KI	GN	RLA II 180
		JE		MWUT				BAʿL	UM	IE-E-MU-UT-BA-LUM-KI	GN	SZLECHTER TJ 16 165
	1			BAWʾ		UM				BA-A-U_2-UM		KISURRA 94 14
				BAWʾ		UM				BA-IA-UM		CT VI 15 III 19
	1			BAWB	AT	UM				BA-BA-TUM	FN	RA LXV 58 I 59
	2			ʾIL	I			BAWB	UM	I_3-LI_2-BA-BU-UM		U UNPUBL.
	1			BAWŠ	AN	UM				BA-ŠA-NU-UM		TA 30 615
				BAWŠ	T	UM				BA-AŠ-TUM	FN	M+
	1			BAWZ	AT	UM				BA-ZA-TUM	FN	B 15+, M+
				BAWZ	AN	UM				BA-ZA-NU-UM		B 43+
	1			BAJN		UM				BA-NU-UM		M
				BAJN	AN	UM				BA-NA-NU-UM		B 43+
				BAJN	AN	UM				BA-A-NA-NU-UM		B 43
				BAJN	AT	UM				BA-NA-TUM	FN	C; EDZARD 58:3
				BAJN	AT	UM				BA-NA-A-TUM	FN	HARRIS 86 1
	1			BAJR		UM				BA-RU-UM		HARRIS 89 2
				BAJR	AT	UM				BA-RA-TUM	FN	CT VIII 6A 3+
	1			BABUL		UM				BA-BU-LU-[UM]	FN	RA LXV 62 V 8
	1			BADID		UM				BA-DI-DU-UM		B 15+
	1			BAGIN		UM				BA-GI-NU-UM		B 15

UM	1	BAKAL		UM			BA-KA-LUM		RUTTEN 38 18+
	1	BAKIL		UM			BA-KI-LUM		B 15+
		BAKIR		UM			BA-KI-RUM		M
	1	BAKŠ	AT	UM			BA-AK-SA-TUM	FN	M
	1	BAKŠIŠ		UM			BA-AK-ŠI-ŠUM		HARRIS 5 3+
	1	BAKUR	AT	UM			BA-KU-RA-TUM	FN	B
	1	BALBAL		UM			BA-AL-BA-LUM		RUTTEN 37 4 8
	1	BALIL		UM			BA-LI-LUM		B 15+
		BALIL	AT	UM			BA-LI-LA?-TUM	MN?	VIII 3 5
	1	BALK		UM			BA-AL-KUM		TIM V 1 23
	1	BANḪ	AT	UM			BA-AN-ḪA-TUM	FN	IX 291 II 19
	1	BANN		UM			BA-AN-NU-UM		M+
	1	BANUQ		UM			BA-NU-KU-UM		CT XXXIII 48A 3
	1	BAQAQ		UM			BA-GA-KUM		KISURRA 75A 21+
	1	BAQQ		UM			BA-AK-KUM		M
		BAQQ		UM			BA-KU-UM		M
		BAQQ		UM			BA-KU-UM	FN	RA LXV 62 V 12
		BAQQ	AN	UM			BA-AQ-QA-NU-UM		M
	1	BARIL	AT	UM			BA-RI-LA-TUM	FN	CT VI 35A 15
	1	BAŠAJ	AT	UM			BA-ŠA-A-IA-[TUM]?	FN	M
	1	BAŠUM		UM			BA-SU-MU-UM		SIMMONS 46 27+
	1	BATQ	AN	UM			BA-AT-GA-NU-UM		ZA XLII 41
	1	BATUL		UM			BA-TU-LUM		HARRIS 15 4+
		BATUL	AT	UM			BA-TU-LA-TUM	FN	XIII 1 II 59
	1	BAZAZ		UM			BA-ZA-ZUM		BM 17072+
	1	BAZBAZ		UM			BA-AZ-BA-ZUM		B 48
	1	BAZIḪ	AN	UM			BA-ZI-ḪA-NU-UM		TA 1931, 230 U
		BAZIN		UM			BA-ZI-NU-UM		B 15+
	1	BAZUR	AT	UM			BA-ZU-RA-TUM	FN	CT XLV 25 11, 20
	1	BEʿD	IT	UM			BE-DI-TUM	MN	EDZARD, DER 145:10
	1	BEʿL		UM			BE-E-LUM		KISURRA 36 4
		BEʿL	AN	UM			BE-LA-NU-UM		M+
		BEʿL	AK	UM			BE-LA-KUM		CT VIII 31A 21+
		BEʿL	AT	UM			BE-LA-TUM	FN	M+
		BEʿL	AT	UM			BE-LA-A-TUM	FN	RA LXV 60 III 26
	2	ḪADUR			BEʿL	UM	A-DU-UR-BE-LUM	GN	SIMMONS 138:10
	1	BELBAN		UM			BE-EL-BA-NU-UM		BM 81108 2
	1	BIḪIR		UM			BI-ḪI-RUM		M+
	1	BIʿD	AN	UM			BI-DA-NU-UM		SIMMONS 98 9+
	1	BIJT	AT	UM			BI-TA-TUM	MN	B 16+
	2	ŠAWB		I	BIJT	UM	ŠA-A-BI-E$_2$		SUMER V 142 NO. 6
	1	BIBIJ	AT	UM			BI-BI-IA-TUM	FN	RA LXV 62 V 25
	1	BIKAN		UM			BI-KA-NU-UM		KISURRA 47A 10+
	1	BIKIN		UM			BI-KI-IN-NU-UM		VAS VIII 15 16
		BIKIN		UM			BI-IK-KI-NU-UM		YOS XIII 306:4
	1	BIKN	AN	UM			BI-IK-NA-NU-UM		VAS VIII 1 21+
	1	BIKUR	T	UM			BI-KU-UR-TUM	MN	BASOR 95 P. 24
	1	BILK	UT	UM			BI-IL-KU-TUM	FN	XIII 1 XIII 17
	1	BILL		UM			BE-EL-LUM		B 15 HANA
		BILL		UM			BIL-LUM		B 15
		BILL	ATAN	UM			BI-LA-TA-NU-UM		HARRIS 49 14
	1	BILUL		UM			BI-LU-LU-UM		HARRIS 7 8+
	1	BIN		UM			BI-NU-UM		BM 82360 M+
		BIN	AT	UM			BI-NA-TUM	MN	BM 16820+
	2 JI	NDIN			BIN	UM	I-DIN-BI-NU-UM		UCP X/1 64 2
		TABʾ		I	BIN	UM	TA-AB-I-BI-NU-UM		BM 82437 4 9
	1	BINQ	ATAN	UM			BI$_2$-GA-TA-NU-UM	MN	TIM III 7:12;39:13
		BINQ	ATAN	UM			BI$_2$-IN-GA-TA-NU-UM	MN	TIM III 45:11
	1	BIQAQ		UM			BI-GA-GU-UM		YOS VIII 64 19
	1	BIRBIR		UM			BI-IR-BI-RU-UM		RUTTEN 7 15+
		BIRBIR		UM			BIR$_4$-BI$_2$-RU-UM		I
	1	BIRKIN		UM			BI-IR-KI-NU-UM		TIM V 2 24
	1	BIRUR	UT	UM			BI-RU-RU-TUM	MN	B 15+
	1	BIZAZ		UM			BI-ZA-ZUM		TA 1931, 327
	1 JA	BLIJ	AT	UM			IA-AB-LI-IA-TUM	FN	B 25+
	1 JA	BLIM		UM			JA-AB-LI-MU-UM		RUTTEN 2 17+

UM	1	JI	BLIM		UM					IB-LI-NU-UM		TA 1930, 615:25 +
	1	TA	BNIJ	T	UM					TAB-NI-TUM	FN	XIII 1 VI 5+
	1		BUʾUL		UM					[B]U-U$_2$-LU-UM		I
			BUʾUL		UM					BU-U$_2$-LUM		TCL I 75 5
			BUʾUL	T	UM					BU-ḪU-UL-TUM	FN	RA LXV 58 I 56
	1		BUḪAZ		UM					BU-ḪA-ZU-UM		BM 80328 12
	1		BUʿD		UM					BU-DU-UM		M
	1		BUWZ		UM					BU-ZU[M]-UM	MN	UCP X/3 2 23
			BUWZ		UM					BU-ZU-UM	FN	C+
	2		KIWN			BUWZ	AN	UM		KI-IN-BU-ZA-NU-UM		HARRIS 68 14
	1		BUDBUD		UM					BU-UD-BU-DU-UM		BM 16551
	1		BUKŠ	AN	UM					BU-UK-SA-NU-UM		PBS XIV 495
	1		BULAṬ		UM					BU-LA-TUM		CT XLV 12 25
			BULAṬ	AT	UM					BU-LA-DA-TUM	MN	BRM III 19E, 22G+
	1		BUN	AN	UM					BU-NA-NU-UM		B 44
			BUN	AT	UM					BU-NA-TUM	MN	A 7699 23+
			BUN		UM	ŠAGIŠ				BU-NU-UM-ŠA-GI-IŠ		EDZARD,DER 73:15
			BUN		UM	ʾEL		UM		BU-NU-UM-E-LU-UM		B 16
			BUN		UM	MA						
						ŠAKR				BU-NU-UM-MA-ŠAR		B 16
	1		BUNAQ		UM					BU-NA-GU-UM		TIM III 98 8+
			BUNAQ		UM					BU-NA-KUM		CT XLVIII 87 REV.
	1		BUQAQ		UM					BU-QA-KUM		M+
			BUQAQ		UM					BU-QA-KU-UM		M
	1		BUQQ	AN	UM					BU-GA-NU-UM		I+
	1		BURAN	AT	UM					BU-RA-NA-TUM	FN	RA LXV 59 II 70
	1		BURBIN		UM					BU-UR$_2$-BI-NU-UM		B 16
			BURBUR		UM					BU-UR$_2$-BU-RU-UM		BIN VII 155 6
			BURBUR		UM					BUR-BUR-RU?-UM		SCHEIL 10 17
	1		BURQ	AN	UM					BU-UR-GA-NU-UM		UET V 482 5
			BURQ	AT	UM					BU-UR-QA-TUM	FN	XIII 1 VII 52+
			BURQ	ATANUM						BU-UR$_2$-GA-TA-NU-UM	MN	SIMMONS 78 11
	1		BUŠAN	UT	UM					BU?-SA?-NU-TUM	MN?	VIII 13 10'
	1		BUṬUM	T	UM					BU-TU-UM-TUM	FN	RA LXV 59 II 39
	1		BUZBUZ		UM					BU-UZ-BU-ZU-UM		B 48+
	1		BUZZ	AN	UM					BU-UZ-ZA-NU-UM		M
	1	JA	DWIR		UM					[IA-DI]-RU-U[M]		B 25
		JA	DWIR	AT	UM					[IA-DI]-RA-TUM		B 25
	1		DAʿ		UM					DA-UM		B 17
	2		ŠAM		I	DAʿ		UM		SA-MI-DA-ḪU-UM		M+
			ŠAM		I	DAʿ	AT	UM		SA-MI-DA-ḪA-TUM	FN	M
	1		DAWD		UM					DA-DUM		RA LXV 52 XI 3
			DAWD	AT	UM					DA-DA-TUM	MN	TCL I 109 16+
			DAWD	AT	UM					[D]A-DA-TUM	FN	M
			DAWD	AN	UM					DA-AW-DA-NU-UM		HARRIS 19A 6+
			DAWD	AN	UM					DA-DA-NU-UM		SIMMONS 92 14 M+
			DAWD	AK	UM					DA-DA-KUM		KISURRA 39A 4+
			DAWD		UM	LU			HU	DA-DU-UM-LU-U$_2$		M
			DAWD		UM	PI						
						ʾIL				DA-DUM-BI$_2$-DINGIR		I
	2		ʾAB		A	DAWD		UM		A-BA-DA-DUM		HARRIS 95 9
			ʿAQB		U	DAWD		UM		AQ-BU-DA-DU-UM		PBS VIII/2 253 7
			ʾAŠD		I	DAWD		UM		AŠ$_2$-DI?-DA-DU-UM		EDZARD, DER 60:11
			JAT		A	DAWD		UM		IA-TA-DA-DUM		B 31
			ḎU			DAWD		UM		ZU-DA-TUM		I
	1		DABIʾ		UM					DA-BI-UM		M
			DABIN		UM					DA-BI-NU-UM		TIM III 18 8+
	1		DADM	IT	UM					DA-AD-MI-TUM	FN	M
	1		DAKŠ	AT	UM					DA-AK-SA-TUM	FN	CT IV 45B 6
	1		DAKUL		UM					DA-KUL-LUM		UET V P. 35+
	2		ʾIL		A	DAKUL		UM		DINGIR-DA-AK-KU-UL-LUM		UET V P. 43
			ʾIL		A	DAKUL		UM		DINGIR-DA-KU-UL-LUM		UET V P. 43+
	1		DALAQ		UM					DA-LA-KÚM		VAS IX 120 13
	1		DALQ		UM					DA-AL-KUM		CT VI 28A 24
	1		DALUM		UM					DA-LU-MU-UM		MEISSNER 24 15
	1		DAM	AN	UM					DA-MA-NU-UM		B 44

UM	1		DAM	AT	UM				DA-MA-TUM	FN	XIII 1 V 30	
	1		DAMIQ	T	UM				DA-ME-IQ-TUM	FN	RA LXV 59 II 60	
	1		DAMQ	AT	UM				DAM-QA-TUM	FN	CT XLV 2 22+	
			DAMQ	AN	UM				DA-AM-QA-NU-UM		SIMMONS 67 7	
			DAMQ	AN	UM				DAM-QA-NU-UM		SIMMONS PASSIM	
	1		DANN		UM	TA	ʾḪAḎ		D-DA-AN-NU-UM-TA-ḪA-AZ		SIMMONS 36 A 22	
			DANN		UM	TA	ʾḪAḎ		DA-AN-NU-UM-TA-ḪA-AZ		SIMMONS 36	CASE 22
			DANN		UM	TA	ʾḪAḎ		DA-NU-UM-TA-ḪA-AZ		A 7634, M	
			DANN		UM	TA	ʾḪAḎ		D-DA-NU-UM-TA-ḪA-[AZ]		TIM V 19 14	
	2		ʾAḪ		I		DANN	UM	A-ḪI-DA-NU-UM		I	
			ʾEB		I		DANN	UM	E-BI-DA-NU-UM		U	
			DAWD		U		DANN	UM	DA-AM-DU-DA-NU-UM		HARRIS 92:14+	
			KUʾM				DANN	UM	KU-UM-DA-NU-UM		U	
			MILK		U		DANN	UM	MI-IL-KU-DA-NU-UM		UET V 549:8	
			QAWM		A		DANN	UM	QA-MA-[D]A-NUM		M	
			SIKIL				DANN	UM	ZI-GI-IL-DA-NU-UM		M+	
	1		DARIK		UM				DA-RI-KUM		B 17+	
			DARIK		UM				DA-RI-KU-UM		CT XLV 117 27	
			DARIK		UM				DA-AR-RI-KU-[UM]		B 17	
	1		DARK	AT	UM				DA-AR-KA-TUM	FN	C	
	1		DAŠIK	T	UM				DA-SI-IK-TUM	MN	MEISSNER 90 27	
	1		DAŠUR		UM				DA-ŠU-RU-UM		B 17+	
			DAŠUR	AT	UM				DA-ŠU-RA-TUM	FN	YOS VIII 51 2,14	
	1	ʾA	DBAR	AT	UM				AD-BA-RA-TUM	MN	A 21946	
	1		DIʾL	AN	UM				DI-LA-NU-UM		B 44	
	1		DIʿ	ATANUM					DI-ḪA-TA-NU-U[M]		CT XLVII 4 3	
	1		DIWD		UM				DI-DU-UM		BIN VII 63 24	
	2		ʾAJAM				DIWD	UM	ḪA-IA-AM-DI-DU-UM		B 18+	
	1		DIWR	IT	UM		KAʾB	I	D-DI-RI-TUM-KA-BI		XIII 1 VI 45	
	2	JA	KWUN				DIWR	UM	IA-KU-UN-DI-RUM		CT XLVIII 115	
		JA	MWUT				DIWR	UM	IA-MU-UT-DI-RUM		WATERMAN 14 9	
	1		DIBDIB		UM				DI-IB-DI-BU-UM		SIMMONS 13 10	
	1		DIDAM	AN	UM				DI-DA-MA-NU-UM		B 44	
	1		DIGAN		UM				DI-GA-NU-UM		RUTTEN 11 2	
	1		DIGDIG		UM				DI-IG-DI-GU-UM		B 48+	
			DIGDIG		UM				DI-DI-GU-UM		UET V 702 R 13	
	1		DIMAḪ		UM				DI-MA-ḪU-UM		B 17	
	1		DITAN		UM				TI-DA-NUM_2	GN	GUDEA	
	2		ʾAB		I		DITAN	UM	A-BI-TI-DA-NU-UM		TA 1931, 538 III,IV	
	2		ŠUM		U		DITN	UM	SU-MU-DI-IT-NU-UM		B 39	
	1	ʾA	DRAK	AT	UM				AD-RA-KA-TUM	FN	M+	
	1		DUWD	AN	UM				DU-DA-NU-UM		CT XLVIII 87	
			DUWD	UT	UM				DU-DU-TUM	FN	M	
	1		DUKUB		UM				DU-KU-BU-UM		SUMER XIV 54 28 6	
	1		DULAQ		UM				DU-LA-KUM		TCL I 56 22+	
	1		DULDUL		UM				DU-UL-DU-LUM		B 48	
	1		DULQ	AN	UM				TU-UL-GA-NUM_2		U	
	1		DULUQ		UM				DU-LU-KUM		RUTTEN 3 16+	
			DULUQ		UM				DU-UL-LU-KUM		RUTTEN 29 5	
			DULUQ	AT	UM				DU-LU-GA-TUM	FN	VAS IX 178 2	
			DULUQ	T	UM				DU-LU-UQ-TUM	FN	MEISSNER 7 26	
	1		DUŠUB	T	UM				DU-ŠU-UB-TUM	FN	TCL XI 244 11, M	
	1		ḎABAB		UM				ZA-BA-BU-UM		HARRIS 98 R. 5	
	1		ḎABB		UM				ZA-AB-BU-UM		BM 17051 7	
	1		ḎABIB		UM				SA-BI-BU-UM		WATERMAN 24 R. 4+	
			ḎABIB		UM				ZA-BI-BU-UM		B 40+	
			ḎABIB	IT	UM				SA-BI-BI-TUM	FN?	HARRIS 100 6	
			ḎABIL		UM				DA-BI-LU-UM		RA LXV 54 XII 20	
	1		ḎAKIR		UM				DA-KI-RU-UM		B 16	
			ḎAKIR		UM				DA-KI-RUM		B 16+	
			ḎAKIR		UM				ZA-KI-RUM		RA LXV 53 XI 22; B 41	
			ḎAKIR		UM				ZA-KI-RU-UM		M	
			ḎAKIR	AT	UM				ZA-KI-RA-TUM?	FN	C	
	1		ḎAKUR		UM				ZA-KU-RU-UM		B 41+	
			ḎAKUR		UM				ZA-KU-RUM		B 41+	
	1		ḎAMAR	AN	UM				ZA-MA-[RA]?-NU-[UM]		TA 1930, 615 28	

SUFFIXES, Class 2

UM	1		ḎAMIR		UM	DA-ME-RU-UM		B 17+
			ḎAMIR		UM	DA-MI-RU-UM		I
	1		ḎANB		UM	ZA-AN-BU-UM		TIM V 33 23
	1		ḎANIB		UM	ZA-NI-BU-UM		BA V 486 NO. 2 5
			ḎANIB		UM	SA-NI-BU-UM		BA V 517 NO. 57 3, 6+
	1		ḎAQAN		UM	ZA-KA-NU-UM		WALTERS,WL 85:4
	1		ḎAQN	IT	UM	DA-AQ-NI-TUM	FN	XIII 1 XIII 22
	1		ḎARʿ	AN	UM	ZA-AR-ḪA-NU-UM	GN	B 48
	1		ḎARAʿ		UM	DA-RA-UM		U
	1		ḎARIʿ		UM	ZA-RI-ḪU-UM		HARRIS 34 12+
	1		ḎIBIB		UM	SI-BI-BU-UM		PBS VIII/2 228 A4
	1		ḎIKR	AT	UM	ZI-IK-RA-TUM	FN	XIII 1 II 50
	1		ḎIMR	AT	UM	ZI-IM-RA-TUM	MN	B 42+, M
	1		ḎINB	AT	UM	ZI-IB-BA-TUM	FN	M+, C P. 38+
	1		ḎIQN		UM	ZI-IQ-NU-UM	FN	RA LXV 61 IV 43
	1	JI	ḎKUR		UM	IZ-KUR-RUM		LANGDON XXIX 24
	1	MA	ḎMAR		UM	MA-AZ-MA-RU-UM		SIMMONS 52 17+, M
		MA	ḎMAR	AT	UM	MA-AZ-MA-RA-TUM	FN	CT VIII 41A 3 4+
		MA	ḎMAR	AT	UM	MA-IZ-MA-RA-TUM	FN	CT II 30 35
	1	JA	ḎRAʿ		UM	IA-AZ-RA-ḪU-UM		XIV 77:8
	1	JA	ḎRIʿ		UM	IA-AZ?-RI-ḪU-[UM]		PBS XIII 56:4
		ME	ḎRIʿ		UM	ME-IZ-RI-JU-UM		M
	1		ḎUHUB		UM	ZU-U_2-BU-UM		VII 194 5'
	1		ḎUBAB		UM	DU-BA-BU-UM		UET V 208 2+
			ḎUBAB		UM	SU-BA-BU-UM		TA 30, 30 32+
			ḎUBAB		UM	SU-PA-BU-UM		RIFTIN 29 23+
			ḎUBAB		UM	ZU-BA-BU-UM		UET V P. 66+
			ḎUBAB	AT	UM	DU-BA-BA-TUM	FN	UCP X/1 87 3+
	1		ḎUNAB		UM	SU-NA-BU-UM		CT IV 44B 5+
			ḎUNAB		UM	ZU-NA-BU-UM		BIN VII 150 9
	1		GAʾAŠ		UM	GA-ḪA-ŠUM		XIV 62:25
	1		GAʾG		UM	GA-GU-UM		HARRIS 5 18+
			GAʾG	AT	UM	GA-GA-TUM	MN?	HARRIS 13 13+
			GAʾG	AN	UM	GA-GA-NU-UM		B 44+
	1		GAʾIL		UM	GA-JI-LUM		RA LXV 51 IX 54
			GAʾIL	AT	UM	GA-I-LA-TUM	MN?	B 17+
			GAʾIL	AT	UM	GA-I-LA-TUM	FN	EDZARD,DER 224:35
	1		GAʾUŠ		UM	GA-U_2-ŠUM		I+
	1		GABAʾ		UM	GA-BA-UM		LANGDON XXX 18
	1		GABIʾ		UM	GA-BI-U[M]		M
			GABIʾ	AT	UM	GA-BI-A-TUM	FN	X 1 3
			GABIʾ	T	UM	GA-BI-TUM		RA LXIV 36 NO. 32
	1		GABN	AN	UM	GA-AB-NA-NU-UM		SIMMONS 107 14
	1		GABUʾ		UM	GA-BU-UM		B 17
			GABUʾ		UM	GA-BU-U_2-UM		M
	1		GAMIR	AN	UM	GA-MI-RA-NU-UM		TA 1931, 538 I, V?
	1		GANAM	AN	UM	GA-NA-MA-NU-UM		TA 1931, 438
	1		GANIN	AN	UM	GA-NI-NA-NU-UM		BIN VII P. 12+
	1		GARAN		UM	GA-RA-NU-UM		B 44+
	1		GARIŠ		UM	GA-RI-SU-UM		B 17
	1		GARUB		UM	GA-RU-BU-UM		B 17+
	1		GAZIZ	AN	UM	GA-ZI-ZA-NU-[UM]		M
	1		GIJD	AN	UM	GI-DA-NUM_2		BIROT,TEA 70 C REV. I 7
			GIJD	AN	UM	GI-DA-NU-UM		SIMMONS 11 1+
	1		GIZZ	AN	UM	GI-ZA-NU-UM		B 93
	1		GUʾAD		UM	GU-ḪA-DU-UM		JCS XXVI 137:24+ HARMAL
	1		GUʾG	AN	UM	GU_2-GA-NU-UM		TA 30, 111 6
	1		GUʾR		UM	GUR-RU-UM MAR-TU		IRAQ MUS. 43488
			GUʾR		UM	GU-RU-UM		UCP X/3 6A 18+
			GUʾR	AT	UM	GU-RA-TUM	FN	C
	1		GUBʾ	AN	UM	GU-UB-ḪA-NU-UM		M
	1		GUBL	AJITUM		GU-UB-LA-JI-TUM	GN FN	SYRIA XX 111
	1		GULL	AT	UM	GUL-LA-TUM	FN	M+
	1		GULZ		UM	GUL-ZUM		TA 1931, 538 VI
			GULZ	AT	UM	GU-UL-ZA-TUM		LANGDON XXIX 22
	1		GUNGUN		UM	GU-UN-GU-NU-UM		B 48+

UM	1	GURGUR		UM			GU-UR$_2$-GU-RU-UM		KISURRA 202 5
	1 ME	KWIN		UM			ME-KI-NU-UM		M+
	1 JA	KWUN		UM			IA-KU-NU-UM		B 27+
	JA	KWUN		UM			IA-A-KU-NU-UM		B 27
	1	KAʾM	AT	UM			KA-MA-TUM	FN	C
	1	KAʾŠ	AN	UM			KA-SA-NU-UM		SIMMONS 128:5
	2	ḪANN		A	KAʾT	UM	AN-NA-KA-TUM		YOS XIII 509:2
	2	ʾEL			KAWN	UM	EL-GA-NU-UM		TA 1931 238
		ʾIL		A	KAWN	UM	DINGIR-KA-NU-UM		MAH II/3 P. 188F
	1	KABAS		UM			GA-BA-ZU-UM		BSM 7900, UR III
		KABAS	AN	UM			GA-BA-ZA-NU-UM		TA 1931,262
	1	KABID	AN	UM			GA-BI-DA-NU-UM		TA 1930,486 OLDER OB
		KABIS		UM			KA-BI-ZUM		B 32
		KABIS	AT	UM			KA-BI-ZA-TUM	FN	C
	1	KABKAB		UM			KA[B-K]A-BU-UM		RA LXV 52 X 77
	1	KABL	AK	UM			KA-AB-LA-KU-UM		B 32
	1	KABŠ	AT	UM			KAB-SA-TUM	FN	M+
		KABŠ	AN	UM			KA-AB-SA-NU-UM		YOS V 18 17
	1	KADAD		UM			KA-DA-DU-UM	FN	BM 17063A 34
	1	KAKK	ATANUM				KA-KA-TA-NU-UM		SIMMONS 104 6
	1	KALAL		UM			KA-LA-LUM		M
	1	KALB		UM			GA?-[AL]?-BU-UM		BIN IX 410 3
		KALB	AT	UM			KA-AL-BA-TUM	FN	RA LXV 61 IV 46
	1	KALK	AT	UM			KA-AL-KA-TUM	MN	CT VIII 12C 1 6 9+
	1	KAMAN		UM			KA-MA-NU-UM		B 45+
		KAMAN	IN	UM			KA-MA-NI-NU-UM		EDZARD,DER 68 IV 11
	1	KAMIN		UM			KA-MI-NU-UM		PBS VIII/1 32 II 6
		KAMIS		UM			GA-MI-ZUM		I
		KAMIS		UM			KA-MI-ZUM		CT VIII 49A 7
		KAMIS		UM			KA-MI-ZU-UM		AJSL XLIV 243 NO. 32
	1	KAMM	AT	UM			KAM-MA-TUM	FN	M+
	1	KANAN		UM			KA-NA-NU-UM		B 45+
		KANAŠ		UM			KA-NA-ŠUM		TIM III 126 15
	1	KANIŠ		UM			KA-NI-ŠUM		RUTTEN 14 23
		KANIŠ	IT	UM			KA-NI-SI-T[UM]	FN	M
		KANIŠ	IT	UM			KA-NI-ŠI-TUM	FN	M+
	1	KANUT		UM			KA-NU-TUM		RA LXIV 43
	1	KAPAŠ		UM			KA?-PA-SU-UM		KISURRA 58 10
	1	KARAN	AT	UM			KA-RA-NA-TUM	FN	CT II 40B 1, M
	1	KAŠER		UM			KA-ŠE-RUM		X 30 3
	1	KAŠIL		UM			KA-ŠI-LUM		HARRIS 69 9
	1	KATR		UM			KA-AT-RU-UM		WATERMAN 14 L.E.+
	1	KIʾL		UM	ʾALLAI		KI-LUM-AL-LA-I	FN	XIII 1 XI 49
	1	KIʾZ		UM			KI-ZU-UM		RA LXV 43 IV 16
	1	KIHIL		UM			KI-ḪI-LUM		M+
	1	KIWN		UM	ʾADAL		KI-NU-UM-A-DA-AL		RA LXV 48 VII 60
	1	KIBS	AT	UM			KI-IB-ZA-TUM	FN	M+
	1	KIBŠ	AT	UM			KI-IB-SA-TUM	FN	RA LXV 56 I 11
	1	KIBUN		UM			KI-BU-NU-UM		TIM III 33 5+
	1	KIKKIN		UM			KI-KI-NU-UM		BM 82437 2 6
		KIKKIN		UM			KI-IK-KI-NUM		B 49
	1	KINAN		UM			KI-NA-NU-UM		UCP X/1 P. 58+
		KINAN	AT	UM			KI-NA-NA-TUM		UCP X/1 27 7+
	1	KIPT		UM			KI-IP-TU-UM		M
	1	KIRB	AN	UM			GIR$_3$-BA-NUM$_2$		U
	1	KIRUʾ		UM			KI-RU-UM	FN	M+
	1	KIRZ		UM			KI-IR-ZU-UM	FN	RA LXV 64 VI 26
	1	KISIBIR	AT	UM			KI-ZI-BI-RA-TUM	FN	RA LXV 61 IV 50
	1 JA	KLIL		UM			A-AK-LI-LUM		HARRIS 28 11
	1	KUʾR		UM			KU-RU-UM		M+
		KUʾR	AN	UM			KU-RA-NU-UM		B 45
	1	KUʾT	AN	UM			KU-TA-NU-UM		RUTTEN 38 20+
		KUʾT	AN	UM			KU-TA-A-NU-UM		SIMMONS 98 14
	1	KUʾUT		UM			KU-ḪU-TUM		UCP X/1 38 9
	1	KUʾZ		UM			KU-ZUM		TA 1931, 327
		KUʾZ	AN	UM			KU-ZA-NU-UM		B 46

UM	1	KUWN		UM				KU-NU-UM		RUTTEN 33 6 SEAL+;M
		KUWN	AT	UM				KU-NA-TUM	FN	C
		KUWN	AN	UM				KU-NA-NU-UM		RUTTEN 1 19+
	1	KUWUN		UM				KU-U$_2$-NU-UM		UCP X/3 1 35
	1	KUBAR		UM				GU-BA-RU-UM		U
		KUBAS	AT	UM				KU-BA-ZA-TUM	FN	RA LXV 58 I 32
	1	KUBB	AN	UM				KU-UB-BA-NU-UM		B 45
	1	KUBS	AT	UM				KU-UB-ZA-TUM		SZLECHTER TJ P. 186
	1	KUBUR		UM				KU-UB-BU-RUM		A.
	1	KUDAD	AN	UM				KU-DA-DA-NU-UM		U
	1	KUKKUB	AT	UM				KU-KU-BA-TUM		VAS IX 175:11
		KUKKUB	AT	UM				KU-KU-BA-TUM	FN	XIII 1 VII 44
		KUKKUN		UM				KU-KU-NU-UM		SIMMONS 111 6 15+
		KUKKUŠ	AN	UM				KU-UK-KU-ZA-NU-UM		M
	1	KULP	AN	UM				KU-UL-BA-NU-UM		TA 1931,148
		KULP	AN	UM				GUL-BA-NU-UM		U
	1	KUMAN		UM				KU-MA-NU-UM		B 45
	1	KUMT	AN	UM				GU-UM-DA-NU-UM		HSM 7936, UR III
	1	KUNAN		UM				KU-NA-A-NU-UM		B 45+
		KUNAN		UM				KU-NA-NU-UM		B 93
		KUNAN	AT	UM				KU-NA-NA-TUM	FN	M
		KUNAB		UM				KU-NA-PU-UM		EDZARD,DER 59:25+
	1	KUNDUL	AT	UM				KU-UN-DU-LA-TUM	FN	M+
	1	KUNZ	AN	UM				KU-UN-ZA-NU-UM		BIROT,TEA 65:17
		KUNZ	AN	UM				KU-UN-ZA-NUM$_2$		TA 1930,181+
	1	KURAŠ	AN	UM				KU-RA-ŠA-NU-UM		LAESSOE P. 53+
	1	KURD	AN	UM				KUR-DA-A-NU-UM		RUTTEN 11 26
	1	KURKUR		UM				KU-UR$_2$-KU-RU-UM		B 49+
		KURKUR	T	UM				KUR$_2$-KUR$_2$-TUM	MN?	PBS VIII/2 178 36
	1	KURŠ	AN	UM				KU-UR$_2$-ŠA-NU-UM		B 45
	1	KUŠAP	AN	UM				KU-SA-PA-NU-UM		TIM III 57 6 66 6
	1	KUŠR	AN	UM				KU-UŠ-RA-NU-UM		SIMMONS 51 17
	1	KUTKUT		UM				KU-UT-KU-TUM		M, KISURRA 37 8+
	1	KUZAB	AT	UM				KU-ZA-BA-TUM	MN	CT VI 30B 23+
		KUZAB	AT	UM				KU-ZA-BA-TUM	FN	CT VIII 43A 4, 10+
	1	LAʾIJ		UM				LA-I-JU-UM		M+
		LAʾIJ	T	UM				LA-I-TUM	FN	RA LXV 58 II 3
		LAʾIŠ	T	UM				LA-ḪI-EŠ$_3$-TUM	FN	C
	1	LAʾL		UM				LA-LU-UM		HARRIS 76 22
		LAʾL		UM				LA-LUM		HARRIS 76 2
	2	GAʾJ		I	LAʾL		UM	GA-I-LA-LUM		M
		KAWJ		A	LAʾL		UM	KA-A-LA-LUM		M
		PAQAḪ		A	LAʾL		UM	BA-GA-A-LA-LUM		HARRIS 69 2+
		ŠUM		U	LAʾL		UM	SU-MU-LA-LUM		PBS XI/2 1 I 16
	1	LAʾUŠ		UM				LA-U$_2$-ŠUM		I
	1	LAḪM	ATANUM					LA-AḪ-MA-TA-NU-UM		SIMMONS 89 10
	1	LAḪAN		UM				LA-ḪA-NU-UM		M+
	1	LAḪN		UM				LA-AḪ?-NU-UM		M
	1	LAWUJ		UM				LA-U$_2$-UM		M+
	2	LA			LABW		UM	LA-LA-BU-[UM]?		M
	1	LABN		UM				LA-AB-NU-UM		TA 1930, 221
	1	LAGIG		UM				LA-GI-GU-UM		UET V 719 2
	1	LAKIŠ		UM				LA-KI-SU-[U]M		UET V 685 28
	1	LALAʾ	AN	UM				LA-LA-A-NU-UM		UCP X/3 2 27
		LALAʾ	AT	UM				LA-LA-A-TUM	FN	M
		LALAʾ	AT	UM				LA-LA-ḪA-TUM	FN	TCL XVIII 121 9
	1	LAMAS	AT	UM				[LA]-MA-ZA-TUM	FN	XIII 1 XIV 6
	2	ʾANN		U	LAMAS	IT	UM	AN-NU-LA-MA-ZI-TUM	FN	RA LXV 59 II 13
	1	LAMR	AT	UM				LA-AM-RA-TUM	FN	YOS XIII 294:18
	1	LAMUM	AN	UM				LA-MU-MA-NU-UM		I; TA 1931,148
	1	LAṬUP		UM				LA-TU-BU-UM		TA 1931,327
		LAṬUP		UM				LA-DU-BU-UM		TA 31, 297
	2	ṢIBʾ		I	LIʾL		UM	ZE$_2$-BI-LI-LUM		HSM 7900, UR III
	1	LIʾR	AT	UM				LI-RA-TUM	FN	A.
	1	LIʾŠ	AT	UM				LI-SA-TUM	MN?	TCL X 38 6
	1	LIWJ		UM				LI-I-UM		TA 1931, 538

UM	1		LIWJ		UM				LI-U_2-UM		M
	1		LUʾL	AT	UM				LU-LA-TUM	MN	BM 16820 2, 11
	1		LUʾUN		UM				LU-U_2-NU-UM		TOTTEN 26 UNPUBL.
	1		LUMM	AN	UM				LU-MA-NU-UM		SIMMONS 94 12+
			LUMM	AN	UM				LU-MA-A-NU-UM		SIMMONS 103 5
			LUMM	AN	UM				LUM-MA-NU-UM		SIMMONS 96 11+
			LUMM	AN	UM				LUM-MA-A-NU-UM		SIMMONS 105 16+
	1	JA	MʾAD		UM				IA-AM-ḪA-DU-UM-KI	GN	M+
		JA	MʾAD	IJ	UM				IA_3-A-MA-TI-UM		U
	1	JA	MWUT		UM				IA_3-A-MU-TUM		U
	1		MAʾJ	AT	UM				MA-IA-TUM	FN	B 34+
	2		ʾAḪ		I		MAʾJ	UM	A-ḪI-MA-IU-UM		MAM III P. 274
	1		MAʾAN		UM				MA-A-NU-UM		KISURRA 22A 17+
			MAʾAN		UM				MA-ḪA-NU-UM		SIMMONS 96 15; M
	1		MAʾD	AN	UM				MA-AḪ-DA-NU-UM		I
	1		MAʾM	AT	UM				MA-MA-TUM		CT XLV 96 18
	1		MAʾN	AN	UM				MA-AḪ-NA-NU-UM		HILPRECHT AV P. 91
	1		MAʾR	AT	UM				MA-RA-TUM	MN?	TIM I 14 3
			MAʾR	IT	UM				MA-RI-TUM	FN	XIII 1 XIII 14
	1		MAʾŠ		UM				MA-ŠUM		M+
	1		MAʾT	AT	UM				MA-TA-TUM	FN	CT II 50 6, 18
			MAʾT	AT	UM				MA-TA-TUM	MN?	LIH 29 9
	2		ʾAHL		UM		MAʾT	UM	[A-LU-UM]-MA-TUM	FN	M
		JA	ḪNUN				MAʾT	UM	IA-UN-MA-TUM	FN	RA L 63
			DANN		U		MAʾT	UM	DA-NU-MA-TUM		CT XLV 12:24
		TA	KWUN				MAʾT	UM	TA-KU-UN-MA-TUM	FN	M, C+
			KIWN		I	Š	MAʾT	UM	KI-NI-IŠ-MA-TUM	FN	M+;C
			KUWN		A		MAʾT	UM	KU-NA-MA-TUM		U
		TA	RʿIŠ				MAʾT	UM	TA-RI-IŠ-MA-TUM	FN	M+, C
			ŠI				MAʾT	UM	ŠI-I-MA-TUM	FN	C+
		TA	TWUR				MAʾT	UM	TA-TU-UR-MA-TUM	FN	M+; C+
		TA	TWUR				MAʾT	UM	TA-DUR-MA-TUM	FN	XIII 1 XIV 34+
	1		MAʾZ	AT	UM				MA-ZA-TUM	FN	KISURRA 21 3, M
			MAʾZ	AN	UM				MA-ZA-NU-UM		UET V 625 9
	1		MAHR	AN	UM				[M]A-AḪ-RA-NU-UM		U
	1		MADAG	AT	UM				MA-DA?-GA-TUM	FN	IX 24 III 22
	1		MAGAN		UM				MA-GA-NU-UM		U
	1		MAGUN	AT	UM				MA-KU-NA-TUM	FN	C+
	1		MAKAL		UM				MA-KA-LUM		BIROT, TEA 72 V 6+
	1		MAKIJ	AT	UM				MA-KI-IA-TUM		A 7724 2
			MAKIJ	AN	UM				MA-KI-A-NU-UM		TA 31, 223
	1		MALIK		UM				MA-LI-KUM		U, B 34+
			MALIK		UM				MA-A-LI-KUM		KISURRA 81A 14
			MALIK	AT	UM				MA-LI-KA-TUM		BM 17060 35+
			MALIK	AT	UM				MA-LI-KA-TUM	FN	EDZARD, DER 91:3
			MALIL		UM				MA-LI-LUM		B 34+
	1		MAMM	AT	UM				[M]A-A[M]-MA-TUM	FN	RA LXV 64 VI 9
	1		MAMN		UM				MA-AM-NU-UM		I
	1		MANAW		UM				MA-NA-UM		I
			MANAN		UM				MA-NA-NU-UM		I
			MANAN	AT	UM				MA-NA-NA-TUM	FN	B 93+
	1		MANIJ		UM				MA-NI-UM		U; TA 30, 615:40+
			MANIJ	AN	UM				MA?-NI-A-NU-UM		TA 1931, 538 II
			MANIN		UM				MA-NI-NU-UM		B 34+
	1		MANMAN		UM				MA-AN-MA-NU-UM		UCP X/3 P. 199+
			MANMAN		UM				MA-MA-NU-UM		B 46+
	1		MANN	AT	UM				MA-AN-NA-TUM	FN	WATERMAN 52 2+, X 2 6
			MANN	AT	UM				MA-NA-TUM	FN	BM 81479 4
	1		MANUW		UM				MA-NU-UM		M+
			MANUW	T	UM				MA-NU-TUM	FN	CT VIII 28A 2, 4+
			MANUW	AT	UM				MA-NU-A-TUM	FN	I (UNPUBL.)
	2		LA				MANUW	UM	LA-MA-NU-UM		I, TIM III 136 4
	1		MARAR		UM				MA-RA-RU-UM		WATERMAN 45 R. 12
			MARAṢ		UM				MA-RA-ZUM		I+, UET V 527 2
	1		MARIʾ	AN	UM				MA-RI-A-NU-UM		B 46
	1		MARṢ	AT	UM				MAR-ZA-TUM	FN	M+

UM	1	MAŠḪ		UM				MA-AŠ-ḪU-UM		M+
		MAŠḪ	AT	UM				MA-AŠ-ḪA-TUM	FN	M
	1	MAŠAL		UM				MA-SA-LUM		EK I P. 40
		MAŠAL		UM				MA-SA-LU-U[M]		HARRIS 95 10
	1	MAŠD	AK	UM				MA-AŠ-DA-KUM		TA 30, 615 6
	1	MAŠIḪ		UM				MA-SI-ḪU-UM		M+
		MAŠIK	T	UM				MA-SI-IK-TUM		BM 17063 26+
		MAŠIK	T	UM				MA-SI-IK-TUM	FN	XIII 1 V 73; YOS XIII 453
	1	MAŠK		UM				MA-AŠ$_2$-KUM		BM 16821 8+
		MAŠK		UM				MAŠ-KUM		EBPN 123+
		MAŠK		UM				MA-AŠ$_2$-KU-UM		M
	1	MAṢIʾ	AT	UM				MA-ZI-A-TUM	FN	WATERMAN 56 R. 8
	1	MAṬAR		UM				MA-TA-RUM		M
	1	MAZN		UM				MA-AZ-NU-UM		MOORTGAT 345
	1	MEʾM	AT	UM				ME-MA-TUM	FN	BASOR 95, 21 I 21
	1	MENG		UM				ME-EN-GU-UM		CT XLVIII 86 REV.+
	1	MENIJ	T	UM				ME-NI-TUM	FN	M
	1	MENN	AT	UM				ME-EN-NA-TUM	FN	XIII 1 V 32
	1	MERḪ		UM				ME-ER-ḪU-UM		M+; YOS XIII 321+
	1	MERR		UM				ME-ER-RUM		M+
	1	MIʾD	AN	UM				MI-DA-NU-UM		U+
	2 JA	MWUT				MIʾR	UM	IA-MU-UT-MI-RUM		RA LXV 52 X 41
		MUT				MIʾR	UM	MU-UT-MI-RUM?		EDZARD, DER 89:4
	1	MIGIJ		UM				MI-GI-JU-UM		RA LXV 40 I 9
	1	MILAL		UM				MI-LA-LUM		BM 16943 36
	1	MILK	AT	UM				MI-IL-KA-TUM		TCL XI 220 11
		MILK	AT	UM				MIL-KA-TUM		YOS XIII 112:16
		MILK	AN	UM				MI-IL-GA-NU-UM		U; TA 31, 148
		MILK	AN	UM				MI-EL-GA-NU-UM		TA 1931, 538 I
		MILK		UM		MA				
						ʾIL		MIL-KUM-MA-DINGIR		A. LATE
	2	ʾIL		A		MILK	UM	DINGIR-MI-IL-KUM		BAHREIN UNP.,POST-UR III
	1	MIMEʾ		UM				MI-ME-U$_2$-UM		M
		MIMEʾ		UM				MI-IM-[ME-U$_2$-UM]		M
	1	MINAN		UM				MI-NA-NU-UM		B 46+
		MINAN		UM				MI-IN-NA-NU-UM		SIMMONS 18 1, 8
		MINAN		UM				ME-NA-NUM		KISURRA 175A 19
	1	MINN	ATANUM					MI-NA-TA-NU-UM		HARRIS 76 11
	1 JA	MRAṢ		UM				A-AM-RA-ZUM		HARRIS 45 10
	1 JA	MṢIʾ		UM				IA-AM-ZI-JU-UM?		M
	JE	MṢIʾ		UM				IE-E-IM-ZU-UM		BIN VII 35:6
	JE	MṢIʾ		UM				E-IM-ṢI-UM		BIN VII P. 11+
	1 JA	MṬAR		UM				IA-AM-TA-RU-[UM]		TIM V 63:12
	2	DINIK				MUʾ	UM	DI-NI-IK-MU-UM		SIMMONS 39 3+
		NANN		A		MUʾ	UM	NA-AN-NA-MU-UM		M
	1	MUʾZ		UM				MU-ZU-[U]M		RA LXV 51 IX 40
	1	MUHR	AN	UM				MU-RA-NU-UM		U
		MUHR	AT	UM				MU-UḪ-RA-TUM		BIROT, TEA 72 I 49'+
	1	MUWIʾ		UM				MU-E-UM		U (MLC 80)
	1	MUNAN		UM				MU-NA-NU-UM		I, B 46+
		MUNAN	AN	UM				MU-NA-NA-NU-UM		B 46
	1 ʾA	MURR		UM				A-MU-RU-UM		U
	ʾA	MURR		UM				A-MUR-RU-UM		CT II 50 21+
	2 JI	DNIK			ʾA	MURR	UM	D-ID-NI-IK-MAR-TU	DN	U
	1	MUŠAḪ		UM				MU-SA-ḪU-UM		UET V P. 50+
		MUŠAḪ		UM				MU-SA-AḪ-ḪU-UM		UET V 722 11
	1	MUT	AN	UM				MU-DA-NU-UM		U+
		MUT	AN	UM				MU-TA-NU-UM		B 46
		MUT		UM		ʾABIḪ		MU-TUM-A-BI-IḪ		TA 1930, 695
		MUT		UM		ʾEL		MU-TUM-E-EL		YOS VIII P. 16+
		MUT		UM		ʾEL		MU-TUM-EL		YOS VIII P. 16+
		MUT		UM		ʾIL		MU-TUM-DINGIR		FRANK 29 4, 10+ M+
		MUT		UM		JARIQ		MU-TUM-JA-RI-IQ		TA 1931, 104, 538
		MUT		UM		MA				
						ʾEL		MU-TUM-MA-EL		TA 1931, 456
		MUT		UM		ME				
						ʾEL		MU-TUM-ME-EL		RUTTEN 32 8+

UM	1		MUT		UM	NIʾŠ	A	MU-TUM-NI-ŠA		TA 1931, 538 III
	1		MUTT	IJ	UM			MU-UT-TI-JU-UM		M
	1	JE	MZUʾ		UM			E-IM-ZU-UM		BIN VII P. 11+
		JE	MZUʾ		UM			IE-E-EM-ZU-UM		B 25+
	1	ME	NḪIM		UM			ME-EN-ḪI-MU-UM		HARRIS 57 17
	1	JA	NḪAB		UM			IA-ḪA-DU-UM		YOS XII
		TA	NḪAB	AT	UM			TA-ḪA-BA-TUM	FN	VAS VIII 127 2, 29
	1	ME	NḪIJ		UM			ME-EN-ḪI-I-UM		XIII 105 8
	1	JA	NḪIB		UM			IA-ḪI-BU-UM		SIMMONS 46 3
	1	JE	NḪIN		UM			IE-EN-ḪI-NU-UM		B 25
	1	JA	NḪUR		UM			IA-AN-ḪU-RU-UM		SIMMONS 103 2
	1	JI N	NWAB	AT	UM			IN-NA-BA-TUM	FN	CT VI 17 13+
		JI N	NWAB	AT	UM			IN-NA-BA-A-TUM	FN	CT VI 1A 3
	1	JE	NWIḪ		UM			E-NI-ḪU-UM		CT VIII 28C 4
		ME	NWIḪ		UM			ME-NI-ḪU-UM		BIN II 94 4+
		MI	NWIḪ		UM			MI-NI-ḪU-UM		YOS XII
	1	JI N	NWIB		UM			IN-NI-BU-UM		M
	1	JA	NWUP		UM			IA-NU-BU-UM		B 29+
	1	JA	NWUR		UM			IA-NU-RU-UM		RUTTEN 11 10+
	1	JA	NWUZ		UM			IA$_2$-A-NU-ZU-UM		U
		JE	NWUZ		UM			E-NU-ZU-UM		I
	1		NAʾJ	AT	UM			NA-JA-TUM	FN	KISURRA 59A:4
	1		NAʾAŠ		UM			NA-A-ŠU-UM	FN	RA LXV 58 I 57
	1		NAʾUL		UM			NA-U$_2$-LU-UM		TA 1931, 297, 538
	1		NAHR	AN	UM			NA-RA-NU-UM		B 47
	2		BIN			NAHR	UM	BI-IN-NA-RUM		CT VI 23 5+
			BIN			NAHR	UM	BI-NA-RU-UM		BIN VII 67 27+
		JA	TWUR			NAHR	UM	IA-DUR-NA-RUM?		RA LXV 48 VII 72
	1		NAʿIM		UM			NA-ḪI-MU-UM		B 36+
	1		NAʿM		UM	DAGAN		NA-AḪ-MU-UM-D-DA-GAN		BM 16824 28+
	1		NAWḪ	AN	UM			NA-ḪA-NU-UM		U
			NAWḪ		UM	DAGAN		NA-ḪU-UM-D-DA-GAN		B 36+
	2	TA	NWUḪ			NAWIJ	UM	TA-NU-UḪ-NA-WI-UM	FN	M
	1		NABAŠ	AN	UM			NA-BA-SA-NUM		BM 17072 9,12+
	1		NABIʾ		UM			NA-BI-UM		TA 1931, 538 V
	1		NABL	AN	UM			NA-AB-LA-NU-UM		U+, B 46+
			NABL	AN	UM			NA-AB-LA-NUM$_2$		U+
	1		NABUṬ		UM			NA-BU-TUM		UET V P. 50+
	2		JIŠʿ		I	NABUʾ	UM	IŠ-ḪI-NA-BU-U[M]		EDZARD, DER 68 III 6
		JI	JṢIʾ			NABUʾ	UM	I-ZI-NA-B[U-U]M?		VAS IX 79 5
	1		NADUB		UM			NA-DU-BU-UM		B 35
	1		NAGIH		UM			NA-KI-ḪU-UM		TIM III 31 17+
			NAGIH	AN	UM			NA-GI$_4$-A-NU-UM		TA 30 615 13
			NAGIŠ	AN	UM			NA-GI$_4$-SA-NU-UM		RUTTEN 2 8+
			NAGIŠ	AN	UM			NA-GI-SA-NU-UM		RUTTEN 5 8
	1		NAKAM	T	UM			NA-KA-AM-TUM	FN	M
			NAKAR		UM			NA-KA-RU-UM		BIROT, TEA 70A II 14+
			NAKAR		UM			NA-KA-RUM		BM 16914 3,11+
			NAKAR	AT	UM			NA-KA-RA-TUM	FN	RA LXV 59 II 71
			NAKAR	T	UM			NA-KA-AR-TUM	FN	M
	1		NAKL		UM			NA-AK-LUM		BIROT, TEA 69 III 2
			NAKL	AT	UM			NA-AK-LA-TUM	FN	YOS XIII 90 REV 22
	1		NAMAL		UM			NA-MA-LUM		HARRIS 7 12
			NAMAL	AT	UM			NA-MA-LA-TUM	MN	B 36+
	1		NAMIŠ		UM			NA?-MI-ŠUM		XIII 1 VIII 47
	1		NAMR	AT	UM			NA-AM-RA-TUM	FN	YOS XIII 163:7
	1		NAN	AT	UM			NA-NA-TUM	FN	RA LXV 65 VI 57
	2		ʾAB		U	NAN	UM	A-BU-NA-NU-UM		B 42+
		ʾA	JPAʿ			NAN	UM	A-BA-AḪ-NA-NU-UM		TA 1931, 374, EARLY OB
			ʿAQB		I	NAN	UM	AQ-BI-NA-NU-UM		B 42+
		JA	JTIR			NAN	UM	JA-TI-IR-NA-NU-UM		M+
			ḪAZAQ			NAN	UM	A-ZA-AQ-NA-NU-UM		CT IV 50A 21
			MUT			NAN	UM	MU-UT-NA-NU-UM		TA 30, 615:39+
	1		NANIB		UM			NA-NI-BU-UM		SIMMONS 138 29
	1		NAPŠ		UM			NA-AP-SU-UM		SIMMONS 36B 6+, M
			NAPŠ		UM			NA-AP-ZUM		SIMMONS 36 7

UM	1		NAPŠ		UM			NA-AP-SU-UM	FN	RA LXV 59 II 47
			NAPŠ	AN	UM			NA-AP-SA-NU-UM		U, B 46+
			NAPŠ	AN	UM			NA-AP-ŠA-NU-UM		U+, I+
			NAPŠ	AN	UM			NA-AP-ZA-NU-UM		CT XLV 115 14
	1		NAQIM		UM			NA-KI-MU-UM		B 36+
	1		NARB	AT	UM			NA-AR-BA-TUM	FN	M+
	1		NASQ	AT	UM			NA-AS-QA-TUM	FN	RA LXV 58 I 38
	1		NAŠʾ	AT	UM			NA-AŠ-ḪA-TUM	FN	RA LXV 61 IV 33
	2		LA			NAŠUʾ	UM	LA-NA-SU-U$_2$-UM		M
			LA			NAŠUʾ	UM	LA-NA-SU-WU-UM		XIV 53:20+
	1		NAŠP	AT	UM			NA-AŠ-PA-TUM	FN	CT II 35 28+
	1		NAṢAB	AN	UM			NA-ZA-BA-NU-UM		TCL I 111 3
	1		NAṢB		UM			NA-AZ-BU-UM	FN	RA LXV 64 VI 25
	1		NATUN		UM			NA-TU-NU-UM		B 36
	1	ME	NDIB		UM			ME-EN-DI-BU-UM		KING LIH I 25 4
	1	JI	NDIN		UM			IN-DIN-NU-UM		I
	1	JA	NDUR		UM			IA-AN-DU-RUM?		TIM II 37 1
	1		NIʾŠ		UM			NI-ŠUM		M+
	1		NIʿIM	AT	UM			NI-ḪI-MA-T[UM]	FN?	C II 42 III 31
	1		NIʿM		UM			NI-IḪ-MU-UM		M+
			NIʿM	AT	UM			NI-IḪ-MA-TUM	FN	M+
	1		NIWḪ	AT	UM			NI-ḪA-TUM	FN	M+
	2		ŠUM		U	NIWḪ	UM	SU-MU-NI-ḪU-UM		B 39
	1		NIGH	AT	UM			NI-IG-ḪA-TUM	FN	M
	1		NIKID	AT	UM			NI-KI-DA-TUM		VAS XIII 65 2,3+
	1		NIKR		UM			NI-IK-RU-UM		RA LXV 45 V 40
	1		NIQM	AN	UM			NI-IQ-MA-NU-UM		B 47+
			NIQM	AN	UM			NI-IQ-MA-A-NU-UM		B 47+
	1	JI	NPIḪ		UM			IB-BI$_2$-ḪU-UM?		VIII 3 19
	1	JE	NQIM		UM			EN-GI-MU-UM		U+
	1	JA	NṢIB		UM			IA-AN-ZI-BU-UM		M+
	1	JA	NTIN		UM			IA-AN-TI-NU-UM		B 29+
		JA	NTIN		UM			A-AN-TI-NU-UM		SIMMONS 79 6'
		JA	NTIN		UM			IA-AN-TE-NU-UM		SIMMONS 104 13
		JI	NTIN		UM			IN-TI-NU-UM		I
		JE	NTIN		UM			E-EN-TI-NU-UM		WALTERS,WL 112:25
		MA	NTIN		UM			MA-AN-TI-NU-UM		HARRIS 31 13+
	2		ʾADAN			NUWḪ	UM	ḪA-DA-NU-U$_2$-UM		M
	1		NUWD	AT	UM			NU-DA-TUM	MN	U
	1		NUWP	AN	UM			NU-PA-NU-UM		SIMMONS 95 10+
			NUWP	AN	UM			NU-PA-A-NU-UM		SIMMONS 103 7+
			NUWP	AT	UM			NU-BA-TUM		YOS XIII 191:8
			NUWP	AT	UM			NU-PA-TUM	FN	BIROT, TEA 70C R II 18
	1		NUWR	T	UM			NU-UR$_2$-TUM	FN	RA LXV 65 VII 21
	1		NUKR	AN	UM			NU-UK-RA-NU-UM		U+
	1		NUMN		UM			NU-UM-NU-UM		BIROT, TEA 65:8
	1		NURNUR	AT	UM			NU-UR$_2$-NU-RA-TUM	MN?	BIN VII 157 7
	1		NUŠUP		UM			NU-ŠU-BU-UM		HARRIS 4 9+
	1		NUṢAB		UM			NU-ZA-BU-UM		M
	1		NUṬUP	AT	UM			NU-DU-PA-TUM	FN	FRANK SKT P. 31+
			NUṬUP	T	UM			NU-DU-UB-TUM	FN	UET V P. 53+
			NUṬUP	T	UM			NU-TU-UP-TUM	FN	UET V P. 53+
	1	ʾA	NZAL	AT	UM			AN-ZA-LA-TUM	FN?	XIII 1 I 14
		MA	NZAL	AN	UM			MA-AN-ZA-LA-NU-UM		UET V 465 17
	1	JA	PḪUR		UM			IA-AP-ḪU-RU-UM		B 24
		JA	PḪUR		UM			IA-AP-ḪU-RUM		TIM IV 33 19, SEAL +
	2		ʾIL		I	PAʾAL	UM	I$_3$-LI$_2$-PA-A-LU-UM		TIM III 44 16+
			ʾIL		I	PAʾAL	UM	I$_3$-LI$_2$-PA-ḪA-LUM		M
	1		PAʾP	AK	UM			PA-PA-KUM		B 37
	1		PAʾR	T	UM			PA-AR-TUM	FN	CT XLV 54 24, M+
	1		PAʾT	AT	UM			PA-TA-TUM	FN	M+
	1		PAGIR		UM			PA-GI-RUM		B 36 HANA
			PAGIR		UM			PA-GI-RU-UM		B 36+ HANA
	1		PAKN		UM			PA-AK-NU-UM		B 37
			PAKN	AN	UM			PA-AK-NA-NU-UM		B 47+
	1		PALAṬ		UM			PA-LA-TUM		TIM III 37 14+

UM	1		PALL	AK	UM			PA-AL-LA-KUM		B 37
			PALL	AK	UM			PA-LA-KUM		YOS XIII 164:1
	1		PALS		UM			PA-AL-ZU-UM		HARRIS 65 18
	1		PALUS		UM			BA-LU-ZUM		TA 30 615 26
	1		PANAN		UM			PA-NA-NU-UM		B 93
			PANAN		UM			PA-NA-NUM		B 47
	1		PANIJ	AT	UM			PA-NI-IA-TUM	MN?	TIM I 11 11
			PANIJ	AT	UM			PA-AN-NI-IA-TUM	MN	UET V 615 9
	1		PANN	AT	UM			PA-AN-NA-TUM	MN?	CT XLV 49 11
	1		PAQAḪ	AT	UM			BA-GA-A-TUM	MN	A 29366:17
	1		PAQID		UM			PA-GI-DU-UM		CT XLV 89 II 32
	1		PARG	AN	UM			PA-AR-GA-NU-UM		B 47
	1		PASAʿ	T	UM			PA-ZA-AḪ-TUM	FN	XIII 1 VIII 81
	2		LA			PAŠIQ	UM	LA-PA-SI-KU-UM		M
	1		PATIḪ		UM			PA-TE-ḪU-UM		HARRIS 53 19+
			PATIḪ	AT	UM			PA-TE-ḪA-TUM	MN?	CARNEGIE CAT. Q B 11
		MU	PATIḪ	T	UM			MU-PA-AT-TI-TUM	FN	C+
	1		PAṬAR		UM			PA-AT-TA-RUM		B 37
			PAṬAR	AN	UM			BA-DA-RA-NU-UM		SIMMONS 31 5
	1		PAṬIR		UM			PA-TI-RUM		M
			PAṬIR		UM			BA-DI-RU-UM		HARRIS 26 7
			PAṬIR		UM			BA-TI-RU-UM		TA 1931,377
	1	JA	PDIJ		UM			IA-AP?-DI-UM		UNPUBL.
	1		PILAḪ		UM			BI-LA-ḪU-[UM]		RA LXV 54 XII 44
	1		PILS	AN	UM			BIL-ZA-NU-UM		BM 80363 8
	1		PIQD	AT	UM			BI-IQ-DA-TUM	FN	XIII 1 X 27
	1	JA	PLAḪ		UM			IA-AP-LA-ḪU-UM		B 24+
	1	JA	PLUS		UM			IA-AP-LU-ZUM		SIMMONS 49 4
	1	JA	PQID		UM			IA-AP-KI?-DU-UM		CT XLVIII 29:2
	1	JA	PTAḪ		UM			IA-AP-TA-ḪU-UM		WALTERS,WL 93:1
	1	ME	PTUḪ		UM			ME-EP-TU-U$_2$-UM		M+
		ME	PTUḪ		UM			ME-EP-TU-UM		M+
	1	ʾA	PTUN	AN	UM			AP-TU-NA-NU-UM		YOS VIII 176 SEAL
	1	JA	PṬIR		UM			IA-AP-DI-RUM		YOS XII
	1	JA	PṬUR		UM			IA-AP-TU-RU-UM	GN	JCS VII 52 II 3
	1		PU		UM	ʾEL		PU-UM-E-EL		BAGH.MITT. IV 291,SEAL
	1		PUḪUR	T	UM			PU-ḪU-UR-TUM	FN	M
	1		PULS	AT	UM			PU-UL-ZA-TUM	MN	TIM III 23 11+
	1		PURUS	AT	UM			PU-RU-ZA-TUM	FN	RA LXV 60 III 60
	1		PUZAR		UM			BU-ZA-RU-UM		TCL I 56 2+
	1	JA	QWIM	AT	UM			IA-KI-MA-TUM	FN	RA LXV 60 III 7
	1	JA	QWUJ		UM			IA-KU-UM		RUTTEN 6:3+; VIII 70:3, 8
		JA	QWUJ		UM			IA-KU-U$_2$-UM		RUTTEN 2:7+
	2		JAMM		U	QAʾD	UM	IA-AM-MU?-QA-DU-UM		III 56 7
	1		QAHIL	AT	UM			QA-ḪI-LA-TUM	FN	C P. 55+
	2		ʾAŠD		U	QAWM	UM	AŠ$_2$-DU-GA-MU-UM		TCL I 130 8+
			BAʿL		UM	QAWM	UM	BA-LUM-QA-MU-UM		RA LXV 40 I 11
	1		QABAL	AT	UM			GA-BA-LA-TUM	FN	CT XLV 117 36
	1		QABIL		UM			GA-BI-LUM		KISURRA 106 15
	1		QADIM	AT	UM			QA-DI-MA-TUM	FN	WATERMAN 39 8+
			QADIŠ		UM			KA-DI-ŠUM		RA LXV 52 XI 2
	1		QADM	AN	UM			GA-AD-MA-NU-UM		U
	1		QANAT	AN	UM			GA-NA-TA-NU-UM		KISURRA 30 7
	1		QANIJ	AT	UM			QA-NI-A-TUM	FN	RA LXV 66 VII 52; C+
		MU	QANIT		UM			MU-GA-NI-TUM	MN?	TIM III 86 6+
	1		QARIʾ		UM			QA-RI-U$_2$-UM		M+
	1		QARN	AN	UM			QAR-NA-NU-UM		B 93+
	1		QAṢIR		UM			QA-ZI-RUM		RA LXV 53 XI 46
	1		QAṬAR		UM			QA-TA-RU-UM		B 37
	1		QAṬR	AN	UM			GA-AT-RA-NU-UM		RUTTEN 14 22
	1	JA	QBIJ		UM			IA-AQ-BU?-UM?		CT IV 30D 11
	1		QIJŠ	AT	UM			KI-SA-TUM	MN	VAS IX 175 5+, M
			QIJŠ	AT	UM			KI-SA-T[U-U]M	MN	M
			QIJŠ	AT	UM			KI-ŠA-TUM	MN	XIII 1 V 19
			QIJŠ	T	UM			KI-IŠ-TUM	FN	XIII 1 III 16
	1		QIDM	AN	UM			KI-ID-MA-NU-UM		U

UM	1 JI	QNIJ		UM				IQ-NI-UM	FN	RA LXV 58 I 34
	TA	QNIJ	T	UM				TA?-AQ-NI-TUM	FN	XIII 1 VIII 74
	1 JI	QRIB	AN	UM				IQ-RI-BA-NU-UM		I
	1 JA	QṢUR		UM				IA-AQ-ZU-RU-UM		BE VI/1 1 22+
	1	QUWJ		UM				KU-IA-UM		YOS XII +
		QUWJ		UM				KU-WU-UM		EDZARD,DER 94:18
		QUWJ	AT	UM				KU-IA-TUM		CT VIII 28A 29+
		QUWJ		UM		HADD	U	KU-UM-D-U		MRS XVI 9:7
	1	QUDAŠ		UM				GU-DA-SU-UM		JCS XXIV 60 NO.51+
	1 JA	RḪAB		UM				IA-AR-ḪA-BU-UM		B 29+
	1 JA	RḪAM		UM				IA-AR-A-MU-UM		M+
	1 JI	RḪAQ		UM				IR-ḪA-KUM		B 22
	JI	RḪAQ		UM				II-IR-ḪA-KUM		SIMMONS 96 10+
	JE	RḪAQ		UM				E-ER-ḪA-KUM		SIMMONS 112 7, SEAL
	1 JA	RḪIB		UM				IA-AR-I-BU-UM		RA LXIV NO.33
	1 JA	RḪIQ		UM				IA-AR-ḪI-KU-UM		A 32133:7
	1 JA	Rʿ IŠ		UM				IA-RI-ŠUM		B 29
	2	LA			JE	RWIḪ	UM	LA-E-RI-ḪU-UM		U
	1 JA	RWIJ		UM				IA-AR-WI-UM	NOM	KUPPER, NOM. P. 199
	1 TA	RJIB		UM				TA-RI-BU-UM		M
	1	RAʾK	AT	UM				RA-KA-TU-UM	FN?	M
	2	MA				RAʾŠ	UM	MA-A-RA-SU-UM		M
	1	RAʾZ		UM				RA-ZU-UM		TA 1931, 538 IV
	1	RAḪIB		UM				RA-I-BU-UM		CT VIII 47A 7
		RAḪIM		UM				RA-I-MU-UM		JCS XXVI 151:21 HARMAL
	1	RAWḪ	AT	UM				RA-ḪA-TUM	FN	XIII 1 XII 6
	2	KANAK				RAWḪ	UM	KA-NA-AK-RA-ḪU-UM		VAS XIII 66A R. 5+
	1	RAWM	AT	UM				RA-MA-TUM	FN	M, CT VIII 1A 2+
		RAWM	AN	UM				RA-MA-NU-UM		B 47
	1	RAJB	AT	UM				RA-BA-TUM	FN	XIII 1 X 59+
		RAJB	AN	UM				RA-BA-NU-UM		RUTTEN 3 6+
		RAJB	AN	UM				RA-BA-A-NU-UM		RUTTEN 13 3, 8, SEAL+
	1	RABAB	AN	UM				RA-BA-BA-NU-UM		KISURRA 187 11+
	1	RAMAM	AN	UM				RA-MA-MA-NU-UM		B 93
	1	RAMIK	AN	UM				RA-MI-GA-NU-UM		TA 1931, 538 II
		RAMIŠ		UM				RA-MI-ŠUM		TA 1931, 538 III, V
	1	RAPAʾ	AN	UM				RA-PA-NU-UM		BM 78768
	1	RAPIʾ		UM				RA-BI-U_2-UM		M+
		RAPIʾ		UM				RA-BI-JU-[UM]?		M
		RAPIʾ	AT	UM				RA-BI-A-TUM	FN	C+
		RAPIʾ	T	UM				RA-BI-TUM	FN	M
	1	RAPUʾ		UM				RA-PU-U_2-UM		RA LXV 41 II 30
		RAPUʾ	AT	UM				RA-PU-A-TUM		A 7660 1
	1 MA	RDAP		UM				MAR-DA-BU-UM		BIN III 546; U+
	MA	RDAP	AN	UM				MAR-DA-BA-NU-UM		U
	1 ʾA	RGAM	AT	UM				AR-GA-MA-TUM	FN	C
	1	RIWḪ	AT	UM				RI-ḪA-DU-UM?		U UNPUBL.
		RIWḪ	AT	UM				RI-ḪA-TUM	FN	XIII 1 I 23+
	1	RIWM	AT	UM				RI-MA-TUM	FN	M+
		RIWM	AN	UM				RI-MA-NU-UM		U
	1	RIJB		UM				RI-I-BU-UM		I
		RIJB	AT	UM				RI-BA-TUM	FN	CT VIII 48B 7+, M+, C+
	1	RIGM	AN	UM				RI-IG-MA-NUM		M
	1 JI	RKAB	T	UM				IR-KAB-TUM	MN	A.+
	1 ʾA	RMAN	UN	UM				AR-MA-NU-NUM_2		TA 1931 , 538 IV
	2	LA			ʾA	RŠIJ	UM	LA-AR-ŠI-U_2-U[M]		TA 1931, 538 IV
	1	RUḪB	AT	UM				RU-UḪ-BA-TUM	FN	XIII 1 IX 46
	2	KANIK				RUWḪ	UM	KA-NI-IK-RU-UM		B 33+
		KANIK				RUWḪ	UM	KA-NI-IK-RUM		B 33
	1	RUWB	AT	UM				RU-BA-TUM	FN	M+
	1	RUWM	AT	UM				RU-MA-TUM	FN	XIII 1 VI 10
	1	RUKAB	AT	UM				RU-KA-BA-TUM	FN	XIII 1 V 33
	1	SANIQ		UM				ZA-NI-ḲUM		M
	1	SATUR		UM				ZA-TU-RU-UM		RA LXIV 34 NO.24
	1	SAṬIʾ	AT	UM				ZA-DI-IA-TUM	FN	XIII 1 I 72
	1	SIKIL		UM				ṢI-KI-LUM		KISURRA 27 11

UM	1		SIKL		UM				ZI-IK-LUM		TIM V 31 19
	1	JI	SRID		UM				IZ-RI-TUM		CT XLV 116 16
	1		SUKIL		UM				ZU-KI-LUM		KISURRA 38 SEAL
	1		SUṬIʾ	AN	UM				ZUM-TI-A-NU-U[M]		TA 1930, 6
	1	JA	ŠḪIR		UM				IA-AŠ-ḪI-RUM		M
	1	JA	ŠJIM	AT	UM				IA-SI-MA-TUM	FN	RA LXV 60 III 8
	1	JA	ŠJIT		UM				IA-SI-TUM		XIII 98 3+
	1		ŠAʾB	AT	UM				SA-BA-TUM		JCS XXIV 57 NO. 42,44
	1		ŠAʾIL	AT	UM				SA-I-LA-TUM	FN	B 37, TIM IV 53 7
			ŠAʾIL	T	UM				ŠA-IL-TUM	FN	U+
			ŠAʾIQ		UM				ŠA-I-GU-UM		RA LXV 54 XII 27
			ŠAʾIR	AT	UM				SA-E-RA-TUM	FN	B 37
	1		ŠAʾL	AT	UM				SA-LA-TUM	FN	CT VIII 20B 9+, M+, C+
			ŠAʾL	AN	UM				ŠA-LA-NU-UM		TA 30, 615 23
	1		ŠAʾQ		UM				SA-KUM		UCP X/1 P. 61+, M
			ŠAʾQ	AT	UM				SA-QA?-TUM	FN	XIII 1 VI 59
	1		ŠAʾR		UM				SA-RU-UM		TIM II 89 2, M
			ŠAʾR	AN	UM				SA-RA-NU-UM		TIM V 19 4
	1		ŠAWIR	AT	UM				SA-WI-RA-TUM		UET V 378 5
	2		ŠUM		U	JA	ŠABAŠ	UM	SU-MU-IA-SA-BA-SU-UM		PBS XI/2 1 I 34
	1		ŠABIM		UM				SA-BI-MU-UM		M+
	1		ŠADID		UM				SA-DI-DU-UM		HARRIS 76 17
			ŠADIR	AT	UM				SA-DI-RA-TUM?	FN	BM 80485 7, 18
	1		ŠADR		UM				SA-AD-[RU]?-UM		RA LXV 53 XI 34
	1		ŠAGAR		UM				SA-GA-RU-UM		GAUTIER 4 R. 4+
			ŠAGAR		UM				SAG-GA-RU-UM		UET V 534 R. 6+
			ŠAGAR		UM				SA-AN-GA-RU-UM		BIN VII 45 12
			ŠAGAR	AT	UM				SA-GA-RA-TUM-KI	GN	M+
	1		ŠAKAN		UM				SA-KA-NU-UM		B 93
			ŠAKAR		UM				SA-KA-RU-UM		HARRIS 39 13
			ŠAKAR		UM				SA-KA-RUM		BIN VII 90 12+
	1		ŠAKIR		UM				SA-KI-RUM		M+
			ŠAKIR		UM				SA-KI-RU-UM		RUTTEN 35 6, SEAL+
	1		ŠAKN		UM				SA-AK-NU-UM		TA 30, 36 2
			ŠAKN	AT	UM				SA-AK-NA-TUM	FN	RA LXV 58 I 27
	1		ŠAKUN	UN	UM				SA-KU-NU-NU-UM		RUTTEN 26 4
	1		ŠALAL		UM				ŠA-LA-LUM		XIII 1 VII 29
			ŠALAM		UM				ŠA-LA-MU-UM		EDZARD, DER 100:16
			ŠALAM	AT	UM				SA-LA-MA-TUM	FN?	M
	1		ŠALIḪ		UM				SA-LI-ḪU-UM		M
			ŠALIL		UM				SA-LI-LUM		TIM III 131 9
		MU	ŠALIM		UM				MU-SA-LI-MU-UM		CT XLVIII 57 2, 3
			ŠALIM	AT	UM				SA-LI-MA-TUM	MN?	CT VIII 49A 46+
			ŠALIM	AT	UM				SA-LI-MA-TUM	FN	XIII 1 VI 46
	1		ŠAM		UM				SA-MU-UM		EBPN 141+, M
			ŠAM	AN	UM				SA-MA-NU-UM		B 47
			ŠAM	AN	UM				ŠA-MA-NUM$_2$		U
			ŠAM	AN	UM				ŠA-MA-NU-UM		I
			ŠAM	T	UM				SA-AM-TUM	FN	TCL I 189 17, M+
	1		ŠAMʿ	AN	UM				SA-AM-ḪA-NU-UM		TCL X 21 21
			ŠAMʿ	AN	UM				ŠA-AM-ḪA-NU-UM		B 93+
	1		ŠAMAK		UM				SA-MA-GU-UM		AJSL XLIV 242 NO. 29
			ŠAMAK	T	UM				ŠA-M[A]-AK-T[UM]	MN	TA 1931, 527
			ŠAMAM		UM				SA-MA-MU-UM		I+, CT VI 44B 12
			ŠAMAM		UM				ŠA-MA-MU-UM		I+
	1		ŠAMIʿ		UM				SA-ME-ḪU-UM		B 38
			ŠAMIʿ		UM				SA-MI-UM		LARSA, KING
			ŠAMIʿ		UM				SA-MU-UM		LARSA, KING
			ŠAMIʿ		UM				SA-MU-U$_2$-UM		RA LII 235, KING
			ŠAMIB	AT	UM				SA-MI-BA-TUM	FN	M
			ŠAMID		UM				SA-MI-TUM		U
			ŠAMIM		UM				SA-MI-MU-UM		BIN VII 154:4+
	3		LU				ḪAJJ	A			
							ŠAMIʿ	UM	LU-ḪA-A-A-SA-MU-UM		UET V 569 8
			LU				ḪAJJ	A			
							ŠAMIʿ	UM	LU-ḪA-A-A-SA-MI-UM		UET V 569 17

UM	1	ŠAMK	AN	UM					ZA-AM?-GA-NU-UM		TA 1931, 538 V
	1	ŠAMŠ		UM					ZA-AM-ZUM		CT IV 47B 20
		ŠAMŠ	AN	UM					SA-AM-SA-NU-UM		SIMMONS 119 23+
	1	ŠAMUK		UM					SA-MU-KUM		CT XLVIII 90 REV.
		ŠAMUK	AN	UM					SA-MU-KA-NU-[UM]		HARRIS 68 21
		ŠAMUL	AT	UM					SA-MU-LA-TUM	FN	M
	1	ŠANAG		UM					SA-NA-GU-UM		JCS IV 109, 3328 2+
		ŠANAGR	AT	UM					SA-NA-AG-RA-TUM	FN	CT IV 47B 27+, M+
	1	ŠANIN		UM					ŠA-NI-NU-UM		SIMMONS 55 13
	1	ŠANQAM		UM					SA-AN-QA-MU-UM		JCS V 89, MAH 15882
	1	ŠAPAQ		UM					SA-BA-KUM		TA 30 28
		ŠAPAR	AK	UM					ŠA-BA-AR-KUM		U
	1	ŠAPIQ		UM					SA-BI-KUM		TCL I 190 4, 5
		ŠAPIR		UM					ŠA-BI-RU-UM		I+
		ŠAPIR		UM					SA-BI-RU-UM		B 37+
		ŠAPIR	AT	UM					SA-BI-RA-TUM	FN	B 37+
		ŠAPIR	AT	UM					SA-PI-RA-TUM		B 37
	1	ŠAPR	AK	UM					ŠA-AP-RA-KUM		M
	1	ŠAPUR		UM					SA-PU-RU-UM		TIM V 19 5
	1	ŠARAM		UM					SA-RA-MU-UM		YOS XII
	1	ŠARIK		UM					SA-RI-KUM		B 38+
	1	ŠARR		UM	ʿADN		U	HU	LUGAL-AD-NU-U$_2$		SIGRIST UNPUBL.
		ŠARR		UM	JAQR	AH			LUGAL-JA-AQ-RA	FN	XIII 1 X 45
		ŠARR		UM	BAWŠ	T	I		LUGAL-BA-AŠ-TI	FN	M
		ŠARR		UM	BAWŠ	T	I		LUGAL-BA-AŠ$_2$-TI	FN	M+
		ŠARR		UM	NIWR		I		LUGAL-NI-RI	FN	XIII 1 XIII 3+
	2	ʾAJA			ŠARR		UM		ḪA-IA-ŠA-RUM		UCP X P. 56+
	JI	JṢIʾ			ŠARR		UM		I-ZI-ŠAR-RUM-KI	GN	SUMER III 79 VI 197+
	JA	KWUN			ŠARR		UM		IA-KU-UN-ŠAR-RU-UM		B 28
	JA	KNUW			ŠARR		UM		IA-AK-NU-ŠA-RU-UM		KISURRA 47A 4+
	1	ŠAṬUḪ		UM					SA-TU-ḪU-UM		UCP X/1 89 28
	1	ŠIJB	AT	UM					ŠI-BA-TUM	FN	M
		ŠIJB	T	UM					ŠI-IB-TU-UM	FN	RA LXV 62 V 50
		ŠIJB	T	UM					ŠI-IB-TUM	FN	M
	1	ŠIJM	AT	UM					ŠI-MA-TUM	FN	M+
	2	ṬAJB			ŠIJM	T	UM		TA-AB-SI-IM-TUM	FN	A. 8 4
	1	ŠIJT	AT	UM					SI-TA-TUM	FN	XIII 1 IV 74+
	1	ŠIBIL		UM					SI-BI-LU-UM		A 21941
	1	ŠIKIR		UM					SI-KI-RUM		YOS XIII 294:4+
	1	ŠILIB		UM					ŠI-LI-BU-UM		HARRIS 36 5
	1	ŠIMʾAL		UM					SI-IM-A-LU-UM	TRIBE	M
	1	ŠINAN		UM					SI-NA-NU-UM		SIMMONS 114 7
	1	ŠIPR	AN	UM					ŠE?-IP?-[RA]?-NU-UM		I
		ŠIPR	AN	UM					ŠI-IP?-RA?-NU-UM		I
	1	ŠIRUN		UM	GAMIL				SI?-RU-NU-UM-GA-MIL?		VII 139 7
	1 MA	ŠKAR		UM					MAŠ-GA-RU-UM		RUTTEN 33 5, SEAL
	1 ʾA	ŠKIN	AN	UM					AŠ$_2$-KI-NA-NU-UM		TA 30 87+
	ME	ŠKIN		UM					ME-EŠ$_3$-KI-NU-UM		WALTERS, WL 95:2
	1 ME	ŠKIR		UM					ME-IŠ-KI-RUM		B 34
	MI	ŠKIR		UM					MI-IŠ-KI-RUM		VAS IX 172 13
	1 JA	ŠKUR		UM					IA-AŠ$_2$-KU-RUM		XIII 1 XI 13
	JA	ŠKUR		UM					IA-AŠ-KU-RUM		XIII 1 XI 19
	JA	ŠKUR		UM					IA-UŠ-KU-RU-UM		TIM III 133 11
	1 TA	ŠLAL		UM					DA-AŠ-LA-LUM		TA 1931, 538 II
	TA	ŠLAL		UM					DA-AŠ-LA-LU-UM		TA 1931, 435
	1 ME	ŠLIB	AT	UM					ME-EŠ$_3$-LI-BA-TUM	FN	YOS V 117 1
	1 ME	ŠLIM		UM					ME-IŠ-LI-MU-UM		HARRIS 31 18
	1 JA	ŠMAʿ		UM					IA-AŠ$_2$-MA-ḪU-UM		M
	1 JI	ŠNUL		UM					IŠ-NU-LU-UM	TRIBE	M
	1 MA	ŠPAR		UM					MAŠ-PA-RU-UM		B 49+
	MA	ŠPAR		UM					MA-AŠ$_2$-PA-RU-UM		SUMER XXIII 153 8, 17, 23
	1 MA	ŠPIR		UM					MAŠ-PI-RU-UM		CT VI 49B 12
	1 JA	ŠPUQ		UM					IA-AŠ$_2$-PU-KU-UM		B 30+
	JA	ŠPUQ		UM					IA-AŠ-PU-KUM		VAS XIII 3 15+
	1 MU	ŠṬAḪ	AT	UM					MU-UŠ-TA-ḪA-[TUM]?	MN	M
	1 MU	ŠṬUḪ	AT	UM					MU-UŠ-TU-A-TUM	FN	C

UM	1		ŠUʾQ	AN	UM				ŠU-GA-NU-UM		EDZARD, DER 90:14
	1		ŠUʾUL		UM				SU-U$_2$-LU-UM		M
	1		ŠUḪ	IT	UM				SU?-ḪI-TUM	FN	XIII 1 II 52
	1		ŠUḪAR		UM				SU-ḪA-RU-UM		TA 30, 249 4
			ŠUḪAR	T	UM				ŠU-ḪA-AR-TUM	FN	M
	1		ŠUBUL		UM				SU-BU-LU-UM		AJSL XXXII 227 4
			ŠUBUL		UM				SU-BU-LUM	FN	RA LXV 58 I 65
	1		ŠUGAG		UM				SU-GA-GU-UM		CT IV 42A 1, 8+
			ŠUGAG		UM				ZU-GA-GU-UM		SIMMONS 72 11+
	1		ŠUKUR	AT	UM				ŠU-KU-[R]A-TUM	FN	XIII 1 V 78
			ŠUKUŠ		UM				SU-KU-SU-UM		M
	1		ŠULAḪ	AT	UM				SU-LA-A-TUM	FN	RA LXV 66 VII 62
			ŠULAM		UM				SU-LA-NU-UM		UET V 608 3
			ŠULAP		UM				SU-LA-PU-UM		PBS XI/2 P. 119
	1		ŠULM	AN	UM				ŠU-U[L]-MA-NU-U[M]		I
	1		ŠULUḪ		UM				SU-LU?-ḪU-UM		UET V 169 18
			ŠULUK		UM				SU-LU-KUM		PBS XI/2 P. 119
			ŠULUL		UM				SU-UL-LU-LUM		PBS XI/2 P. 119
	1		ŠUM		UM				ŠU-MU-UM		TA 30, 615 5
			ŠUM		UM		ʾAB	I			
						JA	RWIM		SU-MU-UN-A-BI-IA-RI-IM		SUMER XXIII 153:9
			ŠUM		UM		ʿAD	U	SU-MU-UM?-ḪA-DU-KI	GN	YOS II 117:17+
			ŠUM		UM		LA				
							ʾAB	I	SU-MU-UM-LA-A-BI	FN	RA LXV 65 VII 24
			ŠUM		UM		MAZAZ		ŠU-MU-UM-MA-ZA-AZ		TA 1931, 538 I, IV
	2		JAʾ		U		ŠUM	UM	IA?-U$_2$-SU?-MU-UM?		XIII 146 13
		JI	JṢIʾ				ŠUM	UM	I-ZI-SU-MU-UM		B 23, M+
			LA			NA	ŠUM	UM	LA-NA-SU-MU-[UM]		CT VIII 26B 22
	1		ŠUMAT	AN	UM				SU-MA-TA-A-NU-UM		GORDON 38 2, 5
	1		ŠUMK	AN	UM				ZUM-GA-NU-UM		TA 1931, 538 IV
	1		ŠUMUḪ		UM				SU-MU-ḪU-UM		BM 16852
			ŠUMUḪ		UM				ZU-MU-ḪU-UM		M
			ŠUMUḪ	AT	UM				ŠU-MU-ḪA-TUM	FN	RA LXV 64 V 58
			ŠUMUḪ	T	UM				ŠU-MU-UḪ-TUM	FN	XIII 1 X 49+
	1		ŠUNAḪ		UM				SU-NA-ḪU-UM		UET V 572 2
			ŠUNAN		UM				SU-NA-NU-UM		TA 30, 30 29
	1		ŠUPUR	T	UM				SU-PU-UR-TUM		PBS VIII/1 45 17
	1		ŠURAR		UM				SU-RA-RU-UM		TIM III 133 14
	1	JA	ŠWUB		UM				IA-ŠU-BU-UM		B 30+
		TA	ŠWUB	AT	UM				TA-ŠU-BA-TUM	FN	M
	1		ŠAʾḪ	AT	UM				ŠA-ḪA-TUM	FN	RA LXV 59 II 75
	1		ŠAWIL		UM				ŠA-WI-LUM		M
			ŠAWIL	AT	UM				ŠA-WI-LA-TUM	FN	M
	1		ŠAWUʾ		UM				ŠA-WU-U$_2$-UM		RA LXV 48 VIII 16
	1		ŠADW		UM		LABW	A	ŠA-DU-UN-LA-BA		M+
			ŠADW		UM		LABW	A	ŠA-DU-UM-LA-BA		M
			ŠADW		UM		LABW	A	ŠA-DU-UM-LA-BU-A		M
			ŠADW		UM		LABW	I	ŠA-DU-UM-LA-BI		M
			ŠADW		UM		ŠARR	I	[Š]A-DU-UM-ŠAR-RI		XIV 106:10, 17
			ŠADW		UM		ŠARR	I	ŠA-DU-UN-ŠAR-RI		M
	1		ŠAKIM		UM				ŠA-KI-MU-UM		HARRIS 91 17+
			ŠAKIM	AN	UM				ŠA-KI-MA-NUM		C
	1		ŠAKUM		UM				SA-KU-MU-UM		B 37+
	1		ŠANIJ		UM				SA-NI-U$_2$-UM		M
	1	T	ŠAQL		UM				ŠA-TA-AQ-LUM		RA LXV 43 III 50
	1		ŠARŠAR	AN	UM				ŠA-ŠA-RA-NU-UM		M
	1		ŠEʾR		UM		MAGUN	U	ŠE-EḪ-RUM-MA-GU-NU	FN	C
	2		NAPŠ		I		ŠEʾR	UM	NA-AP-SI-ŠE?-RUM?		M
	1		ŠIQL	AN	UM				SI-IQ-LA-NU-UM		TA 30, 231+
			ŠIQL	AN	UM				ŠI-IQ-LA-NU-UM		TA 30, 2 4
	1		ŠUʾḪ		UM				ŠU-ḪU-UM		RUTTEN 29 3, 6 SEAL+
			ŠUʾḪ	AT	UM				ŠU-ḪA-TUM		HARRIS 1 3, 6+
	1		ŠUBUL	T	UM				ŠU-BU-UL-TUM	FN	M, C
	1		ŠUKUD		UM				ŠU-KU-DU-UM		M
	1		ŠUQUL	T	UM				ŠU-GUL-TUM	FN	XIII 1 XI 9
	1		ŠURAN	AT	UM				ŠU-RA-NA-TUM	FN	M

SUFFIXES, Class 2

UM	1 JE	ṢJID	AN	UM					E-ZI-DA-NU-UM		I
	TA	ṢJID		UM					TA-ZI-TUM	FN	M
	ME	ṢJID		UM					ME-ṢI-TUM		B 34
	ME	ṢJID		UM					ME-ZI-TUM		XIII 1 VI 29
	ME	ṢJID		UM					ME-ZI-[T]U-UM		M
	1	ṢAJAD		UM					ZA-IA-DU-UM		CT XLV 97 16
	1	ṢAJID	AT	UM					ZA-I-DA-TUM	FN	EDZARD, DER 90:2+
	1	ṢABʾ	AN	UM					ZA-AB-ḪA-NU-UM		CT XLVIII 88 REV.
	1	ṢABIʾ		UM					ZA-BI-UM		OB KING
		ṢABIʾ		UM					ZA-BU-UM		OB KING
		ṢABIʾ		UM					ZA-BI-ḪU-UM		M+
	1	ṢABR		UM					ZA-AB-RUM		YOS VIII 29 3
		ṢABR	AN	UM					ZA-AB-RA-NU-UM		I
	1	ṢABUʾ		UM					ZA-BU-UM	FN	M
		ṢABUʾ		UM					ZA-BU-U_2-UM	MN	M
	1	ṢADUQ		UM					ZA-DU-KUM		B 41
	1	ṢALIL		UM					ZA-LI-LUM		B 41+
	1	ṢAMID		UM					ZA-MI-DU-UM	FN	B 41+
	1	ṢARIP	AT	UM					ZA-RI-PA-TUM	FN	RA LXV 60 III 49
		ṢARIR		UM					ZA-RI-RU-UM		A 7688
	2 JI	JṢIʾ				ṢARIR		UM	I-ZI-ZA-RI-RUM		CT XLV 115 18
	1	ṢARR		UM					ZA-AR-RUM		XIII 1 I 52
		ṢARR		UM					ZA-AR-RU-[UM]		IX 285 1
	2	LA				ṢARR		UM	LA-ZA-RU-UM?		B 33
	1 JA	ṢDUQ		UM					IA-AŠ-DU-KUM		B 30
	1	ṢIJḪ	AT	UM					ZI-ḪA-TUM	FN	XIII 1 VII 35
	2	MAM		A		ṢIJḪ	AT	UM	MA-MA-ZI-A-TUM	FN	RA LXV 61 IV 37
	1	ṢIBʾ	AT	UM					ZI-IB-A-TUM	FN	XIII 1 III 2
	1	ṢIBAR		UM					ZI-BA-RU-UM		RA VIII 69 21+
		ṢIBAR	AT	UM					ṢI-BA-RA-TUM	MN?	OLZ VIII 351 16
	1	ṢIDQ		UM					ZI-ID-KUM		TCL XI 198 23
		ṢIDQ	AN	UM					ṢI-ID-GA-NU-UM		EDZARD, DER 85:45+
		ṢIDQ		UM		MAṢIʾ			ZI-ID-KUM-MA-ZI		X 131 5+
	2	ʾIL		I		ṢIDQ		UM	I_3-LI_2-ZI-ID-KUM		UCP X/1 100 7
		ŠUM		U		ṢIDQ		UM	[SU]-MU-ZI-ID-KUM		B 40
		ŠUM		U		ṢIDQ		UM			
						DITAN		A	[SU]-MU-ZI-ID-KUM-DI-TA-NA		B 40
		ŠARAJ				ṢIDQ		UM	ŠA-RA-ZI-ID-K[UM]		MEISSNER 36 22
	2	KAʾM		A		ṢILL		UM	KA-MA-ZI-LUM	FN	B 33+
	1	ṢIMID	AT	UM					ZI-MI-DA?-TUM	FN	M
	2	ŠARAJ				ṢUWR		UM	ŠA-RA-ṢUR-RU-UM		KISURRA 111 6
	2	LA			KA	ṢUBʾ		UM	LA-KA-ZU-BU-UM		M
	1	ṢUBUʾ		UM					ZU-BU-UM		SIMMONS 50 23+
		ṢUBUʾ		UM					ZU-BU-U_2-UM		SIMMONS 47 21
	1	ṢUPR		UM					ZU-UP-RUM	FN	RA LXV 62 V 9
	1	ṢURAR		UM					ZU-RA-RUM		PBS VIII/2 198 8
	1	ṢURR		UM					ZU-UR-R[U-UM]?		M
	1	TAʾG	IT	UM					TA-GI-TUM	FN	XIII 1 II 45
	1	TAʾL		UM					TA-LU-UM		EDZARD, DER 112:23
	1	TAḪTAḪ		UM					TA-AḪ-TA-ḪU-UM		BIN VII 116 3
	1	TAWIR		UM					TA-E-RUM		KISURRA 73 2+
	1	TABIN		UM					TA-BI-NU-UM		BM 82359
	1	TALAʾ		UM					TA-LA-ḪU-UM		BE VI/2 80 29
	1	TALIʾ	AN	UM					TA-LI-A-NU-UM		TA 1931, 538 VI
	1	TANTAN		UM					TA-AN-TA-NU-UM		SUMER V 141
		TANTAN		UM					TA-TA-NU-UM		HARRIS 11 17, 14 14+
	1	TARAJ	AT	UM					TA-RA-IA-TUM	FN	VAS XIII 14 5+
	1	TIʾAR		UM					TI-A-RUM		B 40
	1	TIʾL	AN	UM					TI-LA-NU-UM		B 47
	1	TIʾŠ	AT	UM					TI-ŠA-TUM	FN	M
	1	TIWR	AT	UM					TI-RA-TUM	FN	M
	2	MATIʿ				TIWR		UM	MA-TI-TI-RUM		BM 67281
	1	TINʾ	AT	UM					TI-IN-A-TUM	FN	XIII 1 VI 4
	1	TISP		UM					[T]I-IS-PU-UM		RA XLI 45 8', HANA
		TISP	AT	UM					TI-IS-PA-TUM	FN	M+, C
		TISP	AT	UM					TI-IS-PA-A-TUM	FN	X 105 3

UM	1	TIŠAN	AT	UM				TI-ŠA-NA-TUM	MN	VAS VIII 58 34+
		TIŠAN	AT	UM				TI-ŠA-NA-TUM	FN	BM 82372, M
	1 ME	TMIH		UM				ME-IT-ME-U_2-UM		M
	ME	TMIH		UM				ME-IT-MU-UM		M
	1	TUʾ	AN	UM				TU-ḪA-NU-UM		UCP X/3 2 26
	1	TUʾM	AN	UM				TU-MA-NU-UM		B 47
	1	TUʾN	AN	UM				TU-NA-NU-UM		TCL XVIII 118 7
		TUʾN	AK	UM				TU-NA-KUM		UET V 285 22
	1	TUBIN		UM				TU-BI-NU-UM		TA 30 103
	1	TUDAR		UM	ʿAŠTAR			TU-DA-RUM-$EŠ_4$-DAR	FN	EDZARD, DER 61:16
	1	TUQAR		UM				TU-GA-RU-UM		UET V 625 10+
		TUQAR		UM				TU-QA-RU-UM		CT XXXIII 42 21
	1	TURM	AT	UM				TU-UR-MA-TUM	FN	M
	1	TUŠAR		UM				TU-ŠA-RU-UM	FN	BM 82212 3
	1	TUŠIM		UM				DU-SI-MU-UM		I
		TUŠIM	AT	UM				TU-ŠI-MA-TUM	FN	RA LXV 61 III 77
	1	TUTUG		UM				TU-TU-GU-UM		SIMMONS 119 21+
	1	TUZAL		UM				TU-ZA-LUM		BM 17049 19+
	1	ṬAJB	AT	UM				DA-BA-TUM	FN	U
		ṬAJB	AT	UM				$ṬA_3$-BA-TUM	FN	M+
	2	LA			ṬAJB		UM	LA-DA-BU-UM		U
		LA			ṬAJB	T	UM	LA-$ṬA_3$-AB-TUM	FN	XIII 1 VI 44+
	1	ṬABIḪ	AT	UM				TA-BI-ḪA-TUM	MN?	BE VI/1 3 3 11
	1	ṬARID		UM				DA-RI-DU-UM		B 17+
		ṬARID		UM				TA-RI-DU-UM		BM 17049 26+
	1	ṬARUD		UM				DA-RU-DU-UM		TCL X 30 11
	1	ṬUḪŠ	AT	UM				DU-UḪ-ŠA-TUM	FN	TCL X 12 12, M
		ṬUḪŠ	AT	UM				TU-$UḪ_3$-ŠA-TUM		UET V 290 2
	1	ṬUBQ	AT	UM				TU-UB-GA-TUM	MN	MEISSNER 11 3
	1	ṬUQM	AT	UM				TU-UK-MA-TUM	FN	RA LXV 65 VII 25
	1	ZAʾAN		UM				ZA-A-NU-UM		SIMMONS 98 8 SEAL
		ZAʾAN		UM				ZA-ḪA-NU-UM		M+
	1	ZAʾR		UM				ZA-RUM		XIII 1 IV 17
		ZAʾR	T	UM				ZA-AR-TUM	FN	M
	2	MALIK			ZAʾT		UM	MA-LIK-ZA-DU-UM		B 34
	1	ZAʾZ	AN	UM				ZA-ZA-NU-UM		RA LXV 47 VII 28; B 48+
		ZAʾZ	AN	UM				ZA-ZA-NUM_2		KISURRA 2A:7+
		ZAʾZ	UN	UM				ZA-ZU-NU-UM		M
	1	ZAḪIL		UM				ZA-ḪI-LUM		HARRIS 12 30
	1	ZAḪZAḪ		UM				ZA-AḪ-ZA-ḪU-UM		B 49
	1	ZABAN		UM				ZA-BA-NU-UM		U UNPUBL., B 47+
	1	ZABIL	AT	UM				ZA-BI-LA-TUM	FN	RA LXV 60 III 50
		ZABIN		UM				ZA-BI-NU-UM		M
		ZABIZ	AT	UM				ZA-BI-ZA-TUM		YOS XIII 175:11
	1	ZABUL		UM				ZA-BU-LUM		A 21950 4 5
	1	ZABZAB		UM				ZA-AB-ZA-BU-UM		B 49
	2	ʿAMM		I	ZAKK		UM	AM-MI-ZA-KU-UM		IRAQ IV 185, A 385
	1	ZAKZAK		UM				ZA-AK-ZA-KU-UM		UNPUBL.
		ZAKZAK		UM				ZA-AK-ZA-KUM		B 49
	1	ZALḪ		UM				ZA-AL-ḪU-UM		RUTTEN 6 23
	1	ZALUḪ		UM				ZA-LU-ḪU-UM		BIN VII 8 5
	1	ZALZAL		UM				ZA-AL-ZA-LUM		B 49+
	1	ZAMIN		UM				ZA-MI-NU-UM		YOS VIII P. 25+
		ZAMIN		UM				ZA-MI-NUM_2		YOS VIII P. 25
	1	ZAMM	AN	UM				ZA-AM-MA-A-NU-UM		B 48
		ZAMM	AN	UM				ZA-AM-MA-NU-UM		B 48+
	1	ZANIJ	AT	UM				ZA-NI-IA-TUM		BM 80496 3'
	1	ZANN		UM				ZA-AN-NU-UM		BIN VII 186 22, M
		ZANN	AT	UM				ZA-AN-NA-TUM	FN	M+
	1	ZAQAT		UM				ZA-KA-TUM		B 41
		ZAQAT		UM				ZA-GA-TUM		KISURRA 112 5+
		ZAQAT		UM				ZA-KA-TUM	FN	RA LXV 61 IV 63
	1	ZARAM		UM				ZA-AR-RA-MU-UM		TIM III 131 4
		ZARAM	AN	UM				ZA-RA-MA-NU-UM		TIM III 24 14
		ZARAM	AN	UM				ZA-RA-MA-A-NU-UM		SIMMONS 99 8 SEAL
	1	ZARNAB		UM				ZA-AR-NA-BU-UM		B 41

UM	1		ZARQ	ATANUM				ZA-AR-GA-TA-NU-UM		JCS IV 110A 19
	1		ZARZAR		UM			ZA-AR-ZA-RU-UM		BM 16835 26+
	1		ZI'Z	AN	UM			ZI-ZA-NU-UM		B 48+
	1		ZIBL	AN	UM			ZI-IB-LA-NU--M		BASOR 95 23
	1		ZIKZIK		UM			ZI-IK-ZI-KUM		B 49
	1		ZILIB		UM			ZI-LI-BU-UM		M
	1		ZINAN		UM			ZI-NA-NU-UM		CT XLV 117 32
	1		ZIRQ	AN	UM			ZE_2-IR-GA-NU-UM		TA 1931,438
	1	MA	ZNIJ	AT	UM			MA-AZ-NI-A-T[UM]	FN	JCS XIX 56
	1	JI	ZNUR		UM			IZ-NU-RU-UM		SIMMONS 48 20+
		JI	ZNUR		UM			IZ-NU-RUM		CT XLV 82 7 25
	1	MA	ZRAQ	AT	UM			MA-AZ-RA-QA-TUM	FN	XIII 1 II 37
	1		ZU'Z	AN	UM			ZU-ZA-NU-UM		B 48
			ZU'Z	AN	UM			ZU-ZA-NUM_2		RUTTEN 9 16
			ZU'Z	AN	UM			ZU-ZA-A-NUM_2		KISURRA 48:12
	1		ZUḪL	AN	UM			ZU-$UḪ_3$-LA-NU-U[M]		TA 1931, 141
	1		ZUBAL	AT	UM			ZU?-BA-LA-TUM	FN	U
	1		ZULAN		UM			ZU-LA-NU-UM		TA 30 35 6
	2	TA	KWUN			ZULAT	UM	TA-KU-UN-ZU?-LA-TUM	FN	RA LXV 62 V 30
	1		ZUNAN		UM			ZU-NA-NU-UM		KISURRA 94 5
	1		ZUNZ		UM			ZU-UN-ZU-UM		RA LXV 48 VIII 4
			ZUNZUN		UM			ZU-UN-ZU-NU-UM		RUTTEN 1 9
	1		ZUQAT		UM	MA		ZU-KA-TUM-MA		EDZARD,DER 152 REV. 11
	1		ZURZUR		UM			ZU-UR-ZU-RU-UM		CT XLV 5 R. 6
			ZURZUR		UM			ZU-UR_2-ZU-RU-UM		KISURRA 20 13+
			ZURZUR	T	UM			ZU-UR_2-ZU-UR-TUM	FN	KISURRA 187 5
			ZURZUR	T	UM			ZU-UR_2-ZU-UR-TUM	FN	KISURRA 187 5

SUFFIXES, Class 3

HA	1			ʾAḪ	AT	A	HA					A-ḪA-TA-A	FN	RA LXV 62 V 52
	1			ʾAJAL		A	HA					A?-IA-LA-A	FN?	M
	1			ʾADM		U	HA					AD-MU-A	FN	U
	1			ʿAD	AT	A	HA					A-DA-TA-A	FN	APN P. 12 LATE
	2	ʾA		RŠIJ					ʿAD	A	HA	AR-ŠI-A-DA?-A	FN	C
	1			BALṬ		A	HA					BA-AL-TA-A	FN	XIII 1 IX 32
	1			KIHIL		A	HA					KI-ḪI-LA-A	FN	M
	2			ḪAʾAN		A			LA		HA	ḪA-A-NA-LA-A	FN	XIII 1 II 53+
	1			MENN		A	HA					ME-IN-NA-A	FN	X 176:8, 15
	1			PAʾL		A	HA					PA-LA-A	FN	B 37
	1			TATT		A	HA					TA-AT-TA-A	FN	RA LXV 60 III 73
	2			KALAL					TULAʿ		HA	KA-LA-AL-TU-LA-A	FN	M, C
HU	2			ʾAJA					ʾAB	U	HU	A-A-A-BU-U_2	FN	DE CLERCQ II 253B
	1			ʾALM		U	HU					ḪA-AL-MU-U_2		SYRIA XXXVII 206 9 HANA
	1			ʾASIN		U	HU					A-ZI-NU-U_2		M
				ʾASIN		U	HU					A-SI-NU-U		APN P. 31 LATE
	2	JI		TWUR					ʾAŠD	U	HU	I-DUR-AŠ-DU-U_2		SIMMONS 90 4
		JI		TWUR					ʾAŠD	U	HU	I-DUR-$AŠ_2$-DU-U_2		M
	2			ḪAʾL		I			ʾIL	U	HU	ḪA-A-LI_2-I-LU-U_2		X 146 5
	1	JA		ʾMUW			HU					IA-AḪ-MU-U_2		B 26
	1	ʾA		ʾMUR		U	HU					A-MU-RU-U_2		PBS VIII/1 98 9
	2			ʾIL		A			ḪAʾL	U	HU	DINGIR-ḪA-LU-U_2		XIII 1 IV 18
			Š	NUʾR		A			ḪAʾL	U	HU	ŠU-NU-UḪ-RA-ḪA-LU-U_2		M+
			Š	NUʾR		A			ḪAʾL	U	HU	ŠU-NU-ḪU-RA-ḪA-LU-U_2		XIV 11:1
			Š	NUʾR		A			ḪAʾL	U	HU	ŠU-NU-UḪ-ḪU-RA-ḪA-LU-U_2		XIV 36:1+
	1			ḪAMBUZ		U	HU					ḪA-AM-BU-ZU-U_2		B 19
	2			ʾIL		I		JI	ḪNUW		HU	I_3-LI_2-IḪ-NU-U_2		UCP X/1 19:4+
	2			RABB		U			ʿAD	U	HU	RA-AB-BU-ḪA-DU-U_2		B 17+
				RABB		U			ʿAD	U	HU	RA-AB-BU-U_2-ḪA-DU-U_2		BM 17051A 30
				ŠUM		U			ʿAD	U	HU	SU-MU-ḪA-DU-U_2		M+
	2			ḪAʾL		I			ʿADN	U	HU	ḪA-LI-ḪA-AD-NU-U_2		M
				ʾIL		A			ʿADN	U	HU	I-LA-ḪA-AD-NU-U_2		M
				ʾIL		A			ʿADN	U	HU	I-LA-ḪA-AD-NU-U_2	FN	C+
				ʾIL		A			ʿADN	U	HU	DINGIR-ḪA-AD-NU-U_2	FN	C+
				JATAR					ʿADN	U	HU	IA-TAR-ḪA-AD-NU-U_2		RA LXV 54 XII 56
				DAWD		I			ʿADN	U	HU	DA-DI-ḪA-AD-NU-U_2		18 R.A. P.61 A 3821+
		JA		MṢIʾ					ʿADN	U	HU	IA-AM-ZI-AD-NU-U_2		BM 81302 4
		JA		MṢIʾ					ʿADN	U	HU	IA-AM-ZI-ḪA-AD-NU-U_2		DELAPORTE CCL II A 385, M+
		JA		MZUʾ					ʿADN	U	HU	IA-AM-ZU-AD-NU-U_2		B 28+
				ŠARR		UM			ʿADN	U	HU	LUGAL-AD-NU-U_2		SIGRIST UNPUBL.
		JI		TWUR					ʿADN	U	HU	I-DUR-ḪA-AD-NU-U_2		TCL XVIII 83 6
	1			ʿAMM		U	HU					A-MU-U_2		EDZARD, DER 90:10+
				ʿAMM		U	HU					ḪA-AM-MU-U_2		EDZARD, DER 68 III 6
				ʿAMM		U	HU		JATAR			ḪA-AM-MU-U_2-TAR		M
				ʿAMM		U	HU		RAPIʾ			ḪA-AM-MU-U_2-RA-BI		M
	2			ʾAJA					ʿAMM	U	HU	A-A-ḪA-AM-MU-U_2		BASOR 95 23
				ʾAJA					ʿAMM	U	HU	A-IA-ḪA-MU-U_2		A 7648, M
				ʾAJA					ʿAMM	U	HU	A-IA-AM-MU-U_2		VAS XIII 34:3
				ʾAJA					ʿAMM	U	HU	A-IA-AM-MU-KU		CT XLV 6 33
				ʾAJA					ʿAMM	U	HU	IA-ḪA-AM-MU-U_2		VAS XVIII 100:19
				JAḤAD					ʿAMM	U	HU	IA-ḪA-AD-ḪA-MU-U_2		M
				ʾALI					ʿAMM	U	HU	A-LI_2-AM-MU-U_2		UCP X/2 58 16
				ʿAQB		A			ʿAMM	U	HU	ḪA-AQ-BA-ḪA-AM-MU-U_2		II 39 14, 16, 24
				ʿAQB		U			ʿAMM	U	HU	AQ-BU-AM-MU-U_2		X 174 3
				ḎAKIR		A			ʿAMM	U	HU	ZA-KI-RA-ḪA-AM-MU-U_2		M+
				ḎIMR		A			ʿAMM	U	HU	ZI-IM-RA-ḪA-MU-U_2		TIM IV 33 SEAL, 34 SEAL
				ṢUWR		A			ʿAMM	U	HU	ZU-RA-ḪA-AM-MU-U_2		M
				ṢUWR		I			ʿAMM	U	HU	ZU-RI-ḪA-AM-MU-U_2		M+
		JI		TWUR					ʿAMM	U	HU	I-DUR-ḪA-MU-U_2		UNPUBL.
	1			ʿAQB		U	HU					AQ-BU-U_2		CT IV 50B 24+
	1	JA		ʿNUW			HU					IA-AḪ-NU-U_2		OIP XLVII 66
	1	JA		ʿZIB		U	HU					IA-AḪ-ZI-BU-U_2		M+
	1			JAMAM			HU					IA_3-MA-AM-U_2		U
	1			JAMM		U	HU					IA-AM-MU-U_2		VAS XVIII 19 R. 6
	1			JAT		U	HU					IA-TU-U_2		YOS XIII 426:14
	2			MATIʿ					JAT	U	HU	MA-TI-IA-TU-U_2		UCP X/3 107 18

HU	3		LA					RIWM					
							JI	JBAL	U	HU	[L]A?-RI-IM-I-BA-LU-U$_2$		M
	1		JID		U	HU					I-DU-U$_2$		RA LXV 65 VI 59
	1		BAʿD	AN	U	HU					BA-AH̲-TA-NU-U$_2$		BM 17060 2
	2		ʾIL		A			BAʿL	U	HU	I-LA-BA-LU-U$_2$		M
			MUT		U			BAʿL	U	HU	MU-TU-BA-LU-U$_2$		RA LXV 44 IV 26
	2		ŠU				JI	BNIJ		HU	ŠU-U$_2$-IB-NI-U$_2$		TA 1931, 636 REV +
	1		BUʾL		U	HU					BU-LU-U$_2$		CT XLV 92 II 13
	1		BUWZ		U	HU					BU-ZU-U$_2$		TCL I 59 16+
	1		BUN		U	HU		PI					
								ʾIL	UM		BU-NU-U$_2$?-BI-I-LUM		UET V 548 2
	1	JA	BZUW			HU					IA-AB-ZU-U$_2$		CT IV 30D 10+
	2		ʾAJA					DAWD	U	HU	A-A-DA-DU-U$_2$		HARRIS 79 5
			ʾAJA					DAWD	U	HU	A-IA-DA-DU-U$_2$		TIM IV 39 15
	1	JA	DLUW			HU					A-AD-LU-U$_2$		HARRIS 70 15+
	1		DUWD		U	HU					DU-DU-U$_2$		M, TCL X 112 8, 22+
	1		D̲IKR		U	HU					ZI-IK-RU-U$_2$		VAS IX 185 12+
	2		ʾIL		A			KABKAB	U	HU	I-LA-KAB-KA-BU-U$_2$		M+
	2	JI	TWUR					KUʾN	U	HU	I-DUR-KU?-NU-U$_2$		VAS XIII 14 R. 10
	1		KUTUL		U	HU					KU-TU-LU-U$_2$		RA LXV 43 III 76
	2		JAʾ		UM			LU		HU	IA-UM-LU-H̲U		UET V 496:10
			H̲AM		UM			LU		HU	U-A-MU-UM-LU-U$_2$		M
			DAWD		UM			LU		HU	DA-DU-UM-LU-U$_2$		M
			D̲IMR		I			LU		HU	ZI-IM-RI-LU-U$_2$	FN	RA LXV 55 XIII 39
		JA	KWIN					LU		HU	IA-KI-IN-LU-U$_2$		TALLQUIST APN 95 LATE
			ŠUWB			NA		LU		HU	ŠU-UB-NA-LU-U$_2$		M+
			TIʾM					LU		HU	TI-IM-LU-U$_2$	FN	XIII 1 VIII 73+
	3		LA					RIWM					
								LU		HU	LA-RI-IM-LU-U$_2$		M
	2		ʾAŠD		I			MAʾK	U	HU	AŠ$_2$-DI-MA-KU-U$_2$		VAS IX 172 30
			MUT		I			MAʾK	U	HU	MU-TI-MA-KU-U$_2$		M+
	2		H̲AM		UM		TA	NWUH̲		HU	A-MU-UM-TA-NU-U$_2$		M
			ŚAQAH̲				TA	NWUH̲		HU	SA-QA-AH̲-TA-NU-U$_2$		CT VI 46 2
	1		NABUʾ			HU		MALIK			U-NA-BU-U$_2$-MA-LIK		M
	2	JI	JṢIʾ					NABUʾ		HU	I-ZI-NA-BU-U$_2$		B 23+, M+
		JI	NBIʾ					NABUʾ		HU	I-BI-NA-BU-U$_2$		A 7685 13
	1		NAMH̲		U	HU					NAM-H̲U-U$_2$		BM 80328 8
	1		NAMZ		U	HU					NAM-ZU-U$_2$		BM 80328 5
	2		MUT		U		JA	NŠUʾ		HU	MU-TU-A-AN-ŠU-U$_2$		KISURRA 91 24
	1		NUMN		U	HU					NU-UM-NU-U$_2$		M
	1		PI			HU					BI-U$_3$		U
	2		ʾAJIŠ					PI		HU	H̲A-II-IŠ-PI$_2$-U$_2$		KISURRA 22+
			ʾAJIŠ					PI		HU	H̲A-A-IŠ-PI$_2$-U$_2$		KISURRA 5+
	1		PU			HU		DAGAN			PU-U$_2$-D-DA-GAN		M
	2		ʾAHL		UM			PU		HU	A-LUM-BI-U$_2$		SIMMONS 129 13
			ʾAHL		UM			PU		HU	H̲A-LAM-BU-U$_2$		RLA II 165 17
			ʾAHL		UM			PU		HU	[A]-LI-IM-BU-MU		OLZ 1958 547 N.1
			ʾAHL		UM			PU		HU	A-LUM-BU-MU		OLZ 1958 547 N.1
	1		QAʾT		U	HU					QA-TU-U$_2$	FN	RA LXV 58 I 47
	1	JE	RBUʾ			HU		ʾEL			E-[IR]-BU-U$_2$-[E]L		KISURRA 152 9
	2		ʾIPQ					RIʿAJ		HU	I-BI-IQ-RI-E-U$_2$		U
			LU					RIʿAJ		HU	LU$_2$-RI-E$_2$-U$_2$		U
			LU					RIʿAJ		HU	LU$_2$-RI-H̲U		U
	1		RIJB		U	HU					RI-BU-U$_2$		KISURRA 187 12
	1		SITR		U	HU					ZI-IT-RU-U$_2$		DE GEN. KICH II C 82
	2		LI			JA		SITR	U	HU	LI-IA-ZI-IT-RU-U$_2$		M+
			RAJB		A			SITR	U	HU	RA-BA-ZI-IT-RU-U$_2$	FN	M
	1		ŚAʾQ		U	HU					SA-GU-U$_2$		SIMMONS 60 31
	1		ŚAM		U	HU					SA-MU-U$_2$		M+
			ŚAM		U	HU		ʾIL	A		SA-MU-U$_2$-I-LA		M
	1		ŚAMIN		U	HU					SA-MI-NU-U$_2$	FN	CT II 46 4
	1		ŚAMUM		U	HU					SA-MU-MU-U$_2$		M
	2		ʾAJA					ŚUM	U	HU	H̲A-IA-SU-MU-U$_2$		XI P.83 N.1+
			ʾAJA					ŚUM	U	HU	H̲A-IA$_3$-SU-MU-U$_2$		M+
			ʾAJA					ŚUM	U	HU	H̲A-IA$_3$-SU-U$_2$-MU		M+
			ʾAJA					ŚUM	U	HU	H̲A-IA$_3$-SU-U$_2$-MU-U$_2$		X 113 4, 11, 14

HU	2		ʿAMM		I			ŠUM	U	HU	ḪA-AM-MI-SU-MU-U$_2$		CT XLVII 30 44
			JATAR					ŠUM	U	HU	IA-TAR-SU-MU-U$_2$		M+
		JI	JṢIʾ					ŠUM	U	HU	I-ZI-SU-MU-U$_2$		A 7646 3+
			MAʾL		I			ŠUM	U	HU	MA-LI-SU-MU-U$_2$		TIM I 29 10
			MALIK					ŠUM	U	HU	MA-LIK-SU-MU-U$_2$		M
		JA	ŜJIM					ŠUM	U	HU	IA-SI-IM-SU-MU-U$_2$		M+
			ṬAJB					ŠUM	U	HU	ṬA$_3$-AB-SU-MU-U$_2$		M+
	3		ʾAJA					LA					
								ŠUM	U	HU	A-IA-LA-SU-MU-U$_2$		M, C
	2		ṬAJB					ṢILL	U	HU	ṬA$_3$-AB-ṢI-LU-U$_2$		TCL X 38 7
	2		ʾABIL					TAʾK	U	HU	A-BI-IL-TA-KU-U$_2$		WALTERS, WL 87:4;105:3+
	1		TURUN		U	HU		GAMIL			D-TU-UR-RU-NU-U$_2$-GA-MIL	FN?	XIII 118 14
	2	JI	ʾLAP					ṬALL	U	HU	I-LA-AP-TA-LU-U$_2$		M
			ʿAMM		I			ṬALL	U	HU	ḪA-MI-TI-LU-U$_2$		M
			ʿAMM		I			ṬALL	U	HU	ḪA-AM-MI-TA-LU-U$_2$		M+
			ʿAMM		I			ṬALL	U	HU	ḪA-AM-MI-TI-LU-U$_2$		M+
	2		ʿAMM		I			ṬILL	U	HU	ḪA-AM-MI-TE-LU-U$_2$		RA LXVI 118:15
	2		MAʾR		U			ZAʾT	U	HU	MA-RU-ZA-TU-U$_2$		CT XLVIII 27
	1		ZAKK		U	HU					ZA-AK-KU-U$_2$		M+
			ZAKK		U	HU					ZA-KU-U$_2$		M
	2		ʿAMM		I			ZAKK	U	HU	ḪA-AM-MI-ZA-KU-U$_2$		M
	1		ZIDAR		U	HU					ZI-DA-RU-U$_2$		VAS XIII 93A R. 8+
	2		ʿAMM		I			ZUʾG	U	HU	ḪA-AM-MI-ZU-GU-U$_2$		BM 17045+
JA	2		ŠUM		U			ʾAḪ	I	JA	[SU]-MU-A-ḪI-IA		PBS XI/2 1 I 27
	2		ʿAD		U	NI		ʾAB	I	JA	A-DU-NI-A-BI-IA		RA XXVII 87 LATE
			ŠUM		U			ʾAB	I	JA	[SU]-MU-A-BI-IA		B 38
	1		ʾADD		I	JA		ʾEL			AD-DI-JA-EL		BAB. III 267 HANA
			ʾADD		I	JA		ʾEL			AD-DI-IA-DINGIR		MAOG IV 2 12 HANA
	2		ʾANN		U			ʾAMR	I	JA	AN-NU-AM-RI-IA	FN	RA LXV 61 IV 47
	2		ʾIL		I			ʾAP	I	JA	I$_3$-LI$_2$-A-PI?-A		TIM III 4 14
	2		ḪAJJ		A			ʾAŠR	A	JA	E$_2$-A-AŠ-RA-IA		M+
			ʾIL		I			ʾAŠR	A	JA	I$_3$-LI$_2$-AŠ-RA-IA		M+
			DAGAN					ʾAŠR	A	JA	D-DA-GAN-AŠ-RA-IA		M+
	2		ʾIL		I			ʾATAJ	A	JA	I$_3$-LI$_2$-A-TA-A-IA		RA VIII 69 26'
	2		BIN					ʾIL	I	JA	BI-IN-I-LI$_2$-IA		RA LXIV 24 NO.8
	1	JA	HWIJ			JA					IA-WI-IA		M
	2		LA				ʾA	HWIJ		JA	LA-WI-IA	FN	RA LXV 60 III 37
	1	JA	ḪJIJ			JA					IA-ḪI-IA		XIV 61:6
	2		ʾIL		I			ḪAṢN	A	JA	I$_3$-LI$_2$-ḪA-AṢ-NA-A-IA		M+
			ʾIL		I			ḪAṢN	I	JA	I$_3$-LI$_2$-ḪA-AṢ-NI-IA		XIII 1 IX 8
	1	JI	ḪLIJ			JA					IḪ-LI-IA		XIII 139 18
	1		ḪABIʾ			JA					ḪA-BI-IA		RA LXV 52 X 71
	2		LA					ʿADN	I	JA	LA-AD-NI-IA		M
	1	ME	ʿANIJ			JA					ME-ḪA-NI-IA	FN	RA LXV 58 I 43+
	2		ʾIL		I			ʿIJN	A	JA	I$_3$-LI$_2$-I-NA-A-A		GAUTIER 40 7
	1	MU	WṢIʾ			JA					MU-ZI-IA		M+
	2		ʾAB		U			JAT	I	JA	A-BU-IA-TI-IA		TCL I 85 10
	1	JI	BWAʾ			JA					I-BA-A-IA		C+
		JI	BWAʾ			JA					I-BA-IA		C II 7 II 3
	2		ʾAJA					BAʿL	A	JA	A-A-BA-LA-IA		SIMMONS 63 9
	2		ʾIL		A			BAWB	I	JA	DINGIR-BA-BI-A		UET V 263 17
	3		ŠUM		U			ʾIL					
								BAWB	I	JA	[SU-MU-I]L-BA-BI-IA		PBS XI/2 1 I 11
	2		ʾIL		I			BIN	A	JA	I$_3$-LI$_2$-BI-NA-A-IA		M+
	1	JA	BLIJ			JA					IA-AB-LI-IA-KI	GN	M+
	2		ʾIL		I			GUML	I	JA	I$_3$-LI$_2$-GU-UM-LI-IA		XIII 1 VIII 45
	2		BIN	T	I			KIʾD	I	JA	BI-IN-TI-KI-DI-IA	FN	A.+
	2		ʾAB		U			LA		JA	A-BU-LA-IA		XIII 101 6
	1		LAʾJ			JA					LA-A-A		U+
	1		LAʾIJ			JA					LA-I-IA		XIII 1 VII 70+
	1		LI			JA		ʾEL			LI-IA-EL		RA LXV 41 II 23
			LI			JA		SITR	U	HU	LI-IA-ZI-IT-RU-U$_2$		M+
	2		ʾAḪ		UM			LI		JA	A-ḪU-UM-LI-A		M
			ʿAŠTAR					LI		JA	EŠ$_4$-DAR-LI?-IA		YOS XIII 12 REV 14
	3		ʾIL		I		JI	ḪTAʾ					
								LI		JA	I$_3$-LI$_2$-IḪ-TA-LI-A		BIROT,TEA 69 I 14

JA	3	ŠUM		A		LA					
						LI		JA	SU-MA-LA-LI-A		BM 80363 1
	1	MAKAJ			JA				MA-KA-A		M+
	1 JI	NDIN			JA				I-DIN-IA		M
	2	KAKK		A		NIʾŠ	U	JA	KA-AK-KA-NI-ŠU-IA		RA LXV 64 VI 35
		KAKK		A		NIʾŠ	U	JA	KA-KA-NI-ŠU-IA	FN	RA LXV 65 VII 44
		ŠUM		U		NIʾŠ	U	JA	SU-MU-NI-ŠU-A		CT VIII 38D:14
	2	DAGAN				NUPAR	A	JA	D-DA-GAN-NU?-PA?-RA-IA		M
	2	ʾIL		A		PAʾŠ	I	JA	DINGIR-PA-ŠI-IA		TCL XVIII 106 9
	2 JA	KWUN				PI	I	JA	IA-KU-UN-BI-IA		XII 14
	JI	KWUN				PI	I	JA	I-KU-BI-IA		SM P. 54
	1 JA	QWUJ			JA				IA-KU-IA		C+
	JA	QWUJ			JA				IA-KU-IA	FN	RA LXV 43 III 49
	2	ʾIL		A		RAWḪ	I	JA	DINGIR-RA[Ḫ]I-A		HARRIS 76 21
		ʾIL		A		RAWḪ	I	JA	I-LA-RA-ḪI-IA		M
	1	RAŠIJ			JA				RA-SI-A		TIM III 134 4
	2	ʾIL		I		ŠIMḪ	A	JA	I$_3$-LI$_2$-ŠI-IM-ḪA-IA		VIII 57 BIS 16
		ʾIL		I		ŠIMḪ	A	JA	I$_3$-LI$_2$-ŠE-IM-ḪA-IA		VIII 57 14
	1	ŠUM		U	JA				SU-MU-IA		B 39+
		ŠUM		U	JA				SU-MU-U$_2$-A		PBS XI/2 1 32
	2 JI	JṢIʾ				ŠUM	U	JA	I-ZI-SU-MU-A		KISURRA 112 7
		QARAʾ				ŠUM	I	JA	QA-RA-SU-MI-IA		CT II 34 5
		QARAʾ				ŠUM	I	JA	GA-RA-SU-MI-IA		CT XLVIII 89 REV.
		QARAʾ				ŠUM	U	JA	QA-RA-SU?-MU-IA		CT VI 43 6
		QARAʾ				ŠUM	U	JA	GA-RA-SU-MU-IA		CT XLV 11 2, 46+
		QARAʾ				ŠUM	U	JA	KA-RA?-SU-MU-IA		CT II 30 3
		QARAʾ				ŠUM	U	JA	KA-RA-SU-LUM		CT II 30 34
	1	ŠI			JA	....			ŠI-IA-N[A-....]	FN	M
		ŠI			JA	TAKAL			ŠI-IA-TA-KA-AL	MN	IX 291 III 37'
	2	ʾAŠIR				ŠI		JA			
						....			A-ŠE-ER-ŠI-IA-[X]	FN	XIII 1 VIII 2
	2	ʾAḪ		I	Š	TUʾ		JA	A-ḪI-IŠ-TU-IA		A. 86 9
	2	ʾIL		I		TUWR	A	JA	I$_3$-LI$_2$-TU-RA-[I]A		RA LXV 40 I 45
		ʾIL		I		TUWR	I	JA	I$_3$-LI$_2$-TU-RI-IA		XII 115 5+
		ʿAŠTAR				TUWR	I	JA	EŠ$_4$-DAR-TU-RI-IA	FN	XIII 1 XIII 33
		KAKK		A		TUWR	I	JA	KA-KA-TU-RI-IA	FN	M
		ŠALAŠ				TUWR	A	JA	ŠA-LA-AŠ-TU-RA-IA	FN	C
JE	1	ʾAḪ		I	JE	MALIK			A-ḪI-E-MA-LIK		M
	2	ʾIL		I		ʾITEJ		JE	I$_3$-LI$_2$-I-TE-E		MEISSNER 110 20, 23+, M
		ŠAMŠ		I		ʾITEJ		JE	D-UTU-I-TE-E		CT IV 44 B 3, 4
	2	ʿAMM		I	Š	ḪARIJ		JE	AM-MI-IS-ḪA-RI?-E?		JEAN, S'A CLXXXVIII R. 3
	2	ʾATTA				BAʿL	I	JE	AT-TA-BA-AḪ-LI-E		JCS XIII 51 293:15,A.LATE
	1	BIN	T	E	JE				BI-IT-TE-E	FN	TCL I 52 11
	2 JI	JṢIʾ				ḎARIʾ		JE	I-ZI-DA-RI-E		B 22+
	JI	JṢIʾ				ḎARIʾ		JE	I-ṢI-DA-RI-E		B 22+
	JI	JṢIʾ				ḎARIʾ		JE	I-ṢI-DA-RI-E-KI	GN	B 22
	JI	JṢIʾ				ḎARIʾ		JE	I-ṢI-DA-RI-I-KI	GN	B 22
	JI	JṢIʾ				ḎARIʾ		JE	I-ZI-DA-RI		TCL XI 218 9
	JI	JṢIʾ				ḎARIʾ		JE	I-ZI-ZA-RI-E		B 23+, M
	JI	JṢIʾ				ḎARIʾ		JE	I-ZI-IZ-ZA-RI-E		B 23
	JI	JṢIʾ				ḎARIʾ		JE	I-ZA-AR-RI-E		UET V 202 15
	1	ḎIMR		I	JE	HADD	U		ZI-IM-RI-E-D-IM		M
	1	KABAS		I	JE				KA-BA-AZ-ZI-E		A.
	2 JI	JṢIʾ				MARIʾ		JE	I-ṢI-MA-RI-E		B 22
	2 TA	KWUN				MITEʿ		JE	TA-KU-UN-MI-TE-E		M
	2	ʾIL		A		RAWḪ	I	JE	I-LA-RA-ḪI-E		M
		ʾIL		A		RAWḪ	I	JE	DINGIR-RA-ḪI-E		HARRIS 85 14
		ʾIL		I		RAWḪ	I	JE	I$_3$-LI$_2$-RA-AḪ-E		VAS XVI 168 9, FRANK 13 9
		KULP		A		RAWḪ	I	JE	KU-UL-PA-RA-ḪI-E		TCL I 14 1, YOS VIII 141 34
	2	LAʾT		I		RAWM	E	JE	LA-TI-RA-ME-E		M
		MUT				RAWM	E	JE	MU-UT-RA-ME-E		BM 81584 3, M+
		MUT		U		RAWM	I	JE	MU-TU-RA-MI-E		CT XLV 63 15
		ŠUM		U		RAWM	E	JE	SU-MU-RA-ME-E		B 40+
	1	SITR		I	JE	HADD	U		ZI-IT-RI-E-D-IM		JCS XXIV 63 NO.56 REV.
	2	ʾAB		I		ŠARIJ		JE	A-BI-SA-RI-E		B 11+; M+
		ʾAB		I		ŠARIJ		JE	A-BI$_2$-SA-RI-E		BIN VII 93 DATE

JE	2	JI		JṢIʾ				ŠARIJ		JE	I-ZI-SA-RI-E		BIN VII 105 12
K	1			ḪIRṢ	U	K					ḪI-IR-ZU-UK		RA LXV 51 IX 44
	1			LA		K		MA					
								ʾIL			LA-AK-MA-AN		B 33
	1			NIQM	U	K					NI-IQ-MU-UK	FN	M
	2	JI		JṢIʾ				PU		K	I-ZI-PU-UK	FN?	M+
	2			ṢIḪAR				ṬALL	U	K	ṢI-ḪAR-TI-LU-UK	FN	PBS VIII/2 252 9, 18
KA	1			ʿAZZ	U	KA					AZ-ZU-KA	FN	M+, C
	1			ʿIZZ	U	KA					I-ZU-KA		XIII 1 III 50
	2			ʾIL	I			JAT		KA	I_3-LI_2-A-AT-KA		TIM III 10 14+
	1			LA		KA		ʾIL			LA-KA-DINGIR		KISURRA 111 5
				LA		KA		ṢUBʾ	UM		LA-KA-ZU-BU-UM		M
	2			ḪIʾD				LA		KA	ḪI-I[D]-LA-A?-KA		XII 141 8
				ḪIʾD				LA		KA			
								ʾIL	I		ḪI-ID-LA-KA-I_3-LI_2		M
				ʾIL	A			LA		KA	I-LA-LA-KA		B 21+
	2			ŠUM	A			LI		KA	SU-MA-LI-KA		BM 80328 13
	1			PA		KA		ʾIL	A		PA-KA-I-LA		B 37+
				PA		KA		ʾIL	A		PA-KA-DINGIR		B 37
				PA		KA		ʾIL	A		PA-A-KA-I-LA		B 37
	1			PASAʿ		KA					PA-ZA-AḪ-GA		HARRIS 31 6
	1			PU		KA		DAGAN			PU-KA-D-DA-GAN		M
	2			ʾAḪ	I	Š		TUʾ		KA	A-ḪI-IŠ-DU-KA		A. 98C 1, 6
				ʾUBUŠ				TUʾ		KA	ḪU-BU-UŠ-TU-KA		A. 268 17
				BAʿL				TUʾ		KA	BA-AL-DU-UḪ-KA		A.
KI	1			ʿAZZ	U	KI					AZ-ZU-UK-KI	FN	XIII 1 VIII 66
NA	1			ʾAŠD	U	NA	JA	RWIM			[$AŠ_2$-D]U-NI-A-RI-IM		CT XXXVI 4 1
				ʾAŠD	U	NA	JE	RWIM			$AŠ_2$-DU-NI-E-RI-IM		RA VIII 65 1
	1			ʾIL	U	NA					I-LU-NA		RA LXV 43 III 80
				ʾIL	U	NA		KIRIŠ	U		I-LU-NA-KI-RI-ŠU		XIII 8 19+
	2			JIŠʿ	I			ʾIL	U	NA	IŠ-ḪI-LU-NA		VII 215 33
				ŠAMŠ	U			ʾIL	U	NA	SA-AM-SU-I-LU-NA		B 38+
				ŠAMŠ	U			ʾIL	U	NA			
								KIMA			SA-AM-SU-I-LU-NA-KI-MA-DINGIR		BM 81047:6
				ŠAMŠ	U			ʾIL	U	NA			
								....			SA-AM-SU-I-LU-NA-QAR-RA-AD		CT XLV 48 5
	1			ʾILL	U	NA					IL-LU-NA	FN	A.
	1			ḪAʾL	A	NA					ḪA-LA?-NA	FN	RA LXV 59 II 74
	1			ʿAD	U	NA		HADD	U		A-DU-NA-D-IM		SYRIA XIX 109
	1			ʿADIJ		NA		ʾIL			A-DI-E-NA-DINGIR		M
	1	JI		ʿZIB		NA					I-ZI-IB-NA		CT XLV 118 24
	1	JA	T	BAḤAR		NA					IA-AB-TA-ḪA-AR-NA	GN	M+
	1			BUWZ	U	NA					BU-ZU-NA	FN	RA LXV 58 I 50
	1			BULM	A	NA		HADD	U		BU-UL-MA-NA-D-IM		M+
	1			KIBS	U	NA					KI-IB-ZU-UN-NA	FN	M+
	1			KUZAR	I	NA					KU-ZA-RI-NA		RA LXV 45 V 22
	1			LA		NA		HADD	U		LA-NA-D-IM		XIII 109 15, 16
				LA		NA		ʾIL			LA-NA-DINGIR		RUTTEN 27 15+
				LA		NA		DAGAN			LA-NA-D-DA-GAN		M+
				LA		NA		ŠUM	UM		LA-NA-SU-MU-[UM]		CT VIII 26B 22
	2			MA				LA		NA			
								DITAN	A		MA-A-LA-NA-DI-TA-NA		B 34
	3			LA			ʾA	HWIJ					
								LA		NA	LA-AḪ-WI-LA-NA		RA LXV 65 VII 19
	1			NAPŠ	U	NA		HADD	U		NA-AP-SU-NA-D-IM		M+
				NAPŠ	U	NA		DAWR	A		NA-AP-SU-NA-D-DA-RA		CT IV 1 8
	1			PUḪR	A	NA					PU-$UḪ_3$-RA-NA		YOS VIII 101B 13
	1			PULS	U	NA		HADD	U		PU-UL-ZU-NA-D-IM		UNPUBL.
	1	JA		ŠJIT		NA					IA-SI-IT-NA		TIM IV 20 SEAL, M
		JI		ŠJIT		NA					I-SI-IT-NA		UCP X/1 58 3
		JA		ŠJIT		NA		ʾAB	U		IA-SI-IT-NA-A-BU		XIII 1 XII 15
	1			ŠAMŠ	U	NA					SA-AM-SU-NA		HARRIS 58 14+
				ŠAMŠ	U	NA		BAʿL	A		SA-AM-SU-NA-BA-LA		A. 77+
	1			ŠIJB	U	NA		ḤARAM			ŠI-BU-NA-A-RA-AM		M
	1			ŠIPQ	U	NA		HADD	A		SI-IP-KU-NA-D-IM		M
				ŠIPQ	U	NA		HADD	A		SI-IP-KU-NA-DA		M

NA	1	ŠUM		NA		JATAR			SU-UM-NA-IA-TAR		RA LXV 52 X 56
		ŠUM	U	NA		ʾAB	I		SU-MU-UN-NA-A-BI	FN	A. 64 7
		ŠUM	U	NA		ʾAB	I		SU-MU-UN-NA-BI	FN	A. 33 3, 34 2+
		ŠUM	U	NA		ʾAB	I		SU-MU-NA-BI	FN	A. 59 8
		ŠUM	U	NA		ʾAB	I		SU-MU-NA-A-BI	FN	A. 244 5, M
		ŠUM	U	NA		ʾAB	I				
					JA	RWIM			SU-MU-NA-BI-IA-RI-IM		SUMER XXIII PL. 7 17+
		ŠUM	U	NA		ʾAB	I				
					JA	RWIM			SU-MU-UN?-A-BI-JA-RI-IM		SUMER XXIII P. 153 9
		ŠUM	U	NA		HALAL			SU-MU-NA-ḪA-LA?-AL		UET V 245 11
		ŠUM	U	NA	JA	JPUʿ	A		SU-MU-NA-IA-PU-ḪA-[....]		M
		ŠUM	U	NA	JA	RWIM			SU-UM-MU-NA-A-RI-IM		HARRIS 57 11
	2	ʾAḪ	I			ŠUM	U	NA	A-ḪI-SU-MU-NA		SIMMONS 83 5
	1	ŠUWB		NA		ʾIL			ŠU-UB-NA-DINGIR		B 40+, M+
		ŠUWB		NA		ʾIL			ŠU-UB-NA-IL		B 40
		ŠUWB		NA		ʾIL	U		ŠU-UB-NA-ḪI-LU		B 40
		ŠUWB		NA		LU		HU	ŠU-UB-NA-LU-U$_2$		M+
	1	TURUM		NA		ḪATK	I		TU-RUM-NA-AT-KI		M+
NI	1	ʾALM	U	NI					AL-MU-NI		RA LXV 48 VIII 7
	1	ʾIL	A	NI					I-LA-A-NI		A. 279 2
		ʾIL	U	NI					I-LU-NI		M+
	1	ḤAŠAK		NI		ʾEL			A-SA-AK-NI-EL		RA LXV 52 XI 6
	1	ḪAWIR		NI					ḪA-WI-IR-NI		RA LXV 45 V 12
	1	ʿAD	U	NI		ʾAB	I	JA	A-DU-NI-A-BI-IA		RA XXVII 87 LATE
		ʿAD	U	NI		HADD	U		A-DU-NI-D-U		MRS VI 15, 42 II 20 UGARIT
		ʿAD	U	NI		ʾIL	A		A-DU-NI-LA		U
	1	ʿAZZ	U	NI					AZ-ZU-UN-NI	FN	M
	1	ʿIZZ	U	NI					IZ-ZU-UN-NI		M
	1	DUWR		NI		ʾIL			DU-UR-NI-DINGIR		M+
	1	LA		NI		ʾIL			LA$_2$-NI-DINGIR		U
	2	ŠUM	U			LA		NI	SU-MU-LA-NI		HARRIS 39 11
		ŠIMAʿ				LA		NI	SI-MA-AḪ-LA-NI		SYRIA XLI 54 N. 1
		ŠIMAʿ				LA		NI	SI-MA-AḪ-LA-A-NI		SYRIA XLI 54 N. 1
		ŠIMAʿ				LA		NI	SI-MA-AḪ-I-LA-A-NI		RA LXVI 112 MARI
	2	ʾALI				ŠARAM		NI	A-LI-ŠA-RA-AM-NI	FN	RA LXV 58 I 54
	1	ŠIMAʿ		NI		ʾIL			ŠI-MA-AḪ-NI-DINGIR		VIII 49 BIS 5'
	2	ʾAḪ	I		JI	ŠMAʿ		NI	A-ḪI-IŠ-MA-NI		VAS VIII 14:41+
	1	ŠUM	U	NI					SU-MU-NI		B 39
	1	ŠUWB	A	NI		ʾIL			ŠU-BA-NI-DINGIR		RUTTEN 41 3, 13
NIA	2	ŠUM	U			LA		NIA	SU-MU-LA-NI-A		CT XLVIII 10 1
	2	ʾIL	I		JI	ŠMAʿ		NIA	I$_3$-LI$_2$-IŠ-MA-NI-A		TA 1930,399
NIE	2	ŠIMAʿ				LA		NIE	SI-MA-AḪ-LA-NI-E		SYRIA XLI 54 N. 1+
		ŠIMAʿ				LA		NIE	SI-MA-AḪ-I-LA-A-NI-E		SYRIA XLI 54 N. 1
		ŠIMAʿ				LA		NIE	SU-MU-ḪA-LA-NI-E		SYRIA XLI 54 N. 1
		ŠIMAʿ				LA		NIE	SU-MU?-ḪI-LA-NI-E		SYRIA XLI 54 N. 1
		ŠIMAʿ				LA		NIE	SI-MA-AḪ-LA-A-NI-E		RA LXVI 115:21;117:11 MARI
		ŠIMAʿ				LA		NIE	SI-MA-AḪ-I-LA-NI-E		RA LXVI 112 MARI
		ŠIMAʿ				LA		NIE	SU-MA-AḪ-I-LA-A-NI-E		RA LXVI 120:7 MARI
Š	1	ʾAḪ	I	Š		TUʾ		JA	A-ḪI-IŠ-TU-IA		A. 86 9
		ʾAḪ	I	Š		TUʾ		KA	A-ḪI-IŠ-DU-KA		A. 98C 1, 6
	1	ʾAB	I	Š		KIWN			A-BI$_2$-IŠ-KI-IN		U
		ʾAB	I	Š		MUM	U		A-BI-IŠ-MU-MU		HARRIS 98 2
		ʾAB	I	Š		TUʾ			A-BI-IŠ-DU		A. LATE
	1	ʾADAN	I	Š		....			ḪA-DA-NI-IŠ-MU-[....]		SIGRIST UNPUBL.
	1	ʾAL	I	Š		TUT	U		A-LI-IŠ-TU-TU		VAS XVI 23 13
	1	ʾAN	I	Š		ḪURB	I		A-NI-IŠ-ḪU-UR-BI		M+
		ʾAN	I	Š		KIBAL			A-NI-IŠ-KI-BA-AL		RA LXV 53 XI 37+
		ʾAN	I	Š		KIBEL			A-NI-IŠ-KI-BE-EL		TCL XX 191 33 CAPP.
		ʾAN	A	Š		KIBAL			[A]?-NA-AŠ-KI-BA-AL		VIII 86 23
	1	ʾANA	I	Š					A-NA-IŠ		RA LXV 52 X 79
	2 JA	NTIN				ʾANN	I	Š	[IA-AN]-TI-IN-A-NI-IŠ		VII 180 8'
	1	ʾELIL	I	Š					E-LI-LI-IŠ		M+
		ʾELIL	I	Š					E-LI-LI-ŠA		M
	1	ʾEN	I	Š		ʾAG	UM		E-NI-IŠ-A-GU-UM		M+
	1	ʾIL	I	Š		BAʾB	A		I$_3$-LI$_2$-IŠ-BA-BA		HSM 7934, UR III
		ʾIL	I	Š		GAʾUL	U		I$_3$-LI$_2$-IŠ-GA-U$_2$-LU		KISURRA 70A 17+

Š	1	ʾIL	I	Š	KUTUL			I$_3$-LI$_2$-IŠ-KU-TU-UL		KISURRA 75A 18+
	1	ḪAʾL	U	Š	MI					
					ʾIL			ḪA-LU-UŠ-MI-DINGIR		M
	1	ʿAMM	I	Š	ḪARIJ		JE	AM-MI-IS-ḪA-RI?-E?		JEAN, S'A CLXXXVIII R. 3
		ʿAMM	U	Š	KI					
					ʾIL			AM-MU-US-KI-DINGIR		A.
		ʿAMM	U	Š	KI					
					ʾIL			AM-MU-UŠ-KI-DINGIR		A.+
	1	BAʿL	I	Š	ʾAG	UM		BA-LI-IŠ-A-GU-UM		RA LXV 45 V 36
	1	BALK	U	Š	RAḪAB			BA-AL-KU-UŠ$_2$-RA-ḪA-AB FN		XIII 1 VIII 61
	2	LABW	A		BIḪR	I	Š	LA-BA-BI$_2$-RI-IŠ		HSM 7936, UR III
	1	BILM	U	Š				BI-IL-MU-UŠ$_2$		RA LXV 45 V 80
	1	DAWD	I	Š	ME					
					ʾEL			DA-DI-EŠ$_3$-ME-EL		UCP X/3 P. 198+
	1	DANN	I	Š	ME					
					ʾIL			DA-NI-IŠ-ME-DINGIR?		I
	1	DUWD	U	Š	ME					
					ʾEL			DU-DU-UŠ-ME-EL		UCP X/3 P. 198+
	1	KIWN	I	Š	LUʾP	A		KI-NI-IŠ-LU-BA		EDZARD,DER 94:17;95:6
		KIWN	I	Š	MAʾT	UM		KI-NI-IŠ-MA-TUM	FN	M+;C
	1	TIWR	I	Š	TUWR			TE-RI-IŠ-TU-UR$_2$		C+
	1	TIBIʾ	A	Š	ME					
					ʾEL			TI-BI$_2$-AŠ$_2$-ME-EL		CT XXXIII 48A 4
	1	TILIʾ	A	Š	GAMIL			TI-LI-AŠ-GA-MIL		UNPUBL.
TA	1	ʾADAM		TA	ʾAR	U		ḪA-DAM-TA-A-RU		WATERMAN 45 EDGE
TI	1	ʾAJAM		TI	ʾIL			ḪA-IA-AM-TI-DINGIR		BIROT, TEA 72 III 5
	1	ʾADAM		TI	ʾEL			ḪA-DAM-TI-EL		HARRIS 61 2
		ʾADAM		TI	ʾEL	UM		A-DAM-TE-LUM		GAUTIER 31 6
	1	ʿANAJ		TI	ʾEL			A-NI-TE-EL		MOORTGAT 309
		ʿANAJ		TI	ʾIL			A-NI-TI-DINGIR		M
	1	JADAʿ		TI	ʾEL			IA-DA-AḪ-TE-DINGIR		UNPUBL.
	1	JAŜAR		TI	ʾIL			IA-SA-AR-TI-DINGIR		M
	1	ŜARAJ		TI	ʾEL			ŠA-RA-TI-EL		TIM III 59 6
		ŜARAJ		TI	ʾEL			ŠA-RA-TE-EL		TIM III 44 18+
	1	ṢABAʾ		TI	ʾEL			ZA-BA-TE-EL		UNPUBL.

4. STEM COUNT

The aim of this chapter (originally called "Root Vocalism") is to present a synthetic picture of all formations or vocalic patterns that occur in Amorite stems. For the definition of "stem" see introductory remarks to chapter 1, "Stems."

Each entry consists of three parts:

1) Lemma, indicated by small consonants and capital vowels, as in cA, cAc, cAcAc, corresponding to the patterns indicated by other scholars as QA, QAT, QATAL or *qa*, *qat*, *qatal* or the like.

2) Stem, plus the number of occurrences of that stem. Thus the stem KA occurs in 10 names (including variants) and ᵓAḪ occurs in 116 names (including variants).

3) Total number of different stems listed that have a given pattern (not the number of occurrences), and the number of times that pattern occurs in the form of a particular stem. Thus the pattern cAcAc occurs in 240 stems. While the main aim of the computer was to count the number of *tokens* (occurring in 240 stems) by *type* (the pattern cAcAc), it also counted the number of its occurrences under each stem, as in the stem *maraṣ*, which occurs in 14 names.

For questionable stem analysis see section 0.3.

Consonantal phonemes are discussed briefly in section 0.4.

We find that there are 1,996 stems altogether, distributed among 1,020 consonantal roots. See also the introductory remarks to chapter 2, "Roots."

The most common patterns are:

cAcAc	240	cIcc	165
cAcIc	225	cUcAc	94
cAcUc	98	cUcIc	15
cAcc	298	cUcUc	74
cAccAc	26	cUcc	144
cIcAc	55	ccAc	67
cIcIc	38	ccIc	146
cIcUc	21	ccUc	97

The lemmata are given in the order of the roman alphabet with some grouping by classes. The stems are listed in the new order discussed in section 0.5:

ᵓ	H	Ḥ	Ḫ	ᶜ	W	J	
A	B	D	D̮	E	G	I	
K	L	M	N	P	Q	R	
S	Ś	Š	Ṣ	T	Ṭ	U	Z

cA	KA	10	LA	133	MA	83	PA	13	ŠA	2								
	Total cA	5																
cAc	ʾAḪ	116	ʾAJ	2	ʾAB	235	ʾAG	3	ʾAK	11	ʾAL	2	ʾAM	5	ʾAN	4	ʾAP	3
	ʾAR	2	ḤAM	40	ʿAD	25	ʿAN	45	JAʾ	19	JAD	4	JAM	5	JAT	40	DAʿ	9
	DAM	3	MAM	15	NAN	15	ŚAM	43	ŠAL	1	ŠAT	2	TAʾ	4				
	Total cAc	25																
cAcA	ʾAJA	51	ʾANA	12	JAJA	2	KALA	2	KAMA	4	LAMA	9						
	Total cAcA	6																
cAcAc	ʾAḪAL	1	ʾAWAʾ	4	ʾAJAK	2	ʾAJAL	10	ʾAJAM	5	ʾAJAN	8	ʾABAB	4	ʾABAL	1	ʾABAN	3
	ʾABAQ	1	ʾABAŚ	1	ʾADAʾ	2	ʾADAD	1	ʾADAL	1	ʾADAM	7	ʾADAN	6	ʾAKAN	1	ʾALAK	1
	ʾALAM	1	ʾALAŚ	2	ʾAMAL	1	ʾAMAN	7	ʾAMAR	6	ʾAMAT	2	ʾANAZ	1	ʾARAḪ	2	ʾARAM	4
	ʾARAŚ	1	ʾAŚAL	1	ʾAŚAŚ	1	ʾAŠAR	14	ʾATAJ	1	ʾATAL	4	ʾATAM	3	ʾATAR	2	ʾATAZ	2
	HALAL	1	ḤABAS	1	ḤAKAM	2	ḤALAJ	1	ḤALAB	2	ḤALAṢ	3	ḤAMAD	4	ḤANAN	6	ḤARAB	3
	ḤARAM	1	ḤASAD	2	ḤAŚAK	1	ḤAṢAN	4	ḤAZAQ	4	ḪAʾAN	2	ḪAʾAZ	1	ḪABAD	3	ḪALAN	1
	ḪAMAŚ	1	ḪAMAṬ	1	ḪANAŠ	1	ḪAQAT	1	ḪARAR	4	ḪAŚAM	1	ḪATAʾ	2	ḪATAN	2	ʿAḎAR	10
	ʿAGAL	3	ʿALAṢ	3	ʿAMAS	2	ʿANAJ	2	ʿANAQ	2	ʿAQAB	1	ʿARAD	1	ʿAZAB	2	ʿAZAL	9
	ʿAZAZ	2	JAʾAN	5	JAʾAR	10	JAḤAD	16	JAʿAL	2	JAJAM	1	JABAL	13	JABAŚ	3	JADAʿ	18
	JAKAL	2	JAMAM	4	JAMAN	1	JAPAR	3	JAQAR	10	JARAḪ	102	JARAN	1	JAŚAR	10	JAŠAB	1
	JATAM	3	JATAR	56	BAʾAN	3	BAʾAT	1	BAḤAR	1	BAJAN	1	BAKAL	2	BALAL	1	BALAṬ	3
	BAQAQ	1	BAŚAJ	1	BAŚAR	5	BAZAZ	1	DAGAN	118	DAGAZ	1	DALAQ	1	DARAB	1	DARAN	1
	ḎABAB	1	ḎAKAJ	1	ḎAMAR	3	ḎANAB	1	ḎAQAN	1	ḎARAʿ	2	GAʾAŠ	1	GABAʾ	1	GALAZ	1
	GANAM	1	GARAN	1	KAʾAM	2	KAHAL	5	KABAR	1	KABAS	3	KADAD	2	KALAL	2	KAMAN	2
	KANAK	3	KANAN	1	KANAP	1	KANAŚ	2	KANAT	2	KAPAŚ	1	KARAN	2	KAŚAJ	1	KAŠAR	1
	KATAZ	1	LAʾAT	1	LAḪAN	2	LABAN	3	LALAʾ	4	LAMAS	9	MAʾAN	4	MAHAR	1	MADAG	1
	MAGAN	2	MAKAJ	2	MAKAL	2	MALAK	5	MANAW	2	MANAN	7	MAQAṬ	1	MARAQ	1	MARAR	1
	MARAṢ	14	MAŚAL	2	MATAʿ	1	MATAN	2	MATAQ	1	MAṬAR	22	MAZAʾ	1	MAZAL	1	MAZAZ	1
	NAʾAŠ	1	NAḪAL	1	NAḪAR	1	NAWAR	6	NAJAL	1	NABAʾ	2	NABAŚ	1	NAKAM	1	NAKAR	5
	NAMAL	2	NAMAŠ	2	NAṢAB	1	PAʾAL	2	PAʾAR	2	PADAL	1	PALAṬ	1	PANAN	3	PAQAḪ	2
	PASAʿ	2	PATAḪ	1	PAṬAR	2	QABAL	1	QANAT	1	QARAʾ	6	QARAD	1	QAṬAN	6	QAṬAR	16
	RAḪAB	2	RAḪAṢ	1	RABAʿ	1	RABAB	2	RAMAM	1	RAMAŠ	2	RAPAʾ	2	RAŚAP	4	RAṢAJ	1
	ŚAʾAD	1	ŚAʾAL	1	ŚABAŚ	1	ŚAGAR	8	ŚAKAN	1	ŚAKAR	2	ŚALAL	1	ŚALAM	3	ŚAMAʿ	4
	ŚAMAK	3	ŚAMAM	2	ŚAMAR	17	ŚAMAŚ	1	ŚAMAT	1	ŚANAG	1	ŚAPAQ	1	ŚAPAR	9	ŚAQAḪ	1
	ŚARAJ	4	ŚARAM	4	ŚATAM	1	ŚAṬAR	1	ŠAWAB	2	ŠALAŠ	4	ŠAMAR	4	ŠAPAṬ	1	ṢAJAD	3
	ṢABAʾ	3	ṢADAQ	1	TADAB	1	TAKAL	1	TALAʾ	1	TAMAR	3	TARAJ	1	ZAʾAN	3	ZAʾAZ	1
	ZABAN	1	ZALAT	2	ZAMAʾ	1	ZANAN	2	ZAQAT	4	ZARAM	3						
	Total cAcAc	240																
cAcAcA	ZABABA	1																
	Total cAcAcA	1																
cAcAcU	ʾANAKU	2																
	Total cAcAcU	1																
cAcAcc	ʾARAPḪ	1	ŚANAGR	1														
	Total cAcAcc	2																
cAcEc	BAʾEL	1	KAŠER	2														
	Total cAcEc	2																
cAcI	ʾAJI	1	ʾALI	18	NAZI	3												
	Total cAcI	3																
cAcIc	ʾAḪIḎ	1	ʾAḪIL	1	ʾAWIJ	6	ʾAWIN	2	ʾAJIŠ	4	ʾABIḪ	5	ʾABIL	1	ʾABIŚ	1	ʾADID	3
	ʾAGIG	2	ʾAKIN	1	ʾAKIR	3	ʾALIK	3	ʾALIM	2	ʾALIP	2	ʾAMIN	8	ʾAMIR	7	ʾARIŚ	1
	ʾASIN	5	ʾAŚIJ	1	ʾAŚIN	2	ʾAŚIR	3	ʾAŠIḪ	2	ʾAŠIR	4	ʾATIM	3	HALIL	8	ḤABIB	2
	ḤABIS	3	ḤALIṢ	3	ḤAMID	2	ḤANIN	2	ḤARIB	3	ḤASID	3	ḤAŚIK	1	ḤATIK	1	ḤAZIQ	1
	ḪAWIR	1	ḪABIʾ	3	ḪABIR	2	ḪAGIR	1	ḪAPIʾ	1	ḪARIJ	1	ḪARIR	3	ḪAŚIJ	1	ḪAŠIŠ	1
	ḪATIʾ	5	ḪAZIM	1	ʿAWIQ	2	ʿADIJ	4	ʿAḎIR	12	ʿALIJ	15	ʿAMIQ	1	ʿAMIS	2	ʿANIJ	4
	ʿARIṢ	2	ʿAZIB	3	ʿAZIZ	1	JAʾIT	1	JAʿIL	12	JADID	9	JAMIN	9	JANIN	1	JARIN	2
	JARIQ	1	JAŠIʿ	1	BAʾIL	3	BAḤIR	1	BADID	1	BAGIN	2	BAKIL	3	BAKIR	1	BALIK	2

	BALIL	3	BALIṬ	2	BANIḪ	1	BANIJ	9	BARIL	1	BAŠIJ	1	BAŠIR	1	BAZIḪ	1	BAZIN	3
	DAWIR	1	DABIʾ	1	DABIN	1	DAMIQ	2	DARIK	3	DAŠIK	1	DAŠIL	1	ḎABIB	4	ḎABIL	1
	ḎAKIR	10	ḎAMIR	3	ḎANIB	2	ḎARIʾ	8	ḎARIʿ	2	GAʾIL	3	GAJID	2	GABIʾ	5	GAMIL	4
	GAMIR	1	GANIB	1	GANIN	1	GARIŠ	2	GAZIZ	1	KABID	6	KABIS	2	KAMIN	1	KAMIS	3
	KANIK	4	KANIŠ	5	KARIT	1	KASIJ	1	KAŠIL	1	KATIR	1	KAZIB	2	KAZIR	1	LAʾIJ	7
	LAʾIP	2	LAʾIŠ	1	LABIN	1	LAGIG	1	LAKIŠ	1	LASIM	3	LAŠIK	1	MAHIR	2	MAKIJ	3
	MALIK	38	MALIL	1	MANIJ	5	MANIN	2	MARIʾ	2	MAŠIḤ	4	MAŠIK	3	MAṢIʾ	2	MATIʿ	7
	MATIN	1	MATIQ	1	NAʿIM	5	NAWIJ	2	NABIʾ	11	NABIB	1	NABIT	2	NADIN	1	NAGIH	4
	NAGIŠ	2	NAMIŠ	3	NANIB	2	NAQIM	4	NAŠIʾ	4	NAṢIR	3	PAḪIR	1	PAGIR	2	PALIS	1
	PANIJ	4	PAQID	1	PAŠIQ	1	PATIḤ	8	PAṬIR	3	QAHIL	1	QABIL	1	QADIM	3	QADIŠ	1
	QANIJ	2	QANIT	1	QARIʾ	2	QAṢIR	1	QAZIJ	1	RAḪIB	1	RAḪIM	2	RAMIK	1	RAMIŠ	1
	RAPIʾ	54	RAŠIJ	1	RAṢIJ	3	RAZIN	1	SANIQ	1	SAṬIʾ	6	ŠAʾIL	2	ŠAʾIQ	1	ŠAʾIR	2
	ŠAḪIR	2	ŠAWIR	2	ŠABIM	3	ŠADID	1	ŠADIR	1	ŠAKIR	5	ŠALIḤ	3	ŠALIL	2	ŠALIM	23
	ŠAMIʿ	7	ŠAMIB	1	ŠAMID	2	ŠAMIM	2	ŠAMIN	1	ŠAMIR	1	ŠANIN	1	ŠAPIQ	1	ŠAPIR	6
	ŠARIḤ	1	ŠARIJ	4	ŠARIK	2	ŠAṬIḤ	1	ŠAWIL	2	ŠAGIŠ	4	ŠAKIM	6	ŠANIJ	5	ṢAJID	2
	ṢABIʾ	6	ṢALIL	2	ṢAMID	2	ṢARIP	1	ṢARIR	2	TAʾIL	1	TAWIR	2	TABIN	1	TALIʾ	1
	ṬABIḪ	1	ṬARID	3	ZAḪIL	1	ZABIL	2	ZABIN	1	ZABIZ	1	ZALIJ	1	ZAMIN	2	ZANIJ	1
	Total cAcIc	225																
cAcU	LAŠU	4																
	Total cAcU	1																
cAcUc	ʾADUD	1	ʾADUN	7	ʾAKUN	6	ʾALUʾ	2	ʾALUN	6	ʾALUP	3	ʾAMUM	1	ʾAMUR	2	ʾARUḪ	1
	ʾARUM	1	ʾARUŠ	5	ʾASUN	1	ʾAŠUD	1	ʾAŠUL	1	ʾAŠUR	2	ʾAŠUZ	1	ʾATUL	1	ḤADUR	4
	ḤANUN	1	ḤARUB	1	ḤAZUQ	1	ḪAḪUN	1	ḪABUR	2	ḪAGUR	1	ḪAMUJ	1	ʿAQUB	3	ʿARUL	2
	JABUB	1	JABUS	2	JABUŠ	3	JAKUK	1	JAŠUN	2	JATUM	2	BAḤUR	1	BABUL	1	BAKUR	2
	BAKUS	1	BAKUŠ	1	BALUL	1	BANUQ	2	BAŠUM	1	BATUL	2	BAZUR	3	DAKUL	5	DALUM	1
	DAŠUR	6	ḎAKUR	12	ḎAMUR	1	GAʾUL	2	GAʾUŠ	1	GABUʾ	4	GARUB	1	KADUL	1	KANUK	1
	KANUT	1	LAʾUŠ	1	LAWUJ	9	LAMUM	1	LAṬUP	2	MAGUN	2	MANUW	5	MARUʾ	2	MARUṢ	2
	MAŠUB	1	MAZUM	1	NAʾUL	1	NABUʾ	5	NABUṬ	3	NADUB	3	NAŠUʾ	8	NATUN	2	PALUS	1
	PAPUZ	1	PARUR	1	RAPUʾ	4	SATUR	1	ŠAKUN	1	ŠAKUR	2	ŠALUḤ	1	ŠAMUʿ	5	ŠAMUK	5
	ŠAMUL	1	ŠAMUM	2	ŠAMUŠ	2	ŠAPUR	1	ŠAṬUḤ	1	ŠAʾUM	1	ŠAWUʾ	1	ŠAKUM	2	ŠAṬUP	2
	ṢABUʾ	2	ṢADUQ	9	TABUB	8	TABUZ	1	ṬARUD	1	ZABUG	2	ZABUL	1	ZALUḪ	1		
	Total cAcUc	98																
cAcc	ʾAHL	14	ʾAḪW	1	ʾAḪN	1	ʾAḪR	1	ʾAWN	11	ʾABB	15	ʾABN	12	ʾADD	3	ʾADM	22
	ʾAKK	19	ʾAKN	1	ʾALL	6	ʾALM	5	ʾALP	1	ʾAMR	11	ʾANN	55	ʾANT	1	ʾANZ	1
	ʾAPK	3	ʾAPP	2	ʾAPR	2	ʾARḪ	4	ʾARK	2	ʾARR	1	ʾARŠ	1	ʾAŠJ	7	ʾAŠD	48
	ʾAŠM	7	ʾAŠR	8	ʾATT	14	ʾAZJ	2	HADD	240	HAND	18	ḤAJJ	31	ḤABS	1	ḤANN	25
	ḤARB	4	ḤAṢN	10	ḤATK	8	ḪAʾD	1	ḪAʾL	77	ḪAʾN	4	ḪAʾR	6	ḪAʾŠ	3	ḪAʾT	6
	ḪAʾZ	1	ḪAWR	4	ḤALD	1	ḪAMR	2	ḪAMŠ	1	ḪANB	1	ḪAND	1	ḪANP	2	ḪANZ	2
	ḪAŠT	1	ḪAŠŠ	1	ʿABD	75	ʿADN	50	ʿAḎR	14	ʿAGL	1	ʿAMM	211	ʿAQB	28	ʿARD	7
	ʿARṢ	3	ʿAZB	1	ʿAZZ	12	WARḪ	1	JAʾN	6	JABS	1	JADN	1	JAMM	5	JAMN	4
	JANT	1	JAPʿ	4	JAQR	5	JARN	1	JARQ	1	JAŠʿ	4	JATM	1	JATR	4	JATT	3
	BAʾB	2	BAʾT	1	BAḤR	4	BAḪŠ	1	BAʿD	12	BAʿL	114	BAWʾ	8	BAWB	6	BAWŠ	20
	BAWZ	5	BAJN	8	BAJR	3	BAKS	1	BAKŠ	1	BALK	2	BALṬ	2	BANḪ	2	BANN	1
	BAQQ	5	BATQ	1	DAʾK	3	DAʾŠ	1	DAWD	52	DAWR	6	DADM	2	DAKŠ	1	DALQ	1
	DAMQ	9	DANN	21	DARK	3	ḎABB	1	ḎAMR	1	ḎANB	1	ḎAQN	2	ḎARʿ	3	GAʾJ	9
	GAʾG	4	GAʾL	1	GAʾN	1	GAʾR	1	GAʾŠ	1	GAJD	1	GABN	1	GALD	1	GALZ	1
	GAML	1	GANN	1	KAʾB	19	KAʾK	2	KAʾL	2	KAʾM	5	KAʾR	1	KAʾŠ	1	KAʾT	1
	KAWJ	4	KAWN	7	KABD	1	KABL	1	KABŠ	2	KAKK	19	KALB	7	KALK	2	KAMB	1
	KAMM	1	KAMN	1	KAMT	1	KANN	2	KANZ	3	KARŠ	1	KAŠP	1	KATR	4	LAʾJ	1
	LAʾL	7	LAʾR	4	LAʾT	1	LAḤM	1	LAḪN	1	LABW	12	LABN	1	LAMM	1	LAMR	1
	LAND	2	LAŠG	1	MAʾJ	3	MAʾD	12	MAʾK	2	MAʾL	3	MAʾM	2	MAʾN	3	MAʾR	8
	MAʾŠ	5	MAʾT	19	MAʾZ	3	MAHR	1	MALK	2	MAMM	2	MAMN	1	MANN	17	MAQṬ	1
	MARṢ	5	MAŠḤ	3	MAŠD	1	MAŠK	4	MATQ	1	MAZN	1	NAʾJ	1	NAʾD	2	NAHR	13
	NAḤL	1	NAḪN	1	NAʿM	26	NAWḪ	11	NAWP	2	NABL	2	NAKL	2	NAKR	1	NAMḪ	2
	NAMR	1	NAMZ	1	NANN	5	NAPŠ	23	NARB	3	NASQ	1	NAŠʾ	1	NAŠP	1	NAṢB	1
	NAṢR	1	NATT	1	PAʾL	1	PAʾP	1	PAʾR	2	PAʾŠ	1	PAʾT	1	PAKN	4	PALL	2
	PALS	2	PALṬ	3	PANN	1	PARG	1	PAŠD	1	PAṬR	1	PAZR	1	QAʾB	1	QAʾD	3
	QAʾN	3	QAʾT	1	QAWL	2	QAWM	9	QADM	1	QARN	3	QAṬR	1	RAʾK	1	RAʾŠ	1
	RAʾZ	1	RAḤM	5	RAWḤ	19	RAWM	24	RAJB	5	RABB	4	RAPŠ	1	ŠAʾB	1	ŠAʾL	5
	ŠAʾQ	5	ŠAʾR	4	ŠAḪR	1	ŠADL	1	ŠADR	1	ŠAKB	2	ŠAKN	4	ŠALD	1	ŠALM	2
	ŠAMḪ	1	ŠAMʿ	2	ŠAMK	3	ŠAMM	6	ŠAMŠ	73	ŠAPR	3	ŠAPŠ	5	ŠAQṬ	1	ŠARB	1
	ŠARR	38	ŠAʾḪ	1	ŠAWB	4	ŠADW	18	ŠAKK	1	ŠALG	2	ŠAQL	1	ŠAṬP	1	ṢABʾ	2

ṢABR 3 ṢABṬ 2 ṢARP 1 ṢARK 4 TAʾG 3 TAʾK 5 TAʾL 1 TAʾM 1 TAḪT 1
TAWR 1 TABʾ 1 TABB 5 TALM 4 TAMB 1 TATT 3 ṬAḪD 1 ṬAJB 25 ṬALL 7
ZAʾN 1 ZAʾR 2 ZAʾT 5 ZAʾZ 7 ZAḪL 1 ZAKK 9 ZALḪ 1 ZAMM 2 ZANN 4
ZARQ 1
Total cAcc 298

cAccA ʾALLA 5 ʾATTA 3
Total cAccA 2

cAccAI ʾALLAI 2
Total cAccAI 1

cAccAc ʾANTAR 1 ʾARNAB 3 ḪANḪAN 3 ḪARḪAR 1 ḪARGAL 2 ḪAŠḪAŠ 1 ʿAŠTAR 68 BALBAL 1 BAZBAZ 1
KABKAB 7 KAKKAR 1 MANMAN 2 MARMAR 1 QAQQAD 1 QAQQAR 1 ŚAMʾAL 2 ŚANQAM 1 ŠARŠAR 3
TAḪTAḪ 1 TANTAN 2 ZAḪZAḪ 1 ZABZAB 1 ZAKZAK 2 ZALZAL 2 ZARNAB 1 ZARZAR 1
Total cAccAc 26

cAccEc ʾANTEL 1 ḪANDEN 1
Total cAccEc 2

cAccI BALTI 5 ZANZI 2
Total cAccI 2

cAccIc ʾARWIJ 10 BAKŠIŠ 1 ŚAMʾIL 1
Total cAccIc 3

cAccUc ʾANDUL 2 ʾAŠQUD 10 ḪABZUR 1 ḪAMBUZ 1 ḪANZUR 1 ḪAŠTUR 1 JALQUṬ 1 MARDUK 1 TAḪTUN 2
Total cAccUc 9

cE ME 15
Total cE 1

cEc ʾEB 3 ʾEK 1 ʾEL 136 ʾEN 2
Total cEc 4

cEcAc ʾEDAK 2 ʾEKAL 1 ʾELAP 1 HELAL 1 BELAʾ 1 NEJAL 1
Total cEcAc 6

cEcEc ʿEMES 1 LEʾEJ 3
Total cEcEc 2

cEcIc ʾEWIN 1 ʾEDID 1 ʾELIL 2 ʿEBIB 1 MENIJ 1 MEŚIL 1 ŠERIR 1
Total cEcIc 7

cEcUc ʾELUR 2 ʿEMUQ 1 TEBUʾ 1 TENUT 1
Total cEcUc 4

cEcc ʾELL 9 ʾELM 2 ʾEŠB 2 HEDD 19 ʿEBB 4 BEʿD 4 BEʿL 30 MEʾM 1 MEʾN 1
MEʾR 12 MENG 1 MENN 3 MERḪ 2 MERR 3 ŠEʾR 3 TEʾḪ 1
Total cEcc 16

cEccAc BELBAN 1
Total cEccAc 1

cEccIc ʾENLIL 1 ʾENTIL 3 BELBIN 2
Total cEccIc 3

cI KI 13 LI 25 MI 6 PI 45 ŠI 12
Total cI 5

cIc ʾIB 2 ʾIL 721 ʾIR 1 JID 7 BIN 45 DIʿ 4 ṢIʾ 1
Total cIc 7

cIcA ʾIJA 2 KIMA 1 MIJA 3 ŠINA 1
Total cIcA 4

STEM COUNT

cIcAc	ʾIDAD	1	ʾIDAR	1	ʾIGAR	1	ʾILAP	2	ʾILAR	3	ʾIMAG	1	ʾIRAḪ	1	ʾIŠAL	1	ʾIŠAW	1
	ʾIZAM	2	HILAL	5	ḪIMAR	2	ḪINAN	1	ḪIRAB	1	ḪIʾAN	1	ḪIBAR	1	ʿINAB	1	BIKAN	3
	BILAL	1	BINAḪ	1	BINAŠ	1	BIQAQ	2	BIZAZ	1	DIDAM	1	DIGAN	1	DIMAḪ	1	DIRAḪ	1
	DITAN	17	KIBAL	3	KIBAR	1	KINAN	3	KIŠAM	1	LILAR	1	MILAL	1	MINAN	5	MISAR	1
	NIṢAB	1	PILAḪ	1	RIʿAJ	3	SINAQ	1	ŠIMAʿ	13	ŠIMAR	1	ŠINAN	2	ŠITAŠ	1	ṢIḪAQ	1
	ṢIḪAR	1	ṢIBAR	2	TIʾAR	1	TIMAN	1	TIŠAN	2	ZIJAD	1	ZIJAN	3	ZIDAR	1	ZINAN	1
	ZIZAB	1																
	Total cIcAc	55																
cIcEc	ʾITEJ	2	KIBEL	1	MIMEʾ	2	MITEʿ	1										
	Total cIcEc	4																
cIcI	ŠINI	3																
	Total cIcI	1																
cIcIc	ʾIBIR	1	ʾIDID	2	ʾIMIR	5	ʾIŠIM	1	ḪININ	2	ḪINIʾ	1	ʿIZIL	1	ʿIZIZ	1	BIḪIR	2
	BIBIJ	1	BIKIN	5	BIŠIR	2	DIWIR	6	DINIK	1	ḎIBIB	2	KIHIL	4	KIBIR	1	KIBIS	1
	KIRIŠ	2	MIGIJ	1	MIQIṬ	2	NIʿIM	2	NIKID	1	NIMIN	1	SIKIL	8	ŠIBIL	1	ŠIKIR	1
	ŠILIB	1	ŠININ	3	ŠIRIB	1	ṢIBIṬ	1	ṢIMID	1	TIBIʾ	1	TIDIQ	1	TILIʾ	1	ZIBIN	1
	ZILIB	3	ZIRIT	1														
	Total cIcIc	38																
cIcIcIc	KISIBIR	1																
	Total cIcIcIc	1																
cIcUc	ʾILUL	2	ʾILUR	6	ʾIŠUL	1	ḪILUṢ	1	ḪINUN	3	ḪIGUL	1	ḪILUK	1	JIBUS	1	JITUM	1
	BIDUM	1	BIKUR	1	BILUL	1	BIRUR	1	ḎINUB	1	ḎIQUN	1	KIBUN	1	KIRUʾ	3	KIZUR	1
	LILUR	1	SINUQ	2	ŠIRUN	1												
	Total cIcUc	21																
cIcc	ʾIBL	2	ʾIBN	1	ʾIDD	3	ʾILL	13	ʾIMM	4	ʾINZ	1	ʾIPQ	10	ʾIRR	13	ʾIRŠ	3
	ʾIŠN	1	ʾITT	2	HILL	1	ḪIJJ	3	ḪIMD	5	ḪINN	14	ḪIRB	2	ḪIṢN	3	ḪIʾD	4
	ḪIʾL	6	ḪIBR	1	ḪIMʾ	1	ḪIML	1	ḪIMR	1	ḪIRD	1	ḪIRṢ	2	ḪIŠŠ	1	ḪIZR	1
	ʿIJN	2	ʿIMD	2	ʿIMS	1	ʿINB	5	ʿIQB	6	ʿIZB	1	ʿIZL	1	ʿIZZ	14	JIPʿ	2
	JIQR	4	JIRʾ	1	JIRR	1	JIŠʿ	30	BIḪR	2	BIʿD	4	BIJT	7	BIKN	1	BILK	1
	BILL	5	BILM	1	BINQ	2	BINZ	1	BIRB	1	BIZZ	2	DIʾL	1	DIWD	3	DIWR	10
	DIJN	7	DITN	2	ḎIKR	18	ḎIMR	51	ḎINB	1	ḎIQN	2	GIJD	4	GIZZ	6	KIʾD	1
	KIʾL	9	KIʾM	2	KIʾR	4	KIʾZ	1	KIWN	13	KIBR	8	KIBS	6	KIBŠ	1	KIMM	2
	KIMR	1	KINZ	1	KIPT	1	KIRB	2	KIRZ	1	KITT	1	LIʾD	2	LIʾL	5	LIʾM	54
	LIʾR	1	LIʾŠ	1	LIWJ	3	LIBB	1	MIʾD	1	MIʾR	2	MIʾŠ	1	MIHR	2	MIWT	1
	MIGN	1	MILʾ	1	MILK	38	MINN	3	MIŠR	1	NIʾG	1	NIʾŠ	5	NIʿM	10	NIWḪ	4
	NIWR	28	NIGH	1	NIKR	1	NILŠ	1	NIMḪ	1	NINN	1	NIPR	1	NIQM	17	NIṢB	2
	PILḪ	1	PILS	2	PIQD	1	QIJŠ	12	QIDM	1	QIMṢ	1	RIḪṢ	1	RIʿŠ	1	RIWḪ	3
	RIWM	19	RIJB	9	RIBK	1	RIGM	2	RIMŠ	4	RIPʾ	8	SIKL	1	SIMT	1	SITR	13
	ŠIJB	7	ŠIJM	7	ŠIJT	1	ŠIKR	1	ŠIMḪ	12	ŠIMM	1	ŠIMR	1	ŠINN	1	ŠIPQ	2
	ŠIPR	5	ŠIʾN	3	ŠIPṬ	5	ŠIQL	5	ŠIRṬ	2	ṢIJḪ	3	ṢIBʾ	9	ṢIDQ	15	ṢILL	11
	ṢIRR	1	TIʾL	1	TIʾM	2	TIʾŠ	2	TIʾT	1	TIWR	11	TILL	2	TINʾ	4	TIRR	2
	TISP	3	ṬILL	1	ZIʾM	1	ZIʾN	1	ZIʾQ	1	ZIʾZ	2	ZIBL	1	ZILḪ	1	ZIMM	1
	ZIPP	1	ZIRQ	2	ZIZN	1												
	Total cIcc	165																
cIccAc	ʾIRŠAP	1	ʾIŠḪAR	21	ʿIŠTAR	1	NINGAL	1	ŠIMʾAL	4	TIŠPAK	1						
	Total cIccAc	6																
cIccIc	ḪILḪIL	2	BIRBIR	2	BIRKIN	3	BIZKIN	1	DIBDIB	1	DIGDIG	2	KIKKIN	6	KIKKIR	1	ŠIMGIN	3
	ZIKZIK	1																
	Total cIccIc	10																
cIccUc	BIRḪUN	1																
	Total cIccUc	1																
cU	ḎU	17	LU	17	PU	10	ŠU	8										
	Total cU	4																
cUc	ʾUM	1	ʾUP	5	BUN	44	LUʾ	3	MUʾ	2	MUM	1	MUT	111	NUN	5	ŠUḪ	1
	ŠUM	191	TUʾ	8	TUT	1												
	Total cUc	12																

STEM COUNT

cUcAc	ʾUGAZ	1	ʾUMAN	1	ʾUNAB	6	ʾURAN	3	ʾURAŚ	1	ʾUŚAL	2	ʾUŚAT	1	ʾUŠAŠ	1	HULAL	1
	ḤUBAS	6	ḤUMAD	1	ḤUṢAN	4	ḪUWAL	2	ḪUBAD	2	ḪULAŠ	1	ḪUNAŠ	1	ḪURAṢ	2	ḪUZAM	1
	ʿUMAS	1	ʿUZAB	4	ʿUZAL	5	BUḪAZ	1	BUDAM	1	BUGAŠ	1	BULAṬ	2	BUNAQ	2	BUQAQ	4
	BURAN	2	BUŚAN	1	DULAQ	1	DUMAR	1	DUMAT	1	ḎUBAB	8	ḎUNAB	3	GUʾAD	1	GULAL	1
	KUBAR	1	KUBAS	2	KUDAD	2	KUMAN	1	KUMAR	1	KUNAB	1	KUNAN	3	KUPAD	1	KURAŚ	1
	KUŚAP	2	KUZAB	3	KUZAR	4	KUZAZ	1	MUNAN	4	MUŚAḤ	2	MUŠAR	1	NUʿAM	1	NUWAP	1
	NUBAṬ	1	NUMAḪ	4	NUPAR	2	NUṢAB	2	NUZAM	1	PULAḪ	1	PUZAR	1	QUDAŚ	1	RUKAB	1
	SUTAR	1	ŚUḪAR	2	ŚUGAG	3	ŚULAḤ	2	ŚULAL	1	ŚULAM	1	ŚULAP	2	ŚUMAT	4	ŚUNAḪ	1
	ŚUNAN	1	ŚURAR	1	ŠUʾAR	1	ŠUʿAL	2	ŠURAN	1	ŠUŠAG	1	ṢURAR	2	TUʾAL	2	TUBAB	1
	TUDAR	2	TULAʿ	1	TUQAR	3	TURAḪ	2	TUŠAR	1	TUZAL	1	ZUḪAL	1	ZUJAN	3	ZUBAL	3
	ZULAN	1	ZULAT	1	ZUNAN	3	ZUQAT	1										
	Total cUcAc	94																
cUcAcA	KUPAPA	2																
	Total cUcAcA	1																
cUcEc	NUMEN	1	TUŠER	1														
	Total cUcEc	2																
cUcIc	ʾUBIR	1	ʾUDIN	1	ʾUŚIL	1	ḪUNIN	3	ḪUZIR	3	ʿUZIL	1	KUKIM	1	KULIM	2	KUMIS	1
	MUWIʾ	1	SUKIL	1	SUṬIʾ	1	TUBIN	1	TUŠIM	2	ZUḪIR	1						
	Total cUcIc	15																
cUcUc	ʾUBUŚ	4	ʾUDUD	1	ʾUḎUN	1	ʾUKUL	1	ʾUNUB	9	ʾUZUL	2	ḤUBUS	1	ḤUMUD	1	ḤUNUN	3
	ḤUSUD	1	ḪUBUR	1	ḪUGUL	1	ḪUMUŚ	1	ḪURUṢ	3	ʿUMUS	1	ʿUZUB	1	ʿUZUL	1	BUʾUL	3
	BULUK	1	BUṬUḤ	1	BUṬUM	1	DUKUP	1	DULUQ	4	DUŚUB	1	DUŠUR	5	ḎUHUB	1	ḎUMUR	1
	ḎUNUB	1	GUʾUD	1	GUMUL	1	GURUD	2	GURUR	1	KUʾUT	1	KUWUN	1	KUBUR	1	KULUP	1
	KURUB	2	KUTUL	2	LUʾUN	1	LUʾUP	1	MUʾUT	1	MULUK	8	MUNUZ	1	NUBUṬ	1	NUPUR	1
	NUŠUP	1	NUṬUP	4	PUḪUR	2	PURUS	1	PUZUR	2	ŚUʾUL	1	ŚUBUL	2	ŚUKUR	1	ŚUKUŚ	1
	ŚULUḤ	2	ŚULUK	1	ŚULUL	1	ŚUMUḪ	5	ŚUMUK	1	ŚUMUM	1	ŚUMUT	5	ŚUPUR	1	ŠUBUL	2
	ŠUKUD	1	ŠUQUL	1	ṢUBUʾ	2	TUKUL	2	TURUM	1	TURUN	1	TUŠUʿ	1	TUTUG	1	ṬUBUQ	1
	ZUʾUM	3	ZUʾUZ	1														
	Total cUcUc	74																
cUcUcAc	SUMUKAN	1																
	Total cUcUcAc	1																
cUcc	ʾUWR	6	ʾUWŠ	4	ʾUDM	1	ʾULP	1	ʾUMM	32	ʾURK	1	ʾURL	1	ʾURR	1	ʾUŚK	2
	ʾUŚM	1	ʾUŚŚ	1	ʾUŚT	1	ʾUTL	1	ḤUNN	14	ḤURB	3	ḪUʾD	1	ḪUʾT	1	ḪUʾZ	1
	ḪUBD	1	ḪUBR	1	ḪULM	1	ḪUMR	1	ḪUPŠ	2	ḪURR	1	ḪURṢ	5	ḪUŠŠ	3	ḪUZM	2
	ʿUWQ	1	ʿUZZ	3	BUʾL	2	BUʿD	3	BUWZ	10	BUKŚ	1	BULM	1	BUNZ	1	BUQQ	3
	BURQ	5	BURR	1	BURŠ	1	BUZZ	1	DUWD	6	DUWR	3	DUDM	1	DULQ	1	DUMQ	1
	DUNN	5	ḎUKR	1	GUʾG	1	GUʾR	7	GUʾZ	2	GUBʾ	1	GUBL	3	GULL	3	GULZ	2
	GUML	2	GURD	1	KUʾB	6	KUʾD	2	KUʾM	6	KUʾN	2	KUʾR	4	KUʾŚ	2	KUʾT	4
	KUʾZ	4	KUWN	12	KUBB	2	KUBS	1	KUDD	1	KULP	3	KUMM	1	KUMR	2	KUMS	1
	KUMT	1	KUND	1	KUNN	4	KUNZ	4	KURD	2	KURŚ	3	KUŠM	1	KUŠR	1	LUʾL	3
	LUʾM	5	LUʾP	2	LUMM	8	MUʾZ	2	MUHR	3	MURR	5	MUŠN	1	MUTT	2	NUʾR	7
	NUʿM	7	NUWḪ	2	NUWD	1	NUWP	8	NUWR	5	NUKR	1	NUMḪ	7	NUMN	2	NUMR	1
	NUNM	1	NUṢR	4	PUḪR	1	PULS	7	PUṬR	2	QUWJ	9	QUDM	3	RUḤB	1	RUWḤ	3
	RUWB	6	RUWM	1	RUŚP	2	ŚUʾQ	1	ŚUḪR	1	ŚULM	1	ŚUMḪ	2	ŚUMK	1	ŠUʾḪ	3
	ŠUʾG	1	ŠUʾM	1	ŠUWB	16	ŠUWR	1	ṢUWR	22	ṢUBʾ	1	ṢUPR	3	ṢURR	2	TUʾM	1
	TUʾN	3	TUʾZ	3	TUḪT	1	TUWR	12	TUKR	1	TULL	1	TUND	1	TUPT	2	TURM	1
	ṬUḪŠ	2	ṬUBQ	2	ṬUQM	1	ZUʾG	1	ZUʾZ	5	ZUḪL	1	ZUMM	2	ZUNN	1	ZUNZ	1
	Total cUcc	144																
cUccAc	ʾURŚAM	1	ḪURŚAN	3														
	Total cUccAc	2																
cUccI	ŠULGI	1																
	Total cUccI	1																
cUccIc	BURBIN	1	TURBIN	1														
	Total cUccIc	2																
cUccUc	BUDBUD	1	BUNZUR	1	BURBUR	3	BUZBUZ	1	DULDUL	1	GUNGUN	1	GURGUR	1	KUKKUB	2	KUKKUN	1
	KUKKUŚ	3	KUNDUL	2	KURKUR	3	KUTKUT	1	MURMUR	1	NURNUR	1	PURʿUŚ	1	TURTUR	2	ZUNZUN	2

	ZURZUR	3																
	Total cUccUc	19																
ccAc	ʾḤAḎ	9	ʾLAP	3	ʾLAŚ	1	ʾMAR	2	ḤBAB	1	ḤBAS	2	ḤLAJ	1	ḤLAM	3	ḤMAD	1
	ḤBAʾ	1	ḤTAN	1	ḤṬAʾ	1	ʿḎAR	6	WDAJ	4	WDAD	2	WMAʾ	7	WQAH	13	WTAʾ	2
	WTAR	3	JBAL	25	JDAʿ	8	JPAʿ	27	JQAH	2	JŚAR	8	JTAR	6	BḤAR	3	BWAʾ	11
	BNAḤ	1	DBAR	1	DRAK	2	ḎMAR	4	ḎRAʿ	5	LʾAʾ	4	MʾAD	11	MRAṢ	5	MṬAR	1
	NḤAB	5	NḤAN	1	NWAḤ	1	NWAB	3	NZAL	2	PLAḤ	10	PTAḤ	2	PTAN	5	QDAM	1
	RḤAB	1	RḤAM	9	RḤAQ	3	RḤAŠ	1	RDAK	1	RDAP	3	RGAM	1	RKAB	3	RMAN	1
	RPAʾ	5	RŚAP	3	ŚKAR	1	ŚLAḤ	1	ŚLAL	2	ŚLAM	2	ŚMAʿ	25	ŚMAR	1	ŚPAR	2
	ŠṬAḤ	1	ŠKAK	1	ṢḤAQ	1	ZRAQ	1										
	Total ccAc	67																
ccEc	ZMEʾ	1																
	Total ccEc	1																
ccIc	ʾḤIḎ	3	ʾWIʾ	1	ʾWIR	5	ʾWIŠ	2	ʾLIP	1	ʾMIʾ	5	ʾMIN	1	ʾNIP	1	ʾZIJ	5
	HWIJ	33	HLIL	1	ḤJIJ	8	ḤBIS	1	ḤLIJ	7	ḤRIM	1	ḤṢIN	4	ḤZIQ	3	ḤBIʾ	1
	ḤŚIJ	2	ḤŚIM	1	ḤŚIR	1	ḤTIN	1	ḤZIM	1	ʿDIJ	1	ʿḎIR	8	ʿMIS	3	ʿNIJ	4
	ʿQIB	4	ʿTIQ	1	ʿZIB	15	WḤIJ	1	WḤIN	1	WBIT	1	WPIʿ	1	WQIH	1	WQIR	1
	WSIL	1	WŠIʿ	2	WŠIB	1	WṢIʾ	10	JʿIL	3	JBIL	2	JBIŚ	11	JDIʿ	20	JPIʿ	3
	JQIR	2	JRID	3	JŚIR	5	JŠIʿ	1	JṢIʾ	67	JTIR	11	BJIN	2	BJIR	2	BLIJ	2
	BLIM	2	BNIJ	12	BNIQ	1	DWIR	3	DJIN	4	DBIR	1	DNIK	1	ḎRIʿ	2	GJIḤ	7
	GJID	2	GMIR	1	GRIN	1	KWIN	9	KLIL	1	KMIN	1	KMIS	1	KSIJ	2	KŚIJ	1
	LʾIJ	9	MʾID	1	MLIʾ	1	MLIK	9	MNID	1	MSIR	1	MŚIḤ	1	MŚIJ	2	MṢIʾ	11
	NḤIM	1	NḤIJ	1	NḤIB	2	NḤIN	1	NḤIR	1	NWIḤ	6	NWIB	4	NBIʾ	7	NBIṬ	2
	NDIB	1	NDIN	31	NGIH	1	NPIḤ	3	NQIM	8	NŚIʾ	17	NṢIB	10	NTIN	31	NṬIʿ	1
	PDIJ	1	PLIḤ	1	PQID	3	PTIḤ	1	PṬIR	1	QWIM	13	QJIŚ	2	QBIJ	4	QNIJ	3
	QRIʾ	1	QRIB	1	RḤIB	12	RḤIQ	2	RʿIJ	2	RʿIŠ	6	RWIḤ	10	RWIJ	2	RWIM	25
	RJIB	4	RBIJ	5	RKIB	1	RŠIJ	12	SNIQ	3	SRID	1	ŚḤIR	1	ŚJIM	17	ŚJIT	11
	ŚBIJ	4	ŚBIM	1	ŚKIN	4	ŚKIR	2	ŚLIJ	1	ŚLIB	1	ŚLIM	2	ŚMIʿ	1	ŚPIQ	1
	ŚPIR	1	ŚQIḤ	1	ŚQIṬ	1	ŠṬIḤ	2	ŠWIB	2	ŠNIJ	8	ṢJID	5	TḤIJ	1	TMIH	3
	ZLIJ	1	ZNIJ	1														
	Total ccIc	146																
ccUc	ʾḤUḎ	2	ʾWUŠ	11	ʾBUQ	1	ʾDUM	1	ʾGUN	6	ʾKUR	6	ʾMUW	2	ʾMUR	8	ʾNUP	6
	ʾQUD	5	ʾRUR	11	ʾRUŚ	1	ʾŚUʾ	1	ʾŚUD	3	ʾŠUR	1	ʾZUW	5	HLUL	1	ḤKUM	1
	ḤNUN	6	ḤṢUN	2	ḤZUQ	1	ḤBUʾ	1	ḤBUD	1	ḤMUM	2	ḤMUṬ	3	ḤNUW	1	ḤZUM	1
	ḤZUR	3	ʿWUQ	1	ʿDUN	5	ʿMUS	3	ʿNUW	1	ʿQUB	12	ʿZUB	1	JʿUL	1	JPUʿ	20
	JŠUʿ	23	BʾUL	1	BLUW	1	BLUṬ	2	BRUW	1	BRUQ	3	BZUW	1	DWUR	5	DLUW	1
	DLUQ	1	DRUK	1	ḎKUR	8	ḎRUʿ	2	GMUR	2	KWUN	55	KBUR	1	KNUW	2	KRUB	8
	KSUW	2	LʾUM	1	MWUʾ	1	MWUŠ	2	MWUT	39	MKUS	1	MQUṬ	2	MRUṢ	3	MZUʾ	5
	NḤUR	1	NWUḤ	20	NWUD	3	NWUP	1	NWUR	1	NWUZ	2	NBUL	1	NDUB	1	NDUR	1
	NŠUʾ	1	NṢUR	3	PḤUR	6	PLUS	2	PRUD	1	PRUS	1	PTUḤ	9	PTUN	2	PṬUR	4
	QWUJ	5	QWUM	2	QṢUR	2	RWUB	1	RBUʾ	2	RMUK	2	ŚKUB	1	ŚKUR	17	ŚNUL	1
	ŚPUQ	3	ŚRUK	1	ŚṬUḤ	2	ŠWUB	23	ṢDUQ	3	TWUR	29	ZNUR	2				
	Total ccUc	97																
		5		2		2		1		2		2		1		17		1

5. PHONEME COUNT

This chapter presents the frequencies of consonantal phonemes as these appear in roots and stems, but not in prefixes and suffixes. If we were to include the 63 prefixes and suffixes discussed in chapter 3, the totals would be mainly affected by the inclusion of the phonemes *j*, *t*, and *n*, and, to a much lesser extent, *m*, *k*, *š*, ʾ, and *h*.

Statistics for each consonant are given in four parts, according to whether the consonant occurs in the first, second, third, or fourth position of a root.

Each root is listed under one of the four positions, and the total number of occurrences of that root is indicated. Thus the root ʾHL occurs in 14 names (including variants) and the root ʾḪ occurs in 116 names (including variants).

Each grouping of roots is followed by the number of times each consonant occurs in a given position in a different root. Thus ʾ occurs in the first position in 121 different roots, and in the second position in 105 different roots.

At the end of a section dealing with a given consonant is given the total number of occurrences of that consonant in all four positions in different roots. Thus the consonant ʾ occurs in 270 different roots—in 121 of them in the first position, in 105 in the second position, in 44 in the third position, and in 0 in the fourth position.

While the main aim of the computer was to count the number of *tokens* (occurring in 270 roots) by *type* (the consonant ʾ), it also counted the number of its occurrences under each root, as in the consonantal root ʾHL, which occurs in 14 names.

For the discussion of points of questionable stem and root analysis see section 0.3.

Problems connected with the definition of consonantal phonemes are discussed briefly in section 0.4.

Taking into account the difficulties of stem, root, and phoneme analysis, we find some very interesting points of statistical significance. Without commenting on them, I present below five small tables only, one showing the overall frequencies of Amorite consonants and the others the frequencies of consonants in each of the four positions. The symbols + or - after a number indicate that, because of uncertainties of phonemic analysis, the actual number is likely to be larger or smaller than the one here given. I do not need to stress that statistical data are of fundamental importance in the decipherment of unknown writings and languages of Semitic peoples.

The frequency order of consonantal phonemes is:

r	274	*š*	103
n	273	*p*	83
ʾ	270-	*q*	80+
b	228	*g*	77-
m	223	*w*	74
l	207	ʿ	51+
k	177	*ḥ*	43+
d	148-	*ṭ*	32+
t	147	*ṣ*	30+
ś	133	*s*	28+
j	125	*ḏ*	14+
z	122-	*h*	14+
ḫ	120-		

The frequency order of consonantal phonemes in first position is:

ʾ	121-	*l*	32
k	82	*p*	32
b	74	ʿ	29+
n	68	*g*	29-
ś	66	*q*	26+
m	66	*ḥ*	21+
ḫ	61-	*w*	16
t	56	*ṣ*	15+
z	44-	*ḏ*	11+
j	43	*ṭ*	8+
d	38-	*s*	7+
r	34	*h*	4+
š	34		

The frequency order of consonantal phonemes in second position is:

r	109	*ḫ*	28-
ʾ	105-	*j*	28
n	90	*p*	27
m	87	*g*	23-
l	79	*q*	21+
b	77	*ṭ*	18+
k	47	*ḥ*	12+
d	43-	*s*	11+
w	42	ʿ	8+
t	40	*ṣ*	8+
ś	37	*h*	6+
z	35-	*ḏ*	2+
š	33		

The frequency order of consonantal phonemes in third position is:

r	111	*ś*	29
n	98	*ẖ*	28-
l	85	*g*	24-
b	71	*p*	23
m	68	*w*	16
d	64-	ᶜ	14+
j	53	*s*	10+
t	50	*ḥ*	10+
k	45	*ṭ*	9+
ᵓ	44-	*ṣ*	7+
z	41-	*h*	4+
q	33+	*ḏ*	1+
š	33		

The frequency order of consonantal phonemes in fourth position is:

r	20	*ś*	1
n	17	*t*	1
l	11	*ṭ*	1+
b	6	ᵓ	0
ẖ	3-	*h*	0+
d	3-	*ḥ*	0+
k	3	ᶜ	0+
š	3	*w*	0
m	2	*ḏ*	0+
z	2-	*q*	0+
j	1	*s*	0+
g	1-	*ṣ*	0+
p	1		

The lemmata and roots are given in the new order of roots discussed in section 0.5:

ᵓ	H	Ḥ	Ḫ	ᶜ	W	J
B	D	Ḏ	G			
K	L	M	N	P	Q	R
S	Ś	Š	Ṣ	T	Ṭ	Z

PHONEME COUNT

Roots Containing ʾ

First Consonant ʾ

ʾHL	14	ʾḪ	116	ʾḪW	1	ʾḪḎ	15	ʾḪL	2	ʾḪN	1	ʾḪR	1	ʾWʾ	5	ʾWJ	6	ʾWN	14
ʾWR	11	ʾWŠ	17	ʾJ	56	ʾJK	2	ʾJL	10	ʾJM	5	ʾJN	8	ʾJŠ	4	ʾB	240	ʾBḪ	5
ʾBB	19	ʾBL	4	ʾBN	16	ʾBQ	2	ʾBR	2	ʾBŚ	6	ʾDʾ	2	ʾDD	16	ʾDK	2	ʾDL	1
ʾDM	31	ʾDN	14	ʾDR	1	ʾḎN	1	ʾG	3	ʾGG	2	ʾGN	6	ʾGR	1	ʾGZ	1	ʾK	12
ʾKK	19	ʾKL	2	ʾKN	9	ʾKR	9	ʾL	877	ʾLʾ	2	ʾLK	4	ʾLL	39	ʾLM	10	ʾLN	6
ʾLP	14	ʾLR	11	ʾLŚ	3	ʾM	6	ʾMʾ	5	ʾMW	2	ʾMG	1	ʾML	1	ʾMM	37	ʾMN	17
ʾMR	41	ʾMT	2	ʾN	18	ʾNB	15	ʾNDL	2	ʾNK	2	ʾNLL	1	ʾNN	55	ʾNP	7	ʾNT	1
ʾNTL	4	ʾNTR	1	ʾNZ	3	ʾP	8	ʾPK	3	ʾPP	2	ʾPQ	10	ʾPR	2	ʾQD	5	ʾR	3
ʾRḪ	8	ʾRWJ	10	ʾRK	3	ʾRL	1	ʾRM	5	ʾRN	3	ʾRNB	3	ʾRPḪ	1	ʾRR	26	ʾRŚ	13
ʾRŚM	1	ʾRŠP	1	ʾSN	6	ʾŚʾ	1	ʾŚJ	8	ʾŚD	52	ʾŚK	2	ʾŚL	7	ʾŚM	9	ʾŚN	3
ʾŚQD	10	ʾŚR	3	ʾŚŚ	2	ʾŚT	2	ʾŠḪ	2	ʾŠḪR	21	ʾŠW	1	ʾŠB	2	ʾŠR	29	ʾŠŠ	1
ʾŠZ	1	ʾTJ	3	ʾTL	6	ʾTM	6	ʾTR	2	ʾTT	19	ʾTZ	2	ʾZW	5	ʾZJ	7	ʾZL	2
ʾZM	2	TOTAL 121																	

Second Consonant ʾ

ḪʾD	6	ḪʾL	83	ḪʾN	7	ḪʾR	6	ḪʾŚ	3	ḪʾT	7	ḪʾZ	3	Jʾ	19	JʾN	11	JʾR	10
JʾT	1	BʾB	2	BʾL	10	BʾN	3	BʾT	2	DʾK	3	DʾL	1	DʾŠ	1	GʾJ	9	GʾD	2
GʾG	5	GʾL	6	GʾN	1	GʾR	8	GʾŠ	3	GʾZ	2	KʾB	25	KʾD	3	KʾK	2	KʾL	11
KʾM	15	KʾN	2	KʾR	9	KʾŚ	3	KʾT	6	KʾZ	5	Lʾ	3	Lʾʾ	5	LʾJ	19	LʾD	2
LʾL	15	LʾM	60	LʾN	1	LʾP	5	LʾR	5	LʾŚ	3	LʾT	2	Mʾ	2	MʾJ	3	MʾD	25
MʾK	2	MʾL	3	MʾM	3	MʾN	8	MʾR	22	MʾŠ	6	MʾT	20	MʾZ	5	NʾJ	1	NʾD	2
NʾG	1	NʾL	1	NʾR	7	NʾŠ	6	PʾL	3	PʾP	1	PʾR	4	PʾŠ	1	PʾT	1	QʾB	1
QʾD	3	QʾN	3	QʾT	1	RʾK	1	RʾŚ	1	RʾZ	1	ŚʾB	1	ŚʾD	1	ŚʾL	9	ŚʾQ	7
ŚʾR	6	ŠʾḪ	4	ŠʾG	1	ŠʾM	2	ŠʾN	3	ŠʾR	4	Ṣʾ	1	Tʾ	12	TʾḪ	1	TʾG	3
TʾK	5	TʾL	5	TʾM	4	TʾN	3	TʾR	1	TʾŠ	2	TʾT	1	TʾZ	3	ZʾG	1	ZʾM	4
ZʾN	5	ZʾQ	1	ZʾR	2	ZʾT	5	ZʾZ	16	TOTAL 105									

Third Consonant ʾ

ʾWʾ	5	ʾDʾ	2	ʾLʾ	2	ʾMʾ	5	ʾŚʾ	1	ḪBʾ	6	ḪMʾ	1	ḪNʾ	1	ḪPʾ	1	ḪTʾ	7
ḪṬʾ	1	WMʾ	7	WṢʾ	10	WTʾ	2	JRʾ	1	JṢʾ	67	BWʾ	19	BLʾ	1	DBʾ	1	ḎRʾ	8
GBʾ	11	KRʾ	3	Lʾʾ	5	LLʾ	4	MWʾ	2	MLʾ	2	MMʾ	2	MRʾ	4	MṢʾ	13	MZʾ	6
NBʾ	25	NŠʾ	30	NŠʾ	1	QRʾ	9	RBʾ	2	RPʾ	73	SṬʾ	7	ŚMʾL	7	ŠWʾ	1	ṢBʾ	25
TBʾ	3	TLʾ	3	TNʾ	4	ZMʾ	2	TOTAL	44										

Fourth Consonant ʾ

TOTAL 0

Total Roots Containing ʾ 270

Roots Containing H

First Consonant H

HWJ	33	HDD	259	HLL	19	HND	18	TOTAL	4

Second Consonant H

ʾHL	14	ḎHB	1	KHL	9	MHR	9	NHR	13	QHL	1	TOTAL	6

Third Consonant H

WQH	14	JQH	2	NGH	6	TMH	3	TOTAL	4

Fourth Consonant H

TOTAL 0

Total Roots Containing H 14

Roots Containing Ḫ

PHONEME COUNT

First Consonant Ḥ

ḤJJ	42	ḤBB	3	ḤBS	15	ḤDR	4	ḤKM	3	ḤLJ	9	ḤLB	2	ḤLM	3	ḤLṢ	7	ḤM	40
ḤMD	14	ḤMR	2	ḤNḤN	3	ḤNN	80	ḤRB	17	ḤRM	2	ḤSD	6	ḤŚK	2	ḤṢN	27	ḤTK	9
ḤZQ	10	TOTAL	21																

Second Consonant Ḥ

WḤJ	1	JḤD	16	BḤR	14	LḤM	1	NḤL	2	NḤM	1	RḤB	17	RḤM	16	RḤQ	5	ṢḤQ	2
TḤT	2	TḤTN	2	TOTAL	12														

Third Consonant Ḥ

ḤNḤN	3	BṬḤ	1	GJḤ	7	MŚḤ	10	PQḤ	2	PTḤ	21	RWḤ	35	ŚLḤ	9	ŚRḤ	1	ŚṬḤ	7
TOTAL	10																		

Fourth Consonant Ḥ

TOTAL 0

Total Roots Containing Ḥ 43

Roots Containing Ḫ

First Consonant Ḫ

ḪʾD	6	ḪʾL	83	ḪʾN	7	ḪʾR	6	ḪʾŚ	3	ḪʾT	7	ḪʾZ	3	ḪḪN	1	ḪWL	2	ḪWR	5
ḪBʾ	6	ḪBD	7	ḪBR	8	ḪBZR	1	ḪGL	2	ḪGR	2	ḪLḪL	2	ḪLD	1	ḪLK	1	ḪLM	1
ḪLN	1	ḪLŠ	1	ḪMʾ	1	ḪMJ	1	ḪMBZ	1	ḪML	1	ḪMM	2	ḪMR	4	ḪMŚ	3	ḪMṬ	4
ḪNʾ	1	ḪNW	1	ḪNE	1	ḪND	1	ḪNDN	1	ḪNP	2	ḪNŠ	2	ḪNZ	2	ḪNZR	1	ḪPʾ	1
ḪPŠ	2	ḪQT	1	ḪRḪR	1	ḪRJ	1	ḪRD	1	ḪRGL	2	ḪRR	8	ḪRŚN	3	ḪRṢ	12	ḪŚJ	3
ḪŚM	2	ḪŚR	1	ḪŚT	1	ḪŠḪŠ	1	ḪŠŠ	6	ḪŠTR	1	ḪTʾ	7	ḪTN	4	ḪṬʾ	1	ḪZM	6
ḪZR	7	TOTAL	61																

Second Consonant Ḫ

ʾḪ	116	ʾḪW	1	ʾḪḎ	15	ʾḪL	2	ʾḪN	1	ʾḪR	1	ḪḪN	1	WḪN	1	BḪŠ	1	BḪZ	1
LḪN	3	NḪJ	1	NḪB	7	NḪN	3	NḪR	3	PḪR	10	RḪŠ	1	RḪṢ	2	ŚḪ	1	ŚḪR	7
ṢḪR	1	TḪJ	1	TḪTḪ	1	ṬḪD	1	ṬḪŠ	2	ZḪL	4	ZḪR	1	ZḪZḪ	1	TOTAL	28		

Third Consonant Ḫ

ʾBḪ	5	ʾRḪ	8	ʾŠḪ	2	ʾŠḪR	21	ḪLḪL	2	ḪRḪR	1	ḪŠḪŠ	1	WRḪ	1	JRḪ	102	BNḪ	5
BRḪN	1	BZḪ	1	DMḪ	1	DRḪ	1	MRḪ	2	NWḪ	44	NMḪ	14	NPḪ	3	PLḪ	14	ŚMḪ	20
ŚNḪ	1	ŚQḪ	2	ŠʾḪ	4	ṢJḪ	3	TʾḪ	1	TRḪ	2	ṬBḪ	1	ZLḪ	3	TOTAL	28		

Fourth Consonant Ḫ

ʾRPḪ	1	TḪTḪ	1	ZḪZḪ	1	TOTAL	3

Total Roots Containing Ḫ 120

Roots Containing ʿ

First Consonant ʿ

ʿWQ	4	ʿJN	2	ʿBB	5	ʿBD	75	ʿD	25	ʿDJ	5	ʿDN	55	ʿḎR	50	ʿGL	4	ʿLJ	15
ʿLṢ	3	ʿMD	2	ʿMM	211	ʿMQ	2	ʿMS	14	ʿN	45	ʿNW	1	ʿNJ	10	ʿNB	6	ʿNQ	2
ʿQB	54	ʿRD	8	ʿRL	2	ʿRṢ	5	ʿŠTR	69	ʿTQ	1	ʿZB	28	ʿZL	18	ʿZZ	33	TOTAL	29

Second Consonant ʿ

JʿL	18	BʿD	23	BʿL	144	Dʿ	13	NʿM	51	RʿJ	5	RʿŠ	7	ŠʿL	2	TOTAL	8

Third Consonant ʿ

WPʿ	1	WŠʿ	2	JDʿ	46	JPʿ	56	JŠʿ	59	ḎRʿ	16	MTʿ	9	NṬʿ	1	PRʿŠ	1	PSʿ	2
RBʿ	1	ŚMʿ	57	TLʿ	1	TŚʿ	1	TOTAL	14										

Fourth Consonant ʿ

TOTAL 0

Total Roots Containing ʿ 51

Roots Containing W

First Consonant W

WḤJ	1	WḪN	1	WBT	1	WDJ	4	WDD	2	WMʾ	7	WPʿ	1	WQH	14	WQR	1	WRḪ	1
WSL	1	WŠʿ	2	WŠB	1	WṢʾ	10	WTʾ	2	WTR	3	TOTAL	16						

Second Consonant W

ʾWʾ	5	ʾWJ	6	ʾWN	14	ʾWR	11	ʾWŠ	17	HWJ	33	ḪWL	2	ḪWR	5	ʿWQ	4	BWʾ	19
BWB	6	BWŠ	20	BWZ	15	DWD	61	DWR	34	KWJ	4	KWN	97	LWJ	12	MWʾ	2	MWŠ	2
MWT	40	NWḪ	44	NWJ	2	NWB	7	NWD	4	NWP	12	NWR	40	NWZ	2	QWJ	14	QWL	2
QWM	24	RWḪ	35	RWJ	2	RWB	7	RWM	69	ŚWR	2	ŠWʾ	1	ŠWB	47	ŠWL	2	ŠWR	1
ṢWR	22	TWR	55	TOTAL	42														

Third Consonant W

ʾḪW	1	ʾMW	2	ʾRWJ	10	ʾŠW	1	ʾZW	5	ḪNW	1	ʿNW	1	BLW	1	BRW	1	BZW	1
DLW	1	KNW	2	KSW	2	LBW	12	MNW	7	ŠDW	18	TOTAL	16						

Fourth Consonant W

TOTAL 0

Total Roots Containing W 74

Roots Containing J

First Consonant J

Jʾ	19	JʾN	11	JʾR	10	JʾT	1	JḤD	16	JʿL	18	JJ	2	JJM	1	JBB	1	JBL	40
JBS	4	JBŚ	17	JD	11	JDʿ	46	JDD	9	JDN	1	JKK	1	JKL	2	JLQṬ	1	JM	5
JMM	9	JMN	14	JNN	1	JNT	1	JPʿ	56	JPR	3	JQH	2	JQR	21	JRʾ	1	JRḪ	102
JRD	3	JRN	4	JRQ	2	JRR	1	JŚR	23	JŠʿ	59	JŠB	1	JŠN	2	JṢʾ	67	JT	40
JTM	7	JTR	77	JTT	3	TOTAL	43												

Second Consonant J

ʾJ	56	ʾJK	2	ʾJL	10	ʾJM	5	ʾJN	8	ʾJŠ	4	ḤJJ	42	ʿJN	2	JJ	2	JJM	1
BJN	11	BJR	5	BJT	7	DJN	11	GJḤ	7	GJD	9	MJ	3	NJL	2	QJŠ	14	RJB	18
ŚJB	7	ŚJM	24	ŚJT	12	ṢJḪ	3	ṢJD	10	ṬJB	25	ZJD	1	ZJN	6	TOTAL	28		

Third Consonant J

ʾWJ	6	ʾŚJ	8	ʾTJ	3	ʾZJ	7	HWJ	33	ḤJJ	42	ḤLJ	9	ḪMJ	1	ḪRJ	1	ḪŚJ	3
ʿDJ	5	ʿLJ	15	ʿNJ	10	WḤJ	1	WDJ	4	BBJ	1	BLJ	2	BNJ	21	BŚJ	2	ḎKJ	1
GʾJ	9	KWJ	4	KSJ	3	KŚJ	2	LʾJ	19	LWJ	12	MʾJ	3	MGJ	1	MKJ	5	MNJ	6
MŚJ	2	NʾJ	1	NḪJ	1	NWJ	2	PDJ	1	PNJ	4	QWJ	14	QBJ	4	QNJ	5	QZJ	1
RʿJ	5	RWJ	2	RBJ	5	RŠJ	13	RṢJ	4	ŚBJ	4	ŚLJ	1	ŚRJ	8	ŠNJ	13	TḪJ	1
TRJ	1	ZLJ	2	ZNJ	2	TOTAL	53												

Fourth Consonant J

ʾRWJ 10 TOTAL 1

Total Roots Containing J 125

Roots Containing B

First Consonant B

BʾB	2	BʾL	10	BʾN	3	BʾT	2	BḤR	14	BḪŠ	1	BḪZ	1	BʿD	23	BʿL	144	BWʾ	19
BWB	6	BWŠ	20	BWZ	15	BJN	11	BJR	5	BJT	7	BBJ	1	BBL	1	BDBD	1	BDD	1

BDM	2	BGN	2	BGŠ	1	BKL	5	BKN	9	BKR	4	BKS	2	BKŚ	3	BKŠŠ	1	BLʾ	1
BLW	1	BLJ	2	BLBL	1	BLBN	3	BLK	6	BLL	12	BLM	4	BLT	5	BLṬ	11	BN	89
BNḪ	5	BNJ	21	BNN	1	BNQ	7	BNŠ	1	BNZ	2	BNZR	1	BQQ	15	BRḪN	1	BRW	1
BRB	1	BRBN	1	BRBR	5	BRKN	3	BRL	1	BRN	2	BRQ	8	BRR	2	BRŠ	1	BŚJ	2
BŚM	1	BŚN	1	BŚR	8	BTL	2	BTQ	1	BT̤Ḫ	1	BṬM	1	BZḪ	1	BZW	1	BZBZ	2
BZKN	1	BZN	3	BZR	3	BZZ	5	TOTAL	74										

Second Consonant B

ʾB	240	ʾBḪ	5	ʾBB	19	ʾBL	4	ʾBN	16	ʾBQ	2	ʾBR	2	ʾBŚ	6	ḤBB	3	ḤBS	15
ḪBʾ	6	ḪBD	7	ḪBR	8	ḪBZR	1	ʿBB	5	ʿBD	75	WBT	1	JBB	1	JBL	40	JBS	4
JBŚ	17	BBJ	1	BBL	1	DBʾ	1	DBDB	1	DBN	1	DBR	2	ḎBB	16	ḎBL	1	GBʾ	11
GBL	3	GBN	1	KBB	2	KBD	7	KBKB	7	KBL	5	KBN	1	KBR	14	KBS	15	KBŚ	3
LBW	12	LBB	1	LBN	5	NBʾ	25	NBB	1	NBL	3	NBŚ	1	NBT	2	NBṬ	7	QBJ	4
QBL	2	RBʾ	2	RBʿ	1	RBJ	5	RBB	6	RBK	1	ŚBJ	4	ŚBL	3	ŚBM	4	ŚBŚ	1
ŠBL	2	ṢBʾ	25	ṢBR	5	ṢBṬ	3	TBʾ	3	TBB	14	TBN	2	TBZ	1	ṬBḪ	1	ṬBQ	3
ZBB	1	ZBG	2	ZBL	7	ZBN	3	ZBZ	1	ZBZB	1	TOTAL	77						

Third Consonant B

ʾBB	19	ʾNB	15	ʾŠB	2	ḤBB	3	ḤLB	2	ḤRB	17	ḪMBZ	1	ḪNB	1	ʿBB	5	ʿNB	6
ʿQB	54	ʿZB	28	WŠB	1	JBB	1	JŠB	1	BʾB	2	BWB	6	BDBD	1	BLBL	1	BLBN	3
BRB	1	BRBN	1	BRBR	5	BZBZ	2	DKB	1	DRB	1	DŚB	1	ḎHB	1	ḎBB	16	ḎNB	10
GNB	1	GRB	1	KʾB	25	KBB	2	KLB	7	KMB	1	KNB	1	KRB	12	KSBR	1	KZB	5
LBB	1	MŚB	1	NḪB	7	NWB	7	NBB	1	NDB	5	NNB	2	NRB	3	NṢB	17	QʾB	1
QRB	1	RḤB	17	RWB	7	RJB	18	RBB	6	RKB	5	ŚʾB	1	ŚJB	7	ŚKB	3	ŚLB	2
ŚMB	1	ŚRB	2	ŠWB	47	TBB	14	TDB	1	TMB	1	TRBN	1	ṬJB	25	ZBB	1	ZLB	3
ZZB	1	TOTAL	71																

Fourth Consonant B

ʾRNB	3	DBDB	1	KBKB	7	KKKB	2	ZBZB	1	ZRNB	1	TOTAL	6

Total Roots Containing B 228

Roots Containing D

First Consonant D

DʾK	3	DʾL	1	DʾŠ	1	Dʿ	13	DWD	61	DWR	34	DJN	11	DBʾ	1	DBDB	1	DBN	1
DBR	2	DDM	4	DGDG	2	DGN	119	DGZ	1	DKB	1	DKL	5	DKŚ	1	DLW	1	DLDL	1
DLM	1	DLQ	9	DM	3	DMḪ	1	DMQ	12	DMR	1	DMT	1	DNK	2	DNN	26	DRḪ	1
DRB	1	DRK	9	DRN	1	DŚB	1	DŚK	1	DŚL	1	DŠR	11	DTN	19	TOTAL	38		

Second Consonant D

ʾDʾ	2	ʾDD	16	ʾDK	2	ʾDL	1	ʾDM	31	ʾDN	14	ʾDR	1	HDD	259	ḤDR	4	ʿD	25
ʿDJ	5	ʿDN	55	WDJ	4	WDD	2	JD	11	JDʿ	46	JDD	9	JDN	1	BDBD	1	BDD	1
BDM	2	DDM	4	KDD	5	KDL	1	MDG	1	NDB	5	NDN	32	NDR	1	PDJ	1	PDL	1
QDM	9	QDŚ	2	RDK	1	RDP	3	ŚDD	1	ŚDL	1	ŚDR	2	ŠDW	18	ṢDQ	28	TDB	1
TDQ	1	TDR	2	ZDR	1	TOTAL	43												

Third Consonant D

ʾDD	16	ʾNDL	2	ʾQD	5	ʾŚD	52	HDD	259	HND	18	ḤMD	14	ḪSD	6	ḪʾD	6	ḪBD	7
ḪLD	1	ḪND	1	ḪNDN	1	ḪRD	1	ʿBD	75	ʿMD	2	ʿRD	8	WDD	2	JḤD	16	JDD	9
JRD	3	BʿD	23	BDD	1	DWD	61	DBDB	1	DGDG	2	DLDL	1	GʾD	2	GJD	9	GLD	1
GRD	3	KʾD	3	KBD	7	KDD	5	KND	1	KNDL	2	KPD	1	KRD	2	LʾD	2	LND	2
MʾD	25	MND	1	MRDK	1	MŚD	1	NʾD	2	NWD	4	NKD	1	PQD	5	PRD	1	PŚD	1
QʾD	3	QRD	1	SRD	1	ŚʾD	1	ŚDD	1	ŚLD	1	ŚMD	2	ŠKD	1	ṢJD	10	ṢMD	3
TND	1	T̤ḪD	1	ṬRD	4	ZJD	1	TOTAL	64										

Fourth Consonant D

ʾŚQD	10	BDBD	1	QQQD	1	TOTAL	3

PHONEME COUNT

Total Roots Containing D 148

Roots Containing Ḏ

First Consonant Ḏ

Ḏ	17	ḎHB	1	ḎBB	16	ḎBL	1	ḎKJ	1	ḎKR	49	ḎMR	64	ḎNB	10	ḎQN	6	ḎRʾ	8
ḎRʿ	16	TOTAL	11																

Second Consonant Ḏ

ʾḎN	1	ʿḎR	50	TOTAL	2

Third Consonant Ḏ

ʾḪḎ	15	TOTAL	1

Fourth Consonant Ḏ

TOTAL 0

Total Roots Containing Ḏ 14

Roots Containing G

First Consonant G

GʾJ	9	GʾD	2	GʾG	5	GʾL	6	GʾN	1	GʾR	8	GʾŠ	3	GʾZ	2	GJḤ	7	GJD	9
GBʾ	11	GBL	3	GBN	1	GLD	1	GLL	4	GLZ	4	GML	8	GMR	4	GNB	1	GNGN	1
GNM	1	GNN	2	GRB	1	GRD	3	GRGR	1	GRN	2	GRR	1	GRŚ	2	GZZ	7	TOTAL	29

Second Consonant G

ʾG	3	ʾGG	2	ʾGN	6	ʾGR	1	ʾGZ	1	ḪGL	2	ḪGR	2	ʿGL	4	BGN	2	BGŠ	1
DGDG	2	DGN	119	DGZ	1	LGG	1	MGJ	1	MGN	5	NGH	6	NGŚ	2	PGR	2	RGM	3
ŚGG	3	ŚGR	8	ŠGŠ	4	TOTAL	23												

Third Consonant G

ʾGG	2	ʾMG	1	ḪRGL	2	GʾG	5	GNGN	1	GRGR	1	LGG	1	LŠG	1	MDG	1	MNG	1
NʾG	1	NNGL	1	PRG	1	ŚGG	3	ŚNG	1	ŚNGR	1	ŠʾG	1	ŠLG	3	ŠMGN	3	ŠŠG	1
TʾG	3	TTG	1	ZʾG	1	ZBG	2	TOTAL	24										

Fourth Consonant G

DGDG	2	TOTAL	1

Total Roots Containing G 77

Roots Containing K

First Consonant K

K	23	KʾB	25	KʾD	3	KʾK	2	KʾL	11	KʾM	15	KʾN	2	KʾR	9	KʾŚ	3	KʾT	6
KʾZ	5	KHL	9	KWJ	4	KWN	97	KBB	2	KBD	7	KBKB	7	KBL	5	KBN	1	KBR	14
KBS	15	KBŠ	3	KDD	5	KDL	1	KKK	19	KKKB	2	KKKN	7	KKKR	2	KKKŚ	3	KKM	1
KL	2	KLB	7	KLK	2	KLL	3	KLM	2	KLP	4	KM	5	KMB	1	KMM	4	KMN	6
KMR	4	KMS	6	KMT	2	KNW	2	KNB	1	KND	1	KNDL	2	KNK	8	KNN	13	KNP	1
KNŚ	7	KNT	3	KNZ	8	KPD	1	KPP	2	KPŚ	1	KPT	1	KRʾ	3	KRB	12	KRD	2
KRKR	3	KRN	2	KRŚ	5	KRŠ	2	KRT	1	KRZ	1	KSW	2	KSJ	3	KSBR	1	KŚJ	2
KŚP	3	KŠL	1	KŠM	2	KŠR	4	KTKT	1	KTL	2	KTR	5	KTT	1	KTZ	1	KZB	5
KZR	6	KZZ	1	TOTAL	82														

Second Consonant K

ʾK	12	ʾKK	19	ʾKL	2	ʾKN	9	ʾKR	9	ḤKM	3	JKK	1	JKL	2	BKL	5	BKN	9
BKR	4	BKS	2	BKŚ	3	BKŠŠ	1	DKB	1	DKL	5	DKŚ	1	ḎKJ	1	ḎKR	49	KKK	19
KKKB	2	KKKN	7	KKKR	2	KKKŚ	3	KKM	1	LKŚ	1	MKJ	5	MKL	2	MKS	1	NKD	1
NKL	2	NKM	1	NKR	8	PKN	4	RKB	5	SKL	10	ŚKB	3	ŚKN	10	ŚKR	32	ŚKŚ	1

ŠKD	1	ŠKK	2	ŠKM	8	TKL	3	TKR	1	ZKK	9	ZKZK	3	TOTAL	47				

Third Consonant K

ʾJK	2	ʾDK	2	ʾKK	19	ʾLK	4	ʾNK	2	ʾPK	3	ʾRK	3	ʾŚK	2	ḤŚK	2	ḤTK	9
ḪLK	1	JKK	1	BLK	6	BRKN	3	BZKN	1	DʾK	3	DNK	2	DRK	9	DŚK	1	KʾK	2
KBKB	7	KKK	19	KKKB	2	KKKN	7	KKKR	2	KKKŚ	3	KLK	2	KNK	8	KRKR	3	KTKT	1
LŠK	1	MʾK	2	MLK	100	MŚK	7	RʾK	1	RBK	1	RDK	1	RMK	3	SMKN	1	ŚLK	1
ŚMK	13	ŚRK	3	ŠKK	2	TʾK	5	ZKK	9	TOTAL	45								

Fourth Consonant K

MRDK	1	TŠPK	1	ZKZK	3	TOTAL	3

Total Roots Containing K 177

Roots Containing L

First Consonant L

L	175	Lʾ	3	Lʾʾ	5	LʾJ	19	LʾD	2	LʾL	15	LʾM	60	LʾN	1	LʾP	5	LʾR	5
LʾŚ	3	LʾT	2	LḤM	1	LḪN	3	LWJ	12	LBW	12	LBB	1	LBN	5	LGG	1	LKŚ	1
LLʾ	4	LLR	2	LM	9	LMM	10	LMR	1	LMS	9	LND	2	LSM	3	LŠ	4	LŠG	1
LŠK	1	LṬP	2	TOTAL	32														

Second Consonant L

ʾL	877	ʾLʾ	2	ʾLK	4	ʾLL	39	ʾLM	10	ʾLN	6	ʾLP	14	ʾLR	11	ʾLŚ	3	HLL	19
ḤLJ	9	ḤLB	2	ḤLM	3	ḤLṢ	7	ḪLḪL	2	ḪLD	1	ḪLK	1	ḪLM	1	ḪLN	1	ḪLŠ	1
ʿLJ	15	ʿLṢ	3	JLQṬ	1	BLʾ	1	BLW	1	BLJ	2	BLBL	1	BLBN	3	BLK	6	BLL	12
BLM	4	BLT	5	BLṬ	11	DLW	1	DLDL	1	DLM	1	DLQ	9	GLD	1	GLL	4	GLZ	4
KL	2	KLB	7	KLK	2	KLL	3	KLM	2	KLP	4	LLʾ	4	LLR	2	MLʾ	2	MLK	100
MLL	2	NLŠ	1	PLḪ	14	PLL	2	PLS	15	PLṬ	4	ŚLḪ	9	ŚLJ	1	ŚLB	2	ŚLD	1
ŚLK	1	ŚLL	7	ŚLM	34	ŚLP	2	ŠL	1	ŠLG	3	ŠLŠ	4	ṢLL	13	TLʾ	3	TLʿ	1
TLL	3	TLM	4	ṬLL	8	ZLḪ	3	ZLJ	2	ZLB	3	ZLN	1	ZLT	3	ZLZL	2	TOTAL	79

Third Consonant L

ʾHL	14	ʾḪL	2	ʾJL	10	ʾBL	4	ʾDL	1	ʾKL	2	ʾLL	39	ʾML	1	ʾNLL	1	ʾRL	1
ʾŚL	7	ʾTL	6	ʾZL	2	HLL	19	ḪʾL	83	ḪWL	2	ḪGL	2	ḪML	1	ʿGL	4	ʿRL	2
ʿZL	18	WSL	1	JʿL	18	JBL	40	JKL	2	BʾL	10	BʿL	144	BBL	1	BKL	5	BLL	12
BRL	1	BTL	2	DʾL	1	DKL	5	DŚL	1	ḎBL	1	GʾL	6	GBL	3	GLL	4	GML	8
KʾL	11	KHL	9	KBL	5	KDL	1	KLL	3	KŠL	1	KTL	2	LʾL	15	MʾL	3	MKL	2
MLL	2	MŚL	3	MZL	1	NʾL	1	NḤL	2	NJL	2	NBL	3	NKL	2	NML	2	NZL	2
PʾL	3	PDL	1	PLL	2	QHL	1	QWL	2	QBL	2	SKL	10	ŚʾL	9	ŚBL	3	ŚDL	1
ŚLL	7	ŚML	1	ŚNL	1	ŠʿL	2	ŠWL	2	ŠBL	2	ŠQL	7	ṢLL	13	TʾL	5	TKL	3
TLL	3	TZL	1	ṬLL	8	ZḪL	4	ZBL	7	TOTAL	85								

Fourth Consonant L

ʾNDL	2	ʾNLL	1	ʾNTL	4	ḪLḪL	2	ḪRGL	2	BLBL	1	DLDL	1	KNDL	2	NNGL	1	ŚMʾL	7
ZLZL	2	TOTAL	11																

Total Roots Containing L 207

Roots Containing M

First Consonant M

M	104	Mʾ	2	MʾJ	3	MʾD	25	MʾK	2	MʾL	3	MʾM	3	MʾN	8	MʾR	22	MʾŠ	6
MʾT	20	MʾZ	5	MHR	9	MWʾ	2	MWŠ	2	MWT	40	MJ	3	MDG	1	MGJ	1	MGN	5
MKJ	5	MKL	2	MKS	1	MLʾ	2	MLK	100	MLL	2	MM	16	MMʾ	2	MMM	2	MMN	1
MNW	7	MNJ	6	MND	1	MNG	1	MNMN	2	MNN	41	MNZ	1	MQṬ	6	MRʾ	4	MRḪ	2
MRDK	1	MRMR	2	MRQ	1	MRR	9	MRṢ	29	MSR	2	MŚḪ	10	MŚJ	2	MŚB	1	MŚD	1
MŚK	7	MŚL	3	MŠN	1	MŠR	2	MṢʾ	13	MT	111	MTʿ	9	MTN	3	MTQ	3	MTT	2
MṬR	23	MZʾ	6	MZL	1	MZM	1	MZN	1	MZZ	1	TOTAL	66						

Second Consonant M

ʾM	6	ʾMʾ	5	ʾMW	2	ʾMG	1	ʾML	1	ʾMM	37	ʾMN	17	ʾMR	41	ʾMT	2	ḤM	40
ḤMD	14	ḤMR	2	ḪMʾ	1	ḪMJ	1	ḪMBZ	1	ḪML	1	ḪMM	2	ḪMR	4	ḪMŚ	3	ḪMṬ	4
ʿMD	2	ʿMM	211	ʿMQ	2	ʿMS	14	WMʾ	7	JM	5	JMM	9	JMN	14	DM	3	DMḪ	1
DMQ	12	DMR	1	DMT	1	ḎMR	64	GML	8	GMR	4	KM	5	KMB	1	KMM	4	KMN	6
KMR	4	KMS	6	KMT	2	LM	9	LMM	10	LMR	1	LMS	9	MM	16	MMʾ	2	MMM	2
MMN	1	NMḪ	14	NML	2	NMN	4	NMR	2	NMŠ	5	NMZ	1	QMṢ	1	RMK	3	RMM	1
RMN	1	RMŠ	7	SMKN	1	SMT	1	ŚM	234	ŚMʾL	7	ŚMḪ	20	ŚMʿ	57	ŚMB	1	ŚMD	2
ŚMK	13	ŚML	1	ŚMM	14	ŚMN	1	ŚMR	21	ŚMŚ	76	ŚMT	10	ŠMGN	3	ŠMR	4	ṢMD	3
TMH	3	TMB	1	TMN	1	TMR	3	ZMʾ	2	ZMM	5	ZMN	2	TOTAL	87				

Third Consonant M

ʾJM	5	ʾDM	31	ʾLM	10	ʾMM	37	ʾRM	5	ʾŚM	9	ʾTM	6	ʾZM	2	ḤKM	3	ḤLM	3
ḤRM	2	ḪLM	1	ḪMM	2	ḪŚM	2	ḪZM	6	ʿMM	211	JJM	1	JMM	9	JTM	7	BDM	2
BLM	4	BŚM	1	BṬM	1	DDM	4	DLM	1	GNM	1	KʾM	15	KKM	1	KLM	2	KMM	4
KŠM	2	LʾM	60	LḤM	1	LMM	10	LSM	3	MʾM	3	MMM	2	MNMN	2	MRMR	2	MZM	1
NḤM	1	NʿM	51	NKM	1	NNM	1	NQM	29	NZM	1	QWM	24	QDM	9	RḤM	16	RWM	69
RGM	3	RMM	1	ŚJM	24	ŚBM	4	ŚLM	34	ŚMM	14	ŚRM	4	ŚTM	1	ŠʾM	2	ŠKM	8
TʾM	4	TLM	4	TRM	2	TŠM	2	ṬQM	1	ZʾM	4	ZMM	5	ZRM	3	TOTAL	68		

Fourth Consonant M

ʾRŚM	1	ŚNQM	1	TOTAL	2

Total Roots Containing M 223

Roots Containing N

First Consonant N

NʾJ	1	NʾD	2	NʾG	1	NʾL	1	NʾR	7	NʾŠ	6	NHR	13	NḤL	2	NḤM	1	NḪJ	1
NḪB	7	NḪN	3	NḪR	3	NʿM	51	NWḪ	44	NWJ	2	NWB	7	NWD	4	NWP	12	NWR	40
NWZ	2	NJL	2	NBʾ	25	NBB	1	NBL	3	NBŚ	1	NBT	2	NBṬ	7	NDB	5	NDN	32
NDR	1	NGH	6	NGŚ	2	NKD	1	NKL	2	NKM	1	NKR	8	NLŠ	1	NMḪ	14	NML	2
NMN	4	NMR	2	NMŠ	5	NMZ	1	NN	20	NNB	2	NNGL	1	NNM	1	NNN	6	NPḪ	3
NPR	4	NPŚ	23	NQM	29	NRB	3	NRNR	1	NSQ	1	NŚʾ	30	NŠʾ	1	NŠP	2	NṢB	17
NṢR	11	NTN	33	NTT	1	NṬʿ	1	NṬP	4	NZ	3	NZL	2	NZM	1	TOTAL	68		

Second Consonant N

ʾN	18	ʾNB	15	ʾNDL	2	ʾNK	2	ʾNLL	1	ʾNN	55	ʾNP	7	ʾNT	1	ʾNTL	4	ʾNTR	1
ʾNZ	3	HND	18	ḤNḤN	3	ḤNN	80	ḪNʾ	1	ḪNW	1	ḪNB	1	ḪND	1	ḪNDN	1	ḪNP	2
ḪNŠ	2	ḪNZ	2	ḪNZR	1	ʿN	45	ʿNW	1	ʿNJ	10	ʿNB	6	ʿNQ	2	JNN	1	JNT	1
BN	89	BNḪ	5	BNJ	21	BNN	1	BNQ	7	BNŠ	1	BNZ	2	BNZR	1	DNK	2	DNN	26
ḎNB	10	GNB	1	GNGN	1	GNM	1	GNN	2	KNW	2	KNB	1	KND	1	KNDL	2	KNK	8
KNN	13	KNP	1	KNŚ	7	KNT	3	KNZ	8	LND	2	MNW	7	MNJ	6	MND	1	MNG	1
MNMN	2	MNN	41	MNZ	1	NN	20	NNB	2	NNGL	1	NNM	1	NNN	6	PNJ	4	PNN	4
QNJ	5	QNT	2	SNQ	7	ŚNḪ	1	ŚNG	1	ŚNGR	1	ŚNL	1	ŚNN	8	ŚNQM	1	ŠN	4
ŠNJ	13	TNʾ	4	TND	1	TNT	1	TNTN	2	ZNJ	2	ZNN	11	ZNR	2	ZNZ	3	ZNZN	2
TOTAL	90																		

Third Consonant N

ʾḪN	1	ʾWN	14	ʾJN	8	ʾBN	16	ʾDN	14	ʾḎN	1	ʾGN	6	ʾKN	9	ʾLN	6	ʾMN	17
ʾNN	55	ʾRN	3	ʾRNB	3	ʾSN	6	ʾŚN	3	ḤNN	80	ḤṢN	27	ḪʾN	7	ḪḪN	1	ḪLN	1
ḪTN	4	ʿJN	2	ʿDN	55	WḪN	1	JʾN	11	JDN	1	JMN	14	JNN	1	JRN	4	JŠN	2
BʾN	3	BJN	11	BGN	2	BKN	9	BNN	1	BRN	2	BŚN	1	BZN	3	DJN	11	DBN	1
DGN	119	DNN	26	DRN	1	DTN	19	ḎQN	6	GʾN	1	GBN	1	GNN	2	GRN	2	KʾN	2
KWN	97	KBN	1	KMN	6	KNN	13	KRN	2	LʾN	1	LḪN	3	LBN	5	MʾN	8	MGN	5
MMN	1	MNN	41	MŠN	1	MTN	3	MZN	1	NḪN	3	NDN	32	NMN	4	NNN	6	NRNR	1
NTN	33	PKN	4	PNN	4	PTN	7	QʾN	3	QRN	3	QṬN	6	RMN	1	RZN	1	ŚKN	10
ŚMN	1	ŚNN	8	ŚRN	1	ŠʾN	3	ŠRN	1	TʾN	3'	TBN	2	TMN	1	TRN	1	TŠN	2
ZʾN	5	ZJN	6	ZBN	3	ZLN	1	ZMN	2	ZNN	11	ZRNB	1	ZZN	1	TOTAL	98		

Fourth Consonant N

ḤNḤN	3	ḪNDN	1	ḪRŚN	3	BLBN	3	BRḪN	1	BRBN	1	BRKN	3	BZKN	1	GNGN	1	KKKN	7
MNMN	2	SMKN	1	ŠMGN	3	TḤTN	2	TNTN	2	TRBN	1	ZNZN	2	TOTAL	17				

Total Roots Containing N 273

Roots Containing P

First Consonant P

P	68	PʾL	3	PʾP	1	PʾR	4	PʾŠ	1	PʾT	1	PḪR	10	PDJ	1	PDL	1	PGR	2
PKN	4	PLḪ	14	PLL	2	PLS	15	PLṬ	4	PNJ	4	PNN	4	PPZ	1	PQḤ	2	PQD	5
PRʿŠ	1	PRD	1	PRG	1	PRR	1	PRS	2	PSʿ	2	PŚD	1	PŚQ	1	PTḤ	21	PTN	7
PṬR	13	PZR	4	TOTAL	32														

Second Consonant P

ʾP	8	ʾPK	3	ʾPP	2	ʾPQ	10	ʾPR	2	ḪPʾ	1	ḪPŠ	2	WPʿ	1	JPʿ	56	JPR	3
KPD	1	KPP	2	KPŚ	1	KPT	1	NPḪ	3	NPR	4	NPŚ	23	PPZ	1	RPʾ	73	RPŠ	1
ŚPQ	8	ŚPR	28	ŚPŚ	5	ŠPṬ	6	ṢPR	3	TPT	2	ZPP	1	TOTAL	27				

Third Consonant P

ʾLP	14	ʾNP	7	ʾPP	2	ʾRPḪ	1	ḪNP	2	KLP	4	KNP	1	KPP	2	KŚP	3	LʾP	5
LṬP	2	NWP	12	NŠP	2	NṬP	4	PʾP	1	RDP	3	RŚP	9	ŚLP	2	ŠṬP	3	ṢRP	2
TSP	3	TŠPK	1	ZPP	1	TOTAL	23												

Fourth Consonant P

ʾRŠP	1	TOTAL	1

Total Roots Containing P 83

Roots Containing Q

First Consonant Q

QʾB	1	QʾD	3	QʾN	3	QʾT	1	QHL	1	QWJ	14	QWL	2	QWM	24	QJŚ	14	QBJ	4
QBL	2	QDM	9	QDŚ	2	QMṢ	1	QNJ	5	QNT	2	QQQD	1	QQQR	1	QRʾ	9	QRB	1
QRD	1	QRN	3	QṢR	3	QṬN	6	QṬR	17	QZJ	1	TOTAL	26						

Second Consonant Q

ʾQD	5	ḪQT	1	ʿQB	54	WQH	14	WQR	1	JQH	2	JQR	21	BQQ	15	ḎQN	6	MQṬ	6
NQM	29	PQḤ	2	PQD	5	QQQD	1	QQQR	1	ŚQḪ	2	ŚQṬ	2	ŠQL	7	TQR	3	ṬQM	1
ZQT	5	TOTAL	21																

Third Consonant Q

ʾBQ	2	ʾPQ	10	ʾŚQD	10	ḤZQ	10	ʿWQ	4	ʿMQ	2	ʿNQ	2	ʿTQ	1	JLQṬ	1	JRQ	2
BNQ	7	BQQ	15	BRQ	8	BTQ	1	DLQ	9	DMQ	12	MRQ	1	MTQ	3	NSQ	1	PŚQ	1
QQQD	1	QQQR	1	RḤQ	5	SNQ	7	ŚʾQ	7	ŚNQM	1	ŚPQ	8	ṢḤQ	2	ṢDQ	28	TDQ	1
ṬBQ	3	ZʾQ	1	ZRQ	4	TOTAL	33												

Fourth Consonant Q

TOTAL 0

Total Roots Containing Q 80

Roots Containing R

First Consonant R

RʾK	1	RʾŚ	1	RʾZ	1	RḤB	17	RḤM	16	RḤQ	5	RḪŠ	1	RḪṢ	2	RʿJ	5	RʿŠ	7
RWḤ	35	RWJ	2	RWB	7	RWM	69	RJB	18	RBʾ	2	RBʿ	1	RBJ	5	RBB	6	RBK	1
RDK	1	RDP	3	RGM	3	RKB	5	RMK	3	RMM	1	RMN	1	RMŠ	7	RPʾ	73	RPŠ	1
RŚP	9	RŠJ	13	RṢJ	4	RZN	1	TOTAL	34										

Second Consonant R

ʾR	3	ʾRḪ	8	ʾRWJ	10	ʾRK	3	ʾRL	1	ʾRM	5	ʾRN	3	ʾRNB	3	ʾRPḪ	1	ʾRR	26
ʾRŚ	13	ʾRŚM	1	ʾRŠP	1	ḤRB	17	ḤRM	2	ḪRḪR	1	ḪRJ	1	ḪRD	1	ḪRGL	2	ḪRR	8
ḪRŚN	3	ḪRṢ	12	ʿRD	8	ʿRL	2	ʿRṢ	5	WRḪ	1	JRʾ	1	JRḪ	102	JRD	3	JRN	4
JRQ	2	JRR	1	BRḪN	1	BRW	1	BRB	1	BRBN	1	BRBR	5	BRKN	3	BRL	1	BRN	2
BRQ	8	BRR	2	BRŠ	1	DRḪ	1	DRB	1	DRK	9	DRN	1	ḎRʾ	8	ḎRʿ	16	GRB	1
GRD	3	GRGR	1	GRN	2	GRR	1	GRŚ	2	KRʾ	3	KRB	12	KRD	2	KRKR	3	KRN	2
KRŚ	5	KRŠ	2	KRT	1	KRZ	1	MRʾ	4	MRḪ	2	MRDK	1	MRMR	2	MRQ	1	MRR	9
MRṢ	29	NRB	3	NRNR	1	PRʿŠ	1	PRD	1	PRG	1	PRR	1	PRS	2	QRʾ	9	QRB	1
QRD	1	QRN	3	SRD	1	ŚRḤ	1	ŚRJ	8	ŚRB	2	ŚRK	3	ŚRM	4	ŚRN	1	ŚRR	39
ŠRN	1	ŠRR	1	ŠRŠR	3	ŠRṬ	2	ṢRP	2	ṢRR	11	TRḪ	2	TRJ	1	TRBN	1	TRM	2
TRN	1	TRR	2	TRTR	2	ṬRD	4	ZRM	3	ZRNB	1	ZRQ	4	ZRT	1	ZRZR	4	TOTAL	109

Third Consonant R

ʾḪR	1	ʾWR	11	ʾBR	2	ʾDR	1	ʾGR	1	ʾKR	9	ʾLR	11	ʾMR	41	ʾPR	2	ʾRR	26
ʾŚR	3	ʾŠR	29	ʾTR	2	ḤDR	4	ḤMR	2	ḪʾR	6	ḪWR	5	ḪBR	8	ḪGR	2	ḪMR	4
ḪRR	8	ḪŚR	1	ḪZR	7	ʿḎR	50	WQR	1	WTR	3	JʾR	10	JPR	3	JQR	21	JRR	1
JŚR	23	JTR	77	BḤR	14	BJR	5	BKR	4	BRR	2	BŚR	8	BZR	3	DWR	34	DBR	2
DMR	1	DŠR	11	ḎKR	49	ḎMR	64	GʾR	8	GMR	4	GRR	1	KʾR	9	KBR	14	KMR	4
KŠR	4	KTR	5	KZR	6	LʾR	5	LLR	2	LMR	1	MʾR	22	MHR	9	MRR	9	MSR	2
MŠR	2	MṬR	23	NʾR	7	NHR	13	NḪR	3	NWR	40	NDR	1	NKR	8	NMR	2	NPR	4
NṢR	11	PʾR	4	PḪR	10	PGR	2	FRR	1	PṬR	13	PZR	4	QṢR	3	QṬR	17	STR	15
ŚʾR	6	ŚḪR	7	ŚWR	2	ŚDR	2	ŚGR	8	ŚKR	32	ŚMR	21	ŚPR	28	ŚRR	39	ŚṬR	1
ŠʾR	4	ŠWR	1	ŠMR	4	ŠRR	1	ṢḪR	1	ṢWR	22	ṢBR	5	ṢPR	3	ṢRR	11	TʾR	1
TWR	55	TDR	2	TKR	1	TMR	3	TQR	3	TRR	2	TŠR	2	ZʾR	2	ZḪR	1	ZDR	1
ZNR	2	TOTAL	111																

Fourth Consonant R

ʾNTR	1	ʾŠḪR	21	ḪBZR	1	ḪNZR	1	ḪRḪR	1	ḪŠTR	1	ʿŠTR	69	BNZR	1	BRBR	5	GRGR	1
KKKR	2	KRKR	3	KSBR	1	MRMR	2	NRNR	1	QQQR	1	ŚNGR	1	ŠRŠR	3	TRTR	2	ZRZR	4
TOTAL	20																		

Total Roots Containing R 274

Roots Containing S

First Consonant S

SKL	10	SMKN	1	SMT	1	SNQ	7	SRD	1	STR	15	SṬʾ	7	TOTAL	7

Second Consonant S

ʾSN	6	ḤSD	6	WSL	1	KSW	2	KSJ	3	KSBR	1	LSM	3	MSR	2	NSQ	1	PSʿ	2
TSP	3	TOTAL	11																

Third Consonant S

ḤBS	15	ʿMS	14	JBS	4	BKS	2	KBS	15	KMS	6	LMS	9	MKS	1	PLS	15	PRS	2
TOTAL	10																		

Fourth Consonant S

TOTAL 0

Total Roots Containing S 28

Roots Containing Ś

First Consonant Ś

ŚʾB	1	ŚʾD	1	ŚʾL	9	ŚʾQ	7	ŚʾR	6	ŚḪ	1	ŚḪR	7	ŚWR	2	ŚJB	7	ŚJM	24
ŚJT	12	ŚBJ	4	ŚBL	3	ŚBM	4	ŚBŚ	1	ŚDD	1	ŚDL	1	ŚDR	2	ŚGG	3	ŚGR	8
ŚKB	3	ŚKN	10	ŚKR	32	ŚKŚ	1	ŚLḤ	9	ŚLJ	1	ŚLB	2	ŚLD	1	ŚLK	1	ŚLL	7
ŚLM	34	ŚLP	2	ŚM	234	ŚMʾL	7	ŚMḪ	20	ŚMʿ	57	ŚMB	1	ŚMD	2	ŚMK	13	ŚML	1

ŚMM	14	ŚMN	1	ŚMR	21	ŚMŚ	76	ŚMT	10	ŚNḪ	1	ŚNG	1	ŚNGR	1	ŚNL	1	ŚNN	8
ŚNQM	1	ŚPQ	8	ŚPR	28	ŚPŚ	5	ŚQḪ	2	ŚQṬ	2	ŚRḪ	1	ŚRJ	8	ŚRB	2	ŚRK	3
ŚRM	4	ŚRN	1	ŚRR	39	ŚTM	1	ŚṬḤ	7	ŚṬR	1	TOTAL	66						

Second Consonant Ś

ʾṢʾ	1	ʾŚJ	8	ʾŚD	52	ʾŚK	2	ʾŚL	7	ʾŚM	9	ʾŚN	3	ʾŚQD	10	ʾŚR	3	ʾŚŚ	2
ʾŚT	2	ḤŚK	2	ḪŚJ	3	ḪŚM	2	ḪŚR	1	ḪŚT	1	JŚR	23	BŚJ	2	BŚM	1	BŚN	1
BŚR	8	DŚB	1	DŚK	1	DŚL	1	KŚJ	2	KŚP	3	MŚḤ	10	MŚJ	2	MŚB	1	MŚD	1
MŚK	7	MŚL	3	NŚʾ	30	PŚD	1	PŚQ	1	RŚP	9	TŚʿ	1	TOTAL	37				

Third Consonant Ś

ʾBŚ	6	ʾLŚ	3	ʾRŚ	13	ʾRŚM	1	ʾŚŚ	2	Ḫʾ Ś	3	ḪMŚ	3	ḪRŚN	3	JBŚ	17	BKŚ	3
DKŚ	1	GRŚ	2	KʾŚ	3	KBŚ	3	KNŚ	7	KPŚ	1	KRŚ	5	LʾŚ	3	LKŚ	1	NBŚ	1
NGŚ	2	NPŚ	23	QJŚ	14	QDŚ	2	RʾŚ	1	ŚBŚ	1	ŚKŚ	1	ŚMŚ	76	ŚPŚ	5	TOTAL	29

Fourth Consonant Ś

KKKŚ	3	TOTAL	1

Total Roots Containing Ś 133

Roots Containing Š

First Consonant Š

Š	22	ŠʾḪ	4	ŠʾG	1	ŠʾM	2	ŠʾN	3	ŠʾR	4	ŠʿL	2	ŠWʾ	1	ŠWB	47	ŠWL	2
ŠWR	1	ŠBL	2	ŠDW	18	ŠGŠ	4	ŠKD	1	ŠKK	2	ŠKM	8	ŠL	1	ŠLG	3	ŠLŠ	4
ŠMGN	3	ŠMR	4	ŠN	4	ŠNJ	13	ŠPṬ	6	ŠQL	7	ŠRN	1	ŠRR	1	ŠRŠR	3	ŠRṬ	2
ŠŠG	1	ŠT	2	ŠTŠ	1	ŠṬP	3	TOTAL	34										

Second Consonant Š

ʾŠḪ	2	ʾŠḪR	21	ʾŠW	1	ʾŠB	2	ʾŠR	29	ʾŠŠ	1	ʾŠZ	1	ḪŠḪŠ	1	ḪŠŠ	6	ḪŠTR	1
ʿŠTR	69	WŠʿ	2	WŠB	1	JŠʿ	59	JŠB	1	JŠN	2	DŠR	11	KŠL	1	KŠM	2	KŠR	4
LŠ	4	LŠG	1	LŠK	1	MŠN	1	MŠR	2	NŠʾ	1	NŠP	2	RŠJ	13	ŠŠG	1	TŠM	2
TŠN	2	TŠPK	1	TŠR	2	TOTAL	33												

Third Consonant Š

ʾWŠ	17	ʾJŠ	4	ʾRŠP	1	ʾŠŠ	1	ḪLŠ	1	ḪNŠ	2	ḪPŠ	2	ḪŠŠ	6	BḪŠ	1	BWŠ	20
BGŠ	1	BKŠŠ	1	BNŠ	1	BRŠ	1	DʾŠ	1	GʾŠ	3	KRŠ	2	MʾŠ	6	MWŠ	2	NʾŠ	6
NLŠ	1	NMŠ	5	PʾŠ	1	RḪŠ	1	RʿŠ	7	RMŠ	7	RPŠ	1	ŠGŠ	4	ŠLŠ	4	ŠRŠR	3
ŠTŠ	1	TʾŠ	2	ṬḪŠ	2	TOTAL	33												

Fourth Consonant Š

ḪŠḪŠ	1	BKŠŠ	1	PRʿŠ	1	TOTAL	3

Total Roots Containing Š 103

Roots Containing Ṣ

First Consonant Ṣ

Ṣʾ	1	ṢḤQ	2	ṢḪR	1	ṢWR	22	ṢJḪ	3	ṢJD	10	ṢBʾ	25	ṢBR	5	ṢBṬ	3	ṢDQ	28
ṢLL	13	ṢMD	3	ṢPR	3	ṢRP	2	ṢRR	11	TOTAL	15								

Second Consonant Ṣ

ḤṢN	27	WṢʾ	10	JṢʾ	67	MṢʾ	13	NṢB	17	NṢR	11	QṢR	3	RṢJ	4	TOTAL	8

Third Consonant Ṣ

ḤLṢ	7	ḪRṢ	12	ʿLṢ	3	ʿRṢ	5	MRṢ	29	QMṢ	1	RḪṢ	2	TOTAL	7

Fourth Consonant Ṣ

TOTAL 0

Total Roots Containing Ṣ 30

Roots Containing T

First Consonant T

Tʾ	12	TʾḪ	1	TʾG	3	TʾK	5	TʾL	5	TʾM	4	TʾN	3	TʾR	1	TʾŠ	2	TʾT	1
TʾZ	3	TḤT	2	TḪTN	2	TḪJ	1	TḪTḪ	1	TWR	55	TBʾ	3	TBB	14	TBN	2	TBZ	1
TDB	1	TDQ	1	TDR	2	TKL	3	TKR	1	TLʾ	3	TLʿ	1	TLL	3	TLM	4	TMH	3
TMB	1	TMN	1	TMR	3	TNʾ	4	TND	1	TNT	1	TNTN	2	TPT	2	TQR	3	TRḪ	2
TRJ	1	TRBN	1	TRM	2	TRN	1	TRR	2	TRTR	2	TSP	3	TŠʿ	1	TŠM	2	TŠN	2
TŠPK	1	TŠR	2	TT	1	TTG	1	TTT	3	TZL	1	TOTAL	56						

Second Consonant T

ʾTJ	3	ʾTL	6	ʾTM	6	ʾTR	2	ʾTT	19	ʾTZ	2	ḤTK	9	ḪTʾ	7	ḪTN	4	ʿTQ	1
WTʾ	2	WTR	3	JT	40	JTM	7	JTR	77	JTT	3	BTL	2	BTQ	1	DTN	19	KTKT	1
KTL	2	KTR	5	KTT	1	KTZ	1	MT	111	MTʿ	9	MTN	3	MTQ	3	MTT	2	NTN	33
NTT	1	PTḤ	21	PTN	7	STR	15	ŠTM	1	ŠT	2	ŠTŠ	1	TT	1	TTG	1	TTT	3
TOTAL	40																		

Third Consonant T

ʾMT	2	ʾNT	1	ʾNTL	4	ʾNTR	1	ʾŚT	2	ʾTT	19	ḪʾT	7	ḪQT	1	ḪŚT	1	ḪŠTR	1
ʿŠTR	69	WBT	1	JʾT	1	JNT	1	JTT	3	BʾT	2	BJT	7	BLT	5	DMT	1	KʾT	6
KMT	2	KNT	3	KPT	1	KRT	1	KTT	1	LʾT	2	MʾT	20	MWT	40	MTT	2	NBT	2
NTT	1	PʾT	1	QʾT	1	QNT	2	SMT	1	ŚJT	12	ŚMT	10	TʾT	1	TḤT	2	TḤTN	2
TḪTḪ	1	TNT	1	TNTN	2	TPT	2	TRTR	2	TTT	3	ZʾT	5	ZLT	3	ZQT	5	ZRT	1
TOTAL	50																		

Fourth Consonant T

KTKT	1	TOTAL	1

Total Roots Containing T 147

Roots Containing Ṭ

First Consonant Ṭ

ṬḪD	1	ṬḪŠ	2	ṬJB	25	ṬBḪ	1	ṬBQ	3	ṬLL	8	ṬQM	1	ṬRD	4	TOTAL	8

Second Consonant Ṭ

ḪṬʾ	1	BṬḤ	1	BṬM	1	LṬP	2	MṬR	23	NṬʿ	1	NṬP	4	PṬR	13	QṬN	6	QṬR	17
SṬʾ	7	ŚṬḤ	7	ŚṬR	1	ŠṬP	3	TOTAL	14										

Third Consonant Ṭ

ḪMṬ	4	BLṬ	11	MQṬ	6	NBṬ	7	PLṬ	4	ŚQṬ	2	ŠPṬ	6	ŠRṬ	2	ṢBṬ	3	TOTAL	9

Fourth Consonant Ṭ

JLQṬ	1	TOTAL	1

Total Roots Containing Ṭ 32

Roots Containing Z

First Consonant Z

ZʾG	1	ZʾM	4	ZʾN	5	ZʾQ	1	ZʾR	2	ZʾT	5	ZʾZ	16	ZḪL	4	ZḪR	1	ZḪZḪ	1
ZJD	1	ZJN	6	ZBB	1	ZBG	2	ZBL	7	ZBN	3	ZBZ	1	ZBZB	1	ZDR	1	ZKK	9
ZKZK	3	ZLḪ	3	ZLJ	2	ZLB	3	ZLN	1	ZLT	3	ZLZL	2	ZMʾ	2	ZMM	5	ZMN	2
ZNJ	2	ZNN	11	ZNR	2	ZNZ	3	ZNZN	2	ZPP	1	ZQT	5	ZRM	3	ZRNB	1	ZRQ	4

ZRT	1	ZRZR	4	ZZB	1	ZZN	1	TOTAL	44

Second Consonant Z

ʾZW	5	ʾZJ	7	ʾZL	2	ʾZM	2	ḪZQ	10	ḪZM	6	ḪZR	7	ʿZB	28	ʿZL	18	ʿZZ	33
BZḪ	1	BZW	1	BZBZ	2	BZKN	1	BZN	3	BZR	3	BZZ	5	GZZ	7	KZB	5	KZR	6
KZZ	1	MZʾ	6	MZL	1	MZM	1	MZN	1	MZZ	1	NZ	3	NZL	2	NZM	1	PZR	4
QZJ	1	RZN	1	TZL	1	ZZB	1	ZZN	1	TOTAL	35								

Third Consonant Z

ʾGZ	1	ʾNZ	3	ʾŠZ	1	ʾTZ	2	Ḫʾ Z	3	ḪBZR	1	ḪNZ	2	ḪNZR	1	ʿZZ	33	BḪZ	1
BWZ	15	BNZ	2	BNZR	1	BZZ	5	DGZ	1	GʾZ	2	GLZ	4	GZZ	7	KʾZ	5	KNZ	8
KRZ	1	KTZ	1	KZZ	1	MʾZ	5	MNZ	1	MZZ	1	NWZ	2	NMZ	1	PPZ	1	RʾZ	1
TʾZ	3	TBZ	1	ZʾZ	16	ZḪZḪ	1	ZBZ	1	ZBZB	1	ZKZK	3	ZLZL	2	ZNZ	3	ZNZN	2
ZRZR	4	TOTAL	41																

Fourth Consonant Z

ḪMBZ	1	BZBZ	2	TOTAL	2

Total Roots Containing Z 122

6. INDEX OF NAMES

This chapter contains a complete list of all the names in the order of their transliteration. The chapter is meant to facilitate reference to the analyses offered in other chapters of this volume.

Each entry consists of three columns:

1) Analysis of the name, preceded by a sequential number that refers to the transliteration given in the second column. The numbers, useful for future citations, are irrelevant for other chapters of this volume.

2) Transliteration of the name, plus some auxiliary indications, as discussed in section 0.3.

3) Reference(s), plus some auxiliary indications, as discussed in section 0.3.

In form, this index is almost identical with the list produced in 1966-67 (see p. 3), but does not have the detailed columns of analysis that appear in the first three chapters (see p. 4).

The order of the index of names is that of the roman-alphabet transliterations of the cuneiform signs as the transliterations appear in column 2, disregarding the semantic indicators (determinatives) but not the index numbers of the homophonous signs.

INDEX OF NAMES

1.	ʾAJA+ʾAB-U-HU	A-A-A-BU-U_2	FN	DE CLERCQ II 253B
2.	ʾAJ-A+ʾARR-I	D-A-A-AR-RI	FN	M
3.	ʾAJA+BAʿL-A-JA	A-A-BA-LA-IA		SIMMONS 63 9
4.	ʾAJA+DAWD-U-HU	A-A-DA-DU-U_2		HARRIS 79 5
5.	ʾAJA+JE-JŠUʿ	A-A-E-ŠU-UḪ?		TCL X 9 3
6.	ʾAJA+ʿAMM-U-HU	A-A-ḪA-AM-MU-U_2		BASOR 95 23
7.	ʾAJ-A+ʿALIJ-AT	D-A-A-ḪA-LI-IA-AT	MN?	CT XLV 92 R. 12
8.	ʾAJAL-AT-UM	D-A-A-LA-TUM	FN	CT VIII 29C 22+
9.	ʾAJAL-UM	A-A-LUM		KISURRA 116
10.	ḪAJJ-AN-UM	A-A-NU-UM		M
11.	ḪAJJ-AT-IJA	A-A-TI-IA		BM 92654 5
12.	JA-BRUQ+ʾAB-UM	A-AB-RU-UK-A-BU-UM		JCS XXVI 151:13, HARMAL
13.	HADD-AJA	A-AD-DA-A		M+
14.	JA-ḎKUR+ʾIL	A-AD-KU-UR-DINGIR		HARRIS 10 18
15.	JA-ḎKUR+ʾIL	A-AD-KUR-DINGIR		SIMMONS 80 13
16.	JA-DLUW-HU	A-AD-LU-U_2		HARRIS 70 15+
17.	JA-ʿQUB+ʾIL	A-AḪ-KU-UB-DINGIR		HARRIS 12 3+
18.	JA-ʾKUR+ʾIL	A-AḪ-KU-UR_2-[DINGIR]?		HARRIS 79 22
19.	JA-ʿZIB-I+ʾIL	A-AḪ-ZI-BI-DINGIR		SIMMONS 70 5
20.	JA-ʿZIB+ʾIL	A-AḪ-ZI-IB-DINGIR		HARRIS 57 2
21.	JA-KLIL-UM	A-AK-LI-LUM		HARRIS 28 11
22.	JA-KSIJ+ʾIL	A-AK-ZI-DINGIR		FIGULLA CAT I 14029
23.	ʾALLA+MUT-IJ-I	A-AL-MU-TI-I	TRIBE	M
24.	JA-MLIʾ+ʾIL	A-AM-LI-DINGIR		YOS XIII 63:3, 6
25.	JA-MLIK+ʾIL	A-AM-LIK-DINGIR		HARRIS 76 22
26.	JA-MRAṢ-UM	A-AM-RA-ZUM		HARRIS 45 10
27.	ʾAJAN+ʾABAL	A-AN-A-BA-AL	FN	XIII 1 IX 38
28.	JA-NḪIR-AJA	A-AN?-ḪI?-RA-A		HARRIS 85 16
29.	JA-NQIM+ʾIL	A-AN-KI-IM-DINGIR		HARRIS 9 14+
30.	ʾAJAN+KURUB	A-AN-KU-RU-UB	FN	RA LXV 51 X 15
31.	ʾAJAN+LIʾM	A-AN-LI-IM		M+
32.	JA-NTIN+ʾIL	[A-A]N-TI-IN-DINGIR		HARRIS 56 15
33.	JA-NTIN-UM	A-AN-TI-NU-UM		SIMMONS 79 6'
34.	JA-RŠIJ+ʾIL-I	A-AR-ŠI-DINGIR		TA 1930,7:6
35.	JA-RWIJ+ʾIL	A-AR-WI-DINGIR		HARRIS 98 R. 7
36.	ʾA-WDAJ+ʾIL	A-AW-TE-IL		U
37.	ʾAB-A+JARAḪ	A-BA-A-RA-AḪ		KICH II D 8 3
38.	ʾA-JPAʿ+NAN-UM	A-BA-AḪ-NA-NU-UM		TA 1931, 374, EARLY OB
39.	ʾAB-A+ʾANN-U	A-BA-AN-NU		M
40.	ʾABAB-AH	A-BA-BA	FN	C+
41.	ʾABAB-AJA	A-BA-BA-A-IA	FN	M
42.	ʾABAB-AN-IM	A-BA-BA-NI-IM	GEN	B 42
43.	ʾABAB-AN-UM	A-BA-BA-NU-UM		B 71+
44.	ʾAB-A+DAWD-UM	A-BA-DA-DUM		HARRIS 95 9
45.	ʾAB-A+ʾIL	A-BA-DINGIR	FN	A. 59 5
46.	ʾAB-A+ʾEL	A-BA-EL		TA 31, 221
47.	ʾABAQ-UM	A-BA-GU-UM		KISURRA 82 9
48.	ʾABAN-AJA	A-BA-NA-A		BM 81660 2
49.	ʾAB-AN-UM	A-BA-NU-UM		U+, SIMMONS 51 18
50.	ʾABAŠ-IN-UM	A-BA-ŠE-NU-UM		M
51.	ʾAB-I+JARAḪ	A-BE-RA-AḪ		B 9
52.	ʾAB-I+ṢUWR-A	A-BE-ZU-RA		TCL IV 87 10 CAPP.
53.	ʾAB-I+JABAL	A-BI-A-BA-AL		FIGULLA CAT. I 14206
54.	ʾAB-I+HADD-U	A-BI-A-DU		A.+
55.	ʾAB-I+JAʾAR	A-BI-A-ḪA-AR		CT XLIII 125 1+
56.	ʾAB-I+ḪAM-A	A-BI-A-MA		SIMMONS 50 22+
57.	ʾAB-I+ʾAMAL	A-BI-A-MA-AL		KISURRA 153 34
58.	ʾAB-I+JARAḪ	A-BI-A-RA-AḪ		B 9+
59.	ʾAB-I+ʾAŠD	A-BI-A-SA-AD		B 10+
60.	ʾAB-I+ʾAZJ-I	A-BI-A-ZI		A.
61.	ʾAB-I+ʿAḎR-I	A-BI-AD-RI		A. LATE
62.	ʾAB-I+ʾANN-IM	A-BI-AN-NIM	GEN	M
63.	ʾAB-I+ʾA-T-ŠAMAR	A-BI-AŠ-TA-MA-AR		YOS XIII 489:4
64.	ḪABIB-IM	A-BI-BI-IM	GEN	KISURRA 62
65.	ʾAB-I+DAGAN	A-BI-D-DA-GAN		M+
66.	ʾAB-I+DARAB	[A]?-BI-DA-RA-AB		RA LXV 43 III 67

133.	ʾAB-I+ŠAMAT-A	A-BI-SA-MA-TA		EDZARD, DER 120:4
134.	ʾAB-I+ŠAMAR	A-BI-SA-MAR		M+
135.	ʾABIŠ-AN-UM	A-BI-SA-NU-UM		CT XLVIII 29 REV.
136.	ʾAB-I+ŠAPAR	A-BI-SA-PA-AR	FN	C
137.	ʾAB-I+ŠAPAR	A-BI-SA-PAR$_2$		CT XLV 82 7+, XIII 1 II 15
138.	ʾAB-I+ŠARIJ	A-BI-SA-RI		LIMET, SCEAUX CASS. P 114
139.	ʾAB-I+ŠARIJ-JE	A-BI-SA-RI-E		B 11+; M+
140.	ʾAB-I+ṢUWR-A	A-BI-ṢU-RA		TIM IV 34 27
141.	ʾAB-I+JA-JŠUʿ	A-BI-ŠU-UḪ		B 10
142.	ʾAB-I+JA-JŠUʿ+....	A-BI-ŠU-UT-LI		B 11
143.	ʾAB-I+DITAN-UM	A-BI-TI-DA-NU-UM		TA 1931, 538 III,IV
144.	ʾAB-I+ṬAJB-A	A-BI-ṬA-BA		A.+
145.	ʾAB-I+ŠAMŠ	A-BI-D-UTU	FN	XIII 24 IV 40
146.	ʾAB-I+ŠAMŠ-I	A-BI-D-UTU-ŠI	FN	XIII 1 IX 40+
147.	ʾAB-I+ṢUWR-I	A-BI-ZU-RI		M
148.	ḪABIS-UM	A-BI-ZU-UM		TIM III 4 3+
149.	ḪABIS-UM	A-BI-ZUM		TIM II 122 3+
150.	ʾAB-I+JA-MWUT-I	A-BI$_2$-A-MU-TI		U
151.	ʾAB-I-Š+KIWN	A-BI$_2$-IŠ-KI-IN		U
152.	ʾAB-I+ŠARIJ-JE	A-BI$_2$-SA-RI-E		BIN VII 93 DATE
153.	ʾAB-I+JATAR	A-BI$_2$-WA-DAR		U
154.	ʾAB-U+ḪAʾL-IM	A-BU-ḪA-LIM	GEN	M+
155.	ʾAB-U+ḪAʾL-UM	A-BU-ḪA-LUM		UCP X P. 53, M
156.	ʾAB-U+JAT-I-JA	A-BU-IA-TI-IA		TCL I 85 10
157.	ʾAB-U+KA+ʾIL	A-BU-KA-DINGIR		M+
158.	ʾAB-U+LA-JA	A-BU-LA-IA		XIII 101 6
159.	ʾAB-U+ME-QWIM	A-BU-ME-KI-IM		M+
160.	ʾAB-U+ME-KWIN	A-BU-ME-KI-IN		X 154 2+
161.	ʾAB-U+NAN-UM	A-BU-NA-NU-UM		B 42+
162.	ʾAB-U+NIWR-A	A-BU-NI-RA		TIM VI 34, U
163.	ʾAB-U+JAQAR	A-BU-QAR		M
164.	ʾAB-U+ŠALIM	A-BU-SA-[LIM]		M
165.	ʾAB-UM+ʾIL	A-BU-UM-DINGIR		U, M+
166.	ʾAB-UM+JE-KWIN	A-BU-UM-E-KI-IN		M
167.	ʾAB-UM+ḪAʾL-UM	A-BU-UM-ḪA-LU-UM		B 11+
168.	ʾAB-UM+ḪAʾL-UM	A-BU-UM-ḪA-LUM		B 11+
169.	ʾAB-UM+ḪIʾL-UM	A-BU-UM-ḪI-LUM		B 11
170.	ʾAB-UM+JAQAR	A-BU-UM-WA-QAR		M
171.	ʾAB-U+JAQAR	A-BU-WA-QAR		M
172.	HADD-AJA	A-DA-A		M
173.	ʾA-JDAʿ+PI+ʾEL	A-DA-AḪ-[BI]?-EL		SIMMONS 51 21
174.	ʾADAN-T-A	A-DA-AT-TA	FN	C+
175.	ʾADAD-I	A-DA-DI	FN	XIII 1 X 30
176.	JI-JDAʿ+MARAṢ	A-DA-MA-RA-AṢ	GN	B 11
177.	ʾADAM-U	A-DA-MU	FN	C+
178.	ʾADAM-U	A-DA-MU	MN	JNES XIII 210+ LATE
179.	ʿAḎAR-UM	A-DA-RU-UM	FN	RA LXV 60 III 25
180.	ʿAD-AT-A-HA	A-DA-TA-A	FN	APN P. 12 LATE
181.	ʿAD-AT-IJA	A-DA-TI-A	FN	MRS IX P. 243 UGARIT
182.	ʿAD-AT-IM	A-DA-TIM	MN GEN	XIII 87 5
183.	ʿAD-AT-UM	A-DA-TUM	FN	M+
184.	ʿAD-AT-UM	A-DA-TUM	MN	I, MEISSNER 51 3
185.	ʾADAM-TI+ʾEL-UM	A-DAM-TE-LUM		GAUTIER 31 6
186.	ʿADIJ+ʾIL	A-DI-DINGIR		M
187.	ʾADID-U	A-DI-DU		B 11
188.	ʾADID-UM	A-DI-DU-UM		B 11+
189.	ʾADID-UM	A-DI-DUM		SIMMONS 69A 5
190.	ʿADIJ-NA+ʾIL	A-DI-E-NA-DINGIR		M
191.	ʿADIJ-UM	A-DI-UM		M
192.	ʿAD-U	A-DU		A. 269 67, 73+
193.	ʾADUD-U	A-DU-DU	FN	XIII 1 X 7+
194.	ʿAD-U-NA+HADD-U	A-DU-NA-D-IM		SYRIA XIX 109
195.	ʾADUN-AT-UM	A-DU-NA-TUM	MN	TA 30 275
196.	ʿAD-U-NI+ʾAB-I-JA	A-DU-NI-A-BI-IA		RA XXVII 87 LATE
197.	ʿAD-U-NI+ʾIL-A	A-DU-NI-LA		U
198.	ʿAD-U-NI+HADD-U	A-DU-NI-D-U		MRS VI 15, 42 II 20 UGARIT

199. ʾADUN-UM	A-DU-NU-UM	FIELD	CT II 23 2
200. ʿAD-U+RAWM-U	A-DU-RA-MU	FN	U
201. ʾADUN	A-DU-UN		A. 237 5+
202. ḪADUR+BAʿL-A-IA	A-DU-UR-BA-LA-IA	GN	SUMER XIV 26
203. ḪADUR+BAʿL-U	A-DU-UR-BA-LU	GN	SUMER XIV 26
204. ḪADUR+BEʿL-UM	A-DU-UR-BE-LUM	GN	SIMMONS 138:10
205. ʾAKK-AT+ʾEL	A-GA?-AD-E-EL		I
206. ʾAKK-ATAN-I	A-GA-DA-NI		TA 1931, 489
207. ʿAGAL-IM	A-GA-LIM	GEN	YOS XIII 426:9
208. ʾAKK-ATAN-I	A-GA-TA-NI		TA 1931, 530 I, III
209. ʾAGIG-U	A-GI-GU		B 12
210. ʾAGIG-UM	A-GI-GU-UM		B 12+
211. ʾAḪ-AM+ʾA-RŠIJ	A-ḪA-AM-AR-ŠI		I+
212. ʾAḪ-AT+JIQR-AH	A-ḪA-AT-IQ-RA	FN	M
213. ʾAḪAL-UM	A-ḪA-LUM		BIROT, TEA 45:12
214. ʾAḪ-I+ʾAŚD	A-ḪA-SA-AD		UET V 539 II 19
215. ʾAḪ-AT-A-HA	A-ḪA-TA-A	FN	RA LXV 62 V 52
216. ʾAḪ-AT-A+ʾAB-I	A-ḪA-TA-A-BI	FN	M+
217. ʾAḪ-AT-A+NAʿM-I	A-ḪA-TA-NA-AḪ-MI	FN	XIII 1 XI 3
218. ʾAḪ-AT-I	A-ḪA-TI	FN	XIII 1 VIII 6
219. ʾAḪ-AT-I+JIQR-AH	A-ḪA-TI-IQ-RA	FN	XIII 1 II 72+
220. ʾAḪ-AT-I+JIQR-AT	A-ḪA-TI-IQ-RA-AT	FN	XIII 1 V 5
221. ʾAḪ-AT-I+MA	A-ḪA-TI-MA	FN	JCS XXVII 135:1
222. ʾAḪ-AT-UJA	A-ḪA-TU-IA	FN	SIMMONS 66 4+
223. ʾAḪ-AT-UM	A-ḪA-TUM	FN	M+
224. ʾAḪ-I+HADD-A	A-ḪI-A-DA		B 12
225. ʾAḪ-I+ʾAŚD	A-ḪI-A-SA-AD		B 12
226. ʾAḪ-I+DANN-UM	A-ḪI-DA-NU-UM		I
227. ʾAḪ-I+DAŠUR	A-ḪI-DA-ŠU-UR_2		PBS XI/2 P. 140 NO. 1128
228. ʾAḪ-I+JABAL	A-ḪI-E-BA-AL		M
229. ʾAḪ-I+JE-QWIM	A-ḪI-E-KI-IM		M
230. ʾAḪ-I-JE+MALIK	A-ḪI-E-MA-LIK		M
231. ʾAḪ-I+JATAR	A-Ḫ[I]-E?-TAR		RA LXV 46 V 86
232. ʾAḪ-I+ḪIʾL	A-ḪI-ḪI-EL		XIII 1 X 17
233. ʾAḪ-I+JI-ʿQUB-A	A-ḪI-I-KU-BA		KISURRA 7A 9
234. ʾAḪ-I+ʾIL-I	A-ḪI-I_3-LI_2	FN	XIII 1 VIII 20
235. ʾAḪ-IJA	A-ḪI-IA		M+
236. ʾAḪ-I+JA-JŠUʿ	A-ḪI-IA-ŠU		BIROT, TEA 28:17+
237. ʾAḪ-I+JA-JŠUʿ	A-ḪI-IA-ŠU-UḪ		SIMMONS 58 16
238. ʾAḪ-I+ʾIL	A-ḪI-[I]L		HARRIS 45 11
239. ʾAḪ-IM	A-ḪI-IM	GEN	M
240. ʾAḪ-I-Š+TUʾ-KA	A-ḪI-IŠ-DU-KA		A. 98C 1, 6
241. ʾAḪ-I+JI-ŚMAʿ-NI	A-ḪI-IŠ-MA-NI		VAS VIII 14:41+
242. ʾAḪ-I-Š+TUʾ-JA	A-ḪI-IŠ-TU-IA		A. 86 9
243. ʾAḪ-I+KAʾB-I	A-ḪI-KA-PI		YOS VIII 64 18
244. ʾAḪ-I+KI+LIʾM	A-ḪI-KI-LI-IM		JEAN T.SIFR 72 5, 6, 13+
245. ʾAḪ-I+LABAN	A-ḪI-LA-BA-AN		RA LXV 43 IV 5+
246. ʾAḪIL-AT-UM	A-ḪI-LA-TUM	FN	XIII 1 I 67
247. ʾAḪ-I+LIʾM	A-ḪI-LI-IM		B 12, M
248. ʾAḪ-I+MAʾJ-UM	A-ḪI-MA-IU-UM		MAM III P. 274
249. ʾAḪ-I+MARAṢ	A-ḪI-MA-RA-AṢ		B 12+, M+
250. ʾAḪ-I+MARAṢ	A-ḪI-MA-RA-AṢ	FN	XIII 1 IX 24
251. ʾAḪ-I+MARAṢ	A-ḪI-MA-RA-UṢ		RUTTEN 1 22
252. ʾAḪ-I+ʾAŚD	A-ḪI-SA-AD		B 12+
253. ʾAḪ-I+JA-ŚJIT	A-ḪI-SI-IT		TA 1931, 636
254. ʾAḪ-I+ŚUM-U-NA	A-ḪI-SU-MU-NA		SIMMONS 83 5
255. ʾAḪ-I+ŠALAŠ	A-ḪI-ŠA-LA-AŠ		EDZARD, DER 104:2
256. ʾAḪ-I+TA-NWUḪ-A	A-ḪI-TA-NU-A		M
257. ʾAḪIḎ-AN	A-ḪI-ZA-AN		M
258. ʾAḪ-I+ṢADUQ	A-ḪI-ZA-DU-UQ		B 12
259. ʾAḪ-U+ʾEL	A-ḪU-EL		RA LXV 50 IX 1
260. ʾAḪ-U+JAḪAD	A-ḪU-IA-ḪA-AD		M+
261. ʾAḪ-U+JAT-UM	A-ḪU-IA-TUM	MN	BIN II 98 4
262. ʾAḪ-U+JAT-UM	A-ḪU-JA-TUM	MN	M
263. ʾAḪ-U+KA+ʾAB-I	A-ḪU-KA-A-BI	FN	XIII 1 VIII 60, C+
264. ʾAḪ-U+LUʾM-U	A-ḪU-LU-MU		M

265.	ʾAḪ-UM	A-ḪU-UM		M+
266.	ʾAḪ-UM+LA+ʾAB-I	A-ḪU-UM-LA-A-BI		YOS XIII 245:17, SEAL
267.	ʾAḪ-UM+LI-JA	A-ḪU-UM-LI-A		M
268.	ʾAḪ-UM+LUʾM-U	A-ḪU-UM-LU-MU		X 166 4+
269.	ʾAḪ-UM+MAṬAR-I	A-ḪU-UM-MA-DA-RI		M
270.	ʾAḪ-UM+MA+ʾIL	A-ḪU-UM-MA-DINGIR		M+
271.		A-ḪU-UN-NA-TA		VII 220 25
272.	ʾAJI+DAWD-I	A-I-DA-TE	FN	A.
273.	ʿAWIQ-AN	A-I-GA-AN		RA LXV 52 X 58
274.	ḪAJJ-AH	A-I-IA	FN	A. LATE+
275.	ḪAJJ-AH	A-IA	FN	XIII 1 X 47
276.	ʾAJA+ʾAB-I	A-IA-A-BI		A.
277.	ʾAJA+ʾAB-U	A-IA-A?-BU?	FN	C+
278.	ʾAJA+ʾAḪ-AT-I	A-IA-A-ḪA-TI	FN	A.
279.	ʾAJA+ʾAḪ-I	A-IA-A-ḪI		X 166 8'+
280.	ʾAJA+ʾAḪ-IM	A-IA-A-ḪI-IM		X 166 4
281.	ʾAJA+ʾAḪ-U	A-IA-A-ḪU		XIII 1 III 52
282.	ʾAJA+ʾAḪW-I	A-IA-A-ḪU-I		JCS V 133
283.	ʾAJA+ʾAḪ-UM	A-IA-A-ḪU-UM		RA LXV 41 II 24
284.	ʾAJAM+ʾIL-T-I	A-IA-AM-IL-TI	FN	XIII 1 X 8
285.	ʾAJA+ʿAMM-U	A-IA-AM-MU		MAOG IV 2 10, 11, A 7740+
286.	ʾAJA+ʿAMM-U-KU	A-IA-AM-MU-KU		CT XLV 6 33
287.	ʾAJA+ʿAMM-U-HU	A-IA-AM-MU-U$_2$		VAS XIII 34:3
288.	ʾAJAN+ŠARR-I	A-IA-AŠ-LUGAL		A. 18 4
289.	ʾAJA+ʾAB-I	A-IA-BI		A.+
290.	ʾAJA+ʾAB-I+ŠARR-I	A-IA-BI-ŠAR-RI		A.
291.	ʾAJA+ʾAB-I+TALM-A	A-IA-BI-TA-AL-MA		A. 239 15
292.	ʾAJA+ʾAB-U	A-IA-BU		A. LATE +
293.	ʾAJA+DAWD-U	A-IA-DA-DU		M
294.	ʾAJA+DAWD-U-KU	A-IA-DA-DU-U$_2$		TIM IV 39 15
295.	ʾAJA+ʾIL	A-IA-DINGIR		A.+
296.	ʾAJA+ḪAʾL-U	A-IA-ḪA-LU		M
297.	ʾAJA+ʿAMM-U-HU	A-IA-ḪA-MU-U$_2$		A 7648, M
298.	ʾAJA+ʾAḪ-U	A-IA-ḪU		A. LATE+
299.	ʾAJA+KALB-AH	A-IA-KA-AL-BA?	FN	C
300.	ʾAJAK-UM	A-IA-KU-UM		RA LXV 52 X 51
301.	ʾAJAL-AH	A-IA-LA	FN	M+
302.	ʾAJAL-A-HA	A?-IA-LA-A	FN?	M
303.	ʾAJA+LA+ŠUM-U-HU	A-IA-LA-SU-MU-U$_2$		M, C
304.	ʾAJAL-AT-UM	A-IA-LA-TUM	FN	VAS VII 3 25
305.	ʾAJAL-IM	A-IA-LIM	GEN	M
306.	ʾAJAL-UM	A-IA-LU-UM		CT XLV 5 9
307.	ʾAJAN+ŠARR-I	A-IA-LUGAL		A. 274 4
308.	ʾAJAN+ŠARR-I	A-IA-LUGAL-RI		A. 243 22
309.	ʾAJAL-UM	A-IA-LUM		M
310.	ʾAJA+MAṬAR	A-IA-MA-[DAR]		YOS XII 360 SEAL
311.	ʾAJA+MA+ʾIL	A-IA-MA-DINGIR		M
312.	ʾAJA+MA+ʾEL	A-IA-MA-EL		RA LXV 42 III 14
313.	ʾAJAN+ʾAB-I	A-IA-NA-BI	FN	A.
314.	ʾAJAN+ʾAB-I+ʾILL-A	A-IA-NA-BI-IL-LA		A.
315.	ʾAJA+NIWR-I	[A]-IA-NI-RI		RA LXV 59 II 36
316.		A-IA-RI-ŠA	FN	XIII 1 VIII 22
317.	ḪAJJ-AT-IJA	A-IA-TI-IA		BM 82440
318.	ʾAJA+ʾUMM-I	A-IA-UM-MI	FN	RA LXV 59 II 27
319.	ʾAJA+ʾAZJ-I	A-IA-ZI		M
320.	ʾAJAK-U	A-JA-KU		RA LXV 52 X 44
321.	ʾAJAL-AH	A-JA-LA	FN	XIII 1 IV 37
322.	ʾAJAL-AN	A-JA-LA-AN		RA LXV 52 X 81
323.	ʾAJIŠ+TULL-A	A-JI-IŠ-TU-UL-LA		M
324.		A-KA-LA-AŠ$_2$-LUM		IRAQ IV 185 A. 386
325.	ʾAKAN-AT-UM	A-KA-NA-TUM		JCS XXIV 62 NO.55+
326.	ʾAKK-ATAN-UM	A-KA-TA-A-NU-UM		SIMMONS 105 7, SEAL
327.	ʾAKK-AT-IJA	A-KA-TI-IA	FN	KISURRA 171 1; M+
328.	ʾAKK-AT-IJA	A-KA-TI-IA-A		KISURRA 178 1
329.	ʾAKK-AT-UM	A-KA-TUM		KISURRA 104 36
330.	ʾAK-I+....	A-KI-[....]	FN	IX 291 13

331.	ʾAK-I+ʾIL	A-KI-DINGIR		M
332.	ʾAK-I+JARAḪ	A-KI-E-RA-AḪ		M
333.	ʾAK-I+ʾEL	A-KI-EL		RA LXV 46 VI 49
334.	ʾAK-IJA	A-KI-IA		M+
335.	ʾAK-IJAN	A-KI-IA-AN		M, A. LATE+
336.	ʾAK-I+LAMA	A-KI-LA-MA		B 12
337.	ʾAKIN-UM	A-KI-NU-UM		TA 1931, 538 I
338.	ʾAKIR-AH	A-KI-RA	FN	M
339.	ʾAKIR-I	A-KI-RI	GEN	VAS VIII 14 37
340.	ʾAKIR-UM	A-KI-RU-UM		KISURRA 8 7+
341.	ʿAQUB-U	A-KU-BU		VAS VIII 14 14
342.	ʾAKUN-AN-IM	A-KU-NA-NIM	GEN	B 92
343.	ʾAKUN-AT-UM	A-KU-NA-TUM	MN?	M+
344.	ʾAKUN-IJA	A-KU-NI-IA		CT XLV 5 R. 3
345.	ʾAKUN-U+QAṬAR	A-KU-NU-GA-DAR		BIN VII 30 5
346.	ʾAKUN-UM	A-KU-NU-UM		KISURRA 58 8
347.	ʾAKUN-UM	A-KU-NUM$_2$		KISURRA 48 4
348.	ʿAQUB-I+ʾEL	A-KU-PI-EL		GORDON 38 16
349.	ʾA-KWUN+PI+ʾEL	A-KU-PI-EL		GORDON, SCT 38 16
350.	ʿAQUB+ʾIL	A-KU-UB-DINGIR		HARRIS 84 13
351.	ʾAK-UM	A-KU-UM		U
352.	ʾAK-UM+LA+ʾIL-A	A-KUM-LA-I-LA		RA LXV 55 XIII 1
353.	ʾALAŠ-I+ʾEL	A-LA-SI-E-EL		UCP X/3 3 17
354.	ḪALAṢ-I	A-LA-ṢI		4E RENC. ASS. P. 178 2
355.	ḪALAṢ-UM	A-LA-ZU-UM		UET V 397 14
356.	ḪALAṢ-UM	A-LA-ZUM		UET V 796 11+
357.	ʾALI+ʾAB-I	A-LI-A-BI	FN	M+
358.	ʾALI+ʾAḪ-AT-I	A-LI-A-ḪA?-TA-TI	FN	M
359.	ʾALI+ʾAḪ-AT-I	A-LI-A-ḪA-TI	FN	XIII 1 IV 71+
360.	ʾALI+ʾAḪ-I	A-LI-A-ḪI	FN	M+
361.	ʿALIJ-UM	A-LI-I-U$_2$-UM		RUTTEN 7 20+
362.	ʾALIP+ŠAMŠ	A-LI-IB-D-UTU		CT VIII 35B 24+
363.	ʾALIM	A-LI-IM	NOM	M, TIM III 43 5
364.	ʾAHL-UM+PU-HU	[A]-LI-IM-BU-MU		OLZ 1958 547 N.1
365.	ʾAL-I-Š+TUT-U	A-LI-IŠ-TU-TU		VAS XVI 23 13
366.	ʿALIJ-UM	A-LI-JU-UM		M
367.	ʾALIK-UM	A-LI-KUM		B+
368.	HALIL-A+ʿAD-UM	A-LI-LA-ḪA-DU-UM		KISURRA 18 12
369.	HALIL-UM	A-LI-LU-UM		B 18
370.	ʾALI+PA+ʾIL	A-LI-PA-DINGIR		TIM III 5 18+
371.	ʾALI+ŠARAM-NI	A-LI-ŠA-RA-AM-NI	FN	RA LXV 58 I 54
372.	ʿALIJ-T-IM	A-LI-TIM	FN GEN	M
373.	ʿALIJ-T-UM	A-LI-TUM	FN	M+
374.	ʿALIJ-UM	A-LI-U$_2$-UM		GAUTIER 33 R. 6
375.	ʾALI+ʾUMM-I	A-LI-UM-MI	FN	M
376.	ḪALIṢ-IT-UM	A-LI-ZI-TUM?		UET V 534 R. 9
377.	ḪALIṢ-UM	A-LI-ZUM		HARRIS 98 R. 5
378.	ʾALI+ʾAḪ-AT-I	A-LI$_2$-A-ḪA-TI	FN	RA LXV 59 II 65+
379.	ʾALI+ʾAḪ-I	A-LI$_2$-A-ḪI	FN	RA LXV 59 II 41
380.	ʾALI+ʿAMM-U	A-LI$_2$-AM-MU		UCP X/1 52 22
381.	ʾALI+ʿAMM-U-HU	A-LI$_2$-AM-MU-U$_2$		UCP X/2 58 16
382.	ʾALI+ʾIL	A-LI$_2$-IL		HARRIS 65 16
383.	ʿALIJ-U	A-LI$_2$-JU-U$_2$		RUTTEN 16 14
384.	ʿALIJ-UM	A-LI$_2$-JU-UM		JCS XXIV 52 NO.27+
385.	ʾALI+PA+ʾIL-UM	A-LI$_2$-KA-LUM		RUTTEN 37 19
386.	ʾALI+LAMA	A-LI$_2$-LA-MA		SIMMONS 118 17+
387.	ʾALI+PA+ʾIL	A-LI$_2$-PA-DINGIR		RUTTEN 6 21+
388.	ʾALI+PA+ŠAMŠ	A-LI$_2$-PA-D-UTU		BE VI/1 15:25
389.	ʾALI+ʾUP-UM	A-LI$_2$-U$_2$-PU-UM		KISURRA 117 5
390.	ʾALUP-I	A-LU-BI	GEN?	CT XLV 92 R. I 14
391.	ʾALUN-IJA	A-LU-NI-IA	FN	EDZARD,DER 91:13
392.	ʾALUP-AT-UM	A-LU-PA-TUM	FN	CT XLVII 7 35, 7A 16'
393.	ʾALUP-UM	A-LU-PU-UM		B+
394.	ʾALUʾ-U	A-LU?-U$_2$	FN	M
395.	ʾALUʾ-UM	A-LU-U$_2$-UM		VAS XVI 131:1
396.	ʾAHL-UM+MAʾT-U	[A-LU]-UM-MA-[TU]	FN	M

397.	ʾAHL-UM+MAʾT-UM	[A-LU-UM]-MA-TUM	FN	M
398.	ʾAHL-UM+PU-HU	A-LUM-BI-U$_2$		SIMMONS 129 13
399.	ʾAHL-UM+PU-HU	A-LUM-BU-MU		OLZ 1958 547 N.1
400.	ʾAM-T+BAʿL-AH	A-MA-AT-D-BA-A-LA	FN	BAGHD. MITT. II 72 5, 9+
401.	ʾAMAN-AN-IM	A-MA-NA-NIM	GEN	B 43
402.	ʾAMAN-AN-UM	A-MA-NA-NU-UM		B 42+
403.	ʾAMAN-UM	A-MA-NU-UM		CT XLV 2 24,SEAL
404.	ʾAMAT-AN	A-MA-TA-AN		M+
405.	ʿAMM-I+JATAR	A-MA-TA-AR		WALTERS, WL 109:9
406.	ʿAMAS-IM	A-MA-ZI-IM	GEN	KISURRA 166 4+
407.	ʿAMAS-UM	A-MA-ZU-UM		KISURRA 98 8
408.	ʾAMAR+ʾIL-I	A-MAR-I$_3$-LI$_2$		MAOG IV 2 3 HANA
409.	ʾAMIR+....	A-ME-IR-[....]		M
410.	ʾAMIR+KAKK-A	A-ME-IR-KA-AK-KA		XIII 1 V 20
411.	ḪAM-I+....	D-A-MI-[....]		M
412.	ḪAM-I+JE-JŠUʿ	D-A-MI-E-ŠU-UḪ		M+
413.	ḪAM-I+JE-JŠUʿ	A-MI-E-ŠU-UḪ		M+
414.	ḪAM-I+JI-JBAL	D-A-MI-I-BA-AL		M+
415.	ḪAM-I+MALIK	A-MI-MA-LIK		C
416.	ʾAMIN-AH	A-MI-NA	FN	RA LXV 64 V 76
417.	ʾAMIN-AN-UM	A-MI-NA-NU-UM		B 43
418.	ʾAMIN-AT-UM	A-MI-NA-TUM		B 12
419.	ʾAMIN-I+ʾANN-U	A-MI-NI-AN-NU		M
420.	ʾAMIN-U	A-MI-NU		JNES XIII 210+ LATE
421.	ʾAMIN-UM	A-MI-NU-UM		B 12+
422.	ʾAMIN-UM	A-MI-NUM		M
423.	ʾAMIR-A+ʾAB-UM	A-MI-RA-A-BU-UM		RA LXV 55 XIII 5
424.	ʾAMIR-AJA	A-MI-RA-IA	FN	C
425.	ʾAMIR-AT-UM	A-MI-RA-TUM	FN	M
426.	ʾAMIR-UM	A-MI-RU-UM		B 13
427.	ʾAMIR-UM	A-MI-RUM		M
428.	ḪAM-I+ŠAMUʿ	D-A-MI-SA-MU-UḪ		M+
429.	ḪAM-I+TA-NWUḪ	D-A-MI-TA-NU		M
430.	ḪAM-I+TA-NWUḪ-A	D-A-MI-TA-NU-A		M
431.	ḪAM-I+TA-NWUḪ	D-A-MI-TA-NU-UḪ		M+
432.	ḪAM-I+JATAR	D-A-MI-T[AR]?		M
433.	ḪAM-I+ṬAJB-I	A-MI-ṬA-BI		RA LXV 45 V 81
434.	ḪAM-I+ṢABṬ-I	A-MI-ZA-AB-TI	FN	CT VIII 35 B 1
435.	ḪAM-I+ṢABṬ-I	A-MI-ZA-AB-TI	MN	B 13
436.	ḪAM-U+DAWD-I	D?-[A?-M]U?-DA-DI		IX 291 16
437.	ḪAM-U+DAWD-U	D-A-MU-DA-DU		M
438.	ḪAM-U+MALIK	D-A-MU-MA-LIK		M
439.	ʾA-ʾMUR-U-HU	A-MU-RU-U$_2$		PBS VIII/1 98 9
440.	ʾA-MURR-UḪI	A-MU-RU-UḪ-ḪI		A.
441.	ʾA-MURR-UM	A-MU-RU-UM		U
442.	ḪAM-U+TA-NWUḪ	D-A-MU-TA-NU		M
443.	ʿAMM-U-HU	A-MU-U$_2$		EDZARD, DER 90:10+
444.	ḪAM-UM+JE-JŠUʿ	D-A-MU-UM-E-ŠU-UḪ		B 13 HANA
445.	ḪAM-UM+LU-HU	D-A-MU-UM-LU-U$_2$		M
446.	ḪAM-UM+MALIK	D-A-MU-UM-MA-LIK		M
447.	ḪAM-UM+TA-NWUḪ-HU	A-MU-UM-TA-NU-U$_2$		M
448.		A-MU-UR-DI	FN	RA LXV 60 III 22
449.	ʾA-MURR-U	A-MU-UR-RU		M+
450.	ʾA-MWUT+PI+ʾIL	A-MU-UT-BI-DINGIR		M+
451.	ʾA-MWUT+PI+ʾIL-A	A-MU-UT-BI-I-LA		M
452.	ʾA-MWUT+PA+ʾIL	A-MU-UT-PA-DINGIR		SYRIA L 7
453.	ʾA-MURR-UM	A-MUR-RU-UM		CT II 50 21+
454.	ʾAMUR+ŠA+DAGAN	A-MUR-ŠA-D-DA-GAN		TCL I 237 31 HANA
455.	ʾAMUR+ŠA+ŠAMŠ	A-MUR-ŠA-D-UTU		A.
456.	ʾANA+ʿAN-A	A-NA-A-NA		A. 36:11
457.	ḪANN-A+ʾABN-UM	A-NA-AB-NU-UM		HARRIS 57 18
458.	ʾANA+ḪANN-I	A-NA-AḪ-ḪA-AN-NI	FN	XIII 1 V 29
459.	ʾAN-A-Š+KIBAL	[A]?-NA-AŠ-KI-BA-AL		VIII 86 23
460.	ʿAN-AT+KUʾB-U	A-NA-AT-KU-BU		TCL I 204:11
461.	ʾANA+BAʿL-U	A-NA-BA-LU	FN	M
462.	ʾANA+BAʿL-U	A-NA-BA-LU	MN?	CT XLVIII 86 REV

463.	ʾANA+DAGAN	A-NA-D-DA-GAN		M
464.	ʿANAQ-UM	A-NA-GU-UM		KISURRA 71A 15+
465.	ʾANA+ḪIJJ-A	A-NA-ḪI?-A?		RUTTEN 20:16
466.	ʾANA+ʾIL-I+MA	A-NA-I-LIM-MA		A.
467.	ʿAN-AJA	A-NA-IA		RA LXV 46 VI 17
468.	ʾANA+HADD-U	A-NA-D-IM		MRS XII NO. 24, 6, UGARIT
469.	ʾANA-I-Š	A-NA-IŠ		RA LXV 52 X 79
470.	ʾANA+KIBAL-I	A-NA?-KI-BA-[L]I	FN	M
471.	ʾANAKU+ʾIL-AM+MA	A-NA-KU-DINGIR-LAM-MA		XIII 1 II 29
472.	ʾANAKU+ʾIL-A+MA	A-NA-KU-I-LA-MA		SIMMONS 46 7+
473.	ʿANAQ-UM	A-NA-KUM		KISURRA 29 8+
474.	ʾANA+MA+ʾIL	A-NA-MA-DINGIR		A 29366:9
475.	ḪANAN-A	A-NA-NA		U
476.	ḪANAN-A+GAʾJ-A	A-NA-NA-GA-A		RA XLIV 112 5 QATNA
477.	ḪANAN-AT-UM	A-NA-NA-TUM	FN	EDZARD, DER 97:14
478.	ḪANAN-IM	A-NA-NI-IM	GEN	B 43
479.	ʾANA+RAḪAB-U	A-NA-RA-A-BU		M+
480.	ʿAN-ATAN	A-NA-TA-AN		RA LXV 53 XI 13
481.	ʿAN-AT-UM	A-NA-TUM		BIROT, TEA 72 III 58+
482.	ʿAN-IJA	A-NI-IA		RUTTEN 31 5+
483.	ʾAN-I-Š+ḪURB-I	A-NI-IŠ-ḪU-UR-BI		M+
484.	ʾAN-I-Š+KIBAL	A-NI-IŠ-KI-BA-AL		RA LXV 53 XI 37+
485.	ʾAN-I-Š+KIBEL	A-NI-IŠ-KI-BE-EL		TCL XX 191 33 CAPP.
486.	ḪANIN-UM	A-NI-NU-UM		EDZARD, DER 73:19
487.	ʿANAJ-TI+ʾEL	A-NI-TE-EL		MOORTGAT 309
488.	ʿANAJ-TI+ʾIL	A-NI-TI-DINGIR		M
489.	ḪANUN-UM	A-NU-NU-UM		HARRIS 79 16
490.	ʿAN-UM+ʾAḪ-I	A-NU-UM-A-ḪI		RA LXV 53 XI 43
491.	ʿAN-UM+ḪIRB-I	A-NU-UM-ḪI-IR-BI		BALKAN, LETTER P. 6
492.	ʾA-JPAʿ+ʾAB-I	A-PA-AḪ-A-BI		YOS VIII 29 13
493.	ʾA-JPAʿ+RAPIʾ	A-PA-AḪ-RA-BI		SUMER XIV 5, IM 52272
494.	ʾAP-AN-UM	A-PA-NU-UM		B 43+
495.	ʾAP-I+ʾAŠAL	A-PI-A-ŠAL		JNES XIII 212F.+ LATE
496.	ʿAQAB+ʾEL	A-QA-BE-EL		UET V 839 23
497.	ʾARAM+MAṬAR-A	A-RA-AM-MA-DA-RA		BM 80328 1
498.	ʾARAM-U	A-RA-AM-MU		A.+
499.	ḪARAB-AT-UM	A-RA-BA-TUM		YOS XIII 389:4+
500.	ʾARAM-A	A-RA-MA		A.+
501.	ʾARAM-U	A-RA-MU		M
502.	ḪARIB-AN-UM	A-RI-BA-A-NU-UM		SIMMONS 103 13+
503.	ḪARIB-AN-UM	A-RI-BA-NU-UM		SIMMONS 96 12+
504.	ʿARIṢ-AN-UM	A-RI-ZA-NU-UM		U
505.	ḪARUB-AH	A-RU-B[A]	FN	XIII 1 III 64+
506.	ʾARUḪ-UM	A-RU-ḪU-UM		B 13
507.	ʿARUL-U	A-RU-LU		STRASSM. 56 29+
508.	ʿARUL-UM	A-RU-LU-UM		B 13+
509.	ʾARUM-A	A-RU-MA	GEN	RA VIII 74 16
510.	ʾARUŠ-I+ʾIL	A-RU-SI-DINGIR		A 7459, M
511.	ʾARUŠ-U	A-RU-SU		JEAN TELL SIFR 72 5+
512.	ʾARUŠ-UM	A-RU-SU-UM		M, JEAN TELL SIFR 72A 3+
513.	ʾARUŠ+PI+ʾIL	A-RU-UŠ-BI-DINGIR		M, RA XLI 45 4' HANA
514.	ʾARUŠ+ʾEL-UM	A-RU-UŠ-E-LUM		UCP X/3 2 25
515.	ḪAŠAK-NI+ʾEL	A-SA-AK-NI-EL		RA LXV 52 XI 6
516.	ʿAZAL-IJA	A-SA-LI-JA		B 14+
517.	ʾAŠAŠ-UM	A-SA-ŠUM		BIROT, TEA 72 IV 17
518.	ʾAŠJ-IM	A-SI-IM	GEN	C
519.	ʾASIN-I	A-SI-NI		APN P. 31 LATE
520.	ʾAŠIN-U	A-SI-NU		B 14
521.	ʾASIN-U-HU	A-SI-NU-U		APN P. 31 LATE
522.	ʾAŠIN-UM	A-SI-NU-UM		B 14+
523.	ʾAŠIR-AT-UM	A-SI-RA-TUM		B 14
524.	ʾAŠIR-UM	A-SI-RU-UM		B 14+
525.	ʾAŠIR-UM	A-SI-RUM		B 14+, M+
526.	ʾAŠUL-U	A-SU-LU		TA 30 36 3
527.	ʾAŠJ-UM	A-SU-UM		M
528.	ʾAŠAR-UM	A-ŠA-RU-UM		EDZARD, DER 68 IV 3

529.	ʾAŠAR+NAṢIR	D-A-ŠAR-NA-ṢIR		M
530.	ʾAŠIR+ŠI-JA+....	A-ŠE-ER-ŠI-IA-[X]	FN	XIII 1 VIII 2
531.	ʾAŠIḪ-UM	A-ŠI-ḪU-UM	FN	RA LXV 62 V 33
532.	ʾAŠIR-AT-UM	D-A-ŠI-RA-TUM	DN FN	RIFTIN 60 SEAL
533.	ʾA-ŠWUB+ʾIL-A	A-ŠU-UB-I-LA		A. LATE
534.	ʾA-ŠWUB+LA+ʾIL	A-ŠU-UB-LA-DINGIR		C+
535.	ʾA-ŠWUB+LA+ʾEL	A-ŠU-UB-LA-EL		TA 1931,765
536.	ʾA-ŠWUB+LI+ʾEL	A-ŠU-UB-LI-EL		OIP XLIII 154 NO. 48+
537.	ʾAŠUZ-I	A-ŠU-ZI		M
538.	T-ʾAMR-IM	A-TA-AM-RI-IM	GEN	M+
539.	T-ʾAMR-UM	A-TA-AM-RU-UM		M+
540.	ʾATAL-AN-UM	A-TA-LA-NU-UM		EDZARD, DER 100:3
541.	ʾATAM-AN-UM	A-TA-MA-NU-UM		UCP X/3 3 22+
542.	JI-JDAʿ+MARAṢ	A-TA-MA-RA-AṢ	PN	CT II 26 3
543.	ʾATTA+NABIT-I	A-TA-NA-BE-TI		JCS XIII 57 306:5+,A LATE
544.	ʾATAR-AN-I	A-TA-RA-NI	GEN	HARRIS 71 12
545.	T-ʾAMR-AH	A-TAM-RA	FN	M+
546.	T-ʾAMR-AM	A-TAM-RA-AM	ACC	M+
547.	T-ʾAMR-AT-UM	A-TAM-RA-TUM	FN	M
548.	T-ʾAMR-I+ʾIL	A-TAM-RI-DINGIR		M+
549.	T-ʾAMR-IM	A-TAM-RI-IM	GEN	M+
550.	T-ʾAMR-UM	A-TAM-RUM		M+
551.	ʾATIM-AM	A-TI-M[A-AM]	ACC	M
552.	ʾATIM-U	A-TI-MU		M
553.	ʾATIM-UM	A-TI-MU-UM		TA 30 7 8, M
554.		A-TU-A-NU-UM		TA 1931, 538 I, IV
555.	ʾA-WDAJ+ʾIL	A-U_3-DA-IL		U
556.	ʾAWAʾ-ATAN	A-WA-TA-AN		RA LXV 47 VII 31+
557.	ʾAWAʾ-AT-I+ʾIL	A-WA-TI-DINGIR	MN	XIII 1 XI 39
558.	ʾAWAʾ-AT-I+ʾEL	A-WA-TI-EL		RA LXV 41 II 37+
559.	ʾAWAʾ-AT-UM	A-WA-TUM	FN	M
560.	ʾAWIJ-AT-UM	A-WI-IA-TUM	MN?	TIM I 11 10+
561.	ʾAWIJ+JA-JṢIʾ	A-WI-IA-ZI		RA LXV 53 XI 49
562.	ʾAWIN	A-WI-IN		M+
563.	ʾAWIJ+KIRIŠ-U	A-WI-KI-RI-IŠ		XIV 106:18
564.	ʾAWIN-UM	A-WI-NU-UM		FLP 516, UR III
565.	ʾAWIJ-UM	A-WI-U_2-UM		GORDON 38 21+
566.	ʿAZAL-UM	A-ZA-AL-LUM		KISURRA 26 6
567.	ḪAZAQ+NAN-UM	A-ZA-AQ-NA-NU-UM		CT IV 50A 21
568.	ʿAZAB-AN-I	A-ZA-BA-NI		TA 1931, 216
569.	ʿAZAB-UM	A-ZA-BU-UM		GAUTIER 23 5+
570.	ḪASAD-UM	A-ZA-DU-UM		CT XLV 77 27
571.	ʿAZAL-AJA	A-ZA-LA-IA		B 14
572.		A-ZA-LA-LUM		KISURRA 206 3
573.	ʿAZAL-IJA	A-ZA-LI-IA		B 14+
574.	ʿAZAL-IM	A-ZA-LIM	GEN	VAS VIII 14 23
575.	ʿAZAL-UM	A-ZA-LU-UM		B 14
576.	ʿAZAL-UM	A-ZA-LUM		EDZARD, DER 60:8
577.	ḪAṢAN-IJA	A-ZA-NI-IA		BM 80363 17
578.	ḪAṢAN-UM	A-ZA-NU-UM		B 43+
579.	ʿAḎAR+ʾAḪ	A-ZA-RA-AḪ		JNES XIII 210+ LATE
580.	ʿAḎAR-IM	A-ZA-RI-IM	GEN	B 14
581.	ʿAḎAR-UM	A-ZA-RU-UM		B 14
582.	ʿAZZ-AT-AM	A-ZA-TAM	FN ACC	CT VIII 37D 3
583.	ʿAZZ-AT-UM	A-ZA-TUM	FN	CT VIII 37D 7, M
584.	ʿAZAZ-AN-UM	A-ZA-ZA-NU-UM		B 92
585.	ʿAZAZ-UM	A-ZA-ZUM		I
586.	ʿAZZ-I+DAGAN	A-ZI-D-DA-GAN		A. LATE
587.	ʿAZZ-I+ʾIL	A-ZI-DINGIR		HARRIS 39 11
588.	ʾASIN-AM	A-ZI-NA-A[M]	ACC	XIV 33:7
589.	ʾASIN-IM	A-ZI-NIM	GEN	XIII 13 13+
590.	ʾASIN-U-HU	A-ZI-NU-U_2		M
591.	ʿAḎIR-A	A-ZI-RA	NOM	A. LATE+
592.	ʿAḎIR-AN	A-ZI-RA-AN		A. P. 131 LATE+
593.	ʿAḎIR-UM	A-ZI-RUM		B 14, M+, C+
594.	ʿAZIZ-AN	A-ZI-ZA-AN		RA LXV 44 IV 45

595.	ʿAZZ-U+ḪAʾL-IM	A-ZU-ḪA-LIM	NOM	M
596.	ʾASUN-AN	A-ZU-NA-AN		RA LXV 48 VIII 29
597.	ḪAJJ-U+ʾIL	A$_2$-U$_2$-DINGIR		U
598.	ʾABB-A	AB-BA		RA LXV 55 XIII 12
599.	ʾABB-A+ʾIL	AB-BA-DINGIR		A.+
600.	ʾABB-A+ʾIL	D-AB-BA-DINGIR	FN	M
601.	ʾABB-A+ʾIL-I	AB-BA-I$_3$-LI$_2$	FN	XIII 1 XI 14
602.	ʾABB-A+ʾIL-I	D-AB-BA-I$_3$-LI$_2$	FN	SIMMONS 112:17
603.	ʾABB-A+ŠARR	AB-BA-LUGAL		A. 86 2
604.	ʾABAN-AN	AB-BA-NA?-AN		M
605.	ʾABB-I+LIʾM+MA	AB-BI-LIM-MA		A.+
606.	ʿABD-AJA	AB-DA-A		GORDON 38 15+
607.	ʿABD-AN	AB-DA-AN		M
608.	ʿABD+ʾEL	AB-DA-EL		TA 30, 615 9, 41
609.	ʿABD-AN-U	AB-DA-NU		CT XLV 59 6
610.	ʿABD-ATAN	AB-[DA?-T]A-AN		RA LXV 44 IV 62
611.	ʿABD+ḪAM-I	AB-DI-A-MI		BAGHD. MITT. II 58 III 21
612.	ʿABD+ʿAN-AT-I	AB-DI-A-NA-TI		A. P. 128B LATE +
613.	ʿABD+JARAḪ	AB-DI-A-RA-AḪ		B 9+
614.	ʿABD+HADD-U	AB-DI-AD-DU		BAGHD. MITT. II 57 28
615.	ʿABD+ʾIL	AB-DI-DINGIR		B 9+
616.	ʿABD+JARAḪ	AB-DI-E-RA-AḪ		M+, UCP X P. 198+
617.	ʿABD+JARAḪ	AB-DI-D-E-RA-AḪ		YOS XIII 199:22+
618.	ʿABD+JARAḪ	AB-DI-D-EN-ZU		PBS VII/1 94 III 28
619.	ʿABD+ʿAŠTAR	AB-DI-D-EŠ$_4$-DAR		A. 19 4, 7
620.	ʿABD-IJA	AB-DI-IA		A.+
621.	ʿABD+HAND-U	AB-DI-IA-DU		KUPPER NOM. P. 231
622.	ʿABD+NAHR	AB-DI-D-ID$_2$		SCHEIL 10 15, 16
623.	ʿABD-IM	AB-DI-IM	GEN	B 9, M
624.	ʿABD+ʾIŠḪAR-AH	AB-DI-D-IŠ-ḪA-RA		A.+
625.	ʿABD+ʾIL-I	AB-DI-LI		A.+
626.	ʿABD+JARAḪ	AB-DI-RA-AḪ		B 9+
627.	ʿABD+ʿAMM-IM	AB-DU-A-MI-IM	GEN	M+
628.	ʿABD+ʿAMM-IM	AB-DU-A-MI-IM	NOM	M+
629.	ʿABD+DAGAN	AB-DU-D-DA-GAN		M
630.	ʿABD+JARAḪ	AB-DU-D-E-RA-AḪ		YOS XIII 218:13+
631.	ʿABD+JARAḪ	AB-DU-E-RA-AḪ		M+
632.	ʿABD+ʿAŠTAR	AB-DU-EŠ$_4$-DAR		M+
633.	ʿABD+HAND-U	AB-DU-IA-AN-DU		KUPPER NOM. P. 231
634.	ʿABD+ʿIŠTAR-AH	AB-DU-IŠ-TA-RA?		B 9
635.	ʿABD+MA+DAGAN	AB-DU-MA-D-DA-GAN		M+
636.	ʿABD+MALIK-I	AB-DU-MA-LI-KI		YOS XIII 54:5
637.	ʿABD+MALIK	AB-DU-MA-LIK		XIII 37 16
638.	ʿABD+NAWAR	AB-DU-NA-W[A-AR]		M
639.	ʿABD+ŠUWR-I	AB-DU-ŠU-RI		IRAQ XXX 94, RIMAH
640.	ʿABD+ʾUTL-I	AB-DU-UT-LI	FN	A. LATE
641.	ʾABN-U+RAPIʾ	AB-NU-RA-BI		C, C II P. 244+
642.	ʿABD-AN-A	AB-TA-NA	NOM	A. LATE
643.	ʿABD+ʿAN-AT-I	AB-TA-NA-TI		A. P. 128A LATE +
644.	ʿABD-AN-U	AB-TA-NU		A. LATE
645.	ʿABD+ʾIL	AB-TE-IL		I
646.	ʿABD+ʿAN-AT-I	AB-TI-A-NA-TI		JCS XIII 54 300, A. LATE
647.	ʾA-DBAR-AT-UM	AD-BA-RA-TUM	MN	A 21946
648.	HADD-A	AD-DA		M+
649.		AD-DA-ḪA-AN		RA LXV 50 VIII 56
650.		AD-DA-ḪA-NI-DINGIR		VIII 11 6
651.	ʾADAM-AN-U	AD-DA-MA-NU		RUTTEN 28 12
652.	ʾADD-I-JA+ʾEL	AD-DI-IA-DINGIR		MAOG IV 2 12 HANA
653.	ʾADD-I-JA+ʾEL	AD-DI-JA-EL		BAB. III 267 HANA
654.	ʾADD-I+ŠAMŠ	AD-DI-D-UTU?		RA LXIV 99:23
655.	HADD-U+MALIK	AD-DU-MA-LIK		A. 268 4
656.	ʾAB-I+ʿALAṢ-I	AD-ḪA-LA-ZI	FN	C
657.	ʾAB-I+ʾIR-A	AD-I-RA	FN	A.
658.	ʾA-DLUQ-IJA	AD-LU-KI-IA		RES 1939, 69
659.	ʾADM-AN-UM	AD-MA-NU-UM		JCS XXIV 69 NO.3
660.	ʾADM-U-HA	AD-MU-A	FN	U

661.	ʾADM-U+BALAṬ-I	D-AD-MU-BA-LA-TI?	FN	M
662.	ʾADM-U+ḪAṢN-I	D-AD-MU-ḪA-AZ-NI	FN	RA LXV 61 IV 21
663.	ʾADM-U+ʿALIJ-AH	D-AD-MU-ḪA-LI-IA	FN	XIII 1 V 55
664.	ʾADM-U+JIŠʿ-AH	AD-MU-IŠ-ḪA	FN	XIII 1 IX 57
665.	ʾADM-U+JIŠʿ-AH	D-AD-MU-IŠ-ḪA	FN	XIII 1 IX 18
666.	ʾADM-U+QUDM-I	AD-MU-KU-UD-MI	FN	XIII 1 IX 55
667.	ʾADM-U+NIWR-I	AD-MU-NE-RI	FN	XIII 1 VIII 13
668.	ʾADM-U+NIWR-I	D-AD-MU-NI-RI	FN?	M
669.	ʾADM-U+RUWB-AH	D-AD-MU-RU-BA	FN	XIII 1 VII 59
670.	ʾADM-U+ŠIMḪ-I	AD-MU-ŠI-IM-ḪI	FN	XIII 1 IV 6
671.	ʾADM-U+ŠIMḪ-I	D-AD-MU-ŠI-IM-ḪI	FN	RA LXV 62 V 28
672.	ʾADM-U+TA-ḪNUN-AN	D-AD-MU-TA-ḪU-NA-AN	FN	RA LXV 61 IV 38
673.	ʿADN-AN-UM	AD-NA-NU-UM		TIM III 44 19+
674.	ʾA-DRAK-AT-IM	AD-RA-KA-TIM	FN GEN	M+
675.	ʾA-DRAK-AT-UM	AD-RA-KA-TUM	FN	M+
676.	ʿAḎR-AN-UM	AD-RA-NU-UM		I., CT XLVIII 88 REV.
677.	ʿAḎR-I+HADD-U	AD-RI-A-DU		A.+
678.	ʿAḎR-I+JAḪAD	AD-RI-E-ḪA-AD		M+
679.	ʿAḎR-I+ḪAʾT-UM	AD-RI-ḪA-TUM		SIMMONS 88 16+
680.	ʿAḎR-I+HAND-U	AD-RI-IA-AN-DU		KUPPER, NOM. 231
681.	ʿAḎR-I+HADD-U	AD-RI-IA-DU		KUPPER, NOM. 231
682.	ʾAKK-ATAN-UM	AG-GA-TA-A-NU-UM		SIMMONS 103 6
683.	ʾAKK-ATAN-UM	AG-GA-TA-NU-UM		SIMMONS 96 6
684.	ʿAGL-AT-UM	AG-LA-TUM	FN	ABB IV 98:2
685.	ʾA-ḪBAB-U	AḪ-BA-BU		U
686.	ʾA-ḪBUD-IJ-UM	AḪ-BU-TE-UM		U
687.	ʾA-ḪLAM-U	AḪ-LA-A-MU		XI 208 2
688.	ʾA-ḪLAM-U	AḪ-LA-AM-MU		XII 508 2
689.	ʾA-ḪLAM-U	AḪ-LA-MU		M+
690.	ʾA-HLUL-AJ-UM	AḪ-LU-LA-UM		CT VIII 38 B 4
691.	ʾAḪN-AN-UM	AḪ-NA-NU-UM		KISURRA 14 4+
692.	ʾAḪR-AM	AḪ-RA-AM	ACC	II 43 13
693.	JA-ʿḎAR+ʾIL	AḪ-ZA-AR-I$_3$-DINGIR		VAS XVIII 20:20
694.	ʾAKK-A	AK-KA		XIII 1 IV 27+
695.	ʾAKK-AT+MAʾT-I	AK-KA-AD-MA-TI	FN	A. 409 22
696.	ʾAKK-A+BANIJ	AK-KA-BA-NI		M
697.	ʾAKK-ATAN-UM	AK-KA-TA-A-NU-UM		SIMMONS 106 6, 10 SEAL
698.	ʾAKK-ATAN-IM	AK-KA-TA-NI-IM	GEN	A 32133:6
699.	ʾAKK-ATAN-UM	AK-KA-TA-NU-UM		SIMMONS 112 6, SEAL
700.	ʾAKN-AN-U	AK-NA-NU		B 42
701.	ʾAL+ʾAḪ-AT-I	AL-A-ḪA-TI	FN	A.
702.	ʾALL-AH	AL-LA	FN	RA LXV 59 II 42
703.		AL-LA-E		M
704.	ʾALLAI+ḪAṢN-U	AL-LA-I-AṢ-NU	FN	M
705.	ʾALLA+MUT-IJ-I	AL-LA-MU-TI-I	TRIBE	4E RENC. ASS. P. 178 9
706.	ʾALLA+RAPIʾ	AL-LA-RA-PI		TCL XVIII 95 12, 15
707.	ʾALLA+ŠUʾḪ-U	AL-LA-ŠU-ḪU		U
708.	ʾALL-I+KUPAPA	AL-LI-KU-PA-PA	FN	A.
709.	ʾALL-I+NIWR-I	AL-LI-NI-RI	FN	A.
710.	ʾALL-I+TALM-A	AL-LI-TA-AL-MA	FN	A.
711.	ʾALL-I+TURAḪ	AL-LI-TU-RA-AḪ?	FN	XIII 1 I 10+
712.	ʾALL-I+TURAḪ-I	AL-LI-TU-RA-ḪI	FN	A.
713.	ʾALM-AN-UM	AL-MA-NU-UM		TA 1931,148
714.	ʾALM-U-NI	AL-MU-NI		RA LXV 48 VIII 7
715.	ʾALP-AN	AL-PA-AN		M+
716.		AL-SU-UM-LA-U$_2$-SA		CT XXXIII 48A 10
717.		AL-TI-EŠ$_3$-QA-AL-LU-TIM		I 45 7, 16
718.		AL-TI-EŠ$_3$-QA-LU		VII 120 3'
719.	ʾAMAN+TAʾ-I	AM-MA-AN-TA-ḪI		M
720.	ʾAMAR-A+HADD-U	AM-MA-RA-A-DU		A.
721.	ʾAMAR+HADD-U	AM-MA-RA-DU		A.+
722.		AM-MA-RI-IK-E		A.+
723.		AM-MA-RI-IK-KI		A.
724.	ʾAMAR-U	AM-MA-RU		M
725.	ʿAMM-I+....	AM-MI-....-LU-UB		A. 95 85
726.	ʿAMM-I+HADD-U	AM-MI-A-DU		A. 60 14

727.	ʿAMM-I+HADD-U	AM-MI-AD-DU		A. 267 17
728.	ʿAMM-I+DANN-U	AM-MI-DA-NU		YOS XII
729.	ʿAMM-I+DAŠUR	AM-MI-DA-ŠUR?		A 7894
730.	ʿAMM-I+DITAN-A	AM-MI-DI-TA-NA		B13+
731.	ʿAMM-I+DUŠUR	AM-MI-DU-ŠU-UR		A7894+
732.	ʿAMM-I+HEDD-A	AM-MI-E-DA		A.
733.	ʿAMM-I+ʾAK-I	AM-MI-E-KI		A.
734.	ʿAMM-I+ʿADN-A	AM-MI-ḪA-AD-NA		GOETZE, KIZZ. P. 8, LATE
735.	ʿAMM-IJA	AM-MI-IA		B 13+
736.	ʿAMM-I+HADD-U	AM-MI-IA-A-DU		A.
737.	ʿAMM-IJAN	AM-MI-IA-AN		A.+
738.	ʿAMM-I+JAT-UM	AM-MI-IA-TUM		A. 273 14
739.	ʾAMIN-AH	AM-MI-IN-NA	FN	RA LXV 64 V 64
740.	ʿAMM-I-Š+ḪARIJ-JE	AM-MI-IS-ḪA-RI?-E?		JEAN, S'A CLXXXVIII R. 3
741.	ʿAMM-I+JI-T-ŠAMAR-U	AM-MI-IS-TAM-RU		MRS VI P. 239 UGARIT+
742.	ʿAMM-I+JI-T-ŠAMAR	AM-MI-IŠ-TA-MAR		M
743.	ʿAMM-I+JI-T-ŠAMAR-U	AM-MI-IŠ-TAM-RU		MRS VI P. 329 UGARIT+
744.	ʿAMM-I+MAṬAR	AM-MI-MA-DAR		B 13 HANA
745.	ʿAMM-I+RAPIʾ	AM-MI-RA-BI-IḪ		RA XXXIV 186 HANA
746.	ʿAMM-I+RAPIʾ	AM-MI-RA-PI		SYRIA XXXVII 206 END HANA
747.	ʿAMM-I+ŠUM-U	AM-MI-SU-MU		CT XLVIII 61 4,5
748.	ʿAMM-I+ŠAGIŠ	AM-MI-ŠA-GI-IŠ		M
749.	ʿAMM-I+TA-QWUM	AM-MI-TA-KU-UM		A.+
750.	ʿAMM-I+TA-QWUM+MA	AM-MI-TA-KU-UM-MA		A. +
751.	ʿAMM-I+DITAN-A	AM-MI-TE-TA-NA		CT XLV 44 24
752.	ʿAMM-I+ṬAJB-A	AM-MI-ṬA-BA		A.+
753.	ʿAMM-I+ṢADUQ-A	AM-MI-ZA-DU-GA		B 13+
754.	ʿAMM-I+ṢADUQ-A+....	AM-MI-ZA-DU-GA-I-LU-NI		B 13+
755.	ʿAMM-I+ZAKK-UM	AM-MI-ZA-KU-UM		IRAQ IV 185, A 385
756.	ʿAMM-I+ṢUWR-A	AM-MI-ZU-RA		CT XLVIII 90 REV.
757.	ʿAMM-U+HADD-A	AM-MU-A-DA		A.+
758.	ʿAMM-U+ʿADAR	AM-MU-A-DAR		TA 30 59
759.	ʿAMM-U+ʾIL	AM-MU-DINGIR		UCP X/1 18 24
760.	ʿAMM-U+ʾEL	AM-MU-E-EL		BM 16931 2
761.	ʿAMM-UJAN	AM-MU-JA-AN		A.+
762.	ʿAMM-U+KUMAR-A	AM-MU-KU-MAR-RA		A.
763.	ʿAMM-U+NIQM-A	AM-MU-NI-IQ-MA		A.+
764.	ʿAMM-U+RAPIʾ	AM-MU-RA-BI		B 19+
765.	ʿAMM-U+RAPIʾ-I	AM-MU-RA-BI-I		A+
766.	ʿAMM-U+RAPIʾ	AM-MU-RA-PI		ABL 255 LATE
767.	ʿAMM-U+RAPIʾ	D-AM-MU-RA-PI		YBC 4362
768.	ʿAMM-U+ŠAM-A	AM-MU-SA-MA		A.+
769.	ʿAMM-U+ḪURB-I	AM-MU-UR-BI		A.
770.	ʿAMM-U-Š+KI+ʾIL	AM-MU-US-KI-DINGIR		A.
771.	ʿAMM-U-Š+KI+ʾIL	AM-MU-UŠ-KI-DINGIR		A.+
772.	ʾA-MWUT+PA+ʾIL	AM-MU-UT-PA-DINGIR		RA XLIII 212 39 QATNA
773.	ʿAMM-U+HADD-A	AM-MU-WA-DA		A.
774.	ʾAWN-AN+JA-ʾRUR	AM-NA-AN-IA-AḪ-RU-UR	TRIBE	BAGHD. MITT. II 56 I 12+
775.	ʾAWN-ANIJ-I	AM-NA-NI-I	TRIBE	M
776.	ʾAWN-AN-U	AM-NA-NU		BM 80328 9
777.	ʾAWN-AN-UM	AM-NA-NU-UM	GN	SAKI P. 222+
778.	ʾAWN-AN-UM	AM-NA-NU-UM	PN	SUMER XIV 49
779.	ʾAMR+ʿAD-UM	AM-RA-DU-UM		M
780.	ʾAMR-AT-UM	AM-RA-TUM		YOS XIII 513:4
781.		AM?-RI-MU-UM		VIII 3 23
782.	ʾAM-T+ʿAŠTAR-AH	AM-TI-AŠ-TA-RA	FN?	A. LATE
783.	ʾAM-T+LABW-A	AM-TI-LA-BA	MN	TIM III 7 5
784.	ʾAM-T-UM	AM-TUM	FN	XIII 1 II 48
785.	HAND-U+MALIK	AN-DU-MA-LIK		A. 252 10
786.		AN-MA?-NA-I-LA		ZA XXXVIII 267
787.	ḪANN-A+ʾAḪ-I	AN-NA-A-ḪI	GEN	M
788.	ḪANN-A+ʾAḪ-IM	AN-NA-A-ḪI-IM	GEN	M
789.	ḪANN-A+ʾAḪ-UM	AN-NA-A-ḪU-UM		RA LXV 52 XI 1
790.	ḪANN-A+ʾABN-UM	AN-NA-AB-NU-UM		KISURRA 8A 14
791.	ḪANN-A+ʾIL	AN-NA-DINGIR		B 13+, C+
792.	ḪANN-AJA	AN-NA-IA	FN	RA LXV 62 V 13

793.	ḪANN-A+HADD-U	AN-NA-D-IM		M+
794.		AN-NA-IŠ-ḪU-MU		M
795.	ḪANN-A+KAʾT-UM	AN-NA-KA-TUM		YOS XIII 509:2
796.	ḪANN-A+KUʾN-I	AN-NA-KU-NI		VAS VIII 14 44
797.	ḪANN-A+MAʾJ-A	AN-NA-MA-A-A		RUTTEN 14 15
798.	ʾANAZ-UM	AN-NA-ZUM		B 13+
799.	ḪANN-I+ʾIL	AN-NI-DINGIR		B 13+, M
800.	ḪANN-I+JI-JŠAR	AN-NI-I-ŠAR?		M
801.	ḪANN-I+KAʾB-I	A[N-N]I-KA-BI	FN	RA LXV 62 V 17
802.	ʾANN-U+ʾAŠJ-AH	AN-NU-A-SI-IA	FN	XIII 1 IV 41+
803.	ʾANN-U+ʾAMR-I-JA	AN-NU-AM-RI-IA	FN	RA LXV 61 IV 47
804.	ʾANN-U+ʾAŠR-I	AN-NU-AŠ-RI	FN	M+
805.	ʾANN-U+BAWŠ-T-I	AN-NU-BA-AŠ-TI	FN	RA LXV 65 VII 27
806.	ʾANN-U+DAMQ-AH	AN-NU-DAM-QA	FN	XIII 1 X 51
807.	ʾANN-U+DUNN-I	AN-NU-DU-NI	FN	RA LXV 65 VII 15
808.	ʾANN-U+DUNN-I	AN-NU-DU-UN-NI	FN	XIII 1 III 37
809.	ʾANN-U+ṬAJB	AN-NU-DUG$_3$		M+
810.	ʾANN-U+GAMIL-T-I	AN-NU-GA-ME-IL-TI	FN	RA LXV 66 VII 66
811.	ʾANN-U+ʾAJAM	AN-NU-[Ḫ]A-A-AM	FN	XIII 1 II 62
812.	ʾANN-U+ḪANN-I	AN-NU-ḪA-AN-NI	FN	M+
813.	ʾANN-U+ḪAṢN-I	AN-NU-ḪA-AṢ-NI	FN	M+
814.	ʾANN-U+T-HILAL	AN-NU-ḪI-IT-LA-AL	FN	RA LXV 60 III 18
815.	ʾANN-U+JAPʿ-AH	AN-NU-IA-AP-ḪA	FN	XIII 1 IV 3+
816.	ʾANN-U+JATR-AH	AN-NU-IA-AT-RA	FN	XIII 1 VI 53+
817.	ʾANN-U+JIPʿ-AH	AN-NU-IP-ḪA	FN	XIII 1 VIII 29
818.	ʾANN-U+JIŠʿ-AH	AN-NU-IŠ-ḪA	FN	XIII 1 V 46+
819.	ʾANN-U+KAMA+ʾAB-I	AN-NU-KA-MA-BI		CT XLV 116 36
820.	ʾANN-U+QUDM-I	AN-NU-KU-UD-MI	FN	XIII 1 VIII 77
821.	ʾANN-U+KUʾM	AN-NU-KUM	FN	XIII 1 VI 8
822.	ʾANN-U+LAMAS-I	AN-NU-LA-MA-ZI	FN	M+
823.	ʾANN-U+LAMAS-IT-UM	AN-NU-LA-MA-ZI-TUM	FN	RA LXV 59 II 13
824.	ʾANN-U+LAMAS-I	AN-NU-D-LAMA	FN	XIII 1 VII 8+
825.	ʾANN-U+MAʾN-A	AN?-NU-MA-NA	FN	M
826.	ʾANN-U+NABIʾ	AN-NU-NA-BI-IḪ	FN	RA LXV 62 V 24
827.	ʾANN-U+NABIT-I	AN-NU-NA-BI-TI		XIII 1 VI 61
828.	ʾANN-U+NIWR-I	AN-NU-NI-RI	FN	M
829.	ʾANN-U+PUṬR-I	AN-NU-PU-UṬ-RI	FN	RA LXV 58 I 19+
830.	ʾANN-U+RAḪM-I	AN-NU-RA-AḪ-MI	FN	XIII 1 V 11+
831.	ʾANN-U+RIMŠ-I	AN-NU-RI-IM-ŠI	FN	M+
832.	ʾANN-U+ŠATAM	AN?-NU?-ŠA-TAM	FN	XIII 1 IV 46
833.	ʾANN-U+ŠIMḪ-I	[A]N-NU-ŠI-IM-ḪI		XIII 1 XIV 24
834.	ʾANN-U+TA-ḪNUN	AN-NU-TA-AḪ-NU-UN	FN	RA LXV 61 IV 15+
835.	ʾANN-U+TA-LʾIJ	AN-NU-TA-AL-E	FN	M+
836.	ʾANN-U+TA-RḪAM	AN-NU-TA-AR-AM	FN	M+
837.	ʾANN-U+TA-ŠMAʿ	AN-NU-TA-AŠ$_2$-MA-AḪ	FN	M
838.	ʾANN-U+TABB-I	AN-NU-TAB-BI	FN	XIII 1 III 36+
839.	ʾANN-U+TA-RBIJ	AN-NU-TAR-BI	FN	XIII 1 XI 47
840.	ʾANN-U+TIWR-I	AN-NU-TI-RI	FN	M+
841.	ʾANN-U+TILL-AT-I	AN-NU-TIL-LA-TI	FN	XIII 1 X 2
842.	ʾANN-U+TUKUL-T-I	AN-NU-TU-GUL-TI	FN	XIII 1 X 3
843.	ʾANN-U+TUKUL-T-I	AN-NU-TU-KU-UL-[TI]	FN	M+
844.		AN-NU-TU-NU-UM		RA LXIV 28 NO. 17
845.	ʾANN-U+ʾUMM-I	AN-NU-UM-MI	FN	XIII 1 IV 48+
846.	ʾANN-U+ʾUMM-I	AN-NU-UN-UM-MI		M
847.	ʾANT-AN-UM	AN-TA-NU-UM		TA 1930, 698
848.	ʾANTAR-UM	AN-TA-RU-UM		CT VIII 47 B 21
849.	ʾA-NZAL-AT-UM	AN-ZA-LA-TUM	FN?	XIII 1 I 14
850.	ʾANZ-AN-UM	AN-ZA-NU-UM		B 43
851.	ʾAPK-AN-UM	AP-KA-NU-UM		SIMMONS 66 28
852.	ʾAPK-ATAN	AP-KA-TA-AN		M+
853.	ʾAPK-AT-UM	AP-KA-TUM	MN	UCP X/1 4 5
854.	ʾA-PQID-A	AP-KI-DA		U
855.	ʾA-PLAḪ+HAND-A	AP-LA-AḪ-[AN]-DA		M
856.	ʾA-PLAḪ+HAND-A	AP-LA-ḪA-AN-DA		M+
857.	ʾA-PLAḪ+HAND-U	AP-LA-ḪA-AN-DU		RA LXV 42 II 65
858.	ʾA-PLAḪ+HAND-A	AP-LA-ḪA-DA		M

859.	ʾA-PLAḪ+HAND-A	AP-LI-ḪA-AN-DA		M
860.		AP-LI-TI-DINGIR[....]		M
861.	ʾAPP-ATAN	AP-PA-TA-AN		RA LXV 43 IV 18
862.	ʾAPP-AT-UM	AP-PA-TUM	FN	A.+
863.	ʾAPR-AN	AP-RA-AN		A. LATE
864.	ʾAPR-IJA	AP-RI-A		A.
865.	ʾA-PTUN-AN-UM	AP-TU-NA-NU-UM		YOS VIII 176 SEAL
866.	ʿAQB-A+ʾAḪ-AM	AQ-BA-A-ḪA-AM	ACC	M
867.	ʿAQB-A+ʾAḪ-I	AQ-BA-A-ḪI	GEN	XII 448 5+
868.	ʿAQB-A+ʾAḪ-IM	AQ-BA-A-ḪI-IM	GEN	M+
869.	ʿAQB-A+ʾAḪ-U	AQ-BA-A-ḪU		M+, C+
870.	ʿAQB-A+ʾAḪ-UM	AQ-BA-A-ḪU-UM		M+
871.	ʿAQB-AN	AQ-BA-AN		M
872.	ʿAQB-A+ʿAMM-U	AQ-BA-ḪA-AM-MU		IRAQ XXX 91, RIMAH
873.	ʿAQB-A+ʿAMM-U	AQ-BA-ḪA-MU		M
874.	ʿAQB-A+ʾAḪ-U	AQ-BA-ḪU		BASOR 95 19+
875.	ʿAQB-A+ḪUNN-UM	AQ-BA-ḪU-NI-UM		B 11
876.	ʿAQB-A+ʾAḪ-UM	AQ-BA-ḪU-UM		B 11+
877.	ʿAQB-AN-UM	AQ-BA-NU-UM		RUTTEN 40 2+
878.	ʿAQB-I+ʾAḪ-U	AQ-BI-A-ḪU		B 11
879.	ʿAQB-I+ʾIL	AQ-BI-DINGIR		BIN VII 156 10+
880.	ʿAQB-I+ʾIL	AQ-BI-IL		B 11
881.	ʿAQB-I+NAN-UM	AQ-BI-NA-NU-UM		B 42+
882.	ʿAQB-U+ʿAMM-U-HU	AQ-BU-AM-MU-U$_2$		X 174 3
883.	ʿAQB-U+DAWD-A	AQ-BU-DA-DA		B 12
884.	ʿAQB-U+DAWD-I	AQ-BU-DA-DI		M
885.	ʿAQB-U+DAWD-UM	AQ-BU-DA-DU-UM		PBS VIII/2 253 7
886.	ʿAQB-U-HU	AQ-BU-U$_2$		CT IV 50B 24+
887.	ʿAQB-UM	AQ-BU-UM		TIM III 82 6
888.	ʾA-QDAM-U	AQ-DA-MU		C P. 35+
889.	ḪARB-ATAN-U	AR-BA-TA-NU		CT IV 22A 19
890.	ḪARB-ATAN-UM	AR-BA-TA-NU-UM		B 43
891.	ḪARB-I+TUWR-AM	AR-BI-TU-RA-AM		BIROT, TEA 65:35
892.	ʾARWIJ-T-UM	AR-BI-TUM		LEGRAIN, TRU 41+, U
893.	ʾARWIJ-T-UM	AR-BI$_2$-TUM		TCL V 6039 REV 17, U
894.	ʾARWIJ-UM	AR-BI$_2$-UM		ITT II/1 P 48, 933, U
895.	ʾA-RDAK+HAND-A	AR-DA-KA-AN-DA		M
896.	ʿARD-U	AR-DU		TCL I 166 2
897.	ʿARD-UM	AR-DU-UM		TCL I 168 4+
898.	ʾARK-ATAN-UM	AR-GA-DA-NU-UM		KISURRA 1A 15+
899.	ʾA-RGAM-AT-UM	AR-GA-MA-TUM	FN	C
900.	ʾARK-ATAN-UM	AR-GA-TA-NU-UM		KISURRA 141 9
901.	ʾARḪ-AN-UM	AR-ḪA-NU-UM		BM 92657+
902.	ʾARḪ-I+ŠAMŠ-I	AR-ḪI-D-UTU-ŠI	FN	XIII 1 XIII 2
903.	ʾARḪ-UM	AR-ḪU-UM	FN	XIII 1 VIII 23
904.	ʾA-RMAN-UN-UM	AR-MA-NU-NUM$_2$		TA 1931 , 538 IV
905.	ʾARNAB-AT-IM	AR-NA-BA-TIM	FN? GEN	MEISSNER 18 3
906.	ʾARNAB-AT-UM	AR-NA-BA-TUM	FN	CT VIII 43C 22+, XIII 1 X 39
907.	ʾARNAB-UM	AR-NA-BU-UM	FN	M+
908.		AR-NU-X-TUM	FN	XIII 1 IX 21
909.		AR-RA-ZA-[....]		XIII 1 XII 22
910.		AR-RI-WU-UK		M+
911.		AR-RU-UT-RUM		TCL I 109 8
912.	ʾA-RŠIJ+ʿAN-UM	AR-SI?-A-NUM$_2$		U
913.	ʾA-RŠIJ+HADD-A	AR-ŠI-A-DA		M
914.	ʾA-RŠIJ+ʿAD-A-HA	AR-ŠI-A-DA?-A	FN	C
915.	ʾA-RŠIJ+ʾAḪ-UM	AR-ŠI-A-ḪU-UM		M+
916.	ʾA-RŠIJ+ʾEDAK-U	AR-ŠI-E-DA-KU	FN	M
917.	ʾARWIJ-EM	AR-WI-E-[EM]	GEN	I 30 10
918.	ʾARWIJ-IM	AR-WI-IM	GEN	TIM V 14 23, M
919.	ʾARWIJ-ATAN-UM	AR-WI-TA-NU-UM		B 43
920.	ʾARWIJ-T-UM	AR-WI-TUM	FN	KISURRA 134 3, M+
921.	ʾARWIJ-U	AR-WI-U$_2$		B 13
922.	ʾARWIJ-UM	AR-WI-U$_2$-UM		B 13+, M
923.	ʾARWIJ-UM	AR-WI-UM		B 13+, M+
924.	ʿARṢ-AN-UM	AR-ZA-NU-UM		B 43+

925.	ʿARṢ-AT-UM	AR-ZA-TUM	FN	C
926.	ʿABD+ʾABN-IM	ARAD$_2$-AB-NIM		BAGHD. MITT. II 72
927.	ʾAŠD-A+ʾAḪ-I	AŠ-DA-A-ḪI		VAS XVI 44 3
928.	ʾAŠD-I+JATAR	AŠ-DI-E-TAR		M
929.	ʾAŠD-IJA	AŠ-DI-IA		BIN VII 32 4
930.	ʾAŠD-I+KIʾR-U	AŠ-DI-KI-E-RU		BM 92654 A
931.	ʾAŠD-I+KIʾR-U	AŠ-DI-KI-RU		BM 92654
932.	ʾAŠD-I+LUMM-A	AŠ-DI-LU-MA		UCP X/3 2 31
933.	ʾAŠD-I+RAWM	AŠ-DI-RA-AM		RA LXV 55 XIII 42
934.	ʾAŠD-U	D-AŠ-DU		RT XIX 48 SEAL
935.	ʾAŠD-U+QAWM-U	AŠ-DU-GA-MU		CT XLV 77 R. 10, 14+
936.	ʾAŠD-UM	AŠ-DU-UM		VAS VIII 60 26
937.	ʾAŠD-UM+ʾAB-I	D-AŠ-DU-UM-A-BI		UET V 483 4
938.	ʾAŠD-UM+PI+JAD-IM	AŠ-DU-UM-BI-IA-DI-IM		RA LXV 55 XIII 44
939.	ʾAŠD-UM+LA+ʾAB-UM	AŠ-DU-UM-LA-A-BU-UM		SUMER V 142
940.	ʾAŠQUD-AN	AŠ-KU-DA-AN		M
941.	ʾAŠQUD-AN-AM	AŠ-KU-DA-NA-AM	ACC	B 43
942.	ʾAŠQUD-AN-UM	AŠ-KU-DA-NU-UM		CT XLVIII 86 REV 10+
943.	ʾAŠQUD-I	AŠ-KU-DI	GEN	M+
944.	ʾAŠQUD-IM	AŠ-KU-DI-IM	GEN	M+
945.	ʾAŠQUD-U	AŠ-KU-DU		M
946.	ʾAŠQUD-UM	AŠ-KU-DU-UM		KISURRA 205 7, M+
947.	ʾA-ŠKUR-AN	AŠ-KU-RA-AN		RA LXV 50 IX 15
948.	ʾAŠQUD-UM	AŠ-KU-TU-UM		KISURRA 88 1, 8+
949.	ʾA-ŠKUR+HEDD-A	AŠ-KUR-E-DA		A. 54 25
950.	ʾA-ŠKUR+HADD-U	AŠ-KUR-D-IM		M+
951.	ʾAŠM-A+HADD-U	AŠ-MA-A-DU		A.+
952.	ʾAŠM-AN	AŠ-MA-AN		BM 81174 11
953.	ʾAŠM-AT	AŠ-MA-AT	MN	M+
954.	ʾAŠM-A+HADD-U	AŠ-MA-DU		BM 80328 14
955.	ʾAŠR-AT-UM+ʾUMM-I	D-AŠ-RA-TUM-UM-MI	FN	TCL I P. 16+
956.	ʾAŠR-I+JATAR	AŠ-RI-E-TAR		RA XLIX 24 N. 9
957.	ʾA-T-ŠAMAR+HADD-U	AŠ-TA-MAR-D-IM		M+
958.	ʿAŠTAR+ʾAB-I	AŠ-TAR-A-BI		MRS VI P. 242
959.	ʾAŠD-I+DAWD-UM	AŠ$_2$-DI?-DA-DU-UM		EDZARD, DER 60:11
960.	ʾAŠD-I+JAŠAR	AŠ$_2$-DI-E-SA-AR		XIII 1 XI 35
961.	ʾAŠD-I+JE-JŠUʿ	AŠ$_2$-DI-E-ŠU-UḪ		M
962.	ʾAŠD-I+MAʾK-U-HU	AŠ$_2$-DI-MA-KU-U$_2$		VAS IX 172 30
963.	ʾAŠD-I+NIʿM	AŠ$_2$-DI-NI-ḪI-IM		M+
964.	ʾAŠD-I+TA-QWIM	AŠ$_2$-DI-TA-KI-IM		M+
965.	ʾAŠD-U+QAWM-UM	AŠ$_2$-DU-GA-MU-UM		TCL I 130 8+
966.	ʾAŠD-U-NA+JA-RWIM	[AŠ$_2$-D]U-NI-A-RI-IM		CT XXXVI 4 1
967.	ʾAŠD-U-NA+JE-RWIM	AŠ$_2$-DU-NI-E-RI-IM		RA VIII 65 1
968.	ʾAŠD-U+RAPIʾ	AŠ$_2$-DU-RA-BI		C+
969.	ʾAŠD-UM+ʾAB-I	AŠ$_2$-DU-UM-A-BI		BE VI/1 1 7+
970.	ʾAŠD-UM+LA+ʾAB-UM	AŠ$_2$-DU-UM-LA-A-BU-UM		SUMER V 142+
971.	ʾA-ŠKIN-AN-UM	AŠ$_2$-KI-NA-NU-UM		TA 30 87+
972.	ʾAŠQUD-UM	AŠ$_2$-KU-DU-UM		X 59 8
973.	ʾA-ŠKUR+HADD-U	AŠ$_2$-KU-UR-D-IM		TCL 1 146 4
974.	ʾAŠM-ATEN	AŠ$_2$-MA-TI-EN		M
975.	ḪATK-AN-UM	AT-GA-NU-UM		U
976.	ʾATAZ-AH	AT-TA-AZ-ZA	FN	XIII 1 III 9+
977.	ʾATTA+BAʿL-I	AT-TA-BA-AḪ-LI		JCS XIII 51 293:8,A. LATE
978.	ʾATTA+BAʿL-I-JE	AT-TA-BA-AḪ-LI-E		JCS XIII 51 293:15,A.LATE
979.	ʾATAM-AN-UM	AT-TA-MA-NU-UM		SIMMONS 122 16
980.	ʾATAR-I+ṢADUQ	[A]T-TA-RI-ZA-DU-UQ		I 103 17
981.	ʾATAZ-AH	AT-TA-ZA	FN	M
982.	ʾATT-I	AT-TI	FN	RA LXV 65 VII 6
983.	ʾATT-I+ʿAMM-A	AT-TI-AM-MA		A. LATE
984.	ʾATT-IJAN	AT-TI-IA-AN		A. 261 14
985.	ʾATT-I+HADD-U	AT-TI-D-IM		M+
986.	ʾATT-I+LIʾM-A	AT-TI-LI-MA		A. LATE
987.	ʾATT-I+MEʾR	AT?-TI-ME-IR?		IX 234 10
988.	ʾAWN-AN-IM	AW-NA-NI-[IM]	GEN	MAM III 320, PSARG MARI
989.	ʾAWN-AN-UM	AW-NA-NU-[UM]	TRIBE	M
990.	ḪAṢN-U+TABB-I	AZ?-NU-TAB-BI	FN	M

991.	ʿAZZ+ʿAMM-I	AZ-ZA-AM-MI		A. 265 19
992.	ʿAZAL-UM	AZ-ZA-LUM		GAUTIER 1 R. 9
993.	ʿAZZ-U	AZ-ZU	FN	M+, C+
994.	ʿAZZ-U-KA	AZ-ZU-KA	FN	M+, C
995.	ʿAZZ-U-KI	AZ-ZU-UK-KI	FN	XIII 1 VIII 66
996.	ʿAZZ-U-NI	AZ-ZU-UN-NI	FN	M
997.	BAʿL-AN	BA-A-LA-AN		RA LXV 46 VI 48
998.	BAʾAN-AN-UM	BA-A-NA-NU-UM		B 43
999.	BAJN-AN-UM	BA-A-NA-NU-UM		B 43
1000.	BAʾAN-UM	BA-A-NU-UM		TA 1931, 434+
1001.	BAWʾ+JARAḪ	BA-A-RA-AḪ		RUTTEN 39 18
1002.	BAWʾ-UM	BA-A-U$_2$-UM		KISURRA 94 14
1003.	BAʿD-AN	BA-AḪ-DA-AN		RUTTEN 7 18+
1004.	BAʿD-AN-UM	BA-AḪ-DA-NUM		HARRIS 106 5
1005.	BAʿD-I+ʾEL	[BA]-AḪ-DI-EL		KISURRA 51 10
1006.	BAʿD-IJA	BA-AḪ-DI-IA		RUTTEN 12A 23+
1007.	BAʿD-I+HADD-U	BA-AḪ-DI-D-IM		M+
1008.	BAʿD-IM	BA-AḪ-DI-IM	GEN	RES 1939 69
1009.	BAʿD-I+LIʾM	BA-AḪ-DI-LI-IM		M+
1010.	BAʿL-AN	BA-AḪ-LA-AN		M
1011.	BAʿL-AT-IM	BA-AḪ-LA-TIM	FN GEN	XIII 1 XIV 37
1012.	BAʿL-AT-UM	BA-AḪ-LA-TUM	FN	M+
1013.	BAʿL-I	BA-AḪ-LI		M
1014.	BAʿL-I+BAWŠ-T-I	BA-AḪ-LI-BA-AŠ-TI	FN	M+
1015.	BAʿL-I+DIWR-I	BA-AḪ-LI-DI-RI	FN	C+
1016.	BAʿL-I+ʾIL	BA-AḪ-LI-DINGIR		B 15
1017.	BAʿL-I+ʾIL-I	BA-AḪ-LI-I$_3$-LI$_2$	FN	M
1018.	BAʿL-IJA	BA-AḪ-LI-IA		KISURRA 24 5, 7
1019.	BAʿL-I+HADD-U	BA-AḪ-LI-D-IM		M+
1020.	BAʿL-I+NIWR-I	BA-AḪ-LI-NI-RI	FN	M+
1021.	BAʿL-I+....	BA-AḪ-LI-RA-[....]	FN	M
1022.	BAʿL-I+ŠAPAR	BA-AḪ-LI-SA-PA-AR	FN	M+
1023.	BAʿL-I+ŠAPAR	BA-AḪ-LI-SA-PAR$_2$	FN	M, C+
1024.	BAʿL-I+ŠAMŠ-I	BA-AḪ-LI-D-UTU-ŠI	FN	M
1025.	BAʿL-U+BAʿD-I	BA-AḪ-LU-BA-DI		EA
1026.	BAʿL-U+GAʾJ-A	BA-AḪ-LU-GA-A	GEN	HOLMA 6 5
1027.	BAʿL-U+GAʾJ-I	BA-AḪ-LU-GA-A-JI	NOM	M
1028.	BAʿL-U+GAʾJ-I	BA-AḪ-LU-GA-I	NOM	M+
1029.	BAʿL-U+GAʾJ-IM	BA-AḪ-LU-GA-I-IM	GEN	M+
1030.	BAʿL-U+GAʾJ-IM	BA-AḪ-LU-GA-JI-IM	GEN	M+
1031.	BAʿL-U+KULIM	BA-AḪ-LU-KU-LI-IM		SYRIA XXXII 7 III 6
1032.	BAʿL-U+LUʾL-I	BA-AḪ-LU-LU-L[I]?		HARRIS 71 14
1033.	BAʿL-UM+ʾIL	BA-AḪ-LU-UM-DINGIR		B 15+
1034.	BAḪŠ-UM	BA-AḪ-ŠUM		RA LXV 43 III 71
1035.	BAʿD-AN-U	BA-AḪ-TA-NU		BM 17060 10
1036.	BAʿD-AN-U-HU	BA-AḪ-TA-NU-U$_2$		BM 17060 2
1037.	BAQQ-UM	BA-AK-KUM		M
1038.	BAKŠ-AT-UM	BA-AK-SA-TUM	FN	M
1039.	BAKŠIŠ-UM	BA-AK-ŠI-ŠUM		HARRIS 5 3+
1040.	BAKS-I	BA-AK-ZI	NOM	BASOR 95 P.23
1041.	BALBAL-UM	BA-AL-BA-LUM		RUTTEN 37 4 8
1042.	BAʿL+TUʾ-KA	BA-AL-DU-UḪ-KA		A.
1043.	BALK-U-Š+RAḪAB	BA-AL-KU-UŠ$_2$-RA-ḪA-AB	FN	XIII 1 VIII 61
1044.	BALK-UM	BA-AL-KUM		TIM V 1 23
1045.	BALṬ-A-HA	BA-AL-TA-A	FN	XIII 1 IX 32
1046.	BALṬ-AN	BA-AL-TA-AN		M
1047.	BANḪ-AT-UM	BA-AN-ḪA-TUM	FN	IX 291 II 19
1048.	BANN-UM	BA-AN-NU-UM		M+
1049.	BAQQ-AN-IM	BA-AQ-QA-NIM	GEN	M
1050.	BAQQ-AN-UM	BA-AQ-QA-NU-UM		M
1051.	BAWŠ-T-I+NUṢR-I	BA-AŠ-TI-NU-IZ-RI	FN	RA LXV 58 I 45
1052.	BAWŠ-T-I+NUṢR-I	BA-AŠ-TI-UZ-RI		RA LXIV 28 NO. 15
1053.	BAWŠ-T-UM	BA-AŠ-TUM	FN	M+
1054.	BAWŠ-T-I+NUṢR-I	BA-AŠ$_2$-TI-NU-UZ-RI	FN	XIII 1 VII 24
1055.	BATQ-AN-UM	BA-AT-GA-NU-UM		ZA XLII 41
1056.	PAṬR-IJA	BA-AṬ-RI-IA		A 21950

1057.	BAZBAZ-UM	BA-AZ-BA-ZUM		B 48
1058.	BAWB-AT-UM	BA-BA-TUM	FN	RA LXV 58 I 59
1059.	BAWB-I+ḪAJJ-A	D-BA-BI-E_2-A?		VIII 31 7
1060.	BABUL-UM	BA-BU-LU-[UM]	FN	RA LXV 62 V 8
1061.	BAWB-U+QAʾN	BA-BU-QA-AN		M
1062.	BAʿD-AN-UM	BA-DA-NU-UM		U
1063.	PAṬAR-AN-UM	BA-DA-RA-NU-UM		SIMMONS 31 5
1064.	BADID-UM	BA-DI-DU-UM		B 15+
1065.	PAṬIR-UM	BA-DI-RU-UM		HARRIS 26 7
1066.	PAQAḪ-A+LAʾL-UM	BA-GA-A-LA-LUM		HARRIS 69 2+
1067.	PAQAḪ-AT-UM	BA-GA-A-TUM	MN	A 29366:17
1068.	BAQAQ-UM	BA-GA-KUM		KISURRA 75A 21+
1069.	BAKAL-A	BA-GA-LA		A. LATE
1070.	BAGIN-U	BA-GI-NU		B 15+
1071.	BAGIN-UM	BA-GI-NU-UM		B 15
1072.	BAʾAN-IM	BA-ḪA-NIM	GEN	EDZARD, DER 71 IV 3
1073.	BAʾIL-IM	BA-ḪI-LIM	NOM	ABB V 157:9'
1074.	BAʾIL-UM	BA-ḪI-LUM		M+
1075.	BAḪUR-A	BA-ḪU-RA		A. LATE
1076.	BAḪIR-UM	BA-I-RUM		M
1077.	BAWʾ+JARAḪ	BA-IA-RA-AḪ		RUTTEN 7 3
1078.	BAWʾ-UM	BA-IA-UM		CT VI 15 III 19
1079.	BAKAL-UM	BA-KA-LUM		RUTTEN 38 18+
1080.	BAKIL-AH	BA-KI-LA	FN	RA LXV 60 III 68
1081.	BAKIL-A	BA-KI-LA_2		TCL XIX 74:18
1082.	BAKIL-UM	BA-KI-LUM		B 15+
1083.	BAKIR-UM	BA-KI-RUM		M
1084.	BAKUR-AJA	BA-KU?-RA-IA		C
1085.	BAKUR-AT-UM	BA-KU-RA-TUM	FN	B
1086.	BAKUŠ-AJA	BA-KU-SA-A-IA	FN	XIII 1 II 63
1087.	BAQQ-UM	BA-KU-UM		M
1088.	BAQQ-UM	BA-KU-UM	FN	RA LXV 62 V 12
1089.	BAKUS-I	BA-KU-ZI		RA LXV 55 XIII 43
1090.	BAʿL-AN	BA-LA-AN		M+
1091.	BAʿL-A+ʿAŠTAR	BA-LA-$EŠ_4$-DAR		M
1092.	BAʿL-A+HAND-U	BA-LA-ḪA-AN-DU		VOIX 187:13 MARI
1093.	BALAL-AT-I	BA-LA-LA-TI		TA 1930, 399+
1094.	BAʿL-A+MI+NAMḪ-U	BA-LA-MI-NA-AM-ḪU		SYRIA XLIV 201 N.1 MARI
1095.	BAʿL-AN-UM	BA-LA-NU-UM		B 43+
1096.	BALAṬ-I+ʾEL	BA-LA-TI-EL		RUTTEN 5 21
1097.	BAʿL-AT-UM	BA-LA-TUM	FN	BM 16944 5
1098.	BAʿL-I+JA-JPUʿ	BA-LI-A-PU-UḪ		HARRIS 96 6+
1099.	BAʿL-I+JARAḪ	BA-LI-A-RA-AḪ		SIMMONS 58 11
1100.	BAʿL-I+ʾIL	BA-LI-DINGIR		EDZARD, DER 68 IV 7
1101.	BAʿL-EJA	BA-LI-E-IA		A.
1102.	BAʿL-I+JE-JPAʿ	BA-LI-E-PA		A.
1103.	BAʿL-I+JARAḪ	BA-LI-E-RA-AḪ		M+, TCL XVIII 92 14
1104.	BAʿL-IJA	BA-LI-IA		A.; M
1105.	BAʿL-I+HADD-U	BA-LI-D-IM		M
1106.	BAʿL-I-Š+ʾAG-UM	BA-LI-IŠ-A-GU-UM		RA LXV 45 V 36
1107.	BALIK-AH	BA-LI-KA	FN	A.
1108.	BALIK-I	BA-LI-KI	GEN	A.
1109.	BALIL-AH	BA-LI-LA	FN	XIII 1 VIII 72
1110.	BALIL-AT-UM	BA-LI-LA?-TUM	MN?	VIII 3 5
1111.	BALIL-UM	BA-LI-LUM		B 15+
1112.	BAʿL-I+JA-JPUʿ	BA-LI-PU-$UḪ_2$		EDZARD, DER 117:38 DATE
1113.	BAʿL-I+JARAḪ	BA-LI-RA-AḪ		TCL XVIII 94 I 14+
1114.	BAʿL-I+ṬAJB	BA-LI-SIG_5?	FN	XIII 1 VIII 36
1115.	BAʿL-U+ʿAŠTAR	BA-LU-$EŠ_4$-DAR		M+
1116.	BAʿL-U+ME+NUMḪ-I	BA-LU-ME-NU-ḪI		M+
1117.	BAʿL-U+ME+NUMḪ-I	BA-LU-ME-NU-UM-ḪI		IX 41 2
1118.	BAʿL-U+ŠAMŠ	BA-LU-D-UTU		M
1119.	PALUS-UM	BA-LU-ZUM		TA 30 615 26
1120.	BALUL-A	BA-LUL-LA	MN	AJSL XXXIII 224 3, 6
1121.	BAʿL-UM	BA-LUM		CT II 35 29
1122.	BAʿL-UM+QAWM-UM	BA-LUM-QA-MU-UM		RA LXV 40 I 11

1123.	BAJN-AT-UM	BA-NA-A-TUM	FN	HARRIS 86 1
1124.	BAJN-AN-IM	BA-NA-NIM	GEN	B 43
1125.	BAJN-AN-UM	BA-NA-NU-UM		B 43+
1126.	BAJN-AT-UM	BA-NA-TUM	FN	C; EDZARD 58:3
1127.	BANIḪ-AN	BA-NI-ḪA-AN		M
1128.	BANIJ-IM	BA-NI-I-IM	GEN	M
1129.	BANIJ+ME+ʾEL	BA-NI-ME-EL		HARRIS 12 15
1130.	BAJN-U+DAGAN	BA-NU-D-DA-GAN		M+
1131.	BANUQ-AN	BA-NU-KA-AN		RA LXV 55 XIII 46
1132.	BANUQ-UM	BA-NU-KU-UM		CT XXXIII 48A 3
1133.	BAJN-UM	BA-NU-UM		M
1134.	BAJR-ATAN	BA-RA-TA-AN	MN	M
1135.	BAJR-AT-UM	BA-RA-TUM	FN	CT VIII 6A 3+
1136.	BARIL-AT-UM	BA-RI-LA-TUM	FN	CT VI 35A 15
1137.	BAJR-UM	BA-RU-UM		HARRIS 89 2
1138.	BAŠAR	BA-SA-AR KUR	MOUNT	RTC 124,SARGONIC
1139.	BAWŠ-AN-U	BA-SA-NU		MAOG 4 440 HANA
1140.	BAŠAR-AN	BA-SA-RA-AN		RA LXV 50 VIII 41
1141.	BAŠUM-UM	BA-SU-MU-UM		SIMMONS 46 27+
1142.	BAŠAJ-AT-UM	BA-ŠA-A-IA-[TUM]?	FN	M
1143.	BAŠAR	ḪUR-SAG BA-ŠA-AR	MOUNT	RA IX 57,UR III
1144.	BAWŠ-AN-UM	BA-ŠA-NU-UM		TA 30 615
1145.	T-BAḪR-AH	BA-TA-AḪ-RA	FN	RA LXV 59 II 40
1146.	T-BAḪR-I	BA-TA-AḪ-RI	GEN	M+
1147.	T-BAḪR-IM	BA-TA-AḪ-RI-IM	GEN	M
1148.	T-BAḪR-UM	BA-TA-AḪ-RUM		M+
1149.	T-BANḪ-IM	BA-TA-AN-ḪI-IM	GEN	M
1150.	BAʿD-AN-UM	BA-TA-NUM$_2$		U
1151.	PAṬIR-UM	BA-TI-RU-UM		TA 1931,377
1152.	BATUL-AT-UM	BA-TU-LA-TUM	FN	XIII 1 II 59
1153.	BATUL-UM	BA-TU-LUM		HARRIS 15 4+
1154.	BAWʾ-U+ʾIL-A	BA-U$_2$-I-LA		MEISSNER 43 45
1155.	BAWZ-A	BA-ZA	MN	B 15
1156.	BAWZ-AN-UM	BA-ZA-NU-UM		B 43+
1157.	BAWZ-AT-IM	BA-ZA-TI[M]	GEN	M+
1158.	BAWZ-AT-UM	BA-ZA-TUM	FN	B 15+, M+
1159.	BAZAZ-UM	BA-ZA-ZUM		BM 17072+
1160.	BAWZ-I+ʿAŠTAR	BA-ZI-EŠ$_4$-DAR		M
1161.	BAZIḪ-AN-UM	BA-ZI-ḪA-NU-UM		TA 1931, 230 U
1162.	BAZIN-IM	BA-ZI-NIM	GEN	B 15
1163.	BAZIN-U	BA-ZI-NU		B 15
1164.	BAZIN-UM	BA-ZI-NU-UM		B 15+
1165.	BAZUR-AH	BA-ZU-R[A]	FN	XIII 1 VII 2
1166.	BAZUR-AT-IM	BA-ZU-RA-TIM	FN GEN	CT XLV 25 17
1167.	BAZUR-AT-UM	BA-ZU-RA-TUM	FN	CT XLV 25 11, 20
1168.	BEʿD-I+ʾIL	BE-DI-DINGIR		TIM III 130 11+
1169.	BEʿD-I+ʾIL-UM	BE-DI-LU-UM		TIM III 62 6+
1170.	BEʿD-I+ʾIL-UM	BE-DI-LUM		TIM III 61 15
1171.	BEʿD-IT-UM	BE-DI-TUM	MN	EDZARD, DER 145:10
1172.	BEʿL-UM	BE-E-LUM		KISURRA 36 4
1173.	BELBAN-UM	BE-EL-BA-NU-UM		BM 81108 2
1174.	BELBIN	BE?-EL-BI-IN		HARRIS 108 4
1175.	BILL-UM	BE-EL-LUM		B 15 HANA
1176.	BEʿL-T-I+MAʾT-I	BE-EL-TI-MA-TI	FN	A. 253 6
1177.		BE-EŠ$_3$-NU	FN	M
1178.	BEʿL-AH	BE-LA	FN	IX 291 3 9'
1179.	BEʿL-AT-UM	BE-LA-A-TUM	FN	RA LXV 60 III 26
1180.	BEʿL-AK-I	BE-LA-KI	GEN	CT VIII 31B 23+
1181.	BEʿL-AK-UM	BE-LA-KUM		CT VIII 31A 21+
1182.	BEʿL-AN-IM	BE-LA-NIM	GEN	M+
1183.	BEʿL-AN-UM	BE-LA-NU-UM		M+
1184.	BEʿL-AT-I	BE-LA-TI	FN? GEN	VIII 63:11
1185.	BEʿL-AT-IM	BE-LA-TI-IM	FN? GEN	VIII 63:2
1186.	BEʿL-AT-UM	BE-LA-TUM	FN	M+
1187.	BEʿL-I+ʾAHL-I	BE-LI-IA-LI$_2$		KISURRA 112 14
1188.	BEʿL-I+BAWŠ-T-I	BE-LI$_2$-[B]A-AŠ-TI	FN	RA LXV 60 III 42

1189.	BEʿL-I+ʾIL-I	BE-LI$_2$-I$_3$-LI$_2$	FN	RA LXV 64 VI 50
1190.	BEʿL-I+HADD-U	BE-LI$_2$-D-IM		RA LXV 52 X 39
1191.	BEʿL-I+KAʾB-I	BE-LI$_2$-KA-BI	FN	XIII 1 V 28+
1192.	BEʿL-I+KIʾR-I	BE-LI$_2$-KI-RI	FN	RA LXV 58 I 15
1193.	BEʿL-I+NIWR-I	BE-LI$_2$-NE-RI	FN	XIII 1 II 55+
1194.	BEʿL-I+NIWR-I	BE-LI$_2$-NI-RI	FN	M+
1195.	BEʿL-I+NUṢR-I	BE-LI$_2$-NU-IZ-RI	FN	RA LXV 64 V 60
1196.	BEʿL-I+RAWM	BE-LI$_2$-RA-AM		RA LXV 54 XII 60
1197.	BEʿL-I+ŠAPAR	BE-LI$_2$-SA-PAR$_2$	FN	M
1198.	BEʿL-I+TA-LEʾEJ	BE-LI$_2$-TA-LI-IḪ		RA LXV 50 VIII 44
1199.	BEʿL-I+ʾUŠIL-I	BE-LI$_2$-U$_2$-SI-LI	FN	RA LXV 56 I 10
1200.	BIBIJ-AT-UM	BI-BI-IA-TUM	FN	RA LXV 62 V 25
1201.	BIʿD-AN-UM	BI-DA-NU-UM		SIMMONS 98 9+
1202.	BIʿD-I+KI+ʾEL	BI-DI-KI-EL		RA LXV 53 XI 54
1203.	BIDUM-U	BI-DU-MU		M
1204.	PILḪ-U+HADD-U	BI-EL-ḪU-D-IM		RA LXV 55 XIII 4
1205.	BILL+MAŠIK-A	BI-EL-MA-SI-KA?		M
1206.	BIKAN	BI-GA-AN		YOS XIII 271:6,7+
1207.	BIQAQ-UM	BI-GA-GU-UM		YOS VIII 64 19
1208.	BIḪIR-AH	BI-ḪI-RA	FN	M
1209.	BIḪIR-UM	BI-ḪI-RUM		M+
1210.	BIKIN-T-I	BI-IK-KI-IT-TI	MN GEN	A.
1211.	BIKIN-UM	BI-IK-KI-NU-UM		YOS XIII 306:4
1212.	BIKN-AN-UM	BI-IK-NA-NU-UM		VAS VIII 1 21+
1213.	BILK-UT-UM	BI-IL-KU-TUM	FN	XIII 1 XIII 17
1214.	BILL+ʾAB-I	BI-IL-LA-BI	FN	XIII 1 X 41
1215.	BILM-U-Š	BI-IL-MU-UŠ$_2$		RA LXV 45 V 80
1216.	PILS-I+HADD-U	BI-IL-ZI-D-IM		XIV 41:14
1217.	BIN+DAM-U	BI-IN-DA-MU		RA LXV 42 II 61
1218.	BIN-T-U+ṬAJB-AH	BI-IN-DU-ṬA$_3$-BA	FN	RA LXV 65 VII 10
1219.	BIN+ʾIL-A	BI-IN-I-LA		A. LATE
1220.	BIN+ʾIL-I-JA	BI-IN-I-LI$_2$-IA		RA LXIV 24 NO.8
1221.	BIN+MA+ʾAḪ-IM	BI-IN-MA-A-ḪI-IM		M
1222.	BIN+NAHR-I	BI-IN-NA-A-R[I]?		M
1223.	BIN+NAHR-UM	BI-IN-NA-RUM		CT VI 23 5+
1224.	BIN-IJA	BI-IN-NI-IA		CT IV 10 39+
1225.	BIN-I+MA+ʾAḪ-UM	BI-IN-NI-MA-ḪU-UM		TLB I 3 28
1226.	BIN-T-I+KIʾD-I-JA	BI-IN-TI-KI-DI-IA	FN	A.+
1227.	BIN+ŠAMŠ	BI-IN-D-UTU		M
1228.	BINZ-IJA	B[I]-IN-ZI-IA		M
1229.	PIQD-AT-UM	BI-IQ-DA-TUM	FN	XIII 1 X 27
1230.	BIRB-AJA	BI-IR-BA-IA		RA LXV 52 X 82
1231.	BIRBIR-UM	BI-IR-BI-RU-UM		RUTTEN 7 15+
1232.	BIRḪUN-AH	BI-IR-ḪU-UN-NA	FN	XIII 1 XII 3+
1233.	BIRKIN-U	BI-IR-KI-IN-NU	MN	XIII 1 VI 26
1234.	BIRKIN-AH	BI-IR-KI-NA	FN	M
1235.	BIRKIN-UM	BI-IR-KI-NU-UM		TIM V 2 24
1236.	BIZZ-I+JARAḪ	BI-IṢ-ṢI-E-RA-AḪ		YOS XIII 245:16
1237.	BIN-T-A+ʾATT-I	BI-IT-TA-AT-TI	FN	A.+
1238.	BIN-T-A+MALK-I	BI-IT-TA-MA-AL-KI	FN	A. LATE
1239.	BIN-T-E-JE	BI-IT-TE-E	FN	TCL I 52 11
1240.	BIN-T-I+DAGAN	BI-IT-TI-D-DA-GAN	FN	B 16+
1241.	BIZKIN-AH	BI-IZ-KI-NA	FN	RA LXV 62 V 22
1242.	BIQAQ-IM	BI-KA-KI-IM	GEN	CT XLV 79 7
1243.	PI+KAMA+ʾIL	BI-KA-MA-DINGIR		XIV 111:10+
1244.	PI+KAMA+ʾEL	BI-KA-MA-EL		M+
1245.	BIKAN-I	BI-KA-NI		KISURRA 30 8
1246.	BIKAN-UM	BI-KA-NU-UM		KISURRA 47A 10+
1247.	BIKIN-AH	BI-KI-IN-NA	FN	XIII 1 VIII 27
1248.	BIKIN-UM	BI-KI-IN-NU-UM		VAS VIII 15 16
1249.	BIKIN-IJA	BI-KI-NI-IA		VAS XIII 20A R. 19
1250.	BIKUR-T-UM	BI-KU-UR-TUM	MN	BASOR 95 P. 24
1251.	PILAḪ-UM	BI-LA-ḪU-[UM]		RA LXV 54 XII 44
1252.	BILAL-A+MA	BI-LA-LA-MA		OIP XLIII 135+
1253.	BILL-ATAN-UM	BI-LA-TA-NU-UM		HARRIS 49 14
1254.	BILUL-UM	BI-LU-LU-UM		HARRIS 7 8+

1255.	BIN+MA+ʾIL	BI-MA-DINGIR		C+
1256.		BI-MU-TI-....		IX 290 6
1257.		BI-MU-TI-BA		M+
1258.	BIN-AH	BI-[N]A	FN	RA LXV 60 III 62
1259.	BIN-A+ʾAḪ-UM	BI-NA-A-ḪU-UM		M+
1260.	PI+NAʿM+ʾEL	BI-NA-AḪ-ME-EL		B 15
1261.	BIN-A+ʿAMM-I	BI-NA-AM-MI		B 15
1262.	BIN-AN	BI-NA-AN		RA LXV 43 IV 14
1263.	BIN-A+ʾANTEL	BI-NA-AN-TE-EL		TLB I 220 26, M+
1264.	BIN-A+ʿAŠTAR	BI-NA-EŠ$_4$-DAR		M+
1265.	BINAḪ-AN	BI-NA-ḪA-AN		M
1266.	BIN-A+ḪANDEN	BI-NA-ḪA-AN-DI-EN		M
1267.	BIN-A+HADD-U	[B]I-NA-D-IM		M
1268.	BIN-A+LIʾM	BI-NA-LI-IM		RA LXV 45 V 54
1269.	BIN+NAHR-UM	BI-NA-RU-UM		BIN VII 67 27+
1270.	BIN-AT-UM	BI-NA-TUM	MN	BM 16820+
1271.	BIN-IJA	BI-NI-IA		M
1272.	BIN-IM	BI-NI-IM	GEN	M
1273.	BIN-I+MA	BI-NI-MA		A. LATE
1274.	BIN-I+MA+....	BI-NI-MA-D-....		UET V 713 7
1275.	BIN-I+MA+BIʿD-I-JE	BI-NI-MA-BI-DI-E		EK I 40
1276.	BIN-I+MA+ʾIL	BI-NI-MA-DINGIR		A. LATE
1277.	BIN-I+MA+ʾAḪ-UM	BI-NI-MA-ḪU-UM		CCT IV 13A 6+ CAPP.
1278.	BIN-I+MARAṢ	BI-NI-MA-RA-AṢ		M
1279.	BIN-I+MARAṢ-I	BI-NI-MA-RA-ZI	FN	XII 265 2
1280.	BIN-U+MA+HADD-U	BI-NU-MA-D-IM		4E RENCONTRE 21 NO. 25
1281.	BIN-UM	BI-NU-UM		BM 82360 M+
1282.	BIRUR-UT-UM	BI-RU-RU-TUM	MN	B 15+
1283.	BIJT-AT-UM	BI-TA-TUM	MN	B 16+
1284.	BIN-T-I+ḪIJJ-A	BI-TI-ḪI?-A	FN	HARRIS 85 3
1285.	PI-HU	BI-U$_3$		U
1286.	BIZAZ-UM	BI-ZA-ZUM		TA 1931, 327
1287.	PI+ʿAN-UM	BI$_2$-A-NU-UM		I
1288.	BINQ-ATAN-UM	BI$_2$-GA-TA-NU-UM	MN	TIM III 7:12;39:13
1289.	BINQ-ATAN-UM	BI$_2$-IN-GA-TA-NU-UM	MN	TIM III 45:11
1290.	BILL-UM	BIL-LUM		B 15
1291.	PILS-AN-UM	BIL-ZA-NU-UM		BM 80363 8
1292.	BIRBIR-UM	BIR$_4$-BI$_2$-RU-UM		I
1293.	BUʿD-AN	BU-DA-AN		M
1294.	BUDAM-AN	BU-DA-MA-AN		RA LXV 51 X 4
1295.	BUʿD-AT-IM	BU-DA-TIM	GEN	EDZARD, DER 152 REV 6
1296.	BUṬUḪ-IM	BU-DU-ḪI-IM	GEN	M
1297.	BUʿD-UM	BU-DU-UM		M
1298.	BUQQ-AN-UM	BU-GA-NU-UM		I+
1299.	BUḪAZ-UM	BU-ḪA-ZU-UM		BM 80328 12
1300.	BUʾUL-T-UM	BU-ḪU-UL-TUM	FN	RA LXV 58 I 56
1301.	BULAṬ-AT-UM	BU-LA-DA-TUM	MN	BRM III 19E, 22G+
1302.	BULAṬ-UM	BU-LA-TUM		CT XLV 12 25
1303.	BUʾL-I+HADD-U	BU-LI-A-DU		A. 60 12
1304.	BULUK-AN	B[U]-LU-GA-AN		RA LXV 46 VI 22
1305.	BUʾL-U-HU	BU-LU-U$_2$		CT XLV 92 II 13
1306.	BUN-A+ʿAN-UM	BU-NA-A-NU-UM		U
1307.	BUNAQ-UM	BU-NA-GU-UM		TIM III 98 8+
1308.	BUN-A+ʿAŠTAR	BU-NA-D-INNIN		BASOR 95, 19
1309.	BUNAQ-UM	BU-NA-KUM		CT XLVIII 87 REV.
1310.	BUN-A+MA+ʾIL	BU-NA-MA-DINGIR		XII 1 X 36
1311.		BU-NA-NU-ŠU		TCL I 27 3
1312.	BUN-AN-UM	BU-NA-NU-UM		B 44
1313.	BUN-AT-UM	BU-NA-TUM	MN	A 7699 23+
1314.	BUN-I+ʾIL	BU-NI-DINGIR		B 16
1315.	BUN-I+ʾIL-A	BU-NI-I-LA		B 16+
1316.	BUN-IJA	BU-NI-IA		RA LXV 54 XII 31
1317.	BUN+ʾIL-UM	BU-NI-LUM		TIM III 33 15+
1318.	BUN-I+MA+ʾAḪ-UM	BU-NI-MA-ḪU-UM		TCL XX 96 8
1319.	BUN-I+MARAṢ	BU-NI-MA-RA-AṢ		C+
1320.	BUN-U+ḪAM-I	BU-NU-D-A-MI		M+

1321.	BUN-U+ḪAM-IM	BU-NU-D-A-MI-IM		RA LXV 41 II 27+
1322.	BUN-U+ʿAN-AT-I	BU-NU-A-NA-TI		B 16
1323.	BUN-U+ʾA-BLUṬ	BU-NU-AB-LU-UṬ		BIROT,TEA 64:4
1324.	BUN-U+ʿAMM-U	BU-NU-AM-MU		B 16+
1325.	BUN-U+ʾA-ŠKUR	BU-NU-AŠ$_2$-KU-UR		SYRIA XXXVII 206 29 HANA
1326.	BUN-U+BAʿL-AN-U	BU-NU-BA-AḪ-LA-NU		M
1327.	BUN-U+BAʿL-UM	BU-NU-BA-LUM		B 16+
1328.	BUN-U+JARAḪ	BU-NU-E-RA-AḪ		M
1329.	BUN-U+ʿAŠTAR	BU-NU-EŠ$_4$-DAR		M+, C+
1330.	BUN-U+ʿAMM-I	BU-NU-ḪA-AM-MI	FN	M+
1331.	BUN-U+ʾIL-A	BU-NU-I-LA		CT XLV 115 24
1332.	BUN-U+JAŠʿ-AH	BU?-NU-IA-AŠ-[ḪA]	FN	XII 1 VII 67
1333.	BUN-U+KALA+ʾIL-I	BU-NU-KA-LA-I-LI		B 16
1334.	BUN-U+KAMA+ʾIL-A	BU-NU-KA-MA-I-LA		B 16
1335.	BUN-U+KI+ʾIL	BU-NU-KI-DINGIR		M
1336.	BUN-U+LAʾR-A	BU-NU-LA-RA		B 16
1337.	BUN-U+MA+ʾAḪ-UM	BU-NU-MA-A-ḪU-UM		B 16
1338.	BUN-U+MA+ʾAŠAR	BU-NU-MA-A-ŠA-AR		KISURRA 93 4
1339.	BUN-U+MA+ʾIL	BU-NU-MA-DINGIR		M
1340.	BUN-U+MA+HADD-U	BU-NU-MA-D-IM		M+
1341.	BUN-U+MA+ʾAŠAR	BU-NU-MA-ŠAR		B 16+
1342.	BUN-U+NAWIJ-E	BU-NU-NA-WI-E		CT XLVIII 56 REV.11
1343.	BUN-U+ŠALG-I	BU-NU-ŠA?-AL?-GI		B 16
1344.	BUN-U+TAḪTUN+ʾIL-A	BU-NU-TAḪ-TU-UN-I-LA		B 16+
1345.	BUN-U-HU+PI+ʾIL-UM	BU-NU-U$_2$?-BI-I-LUM		UET V 548 2
1346.	BUN-UM+ʾEL-UM	BU-NU-UM-E-LU-UM		B 16
1347.	BUN-UM+MA+ŠARR	BU-NU-UM-MA-ŠAR		B 16
1348.	BUN-UM+ŠAGIŠ	BU-NU-UM-ŠA-GI-IŠ		EDZARD,DER 73:15
1349.	BUQQ-AN	BU-QA-AN		C+
1350.	BUQAQ-IM	BU-QA-KI-IM	GEN	M+
1351.	BUQAQ-UM	BU-QA-KU-UM		M
1352.	BUQAQ-UM	BU-QA-KUM		M+
1353.	BUQAQ-AM	BU-QA-QA-AM	ACC	M
1354.	BURAN-AH	BU-RA-NA	FN	XIII 1 VI 58
1355.	BURAN-AT-UM	BU-RA-NA-TUM	FN	RA LXV 59 II 70
1356.	BUŠAN-UT-UM	BU?-SA?-NU-TUM	MN?	VIII 13 10'
1357.	BUṬUM-T-UM	BU-TU-UM-TUM	FN	RA LXV 59 II 39
1358.	BUʾUL-UM	[B]U-U$_2$-LU-UM		I
1359.	BUʾUL-UM	BU-U$_2$-LUM		TCL I 75 5
1360.	BUDBUD-UM	BU-UD-BU-DU-UM		BM 16551
1361.	BUQQ-AN	BU-UK-KA-AN		M
1362.	BUKŠ-AN-UM	BU-UK-SA-NU-UM		PBS XIV 495
1363.	BULM-A-NA+HADD-U	BU-UL-MA-NA-D-IM		M+
1364.	BUN+BAŠAR	BU-UN-BA-SAR		EDZARD,DER 68 IV 7
1365.	BUN-I+ʾEL-UM	BU-UN?-NE-E-LUM		TCL I 220 42
1366.	BUN+TAḪTUN+ʾIL-A	BU-UN-TAḪ-UN-I-LA		B 16
1367.	BUN+TENUT-A	BU-UN-TE-NU?-TA?		MEISSNER 68 13
1368.	BUNZ-I	BU-UN-ZI	FN	XIII 1 X 25
1369.	BUNZUR-I	BU-UN-ZU-RI	FN	XIII 1 III 13
1370.	BURBUR-AN	BU-UR-BU-RA-AN		RA LXV 50 VIII 69
1371.	BURQ-AN-UM	BU-UR-GA-NU-UM		UET V 482 5
1372.	BURQ-AN	BU-UR-QA-AN		M+
1373.	BURQ-AT-UM	BU-UR-QA-TUM	FN	XIII 1 VII 52+
1374.	BURR-AN	BU-UR-RA-AN		RA LXV 47 VII 43
1375.	BURBIN-UM	BU-UR$_2$-BI-NU-UM		B 16
1376.	BURBUR-UM	BU-UR$_2$-BU-RU-UM		BIN VII 155 6
1377.	BURQ-AN-U	BU-UR$_2$-GA-NU		BM 17028 5
1378.	BURQ-ATAN-UM	BU-UR$_2$-GA-TA-NU-UM	MN	SIMMONS 78 11
1379.	BUZBUZ-UM	BU-UZ-BU-ZU-UM		B 48+
1380.	BUZZ-AN-UM	BU-UZ-ZA-NU-UM		M
1381.	PUZAR-UM	BU-ZA-RU-UM		TCL I 56 2+
1382.	BUWZ-I	BU-ZI	FN	M+, C+
1383.	BUWZ-IJA	BU-ZI-IA		M+
1384.	BUWZ-U	BU-ZU		RA LXV 50 VIII 75
1385.	BUWZ-UJA	BU-ZU-A-IA	FN	RA LXV 62 V 27
1386.	BUWZ-U-NA	BU-ZU-NA	FN	RA LXV 58 I 50

1387.	PUZUR-AN	BU-ZU-RA-AN		RA LXV 53 XI 10
1388.	BUWZ-U-HU	BU-ZU-U$_2$		TCL I 59 16+
1389.	BUWZ-UM	BU-ZU-UM	FN	C+
1390.	BUWZ-UM	BU-ZU[M]-UM	MN	UCP X/3 2 23
1391.	BURBUR-UM	BUR-BUR-RU?-UM		SCHEIL 10 17
1392.	DAWD-A	DA-A-DA	MN	A.
1393.	DADM-IM	DA-AD-MI-IM	GEN	M
1394.	DADM-IT-UM	DA-AD-MI-TUM	FN	M
1395.	DAKŠ-AT-UM	DA-AK-SA-TUM	FN	CT IV 45B 6
1396.	DALQ-UM	DA-AL-KUM		CT VI 28A 24
1397.	DAWD-AN-IM	DA-AM-DA?-NIM	GEN	CT XLVII 78:37
1398.	DAWD-U+DANN-UM	DA-AM-DU-DA-NU-UM		HARRIS 92:14+
1399.	DAMQ-AN-UM	DA-AM-QA-NU-UM		SIMMONS 67 7
1400.	DANN-UM+TA-ʾḪAḎ	D-DA-AN-NU-UM-TA-ḪA-AZ		SIMMONS 36 A 22
1401.	DANN-UM+TA-ʾḪAḎ	DA-AN-NU-UM-TA-ḪA-AZ		SIMMONS 36 CASE 22
1402.	ḎAQN-IT-UM	DA-AQ-NI-TUM	FN	XIII 1 XIII 22
1403.	DARK-AT-UM	DA-AR-KA-TUM	FN	C
1404.	DARIK-UM	DA-AR-RI-KU-[UM]		B 17
1405.	TA-ŠLAL-UM	DA-AŠ-LA-LU-UM		TA 1931, 435
1406.	TA-ŠLAL-UM	DA-AŠ-LA-LUM		TA 1931, 538 II
1407.	DAWD-AN-IM	DA-AW-DA-NIM	GEN	B 17+
1408.	DAWD-AN-UM	DA-AW-DA-NU-UM		HARRIS 19A 6+
1409.	ṬAJB-AT-UM	DA-BA-TUM	FN	U
1410.	ḎABIL-UM	DA-BI-LU-UM		RA LXV 54 XII 20
1411.	DABIN-UM	DA-BI-NU-UM		TIM III 18 8+
1412.	DABIʾ-UM	DA-BI-UM		M
1413.	DAWD-A	DA-DA	MN	M+, A.
1414.	DAWD-AJA	DA-DA-A	FN	RA LXV 61 IV 2
1415.	DAWD-AK-UM	DA-DA-KUM		KISURRA 39A 4+
1416.	DAWD-AN-I	DA?-DA-NI	FN NOM	M
1417.	DAWD-AN-IM	DA-DA-NI-IM	GEN	HARRIS 60:6
1418.	DAWD-AN-U	DA-DA-NU		M
1419.	DAWD-AN-UM	DA-DA-NU-UM		SIMMONS 92 14 M+
1420.	DAWD-AT-UM	DA-DA-TUM	MN	TCL I 109 16+
1421.	DAWD-AT-UM	[D]A-DA-TUM	FN	M
1422.	DAWD-I+JABAL	DA-DI-E-BA-AL		UNPUBL.
1423.	DAWD-I+JAŠAR	DA-DI-E-SA-AR		RA LXV 50 VIII 48+
1424.	DAWD-I+JE-JŠUʿ	DA-DI-E-ŠU-UḪ		M+
1425.	DAWD-I-Š+ME+ʾEL	DA-DI-EŠ$_3$-ME-EL		UCP X/3 P. 198+
1426.	DAWD-I+ʿADN-U-HU	DA-DI-ḪA-AD-NU-U$_2$		18 R.A. P.61 A 3821+
1427.	DAWD-I+ʿADN	DA-DI-ḪA-DU-UN		M+
1428.	DAWD-IJA	DA-DI-IA		B 16+, M+
1429.	DAWD-IJAN	DA-DI-IA-AN		RA LXV 44 IV 75
1430.	DAWD-IM	DA-DI-IM	GEN	M
1431.	DAWD-I+ŠAMUʿ	DA-DI-SA-MU-UḪ		RA LXV 47 VII 44
1432.	DAWD-UJAN	DA-DU-JA-AN		RA LXV 51 IX 75
1433.	DAWD-U+MA	DA-DU-MA		HARRIS 49 5
1434.	DAWD-U+MALIK	DA-DU-MA-LIK		XIII 1 VI 27
1435.	DAWD-U+RAPIʾ	DA-DU-RA-BI		B 16+
1436.	DAWD-UM+LU-HU	DA-DU-UM-LU-U$_2$		M
1437.	DAWD-UM	DA-DUM		RA LXV 52 XI 3
1438.	DAWD-UM+PI+ʾIL	DA-DUM-BI$_2$-DINGIR		I
1439.	DAGAZ-I	DA-GA-ZI	FN	RA LXV 56 I 6
1440.	DAGAN+ʾA-JPUʿ	D-DA-GAN-A-PU-UḪ		M
1441.	DAGAN+ʾAŠR-A-JA	D-DA-GAN-AŠ-RA-IA		M+
1442.	DAGAN+BAWŠ-T-I	D-DA-GAN-BA-AŠ-TI	FN	M+
1443.	DAGAN+GAML-I	D-DA-GAN-GA-AM-LI		M
1444.	DAGAN+ʾIL-I	D-DA-GAN-I$_3$-LI$_2$	FN	RA LXV 62 V 51
1445.	DAGAN+KIBR-I	D-DA-GAN-KI-IB-RI	FN	M+
1446.	DAGAN+MALAK-U	D-DA-GAN-MA-LA-KU	FN	RA LXV 60 III 3
1447.	DAGAN+MALIK	D-DA-GAN-MA-LIK		M+
1448.	DAGAN+NAʿM-I	D-DA-GAN-NA-AḪ-MI	FN	X 116 1, 22
1449.	DAGAN+NAʾD-I	D-DA-GAN-NA-DI	FN	XIII 1 III 17+
1450.	DAGAN+NAṢIR	D-DA-GAN-NA-ṢIR		RA LXV 52 X 76
1451.	DAGAN+NIWR-I	D-DA-GAN-NE-RI	FN	M+
1452.	DAGAN+NIWR-I	D-DA-GAN-NI-RI	FN	M+

1453.	DAGAN+NIWR-I	D-DA-GAN-NI-RI	MN	RA LXV 47 VII 38
1454.	DAGAN+NUPAR-A-JA	D-DA-GAN-NU?-PA?-RA-IA		M
1455.	DAGAN+TIWR-I	D-DA-GAN-TI-RI	FN	RA LXV 61 IV 51
1456.	DAGAN+ŠAMŠ-I	D-DA-GAN-D-UTU-ŠI	FN	RA LXV 58 I 23+
1457.	DAWIR-AH	DA-I-RA	FN	M
1458.	DAʾK-A+BIJT-I	DA?-KA-BI-TI		A.
1459.	ḎAKIR-UM	DA-KI-RU-UM		B 16
1460.	ḎAKIR-UM	DA-KI-RUM		B 16+
1461.	DAKUL-UM	DA-KUL-LUM		UET V P. 35+
1462.	DALAQ-UM	DA-LA-KUM		VAS IX 120 13
1463.	DALUM-UM	DA-LU-MU-UM		MEISSNER 24 15
1464.	DAM-AN-UM	DA-MA-NU-UM		B 44
1465.	DAM-AT-UM	DA-MA-TUM	FN	XIII 1 V 30
1466.	DAMIQ-T-UM	DA-ME-IQ-TUM	FN	RA LXV 59 II 60
1467.	ḎAMIR-IM	DA-ME-RI-IM	GEN	HARRIS 77 13
1468.	ḎAMIR-UM	DA-ME-RU-UM		B 17+
1469.	ḎAMIR-UM	DA-MI-RU-UM		I
1470.	DANN-A+BIJT	DA-NA-BI$_2$-IT		U
1471.	DANN-I+ʾIL	DA?-NI-DINGIR		M
1472.	DANN-I-Š+ME+ʾIL	DA-NI-IŠ-ME-DINGIR?		I
1473.	DANN-U+MAʾT-UM	DA-NU-MA-TUM		CT XLV 12:24
1474.	DANN-U+TA-ʾḪAḎ	DA-NU-TA-ḪA-AZ		SIMMONS 36 23
1475.	DANN-U+TA-ʾḪAḎ	D-DA-NU-TA-ḪA-AZ		SIMMONS 84 15
1476.	DANN-UM+TA-ʾḪAḎ	DA-NU-UM-TA-ḪA-AZ		A 7634, M
1477.	DANN-UM+TA-ʾḪAḎ	D-DA-NU-UM-TA-ḪA-[AZ]		TIM V 19 14
1478.	ḎARAʿ-UM	DA-RA-UM		U
1479.	ṬARID-UM	DA-RI-DU-UM		B 17+
1480.	DAWR-IJA	DA-RI-IA		M+
1481.	DARIK-UM	DA-RI-KU-UM		CT XLV 117 27
1482.	DARIK-UM	DA-RI-KUM		B 17+
1483.	TA-RʿIŠ-AH	DA-RI$_2$-ŠA	FN	U
1484.	ṬARUD-UM	DA-RU-DU-UM		TCL X 30 11
1485.	DAŠIK-T-UM	DA-SI-IK-TUM	MN	MEISSNER 90 27
1486.	DAŠIL-AJA	DA-SI-LA-A-A		HARRIS 79 24
1487.	DAʾŠ-U	DA-ŠU		U
1488.	DAŠUR-AH+ʿAŠTAR	DA-ŠU-RA-EŠ$_4$-DAR	FN	YOS VIII 51 5
1489.	DAŠUR-AT-UM	DA-ŠU-RA-TUM	FN	YOS VIII 51 2,14
1490.	DAŠUR-UM	DA-ŠU-RU-UM		B 17+
1491.	DAʿ-UM	DA-UM		B 17
1492.	DAMQ-AN-U	DAM-QA-NU		XIII 1 II 1
1493.	DAMQ-AN-UM	DAM-QA-NU-UM		SIMMONS PASSIM
1494.	DAMQ-AT-UM	DAM-QA-TUM	FN	CT XLV 2 22+
1495.	DANN+ʾIL	DAN-DINGIR		U
1496.	DANN-U+TA-ʾḪAḎ	DAN-NU-TA-ḪA-AZ		M+
1497.	DARK-I+MA	DAR-KI-MA	FN	RA LXV 61 IV 14
1498.	DARK-U	DAR-KU		C
1499.	DIWIR+ʾAB-I	DI-BI-IR-A-BI		PBS XI/1 P. 55+
1500.	DIWIR+ʾAḪ-I	DI-BI-IR-A-ḪI		PBS XI/1 P. 55+
1501.	DIWIR+MUT-I	DI-BI-IR-A-MU-TI		PBS XI/1 P. 55+
1502.	DITAN-U	DI-DA-A-NU		JNES XIII 210+ LATE
1503.	DIDAM-AN-UM	DI-DA-MA-NU-UM		B 44
1504.	DIGDIG-UM	DI-DI-GU-UM		UET V 702 R 13
1505.	DIWD-UM	DI-DU-UM		BIN VII 63 24
1506.	DIGAN-UM	DI-GA-NU-UM		RUTTEN 11 2
1507.	DIʿ-ATAN-UM	DI-ḪA-TA-NU-U[M]		CT XLVII 4 3
1508.	DIBDIB-UM	DI-IB-DI-BU-UM		SIMMONS 13 10
1509.	DIGDIG-UM	DI-IG-DI-GU-UM		B 48+
1510.	DIʾL-AN-UM	DI-LA-NU-UM		B 44
1511.	DIMAḪ-UM	DI-MA-ḪU-UM		B 17
1512.	DIJN-I+HADD-U	DI-NA-A-DU		A. LATE
1513.	DIJN-I+HADD-U	DI-NI-A-DU		A.+
1514.	DINIK+MUʾ-UM	DI-NI-IK-MU-UM		SIMMONS 39 3+
1515.	DIWR-IT-UM+KAʾB-I	D-DI-RI-TUM-KA-BI		XIII 1 VI 45
1516.	DITAN-U	DI-TA-NU		BM 80328 6
1517.	DIWIR+ʾAB-I	DI-WI-IR-A-BI		PBS XI/1 P. 55+
1518.	DIWIR+ʾAḪ-I	DI-WI-IR-A-ḪI		PBS XI/1 P. 55+

1519.	DIWIR+MUT-I	DI-WI-IR-MU-TI		PBS XI/1 P. 55+
1520.	ʾIL-I+ʾA-PTAN	DINGIR-AP-TAN		TIM III 150 12
1521.	ʾIL-A+BAWB-I-JA	DINGIR-BA-BI-A		UET V 263 17
1522.	ʾIL-A+BIN-I	DINGIR-BI-NI		UCP X/3 1 7
1523.	ʾIL-A+DAKUL	DINGIR-DA-AK-KU-UL		UET V P. 43
1524.	ʾIL-A+DAKUL-UM	DINGIR-DA-AK-KU-UL-LUM		UET V P. 43
1525.	ʾIL-I+DAʿ-AT	DINGIR-DA-ḪA-AT		A 7650:2
1526.	ʾIL-A+DAʿ-AT	BAD$_3$-DINGIR-DA-ḪA-AT	GN	A 7650
1527.	ʾIL-A+DAKUL	DINGIR-DA-KU-UL		UET V P. 43
1528.	ʾIL-A+DAKUL-UM	DINGIR-DA-KU-UL-LUM		UET V P. 43+
1529.	ʾIL-A+DARAN	DINGIR-DA-RA-AN		M+
1530.	ʾIL-A+GULL-A	DINGIR-GU-UL-LA	FN	C+
1531.	ʾIL-A+GULL-A+ʿAḎIR-AT	DINGIR-GUL-LA$_2$-ḪA-ZI-RA-AT	FN	M+
1532.	ʾIL-A+ʿADN-U-HU	DINGIR-ḪA-AD-NU-U$_2$	FN	C+
1533.	ʾIL-A+ḪABAD	DINGIR-ḪA-BA-AD		M+
1534.	ʾIL-A+ḪAʾL-U-HU	DINGIR-ḪA-LU-U$_2$		XIII 1 IV 18
1535.	ʾIL-A+ḪAʾL-UM	DINGIR-ḪA-LUM		B 21
1536.	ʾIL-A+JI-JBAL	DINGIR?-I-BA-AL		M
1537.	ʾIL-A+KAʾAM	DINGIR-KA-A-AM		TIM III 101 7
1538.	ʾIL-A+KA+ʾAB-UM	DINGIR-KA-A-BU-UM		CT XLV 100 17
1539.	ʾIL-A+KAWN	DINGIR-KA-AN	FN	M
1540.	ʾIL-A+KAWN	DINGIR-KA-AN	MN	M+
1541.	ʾIL-A+KAWN-IM	DINGIR-KA-NI-IM	GEN	M
1542.	ʾIL-A+KAWN-IM	DINGIR-KA-NIM	GEN	M+
1543.	ʾIL-A+KAWN-UM	DINGIR-KA-NU-UM		MAH II/3 P. 188F
1544.	ʾIL-A+KABKAB-I	DINGIR-KAB-KA-BI		JNES XIII 210+ LATE
1545.	ʾIL-A+LA+ʾIL	DINGIR-LA-IL		U
1546.	ʾIL-AM+DIʿ-I	DINGIR-LAM-DI-I		SIMMONS 24 10+
1547.	ʾIL-A+MA+ʾAB-I	DINGIR-MA-A-BI		M
1548.	ʾIL-A+MALK-I	DINGIR-MA-AL-KI		A. LATE
1549.	ʾIL-I+MAʾD-I+ʾAḪ	DINGIR?-MA-DA-AḪ		RA LXV 42 III 21
1550.	ʾIL-A+MAṮAR	DINGIR-MA-DA-AR		OR. N.S. XXVI 28 N.4 CAPP
1551.	ʾIL-A+MAʾD-I	DINGIR-MA-DI		M
1552.	ʾIL-A+MA+ʾIL-A	DINGIR-MA-D-I-LA		B 21
1553.	ʾIL-A+MA+ʾIL-A	DINGIR-MA-I$_3$-LA		B 21+
1554.	ʾIL-A+MAṮAR	DINGIR-MA-TAR		M+
1555.	ʾIL-A+MEʾR	DINGIR-ME-IR		JNES XIII 210+ LATE
1556.	ʾIL-A+MILK-UM	DINGIR-MI-IL-KUM		BAHREIN UNP.,POST-UR III
1557.	ʾIL-UM+MULUK-AJ-I	DINGIR-MU-LU-KA-JI-KI	GN	XV 127
1558.	ʾIL-UM+MULUK	DINGIR-MU-LU-UK-KI	GN	XV 127
1559.	ʾIL-A+NABUṮ	DINGIR-NA-BU-UṮ		VAS VIII 14 31
1560.	ʾIL-A+NAʿM-A	DINGIR-NA-MA-....		VAS VIII 14 44
1561.	ʾIL-A+PAʾŠ-I-JA	DINGIR-PA-ŠI-IA		TCL XVIII 106 9
1562.	ʾIL-A+QAʾB	DINGIR-QA-AB		TIM III 130 12, SEAL
1563.	ʾIL-A+RAWḪ-I-JE	DINGIR-RA-ḪI-E		HARRIS 85 14
1564.	ʾIL-A+RAWḪ-I-JA	DINGIR-RA[Ḫ]I-A		HARRIS 76 21
1565.	ʾIL-A+Š-BAʿL-UM	DINGIR-ŠU-BA-A-LUM		CT II 15 9
1566.	ʾIL-A+ʾUWR-I	DINGIR-U$_2$-RI		RA LXVIII 28:13 MARI
1567.	ʾIL-A+ʾUMM-A	DINGIR-UM-MA		RA LXV 45 V 31
1568.	ḎUBAB-AT-UM	DU-BA-BA-TUM	FN	UCP X/1 87 3+
1569.	ḎUBAB-U	DU-BA-BU		YOS XII
1570.	ḎUBAB-UM	DU-BA-BU-UM		UET V 208 2+
1571.	DUWD-AN-IM	DU-DA-NIM		M
1572.	DUWD-AN-UM	DU-DA-NU-UM		CT XLVIII 87
1573.	DUWD-UT-UM	DU-DU-TUM	FN	M
1574.	DUWD-U-HU	DU-DU-U$_2$		M, TCL X 112 8, 22+
1575.	DUWD-U-Š+ME+ʾEL	DU-DU-UŠ-ME-EL		UCP X/3 P. 198+
1576.	DUKUB-UM	DU-KU-BU-UM		SUMER XIV 54 28 6
1577.	DULAQ-UM	DU-LA-KUM		TCL I 56 22+
1578.	DULUQ-AT-UM	DU-LU-GA-TUM	FN	VAS IX 178 2
1579.	DULUQ-UM	DU-LU-KUM		RUTTEN 3 16+
1580.	DULUQ-T-UM	DU-LU-UQ-TUM	FN	MEISSNER 7 26
1581.	DUMAT-AN	DU-MA-TA-AN		XIV 47:19
1582.	DUNN-I+HADD-U	DU-NI-A-DU		A. LATE
1583.	DUNN-I+....	DU-NI-PA-DU		A.
1584.	TUŠIM-UM	DU-SI-MU-UM		I

1585.	DUŠUB-T-UM	DU-ŠU-UB-TUM	FN	TCL XI 244 11, M
1586.	ṬUḪŠ-AT-UM	DU-UḪ-ŠA-TUM	FN	TCL X 12 12, M
1587.	DULDUL-UM	DU-UL-DU-LUM		B 48
1588.	DULUQ-UM	DU-UL-LU-KUM		RUTTEN 29 5
1589.	DUWR-NI+ʾIL	DU-UR-NI-DINGIR		M+
1590.	BIN+HADD-U	DUMU-D-IM		M+
1591.	TUWR-U+ʿAMM-I	DUR-RU-AM-MI		MAOG IV 2 6 HANA
1592.		E-A-LI		XI 3 11
1593.	ʾEB-ATAN	E-BA-TA-AN		M+
1594.	ʿEBIB-UM	E-BI-BU-UM		SIMMONS 76 6
1595.	ʾEB-I+DANN-UM	E-BI-DA-NU-UM		U
1596.	ʾEB-I+ʾIL	E-BI-IL		M
1597.	ʾEDAK-UM	E-DA-KUM		CT VIII 4A 4
1598.	ʾEDID-UM	E-DI-DU-UM		SIMMONS 138 7
1599.		E-DU-NA-SA		KISURRA 76 3
1600.	JE-ʾZIJ+ʾIL-UM	E-EḪ-ZI-LUM		VIII 3 25
1601.	ʾELL-AN-U	E-EL-LA-NU		C
1602.	ʾELL-AN-UM	E-EL-LA-NUM		C
1603.	ʾELL-I	E-EL-LI		A. 377 8
1604.	JE-NQIM+ʾIL	E-EN-KI-IM-DINGIR		CT VI 49B 4
1605.	JE-NTIN-UM	E-EN-TI-NU-UM		WALTERS,WL 112:25
1606.	JE-RḪAQ-UM	E-ER-ḪA-KUM		SIMMONS 112 7, SEAL
1607.	JE-GJIḪ+LUʾ+MA	E-GI-IḪ-LU-MA		SUMER XXIII 192
1608.	ʾELL-UM	E-IL-LUM		RA LXV 50 VIII 70
1609.	JE-MṢIʾ-UM	E-IM-ṢI-UM		BIN VII P. 11+
1610.	JE-MZUʾ-UM	E-IM-ZU-UM		BIN VII P. 11+
1611.	JE-RBIJ+ʾIL	E-IR-BI-DINGIR		KISURRA 22A 15
1612.	JE-RBUʾ-HU+ʾEL	E-[IR]-BU-U_2-[E]L		KISURRA 152 9
1613.	ʾEK-I+LA+ʾA-HWIJ	E-KI-LA-AḪ-WI		M
1614.	JE-KWUN+PI	E-KU-PI		B 17
1615.		E-LA-AḪ-TI		RA LXV 46 VI 23
1616.	ʾELL-AN	E-LA-AN		MAD V, SARG.
1617.	ʾELAP-I	E-LA-BI	FN	RA LXV 65 VI 62
1618.	HELAL-I	E-LA-LI		RA LXV 50 IX 25
1619.	ʾEL-AN-I	E-LA-NI		M
1620.	ʾEL-AN-UM	E-LA-NU-UM		U
1621.	ʾELL-AN-UM	E-LA-NUM		C
1622.	ʾELIL-I-Š	E-LI-LI-IŠ		M+
1623.	ʾELIL-I-Š	E-LI-LI-ŠA		M
1624.	ʿEMES-UM	E-ME-ZUM		I+
1625.	ʿEMUQ-I+ʾEL	E-[M]U-QI_2-EL		RA LXV 40 I 3
1626.	JE-MWUT+BAʿL-UM	E-MU-UT-BA-A-LUM-KI	GN	RLA II 180
1627.	JE-MWUT+BAʿL-A	E-MU-UT-BA-LA	GN GEN	SAKI P. 212+
1628.	JE-MWUT+BAʿL-IM	E-MU-UT-BA-LI-IM	GN GEN	KING 34 6+
1629.	JE-MWUT+BAʿL-UM	E-MU-UT-BA-LUM-KI	GN	B 28+
1630.	JE-ʿMUS-UM	E-MU-ZUM		I UNPUBL.
1631.	ḪINN-A+BAWŠ-AT	E-NA-BA-ŠA-AT		ICK 63 2+ CAPP.
1632.	ḪINN-A+BAWŠ-AT-A	E-NA-BA-ŠA-TA		EL II P. 171 N. CAPP.
1633.	ḪINN-I+BAWŠ-AT	E-NI-BA-ŠA-AT		ICK 113 10 CAPP.
1634.	ḪINN-I+BAWŠ-AT-A	E-NI-BA-ŠA-TA		KTS 47C 1 CAPP.
1635.	JE-NWIḪ-UM	E-NI-ḪU-UM		CT VIII 28C 4
1636.	ʾEN-IJA	E-NI-IA		M+
1637.	ʾEN-I-Š+ʾAG-UM	E-NI-IŠ-A-GU-UM		M+
1638.	ḪINUN-UM	E-NU-NU-UM		SIMMONS 112 20
1639.	JE-NWUZ-UM	E-NU-ZU-UM		I
1640.		E-RI-....	FN	M
1641.	JE-RWIḪ-I+ʾIL	E-RI-ḪI-DINGIR		U
1642.	JIŠʿ+BAʿL-A	E-ŠE-EḪ-BA-LA?		VAS VII 160 7
1643.	JAŠUN-UM	E-ŠU-NU-UM		U
1644.	JE-ŠWUB+ʾIL	E-ŠU-UB-DINGIR		BIN VII P. 12+
1645.	JE-JDIʿ-UM	E-TI-UM		I
1646.	JE-HWIJ+MALIK	E-WI-MA-LIK		A.
1647.	ʾEWIN-I	E-[W]I-NI		RA LXV 47 VII 22
1648.	JE-ʾWUŠ+ʾIL	E-WU-ŠI-DINGIR		BIRCT, TEA 48:20
1649.	JE-ṢJID-AN-UM	E-ZI-DA-NU-UM		I
1650.	ḪAJJ-A+ʾAŠR-A-JA	E_2-A-AŠ-RA-IA		M+

1651.	ḪAJJ-A+NIWR-I	E$_2$-A-NE-RI	FN	XIII 1 VII 26
1652.	ḪAJJ-A+NIWR-I	E$_2$-A-NI-RI	FN	RA LXV 58 II 2
1653.	ḪAJJ-A+ŠIMḪ-I	E$_2$-A-ŠI-IM-ḪI	FN	XIII 1 II 44
1654.	BIJT+ʾIL	D-E$_2$-IL		U
1655.	ʾEL+KAWN-UM	EL-GA-NU-UM		TA 1931 238
1656.	JE-LʾIJ+DAGAN	EL-I-D-DA-GAN		M
1657.	ʾELL-AN	EL-LA-AN		M
1658.	ʾELL-AT+....	EL-LA-AT-[....]		M
1659.	ʾELL-ATAN	EL-LA-TA-AN		C II 39:8
1660.	ʾELUR-AT-UM	EL-LU-RA-TUM	MN?	WATERMAN 38 9
1661.	ʾELUR-UM	EL-LU-RUM		CT VIII 43B21
1662.	ʾELM-AN-UM	EL-MA?-NU-UM		TA 1931, 538 I
1663.	ʾELM-ATAN	EL-MA-TA-AN		M
1664.	JE-NQIM-UM	EN-GI-MU-UM		U+
1665.	ḪININ-UM	EN-NE-NU-UM		B 44+
1666.	ḪINN-I+ʿAŠTAR	EN-NI-D-EŠ$_4$-DAR		A. 247 23
1667.	ḪININ-UM	EN-NI-NU-UM		SIMMONS 48 5+
1668.	JARAḪ+ʾAŠD-UM	D-EN-ZU-AŠ-DU-UM		WALTERS, WL 114:2
1669.	ZIJAN-I	D-EN-ZU-I-A-NI		KISURRA 72:6
1670.	JARAḪ+TIWR-I	D-EN-ZU-TI-RI		M+
1671.	JARAḪ+TIWR-IM	D-EN-ZU-TI-RI-IM	GEN	M
1672.	ʾEŠB-I+ʾADAN-T-A	EŠ-BI-A-DA-AT-TA		A. 455 31, 55
1673.	ʾEŠB-I+HADD-U	EŠ-BI-D-IM		A.+
1674.	ʿAŠTAR+ʾAŠJ-AH	EŠ$_4$-DAR-A-SI-IA	FN	XIII 1 IX 3+
1675.	ʿAŠTAR+ʾAŠJ-AH	EŠ$_4$-DAR-A-ZU-IA	FN	M
1676.	ʿAŠTAR+ʾANDUL-I	EŠ$_4$-DAR-AN-DUL$_3$-LI$_2$	FN	M
1677.	ʿAŠTAR+BAʿL-AH	EŠ$_4$-DAR-BA-AḪ?-LA	FN	M
1678.	ʿAŠTAR+DAMQ-AH	EŠ$_4$-DAR-DAM-QA	FN	XIII 1 V 50+
1679.	ʿAŠTAR+ḪAṢN-I	EŠ$_4$-DAR-ḪA-AZ-NI	FN	XIII 1 II 41
1680.	ʿAŠTAR+ʾIL-I	EŠ$_4$-DAR-I$_3$-LI$_2$	FN	RA LXV 56 I 3
1681.	ʿAŠTAR+JAŠʿ-AH	EŠ$_4$-DAR-IA-AŠ-ḪA	FN	M
1682.	ʿAŠTAR+JA-HWIJ	EŠ$_4$-DAR-IA-WI		VAS VII 157 7
1683.	ʿAŠTAR+JIPʿ-AH	EŠ$_4$-DAR-IP-ḪA	FN	XIII 1 VI 19+
1684.	ʿAŠTAR+KAWN	EŠ$_4$-DAR-KA-AN		IX 237 II 4+
1685.	ʿAŠTAR+KABAR	EŠ$_4$-DAR-KA-BAR		RA LXV 41 II 39
1686.	ʿAŠTAR+LAMAS-I	EŠ$_4$-DAR-LA-MA-ZI	FN	M
1687.	ʿAŠTAR+LAMAS-I	EŠ$_4$-DAR-D-LAMA	FN	XIII 1 I 69+
1688.	ʿAŠTAR+LI-JA	EŠ$_4$-DAR-LI?-IA		YOS XIII 12 REV 14
1689.	ʿAŠTAR+MILK-I	EŠ$_4$-DAR-ME-IL-KI	FN	RA LXV 62 V 10
1690.	ʿAŠTAR+NIWR-I	EŠ$_4$-DAR-NE-RI	FN	XIII 1 IX 48
1691.	ʿAŠTAR+PUṬR-I	EŠ$_4$-DAR-PU-UṬ-RI	FN	M+
1692.	ʿAŠTAR+RAḪM-I	EŠ$_4$-DAR-RA-AḪ-MI	FN	XIII 1 VIII 83
1693.	ʿAŠTAR+ŠARR-AH	EŠ$_4$-DAR-ŠAR-RA	FN	XIII 1 II 67
1694.	ʿAŠTAR+ŠIMḪ-I	EŠ$_4$-DAR-ŠI-IM-ḪI	FN	XIII 1 XII 2
1695.	ʿAŠTAR+TA-LʾIJ	EŠ$_4$-DAR-TA-AL-E	FN	XIII 1 V 41+
1696.	ʿAŠTAR+TA-JṢIʾ	EŠ$_4$-DAR-TA-ZI	FN	XIII 1 IV 79
1697.	ʿAŠTAR+TABB-I	EŠ$_4$-DAR-TAB-BI	FN	M+, C
1698.	ʿAŠTAR+TIWR-AH	D-EŠ$_4$-DAR-TE-IR-RA		A.
1699.	ʿAŠTAR+TUWR-I-JA	EŠ$_4$-DAR-TU-RI-IA	FN	XIII 1 XIII 33
1700.	ʿAŠTAR+ʾUMM-I	EŠ$_4$-DAR-UM-MI	FN	XIII 1 II 38 +
1701.	ʿAŠTAR+ŠAMŠ-I	EŠ$_4$-DAR-D-UTU-ŠI	FN	M
1702.		EŠ$_4$-DAR?-...-KA-RI-E	FN	XIII 1 V 77
1703.	GABN-AN-UM	GA-AB-NA-NU-UM		SIMMONS 107 14
1704.	QADM-AN-UM	GA-AD-MA-NU-UM		U
1705.	GAʾŠ-U	GA-AḪ-ŠU		M
1706.	KALB+ʾIL	GA-AL-BA-IL		I
1707.	KALB-UM	GA?-[AL]?-BU-UM		BIN IX 410 3
1708.	GALD-AN-U	GA-AL-DA-NU		B 44+
1709.	GALZ-....	GA-AL-ZI-....		M
1710.	GANN-I	GA-AN-NI		M
1711.	QAṬR-AN-UM	GA-AT-RA-NU-UM		RUTTEN 14 22
1712.	QABAL-AT-UM	GA-BA-LA-TUM	FN	CT XLV 117 36
1713.	GABAʾ-UM	GA-BA-UM		LANGDON XXX 18
1714.	KABAS-AN-UM	GA-BA-ZA-NU-UM		TA 1931,262
1715.	KABAS-UM	GA-BA-ZU-UM		HSM 7900, UR III
1716.	GABIʾ-AT-UM	GA-BI-A-TUM	FN	X 1 3

1717.	KABID-AN-UM	GA-BI-DA-NU-UM		TA 1930,486 OLDER OB
1718.	GABIʾ+ʾIL	GA-BI-DINGIR		C 39+
1719.	GABUʾ-IM	GA-BI-I-IM	GEN	M+
1720.	GABIʾ+ʾIL	GA-BI-IL		TIM III 12 16A
1721.	GABUʾ-IM	GA-BI-IM	GEN	B 17
1722.	QABIL-UM	GA-BI-LUM		KISURRA 106 15
1723.	GABIʾ-T-UM	GA-BI-TUM		RA LXIV 36 NO. 32
1724.	GABIʾ-UM	GA-BI-U[M]		M
1725.	GABUʾ-UM	GA-BU-U_2-UM		M
1726.	GABUʾ-UM	GA-BU-UM		B 17
1727.	GAJD-AN-IM	GA-DA-NIM	GEN	B 44
1728.	QAṮAR-I	GA?-DA-RI		RA LXV 51 IX 72
1729.	KABKAB-AN	GA-GA-BA-AN-KI	GN	IRAQ VII 66 SARGONIC
1730.	GAʾG-AN-UM	GA-GA-NU-UM		B 44+
1731.	GAʾG-AT-UM	GA-GA-TUM	MN?	HARRIS 13 13+
1732.	GAʾG-IJA	GA-GI-IA		HARRIS 13 12
1733.	GAʾG-UM	GA-GU-UM		HARRIS 5 18+
1734.	GAʾAŠ-UM	GA-ḪA-ŠUM		XIV 62:25
1735.	GAJID-AH	GA-I-DA	FN	C; RA LXV 65
1736.	GAʾJ-I+LAʾL-UM	GA-I-LA-LUM		M
1737.	GAʾIL-AT-UM	GA-I-LA-TUM	FN	EDZARD, DER 224:35
1738.	GAʾIL-AT-UM	GA-I-LA-TUM	MN?	B 17+
1739.	GAJID-E	GA-I-TE		A.
1740.	GAʾIL-UM	GA-JI-LUM		RA LXV 51 IX 54
1741.	GAʾJ-I+JARAḪ	GA-JI-RA-A[Ḫ]		HARRIS 39 15
1742.	GALAZ-IM	GA-LA-ZI-IM	GEN	HARRIS 83 2
1743.	QAWM-I+ʾIL	GA-MI-DINGIR		TIM III 12 16+
1744.	GAMIR-AN-UM	GA-MI-RA-NU-UM		TA 1931, 538 I, V?
1745.	KAMIS-UM	GA-MI-ZUM		I
1746.	QAWM-U+HADD-U	GA-MU-D-IM		M
1747.	GAʾN-AN	GA-NA-AN		RA LXV 54 XII 5
1748.	GANAM-AN-UM	GA-NA-MA-NU-UM		TA 1931, 438
1749.	QANAT-AN-UM	GA-NA-TA-NU-UM		KISURRA 30 7
1750.	GANIB-AN	GA-NI-BA-AN		RA LXV 42 II 80+
1751.	GANIN-AN-UM	GA-NI-NA-NU-UM		BIN VII P. 12+
1752.	GARAN-UM	GA-RA-NU-UM		B 44+
1753.	QARAʾ+ŠUM-I-JA	GA-RA-SU-MI-IA		CT XLVIII 89 REV.
1754.	QARAʾ+ŠUM-U-JA	GA-RA-SU-MU-IA		CT XLV 11 2, 46+
1755.	GAʾR-IJA	GA-RI-IA		RA LXV 44 IV 58
1756.	GARIŠ-U	GA-RI-SU		B 17
1757.	GARIŠ-UM	GA-RI-SU-UM		B 17
1758.	GARUB-UM	GA-RU-BU-UM		B 17+
1759.	KAŠER-AH	GA-ŠE-RA	FN	M
1760.	QAṮAR+ʾIL	GA-TA-AR-DINGIR		B 17
1761.	QAṮAR+ʾAB-I	GA-TAR-A-BI		BASOR 95 22
1762.	GAʾUL-A	GA-U_2-LA		JCS XIII 56, ALA. LATE
1763.	GAʾUŠ-UM	GA-U_2-ŠUM		I+
1764.	GAZIZ-AN-UM	GA-ZI-ZA-NU-[UM]		M
1765.	KALB+....	GAL-BA-....		MCS V 120
1766.	ʾAM-T+ʾEL	$GEME_2$-E-IL		RIFTIN 44 10
1767.	GIJD-AN-IM	GI-DA-NI-IM	GEN	SIMMONS 12 6
1768.	GIJD-AN-IM	GI-DA-NIM	GEN	M, SIMMONS 16 4
1769.	GIJD-AN-UM	GI-DA-NU-UM		SIMMONS 11 1+
1770.	GIJD-AN-UM	GI-DA-NUM_2		BIROT, TEA 70 C REV. I 7
1771.	GIZZ-I	GI-IZ-ZI		A. 32 3
1772.	GIZZ-AN-IM	GI-ZA-NI-IM	GEN	B 44
1773.	GIZZ-AN-U	GI-ZA-NU		B 93
1774.	GIZZ-AN-UM	GI-ZA-NU-UM		B 93
1775.	GIZZ-IT-IM	GI-ZI-TIM	FN GEN	M
1776.	KIRB-AN-UM	GIR_3-BA-NUM_2		U
1777.	SUMUKAN+JI-JBAL	D-GIR_3-I-BA-AL		C
1778.	KUBAR-UM	GU-BA-RU-UM		U
1779.	QUDAŠ-UM	GU-DA-SU-UM		JCS XXIV 60 NO.51+
1780.	GUʾAD-UM	GU-ḪA-DU-UM		JCS XXVI 137:24+ HARMAL
1781.	GULAL-AN	GU-LA-LA-AN		RA LXV 47 VII 55
1782.	GUMUL+JARAḪ	GU-MU-UL-D-EN-ZU		M+

1783.	GUʾR-AT-IM	GU-RA-TIM	FN GEN	B 17
1784.	GUʾR-AT-UM	GU-RA-TUM	FN	C
1785.	GUʾR-I	GU-RI	GEN	B 17
1786.	GUʾR-IJA	GU-RI-IA		BARRIS 8 5+
1787.	GURUD-IM	GU-RU-DI-IM	GEN	M
1788.	GURUD-U	GU-RU-DU		XIII 1 III 41
1789.	GUʾR-U+HADD-U	GU-RU-D-IM		M+
1790.	GUʾR-UM	GU-RU-UM		UCP X/3 6A 18+
1791.	GUʾUD-A	GU-U_2-DA		U
1792.	GUBʾ-AN-UM	GU-UB-ḪA-NU-UM		M
1793.	GUBL-AJ-I	GU-UB-LA-A-JI	GN PL NOM	SYRIA XX 111
1794.	GUBL-AJ-I	GU-UB-LA-JI	GN NOM	SYRIA XX 111
1795.	GUBL-AJIT-UM	GU-UB-LA-JI-TUM	GN FN	SYRIA XX 111
1796.	GULZ-AT-UM	GU-UL-ZA-TUM		LANGDON XXIX 22
1797.	KUMT-AN-UM	GU-UM-DA-NU-UM		HSM 7936, UR III
1798.	GUNGUN-UM	GU-UN-GU-NU-UM		B 48+
1799.	GURD-AN	GU-UR-DA-AN		M
1800.	GURUR-U	GU-UR-RU-RU		M
1801.	GURGUR-UM	GU-UR_2-GU-RU-UM		KISURRA 202 5
1802.	GUʾZ-AN	GU-ZA-AN		RA LXV 53 XI 57;64
1803.	GUʾZ-I	GU-ZI	FN	RA LXV 55 XIII 8
1804.	GUʾG-AN-UM	GU_2-GA-NU-UM		TA 30, 111 6
1805.	KULP-AN-UM	GUL-BA-NU-UM		U
1806.	GULL-AT-UM	GUL-LA-TUM	FN	M+
1807.	GULZ-UM	GUL-ZUM		TA 1931, 538 VI
1808.	GUʾR-UM	GUR-RU-UM MAR-TU		IRAQ MUS. 43488
1809.	ḤAJJ-AT-UM	[Ḫ]A-A-A-IA-TUM	FN	XIII 1 XIV 13
1810.	ʾAJA+ʾAB-AM	ḪA-A-IA-A-BA-AM	ACC	M+
1811.	ʾAJA+ʾAB-UM	ḪA-A-IA-A-BU-UM		M
1812.	ʾAJIŠ+PI-HU	ḪA-A-IŠ-PI_2-U_2		KISURRA 5+
1813.	ʾALI+PA+ʾIL	ḪA-A-LI-PA-DINGIR		EDZARD, DER 152 REV.16
1814.	ḪAʾL-I+ʾEL	ḪA-A-LI_2-EL		RA LXV 42 III 20
1815.	ḪAʾL-I+ʾIL-U-HU	ḪA-A-LI_2-I-LU-U_2		X 146 5
1816.	ḪAʾL-U	ḪA-A-LU		A
1817.	ḪAʾL-UM	ḪA-A-LUM		UCP X/1 34 12
1818.	ḪAʾAN-AN	ḪA-A-NA-AN		C+
1819.	ḪAʾAN-A+LA-HA	ḪA-A-NA-LA-A	FN	XIII 1 II 53+
1820.	ḪAʾAZ-U+ʾIL	ḪA?-A-ZU-DINGIR		M
1821.	ʿABD-AN	ḪA-AB-DA-AN		M, C+
1822.	ʿABD-AN-UM	ḪA-AB-DA-[NUM]?		PBS VIII/2 260 4
1823.	ʿABD-ATAN	ḪA-AB-DA-TA-AN		M+
1824.	ʿABD-AT-UM	ḪA-AB-DA-TUM	FN	XIII 1 XIV 39
1825.	ʿABD+JARAḪ	ḪA-AB-DI-A-RA-AḪ		B 9
1826.	ʿABD+ʾIL	ḪA-AB-DI-DINGIR		B 9
1827.	ʿABD+HEDD-A	ḪA-AB-DI-E-D-IM		RS XIX 338F.
1828.	ʿABD+JARAḪ	ḪA-AB-DI-E-RA-AḪ		M+, C+
1829.	ʿABD+ʾEL	ḪA-AB-DI-EL		KISURRA 74 17
1830.	ʿABD-IJA	ḪA-AB-DI-IA		B 9+, M, C+
1831.	ʿABD+HAND-U	ḪA-AB-DI-IA-AN-DU		KUPPER NOM. P. 231
1832.	ʿABD+JARAḪ	ḪA-AB-DI-RA-AḪ		SUMER XXIII 162 46
1833.	ʿABD+ḤAM-I	ḪA-AB-DU-D-A-MI		M+
1834.	ʿABD+ḤAM-I	ḪA-AB-DU-A-MI		M
1835.	ʿABD+ʿAMM-IM	ḪA-AB-DU-A-MI-IM		M
1836.	ʿABD+ʿAMM-UM	ḪA-AB-DU-A-MU-UM		M
1837.	ʿABD+ʾAŠUR-A	ḪA-AB-DU-A-ŠU-RA		M
1838.	ʿABD+BAʿL-AH	ḪA-AB-DU-BA-AḪ-LA		M
1839.	ʿABD+BAʿL-AT-I	ḪA-AB-DU-BA-AḪ-LA-TI		M+
1840.	ʿABD+DAGAN	ḪA-AB-DU-D-DA-GAN		M
1841.	ʿABD+JARAḪ	ḪA-AB-DU-E-RA-AḪ		DELAPORTE CCL II A 418 M
1842.	ʿABD+ʿAŠTAR	ḪA-AB-DU-$EŠ_4$-DAR		M+, C+
1843.	ʿABD+ʿAḎR-A	ḪA-AB-DU-ḪA-AD-RA		M
1844.	ʿABD+ʿAN-AT	ḪA-AB-DU-D-ḪA-NA-AT		M+
1845.	ʿABD+HADD-U	ḪA-AB-DU-D-IM		RA LXV 48 VIII 34
1846.	ʿABD+ʾIRŠAP-A	ḪA-AB-DU-IR?-ŠA-PA?		M
1847.	ʿABD+ʾIŠḪAR-AH	ḪA-AB-DU-D-IŠ-ḪA-RA		XIII 1 II 79+
1848.	ʿABD+KUʾB-I	ḪA-AB-DU-KU-BI		M+

1849.	ʿABD+MA+DAGAN	ḪA-AB-DU-MA-D-DA-GAN		M+
1850.	ʿABD+MALIK	ḪA-AB-DU-MA-LIK		M+
1851.	ʿABD+NAWAR	ḪA-AB-DU-NA-WA-AR		M
1852.	ʿABD-U+TA-RWIM	[ḪA-A]B-DU-TA-RI-IM		M
1853.	ʿABD-UM	ḪA-AB-DU-UM		B 9+, M+
1854.	ʾABN-A+JARAḪ	ḪA?-AB-NA-A-RA-AḪ		UET V 476 SEAL 6
1855.	ʾABN-I+ʾIL	ḪA-AB-NI-DINGIR		M
1856.	ʾABN-UM	ḪA-AB-NU-UM		GAUTIER 10 R. 10+
1857.	ḪABS-AT-UM	ḪA-AB-ZA-TUM		BM 17049+
1858.	ḪABZUR-AN	ḪA-AB-ZU-RA-AN		RA LXV 48 VIII 21+
1859.	ʾADM-AN-IM	ḪA-AD-MA?-NIM	GEN	B 44
1860.	ʾADM-AN-UM	ḪA-AD-MA?-NU-UM		VIII 85:29
1861.	ʿADN-A+ʾAB-I	ḪA?-AD-NA-A-BI		TTKB XIX 304
1862.	ʿADN-A+ʾA-ʾMUR	ḪA-AD-NA-AM?-MU-UR		X 75 18
1863.	ʿADN-AN	ḪA-AD-NA-AN		M, C
1864.	ʿADN-I+HADD-U	ḪA-AD-NI-A-D[U]		DELAPORTE CCL II A 914
1865.	ʿADN-I+DAGAN	ḪA-AD-NI-D-DA-GAN		M
1866.	ʿADN-I+ʾIL	ḪA-AD-NI-DINGIR		M+
1867.	ʿADN-I+ʾIL-U+MA	ḪA-AD-NI-DINGIR-MA		M
1868.	ʿADN-I+JARAḪ	ḪA-AD-NI-E-RA-AḪ		M
1869.	ʿADN-I+ʿAMM-U	ḪA-AD-NI-ḪA-MU		RA LXV 50 VIII 49
1870.	ʿADN-I+HADD-U	ḪA-AD-NI-D-IM		M, C+
1871.	ʿADN-I+ŠAMŠ	ḪA-AD-NI-SA-MA-AŠ$_2$		M
1872.	ʿADN-U	ḪA-AD-NU		KISURRA 81A 20
1873.	ʿADN-U+MA+JATAR	ḪA-AD-NU-ME-TAR		M+
1874.	ʿADN-U+RAPIʾ	ḪA-AD-NU-RA-BI		XIV 109:18+
1875.	ʿADN-UM+MAZAʾ-A	ḪA-[A]D?-NU-UM-MA-ZA-A		RA LXV 41 II 52
1876.	ʿAḎR-I+HAND-U	ḪA-AD-RI-IA-AN-DU		KUPPER, NOM. 231
1877.	ḪALD-A+MULUK	ḪA?-AL-DA-MU-LU-UK		BASOR 95 21
1878.	ʾALM-AN-UM	ḪA-AL-MA-NU-UM		HARRIS 62 14+
1879.	ʾALM-AT-UM	ḪA-AL-MA-TUM	MN?	HARRIS 66 13
1880.	ʾALM-U-HU	ḪA-AL-MU-U$_2$		SYRIA XXXVII 206 9 HANA
1881.	ḪAMBUZ-U-HU	ḪA-AM-BU-ZU-U$_2$		B 19
1882.	ʿAMM-AN	ḪA-AM-MA-AN		M+
1883.	ʿAMM-AN-IM	ḪA-AM-MA-NIM	GEN	M
1884.	ʿAMM-AN-U	ḪA-AM-MA-NU		M
1885.	ʿAMM-AN-UM	ḪA-AM-MA-NU-UM		M
1886.	ʿAMM-ATAN	ḪA-AM-MA-TA-AN		M+
1887.	ʿAMM-I+JATAR	ḪA-AM-MA-TA-AR		B 19
1888.	ʿAMM-I+JATAR	ḪA-AM-MI-A-TAR		B 19+
1889.	ʿAMM-I+ʾANDUL-I	ḪA-AM-MI-AN-DUL$_3$-LI$_2$		M+
1890.	ʿAMM-I+DUŠUR	ḪA-AM-MI-DU-ŠU-UR		HARRIS 18 15+
1891.	ʿAMM-I+DUŠUR	ḪA-AM-MI-DU-ŠU-UR$_2$		HARRIS 27 17+
1892.	ʿAMM-I+JE-JPUʿ	ḪA-AM-MI-E-PU-UḪ		M+
1893.	ʿAMM-I+JAŠAR	ḪA-AM-MI-E-SA-AR?		M
1894.	ʿAMM-IJA	ḪA-AM-MI-IA		M
1895.	ʿAMM-I+JI-T-ŠAMAR	ḪA-AM-MI-IŠ-TA-MAR		M+
1896.	ʿAMM-I+RAPIʾ	ḪA-AM-MI-RA-BI		B 19
1897.	ʿAMM-I+ŠUM-U-HU	ḪA-AM-MI-SU-MU-U$_2$		CT XLVII 30 44
1898.	ʿAMM-I+ŠAGIŠ	ḪA-AM-MI-ŠA-GI-IŠ		M+
1899.	ʿAMM-I+TA-QWIM	ḪA-AM-MI-TA-KI-IM	NOM	M
1900.	ʿAMM-I+ṬALL-U-HU	ḪA-AM-MI-TA-LU-U$_2$		M+
1901.	ʿAMM-I+ṬILL-U-HU	ḪA-AM-MI-TE-LU-U$_2$		RA LXVI 118:15
1902.	ʿAMM-I+ṬALL-U-HU	ḪA-AM-MI-TI-LU-U$_2$		M+
1903.	ʿAMM-I+ṢADUQ	ḪA-AM-MI-ZA-DU-UQ		M
1904.	ʿAMM-I+ZAKK-U-HU	ḪA-AM-MI-ZA-KU-U$_2$		M
1905.	ʿAMM-I+ZUʾG-U-HU	ḪA-AM-MI-ZU-GU-U$_2$		BM 17045+
1906.	ʿAMM-U+DAGAN	ḪA-AM-MU-D-DA-GAN		M
1907.	ʿAMM-U+ḪAʾL-UM	ḪA-AM-MU-ḪA-LUM		M+
1908.	ʿAMM-U+LABW-A	ḪA-AM-MU-LA-BA-A		XIV 114:6
1909.	ʿAMM-U+NIʿM	ḪA-AM-MU-NI-ḪI-IM	NOM	M
1910.	ʿAMM-U+PATAḪ-A	ḪA-AM-MU-PA-TA-A		M
1911.	ʿAMM-U+RAPIʾ	ḪA-AM-MU-RA-BI		B 19+, M+, A.+
1912.	ʿAMM-U+RAPIʾ	D-ḪA-AM-MU-RA-BI		B 19+
1913.	ʿAMM-U+RAPIʾ+BANIJ	ḪA-AM-MU-RA-BI-BA-NI		B 19
1914.	ʿAMM-U+RAPIʾ+ʾIL	ḪA-AM-MU-RA-BI-DINGIR		B 19

1915.	ʿAMM-U+RAPIʾ	ḪA-AM-MU-RA-BI-IḪ		B 19 HANA
1916.	ʿAMM-U+RAPIʾ+....	ḪA-AM-MU-RA-BI-LU-DA-RI		B 19
1917.	ʿAMM-U+ŠARR	ḪA-AM-MU-SA-AR		XIV 108:6
1918.	ʿAMM-U+JATAR	[Ḫ]A-AM-MU-TA-[A]R		M
1919.	ʿAMM-U-HU	ḪA-AM-MU-U$_2$		EDZARD, DER 68 III 6
1920.	ʿAMM-U-HU+RAPIʾ	ḪA-AM-MU-U$_2$-RA-BI		M
1921.	ʿAMM-U-HU+JATAR	ḪA-AM-MU-U$_2$-TAR		M
1922.	ʿAMM-UM+RAPIʾ	ḪA-AM-MU-UM-RA-BI		B 19+
1923.	ʿAMM-UM+RAPIʾ	ḪA-AM-MU-UM-RA-PI		YBC 6496, 6508
1924.	ʿAMM-UM+RAPIʾ+....	[ḪA-AM]-MU-UM-RA-PI-LI-WI-IR		UNPUBL.
1925.	ḪAMR-U	ḪA-AM-RU		C
1926.	ḪAMR-U+RAPIʾ	ḪA-AM-RU-RA-BI		M
1927.	ḪAMŠ-AT-UM	ḪA-AM-SA-TUM	FN	BM 16844+
1928.	ḪANB-AT-UM	ḪA-AN-BA-TUM	FN	CT XLV 91 18+
1929.	ḪAND-IJA	ḪA-AN-DI-IA		BIN VII 63 28
1930.	ḪANḪAN-U	ḪA-AN-ḪA-NU		CT XLV 11 42
1931.	ḪANḪAN-UM	ḪA-AN-ḪA-NU-UM		B 48+
1932.	ḪANN-A+ʾABN-AT	ḪA-AN-NA-AB-NA-AT		A 7763, ISHCHALI
1933.	ḪANN-A+JARAḪ	ḪA-AN-NA-D-EN-ZU		M
1934.	ḪANN-A+JI-TWUR+MEʾR	ḪA-AN-NA-D-I-DUR-ME-ER		M
1935.	ḪANN-A+HADD-U	ḪA-AN-NA-D-IM		M
1936.	ḪANN-IJA	ḪA-AN-NI-A	FN	RA LXV 60 III 48
1937.	ḪANN-I+ʾIL	ḪA-AN-NI-DINGIR	FN	XIII 1 II 7
1938.	ḪANN-I+ʾIL-A	ḪA-AN-NI-I-LA		A. LATE
1939.	ḪANN-I+....	ḪA-AN-NI-D-NIN-ŠE-X-RA?	FN	RA LXV 61 IV 63
1940.	ḪANP-AT-IM	ḪA-AN-PA-TIM	FN GEN	A 3521 31
1941.	ḪANP-AT-UM	ḪA-AN-PA-TUM	FN	A 3521 29
1942.	ḪANZ-A+HADD-U	ḪA-AN-ZA-D-IM		M
1943.	ḪANZ-I	ḪA-AN-ZI		TA 1931, 434
1944.	ḪANZUR-A	ḪA-AN-ZU-RA		VAS IX 172 39+
1945.	ʿAQB-A+ʾAḪ-IM	ḪA-AQ-BA-A-ḪI-IM	GEN	M+
1946.	ʿAQB-A+ʾAḪ-UM	ḪA-AQ-BA-A-ḪU-UM		RA LXV 43 III 57+
1947.	ʿAQB-AN	ḪA-AQ-BA-AN		M+
1948.	ʿAQB-A+ʿAMM-U	ḪA-AQ-BA-ḪA-AM-MU		II 39 19, 58, 80
1949.	ʿAQB-A+ʿAMM-U-HU	ḪA-AQ-BA-ḪA-AM-MU-U$_2$		II 39 14, 16, 24
1950.	ʿAQB-U+DAWD-I	ḪA-AQ-BU-DA-DI		M+
1951.	ḪARB-AH	ḪA-AR-B[A]?	FN	RA LXV 62 V 41
1952.	ʿARD-AJA	ḪA-AR-DA-IA	FN	XIII 1 IV 70
1953.	ʿARD-AN-UM	ḪA-AR-DA-NU-UM		M+
1954.	ʿARD-AT-UM	ḪA-AR-DA-TUM	FN	M+
1955.	ʿARD-IM	ḪA-AR-DI-IM	GEN	M
1956.	ʿARD-UM	ḪA-AR-DU-UM		M+
1957.	ḪARGAL	ḪA-AR-GA-AL		M
1958.	ḪARGAL-UM	ḪA-AR-GA-LUM		VAS VIII 14 26
1959.	ḪARIR-UM	ḪA-AR-RI-RUM		B 20
1960.	ʾARŠ-UM+MALIK	ḪA-AR?-ŠUM?-MA-LIK		M
1961.	ʾAŠD-AH	ḪA-AŠ-DA	FN	RA LXV 58 I 62
1962.	ḪAŠḪAŠ-UM	ḪA-AŠ-ḪA-ŠUM		KISURRA 62 3
1963.	ʾAŠQUD-AN	ḪA-AŠ-KU-DA-AN		M
1964.	ʾAŠM-AN-I	ḪA-AŠ-MA-NI	GEN	B 44
1965.	ʾAŠM-AN-UM	ḪA-AŠ-MA-NU-UM		U
1966.	ḪAŠŠ-UM	ḪA-AŠ-ŠUM		RA LXV 47 VII 27
1967.	ḪAŠT-AT-UM	ḪA-AŠ-TA-TUM	FN	XIII 1 III 62
1968.	ḪAŠTUR-UM	ḪA-AŠ-TU-RU-UM		YOS VIII 139 15 CASE 13
1969.	ʾAŠR-I	ḪA-AŠ$_2$-RI		CT XLV 92 R. 9
1970.	ḪATK-UM	ḪA-AT-KU-UM		M
1971.	ʾATT-A	D-ḪA-AT-TA	DN	M+
1972.	ʾATAL-UM	ḪA-AT-TA-LUM		CT XXXIII 43A 6
1973.	ʾATT-I	ḪA-AT-TI		RA LXV 40 I 32
1974.	ʾATT-IM	ḪA-AT-TI-IM	GEN	M+
1975.	ʾATT-U	ḪA-AT-TU		C+
1976.	ʾATT-UM	ḪA-AT-TU-UM		M
1977.	ḪAWR-AN+ʾAB-I	ḪA-AW-RA-AN-A-BI		M
1978.	ḪAWR+ʾAB-I	ḪA-AW-RA-BI		TIM IV 33 21, 34 14
1979.	ḪAWR-AN+ʾAB-I	ḪA-AW-RA-NA-A-BI		M+
1980.	ḪAWR-AN-IM	ḪA-AW-RA-NIM	GEN	B 44

1981.	ʿAZB-UM	ḪA-AZ-BU-UM		RA LXV 53 XI 20
1982.	ḪAṢN-AT-UM	ḪA-AZ-NA-TU[M]	FN	M
1983.	ʿAḎR-AN	ḪA-AZ-RA-AN		M
1984.	ʿAḎR+ʾAḪ-I	ḪA-AZ-RA-ḪI?		CT XLV 54 9
1985.	ʿAḎR-I+ʿAMM-IM	ḪA-AZ-RI-A-MI-IM	GEN	M
1986.	ʿAḎR-IJA	ḪA-AZ-RI-IA		RA LXV 41 II 21+
1987.	ʿAZZ-U	ḪA-AZ-ZU		C+
1988.	ḪABAD-U+ʾIL	ḪA-BA-DU-DINGIR		M
1989.		ḪA-BA-LU-UK		RA LXV 45 V 18
1990.	ʾABAN-UM	ḪA-BA-NU-UM		TA 30, 191+
1991.	ḪABAD-UM	ḪA-BA-TUM	FN	RA LXV 59 II 76
1992.	ḪABAS-U	ḪA-BA?-ZU	FN	XIII 1 I 1
1993.	ḪABIʾ-AN-U	ḪA-BI-A-NU		YOS XIII 175:12
1994.	ḪABIB-UM	ḪA-BI-BU-UM		RUTTEN 27 14+
1995.	ḪABIʾ-JA	ḪA-BI-IA		RA LXV 52 X 71
1996.	ḪABIʾ+HADD-U	ḪA-BI-D-IM		M
1997.	ḪABIR-AN	ḪA-BI-RA-AN		RA LXV 54 XII 21
1998.	ḪABIR-IM	ḪA-BI-RI-IM	GEN	M
1999.	ḪABIS-AN-I	ḪA-BI-ZA-NI	GEN	CT VIII 42 B 17
2000.	ḪABUR-I	ḪA-BU-UR-RI	FN	RA LXV 63 III 1
2001.	ḪABUR+JI-JBAL+BUGAŠ	ID$_2$-ḪA-BUR-I-BA-AL-BU-GA-AŠ$_2$		BRM IV 52 HANA
2002.	ʾADAN+ʾIL	ḪA-DA-AN-DINGIR		B 18
2003.	ʾADAN-AT-UM	ḪA-DA-AN-N[A]?-TUM?	FN	RA LXV 62 V 7
2004.	ʾADAM-U	ḪA-DA-MU	MN	RUTTEN 19 19+
2005.	ʾADAN-I-Š+....	ḪA-DA-NI-IŠ-MU-[....]		SIGRIST UNPUBL.
2006.	ʾADAN+NUWḪ-UM	ḪA-DA-NU-U$_2$-UM		M
2007.	ḪAʾD-ATAN	ḪA-DA-TA-AN		M+
2008.	ʾADAM-TA+ʾAR-U	ḪA-DAM-TA-A-RU		WATERMAN 45 EDGE
2009.	ʾADAM-TI+ʾEL	ḪA-DAM-TI-EL		HARRIS 61 2
2010.	ʿADIJ+ʾEL	ḪA-DI-EL		KISURRA 113 12+
2011.	ʾADUN+LUʾM-U	ḪA-DU-LU-MU		M
2012.	ʾADUN-AH	ḪA-DU-NA	FN	XIII 1 III 65
2013.	ʾADUN+LUʾM-U	ḪA-DU-UN-LU-MU		M
2014.	ʿAGAL-IJA	ḪA-GA-LI-IA		HARRIS 88:3
2015.	ʿAGAL-IM	ḪA-GA-LIM	GEN	M
2016.	ḪAGIR-UM	ḪA-GI-RUM		M
2017.	ḪAGUR-AH	ḪA-GU-RA	FN	RA LXV 64 V 63
2018.	ḪANḪAN-UM	ḪA-ḪA-NU-UM		SPELEERS 224 10
2019.	ḪAḪUN-A	ḪA-ḪU-NA		CT II 23 33
2020.	ʿAWIQ-AT-UM	ḪA-I-KA-TUM	FN	SIMMONS 112:17
2021.	ḪAJJ-AN-I	ḪA-IA-A-NI		JNES XIII 210FF.+ LATE
2022.	ʾAJA+ʾAB+ʾIL	ḪA-IA-AB-DINGIR		B 18
2023.	ʾAJA+ʾABN-I+ʾIL	ḪA-IA-AB-NI-DINGIR		B 18+
2024.	ʾAJAM+DIWD-U	ḪA-IA-AM-DI-DU		B 18
2025.	ʾAJAM+DIWD-UM	ḪA-IA-AM-DI-DU-UM		B 18+
2026.	ʾAJAM-TI+ʾIL	ḪA-IA-AM-TI-DINGIR		BIROT, TEA 72 III 5
2027.	ʾAJA+ʾAB-UM	ḪA-IA-BU-UM		B 18+
2028.	ʾAJA+MAṬAR	ḪA-IA-MA-DAR		YOS XII 360 17
2029.	ʾAJA+MUT-I	ḪA-IA-MU-TI		BAGHD. MITT. II 7 2, 4, 8
2030.	ḪAJJ-AN-UM	ḪA-IA-NU-UM		VAS XVI 62 12
2031.	ʾAJA+ŠUM-U+ʾAB-IM	ḪA-IA-SU-MU-A-BI-IM		M
2032.	ʾAJA+ŠUM-U-HU	ḪA-IA-SU-MU-U$_2$		XI P.83 N.1+
2033.	ʾAJA+ŠARR-UM	ḪA-IA-ŠA-RUM		UCP X P. 56+
2034.	ḪAJJ-ATAN	ḪA-IA-TA-AN		M+
2035.	ḪAJJ-AT-UM	ḪA-IA-TUM	MN	B 18+
2036.	ʾAJA+MA+ʾIL	ḪA-IA$_3$-MA-DINGIR		XIV 93:8+
2037.	ʾAJA+ŠUM-U	ḪA-IA$_3$-SU-MU		DELAPORTE CCL II A 337+
2038.	ʾAJA+ŠUM-U-HU	ḪA-IA$_3$-SU-MU-U$_2$		M+
2039.	ʾAJA+ŠUM-U-HU	ḪA-IA$_3$-SU-U$_2$-MU		M+
2040.	ʾAJA+ŠUM-U-HU	ḪA-IA$_3$-SU-U$_2$-MU-U$_2$		X 113 4, 11, 14
2041.	ʾAJA+ŠUM	ḪA-IA$_3$-SU?-UM		M
2042.	ʾAJIŠ+PI-HU	ḪA-II-IŠ-PI$_2$-U$_2$		KISURRA 22+
2043.	ʾAJIŠ-UM	ḪA-II-ŠUM		KISURRA 101 6+
2044.	ḪAJJ-UM	ḪA-IU-UM		B 18+
2045.	ḪAJJ-UM+RAPIʾ	ḪA-JU-UM-RA-BI		M
2046.	ḪAKAM-AJA	ḪA-KA-MA-A-IA	FN	XIII 1 V 44

2047.	ḪAKAM-AT-UM	ḪA-KA-MA-TUM	FN	C+
2048.	ḪAʾL-AJA	ḪA-LA-A-A		B 18
2049.	ḪALAJ-A+KUʾM-U	ḪA-LA-A-KU-MU		XIV 79:5+
2050.	ʾALAK-UM	ḪA-LA-KUM		CT XLV 2 22+
2051.	ḪAʾL-A-NA	ḪA-LA?-NA	FN	RA LXV 59 II 74
2052.	ḪALAN-I+JATAR	ḪA-LA-NI-E-TAR		M
2053.	ḪAʾL-AN-UM	ḪA-LA-NU-UM		KISURRA 57 4, SEAL
2054.	ḪAʾL-AN-UM	ḪA-LA-NUM$_2$		KISURRA 24 2
2055.	ḪAʾL-ATAN	ḪA-LA-TA-AN		M+
2056.	ḪAʾL-AT-UM	ḪA-LA-TUM		KISURRA 104 8
2057.	ʾAHL-UM+PU-HU	ḪA-LAM-BU-U$_2$		RLA II 165 17
2058.	ḪAʾL-I+HADD-U	ḪA-LI-A-DU		A.+
2059.	ḪAʾL-I+ʿAḎIR-UM	ḪA-LI-A-ṢI-RUM		UNPUBL.
2060.	ʾALIP-AH	ḪA-LI-BA	FN	XIII 1 VIII 37
2061.	ḪAʾL-I+ʿADN-U-HU	ḪA-LI-ḪA-AD-NU-U$_2$		M
2062.	ḪAʾL-I+ʿADN	ḪA-LI-ḪA-DU-UM?		M
2063.	ḪAʾL-I+ʿADN	ḪA-LI-ḪA-DU-UN		M+
2064.	ʿALIJ-UM	ḪA-LI-I-JU-UM		CT XLVIII 31 7, 10
2065.	ḪAʾL-IJA	ḪA-LI-IA		C, A. LATE
2066.	ḪAʾL-IJAN	ḪA-LI-IA-AN		A. LATE
2067.	ḪAʾL-I+HADD-U	ḪA-LI-IA-[D]U		M
2068.	ʿALIJ-AT-UM	ḪA-LI-IA-TUM	FN	B 18+, XIII 1 VII 1
2069.	ʿALIJ-UM	ḪA-LI-IU-UM		B 19+
2070.	ʿALIJ-UM	ḪA-LI-JU-UM		B 19+
2071.	ʾALIK-UM	ḪA-LI-KU-UM		B 12+
2072.	ʾALIK-UM	ḪA-LI-KUM		B 12+
2073.	HALIL-AT-UM	ḪA-LI-LA-TUM		KISURRA 211 4
2074.	HALIL-IJA	ḪA-LI-LI-IA		B 18+
2075.	HALIL-IM	ḪA-LI-LI-IM	GEN	B 18
2076.	HALIL-IM	ḪA-LI-LIM	GEN	SIMMONS 57 14
2077.	HALIL-UM	ḪA-LI-LU-UM		B 18+
2078.	HALIL-UM	ḪA-LI-LUM		B 18+, M
2079.	ḪAʾL-I+MA	ḪA-LI-MA	FN	RA LXV 59 II 43
2080.	ʾALIM-AH	ḪA-LI-MA	FN	M+
2081.	ḪAʾL-I+MARAṢ	ḪA-LI-MA-RA-AṢ		GEN, KICH I P. 59 NO. 219
2082.	ḪAʾL-I+MARAṢ	ḪA-LI-MA-RA-AṢ		UET V 521 1
2083.	ḪAʾL-I+ŠADW-A	ḪA-LI-SA-DA		B 19
2084.	ḪAʾL-I+TA-NWUḪ-A	ḪA-LI-TA-NU-A		A.+
2085.	ʿALIJ-UM	ḪA-LI-U$_2$-UM		B 19+, M
2086.	ḪALIṢ-UM	ḪA-LI-ZUM		SUMER V 141 3
2087.	ḪAʾL-I+ʾIL	ḪA-LI$_2$-DINGIR		B 18
2088.	ḪAʾL-I+ʾEL	ḪA-LI$_2$-EL		RA LXV 42 III 18+
2089.	ḪAʾL-I+ʿAŠTAR	ḪA-LI$_2$-EŠ$_4$-DAR		RA LXV 53 XII 1
2090.	ḪAʾL-I+ʿADN	ḪA-LI$_2$-ḪA-DU-UN		M+
2091.	ḪAʾL-IJA	ḪA-LI$_2$-IA		C+
2092.	ḪAʾL-IJA	ḪA-LI$_2$-IA		RA LXV 47 VI 64; C+
2093.	ḪAʾL-I+HADD-U	ḪA-LI$_2$-D-IM		M+
2094.	ḪAʾL-I+KUPAPA	ḪA-LI$_2$-KU-BA-BA	FN	RA LXV 58 I 14
2095.	ḪAʾL-I+MAMM-A	ḪA-LI$_2$-D-M[A-A]M-M[A]		M
2096.	ḪAʾL-I+MA+ʾIL	ḪA-LI$_2$-MA-DINGIR		M
2097.	ḪAʾL-I+MALIK	ḪA-LI$_2$-MA-LIK		M+
2098.	ḪAʾL-I+MU-WTAR	ḪA-LI$_2$-MU-TAR		M
2099.	ʾALUN+PI+JAM-U	ḪA-LU-BI-JA-MU		M
2100.	ḪAʾL-U+ʾIL	ḪA-LU-DINGIR		M
2101.	ḪAʾL-U+ʿADN-U	ḪA-LU-ḪA-AD-NU		M+
2102.	ḪAʾL-UJAN	ḪA-LU-JA-AN		RA LXV 41 II 33+
2103.	ḪAʾL-U+MAṮAR	ḪA-LU-MA-DA-AR		M+
2104.	ʾALUN-A+HADD-U	ḪA-LU-NA-D-IM		M
2105.	ḪAʾL-U+NIʿM	ḪA-LU-NI-ḪI-IM		RA LXV 52 X 74
2106.	ḪAʾL-U+RAPIʾ	ḪA-LU-RA-PI		M+
2107.	ḪAʾL-UM	ḪA-LU-UM		B 19
2108.	ʾALUN+PI+JAM-U	ḪA-LU-UM-BI-JA-MU		RA LXV 43 III 78
2109.	ʾALUN+PI+JAM-U	ḪA-LU-UN-BI-JA-MU		M
2110.	ʾALUN+HADD-U	ḪA-LU-UN-D-IM		M; JCS XIV 203
2111.	ḪAʾL-U-Š+MI+ʾIL	ḪA-LU-UŠ-MI-DINGIR		M
2112.	ḪAʾL-UM+MAṮAR-I	ḪA-LUM-MA-DA-RI		SIMMONS 67 B 11

2113.	ḪAʾL-UM+MAṬAR	ḪA-LUM-MA-DAR		C, SIMMONS 67 SEAL
2114.	ḪAʾL-UM+MAṬAR-I	ḪA-LUM-MA-DAR-RI		SIMMONS 67 11
2115.	ḤAMAD-U	ḪA-MA-DU	FN	XIII 1 XIII 20
2116.	ḤAMAD-UM	ḪA-MA-DU-UM	FN	M+
2117.	ʿAMM-A+JI-ḎRUʿ	ḪA-MA-IZ-RU		RUTTEN 28 5+
2118.	ʿAMM-AN-IM	ḪA-MA-NIM	GEN	M
2119.	ʾAMAN-U	ḪA-MA-NU		X 151 4+, KISURRA 21 9
2120.	ʾAMAN-U	ḪA-MA-NU	FN	RA LXV 66 VIII 6
2121.	ḪAMAŚ-AT-UM	ḪA-MA-SA-TUM	MN	CT XLV 91 20
2122.	ʾAMAT-AN	ḪA-MA-TA-AN		RA LXV 43 III 43
2123.	ḪAMAṬ-I+ʾIL	ḪA-MA-TI-IL		FIGULLA, CAT. I 14135
2124.	ʿAMIS-AH	ḪA-ME-ZA	FN	RA LXV 58 I 24
2125.	ḤAMID-AH	ḪA-MI-DA	FN	RA LXV 58 I 20
2126.	ʿAMM-I+DAGAN	ḪA-MI-D-DA-GAN		RA LXV 53 XI 33
2127.	ʿAMM-I+DUŠUR	ḪA-MI-DU-ŠU-UR		SIMMONS 46 18+
2128.	ʿAMM-I+DUŠUR	ḪA-MI-DU-ŠU-UR$_2$		SIMMONS 50 14
2129.	ḤAMID-UM	ḪA-MI-DU-UM		M
2130.	ʿAMM-I+JE-JPUʿ	ḪA-MI-E-PU-UḪ		M+
2131.	ʿAMM-I+JE-JŠUʿ	ḪA-MI-E-ŠU-UḪ		M
2132.	ʿAMM-I+ʿAN-AT	ḪA-MI-D-ḪA-NA-AT		M
2133.	ʿAMM-I+JI-JBAL	ḪA-MI-I-BA-AL		M
2134.	ʿAMM-I+ʾIL-I	ḪA-MI-I$_3$-LI$_2$		MDP XXIII 307 16
2135.	ʿAMM-IJA	ḪA-MI-IA		C+
2136.	ʿAMM-I+KUWN	ḪA-MI-KU-UN		RA LXV 54 XII 15
2137.		ḪA-MI-KU-UN		M
2138.	ʿAMM-I+MAṬAR	ḪA-MI-MA-DAR	FN	C
2139.	ʿAMIQ-AT-IM	ḪA-MI-QA-TIM-KI	GN GEN	M+
2140.	ʿAMM-I+ṬALL-U-HU	ḪA-MI-TI-LU-U$_2$		M
2141.		ḪA-MI-UR-KU-X-X-X-UM		M
2142.	ʿAMM-I+ṢADUQ	ḪA-MI-ZA-DU-[UQ]		M
2143.	ʿAMIS-AN-U	ḪA-MI-ZA-NU		M
2144.	ʿAMM-I+ZAʾT-I	ḪA-MI-ZA-TI		HARRIS 103 1
2145.	ʿAMM-U+ʾIL	ḪA-MU-DINGIR		M
2146.	ʿAMM-U+DUMAR	ḪA-MU-DU-MAR		RA LXV 51 IX 66
2147.	ʿAMM-U+JE-JPUʿ	ḪA-MU-E-PU-UḪ	FN	C+
2148.	ʿAMM-U+JAQAR	ḪA-MU-IA-QAR		RA LXV 52 X 62
2149.	ʿAMM-U+JAŚAR	ḪA-MU-JA-ŠAR		M
2150.	ʿAMM-U+LA+RIWM	ḪA-MU-L[A]-RI-IM		RA LXV 46 VI 40
2151.	ʿAMM-U+LIʾM	ḪA-MU-LI-IM		RA LXV 52 X 22
2152.	ʿAMM-U+MAṬAR	ḪA-MU-MA-DAR	FN	C
2153.	ʿAMM-U+RAPIʾ	ḪA-MU-RA-BI		B 19+, M+
2154.	ʿAMM-U+RAWM-A	ḪA-MU-RA-MA		M
2155.	ʿAMM-U+ŚARR	ḪA-MU-SA-AR		RA LXV 40 I 42
2156.	ʿAMM-U+ŚARR	ḪA-MU-SA-AR	FN	C+
2157.	ʿAMM-U+ŚALIM	ḪA-MU-SA-L[IM]?		M
2158.	ʿAMM-U+ŚAMAR	ḪA-MU-SA-MAR		RA LXIV 36 NO. 31
2159.	ʿAMM-U+ŚAMAR	ḪA-MU-SA-MAR	FN	C+
2160.	ʿAMM-U+ŠAGIŠ	ḪA-MU-ŠA-KI-IŠ		X 174 13
2161.	ʿAMM-U+JATAR	ḪA-MU-TAR		M
2162.	ʿAMM-U+RAPIʾ	ḪA-MU-U$_2$-RA-BI		FIGULLA, CAT. 14138
2163.	ʿAMM-UM+RAPIʾ	ḪA-MU-UM-RA-BI		BM 17046+
2164.	ʿAMM-U+RAPIʾ	ḪA-MU-UR$_2$-RA-BI		CT XLVII 31 32+
2165.	ʿAMM-U+ḎAKAJ-A	Ḫ[A]-MU-ZA-KA-A		RA LXV 43 III 75
2166.	ḪAʾN-A+ʾAB-I	ḪA-NA-A-BI		TIM II 113 2, 8
2167.	ḤANAN-AH	ḪA-NA-AN-NA	FN	C
2168.	ʿAN-AT	D-ḪA-NA-AT	DN FN	M+
2169.	ʿAN-AT	ḪA-NA-AT-KI	GN FN	M+
2170.	ʿAN-AJA	ḪA-NA-IA		RA LXV 50 IX 19
2171.	ḪAʾN-A	ḪA-NA-KI	GN	M+
2172.	ḤANAN-IM	ḪA-NA-NI-IM	GEN	B 44
2173.	ḪANAŠ-I	ḪA-NA-ŠI	GEN	HARRIS 3916
2174.	ʿAN-ATAN	ḪA-NA-TA-AN		M+
2175.	ʿAN-AT-I+JI-JBAL	ḪA-NA-TI-I-BA-AL		RA LXV 40 I 12
2176.	ʿAN-AT-UM	ḪA-NA-TUM	FN	XIII 1:34+
2177.	ḤANIN-UM	ḪA-NI-NU-UM		B 19+
2178.	ḪAʾN-IJ-U	ḪA-NU-U$_2$		JNES XIII 210+ LATE

2179.	ḪAQAT-A	ḪA-QA-TA		DELAPORTE CCL II A 914
2180.	ḪARAB-AH	ḪA-RA-BA	FN	M
2181.	ʿARAD-AN	ḪA-RA-DA-AN		M
2182.	ʾARAŠ-UM	ḪA-RA-ŠUM		M
2183.	ḪAʾR-I+ʾATT-A	ḪA-RI-A-TA		C II 5 7
2184.	ḪARIB-AN	ḪA-RI-BA-AN		M+
2185.	ḪAʾR-I+ʾIL	ḪA-RI-DINGIR		BM 82372 27
2186.	ḪAʾR-IJA	ḪA-RI-IA		M+
2187.	ḪAʾR-I+MALIK-I	ḪA-RI-MA-LI-KI	GEN	B 20
2188.	ḪAʾR-I+MALIK	ḪA-RI-MA-LIK		BE VI/1 46 5
2189.	ḪARIR-UM	ḪA-RI-RUM		B 20
2190.	ʾARIŠ-AN	ḪA-RI-ŠA-AN		M
2191.	ʿARIṢ-AN-U	ḪA-RI-ZA-NU		PBS II/1 P. 23+ LATE
2192.	ḪAʾŠ-AN-U	ḪA-SA-NU		M
2193.	ḪAʾŠ-AT-UM	ḪA-SA-TUM	MN	RUTTEN 15 6 SEAL
2194.	ḪAŠIK-UM	ḪA-SI-KUM		B 20+
2195.	ʾAŠUD-UM	ḪA-SU-DU-UM		A 7660 2
2196.	ḪAŠIJ-AN-UM	ḪA-ŠI-A-NU-UM		TA 1931, 538 III
2197.	ʾAŠIR	ḪA-ŠI-IR?		HARRIS 38 5
2198.	ḪAŠIŠ-UM	ḪA-ŠI-ŠUM		B 20+
2199.	ḪATAʾ-A+ʾAR-UM	ḪA-TA-A-A-RUM?		CT XXIX 8A 1
2200.	ḪATAN+PI+ʾIL	ḪA-TA-AN-BI-DINGIR		M
2201.	ʾATAL-I+ʾEL	ḪA-TA-LI-EL		M
2202.	ʾATAL-UM	ḪA-TA-LU-UM		CT XXXIII 42 23+
2203.	ʾATAM-UM	ḪA-TA-MU-UM		B 20
2204.	ḪATAʾ+ʾUMAN-UM	ḪA-TA-UM-MA-NU-UM		RA VIII 74 19
2205.	ḪATIK-U	ḪA-TI-KU		M
2206.	ʾATUL-AH	ḪA-TU-LA	FN	RA LXV 65 VII 4
2207.	ḪAJJ-UM	ḪA-U_2-UM		CT VI 46 5
2208.	ʾAWIJ-AT-UM	ḪA-WI-IA-TUM		BIROT TEA 39:4
2209.	ḪAWIR-NI	ḪA-WI-IR-NI		RA LXV 45 V 12
2210.	ʾAWIJ-T-UM	ḪA-WI-TUM		BIROT TEA 72 I 28+
2211.	ḪAṢAN+ʾIL-UM	ḪA-ZA-AN-I-LU-UM		M+
2212.	ḪASAD-UM	ḪA-ZA-DU-U[M]?		M
2213.	ḪAZAQ-AN	ḪA-ZA-KA-AN-KI	GN	M
2214.	ḪAZAQ-AN-IM	ḪA-ZA-KA-AN-NIM-KI	GN GEN	C
2215.	ḪAZAQ-AN-IM	ḪA-ZA-KA-NIM-KI	GN GEN	C II 39 13
2216.	ʿAZAL-AH	ḪA-ZA-LA	FN	M+
2217.		ḪA-ZA-MU-LA		M+
2218.	ḪAṢAN-AT-UM	ḪA-[Z]A-NA-TUM	FN	M
2219.	ʿAḎAR-AN-IM	ḪA-ZA-RA-NIM	GEN	B 44
2220.	ʿAZZ-ATAN-IM	ḪA-ZA-TA-NIM	MN GEN	C II 6
2221.	ʿAZIB-AH	ḪA-ZI-BA	FN	XIII 1 IV 35
2222.	ʿAZIB-AT-UM	ḪA-ZI-BA-TUM	MN	GAUTIER 65 5
2223.	ḪASID-AN-IM	ḪA-ZI-DA-NIM	GEN	M+
2224.	ḪASID-AN-U	ḪA-ZI-DA-NU		M+
2225.	ḪASID-U	ḪA-ZI-DU	FN	XIII 1 VII 42
2226.	ʿAḎIR+ŠAMŠ	ḪA-ZI-IR-D-UTU		M
2227.	ḪAZIM-UM	ḪA-ZI-MU-UM		HARRIS 63 16
2228.	ʿAZIB-AN	ḪA-ZI-PA-AN		RA LXV 44 IV 25
2229.	ḪAZIQ-AJA	ḪA-ZI-QA-IA		UCP X/1 87 12
2230.	ʿAḎIR-AH	ḪA-ZI-RA	FN	RA LXV 62 V 26
2231.	ʿAḎIR-IM	ḪA-ZI-RI-IM	GEN	B 20+
2232.	ʿAḎIR-UM	ḪA-ZI-RU-UM		B 20, M
2233.	ʿAḎIR-UM	ḪA-ZI-RUM	FN	M+
2234.	ʿAḎIR-UM	ḪA-ZI-RUM	MN	B 20+, M+
2235.	ḪAZUQ-AN	ḪA-ZU-GA-AN		RA LXV 54 XII 22
2236.	ḪAʾZ-UT-UM	ḪA-ZU-TUM	FN	RA LXV 58 II 1
2237.	ḪANN-A+JARAḪ	ḪAN-NA-D-EN-ZU		XIII 1 V 27
2238.	ḪARḪAR-U	ḪAR-ḪA-RU		JNES XIII 210+ LATE
2239.	ʿARṢ-U	ḪAR-ṢU		JNES XIII 210+ LATE
2240.	ḪIʾAN-A	ḪI-A-NA		BM 80328 4
2241.	ḪIBAR-AT-I	ḪI-BA-RA-TI	MN NOM	VIII 6 31
2242.	ḪIʾD-AT-UM	ḪI-DA-TUM	FN	XIII 1 V 54
2243.	ḪILḪIL-UM	ḪI-EL-ḪI-LUM		SIMMONS 111 3
2244.	HILL-U	ḪI-EL-LU		M

2245.	ḪIGUL-AH	ḪI-GU-LA	FN	M+
2246.	ḪIBR-AN	Ḫ[I-I]B-RA-AN		RA LXV P. 42 III 6
2247.	ʾIDD-IM	ḪI-ID-DI-IM		XIV 56:28
2248.	ḪIʾD+LA-KA	ḪI-I[D]-LA-A?-KA		XII 141 8
2249.	ḪIʾD+LA-KA+ʾIL-I	ḪI-ID-LA-KA-I_3-LI_2		M
2250.	ḪIʾD+LA-....	ḪI-ID-L[A]-NAM		XIII 38 27
2251.	ḪILḪIL-UM	ḪI-IL-ḪI-LUM		B 48+
2252.	HILAL-IM	ḪI-IL-LA-LIM	GEN	M+
2253.	HILAL-UM	ḪI-IL-LA-LUM		M+
2254.	ḪIMʾ-AT-UM	ḪI-IM-A-TUM	FN	XIII 1 X 40
2255.	ḪIMD-IJA	ḪI-IM-DI-IA		M+
2256.	ḪIMD-I+MALIK	ḪI-IM-DI-MA-LIK		M
2257.	ḪIML-UM+....	Ḫ[I-I]M-LU-UM-[....]	FN	M
2258.	ʾIMM-AH	ḪI-IM-MA	FN	XIII 1 VI 75
2259.	ḪINN-I+ʾIL	ḪI-IN-NE-DINGIR		XIII 1 I 53
2260.	ʿIQB-AN	ḪI-IQ-BA-AN		M+
2261.	ḪIRD-IJA	ḪI-IR-DI-IA		RA LXV 53 XI 50
2262.	ḪIRṢ-U-K	ḪI-IR-ZU-UK		RA LXV 51 IX 44
2263.	ḪIRṢ-UM	ḪI-IR-ZU-UM		RA LXV 48 VIII 6
2264.	ḪIŠŠ-AT-UM	ḪI-IŠ-ŠA-TUM	FN	WATERMAN
2265.	T-HILAL+ʾAKK-A	ḪI-IT-LA-AL-AK-KA		RA LXV 54 XII 36,71
2266.	ʾITT-A+ʾABB-A	ḪI-IT-TA-D-AB-BA		M
2267.	ʿIZB-A+....	ḪI-IZ-BA-.[....]		VAS XIII 62 R. 1
2268.	ʿIZL-AH	ḪI-IZ-LA	FN	C+
2269.	ḪIṢN-AN-UM	ḪI-IZ-NA-NU-UM		WALTERS, WL 93:2, 14
2270.	ḪIṢN-I	ḪI-IZ-NI		B 20 HANA
2271.	ḪIṢN-I+DAGAN	ḪI-IZ-NI-D-DA-GAN		B 20+ HANA
2272.	ḪIZR-IJAN	ḪI-IZ-RI-IA-AN		M
2273.	HILAL-IM	ḪI-LA-LI-IM	GEN	BARRIS 71 10
2274.	ḪIʾL-AT-UM	ḪI-LA-TUM	FN	XIII 1 II 71
2275.	ḪILUK-AH	ḪI-LU?-KA	FN	XIII 1 V 81
2276.	ḪIMAR-AN	ḪI-MA-RA-AN-KI	GN	M+
2277.	ḪIMAR-UM	ḪI-MA-RUM		RA LXV 45 V 56
2278.	ḪIMD+ʾIRR-A	ḪI-ME-ID-IR_3-RA		M+
2279.	ḪIMD+ʾIRR-A	ḪI-MI-ID-D-IR_3-RA		M+
2280.	ḪIMD+KAKK-A	ḪI-MI-ID-KA-AK-KA		M
2281.	ḪINN-AN-U	ḪI-NA-NU		KISURRA 62 SEAL
2282.	ḪINN-AT-UM	ḪI-NA-TUM	FN	RA LXV 59 II 66
2283.	ḪINIʾ-I	ḪI-NI-I		XII 1 VIII 51
2284.	ḪINN-IJA	ḪI-NI-IA	FN	X 116 3
2285.	ḪIRAB-AN	ḪI-RA-BA-AN		RA LXV 42 II 57
2286.	ʾIŠUL-UM	ḪI-SU-LUM		SIMMONS 79 4'
2287.		ḪI-ŠA-LA-DA?		M+
2288.	ʿIZIL-I	ḪI-ZI-LI		C II 45 II 35
2289.	ḪUBAS-A	ḪU-BA-AZ-ZA		M+
2290.	ḪUBAS-AN	ḪU-BA-ZA-AN		M
2291.	ḪUBAS-UM	ḪU-BA-ZU-UM		TA 1931, 218
2292.	ḪUBAS-UM	ḪU-BA-ZUM		VAS VIII 14 33
2293.		ḪU-BI_2-....		I
2294.	ʾUBUŠ-UM	ḪU-BU-ŠUM		UCP X/1 34 13
2295.	ʾUBUŠ+TUʾ-KA	ḪU-BU-UŠ-TU-KA		A. 268 17
2296.	ḪUBUS	ḪU-BU-UZ		M
2297.	ḪUʾD-AN-UM	ḪU-DA-A-NU-UM		SIMMONS 83 8
2298.	ʾUDUD-UM	ḪU-DU-DU-UM		TLB I/2, 15 18+
2299.	ḪUGUL-UM	ḪU-GU-LU[M]		HARRIS 79 4
2300.	ḪUZM-ATAN	ḪU-IZ-MA-TA-AN		M
2301.	ʿIZZ-I	ḪU-IZ-ZI	FN	M
2302.	ʿUWQ-UM	ḪU-KU-UM	FN	RA LXV 58 I 51
2303.	HULAL-UM	ḪU-LA-LUM		M
2304.	ḪULAŠ-AJA	ḪU-LA-ŠA-A		HARRIS 75 22
2305.	ḪUMAD-I	ḪU-MA-DI		PINCHES, PEEK 1 4
2306.	ʿUMAS-UM	ḪU-MA-ZUM		VAS VIII 14 33
2307.	ḪUMUŠ-AT-UM	ḪU-MU-SA-TUM	MN	TCL I 62 3
2308.	ʾUNAB-AH	ḪU-NA-BA	FN	XIII 1 VI 50
2309.	ʾUNAB-AT-UM	ḪU-NA-BA-TUM	FN	WATERMAN 54 2, 3+
2310.	ʾUNAB-I	ḪU-NA-BI	NOM	GAUTIER 11 8, R. 2

2311.	ʾUNAB-UM	ḪU-NA-BU-UM		KISURRA 17 5
2312.	ḪUNN-AN-IM	ḪU-NA-NIM	GEN	B 93
2313.	ḪUNN-AN-UM	ḪU-NA-NU-UM		TA 30 615 18+
2314.	ḪUNAŠ-UM	ḪU-NA-ŠUM		BM 82432
2315.	ḪUNN-IJA	ḪU-NI-IA		UCP X/3 2:22; M
2316.	ḪUNIN-AN-UM	ḪU-NI-NA-NU-UM		I
2317.	ʾUNUB-AT-UM	ḪU-NU-BA-TUM	FN	EDZARD, DER 134:4
2318.	ʾUNUB-IM	ḪU-NU-BI-I[M]	GEN	M
2319.	ʾUNUB-UM	ḪU-NU-BU-UM		GORDON 39 5, 10
2320.	ʾUNUB-AT-UM	ḪU-NU-PA-TUM	FN?	BM 17060 35
2321.	ʾUNUB-T-UM	ḪU-NU-UB-TUM	FN	EDZARD, DER 99:8
2322.	ḪUBAD-I	ḪU-PA-DI		EDZARD, DER 101:12
2323.	ḪUBAD-UM	ḪU-PA-DU-UM		WATERMAN 14 R. 14
2324.	ḪURAṢ-AJA	ḪU-RA-ZA-A-IA	FN	XIII 1 VIII 84
2325.	ḪURAṢ-AT-UM	ḪU-RA-ZA-TUM	FN	XIII 1 I 73+
2326.	ḪURUṢ-AN	ḪU-RU-ZA-AN		RA LXV 44 IV 53+
2327.	ḪURUṢ-AN-UM	ḪU-RU-ZA-NU-UM		B 44
2328.	ḪURUṢ-UM	ḪU-RU-ZUM		RA LXV 53 XI 16
2329.	ʾUWŠ-AN-U	ḪU-SA-NU		4E RENC. ASS. P. 178 4
2330.	ʾUWŠ-AN-UM	ḪU-ŠA-A-NU-UM		KISURRA 48 8
2331.	ʾUŠAL-UM	ḪU-ŠA-LUM		HARRIS 105 5
2332.	ʾUWŠ-AN-UM	ḪU-ŠA-NU-UM		B 45+
2333.	ḪUŠŠ-UT-IM	ḪU-ŠU-TIM	FN GEN	X 27 8
2334.	ḪUŠŠ-UT-UM	ḪU-ŠU-TUM	FN	CT VI 43 6, 34
2335.	ḪUʾT-AN-UM	ḪU-TA-NU-UM		B 45
2336.	ḪUBR-AT-UM	ḪU-UB-RA-TUM	FN	XIII 1 IX 31
2337.	ʾUDM-AN-UM	ḪU-UD-MA?-NU		XII 712 R 9
2338.	ḪULM-EJA	ḪU-UL-ME-I[A]		RA LXV 41 II 46
2339.	ʾULP-AH	ḪU-UL-PA	FN	C
2340.	ḪUMR-AN-UM	ḪU-UM-RA-NU-UM		U
2341.	ḪUNN+PI+ʾEL	ḪU-UN-BI-EL		SIMMONS 82 7
2342.	ḪUNN+ḪUPŠ-I	ḪU-UN-ḪU-UP-ŠE		U
2343.	ḪUNN-AT-UM	ḪU-UN-NA-TUM	MN	CT XLV 49 8+
2344.	ḪUNN+ŠULGI	ḪU-UN-D-ŠUL-GI		U
2345.	ḪUNN+ZANZI	ḪU-UN-ZA-AN-ZI	FN	XIII 1 IX 42
2346.	ḪUNN+ZANZI	ḪU-UN-ZA-ZI	FN	XIII 1 IX 34, C
2347.	ḪUBD-AT-UM	ḪU-UP-DA-T[UM]	FN	XIII 1 VII 65
2348.	ḪUPŠ-UM	ḪU-UP-ŠUM		CT XLVIII 91 REV.
2349.	ḪURR-AN-UM	ḪU-UR-RA-NU-UM		CT IV 25C 15
2350.	ḪURṢ-AN-IM	ḪU-UR-ZA-NIM	GEN	B 44
2351.	ḪURṢ-AN-U	ḪU-UR-ZA-NU-KI	GN	A.
2352.	ḪURṢ-AN-UM	ḪU-UR-ZA-NU-UM		B 44
2353.	ḪUŠŠ-UT-UM	ḪU-UŠ$_2$-ŠU-TUM	FN	X 96 3
2354.	ḪUZM-AN-UM	ḪU-UZ-MA-N[U-UM]		TA 1931, 265
2355.	ʿUZZ-AM	ḪU-UZ-ZA-AM	ACC	XIII 100 9
2356.	ʾUZUL-IM	ḪU-UZ-ZU-LIM	GEN	GORDON 38 21+
2357.	ḪUWAL-IM	ḪU-WA-LI-IM	GEN	B 20
2358.	ḪUWAL-UM	ḪU-WA-LUM		B 20
2359.	ḪUṢAN-UM	ḪU-ZA-A-NU-UM		BIN VII 101:3
2360.	ʿUZAB-U	[ḪU]-ZA-BU	FN	XIII 1 XIV 14
2361.	ʿUZAL-AT-UM	ḪU-ZA-LA-TUM	FN	WATERMAN 12 R. 7+
2362.	ʿUZAL-AT-UM	ḪU-ZA-LA-TUM	MN	UCP X/1 86 4+
2363.	ʿUZAL-IJA	ḪU-ZA-LI-IA		BIROT, TEA 70BIS:36'
2364.	ʿUZAL-UM	ḪU-ZA-LUM		UCP X/1 17 14+
2365.	ḪUZAM-I	ḪU-ZA-MI		BE VI/2 138 18
2366.	ḪUṢAN-I	ḪU-ZA-NI	NOM	B 45
2367.	ḪUṢAN-U	ḪU-ZA-NU		M
2368.	ḪUʾZ-AN-UM	ḪU-ZA-NU-UM		RA LXV 55 XIII 13+
2369.	ḪUZIR-AN	ḪU-ZI-RA-AN		RA LXV 50 VIII 67+
2370.	ḪUZIR-AN-UM	ḪU-ZI-RA-NU-UM		B 45
2371.	ḪUZIR-AT-UM	ḪU-ZI-RA-TUM		EDZARD, DER 99 REV 8
2372.		ḪU-ZU-[....]		M
2373.	ʿUZUB-UM	ḪU-ZU-BU-UM		RA VIII 75
2374.	ḪUSUD-UM	ḪU-ZU-DU-UM	FN	RA LXV 60 III 41
2375.	ḪURṢ-AN-IM	ḪUR-ZA-A-NIM	GEN	B 44
2376.	ḪURṢ-AN-IM	ḪUR-ZA-NIM	GEN	B 44

2377.	ʾIJA+ʾAB+ʾIL	I-A-AB-DINGIR		OIP XXII 262
2378.	JA-NBIʾ+NAʿIM	I-A-BI-NA-IM	NOM, GEN	BAHREIN UNPUB, POST U.
2379.	JAʾ-UM	I-A-UM		U
2380.	JA-MQUṬ-U	I-AM-KU-DU		M
2381.	JA-RBIJ+ʾIL	I-AR-BI-DINGIR		KISURRA 5A 8+
2382.	JI-BWAʾ-JA	I-BA-A-IA		C+
2383.	JI-BWAʾ+ʾIL	I-BA-AḪ-DINGIR		KISURRA 6 15
2384.	JI-JBAL+....	I-BA-AL-D-[....]		M
2385.	JI-JBAL+....	I-BA-AL-[....]	FN	M
2386.	JI-JBAL+ḤAM-UM	I-BA-AL-D-A-MU-UM		RA LXV 52 X 43
2387.	JI-JBAL+....	I-BA-AL-AN-ḪAR		XIII 1 X 43
2388.	JI-JBAL+PI+ʾIL	I-BA-AL-BI-DINGIR		M+
2389.	JI-JBAL+PI+ʾEL	I-BA-AL-BI-EL		M+
2390.	JI-JBAL+DAGAN	I-BA-AL-D-DA-GAN		M
2391.	JI-JBAL+ʾIL	I-BA-AL-DINGIR		EEMY III/4 P. 130, M+
2392.	JI-JBAL+JARAḪ	I-BA-AL-E-RA-AḪ		B 20; RA LXV 52 X 27
2393.	JI-JBAL+ʿAŠTAR	I-BA-AL-EŠ$_4$-DAR		M
2394.	JI-JBAL+HADD-U	I-BA-AL-D-IM		M+, C+
2395.	JI-JBAL+LA+ʾIL	I-BA-AL-LA-DINGIR		RA LXV 47 VII 26
2396.	JI-JBAL+PI+ʾEL	I-BA-AL-PI-EL		UCP X P. 56+
2397.	JI-BAŚIR	I-BA-AS$_2$-SI-IR		M
2398.	JI-BAʾEL+ʾABN-U	I-BA-EL-A-AB-NU		III 46 13
2399.	JI-BWAʾ-JA	I-BA-IA		C II 7 II 3
2400.	JI-JBAL-U	I-BA-LU		CT VIII 17C 11
2401.	JI-JBAL-UM	I-BA-LUM		B 21, M
2402.		I-BA-NU-UM		TA 1931, 148
2403.		I-BA-SA-X		SIMMONS 130 7
2404.	JI-BWAʾ-UM	I-BA-UM		TA 30 615
2405.	JI-JBAL+DAGAN	I-BAL-D-DA-GAN		B 20
2406.	JI-NBIʾ+DAGAN	I-BI-D-DA-GAN		M
2407.	JI-NPIḪ-U	I-BI-ḪU	FN	C
2408.	ʾIB-I+JAT-UM	I-BI-IA-TUM		TIM II 27 4
2409.	ʾIPQ+JARAḪ	I-BI-IQ-D-[EN]-ZU		M
2410.	ʾIPQ+RIʿAJ-HU	I-BI-IQ-RI-E-U$_2$		U
2411.	JI-JBIŚ+JARAḪ	I-BI-IŠ-A-RA-AḪ		DELAPORTE CCL I A 446
2412.	JI-JBIŚ+ʾIL	I-BI-IŠ-DINGIR		TA 1930, 261
2413.	JI-JBIŚ+KABID	I-BI-IŠ-GA-BI-ID		KISURRA 63A
2414.	JI-JBIŚ+ʾEL	I-BI-IŠ-I$_3$-EL		SIMMONS 70 12
2415.	JI-NBIṬ+LIʾM	I-BI-IṬ-LI-IM		ANN. ARCH. SYR. XX 74:2
2416.	ʾIB-I+LA+ʾIL-UM	I-BI-LA-I$_3$-LUM		U
2417.	JI-NBIʾ+NABUʾ-HU	I-BI-NA-BU-U$_2$		A 7685 13
2418.	ʾIBIR-AN	I-BI-RA-AN		RA LXV XIII 34
2419.	JI-BJIR-UM	I-BI-RUM		M
2420.	JI-JBIŚ-U	I-BI-ŠU	FN	BM 82359
2421.		I-BI-TUM?		M
2422.	JI-JBIŚ+ʾIL	[I-B]I$_2$-IŠ-I$_3$-IL		I
2423.	JIBUS-AT-UM	I-BU-ZA-TUM		EDZARD, DER 87:11
2424.	JI-JDAʿ+PI+ʾIL	I-DA-BI$_2$-DINGIR		I
2425.	ʾIDAD-UM	I-DA-DU-UM		WATERMAN 34 R. 13+
2426.	JI-JDAʿ+LIʾM+MA	I-DA-LIM-MA		B 21
2427.	JI-JDAʿ+MARAṢ	I-DA-MA-RA-AṢ	GN	B 21+, M
2428.	JID-AN-UM	I-DA-NU-UM		I+
2429.	ʾIDAR-AN	I-DA-RA-AN		M
2430.	JI-JDAʿ+ŚUM	I-DA-SU-UM		M
2431.	JI-JDAʿ+RAWM	I-DAḪ-RA-AM		MEISSNER 91 17
2432.	JID-I	I-DI		RA LXV 40 I 22
2433.	JI-NDIN+ʾANN-U	I-DI-AN-NU		RA LXV 51 IX 31
2434.	ʾIDID-A	I-DI-DA	MN	BE VI/1 14 30
2435.	JID-I+ʾIL	I-DI-DINGIR		M
2436.	ʾIDID-UM	I-DI-DUM		XIII 1 I 22
2437.	JID-IJA	I-DI-IA		M
2438.	JID-I+JAT-UM	I-DI-IA-TUM		M
2439.		I-DI-IM-ME-NI	FN	M+
2440.	JID-IJAN	I-DI-JA-AN		RA LXV 47 VII 54
2441.	JI-DJIN-IM	I-DI-NIM	GEN	M
2442.	JI-NDIN+ʾABB-A	I-DIN-AB-BA		XIII 1 VIII 46

2443.	JI-NDIN+ʾADM-U	I-DIN-D-AD-MU		M+
2444.	JI-NDIN+ʾAKK-A	I-DIN-AK-KA		XIII 1 I 54+
2445.	JI-NDIN+ʾANN-U	I-DIN-AN-NU		M+
2446.	JI-NDIN+ʾANN-UM	I-DIN-AN-NU-UM		M+
2447.	JI-NDIN+ʾA-ŠKUR	I-DIN-D-AŠ$_2$-KU-UR		SYRIA XXXVII 206 8 HANA
2448.	JI-NDIN+BIN-UM	I-DIN-BI-NU-UM		UCP X/1 64 2
2449.	JI-NDIN+DAGAN	I-DIN-D-DA-GAN		M+
2450.	JI-NDIN+DIWR-IT-IM	I-DIN-D-DI-RI-TIM	GEN	M
2451.	JI-NDIN+JI-TWUR+MEʾR	I-DIN-D-I-DUR-ME-ER		XIII 1 III 49+
2452.	JI-NDIN-JA	I-DIN-IA		M
2453.	JI-NDIN+JAT-AM	I-DIN-IA-TAM	ACC	XIV 64:7
2454.	JI-NDIN+JAT-IM	I-DIN-IA-TIM	GEN	M+
2455.	JI-NDIN+JAT-UM	I-DIN-IA-TUM		M+
2456.	JI-NDIN+....	I-DIN-D-IGI-KUR		M+
2457.	JI-NDIN+KAKK-A	I-DIN-KA-AK-KA		M+
2458.	JI-NDIN+KAKK-A	I-DIN-D-KA-KA		M+
2459.	JI-NDIN+LABW-A	I-DIN-D-LA-BA		M
2460.	JI-NDIN+MAM-A	I-DIN-D-MA-MA		M+
2461.	JI-NDIN+MEʾR	I-DIN-D-ME-ER		MAOG IV 2 2 HANA
2462.	JI-NDIN+RIWM	I-DIN-D-RI-IM		TCL I 238 16 HANA
2463.	JI-NDIN+RUŠP-AN	I-DIN-D-RU-UŠ-PA-AN		MAOG IV 2 5 HANA+
2464.	JI-NDIN+RUŠP-AN	I-DIN-D-RU-UŠ$_2$-PA-AN		MEL. SYR. I 275
2465.	JI-NDIN+TABUB-U	I-DIN-TA-BU-BU		M
2466.		I-DU-NA-SA		KISURRA 112 5
2467.	JID-U-HU	I-DU-U$_2$		RA LXV 65 VI 59
2468.	JI-TWUR+ʾAŠD-UM	I-DUR-A-AŠ-DU-UM		B 23
2469.	JI-TWUR+ʾAHL-I	I-DUR-A-LI		JCS XXIV 46 NOS. 5, 6
2470.	JI-TWUR+ʾAŠD-U	I-DUR-AŠ-DU		B 23+
2471.	JI-TWUR+ʾAŠD-U-HU	I-DUR-AŠ-DU-U$_2$		SIMMONS 90 4
2472.	JI-TWUR+ʾAŠD-UM	I-DUR-AŠ-DU-UM		B 23+
2473.	JI-TWUR+ʾAŠD-UM	I-DUR-AŠ-DUM		B 23
2474.	JI-TWUR+ʾAŠD-U	I-DUR-AŠ$_2$-DU		VAS IX 172 5, M+
2475.	JI-TWUR+ʾAŠD-U-HU	I-DUR-AŠ$_2$-DU-U$_2$		M
2476.	JI-TWUR+ʾAŠD-UM	I-DUR-AŠ$_2$-DU-UM		M+
2477.	JI-TWUR+PI+ʾIL	I-DUR-[BI]?-DINGIR		I
2478.	JI-TWUR+ḪAJJ-A	I-DUR-E$_2$-A		M
2479.	JI-TWUR+ʿADN-U	I-DUR-ḪA-AD-[NU]		B 24
2480.	JI-TWUR+ʿADN-U-HU	I-DUR-ḪA-AD-NU-U$_2$		TCL XVIII 83 6
2481.	JI-TWUR+ʿAMM-U-HU	I-DUR-ḪA-MU-U$_2$		UNPUBL.
2482.	JI-TWUR+KUʾN-U-HU	I-DUR-KU?-NU-U$_2$		VAS XIII 14 R. 10
2483.	JI-TWUR+MEʾR	D-I-DUR-ME-IR	DN	M+
2484.	JI-TWUR+NINGAL	I-DUR-D-NIN-GAL		M
2485.	JI-TWUR+ŠALIM	I-DUR-SA-LIM		YOS II 84 21 22
2486.	JI-TWUR+ŠUM-U+ʾEL	I-DUR-SU-ME-EL		KISURRA 43 5+
2487.	JE-NBIṬ+TIŠPAK	I-EN-BI-IṬ-D-TIŠPAK		JCS XXIV 49 NO. 15:3
2488.	ʾIGAR-AN	I-GA-RA-AN		RA LXV 42 III 15
2489.	JI-GJIḪ+LUʾ+MA	I-GI-E-EḪ-LU-MA		JCS XXVI 143:21 HARMAL
2490.	JI-GJID+LIʾM	I-GI-ID-LI-IM		B 21 HANA
2491.	JI-GJIḪ+LUʾ+MA	I-GI-IḪ-LU-MA		SIMMONS 60 8, 14+
2492.	JI-JʿIL+PI+ʾIL	I-ḪI-IL-BI-DINGIR		M
2493.	JI-JʿIL+DIJN-I	I-ḪI-IL-DI-NI-X?		RA LXV 48 VIII 1
2494.	JA-MRUṢ-I+ʾIL-UM	I-IA-AM-RU-UṢ-ZI-I-LU-UM		B 21
2495.	ʾIJA+ʾUMM-U	I-IA-AMA		MRS VI P. 328+
2496.	JAT+KALA	I-IA-AT-KA-LA		VAS XVI 165 5
2497.	JA-ʾGUN-UM	I-IA-GU-NU-UM		YOS XII
2498.	JAMIN-A	I-IA-MI-NA	TRIBE	M
2499.	JAT-UM	I-IA-TUM	FN	RA LXV 64 VI 31
2500.	JAT-UM+MARṢ-AT	I-IA-TUM-MA-AR-ZA-AT	FN	RA LXV 62 V 15
2501.	JA-WṢIʾ	I-IA-U$_2$-ZI	FN	XIII 1 X 29
2502.	JI-LʾIJ+DAGAN	I-IL-ḪI-D-DA-G[AN]		M
2503.	JI-JQAH+ʾIL	I-KA-AḪ-DINGIR		B 21
2504.	JI-ʿQIB-UM	I-KI-BU-UM		CT VIII 19 19+
2505.	JI-KWUN+PI-I-JA	I-KU-BI-IA		SM P. 54
2506.	JI-ʿQUB-UM	I-KU-BU-UM		KISURRA 117 7, 9+
2507.	JI-KWUN+ʾAŠAR	I-KU-UN-A-ŠAR		GORDON 38 6
2508.	JI-KWUN+BAʿL-I	I-KU-UN-BA-AḪ-LI		A. 246 33

2509.	JI-KWUN+BAʿL-I	I-KU-UN-BA-LI		A.
2510.	JI-KWUN+PI-I	I-KU-UN-BI-I		C II 2 11
2511.	JI-KWUN+ḪARAR-I	I-KU-UN-ḪA-RA-RI?	GEN	TCL I 151 4
2512.	JI-ʾKUR+BAʿL-I	I-KU-UR-BA-LI		EDZARD, DER 102:9
2513.	ʾIL-A+ʾAB-I	I-LA-A-BI		C
2514.	ʾIL-A-NI	I-LA-A-NI		A. 279 2
2515.	ʾIL-AN-UM	I-LA-A-NU-UM		B 93
2516.	JI-ʾLAP+ṮALL-U-HU	I-LA-AP-TA-LU-U$_2$		M
2517.	JI-ʾLAP+ṮALL	I-LA-AP-TI-IL		U
2518.	ʾILAR+ŠUM	I-LA-AR-ŠUM		I
2519.	ʾILAR+TAʾ-A	I-LA-AR-TA-A		M
2520.	ʾILAR+TAʾ-A	I-LA-AR-TA-ḪA		M
2521.		I-LA-AT-ḪA-[X]		HARRIS 61 7
2522.	ʾIL-A+PA-I	I-LA-BA-I		TA 1931, 499
2523.	ʾIL-A+BAʿL-U-HU	I-LA-BA-LU-U$_2$		M
2524.	ʾIL-A+BIN-I	I-LA-BI$_2$-NI		I
2525.	ʾIL-A+DAʿ-AT	I-LA-DA-ḪA-AT		SUMER V 141,3+
2526.	ʾIL-A+ʾIL	I-LA-DINGIR		B 21
2527.		I-LA-DU		A. LATE
2528.	ʾIL-A+ʾEL	I-LA-EL		RA LXV 43 IV 3
2529.	ʾIL-A+ʿAŠTAR	I-LA-EŠ$_4$-DAR		RA LXV 42 III 16+
2530.	ʾIL-A+ʿADN-U-HU	I-LA-ḪA-AD-NU-U$_2$		M
2531.	ʾIL-A+ʿADN-U-HU	I-LA-ḪA-AD-NU-U$_2$	FN	C+
2532.	ʾIL-A+ʿAMM-U	I-LA-ḪA-MU		RA LXV 42 II 77+
2533.	ʾIL-A+ʾIRR-A	[I-L]A?-IR$_3$-RA		RA LXV 47 VII 18
2534.	ʾIL-A+KABKAB-U-HU	I-LA-KAB-KA-BU-U$_2$		M+
2535.	ʾIL-A+LAʾIJ	I-LA-LA-AḪ		RA LXV IX 38,X 10
2536.	ʾIL-A+LAʾIJ	I-LA-LA-E		TA 1931,609,UR III
2537.	ʾIL-A+LAʾIJ	I-LA-LA-E-KI	GN	LAESSOE,SHEMSHARA P.77
2538.	ʾIL-A+LAʾIJ	I-LA-LA-I		TA 1931,395,UR III
2539.	ʾIL-A+LA-KA	I-LA-LA-KA		B 21+
2540.	ʾIL-A+NUN-U	I-LA-NU-NU		FIGULLA CAT. I 14029
2541.	ʾIL-AN-UM	I-LA-NU-UM		I+, B 45+
2542.	ʾIL-A+RAWḪ-I-JE	I-LA-RA-ḪI-E		M
2543.	ʾIL-A+RAWḪ-I-JA	I-LA-RA-ḪI-IA		M
2544.	ʾIL-A+ŠALIM	I-LA-SA-LIM		M, C
2545.	ʾIL-A+ŠAMAR	I-LA-ŠA-MA-AR		U
2546.	ʾIL-ATAN	I-LA-TA-AN		M
2547.	ʾIL-A+TA-RʿIŠ	I-LA-TA-RI-IŠ		B 21
2548.	ʾIL-AT-I	I-LA-TI	MN	M
2549.	JI-LEʾEJ+HADD-U	I-LE-E-D-IM		XIII 93 5
2550.	ʾIL-I+ʾILL-A	I-LI-IL-LA		A. LATE
2551.	ʾIL-I+QAʾN	I-LI-QA-AN		A. LATE
2552.	ʾIL-I+ʾUWR-I	I-LI-U$_2$-RI	FN	A.
2553.	ʾIL-I+ʾIMM-AH	I-LI$_2$-IM-MA	FN	C II 41 56, 44 57
2554.	ʾIL-U+MALIK-AJ-I	I-LU-MA-LI-KA-JI-KI	GN	XV 127
2555.	ʾIL-U-NA	I-LU-NA		RA LXV 43 III 80
2556.	ʾIL-U-NA+KIRIŠ-U	I-LU-NA-KI-RI-ŠU		XIII 8 19+
2557.	ʾIL-U-NI	I-LU-NI		M+
2558.	ʾILUR-A	I-LU-RA	GEN	A.
2559.	ʾILUR-AN	I-LU-RA-AN		A. 378 10
2560.	ʾILUR-IM	I-LU-RI-IM	GEN	B 22
2561.	ʾILUR-U	I-LU-RU		B 22
2562.	ʾILUL-A	I-LU-UL-LA		M
2563.	ʾILUL-I	I-LU-UL-LI		M
2564.	ʾIL-UM+KATAZ-I	I-LU-UM-KA-TA-ZI		RUTTEN 40 1
2565.	ʾIL-UM+MULUK	I-LU-UM-MU-LU-UK-KI	GN	XV 127
2566.	ʾIL-UM+ŠALM-A	I-LU-UM-ŠA-AL-MA		RA LXV 45 V 51
2567.	ʾIL-UM+TUŠUʿ-U	D-I-LU-UN-TU-SU-U$_2$	DN	KISURRA
2568.	ḪILUṢ-AT-UM	I-LU-ZA-TUM	FN	CT II 30 29
2569.	ʾIL-UM+ʾAB-I	I-LUM-A-BI		A.
2570.	ʾIL-UM+ʾAB-UM	I-LUM-A-BU-UM		U
2571.	ʾIMAG-U	I-MA-GU	FN	M
2572.	ʾIMIR-IN-UM	I-ME-RI-NU-UM		TA 30 615 12
2573.	ʾIMIR-UM	I-MI-RU-UM		UCP X/3 2 21
2574.		I-MU?-UT?-KI-MA-ME-ET		VIII 87 5'

2575.	ʿINAB-AN-UM	I-NA-BA-NU-UM		U
2576.	ḪINAN-UM	I-NA-NU-UM		I
2577.	JI-N-RMUK	I-NE-IR-MU-UK		M
2578.	JI-N-RMUK	I-NI-IR-MU-UK		M+
2579.	ḪINUN-AM	I-NU-NAM	NOM	SIMMONS 51 3+
2580.	JI-NWUḪ+DITAN	I-NU-UḪ-DI-TA-AN		GORDON 38 20+
2581.	JI-NWUḪ+LIBB-I	I-NU-UḪ-LI-BI		M
2582.	JI-NWUḪ+ŠAMAR	I-NU-UḪ-SA-MAR		TCL I 74 5,18
2583.	JI-NWUḪ+ŠAMAR	I-NU-UḪ$_3$-SA-MAR		BIN VII 7 4,9+
2584.	ḪINUN+ʾEL	I-NU-UN-E-EL		UET V 569 2
2585.	JI-PANIJ+ʾEL-UM	I-PA-AN-NI-E-LUM		UNPUBL.
2586.	ʾIRAḪ-I	I-RA-ḪI		RA LXV 47 VII 49+
2587.	ʾIRR-I+HADD-U	I-RI-A-DU		A.+
2588.	JI-JRID-AN-UM	I-RI-DA-NU-UM		M
2589.	JI-RḪIB	I-RI-IB		I
2590.	JI-RWIM+DAGAN	I-RI-IM-D-DA-GAN		SYRIA XXXVII 206 2 HANA
2591.	JI-RWIM+ʾILL-A	I-RI-IM-IL-LA		A. LATE
2592.	ʾIRŠ+MA+ʾAB-I	I-RI-IŠ-MA-A-BI		A.
2593.	ʾIRŠ+MA+ʾAB-I	I-RI-IŠ-MA-BI		A.
2594.	ʾIRR-I+MAʾT-U	I-RI-MA-TU		A.
2595.	JI-RWIM+ʾILL-A	I-RI-MI-IL-LA		A. LATE
2596.	JI-RWIM+ʾILL-A	I-RI-MIL-LA		A. 87 30 LATE
2597.	ʾIŠAL-I	I-SA-LI	GEN	CT VIII 44A+
2598.	JIŠʿ+DAGAN	I-SI-IḪ-D-DA-GAN		RA XLI 43 HANA
2599.	JI-NŠIʾ+DAGAN	I-SI-IḪ-D-DA-GAN		RA XLI 44 R. 6 HANA
2600.	JI-ŠJIT-NA	I-SI-IT-NA		UCP X/1 58 3
2601.	ʾIŠIM-AN-AJA	I-SI-MA-NA-A		B 22
2602.	JI-JṢIʾ+ʾAŠAR	I-ṢI-A-ŠAR		YOS VIII 108 SEAL
2603.	JI-JṢIʾ+D̠ARIʾ-JE	I-ṢI-DA-RI-E		B 22+
2604.	JI-JṢIʾ+D̠ARIʾ-JE	I-ṢI-DA-RI-E-KI	GN	B 22
2605.	JI-JṢIʾ+D̠ARIʾ-JE	I-ṢI-DA-RI-I-KI	GN	B 22
2606.	JI-JṢIʾ+QAṬAR	I-ṢI-GA-TA-AR		B 22+
2607.	JI-JṢIʾ+QAṬAR	I-ṢI-GA-TAR		B 22+
2608.	JI-JṢIʾ+ŠARR	I-ṢI-LUGAL-KI	GN	TIM III 75:3
2609.	JI-JṢIʾ+MARIʾ-JE	I-ṢI-MA-RI-E		B 22
2610.	JI-JṢIʾ+ŠALIM	I-ṢI-SA-LIM		RUTTEN 4 19+
2611.	JI-JŠAR-I	I-ŠA-RI	FN	A.
2612.	JI-JŠAR-UM	I-ŠA-RUM		C
2613.	ʾIŠAW-UM	I-ŠA-WU-UM		M
2614.	JI-JŠAR+LIʾM	I-ŠAR-LI-IM		M+, C+, CT VI 47B 17
2615.	JI-ŠJIM+ḪAJJ-A	I-ŠI-IM-E$_2$-A		M
2616.	JI-JTAR-UM	I-TA-RU-UM		B 23+
2617.	JI-JTAR+ʿADN-I	I-TAR-AD-AN		WATERMAN 41 R. 10
2618.	JI-JTAR+BEʿL-I	I-TAR-BE-LI$_2$		RA LXV 47 VII 39
2619.	JI-JTAR+ʾIL-I	I-TAR-I-LI		B 23
2620.	JI-JTAR+....	I-TAR-MA-[....]		AJSL XXXIII 229 SEAL+
2621.	JI-JTAR+MULUK	I-TAR-MU-LU-UK		B 23
2622.	JI-NTIN+HADD-U	I-TI-IN-D-IM		M
2623.	JITUM-AN-IM	I-TU-MA-NIM	GEN	B 45
2624.	JI-ʾWUŠ+ŠALIM	I-UŠ?-SA-LIM		RUTTEN 1 3
2625.	JI-HWIJ+MUT-I	I-WI-MU-TI		U
2626.	ʿIZZ-AN	I-ZA-AN		RA LXV 44 IV 35
2627.	JI-JṢIʾ+D̠ARIʾ-JE	I-ZA-AR-RI-E		UET V 202 15
2628.	ʿIZZ-AK-UM	I-ZA-KUM		B 24
2629.	ʾIZAM-AN-UM	I-ZA-MA-NU-UM		B 45
2630.	ʾIZAM-U	I-ZA?-MU	FN	M
2631.	ʿIZZ-AN-UM	I-ZA-NU-UM		U
2632.	ʿIZZ-AN-UM	I-ZA-NUM$_2$		U
2633.	JI-JṢIʾ+ʿAD-UM	I-ZI-A-DU-UM		M
2634.	JI-JṢIʾ+ʾAḪ-U	I-ZI-A-ḪU?		X 53:6
2635.	JI-JṢIʾ+ʾAḪ-UM	I-ZI-A-ḪU-UM		M+
2636.	JI-JṢIʾ+JA-JPAʿ	I-ZI-A-PA-AḪ		B 22
2637.	JI-JṢIʾ+JAPAR	I-ZI-A-PA-AR		B 22
2638.	JI-JṢIʾ+ʾAŠAR	I-ZI-A-ŠAR		B 22+
2639.	JI-JṢIʾ+ḪAJJ-UM	I-ZI-A-UM		MOORTGAT 488
2640.	JI-JṢIʾ+BANIJ-IM	I-ZI-BA-NI-IM	GEN	B 45

2641.	JI-ʿZIB-UM	I-ZI-BU-UM		KISURRA 10A 5+
2642.	JI-JṢIʾ+DAGAN	I-ZI-D-DA-GAN		B 22 HANA
2643.	JI-JṢIʾ+ḎARIʾ-JE	I-ZI-DA-RI		TCL XI 218 9
2644.	JI-JṢIʾ+ḎARIʾ-JE	I-ZI-DA-RI-E		B 22+
2645.	JI-JṢIʾ+QAṬAR	I-ZI-GA-DAR		B 22
2646.	JI-JṢIʾ+QAṬAR-I	I-ZI-GA-DAR-I		B 22
2647.	JI-JṢIʾ+QAṬAR	I-ZI-GA-TA-AR		B 22+
2648.	JI-JṢIʾ+QAṬAR	I-ZI-GA-TAR		B 22+
2649.	JI-JṢIʾ+ḪAʾL-U	I-ZI-ḪA-LU		XIV 96:9+
2650.	JI-JṢIʾ+ḪAʾR-U	I-ZI-ḪA-RU		XIV 52:5, 16+
2651.	JI-JṢIʾ+....	I-ZI-ḪI-X		B 23
2652.	JI-JṢIʾ+ʾIL-U+MA	I-ZI-I-LU-MA		B 23+
2653.	ʿIZZ-IJA	I-ZI-IA		RA LXV 51 IX 41
2654.	JI-JṢIʾ+....	I-ZI-IA-[....]		PBS XI/2 1 IX 15
2655.	JI-JṢIʾ+....	I-ZI-IA-AN?		PBS XI/2 1 IX 16
2656.	JI-JṢIʾ+JAT-UM	I-ZI-IA-TUM		B 23+
2657.	JI-JṢIʾ+....	I-ZI-IA-ZI-[....]		B 23
2658.	JI-ʿZIB-NA	I-ZI-IB-NA		CT XLV 118 24
2659.	JI-JṢIʾ+....	I-ZI-IŠ-MA-AḪ		HARRIS 7 11
2660.	JI-JṢIʾ+ḎARIʾ-JE	I-ZI-IZ-ZA-RI-E		B 23
2661.	JI-JṢIʾ+KURUB	I-ZI-KU-RU-UB		RA LXV 53 XI 11
2662.	JI-JṢIʾ+NABUʾ-HU	I-ZI-NA-BU-U$_2$		B 23+, M+
2663.	JI-JṢIʾ+NABUʾ-UM	I-ZI-NA-B[U-U]M?		VAS IX 79 5
2664.	JI-JṢIʾ+PU-K	I-ZI-PU-UK	FN?	M+
2665.	JI-JṢIʾ+QAṬAR	I-ZI-QA-TAR		XIII 1 IV 59
2666.	JI-JṢIʾ+ŠAM-U+ʾAB-UM	I-ZI-SA-MU-A-BU-UM		B 23
2667.	JI-JṢIʾ+ŠARIJ-JE	I-ZI-SA-RI-E		BIN VII 105 12
2668.	JI-JṢIʾ+ŠUM-U-JA	I-ZI-SU-MU-A		KISURRA 112 7
2669.	JI-JṢIʾ+ŠUM-U+ʾAB-IM	I-ZI-SU-MU-A-BI-IM	GEN	B 23
2670.	JI-JṢIʾ+ŠUM-U+ʾAB-UM	I-ZI-SU-MU-A-BU-UM		B 23+
2671.	JI-JṢIʾ+ŠUM-U-HU	I-ZI-SU-MU-U$_2$		A 7646 3+
2672.	JI-JṢIʾ+ŠUM-UM	I-ZI-SU-MU-UM		B 23, M+
2673.	JI-JṢIʾ+ŠARR	I-ZI-ŠAR		B 22
2674.	JI-JṢIʾ+ŠARR-UM	I-ZI-ŠAR-RUM-KI	GN	SUMER III 79 VI 197+
2675.	JI-JṢIʾ+TAMB-U	I-ZI-TA-AM-BU		BAHREIN UNPUB, POST-U.
2676.	JI-JṢIʾ+....	I-ZI-TA?-KAM		B 23
2677.	ʿIZIZ-AH	I-ZI-ZA	FN	RA LXV 58 I 28
2678.	JI-JṢIʾ+ḎARIʾ-JE	I-ZI-ZA-RI-E		B 23+, M
2679.	JI-JṢIʾ+ṢARIR-UM	I-ZI-ZA-RI-RUM		CT XLV 115 18
2680.	ʿIZZ-U-KA	I-ZU-KA		XIII 1 III 50
2681.	ʿIZZ-U+ŠAPAR	I-ZU-SA-PAR$_2$		U+
2682.	JI-NṢUR+ʾAŠD-UM	I-ZUR-A-AŠ-DU-UM		CT II 42 25
2683.	JI-NṢUR+ʾAŠD-UM	I-ZUR-AŠ-DU-UM		A 7685 5
2684.	ʾIL-I+HEDD-A	I$_3$-LI-E-DA		A.
2685.	ʾIL-I+MA+ʾAB-I	I$_3$-LI-MA-A-BI		M+
2686.	ʾIL-I+JA-MLIK	I$_3$-LI$_2$-A-AM-LIK		HARRIS 49 12
2687.	ʾIL-I+JAT	I$_3$-LI$_2$-A-AT?		TA 1931, 261
2688.	ʾIL-I+JAT-KA	I$_3$-LI$_2$-A-AT-KA		TIM III 10 14+
2689.	ʾIL-I+HADD-U	I$_3$-LI$_2$-A-DU		A. 57 47
2690.	ʾIL-I+ʾAP-I-JA	I$_3$-LI$_2$-A-PI?-A		TIM III 4 14
2691.	ʾIL-I+ʾAŠIJ-AH	I$_3$-LI$_2$-A-SI-IA	FN	XIII 1 VII 55
2692.	ʾIL-I+ʾATAJ-A-JA	I$_3$-LI$_2$-A-TA-A-IA		RA VIII 69 26
2693.	ʾIL-I+JATAR	I$_3$-LI$_2$-A-TAR		B 21+
2694.	ʾIL-I+JAʾ-UM	I$_3$-LI$_2$-A-UM		B 21
2695.	ʾIL-I+ʾA-ḪTAN	I$_3$-LI$_2$-AḪ-TA-AN		RUTTEN 6 16+
2696.	ʾIL-I+ʾA-PTAN	I$_3$-LI$_2$-AP-TA-AN		B 21
2697.	ʾIL-I+JAQR-A	I$_3$-LI$_2$-AQ-RA		IRAQ XXX 90, RIMAH
2698.	ʾIL-I+ʾAŠR-A-JA	I$_3$-LI$_2$-AŠ-RA-IA		M+
2699.	ʾIL-I+BAWŠ-T-I	I$_3$-LI$_2$-BA-AŠ$_2$-TI	FN	M+
2700.	ʾIL-I+BAWB-UM	I$_3$-LI$_2$-BA-BU-UM		U UNPUBL.
2701.	ʾIL-I+BIN-A-JA	I$_3$-LI$_2$-BI-NA-A-IA		M+
2702.	ʾIL-I+ṬAJB-A	I$_3$-LI$_2$-DA-[B]A		A. 96 R. 10
2703.	ʾIL-I+DAGAN	I$_3$-LI$_2$-D-DA-GAN		M+
2704.	ʾIL-I+DIʿ-AT	I$_3$-LI$_2$-DI-ḪA-[AT]		HARRIS 39 19
2705.	ʾIL-I+DITAN	I$_3$-LI$_2$-DI-TA-AN		BM 82424 R. 18
2706.	ʾIL-I+JE-JPAʿ	I$_3$-LI$_2$-E-PA		A.+

2707.	ʾIL-I+JE-JPUʿ	I$_3$-LI$_2$-E-PU-UḪ		M+
2708.	ʾIL-I+JARAḪ	I$_3$-LI$_2$-E-RA-AḪ		M+, TIM III 133 4, SEAL
2709.	ʾIL-I+JE-JŠUʿ	I$_3$-LI$_2$-E-ŠU-UḪ		B 21 M
2710.	ʾIL-I+JATAR	I$_3$-LI$_2$-E-TAR		M+
2711.	ʾIL-I+ʿAŠTAR	I$_3$-LI$_2$-EŠ$_4$-DAR		M+
2712.	ʾIL-I+GUML-I-JA	I$_3$-LI$_2$-GU-UM-LI-IA		XIII 1 VIII 45
2713.	ʾIL-I+ʿADN-I	I$_3$-LI$_2$-ḪA-AD-NI	FN	M
2714.	ʾIL-I+ḪAṢN-A-JA	I$_3$-LI$_2$-ḪA-AṢ-NA-A-IA		M+
2715.	ʾIL-I+ḪAṢN-I-JA	I$_3$-LI$_2$-ḪA-AṢ-NI-IA		XIII 1 IX 8
2716.	ʾIL-I+ḪAʾL-UM	I$_3$-LI$_2$-ḪA-LU-UM		CT XLV 3 10
2717.	ʾIL-I+ʿAMM-U	I$_3$-LI$_2$-ḪA-MU		RA LVII 178
2718.	ʾIL-I+ḪUMUD-I	I$_3$-LI$_2$-ḪU-MU-DI		M
2719.	ʾIL-I+JAT-UM	I$_3$-LI$_2$-I-IA-TUM		VAS XVIII 83:15
2720.	ʾIL-I+ʾIL-A	I$_3$-LI$_2$-I-LA		A. LATE
2721.	ʾIL-I+ʿIJN-A-JA	I$_3$-LI$_2$-I-NA-A-A		GAUTIER 40 7
2722.	ʾIL-I+ʾITEJ-JE	I$_3$-LI$_2$-I-TE-E		MEISSNER 110 20, 23+, M
2723.	ʾIL-I+JAʾ-UM	I$_3$-LI$_2$-I-U$_2$-UM		KISURRA 56 3+
2724.	ʾIL-I+JAʾ-UM	I$_3$-LI$_2$-I-UM		KISURRA 4A 12+
2725.	ʾIL-IJA	I$_3$-LI$_2$-IA		M+
2726.	ʾIL-I+JA-MWUT	I$_3$-LI$_2$-IA-MU-[UT]		RA LXV 40 I 29
2727.	ʾIL-I+JAʾN-UM	I$_3$-LI$_2$-IA-NU-UM		TIM I 29 3
2728.	ʾIL-I+JARAḪ	I$_3$-LI$_2$-IA-RA-AḪ		SIMMONS 131 20
2729.	ʾIL-I+JAʾ-UM	I$_3$-LI$_2$-IA-UM		KISURRA 71A 5+
2730.	ʾIL-I+JI-ḪNUW-HU	I$_3$-LI$_2$-IḪ-NU-U$_2$		UCP X/1 19:4+
2731.	ʾIL-I+JI-ḪTAʾ+LI-JA	I$_3$-LI$_2$-IḪ-TA-LI-A		BIROT,TEA 69 I 14
2732.	ʾIL-I+HADD-U	I$_3$-LI$_2$-D-IM		M+
2733.	ʾIL-I-Š+BAʾB-A	I$_3$-LI$_2$-IŠ-BA-BA		HSM 7934, UR III
2734.	ʾIL-I+JI-ŠPIQ	I$_3$-LI$_2$-IŠ-BI-IK		TA 1931, 71
2735.	ʾIL-I-Š+GAʾUL-U	I$_3$-LI$_2$-IŠ-GA-U$_2$-LU		KISURRA 70A 17+
2736.	ʾIL-I-Š+KUTUL	I$_3$-LI$_2$-IŠ-KU-TU-UL		KISURRA 75A 18+
2737.	ʾIL-I+JI-ŠMAʿ-NIA	I$_3$-LI$_2$-IŠ-MA-NI-A		TA 1930,399
2738.	ʾIL-I+JI-T-ŠAMAR	I$_3$-LI$_2$-IŠ-TA-MAR		EDZARD,DER 67:11
2739.	ʾIL-I+KABKAB-U	I$_3$-LI$_2$-KA-AB-KA-BU		A 21914 3
2740.	ʾIL-I+KAʾB-I	I$_3$-LI$_2$-KA-PI		BIROT, TEA 69:28
2741.	ʾIL-I+KAŠAR	I$_3$-LI$_2$-KA-ŠA-AR		M
2742.	ʾIL-I+KUWN	I$_3$-LI$_2$-KU-UN		RA LXV 55 XIII 32
2743.	ʾIL-I+LIʾM	I$_3$-LI$_2$-LI-IM		M+, C
2744.	ʾIL-I+MAʾD-A	I$_3$-LI$_2$-MA-DA		TA 30 615 6
2745.	ʾIL-I+MAṬAR	I$_3$-LI$_2$-MA-DA-AR		M
2746.	ʾIL-I+MAʾD-I+ʾAḪ-A	I$_3$-LI$_2$-MA-DA-ḪA		VAS VIII 14 4
2747.	ʾIL-I+MAʾD-I+ʾAḪ-I	I$_3$-LI$_2$-MA-DA-ḪI		RUTTEN 14 7
2748.	ʾIL-I+MAʾD-I	I$_3$-LI$_2$-MA-DI		SIMMONS 33 19
2749.	ʾIL-I+MAʾD-I+ʾAḪ	I$_3$-LI$_2$-MA-DI-A-AḪ		RUTTEN 1 8
2750.	ʾIL-I+MALIK	I$_3$-LI$_2$-MA-LIK		M
2751.	ʾIL-I+MAṬAR	I$_3$-LI$_2$-MA-TA-AR		B 21
2752.	ʾIL-I+MAṬAR	I$_3$-LI$_2$-MA-TAR		M
2753.	ʾIL-I+MAʾD-I+ʾAḪ	I$_3$-LI$_2$-MI-DI-AḪ		EDZARD,DER 146:14
2754.	ʾIL-I+MIWT-I	I$_3$-LI$_2$-MI-TI		I
2755.	ʾIL-I+MILK-U	I$_3$-LI$_2$-MIL-KU	FN	RA LXV 58 I 31
2756.	ʾIL-I+NATUN	I$_3$-LI$_2$-NA-TU-UN		M
2757.	ʾIL-I+NIʿM	I$_3$-LI$_2$-NE-ḪI-IM		M
2758.	ʾIL-I+NIWR-I	I$_3$-LI$_2$-NE-RI	FN	XIII 1 II 6+
2759.	ʾIL-I+PAʾAL-UM	I$_3$-LI$_2$-PA-A-LU-UM		TIM III 44 16+
2760.	ʾIL-I+PAʾAL-UM	I$_3$-LI$_2$-PA-ḪA-LUM		M
2761.	ʾIL-I+RAWḪ-I-JE	I$_3$-LI$_2$-RA-AḪ-E		VAS XVI 168 9, FRANK 13 9
2762.	ʾIL-I+RAWM	I$_3$-LI$_2$-RA-AM		M
2763.	ʾIL-I+RAPIʾ	I$_3$-LI$_2$-RA-BI		M+
2764.	ʾIL-I+RAŠAP	I$_3$-LI$_2$-D-RA-SA-[AP]		XIII 66 5
2765.	ʾIL-I+RIḪṢ-I	I$_3$-LI$_2$-RI-IḪ-ZI	FN	XIII 1 IX 39
2766.	ʾIL-I+ŠAMŠ	I$_3$-LI$_2$-SA-MA-AŠ$_2$		M
2767.	ʾIL-I+ŠAMUʿ	I$_3$-LI$_2$-SA-MU-UḪ		XIII 21 11'
2768.	ʾIL-I+ŠUM-U	I$_3$-LI$_2$-SU-U$_2$-MU		M
2769.	ʾIL-I+ŠAKIM	I$_3$-LI$_2$-ŠA-KI-IM		RA LXV 40 I 44+
2770.	ʾIL-I+ŠIMḪ-A-JA	I$_3$-LI$_2$-ŠE-IM-ḪA-IA		VIII 57 14
2771.	ʾIL-I+ŠIMḪ-A-JA	I$_3$-LI$_2$-ŠI-IM-ḪA-IA		VIII 57 BIS 16
2772.	ʾII-I+ŠIMḪ-I	I$_3$-LI$_2$-ŠI-IM-ḪI		M+

2773.	ʾIL-I+TA-NWUḪ	I$_3$-LI$_2$-TA-NU		RA LXV 45 V 52
2774.	ʾIL-I+TA-NWUḪ	I$_3$-LI$_2$-TA-NU-UḪ		XIII I IV 19
2775.	ʾIL-I+TUWR-A	I$_3$-LI$_2$-TU-RA		M+
2776.	ʾIL-I+TUWR-A-JA	I$_3$-LI$_2$-TU-RA-[I]A		RA LXV 40 I 45
2777.	ʾIL-I+TUWR-I-JA	I$_3$-LI$_2$-TU-RI-IA		XII 115 5+
2778.	ʾIL-I+JAʾ-UM	I$_3$-LI$_2$-U$_2$-A-UM		KISURRA 186 5
2779.	ʾIL-I+ḪUNIN-I	I$_3$-LI$_2$-U$_2$-NE-NI		RUTTEN 6 20
2780.	ʾIL-I+ZANN-I	I$_3$-LI$_2$-ZA-AN-NI	FN	M+
2781.	ʾIL-I+ṢADUQ	I$_3$-LI$_2$-ZA-DU-UQ		M+
2782.	ʾIL-I+ṢIDQ-I	I$_3$-LI$_2$-ZI-ID-KI		DELAPORTE CCL II A 337
2783.	ʾIL-I+ṢIDQ-UM	I$_3$-LI$_2$-ZI-ID-KUM		UCP X/1 100 7
2784.	JAʾ-A+ʿAN-UM	IA-A-A-NU-UM		YOS V 134 16
2785.	JAʾ-AT-UM	IA-A-A-TUM	MN	A 29366:3
2786.	JAʾAR	IA-A-AR		M
2787.	JA-ḪJIJ+ʾIL	IA-A-ḪI-DINGIR		XIII 65 5
2788.	JA-KWUN-UM	IA-A-KU-NU-UM		B 27
2789.	JA-MWUŠ-I+ʾIL	IA-A-MU-ŠI-DINGIR		VAS VII 166 4 LATE
2790.	JAʾAN-AM	IA-A-NA-AM		M
2791.	JAʾAN-UM	IA-A-NU-UM		BIN VII 67 9
2792.	JA-JPAʿ	IA-A-PA-AḪ		M+
2793.	JA-JPAʿ+HADD-U	IA-A-PA-AḪ-D-IM		M+
2794.	JA-JPAʿ+LIʾM	IA-A-PA-AḪ-LI-IM		M+
2795.	JAʾAR-UM	IA-A-RUM		VAS VII 183 I 7, II 12+
2796.	JAʾ-UM	IA-A-UM		BIN VII 67 27
2797.	JAʾ-UM+ʾIL	IA-A-UM-[DINGIR]		B 31
2798.	JA-ʿZIB-I+ʾIL	IA-A-ZI-BI-DINGIR		KAJ 34 18, 25 LATE
2799.	JA-BANIJ+ʾIL	IA-AB-BA-AN-NI-DINGIR		M
2800.	JA-NBIʾ+DAGAN	IA-AB-BI-D-DA-GAN		M+
2801.	JA-NBIʾ+HADD-U	IA-AB-BI-D-IM		M
2802.	JA-BḪAR+....	IA-AB-ḪA-AR-[....]		M
2803.	JA-BḪAR+HADD-U	IA-AB-ḪA-AR-D-IM		M
2804.	JA-BḪAR-UM	IA-AB-ḪA-RU-UM		B 24
2805.		IA-AB-KU-BA-AT		VAS XVI 58:3
2806.	JA-BLIJ-JA	IA-AB-LI-IA-KI	GN	M+
2807.	JA-BLIJ-AT-UM	IA-AB-LI-IA-TUM	FN	B 25+
2808.	JA-BLUW+DAGAN	IA-AB-LU-D-DA-GAN		M
2809.	JA-BLUṬ-AN-U	IA-AB-LU-TA-NU		MRS VI P. 261+
2810.	JA-BNIJ+DAGAN	IA-AB-NI-D-DA-GAN		M+
2811.	JA-BNIJ+HADD-U	IA-AB-NI-D-IM		M
2812.	JA-BNIQ+ʾIL	IA-AB-NI-IQ-DINGIR		B 25
2813.	JA-BRUQ+ʾIL	IA-AB-RU-UQ-DINGIR		BASOR 95, 19
2814.	JA-BRUQ+LIʾM	IA-AB-RU-UQ-LI-IM		TCL XI 156 12
2815.	JA-T-BAḪAR-NA	IA-AB-TA-ḪA-AR-NA	GN	M+
2816.	JABS-AT-UM	IA-AB-ZA?-TUM	MN?	VAS VIII 121 5
2817.	JA-BZUW-HU	IA-AB-ZU-U$_2$		CT IV 30D 10+
2818.	JA-ḎKUR+ʾIL	IA-AD-GUR-DINGIR		SUMER V 142 8+
2819.	JA-ḎKUR+ʾIL	IA-AD-KU?-UR?-DINGIR		VAS IX 58 15
2820.	JA-ḎKUR+ʾIL	IA-AD-KUR-DINGIR		SUMER V 141
2821.	JADN-U	IA-AD-NU		M
2822.	JA-DRUK-A	IA-AD-RU-QA		A. LATE
2823.	JA-GMUR+....	IA-AG-MU-UR-[....]		M
2824.	JA-GMUR+ʾIL	IA-AG-MU-UR-DINGIR		M
2825.	JA-ʿZIB+ʾIL	IA-AH-ZI-IB-DINGIR		RUTTEN 21 7+, M
2826.	JA-ḪBAS+ʾIL	IA-AḪ-BA-AZ-DINGIR		CT II 39 18+
2827.	JA-ḪBAʾ+RAŠAP	IA-AḪ-BA-D-RA-SA-AP		XIII 94 5
2828.	JA-ḪBIʾ+ʾIL-A	IA-AḪ-BI-LA-KI	GN	M+
2829.	JA-ḪBIS-UM	IA-AḪ-BI-ZUM		GORDON 38 3
2830.	JA-ḪBUʾ-UM	IA-AḪ-BU-U$_2$-UM		M
2831.	JA-ʿDUN+LIʾM	IA-AḪ-DU-LI-IM		M+
2832.	JA-ʿDUN-AN-UM	IA-AḪ-DU-NA-NU-UM		JCS XXIV 60 NO.51 REV.
2833.	JA-ʿDUN-UM	IA-AḪ-DU-NU-UM		B 26
2834.	JA-ʿDUN+LIʾM	IA-AḪ-DU-UL-LI-IM		M
2835.	JA-ʿDUN+LIʾM	IA-AḪ-DU-UN-LI-IM		M+
2836.	JA-ʾGUN-UM	IA-AḪ-GU-NU-UM		TLB IV 82:1
2837.	JA-ʾGUN	IA-AḪ-GU-UN		TCL XVII 25 1
2838.	JA-ʾGUN-I	IA-AḪ-GU-UN-NI	GEN	TCL XVII 26 1

2839.	JA-ʾGUN-UM	IA-AḪ-GU-UN-NU-UM		TCL XVII 24 1
2840.	JA-NḪAB+ʾIL	IA-AḪ-ḪA-AB-DINGIR		C+
2841.	JA-ʿQUB-I+ʾIL	IA-AḪ-KU-BI-DINGIR		CT II 39 18
2842.	JA-ʾQUD-UM	IA-AḪ-KU-DU-UM		CT XXXIII 29 14
2843.	JA-ḪKUM-UM	IA-AḪ-KU-MU-UM		B 26
2844.	JA-ʿQUB+ʾIL	IA-AḪ-KU-UB-DINGIR		XIII 1 VII 17, C+
2845.	JA-ʾKUR+ʾIL	IA-AḪ-KU-UR-DINGIR		CT XLV 6 24
2846.	JA-ḪLIJ+ʾIL	IA-AḪ-LI-DINGIR		B 26
2847.	JA-ḪMAD-UM	IA-AḪ-MA-DU-UM		CT XLV 5 7
2848.	JA-ʾMIʾ+ʾIL	IA-AḪ-MI-DINGIR		PBS XI/2 P. 120 NO. 92
2849.	JA-ʿMIS+ʾIL	IA-AḪ-MI-IS-DINGIR		RUTTEN 2 23+
2850.	JA-ʿMIS+JARAḪ	IA-AḪ-MI-IS-D-SIN		M
2851.	JA-ʿMIS+ʾIL-UM	IA-AḪ-MI-ZI-LUM		RUTTEN 16 17
2852.	JA-ḪMUṬ-AN	IA-AḪ-MU-DA-AN		M
2853.	JA-ʾMUW+DAGAN	IA-AḪ-MU-D-DA-GAN	GN	B 26
2854.	JA-ʿMUS+....	IA-AḪ-MU-IS-[....]		XIV 129:5
2855.	JA-ḪMUM-AM	IA-AḪ-MU-MA-AM-KI	GN ACC	M
2856.	JA-ḪMUM-IM	IA-AḪ-MU-MI-IM	GN GEN	M
2857.	JA-ḪMUṬ-U	IA-AḪ-MU-TU		JEAN, TELL SIFR 13 15
2858.	JA-ḪMUṬ-UM	IA-AḪ-MU-TU-UM-KI	GN	UET V 9721
2859.	JA-ʾMUW-HU	IA-AḪ-MU-U_2		B 26
2860.	JA-ʿMUS+ʾIL	IA-AḪ-MU-US-DINGIR		M
2861.	JA-ʿNIJ+ʾIL	IA-AḪ-NI-DINGIR		A 7630 6
2862.	JA-ʿNUW-HU	IA-AḪ-NU-U_2		OIP XLVII 66
2863.	JA-ʾRUR-A	IA-AḪ-RU-RA-KI	GN	B 26, M
2864.	JA-ʾRUR-IJ-I	IA-AḪ-RU-RI-I-KI	GN	M
2865.	JA-ʾRUR-UM	IA-AḪ-RU-RU-UM	GN	B 26+
2866.	JA-ʾRUR-UM	IA-AḪ-RU-RUM		BM 80328 10
2867.	JA-ʾRUR-UM	IA-AḪ-RU-RUM	GN	B 26+
2868.	JA-ʾRUR	IA-AḪ-RU-UR-KI	GN	M
2869.	JA-ʾRUŠ	IA-AḪ-RU-UŠ		RA LXV 55 XIII 52
2870.	JA-ḪŠIJ+ʾIL	IA-AḪ-SI-DINGIR		OLZ VIII 350 2
2871.	JA-HWIJ+ʾIL	IA-AḪ-WI-DINGIR		B 27+
2872.	JA-HWIJ+ʾIL-I	IA-AḪ-WI-DINGIR-LI_2		KISURRA 6+
2873.	JA-HWIJ+KI+HADD-U	[IA-A]Ḫ-WI-KI-D-IM		M
2874.	JA-HWIJ+NAŠIʾ	IA-AḪ-WI-NA-SI		M+
2875.	JA-HWIJ-UM	IA-AḪ?-WI?-UM?		B 32
2876.	JA-ʿḎAR+ʾIL	IA-AḪ-ZA-AR-DINGIR		B 26
2877.	JA-ʿḎAR+ʾIL	IA-AḪ-ZA-AR-I_3-IL		B 26
2878.	JA-ʿZIB-A+ʾEL	IA-AḪ-ZI-BA-EL?		RA LXV 50 VIII 77
2879.	JA-ʿZIB-I+ʾIL	IA-AḪ-ZI-BI-DINGIR		KISURRA 86A 11
2880.	JA-ʿZIB-U-HU	IA-AḪ-ZI-BU-U_2		M+
2881.	JA-ʾZIJ+DAGAN	IA-AḪ-ZI-D-DA-GAN		RA LXV 54 XII 52
2882.	JA-ʾZIJ+ʾIL	IA-AḪ-ZI-DINGIR		M
2883.	JA-ʾZIJ+ʾIL-I	IA-AḪ-ZI-I_3-LI_2		TCL X 21 13
2884.	JA-ʿZIB+....	IA-AḪ-ZI-IB-[....]		M
2885.	JA-ʿZIB+HADD-U	IA-AḪ-ZI-IB-D-IM		M+
2886.	JA-ḪZIM+....	IA-AḪ-ZI-IM-[....]		M
2887.	JA-ḤṢIN+DAGAN	IA-AḪ-ZI-IN-D-DA-GAN		M
2888.	JA-ḤṢIN+ḤAJJ-A	IA-AḪ-ZI-IN-E_2-A		XIII 1 VII 23
2889.	JA-ḤṢIN+ʾIRR-A	IA-AḪ-ZI-IN-IR_3-RA		M
2890.	JA-ʿḎIR	IA-AḪ-ZI-IR		YOS VIII 76 26
2891.	JA-ʿḎIR+ʾIL	IA-AḪ-ZI-IR-DINGIR		B 26+
2892.	JA-ʿḎIR+ʾIL	IA-AḪ-ZI-IR-I_3-DINGIR		CT XLV 8 6
2893.	JA-ʿḎIR+ʾIL	IA-AḪ-ZI-IR-I_3-IL		SUMER V 137
2894.	JA-ʿḎIR-I	IA-AḪ-ZI-RI	GEN	BM 16943 34
2895.	JA-ʿḎIR-U	IA-AḪ-ZI-RU		CT XLV 63 34
2896.	JA-ʿḎIR-UM	IA-AḪ-ZI-RUM		B 26+
2897.	JA-ḪZUM-U	IA-AḪ-ZU?-MU		BM 78799 12
2898.	JA-ʾZUW+RAŚAP	IA-AḪ-ZU-D-RA-SA-AP		M
2899.	JA-ʿZUB+ʾIL	IA-AḪ-ZU-UB-DINGIR		B 26+
2900.	JA-ḤṢUN+ʾIL	IA-AḪ-ZU-UN-DINGIR		BE VI/1 7 18
2901.	JA-ḪZUQ+ʾIL	IA-AḪ-ZU?-UQ-DINGIR		CT XLVIII 10 3
2902.	JA-ḪZUR+ʾIL	IA-AḪ-ZU-UR-DINGIR		JCS XXIV 57 NO 39 AND 51
2903.	JA-ḪZUR+ʾIL	IA-AḪ-ZU-UR-IL		TIM III 34 15A
2904.	JA-ḪZUR+HADD-U	IA-AḪ-ZU-UR-D-IM		M

2905.	JA-KBUR-IM	IA-AK-BU-RI-IM	GEN	B 27
2906.	JA-NQIM+HADD-U	IA-AK-KI-IM-D-IM		M+
2907.	JA-NQIM+LIʾM	IA-AK-KI-IM-LI-IM		M
2908.	JA-ʿQUB+HEDD-A	IA-AK-KU-UB-E-DA		JEA VIII 207F.
2909.	JA-KMIN-I	IA-AK-ME-NI		JNES XIII 210+ LATE
2910.	JA-KMIS-I	IA-AK-ME-SI		JCS XIII 210+ LATE
2911.	JA-KNUW+ŠARR-U	IA-AK-NU-ŠA-RU		TIM III 133 9
2912.	JA-KNUW+ŠARR-UM	IA-AK-NU-ŠA-RU-UM		KISURRA 47A 4+
2913.	JA-KRUB+ʾIL	D-IA-AK-RU-UB-DINGIR	DN	M+
2914.	JA-KRUB+ʾIL+TILL-AT-I	D-IA-AK-RU-UB-DINGIR-TIL-LA-TI		M
2915.	JA-KRUB+ʾEL	D-IA-AK-RU-UB-EL	DN	M+
2916.	JA-KRUB+ʾIL	D-IA-AK-RU-UB-IL	DN	M+
2917.	JA-KŠIJ+....	IA-AK-SI-DINGIR-....		DE GEN. KICH II D47+
2918.	JA-KSIJ+ʾIL	IA-AK-ZI-DINGIR		SIMMONS 92 16
2919.	JA-LʾAʾ+KULIM	IA-AL-A-KU-LIM		RA LXV 55 XIII 18
2920.	JA-LʾIJ	IA-AL-E		RA LXV 46 VI 50
2921.	JA-LʾIJ+DAGAN	IA-AL-E-D-DA-GAN		M+
2922.	JA-LʾIJ+JA-JPAʿ	IA-AL-E-PA-AḪ		M
2923.	JALQUṮ-UM	IA-AL-GU-TUM		BIN II 68 18
2924.	JA-LʾIJ+DAGAN	IA-[AL]?-I-D-DA-GAN		RA LXV 47 VII 23
2925.	JA-LʾUM-U	IA-AL-U$_2$-MU		XIII 36 20
2926.	JA-MʾAD	IA-AM-A-AD	GN	A. 377 8
2927.	JA-T-MAQAṮ	IA-AM-DA-GA-AD		B 28
2928.	JA-MʾAD	IA-AM-ḪA-AD-KI	GN	M+
2929.	JA-MʾAD-AJ-I	IA-AM-ḪA-DA-I-KI	GN GEN	M
2930.	JA-MʾAD-IJ-I	IA-AM-ḪA-DI-I-KI	GN NOM	M
2931.	JA-MʾAD-IM	IA-AM-ḪA-DI-IM-KI	GN GEN	M+
2932.	JA-MʾAD-IJ-I	IA-AM-ḪA-DI-JI	GN NOM	M
2933.	JA-MʾAD-U	IA-AM-ḪA-DU	GN	XII 747 4
2934.	JA-MʾAD-UM	IA-AM-ḪA-DU-UM-KI	GN	M+
2935.	JA-MʾID+ʾADM-I	IA-AM-I-ID-D-AD-MI		A. 60 4
2936.	JA-MQUṮ-U	IA-AM-KU-DU		M
2937.	JA-MKUS-U+....	IA-AM-KU-UZ-ZU-....		BM 80328 3
2938.	JA-MLIK+ʾIL	IA-AM-LI-IK-DINGIR		B 28+
2939.	JA-MLIK-AN	IA-AM-LI-KA-AN		M
2940.	JA-MLIK+ʾIL	IA-AM-LIK-DINGIR		B 28+, M
2941.	JA-MLIK+HADD-U	IA-AM-LIK-D-IM		RA LXV 40 I 31
2942.	JAMM-AJA	IA-AM-MA-A		B 28+
2943.	JAMM-AJA	IA-AM-MA-A-IA	FN	C+
2944.	JAMM-AN	IA-AM-MA-AN		YOS XIII 514:6
2945.	JAMM-U+QAʾD-UM	IA-AM-MU?-QA-DU-UM		III 56 7
2946.	JAMM-U-HU	IA-AM-MU-U$_2$		VAS XVIII 19 R. 6
2947.	JAMN-ATAN	IA-AM-NA-TA-AN		RA LXV 52 X 48
2948.	JAMN-IJA	IA-AM-NI-IA		RA LXV 54 XII 63
2949.	JAMN-UN-UM	IA-AM-NU-NU-UM		TIM III 26 13, 39 16
2950.	JAMN-UM	IA-AM-NU-UM		B 28+
2951.	JA-MRAṢ	IA-AM-RA-AṢ		BM 81591 6
2952.	JA-MRAṢ+ʾIL	IA-AM-RA-AṢ-DINGIR		M+
2953.	JA-MRAṢ-I+ʾIL	IA-AM-RA-ZI-DINGIR		M
2954.	JA-MRUṢ+ʾIL	IA-AM-RU-IṢ-DINGIR		M
2955.	JA-MRUṢ+ʾIL	IA-AM-RU-UṢ-DINGIR		B 28
2956.	JA-MŠIJ+ʾIL	IA-AM-SI-DINGIR		B 28+
2957.	JA-MṢIʾ+ʿADN-U	IA-AM-ṢI-AD-NU		BM 16914 31
2958.	JA-MṢIʾ+ʾIL	IA-AM-ṢI-DINGIR		B 28+
2959.	JA-T-MAQṮ-AM	IA-AM-TA-AQ-TA-AM	ACC	ABB V 39 REV 8'
2960.	JA-MṮAR-UM	IA-AM-TA-RU-[UM]		TIM V 63:12
2961.	JA-MṢIʾ+ʿADN-U	IA-AM-ZI-AD-[NU]		CT VI 33A 33
2962.	JA-MṢIʾ+ʿADN-U-HU	IA-AM-ZI-AD-NU-U$_2$		BM 81302 4
2963.	JA-MṢIʾ+ʾIL	IA-AM-ZI-DINGIR		B 28, M
2964.	JA-MṢIʾ+ʿADN-U	IA-AM-ZI-ḪA-AD-NU		M+
2965.	JA-MṢIʾ+ʿADN-U-HU	IA-AM-ZI-ḪA-AD-NU-U$_2$		DELAPORTE CCL II A 385, M+
2966.	JA-MṢIʾ-UM	IA-AM-ZI-JU-UM?		M
2967.	JA-MSIR-U	IA-AM-ZI-RU		UCP X/1 50 9
2968.	JA-MZUʾ+ʿADN-U-HU	IA-AM-ZU-AD-NU-U$_2$		B 28+
2969.	JA-MZUʾ+ʿADN-IM	[IA?-AM?-Z]U?-ḪA-AD-NIM	GEN	XIII 129 5
2970.	JA-MZUʾ+MALIK	IA-AM-ZU-MA-LIK		B 28

2971.	JAʾAN-....	IA-AN-[....]		IX 257 2
2972.	JA-NṬIʿ-A	IA-AN-DI-ḪA-KI	GN	M
2973.	JAʾAN+ʾIL	IA-AN-DINGIR		M
2974.	JA-NDUR-UM	IA-AN-DU-RUM?		TIM II 37 1
2975.	JA-NGIH	IA-AN-GI		JNES XIII 210+ LATE
2976.	JA-NḪAN-A	IA-AN-ḪA-NA	GEN	MRS VI P. 334
2977.	JA-NḪUR-UM	IA-AN-ḪU-RU-UM		SIMMONS 103 2
2978.	JA-NQIM+ʾIL	IA-AN?-KI-IM-DINGIR		RA VIII 69 22
2979.	JAʾAN+ŠARR-I	IA-AN-ŠAR-RI		M XIII 1 X 16
2980.	JA-T-NAQIM	IA-AN-TA-KI-IM		M+
2981.	JA-NTIN-UM	IA-AN-TE-NU-UM		SIMMONS 104 13
2982.	JANT-IJA	IA-AN-TI-IA		M+
2983.	JA-NTIN+....	IA-AN-TI-IN-D-[....]		M
2984.	JA-NTIN+ʾANN-I-Š	[IA-AN]-TI-IN-A-NI-IŠ		VII 180 8'
2985.	JA-NTIN+JARAḪ	IA-AN-TI-IN-A-RA-AḪ		RA LXV 62 V 34
2986.	JA-NTIN+DAGAN	IA-AN-TI-IN-D-DA-GAN		M+
2987.	JA-NTIN+ʾIL	IA-AN-TI-IN-DINGIR		B 29+, M+
2988.	JA-NTIN+JARAḪ	IA-AN-TI-IN-E-RA-AḪ		M+
2989.	JA-NTIN+ʿAMM-U	IA-AN-TI-IN-ḪA-MU		M
2990.	JA-NTIN+HADD-U	IA-AN-TI-IN-D-IM		M+
2991.	JA-NTIN+JARAḪ	IA-AN-TI-LA-RA-AḪ		VAS XVI 91 3
2992.	JA-NTIN+HADD-U	IA-AN-TI-NA-DU		ZDPV XLIX PL. 45 LATE
2993.	JA-NTIN+JARAḪ	IA-AN-TI-NA-RA-AḪ		RUTTEN 11 20+
2994.	JA-NTIN-I+ʾIL	IA-AN-TI-NI-DINGIR		BM 17084
2995.	JA-NTIN-IM	IA-AN-TI-NIM	GEN	M
2996.	JA-NTIN-U	IA-AN-TI-NU		M
2997.	JA-NTIN-UM	IA-AN-TI-NU-UM		B 29+
2998.	JA-NṢIB-AN	IA-AN-ZI-BA-AN		M
2999.	JA-NṢIB-IM	IA-AN-ZI-BI-IM	GEN	M+
3000.	JA-NṢIB-UM	IA-AN-ZI-BU-UM		M+
3001.	JA-NṢIB+....	IA-AN-ZI-IB-[....]		M+
3002.	JA-NṢIB+....	IA-AN-ZI-IB-D-[....]		M
3003.	JA-NṢIB+DAGAN	IA-AN-ZI-IB-D-DA-GAN		M+
3004.	JA-NṢIB+ʾIL	IA-AN-Z[I-I]B-DINGIR		XII 683 4
3005.	JA-NṢIB+HADD-U	IA-AN-ZI-IB-D-IM		M+
3006.	JA-NṢIB-AN	IA-AN-ZI-PA-AN		M
3007.	JA-PṬIR-UM	IA-AP-DI-RUM		YOS XII
3008.	JA-PDIJ-UM	IA-AP?-DI-UM		UNPUBL.
3009.		IA-AP-DU-UM		KISURRA 19:4 +
3010.	JAPʿ-AT-UM	IA-AP-ḪA-TUM	FN	YOS VIII 12 2+
3011.	JAPʿ-AT-UM	IA-AP-ḪA-TUM	MN	B 24+
3012.	JA-PḪUR-AN-U	IA-AP-ḪU-RA-NU		M
3013.	JA-PḪUR-UM	IA-AP-ḪU-RU-UM		B 24
3014.	JA-PḪUR-UM	IA-AP-ḪU-RUM		TIM IV 33 19, SEAL +
3015.	JAPʿ-UM	IA-AP-ḪU-UM		M+
3016.	JA-PḪUR+HADD-U	IA-AP-Ḫ[U-UR]-A-DU		M
3017.	JA-PḪUR+LIʾM	IA-AP-ḪU-UR-LI-IM		M+, A 7630
3018.	JA-PḪUR+JARAḪ	IA-AP-ḪU-UR-SIN		M
3019.	JA-PQID-IM	IA-AP-KI?-DI-IM	GEN	BE VI/1 8 34
3020.	JA-PQID-UM	IA-AP-KI?-DU-UM		CT XLVIII 29:2
3021.	JA-PLAḪ+....	IA-AP-LA-[AḪ?-....]		XIII 1 XII 23
3022.	JA-PLAḪ+ʾIL	IA-AP-LA-AḪ-DINGIR		M, TIM III 56 5+
3023.	JA-PLAḪ+ʾIL-IM	IA-AP-LA-AḪ-I-LI-IM	GEN	RA LXIV 43
3024.	JA-PLAḪ-U	IA-AP-LA-ḪU		B 24+
3025.	JA-PLAḪ-UM	IA-AP-LA-ḪU-UM		B 24+
3026.	JA-PLIḪ+ʾIL	[I]A-AP-LI?-I[Ḫ?-DINGIR]		VII 215 32
3027.	JA-PLUS-I+ŠUM-I	IA-AP-LU-SI-SU-U_2-MI		BIRCT, TEA 31:6
3028.	JA-PLUS-UM	IA-AP-LU-ZUM		SIMMONS 49 4
3029.	JA-PRUS+ʾAB-I	IA-AP-RU-US-A-BI		BAGHD. MITT. II 23
3030.	JA-PTAḪ-U	IA-AP-TA-ḪU		YOS VIII 156 2, A. LATE
3031.	JA-PTAḪ-UM	IA-AP-TA-ḪU-UM		WALTERS, WL 93:1
3032.	JA-PṬUR-AJ-I	IA-AP-TU-RA-A-JI-KI	GN	M
3033.	JA-PṬUR-AJ-I	IA-AP-TU-RA-JI-KI	GN	M
3034.	JA-PṬUR-I	IA-AP-TU-RI	GN GEN	M
3035.	JA-PṬUR-UM	IA-AP-TU-RU-UM	GN	JCS VII 52 II 3
3036.	JA-QBIJ+HADD-U	IA-AQ-BI-D-IM		RA LXV 43 III 38

3037.	JA-QBIJ-IM	IA-AQ-BI-IM	GEN	M
3038.	JA-QBIJ-UM	IA-AQ-BU?-UM?		CT IV 30D 11
3039.	JA-QNIJ+ʾIL	IA-AQ-NI-DINGIR		CT XLV 92 I 10+
3040.	JAQR-AN	[I]A-AQ-RA-AN		RA LXV 44 IV 37
3041.	JA-QRIʾ+ʾIL	IA-AQ-RI-DINGIR		B 27
3042.	JAQR-IT-UM	IA-AQ-RI-TUM		EDZARD, DER 155 REV 15
3043.	JAQR-UM+ʾIL	IA-AQ-RUM-DINGIR		A 22010
3044.	JA-QṢUR-UM	IA-AQ-ZU-RU-UM		BE VI/1 1 22+
3045.	JA-QṢUR+ʾIL	IA-AQ-ZU-UR-DINGIR		B 29+
3046.	JA-RḪAM-UM	IA-AR-A-MU-UM		M+
3047.	JA-RBIJ+ʾIL	IA-AR-BI-DINGIR		B 29+
3048.	JA-RBIJ+ʾEL	IA-AR-BI-EL		CT XLV 12 23
3049.	JA-RBUʾ+ʾIL	IA-AR-BU-DINGIR		KISURRA 9A 9+
3050.	JA-RḪAM+ʾIL	IA-AR-ḪA-AM-DINGIR		B 29
3051.	JA-RḪAB-UM	IA-AR-ḪA-BU-UM		B 29+
3052.	JA-RḪAM-AN	IA-AR-ḪA-MA-AN	FN	RA LXV 55 XIII 51
3053.	JA-RḪAM-I+ʾIL	IA-AR-ḪA-MI-DINGIR		KISURRA 5A 15+
3054.	JA-RḪAM-U	IA-AR-ḪA-MU		B 29+, M
3055.	JA-RʿIJ+ʾIL	IA-AR-ḪI-DINGIR		CT XLVIII 27
3056.	JA-RḪIQ-UM	IA-AR-ḪI-KU-UM		A 32133:7
3057.	JAʾAR+ʾIPQ	IA-AR-I-BI-IQ		M
3058.	JA-RḪIB-U	IA-AR-I-BU		XIII 1 VI 63
3059.	JA-RḪIB-UM	IA-AR-I-BU-UM		RA LXIV NO.33
3060.	JA-RḪIB+ʾIL	IA-AR-I-IB-DINGIR		M+
3061.	JA-RḪIB+ʾIRR-A	IA-AR-I-[IB]-IR$_3$-RA		M
3062.	JAʾAR+ʾIL	IA-AR-I-I[L-....]		XIII 69 5
3063.	JA-RḪIB+ʾABB-A	IA-AR-IB-D-AB-BA		M
3064.	JA-RḪIB+DAGAN	IA-AR-IB-D-DA-GAN		M+
3065.	JA-RḪIB+ʾIL	IA-AR-IB-DINGIR		M+
3066.	JA-RḪIB+ḪAJJ-A	IA-AR-IB-D-E$_2$-A		M+
3067.	JA-RḪIB+HADD-U	IA-AR-IB-D-IM		M+
3068.	JA-RḪIB+ʾIRR-A	IA-AR-IB-D-IR$_3$-RA		M
3069.	JA-RKAB+HADD-U	IA-AR-KA-AB-D-IM		4E RENCONTRE 23
3070.	JA-RKIB-A+HADD-U	IA-AR-KI-BA-D-IM		XIII 145 6
3071.	JA-RPAʾ+HADD-U	IA-AR-PA-D-IM		M+
3072.	JARQ-AN	IA-AR-QA-A[N]		M
3073.	JA-RŠAP+LA+ʾIL	IA-AR-SA-AP-LA-DINGIR		M+
3074.	JA-RŠAP+LA+ʾIL-A	IA-AR-SA-AP-LA-I-[LA]?		M
3075.	JA-RŠIJ+ʾAŠAR-I	IA-AR-ŠI-A-ŠA-RI		M
3076.	JA-RŠIJ+ʾIL	IA-AR-ŠI-DINGIR		B 29+, M
3077.	JA-RŠIJ+ʾIL-UM	IA-AR-ŠI-DINGIR-UM		UCP X/1 P. 58+
3078.	JA-RŠIJ+ʿAMM-U	IA-AR-ŠI-ḪA-MU		M, C+
3079.	JA-RWIJ-UM	IA-AR-WI-UM	NOM	KUPPER, NOM. P. 199
3080.	JA-SNIQ+ʾIL	IA-AS-NI-IQ-DINGIR		RA LXV 48 VII 66
3081.	JA-SNIQ-AN	IA-AS-NI-KA-AN		RA LXV 50 VIII 51
3082.	JA-NṢUR+HADD-U	IA-AṢ-ṢU-UR-D-IM		X 12 6, 21+
3083.	JA-ŠBIJ+ʾIL	IA-AŠ-BI-DINGIR		B 32
3084.	JA-ŠBIJ+ʾIL-A	IA-AŠ-BI-I-LA		B 30
3085.	JA-ŠṬIḪ+ʿAMM-U	IA-AŠ-DI-ḪA-AM-MU		B 30
3086.	JA-ṢDUQ-UM	IA-AŠ-DU-KUM		B 30
3087.	JA-ṢDUQ+ʾIL	IA-AŠ-DU-UQ-DINGIR		JEAN 164 R. 4+
3088.	JA-ŠḪIR-UM	IA-AŠ-ḪI-RUM		M
3089.	JA-ŠQIṬ+ʾIL	IA-AŠ-KI-IṬ-DINGIR		B 30, M+
3090.	JA-ŠKUR-UM	IA-AŠ-KU-RUM		XIII 1 XI 19
3091.	JA-ŠKUR+ʾIL	[IA]-AŠ-KU-UR-DINGIR		VIII 38 7'
3092.	JA-ŠLIJ+ḪAʾL	IA-AŠ?-LI?-ḪA-AL		M
3093.	JA-ŠPUQ-UM	IA-AŠ-PU-KUM		VAS XIII 3 15+
3094.	JA-JŠIR+HEDD-A	IA-AŠ-RI-E-DA		A.+
3095.	JA-ŠṬIḪ+ʾIL	IA-AŠ-TI-DINGIR		XIII 1 IX 7
3096.	JA-ṢDUQ+ʾIL	[IA]-AŠ$_2$-DU-UQ-DINGIR		BASOR 95, 19
3097.	JA-ŠKIN+ʾIL	IA-AŠ$_2$-KI-IN-DINGIR-[....]?		M
3098.	JA-ŠKUR-IM	IA-AŠ$_2$-KU-RI-IM	GEN	M+
3099.	JA-ŠKUR-UM	IA-AŠ$_2$-KU-RUM		XIII 1 XI 13
3100.	JA-ŠKUR+ʾIL	IA-AŠ$_2$-KU-UR-DINGIR		B 30+
3101.	JA-ŠKUR+ʾIL	IA-AŠ$_2$-KU-UR$_2$-DINGIR		B 81
3102.	JA-ŠKUR+ʾIL	IA-AŠ$_2$-KUR-DINGIR		JNES XIII 210+ LATE

3103.	JA-ŠLAḪ+....	IA-AŠ$_2$-LA-A[Ḫ-....]		M
3104.	JA-ŠLAM+ʾIL	IA-AŠ$_2$-LAM-DINGIR		XIV 47:11
3105.	JA-ŠLIM+HADD-U	IA-AŠ$_2$-LI-IM-IA-[AN-D]U		M
3106.	JA-ŠMAʿ+BAʿL	[IA-A]Š$_2$-MA-AḪ-BA-AL		VIII 101 L.E.
3107.	JA-ŠMAʿ+DAGAN	IA-AŠ$_2$-MA-AḪ-D-DA-GAN		B 30 HANA+, M+
3108.	JA-ŠMAʿ+ʾIL	IA-AŠ$_2$-MA-AḪ-DINGIR		SIMMONS 55 11, M
3109.	JA-ŠMAʿ+ʾEL	IA-AŠ$_2$-MA-AḪ-I$_3$-EL		B 30
3110.	JA-ŠMAʿ+HADD-U	IA-AŠ$_2$-MA-AḪ-D-IM		M+, C+
3111.	JA-ŠMAʿ-U	IA-AŠ$_2$-MA-ḪU		B 30 HANA
3112.	JA-ŠMAʿ+ʾUP-I	IA-AŠ$_2$-MA-ḪU-PI		BULL. ACAD. BELG. 1974 228
3113.	JA-ŠMAʿ-UM	IA-AŠ$_2$-MA-ḪU-UM		M
3114.	JA-ŠMAʿ+HADD-U	IA-AŠ$_2$-MI-IḪ-D-IM		M
3115.	JA-SNIQ+ʾIL	IA-AŠ$_2$-NI-IQ-DINGIR		SIMMONS 55 14
3116.	JA-ŠPUQ-UM	IA-AŠ$_2$-PU-KU-UM		B 30+
3117.	JA-ŠPUQ+ʾIL	IA-AŠ$_2$-PU-UK-DINGIR		M
3118.	JA-ŠRUK-AN	IA-AŠ$_2$-RU-KA-AN		RA XLI 45 6' HANA+
3119.	JA-NŠIʾ+DAGAN	IA-AŠ$_2$-SI-D-DA-GAN		M+
3120.	JA-NŠIʾ-AN	IA-AŠ$_2$-SI-IA-AN		M
3121.	JA-NŠIʾ+HADD-U	IA-AŠ$_2$-ŠI-D-IM		RA LXV 42 III 13
3122.	JA-TḪIJ+DAGAN	IA-AT-ḪI-D-DA-GAN		M
3123.	JATR-AT-UM	IA-AT-RA-TUM	MN	VAS VIII 105 4, 7, 12+
3124.	JATR-IM	IA-AT-RI-IM	GEN	CT XLVIII 29 REV.
3125.	JATT-A+LIʾM	IA-AT-TA-LI-IM		ZA XXXVI 95, BJ 88 12
3126.	JATT-IJA	IA-AT-TI-IA		M
3127.	JATT-I+HADD-U	IA-AT-TI-D-IM		M
3128.	JA-NTIN+ʾIL	IA-AT-TI-IN-DINGIR		M
3129.	JA-NTIN+JARAḪ	IA-AT-TI-IN-E-RA-AḪ		M+
3130.	JA-NTIN-IM	IA-AT-TI-NIM	GEN	M+
3131.	JA-NTIN-U	IA-AT-TI-NU		YOS XIII 280:13
3132.	JA-WMAʾ+ʿAMM-AJ-I	IA-AW-MA-ḪA-MA-JI-KI	GN	M
3133.	JA-WŠIB-U	IA-AW-ŠI-BU		M
3134.	JA-WṢIʾ+ʾIL	IA-AW-ZI-DINGIR		M+
3135.	JA-WṢIʾ+ʾEL	IA-A[W-Z]I-EL?		VIII 87 8'
3136.	JA-ṢḪAQ-IM	IA-AZ-ḪA-KI?-IM	GEN	IX 291 I 38
3137.	JA-ZLIJ+ʾIL	IA-AZ-LI-DINGIR		M
3138.	JA-ḎRAʿ+DAGAN	IA-AZ-RA-AḪ-D-DA-GAN		XIII 123 26
3139.	JA-ḎRAʿ+ʾIL	IA-AZ-RA-AḪ-DINGIR		VIII 100 15+
3140.	JA-ḎRAʿ+HADD-U	IA-AZ-RA-AḪ-D-IM		M+
3141.	JA-ḎRAʿ-UM	IA-AZ-RA-ḪU-UM		XIV 77:8
3142.	JA-ḎRIʿ-UM	IA-AZ?-RI-ḪU-[UM]		PBS XIII 56:4
3143.	JA-NṢIB+DAGAN	IA-AZ-ZI-IB-D-DA-GAN		B 29
3144.	JA-BWAʾ	IA-BA-A		WATERMAN 36 R. 14
3145.	JA-BWAʾ+ʾIL	IA-BA-A?-DINGIR		M
3146.	JA-BWAʾ+ʿAN-UM	IA-BA-A-NU-UM		B 45
3147.	JABAL+HADD-U	IA-BA-AL-D-IM		M
3148.	JA-BANIJ+ʾIL	IA-BA-AN-NI-DINGIR		M+
3149.	JA-BWAʾ+ʾIL	IA-BA-DINGIR?		MEISSNER 36 25
3150.	JA-BAŠIJ+DAGAN	IA-BA-SI-D-DA-GAN		M
3151.	JA-BWAʾ-AT-UM	IA-BA-TUM		AJSL XXXIII 237 16
3152.	JA-NBIʾ+DAGAN	IA-BI-D-DA-GAN		M
3153.	JA-JPIʿ+HADD-U	IA-BI-IḪ-D-IM		M
3154.	JA-JBIL+JIRR-A	IA-BI-IL-WI-IR-RA		B 24
3155.	JA-JBIL-I+....	IA-BI-LI-[....]		FM 3998 SEAL
3156.	JA-BJIN-IM	IA-BI-NI-IM	GEN	M+
3157.	JA-BJIN-UM	IA-BI-NU-UM		XIII 38 13
3158.	JA-BJIR-UM	IA-BI-RUM		M
3159.	JA-JBIŠ-U	IA-BI-ŠU		A 29366:10
3160.	JA-JBIŠ-UM	IA-BI-ŠUM		B 24+
3161.	JABUB-U	IA-BU-BU		CT XLIII 29 1
3162.	JA-ʾBUQ-UM	IA-BU-KUM		KISURRA 83 14
3163.	JABUŠ-UM	[I]A-BU-SU-UM		VIII 85 41, 44
3164.	JABUŠ-UM	IA-BU-ŠUM	GN	KING LIH II NO. 97 III 1
3165.	JABUŠ	IA-BU-UŠ		CT VIII 29A 28
3166.	JABUS-AT-IM	IA-BU-ZA-TIM	FN GEN	B 25+
3167.	JABUS-AT-UM	IA-BU-ZA-TUM	FN	CT XLVIII 31 5, 9
3168.	JADAʿ+JAT-UM	IA-DA-A-A-TUM		B 25

3169. JADAʿ+ʾIL	IA-DA-AḪ-DINGIR		CT XLVIII 21 SEAL
3170. JADAʿ+ḪAʾL-UM	IA-DA-AḪ-ḪA-LUM		B 25
3171. JADAʿ-TI+ʾEL	IA-DA-AḪ-TE-DINGIR		UNPUBL.
3172. JADAʿ+ʿAMM-U	IA-DA-AM-MU		C II 5 4
3173. JADAʿ+PI+ʾIL	IA-DA-BI-DINGIR		AJSL XXXIII 224 3
3174. JADAʿ+ʾIL	IA-DA-DINGIR		M
3175. JADAʿ-UM	IA-DA-ḪU-UM		YOS XII
3176. JAD-AN-UM	IA-DA-NU-UM		SIMMONS 131 17
3177. JADAʿ+ʾIL	IA-DAḪ-DINGIR		B 25+
3178. JADAʿ+LIʾM	IA-DAḪ-LI-IM		YOS XII
3179. JA-ʿḎAR+ʾIL	IA-DAR-DINGIR		RUTTEN 5 9+
3180. JA-JDIʿ+....	IA-DI-[....]	FN	M
3181. JA-JDIʿ+ʾAB-U	IA-DI-A-BU		YOS XII+
3182. JA-JDIʿ+ʾAB-UM	IA-DI-A-BU-UM		M, YOS XII+
3183. JADID-AH	IA-DI-DA	FN	M+
3184. JADID-A	IA-DI-DA	MN GEN	VII 206 2, 13
3185. JA-JDIʿ+DAGAN	I[A]-DI-D-DA-GAN		B 25
3186. JADID-AT-IM	IA-DI-DA-TIM	MN GEN	B 25+
3187. JADID-AT-UM	IA-DI-DA-TUM	MN	B 25+
3188. JADID-IM	IA-DI-D[I-IM]	GEN	M
3189. JADID-IM	IA-DI-DIM	GEN	JCS IV 95 1612 13
3190. JA-JDIʿ+ʾIL	IA-DI-DINGIR		M
3191. JADID-U	IA-DI-DU		FIGULLA CAT. I 13371 M
3192. JADID-UM	IA-DI-DU-UM		B 25+, M+
3193. JADID-UM	IA-DI-DUM		CT XLI A 10+
3194. JA-JDIʿ-AH	IA-DI-ḪA	FN	M+
3195. JA-JDIʿ+ʾAB-IM	IA-DI-ḪA-A-BI-IM	GEN	M+
3196. JA-JDIʿ+ʾAB-UM	IA-DI-ḪA-A-BU-U[M]		RA LXV 45 V 9
3197. JA-JDIʿ+ʾAB-U	IA-DI-ḪA-BU		PBS XIV 1084
3198. JA-JDIʿ+ʾAB-UM	IA-DI-ḪA-BU-UM		B 25+
3199. JA-JDIʿ-A+ʾEL	IA-DI-ḪA-EL		KISURRA 10A 4
3200. JA-JDIʿ-AT-UM	IA-DI-ḪA-TUM	FN	B 25+
3201. JA-JDIʿ+ʾEL-UM	IA-DI-ḪI-E-LUM		UNPUBL.
3202. JA-JDIʿ-IM	IA-DI-ḪI-IM	GEN	M+
3203. JA-JDIʿ-UM	IA-DI-ḪU-UM		B 25+
3204. JA-JDIʿ+ʾIL	IA-DI-IḪ-DINGIR		B 25+
3205. JAD-IM	IA-DI-IM	GEN	TIM V 35 6
3206. JA-DJIN+HADD-U	IA-DI-IN-D-IM		RA LXV 44 IV 51+
3207. JAD-I+NAṢIR	IA-DI-NA-ṢIR		BM 17051, 17052
3208. JA-DJIN-IM	IA-DI-NIM	GEN	M+
3209. JA-DWIR-AT-UM	[IA-DI]-RA-TUM		B 25
3210. JA-DWIR-I	IA-DI-RI	NOM	B 25 HANA
3211. JA-DWIR-UM	[IA-DI]-RU-U[M]		B 25
3212. JA-JDIʿ-U	IA-DI-U_2		CT VIII 10 B 7+
3213. JA-JDIʿ+ʾAB-UM	IA-DU-A-BU-UM		YOS XII+
3214. JA-DWUR-AN	IA-DU-RA-AN		M
3215. JA-DWUR-IM	IA-DU-RI-IM	GEN	M
3216. JA-DWUR+ʾIL	IA-DU-UR-DINGIR		M
3217. JA-DWUR+LIʾM	IA-DU-UR-LI-I[M]		RA LXV 45 V 82
3218. JA-DWUR+NAŠIʾ	IA-DU-UR-NA-SI		M+
3219. JA-TWUR+NAHR-UM	IA-DUR-NA-RUM?		RA LXV 48 VII 72
3220. JA-ʾḪIḎ-A	IA-E-DA		YOS XIII 343:4
3221. JAQAR-UM	IA-GA-RU-UM		KISURRA 59A 24
3222. JA-GJIḪ-AN	IA-G[I]-ḪA-A[N]		M
3223. JA-GJIḪ+HADD-U	IA-GI-ḪA-D-IM		M
3224. JA-GJIḪ+ḪAʾL-UM	IA-GI?-ḪA-LUM		RUTTEN 16 18
3225. JA-GJID+LIʾM	IA-GI-ID-LI-IM		M+
3226. JA-GJIḪ+HADD-U	IA-GI-IḪ-D-IM		M+
3227. JA-QWIM+HADD-U	IA-GI-I[M]?-D-IM		IX 291 III 29'
3228. JA-ʾQUD-AN-IM	IA-GU-DA-NIM	GEN	BM 16823A 1
3229. JA-ʾGUN-IM	IA-GU-NI-IM	GEN	BM 16485
3230. JA-ʾGUN-UM	IA-GU-NU-UM		YOS XII
3231. JA-NḪAB+ʿAMM-U	IA-ḪA-AB-ḪA-MU		M
3232. JAḪAD+ʾIL	IA-ḪA-AD-DINGIR		M
3233. JAḪAD+ʾEL-UM	IA-ḪA-AD-E-LUM		RIFTIN 136 26
3234. JAḪAD+JARAḪ	IA-ḪA-AD-E-RA-AḪ		M

3235.	JAḪAD+ʿAMM-U	IA-ḪA-AD-ḪA-AM-MU		M
3236.	JAḪAD+ʿAMM-U	IA-ḪA-AD-ḪA-MU		M+
3237.	JAḪAD+ʿAMM-U-HU	IA-ḪA-AD-ḪA-MU-U_2		M
3238.	JAʿAL+PI+ʾIL-UM	IA-ḪA-AL-PI-LUM		3NT867:5, 12, 21
3239.	ʾAJA+ʿAMM-U-HU	IA-ḪA-AM-MU-U_2		VAS XVIII 100:19
3240.	JA-ḪAPIʾ+ʾIL	IA-ḪA-AP-PI-I-IL_5	GN	JCS XVIII 59 12+
3241.	JAʾAR+HADD-U	IA-ḪA-AR-D-IM		M
3242.	JA-ḪATIʾ+ʾIL	IA-ḪA-AT-TI-DINGIR		M+, C
3243.	JA-ḪATIʾ+ŠAMŠ	IA-ḪA-AT-TI-D-UTU		UCP X/1 89 15
3244.	JA-NḪAB-UM	IA-ḪA-BU-UM		YOS XII
3245.	JAḪAD-A+....	IA-ḪA-DA-[....]		RA LXV 45 V 74
3246.	JAḪAD-IM	IA-ḪA-DI-IM	GEN	XIII 1 IX 30
3247.	JAḪAD-U	IA-ḪA-DU		M
3248.	JAḪAD-UM	IA-ḪA?-DU-UM		VII 199 8
3249.	JAḪAD-UM	IA-ḪA-DUM		BIN VII 155 1
3250.	JAʿAL-A	IA-ḪA-LA		YOS XIII 513:9
3251.	JAḪAD+ʾEL-UM	IA-ḪA-TE-LUM?		UET V 605 13
3252.	JA-ḪATIʾ+ʾIL	IA-ḪA-TI-DINGIR		RUTTEN 15:2+; M
3253.	JA-ḪATIʾ+ʾEL	IA-ḪA-TI-EL		RA LXV 44 IV 46
3254.	JA-ḪATIʾ+ʾIL-UM	IA-ḪA-TI-LUM		YOS XII
3255.	JAḪAD-U	IA-ḪA-TU		B 26
3256.	JA-NḪIB-UM	IA-ḪI-BU-UM		SIMMONS 46 3
3257.	JA-ḪJIJ+ʾIL	IA-ḪI-DINGIR		B 26+
3258.	JA-ʾḪID̲+ʾUMM-I	IA-ḪI-DU-UM-ME	FN	RA LXV 65 VII 34
3259.	JA-ḪJIJ-JA	IA-ḪI-IA		XIV 61:6
3260.	JA-ḪJIJ-AN	[I]A?-Ḫ[I]?-IA-AN		RA LXV 41 II 54
3261.	JA-JʿIL+LIʾM	IA-ḪI-IL-LI-IM		M
3262.	JA-ʾWIŠ+....	IA-ḪI-IŠ-[....]		TIM IV 33 SEAL, 34 SEAL
3263.	JAʿIL-AH	IA-ḪI-LA	FN	M
3264.	JAʿIL-AT-IM	IA-ḪI-LA-TIM	GEN	CT XLVIII 27 CASE
3265.	JAʿIL-AT-UM	IA-ḪI-LA-TUM	FN	B 26
3266.	JA-JʿUL+DAGAN	IA-ḪU-UL-D-DA-GAN		RA LXV 48 VII 75
3267.	JA-ḪNUN+ʾIL	IA-ḪU-UN-DINGIR		M+
3268.	JA-ḪNUN+PI+ʾEL	IA-ḪU-UN-PI-EL		SIMMONS 54 18
3269.	JA-ʾRUR-A	IA-ḪU-UR-RA-KI	GN	M+
3270.	JA-ʾRUR-UM	IA-ḪU-UR-RU-UM-KI	GN	M
3271.	JA-ʾḪUD̲-AN	IA-ḪU-ZA-AN		RA LXV 43 IV 21
3272.	JAʿIL-A	IA-I-LA	MN	RA LXV 40 I 27
3273.	JAʿIL-AT-UM	IA-I-LA?-TUM	FN	B 26
3274.	JAʾIT-I+JI-JBAL	IA-I-TI-I-BA-AL		M
3275.	JAJAM-U	IA-IA-MU		B 26
3276.	JAJA-AT-UM	IA-IA-TUM		B 26
3277.	JAJA-UM	IA-IA-UM		B 27+
3278.		IA-KA-A-TUM		YOS XIII 169:11
3279.	JA-ʿQIB+ʾIL	IA-KI-IB-DINGIR		TIM V 33 23
3280.	JA-NQIM+HADD-U	IA-KI-IM-D-IM		M+
3281.	JA-QWIM+HADD-U	IA-KI-IM-D-IM		M+
3282.	JA-NQIM+LIʾM	IA-KI-IM-LI-IM		M
3283.	JA-QWIM+LIʾM	IA-KI-IM-LI-IM		M+
3284.	JA-KWIN+HADD-U	IA-KI-IN-D-IM		M
3285.	JA-KWIN+LU-HU	IA-KI-IN-LU-U_2		TALLQUIST APN 95 LATE
3286.	JA-QWIM-AH	IA-KI-MA	FN	M+
3287.	JA-QWIM-AT-UM	IA-KI-MA-TUM	FN	RA LXV 60 III 7
3288.	JA-JQIR-A+ʾAB-UM	IA-KI-RA-A-BU-UM		RA LXV 47 VII 30
3289.	JA-JQIR-AN-U	IA-KI-RA-NU		M
3290.	JA-KWUN+BAʿL	IA-KU-BA-AL		RA LXV 44 V 7
3291.	JA-ʿQUB-AM	IA-KU-BA-[A]M?	NOM	RA LXV 46 V 84
3292.	JA-ʿQUB-AN	IA-KU-B[A]-AN		RA LXV 45 V 57
3293.	JA-KWUN+PI	IA-KU-BI		B 27
3294.	JA-ʿQUB-I+ʾIL	IA-KU-BI-DINGIR		KISURRA 41 10
3295.	JA-ʿQUB-U	IA-KU-BU		CT II 9 26
3296.	JA-KWUN+DIWR	IA-KU-DI-IR		RA LXV 45 V 14
3297.	JA-ʾQUD-U	IA-KU-DU-KI	GN	UCP IX/4 5 1
3298.	JA-ʾQUD-UM	IA-KU-DU-UM		CT VIII 44A 28, UET V 523
3299.	JA-ʾQUD-UM	IA-KU-DU-UM-KI	GN	BRM IV 53 III 47+
3300.	JA-QWUJ-JA	IA-KU-IA		C+

3301.	JA-QWUJ-JA	IA-KU-IA	FN	RA LXV 43 III 49
3302.	JAKUK-UM	IA-KU?-KU-UM		B 27
3303.	JA-KWUN+LIʾM	IA-KU-LI-IM		M+
3304.	JA-KWUN+MAṬAR	IA-KU-MA-DAR		SYMB.BOHL P.361:6
3305.	JA-KWUN-AM	IA-KU-NA-AM	ACC	CT VIII 36D 7
3306.	JA-KWUN-AN	IA-KU-NA-AN		M+
3307.	JA-KWUN-I	IA-KU-NI	GEN	TIM III 58 16+
3308.	JA-KWUN-IM	IA-KU-NIM	GEN	B 28, M+
3309.	JA-KWUN-U	IA-KU-NU		B 27+
3310.	JA-KWUN-UM	IA-KU-NU-UM		B 27+
3311.	JA-KWUN+PI	IA-KU-PI		B 27
3312.	JA-ʾKUR-AN	IA-KU-RA-AN		M
3313.	JA-ʾKUR-IM	IA-KU-RI?-IM?	GEN	VIII 2 23
3314.	JA-QWUJ-U	IA-KU-U_2		RUTTEN 16:16
3315.	JA-QWUJ-UM	IA-KU-U_2-UM		RUTTEN 2:7+
3316.	JA-ʿQUB+ʾIL	IA-KU-UB-DINGIR		B 27+
3317.	JA-QWUJ-UM	IA-KU-UM		RUTTEN 6:3+; VIII 70:3, 8
3318.	JA-KWUN+ʾAHL-I	IA-KU-UN-A-LI		B 92
3319.	JA-KWUN+ʾAŠAR-I	IA-KU-UN-A-ŠA-RI	NOM	CT XLVIII 10 6
3320.	JA-KWUN+ʾAŠAR-UM	IA-KU-UN-A-ŠA-RU-UM		B 27
3321.	JA-KWUN+ʾAŠAR	IA-KU-UN-A-ŠAR		B 92+, M+
3322.	JA-KWUN+ʿAMM-U	IA-KU-UN-AM-MU		B 27
3323.	JA-KWUN+ʾAŠD-UM	IA-KU-UN-AŠ-DU-UM		B 27
3324.	JA-KWUN+PI-I-JA	IA-KU-UN-BI-IA		XII 14
3325.	JA-KWUN+PI+MAM-A	IA-KU-UN-BI-D-MA-MA	FN	RA LXV 66 VII 61
3326.	JA-KWUN+DAGAN	IA-KU-UN-D-DA-GAN		X 171 3
3327.	JA-KWUN+DIWR	IA-KU-UN-DI-IR		M+
3328.	JA-KWUN+DIWR-I	IA-KU-UN-DI-RI	GEN	CT XLVIII 115 CASE
3329.	JA-KWUN+DIWR-IM	IA-KU-UN-DI-[R]I-IM	GEN	M
3330.	JA-KWUN+DIWR-UM	IA-KU-UN-DI-RUM		CT XLVIII 115
3331.	JA-KWUN+ʾIL	IA-KU-UN-DINGIR		M
3332.	JA-KWUN+ʿALAṢ-I	IA-KU-UN-ḪA-LA-ZI		RA LXV 44 IV 41;43
3333.	JA-KWUN+ḪARAR	IA-KU-UN-ḪA-RA-AR		VAS IX 172 4+
3334.	JA-KWUN+ḪARAR-I	IA-KU-[UN-ḪA]-RA-RI	GEN	BM 81641 6
3335.	JA-KWUN+HADD-U	IA-KU-UN-D-IM		B 27, M+
3336.	JA-KWUN+LIʾM	IA-KU-UN-LI-IM		M+
3337.	JA-KWUN+MEʾR	IA-KU-UN-ME-IR		M+
3338.	JA-KWUN+PI	IA-KU-UN-PI		CT VIII 43C 8
3339.	JA-KWUN+RAPIʾ	IA-KU-UN-RA-BI		M
3340.	JA-KWUN+ŠUM-U+ʾAB-IM	IA-KU-UN-SU-MU-A-BI-IM		M
3341.	JA-KWUN+ŠARR-UM	IA-KU-UN-ŠAR-RU-UM		B 28
3342.	JA-ʾKUR+DAGAN	IA-KU-UR-D-DA-GAN		M+
3343.	JA-KWUN+ḪARAR-I	IA-KUN_3-ḪA-RA-RI		CT XLVIII 3:3
3344.	JAMAN	IA?-MA-AN		XII 5 6
3345.	JA-MATIʿ+ʾIL	IA-MA-AT-TI-DINGIR		M+
3346.	JA-WMAʾ+ʿAMM-UM	IA-MA-ḪA-MU-UM		M
3347.	JAMAM-AH	IA-MA-MA?	FN	M
3348.	JA-ʾMAR-AH	IA-MA-RA	FN	XIII 1 XIV 26
3349.	JA-MATIʿ+ʾIL	IA-MA-TI-DINGIR		XII 5 3
3350.	JAMIN-A	IA-ME-NA	TRIBE	M
3351.	JA-ʾMIʾ+ʾIL-A	IA-MI-I-LA		M
3352.	JAMIN	IA-MI-IN	TRIBE	M
3353.	JAMIN-A	IA-MI-NA	PN	RA LXV 45 V 21
3354.	JAMIN-A	IA-MI-NA	TRIBE	M+
3355.	JAMIN-A	IA-MI-NA-A	TRIBE	M
3356.	JAMIN-I	IA-MI-NI	TRIBE	M
3357.	JAMIN-IM	IA-MI-NIM	TRIBE	M
3358.	JA-ʾMUR-IM	IA-MU-RI-IM	GEN	B 28+
3359.	JA-MWUŠ-I+ʾIL	IA-MU-ŠI-DINGIR		B 28
3360.	JA-MWUʾ-A	IA-MU-U_2-A		KISURRA 33 3
3361.	JA-ʾMUR+HADD-U	IA-MU-UR-AD-DU		M
3362.	JA-MWUT+BAʿL-UM	IA-MU-UT-BA-A-LUM-KI	GN	RLA II 194
3363.	JA-MWUT+BAʿL	IA-MU-UT-BA-AL	GN	M+
3364.	JA-MWUT+BAʿL-AJ-I	IA-MU-UT-BA-LA-I	GN NOM	M
3365.	JA-MWUT+BAʿL-AJ-I	IA-MU-UT-BA-LA-JI	GN NOM	M
3366.	JA-MWUT+BAʿL-IJ-I	IA-MU-UT-BA-LI-I	GN ACC	M

3367.	JA-MWUT+BAʿL-IM	IA-MU-UT-BA-LI-IM	GN GEN	YOS II 49 12+
3368.	JA-MWUT+BAʿL-IM	IA-MU-UT-BA-LIM	GN GEN	BAGHD. MITT. II 56+
3369.	JA-MWUT+BAʿL-UM	IA-MU-UT-BA-LUM-KI	GN	B 28+
3370.	JA-MWUT+DAWD-U	IA-MU-UT-DA-DU		RA LXV 51 X 11
3371.	JA-MWUT+DIWR-UM	IA-MU-UT-DI-RUM		WATERMAN 14 9
3372.	JA-MWUT+ḪAMAD	IA-MU-UT-ḪA-MA-AD		X 174 18
3373.	JA-MWUT+ḪAMAD-I	IA-MU-UT-ḪA-MA-DI	FN	XIII 1 VI 51
3374.	JA-MWUT+KULUP	IA-MU-UT-KU-LU-UP		DELAPORTE, CCL II A 418
3375.	JA-MWUT+LIʾM	IA-MU-UT-LI-IM		B 28+
3376.	JA-MWUT+LIʾM-U	IA-MU-UT-LI-MU		TCL XI 182 10
3377.	JA-MWUT+MIʾR-UM	IA-MU-UT-MI-RUM		RA LXV 52 X 41
3378.	JA-MWUT+NIWR-I	IA-MU-UT-NI-RI	FN	A.
3379.	JA-ʾMUR+JARAḪ	IA-MUR-D-EN-ZU		UET V 583 19
3380.	JA-NABIʾ+ʾIL	IA-NA-AB-BI-DINGIR		M+
3381.	JA-NABIʾ+ʾIL	IA-NA-BI-DINGIR		M
3382.	JA-NABIʾ+ʾEL	IA-NA-BI-EL		M+
3383.	JA-NABIʾ-IM	IA-NA-BI-IM	GEN	M
3384.	JA-NWIḪ-AH	IA-NI-ḪA	FN	RA LXV 58 I 55
3385.	JANIN-UM	IA-NI-NU-UM		TIM V 18 22
3386.	JA-NWUP-UM	IA-NU-BU-UM		B 29+
3387.	JA-NWUḪ-AN	IA-NU-ḪA-AN		RA LXV 40 I 43
3388.	JA-NWUR-UM	IA-NU-RU-UM		RUTTEN 11 10+
3389.	JA-NWUD+....	IA-NU-UD-[....]		M
3390.	JA-NWUD+LIʾM	IA-NU-UD-LI-IM		M
3391.	JA-NWUḪ+LIʾM	IA-NU-UḪ-LI-IM		RA LXV 44 V 8
3392.	JA-NWUḪ+ŠAMAR	IA-NU-UḪ-SA-MAR		CT XLIII 58 3, M
3393.	JAʾN-UM	IA-NU-UM		B 29
3394.	JA-ḪNUN+ʾIL	IA-NU-UN-DINGIR		RA LXV 51 IX 65
3395.	JA-JPAʿ	IA-PA		A.
3396.	JA-JPAʿ+DAGAN	IA-PA-AḪ-D-DA-GAN		XIII 58 5+
3397.	JA-JPAʿ+ʾIL	IA-PA-AḪ-DINGIR		RA LXV 51 IX 74
3398.	JA-JPAʿ+HADD-U	IA-PA-AḪ-D-IM		M+
3399.	JA-JPAʿ+LIʾM	IA-PA-AḪ-LI-IM		M+
3400.	JA-JPAʿ+ŠUM-U+ʾAB-I	IA-PA-AḪ-SU-MU-A-BI		A. 56 47
3401.	JA-JPAʿ+ʾIL	IA-PA-DINGIR		B 29
3402.	JA-JPAʿ-AH	IA-PA-ḪA	FN	M+
3403.	JA-JPAʿ+HADD-U	IA-PA-ḪA-D-IM		M
3404.	JA-JPAʿ-AT-UM	IA-PA-ḪA-TUM	FN	M+
3405.	JA-JPAʿ-UM	IA-PA-ḪU-UM		RA LXVI 118:16
3406.	JA-JPAʿ-UM	[I]A-PA-ḪU-UM	FN	RA LXV 64 VI 8
3407.	JAPAR-IM	IA-PA-RI-IM	GEN	M
3408.	JA-PATIḪ+....	IA-PA-TE-X		KISURRA 100 8
3409.	JA-JPUʿ-AJA	IA-PU-ḪA-IA	FN	C+
3410.	JA-JPUʿ-AT-UM	IA-PU-ḪA-TUM	FN	C+
3411.	JA-JPUʿ-U	IA-PU-ḪU		B 25
3412.	JA-JPUʿ-UM	IA-PU-ḪU-UM		B 25+
3413.	JA-JQAH+ʿAMM-U	IA-QA-AM-MU		A.+
3414.	JAQAR-UM	IA-QA-RUM		M+
3415.	JAQAR	IA-QAR		WATERMAN 72 4
3416.	JAQAR+ʾIL	IA-QAR-DINGIR		CT VI 49 A 23
3417.	JAQAR-T-UM	IA-QAR-TUM	FN	M
3418.	JARAḪ-T-IM	IA-RA-AḪ-TIM	MN GEN	YOS XII
3419.	JARAḪ-T-UM	IA-RA-AḪ-TUM	MN	B 29+
3420.	JA-JRID-UM	IA-RI-DU-UM		UCP X/1 109 3
3421.	JARIN	IA-RI-EN		TA 1931, 241
3422.	JA-RWIḪ-A+ʾAB-AM	IA-RI-ḪA-A-BA-AM	ACC	XIV 101:8
3423.	JA-RWIḪ-A+ʾAB-AM	IA-RI-ḪA-A-BA-AN	ACC	VII P. 234 N. 4
3424.	JA-RWIḪ-A+ʾAB-IM	IA-RI-ḪA-A-BI-IM	GEN	M+
3425.	JA-RWIḪ-A+ʾAB-UM	IA-RI-ḪA-A-BU-UM		VII P. 234 N. 4
3426.	JA-RWIḪ-A+ḪAM-U	IA-RI-ḪA-A-MU		M+
3427.	JA-RWIḪ-AJ-I	IA-RI-ḪA-JI-KI	GN	M
3428.	JA-RWIḪ-IJ-I	IA-RI-ḪI-I-KI	GN	M+
3429.	JA-RJIB+DAGAN	IA-RI-IB-D-D[A-GAN]?		M
3430.	JA-RJIB+HADD-U	IA-RI-IB-D-IM		B 29+
3431.	JA-RWIḪ	IA-RI-IḪ	GN	M
3432.	JA-RWIM+DAWD-U	IA-RI-IM-DA-DU		RA LXV 40 I 38+

3433.	JA-RWIM+DAGAN	IA-RI-IM-D-DA-GAN		M+
3434.	JA-RWIM+JARAḪ	IA-RI-IM-E-RA-AḪ		M
3435.	JA-RWIM+ḪAʾL	IA-RI-IM-ḪA-AL		M+
3436.	JA-RWIM+ʿAMM-U	IA-RI-IM-ḪA-AM-MU		M
3437.	JA-RWIM+ʿAMM-U	IA-RI-IM-ḪA-MU		M
3438.	JA-RWIM+JARAḪ	IA-RI-IM-IA-RA-AḪ		RA LXV 41 II 28
3439.	JA-RWIM+HADD-U	IA-RI-IM-D-IM		M+
3440.	JA-RWIM+LIʾM	IA-RI-IM-LI-IM		SIMMONS 66 77, M+, C+, A.+
3441.	JA-RWIM+MALIK	IA-RI-IM-MA-LIK		A 3580:2+
3442.	JA-RWIM+ŠUM-U+ʾAB-I	IA-RI-IM-SU-MU-A-BI		RA LXV 42 III 8
3443.	JA-RʿIŠ-UM	IA-RI-ŠUM		B 29
3444.	JA-ʾRUR-UM	IA-RU-RUM-KI	GN	YOS XII
3445.	JA-SAṬIʾ+ʾIL	IA-SA-AD-DI-DINGIR		M
3446.	JAŠAR-TI+ʾIL	IA-SA-AR-TI-DINGIR		M
3447.	JAŠAR-AH	IA-SA-RA	FN	XIII 1 II 64+
3448.	JAŠAR-AM	IA-SA-RA-AM	ACC	M
3449.	JAŠAR-UM	IA-SA-RU-UM		PINCHES BERENS 101 10, M+
3450.	JA-SAṬIʾ+ʾIL	IA-S[A]-TI-DINGIR		M
3451.		IA-SI-[....]-TI		CT VIII 17C 12
3452.	JA-NŠIʾ+JARAḪ	IA-SI-A-RA-AḪ		GRANT, HAV. 242:2+
3453.	JA-NŠIʾ+DAGAN	IA-SI-D-DA-GAN		M+
3454.	JA-NŠIʾ+ʾIL	IA-SI-DINGIR		B 29+
3455.	JA-NŠIʾ+JARAḪ	IA-SI-E-RA-AḪ		B 28
3456.	JA-NŠIʾ+ʿAMM-U	IA-SI-ḪA-MU		M
3457.	JA-NŠIʾ+ʾIL-I	IA-SI-I-LI_2		TCL X 5 3
3458.	JA-NŠIʾ+HADD-U	IA-SI-D-IM		B 29
3459.	JA-ŠJIM+ʾAB-IM	IA-SI-IM-A-BI-IM	GEN	M
3460.	JA-ŠJIM+DAGAN	IA-SI-IM-D-DA-GAN		M+
3461.	JA-ŠJIM+ʾIL	IA-SI-IM-DINGIR		M+
3462.	JA-ŠJIM+ʿAMM-U	IA-SI-IM-ḪA-AM-MU		M
3463.	JA-ŠJIM+ʿAMM-U	IA-SI-IM-ḪA-MU		M
3464.	JA-ŠJIM+HADD-U	IA-SI-IM-D-IM		M
3465.	JA-ŠJIM+KI+ʾIL	IA-SI-IM-KI-DINGIR		M
3466.	JA-ŠJIM+MAHAR	IA-SI-IM-MA-ḪA-AR		M
3467.	JA-ŠJIM+ŠUM-U-HU	IA-SI-IM-SU-MU-U_2		M+
3468.	JA-ŠJIT+ʾAB-I	IA-SI-IT-A-BI		M
3469.	JA-ŠJIT+ʾAB-U	IA-SI-IT-A-BU		M+
3470.	JA-ŠJIT-NA	IA-SI-IT-NA		TIM IV 20 SEAL, M
3471.	JA-ŠJIT-NA+ʾAB-U	IA-SI-IT-NA-A-BU		XIII 1 XII 15
3472.	JA-ŠJIT-AN	IA-SI-IT-TA-AN		M
3473.	JA-NŠIʾ+ʾIL-I	IA-SI-LI		B 29+
3474.	JA-NŠIʾ+ʾIL-UM	IA-SI-LUM		RA IX 22 2+
3475.	JA-ŠJIM-AT-UM	IA-SI-MA-TUM	FN	RA LXV 60 III 8
3476.	JA-NŠIʾ+JARAḪ	IA-SI-RA-AḪ		B 30
3477.	JA-JŠIR-UM	IA-SI-RUM		B 30+
3478.	JA-NŠIʾ+JA-JŠUʿ	IA-SI-SU-UḪ		BIN II 104 15
3479.	JA-ŠJIT-AN	IA-SI-TA-AN		M+
3480.	JA-ŠJIT-UM	IA-SI-TUM		XIII 98 3+
3481.	JA-ʾŠUD-UM	IA-SU?-DU-UM		CT II 28 19
3482.	JA-ʾŠUʾ+HADD-U	IA-SU-D-IM		TCL I 238 4 HANA+
3483.	JA-ʾŠUD+PI+ʾEL	IA-SU-UD-PI-EL		SIMMONS 46 31
3484.	JA-JṢIʾ+ʾIL	IA-ṢI-DINGIR		JCS IV 109 4311 21
3485.	JA-JṢIʾ+QAṬAR	IA-ṢI-QA-TAR		B 30
3486.	JAŠAB-AN	IA-ŠA-BA-AN		RA LXV 45 V 35
3487.	JAŠAR-UM	IA-ŠA-RU-UM		B 30
3488.	JA-JŠIR+HEDD-A	IA-ŠE-RE-DA		A. 367 5
3489.	JA-ŠWIB-I+ʾILL-A	IA-ŠI-BI-IL-LA		A.
3490.	JA-ŠWIB+ʾIL	IA-ŠI-IB-DINGIR		A.
3491.	JA-ŠJIM+DAGAN	IA-ŠI-IM-D-DA-GAN		VIII 11 33
3492.	JA-ŠJIM+ḪAJJ-A	[I]A-ŠI-IM-E_2-A		M
3493.	JA-ŠJIM+ʾIRR-A	IA-ŠI-IM-IR_3-RA		M
3494.	JA-JŠIR-UM	IA-ŠI-RU-[UM]		A 22002
3495.	JA-JŠIR-T-IM	IA-ŠIR-TI-IM	MN GEN	WATERMAN 45 R. 10
3496.	JA-ŠWUB-AN	IA-ŠU-BA-AN		M
3497.	JA-ŠWUB-IM	IA-ŠU-BI-IM	GEN	M+
3498.	JA-ŠWUB-UM	IA-ŠU-BU-UM		B 30+

3499.	JA-JŠUʿ+ʾIL	IA-ŠU-DINGIR		RA LXIV 36 NO. 31
3500.	JA-JŠUʿ-AH	IA-ŠU-ḪA	FN	M+
3501.	JA-JŠUʿ-AT-UM	IA-ŠU-ḪA-TUM	FN	RA LXV 58 I 17; B 30+
3502.	JA-JŠUʿ-UM	IA-ŠU-ḪU-UM		B 30+
3503.	JAŠUN-A	IA-ŠU-NA		A.
3504.	JA-ʾŠUR-UM	IA-ŠU-RU-UM		RA LXV 54 XII 38
3505.	JA-ŠWUB+....	IA-ŠU-UB-[....]		A.
3506.	JA-ŠWUB+ʾAŠAR	IA-ŠU-UB-A-ŠAR		M+
3507.	JA-ŠWUB+DAGAN	IA-ŠU-UB-D-DA-GAN		B 30 HANA+, M+
3508.	JA-ŠWUB+ʾIL	IA-ŠU-UB-DINGIR		CT II 23 15+, M+
3509.	JA-ŠWUB+ḪAʾL	IA-ŠU-UB-ḪA-AL		RA LXV 44 IV 28
3510.	JA-ŠWUB+JI-JPUʿ	IA-ŠU-UB-D-I-PU-UḪ		M
3511.	JA-ŠWUB+JAḪAD	IA-ŠU-UB-IA-ḪA-AD		M
3512.	JA-ŠWUB+HADD-U	IA-ŠU-UB-D-IM		LAESSOE P. 90+, C+
3513.	JA-ŠWUB+LIʾM	IA-ŠU-UB-LI-IM		M+
3514.	JA-ŠWUB+MALIK	IA-ŠU-UB-D-MA-[LIK]		M
3515.	JA-ŠWUB+NAHR	IA-ŠU-UB-NA-AR		M+
3516.	JA-ŠWUB+RAPIʾ	IA-ŠU-UB-RA-BI		A.
3517.	JATAR+ʾIL	IA-TA-AR-DINGIR		B 31+ +
3518.	T-JAŠʿ-AH	IA?-TA-AŠ-ḪA?	FN	M
3519.	JAT-A+DAWD-UM	IA-TA-DA-DUM		B 31
3520.	JATAM-U	IA-TA-MU		JCS XIII 51 292, A. LATE
3521.	JATAM-UM	IA-TA-MU-UM		YOS VIII 153 5
3522.	JATAR-AH	IA-TA-RA	FN	M+
3523.	JATAR-AJA	IA-TA-RA-A-IA	FN	XIII 1 X 54
3524.	JATAR-AJA	IA-TA-RA-IA	FN	M
3525.	JATAR-AT-IM	IA-TA-RA-TIM	MN GEN	B 31+
3526.	JATAR-AT-UM	IA-TA-RA-TUM	FN	B 31
3527.	JATAR-AT-UM	IA-TA-RA-TUM	MN	B 31
3528.	JATAR-I	IA-TA-RI	GEN	M
3529.	JATAR-IM	IA-TA-RI-IM	GEN	B 31, M+
3530.	JATAR-U	IA-TA-RU		KISURRA 106 16
3531.	JATAR-UM	IA-TA-RU-UM		B 31
3532.	JATAR-UM	IA-TA-RUM		B 31, M+
3533.	JATAM+MA+ʾIL	IA-TAM-MA-DINGIR		UET V 172 5'
3534.	JATAR+ḪAM-I	IA-TAR-D-A-MI		M+
3535.	JATAR+ʾAKK-A	IA-TAR-AK-KA		M
3536.	JATAR+ʾAŠD-I	IA-TAR-AŠ-DI		M
3537.	JATAR+ʾIL	IA-TAR-DINGIR		M
3538.	JATAR+ʿADN-U	IA-TAR-ḪA-AD-NU		M+
3539.	JATAR+ʿADN-U-HU	IA-TAR-ḪA-AD-NU-U_2		RA LXV 54 XII 56
3540.	JATAR+ʿAMM-U	IA-TAR-ḪA-MU		M
3541.	JATAR+ʿAMM-U	IA-TAR-ḪA-MU	FN	C II P. 247+
3542.	JATAR+HADD-U	IA-TAR-D-IM		M+
3543.	JATAR+LIʾM	IA-TAR-LI-IM		M+
3544.	JATAR+MALIK	IA-TAR-MA-LIK		A.+
3545.	JATAR-UM	IA-TAR-RUM		B 31
3546.	JATAR+ŠALIM	IA-TAR-SA-LIM		M+
3547.	JATAR+ŠUM-U	IA-TAR-SU-MU		XII 456 10
3548.	JATAR+ŠUM-U-HU	IA-TAR-SU-MU-U_2		M+
3549.	JA-JTIR+HEDD-A	IA-TE-IR-E-DA		A.+
3550.	JA-JTIR-A	IA-TE-RA	GEN	A.
3551.	JA-JTIR+HEDD-A	IA-TE-RI-DA		A.+
3552.	JAT-I+ʾIL	IA-TI-DINGIR		B 31
3553.	JAT-I+ʾAMAN	IA-TI-ḪA-MA-AN	FN	RA LXV 42 II 55
3554.	JAT-IJA	IA-TI-IA		M+
3555.	JA-NTIN+DAGAN	IA-TI-IN-D-DA-GAN		M
3556.	JA-NTIN+JARAḪ	IA-T[I-I]N-E-RA-AḪ		M
3557.	JA-NTIN-U	IA-TI-NU		B 31
3558.	JA-JTIR+ḪAM-U	IA-TI-RA-MU		A. 235 4 LATE
3559.	JATUM-U	IA-TU-MU		HARRIS 104 5
3560.	JATUM-UM	IA-TU-MU-UM		B 31
3561.	JAT-U-HU	IA-TU-U_2		YOS XIII 426:14
3562.	JA-TWUR+MEʾR	D-IA-TU-[U]R-ME-I[R]	DN	M
3563.	JAT-UM+MARṢ-AH	IA-TUM-MAR-ZA		A 21899+
3564.	JAT-UM+ṢIʾ-A	IA-TUM-ZI-A		CT XLV 97 5

3565.	JADAʿ+HADD-U	[IA]-ṬA$_3$-AḪ-D-IM		VI 76 10
3566.	JADAʿ+LIʾM	IA-ṬA$_3$-AḪ-LI-IM		YOS XII
3567.	JADAʿ-UM	IA-ṬA$_3$-ḪU-UM		YOS XII
3568.	JAʾ-U+ʾIL-I	IA-U-I-LI$_2$		SUMER V 143 NO. 2
3569.	JAʾ-U+ʾAHL-I	IA-U$_2$-A-LI$_2$		KISURRA 85 19
3570.	JA-WḪIJ+ʾIL	IA-U$_2$-ḪI-DINGIR		B 31
3571.	JA-ʿWUQ-UM	IA-U$_2$-KU-UM		B 31+
3572.	JA-ʾWUŠ-AN	IA-U$_2$-SA-AN		RA LXV 43 IV 15
3573.	JAʾ-U+ŠUM-UM	IA?-U$_2$-SU?-MU-UM?		XIII 146 13
3574.	JA-WṢIʾ+ʾIL	IA-U$_2$-ṢI-DINGIR		BAGHD. MITT. II 23
3575.	JA-ʾWUŠ-U	IA-U$_2$-ŠU		B 31
3576.	JAʾ-UM+ʾIL	IA-U$_2$-UM-DINGIR		B 31
3577.	JA-ʾWUŠ+ḪAM-U	IA-U$_2$-UŠ-D-A-MU		M
3578.	JA-ʾWUŠ+ʾIL	IA-U$_2$-UŠ-DINGIR		RA LXV 42 III 10+
3579.	JA-ʾWUŠ+HADD-U	IA-U$_2$-UŠ-D-IM		M+
3580.	JA-ʾWUŠ+ʾIL	IA-U$_2$-UŠ$_2$-DINGIR		C II 35 28
3581.	JA-WṢIʾ+ʾIL	IA-U$_2$-ZI-DINGIR		B 31
3582.	JA-WṢIʾ+ʾIL-UM	IA-U$_2$-ZI-LUM		B 31
3583.	JAʾ-UM+LU-HU	IA-UM-LU-ḪU		UET V 496:10
3584.	JA-ḪNUN+MAʾT-UM	IA-UN-MA-TUM	FN	RA L 63
3585.		IA-UR-ḪA-TUM		RA L 63
3586.	JA-ʾWUŠ+ʾIL	IA-UŠ-DINGIR		M+
3587.	JA-ʾWUŠ+HADD-U	IA-UŠ-D-IM		M+
3588.	JA-ŠKUR-UM	IA-UŠ-KU-RU-UM		TIM III 133 11
3589.	JA-ʾWUŠ+HADD-U	IA-UŠ$_2$-D-IM		M
3590.	JA-HWIJ+DAGAN	IA-WI-D-DA-GAN		B 31
3591.	JA-HWIJ+ʾIL	IA-WI-DINGIR		B 31+, M+
3592.	JA-HWIJ-JA	IA-WI-IA		M
3593.	JA-HWIJ+HADD-U	IA-WI-D-IM		M+
3594.	JA-HWIJ+ʾIL-I	IA-WI-LI		A 7695 10
3595.	JA-ʾWIR-UM	IA-WI-RU-UM		B 31
3596.	JA-HWIJ+TA-NWUḪ	IA-WI?-TA-NU		RA LXV 43 III 64
3597.	JA-HWIJ-UM	IA?-WI-U$_2$-UM		M
3598.	JAʾ-UM+ʾIL	IA-WU-UM-DINGIR		B 31
3599.	JA-SAṬIʾ+ʾIL	IA-ZA-AD-DI-DINGIR		M+
3600.	JA-SAṬIʾ+ʾEL	[I]A-ZA-AD-DI-EL		M
3601.	JA-ʿḌAR+ʾIL	IA-ZA-AR-DINGIR?		IX 291 II 21,30
3602.	JA-SAṬIʾ+ʾIL	IA-ZA-AT-TI-DINGIR		M
3603.	JA-JṢIʾ+ʾAŠAR	IA-ZI-A-ŠAR		SZLECHTER TJ P. 186
3604.	JA-ʿZIB-IM	IA-ZI-BI-IM	GEN	XIV 92:26+
3605.	JA-ʿZIB-UM	IA-ZI-BU-UM		M+
3606.	JA-JṢIʾ+DAGAN	IA-ZI-D-DA-GAN		B 31 HANA, M
3607.	JA-JṢIʾ+ʾIL	IA-ZI-DINGIR		M+
3608.	JA-JṢIʾ+JARAḪ	IA-ZI-E-RA-AḪ		B 32, C
3609.	JA-ʿZIB+DAGAN	IA-ZI-IB-D-DA-GAN		M+
3610.	JA-ʿZIB+HADD-U	IA-ZI-IB-D?-IM?		M
3611.	JA-JṢIʾ+HADD-U	IA-ZI-D-IM		M
3612.	JA-JṢIʾ+ʾIL-UM	IA-ZI-LUM-KI	GN	B 32
3613.	JA-ʾZUW+DAGAN	IA-ZU-D-DA-GAN		M+, SYRIA V 273, HANA
3614.	JA-ʾZUW+HADD-U	IA-ZU-D-IM		M
3615.	JA-ḪṢUN-UM	IA-ZU-NU-UM		SIMMONS 125 13+
3616.	JA-ʾZUW+JARAḪ	IA-ZU-RA-AḪ		M+
3617.	JA-ʾZUW-UM	IA-ZU-UM		UET V 714 +
3618.	JA-NWUZ-UM	IA$_2$-A-NU-ZU-UM		U
3619.	JA-NBIʾ+ʾIL-UM	IA$_2$-AN-BI$_2$-I$_3$-LUM		U
3620.	JA-NBUL-I	IA$_2$-AN-BU-LI		U
3621.	JA-NŠIʾ+LIʾM	IA$_2$-ŠI-LI-IM		U+
3622.	JA-MʾAD-I	IA$_3$-A-MA-TI		U
3623.	JA-MʾAD-IJ-UM	IA$_3$-A-MA-TI-UM		U
3624.	JA-MʾAD-U	IA$_3$-A-MA-TU		U
3625.	JA-MWUT-UM	IA$_3$-A-MU-TUM		U
3626.	JAʾ-UM	IA$_3$-A-UM		U
3627.	JA-LEʾEJ	IA$_3$-LE-E		U
3628.	JAMAM-HU	IA$_3$-MA-AM-U$_2$		U
3629.	ʿEBB-ATAN-UM	IB-BA-TA-NU-UM		BE VI/2 26 III 1
3630.	ʿEBB-AT-IM	IB-BA-TIM	FN GEN	M

3631.	ʿEBB-AT-UM	IB-BA-TUM	FN	M+
3632.	JI-NPIḪ+LI+DIJN-I	IB-BI-IḪ-LI-DI-NI	FN	C
3633.	ʿEBB-IM	IB-BI-IM	GEN	M+
3634.	JI-NPIḪ-UM	IB-BI$_2$-ḪU-UM?		VIII 3 19
3635.	ʾIBL-AN-UM	IB-LA-A-NU-UM		HAV. SYMP. 237 13
3636.	ʾIBL-AN-UM	IB-LA-NU-UM		I
3637.	JI-BLIM-UM	IB-LI-NU-UM		TA 1930, 615:25 +
3638.	ʾIBN-AT-UM	IB-NA-TUM	MN	BM 16939 27+
3639.	JI-BNIJ+DAGAN	[I]B?-NI-D-DA-GAN		A. 6 34
3640.	JI-BNIJ+JARAḪ	IB-NI-E-RA-AḪ		SIMMONS 62 14'+
3641.	JI-BNIJ+HADD-U	IB-NI-D-IM		M+
3642.	JI-BʾUL-UM	IB-U$_2$-LUM		I
3643.	ʾIDD-AT-UM	ID-DA-TUM	MN	B 21, M
3644.	ʾIDD-I	ID-DI		XIII 1 IX 69+
3645.	JI-NDIN+JAT-IM	ID-DI-IA-TIM	GEN	M
3646.	JI-NDIN-A	ID-DI-NA		A.
3647.	JI-NDIN+ʾABB-A	ID-DI-NA-AB-BA		A.
3648.	JI-NDIN+ʾABB-A	ID-DI-NA-BA		A. LATE
3649.	JI-NDIN-U	ID-DI-NU		XIII 1 I 47
3650.	JI-DNIK+ʾA-MURR-UM	D-ID-NI-IK-MAR-TU	DN	U
3651.	NAHR+BAJAN	D-ID$_2$-BA-IA-AN		A 21929 5,12
3652.	NAHR+ṢUWR-I	D-ID$_2$-ZU-RI		M
3653.	JE-MṢIʾ+ʾIL	IE-E-EM-ZI-DINGIR		B 25
3654.	JE-MZUʾ-UM	IE-E-EM-ZU-UM		B 25+
3655.	JE-MṢIʾ-UM	IE-E-IM-ZU-UM		BIN VII 35:6
3656.	JE-MWUT+BAʿL-UM	IE-E-MU-UT-BA-LUM-KI	GN	SZLECHTER TJ 16 165
3657.	JE-ŠWUB-I+ʾIL	IE-E-ŠU-BI-DINGIR		B 26
3658.	JE-NḪIN-UM	IE-EN-ḪI-NU-UM		B 25
3659.	JI-GMIR+HADD-U	IG-MI-RA-A-DU		A.+
3660.	JI-ʾLAP+HADD-U	IḪ-LA-AP-A-DU		A.
3661.	JI-ḪLAJ+HADD-U	IḪ-LA-D-IM		XIII 1 II 76
3662.	JI-ḪLIJ+HADD-U	IḪ-LI-A-DU		A. P. 133+
3663.	JI-ḪLIJ+ʿAŠTAR	IḪ-LI-AŠ-TAR		A. 55 35
3664.	JI-ʾLIP+HADD-A	IḪ-LI-BA-DA		TCL I 222 13
3665.	JI-ḪLIJ+ʿAŠTAR	IḪ-LI-EŠ$_4$-DAR		A. P. 133+
3666.	JI-ḪLIJ-JA	IḪ-LI-IA		XIII 139 18
3667.	JI-ḪLIJ-AN	IḪ-LI-IA-AN		RA LXV 42 II 73+
3668.	JI-ḪLIJ+HADD-U	IḪ-LI$_3$-A-DU		A. P. 133
3669.	JI-MLIK+ʾIL	II-IM-LIK-DINGIR		B 28+
3670.	JI-RḪAQ-UM	II-IR-ḪA-KUM		SIMMONS 96 10+
3671.	JI-ḎKUR+ʾIL	II-IZ-KUR-DINGIR		SIMMONS 67 18
3672.	JI-ḎRUʿ+ʾIL	II-IZ?-RU-UḪ-DINGIR		TCL XI 156 17
3673.	JI-KRUB+ʾIL	D-IK-RU-BI-DINGIR	DN	M
3674.	JI-KRUB+ʾIL	D-IK-RU-UB-DINGIR	DN	M+
3675.	JI-KRUB+ʾEL	D-IK-RU-UB-EL	DN	M+
3676.	JI-KRUB+ʾIL	D-IK-RU-UB-IL	DN	M
3677.	JI-KSUW+ʾEL	IK-ZU-EL		TA 30 615 10, 20+
3678.	JI-KSUW+ʾIL	IK-ZU-IL		TA 1931 ,435 REV.2
3679.		IL-A-DU		A.
3680.	JI-LʾAʾ+HADD-U	IL-A-DU		A. 78 20
3681.		IL-A-GUL-LAM		VII 140 10'
3682.	JI-LʾAʾ+HADD-U	IL-A-D-IM		X 83 4, 7'
3683.	JI-LʾAʾ+....	IL-A-KUL$_2$-LAM?		VII 140:10
3684.		IL-BA-BI-LA		HARRIS 71 13
3685.	ʾILAP-AN	IL-LA-BA-AN		RA LXV 51 X 9
3686.	ʾILL-A+JAT-I	IL-LA-I-IA-TI	FN NOM	XIII 1 IX 51
3687.	ʾILL-A+JAT-IM	IL-LA-I-IA-TIM	FN NOM	XIII 1 IV 75
3688.	ʾILAP-UM	IL-LA-PU-UM		RA LXV 46 VI 1,10
3689.	ʾILL-AT-UM	IL-LA-TUM	FN	XIII 1 X 46
3690.	ʾILL-U-NA	IL-LU-NA	FN	A.
3691.	ʾILUR-AT	IL-LU-RA-AT	FN	JACOBSEN CTC P. 49+
3692.	ʾILUR-AT-UM	IL-LU-RA-TUM	FN	CT IV 26A 3+
3693.	HADD-U+BAʿL-I	D-IM-BA-AḪ-LI		M+
3694.	HADD-U+BANIJ	D-IM-BA-NI		M+
3695.	HADD-U+DUWR-I	D-IM-DU-RI		M+
3696.		IM-LA-TA-AL		TCL I 222 5, 6

3697.	ʾIMM-AN	IM-MA-AN		M
3698.	HADD-U+MALIK	D-IM-MA-LIK		M+
3699.	ʾIMIR+ḪUNN-A	IM-ME-IR?-ḪU-UN-NA		A. 43 9
3700.	ʾIMIR+ʾIL-I	IM-ME-IR-I_3-LI_2		UNPUBL.
3701.	ʾIMIR-I	IM-ME-RI		A.+
3702.	HADD-U+NIWR-I	D-IM-NI-RI	FN	RA LXV 61 IV 17
3703.	ʿIMS-U	IM-ṢU		JNES XIII 210+ LATE
3704.	HADD-U+ŠADW-A	D-IM-ŠA-DA		PSBA XXIX 273 NO. 9 R. 10
3705.	ʿIJN+BAʿL-I	IN-BA-AḪ-LI	FN	A.
3706.	ʿINB-AT-UM	IN-BA-TUM	FN	BM 78768 3', X 84 3+
3707.	ʿINB-I+JARAḪ	IN-BI-RA-AḪ		KISURRA 6 15
3708.	ʿINB-I+ʾIL	IN-BI_2-IL		U UNPUBL.
3709.	ʿINB-U	IN-BU	FN	C+
3710.	ʿINB-UM	IN-BU-UM		M
3711.	JI-NDIN-UM	IN-DIN-NU-UM		I
3712.	JI-NDUB+ŠALIM	IN-DU-UB-ŠA-LIM		TA 1931, 265:10
3713.	JI-N-NWAB-AT-UM	IN-NA-BA-A-TUM	FN	CT VI 1A 3
3714.	JI-N-NWAB-AT-IM	IN-NA-BA-TIM	FN GEN	CT VI 17 2
3715.	JI-N-NWAB-AT-UM	IN-NA-BA-TUM	FN	CT VI 17 13+
3716.	JI-N-NWAḪ-AN	IN-NA-ḪA-AN		M+
3717.	ḪINN-ATAN-UM	IN-NA-TA-NU-UM		TA 1931, 294
3718.	JI-N-NWIB-U	IN-NE-BU		M
3719.		IN-NE-ER-RI	NOM	VII 221 3
3720.	ḪINN-I+BAJN-AH	IN-NI-BA-NA	FN NOM	X 81 4
3721.	JI-N-NWIB-I	IN-NI-BI		CLAY PNCP 90+
3722.	JI-N-NWIB-U	IN-NI-BU		YOS XIII 191:2+
3723.	JI-N-NWIB-UM	IN-NI-BU-UM		M
3724.	ḪINN-I+HADD-U	IN-NI-D-IM		A.
3725.		IN-NI-IR-RI	NOM	VI 19 31
3726.	JI-NTIN-UM	IN-TI-NU-UM		I
3727.	ʾINZ-AH	IN-ZA	FN	XIII 1 XII 7
3728.	ʾIPQ-AT-UM	IP-GA-TUM	MN	CT XLV 23 R. 13
3729.	ʾIPQ-U+JI-TWUR+MEʾR	IP-KU-D-I-DUR-ME-ER		M
3730.	ʾIPQ-U+NAZI	IP-KU-D-NA-AZ-ZI		M
3731.	ʾIPQ-U+ŠAL-A	IP-KU-D-ŠA-LA		M
3732.	JI-N-PALIS-U	IP-PA-LI-ZU?		MAOG IV 2 3 HANA
3733.	ʾIPQ-AT-IM	IP-QA-TI-IM	MN? GEN	M
3734.	ʾIPQ-AT-IM	IP-QA-TIM	MN GEN	M+
3735.	ʾIPQ-AT-UM	IP-QA-TUM	MN	M+
3736.	JI-PRUD-U	IP-RU-DU		CT XLV 59 22 SEAL
3737.	JI-PTAN	IP-TA-AN		C II 39 22; M
3738.	JI-PTIḪ+JA-MWUT-A	IP-TI-IA-MU-TA		BM 80328 11
3739.	ʿIQB-A+ʾAḪ-UM	IQ-BA-A-ḪU-UM		KISURRA 4A 11, M
3740.	ʿIQB-A+ʿAMM-U	IQ-BA?-AM-MU		A. 8 35
3741.	ʿIQB-A+ʾAḪ-UM	IQ-BA-ḪU-UM		KISURRA 121 6
3742.	ʿIQB-AN-UM	IQ-BA-NU-UM		I+
3743.	ʿIQB-I+HADD-U	IQ-BI-D-IM		KISURRA 114 7
3744.	JI-QNIJ-UM	IQ-NI-UM	FN	RA LXV 58 I 34
3745.	JI-QRIB-AN-UM	IQ-RI-BA-NU-UM		I
3746.	JI-RḪAQ-UM	IR-ḪA-KUM		B 22
3747.	JI-RḪAM-I+ʾIL	IR-ḪA-MI-DINGIR		A.
3748.	JI-RḪAM+ʾILL-A	IR-ḪA-MI-IL-LA		A. 274 26
3749.	JI-RḪAM+ʾIL-A	IR-ḪA-MI-LA		A.+
3750.	JI-RḪIQ-A	IR-ḪI-GA		M
3751.	JI-RḪIB	IR-IB		U
3752.	JI-RKAB-T-U	IR-KAB-DU	MN	A.+ LATE
3753.	JI-RKAB-T-UM	IR-KAB-TUM	MN	A.+
3754.	JI-RPAʾ+ʾAB-I	IR-PA-A-BI		A.+
3755.	JI-RPAʾ+HADD-A	IR-PA-A-DA		A. 76 8+
3756.	JI-RPAʾ+HADD-A	IR-PA-DA		A. 41 14
3757.	JI-RPAʾ+HADD-U	IR-PA-D-IM		A.+
3758.	ʾIRR-I+HADD-U	IR-RI-A-DU		A.
3759.	ʾIRŠ-U+MA+ʾAB-I	IR-ŠU-MA-BI		A.
3760.	ʾIRR-A+ʾAB-I	IR_3-RA-A-BI		M
3761.	JI-ŠMAʿ+ʾIL	IS-MA-AḪ-DINGIR		CT XLV 3 7
3762.	JI-JṢIʾ+DAGAN	IS-SI-D-DA-GAN		CT IV 1 14

3763.	JI-NŠIʾ+DAGAN	IS-SI-D-DA-GAN		B 22 HANA
3764.	JIŠʿ-AT-I	IŠ-A-TI	MN? GEN	PBS VIII/2 238 5, 8
3765.	JI-ŠBIJ+ʾIRR-A	IŠ-BI-D-IR$_3$-RA		M+
3766.	JI-ŠBIJ+ʾIRR-A	IŠ-BI-IR$_3$-RA		M+
3767.	JI-ŠBIM-U	IŠ-BI-MU		CT IV 30D 10
3768.	JIŠʿ-IJA	IŠ-HI-IA		M, C
3769.	JIŠʿ-AH	IŠ-ḪA	FN	XIII 1 VIII 25+
3770.	JIŠʿ-A+BAʿL	IŠ-ḪA-B[A-A]L		HARRIS 39 14
3771.	JIŠʿ-A+GAʾL	IŠ-ḪA-GA-AL		A 7459 10
3772.	ʾIŠḪAR-AH+ʾAŠJ-AH	D-IŠ-ḪA-RA-A-SI-IA	FN	XIII 1 XI 43
3773.	ʾIŠḪAR-AH+DAMQ-AH	D-IŠ-ḪA-RA-DAM-QA	FN	RA LXV 58 I 18
3774.	ʾIŠḪAR-AH+DANN-AT	IŠ-ḪA-RA-DAN-NA-AT	FN	M
3775.	ʾIŠḪAR-AH+DUMQ-I	D-IŠ-ḪA-RA-DU-UM-KI	FN	XII 265 3
3776.	ʾIŠḪAR-AH+GUML-I	D-IŠ-ḪA-RA-GU-UM-LI	FN	XIII 1 IV 39
3777.	ʾIŠḪAR-AH+LAMAS-I	D-IŠ-ḪA-RA-D-LAMA	FN	XIII 1 IX 23
3778.	ʾIŠḪAR-AH+MALAK-I	D-IŠ-ḪA-RA-M[A-L]A-KI	FN	RA LXV 61 IV 61
3779.	ʾIŠḪAR-AH+NAʿM-I	D-IŠ-ḪA-RA-NA-AḪ-ME	FN	RA LXV 64 VI 37
3780.	ʾIŠḪAR-AH+NAPŠ-I	D-IŠ-ḪA-RA-NA-AP-SI	FN	XIII 1 VII 13
3781.	ʾIŠḪAR-AH+NIWR-I	D-IŠ-ḪA-RA-NI-RI	FN	RA LXV 59 II 22
3782.	ʾIŠḪAR-AH+ŠARR-AT	D-IŠ-ḪA-RA-ŠAR-RA-AT	FN	M
3783.	ʾIŠḪAR-AH+TA-ŠKUB	D-IŠ-ḪA-RA-TA-AŠ-KU-UB	FN	RA LXV 56 V 21+
3784.	ʾIŠḪAR-AH+ʾUMM-I	D-IŠ-ḪA-RA-UM-MI	FN	XIII 1 II 47+
3785.	ʾIŠḪAR-AH+ŠAMŠ-I	D-IŠ-ḪA-RA-D-UTU-ŠI	FN	XII 265 6
3786.	ʾIŠḪAR-AH+ḎAMR-AT-I	D-IŠ-ḪA-RA-ZA-AM-RA-TI	FN	M
3787.	JIŠʿ-AT-IJA	IŠ-ḪA-TI-IA	MN?	B 24+
3788.	JIŠʿ-AT-UM	IŠ-ḪA-TUM	FN	RA LXV 60 III 57
3789.	JIŠʿ-I+ʿAN-UM	IŠ-ḪI-A-NU-UM		B 45
3790.	JIŠʿ-I+DAGAN	IŠ-ḪI-D-DA-GAN		M+
3791.	JIŠʿ-I+ʾIL	IŠ-ḪI-DINGIR		WALTERS, WL 109:5+
3792.	JIŠʿ-I+ʾIL-A+MA	IŠ-ḪI-DINGIR-LA-MA		M
3793.	JIŠʿ-I+ʾIL-A+MA	IŠ-ḪI-DINGIR-MA		M
3794.	JIŠʿ-I+JABAL	IŠ-ḪI-E-BA-AL		M
3795.	JIŠʿ-I+HEDD-A	IŠ-ḪI-E-D-IM		TIM IV 33 SEAL, 34 SEAL
3796.	JIŠʿ-I+JARAḪ	IŠ-ḪI-E-RA-AḪ		RA LXV 41 II 25
3797.	JIŠʿ-I+HADD-U	IŠ-ḪI-D-IM		M+, C+
3798.	JIŠʿ-I+LI+ʾEL	IŠ-ḪI-LI-EL		JCS XXIV 69 NO. 3 SEAL
3799.	JIŠʿ-I+LIʾM	IŠ-ḪI-LI-IM		M
3800.	JIŠʿ-I+ʾIL-U+MA	IŠ-ḪI-LU-MA		YOS VIII 176 20
3801.	JIŠʿ-I+ʾIL-U-NA	IŠ-ḪI-LU-NA		VII 215 33
3802.	JIŠʿ-I+MAṬAR	IŠ-ḪI-MA-DAR		V 40 5, 16
3803.	JIŠʿ-I+NABUʾ-UM	IŠ-ḪI-NA-BU-U[M]		EDZARD, DER 68 III 6
3804.	JIŠʿ-IT-IJA	IŠ-ḪI-TI-IA	MN?	CT XLVIII 91 REV.+
3805.	JIŠʿ-I+JARAḪ	IŠ-I-RA-AḪ		TIM III 28 12
3806.	JI-ŠKUR+ʾEL-I	IŠ-KUR-E-LI	FN	XIII 1 VII 41
3807.	JI-ŠLAM-AN-A	IŠ-LA-MA-NA	GEN	MRS VI P. 202 UGARIT
3808.	JI-ŠMAʿ+HADD-A	IŠ-MA-A-DA		A.+
3809.	JI-ŠMAʿ+DAGAN	IŠ-MA-AḪ-D-DA-GAN		RA XXXIV 186 R. 2 HANA+
3810.	JI-ŠMAʿ+HADD-U	IŠ-MA-D-IM		M
3811.	JI-ŠMAʿ+ʾAMUM-I	IŠ-ME-A-MU-MI	FN	M
3812.	JI-ŠMAʿ+BAʿL-A	IŠ-ME-BA-LA		TA 30, 122 2
3813.	JI-ŠMAʿ+BAʿL-I	IŠ-ME-BA-LI		HARRIS 71 6+
3814.	JI-ŠMAʿ+DAGAN	IŠ-ME-D-DA-GAN		M+
3815.	JI-ŠMAʿ+BAʿL	IŠ-ME-EḪ-BA-AL		M
3816.	JI-ŠMAʿ+BAʿL-A	IŠ-ME-EḪ-BA-LA		TA 30, 71
3817.	JI-ŠMAʿ+ʾIL	IŠ-ME-EḪ-DINGIR		KISURRA 40 9
3818.	JI-ŠMAʿ+HADD-U	IŠ-ME-D-IM		M+
3819.	JI-ŠMAʿ+ʾILL-A	IŠ-MI-IL-LA		A.
3820.	ʾIŠN-AN-U	IŠ-NA-NU		B 45+
3821.	JI-ŠNIJ+HADD-U	IŠ-NI-D-IM		A.
3822.	JI-ŠNUL-UM	IŠ-NU-LU-UM	TRIBE	M
3823.	JI-T-ŠAWAB-U	IŠ-TA-A-BU		MAOG IV 3 36 HANA
3824.	JI-ŠT-ŠNIJ+ʾIL	IŠ-TA-AŠ-NI-DINGIR		VAS IX 156 11+
3825.	JI-ŠT-ŠNIJ+ʾEL	IŠ-TA-AŠ-NI-EL		SIMMONS 46 30
3826.	JI-ŠT-ŠNIJ+ʾIL	IŠ-TA-AŠ-NI-IL		SYRIA V 274 HANA
3827.	JI-T-ŠAWAB-U	IŠ-TA-BU		B 24 HANA
3828.		IT-NU-ŠA		M

3829.	ʾITT-A+ʾIL-I	IT-TA-I_3-LI_2		M
3830.	JI-NTIN	IT-TI-IN		M
3831.		IT-TU-NU-UM		M
3832.	JI-ḎKUR+RAPIʾ	IZ-KUR-RA-BI		BM 81591 7
3833.	JI-ḎKUR-UM	IZ-KUR-RUM		LANGDON XXIX 24
3834.	JI-ZMEʾ+ʾIL	IZ-ME-DINGIR		VAS IX 141 2
3835.	JI-ZNUR-UM	IZ-NU-RU-UM		SIMMONS 48 20+
3836.	JI-ZNUR-UM	IZ-NU-RUM		CT XLV 82 7 25
3837.	JI-ḎRAʿ+DAGAN	IZ-RA-AH̱-D-DA-GAN		B 24 HANA+
3838.	JI-SRID-UM	IZ-RI-TUM		CT XLV 116 16
3839.	ʿIZZ-AJA	IZ-ZA-A-IA	FN	XIII 1 III 68
3840.	ʿIZZ-AN	IZ-ZA-AN		M
3841.	ʿIZZ+ʾAB-I	IZ-ZA-BI		C+
3842.	ʿIZZ-AN-I	IZ-ZA-NI		M
3843.		IZ-ZI-BI-LA-TUM	FN	M
3844.	ʿIZZ-U+ŠAPAR	IZ?-ZU?-ŠA-PA-AR		BIN II 98 5
3845.	ʿIZZ-U-NI	IZ-ZU-UN-NI		M
3846.	JAʿIL	JA-A-IL-KI	GN	M+
3847.	JA-BLIM-UM	JA-AB-LI-MU-UM		RUTTEN 2 17+
3848.	JA-BNAH̱	JA-AB-NA-AH̱		M
3849.	JA-ʿDIJ+....	JA-AH̱-DI-[....]		M
3850.	JA-H̱ŠIJ+ʾIL	JA-AH̱-SI-DINGIR		M
3851.	JA-HWIJ+ʾIL	JA-AH̱-WI-DINGIR		M
3852.	JARN-UM	JA-AR-NU-UM		RUTTEN 22 17
3853.	JATR-A+ʾIL	JA-AT-RA-IL		I
3854.	JABAŠ-IJ-I	JA-BA-SI-I	TRIBE	M
3855.	JABAŠ-IJ-IM	JA-BA-SI-IM	TRIBE	M
3856.	JABAŠ-IJ-I	JA-BA-SI-JI	TRIBE	M
3857.	JA-KWUN-AN	JA-GU-NA-AN		U
3858.	JAʿIL	JA-I-IL-KI	GN	M+
3859.	JAʿIL-AN	JA-I-LA-AN		M
3860.	JAʿIL-AJ-I	JA-I-LA-JI-KI	GN	M
3861.	JAʿIL-AN-I	JA-I-LA-NI	TRIBE	SHEMSHARA P.100
3862.	JAʿIL-AN-IM	JA-I-LA-NIM	TRIBE GEN	M+, SHEMSHARA P. 100+
3863.	JAʿIL-AN-U	JA-I-LA-NU	TRIBE	C
3864.	JAKAL-ITIJ-IM	JA-KA-LI-TE-IM	TRIBE GEN	M
3865.	JAKAL-ITIJ-I	[JA]-KA-LI-TI-I	TRIBE GEN	M
3866.	JA-KWIN+ʾIL	JA-KI-IN-DINGIR		JEA VII 196
3867.	JA-WMAʾ+ʾAH̱-UM	JA-MA-A-H̱U-UM		RA LXV 52 X 49
3868.	JA-WMAʾ+ʿAMM-I	JA-MA-H̱A-MI-KI	GN	M
3869.	JA-WMAʾ+ʿAMM-UM	JA-MA-H̱A-MU-UM		M
3870.	JAMIN-UM	JA-ME-NU-UM		TA 1931, 538 IV 1, 13
3871.	JA-ʾMIʾ+ʾIL-A	JA-MI-I-LA		M
3872.	JAʾN-A+ʾAHL-UM	JA-NA-A-LUM	GN	MRS VI P.125 61
3873.	JAʾN-AN	JA-NA-AN-KI	GN	M+
3874.	JAʾN-UM+PI	JA-NU-UM-BI-KI	GN	M
3875.	JARAN-I	JA-RA-A-NI	FN	A. 21 9
3876.	JA-RʿIJ+HADD-U	JA-RI-A-DU		RA LXV 50 VIII 64
3877.	JARIN-IM	JA-RI-NI-IM	GEN	CT XLV 89 III 9
3878.	JATAR+ʾAH̱-UM	JA-TA-AR-H̱U-UM		I
3879.	JA-JTIR+NAN-AM	JA-TE-IR-NA-NAM	ACC	M
3880.	JA-JTIR+NAN-IM	JA-TE-IR-NA-NIM	GEN	M
3881.	JA-JTIR+NAZI	JA-TE-IR-NA-ZI		SYRIA XX 174 MARI
3882.	JA-JTIR+NAN-AM	JA-TI-IR-NA-NAM	ACC	M
3883.	JA-JTIR+NAN-IM	JA-TI-IR-NA-NIM	GEN	M+
3884.	JA-JTIR+NAN-UM	JA-TI-IR-NA-NU-UM		M+
3885.	JI-JBAL-AT-UM	JI-BA-LA-TUM	FN	U
3886.	JI-MŠIJ+ʾIL	JI-IM-SI-DINGIR		M
3887.	JIRʾ-I	JI-IR-I	TRIBE	IX 248 15'
3888.	JU-MRAS̱+ʾIL	JU-UM-RA-AS̱-DINGIR		M+
3889.	KAWJ-AJA	KA-A-IA-A-IA		M+
3890.	KAWJ-AN	KA-A-IA-AN		RA LXV 51 IX 58
3891.	KAWJ-AN	KA-A-IA-AN	FN	C
3892.	KAʾK-A	KA-A-KA		A.
3893.	KAHAL-AN	KA-A-LA-AN		M+
3894.	KAWJ-A+LAʾL-UM	KA-A-LA-LUM		M

3895.	KAHAL-I+ʾIL-U+MA	KA-A-LI-DINGIR-MA		M+
3896.	KAHAL-I+ʾIL-U+MA	KA-A-LI-I-LU-MA		XIV 62:4+
3897.	KAHAL-IJA	KA-A-LI-IA		M
3898.	KAHAL-I+HADD-U	KA-A-LI-D-IM		M+
3899.	KAʾAM-I	KA-A-MI		A.
3900.	KABKAB-AH	KA-AB-KA-BA	FN	M+
3901.	KABL-AK-UM	KA-AB-LA-KU-UM		B 32
3902.	KABŠ-AN-UM	KA-AB-SA-NU-UM		YOS V 18 17
3903.	KABD-U+KA+ʾAB-I	KA-AB-TU-KA-A-BI		UET V 688:8,12
3904.	KAKK-AH	KA-AK-KA	FN	M
3905.	KAKK-A+ʾAŚJ-AH	KA-AK-KA-A-SI-IA	FN	XIII 1 VI 11
3906.	KAKK-A+ʾAŠR-I	KA-AK-KA-AŠ-RI	FN	XIII 1 V 1
3907.	KAKK-A+LIʾD-I	KA-AK-KA-LI-DI	FN	X 10 5
3908.	KAKK-A+MANN-U	KA-AK-KA-MA-AN-NU		M
3909.	KAKK-A+NAʿM-I	KA-AK-KA-NA-AḪ-MI	FN	XIII 1 VII 30
3910.	KAKK-A+NILŠ-I	KA-A[K]-KA-NI-EL?-ŠI?	FN	XIII 1 VIII 41
3911.	KAKK-A+NIʾŠ-U-JA	KA-AK-KA-NI-ŠU-IA		RA LXV 64 VI 35
3912.	KAKK-A+RIMŠ-I	KA-AK-KA-RI-IM-ŠI	FN	RA LXV 60 III 5
3913.	KAKK-U	KA-AK-KU	FN	C+
3914.	KALB+ʾIL	KA-AL-BA-DINGIR		M
3915.	KALB-AT-UM	KA-AL-BA-TUM	FN	RA LXV 61 IV 46
3916.	KALB+ḪAM-I	K[A]-AL-BU-D-A-MI		XIII 1 X 20
3917.	KALK-AJA	KA-AL-KA-IA		CT XLVIII 89 REV.
3918.	KALK-AT-UM	KA-AL-KA-TUM	MN	CT VIII 12C 1 6 9+
3919.	KAMN-IJA	KA-AM-NI-IA		VAS XVI 78:0
3920.	KAMT-AN	KA-AM-TA-AN		M
3921.	KANN-A+MA+ʾIL	KA-AN-NA-MA-DINGIR		M
3922.	KANN-I	KA-AN-NI		XIII 1 IX 62
3923.	KANUK-A	KA-AN-NU-UK-KA		M
3924.	KANZ-AN	KA-AN-ZA-AN	FN	C+
3925.	KANZ-U	KA-AN-ZU	FN	M+; C II 45 II 40
3926.	KANZ-....	KA-AN-ZU-UN-[....]	FN	M
3927.	KARŠ-AN	KA-AR-ŠA-AN		RA LXV 54 XII 23
3928.	KAŚP-AN-U	KA-AŠ$_2$-BA-NU		M
3929.	KATR-AJA	KA-AT-RA-IA	FN	XIII 1 III 8
3930.	KATR-IM	KA-AT-R[I-I]M	GEN	HARRIS 75 17
3931.	KATR-U	KA-AT-RU		B 33+
3932.	KATR-UM	KA-AT-RU-UM		WATERMAN 14 L.E.+
3933.	KABAS-I-JE	KA-BA-AZ-ZI-E		A.
3934.	KAʾB-I+ʾATT-A	KA-BI-A-TA		M
3935.	KAʾB-I+BEʿL	KA-BI-BE-EL		YOS XIII 432:12
3936.	KAʾB-I+BURŠ-A	KA-BI-BU-UR-ŠA	FN	XIII 1 XIV 53
3937.	KABID-AH	KA-BI-DA	FN	M+
3938.	KAʾB-I+DAGAN	KA-BI-D-DA-GAN		M+
3939.	KABID-AJA	KA-BI-DA-IA	FN	M
3940.	KAʾB-I+JADAʿ	KA-BI-E-DA-AḪ		XIII 1 XI 54
3941.	KAʾB-I+HEDD-A	KA-BI-E-D-IM		M+
3942.	KAʾB-I+JE-JPUʿ	KA-BI-E-PU-UḪ		M
3943.	KAʾB-I+JARAḪ	KA-BI-E-RA-AḪ		RA LXV 41 II 29+;B 32+
3944.	KAʾB-IJA	KA-BI-IA		M+
3945.	KAʾB-I+HADD-U	KA-BI-D-IM		B 32, M+, C
3946.	KABID-T-A	KA-BI-IT-TA	MN	C II 6
3947.	KAʾB-I+LA+RIWM	KA-BI-LA-RI-IM		RA LXV 47 VI 65+; C+
3948.	KABIS-AT-UM	KA-BI-ZA-TUM	FN	C
3949.	KABIS-UM	KA-BI-ZUM		B 32
3950.	KADAD-A	KA-DA-DA	GEN	BM 17060 30+
3951.	KADAD-UM	KA-DA-DU-UM	FN	BM 17063A 34
3952.	QADIŠ-UM	KA-DI-ŠUM		RA LXV 52 XI 2
3953.	KADUL-I	KA-DU-LI	FN	M
3954.	KAʾK-A	KA-KA		A.
3955.	KAKK-A+JIŠʿ-AH	KA-KA-IŠ-ḪA	FN	M+
3956.	KAKK-A+NIʾŠ-U-JA	KA-KA-NI-ŠU-IA	FN	RA LXV 65 VII 44
3957.	KAKKAR-I	KA-KA-RI		RA LXV 50 IX 7
3958.	KAKK-ATAN-UM	KA-KA-TA-NU-UM		SIMMONS 104 6
3959.	KAKK-A+TUWR-I-JA	KA-KA-TU-RI-IA	FN	M
3960.	KALAL+TULAʿ-HA	KA-LA-AL-ṬU-LA-A	FN	M, C

3961.	KALAL-UM	KA-LA-LUM		M
3962.	KAʾL-IJA	KA-LI-IA		RA LXV 53 XI 48
3963.	KAʾL-IJA	KA-LI-IA	FN	C
3964.	KAMAN-IN-UM	KA-MA-NI-NU-UM		EDZARD, DER 68 IV 11
3965.	KAMAN-UM	KA-MA-NU-UM		B 45+
3966.	KAʾM-AT-UM	KA-MA-TUM	FN	C
3967.	KAʾM-A+ṢILL-U	KA-MA-ZI-LU?	FN	VAS XIII 9 R. 2
3968.	KAʾM-A+ṢILL-UM	KA-MA-ZI-LUM	FN	B 33+
3969.	KAʾM-I+JAʾAR-UM	KA-MI-IA-A-RUM		VAS VII 128 46
3970.	KAMIN-UM	KA-MI-NU-UM		PBS VIII/1 32 II 6
3971.	KAMIS-UM	KA-MI-ZU-UM		AJSL XLIV 243 NO. 32
3972.	KAMIS-UM	KA-MI-ZUM		CT VIII 49A 7
3973.	KANAK+RAWḪ-I	KA-NA-AK-RA-ḪI		VAS XIII 79 R. 7
3974.	KANAK+RAWḪ-U	KA-NA-AK-RA-ḪU		VAS XIII 66 R. 6
3975.	KANAK+RAWḪ-UM	KA-NA-AK-RA-ḪU-UM		VAS XIII 66A R. 5+
3976.	KANAN-UM	KA-NA-NU-UM		B 45+
3977.	KANAP-AN	KA-NA-PA-AN		M+
3978.	KANAŠ-UM	KA-NA-ŠUM		TIM III 126 15
3979.	KANAT-I	KA-NA-TI		LIMET, SCEAUX CASS. P. 114
3980.	QANIJ-AN-U	KA-NI-IA-NU		M
3981.	KANIK+RUWḪ-IM	KA-NI-IK-RI-IM	GEN	B 33
3982.	KANIK+RUWḪ-UM	KA-NI-IK-RU-UM		B 33+
3983.	KANIK+RUWḪ-UM	KA-NI-IK-RUM		B 33
3984.	KANIK-AN	KA-NI-KA-AN		M
3985.	KANIŠ-AH	KA-NI-SA		RA LXV 60 III 12+
3986.	KANIŠ-AN	KA-NI-SA-AN		M+
3987.	KANIŠ-IT-UM	KA-NI-SI-T[UM]	FN	M
3988.	KANIŠ-IT-UM	KA-NI-ŠI-TUM	FN	M+
3989.	KANIŠ-UM	KA-NI-ŠUM		RUTTEN 14 23
3990.	KANUT-UM	KA-NU-TUM		RA LXIV 43
3991.	KAPAŠ-UM	KA?-PA-SU-UM		KISURRA 58 10
3992.	KAʾB-I+ʾAHL-UM	KA-PI-IA-LUM		UET V 626 11, 702 REV. 5
3993.	KARAN-AT-IM	KA-RA-NA-[T]IM	FN	M
3994.	KARAN-AT-UM	KA-RA-NA-TUM	FN	CT II 40B 1, M
3995.	QARAʾ+ŠUM-U-JA	KA-RA-SU-LUM		CT II 30 34
3996.	QARAʾ+ŠUM-U-JA	KA-RA?-SU-MU-IA		CT II 30 3
3997.	KAʾR-IJA	KA-RI-IA		RA LXV 52 X 25
3998.	KARIT-AN	KA-RI-TA-AN		RA LXV 41 II 36
3999.	KAʾŠ-AN-UM	KA-SA-NU-UM		SIMMONS 128:5
4000.	KAŠER-UM	KA-ŠE-RUM		X 30 3
4001.	KAŠIL-UM	KA-ŠI-LUM		HARRIS 69 9
4002.	KATIR-I	KA-TI-RI	GEN	UET V 88 2, SEAL, A. 37 12
4003.	KAZIB-IM	KA-ZI-BI-IM	GEN	M+
4004.	KAZIB-U	KA-ZI-BU		M
4005.	KAZIR-AM	KA-ZI-RA-AM	NOM	RA LXV 52 X 24
4006.	KA+ṢUWR-A+ʾIL	KA-ZU-RA-DINGIR		M
4007.	KA+ṢUWR-I+ḪAʾL-A	KA-ZU-RI-ḪA-LA		M
4008.	KABKAB-IM	KAB-KA-BI-IM	GEN	C
4009.	KABKAB-UM	KA[B-K]A-BU-UM		RA LXV 52 X 77
4010.	KABŠ-AT-UM	KAB-SA-TUM	FN	M+
4011.	KAMM-AT-UM	KAM-MA-TUM	FN	M+
4012.	KIBAR	KI-BA-AR		RA LXV 47 VII 19
4013.	KIBR+ʾABB-A	KI-BI-IR-D-AB-BA		M+
4014.	KIBR+ḪAJJ-A	KI-BI-IR-E$_2$-A		XIV 62:23
4015.	KIBR+JARAḪ	KI-BI-IR-D-EN-ZU		RUTTEN 11 25
4016.	KIBIR-I	[K]I-BI-RI		RA LXV 43 III 77
4017.	KIBIS-AN	KI-BI-ZA-AN		M
4018.	KIBUN-UM	KI-BU-NU-UM		TIM III 33 5+
4019.		KI-DA-ḪU-MU		RA LXV 41 II 31
4020.	KIHIL-AH	KI-ḪI-LA	FN	M+
4021.	KIHIL-A-HA	KI-ḪI-LA-A	FN	M
4022.	KIHIL-IM	KI-ḪI-LIM	GEN	M
4023.	KIHIL-UM	KI-ḪI-LUM		M+
4024.	KIBR+ʾABB-A	KI-IB-RA-AB-BA		CT XXIX 14 16
4025.	KIBR+ʾABB-A	KI-IB-RA-BA		CT XXIX 14 29
4026.	KIBR-I+DAGAN	KI-IB-RI-D-DA-GAN		M+

4027.	KIBR-I+ʿAŠTAR	KI-IB-RI-EŠ$_4$-DAR		M+
4028.	KIBŚ-AT-UM	KI-IB-SA-TUM	FN	RA LXV 56 I 11
4029.	KIBS+HADD-U	KI-IB-ZA-DU	FN	A.
4030.	KIBS-AT-UM	KI-IB-ZA-TUM	FN	M+
4031.	KIBS-I+HEDD-A	KI-IB-ZI-E-D-IM		M
4032.	KIBS-I+JARAḪ	KI-IB-ZI-E-RA-AḪ		RA LXV 43 III 44+
4033.	KIBS-I+HADD-U	KI-IB-ZI-D-IM		M+
4034.	KIBS-U-NA	KI-IB-ZU-UN-NA	FN	M+
4035.	QIDM-AN-UM	KI-ID-MA-NU-UM		U
4036.	KIKKIN-I	KI-IK-KI-NI	GEN	B 49+
4037.	KIKKIN-U	KI-IK-KI-NU		B 49+
4038.	KIKKIN-UM	KI-IK-KI-NUM		B 49
4039.	KIKKIR-IM	KI-IK-KI-RI-IM	GEN	M
4040.	KIMM-AH	KI-IM-MA	FN	M
4041.	KIMM-AN	KI-IM-MA-AN	FN	C
4042.	KIMR-AN-U	KI-IM-RA-NU		M
4043.	QIMṢ-I+JARAḪ	KI?-IM-ZE$_2$-RA-AḪ		EDZARD, DER 231:2
4044.	KIWN+BUWZ-AN-UM	KI-IN-BU-ZA-NU-UM		HARRIS 68 14
4045.	KIWN+NAHR-IM	KI-IN-NA-RI-IM	GEN	M+
4046.	KINZ-IJA	KI-IN-ZI-IA		M
4047.	KIPT-UM	KI-IP-TU-UM		M
4048.	KIRB-AN	KI-IR-BA-AN		RA LXV 51 IX 36
4049.	KIRZ-UM	KI-IR-ZU-UM	FN	RA LXV 64 VI 26
4050.	QIJŚ+ʾAG-U	KI-IŠ-A-GU	FN	XIII 1 I 70
4051.	QIJŚ-T-I+ʾADM-U	KI-IŠ-TI-AD-MU		M+
4052.	QIJŚ-T-I+LIʾL-IM	KI-IŠ-TI-LI-LIM	GEN	RA LXIV 34 NO.26
4053.	QIJŚ-T-I+MAM-A	KI-IŠ-TI-D-MA-AM-MA		XIV 61:5
4054.	QIJŚ-T-I+MAM-A	KI-IŠ-TI-D-MA-MA		M+
4055.	QIJŚ-T-I+NUN-U	KI-IŠ-TI-D-NU-NU		M+
4056.	QIJŚ-T-UM	KI-IŠ-TUM	FN	XIII 1 III 16
4057.	KITT-AN-IM	KI-IT-TA-NI-IM	GEN	SIMMONS 63 2
4058.	GIZZ-I	KI-IZ-ZI		A.+
4059.	KIKKIN-IM	KI-KI-NI-IM	GEN	B 49
4060.	KIKKIN-IM	KI-KI-NIM	GEN	B 49+
4061.	KIKKIN-UM	KI-KI-NU-UM		BM 82437 2 6
4062.	KIʾL-AN	KI-LA-AN		M
4063.	KIʾL-I+ʿAMM-I	KI-LI-AM-MI	GEN	MRS XVI 12:2
4064.	KIʾL-I+BELAʾ-I	KI-LI-BE-LA-I		M
4065.	KIʾL-I+ʾIL	KI-LI-DINGIR		CT IV 33B 19
4066.	KIʾL-I+ʾIL-UM	KI-LI-DINGIR-LUM		XIII 106 14
4067.	KIʾL-IJA	KI-LI-IA		RA LXV 45 V 55
4068.	KIʾL-U+MAʾN-A	KI-LU-MA-NA	FN	RA LXV 56 I 9
4069.	KIʾL-UM+ʾALLAI	KI-LUM-AL-LA-I	FN	XIII 1 XI 49
4070.	KI+MARUṢ	KI-MA-RU-UṢ		A 3549+
4071.	KIʾM-AT-IM	KI-MA-TIM	FN GEN	M
4072.	KIʾM-I+ʾEL	KI-MI-EL		UCP X/3 2 2
4073.	KI+MILK-I+ʾEL	KI-MI-IL-KI-EL		KISURRA 112:8
4074.		KI-NA-AT-RA-....		M
4075.	KIWN-A+ʾIL-I	KI-NA-I$_3$-LI$_2$		M
4076.	KINAN-AT-UM	KI-NA-NA-TUM		UCP X/1 27 7+
4077.	KINAN-U	KI-NA-NU		B 45+
4078.	KINAN-UM	KI-NA-NU-UM		UCP X/1 P. 58+
4079.	KIWN-I+BAWŠ-I	KI-NI-BA-ŠI	FN	HARRIS 45 8
4080.	KIWN-I-Š+LUʾP-A	KI-NI-IŠ-LU-BA		EDZARD, DER 94:17;95:6
4081.	KIWN-I-Š+MAʾT-UM	KI-NI-IŠ-MA-TUM	FN	M+; C
4082.		KI-NI-IT-[TUM]		XIII 1 I 7
4083.	KIWN-U+BAWŠ-I	KI-NU-BA-ŠI		LANGDON XXVIII 12
4084.	KIWN-UM+ʾADAL	KI-NU-UM-A-DA-AL		RA LXV 48 VII 60
4085.	KIʾR-I+DAGAN	KI-RI-D-DA-GAN		RA LXV 52 X 21
4086.	KIRUʾ-IM	KI-RI-E-IM	FN GEN	X 135 3
4087.	KIRUʾ-U	KI-RU-U$_2$	FN NOM	X 32 3+
4088.	KIRUʾ-UM	KI-RU-UM	FN	M+
4089.	QIJŚ-AT-UM	KI-SA-T[U-U]M	MN	M
4090.	QIJŚ-AT-UM	KI-SA-TUM	MN	VAS IX 175 5+, M
4091.	KIŠAM-AN-U	KI-ŠA?-MA-NU		XIII 1 V 60
4092.	QIJŚ-AT-IM	KI-ŠA-TIM	MN GEN	M+

4093.	QIJŠ-AT-UM	KI-ŠA-TUM	MN	XIII 1 V 19
4094.	QIJŠ-IM	KI-ŠI-IM	GEN	M
4095.	KISIBIR-AT-UM	KI-ZI-BI-RA-TUM	FN	RA LXV 61 IV 50
4096.	KIZUR-I	KI-ZU-RI		RA LXV 43 III 41,42
4097.	KIʾZ-UM	KI-ZU-UM		RA LXV 43 IV 16
4098.	KUʾB-A+BUWZ-I	KU-BA-BU-ZI	FN	M
4099.	KUʾB-A+ʾEL	KU-BA-DINGIR		M
4100.	KUʾB-A+ʾEL	KU-BA-EL		X 91 4'
4101.	KUBAS-AT-UM	KU-BA-ZA-TUM	FN	RA LXV 58 I 32
4102.	KUBAS-U+....	KU-BA-ZU-[....]		RA LXV 50 VIII 83
4103.	KUDAD-AN-UM	KU-DA-DA-NU-UM		U
4104.	KUDAD-I	KU-DA-DI	FN	RA LXV 61 IV 5
4105.	KUʾD-IJA	KU-DI-IA	FN	XIII 1 III 35
4106.	KUʾD-U+BIZZ-U	KU-DU-BI-IZ-ZU		A.
4107.	KUʾUT-UM	KU-ḪU-TUM		UCP X/1 38 9
4108.	QUWJ-AT-UM	KU-IA-TUM		CT VIII 29A 29+
4109.	QUWJ-UM	KU-IA-UM		YOS XII +
4110.	KUKKUB-AT-UM	KU-KU-BA-TUM		VAS IX 175:11
4111.	KUKKUB-AT-UM	KU-KU-BA-TUM	FN	XIII 1 VII 44
4112.	KUKKUN-UM	KU-KU-NU-UM		SIMMONS 111 6 15+
4113.	KUKKUŠ-AN	KU-KU-SA-AN		RA LXV 46 VI 3
4114.		KU-LA-IL-E		TCL I 182 7
4115.	KUMAN-UM	KU-MA-NU-UM		B 45
4116.	KUMIS-AN	KU-ME-ZA-AN		RA LXV 50 VIII 53
4117.	KUʾM-U+LIʾL-U	KU-MU-LI-LU		CT IV 22A 14
4118.	KUʾM-U+ṢILL-I	KU-MU-ZI-LI	FN	B 33+
4119.	KUNAN-UM	KU-NA-A-NU-UM		B 45+
4120.	KUWN-AM	KU-NA-AM	MN NOM	TIM III 17 7, M+
4121.	KUWN-A+MAʾT-UM	KU-NA-MA-TUM		U
4122.	KUNAN-AT-UM	KU-NA-NA-TUM	FN	M
4123.	KUWN-AN-IM	KU-NA-NI-IM	GEN	M
4124.	KUWN-AN-UM	KU-NA-NU-UM		RUTTEN 1 19+
4125.	KUNAN-UM	KU-NA-NU-UM		B 93
4126.	KUNAB-UM	KU-NA-PU-UM		EDZARD,DER 59:25+
4127.	KUWN-AT-UM	KU-NA-TUM	FN	C
4128.	KUWN-I+DAʾK-A	KU-NI-DA-KA		A. 367 11
4129.	KUWN-UM	KU-NU-UM		RUTTEN 33 6 SEAL+;M
4130.	KUPAD-IM	KU-PA-DI-IM	GEN	M
4131.	KUʾR-AN-U	KU-RA-NU		B 45, M, C+
4132.	KUʾR-AN-UM	KU-RA-NU-UM		B 45
4133.	KURAŠ-AN-UM	KU-RA-ŠA-NU-UM		LAESSOE P. 53+
4134.	KUʾR-U+HADD-U	KU-RU-D-IM		M
4135.	KUʾR-UM	KU-RU-UM		M+
4136.	KUʾŠ-AN	KU-SA-AN		M+
4137.	KUŠAP-IJA	KU-SA-BI-IA		M
4138.	KUŠAP-AN-UM	KU-SA-PA-NU-UM		TIM III 57 6 66 6
4139.	KUʾŠ-I+ḪIMR-I	KU-ŠI-ḪI-IM-RI		SIMMONS 87 19
4140.	KUʾT-AN-UM	KU-TA-A-NU-UM		SIMMONS 98 14
4141.	KUʾT-AN	KU-TA-AN		M
4142.	KUʾT-AN-UM	KU-TA-NU-UM		RUTTEN 38 20+
4143.	KUʾT-AT-U	KU-TA-TU	MN	B 33
4144.	KUTUL-U-HU	KU-TU-LU-U_2		RA LXV 43 III 76
4145.	QUWJ-U+DAGAN	KU-U_2-D-DA-GAN		RA LXV 41 II 43+
4146.	QUWJ-U+HADD-U	KU-U_2-D-IM		M
4147.	KUWUN-UM	KU-U_2-NU-UM		UCP X/3 1 35
4148.	KUBB-AN-UM	KU-UB-BA-NU-UM		B 45
4149.	KUBB-IJA	KU-UB-BI-IA		M
4150.	KUBUR-UM	KU-UB-BU-RUM		A.
4151.	KUBS-AT-UM	KU-UB-ZA-TUM		SZLECHTER TJ P. 186
4152.	KUDD-I	[K]U-UD-DI		RA LXV 40 I 18
4153.	KUKIM+ḪIJJ-A	KU-UK-KI-IM?-ḪI-IA	FN	X 100 5
4154.	KUKKUŠ-AN-IM	KU-UK-KU-ZA-NIM	GEN	M
4155.	KUKKUŠ-AN-UM	KU-UK-KU-ZA-NU-UM		M
4156.	KULP-AN-UM	KU-UL-BA-NU-UM		TA 1931,148
4157.	KULP-A+RAWḪ-I-JE	KU-UL-PA-RA-ḪI-E		TCL I 14 1, YOS VIII 141 34
4158.	KUʾM+DANN-UM	KU-UM-DA-NU-UM		U

4159.	KUMM-I+NAʾD-A	KU-UM-MI-NA-DA		JCS IV 113
4160.	KUʾM+NUWP-I	KU-UM-NU-BI		M
4161.	KUMR-I	KU-UM-RI		RA LXV 42 II 59
4162.	QUWJ-UM+HADD-U	KU-UM-D-U		MRS XVI 9:7
4163.	KUMS-AJA	KU-UM-ZA-A-A		HARRIS 66 16
4164.	KUWN+ʿAMM-U	KU-UN-AM-MU		MRS VI P. 249
4165.	KUND-I	KU-UN-DI	FN	XIII 1 IV 76, C
4166.	KUNDUL-AH	KU-UN-DU-LA	FN	XIII 1 III 21, CT XLIV 54 29
4167.	KUNDUL-AT-UM	KU-UN-DU-LA-TUM	FN	M+
4168.	KUWN+ʾIL-A	KU-UN-I-LA		RA LXV 53 XI 31
4169.	KUNN-A	KU-UN-NA		WO V 59+ ALA. LATE
4170.	KUNN-A+MA	[K]U-UN-NA-MA		XIV 101:8
4171.	KUNN-AM	KU-UN-NAM	NOM	XIV 102:8, 15, 24
4172.	KUNN-I	KU-UN-NI		RA LXV 52 XI 4
4173.	KUNZ-AN-AM	KU-UN-ZA-NAM	ACC	TA 1930,181
4174.	KUNZ-AN-UM	KU-UN-ZA-NU-UM		BIROT,TEA 65:17
4175.	KUNZ-AN-UM	KU-UN-ZA-NUM$_2$		TA 1930,181+
4176.	KUNZ-I	KU-UN-ZI	FN	XIII 1 V 39; C
4177.	KURKUR-IM	KU-UR-KU-RI-IM	GEN	M
4178.	KURŠ-AN-U	KU-UR-[S]A-NU		M
4179.	KURKUR-UM	KU-UR$_2$-KU-RU-UM		B 49+
4180.	KURŠ-AN-I	KU-UR$_2$-SA-NI	NOM	M
4181.	KURŠ-AN-UM	KU-UR$_2$-ŠA-NU-UM		B 45
4182.	KUŠR-AN-UM	KU-UŠ-RA-NU-UM		SIMMONS 51 17
4183.	KUŠM-I+ʾEL	KU-UŠ$_2$-MI-EL		RA LXV 48 VII 74
4184.	KUTKUT-UM	KU-UT-KU-TUM		M, KISURRA 37 8+
4185.	KUZAR-I	KU-UZ-ZA-RI		IX 259:5
4186.	KUZAR-I	KU-UZ$_2$-ZA-RI		XIII 90:5
4187.	QUWJ+JARAḪ	KU-WE-RA-AḪ		A 32133 REV.4
4188.	QUWJ-UM	KU-WU-UM		EDZARD, DER 94:18
4189.	KUʾZ-AN	KU-ZA-AN		XIV 86:5+
4190.	KUZAZ-I	KU-ZA-AZ-ZI	FN	RA LXV 60 III 52
4191.	KUZAB-AT-UM	KU-ZA-BA-TUM	FN	CT VIII 43A 4, 10+
4192.	KUZAB-AT-UM	KU-ZA-BA-TUM	MN	CT VI 30B 23+
4193.	KUZAB-U	KU-ZA-BU	FN	VAS VII 166 11
4194.	KUʾZ-AN-U	KU-ZA-NU		B 46
4195.	KUʾZ-AN-UM	KU-ZA-NU-UM		B 46
4196.	KUZAR-I	KU-ZA-RI		RA LXV 45 V 15+
4197.	KUZAR-I-NA	KU-ZA-RI-NA		RA LXV 45 V 22
4198.	KUʾZ-UM	KU-ZUM		TA 1931, 327
4199.	KURD-AN-UM	KUR-DA-A-NU-UM		RUTTEN 11 26
4200.	KURD-A+KAMB-I	KUR-DA-KA-AM-BI	FN	XIII 1 III 25
4201.	KURKUR-T-UM	KUR$_2$-KUR$_2$-TUM	MN?	PBS VIII/2 178 36
4202.	LAʾJ-JA	LA-A-A		U+
4203.	LA+ʾAB-A	LA-A-BA		U
4204.	LA+ʾA-ʾMUR-IM	LA-A-MU-RI-IM	GEN	M
4205.	LA+NAŠUʾ-IM	LA-A-NA-SU-I-IM	GEN	M
4206.	LA+ʿAN-UM	LA-A-NU-UM		U
4207.	LABIN-A	LA-AB-BI-NA		A.+
4208.	LABN-UM	LA-AB-NU-UM		TA 1930, 221
4209.	LA+ʿADN-I-JA	LA-AD-NI-IA		M
4210.	LA+ʾA-ʾDUM-U	LA-AḪ-DU-MU		4E RENC. ASS. P. 178 4
4211.	LAḪM-ATAN-UM	LA-AḪ-MA-TA-NU-UM		SIMMONS 89 10
4212.	LAḪN-UM	LA-AḪ?-NU-UM		M
4213.	LA+ʾA-ḪŠIR-UM	LA-AḪ-SI-RU-UM		BM 80368 2
4214.	LA+ʾA-ʾŠUD-I+ʾIL	LA-AḪ-SU-DI-DINGIR		XIII 4 14
4215.	LA+ʾA-HWIJ+ʾAB-I	LA-AḪ-WI-A-BI	FN	XIII 1 XIII 6
4216.	LA+ʾA-HWIJ+HADD-U	LA-AḪ-WI-A-DU		A. 95 36
4217.	LA+ʾA-HWIJ+ʾAḪ-I	LA-AḪ-WI-A-ḫI	FN	XIII 1 VII 3
4218.	LA+ʾA-HWIJ+BAʿL-U	LA-AḪ-WI-BA-AḪ-LU		XIV 29:28
4219.	LA+ʾA-HWIJ+BAʿL-U	LA-AḪ-WI-BA-LU		C
4220.	LA+ʾA-HWIJ+BEʿL-I	LA-AḪ-WI-BE-LI$_2$	FN	RA LXV 59 II 73
4221.	LA+ʾA-HWIJ+ʾIL	LA-[AḪ]?-WI-DINGIR		M
4222.	LA+ʾA-HWIJ+JAŠAR	LA-AḪ-WI-E-SA-AR		RA LXV 40 I 21
4223.	LA+ʾA-HWIJ+LA-NA	LA-AḪ-WI-LA-NA		RA LXV 65 VII 19
4224.	LA+ʾA-HWIJ+MALIK-U	LA-AḪ-WI-MA-LI-KU		M

4225.	LA+ʾA-HWIJ+MALIK	LA-AḪ-WI-MA-LIK		X 141 2
4226.	LA+ʾA-HWIJ+NIWR-I	LA-AḪ-WI-NE-RI	FN	XIII 1 II 11
4227.	LA-K+MA+ʾIL	LA-AK-MA-AN		B 33
4228.	LA+ʾA-MLIK+ʾIL	LA-AM-LI-IK-DINGIR		RUTTEN 5 22
4229.	LAMR-AT-UM	LA-AM-RA-TUM	FN	YOS XIII 294:18
4230.	LAND-AN	LA-AN-DA-AN		C
4231.	LAND-U	LA-AN-TU		TA 1931, 148
4232.	LAʾR+MULUK	LA-AR-MU-LU-UK	FN	XIII 1 IX 33
4233.	LAʾR+NAPŠ-U	LA-AR-NA-AP-SU	FN	XIII 1 I 71
4234.	LA+ʾA-RŠIJ-UM	LA-AR-ŠI-U$_2$-U[M]		TA 1931, 538 IV
4235.	LA+ʾA-ŠNIJ+ʾIL	LA-AŠ-NI-DINGIR		M
4236.	LA+BAWʾ-U	LA-BA-ʾU-U		TALLQUIST, APN P.120 LATE
4237.	LABAN	LA-BA-AN		RA LXV 41 II 32
4238.	LABW-A+BIḪR-I-Š	LA-BA-BI$_2$-RI-IŠ		HSM 7936, UR III
4239.	LA+BAŠAR	LA-BA-ŠA-AR		RA LXV 42 II 58
4240.	LA+BAWʾ-U	LA-BA-U$_2$		JCS XIII 51 292:5' A.LATE
4241.	LABW-I+ŠAM-A	LA-BI-SA-MA		UCP X/3 P. 199+
4242.	LA+ṬAJB-UM	LA-DA-BU-UM		U
4243.	LA+DJIN+JARAḪ	LA-DI-IN-E-RA-AḪ		RA LXV 46 VI 26+
4244.	LA+DIJN-AM	LA-DI-NAM	ACC	M
4245.	LAṬUP-UM	LA-DU-BU-UM		TA 31, 297
4246.	LA+ʾADUN-IM	LA-DU-NIM	GEN	M
4247.	LAWUJ-EM	LA-E-EM	ACC	M+
4248.	LA+JE-N-JBIŠ-U	LA-E-NI-BI-ŠU		YOS XII
4249.	LA+JE-RWIḪ-UM	LA-E-RI-ḪU-UM		U
4250.	LAGIG-UM	LA-GI-GU-UM		UET V 719 2
4251.	LA+ʿADN-A+ʾA-MWUT	LA-ḪA-AD-NA-A-MU-UT		M
4252.	LA+ʿANM-U	LA-ḪA-AM-MU		HARRIS 18 14
4253.	LA+ḪAMUJ-IM	LA-ḪA-MU-JI-IM	GEN	M
4254.	LAḪAN-I+KIWN-IM	LA-ḪA-NI-KI-IN-IM	GEN	UCP X/3 2 5
4255.	LAḪAN-UM	LA-ḪA-NU-UM		M+
4256.	LAʾAT-AN	LA-ḪA-TA-AN		RA LXV 51 IX 68
4257.	LA+ʾA-ḪJIJ+HADD-U	LA-ḪI-A-DU		A. 57 11, 13
4258.	LA+ʾA-ḪJIJ+ʿAN-UM	LA-ḪI-A-NU-UM		U
4259.	LA+ʾA-ḪJIJ+BIḪR-U	LA-ḪI-BI-RU		WATERMAN 25 R. 5
4260.	LAʾIŠ-T-UM	LA-ḪI-EŠ$_3$-TUM	FN	C
4261.	LAʾIP-AH	LA-ḪI-PA	FN	XIII 1 II 65+
4262.	LAʾIP-AN	LA-ḪI-PA-AN		M+
4263.	LA+ʾA-ḪJIJ+ṢADUQ	LA-ḪI-ZA-DU-UQ		A.+
4264.	LA+ḪUNN-IM	LA-ḪU-NI-IM	GEN	M
4265.		LA-ḪU-UM		TA 1931, 538 I, IV?
4266.	LAʾIJ-JA	LA-I-IA		XIII 1 VII 70+
4267.		LA-I-IA-WI		SYRIA XV 138 5, UGARIT
4268.	LAWUJ-IM	LA-I-IM	GEN	M+
4269.	LAʾIJ-UM	LA-I-JU-UM		M+
4270.	LA+ʾIL-A	[L]A?-I-LA		RA LXV 44 IV 36
4271.	LA+ʾIL-A+MILK-I	LA-I-LA-MI-IL-KI		TA 30, 75 2
4272.	LAʾIJ-T-UM	LA-I-TUM	FN	RA LXV 58 II 3
4273.		LA-KA-A-MA?-ZU?		VII 212 9
4274.	LA-KA+ʾIL	LA-KA-DINGIR		KISURRA 111 5
4275.		LA-KA-ŠI-....		B 33
4276.		LA-KA-ZA-ME-....		VIII 63 3, 15
4277.	LA-KA+ṢUBʾ-UM	LA-KA-ZU-BU-UM		M
4278.	LA+KIWN+HADD-U	LA-KI-IN-A-DU		A.
4279.	LA+KIWN-U	LA-K[I]-NU		M
4280.	LAKIŠ-UM	LA-KI-SU-[U]M		UET V 685 28
4281.	LALAʾ-AN-UM	LA-LA-A-NU-UM		UCP X/3 2 27
4282.	LALAʾ-AT-UM	LA-LA-A-TUM	FN	M
4283.	LA+LABW-UM	LA-LA-BU-[UM]?		M
4284.	LALAʾ-AT-UM	LA-LA-ḪA-TUM	FN	TCL XVIII 121 9
4285.	LALAʾ-IM	LA-LA-I-IM	GEN	XIII 85 5
4286.	LAʾL-I+ʾEL	LA-LI-E-EL		SIMMONS 70 15
4287.	LAʾL-UM	LA-LU-UM		HARRIS 76 22
4288.	LAʾL-UM	LA-LUM		HARRIS 76 2
4289.	LAMA+ʾADAʾ-E	LA-MA-A-DA-E	FN	A.
4290.	LAMA+ʾIL	LA-MA-DINGIR		B 33+, M+

4291.	LAMA+DUWD-U	LA-MA-DU-DU		M
4292.	LAMA+ʾIL-A	LA-MA-I-LA		YOS XIII 244:2+
4293.	LAMA+LA+ʾIL	LA-MA-LA-DINGIR		KAJ 72 18, LATE
4294.	LA+MANUW-IM	LA-MA-NI-IM	GEN	B 46
4295.	LA+MANUW-UM	LA-MA-NU-UM		I, TIM III 136 4
4296.	LA+ʾA-ʾMAR-UM	LA-MA-RUM		BM 80644
4297.	LAMA+ʾADAʾ-E	LA-MA-TA-E	FN	A.+
4298.	LAMAS-AH	LA-MA-ZA	FN	M
4299.	LAMAS-AT-UM	[LA]-MA-ZA-TUM	FN	XIII 1 XIV 6
4300.	LAMAS-I	LA-MA-ZI	GEN	IV 68 18, 20, 21
4301.	LAMUM-AN-UM	LA-MU-MA-NU-UM		I; TA 1931,148
4302.	LA+ʾA-ʾMUR-A	LA-MU-RA		B 33+
4303.	LA-NA+DAGAN	LA-NA-D-DA-GAN		M+
4304.	LA-NA+ʾIL	LA-NA-DINGIR		RUTTEN 27 15+
4305.	LA-NA+HADD-U	LA-NA-D-IM		XIII 109 15, 16
4306.	LA+NAŠUʾ-IM	LA-NA-SU-I-IM	GEN	M
4307.	LA+NAŠUʾ-I	LA-NA-SU-JI	GEN	M
4308.	LA-NA+ŠUM-UM	LA-NA-SU-MU-[UM]		CT VIII 26B 22
4309.	LA+NAŠUʾ-U	LA-NA-SU-U$_2$		B 33, 4E RENC. ASS. P. 178 8
4310.	LA+NAŠUʾ-UM	LA-NA-SU-U$_2$-UM		M
4311.	LA+NAŠUʾ-UM	LA-NA-SU-WU-UM		XIV 53:20+
4312.	LA+NAŠUʾ-I	LA-NI-SU-JI	FN NOM	M
4313.	LABAN-A+ʾIL-A	LA-PA-NA-I-LA		ZA XXXVIII 267
4314.	LA+PAŠIQ-UM	LA-PA-SI-KU-UM		M
4315.		LA-PA-X-LA		SIMMONS 107 11
4316.	LAʾR-A+JARAḪ	LA-RA-D-SIN		KAJ 167 23+, LATE
4317.	LA+RIWM+ḪAM-I	LA-RI-IM-D-A-MI		M
4318.	LA+RIWM+BAʿL-I	LA-RI-IM-BA-AḪ-LI		M+
4319.	LA+RIWM+BEʿL-I	LA-RI-IM-BE-LI$_2$		X 69 5
4320.	LA+RIWM+DIWR	LA-RI-IM-DI-IR		RA LXV 50 IX 22
4321.	LA+RIWM+ʿAḎIR	LA-RI-IM-ḪA-ZI-IR		DELAPORTE, CAT. BN 207
4322.	LA+RIWM+JI-JBAL-U-HU	[L]A?-RI-IM-I-BA-LU-U$_2$		M
4323.	LA+RIWM+LU-EU	LA-RI-IM-LU-U$_2$		M
4324.	LA+RIWM+NUMAḪ-A	LA-RI-IM-NU-MA-A		M
4325.	LA+RIWM+NUMAḪ-A	LA-RI-IM-NU-MA-ḪA-A		M+
4326.	LA+ŠIJM-A	LA-SI-MA		M
4327.	LAŠU+ʾEL+KA+ʾAB-IM	LA-ŠI-EL-KA-A-BI-IM		B 33
4328.	LAŠIK-U	LA-ŠI-KU	FN	EDZARD, DER 91:17
4329.	LAŠU+ʾIL	LA-ŠU-IL		U
4330.	LAŠU+MIQIṬ	LA-ŠU-MI-GI-IT		B 33
4331.	LAŠU+MIQIṬ	LA-ŠU-MI-KI-IT		B 33
4332.	LA+TEBUʾ-U	LA-TE-BU-U$_2$		B 33
4333.	LA+TEʾḪ-U	LA-TE-ḪU		MRS VI P. 196 22, LATE
4334.	LAʾT-I+RAWM-E-JE	LA-TI-RA-ME-E		M
4335.	LAṬUP-UM	LA-TU-BU-UM		TA 1931,327
4336.	LA+ṬAJB-T-UM	LA-ṬA$_3$-AB-TUM	FN	XIII 1 VI 44+
4337.	LAWUJ+HADD-U	LA-U$_2$-D-IM		A.
4338.	LAWUJ+LA+HADD-A	LA-U$_2$-LA-A-DA		A.
4339.	LAʾUŠ-UM	LA-U$_2$-ŠUM		I
4340.	LAWUJ-UM	LA-U$_2$-UM		M+
4341.	LA+ʾA-HWIJ+ʾIL	LA-WI-DINGIR		XIV 109:7
4342.	LA+ʾA-HWIJ-JA	LA-WI-IA	FN	RA LXV 60 III 37
4343.	LA+ʾA-ʾWIʾ+ʾIL	LA-WI-IḪ?-DINGIR		TIM IV 33,34, SEALS
4344.	LA+ʾA-ʾWIR-UM	LA-WI-RUM		RA XXIV 58 9 4
4345.	LAWUJ+ʾIL	LA-WU-DINGIR		M
4346.	LAWUJ+HADD-U	LA-WU-D-IM		M+
4347.	LAWUJ+LA+ʾIL	LA-WU-LA-DINGIR		M+
4348.	LAWUJ+LA+HADD-U	LA-WU-LA-D-IM		M+, C
4349.	LA+ṢABIʾ-IM	LA-ZA-BI-IM	GEN	M+
4350.	LA+ṢARR-AJA	LA-ZA-RA-A		YOS XIII 244:14
4351.	LA+ṢARR-UM	LA-ZA-RU-UM?		B 33
4352.	LASIM+ʿAN-UM	LA-ZE$_2$-IM-A-NU-UM		FLP 590:6, U
4353.	LASIM-A	LA-ZI-MA	NOM	BIN VII 31 6
4354.	LASIM+ʿAN-UM	LA-ZI-MA-NU-UM		MVN III 338:17, U
4355.	LAŠG-AN	LA$_2$-AŠ$_2$-GA-AN		RA XXXIV 176
4356.	LA-NI+ʾIL	LA$_2$-NI-DINGIR		U

4357.	LIʾD-AJA	LI-DA-A-IA		M+
4358.	LIWJ-I+DAGAN	LI-I-D-DA-GAN		M
4359.	LIWJ-UM	LI-I-UM		TA 1931, 538
4360.	LI-JA+ʾEL	LI-IA-EL		RA LXV 41 II 23
4361.	LI-JA+SITR-U-HU	LI-IA-ZI-IT-RU-U$_2$		M+
4362.	LI+JI-MLIK+....	LI-IM-LI$_2$-LI-IK-ḪI-LI-GAL$_2$		HSM 7934, UR III
4363.	LI+JI-T-ŠAMAʿ(+)ʾIL	LI?-IŠ?-TA-MI-DINGIR		IX 291 I 18
4364.		LI-LA-MI-....		SIMMONS 82 8+
4365.	LILAR-U	LI-LA-RU		SIMMONS 30 10
4366.	LIʾL-IM	LI-LI-IM	GEN	XIII 73 5
4367.	LILUR-I	LI-LU-RI	FN	RA LXV 62 IV 66
4368.	LIʾM-A+HADD-U	LI-MA-A-DU		A.
4369.	LIʾM-I+HADD-U	LI-ME-D-IM		M+
4370.	LIʾM-I+HADD-U	LI-MI-D-IM		M+
4371.	LIʾR-AT-UM	LI-RA-TUM	FN	A.
4372.	LIʾŠ-AT-UM	LI-SA-TUM	MN?	TCL X 38 6
4373.	LI+JI-TWUR+ʾAHL-I	LI-TU-UR-A-LI		JCS XXIV 62 NO.55+
4374.	LIWJ-UM	LI-U$_2$-UM		M
4375.	LI+JI-JṢIʾ+ʾAŠD-UM	LI-ZI-AŠ-DU-UM		VAS XIII 104 R. II 24
4376.	LUʾP-U+ʾEL	LU-BU-E-EL		I
4377.	LU+ḪAJJ-A+ŠAMIʿ-UM	LU-ḪA-A-A-SA-MI-UM		UET V 569 17
4378.	LU+ḪAJJ-A+ŠAMIʿ-UM	LU-ḪA-A-A-SA-MU-UM		UET V 569 8
4379.	LU+ʿAD-UM	LU-ḪA-DU-UM		YOS XIII 497:2
4380.	LUʾL-AT-UM	LU-LA-TUM	MN	BM 16820 2, 11
4381.	LUMM-AN-UM	LU-MA-A-NU-UM		SIMMONS 103 5
4382.	LUMM-A+ʾIL	LU-MA-DINGIR		KISURRA 104 29+
4383.	LUMM-AN-UM	LU-MA-NU-UM		SIMMONS 94 12+
4384.	LUʾUN-UM	LU-U$_2$-NU-UM		TOTTEN 26 UNPUBL.
4385.	LUʾUP-U	LU-U$_2$-PU		A.
4386.	LU+ʿAN-UM	LU$_2$-A-NU-UM		U
4387.	LU+KIʾL-A	LU$_2$-KI-LA		BASOR 95, 19
4388.	LU+RAPIʾ	LU$_2$-RA-BI$_2$		I
4389.	LU+RIʿAJ-HU	LU$_2$-RI-E$_2$-U$_2$		U
4390.	LU+RIʿAJ-HU	LU$_2$-RI-ḪU		U
4391.	ŠARR-UM+ʿADN-U-HU	LUGAL-AD-NU-U$_2$		SIGRIST UNPUBL.
4392.	ŠARR-UM+BAWŠ-T-I	LUGAL-BA-AŠ-TI	FN	M
4393.	ŠARR-UM+BAWŠ-T-I	LUGAL-BA-AŠ$_2$-TI	FN	M+
4394.	ŠARR-UM+JAQR-AH	LUGAL-JA-AQ-RA	FN	XIII 1 X 45
4395.	ŠARR-UM+NIWR-I	LUGAL-NI-RI	FN	XIII 1 XIII 3+
4396.	LUMM-AN-UM	LUM-MA-A-NU-UM		SIMMONS 105 16+
4397.	LUMM-A+ʾIL	LUM-MA-DINGIR		KISURRA 100 7+
4398.	LUMM-A+ʾIL	LUM-MA-IL		M+
4399.	LUMM-AN-UM	LUM-MA-NU-UM		SIMMONS 96 11+
4400.	MA+LA-NA+DITAN-A	MA-A-LA-NA-DI-TA-NA		B 34
4401.	MALIK-UM	MA-A-LI-KUM		KISURRA 81A 14
4402.	MAʾAN-UM	MA-A-NU-UM		KISURRA 22A 17+
4403.	MA+RAʾŠ-UM	MA-A-RA-SU-UM		M
4404.	MA-GRIN	MA-AG-RI-IN		HARRIS 76 15
4405.	MAʾD-AN-UM	MA-AḪ-DA-NU-UM		I
4406.	MA-HLIL-UM	MA-AḪ-LI-LUM		SIMMONS 46 34 124 16+
4407.	MA-ʾMIN-UM	MA-AḪ-MI-NU-UM		CT XLVIII 89 REV.
4408.	MAʾN-AN-UM	MA-AḪ-NA-NU-UM		HILPRECHT AV P. 91
4409.	MA-ʾNUP+ʾIL	MA-AḪ-NU-BI-DINGIR		B 33+, M+
4410.	MA-ʾNUP-U	MA-AḪ-NU-KA		VAS IX 193 18
4411.	MA-ʾNUP-UM	[MA]-AḪ-NU-KA-UM		VAS IX 192 18
4412.	MA-ʾNUP-U	MA-AḪ-NU-PU		M
4413.	MA-ʾNUP+ʾIL	MA-AḪ-NU-UP-DINGIR		B 33+, M+
4414.	MA-ʾNUP+ʾIL-I	MA-AḪ-NU-UP-I$_3$-LI$_2$		B 33+
4415.	MAHR-AN-UM	[M]A-AḪ-RA-NU-UM		U
4416.	MA-ḪŠIM-AN-UM	MA-AḪ-ŠI-MA-NU-UM		B 46+
4417.	MAMM-AT-UM	[M]A-A[M]-MA-TUM	FN	RA LXV 64 VI 9
4418.	MAMN-UM	MA-AM-NU-UM		I
4419.	MANN+BALTI+ʾIL	MA-AN-BA-AL-TI-DINGIR		RA LXIV 34 NO. 24
4420.	MANMAN-UM	MA-AN-MA-NU-UM		UCP X/3 P. 199+
4421.	MANN-A+....	MA-AN-N[A-....]		M
4422.	MANN-A+BALTI+ʾIL	MA-AN-NA-BA-AL-TI-DINGIR		M

4423.	MANN-AJA	MA-AN-NA-IA	FN	RA LXV 62 V 49
4424.	MANAN-IM	MA-AN-NA-NIM	GEN	B 46
4425.		MA-AN-NA-ŠE	FN	RA LXV 58 I 60
4426.	MANN-AT-UM	MA-AN-NA-TUM	FN	WATERMAN 52 2+, X 2 6
4427.	MANN-IJA	MA-AN-NI-IA		M+
4428.	MA-NTIN-U	URU-MA-AN-TI-NU	GN	BM 16387
4429.	MA-NTIN-UM	MA-AN-TI-NU-UM		HARRIS 31 13+
4430.	MA-NZAL-AN-UM	MA-AN-ZA-LA-NU-UM		UET V 465 17
4431.	MARMAR-AN-IM	MA-AR-MA-RA-NIM	GEN	B 93
4432.	MARṢ-AJA	MA-AR-ZA-IA	FN	M
4433.	MAŠD-AK-UM	MA-AŠ-DA-KUM		TA 30, 615 6
4434.	MAŠḪ-AT-UM	MA-AŠ-ḪA-TUM	FN	M
4435.	MAŠḪ-IM	MA-AŠ-ḪI-IM	GEN	M+
4436.	MAŠḪ-UM	MA-AŠ-ḪU-UM		M+
4437.	MA-ŠKAK-IM	MA-AŠ-KA-KI-[I]M	GEN	M
4438.	MA-ŠMAR-IM	MA-AŠ-MA-RI-IM	GEN	M
4439.	MA-ŠMIʿ-AN-AM	MA-AŠ-MI-A-NA-AM	ACC	M
4440.	MAŠK-U	[M]A-AŠ$_2$-KU		M
4441.	MAŠK-UM	MA-AŠ$_2$-KU-UM		M
4442.	MAŠK-UM	MA-AŠ$_2$-KUM		BM 16821 8+
4443.	MA-ŠPAR-UM	MA-AŠ$_2$-PA-RU-UM		SUMER XXIII 153 8, 17, 23
4444.	MATQ-U+NAN-A	MA-AT-KU-NA-NA	FN	RA LXV 60 III 33
4445.	MATAN-I	MA-AT-TA-NI		TIM II 99:3
4446.	MA-ḎMAR-AH	MA-AZ-MA-RA	FN	M+
4447.	MA-ḎMAR-AT-UM	MA-AZ-MA-RA-TUM	FN	CT VIII 41A 3 4+
4448.	MA-ḎMAR-UM	MA-AZ-MA-RU-UM		SIMMONS 52 17+, M
4449.	MA-ZNIJ-AT-UM	MA-AZ-NI-A-T[UM]	FN	JCS XIX 56
4450.	MAZN-UM	MA-AZ-NU-UM		MOORTGAT 345
4451.	MA-ZRAQ-AT-UM	MA-AZ-RA-QA-TUM	FN	XIII 1 II 37
4452.	MADAG-AT-UM	MA-DA?-GA-TUM	FN	IX 24 III 22
4453.	MAʾD-IJA	MA-DI-IA		RA LXV 55 XIII 49
4454.	MAʾD-I+JAM-A	MA-DI-IA-MA		UCP X/1 33 10
4455.	MAʾD-I+JAT-UM	MA-DI-IA-TUM		UCP X/1 P. 59+
4456.	MAGAN-I	MA-GA-NI	GEN	MRS XVI P. 329 UGARIT
4457.	MAGAN-UM	MA-GA-NU-UM		U
4458.	MAʾAN-IJA	MA-ḪA-NI-IA	FN	M+
4459.	MAʾAN-IM	MA-ḪA-NIM	GEN	BM 72766
4460.	MAʾAN-UM	MA-ḪA-NU-UM		SIMMONS 96 15; M
4461.	MAHIR-AH	MA-ḪI-RA	FN	XIII 1 VII 34
4462.	MAHIR-AN-IM	MA-ḪI-RA-NIM	GEN	C II 2 8
4463.	MAʾJ-AT-UM	MA-IA-TUM	FN	B 34+
4464.	MA-ḎMAR-AT-UM	MA-IZ-MA-RA-TUM	FN	CT II 30 35
4465.	MAKAJ-JA	MA-KA-A		M+
4466.	MAKAJ-AN	MA-KA-A-AN		RA LXV 43 IV 2+
4467.	MAKAL-AN-U	MA-KA-LA-NU		VAS IX 34 6
4468.	MAKAL-UM	MA-KA-LUM		BIRCT, TEA 72 V 6+
4469.	MAKIJ-AN-UM	MA-KI-A-NU-UM		TA 31, 223
4470.	MA-KWIN	MA?-KI-EN		C
4471.	MAKIJ-AH	MA-KI-IA	FN	M
4472.	MAKIJ-AT-UM	MA-KI-IA-TUM		A 7724 2
4473.	MAGUN-AT-UM	MA-KU-NA-TUM	FN	C+
4474.	MALAK+ʾIL-I	MA-LA-AK-I$_3$-LI$_2$		M
4475.	MALAK-U+ʾIL	MA-LA-KU-IL		M
4476.	MAʾL-I+ḪARAB-A	MA-LI-A-RA-BA?		CT II 30 29
4477.	MAʾL-IJA	MA-LI-IA		M
4478.	MALIK+DAGAN	MA-LI-IK-D-DA-GAN		M
4479.	MALIK-AH	MA-LI-KA	FN	M
4480.	MALIK-AT-UM	MA-LI-KA-TUM		BM 17060 35+
4481.	MALIK-AT-UM	MA-LI-KA-TUM	FN	EDZARD, DER 91:3
4482.	MALIK-I	MA-LI-KI	GEN	B 34, A. 77 6
4483.	MALIK-UM	MA-LI-KUM		U, B 34+
4484.	MALIL-UM	MA-LI-LUM		B 34+
4485.	MAʾL-I+ŠUM-U-HU	MA-LI-SU-MU-U$_2$		TIM I 29 10
4486.	MALIK+ŠUM-U-HU	MA-LIK-SU-MU-U$_2$		M
4487.	MALIK+ZAʾT-UM	MA-LIK-ZA-DU-UM		B 34
4488.	MAM-A+DUNN-I	D-MA-MA-DU-UN-NI	FN	M

4489.	MAM-A+ḪAṢN-I	D-MA-MA-ḪA-AZ-NI	FN	RA LXV 56 I 7
4490.		D-MA-MA-KU	FN	M
4491.	MAM-A+QUDM-I	D-MA-MA-KU-UD-ME	FN	RA LXV 59 II 18
4492.	MANMAN-UM	MA-MA-NU-UM		B 46+
4493.	MAM-A+NUMR-I	D-MA-MA-NU-UM-RI	FN	RA LXV 65 VII 30
4494.	MAM-A+ŠARR-AH	D-MA-MA-ŠAR-RA	FN	M
4495.	MAM-A+TA-Lʾ IJ	D-MA-MA-TA-AL-E	FN	M
4496.	MAM-A+TUʾ AL-I	D-MA-MA-TU-ḪA-LI	FN	M
4497.	MAʾ M-AT-UM	MA-MA-TUM		CT XLV 96 18
4498.	MAM-A+ṢIJḪ-AT-UM	MA-MA-ZI-A-TUM	FN	RA LXV 61 IV 37
4499.	MAʾ M-IJA	MA-MI-IA		M
4500.	MANAN-A	MA-NA-AN-NA		M+
4501.	MANN-A+BALTI+ʾ EL	MA-NA-BA-AL-TE-EL		B 28+
4502.	MANN-A+BALTI+ʾ EL	MA-NA-BA-AL-TI-EL		KISURRA 70A 14+
4503.	MANN-A+BALTI+ʾ EL	MA-NA-BA-AŠ-TE-EL		M+
4504.	MANN-A+BAʿ L-A	MA-NA-BA-LA		M
4505.	MANN-A+BIʿ D-IM	MA-NA-BI-IḪ-DI-IM	GEN	HARRIS 3 18
4506.	MANAN-AJA	MA-NA-NA-A		B 34+
4507.	MANAN-AT-UM	MA-NA-NA-TUM	FN	B 93+
4508.	MANAN-IM	MA-NA-NI-IM	GEN	B 46+
4509.	MANAN-IM	MA-NA-NIM	GEN	B 46
4510.	MANAN-UM	MA-NA-NU-UM		I
4511.	MANN-ATAN	MA-NA-TA-AN		M+
4512.	MANN-ATAN-U	MA-NA-TA-NU		M
4513.	MANN-A+TAWR-I	MA-NA-TA-RI		B 34
4514.	MANN-AT-UM	MA-NA-TUM	FN	BM 81479 4
4515.	MANAW-UM	MA-NA-UM		I
4516.	MANAW-AH	MA-NA-WA	FN	XIII 1 VII 45
4517.	MANIJ-AN-UM	MA?-NI-A-NU-UM		TA 1931, 538 II
4518.	MA-ʾ NIP-UM	MA-NI-PU-UM		SIMMONS 119 10 S
4519.	MANIJ+DAGAN	MA?-NI-D-DA-GAN		A. 6 34
4520.	MANIJ+ʾ EL	MA-NI-EL		RA VIII 72 7
4521.	MA-NWIḪ-AH	MA-NI-ḪA	FN	RA LXV 58 I 36+
4522.	MANIJ+ʾ IL	MA-NI-IL		U
4523.	MANIN-I	MA-NI-NI	GEN	B 34+
4524.	MANIN-UM	MA-NI-NU-UM		B 34+
4525.	MANIJ-UM	MA-NI-UM		U; TA 30, 615:40+
4526.	MANUW-AT-UM	MA-NU-A-TUM	FN	I (UNPUBL.)
4527.	MANN-U+ŠAM-A	MA-NU-SA-MA		B 34
4528.	MANUW-T-UM	MA-NU-TUM	FN	CT VIII 28A 2, 4+
4529.	MANUW-UM	MA-NU-UM		M+
4530.	MAʾ R-A+ʾ EL	URU-MA-RA-DINGIR	GN	MRS IX 17340:7
4531.	MAʾ R-A+ʾ EL	MA-RA-EL		TA 1931, 298
4532.	MAʾ R-A+ʾ EL	URU-MA-RA-EL	GN	MRS VI 11830:10
4533.	MARAQ-A	MA-RA-QA	GEN	B 34
4534.	MARAR-UM	MA-RA-RU-UM		WATERMAN 45 R. 12
4535.	MAʾ R-AT-IJA	MA-RA-TI-IA		HARRIS 99 13
4536.	MAʾ R-AT-UM	MA-RA-TUM	MN?	TIM I 14 3
4537.	MARAṢ-UM	MA-RA-ZUM		I+, UET V 527 2
4538.	MARIʾ-AN-UM	MA-RI-A-NU-UM		B 46
4539.	MA-JRID-UN-UM	MA-RI-DU-NU-UM		SIMMONS 124 17
4540.	MAʾ R-IJAN	MA-RI-IA-AN		RA LXV 43 III 81
4541.	MAʾ R-IT-UM	MA-RI-TUM	FN	XIII 1 XIII 14
4542.	MARUʾ+JAT-UM	MA-RU-IA-TUM		DE GEN., KICH II D 43 R. 2, 4
4543.	MARUʾ+LI+ʾ EL	MA-RU-LI-EL		SIMMONS 47 18, 49 22
4544.	MARUṢ-AJA	MA-RU-ZA-IA	FN	RA LXV 61 IV 64
4545.	MAʾ R-U+ZAʾ T-U-HU	MA-RU-ZA-TU-U$_{2}$		CT XLVIII 27
4546.	MAŠAL-UM	MA-SA-LU-U[M]		HARRIS 95 10
4547.	MAŠAL-UM	MA-SA-LUM		EK I P. 40
4548.	MAʾ Š-AN-IM	MA-SA-NIM	GEN	CT XLV 93 6
4549.	MAŠIḪ-A	MA-SI-ḪA	MN NOM	M
4550.	MAŠIḪ-AN	MA-SI-ḪA-AN		XIII 1 XI 58+
4551.	MAŠIḪ-IM	MA-SI-ḪI-IM	GEN	M
4552.	MAŠIḪ-UM	MA-SI-ḪU-UM		M+
4553.	MAŠIK-T-UM	MA-SI-IK-TUM		BM 17063 26+
4554.	MAŠIK-T-UM	MA-SI-IK-TUM	FN	XIII 1 V 73; YOS XIII 453

4555.	MA-ŚJIT+ʿAN-UM	MA-SI-IT-A-NU-UM		I
4556.	MAŚUB-AH	MA?-SU-BA?	FN	XIII 1 III 24
4557.	MAʾŠ-AM	MA-ŠA-AM	ACC	M+
4558.	MAʾŠ-IJA	MA-ŠI-IA		M+
4559.	MAʾŠ-IM	MA-ŠI-IM	GEN	M+
4560.	MAʾŠ-UM	MA-ŠUM		M+
4561.	MATAʿ-A+KI+ʾEL	MA-TA-A-KI-EL		RA LXV 50 IX 20;HARRIS 19:5,SEAL+
4562.	MATAQ-I	MA-TA-KI	FN	CT IV 26A 1
4563.	MATAN-I	MA-TA-NI	FN	EDZARD, DER 33:3
4564.	MAṬAR-UM	MA-TA-RUM		M
4565.	MAʾT-AT-IM	MA-TA-TIM	MN? GEN	VAS XVI 118 2
4566.	MAʾT-AT-UM	MA-TA-TUM	FN	CT II 50 6, 18
4567.	MAʾT-AT-UM	MA-TA-TUM	MN?	LIH 29 9
4568.	MATIʿ+ʾIL	MA-TI-DINGIR		M
4569.	MATIQ-I	MA-TI-GI	FN	M+
4570.	MATIʿ+ʾAHL-I	MA-TI-IA-LI		UCP X/1 1 16
4571.	MATIʿ+JAT-U-HU	MA-TI-IA-TU-U_2		UCP X/3 107 18
4572.	MATIN-AT	MA-TI-NA-AT		U
4573.	MATIʿ+TIWR-UM	MA-TI-TI-RUM		BM 67281
4574.	MATIʿ+....	MA-TI-UT-TA-A-LI		SIMMONS 61 11
4575.	MAʾT-U+BANIJ	MA-TU-BA-NI		KISURRA 112 6
4576.	MAZAL-AH	MA-ZA-AL-LA	FN	XIII 1 IV 40+
4577.	MAʾZ-AN-I	MA-ZA-NI		KISURRA 68A 10+
4578.	MAʾZ-AN-UM	MA-ZA-NU-UM		UET V 625 9
4579.	MAʾZ-AT-UM	MA-ZA-TUM	FN	KISURRA 21 3, M
4580.	MAṢIʾ-AT-UM	MA-ZI-A-TUM	FN	WATERMAN 56 R. 8
4581.	MA-ḪZIQ-UM	MA-ZI-GU-UM		CT XLVIII 27 CASE
4582.	MAZUM-AH	MA-ZU-MA	FN	XIII 1 III 22
4583.	MA-RDAP-AN	MAR-DA-BA-AN		ITT P.4, 7031 UR III
4584.	MA-RDAP-AN-UM	MAR-DA-BA-NU-UM		U
4585.	MA-RDAP-UM	MAR-DA-BU-UM		BIN III 546; U+
4586.	MA-RḪAŠ-AN	MAR-ḪA-ŠA-AN		RA LXV 54 XII 12
4587.	MARṢ-AT-UM	MAR-ZA-TUM	FN	M+
4588.	MA-ŚKAR-UM	MAŠ-GA-RU-UM		RUTTEN 33 5, SEAL
4589.	MAŚK-UM	MAŠ-KUM		EBPN 123+
4590.	MA-ŚPAR-UM	MAŠ-PA-RU-UM		B 49+
4591.	MA-ŚPIR-UM	MAŠ-PI-RU-UM		CT VI 49B 12
4592.	ME-JPIʿ-UM	ME-BI-ḪU-UM		M
4593.	ME-JBIŚ-A	ME-BI-SA	MN	M
4594.	ME-JBIŚ-UM	ME-BI-ŠUM		M+
4595.	....+DITAN	ME-D-DI-TA-AN		UET V 497 11, 581 11
4596.		ME-E-IM-MA	FN	XIII 1 II 39
4597.	ME-DBIR	ME-ED-BI-IR		BASOR 95, 24
4598.	ME-ʿNIJ-IM	ME-EḪ-NI-IM	GEN	KISURRA 80A
4599.	ME-ʿNIJ-UM	ME-EḪ-NI-JU-UM		M
4600.	ME-ʿNIJ-UM	ME-EḪ-NU-UM		KISURRA 36 4
4601.	MIHR-I+....	ME-EḪ-RI-[....]		M
4602.	MIHR-I+HADD-U	ME-EḪ-RI-D-IM		C+
4603.	ME-ḪRIM-IM	ME-EḪ-RI-MI-IM	GEN	M+
4604.	ME-NDIB-UM	ME-EN-DI-BU-UM		KING LIH I 25 4
4605.	MENG-UM	ME-EN-GU-UM		CT XLVIII 86 REV.+
4606.	ME-NḪIB-AH	ME-EN-ḪI-BA	EN	XIII 1 I 24
4607.	ME-NḪIJ-UM	ME-EN-ḪI-I-UM		XIII 105 8
4608.	ME-NḪIM-UM	ME-EN-ḪI-MU-UM		HARRIS 57 17
4609.	MENN-AH	ME-EN-NA	FN	XIII 1 I 68+
4610.	MENN-AT-UM	ME-EN-NA-TUM	FN	XIII 1 V 32
4611.	ME-PTUḪ-IM	ME-EP-TE-IM	GEN	XIII 43 15
4612.	ME-PTUḪ-IM	ME-EP-TI-I-IM	GEN	M+
4613.	ME-PTUḪ-IM	ME-EP-TI-IM	GEN	M+
4614.	ME-PTUḪ-U	ME-EP-TU-U_2		M+
4615.	ME-PTUḪ-UM	ME-EP-TU-U_2-UM		M+
4616.	ME-PTUḪ-UM	ME-EP-TU-UM		M+
4617.	MERḪ-IM	ME-ER-ḪI-IM	GEN	M+
4618.	MERḪ-UM	ME-ER-ḪU-UM		M+; YOS XIII 321+
4619.	MERR-AM	ME-ER-RA-AM	ACC	M
4620.	MERR-IM	ME-ER-RI-IM	GEN	M+

4621.	MERR-UM	ME-ER-RUM		M+
4622.	ME-ŚKIN-IM	ME-EŠ$_3$-KI-NIM	GEN	M+
4623.	ME-ŚKIN-UM	ME-EŠ$_3$-KI-NU-UM		WALTERS, WL 95:2
4624.	ME-ŚLIB-AT-UM	ME-EŠ$_3$-LI-BA-TUM	FN	YOS V 117 1
4625.	ME-QWIM	ME-[G]I-IM	GEN	IX 291 III 16'
4626.	ME-ʿANIJ-I	ME-ḪA-A-NI?	GEN	VAS VIII 14 43
4627.	ME-ʿANIJ-U	ME-ḪA-A-NU		KISURRA 81A
4628.	ME-ʾḪAḎ-UM	ME-ḪA-DUM		UCP X/3 3:18; YONDORF 4
4629.	ME-ʿANIJ-JA	ME-ḪA-NI-IA	FN	RA LXV 58 I 43+
4630.	ME-ʿANIJ-IM	ME-ḪA-NI-IM	GEN	KISURRA 80B
4631.	ME-ʾḪIḎ-UM	ME-ḪI-DU-UM		RA LXV 54 XII 64
4632.	ME-ʾWIR-I	ME-ḪI-RI		C
4633.	ME-ʾWIR-I+ʾEL	ME-ḪI-RI-E-EL		JCS IV 109 4311 7
4634.	ME-ʾWIŠ-UM	ME-I-SU-UM		CT VI 7 21+
4635.	MIJA+MUT-A	ME-IA-MU-TA		B 34
4636.	MILK-U	ME-IL-KU	FN	RA LXV 61 IV 3+
4637.	MENN-A-HA	ME-IN-NA-A	FN	X 176:8, 15
4638.	ME-ŚKIR-UM	ME-IŠ-KI-RUM		B 34
4639.	ME-ŚLIM-UM	ME-IŠ-LI-MU-UM		HARRIS 31 18
4640.	MIŠR-IJA	ME-IŠ?-RI-IA	FN	RA LXV 60 III 35
4641.	ME-TMIH-UM	ME-IT-ME-U$_2$-UM		M
4642.	ME-TMIH-U	ME-IT-MI-JU		M+
4643.	ME-TMIH-UM	ME-IT-MU-UM		M
4644.	ME-ḎRIʿ-UM	ME-IZ-RI-JU-UM		M
4645.	ME-ʿQIB-IM	ME-KI-BI-IM	GEN	M+
4646.	ME-ʿQIB-UM	ME-KI-BU-UM		U, M+
4647.		ME-KI-I[A-....]	FN	M
4648.	ME-QWIM	ME-KI-IM		RA XXXV 119, MARI
4649.	ME-KWIN	ME-KI-IN	FN	A.
4650.	ME-KWIN-UM	ME-KI-NU-UM		M+
4651.	MEʾM-AT-UM	ME-MA-TUM	FN	BASOR 95, 21 I 21
4652.	ME-ʾMIʾ-IM	ME-MI-ḪI-IM	GEN	C
4653.	MINAN-AH	ME-NA-AN-NA	FN	RA LXV 60 III 11
4654.	MINAN-UM	ME-NA-NUM		KISURRA 175A 19
4655.	MEʾN-I+ʾEL	ME-NI-EL		RA LXV 52 X 18
4656.	ME-NWIḪ-UM	ME-NI-ḪU-UM		BIN II 94 4+
4657.	MENIJ-T-UM	ME-NI-TUM	FN	M
4658.	ME-JPIʿ-UM	ME-PI-UM		I
4659.	ME-JŠIʿ-UM	ME-SI-UM		SIGRIST UNPUBL.
4660.	ME-ṢJID-UM	ME-ṢI-TUM		B 34
4661.	ME-JŚAR-UM	ME-ŠA-RUM		A.
4662.		ME-TE-BA-AN		TA 1931, 304
4663.	ME-JTIR-AN-UM	ME-TE-RA-NU-UM		TA 1930, 489
4664.	ME-JDIʿ-UM	ME-TE-UM		I
4665.	ME-ḤZIQ-A	ME-ZI-QA		M
4666.	ME-ḤZIQ-AN	ME-ZI-QA-AN		RA LXV 44 IV 30
4667.	ME-ʿḎIR-I	ME-ZI-RI		M
4668.	ME-ṢJID-UM	ME-ZI-[T]U-UM		M
4669.	ME-ṢJID-UM	ME-ZI-TUM		XIII 1 VI 29
4670.	MIʾD-AN-UM	MI-DA-NU-UM		U+
4671.	MILK-AN-UM	MI-EL-GA-NU-UM		TA 1931, 538 I
4672.	MILK-I+ʾIL-A	MI-EL-KI-I-[LA]		UCP X/3 1 29
4673.	MILK-I+LI+ʾIL	[MI]-EL-KI-LI-IL		I
4674.	MIGIJ-UM	MI-GI-JU-UM		RA LXV 40 I 9
4675.	MI-ʾḪAḎ-UM	MI-ḪA-[TUM]?	TRIBE	IX 244:5
4676.	MI-ʾWIR-UM	MI-I-RUM		RA LXV 46 V 83
4677.	MIJA+MUT-U	MI-IA-MU-DU		KISURRA 25 11
4678.	MIJA+NAŚUʾ	MI-IA-NA-SU		XIII 1 I 18
4679.	MILʾ-A+BIJT-I	MI-IL-A-BI-TI		A. 60 2
4680.	MILK-AN-UM	MI-IL-GA-NU-UM		U; TA 31, 148
4681.	MILK-A+HADD-U	MI-IL-KA-D-IM		SYRIA XXXVII 206 27 HANA
4682.	MILK-AT-UM	MI-IL-KA-TUM		TCL XI 220 11
4683.	MILK-I+ʾIL	MI-IL-KI-DINGIR		B 34
4684.	MILK-I+HADD-U	MI-IL-KI-D-IM		M
4685.	MILK-IM	MI-IL-KI-IM	GEN	B 35
4686.	MILK-I+LA+ʾEL	MI-IL-KI-LA-EL		TA 30 615 21

4687.	MILK-I+LI+ʾEL-UM	MI-IL-KI-LI-E-LUM		A 32065:3
4688.	MILK-I+LI+ʾEL	MI-IL-KI-LI-EL		B 34, M+
4689.	MILK-I+LI+ʾIL	MI-IL-KI-LI$_2$-IL		I
4690.	MILK-I+ʾIL-U	MI-IL-KI-LU		B 34
4691.	MILK-I+LU+ʾIL-A	MI-IL-KI-LU-I-LA		VAS XVI 10 5, 9
4692.	MILK-I+ʾIL-UM	MI-IL-KI-LUM		B 34
4693.	MILK-I+TAʾG-A	MI-IL-KI-TA-GA		A. LATE
4694.	MILK-U+DANN-UM	MI-IL-KU-DA-NU-UM		UET V 549:8
4695.	MILK-U+MA	MI-IL-KU-MA		JCS XIII 51 292 R 10,A.LATE
4696.	MILK-U+MA+ʾIL	MI-IL-KU-MA-DINGIR		C+
4697.	MILK-U+MA+ʾIL	MI-IL-KU-MA-IL		B 35+
4698.	MILK-UN-IM	MI-IL-KU-NI-IM	GEN	SIMMONS 46 33
4699.	MILK-UN-IM	MI-IL-KU-NIM	GEN	SIMMONS 70 17
4700.	MIMEʾ-UM	MI-IM-[ME-U$_2$-UM]		M
4701.	MINN-AH+MINN-AH	MI-IN-NA-MI-IN-NA	FN	XIII 1 XII 1
4702.	MINAN-UM	MI-IN-NA-NU-UM		SIMMONS 18 1, 8
4703.	MI-PTUḪ-I	MI-IP-TI-I	GEN	XII 406 5
4704.	MI-PTUḪ-IM	MI-IP-TI-IM	GEN	M+
4705.	MI-PTUḪ-U	MI-IP-TU-U$_2$		RA LXIV 104:3
4706.	MI-ŠQIḪ-I	MI-IS-KI-ḪI	NOM	UET V 605 20
4707.	MI-ŠKIR-UM	MI-IŠ-KI-RUM		VAS IX 172 13
4708.	MILAL-UM	MI-LA-LUM		BM 16943 36
4709.	MIMEʾ-UM	MI-ME-U$_2$-UM		M
4710.	MINAN-I	MI-NA-NI	GEN	B 46+
4711.	MINAN-UM	MI-NA-NU-UM		B 46+
4712.	MINN-ATAN-UM	MI-NA-TA-NU-UM		HARRIS 76 11
4713.	ṢILL+ʾAKK-A	MI-NI-AK-KA		M
4714.	ṢILL+ʾANN-U	MI-NI-AN-NU		M
4715.	ṢILL+BAʿL-I	MI-NI-BA-AḪ-LI		M+
4716.	ṢILL+ʿAN-AT	MI-NI-D-ḪA-NA-AT		XIII 83 8
4717.	MI-NWIḪ-U	MI-NI-ḪU		TIM V 62 13
4718.	MI-NWIḪ-UM	MI-NI-ḪU-UM		YOS XII
4719.	MIʾŠ-AJA	MI-ŠA-IA		M+
4720.	MISAR-I	MI?-ZA-RI	FN	RA LXV 65 VI 71
4721.	MILK-AT-UM	MIL-KA-TUM		YOS XIII 112:16
4722.	MILK-I+DAGAN	MIL-KI-D-DA-GAN		TCL I 237 12 HANA
4723.	MILK-I+JARAḪ	MIL-KI-E-RA-AḪ		AJSL XLIV 243 NO. 33
4724.	MILK-I+ḪAJJ-A	MIL-KI-ḪA-A-IA	FN	IRAQ XVI 40 NA
4725.	MILK-I+HADD-U	MIL-KI-D-IM		M
4726.	MILK-I+LI+ʾEL	MIL-KI-LI-EL		VAS VIII 128 16+
4727.	MILK-I+ʾIL-U	MIL-KI-LU		B 34+
4728.	MILK-UM+MA+ʾIL	MIL-KUM-MA-DINGIR		A. LATE
4729.	MU-WPIʿ-I	MU-BI-ḪI		TA 30, 7 10
4730.	MU-WBIT-UM	MU-BI-TU-UM		LANGDON XXVII 4
4731.	MU-WDAD-U	MU-DA-DU		YOS XIII 513:9
4732.	MU-WDAD-UM	MU-DA-DU-UM		I, VAS VIII 60 5, 18+
4733.	MUT-AN-UM	MU-DA-NU-UM		U+
4734.	MUWIʾ-UM	MU-E-UM		U (MLC 80)
4735.		MU-EL-LI-[U]M		TA 1931, 698
4736.	MU-QADIM-U	MU-GA-DI-MU		CT XLV 6 33
4737.	MU-QANIT-UM	MU-GA-NI-TUM	MN?	TIM III 86 6+
4738.	MU-WQIR-AN-UM	MU-GI-RA-NU-UM		U
4739.	MU-ḪARIR-IM	MU-ḪA-RI-RI-IM	GEN	M
4740.	MU-WḪIN-UM	MU-ḪI-NU-UM		HAGER DISSERT. PL II/3
4741.		MU-ḪU-UŠ-KI		SZLECHTER TJ MAH 16194 4,SEAL
4742.	MU-KAŠAJ-EM	MU-KA-SA-A-JE-EM	ACC	M
4743.	MULUK-AN	MU-LU-GA-AN		RA LXV 41 II 35
4744.	MUNAN-AN-UM	MU-NA-NA-NU-UM		B 46
4745.	MUNAN-IM	MU-NA-NI-IM	GEN	B 46
4746.	MUNAN-IM	MU-NA-NIM	GEN	B 46
4747.	MUNAN-UM	MU-NA-NU-UM		I, B 46+
4748.		MU-NA-RU-RUM		VAS VIII 66 17 67 15
4749.	MUNUZ-I	MU-NU-ZI	FN	RA LXV 64 V 59
4750.	MU-PATIḪ-AH	MU-PA-AT-TI-IA	FN	XIII 1 VIII 38+
4751.	MU-PATIḪ-T-UM	MU-PA-AT-TI-TUM	FN	C+
4752.	MU-PAḪIR-AH	MU-PA-ḪI-ŘA	FN	XIII 1 VII 47

4753.	MU-PATIḤ-AH	MU-PA-TI-IA	FN	XIII 1 XIII 19+
4754.	MUHR-AN-UM	MU-RA-NU-UM		U
4755.	....+DITN-IM	MU-RI-IQ-TI-IT-NI-IM	GN GEN	U
4756.	MUHR-U+DAGAN	MU-RU-D-DA-GAN		RA LXV 53 XI 53
4757.	MUŜAḤ-UM	MU-SA-AḪ-ḪU-UM		UET V 722 11
4758.	MU-ŜARIK-AH	MU-SA-AR-RI-KA	FN	XIII 1 VIII 75
4759.	MUŜAḤ-UM	MU-SA-ḪU-UM		UET V P. 50+
4760.	MU-ŜALIM-AT-IM	MU-SA-LI-MA-TIM	FN GEN	BE VI/1 8 14
4761.	MU-ŜALIM-I	MU-SA-LI-MI	NOM	UCP X/1 87 11
4762.	MU-ŜALIM-IM	MU-SA-LI-MI-IM	GEN	CT VIII 47B 28
4763.	MU-ŜALIM-U	MU-SA-LI-MU		CT IV 47B 28
4764.	MU-ŜALIM-UM	MU-SA-LI-MU-UM		CT XLVIII 57 2, 3
4765.	MUŠAR-AN	MU-ŠA-RA-AN		RA LXV 50 VIII 65
4766.		MU-ŠI-[....]		M
4767.		MU-TA-[....]-AN		XIII 1 III 55
4768.	MUT+HADD-I	MU-TA-AD-DI		VAS XVI 165:4
4769.	MU-WTAR	MU?-TA-AR		IX 290 1
4770.	MUT-I+JABAL	MU-TA-BA-AL-KI	GN	OIP XI 216 IV 3
4771.		MU-TA-MU-[....]		M
4772.	MUT-AN-I	MU-TA-NI		A. 52 28
4773.	MUT-A+NIʿM	MU-TA-NI-ḪI-IM		RA LXV 43 III 51
4774.	MUT-AN-UM	MU-TA-NU-UM		B 46
4775.	MUT-A+JŠUʿ	MU-TA-ŠU-UḪ		M+
4776.	MUT-A+TA-KWIN	MU-TA-TA-KI-IN		RA LXV 51 IX 78
4777.		MU-TA-TA-RUM		M
4778.	MUT-I+JARAḪ	MU-TE-E-RA-AḪ		A 7804 13
4779.	MUT-I+JABAL	MU-TI-A-BA-AL-KI	GN	B 35+
4780.	MUT-I+JABAL-A	MU-TI-A-BA-LA-KI	GN	B 35
4781.	MUT-I+ʾAḪ-I	MU-TI-A-ḪI	GEN	B 35
4782.	MUT-I+ʿAN-AT-A	MU-TI-A-N[A-T]A		B 35
4783.	MUT-I+JARAḪ	MU-TI-A-RA-AḪ		B 35
4784.	MUT-I+JABAL	MU-TI-BA-AL-KI	GN	B 35+
4785.	MUT-I+....	MU-TI-DA-ZI-U_2		TA 1930, 489 I
4786.	MUT-I+JE-ʾMIʾ	MU-TI-E-MI-IḪ		M
4787.	MUT-I+JARAḪ	MU-TI-E-RA-AḪ		M; TCL XI 224:69+
4788.	MUT-I+ḤATK-IM	MU-TI-ḪA-AD-KI-IM	NOM	IRAQ XXX 92+ RIMAH
4789.	MUT-I+ḪURŜAN-A	MU-TI-ḪU-UR-ŠA-NA		B 35+
4790.	MUT-I+ḪURŜAN-I	MU-TI-ḪU-UR-ŠA-NI		YOS XII
4791.	MUT-I+ḪURŜAN	MU-TI-ḪUR-SAG		YOS XII+
4792.	MUT-I+JAʾN-A	MU-TI-I-IA-NA		B 35
4793.	MUT-IJA	MU-TI-IA		B 35, A.+
4794.	MUT-I+HADD-U	MU-TI-D-IM		M
4795.	MUT-I+....	[M]U?-TI-KA-ṢI-E		PBS XIII 56:8
4796.	MUT-I+ʾIL-UM	MU-TI-LUM		YOS XIII 151:4+
4797.	MUT-I+MAʾK-U-HU	MU-TI-MA-KU-U_2		M+
4798.	MUT-I+ME+ʾEL	MU-TI-ME-EL		TA 30, 615:4+
4799.	MUT-I+ŜAMŜ	MU-TI-D-UTU		A.
4800.	MUT-U+JA-NŠUʾ-HU	MU-TU-A-AN-ŠU-U_2		KISURRA 91 24
4801.	MUT-U+ʾABIḪ-IM	MU-TU-A-BI-ḪI-IM		C
4802.	MUT-U+ʾABIḪ	MU-TU-A-BI-I[Ḫ]		M
4803.	MUT-U+ḤAM-I	MU-TU-D-A-MI		RA LXV 51 IX 49
4804.	MUT-U+ḤATK-IM	MU-TU-AD-KI-IM		M
4805.	MUT-U+ʾAWN-AN-UM	MU-TU-AM-NA-NU-UM		BM 81641 3, 8
4806.	MUT-U+ʾARAPḪ-IM	MU-TU-AR-RA-AP-ḪI-IM		C+
4807.	MUT-U+ʾAŜD-I	[MU]-TU-AŠ-DI		VIII 17 13'
4808.	MUT-U+BAʿL-U-HU	MU-TU-BA-LU-U_2		RA LXV 44 IV 26
4809.	MUT-U+BAWŠ-A	MU-TU-BA-SA		B 35+
4810.	MUT-U+BIŜIR	MU-TU-BI-SI-IR		M+
4811.	MUT-U+DAGAN	MU-TU-D-DA-GAN		CT XLIII 29 1 M+
4812.	MUT-U+JARAḪ	MU-TU-E-RA-AḪ		JCS XXIV 60 NO. 51 REV
4813.	MUT-U+JE-JŠUʿ	M[U-T]U-E-ŠU-UḪ		RA LXV 47 VII 21
4814.	MUT-U+ḤATK-I	MU-TU-ḪA-AD-KI		M
4815.	MUT-U+ḤATK-IM	MU-TU-ḪA-AD-KI-IM		M+
4816.	MUT-U+ʾIL-A	MU-TU-I-LA		RA LXV 43 III 68
4817.	MUT-U+JAM-A	MU-TU-IA-MA		M
4818.	MUT-U+HADD-U	MU-TU-D-IM		M

4819.	MUT-UJAN	MU-TU-JA-AN		C+
4820.	MUT-U+KANAT-A	MU-TU-KA-NA-TA		M
4821.	MUT-U+KUʾB-I	MU-TU-KU-BI		RA LXV 42 II 66
4822.	MUT-U+KUMR-I	MU-TU-KU-UM-RI		X 166 10', 13'
4823.	MUT-U+MALAK-A	MU-TU-MA-LA-KA		M
4824.	MUT-U+ME+ʾEL	MU-TU-ME-EL		CT VIII 31A 25+
4825.	MUT-U+MEʾR	MU-TU-ME-ER		M
4826.	MUT-U+RAWM-I-JE	MU-TU-RA-MI-E		CT XLV 63 15
4827.	MUT-UM+ʾABIḪ	MU-TUM-A-BI-IḪ		TA 1930, 695
4828.	MUT-UM+ʾIL	MU-TUM-DINGIR		FRANK 29 4, 10+ M+
4829.	MUT-UM+ʾEL	MU-TUM-E-EL		YOS VIII P. 16+
4830.	MUT-UM+ʾEL	MU-TUM-EL		YOS VIII P. 16+
4831.	MUT-UM+JARIQ	MU-TUM-JA-RI-IQ		TA 1931, 104, 538
4832.	MUT-UM+MA+ʾEL	MU-TUM-MA-EL		TA 1931, 456
4833.	MUT-UM+ME+ʾEL	MU-TUM-ME-EL		RUTTEN 32 8+
4834.	MUT-UM+NIʾŠ-A	MU-TUM-NI-ŠA		TA 1931, 538 III
4835.	MUʾUT-IJA	MU-U_2-TI-IA	FN	XIII 1 VII 48
4836.	MUHR-AT-UM	MU-UḪ-RA-TUM		BIROT, TEA 72 I 49'+
4837.	MURMUR-T-IM	MU-UR-MU-UR-TIM	FN GEN	B 49
4838.	MUŠN-A+HADD-U	MU-UŠ-NA-A-DU		A.+
4839.	MU-ŠṬAḪ-AT-UM	MU-UŠ-TA-ḪA-[TUM]?	MN	M
4840.	MU-ŠṬUḪ-AT-UM	MU-UŠ-TU-A-TUM	FN	C
4841.	MU-ŠṬUḪ+KAʾM-I	MU-UŠ-TU-KA-M[I]		M+
4842.	MUT+ʾARḪ-U	MU-UT-AR-ḪU		M
4843.	MUT+ʾAŠD-IM	MU-UT-AŠ-DI-IM		M
4844.	MUT+ʾA-ŠKUR	MU-UT-AŠ-KUR		M+
4845.	MUT+ʾAWN-AN	MU-UT-AW-NA-AN		B 35 HANA
4846.	MUT+BIŠIR	MU-UT-BI-SI-IR		M+
4847.	MUT+DAGAN	MU-UT-D-DA-GAN		M+
4848.	MUT+ʾIL	MU-UT-DINGIR		MAOG IV 2 4 HANA
4849.	MUT+ʾEKAL-IM	MU-UT-E_2-GAL-LIM		M
4850.	MUT+KABID	MU-UT-GA-BI-ID		TA 30, 615 24
4851.	MUT+ḪATK-IM	MU-UT-ḪA-AT-KI-IM		RA LXV 44 IV 57
4852.	MUT+ḪALAB	MU-UT-ḪA-LA-AB		A. 271 3
4853.	MUT+ʾALAM-I	MU-UT-ḪA-LA-MI		C+
4854.	MUT+ḪAʾL-I	MU-UT-ḪA-LI		B 35 HANA
4855.	MUT+ḪAʾL-I+MA	MU-UT-ḪA-LI-MA		M
4856.	MUT+ḪAʾN-A	MU-UT-ḪA-NA		XIV 47:31
4857.	MUT+ʿAN-AT	MU-UT-D-ḪA-NA-AT		RA LXV 52 X 65
4858.	MUT+ḪAʾŠ-UM	MU-UT-ḪA-SU-UM		A.
4859.	MUT+ḪIRB-AN	MU-UT-ḪI-IR-BA?-AN		VIII 11 4
4860.	MUT+ḪUBUR	MU-UT-ḪU-BUR		SYRIA V 271, 275
4861.	MUT+ʿUMUS-IM	MU-UT-ḪU-MU-ZI-IM		XIV 122:6+
4862.	MUT+....	MU-UT-D-IGI-KUR		M
4863.	MUT+HADD-U	MU-UT-[D]?-IM		RA LXV 41 II 17
4864.	MUT+KASIJ-....	MU-UT-KA-ZI-....		VIII 6 35'
4865.	MUT+MEŠIL-I	MU-UT-ME-SI-LI		RIFTIN 45 14
4866.	MUT+MIʾR-UM	MU-UT-MI-RUM?		EDZARD, DER 89:4
4867.	MUT+NAWḪ-A	MU-UT-NA-ḪA		B 35 HANA
4868.	MUT+NAN-UM	MU-UT-NA-NU-UM		TA 30, 615:39+
4869.	MUT+NAHR-IM	MU-UT-NA-RI-IM		RA LXV 51 IX 59
4870.	MUT+PA+NAZI	MU-UT-PA-A-NA-ZI		RA LXV 40 I 10
4871.	MUT+RAWḪ	MU-UT-RA-AḪ		M
4872.	MUT+RAPŠ-IM	MU-UT-RA-AP-ŠI-IM		RA LXV 53 XI 7
4873.	MUT+RAPIʾ	MU-UT-[R]A-BI		M
4874.	MUT+RAWM-A	MU-UT-RA-MA		CT II 23 13
4875.	MUT+RAWM-E-JE	MU-UT-RA-ME-E		BM 81584 3, M+
4876.	MUT+RAWM-EM	MU-UT-RA-ME-IM		M
4877.	MUT+ŠALIM	MU-UT-SA-LIM		M
4878.	MUT+ŠAKIM	MU-UT-ŠA-KI-IM		RA LXV 55 XIII 35
4879.	MUTT-IJ-UM	MU-UT-TI-JU-UM		M
4880.	MUTT-UJAN	MU-UT-TU-IA-AN		RA LXV 50 IX 18
4881.	MUʾZ-AN-I	MU-ZA-NI		KISURRA 1A 3+; M
4882.	MU-WṢIʾ-JA	MU-ZI-IA		M+
4883.	MU-WSIL-AT-UM	MU-ZI-LA-TUM	FN	B 35
4884.	MUʾZ-UM	MU-ZU-[U]M		RA LXV 51 IX 40

4885.		NA-A-BI-ZI-....		M
4886.	NAʾAŠ-UM	NA-A-ŠU-UM	FN	RA LXV 58 I 57
4887.	NABL-AN-UM	NA-AB-LA-NU-UM		U+, B 46+
4888.	NABL-AN-UM	NA-AB-LA-NUM_2		U+
4889.	NAḪL-I+ʾIL-UM	NA-AḪ-LI-LUM		B 36+
4890.	NAʿM-AN-U	NA-AḪ-MA-NU		M+
4891.	NAʿM-I+ʾAŠD-U	NA-AḪ-ME-AS-DU	FN	RA LXV 60 III 2
4892.	NAʿM-I+DAGAN	NA-AḪ-ME-D-DA-GAN		RA LXV 48 VIII 33
4893.	NAʿM-I	NA-AḪ-MI	GEN	M
4894.	NAʿM-I+DAGAN	NA-AḪ-MI-D-DA-GAN		A.+
4895.	NAʿM-I+JARAḪ	NA-AḪ-MI-E-RA-AḪ		JCS XI 29 NO.17 5
4896.	NAʿM-IJA	NA-AḪ-MI-IA		JCS XXVI 142:8 HARMAL
4897.	NAʿM-IM	NA-AḪ-MI-IM	GEN	M
4898.	NAʿM-UM+DAGAN	NA-AḪ-MU-UM-D-DA-GAN		BM 16824 28+
4899.	NAḪN-I+ʾIL	NA-AḪ-NI-DINGIR		TIM III 86:5
4900.	NAKL-AT-UM	NA-AK-LA-TUM	FN	YOS XIII 90 REV 22
4901.	NAKL-UM	NA-AK-LUM		BIROT, TEA 69 III 2
4902.	NAKR+ʾAḪ-UM	NA-AK-RA-ḪU-UM		RUTTEN 2 19+
4903.		NA-AL-LA-ME	FN	M+
4904.	NAMR-AT-UM	NA-AM-RA-TUM	FN	YOS XIII 163:7
4905.	N-MŠIḪ+HEDD-A	NA-AM-SI-E-D-IM		A 7646 6
4906.	NANN-AH	NA-AN-NA	FN	M+
4907.	NANN-A+MUʾ-UM	NA-AN-NA-MU-UM		M
4908.	NANN-IJA	NA-AN-NI-IA	FN	XIII 1 I 66
4909.	NANN-I+ŠARR-AH	D-NA-AN-NI-ŠAR-RA	FN	XIII 1 V 31
4910.	NAWP+LIʾM+MA	NA-AP-LIM-MA		RA XLIV 122+ QATNA
4911.	NAPŠ-AN-U	NA-AP-SA-NU-KI	GN	B 46
4912.	NAPŠ-AN-UM	NA-AP-SA-NU-UM		U, B 46+
4913.	NAPŠ-I+PI+ʾIL	NA-AP-SI-BI-DINGIR		SYRIA XLVIII 9:22
4914.	NAPŠ-I+DAGAN	NA-AP-SI-D-DA-GAN		M+
4915.	NAPŠ-I+JARAḪ	NA-AP-SI-E-RA-AḪ		M+
4916.	NAPŠ-IJA	NA-AP-SI-IA		M
4917.	NAPŠ-I+HAND-U	NA-AP-SI-IA-AN-DU		M
4918.	NAPŠ-I+HADD-U	NA-AP-SI-D-IM		M+
4919.	NAPŠ-I+ḪINN-I	NA-AP-SI-IN-NI	FN	XIII 1 IV 72
4920.	NAPŠ-I+ŠEʾR-UM	NA-AP-SI-ŠE?-RUM?		M
4921.	NAPŠ-U+HADD-U	NA-AP-SU-D-IM		M
4922.	NAPŠ-U-NA+DAWR-A	NA-AP-SU-NA-D-DA-RA		CT IV 1 8
4923.	NAPŠ-U-NA+HADD-U	NA-AP-SU-NA-D-IM		M+
4924.	NAPŠ-UM	NA-AP-SU-UM		SIMMONS 36B 6+, M
4925.	NAPŠ-UM	NA-AP-SU-UM	FN	RA LXV 59 II 47
4926.	NAPŠ-AN-UM	NA-AP-ŠA-NU-UM		U+, I+
4927.	NAPŠ-I+HADD-U	NA-AP-ŠI-A-DU		A.+
4928.	NAWP+ŠAMŠ	NA-AP-D-UTU		M
4929.	NAPŠ-AN-UM	NA-AP-ZA-NU-UM		CT XLV 115 14
4930.	NAPŠ-UM	NA-AP-ZUM		SIMMONS 36 7
4931.	NARB-AN-IM	NA-AR-BA-NIM	GEN	A 21950
4932.	NARB-AT-UM	NA-AR-BA-TUM	FN	M+
4933.	NARB-U	NA-AR-BU		XIII 1 II 32
4934.	NASQ-AT-UM	NA-AS-QA-TUM	FN	RA LXV 58 I 38
4935.	NAṢR-IJA	NA-AṢ-RI-IA		RA LXV 44 IV 47+
4936.	NAŠʾ-AT-UM	NA-AŠ-ḪA-TUM	FN	RA LXV 61 IV 33
4937.	NAŠP-AT-UM	NA-AŠ-PA-TUM	FN	CT II 35 28+
4938.	NATT-A	NA-AT-TA		M
4939.	NAṢB-UM	NA-AZ-BU-UM	FN	RA LXV 64 VI 25
4940.	NABAʾ-IM	NA-BA-I-IM	GEN	M+
4941.	NABAʾ-IM	NA-BA-JI-IM	GEN	VIII 39 4
4942.	NABAŠ-AN-UM	NA-BA-SA-NUM		BM 17072 9,12+
4943.	NABIʾ+ʾANN-U	NA-BI-AN-NU		M
4944.	NABIB-I	NA-BI-BI		M
4945.	NABIʾ+ʾIL-I	NA-BI-I_3-LI_2		XIII 1 III 61
4946.	NABIʾ+ʾILL-I	NA-BI-IL-LI		SYRIA V 274 HANA
4947.	NABIʾ+KAKK-A	NA-BI-KA-KA		M+
4948.	NABIʾ-UM	NA-BI-UM		TA 1931, 538 V
4949.	NABIʾ+ŠAMŠ	NA-BI-D-UTU		M+
4950.	NABUṬ-IJA	NA-BU-DI-IA		TCL XVIII 125 3

4951.	NABUṬ-UM	NA-BU-TUM		UET V P. 50+
4952.	NABUʾ-HU+MALIK	D-NA-BU-U_2-MA-LIK		M
4953.	NADIN-A	NA-DI-NA	GEN	A.+
4954.	NADUB-AH	NA-DU-BA?	FN	XIII 1 VIII 32+
4955.	NADUB+ʾEL-I	NA-DU-BE-LI_2		U
4956.	NADUB-UM	NA-DU-BU-UM		B 35
4957.	NAGIH-AH	NA-GI-IA	FN	XIII 1 V 82
4958.	NAGIŠ-AN-UM	NA-GI-SA-NU-UM		RUTTEN 5 8
4959.	NAGIH-AN-UM	NA-GI_4-A-NU-UM		TA 30 615 13
4960.	NAGIŠ-AN-UM	NA-GI_4-SA-NU-UM		RUTTEN 2 8+
4961.	NAWḪ-AN	NA-ḪA-AN	TRIBE	M
4962.	NAWḪ-AJA	NA-ḪA-IA		B 35
4963.	NAḪAL-I	NA-ḪA-LI	FN	IX 291 30
4964.	NAWḪ-AN-UM	NA-ḪA-NU-UM		U
4965.	NAḪAR-AH	NA-ḪA-RA	FN	RA LXV 60 III 36
4966.		NA-ḪI-DA-[....]		M
4967.	NAWḪ-I+ʾIL	NA-ḪI-DINGIR		B 35+
4968.		NA-ḪI-DU-ŠI		TCL I 49 13
4969.	NAWḪ-I+ʾIMM-I	D-NA-ḪI-IM-MI		YOS II 112 11
4970.	NAWḪ+ʾIL-I	NA-ḪI-LI		B 35
4971.	NAWḪ+ʾIL-IM	NA-ḪI-LI-IM	GEN	B 35
4972.	NAWḪ+ʾIL-UM	NA-ḪI-LU-UM		B 35
4973.	NAWḪ+ʾIL-UM	NA-ḪI-LUM		B 35+
4974.	NAʿIM-I	NA-ḪI-MI	GEN	B 36
4975.	NAʿIM-IM	NA-ḪI-MI-IM	GEN	B 36
4976.	NAʿIM-UM	NA-ḪI-MU-UM		B 36+
4977.	NAWḪ-UM+DAGAN	NA-ḪU-UM-D-DA-GAN		B 36+
4978.	NAʿIM-U	NA-I-MU		B 36+
4979.	NAJAL-AM	NA-JA-LAM		RA LXV 40 I 33
4980.	NAʾJ-AT-UM	NA-JA-TUM	FN	KISURRA 59A:4
4981.	NAKAM-T-UM	NA-KA-AM-TUM	FN	M
4982.	NAKAR-T-UM	NA-KA-AR-TUM	FN	M
4983.	NAKAR-AH	NA-KA-RA	FN	XIII 1 VIII 19
4984.	NAKAR-AT-UM	NA-KA-RA-TUM	FN	RA LXV 59 II 71
4985.	NAKAR-UM	NA-KA-RU-UM		BIROT, TEA 70A II 14+
4986.	NAKAR-UM	NA-KA-RUM		BM 16914 3,11+
4987.	NAGIH-IM	NA-KI-ḪI-IM	GEN	TIM III 77 5A
4988.	NAGIH-UM	NA-KI-ḪU-UM		TIM III 31 17+
4989.	NAQIM-IM	NA-KI-MI-IM	GEN	B 36+
4990.	NAQIM-U	NA-KI-MU		B 36+
4991.	NAQIM-UM	NA-KI-MU-UM		B 36+
4992.	NAʿM-A+ʾEL	NA-MA-EL		TA 30 615:11+
4993.	NAMAL-AT-UM	NA-MA-LA-TUM	MN	B 36+
4994.	NAMAL-UM	NA-MA-LUM		HARRIS 7 12
4995.	NAʿM-AN-IM	NA-MA-NI-IM	GEN	TIM III 46 15
4996.	NAMAŠ-I	NA-MA-ŠI		MAOG IV 3 30 HANA
4997.	NAMAŠ-U	NA-MA-ŠU		B 36 HANA
4998.	NAʿM-I+ʿAN-IM	NA-MI-A-NIM		A. 142
4999.	NAʿM-I+DAGAN	NA-MI-D-DA-GAN		A.+
5000.	NAʿM-I+DAʾK-A	NA-MI-DA-KA		A. 242 7
5001.	NAʿM-IJA	NA-MI-IA	FN	CT XLV 3 8,15,23
5002.	NAʿM-I+JAT-UM	NA-MI-IA-TUM	MN	MEISSNER 100 2
5003.	NAMIŠ-A	NA-MI-ŠA	GEN	MAOG IV 3 34 HANA
5004.	NAMIŠ-U	NA-MI-ŠU		B 36 HANA
5005.	NAMIŠ-UM	NA?-MI-ŠUM		XIII 1 VIII 47
5006.	NANN-ATAN	NA-NA-TA-AN		M
5007.	NAN-AT-UM	NA-NA-TUM	FN	RA LXV 65 VI 57
5008.	NAN-I	D-NA-NI	DN	M
5009.	NANIB-U+MA	NA-NI-BU-MA		SIMMONS 138 4+
5010.	NANIB-UM	NA-NI-BU-UM		SIMMONS 138 29
5011.	NAN-IJA	NA-NI-IA	FN	RA LXV 60 III 66
5012.	NAHR-AN-UM	NA-RA-NU-UM		B 47
5013.	NAHR-IM	NA-RI-IM	GEN	A.
5014.	NATUN-UM	NA-TU-NU-UM		B 36
5015.	NAʾUL-UM	NA-U_2-LU-UM		TA 1931, 297, 538
5016.	NAWAR+JE-JŠAR	NA-WA-AR-E-ŠAR	FN	XIII 1 VI 40

5017.	NAWAR+HADD-U	NA-WA-AR-D-IM		RA LXV 50 VIII 55+
5018.	NAWAR-I	NA-WA-RI?		RA LXV 53 XI 55
5019.	NAṢAB-AN-UM	NA-ZA-BA-NU-UM		TCL I 111 3
5020.	NAMḪ-U-HU	NAM-ḪU-U_2		BM 80328 8
5021.	NAMZ-U-HU	NAM-ZU-U_2		BM 80328 5
5022.	NEJAL-AH	NE-IA-LA	FN	XIII 1 VII 51
5023.	NIṢB-I+ʾEL	NE-IZ-BI-EL		TA 1930, 747 +
5024.	NIṢB-I+ʾIL	NE-IZ-BI-IL		TA 1931, 172
5025.	NIWR-AH	NI-E-RA	FN	A.
5026.	NIWR-U	NI-E-RU		A.
5027.	NIWḪ-AT-UM	NI-ḪA-TUM	FN	M+
5028.	NIʿIM-AH	NI-ḪI-MA	FN	M
5029.	NIʿIM-AT-UM	NI-ḪI-MA-T[UM]	FN?	C II 42 III 31
5030.	NIGH-AT-UM	NI-IG-ḪA-TUM	FN	M
5031.	NIʿM-AT-UM	NI-IḪ-MA-TUM	FN	M+
5032.	NIʿM-UM	NI-IḪ-MU-UM		M+
5033.	NIKR-UM	NI-IK-RU-UM		RA LXV 45 V 40
5034.	NIMḪ-AM+PI+ʾIL	NI-IM?-ḪA-AM-BI-DINGIR		A. 95 17 (=JCS VIII 8)
5035.	NINN-U	NI-IN-NU		M
5036.	NIPR-AM	NI-IP-RA-AM		RA LXV 50IX 26
5037.		NI-IP-RA-ḪU		M
5038.	NIQM+ʾAB-I	NI-IQ-MA-A-BI		A. 86 7+
5039.	NIQM+HADD-U	NI-IQ-MA-A-DU		A.+
5040.	NIQM-AN-UM	NI-IQ-MA-A-NU-UM		B 47+
5041.	NIQM-AN	NI-IQ-MA-AN		M
5042.	NIQM+HADD-U	NI-IQ-MA-DU		A.
5043.	NIQM-AN-UM	NI-IQ-MA-NU-UM		B 47+
5044.	NIQM+HADD-U	NI-IQ-MA_2-A-DU		B 36
5045.	NIQM-EJA	NI-IQ-ME-IA		M+
5046.	NIQM-I+JA-JPAʿ	NI-IQ-ME-PA		A.+
5047.	NIQM-I+HADD-U	NI-IQ-MI-A-DU		A.+
5048.	NIQM-I+JE-JPUʿ	NI-IQ-MI-E-PU-UḪ		M+, A.+
5049.	NIQM-I+JATAR	NI-IQ-MI-E-TAR		C II 39 3
5050.	NIQM-I+HADD-U	NI-IQ-MI-IA-AD-DU		M
5051.	NIQM-I+LA+NAŠIʾ	NI-IQ-MI-LA-NA-SI		M
5052.	NIQM-I+JA-JPAʿ	NI-IQ-MI-PA		A. 27 12
5053.	NIQM-U-K	NI-IQ-MU-UK	FN	M
5054.	NIWR-I+HADD-U	NI-IW-RI-A-DU		A.+
5055.	NIKID-AT-UM	NI-KI-DA-TUM		VAS XIII 65 2,3+
5056.		NI-LU-UK		M
5057.	NIʿM-A+HADD-U	NI-MA-A-DU		A.
5058.	NIMIN-A+HADD-U	NI-MI-NA-A-DU		A.+
5059.	NIʾŠ-UM	NI-ŠUM		M+
5060.	NIWR+MEʾR	NI-WA-AR-ME-ER		M
5061.	NIṢAB-AH	NI-ZA-BA?	FN	RA LXV 68 V 9A
5062.	BEʿL-T-I+JARAḪ	NIN?-TI-E-RA-AḪ		RA LXV 52 X 54
5063.	NUWAP-U	NU-A-BU		JNES XIII 210+ LATE
5064.	NUWP-AJA	NU-BA-IA		RA LXV 48 VIII 28
5065.	NUBAṬ-AH	NU-BA-TA	FN	M
5066.	NUWP-AT-UM	NU-BA-TUM		YOS XIII 191:8
5067.	NUPAR+ŠARR-IM	NU-BAR-LUGAL		A.
5068.	NUWP-I+ʾIL	NU-BI-DINGIR		C+
5069.	NUBUṬ-AH	NU-BU-TA	FN	XIII 1 XIV 9
5070.	NUWD-AT-UM	NU-DA-TUM	MN	U
5071.	NUṬUP-AT-UM	NU-DU-PA-TUM	FN	FRANK SKT P. 31+
5072.	NUṬUP-T-UM	NU-DU-UB-TUM	FN	UET V P. 53+
5073.	NUʿAM-AH	NU-ḪA-MA	FN	M
5074.	NUWḪ-I+ʾIL	NU-ḪI-DINGIR		I
5075.	NUMAḪ-A	NU-MA-ḪA-A	GN	M
5076.	NUMEN-AH	NU-ME-EN-NA	FN	XIII 1 IV 32
5077.	NUN-U+NIWR-I	D-NU-NU-NE?-RI	FN	RA LXV 66 VII 56
5078.	NUN-U+TA-BNIJ	D-NU-NU-TA-AB-NI	FN	XII 265 1
5079.	NUWP-AN-UM	NU-PA-A-NU-UM		SIMMONS 103 7+
5080.	NUWP-AN-UM	NU-PA-NU-UM		SIMMONS 95 10+
5081.	NUWP-AT-IJA	NU-PA-TI-IA	FN	M
5082.	NUWP-AT-UM	NU-PA-TUM	FN	BIROT, TEA 70C R II 18

5083.	NUPUR-I	NU-PU-RI		XIII 1 IV 12
5084.		NU-PU-RI-IK-KU		M
5085.	NUWR-AH	NU-RA	FN	M
5086.	NUWR-U+ʾAMAR	NU-RU-A-MA-AR		HARRIS 68 19
5087.	NUŠUP-UM	NU-ŠU-BU-UM		HARRIS 4 9+
5088.	NUṬUP-AJA	NU-TU-PA-A-A		UET V 480 3
5089.	NUṬUP-T-UM	NU-TU-UP-TUM	FN	UET V P. 53+
5090.	NUʿM-I+JABAL	NU-UḪ-ME-E-BA-AL	FN	RA LXV 62 V 19
5091.	NUʿM-I+ʾAB-I	NU-UḪ-MI-A-BI		XIII 1 I 38
5092.	NUʿM-I+DAGAN	NU-UḪ-MI-D-DA-GAN		M
5093.	NUʿM-I+ʾIL	NU-UḪ-MI-DINGIR		M+
5094.	NUʿM-I+ʾIL-I	NU-UḪ-MI-I$_3$-LI$_2$		XIII 1 XIII 26
5095.	NUʿM-I+LIʾM	NU-UḪ-MI-LI-IM		M+
5096.	NUʿM-U+BAʾAT-IM	NU-UḪ-MU-BA-A-TIM	FN	C+
5097.	NUKR-AN-UM	NU-UK-RA-NU-UM		U+
5098.	NUMḪ-A	NU-UM-ḪA-A(-KI)	GN	M+
5099.	NUMḪ-AJ-I	NU-UM-ḪA-A-JI	GN	X 5 4
5100.	NUMḪ-AJ-I	NU-UM-ḪA-I	GN	IX 48 3+
5101.	NUMN-U-HU	NU-UM-NU-U$_2$		M
5102.	NUMN-UM	NU-UM-NU-UM		BIROT, TEA 65:8
5103.	NUNM-AN	NU-UN-MA-AN		RUTTEN 26 9
5104.	NUWR+MEʾR	NU-UR-ME-ER		M
5105.	NURNUR-AT-UM	NU-UR$_2$-NU-RA-TUM	MN?	BIN VII 157 7
5106.	NUWR-T-UM	NU-UR$_2$-TUM	FN	RA LXV 65 VII 21
5107.	NUṢAB-U	NU-ZA-BU		XIV 61:7
5108.	NUṢAB-UM	NU-ZA-BU-UM		M
5109.	NUZAM-AN	NU-ZA-MA-AN		XIII 1 V 22
5110.	PA-KA+ʾIL-A	PA-A-KA-I-LA		B 37
5111.	PAʾAR-AT-IM	PA-A-RA-TIM	FN GEN	X 170:1
5112.		PA-A-ŠUM-I?-L[A]?		BASOR 95, 21 II 24
5113.	PAKN-AN-A	PA-AK-NA-NA	GEN	BE VI/2 81 14
5114.	PAKN-AN-IM	PA-AK-NA-NIM	GEN	B 47
5115.	PAKN-AN-UM	PA-AK-NA-NU-UM		B 47+
5116.	PAKN-UM	PA-AK-NU-UM		B 37
5117.	PALṮ-A+BIJT-U	PA-AL-DA-BI-TU		A. LATE
5118.	PALL-AK-UM	PA-AL-LA-KUM		B 37
5119.	PALṮ-A+ʿAN-UM	PA-AL?-TA-A-NU-UM		LANGDON IV 15
5120.	PALṮ-IJA	PA-AL-TI-IA		YONDORF 2
5121.	PALS-IJA	PA-AL-ZI-IA		SIMMONS 44 6+
5122.	PALS-UM	PA-AL-ZU-UM		HARRIS 65 18
5123.	PANN-AT-UM	PA-AN-NA-TUM	MN?	CT XLV 49 11
5124.	PANIJ-AT-UM	PA-AN-NI-IA-TUM	MN	UET V 615 9
5125.	PARG-AN-UM	PA-AR-GA-NU-UM		B 47
5126.	PAʾR-T-UM	PA-AR-TUM	FN	CT XLV 54 24, M+
5127.	PAŠD-IJA	PA-AŠ-DI-IA		B 37
5128.	PAṮAR-UM	PA-AT-TA-RUM		B 37
5129.	PAZR-I	PA-AZ-RI		M
5130.	PADAL-AN	PA-DA-LA-AN		RA LXV 51 IX 33
5131.		PA-DA-NI-TE	FN	XIII 1 III 67
5132.	PAQID-UM	PA-GI-DU-UM		CT XLV 89 II 32
5133.	PAGIR-UM	PA-GI-RU-UM		B 36+ HANA
5134.	PAGIR-UM	PA-GI-RUM		B 36 HANA
5135.	PAʾAR+MI	PA-ḪA-AR-MI	FN	RA LXV 59 II 23
5136.	PA+ʾIL-A	PA-I-LA		XIII 1 VII 16
5137.	BAWʾ+JARAḪ	PA-IA-RA-AḪ		RUTTEN 7 7
5138.	PA-KA+ʾIL-A	PA-KA-DINGIR		B 37
5139.	PA-KA+ʾIL-A	PA-KA-I-LA		B 37+
5140.		PA-KA-IA		B 37
5141.		PA-KI-AN-NA-E$_2$		M
5142.		PA?-KI-IA-DINGIR		SPELEERS 227 3
5143.	PAʾL-A-HA	PA-LA-A	FN	B 37
5144.	PALL-AK-UM	PA-LA-KUM		YOS XIII 164:1
5145.	PALAṮ-UM	PA-LA-TUM		TIM III 37 14+
5146.		PA-LI-AŠ-ŠI-RU?		VII 56 4
5147.	PANAN-IM	PA-NA-NIM	GEN	B 47
5148.	PANAN-UM	PA-NA-NU-UM		B 93

5149.	PANAN-UM	PA-NA-NUM		B 47
5150.	PANIJ-AT-UM	PA-NI-IA-TUM	MN?	TIM I 11 11
5151.	PANIJ+ʾIL-A	PA-NI-LA		IX 252 17, A. LATE
5152.	PAʾP-AK-UM	PA-PA-KUM		B 37
5153.	PAPUZ-I	PA-PU-ZI	FN	XIII 1 III 14
5154.	PAʾR-AT-IJA	PA-RA-TI-IA		UCP X/3 3 8
5155.	PARUR-I	PA-RU-RI		XIII 1 V 64
5156.		PA-TA-AL-LA	MN	DELAPORTE, CCL II A 914
5157.	PAʾT-AT-UM	PA-TA-TUM	FN	M+
5158.	PATIḪ-IM	PA-TE-E-IM	GEN	CT IV 21B 6, 22
5159.	PATIḪ-AT-UM	PA-TE-ḪA-TUM	MN?	CARNEGIE CAT. Q B 11
5160.	PATIḪ-UM	PA-TE-ḪU-UM		HARRIS 53 19+
5161.	PATIḪ-AH	PA-TI-ḪA	FN	M+
5162.	PAṬIR-UM	PA-TI-RUM		M
5163.	PASAʿ-KA	PA-ZA-AḪ-GA		HARRIS 31 6
5164.	PASAʿ-T-UM	PA-ZA-AḪ-TUM	FN	XIII 1 VIII 81
5165.	PI+ʿAN-UM	PI-A-NUM$_2$		I
5166.	PI+ʾIL-A	PI-I-LA		A. LATE
5167.	PUḪUR+NUN-U	PU-ḪU-UR-D-NU-NU		M
5168.	PUḪUR-T-UM	PU-ḪU-UR-TUM	FN	M
5169.	PU-KA+DAGAN	PU-KA-D-DA-GAN		M
5170.	PULAḪ-AN	PU-LA-ḪA-AN		M
5171.	PU+MA+ʾEL	PU-MA-[E]L		TA 1931,538 I
5172.	PU+ME+ʾIL	PU-ME-IL		I
5173.	PURUS-AT-UM	PU-RU-ZA-TUM	FN	RA LXV 60 III 60
5174.	PU-HU+DAGAN	PU-U$_2$-D-DA-GAN		M
5175.	PUḪR-A-NA	PU-UḪ$_3$-RA-NA		YOS VIII 101B 13
5176.	PULS-I+JARAḪ	PU-UL-SI-E-RA-AḪ		TIM V 69 16+
5177.	PULS-AN	PU-UL-ZA-AN		M
5178.	PULS-AT-UM	PU-UL-ZA-TUM	MN	TIM III 23 11+
5179.	PULS-IJA	PU-UL-ZI-IA		M
5180.	PULS-I+HADD-U	PU-UL-ZI-D-IM		M+
5181.	PULS-I+JARAḪ	PU-UL-ZI-RA-AḪ		HARRIS 18 14
5182.	PULS-U-NA+HADD-U	PU-UL-ZU-NA-D-IM		UNPUBL.
5183.	PU-UM+ʾEL	PU-UM-E-EL		BAGH.MITT. IV 291,SEAL
5184.	PURʿUŠ-AN-U	PU-UR-ḪU-ŠA-NU		M
5185.	PUZUR+ʿAN-A	PUZUR-A-NA		BIN IV 61 29+ CAPP.
5186.	QAʾN+HADD-U	QA-AN-A-DU		A.
5187.	QADIM-AT-IM	QA-DI-MA-TIM	FN GEN	WATERMAN 39 11
5188.	QADIM-AT-UM	QA-DI-MA-TUM	FN	WATERMAN 39 8+
5189.	QAHIL-AT-UM	QA-ḪI-LA-TUM	FN	C P. 55+
5190.	QAWL-A+ḪAM-I	QA-LA-D-A-M[I]		M
5191.	QAWL-U+ḪAM-I	QA-L[U]-D-A-MI		M
5192.	QAWM-A+DANN-UM	QA-MA-[D]A-NUM		M
5193.	QAWM-U+MA+ʾAḪ-I	QA-MU-MA-A-ḪI		RA LXV 41 II 22
5194.	QAWM-U+MA+ʾAḪ-UM	QA-MU-MA-A-ḪU-UM		M
5195.	QAWM-U+MA+ʾIL	QA-MU-MA-DINGIR		M
5196.	QANIJ-AT-UM	QA-NI-A-TUM	FN	RA LXV 66 VII 52; C+
5197.	QAQQAD-AN	QA-QA-DA-AN		XIV 47:20
5198.	QAQQAR-AN	QA?-QA-RA?-AN		VII 198:11
5199.	QARAʾ+ŠUM-I-JA	QA-RA-SU-MI-IA		CT II 34 5
5200.	QARAʾ+ŠUM-U-JA	QA-RA-SU?-MU-IA		CT VI 43 5
5201.	QARIʾ+ʾEL	QA-R[I]-E[L]		M
5202.	QARIʾ-UM	QA-RI-U$_2$-UM		M+
5203.	QAṬAN-AJ-I	QA-TA-NA-A-JI-KI	GN	M
5204.	QAṬAN-AJ-IM	QA-TA-NA-IM-KI	GN GEN	M
5205.	QAṬAN-AJ-I	QA-TA-NA-JI-KI	GN	M+
5206.	QAṬAN-A	QA-TA-NA-KI	GN	M
5207.	QAṬAN-IM	QA-TA-NIM-KI	GN GEN	M+
5208.	QAṬAR-A	QA-TA-RA-KI	GN	M
5209.	QAṬAR-UM	QA-TA-RU-UM		B 37
5210.	QAʾT-U-HU	QA-TU-U$_2$	FN	RA LXV 58 I 47
5211.	QAṬAN-IM	QA-ṬA$_3$-NIM-KI	GN GEN	M+
5212.	QAṬAR-A	QA-ṬA$_3$-RA-A-KI	GN	M+
5213.	QAṬAR-A	QA-ṬA$_3$-RA-KI	GN	M
5214.	QAZIJ+RAWM-A	QA-ZI-RA-MA		A. LATE

5215.	QAṢIR-UM	QA-ZI-RUM		RA LXV 53 XI 46
5216.	QARN-AN-A	QAR-NA-NA	GEN	SIMMONS 13 5
5217.	QARN-AN-UM	QAR-NA-NU-UM		B 93+
5218.	QARN-I+LIʾM	QAR-NI-LI-IM		M+
5219.	QUWJ+MILK-U	QU-U$_2$-LUGAL		MRS XII 31:24
5220.	RABB-I+JARAḪ	RA-AB-BI-E-RA-AḪ		B 37+
5221.	RABB-U+ʿAD-U-HU	RA-AB-BU-ḪA-DU-U$_2$		B 17+
5222.	RABB-U+ʿAD-U-HU	RA-AB-BU-U$_2$-ḪA-DU-U$_2$		BM 17051A 30
5223.	RAḪM-AJA	RA-AḪ-MA-IA		M+
5224.	RAḪM-I+....	RA-AḪ-MI-....	FN	M
5225.	RAḪM-I+ʾIL-I	RA-AḪ-MI-I$_3$-LI$_2$		XIII 1 VIII 79+
5226.	RAWM	RA-AM	DN	PBS XIV 360
5227.	RAJB-AN-UM	RA-BA-A-NU-UM		RUTTEN 13 3, 8, SEAL+
5228.		RA-BA?-AD-DU-TUM		XIII 1 V 76
5229.	RABAʿ+DUDM-U	RA-BA?-AḪ-DU-UD-MU		M
5230.	RAJB-AN	RA-[BA]?-AN		RA LXV 47 VI 67
5231.	RABAB-AN	RA-BA-BA-AN		M
5232.	RABAB-AN-UM	RA-BA-BA-NU-UM		KISURRA 187 11+
5233.	RAJB-AN-UM	RA-BA-NU-UM		RUTTEN 3 6+
5234.	RAJB-AT-UM	RA-BA-TUM	FN	XIII 1 X 59+
5235.	RAJB-A+SITR-U-HU	RA-BA-ZI-IT-RU-U$_2$	FN	M
5236.	RAPIʾ-AH	RA-BI-A	FN	XIII 1 VII 32+
5237.	RAPIʾ-AT-UM	RA-BI-A-TUM	FN	C+
5238.	RAPIʾ-UM	RA-BI-JU-[UM]?		M
5239.	RAPIʾ+MI+ʾIL	RA-BI-MI-IL		BIROT,TEA 72 VI 19
5240.	RAPIʾ+MI+ʾIL-UM	RA-BI-MI-LUM		BIROT,TEA 72 IX 29
5241.	RAPIʾ+TA-ʾLAŠ	RA-BI-TA-AḪ-LA-AŠ		BASOR 95 22
5242.	RAPIʾ-I-UM	RA-BI-TUM	FN	M
5243.	RAPIʾ-UM	RA-BI-U$_2$-UM		M+
5244.	RAWḪ-A+ʾANN-UM	RA-ḪA-AN-NU-UM		M
5245.	RAWḪ-AT-UM	RA-ḪA-TUM	FN	XIII 1 XII 6
5246.	RAḪAṢ-U	RA-ḪA-ZU		WALTERS,WL 114:12
5247.	RAḪIM-AH	RA-ḪI-MA	FN	XIII 1 II 4+
5248.	RAḪIB-UM	RA-I-BU-UM		CT VIII 47A 7
5249.	RAḪIM-UM	RA-I-MU-UM		JCS XXVI 151:21 HARMAL
5250.	RAʾK-AT-UM	RA-KA-TU-UM	FN?	M
5251.	RAWM+...	RA-MA-[....]		M
5252.	RAMAŠ-I	RA-MA-A-ŠI	FN	EDZARD,DER 224:42
5253.	RAWM-A+JAT-UM	RA-MA-IA-TUM		B 22+
5254.	RAMAM-AN-UM	RA-MA-MA-NU-UM		B 93
5255.	RAWM-AN-UM	RA-MA-NU-UM		B 47
5256.	RAMAŠ-I	RA-MA-ŠI	FN	M
5257.	RAWM-AT-UM	RA-MA-TUM	FN	M, CT VIII 1A 2+
5258.	RAWM-E+ʾEL	R[A]-ME-EL		RA LXV 42 II 56
5259.	RAMIK-AN-UM	RA-MI-GA-NU-UM		TA 1931, 538 II
5260.	RAMIŠ-UM	RA-MI-ŠUM		TA 1931, 538 III, V
5261.	RAPAʾ-AN-UM	RA-PA-NU-UM		BM 78768
5262.	RAPUʾ-AT-UM	RA-PU-A-TUM		A 7660 1
5263.	RAPUʾ-UM	RA-PU-U$_2$-UM		RA LXV 41 II 30
5264.	RAŠIJ-JA	RA-SI-A		TIM III 134 4
5265.	RAṢAJ+DAGAN	RA-ZA-D-DA-GAN		M
5266.	RAṢIJ-EM	RA-ZI-E-IM-KI	GN	M+
5267.	RAṢIJ-IM	RA-ZI-IM-KI	GN	M
5268.	RAZIN-IM	RA-ZI-NI-IM	GEN	HARRIS 71 9
5269.	RAʾZ-UM	RA-ZU-UM		TA 1931, 538 IV
5270.	RIJB-A+ʿAMM-U	RI-BA-AM-MU		A. 97 4+
5271.	RIJB-AT-UM	RI-BA-TUM	FN	CT VIII 48B 7+, M+, C+
5272.	RIPʾ-I+DAGAN	RI-BI-D-DA-GAN		M
5273.	RIJB-U+DAGAN	RI-BU-D-DA-GAN		RA LXV 47 VII 52
5274.	RIJB-U-HU	RI-BU-U$_2$		KISURRA 187 12
5275.	RIWḪ-AN	RI-ḪA-AN		C
5276.	RIWḪ-AT-UM	RI-ḪA-DU-UM?		U UNPUBL.
5277.	RIWḪ-AT-UM	RI-ḪA-TUM	FN	XIII 1 I 23+
5278.	RIJB-UM	RI-I-BU-UM		I
5279.	RIBK-U	RI-IB-KU	FN	XIII 1 IX 56+
5280.	RIGM-AN-U	RI-IG-MA-NU		M

5281.	RIGM-AN-UM	RI-IG-MA-NUM		M
5282.	RIWM+DAGAN	RI-IM-D-DA-GAN		M
5283.	RIWM+ʾIL-A	RI-IM-I-LA		TCL XIV 54 17 CAPP.
5284.	RIWM+HADD-U	RI-IM-D-IM		M+, A. 57 46
5285.	RIMŠ-I+ʾIL	RI-IM-ŠI-DINGIR		M+
5286.	RIMŠ-I+ʾIL-I	RI-IM-ŠI-I_3-LI_2		M
5287.	RIPʾ-A+ʾIL-A	RI-IP-A-DINGIR		M+
5288.	RIPʾ-A+MALIK	RI-IP-A-MA-LIK		M
5289.	RIPʾ-I+HEDD-A	RI-IP-E-D-IM		M
5290.	RIPʾ-I+DAGAN	RI-IP-I-D-DA-GAN		M+
5291.	RIPʾ-I+HADD-U	RI-IP-I-D-IM		M+
5292.	RIPʾ-IM	RI-IP-I-IM	GEN	M+
5293.	RIPʾ-I+LIʾM	RI-IP-I-LI-IM		M
5294.	RIWM-AN	[R]I?-MA-AN		RA LXV 41 II 8
5295.	RIWM-AN-UM	RI-MA-NU-UM		U
5296.	RIWM-AT-UM	RI-MA-TUM	FN	M+
5297.	RIWM-U+HADD-U	RI-MU-D-IM		M
5298.	RIʿŠ-AT+....	RI-ŠA-A[T-....]	FN	I 89 5
5299.	RUWB-AJA	RU-BA-A-IA	FN	RA LXIV 43
5300.	RUWB-AN	RU-BA?-AN		RA LXV 45 V 34
5301.	RUWB-AJA	RU-BA-IA	FN	XIII 1 II 10+
5302.	RUWB-AT-IM	RU-BA-TIM	FN GEN	M
5303.	RUWB-AT-UM	RU-BA-TUM	FN	M+
5304.	RABB-U+ʿAD-UM	RU-BU-ḪA-DU-UM		BM 17055 26
5305.	RUKAB-AT-UM	RU-KA-BA-TUM	FN	XIII 1 V 33
5306.	RUWM-AT-UM	RU-MA-TUM	FN	XIII 1 VI 10
5307.		RU-ŠU-UM		TA 1931,148
5308.	RUḪB-AT-UM	RU-UḪ-BA-TUM	FN	XIII 1 IX 46
5309.	ŠAʾAD-IJA	SA-A-DI-IA		C+
5310.	ŠAʾAL-A	SA-A-LA	NOM	CT II 42 2, 5
5311.	ŠADL-U+MA	SA-AD-LU-MA		UCP X/1 P. 61+
5312.	ŠADR-UM	SA-AD-[RU]?-UM		RA LXV 53 XI 34
5313.	ŠAKB-IJA	SA-[A]K-BI-IA		RA LXV 44 IV 34
5314.	ŠAKB-I+HADD-U	SA-AK-BI-D-IM		ARMT V P. 123
5315.	ŠAKN-AT-UM	SA-AK-NA-TUM	FN	RA LXV 58 I 27
5316.	ŠAKN-U	SA-AK-NU	FN	M
5317.	ŠAKN-UM	SA-AK-NU-UM		TA 30, 36 2
5318.	ŠALD-IJA	SA-AL-DI-IA		TCL I 80 16
5319.	ŠALUḪ-I	SA-AL-LU-ḪI	GEN	BE VI/2 138 2, 5
5320.	ŠAMʾAL	SA-AM-A-AL		M
5321.	ŠAMʾAL-A+ʾIL	SA-AM-A-LA-DINGIR		M+
5322.	ŠAMʿ-AN-UM	SA-AM-ḪA-NU-UM		TCL X 21 21
5323.	ŠAMḪ-ATAN-I	SA-AM-ḪA-TA-NI		VAS VIII 14 5
5324.	ŠAMʾIL-I+ʾIL	SA-AM-ḪI-LI-DINGIR		M
5325.	ŠAMK-AJA	SA-AM-KA-IA		RA LXV 53 XII 4
5326.	ŠAMM-I+JATAR	SA-AM-ME-E-TAR		M+
5327.	ŠAMM-I+JATAR	SA-AM-ME-TAR		M+
5328.	ŠAMM-I+JATAR	SA-AM-MI-A-TA-AR		TIM I 28 34, 38, 49
5329.	ŠAMM-I+JATAR	SA-AM-MI-E-TAR		M+
5330.	ŠAMM-I+JATAR	SA-AM-MI-TAR		M+
5331.	ŠAMŠ-AN-UM	SA-AM-SA-NU-UM		SIMMONS 119 23+
5332.	ŠAMŠ-I+HADD-U	SA-AM-SI-A-DU		M+
5333.	ŠAMŠ-I+ʾAḪ-I	SA-AM-SI-A-ḪI		RA LXV 54 XII 26
5334.	ŠAMŠ-I+DAGAN	SA-AM-SI-D-DA-GAN		M+
5335.	ŠAMŠ-I+DIʿ-AT	SA-AM-SI-DI-ḪA-AT?		TIM II 49 5
5336.	ŠAMŠ-I+DITAN-A	SA-AM-SI-DI-TA-NA		B 38
5337.	ŠAMŠ-I+HEDD-A	SA-AM-SI-E-DA		A. 455 36
5338.	ŠAMŠ-I+HEDD-A	SA-AM-SI-E-D-IM		SIMMONS 4 20
5339.	ŠAMŠ-I+JARAḪ	SA-AM-SI-E-RA-AḪ		BASOR 95, 19+, M+
5340.	ŠAMŠ-IJA	SA-AM-SI-IA		X 166 9, 13
5341.	ŠAMŠ-I+HADD-U	SA-AM-SI-IA-AD-DU		M
5342.	ŠAMŠ-I+HADD-U	SA-AM-SI-D-IM		M+, A.+
5343.	ŠAMŠ-I+HADD-U+ʾIL-I	SA-AM-SI-D-IM-I_3-LI_2		C+
5344.	ŠAMŠ-I+HADD-U+....	SA-AM-SI-D-IM-TU-GUL-TI		M
5345.	ŠAMŠ-I+LIʾM	SA-AM-SI-LI-IM		M
5346.	ŠAMŠ-U	SA-AM-SU		YOS XII

5347.	ŠAMŠ-U+BAʿL-I	SA-AM-SU-BA-AḪ-LI		ABB I 59 8
5348.	ŠAMŠ-U+BAʿL-A	SA-AM-SU-BA-LA		SIMMONS 35 14+
5349.	ŠAMŠ-U+DITAN-A	SA-AM-SU-DI-TA-NA		B 38+
5350.	ŠAMŠ-U+JARAḪ	SA-AM-SU-E-RA-AḪ		B 38
5351.	ŠAMŠ-U+ʾIL-U-NA	SA-AM-SU-I-LU-NA		B 38+
5352.	ŠAMŠ-U+ʾIL-U-NA+KIMA	SA-AM-SU-I-LU-NA-KI-MA-DINGIR		BM 81047:6
5353.	ŠAMŠ-U+ʾIL-U-NA+....	SA-AM-SU-I-LU-NA-QAR-RA-AD		CT XLV 48 5
5354.	ŠAMŠ-U+JI-JŠAR	SA-AM-SU-D-I-[Š]AR		M
5355.	ŠAMŠ-U+....	SA-AM-SU-MA-[....]		YOS XIII 446:3
5356.	ŠAMŠ-U-NA	SA-AM-SU-NA		HARRIS 58 14+
5357.	ŠAMŠ-U-NA+BAʿL-A	SA-AM-SU-NA-BA-LA		A. 77+
5358.	ŠAMŠ-I+HADD-U	SA-AM-ŠI-D-IM		C
5359.	ŠAMŠ-U+HADD-U	SA-AM-ŠU-D-IM		COLLON, SEALS NO. 141
5360.	ŠAM-T-UM	SA-AM-TUM	FN	TCL I 189 17, M+
5361.	ŠAGAR-AT-IM	SA-AN-GA-RA-TIM-KI	GN GEN	M
5362.	ŠAGAR-UM	SA-AN-GA-RU-UM		BIN VII 45 12
5363.	ŠANQAM-UM	SA-AN-QA-MU-UM		JCS V 89, MAH 15882
5364.	ŠAPR-A+HADD-U	SA-AP-RA-A-DU		A. 96 R. 12
5365.	ŠAPR-AJA	SA-AP-RA-IA		A.
5366.	ŠAPŠ-I+HADD-U	SA-AP-SI-A-DU		A.+
5367.	ŠAPŠ-I+HEDD-A	SA-AP-SI-E-DA		A.+
5368.	ŠAPŠ-IJA	SA-AP-SI-IA		A. 53 R. 9
5369.	ŠARB-AN	SA-AR-BA-AN		M
5370.	ŠAWB-A+ḤAJJ-UM	SA-BA-A-U_2-UM		OIP XLVII 66
5371.	ŠAPAQ-UM	SA-BA-KUM		TA 30 28
5372.	ŠAʾB-AT-UM	SA-BA-TUM		JCS XXIV 57 NO. 42,44
5373.	D̠ABIB-I+ʾIL	SA-BI-BI-DINGIR		M
5374.	D̠ABIB-IT-UM	SA-BI-BI-TUM	FN?	HARRIS 100 6
5375.	D̠ABIB-UM	SA-BI-BU-UM		WATERMAN 24 R. 4+
5376.	ŠAPIQ-UM	SA-BI-KUM		TCL I 190 4, 5
5377.	ŠABIM-AT-IM	SA-BI-MA-TIM	FN NOM	RA LXIV 43
5378.	ŠABIM-U	SA-BI-MU		C+
5379.	ŠABIM-UM	SA-BI-MU-UM		M+
5380.	ŠAPIR-AJA	SA-BI-RA-A-IA	FN	X 166 11, 12+
5381.	ŠAPIR-AT-UM	SA-BI-RA-TUM	FN	B 37+
5382.	ŠAPIR-U	SA-BI-RU		YOS XIII 166:14
5383.	ŠAPIR-UM	SA-BI-RU-UM		B 37+
5384.	ŠADW-I+ʾIL	SA-DI-DINGIR		JCS IV 110, 2040 16
5385.	ŠADID-UM	SA-DI-DU-UM		HARRIS 76 17
5386.	ŠADIR-AT-UM	SA-DI-RA-TUM?	FN	BM 80485 7, 18
5387.	ŠAʾIR-AT-IM	SA-E-RA-TIM	FN GEN	B 37+
5388.	ŠAʾIR-AT-UM	SA-E-RA-TUM	FN	B 37
5389.	ŠAʾQ-A+ʿAN-UM	SA-GA-A-NU-UM		B 47
5390.	ŠAGAR-AT-IM	SA-GA-RA-TIM-KI	GN GEN	M+
5391.	ŠAGAR-AT-UM	SA-GA-RA-TUM-KI	GN	M+
5392.	ŠAGAR-UM	SA-GA-RU-UM		GAUTIER 4 R. 4+
5393.	ŠAʾQ-U-HU	SA-GU-U_2		SIMMONS 60 31
5394.	ŠAʾIL-AT-UM	SA-I-LA-TUM	FN	B 37, TIM IV 53 7
5395.	ŠAKAN-UM	SA-KA-NU-UM		B 93
5396.	ŠAKAR-UM	SA-KA-RU-UM		HARRIS 39 13
5397.	ŠAKAR-UM	SA-KA-RUM		BIN VII 90 12+
5398.	ŠAKIR-AH	SA-KI-RA	FN	M
5399.	ŠAKIR-AM	SA-KI-RA-AM	ACC	M
5400.	ŠAKIR-U	SA-KI-RU		B 37
5401.	ŠAKIR-UM	SA-KI-RU-UM		RUTTEN 35 6, SEAL+
5402.	ŠAKIR-UM	SA-KI-RUM		M+
5403.	ŠAKUM-I+ʾIL	SA-KU-MI-DINGIR		M+
5404.	ŠAKUM-UM	SA-KU-MU-UM		B 37+
5405.	ŠAKUN-UN-UM	SA-KU-NU-NU-UM		RUTTEN 26 4
5406.	ŠAKUR-AN	SA-KU-RA-AN		RA LXV 54 XII 24
5407.	ŠAKUR-AN-U	SA-KU-RA-NU		M+
5408.	ŠAʾQ-UM	SA-KUM		UCP X/1 P. 61+, M
5409.	ŠALAM-AN	SA-LA-MA-AN		RA LXV 43 III 55
5410.	ŠALAM-AT-UM	SA-LA-MA-TUM	FN?	M
5411.	ŠAʾL-AT-UM	SA-LA-TUM	FN	CT VIII 20B 9+, M+, C+
5412.	ŠAʾL-I+ʾIL	SA-LI-DINGIR		B 37+

5413.	ŠALIḪ-AH	SA-LI-ḪA	FN	M+
5414.	ŠALIḪ-U	SA-LI-ḪU		M, SYRIA V 274+ HANA
5415.	ŠALIḪ-UM	SA-LI-ḪU-UM		M
5416.	ŠAʾL-IJA	SA-LI-IA		B 37
5417.	ŠALIL-UM	SA-LI-LUM		TIM III 131 9
5418.	ŠALIM-AH	SA-LI-MA	FN	XIII 1 III 29+
5419.	ŠALIM-AN	SA-LI-MA-AN		M+
5420.	ŠALIM-AN-IM	SA-LI-MA-NIM	GEN	M
5421.	ŠALIM-AN-U	SA-LI-MA-NU		A 7733 4, C+
5422.	ŠALIM-AT-IM	SA-LI-MA-TIM	FN GEN	CT VIII 28C 13
5423.	ŠALIM-AT-UM	SA-LI-MA-TUM	FN	XIII 1 VI 46
5424.	ŠALIM-AT-UM	SA-LI-MA-TUM	MN?	CT VIII 49A 46+
5425.	ŠAʾL-U+MAṬAR	SA-LU-MA-DAK		RA LXV 52 X 68+
5426.	ŠAM-A+JADAʿ-IM	SA-MA-A-DA-Ḫ[I-I]M	GEN	M
5427.	ŠAM-A+JADAʿ-U	SA-MA-A-DA-ḪU		M
5428.	ŠAM-A+JADAʿ-UM	SA-MA-A-DA-ḪU-UM		M+
5429.	ŠAM-AN-I	SA-MA-A-NI		JNES XIII 212F.+ LATE
5430.	ŠAM-AM	SA-MA-AM	ACC	XIII 38 7+
5431.	ŠAM-AN	SA-MA-AN		B 39+, M
5432.	ŠAMAK-UM	SA-MA-GU-UM		AJSL XLIV 242 NO. 29
5433.	ŠAM-A+MEʾ+ʾEL	SA-MA-ME-EL		M
5434.	ŠAMAM-UM	SA-MA-MU-UM		I+, CT VI 44B 12
5435.	ŠAM-AN-U	SA-MA-NU		JNES XIII 212F. LATE
5436.	ŠAM-AN-UM	SA-MA-NU-UM		B 47
5437.	ŠAMAR-A	SA-MA-RA?		HARRIS 35 11
5438.	ŠAM-A+RAWḪ	SA-MA-RA-AḪ		B 38+, XII 385 8
5439.	ŠAMAR-AN-U	SA-MA-RA?-NU		X 20 11
5440.	ŠAMAR-I+HADD-U	SA-MA-RI-A-DU		A. 57 45
5441.	ŠAMAR-I+ʾIL	SA-MA-RI-DINGIR		A. 455 46
5442.	ŠAM-I+JARAḪ	SA-ME-E-RA-AḪ		M
5443.	ŠAMIʿ-AH	SA-ME-ḪA	FN	RA LXV 60 III 54
5444.	ŠAMIʿ-UM	SA-ME-ḪU-UM		B 38
5445.	ŠAM-I+JARAḪ	SA-ME-RA-AḪ		YOS VIII 64 19+
5446.	ŠAMIB-AT-UM	SA-MI-BA-TUM	FN	M
5447.	ŠAM-I+DAʿ-AT-IM	SA-MI-DA-ḪA-TIM	FN? GEN	XII 741 6
5448.	ŠAM-I+DAʿ-AT-UM	SA-MI-DA-ḪA-TUM	FN	M
5449.	ŠAM-I+DAʿ-IM	SA-MI-DA-ḪI-IM	GEN	M+
5450.	ŠAM-I+DAʿ-UM	SA-MI-DA-ḪU-UM		M+
5451.	ŠAMID-U	SA-MI-DU		CT VIII 9A 1
5452.	ŠAMM-I+JATAR	SA-MI-E-TA-AR		M+
5453.	ŠAM-I+JATAR	SA-MI-E-TAR		XII 601 6
5454.	ŠAM-IJA	SA-MI-IA		EBPN 140+, MAM II/3 PL. XXXIX+
5455.	ŠAM-IM	SA-MI-IM	GEN	CT XLVIII 91, XIII 142 40+
5456.	ŠAM-I+MA+JA-ŠJIM	SA-MI-MA-IA-SI-IM	FN	C+
5457.	ŠAM-I+MEʾ+ʾEL	SA-MI-ME-EL		CT XLV 117 33
5458.	ŠAMIM-U	SA-MI-MU		WALTERS, WL 109:10
5459.	ŠAMIM-UM	SA-MI-MU-UM		BIN VII 154:4+
5460.	ŠAMIN-U-HU	SA-MI-NU-U_2	FN	CT II 46 4
5461.	ŠAMID-UM	SA-MI-TUM		U
5462.	ŠAMIʿ-UM	SA-MI-UM		LARSA, KING
5463.	ŠAM-U+ʾAB-IM	SA-MU-A-BI-IM	GEN	SUMER XXIII 153+
5464.	ŠAM-U+ʾAB-IM	SA-MU-A-BI-IM	NOM	RA VIII 71
5465.	ŠAM-U+JARAḪ	SA-MU-A-RA-AḪ		SIMMONS 98 3
5466.	ŠAM-U+BALIṬ	SA-MU-BA-LI_2-IṬ?		RUTTEN 34 11
5467.	ŠAM-U+DAGAN	SA-MU-D-DA-GAN		M
5468.	ŠAM-U+JARAḪ	SA-[M]U-E?-RA-A[Ḫ]?		RA LXV 47 VII 13
5469.	ŠAMUʿ-I+ʾEL	SA-MU-ḪI-EL		M
5470.	ŠAMUʿ-I+ʾIL	SA-MU-ḪI-IL		XIV 76:19
5471.	ŠAM-U+ʾIL-A	SA-MU-I-LA		M
5472.	ŠAM-U+HADD-U	SA-MU-D-IM		M+
5473.	ŠAMUK-AN-UM	SA-MU-KA-NU-[UM]		HARRIS 68 21
5474.	ŠAMUK-I+ʾEL	SA-MU-KI-EL		B 38+
5475.	ŠAMUK-IM	SA-MU-KI-IM	GEN	CT VIII 47B 22
5476.	ŠAMUK-UM	SA-MU-KUM		CT XLVIII 90 REV.
5477.	ŠAM-U+LA+ʾIL	SA-MU-LA-DINGIR		B 39+
5478.	ŠAMUL-AT-UM	SA-MU-LA-TUM	FN	M

5479.	ŚAMUM-AN-IM	SA-MU-MA-NIM	GEN	PBS XIV 357
5480.	ŚAMUM-U-HU	SA-MU-MU-U$_2$		M
5481.	ŚAM-U+RAWḪ	SA-MU-RA	NOM	CT XLVIII 29 REV.
5482.	ŚAM-U+RAWḪ	SA-MU-RA-A-AḪ		SIMMONS 46 28, 47 23
5483.	ŚAMUŚ-IM	SA-MU-SI-IM	GEN	BM 78366 3
5484.	ŚAMUŚ-A	SA-MU-ŠA	NOM	M+
5485.	ŚAM-U-HU	SA-MU-U$_2$		M+
5486.	ŚAM-U-HU+ʾIL-A	SA-MU-U$_2$-I-LA		M
5487.	ŚAMIʿ-UM	SA-MU-U$_2$-UM		RA LII 235, KING
5488.	ŚAMUK	SA-MU-UK		HARRIS 41 12
5489.	ŚAM-UM	SA-MU-UM		EBPN 141+, M
5490.	ŚAMIʿ-UM	SA-MU-UM		LARSA, KING
5491.	ŚANAGR-AT-UM	SA-NA-AG-RA-TUM	FN	CT IV 47B 27+, M+
5492.	ŚANAG-UM	SA-NA-GU-UM		JCS IV 109, 3328 2+
5493.	ḎANIB-UM	SA-NI-BU-UM		BA V 517 NO. 57 3, 6+
5494.	ŠANIJ-I	SA-NI-I		YOS II 139 3
5495.	ŠANIJ-UM	SA-NI-U$_2$-UM		M
5496.	ŚAPAR-AN	[S]A-PA-RA-AN		RA LXV 40 I 7
5497.	ŚAPIR-AT-UM	SA-PI-RA-TUM		B 37
5498.	ŚAPUR-UM	SA-PU-RU-UM		TIM V 19 5
5499.	ŚAQAḪ+TA-NWUḪ-HU	SA-QA-AḪ-TA-NU-U$_2$		CT VI 46 2
5500.	ŚAʾQ-AT-UM	SA-QA?-TUM	FN	XIII 1 VI 59
5501.	ŚARAM-AN-U	SA-RA-MA-NU		SZLECHTER TJ P. 25
5502.	ŚARAM-UM	SA-RA-MU-UM		YOS XII
5503.	ŚAʾR-AN-UM	SA-RA-NU-UM		TIM V 13 4
5504.	ŚAʾR-I	SA-RI	GEN	VAS VIII 14 28
5505.	ŚARIḪ-AH	SA-RI-ḪA	FN	RA LXV 60 III 39
5506.	ŚAʾR-IJA	SA-RI-IA		UCP X/1 108 10+
5507.	ŚARIK-UM	SA-RI-KUM		B 38+
5508.	ŚAʾR-UM	SA-RU-UM		TIM II 89 2, M
5509.	ŚAṬIḪ-I	SA-TI-I	GEN	SYRIA XXXVII 206 10 HANA
5510.	ŚAṬUḪ-UM	SA-TU-ḪU-UM		UCP X/1 89 28
5511.	ŚAWIR-AN-IM	SA-WI-RA-NI-IM	GEN	TA 1930, 558
5512.	ŚAWIR-AT-UM	SA-WI-RA-TUM		UET V 378 5
5513.	ŚAGAR-AT-IM	SAG-GA-RA-TIM	GN GEN	M+
5514.	ŚAGAR-AT-IM	SAG-GA-RA-TIM	MN GEN	M
5515.	ŚAGAR-UM	SAG-GA-RU-UM		UET V 534 R. 6+
5516.	ŚIJB-ATAN-U	SI-BA-TA-NU		SIMMONS 88 1
5517.	ŚIJB-AT-IJA	SI-BA-TI-IA	FN?	BM 80363 7
5518.	ḎIBIB-U	SI-BI-BI-BU		PBS VIII/2 228 4
5519.	ḎIBIB-UM	SI-BI-BU-UM		PBS VIII/2 228 A4
5520.	ŚIBIL-UM	SI-BI-LU-UM		A 21941
5521.	ŠI+RAWM-A	SI-I-RA-MA		A. 28 3, 16
5522.	ŚIKR-I+HADD-A	SI-IK-RI-ḪA-DA		BE VI/1 6 19
5523.	ŚIMʾAL	SI-IM-A-AL	TRIBE	M+
5524.	ŚIMʾAL-UM	SI-IM-A-LU-UM	TRIBE	M
5525.	ŚIMʾAL	SI-IM-ḪA-AL	TRIBE	M
5526.	ŚIMḪ-I+DAGAN	SI-IM-ḪI-D-DA-GAN		M
5527.	ŚIMM-I+JATAR	SI-IM-ME-A-TAR		A 7537 16, 21+
5528.	ŚINN-AH	SI-IN-NA	FN	RA LXV 58 I 61
5529.	ŚIPQ-U-NA+HADD-A	SI-IP-KU-NA-DA		M
5530.	ŚIPQ-U-NA+HADD-A	SI-IP-KU-NA-D-IM		M
5531.	ŠIQL-AN-IM	SI-IQ-LA-NIM	GEN	TA 1930, 189
5532.	ŠIQL-AN-UM	SI-IQ-LA-NU-UM		TA 30, 231+
5533.		SI-IT-ḪA-RA-MA-AM		RA LXV 42 III 12
5534.	SITR-I+HADD-U	SI-IT-RI-D-IM		JCS XXIV 60 NO.51 REV.
5535.	ŚIKIR-UM	SI-KI-RUM		YOS XIII 294:4+
5536.	ŚIMAʿ+LA-NI	SI-MA-AḪ-I-LA-A-NI		RA LXVI 112 MARI
5537.	ŚIMAʿ+LA-NIE	SI-MA-AḪ-I-LA-A-NI-E		SYRIA XLI 54 N. 1
5538.	ŚIMAʿ+LA-NIE	SI-MA-AḪ-I-LA-NI-E		RA LXVI 112 MARI
5539.	ŚIMAʿ+LA-NI	SI-MA-AḪ-LA-A-NI		SYRIA XLI 54 N. 1
5540.	ŚIMAʿ+LA-NIE	SI-MA-AḪ-LA-A-NI-E		RA LXVI 115:21;117:11 MARI
5541.	ŚIMAʿ+LA-NI	SI-MA-AḪ-LA-NI		SYRIA XLI 54 N. 1
5542.	ŚIMAʿ+LA-NIE	SI-MA-AḪ-LA-NI-E		SYRIA XLI 54 N. 1+
5543.	ŚIMʾAL	SI-MA-AL	TRIBE	M
5544.	ŚIMAʿ+ʾIL-A	SI-MA-I-LA		X 5 4, 5

5545.	ŠIJM-U+DAWR-A	SI-MU-DA-RA		TA 30, 186+
5546.	ŠINAN-UM	SI-NA-NU-UM		SIMMONS 114 7
5547.	ŠININ-AH	SI-NE-NA	FN	XIII 1 V 51+
5548.	ŠININ-AH	SI-NI-NA	FN	M+
5549.	ŠININ-AJA	SI-NI-NA-A-IA	FN	X 166 1+
5550.	SINUQ-A	SI-NU-GA		BIROT,TEA 16:11
5551.	ŠIʾN-U+RAPIʾ	SI-NU-RA-BI		A.+
5552.	ŠIRIB-I	SI-RI-BI		SYRIA XXXVII 206 29 HANA
5553.	ŠIRUN-UM+GAMIL	SI?-RU-NU-UM-GA-MIL?		VII 139 7
5554.	T-ŠAḪR-AH	SI?-TA-AḪ-RA	FN	IX 291 III 29'
5555.	ŠIJṮ-AT-UM	SI-TA-TUM	FN	XIII 1 IV 74+
5556.	JARAḪ+ʿAD-U	SIN-A-DU		RA XLIII 8 QATNA
5557.	JARAḪ+DAŠUR	SIN-DA-ŠUR		VAS IX 185 12+
5558.	JARAḪ+KIWN-A	SIN-KI-NA		TCL I 237 31
5559.		SU-A-ḪA-AM-MI-I-ŠA		VIII 85 17
5560.	ḎUBAB-IJA	SU-BA-BI-IA		SIMMONS P. 71 N. 5 3
5561.	ḎUBAB-UM	SU-BA-BU-UM		TA 30, 30 32+
5562.	ŠUWB-A+ḪAʾL-I	SU-BA-ḪA-LI		A. 6 29
5563.	ŠUBUL-UM	SU-BU-LU-UM		AJSL XXXII 227 4
5564.	ŠUBUL-UM	SU-BU-LUM	FN	RA LXV 58 I 65
5565.	ŠUGAG-I	SU-GA-GI	GEN	CT IV 31A 5+
5566.	ŠUGAG-UM	SU-GA-GU-UM		CT IV 42A 1, 8+
5567.	ŠUḪAR-UM	SU-ḪA-RU-UM		TA 30, 249 4
5568.	ŠUḪ-IT-UM	SU?-ḪI-TUM	FN	XIII 1 II 52
5569.	ŠUKUŠ-UM	SU-KU-SU-UM		M
5570.	ŠULAḪ-AT-UM	SU-LA-A-TUM	FN	RA LXV 66 VII 62
5571.	ŠULAḪ-AN-U	SU-LA-ḪA-NU		A 7702 13
5572.	ŠULAM-UM	SU-LA-MU-UM		UET V 608 3
5573.	ŠULAP-I	SU-LA-PI		PBS XI/2 P. 119
5574.	ŠULAP-UM	SU-LA-PU-UM		PBS XI/2 P. 119
5575.	ŠULUḪ-U	SU-LU-ḪU		UET V 427 16
5576.	ŠULUḪ-UM	SU-LU?-ḪU-UM		UET V 169 18
5577.	ŠULUK-UM	SU-LU-KUM		PBS XI/2 P. 119
5578.	ŠUM-U+ʾAB-I	SU-MA-A-BI		A.
5579.	ŠIMAʿ+LA-NIE	SU-MA-AḪ-I-LA-A-NI-E		RA LXVI 120:7 MARI
5580.	ŠUM-AN	SU-MA-AN		B 39
5581.	ŠUMAT+JARAḪ	SU-MA-AT-E-RA-AḪ		M+
5582.	ŠUMAT+ʾIL-I	SU-MA-AT-I_3-LI_2		XIII 1 II 85
5583.	ŠUM-U+ʿAḎAR	SU-MA-DAR		SIMMONS 50 26 DATE+
5584.	ŠUM-A+ʾIL-A	SU-MA-I-LA		YOS XIII 244:15+
5585.	ŠUM-A+LA+LI-JA	SU-MA-LA-LI-A		BM 80363 1
5586.	ŠUM-A+LI-KA	SU-MA-LI-KA		BM 80328 13
5587.	ŠUM-A+RAPIʾ	SU-MA-RA-BI		KAJ 39 17 LATE
5588.	ŠUMAT-AN-UM	SU-MA-TA-A-NU-UM		GORDON 38 2, 5
5589.	ŠUMAT-AN	SU-MA-TA-AN		M
5590.	ŠUM-I+ʾAB-UM	SU-ME-A-BU-UM		A. 12 4
5591.	ŠUM-I+ʾENLIL	SU-ME-D-EN-LIL_2		KISURRA 197A 12
5592.	ŠUM-I+ʾENTIL	SU-ME-EN-TI-[IL]?		B 38
5593.	ŠUM-I+HADD-U	SU-MI-A-DU		A.+
5594.	ŠUM-I+DAWR-U	SU?-MI-DA-AR-RU		A. 322 9
5595.	ŠUM-I+ṬAJB-A	SU?-MI-DA-BA		A. 7 44+
5596.	ŠUM-I+HEDD-A	SU-MI-E-DA		YOS XIII 486:1
5597.	ŠUM-IJA	SU-MI-IA		M+
5598.	ŠUM-I+JAMAM	SU-MI-IA-MA-AM		XII 61 5
5599.	ŠUM-I+LAMM-U	SU-MI-LAM-MU		VAS XVI 24 4, A.+
5600.	ŠUM-I+ʾIL-UM	SU-MI-LU-UM		WALTERS, WL 114:13
5601.	ŠUM-I+RAPAʾ	SU-MI-RA-PA		RA LVI 169, A.+
5602.	ŠUM-I+RIJB-A	SU-MI-RI-BA		A. 98C 10
5603.	ŠUM-U+ʾAB-I+JA-RWIM	SU-MU-A-BI-A-RI-IM		TA 30 9, 14, 15+
5604.	ŠUM-U+ʾAB-I-JA	[SU]-MU-A-BI-IA		B 38
5605.	ŠUM-U+ʾABIḪ	SU-MU-A-BI-IḪ		TIM V 1 16
5606.	ŠUM-U+ʾAB-IM	SU-MU-A-BI-IM	GEN	SUMER XXIII PL. 12 19
5607.	ŠUM-U+ʾAB-IM	[S]U-MU-A-BI-IM	NOM	EDZARD, DER 111:5
5608.	ŠUM-U+ʾAB-UM	SU-MU-A-BU-UM		B 38+
5609.	ŠUM-U+ʾAB-UM	D-SU-MU-A-BU-UM		KISURRA 93 22
5610.	ŠUM-U+JADAʿ-UM	SU-MU-A-DA-ḪU-UM		KISURRA 78A 15

5611.	ŠUM-U+ʿAḎAR	SU-MU-A-DAR		GORDON 38 DATE+
5612.	ŠUM-U+ʾAḪ-I-JA	[SU]-MU-A-ḪI-IA		PBS XI/2 1 I 27
5613.	ŠUM-U+ḤALAB	SU-MU-A-LA-AB		A.
5614.	ŠUM-U+ḤAM-I	SU-MU-A-MI		M
5615.	ŠUM-U+ḤAM-IM	SU-MU-D-A-MI-IM		RA LXV 40 I 25+
5616.	ŠUM-U+....	[SU-M]U-A-NI-....		PBS XI/2 1 I 12
5617.	ŠUM-U+JA-JPAʿ	[SU-MU]-A-PA-AḪ		B 38
5618.	ŠUM-U+JAPAR	[SU-MU]-A-PA-AR		B 38
5619.	ŠUM-U+JARAḪ	SU-MU-A-RA-AḪ		B 38+
5620.	ŠUM-U+ʿAḎAR	SU-MU-A-TAR		GORDON 38 DATE+
5621.	ŠUM-U+ʾAWN-AN-UM	SU-MU-AM-NA-NU-UM		B 38+
5622.	ŠUM-U+ʾA-MNID-IM	[SU-M]U-AM-NI-DI-IM		B 38
5623.	ŠUM-U+ʾAWN-AN-IM	SU-MU-AW-NA-NIM		SUMER XXIII ARABIC 178
5624.	ŠUM-U+BAʿL-A	SU-MU-BA-LA		UNPUBL.
5625.	ŠUM-U+BALIṬ	SU-MU-BA-LI$_2$-IṬ?		RUTTEN 26 12+
5626.	ŠUM-U+BELBIN	SU-MU-BE-EL-BI-IN		JCS IV 108, YBC 5198
5627.	ŠUM-U+BINAŠ-U	SU-MU-BI-NA-ŠU		A 7630 2
5628.	ŠUM-U+ṬAJB-I	SU-MU-DA-BI		X 90 10+
5629.	ŠUM-U+DAGAN	SU-MU-D-DA-GAN		B 39+
5630.	ŠUM-U+DITN-UM	SU-MU-DI-IT-NU-UM		B 39
5631.	ŠUM-U+....	SU-MU-DI-NA-....		B 39
5632.	ŠUM-U+DIJN-I	[SU-M]U-DI-NI		PBS XI/2 P. 119
5633.	ŠUM-U+DITAN	[SU]?-MU?-DI?-TA-A-AN		VAS XVI 24 3
5634.	ŠUM-U+DITAN	SU-MU-DI-TA-AN		SIMMONS 126 17+
5635.	ŠUM-U+DITAN-A	SU-MU-DI-TA-NA		B 39+, M
5636.	ŠUM-U+ʾIL	SU-MU-DINGIR		B 39+
5637.	ŠUM-U+ʾIL	D-SU-MU-DINGIR		KISURRA 85 15, 22+
5638.	ŠUM-U+ʾIL+....	SU-MU-DINGIR-LI-BUR-RA-AM		FRANK 27 4
5639.	ŠUM-U+ʾIL+ŠARR	SU-MU-[DINGIR]-LUGAL		UCP X/1 17 15
5640.	ŠUM-U+JE-MWUT+BAʿL-A	SU-MU-E-MU-UT-BA-LA	GEN	JCS IV 68 17
5641.	ŠUM-U+JE-MWUT+BAʿL-A	SU-MU-E-MU-UT-BA-LA	NOM	JCS IV 66 22
5642.	ŠUM-U+JE-MWUT+BAʿL-IM	SU-MU-E-MU-UT-BA-LIM?	GEN	JCS IV 71 9
5643.	ŠUM-U+JE-JPUʿ	SU-MU-E-PU-UḪ		M+
5644.	ŠUM-U+JARAḪ	SU-MU-E-RA-AḪ		M+
5645.	ŠUM-U+ʾEL	SU-MU-EL		TA 30, 34 6
5646.	ŠUM-U+ʾENTIL	SU-MU-EN-TE-IL		B 39
5647.	ŠUM-U+ʾENTIL	SU-MU-EN-TI-[IL]?		KISURRA 95 15
5648.	ŠUM-U+ʿAŠTAR	SU-MU-EŠ$_4$-DAR		PBS VIII/2 207 5, M
5649.	ŠUM-U+KANAŠ-A	SU-MU-GA-NA-SA		KISURRA 19 9
5650.	ŠUM-U+ʿADN-U	SU-MU-ḪA-AD-NU		B 39
5651.	ŠUM-U+ʿAMM-U	SU-MU-ḪA-AM-MU		B 39+
5652.	ŠUM-U+ʿAD-I	SU-MU-ḪA-DI-I	GEN	XIII 13:8
5653.	ŠUM-U+ʿAD-IM	SU-MU-ḪA-DI-IM		X 57 8
5654.	ŠUM-U+ʿAD-U-HU	SU-MU-ḪA-DU-U$_2$		M+
5655.	ŠUM-U+ḪAʾL-A	SU-MU-ḪA-LA		B 39
5656.	ŠIMAʿ+LA-NIE	SU-MU-ḪA-LA-NI-E		SYRIA XLI 54 N. 1
5657.	ŠUM-U+ʿAMM-U	SU-MU-ḪA-MU		M
5658.	ŠUM-U+ʿAMM-U	SU-MU-ḪA-MU	FN	C+
5659.	ŠUM-U+ʿADN-U	SU-MU-ḪI-AD-NU		KISURRA 29 12
5660.	ŠIMAʿ+LA-NIE	SU-MU?-ḪI-LA-NI-E		SYRIA XLI 54 N. 1
5661.	ŠUMUḪ-UM	SU-MU-ḪU-UM		BM 16852
5662.	ŠUM-U+ʾIL-A	SU-MU-I-LA		B 39; M+
5663.	ŠUM-U-JA	SU-MU-IA		B 39+
5664.	ŠUM-U+JA-ʾRUR-A	[SU-MU-I]A-AḪ-RU-RA		B 39
5665.	ŠUM-U+JAMAM	SU-MU-IA-MA-AM		M+
5666.	ŠUM-U+JA-MWUT-U+BAʿL-A	[SU]-MU-IA-MU-TU-BA-LA		PBS XI/2 1 I 19
5667.	ŠUM-U+JA-MWUT+BAʿL-A	SU-MU-IA-MU-UT-BA-[LA]		RUTTEN 3 21
5668.	ŠUM-U+JA-MWUT+BAʿL-IM	SU-MU-IA-MU-UT-BA-LIM	GEN	CT XLIII 86 1
5669.	ŠUM-U+JA-ŠABAŠ-UM	SU-MU-IA-SA-BA-SU-UM		PBS XI/2 1 I 34
5670.	ŠUM-U+JA-ŠJIM	SU-MU-IA-SI-IM		M+
5671.	ŠUM-U+JA-ŠJIT	SU-MU-IA-SI-IT		B 39
5672.	ŠUM-U+JAT-UM	SU-MU-IA-TUM		TLB IV 40 9, 12, 14
5673.	ŠUM-U+ʾIL+BAWB-I-JA	[SU-MU-I]L-BA-BI-IA		PBS XI/2 1 I 11
5674.	ŠUM-U+LABW-A	SU-MU-LA-BA		M
5675.	ŠUM-U+LA+ʾIL	SU-MU-LA-DINGIR		B 39+
5676.	ŠUM-U+LA+ʾEL	SU-MU-LA-EL		SUMER XXIII 160 5

5677.	ŠUM-U+LA+ʾIL-I	SU-MU-LA-I$_3$-LI$_2$		UCP X/1 34 2
5678.	ŠUM-U+LAʾL-UM	SU-MU-LA-LUM		PBS XI/2 1 1 16
5679.	ŠUM-U+LA-NI	SU-MU-LA-NI		HARRIS 39 11
5680.	ŠUM-U+LA-NIA	SU-MU-LA-NI-A		CT XLVIII 10 1
5681.	ŠUM-U+LI+ʾEL	SU-MU-LI-EL		B 39+
5682.	ŠUM-U+LI+ʾEL+DUWRI	SU-MU-LI-EL-DU-RI		A 7630 3
5683.	ŠUM-U+LIʾL-U	SU-MU-LI-LU		B 39
5684.	ŠUM-U+LI+JI-JṢIʾ	SU-MU-LI-ZI		MEISSNER 37 15+
5685.	ŠUM-U+ME+ʾEL	SU-MU-ME-EL		JCS IV 107, YBC 4968
5686.	ŠUMUM-U	SU-MU-MU		RA LXIV 22 NO. 2+
5687.	ŠUM-U+MUT-I+JABAL-A	SU-MU-MU-TI-A-BA-LA		B 39
5688.	ŠUM-U-NA+ʾAB-I	SU-MU-NA-A-BI	FN	A. 244 5, M
5689.	ŠUM-U-NA+ʾAB-I	SU-MU-NA-BI	FN	A. 59 8
5690.	ŠUM-U-NA+ʾAB-I+JA-RWIM	SU-MU-NA-BI-IA-RI-IM		SUMER XXIII PL. 7 17+
5691.	ŠUM-U-NA+HALAL	SU-MU-NA-ḪA-LA?-AL		UET V 245 11
5692.	ŠUM-U-NA+JA-JPUʿ-A	SU-MU-NA-IA-PU-ḪA-[....]		M
5693.		SU-MU-NE?-BI?-EL?		B 39
5694.	ŠUM-U-NI	SU-MU-NI		B 39
5695.	ŠUM-U+NIWḪ-A	SU-MU-NI-A		GORDON 39 9, 13
5696.	ŠUM-U+NIWḪ-IM	SU-MU-NI-ḪI-IM	GEN	SIMMONS 121 18, M+
5697.	ŠUM-U+NIWḪ-UM	SU-MU-NI-ḪU-UM		B 39
5698.	ŠUM-U+NIWR-I	SU-MU-NI-RI	FN	XIII 1 XI 46
5699.	ŠUM-U+NIʾŠ-U-JA	SU-MU-NI-ŠU-A		CT VIII 38D:14
5700.	ŠUM-U+NUMAḪ-A	SU-MU-NU-MA-ḪA		M
5701.	ŠUM-U+NUMḪ-A	SU-M[U-N]U-UM-ḪA		RA LXIV 43
5702.	ŠUM-U+NUMḪ-IM	SU-MU-NU-UM-ḪI-IM		RIFTIN 44 12,16+
5703.	ŠUM-U+RAWḪ	SU-MU-RA-A		B 40
5704.	ŠUM-U+RAWḪ	SU-MU-RA-A-AḪ		CT II 39 1, 15
5705.	ŠUM-U+RAWḪ	SU-MU-RA-AḪ		B 38+
5706.	ŠUM-U+RAPIʾ	SU-MU-RA-BI		M
5707.	ŠUM-U+RAWḪ-EM	[SU]-MU-RA-ḪI-E-IM		B 40
5708.	ŠUM-U+RAWM-E-JE	SU-MU-RA-ME-E		B 40+
5709.	ŠUM-U+RAWM-EM	SU-MU-RA-ME-IM		M
5710.	ŠUM-U+RAṢIJ-EM	[SU]-MU-RA-ZI-E-IM		B 40
5711.	ŠUM-U+....	SU-MU-SI-MU-....		A 7457 3
5712.	ŠUMUT-AN	SU-MU-TA-AN		RA LXV 46 VI 4+
5713.	ŠUM-U+TA-QWIM	SU-MU-TA-KI-IM		XIII 131 4'
5714.	ŠUM-U+TA-QJIŠ	SU-MU-TA-KI-IŠ		M
5715.	ŠUM-U+TAMAR-U	SU-MU-TA-MA-RU		RA LXIV 43
5716.	ŠUM-U+TAMAR	SU-MU-TA-MAR		B 40+
5717.	ŠUMUT-I	SU-MU-TI		B 40
5718.	ŠUMUT-I+JABAL-A	SU-MU-TI-A-BA-LA?		PBS XI/2 1 I 35
5719.	ŠUMUT-I+BAʿL	SU-MU-TI-BA-AL		M
5720.	ŠUM-U-JA	SU-MU-U$_2$-A		PBS XI/2 1 32
5721.	ŠUMUḪ+BAʿL-A	SU-MU-UḪ-BA-LA		PBS XI/2 1 I 18
5722.	ŠUM-U+ʾUP-I	SU-MU-UḪ$_2$-KI		JCS XI 23 NO. 10 14+
5723.	ŠUMUK+LIʾM	SU-MU-UK-LI-IM		C P. 42+
5724.	ŠUM-UM+ʿAD-U	SU-MU-UM?-ḪA-DU-KI	GN	YOS II 117:17+
5725.	ŠUM-UM+LA+ʾAB-I	SU-MU-UM-LA-A-BI	FN	RA LXV 65 VII 24
5726.	ŠUM-UM+ʾAB-I+JA-RWIM	SU-MU-UN-A-BI-IA-RI-IM		SUMER XXIII 153:9
5727.	ŠUM-U-NA+ʾAB-I+JA-RWIM	SU-MU-UN?-A-BI-JA-RI-IM		SUMER XXIII P. 153 9
5728.	ŠUM-U-NA+ʾAB-I	SU-MU-UN-NA-A-BI	FN	A. 64 7
5729.	ŠUM-U-NA+ʾAB-I	SU-MU-UN-NA-BI	FN	A. 33 3, 34 2+
5730.	ŠUM-U+JI-T-ŠAMAR	SU-MU-UŠ-TA-MAR		TIM II 14 21
5731.	ŠUMUT+ʾIL	SU-MU-UT-DINGIR		VAS VII 148 5+
5732.	ŠUM-U+ŠAMŠ	SU-MU-D-UTU		CT XLVIII 83 SEAL
5733.	ŠUM-U+ṢIDQ-UM	[SU]-MU-ZI-ID-KUM		B 40
5734.	ŠUM-U+ṢIDQ-UM+DITAN-A	[SU]-MU-ZI-ID-KUM-DI-TA-NA		B 40
5735.	ḎUNAB-IM	SU-NA-BI-IM	GEN	SUMER XIV 51 NO. 26 23
5736.	ḎUNAB-UM	SU-NA-BU-UM		CT IV 44B 5+
5737.	ŠUNAḪ-UM	SU-NA-ḪU-UM		UET V 572 2
5738.	ŠUNAN-UM	SU-NA-NU-UM		TA 30, 30 29
5739.	ḎUBAB-IJA	SU-PA-BI-IA		UCP X/1 108 1
5740.	ḎUBAB-UM	SU-PA-BU-UM		RIFTIN 29 23+
5741.	ŠUWB-A+ḪAʾL-I	SU-PA-ḪA-LI		A. 252 12+
5742.	ŠUPUR-T-UM	SU-PU-UR-TUM		PBS VIII/1 45 17

5743.	ŠURAR-UM	SU-RA-RU-UM		TIM III 133 14
5744.	ŠUʾUL-UM	SU-U_2-LU-UM		M
5745.	ŠUWB+ḪAʾL-I	SU-UB-ḪA-LI		A. 268 5
5746.	ŠULAL-I	SU-UL-LA-LI	GEN	TCL XVIII 95 1
5747.	ŠULUL-UM	SU-UL-LU-LUM		PBS XI/2 P. 119
5748.	ŠUMḪ-U+BAʿL	SU-UM-ḪU-BA-AL		YOS XII 390 2,9
5749.	ŠUMḪ-U+RAPIʾ	SU-UM-ḪU-RA-BI		M+
5750.	ŠUM+LI+JI-JṢIʾ-IM	SU-UM-LI-ZI-IM	GEN	WATERMAN 25 R 9
5751.		SU-UM-MA-BU		YOS XIII 352:7
5752.	ŠUM-U-NA+JA-RWIM	SU-UM-MU-NA-A-RI-IM		HARRIS 57 11
5753.	ŠUM-NA+JATAR	SU-UM-NA-IA-TAR		RA LXV 52 X 56
5754.	ṢIBAR-AT-UM	ṢI-BA-RA-TUM	MN?	OLZ VIII 351 16
5755.	ṢIḪAR+ṬALL-U-K	ṢI-ḪAR-TI-LU-UK	FN	PBS VIII/2 252 9, 18
5756.	ṢIDQ-AN-UM	ṢI-ID-GA-NU-UM		EDZARD, DER 85:45+
5757.	SIKIL-UM	ṢI-KI-LUM		KISURRA 27 11
5758.	ṢURAR-U	ṢU-RA-RU		KISURRA 104 36
5759.	ŠAWB-I+BIJT-UM	ŠA-A-BI-E_2		SUMER V 142 NO. 6
5760.	ŠAKK-I	ŠA-AK-KI		RA LXV 45 V 13
5761.	ŠAKN-U	ŠA-AK-NU		M
5762.	ŠALG-AN	ŠA-AL-GA-AN		RA LXV 40 I 49
5763.	ŠALM-U+ṬAJB-A	ŠA-AL-MU-ṬA_3-BA	FN	RA LXV 66 VII 64
5764.		ŠA-AL-MU-ZI	FN	M
5765.	ŠAMʿ-AN-UM	ŠA-AM-ḪA-NU-UM		B 93+
5766.	ŠAMK-AN-IM	ŠA-AM-KA-NIM	GEN	LIH 81 7,17, 23
5767.	ŠAMAR+HADD-U	ŠA-AM-MA-RA-DU		A.
5768.	ŠAMŠ-I+HADD-U	ŠA-AM-SI-D-IM		M+
5769.	ŠAMŠ-I+RAPIʾ	ŠA-AM-[SI]-RA-BI		M
5770.		ŠA-AN-QA-I	FN	RA LXV 60 III 56
5771.	ŠAPR-AK-UM	ŠA-AP-RA-KUM		M
5772.	ŠAPŠ-I	ŠA-AP-ŠI		A.
5773.	ŠAPŠ-I+ʾAB-I	ŠA-AP-ŠI-A-BI	FN	A.
5774.	ŠAQṬ-I	ŠA-AQ-TI	GEN	CT VIII 10B 7+
5775.	ŠAT+ʿAN-A	ŠA-AT-A-NA		TCL XXI 220A 4+ CAPP.
5776.	ŠAṬP-AH	ŠA-AṬ-BA	FN	RA LXV 65 VII 39
5777.	ŠAPAR-AK-UM	ŠA-BA-AR-KUM		U
5778.	ŠAWB-I+DAWD-I	[Š]A?-BI-DA-DI		RA LXV 43 I 13
5779.	ŠAWB-I+ʾIL	ŠA-BI-DINGIR		M, C+
5780.	ŠAPIR-UM	ŠA-BI-RU-UM		I+
5781.	ŠADW-IJA	ŠA?-DI?-IA		XIII 1 I 3
5782.	ŠADW-I+HADD-U	ŠA-DI-D-IM		M
5783.	ŠADW-I+MA+ʾIL	ŠA-DI-MA-DINGIR		RA LXV 48 VIII 20
5784.	ŠADW-U+ʾIL-A	ŠA-DU-[I]-LA		RA LXV 45 V 50
5785.	ŠADW-U+LABW-A	ŠA-DU-LA-BA		M
5786.	ŠADW-U+ŠARR-I	ŠA-DU-LUGAL		M
5787.	ŠADW-U+ŠARR-I	ŠA-DU-ŠA-AR-RI		M
5788.	ŠADW-U+ŠARR-I	ŠA-DU-ŠAR-RI		XIV 109:6
5789.		ŠA-DU?-UL?-LA-....		M
5790.	ŠADW-UM+LABW-A	ŠA-DU-UM-LA-BA		M
5791.	ŠADW-UM+LABW-I	ŠA-DU-UM-LA-BI		M
5792.	ŠADW-UM+LABW-A	ŠA-DU-UM-LA-BU-A		M
5793.	ŠADW-UM+ŠARR-I	[Š]A-DU-UM-ŠAR-RI		XIV 106:10, 17
5794.	ŠADW-UM+LABW-A	ŠA-DU-UN-LA-BA		M+
5795.	ŠADW-UM+ŠARR-I	ŠA-DU-UN-ŠAR-RI		M
5796.	ŠAʾQ-IJAN	ŠA-GI-IA-AN		RA LXV 54 XII 11+
5797.	ŠAʾḪ-AT-UM	ŠA-ḪA-TUM	FN	RA LXV 59 II 75
5798.	ŠAḪIR-A	ŠA-ḪI-RA	GEN	CT VIII 37D 6, 13
5799.	ŠAḪIR-A	ŠA-ḪI-RA	NOM	CT VIII 37D 1, 9
5800.	ŠAʾIQ-UM	ŠA-I-GU-UM		RA LXV 54 XII 27
5801.	ŠAʾIL-T-UM	ŠA-IL-TUM	FN	U+
5802.		ŠA-JA-MU-RU		RA LXV 45 V 79
5803.	ŠAKIM-AN-UM	ŠA-KI-MA-NUM		C
5804.	ŠAKIM-UM	ŠA-KI-MU-UM		HARRIS 91 17+
5805.	ŠALAŠ+NIʾG-I	ŠA-LA-AŠ-NI-GI	FN	C+
5806.	ŠALAŠ+TABB-I	D-ŠA-LA-AŠ-TAB-BI	FN	XIII 1 III 26
5807.	ŠALAŠ+TUWR-A-JA	ŠA-LA-AŠ-TU-RA-IA	FN	C
5808.	ŠALAL-UM	ŠA-LA-LUM		XIII 1 VII 29

5809.	ŠALAM-UM	ŠA-LA-MU-UM		EDZARD, DER 100:16
5810.	ŠAʾL-AN-UM	ŠA-LA-NU-UM		TA 30, 615 23
5811.	ŠALIM+ʿAN-UM	ŠA-LIM-A-NU-UM		M
5812.	ŠALIM+ʾAŠAR	ŠA-LIM-D-A-ŠAR		M
5813.	ŠAMAʿ-A+JAT-UM	ŠA-MA-A-IA-TUM	MN	WATERMAN 21 R. 6
5814.	ŠAMAK-T-UM	ŠA-M[A]-AK-T[UM]	MN	TA 1931, 527
5815.	ŠAMAʿ+ḪAʾT-IM	ŠA-MA-ḪA-TIM	GEN	XIII 1 VIII 44
5816.	ŠAMAʿ+JAT-UM	ŠA-MA-IA-TUM	MN	CT IV 43B 6+
5817.	ŠAM-A+ME+ʾEL	ŠA-MA-ME-EL		TA 1931, 421
5818.	ŠAMAM-UM	ŠA-MA-MU-UM		I+
5819.	ŠAM-AN-UM	ŠA-MA-NU-UM		I
5820.	ŠAM-AN-UM	ŠA-MA-NUM$_2$		U
5821.	ŠAMAŠ-I	ŠA-MA-ŠI		CT IV 43B 7
5822.	ŠAMIR+Š-BAʿL	ŠA-MI-IR-ŠU-BI-EL		TCL XVIII 125 30
5823.		ŠA-MU-U$_2$	FN	RA LXV 65 VI 72
5824.	ŠANIN-UM	ŠA-NI-NU-UM		SIMMONS 55 13
5825.	ŠAPAṬ-AN	ŠA-PA-TA-AN		M
5826.	ŠARAM-AJA	ŠA-RA-MA-A		M
5827.	ŠARAJ+ṢUWR-UM	ŠA-RA-ṢUR-RU-UM		KISURRA 111 6
5828.	ŠARAJ-TI+ʾEL	ŠA-RA-TE-EL		TIM III 44 18+
5829.	ŠARAJ-TI+ʾEL	ŠA-RA-TI-EL		TIM III 59 6
5830.	ŠARAJ+ṢIDQ-UM	ŠA-RA-ZI-ID-K[UM]		MEISSNER 36 22
5831.	ŠARŠAR-AN-IM	ŠA-ŠA-RA-NIM	GEN	M+
5832.	ŠARŠAR-AN-U	ŠA-ŠA-RA-NU		M
5833.	ŠARŠAR-AN-UM	ŠA-ŠA-RA-NU-UM		M
5834.	ŠT-ḪTIN+ʾIL	(E$_2$-)ŠA-TA-AḪ-TI-IN-DINGIR	GN	KISURRA
5835.	T-ŠAQL-UM	ŠA-TA-AQ-LUM		RA LXV 43 III 50
5836.	ŠT-ŠNIJ+ʾIL	ŠA-TA-AŠ-NI-IL		SUMER V 139 NO. 4
5837.	ŠAṬUP-I+ʾIL	ŠA-TU-BI-DINGIR		M+
5838.	ŠAṬUP-I+ʾEL	ŠA-TU-BI-EL		RA LXV 44 IV 74
5839.	ŠAṬAR-AH	ŠA-ṬA$_3$-AR-RA	FN	M
5840.	ŠAʾUM-I	ŠA-U$_2$-MI		BAB. III 267 HANA
5841.	ŠAWIL-AT-UM	ŠA-WI-LA-TUM	FN	M
5842.	ŠAWIL-UM	ŠA-WI-LUM		M
5843.	ŠAWUʾ-UM	ŠA-WU-U$_2$-UM		RA LXV 48 VIII 16
5844.		ŠA-ZI-ḪU-UM		B 40
5845.	ŠARR-AJA	ŠAR-RA-A-IA		M
5846.	ŠARR-A+ʾIL	ŠAR-RA-DINGIR		A. LATE+
5847.	ŠARR-AJA	ŠAR-RA-IA		M+
5848.	ŠARR-IJA	ŠAR-RI-IA		M+
5849.	ŠEʾR-UM+MAGUN-U	ŠE-EḪ-RUM-MA-GU-NU	FN	C
5850.	ŠIRṬ-IJA	ŠE-ER-DI-IA		A.
5851.	ŠIPR-AN-UM	ŠE?-IP?-[RA]?-NU-UM		I
5852.	ŠIPR-AT-U	ŠE-IP-RA-TU	MN	LAESSOE P. 99+
5853.		ŠE-MU-BA		A.
5854.	ŠEʾR-AH+MAM-A	ŠE-RA-D-MA-MA	FN	X 110 3
5855.	ŠERIR-AN-IM	ŠE-RI-RA-NIM	GEN	M
5856.	ŠIJB-AT-UM	ŠI-BA-TUM	FN	M
5857.	ŠIJB-U-NA+ḪARAM	ŠI-BU-NA-A-RA-AM		M
5858.	ŠI+DUWR-I	ŠI-DU-RI	FN	RA LXV 58 I 68+
5859.	ŠI+QUWJ-I	ŠI-I-KU-WI	FN	A. 8 12, 34
5860.	ŠI+MAʾT-UM	ŠI-I-MA-TUM	FN	C+
5861.	ŠI-JA+....	ŠI-IA-N[A-....]	FN	M
5862.	ŠI-JA+TAKAL	ŠI-IA-TA-KA-AL	MN	IX 291 III 37'
5863.	ŠIJB-T-U	ŠI-IB-TU	FN	M+
5864.	ŠIJB-T-UM	ŠI-IB-TU-UM	FN	RA LXV 62 V 50
5865.	ŠIJB-T-UM	ŠI-IB-TUM	FN	M
5866.	ŠIMGIN-AH	ŠI-IM-GI-EN-NA	FN	M
5867.	ŠIMGIN-AH	ŠI-IM-GI-IN-NA	FN	M
5868.	ŠIMGIN-AH	ŠI-IM-GI-NA	FN	M+, C
5869.	ŠIMḪ-AJA	ŠI-IM-ḪA-A-IA	FN	M
5870.	ŠIMḪ-U+ʾIL-UM	ŠI-IM-ḪU-LUM?		A. 265 8
5871.	ŠIMAR+HADD-U	ŠI-IM-MA-RA-DU?		A.
5872.	ŠIMR+ʾALLA	ŠI-IM-RA-AL-LA		A.
5873.	ŠIPR-AN	ŠI-IP-RA-AN		A. LATE
5874.	ŠIPR-AN-UM	ŠI-IP?-RA?-NU-UM		I

5875.	ŠIPR-I+HAND-A	ŠI-IP-RI-AN-TA		A. LATE
5876.	ŠIPṮ-A+ʾAḪ-UM	ŠI-IP-TA-A-ḪU-UM		RA LXV 46 VI 27
5877.	ŠIPṮ-I+JAʾAR	ŠI-IP-TI-A-ḪA-AR	FN	C
5878.	ŠIPṮ-I+HAND-A	ŠI-IP-TI-AN-TA		A. LATE
5879.	ŠIPṮ-I+HAND-A	ŠI-IP-TI-IA-AN-TA		A. LATE
5880.	ŠIPṮ-I+HADD-U	ŠI-IP-TI-D-IM		A. LATE
5881.	ŠIQL-AN-U	ŠI-IQ-LA-NU		B 47
5882.	ŠIQL-AN-UM	ŠI-IQ-LA-NU-UM		TA 30, 2 4
5883.	ŠIQL-IM	ŠI-IQ-LI-IM	GEN	CT XLVIII 80
5884.	ŠIRṮ-I+ʾIL-I	ŠI-IR-TE-I_3-LI_2		A. LATE
5885.	ŠITAŠ+ʾIL-I	ŠI-IT-TA-AŠ-I_3-LI_2		MEL. SYR. 994
5886.	ŠILIB-UM	ŠI-LI-BU-UM		HARRIS 36 5
5887.	ŠIMAʿ-NI+ʾIL	ŠI-MA-AḪ-NI-DINGIR		VIII 49 BIS 5'
5888.	ŠIJM-AT+DAGAN	ŠI-MA-AT-D-DA-GAN	FN	XIII 1 VIII 33+
5889.	ŠIJM-AT+ʿAŠTAR	ŠI-MA-AT-E$Š_4$-DAR	FN	XIII 1 V 75+
5890.		ŠI-MA-ḪA-[....]		VAS IX 172 42, 174 29
5891.	ŠI+MALIK-T-I	ŠI-MA-LI-IK-TI		IX 294:7'
5892.	ŠIJM-AT-IM	ŠI-MA-TIM	FN GEN	XIII 1 V 15+
5893.	ŠIJM-AT-UM	ŠI-MA-TUM	FN	M+
5894.	ŠI+MIGN-I	ŠI-ME-IG-NI	FN	RA LXV 60 III 24
5895.	ŠIMAʿ+TA-ʿQUB	ŠI-ME-TA-GU-UB		M+
5896.	ŠINAN-A	ŠI-NA-AN-NA		XIII 1 I 19
5897.	ŠINA+DAMQ-A	ŠI-NA-DAM-QA	FN	XIII 1 IV 29+
5898.	ŠIʾN-AT-IM	ŠI-NA-TIM	FN GEN	XIII 1 V 83
5899.	ŠINI+ʿAḎR-I	ŠI-NI-AD-RI		M
5900.	ŠINI+DAMQ-A	ŠI-NI-DAM-QA	FN	RA LXV 61 IV 48
5901.	ŠINI+HADD-U	ŠI-NI-D-U		MRS XVI 44:3
5902.	ŠIʾN-U+RAPIʾ	ŠI-NU-RA-BI		A.+
5903.	ŠI+NUWR-I	ŠI-NU-RI	FN	A. LATE
5904.	ŠI+TA-BNIJ	ŠI-TAB-NI	FN	RA LXV 64 VI 18
5905.	ŠI+TA-BNIJ	ŠI-TAB-NI-A-JA	FN	RA LXV 66 VII 57
5906.	ŠUʾAR-I+....	ŠU-A-RI-[....]		M
5907.	ŠUWB-A+ʿAMM-I	ŠU-BA-AM-MI		A. 270 22
5908.	ŠU+BAʾB-A	ŠU-BA-BA		U
5909.	ŠUWB-A+ʾIL-A	ŠU-BA-D-DINGIR		B 23+
5910.	ŠUWB-A+ḪAʾL-I	ŠU-BA-ḪA-LI		A. 97 16, 18+
5911.	ŠUWB-A-NI+ʾIL	ŠU-BA-NI-DINGIR		RUTTEN 41 3, 13
5912.	ŠUWB-I+QARAD	ŠU-BI-GA-RA-AD		I
5913.	ŠUWB-I+HADD-U	ŠU-BI-D-IM		M
5914.	Š-BAʿL-AN-UM	ŠU-BI-LA-NU-UM		B 47
5915.	ŠUWB-U+RAPUʾ	ŠU-BU-RA-BU		TCL X 4A 25, B 15
5916.	ŠUBUL+ʾAB-I	ŠU-BU-UL-A-BI		M
5917.	ŠUBUL-T-UM	ŠU-BU-UL-TUM	FN	M, C
5918.	ŠU+DAMIQ	ŠU-DA-ME-IQ		RA LXV 41 II 16
5919.	ŠU+ʾEL-UM	ŠU-E-LUM		B 40
5920.	ŠUʾQ-AN-UM	ŠU-GA-NU-UM		EDZARD, DER 80:14
5921.	ŠUʾG-U+JAT-UM	ŠU-GU-IA-TUM		B 40
5922.	ŠUQUL-T-UM	ŠU-GUL-TUM	FN	XIII 1 XI 9
5923.	ŠU+ʿABD-I	ŠU-ḪA-AB-DI		CT XLVIII 43:15,19
5924.	ŠU+ʿAMM-U	ŠU-ḪA-AM-MU		M+
5925.	ŠUḪAR-T-UM	ŠU-ḪA-AR-TUM	FN	M
5926.	ŠUʿAL-AN	ŠU-ḪA-LA-AN		M
5927.	ŠUʿAL-AN-U	ŠU-ḪA-LA-NU		M
5928.	ŠUʾḪ-AT-UM	ŠU-ḪA-TUM		HARRIS 1 3, 6+
5929.	ŠUʾḪ-UM	ŠU-ḪU-UM		RUTTEN 29 3, 6 SEAL+
5930.	ŠUKUD-UM	ŠU-KU-DU-UM		M
5931.	ŠUKUR-AT-UM	ŠU-KU-[R]A-TUM	FN	XIII 1 V 78
5932.		ŠU-LUM-ŠU-RA-MA	FN	RA LXV 58 I 13
5933.	ŠUM-A+HADD-U	ŠU-MA-A-DU		A.
5934.	ŠUM-I+RIJB-A	ŠU-ME-RI-PA		A. LATE
5935.	ŠUM-I+ḪINN-I	ŠU-MI-IN-NI		U
5936.	ŠUM-I+RIJB-A	ŠU-MI-RI-PA		A. LATE
5937.	ŠUM-I+DAWR-U	ŠU-MI-TA-RU		A. LATE
5938.	ŠUM-U+ʾA-ŠKUR-A	ŠU-MU-$AŠ_2$-KU-RA		TA 30, 299
5939.	ŠUMUḪ-AT-UM	ŠU-MU-ḪA-TUM	FN	RA LXV 64 V 58
5940.	ŠUMUḪ-T-UM	ŠU-MU-UḪ-TUM	FN	XIII 1 X 49+

5941.	ŚUM-UM	ŠU-MU-UM		TA 30, 615 5
5942.	ŚUM-UM+MAZAZ	ŠU-MU-UM-MA-ZA-AZ		TA 1931, 538 I, IV
5943.	Š-NUʾR-A+ḪAʾL-U-HU	ŠU-NU-ḪU-RA-ḪA-LU-U_2		XIV 11:1
5944.	Š-NUʾR-A+ḪAʾL-U-HU	ŠU-NU-UḪ-ḪU-RA-ḪA-LU-U_2		XIV 36:1+
5945.	Š-NUʾR-A+ʿAMM-U	ŠU-NU-UḪ-RA-AM-MU		B 40 HANA+
5946.	Š-NUʾR-A+ḪAʾL-U	ŠU-NU-UḪ-RA-ḪA-LU		M+
5947.	Š-NUʾR-A+ḪAʾL-U-HU	ŠU-NU-UḪ-RA-ḪA-LU-U_2		M+
5948.	Š-NUʾR-U+ḪAʾL-U	ŠU-NU-UḪ-RU-ḪA-LU		M+
5949.	Š-NUʾR+ḪAʾL-I	ŠU-NU-UR-ḪA-LI		KING LIH I 22 4, R. 2
5950.	ŠU+RAWM-A	ŠU-RA-MA		A. LATE+
5951.	ŠU+RAWM-U	ŠU-RA-MU		A. LATE+
5952.	ŠURAN-AT-UM	ŠU-RA-NA-TUM	FN	M
5953.	ŠUŠAG-I	ŠU-ŠA-GI	FN	M
5954.	ŠU+JI-BNIJ-HU	ŠU-U_2-IB-NI-U_2		TA 1931, 636 REV +
5955.	ŠUWB+ʿAMM-U	ŠU-UB-AM-MU		MRS VI P. 257+
5956.	ŠUWB+ʾIL-A	ŠU-UB-D-I-LA		RA LXV 52 X 66
5957.	ŠUWB-NA+ʾIL	ŠU-UB-NA-DINGIR		B 40+, M+
5958.	ŠUWB-NA+ʾIL-U	ŠU-UB-NA-ḪI-LU		B 40
5959.	ŠUWB-NA+ʾIL	ŠU-UB-NA-IL		B 40
5960.	ŠUWB-NA+LU-HU	ŠU-UB-NA-LU-U_2		M+
5961.	ŠUʾM-A+BAʾIL	ŠU-UḪ-MA-BA-IL		RA LXV 51 IX 60
5962.	ŚUḪR-AJA	ŠU-UḪ-RA-IA	FN	SIMMONS 138 5, 14
5963.	ŚULM-AN-UM	ŠU-U[L]-MA-NU-U[M]		I
5964.	ṬAJB-AH	TA-A-BA	FN	M+
5965.	TABʾ-I+BIN-UM	TA-AB-I-BI-NU-UM		BM 82437 4 9
5966.	ṬAJB+ŚIJM-T-UM	TA-AB-SI-IM-TUM	FN	A. 8 4
5967.	ṬAḤD-I+LIʾM	TA-AḪ-DI-LI-IM		M
5968.	TA-ḤBAS-I	TA-AḪ-PA-ZI		A. 28 4, 17
5969.	TAḪTAḪ-UM	TA-AḪ-TA-ḪU-UM		BIN VII 116 3
5970.	TA-T-ʾAMAR	TA-AḪ-TA-MAR		M
5971.	TAḤT-U+PI+ʾIL	TA-AḪ-TU-BI-DINGIR		M+
5972.	TA-HWIJ+JARAḪ	TA-AḪ-WI?-D-EN-ZU		RA LXIV 28 NO. 16
5973.	TA-HWIJ+NAPŠ-U	TA-AḪ-WI-NA-AP-SU		RA LXIV 28 NO. 14
5974.	TA-ḤṢIN+ʾADM-U	TA-AḪ-ZI-IN-AD-MU	FN	M
5975.	TA-ʾZIJ+ʾADM-U	TA-AḪ-ZI-D-AD-MU	FN	M
5976.	TALM-A+ʿAMM-U	TA-AL-MA-AM-MU		A.+
5977.	TALM-U+ʾAŠIḪ-I	TA-AL-MU-A-ŠI-ḪI	FN	XIII 1 III 63
5978.	TANTAN-UM	TA-AN-TA-NU-UM		SUMER V 141
5979.	TA-QBIJ-IM	TA-AQ-BI-IM	GEN?	M+
5980.	TA-QNIJ-T-UM	TA?-AQ-NI-TUM	FN	XIII 1 VIII 74
5981.		TA-AR-MA-RI-IŠ		M
5982.	TA-RŚAP-AH	TA-AR-SA-BA	FN	RA LXV 64 VI 28
5983.	TATT-AH	TA-AT-TA	FN	RA LXV 62 V 55
5984.	TATT-A-HA	TA-AT-TA-A	FN	RA LXV 60 III 73
5985.	TATT-I+BAʾT-UM	TA-AT-TI-BA-TUM		TCL I 204:10
5986.	ṬABIḪ-AT-UM	TA-BI-ḪA-TUM	MN?	BE VI/1 3 3 11
5987.	TABB-I+MAM-A	TA-BI-D-MA-MA	FN	M
5988.	TABIN-UM	TA-BI-NU-UM		BM 82359
5989.	TABUB-U	TA-BU-BU	FN	XIII 1 VIII 35
5990.	TABUB-U+ḤAṢN-I	TA-BU-BU-ḪA-AṢ-NI	FN	RA LXV 60 III 19
5991.	TABUB-U+ʿALIJ-AH	D-TA-BU-BU-ḪA-LI-IA	FN	XIII 1 VI 13
5992.	TABUB-U+ŠIMḪ-I	TA-BU-BU-ŠI-IM-ḪI	FN	XII 265 4
5993.	TABUB-U+ʾUMM-I	TA-BU-BU-UM-MI	FN	XIII 1 VI 57
5994.	TABUB-I+ʿIMD-I	TA-BU-TI?-IM-DI	FN	VIII 31 10 15
5995.	TABUB+ʿIMD-I	TA-BU-UB-IM-[DI]?	FN	VIII 33 7
5996.	TABUZ-I	TA-BU-ZI		RA LXV 45 V 33
5997.	TADAB+JE-JŚAR	TA-DA-AB-E-ŠAR	FN	XIII 1 VI 42
5998.	TA-ʿḎAR-AH	TA-DA-RA	FN	M
5999.	TA-TWUR+ḪAʾT-UM	TA-DUR-ḪA-TUM		TA 1931, 489
6000.	TA-TWUR+MAʾT-UM	TA-DUR-MA-TUM	FN	XIII 1 XIV 34+
6001.	TAWIR-U	TA-E-RU		KISURRA 81A 4+
6002.	TAWIR-UM	TA-E-RUM		KISURRA 73 2+
6003.	TAʾG-I	TA-GI		RA LXV 43 III 40+
6004.	TAʾG-IT-UM	TA-GI-TUM	FN	XIII 1 II 45
6005.	TA-NḪAB-AT-I	TA-ḪA-BA-TI	FN GEN	VAS VIII 127 2
6006.	TA-NḪAB-AT-UM	TA-ḪA-BA-TUM	FN	VAS VIII 127 2, 29

6007.	TAʾ-I	TA-H̱I		M+
6008.	TAʾIL-U	TA-H̱I-LU?	FN	RA LXV 65 VII 33
6009.	TA-ʾH̱UḎ-AN	TA-H̱U-ZA-AN		RA LXV 52 X 33
6010.	TAʾK-I	TA-KI		RA LXV 55 XIII 19
6011.	TAʾK-I+ʾIŠH̱AR-AH	TA-KI-D-IŠ-H̱A-RA		JCS XIII 52 293 LE,A.LATE
6012.	TA-QJIŠ+NAN-I	TA-KI-IŠ-NA-NI	FN?	TIM III 41 6
6013.	TAʾK-U+ʾIL	TA-KU-DINGIR		VAS VIII 14 27
6014.	TAʾK-U+ʾIŠH̱AR-AH	TA-KU-D-IŠ-H̱A-R[A]		JCS XIII 52 293 R, A.LATE
6015.	TA-KWUN-AH	TA-KU-NA	FN	XIII 1 VIII 18+
6016.	TA-KWUN-AJA	TA-KU-NA-IA	FN	C
6017.	TA-KWUN+H̱Aʾ T-UM	TA-KU-UN-H̱A-TUM	FN	M+
6018.	TA-KWUN+MAʾT-UM	TA-KU-UN-MA-TUM	FN	M, C+
6019.	TA-KWUN+MITEʿ-JE	TA-KU-UN-MI-TE-E		M
6020.	TA-KWUN+ZULAT-UM	TA-KU-UN-ZU?-LA-TUM	FN	RA LXV 62 V 30
6021.	TA-KWUN+MAʾT-I	TA-KUM-MA-TI	FN	A.+
6022.	TALAʾ-UM	TA-LA-H̱U-UM		BE VI/2 80 29
6023.	TALIʾ-AN-UM	TA-LI-A-NU-UM		TA 1931, 538 VI
6024.	ṬALL-I+JI-BNIJ	TA-LI-IB-NI	FN	CT II 5 3 9
6025.	TAʾL-UM	TA-LU-UM		EDZARD, DER 112:23
6026.		TA-MA-KU?-ME-NI		M
6027.	TAMAR-U	TA-MA-RU		RA LXV 50 VIII 71
6028.	TAʾM-I	TA-MI		RA LXV 50 IX 13
6029.	TA-ʾMUR	TA-MU-UR	FN	M
6030.	TA-NWUD-AH	TA-NU-DA	FN	RA LXV 61 IV 45
6031.	TA-NWUH̱-AH	TA-NU-H̱A	FN	M
6032.	TA-NWUH̱+NAWIJ-UM	TA-NU-UH̱-NA-WI-UM	FN	M
6033.	ṬAJB-A+ʾAŠUR-A	TA-PA-AŠ-ŠU-RA		A.
6034.		TA-RA-AH̱-TU-UK		RA LXV 48 VIII 22
6035.		TA-RA-AM-NU	FN	XIII 1 XIII 11
6036.	TARAJ-AT-UM	TA-RA-IA-TUM	FN	VAS XIII 14 5+
6037.	TA-RJIB-IM	TA-RI-BI-IM	GEN	M
6038.	TA-RJIB-UM	TA-RI-BU-UM		M
6039.	ṬARID-A+ʾADM-U	TA-RI-DA-AD-MU		XIII 1 16
6040.	ṬARID-UM	TA-RI-DU-UM		BM 17049 26+
6041.	TA-RWIM+ʿAŠTAR	TA-RI-IM-EŠ$_4$-DAR	FN	XIII 1 II 13
6042.	TA-RWIM+ŠAKIM	TA-RI-IM-ŠA-KI-IM		M+
6043.	TA-RʿIŠ+ʿAŠTAR	T[A-R]I-IŠ-EŠ$_4$-DAR	FN	RA LXV 65 VII 36
6044.	TA-RʿIŠ+H̱Aʾ T-U	TA-RI-IŠ-H̱A-AT-TU	FN	M+
6045.	TA-RʿIŠ+MAʾT-UM	TA-RI-IŠ-MA-TUM	FN	M+, C
6046.	TA-RWUB-AH	TA-RU-BA	FN	M
6047.	TA-ŠJIM+ʿAŠTAR	TA-ŠI-IM-EŠ$_4$-DAR	FN	XIII 1 IV 28
6048.	TA-ŠWUB-AH	TA-ŠU-BA	FN	M+
6049.	TA-ŠWUB-AT-UM	TA-ŠU-BA-TUM	FN	M
6050.	TANTAN-UM	TA-TA-NU-UM		HARRIS 11 17, 14 14+
6051.	TA-ʿTIQ+ʾABN-U	TA-TI-QA-AB-NU		RES 1938 128
6052.	TA-TWUR+ʿAŠTAR	TA-TU-UR-EŠ$_4$-DAR	FN	M
6053.	TA-TWUR+MAʾT-UM	TA-TU-UR-MA-TUM	FN	M+; C+
6054.	TA-ṢJID-UM	TA-ZI-TUM	FN	M
6055.	TA-BNIJ+ʿAŠTAR	TAB-NI-EŠ$_4$-DAR	FN	XIII 1 XIII 15+
6056.	TA-BNIJ-T-UM	TAB-NI-TUM	FN	XIII 1 VI 5+
6057.	TA-BRUW+ʿAŠTAR	TAB-RU?-EŠ$_4$-DAR	FN	XIII 1 V 43
6058.	TA-PTAN+HADD-A	TAP-DA-NA-TA		A. LATE
6059.	TA-PTAN+HADD-A	TAP-TA-NA-A-DA		A. 206 5
6060.	TA-PTUN+HADD-A	TAP-TU-NA-A-DA		A. 33 26
6061.	TIRR-U	TE-IR-RU		M+
6062.	TIWR-I-Š+TUWR	TE-RI-IŠ-TU-UR$_2$		C+
6063.		TE-ZI-ID?-DI-MI		VII 127 4
6064.	TIʾAR-UM	TI-A-RUM		B 40
6065.	TIBIʾ-A-Š+ME+ʾEL	TI-BI$_2$-AŠ$_2$-ME-EL		CT XXXIII 48A 4
6066.	DITAN-UM	TI-DA-NUM$_2$	GN	GUDEA
6067.	TIDIQ-AN	TI-DI-QA-AN		RA LXV 48 VIII 18+
6068.		TI-IH̱-ME-DU		RA LXV 53 XI 19
6069.	TIʾM+LU-HU	TI-IM-LU-U$_2$	FN	XIII 1 VIII 73+
6070.	TIʾM+RIJB-A	TI-IM-RI-PA		A.
6071.		TI-IM-ZU-NA-....		HARRIS 5 21
6072.	TINʾ-AT-UM	TI-IN-A-TUM	FN	XIII 1 VI 4

6073.	TINʾ-I+JARAḪ	TI-IN-E-RA-AḪ		C
6074.	TINʾ-I+JARAḪ	TI-IN-I-E-RA-AḪ		C
6075.	TINʾ-IJAN	TI-IN-I-IA-AN		RA LXV 51 IX 76+
6076.	TIWR+ḪAJJ-A	TI-IR-E$_2$-A		M+
6077.	TIWR+ʿAŠTAR	TI-IR-EŠ$_4$-DAR		M+
6078.	TIWR+MAM-A	TI-IR-MA-MA		M+
6079.	TIRR-U	TI-IR-RU		M
6080.	TISP-AT-UM	TI-IS-PA-A-TUM	FN	X 105 3
6081.	TISP-AT-UM	TI-IS-PA-TUM	FN	M+, C
6082.	TISP-UM	[T]I-IS-PU-UM		RA XLI 45 8', HANA
6083.	TIʾŠ+LUʾM-U	TI-IŠ-LU-MU		M
6084.	TIʾL-AN-UM	TI-LA-NU-UM		B 47
6085.	TILIʾ-A-Š+GAMIL	TI-LI-AŠ-GA-MIL		UNPUBL.
6086.	TIMAN-AJA	TI-MA-NA-A-A		HARRIS 66 14
6087.	DIJN-I+HADD-U	TI-NI-A-DU		A. 59 2
6088.		TI-NI-LA-NU-UM		TA 1931, 538 I, V
6089.	TIWR-AT-UM	TI-RA-TUM	FN	M
6090.		TI-RI-IS-RA		A. LATE+
6091.		TI-RI-IŠ-RA		A. 224 R. 5 LATE
6092.	TIŠAN-AT-UM	TI-ŠA-NA-TUM	FN	BM 82372, M
6093.	TIŠAN-AT-UM	TI-ŠA-NA-TUM	MN	VAS VIII 58 34+
6094.	TIʾŠ-AT-UM	TI-ŠA-TUM	FN	M
6095.	TIʾT-AJA	TI-TA-A-A		RUTTEN 28 10+
6096.		TI-ZI-ḪA-AM		RA LXV 41 II 38
6097.	TUʾAL-U	TU-A-LU		RA LXV 48 VIII 17
6098.	TUBAB-I	TU-BA-BI		RA LXV 41 II 26
6099.		TU-BI-BA?-AR-RA	FN	XIII 1 VIII 59
6100.	TUBIN-UM	TU-BI-NU-UM		TA 30 103
6101.	ṮUBUQ-AH	TU-BU-QA	FN	M
6102.	TUDAR-I+ʿAŠTAR	TU-DA-RI-EŠ$_4$-DAR	FN	EDZARD, DER 58:7
6103.	TUDAR-UM+ʿAŠTAR	TU-DA-RUM-EŠ$_4$-DAR	FN	EDZARD, DER 61:16
6104.		TU-DI-EN		M
6105.	TUQAR-IM	TU-GA-RI-IM	GEN	HARRIS 64 7
6106.	TUQAR-UM	TU-GA-RU-UM		UET V 625 10+
6107.	TUʾ-AN-UM	TU-ḪA-NU-UM		UCP X/3 2 26
6108.	TUʾ-ATAN	TU-ḪA-TA-AN		M
6109.	TUʾ-I	TU-I		XIII 60 5
6110.		TU-KA-ZU-[....]		M
6111.		TU-LI-IA-ŠUM		CT XLV 54 18
6112.		TU-LI-IŠ		M+
6113.		TU-LI-IŠ-TA-A-NIM		UCP X/1 105 3 9
6114.	TUʾM-AN-UM	TU-MA-NU-UM		B 47
6115.	TUʾN-AK-UM	TU-NA-KUM		UET V 285 22
6116.	TUʾN-AN-U	TU-NA-NU		BM 81617 5
6117.	TUʾN-AN-UM	TU-NA-NU-UM		TCL XVIII 118 7
6118.	TUQAR-UM	TU-QA-RU-UM		CT XXXIII 42 21
6119.	TUWR-A+DAGAN	TU-RA-D-DA-GAN		M+
6120.	TUWR-A+ʾIL-I	TU-RA-I$_3$-LI$_2$		SAUREN, WUG 285 V, U.
6121.	TUWR-I+DAGAN	TU-RI-D-DA-GAN		B 40+ HANA
6122.	TURUM-NA+ḪATK-I	TU-RUM-NA-AT-KI		M+
6123.	TUŠAR-UM	TU-ŠA-RU-UM	FN	BM 82212 3
6124.	TUŠER-U	TU-ŠE?-RU?		M
6125.	TUŠIM-AT-UM	TU-ŠI-MA-TUM	FN	RA LXV 61 III 77
6126.	TU-WTAR+ʾABN-U	TU-TAR-AB-NU		M
6127.	TUTUG-UM	TU-TU-GU-UM		SIMMONS 119 21+
6128.	TURTUR-AH	TU-TU-RA	FN	RA LXV 60 III 67
6129.	ṮUBQ-AT-UM	TU-UB-GA-TUM	MN	MEISSNER 11 3
6130.	ṮUBQ-I	TU-UB-KI		RA LXV 40 I 24
6131.	TUḪT-U+....	TU-UḪ-TU-[....]		M
6132.	ṮUḪŠ-AT-UM	TU-UḪ$_3$-ŠA-TUM		UET V 290 2
6133.		TU-UK-BI-IA-AŠ-RUM	FN	XIII 1 VIII 9
6134.	ṮUQM-AT-UM	TU-UK-MA-TUM	FN	RA LXV 65 VII 25
6135.	DULQ-AN-UM	TU-UL-GA-NUM$_2$		U
6136.	TUND-I	TU-UN-DI	FN	M+
6137.	TUPT-I+JA-MWUT-A	TU-UP-TI-IA-MU-TA		BM 80328 2
6138.	TURBIN-AH	TU-UR-BI-NA	FN	IX 291 II 17

6139.	TURM-AT-UM	TU-UR-MA-TUM	FN	M
6140.	TURUN-U-HU+GAMIL	D-TU-UR-RU-NU-U$_2$-GA-MIL	FN?	XIII 118 14
6141.	TURTUR-AN	TU-UR-TU-RA-AN		RA LXV 42 II 76
6142.	TUʾZ-AJA	TU-ZA-A	FN	XIII 1 XIII 29
6143.	TUʾZ-AJA	TU-ZA-[I]A	FN	M
6144.	TUZAL-UM	TU-ZA-LUM		BM 17049 19+
6145.	TUʾZ-ATAN	TU-ZA-TA-AN		M
6146.	TUKR-ATIJ-I	TUK-RA-TI-I	GEN	UCP X/3 2 19
6147.	TUPT-U+ʿAŠTAR	TUP-TU-EŠ$_4$-DAR		M
6148.	ṬAJB-A+ʾIL	ṬA-BA-DINGIR		A. 60 11
6149.	ṬAJB+ŠUM-U-HU	ṬA$_3$-AB-SU-MU-U$_2$		M+
6150.	ṬAJB+ṢILL-U-HU	ṬA$_3$-AB-ṢI-LU-U$_2$		TCL X 38 7
6151.	ṬAJB-AH	ṬA$_3$-BA	FN	M+
6152.	ṬAJB-AT-UM	ṬA$_3$-BA-TUM	FN	M+
6153.	ṬAJB-IJA	ṬA$_3$-BI-A	FN	RA LXV 66 VII 54
6154.	ʾU-BWAʾ+ʾIL	U$_2$-BA-DINGIR		M
6155.	ʾU-BWAʾ+ʾIL-A	U$_2$-BA-D-DINGIR		VAS VIII 14:22
6156.	ḪUBAS-IM	U$_2$-BA-ZI-IM	GEN	SIMMONS 118 2
6157.	ḪUBAS-UM	U$_2$-BA-ZU-UM		SIMMONS 118 17+
6158.	ʾUBIR-A	U$_2$-BI-RA		M
6159.	ʾUBUŠ-I	U$_2$-BU-SI		M
6160.	ʾUBUŠ+ʿAŠTAR	U$_2$-BU-UŠ$_3$-EŠ$_4$-DAR		RES 1938 P. 128
6161.	ʾU-WDAJ+....	U$_2$-DA-[....]		TA 30, 615 29
6162.	ʾU-WDAJ+MA	U$_2$-DA-MA		I
6163.	ʾUDIN-AH	U$_2$-DI-NA	FN	XIII 1 IV 67
6164.		U$_2$-DU-NA-SA		KISURRA 1 3+
6165.	ʾU-WQAH+ŠAMŠ	U$_2$-GA-A-D-UTU		SZLECHTER TJ 15944 SEAL
6166.	ʾU-WQAH+ʾIL	U$_2$-GA-DINGIR		GAUTIER 41 5
6167.	ʾU-WQAH+ʾIL-UM	U$_2$-GA-DINGIR-LUM		FRANK 29 9
6168.	ʾU-WQAH+HADD-U	U$_2$-GA-D-IM		BIROT, TEA 24:6
6169.	ʾU-WQAH+ŠAMŠ	U$_2$-GA-D-UTU		BIROT, TEA 72 V 16'
6170.	ʾUGAZ-UM	U$_2$-GA-ZUM		TA 30 615 22
6171.	ʾUKUL-IN-UM	U$_2$-KU-LI-NU-UM		RA LXV 43 III 54
6172.		U$_2$-LA-ŠU-DA		RA XLIII 29 QATNA
6173.		U$_2$-LI-[....]		M
6174.		U$_2$-MA-AN-NI-SU-TA		VIII 1 35
6175.	ʾU-WMAʾ+ʾIL-A	U$_2$-MA-D-DINGIR		B 40
6176.	ʾUM-U+ŠAKIM	U$_2$-MU-ŠA-KI-IM		M+
6177.		U$_2$-NA-AK-KA	FN	XIII 1 VIII 15
6178.	ʾUNAB-AT-UM	U$_2$-NA-BA-TUM	FN	TIM III 26 7
6179.	ʾUNAB-UM	U$_2$-NA-BU-UM		TIM III 42 13
6180.		U$_2$-NA-TI?-X	FN	XIII 1 VIII 85
6181.	ḪUNIN-AH	U$_2$-NI-NA	FN	M+
6182.	ʾUNUB-UM	U$_2$-NU-BU-UM		EDZARD, DER 74:11+
6183.	ḪUNUN-I+ʾIL	U$_2$-NU-NI-DINGIR		PBS XI/2 P. 125 NO. 347
6184.	ḪUNUN-I+ʾEL	U$_2$-NU-NI-EL		B 40
6185.	ʾU-WQAH+ʾIL	U$_2$-QA-DINGIR		M+
6186.	ʾU-WQAH+ʾIL-A	U$_2$-Q[A]-I-LA		A 7699:14, ISCHCHALI
6187.	ʾU-WQAH+ʾIL	U$_2$-QA-IL		SYRIA V 274 HANA
6188.	ʾU-WQAH+HADD-U	U$_2$-QA-D-IM		RA LXV 44 IV 51
6189.	ʾU-WQAH+KI+ʾEL	U$_2$-QA-KI-EL		RA LXV 51 IX 69
6190.	ʾU-WQIH+ʾEL	U$_2$-QI$_2$-E[L]		RA LXV 41 II 44
6191.	ʾUWR-A+HADD-U	U$_2$-RA-A-DU		A.
6192.	ʾURAN-AT-UM	U$_2$-RA-NA-TUM	FN	HARRIS 83 1
6193.	ʾURAN-UM	U$_2$-RA-NU-UM		M+
6194.	ʾURAŠ-IJA	U$_2$-RA-SI-IA		M
6195.		U$_2$-RA-X-GI	FN	XIII 1 75
6196.	ʾUWR-I+HADD-U	U$_2$-RI-A-DU		A.
6197.	ʾUWR-I+JARAḪ	U$_2$-RI-E-RA-AḪ		M
6198.	ʿUZAB-UM	U$_2$-SA-BU-UM		SIMMONS 52 16
6199.	ʾUŠAL-UM	U$_2$-SA?-LUM		WATERMAN 21 R. 10
6200.	ʾUŠAT-AN	U$_2$-SA-TA-AN		M+
6201.	ʾU-WŠIʿ-I	U$_2$-SI-I		I+
6202.	ʾU-WŠIʿ-UM	U$_2$-SI-UM		I
6203.	JA-WṢIʾ+ŠUM-U+ʾAB-UM	U$_2$-ṢI-SU-MU-A-BU-UM		AJSL XXVIII 244 19
6204.	ʾUWŠ-AN	U$_2$-ŠA-AN		M+

6205.	ʾUŠAŠ-UM	U$_2$-ŠA-ŠUM		I
6206.	ʾU-WTAʾ+ʾAḪ-I	U$_2$-TA-A-ḪI		M
6207.	ʾU-WTAʾ-T-UM	U$_2$-TA-TUM	FN	C
6208.	ʾUMM-U+JARAḪ	U$_2$?-UM-MU-E-RA-AḪ		B 40+
6209.	ʿUZAB-IM	U$_2$-ZA-BI-IM	GEN	SIMMONS 70 16
6210.	ʿUZAB-UM	U$_2$-ZA-BU-UM		SIMMONS 46 32
6211.	ʿUZZ+HADD-U	U$_2$-ZA-DU		U
6212.	ʿUZAL-UM	U$_2$-ZA-LUM		CT XXXIII 46A 3+
6213.	ḪUṢAN-AH	U$_2$-ZA-NA	FN	XIII 1 II 68
6214.	JA-WṢIʾ	U$_2$-ZI		M
6215.	JA-WṢIʾ+ʾALAŠ-UM	U$_2$-ZI-A-LA-ŠUM		M
6216.	ʿUZIL-A	U$_2$-ZI-LA		RA LXV 50 IX 6
6217.	ʿUZUL-I	U$_2$-ZU-LI		RA LXV 51 X 6
6218.	ʾUḎUN-AN	U$_2$-ZU-NA-AN		M+
6219.	ʾUZUL-I	U$_2$-ZU-UL-LI	FN	XIII 1 III 66
6220.	ʾU-WQAH	U$_3$-GA		U
6221.	ʾU-WQAH	U$_3$-GA-A		SAUREN, WUG 114 REV, U
6222.	ʾU-WMAʾ+ʾIL	U$_3$-MA-IL		U
6223.	ḪUNN-U+ʾEL	U$_3$-NU-EL		TA 31 223
6224.	ʾU-WQAH+ʾIL	U$_3$-QA-DINGIR		SIMMONS 1 3+
6225.	ʾURAN-UM	U$_3$-RA-NU-UM		TA 1931, 538 IV
6226.		UK-LU-UL-LU		M
6227.		UL-LU-NI		M
6228.	ʾUMM-I+ʾAŠIR-AH	UM-MI-A-ŠI-RA	FN	VAS XIII 73 6,13
6229.	ʾUMM-I+BAʿL-AH	UM-MI-BA-A-LA	FN	A. LATE
6230.	ʾUMM-I+ḪAʾT-UM	UM-MI-ḪA-TUM	FN	M+
6231.	ʾUMM-I+ʾIL-I	UM-MI-I$_3$-LI$_2$	FN	XIII 1 VIII 64
6232.	ʾUMM-IJA	UM?-MI-IA	FN	XIII 1 XIV 18
6233.	ʾUMM-I+JAT-UM	UM-MI-IA-TUM		UCP X/1 89 24
6234.	ʾUMM-I+JIQR-AH	UM-MI-IQ-RA	FN	M+
6235.	ʾUMM-I+ʾIŠḪAR-AH	UM-MI-IŠ-ḪA-RA	FN	XIII 1 V 74, A.+
6236.	ʾUMM-I+MARṢ-AT	UM-MI-MAR-ṢA-AT	FN	XIII 1 III 5
6237.	ʾUMM-I+NAʿM-I	UM-MI-NA-AḪ-ME	FN	RA LXV 59 II 17
6238.	ʾUMM-I+NAʿM-I	UM-MI-NA-MI	FN	A.
6239.	ʾUMM-I+NAHR-U	UM-MI-NA-RU	FN	M
6240.	ʾUMM-I+NAWAR	UM-MI-NA-WA-AR	FN	XIII 1 IV 73
6241.	ʾUMM-I+ṬAJB-AH	UM-MI-ṬA$_3$-BA	FN	M+
6242.	ʾUMM-I+ṬAJB-AH	UM-MI-ṬA$_3$-BA-NU	FN	RA LXV 64 VI 34
6243.	ʾUMM-I+ŠAMŠ-I	UM-MI-D-UTU-ŠI	FN	RA LXV 65 VII 38
6244.	ʾUMM-U+KA+ʾAB-I	UM-MU-KA-A-BI	FN	RA LXV 62 V 16
6245.	ʾUMM-U+ŠARR-AH	UM-MU-ŠAR-RA	FN	IX 291 33
6246.	ʾUMM-UM+KA+ʾAB-I	UM-MU-UM-KA-A-BI	FN	XIII 1 VII 56
6247.	ʾUMM-UM+KA+ʾAB-IM	UM-MU-UM-KA-A-BI-IM	FN	M
6248.		UN-DA-AN-KI	FN	XIII 1 VIII 26
6249.	ʾUNUB-AT-UM	UN-NU-BA-TUM	FN	WATERMAN 24 R. 24
6250.	ʾUNUB-UM	UN-NU-BU-UM		EDZARD, DER 68 III 10
6251.	ḪUNUN-U	UN-NU-NU		YOS XIII 139:9+
6252.	ʾUNUB-T-UM	UN-NU-UB-TUM	FN	EDZARD, DER 33:11+
6253.	ʾUP+ʾIL-A	UP-I-LA		BULL. ACAD. BELG. 1974 227
6254.	ḪURB-ATAN-U	UR-BA-TA-NU		KISURRA 24 6
6255.	ʾURK-UTAN-IM	UR-KU-TA-NIM	GEN	CT VIII 20B 10
6256.	ʾURL-IJ-UM	UR-LI-U$_2$-UM		M
6257.	ʾURR-AN	UR-RA-AN		RA LXV 53 XI 15
6258.	ʾURŠAM-AN-AM	UR-SA-MA-NAM	ACC	M+
6259.	ʾUŠK-ATAN-IM	UŠ-KA-TA-NIM	MN GEN	XIII 61 5+
6260.	ʾUŠK-ATAN-UM	UŠ-KA-TA-NU-UM		XIII 92 11
6261.	ʾUŠM-A+ʿAMM-I	UŠ-MA-AM-MI		CT XXXIII 46A 4
6262.	ʾUŠŠ-AT-I+ʾEL	UŠ-SA-TE-EL		TIM III 43 6
6263.		UŠ?-ŠU-UL-TU		M
6264.	JU-T-ŠANIJ	UŠ-TA-AN-NI		RA LXV 44 IV 55; A.+
6265.	JU-ŠT-ŠNIJ+ʾIL	UŠ-TA-AŠ-NI-DINGIR		VAS IX 131 21+
6266.	ʾUŠT-AJA	UŠ-TA-IA		RA LXV 55 XIII 14
6267.	JU-T-ŠALIL-I	UŠ-TA-LI-LI	NOM	M+
6268.	JU-T-ŠANIJ+ʾIL-A	UŠ-TA-NI-I-LA		A. 33 22
6269.	JU-ŠT-ŠNIJ+ʾIL	UŠ-TAŠ-NI-DINGIR		VAS IX 130 21+
6270.	JU-T-ŠANIJ+HADD-U	UŠ-TI-NI-D-IM?		A. 36 9+

6271.	ŜAMŜ-I+ʾAB-I	D-UTU-A-BI		M+
6272.	ŜAMŜ-I+DAʿ-I	D-UTU-DA-ḪI-I		LANGDON XV 2
6273.	ŜAMŜ-I+ʾITEJ-JE	D-UTU-I-TE-E		CT IV 44 B 3, 4
6274.	ŜAMŜ-I+JAŠʿ-AH	D-[UT]U-IA-AŠ-ḪA	FN	XIII 1 IV 43
6275.	ŜAMŜ-I+JA-JPUʿ-AT	D-UTU-IA-PU-ḪA-AT	FN?	BM 17075
6276.	ŜAMŜ-I+HADD-U	D-UTU-ŠI-A-DU		A.
6277.	ŜAMŜ-I+HADD-U	D-UTU-ŠI-D-IM		M+, C+
6278.	ʿUZZ-U	UZ-ZU	FN	XIII 1 XIV 31
6279.	WARḪ+ʾIL-A	WA-AR-ḪI-LA$_{2}$		CCT I 38C 2 CAPP.
6280.	JATM-UM	WA-AT-MU-UM?		CT XLV 5 R. 4
6281.	ʾUWR-I+HADD-U	WU-RI-A-DU		A.
6282.	ṢAJAD-AN	ZA-A-DA-AN		RA LXV 43 III 45; C+
6283.	ZAʾAN-UM	ZA-A-NU-UM		SIMMONS 98 8 SEAL
6284.	ḎABB-UM	ZA-AB-BU-UM		BM 17051 7
6285.	ṢABʾ-AN-UM	ZA-AB-ḪA-NU-UM		CT XLVIII 88 REV.
6286.	ṢABR-AN-UM	ZA-AB-RA-NU-UM		I
6287.	ṢABR-IJA	ZA-AB-RI-IA		YOS VIII 120 22
6288.	ṢABR-UM	ZA-AB-RUM		YOS VIII 29 3
6289.	ZABZAB-UM	ZA-AB-ZA-BU-UM		B 49
6290.	ZAḪL-AT-IM	ZA-AḪ-LA-TIM	GEN	CT VIII 31B 25
6291.	ZAʾN-AN	ZA-AḪ-NA-AN		M
6292.	ZAḪZAḪ-UM	ZA-AḪ-ZA-ḪU-UM		B 49
6293.	ZAKK+DAWD-I	ZA-AK-DA-TI		TA 1931,377+ EARLY OB
6294.	ZAKK+ʾIL-I	ZA-AK-I$_{3}$-LI$_{2}$		TA 1931,389 UR III
6295.	ZAKK-A+BALAṬ	ZA-AK-KA-BA-LA-AṬ?		M+
6296.	ZAKK-U	ZA-AK-KU		M
6297.	ZAKK-U-HU	ZA-AK-KU-U$_{2}$		M+
6298.	ZAKK+PI+ʾEL	ZA-AK-PI-EL		TA 1931,198 EARLY OB
6299.	ZAKZAK-UM	ZA-AK-ZA-KU-UM		UNPUBL.
6300.	ZAKZAK-UM	ZA-AK-ZA-KUM		B 49
6301.	ZALḪ-UM	ZA-AL-ḪU-UM		RUTTEN 6 23
6302.	ZALZAL-IM	ZA-AL-ZA-LIM	GEN	M+
6303.	ZALZAL-UM	ZA-AL-ZA-LUM		B 49+
6304.	ŜAMK-AN-UM	ZA-AM?-GA-NU-UM		TA 1931, 538 V
6305.	ZAMM-AN-UM	ZA-AM-MA-A-NU-UM		B 48
6306.	ZAMM-AN-UM	ZA-AM-MA-NU-UM		B 48+
6307.	ḎAMAR-AN-IM	ZA-AM-MA-RA-NIM-KI	GN GEN	C II 39 8
6308.	ŜAMŜ-I+ŜAMŜ	ZA-AM-SI-D-UTU		YOS XII 39 END
6309.	ŜAMŜ-AN-U	ZA-AM-ZA-NU		M
6310.	ŜAMŜ-UM	ZA-AM-ZUM		CT IV 47B 20
6311.	ḎANB-UM	ZA-AN-BU-UM		TIM V 33 23
6312.	ZANN-AT-UM	ZA-AN-NA-TUM	FN	M+
6313.	ZANN-I	ZA-AN-NI		B 41
6314.	ZANN-UM	ZA-AN-NU-UM		BIN VII 186 22, M
6315.	ḎAQN-IJA	ZA-AQ-NI-IA		WALTERS,WL 100:4+
6316.	ṢARP-I+....	ZA-AR-BI-[....]		M
6317.	ZARQ-ATAN-UM	ZA-AR-GA-TA-NU-UM		JCS IV 110A 19
6318.	ḎARʿ-AN	(E$_{2}$)-ZA-AR-ḪA-AN-KI	GN	M+
6319.	ḎARʿ-AN-UM	ZA-AR-ḪA-NU-UM	GN	B 48
6320.	ḎARʿ-IM	ZA-AR-IM	GEN	M
6321.		ZA-AR-KU-IŠ		M
6322.	ZARNAB-UM	ZA-AR-NA-BU-UM		B 41
6323.	ZARAM-UM	ZA-AR-RA-MU-UM		TIM III 131 4
6324.	ṢARR-UM	ZA-AR-RU-[UM]		IX 285 1
6325.	ṢARR-UM	ZA-AR-RUM		XIII 1 I 52
6326.	ZAʾR-T-UM	ZA-AR-TUM	FN	M
6327.	ZARZAR-UM	ZA-AR-ZA-RU-UM		BM 16835 26+
6328.	ZAʾT+ʿAMM-U	ZA-AT-AM-MU	MN	A. 279 2 3
6329.	ṢABAʾ+HADD-U	ZA-BA-AD-DU		M
6330.	ḎABAB-UM	ZA-BA-BU-UM		HARRIS 98 R. 5
6331.	ṢABAʾ+JAT-UM	ZA-BA-IA-TUM	MN	BM 16835 19+
6332.	ZABAN-UM	ZA-BA-NU-UM		U UNPUBL., B 47+
6333.	ṢABAʾ-TI+ʾEL	ZA-BA-TE-EL		UNPUBL.
6334.	ḎABIB-UM	ZA-BI-BU-UM		B 40+
6335.	ṢABIʾ-IM	ZA-BI-ḪI-IM	GEN	M+
6336.	ṢABIʾ-UM	ZA-BI-ḪU-UM		M+

6337. ṢABIʾ-IM	ZA-BI-I-IM	GEN	C P.39 N. 8+
6338. ZABIL-AT-UM	ZA-BI-LA-TUM	FN	RA LXV 60 III 50
6339. ZABIL-IM	ZA-BI-LIM	GEN	M+
6340. ZABIN-UM	ZA-BI-NU-UM		M
6341. ṢABIʾ-UM	ZA-BI-UM		OB KING
6342. ZABIZ-AT-UM	ZA-BI-ZA-TUM		YOS XIII 175:11
6343. ṢABʾ-I	ZA-BI$_2$	FN	U
6344. ZABUG-A	ZA-BU-GA		JCS XIII 57 NO.305 A.LATE
6345. ZABUG-AN	ZA-BU-GA-AN		RA LXV 45 V 23,30
6346. ZABUL-UM	ZA-BU-LUM		A 21950 4 5
6347. ṢABUʾ-UM	ZA-BU-U$_2$-UM	MN	M
6348. ṢABIʾ-UM	ZA-BU-UM		OB KING
6349. ṢABUʾ-UM	ZA-BU-UM	FN	M
6350. ṢADAQ-AH	ZA-DA-GA	FN	U
6351. SAṬIʾ-AT-UM	ZA-DI-IA-TUM	FN	XIII 1 I 72
6352. ṢADUQ-UM	ZA-DU-KUM		B 41
6353. ZAQAT-I	ZA-GA-TI	GEN	B 41
6354. ZAQAT-UM	ZA-GA-TUM		KISURRA 112 5+
6355. ḪADUR+BAʿL-A-IA	D-ZA-GAR$_3$-BA-LA-IA	GN	SUMER XIV 26
6356. ZAʾAZ-AH	ZA-ḪA-AZ-ZA	FN	XIII 1 IX 22
6357. ZAʾAN-IM	ZA-ḪA-NIM	GEN	M
6358. ZAʾAN-UM	ZA-ḪA-NU-UM		M+
6359. ZAḪIL-UM	ZA-ḪI-LUM		HARRIS 12 30
6360. ṢAJID-AT-UM	ZA-I-DA-TUM	FN	EDZARD, DER 90:2+
6361. ṢAJID-IM	ZA-I-DI-IM	GEN	VAS IX 172 18+
6362. ṢAJAD-UM	ZA-IA-DU-UM		CT XLV 97 16
6363. ṢAJAD-AN	ZA-JA-DA-AN		M+
6364. ḎAQAN-UM	ZA-KA-NU-UM		WALTERS,WL 85:4
6365. ZAQAT-UM	ZA-KA-TUM		B 41
6366. ZAQAT-UM	ZA-KA-TUM	FN	RA LXV 61 IV 63
6367. ḎAKIR-A+ʿAMM-U	ZA-KI-RA-ḪA-AM-MU		M+
6368. ḎAKIR-A+ʿAMM-U-HU	ZA-KI-RA-ḪA-AM-MU-U$_2$		M+
6369. ḎAKIR-A+ʿAMM-I	ZA-KI-RA-ḪA-MI		M
6370. ḎAKIR-A+ʿAMM-U	ZA-KI-RA-ḪA-MU		M
6371. ḎAKIR-AT-UM	ZA-KI-RA-TUM?	FN	C
6372. ḎAKIR-IM	ZA-KI-RI-IM	GEN	BM 17069 8+, M
6373. ḎAKIR-UM	ZA-KI-RU-UM		M
6374. ḎAKIR-UM	ZA-KI-RUM		RA LXV 53 XI 22; B 41
6375. ḎAKUR-AH	ZA-KU-RA	FN	XIII 1 II 40
6376. ḎAKUR-A+ʾAB-I	ZA-KU-RA-A-BI	GEN	B 41
6377. ḎAKUR-A+ʾAB-U	ZA-KU-RA-A-BU		M
6378. ḎAKUR-A+ʾAB-UM	ZA-KU-RA-A-BU-UM		X 79 5
6379. ḎAKUR-A+ʾAḪ-UM	ZA-KU-RA-A-ḪU-UM		M+
6380. ḎAKUR-A+ʾIL	ZA-KU-RA-DINGIR		M+
6381. ḎAKUR-A+KUWN-U	ZA-KU-RA-KU-NU		VII 85 12
6382. ḎAKUR-I+ʾEL	ZA-KU-RI-E-EL		UCP X/1 86 15
6383. ḎAKUR-I+ʾEL-UM	ZA-KU-RI-E-LUM		UNPUBL.
6384. ḎAKUR-UM	ZA-KU-RU-UM		B 41+
6385. ḎAKUR-UM	ZA-KU-RUM		B 41+
6386. ZAKK-U-HU	ZA-KU-U$_2$		M
6387. ḎAKUR+ʾAB-I	ZA-KU-UR-A-BI	GEN	B 41
6388. ZALAT-AN	ZA-LA-TA-AN		RA LXV 55 XIII 38
6389. ZALAT-IJA	ZA-LA-TI-IA		BM 17060 35+
6390. ZALIJ+ʾIL	ZA-LI-DINGIR		B 41
6391. ṢALIL-I	ZA-LI-LI	GEN	B 41
6392. ṢALIL-UM	ZA-LI-LUM		B 41+
6393. ZALUḪ-UM	ZA-LU-ḪU-UM		BIN VII 8 5
6394. ZAMAʾ+JAT-UM	ZA-MA-A-A-TUM	MN?	TCL X 38 1
6395.	ZA-MA-AR-GA		M+
6396. ḎAMAR-AN-UM	ZA-MA-[RA]?-NU-[UM]		TA 1930, 615 28
6397. ḎAMAR-I+ʾEL-UM	ZA-MA-RI-E-LUM		B. 92+
6398. ṢAMID-UM	ZA-MI-DU-UM	FN	B 41+
6399. ṢAMID+ʾAḪ-I	ZA-MI-ID-A-ḪI		CT IV 8B 17
6400. ZAMIN-UM	ZA-MI-NU-UM		YOS VIII P. 25+
6401. ZAMIN-UM	ZA-MI-NUM$_2$		YOS VIII P. 25
6402. ḎAMUR-AN	ZA-MU-RA-AN		M

6403.	ḎANAB-AN	ZA-NA-BA-AN		RA LXV 41 II 51+
6404.	ZANAN-AH	ZA-NA-NA	FN	RA LXV 64 V 61
6405.	ZANAN-I	ZA-NA-NI	GEN	B 48
6406.	ḎANIB-UM	ZA-NI-BU-UM		BA V 486 NO. 2 5
6407.		ZA-NI-DAḪ		HARRIS 20 5
6408.	ZANIJ-AT-UM	ZA-NI-IA-TUM		BM 80496 3'
6409.	SANIQ-UM	ZA-NI-KUM		M
6410.	ḎARAʿ+LI+ʾIL	ZA-RA-AḪ?-LI-DINGIR		M
6411.	ZARAM-AN-UM	ZA-RA-MA-A-NU-UM		SIMMONS 99 8 SEAL
6412.	ZARAM-AN-UM	ZA-RA-MA-NU-UM		TIM III 24 14
6413.	ḎARIʿ-IM	ZA-RI-ḪI-IM	GEN	HARRIS 3 17
6414.	ḎARIʿ-UM	ZA-RI-ḪU-UM		HARRIS 34 12+
6415.	ṢARIP-AT-UM	ZA-RI-PA-TUM	FN	RA LXV 60 III 49
6416.	ṢARIR-UM	ZA-RI-RU-UM		A 7688
6417.	ZAʾR-UM	ZA-RUM		XIII 1 IV 17
6418.		ZA-ŠA-U$_2$-DA		A. 34 8
6419.	ZAʾT-AN	ZA-TA-AN		RA LXV 45 V 38
6420.	SATUR-UM	ZA-TU-RU-UM		RA LXIV 34 NO.24
6421.		ZA-U$_2$-TA		A.
6422.	ZAʾZ-AN-AJA	ZA-ZA-NA-IA	FN	RA LXV 58 I 52
6423.	ZAʾZ-AN-IM	ZA-ZA-NI-IM	GEN	B 48
6424.	ZAʾZ-AN-UM	ZA-ZA-NU-UM		RA LXV 47 VII 28; B 48+
6425.	ZAʾZ-AN-UM	ZA-ZA-NUM$_2$		KISURRA 2A:7+
6426.	ZAʾZ-I+ʾANN-U	ZA-ZI-AN-NU		B 41+
6427.	ZAʾZ-IJA	ZA-ZI-IA		M+
6428.	ZAʾZ-UN-UM	ZA-ZU-NU-UM		M
6429.	ṢIBʾ-I+LIʾL-UM	ZE$_2$-BI-LI-LUM		BSM 7900, UR III
6430.	ZIRQ-AN-UM	ZE$_2$-IR-GA-NU-UM		TA 1931,438
6431.	ṢIBʾ-AN	ZI-BA-AN		BM 16836 27; M+
6432.	ṢIBAR-UM	ZI-BA-RU-UM		RA VIII 69 21+
6433.	ṢIBʾ-ATAN	[Z]I-BA-TA-AN		VII 185 10
6434.	ṢIBʾ-IJA	ZI-BI-IA		XIV 106:6
6435.	ṢIBʾ-IJAN	ZI-BI-IA-AN		RA LXV 42 III 24
6436.	ṢIBIṬ-AH	ZI-BI-IT-TA	FN	C P. 41+
6437.	ṢIBʾ-I+LIʾM	ZI-BI-LI-IM		M
6438.	ZIBIN-I	ZI-BI-NI		B 42
6439.	ṢIBʾ-I+NIʿM	ZI-BI-NI-ḪI-I[M]		M
6440.	ṢIBʾ-U	ZI-BU		B 42
6441.	ZIDAR-U-HU	ZI-DA-RU-U$_2$		VAS XIII 93A R. 8+
6442.	SIKIL+DANN-UM	ZI-GI-IL-DA-NU-UM		M+
6443.	SIKIL-T-F	ZI-GI-IL-TE	MN	A.
6444.	ṢIJḪ+HADD-A	ZI-ḪA-DA		TA 1933,7 EARLY OB
6445.	ṢIḪAQ-AJA	ZI-ḪA-KA-A-A		KISURRA 82 2
6446.	ṢIJḪ-AT-UM	ZI-ḪA-TUM	FN	XIII 1 VII 35
6447.	ZIJAD-AH	ZI?-IA?-DA	FN	XIII 1 XIII 25
6448.	ZIJAN-I	ZI-IA-NI		KISURRA 4A:11+
6449.		ZI-IA-RU-TU-RA-KI-A		OLZ VII 351 28
6450.	ṢIBʾ-AT-UM	ZI-IB-A-TUM	FN	XIII 1 III 2
6451.	ḎINB-AT-UM	ZI-IB-BA-TUM	FN	M+, C P. 38+
6452.	ZIBL-AN-UM	ZI-IB-LA-NU--M		BASOR 95 23
6453.	ṢIDQ-I+JE-JPAʿ	ZI-ID-KI-E-PA		RA XLIII 37 QATNA
6454.	ṢIDQ-I+JE-JPUʿ	ZI-ID-KI-E-PU-UḪ		M+, C+
6455.	ṢIDQ-I+JATAR	ZI-ID-KI-E-TAR		M+
6456.	ṢIDQ-IJA	ZI-ID-KI-IA		RA LXV 55 XIII 9
6457.	ṢIDQ-U+LA+NAŠIʾ	ZI-ID-KU-LA-NA-SI		M+
6458.	ṢIDQ-UM	ZI-ID-KUM		TCL XI 198 23
6459.	ṢIDQ-UM+MAṢIʾ	ZI-ID-KUM-MA-ZI		X 131 5+
6460.	ṢIDQ-AN	ZI-ID-QA-AN		M
6461.	ṢIDQ-A+HADD-U	ZI-ID-QA-D-IM		M
6462.	SIKL-UM	ZI-IK-LUM		TIM V 31 19
6463.	ḎIKR-AN	ZI-IK-RA-AN		RA LXV 51 IX 34
6464.	ḎIKR-A+ʿAŠTAR	ZI-IK-RA-EŠ$_4$-DAR		M+
6465.	ḎIKR-ATAN	ZI-IK-RA-TA-AN		M+
6466.	ḎIKR-AT-IM	ZI-IK-RA-TIM	MN? GEN	XII 263 10
6467.	ḎIKR-AT-UM	ZI-IK-RA-TUM	FN	XIII 1 II 50
6468.	ḎIKR-I+JARAḪ	ZI-IK-RI-E-RA-AḪ		TIM V 69 7, 17+

6469.	ḎIKR-I+ʿAŠTAR	ZI-IK-RI-EŠ$_4$-DAR		M+
6470.	ḎIKR-I+ʿAN-AT	ZI-IK-RI-ḪA-NA-AT		M
6471.	ḎIKR-I+ʿAN-AT	ZI-IK-RI-D-ḪA-N[A-AT]		M
6472.	ḎIKR-IJA	ZI-IK-RI-IA		RA LXV 43 IV 20
6473.	ḎIKR-I+HADD-U	ZI-IK-RI-D-IM		M+
6474.	ḎIKR-IM	ZI-IK-RI-IM	GEN	M
6475.	ḎIKR-I+LIʾM	ZI-IK-RI-LI-IM		M+
6476.	ḎIKR-ITAN-U	ZI-IK-RI-TA-NU		M
6477.	ḎIKR+MARDUK	[Z]I?-IK-RU-D-AMAR-UD		KUPFER, L'ICON PL II NO 8
6478.	ḎIKR+MARAṢ	ZI-IK-RU-MA-RA-AZ	FN	RA LXV 55 XIII 33
6479.	ḎIKR-U-HU	ZI-IK-RU-U$_2$		VAS IX 185 12+
6480.	ZIKZIK-UM	ZI-IK-ZI-KUM		B 49
6481.	ZILḪ-AN	ZI-IL-ḪA-AN		M+, C
6482.	ṢILL+HADD-U	ZI-IL-LA-AD-DU		A. 81
6483.	ṢILL-AN	Z[I]-IL-LA-AN		RA LXV 55 XIII 15
6484.	ZIMM-I+DAWD-I	ZI-IM-MI-DA-DI	FN	C II 44 33+
6485.	ḎIMR-A+ʿAMM-U	ZI-IM-RA-AM-MU		TIM IV 33 20, 34 13
6486.	ḎIMR-AN	ZI-IM-RA-AN		M+
6487.	ḎIMR-A+ʿAŠTAR	ZI-IM-RA-EŠ$_4$-DAR		M+
6488.	ḎIMR-A+ʿAMM-U	ZI-IM-RA-ḪA-AM-MU		M
6489.	ḎIMR-A+ʿAMM-U	ZI-IM-RA-ḪA-MU		CT XLIV 54 20, C
6490.	ḎIMR-A+ʿAMM-U-HU	ZI-IM-RA-ḪA-MU-U$_2$		TIM IV 33 SEAL, 34 SEAL
6491.	ḎIMR-AN-AM	ZI-IM-RA-NAM	ACC	M+
6492.	ḎIMR-ATAN	ZI-IM-RA-TA-AN		M
6493.	ḎIMR-AT-IM	ZI-IM-RA-TIM	MN? GEN	M
6494.	ḎIMR-AT-UM	ZI-IM-RA-TUM	MN	B 42+, M
6495.	ḎIMR-I+....	ZI-IM-RI-D-[....]		M
6496.	ḎIMR-I+ʾAB-UM	ZI-IM-RI-A-BU-UM		B 42
6497.	ḎIMR-I+ʿAMM-U	ZI-IM-RI-AM-MU		TIM III 94 4
6498.	ḎIMR-I+DAGAN	ZI-IM-RI-D-DA-GAN		M+
6499.	ḎIMR-I+ʾIL	ZI-IM-RI-DINGIR		B 42+
6500.	ḎIMR-I+ʾIL-U+MA	ZI-IM-RI-DINGIR-MA		M
6501.	ḎIMR-I+HEDD-A	ZI-IM-RI-E-ID-DA		B 42
6502.	ḎIMR-I-JE+HADD-U	ZI-IM-RI-E-D-IM		M
6503.	ḎIMR-I+JARAḪ	ZI-IM-RI-E-RA-AḪ		B 42+, C+, M+
6504.	ḎIMR-I+ʿAŠTAR	ZI-IM-RI-D-EŠ$_4$-DAR		M, A.+
6505.	ḎIMR-I+ʿAMM-U	ZI-IM-RI-ḪA-AM-MU		B 42+, X 35 12
6506.	ḎIMR-I+ʿAMM-U	ZI-IM-RI-ḪA-MU		C
6507.	ḎIMR-I+ʿAN-AT-A	ZI-IM-RI-ḪA-NA-TA		B 42
6508.	ḎIMR-I+ḪAŠAM	ZI-IM-RI-ḪA-SA-AM	NOM	C+
6509.	ḎIMR-I+ʾIL-U+MA	ZI-IM-RI-I-LU-MA		M
6510.	ḎIMR-IJA	ZI-IM-RI-IA		M+, C+
6511.	ḎIMR-IJAN	ZI-IM-RI-IA-AN		RA LXV 44 IV 76
6512.	ḎIMR-I+HADD-U	ZI-IM-RI-D-IM		M+
6513.	ḎIMR-I+LIʾM	ZI-IM-RI-LI-IM		M+
6514.	ḎIMR-I+ʾIL-U+MA	ZI-IM-RI-LU-MA		SIMMONS 67 12
6515.	ḎIMR-I+LU-HU	ZI-IM-RI-LU-U$_2$	FN	RA LXV 55 XIII 39
6516.	ḎIMR-I+RAPUʾ	ZI-IM-RI-RA-BU		M
6517.	ḎIMR-I+ŠAMŠ	ZI-IM-RI-SA-MA-AŠ$_2$		M+
6518.	ḎIMR-I+ŠAMŠ	ZI-IM-RI-SA-MAŠ		A.
6519.	ḎIKR+ŠAMŠ	ZI-IM-RI-D-UTU		BIN VII 206 23+
6520.	ḎIMR-U+ʾARAḪ	ZI-IM-RU-A-RA-AḪ		BM 17045A 13
6521.	ḎIMR-U+ʿAŠTAR	ZI-IM-RU-EŠ$_4$-DAR		IRAQ IV 185 A. 385
6522.	ḎIMR-U+ʿAMM-I	ZI-IM-RU-ḪA-AM-MI		B 42
6523.	ḎIMR-U+ʿAMM-U	ZI-IM-RU-ḪA-AM-MU		JCS XI 23 10 13
6524.	ḎIMR-U+ḪAʾL-A	ZI-IM-RU-ḪA-LA		BM 17045
6525.	ḎIMR-U+ʾARAḪ	ZI-IM-RU-ḪA-RA-AḪ		BM 17045 13
6526.	ḎIMR-U+ʾIL-A	ZI-IM-RU-I-L[A]?		II 5 7
6527.	ḎIMR-U+HADD-U	ZI-IM-RU-D-IM		CT XLVIII 22 REV
6528.	ḎIMR-U+LA+ʾAB-I	ZI-IM-RU-LA-A-BI		RA LXV 42 III 7
6529.	ḎIMR-U+RAPIʾ	ZI-IM-RU-RA-BI		TA 30 82
6530.	ḎIMR-U+ʾUP-I	ZI-IM-RU-UḪ$_2$-KI		TCL VII 23 14 21+
6531.	ḎIMR+ŠAMŠ	ZI-IM-RU-D-UTU		BIN VII 190 18
6532.	ḎIMR-U+ŠAMŠ	ZI-IM-RU-D-UTU		BIROT,TEA 70 B I 9
6533.	SIMT-I+JARAḪ	ZI-IM-TI-E-RA-AḪ		M+
6534.	ZIPP-ATAN-IM	ZI-IP-PA-TA-NIM	GEN	M

6535.	ḌIQN-U	ZI-IQ-NU	FN	XIII 1 V 36
6536.	ḌIQN-UM	ZI-IQ-NU-UM	FN	RA LXV 61 IV 43
6537.	ZIRQ-AN-IM	ZI-IR-GA-NIM	GEN	TA 1930,221 EARLY OB
6538.	ṢIRR-I	ZI-IR-RI	NOM	M, A.+
6539.	SITR-A+HADD-U	ZI-IT-RA-A-DU		A. 456 19
6540.	SITR-I+ʾIL	ZI-IT-RI-DINGIR		B 42
6541.	SITR-I+JABAL	ZI-IT-RI-E-BA-AL		M+
6542.	SITR-I-JE+HADD-U	ZI-IT-RI-E-D-IM		JCS XXIV 63 NO.56 REV.
6543.	SITR-I+ʾEL-UM	ZI-IT-RI-E-LUM		B 42
6544.	SITR-IJA	ZI-IT-RI-IA		M+, C+
6545.	SITR-I+HADD-U	ZI-IT-RI-D-IM		M
6546.	SITR-IJA	ZI-IT-RI-JA		M
6547.	SITR-I+KI+ʾEL	ZI-IT-RI?-KI-EL?		B 42
6548.	SITR-U-HU	ZI-IT-RU-U$_2$		DE GEN. KICH II C 82
6549.	ZIZN-I+ʾEL	ZI-IZ-NI-EL		RA LXV 55 XIII 11
6550.	ZIJAN-I	ZI-JA-NI	FN	M
6551.	SIKIL-T-A	ZI-KI-EL-TA	MN	A. LATE
6552.	SIKIL-T-A	ZI-KI-IL-DA	MN	A. 24 3
6553.	SIKIL-T-A	ZI-KI-IL-TA	MN	A. LATE+
6554.	ḌIKR+ʿAŠTAR	ZI-KI-IR-EŠ$_4$-[DAR]		M
6555.	SIKIL-IJA	ZI-KI-LI-IA		CT XLVIII 89
6556.	SIKIL-IM	ZI-KI-LI-IM	GEN	TCL I 185 3
6557.	ḌIQUN-A+ṬAJB	ZI-KU-NA-ṬA$_3$-AB	FN	RA LXV 59 II 77
6558.	ṢILL-AN	ZI-LA-AN		RA LXV 55 XIII 47
6559.	ZILIB-AN	ZI-LI-BA-AN		I 14 10
6560.	ZILIB-IJA	ZI-LI-BI-IA		RUTTEN 19 21
6561.	ZILIB-UM	ZI-LI-BU-UM		M
6562.	ḌIMR+RAPIʾ-I	ZI-ME-IR-RA-BI-I		TA 30 34
6563.	ḌIMR+ŠAMŠ	ZI-ME-IR-D-UTU		B 42+
6564.	ḌIMR+ZABABA	ZI-ME-IR-D-ZA-BA$_4$-BA$_4$		CIG P. 155
6565.	ṢIMID-AT-UM	ZI-MI-DA?-TUM	FN	M
6566.	ZIʾM-U+DAWR-A	ZI-MU-DA-RA		RA VIII 75 R. 2
6567.	SINAQ-I	ZI-NA-GI		M
6568.	ZINAN-UM	ZI-NA-NU-UM		CT XLV 117 32
6569.	ZIʾN-ATAN-U	ZI-NA-TA-NU		BM 16984 24
6570.	ḌINUB-I+ʾIL	ZI-NU-BI-DINGIR		RA LXV 48 VIII 12
6571.	SINUQ-A	ZI-NU-GA		M+
6572.	ZIʾQ-AN	ZI-QA-AN		RA LXV 54 XII 14
6573.	ZIRIT-AN	ZI-RI-IT-TA-A[N]		M
6574.	ZIZAB-AN	ZI-ZA-BA-AN		RA LXV 52 X 38
6575.	ZIʾZ-AN-UM	ZI-ZA-NU-UM		B 48+
6576.	ZIʾZ-U	ZI-ZU	FN	RA LXV 65 VII 43
6577.	ḌUBAB-UM	ZU-BA-BU-UM		UET V P. 66+
6578.	ZUBAL-AN	ZU-BA-LA-AN		M
6579.	ZUBAL-AT-UM	ZU?-BA-LA-TUM	FN	U
6580.	ZUBAL-IM	ZU-BA-LI-IM	GEN	EDZARD,DER 152:18
6581.	ṢUBUʾ-UM	ZU-BU-U$_2$-UM		SIMMONS 47 21
6582.	ṢUBUʾ-UM	ZU-BU-UM		SIMMONS 50 23+
6583.	ḌU+DAWD-I	ZU-DA-DI		XIV 91:5, 13
6584.	ḌU+DAWD-UM	ZU-DA-TUM		I
6585.	ḌU+DAWD-A	ZU-E-TA-TA		BIN IV 100 1 CAPP
6586.	ŠUGAG-UM	ZU-GA-GU-UM		SIMMONS 72 11+
6587.	ḌU+ʿADN-I	ZU-ḪA-AD-NI	GEN	M+
6588.	ḌU+ʿADN-I	ZU-ḪA-AD-NI	NOM	M+
6589.	ḌU+ʿADN-IM	ZU-ḪA-AD-NIM	GEN	M+
6590.	ḌU+ʿADN-U	ZU-ḪA-AD-NU		M+
6591.	ḌU+ʿAD-IM	ZU-ḪA-DI-IM	GEN	M
6592.	ZUḪAL-AN	ZU-ḪA-LA-AN		RA LXV 51 X 2
6593.		ZU-ḪI-GA-X	FN	M
6594.	ZUḪIR-I	ZU-ḪI-RI		M
6595.	ZUJAN	ZU-I-IA-AN		RA LXV 50 IX 3
6596.	ḌU+ʾIL-A	ZU-I-LA		B 42+
6597.	ḌU+JAŠIʿ-A	ZU-IA-ŠE-IA		A. 64 9
6598.	ḌU+ʾIŠḪAR-AH	ZU-D-IŠ-ḪA-RA		XIII 64 5
6599.	ZUJAN-E	ZU-JA-NE	FN	XIII 1 VIII 11
6600.	ZUJAN-I	ZU-JA-NI	FN	C

6601.	ZUQAT-UM+MA	ZU-KA-TUM-MA		EDZARD, DER 152 REV. 11
6602.	SUKIL-UM	ZU-KI-LUM		KISURRA 38 SEAL
6603.	ZULAN-UM	ZU-LA-NU-UM		TA 30 35 6
6604.		ZU-LU?-ŠA?-RA-TIM	GEN	I 80 6
6605.	ŠUMUḪ-UM	ZU-MU-ḪU-UM		M
6606.	ḌUMUR-ATAN-U	ZU-MUR?-TA-NU		ZA XLII 41
6607.	ZUNAN	ZU-NA-AN		M
6608.	ḌUNAB-UM	ZU-NA-BU-UM		BIN VII 150 9
6609.	ZUNAN-U	ZU-NA-NU		B 48
6610.	ZUNAN-UM	ZU-NA-NU-UM		KISURRA 94 5
6611.	ḌUNUB-I+ʾIL	ZU-NU-BI-DINGIR		RA LXV 51 X 14
6612.	ṢUWR-AJA	ZU-RA-A		M
6613.	ṢUWR-A+ʾIL	ZU-RA-DINGIR		M+
6614.	ṢUWR-A+ʿAMM-U	ZU-RA-ḪA-AM-MU		M+
6615.	ṢUWR-A+ʿAMM-U-HU	ZU-RA-ḪA-AM-MU-U_2		M
6616.	ṢUWR-A+ʿAMM-U	Z[U]-RA-ḪA-M[U]		XIII 132 7
6617.	ṢURAR-UM	ZU-RA-RUM		PBS VIII/2 198 8
6618.	ṢUWR-ATAN-U	ZU-RA-TA-NU		M
6619.	ṢUWR-AT-IM	ZU?-RA?-TIM	GEN	M
6620.	ṢUWR-I+DAGAN	ZU-RI-D-DA-GAN		M
6621.	ṢUWR-I+ʾIL	ZU-RI-DINGIR		M
6622.	ṢUWR-I+JARAḪ	ZU-RI-E-RA-AḪ		M
6623.	ṢUWR-I+ʿAMM-U	ZU-RI-ḪA-AM-MU		M
6624.	ṢUWR-I+ʿAMM-U-HU	ZU-RI-ḪA-AM-MU-U_2		M+
6625.	ṢUWR-IJA	ZU-RI-IA		XIV 98:11
6626.	ṢUWR-I+HADD-U	ZU-RI-D-IM		M+
6627.	ḌU+ŠAT-I	ZU-ŠA-TI		HARRIS 56 12
6628.	SUTAR-AH	ZU?-TA-RA	FN	RA LXV 61 IV 42
6629.	ḌUHUB-UM	ZU-U_2-BU-UM		VII 194 5'
6630.	ḌU+ʿADN-IM	ZU-U_2-ḪA-AD-NIM		VOIX 187:18 MARI
6631.	ḌU+ʾIL-A	ZU-U_2-I-LA		B 42
6632.	ḌU+MA+ʾAB-I	ZU-U_2-MA-A-BI		XIV 77:17
6633.	ḌU+MA+ʾAB-I	ZU-U_2-MA?-A-BI		M
6634.	ZUʾUM-I	ZU-U_2-MI	GEN	PBS VIII/2 236 6
6635.	ZUʾUM-IM	ZU-U_2-MI-IM	GEN	M
6636.	ZUʾUM-IM	ZU-[U_2]?-MI-IM	GEN	M
6637.	ḌU+ŠUM-IM	ZU-U_2-ŠU?-MI-IM		M
6638.	ZUʾUZ-U	ZU-U_2-ZU		M
6639.	ZUḪL-AN-UM	ZU-$UḪ_3$-LA-NU-U[M]		TA 1931, 141
6640.	ḌUKR-A+ʿAŠTAR	[Z]U-UK-RA-$EŠ_4$-DAR		RA LXV 46 VI 21
6641.	ZUMM-AN	ZU-UM-MA-AN		XIII 95 6
6642.	ZUMM+ʾAB-U	ZU-UM-MA-BU		BM 80328 7
6643.	ZUNN-AH	ZU-UN-NA	FN	XIII 1 IV 51
6644.	ZUNZUN-A	ZU-UN-ZU-NA		B 49
6645.	ZUNZUN-UM	ZU-UN-ZU-NU-UM		RUTTEN 1 9
6646.	ZUNZ-UM	ZU-UN-ZU-UM		RA LXV 48 VIII 4
6647.	ṢUPR-AM	ZU-UP-RA-AM		RA LXV 51 IX 70
6648.	ṢUPR-I+JARAḪ	ZU-UP-RI-E-RA-AḪ		M+
6649.	ṢUPR-UM	ZU-UP-RUM	FN	RA LXV 62 V 9
6650.	ṢURR-I	ZU-UR-RI	NOM	M
6651.	ṢURR-UM	ZU-UR-R[U-UM]?		M
6652.	ZURZUR-UM	ZU-UR-ZU-RU-UM		CT XLV 5 R. 6
6653.	ZURZUR-UM	ZU-UR_2-ZU-RU-UM		KISURRA 20 13+
6654.	ZURZUR-T-UM	ZU-UR_2-ZU-UR-TUM	FN	KISURRA 187 5
6655.	ZUʾZ-AN-UM	ZU-ZA-A-NUM_2		KISURRA 48:12
6656.	ZUʾZ-AN	ZU-ZA-AN		M+
6657.	ZUʾZ-AN-U	ZU-ZA-NU		B 48
6658.	ZUʾZ-AN-UM	ZU-ZA-NU-UM		B 48
6659.	ZUʾZ-AN-UM	ZU-ZA-NUM_2		RUTTEN 9 16
6660.		ZU-ZU-GA		VAS VIII 14 5
6661.	ŠUMK-AN-UM	ZUM-GA-NU-UM		TA 1931, 538 IV
6662.	SUṬIʾ-AN-UM	ZUM-TI-A-NU-U[M]		TA 1930, 6

7. UNANALYZED NAMES

This small collection brings together all the unanalyzed names of chapter 6, "Index of Names," but presents them in the work order, as explained in section 0.5.

A-ḪU-UN-NA-TA		VII 220 25
E-A-LI		XI 3 11
U$_2$-RA-X-GI	FN	XIII 1 75
A-IA-RI-ŠA	FN	XIII 1 VIII 22
I-BI-TUM?		M
ḪU-BI$_2$-....		I
IA-AB-KU-BA-AT		VAS XVI 58:3
ḪA-BA-LU-UK		RA LXV 45 V 18
I-BA-NU-UM		TA 1931, 148
AD-DA-ḪA-AN		RA LXV 50 VIII 56
AD-DA-ḪA-NI-DINGIR		VIII 11 6
I-DI-IM-ME-NI	FN	M+
E-DU-NA-SA		KISURRA 76 3
I-DU-NA-SA		KISURRA 112 5
U$_2$-DU-NA-SA		KISURRA 1 3+
IA-KA-A-TUM		YOS XIII 169:11
UK-LU-UL-LU		M
A-KA-LA-AŠ$_2$-LUM		IRAQ IV 185 A. 386
IL-A-GUL-LAM		VII 140 10'
AN-MA?-NA-I-LA		ZA XXXVIII 267
U$_2$-LI-[....]		M
E-LA-AḪ-TI		RA LXV 46 VI 23
IL-BA-BI-LA		HARRIS 71 13
II-A-DU		A.
I-LA-DU		A. LATE
AL-LA-E		M
UL-LU-NI		M
U$_2$-LA-ŠU-DA		RA XLIII 29 QATNA
AL-SU-UM-LA-U$_2$-SA		CT XXXIII 48A 10
I-LA-AT-ḪA-[X]		HARRIS 61 7
AL-TI-EŠ$_3$-QA-AL-LU-TIM		I 45 7, 16
AL-TI-EŠ$_3$-QA-LU		VII 120 3'
ḪA-MI-UR-KU-X-X-X-UM		M
ḪA-MI-KU-UN		M
IM-LA-TA-AL		TCL I 222 5, 6
U$_2$-MA-AN-NI-SU-TA		VIII 1 35
AM-MA-RI-IK-KI		A.
AM-MA-RI-IK-E		A.+
A-MU-UR-DI	FN	RA LXV 60 III 22
AM?-RI-MU-UM		VIII 3 23
UN-DA-AN-KI	FN	XIII 1 VIII 26
U$_2$-NA-AK-KA	FN	XIII 1 VIII 15
AN-NA-IŠ-ḪU-MU		M
U$_2$-NA-TI?-X	FN	XIII 1 VIII 85
AN-NU-TU-NU-UM		RA LXIV 28 NO. 17
AP-LI-TI-DINGIR[....]		M
E-RI-....	FN	M
AR-NU-X-TUM	FN	XIII 1 IX 21
IN-NI-IR-RI	NOM	VI 19 31
IN-NE-EK-RI	NOM	VII 221 3
AR-RI-WU-UK		M+
AR-RU-UT-RUM		TCL I 109 8
AR-RA-ZA-[....]		XIII 1 XII 22
IA-SI-[....]-TI		CT VIII 17C 12
ḪI-ŠA-LA-DA?		M+
UŠ?-ŠU-UL-TU		M
EŠ$_4$-DAR?-...-KA-RI-E	FN	XIII 1 V 77
A-TU-A-NU-UM		TA 1931, 538 I, IV
IT-NU-ŠA		M
ḪU-ZU-[....]		M
A-ZA-LA-LUM		KISURRA 206 3
ḪA-ZA-MU-LA		M+
IZ-ZI-BI-LA-TUM	FN	M
BI-MU-TI-....		IX 290 6
BI-MU-TI-BA		M+
BU-NA-NU-ŠU		TCL I 27 3

I-BA-SA-X		SIMMONS 130 7
BE-EŠ$_3$-NU	FN	M
KU-LA-IL-E		TCL I 182 7
KI-DA-ḪU-MU		RA LXV 41 II 31
KI-NI-IT-[TUM]		XIII 1 I 7
KI-NA-AT-RA-....		M
LA-KA-ŠI-....		B 33
LA-ḪU-UM		TA 1931, 538 I, IV?
LA-I-IA-WI		SYRIA XV 138 5, UGARIT
LA-KA-A-MA?-ZU?		VII 212 9
LA-KA-ZA-ME-....		VIII 63 3, 15
LI-LA-MI-....		SIMMONS 82 8+
LA-PA-X-LA		SIMMONS 107 11
MU-EL-LI-[U]M		TA 1931, 698
ME-E-IM-MA	FN	XIII 1 II 39
MU-ḪU-UŠ-KI		SZLECHTER TJ MAH 16194 4,SEAL
I-MU?-UT?-KI-MA-ME-ET		VIII 87 5'
ME-KI-I[A-....]	FN	M
D-MA-MA-KU	FN	M
MA-AN-NA-ŠE	FN	RA LXV 58 I 60
MU-NA-RU-RUM		VAS VIII 66 17 67 15
MU-ŠI-[....]		M
MU-TA-[....]-AN		XIII 1 III 55
MU-TA-MU-[....]		M
MU-TA-TA-RUM		M
ME-TE-BA-AN		TA 1931, 304
NA-A-BI-ZI-....		M
NA-ḪI-DA-[....]		M
NA-ḪI-DU-ŠI		TCL I 49 13
NI-LU-UK		M
NA-AL-LA-ME	FN	M+
NI-IP-RA-ḪU		M
NU-PU-RI-IK-KU		M
IT-TU-NU-UM		M
IA-UR-ḪA-TUM		RA L 63
PA-KI-AN-NA-E$_2$		M
PA-A-ŠUM-I?-L[A]?		BASOR 95, 21 II 24
IA-AP-DU-UM		KISURRA 19:4 +
PA-DA-NI-TE	FN	XIII 1 III 67
PA-KA-IA		B 37
PA?-KI-IA-DINGIR		SPELEERS 227 3
PA-LI-AŠ-ŠI-RU?		VII 56 4
PA-TA-AL-LA	MN	DELAPORTE, CCL II A 914
RU-ŠU-UM		TA 1931,148
RA-BA?-AD-DU-TUM		XIII 1 V 76
SU-A-ḪA-AM-MI-I-ŠA		VIII 85 17
ŠA-JA-MU-RU		RA LXV 45 V 79
ŠA-DU?-UL?-LA-....		M
ŠU-LUM-ŠU-RA-MA	FN	RA LXV 58 I 13
ŠA-AL-MU-ZI	FN	M
SU-UM-MA-BU		YOS XIII 352:7
SU-MU-NE?-BI?-EL?		B 39
ŠI-MA-ḪA-[....]		VAS IX 172 42, 174 29
ŠA-MU-U$_2$	FN	RA LXV 65 VI 72
ŠE-MU-BA		A.
ŠA-AN-QA-I	FN	RA LXV 60 III 56
SI-IT-ḪA-RA-MA-AM		RA LXV 42 III 12
ŠA-ZI-ḪU-UM		B 40
TI-IḪ-ME-DU		RA LXV 53 XI 19
TU-BI-BA?-AR-RA	FN	XIII 1 VIII 59
TU-DI-EN		M
TU-UK-BI-IA-AŠ-RUM	FN	XIII 1 VIII 9
TU-KA-ZU-[....]		M
TU-LI-IŠ		M+
TU-LI-IŠ-TA-A-NIM		UCP X/1 105 3 9
TU-LI-IA-ŠUM		CT XLV 54 18

TA-MA-KU?-ME-NI		M
TI-IM-ZU-NA-....		HARRIS 5 21
TI-NI-LA-NU-UM		TA 1931, 538 I, V
TA-RA-AḪ-TU-UK		RA LXV 48 VIII 22
TA-RA-AM-NU	FN	XIII 1 XIII 11
TA-AR-MA-RI-IŠ		M
TI-RI-IS-RA		A. LATE+
TI-RI-IŠ-RA		A. 224 R. 5 LATE
TI-ZI-ḪA-AM		RA LXV 41 II 38
TE-ZI-ID?-DI-MI		VII 127 4
ZU-ḪI-GA-X	FN	M
ZI-IA-RU-TU-RA-KI-A		OLZ VII 351 28
ZA-U_2-TA		A.
ZU-LU?-ŠA?-RA-TIM	GEN	I 80 6
ZA-MA-AR-GA		M+
ZA-NI-DAḪ		HARRIS 20 5
ZA-AR-KU-IŠ		M
ZA-ŠA-U_2-DA		A. 34 8
ZU-ZU-GA		VAS VIII 14 5